TRAVELING WITH YOUR PET
THE AAA PETBOOK®

The AAA guide to more than 10,000
pet-friendly, AAA-RATED® lodgings
across the United States and Canada

4th Edition

AAA PUBLISHING

AAA wishes to acknowledge the following for their assistance:
American Boarding Kennels Association, American Veterinary Medical Association, Birds and Animals Unlimited, Dogpark.com®, Humane Society of the United States, National Association of Professional Pet Sitters, Pet Sitters International, U.S. Department of Agriculture-Animal & Plant Health Inspection Services
Printed in the USA by Quebecor World Inc.

FOREWORD

One of my favorite things about being a canine actor is traveling to new and exciting places. I am fortunate to get to visit many bustling cities, quaint towns and beautiful parks across North America. I travel by car and plane, and have even crossed borders to travel internationally. Most of my travel involves acting or making personal appearances, but like many other dogs, cats and other pets, I also love to go on vacation with my best friend.

Every year more pets are traveling to great places and enjoying special time with *their* best friends, people just like you! And when you decide to take a trip with your favorite furry companion, you'll want to make sure both of you have a wonderful time. Traveling with dogs, cats and other pets requires special care and attention to their particular needs. Finding pet-friendly lodgings, points of interest and emergency vet clinics is particularly important.

AAA Publishing has spent several years researching and compiling information on pet travel. The result is the 4th edition of *Traveling with Your Pet — The AAA Pet-Book®*. All the information you and your pet need when traveling together is here, from trip preparation, to selecting an appropriate carrier, to flying and driving tips. The PetBook also features national parks and other public lands that allow pets, dog parks, pet-friendly attractions and listings for more than 10,000 AAA-RATED® lodgings that accept pets. There is even a section that describes what to do in case of an emergency.

If your pet loves to travel as much as I do, you'll be pleased to find that more and more places are not only welcoming animals, but also offering special programs for pets to enhance your visit. So read on, and begin planning a great trip with your pet!

Moose

ABOUT THIS BOOK

Welcome to the 4th edition of ***Traveling With Your Pet — The AAA PetBook*®**. *Traveling With Your Pet* is a must for the traveler who's also an animal lover. This comprehensive book provides all the information you need to know about taking a four-legged friend on the road. Will Spot be a good car passenger? Is it safe to take Snowball on a plane? What are the important rules of pet etiquette? Is pet insurance a good idea? *Traveling With Your Pet* answers all of these questions and more. Here are just some of the features covered:

- Dog parks where you and your furry friends can play, exercise or just relax.

- An extensive listing of animal clinics compiled by the Veterinary Emergency & Critical Care Society. Names, addresses and phone numbers offer an at-your-fingertips way to plan for unexpected or emergency situations, both en route and at your destination.

- A roundup of pet-friendly attractions.

- National public lands in the United States and Canada that allow pets, along with recreation information.

- Border crossing procedures and tips for travelers — both entering Canada from the United States and vice versa.

- Policies pertaining to service animals.

Traveling With Your Pet lists more than 10,000 AAA-RATED® lodgings. And the listings show AAA's trustworthy diamond ratings, the traveler's assurance of quality. Other handy features include:

- Informative highway directions.

- Specific information about lodgings' pet policies: deposits and fees, housekeeping service, designated rooms and other stipulations relating to travelers with pets.

- Additional details about the lodgings themselves, including icons for amenities, recreation, dining and accessibility.

- Icons designating AAA's member discount programs.

All of this valuable information is packaged in a contemporary, easy-to-read format, making *Traveling With Your Pet — The AAA PetBook* as indispensable an on-the-road companion as Spot's water dish or Snowball's litter box. Don't leave home without it, and remember: It always pays to *Travel With Someone You Trust*®.

TABLE OF CONTENTS

Traveling With Pets

Pet-Friendly Places in the U.S. and Canada

Pet-Friendly Accommodations

United States

United States (continued)

Canada

Many people view their pets as full-fledged members of the family. Spot and Snowball often have their own beds, premium-quality foods, a basketful of toys and a special place in their humans' hearts.

Until it's time to go on vacation, that is. Then the family dog or cat is consigned to "watching the fort" at home while everyone else experiences the joy of traveling. Many pet lovers hesitate to take their animals with them because they don't think they'll be able to find accommodations that accept four-legged guests. Others aren't sure how — or if — their furry friends will adapt.

The truth is, including a pet in the family vacation is fairly easy, so long as you plan ahead. Most pets respond well to travel, a fact that isn't lost on the tourism industry. More than 10,000 AAA-RATED® hotels and motels from coast to coast are pet-friendly, and airline bookings for pet passengers are on the rise. Great companions at home, pets are earning their stripes on the road, too.

So if you've been longing to hit the trail with a canine or feline companion, read the tips on the following pages. You may find that a getaway can be far more enjoyable with than without your pet.

Should Your Pet Travel?

Before you make reservations, determine if your pet is able to travel. Most animals can and do make the most of the experience, but a small percentage simply are not cut out for traveling. Illness, physical condition and temperament are important factors, as is your pet's ability to adjust to such stresses as changes to his environment and routine. When in doubt, check with your veterinarian. If you feel your pet isn't up to the trip, it's better for everyone if he stays home.

❧ **Rule 1: Pets who are very young, very old, pregnant, sick, injured, prone to biting or excessive vocalizing, or who cannot follow basic obedience commands should not travel.**

Even if Spot and Snowball are seasoned travelers, take into account the type of vacation and activities you have planned. No pet is going to be happy (or safe) cooped up in a car or hotel room. Likewise, the family dog may love camping and hiking, but the family cat may not. Putting a little thought toward your animal's needs and safety will pay off in a more enjoyable vacation for everyone.

❧ **Rule 2: If your pet can't actively participate in the trip, she should stay home.**

Most of the information in this book pertains to cats and dogs. If you own a bird, hamster, pig, ferret, lizard or other exotic creature, remember that unusual animals are not always accepted as readily as more conventional pets. Always specify the type of pet you have when making arrangements.

Also check states' animal policies. **Hawaii** imposes 30- and 120-day quarantines for all imported carnivorous animals to prevent the importation of rabies. Guide dogs and other service animals are exempt from the quarantine provided they have a current rabies vaccination, although upon arrival they still must be examined for external parasites and undergo serum antibody testing and microchip identification. For additional details, obtain the brochure Animal Quarantine Station Rabies Information Brochure from the Hawaii Department of Agriculture, Animal Quarantine Station, 99-951 Halawa Valley St., Aiea, HI 96701-5602; phone (808) 483-7151, fax (808) 483-7161. The website address is www.hawaiiag.org/hdoa/ai_aqs_info.htm. Guide and service dog owners should request information about the exemption program.

North Carolina has stringent restrictions regarding pets in lodgings. Make certain you understand an accommodation's specific policies before making reservations.

❧ **Rule 3: Be specific when making travel plans that include your pet. Nobody wants unpleasant surprises on vacation.**

If Spot and Snowball stay behind, leave them in good hands while you're gone. **Family, friends and neighbors** make good sitters (provided they're willing), especially if they know your pet and can care for him in your home. Provide detailed instructions for feeding, exercise and medication, as well as phone numbers for your destination, your veterinarian and your local animal emergency clinic.

Professional pet sitters offer a range of services, from feeding and walking your pet daily to full-time house sitting while you are gone. Interview several candidates, and always check credentials and references. For additional information, contact the National Association of

Professional Pet Sitters or Pet Sitters International. *(See sidebars below and on p. 9.)*

Kennels board many animals simultaneously and generally are run by professionals who will provide food and exercise according to your instructions. Pets usually are kept in a run (dogs) or cage (cats and small dogs) and may not get the same level of human interaction as at home. **Veterinary clinics** also board pets and may be the best choice if yours is sick, injured or needs special medical care. For further information on how to select a kennel, contact the American Boarding Kennels Association.

Veterinarians, fellow pet owners and professional associations are a good source of referrals for sitters and kennels.

🐾 **Rule 4: Never leave your pet with someone you don't trust.**

CHOOSING A PET SITTER

Before hiring a pet sitter, ask:

- Are they insured (for commercial liability) and bonded?
- What is included in the fee?
- Do they require that your pet have a current vaccination?
- What kind of animals do they typically care for?
- How will they handle a medical, weather or home emergency?
- Do they fully understand your pet's medical or dietary needs?
- How much time will they spend with your pet?

The pet sitter should:

- Have a polished, professional attitude.
- Provide references.
- Have a standard contract outlining terms of service.
- Have experience in caring for animals.
- Insist on current vaccinations.
- Ask about your pet's health, temperament, schedule and needs.
- Visit and interact with your pet before you leave.
- Devote time and attention to your pet.
- Be affiliated with pet care organizations.

Be sure you:

- Explain your pet's personality — favorite toys, good and bad habits, hiding spots, general health, etc.
- Leave care instructions, keys, food and water dishes, extra supplies (food, medication, etc.), and phone numbers for your veterinarian and an emergency contact.
- Bring pets inside before leaving.

CHOOSING A KENNEL

Before reserving a kennel, ask:

- What is included in the fee?
- Do they require current vaccinations?
- What kind of animals do they board?
- How will they handle a medical or weather emergency?
- Will your pet be kept in a cage or run?
- Will your pet receive daily exercise?
- Do they fully understand your pet's medical or dietary needs?
- How and how often will they interact with your pet?

The kennel should:

- Require proof of current vaccinations.
- Be clean, well-ventilated and offer adequate protection from the elements.
- Have separate areas for dogs, cats and other animals, with secure fencing and caging.
- Clean and disinfect facilities daily.
- Give your pet his regular food on his regular schedule.
- Provide soft bedding in runs/cages.
- Understand your pet's medical needs.
- Provide or obtain veterinary care if necessary.
- Offer sufficient supervision.
- Have a friendly, animal-loving staff.

Be sure you:

- Notify staff of behavior quirks (dislike of other animals, children, etc.).
- Provide food and medication.
- Leave a familiar object with your pet.
- Leave phone numbers for your veterinarian and an emergency contact.
- Spend time with your pet before boarding him.

Travelers Who Have Disabilities

Individuals with disabilities who own service animals to assist them with everyday activities undoubtedly face challenges, but traveling should not be one of them. Service animals (the accepted term for animals trained to help people with disabilities) are not pets and thus are not subject to many of the laws or policies pertaining to pets.

The Americans With Disabilities Act (ADA) defines a service animal as "any guide dog, signal dog or other animal individually trained to provide assistance to an individual with a disability." ADA regulations stipulate that public accommodations are required to modify policies, practices and procedures to permit the use of a service animal by an individual with a disability.

The purpose of these regulations is to provide equal access opportunities for people with disabilities and to ensure that they are not separated from their service animals. A tow truck operator, for example, must allow a service animal to ride in the truck with her owner rather than in the towed vehicle.

Public accommodations may charge a fee or deposit to an individual who has a disability — provided that fee or deposit is required of all customers — but no fees or deposits may be charged for the service animal, even those normally charged for pets.

The handler (the animal's owner) is responsible for her care and behavior; if she creates an altercation or poses a direct threat, the handler may be required to remove the animal from the premises and pay for any resulting damages.

The **Delta Society,** an organization devoted to companion and service animals, has information about laws that affect people and service animals in public accommodations. Phone (425) 226-7357 for a catalog, or visit Delta's website: www.deltasociety.org.

Preparing Your Pet for Travel

Happily, many vacations can be planned to include fun activities for pets. Trips to parks, nature trails, the ocean or lakes offer exposure to the world beyond the window or fence at home, as well as the chance to explore new

CONTACT INFORMATION

The following organizations offer information, tips, brochures and other travel materials designed to help you and your pet enjoy a happy and safe vacation.

American Animal Hospital Association
12575 W. Bayaud Ave., Lakewood, CO 80228
(303) 986-2800 — www.healthypet.com

American Boarding Kennels Association
1702 East Pikes Peak Ave.
Colorado Springs, CO 80909
(719) 667-1600 — www.abka.com

American Society for the Prevention of Cruelty to Animals
424 E. 92nd St., New York, NY 10128
(212) 876-7700 — www.aspca.org

American Veterinary Medical Association
1931 N. Meacham Rd., Suite 100
Schaumburg, IL 60173
(847) 925-8070 — www.avma.org

Dogpark.com ®
716 Fourth St., San Rafael, CA 94901
www.dogpark.com

Humane Society of the United States
2100 L St. NW, Washington, DC 20037
(202) 452-1100 — www.hsus.org

National Association of Professional Pet Sitters
6 State Rd., Suite 113
Mechanicsburg, PA 17050
(717) 691-5565 — www.petsitters.org

PetGroomer.com
13775 A Mono Way, Suite 224
Sonora, CA 95370
(209) 532-5222 — www.petgroomer.com

Pet Sitters International
201 E. King St., King, NC 27021-9161
(336) 983-9222 — www.petsit.com

USDA-APHIS
Deputy Administrator
USDA-APHIS-Animal Care
4700 River Rd., Unit 84
Riverdale, MD 20737
(301) 734-4981 — www.aphis.usda.gov

sights and sounds. Even the streets of an unfamiliar city can provide a smorgasbord of discoveries for your animal friend to enjoy.

Once you decide Spot and Snowball are ready to hit the road, plan accordingly:

❧ **Get a clean bill of health from the veterinarian.** Update your pet's vaccinations, check his general physical condition and obtain a health certificate showing proof of up-to-date inoculations, particularly rabies, distemper and kennel cough. Such documentation will be necessary if you cross state or country lines, and also may come in handy in the unlikely event your pet gets lost and must be retrieved from the local shelter. Don't forget to ask the doctor about potential health risks at your destination (Lyme disease, heartworm infection) and the necessary preventive measures.

If your pet is taking prescribed medicine pack a sufficient supply, plus a few days' extra. Also take the prescription in case you need a refill. Be prepared for emergencies by getting the names and numbers of clinics or doctors at your destination from your veterinarian or the American Animal Hospital Association **Hint:** Obtain these references before you leave and keep them handy throughout the trip.

Make sure your pet is in good physical shape overall, especially if you are planning an active vacation. If your animal is primarily sedentary or overweight, he may not be up to lengthy hikes through the woods.

Note: Some owners believe a sedated animal will travel more easily than one that is fully aware, but this is rarely the case. In fact, tranquilizing an animal can make travel much more stressful. Always consult a veterinarian about what is best for your pet, and administer sedatives only under the doctor's direction. In addition, never give an animal medication that is specifically prescribed for humans. The dosage may be too high for an animal's much smaller body mass, or may cause dangerous side effects.

❧ **Acclimate your pet to car travel.** Even if you're flying, your pet will have to ride in the car to get to the airport or terminal, and you don't want any unpleasant surprises before departure.

Some animals are used to riding in the car and even enjoy it. But most associate the inside of the carrier or the car with one thing only: the annual visit to the V-E-T. Considering that these visits usually end with a jab from a sharp needle, it's no wonder that some pets forget their training and act up in the car. If this is your situation, you will have to re-train your animal to view a drive as a reward, not a punishment.

Begin by allowing your pet to become used to the car without actually going anywhere. Then take short trips to places that are fun for animals, such as the park or the drive-through window at a fast-food restaurant. (Keep those indulgent snacks to a minimum!) Be sure to praise her for good behavior with words, petting and healthy treats. It shouldn't take long before you and your furry friend are enjoying leisurely drives without incident. *(See Traveling by Car, p. 13.)*

❧ **Brush up on behavior.** Will Snowball make a good travel companion? Or will he be an absolute terror on the road? Don't wait until the vacation is already under way to find out; review general behavioral guidelines with respect to your animal, keeping in mind that the unfamiliarity of travel situations may test the temperament of even the most well-behaved pet.

It's a good idea to socialize Spot by exposing her to other people and animals (especially if she normally stays inside). You're likely to encounter both on your trip, and it is important that she learns to behave properly in the company of strangers. Make her introduction to the outside world gradual, such as a walk in a new neighborhood or taking her along while you run errands. Exposure to new situations will help reduce fear of the unknown and result in more socially acceptable behavior.

Is your pet housebroken? How is he around children? Does he obey vocal commands? Be honest about your animal's ability to cope in unfamiliar surroundings. Depending on the length and nature of the trip and your pet's level of command response, an obedience refresher course might be a good idea.

❧ **Learn about your destination.** Check into quarantines or other restrictions well in advance, and make follow-up calls as your departure date approaches. Find out what types of documentation will be required — not just en route, but on the way home as well.

Be aware of potential safety or health risks where you're going, and plan accordingly. For example, the southeastern United States — particularly Florida — is home to alligators and heartworm-carrying mosquitoes, and many mountainous and wooded areas may harbor ticks that transmit Lyme disease.

Confirm all travel plans within a few days of your departure, especially with lodgings and airlines; their policies may have changed after you made the reservations. If you plan to visit state parks or attractions that accept pets on the premises, obtain their animal regulations in advance.

❧ **Determine the best mode of transportation.** Most people traveling with pets drive. Many airlines do accept animals in the passenger cabin or cargo hold, and as more people choose to fly with their pet these airlines are becoming more pet-conscious. Restrictions vary as to the type and number of pets an airline will carry, however, so inquire about animal shipping and welfare policies before making reservations. If your pet must travel in the cargo hold, heed the cautionary advice in the Traveling by Air section of this book. *(See p. 14.)*

Flying is really the only major option to car travel. Amtrak, as well as Greyhound and other interstate bus lines, do not accept pets. Local rail and bus companies may allow pets in small carriers, but this is an exception rather than a rule. The only cruise ship that permits pets is the Cunard Line's *Queen Elizabeth 2* (on trans-Atlantic crossings), and animals are restricted to the cargo area.

Note: Seeing-eye dogs and other service animals are exempt from the regulations prohibiting pets on Amtrak and interstate bus lines.

A word of advice: Never try to sneak your pet onto any mode of public transportation where she is not permitted. You may face legal action or fines, and the animal may be confiscated if discovered.

❧ **Pack as carefully for your pet as you do for yourself.** *(See checklist, below.)* Make sure she has a collar with a license tag and ID tag(s) listing her name and yours, along with your address and phone number. As an added precaution, some owners outfit their dog with a second tag listing the name and number of a

---

WHAT TO TAKE

- ❑ Carrier or crate. *(See Selecting a Carrier or Crate, p. 12, for specifications.)*
- ❑ Nylon or leather collar or harness, license tag, ID tag(s) and leash. All should be sturdy and should fit your pet properly.
- ❑ Food and water dishes.
- ❑ Can opener and spoon (for canned food).
- ❑ An ample supply of food, plus a few days' extra.
- ❑ Bottled water from home. (Many animals are finicky about their drinking water.)
- ❑ Cooler with ice.
- ❑ Healthy treats.
- ❑ Medications, if necessary.
- ❑ Health certificate and other required documents.
- ❑ A blanket or other bedding. (If your pet is used to sleeping on the furniture, bring an old blanket or sheet to place on top of the hotel's bedding.)
- ❑ Litter supplies (for cats or other small animals), a scooper and plastic bags (for dogs).
- ❑ Favorite toys.
- ❑ Carpet deodorizer.
- ❑ Chewing preventative.

- ❑ A recent photograph and a written description including name, breed, gender, height, weight, coloring and distinctive markings.
- ❑ Grooming supplies:
  comb/brush
  nail clippers
  shampoo
  towels
  cotton balls/tissues
  paper towels
- ❑ First-aid kit:
  gauze
  bandages and adhesive tape
  towels
  hydrogen peroxide
  rubbing alcohol
  ointment
  muzzle
  scissors
  tweezers (for removing ticks, burrs, splinters, etc.)
  local emergency phone numbers
  first-aid guide (such as *Pet First Aid: Cats & Dogs*, published by The Humane Society of the United States and the American Red Cross)

contact person at home. Popular backup identification methods are to have your animal tattooed with an ID number (usually a social security number) or to implant a microchip under her skin.

If your pet requires medication, make sure that is specified on his tag. This helps others understand your animal's needs and also may prevent people from keeping a found pet or from stealing one to sell.

Note: Choke chains, collars that tighten when they are pulled, may be useful during training sessions, but they do not make good full-time collars. If the chain catches on something, your pet could choke herself trying to pull free. For regular wear, use a harness or a conventional collar made of nylon or leather.

Selecting a Carrier or Crate

This is one of the most important steps in ensuring your pet's safety when traveling. A good-quality carrier not only contains your pet during transit, it also gives him a safe, reassuring place to stay when confinement is necessary at your destination. Acclimate the animal before the trip so he views the crate as a cozy den, not a place of exile.

If you plan to travel by car, a carrier will confine your pet en route, and also may come in handy if Spot or Snowball must stay in the room unsupervised. A secured crate will prevent your pet from escaping from the room when the cleaning staff arrives, or at night if camping in the open. *(See At Your Destination, p. 17.)*

Some airlines allow small pets to travel in the passenger cabin as carry-on luggage. There are

no laws dictating the type of carrier to use, but remember that it must be small enough to fit under a standard airplane seat, usually **13 by 9 by 23 inches or 10 by 16 by 24 inches.** If your pet will be flying in the cargo hold, you must use a carrier that meets U.S. Department of Agriculture Animal and Plant Health Inspection Service (USDA-APHIS) specifications. *(See Traveling by Air, p. 14.)*

Crates are available at pet supply stores; some airlines also sell carriers. Soft-sided travel bags are handy for flyers with small pets. The Sherpa Bags sold by Sherpa's Pet Trading Co. are approved by most major airlines and are available for 6-, 16- and 22-pound animals; phone (800) 743-7723 for information, or visit their website: www.sherpapet.com.

Even if you never take to the skies, these common-sense guidelines provide a good rule of thumb in selecting a crate for other uses. USDA-APHIS rules stipulate the following:

❧ The crate must be enclosed, but with ventilation openings occupying at least 14 percent of total wall space, at least one-third of which must be located on the top half of the kennel. A three-fourths of an inch lip or rim must surround the exterior to prevent air holes from being blocked.

❧ The crate must open easily, but must be sufficiently strong to hold up during normal cargo transit procedures (loading, unloading, etc.).

❧ The floor must be solid and leakproof, and must be covered with an absorbent lining or material (such as an old towel or litter).

❧ The crate must be just large enough to allow the animal to turn freely while standing, and to have a full range of normal movement while standing or lying down.

❧ The crate must offer exterior grips or handles so that handlers do not have to place their hands or fingers inside.

❧ If the carrier has wheels, they must be removed or immobilized prior to loading.

❧ One-inch lettering stating "Live Animal" or "Wild Animal" must be placed visibly on the exterior, and must be accompanied by directional arrows showing the crate's proper orientation. It also is a good idea to

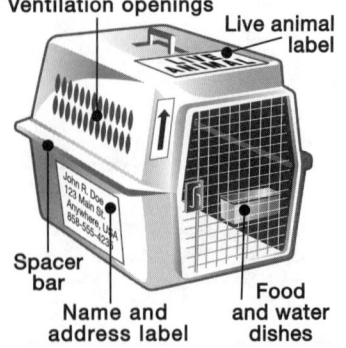

Ventilation openings

Live animal label

Spacer bar

Name and address label

Food and water dishes

label the crate with your name, home address and home phone number, as well as an address and phone number where you can be reached during the trip. (Hint: Use an adhesive label or an indelible marker and write directly on the crate, as paper may be ripped off accidentally in transit.)

❧ Attach a list of care instructions (feeding, watering, etc.) for a 24-hour period to the exterior of the carrier. This will help airport workers care for your pet if he is sent to the wrong destination.

❧ If you are traveling with multiple pets, note that crates may contain only one animal whose weight exceeds 20 pounds. Smaller animals may travel together under the following guidelines: one species to a crate, except compatible dogs and cats of similar size; two puppies or kittens under 6 months of age; 15 guinea pigs or rabbits; 50 hamsters. **Note:** These are federal limits; airlines may impose more stringent regulations.

Traveling by Car

The first step in ensuring your pet's well-being during a vacation is to train her to ride in the car. For safety reasons, pets should be confined to the back seat, either in a carrier or a harness attached to the car's seat belt. This keeps the animal from interfering with or distracting the driver, and also may save her life in the event of an accident. And a restrained animal will not be able to break free and run away the second the car door is opened.

To help prevent car sickness, feed your pet a light meal four to six hours before departing. Do not give an animal food or water in a moving vehicle.

Never allow your pet to ride in the bed of a pickup truck. It's illegal in some states; he also can jump out or be thrown, endangering himself and others on the road. Harnessing or leashing him to the truck bed is not advisable either: If he tries to jump out, he could be dragged along the road or the restraint could become a noose. Avoid placing animals in campers or trailers as well. **If your pet cannot ride in the car with you, leave him at home.**

Don't let your dog stick her head out the window, no matter how enjoyable it seems. Road

HEATSTROKE AND HYPOTHERMIA

The best way to treat heatstroke or hypothermia is to prevent it. Do not leave pets unattended in a car, even if only for a few minutes. Also heed airlines' restrictions on pet travel, and carefully investigate animal welfare policies to make certain the airline has safeguards to protect your pet from both conditions.

Other preventive measures are to avoid strenuous exercise — including such activities as hiking and "fetch" — when the sun is strongest (10 a.m.-2 p.m.), and to provide your pet access to clean, fresh drinking water at all times.

Following are the warning signs and basic first aid for heatstroke and hypothermia. Always be alert to your pet's physical condition and watch for symptoms — immediate attention to the situation may mean the difference between life and death. If your pet is struck with either disorder, take him to an animal hospital or veterinarian as fast as safely possible.

HEATSTROKE

Symptoms
- rapid, shallow breathing
- excessive salivation
- heavy panting
- hot to the touch
- glazed eyes
- unsteadiness, dizziness
- deep red or purple tongue or gums
- vomiting
- body temperature of 104 F or higher

First Aid
- place pet in the shade
- quickly dampen with cool water, especially on the head and neck
- give small amounts of water

HYPOTHERMIA

Symptoms
- shivering
- weakness
- lethargy
- cold to the touch
- body temperature of 95 F or lower

First Aid
- place in a warm area
- wrap in towels or a blanket
- quickly warm by gently massaging the head, chest and extremities

debris and other flying objects can injure delicate eyes and ears, and the animal is at greater risk for severe injury if the vehicle should stop suddenly or be struck. If it is hot outside, run the air conditioner instead of opening the windows, and be sure that the air flow is reaching your pet.

AAA recommends that drivers stop every two hours to stretch their legs and take a quick break from driving. Your pet will appreciate the same break. Plan to visit a rest stop every four hours or so to let him have a drink and a chance to answer the call of nature. (Cat owners should bring along a litter box; dog owners should clean up afterward.)

Be sure your pet is leashed before opening the car door. This is not merely a courtesy to fellow travelers; it will prevent her from unexpectedly breaking free and running away. Keep in mind that even the most obedient pet may become disoriented during travel or in strange places and set off for home. **Hint:** If your pet is not used to traveling, use a harness instead of a collar; it is more difficult for an animal to wriggle out of a harness.

NEVER leave an animal in a parked car, even if the windows are partially open. Even on pleasant days the temperature inside a car can soar to well over 100 degrees in less than 10 minutes, placing your pet at risk for heatstroke and possibly death. On very cold days, hypothermia is a risk. Also, animals left unattended in parked cars frequently are stolen.

Traveling by Air

(Service animals are normally exempt from most of the regulations and fees specified in this section. Check policies with the airline when making reservations.)

Opinion is divided as to whether air travel is truly safe for pets. Statistically, it is less dangerous than being a passenger in a car, but some experts warn of potentially deadly conditions for animals. The truth lies somewhere in between: Most pets arrive at their destination in fine condition, but death or injury is always a possibility. Before you decide to fly, know the risk factors and the necessary precautions to keep your pet safe.

❧ **Determine whether your pet is fit to fly.** The Animal Welfare Act (AWA), administered by USDA-APHIS, specifies that dogs and cats must be at least eight weeks old and weaned at least five days before air travel. Animals that are very young, very old, pregnant, ill or injured should not fly at all. Cats, snub-nosed dogs (pugs, boxers, etc.) and long-nosed dogs (shelties, collies, etc.) are prone to severe respiratory difficulties in an airplane's poorly ventilated cargo hold and should travel only in the passenger cabin (if size allows) with their owner.

❧ **Decide where your pet will fly.** Most animals fly in the hold as checked baggage when traveling with their owners, or as cargo when they are unaccompanied. The AWA was enacted to ensure animals traveling in this manner are treated humanely and are not subjected to dangerous or life-threatening conditions. For specific requirements pertaining to your animal, check with the airline in advance, as policies vary. Some airlines will not ship dogs as checked baggage, and United Airlines will only accept dogs shipped as cargo from "known shippers"; i.e., commercial shippers or licensed pet breeders.

Items classified as "dangerous goods" (dry ice or toxic chemicals, for example) must be transported in a different part of the hold from where live animals are carried. Some planes are designed to have separate hold areas, but so-called "people mover" airlines that are primarily interested in getting human passengers from one point to another as quickly as possible may not give priority to this feature. Check your airline's specific baggage policies so you know exactly where in the hold your pet will be traveling.

Small pets may be taken into the passenger cabin with you as carry-on luggage. This places the animal's welfare squarely in your hands but is feasible only if he is very well-behaved and fits comfortably in a container that meets standard carry-on regulations. *(See Selecting a Carrier or Crate, p. 12.)* Keep in mind that the carrier — with the animal inside — must be kept under the seat in front of you throughout the flight. **Note:** AWA regulations do not apply to animals traveling in the cabin.

❧ **Do your homework.** Investigate the airline's animal transport and welfare policies, especially if you are flying with a small or commuter airline. All airlines are subject to the basic regulations of the AWA, but specific standards of care vary greatly from one company to another. Do your research well in advance and confirm the information 24-48 hours before departing.

The more information an airline provides, the better care your pet is likely to receive. Beware of companies that have vague animal welfare guidelines, or none at all. All major airlines provide information about pet transport on their websites. Also talk to fellow travelers and pet owners about their experiences. Finally, keep in mind that airlines are not required to transport live animals and can refuse to carry them for any reason.

❧ **Protect your investment.** Most people think of their pets as part of the family, but the legal system assigns them the same value as a piece of luggage. Inquire about insurance — an airline that won't insure animals in its care may not be the right one for your pet. (Always read the fine print before purchasing any insurance policy.) Also ask if the airline's workers are trained to handle animals. Few are, but it doesn't hurt to check. Remember, it's up to you to choose an airline that values pets and will treat yours with care.

❧ **Understand the potential hazards.** Because a plane's cargo hold is neither cooled nor heated until takeoff, the most dangerous time for your pet is that spent on the ground in this unventilated compartment. In summer, the space absorbs heat while the plane sits on the tarmac; the reverse is true in winter, when it is no warmer inside the hold than outside. Both instances expose pets to the possibility of serious injury or death from heatstroke or hypothermia. **Note:** The latter also may be a concern during flight if the hold's heater is disabled or turned off, allowing the temperature to drop to near-freezing levels.

❧ To minimize these risks, USDA-APHIS rules prohibit animals from being kept in the hold or on the tarmac for more than 45 minutes when temperatures are above 85 F or below 45 F. Some airlines impose even tighter temperature restrictions and may not permit animals to fly on planes going to cities where the ground temperatures may exceed these limits. American and Delta, for example, do not carry animals in their cargo holds May 15 through Sept. 15. (Exceptions may be made for animals whose veterinarians certify they are acclimated to colder temperatures, but never warmer.)

❧ **Make stress-free travel arrangements.** Once you decide to fly, reserve space for Spot or Snowball when you arrange your own tickets, preferably well in advance of your travel date.

Airlines accept only a limited number of animals per flight — usually two to four in the passenger cabin and one pet per passenger — on a first-come, first-served basis. More animals are generally allowed in the cargo hold.

Prepare to pay an additional fee, about $50 each way; the cost is often greater for large animals traveling on a flight without their owner. (Unfortunately, pets are not eligible for frequent flyer miles.) Always reconfirm your reservations and flight information 24-48 hours before departure.

If your pet will be flying in the hold, travel on the same plane and reserve a nonstop flight. This not only reduces the danger of heatstroke or hypothermia during layovers, it also eliminates the possibility that she will be placed on the wrong connecting flight. In summer, fly during

Pet Insurance

Just like their owners, pets can experience major medical problems at some point in their lifetime—even those that live indoors. And if illness strikes while you're on the road, it may be necessary to obtain care quickly. As a result, more and more people who travel with their devoted companion are considering pet health insurance.

Insurance plans run the gamut from basic coverage and routine care for illness and injury to comprehensive health maintenance, vaccinations and exams. Annual premiums range from less than $100 to more than $350, depending on the type of pet and plan. When choosing your plan, consider the following:

- What are the enrollment guidelines (age, breed, specific restrictions, etc.)?
- Which expenses are covered and which are excluded?
- What is the plan's policy concerning existing health problems?
- Does the plan allow you to use your own veterinarian?
- How are veterinary fees paid?
- Is a multiple pet discount offered?

If you're thinking about pet insurance for your dog or cat, contact AAA Insurance Services for more information; phone (407) 444-8608.

the early morning or late evening when temperatures are cooler. Because of large crowds and the chance of heavy air traffic causing delays, avoid holiday travel whenever possible.

Additional precautions may be necessary when traveling outside the United States and Canada. Other countries may impose lengthy quarantines, and airline workers outside North America may not be bound by animal welfare laws. *(See International Travel, p. 20.)*

AIRLINE CONTACT INFORMATION

Following is a list of the major North American airlines and their toll-free reservation numbers.

Website addresses have been given for those airline websites that include information about flying with animals. Hint: Look under links for baggage, cargo or programs and services, or do a site search for "pets."

Air Canada . . . . (888) 247-2262
www.aircanada.ca

Alaska Airlines . . . . (800) 225-2752
www.alaskaair.com

(Accepts carry-on animals only, except America West Express flights.)

America West Airlines. . . (800) 235-9292
www.americawest.com

American Airlines . . . . . . (800) 433-7300
www.americanair.com

Continental Airlines. . . . . (800) 525-0280
www.continental.com

Delta Airlines. . . . . (800) 221-1212
www.delta.com

Northwest Airlines. . . . . . (800) 225-2525
www.nwa.com

Southwest Airlines . . . . . (800) 435-9792
www.iflyswa.com

(Accepts service animals only.)

United Airlines . . . . (800) 241-6522
www.ual.com

US Airways . . . . (800) 428-4322
www.usair.com

✤ **Play an active role in your pet's well-being.** Flying safely with your pet requires careful planning and attention to his welfare. See the veterinarian within 10 days of departure for a health certificate (required by most airlines) and a pre-flight check-up.

Address any concerns you have about your pet traveling by air, especially if you are considering tranquilization. Sedation usually is not recommended for cats and dogs, regardless of whether they fly in the cabin or in the hold. Exposure to increased altitude pressure can create respiratory and cardiovascular problems; animals with short, wide heads are particularly susceptible to disorientation and possible injury. Sedation should never be administered without your veterinarian's approval.

Obtain an airline-approved carrier and acclimate your pet to its presence by leaving it open with a familiar object inside. A sturdy, well-ventilated crate adds an additional measure of protection.

Because animals are classified as luggage, they may be loaded on the plane via conveyor belt. If the crate falls off the belt, your pet could be injured or released. Ask that she be hand-carried on and off the plane, and that you be permitted to watch both procedures. Also ask about "counter-to-counter" shipping, in which the animal is loaded immediately before departure and unloaded immediately after arrival. There usually is an additional fee for this service.

Make sure you will have access to your pet if there is a lengthy layover or delay. Think twice about flying on an airline that won't allow you to check on your animal under such circumstances.

✤ **Prepare for the flight.** Keep in mind that traveling with an animal will require additional pre-flight time and preparation on your part. Exercise your pet before the flight, and arrive at least two but not more than four hours before departure. If he is traveling as carry-on luggage, check-in is normally at the passenger terminal; if he is traveling as checked baggage or as cargo in the cargo hold, proceed to the airline's cargo terminal, which is often in a different location. Find this out when making reservations and again when confirming flight information.

Make sure your animal's crate is properly labeled and secured, but do not lock it in case airline personnel have to provide emergency care. Include an ice pack for extra comfort on a hot day, a hot water bottle on a cold one. **Hint:** Wrap in a towel to prevent leaking.

Do not feed your pet less than four hours before departure, but provide water up until boarding. **Hint:** Freeze water in the bowl so that it melts throughout the trip, providing a constant drinking source.

Spot or Snowball should wear a sturdy collar (breakaway collars are recommended for cats) and two identification tags marked with your name, home address and phone number, and travel address and phone number. It's also a good idea to clip your pet's nails before departure so they won't accidentally get caught on any part of the carrier.

Note: You may be required to take your pet out of the carrier as you pass through security on your way to the gate. Make sure the animal is wearing a collar and leash or harness.

Attach food and water dishes inside the carrier so that airline workers can reach them without opening the door. If the trip will take longer than 12 hours, also attach a plastic bag with at least one meal's worth of dry food. Animals under 16 weeks of age must be fed every 12 hours, adult animals every 24 hours. Water must be provided at least every 12 hours, regardless of the animal's age.

Allow your pet to answer the call of nature before boarding, but do not take her out of the carrier while in the terminal. As a courtesy, wait until you are outside and away from fellow travelers. Keep her leash with you — do not leave it inside or attached to the kennel.

If your pet is traveling as carry-on luggage, let the passenger sitting next to you know. Someone with allergies may want to change seats.

Perhaps the most important precaution is to alert the flight crew and the captain that your pet is aboard. The pilot must activate the heater for the cargo hold; make sure this is done once you are in the air. If there are layovers or delays, ask the flight crew to be sure your pet has adequate shelter and/or ventilation; better yet, ask them to allow you to check in person.

If you have arranged to watch your pet being unloaded, ask a flight attendant to call the baggage handlers and let them know you are on the way. Above all, do not hesitate to voice any concerns you have for your pet's welfare — it is your responsibility to do so.

🐾 **Be prepared for emergencies.** In the unlikely event your pet gets lost en route, contact the airline, local humane shelters, animal control agencies or USDA-APHIS. Many airlines can trace a pet that was transferred to the wrong flight. If your pet is injured in transit, proceed to the nearest animal hospital; register any complaints with USDA-APHIS. **Hint:** Carry a list of emergency contact numbers and a current photograph of your pet in your wallet or purse, just in case.

At Your Destination

How well you and your companion behave on the road directly affects the way future furry travelers will be treated. Always clean up after your pet and keep him under your control. This is not only a courtesy to fellow human travelers; it's the surest way to enjoy a safe and happy vacation.

Inquire about pet policies before making lodging reservations. Properties may impose restrictions on the type or size of pet allowed, or they may designate only certain rooms, such as smoking rooms, for travelers with animals. If you have a dog, get a room on the first floor with direct access outside, preferably near a walking area; keep her leashed on any excursion.

Lodgings may have supervision policies requiring that pets be crated when unattended or that they may not be left alone at all. Allow your pet only in designated exercise or animal-approved areas; never take him into such off-limits places as the lobby, pool area, patio or restaurant. Prepare to receive limited housekeeping service, or none at all.

Expect to pay some type of additional charge, which may be per room or per pet and may include any of the following: refundable deposit, non-refundable deposit, daily fee, weekly fee.

If staying with friends or relatives, make certain your pet is a welcome guest. Know and respect their "house rules," especially if they have small children or pets of their own.

Once in the room, check for such hazards as chemically treated toilet water, hiding spaces and electrical cords before freeing your pet. Give her time to adjust to her new surroundings under your supervision.

Above all, practice good "petiquette":

❧ Try not to leave your pet alone, but if you must, crate or otherwise confine her.

❧ Crate at night as well.

❧ To keep your pet and the housekeeper from having an unexpected encounter, leave the "Do Not Disturb" sign on the door when you go out without him.

❧ Barking dogs make poor hotel neighbors — keep your pet quiet.

❧ Don't allow your pet on the furniture. If she insists on sleeping on the bed, bring a bedspread or sheet from home and place that on top of the hotel bedding.

❧ Clean up after your pet immediately — inside the room and out — and leave no trace of him behind when checking out.

❧ Dispose of litter and other "accidents" properly — check with housekeeping.

❧ Notify the management immediately if something is damaged, and be ready to pay for repairs.

❧ Add a little extra to the housekeeping tip.

❧ When you take your pet out of the room, keep her leashed, especially in wilderness areas and around small children. No matter how obedient she is at home, new stimuli and distractions may cause her to forget or ignore vocal commands. Know and obey animal policies at parks, beaches and other public areas. Check before arriving to make certain animals still are welcome, even if you've been there before — the rules may have changed.

❧ Look for outdoor cafes when selecting restaurants. For health reasons, pets are not permitted inside eating establishments, but many restaurants allow animals to sit quietly with their owners at outdoor tables. Drive-through restaurants are another alternative.

In Case of Emergency

Be prepared for any turn of events by knowing how to get to the nearest animal hospital. *(See Animal Clinics, p. 49.)* Also have the name and number of a local animal shelter and a local veterinarian handy — ask your veterinarian for a recommendation. Take first-aid supplies with you and know how to use them. An animal in pain may become aggressive, so exercise caution at all times.

Emergency evacuation shelters do not accept pets, and domesticated animals do not fare well if left to weather an emergency on their own, especially when far from home. Avert a potential tragedy by planning in advance where you will go with your pet in case of evacuation. Use the listings in this book to find other lodgings willing to take you and your pet. Above all, don't wait for disaster to strike. Leave as soon as the evacuation order is announced, and take your animal with you.

The Great Outdoors

Travelers planning an active or camping vacation should make some additional preparations. Check in advance to be sure your pet is permitted at campgrounds, parks, beaches, trails and anywhere else you will be visiting. If there are restrictions — and there usually are — follow them. Remember that pets other than service animals usually are not allowed in public buildings.

Note: It is not advisable to take animals other than dogs into wilderness areas. For example, bringing a pet is not recommended at some national parks in Alaska. Also keep in mind that rural areas often have few veterinarians and even fewer boarding kennels.

Use common sense. Clean up after your pet, do not allow excessive vocalizing and keep her under your control. If the property requires your pet to be leashed or crated at all times, do so. Few parks or natural areas will allow a pet to be unattended, even when chained — the risk of disagreeable encounters with other travelers or wildlife is too great. The National Park Service may confiscate pets that harm wildlife or other visitors.

If camping, crate your pet at night to protect him from the elements and predators. (Chaining confines the animal but won't keep him from becoming a midnight snack.)

When hiking, stick to the trail and keep your pet on a short leash. It is all too easy for an unleashed pet to wander off and get lost or fall prey to a larger animal. Keep an eye out for such wildlife as alligators, bears, big cats, porcupines and skunks, and avoid other dogs and small children. Be aware of indigenous poisonous plants, such as English ivy and oleander, or those causing physical injury, such as cactus, poison ivy or stinging nettle. Your veterinarian or local poison control center should be able to give you a full list of hazardous flora.

Before setting out on the trail, make sure both of you are in good physical shape. An animal that rarely exercises at home will not suddenly be ready for a 10-mile trek across uneven terrain. Plan a hike well within the limits of your pet's endurance, and don't push — remember, if Spot gets too tired to make it back on her own, you'll have to carry her.

Carry basic first-aid supplies, including a first-aid guide. *(See "What to Take," p. 11.)* Also carry fresh drinking water for both of you — "found" water may contain harmful germs or toxins. Drink often, not just when thirst strikes, and have your pet do the same. Watch for signs of dehydration, leg or foot injuries, heat exhaustion or heatstroke. Stop immediately and return home or to camp if any of these occur.

Note: Dogs can carry their own backpacks (check your local pet store for specially designed packs), but should never carry more than one-third of their body weight. Train the dog to accept the pack beforehand, and only use it with a strong, healthy animal in excellent physical condition.

No matter where or how you spend your vacation, visit the veterinarian when you return home to check for injuries, parasites and general health.

Note: Most campgrounds accept pets. The AAA CampBook® guides are an excellent source for obtaining detailed information regarding pet policies, restrictions and extra charges for campgrounds in the United States and Canada. AAA members may obtain complimentary copies of the CampBook® guides at their local AAA club.

Traveling Between the U.S. and Canada

Traveling across the international border with your pet — either from the United States into Canada or from Canada into the United States — should prove largely hassle-free, although some basic regulations need to be kept in mind.

Passports to enter Canada or return to the United States are not required for native-born citizens of either country. Proof of citizenship is required; a birth or baptismal certificate and a photo ID (a driver's license, which also establishes proof of residence) normally are sufficient. Naturalized citizens should carry their naturalization certificate, and U.S. resident aliens must have an Alien Registration Receipt Card (Green Card).

U.S. Customs grants returning U.S. citizens who stay in Canada more than 48 hours an individual $400 exemption (if not used within the prior 30 days). Any amount over the $400 exemption is subject to duty.

The exemption is based on fair retail value and applies to goods acquired for personal or household use or as gifts but not intended for sale. All items for which the exemption is claimed must accompany you upon return. A $200 exemption is granted for stays of less than 48 hours.

A 7 percent Goods and Service Tax (GST) is levied on most items sold and most services rendered in Canada. In Nova Scotia, New Brunswick and Newfoundland, a Harmonized Sales Tax (HST) of 15 percent (which includes the GST) is charged on goods and services. Rebates can be claimed on some items. Brochures that explain the GST and contain a rebate form are available at tourist information centers, customs offices and duty free shops at the border and in airports.

U.S. citizens taking pet cats and dogs three months of age and older into Canada must carry a health certificate signed by a licensed veterinarian that describes the animal and provides proof of rabies vaccination within the past 36 months. Collar tags are not sufficient proof of immunization. The certificate also is needed to bring a pet back into the United States; make sure the vaccination doesn't expire while you're in Canada.

Service animals are exempt from these rules. Also exempt are up to two puppies or kittens under three months old; obtain a certificate of health from your veterinarian indicating that the animal is too young to vaccinate. **Note:** Pets entering Canada through Newfoundland require a certificate and entry permit, which must be obtained in advance. For details, contact the Canadian Embassy; 501 Pennsylvania Ave. N.W., Washington, DC 20001; phone (202) 682-1740. The website address is www.canadianembassy.org.

The Canadian Food Inspection Agency (CFIA) provides additional pet information; phone (613) 225-2342. If you need assistance while in Canada, contact the U.S. Embassy, 490 Sussex Dr., Ottawa, ON, Canada K1N 1G8; phone (613) 238-5335.

Canadian Customs allows Canadian citizens to bring back from the United States, duty and tax free, goods valued up to $200 any number of times per year, provided the visit is 48 hours or more. A $50 exemption, excluding alcoholic beverages and tobacco products, may be claimed if the visit is 24 hours or more and no other exemption is being used. If returning from a visit of seven days or more (not counting the day of departure from Canada), the exemption goes up to $500.

Canadian travelers may take pet cats and dogs into the United States with no restrictions, but U.S. Customs requires that dogs have proof of rabies vaccination no less than 30 days before arrival. For additional information on U.S. regulations, contact the Animal and Veterinary Services department of the USDA-APHIS National Center for Import and Export, (301) 734-7830.

International Travel

If you plan to travel abroad with Spot or Snowball, prepare for a lengthy flight and at least a short quarantine period. Be aware that airline and animal workers in other countries may not be bound by the same animal welfare laws that exist in the United States and Canada. Contact the embassy or consulate at your destination for information about documentation and quarantine requirements, animal control laws and animal welfare regulations.

As with any trip, have your pet checked by your regular veterinarian within 10 days of departure to obtain a health certificate showing proof of rabies and other inoculations. If you are traveling with an animal other than a domesticated dog or cat, check with USDA-APHIS for restrictions or additional documentation required.

The leaflet "Pets, Wildlife and U.S. Customs" has general information about traveling abroad with animals; write U.S. Customs Service, P.O. Box 7407, Washington, DC 20044, or visit www.customs.gov/travel/travel.htm.

Note: Many island nations, such as Australia and the United Kingdom, are rabies-free and impose a quarantine on animals brought in from the United States and Canada. Hawaii imposes 30- and 120-day quarantines for all imported animals except guide dogs.

Loss Prevention Tips

Searching the woods or an unfamiliar town for a missing pet is easily prevented by following these helpful tips:

❧ Have your pet wear a sturdy nylon or leather collar with current ID and rabies tags firmly attached. Be sure the ID tag

includes the phone number of an emergency contact.

❧ Keep your pet on a leash or harness. Even trained animals can become agitated or disoriented in unfamiliar surroundings and fail to obey vocal commands.

❧ Attach the leash or harness while your pet is still inside the closed car or crate.

❧ Do not leave your pet unattended at any time, anywhere. A stolen pet is extremely difficult to recover.

❧ Escape-proof your hotel room by crating your pet and asking hotel management to make certain no one enters your room while you are gone. (Inform the property that you're traveling with an animal when making reservations.)

❧ Take along a recent picture and a detailed written description of your pet.

If your pet gets lost these steps will improve your chances of recovery:

❧ If your pet is lost in transit, contact the airline immediately. Ask to trace the animal via the airline's automated baggage tracking system.

❧ Contact local police, animal control, animal shelters, humane organizations and veterinary clinics with a description and a recent photograph. Stay in contact until your pet is found, and provide your home and destination phone numbers.

❧ Post signs and place an ad in the local newspaper so that anyone who comes across your pet knows she is lost and how to reach you.

The Last Word

You are ultimately responsible for your pet's welfare and behavior while traveling. Since animals cannot speak for themselves, it is up to you to focus on your pet's well-being every step of the way. It also is important to make sure he conducts himself properly so that other pets will be welcome visitors in the future. Following the common-sense information in this book will help ensure that both you and your animal companion have a safe and happy trip.

PET-FRIENDLY PLACES

Dog Parks
Attractions
National Public Lands
Animal Clinics

DOG PARKS

A dog park is a place where people and their dogs can play together. These places offer dogs an area to play, exercise and socialize with other dogs while their owners enjoy the park-like setting. Dog park size and features vary greatly from location to location, from several hundred square feet in urban areas to several hundred acres in the suburbs and rural locations. Dog owners should remember to always keep their animal leashed until they reach the dog park entrance, to maintain voice control of their animal at all times, to bring their own supply of bags for picking up after their pet (and to be diligent in doing so), and to always have fresh water available for their dog. Please observe all dog park rules.

This list of dog parks in the United States and Canada is provided by Dogpark.com®. Dogpark.com is all about dogs — all breeds, all mixes of breeds, and all shapes, sizes and dispositions. It provides articles and information about dogs and their care, health and play. Online, visit www.dogpark.com.

The dog parks listed here welcome people who travel with their dogs; private parks or parks requiring local residency are not included. **Note:** Fence types and heights vary, and some areas have no fencing at all, requiring that the dog be under firm voice control.

United States

Arizona

Vista del Camino Park, Scottsdale
7700 East Pierce St.; take Pierce Street heading east from Hayden Road
Daily sunrise-10:30 p.m.
Drinking fountains (one for people and one for pooches), benches, mutt mitt stations, lighted. The fenced-in area is all turf and just under an acre in size. Restroom facilities nearby.

Horizon Park, Scottsdale
15444 N. 100th St. (Thompson Peak Parkway and 100th Street, east of SR 101 off Frank Lloyd Wright Boulevard)
Daily sunrise-10:30 p.m.
Fenced, benches, tables, disposal bags, parking, phones, restrooms, lighted, trash cans, bring your own water, little shade.

Creamery Park, Tempe
tempe.gov/pkrec/parkfacil/offleash.htm
8th Street and Una Avenue (just south of University near Rural)
Daily 6 a.m.-midnight

Mitchell Park, Tempe
tempe.gov/pkrec/parkfacil/offleash.htm
Mitchell Drive and 9th Street
Daily 6 a.m.-midnight
Fenced, benches, disposal bags, trees, parking, lighted, water, trash cans. Access for the disabled.

Papago Park, Tempe
tempe.gov/pkrec/parkfacil/offleash.htm
Curry Road and College Avenue
Daily 6 a.m.-midnight

California

Calabasas Bark Park, Calabasas
ci.calabasas.ca.us/recreation/barkpark.html
4232 Las Virgines Rd., south of the Las Virgenes Municipal Water District (approximately 2 miles west of US 101 on the south side)
Daily 5 a.m.-9 p.m.
Fenced, benches, trees, parking, lighted, water, trash cans, scoops, doggie drinking fountain.

Claremont Pooch Park, Claremont
ClaremontPOOCHPark.org
100 S. College Ave. (just north of Arrow Highway)
Daily 7 a.m.-9 p.m.
Tree-lined park, fully fenced with double-gated entry. Ample parking, lots of benches, water, disposal bags and trash cans provided. Access for the disabled.

Costa Mesa Bark Park, Costa Mesa
cmbarkpark.org
Arlington Drive and Newport Boulevard, across from the Orange County Fairgrounds
Wed.-Mon. dawn-dusk; closed rainy days
Fenced, benches, tables, disposal bags, trees, parking, telephones, restrooms, water, trash cans, grass surface, 2 1/2 acres. Access for the disabled.

Sepulveda Basin Off-Leash Dog Park, Encino
dog-park.com
17550 Victory Blvd.
Daily sunrise-sunset
Fully fenced, benches, tables, trees, scoopers, trash cans, portapotty, parking, 4 acres for larger dogs, separate fenced acre for small dogs, water fountains and mud-free dog watering stations, "fake" fire hydrants.

Elizabeth Anne Perrone Dog Park, Glen Ellen
sonoma-county.org/parks/table.htm
13630 Sonoma Hwy. in Sonoma Valley Regional Park (SR 12 between Arnold Drive and Madrone Road)
Daily sunrise-sunset
Fully fenced, 1 acre, double-gated entry, doggy drinking fountain.

Huntington Dog Beach, Huntington Beach
dogbeach.org
Pacific Coast Highway between 21st and Seapoint
streets
Daily 5 a.m.-8 p.m.
Benches and tables on the bluffs above the beach,
disposal bags, metered parking, restrooms, trash cans.
Dogs may be off leash in the water and on the wet
sand. Access for the disabled to the sand.

Laguna Niguel Dog Park, Laguna Niguel
lagunanigueldogpark.com
Golden Lantern near Chapparosa Park
Tues.-Thurs. and Sat. 7 a.m.-dusk, Sun. 8 a.m.-dusk,
Mon. and Fri. noon-dusk
Fenced, landscaped, water source, 1.1 acres.

Long Beach Recreation Dog Park, Long Beach
geocities.com/lbdogpark
5201 East 7th St. at Park
Daily sunrise-10 p.m.; closed Mon. until noon for
regular maintenance
Fenced, benches, tables, disposal bags, trees,
parking, lighted, water, trash cans, separate fenced
area for small dogs, crushed-granite ground cover.
Access for the disabled.

Silverlake Dogpark, Los Angeles
canineworld.com/silverlakedogpark
1850 Silverlake Blvd. at Easterly Terrace
Daily 6 a.m.-10 p.m.
Fenced, benches, tables, disposal bags, trees, lighted,
water, trash cans, special dog water fountain, 1/4
acre. Access for the disabled.

Palm Springs Dog Park, Palm Springs
traveler.com/palmspri/points/dogpark
222 Civic Dr. North, behind City Hall
Daily dawn-10 p.m.
Fenced, benches, tables, disposal bags, trees,
parking, phones, lighted, water, trash cans, shelter.
Beautiful fence designed and built by sculptor Phill
Evans; dual-level drinking fountains, large- and
small-dog areas, antique fire hydrants. Access for the
disabled.

**Rancho Cucamonga Dog Park, Rancho
Cucamonga**
North end of East Avenue north of Summit Avenue;
the dog park is part of Etiwanda Creek Park
Daily dawn-dusk
Fences, trees, parking, telephones, restrooms, water,
dog washing facility, puppy/small dog area.

Redondo Beach Dog Park, Redondo Beach
rbdogpark.com
Located on the southeast corner of 190th Street and
Flagler Lane
Daily sunrise-9 p.m.; closed Wed. dawn-noon for
maintenance
Fences, benches, disposal bags, trees, parking,
telephones, water, trash cans, separate fenced
small-dog area. Access for the disabled.

Bannon Creek Dog Park, Sacramento
cityofsacramento.org/parks/dogpark1.htm
In Bannon Creek Park on Bannon Creek Drive, off of
Azevedo Drive (near West El Camino)
Daily sunrise-10 p.m.
Well-fenced, about a half-acre, bench, water spigot for
dogs, trash cans, disposal bags. Access for the
disabled.

Granite Dog Park, Sacramento
cityofsacramento.org/parks/dogpark1.htm
On Ramona Avenue off Power Inn Road (in Granite
Regional Park)
Daily sunrise-10 p.m.
Well-fenced, two acres, bench, water spigot for dogs,
trash cans, disposal bags. Access for the disabled.

Partner Park, Sacramento
cityofsacramento.org/parks/dogpark1.htm
5699 South Land Park Dr. (at Fruitridge Road), behind
Belle Cooledge Community Center
Daily sunrise-10 p.m.
Well-fenced, lighted, over two acres, landscaped with
turf and mature trees, bench, water spigot for dogs,
trash cans, disposal bags. Access for the disabled.

Balboa Park, San Diego
*ci.san-diego.ca.us/park-and-recreation/general-info/
dogs.shtml*
There are two off-leash areas within Balboa Park:
Nate's Point at El Prado, on the south side of Cabrillo
Bridge; and Morley Field, northwest of the tennis
courts.
Daily 24 hours
Large field.

Dog Beach, San Diego
*ci.san-diego.ca.us/park-and-recreation/general-info/
dogs.shtml*
Beach area is located in Ocean Beach at the west
end of Voltaire Street; enter the parking lot at the west
end of Voltaire Street.
Daily 24 hours
Disposal bags, trash cans, water, restrooms nearby.
Access for the disabled.

Fiesta Island, San Diego
*ci.san-diego.ca.us/park-and-recreation/general-info/
dogs.shtml*
This island in Mission Bay Park allows dogs anywhere
outside the fenced areas.
Daily 6 a.m.-10 p.m.

Grape Street Park, San Diego
*ci.san-diego.ca.us/park-and-recreation/general-info/
dogs.shtml*
Grape Street and Granada Avenue
Mon.-Fri. 7:30-10 a.m. and 4-9 p.m., Sat.-Sun. and
holidays 9-11 a.m. and 4-9 p.m.
Benches, tables, trees, parking, restrooms, lighted,
water, trash cans.

Alta Plaza Park, San Francisco
parks.sfgov.org
Second terrace of park, on Clay Street between Scott
and Steiner streets
Daily 6 a.m.-10 p.m.
Unfenced; dogs must be under firm voice control.

Bernal Heights, San Francisco
parks.sfgov.org
Top of the hill (the entire section bounded by Bernal
Heights Boulevard)
Daily 6 a.m.-10 p.m.
Unfenced; dogs must be under firm voice control.

Buena Vista Park, San Francisco
parks.sfgov.org
Buena Vista West at Central Avenue
Daily 6 a.m.-10 p.m.
Unfenced; dogs must be under firm voice control.

Corona Heights, San Francisco
parks.sfgov.org
Field area next to Randall Museum at Roosevelt Way
and Museum Way
Daily 6 a.m.-10 p.m.
Fenced area.

Dolores Park, San Francisco
parks.sfgov.org
South of the tennis courts between Church and
Dolores streets
Daily 6 a.m.-10 p.m.
Unfenced; dogs must be under firm voice control.

Golden Gate Park, San Francisco
parks.sfgov.org
Southeast section bounded by Lincoln Way, King
Drive and 2nd and 7th avenues
Northeast section at Stanyan and Grove streets
South-central area bounded by Martin Luther King Jr.
Drive, Middle Drive and 34th and 38th avenues
Fenced dog training area near 38th Avenue and
Fulton Street

Lafayette Park, San Francisco
parks.sfgov.org
Near Sacramento Street, between Octavia and Gough
streets
Daily 6 a.m.-10 p.m.
Unfenced; dogs must be under firm voice control.

Lake Merced, San Francisco
parks.sfgov.org
Northern lake area at Lake Merced Boulevard and
Middlefield Drive
Daily 6 a.m.-10 p.m.
Unfenced area; dogs must be under firm voice control.

McKinley Square, San Francisco
parks.sfgov.org
San Bruno Avenue and 20th Street, on the west slope
Daily 6 a.m.-10 p.m.
Unfenced area; dogs must be under firm voice control.

McLaren Park, San Francisco
parks.sfgov.org
Top of the hill at Shelley Drive and Mansell Street (the
park's southern section, reached via the 1600 block of
Geneva or the 1600 block of Sunnydale, exclusive of
significant natural resource areas)
Daily 6 a.m.-10 p.m.
Unfenced area; dogs must be under firm voice control.

Mountain Lake Park, San Francisco
parks.sfgov.org
East end of park, north of Lake Street at 8th Avenue
Daily 6 a.m.-10 p.m.
Unfenced area; dogs must be under firm voice control.

Potrero Hill Mini Park, San Francisco
parks.sfgov.org
22nd Street between Arkansas and Connecticut
streets
Daily 6 a.m.-10 p.m.
Unfenced area; dogs must be under firm voice control.

Stern Grove, San Francisco
parks.sfgov.org
North side, along Wawona Street between 21st and
23rd avenues
Daily 6 a.m.-10 p.m.
Unfenced area; dogs must be under firm voice control.

Field of Dogs, San Rafael
mariodimsn.com
3540 Civic Center Dr. near the intersection of US 101
and North San Pedro Road
Daily sunrise-sunset
Fenced, double-gated entry, parking, benches, tables,
disposal bags, trees, parking, water, trash cans,
shelter. Access for the disabled.

DeTurk Roundbarn Park, Santa Rosa
ci.santa-rosa.ca.us/econnect/Facilities/
819 Donahue St. between West 8th and 9th streets
Daily during daylight hours
Fenced, water. This is a small neighborhood park.

Doyle Park Dog Park, Santa Rosa
ci.santa-rosa.ca.us/econnect/Facilities/
700 Hoen Ave. within Doyle Park (Enter via Hoen
Avenue, go west on Sonoma, turn left on Hoen and
then turn right into the parking lot. The fenced dog
park is behind the stadium.)
Daily during daylight hours
Approximately 1/4 acre, fully fenced, bench, water,
disposal bags, bathroom nearby.

Galvin Dog Park, Santa Rosa
ci.santa-rosa.ca.us/econnect/Facilities/
3330 Yulupa Ave. (within Don Galvin Park, next to
Bennet Valley Golf Course)
Daily during daylight hours
Fenced, trees, parking, water, trash cans. Has double
gate at main entrance for easier coming and going
with your dog. Access for the disabled.

Northwest Community Dog Park, Santa Rosa
ci.santa-rosa.ca.us/econnect/Facilities/
Part of Northwest Community Park (Go west on
Gurneville Road, turn right on Marlow and then turn
right into the park's parking lot, at the first traffic light.
Walk east along the path; the dog park is on the left.)
Daily during daylight hours
Approximately 1/2 acre, fenced, separate small-dog
park adjacent, benches, bathrooms nearby, trash
cans, disposal bags. Bring a container to hold water,
as drinking fountains are nearby.

Rincon Valley Dog Park, Santa Rosa
ci.santa-rosa.ca.us/econnect/Facilities/
5108 Badger Rd. (within Rincon Valley Community
Park)
Daily during daylight hours
Approximately 1/2 acre, fenced, benches, tables,
access for the disabled, disposal bags, trees, parking,
phones, restrooms, water, trash cans, fenced pond
area for dogs, separate fenced large- and small-dog
areas. Large-dog area closes during the winter; pond
and small-dog exercise area are open year-round.
Monitors are present during peak hours to enforce
rules.

Off-leash, unfenced, under voice control areas:

Doyle Park, Santa Rosa
ci.santa-rosa.ca.us/econnect/Facilities/
Mon.-Fri. 6-8 a.m. and 4-7 p.m., early Apr.-late Oct.;
6-8 a.m. and 4-6 p.m., rest of year
Dogs may be off leash but under voice control in the
area in front of the caretaker's residence (designated
by signs and maps in the parking lot).

700 Doyle Park Drive, Santa Rosa
ci.santa-rosa.ca.us/econnect/Facilities/
Enter on Hoen Avenue, go west on Sonoma, turn left
on Hoen and then turn right into the parking lot. There
is an unfenced, off-leash area to the right of the
fenced dog park.
Daily 6-8 a.m.

Franklin Park, Santa Rosa
ci.santa-rosa.ca.us/econnect/Facilities/
2095 Franklin Ave.
Daily 6-8 a.m.

Southwest Community, Santa Rosa
ci.santa-rosa.ca.us/econnect/Facilities/
1698 Hearn Ave.
Daily 6-8 a.m.

Youth Community, Santa Rosa
ci.santa-rosa.ca.us/econnect/Facilities/
1725 Fulton Rd.
Daily 6-8 a.m.

Remington Dog Park, Sausalito
dogpark-sausalito.com
Ebbtide at Bridgeway
Mon.-Fri. 7-7, Sat.-Sun. 8-7
Fully fenced with safety gated entrance, water, tents
for shelter, parking, scoops and scooper cleaning
station, trash cans, lighted, tennis balls and racquets
provided, picnic tables and benches.

Sierra Madre Dog Park, Sierra Madre
611 East Sierra Madre Blvd.
Daily 6 a.m.-10 p.m.
Fenced, double-gated entry, benches, access for the
disabled, disposal bags, trees, parking, phones,
restrooms, lighted, water, trash cans, separate fenced
areas for large/active dogs and "special needs" dogs.

Ernest Holman Memorial Dog Park, Sonoma
First Street West, north of Depot Park (next to the
police station and across from the Veteran's Memorial
Building)
Daily sunrise-sunset; subject to closure on rainy days
Fenced, benches, tables, disposal bags, trees, lighted,
parking, water, trash cans, double-gated entry. Access
for the disabled.

Colorado

Grandview Off-Leash Dog Park, Aurora
For additional information phone (303) 739-7160
17900 E. Quincy Ave. (west of Quincy Reservoir and
just east of Pitkin Street)
Daily dawn-dusk
Fenced, parking, water, trash cans.

Dog Park, Boulder
fidos.org
Valmont and Airport roads
Daily dawn-dusk
Fenced, disposal bags, parking, trash cans, water.
Access for the disabled.

East Boulder Community, Boulder
fidos.org
5660 Sioux Dr.
Daily dawn-dusk
Fenced, disposal bags, parking, water, trash cans,
fenced-off swimming area. Access for the disabled.

Howard H. Hueston Park, Boulder
fidos.org
34th Street near O'Neal Parkway
Daily dawn-dusk
Benches, tables, trees, parking, trash cans. Access for
the disabled.

Palmer Park, Colorado Springs
At Maizeland Road and Academy Boulevard
Daily 5 a.m.-11 p.m., May-Oct.; 5 a.m.-9 p.m., rest of
year
Fenced, benches, tables, parking, water, trash cans,
disposal bags, phones, restrooms. Access for the
disabled.

Rampart Dog Park, Colorado Springs
8270 Lexington Dr. (from the intersection of Lexington
Drive and N. Union Boulevard, go north on Lexington,
then turn left into the park entrance)
Daily 5 a.m.-11 p.m., May-Oct.; 5 a.m.-9 p.m., rest of
year
Fenced, benches, trees, parking, disposal bags, water,
trash cans. Access for the disabled.

Denver Off-Leash Dog Park, Denver
*denvergov.com or email kelledl@ci.denver.co.us for
additional information*
666 South Jason St. (the large field behind the
Division of Animal Control)
Daily sunrise-sunset
Fenced, parking. Access for the disabled.

Florida

Happy Tails Canine Park, Bradenton
51st Street West at G.T. Bray Park, about halfway
between Manatee Avenue and Cortez Road
Daily dawn-dusk
Approximately 3 acres, 8-foot fence, benches, tables,
parking (including handicapped spaces), disposal
bags, trees, restrooms (a short walk outside the park),
water, trash cans.

**Dr. Paul's Pet Care Center Dog Park, Coral
Springs**
TopPetCare.com
Off Sportsplex Drive in the Sportsplex Regional Park
Complex (park off Sportsplex Drive at the west
pedestrian entrance)
Daily sunrise-sunset
Enclosed, paved running path, watering area, dog
shower, dog statues, landscaping, disposal bag
dispensers, trash barrels, picnic table, dog agility
equipment, gazebo, trees, shaded area.

The Dog Park in Lake Ida Park, Delray Beach
co.palm-beach.fl.us/parks/Dogpark.htm
2929 Lake Ida Rd. (take the Atlantic Avenue West exit
off I-95, proceed west to Congress Avenue, go north
on Congress for 1 mile, turn right onto Lake Ida
Road, proceed east just past I-95, park entrance is on
the left)
Daily sunrise-sunset
2.5 acres, separate fenced areas for large and small
dogs, two canine drinking stations, dog washing area,
eight shaded sitting areas, paved pathway, dispensers
and receptacles for disposal bags, restrooms and
parking areas nearby, information kiosk.

Bark Park at Snyder Park, Fort Lauderdale
ci.fort-lauderdale.fl.us/cityparks/snyder/barkpark
3299 S.W. 4th Ave. (dogs must remain in the car until
arrival at the Bark Park and are not permitted in the
remainder of Snyder Park)
Daily 7-7, early Apr.-late Oct.; 7-6:30, rest of year
Fee Mon.-Fri. $1.50; ages 6-12, $1. Fee Sat.-Sun.
and holidays $2; ages 6-12, $1.50.
Fenced, benches, trees, disposal bags, parking,
restrooms, water, trash cans, agility equipment,
separate small-dog area, two hose stations, drinking
fountains, two open-air pavilions, small nature area
with more than 20 labeled native trees. Access for the
disabled.

Dog Wood Off-Leash Park, Gainesville
dogwoodpark.com
5505 S.W. Archer Rd., 1 mile west of I-75
Sat.-Sun. 10-5
Fee $1.50, plus $5 for the first dog and $2 for each
additional dog
Approximately 15 acres, 6-foot-high chain link fence,
double-gated entrances and exits, jogging trail,
hammocks, picnic tables, lounge chairs, swinging
benches, regular benches, two huge dog swimming
ponds, kiddie pools, fountain, gazebo, agility course,
sunny and shady small-dog areas, dog shower, indoor
restrooms, soft drinks for sale, free bottled water,
agility equipment, park-provided tennis balls, multiple
clean-up stations with disposal bags. Dog Wood Park
also offers a do-it-yourself dog wash, a doggie
boutique, dog day care, and agility and obedience
training.

St. Johns County Paw Park, St. Augustine
sjcpawpark@cs.com
Located just inside Treaty Park, a 40-acre multi-use
park in southern St. Johns County (take I-95 exit 94
and proceed north to Wildwood Drive; the park is
situated between US 1 and SR 207 on Wildwood
Drive)
Daily sunrise-sunset
Approximately 1 acre, completely fenced off-leash
exercise area, shade trees, parking, restrooms, mutt
mitts and scoopers, trash cans, automatic refillable
water bowls, benches, agility equipment, separate
small-dog area.

Paw Park of Historic Sanford, Sanford
pawparksanford.org
427 French Ave. (US 17/92) in Sanford's Historic
District. From I-4, take the SR 46 exit (exit 51,
Sanford/Mount Dora), proceed east on SR 46
approximately 4 miles to French Avenue, turn right
(southbound) and get into the left-thru lane; the Paw
Park is on the left just past the Burger King.
Daily 7:30-7:30
Fenced, double-gated entrance, benches, tables,
self-watering bowls, dog showers, small-dog area,
disposal bag dispensers, parking, community bulletin
board, nicely shaded with mature oak trees, 20
minutes north of downtown Orlando. Access for the
disabled.

Lakeview Park, Sarasota
co.sarasota.fl.us/parks/pawpark.asp
7150 Lago St.
Daily dawn-dusk
Six-foot fence, benches, tables, disposal bags, many
trees, parking, restrooms, water, trash cans, dog
shower, community bulletin board, small-dog area,
double-gated entrance. Access for the disabled.

Sarasota Paw Park, Sarasota
co.sarasota.fl.us/parks/pawpark.asp
4570 17th St.
Daily dawn-midnight (lighted)
Approximately 6 acres, 6-foot fence, lighted, benches,
tables, disposal bags, trees, parking, restrooms, water,
trash cans, dog shower, small-dog area, double-gated
entrance, community bulletin board. Access for the
disabled.

Brohard Beach, Venice
co.sarasota.fl.us/parks/pawpark.asp
1600 Harbor Dr.
Daily dawn-dusk
Boardwalk to beach, parking, trash cans.

Brohard Paw Park, Venice
co.sarasota.fl.us/parks/pawpark.asp
1600 Harbor Dr.
Daily dawn-dusk
Six-foot fence, benches, tables, shelter, disposal bags,
trees, parking, water, trash cans, small-dog area, dog
shower, community bulletin board. Access for the
disabled.

Woodmere Paw Park, Venice
co.sarasota.fl.us/parks/pawpark.asp
3951 Merewood Blvd. (at Alligator Creek near
Jacaranda)
Daily dawn-dusk
Fenced, double-gated entrance, benches, tables,
disposal bags, trees, parking, restrooms, water, trash
cans, double-gated small-dog section near the front
gate, dog shower, community bulletin board. Access
for the disabled.

Michigan

Lyon Oaks Bark Park, Lyon Township
co.oakland.mi.us/arc/c_serv/parks/orionoks.html
Pontiac Trail, between Wixom and Old Plank roads
Daily half an hour before sunrise-half an hour after
sunset
A park pass is required; daily and annual passes are
available at the park. Non-resident fee $8 per vehicle
for daily entry, $46 for an annual pass; over 61, $3
per vehicle for daily entry, $17 for an annual pass.
13 acres, fenced, benches, tables, disposal bags,
parking, restrooms, trash cans, open fields. (opening
May 2002)

Orion Oaks Bark Park, Lake Orion
co.oakland.mi.us/arc/c_serv/parks/orionoks.html
Off Joslyn Road, south of Clarkston Road (park at the
north Joslyn Road entrance and follow the signs)
Daily half an hour before sunrise-half an hour after
sunset
A park pass is required. A daily pass is available at
the Lake Orion Township office (open Mon.-Fri.),
located on Joslyn Road south of the park, or at
Independence Oaks County Park (open daily), located
on Sashabaw Road 2 1/2 miles north of I-75.
Non-resident fee $8 per vehicle for daily entry, $46 for
an annual pass; over 61, $3 per vehicle for daily
entry, $17 for an annual pass.
Fenced, benches, tables, disposal bags, trees, water
source, parking, Portajohns, trash cans. Access for the
disabled. A portion of Lake Sixteen is reserved for
canine swimmers.

Minnesota

Bloomington Off-Leash Area, Bloomington
*ci.bloomington.mn.us/cityhall/dept/commserv/parkrec/
offbromp.htm*
111th and Nesbitt streets
Daily dawn-10 p.m.
Approximately 25 acres, partially fenced, tables,
disposal bags, trees, parking, trash cans, swimming
hole available. Access for the disabled.

Columbia Park, Minneapolis
mromp.org
St. Anthony Parkway off Central Avenue
Daily 6 a.m.-10 p.m.
Approximately 2 acres, double-gated entry at the east
and west ends of the park, fully fenced, parking,
disposal bag dispensers, bench.

Franklin Terrace, Minneapolis
mromp.org
Franklin Terrace and 30th Avenue S.
Daily 6 a.m.-10 p.m.
2.6 acres, fully fenced, double-gated entry at the east
and west ends of the site, disposal bag dispensers,
bench, on-street parking.

Lake of the Isles Park, Minneapolis
mromp.org
Lake of the Isles Parkway and W. 28th Street
Daily 6 a.m.-10 p.m.
2.6 acres, fully fenced, two double-gated entry
vestibules at the northern end of the site, lighted at
the southern end, disposal bag dispensers, benches.

Minnehaha Park, Minneapolis
mromp.org
Minnehaha Avenue and E. 54th Street
Daily 6 a.m.-10 p.m.
Approximately 4.2 acres along the Mississippi River
(where dogs can swim), fenced, disposal bag
dispensers, lighted parking area, Portajohn in parking
area.

Nevada

Desert Breeze Park, Las Vegas
co.clark.nv.us/parks/Dog_Parks.htm
8425 W. Spring Mountain Road (at Durango)
Fenced, benches, disposal bags, trees, parking,
phones, lighted, restrooms, trash cans, water. The dog
park is a couple of fenced acres (with two or three
palm trees) within a larger park. There are three
separate areas for different sized dogs.

Desert Inn Dog Park, Las Vegas
co.clark.nv.us/parks/Dog_Parks.htm
3570 Vista del Monte
Daily 6 a.m.-11 p.m.
Fenced, water, benches, minimal lighting.

Dog Fancier's Park, Las Vegas
co.clark.nv.us/parks/Dog_Parks.htm
5800 E. Flamingo Rd., near Stephanie Street
Daily 6 a.m.-11 p.m., early Apr.-late Oct. (summer
hours)
Approximately 12 acres, fenced, benches, tables,
trees, parking, phones, lighted, restrooms, trash cans,
water. Access for the disabled.

Shadow Rock Dog Park, Las Vegas
co.clark.nv.us/parks/Dog_Parks.htm
2650 Los Feliz, near Lake Mead and N. Hollywood
boulevards
Daily dawn-dusk
Fenced, benches, disposal bags, trees, parking, trash
cans, water, shaded shelters with benches.

Sunset Park, Las Vegas
co.clark.nv.us/parks/Dog_Parks.htm
2601 E. Sunset Rd.
Daily 6 a.m.-11 p.m.
Approximately 9 acres, fenced, benches, tables, trees,
disposal bags, parking, restrooms, lighted, phones (in
the main park), water, trash cans. Access for the
disabled. The dog park is a special fenced-in area in
the southwest corner of Sunset Park. The closest
parking to the dog park is off Eastern Avenue
between Sunset and Warm Springs roads.

New York

New York City (Manhattan and boroughs)
urbanhound.com
*nycparks.completeinet.net/sub_things_to_do/facilities/
af_dog_runs.html*

Brooklyn

Owl's Head Park, Bay Ridge
68th Street and Shore Road
Disposal bags, tree, grass surface.

Hillside Park, Brooklyn Heights
Columbia Heights and Middagh Street
Daily 24 hours
Fenced.

Palmetto Playground, Brooklyn Heights
Columbia Place and State Street (in a corner by the
BQE)
Daily 24 hours
Water supply, four benches, one park light.

Prospect Park, Brooklyn Heights
fidobrooklyn.org
Grand Army Plaza and Flatbush; off-leash areas may
be accessed from all park entrances
Daily 9-9, Apr.-Oct.; 9-5, rest of year (in the 80-acre
Long Meadow and 6-acre Peninsula Meadow). Dogs
may be off-leash in the 15-acre Nethermead Mon.-Fri.
9-5 year-round (except holidays). On holidays and
weekends, the hours above apply to Nethermead as
well. At all other times, dogs must be on a leash.
Trees, restrooms (at Long Meadow only; may not be
available early in the morning), water; some fountains
equipped with troughs for dogs.
Note: There are no fenced dog areas. Dogs may be
off-leash with appropriate supervision in three large
meadows at the hours specified above; please
observe all off-leash rules. Dogs must be on a leash
at all other places and times.

Bronx

Ewen Park ("John's Run"), Riverdale
Riverdale to Johnson avenues, south of West 232nd
Street and down the steps in the clearing on the right.
Daily dawn-dusk
Plastic lawn furniture, scenic views.

Seton Park, Riverdale
West 235th Street and Independence Avenue (west of
Independence on 235th Street, near the Spuyten
Duyvil Library)
Daily dawn-dusk

Canine Court, Van Cortlandt Park
West 252nd Street and Broadway (enter on the path
on 252nd and follow it about 100 feet to the left)
Daily dawn-dusk
Two huge runs, a basic dog run and a canine agility
playground with a teeter-totter, hurdles, a ladder, three
chutes and a hanging tire.

Manhattan

Tompkins Square Park, East Village
East 9th Street at Avenue B
Daily 6 a.m.-midnight
Benches, picnic tables, water, a dog memorial.

Madison Square Park, Gramercy/Flatiron/Union Square
East 24th Street at Fifth Avenue
Daily 6 a.m.-midnight
Disposal bags, water supply, benches, trees.

Union Square Dog Run, Gramercy/Flatiron/Union Square
West 15th Street and Union Square West
Daily dawn-dusk
Benches, two picnic tables, scoopers.

Thomas Jefferson Park, Harlem
East 112th Street at First Avenue
Daily 24 hours
Benches, wood chips.

J. Hood Wright Park, Inwood/Ft George/ Washington Heights
West 173rd Street between Fort Washington Avenue
and Haven Avenue

Fishbridge Park, Lower East Side
Dover Street at Pearl Street. just south of the
Brooklyn Bridge
Daily dawn-dusk
Water hose, wading pool (summer only), benches,
lock-box for toys, lock-box with newspapers for picking
up after your dog.

Peter Detmold Park, Midtown East
East 49th Street at FDR Drive (behind Beekman
Place)
Daily dawn-9 p.m., June-Sept.; dawn-8 p.m., Mar.-May
and Oct.-Nov.; dawn-7 p.m., rest of year
Benches, disposal bags, trees, historical lamps.

Carl Shurz Park, Upper East Side
East 86th Street at East End Avenue
Daily dawn-1 a.m.
Benches, scoops, pea gravel surface. Past the main
run, toward the East River, is a second run for small
dogs that has a superb view of the river and the 59th
Street Bridge.

Riverside Park at 72nd Street, Upper West Side/Morningside Heights
rspfloral.org
West 72nd Street
Daily 6 a.m.-1 a.m.
Bench, disposal bags, scoopers, hanging flowerpots.

Riverside Park at 105th Street, Upper West Side/Morningside Heights
riversidedog.org
West 105th Street, Riverside Park Central Promenade
Daily dawn-dusk
Water fountain for dogs, small-dog area, disposal bag
dispensers, benches, trees, crushed granite surface.

Theodore Roosevelt Park, Upper West Side/ Morningside Heights
West 81st Street at Columbus Avenue
Daily 8 a.m.-10 p.m.
Water faucets for dogs, a water fountain for humans,
many benches, a separate run for small dogs, shade
trees.

Washington Square Park, West Village
West 4th Street at Thompson Street
Daily 6 a.m.-midnight
Benches, trees, water hose, water bowls, scoopers,
pea gravel surface.

Queens

Doughboy Plaza, Woodside
Windmuller Park
Woodside Avenue from 54th to 56th streets (also
south of Woodside at 56th Street)
Daily dawn-dusk
Fenced, trash can.

North Carolina

French Broad River Link Dog Park, Asheville
ci.asheville.nc.us/parks/parks&play_areas.htm
Within French Broad River Link Park (closest cross
streets are Amboy and Lyman)
Daily dawn-dusk
Fenced, benches, disposal bags, trees, parking,
restrooms, water, trash cans, scenic views of the
French Broad River, convenient to downtown
Asheville.

Ohio

Mt. Airy Dog Park, Cincinnati
cinci-parks.org
Located within Mt. Airy Forest's Highpoint Picnic Area on Westwood Northern Boulevard, between Montana Avenue and North Bend Road
Daily dawn-dusk
Fenced, benches, tables, trees, parking, restrooms, water, trash cans, shelter. Access for the disabled.
Upper Arlington (all city public parks)
ua-ohio.net
Daily 8-8, Apr.-Oct.; 8-5, rest of year
No fenced areas, dogs must be under voice control at all times when off-leash, owners must bring their own disposal bags.

Oregon

Alton Baker Park, Eugene
ci.eugene.or.us
South side of Day Island Road
Daily 6 a. m.-11 p.m.
Fenced, parking, water, disposal bag receptacles, benches and/or tables and simple shelters for protection from sun/rain.
Amazon Park, Eugene
ci.eugene.or.us
East of 29th Street and Amazon Parkway until summer 2002, thereafter south of Leo Harris Parkway near Autzen Stadium
Daily 6 a.m.-11 p.m.
Fenced, water, disposal bag receptacles, benches and/or tables and simple shelters for protection from sun/rain, parking nearby.
Morse Ranch, Eugene
ci.eugene.or.us
Crest Drive and Lincoln Street
Park in the main parking area at 595 Crest Dr. and take the trail east
Daily 6 a.m.-11 p.m.
Fenced, water, disposal bag receptacles, benches and/or tables and simple shelters for protection from sun/rain.
Chimney Park, Portland
parks.ci.portland.or.us/DogsinParks/offLeashAreas.htm
9360 N. Columbia Blvd.
16 acres of off-leash meadow and trails. Partial fencing along a busy road; dogs should be under excellent voice command.
West Delta Park, Portland
parks.ci.portland.or.us/DogsinParks/offLeashAreas.htm
North Expo and Broadacre roads (located just north of Portland International Raceway)
Off-leash site, large open field that can be used only when there are no official events taking place in the park. Guardrail fencing only; dogs should be under excellent voice command.

Pennsylvania

Orianna Hill Park, Philadelphia
oriannahill.org
901-913 N. Orianna St.
Daily 24 hours
Fenced, benches, disposal bags, trees, trash cans. Please remember to pick up after your dog.

Schuylkill River Dog Run, Philadelphia
phillyfido.net
25th Street between Locust and Spruce streets
Daily 24 hours
Fenced, benches, trees, trash cans.

Texas

White Rock Lake Dog Park, Dallas
dallasdogparks.org
Mockingbird Point within White Rock Lake Park
Tues.-Sun. 5 a.m.-midnight
Approximately two acres, fenced, benches, disposal bags, trees, parking, restrooms, trash cans, water fountains.

Virginia

Ben Brenman Park, Alexandria
ci.alexandria.va.us/rpca/rpca__dogpark.html
Along Backlick Creek
Daily 6 a.m.-10 p.m.
Fenced, trash bins, parking, disposal bag dispensers.
Chetworth Park, Alexandria
ci.alexandria.va.us/rpca/rpca__dogpark.html
At Chetworth Place
Daily 6 a.m.-10 p.m.
Fenced, trash bins, parking, disposal bag dispensers.
Dog Park, Alexandria
ci.alexandria.va.us/rpca/rpca__dogpark.html
5000 block of Duke Street east of the Charles E. Beatley, Jr. Library
Daily 6 a.m.-10 p.m.
Fenced, trash bins, parking, disposal bag dispensers.
Montgomery Park, Alexandria
ci.alexandria.va.us/rpca/rpca__dogpark.html
At the corner of Fairfax and 1st streets
Daily 6 a.m.-10 p.m.
Fenced, trash bins, parking, disposal bag dispensers.
Simpson Stadium Park, Alexandria
ci.alexandria.va.us/rpca/rpca__dogpark.html
At Monroe Avenue
Daily 6 a.m.-10 p.m.
Fenced, trash bins, parking, disposal bag dispensers, dog-accessible water fountains.

Off-leash, unfenced, under voice control areas:

Chinquapin Park, Alexandria
ci.alexandria.va.us/rpca/rpca__dogpark.html
At the east end of the loop road
Daily 6 a.m.-10 p.m.
Unfenced site.
Hooff's Run, Alexandria
ci.alexandria.va.us/rpca/rpca__dogpark.html
East of Commonwealth Avenue between Oak and Chapman streets
Daily 6 a.m.-10 p.m.
Unfenced site.
Monticello Park, Alexandria
ci.alexandria.va.us/rpca/rpca__dogpark.html
Area to the east of the entrance
Daily 6 a.m.-10 p.m.
Unfenced 50-foot by 200-foot site.

Pommander Park, Alexandria
ci.alexandria.va.us/rpca/rpca_dogpark.html
Southwest corner of Gibbon and Union streets
Daily 6 a.m.-10 p.m.
Unfenced site.

Tarleton Park, Alexandria
ci.alexandria.va.us/rpca/rpca_dogpark.html
Along Old Mill Run west of Gordon Street
Daily 6 a.m.-10 p.m.
Unfenced site.

Dog exercise area, Alexandria
ci.alexandria.va.us/rpca/rpca_dogpark.html
Northeast corner of Founders Park (at Oronoco Street
and the Potomac River)
Daily 6 a.m.-10 p.m.
Unfenced 100-foot by 100-foot site.

Dog exercise area, Alexandria
ci.alexandria.va.us/rpca/rpca_dogpark.html
Southeast corner of Braddock Road and
Commonwealth Avenue
Daily 6 a.m.-10 p.m.
Unfenced site.

Dog exercise area, Alexandria
ci.alexandria.va.us/rpca/rpca_dogpark.html
Area between Ft. Williams and New Ft. Williams
Parkway
Daily 6 a.m.-10 p.m.
Unfenced site.

Dog exercise area, Alexandria
ci.alexandria.va.us/rpca/rpca_dogpark.html
Southeast corner of Armistead and Beauregard streets
Daily 6 a.m.-10 p.m.
Unfenced site.

Dog exercise area, Alexandria
ci.alexandria.va.us/rpca/rpca_dogpark.html
Along Chambliss Street, south of the tennis courts at
Grigsby Avenue
Daily 6 a.m.-10 p.m.
Unfenced site.

Dog exercise area, Alexandria
ci.alexandria.va.us/rpca/rpca_dogpark.html
East side of entrance to Fort Ward Park
Daily 6 a.m.-10 p.m.
Unfenced 100-foot by 100-foot site

Dog exercise area, Alexandria
ci.alexandria.va.us/rpca/rpca_dogpark.html
From Median to Timberbranch Parkway between
Braddock Road and Oakley Place
Daily 6 a.m.-10 p.m.
Unfenced site.

Dog exercise area, Alexandria
ci.alexandria.va.us/rpca/rpca_dogpark.html
Area west of the Edison Street cul-de-sac, between
the bike trail and Berkey Photo Processing
Daily 6 a.m.-10 p.m.
Unfenced site.

Dog exercise area, Alexandria
ci.alexandria.va.us/rpca/rpca_dogpark.html
200 feet of the W&OD Railroad right-of-way
located south of Raymond Avenue
Daily 6 a.m.-10 p.m.
Unfenced site.

Benjamin Banneker Park, Arlington County
arlingtondogs.org
1600 block of North Sycamore Street (Take I-66 west
to Sycamore Street/exit 69. Turn left on Sycamore
and proceed past the East Falls Church Metro Station.
Turn right onto North 16th Street and take the first
right, which dead ends at the dog exercise area.)
Daily sunrise to a half-hour after sunset
Fully fenced, water source.

Fort Barnard Park, Arlington County
arlingtondogs.org
Corner of South Pollard Street and South Walter Reed
Drive (From Route 50, take Glebe Road south. Turn
right on South Walter Reed Drive and proceed to
Pollard Street; the park is on the right-hand side.)
Daily sunrise to a half-hour after sunset
Fully fenced, water source, picnic table and benches.

Glencarlyn Park, Arlington County
arlingtondogs.org
301 South Harrison St. (From Route 50, head west to
the Carlin Springs Road exit. Exit right and then turn
left at the stop sign. Pass under Route 50 and follow
Carlin Springs to 4th Street. Turn left on 4th Street
and proceed five blocks until the road ends at the
Glencarlyn Park sign. Follow the park road until it
ends. Park and walk over a small bridge and stream
to the exercise area.)
Daily sunrise to a half-hour after sunset
Unfenced area located near a creek and woods.

Madison Community Center, Arlington County
arlingtondogs.org
3829 North Stafford St. (From Lee Highway/US 29
northbound or southbound, turn onto Military Road
and follow it to the end. Turn left onto Old Glebe
Road; the exercise area is on the left. Drive past and
turn left into the Community Center entrance. Park in
the center's front lot and walk to the left of the
building to enter the area.)
Daily sunrise to a half-hour after sunset
Fully fenced.

Shirlington Park, Arlington County
arlingtondogs.org
2601 S. Arlington Mill Dr. (The dog area is located
along the bicycle path behind a storage facility that
borders South Four Mile Run, between Shirlington
Road and South Walter Reed Drive; it is close to but
not in Jennie Dean Park. Heading east on South Four
Mile Run, take a right on Nelson; heading west, take
a left. Proceed on Nelson and park behind the
storage facility. The dog area is between the facility
and the water; there is no signage indicating its
location.)
Daily sunrise to a half-hour after sunset
Partially fenced, water source.

Towers Park, Arlington County
arlingtondogs.org
801 South Scott St. (From I-395 North or South, take
Columbia Pike west toward Bailey's Crossroads. Stay
in the right-hand lane and take a right on Scott Street
at the white church. Proceed until the road ends at
the parking lot. The exercise area is behind the tennis
courts.)
Daily sunrise to a half-hour after sunset
Fully fenced, water source, limited parking.

Utah Park, Arlington County
arlingtondogs.org
3308 S. Stafford St. (From I-395 North or South, take the Shirlington exit and follow signs to Quaker Lane. From Quaker Lane, take the first right onto 32nd Road S. Take the next right onto S. Stafford Street and follow the curve to the yield sign. At the sign, turn left onto 32nd Street. Park at the bottom of the hill or along the street. The dog exercise area is on the far side of the softball diamond from the parking lot.)
Daily sunrise to a half-hour after sunset
Fully fenced, water source.

Blake Lake Park, Oakton
10033 Blake Lane (near Bushman Drive)
Daily sunrise-sunset
Approximately 1/3 acre, fully fenced, benches, parking, trash cans. Children under 9 are not permitted. Capacity limited to 25 dogs. Please bring water and disposal bags. Parking is available at the Recycling Center on Blake Lane.

Red Wing Park, Virginia Beach
vbgov.com/dept/parks/dogpark.asp
1398 General Booth Blvd.
Daily 7:30 a.m.-sunset; closed Jan. 1, Lee-Jackson-Kind Day, Veterans Day, Thanksgiving and Dec. 25
Fenced, benches, disposal bags, parking, restrooms, water. Access for the disabled. Fee $3 for first-time visitors, who must register at the park office, show proof of their pet's rabies shot and vaccines, and obtain a city dog license.

Woodstock Community Park, Virginia Beach
vbgov.com/dept/parks/dogpark.asp
5709 Providence Rd.
Daily 7:30 a.m.-sunset; closed Jan. 1, Lee-Jackson-Kind Day, Veterans Day, Thanksgiving and Dec. 25
Fenced, benches, disposal bags, parking, restrooms, water. Access for the disabled. Fee $3 for first-time visitors, who must register at the park office, show proof of their pet's rabies shot and vaccines, and obtain a city dog license.

Washington

Dr. Jose Rizal Park, Seattle
coladog.org
1008 12th Ave. South on North Beacon Hill (off-leash area is in the lower portion of the park)
Daily 6 a.m.-11 p.m.
4 acres, fenced, double-gated entry, parking, beautiful view of downtown.

Genesee Park, Seattle
coladog.org
46th Avenue South and South Genesee Street
Daily 6 a.m.-11 p.m.
Fenced, double-gated entry, disposal bags, doggie drinking fountain, parking.

Golden Gardens Park, Seattle
coladog.org
8498 Seaview Place N.W. in Ballard
Daily 6 a.m.-11 p.m.
Fenced, lighted, parking. The off-leash area is located in the upper (eastern) portion of the park, not in the lower beach area. Please note that dogs are not allowed on the beach.

I-90 "Blue Dog Pond," Seattle
coladog.org
Martin Luther King Jr. Way and South Massachusetts Street, on the northwest corner
Daily 6 a.m.-11 p.m.
Fenced, parking, sculpture of large blue dog. Note: There are no off-leash areas in I-90 Lid Park, located just east of Blue Dog Pond.

Magnuson Park, Seattle
coladog.org
6500 Sandpoint Way N.E.
Daily 6 a.m.-11 p.m.
The off-leash area is located along the eastern and northern boundary of the park, with some beach access in the park's northeast corner.

Northacres Park, Seattle
coladog.org
West of I-5 at North 130th Street
Daily 6 a.m.-11 p.m.
Fenced, parking. The off-leash area is in the northeast corner of the park at 12530 Third Ave. N.E., north of the ball field. Parking is available on the west side of the park along 1st Street N.E. and on the south side along North 125th Street.

Westcrest Park, Seattle
coladog.org
8806 8th Ave. S.W. in West Seattle
Daily 6 a.m.-11 p.m.
Unfenced site, parking. The off-leash area is located along the southern and western border of the reservoir.

Woodland Park, Seattle
coladog.org
West of the tennis courts on West Green Lake Way North
Daily 6 a.m.-11 p.m.
Fenced, doggie drinking fountain, parking.

Canada

Alberta

91 Street Right of Way, Edmonton
gov.edmonton.ab.ca/comm_services/parkland_services/parks/parks_for_paws.html
Berm east of 91 Street, starting at 10 Avenue and extending north to Whitemud Freeway and east to 76 Street
Unfenced site.

Buana Vista Great Meadow, Edmonton
gov.edmonton.ab.ca/comm_services/parkland_services/parks/parks_for_paws.html
North of Laurier Park and Buena Vista Drive and south of Melton Ravine (in the vicinity of 88 Avenue)
Unfenced site. Does not include the pedestrian bridge access trail, Yorath property or the trail north to McKenzie Ravine. This is a hot-air balloon site, so please leash your dog when balloons launch.

Hermitage Park North, Edmonton
gov.edmonton.ab.ca/comm_services/parkland_services/parks/parks_for_paws.html
129 Avenue to 137 Avenue, also 22 Street along the riverbank where signs designate an off-leash area.
Unfenced site. This is a multi-use area in the valley north of the park's fishing pond and picnic area.

Jackie Parker Park, Edmonton
gov.edmonton.ab.ca/comm_services/parkland_services/parks/parks_for_paws.html
Whitemud Freeway and 50 Street
Unfenced site. Includes the area south of the 44 Avenue entrance. Does not include golf course.

Keehewin Blackmud, Edmonton
gov.edmonton.ab.ca/comm_services/parkland_services/parks/parks_for_paws.html
Pipeline corridor, 104 Street and 20 Avenue to the south end of 109 Street (excludes Bearspaw Drive West and Blackmud Creek and Ravine)
Unfenced site.

Kennydale, Edmonton
gov.edmonton.ab.ca/comm_services/parkland_services/parks/parks_for_paws.html
Ravine west of the 40 Street loop, west to 47 Street and the top of the bank
Unfenced site.

Lauderdale, Edmonton
gov.edmonton.ab.ca/comm_services/parkland_services/parks/parks_for_paws.html
South end of Grand Trunk Park, from 127 to 129 Avenue and 113A to 109 Street
Unfenced site.

Mill Creek Ravine, Edmonton
gov.edmonton.ab.ca/comm_services/parkland_services/parks/parks_for_paws.html
Access is from 68 Avenue and 93 Street (west side of Argyll Park) or from the north side of Argyll Park
Unfenced site. A granular trail along the bottom of the ravine leads to the Whyte (82) Avenue overpass.

Saddleback Road, Edmonton
gov.edmonton.ab.ca/comm_services/parkland_services/parks/parks_for_paws.html
29 A Avenue along the powerline, and across 119 Street to the edge of Whitemud Park
Unfenced site.

Terwillegar Park, Edmonton
gov.edmonton.ab.ca/comm_services/parkland_services/parks/parks_for_paws.html
Park access via Rabbit Hill Road
Unfenced site. This is a multi-use area.

Manitoba

Bourkevale Park, Winnipeg
city.winnipeg.mb.ca/interhom/news/1998/jul28%5F98.htm
Area south of the dike, along the riverbank
Daily 6 a.m.-10 p.m.
Unfenced site, trash cans, parking, bring your own disposal bags.

Juba Park & Pioneer Avenue, Winnipeg
city.winnipeg.mb.ca/interhom/news/1998/jul28%5F98.htm
All vacant land west of the walkway to Juba Park
Daily 6 a.m.-10 p.m.
Unfenced site, trash cans, parking, bring your own disposal bags.

Kil-Cona Park, Winnipeg
city.winnipeg.mb.ca/interhom/news/1998/jul28%5F98.htm
The area north of the west parking lot
Daily 6 a.m.-10 p.m.
Unfenced site, trash cans, parking, bring your own disposal bags.

King[0092]s Park, Winnipeg
city.winnipeg.mb.ca/interhom/news/1998/jul28%5F98.htm
South end of park, south of the lake
Daily 6 a.m.-10 p.m.
Unfenced site, trash cans, parking, bring your own disposal bags.

Maple Grove Park, Winnipeg
city.winnipeg.mb.ca/interhom/news/1998/jul28%5F98.htm
North area of park
Daily 6 a.m.-10 p.m.
Unfenced site, trash cans, parking, bring your own disposal bags.

Westview Park, Winnipeg
city.winnipeg.mb.ca/interhom/news/1998/jul28%5F98.htm
Entire park is an off-leash area
Daily 6 a.m.-10 p.m.
Unfenced site, trash cans, parking, bring your own disposal bags.

California

 Disneyland® Resort

(714) 781-4565, 1313 Harbor Blvd. via I-5
Disneyland Drive and Disney Way exits,
Anaheim
Disneyland® Resort consists of two
family-oriented theme parks — Disneyland Park
and Disney's California Adventure Park — and
the shops, restaurants and entertainment of
Downtown Disney®. Indoor kennel facilities $10.
Mon.-Fri. 10-8, Sat. 9 a.m.-midnight, Sun. 9
a.m.-10 p.m.; extended hours in summer.
Admission to either park $43; over 60, $41;
ages 3-9, $33. Parking fee.

 SeaWorld Adventure Park

(619) 226-3901, (714) 939-6212 or (800)
257-4268, 1720 South Shores Rd., San Diego
SeaWorld offers four major animal shows, rides
and playgrounds, a marina and exhibits
featuring marine creatures from around the
world. Pet facility provided for a nominal charge
on a first-come, first-serve basis. Opens daily at
9, mid-June through Labor Day; at 10, rest of
year. Closing times vary. Admission $41.95;
over 54, $38.95; ages 3-11, $31.95.
Parking fee.

 Universal Studios Hollywood

(800) 864-8377, 100 Universal Dr., Universal
City
In addition to thrill rides and arcade games,
Universal Studios gives visitors a
behind-the-scenes look at the workings of a
major film and TV studio. Complimentary kennel
service. Daily 8 a.m.-10 p.m., in summer; 9-7
rest of year. Box office closes at 5 in summer,
at 4 rest of year. Closed Thanksgiving and Dec.
25. Admission $43; over 59, $37; ages 3-11,
$33. Parking fee.

District of Columbia

 Washington Monument

(202) 426-6841, off 14th Street N.W. at the
west end of the National Mall, Washington, D.C.
This instantly recognizable 555-foot marble
obelisk commemorates our nation's first
president and is surrounded by grounds that
extend for several blocks. Pets on leash. Daily
8 a.m.-11:45 p.m., Apr. 1-Labor Day; 9-5, rest of
year. Closed Dec. 25. Free.

Florida

 Walt Disney World® Resort

(407) 824-4321, theme parks accessible from
US 192, Osceola Parkway and several I-4 exits,
Lake Buena Vista
Walt Disney World has — count 'em — four
theme parks: Magic Kingdom® Park, Epcot®,
Disney's Animal Kingdom® Theme Park and
Disney-MGM Studios, plus shopping, dining and
entertainment at the Downtown Disney® Area.
Air-conditioned kennels. Theme parks generally
open daily at 9 a.m., closing times vary.
One-day, one-park admission $48; ages 3-9,
$38. Parking fee.

 SeaWorld Orlando

(407) 351-3600, 7007 Sea World Dr. at I-4 and
SR 528 (Bee Line Expressway), Orlando
A research facility as well as a theme park,
SeaWorld Orlando presents crowd-pleasing
animal shows starring a family of seven
performing killer whales. Air-conditioned kennels.
Generally opens daily at 9; closing times vary.
Admission $49.95; ages 3-9, $40.95.
Parking fee.

 Universal Orlando

(407) 363-8000, off I-4 exit 30A (eastbound) or
29B (westbound), Orlando
At Universal Orlando you can "ride the movies"
at the Universal Studios theme park, cavort with
superheroes and cartoon characters at the
Islands of Adventure theme park, or visit the
specialty shops, celebrity-themed restaurants
and entertainment venues at CityWalk.
Air-conditioned kennels. Theme parks open
daily at 9 a.m.; closing times vary by season.
CityWalk open daily 11 a.m.-2 a.m. Admission
to either park $49.95; ages 3-9, $40.95.
Parking fee.

 Busch Gardens Tampa Bay

(813) 987-5082, 3000 E. Busch Blvd., Tampa
This African-themed family entertainment park
and outstanding zoological facility features all
kinds of thrill rides and numerous opportunities
for animal observation. Outdoor kennel facilities.
Generally open daily at 9 a.m.; closing times
vary. Admission $47.95; ages 3-9, $38.95.
Parking fee.

Georgia

 Six Flags Over Georgia

(770) 739-3400, 7561 Six Flags Pkwy. (off I-20), Austell
Six Flags offers more than 100 rides, attractions and shows, a 12,000-seat concert amphitheater, Broadway-style musical shows and a nightly summer fireworks display. Kennel facilities (water provided, but no food). Open daily at 10 a.m., late May to mid-Aug.; Sat.-Sun. at 10, mid-Mar. to late May and mid-Aug. to late Oct. Closing times vary. Admission $39.05, over 54 and under 49 inches tall $19.52, under 3 free. Parking fee.

Illinois

 Six Flags Great America

(847) 249-4636, 1 mile east of I-94 on Grand Avenue (SR 132), Gurnee
Batman the Ride, Iron Wolf and Raging Bull are among the thrill rides at this family theme park, which also has a section of rides and attractions for children under 55 inches tall. Kennel facilities. Open daily at 10 a.m., late May-late Aug.; Sat.-Sun. at 10, early-late May and first 2 weekends in Sept.; Fri.-Sun. at 10, in Oct. Closing times vary. Admission $40.99; under 55 inches tall $30.99; over 59, $20.49; under 4 free. Parking fee.

Iowa

 Pella Historical Village

(641) 628-2409 or 628-4311, 507 Franklin St., Pella
A country store, log cabin, grist mill, windmill, smithy and other buildings (including Wyatt Earp's boyhood home) are reminders of this town's Dutch Heritage. Pets on leash (grounds only). Mon.-Fri. 9-5 (also Sat. 9-5, Apr.-Dec.). Admission $7; ages 5-18, $2.

Massachusetts

 Bunker Hill Monument

(617) 242-5641, in Monument Square on Breed's Hill, Charlestown
Part of Boston National Historical Park, this 221-foot-tall granite obelisk commemorates the site of the Battle of Bunker Hill on June 17, 1775. Pets on leash (grounds only). Daily 9-4:30. Free.

Mississippi

 Vicksburg National Military Park

(601) 636-0583, entered on the eastern edge from US 80
More than 1,260 memorials, monuments, statues and markers honor the Union and Confederate troops who engaged in the siege of Vicksburg in 1863. Pets on leash. Grounds open daily dawn-dusk; visitor center daily 8-5. Admission $4 per private vehicle.

Missouri

 The Gateway Arch

(877) 982-1410, Memorial Drive and Market Street, St. Louis
This curved, stainless steel monument soars 630 feet high and symbolizes the gateway to the West. A tram ride takes visitors to an observation deck. Pets on leash (grounds only). Tram ticket center open daily 8 a.m.-10 p.m., Memorial Day-Labor Day; 9-6, rest of year. Closed Jan. 1, Thanksgiving and Dec. 25. Tram ride $8; ages 13-16, $5; ages 3-12, $3.

New York

 Fort Ticonderoga

(518) 585-2821, about 1 mile east on SR 74, Ticonderoga
Built by the French in 1755, this restored fort on Lake Champlain once controlled the connecting waterway between Canada and the American Colonies. Pets on leash (designated areas only).
Site open daily 9-6, July-Aug.; 9-5, early May-June 30 and Sept. 1 to late Oct. Admission $10; over 60, $9; ages 7-12, $6.

North Carolina

 Paramount's Carowinds Theme Park

(704) 588-2600, (803) 548-5300 or (800) 888-4386, 10 miles south on I-77 to exit 90, Charlotte
Themed areas at this park depict the past and present of the Carolinas, and offer roller coasters and water rides, children's play areas and other family entertainment. Air-conditioned kennels. Open daily at 10 a.m., early June to mid-Aug.; Sat.-Sun. at 10, mid-Mar. to early June and mid-Aug. to early Oct. Closing times vary. Admission $38.99; over 55 and ages 3-6 or under 48 inches tall, $26.99. Parking fee.

Ohio

 Paramount's Kings Island

(513) 754-5700 or (800) 288-0808, Kings Island Drive (a half-mile southwest via I-71 exit 25A), Kings Mills

Kings Island is a family entertainment park featuring 13 hair-raising roller coasters; WaterWorks, a water recreation playground; costumed cartoon characters; and a variety of live shows. Free outdoor kennel facilities. Open daily at 9 a.m., late May-late Aug. and Aug. 31-Sept. 2; Sat.-Sun. at 10, early Apr. to mid-May and late Sept.-early Nov. Admission $41.99; over 59, ages 3-6 or under 48 inches tall, $20.99. Parking fee.

Pennsylvania

 Hersheypark

(800) 437-7439, just off SR 743 and US 422, Hershey

The emphasis is on thrill rides at Hersheypark, plus live entertainment that includes a marine mammal show, song and dance reviews and big-name performers. Air-conditioned kennels. Open daily at 10 a.m., late May-early Sept.; Fri.-Sun. at 10, selected weekends in May; Sat.-Sun at 10, selected weekends in Sept. Closing times vary. Admission $32.95; over 54 and ages 3-8, $17.95.

Texas

 Six Flags Over Texas

(817) 640-8900, 2201 Road to Six Flags (at the junction of I-30 and SR 360 exit 30), Arlington

Themed areas, each featuring thrill rides, food and entertainment, depict Texas under six different flags: Spain, France, Mexico, the Republic of Texas, the Confederate States of America and the United States. Air-conditioned kennels. Open daily, June 1 to mid-Aug. and mid- to late Dec.; Sat.-Sun and Labor Day, late Mar. through May 31, mid-Aug. through Oct. 31 and early to mid-Dec. Hours vary; phone ahead to confirm schedule. Admission $40.99; over 54, the physically impaired and under 48 inches tall, $20.49; under 3 free. Parking fee.

 Seaworld San Antonio

(210) 523-3611 or (800) 722-2762, 10500 Sea World Dr. (off SR 151 at the junction of Westover Hills Boulevard and Ellison Drive), San Antonio

Killer and beluga whales, sea lions, otters, walruses and dolphins perform at this marine life park, which also has shark exhibits, a penguin habitat and a children's playground. Outdoor kennel facilities (owner must provide food and water). Open daily at 10 a.m., late May to mid-Aug; Sat.-Sun. and some weekdays at 10, mid-Mar. to late May; Sat.-Sun. at 10, mid-Aug. through Thanksgiving weekend. Closing times vary. Admission $34.95; ages 3-11, $24.95 (phone to confirm times and admission).

Virginia

 Paramount's Kings Dominion

(804) 876-5000, 16000 Theme Park Way (on SR 30 5 miles east of I-95 exit 98), Doswell

Eight themed areas make up Kings Dominion, a full-scale theme park with thrill rides, kiddie play areas, costumed characters, live shows and specialty shopping. Air-conditioned kennels. Park open daily, Memorial Day-Labor Day; Sat.-Sun., late Mar.-day before Memorial Day and first Sat. after Labor Day-early Oct. Hours vary seasonally; phone ahead. Admission $38.99; over 54, $33.99; ages 3-6, $26.99. Parking fee.

Washington

 Hovander Homestead

(360) 384-3444, 1 mile south via Hovander Road, Ferndale

This restored house, dating from 1903 and furnished with antiques, is within a large park encompassing gardens, picnic sites and a children's farm zoo. Pets on leash (grounds only). Grounds open daily 8 a.m.-dusk; house open Thurs.-Sun. noon-4:30, June 1-Labor Day. Grounds $3 per private vehicle. House $1; ages 5-12, 50c.

Canada

Ontario

 Upper Canada Village

(613) 543-4328 or (800) 437-2233, 7 miles (11 kilometers) east on CR 2 off Hwy. 401, Morrisburg

Upper Canada Village re-creates life during the 1860s through a working community of artisans and costumed interpreters who perform chores typical of the era. Pets on leash (grounds only). Daily 9:30-5, Victoria Day weekend-Oct. 6. Village admission $15.95; over 65, $14.95; students with ID $9.95; ages 5-12, $6.95.

 Paramount Canada's Wonderland

(905) 832-7000 or 832-8131, off Hwy. 400 (Rutherford Road exit northbound or Major Mackenzie Drive E. exit southbound) at 9580 Jane St., Vaughan

Thrill rides at this theme park include the Top Gun coaster and Drop Zone, a free-fall plunge, while Scooby Doo's Haunted Mansion and Hanna-Barbera Land will entertain little ones. Air-conditioned kennels. Open daily at 10 a.m., late May-Labour Day; some weekends early to late May and day after Labour Day-second Mon. in Oct. Closing times vary. Grounds admission $24.99. Grounds and rides passport $44.99; over 59 and ages 3-6, $22.49.

The National Public Lands listed below permit pets on a leash. Keep in mind that animals may be prohibited from entering public buildings and even some areas outdoors, particularly those that are ecologically sensitive. Specific pet policies vary from park to park and are subject to change. Always check in advance regarding any applicable regulations and to confirm that pets are still permitted where you are going.

Never leave your pet unattended. Keep him leashed or crated at all times. Follow park guidelines faithfully, and monitor your pet's behavior; the National Park Service may confiscate pets that harm wildlife or other visitors. *For additional information on outdoor vacations, see The Great Outdoors, p. 18.*

United States

Alabama

Conecuh National Forest
On the Alabama-Florida border.
(334) 222-2555
🚲 🅰 🥾 🏕 🏊

Horseshoe Bend National Military Park
12 mi. north of Dadeville on SR 49.
(256) 234-7111
🥾 🏕 🏊 👥

Talladega National Forest
In central Alabama.
(334) 832-4470
🅰 🥾 🏕 🏊

Tuskegee National Forest
Northeast of Tuskegee.
(334) 727-2652
🅰 🥾 🏕

William B. Bankhead National Forest
In northwestern Alabama.
(205) 489-5111
🚲 🅰 🥾 🏕 🏊

Alaska

Chugach National Forest
Along the Gulf of Alaska from Cape Suckling to Seward.
(907) 271-2500
🅰 🥾 🏕 👥

Denali National Park and Preserve
In south-central Alaska.
(907) 683-2294
🅰 🥾 🏕 👥 🍽

Glacier Bay National Park and Preserve
North of Cross Sound to the Canadian border.
(907) 697-2230
🅰 🥾 👥 🍽

Kenai Fjords National Park
Southeastern side of the Kenai Peninsula.
(907) 224-3175 or 224-2132
🅰 🥾 🏕 👥

Lake Clark National Park and Preserve
In southern Alaska.
(907) 271-3751
🅰 👥

Tongass National Forest
In southeastern Alaska.
(907) 586-8751 or 228-6220
🅰 🥾 🏕 👥

Wrangell-St. Elias National Park and Preserve
In southeastern Alaska, northwest of Tongass National Forest.
(907) 822-5234
🅰 🥾 🏕 👥

Arizona

Apache-Sitgreaves National Forests
In east-central Arizona.
(928) 333-4301
🚲 🅰 🥾 🏕 👥 🍽

Coconino National Forest
In northern Arizona.
(928) 527-3600
🅰 🥾 🏕 🏊 🍽

Coronado National Forest
In southeastern Arizona and southwestern New Mexico.
(520) 670-4552
🚲 🅰 🥾 🏕 👥

Glen Canyon National Recreation Area
In north-central Arizona.
(928) 608-6404 or 608-6200
🅰 🥾 🏕 🏊 👥 🍽

🚲 Bicycling   🅰 Camping   🥾 Hiking   🏕 Picnicking
🏊 Swimming   👥 Visitor center   🍽 Food service

Grand Canyon National Park
In northwestern Arizona.
(928) 638-7888
[icons]

Kaibab National Forest
In north-central Arizona.
(928) 635-4061 or (800) 863-0546
[icons]

Lake Mead National Recreation Area
In northwestern Arizona.
(702) 293-8906
[icons]

Petrified Forest National Park
In east-central Arizona, east of Holbrook.
(928) 524-6228
[icons]

Prescott National Forest
In central Arizona.
(928) 771-4700 or TDD (928) 771-4792
[icons]

Saguaro National Park
Two districts, 15 mi. east and west of Tucson.
(520) 733-5153
[icons]

Tonto National Forest
In central Arizona.
(602) 225-5200
[icons]

Arkansas

Buffalo National River
In northwestern Arkansas.
(870) 741-5443
[icons]

Felsenthal National Wildlife Refuge
7 mi. west of Crossett on US 82.
(870) 364-3167
[icons]

Hot Springs National Park
In western Arkansas.
(501) 624-3383
[icons]

Ouachita National Forest
In west-central Arkansas and southeastern Oklahoma.
(501) 321-5202
[icons]

Ozark National Forest
In northwestern Arkansas.
(501) 968-2354
[icons]

St. Francis National Forest
In east-central Arkansas.
(870) 295-5278
[icons]

California

Angeles National Forest
In southern California.
(626) 574-5200
[icons]

Cleveland National Forest
In southwestern California.
(858) 673-6180
[icons]

Death Valley National Park
Along the Nevada border in east-central California.
(760) 786-2331
[icons]

Eldorado National Forest
In central California.
(530) 644-6048
[icons]

Golden Gate National Recreation Area
North of the Golden Gate Bridge and in northern and western San Francisco.
(415) 556-0560
[icons]

Inyo National Forest
In central California.
(760) 873-2400
[icons]

Joshua Tree National Park
East of Desert Hot Springs.
(760) 367-5500
[icons]

King Range National Conservation Area
On the northern California coast west of Garberville.
(530) 758-0380
[icons]

Klamath National Forest
In northern California.
(530) 842-6131
[icons]

Lassen National Forest
In northern California.
(530) 257-2151
[icons]

Lassen Volcanic National Park
In northeastern California.
(530) 595-4444
[icons]

Los Padres National Forest
In southern California.
(805) 968-6640
[icons]

Mendocino National Forest
In northwestern California.
(530) 934-2350 or 934-3316
[icons]

Modoc National Forest
In northeastern California.
(530) 233-5811
🚲 ⛺ 🥾 🪑 🏠

Mojave National Preserve
Between I-15 and I-40 in southeastern California.
(760) 733-4040
⛺ 🥾 🪑 🏠 🍴

Plumas National Forest
In northern California.
(530) 283-2050
🚲 ⛺ 🥾 🪑 🏊 🏠 🍴

Point Reyes National Seashore
Along the California coast just north of San Francisco.
(415) 464-5100
🚲 ⛺ 🥾 🪑 🏠 🍴

Redwood National Park
On the northern California coast.
(707) 464-6101, ext. 5064 or 5265
🚲 ⛺ 🥾 🪑 🏊 🏠 🍴

San Bernardino National Forest
In southern California.
(909) 383-5588
🚲 ⛺ 🥾 🪑 🏊 🏠 🍴

Santa Monica Mountains National Recreation Area
West from Griffith Park in Los Angeles to the Ventura County line.
(805) 370-2301 or (805) 370-2300 in Calif.
🚲 ⛺ 🥾 🪑 🏊 🏠 🍴

Sequoia and Kings Canyon National Parks
In east-central California.
(559) 565-3341
⛺ 🥾 🪑 🏠 🍴

Sequoia National Forest
In south-central California.
(559) 784-1500
🚲 ⛺ 🥾 🪑 🏊 🏠 🍴

Shasta-Trinity National Forests
In northern California.
(530) 244-2978
⛺ 🥾 🪑 🏊 🏠 🍴

Sierra National Forest
In central California.
(559) 297-0706
🚲 ⛺ 🥾 🪑 🏊 🏠 🍴

Six Rivers National Forest
In northwestern California.
(707) 441-3523
🚲 ⛺ 🥾 🪑 🏊 🏠 🍴

Smith River National Recreation Area
Within Six Rivers National Forest in northwestern California.
(707) 441-3523
🚲 ⛺ 🥾 🪑 🏊

Stanislaus National Forest
In central California.
(209) 532-3671
🚲 ⛺ 🥾 🪑 🏊 🍴

Tahoe National Forest
In north-central California.
(530) 265-4531
⛺ 🥾 🪑 🏊 🏠 🍴

Whiskeytown-Shasta-Trinity National Recreation Area
North and west of Redding.
(530) 242-3400
🚲 ⛺ 🥾 🪑 🏊 🏠 🍴

Yosemite National Park
In central California.
(209) 372-0200
🚲 ⛺ 🥾 🪑 🏊 🏠 🍴

Colorado

Arapaho and Roosevelt National Forests
In north-central Colorado.
(970) 498-2770 or TDD 498-2707
🚲 ⛺ 🥾 🪑 🏊 🏠

Arapaho National Recreation Area
In north-central Colorado.
(970) 887-4100 or TDD 887-4101
🚲 ⛺ 🥾 🪑 🏊 🏠

Black Canyon of the Gunnison National Park
In western Colorado.
(970) 641-2337
⛺ 🥾 🪑 🏠 🍴

Curecanti National Recreation Area
In south-central Colorado between Gunnison and Montrose, paralleling US 50.
(970) 641-2337
⛺ 🥾 🪑 🏊 🏠 🍴

Grand Mesa-Uncompahgre-Gunnison National Forests
In west-central Colorado.
(970) 874-6600
🚲 ⛺ 🥾 🪑 🍴

Mesa Verde National Park
In southwestern Colorado.
(970) 529-4465
⛺ 🥾 🪑 🏠 🍴

🚲 Bicycling ⛺ Camping 🥾 Hiking 🪑 Picnicking
🏊 Swimming 🏠 Visitor center 🍴 Food service

Pike National Forest
In central Colorado.
(719) 545-8737
[icons]

Rio Grande National Forest
In south-central Colorado.
(719) 852-5941
[icons]

Rocky Mountain National Park
In north-central Colorado.
(970) 586-1206 or 586-1333
[icons]

Routt National Forest
In northwestern Colorado.
(970) 879-1870
[icons]

San Isabel National Forest
In south-central Colorado.
(719) 545-8737
[icons]

San Juan National Forest
In southwestern Colorado.
(970) 247-4874
[icons]

White River National Forest
In west-central Colorado.
(970) 945-2521
[icons]

Florida

Ocala National Forest
In north-central Florida.
(352) 625-2520
[icons]

Georgia

Chattahoochee and Oconee National Forests
In central and northern Georgia.
(770) 297-3000
[icons]

Chattahoochee River National Recreation Area
North of Atlanta.
(770) 399-8070, ext. 236
[icons]

Idaho

Boise National Forest
In south-central Idaho.
(208) 373-4007
[icons]

Caribou National Forest
In southeastern Idaho.
(208) 524-7500
[icons]

Clearwater National Forest
In northeastern Idaho.
(208) 476-4541
[icons]

Hells Canyon National Recreation Area
In western Idaho and northeastern Oregon.
(509) 758-0616 or 758-1957
[icons]

Idaho Panhandle National Forest
In northern and northwestern Idaho.
(208) 765-7223
[icons]

Nez Perce National Forest
In north-central Idaho.
(208) 983-1950
[icons]

Payette National Forest
In west-central Idaho.
(208) 634-0700
[icons]

Salmon-Challis National Forest
In east-central Idaho.
(208) 756-5100
[icons]

Sawtooth National Forest
In south-central Idaho.
(208) 737-3200 or TDD (208) 737-3235
[icons]

Sawtooth National Recreation Area
In south-central Idaho.
(208) 727-5013 or (800) 260-5970
[icons]

Targhee National Forest
In southeastern Idaho.
(208) 624-3151
[icons]

Illinois

Shawnee National Forest
In southern Illinois.
(618) 253-7114 or (800) 699-6637
[icons]

Indiana

Hoosier National Forest
In southern Indiana.
(812) 275-5987
[icons]

Indiana Dunes National Lakeshore
On the southern shore of Lake Michigan.
(219) 926-7561, ext. 225
[icons]

Kentucky

Big South Fork National River and Recreation Area
In southeastern Kentucky and northeastern Tennessee.
(931) 879-3625
[⬥] [⛺] [🚶] [🛆] [🏊] [👥]

Daniel Boone National Forest
In eastern Kentucky.
(859) 745-3100
[⛺] [🚶] [🛆] [🏊] [👥]

Daniel Boone National Forest (Laurel River Lake)
In southeastern Kentucky west of Corbin.
(859) 745-3100
[⛺] [🚶] [🛆] [🏊]

Daniel Boone National Forest (Rockcastle)
In southeastern Kentucky 22 mi. southwest of London via SR 192/3497.
(859) 745-3100
[⛺] [🚶] [🛆] [🏊]

Land Between the Lakes National Recreation Area
In western Kentucky and Tennessee.
(270) 924-2000 or (800) 525-7077
[⬥] [⛺] [🚶] [🛆] [🏊] [👥]

Mammoth Cave National Park
In south-central Kentucky 8 mi. west of Cave City.
(270) 758-2328
[⬥] [⛺] [🚶] [🛆] [👥] [🍴]

Louisiana

Bayou Sauvage National Wildlife Refuge
Within the New Orleans city limits.
(985) 646-7555
[🚶] [🛆]

Kisatchie National Forest
In central and northern Louisiana.
(318) 473-7160
[⛺] [🚶] [🛆] [🏊]

Sabine National Wildlife Refuge
8 mi. south of Hackberry on SR 27.
(337) 762-3816
[🚶] [👥]

Maine

Acadia National Park
Along the Atlantic coast southeast of Bangor.
(207) 288-3338
[⬥] [⛺] [🚶] [🛆] [🏊] [👥] [🍴]

Maryland

Assateague Island National Seashore
In southeastern Maryland south of Ocean City.
(410) 641-1441 or 641-3030
[⬥] [⛺] [🚶] [🛆] [🏊] [👥]

Michigan

Hiawatha National Forest
In Michigan's Upper Peninsula.
(906) 786-4062
[⬥] [⛺] [🚶] [🛆] [🏊] [👥]

Huron-Manistee National Forests
In the northern part of the Lower Peninsula.
(231) 775-2421 or (800) 821-6263
[⬥] [⛺] [🚶] [🛆] [🏊] [👥]

Ottawa National Forest
In Michigan's Upper Peninsula.
(906) 932-1330
[⬥] [⛺] [🚶] [🛆] [🏊] [👥]

Pictured Rocks National Lakeshore
Along Lake Superior in Michigan's Upper Peninsula.
(906) 387-2607
[⛺] [🚶] [🛆] [🏊] [👥]

Sleeping Bear Dunes National Lakeshore
Along Lake Michigan in the northwestern part of the Lower Peninsula.
(231) 326-5134
[⛺] [🚶] [🛆] [🏊] [👥]

Minnesota

Chippewa National Forest
In north-central Minnesota.
(218) 335-8600 or TDD (218) 335-8632
[⬥] [⛺] [🚶] [🛆] [🏊] [👥] [🍴]

Superior National Forest
In northeastern Minnesota.
(218) 626-4300
[⬥] [⛺] [🚶] [🛆] [🏊] [👥] [🍴]

Mississippi

Bienville National Forest
In central Mississippi.
(601) 469-3811
[⛺] [🚶] [🛆] [🏊] [👥]

Gulf Islands National Seashore
Along the Gulf of Mexico in southern Mississippi.
(228) 875-9057
[⛺] [🛆] [🏊] [👥] [🍴]

[⬥] Bicycling   [⛺] Camping   [🚶] Hiking   [🛆] Picnicking
[🏊] Swimming   [👥] Visitor center   [🍴] Food service

Missouri

Mark Twain National Forest
In southern Missouri.
(573) 364-4621
♿ ▲ 🥾 ⛱ ⚓

Mark Twain National Forest (Big Bay)
1 mi. southeast of Shell Knob on SR 39, then 3 mi.
southeast on CR YY.
(573) 364-4621
▲ ⛱ ⚓

Mark Twain National Forest (Crane Lake)
12 mi. south of Ironton off SR 49 and CR E.
(573) 364-4621
♿ 🥾 ⛱

Mark Twain National Forest (Fourche Lake)
18 mi. west of Doniphan on SR 160.
(573) 364-4621
🥾 ⛱

Mark Twain National Forest (Noblett Lake)
8 mi. west of Willow Springs on SR 76, then 1.5 mi.
south on SR 181, 3 mi. southeast on CR AP and 1
mi. southwest on FR 857.
(573) 364-4621
♿ ▲ 🥾 ⛱

Mark Twain National Forest (Pinewoods Lake)
7 mi. north of Ellsinore on SR 67, then 2 mi. west on
CR 60.
(573) 364-4621
♿ 🥾 ⛱ ⚓

Mark Twain National Forest (Red Bluff)
1 mi. east of Davisville on CR V, then 1 mi. north on
FR 2011.
(573) 364-4621
▲ 🥾 ⛱ ⚓

Ozark National Scenic Riverways
In southeastern Missouri.
(573) 323-4236
▲ 🥾 ⛱ ⚓ 🏕 🍴

Montana

Beaverhead-Deerlodge National Forest Area
In southwestern Montana.
(406) 683-3900
♿ ▲ 🥾 ⛱ ⚓

Bighorn Canyon National Recreation Area
In southern Montana and northern Wyoming.
(406) 666-2412
▲ 🥾 ⛱ ⚓ 🏕 🍴

Bitterroot National Forest
In western Montana.
(406) 363-7161
▲ 🥾 ⛱ ⚓ 🏕

Custer National Forest/Dakota Prairie Grasslands
In southeastern Montana.
(406) 248-9885
♿ ▲ 🥾 ⛱ ⚓ 🍴

Flathead National Forest
In northwestern Montana.
(406) 758-5204
♿ ▲ 🥾 ⛱ ⚓ 🏕

Gallatin National Forest
In south-central Montana.
(406) 522-2520
♿ ▲ 🥾 ⛱ ⚓ 🏕 🍴

Glacier National Park
In northwestern Montana.
(406) 888-7800
▲ 🥾 ⛱ ⚓ 🏕 🍴

Helena National Forest
In west-central Montana.
(406) 449-5201
▲ 🥾 ⛱ ⚓

Kootenai National Forest
In northwestern Montana.
(406) 293-6211
♿ ▲ 🥾 ⛱ ⚓ 🏕 🍴

Lewis and Clark National Forest
In central Montana.
(406) 791-7700
▲ 🥾 ⛱ ⚓

Nebraska

Nebraska National Forest
In central and northwestern Nebraska.
(308) 432-0300 or TDD (308) 432-0304
♿ ▲ 🥾 ⛱ ⚓

Oglala National Grassland
In northwestern Nebraska, 6 mi. north of Crawford via
SR 2.
(308) 432-4475
▲ 🥾 ⛱ 🏕

Nevada

Great Basin National Park
In central Nevada, 5 mi. west of Baker near the
Nevada-Utah border.
(775) 234-7331
▲ 🥾 ⛱ 🏕 🍴

Lake Mead National Recreation Area
In southeastern Nevada.
(702) 293-8906
♿ ▲ 🥾 ⛱ ⚓ 🏕 🍴

Humboldt-Toiyabe National Forest
In central, western, northern and southern Nevada
and eastern California.
(775) 331-6444
♿ ▲ 🥾 ⛱

New Hampshire

White Mountain National Forest
In northern New Hampshire.
(603) 528-8721 or TDD (603) 528-8722
[⚹] [▲] [𝆺] [⇴] [⚐] [♠♠]

New Jersey

Gateway National Recreation Area
In northeastern New Jersey (Sandy Hook Unit).
(732) 872-5970
[𝆺] [⇴] [⚐] [♠♠] [⦿]

New Mexico

Carson National Forest
In north-central New Mexico.
(505) 758-6200
[⚹] [▲] [𝆺] [⇴] [♠♠]

Chaco Culture National Historical Park
In northwestern New Mexico.
(505) 786-7014
[⚹] [▲] [𝆺] [⇴] [♠♠]

Cibola National Forest
In central New Mexico.
(505) 346-3900
[⚹] [▲] [𝆺] [⇴] [⚐] [♠♠] [⦿]

Gila National Forest
In southwestern New Mexico.
(505) 388-8201
[▲] [𝆺] [⇴] [⚐] [♠♠]

Lincoln National Forest
In south-central New Mexico.
(505) 434-7200 or TTY (505) 434-7296
[⚹] [▲] [𝆺] [⇴] [⦿]

Santa Fe National Forest
In north-central New Mexico between the San Pedro Mountains and the Sangre de Cristo Mountains.
(505) 438-7840
[⚹] [▲] [𝆺] [⇴] [♠♠]

New York

Finger Lakes National Forest
In north-central New York on a ridge between Seneca and Cayuga lakes, via I-90, I-81 and SR 17.
(607) 546-4470
[▲] [𝆺] [⇴]

Fire Island National Seashore
In southeastern New York on Fire Island, off the south shore of Long Island.
(631) 289-4810
[▲] [𝆺] [⇴] [⚐] [♠♠] [⦿]

Gateway National Recreation Area (Jamaica Bay District)
On Brooklyn and Queens boroughs in New York City.
(718) 338-3687 or 338-3688
[⚹] [𝆺] [⇴] [♠♠] [⦿]

Gateway National Recreation Area (Staten Island Unit)
On Staten Island borough in New York City.
(718) 338-3687 or 338-3688
[⚹] [𝆺] [⇴] [⚐] [♠♠] [⦿]

North Carolina

Cape Hatteras National Seashore
In eastern North Carolina along the Outer Banks.
(252) 473-2111 or 441-5711
[▲] [𝆺] [⇴] [⚐] [♠♠]

Croatan National Forest
In southeastern North Carolina.
(252) 638-5628
[▲] [𝆺] [⇴] [⚐]

Great Smoky Mountains National Park
In western North Carolina.
(865) 436-1200
[▲] [𝆺] [⇴] [⚐] [♠♠]

Nantahala National Forest
At North Carolina's southwestern tip.
(828) 257-4200
[⚹] [▲] [𝆺] [⇴] [⚐]

Nantahala National Forest (Hanging Dog)
5 mi. northwest of Murphy on SR 1326.
(828) 257-4200
[▲] [𝆺]

Nantahala National Forest (Jackrabbit Mountain)
10 mi. northeast of Hayesville via US 64, SR 175 and SR 1155.
(828) 257-4200
[▲] [𝆺] [⇴] [⚐]

Nantahala National Forest (Standing Indian Mountain)
12 mi. west of Franklin on US 64, then 2 mi. east on old US 64 and 2 mi. south on FR 67.
(828) 257-4200
[▲] [𝆺] [⇴]

Pisgah National Forest
In western North Carolina.
(828) 257-4200
[⚹] [▲] [𝆺] [⇴] [⚐] [♠♠] [⦿]

Pisgah National Forest (Lake Powhatan)
7 mi. southwest of Asheville on SR 191 and FR 3484.
(828) 257-4200
[⚹] [▲] [𝆺] [⇴] [⚐]

[⚹] Bicycling [▲] Camping [𝆺] Hiking [⇴] Picnicking
[⚐] Swimming [♠♠] Visitor center [⦿] Food service

Pisgah National Forest (Rocky Bluff)
3 mi. south of Hot Springs on SR 209.
(828) 257-4200
[A] [派] [굤]

Uwharrie National Forest
In central North Carolina.
(910) 576-6391
[A] [派] [굤] [초]

North Dakota

Theodore Roosevelt National Park (North Unit)
In western North Dakota.
(701) 623-4466
[A] [派] [굤] [￼]

Theodore Roosevelt National Park (South Unit)
In western North Dakota.
(701) 623-4466
[A] [派] [굤] [￼]

Note: Leashed pets allowed in front country only;
some restrictions apply.

Ohio

Cuyahoga Valley National Park
In northeastern Ohio.
(216) 524-1497
[ふ] [派] [굤] [￼]

Oklahoma

Chickasaw National Recreation Area
In southern Oklahoma.
(580) 622-3165
[A] [派] [굤] [초] [￼]

Ouachita National Forest
In southeastern Oklahoma and west-central Arkansas.
(501) 321-5202
[ふ] [A] [派] [굤] [초] [￼] [￼]

Oregon

Crater Lake National Park
On the crest of the Cascade Range off SR 62.
(541) 594-2211, ext. 402
[ふ] [A] [派] [굤] [￼] [￼]

Deschutes National Forest
In central Oregon 6 mi. south of Bend via US 97.
(541) 383-5300
[ふ] [A] [派] [굤] [초] [￼] [￼]

Fremont National Forest
In south-central Oregon.
(541) 947-2151
[ふ] [A] [派] [굤] [초]

Hells Canyon National Recreation Area
In northeastern Oregon and western Idaho.
(541) 523-3356 or (800) 523-1235
[A] [派] [굤] [￼]

Malheur National Forest
In eastern Oregon.
(541) 575-3000
[ふ] [A] [派] [굤] [초]

Mount Hood National Forest
In northwestern Oregon.
(888) 622-4822
[ふ] [A] [派] [굤] [초] [￼] [￼]

Ochoco National Forest
In central Oregon off US 26.
(541) 416-6500
[ふ] [A] [派] [굤] [초]

Oregon Dunes National Recreation Area
Between North Bend and Florence.
(541) 271-3611
[A] [派] [굤] [초] [￼]

Rogue River National Forest
In southwestern Oregon off I-5 from Medford.
(541) 858-2200
[ふ] [A] [派] [굤] [초] [￼]

Siskiyou National Forest
In southwestern Oregon.
(541) 471-6500
[ふ] [A] [派] [굤] [초] [￼]

Siuslaw National Forest
In western Oregon.
(541) 750-7000
[ふ] [A] [派] [굤] [초] [￼]

Umatilla National Forest
In northeastern Oregon.
(541) 278-3716
[ふ] [A] [派] [굤] [초] [￼]

Umpqua National Forest
In southwestern Oregon 33 mi. east of Roseburg on
SR 138.
(541) 672-6601 or TDD (541) 957-3459
[ふ] [A] [派] [굤] [초] [￼] [￼]

Wallowa-Whitman National Forest
In northeastern Oregon.
(541) 523-1205
[A] [派] [굤] [초]

Willamette National Forest
In western Oregon.
(541) 465-6521
[ふ] [A] [派] [굤] [초] [￼]

Winema National Forest
In south-central Oregon off US 97N or 140W from
Klamath Falls.
(541) 883-6714
[ふ] [A] [派] [굤] [초] [￼] [￼]

Pennsylvania

Allegheny National Forest
In northwestern Pennsylvania.
(814) 723-5150 or TDD (814) 726-2710
🚴 🔺 🥾 ⛱ 🏊 👫 🍴

Delaware Water Gap National Recreation Area
In eastern Pennsylvania and northwestern New Jersey.
(570) 588-2451
🔺 🥾 ⛱ 🏊 👫

South Carolina

Francis Marion National Forest
On the Coastal Plain north of Charleston.
(803) 561-4000
🚴 🔺 🥾 ⛱

Sumter National Forest
In western South Carolina.
(803) 561-4000
🚴 🔺 🥾 ⛱ 🏊

South Dakota

Badlands National Park
In southwestern South Dakota.
(605) 433-5361, ext. 100
🔺 🥾 ⛱ 👫 🍴

Black Hills National Forest
In southwestern South Dakota.
(605) 673-2251 or TDD (605) 673-4954
🚴 🔺 🥾 ⛱ 🏊 👫 🍴

Custer National Forest/Dakota Prairie Grasslands
In northwestern South Dakota.
(605) 797-4432
🔺 🥾 ⛱

Wind Cave National Park
In southwestern South Dakota.
(605) 745-4600
🔺 🥾 ⛱ 👫 🍴

Tennessee

Big South Fork National River National Recreation Area
In northeastern Tennessee and southeastern Kentucky.
(931) 879-3625
🚴 🔺 🥾 ⛱ 🏊 👫

Cherokee National Forest
In eastern Tennessee.
(423) 476-9700
🚴 🔺 🥾 ⛱ 🏊 👫

Great Smoky Mountains National Park
In eastern Tennessee.
(865) 436-1200
🔺 🥾 ⛱ 👫

Land Between the Lakes National Recreation Area
In western Kentucky and Tennessee.
(270) 924-2000 or (800) 525-7077
🚴 🔺 🥾 ⛱ 🏊 👫 🍴

Texas

Amistad National Recreation Area
Northwest of Del Rio via US 90.
(830) 775-7491
🔺 🥾 ⛱ 🏊

Angelina National Forest
In east Texas.
(936) 639-8620
🔺 🥾 ⛱ 🏊

Big Bend National Park
Southeast of Alpine on SR 118 and US 385.
(915) 477-2251
🔺 🥾 ⛱ 👫 🍴

Davy Crockett National Forest
In east Texas.
(936) 655-2299
🔺 🥾 ⛱ 🏊 🍴

Guadalupe Mountains National Park
110 mi. east of El Paso on US 62/180.
(915) 828-3251
🔺 🥾 ⛱ 👫

Lake Meredith National Recreation Area
45 mi. northeast of Amarillo and 9 mi. west of Borger via SR 136.
(806) 857-3151
🔺 ⛱ 🏊

Padre Island National Seashore
On Padre Island paralleling the Texas coast between Port Isabel and Corpus Christi.
(361) 949-8068
🔺 🥾 ⛱ 🏊 👫 🍴

Sabine National Forest
In east Texas.
(409) 787-3870 or (936) 275-2632
🔺 🥾 ⛱ 🏊

Sam Houston National Forest
40 mi. north of Houston in east Texas.
(281) 344-6205 or 592-6461
🚴 🔺 🥾 ⛱ 🏊 🍴

🚴 Bicycling   🔺 Camping   🥾 Hiking   ⛱ Picnicking
🏊 Swimming   👫 Visitor center   🍴 Food service

Utah

Arches National Park
5 mi. northwest of Moab on US 191.
(435) 719-2100 or TTY (435) 259-5279
⬛ 🚶 🏕 👥

Ashley National Forest
In northeastern Utah.
(435) 789-1181
♿ ⬛ 🚶 🏕 🚤 👥 🍴

Bryce Canyon National Park
26 mi. southeast of Panguitch via US 89 and SRs 12 and 63.
(435) 834-5322
⬛ 🚶 🏕 👥 🍴

Canyonlands National Park
In southeastern Utah.
(435) 259-7164
⬛ 🚶 🏕 👥

Capitol Reef National Park
5 mi. east of Torrey on SR 24.
(435) 425-3791
♿ ⬛ 🚶 🏕 👥

Dixie National Forest
In southwestern Utah.
(435) 865-3700
♿ ⬛ 🚶 🏕 🚤 👥 🍴

Fishlake National Forest
In south-central Utah.
(435) 896-9233
♿ ⬛ 🚶 🏕 👥 🍴

Flaming Gorge National Recreation Area
In northeastern Utah.
(435) 784-3445
♿ ⬛ 🚶 🏕 🚤 👥 🍴

Glen Canyon National Recreation Area
In south-central Utah.
(520) 608-6404 or 608-6200
⬛ 🚶 🏕 🚤 👥 🍴

Manti-La Sal National Forest
In southeastern Utah.
(435) 637-2817
⬛ 🚶 🏕 🍴

Uinta National Forest
In central Utah.
(801) 377-5780
♿ ⬛ 🚶 🏕 🚤 👥

Wasatch-Cache National Forest
In north-central and northeastern Utah.
(801) 524-3900
♿ ⬛ 🚶 🏕 🚤

Zion National Park
In southwestern Utah.
(435) 772-3256
⬛ 🚶 🏕 👥 🍴

Vermont

Green Mountain National Forest
In south-central Vermont.
(802) 747-6700
⬛ 🚶 🏕 🚤

Virginia

George Washington and Jefferson National Forests
In western Virginia and the eastern edge of West Virginia.
(888) 265-0019
♿ ⬛ 🚶 🏕 🚤 👥

Mount Rogers National Recreation Area
In southwestern Virginia.
(540) 783-5196 or (800) 628-7202
♿ ⬛ 🚶 🏕 🚤 👥

Shenandoah National Park
In western Virginia.
(540) 999-3500
⬛ 🚶 🏕 👥 🍴

Washington

Gifford Pinchot National Forest
In southwestern Washington.
(360) 891-5000
♿ ⬛ 🚶 🏕 🚤 👥 🍴

Lake Roosevelt National Recreation Area
In northeastern Washington.
(509) 633-9441
⬛ 🏕 🚤 👥 🍴

Mount Baker-Snoqualmie National Forest (Douglas Fir)
2 mi. east of Glacier on SR 542.
(425) 775-9702 or (800) 627-0062, ext. 0
⬛ 🚶 🏕

Mount Baker-Snoqualmie National Forest (Horseshoe Cove)
14 mi. north of Concrete on Baker Lake.
(425) 775-9702 or (800) 627-0062, ext. 0
⬛ 🚶 🚤

Mount Baker-Snoqualmie National Forest (Shannon Creek)
24 mi. north of Concrete on Baker Lake.
(425) 775-9702 or (800) 627-0062, ext.0
⬛ 🚶 🏕 🚤

Olympic National Forest
In northwestern Washington.
(360) 956-2400
♿ ⬛ 🚶 🏕 🚤 👥 🍴

West Virginia

Monongahela National Forest
In eastern West Virginia.
(304) 636-1800 (voice and TDD)
🅰 👣 🏕 🏊 👥

New River Gorge National River
Between Fayetteville and Hinton.
(304) 465-0508
👣 🏕 🏊 👥

Spruce Knob-Seneca Rocks National Recreation Area
In east-central West Virginia.
(304) 567-2827
🅰 👣 🏕 🏊 👥

Wisconsin

Apostle Islands National Lakeshore
Off northern Wisconsin's Bayfield Peninsula in Lake Superior.
(715) 779-3397
🅰 👣 🏕 🏊 👥

Chequamegon-Nicolet National Forest
In north-central and northeastern Wisconsin.
(715) 762-2461 or TTY (715) 762-5701 (Chequamegon), (715) 362-1300 or TTY (715) 362-1383 (Nicolet)
🚲 🅰 👣 🏕 🏊 🍽

St. Croix National Scenic Riverway
Running 252 mi. from Cable to Prescott.
(715) 483-3284
🅰 👣 🏕 🏊 👥

Wyoming

Bighorn Canyon National Recreation Area
In Montana and northern Wyoming.
(307) 548-2251
🅰 👣 🏕 🏊 👥 🍽

Bighorn National Forest
In north-central Wyoming.
(307) 672-0751
🅰 👣 🏕 🍽

Devils Tower National Monument
Between Sundance and Hulett.
(307) 467-5283
🅰 👣 🏕 🏊 👥

Flaming Gorge National Recreation Area
On the Wyoming-Utah border.
(435) 784-3445
🚲 🅰 👣 🏕 🏊 👥 🍽

Fossil Butte National Monument
14 mi. west of Kemmerer on US 30.
(307) 877-4455
👣 🏕 👥

Grand Teton National Park
In northwestern Wyoming.
(307) 739-3410
🚲 🅰 👣 🏕 🏊 👥 🍽

Medicine Bow National Forest
In eastern Wyoming.
(307) 745-2300
🚲 🅰 👣 🏕 🏊 👥

Shoshone National Forest
In northwestern Wyoming.
(307) 527-6241
🚲 🅰 👣 🏕 🏊 👥 🍽

Yellowstone National Park
In northwestern Wyoming.
(307) 344-7311
🅰 👣 🏕 👥 🍽

Canada

Alberta

Elk Island National Park
In central Alberta, east of Edmonton.
(780) 992-2950
🅰 👣 🏕 👥 🍽

Jasper National Park
In west-central Alberta along the British Columbia border.
(780) 852-6161
🚲 🅰 👣 🏕 🏊 👥 🍽

Waterton Lakes National Park
In Alberta's southwestern corner.
(403) 859-5133, or 859-2224 during the winter
🅰 👣 🏕 🏊 👥 🍽

British Columbia

Glacier National Park
In southeastern British Columbia.
(250) 837-7500
🅰 👣 🏕 👥 🍽

🚲 Bicycling   🅰 Camping   👣 Hiking   🏕 Picnicking
🏊 Swimming   👥 Visitor center   🍽 Food service

Kootenay National Park
In southeastern British Columbia.
(250) 347-9615 or (800) 748-7275

Mount Revelstoke National Park
In southeastern British Columbia.
(250) 837-7500

Pacific Rim National Park Reserve
On the southwestern coast of Vancouver Island.
(250) 726-7721 or 726-4212, mid-Mar. to mid-Oct.

Yoho National Park
On the British Columbia-Alberta border.
(250) 343-6783

Manitoba

Riding Mountain National Park
In western Manitoba.
(204) 848-7275 or (800) 707-8480

New Brunswick

Fundy National Park
On Hwy. 114, 130 km. southwest of Moncton.
(506) 887-6000

Kouchibouguac National Park
On Hwy. 134, north of Moncton.
(506) 876-2443 or TDD (506) 876-4205

Newfoundland

Gros Morne National Park
On Newfoundland's western coast.
(709) 458-2417, 458-2066 or TDD (709) 458-2996

Terra Nova National Park
In eastern Newfoundland.
(709) 533-2801 or (800) 213-7275

Northwest Territories

Nahanni National Park Reserve
145 km. west of Fort Simpson in western Northwest
Territories.
(867) 695-3151

Wood Buffalo National Park
On the Northwest Territories-Alberta border.
(867) 872-7960

Nova Scotia

Cape Breton Highlands National Park
5 km. northeast of Chéticamp on Cabot Tr.
(902) 224-2306 or (888) 773-8888

Kejimkujik National Park and National Historic Site
In southwestern Nova Scotia off Hwy. 8 at Maitland
Bridge.
(902) 682-2772

Ontario

Bruce Peninsula National Park
In southwestern Ontario.
(519) 596-2233

Prince Edward Island

Prince Edward Island National Park
Along the island's northern shore.
(902) 566-7050

Quebec

Forillon National Park
20 km. northeast of Gaspé via Hwy. 132.
(418) 368-5505 or (800) 463-6769

La Mauricie National Park
North of Trois Rivières via Hwy. 55.
(819) 538-3232 or (800) 463-6769

Saskatchewan

Grasslands National Park
Between Val Marie and Killdeer in southern
Saskatchewan.
(306) 298-2257

Prince Albert National Park
In central Saskatchewan.
(306) 663-4522

This list of animal clinics in the United States and Canada is provided by the Veterinary Emergency & Critical Care Society as a service to the community for information purposes only. This is not to be construed as a certification or an endorsement of any clinic listed. For further information, contact the society at (210) 698-5575 or online at http://veccs.org.

If you are traveling to an area not covered in this list, be prepared for an emergency by asking your regular veterinarian to recommend a clinic or veterinarian at your destination. The American Animal Hospital Association also provides a veterinary locator service to clinics that meet the association's high standards for veterinary care. Contact the association at (303) 986-2800 or online at www.healthypet.com.

United States

Alabama

Village Veterinary Clinic
403 Opelika Rd., Auburn
(334) 821-7730

Emergency Pet Care
4524 Southlake Pkwy., Birmingham
(205) 988-5988

Kent's Animal Hospital
3222 6th Ave. S., Birmingham
(205) 323-1536

Emergency Clinic of North Alabama
2306-A Memorial Pkwy. SW, Huntsville
(256) 533-7600

Rehm Animal Clinic
951 Hillcrest Rd., Mobile
(251) 639-9120

Carriage Hills Animal Clinic
3200 E. Bypass, Montgomery
(334) 277-2867

Alaska

Pet Emergency
3315 Fairbanks St., Anchorage
(907) 274-5636

Arizona

East Valley Veterinary Hospital
1721 E. University Dr., Mesa
(480) 890-8283

Mesa Veterinary Hospital
858 N. Country Club Dr., Mesa
(480) 833-7330

Emergency Animal Clinic
2260 West Glendale Ave., Phoenix
(602) 995-3757

Palo Verde Animal Hospital
1215 E. Northern Ave., Phoenix
(602) 944-9661

Emergency Animal Clinic
14202 N. Scottsdale Rd., Suite 163, Scottsdale
(480) 949-8001

Paradise Valley Emergency Animal Clinic
10614 N. 71st Pl., Scottsdale
(480) 991-1845

Animal Emergency Service
4832 E. Speedway St., Tucson
(520) 327-5624

Grant Road Small Animal Hospital
1675 West Grant Rd., Tucson
(520) 792-1858

Arkansas

Animal Emergency Clinic
801 John Barrow Rd., #6, Little Rock
(501) 224-3784

California

Animal Hospital of Antioch
2204 A St., Antioch
(925) 754-6700

Antioch Veterinary Hospital
1432 West 10th St., Antioch
(925) 757-2233

Central Coast Pet Emergency Clinic
1558 W. Branch St., Arroyo Grande
(805) 489-6573

Kern Animal Emergency Clinic
4300 Easton Dr., #1, Bakersfield
(661) 322-6019

Pet Emergency Treatment Service Inc.
1048 University Ave., Berkeley
(510) 548-6684

United Emergency Animal Clinic
1657 S. Bascom Ave., Campbell
(408) 371-6282

AKA Sacramento Animal Medical Group
4990 Manzanita Ave., Carmichael
(916) 331-2059

Acacia Veterinary Hospital
479 East Ave., Chico
(530) 345-1338

Contra Costa Veterinary Emergency Clinic
1410 Monument Blvd., Concord
(925) 798-2900

Solano Pet Emergency Clinic
4437 Central Pl., Cordelia
(707) 864-1444

East Valley Emergency Pet Clinic
938 N. Diamond Bar Blvd., Diamond Bar
(909) 861-5737

Dublin Veterinary Hospital
7410 Amador Valley Blvd., #D, Dublin
(510) 828-5520

Tri-Valley Veterinary Emergency Clinic
6743 Dublin Blvd., Dublin
(510) 828-0654

Emergency Pet Clinic of San Gabriel Valley
3254 Santa Anita Ave., El Monte
(626) 579-4550

Greenback Veterinary Hospital
8311 Greenback Ln., Fair Oaks
(916) 725-1541

All Care Animal Referral Center
18440 E. Amistad St., Fountain Valley
(714) 963-0909

Central Veterinary Hospital & Emergency Service
5245 Central Ave., Fremont
(510) 797-7387

Veterinary Emergency Services
1639 N. Fresno St., Fresno
(559) 486-0520

Orange County Emergency Pet Clinic
127501 Garden Grove Blvd., Garden Grove
(714) 537-3032

Chatoak Pet Clinic
17659 Chatsworth St., Granada Hills
(818) 363-7444

Animal Emergency Clinic
12022 La Crosse Ave., Grand Terrace
(909) 825-9350

Animal Emergency Clinic of Victor Valley
17085 Main St., Hesperia
(760) 948-2868

North Orange County Pet Clinic
1472 S. Harbor Blvd., La Habra
(714) 537-3032

Pet Emergency Clinic of East County
5232 Jackson Dr., #105, La Mesa
(619) 462-4800

Loomis Basin Veterinary Clinic
3901 Sierra College Blvd., Loomis
(916) 652-5816

Adobe Animal Hospital
398 First St., Los Altos
(650) 948-9661

Animal Emergency Facility
1736 South Sepulveda Blvd., #A, Los Angeles
(310) 473-1561

Eagle Rock Emergency Pet Clinic
4254 Eagle Rock Blvd., Los Angeles
(323) 254-7382

West Los Angeles Animal Hospital
1818 South Sepulveda Blvd., Los Angeles
(310) 473-2951

Animal Urgent Care
28085 Hillcrest, Mission Viejo
(949) 364-6228

Monterey Animal Hospital Inc.
725 Foam St., Monterey
(408) 373-0711

Central Orange County Emergency Animal Clinic
3720 Campus Dr., Newport Beach
(949) 261-7979

Crossroads Animal Emergency & Referral Center
11057 E. Rosencrans Ave., Norwalk
(562) 863-2522

South Peninsula Veterinary Emergency Clinic
3045 Middlefield Rd., Palo Alto
(650) 494-1461

Animal Emergency Clinic of Pasadena
2121 Foothill Blvd., Pasadena
(626) 564-0704

McClave Vet Hospital
6950 Reseda Blvd., Reseda
(818) 881-5102

Rim Forest Animal Hospital
1299 Bear Springs Rd., Rimforest
(909) 337-8589

Animal Care Center of Sonoma County
6620 Redwood Dr., Rohnert Park
(707) 584-4343

Emergency Animal Clinic of Sacramento
9700 Business Park Dr., #404, Sacramento
(916) 362-3111

Sacramento Emergency Veterinary Clinic
2201 El Camino Ave., Sacramento
(916) 922-3425

San Clemente Veterinary Hospital
1833 South El Camino Real, San Clemente
(949) 492-5777

Animal Center of San Diego
246 W. Washington St., San Diego
(619) 299-7387

Emergency Animal Hospital & Referral Center
2317 Hotel Cir. South, San Diego
(619) 299-2400

All Animals Emergency Hospital
1333 9th Ave., San Francisco
(415) 566-0531

Mission Pet Hospital
720 Valencia St., San Francisco
(415) 552-1969

South Bay Veterinary Specialists
5440 Thornwood Dr., #E, San Jose
(408) 363-8066

Alameda County Emergency Pet
14790 Washington Ave., San Leandro
(510) 352-6080

Northern Peninsula Veterinary Emergency Clinic
227 N. Amphlett Blvd., San Mateo
(650) 348-2575

Santa Cruz Veterinary Hospital
2585 Soquel Dr., Santa Cruz
(831) 475-5400

North Bay Animal Emergency Hospital
1304 Wilshire Blvd., Santa Monica
(310) 451-8962

Pet Care Veterinary Hospital
1370 Fulton Rd., Santa Rosa
(707) 579-5900

Beverly Oaks Animal Hospital
14302 Ventura Blvd., Sherman Oaks
(818) 788-2022

American Veterinary Hospital
2109 Tapo St., #3, Simi Valley
(805) 581-9111

Rancho Sequoia Veterinary Hospital
3380 Los Angeles Ave., Simi Valley
(805) 522-7476

Associated Veterinary Emergency Services
3008 E. Hammer Ln., #115, Stockton
(209) 952-8387

Animal Emergency Center
11740 Ventura Blvd., Studio City
(818) 760-3882

Emergency Pet Clinic of the Inland Empire
27443 Jefferson Ave., Temecula
(909) 695-5044

Pet Emergency Clinic of Thousand Oaks
2967 North Moorpark Rd., Thousand Oaks
(805) 492-2436

Animal Emergency Clinic of the Desert
72-374 Ramon Rd., Thousand Palms
(760) 343-3438

Emergency Pet Clinic of South Bay
2325 Torrance Blvd., Torrance
(310) 320-8300

Central Veterinary Hospital
281 North Central Ave., Upland
(909) 981-2855

Pet Emergency Clinic of Ventura
2301 S. Victoria Ave., Ventura
(805) 642-8562

North County Emergency Animal Clinic/Cal Vet Specialist
1925 West Vista Way, Vista
(760) 724-7444

Washington Blvd. Animal Hospital
12116 East Washington Blvd., Whittier
(562) 693-8233

Colorado

All Pets Veterinary Clinic
5290 Manhattan Cir., Boulder
(303) 499-5335

Boulder Emergency Pet Clinic
1658 30th St., Boulder
(303) 440-7722

Animal Emergency Care, P.C.
5752 North Academy Blvd., Colorado Springs
(719) 260-7141

Animal Emergency Center
2812 East Pikes Peak Ave., Colorado Springs
(719) 578-9300

Alameda East Animal Hospital
9870 E. Alameda Ave., Denver
(303) 366-3527

Veterinary Teaching Hospital
300 W. Drake Rd., Fort Collins
(970) 221-4535

Centennial Veterinary Clinic
2731 W. Belleview Ave., Littleton
(303) 795-0130

Wheat Ridge Animal Hospital
3695 Kipling St., Wheat Ridge
(303) 424-3325

Connecticut

East of the River Veterinary Emergency Clinic
222 Boston Tpk., Bolton
(860) 646-6134

Shoreline Animal Emergency Clinic
843 State St., New Haven
(203) 375-6500

Animal Emergency and Critical Care
41 Prospect Ave., West Hartford
(860) 233-8387

Florida

Animal Emergency Clinic
103 N. Powerline Rd., Deerfield Beach
(954) 428-9888

Animal Emergency and Referral Center
3984 S. US 1, Fort Pierce
(561) 466-3441

AA Pet Emergency Services
4000-B Newberry Rd., Gainesville
(352) 268-0477

Chasewood Animal Clinic
6779 W. Indiantown Rd., Jupiter
(561) 745-4944

Veterinary Emergency Clinic
3609 Hwy. 98 S., Lakeland
(863) 665-3199

Lantana Animal Clinic
3530 Lantana Rd., Lantana
(561) 439-0694

Promenade Animal Hospital
4424 N. University Dr., Lauderhill
(954) 748-9600

Animal Emergency Clinic South
8429 S.W. 132nd St., Miami
(305) 251-2096

Knowles Emergency Clinic
1000 N.W. 27th Ave., Miami
(305) 649-1234

Snapper Creek Emergency Clinic
9933 Sunset Dr., Miami
(305) 279-2323

Emergency Veterinary Clinic Okaloosa/Walton
210 A Government Ave., Niceville
(850) 729-3335

Veterinary Emergency Clinic
9500 Satellite Blvd., Orlando
(407) 644-4449

Pet Emergency & Critical Care Clinic
3816 Northlake Blvd., Palm Beach Gardens
(561) 691-9999

After Hours Emergency Animal Clinic of Hollywood
6602 Pines Blvd., Pembroke Pines
(305) 962-0300

West Florida Animal Hospital
8560 N. Davis Hwy., Pensacola
(850) 479-9484

Animal Emergency Clinic of Pasco
8740 US Hwy. 19 N., Port Richey
(727) 841-6575

Emergency Veterinary Clinic of Sarasota
7517 S. Tamiami Tr., #107, Sarasota
(941) 923-7260

Animal Emergency of Hernando
3496 Deltona Blvd., Spring Hill
(352) 666-0904

Animal Emergency Clinic of St. Petersburg
3165 22nd Ave. N., St. Petersburg
(727) 323-1311

Allied Veterinary Emergency
401 9th Ave., Tallahassee
(850) 222-0123

Northwood Animal Hospital
1881-B North Martin Luther King Jr. Blvd., Tallahassee
(850) 385-8181

Murphy Animal Hospital
6845 N. Dale Mabry, Tampa
(813) 879-6090

Animal Emergency Clinic
3425 Forest Hill Blvd., West Palm Beach
(561) 433-2244

Summit Boulevard Animal Hospital
1000 S. Military Tr., #B and C, West Palm Beach
(561) 439-7900

Veterinary Emergency Clinic
882 Jackson Ave., Winter Park
(407) 644-4449

Georgia

Animal Emergency Clinic
228 Sandy Springs Pl., Atlanta
(404) 252-7881

Augusta Emergency Clinic
208 Hudson Trace, Augusta
(706) 733-7458

Animal Emergency Care
2009 Mercer University Dr., Macon
(478) 750-0911

Cobb Emergency Veterinary Clinic
630 Cobb Pkwy. N., Marietta
(770) 424-9157

Peachtree Corners Animal Clinic
4020 Holcomb Bridge Rd., Norcross
(770) 448-0700

Animal Emergency Center of North Fulton
900 Mansell Rd., #19, Roswell
(770) 594-2266

Chattahoochee Animal Clinic
1176 Alpharetta St., Roswell
(770) 993-6329

Savannah Veterinary Emergency and Specialty Referral Center
317 Eisenhower Dr., Savannah
(912) 355-6113

Illinois

Animal Emergency Center
2005 Mall St., Collinsville
(618) 346-1843

Emergency Veterinary Care South
13815 S. Cicero Ave., Crestwood
(708) 388-3771

All Creatures Emergency
1806 Belvidere Rd., Grayslake
(708) 548-5300

Emergency Veterinary Service
820 Ogden Ave., Lisle
(630) 960-2900

Animal Emergency and Critical Care Center
1810 Frontage Rd., Northbrook
(847) 564-5775

Emergency Pet Care Center
530 Dunham Rd., St. Charles
(708) 377-2102

Animal Emergency of Lake County
131 Townline Rd., Vernon Hills
(847) 680-8600

Indiana

Emergency Animal Clinic
1313 Broadway, Fort Wayne
(219) 426-1062

Indianapolis Vet Emergency Clinic
5245 Victory Dr., Indianapolis
(317) 782-4418

Veterinary Clinics of America
4030 W. 86th St., Indianapolis
(317) 872-0200

All Pet Emergencies
5044 State Rte. 261, Newburgh
(812) 422-3300

New Carlisle Animal Clinic
8935 East US 20, New Carlisle
(219) 654-3129

Calumet Emergency Veterinary Clinic
216 W. Lincoln Hwy., Schererville
(219) 865-0970

Arbor View Animal Hospital
244 W. US Hwy. 6, Valparaiso
(219) 762-6586

Iowa

Animal Emergency Clinic
1330 2nd Ave., Des Moines
(515) 280-3051

Kansas

Mission Medvet
5501 Johnson Dr., Mission
(913) 722-5566

Emergency Veterinary Clinic
10333 Metcalf, Overland Park
(913) 649-6850

Wichita Emergency Veterinary Clinic
737 S. Washington, Wichita
(316) 262-5321

Kentucky

Colonial Animal Clinic
1601 Argillite Rd., Flatwoods
(606) 836-8112

Hagyard Davidson McGee Veterinarians
4250 Ironworks Pike, Lexington
(859) 255-8741

Jefferson Animal & Emergency Hospital
4504 Outer Loop, Louisville
(502) 966-4104

Louisiana

Westbank Pet Emergency Clinic, Inc.
403 Lapalco Blvd., Gretna
(504) 392-1932

Animal Emergency Clinic
1955 Veterans Memorial Blvd., Metairie
(504) 271-1234

Pet Corner
9954 Lake Forest Blvd., New Orleans
(504) 244-8550

Maine

Norway Veterinary Hospital
Route 26, Lower Main St., Norway
(207) 743-6384

Animal Emergency Clinic
352 Warren Ave., Portland
(207) 878-3121

Maryland

Anne Arundel Veterinary Emergency Clinic, Inc.
2138 B Generals Hwy., Annapolis
(410) 224-0331

Emergency Veterinary Clinic
32 Mellor Ave., Catonsville
(410) 788-7040

Veterinary Referral Associates, Inc.
15021 Dufief Mill Rd., Gaithersburg
(301) 340-3129

Beltway Emergency Hospital
11660 Annapolis Rd., Rt. 450, Glenn Dale
(301) 464-3737

Emergency Animal Center, Inc.
1896 Urbana Pike, #23, Hyattstown
(301) 831-1088

Metropolitan Emergency Animal Clinic
12106 Nebel St., Rockville
(301) 770-5225

Animal Emergency Clinic
1711 York Rd., Timonium
(410) 252-8387

Veterinary Emergency Treatment Service
3 Rockefeller Ct., Waldorf
(301) 638-0988

Westminster Veterinary Hospital-Emergency Trauma Center
269 W. Main St., Westminster
(410) 848-3363

Massachusetts

Angell Memorial Animal Hospital
350 S. Huntington Ave., Boston
(617) 522-7282

Roberts Animal Hospital
516 Washington St., Hanover
(781) 826-2306

Holyoke Animal Hospital
320 Easthampton Rd., Holyoke
(413) 538-8700

Animal Health Care Associates
Martha's Vineyard Airport, Martha's Vineyard
(508) 693-6515

Veterinary Emergency Center
1299 Highland Ave., Needham
(617) 453-0143

Tufts University School Of Veterinary Medicine
200 Westboro Rd., North Grafton
(508) 839-5395

South Deerfield Veterinary Clinic
I-91 (Elm Street Exit), South Deerfield
(413) 665-5107

Veterinary Associates of Cape Cod
16 Commonwealth Ave., South Yarmouth
(508) 394-3566

Rowley Memorial Animal Hospital
53 Bliss St., Springfield
(413) 785-1221

Animal Extra Care
19 Main St., Wakefield
(781) 245-0045

Animal Emergency Center
595 West Center St., West Bridgewater
(508) 583-4220

Michigan

Veterinary Emergency Service West
24400 Ford Rd., Dearborn Heights
(313) 274-3300

Lansing Veterinary Urgent Care
5133 S. Martin Luther King Jr. Blvd., Lansing
(517) 393-9200

Veterinary Medical Center
243 N. Jebauy Dr., Ludington
(231) 845-0585

Veterinary Emergency Service & Critical Care
28223 John R Rd., Madison Heights
(248) 547-4677

Michigan Veterinary Emergency Care
21600 West 11 Mile Rd., Southfield
(248) 354-0303

Affiliated Veterinary Emergency Clinic
14085 Northline Rd., Southgate
(734) 284-1700

Union Lake Veterinary Hospital
6545 Looley Lake Rd., Waterford
(248) 363-1508

Minnesota

South Metro Animal Emergency Clinic
14520 Pennock Ave., Apple Valley
(952) 953-3737

Coon Rapids Clinic
1615 Coon Rapids Blvd., Coon Rapids
(612) 754-9434

Emergency Veterinary Service
4708 Olson Memorial Hwy., Golden Valley
(763) 529-6560

Animal Emergency Clinic
301 University Ave., St. Paul
(651) 293-1800

Mississippi

Bienville Animal Hospital
1524 US 90 East, Ocean Springs
(228) 872-1231

Missouri

Animal Emergency Clinic
12501 Natural Bridge Rd., Bridgeton
(314) 739-1500

Animal Emergency Clinic St. Louis
9937 Big Bend Blvd., St. Louis
(314) 822-7600

Montana

Animal Medical Clinic
5100 9th Ave. South, Great Falls
(406) 761-8183

Nebraska

VCA-Rohrig Animal Hospital
8022 W. Dodge Rd., Omaha
(402) 399-8100

Nevada

Carson Tahoe Veterinary Hospital
3389 S. Carson St., Carson City
(775) 883-8238

Animal Emergency Center
1914 E. Sahara Ave., Las Vegas
(702) 457-8050

Lake Mead Animal Hospital
4805 E. Lake Mead Blvd., Las Vegas
(702) 453-5906

Painted Desert Animal Hospital
4601 N. Rancho Dr., Las Vegas
(702) 645-2543

Animal Emergency Center
6427 S. Virginia St., Reno
(775) 851-3600

New Hampshire

Animal Emergency Clinic
2626 Brown Ave., Pine Island Plaza, Manchester
(603) 666-6677

State Line Veterinary Hospital
325 S. Daniel Webster Hwy., Nashua
(603) 888-2751

Animal Medical Center
1550 Woodbury Ave., Portsmouth
(603) 436-4922

New Jersey

Ocean County Veterinary Hospital
838 River Ave., Lakewood
(732) 363-7202

Oradell Animal Hospital
481 Kinderkamack Rd., Oradell
(201) 262-0010

Alliance Emergency Veterinary Clinic
540 Route 10 West, Randolph
(973) 328-2844

New Mexico

Albuquerque Animal Emergency Clinic
5005 Prospect Ave. N.E., Albuquerque
(505) 884-3433

Great Plains Veterinary Clinic
2720 Lovington Hwy., Hobbs
(505) 392-5513

Ruidoso Animal Clinic
160 Sudderth, Ruidoso
(505) 257-4027

Emergency Veterinary Clinic of Santa Fe
1911 St. Michael's Dr., Santa Fe
(505) 984-0625

New York

Central Veterinary Hospital
388 Central Ave., Albany
(518) 434-2115

Greater Buffalo Veterinary Services
4949 Main St., Amherst
(716) 839-4043

Bayside Animal Clinic
36-43 Bell Blvd., Bayside
(718) 224-4451

Bellerose Animal Hospital
242-01 Jamaica Ave., Bellerose
(718) 347-1057

Brooklyn Veterinary Emergency Service
453 Bay Bridge Ave., Brooklyn
(718) 748-5180

Crawford Far Rockaway Animal Hospital
708 Beach-19th St., Far Rockaway
(718) 327-0256

Boulevard Animal Clinic
112-49 Queens Blvd., Forest Hills
(718) 261-1231

Great Neck Animal Clinic
501 Great Neck Rd., Great Neck
(516) 466-9191

Homer/Tully Animal Clinics
66 S. West St., Homer
(607) 749-7223

Queens Veterinary Emergency Clinic
187-11 Hillside Ave., Jamaica
(718) 454-4141

Hilton Hospital for Animals
120 Merrick Rd., Lynbrook
(516) 887-2914

Animal Medical Center
510 East 62nd St., New York
(212) 838-8100

Manhattan Veterinary Group
240 East 80th St., New York
(212) 988-1000

West End Veterinary Emergency Center
250 West 100th St., New York
(212) 666-7387

Orchard Park Veterinary Medical Center
3507 Orchard Park Rd., Orchard Park
(716) 662-6660

Animal Emergency Clinic of Hudson Valley
328 Manchester Rd., Poughkeepsie
(845) 471-8242

Animal Hospital Group
5 Boone St., Staten Island
(718) 494-0050

Veterinary Emergency Center
1293 Clove Rd., Staten Island
(718) 720-4211

Animal Emergency Clinic
2612 Erie Blvd. East, Syracuse
(315) 446-7933

Valley Cottage Animal Hospital
202 Route 303, Valley Cottage
(845) 268-9263

Central Veterinary Associates
73 W. Merrick Rd., Valley Stream
(516) 825-3066

Animal Care Hospital
4535 Old Vestal Rd., Vestal
(607) 770-9999

Schroon River Animal Hospital
Horicon Avenue, Warrensburg
(518) 623-3181

Nassau Animal Emergency Clinic
740 Old County Rd., Westbury
(516) 333-6262

North Carolina

Emergency Veterinary Clinic
2440 Plantation Center Dr., Charlotte
(704) 376-9622

Freedom Animal Hospital
3055 Freedom Dr., Charlotte
(704) 399-6534

Triangle Pet Emergency Treatment Service
3319 Chapel Hill Blvd., Durham
(919) 489-0615

Veterinary Emergency Clinic of Gaston County
728 E. Franklin Blvd., Gastonia
(704) 866-7918

Cabarrow Emergency Veterinary Clinic
1317 S. Cannon Blvd., Kannapolis
(704) 932-1182

After Hours Small Animal Emergency Clinic
409 Vick Ave., Raleigh
(919) 781-5145

Animal Emergency Clinic at Tryon Hills
3535 South Wilmington St., Raleigh
(919) 622-5559

Wilmington Animal Emergency Clinic
5739 Oleander Dr., Wilmington
(910) 791-7387

Forsyth After Hours Veterinary Emergency Clinic
7781 Northpoint Blvd., Winston-Salem
(336) 896-0902

Ohio

County Animal Hospital
11605 Stablewatch Ct., Cincinnati
(513) 398-8000

Emergency Veterinary Clinic of Cincinnati
4779 Red Bank Rd., Cincinnati
(513) 561-5688

Cleveland Animal Emergency & Specialty Clinic
5320 West 140th St., Cleveland
(216) 362-6000

Columbus Veterinary Emergency Service
5747 Cleveland Ave., Columbus
(614) 890-2545

Dayton Emergency Vet Clinic
2714 Springboro West, Dayton
(937) 293-2714

Animal Medical & Emergency Hospital
3859 West Dublin-Granville Rd., Dublin
(614) 889-2556

Lorain County Animal Emergency Center
1909 North Ridge Rd., Lorain
(440) 240-1400

Aaron Animal Clinic and Emergency Hospital
6210 Broadview Rd., Parma
(216) 901-9980

Oklahoma

Midtown Animal Hospital
1101 S.W. Park Ave., Lawton
(580) 353-3438

Veterinary Emergency and Critical Care Hospital
1800 W. Memorial Rd., Oklahoma City
(405) 749-6989

Animal Emergency Center
7220 E. 41st St., Tulsa
(918) 665-0508

Oregon

Willamette Veterinary Clinic
650 S.W. Third St., Corvallis
(541) 753-2223

Dove Lewis Emergency Animal Hospital
1984 N.W. Pettygrove St., Portland
(503) 228-7281

Salem Veterinary Emergency Clinic
450 Pine St. N.E., Salem
(503) 588-8082

Emergency Veterinary Clinic of Tualatin
19314 S.W. Mohave Ct., Tualatin
(503) 691-7922

Pennsylvania

Providence Veterinary Hospital
24th and Providence Ave., Chester
(610) 872-4000

Valley Central Emergency Veterinary Hospital
210 Fullerton Ave., Fullerton
(610) 435-5588

Animal Emergency & Critical Care Service
1900 W. Old Lincoln Hwy., Langhorne
(215) 750-2774

Langdon & Leveto Veterinary Hospital & Emergency Center
316 Conneaut Lake Rd., Meadville
(814) 337-3271

Metropolitan Veterinary Center
560 McNeilly Rd., Pittsburgh
(412) 344-6888

Allegheny Veterinary Emergency Association
1835 Rte. 286, Pittsburgh
(724) 325-1881

Castle Shannon Veterinary Hospital
3610 Library Rd., Pittsburgh
(412) 885-2500

Tri-County Veterinary Emergency Service
2250 Old Bethlehem Pike, Quakertown
(215) 536-6245

Animal Emergency Clinic
3256 Susquehanna Tr., York
(717) 767-5355

Rhode Island

North Kingstown Animal Hospital
3637 Quaker Ln., North Kingstown
(401) 295-9777

Animal Care Services
135 Meadow St., Warwick
(401) 738-6695

Warwick Animal Hospital
1950 Elmwood Ave., Warwick
(401) 785-2222

South Carolina

South Carolina Veterinary Emergency Care Center
132 Stonemark Ln., Columbia
(803) 798-3837

Animal Hospital of North Myrtle Beach
2501 Hwy. 17 S., North Myrtle Beach
(843) 272-8121

Veterinary Emergency Clinic of Spartanburg
1291 Ashville Hwy., Spartanburg
(864) 591-1923

Tennessee

Keith Street Animal Clinic
1990 Keith St., Cleveland
(423) 476-1804

After Hours Pet Emergency Clinic
215 Center Park Dr., Knoxville
(865) 966-3888

Fox Meadows Pet Emergency Hospital
5650 Mt. Moriah, Memphis
(901) 365-9690

Texas

I-20 Animal Medical Center
5750 I-20 West, Arlington
(817) 478-9238

Animal Emergency Hospital of Austin
4106 N. Lamar Blvd., Austin
(512) 459-4336

Emergency Animal Hospital of Austin
4544 S. Lamar Blvd., #760, Austin
(512) 899-0955

Emergency Animal Hospital of Austin
12034 Research Blvd., Austin
(512) 331-6121

North Texas Emergency Pet Clinic
1712 W. Frankford Rd., Carrollton
(972) 323-1310

Emergency Animal Clinic
12101 Greenville Ave., #118, Dallas
(972) 994-9110

Whiterock Animal Hospital
11414 East Northwest Hwy., Dallas
(214) 328-3255

El Paso Animal Emergency Center
2101 Texas Ave., El Paso
(915) 545-1148

Airport Freeway Animal Emergency Clinic
209 S. Main St., Euless
(817) 571-2088

Animal Emergency Clinic
8921 Katy Frwy., Houston
(713) 932-9589

Animal Emergency Clinic Southeast
10331 Gulf Frwy., Houston
(713) 941-8460

Animal Emergency Clinic Southeast
1100 Gulf Frwy. S., #104, League City
(281) 332-1678

Lake Olympia Animal Hospital
6311 Hwy. 6, Missouri City
(281) 499-7242

Permian Basin Emergency Veterinary Clinic
13528 W. US Hwy. 80, Odessa
(915) 561-8301

Emergency Pet Clinic
8503 Broadway, #101, San Antonio
(210) 822-2873

Southwest Freeway Animal Hospital & Emergency Center
15575 Southwest Frwy., Sugarland
(281) 491-8387

Ridgmar Animal Hospital
2020 S. Las Vegas Tr., White Settlement
(817) 246-2431

Utah

Animal Medical Services
469 W. Center St., Orem
(801) 225-3346

Central Valley Emergency Animal Clinic
55 E. Miller Ave., Salt Lake City
(801) 487-1325

Vermont

Lamoille Valley Veterinary Services
P.O. Box 41, Hyde Park
(802) 888-7911

Virginia

Virginia-Maryland Veterinary Emergency Service
2660 Duke St., Alexandria
(703) 823-3601

Albemarle Veterinary Hospital
445 Westfield Rd., Charlottesville
(434) 973-6146

Animal Emergency Clinic
1210 Snowden St., Fredericksburg
(540) 371-0554

Animal Emergency Hospital
2 Cardinal Park Dr., #101B, Leesburg
(703) 777-5755

Animal Emergency Clinic of Central Virginia
1000 Miller Park Sq., Lynchburg
(804) 846-1504

Veterinary Referral of Northern Virginia
610 Centreville Rd., Manassas
(703) 631-1030

Veterinary Emergency Center
3312 W. Gary St., Richmond
(804) 353-9000

Springfield Emergency Veterinary Hospital
6651-F Backlick Rd., Springfield
(703) 451-8900

Silver Spring Veterinary Hospital
241 Garber Ln., Winchester
(540) 662-2301

Washington

Auburn Veterinary Hospital
718 Auburn Way N., Auburn
(253) 833-4510

Aerowood Animal Hospital
2975 156th St. S.E., Bellevue
(425) 746-6557

Snoqualmie Valley Animal Hospital
32020 S.E. 40th St., Fall City
(425) 222-7220

Vista Veterinary Hospital
5603 W. Canal Dr., Kennewick
(509) 783-2131

Animal Emergency & Referral Center
19511 24th Ave. W., Lynnwood
(425) 745-6745

Animal Emergency/Trauma Center
19494 7th Ave. N.E., #F, Poulsbo
(360) 697-7771

Emerald City Emergency Clinic
4102 Stone Way N., Seattle
(206) 634-9000

Five Corners Veterinary Hospital
15707 1st Ave. S., Seattle
(206) 243-2982

Pet Emergency Clinic
21 Mission Ave. E., Spokane
(509) 326-6670

Animal Emergency Clinic
5608 South Durango, Tacoma
(253) 474-0791

Emergency Veterinary Service
6818 E. 4th Plain Blvd., Vancouver
(360) 694-3007

West Virginia

Middletown Animal Clinic
Route 5, Fairmont
(304) 366-6130

Kanawha Valley Animal Emergency Clinic
5304 MacCorkle Ave. S.W., South Charleston
(304) 768-2911

Wisconsin

Fox Valley Animal Referral Center
842 Westhill Blvd., Appleton
(920) 993-9193

Animal Emergency Center
2100 W. Silver Spring Ave., Glendale
(414) 540-6710

Emergency Clinic for Animals
229 W. Beltline Hwy., Madison
(608) 274-7772

Animal Clinic & Hospital
2734 Calumet Dr., Sheboygan
(920) 565-2125

Emergency Veterinary Service
360 Bluemound Rd., Waukesha
(262) 542-3241

Canada

British Columbia

Animal Emergency Clinic
#103-6337 198th St., Langley
(604) 514-1711

Animal Emergency Clinic
1590 West 4th Ave., Vancouver
(604) 734-5104

Ontario

Park Animal Hospital
1958 Burnham Thorpe Rd. E., Mississauga
(905) 625-5222

Niagara Veterinary Emergency Clinic
210 Glendale Ave., St. Catherines
(905) 641-3185

PET-FRIENDLY LODGINGS

How to Use the Listings
U.S. Lodgings
Canadian Lodgings

Some 10,000 AAA-RATED® properties across North America accept traveling pets. This guide provides listings for those lodgings in the United States and Canada that roll out the welcome mat for pets as well as the people who love them.

For the purpose of this book, "pets" are domestic cats or dogs. If you are planning to travel with any other kind of animal — particularly such exotic pets as birds or reptiles — check with the property before making definite plans. If you are taking a nontraditional pet, expect to keep her crated at all times.

Note: Always inform the management that you are traveling with an animal; you may be fined if you do not declare your pet. Many properties require guests with pets to sign a waiver or release form and to pay for the room with a credit card. Of course, whether you pay in cash or by credit card, you will be held liable for any damages caused by your pet, even if the property does not charge a deposit or pet fee. It is not a good idea to leave your pet unattended in the room, but if you must, crate him and notify the management. When in public areas, keep your pet leashed and do not allow him to disturb other guests.

About the Listings

Geographic listings are used for accuracy and consistency; lodgings are listed under the city or town in which they physically are located — or in some cases under the nearest recognized city or town. For a complete list of all cities within a state or province, see the comprehensive City Index at the beginning of the corresponding section.

U.S. properties are given first, followed by Canadian properties. Most listings are alphabetically organized by state or province, city and establishment name. Reflecting contemporary travel patterns, properties in some cities or towns may instead be listed within destination cities or areas. Such "vicinity cities" and their listings will be shown alphabetically in the destination city or area, and the vicinity city also will appear in alphabetical order in the City Index, along with the page number on which the listings begin.

Each listing provides the following information *(see sample listing, next page)*:

❶ Symbol denoting Official Appointment (OA) properties. The OA program permits properties to display and advertise the 4- or 5-diamond emblem. OAs have a special interest in serving AAA/CAA members. Ask if they offer special member amenities such as free breakfast, early check-in/late check-out, free room upgrade, free local phone calls, etc.

❷ Diamond rating.

❸ Property name.

❹ Lodging classification.

❺ Special amenities offered. These properties provide an additional benefit to pets, such as treats, toys or gifts, pet sitting and/or walking, a pet menu, food/water dishes, pet sheets or pillows, pet beds or other extras.

❻ Telephone number.

❼ Two-person (2P) rate year-round, and cancellation notice validity period (if more than 48 hrs.). Rates listed are usually daily, but weekly rates also may be listed. **Note:** Most properties accept any or all of the major credit cards, including American Express, MasterCard and VISA. If a property accepts only cash, the phrase "(no credit cards)" follows the rates.

❽ Physical address and highway directions. If no physical address was available, the phrase "call for directions" appears.

❾ Exterior or interior corridors.

❿ Pet policies. If the phrase "pets accepted" appears, the property does accept pets but specific information was unavailable at press time. Otherwise, pet-specific policies are denoted as follows:

Size. "Very small" denotes pets weighing up to 10 pounds; "small," up to 25 pounds; "medium," up to 50 pounds; and "large," up to 100 pounds. If no size is specified, the property accepts pets of all sizes.

Species. "Other" indicates the property accepts animals other than dogs and cats. Always call ahead and specify the type of pet you plan to bring.

Deposits and fees. Includes the dollar amount, the type of charge (refundable deposit or nonrefundable fee), the frequency of the charge and whether the charge is per pet or per room.

Designated rooms. Guests with pets are placed in certain rooms, often smoking rooms or those on the ground floor.

Housekeeping service. The phrase "service with restrictions" denotes properties that require the pet to be crated, removed or attended by the owner during housekeeping service.

Supervision. The pet is required to be supervised at all times.

Crate. The pet must be crated when the owner is not present. If this policy applies only to cats, the phrase "(cats only)" will follow.

❿ Property discounts and amenities:

〔SAVE〕 Minimum 10% discount.

〔SAVE〕 Show Your Card & Save partners.

〔ASK〕 May offer discount.

〔S₫〕 Senior discount.

✕ Non-smoking rooms.

〔&M〕 Semi-accessible or 〔&M〕 fully accessible.

〔⬙〕 Hearing impaired.

〔⬙〕 Roll-in showers.

⬛ Refrigerator.

⬛ Coffee maker.

⬛ Restaurant on premises.

⬛ Outdoor pool.

⬛ Indoor pool.

⬛ Indoor/outdoor pool.

✕ Recreational activities.

〔⍼〕 No air conditioning.

〔⍼〕 No TV.

⬛ No telephones.

Please note, some in-room amenities represented by the icons in the listings may be available only in selected rooms, and may incur an extra fee. Please inquire when making your reservations.

It is important to remember that animal policies do change; always confirm policies, restrictions and fees with the lodging when making reservations and again 1-2 days before departure.

Listing information is subject to change. All listing information was accurate at press time. However, lodging rates and policies change and the publisher cannot be held liable for changes occurring after publication.

AAA Diamond Ratings

Before a property is listed by AAA, it must satisfy a set of minimum standards regarding basic lodging needs as identified by AAA members. If a property meets those requirements, it is assigned a diamond rating reflecting the overall quality of the establishment.

AAA ratings range from one to five diamonds and indicate the property's physical and service standards as measured against the standards of each diamond level. The rating process takes into account the property's classification; i.e., its physical structure and style of operation.

◈ Properties meet all listing requirements. They are clean and well-maintained.

◈◈ Properties maintain the attributes offered at the 1-diamond level while showing noticeable enhancements in room decor and quality of furnishings.

(continued next page)

▼▼▼ Properties show a marked upgrade in physical attributes, services and comfort. Additional amenities, services and facilities may be offered.

▼▼▼ ▼ Properties reflect an exceptional degree of hospitality, service and attention to detail while offering upscale facilities and a variety of amenities.

▼▼▼ ▼▼ Property facilities and operations exemplify an impeccable standard of excellence while exceeding guest expectations in hospitality and service. These renowned properties are both striking and luxurious, offering many extra amenities.

Lodging Classifications

A Apartment: Establishments that primarily offer transient guest accommodations with one or more bedrooms, a living room, a full kitchen and an eating area. Studio-type apartments may combine the sleeping and living areas into one room.

BB Bed & Breakfast: Usually smaller establishments emphasizing a more personal relationship between operators and guests, leading to an "at home" feeling. Guest units tend to be individually decorated. Rooms may not include some modern amenities such as televisions and telephones, and may have a shared bathroom. Usually owner-operated, with a common room or parlor separate from the innkeeper's living quarters, where guests and operators can interact during evening and breakfast hours. Evening office closures are normal. A continental or full, hot breakfast is served and is included in the room rate.

X Complex: A combination of two or more types of lodging classifications.

CO Condominium: Establishments that primarily offer guest accommodations that are privately owned by individuals and available for rent. These can include apartment-style units or homes. A variety of room styles and decor treatments as well as limited housekeeping service is typical. May have off-site registration.

C Cottage: Establishments that primarily provide individual housing units that may offer one or more separate sleeping rooms, a living room and cooking facilities. Usually incorporate rustic decor treatments and are geared to vacationers.

CI Country Inn: Although similar in definition to a bed and breakfast, country inns are usually larger in size, provide more spacious public areas and offer a dining facility that serves at least breakfast and dinner. May be located in a rural setting or downtown area.

H Hotel: Usually high-rise establishments offering a full range of on-premises food and beverage service, cocktail lounge, entertainment, conference facilities, business services, shops and recreational activities. Wide range of services provided by uniformed staff on duty 24 hours. Parking arrangements vary.

L Lodge: Typically two or more stories with all facilities in one building, rustic decor. Located in vacation, ski, fishing areas, etc. Usually has food and beverage service.

M Motel: Low-rise or multistory establishment offering limited public and recreational facilities.

MI Motor Inn: Single or multistory establishment offering on-premises food and beverage service. Meeting and banquet facilities and some recreational activities. Usually complimentary on-site parking.

RA Ranch: Often offers rustic decor treatments and food and beverage facilities. Entertainment and recreational activities are geared to a Western-style adventure vacation. May provide some meeting facilities.

R Resort: Geared to vacation travelers. It is a destination offering varied food and beverage outlets, specialty shops, meeting or conference facilities, entertainment and extensive recreational facilities for special interests such as golf, tennis, skiing, fishing and water sports. Assorted social and recreational programs are typically offered in season, and a variety of package plans are usually available, including meal plans incorporated into the rates. Larger resorts may offer a variety of guest accommodations.

United States

CITY INDEX

ANDALUSIA

▼▼ Days Inn M
(334) 427-0050. **$56, 7 days notice.** 1604 E Bypass Hwy 84. Just s of US 84. Ext corridors. **Pets:** Medium, other species. $6 daily fee/pet. Designated rooms, service with restrictions, supervision.

SAVE S⬦ ✕ 🛏 🖵 ⇌

ARDMORE

⟨AAA⟩ ▼▼ Budget Inn M
(256) 423-6699. **$39-$69.** 28555 Boyds Chapel Rd. I-65, exit 365. Ext corridors. **Pets:** Accepted.

SAVE S⬦ ✕ 🛏

ATHENS

⟨AAA⟩ ▼▼▼ Best Western Inn M
(256) 233-4030. **$54-$99.** 1329 Hwy 72 E. I-65, exit 351, just nw. Ext corridors. **Pets:** Very small. $7 daily fee/pet. Service with restrictions, supervision.

SAVE S⬦ ✕ 🛏 🖵 ⇌

▼▼ Days Inn Athens M
(256) 233-7500. **$45-$50.** 1322 Hwy 72 E. Just w of jct I-65 (US 72). Ext corridors. **Pets:** Accepted.

SAVE S⬦ ✕ 🛏 🖵 ⇌

▼▼▼ Hampton Inn-Athens M
(256) 232-0030. **$79-$85.** 1488 Thrasher Blvd. I-65, exit 351, just ne. Ext corridors. **Pets:** Accepted.

SAVE S⬦ ✕ 🛏 🖵 ⇌

ATTALLA

⟨AAA⟩ ▼▼▼ Holiday Inn Express
        Gadsden M ❀
(256) 538-7861. **$60.** 801 Cleveland Ave. I-59, exit 183, just e on US 278 and 431. Ext corridors. **Pets:** Small. Service with restrictions, supervision.

SAVE S⬦ ✕ ⟨⟩ 🛏 🖵 ⇌

AUBURN

⟨AAA⟩ ▼▼▼ Auburn University Hotel & Dixon
        Conference Center 🏨
(334) 821-8200. **$69-$99.** 241 S College St. I-85, exit 51, 3.5 mi w. Int corridors. **Pets:** Large, other species. Supervision.

SAVE S⬦ ✕ ⬟M 🅿 🛏 🖵 🍴 ⇌

BESSEMER

▼▼ Jameson Inn M
(205) 428-3194. **$55-$70.** 5021 Academy Ln. I-59/20, exit 108. Ext corridors. **Pets:** Accepted.

✕ ⬟M 🅿 ⟨⟩ ⇌

BIRMINGHAM

⟨AAA⟩ ▼▼▼ AmeriSuites
        (Birmingham/Inverness) M
(205) 995-9242. **$109-$129, 7 days notice.** 4686 Hwy 280 E. I-459, exit 19, 1.5 mi s. Int corridors. **Pets:** Accepted.

SAVE S⬦ ✕ ⬟M ⟨⟩ 🛏 🖵 ⇌

⟨AAA⟩ ▼▼ Baymont Inn &
        Suites-Birmingham M
(205) 995-9990. **$59-$69.** 513 Cahaba Park Cir. I-459, exit 19, 1.5 mi s off US 280. Int corridors. **Pets:** Accepted.

SAVE S⬦ ✕ 🛏 🖵

⟨AAA⟩ ▼▼▼ Best Suites of America M
(205) 940-9990. **$93-$130.** 140 State Farm Pkwy. I-65, exit 255, 0.5 mi nw. Int corridors. **Pets:** Accepted.

SAVE S⬦ ✕ 🅿 ⟨⟩ 🛏 🖵 ⇌

⟨AAA⟩ ▼▼▼ Best Western Rime Garden Inn &
        Suites M
(205) 951-1200. **$89, 7 days notice.** 5320 Beacon Dr. I-20 W, exit 133, just s. Ext corridors. **Pets:** Accepted.

SAVE S⬦ ✕ 🛏 🖵 🍴 ⇌

▼▼▼▼ **Crowne Plaza Birmingham-The Redmont** H
(205) 324-2101. **$99-$159.** 2101 Fifth Ave N. Corner of Fifth Ave and 21st St; I-65, exit 22nd St, then s. Int corridors. **Pets:** Accepted.

ASK SÓ ✕ ▣ ⑪

▼▼▼▼ **Drury Inn & Suites-Birmingham** M
(205) 967-2450. **$75-$95.** 3510 Grandview Pkwy. I-459, exit 19, southeast corner. Int corridors. **Pets:** Accepted.

✕ ⟨⟩ 🖬 ▣ ⬲

▼▼▼▼ **Embassy Suites Birmingham** H
(205) 879-7400. **$109-$152.** 2300 Woodcrest Pl. Just n of jct US 31 and 280, exit 21st Ave southbound, then 0.3 mi s. Int corridors. **Pets:** Accepted.

SAVE SÓ ✕ ⟨⟩ 🖬 ▣ ⑪ ⬲

▼▼▼▼ **Holiday Inn-Airport** MI
(205) 591-6900. **$79-$99.** 5000 10th Ave N. I-59/20, exit 129, just s. Int corridors. **Pets:** Small. $25 one-time fee/room. No service, supervision.

ASK SÓ ✕ ▣ ⑪ ⬲

▼▼▼▼ **La Quinta Inn & Suites-Birmingham Homewood** M
(205) 290-0150. **$85-$115.** 60 State Farm Pkwy. I-65, exit 255, 0.9 mi on northwest frontage road. Int corridors. **Pets:** Accepted.

SAVE ✕ ⟨⟩ 🖬 ▣ ⬲

▼▼▼▼ **Pickwick Hotel** H
(205) 933-9555. **$94-$159.** 1023 20th St S. 1.5 mi s of downtown. Int corridors. **Pets:** Large, other species. $25 daily fee/pet. Service with restrictions.

ASK SÓ ✕ 🖬 ▣

⟨AAA⟩ ▼▼▼▼ **Residence Inn By Marriott** A ❀
(205) 991-8686. **$69-$115.** 3 Green Hill Pkwy at US 280. 2 mi s of jct I-459 and US 280. Ext corridors. **Pets:** Other species. $100 one-time fee/room. Service with restrictions.

SAVE ✕ 🖬 ▣ ⬲

⟨AAA⟩ ▼▼▼▼ **Residence Inn by Marriott** M
(205) 943-0044. **$107-$139.** 50 State Farm Pkwy. I-65, exit 255, 1 mi nw. Int corridors. **Pets:** $165 one-time fee/room. Service with restrictions, crate.

SAVE SÓ ✕ 🖬 ▣ ⬲

⟨AAA⟩ ▼▼▼▼ **The Tutwiler-A Wyndham Historic Hotel** H
(205) 322-2100. **$109-$134.** 2021 Park Place N. Downtown. Int corridors. **Pets:** Accepted.

SAVE SÓ ✕ ⟨⟩ 🖬 ▣ ⑪

CALERA

▼▼▼▼ **Holiday Inn Express** M
(205) 668-3641. **$69-$79.** 357 Hwy 304. I-65, exit 231, just se. Ext corridors. **Pets:** Accepted.

ASK SÓ ✕ ⟨⟩ ▣ ⬲

HOMEWOOD

▼▼ ▼▼ **Microtel** M
(205) 945-5550. **$34-$51, 5 days notice.** 251 Summit Pkwy. I-65, exit 256, 0.3 mi w. Int corridors. **Pets:** Accepted.

ASK SÓ ✕ ⟨⟩

▼▼▼▼ **The Mountain Brook Inn** MI
(205) 870-3100. **$89-$115.** 2800 Hwy 280. 5 mi se on US 280. Int corridors. **Pets:** Accepted.

ASK SÓ ✕ 🖬 ▣ ⑪ ⬲

⟨AAA⟩ ▼▼▼ **Red Roof Inn** M
(205) 942-9414. **$44-$59.** 151 Vulcan Rd. I-65, exit 256 northbound; exit 256A southbound, just nw. Ext corridors. **Pets:** Accepted.

SAVE ✕

⟨AAA⟩ ▼▼▼▼ **Shoney's Inn & Suites** M
(205) 916-0464. **$69-$89.** 226 Summit Pkwy. I-65, exit 256, 0.3 mi w; exit 256A southbound. Int corridors. **Pets:** Small. Service with restrictions, crate.

SAVE SÓ ✕ 🖬 ▣ ⬲

HOOVER

⟨AAA⟩ ▼▼▼▼ **AmeriSuites (Birmingham/Riverchase)** M
(205) 988-8444. **$115-$125, 7 days notice.** 2980 Hwy 150. Jct I-459 and US 31, 0.5 mi s on US 31, 0.8 mi w on SR 150. Int corridors. **Pets:** Small. Service with restrictions, supervision.

SAVE SÓ ✕ ⟨⟩ 🖬 ▣ ⬲

⟨AAA⟩ ▼▼▼▼ **La Quinta Inn & Suites-Birmingham Hoover** M
(205) 403-0096. **$76-$96.** 120 Riverchase Pkwy E. I-65, exit 247 (Valleydale Rd). Int corridors. **Pets:** Small, other species. Service with restrictions, supervision.

SAVE SÓ ✕ ⟨⟩ 🖬 ▣ ⬲

LEEDS

⟨AAA⟩ ▼▼▼ **Days Inn of Leeds** M
(205) 699-9833. **$50-$150.** 1835 Ashville Rd. On US 411; 0.3 mi s of I-20, exit 144B westbound; exit 144A eastbound. Ext corridors. **Pets:** Medium, other species. $5 daily fee/pet. Designated rooms, service with restrictions, crate.

SAVE ✕ 🖬 ⬲

PELHAM

⟨AAA⟩ ▼▼▼ **Best Western Oak Mountain Inn** M
(205) 982-1113. **$69, 7 days notice.** 100 Bishop Cir. I-65, exit 246, just sw, then just s on State Park Rd. Int corridors. **Pets:** Accepted.

SAVE SÓ ✕ ⟨⟩ 🖬 ▣ ⬲

❀ **END METROPOLITAN AREA** ❀

BOAZ

▼▼ ▼▼ Key West Inn M
(256) 593-0800. **$51-$150, 30 days notice.** 10535 SR 168.
0.5 mi w of jct US 431. Ext corridors. **Pets:** Small. $5 daily
fee/pet. Service with restrictions, supervision.
A$K S🐾 ⊠ 🖥 🖳

▼▼ ▼▼ Rodeway Inn M
(256) 593-8410. **$48-$75, 3 days notice.** 751 Hwy 431 S.
SR 431. Ext/int corridors. **Pets:** Small. $10 daily fee/pet.
Designated rooms, service with restrictions, supervision.
SAVE S🐾 ⊠ ➿

CLANTON

▲▲▲ ▼▼▼▼ Best Western Inn M
(205) 280-1006. **$65-$80, 5 days notice.** 801 Bradberry Ln.
I-65, exit 205, 0.5 mi e. Ext corridors. **Pets:** $6 daily fee/
room. Service with restrictions.
SAVE S🐾 ⊠ 🖧 🖥 🖳 ➿

▼▼ ▼▼ Days Inn M
(205) 755-0510. **$55, 3 days notice.** 2000 Big M Blvd. I-65,
exit 205, just ne on US 31 and SR 22. Ext corridors.
Pets: Accepted.
SAVE S🐾 ⊠ ➿

▼▼ ▼▼ Key West Inn M
(205) 755-8500. **$55-$60, 5 days notice.** 2045 7th St S.
I-65, exit 205, just w on US 31 and SR 22. Ext corridors.
Pets: Accepted.
A$K S🐾 ⊠ 🖥 🖳

▼▼ ▼▼ Shoney's Inn MI
(205) 280-0306. **$48-$53.** 946 Lake Mitchell Rd. I-65, exit
208, just w. Ext corridors. **Pets:** Medium, other species. $20
deposit/room. Service with restrictions, supervision.
A$K ⊠ ⑪ ➿

CULLMAN

▲▲▲ ▼▼▼▼ Best Western Fairwinds Inn M
(256) 737-5009. **$59-$98.** 1917 Commerce Ave NW. I-65,
exit 310, just e. Ext corridors. **Pets:** Small. $9 one-time
fee/room. Crate.
SAVE S🐾 ⊠ 🖥 🖳 ➿

▼▼ ▼▼ Days Inn MI
(256) 739-3800. **$50-$75.** 1841 4th St SW. I-65, exit 308
(US 278). Ext corridors. **Pets:** Medium. $4 daily fee/room.
Service with restrictions, supervision.
SAVE S🐾 ⊠ 🖥 ⑪ ➿

DALEVILLE

▼▼ ▼▼ Econo Lodge M
(334) 598-6304. **$47-$57.** 444 N Daleville Ave. 1 mi n jct
US 84 and SR 85. Ext corridors. **Pets:** Other species. $15
one-time fee/room. Service with restrictions.
SAVE S🐾 ⊠ 🖥 🖳 ➿

DECATUR

▲▲▲ ▼▼▼▼ Key West Inn & Suites M
(256) 355-1999. **$82.** 2212 Danville Rd. SR 67; at intersec-
tion with Beltline. Int corridors. **Pets:** Other species. $35
deposit/room. Service with restrictions, supervision.
SAVE ⊠ 🖧 🖥 🖳 ➿

▼▼ ▼▼ Ramada Limited M 🐾
(256) 353-0333. **$47.** 1317 E Hwy 67. On SR 67; 4 mi nw
of I-65, exit 334, 0.3 mi e of jct US 31. Ext corridors.
Pets: Small. $10 one-time fee/pet. Service with restrictions,
supervision.
A$K S🐾 ⊠ 🖥 🖳 ➿

DOTHAN

▲▲▲ ▼▼▼▼ Comfort Inn M
(334) 793-9090. **$74-$91.** 3593 Ross Clark Cir. 3 mi nw on
US 231; at jct US 84 W. Int corridors. **Pets:** Small, other
species. $5 daily fee/room. Designated rooms, service with
restrictions, supervision.
SAVE S🐾 ⊠ 🖧M 🖋 🖥 🖳 ➿

▼▼ ▼▼ Days Inn M 🐾
(334) 793-2550. **$41-$47, 7 days notice.** 2841 Ross Clark
Cir. 2 mi sw on US 231 Bypass. Ext corridors. **Pets:** Other
species. $5 daily fee/pet. Service with restrictions.
SAVE S🐾 ⊠ 🖥 🖳 ➿

▲▲▲ ▼▼▼▼ Econo Lodge M
(334) 673-8000. **$49-$60, 7 days notice.** 2910 Ross Clark
Cir. 2 mi sw on US 231 Bypass. Ext corridors. **Pets:** Very
small, dogs only. $10 daily fee/room. Designated rooms,
service with restrictions, supervision.
SAVE S🐾 ⊠ 🖧M 🖧 🖥 🖳 ➿

▲▲▲ ▼▼▼▼ Hampton Inn M
(334) 671-3700. **$59.** 3071 Ross Clark Cir. On US 231
Bypass; at jct US 84 W. Ext corridors. **Pets:** Other species.
$15 one-time fee/room. Service with restrictions.
SAVE S🐾 ⊠ 🖧M 🖋 🖥 🖳

▼▼▼▼ Holiday Inn-South MI
(334) 794-8711. **$52-$85.** 2195 Ross Clark Cir SE. 2 mi s
on US 231 Bypass; at jct US 84 W. Ext corridors.
Pets: Service with restrictions, supervision.
A$K S🐾 ⊠ 🖧M 🖧 🖥 🖳 ⑪ ➿

▲▲▲ ▼▼▼▼ Holiday Inn-West MI
(334) 794-6601. **$75-$80.** 3053 Ross Clark Cir. 2 mi w on
US 231 Bypass; just s of jct US 84 W. Ext corridors.
Pets: Accepted.
SAVE ⊠ 🖧M 🖋 🖧 🖥 🖳 ⑪ ➿

ENTERPRISE

▼▼ ▼▼ Comfort Inn M
(334) 393-2304. **$68-$73.** 615 Boll Weevil Cir. On SR 16;
0.5 mi n of jct SR 134 and US 84 Bypass. Ext corridors.
Pets: Other species. $25 one-time fee/pet. Service with
restrictions.
SAVE S🐾 ⊠ 🖋 🖥 🖳 ➿

▼▼▼▼ **Ramada Inn** M
(334) 347-6262. **$57-$62.** 630 Glover Ave. On SR 248; 0.5 mi w of US 84 Bypass. Ext corridors. **Pets:** Accepted.
(ASK) (S) ⊠ ⊘ (c) █ ▣ ⇌

EUFAULA

▼▼▼ **Ramada Inn** MI
(334) 687-2021. **$52.** 631 E Barbour St. On US 82; 0.5 mi e of jct US 431. Ext corridors. **Pets:** $10 one-time fee/room. Service with restrictions, supervision.
⊠ █ ▣ ⊺⊺ ⇌

EVERGREEN

▲▲▲ ▼▼▼▼ **Comfort Inn** M
(251) 578-4701. **$58-$78.** I-65/Bates Rd. I-65, exit 96 (SR 83), on southwest service road. Ext corridors. **Pets:** Small, other species. $5 daily fee/pet. Service with restrictions, supervision.
(SAVE) (S) ⊠ ⊘ █ ▣ ⇌

▼▼▼ **Days Inn of Evergreen** M
(251) 578-2100. **$50.** I-65, exit 96, just w on SR 83. Ext corridors. **Pets:** Accepted.
(SAVE) (S) ⊠ █

FLORENCE

▼ **Days Inn-Florence** M
(256) 766-2620. **$50-$70, 7 days notice.** 1915 Florence Blvd. US 72. Ext corridors. **Pets:** Small, other species. $50 deposit/pet. Designated rooms, service with restrictions, supervision.
(SAVE) (S) ⊠ █ ⇌

▼▼ **Homestead Executive Inn** MI
(256) 766-2331. **$38-$59, 3 days notice.** 505 S Court St. On US 43 and 72; at jct SR 17 and 157. Ext corridors. **Pets:** Other species. $10 daily fee/room. Service with restrictions, crate.
(ASK) (S) ⊠ █ ▣ ⊺⊺ ⇌

▲▲▲ ▼ **Super 8 Motel** M ☙
(256) 757-2167. **$50-$68.** 101 Hwy 72 & 43 E. E on US 72, 0.3 mi w of jct US 43. Ext corridors. **Pets:** Medium. $20 deposit/room, $5.50 daily fee/pet. Designated rooms, service with restrictions, supervision.
(SAVE) (S) ⊠ █ ⇌

FOLEY

▼▼▼▼ **Holiday Inn Express** M
(251) 943-9100. **Call for rates.** 2682 S Mackenzie St. On SR 59, 1.9 mi s of jct US 98. Ext corridors. **Pets:** Small, other species. $21.60 one-time fee/room. Service with restrictions.
⊠ (M) ⊘ (c) █ ⇌

▼▼ **Key West Inn** M
(251) 943-1241. **$58-$89, 7 days notice.** 2520 S McKenzie St. On SR 59; 1.8 mi s of jct US 98. Ext corridors. **Pets:** Accepted.
(ASK) (S) ⊠ █ ▣ ⇌

▼▼ **Riviera Lodge** M ☙
(251) 943-3339. **$45-$88.** 126 CR 20 W. SR 59, just e. Ext corridors. **Pets:** Large. $10 one-time fee/room. No service.
(ASK) (S) ⊠ ⊘ █ ▣ ⇌

GADSDEN

▲▲▲ ▼▼▼ **Red Roof Inn** M
(256) 382-9200. **$49-$61.** 1600 Rainbow Dr. I-59, exit 182; 4 mi e on I-759, exit 4A, just s on US 411. Ext corridors. **Pets:** Accepted.
(SAVE) ⊠ ⊘ █ ⇌

GREENVILLE

▲▲▲ ▼▼▼ **Best Western Inn** M
(334) 382-9200. **$50-$70, 7 days notice.** 56 Cahaba Rd. I-65, exit 130, just w on SR 185. Ext corridors. **Pets:** Medium, other species. $5 daily fee/room. Service with restrictions, crate.
(SAVE) (S) ⊠ ⊘ █ ⇌

▲▲▲ ▼▼▼ **Econo Lodge** M
(334) 382-3118. **$50-$65, 7 days notice.** 946 Fort Dale Rd. I-65, exit 130, just ne on SR 185. Ext corridors. **Pets:** $10 daily fee/pet. Service with restrictions, supervision.
(SAVE) (S) ⊠ █ ▣

▼▼▼▼ **Hampton Inn-Greenville** M
(334) 382-9631. **Call for rates.** 219 Interstate Dr. I-65, exit 130, 0.5 mi nw. Int corridors. **Pets:** Accepted.
(ASK) ⊠ (M) (c) █ ▣ ⇌

GUNTERSVILLE

▲▲▲ ▼▼▼ **Super 8 Motel-Guntersville** M
(256) 582-8444. **$46-$60.** 14341 Hwy 431 S. 2 mi s from jct SR 69. Ext corridors. **Pets:** Accepted.
(SAVE) ⊠ █

HAMILTON

▼▼ **Days Inn** M
(205) 921-1790. **$59-$69.** 1849 Military St S. US 78, exit 14, 1.1 mi ne on US 43. Ext corridors. **Pets:** Accepted.
(SAVE) (S) ⊠ (c) █ ▣ ⇌

▼▼ **Riverchase Inn** MI
(205) 921-7831. **$55-$60.** 2031 Military St S. US 78, exit 14. Ext corridors. **Pets:** Small, other species. Service with restrictions, supervision.
(ASK) (S) ⊠ █ ▣ ⊺⊺ ⇌

HUNTSVILLE

▲▲▲ ▼▼▼ **Baymont Inn & Suites-Huntsville** M
(256) 830-8999. **$69-$79.** 4890 University Dr. US 72, 5 mi w of jct US 231/431. Int corridors. **Pets:** Large, other species. $50 deposit/room. Designated rooms, no service, crate.
(SAVE) (S) ⊠ █ ▣ ⇌

▼▼▼ **Hilton Huntsville** 🅷
(256) 533-1400. **$99-$129.** 401 Williams Ave. Downtown.
Int corridors. **Pets:** Accepted.
〔SAVE〕 ⊠ 🔋 💻 ⑪ ⤳

▼▼▼▼ **La Quinta Inn-Huntsville Research Pk** 🅼
(256) 830-2070. **$62-$87, 14 days notice.** 4870 University
Dr. US 72, 5 mi w of US 231. Ext corridors. **Pets:** Accepted.
〔SAVE〕 🆂ó ⊠ 🔋 💻 ⤳

🅐🅐🅐 ▼▼▼▼ **La Quinta Inn-Huntsville Space
                Center** 🅼
(256) 533-0756. **$56-$71.** 3141 University Dr. US 72, 1.3 mi
w of jct US 231/431. Ext corridors. **Pets:** Small, other species. Service with restrictions.
〔SAVE〕 🆂ó ⊠ 🔋 💻 ⤳

MADISON

▼ **Motel 6–1087** 🅼
(256) 772-7479. **Call for rates.** 8995 Madison Blvd. I-565,
exit 8, just w. Ext corridors. **Pets:** Accepted.
⊠ 〔👟〕 🔋 ⤳

MOBILE

🅐🅐🅐 ▼▼▼ **Best Inns** 🅼
(251) 343-4911. **$52-$62.** 156 Beltline Hwy S. I-65, exit 4,
0.5 mi s on west frontage road. Int corridors.
Pets: Accepted.
〔SAVE〕 🆂ó ⊠ 〔👟〕 🔋 ⤳

🅐🅐🅐 ▼▼▼▼ **Best Suites of America** 🅼
(251) 343-4949. **$69-$100.** 150 S Beltline Hwy. I-65, exit 4,
0.5 mi sw on west service road. Int corridors.
Pets: Accepted.
〔SAVE〕 ⊠ 🔋 💻 ⤳

▼▼▼▼ **Drury Inn** 🅼
(251) 344-7700. **$78-$98.** 824 S Beltline Hwy. I-65, exit 3,
to Airport Blvd, just sw on service road. Int corridors.
Pets: Accepted.
⊠ 🔋 💻 ⤳

▼▼▼ **GuestHouse International Inn** 🅼
(251) 471-2402. **$35-$70.** 3132 Government Blvd. I-65, exit
1, just ne on service road. Int corridors. **Pets:** Accepted.
〔ASK〕 🆂ó ⊠ 💻 ⤳

▼▼▼▼ **Holiday Inn-Bellingrath Gardens** 🅼🅸
(251) 666-5600. **Call for rates, 30 days notice.** 5465 Hwy
90 W. I-10, exit 15B, just ne. Int corridors. **Pets:** Accepted.
〔ASK〕 ⊠ 🖉 🔋 💻 ⑪ ⤳

▼▼▼ **Holiday Inn-I-65** 🅼🅸 🐾
(251) 342-3220. **$65-$74.** 850 S Beltline Hwy. I-65, exit 3,
0.5 mi sw on west service road. Ext corridors. **Pets:** Large,
other species. $25 deposit/room. Service with restrictions,
crate.
〔ASK〕 🆂ó ⊠ 🔋 💻 ⑪ ⤳

▼▼ **Lafayette Plaza Hotel** 🅷
(251) 694-0100. **$70-$175, 3 days notice.** 301 Government
St. Downtown. Int corridors. **Pets:** Accepted.
〔ASK〕 🆂ó ⊠ 🔋 💻 ⑪ ⤳

🅐🅐🅐 ▼▼▼▼ **La Quinta Inn-Mobile** 🅼
(251) 343-4051. **$55-$85.** 816 Beltline Hwy S. I-65, exit 3,
to Airport Blvd, just sw on service road. Ext corridors.
Pets: Small. Service with restrictions, crate.
〔SAVE〕 ⊠ 🔋 💻 ⤳

🅐🅐🅐 ▼▼ **Olsson's Motel** 🅼
(251) 661-5331. **$36, 10 days notice.** 4137 Government
Blvd. I-65, exit 1, 2 mi w on US 90. Ext corridors.
Pets: Very small, dogs only. $10 daily fee/pet. Designated
rooms, service with restrictions, supervision.
〔SAVE〕 🆂ó ⊠ 🔋

🅐🅐🅐 ▼▼▼▼ **Radisson Admiral Semmes
                Hotel** 🅷
(251) 432-8000. **$109-$165.** 251 Government St. Downtown. Int corridors. **Pets:** Accepted.
〔SAVE〕 🆂ó ⊠ 🖉 🔋 💻 ⑪ ⤳

🅐🅐🅐 ▼▼▼ **Red Roof Inn-North** 🅼
(251) 476-2004. **$40-$53.** 33 S Beltline Hwy. I-65, exit 4,
just se. Ext corridors. **Pets:** Small, other species. No service, crate.
〔SAVE〕 ⊠

🅐🅐🅐 ▼▼▼ **Red Roof Inn-South** 🅼
(251) 666-1044. **$44-$56.** 5450 Coca Cola Rd. I-10, exit
15B, 0.3 mi e on US 90. Ext corridors. **Pets:** Small, other
species. Service with restrictions, crate.
〔SAVE〕 ⊠ 🖉

🅐🅐🅐 ▼▼▼ **Shoney's Inn of Mobile** 🅼🅸
(251) 660-1520. **$59-$79.** 5472A Inn Rd. I-10, exit 15B; at
jct US 90. Ext corridors. **Pets:** Other species. No service.
〔SAVE〕 🆂ó ⊠ 🔋 💻 ⤳

MONTGOMERY

🅐🅐🅐 ▼▼▼ **Baymont Inn &
                Suites-Montgomery** 🅼
(334) 277-6000. **$66-$76.** 5225 Carmichael Rd. I-85, exit 6,
just sw at East Blvd. Int corridors. **Pets:** Small. $50 deposit/
room. Designated rooms, service with restrictions, supervision.
〔SAVE〕 🆂ó ⊠ ♿M 🖉 🔋 💻 ⤳

🅐🅐🅐 ▼▼▼ **Best Inns of
                America-Montgomery** 🅼
(334) 270-9199. **$58-$63, 7 days notice.** 5135 Carmichael
Rd. I-85, exit 6, just sw. Int corridors. **Pets:** Other species.
〔SAVE〕 🆂ó ⊠ 🖉 〔👟〕 🔋 💻 ⤳

🅐🅐🅐 ▼▼▼▼ **Best Suites of America** 🅼
(334) 270-3223. **$69-$100.** 5155 Carmichael Rd. I-85, exit
6, just sw at East Blvd. Int corridors. **Pets:** Accepted.
〔SAVE〕 🆂ó ⊠ ♿M 🖉 〔👟〕 🔋 💻 ⤳

▼▼/▼▼ Econo Lodge M
(334) 284-3400. **$50-$52.** 4135 Troy Hwy. On US 82 and 231, 0.5 mi se of jct South and East blvds. Ext corridors. **Pets:** Very small. $8 daily fee/pet. Designated rooms, service with restrictions.
(SAVE) (×) 🖬 💻 ⊋

▼▼/▼▼ Holiday Inn-East M
(334) 272-0370. **$89-$99, 14 days notice.** 1185 Eastern Bypass. I-85, exit 6, just ne on US 80 and 231. Ext/int corridors. **Pets:** Accepted.
(ASK) (×) (&M) (⌀) (&) 🖬 💻 (¶) ⊋

(AAA) ▼▼/▼▼ La Quinta Inn-Montgomery M
(334) 271-1620. **$55-$85.** 1280 East Blvd. I-85, exit 6. Ext corridors. **Pets:** Small, other species. Service with restrictions, supervision.
(SAVE) (×) (⌀) 🖬 💻 ⊋

(AAA) ▼▼/▼▼ Residence Inn by Marriott A
(334) 270-3300. **$129.** 1200 Hilmar Ct. I-85, exit 6, 0.3 mi se on Carmichael Rd. Ext/int corridors. **Pets:** Medium, other species. $135 one-time fee/room. Service with restrictions, supervision.
(SAVE) (S6) (×) (⌀) (&) 🖬 💻 ⊋

NORTHPORT

(AAA) ▼▼/▼▼ Best Western Catalina Inn M
(205) 339-5200. **$55-$85, 7 days notice.** 2015 McFarland Blvd. I-59/20, exit 71 to I-359/SR 69, n to US 82, just w. Ext corridors. **Pets:** Very small. $5 daily fee/pet. Service with restrictions, supervision.
(SAVE) (S6) (×) 🖬 💻 ⊋

OPELIKA

▼▼/▼▼ Travelodge M
(334) 749-1461. **$40-$43, 14 days notice.** 1002 Columbus Pkwy. I-85, exit 62, just w. Ext corridors. **Pets:** Accepted.
(ASK) (S6) (×) 🖬 💻 ⊋

OXFORD

**(AAA) ▼▼/▼▼ Best
Western-Anniston/Oxford** M ❧
(256) 831-3410. **$49-$79.** US 78 & SR 21. I-20, exit 185, just n. Ext corridors. **Pets:** Other species. Designated rooms, supervision.
(SAVE) (S6) (×) 🖬 💻 (¶) ⊋

OZARK

(AAA) ▼▼/▼▼ Best Western Ozark Inn M
(334) 774-5166. **$54, 7 days notice.** Deese Rd, US 231 S. 0.5 mi s of jct US 231 and SR 249. Ext corridors. **Pets:** Small. Service with restrictions, supervision.
(SAVE) (S6) (×) 💻 ⊋

▼▼/▼▼ Holiday Inn-Ozark, Ft Rucker M
(334) 774-7300. **$52-$65.** 151 Hwy 231 N. On US 231, 0.3 mi n of jct SR 249. Ext corridors. **Pets:** Small. $25 one-time fee/room. Designated rooms, service with restrictions, supervision.
(ASK) (S6) (×) 🖬 💻 (¶) ⊋

▼▼/▼▼ Jameson Inn M
(334) 774-0233. **$55-$70.** 120 Hwy 231 S. 0.4 mi s of jct SR 249 and 231. Ext corridors. **Pets:** Very small. Service with restrictions, supervision.
(×) (&M) 🖬 💻 ⊋

SELMA

▼▼/▼▼ Holiday Inn M
(334) 872-0461. **$63-$68, 14 days notice.** 1710 W Highland Ave. 2.3 mi w on US 80. Ext corridors. **Pets:** No service, supervision.
(ASK) (S6) (×) (⌀) 🖬 💻 (¶)

TROY

▼▼/▼▼ Holiday Inn Express M
(334) 670-0012. **$55.** Hwy 231, US 29. 0.3 mi n of jct US 29. Ext corridors. **Pets:** Accepted.
(ASK) (S6) (×) 🖬 💻

▼▼/▼▼ Holiday Inn-of Troy M
(334) 566-1150. **$73, 3 days notice.** Hwy 231 at Hwy 29. Just n of jct US 29. Ext corridors. **Pets:** Medium, other species. Service with restrictions, supervision.
(ASK) (S6) (×) 🖬 💻 (¶) ⊋

TUSCALOOSA

▼▼/▼▼ Jameson Inn M
(205) 345-5018. **$55-$70.** 5021 Oscar Baxter Rd. I-59/20, exit 71A. Ext corridors. **Pets:** Accepted.
(×) 🖬 💻 ⊋

▼▼/▼▼ Key West Inn M
(205) 556-3232. **$45-$65.** 4700 Doris Pate Dr. I-59/20, exit 76, just n. Int corridors. **Pets:** Accepted.
(ASK) (S6) (×) 🖬 💻 ⊋

(AAA) ▼▼/▼▼ La Quinta Inn-Tuscaloosa M
(205) 349-3270. **$55-$75.** 4122 McFarland Blvd E. I-59/20, exit 73, just sw on US 82. Ext corridors. **Pets:** Other species.
(SAVE) (×) 🖬 💻 ⊋

(AAA) ▼▼ Masters Inn M
(205) 556-2010. **$40-$60.** 3600 McFarland Blvd. I-59/20, exit 73, just nw on US 82. Ext corridors. **Pets:** Medium. $6 one-time fee/room. Service with restrictions, supervision.
(SAVE) (S6) (×) 🖬 ⊋

VANCE

▼▼/▼▼ Hawthorn Suites Limited M
(205) 556-3606. **$79-$129, 7 days notice.** 11170 Will Walker Rd. I-59/20, exit 89 southbound, just n. Int corridors. **Pets:** Accepted.
(ASK) (S6) (×) (&M) (&) 🖬 💻

YORK

▼▼/▼▼ Days Inn-York M
(205) 392-9675. **$44, 7 days notice.** 17700 SR 17. I-59/20, exit 8, just se. Ext corridors. **Pets:** Accepted.
(SAVE) (S6) (×) (&M) 🖬 💻

ALASKA

CITY INDEX

ANCHORAGE

▼ A to Zzzz.... B & B BB
(907) 248-3436. **$99-$109, 15 days notice.** 2701 W 80th Ave. International Airport Rd, 1.9 mi s on Jewel Lake Rd, 0.8 mi e on Strawberry Rd, just s on Arlene St. Int corridors. **Pets:** Large, dogs only. $100 deposit/pet. Designated rooms, no service.

[ASK] [S🐾] [✕] [🐾] [🏊] [🐾]

⚑ ▼▼▼ Aurora Winds Resort BB
(907) 346-2533. **$79-$249.** 7501 Upper O'Malley Rd. 6.5 mi s on US 1 (New Seward Hwy), 4 mi e on O'Malley Rd, just n on Hillside Dr, just e. Int corridors. **Pets:** Accepted.

[SAVE] [✕] [🛏] [💻] [🏊] [🐾]

⚑ ▼▼▼ Best Western Barratt Inn M ✿
(907) 243-3131. **$89-$199.** 4616 Spenard Rd. International Airport Rd, just ne of jct Jewel Lake and Spenard rds. Ext/int corridors. **Pets:** $50 deposit/pet, $10 daily fee/pet. Designated rooms, service with restrictions, crate.

[SAVE] [✕] [⌖M] [🐾] [🛏] [💻] [🍴]

▼▼▼ Comfort Inn Ship Creek M
(907) 277-6887. **Call for rates.** 111 W Ship Creek Ave. Downtown; at 3rd and E sts, 0.3 mi n on E St, across the railway, just e on Ship Creek Ave (formerly Warehouse Ave). Int corridors. **Pets:** Medium. $10 daily fee/room. Designated rooms, service with restrictions, supervision.

[ASK] [✕] [⌖M] [🐾] [🏊] [🛏] [💻]

⚑ ▼▼▼ Days Inn Downtown M
(907) 276-7226. **$79-$250.** 321 E 5th Ave. Downtown; at Cordova and E 5th Ave. Ext/int corridors. **Pets:** Other species. $25 deposit/pet. Designated rooms, service with restrictions, crate.

[SAVE] [✕] [⌖M] [🐾] [🏊] [🛏] [💻]

▼▼▼ Holiday Inn Express Anchorage Airport M
(907) 248-8848. **$89-$199.** 4411 Spenard Rd. 0.5 mi ne of Jewell Lake and International Airport rds. Int corridors. **Pets:** Small, dogs only. $10 daily fee/room. Designated rooms, service with restrictions, supervision.

[ASK] [S🐾] [✕] [🐾] [🏊] [🛏] [💻] [🐾]

⚑ ▼▼▼ Long House Alaskan Hotel M ✿
(907) 243-2133. **$62-$139.** 4335 Wisconsin St. From International Airport Rd, 1.5 mi ne on Spenard Rd, nw on Wisconsin St at 43rd Ave, just e. Int corridors. **Pets:** Large, other species. $50 deposit/pet, $10 daily fee/pet. Designated rooms, service with restrictions, supervision.

[SAVE] [✕] [⌖M] [🏊] [🛏] [💻] [🐾]

⚑ ▼▼ Merrill Field Inn M
(907) 276-4547. **$65-$132.** 420 Sitka St. 1 mi e via US 1 (Glenn Hwy); directly opposite Merrill Field Airstrip. Ext corridors. **Pets:** Other species. $7 daily fee/pet. Service with restrictions.

[SAVE] [S🐾] [✕] [🛏] [🐾]

⚑ ▼ Parkwood Inn M ✿
(907) 563-3590. **$68-$190.** 4455 Juneau St. Jct of International Airport Rd and Old Seward Hwy, 0.4 mi n on Old Seward Hwy, just e on 45th St. Ext corridors. **Pets:** Other species. $50 deposit/room, $5 one-time fee/pet. Designated rooms, supervision.

[SAVE] [S🐾] [✕] [🛏] [💻] [🐾]

⚑ ▼▼▼ Residence Inn by Marriott A
(907) 563-9844. **$133-$298.** 1025 35th Ave. Corner of SR 1/New Seward Hwy and 36th Ave. Int corridors. **Pets:** Accepted.

[SAVE] [S🐾] [✕] [🐾] [🏊] [🛏] [💻] [🐾]

▼▼ Super 8 Motel-Anchorage M
(907) 276-8884. **$63-$135.** 3501 Minnesota Dr. At 36th Ave, just n of Spenard Rd. Int corridors. **Pets:** Other species. $25 deposit/room. Designated rooms, service with restrictions, supervision.

[ASK] [S🐾] [✕] [🐾] [🏊] [🛏] [💻]

⚑ ▼ Westmark Inn Anchorage M
(907) 272-7561. **$116.** 115 E 3rd Ave. Downtown; e at Barrow St. Ext/int corridors. **Pets:** $50 deposit/room, $15 daily fee/pet. Service with restrictions.

[SAVE] [✕] [🍴] [🐾]

CANTWELL

⚑ ▼▼ Backwoods Lodge M ✿
(907) 768-2232. **$90-$120, 7 days notice.** Denali Hwy milepost 133.8. George Parks Hwy, milepost 210, just e on Denali Hwy. Ext corridors. **Pets:** Medium. Service with restrictions, supervision.

[SAVE] [✕] [🛏] [💻] [🐾]

EAGLE RIVER

⚑ ▼ Eagle River Motel M
(907) 694-5000. **$60-$90, 3 days notice.** 11111 Old Eagle River Rd. Glenn Hwy, exit Eagle River, just e; in town centre. Ext corridors. **Pets:** Other species. $7 daily fee/room. Designated rooms, service with restrictions, crate.

[SAVE] [✕] [🛏] [🐾]

FAIRBANKS

▼▼ Comfort Inn-Chena River M
(907) 479-8080. **$79-$189.** 1908 Chena Landings Loop.
Airport Way, just n on Peger Rd, just e on Phillips Field Rd,
follow signs in wooded area south of road. Int corridors.
Pets: Large, other species. $10 daily fee/pet. Designated
rooms, service with restrictions, crate.
SAVE ✕ &M ⚷ ⊟ ⊇ ⇲

▼ Regency Fairbanks Hotel M
(907) 452-3200. **Call for rates.** 95 Tenth Ave. Center; just w
of US 2 (Steese Expwy). Int corridors. **Pets:** Accepted.
✕ ⊟ ⊇ ⚏

▼ Super 8 Motel M
(907) 451-8888. **$69-$149.** 1909 Airport Way. Just e of
Peger; across from Alaskaland. Int corridors. **Pets:** $25
deposit/room. Designated rooms, service with restrictions,
crate.
ASK S✕ ✕ ⊟

GUSTAVUS

▼▼▼ Glacier Bay's Bear Track Inn L
(907) 697-3017. **$450, 60 days notice.** 255 Rink Creek Rd.
7 mi e of airport; at the end of Rink Creek Rd. Int corridors.
Pets: Accepted.
ASK S✕ ✕ ⚏ ⚏ ⚏ ⚏

HAINES

⚑ ▼ Captain's Choice Inc Motel M
(907) 766-3111. **$87-$165.** 108 2nd Ave N. 2nd and Dalton
sts. Ext corridors. **Pets:** Other species. $10 one-time fee/
room. Service with restrictions, supervision.
SAVE ✕ ⊟ ⊇ ⚏

HOMER

⚑ ▼▼ Best Western Bidarka Inn M
(907) 235-8148. **$72-$169.** 575 Sterling Hwy. 0.3 mi n on
SR 1. Ext/int corridors. **Pets:** Accepted.
SAVE S✕ ✕ ⊟ ⊇ ⚏ ⚏

JUNEAU

⚑ ▼▼▼ Frontier Suites Airport Hotel M
(907) 790-6600. **$80-$134.** 9400 Glacier Hwy. At Juneau
International Airport. Ext/int corridors. **Pets:** Small, dogs
only. $50 one-time fee/room. Service with restrictions, crate.
SAVE S✕ ✕ &M ⊟ ⊇ ⚏ ⚏

▼ Super 8 M
(907) 789-4858. **Call for rates.** 2295 Trout St. At airport,
just nw to Glacier Hwy, just e. Int corridors. **Pets:** Accepted.
✕ ⊟ ⚏

KETCHIKAN

⚑ ▼▼▼ Best Western Landing M
(907) 225-5166. **$-$150, 5 days notice.** 3434 Tongass Ave.
Across from the Alaska Marine Hwy Ferry Terminal. Ext/int
corridors. **Pets:** Other species. $50 deposit/room, $10 daily
fee/room. Designated rooms, service with restrictions,
supervision.
SAVE S✕ ✕ ⊟ ⊇ ⚏

▼ Super 8 M
(907) 225-9088. **$71-$112, 14 days notice.** 2151 Sea
Level Dr. From Alaska Marine Hwy ferry terminal, 0.9 mi se
to Washington St, then just s; from airport ferry terminal, 1.3
mi se. Int corridors. **Pets:** Accepted.
ASK S✕ ✕ ⊟ ⚏

KODIAK

⚑ ▼▼▼ Best Western Kodiak Inn M ❀
(907) 486-5712. **$99-$149.** 236 W Rezanof Dr. Center; 0.3
mi w of ferry terminal. Ext/int corridors. **Pets:** $50 deposit/
room, $25 one-time fee/room. Designated rooms, service
with restrictions, supervision.
SAVE S✕ ✕ ⚏ ⊟ ⊇ ⚏ ⚏

TOK

⚑ ▼▼ Cleft of the Rock Bed &
Breakfast X
(907) 883-4219. **$60-$130, 3 days notice.** Mile 0.5 Sundog
Tr. From jct SR 1 and 2, 3 mi w on SR 2 to Sundog Tr, then
0.5 mi n. Ext/int corridors. **Pets:** Service with restrictions,
supervision.
SAVE ✕ ⊟ ⊇ ✕ ⚏

⚑ ▼▼▼ Westmark Tok M
(907) 883-5174. **$116.** On SR 1; at jct SR 2. Ext corridors.
Pets: Accepted.
SAVE ✕ ⊇ ⚏ ⚏

WASILLA

⚑ ▼▼▼▼ Pioneer Ridge Bed and Breakfast
Inn BB
(907) 376-7472. **$100-$120, 14 days notice.** 2221 Yukon
Cir. Jct Parks Hwy, 1.5 mi s on Fairview Loop Rd, follow
signs onto Lin-Lu Rd and onto Yukon. Int corridors.
Pets: Other species. Designated rooms, service with
restrictions, supervision.
SAVE S✕ ✕ ⊟ ⊇ ⚏

ARIZONA

CITY INDEX

AJO

♦ **La Siesta Motel** [M]
(520) 387-6569. **$46-$60, 3 days notice.** 2561 N Ajo-Gila Bend Hwy. 1.8 mi n of town plaza; on SR 85. Ext corridors. **Pets:** Accepted.
✕ 🧊 📺 🏊

AAA ♦ **Marine Motel** [M]
(520) 387-7626. **$44-$69.** 1966 N 2nd Ave. 1 mi n of town plaza on SR 85. Ext corridors. **Pets:** Accepted.
[SAVE] [S/D] ✕ 🧊 📺

BENSON

AAA ♦♦ **Best Western Quail Hollow Inn** [M]
(520) 586-3646. **$65-$85, 14 days notice.** 699 N Ocotillo St. I-10, exit 304, just s. Ext corridors. **Pets:** Medium. Designated rooms, service with restrictions, supervision.
[SAVE] [S/D] ✕ ♿ 🧊 📺 🏊

AAA ♦♦ **Super 8 Motel** [M]
(520) 586-1530. **$49-$61.** 855 N Ocotillo Rd. I-10, exit 304, just n. Ext corridors. **Pets:** Accepted.
[SAVE] [S/D] ✕ 🧊 🏊

BISBEE

AAA ♦♦ **San Jose Lodge** [M]
(520) 432-5761. **$65-$75.** 1002 Naco Hwy. From SR 80, take SR 92, 2.5 mi sw, then 1.5 mi s. Ext corridors. **Pets:** $10 daily fee/pet. Designated rooms, service with restrictions, supervision.
[SAVE] ✕ 🧊 🍴 🏊

BULLHEAD CITY

AAA ♦♦♦ **Best Western Bullhead City Inn** [M]
(928) 754-3000. **$99, 3 days notice.** 1126 Hwy 95. 1.8 mi s of Laughlin Bridge. Ext corridors. **Pets:** $10 one-time fee/pet. Service with restrictions, supervision.
[SAVE] [S/D] ✕ 👂 🧊 🏊

AAA ♦ **Lake Mohave Resort** [M]
(928) 754-3245. **$80-$110, 3 days notice.** Katherine Landing. 1.5 mi n of Laughlin Bridge on SR 95 to 68, then 4.6 mi on Lake Mead/Katharine Landing turnoff, follow signs. Ext corridors. **Pets:** Accepted.
[SAVE] 🧊 🎾

AAA ♦ **Lodge on The River** [M]
(928) 758-8080. **$31-$64.** 1717 Hwy 95. 3.8 mi s of Laughlin Bridge. Ext corridors. **Pets:** Accepted.
[SAVE] ✕ ♿ 🧊 📺 🏊

♦♦ **Shangri-la Lodge** [A]
(928) 758-1117. **$33.** 1767 Georgia Ln. 2 mi s of Laughlin Bridge. Ext corridors. **Pets:** Small, dogs only. Service with restrictions, supervision.
[A$K] ✕ 🧊

CAMP VERDE

AAA ♦♦♦ **Comfort Inn** [M]
(928) 567-9000. **$79-$99.** 340 N Industrial Dr. I-17, exit 287, just e, then just s. Int corridors. **Pets:** Other species. $15 one-time fee/room. Designated rooms, service with restrictions, supervision.
[SAVE] [S/D] ✕ 👂 ♿ 🧊 📺 🏊

AAA ♦♦ **Microtel Inn & Suites of Camp Verde** [M] 🐾
(928) 567-3700. **$49-$74.** 504 Industrial Dr. I-17, exit 287, just e, then just n. Int corridors. **Pets:** Other species. $10 daily fee/room. Service with restrictions, supervision.
[SAVE] [S/D] ✕ ♿ 🧊 📺 🏊

CASA GRANDE

♦♦♦ **Best Western Casa Grande Suites** [M]
(520) 836-1600. **$59-$99, 7 days notice.** 665 Via Del Cielo. I-10, exit 194 (SR 287), 1 mi w. Ext corridors. **Pets:** Medium. $10 one-time fee/pet. Designated rooms, service with restrictions, supervision.
[SAVE] [S/D] ✕ ♿M 👂 🧊 📺 🏊

▼▼▼ **Holiday Inn Casa Grande** Ⓜ️
(520) 426-3500. **$69-$97, 3 days notice.** 777 N Pinal Ave.
I-10, exit 194 (SR 287), 3.9 mi w. Int corridors.
Pets: Accepted.
(ASK) (S🐾) ✕ (🦽) (🐿) 🖥️ 💻 🍴 🏊

▼ **Motel 6–1263** Ⓜ
(520) 836-3323. **$37-$61.** 4965 N Sunland Gin Rd. I-10,
exit 200. Ext corridors. **Pets:** Accepted.
(S🐾) ✕ 🖥️ 🏊

▼ **Super 8 Motel** Ⓜ
(520) 836-8800. **$49-$110.** 2066 E Florence Blvd. I-10, exit
194 (SR 287), 0.6 mi w on SR 187. Int corridors. **Pets:** $5
daily fee/pet, $5 one-time fee/pet. Service with restrictions,
supervision.
(ASK) ✕ (🐾) 🖥️ 🏊

CHAMBERS

🅰️ ▼▼▼ **Best Western Chieftain** Ⓜ️
(928) 688-2754. **$78-$150, 3 days notice.** I-40, exit 333,
just n at jct US 191. Ext corridors. **Pets:** Small, other species. $10 daily fee/pet. Service with restrictions, supervision.
(SAVE) (S🐾) ✕ 🍴 🏊

COTTONWOOD

🅰️ ▼▼▼ **Best Western Cottonwood Inn** Ⓜ️
(928) 634-5575. **$69-$99.** 993 S Main. On SR 89A at jct SR
260. Ext corridors. **Pets:** Accepted.
(SAVE) (S🐾) ✕ (🐾) 🖥️ 💻 🍴 🏊

🅰️ ▼ **Little Daisy Motel** Ⓜ
(928) 634-7865. **$48-$58.** 34 S Main St. Historic SR 89A
(Main St), just n of jct SR 89A. Ext corridors. **Pets:** Other
species. $20 deposit/room, $3 daily fee/pet. Service with
restrictions, crate.
(SAVE) (S🐾) ✕ 🖥️

🅰️ ▼ **The Pines Motel** Ⓜ 🐾
(928) 634-9975. **$44-$69.** 920 S Camino Real. Just s of jct
SR 89 and 260, just w of Main St. Ext corridors. **Pets:** $10
one-time fee/room. Supervision.
(SAVE) (S🐾) ✕ 🖥️

🅰️ ▼ **The View Motel** Ⓜ
(928) 634-7581. **$40-$50.** 818 S Main St. Just w of jct SR
260/89A. Ext corridors. **Pets:** Accepted.
(SAVE) ✕ 🖥️ 🏊

EAGAR

▼▼▼ **Best Western Sunrise Inn** Ⓜ
(928) 333-2540. **$59-$99, 7 days notice.** 128 N Main St.
From SR 260, just n; from US 60, 1.5 mi s. Ext corridors.
Pets: Accepted.
(SAVE) (S🐾) ✕ (🐾) 🖥️ 💻

EHRENBERG

🅰️ ▼▼ **Best Western Flying J Motel** Ⓜ️
(928) 923-9711. **$69-$119.** I-10, exit 1, just s; 0.5 mi e of
the Colorado River. Int corridors. **Pets:** Other species. $10
deposit/pet. Service with restrictions, supervision.
(SAVE) (S🐾) ✕ 🖥️ 🍴 🏊

FLAGSTAFF

🅰️ ▼▼▼▼ **AmeriSuites (Flagstaff/Interstate
Highway)** Ⓜ
(928) 774-8042. **$69-$159.** 2455 S Beulah Blvd. I-40, exit
195B, just n to Forest Meadows, just w, then just s. Int
corridors. **Pets:** Accepted.
(SAVE) (S🐾) ✕ (🐿) (🐾) 🖥️ 💻 🏊

🅰️ ▼▼ **Best Western Kings House Motel** Ⓜ
(928) 774-7186. **$49-$99, 7 days notice.** 1560 E Route 66.
I-40, exit 198 (Butler), just w on Butler, then 1 mi n on
Enterprise. Ext corridors. **Pets:** Accepted.
(SAVE) (S🐾) ✕ 🖥️ 🏊

🅰️ ▼ **Canyon Inn** Ⓜ
(928) 774-7301. **$26-$125.** 500 S Milton Rd. I-40, exit
195B, 1.5 mi n. Ext corridors. **Pets:** Accepted.
(SAVE) (S🐾) ✕

🅰️ ▼▼ **Comfort Inn** Ⓜ
(928) 774-7326. **$47-$109.** 914 S Milton Rd. I-40, exit
195B, 1.2 mi n. Ext corridors. **Pets:** Medium. Designated
rooms, service with restrictions, supervision.
(SAVE) (S🐾) ✕ 🖥️ 🏊

🅰️ ▼▼ **Comfort Inn I-17/I-40** Ⓜ 🐾
(928) 774-2225. **$50-$90.** 2355 S Beulah Blvd. I-40, exit
195B, just n to Forest Meadows, then 1 blk w. Int corridors.
Pets: Other species. $5 daily fee/pet. Supervision.
(SAVE) (S🐾) ✕ (🐿) 🖥️ 💻 🏊

🅰️ ▼▼ **Days Inn Flagstaff Hwy 66** Ⓜ
(928) 774-5221. **$35-$139, 3 days notice.** 1000 W Route
66. I-40, exit 195B, 1.5 n on Milton Rd, then just w. Ext
corridors. **Pets:** Large, other species. $10 daily fee/room.
Designated rooms, service with restrictions, supervision.
(SAVE) (S🐾) ✕ (🐿) 🏊

🅰️ ▼▼▼ **Embassy Suites-Flagstaff/Grand
Canyon** Ⓜ
(928) 774-4333. **$89-$179.** 706 S Milton Rd. I-40, exit
195B, 1.5 mi n. Int corridors. **Pets:** Accepted.
(SAVE) (S🐾) ✕ (🐿) 🖥️ 💻 🏊

▼▼ **Flagstaff Travelodge** Ⓜ️ 🐾
(928) 526-1399. **$25-$99.** 2610 E Route 66. I-40, exit 201,
1.3 mi w on US 180, 89 and I-40 business loop. Ext corridors. **Pets:** Medium, other species. $10 daily fee/pet. Serv-
ice with restrictions, supervision.
(ASK) (S🐾) ✕ 🖥️ 💻 🍴 🏊

Holiday Inn Flagstaff/Grand Canyon M
(928) 714-1000. **$89-$109, 7 days notice.** 2320 E Lucky Ln. I-40, exit 198, just n. Int corridors. **Pets:** Other species. $25 one-time fee/room. Service with restrictions, supervision.

Howard Johnson Inn M
(928) 526-1826. **$39-$79.** 3300 E Route 66. I-40, exit 201, 1.7 mi w. Ext corridors. **Pets:** Other species. $5 daily fee/pet. Service with restrictions.

Inn Suites Hotel M
(928) 774-7356. **$52-$129.** 1008 E Route 66. I-40, exit 198, 1 mi n on Milton Rd/SR 89A, then just e. Ext corridors. **Pets:** Small. $25 deposit/room. Designated rooms, service with restrictions, supervision.

La Quinta Inn & Suites M
(928) 556-8666. **$66-$116.** 2015 S Beulah Blvd. I-40, exit 195B, just n to Forest Meadow, then just w. Int corridors. **Pets:** Large, other species. Service with restrictions, supervision.

Ramada Limited-Lucky Lane M
(928) 779-3614. **$42-$79, 7 days notice.** 2350 E Lucky Ln. I-40, exit 198. Ext corridors. **Pets:** Medium, other species. $5 daily fee/room. Service with restrictions, supervision.

Ramada Limited West M
(928) 773-1111. **$39-$129, 7 days notice.** 2755 S Woodlands Village Blvd. I-40, exit 195B, just n to Forest Meadows St, then w to Beulah Rd, then just w. Ext corridors. **Pets:** Medium. $10 daily fee/room. Designated rooms, service with restrictions, supervision.

Residence Inn by Marriott Flagstaff
(928) 526-5555. **$99-$229.** 3440 N Country Club Dr. I-40, exit 201, just s. Ext corridors. **Pets:** Other species. $20 daily fee/room. Designated rooms.

Rodeway Inn East M
(928) 526-2200. **$35-$79.** 2650 E Route 66. I-40, exit 201, 0.5 mi n, then 0.5 mi w. Ext corridors. **Pets:** Small. $5 daily fee/pet. Service with restrictions, supervision.

Super 8 Motel M
(928) 774-4581. **$39-$125.** 602 W Route 66. I-40, exit 195B, 1.5 mi n on SR 89A (Milton Rd), then just w. Ext corridors. **Pets:** $10 daily fee/pet. Service with restrictions, supervision.

Super 8 Motel M
(928) 526-0818. **$39-$74.** 3725 N Kasper Ave. I-40, exit 201, 0.5 mi w on I-40 business loop. Int corridors. **Pets:** Other species. Service with restrictions, supervision.

Travelodge Hotel M
(928) 779-6944. **$29-$139.** 2200 E Butler Ave. I-40, exit 198, just nw. Int corridors. **Pets:** Small, other species. $10 one-time fee/pet. Designated rooms, service with restrictions, supervision.

University/Grand Canyon Travelodge M
(928) 774-3381. **$22-$99.** 801 W Highway 66. I-40, exit 191, 2 mi e. Ext corridors. **Pets:** Small, other species. $10 one-time fee/pet. Designated rooms, service with restrictions, supervision.

FLORENCE

Rancho Sonora Inn M
(520) 868-8000. **$64-$150, 3 days notice.** 9198 N Hwy 79. On SR 79, 5 mi s of SR 287. Ext corridors. **Pets:** Accepted.

FOREST LAKES

Forest Lakes Lodge M
(928) 535-4727. **$54-$74.** On SR 260. Ext corridors. **Pets:** Accepted.

GILA BEND

Best Western Space Age Lodge M
(928) 683-2273. **$69-$109.** 401 E Pima St. Business loop I-8; center of town. Ext corridors. **Pets:** Service with restrictions, supervision.

Super 8 Motel M
(928) 683-6311. **$55-$65, 3 days notice.** 2888 Butterfield Tr. I-8, exit 119, just w. Int corridors. **Pets:** Accepted.

GLOBE

Comfort Inn M
(928) 425-7575. **$49-$59.** 1515 South St. On US 60, 1 mi e of town. Ext corridors. **Pets:** Accepted.

Holiday Inn Express-Globe M
(928) 425-7008. **$50-$85.** 2119 Hwy 60. 4 mi w of town. Int corridors. **Pets:** Accepted.

Ramada Limited M
(928) 425-5741. **$45-$55.** 1699 E Ash St. On US 60, 1.3 mi e of town. Ext/int corridors. **Pets:** Dogs only. $10 one-time fee/pet. Service with restrictions, supervision.

GRAND CANYON NATIONAL PARK AREA

GRAND CANYON

(AAA) ♦♦♦ Rodeway Inn-Red Feather Lodge [M]
(928) 638-2414. **$59-$159.** On SR 64, 2 mi s of south rim
entrance. Ext/int corridors. **Pets:** Accepted.
[SAVE] [❄] [✕] [🅿] [🛏] [💻] [🏊]

❀ END AREA ❀

HOLBROOK

(AAA) ♦♦♦ Best Inn [M]
(928) 524-2654. **$41-$52.** 2211 E Navajo Blvd. I-40, exit
289, 1 mi w. Ext corridors. **Pets:** Medium. $5 daily fee/
room. Service with restrictions, supervision.
[SAVE] [❄] [✕] [🛏]

(AAA) ♦♦♦ Best Western Adobe Inn [M]
(928) 524-3948. **$40-$55.** 615 W Hopi Dr. I-40, exit 285, 1
mi e on US 180. Ext corridors. **Pets:** Accepted.
[SAVE] [❄] [✕] [🏊]

(AAA) ♦♦♦♦ Best Western Arizonian Inn [M]
(928) 524-2611. **$50-$76.** 2508 E Navajo Blvd. I-40, exit
289, 0.5 mi w. Ext corridors. **Pets:** Medium. $30 deposit/
room. Designated rooms, crate.
[SAVE] [❄] [✕] [🛏] [💻] [🏊]

(AAA) ♦♦ Budget Host Holbrook Inn [M]
(928) 524-3809. **$26-$30.** 235 W Hopi Dr. I-40, exit 285, 1.5
mi e on US 180. Ext corridors. **Pets:** Other species. $10
deposit/room. Supervision.
[SAVE] [❄] [✕] [🛏] [💻]

(AAA) ♦♦♦ Comfort Inn [M]
(928) 524-6131. **$54-$79.** 2602 E Navajo Blvd. I-40, exit
289, just w. Ext corridors. **Pets:** Accepted.
[SAVE] [❄] [✕] [🛏] [💻] [🏊]

(AAA) ♦♦ Econo Lodge [M]
(928) 524-1448. **$44-$54.** 2596 E Navajo Blvd. I-40, exit
289, just w. Ext corridors. **Pets:** Other species. $25 deposit/
pet. Designated rooms, service with restrictions, supervision.
[SAVE] [❄] [✕] [🛏] [💻] [🏊]

♦♦♦ Holbrook Holiday Inn Express [M]
(928) 524-1466. **$69-$77, 12 days notice.** 1308 E Navajo
Blvd. I-40, exit 286, just n. Int corridors. **Pets:** Small, other
species. $10 one-time fee/pet. Service with restrictions,
supervision.
[ASK] [❄] [✕] [🛏] [💻] [🏊]

(AAA) ♦♦♦ Relax Inn [M]
(928) 524-6815. **$35.** 2418 E Navajo Blvd. I-40, exit 289,
0.4 mi w. Ext corridors. **Pets:** Accepted.
[SAVE] [❄] [✕] [🛏]

JEROME

♦♦ Connor Hotel of Jerome [H]
(928) 634-5006. **$85-$125, 3 days notice.** 164 Main St.
Downtown. Int corridors. **Pets:** Other species. Service with
restrictions, supervision.
[ASK] [❄] [✕] [🛏] [💻]

KAYENTA

♦♦♦ Hampton Inn of Kayenta [MI]
(928) 697-3170. **$79-$112, 14 days notice.** Hwy 160. W on
Hwy 160. Int corridors. **Pets:** Other species. Service with
restrictions, supervision.
[SAVE] [❄] [✕] [♿] [💻] [🍴] [🏊]

KINGMAN

(AAA) ♦♦♦ Best Western A Wayfarer's Inn [M]
(928) 753-6271. **$65-$82, 7 days notice.** 2815 E Andy
Devine Ave. I-40, exit 53, 0.5 mi sw on I-40 business loop
(US 93 and SR 66). Ext corridors. **Pets:** Accepted.
[SAVE] [❄] [✕] [🅿] [🛏] [💻] [🏊]

(AAA) ♦♦♦ Best Western King's Inn &
Suites [M]
(928) 753-6101. **$65-$82, 7 days notice.** 2930 E Andy
Devine Ave. I-40, exit 53, 0.3 mi sw on I-40 business loop
and SR 66. Ext corridors. **Pets:** Accepted.
[SAVE] [❄] [✕] [🅿] [♿] [🛏] [💻] [🏊]

(AAA) ♦♦♦ Brunswick Hotel & Hubb's Bistro [H]
(928) 718-1800. **$25-$115.** 315 E Andy Devine Ave. on SR
66. Int corridors. **Pets:** $25 deposit/room, $10 daily fee/
room. No service.
[SAVE] [❄] [✕] [♿] [🛏] [🍴]

(AAA) ♦♦♦ Days Inn West [M]
(928) 753-7500. **$29-$89, 3 days notice.** 3023 E Andy
Devine Ave. I-40, exit 53, just sw on I-40 business loop (US
93 and SR 66). Ext corridors. **Pets:** Accepted.
[SAVE] [❄] [✕] [🛏] [🏊]

(AAA) ♦♦ Hill Top Motel [M]
(928) 753-2198. **$28-$50.** 1901 E Andy Devine Ave. I-40,
exit 53, 2 mi sw on I-40 business loop/SR 66 and US 93.
Ext corridors. **Pets:** Dogs only. Service with restrictions,
supervision.
[SAVE] [❄] [✕] [🛏] [🏊]

▼▼ Motel 6–1114 **M**
(928) 753-9222. **$36-$51.** 424 W Beale St. I-40, exit 48, just se on busines loop I-40/US 93. Ext corridors. **Pets:** Medium, other species. Supervision.

⬛⬛ ⬛ ⬛ ⬛ ⬛

⬛⬛⬛ ▼▼▼ Quality Inn **M**
(928) 753-4747. **$48-$70, 10 days notice.** 1400 E Andy Devine Ave. I-40, exit 48, 2 mi se on I-40 business loop/SR 66 and US 93. Ext corridors. **Pets:** Other species. $10 one-time fee/pet. Designated rooms.

⬛ ⬛ ⬛ ⬛ ⬛ ⬛ ⬛

⬛⬛⬛ ▼▼▼ Super 8 Motel **M**
(928) 757-4808. **$35-$79, 3 days notice.** 3401 E Andy Devine Ave. I-40, exit 53, 0.3 mi ne on SR 66. Int corridors. **Pets:** Other species. $10 daily fee/pet. Designated rooms, service with restrictions, supervision.

⬛ ⬛ ⬛ ⬛

LAKE HAVASU CITY

⬛⬛⬛ ▼▼▼ Best Western Lake Place Inn **MI**
(928) 855-2146. **$55-$256, 7 days notice.** 31 Wing's Loop. 1 mi e of SR 95 via Swanson Ave. Ext corridors. **Pets:** Accepted.

⬛ ⬛ ⬛ ⬛ ⬛ ⬛ ⬛

⬛⬛⬛ ▼▼▼ Havasu Travelodge **M**
(928) 680-9202. **$59-$109, 14 days notice.** 480 London Bridge Rd. 1 mi n of London Bridge. Int corridors. **Pets:** Small. $50 deposit/room. Service with restrictions, supervision.

⬛ ⬛ ⬛ ⬛ ⬛

▼▼▼▼ Holiday Inn **MI**
(928) 855-4071. **$57-$92.** 245 London Bridge Rd. 0.5 mi n of London Bridge. Int corridors. **Pets:** Other species. $10 daily fee/room. Service with restrictions, supervision.

⬛ ⬛ ⬛ ⬛ ⬛ ⬛ ⬛ ⬛

⬛⬛⬛ ▼▼▼ Island Inn Hotel **MI**
(928) 680-0606. **$55-$256, 14 days notice.** 1300 W McCulloch Blvd. 0.7 mi w of London Bridge/SR 95. Int corridors. **Pets:** Other species. $10 one-time fee/pet. Service with restrictions, supervision.

⬛ ⬛ ⬛ ⬛ ⬛

▼▼ Lake Havasu City Super 8 **M**
(928) 855-8844. **$56-$85.** 305 London Bridge Rd. Just w of US 95, exit Palo Verde; 0.5 mi n of London Bridge. Int corridors. **Pets:** Accepted.

⬛ ⬛ ⬛ ⬛

MUNDS PARK

⬛⬛⬛ ▼▼▼ Motel In The Pines **M**
(928) 286-9699. **$35-$89.** 80 W Pinewood Rd. I-17, exit 322, just e. Ext corridors. **Pets:** Small, other species. $30 deposit/room, $3 daily fee/pet. Designated rooms, service with restrictions, supervision.

⬛ ⬛ ⬛ ⬛ ⬛

NOGALES

▼▼ ▼▼ Super 8 Motel **MI**
(520) 281-2242. **$50-$65, 3 days notice.** 547 W Mariposa Rd. I-19, exit 4, just e. Ext/int corridors. **Pets:** $15 one-time fee/pet. Service with restrictions, supervision.

⬛ ⬛ ⬛ ⬛ ⬛ ⬛

PAGE

⬛⬛⬛ ▼▼▼▼ Best Western Arizonainn **MI**
(928) 645-2466. **$59-$99, 3 days notice.** 716 Rimview Dr. 0.7 mi e of US 89 via SR 89L, Lake Powell Blvd. Int corridors. **Pets:** Medium. $10 one-time fee/room. Service with restrictions.

⬛ ⬛ ⬛ ⬛ ⬛ ⬛ ⬛ ⬛

⬛⬛⬛ ▼▼ Economy Inn Budget Host **M**
(928) 645-2488. **$35-$69.** 121 S Lake Powell Blvd. 1.3 mi s of US 89/SR 89L. Ext corridors. **Pets:** Small. $50 deposit/room. Designated rooms, service with restrictions, supervision.

⬛ ⬛ ⬛ ⬛ ⬛

▼▼▼▼ Lake Powell Days Inn **M**
(928) 645-2800. **$49-$109.** 961 N Hwy 89. Just s on US 89. Int corridors. **Pets:** $10 daily fee/pet. Service with restrictions, supervision.

⬛ ⬛ ⬛ ⬛ ⬛ ⬛ ⬛

▼▼▼ Linda's Lake Powell Condos **C**
(928) 353-4591. **$78-$111, 5 days notice.** 1019 Tower Butte. 6 mi n of town on US 89. Ext corridors. **Pets:** Accepted.

⬛ ⬛ ⬛ ⬛

⬛⬛⬛ ▼▼ ▼▼ Motel 6–Page/Lake Powell–4013 **M**
(928) 645-5888. **$35-$69.** 637 S Lake Powell Blvd. Just e of US 89, on Business Loop SR 89L (Lake Powell Blvd). Int corridors. **Pets:** Small. $50 deposit/room. Designated rooms, service with restrictions, supervision.

⬛ ⬛ ⬛ ⬛ ⬛

⬛⬛⬛ ▼▼▼▼ Quality Inn, Page Lake Powell **MI**
(928) 645-8851. **$69-$89.** 287 N Lake Powell Blvd. 0.8 mi e of US 89/SR 89L. Int corridors. **Pets:** Large. $5 daily fee/room. Service with restrictions.

⬛ ⬛ ⬛ ⬛ ⬛ ⬛ ⬛ ⬛

⬛⬛⬛ ▼▼▼▼ Wahweap Lodge **R**
(928) 645-2433. **$105-$161.** 100 Lakeshore Dr. 4 mi n of Glen Canyon Dam via US 89. Int corridors. **Pets:** Accepted.

⬛ ⬛ ⬛ ⬛ ⬛ ⬛ ⬛ ⬛

PARKER

⬛⬛⬛ ▼▼▼▼ Best Western Parker Inn **M**
(928) 669-6060. **$49-$99.** 1012 Geronimo Ave. E of US 95. Int corridors. **Pets:** Small, other species. Designated rooms, service with restrictions, crate.

⬛ ⬛ ⬛ ⬛ ⬛ ⬛ ⬛

PAYSON

(AAA) ▼▼◆▼▼ Days Inn & Suites M ✿
(928) 474-9800. **$59-$129.** 301A S Beeline Hwy. SR 87 just s of SR 260. Int corridors. **Pets:** Medium. $10 daily fee/pet. Designated rooms, service with restrictions, supervision.
[SAVE] [S⌀] [✕] [🐾] [🛏] [📶] [💻] [⌒]

(AAA) ▼▼◆▼▼ GuestHouse Inn & Suites M
(928) 474-5241. **$59-$139.** 809 E Hwy 260. 0.8 mi e of SR 87. Ext corridors. **Pets:** Accepted.
[SAVE] [✕] [📶] [💻]

(AAA) ▼▼◆▼ Inn of Payson M
(928) 474-3241. **$69-$109.** 801 N Beeline Hwy. On SR 87, 0.3 mi n of SR 260. Ext corridors. **Pets:** Medium. $10 daily fee/room. Service with restrictions, supervision.
[SAVE] [S⌀] [✕] [&M] [🐾] [📶] [📶] [💻]

(AAA) ▼▼◆▼ Paysonglo Lodge M
(928) 474-2382. **$75-$140.** 1005 S Beeline Hwy. SR 87, 1 mi s of SR 260. Ext corridors. **Pets:** Small. $30 deposit/room. Designated rooms, service with restrictions, supervision.
[SAVE] [S⌀] [✕] [📶] [💻] [⌒]

(AAA) ▼▼◆▼ Rim Country Inn M
(928) 474-4526. **$37-$120.** 101 W Phoenix St. On SR 87 (Beeline Hwy), 1.3 mi s of SR 260. Int corridors. **Pets:** Accepted.
[SAVE] [S⌀] [✕] [📶]

▼▼ Trails End Motel M
(928) 474-2283. **$49-$89.** 811 S Beeline Hwy. On SR 87, 0.5 mi s of SR 260. Ext/int corridors. **Pets:** Accepted.
[ASK] [S⌀] [✕] [📶] [💻]

PHOENIX METROPOLITAN AREA

APACHE JUNCTION

(AAA) ▼▼ Apache Junction Motel M ✿
(480) 982-7702. **$34-$66, 7 days notice.** 1680 W Apache Tr. US 60, exit 195, 2 mi n. Ext corridors. **Pets:** Very small, dogs only. $20 one-time fee/pet. Designated rooms, service with restrictions, supervision.
[SAVE] [S⌀] [✕] [📶]

▼▼▼ Apache Junction Super 8 M
(480) 288-8888. **$55-$115.** 251 E 29th Ave. US 60, exit 196, just n. Ext/int corridors. **Pets:** Accepted.
[ASK] [S⌀] [✕] [🐾] [🐾] [📶] [⌒]

BUCKEYE

▼▼◆▼ Days Inn-Buckeye M
(623) 386-5400. **$69-$159.** 25205 W Yuma Rd. I-10, exit 114 (Miller Rd), just sw. Ext corridors. **Pets:** Large, other species. $20 deposit/room. Service with restrictions, supervision.
[SAVE] [S⌀] [✕] [🐾] [📶] [💻] [⌒]

CAREFREE

(AAA) ▼▼◆▼◆▼ The Boulders Resort and Golden Door Spa R
(480) 488-9009. **$260-$565, 21 days notice.** 34631 N Tom Darlington Dr. Scottsdale Rd, 11 mi n of Bell Rd to Carefree Hwy, then just n. Ext corridors. **Pets:** Other species. $100 one-time fee/room. Service with restrictions, crate.
[SAVE] [✕] [🐾] [💻] [🍴] [⌒] [✕⌒]

CHANDLER

(AAA) ▼▼◆▼▼ Chandler Residence Inn M
(480) 782-1551. **$139-$169, 3 days notice.** 200 N Federal St. I-10, exit 160 (Chandler Blvd), 4.2 mi e. Int corridors. **Pets:** Medium, other species. $150 one-time fee/room. Service with restrictions, supervision.
[SAVE] [S⌀] [✕] [🐾] [📶] [💻] [⌒]

▼▼◆▼ Chandler Super 8 M
(480) 961-3888. **$55-$86.** 7171 W Chandler Blvd. I-10, exit 160 (Chandler Blvd), just e. Int corridors. **Pets:** $5.58 daily fee/pet. Service with restrictions, supervision.
[ASK] [S⌀] [✕] [📶] [⌒]

(AAA) ▼▼◆▼ Comfort Inn M
(480) 705-8882. **$59-$139.** 255 N Kyrene Rd. I-10, exit 160 (Chandler Blvd), 1.5 mi e, just n. Int corridors. **Pets:** Other species. $50 deposit/room.
[SAVE] [S⌀] [✕] [&M] [🐾] [📶] [⌒]

▼▼◆▼▼ Hawthorn Suites Ltd M
(480) 705-8881. **$79-$119.** 5858 W Chandler Blvd. I-10, exit 160 (Chandler Blvd), 1.5 mi e. Int corridors. **Pets:** Accepted.
[ASK] [S⌀] [✕] [🐾] [📶] [💻] [⌒]

▼▼◆▼▼ Homewood Suites by Hilton M
(480) 753-6200. **$94-$184.** 7373 W Detroit St. I-10, exit 160 (Chandler Blvd), 0.4 mi e, n on 54th. Int corridors. **Pets:** Small, dogs only. $100 one-time fee/pet. Service with restrictions, supervision.
[SAVE] [S⌀] [✕] [&M] [🐾] [📶] [💻] [⌒]

(AAA) ▼▼◆▼ Red Roof Inn-Chandler M
(480) 857-4969. **$46-$69.** 7400 W Boston St. I-10, exit 160 (Chandler Blvd), just e, then s on Southgate. Int corridors. **Pets:** Service with restrictions, supervision.
[SAVE] [✕] [&M] [🐾] [🐾] [📶] [💻] [⌒]

▼▼◆▼▼ Sheraton San Marcos Golf Resort and Conference Center H
(480) 812-0900. **$55-$169, 3 days notice.** 1 San Marcos Pl. Just s of Chandler Blvd on Arizona Ave. Ext corridors. **Pets:** Medium. $50 deposit/room. Service with restrictions, supervision.
[ASK] [S⌀] [✕] [📶] [💻] [🍴] [⌒] [✕⌒]

(AAA) ▼▼◆▼▼ Windmill Suites of Chandler M
(480) 812-9600. **$69-$149.** 3535 W Chandler Blvd. I-10, exit 160 (Chandler Blvd), 3.9 mi e, corner of Country Club Way. Int corridors. **Pets:** Other species. Service with restrictions, supervision.
[SAVE] [S⌀] [✕] [🐾] [📶] [⌒]

GLENDALE

▼▼▼ Holiday Inn Express Arrowhead Ⓜ
(623) 412-2000. **$59-$139, 7 days notice.** 7885 W Arrowhead Towne Ctr Dr. Loop 101, exit Bell, 0.3 mi e, then just n on 79th Ave. Ext corridors. **Pets:** Medium. $10 daily fee/room. Designated rooms, service with restrictions, supervision.

ASK S◻ ☒ 🐾 ♿ 🖥 💻 ⊶

GOODYEAR

▲▲▲ ▼▼▼ Best Western Phoenix Goodyear Inn Ⓜ
(623) 932-3210. **$69-$109.** 55 N Litchfield Rd. I-10, exit 128, 0.8 mi s. Ext/int corridors. **Pets:** Accepted.

SAVE S◻ ☒ 🖥 💻 🍽 ⊶

▼▼▼▼ Hampton Inn & Suites Ⓜ
(623) 536-1313. **$89-$179, 3 days notice.** 2000 N Litchfield Rd. I-10, exit 128, 0.5 mi n. Int corridors. **Pets:** Medium, other species. $25 deposit/room. Service with restrictions.

SAVE S◻ ☒ ♿M ♿ 🖥 💻 ⊶

▼▼▼▼ Holiday Inn Express Ⓜ
(623) 535-1313. **$89-$179, 3 days notice.** 1313 Litchfield Rd. I-10, exit 128, just n. Int corridors. **Pets:** Medium, other species. $25 deposit/room. Service with restrictions.

ASK S◻ ☒ ♿ 🖥 💻 ⊶

LITCHFIELD PARK

▼▼▼ ▼▼▼ The Wigwam Resort Ⓡ
(623) 935-3811. **$139-$411, 7 days notice.** 300 Wigwam Blvd. I-10, exit 128 (Litchfield Rd), 2.4 mi n, 0.4 mi e. Ext corridors. **Pets:** Small, dogs only. $25 one-time fee/room. Service with restrictions.

ASK S◻ ☒ ♿ 🖥 💻 🍽 ⊶ ☒

MESA

▲▲▲ ▼▼▼ Arizona Golf Resort & Conference Center Ⓡ ☸
(480) 832-3202. **$99-$179.** 425 S Power Rd. 1.3 mi n of US 60 (Superstition Frwy), exit Power Rd; southeast corner of Broadway and Power rds, entrance on Broadway Rd. Ext corridors. **Pets:** Other species. Service with restrictions.

SAVE ☒ 🖥 💻 🍽 ⊶ ☒

▲▲▲ ▼▼▼ Best Western Mesa Inn Ⓜ
(480) 964-8000. **$49-$99.** 1625 E Main St. 2 mi n of US 60 (Superstition Frwy), exit Stapley Dr, 0.5 mi e. Ext corridors. **Pets:** Medium, other species. $5 one-time fee/pet. Service with restrictions, supervision.

SAVE S◻ ☒ 🖥 💻 ⊶

▲▲▲ ▼▼▼ Best Western Mezona Inn Ⓜ
(480) 834-9233. **$54-$119.** 250 W Main St. Just e of Country Club Dr. Ext corridors. **Pets:** Medium, other species. Service with restrictions, supervision.

SAVE S◻ ☒ 🖥 💻 ⊶

▲▲▲ ▼▼▼ Holiday Inn Hotel & Suites Ⓜ ☸
(480) 964-7000. **$57-$99, 3 days notice.** 1600 S Country Club Dr. US 60 (Superstition Frwy), exit Country Club Dr. Ext/int corridors. **Pets:** Small. $25 deposit/pet. Service with restrictions, supervision.

SAVE S◻ ☒ 🖥 💻 🍽

▼▼▼ Homestead Studio Suites-Mesa/Tempe Ⓜ
(480) 752-2266. **$48-$69.** 1920 W Isabella. Just s of US 60, exit Dobson Rd. Ext corridors. **Pets:** Other species. $75 one-time fee/room.

ASK S◻ ☒ ♿ 🖥 💻

▲▲▲ ▼▼▼▼ La Quinta Inn & Suites-Mesa Ⓜ
(480) 844-8747. **$66-$126.** 902 W Grove Ave. US 60, exit Alma School Rd, 0.5 mi n to Southern Ave, 0.5 mi e to Extension Rd, then just s. Int corridors. **Pets:** Small. Service with restrictions, supervision.

SAVE S◻ ☒ 🐾 ♿ 🖥 💻

▼▼▼▼ La Quinta Inn & Suites-Superstition Springs Ⓜ
(480) 654-1970. **$69-$126.** 6530 E Superstition Springs Blvd. US 60 (Superstition Frwy), exit Power Rd, just s. Int corridors. **Pets:** Accepted.

SAVE ☒ ♿M 🐾 ♿ 🖥 💻 ⊶

▼▼▼ Motel 6–1030 Ⓜ
(480) 834-0066. **$45-$63.** 1511 S Country Club Dr. SR 60, exit 179 (Country Club Dr), just n. Ext corridors. **Pets:** Accepted.

S◻ ☒ 🖥

▲▲▲ ▼▼▼ Residence Inn by Marriott Mesa Ⓜ ☸
(480) 610-0100. **$59-$179.** 941 W Grove Ave. From US 60 (Superstition Frwy), exit Alma School Rd, just n to Grove Ave, then just e. Int corridors. **Pets:** Other species. $10 daily fee/room, $50 one-time fee/room.

SAVE S◻ ☒ ♿M 🐾 ♿ 🖥 💻 ⊶

▲▲▲ ▼▼▼▼ Sheraton Phoenix East/Mesa Hotel Ⓗ
(480) 898-8300. **$59-$90, 3 days notice.** 200 N Centennial Way. 2 mi n of US 60 (Superstition Frwy), exit Mesa Dr, just n and w of Mesa Dr. Int corridors. **Pets:** Other species. $50 one-time fee/room. Service with restrictions, crate.

SAVE ☒ 🖥 💻 🍽 ⊶

▼▼▼ Sleep Inn of Mesa Ⓜ ☸
(480) 807-7760. **$64-$119.** 6347 E Southern Ave. US 60 (Superstition Frwy), exit Power Rd, 0.8 mi n, just w to Mall Entrance West. Int corridors. **Pets:** Medium, other species. $25 one-time fee/room. Designated rooms, service with restrictions, crate.

SAVE S◻ ☒ 🖥 💻 ⊶

▼▼▼ Super 8 Motel-Mesa/Gilbert Rd Ⓜ
(480) 545-0888. **$45-$81.** 1550 S Gilbert Rd. From jct SR 101, 6.1 mi e on US 60 E, exit 182, just n. Int corridors. **Pets:** Small. $5 daily fee/pet. Service with restrictions, supervision.

ASK S◻ ☒ ♿ 🖥 ⊶

▼▼ ▼▼ Travelodge Suites Mesa M ❖
(480) 832-5961. **$49-$109.** 4244 E Main St. I-60, exit 185 (Greenfield Rd), 2 mi n, just w. Ext corridors. **Pets:** Medium, other species. $5 daily fee/room. Service with restrictions, supervision.

ASK 🔊 ✕ 🔋 💻 🏊

PARADISE VALLEY

▼▼▼▼ Hermosa Inn M
(602) 955-8614. **$105-$715, 7 days notice.** 5532 N Palo Cristi Rd. 1 mi s of Lincoln Dr, corner of Stanford Dr. Ext corridors. **Pets:** Medium, other species. $50 one-time fee/ room. Supervision.

ASK 🔊 ✕ 💻 🍴 🏊

PEORIA

▼▼▼ Comfort Suites of Peoria M
(623) 334-3993. **$59-$139.** 8473 W Paradise Ln. Loop 101, exit Bell Rd, just e to 83rd Ave, then just s. Int corridors. **Pets:** Small. $50 one-time fee/pet. Designated rooms, service with restrictions, supervision.

SAVE 🔊 ✕ 🏞 🔋 💻 🏊

▲▲▲ ▼▼▼▼ La Quinta Inn & Suites Phoenix West/Peoria M
(623) 487-1900. **$66-$162.** 16321 N 83 Ave. From Loop 101, exit Bell Rd, just e, then just s. Int corridors. **Pets:** Other species. Service with restrictions, supervision.

SAVE 🔊 ✕ 🏞 🔋 💻 🏊

▲▲▲ ▼▼▼▼ Residence Inn by Marriott M
(623) 979-2074. **$72-$216.** 8435 W Paradise Ln. Loop 101, exit Bell Rd, just e, then just s on 83rd Ave. Int corridors. **Pets:** Small. $100 one-time fee/room. Designated rooms, service with restrictions, crate.

SAVE 🔊 ✕ 🔋 💻 🏊

PHOENIX

▲▲▲ ▼▼▼ AmeriSuites-Phoenix Metro Center M
(602) 997-8800. **$89-$159.** 10838 N 25th Ave. I-17, exit 208 (Peoria Ave), just e, then 0.3 mi n. Int corridors. **Pets:** Small, other species. Service with restrictions, supervision.

SAVE 🔊 ✕ 🦽 🔋 💻 🏊

▲▲▲ ▼▼▼ Best Western Airport Inn MI
(602) 273-7251. **$59-$119.** 2425 S 24th St. I-10, exit 150B westbound, just s; exit 151 eastbound (University Dr), just n to I-10 westbound, 1 mi w to exit 150B (24th St), just s. Ext/int corridors. **Pets:** Accepted.

SAVE 🔊 ✕ 🏞 🔋 🍴 🏊

▲▲▲ ▼▼▼ Best Western Bell Hotel M
(602) 993-8300. **$59-$129.** 17211 N Black Canyon Hwy. I-17, exit 212, just e, then just n. Ext corridors. **Pets:** Small, dogs only. $25 one-time fee/room. Service with restrictions.

SAVE 🔊 ✕ 🏞 🔋 💻 🏊

▲▲▲ ▼▼▼▼ Best Western InnSuites Hotel & Suites M
(602) 997-6285. **$69-$119.** 1615 E Northern Ave. Loop 51, 0.3 mi w. Ext corridors. **Pets:** Medium. $25 one-time fee/ pet. Designated rooms, service with restrictions, supervision.

SAVE 🔊 ✕ 🏞 🔋 💻 🏊

▲▲▲ ▼▼▼ Comfort Inn Black Canyon M
(602) 242-8011. **$50-$110.** 5050 N Black Canyon Hwy. I-17, exit 203 (Camelback Rd), just w, then just n on westside of frwy. Ext corridors. **Pets:** Small, dogs only. $25 deposit/pet. Designated rooms, service with restrictions, supervision.

SAVE 🔊 ✕ 🔋 🏊

▲▲▲ ▼▼▼ Comfort Inn Turf Paradise M
(602) 866-2089. **$59-$129, 7 days notice.** 1711 W Bell Rd. I-17, exit 212, 1 mi e. Ext corridors. **Pets:** Accepted.

SAVE 🔊 ✕ 🏞 🔋 💻 🏊

▼▼▼ Comfort Suites M
(602) 861-3900. **$45-$125, 14 days notice.** 10210 N 26th Dr. I-17, exit 208, just e, just s on 25th Ave, then 0.3 mi w on W Beryl Ave. Int corridors. **Pets:** Small. $5 daily fee/ room, $50 one-time fee/room. Designated rooms, service with restrictions, supervision.

SAVE 🔊 ✕ 🔋 💻 🏊

▲▲▲ ▼▼▼ Crowne Plaza North Phoenix H
(602) 943-2341. **$59-$99.** 2532 W Peoria Ave. I-17, exit 208, just e. Int corridors. **Pets:** Accepted.

SAVE 🔊 ✕ 🦽 🏞 🎿 🔋 💻 🍴 🏊

▲▲▲ ▼▼▼ Days Inn-Airport MI
(602) 244-8244. **$42-$79.** 3333 E Van Buren. Loop 202, exit 1C, 0.6 mi s, then just e. Ext/int corridors. **Pets:** Other species. $20 one-time fee/room. Service with restrictions, supervision.

SAVE 🔊 ✕ 🏞 🔋 💻 🍴

▲▲▲ ▼▼▼ Embassy Suites Airport at 44th St H
(602) 244-8800. **$69-$209.** 1515 N 44th St. Loop 202, exit 2, 0.3 mi n. Ext corridors. **Pets:** Medium. $50 one-time fee/room. Service with restrictions, crate.

SAVE 🔊 ✕ 🏞 🔋 💻 🍴 🏊

▼▼▼▼ Embassy Suites Hotel Airport West H
(602) 957-1910. **$84-$159.** 2333 E Thomas Rd. Just w of 24th St. Ext corridors. **Pets:** Medium, other species. $15 daily fee/room. Service with restrictions, supervision.

SAVE 🔊 ✕ 🦽 🔋 💻 🍴 🏊

▼▼▼▼ Embassy Suites Phoenix-Biltmore H
(602) 955-3992. **$98-$260.** 2630 E Camelback Rd. Just n of Camelback Rd on 26th St. Int corridors. **Pets:** Other species. $25 one-time fee/room. Service with restrictions, crate.

SAVE 🔊 ✕ 🏞 🔋 💻 🍴 🏊

Hampton Inn I-17 Phoenix Metro Center M
(602) 864-6233. **$54-$94, 7 days notice.** 8101 N Black Canyon Hwy. I-17, exit 206 (Northern Ave), just e, then just n; on east side of freeway. Ext corridors. **Pets:** Large, other species. $25 deposit/pet, $25 one-time fee/room.

Hilton Suites-Phoenix H
(602) 222-1111. **$69-$239.** 10 E Thomas Rd. Just e of Central Ave; in Phoenix Plaza. Int corridors. **Pets:** Small, dogs only. $300 deposit/room. Service with restrictions, supervision.

Holiday Inn Express Hotel & Suites M
(480) 785-8500. **$59-$109.** 15221 S 50th St. I-10, exit 160 (Chandler Blvd), just w. Int corridors. **Pets:** $5 daily fee/pet. Designated rooms, service with restrictions, supervision.

Holiday Inn Express Hotel & Suites MI
(602) 453-9900. **$89-$169.** 3401 E University Dr. I-10, exit 151 (University Dr), just n. Int corridors. **Pets:** Accepted.

Holiday Inn Select-Airport H
(602) 273-7778. **$71-$138.** 4300 E Washington St. From Loop 202, exit 2, 0.7 mi s. Int corridors. **Pets:** Accepted.

Holiday Inn West H
(602) 484-9009. **$69-$129.** 1500 N 51st Ave. I-10, exit 139, just n. Int corridors. **Pets:** Medium. $25 one-time fee/pet. Service with restrictions, supervision.

Homestead Studio Suites-Phx/Metro M
(602) 944-7828. **$44-$94.** 2102 W Dunlap Ave. I-17, exit 207, 0.6 mi e. Ext corridors. **Pets:** Other species. $75 one-time fee/pet. Service with restrictions, crate.

Homewood Suites Hotel M
(602) 674-8900. **$99-$179.** 2536 W Beryl Ave. I-17, exit 208, just e, just s on 25th Ave, then just w. Int corridors. **Pets:** Other species. $200 deposit/room, $50 one-time fee/room. Service with restrictions.

La Quinta Inn & Suites-Chandler M
(480) 961-7700. **$86-$117.** 15241 S 50th St. I-10, exit 160 (Chandler Blvd), just w, just n. Int corridors. **Pets:** Accepted.

La Quinta Inn Thomas Rd M
(602) 258-6271. **$56-$76.** 2725 N Black Canyon Hwy. I-17, exit 201 (Thomas Rd), just e, then just s, on east side of freeway. Ext corridors. **Pets:** Accepted.

La Quinta Phoenix North M
(602) 993-0800. **$56-$102.** 2510 W Greenway Rd. I-17, exit 211, just e. Ext corridors. **Pets:** Accepted.

Lexington Hotel and Sports Club at City Square H
(602) 279-9811. **$80-$134, 3 days notice.** 100 W Clarendon Ave. Just w of Central Ave, 0.3 mi s of Indian School Rd. Int corridors. **Pets:** Medium, other species. $100 deposit/room. Service with restrictions, crate.

Los Olivos Hotel & Suites MI
(602) 528-9100. **$59-$129.** 202 E McDowell Rd. Just e of Central Ave. Int corridors. **Pets:** Accepted.

Pointe Hilton Tapatio Cliffs Resort R
(602) 866-7500. **$114-$324, 3 days notice.** 11111 N 7th St. I-17, exit 207, 2 mi e, then 2 mi n. Ext corridors. **Pets:** Accepted.

Premier Inns M ❧
(602) 943-2371. **$40-$90.** 10402 N Black Canyon Hwy. I-17, exit 208, 0.3 mi w to 28th Dr, just s, just e on Metro Pkwy E, just n on 27th Ave. Ext corridors. **Pets:** Large. Designated rooms, service with restrictions, supervision.

Quality Inn Airport MI
(480) 893-3900. **$53-$93.** 5121 E La Puenta Ave. I-10, exit 157 (Elliot Rd), just w, just n on 51st St, then just e. Ext corridors. **Pets:** Medium, other species. $25 one-time fee/room. Service with restrictions, crate.

Red Lion Hotel Phoenix North H
(602) 866-7000. **$53-$119.** 12027 N 28th Dr. I-17, exit 209 (Cactus Rd), just w, then just s. Int corridors. **Pets:** Small. $50 deposit/room. Service with restrictions, supervision.

Red Roof Inn M
(602) 233-8004. **$46-$74.** 5215 W Willetta. I-10, exit 139 (51st Ave), just n, just e on McDowell, then just s. Int corridors. **Pets:** Accepted.

Residence Inn By Marriott M ❧
(602) 864-1900. **$69-$188.** 8242 N Black Canyon Hwy. I-17, exit 207, just w, then 0.5 mi n. Ext/int corridors. **Pets:** Medium, other species. $200 deposit/room, $50 one-time fee/room. Service with restrictions, supervision.

Residence Inn by Marriott Phoenix Airport M
(602) 273-9220. **$89-$179.** 801 N 44th St. From Loop 202, exit 152 (40th and 44th), just s. Int corridors. **Pets:** Accepted.

▼▼ **Royal Suites Villager Premeire** **M**
(602) 942-1000. **$49-$105.** 10421 N 33rd Ave. I-17, exit 208, 1 mi w, then just s. Ext corridors. **Pets:** Small, other species. $50 deposit/pet, $5 daily fee/pet. Designated rooms, service with restrictions, supervision.

🆂🅾 ✖ 🖉 🖉 🍴 📺 🏊

▼▼▼ **Sheraton Crescent Hotel** **H**
(602) 943-8200. **$59-$189.** 2620 W Dunlap Ave. I-17, exit 207, just e. Int corridors. **Pets:** Small. Service with restrictions, supervision.

🆂🅾 ✖ 🔥M 🖉 🖉 🍴 📺 🍽 🏊 ⊗

▼▼▼ **Sierra Suites Hotel-Phoenix/Biltmore** **M**
(602) 265-6800. **$69-$189.** 5235 N 16th St. Just n of Camelback Rd. Int corridors. **Pets:** Small. $150 one-time fee/room. Service with restrictions, crate.

A$K 🆂🅾 ✖ 🖉 🍴 📺 🏊

▼▼▼ **Sierra Suites Hotel-Phoenix/Metro
Center** **M** ❀
(602) 395-0900. **$49-$124.** 9455 N Black Canyon Hwy. I-17, exit 207, just e, then 0.4 mi n. Int corridors. **Pets:** Large, other species. $150 one-time fee/room. Service with restrictions, supervision.

A$K 🆂🅾 ✖ 🍴 📺 🏊

▼▼ **Sleep Inn Phoenix North** **M**
(602) 504-1200. **$49-$109.** 18235 N 27th Ave. I-17, exit 214A, just w, then just s. Int corridors. **Pets:** Other species. $25 one-time fee/room. Designated rooms, supervision.

SAVE 🆂🅾 ✖ 🔥M 🖉 🍴 📺 🏊

▲▲▲ ▼▼▼ **Sleep Inn Sky Harbor Airport** **M**
(480) 967-7100. **$54-$99.** 2621 S 47th Pl. I-10, exit 151 (University Dr), 2 mi n, then just w. Int corridors. **Pets:** Medium, other species. $25 one-time fee/room. Service with restrictions, supervision.

SAVE 🆂🅾 ✖ 🖉 🍴 📺 🏊

▲▲▲ ▼▼▼ **TownePlace Suites-Phoenix** **M**
(602) 943-9510. **$49-$75.** 9425-B N Black Canyon Hwy. I-17, exit 207, just e, then 0.3 mi n. Int corridors. **Pets:** Accepted.

SAVE 🆂🅾 ✖ 🍴 📺 🏊

▲▲▲ ▼ **Travelodge-Fairgrounds** **M**
(602) 269-6281. **$55-$65.** 1624 N Black Canyon Hwy. I-17, exit 200B (McDowell/Van Buren) southbound, 3 mi s, then just w, just n; on west side of freeway. Ext corridors. **Pets:** Small, dogs only. $40 deposit/pet. Designated rooms, service with restrictions, supervision.

SAVE 🆂🅾 ✖ 🍴 📺 🏊

▲▲▲ ▼▼▼ **Wellesley Inn & Suites
(Phoenix/Airport)** **M**
(602) 225-2998. **$67-$119.** 4357 E Oak St. Loop 202, exit 2, 0.8 mi n. Ext corridors. **Pets:** Other species. Service with restrictions, supervision.

SAVE 🆂🅾 ✖ 🔥M 🍴 📺 🏊

▲▲▲ ▼▼▼ **Wellesley Inn & Suites
(Phoenix/Chandler)** **M**
(480) 753-6700. **$59-$109.** 5035 E Chandler Blvd. I-10, exit 160 (Chandler Blvd), just w. Ext corridors. **Pets:** Small, other species. $25 deposit/pet. Service with restrictions, supervision.

SAVE 🆂🅾 ✖ 🖉 🍴 📺 🏊

▲▲▲ ▼▼▼▼ **Wellesley Inn & Suites (Phoenix/Metro
Center)** **M**
(602) 870-2999. **$59-$109.** 11211 N Black Canyon Hwy. I-17, exit 208 (Peoria Ave), just e, then 0.3 mi n; on east side of frwy. Ext corridors. **Pets:** Small. Service with restrictions, supervision.

SAVE 🆂🅾 ✖ 🍴 📺 🏊

▲▲▲ ▼▼▼▼ **Wellesley Inn & Suites (Phoenix/Park
Central Mall)** **M**
(602) 279-9000. **$74-$134.** 217 W Osborn Rd. 0.7 mi s of Indian School Rd. Int corridors. **Pets:** Small, other species. Service with restrictions, supervision.

SAVE 🆂🅾 ✖ 🔥M 🖉 🍴 📺 🏊

SCOTTSDALE

▲▲▲ ▼▼▼▼ **AmeriSuites (Scottsdale/Civic
Center)** **H**
(480) 423-9944. **$69-$199.** 7300 E Third Ave. Just e of Scottsdale Rd. Int corridors. **Pets:** Accepted.

SAVE 🆂🅾 ✖ 🔥M 🖉 🍴 📺 🏊

▼▼▼▼ **Best Western-Scottsdale Airpark
Suites** **MI**
(480) 951-4000. **$69-$149.** 7515 E Butherus Dr. 0.8 mi n of Thunderbird Rd, 0.5 mi e of Scottsdale Rd, on the south side of Butherus Dr. Ext corridors. **Pets:** Small. $25 daily fee/room. Designated rooms, service with restrictions, supervision.

SAVE ✖ 🖉 🍴 📺 🍽 🏊

▲▲▲ ▼▼▼▼ **Chaparral Suites Resort** **H**
(480) 949-1414. **$99-$319.** 5001 N Scottsdale Rd. At Chaparral Rd. Ext corridors. **Pets:** Accepted.

SAVE 🆂🅾 ✖ 🖉 🖉 🍴 📺 🍽 🏊

▲▲▲ ▼▼▼▼ **Country Inn & Suites By
Carlson** **M**
(480) 314-1200. **$61-$159.** 10801 N 89th Pl. Just n of Shea Blvd, just e of Pima Rd. Int corridors. **Pets:** Medium. $50 one-time fee/pet. Designated rooms, service with restrictions, crate.

SAVE 🆂🅾 ✖ 🖉 🖉 🍴 📺 🏊

▼▼▼▼ **Doubletree La Posada
Resort–Scottsdale** **R**
(602) 952-0420. **$59-$189, 3 days notice.** 4949 E Lincoln Dr. Southeast corner of Lincoln Dr and Tatum Blvd, enter from Lincoln Dr. Ext corridors. **Pets:** Other species. Service with restrictions, supervision.

SAVE 🆂🅾 ✖ 🖉 📺 🍽 🏊 ⊗

The Fairmont Scottsdale Princess **R** ❖
(480) 585-4848. **$189-$529, 14 days notice.** 7575 E Princess Dr. 0.6 mi n of Bell Rd, 0.5 e of Scottsdale Rd, on south side of Princess Dr. Ext/int corridors. **Pets:** Small, other species. $25 one-time fee/room. Designated rooms, supervision.

Four Seasons Resort Scottsdale at Troon North **R** ❖
(480) 515-5700. **$185-$4500, 7 days notice.** 10600 E Crescent Moon Dr. Pima Rd, 2 mi e on Happy Valley, then 1.5 mi n on Alma School Pkwy. Ext corridors. **Pets:** Small. Service with restrictions.

Hampton Inn-Oldtown/Fashion Square Scottsdale **M**
(480) 941-9400. **$59-$159.** 4415 N Civic Center Plaza. From Scottsdale Rd, just e on Camelback Rd, just s on 75th St. Ext/int corridors. **Pets:** Accepted.

Homestead Studio Suites-Scottsdale **M**
(480) 994-0297. **$47-$99.** 3560 N Marshall Way. Just w of Scottsdale Rd, just s of Goldwater. Ext corridors. **Pets:** Accepted.

Hospitality Suite Resort **MI**
(480) 949-5115. **$49-$129.** 409 N Scottsdale Rd. Just n of McKellips, on east side of Scottsdale Rd. Ext corridors. **Pets:** Medium, dogs only. $100 deposit/room. Service with restrictions, supervision.

La Quinta Inn & Suites **M**
(480) 614-5300. **$67-$136.** 8888 E Shea Blvd. Loop 101, exit Shea Blvd, northeast corner. Int corridors. **Pets:** Accepted.

Marriott's Camelback Inn Resort, Golf Club & Spa **R**
(480) 948-1700. **$139-$500, 10 days notice.** 5402 E Lincoln Dr. 0.5 mi e of Tatum Blvd, on north side of Lincoln Dr. Ext corridors. **Pets:** Other species. Service with restrictions, crate.

Marriott's Mountain Shadows Resort and Golf Club **R**
(480) 948-7111. **$69-$289, 3 days notice.** 5641 E Lincoln Dr. 1 mi e of Tatum Blvd, on south side of Lincoln Dr. Ext corridors. **Pets:** Accepted.

Old Town Hotel & Conference Center Scottsdale **M**
(480) 994-9203. **$-$59, 3 days notice.** 7353 E Indian School Rd. Just e of Scottsdale Rd, on south side of Indian School Rd. Ext corridors. **Pets:** $10 daily fee/room. Designated rooms, service with restrictions, crate.

Park Inn Suites-Scottsdale South **A**
(480) 949-8637. **$109-$159.** 1251 N Miller Rd. SR 202, exit 7, 0.6 mi n to E McDowell Rd, just e to Miller Rd, then just s. Ext corridors. **Pets:** Accepted.

The Phoenician **R**
(480) 941-8200. **$208-$506, 7 days notice.** 6000 E Camelback Rd. 0.5 mi w of 64th St. Int corridors. **Pets:** Accepted.

Quality Suites **M**
(480) 675-7665. **$129-$209.** 3131 N Scottsdale Rd. Northeast corner of Scottsdale Rd and Earll Dr. Int corridors. **Pets:** Accepted.

Ramada Valley Ho Resort **MI**
(480) 945-6321. **$49-$109, 3 days notice.** 6850 Main St. 0.4 mi w of Scottsdale Rd, just s of Indian School Rd, on north side of Main St. Ext/int corridors. **Pets:** Accepted.

Renaissance Scottsdale Resort **R**
(480) 991-1414. **$79-$249.** 6160 N Scottsdale Rd. Just n of McDonald Dr, on west side of Scottsdale Rd. Ext corridors. **Pets:** Accepted.

Residence Inn by Marriott **M**
(480) 948-8666. **$59-$199.** 6040 N Scottsdale Rd. Just n of McDonald Dr. Ext/int corridors. **Pets:** Accepted.

Scottsdale Pima Inn & Suites **M** ❖
(480) 948-3800. **$45-$228.** 7330 N Pima Rd. 0.4 mi n of Indian Bend Rd; on west side of Pima Rd. Ext/int corridors. **Pets:** Large, other species. $10 daily fee/room. Designated rooms, service with restrictions, crate.

Sleep Inn **M**
(480) 998-9211. **$57-$139.** 16630 N Scottsdale Rd. Just s of Bell Rd. Int corridors. **Pets:** Large. $10 daily fee/room. Service with restrictions, supervision.

Summerfield Suites by Wyndham-Scottsdale **M**
(480) 946-7700. **$99-$199, 3 days notice.** 4245 N Drinkwater Blvd. 0.3 mi e of Scottsdale Rd. Ext corridors. **Pets:** Accepted.

(AAA) ▼▼▼ TownePlace Suites by Marriott 🅰
(480) 551-1100. **$69-$139.** 10740 N 90th St. Loop 101, exit Shea Blvd, just e to 90th St, just n. Int corridors. **Pets:** Other species. $75 deposit/room, $15 daily fee/room. Service with restrictions.
[SAVE] [S🐾] [✕] [&M] [📷] [🛢] [🔌] [🖥] [⇋]

SURPRISE

(AAA) ▼▼▼ Quality Inn & Suites 🅼
(623) 583-3500. **$62-$120.** 16741 N Greasewood St. US 60 (Grand Ave), 1.1 mi e on Bell Rd, then just s. Int corridors. **Pets:** Accepted.
[SAVE] [S🐾] [✕] [🔌] [🖥] [⇋]

(AAA) ▼▼▼ Windmill Suites at Sun City West 🅼
(623) 583-0133. **$73-$145.** 12545 W Bell Rd. US 60 (Grand Ave), 1 mi e. Int corridors. **Pets:** Accepted.
[SAVE] [S🐾] [✕] [📷] [🔌] [🖥] [⇋]

TEMPE

(AAA) ▼▼▼ AmeriSuites (Tempe/Arizona Mills) 🅼
(480) 831-9800. **$69-$139.** 1520 W Baseline Rd. I-10, exit 155 (Baseline Rd), 0.4 mi e. Int corridors. **Pets:** Accepted.
[SAVE] [S🐾] [✕] [🛢] [🔌] [🖥] [⇋]

(AAA) ▼▼▼ Best Western Inn of Tempe 🅼
(480) 784-2233. **$49-$134.** 670 N Scottsdale Rd. SR 202 Loop (Red Mountain Frwy), exit 7, just s. Int corridors. **Pets:** Accepted.
[SAVE] [S🐾] [✕] [🛢] [🔌] [🖥] [⇋]

▼▼▼ Country Inn & Suites By Carlson 🅼
(480) 345-8585. **$54-$99.** 1660 W Elliot Rd. I-10, exit 157, just e. Ext corridors. **Pets:** Accepted.
[ASK] [S🐾] [✕] [📷] [🛢] [🔌] [🖥] [⇋]

(AAA) ▼▼▼ Fiesta Inn Resort 🅼
(480) 967-1441. **$79-$139.** 2100 S Priest Dr. I-10, exit 153 (Broadway Rd), 0.5 mi e. Ext corridors. **Pets:** Accepted.
[SAVE] [S🐾] [✕] [📷] [🛢] [🔌] [🖥] [🍴] [⇋] [✕]

▼▼▼ Hampton Inn & Suites 🅼
(480) 675-9799. **Call for rates.** 1429 N Scottsdale Rd. SR 202 (Red Mountain Frwy), exit 7, 0.5 mi n. Ext corridors. **Pets:** Accepted.
[ASK] [✕] [📷] [🛢] [🔌] [🖥] [⇋] [✕]

▼▼▼ Holiday Inn 🅼
(480) 968-3451. **$49-$129.** 915 E Apache Blvd. US 60 (Superstition Frwy), exit 153 (Rural Rd), 2 mi n. Int corridors. **Pets:** Accepted.
[ASK] [S🐾] [✕] [📷] [🛢] [🔌] [🖥] [🍴] [⇋]

▼▼ Holiday Inn Express/Tempe 🅼
(480) 820-7500. **$59-$119.** 5300 S Priest Dr. I-10, exit 155 (Baseline Rd), 0.4 mi e, then just s. Int corridors. **Pets:** Accepted.
[ASK] [S🐾] [✕] [🔌] [🖥] [⇋]

(AAA) ▼▼▼ InnSuites Hotel Tempe/Phoenix Airport 🅼
(480) 897-7900. **$59-$105.** 1651 W Baseline Rd. I-10, exit 155 (Baseline Rd), just e. Ext corridors. **Pets:** Accepted.
[SAVE] [S🐾] [✕] [🔌] [🖥] [🍴] [⇋] [✕]

(AAA) ▼▼▼ La Quinta Inn 🅼
(480) 967-4465. **$66-$106.** 911 S 48th St. I-10, exit 153 (SR 143) eastbound; exit 153A (SR 143) westbound; exit University Dr, 0.8 mi n, on south side of University Dr and e side of SR 143 (Hohokam Expwy). Ext corridors. **Pets:** Accepted.
[SAVE] [S🐾] [✕] [📷] [🔌] [🖥] [⇋]

(AAA) ▼▼▼ Mainstay Suites-Tempe 🅼
(480) 557-8880. **$39-$169.** 2165 W 15th St. I-10, exit 153 (Broadway Rd), 0.3 mi ne, then just nw on S 52nd St. Int corridors. **Pets:** Accepted.
[SAVE] [S🐾] [✕] [🛢] [🖥] [⇋]

(AAA) ▼▼▼ Quality Inn 🅼
(480) 774-2500. **$65-$109.** 1375 E University Dr. 0.5 mi e of Rural Rd. Int corridors. **Pets:** Accepted.
[SAVE] [S🐾] [✕] [🛢] [🔌] [🖥] [⇋]

(AAA) ▼▼▼ Red Roof Inn 🅼
(480) 413-1188. **$46-$76.** 1701 W Baseline Rd. I-10, exit 155 (Baseline Rd), just e. Ext corridors. **Pets:** Accepted.
[SAVE] [S🐾] [✕] [📷] [🛢] [🔌] [⇋]

(AAA) ▼▼▼ Red Roof Inn Phoenix Airport 🅼
(480) 449-3205. **$49-$72.** 2135 W 15th St. I-10, exit 153, just nw on S 52nd St. Int corridors. **Pets:** Accepted.
[SAVE] [✕] [🛢] [🔌] [⇋]

(AAA) ▼▼▼ Residence Inn by Marriott 🅰
(480) 756-2122. **$69-$179.** 5075 S Priest Dr. I-10, exit 155 (Baseline Rd), 0.4 mi e, then just n. Ext/int corridors. **Pets:** Accepted.
[SAVE] [S🐾] [✕] [🛢] [🔌] [🖥] [⇋]

(AAA) ▼▼▼ Rodeway Inn Tempe Airport East 🅼
(480) 967-3000. **$55-$79.** 1550 S 52nd St. I-10, exit 153 (Broadway Rd), 0.3 mi ne. Ext corridors. **Pets:** Accepted.
[SAVE] [S🐾] [✕] [📷] [🔌] [🖥] [⇋]

▼▼▼ Studio 6 Extended Stay 🅼
(602) 414-4470. **$48-$73.** 4909 S Wendler Dr. I-10, exit 155 (Baseline Rd), just w, then 0.4 mi n. Ext corridors. **Pets:** Accepted.
[✕] [🛢] [🔌] [🖥]

(AAA) ▼▼▼ Tempe Mission Palms Hotel 🅷
(480) 894-1400. **$139-$289.** 60 E Fifth St. Just e of Mill Ave and 0.3 mi n of University Dr. Int corridors. **Pets:** Accepted.
[SAVE] [S🐾] [✕] [📷] [🛢] [🔌] [🖥] [🍴] [⇋]

▼▼▼ Tempe Super 8 🅼
(480) 967-8891. **$41-$109, 14 days notice.** 1020 E Apache Blvd. Just e of Rural Rd. Ext corridors. **Pets:** Accepted.
[ASK] [S🐾] [✕] [🔌]

◆◆◆ ▼▼▼▼ Wyndham Buttes Resort R
(602) 225-9000. **$99-$249.** 2000 Westcourt Way. I-10, exit
153 (Broadway Rd) westbound, 0.8 mi w to 48th St, 0.3 mi
s; exit 48th St eastbound, 0.5 mi s. Int corridors.
Pets: Accepted.
[SAVE] [✕] [📶] [💻] [🍴] [🏊]

YOUNGTOWN

**◆◆◆ ▼▼▼▼ Best Western Inn & Suites of Sun
City M**
(623) 933-8211. **$57-$118, 14 days notice.** 11201 Grand
Ave. On US 60, just se of 113th Ave. Ext/int corridors.
Pets: Accepted.
[SAVE] [S📶] [✕] [📶] [🛏] [💻] [🏊]

❀   END METROPOLITAN AREA   ❀

PINETOP LAKESIDE

◆◆◆ ▼▼ Comfort Inn M
(928) 368-6600. **$65-$89.** 1637 W White Mountain Blvd. On
SR 260. Int corridors. **Pets:** Accepted.
[SAVE] [S📶] [✕] [🛏] [💻]

◆◆◆ ▼▼▼▼ Holiday Inn Express M
(928) 367-6077. **$69-$129, 3 days notice.** 431 E White
Mountain Blvd. On SR 260. Int corridors. **Pets:** Accepted.
[SAVE] [S📶] [✕] [🛏] [💻]

▼▼▼▼ Lazy Oaks Resort C
(928) 368-6203. **$64-$80 (no credit cards), 21 days
notice.** 1075 Larson Rd. From SR 260, 1.3 mi s on Rainbow Lake Dr, 0.8 mi nw of Lakeside. Ext corridors.
Pets: Medium. No service, supervision.
[🛏] [💻] [✕] [🎾] [🐾]

▼▼▼▼ Northwoods Resort C
(928) 367-2966. **$79-$149, 14 days notice.** 165 E White
Mountain Blvd. On SR 260. Ext corridors. **Pets:** Accepted.
[✕] [🛏] [💻] [🎾] [🐾]

◆◆◆ ▼▼▼ Woodland Inn & Suites M
(928) 367-3636. **$59-$119, 7 days notice.** 458 E White
Mountain Blvd. On SR 260. Ext corridors. **Pets:** Medium.
$10 daily fee/pet. Service with restrictions, supervision.
[SAVE] [S📶] [✕] [🛏] [💻]

PRESCOTT

▼▼▼▼ Arizona Vacation Lodging C
(928) 778-9573. **$110-$190, 14 days notice.** 5555 Onyx
Dr. From jct SR 89, 5 mi e on SR 69 to Onyn Dr, then 0.5
mi s on dirt/gravel road. Ext corridors. **Pets:** Other species.
$10 daily fee/pet. No service, crate.
[✕] [🛏] [💻] [🐾]

▼▼▼ Best Western Prescottonian Motel MI
(928) 445-3096. **$59-$125, 3 days notice.** 1317 E Gurley
St. On SR 89 (Gurley St), 1.2 mi e of Montezuma St. Ext
corridors. **Pets:** Accepted.
[SAVE] [S📶] [✕] [📶] [🛏] [💻] [🍴] [🏊]

◆◆◆ ▼▼▼▼ Forest Villas Inn M
(928) 717-1200. **$79-$208.** 3645 Lee Cir. 2.5 mi e of jct SR
89 and 69, just n. Int corridors. **Pets:** Small. $10 daily
fee/pet. Designated rooms, service with restrictions, supervision.
[SAVE] [S📶] [✕] [🧎] [🛏] [💻] [🏊]

▼▼▼ Lynx Creek Farm Bed & Breakfast BB
(928) 778-9573. **$75-$160, 14 days notice.** 5555 Onyx Dr.
From jct SR 89, 5 mi e on SR 69 to Onyx Dr, then 0.5 mi s
on dirt/gravel road. Ext corridors. **Pets:** Other species. $10
daily fee/pet. No service, crate.
[✕] [🛏] [💻] [🏊] [W] [🐾]

▼▼▼ Prescott Super 8 Motel M ❀
(928) 776-1282. **$55-$68, 3 days notice.** 1105 E Sheldon
St. East end of town off Gurley. Int corridors. **Pets:** Dogs
only. $10 one-time fee/room. Service with restrictions,
supervision.
[ASK] [S📶] [✕] [📶] [🛏] [💻] [🏊]

PRESCOTT VALLEY

◆◆◆ ▼▼▼ Days Inn/Prescott Valley M
(928) 772-8600. **$69-$99.** 7875 E Hwy 69. 0.3 mi w of
Robert Rd. Ext corridors. **Pets:** Other species. $50 deposit/
room.
[SAVE] [S📶] [✕] [🛏] [🏊]

▼▼▼ Motel 6—4048 M
(928) 772-2200. **Call for rates.** 8383 E Hwy 69. Center; on
SR 69. Int corridors. **Pets:** Other species. $10 daily fee/
room. Service with restrictions, supervision.
[ASK] [✕] [🏊]

RIO RICO

**◆◆◆ ▼▼▼▼ Rio Rico Resort & Country
Club R**
(520) 281-1901. **$110-$235.** 1069 Camino Caralampi. I-19,
exit 17 (Rio Rico Dr), 0.5 mi w. Ext corridors. **Pets:** Small,
other species. $25 deposit/room. Service with restrictions.
[SAVE] [S📶] [✕] [🛏M] [🧎] [🛏] [💻] [🍴] [🏊] [✕]

SAFFORD

◆◆◆ ▼▼▼ Best Western Desert Inn M
(928) 428-0521. **$60-$75.** 1391 W Thatcher Blvd. US 191,
1 mi w of US 70. Ext corridors. **Pets:** Medium. $6 daily
fee/pet. Service with restrictions, supervision.
[SAVE] [S📶] [✕] [🛏] [💻] [🏊]

▼▼▼ Comfort Inn M
(928) 428-5851. **$55-$75.** 1578 W Thatcher Blvd. From US
191, 1.3 mi w on US 70. Ext corridors. **Pets:** Medium. $10
daily fee/pet. Designated rooms, service with restrictions,
supervision.
[SAVE] [S📶] [✕] [🛏] [💻] [🏊]

⨹ ▼▼▼▼ Days Inn Ⓜ
(928) 428-5000. **$65-$85.** 520 E Hwy 70. 0.5 mi e of town on US 70 and US 171. Ext corridors. **Pets:** Other species. $20 deposit/room. Service with restrictions.
SAVE S⊠ ✕ �&M 🦮 🐾 🖥 🖳 ⇌

⨹ ▼▼▼▼ Ramada Inn-Spa Resort Ⓜ!
(928) 428-3200. **$85-$125.** 420 E Hwy 70. From US 191, 0.5 mi e. Ext/int corridors. **Pets:** Other species. $20 deposit/room. Service with restrictions.
SAVE S⊠ ✕ ⛾ 🖥 🖳 🍴 ⇌

SEDONA

▼▼▼▼ Bell Rock Inn & Suites Ⓜ! 🐾
(928) 282-4161. **$100-$179.** 6246 Hwy 179. From SR 89A, 6 mi s. Ext/int corridors. **Pets:** Medium, other species. $20 daily fee/pet. Designated rooms, supervision.
ASK ✕ 🦮 🖥 🖳 🍴 ⇌

⨹ ▼▼▼▼ Best Western Inn of Sedona Ⓜ
(928) 282-3072. **$110-$155.** 1200 W Hwy 89A. From SR 179, 1.2 mi w. Ext corridors. **Pets:** Large, other species. $10 one-time fee/room. Designated rooms, service with restrictions, supervision.
SAVE S⊠ ✕ 🦮 🖥 🖳 ⇌

⨹ ▼▼▼▼ Desert Quail Inn Ⓜ
(928) 284-1433. **$59-$99.** 6626 Hwy 179. 6.5 mi sw of jct SR 89A and 179, on west side of SR 179. Ext corridors. **Pets:** Small, dogs only. $10 daily fee/pet. Designated rooms, service with restrictions, supervision.
SAVE ✕ 🦮 🖥 🖳 ⇌

⨹ ▼▼▼▼ Matterhorn Lodge Ⓜ
(928) 282-7176. **$59-$119.** 230 Apple Ave. SR 89A, just w. Ext corridors. **Pets:** Large, other species. Designated rooms, service with restrictions, crate.
SAVE S⊠ ✕ 🖥 🖳 ⇌

⨹ ▼▼▼▼ Quality Inn-King's Ransom Ⓜ!
(928) 282-7151. **$62-$125.** 771 Hwy 179. From SR 89A, 0.8 mi s. Ext/int corridors. **Pets:** Small. Designated rooms, service with restrictions, supervision.
SAVE S⊠ ✕ 🖥 🖳 🍴 ⇌

⨹ ▼▼▼▼ Sedona Super 8 Ⓜ
(928) 282-1533. **$55-$89.** 2545 W Hwy 89A. From SR 179, 2.8 mi w. Int corridors. **Pets:** Small, dogs only. Designated rooms, service with restrictions, supervision.
SAVE ✕ 🦮 🖥 ⇌

⨹ ▼▼▼▼ Sky Ranch Lodge Ⓜ 🐾
(928) 282-6400. **$75-$179.** Airport Rd. SR 179, 1 mi w on SR 89A, 1 mi s on Airport Rd, on west side. Ext corridors. **Pets:** Other species. $10 daily fee/pet. Service with restrictions, supervision.
SAVE ✕ 🖥 🖳 ⇌

⨹ ▼▼▼ Village Lodge Ⓜ
(928) 284-3626. **$49-$59, 3 days notice.** 78 Bell Rock Blvd. From SR 89A, 6 mi s on SR 179, then just w. Ext/int corridors. **Pets:** Medium, other species. Supervision.
SAVE S⊠ ✕ 🖥 🖳

SELIGMAN

⨹ ▼▼ Historic Route 66 Motel Ⓜ
(928) 422-3204. **$57-$67.** 500 W Hwy 66. I-40, exit 121, 1.1 mi n, follow signs to I-40 business loop and SR 66, then 0.3 mi e. Ext corridors. **Pets:** Accepted.
SAVE S⊠ ✕ 🖥 🖳

SHOW LOW

⨹ ▼▼▼▼ Best Western Paint Pony
      Lodge Ⓜ!
(928) 537-5773. **$64-$89.** 581 W Deuce of Clubs. on SR 60 and 260. Ext corridors. **Pets:** Other species. $5 daily fee/pet. Service with restrictions.
SAVE S⊠ ✕ 🖥 🖳 🍴

⨹ ▼▼▼ Days Inn Ⓜ!
(928) 537-4356. **$59-$74.** 480 W Deuce of Clubs Ave. On US 60 and SR 260. Ext/int corridors. **Pets:** Accepted.
SAVE S⊠ ✕ 🦮 🖥 🍴 ⇌

⨹ ▼▼ Kiva Motel Ⓜ
(928) 537-4542. **$45-$46.** 261 E Deuce of Clubs Ave. On US 60 and SR 260. Ext corridors. **Pets:** Medium, dogs only. $5 daily fee/pet. Service with restrictions, supervision.
SAVE S⊠ ✕ 🖥 🖳

⨹ ▼▼ Snowy River Motel Ⓜ
(928) 537-2926. **$39.** 1640 E Deuce of Clubs Ave. On US 60, just e of jct SR 260. Ext corridors. **Pets:** Small, dogs only. $5 one-time fee/room. Service with restrictions, supervision.
SAVE S⊠ ✕ 🖥 🖳

SIERRA VISTA

⨹ ▼▼▼ Best Western Mission Inn Ⓜ
(520) 458-8500. **$70-$80.** 3460 E Fry Blvd. Just w of jct SR 90 and 92. Ext corridors. **Pets:** Medium, other species. $5 daily fee/pet. Service with restrictions, supervision.
SAVE S⊠ ✕ ⛾M 🖥 🖳 ⇌

▼▼▼ Sierra Suites Ⓜ
(520) 459-4221. **$87-$99.** 391 E Fry Blvd. 2.5 mi w of jct SR 90 and 92. Ext corridors. **Pets:** Small. $25 one-time fee/room. Service with restrictions, supervision.
ASK S⊠ ✕ 🖥 🖳 ⇌

▼▼ Super 8 Motel Ⓜ
(520) 459-5380. **$45-$55, 3 days notice.** 100 Fab Ave. From jct Business SR 90 and Fry Blvd, then just e; east of main entrance to Ft Huachuca. Ext corridors. **Pets:** Dogs only. $10 one-time fee/room. Service with restrictions, supervision.
ASK S⊠ ✕ 🦮 🖥 🖳 ⇌

▼▼ Thunder Mountain Inn-Hotel Ⓜ!
(520) 458-7900. **$56-$85.** 1631 S Hwy 92. SR 92, 1 mi s of jct SR 90. Int corridors. **Pets:** Accepted.
ASK S⊠ ✕ 🖥 🖳 🍴 ⇌

▼▼ Windemere Hotel & Conference Center Ⓜ!
(520) 459-5900. **$89.** 2047 S Hwy 92. 1.5 mi s of jct SR 90. Int corridors. **Pets:** Other species. $50 deposit/pet. Crate.
ASK S⊠ ✕ 🖥 🖳 🍴 ⇌

SNOWFLAKE

(AAA) ▼▼▼▼ Comfort Inn M
(928) 536-3888. **$49-$119.** 2055 S Main. On SR 77, just s of town. Int corridors. **Pets:** Accepted.
[SAVE] [S&] [X] [&] [📶] [💻] [🏊]

SPRINGERVILLE

▼▼ ▼▼ Rode Inn Motel & Suites M
(928) 333-4365. **$60-$70.** 242 E Main St. On US 60/180. Ext/int corridors. **Pets:** Accepted.
[ASK] [S&] [X] [📶] [💻]

TAYLOR

(AAA) ▼▼ ▼▼ Silver Creek Inn M
(928) 536-2600. **$53-$65.** 825 N Main St. On SR 77. Ext corridors. **Pets:** Accepted.
[SAVE] [S&] [X] [📶] [💻]

TOMBSTONE

(AAA) ▼▼ ▼▼ Best Western Lookout Lodge M
(520) 457-2223. **$78-$109.** US Hwy 80 W. 1 mi n on SR 80. Ext corridors. **Pets:** Other species. $5 daily fee/pet. Service with restrictions, supervision.
[SAVE] [S&] [X] [📶] [🏊]

▼▼ Tombstone Motel M
(520) 457-3478. **$45-$70.** 502 E Fremont St. On SR 80, in center of town. Ext corridors. **Pets:** Small. $25 deposit/pet. No service, supervision.
[ASK] [S&] [X] [📶]

TUBA CITY

▼▼ ▼▼ Dine Inn Motel M
(928) 283-6107. **$55-$95.** Hwy 160 & Peshlakai. US 160. Ext corridors. **Pets:** Accepted.
[ASK] [X] [📶]

(AAA) ▼▼ ▼▼ Quality Inn MI
(928) 283-4545. **$105-$135.** Main St & Moenave Rd. 1 mi n of US 160. Int corridors. **Pets:** Medium. $20 deposit/pet. Designated rooms, service with restrictions, supervision.
[SAVE] [S&] [X] [📶] [💻] [🍴]

TUCSON METROPOLITAN AREA

GREEN VALLEY

(AAA) ▼▼▼▼ Best Western Green Valley MI
(520) 625-2250. **$74-$114, 3 days notice.** 111 S La Canada Dr. I-119, exit 65 (Esperanza Rd), just w, then just s. Int corridors. **Pets:** $25 one-time fee/pet. Designated rooms, service with restrictions, supervision.
[SAVE] [S&] [X] [📶] [💻] [🍴] [🏊]

ORO VALLEY

(AAA) ▼▼▼ ▼▼▼ The Golf Villas at Oro Valley CO
(520) 498-0098. **$119-$499, 10 days notice.** 10950 N La Canada. I-10, exit 248 (Ina Rd), 4 mi e, then 4.5 mi n. Ext corridors. **Pets:** Medium. Service with restrictions.
[SAVE] [S&] [X] [📶] [💻] [🏊]

(AAA) ▼▼▼ ▼▼▼ Sheraton El Conquistador R
(520) 544-5000. **$250-$480, 7 days notice.** 10000 N Oracle Rd. I-10, exit 248 (Ina Rd), 5.4 mi e, then 4.4 mi n. Ext/int corridors. **Pets:** Very small, dogs only. $100 deposit/room. Designated rooms, service with restrictions, supervision.
[SAVE] [S&] [X] [&] [📶] [💻] [🍴] [🏊] [✂]

TUCSON

(AAA) ▼▼▼▼ Baymont Inn M
(520) 624-3200. **$49-$149.** 1560 W Grant Rd. I-10, exit 256, just w. Int corridors. **Pets:** Accepted.
[SAVE] [S&] [X] [&] [📶] [💻] [🏊]

(AAA) ▼▼▼▼ Baymont Inn & Suites-Tucson Airport M
(520) 889-6600. **$40-$70, 15 days notice.** 2548 E Medina Rd. Just n of entrance to Tucson International Airport. Int corridors. **Pets:** $50 deposit/room. Service with restrictions, supervision.
[SAVE] [S&] [X] [&M] [&] [📶] [💻] [🏊]

(AAA) ▼▼▼▼ Best Western Executive Inn MI
(520) 791-7551. **$49-$79, 30 days notice.** 333 W Drachman St. I-10, exit 257 (Speedway Blvd), 0.5 mi e to Main St, then 0.3 mi n. Int corridors. **Pets:** $25 deposit/room, $25 one-time fee/pet. Service with restrictions, crate.
[SAVE] [S&] [X] [📶] [🍴] [🏊]

(AAA) ▼▼▼▼ Best Western InnSuites-Catalina M
(520) 297-8111. **$69-$169.** 6201 N Oracle Rd. I-10, exit 250 (Orange Grove Rd), 4 mi e, then just s. Ext corridors. **Pets:** Accepted.
[SAVE] [S&] [X] [📶] [💻] [🏊]

▼▼ Candlelight Suites M
(520) 747-1440. **$45-$90.** 1440 S Craycroft Rd. I-10, exit 265 (Alvernon Way), 4 mi n to Golf Links Rd, 2 mi e, just n. Ext corridors. **Pets:** Accepted.
[ASK] [S&] [X] [&] [📶] [🏊]

▼▼ ▼▼ Clarion Hotel-Randolph Park M
(520) 795-0330. **$71-$129.** 102 N Alvernon. I-10, 8 mi e, then just n. Ext/int corridors. **Pets:** Small. $10 daily fee/ room. Service with restrictions, supervision.
[SAVE] [S&] [X] [📶] [💻] [🏊]

▼▼▼▼ **Comfort Suites at Tuscon Mall** Ⓜ
(520) 888-6676. **$69-$140.** 515 W Auto Mall Dr. I-10, exit 254 (Prince Rd), 1.9 mi e, then 1.2 mi n. Int corridors. **Pets:** Other species. $10 one-time fee/pet. Designated rooms, service with restrictions, crate.
🆂🅰🆅🅴 🆂🔟 ☒ 🄺 🗄 💻 ⤳

Ⓐⓐⓐ ▼▼▼▼ **Days Inn & Suites** Ⓜ
(520) 744-6677. **$49-$129.** 8370 N Cracker Barrel Rd. I-10, exit 246 (Cortaro Rd), just w. Int corridors. **Pets:** Accepted.
🆂🅰🆅🅴 🆂🔟 ☒ 🄺 🗄 💻 ⤳

▼▼▼▼ **Doubletree Guest Suites-Tucson** Ⓜ
(520) 721-7100. **$59-$135.** 6555 E Speedway Blvd. I-10, exit 257 (Speedway Blvd), 8 mi e. Ext corridors. **Pets:** Small, other species. $25 one-time fee/room. Service with restrictions.
🆂🅰🆅🅴 🆂🔟 ☒ 🗄 💻 🍴 ⤳

▼▼▼ **Doubletree Hotel at Reid Park** Ⓗ
(520) 881-4200. **$64-$155.** 445 S Alvernon Way. I-10, exit 259 (22nd St), 4 mi e, then just n. Ext/int corridors. **Pets:** Medium. $50 one-time fee/room. Designated rooms, service with restrictions.
🆂🅰🆅🅴 🆂🔟 ☒ 🗄 🄺 🗄 💻 🍴 ⤳

Ⓐⓐⓐ ▼▼▼▼ **Embassy Suites**
Tucson-Broadway Ⓜ
(520) 745-2700. **$63-$179.** 5335 E Broadway. Jct of Campbell Rd, 3.9 mi e. Ext corridors. **Pets:** Accepted.
🆂🅰🆅🅴 🆂🔟 ☒ 🄺 🗄 💻 ⤳

▼▼▼ **Ghost Ranch Lodge** Ⓜ
(520) 791-7565. **$46-$106.** 801 W Miracle Mile. I-10, exit 255 (Miracle Mile), 1 mi e just w of Oracle Rd (SR 77). Ext corridors. **Pets:** Accepted.
🄰🆂🄺 🆂🔟 ☒ 🗄 💻 🍴 ⤳

Ⓐⓐⓐ ▼▼▼▼ **Hampton Inn North** Ⓜ
(520) 206-0602. **$69-$149.** 1375 W Grant Rd. I-10, exit 256 (Grant Rd), just w. Int corridors. **Pets:** Accepted.
🆂🅰🆅🅴 🆂🔟 ☒ 🄼 🄺 🗄 💻 ⤳

▼▼▼ **Hawthorn Suites LTD** Ⓜ
(520) 298-2300. **$59-$139.** 7 E Tanque Verde Rd. 2.6 mi e on Grant Rd, 0.4 mi ne. Ext corridors. **Pets:** Medium. $25 one-time fee/pet. Service with restrictions, supervision.
🄰🆂🄺 🆂🔟 ☒ 🗄 💻 ⤳

Ⓐⓐⓐ ▼▼▼ **Inn Suites Tucson St Mary's** Ⓜ
(520) 622-3000. **$79-$159.** 475 N Granada Ave. I-10, exit 258 (Congress and Broadway), just e, then 0.4 mi n. Ext/int corridors. **Pets:** Accepted.
🆂🅰🆅🅴 🆂🔟 ☒ 🗄 💻 🍴 ⤳

Ⓐⓐⓐ ▼▼▼▼ **La Quinta Inn & Suites Airport** Ⓜ
(520) 573-3333. **$76-$136.** 7001 S Tucson Blvd. Just n of Tucson International Airport. Int corridors. **Pets:** Accepted.
🆂🅰🆅🅴 🆂🔟 ☒ 🄼 🗄 🄺 🗄 💻 ⤳

▼▼▼▼ **La Quinta Inn-East** Ⓜ
(520) 747-1414. **$62-$126.** 6404 E Broadway. I-10, exit 259 (Congress Rd) eastbound, 7.5 mi e; exit 270 (Kolb Rd) westbound, 7.5 mi n, then 1 mi e. Ext corridors. **Pets:** Accepted.
🆂🅰🆅🅴 ☒ 🗄 💻 ⤳

Ⓐⓐⓐ ▼▼▼ **La Quinta Inn-West** Ⓜ
(520) 622-6491. **$62-$106.** 665 N Frwy. I-10, exit 257 (St Mary's Rd/Speedway), just s. Ext corridors. **Pets:** Accepted.
🆂🅰🆅🅴 🆂🔟 ☒ 🗄 💻 ⤳

▼▼▼▼ **Lodge on the Desert** Ⓜ
(520) 325-3366. **$79-$289, 3 days notice.** 306 N Alvernon Way. I-10, 4 mi e, then just n. Ext corridors. **Pets:** Accepted.
🄰🆂🄺 🆂🔟 ☒ 🗄 💻 🍴 ⤳

Ⓐⓐⓐ ▼▼▼▼ **Loews Ventana Canyon**
Resort Ⓡ ❀
(520) 299-2020. **$99-$375, 7 days notice.** 7000 N Resort Dr. I-10, exit 256 (Grant Rd), 8 mi e, 0.5 mi ne on Tanque Verde Rd, 2 mi n on Sabino Canyon Rd, then 3 mi n on Kolb Rd. Ext/int corridors. **Pets:** Large, other species. Designated rooms, service with restrictions.
🆂🅰🆅🅴 🆂🔟 ☒ 🄼 🄲 🗄 🗄 🍴 ⤳ ☒

▼▼▼ **Radisson Hotel City Center Tucson** Ⓗ
(520) 624-8711. **$119-$195.** 181 W Broadway. I-10, exit 258 (Congress St/Broadway), just e. Int corridors. **Pets:** Accepted.
🄰🆂🄺 🆂🔟 ☒ 🗄 💻 🍴 ⤳

Ⓐⓐⓐ ▼▼▼▼ **Ramada Inn & Suites/Airport** Ⓜ
(520) 294-5250. **$49-$159, 3 days notice.** 5251 S Julian Dr. I-10, exit 264A (Palo Verde Rd), 0.4 mi s. Ext/int corridors. **Pets:** Other species. $10 one-time fee/room. Service with restrictions, crate.
🆂🅰🆅🅴 🆂🔟 ☒ 🗄 🗄 💻 🍴 ⤳

▼▼▼ **Ramada Inn & Suites Foothills Resort** Ⓜ
(520) 886-9595. **$50-$130.** 6944 E Tanque Verde Rd. I-10, exit 256 (Grant Rd), 8 mi e, then 1 mi ne. Ext corridors. **Pets:** Small. $25 one-time fee/pet. Service with restrictions, crate.
🄰🆂🄺 🆂🔟 ☒ 🗄 💻 ⤳

Ⓐⓐⓐ ▼▼▼ **Red Roof Inn Tucson North** Ⓜ
(520) 744-8199. **$40-$69.** 4940 W Ina Rd. I-10, exit 248, just w. Int corridors. **Pets:** Accepted.
🆂🅰🆅🅴 ☒ 🗄 ⤳

Ⓐⓐⓐ ▼▼▼ **Red Roof Inn-Tucson South** Ⓜ
(520) 571-1400. **$39-$69.** 3700 E Irvington Rd. I-10, exit 264 westbound; exit 264B eastbound. Ext corridors. **Pets:** Small. Designated rooms, no service, supervision.
🆂🅰🆅🅴 ☒ 🗄 🗄 ⤳

Ⓐⓐⓐ ▼▼▼▼ **Residence Inn By Marriott** Ⓐ
(520) 721-0991. **$79-$199, 10 days notice.** 6477 E Speedway Blvd. I-10, exit 257 (Speedway Blvd), 8 mi e. Ext corridors. **Pets:** Accepted.
🆂🅰🆅🅴 🆂🔟 ☒ 🗄 🗄 🗄 💻 ⤳

Ⓐⓐⓐ ▼▼▼ **Rodeway Inn I-10 & Grant Rd** Ⓜ
(520) 622-7791. **$49-$89.** 1365 W Grant Rd. I-10, exit 256 (Grant Rd), just w. Ext corridors. **Pets:** Large, other species. $10 one-time fee/pet. Service with restrictions, supervision.
🆂🅰🆅🅴 🆂🔟 ☒ 🗄 🗄 💻 ⤳

Rodeway Inn-Park Ave at I-10 M
(520) 884-5800. **$48-$120.** 810 E Benson Hwy. I-10, exit 262, just s. Ext corridors. **Pets:** Large, other species. $25 deposit/pet. Service with restrictions, supervision.

Studio 6 Extended Stay M
(520) 746-0030. **$45-$63.** 4950 S Outlet Center Rd. I-10, just s, then just n; exit 264A westbound, just e. Ext corridors. **Pets:** Accepted.

Super 8 Motel M
(520) 622-8089. **$65-$110.** 1000 S Freeway. I-10, exit 259 (22nd St), just w, then just n. Int corridors. **Pets:** Accepted.

Super 8 Motel M
(520) 572-0300. **$59-$99.** 8351 N Cracker Barrel Rd. I-10, exit 246, just w. Int corridors. **Pets:** Accepted.

TownePlace Suites by Marriott M
(520) 292-9697. **$54-$179, 10 days notice.** 405 W Rudasill Rd. Jct of Orange Grove, 0.5 mi s on Oracle, just e. Int corridors. **Pets:** Accepted.

Westward Look Resort R ❀
(520) 297-1151. **$109-$349, 14 days notice.** 245 E Ina Rd. I-10, exit exit 248 (Ina Rd), 6 mi e, then just n on Westward Look Dr. Ext corridors. **Pets:** Medium. $50 one-time fee/room. Designated rooms, service with restrictions.

Windmill Suites at St. Philip's Plaza M
(520) 577-0007. **$70-$165.** 4250 N Campbell Ave. I-10, exit 254 (Prince Rd), 4 mi e, then 1 mi n. Int corridors. **Pets:** Large, other species. Service with restrictions, supervision.

❀ **END METROPOLITAN AREA** ❀

WICKENBURG

Best Western Rancho Grande M ❀
(928) 684-5445. **$67-$119.** 293 E Wickenburg Way. Center of town; on US 60 (Wickenburg Way). Ext corridors. **Pets:** Other species. Supervision.

Super 8 Motel M
(928) 684-0808. **$60-$65.** 975 N Tegner. 1 mi n of US 60 and 93. Ext/int corridors. **Pets:** Other species. $5 daily fee/pet. Designated rooms, service with restrictions, supervision.

WILLCOX

Days Inn M
(520) 384-4222. **$50-$54.** 724 N Bisbee Ave. I-10, exit 340, adjacent. Ext corridors. **Pets:** Other species. $5 daily fee/pet. No service, supervision.

WILLIAMS

Arizona Welcome Inn & Suites M
(928) 635-9127. **$25-$59.** 750 N Grand Canyon Blvd. I-40, exit 163, just s. Int corridors. **Pets:** Very small, dogs only. $5 daily fee/pet. Service with restrictions, supervision.

A Westerner Motel M ❀
(928) 635-4312. **$29-$48.** 530 W Route 66. I-40, exit 161, 1.3 mi e. Ext corridors. **Pets:** Other species.

Budget Host Inn M
(928) 635-4415. **$20-$48.** 620 W Route 66. I-40, exit 161, 1 mi e. Ext corridors. **Pets:** Very small. $5 daily fee/pet. No service, supervision.

The Canyon Motel M
(928) 635-9371. **$50-$90.** 1900 Rodeo Rd. I-40, exit 165 (Grand Canyon), mi s on Buisness Loop 40, just w. Ext corridors. **Pets:** Other species. $5 daily fee/pet. Designated rooms, no service, supervision.

El Rancho Motel M ❀
(928) 635-2552. **$29-$63.** 617 E Route 66. I-40, exit 163, 0.8 mi s on I-140 business loop, then just e. Ext corridors. **Pets:** Dogs only. $5 one-time fee/pet. Designated rooms, service with restrictions, supervision.

Highlander Motel M
(928) 635-2541. **$23-$47.** 533 W Route 66. I-40, exit 161, 1.2 mi e. Ext corridors. **Pets:** Medium. $5 daily fee/pet. Service with restrictions, supervision.

Holiday Inn Williams MI
(928) 635-4114. **$49-$99.** 950 N Grand Canyon Blvd. I-40, exit 163. Int corridors. **Pets:** Large, other species. Service with restrictions, supervision.

Motel 6-4010 M
(928) 635-9000. **$35-$51.** 831 W Route 66 Ave. I-40, exit 161, 1 mi e on I-40 business loop. Int corridors. **Pets:** Other species. Service with restrictions, supervision.

Mountain Ranch Resort MI
(928) 635-2693. **$69-$119, 7 days notice.** 6701 E Mountain Ranch Rd. I-40, exit 171 (Deer Farm Rd), just s. Ext corridors. **Pets:** Medium. $20 one-time fee/pet. Designated rooms, service with restrictions, supervision.

▼▼▼ **Mountain Side Inn** Ⓜ ❀
(928) 635-4431. **$56-$86.** 642 E Route 66. I-40, exit 163, 0.6 mi s, then just e on Rt 66. Ext corridors. **Pets:** Small. $15 deposit/room. Designated rooms, service with restrictions, supervision.

Ⓐ🆂🅺 🆂 ⓧ 🕭 🚪 🖳 🍴 ⬯

⚫⚫⚫ ▼ **Route 66 Inn** Ⓜ
(928) 635-4791. **$28-$65.** 128 E Route 66. I-40, exit 163, 0.5 mi s to Route 66, then just e. Ext corridors. **Pets:** Small, other species. $5 one-time fee/room. Designated rooms, service with restrictions, crate.

🆂🅰🆅🅴 🆂 ⓧ 🕭

⚫⚫⚫ ▼▼ **Super 8 Motel West** Ⓜ
(928) 635-4045. **$30-$100.** 911 W Route 66 Ave. On w side of I-40 business loop; I-40, exit 61, 1 mi e. Int corridors. **Pets:** Accepted.

🆂🅰🆅🅴 🆂 ⓧ ♿ ⬯

⚫⚫⚫ ▼ **Travelodge Williams** Ⓜ
(928) 635-2651. **$35-$60.** 430 E Route 66. I-40, exit 161, 2 mi e on I-40 business loop. Ext corridors. **Pets:** Accepted.

🆂🅰🆅🅴 ⓧ 🕭 🖳 ⬯

WINSLOW

⚫⚫⚫ ▼▼▼ **Best Western Adobe Inn** Ⓜ
(928) 289-4638. **$120.** 1701 North Park Dr. I-40, exit 253, adjacent. Int corridors. **Pets:** Accepted.

🆂🅰🆅🅴 🆂 ⓧ ♿ 🍴 ⬯

⚫⚫⚫ ▼▼▼ **Days Inn** Ⓜ
(928) 289-1010. **$49-$85, 3 days notice.** 2035 W Hwy 66. I-40, exit 252, just s. Int corridors. **Pets:** Accepted.

🆂🅰🆅🅴 🆂 ⓧ ♿ ⬯

⚫⚫⚫ ▼▼▼ **Econo Lodge** Ⓜ
(928) 289-4687. **$49-$89.** 1706 North Park Dr. I-40, exit 253. Ext corridors. **Pets:** Medium, other species. $5 daily fee/room. Service with restrictions, crate.

🆂🅰🆅🅴 🆂 ⓧ 🎨 🕭 🖳 ⬯

⚫⚫⚫ ▼▼▼ **Holiday Inn Express- Winslow** Ⓜ
(928) 289-2960. **$89-$99.** 816 Transcon Ln. I-40, exit 255, just n. Int corridors. **Pets:** $10 daily fee/pet. Designated rooms, service with restrictions, supervision.

🆂🅰🆅🅴 🆂 ⓧ ♿ 🕭 🖳 ⬯

▼▼▼ **La Posada Hotel** Ⓗ
(928) 289-4366. **$79-$120, 3 days notice.** 303 E 2nd St. I-40, exit 252, s to Rt 66, then 0.5 mi e. Int corridors. **Pets:** Accepted.

Ⓐ🆂🅺 ⓧ 🕭 🍴 🇿

▼▼ **Motel 6 Winslow** Ⓜ
(928) 289-9581. **$39-$57.** 520 W Desmond St. I-40, exit 253, just w on North Park Dr. Int corridors. **Pets:** Accepted.

Ⓐ🆂🅺 🆂 ⓧ ♿ ⬯

⚫⚫⚫ ▼▼▼ **Super 8 Motel** Ⓜ
(928) 289-4606. **$44-$60.** 1916 W Third St. I-40, exit 252, just e. Int corridors. **Pets:** Medium, other species. $10 deposit/pet. Designated rooms, service with restrictions, supervision.

🆂🅰🆅🅴 🆂 ⓧ

▼▼ **Travelodge Townhouse** Ⓜ
(928) 289-4611. **$45-$57.** 1914 W Third St. I-40, exit 252, 0.5 mi e. Ext corridors. **Pets:** Accepted.

Ⓐ🆂🅺 🆂 ⓧ 🕭 🖳 ⬯

YUMA

⚫⚫⚫ ▼▼ **Airport Travelodge** Ⓜ
(928) 726-4721. **$39-$69, 14 days notice.** 711 E 32nd St. I-8, exit 3 (SR 280), 1 mi s, then 1.5 mi w. Ext corridors. **Pets:** Accepted.

🆂🅰🆅🅴 🆂 ⓧ ♿ 🕭 🖳 🍴 ⬯

⚫⚫⚫ ▼▼▼ **Best Western InnSuites Hotel & Suites** Ⓜ
(928) 783-8341. **$84-$99.** 1450 Castle Dome Ave. I-8, exit 2 (16th St), just ne. Ext corridors. **Pets:** Accepted.

🆂🅰🆅🅴 🆂 ⓧ 🎨 🕭 🖳 🍴 ⬯

▼▼▼ **Comfort Inn** Ⓜ
(928) 782-1200. **$49-$99.** 1691 S Riley Ave. I-8, exit 2 (16th St), just w. Int corridors. **Pets:** Accepted.

🆂🅰🆅🅴 🆂 ⓧ 🅶🅼 ♿ 🕭 🖳 ⬯

▼▼▼ **Holiday Inn Express** Ⓜ
(928) 344-1420. **$94-$129, 7 days notice.** 3181 S 4th Ave. I-8, exit 3 (SR 280), 1 mi s, then 2 mi w. Ext corridors. **Pets:** Medium, other species. $10 daily fee/room. Service with restrictions, supervision.

Ⓐ🆂🅺 🆂 ⓧ ♿ 🕭 🖳 ⬯

▼▼◆ **Mictrotel Inn & Suites** Ⓜ
(928) 345-1777. **$50-$92.** 11274 S Fortuna Rd, Suite H. I-8, exit 12 (Fortuna Rd), just s, then w on Frontage Rd. Int corridors. **Pets:** Small. Service with restrictions, supervision.

Ⓐ🆂🅺 🆂 ⓧ ♿ 🕭 🖳 ⬯

▼▼▼ **Radisson Suites Inn Yuma** Ⓜ
(928) 726-4830. **$79-$159, 3 days notice.** 2600 S 4th Ave. I-8, exit 2 (16th St) eastbound, 1 mi w, then 1 mi s; exit 3 (SR 280) westbound, 0.5 mi s, then 2 mi w. Ext corridors. **Pets:** Medium, other species. Service with restrictions, supervision.

Ⓐ🆂🅺 🆂 ⓧ ♿ 🕭 🖳 ⬯

⚫⚫⚫ ▼▼ **Ramada Inn Chilton Conference Center** Ⓜ
(928) 344-1050. **$69-$99, 3 days notice.** 300 E 32nd St. I-8 business loop, 2.3 mi s of jct US 95. Ext corridors. **Pets:** Accepted.

🆂🅰🆅🅴 🆂 ⓧ 🕭 🖳 🍴 ⬯

⚫⚫⚫ ▼▼ **Yuma Cabana Motel** Ⓜ
(928) 783-8311. **$40-$74.** 2151 S 4th Ave. I-8, exit 2 (16th St), 1 mi w, then 0.5 mi s. Int corridors. **Pets:** Small, other species. $6 daily fee/pet. Service with restrictions, supervision.

🆂🅰🆅🅴 🆂 ⓧ 🕭 ⬯

▼▼ **Yuma Super 8 Motel** Ⓜ
(928) 782-2000. **$44-$99.** 1688 S Riley Ave. I-8, exit 2 (16th St), just w. Int corridors. **Pets:** Other species. $5 one-time fee/room. Service with restrictions, supervision.

Ⓐ🆂🅺 🆂 ⓧ 🅶🅼 ♿ 🕭 ⬯

ARKADELPHIA

◆◆◆ ▼▼▼▼ Best Western-Continental Inn M ❀
(870) 246-5592. **$55-$80.** 136 Valley St. I-30, exit 78. Ext corridors. **Pets:** Other species. Service with restrictions, crate.
SAVE S X ♿ ⬛ 💻

◆◆◆ ▼▼▼▼ Super 8 Motel M
(870) 246-8585. **$45-$90, 7 days notice.** 118 Valley. I-30, exit 78. Ext corridors. **Pets:** Medium. Service with restrictions, supervision.
SAVE S X ⬛ 🐾

BATESVILLE

▼▼▼▼ Ramada Inn of Batesville MI
(870) 698-1800. **$70.** 1325 N St Louis St. 1 mi n on US 67/167. Ext corridors. **Pets:** Medium. Service with restrictions, crate.
ASK S X ♦ ⬛ 💻 🍴 🐾

BEEBE

▼▼▼▼ Oxford Inn M ❀
(501) 882-2008. **$51.** 100 Tammy Ln. US 67/167, exit 28. Ext corridors. **Pets:** Medium. $10 daily fee/room. Service with restrictions.
ASK S X ♿ ⬛ 🐾

BENTON

▼▼ Days Inn M
(501) 776-3200. **$53.** 17701 I-30. I-30, exit 118, on east service road. Ext corridors. **Pets:** Dogs only. $5 one-time fee/room. Service with restrictions.
SAVE S X ♦ ⬛ 🐾

◆◆◆ ▼▼ Econo Lodge M
(501) 776-1515. **$36-$40.** 1221 Hot Springs Rd. I-30, exit 117. Int corridors. **Pets:** Accepted.
SAVE S X ⬛ 💻

◆◆◆ ▼ Scottish Inn M ❀
(501) 778-4591. **$32-$42, 7 days notice.** 17900 I-30. I-30, exit 118, 0.5 mi w on north frontage road. Ext corridors. **Pets:** Medium. $10 deposit/room. Designated rooms, service with restrictions, supervision.
SAVE S X ⬛ 🐾

◆◆◆ ▼ Troutt Motel M
(501) 778-3633. **$32-$38, 7 days notice.** 15438 I-30. I-30, exit 116, just s on west service road. Ext corridors. **Pets:** Small, dogs only. $5 daily fee/pet. Designated rooms, service with restrictions, supervision.
SAVE S X

BLYTHEVILLE

▼▼▼ Comfort Inn of Blytheville M
(870) 763-7081. **$54.** 1520 E Main. I-55, exit 67. Ext corridors. **Pets:** Accepted.
SAVE S X ⬛ 💻 🍴 🐾

▼▼ Drury Inn-Blytheville M
(870) 763-2300. **$52-$78.** 201 Access Rd. I-55, exit 67. Int corridors. **Pets:** Accepted.
X ♦ ⬛ 💻

▼▼▼ Holiday Inn MI
(870) 763-5800. **$68-$85.** 1121 E Main. I-55, exit 67. Ext/int corridors. **Pets:** Medium, other species. $60 deposit/room. Designated rooms, service with restrictions, crate.
ASK S X ⬛ 💻 🍴 🐾

BRINKLEY

▼▼▼ Best Western Brinkley MI
(870) 734-1650. **$55-$65.** 1306 Hwy 17 N. I-40, exit 216. Ext corridors. **Pets:** Small, dogs only. Designated rooms, service with restrictions, supervision.
SAVE S X 💻 🍴 🐾

▼▼▼ Super 8 Motel M
(870) 734-4680. **$42, 3 days notice.** I-40 & Hwy 49 N. I-40, exit 216. Ext corridors. **Pets:** Designated rooms, no service, supervision.
ASK S X 🐾

BRYANT

▼▼ Super 8 Motel Ⓜ
(501) 847-7888. **$52-$56, 5 days notice.** 201 Dell Dr. I-30, exit 123. Ext corridors. **Pets:** Dogs only. $20 deposit/pet. Service with restrictions, supervision.
Ⓐ̶S̶K̶ S̶ ☒ 🔋

CABOT

▼▼ Days Inn of Cabot Ⓜ
(501) 843-0145. **$55-$65.** 1114 W Main St. US 67/167, exit 19 (SR 89), just e. Ext corridors. **Pets:** Medium, other species. $5 daily fee/pet. Designated rooms, service with restrictions, crate.
S̶A̶V̶E̶ S̶ ☒ 🔋 🏊

▼▼ Super 8 of Cabot Ⓜ
(501) 941-3748. **$51-$66.** 15 Ryeland Dr. US 67/167, exit 19 (SR 89), just e. Ext corridors. **Pets:** Medium, other species. $5 daily fee/pet. Designated rooms, service with restrictions, crate.
Ⓐ̶S̶K̶ S̶ ☒ 🔋 🏊

CARLISLE

Ⓐ̶Ⓐ̶Ⓐ̶ ▼▼ Best Western Carlisle Ⓜ
(870) 552-7566. **$55-$70.** 1505 Bankhead Dr. I-40, exit 183. Ext corridors. **Pets:** Accepted.
S̶A̶V̶E̶ S̶ ☒ 🏊

CLARKSVILLE

Ⓐ̶Ⓐ̶Ⓐ̶ ▼▼▼ Best Western Sherwood Motor Inn Ⓜ
(479) 754-7900. **$39-$59, 10 days notice.** 1203 S Rogers Ave. I-40, exit 58. Ext corridors. **Pets:** Other species. Service with restrictions.
S̶A̶V̶E̶ S̶ ☒ 🔋 💻 🏊

Ⓐ̶Ⓐ̶Ⓐ̶ ▼▼▼ Comfort Inn Ⓜ
(479) 754-3000. **$49-$85.** 1167 S Rogers Ave. I-40, exit 58, just n. Ext corridors. **Pets:** $5 daily fee/pet. Designated rooms, service with restrictions, supervision.
S̶A̶V̶E̶ S̶ ☒ 🔋 💻 🏊

CONWAY

▼ Motel 6 Ⓜ
(501) 327-6623. **Call for rates.** 1105 Hwy 65 N. I-40, exit 125, 0.3 mi e. Ext corridors. **Pets:** Accepted.
☒ 🐾 🛎 🏊

Ⓐ̶Ⓐ̶Ⓐ̶ ▼▼▼ Ramada Inn Ⓜ
(501) 329-8392. **$55-$75, 30 days notice.** 815 E Oak St. I-40, exit 127. Ext corridors. **Pets:** Very small. $50 deposit/room. Designated rooms, service with restrictions, supervision.
S̶A̶V̶E̶ S̶ ☒ 🐾 🔋 💻 🍴 🏊

DARDANELLE

Ⓐ̶Ⓐ̶Ⓐ̶ ▼ Economy Inn Ⓜ
(479) 229-4118. **$45.** 503 Hwy 22. I-40, exit 81, 7 mi s on US 7; at jct SR 7, 22 and 27. Ext corridors. **Pets:** $5 daily fee/pet. Service with restrictions, supervision.
S̶A̶V̶E̶ S̶ ☒ 🔋 🏊

DUMAS

▼▼ Days Inn Ⓜ
(870) 382-4449. **$70.** 501 Hwy 65 S. On US 65. Ext corridors. **Pets:** Accepted.
S̶A̶V̶E̶ S̶ ☒ 🛎 🔋 🏊

EL DORADO

▼▼ Comfort Inn Ⓜ
(870) 863-6677. **$70-$150.** 2303 Junction City Rd. On US 167, 0.5 mi n of US 82 Bypass, at jct US 82B. Ext/int corridors. **Pets:** Large, other species. $25 one-time fee/room. Designated rooms, service with restrictions.
S̶A̶V̶E̶ S̶ ☒ 🐾 💻 🏊

EUREKA SPRINGS

▼▼▼ A Cliff Cottage Inn-Luxury B&B Suites & Cottages Ⓑ̶Ⓑ̶ 🐾
(479) 253-7409. **$159-$199, 10 days notice.** 42 Armstrong St. Downtown; just n from jct SR 23. Ext/int corridors. **Pets:** Very small, dogs only. $30 one-time fee/pet. Designated rooms, no service, crate.
☒ 🔋 💻 ☎

▼▼ Basin Park Hotel Ⓗ
(479) 253-7837. **$89-$109, 3 days notice.** 12 Spring St. Downtown; 0.7 mi n of jct US 62 via SR 23 N. Int corridors. **Pets:** Small.
Ⓐ̶S̶K̶ S̶ ☒ 🔋 💻 🍴

Ⓐ̶Ⓐ̶Ⓐ̶ ▼▼▼ Best Western Inn of the Ozarks Ⓜ̶
(479) 253-9768. **$39-$89.** 207 W Van Buren St. On US 62, 0.5 mi w of jct SR 23. Ext corridors. **Pets:** Medium. Service with restrictions, supervision.
S̶A̶V̶E̶ ☒ 🐾 🐾 🔋 💻 🍴 🏊 ☒

Ⓐ̶Ⓐ̶Ⓐ̶ ▼▼▼ Colonial Mansion Inn Ⓜ
(479) 253-7300. **$32-$85.** 154 Huntsville Rd. On SR 23, just s of jct US 62. Ext/int corridors. **Pets:** Small. Designated rooms, supervision.
S̶A̶V̶E̶ S̶ ☒ 🔋 💻 🏊

Ⓐ̶Ⓐ̶Ⓐ̶ ▼▼▼ The Crescent Hotel & Spa Ⓗ
(479) 253-9766. **$109-$129, 3 days notice.** 75 Prospect Ave. 1.3 mi n from jct SR 12; on US 62B Historic Loop. Int corridors. **Pets:** Small, other species. Service with restrictions, crate.
S̶A̶V̶E̶ S̶ ☒ 🔋 💻 🍴 🏊

▼▼ Days Inn Ⓜ
(479) 253-8863. **$40-$170.** 120 W Van Buren St. On US 62, just w of jct SR 23 N. Ext corridors. **Pets:** Small. $10 daily fee/room. Designated rooms, service with restrictions, supervision.
S̶A̶V̶E̶ S̶ ☒ 🔋 💻 🏊

▼▼ **Dogwood Inn** Ⓜ
(479) 253-7200. **$32-$52, 3 days notice.** 170 Huntsville Rd. On SR 23, 0.3 mi s of jct US 62. Ext corridors. **Pets:** Other species. $10 one-time fee/room. Service with restrictions, crate.

⊠ ⇌

⑭ ▼▼▼ **Howard Johnson Express** Ⓜ
(479) 253-6665. **$38-$99.** 4042 E Van Buren St. On US 62, 1.8 mi e of jct SR 23. Ext corridors. **Pets:** Accepted.

[SAVE] Ⓢ ⊠ ⇌

▼▼▼ **Lazee Daze Log Cabin Resort** 🅒
(479) 253-7026. **$95-$160, 14 days notice.** 5432 Hwy 23 S. On SR 23, 6.3 mi s of jct US 62. Ext corridors. **Pets:** Dogs only. $50 deposit/room. No service, crate.

⊠ ◨ ⬜ ⬚

▼▼ **Road Runner Inn** Ⓜ
(479) 253-8166. **$35-$49, 3 days notice.** 3034 Mundell Rd. On US 62, 4.3 mi w, 3.9 mi s on SR 187, then 3 mi se. Ext corridors. **Pets:** Medium, dogs only. Designated rooms, service with restrictions, supervision.

◨ ⬜ ⬚

⑭ ▼▼ **Travelers Inn** Ⓜ
(479) 253-8386. **$32-$58, 3 days notice.** 2044 E Van Buren St. On US 62, 0.3 mi e of jct SR 23. Ext corridors. **Pets:** Small, dogs only. Service with restrictions, crate.

[SAVE] Ⓢ ⊠ ⬜ ⇌

⑭ ▼▼ **Travelodge** Ⓜ
(479) 253-8992. **$38-$120.** 110 Huntsville Dr. On SR 23, at jct US 62. Ext corridors. **Pets:** Accepted.

[SAVE] Ⓢ ⊠ ◨ ⬜ ⇌

FAYETTEVILLE

▼▼ **Quality Inn** Ⓜ
(479) 444-9800. **$64-$100, 10 days notice.** 523 S Shiloh Dr. I-540, exit 62, just w. Ext corridors. **Pets:** Small. $15 one-time fee/room. Designated rooms, service with restrictions, supervision.

[SAVE] Ⓢ ⊠ ◪ ◨ ⬜ ⇌

▼▼▼ **Radisson Hotel Fayetteville** 🅗
(479) 442-5555. **$75-$83.** 70 N East Ave. Downtown; just w of US 71B and SR 471. Int corridors. **Pets:** Supervision.

[ASK] Ⓢ ⊠ ◪ ◨ ⬜ 🍽 ⇌

▼▼ **Sleep Inn** Ⓜ
(479) 587-8700. **$60-$119.** 728 Millsap Rd. I-540, exit 67, 1.6 mi e, just s on US 71B. Int corridors. **Pets:** Accepted.

[SAVE] Ⓢ ⊠ ◪ ◨ ⬜

FORREST CITY

⑭ ▼▼ **Best Western Colony Inn** Ⓜ
(870) 633-0870. **$85-$115, 14 days notice.** 2333 N Washington. I-40, exit 241A. Ext corridors. **Pets:** Medium, other species. Service with restrictions, supervision.

[SAVE] Ⓢ ⊠ ◨ ⬜

▼▼ **Days Inn** Ⓜ
(870) 633-0777. **$59.** 350 Barrow Hill Rd. I-40, exit 241B, just n. Ext corridors. **Pets:** $5 daily fee/pet. Service with restrictions, supervision.

[SAVE] Ⓢ ⊠ ◨ ⬜ ⇌

▼▼▼ **Holiday Inn** Ⓜ
(870) 633-6300. **$60-$75.** 200 Holiday Dr. I-40, exit 241B. Ext corridors. **Pets:** Small. Service with restrictions, supervision.

[ASK] Ⓢ ⊠ ◨ ⬜ 🍽 ⇌

▼▼ **Luxury Inn** Ⓜ
(870) 633-8990. **$39-$42, 7 days notice.** 315 Barrow Hill Rd. I-40, exit 241B, 0.5 mi n on SR 1. Ext corridors. **Pets:** Accepted.

Ⓢ ⊠ ◨

FORT SMITH

⑭ ▼▼ **Baymont Inn & Suites-Fort Smith** Ⓜ
(479) 484-5770. **$64-$69.** 2123 Burnham Rd. I-540, exit 8A (Rogers Ave), just w off SR 22. Int corridors. **Pets:** Medium, other species. Service with restrictions, supervision.

[SAVE] Ⓢ ⊠ ◪ ⬚ ◨ ⬜ ⇌

⑭ ▼▼ **Best Western Kings Row Inn** Ⓜ
(479) 452-4200. **$58-$73.** 5801 Rogers Ave. I-540, exit 8A (Rogers Ave), just w. Ext corridors. **Pets:** Small. $20 deposit/room. Service with restrictions, supervision.

[SAVE] Ⓢ ⊠ ⬚ ◨ ⬜

▼▼ **Days Inn** Ⓜ
(479) 783-0548. **$38-$46.** 1021 Garrison Ave. Center. Ext corridors. **Pets:** Accepted.

[SAVE] Ⓢ ⊠ ◪ ◨ ⇌

▼▼ **Fifth Season Inn** Ⓜ
(479) 452-4880. **$99.** 2219 S Waldron Rd. I-540, exit 8A (Rogers Ave W), just s of Rogers Ave and Waldron Rd. Ext/int corridors. **Pets:** Other species. $10 daily fee/room. Service with restrictions.

[ASK] Ⓢ ⊠ ◨ ⬜ ⇌

▼▼▼ **Holiday Inn Fort Smith City Center** 🅗
(479) 783-1000. **$99-$129.** 700 Rogers Ave. Downtown; just s of US 64 (Garrison Ave). Int corridors. **Pets:** Large. $10 one-time fee/room. Designated rooms, service with restrictions, supervision.

[ASK] Ⓢ ⊠ ⬚ ⬚ ◪ ◨ ⬜ 🍽 ⇌

▼▼ **Ramada Inn** Ⓜ
(479) 646-2931. **$53-$63.** 5103 Towson Ave. On US 71B, 3 mi s. Int corridors. **Pets:** Very small. Service with restrictions, supervision.

[ASK] Ⓢ ⊠ ◪ ◨ 🍽 ⇌

⑭ ▼▼ **Super 8** Ⓜ
(479) 646-3411. **$45-$55, 4 days notice.** 3810 Towson Ave. On US 71B, 3 mi s. Ext corridors. **Pets:** Very small, dogs only. $20 deposit/room. Designated rooms, service with restrictions, supervision.

[SAVE] Ⓢ ⊠ ⬚ ⬚ ◨ ⇌

GAMALIEL

▼ **Twin Gables Resort** C
(870) 467-5686. **$50, 7 days notice.** 3166 Hwy 101. SR 101 at jct CR 806. Ext corridors. **Pets:** Accepted.
ASK S✗ ✗ 🛏 📶

GENTRY

▼▼▼ **Apple Crest Inn Bed & Breakfast** BB
(479) 736-8201. **$100-$155, 14 days notice.** 12758 S Hwy 59. SR 59, 1 mi s. Int corridors. **Pets:** Accepted.
ASK S✗ ✗ 🛏

GLENWOOD

▼▼ **Riverwood Inn** M
(870) 356-4567. **$45-$55.** 363 Hwy 70 E. On US 70, 0.5 mi e. Ext corridors. **Pets:** Accepted.
✗ 📠 🐾

HARRISON

⚫⚫⚫ ▼▼▼ **Family Budget Inn** M ❀
(870) 743-1000. **$34-$37, 3 days notice.** 401 S Main (Hwy 65B S). 1 mi s on US 65B from jct SR 7. Ext corridors. **Pets:** Small. $50 deposit/room, $4 one-time fee/room. Designated rooms, service with restrictions, supervision.
SAVE S✗ ✗ 🛏 🐾

▼▼ **Super 8 Motel Harrison** M
(870) 741-1741. **$39-$50, 5 days notice.** 1330 Hwy 62/65 N. 1.4 mi n on US 62/65/412. Int corridors. **Pets:** Dogs only. $7 daily fee/pet. Service with restrictions, supervision.
ASK S✗ ✗ 🛏 📶 🐾

HETH

▼▼ **West Memphis, Shell Lake KOA** M
(870) 657-2101. **$22-$30.** 453 Hwy 149 N. I-40, exit 260. Ext corridors. **Pets:** Accepted.
ASK ✗ 🛏 📶

HOPE

⚫⚫⚫ ▼▼▼ **Best Western of Hope** M
(870) 777-9222. **$55-$59, 10 days notice.** I-30 & US 278. I-30, exit 30. Ext corridors. **Pets:** Other species. Service with restrictions.
SAVE S✗ ✗ 🛏 📶 🐾

▼▼▼ **Holiday Inn Express** M
(870) 722-6262. **$71-$73.** 2600 N Hervey. I-30, exit 30. Int corridors. **Pets:** Service with restrictions, supervision.
ASK S✗ ✗ 📱 📠 🛏 📶 🐾

⚫⚫⚫ ▼▼▼ **Relax Inn & Suites** M ❀
(870) 777-0777. **$40-$60, 3 days notice.** 2504 N Hazel. I-30, exit 31, just n on SR 29. Ext corridors. **Pets:** Very small. $5 daily fee/pet. Designated rooms, service with restrictions, crate.
SAVE S✗ ✗ 🛏 📶

SUPER 8 MOTEL

▼▼ **Super 8 Motel** M
(870) 777-8601. **$37-$41.** 2000 Holiday Dr. I-30, exit 30, just ne on frontage road. Ext corridors. **Pets:** Medium. Service with restrictions.
ASK S✗ ✗ 🛏 📶 🐾

HOT SPRINGS NATIONAL PARK

⚫⚫⚫ ▼▼▼ **Clarion Resort** MI ❀
(501) 525-1391. **$70-$145.** 4813 Central Ave. 5.5 mi s on SR 7. Int corridors. **Pets:** Medium, other species. $10 daily fee/room. Service with restrictions, supervision.
SAVE S✗ ✗ 📠 🛏 📶 🍴 🐾 📶

▼▼▼ **Lake Hamilton Resort** MI
(501) 767-5511. **$109-$225.** 2803 Albert Pike Rd. 5 mi w on US 270. Int corridors. **Pets:** Accepted.
ASK S✗ ✗ 🛏 📶 🍴 🐾 📶

⚫⚫⚫ ▼ **Margarete Motel** M
(501) 623-1192. **$40-$65, 10 days notice.** 217 Fountain St. Just off SR 7, near bathhouse row. Ext corridors. **Pets:** $5 one-time fee/room. Service with restrictions, supervision.
SAVE S✗ 🛏 📶

⚫⚫⚫ ▼▼▼ **Quality Inn** MI
(501) 624-3321. **$70-$150.** 1125 E Grand Ave. On US 70, 1.3 mi e of jct US 270. Ext corridors. **Pets:** Accepted.
SAVE S✗ ✗ 📱 📠 🛏 📶 🍴 🐾

⚫⚫⚫ ▼ **Travelier Inn** MI
(501) 624-4681. **$39-$62.** 1045 E Grand Ave. On US 70, 1.2 mi e on SR 7. Ext corridors. **Pets:** Other species. Service with restrictions.
SAVE S✗ ✗ 🛏 📶 🐾

⚫⚫⚫ ▼▼▼ **Velda Rose Resort Hotel & Spa** H
(501) 623-3311. **$78-$100.** 217 Park Ave. Center; on US 70B and SR 7. Int corridors. **Pets:** Small. Service with restrictions, crate.
SAVE S✗ ✗ 🛏 📶 🍴 🐾

JACKSONVILLE

▼▼ **Days Inn** M
(501) 982-1543. **$50-$60, 3 days notice.** 1414 John Harden Dr. US 67/167, exit 10B southbound; exit 11 northbound. Ext/int corridors. **Pets:** Large, other species. $5 daily fee/pet. Service with restrictions, supervision.
SAVE S✗ ✗ 🛏 🐾

JONESBORO

▼▼▼ **Holiday Inn of Jonesboro** MI
(870) 935-2030. **$75.** 3006 S Caraway Rd. US 63, exit Stadium/Caraway, just n. Ext/int corridors. **Pets:** Accepted.
ASK S✗ ✗ 📠 🛏 📶 🍴 🐾

⚫⚫⚫ ▼▼▼ **Jonesboro Best Western** M
(870) 932-6600. **$49-$53.** 2901 Phillips Dr. US 63, exit Stadium/Caraway, just n on Stadium. Ext corridors. **Pets:** Accepted.
SAVE S✗ ✗ 🛏 📶 🐾

▼▼ ▼▼ **Ramada Limited** Ⓜ
(870) 932-5757. **$64.** 3000 Apache Dr. US 63, exit Stadium/
Caraway, just n on Stadium. Ext/int corridors. **Pets:** Other
species. Service with restrictions, supervision.

A$K Ⓢ ⊠ 🛏 🐾

▼▼ ▼▼ **Super 8 Motel** Ⓜ
(870) 972-0849. **$40-$49.** 2500 S Caraway Rd. US 63, exit
Stadium/Caraway, 0.5 mi n. Int corridors. **Pets:** Accepted.

A$K Ⓢ ⊠ 🛏 💻

LITTLE ROCK

🆔🆔 ▼▼▼▼ **AmeriSuites (Little Rock/Financial
Center)** Ⓜ
(501) 225-1075. **$76.** 10920 Financial Center Pkwy. Jct
I-430 and 630, exit Shackleford Rd. Int corridors.
Pets: Medium. Service with restrictions, crate.

SAVE Ⓢ ⊠ 🛏 💻 🐾

🆔🆔 ▼▼ ▼▼ **Baymont Inn & Suites-Little Rock
West** Ⓜ
(501) 225-7007. **$64-$74.** 1010 Breckenridge Rd. I-430, exit
8, just e to Breckenridge Rd, just s. Int corridors.
Pets: Accepted.

SAVE Ⓢ ⊠ 🐟 🛏 💻

▼▼▼▼ **Hampton Inn Little Rock I-30** Ⓜ
(501) 562-6667. **$68-$70, 14 days notice.** 6100 Mitchell Dr.
I-30, exit 133. Int corridors. **Pets:** $10 daily fee/pet. Service
with restrictions, crate.

SAVE Ⓢ ⊠ 💻 🐾

▼▼▼▼ **Holiday Inn Select** Ⓜ
(501) 223-3000. **$109.** 201 S Shackleford Rd. Jct of I-430
and 630. Ext/int corridors. **Pets:** Small, dogs only. $15 daily
fee/room. Designated rooms, service with restrictions,
supervision.

A$K ⊠ 💻 🍽 🐾

🆔🆔 ▼▼▼▼ **La Quinta Inn-Fair Park** Ⓜ
(501) 664-7000. **$62-$75.** 901 Fair Park Blvd. I-630, exit 4.
Ext corridors. **Pets:** Accepted.

SAVE ⊠ ♿ 🐟 🛏 💻 🐾

🆔🆔 ▼▼▼▼ **La Quinta Inn-Otter Creek** Ⓜ
(501) 455-2300. **$66-$76.** 11701 I-30. I-30, exit 128. Ext
corridors. **Pets:** Accepted.

SAVE Ⓢ ⊠ 🛏 💻 🐾

🆔🆔 ▼▼▼▼ **Residence Inn** Ⓐ
(501) 312-0200. **$109-$139.** 1401 S Shackleford Rd. I-430,
exit 5, just n. Int corridors. **Pets:** Accepted.

SAVE ⊠ ♿ 🐟 ♿ 🛏 💻 🐾

LONOKE

🆔🆔 ▼▼ ▼▼ **Days Inn** Ⓜ
(501) 676-5138. **$50-$65.** 105 Dee Dee Ln. I-40, exit 175.
Ext corridors. **Pets:** Small. $5 one-time fee/pet. Designated
rooms, service with restrictions, supervision.

SAVE Ⓢ ⊠ 🛏

MAGNOLIA

▼▼ ▼▼ **Best Western-Coachman's Inn** Ⓜ
(870) 234-6122. **$69.** 420 E Main St. Just e of square on
US Business Rt 82B. Ext corridors. **Pets:** Other species.
Service with restrictions, supervision.

SAVE ⊠ 🛏 💻 🍽 🐾

MARION

▼▼ ▼▼ **Best Western-Regency Motor Inn** Ⓜ
(870) 739-3278. **$60-$65, 7 days notice.** 3635 I-55. I-55,
exit 10, via west service road. Ext corridors.
Pets: Accepted.

SAVE Ⓢ ⊠ 🐟 💻 🐾

MAUMELLE

🆔🆔 ▼▼▼▼ **Comfort Suites** Ⓜ
(501) 851-8444. **$69-$155.** 14322 Frontier Dr. I-40, exit 142.
Int corridors. **Pets:** $20 one-time fee/pet. Service with
restrictions, supervision.

SAVE Ⓢ ⊠ 🐟 ♿ 🛏 💻 🐾

▼▼ ▼▼ **Super 8 Motel of Maumelle** Ⓜ 🐾
(501) 851-3500. **$55-$60.** 14325 Frontier Dr. I-40, exit 142.
Ext corridors. **Pets:** Medium. $10 one-time fee/room. Des-
ignated rooms, service with restrictions.

A$K Ⓢ ⊠ ♿ 🛏 🐾

MENA

🆔🆔 ▼▼ **Ozark Inn** Ⓜ 🐾
(479) 394-1100. **$35-$39.** 2102 US 71 S. 2 mi s. Ext corridors. **Pets:** Medium, other species. $5 one-time fee/pet.
Service with restrictions, supervision.

SAVE ⊠ 🐾

MOUNTAIN HOME

▼▼ **Buzzard Roost Inn** Ⓜ
(870) 492-5187. **$44, 30 days notice.** 4271 Buzzard Roost
Rd. SR 178, 2.3 mi se of jct US 62/412. Ext corridors.
Pets: Medium, other species. $5 daily fee/pet. No service,
supervision.

🛏 💻 🍽 ⊠ 🏊

🆔🆔 ▼▼▼▼ **Teal Point Resort** Ⓒ
(870) 492-5145. **$63-$72, 45 days notice.** 715 Teal Point
Rd. 7 mi e on US 62, 0.6 mi n on CR 406, follow signs. Ext
corridors. **Pets:** $7 daily fee/pet. Designated rooms, no
service, crate.

SAVE 🛏 🐾 ⊠ 🏊

MOUNTAIN VIEW

▼▼ ▼▼ **Best Western Fiddlers Inn** Ⓜ 🐾
(870) 269-2828. **$48-$85.** 106 Sylomore. 1 mi n on SR 5, 9
and 14. Ext corridors. **Pets:** Small, dogs only. $5 daily
fee/pet. Designated rooms, service with restrictions, supervision.

SAVE Ⓢ ⊠ 🛏 💻 🐾

NEWPORT

AAA ⩔⩔ Park Inn International M
(870) 523-5851. **$60-$65.** 901 Hwy 367 N. US 67, exit 83, 1 mi w, 0.3 mi n. Ext corridors. **Pets:** Other species. Service with restrictions, supervision.
SAVE 🛇 ✕ 🛏 ▣ 🍽 ⇌

NORTH LITTLE ROCK

AAA ⩔⩔ Baymont Inn & Suites-North Little Rock M
(501) 758-8888. **$64-$74.** 4311 Warden Rd. US 67/167, exit 1B northbound; exit 1 southbound. Int corridors. **Pets:** Medium, other species. $50 deposit/room. Service with restrictions, crate.
SAVE 🛇 ✕ 🐾 🛁 🛏 ▣ ⇌

⩔⩔ Days Inn M
(501) 945-4100. **$55-$65.** 5800 Pritchard Dr. I-40, exit 157. Ext corridors. **Pets:** Very small. $10 daily fee/pet. Service with restrictions, supervision.
SAVE 🛇 ✕

⩔⩔⩔ Days Inn M
(501) 851-3297. **$59, 7 days notice.** 7200 Bicentennial Rd. I-40, exit 142. Ext corridors. **Pets:** Very small, dogs only. $10 daily fee/pet. Designated rooms, service with restrictions, supervision.
SAVE 🛇 ✕ 🛎 🐾 🗏 🛏

⩔⩔⩔ Hampton Inn M
(501) 771-2090. **$62.** 500 W 29th St. I-40, exit 152. Int corridors. **Pets:** Very small. $25 one-time fee/room. Service with restrictions, supervision.
SAVE 🛇 ✕ 🐾 ▣ ⇌

AAA ⩔⩔⩔ La Quinta North M
(501) 945-0808. **$56-$66.** 4100 E McCain Blvd. At jct US 67/167, exit 1A northbound; exit 1 southbound. Ext corridors. **Pets:** Accepted.
SAVE 🛇 ✕ 🐾 🛏 ▣ ⇌

AAA ⩔⩔⩔ Super 8 North M
(501) 945-0141. **$47-$53.** 1 Gray Rd. I-40, exit 157. Ext/int corridors. **Pets:** Accepted.
SAVE 🛇 ✕ ⇌

OSCEOLA

⩔⩔ Best Western Inn M
(870) 563-3222. **$59-$69, 7 days notice.** 4635 W Keiser. I-55, exit 48. Ext corridors. **Pets:** Accepted.
SAVE 🛇 ✕ 🛏 ▣ 🍽 ⇌

OZARK

⩔⩔ Oxford Inn M
(479) 667-1131. **$39-$43.** 305 N 18th St. I-40, exit 35, 3 mi s on SR 23, just n of jct US 64. Ext corridors. **Pets:** Small. $10 daily fee/pet. Service with restrictions, supervision.
✕ 🛏 ⇌

PINE BLUFF

⩔⩔ Best Western Pines M
(870) 535-8640. **$61-$63.** 2700 E Harding. 2.5 mi se on US 65B. Ext corridors. **Pets:** Accepted.
SAVE 🛇 ✕ ▣ 🍽 ⇌

⩔⩔⩔ Hampton Inn Pine Bluff M
(870) 850-0444. **$74-$79.** 3103 E Market St. US 65 Bypass; next to the Pines Mall. Int corridors. **Pets:** Small. Service with restrictions, supervision.
SAVE ✕ 🛎 🐾 🗏 🛏 ▣

RUSSELLVILLE

AAA ⩔⩔⩔ Best Western Inn M
(479) 967-1000. **$52-$56.** 2326 N Arkansas Ave. I-40, exit 81. Ext corridors. **Pets:** Accepted.
SAVE 🛇 ✕ 🛏 ▣ ⇌

AAA ⩔⩔⩔ Holiday Inn M
(479) 968-4300. **$70-$79, 10 days notice.** 2407 N Arkansas Ave. I-40, exit 81. Ext corridors. **Pets:** Large. Service with restrictions.
SAVE 🛇 ✕ 🛏 ▣ 🍽 ⇌

⩔ Park Motel M
(479) 968-4862. **$27-$33.** 2615 W Main St. I-40, exit 81, 2 mi s on SR 7, 1.6 mi w on US 64. Ext corridors. **Pets:** Other species. Service with restrictions, supervision.
✕ 🛏 ⇌

SEARCY

⩔⩔ Comfort Inn M
(501) 279-9100. **$50-$70, 10 days notice.** 107 N Rand St. US 67, exit 46. Ext corridors. **Pets:** Accepted.
SAVE 🛇 ✕ 🛏 ▣ ⇌

AAA ⩔ Royal Inn M
(501) 268-3511. **$40-$45.** 2203 E Race Ave. US 67, exit 46, 1.1 mi w. Ext corridors. **Pets:** Dogs only. $5 daily fee/pet. Designated rooms, service with restrictions, supervision.
SAVE 🛇 ✕ 🛏

⩔⩔⩔ Searcy Hampton Inn M
(501) 268-0654. **$67-$77.** 3204 E Race Ave. US 67, exit 46. Ext/int corridors. **Pets:** Medium. $5 daily fee/pet. Designated rooms, service with restrictions, supervision.
SAVE ✕ 🐾 🛏 ▣ ⇌

SILOAM SPRINGS

⩔⩔ Super 8 Motel M
(479) 524-8898. **$55.** 1800 Hwy 412 W. On US 412, 0.3 mi e. Ext corridors. **Pets:** Accepted.
ASK 🛇 ✕ 🗏 ▣ ⇌

SPRINGDALE

Baymont Inn & Suites-Springdale M
(479) 751-2626. **$59-$69.** 1300 S 48th St. I-540, exit 72, just e on US 412. Int corridors. **Pets:** Small. $50 deposit/ room. Designated rooms, service with restrictions, supervision.

Hampton Inn & Suites M
(479) 756-3500. **$101-$136, 3 days notice.** 1700 S 48th St. I-540, exit 72, just e on US 412. Int corridors. **Pets:** Small, other species. Designated rooms, service with restrictions, crate.

Holiday Inn Northwest AR Hotel & Convention Center H
(479) 751-8300. **$102, 14 days notice.** 1500 S 48th St. I-540, exit 72, just e on US 412. Int corridors. **Pets:** Other species. No service, supervision.

STUTTGART

Holiday Inn Express M
(870) 673-3616. **$58-$109, 3 days notice.** 708 W Michigan. On US 79, just w. Ext corridors. **Pets:** $5 daily fee/pet. Designated rooms, service with restrictions, supervision.

TEXARKANA

Baymont Inn & Suites-Texarkana M ❀
(870) 773-1000. **$59-$69.** 5102 N State Line Ave. Jct I-30, US 59 and 71, exit 223B. Int corridors. **Pets:** Medium, other species. Supervision.

Best Western Kings Row Inn & Suites MI
(870) 774-3851. **$65-$80.** 4200 N State Line Ave. I-30, exit 223A, 0.3 mi s on US 71 and 59. Ext/int corridors. **Pets:** Very small. $20 deposit/pet. Service with restrictions, supervision.

Holiday Inn Texarkana MI
(870) 774-3521. **$94.** 5100 N State Line Ave. Jct I-30, US 59 and 71, exit 223B. Int corridors. **Pets:** Other species. $25 one-time fee/room. Service with restrictions, supervision.

Quality Inn M
(870) 772-0070. **$62, 10 days notice.** 5210 N State Line Ave. Jct I-30, US 59 and 71, exit 223B. Ext corridors. **Pets:** Medium. $25 one-time fee/room. Service with restrictions, supervision.

VAN BUREN

Comfort Inn M
(479) 474-2223. **$65-$85.** 3131 Cloverleaf. I-540, exit 2A, just s. Int corridors. **Pets:** Accepted.

Holiday Inn Express M
(479) 474-8100. **$65.** 1903 N 6th St. I-40, exit 5. Ext corridors. **Pets:** Accepted.

Super 8 Motel M
(479) 471-8888. **$47-$55.** 106 North Plaza Ct. I-40, exit 5, s of jct US 59. Ext/int corridors. **Pets:** Accepted.

WARREN

Super 8 M
(870) 226-9888. **$50-$65.** 1408 E Church St. 1 mi e on US 278. Ext corridors. **Pets:** Small. $50 deposit/room. Designated rooms, service with restrictions, supervision.

WEST HELENA

Best Western Inn M
(870) 572-2592. **$55-$75.** 1053 Hwy 49 W. US 49, 3 mi w. Ext corridors. **Pets:** Accepted.

WHEATLEY

Ramada Limited M
(870) 457-2202. **$45-$70.** 129 Lawson Rd. I-40, exit 221. Ext corridors. **Pets:** Small, other species. $5 daily fee/pet. Service with restrictions, crate.

CITY INDEX

ALTURAS

Best Western Trailside Inn M
(530) 233-4111. **$60-$65, 14 days notice.** 343 N Main St. On US 395. Ext corridors. **Pets:** Small, dogs only. $10 one-time fee/pet. Designated rooms, service with restrictions, supervision.

ANAHEIM

Anaheim Marriott Hotel H
(714) 750-8000. **$220-$300.** 700 W Convention Way. I-5, exit Katella Ave, 0.6 mi w to Harbor Blvd, 0.3 mi s, then just w. Int corridors. **Pets:** Accepted.

Anaheim Towneplace Suites By Marriott M
(714) 939-9700. **$99-$134.** 1730 S State College Blvd. I-5, exit Katella Ave, 0.5 mi e, then just n. Int corridors. **Pets:** Accepted.

Best Western Anaheim Stardust M
(714) 774-7600. **$69-$107.** 1057 W Ball Rd. I-5, exit Ball Rd, just w. Ext corridors. **Pets:** Accepted.

Hawthorn Suites, Ltd Anaheim M
(714) 635-5000. **$79-$145.** 1752 S Clementine St. I-5, exit Katella Ave, just n. Int corridors. **Pets:** Accepted.

Hilton Anaheim H
(714) 750-4321. **$79-$299, 7 days notice.** 777 Convention Way. I-5, exit Katella Ave, just w to Harbor Blvd, just s, then just w. Int corridors. **Pets:** Accepted.

Quality Hotel Maingate MI
(714) 750-3131. **$119-$149.** 616 Convention Way. I-5, exit Katella Ave, 0.6 mi w to Harbor Blvd, then 0.3 mi s. Int corridors. **Pets:** Medium. $10 daily fee/pet, $25 one-time fee/pet. Service with restrictions.

Residence Inn By Marriott A
(714) 533-3555. **$178-$349.** 1700 S Clementine St. I-5, exit Katella Ave, just sw. Ext corridors. **Pets:** Medium, other species. $60 one-time fee/room. Designated rooms, service with restrictions.

ANAHEIM HILLS

Best Western Anaheim Hills M
(714) 779-0252. **$80-$115.** 5710 E La Palma Ave. SR 91, exit Imperial Hwy, 0.3 mi n. Ext/int corridors. **Pets:** Other species. Designated rooms, service with restrictions, supervision.

ANDERSON

AmeriHost Inn-Anderson M
(530) 365-6100. **$69-$86.** 2040 Factory Outlet Dr. I-5, exit Factory Outlet Dr, just w. Int corridors. **Pets:** Other species. $10 one-time fee/pet. Service with restrictions, supervision.

Anderson Valley Inn M ❀
(530) 365-2566. **$55-$75.** 2861 Mc Murry Dr. I-5, exit Central Anderson, just e. Ext corridors. **Pets:** Medium, other species. $10 daily fee/pet. Designated rooms, service with restrictions, supervision.
[SAVE] [S&] [X] [B] [≥]

Best Western Knights Inn M
(530) 365-2753. **$56-$66.** 2688 Gateway Dr. I-5, E of I-5 exit Central Anderson, exit Lassen Park. Ext corridors. **Pets:** Accepted.
[SAVE] [S&] [X] [B] [≥] [≥]

ANGELS CAMP

Best Western Cedar Inn & Suites M
(209) 736-4000. **$68-$148.** 444 S Main St. On SR 49; center of town. Ext/int corridors. **Pets:** Accepted.
[SAVE] [S&] [X] [&M] [&'] [B] [≥] [≥]

Gold Country Inn M
(209) 736-4611. **$65-$70.** 720 S Main St. 1 mi s of jct SR 49 and 4. Ext corridors. **Pets:** Small, other species. $50 deposit/pet. Designated rooms, service with restrictions, supervision.
[SAVE] [X] [≥]

ARCATA

Arcata Super 8 M
(707) 822-8888. **$49-$89.** 4887 Valley West Blvd. US 101, exit Guintoli Ln E, 2 mi n. Int corridors. **Pets:** $50 deposit/room. Designated rooms, service with restrictions, supervision.
[SAVE] [S&] [X] [B]

Best Western Arcata Inn M ❀
(707) 826-0313. **$62-$103, 14 days notice.** 4827 Valley West Blvd. US 101, exit Guintoli Ln, 2 mi n. Ext corridors. **Pets:** Medium, other species. $10 daily fee/pet. Designated rooms, service with restrictions, supervision.
[SAVE] [S&] [X] [⌐] [&'] [B] [≥] [≥]

Comfort Inn M
(707) 826-2827. **$55-$95.** 4701 Valley West Blvd. US 101, exit Guintoli Ln, 2 mi n. Ext corridors. **Pets:** Small, dogs only. $5 daily fee/pet. Designated rooms, service with restrictions, supervision.
[SAVE] [S&] [X] [&M] [&'] [B] [≥] [≥]

Hotel Arcata H
(707) 826-0217. **$75-$95.** 708 9th St. At Central Plaza. Int corridors. **Pets:** Other species. $50 deposit/pet. Service with restrictions, supervision.
[SAVE] [S&] [X] [≥] [¶] [A℃]

AUBURN

Best Western Golden Key Motel M
(530) 885-8611. **$69-$100.** 13450 Lincoln Way. I-80, exit Foresthill Rd, exit Foresthill Rd. Ext corridors. **Pets:** Accepted.
[SAVE] [S&] [X] [&M] [B] [≥] [≥]

Holiday Inn-Auburn MI
(530) 887-8787. **$109-$139.** 120 Grass Valley Hwy. Jct I-80 and SR 49. Int corridors. **Pets:** Medium, dogs only. $20 one-time fee/pet. Service with restrictions, supervision.
[SAVE] [S&] [X] [&M] [&'] [≥] [≥]

BAKER

Bun Boy Motel M
(760) 733-4363. **$60-$73.** 72155 Baker Blvd. I-15, exit SR 127 (Baker Blvd), Jct SR 127. Ext corridors. **Pets:** Accepted.
[SAVE] [S&] [X] [B] [¶]

BAKERSFIELD

Bakersfield Red Lion Hotel MI ❀
(661) 327-0681. **$49-$169.** 2400 Camino Del Rio Ct. SR 99, exit SR 58 (Rosedale Hwy), just s. Ext/int corridors. **Pets:** Other species. $25 daily fee/room. Service with restrictions.
[ASK] [S&] [X] [B] [≥] [≥]

Best Inn M
(661) 764-5221. **$49-$54.** 200 Trask St. I-5, exit Stockdale Hwy, 15 mi w. Ext corridors. **Pets:** Medium, other species. $5 daily fee/pet. Designated rooms, service with restrictions, supervision.
[SAVE] [S&] [X] [≥]

Best Western Heritage Inn-Buttonwillow M
(661) 764-6268. **$65-$70.** 253 Trask St. I-5, exit Stockdale Hwy, 15 mi w of Bakersfield. Ext corridors. **Pets:** Accepted.
[SAVE] [S&] [X] [&'] [≥] [≥]

Best Western Hill House MI ❀
(661) 327-4064. **$59-$99, 14 days notice.** 700 Truxtun Ave St. SR 99, exit California Ave, 1.2 mi e, then 0.4 mi n on Chester Ave. Int corridors. **Pets:** Medium. $7 daily fee/pet. Service with restrictions, supervision.
[SAVE] [S&] [X] [B] [≥] [¶] [≥]

Best Western Inn-Bakersfield MI
(661) 327-9651. **$59-$99, 30 days notice.** 2620 Buck Owens Blvd. SR 99, exit Buck Owens Blvd northbound; exit Rosedale Hwy southbound. Int corridors. **Pets:** Accepted.
[SAVE] [S&] [X] [B] [≥] [¶] [≥]

Days Inn M
(661) 324-5555. **$51-$91.** 4500 Buck Owens Blvd. SR 99, exit Rosedale Hwy southbound, just e to Pierce Rd, then 0.7 mi n; exit Airport Dr northbound, to Buck Owens Blvd, then just s. Ext corridors. **Pets:** Dogs only. $25 one-time fee/room. Service with restrictions, supervision.
[SAVE] [S&] [X] [B] [≥] [≥]

▼▼▼▼ **Doubletree Hotel** 🅷 ❄
(661) 323-7111. **$84.** 3100 Camino Del Rio Ct. SR 58, exit Rosedale Hwy, just w. Int corridors. **Pets:** Other species. $15 one-time fee/room. Supervision.
(SAVE) 🔲 ⊠ 🔲 🔲 🔲 🔲 🔲 🔲

(AAA) ▼▼▼ **GuestHouse International Inn** Ⓜ
(661) 833-8000. **$45-$60, 5 days notice.** 2514 White Ln. SR 99, exit White Ln, just e. Ext corridors. **Pets:** Accepted.
(SAVE) 🔲 ⊠ 🔲 🔲 🔲

▼▼▼▼ **La Quinta Inn** Ⓜ
(661) 325-7400. **$76-$96.** 3232 Riverside Dr. SR 99, exit Rosedale Hwy southbound; exit Buck Owens Blvd northbound, just n of Rosedale Hwy. Ext corridors. **Pets:** Medium. Service with restrictions, supervision.
(SAVE) 🔲 ⊠ 🔲 🔲 🔲

(AAA) ▼▼▼▼ **Quality Inn** Ⓜ ❄
(661) 325-0772. **$71-$125.** 1011 Oak St. SR 99, exit California Ave, just e, then just s. Ext/int corridors. **Pets:** Medium. $10 one-time fee/pet. Service with restrictions, supervision.
(SAVE) 🔲 ⊠ 🔲 🔲 🔲

(AAA) ▼▼▼ **Ramada Limited-Central** Ⓜ
(661) 831-1922. **$50-$70.** 830 Wible Rd. SR 99, exit Ming Ave, 0.8 mi ne. Ext corridors. **Pets:** Large, other species. $5 daily fee/pet. Service with restrictions, supervision.
(SAVE) 🔲 ⊠ 🔲 🔲 🔲 🔲

(AAA) ▼▼▼▼ **Residence Inn by Marriott** 🄰 ❄
(661) 321-9800. **$114-$139.** 4241 Chester Ln. SR 99, exit California Ave, just w, then just n. Ext corridors. **Pets:** Large, other species. $6 daily fee/pet, $60 one-time fee/room. Service with restrictions.
(SAVE) 🔲 ⊠ 🔲 🔲 🔲 🔲 🔲

▼▼ **Royal Oak Inn** Ⓜ
(661) 324-9686. **$40-$80.** 889 Oak St. SR 99, exit California Ave, then just se. Ext corridors. **Pets:** Medium. $5 daily fee/pet. Service with restrictions, supervision.
(ASK) 🔲 ⊠ 🔲 🔲 🔲

▼▼ **Travel Rite Hotel** Ⓜ
(661) 324-6666. **$67.** 818 Real Rd. SR 99, exit California Ave, then just sw. Ext/int corridors. **Pets:** Accepted.
(ASK) 🔲 ⊠ 🔲 🔲 🔲 🔲

(AAA) ▼▼▼ **Vagabond Inn** Ⓜ
(661) 392-1800. **$39-$49.** 6100 Knudsen Dr. West side of SR 99, exit Olive Dr. Ext corridors. **Pets:** Dogs only. $5 daily fee/pet. Service with restrictions, supervision.
(SAVE) 🔲 ⊠ 🔲 🔲

BANNING

(AAA) ▼▼▼ **Days Inn** Ⓜ
(909) 849-0092. **$62-$165, 7 days notice.** 2320 W Ramsey St. I-10, exit 22nd St, just n, then just w. Int corridors. **Pets:** Small, other species. $10 daily fee/pet. Designated rooms, supervision.
(SAVE) 🔲 ⊠ 🔲 🔲 🔲

(AAA) ▼▼▼ **Super 8 Motel** Ⓜ
(909) 849-6887. **$50-$80.** 1690 W Ramsey St. I-10, exit 22nd St, just n, then 0.4 mi e. Int corridors. **Pets:** Medium. $5 daily fee/pet. Service with restrictions, supervision.
(SAVE) 🔲 ⊠ 🔲 🔲

BARSTOW

(AAA) ▼▼▼ **Barstow-Super 8 Motel** Ⓜ
(760) 256-8443. **$55-$69.** 170 Coolwater Ln. I-15, exit E Main St, 0.3 mi w, then just s. Ext corridors. **Pets:** $5 daily fee/pet. Service with restrictions, supervision.
(SAVE) 🔲 ⊠ 🔲 🔲 🔲

(AAA) ▼▼ **Best Motel** Ⓜ
(760) 256-6836. **$33-$36.** 1281 E Main St. I-15/40, exit E Main St, 0.5 mi w. Ext corridors. **Pets:** Other species. $5 daily fee/pet. No service, supervision.
(SAVE) ⊠ 🔲 🔲

(AAA) ▼▼▼ **Days Inn** Ⓜ
(760) 256-1737. **$44-$100.** 1590 Coolwater Ln. I-15, exit E Main St, just w, then 0.1 mi s on Roberta St. Ext corridors. **Pets:** $10 daily fee/room. Supervision.
(SAVE) 🔲 🔲 🔲

(AAA) ▼▼ **Econo Lodge** Ⓜ
(760) 256-2133. **$32-$99, 3 days notice.** 1230 E Main St. I-15, exit E Main St, 0.8 mi w. Ext corridors. **Pets:** Accepted.
(SAVE) 🔲 ⊠ 🔲 🔲 🔲

(AAA) ▼▼ **Executive Inn** Ⓜ
(760) 256-7581. **$45-$70, 3 days notice.** 1261 E Main St. I-15/40, exit E Main St, 0.8 mi w. Ext corridors. **Pets:** Medium, dogs only. Designated rooms, service with restrictions, supervision.
(SAVE) 🔲 ⊠ 🔲

(AAA) ▼▼ **Gateway Motel** Ⓜ
(760) 256-8931. **$45-$65, 3 days notice.** 1630 E Main St. I-15, exit E Main St, just e. Ext corridors. **Pets:** Medium, dogs only. $5 daily fee/room. Designated rooms, service with restrictions, supervision.
(SAVE) 🔲 ⊠ 🔲 🔲

▼▼ **Holiday Inn Express, Barstow-Historic Rte 66** Ⓜ
(760) 256-1300. **$89-$109.** 1861 W Main St. I-15, exit W Main St, 0.8 mi ne. Int corridors. **Pets:** Other species. $20 deposit/room. Service with restrictions, supervision.
(ASK) 🔲 ⊠ 🔲 🔲

(AAA) ▼▼▼ **Quality Inn** Ⓜ❗ ❄
(760) 256-6891. **$64-$79, 7 days notice.** 1520 E Main St. I-15/40 westbound, E Main St exit, 0.3 mi w. Ext corridors. **Pets:** Small. $10 one-time fee/pet. Designated rooms, service with restrictions, supervision.
(SAVE) 🔲 ⊠ 🔲 🔲 🔲 🔲

BEAUMONT

▼▼ Best Western El Rancho Motel Ⓜ
(909) 845-2176. **$120.** 480 E Fifth St. I-10, exit Beaumont Ave, just n, then just e. Ext corridors. **Pets:** Very small, other species. $10 one-time fee/pet. Designated rooms, service with restrictions, supervision.

(SAVE) (✕) (🛏) (💻) (🏊)

🐾 ▼ Budget Host Inn Ⓜ
(909) 845-2185. **$50-$60.** 625 E 5th St. I-10, exit Beaumont Ave, just n. Ext corridors. **Pets:** Medium. $2 daily fee/pet. Service with restrictions, supervision.

(SAVE) (🌡) (✕) (🛏) (🏊)

BENICIA

🐾 ▼▼▼ Best Western Heritage Inn Ⓜ
(707) 746-0401. **$89-$120, 5 days notice.** 1955 E 2nd St. I-780, exit Central Benicia/E 2nd St, just e. Int corridors. **Pets:** Very small. $25 one-time fee/pet. Service with restrictions, supervision.

(SAVE) (🌡) (✕) (🛏) (💻) (🏊)

BERKELEY

▼▼▼ ▼▼▼ The Claremont Resort and Spa Ⓡ
(510) 843-3000. **$199-$329.** 41 Tunnel Rd. SR 13 and 24, 1 mi n, exit SR 24 (Claremont Ave); in Berkeley Hills. Int corridors. **Pets:** Accepted.

(ASK) (🌡) (✕) (💻) (🍴) (🏊) (🚫)

BERRY CREEK

▼▼▼ Lake Oroville Bed & Breakfast ⒷⒷ 🐾
(530) 589-0700. **$75-$150, 5 days notice.** 240 Sunday Dr. Exit SR 70 at SR 162, 15 mi e on SR 162 to Bell Ranch Rd, 0.5 mi w. Int corridors. **Pets:** Other species. $10 daily fee/pet. Service with restrictions, supervision.

(ASK) (🌡) (✕) (LM) (cart)

BIG BEAR LAKE

🐾 ▼▼ Alpine Village Suites Lodge Ⓜ 🐾
(909) 866-5460. **$98-$169, 3 days notice.** 546 Pine Knot Ave. SR 18 Business Route. Ext/int corridors. **Pets:** Medium, other species. $100 deposit/room. Service with restrictions.

(SAVE) (🌡) (✕) (💻) (AK)

🐾 ▼▼ Cozy Hollow Lodge Ⓒ
(909) 866-9694. **$79-$179, 15 days notice.** 40409 Big Bear Blvd. SR 18, 0.8 mi w. Ext corridors. **Pets:** Accepted.

(SAVE) (🌡) (🛏) (💻) (AK)

▼▼ Eagle's Nest Bed & Breakfast ⒷⒷ
(909) 866-6465. **$85-$175, 5 days notice.** 41675 Big Bear Blvd. 1 mi e of Pine Knot Ave on SR 18. Ext/int corridors. **Pets:** $10 one-time fee/pet. Designated rooms, service with restrictions, crate.

(ASK) (🌡) (✕) (🛏) (💻) (AK)

🐾 ▼▼ Golden Bear Cottages Ⓒ
(909) 866-2010. **$79-$109, 30 days notice.** 39367 Big Bear Blvd. SR 18, 2 mi w of village. Ext corridors. **Pets:** Accepted.

(SAVE) (✕) (🛏) (💻) (🏊) (AK)

🐾 ▼▼▼ Grey Squirrel Resort Ⓒ
(909) 866-4335. **$76-$125, 14 days notice.** 39372 Big Bear Blvd. SR 18, 2.5 mi w of village. **Pets:** Other species. $100 deposit/room, $10 daily fee/pet. Service with restrictions, supervision.

(SAVE) (🌡) (✕) (🛏) (💻) (🏊) (AK)

▼▼▼ Holiday Inn-Big Bear Chateau Ⓗ
(909) 866-6666. **$109-$299.** 42200 Moonridge Rd. SR 18, 1.5 mi e of Pine Knot Ave, then 0.5 mi s. Int corridors. **Pets:** Accepted.

(ASK) (🌡) (✕) (🛏) (💻) (🍴) (🏊)

▼▼ Honey Bear Lodge Ⓜ
(909) 866-7825. **$49-$199, 7 days notice.** 40994 Pennsylvania Ave. SR 18 business route (Pine Knot Ave), just e. Ext corridors. **Pets:** Accepted.

(ASK) (✕) (🛏) (💻) (AK)

🐾 ▼▼ Shore Acres Lodge Ⓒ 🐾
(909) 866-8200. **$95-$295, 14 days notice.** 40090 Lakeview Dr. SR 18, 0.5 mi w of Pine Knot Ave, then 0.7 mi nw. Ext corridors. **Pets:** Other species. $10 daily fee/pet.

(SAVE) (🌡) (🛏) (💻) (🏊) (AK)

🐾 ▼▼ Stage Coach Lodge Ⓒ
(909) 878-3008. **$89-$165, 14 days notice.** 652 Jeffries. SR 18, 0.5 mi e of Pine Knot Blvd, then just s. Ext corridors. **Pets:** Other species. $75 deposit/room, $10 daily fee/pet. Designated rooms, service with restrictions, supervision.

(SAVE) (🌡) (✕) (🛏) (💻) (AK)

🐾 ▼▼ Timber Haven Lodge Ⓒ
(909) 866-3568. **$99-$189, 14 days notice.** 877 Tulip Ln. SR 18, 1.8 mi w of Pine Knot Blvd, then just s. Ext corridors. **Pets:** Accepted.

(SAVE) (🌡) (✕) (🛏) (💻) (AK)

🐾 ▼▼▼ The Timberline Lodge Ⓒ
(909) 866-4141. **$71-$200, 10 days notice.** 39921 Big Bear Blvd. SR 18, 1.5 mi w of Pine Knot Blvd. Ext corridors. **Pets:** Accepted.

(SAVE) (🌡) (✕) (🛏) (💻) (🏊) (AK)

BIG PINE

🐾 ▼ Big Pine Motel Ⓜ
(760) 938-2282. **$38-$60.** 370 S Main. US 395. Ext corridors. **Pets:** Medium. $4 daily fee/pet. Service with restrictions, supervision.

(SAVE) (✕) (🛏) (💻)

🐾 ▼ Bristlecone Motel Ⓜ
(760) 938-2067. **$40-$68, 4 days notice.** 101 N Main. US 395. Ext corridors. **Pets:** Other species. Service with restrictions, supervision.

(SAVE) (🌡) (✕) (🛏) (💻)

BISHOP

◆◆◆ ▼▼▼▼ Best Western Bishop Holiday Spa Lodge M
(760) 873-3543. **$75-$105.** 1025 N Main St. US 395. Ext corridors. **Pets:** Medium, other species. Designated rooms, service with restrictions, supervision.
SAVE ⬛ ✕ 🛏 💻 🏊

◆◆◆ ▼▼▼▼ Comfort Inn M
(760) 873-4284. **$69-$109.** 805 N Main St. US 395. Ext corridors. **Pets:** Small. Designated rooms, service with restrictions, supervision.
SAVE ⬛ ✕ 🛏 💻 🏊

◆◆◆ ▼▼ Motel 6–4094 M
(760) 873-6426. **$40-$70.** 1005 N Main St. On US 395. Ext corridors. **Pets:** Accepted.
SAVE ⬛ ✕ 🛏

▼▼▼ Ramada Limited M
(760) 872-1771. **$55-$139.** 155 E Elm St. US 395, just e. Ext corridors. **Pets:** Dogs only. Designated rooms, supervision.
ASK ⬛ ✕ 🛏 💻 🏊

▼▼ ▼ Rodeway Inn M
(760) 873-3564. **$65-$100, 3 days notice.** 150 E Elm St. US 395, just w. Ext/int corridors. **Pets:** Accepted.
SAVE ⬛ ✕ 🛏 💻 🏊

▼ Thunderbird Motel M
(760) 873-4215. **$50-$99.** 190 W Pine St. US 395, just w. Ext corridors. **Pets:** Accepted.
ASK ⬛ ✕ 🛏 💻

◆◆◆ ▼▼◈ Vagabond Inn M
(760) 873-6351. **$81.** 1030 N Main St. On US 395. Ext corridors. **Pets:** Other species. $5 daily fee/pet. Service with restrictions, supervision.
SAVE ⬛ ✕ 🛏 💻 🏊

BLYTHE

◆◆◆ ▼▼▼ Best Western Sahara Motel M
(760) 922-7105. **$59-$139.** 825 W Hobsonway. I-10, exit Lovekin Blvd, just n, then just w. Ext corridors. **Pets:** Medium. Service with restrictions, supervision.
SAVE ⬛ ✕ 🛏 💻 🏊

◆◆◆ ▼▼▼ Legacy Inn M
(760) 922-4146. **$48-$54.** 903 W Hobsonway. I-10, exit Lovekin Blvd, just n, then just w. Ext corridors. **Pets:** Accepted.
SAVE ⬛ ✕ 🛏 💻 🏊

BRAWLEY

◆◆◆ ▼▼ Town House Lodge M
(760) 344-5120. **$55-$65.** 135 Main St. At jct SR 78 and 86. Ext corridors. **Pets:** Accepted.
SAVE ⬛ ✕ 🛏 💻 🏊

BREA

▼▼◈▼ Homestead Studio Suites-Brea/Anaheim M
(714) 528-2500. **$84.** 3050 E Imperial Blvd. SR 57, 1.4 mi e. Ext corridors. **Pets:** Small, other species. $75 one-time fee/room. Service with restrictions, crate.
ASK ⬛ ✕ 🛏 💻

◆◆◆ ▼ Hyland Motel M
(714) 990-6867. **$45-$55, 7 days notice.** 727 S Brea Blvd. SR 57, exit Imperial Hwy, 1 mi w, 0.7 mi s. Ext corridors. **Pets:** Small, dogs only. Service with restrictions, supervision.
SAVE ✕ 🛏 💻

▼▼◈▼ Woodfin Suite Hotel M
(714) 579-3200. **$115-$165.** 3100 E Imperial Hwy. SR 57, 1.5 mi e. Ext corridors. **Pets:** Other species. $150 deposit/pet, $5 daily fee/pet. Service with restrictions.
ASK ⬛ ✕ 🛏 💻 🏊

BRIDGEPORT

◆◆◆ ▼▼◈▼ Best Western Ruby Inn M
(760) 932-7241. **$85-$150.** 333 Main St. US 395, at the center of town. Ext corridors. **Pets:** Accepted.
SAVE ⬛ ✕ 🛏 💻

◆◆◆ ▼ Redwood Motel M
(760) 932-7060. **$50-$129.** 425 Main St. On US 395, at the north side of town. Ext corridors. **Pets:** Other species. $5 daily fee/pet. Service with restrictions, supervision.
SAVE ⬛ ✕ 🖼 🛏 💻

◆◆◆ ▼▼◈ Silver Maple Inn M
(760) 932-7383. **$70-$95.** 310 Main St. US 395, at the center of town. Ext corridors. **Pets:** Accepted.
SAVE ⬛ ✕ 🛏 💻 🎿

BUELLTON

◆◆◆ ▼▼▼ Rodeway Inn M
(805) 688-0022. **$50-$120, 30 days notice.** 630 Ave of Flags. US 101, exit first Buellton southbound; exit Frontage Rd northbound, just w over the freeway. Ext/int corridors. **Pets:** Medium, other species. $25 one-time fee/room. Designated rooms, service with restrictions, supervision.
SAVE ⬛ ✕

BUENA PARK

◆◆◆ ▼▼▼ Innsuites Hotels Buena Park Suite Hotel M
(714) 522-7360. **$64-$114, 7 days notice.** 7555 Beach Blvd. SR 91, exit Beach Blvd, just s. Ext corridors. **Pets:** Accepted.
SAVE ⬛ ✕ 🛏 💻 🏊

BURNEY

(AAA) ▼▼▼ Burney Motel M
(530) 335-4500. **$38-$85, 3 days notice.** 37448 Main St. 0.8 mi e on SR 299. Ext corridors. **Pets:** Small. $7 daily fee/pet. Service with restrictions, supervision.

[SAVE] [✕] [📶] [💻]

(AAA) ▼ Charm Motel M
(530) 335-2254. **$60-$80.** 37363 Main St. 0.8 mi e on SR 299. Ext corridors. **Pets:** Dogs only. $5 daily fee/pet. Service with restrictions, supervision.

[SAVE] [S📶] [✕] [📶] [💻]

(AAA) ▼ Green Gables Motel M
(530) 335-2264. **$66-$108.** 37385 Main St. 0.8 mi e on SR 299. Ext corridors. **Pets:** $5 daily fee/pet. Service with restrictions, supervision.

[SAVE] [S📶] [✕] [📶] [💻] [🏊]

(AAA) ▼▼▼ Shasta Pines Motel M
(530) 335-2201. **$46-$79, 5 days notice.** 37386 Main St. 0.8 mi e on SR 299. Ext corridors. **Pets:** Small. $20 deposit/pet, $6 daily fee/pet. Designated rooms, service with restrictions, supervision.

[SAVE] [S📶] [✕] [🅼] [📶] [💻] [🏊]

BUTTONWILLOW

▼ Super 8 Motel M
(661) 764-5117. **$41-$46, 3 days notice.** 20681 Tracy Ave. I-5, exit SR 58. Ext corridors. **Pets:** Accepted.

[ASK] [S📶] [✕] [🖥] [📶] [🏊]

CALIMESA

(AAA) ▼▼ Calimesa Inn Motel M
(909) 795-2536. **$65-$70.** 1205 Calimesa Blvd. I-10, exit Calimesa Blvd, just nw. Ext corridors. **Pets:** Accepted.

[SAVE] [✕] [📶] [🏊]

CALIPATRIA

(AAA) ▼▼▼ Calipatria Inn M
(760) 348-7348. **$69-$84.** 700 N Sorenson. On SR 111. Ext corridors. **Pets:** Other species. Service with restrictions, supervision.

[SAVE] [S📶] [✕] [📶] [💻] [🏊]

CAMBRIA

(AAA) ▼▼ Cambria Shores Inn M 🐾
(805) 927-8644. **$95-$160, 7 days notice.** 6276 Moonstone Beach Dr. 2 mi n of town; at Moonstone Beach. Ext corridors. **Pets:** Dogs only. $10 daily fee/pet. Designated rooms, supervision.

[SAVE] [✕] [📶] [💻] [🅰]

CAMERON PARK

(AAA) ▼▼▼ Best Western Cameron Park Inn M
(530) 677-2203. **$89.** 3361 Coach Ln. 12 mi w of Placerville on US 50, exit Cameron Park Dr. Ext corridors. **Pets:** Small. $20 daily fee/room. Service with restrictions, supervision.

[SAVE] [S📶] [✕] [💻] [🏊]

CAMPBELL

(AAA) ▼▼▼ Residence Inn By Marriott-San Jose M
(408) 559-1551. **$119-$269.** 2761 S Bascom Ave. SR 17, exit Camden Ave E, just n. Ext corridors. **Pets:** Other species. $10 daily fee/pet, $75 one-time fee/room. Service with restrictions.

[SAVE] [S📶] [✕] [💻] [🏊]

CAPITOLA

(AAA) ▼▼▼ Best Western Capitola By-the-Sea Inn & Suites M
(831) 447-0607. **$88-$198.** 1435 41st Ave. SR 1, exit 41st Ave, 4 blks w. Int corridors. **Pets:** Accepted.

[SAVE] [S📶] [✕] [🅼] [🖥] [📶] [💻] [🏊]

▼▼▼ Capitola Inn M
(831) 462-3004. **$75-$135.** 822 Bay Ave. SR 1, exit Bay Ave, just w. Ext/int corridors. **Pets:** Accepted.

[ASK] [S📶] [✕] [📶] [💻] [🏊]

CARLSBAD

(AAA) ▼▼▼▼ Four Seasons Resort Aviara R 🐾
(760) 603-6800. **$405-$530, 3 days notice.** 7100 Four Seasons Point. I-5, exit Poinsettia Ln/Aviara Pkwy, 2 mi se on Batiquitos Lagoon. Int corridors. **Pets:** Very small, dogs only. $100 one-time fee/pet. Designated rooms, service with restrictions, supervision.

[SAVE] [✕] [💻] [🍽] [🏊] [🎾]

(AAA) ▼▼ Inns of America M
(760) 931-1185. **$92-$101.** 751 Raintree Dr. I-5, exit Poinsetta Ln, just w to Ave Encinas, then just n. Ext corridors. **Pets:** Accepted.

[SAVE] [S📶] [✕] [📶] [🍽] [🏊]

▼▼ Motel 6–1021 M
(760) 434-7135. **$47-$61.** 1006 Carlsbad Village Dr. I-5, exit Carlsbad Village Dr, just w. Ext corridors. **Pets:** Accepted.

[S📶] [✕]

CARPINTERIA

(AAA) ▼▼▼ Comfort Suites M
(805) 566-9499. **$99-$179.** 5606 Carpinteria Ave. US 101, exit Casitas Pass Rd, just s, then just e. Int corridors. **Pets:** Small, other species. $10 daily fee/room. Designated rooms, service with restrictions, supervision.

[SAVE] [S📶] [✕] [📶] [💻] [🏊]

CASTAIC

▼▼ Comfort Inn M
(661) 295-1100. **$49-$79.** 31558 Castaic Rd. I-5, exit Parker Rd northbound, 0.3 mi ne; exit Lake Hughes Rd southbound, 0.5 mi se. Ext corridors. **Pets:** $10 one-time fee/room. Designated rooms, no service.

⬛ 🟦 ❌ 🔳 ⬛ 💻 🔜

CATHEDRAL CITY

◈ ▼▼ Comfort Suites M
(760) 324-5939. **$49-$199, 3 days notice.** 69-151 E Palm Canyon Dr. I-10, exit Date Palm Dr, 5 mi s, then just e. Ext corridors. **Pets:** Accepted.

⬛ 🟦 ❌ ⬛ 💻 🏊

◈ ▼▼▼ Doral Palm Springs Resort ▣
(760) 322-7000. **$69-$169, 3 days notice.** 67-967 Vista Chino. I-10, exit Date Palm Dr, 0.5 mi s, 1 mi w. Int corridors. **Pets:** Medium. $50 one-time fee/room. Designated rooms, service with restrictions, supervision.

⬛ 🟦 ❌ ⬛ 💻 🍴 🔜 ❌

CAYUCOS

▼▼▼ Cayucos Beach Inn M 🐾
(805) 995-2828. **$85-$180, 3 days notice.** 333 S Ocean Ave. Ext corridors. **Pets:** Other species. $5 daily fee/room, $10 one-time fee/room.

❌ ⬛ 💻

◈ ▼ Cypress Tree Motel M 🐾
(805) 995-3917. **$39-$97.** 125 S Ocean Ave. On SR 1 business route. Ext corridors. **Pets:** Large. $10 one-time fee/room. Service with restrictions, crate.

⬛ 🟦 ❌ 💻 🐾

◈ ▼ Estero Bay Motel M
(805) 995-3614. **$45-$125, 3 days notice.** 25 S Ocean Ave. On SR 1 business route. Ext corridors. **Pets:** Small. $10 one-time fee/pet. Service with restrictions, crate.

⬛ ❌ ⬛ 💻 🐾

◈ ▼ Shoreline Inn M
(805) 995-3681. **$80-$160.** # 1 N Ocean Ave. Ext corridors. **Pets:** $15 one-time fee/pet. Designated rooms, service with restrictions, supervision.

⬛ 🟦 ❌ ⬛ 💻 🐾

CEDARVILLE

◈ ▼ Sunrise Motel M
(530) 279-2161. **$50-$55.** 54889 Hwy 299. 0.5 mi w on Hwy 299. Ext corridors. **Pets:** Medium, dogs only. $5 daily fee/pet. Designated rooms, service with restrictions, supervision.

⬛ ❌ ⬛ 💻

CHICO

◈ ▼ Deluxe Inn M
(530) 342-8386. **$45-$69.** 2507 Esplanade. 2 mi n on SR 99 business route. Ext corridors. **Pets:** Accepted.

⬛ 🟦 ❌ ⬛

▼▼▼ Holiday Inn of Chico M!
(530) 345-2491. **$120-$130.** 685 Manzanita Ct. Just w of SR 99, via Cohasset Rd. Int corridors. **Pets:** Other species. $25 one-time fee/room. Service with restrictions.

🅰🆂🅺 🟦 ❌ 🔳 🔳 ⬛ 💻 🍴

▼▼▼ Oxford Suites M!
(530) 899-9090. **$79-$125.** 2035 Business Ln. SR 99, exit 20th St e. Int corridors. **Pets:** Small. $15 one-time fee/pet. No service, supervision.

🅰🆂🅺 🟦 ❌ 🔳 🔳 ⬛ 💻 🔜

◈ ▼ Safari Garden Motel M
(530) 343-3201. **$51-$55.** 2352 Esplanade. 2 mi n on SR 99 business route. Ext corridors. **Pets:** Medium, dogs only. $25 deposit/room. Designated rooms, service with restrictions, supervision.

⬛ 🟦 ❌ ⬛ 💻 🔜

◈ ▼▼ Super 8 Motel M
(530) 345-2533. **$55-$95.** 655 Manzanita Ct. Just w of SR 99, via Cohasset Rd. Int corridors. **Pets:** Medium. $4 daily fee/pet. Service with restrictions, supervision.

⬛ 🟦 ❌ ⬛ 🔜

CHOWCHILLA

◈ ▼▼ Days Inn M
(559) 665-4821. **$58-$68, 3 days notice.** 220 E Robertson Blvd. SR 99, exit Robertson Blvd W. Ext corridors. **Pets:** Accepted.

⬛ 🟦 ❌ ⬛ 💻 🔜

CLIO

▼▼ Molly's Bed & Breakfast ▣▣ 🐾
(530) 836-4436. **$85-$110, 7 days notice.** 276 Lower Main St. Just e of SR 89. Int corridors. **Pets:** $15 daily fee/pet. Designated rooms, service with restrictions, supervision.

🅰🆂🅺 🟦 ❌ 🔳 🔳

COALINGA

◈ ▼▼ Big Country Inn M
(559) 935-0866. **$70-$86.** 25020 W Dorris Ave. W of and adjacent to I-5, at SR 198, Hanford-Lemoore off-ramp. Ext corridors. **Pets:** Very small. $10 one-time fee/pet. Designated rooms, service with restrictions, supervision.

⬛ 🟦 ❌ ⬛ 💻 🔜

◈ ▼▼▼ The Inn at Harris Ranch M!
(559) 935-0717. **$115-$135.** 24505 W Dorris Ave. East side and adjacent to I-5; at SR 198, Hanford-Lemoore off-ramp. Ext/int corridors. **Pets:** Accepted.

⬛ 🟦 ❌ 🔳 💻 🍴 🔜

COLUMBIA

▼ Columbia Gem Motel ▣ 🐾
(209) 532-4508. **$59-$150, 7 days notice.** 22131 Parrotts Ferry Rd. 3 mi n of Sonora; 1 mi from Columbia State Historic Park. Ext corridors. **Pets:** Dogs only. Service with restrictions, supervision.

❌ ⬛ 💻 🔳

CONCORD

◆◆◆◆ Holiday Inn Concord M
(925) 687-5500. **$58-$148.** 1050 Burnett Ave. I-680, exit E
Concord Ave, Diamond Ave S, Burnett Ave W. Ext/int corridors. **Pets:** Other species. $100 deposit/room, $5 daily fee/
room. Service with restrictions, supervision.

🗙 🖪 💻 🍴 ⋙

◆◆ ◆◆◆ Premier Inns M
(925) 674-0888. **$76-$92.** 1581 Concord Ave. Exit SR 242,
Clayton Ave E. Ext corridors. **Pets:** Accepted.

SAVE 🗃 🗙 🖎 🖪 ⋙

CORNING

◆◆ ◆◆◆◆ Amerihost Inn-Corning M
(530) 824-5200. **$62-$69.** 910 Hwy 99 W. I-5, exit Solano
St, Just e of and adjacent to I-5, exit Solano St. Int corridors. **Pets:** Small. $10 one-time fee/pet. Service with
restrictions, supervision.

SAVE 🗃 🗙 ᴦᴹ 🖎 🖪 💻 ⋙

◆◆ ◆◆◆◆ Best Western Inn-Corning M
(530) 824-2468. **$65-$89.** 2165 Solano St. I-5 E, exit Corning, Exit I-5 e via Corning exit, 1 blk e. Ext corridors.
Pets: Accepted.

SAVE 🗃 🗙 ᴦᴹ 🖪 💻 ⋙

◆◆ ◆◆ Days Inn M ❀
(530) 824-2000. **$50-$100.** 3475 Hwy 99 W. I-5, exit South
Ave, Exit I-5 at South Ave, 0.3 mi s. Int corridors.
Pets: Other species. $5 daily fee/pet. Service with restric-
tions, supervision.

SAVE 🗃 🗙 ᴦᴹ 🖎 🖪 ⋙

◆◆ ◆◆◆◆ Shilo Inn M ❀
(530) 824-2940. **$69-$89.** 3350 Sunrise Way. I-5, exit South
Ave, Just e and adjacent to I-5, exit South Ave, 1 mi s. Int
corridors. **Pets:** Other species. $10 daily fee/pet. Service
with restrictions, supervision.

SAVE 🗃 🗙 ᴦᴹ 🖪 💻 ⋙

CORONA

◆◆◆ ◆◆◆◆ Dynasty Suites Corona M
(909) 371-7185. **$57-$64.** 1805 W 6th St. From SR 91, exit
6th St eastbound; exit Maple St westbound, just s. Ext
corridors. **Pets:** Accepted.

SAVE 🗃 🗙 🖪 💻 ⋙

COSTA MESA

◆◆◆◆ Hilton Costa Mesa H
(714) 540-7000. **$99-$299, 3 days notice.** 3050 Bristol St.
I-405, exit Bristol St, just s. Int corridors. **Pets:** $25 one-time
fee/room. Service with restrictions, crate.

SAVE 🗃 🗙 🖪 💻 🍴 ⋙

◆◆ ◆◆ La Quinta Inn M
(714) 957-5841. **$-$86.** 1515 South Coast Dr. I-405, exit
Harbor Blvd, just n, then just w. Ext corridors.
Pets: Accepted.

SAVE 🗃 🗙 🖪 💻 ⋙

◆◆◆ ◆◆◆◆ Residence Inn by Marriott ▲
(714) 241-8800. **$144-$169.** 881 W Baker St. From SR 73,
exit Bear St; from SR 55, exit Baker St. Ext corridors.
Pets: Other species. $10 daily fee/pet, $80 one-time fee/
room. Service with restrictions, crate.

SAVE 🗃 🗙 💻 ⋙

◆◆◆ ◆◆ Vagabond Inn M
(714) 557-8360. **$70-$125.** 3205 Harbor Blvd. I-405, exit
Harbor Blvd, just s; entrance from Gisler, just w of Harbor.
Ext corridors. **Pets:** Accepted.

SAVE 🗃 🗙 🖪 💻 ⋙

◆◆◆◆ The Westin South Coast Plaza Hotel H
(714) 540-2500. **$175.** 686 Anton Blvd. I-405, exit Bristol St,
just n, then just e. Int corridors. **Pets:** Small. Designated
rooms, service with restrictions, crate.

ASK 🗃 🗙 💻 🍴 ⋙

**◆◆◆ ◆◆◆◆ Wyndham Orange County
Airport H**
(714) 751-5100. **$94-$154.** 3350 Ave of the Arts. I-405, exit
Bristol St, n to Anton Blvd, 2 blks e, just n. Int corridors.
Pets: Other species. $25 one-time fee/room. Service with
restrictions.

SAVE 🗃 🗙 🖉 🖪 💻 🍴 ⋙

CRESCENT CITY

◆◆◆ ◆◆◆◆ Anchor Beach Inn M
(707) 464-2600. **$59-$140.** 880 Hwy US 101 S. US 101 at
Anchor Way. Ext corridors. **Pets:** Small, dogs only. $20
deposit/room, $10 daily fee/pet. Designated rooms, service
with restrictions, supervision.

SAVE 🗃 🗙 ⋙

◆◆◆ ◆◆ Best Value Inn M ❀
(707) 464-4141. **$52-$69, 3 days notice.** 440 Hwy 101 N.
On US 101. Ext corridors. **Pets:** Medium, dogs only. $5
daily fee/room. Designated rooms, supervision.

SAVE 🗃 🗙 🖪 💻 🎬

◆◆◆ ◆◆ Super 8 M ❀
(707) 464-4111. **$45-$85, 7 days notice.** 685 Hwy 101 S. E
of US 101 S; opposite harbor. Ext corridors. **Pets:** Small,
dogs only. $10 daily fee/pet. Designated rooms, supervi-
sion.

SAVE 🗃 🗙 💻 🎬

CYPRESS

◆◆◆◆ Woodfin Suite Hotel-Cypress M
(714) 828-4000. **$129.** 5905 Corporate Ave. I-605, exit
Katella Ave, 3 mi e, then 0.4 mi n on Valley View. Int
corridors. **Pets:** Accepted.

ASK 🗃 🗙 🖪 💻 ⋙

DANA POINT

△△△ ▽▽▽▽ Laguna Cliffs Marriott
Resort **H** ❀
(949) 661-5000. **$229-$269, 3 days notice.** 25135 Park Lantern. I-5, From SR 1 (Pacific Coast Hwy), just w on Harbor Dr. Int corridors. **Pets:** Large, other species. Service with restrictions, supervision.
[SAVE] [S6] [X] [H] [▢] [¶] [≈] [X]

DANVILLE

△△△ ▽▽ Danville Inn **M**
(925) 838-8080. **$95.** 803 Camino Ramon. E of and adjacent to I-680, exit via Sycamore Valley Rd. Ext/int corridors. **Pets:** Small, dogs only. Service with restrictions, supervision.
[SAVE] [S6] [X] [▢] [≈]

DAVIS

△△△ ▽▽▽ Best Western University Lodge **M**
(530) 756-7890. **$50-$95, 7 days notice.** 123 B St. Just e of University of California Campus. Ext corridors. **Pets:** Small. $10 daily fee/pet. Service with restrictions, supervision.
[SAVE] [S6] [X] [H] [▢]

▽▽▽▽ Howard Johnson Hotel **M**
(530) 792-0800. **$84-$129.** 4100 Chiles Rd. I-80, exit Mace Blvd, exit Mace Blvd, just s, then 0.3 mi w. Int corridors. **Pets:** Accepted.
[ASK] [S6] [X] [&M] [&] [H] [▢] [≈]

DELANO

△△△ ▽▽▽ Comfort Inn **M**
(661) 725-1022. **$60-$65.** 2211 Girard St. Just e of SR 99; exit County Line. Ext corridors. **Pets:** Medium. $10 daily fee/room. Service with restrictions, supervision.
[SAVE] [S6] [X] [▢] [≈]

▽▽ Shilo Inn **M** ❀
(661) 725-7551. **$75.** 2231 Girard St. From SR 99, exit County Line, just e. Int corridors. **Pets:** Other species. $10 daily fee/pet. Service with restrictions, supervision.
[ASK] [S6] [X] [H] [▢] [≈]

DINUBA

△△△ ▽▽▽▽ Best Western Americana **M**
(559) 595-8401. **$65-$98.** 1450 S Alta Ave. 0.6 mi sw of downtown. Int corridors. **Pets:** Small, dogs only. $50 deposit/room. Service with restrictions, supervision.
[SAVE] [S6] [X] [&] [H] [▢] [≈]

DIXON

△△△ ▽▽▽▽ Best Western Inn **M**
(707) 678-1400. **$68-$110.** 1345 Commercial Way. I-80, exit Pitt School Rd, exit Pitt School Rd, 8 mi w of U.C. Davis Campus. Ext/int corridors. **Pets:** Medium. $50 deposit/room, $10 one-time fee/room. Service with restrictions, supervision.
[SAVE] [S6] [X] [&M] [&] [H] [▢] [≈]

DUNNIGAN

△△△ ▽▽▽ Best Value Inn **M**
(530) 724-3333. **$54-$64.** 3930 Road 89. I-5, exit Dunnigan, exit Dunnigan. Int corridors. **Pets:** Service with restrictions, supervision.
[SAVE] [S6] [X] [H] [≈]

△△△ ▽▽▽▽ Best Western Country **M**
(530) 724-3471. **$64-$82.** 3930 Road 89. I-5, exit Dunnigan, exit Dunnigan. Ext corridors. **Pets:** Service with restrictions, supervision.
[SAVE] [S6] [X] [&M] [H] [≈]

▽▽ Budget 8 Motel **M**
(530) 724-3411. **$42-$60.** 4930 CR 99 W. I-5, exit CR 8, exit at CR-8, just e. Ext corridors. **Pets:** Medium. $5 daily fee/pet. Designated rooms, service with restrictions, supervision.
[ASK] [S6] [H] [≈]

DUNSMUIR

△△△ ▽▽▽▽ Caboose Motel-Railroad Park
Resort **M** ❀
(530) 235-4440. **$75-$100.** 100 Railroad Park Rd. I-5, exit Railroad Park Rd, 1 mi s. **Pets:** Large. $10 daily fee/pet. Service with restrictions, supervision.
[SAVE] [X] [H] [▢] [¶]

△△△ ▽▽▽ Cedar Lodge Motel **M**
(530) 235-4331. **$47-$130, 4 days notice.** 4201 Dunsmuir Ave. I-5, exit Dunsmuir/Siskiyou, 0.5 mi w. Ext corridors. **Pets:** Medium, dogs only. $5 daily fee/pet. Designated rooms, service with restrictions, supervision.
[SAVE] [S6] [X] [H] [▢]

EL CENTRO

△△△ ▽▽▽▽ Barbara Worth Golf Resort and
Convention Center **M**
(760) 356-2806. **$85-$89.** 2050 Country Club Dr. I-8, exit Bowker Rd, 2 mi n, then 3 mi e on CRS-80; 9 mi e of SR 86. Ext/int corridors. **Pets:** Accepted.
[SAVE] [S6] [X] [H] [▢] [¶] [≈]

△△△ ▽▽▽ Brunner's **M**
(760) 352-6431. **$68-$78.** 215 N Imperial Ave. I-8, exit Imperial Ave, 1 mi n. Ext corridors. **Pets:** Accepted.
[SAVE] [S6] [X] [H] [▢] [¶]

▽▽ Days Inn **M**
(760) 352-5511. **$60-$80.** 1425 Adams Ave. I-8, exit Imperial Ave, 1.4 mi n, just w on SR 86 and I-8 Business Loop. Ext corridors. **Pets:** Accepted.
[SAVE] [S6] [X] [H] [≈]

▽▽ Vacation Inn **M**
(760) 352-9523. **$57, 10 days notice.** 2015 Cottonwood Cir. I-8, exit Imperial Ave, just n, then just w. Ext corridors. **Pets:** Small. $40 deposit/room. Designated rooms, service with restrictions, supervision.
[ASK] [S6] [X] [H] [▢] [¶] [≈]

EL PORTAL

Yosemite View Lodge M
(209) 379-2681. **$154-$204, 7 days notice.** 11136 Hwy 140. Just w of YNP Westgate. **Pets:** Other species. $5.50 daily fee/pet. Service with restrictions, supervision.

ENCINITAS

Best Western Encinitas Inn & Suites M
(760) 942-7455. **$110-$229, 3 days notice.** 85 Encinitas Blvd. I-5, exit Encinitas Blvd, just w. Ext corridors. **Pets:** Dogs only. $50 one-time fee/pet. Designated rooms, service with restrictions, supervision.

Days Inn Encinitas/Moonlight Beach M
(760) 944-0260. **$69-$109.** 133 Encinitas Blvd. I-5, exit Encinitas Blvd, just w. Ext corridors. **Pets:** Medium, other species. $25 one-time fee/room. Designated rooms, service with restrictions.

ESCONDIDO

Best Western Escondido M
(760) 740-1700. **$79-$109.** 1700 Seven Oaks Rd. I-15, exit El Norte Pkwy, just e. Int corridors. **Pets:** Small. $25 one-time fee/room. Designated rooms, service with restrictions, supervision.

The Sheridan Inn M
(760) 743-8338. **$75-$114.** 1341 N Escondido Blvd. I-15, exit El Norte Pkwy, 0.8 mi e, then just n. Ext corridors. **Pets:** Accepted.

Welk Resort-San Diego R
(760) 749-3000. **$190-$210, 3 days notice.** 8860 Lawrence Welk Dr. I-15, exit Deer Springs Rd northbound, just e, 2.7 mi n on Champagne Ave, then just e; exit Old Castle Rd southbound, just e, 1.5 mi s on Champagne Ave, then just e. Ext corridors. **Pets:** $25 one-time fee/room. Designated rooms, service with restrictions.

ETNA

Motel Etna M
(530) 467-5330. **$40.** 317 Collier Way. Just w of SR 3. Ext corridors. **Pets:** Accepted.

EUREKA

Bayview Motel M
(707) 442-1673. **$75-$105.** 2844 Fairfield St. E of US 101, exit Henderson, at top of hill, just n. Ext corridors. **Pets:** Small. $5 daily fee/room. Designated rooms, service with restrictions, supervision.

Best Western Bayshore Inn M
(707) 268-8005. **$92-$149.** 3500 Broadway. On US 101, s of Bayshore Mall. Ext corridors. **Pets:** $100 deposit/pet. Service with restrictions, supervision.

Eureka Inn H
(707) 442-6441. **$109-$145.** 518 7th St. E of US 101 N. Int corridors. **Pets:** Accepted.

Eureka Ramada Limited M
(707) 443-2206. **$69-$89.** 270 5th St. On US 101 northbound. Int corridors. **Pets:** Small. $25 deposit/room, $8 daily fee/pet. Designated rooms, service with restrictions, supervision.

Eureka Town House Motel M
(707) 443-4536. **$40-$65.** 933 4th St. US 101 southbound, corner of 4th and K sts. Ext corridors. **Pets:** Small, dogs only. $5 daily fee/pet. Designated rooms, service with restrictions, supervision.

Quality Inn Eureka M
(707) 443-1601. **$78-$200, 14 days notice.** 1209 4th St. On US 101 southbound, between M and N sts. Ext corridors. **Pets:** Accepted.

Red Lion Hotel M
(707) 445-0844. **$79-$109.** 1929 4th St. On US 101 southbound; between T and V sts. Int corridors. **Pets:** $35 one-time fee/room. Designated rooms, service with restrictions, supervision.

Sunrise Inn & Suites M
(707) 443-9751. **$39-$59.** 129 4th St. On US 101, exit C St southbound; exit C St W northbound. Ext corridors. **Pets:** Small. $5 daily fee/pet. Service with restrictions, supervision.

FALL RIVER MILLS

Hi-Mont Motel M
(530) 336-5541. **$74-$82.** 43021 Bridge St. 1 mi w on Hwy 299 at Bridge St. Ext corridors. **Pets:** Accepted.

▼▼▼ Lava Creek Lodge 🗙
(530) 336-6288. **$40-$60, 7 days notice.** One Island Rd.
12 mi n of SR 299 via Glenburn Rd, e on Brown Rd, n on
CR A19; bear right on Island Rd to gravel driveway. Ext
corridors. **Pets:** Other species. $10 daily fee/pet.
🅰🆂🅺 🆂🛅 ✖ 🍴 🛅 🎿 🎦 🈂

FALLBROOK

🆔 ▼▼▼ Best Western Franciscan Inn M
(760) 728-6174. **$83-$103.** 1635 S Mission Rd. I-15, exit
CR S13, 6.5 mi sw. Ext corridors. **Pets:** Small. $10 one-
time fee/room. Designated rooms, service with restrictions,
supervision.
SAVE 🆂🛅 ✖ 🛢 💻 🈂

FISH CAMP

▼▼▼ The Narrow Gauge Inn Mℹ
(559) 683-7720. **$79-$195, 4 days notice.** 48571 Hwy 41.
4 mi from South Gate to Yosemite National Park. Ext corridors. **Pets:** Medium. $27.25 one-time fee/pet. Designated
rooms, service with restrictions, supervision.
✖ 💻 🍴 🈂

FORTUNA

🆔 ▼▼▼▼ Best Western Country Inn M
(707) 725-6822. **$69-$94.** 2025 Riverwalk Dr. US 101, exit
Kenmar Rd/Riverwalk, just w. Ext corridors. **Pets:** Other
species. $100 deposit/room. Designated rooms, service
with restrictions, supervision.
SAVE 🆂🛅 ✖ 🆖 🕗 🈂 🛢 💻 🈂

🆔 ▼▼ Fortuna Super 8 M
(707) 725-2888. **$55-$75.** 1805 Alamar Way. US 101, exit
Kenmar Rd/Riverwalk, just w. Ext corridors. **Pets:** Dogs
only. $10 daily fee/pet. Designated rooms, service with
restrictions, supervision.
SAVE 🆂🛅 ✖ 🈂 🛢 💻

🆔 ▼▼▼▼ Holiday Inn Express M ꙮ
(707) 725-5500. **$84-$139.** 1859 Alamar Way. US 101, exit
Kenmar Rd/Riverwalk, just w. Ext corridors. **Pets:** Other
species. $20 deposit/pet, $10 daily fee/pet. Designated
rooms, service with restrictions, supervision.
SAVE 🆂🛅 ✖ 🛢 💻 🈂

FOUNTAIN VALLEY

**🆔 ▼▼▼ Ramada Limited-Huntington Beach/
Fountain Valley M**
(714) 847-3388. **$89-$94, 7 days notice.** 9125 Recreation
Cir. I-405, exit Warner Ave W northbound; exit Magnolia
southbound, just w. Ext corridors. **Pets:** Medium, other species. $25 deposit/room, $20 daily fee/pet. Designated
rooms, service with restrictions, supervision.
SAVE 🆂🛅 ✖ 🛢 🈂

🆔 ▼▼▼▼ Residence Inn by Marriott 🅰
(714) 965-8000. **$149-$189.** 9930 Slater Ave. I-405, exit
Brookhurst St, just n, then just w. Ext corridors. **Pets:** Small,
other species. $10 daily fee/room, $100 one-time fee/room.
Service with restrictions, crate.
SAVE 🆂🛅 ✖ 🛢 💻 🈂

FREMONT

🆔 ▼▼▼▼ Best Western Garden Court Inn M
(510) 792-4300. **$139-$159, 3 days notice.** 5400 Mowry
Ave. I-880, exit Mowry Ave, just e. Int corridors. **Pets:**
Small. $50 deposit/room. Service with restrictions,
supervision.
SAVE 🆂🛅 ✖ 💻 🈂

🆔 ▼▼▼▼ Fremont Marriott 🅷
(510) 413-3700. **$79-$249.** 46100 Landing Pkwy. I-880, exit
Fremont Blvd/Cushing Pkwy, W of I-880, exit Fremont Blvd/
Cushing Pkwy. Int corridors. **Pets:** Small, other species.
Service with restrictions.
SAVE ✖ 🆖 🛢 💻 🍴 🈂

▼▼▼ Homestead Studio Suites-Fremont M
(510) 353-1664. **$69-$139.** 46080 Fremont Blvd. I-880, exit
Fremont Blvd/Cushing Pkwy, just w. Int corridors.
Pets: Accepted.
🅰🆂🅺 ✖ 🆖 💻

▼▼▼ La Quinta Inn & Suites M ꙮ
(510) 445-0808. **$139-$169.** 46200 Landing Pkwy. I-880,
exit Fremont Blvd/Cushing Pkwy, just w. Int corridors.
Pets: $25 deposit/room. Service with restrictions.
SAVE 🆂🛅 ✖ 🆖 🛢 💻 🈂

🆔 ▼▼▼▼ Residence Inn By Marriott M
(510) 794-5900. **$189-$219.** 5400 Farwell Pl. I-880, exit
Mowry Ave, just e. Ext corridors. **Pets:** Other species. $10
daily fee/room, $75 one-time fee/room. Service with restric-
tions, crate.
SAVE 🆂🛅 ✖ 🈂

FRESNO

▼▼ Ambassador Inn & Suites M
(559) 442-1082. **$40-$140.** 1804 W Olive Ave. Just w of SR
99, exit Olive Ave. Ext corridors. **Pets:** Accepted.
🅰🆂🅺 🆂🛅 ✖ 🛢 🈂

**🆔 ▼▼▼▼ Best Western Garden Court
Inn M ꙮ**
(559) 237-1881. **$59-$119.** 2141 N Parkway Dr. Just w of
SR 99, exit Clinton Ave, just s. Ext corridors. **Pets:** Medium,
other species. $10 daily fee/pet. Service with restrictions,
supervision.
SAVE 🆂🛅 ✖ 🕗 🛢 💻 🍴 🈂

🆔 ▼▼ Days Inn-Parkway M ꙮ
(559) 268-6211. **$47-$89, 15 days notice.** 1101 N Parkway
Dr. SR 99, exit Olive St, just w. Ext corridors.
Pets: Medium. $5 daily fee/pet. Service with restrictions,
supervision.
SAVE 🆂🛅 ✖ 🛢 🈂

🆔 ▼▼▼ Holiday Inn Express-Barcus M
(559) 277-5700. **$89-$105.** 5046 N Barcus. SR 99, exit
Shaw Ave, just e. Int corridors. **Pets:** Small. $20 one-time
fee/room. Designated rooms, service with restrictions,
supervision.
SAVE 🆂🛅 ✖ 🆖 🕗 🛢 💻 🈂

Knights Inn M
(559) 275-7766. **$59-$69.** 3093 N Parkway. SR 99, eastbound exit Shields Ave; northbound exit Clinton, just w. Ext corridors. **Pets:** Accepted.

La Quinta Inn M
(559) 442-1110. **$71-$87.** 2926 Tulare St. Just w of SR 41, exit Tulare St. Ext corridors. **Pets:** Small, other species. Designated rooms, service with restrictions, crate.

Radisson Hotel H
(559) 268-1000. **$129-$149.** 2233 Ventura St. SR 99, exit Ventura St, just e. Int corridors. **Pets:** Medium, other species. $50 one-time fee/room. Designated rooms, service with restrictions, supervision.

Ramada Inn-Ashlan M
(559) 275-2727. **$68-$92, 8 days notice.** 4278 W Ashlan Ave. SR 99, exit Ashlan Ave, just w. Ext corridors. **Pets:** Accepted.

Red Roof Inn M
(559) 276-1910. **$49-$79, 7 days notice.** 5021 N Barcus Ave. SR 99, exit Shaw. Ext corridors. **Pets:** Accepted.

Red Roof Inn M
(559) 431-3557. **$50-$70.** 6730 N Blackstone. W of SR 41 at Herndon. Ext corridors. **Pets:** Medium, other species. $25 deposit/room. Service with restrictions, supervision.

Residence Inn by Marriott M
(559) 222-8900. **$119.** 5322 N Diana Ave. 0.3 mi w of SR 41, exit Shaw Ave, n on Blackstone, e on Barstow. Int corridors. **Pets:** Other species. $5 daily fee/pet, $50 one-time fee/pet. Service with restrictions, supervision.

Super 8-Downtown M
(559) 268-0621. **$45-$90, 3 days notice.** 2127 Inyo St. SR 99, exit Ventura St, 0.5 mi e. Ext corridors. **Pets:** Medium, other species. $10 daily fee/pet. Designated rooms, service with restrictions, supervision.

Super 8-Parkway M
(559) 268-0741. **$45-$99.** 1087 N Parkway Dr. SR 99, exit Olive Ave, just w. Ext corridors. **Pets:** Medium. $10 daily fee/pet. Supervision.

Super 8-University M
(559) 294-0224. **$52-$66.** 2655 E Shaw Ave. SR 41, exit Shaw Ave, 1.5 mi e. Ext corridors. **Pets:** Accepted.

Towne Place Suites by Marriott M ❀
(559) 435-4600. **$65-$98 (no credit cards).** 7127 N Fresno St. SR 41, exit Herndon St E. **Pets:** Medium. $150 deposit/pet, $50 one-time fee/pet. Service with restrictions, supervision.

Travelodge M
(559) 276-7745. **$59-$69.** 3093 N Parkway. SR 99, southbound exit Sheilds Ave; northbound exit Clinton, just w. Ext corridors. **Pets:** Accepted.

Travelodge Blackstone M
(559) 229-9840. **$40-$45.** 3876 N Blackstone Ave. 0.3 mi w of SR 41, exit Shields Ave. Ext corridors. **Pets:** Accepted.

Villager Lodge M
(559) 233-3913. **$38-$42.** 933 N Parkway Dr. SR 99 exit Olive Ave, then w to Parkway Dr. Ext corridors. **Pets:** Small, dogs only. $20 deposit/room. Service with restrictions, crate.

FULLERTON

Fullerton Inn M
(714) 773-4900. **$65-$75.** 2601 W Orangethorpe Ave. From SR 91, exit Magnolia Ave, just n, then just e. Ext corridors. **Pets:** Very small, dogs only. $10 daily fee/pet. No service, supervision.

Fullerton Marriott Hotel at California State Univ MI
(714) 738-7800. **$124-$149.** 2701 E Nutwood Ave. From SR 57, just w. Int corridors. **Pets:** Accepted.

GARBERVILLE

Best Western Humboldt House Inn M
(707) 923-2771. **$79-$104.** 701 Redwood Dr. US 101, 1st exit. Ext corridors. **Pets:** Large, other species. $100 deposit/room. Designated rooms, service with restrictions, supervision.

Motel Garberville M
(707) 923-2422. **$49-$79.** 948 Redwood Dr. On US 101 business route. Ext corridors. **Pets:** Small. Designated rooms, service with restrictions, supervision.

Sherwood Forest Motel M
(707) 923-2721. **$70-$86.** 814 Redwood Dr. On US 101 business route. Ext corridors. **Pets:** Other species. Service with restrictions, supervision.

GARDEN GROVE

▼▼▼▼ **Candlewood Suites Anaheim-South** Ⓜ
(714) 539-4200. **$74-$109.** 12901 Garden Grove Blvd. From SR 22, exit Haster St westbound, just w; exit Fairview eastbound, just nw. Int corridors. **Pets:** Medium. $250 one-time fee/room. Service with restrictions, supervision.
ⒶⓈⓀ Ⓢ Ⓧ Ⓗ ⬛

GILROY

ⒶⒶⒶ ▼▼▼ **Leavesley Inn** Ⓜ
(408) 847-5500. **$68-$75.** 8430 Murray Ave. Just w of US 101, exit Leavesley Rd. Ext corridors. **Pets:** Accepted.
Ⓢ Ⓢ Ⓧ Ⓗ ⌘

GLENNVILLE

▼▼ **The Bunkhouse Motel** Ⓜ
(661) 536-9100. **$65-$75.** 12044 Hwy 15 S. On SR 155 at Granite Rd. Ext corridors. **Pets:** Accepted.
ⒶⓈⓀ Ⓢ Ⓧ Ⓗ ⬛ ⓣⓘ

GRASS VALLEY

ⒶⒶⒶ ▼▼▼ **Alta Sierra Village Inn** Ⓜ ❀
(530) 273-9102. **$69-$185, 10 days notice.** 11858 Tammy Way. 6 mi s, 1.1 mi e on Alta Sierra Dr, 0.8 mi w on Norlene, 0.5 mi e on Tammy, follow signs to Alta Sierra Country Club. Ext corridors. **Pets:** Dogs only. $10 one-time fee/room. Designated rooms, service with restrictions, supervision.
Ⓢ Ⓧ Ⓗ ⬛ Ⓩ

ⒶⒶⒶ ▼▼▼ **Best Western Gold Country Inn** Ⓜ
(530) 273-1393. **$75-$119, 7 days notice.** 11972 Sutton Way. 1 mi e, off and adjacent to SR 20 and 49, midway between Grass Valley and Nevada City, exit Brunswick Rd. Ext corridors. **Pets:** Accepted.
Ⓢ Ⓢ Ⓧ Ⓗ ⬛ ⌘

ⒶⒶⒶ ▼▼ **Coach N' Four Motel** Ⓜ
(530) 273-8009. **$55-$82, 3 days notice.** 628 S Auburn St. SR 49, exit E Empire St, 0.3 mi e, then just s. Ext corridors. **Pets:** Medium, other species. $50 deposit/pet, $10 one-time fee/pet. Designated rooms, service with restrictions, supervision.
Ⓢ Ⓢ Ⓧ Ⓗ

ⒶⒶⒶ ▼▼▼ **Golden Chain Resort Motel** Ⓜ
(530) 273-7279. **$56-$98, 3 days notice.** 13363 SR 49. 2.5 mi s on SR 49. Ext corridors. **Pets:** Small. $10 daily fee/pet. Designated rooms, service with restrictions, supervision.
Ⓢ Ⓧ ⌘

GRIDLEY

ⒶⒶⒶ ▼▼▼ **Gridley Inn** Ⓜ ❀
(530) 846-4520. **$57-$62.** 1490 Hwy 99, Suite A. On SR 99, 1 mi s. Ext corridors. **Pets:** $50 deposit/pet. Service with restrictions, supervision.
Ⓢ Ⓢ Ⓧ Ⓗ ⬛ ⌘

ⒶⒶⒶ ▼▼▼ **Pacific Motel** Ⓜ ❀
(530) 846-4580. **$53-$63, 3 days notice.** 1308 Hwy 99. 1 mi s on SR 99. Ext corridors. **Pets:** $5 daily fee/room. Service with restrictions, supervision.
Ⓢ Ⓢ Ⓧ Ⓗ ⬛ ⌘

GROVELAND

ⒶⒶⒶ ▼▼▼ **Best Value Yosemite Westgate BuckMeadows Lodge** Ⓜ
(209) 962-5281. **$69-$179, 3 days notice.** 7633/7647 Hwy 120. 12 mi e on SR 120. Ext corridors. **Pets:** Other species. $10 daily fee/room. Service with restrictions, supervision.
Ⓢ Ⓢ Ⓧ Ⓗ ⬛ ⓣⓘ ⌘

ⒶⒶⒶ ▼▼▼ **Groveland Hotel** Ⓒ❙ ❀
(209) 962-4000. **$135-$155.** 18767 Main St. Center. Int corridors. **Pets:** Other species. $10 daily fee/pet. Service with restrictions, crate.
Ⓢ Ⓧ ⬛ ⓣⓘ

HANFORD

ⒶⒶⒶ ▼▼▼▼ **Sequoia Inn** Ⓜ
(559) 582-0338. **$61-$95.** 1655 Mall Dr. Exit SR 198 at 12th Ave, n to Mall Dr. Int corridors. **Pets:** Other species. $100 deposit/room. Service with restrictions, supervision.
Ⓢ Ⓢ Ⓧ Ⓗ ⬛ ⌘

HEMET

ⒶⒶⒶ ▼▼▼ **Best Western Inn of Hemet** Ⓜ
(909) 925-6605. **$64-$82.** 2625 W Florida Ave. 2.4 mi w of SR 79 N (San Jacinto St) on SR 74/79. Ext corridors. **Pets:** Small. $10 one-time fee/room. Service with restrictions, supervision.
Ⓢ Ⓢ Ⓧ Ⓗ ⬛ ⌘

ⒶⒶⒶ ▼▼ **Coach Light Motel** Ⓜ
(909) 658-3237. **$48-$55.** 1640 W Florida Ave. 1.7 mi w of SR 74 N (San Jacinto St) on SR 74/79. Ext corridors. **Pets:** Dogs only. $6 daily fee/pet. No service, supervision.
Ⓢ Ⓧ Ⓗ ⌘

▼▼ **Hemet Travelodge** Ⓜ
(909) 766-1902. **$48-$58.** 1201 W Florida Ave. 1.5 mi w of SR 79 N (San Jacino St), on SR 74/79. Ext corridors. **Pets:** Medium. $10 daily fee/pet. Service with restrictions, supervision.
ⒶⓈⓀ Ⓢ Ⓧ Ⓗ ⬛ ⌘

HESPERIA

ⒶⒶⒶ ▼▼▼ **Days Inn Suites** Ⓜ
(760) 948-0600. **$65-$75.** 14865 Bear Valley Rd. I-15, exit Bear Valley Rd, 0.5 mi e of Victor Valley Mall. Ext corridors. **Pets:** Accepted.
Ⓢ Ⓢ Ⓧ Ⓗ ⬛

IDYLLWILD

▼▼▼ **Fireside Inn** 🄲
(909) 659-2966. **$60-$125, 10 days notice.** 54540 N Circle Dr. From SR 243 and town center, 0.3 mi ne. Ext corridors. **Pets:** Small, dogs only. Designated rooms, service with restrictions, supervision.
⊠ 🛢 💻 🗷

IMPERIAL

🆑 ▼▼ **Best Western Imperial Valley Inn** 🄼 🐾
(760) 355-4500. **$63-$96.** 1093 Airport Blvd. On SR 86. Ext corridors. **Pets:** Other species. Service with restrictions.
🆂🆅 🆂🅾 ⊠ 🛢 💻 🍴 ⌚

INDEPENDENCE

🆑 ▼ **Ray's Den Motel** 🄼
(760) 878-2122. **$41-$63.** 405 N Edwards. On US 395. Ext corridors. **Pets:** $6 daily fee/room. Service with restrictions, supervision.
🆂🆅 🆂🅾 ⊠ 🛢 💻

INDIAN WELLS

▼▼▼ **Miramonte Resort** 🄷
(760) 341-2200. **$109-$899, 7 days notice.** 45000 Indian Wells Ln. I-10, exit Cook, 4.4 mi s, then 1.5 mi e. Ext/int corridors. **Pets:** Medium. $75 one-time fee/room. Designated rooms, service with restrictions, supervision.
🅰🆂🅺 🆂🅾 ⊠ 🛢 💻 🍴 ⌚

INDIO

🆑 ▼▼ **Best Western Date Tree Hotel** 🄼
(760) 347-3421. **$69-$139.** 81-909 Indio Blvd. I-10, exit Monroe St westbound, 0.5 mi s; exit Indio Blvd eastbound, 2.4 mi s. Int corridors. **Pets:** Accepted.
🆂🆅 🆂🅾 ⊠ 🛢 💻 ⌚

▼▼ **Holiday Inn Express** 🄼
(760) 342-6344. **$59-$109.** 84096 Indio Springs Pkwy. I-10, exit Golf Center Pkwy, 0.3 mi ne. Ext corridors. **Pets:** Accepted.
🅰🆂🅺 🆂🅾 ⊠ 🛢 ⌚

🆑 ▼▼ **Palm Shadow Inn** 🄼
(760) 347-3476. **$59-$144.** 80-761 Hwy 111. I-10, exit Jefferson Ave, 2.5 mi s, then 0.7 mi e. Ext corridors. **Pets:** Accepted.
🆂🆅 ⊠ 🛢 💻

🆑 ▼▼ **Quality Inn** 🄼
(760) 347-4044. **$64-$149.** 43-505 Monroe St. I-10, exit Monroe St, 0.5 mi s. Int corridors. **Pets:** Accepted.
🆂🆅 🆂🅾 ⊠ 🛢 💻 ⌚

▼▼ **Royal Plaza Inn** 🄼🄸
(760) 347-0911. **$55-$119, 3 days notice.** 82-347 Hwy 111. I-10, exit Monroe St, 1.8 mi s, then 0.4 mi e. Int corridors. **Pets:** Accepted.
🅰🆂🅺 ⊠ 🛢 🍴 ⌚

🆑 ▼ **Super 8 Motel** 🄼
(760) 342-0264. **$50-$79.** 81753 Hwy 111. I-10, exit Monroe St, 1.8 mi s, 0.5 mi w. Ext corridors. **Pets:** $25 deposit/pet, $5 daily fee/pet, $5 one-time fee/pet. Designated rooms, service with restrictions, crate.
🆂🆅 🆂🅾 ⊠ 🛢 ⌚

IRVINE

🆑 ▼▼▼ **Irvine Marriott Hotel** 🄷
(949) 553-0100. **$189-$239.** 18000 Von Karman Ave. I-405, exit Jamboree Rd, 0.3 mi s to Michelson Dr, 0.4 mi w, then just n. Int corridors. **Pets:** Small. $50 deposit/room. Service with restrictions, supervision.
🆂🆅 🆂🅾 ⊠ 🛢 💻 🍴 ⌚

🆑 ▼▼▼ **Residence Inn by Marriott-Irvine Spectrum** 🄰
(949) 380-3000. **$144-$169.** 10 Morgan. I-5, exit Alton Pkwy, 2 mi e. Ext corridors. **Pets:** Accepted.
🆂🆅 🆂🅾 ⊠ 🛢 💻 ⌚

JACKSON

🆑 ▼ **Amador Motel** 🄼 🐾
(209) 223-0970. **$47-$75, 3 days notice.** 12408 Kennedy Flat Rd. 1.5 mi n at jct SR 49 and 88 on Frontage Rd. Ext corridors. **Pets:** Large, dogs only. Service with restrictions, supervision.
🆂🆅 ⊠ 🛢 💻 ⌚

🆑 ▼▼ **Jackson Gold Lodge** 🄼
(209) 223-0486. **$50-$150.** 850 N SR 49. 0.5 mi w on SR 49 and 88. Ext corridors. **Pets:** Medium. $10 daily fee/pet. Service with restrictions, supervision.
🆂🆅 🆂🅾 ⊠ 💻 ⌚

JAMESTOWN

🆑 ▼▼▼ **1859 Historic National Hotel, A Country Inn** 🄲🄸 🐾
(209) 984-3446. **$110-$130, 3 days notice.** 18183 Main St. Downtown. Int corridors. **Pets:** Medium, other species. $10 daily fee/pet. Supervision.
🆂🆅 ⊠ 🍴

🆑 ▼ **Jamestown Railtown Motel** 🄼 🐾
(209) 984-3332. **$45-$75, 3 days notice.** 10301 Willow St. Just s of Main St. Ext corridors. **Pets:** Medium, dogs only. $5 one-time fee/pet. Crate.
🆂🆅 🆂🅾 ⊠ 🛢 ⌚

▼▼ **Sonora Quality Inn** 🄼
(209) 984-0315. **$64-$160.** 18730 Hwy 108. 1 mi e of Jamestown on SR 108 and 49. Ext corridors. **Pets:** Medium, dogs only. $10 daily fee/pet. Service with restrictions, supervision.
🆂🆅 🆂🅾 ⊠ 🛢 💻 ⌚

JULIAN

ⓐ ▽▽ Apple Tree Inn Ⓜ
(760) 765-0222. **$79-$99.** 4360 Hwy 78. 3 mi w of town. Ext corridors. **Pets:** $50 deposit/pet, $10 daily fee/pet. Service with restrictions, supervision.
⟦SAVE⟧ ⟦Sᴅ⟧ ⟦✕⟧ ⟦▣⟧ ⟦↝⟧

JUNE LAKE

ⓐ ▽▽▽ Double Eagle Resort/Spa, Inc Ⓒ
(760) 648-7004. **$216-$298, 14 days notice.** 5587 Hwy 158. On SR 158, 3 mi w of the village. Ext corridors. **Pets:** $200 deposit/room. Designated rooms, service with restrictions, supervision.
⟦SAVE⟧ ⟦Sᴅ⟧ ⟦✕⟧ ⟦⊟⟧ ⟦▣⟧ ⟦⊤⊤⟧ ⟦⊠⟧ ⟦Ⓚ⟧

▽ Gull Lake Lodge Ⓐ
(760) 648-7516. **$65-$103, 21 days notice.** 132 Leonard Ave. Just n of SR 158; via Knoll and Bruce sts. Ext corridors. **Pets:** Other species. $6 daily fee/room. Designated rooms, service with restrictions, supervision.
⟦✕⟧ ⟦⊟⟧ ⟦▣⟧ ⟦Ⓚ⟧ ⟦☎⟧

ⓐ ▽▽ June Lake Motel & Cabins Ⓜ
(760) 648-7547. **$66-$134, 14 days notice.** 2716 Boulder Dr. On SR 158, in center of village. Ext corridors. **Pets:** Accepted.
⟦SAVE⟧ ⟦✕⟧ ⟦⊟⟧ ⟦▣⟧ ⟦Ⓚ⟧

KERNVILLE

▽ Hi-Ho Resort Lodge Ⓜ
(760) 376-2671. **$55-$95, 5 days notice.** 11901 Sierra Hwy. 1.2 mi s of town. Ext corridors. **Pets:** $10 one-time fee/pet. Service with restrictions, supervision.
⟦ASK⟧ ⟦Sᴅ⟧ ⟦✕⟧ ⟦⊟⟧ ⟦▣⟧ ⟦↝⟧ ⟦☎⟧

ⓐ ▽ River View Lodge Ⓜ
(760) 376-6019. **$55-$89.** 2 Sirretta St. In center of town, on Kernville Rd, at the bridge. Ext corridors. **Pets:** Accepted.
⟦SAVE⟧ ⟦Sᴅ⟧ ⟦✕⟧ ⟦⊟⟧ ⟦Ⓚ⟧

KETTLEMAN CITY

ⓐ ▽▽ Best Western Inn Ⓜ 🐾
(559) 386-0804. **$60-$109.** 33410 Powers Dr. E of and adjacent to I-5, exit SR 41 N, 0.3 mi to Bernard, then 0.3 mi n. Ext corridors. **Pets:** Medium, other species. $4 daily fee/pet. Service with restrictions, supervision.
⟦SAVE⟧ ⟦Sᴅ⟧ ⟦✕⟧ ⟦⊟⟧ ⟦▣⟧ ⟦↝⟧

ⓐ ▽▽ Super 8 Ⓜ
(559) 386-9530. **$55-$79.** 33415 Powers Dr. 2 mi sw; 0.5 blk e off I-5, jct SR 41; exit Kettleman City-Paso Robles. Ext corridors. **Pets:** Accepted.
⟦SAVE⟧ ⟦Sᴅ⟧ ⟦✕⟧ ⟦▣⟧ ⟦↝⟧

KING CITY

ⓐ ▽▽ Courtesy Inn Ⓜ
(831) 385-4646. **$39-$119, 7 days notice.** 4 Broadway Cir. Just w of US 101; exit Broadway. Ext corridors. **Pets:** Accepted.
⟦SAVE⟧ ⟦Sᴅ⟧ ⟦✕⟧ ⟦⊾M⟧ ⟦▨⟧ ⟦◎⟧ ⟦⊟⟧ ⟦▣⟧ ⟦↝⟧

KINGSBURG

▽▽ Swedish Inn Ⓜ
(559) 897-1022. **$58-$62.** 401 Conejo St. Just w of SR 99, Conejo exit. Ext corridors. **Pets:** $50 deposit/room. Designated rooms, service with restrictions, supervision.
⟦ASK⟧ ⟦Sᴅ⟧ ⟦✕⟧ ⟦⊟⟧ ⟦▣⟧ ⟦↝⟧

KLAMATH

ⓐ ▽▽ Motel Trees Ⓜ
(707) 482-3152. **$46-$52.** 15495 Hwy 101 N. 4 mi n on US 101. Ext corridors. **Pets:** $20 daily fee/pet. Supervision.
⟦SAVE⟧ ⟦Sᴅ⟧ ⟦✕⟧ ⟦⊟⟧ ⟦▣⟧ ⟦Ⓚ⟧

KYBURZ

ⓐ ▽▽ Kyburz Resort Motel Ⓜ
(530) 293-3382. **$50-$75, 5 days notice.** 13666 Hwy 50. On US 50, halfway between Placerville and South Lake Tahoe. Ext corridors. **Pets:** Accepted.
⟦SAVE⟧ ⟦Sᴅ⟧ ⟦✕⟧ ⟦Ⓚ⟧

LAGUNA BEACH

▽▽▽ The Carriage House-Bed & Breakfast Ⓑ Ⓑ
(949) 494-8945. **$125-$165, 7 days notice.** 1322 Catalina St. From SR 133, 1 mi s on Pacific Coast Hwy to Cress St, then just e. Ext corridors. **Pets:** Medium. $10 daily fee/pet. Service with restrictions, supervision.
⟦✕⟧ ⟦⊟⟧ ⟦▣⟧ ⟦Ⓚ⟧ ⟦☎⟧

▽▽ Casa Laguna Inn Ⓑ Ⓑ 🐾
(949) 494-2996. **$120-$225, 5 days notice.** 2510 S Coast Hwy. From SR 133, 1.3 mi s. Ext corridors. **Pets:** Other species. $10 daily fee/pet. Service with restrictions, supervision.
⟦ASK⟧ ⟦Sᴅ⟧ ⟦✕⟧ ⟦⊟⟧ ⟦↝⟧

LAKE ARROWHEAD

ⓐ ▽▽▽ Arrowhead Saddleback Inn Ⓒ Ⓘ
(909) 336-3571. **$89-$192, 7 days notice.** On SR 173 at jct SR 189, across from entrance to Lake Arrowhead Village. Ext/int corridors. **Pets:** Other species. $8 daily fee/pet. Designated rooms, service with restrictions, supervision.
⟦SAVE⟧ ⟦Sᴅ⟧ ⟦✕⟧ ⟦⊟⟧ ⟦▣⟧ ⟦⊤⊤⟧

ⓐ ▽▽ Arrowhead Tree Top Lodge Ⓜ
(909) 337-2311. **$99-$241.** 27992 Rainbow Dr. 0.3 mi s of Lake Arrowhead Village on SR 173. Ext corridors. **Pets:** Accepted.
⟦SAVE⟧ ⟦Sᴅ⟧ ⟦✕⟧ ⟦⊟⟧ ⟦▣⟧ ⟦↝⟧ ⟦Ⓚ⟧ ⟦☎⟧

▽▽▽ Storybook Inn Ⓑ Ⓑ 🐾
(909) 337-0011. **$89-$179, 7 days notice.** 28717 SR 18. On SR 18, 1.1 mi e of jct 173. Ext/int corridors. **Pets:** Other species. Designated rooms.
⟦ASK⟧ ⟦Sᴅ⟧ ⟦✕⟧ ⟦Ⓚ⟧

LAKE TAHOE AREA

KINGS BEACH

AAA ▼▼ Stevenson's Holliday Inn **M**
(530) 546-2269. **$69-$129, 5 days notice.** 8742 N Lake Blvd. SR 28, 1 mi e of SR 267. Ext corridors. **Pets:** $10 one-time fee/room. No service, supervision.
SAVE ✕ ▯ ➥ ℀

SOUTH LAKE TAHOE

AAA ▼▼▼ Alder Inn **M** ❀
(530) 544-4485. **$58-$130, 15 days notice.** 1072 Ski Run Blvd. 2.5 blks s off US 50 on Ski Run Blvd; 0.8 mi below Heavenly Valley ski lift terminal. Ext corridors. **Pets:** $12 daily fee/pet. Service with restrictions, supervision.
SAVE ℁ ✕ ▯ ▭ ➥ ℀

AAA ▼▼▼ Alpenrose Inn **M**
(530) 544-2985. **$50-$130, 7 days notice.** 4074 Pine Blvd. 0.3 mi n of US 50 via Park Ave. Ext corridors. **Pets:** Medium. $50 deposit/pet, $10 daily fee/pet. Designated rooms, service with restrictions, crate.
SAVE ℁ ✕ ▯ ▭

AAA ▼▼ Blue Jay Lodge **M**
(530) 544-5232. **$54-$149.** 4133 Cedar Ave. 2 blks from casino center. Ext corridors. **Pets:** Accepted.
SAVE ℁ ✕ ℁M ♿ ▯ ▭ ➥

AAA ▼▼ Budget Inn **M**
(530) 544-2834. **$35-$195, 3 days notice.** 3496 Lake Tahoe Blvd. On US 50, 1.5 mi w of casino center. Ext corridors. **Pets:** Small, dogs only. $50 deposit/pet. Service with restrictions, supervision.
SAVE ✕ ▯ ➥

AAA ▼▼ Cal Va Rado Motel **M**
(530) 541-3900. **$49-$89.** 988 Stateline Ave. Just n of US 50; near casino center. Ext corridors. **Pets:** Medium, other species. Service with restrictions.
SAVE ℁ ✕ ▯ ℀

AAA ▼▼▼ Cedar Lodge **M**
(530) 544-6453. **$40-$95.** 4069 Cedar Ave. N off US 50, toward the lake; at Cedar and Friday aves; 3 blks from the casino center. Ext corridors. **Pets:** Small, dogs only. $40 deposit/room, $10 one-time fee/pet. Designated rooms, service with restrictions, supervision.
SAVE ✕ ▯ ▭ ➥

AAA ▼▼▼ Days Inn-Casino Area/South Lake Tahoe **M**
(530) 541-4800. **$49-$150, 3 days notice.** 968 Park Ave. 3 blks w of casino center, 1 blk n off US 50 toward lake at Park and Cedar aves. Int corridors. **Pets:** Medium. $25 deposit/pet, $8 daily fee/pet. Designated rooms, service with restrictions, supervision.
SAVE ℁ ✕ ▭ ➥

AAA ▼▼ High Country Lodge **M**
(530) 541-0508. **$35-$150.** 1227 Emerald Bay Rd. 0.5 mi n of airport; on US 50. Ext corridors. **Pets:** Accepted.
SAVE ℁ ✕ ▯ ▭ ℀

▼▼ Lampliter Inn **M**
(530) 544-2936. **Call for rates.** 4143 Cedar Ave. 2 blks n of US 50. Ext corridors. **Pets:** Accepted.
ASK ℁ ✕ ▯ ▭ ℀

AAA ▼▼ Ridgewood Inn **M**
(530) 541-8589. **$49-$84, 3 days notice.** 1341 Emerald Bay Rd. US 50, 0.5 mi n of airport. Ext corridors. **Pets:** Other species. $50 deposit/room, $10 daily fee/pet. Designated rooms, service with restrictions, supervision.
SAVE ✕ ▭ ℀

AAA ▼▼▼ Tahoe Keys Resort ☒
(530) 544-5397. **$113-$1100.** 599 Tahoe Keys Blvd. Exit US 50 at Tahoe Keys Blvd, 1 mi w. Ext corridors. **Pets:** $100 deposit/pet, $25 one-time fee/pet. Designated rooms, service with restrictions, supervision.
SAVE ℁ ✕ ▭ ➥ ✕ ℀

AAA ▼▼ Tahoe Sundowner Motel **M**
(530) 541-2282. **$35-$175, 7 days notice.** 1211 Emerald Bay Rd. On US 50, 0.5 mi n of airport. Ext corridors. **Pets:** Medium, dogs only. $50 deposit/pet, $5 daily fee/pet. Designated rooms, service with restrictions, supervision.
SAVE ℁ ✕ ℀

AAA ▼▼▼ Tahoe Valley Lodge **M**
(530) 541-0353. **$85-$225, 7 days notice.** 2241 Lake Tahoe Blvd. 0.5 mi e of jct US 50 and SR 89, at Tahoe Keys Blvd. Ext corridors. **Pets:** Small, dogs only. $10 daily fee/pet. Designated rooms, no service, supervision.
SAVE ℁ ✕ ▯ ▭ ➥

TRUCKEE

▼▼ Alpine Country Lodge **M**
(530) 587-3801. **Call for rates.** 12260 Deerfield Dr. I-80, exit Donner Pass Rd, just s. Ext corridors. **Pets:** $10 daily fee/pet. Designated rooms, service with restrictions, supervision.
✕ ▭ ℀

▼▼ The Inn at Truckee **M**
(530) 587-8888. **$80-$130.** 11506 Deerfield Dr. I-80, exit SR 89, just s. Int corridors. **Pets:** Accepted.
ASK ℁ ✕

❀ **END AREA** ❀

LANCASTER

Best Western Antelope Valley Inn Ⓜ️
(661) 948-4651. **$69-$91.** 44055 N Sierra Hwy. From SR 14, exit Ave K, 2.3 mi e. Ext/int corridors. **Pets:** Accepted.

Oxford Inn & Suites Ⓜ️
(661) 949-3423. **$89.** 1651 West Avenue K. From SR 14, exit Ave K, then just w. Int corridors. **Pets:** Other species. $15 one-time fee/room. Service with restrictions, supervision.

LATHROP

Days Inn Ⓜ️
(209) 982-1959. **$84.** 14750 S Harlan Rd. I-5, exit Lathrop Rd, exit Lathrop Rd. Int corridors. **Pets:** Accepted.

LEBEC

Best Rest Inn Ⓜ️
(661) 248-2700. **$90.** 51541 N Peace Valley Rd. I-5, exit Frazier Park, just w. Int corridors. **Pets:** Accepted.

LEE VINING

Murphey's Motel Ⓜ️
(760) 647-6316. **$48-$103.** On US 395, in town. Ext corridors. **Pets:** Medium. $5 one-time fee/room. Designated rooms, service with restrictions, supervision.

LEMOORE

Best Western Vineyard Inn Ⓜ️ 🐾
(559) 924-1261. **$71-$81.** 877 East D St. 0.8 mi nw of SR 198, exit Houston St eastbound; exit D St westbound. Ext corridors. **Pets:** Supervision.

LINDSAY

Super 8 Motel Ⓜ️
(559) 562-5188. **$59-$69.** 390 N Hwy 65. On SR 65. Ext corridors. **Pets:** Small. $10 one-time fee/room. Service with restrictions, supervision.

LIVERMORE

Hampton Inn Ⓜ️
(925) 606-6400. **$129.** 2850 Constitution Dr. I-580, exit Airway/Collier Canyon Rd N. Int corridors. **Pets:** Accepted.

Residence Inn By Marriott Ⓜ️
(925) 373-1800. **$152-$202.** 1000 Airway Blvd. I-580, exit Airway/Collier Canyon Rd, just n. Ext corridors. **Pets:** Accepted.

LOMPOC

Inn of Lompoc Ⓜ️ 🐾
(805) 735-7744. **$59-$129.** 1122 North H St. 1.2 mi n on SR 1. Ext/int corridors. **Pets:** $25 one-time fee/pet. Designated rooms, service with restrictions, supervision.

Quality Inn & Executive Suites Ⓜ️
(805) 735-8555. **$89-$109, 7 days notice.** 1621 North H St. 1.8 mi n on SR 1. Int corridors. **Pets:** Small, other species. $200 deposit/room, $25 one-time fee/pet. Designated rooms, service with restrictions, crate.

LONE PINE

Alabama Hills Inn Ⓜ️ 🐾
(760) 876-8700. **$68-$98.** 1920 S Main St. On US 395, 1.5 mi s of town. Int corridors. **Pets:** Other species. $10 one-time fee/room. Designated rooms, service with restrictions, supervision.

Best Western Frontier Motel Ⓜ️
(760) 876-5571. **$44-$103.** 1008 S Main St. On US 395, at south end of town. Ext corridors. **Pets:** Other species. Service with restrictions, supervision.

Dow Villa Motel Ⓜ️
(760) 876-5521. **$58-$90.** 310 S Main St. On US 395. Ext corridors. **Pets:** Other species. $50 deposit/room. Designated rooms, service with restrictions, supervision.

National 9 Trails Motel Ⓜ️
(760) 876-5555. **$45-$89, 3 days notice.** 633 S Main St. On US 395. Ext corridors. **Pets:** Medium, dogs only. $10 daily fee/pet. Designated rooms, service with restrictions, supervision.

LOS ANGELES METROPOLITAN AREA

ARCADIA

Residence Inn by Marriott A ❖
(626) 446-6500. **$99-$185.** 321 E Huntington Dr. I-210, exit Huntington Dr, 0.5 mi w. Ext corridors. **Pets:** Other species. $75 one-time fee/room. Service with restrictions, supervision.
[SAVE] [S] [X] [M] [] [] [] [] []

BEVERLY HILLS

Avalon Hotel M
(310) 277-5221. **Call for rates.** 9400 W Olympic Blvd. I-10, exit Robertson Blvd, 1.7 mi n, then 0.8 mi w. Ext/int corridors. **Pets:** Accepted.
[ASK] [S] [X] [] [] []

Beverly Hilton H
(310) 274-7777. **$189.** 9876 Wilshire Blvd. I-405, exit Wilshire Blvd, 2.2 mi e. Int corridors. **Pets:** Small, dogs only. Service with restrictions, supervision.
[SAVE] [X] [] [] []

Raffles L'Ermitage Beverly Hills H ❖
(310) 278-3344. **$418-$448.** 9291 Burton Way. I-10, exit Robertson Blvd, 3.1 mi n, then just w. Ext corridors. **Pets:** Small. $150 one-time fee/room. Designated rooms, service with restrictions, supervision.
[SAVE] [S] [X] [M] [] [] []

Regent Beverly Wilshire H ❖
(310) 275-5200. **$415-$555.** 9500 Wilshire Blvd Dr. I-405, exit Wilshire Blvd, 4.5 mi e. Int corridors. **Pets:** Small. $100 deposit/room. Service with restrictions, supervision.
[X] [M] [] [] [] []

BURBANK

The Anabelle MI
(818) 845-7800. **$129-$209.** 2011 W Olive Ave. I-5, exit Olive Ave, 1.3 mi sw. Int corridors. **Pets:** Other species. $100 deposit/pet. Service with restrictions, supervision.
[SAVE] [S] [X] [M] [] [] [] [] []

Burbank Airport Hilton & Convention Center H
(818) 843-6000. **$99-$206.** 2500 Hollywood Way. I-5, exit Hollywood Way, 1 mi s. Int corridors. **Pets:** Small, other species. $25 daily fee/pet. Designated rooms, service with restrictions, supervision.
[SAVE] [S] [X] [] [] [] []

Safari Inn MI
(818) 845-8586. **$95-$129.** 1911 W Olive Ave. I-5, exit Olive Ave, 1.3 mi sw. Ext corridors. **Pets:** Other species. $100 deposit/room. Service with restrictions, supervision.
[SAVE] [S] [X] [] [] [] [] []

CHATSWORTH

Ramada Inn M
(818) 998-5289. **$77-$89, 7 days notice.** 21340 Devonshire St. From SR 118, exit De Soto Ave, 1.5 mi s, then 0.5 mi w. Int corridors. **Pets:** Small. $10 daily fee/pet. Designated rooms, service with restrictions, supervision.
[ASK] [X] [] [] [] []

Summerfield Suites by Wyndham-Chatsworth M
(818) 773-0707. **$99-$159.** 21902 Lassen St. From SR 118, exit Topanga Canyon Blvd, 2 mi s, then just e. Ext corridors. **Pets:** Accepted.
[SAVE] [S] [X] [] [] []

CULVER CITY

Four Points by Sheraton Culver City H
(310) 641-7740. **$79-$119.** 5990 Green Valley Cir. I-405, exit Sepulveda Blvd, just n, then just e. Int corridors. **Pets:** Accepted.
[ASK] [S] [X] [] [] [] []

Radisson Hotel-LA Westside H
(310) 649-1776. **$99-$134, 14 days notice.** 6161 W Centinela Ave. I-405, exit Jefferson Blvd, just s, then just nw. Int corridors. **Pets:** Other species. $150 deposit/room, $50 one-time fee/room. Designated rooms, service with restrictions, crate.
[SAVE] [S] [X] [] [] [] []

DOWNEY

Embassy Suites Hotel H
(562) 861-1900. **$151-$171.** 8425 Firestone Blvd. I-605, exit Firestone Blvd, 2 mi w. Int corridors. **Pets:** Accepted.
[SAVE] [X] [] [] [] []

EL SEGUNDO

Embassy Suites-LAX South H
(310) 640-3600. **$119-$239.** 1440 E Imperial Ave. I-405, exit Imperial Hwy, 1.6 mi w. Int corridors. **Pets:** Medium. $30 daily fee/pet. Service with restrictions.
[SAVE] [S] [X] [] [] [] []

Homestead Studio Suites Hotel M
(310) 607-4000. **$74-$124.** 1910 E Mariposa Ave. I-105, exit Sepulveda Blvd, 1 mi s. Ext corridors. **Pets:** Other species. $75 one-time fee/pet. Service with restrictions, supervision.
[ASK] [S] [X] [] []

Summerfield Suites by Wyndham-El Segundo M
(310) 725-0100. **$89-$179.** 810 S Douglas St. I-405, exit Rosecrans Ave, 0.5 mi e, then just n. Ext/int corridors. **Pets:** Accepted.
[SAVE] [S] [X] [] []

GLENDALE

⬥⬥⬥ ▼▼▼ Vagabond Inn M
(818) 240-1700. **$89.** 120 W Colorado St. From SR 134, exit Brand Blvd, 1 mi s, then just w. Ext corridors. **Pets:** Other species. $10 daily fee/pet. Designated rooms, service with restrictions, supervision.
SAVE S⬥ ✕ 🛏 💻 ⇌

HAWTHORNE

⬥⬥⬥ ▼▼▼ TownePlace Suites by Marriott M
(310) 725-9696. **$59-$99.** 1440 Aviation Blvd. I-405, exit Rosecrans Ave, 0.4 mi w. Int corridors. **Pets:** Accepted.
SAVE ✕ 🛏 💻 ⇌

HOLLYWOOD

⬥⬥⬥ ▼▼▼ Best Western Hollywood Hills MI
(323) 464-5181. **$99-$159.** 6141 Franklin Ave. From US 101, exit Franklin Ave southbound, just e; northbound, just w. Ext/int corridors. **Pets:** Accepted.
SAVE S⬥ ✕ 🛏 💻 ❚❙ ⇌

LA MIRADA

⬥⬥⬥ ▼▼▼ Residence Inn by Marriott A
(714) 523-2800. **$119-$159.** 14419 Firestone Blvd. I-5, exit Valley View, just n, then 0.5 mi e. Ext corridors. **Pets:** Other species. $6 daily fee/pet, $75 one-time fee/pet. Service with restrictions.
SAVE S⬥ ✕ 🛏 💻 ⇌

LONG BEACH

⬥⬥⬥ ▼▼▼ Days Inn-City Center M
(562) 591-0088. **$80-$95, 30 days notice.** 1500 E Pacific Coast Hwy. I-710, exit SR 1(Pacific Coast Hwy), 2 mi e. Ext corridors. **Pets:** Small. $10 daily fee/pet. Designated rooms, service with restrictions, supervision.
SAVE S⬥ ✕ 🛏 💻

⬥⬥⬥ ▼▼▼ GuestHouse Hotel Long Beach MI
(562) 597-1341. **$75-$89.** 5325 E Pacific Coast Hwy. I-405 N, exit SR 22 (Long Beach), 2 mi nw; I-405 S, Lakewood Blvd exit, 2 mi se on SR 1. Ext corridors. **Pets:** Accepted.
SAVE S⬥ ✕ 🛏 💻 ❚❙ ⇌

⬥⬥⬥ ▼▼▼ Hilton Long Beach H
(562) 983-3400. **$124-$400.** Two World Trade Center. I-710, exit Broadway/Downtown, just e to Daisy Ave, just s to Ocean Blvd, then just w. Int corridors. **Pets:** Small. $100 deposit/room. Service with restrictions.
SAVE S⬥ ✕ 💻 ❚❙ ⇌

LOS ANGELES

⬥⬥⬥ ▼ Beverly Laurel Motor Hotel MI
(323) 651-2441. **$84-$94.** 8018 Beverly Blvd. I-10, exit Fairfax Ave, 2.8 mi n, then just w. Ext corridors. **Pets:** Medium. $50 deposit/room, $10 daily fee/pet. Service with restrictions, supervision.
SAVE S⬥ ✕ 🛏 ❚❙ ⇌

▼▼ ▼▼ Century Plaza Hotel & Spa H
(310) 277-2000. **$240.** 2025 Avenue of the Stars. I-10, exit Robertson Blvd, 2.7 mi n to Olympic Blvd, 1.9 mi w, then just w. Int corridors. **Pets:** Accepted.
ASK S⬥ ✕ ⬥M 🌀 🐾 💻 ❚❙ ⇌

▼▼▼ ▼▼ Four Points by Sheraton LAX H 🐾
(310) 645-4600. **$89-$99.** 9750 Airport Blvd. I-405, exit Century Blvd, 1.5 mi w, then just n. Ext/int corridors. **Pets:** Other species. $50 deposit/room. Supervision.
ASK S⬥ ✕ 🛏 💻 ❚❙ ⇌

⬥⬥⬥ ▼▼▼▼ Four Seasons Hotel H
(310) 273-2222. **$350-$460.** 300 S Doheny Dr. I-10, exit Robertson Blvd, 3 mi n to Burton Way, then just w. Int corridors. **Pets:** Accepted.
SAVE ✕ 💻 ❚❙ ⇌

▼▼▼ ▼▼ Furama Hotel Los Angeles H
(310) 670-8111. **$89-$139.** 8601 Lincoln at Manchester Blvd. I-405, exit La Tijera Blvd, 1.2 mi sw, then 1.6 mi w. Int corridors. **Pets:** $75 deposit/room, $10 daily fee/pet. Designated rooms, service with restrictions, supervision.
ASK S⬥ ✕ 🛏 💻 ❚❙ ⇌

⬥⬥⬥ ▼▼▼ Holiday Inn Brentwood/Bel-Air H
(310) 476-6411. **$169-$189.** 170 N Church Ln. I-405, exit Sunset Blvd, just w, then just n. Int corridors. **Pets:** Small. $100 deposit/room, $50 one-time fee/room. Service with restrictions, supervision.
SAVE S⬥ ✕ 🛏 💻 ❚❙ ⇌

⬥⬥⬥ ▼▼▼ Holiday Inn City Center H
(213) 748-1291. **$90-$170, 3 days notice.** 1020 S Figueroa St. From SR 110, exit Olympic southbound, just e; exit 9th St northbound, just e to Flower St, just s to 11 St, just w, then just n. Int corridors. **Pets:** Accepted.
SAVE S⬥ ✕ 🛏 💻 ❚❙ ⇌

⬥⬥⬥ ▼▼▼ Holiday Inn-Downtown H
(213) 628-9900. **$89-$99.** 750 Garland Ave. From SR 110, exit 8th St southbound, just w; exit 9th St northbound, just e to Figueroa St, just n, then just w. Int corridors. **Pets:** Accepted.
SAVE S⬥ ✕ 🛏 💻 ❚❙ ⇌

⬥⬥⬥ ▼▼▼▼ Hotel Sofitel H 🐾
(310) 278-5444. **$159-$219.** 8555 Beverly Blvd. I-10, exit La Cienega Blvd, 2.5 mi n. Int corridors. **Pets:** Other species. Service with restrictions, supervision.
SAVE S⬥ ✕ ❚❙ ⇌

▼▼ ▼▼ Kawada Hotel H
(213) 621-4455. **$109-$129.** 200 S Hill St. From SR 110, exit 2nd St southbound, 0.5 mi e; exit 3rd St northbound, just n on Figueroa St, then 0.5 mi e. Int corridors. **Pets:** Accepted.
ASK S⬥ ✕ 🛏 💻 ❚❙

▼▼▼ ▼ Le Meridien at Beverly Hills H
(310) 247-0400. **$220-$285.** 465 S La Cienega Blvd. I-10, exit La Cienega Blvd, 2.5 mi n. Ext corridors. **Pets:** Medium. $100 deposit/pet, $25 daily fee/pet. Service with restrictions.
ASK S⬥ ✕ ⬥M 🌀 🐾 💻 ❚❙ ⇌

▼▼▼ Los Angeles Airport Hilton & Towers **H**
(310) 410-4000. **$88-$208.** 5711 W Century Blvd. I-405, exit Century Blvd, 0.8 mi w. Int corridors. **Pets:** $15 daily fee/pet. Service with restrictions, supervision.
🈂 🏊 ✕ 🅿 💻 🍴

AAA ▼▼▼ Los Angeles Airport Marriott
Hotel **H** ❀
(310) 641-5700. **$119-$199.** 5855 W Century Blvd. I-405, exit Century Blvd, 1 mi w. Int corridors. **Pets:** Other species. Designated rooms, service with restrictions, supervision.
🈂 ✕ 🎣 🏌 🅿 🍴 ➥

▼▼▼ Luxe Summit Hotel Bel-Air **MI**
(310) 476-6571. **$155.** 11461 Sunset Blvd. I-405, exit Sunset Blvd, just w. Int corridors. **Pets:** Accepted.
ASK 🏊 ✕ 🅿 💻 🍴 ➥

AAA ▼▼▼ Quality Hotel-Los Angeles Airport **H**
(310) 645-2200. **$90-$161.** 5249 W Century Blvd. I-405, exit Century Blvd, just w. Int corridors. **Pets:** Accepted.
🈂 ✕ 🅿 💻 🍴

AAA ▼▼▼ Residence Inn by Marriott-Beverly
Hills **A**
(310) 277-4427. **$179-$189.** 1177 S Beverly Dr. I-10, exit Robertson Blvd, 1.6 mi n to Pico Blvd, then 0.6 mi w. Int corridors. **Pets:** Small. $10 daily fee/pet, $80 one-time fee/room. Service with restrictions, crate.
🈂 ✕ 🅿 💻

AAA ▼▼▼▼ Travelodge Hotel at Lax **MI** ❀
(310) 649-4000. **$64-$109.** 5547 W Century Blvd. I-405, exit Century Blvd, 0.5 mi w. Ext/int corridors. **Pets:** Other species. $10 daily fee/pet. Designated rooms, service with restrictions, supervision.
🈂 🏊 ✕ 🅿 💻 🍴 ➥

AAA ▼▼▼ Vagabond Inn **MI**
(213) 746-1531. **$89.** 3101 S Figueroa St. I-110, exit Adams Blvd, 0.5 mi s. Ext corridors. **Pets:** Accepted.
🈂 🏊 ✕ 🅿 💻 ➥

▼▼▼ The Westin Hotel-Los Angeles
Airport **H**
(310) 216-5858. **$109-$149.** 5400 W Century Blvd. I-405, exit Century Blvd, just w. Int corridors. **Pets:** Small, other species. Service with restrictions, supervision.
ASK 🏊 ✕ 💻 🍴 ➥

MALIBU

▼▼ Malibu Shores Motel **M**
(310) 456-6000. **Call for rates.** 23033 Pacific Coast Hwy. On SR 1. Ext corridors. **Pets:** Medium, dogs only. $100 deposit/pet.
ASK ✕ 🐾

MANHATTAN BEACH

AAA ▼▼▼ Barnabey's Hotel **H**
(310) 750-0300. **$99-$169, 3 days notice.** 3501 N Sepulveda Blvd. I-405, exit Rosecrans Ave, 1.5 mi w, then just s. Int corridors. **Pets:** Accepted.
🈂 🏊 ✕ 🅿 💻 🍴

AAA ▼▼▼ Residence Inn by Marriott **A**
(310) 546-7627. **$258-$298.** 1700 N Sepulveda Blvd. I-405, exit Rosecrans Ave, 1.5 mi w, then 1 mi s on SR 1. Ext corridors. **Pets:** Medium, other species. $8 daily fee/pet, $75 one-time fee/room. Service with restrictions.
🈂 🏊 ✕ 🅿 💻 ➥

MISSION HILLS

▼▼ Best Western Mission Hill Inn **M**
(818) 891-1771. **$80-$83.** 10621 Sepulveda Blvd. I-405, exit Devonshire St, just e, then just n; from SR 118 (Simi Valley Frwy), just s. Ext/int corridors. **Pets:** Small. $10 daily fee/pet. Designated rooms, supervision.
🈂 🏊 ✕ 🎣 🅿 💻 ➥

MONROVIA

▼▼▼ Holiday Inn **H**
(626) 357-1900. **$89-$179, 15 days notice.** 924 W Huntington Dr. I-210, exit Huntington Dr, just s. Int corridors. **Pets:** Accepted.
ASK 🏊 ✕ 🏧 🅿 💻 🍴 ➥

▼▼▼ Homestead Studio
Suites-Monrovia/Pasadena **M**
(626) 256-6999. **$94-$104.** 930 S Fifth Ave. I-210, exit Huntington Dr, just w, then just n. Int corridors. **Pets:** Accepted.
ASK 🏊 ✕ 🏧 🚹 🅿 💻

PASADENA

AAA ▼▼▼ Quality Inn Pasadena **M**
(626) 796-9291. **$69-$79.** 3321 E Colorado Blvd. I-210, exit Madre St, just s, then 0.3 mi e. Ext corridors. **Pets:** Medium, other species. $10 daily fee/pet. Designated rooms, service with restrictions, supervision.
🈂 ✕ 🅿 💻 ➥

AAA ▼▼▼ Vagabond Inn **M**
(626) 449-3170. **$60-$330.** 1203 E Colorado Blvd. I-210, exit Hill St, just s, then just w. Ext/int corridors. **Pets:** Accepted.
🈂 ✕ 🅿 💻 ➥

AAA ▼▼▼ Westway Inn **M**
(626) 304-9678. **$72-$950, 7 days notice.** 1599 E Colorado Blvd. I-210, exit Allen Ave westbound; exit Hill Ave eastbound, 0.8 mi s. Ext corridors. **Pets:** Medium. $10 daily fee/pet. Designated rooms, service with restrictions, crate.
🈂 ✕ 🅿 💻 ➥

PICO RIVERA

AAA ▼▼▼ Pico Rivera Travelodge **M**
(562) 949-6648. **$60-$70.** 7222 Rosemead Blvd. I-5, exit Rosemead Blvd, 1.6 mi n. Ext corridors. **Pets:** Accepted.
🈂 🏊 ✕ 🅿 ➥

POMONA

▼▼▼ Sheraton Suites Fairplex **H**
(909) 622-2220. **$199.** 601 W McKinley Ave. I-10, exit White Ave eastbound, 1 mi n, just w; exit Faiplex Dr westbound, 1 mi n, 0.7 mi e. Int corridors. **Pets:** Other species. $50 one-time fee/room. Crate.
ASK 🏊 ✕ 🅿 💻 🍴 ➥

▼▼ Shilo Hotel-Pomona **M** ✿
(909) 598-0073. **$69-$145.** 3200 Temple Ave. From SR 57,
just w. Int corridors. **Pets:** Other species. $10 daily fee/
room. Service with restrictions, supervision.

(ASK) (Sₒ) (✕) (▤) (▢) (▥) (➤)

SAN PEDRO

Vagabond Inn **M**
(310) 831-8911. **$58-$65.** 215 S Gaffey. I-110, exit Gaffey
St, just s from terminus. Ext corridors. **Pets:** Other species.
$8 daily fee/pet. Designated rooms, service with restrictions,
supervision.

(SAVE) (Sₒ) (✕) (▤) (▢) (➤)

SANTA MONICA

▼▼▼ The Fairmont Miramar Hotel Santa
Monica **H**
(310) 576-7777. **$242-$296.** 101 Wilshire Blvd. I-10, exit
Lincoln Blvd, 0.6 mi n, then 0.6 mi w. Ext/int corridors.
Pets: Accepted.

(ASK) (Sₒ) (✕) (▢) (▥) (➤)

▼▼▼ Le Merigot, A JW Marriott Beach Hotel
and Spa **H** ✿
(310) 395-9700. **$269-$1200.** 1740 Ocean Ave. I-10, exit
Lincoln Blvd, 0.3 mi s, 0.6 mi w on Pico Blvd, then just n.
Int corridors. **Pets:** Large, other species. $150 deposit/
room, $35 one-time fee/room. Service with restrictions.

(SAVE) (Sₒ) (✕) (▥) (➤)

▼▼▼ ▼▼ Loews Santa Monica Beach
Hotel **H** ✿
(310) 458-6700. **$310-$485.** 1700 Ocean Ave. I-10, exit
Lincoln Blvd, 0.3 mi s, 0.6 mi w on Pico Blvd, then just n.
Int corridors. **Pets:** Large, other species. $50 deposit/pet.
Supervision.

(✕) (ᕫM) (⊘) (ᕫ) (▥) (➤)

TARZANA

St. George Motor Inn **M**
(818) 345-6911. **$71-$79.** 19454 Ventura Blvd. From US
101, exit Tampa Ave, just s, then just w. Ext corridors.
Pets: Accepted.

(SAVE) (Sₒ) (✕) (▤) (➤)

TORRANCE

Residence Inn by Marriott **A**
(310) 543-4566. **$79-$169.** 3701 Torrance Blvd. I-405, exit
Hawthorne Blvd, 3.2 mi s, then just e. Ext corridors.
Pets: Accepted.

(SAVE) (Sₒ) (✕) (▤) (▢) (➤)

▼▼▼ Summerfield Suites by
Wyndham-Torrance **M**
(310) 371-8525. **$89-$159.** 19901 Prairie Ave. I-405, exit
Crenshaw Blvd, just s to 190th St, 1 mi w, then just s.
Ext/int corridors. **Pets:** Accepted.

(SAVE) (Sₒ) (✕) (▤) (▢) (➤)

WEST COVINA

Hampton Inn **M**
(626) 967-5800. **$89.** 3145 E Garvey Ave N. I-10, exit Bar-
ranca St, just n, then just e. Int corridors. **Pets:** Other
species.

(SAVE) (Sₒ) (✕) (ᕫM) (⊘) (▤) (▢) (➤)

WEST HOLLYWOOD

▼▼▼ Le Montrose Suite Hotel **H** ✿
(310) 855-1115. **$295-$575.** 900 Hammond St at Cynthia.
I-10, exit La Cienega Blvd, 2.6 mi n to San Vicente Blvd,
1.3 mi nw, then just w on Cynthia St. Int corridors.
Pets: Small. $100 one-time fee/room.

(ASK) (Sₒ) (✕) (▤) (▢) (▥) (➤) (✕)

▼▼▼ Le Parc Suite Hotel **M**
(310) 855-8888. **$165-$220.** 733 N West Knoll Dr. I-10, exit
La Cienega Blvd, 3.5 mi n, just w on Melrose Ave, then just
n. Int corridors. **Pets:** Other species. $75 one-time fee/
room.

(ASK) (Sₒ) (✕) (▤) (▢) (▥) (➤)

▼▼▼ Summerfield Suites by
Wyndham-West Hollywood **M**
(310) 657-7400. **$129-$149.** 1000 Westmount Dr. I-10, exit
La Cienega Blvd, 4 mi n to Santa Monica Blvd, just w, then
just n. Int corridors. **Pets:** Large. $10 daily fee/room, $150
one-time fee/pet. Service with restrictions, supervision.

(SAVE) (Sₒ) (✕) (▤) (▢) (➤)

WHITTIER

Vagabond Inn **M**
(562) 698-9701. **$68-$70.** 14125 E Whittier Blvd. I-605, exit
Whittier Blvd, 3.5 mi e. Ext corridors. **Pets:** Very small. $10
daily fee/pet. Designated rooms, service with restrictions,
crate.

(SAVE) (Sₒ) (✕) (▤) (▢) (➤)

WOODLAND HILLS

▼▼▼ Holiday Inn-Woodland Hills **M**
(818) 883-6110. **$129-$169.** 21101 Ventura Blvd. From US
101, exit DeSoto St, just s, then just w. Int corridors.
Pets: Medium. $25 one-time fee/room. Designated rooms,
service with restrictions.

(ASK) (Sₒ) (✕) (▤) (▢) (▥) (➤)

✿ **END METROPOLITAN AREA** ✿

LOS BANOS

Best Western John Jay Inn MI
(209) 827-0954. **$56-$111, 7 days notice.** 301 W Pacheco Blvd. On SR 152. Int corridors. **Pets:** Small, dogs only. Designated rooms, supervision.

Days Inn-Los Banos MI ✿
(209) 826-9690. **$49-$79.** 2169 E Pacheco Blvd. East end of town. Ext corridors. **Pets:** Small. $5 daily fee/pet, $5 one-time fee/pet. Designated rooms, service with restrictions, supervision.

Regency Inn MI
(209) 826-3871. **$52-$55.** 349 W Pacheco Blvd. On SR 152. Ext corridors. **Pets:** Medium. $20 deposit/pet, $4 daily fee/pet. Service with restrictions, supervision.

LOS GATOS

Los Gatos Lodge MI ✿
(408) 354-3300. **$130-$170.** 50 Los Gatos-Saratoga Rd. Just e of SR 17, E Los Gatos exit. Ext/int corridors. **Pets:** Medium. Service with restrictions, supervision.

LOS OLIVOS

Fess Parker's Wine Country Inn & Spa CI
(805) 688-7788. **$325-$500, 7 days notice.** 2860 Grand Ave. From SR 154, 0.5 mi s. Ext/int corridors. **Pets:** Accepted.

MADERA

Best Western Madera Valley Inn MI
(559) 664-0100. **$77-$89.** 317 North G St. Just e of SR 99, Central Madera exit. Int corridors. **Pets:** Medium, other species. $5 daily fee/pet, $20 one-time fee/room. Service with restrictions, supervision.

Liberty Inn MI ✿
(559) 675-8697. **$55-$65.** 22683 Ave 18 1/2. SR 99, exit Ave 18 1/2, just w. Int corridors. **Pets:** $25 deposit/pet, $5 daily fee/pet. Supervision.

Super 8 MI
(559) 661-1131. **$55-$65.** 1855 W Cleveland Ave. Just w of SR 99, exit Cleveland Ave. Ext corridors. **Pets:** $5 daily fee/pet. Service with restrictions, supervision.

MAMMOTH LAKES

Austria Hof Lodge LI
(760) 934-2764. **$69-$163, 15 days notice.** 924 Canyon Blvd. From Old Mammoth Rd, take SR 203 (Main St), 1 mi w, SR 203 (Minaret Rd), just n, then 1 mi w. Int corridors. **Pets:** Accepted.

Econo Lodge Wildwood Inn MI
(760) 934-6855. **$59-$129, 7 days notice.** 3626 Main St. On SR 203, 0.7 mi w of Old Mammoth Rd. Ext corridors. **Pets:** Large. $10 daily fee/pet. Service with restrictions, supervision.

Executive Inn MI
(760) 934-8892. **$59-$129, 5 days notice.** 54 Sierra Blvd. Just n of SR 203 (Main St), 0.6 mi w of Old Mammoth Rd. Int corridors. **Pets:** Accepted.

Shilo Inn MI ✿
(760) 934-4500. **$112-$155.** 2963 Main St. On SR 203, just e of Old Mammoth Rd. Int corridors. **Pets:** Other species. $10 daily fee/pet. Service with restrictions, supervision.

Sierra Lodge MI
(760) 934-8881. **$75-$159, 3 days notice.** 3540 Main St. On SR 203, 0.6 mi w of Old Mammoth Rd. Int corridors. **Pets:** Other species. $100 deposit/pet, $10 daily fee/pet. Designated rooms.

Sierra Nevada Rodeway Inn MI
(760) 934-2515. **$169, 7 days notice.** 164 Old Mammoth Rd. Just s of SR 203. Ext/int corridors. **Pets:** Large. $25 one-time fee/pet. Designated rooms, service with restrictions, crate.

MANTECA

Best Western Inn & Suites MI
(209) 825-1415. **$74-$84, 7 days notice.** 1415 E Yosemite Ave. At jct of SR 99 and 120, exit Yosemite Ave. Ext corridors. **Pets:** Accepted.

MARIPOSA

Best Value Mariposa Lodge MI
(209) 966-3607. **$49-$85.** 5052 Hwy 140. Center. Ext corridors. **Pets:** Medium. $10 daily fee/pet. Supervision.

Best Western Yosemite Way Station MI
(209) 966-7545. **$44-$99.** 4999 Hwy 140. SR 140 at SR 49S. Ext corridors. **Pets:** Medium, other species. $5 daily fee/room. Supervision.

Miners Inn MI
(209) 742-7777. **$55-$75.** 5181 Hwy 49 N. SR 49, n at SR 140. Ext/int corridors. **Pets:** Other species. $5 daily fee/pet. Service with restrictions, supervision.

MARYSVILLE

AAA ◆◆◆◆ **Amerihost Inn-Marysville** **M**
(530) 742-2700. **$69-$99, 7 days notice.** 1111 N Beale Rd.
0.5 mi s on SR 70, exit at N Beale Rd (Yuba College). Int
corridors. **Pets:** Accepted.
[SAVE] [S❄] [✕] [ሬM] [⚒] [🅗] [🖵] [⊇]

MERCED

AAA ◆◆◆◆ **Best Western Sequoia Inn** **M**
(209) 723-3711. **$74-$89, 10 days notice.** 1213 V St. SR
99, exit Gustine-Sonora, just w. Ext corridors. **Pets:** $10
daily fee/pet. Service with restrictions, supervision.
[SAVE] [S❄] [✕] [🅗] [🖵] [⊇]

AAA ◆◆◆ **Days Inn** **M**
(209) 722-2726. **$58-$98.** 1199 Motel Dr. SR 99, exit Childs
Ave or SR 140, just e. Ext corridors. **Pets:** Accepted.
[SAVE] [S❄] [✕] [🅗] [🖵] [⊇]

AAA ◆◆◆ **Merced-Yosemite Travelodge** **M**
(209) 722-6224. **$55-$85.** 1260 Yosemite Pkwy. SR 99, exit
SR 140, just e. Ext corridors. **Pets:** Medium. $25 deposit/
pet, $10 daily fee/pet. No service, supervision.
[SAVE] [S❄] [✕] [ሬM] [⚒] [🅗] [🖵] [⊇]

MI WUK VILLAGE

AAA ◆◆◆ **Mi-Wuk Village Inn & Resort** **M** 🐾
(209) 586-3031. **$69-$135, 7 days notice.** 24680 SR 108.
15 mi e of Sonora; on SR 108. Ext corridors. **Pets:** Other
species. $10 daily fee/pet. Designated rooms, service with
restrictions, supervision.
[SAVE] [S❄] [✕] [🖵] [⊇]

MILPITAS

AAA ◆◆◆ **Best Western Brookside Inn** **M**
(408) 263-5566. **$89-$189.** 400 Valley Way. I-880, exit Calaveras Blvd/SR 237 (N Abbott Ave), just e. Int corridors.
Pets: Large. $15 one-time fee/pet. Service with restrictions,
supervision.
[SAVE] [S❄] [✕] [⚒] [🅗] [🖵] [⊇]

◆◆◆ **Candlewood Suites-Milpitas/Silicon**
Valley **M**
(408) 719-1212. **$79-$169.** 40 Ranch Dr. Northeast quad-
rant I-880 and SR 237, exit SR 237 (McCarthy Ranch Rd).
Int corridors. **Pets:** Large, other species. $10 daily fee/pet,
$75 one-time fee/room. Service with restrictions.
[ASK] [S❄] [✕] [ሬM] [⚒] [🖵]

AAA ◆◆◆ **Inns of America** **M**
(408) 946-8889. **$119-$149.** 270 S Abbott Ave. I-880, exit
Calaveras Blvd. Ext corridors. **Pets:** Accepted.
[SAVE] [S❄] [✕] [🅗] [🖵] [⊇]

AAA ◆◆◆◆ **Residence Inn By Marriott** **M**
(408) 941-9222. **$289-$319.** 1501 California Cr. I-880, exit
Dixon Landing Rd E, just s. Int corridors. **Pets:** Other species. $10 daily fee/pet, $75 one-time fee/pet.
[SAVE] [S❄] [✕] [⚒] [⊇]

MIRANDA

AAA ◆◆◆◆ **Miranda Gardens Resort** **C**
(707) 943-3011. **$230, 7 days notice.** 6766 Avenue of the
Giants. US 101, exit Avenue of the Giants e.
Pets: Accepted.
[SAVE] [S❄] [🅗] [🖵] [⊇] [🐾] [✉]

MODESTO

AAA ◆◆◆ **Best Western Town House Lodge** **M**
(209) 524-7261. **$72-$79, 7 days notice.** 909 16th St. Frwy
99, 1 mi e, exit via Central Modesto at I St. Ext corridors.
Pets: Other species. $25 deposit/room. Designated rooms,
service with restrictions, supervision.
[SAVE] [S❄] [✕] [🅗] [🖵] [⊇]

◆◆◆ **DoubleTree** **H**
(209) 526-6000. **$79-$169.** 1150 9th St. SR 99 northbound
exit central Modesto; southbound exit Maze Blvd. Int corridors. **Pets:** Large. $20 one-time fee/pet. Designated rooms,
service with restrictions, supervision.
[SAVE] [S❄] [✕] [🍴] [🅗] [🖵] [🍽] [⊇]

AAA ◆◆◆ **Howard Johnson Express Inn** **M**
(209) 537-4821. **$65-$90.** 1672 Herndon Rd. SR 99, exit
Hatch Rd, s on Herndon. Ext corridors. **Pets:** Small, other
species. $50 deposit/pet. Designated rooms, service with
restrictions, supervision.
[SAVE] [S❄] [✕] [🅗] [🖵] [⊇]

AAA ◆◆◆ **Travelodge** **M**
(209) 524-3251. **$75.** 722 Kansas Ave. Exit SR 99 (Kansas
Ave), w. Ext corridors. **Pets:** Accepted.
[SAVE] [S❄] [✕] [🖵] [⊇]

AAA ◆◆◆ **Vagabond Inn** **M**
(209) 521-6340. **$57-$75, 7 days notice.** 1525 McHenry
Ave. 2 mi n on SR 108; from SR 99, exit Briggsmore Ave;
2.3 mi e to McHenry Ave, then just s. Ext corridors.
Pets: Accepted.
[SAVE] [S❄] [✕] [🅗] [🖵] [⊇]

◆◆◆ **Vagabond Inns** **M**
(209) 577-8008. **$56-$61.** 2025 W Orangeburg Ave. SR 99,
exit Briggsmore Ave. Int corridors. **Pets:** Accepted.
[ASK] [S❄] [✕] [🅗] [⊇]

MOJAVE

AAA ◆◆ **Desert Inn** **M**
(661) 824-2518. **$45-$49.** 1954 Hwy 58. Just e of jct SR
14. Ext corridors. **Pets:** Service with restrictions, crate.
[SAVE] [S❄] [✕] [🅗]

AAA ◆◆ **Econo Lodge** **M** 🐾
(661) 824-2463. **$39-$69.** 2145 Hwy 58. Just e of SR 14.
Ext corridors. **Pets:** Other species. $5 daily fee/pet. Service
with restrictions, supervision.
[SAVE] [S❄] [✕] [🅗] [🖵] [⊇]

AAA ◆◆◆ **Scottish Inns** **M**
(661) 824-9317. **$55-$65.** 16352 Sierra Hwy. On SR 14 and
58. Ext corridors. **Pets:** Other species. $5 daily fee/pet.
Service with restrictions, supervision.
[SAVE] [✕] [🅗] [⊇]

MONTEREY PENINSULA AREA

CARMEL VALLEY

AAA ▼▼▼▼ **Carmel Valley Lodge X ❀**
(831) 659-2261. **$139-$199, 7 days notice.** 8 Ford Rd. 11.5 mi e of SR 1; Carmel Valley Rd, at Ford Rd. Ext corridors. **Pets:** Dogs only. $10 daily fee/pet. Supervision.
[SAVE] [S₆] [✕] [🚭] [🔒] [💻] [🛌] [ĸ]

AAA ▼▼▼ **Los Laureles Lodge MI**
(831) 659-2233. **$90-$595, 3 days notice.** 313 W Carmel Valley Rd. 10.5 mi e of SR 1. Ext corridors. **Pets:** Accepted.
[SAVE] [S₆] [✕] [🔒] [💻] [🍴] [🛌] [ĸ]

CARMEL BY THE SEA

AAA ▼▼▼▼ **Best Western Carmel Mission Inn MI ❀**
(831) 624-1841. **$89-$349.** 3665 Rio Rd. 1 mi s on SR 1, at Rio Rd. Ext/int corridors. **Pets:** Medium. $35 one-time fee/pet. Designated rooms, supervision.
[SAVE] [S₆] [✕] [🔒] [💻] [🍴] [🛌]

▼▼▼▼ **Carmel Country Inn BB ❀**
(831) 625-3263. **$125-$245, 7 days notice.** 4 blks n of Ocean Ave at Dolores and 3rd Ave. Ext corridors. **Pets:** $20 daily fee/pet. Designated rooms, service with restrictions, supervision.
[🔒] [💻] [ĸ]

AAA ▼▼▼▼ **Carmel Garden Court BB**
(831) 624-6926. **$170-$245, 7 days notice.** 3 blks n off Ocean Ave, at 4th Ave and Torres St. Ext corridors. **Pets:** Medium. $50 one-time fee/room. Designated rooms, service with restrictions, supervision.
[SAVE] [🔒] [💻] [ĸ]

AAA ▼▼▼ **Carmel River Inn X**
(831) 624-1575. **$75-$215, 3 days notice.** 1 mi s on SR 1, n of Carmel River Bridge at Oliver Rd. Ext corridors. **Pets:** Other species. $25 daily fee/pet. Designated rooms, service with restrictions, supervision.
[SAVE] [S₆] [✕] [🔒] [💻] [🛌] [ĸ]

▼▼▼▼ **Carmel Tradewinds Inn MI**
(831) 624-2776. **$99-$295, 3 days notice.** 4 blks n off Ocean Ave; at Mission St and 3rd Ave. Ext corridors. **Pets:** Medium. $25 daily fee/pet. Designated rooms, service with restrictions, supervision.
[🔒] [💻] [🛌] [ĸ]

AAA ▼▼▼▼ **Coachman's Inn MI**
(831) 624-6421. **$135-$350, 3 days notice.** Just s of Ocean Ave, San Carlos St between 7th and 8th aves. Ext corridors. **Pets:** Medium, dogs only. $15 daily fee/pet. Designated rooms, service with restrictions, supervision.
[SAVE] [S₆] [✕] [🅼] [🔒] [💻] [ĸ]

▼▼▼▼ **Cypress Inn H ❀**
(831) 624-3871. **$125-$395, 3 days notice.** Just s off Ocean Ave at Lincoln St and 7th Ave. Ext/int corridors. **Pets:** $20 daily fee/pet. Service with restrictions, supervision.
[✕] [ĸ]

AAA ▼▼▼ ▼▼▼ **Quail Lodge Resort & Golf Club R**
(831) 624-2888. **$220-$685, 3 days notice.** 8205 Valley Greens Dr. 3.5 mi e of SR 1; via Carmel Valley Rd. Ext corridors. **Pets:** Accepted.
[SAVE] [✕] [🚭] [🦽] [💻] [🍴] [🛌] [✕] [ĸ]

AAA ▼▼▼▼ **Sunset House BB ❀**
(831) 624-4884. **$210-$230.** Just s off Ocean on Camino Real. Ext/int corridors. **Pets:** Large, dogs only. $20 daily fee/pet. Crate.
[SAVE] [S₆] [✕] [🔒] [ĸ]

AAA ▼▼▼▼ **Wayside Inn MI ❀**
(831) 624-5336. **$119-$299, 7 days notice.** 1 blk s off Ocean Ave, at Mission St and 7th Ave. Ext corridors. **Pets:** Other species. Designated rooms, service with restrictions, supervision.
[SAVE] [S₆] [✕] [🔒] [💻] [ĸ]

MONTEREY

AAA ▼▼▼▼ **Bay Park Hotel MI ❀**
(831) 649-1020. **$169-$229.** 1425 Munras Ave. SR 1, exit Munras Ave, just w. Int corridors. **Pets:** Other species. $15 daily fee/pet. Designated rooms, service with restrictions, supervision.
[SAVE] [S₆] [✕] [🅼] [🚭] [🦽] [🔒] [💻] [🍴] [🛌]

AAA ▼▼▼▼ **The Beach Resort-Best Western MI ❀**
(831) 394-3321. **$119-$319, 3 days notice.** 2600 Sand Dunes Dr. SR 1, exit Del Rey Oaks, just w. Ext corridors. **Pets:** Large, other species. $25 daily fee/room. Designated rooms, service with restrictions, crate.
[SAVE] [S₆] [✕] [🔒] [💻] [🍴] [🛌]

AAA ▼▼▼▼ **Best Western Victorian Inn MI ❀**
(831) 373-8000. **$139-$419.** 487 Foam St. SR 1, exit Monterey, 3.4 mi w. Ext/int corridors. **Pets:** $100 deposit/room, $25 one-time fee/room. Designated rooms.
[SAVE] [S₆] [✕] [🅼] [🚭] [🦽] [🔒] [💻] [ĸ]

AAA ▼▼▼ **El Adobe Inn MI**
(831) 372-5409. **$45-$195, 3 days notice.** 936 Munras Ave. SR 1, exit Munras Ave, 0.6 mi w. Ext corridors. **Pets:** Accepted.
[SAVE] [✕] [🚭] [🔒] [💻] [ĸ]

Hyatt Regency-Monterey Resort & Conference Center X ❀
(831) 372-1234. **$134-$250.** 1 Old Golf Course Rd. SR 1, exit Aguajito Rd northbound; exit Monterey southbound, just e. Int corridors. **Pets:** Other species. $50 one-time fee/room. Designated rooms, service with restrictions.
SAVE ✕ &M 🐾 🐾 🖬 🖵 🍴 🍴 ✕ 🐾

Monterey Bay Lodge M ❀
(831) 372-8057. **$59-$250.** 55 Camino Aguajito. SR 1, exit Aguajito Rd, just w. Ext corridors. **Pets:** Medium. $10 daily fee/pet. Service with restrictions, supervision.
SAVE S6 ✕ 🖬 🖵 🍴 ➳

Monterey Fireside Lodge M
(831) 373-4172. **$70-$320, 3 days notice.** 1131 10th St. SR 1, exit Aguajito Rd or Monterey, just w. Ext corridors. **Pets:** Large, other species. $20 daily fee/pet. Service with restrictions, supervision.
SAVE ✕ 🖬 🐾

PEBBLE BEACH

The Lodge at Pebble Beach X ❀
(831) 624-3811. **$475-$800, 10 days notice.** Seventeen Mile Dr. Off SR 1, on 17 Mile Dr. Ext/int corridors. **Pets:** Medium, dogs only. $75 one-time fee/room. Service with restrictions, supervision.
✕ &M 🐾 🐾 🖬 🖵 🍴 ➳ ✕ 🐾

❀ **End Area** ❀

MORGAN HILL

Best Western Country Inn M ❀
(408) 779-0447. **$109-$129.** 16525 Condit Rd. US 101, exit Tennant Ave or E Dunne Ave, just e. Int corridors. **Pets:** Other species. $10 one-time fee/pet. Supervision.
SAVE S6 ✕ 🖬 🖵 ➳

MORRO BAY

Best Western El Rancho MI
(805) 772-2212. **$49-$129.** 2460 Main St. From SR 1, exit SR 41 northbound; exit San Jacinto St southbound, e on east side. Ext corridors. **Pets:** Other species. $10 one-time fee/pet. Service with restrictions, supervision.
SAVE S6 ✕ 🖬 🖵 🍴 ➳ 🐾

Days Inn M
(805) 772-2711. **$69-$155, 3 days notice.** 1095 Main St. From SR 1, 0.4 mi southbound; exit Morro Bay Blvd northbound, 0.7 mi w, then just n. Ext corridors. **Pets:** Medium, dogs only. $10 daily fee/pet. Designated rooms, service with restrictions.
SAVE S6 ✕ 🖬 🖵 🐾

Sundown Motel M
(805) 772-7381. **$36-$129.** 640 Main St. From SR 1, exit Main St southbound, 0.6 mi s; exit Morro Bay Blvd northbound, 0.7 mi w, then just s. Ext corridors. **Pets:** Accepted.
SAVE ✕ 🖬 🖵 🐾

Villager Motel M
(805) 772-1235. **$50-$150, 3 days notice.** 1098 Main St. From SR 1 southbound, 0.4 mi s; exit Morro Bay Blvd northbound, 0.7 mi w, then just n. Ext corridors. **Pets:** Small, dogs only. $20 one-time fee/pet. Designated rooms, service with restrictions, supervision.
SAVE S6 ✕ 🖬 🖵 🐾

MOUNT SHASTA

A-1 Choice Inn M
(530) 926-4811. **$49-$79, 3 days notice.** 1340 S Mt Shasta Blvd. I-5, exit McCloud/SR 89, just n at first left then 1 mi. Ext corridors. **Pets:** Very small, other species. $6 daily fee/pet. Designated rooms, service with restrictions, supervision.
SAVE S6 ✕ 🖬 🖵 ➳

Best Western Tree House Motor Inn MI
(530) 926-3101. **$90-$114.** 111 Morgan Way. I-5, E off and adjacent to I-5, exit Central Mt Shasta, 2nd exit. Ext/int corridors. **Pets:** Accepted.
SAVE S6 ✕ 🐾 🖬 🖵 🍴 ➳

Econo Lodge M
(530) 926-3145. **$45-$89, 3 days notice.** 908 S Mt Shasta Blvd. I-5, exit Central, 0.5 mi e, then 0.5 mi s. Ext corridors. **Pets:** Accepted.
SAVE S6 ✕ 🖬 🖵 ➳

Evergreen Lodge M
(530) 926-2143. **$49-$79, 3 days notice.** 1312 S Mount Shasta Blvd. I-5, exit McCloud/SR 89, just n at first left then 1 mi. Ext corridors. **Pets:** $6 daily fee/pet. Service with restrictions, supervision.
SAVE S6 ✕ 🖬 ➳

Mountain Air Lodge M ❀
(530) 926-3411. **$49-$89.** 1121 S Mount Shasta Blvd. I-5, exit Central, 0.5 mi e, then 0.5 mi s. Ext corridors. **Pets:** Medium, other species. $10 daily fee/pet. Designated rooms, service with restrictions, supervision.
SAVE S6 ✕ 🖬

Swiss Holiday Lodge M
(530) 926-3446. **$40-$60.** 2400 S Mt. Shasta Blvd. I-5, exit McCloud/SR 89, just n at first left. Ext corridors. **Pets:** Small, other species. $5 daily fee/pet. Designated rooms, service with restrictions, supervision.
SAVE S6 ✕ 🖬 ➳

MOUNTAIN VIEW

▼▼▼▼ Homestead Studio Suites-Mountain View/
Silicon Valley **M**
(650) 962-1500. **$124-$144.** 190 E El Camino Real. On SR
82, just w of SR 85. Int corridors. **Pets:** Small, other species. $150 one-time fee/pet. Service with restrictions.

ASK S⬤ ✕ 🅼 📧 💻

⚠ ▼▼▼▼ Tropicana Lodge **M** ❀
(650) 961-0220. **$100-$120.** 1720 El Camino Real W. US
101, exit Shoreline Blvd, 2 mi to SR 82, just n. Ext/int
corridors. **Pets:** Other species. Designated rooms, service
with restrictions, supervision.

SAVE S⬤ ✕ 📧 💻 ≈

NEEDLES

⚠ ▼▼◆▼ Best Western Colorado River
Inn **M**
(760) 326-4552. **$50-$75, 14 days notice.** 2371 W Broadway. I-40, exit W Broadway/River Rd, 0.3 mi e; on Business
Loop I-40. Ext corridors. **Pets:** Accepted.

SAVE S⬤ ✕ 📧 💻 ≈

⚠ ▼▼◆▼ Best Western Royal Inn **M**
(760) 326-5660. **$55-$75, 14 days notice.** 1111 Pashard
St. I-40, exit J St, just e to Broadway, 0.5 mi n via North St
to Bush St, just w to South St, then just n. Ext corridors.
Pets: Accepted.

SAVE S⬤ ✕ 📧 ≈

▼▼◆▼ Days Inn & Suites **M**
(760) 326-5836. **$45-$75, 7 days notice.** 1215 Hospitality
Ln. I-40, exit J St, just se. Ext corridors. **Pets:** Accepted.

SAVE S⬤ ✕ 📧 ≈

⚠ ▼ Imperial 400 Motor Inn **M**
(760) 326-2145. **$35-$49, 3 days notice.** 644 W Broadway.
I-40, exit J St eastbound; exit E Broadway westbound; on
Business Loop I-40. Ext corridors. **Pets:** Very small. No
service, crate.

SAVE ✕ 📧 ≈

⚠ ▼ River Valley Motor Lodge **M**
(760) 326-3839. **$31-$40.** 1707 Needles Hwy. I-40, exit J St
westbound; exit W Broadway eastbound, 1 mi nw; on I-40
business loop. Ext corridors. **Pets:** Medium. Designated
rooms, service with restrictions, supervision.

SAVE S⬤ ✕ 📧 ≈

▼▼ Super 8 Motel of Needles **M**
(760) 326-4501. **$48-$65.** 1102 E Broadway. I-40, exit US
95 (E Broadway), just sw. Ext corridors. **Pets:** Accepted.

ASK S⬤ ✕ 📧 ≈

NEWARK

▼▼▼▼ Hawthorn Suites-Newark **M**
(510) 791-7700. **$139-$199.** 39270 Cedar Blvd. I-880, exit
Mowry, w to Cedar, 0.3 mi s. Int corridors. **Pets:** Accepted.

ASK S⬤ ✕ 📧 📧 💻 ≈

NEWBURY PARK

⚠ ▼ Premier Inns **M**
(805) 499-0755. **$45-$85.** 2434 W Hillcrest Dr. From US
101, exit Borchard Rd just e, then just s. Ext corridors.
Pets: Medium, other species. Service with restrictions,
supervision.

SAVE S⬤ ✕ 📧 ≈

NEWPORT BEACH

⚠ ▼▼◆▼▼ Four Seasons Hotel Newport
Beach **H** ❀
(949) 759-0808. **$345-$400.** 690 Newport Center Dr. From
SR 73, exit MacArthur Blvd northbound, 3 mi s to San
Joaquin Hills Rd, then 0.5 mi w; exit Jamboree Rd southbound, 2.5 mi s to San Joaquin Hills Rd, then 0.5 mi e. Int
corridors. **Pets:** Very small. Service with restrictions.

SAVE ✕ 🍴 ≈ ✕⃠

⚠ ▼◆▼ Hyatt Newporter **H**
(949) 729-1234. **$164-$220.** 1107 Jamboree Rd. From SR
73, exit Jamboree Rd, 3 mi s. Ext/int corridors.
Pets: Accepted.

SAVE ✕ 📧 💻 🍴 ≈ ✕⃠

⚠ ▼◆▼ Newport Beach Marriott Hotel &
Tennis Club **H**
(949) 640-4000. **$169-$209.** 900 Newport Center Dr. From
SR 73, exit Jamboree Rd, 2.5 mi s to Santa Barbara Dr,
then 0.5 mi e. Ext/int corridors. **Pets:** Accepted.

SAVE S⬤ ✕ 📧 💻 🍴 ≈

NOVATO

⚠ ▼▼ Inn Marin **M**
(415) 883-5952. **$94-$134.** 250 Entrada Dr. Just w of US
101 at Ignacio Blvd exit, then just n on Enfrente Rd. Ext
corridors. **Pets:** Other species. $40 daily fee/pet, $20 one-
time fee/pet. Service with restrictions, crate.

SAVE S⬤ ✕ 🅼 📧 ≈

⚠ ▼ Novato Travelodge **M**
(415) 892-7500. **$69-$99.** 7600 Redwood Blvd. US 101,
exit San Marin Dr, just w. Ext corridors. **Pets:** Small. $10
daily fee/pet. Designated rooms, service with restrictions,
supervision.

SAVE S⬤ ✕ 📧 💻 ≈

OAKHURST

⚠ ▼▼◆▼ Best Western Yosemite Gateway
Inn **MI**
(559) 683-2378. **$49-$99.** 40530 Hwy 41. 0.8 mi n of jct SR
49. Ext corridors. **Pets:** Medium, dogs only. Service with
restrictions, supervision.

SAVE S⬤ ✕ 🅼 🏊 🅿 📧 💻 ≈

⚠ ▼▼ Comfort Inn-Oakhurst **M**
(559) 683-8282. **$59-$99.** 40489 Hwy 41. 0.5 mi n of jct SR
49. Ext corridors. **Pets:** Accepted.

SAVE ✕ 🏊 📧 💻 ≈

OAKLAND

▼▼▼▼ Clarion Suites Lake Merritt Hotel H
(510) 832-2300. **$199-$359.** 1800 Madison St. I-880, exit Broadway, 0.8 mi e to 17th St, then just s. Int corridors. **Pets:** Large. $75 deposit/room, $75 one-time fee/room. Designated rooms, service with restrictions, supervision.

SAVE Sᴅ ✕ 🖥 💻 ❌

▼▼▼ Hilton Oakland Airport MI
(510) 635-5000. **$109-$229.** 1 Hegenberger Rd. I-880, exit Hegenberger Rd, 1 mi w, 1.3 mi e of Oakland Airport. Int corridors. **Pets:** Accepted.

SAVE ✕ 🖥 💻 ❌ 🍴 ≈

OJAI

⊛ ▼▼ Best Western Casa Ojai M
(805) 646-8175. **$79-$199.** 1302 E Ojai Ave. 0.8 mi e on SR 150. Ext corridors. **Pets:** Accepted.

SAVE Sᴅ ✕ 🖥 💻 ≈

▼▼▼ Blue Iguana Inn M
(805) 646-5277. **$105-$145, 7 days notice.** 11794 N Ventura Ave. 2.5 mi w of town, on SR 33. Ext corridors. **Pets:** Small, dogs only. $20 daily fee/pet. Supervision.

ASK Sᴅ ✕ 🖥 💻 ≈

⊛ ▼▼ Oakridge Inn M
(805) 649-4018. **$75-$125.** 780 N Ventura Ave. In Oak View, 4 mi s on SR 33, 2 mi e of Lake Casitas. Ext corridors. **Pets:** Medium, dogs only. $50 deposit/pet, $10 daily fee/pet. Service with restrictions, supervision.

SAVE Sᴅ ✕ 🖥 💻

▼▼▼▼ Ojai Valley Inn & Spa R ❀
(805) 646-5511. **$275-$330, 3 days notice.** 905 Country Club Rd. 1 mi w of town on SR 150, 0.3 mi s. Ext/int corridors. **Pets:** Medium. $35 daily fee/pet. Designated rooms, service with restrictions, supervision.

✕ 🖥 🚫 🐾 🖥 💻 🍴 ≈ ✕

ONTARIO

⊛ ▼▼▼ AmeriSuites M
(909) 980-2200. **$89-$149, 7 days notice.** 4760 E Mills Cir. I-10, exit Milliken Ave, just n, then 0.5 mi e on Ontario Mills Dr. Int corridors. **Pets:** Small. $50 one-time fee/room. Designated rooms, service with restrictions, crate.

SAVE Sᴅ ✕ 🖥 🐾 🖥 💻 ≈

⊛ ▼▼▼ Holiday Inn Hotel & Suites MI
(909) 466-9600. **$129-$149, 3 days notice.** 3400 Shelby St. I-10, exit Haven Ave, just n to Inland Empire Blvd, w to Lotus Ave, then just s. Ext/int corridors. **Pets:** Large. $25 deposit/room, $25 one-time fee/room. Designated rooms, service with restrictions, supervision.

SAVE Sᴅ ✕ 🖥 💻 🍴 ≈

▼▼▼ La Quinta Inn & Suites M
(909) 476-1112. **$110-$130.** 3555 Inland Empire Blvd. I-10, exit Haven Ave, just n, then just e. Int corridors. **Pets:** Small, other species. Service with restrictions, supervision.

SAVE Sᴅ ✕ 🐾 🖥 🖥 💻 ≈

⊛ ▼▼▼ Residence Inn by Marriott A
(909) 937-6788. **$179-$224.** 2025 Convention Center Way. I-10, exit Vineyard Ave, just s, then 1 blk e. Ext corridors. **Pets:** $10 daily fee/room, $75 one-time fee/room. Service with restrictions, crate.

SAVE Sᴅ ✕ 🖥 💻 ≈

ORANGE

⊛ ▼▼▼ Hilton Suites Anaheim/Orange H
(714) 938-1111. **$144-$154, 3 days notice.** 400 North State College Blvd. I-5, exit State College Blvd, just s. Int corridors. **Pets:** Accepted.

SAVE Sᴅ ✕ 🖥 💻 🍴 ≈

ORLAND

⊛ ▼▼ Amber Light Inn Motel M ❀
(530) 865-7655. **$42-$50.** 828 Newville Rd. I-5, exit Chico (SR 32), SR 32 off-ramp, then 0.3 mi e. Ext corridors. **Pets:** Small. $5 one-time fee/pet. Service with restrictions, supervision.

SAVE Sᴅ ✕ ≈

⊛ ▼▼ Orland Inn M
(530) 865-7632. **$47-$52.** 1052 South St. I-5, 0.5 mi s; northbound exit I-5 E via Orland-Fairgrounds; southbound exit I-5 E via CR 16; adjacent to I-5. Ext corridors. **Pets:** Other species. $5 one-time fee/pet. Service with restrictions, crate.

SAVE Sᴅ ✕ 🐾 🖥 ≈

OROVILLE

⊛ ▼▼▼ Best Inn & Suites M
(530) 533-9673. **$79-$139.** 1470 Feather River Blvd. SR 70, exit E Montgomery. Int corridors. **Pets:** Other species. $100 deposit/room, $5 daily fee/room. Designated rooms, service with restrictions, supervision.

SAVE Sᴅ ✕ 🐾 🖥 🖥 💻 ≈

▼▼ Days Inn-Oroville M
(530) 533-3297. **Call for rates.** 1745 Feather River Blvd. SR 70 exit E Montgomery St, just e to Feather River Blvd, 0.5 mi s. Ext corridors. **Pets:** Medium. $7 daily fee/pet. Designated rooms, service with restrictions, supervision.

ASK Sᴅ ✕ 🖥 💻 ≈

⊛ ▼▼ Oroville Travelodge M ❀
(530) 533-7070. **$60-$99.** 580 Oro Dam Blvd. Exit SR 70 at Oro Dam Blvd, 0.3 mi e. Ext corridors. **Pets:** Other species. $50 deposit/room, $3 daily fee/room. Designated rooms, service with restrictions, supervision.

SAVE Sᴅ ✕ 🖥 💻 ≈

⊛ ▼ Sunset Inn M
(530) 533-8201. **$50-$99.** 1835 Feather River Blvd. exit SR 70 at E Montegomery St, 0.5 mi s. Ext corridors. **Pets:** Accepted.

SAVE Sᴅ ✕ 🖥 ≈

OXNARD

Best Western Oxnard Inn M
(805) 483-9581. **$99-$109.** 1156 S Oxnard Blvd. From US 101, exit Vineyard Ave northbound; exit Oxnard Blvd southbound, 3 mi s. Ext corridors. **Pets:** Small, dogs only. Designated rooms, service with restrictions, supervision.
SAVE) (S) (X) (B) (D) (A)

Radisson Hotel-Oxnard H
(805) 485-9666. **$89-$139.** 600 Esplanade Dr. From US 101 exit Vineyard Ave, just s. Int corridors. **Pets:** Accepted.
SAVE) (S) (X) (M) (A) (E) (B) (D) (TI) (A)

Residence Inn At River Ridge A ❀
(805) 278-2200. **$113-$140.** 2101 W Vineyard Ave. From US 101, exit Vineyard Ave, 1.8 mi w. Ext corridors. **Pets:** $200 deposit/pet, $6 daily fee/pet, $100 one-time fee/pet.
SAVE) (S) (X) (A) (B) (D) (A) (X)

Vagabond Inn M
(805) 983-0251. **$60-$85.** 1245 N Oxnard Blvd. From US 101, exit Vineyard northbound, 1.5 mi s; exit Oxnard Blvd southbound, 1.5 mi s. Ext corridors. **Pets:** Other species. $5 daily fee/pet. Service with restrictions, supervision.
SAVE) (S) (X) (B) (D) (A)

PALM DESERT

Casa Larrea Resort M
(760) 568-0311. **$55-$114, 30 days notice.** 73-771 Larrea St. I-10, exit Cook St, 4.4 mi s to SR 111, 1.2 mi w to San Luis Rey Ave, just s, then just e. Ext corridors. **Pets:** Small. $100 deposit/pet. Designated rooms, service with restrictions, supervision.
(X) (B) (D) (A)

Comfort Suites M
(760) 360-3337. **$69-$189.** 39-585 Washington St. I-10, exit Washington St, just n. Int corridors. **Pets:** Medium. $50 deposit/pet. Designated rooms, service with restrictions, supervision.
SAVE) (S) (X) (B) (D) (A)

Desert Patch Inn M ❀
(760) 346-9161. **$47-$124, 14 days notice.** 73758 Shadow Mountain Dr. I-10, exit Cook St, 4.4 mi s to SR 111, 1.2 mi w to San Luis Rey Ave, just s, then just e. Ext corridors. **Pets:** Other species. $25 deposit/room. Designated rooms, supervision.
(X) (B) (D) (A)

The Inn at Deep Canyon M
(760) 346-8061. **$47-$167, 3 days notice.** 74470 Abronia Tr. I-10, exit Cook St, 4.4 mi s to SR 111, 0.5 mi w, just s on Deep Canyon Rd. Ext corridors. **Pets:** Large, other species. $10 daily fee/room. Designated rooms, service with restrictions.
SAVE) (S) (X) (B) (D) (A)

Residence Inn by Marriott A
(760) 776-0050. **$85-$319, 7 days notice.** 38-305 Cook St. I-10, exit Cook St, 0.8 mi s. Ext corridors. **Pets:** Small. $5 daily fee/pet, $100 one-time fee/room. Service with restrictions, supervision.
SAVE) (S) (X) (B) (D) (A) (X)

PALM SPRINGS

Casa Cody Country Inn M
(760) 320-9346. **$59-$149, 3 days notice.** 175 S Cahuilla Rd. From SR 111, just w on Tahquitz Canyon Way, then just s. Ext corridors. **Pets:** Accepted.
(B) (D) (A)

Comfort Inn Resort M
(760) 778-3699. **$119-$139.** 390 S Indian Canyon Dr. 0.5 mi s of Tahquitz Canyon Way. Ext corridors. **Pets:** Accepted.
SAVE) (S) (X) (B) (D) (A)

Estrella Inn & Villas X
(760) 320-4117. **$135-$385, 7 days notice.** 415 S Belardo Rd. From Tahquitz Canyon Way, just w of Palm Canyon Dr, then just s. Ext/int corridors. **Pets:** Accepted.
ASK) (S) (X) (B) (D) (A)

Hilton Palm Springs Resort H
(760) 320-6868. **$88-$169, 3 days notice.** 400 E Tahquitz Canyon Way. Just e of Indian Canyon Dr. Int corridors. **Pets:** Accepted.
SAVE) (X) (B) (D) (TI) (A)

Hotel California M
(760) 322-8855. **Call for rates, 3 days notice.** 424 E Palm Canyon Dr. 1.5 mi s of Tahquitz Canyon Way. Ext corridors. **Pets:** Accepted.
ASK) (S) (X) (B) (D) (A)

Merv Griffin's Resort Hotel & Givenchy Spa R
(760) 770-5000. **$99-$629, 3 days notice.** 4200 E Palm Canyon Dr. Ext/int corridors. **Pets:** Accepted.
ASK) (X) (B) (D) (TI) (A)

Palm Springs Riviera Resort H
(760) 327-8311. **$85-$149, 3 days notice.** 1600 N Indian Canyon Dr. 1.5 mi n of Tahquitz Canyon Way. Int corridors. **Pets:** Medium. $200 deposit/room, $20 daily fee/room. Designated rooms, service with restrictions, supervision.
(X) (E) (B) (D) (TI) (A) (X)

Quality Inn Resort M ❀
(760) 323-2775. **$49-$139.** 1269 E Palm Canyon Dr. 2.3 mi se of Tahquitz Canyon Way. Ext corridors. **Pets:** Medium. $50 deposit/room. Supervision.
SAVE) (S) (X) (B) (D) (A)

Ramada Resort Inn & Conference Center M
(760) 323-1711. **$49-$179.** 1800 E Palm Canyon Dr. 2.7 mi se of Tahquitz Canyon Way. Ext/int corridors. **Pets:** Medium. $50 deposit/room, $20 daily fee/room. Service with restrictions, supervision.
ASK) (S) (X) (B) (D) (TI) (A)

▼▼ ▼▼ Royal Sun Inn M
(760) 327-1564. **$59-$99.** 1700 S Palm Canyon Dr. 1.5 mi
s of Tahquitz Canyon Way. Ext corridors. **Pets:** Accepted.

ASK S⌀ ✕ 🛏 ▣ ⊒

▼▼ San Marino Hotel M
(760) 325-6902. **$69-$189, 3 days notice.** 225 W Baristo
Rd. Just s of Tahquitz Canyon Way. Ext corridors.
Pets: Dogs only. $10 daily fee/pet. Service with restrictions,
supervision.

✕ 🛏 ▣ ⊒

▼▼ Super 8 Lodge M
(760) 322-3757. **$55-$75.** 1900 N Palm Canyon Dr. 1.4 mi
n of Tahquitz Canyon Way. Ext corridors. **Pets:** Dogs only.
$10 one-time fee/room. Service with restrictions, supervi-
sion.

ASK S⌀ ✕ 🛏 ▣ ⊒

▼▼ ▼▼ Villa Rosa Inn M ☙
(760) 327-5915. **$69-$145, 7 days notice.** 1577 S Indian
Tr. 2 mi se of Tahquitz Canyon Way, then just n. Ext corridors. **Pets:** Small. $100 deposit/pet. Service with restric-
tions, supervision.

ASK S⌀ ✕ 🛏 ▣ ⊒

PALO ALTO

▼▼▼▼ Crowne Plaza Cabana Hotel 🄷 ☙
(650) 857-0787. **$143-$299.** 4290 El Camino Real. US 101,
exit San Antonio Rd, 0.4 mi n. Ext/int corridors. **Pets:** Small,
other species. $100 deposit/room. Designated rooms, serv-
ice with restrictions, supervision.

ASK S⌀ ✕ ⓜ 🖉 🖉 🛏 ▣ 🍴 ⊒

▼▼▼▼ Sheraton Palo Alto Hotel M
(650) 328-2800. **$269.** 625 El Camino Real. Exit US 101
Embarcadero W, to SR 82, 0.5 mi n. Int corridors.
Pets: Accepted.

ASK S⌀ ✕ 🛏 ▣ 🍴 ⊒

▲▲▲ ▼▼ ▼▼ Travelodge Palo Alto M
(650) 493-6340. **$125-$135.** 3255 El Camino Real. Ext corridors. **Pets:** Accepted.

SAVE S⌀ ✕ 🛏 ▣ ⊒

PARADISE

▲▲▲ ▼▼▼▼ Best Inn & Suites M
(530) 876-0191. **$75-$114.** 5475 Clark Rd. On SR 191, 0.5
mi s of Pearson Rd. Int corridors. **Pets:** Other species.
$100 deposit/pet, $6 daily fee/pet. Designated rooms, service with restrictions, supervision.

SAVE S⌀ ✕ ⓜ 🖉 🛏 ▣ ⊒

▲▲▲ ▼▼ ▼▼ Paradise Inn M
(530) 877-2127. **$45-$69.** 5423 Skyway. 1.5 mi w. Ext corridors. **Pets:** Small. $5 daily fee/pet. Service with restric-
tions, supervision.

SAVE S⌀ ✕ 🛏 ▣ ⊒

▲▲▲ ▼▼▼▼ Ponderosa Gardens Motel M
(530) 872-9094. **$65-$95.** 7010 Skyway. Center; 2 blks e.
Ext corridors. **Pets:** $5 daily fee/pet. Service with restric-
tions, supervision.

SAVE ✕ ⓜ 🖉 🛏 ▣ ⊒

PISMO BEACH

▲▲▲ ▼▼▼▼ Oxford Suites Resort M ☙
(805) 773-3773. **$99-$159.** 651 Five Cities Dr. From US
101, exit 4th St, just w, then just n. Ext corridors.
Pets: Medium, other species. $5 daily fee/pet. Designated
rooms, service with restrictions, supervision.

SAVE S⌀ ✕ 🛏 ▣ ⊒

▲▲▲ ▼▼▼▼ Sandcastle Inn M
(805) 773-2422. **$99-$229.** 100 Stimson Ave. From US 101,
exit Hinds Ave southbound, just w, then just s; exit Price St
northbound, 0.3 mi, then just w. Int corridors.
Pets: Accepted.

SAVE S⌀ ✕ 🛏 ▣

▼▼ ▼▼ Sea Gypsy Motel CO
(805) 773-1801. **$50-$140.** 1020 Cypress. US 101, exit
Price St northbound, 0.5 mi n to Pismo Ave, then just w;
exit Hines Ave southbound, 0.3 mi w, then just n. Ext/int
corridors. **Pets:** Accepted.

✕ 🛏 ▣ ⊒ ✗

PLACENTIA

▲▲▲ ▼▼▼▼ Residence Inn by Marriott M
(714) 996-0555. **$139.** 700 W Kimberly Ave. From SR 57,
exit Orangethorpe Ave, just w, just n on Placentia Ave, then
just e. Ext corridors. **Pets:** Accepted.

SAVE ✕ 🛏 ▣ ⊒

PLACERVILLE

▲▲▲ ▼▼ ▼▼ Mother Lode Motel M ☙
(530) 622-0895. **$50-$68, 3 days notice.** 1940 Broadway.
2 mi e, adjacent to US 50, exit Point View Dr. Ext corridors.
Pets: Small. $10 daily fee/pet. Designated rooms, service
with restrictions, supervision.

SAVE ✕ ⓜ 🖉 🛏 ▣ ⊒

PLEASANT HILL

**▲▲▲ ▼▼▼▼ Residence Inn By Marriott-Pleasant
Hill M ☙**
(925) 689-1010. **$219.** 700 Ellinwood Way. I-680, exit Wil-
low Pass Rd to Taylor W; S Contra Costa Blvd, e on
Ellinwood Dr, then n. Ext/int corridors. **Pets:** Other species.
$6 daily fee/pet, $75 one-time fee/room. Service with
restrictions, supervision.

SAVE ✕ ▣ ⊒

PLEASANTON

▼▼▼▼ Candlewood Suites M
(925) 463-1212. **$159-$179.** 5535 Johnson Dr. I-580, exit
Hopyard Rd S, w on Owen. Int corridors. **Pets:** Accepted.

ASK S⌀ ✕ ▣

▼▼▼▼ **Crowne Plaza-Pleasanton** 🅷
(925) 847-6000. **$69-$189.** 11950 Dublin Canyon Rd. I-580, exit Foothill Rd, 0.3 mi s. Int corridors. **Pets:** Other species. $25 one-time fee/pet. Designated rooms, service with restrictions, crate.

[ASK] [S] [✕] [⌂] [🛏] [▣] [🍴] [≋]

▼▼▼▼ **Hilton Pleasanton at the Club** 🅷
(925) 463-8000. **$94-$294.** 7050 Johnson Dr. In se quadrant at jct I-580 and 680. Int corridors. **Pets:** Accepted.

[SAVE] [S] [✕] [🛏] [▣] [🍴] [≋] [✕]

▼▼▼▼ **Ramada Inn** 🅼
(925) 463-1300. **$108-$134.** 5375 Owens Ct. I-580, exit Hopyard Rd, just s. Ext corridors. **Pets:** Accepted.

[ASK] [S] [✕] [🛏] [▣] [≋]

🅐🅐🅐 ▼▼▼▼ **Residence Inn by Marriott** 🅼
(925) 227-0500. **$89-$185.** 11920 Dublin Canyon Rd. I-580, exit Foothill Blvd S, then w. Int corridors. **Pets:** Accepted.

[SAVE] [S] [✕] [⌂M] [⌂] [▣] [≋]

POLLOCK PINES

🅐🅐🅐 ▼▼▼▼ **Stagecoach Motor Inn** 🅼
(530) 644-2029. **$78-$88, 7 days notice.** 5940 Pony Express Tr. 12 mi e of Placerville; eastbound exit US 50 at Pollock Pines, 1 mi e; westbound exit Sly Park. **Pets:** Accepted.

[SAVE] [S] [≋]

🅐🅐🅐 ▼▼▼▼ **Westhaven Inn** 🅼
(530) 644-7800. **$68.** 5658 Pony Express Tr. Exit US 50 at Pollock Pines, just n. Ext corridors. **Pets:** Accepted.

[SAVE] [S] [✕] [⌂M] [🛏] [▣]

PORTOLA

▼▼▼ **Sleepy Pines Motel** 🅼
(530) 832-4291. **$60-$80.** 74631 Hwy 70. Ext corridors. **Pets:** Dogs only. Service with restrictions, supervision.

[✕] [🛏] [▣] [🎣]

RANCHO CORDOVA

🅐🅐🅐 ▼▼▼▼ **AmeriSuites (Sacramento/Rancho Cordova)** 🅼🅸
(916) 635-4799. **$79-$139.** 10744 Gold Center Dr. Exit US 50 at Zinfandel Dr, just s. Int corridors. **Pets:** Other species. Service with restrictions.

[SAVE] [S] [✕] [⌂M] [⌂] [🛏] [▣] [≋]

🅐🅐🅐 ▼▼▼▼ **Best Western Heritage Inn** 🅼🅸
(916) 635-4040. **$89-$99.** 11269 Point East Dr. 12 mi e of Sacramento, exit US 50 (Sunrise Blvd S). Int corridors. **Pets:** Medium, other species. $75 one-time fee/room. Service with restrictions, supervision.

[SAVE] [S] [✕] [🛏] [▣] [🍴] [≋]

🅐🅐🅐 ▼▼▼ **Inns of America** 🅼
(916) 351-1213. **$63-$80.** 12249 Folsom Blvd. then just s. Ext corridors. **Pets:** Accepted.

[SAVE] [S] [✕] [🛏] [≋]

🅐🅐🅐 ▼▼▼▼ **Residence Inn** 🅼
(916) 851-1550. **$126-$153.** 2779 Prospect Park Dr. US 50 at Zinfandel Dr. Int corridors. **Pets:** Other species. $10 daily fee/room, $50 one-time fee/room. Service with restrictions, supervision.

[SAVE] [S] [✕] [⌂M] [⌂] [▣] [≋]

RED BLUFF

🅐🅐🅐 ▼▼▼ **Best Value Inn & Suites** 🅼 ❀
(530) 529-2028. **$45-$55, 7 days notice.** 30 Gilmore Rd. I-5, (Central District), just s on Gilmore Rd. Ext corridors. **Pets:** Medium. $5 daily fee/pet. Designated rooms, service with restrictions, supervision.

[SAVE] [S] [✕] [🛏] [▣] [≋]

🅐🅐🅐 ▼▼ **Cinderella Riverview Motel** 🅼
(530) 527-5490. **$38-$50, 3 days notice.** 600 Rio St. I-5, (Central District), 0.4 mi w on Antelope Blvd. Ext corridors. **Pets:** Accepted.

[SAVE] [✕] [≋]

🅐🅐🅐 ▼▼ **Days Inn & Suites** 🅼
(530) 527-6130. **$47-$60.** 5 John Sutter St. I-5, exit S Main St. Ext corridors. **Pets:** Large. $5 daily fee/pet. Designated rooms, service with restrictions, supervision.

[SAVE] [S] [✕] [🛏] [≋]

🅐🅐🅐 ▼ **Sportsman Lodge** 🅼
(530) 527-2888. **$48-$68, 3 days notice.** 768 Antelope Blvd. I-5, (Susanville/Lassen Park), 1.5 mi e. Ext corridors. **Pets:** $5 daily fee/pet. No service, supervision.

[SAVE] [S] [✕] [🛏] [≋]

🅐🅐🅐 ▼▼ **Super 8 Motel** 🅼
(530) 527-8882. **$59-$99.** 203 Antelope Blvd. I-5, (Susanville/Lassen Park). Int corridors. **Pets:** Accepted.

[SAVE] [S] [✕] [🛏] [≋]

🅐🅐🅐 ▼▼▼ **Travelodge Red Bluff** 🅼 ❀
(530) 527-6020. **$48-$65.** 38 Antelope Blvd. I-5, (Central District), just 0.2 mi w on Antelope Blvd. Ext corridors. **Pets:** Other species. $5 daily fee/pet. Service with restrictions, supervision.

[SAVE] [S] [✕] [🛏] [▣] [≋]

REDCREST

🅐🅐🅐 ▼▼▼ **Redcrest Resort** 🅲 ❀
(707) 722-4208. **$45-$100, 7 days notice.** 26459 Avenue of the Giants. US 101, exit Redcrest, just n. Ext corridors. **Pets:** $5 daily fee/pet. No service, supervision.

[SAVE] [🛏] [▣] [🎣] [☎]

REDDING

🅐🅐🅐 ▼▼▼ **Best Western Hospitality House** 🅼
(530) 241-6464. **$65-$105.** 532 N Market St. W of I-5 exit Lake Blvd northbound, 0.5 mi to Market, 0.5 mi s; exit Market St southbound, 2 mi s. Ext corridors. **Pets:** Medium, dogs only. $50 deposit/room, $10 daily fee/pet. Designated rooms, service with restrictions.

[SAVE] [S] [✕] [🛏] [▣] [🍴] [≋]

△△△ ▼▼▼ Best Western Ponderosa Inn Ⓜ
(530) 241-6300. **$59-$70.** 2220 Pine St. I-5, exit Cypress Ave, 1.5 mi w. Ext corridors. **Pets:** Other species. $100 deposit/room. Service with restrictions, supervision.
[SAVE] [S☎] [✕] [🛏] [🖼]

△△△ ▼▼▼ Comfort Inn Ⓜ ❀
(530) 221-6530. **$63-$149.** 2059 Hilltop Dr. I-5, exit Cypress Ave E, 0.3 mi n. Ext corridors. **Pets:** Small. $15 one-time fee/pet. Service with restrictions, supervision.
[SAVE] [S☎] [✕] [🛏] [🖼] [🖼]

△△△ ▼▼▼ Holiday Inn Express Ⓜ
(530) 241-5500. **$89-$99.** 1080 Twin View Blvd. I-5, exit Twin View Blvd, just w. Int corridors. **Pets:** Medium, other species. $30 one-time fee/room. Designated rooms, service with restrictions, supervision.
[SAVE] [S☎] [✕] [&M] [🛏] [🖼] [🖼]

△△△ ▼▼▼▼ La Quinta Inn Ⓜ
(530) 221-8200. **$69-$85.** 2180 Hilltop Dr. I-5, exit Cypress Ave E, 0.5 mi n. Int corridors. **Pets:** Accepted.
[SAVE] [S☎] [✕] [&] [🛏] [🖼] [🖼]

▼▼▼▼ Oxford Suites Ⓜ
(530) 221-0100. **$85-$119.** 1967 Hilltop Dr. I-5, exit Cypress E, 0.5 mi n. Ext/int corridors. **Pets:** Small. $20 one-time fee/room. Service with restrictions, supervision.
[ASK] [S☎] [✕] [🛏] [🖼] [🖼]

△△△ ▼▼▼▼ Ramada Limited Ⓜ
(530) 246-2222. **$69-$99.** 1286 Twin View Blvd. I-5, exit Twin View Blvd E, just n. Int corridors. **Pets:** Other species. $15 one-time fee/room. Designated rooms, service with restrictions, crate.
[SAVE] [S☎] [✕] [&M] [&] [🛏] [🖼] [🖼]

△△△ ▼▼▼ River Inn Ⓜ
(530) 241-9500. **$62-$85, 7 days notice.** 1835 Park Marina Dr. I-5, exit SR 299 W, exit SR 299 W; 1 mi w, exit at Park Marina Dr. Ext corridors. **Pets:** Accepted.
[SAVE] [S☎] [✕] [🛏] [🖼] [🖼]

▼▼▼ Vagabond Inn Ⓜ
(530) 223-1600. **$59-$68.** 536 E Cypress Ave. I-5, exit Cypress Ave, just w. Ext corridors. **Pets:** Accepted.
[ASK] [S☎] [✕] [🛏] [🖼] [🖼]

REDLANDS

△△△ ▼▼▼ Best Western Sandman Motel Ⓜ
(909) 793-2001. **$45-$69.** 1120 W Colton Ave. I-10, exit Tennessee St, just s, then just e. Ext corridors. **Pets:** Accepted.
[SAVE] [S☎] [✕] [🛏] [🖼] [🖼]

△△△ ▼▼▼▼ Dynasty Suites-Redlands Ⓜ
(909) 793-6648. **$57-$66.** 1235 W Colton Ave. I-10, exit Tennessee St, just s, then just w. Ext corridors. **Pets:** Accepted.
[SAVE] [S☎] [✕] [🛏] [🖼]

REDWOOD CITY

▼▼▼ ▼▼▼ Hotel Sofitel San Francisco Bay at Redwood Shores Ⓗ
(650) 598-9000. **$269.** 223 Twin Dolphin Dr. US 101, exit Marine World Pkwy E, 0.5 mi s. Int corridors. **Pets:** Accepted.
[ASK] [S☎] [✕] [&] [🖼] [🍴] [🖼]

REEDLEY

△△△ ▼▼▼▼ Edgewater Inn Ⓜ
(559) 637-7777. **$71-$77.** 1977 W Manning Ave. 12 mi e of SR 99 via Manning Hwy. Ext corridors. **Pets:** Dogs only. $7 daily fee/pet. Service with restrictions, supervision.
[SAVE] [✕] [🛏] [🖼] [🖼]

RIALTO

△△△ ▼▼▼▼ Best Western Empire Inn Ⓜ
(909) 877-0690. **$69-$139, 3 days notice.** 475 W Valley Blvd. I-10, exit Riverside Ave, just n, then 0.5 mi w. Ext corridors. **Pets:** Medium. $10 daily fee/pet. Designated rooms, service with restrictions, supervision.
[SAVE] [S☎] [✕] [🍴] [🖼]

RIDGECREST

△△△ ▼▼▼▼ Best Western China Lake Inn Ⓜ
(760) 371-2300. **$77-$85.** 400 S China Lake Blvd. On US 395 business route. Ext corridors. **Pets:** Medium. $10 one-time fee/pet. Designated rooms, service with restrictions, supervision.
[SAVE] [✕] [🛏] [🖼] [🖼]

△△△ ▼▼▼▼ Carriage Inn Ⓜ
(760) 446-7910. **$95-$160.** 901 N China Lake Blvd. On SR 178 and US 395 business route. Ext corridors. **Pets:** Accepted.
[SAVE] [S☎] [✕] [🛏] [🖼] [🍴] [🖼]

△△△ ▼▼▼ Econo Lodge Ⓜ
(760) 446-2551. **$50-$70.** 201 Inyokern Rd. On SR 178 and US 395 business route, just w of China Lake Blvd. Ext corridors. **Pets:** Small, dogs only. Service with restrictions, supervision.
[SAVE] [S☎] [✕] [🛏] [🖼] [🖼]

△△△ ▼▼▼▼ Heritage Inn & Suites Ⓜ
(760) 446-7951. **$95-$105.** 1050 N Norma. US 395 business route, just w. Int corridors. **Pets:** Medium. $100 deposit/room. Service with restrictions, crate.
[SAVE] [✕] [🛏] [🖼] [🍴] [🖼]

△△△ ▼▼▼ Quality Inn Ⓜ
(760) 375-9731. **$69.** 507 S China Lake Blvd. On US 395 business route. Ext corridors. **Pets:** Accepted.
[SAVE] [S☎] [✕] [🛏] [🖼] [🖼]

▼▼▼ Vagabond Inn Ⓜ
(760) 375-2220. **$50.** 426 China Lake Blvd. On US 395 business route. Ext corridors. **Pets:** Accepted.
[ASK] [S☎] [✕] [🛏] [🖼]

RIO DELL

Humboldt Gables Motel M
(707) 764-5609. **$46-$56.** 40 W Davis St. US 101, exit Rio Dell/Davis St W. Ext corridors. **Pets:** Medium, dogs only. $25 deposit/room. Service with restrictions, supervision.

RIVERSIDE

Best Western of Riverside M
(909) 359-0770. **$85-$140.** 10518 Magnolia Ave. From SR 91, exit Tyler St, 0.5 mi nw, then 0.3 mi sw. Ext corridors. **Pets:** Other species. $100 deposit/pet. Designated rooms, service with restrictions, crate.

Dynasty Suites-Riverside M
(909) 369-8200. **$57-$65.** 3735 Iowa Ave. I-215 and SR 60, just w, then just n. Ext corridors. **Pets:** Accepted.

ROCKLIN

Howard Johnson Hotel M
(916) 624-4500. **$69-$129.** 4420 Rocklin Rd. US 80 E, exit Rocklin Rd; westbound exit Rocklin. Int corridors. **Pets:** Small. $100 deposit/room, $20 one-time fee/room. Designated rooms, service with restrictions, supervision.

Microtel Inn & Suites M
(916) 632-3366. **$70-$90.** 4480 Rocklin Rd. I-80, exit Rocklin Rd. Int corridors. **Pets:** Other species. $25 one-time fee/pet. Service with restrictions, supervision.

ROSAMOND

Devonshire Inn Motel M
(661) 256-3454. **$75-$85.** 2076 Rosamond Blvd. From SR 14, exit Edwards/Rosamond, just e. Ext corridors. **Pets:** $10 daily fee/pet. Designated rooms, service with restrictions, supervision.

ROSEVILLE

Best Western Roseville Inn M
(916) 782-4434. **$73-$78.** 220 Harding Blvd. Exit w off I-80 via Douglas, just n. Ext corridors. **Pets:** Large, other species. $10 one-time fee/room. Service with restrictions, supervision.

Oxford Suites MI
(916) 784-2222. **$89, 3 days notice.** 130 N Sunrise Ave. I-80, exit Douglas Blvd, Exit e off I-80 via Douglas Blvd, 0.3 mi n. Ext/int corridors. **Pets:** Large, other species. $15 one-time fee/room. Service with restrictions, supervision.

Residence Inn M ❧
(916) 772-5500. **$150, 7 days notice.** 1930 Taylor Rd. I-80, exit Eureka-Taylor Rd, exit Eureka Taylor Rd, just s. Int corridors. **Pets:** Small. $10 daily fee/pet, $100 one-time fee/room. Service with restrictions, supervision.

SACRAMENTO

Best Western Expo Inn M
(916) 922-9833. **$80-$100.** 1413 Howe Ave. 2.5 mi n of jct SR 16 and US 50, exit Howe Ave. Int corridors. **Pets:** Medium, other species. $100 deposit/room. Designated rooms, service with restrictions, supervision.

Best Western Harbor Inn & Suites M
(916) 371-2100. **$94.** 1250 Halyard Dr. 4 mi w; exit Business Loop 80 via Harbor Blvd. Ext/int corridors. **Pets:** Accepted.

Candlewood Suites MI
(916) 646-1212. **$-$134.** 555 Howe Ave. US 50, exit Howe Ave, 1.5 mi n. Int corridors. **Pets:** Accepted.

Clarion Hotel H
(916) 444-8000. **$99-$139, 14 days notice.** 700 16th St. On SR 160; 1.3 mi n of Business Loop 80, 16th St exit. Int corridors. **Pets:** Small. $35 one-time fee/room. Designated rooms, service with restrictions, supervision.

Econo Lodge M
(916) 443-6631. **$55-$109.** 711 16th St. SR 160, 1 mi n of Business Loop 80, I-80 business loop eastbound exit 15th St; westbound 16th St, I-5 exit J St. Ext corridors. **Pets:** Other species. $6 daily fee/pet. Designated rooms, service with restrictions.

Host Airport Hotel M
(916) 922-8071. **$90-$145.** 6945 Airport Blvd. 11 mi nw from capitol; 6 mi nw of I-80, off I-5. Ext corridors. **Pets:** $50 one-time fee/room. Designated rooms, service with restrictions, supervision.

Inns of America M
(916) 386-8408. **$68-$73.** 25 Howe Ave. Sw corner of jct SR 50 and Howe Ave. Ext corridors. **Pets:** Accepted.

La Quinta Inn-North M
(916) 348-0900. **$66.** 4604 Madison Ave. I-80, exit Madison Ave, exit Madison Ave, 9 mi e. Ext corridors. **Pets:** Accepted.

▼▼▼▼ La Quinta Inn-Sacramento Downtown Ⓜ
(916) 448-8100. **$96-$106.** 200 Jibboom St. I-5, exit Richards Blvd W, exit Richards Blvd w, 2.3 mi nw of Business Loop 80. Ext corridors. **Pets:** Accepted.

SAVE S🐾 ⊗ 🔥M 🔋 💻 🌊

⚠ ▼▼▼▼ Marriott Residence Inn Ⓜ
(916) 920-9111. **$149-$179, 3 days notice.** 1530 Howe Ave. 2.5 mi n of jct SR 16 and US 50, exit Howe Ave. Ext corridors. **Pets:** Large, other species. $100 one-time fee/room. Service with restrictions.

SAVE S🐾 ⊗ 🔥M 🍴 🔋 💻 🌊

▼▼▼ Radisson Hotel Ⓗ
(916) 922-2020. **$99-$149.** 500 Leisure Ln. Exit Business Route 80 at Exposition Blvd, 0.4 mi w. Ext corridors. **Pets:** Medium. $100 deposit/room. Service with restrictions, supervision.

ASK S🐾 ⊗ 🔥M 🍴 🔋 💻 🍴 🌊

⚠ ▼▼▼ Ramada Inn Ⓜ
(916) 487-7600. **$89-$115.** 2600 Auburn Blvd. Exit Business route 80 at Fulton Ave. Int corridors. **Pets:** Medium. $100 deposit/pet. Designated rooms, service with restrictions, supervision.

SAVE ⊗ 🔋 💻 🍴 🌊

▼▼▼▼ Red Lion Hotel Sacramento Ⓜ
(916) 922-8041. **$84-$109.** 1401 Arden Way. Exit Business Loop 80 via Arden Way. Ext/int corridors. **Pets:** Accepted.

ASK S🐾 ⊗ 🔋 💻 🍴 🌊

⚠ ▼▼▼▼ Residence Inn by Marriott Ⓜ ✿
(916) 649-1300. **$99.** 2410 W El Camino. I-5, exit W El Camino, exit W El Camino. Ext corridors. **Pets:** $6 daily fee/pet, $50 one-time fee/pet. No service.

SAVE S🐾 ⊗ 🔥M 🔋 💻 🌊

⚠ ▼▼▼ Vagabond Inn Ⓜ
(916) 446-1481. **$95-$110, 15 days notice.** 909 3rd St. I-5, exit J St (Old Sacramento), 8 blks w of Capitol; exit J St. Ext corridors. **Pets:** Small. $20 daily fee/pet. Designated rooms, service with restrictions, supervision.

SAVE S🐾 ⊗ 🔥M 🔋 🔋 💻 🌊

SALINAS

⚠ ▼▼▼▼ Barlocker's Rustling Oaks
    Ranch ⓇⒶ
(831) 675-9121. **$90-$150, 3 days notice.** 25252 Limeklin Rd. US 101, exit Chualar, 6 mi w, w on River Rd, s (left) after bridge, to Limekiln, right at sign. Ext/int corridors. **Pets:** Accepted.

SAVE S🐾 ⊗ 🌊 🎾 Ⓦ ☎

▼▼▼ Vagabond Inn Ⓜ
(831) 758-4693. **$85-$180.** 131 Kern St. US 101, exit Market St, just e. Ext corridors. **Pets:** Medium, other species. $5 daily fee/pet. Designated rooms, service with restrictions, supervision.

ASK S🐾 ⊗ 🔥M 🔋 💻 🌊

SAN BERNARDINO

▼▼▼▼ La Quinta Inn Ⓜ
(909) 888-7571. **$76-$96.** 205 E Hospitality Ln. I-10, exit Waterman Ave, just n, then 0.3 mi w. Ext corridors. **Pets:** Accepted.

SAVE S🐾 ⊗ 🔋 💻 🌊

SAN CLEMENTE

▼▼▼▼ Holiday Inn-San Clemente
    Resort Ⓜ ✿
(949) 361-3000. **$119-$159.** 111 S Avenida de la Estrella. I-5, exit Avenida Palizada southbound; exit Avenida Presidio northbound, just s, then just w. Int corridors. **Pets:** Other species. $10 daily fee/pet. Crate.

ASK S🐾 ⊗ 🔋 💻 🌊

SAN DIEGO METROPOLITAN AREA

CHULA VISTA

▼▼▼▼ La Quinta Inn Ⓜ
(619) 691-1211. **$102-$122.** 150 Bonita Rd. I-805, exit E St/Bonita Rd, just w. Ext corridors. **Pets:** Small. Service with restrictions, crate.

SAVE S🐾 ⊗ 💻 🌊

CORONADO

⚠ ▼▼▼ ▼▼▼ Coronado Island Marriott
    Resort Ⓗ ✿
(619) 435-3000. **$189-$269.** 2000 2nd St. I-5, exit Coronado Bridge (toll), 1.5 mi w to Glorietta Blvd, then just ne. Ext corridors. **Pets:** Small, dogs only. Designated rooms.

SAVE S🐾 ⊗ 🔋 💻 🍴 🌊 ⊠

▼▼▼ Crown City Inn Ⓜ
(619) 435-3116. **$89-$149.** 520 Orange Ave. I-5, exit SR 75 (Coronado Bay toll bridge), 1.5 mi w, then just s. Ext corridors. **Pets:** Other species. $8 daily fee/pet. Designated rooms, service with restrictions, supervision.

⊗ 🔋 💻 🍴

⚠ ▼▼▼ ▼▼▼ Loews Coronado Bay
    Resort Ⓗ ✿
(619) 424-4000. **$195-$279.** 4000 Coronado Bay Rd. I-5, exit Coronado Bridge (toll), 1.7 mi w to Orange Ave, 1 mi sw to Silver Strand Blvd, then 4.5 mi s to Coronado Cays. Int corridors. **Pets:** Other species. Service with restrictions.

SAVE S🐾 ⊗ 🔋 💻 🍴 🌊 ⊠

DEL MAR

⚑ ▼▼▼▼ Best Western Stratford Inn M
(858) 755-1501. **$99-$199, 3 days notice.** 710 Camino Del Mar. I-5, exit Del Mar Heights Rd, 1 mi w, then 0.3 mi n. Int corridors. **Pets:** Designated rooms, supervision.
[SAVE] [S✿] [✕] [▣] [➤]

⚑ ▼▼▼▼ Del Mar Inn, A Clarion Carriage House M
(858) 755-9765. **$104-$189, 3 days notice.** 720 Camino Del Mar. I-5, exit Del Mar Heights Rd, 1 mi w, 0.3 mi n. Int corridors. **Pets:** Accepted.
[SAVE] [S✿] [✕] [🛏] [➤]

LA JOLLA

⚑ ▼▼▼▼ Hyatt Regency La Jolla H
(858) 552-1234. **$164-$250.** 3777 La Jolla Village Dr. I-5, exit La Jolla Village Dr, just e. Int corridors. **Pets:** Accepted.
[SAVE] [✕] [🛏] [▣] [¶] [➤]

⚑ ▼▼▼▼ La Jolla Marriott H
(858) 587-1414. **$139-$219.** 4240 La Jolla Village Dr. I-5, exit La Jolla Village Dr, 0.5 mi e. Int corridors. **Pets:** Accepted.
[SAVE] [S✿] [✕] [🛏] [▣] [¶] [➤]

⚑ ▼▼▼▼ Residence Inn by Marriott A ❀
(858) 587-1770. **$129-$209.** 8901 Gilman Dr. I-5, exit Gilman Dr, 1.5 mi nw. Ext corridors. **Pets:** Medium, other species. $10 daily fee/pet, $50 one-time fee/room. Designated rooms, service with restrictions, supervision.
[SAVE] [S✿] [✕] [▣] [➤]

NATIONAL CITY

⚑ ▼▼▼▼ Red Lion Inn & Suites San Diego/ South Bay M
(619) 336-1100. **$139-$159.** 801 National City Blvd. I-5, exit 8th St southbound; exit Plaza Blvd northbound. Ext corridors. **Pets:** Other species. $50 deposit/room. Designated rooms, service with restrictions, crate.
[SAVE] [S✿] [✕] [♿M] [✿] [🛏] [▣]

POWAY

⚑ ▼▼▼ Poway Country Inn M ❀
(858) 748-6320. **$62-$99.** 13845 Poway Rd. I-15, exit Poway Rd, 4 mi e. Ext corridors. **Pets:** Small. $50 deposit/room, $10 daily fee/room. Designated rooms, service with restrictions, supervision.
[SAVE] [S✿] [✕] [🛏] [▣] [➤]

⚑ ▼▼▼ Ramada Limited M
(858) 748-7311. **$79-$109.** 12448 Poway Rd. I-15, exit Poway Rd, 3 mi e. Ext corridors. **Pets:** Small, other species. $10 daily fee/room. Service with restrictions.
[SAVE] [S✿] [✕] [🛏] [▣] [➤]

RANCHO BERNARDO

▼▼▼▼ La Quinta Inn M
(858) 484-8800. **$87-$99.** 10185 Paseo Montril. I-15, exit Rancho Penasquitos Blvd/Poway Rd, just w. Ext corridors. **Pets:** Accepted.
[SAVE] [S✿] [✕] [♿M] [🛏] [▣] [➤]

⚑ ▼▼▼▼ Residence Inn by Marriott A ❀
(858) 673-1900. **$139-$189.** 11002 Rancho Carmel Dr. I-15, exit Carmel Mountain Rd, just e. Ext/int corridors. **Pets:** Medium, other species. $10 daily fee/room, $150 one-time fee/room. Service with restrictions, supervision.
[SAVE] [S✿] [✕] [▣] [➤]

RANCHO SANTA FE

▼▼▼▼ The Inn at Rancho Santa Fe X
(858) 756-1131. **$150-$230, 3 days notice.** 5951 Linea del Cielo. I-5, exit Lomas Sante Fe Dr, 4 mi e on CR S-8. Ext/int corridors. **Pets:** Accepted.
[ASK] [🛏] [▣] [¶] [➤]

▼▼▼▼ Rancho Valencia Resort R
(858) 756-1123. **$450-$5000, 7 days notice.** 5921 Valencia Cir. I-5, exit Via De La Valle, 1.3 mi e, 0.5 mi s on El Camino Real, 2.5 mi e on San Dieguito Rd, 1 mi nw on Rancho Diegueno Rd and Rancho Valencia. Ext corridors. **Pets:** Accepted.
[✕] [▣] [¶] [➤] [✕]

SAN DIEGO

⚑ ▼ Beach Haven Inn M
(858) 272-3812. **$75-$160, 3 days notice.** 4740 Mission Blvd. I-5, exit Garnet Ave, 2.5 mi w, then just n; in Pacific Beach area. Ext corridors. **Pets:** Accepted.
[SAVE] [S✿] [✕] [➤]

⚑ ▼▼ Best Western Lamplighter Inn & Suites M
(619) 582-3088. **$75-$130.** 6474 El Cajon Blvd. I-8, exit 70th St, 0.5 mi s, then 1 mi w. Ext corridors. **Pets:** Accepted.
[SAVE] [✕] [🛏] [▣] [➤]

⚑ ▼▼▼ Crown Point View Suite-Hotel A
(858) 272-0676. **$125-$250, 14 days notice.** 4088 Crown Point Dr. I-5, exit Garnet Ave, 1 mi e to Morrell St, then 0.5 mi s; in Pacific Beach area. Ext corridors. **Pets:** Accepted.
[SAVE] [🛏] [▣] [AC]

⚑ ▼▼▼ Diamond Head Inn M
(858) 273-1900. **$89-$169, 3 days notice.** 605 Diamond St. I-5, exit Garnet Ave, 2.5 mi w, just n on Mission Blvd, then just w; in Pacific Beach area. Ext corridors. **Pets:** Other species. $25 one-time fee/room. Designated rooms, service with restrictions, crate.
[SAVE] [S✿] [▣]

[AAA] ♦♦♦ **Doubletree Hotel-San Diego Mission Valley** [H]
(619) 297-5466. **$148-$209.** 7450 Hazard Center Dr. From SR 163, exit Friars Rd, 0.3 mi e to Frazee Rd, then just s. Int corridors. **Pets:** Medium, other species. $50 deposit/room. Designated rooms, service with restrictions, supervision.
[SAVE] [SD] 🚭 ▣ ☕ 🍴 🏊

[AAA] ♦♦♦ **Hilton San Diego Mission Valley** [H]
(619) 543-9000. **$129-$159.** 901 Camino del Rio S. I-8, exit Mission Center Rd, just s. Int corridors. **Pets:** Accepted.
[SAVE] [SD] 🚭 ☕ 🍴 🏊

♦♦ **Homestead Studio Suites-San Diego/Mira Mesa** [M]
(858) 623-0100. **$119-$129.** 9880 Pacific Heights Blvd. I-805, exit Mira Mesa Blvd, 1 mi e. Ext corridors. **Pets:** Large, other species. $75 one-time fee/room. Service with restrictions.
[A$K] [SD] 🚭 ♿ 👂 📟 ▣ ☕

♦♦♦ **Horton Grand Hotel** [H]
(619) 544-1886. **$159-$289, 3 days notice.** 311 Island Ave. I-5, exit Front St southbound, 1.2 mi s, then just e; exit J St northbound, 1 mi w, just n on 3rd Ave, then just e. Int corridors. **Pets:** Accepted.
[A$K] [SD] 🚭 ▣ ☕ 🍴

[AAA] ♦ **Old Town Inn** [M]
(619) 260-8024. **$56-$140.** 4444 Pacific Hwy. I-5, exit Seaworld, just w, then 1 mi s. Ext corridors. **Pets:** Accepted.
[SAVE] 🚭 🏊

[AAA] ♦♦ **Pacific Inn Hotel & Suites-By the Bay** [M]
(619) 232-6391. **$49-$159.** 1655 Pacific Hwy. I-5, exit Front St southbound, just s to Cedar St, 0.3 mi w, then just n; exit Hawthorn St northbound, 0.4 mi w, then just s. Ext corridors. **Pets:** Other species. $10 daily fee/pet. Service with restrictions, crate.
[SAVE] [SD] 🚭 ▣ ☕ 🏊

[AAA] ♦♦ **Premier Inns** [M]
(619) 291-8252. **$49-$89.** 2484 Hotel Circle Pl. I-8, exit Taylor St, just n. Ext corridors. **Pets:** Small. Service with restrictions, supervision.
[SAVE] 🚭 ▣

♦♦♦ **Red Lion Hanalei Hotel** [H]
(619) 297-1101. **$119-$159.** 2270 Hotel Cir. I-8, exit Tayor St, just n, then just e. Ext corridors. **Pets:** Other species. $50 deposit/room. Service with restrictions, supervision.
[A$K] [SD] 🚭 ♿ 👂 📟 ▣ ☕ 🍴 🏊

[AAA] ♦♦♦ **Residence Inn by Marriott-San Diego Central** [A]
(858) 278-2100. **$152-$200.** 5400 Kearny Mesa Rd. From to SR 163, exit Clairemont Mesa. Ext corridors. **Pets:** Accepted.
[SAVE] [SD] 🚭 ▣ ☕ 🏊

[AAA] ♦♦♦ **Residence Inn by Marriott San Diego Downtown** [A] 🐾
(619) 338-8200. **$189-$199.** 1747 Pacific Hwy. I-5, exit Front St southbound, just s to Grape St, 0.3 mi w, then just n; exit Hawthorn St northbound, 0.4 mi w, then just s. Int corridors. **Pets:** Small. $7 daily fee/pet, $100 one-time fee/pet.
[SAVE] [SD] 🚭 ▣ ☕ 🏊

[AAA] ♦♦♦ **Residence Inn San Diego-Sorrento Mesa** [A] 🐾
(858) 552-9100. **$119-$199.** 5995 Pacific Mesa Ct. I-805, exit Mira Mesa Blvd, 1.5 mi e. Int corridors. **Pets:** Medium, other species. $10 daily fee/pet, $150 one-time fee/room. No service.
[SAVE] [SD] 🚭 ▣ ☕ 🏊

[AAA] ♦♦♦♦ **San Diego Marriott Hotel & Marina** [H] 🐾
(619) 234-1500. **$215-$285.** 333 W Harbor Dr. I-5, exit J St northbound, 1.2 mi w to 1st Ave, then just s; exit 1st Ave southbound, 1 mi s. Int corridors. **Pets:** Other species. Service with restrictions, supervision.
[SAVE] [SD] 🚭 ▣ ☕ 🍴 🏊 🎾

[AAA] ♦♦♦ **San Diego Marriott Mission Valley** [H]
(619) 692-3800. **$129-$179.** 8757 Rio San Diego Dr. I-8, exit Qualcomm Way, just n. Int corridors. **Pets:** Accepted.
[SAVE] [SD] 🚭 ☕ 🍴 🏊

[AAA] ♦♦♦ **San Diego Marriott Suites-Downtown** [H]
(619) 696-9800. **$159-$169, 3 days notice.** 701 A St/7th Ave. I-5, exit Front St, 0.5 mi s. Int corridors. **Pets:** Accepted.
[SAVE] [SD] 🚭 ☕ 🍴 🏊

[AAA] ♦♦ **Vagabond Inn Mission Bay** [M]
(858) 274-7888. **$70-$92.** 4540 Mission Bay Dr. I-5, exit Grand Ave/Garnet Ave northbound, 0.5 mi n; exit Balboa Ave southbound, 0.3 mi s. Int corridors. **Pets:** Accepted.
[SAVE] [SD] 🚭 ▣ ☕ 🏊

[AAA] ♦ **Vagabond Inn-Point Loma** [M]
(619) 224-3371. **$61-$89.** 1325 Scott St. I-8, exit Nimintz Blvd, 2 mi s to Rosecrans St, just w to Jarvis St, then just s; in Point Loma area. Ext corridors. **Pets:** Medium. $10 daily fee/pet. Service with restrictions, supervision.
[SAVE] [SD] 🚭 ▣ ☕ 🏊

SAN YSIDRO

[AAA] ♦♦ **International Motor Inn** [M]
(619) 428-4486. **$70-$100.** 190 E Calle Primera. I-5, exit Via de San Ysidro, then just se. Ext corridors. **Pets:** Accepted.
[SAVE] [SD] 🚭 ▣ ☕ 🏊

🐾 **END METROPOLITAN AREA** 🐾

SAN FRANCISCO METROPOLITAN AREA

BURLINGAME

▼▼▼▼ Embassy Suites-SFO �H ❀
(650) 342-4600. **$149-$239.** 150 Anza Blvd. Just e of US 101, exit Broadway-Burlingame or Anza Blvd. Int corridors. **Pets:** Large. $50 one-time fee/pet. Service with restrictions, crate.

SAVE ✕ 🖳M ⌁ ⟨ ✦ 🖳 ¶ ⌇

◆◆◆ ▼▼▼ Red Roof Inn Ⓜ
(650) 342-7772. **$84-$114.** 777 Airport Blvd. Just s of airport; US 101, exit Broadway-Burlingame or E Anza Blvd. Ext corridors. **Pets:** Medium, other species. Service with restrictions, supervision.

SAVE ✕ ⌁ ⟨ ⌇

◆◆◆ ▼▼▼ ▼▼ San Francisco Airport Marriott
(650) 692-9100. **$99-$259.** 1800 Old Bayshore Hwy. Just e of US 101, exit Millbrae Ave. Int corridors. **Pets:** Other species. Service with restrictions.

SAVE 🔊 ✕ 🖳M ⌁ ⟨ ✦ 🖳 ¶ ⌇

◆◆◆ ▼▼ ▼▼ Vagabond Inn-Airport Ⓜ
(650) 692-4040. **$89-$119.** 1640 Bayshore Hwy. Just e of US 101, exit Millbrae Ave. Ext corridors. **Pets:** Accepted.

SAVE 🔊 ✕ ✦ 🖳

HALF MOON BAY

◆◆◆ ▼▼ ▼▼ Harbor View Inn Ⓜ
(650) 726-2329. **$105-$160.** 51 Ave Alhambra. 4 mi n of jct SR 92 and 1; e of SR 1. Ext corridors. **Pets:** Accepted.

SAVE 🔊 ✦ 🜛

MILLBRAE

▼▼▼▼ The Westin Hotel-San Francisco Airport �H
(650) 692-3500. **$379-$439.** 1 Old Bayshore Hwy. Just e of US 101, exit Millbrae Ave. Int corridors. **Pets:** Accepted.

ASK 🔊 ✕ 🖳M ⌁ ⟨ ✦ 🖳 ¶ ⌇

SAN BRUNO

◆◆◆ ▼▼ ▼▼ Regency Inn Ⓜ
(650) 589-7535. **$89-$159.** 411 E San Bruno Ave. Ext corridors. **Pets:** Small. $50 deposit/pet, $10 one-time fee/pet. Service with restrictions, supervision.

SAVE 🔊 ✕ ✦ 🖳

◆◆◆ ▼▼▼▼ Summerfield Suites by Wyndham-San Francisco Ⓜ
(650) 588-0770. **$89-$179.** 1350 Huntington Ave. I-380, exit El Camino Real N, I-380, exit El Camino Real N, e on Sneath Ln. Ext corridors. **Pets:** $10 daily fee/room, $150 one-time fee/room. Service with restrictions.

SAVE 🔊 ✕ ✦ 🖳 ⌇

SAN CARLOS

▼▼▼▼ Homestead Studio Suites Hotel Ⓜ
(650) 368-2600. **$134-$164.** 3 Circle Star Way. W of US 101, exit Whipple Ave, w to Industrial, just n. Int corridors. **Pets:** Small. $75 one-time fee/pet. Service with restrictions.

ASK 🔊 ✕ ⟨ ✦ 🖳

◆◆◆ ▼▼▼▼ Inns of America Ⓜ
(650) 631-0777. **$199-$259.** 555 Skyway Rd. US 101, exit Holly St/Redwood Shores, e to Airport Blvd, then just s. Int corridors. **Pets:** Medium, other species. $40 deposit/pet. Service with restrictions, supervision.

SAVE 🔊 ✕ ⟨ ✦ 🖳 ⌇

SAN FRANCISCO

◆◆◆ ▼▼▼▼ Beresford Arms �H
(415) 673-2600. **$145.** 701 Post St. 3 blks w of Union Square. Int corridors. **Pets:** Accepted.

SAVE 🔊 ✕ ✦ ⟨Ⓚ⟩

◆◆◆ ▼▼▼▼ Best Western Tuscan Inn at Fisherman's Wharf �H
(415) 561-1100. **$249-$309.** 425 Northpoint St. Just s of the wharf at Mason St. Int corridors. **Pets:** Medium. $50 daily fee/room. Service with restrictions, supervision.

SAVE 🔊 ✕ ⌁ 🖳 ¶

▼▼▼▼ Campton Place Hotel �H ❀
(415) 781-5555. **$335-$460.** 340 Stockton St. Just n of Union Square. Int corridors. **Pets:** Other species. $35 deposit/pet. Supervision.

ASK 🔊 ✕ ⟨ ¶

◆◆◆ ▼▼▼ Clarion Bedford Hotel �H ❀
(415) 673-6040. **$149-$199.** 761 Post St. 3 1/2 blks w of Union Square. Int corridors. **Pets:** Medium, other species. Service with restrictions, crate.

SAVE 🔊 ✕ ✦ 🖳 ¶ ⟨Ⓚ⟩

▼▼▼▼ The Fairmont San Francisco �H
(415) 772-5000. **$219-$449.** 950 Mason St. Atop Nob Hill at California St. Int corridors. **Pets:** Accepted.

ASK 🔊 ✕ 🖳M ⌁ ¶

▼▼▼▼ Holiday Inn-Civic Center Ⓜ
(415) 626-6103. **$189-$229.** 50 8th St. 2 blks from Civic Auditorium; just s of Market St and BART Station. Int corridors. **Pets:** Accepted.

ASK 🔊 ✕ 🖳M ⟨ ¶

▼▼▼▼ Holiday Inn-Financial District �H
(415) 433-6600. **$249-$289.** 750 Kearny St. 1 blk from Chinatown. Int corridors. **Pets:** Accepted.

ASK 🔊 ✕ ✦ 🖳 ¶

AAA ▼▼▼ Hotel Beresford H
(415) 673-9900. **$45-$165.** 635 Sutter St. 1 blk nw of Union Square at Mason St. Int corridors. **Pets:** Accepted.
[SAVE] [S✆] [✕] [🛏] [❢] [🏊]

AAA ▼▼▼▼ Hotel Monaco H ☙
(415) 292-0100. **$399.** 501 Geary St. Just w of Union Square at Taylor St. Int corridors. **Pets:** Other species. Designated rooms, service with restrictions, supervision.
[SAVE] [S✆] [✕] [💻] [❢]

AAA ▼▼▼▼ Hotel Palomar H ☙
(415) 348-1111. **$355-$400.** 12 Fourth St. At Market St. Int corridors. **Pets:** Medium, dogs only. $200 deposit/pet, $50 daily fee/pet. Designated rooms, service with restrictions, supervision.
[SAVE] [✕] [&M] [&♿] [🛏] [❢]

AAA ▼▼▼▼ Hotel Triton H ☙
(415) 394-0500. **$249.** 342 Grant St. Near Union Square at Bush St. Int corridors. **Pets:** Other species. Designated rooms, service with restrictions, supervision.
[SAVE] [S✆] [✕] [🛏] [💻]

AAA ▼▼▼▼ The Laurel Inn M ☙
(415) 567-8467. **$150-$175.** 444 Presidio Ave. 1 mi w of US 101 (Van Ness Ave), 1 mi e of Park Presidio Blvd (SR 1) at California St. Int corridors. **Pets:** Service with restrictions, supervision.
[SAVE] [S✆] [✕] [🐾] [💻] [🏊]

AAA ▼▼▼ Pacific Heights Inn M ☙
(415) 776-3310. **$85-$175.** 1555 Union St. Just w of US 101 (Van Ness Ave). Ext corridors. **Pets:** Supervision.
[SAVE] [S✆] [✕] [🛏] [💻] [🏊]

▼▼▼▼ The Pan Pacific Hotel H
(415) 771-8600. **$310-$340.** 500 Post St. Just w of Union Square at Mason St. Int corridors. **Pets:** Medium. $75 one-time fee/pet. Designated rooms, service with restrictions, crate.
[A$K] [S✆] [✕] [&♿] [❢]

AAA ▼▼▼▼ The Prescott Hotel H
(415) 563-0303. **$290-$450.** 545 Post St. Just w of Union Square. Int corridors. **Pets:** Accepted.
[SAVE] [S✆] [✕] [❢]

AAA ▼▼▼▼ San Francisco Marriott Fisherman's Wharf H
(415) 775-7555. **$239-$309.** 1250 Columbus Ave. Just s of the wharf at Bay St. Int corridors. **Pets:** Medium. $5 daily fee/pet, $50 one-time fee/room. Service with restrictions, supervision.
[SAVE] [✕] [&M] [🐾] [&♿] [🛏] [💻] [❢]

AAA ▼▼▼▼ Serrano Hotel H ☙
(415) 885-2500. **$179-$319.** 405 Taylor St. Just w of Union Square. Int corridors. **Pets:** Dogs only. Designated rooms, service with restrictions, crate.
[SAVE] [S✆] [✕] [&M] [&♿] [❢]

AAA ▼▼▼ Travelodge By The Bay M
(415) 673-0691. **$85-$165, 14 days notice.** 1450 Lombard St. On US 101 (Van Ness Ave). Ext corridors. **Pets:** Medium. $20 daily fee/pet. Designated rooms, service with restrictions, supervision.
[SAVE] [S✆] [✕] [&M] [&♿] [💻]

▼▼▼▼ The Westin St. Francis H
(415) 397-7000. **$199-$439.** 335 Powell St. On Union Square. **Pets:** Accepted.
[A$K] [S✆] [✕] [💻] [❢]

SAN MATEO

AAA ▼▼▼ Residence Inn by Marriott M
(650) 574-4700. **$209.** 2000 Winward Way. 0.8 mi se from jct US 101 and SR 92; exit SR 92 via Edgewater Blvd. Ext corridors. **Pets:** Accepted.
[SAVE] [S✆] [✕] [💻] [🏊]

SAN RAFAEL

▼▼▼ Villa Inn M
(415) 456-4975. **$75-$95.** 1600 Lincoln Ave. Off US 101, Lincoln Ave off-ramp; exit Central San Rafael northbound, 0.3 mi w on Fourth St, 0.5 mi n. Ext corridors. **Pets:** Medium, dogs only. $20 deposit/pet. Designated rooms, supervision.
[✕] [🛏] [💻] [🏊]

SOUTH SAN FRANCISCO

AAA ▼▼ Howard Johnson Express Inn M
(650) 589-9055. **$49-$199.** 222 S Airport Blvd. Just e of US 101, exit S Airport Blvd. Ext corridors. **Pets:** Other species. $10 daily fee/pet. Service with restrictions, crate.
[SAVE] [S✆] [✕] [🛏] [💻]

▼▼▼▼ La Quinta Inn M
(650) 583-2223. **$129-$159.** 20 S Airport Blvd. Just w of US 101 at S Airport Blvd exit. Int corridors. **Pets:** Accepted.
[SAVE] [S✆] [✕] [&♿] [🛏] [💻]

☙   **END METROPOLITAN AREA**   ☙

SAN JOSE

Doubletree Hotel ☒
(408) 453-4000. **$159-$369.** 2050 Gateway Pl. 0.3 mi e of
San Jose International Airport via Airport Blvd; w of US 101,
exit N 1st St; US 101 northbound, exit Brokaw Rd.. Int
corridors. **Pets:** Accepted.

Hilton San Jose & Towers ☒
(408) 287-2100. **$319.** 300 Almaden Blvd. Int corridors.
Pets: Medium. $200 deposit/room. Service with restrictions.

Homestead Studio Suites-San Jose Ⓜ
(408) 573-0648. **$124-$154.** 1560 N First St. 1 mi e of San
Jose International Airport; s off US 101, exit N 1st St. Int
corridors. **Pets:** Small. $75 one-time fee/pet. Service with
restrictions, crate.

Homewood Suites by Hilton Ⓜ
(408) 428-9900. **$229-$279.** 10 W Trimble Rd. US 101, exit
Trimble Rd, 1.3 mi e, then 2mi ne San Jose International
Airport. Ext/int corridors. **Pets:** Accepted.

**Summerfield Suites by Wyndham-San
Jose/Silicon Valley** Ⓜ
(408) 436-1600. **$89-$239.** 1602 Crane Ct. US 101, exit
Brokaw E, 0.4 mi to Bering S, then 0.5 mi. Ext corridors.
Pets: Accepted.

Vagabond Ⓜ
(408) 453-8822. **$129.** 1488 N First St. I-880, exit N First
St, then w. Ext corridors. **Pets:** Accepted.

SAN JUAN BAUTISTA

San Juan Inn Ⓜ
(831) 623-4380. **$79-$99.** 410 The Alameda. Jct SR 156.
Ext corridors. **Pets:** Accepted.

SAN JUAN CAPISTRANO

Best Western Capistrano Inn Ⓜ
(949) 493-5661. **$89-$179, 3 days notice.** 27174 Ortega
Hwy. I-5, exit SR 74 (Ortega Hwy), just e. **Pets:** Accepted.

SAN LUIS OBISPO

Best Western Royal Oak Hotel Ⓜ
(805) 544-4410. **$69-$139.** 214 Madonna Rd. From US
101, just s. Ext/int corridors. **Pets:** Medium. $10 one-time
fee/room. Service with restrictions, supervision.

Days Inn Ⓜ
(805) 549-9911. **$59-$189.** 2050 Garfield St. From US 101,
exit Monterey St. Ext corridors. **Pets:** Very small, dogs only.
$50 deposit/pet, $10 daily fee/pet. Designated rooms, service with restrictions, supervision.

Heritage Inn Bed & Breakfast ☒ ☀
(805) 544-7440. **$85-$150, 7 days notice.** 978 Olive St.
From US 101, just w, exit Santa Rosa southbound; exit
Morro Bay northbound. Int corridors. **Pets:** Small, other
species. $35 one-time fee/pet. Service with restrictions,
supervision.

Olive Tree Ramada Inn Ⓜ
(805) 544-2800. **$65-$199.** 1000 Olive St. US 101 exit
Morro Bay northbound; exit Santa Rosa southbound, just e.
Ext corridors. **Pets:** Accepted.

Sands Suites & Motel Ⓜ
(805) 544-0500. **$59-$169.** 1930 Monterey St. From US
101, exit Monterey St, just e. Ext corridors. **Pets:** Other
species. $10 one-time fee/pet. Designated rooms, no serv-
ice.

Vagabond Inn Ⓜ
(805) 544-4710. **$65-$185.** 210 Madonna Rd. From US
101, just e. Ext corridors. **Pets:** Small, dogs only. $5 daily
fee/pet. Designated rooms, service with restrictions, supervision.

SAN MARCOS

**Quails Inn Hotel at Lake San Marcos
Resort** Ⓜ
(760) 744-0120. **$99-$299.** 1025 La Bonita Dr. From SR 78,
exit Rancho Santa Fe Rd, 2 mi s, 0.5 mi e via Lake San
Marcos Dr and San Marino Dr; at Lake San Marcos. Ext/int
corridors. **Pets:** Other species. $10 daily fee/pet. Service
with restrictions.

SAN RAMON

Homestead Studio Suites-San Ramon Ⓜ
(925) 277-0833. **Call for rates.** 18000 San Ramon Valley
Blvd. I-680, exit Bollinger Canyon E, just n. Ext corridors.
Pets: Medium, other species. $75 one-time fee/room. Serv-
ice with restrictions, supervision.

Residence Inn by Marriott Ⓜ
(925) 277-9292. **$197.** 1071 Market Pl. I-680, exit Bollinger
Canyon Rd E, just e. **Pets:** Accepted.

▲▲▲ ▽▽▽▽ San Ramon Marriott at Bishop
Ranch H
(925) 867-9200. **$79-$209.** 2600 Bishop Dr. I-680, exit Bollinger Canyon E, n on Sunset, just w. Int corridors. **Pets:** Accepted.

[SAVE] [✕] [📧] [💻] [🍴]

SAN SIMEON

▽▽▽▽ Motel 6 Premiere M1
(805) 927-8691. **$45-$87.** 9070 Castillo Dr. On SR 1. Int corridors. **Pets:** Accepted.

[S🔒] [✕] [🍴] [🐾]

▲▲▲ ▽▽▽▽ Silver Surf Motel M ❖
(805) 927-4661. **$39-$104.** 9390 Castillo Dr. On SR 1. Ext corridors. **Pets:** Medium, other species. $10 daily fee/pet. Designated rooms, service with restrictions, supervision.

[SAVE] [S🔒] [✕] [🐾] [Ⓧ]

SANGER

▲▲▲ ▽▽ Town House Motel M
(559) 875-5531. **$46-$51.** 1308 Church Ave. 1.3 mi s of SR 180 at Academy Ave, then 0.7 mi n. Ext corridors. **Pets:** Accepted.

[SAVE] [S🔒] [✕] [🐾]

SANTA BARBARA

▲▲▲ ▽▽ Blue Sands Motel M
(805) 965-1624. **$65-$195, 3 days notice.** 421 S Milpas St. From US 101, exit Milpas St, 0.3 mi s. Ext corridors. **Pets:** Accepted.

[SAVE] [✕] [📧] [💻] [🐾] [Ⓧ]

▽▽▽▽ Fess Parker's Doubletree Resort H ❖
(805) 564-4333. **$370-$401, 3 days notice.** 633 E Cabrillo Blvd. From US 101, exit Milpas St, just s, then just w. Ext/int corridors. **Pets:** Designated rooms, service with restrictions, supervision.

[SAVE] [S🔒] [✕] [📧] [💻] [🍴] [🐾] [Ⓧ]

▽▽▽ ▽▽▽ Four Seasons Biltmore R ❖
(805) 969-2261. **$470-$650, 3 days notice.** 1260 Channel Dr. From US 101, exit Olive Mill Rd northbound, 0.3 mi s; exit Carrillo Blvd southbound, 0.8 mi e to Olive Mill Rd, then 0.3 mi s. Ext/int corridors. **Pets:** Small, other species. Designated rooms, service with restrictions, supervision.

[ASK] [✕] [📧] [💻] [🍴] [🐾] [Ⓧ]

▲▲▲ ▽▽▽▽ Pacifica Suites M
(805) 683-6722. **$139-$249.** 5490 Hollister Ave. From US 101, exit Patterson Ave, 0.5 mi s, then 0.5 mi w; in the Goleta area. Ext/int corridors. **Pets:** Small. $10 daily fee/pet. Designated rooms, service with restrictions, supervision.

[SAVE] [S🔒] [✕] [📧] [💻] [🐾]

SANTA CATALINA ISLAND

▲▲▲ ▽▽▽ Best Western Catalina Canyon Resort
& Spa M
(310) 510-0325. **$89-$250, 3 days notice.** 888 Country Club Dr. 0.5 mi from the harbor. Ext corridors. **Pets:** Medium, other species. $25 one-time fee/room. Designated rooms, service with restrictions, crate.

[SAVE] [S🔒] [✕] [💻] [🍴] [🐾]

SANTA CLARA

▲▲▲ ▽▽▽ GuestHouse International Inn &
Suites-Silicon Valley USA M
(408) 241-3010. **$100-$220.** 2930 El Camino Real. SR 82, 0.5 mi w of San Tomas Expwy; US 101, exit S Bowers Ave. Ext corridors. **Pets:** Accepted.

[SAVE] [S🔒] [✕] [♿M] [📧] [💻] [🐾]

▲▲▲ ▽▽▽▽ Santa Clara Marriott Hotel H ❖
(408) 988-1500. **$75-$239.** 2700 Mission College. 0.5 mi e off US 101, exit Great America Pkwy; 0.8 mi s of Great America Theme Park. Int corridors. **Pets:** Other species. $100 deposit/room. Designated rooms, service with restrictions, crate.

[SAVE] [✕] [📧] [💻] [🍴] [🐾] [Ⓧ]

▲▲▲ ▽▽▽ The Vagabond Inn M
(408) 241-0771. **$49-$199.** 3580 El Camino Real. On SR 82; southeast corner of Lawrence Expwy cloverleaf. Ext corridors. **Pets:** Other species. $10 daily fee/pet. Service with restrictions.

[SAVE] [S🔒] [✕] [📧] [💻] [🐾]

▲▲▲ ▽▽▽▽ Wellesley Inn M
(408) 257-8600. **$139.** 5405 Stevens Creek Blvd. I-280 and Lawrence Expwy, exit Stevens Creek Blvd, just w. Int corridors. **Pets:** Other species. Service with restrictions, crate.

[SAVE] [S🔒] [✕] [📧] [💻] [🐾]

▽▽▽ ▽▽▽▽ The Westin Hotel-Santa Clara H
(408) 986-0700. **$89-$329.** 5101 Great America Pkwy. 0.8 mi e off US 101, exit Great America Pkwy. Int corridors. **Pets:** Medium. $50 one-time fee/room. Service with restrictions, crate.

[ASK] [S🔒] [✕] [♿M] [🍽] [📧] [💻] [🍴] [🐾] [Ⓧ]

SANTA CRUZ

▲▲▲ ▽▽▽ Continental Inn M
(831) 429-1221. **$85-$260, 7 days notice.** 414 Ocean St. 5 blks from beach; between Broadway and Soquel aves. Ext corridors. **Pets:** Medium. Designated rooms, service with restrictions, supervision.

[SAVE] [S🔒] [✕] [📧] [💻] [🐾]

▲▲▲ ▽▽▽ Days Inn M
(831) 423-8564. **$58-$185.** 325 Pacific. 6 blks se of SR 1. Ext corridors. **Pets:** Accepted.

[SAVE] [✕] [📧] [🐾]

(AAA) ▼▼ GuestHouse International Pacific Inn M
(831) 425-3722. **$80-$200, 3 days notice.** 330 Ocean St. 1 mi from jct SR 1 and 17. Int corridors. **Pets:** Medium, dogs only. $10 daily fee/pet. Designated rooms, service with restrictions, supervision.
SAVE S❄ ✕ 📶 💻 🏊

(AAA) ▼▼ Ocean Pacific Lodge M
(831) 457-1234. **$78-$187.** 120 Washington. SR 17/1 W, exit Ocean St, 1 mi w to Broadway, turn right, left on Front St to Pacific St, just right. Ext corridors. **Pets:** Accepted.
SAVE S❄ ✕ 📶 🏊

SANTA MARIA

(AAA) ▼▼▼ Best Western Big America MI
(805) 922-5200. **$77-$99.** 1725 N Broadway. From US 101, exit Broadway, 0.5 mi w. Ext corridors. **Pets:** Small, other species. Service with restrictions, supervision.
SAVE S❄ ✕ 📶 💻 🍴 🏊

(AAA) ▼◆▼ Comfort Inn M
(805) 922-5891. **$74-$109.** 210 S Nicholson Ave. From US 101, exit Main St, 0.5 mi e. Int corridors. **Pets:** Small. $10 deposit/pet. Designated rooms, service with restrictions, supervision.
SAVE S❄ ✕ 📶 🏊

▼◆▼ Historic Santa Maria Inn H
(805) 928-7777. **$119-$149, 7 days notice.** 801 S Broadway. From US 101, exit Main St, 1 mi w, then 0.5 mi s. Int corridors. **Pets:** Small. $50 one-time fee/room. Service with restrictions, supervision.
ASK S❄ ✕ 📶 💻 🍴 🏊

SANTA NELLA

(AAA) ▼▼▼ Best Western Andersen's Inn M
(209) 826-5534. **$64-$85, 5 days notice.** 12367 Hwy 33 S. E of I-5; 4 mi n of SR 152 (Pacheco Pass Rd); I-5, exit SR 33 (Santa Nella-Gustine). Ext corridors. **Pets:** Small, dogs only. $10 daily fee/pet. Designated rooms, no service, supervision.
SAVE S❄ ✕ 💻 🏊

(AAA) ▼◆▼ Holiday Inn Express M
(209) 826-8282. **$65-$85.** 28976 W Plaza Dr. I-5, exit SR 33, exit SR 33, 2 blks e. Ext corridors. **Pets:** Designated rooms, service with restrictions, supervision.
SAVE S❄ ✕ 📶 💻 🏊

▼▼ Ramada Inn Mission de Oro MI
(209) 826-4444. **$75-$125, 7 days notice.** 13070 Hwy 33 S. Jct I-5 and SR 33; 4 mi n of SR 152. Ext/int corridors. **Pets:** Medium. $10 one-time fee/room. Service with restrictions, supervision.
ASK S❄ ✕ 📶 🍴 🏊

SCOTTS VALLEY

▼◆▼ Hilton San Jose South/Scotts Valley H
(831) 440-1000. **$189-$379.** 6001 La Madrona Dr. SR 17, exit Mt Hermon Rd. Int corridors. **Pets:** $25 daily fee/pet. Supervision.
SAVE S❄ ✕ ⚒M 📶 💻 🍴 🏊

SELMA

(AAA) ▼▼ Super 8 Motel M
(559) 896-2800. **$50-$60.** 3142 S Highland Ave. SR 99, exit Floral Ave. Int corridors. **Pets:** $20 deposit/pet, $5 one-time fee/pet. Designated rooms, service with restrictions, supervision.
SAVE S❄ ✕ 🏊

SHASTA LAKE

(AAA) ▼▼ Bridge Bay Resort M
(530) 275-3021. **$69-$98.** On Lake Shasta, E of I-5, exit Bridge Bay Rd, 12 mi n of Redding. Ext corridors. **Pets:** Medium. $25 deposit/pet, $5 daily fee/pet. Designated rooms, service with restrictions, supervision.
SAVE ✕ 📶 💻 🍴 🏊 🗙

(AAA) ▼▼▼ Fawndale Lodge & RV Resort M
(530) 275-8000. **$66-$84, 4 days notice.** 1 mi s of Shasta Lake; e of I-5, exit Fawndale Rd (10 mi n of Redding). Ext corridors. **Pets:** Other species. $50 deposit/pet, $6 daily fee/pet. Service with restrictions, supervision.
SAVE S❄ ✕ 📶 💻 🏊

SHELTER COVE

(AAA) ▼ Shelter Cove Motor Inn M
(707) 986-7521. **$75-$120.** 205 Wave Dr. 23 mi w of US 101 via Shelter Cove Rd, 1 mi n on Upper Pacific Rd, w on Lower Pacific Rd. Ext corridors. **Pets:** Other species. Service with restrictions, supervision.
SAVE S❄ 📶 💻 🎿 🗷

SIERRA CITY

(AAA) ▼▼▼ Herrington's Sierra Pines MI
(530) 862-1151. **$55-$80, 10 days notice.** 104 Main St. 0.5 mi w on SR 49. Ext corridors. **Pets:** Other species. $5 one-time fee/room. Supervision.
SAVE S❄ 💻 🍴 🎿 🗷

SMITH RIVER

▼▼ Best Western Ship Ashore Motel MI
(707) 487-3141. **$55-$88.** 12370 Hwy 101. 2.8 mi n on US 101; 3 mi s of OR-CA stateline. Ext corridors. **Pets:** Very small. Service with restrictions, supervision.
SAVE S❄ ✕ 📶 💻 🍴 🎿

SOLVANG

(AAA) ▼ Viking Motel M
(805) 688-1337. **$45-$160, 3 days notice.** 1506 Mission Dr. On SR 246. Ext corridors. **Pets:** Small. $10 daily fee/room. Service with restrictions, supervision.
SAVE S❄ ✕ 📶

SONORA

(AAA) ▼▼▼ Aladdin Motor Inn M
(209) 533-4971. **$68-$76, 30 days notice.** 14260 Mono (Hwy 108) Way. 3.5 mi e on SR 108. Ext/int corridors. **Pets:** Medium. $5 one-time fee/pet. Designated rooms, service with restrictions, supervision.

SAVE ⊠ 🛋 💻 🐾

(AAA) ▼▼▼ Best Western Sonora Oaks M ❀
(209) 533-4400. **$79-$95.** 19551 Hess Ave. 3.5 mi e on SR 108; corner of Hess Ave. Ext/int corridors. **Pets:** Small. $10 daily fee/pet. Designated rooms, service with restrictions, supervision.

SAVE S⊠ ⊠ 🐾 💻 🐾

(AAA) ▼ Miners Motel M
(209) 532-7850. **$44-$75, 3 days notice.** 18740 SR 108. 1 mi e of Jamestown on SR 108 and 49. Ext corridors. **Pets:** Medium, dogs only. $5 daily fee/pet. Service with restrictions, supervision.

SAVE S⊠ ⊠ 🛋 💻 🐾

(AAA) ▼▼▼ Sonora Days Inn M ❀
(209) 532-2400. **$59-$149, 7 days notice.** 160 S Washington St. Downtown. Ext/int corridors. **Pets:** Other species. $10 daily fee/pet. Designated rooms, service with restrictions, crate.

SAVE S⊠ ⊠ 🛋 💻 🍴 🐾

▼ Sonora Gold Lodge M ❀
(209) 532-3952. **Call for rates.** 480 Stockton St. 0.5 mi sw on SR 108 business route and 49. Ext corridors. **Pets:** Other species. $10 one-time fee/room. Designated rooms, service with restrictions, supervision.

ASK S⊠ ⊠ 🐾

STOCKTON

▼▼▼ Days Inn of Stockton M
(209) 948-6151. **$65-$95.** 33 N Center St. 1 blk n; w off El Dorado St via Weber; SR 99 southbound, exit Wilson Way; SR 99 northbound, w via Mariposa Rd to Charter Way; I-5, exit downtown. Ext corridors. **Pets:** Accepted.

SAVE S⊠ ⊠ 🐾

(AAA) ▼ Econo Lodge of Stockton M
(209) 466-5741. **$48-$60.** 2210 S Manthey Rd. I-5 W, exit 8th St, exit 8th St, 0.3 mi s of jct SR 4. Int corridors. **Pets:** Small. $25 deposit/room. Designated rooms, service with restrictions, supervision.

SAVE S⊠ ⊠ 🛋 🐾

▼▼▼ La Quinta Inn M
(209) 952-7800. **$78-$91.** 2710 W March Ln. I-5, exit March Ln, exit March Ln, just w. Ext corridors. **Pets:** Small. Service with restrictions, supervision.

SAVE S⊠ ⊠ 🖐M 💻 🐾

(AAA) ▼▼▼▼ Residence Inn by Marriott M
(209) 472-9800. **$124-$199.** 3240 W March Ln. I-5, exit March Ln, exit March Ln, 0.5 mi w. Int corridors. **Pets:** Small. $15 daily fee/pet, $80 one-time fee/room. Service with restrictions, supervision.

SAVE S⊠ ⊠ 🖐M 🐾 💻 🐾

SUN CITY

(AAA) ▼ Travelodge M
(909) 679-1133. **$62-$68.** 27955 Encanto DR. I-215, exit McCall Blvd, just e, then just s. Ext corridors. **Pets:** Accepted.

SAVE S⊠ ⊠ 🛋 💻 🐾

SUNNYVALE

▼▼▼ Homestead Studio Suites Hotel M
(408) 734-3431. **$124-$154, 7 days notice.** 1255 Orleans Dr. N of SR 237, exit Mathilda Ave, then e on Moffett Park Dr to Orleans Dr. Ext corridors. **Pets:** Accepted.

ASK S⊠ ⊠ 💻

(AAA) ▼▼▼ Residence Inn by Marriott M
(408) 720-1000. **$199.** 750 Lakeway Dr. US 101, exit Lawrence Expwy S, then e on Oakmead. Ext corridors. **Pets:** Other species. $75 deposit/pet. Service with restrictions.

SAVE ⊠ 💻 🐾

(AAA) ▼▼▼ Residence Inn by Marriott M
(408) 720-8893. **$329.** 1080 Stewart Dr. US 101, exit Lawrence Expwy S, Duane Ave W, Stewart Dr S. Ext corridors. **Pets:** Small, other species. $10 daily fee/pet, $75 one-time fee/pet. Service with restrictions, supervision.

SAVE S⊠ ⊠ 🛋 💻 🐾

(AAA) ▼▼▼ Summerfield Suites by Wyndham-Sunnyvale/Silicon Valley M
(408) 745-1515. **$89-$209.** 900 Hamlin Ct. SR 237, exit Mathilda Ave S, w on Ross. Ext corridors. **Pets:** Accepted.

SAVE S⊠ ⊠ 🛋 💻 🐾

▼▼▼ Vagabond Inn M
(408) 734-4607. **$69-$209.** 816 Ahwanee Ave. S off US 101, exit via Mathilda Ave S. Ext corridors. **Pets:** Medium, other species. $10 daily fee/pet. Designated rooms, service with restrictions, supervision.

ASK S⊠ ⊠ 🛋 💻 🐾

▼▼▼ Woodfin Suites M
(408) 738-1700. **$89-$249.** 635 E El Camino Real. US 101, exit Fair Oaks; 2.5 mi w to SR 82 E. Ext corridors. **Pets:** Accepted.

ASK S⊠ ⊠ 💻 🐾

SUSANVILLE

▼ America's Best Inns M
(530) 257-4522. **$44-$60.** 2705 Main St. 1.5 mi e on SR 36. Ext corridors. **Pets:** $5 daily fee/pet. Service with restrictions, supervision.

ASK S⊠ ⊠ 🛋

River Inn M
(530) 257-6051. **$48-$58.** 1710 Main St. 0.8 mi e on SR 36. Ext corridors. **Pets:** Accepted.

Super 8 Motel M
(530) 257-2782. **$56-$64.** 2975 Johnstonville Rd. Off SR 36, 1.8 mi e. Ext corridors. **Pets:** Accepted.

TEHACHAPI

Best Western Mountain Inn M
(661) 822-5591. **$65-$80.** 416 W Tehachapi Blvd. From SR 58, exit SR 202, then 1 mi e. Ext corridors. **Pets:** Other species. Service with restrictions, crate.

Tehachapi Summit Travelodge MI
(661) 823-8000. **$67.** 500 Steuber Rd. From SR 58, exit Monolith eastbound; exit Tehachapi westbound. Int corridors. **Pets:** Other species. $7 one-time fee/room. Designated rooms, service with restrictions, supervision.

THOUSAND OAKS

Thousand Oaks Inn MI
(805) 497-3701. **$85-$105.** 75 W Thousand Oaks Blvd. From US 101, exit Moorpark Rd, just n, then just w. Ext corridors. **Pets:** Small. $75 one-time fee/pet. Designated rooms, service with restrictions, crate.

THOUSAND PALMS

Red Roof Inn M
(760) 343-1381. **$52-$72.** 72-215 Varner Rd. I-10, exit Ramon Rd, just n, then just w. Ext corridors. **Pets:** Medium. Designated rooms, service with restrictions, supervision.

THREE RIVERS

Best Western Holiday Lodge M
(559) 561-4119. **$61-$119.** 40105 Sierra Drive. On SR 198, 2 mi sw of town Center. Ext corridors. **Pets:** Accepted.

Buckeye Tree Lodge M
(559) 561-5900. **$66-$115, 3 days notice.** 46000 Sierra Dr. On SR 198, 6 mi ne of town center, 0.5 mi sw of entrance to Sequoia National Park. Ext corridors. **Pets:** Other species. $5 daily fee/pet. Service with restrictions, supervision.

Lazy J Ranch Motel M
(559) 561-4449. **$80-$105, 3 days notice.** 39625 Sierra Dr. On SR 198, 2.5 mi sw of town center. Ext corridors. **Pets:** $5 one-time fee/pet. Service with restrictions, supervision.

The River Inn M
(559) 561-4367. **Call for rates, 3 days notice.** 45176 Sierra Dr. On SR 198, 5 mi ne of town center, 1.5 mi sw of entrance to Sequoia National Park. Ext corridors. **Pets:** Accepted.

Sequoia Village Inn C
(559) 561-3652. **$69-$115, 7 days notice.** 45971 Sierra Dr. 6 mi ne of town center on SR 198, 0.5 mi sw of entrance to Sequoia National Park. Ext corridors. **Pets:** $5 daily fee/pet. Service with restrictions, supervision.

Sierra Lodge M
(559) 561-3681. **$46-$82, 7 days notice.** 43175 Sierra Dr. On SR 198, 1 mi se of town center, 3 mi sw of entrance to Sequoia National Park. Ext corridors. **Pets:** Other species. $20 deposit/pet. Service with restrictions, supervision.

TRACY

Best Western Luxury Inn M
(209) 832-0271. **$69-$109, 7 days notice.** 811 W Clover Rd. I-205, exit Central Tracy, exit Central Tracy. Int corridors. **Pets:** Accepted.

Phoenix Lodge M
(209) 835-1335. **$55-$85, 7 days notice.** 3511 N Tracy Blvd. I-205, exit Central Tracy. Int corridors. **Pets:** Accepted.

TRINIDAD

Bishop Pine Lodge C
(707) 677-3314. **$80-$110, 7 days notice.** 1481 Patricks Point Dr. Just w on US 101, exit Trinidad northbound, then 2 mi n; exit Seawood southbound, then 1 mi s. Ext/int corridors. **Pets:** $10 daily fee/pet. Designated rooms, no service, supervision.

TULARE

Best Western Town & Country Lodge M
(559) 688-7537. **$66.** 1051 N Blackstone. From SR 99, exit Prosperity Ave, just w. Int corridors. **Pets:** Accepted.

Days Inn M
(559) 686-0985. **$69.** 1183 N Blackstone St. From SR 99, exit Prosperity Ave, just w. Ext corridors. **Pets:** Medium. $5 daily fee/pet. Service with restrictions, supervision.

Hawthorn Inn & Suites M
(559) 685-9500. **$80, 3 days notice.** 1016 E Prosperity Ave. From SR 99, just e. Int corridors. **Pets:** Other species. $100 deposit/room, $5 daily fee/pet. Service with restrictions, supervision.

Quality Inn M
(559) 686-3432. **$63-$69.** 1010 E Prosperity Ave. From SR 99, exit Prosperity Ave, just e. Int corridors. **Pets:** Small, dogs only. $5 daily fee/room. Service with restrictions, supervision.

TURLOCK

The Tree Inn M
(209) 668-3400. **$64-$72.** 201 W Glenwood Ave. SR 99, exit Lander. Ext corridors. **Pets:** Small, dogs only. Designated rooms, service with restrictions, supervision.

TWAIN HARTE

Eldorado Motel M
(209) 586-4479. **$54-$80, 3 days notice.** 22678 Blackhawk Dr. SR 108 exit Twain Harte; corner of Twain Harte and Blackhawk drs; opposite golf course. Ext corridors. **Pets:** Accepted.

TWENTYNINE PALMS

Best Western Gardens Inn & Suites M
(760) 367-9141. **$79.** 71487 Twentynine Palms Hwy. On SR 62, 1.8 mi w of town center. Ext/int corridors. **Pets:** Medium, other species. $100 deposit/room, $10 daily fee/room. Designated rooms, service with restrictions, supervision.

Circle C Lodge M
(760) 367-7615. **$81-$90.** 6340 El Rey Ave. On SR 62, just n, 1.5 mi w of town center. Ext corridors. **Pets:** Accepted.

Sunnyvale Garden Suites Hotel A
(760) 361-3939. **$79-$125, 7 days notice.** 73843 Sunnyvale Dr. From SR 62, 0.7 mi n on Adobe Rd, just e on South Slope, just n on Ocotillo, then just e. Ext corridors. **Pets:** Accepted.

VACAVILLE

Best Western Heritage Inn M
(707) 448-8453. **$86-$125.** 1420 E Monte Vista Ave. I-80, exit Monte Vista Ave, just n. Ext corridors. **Pets:** Small. Designated rooms, service with restrictions, supervision.

Residence Inn by Marriott M
(707) 469-0300. **$120-$180.** 360 Orange Dr. S of I-80, exit Orange Dr eastbound, 0.5 mi; exit Monte Vista westbound, freeway overpass to E Nut Tree Pkwy. Int corridors. **Pets:** Other species. $10 daily fee/pet, $100 one-time fee/pet. Service with restrictions, supervision.

Vacaville Super 8 M
(707) 449-8884. **$63-$93.** 101 Allison Ct. I-80, exit Monte Vista Ave, just n. Int corridors. **Pets:** Cats only. $10 one-time fee/room. Service with restrictions, supervision.

VALLEJO

Holiday Inn at Napa Gateway MI
(707) 644-1200. **$99-$129.** 1000 Fairgrounds Dr. N of I-80, exit Marine World Pkwy (SR 37), 0.3 mi. Int corridors. **Pets:** Accepted.

Ramada Inn M
(707) 643-2700. **$95-$135.** 1000 Admiral Callaghan Ln. I-80 S, exit Columbus Pkwy, 0.5 mi w. Ext corridors. **Pets:** Other species. $25 one-time fee/room. Service with restrictions, crate.

VENTURA

Best Western Inn of Ventura M
(805) 648-3101. **$79-$139.** 708 E Thompson Blvd. From US 101, exit California St northbound, just e; exit Ventura Ave southbound, then 0.5 mi e. Ext corridors. **Pets:** Other species. $20 daily fee/pet. Service with restrictions, crate.

Clarion Ventura Beach Hotel H
(805) 643-6000. **Call for rates.** 2055 Harbor Blvd. US 101, exit Seaward Ave, just w, then 0.5 mi n. Int corridors. **Pets:** Accepted.

La Quinta Inn M
(805) 658-6200. **$66-$95.** 5818 Valentine Rd. US 101, exit Victoria Ave, just s, then n. Ext/int corridors. **Pets:** Accepted.

Vagabond Inn MI
(805) 648-5371. **$59-$129.** 756 E Thompson Blvd. US 101, exit California St northbound, just n; exit Ventura Ave southbound, then 0.6 mi e. Ext corridors. **Pets:** Accepted.

VICTORVILLE

Budget Inn M
(760) 241-8010. **$42-$49.** 14153 Kentwood Blvd. I-15, exit SR 18 W (Palmdale Rd), just w. Ext corridors. **Pets:** Very small. $10 deposit/pet. Designated rooms, service with restrictions, supervision.

Ramada Inn H
(760) 245-6565. **$92.** 15494 Palmdale Rd. I-15, exit SR 18 W (Palmdale Rd), just w. Int corridors. **Pets:** Accepted.

▼▼ Red Roof Inn M
(760) 241-1577. **$46-$67.** 13409 Mariposa Rd. I-15, exit
Bear Valley Rd northbound, just e, then 1.5 mi n; I-15 S,
Green Tree Blvd exit, just e, then 1.5 mi s. Ext corridors.
Pets: Medium. $10 one-time fee/room. Service with restrictions, supervision.

ASK S⊘ ✕ 🖬 💻 ⤳

VISALIA

AAA ▼▼▼ Best Western Visalia Inn M
(559) 732-4561. **$76-$86.** 623 W Main St. From SR 198,
exit Central Visalia, just n. Ext corridors. **Pets:** Accepted.

SAVE S⊘ ✕ 🖬 💻 ⤳

VISTA

▼▼▼ La Quinta Inn M
(760) 727-8180. **$81-$105.** 630 Sycamore Ave at Thibodo
Rd. From SR 78, exit Sycamore Ave, just sw. Ext/int corridors. **Pets:** Accepted.

SAVE S⊘ ✕ 🖬 💻 ⤳

WALNUT CREEK

▼▼▼ Holiday Inn Walnut Creek MI
(925) 932-3332. **$89-$169.** 2730 N Main St. I-680, exit N
Main St, just n. Int corridors. **Pets:** Accepted.

✕ 🖬 💻 ⑪ ⤳

WATSONVILLE

AAA ▼▼▼ Best Western Inn M
(831) 724-3367. **$68-$158.** 740 Freedom Blvd. On SR 152.
Ext corridors. **Pets:** Dogs only. $5 daily fee/pet. Service with
restrictions, supervision.

SAVE S⊘ ✕ 🖬 💻 ⤳

▼▼ Red Roof Inn M
(831) 740-4520. **$79-$129.** 1620 W Beach St. Just w of SR
1, exit Riverside Dr (SR 129). Int corridors. **Pets:** Accepted.

ASK S⊘ ✕ 🖬 ⤳

WEAVERVILLE

AAA ▼▼▼ 49er Gold Country Inn M
(530) 623-4937. **$42-$98.** 718 Main St. On SR 299. Ext
corridors. **Pets:** Other species. Service with restrictions,
supervision.

SAVE S⊘ ✕ 🖬 💻 ⤳

**AAA ▼▼▼ Best Western Weaverville Victorian
Inn M**
(530) 623-4432. **$69-$119.** 1709 Main St. On SR 299. Ext
corridors. **Pets:** Accepted.

SAVE S⊘ ✕ 🐲 🖬 💻 ⑪ ⤳

AAA ▼ Motel Trinity M
(530) 623-2129. **$40-$120, 3 days notice.** 1112 Main St.
Ext corridors. **Pets:** Other species. $100 deposit/room.
Service with restrictions, supervision.

SAVE S⊘ ✕ 🖬 ⤳

▼ Red Hill Motel C
(530) 623-4331. **$35-$75.** Red Hill Rd. On SR 299; just w
of SR 3. Ext corridors. **Pets:** Medium, other species. $5
one-time fee/pet. Service with restrictions, supervision.

🖬 💻

WEED

AAA ▼▼▼ Best Inn & Suites M
(530) 938-1982. **$79-$144.** 1844 Shastina Dr. I-5, exit S
Weed, just e. Int corridors. **Pets:** Accepted.

SAVE S⊘ ✕ 🖫 🖬 💻 ⤳

AAA ▼▼▼ Holiday Inn Express M
(530) 938-1308. **$72-$79.** 1830 Black Butte Dr. Just e of
I-5; in town. Int corridors. **Pets:** Other species. $10 one-time
fee/room. Supervision.

SAVE S⊘ ✕ 🖬

AAA ▼ Sis-Q-Inn Motel M
(530) 938-4194. **$54-$66.** 1825 Shastina Dr. I-5, exit S
Weed, I-5, exit S Weed. Int corridors. **Pets:** Accepted.

SAVE S⊘ ✕ 🖬

WESTLEY

AAA ▼▼▼ Econo Lodge M
(209) 894-3900. **$52-$65.** 7100 McCracken Rd. I-5, exit
Westley E. Ext corridors. **Pets:** $10 daily fee/pet. No service, supervision.

SAVE S⊘ ✕ 🖬 💻 ⤳

WILLIAMS

AAA ▼▼▼ Comfort Inn M
(530) 473-2381. **$68-$73.** 400 C St. I-5, exit Williams, just w
on E St, then just n on 4th St. Ext corridors.
Pets: Accepted.

SAVE S⊘ ✕ 🖫M 🖬 ⤳

AAA ▼▼▼ Granzella's Inn MI
(530) 473-3310. **$70-$100.** 391 6th St. I-5, exit Williams, 0.5
mi w. Int corridors. **Pets:** Other species. $10 one-time fee/
room. Service with restrictions, supervision.

SAVE S⊘ ✕ 🖫M 🖫 🖬 💻 ⑪ ⤳

AAA ▼ Stage Stop Motel M
(530) 473-2281. **$40-$45.** 300 N 7th St. I-5, exit SR 20
business route, Exit I-5 via SR 20 business route, then 3
blks w. Ext corridors. **Pets:** Accepted.

SAVE S⊘ ✕ 🖬 ⤳

WILLOWS

AAA ▼▼▼ Best Value Inn M 🐾
(530) 934-7026. **$44-$80.** 452 N Humboldt Ave. East side
of I-5, exit via Willow-Elk Creek-Glenn Rd. Ext corridors.
Pets: Medium, other species. $7 daily fee/pet. Designated
rooms, service with restrictions, supervision.

SAVE S⊘ ✕ 🖬 ⤳

(AAA) ▼▼▼ **Best Western Golden Pheasant Inn** M
(530) 934-4603. **$90-$120.** 249 N Humboldt Ave. East side of I-5, exit freeway via Willow-Elk Creek-Glenn Rd. Ext corridors. **Pets:** Small. $10 one-time fee/pet. Designated rooms, service with restrictions, crate.
SAVE S X &M ⊟ ⊑ ¶1 ⇝

▼▼ **Super 8 Motel of Willows** M
(530) 934-2871. **$50-$60.** 457 Humboldt Ave. I-5, exit Willow-Elk Creek-Glenn Rd, I-5, exit Willow-Elk Creek-Glenn Rd. Int corridors. **Pets:** Dogs only. $20 deposit/room. Designated rooms, service with restrictions, supervision.
ASK S X ⊟ ⇝

WINE COUNTRY AREA

CALISTOGA

▼▼ **Washington Street Lodging** BB ❖
(702) 942-6968. **$90-$150 (no credit cards), 3 days notice.** 1605 Washington St. 29. Ext corridors. **Pets:** Other species. $15 one-time fee/pet. Service with restrictions.
X ⊟ ⊑ Z

FORT BRAGG

(AAA) ▼▼▼ **Beachcomber Motel** M
(707) 964-2402. **$59-$250.** 1111 N Main St. Ext corridors. **Pets:** Large, other species. $10 daily fee/pet. Designated rooms, service with restrictions, supervision.
SAVE X ⊟ ⊑ AC

(AAA) ▼▼▼ **Beach House Inn** M
(707) 961-1700. **$79-$175, 3 days notice.** 100 Pudding Creek Rd. 0.7 mi n on SR 1. Int corridors. **Pets:** $10 daily fee/pet. Service with restrictions, supervision.
SAVE X ⊟ ⊑ AC

▼▼ **Cleone Gardens Inn** M ❖
(707) 964-2788. **$92-$172, 3 days notice.** 24600 N Hwy 1. 3 mi n on SR 1. Ext corridors. **Pets:** Dogs only. $6 daily fee/pet. Designated rooms, service with restrictions, supervision.
X ⊟ ⊑ AC

▼▼ **Old Stewart House Inn** BB ❖
(707) 961-0775. **$95-$145, 7 days notice.** 511 Stewart St. Just w of SR 1 via Pine St. Ext/int corridors. **Pets:** Other species. Designated rooms, supervision.
ASK X ⊟ ⊑ AC Z

(AAA) ▼▼▼ **Seabird Lodge** M
(707) 964-4731. **$70-$110, 3 days notice.** 191 South St. 0.8 mi n of Noyo Bridge; 1 blk e off SR 1. Ext corridors. **Pets:** Small. $8 daily fee/pet. Designated rooms, service with restrictions, supervision.
SAVE S X ⊟ ⊑ ⇝ AC

GUALALA

▼▼ **Gualala Country Inn** M
(707) 884-4343. **$92-$159, 3 days notice.** 47955 Center St. East side of SR 1. Ext/int corridors. **Pets:** Accepted.
X ⊟ ⊑ AC

▼▼ **Surf Motel** M
(707) 884-3571. **$92-$179.** 39170 S Hwy 1. West side of SR 1. Ext corridors. **Pets:** Accepted.
X ⊟ ⊑ AC

GUERNEVILLE

▼▼ **Ferngrove Cottages** C
(707) 869-8105. **$79-$209, 3 days notice.** 16650 Hwy 116. On SR 116. Ext corridors. **Pets:** Other species. $15 daily fee/pet. Supervision.
X ⊟ ⊑ ⇝ X AC Z

HEALDSBURG

(AAA) ▼▼ **Best Western Dry Creek Inn** M
(707) 433-0300. **$79-$165.** 198 Dry Creek Rd. US 101, exit Dry Creek Rd, just e. Ext corridors. **Pets:** $20 daily fee/room. Service with restrictions, supervision.
SAVE S X Z ⊟ ⊑ ⇝

▼▼▼ **Duchamp** H
(707) 431-1300. **$250-$375, 14 days notice.** 421 Foss St. US 101, exit Central Healdsburg. **Pets:** Small, dogs only. $500 deposit/room, $50 daily fee/pet. Designated rooms, service with restrictions, supervision.
X ⊟ ⇝

(AAA) ▼▼▼ **Fairview Motel** M
(707) 433-5548. **$59-$139, 3 days notice.** 74 Healdsburg Ave. S US 101, exit Central Healdsburg, just e; exit N Guernville/Westside Rd. Ext corridors. **Pets:** Medium, dogs only. $10 daily fee/pet. Service with restrictions, supervision.
SAVE S X ⊟ ⊑ ⇝

JENNER

▼▼ **Jenner Inn** C
(707) 865-2377. **$88-$258, 10 days notice.** 10400 Hwy 1. Ext corridors. **Pets:** Other species. $25 one-time fee/pet. Designated rooms, service with restrictions, supervision.
S X ⊟ ⊑ AC W

KELSEYVILLE

▼▼ **Bell Haven Resort** C
(707) 279-4329. **$125, 14 days notice.** 3415 White Oak Way. 6 mi e of SR 29, exit SR 281. Ext corridors. **Pets:** Medium, other species. $10 daily fee/pet. No service, supervision.
ASK X ⊟ ⊑ X AC Z

LITTLE RIVER

AAA ▼▼▼▼ The Inn at Schoolhouse Creek **BB**
(707) 937-5525. **$135-$250, 14 days notice.** 7051 N Hwy
1. 3 mi s of Mendocino; e of Coast Hwy. Ext corridors.
Pets: Other species. $40 one-time fee/pet. Designated
rooms, service with restrictions, supervision.
SAVE S X ☎ 💻 ✗

MENDOCINO

AAA ▼▼▼ Blackberry Inn **M** ✿
(707) 937-5281. **$85-$180, 7 days notice.** 44951 Larkin
Rd. SR 1, exit Larkin Rd, just e. Ext corridors. **Pets:** Small,
other species. $10 daily fee/pet. Designated rooms, service
with restrictions, supervision.
SAVE X ☎ 💻 ✗

AAA ▼▼▼ Mendocino Seaside
Cottages **BB** ✿
(707) 485-0239. **$145-$391 (no credit cards), 14 days
notice.** 10940 Lansing St. SR 1, exit Little Lake Rd; exit
Lansing St, 0.6 mi nw. Ext/int corridors. **Pets:** Other species. $80 deposit/room. Designated rooms, supervision.
SAVE S X ☎ 💻 ✗

AAA ▼◆▼▼ Stanford Inn by the Sea-Big River
Lodge **X** ✿
(707) 937-5615. **$215-$425, 7 days notice.** Comptche
Highway 1-Ukiah Rd. SR 1, exit Comptche-Ukiah Rd, 0.5
mi e. Ext corridors. **Pets:** Other species. $25 one-time fee/
room.
SAVE X &M ☎ ☎ 💻 ⑪ ✕ ✗

NAPA

▼▼▼ Napa River Inn **M** ✿
(707) 251-8500. **$159-$499.** 500 Main St. Downtown. Int
corridors. **Pets:** Medium. $25 daily fee/pet. Designated
rooms, service with restrictions, supervision.
ASK S X &M ☎ 💻

AAA ▼ Napa Valley Budget Inn **M**
(707) 257-6111. **$67-$137.** 3380 Solano Ave. Just w off SR
29 via Redwood Rd, then just s. Ext corridors. **Pets:** $10
one-time fee/room. Service with restrictions, supervision.
SAVE X &M ☎ ☎

OCCIDENTAL

AAA ▼▼ Occidental Lodge **M**
(707) 874-3623. **$48-$120, 3 days notice.** 3610 Bohemian
Hwy. In the village. Ext corridors. **Pets:** Medium. Service
with restrictions, supervision.
SAVE S X ✗

ROHNERT PARK

▼▼ Good Nite Inn **M**
(707) 584-8180. **Call for rates.** 5040 Redwood Dr. Just w
of US 101, exit Golf Course Dr. Ext corridors.
Pets: Accepted.
ASK S X ☎

SANTA ROSA

AAA ▼▼▼ Best Western Garden Inn **M**
(707) 546-4031. **$75-$120, 7 days notice.** 1500 Santa
Rosa Ave. US 101, exit Baker Ave northbound; exit Corby
Ave southbound. Ext corridors. **Pets:** Accepted.
SAVE S X &M ☎ ☎ 💻 ⑪ ☎

AAA ▼▼▼ Hillside Inn Motel **M**
(707) 546-9353. **$82-$98.** 2901 4th St. 2.5 mi e off US 101
on SR 12; at Farmers Ln and 4th St. Ext corridors.
Pets: Accepted.
SAVE X 💻 ⑪ ☎

AAA ▼▼▼ Santa Rosa Travelodge **M**
(707) 542-3472. **$65-$90.** 1815 Santa Rosa Ave. 1.5 mi s
on US 101 business route; exit US 101 via Baker Ave
northbound; southbound Santa Rosa Ave-Corby. Ext corridors. **Pets:** Accepted.
SAVE S X ☎ 💻 ☎

SONOMA

AAA ▼▼▼ Best Western Sonoma Valley
Inn **M** ✿
(707) 938-9200. **$150-$400, 3 days notice.** 550 2nd St W.
1 blk w of Town Plaza. Ext corridors. **Pets:** Large. $20
one-time fee/pet. Designated rooms, service with restrictions.
SAVE S X &M ☎ 💻 ☎

ST. HELENA

▼▼▼ El Bonita Motel **M** ✿
(707) 963-3216. **$95-$229, 3 days notice.** 195 Main St. 0.8
mi s on SR 29. Ext corridors. **Pets:** Medium, other species.
$5 daily fee/pet. Service with restrictions, supervision.
X ☎ ☎ 💻 ☎

AAA ▼▼▼ Harvest Inn **M**
(707) 963-9463. **$200-$460, 7 days notice.** One Main St.
1.5 mi s on SR 29. Ext corridors. **Pets:** Accepted.
SAVE S X &M ☎ ☎ 💻 ☎

UKIAH

AAA ▼▼ Days Inn **M**
(707) 462-7584. **$60-$125, 7 days notice.** 950 N State St.
US 101, exit N State St, 0.5 mi s on N State St. Ext
corridors. **Pets:** Other species. $5 daily fee/pet. Service with
restrictions, supervision.
SAVE S X ☎ 💻 ☎

AAA ▼▼ Rodeway Inn **M**
(707) 462-2906. **$79-$89.** 1050 S State St. US 101, exit
Talmage Rd off-ramp, 0.5 mi w. Ext corridors.
Pets: Accepted.
SAVE S X ☎ 💻 ☎

Super 8 Motel M
(707) 462-6657. **$58-$98, 15 days notice.** 1070 S State St. US 101, exit Talmage exit, 1 mi w. Ext corridors. **Pets:** Accepted.
SAVE S✺ ✕ 🛏 ➰

Western Traveler Motel M
(707) 468-9167. **$59-$79.** 693 S Orchard Ave. US 101, exit Gobbi St W. Ext corridors. **Pets:** Medium, other species. $5 daily fee/pet. Designated rooms, service with restrictions, supervision.
SAVE S✺ ✕ 🛏 🖵 ➰

WILLITS

Baechtel Creek Inn & Spa M
(707) 459-9063. **$65-$120.** 101 Gregory Ln. US 101, just w. Ext corridors. **Pets:** Small, service only. $15 one-time fee/pet. Designated rooms, service with restrictions, supervision.
SAVE S✺ ✕ 🛏 ➰

YOUNTVILLE

Vintage Inn M ❀
(707) 944-1112. **$275-$485, 7 days notice.** 6541 Washington St. Center; SR 29, exit Yountville. Ext corridors. **Pets:** Large. $35 one-time fee/room. Service with restrictions, supervision.
SAVE ✕ 🔥 🔥 🛏 🖵 ➰

❀ END AREA ❀

YOSEMITE NATIONAL PARK

The Redwoods In Yosemite C ❀
(209) 375-6666. **$112-$655, 10 days notice.** 8038 Chilnualna Falls Rd. 6 mi inside the southern entrance via SR 41 and Chilnualna Falls Rd. Ext corridors. **Pets:** Other species. $10 daily fee/pet. Designated rooms.
ASK S✺ ✕ 🛏 🖵 ✕

YREKA

AmeriHost Inn-Yreka M
(530) 841-1300. **$71-$90.** 148 Moonlit Oaks Ave. I-5, exit SR 3 (Fort Jones Rd). Int corridors. **Pets:** Small. Service with restrictions, supervision.
SAVE S✺ ✕ 🔥 🛏 🖵 ➰

Best Western Miner's Inn M
(530) 842-4355. **$64-$92.** 122 E Miner St. I-5, exit Central Yreka, just w. Ext corridors. **Pets:** Medium, other species. Service with restrictions, supervision.
SAVE S✺ ✕ 🔥 🛏 🖵 ➰

Days Inn M
(530) 842-1612. **$53-$75.** 1804-B Fort Jones Rd. I-5, exit SR 3 (Fort Jones Rd). Int corridors. **Pets:** Medium, other species. $20 deposit/pet, $6 daily fee/pet. Designated rooms, service with restrictions, supervision.
SAVE S✺ ✕ 🛏 ➰

Economy Inn M
(530) 842-4404. **$40-$95.** 526 S Main St. I-5, exit Central Yreka, 0.3 mi s. Ext corridors. **Pets:** Medium, other species. $5 daily fee/pet. Designated rooms, service with restrictions, supervision.
SAVE ✕ 🛏 ➰

Super 8-Yreka M
(530) 842-5781. **$49-$59.** 136 Montague Rd. I-5, exit Montague Rd, just w. Ext corridors. **Pets:** $5 one-time fee/room. Designated rooms, service with restrictions, supervision.
SAVE ✕ 🛏 🖵 ➰

Wayside Inn M
(530) 842-4412. **$45-$78.** 1235 S Main St. I-5, exit Fort Jones Rd northbound, 1 mi s; exit Central Yreka southbound, 1 mi s. Ext corridors. **Pets:** Other species. $3 daily fee/pet. Service with restrictions, supervision.
SAVE S✺ ✕ 🛏 🖵 ➰

YUBA CITY

Comfort Inn M
(530) 674-1592. **$50-$65, 21 days notice.** 730 Palora Ave. E of and adjacent to SR 99, 0.5 mi s of jct SR 20, exit SR 99 at Bridge St. Int corridors. **Pets:** Accepted.
SAVE S✺ ✕ 🔥 🛏 🖵 ➰

Days Inn M
(530) 674-1711. **$45-$70.** 700 N Palora Ave. SR 99, exit Bridge St, 0.5 mi s of SR 20. Ext corridors. **Pets:** Other species. $7 daily fee/pet. Service with restrictions, supervision.
SAVE S✺ ✕ 🔥 🔥 🛏 🖵 ➰

YUCCA VALLEY

Oasis of Eden Inn & Suites M
(760) 365-6321. **$60-$399.** 56377 Twentynine Palms Hwy. 1 mi w of Jct SR 62 and 247. Ext corridors. **Pets:** Small. $25 deposit/pet, $10 daily fee/pet. Designated rooms, service with restrictions, supervision.
SAVE S✺ ✕ 🛏 🖵 ➰

Super 8 Motel M
(760) 228-1773. **$49-$64.** 57096 29 Palms Hwy. On SR 62, 0.3 mi w of jct SR 247. Int corridors. **Pets:** Accepted.
SAVE S✺ ✕ 🛏 🖵 ➰

CITY INDEX

ALAMOSA

Best Western Alamosa Inn M
(719) 589-2567. **$68-$109.** 1919 Main St. 1 mi w on US 160 and 285. Ext corridors. **Pets:** Medium. $6 daily fee/pet. Service with restrictions, supervision.

Comfort Inn of Alamosa M
(719) 587-9000. **$60-$105, 30 days notice.** 6301 Rd 107 S. 2.3 mi w on US 160. Int corridors. **Pets:** Medium, other species. $15 one-time fee/room. Designated rooms, service with restrictions, supervision.

Days Inn M
(719) 589-9037. **$35-$59, 5 days notice.** 224 O'Keefe Pkwy. Just e of jct SR 17 and US 160. Int corridors. **Pets:** Accepted.

Holiday Inn MI
(719) 589-5833. **$69-$99.** 333 Sante Fe Ave. Just e of jct SR 17 on US 160. Int corridors. **Pets:** Other species. $25 deposit/pet.

ASPEN

Hotel Aspen M
(970) 925-3441. **$89-$399, 30 days notice.** 110 W Main St. On SR 82, just w. Ext/int corridors. **Pets:** $20 daily fee/pet. Designated rooms, service with restrictions.

Hotel Jerome H
(970) 920-1000. **$225-$1280, 30 days notice.** 330 E Main St. Downtown; on SR 82. Int corridors. **Pets:** Other species. $75 one-time fee/room, supervision.

Hotel Lenado BB
(970) 925-6246. **$115-$375, 30 days notice.** 200 S Aspen St. Just s of SR 82 via Aspen St at jct of Hopkins St. Ext/int corridors. **Pets:** Accepted.

Limelite Lodge M
(970) 925-3025. **$68-$375, 30 days notice.** 228 E Cooper St. Just s of SR 82 at Monarch and Cooper sts; opposite Wagner Park. Ext corridors. **Pets:** Other species. Designated rooms, service with restrictions, supervision.

The Little Nell H
(970) 920-4600. **$250-$825, 30 days notice.** 675 E Durant Ave. Beside the gondola at the base of Aspen Mountain. Int corridors. **Pets:** Other species. Service with restrictions, supervision.

St. Regis Aspen H
(970) 920-3300. **$225-$1400.** 315 E Dean St. SR 82, s on Monarch St, then just e. Int corridors. **Pets:** Accepted.

BEAVER CREEK

Comfort Inn-Vail/Beaver Creek M
(970) 949-5511. **$69-$199.** 161 W Beaver Creek Blvd. I-70, exit 167, just s. Int corridors. **Pets:** Large. $15 one-time fee/room. Designated rooms, service with restrictions, supervision.

BOULDER

Best Western Boulder Inn MI
(303) 449-3800. **$79-$119.** 770 28th St. Off US 36 at Baseline Rd; opposite University of Colorado. Int corridors. **Pets:** Medium. $100 deposit/pet. Designated rooms, service with restrictions, crate.

Boulder Broker Inn MI
(303) 444-3330. **$119.** 555 30th St. US 36, exit Baseline Rd, 0.3 mi e to 30th Street, then just s. Int corridors. **Pets:** Accepted.

Foot of The Mountain Motel M
(303) 442-5688. **$75-$85.** 200 Arapahoe Ave. 1.8 mi w of US 36. Ext corridors. **Pets:** $50 deposit/room, $5 daily fee/pet. Service with restrictions, supervision.

Homewood Suites by Hilton M
(303) 499-9922. **$139-$157.** 4950 Baseline Rd. 0.3 mi e of US 36; behind Meadows Shopping Center; or Foothills Pkwy (Hwy 150), exit Baseline, just w; entry off Baseline Rd. Ext/int corridors. **Pets:** Accepted.

Ramada Inn MI
(303) 443-3322. **$86-$120.** 800 28th St. US 36, exit Baseline Rd via Frontage Rd; opposite Colorado University campus. Ext/int corridors. **Pets:** Accepted.

Residence Inn by Marriott A
(303) 449-5545. **$149.** 3030 Center Green Dr. 0.5 mi e of US 36; on Valmont Rd at corner of Foothills Pkwy. Ext corridors. **Pets:** Accepted.

Super 8 of Boulder M
(303) 443-7800. **$80-$155.** 970 28th St. US 36; opposite Colorado University. Ext corridors. **Pets:** $50 deposit/room, $5 daily fee/pet. Designated rooms, service with restrictions, supervision.

BROOMFIELD

TownePlace Suites by Marriott Broomfield M ❖
(303) 466-2200. **$125.** 480 Flat Iron Blvd. US 36 W, exit Interlocken Loop, to first traffic light, w on Interlocken Blvd, then s. Int corridors. **Pets:** Other species. $10 daily fee/room. Service with restrictions.

BRUSH

Best Western Brush M
(970) 842-5146. **$61-$88, 14 days notice.** 1208 N Colorado Ave. I-76, exit 90B, just n. Ext/int corridors. **Pets:** Accepted.

BUENA VISTA

Best Western Vista Inn M
(719) 395-8009. **$67-$129.** 733 US Hwy 24 N. 0.5 mi n. Int corridors. **Pets:** Medium, dogs only. $50 deposit/room, $7 daily fee/pet. Designated rooms, service with restrictions, supervision.

BURLINGTON

Burlington Comfort Inn M
(719) 346-7676. **$59-$120.** 282 S Lincoln St. I-70, exit 437, just n on US 385. Int corridors. **Pets:** Large, other species. $50 deposit/room, $10 one-time fee/room. Designated rooms, service with restrictions, supervision.

Chaparral Motor Inn M
(719) 346-5361. **$38-$55, 5 days notice.** 405 S Lincoln St. I-70, exit 437, just n at jct US 385. Ext corridors. **Pets:** Small. $10 daily fee/pet. Service with restrictions, supervision.

Sloans Motel M
(719) 346-5333. **$36-$47.** 1901 Rose Ave. I-70, exit 437, 0.5 mi n on US 385, just e on US 24; exit 438 westbound, 1 mi w on US 24. Ext corridors. **Pets:** Other species. Service with restrictions, supervision.

CANON CITY

Best Western Royal Gorge Motel MI ❖
(719) 275-3377. **$44-$109.** 1925 Fremont Dr. 0.8 mi e on US 50. Ext/int corridors. **Pets:** Medium. $15 one-time fee/pet. Designated rooms, service with restrictions, supervision.

Canon Inn MI
(719) 275-8676. **$58-$89.** 3075 E Hwy 50. Center; 2 mi e of jct SR 115 and US 50. Int corridors. **Pets:** Large, other species. $50 deposit/pet. Service with restrictions, supervision.

Comfort Inn M
(719) 276-6900. **$52-$95.** 311 Royal Gorge Blvd. On US 50, just w of downtown; opposite Dinosaur Depot. Int corridors. **Pets:** Medium, other species. $10 one-time fee/pet. Designated rooms, service with restrictions, supervision.

CARBONDALE

⚫⚫⚫ ◥◤◥◤◥◤ Days Inn-Carbondale Ⓜ
(970) 963-9111. **$65-$129, 3 days notice.** 950 Cowen Dr. Jct of SR 82 and 133. Int corridors. **Pets:** Accepted.

⟦SAVE⟧ ⟦S⟧ ⟦✕⟧ ⟦☐⟧ ⟦☐⟧ ⟦⤳⟧

◥◤◥◤ Thunder River Lodge Ⓜ
(970) 963-2543. **$39-$75.** 179 Hwy 133. Just s on SR 133 from jct SR 82. Ext corridors. **Pets:** Accepted.

⟦✕⟧

CASTLE ROCK

⚫⚫⚫ ◥◤◥◤◥◤ Best Western Inn & Suites of Castle Rock Ⓜ
(303) 814-8800. **$69-$99.** 595 Genoa Way. I-25, exit 184 (Meadows Pkwy), just w to Castleton, then left. Int corridors. **Pets:** Medium, other species. $10 daily fee/pet. Designated rooms, service with restrictions, supervision.

⟦SAVE⟧ ⟦S⟧ ⟦✕⟧ ⟦☐⟧ ⟦☐⟧ ⟦☐⟧ ⟦☐⟧ ⟦⤳⟧

◥◤◥◤◥◤ Comfort Suites Ⓜ
(303) 814-9999. **$74-$104.** 4755 Castleton Way. I-25, exit 184 (Meadows Pkwy). Int corridors. **Pets:** Medium, other species. $10 daily fee/pet. Service with restrictions, supervision.

⟦SAVE⟧ ⟦S⟧ ⟦✕⟧ ⟦M⟧ ⟦☐⟧ ⟦☐⟧ ⟦☐⟧ ⟦☐⟧ ⟦⤳⟧

◥◤◥◤◥◤ Holiday Inn Express Ⓜ
(303) 660-9733. **$89-$119.** 884 Park St. I-25, exit 182, just w. Int corridors. **Pets:** Accepted.

⟦✕⟧ ⟦☐⟧ ⟦☐⟧ ⟦☐⟧ ⟦⤳⟧

CEDAREDGE

⚫⚫⚫ ◥◤◥◤◥◤ Super 8 of Cedaredge Ⓜ
(970) 856-7824. **$52-$99.** 530 S Grand Mesa Dr. Just s on SR 65. Int corridors. **Pets:** Accepted.

⟦SAVE⟧ ⟦S⟧ ⟦✕⟧ ⟦☐⟧ ⟦☐⟧ ⟦☐⟧ ⟦⤳⟧

COLORADO SPRINGS METROPOLITAN AREA

COLORADO SPRINGS

⚫⚫⚫ ◥◤◥◤◥◤ AmeriSuites (Colorado Springs/ Garden of the Gods) Ⓜ
(719) 265-9385. **$81-$107, 7 days notice.** 503 W Garden of the Gods Rd. I-25, exit 146, just w. Int corridors. **Pets:** Small. Service with restrictions, supervision.

⟦SAVE⟧ ⟦S⟧ ⟦✕⟧ ⟦☐⟧ ⟦☐⟧ ⟦☐⟧ ⟦⤳⟧

⚫⚫⚫ ◥◤◥◤ Apollo Park Executive Suites ▲
(719) 634-0286. **$55-$105, 3 days notice.** 805 S Circle Dr, 2-B. I-25, exit 138, 2.5 mi e. Int corridors. **Pets:** Other species. Designated rooms.

⟦SAVE⟧ ⟦S⟧ ⟦✕⟧ ⟦☐⟧ ⟦⤳⟧

⚫⚫⚫ ◥◤ Chief Motel Ⓜ
(719) 473-5228. **$42-$85.** 1624 S Nevada Ave. I-25, exit 140A northbound; exit 140B southbound. Ext corridors. **Pets:** Accepted.

⟦SAVE⟧ ⟦S⟧ ⟦✕⟧ ⟦☐⟧

◥◤◥◤◥◤ Comfort Suites Ⓜ
(719) 536-0731. **$79-$129.** 1055 Kelly Johnson Blvd. I-25, exit 150, just s on Academy Blvd to Kelly Johnson Blvd, then w. Int corridors. **Pets:** Accepted.

⟦SAVE⟧ ⟦S⟧ ⟦✕⟧ ⟦M⟧ ⟦☐⟧ ⟦☐⟧ ⟦☐⟧ ⟦⤳⟧

⚫⚫⚫ ◥◤◥◤ Days Inn Ⓜ
(719) 266-1317. **$49-$94.** 8350 Razorback Rd. I-25, exit 150, just s, then e. Int corridors. **Pets:** Small, dogs only. $100 deposit/room. No service, supervision.

⟦SAVE⟧ ⟦S⟧ ⟦✕⟧ ⟦M⟧ ⟦☐⟧ ⟦⤳⟧

◥◤◥◤◥◤ Doubletree Hotel Colorado Springs, World Arena ⬛
(719) 576-8900. **$179.** 1775 E Cheyenne Mountain Blvd. I-25, exit 138, just w. Int corridors. **Pets:** Other species. $10 daily fee/pet. Service with restrictions, crate.

⟦SAVE⟧ ⟦S⟧ ⟦✕⟧ ⟦M⟧ ⟦☐⟧ ⟦☐⟧ ⟦☐⟧ ⟦☐⟧ ⟦⤳⟧

◥◤◥◤◥◤ Drury Inn-Pikes Peak Ⓜ
(719) 598-2500. **$65-$100.** 8155 N Academy Blvd. I-25, exit 150, just s, then e. Int corridors. **Pets:** Medium, other species. Service with restrictions, crate.

⟦✕⟧ ⟦☐⟧ ⟦☐⟧ ⟦☐⟧ ⟦⤳⟧

⚫⚫⚫ ◥◤◥◤◥◤ Holiday Inn Garden of the Gods Ⓜ
(719) 598-7656. **$99-$139, 3 days notice.** 505 Pope's Bluff Tr. I-25, exit 146, just w, then n on Hilton Pkwy. Int corridors. **Pets:** Accepted.

⟦SAVE⟧ ⟦S⟧ ⟦✕⟧ ⟦M⟧ ⟦☐⟧ ⟦☐⟧ ⟦☐⟧ ⟦☐⟧ ⟦⤳⟧

◥◤◥◤◥◤ Homewood Suites Ⓜ ❀
(719) 265-6600. **$89-$125.** 9130 Explorer Dr. I-25, exit 151, 0.8 mi e; across from Focus on the Family. Int corridors. **Pets:** Medium. $100 one-time fee/room. Service with restrictions, supervision.

⟦SAVE⟧ ⟦S⟧ ⟦✕⟧ ⟦M⟧ ⟦☐⟧ ⟦☐⟧ ⟦☐⟧ ⟦☐⟧

⚫⚫⚫ ◥◤◥◤ Howard Johnson Express Inn Ⓜ
(719) 634-1545. **$35-$85.** 1231 S Nevada Ave. I-25, exit 140A northbound; exit 140B southbound, just n. Ext corridors. **Pets:** Very small. $10 daily fee/pet. Designated rooms, service with restrictions, supervision.

⟦SAVE⟧ ⟦S⟧ ⟦✕⟧ ⟦☐⟧ ⟦☐⟧ ⟦⤳⟧

⚫⚫⚫ ◥◤◥◤◥◤ La Quinta Inn Garden of the Gods Ⓜ
(719) 528-5060. **$56-$96.** 4385 Sinton Rd. I-25, exit 146, just e. Ext corridors. **Pets:** Small. Service with restrictions, supervision.

⟦SAVE⟧ ⟦S⟧ ⟦✕⟧ ⟦☐⟧ ⟦☐⟧ ⟦⤳⟧

La Quinta Inns & Suites M
(719) 527-4788. **$66-$120.** 2750 Geyser Dr. I-25, exit 138 (Circle Dr), just w to Cheyenne Mountain Blvd, just s. Int corridors. **Pets:** Small. $20 deposit/pet. Service with restrictions.

Quality Inn & Suites M
(719) 576-2371. **$59-$160.** 1440 Harrison Rd. I-25, exit 138, just w, on northwest corner of interchange; entry through restaurant. Int corridors. **Pets:** Other species. $50 deposit/pet, $5 daily fee/pet. Designated rooms.

Quality Inn-Garden of the Gods M
(719) 593-9119. **$59-$139.** 555 W Garden of the Gods Rd. I-25, exit 146, just w. Int corridors. **Pets:** Large, other species. $50 deposit/room. Designated rooms, service with restrictions, crate.

Radisson Inn & Suites M
(719) 597-7000. **$119-$139.** 1645 N Newport Rd. I-25, exit 139, 4 mi e on US 24 Bypass (Fountain Blvd). Int corridors. **Pets:** Medium. $100 deposit/room. Service with restrictions, crate.

Radisson Inn Colorado Springs North M
(719) 598-5770. **$79-$169.** 8110 N Academy Blvd. I-25, exit 150, just s. Int corridors. **Pets:** Small. $50 deposit/pet. Service with restrictions, crate.

Ramada Inn-North M
(719) 633-5541. **$59-$109.** 3125 Sinton Rd. I-25, exit 145, just e, then just n. Ext/int corridors. **Pets:** Small. $15 one-time fee/room. Designated rooms, supervision.

Red Lion Hotel Downtown M
(719) 471-8680. **$69-$159.** 314 W Bijou St. I-25, exit 142, northwest corner. Int corridors. **Pets:** Medium. $50 deposit/room. Service with restrictions, supervision.

Residence Inn by Marriott-North A
(719) 574-0370. **$89-$129.** 3880 N Academy Blvd. I-25, exit 146, 6 mi e on Austin Bluffs Pkwy to Academy Blvd (SR 83), 0.3 mi s. Ext corridors. **Pets:** Other species. $50 one-time fee/room. Service with restrictions, crate.

Residence Inn by Marriott-South A
(719) 576-0101. **$99-$189.** 2765 Geyser Dr. I-25, exit 138 (Circle Dr), just w to E Cheyenne Mountain Blvd, then just s. Int corridors. **Pets:** Other species. $50 one-time fee/room. No service.

Rodeway Inn M
(719) 471-0990. **$66-$147.** 2409 E Pikes Peak Ave. I-25, exit 143, e on Uintah to Union, s to Pikes Peak, then e; exit 138, ne on Circle to Pikes Peak, then w. Ext corridors. **Pets:** Accepted.

Sleep Inn M
(719) 260-6969. **$59-$89.** 1075 Kelly Johnson Blvd. I-25, exit 150, just s on Academy Blvd to Kelly Johnson Blvd, then w. Int corridors. **Pets:** Accepted.

Stagecoach Motel M
(719) 633-3894. **$36-$69, 3 days notice.** 1647 S Nevada Ave. I-25, exit 140A or 140B, just s. Ext corridors. **Pets:** Accepted.

TownePlace Suites by Marriott Colorado Springs M
(719) 594-4447. **$89-$139.** 4760 Centennial Blvd. I-25, exit 146, Garden of the Gods Rd w to Centennial, right first left behind 7-11. Int corridors. **Pets:** $15 daily fee/room. Supervision.

Travelodge M
(719) 632-4600. **$40-$80, 5 days notice.** 2625 Ore Mill Rd. I-25, exit 141, 2.3 mi nw on US 24, entry via 26th St. Int corridors. **Pets:** Accepted.

Wyndham Colorado Springs H
(719) 260-1800. **$99-$155.** 5580 Tech Center Dr. I-25, exit 147 (Rockrimmon Blvd), 0.5 mi w. Int corridors. **Pets:** $250 deposit/room. Service with restrictions, supervision.

MANITOU SPRINGS

Red Wing Motel M ❁
(719) 685-5656. **$42-$58.** 56 El Paso Blvd. I-25, exit 141, 4 mi w on US 24, just e to Beckers Ln, then n. Ext corridors. **Pets:** Other species. $10 daily fee/pet. Designated rooms, service with restrictions, supervision.

❁ **END METROPOLITAN AREA** ❁

CORTEZ

[AAA] ◆◆ **Anasazi Motor Inn** [MI]
(970) 565-3773. **$55-$71.** 640 S Broadway. 0.5 mi sw on US 160 and 666. Ext corridors. **Pets:** Large, other species. $50 deposit/room. Service with restrictions, supervision.
[SAVE] [SD] ☒ ♿ 🍴 🏊

[AAA] ◆◆◆ **Best Western Turquoise Inn & Suites** [M] 🐾
(970) 565-3778. **$99-$129, 14 days notice.** 535 E Main St. On US 160. Ext corridors. **Pets:** Medium. $15 one-time fee/room. Service with restrictions, supervision.
[SAVE] [SD] ☒ ♿ ▣ ☕ 🏊

[AAA] ◆◆ **Budget Host Inn** [M]
(970) 565-3738. **$38-$78.** 2040 E Main St. 1.3 mi e on US 160, w of jct SR 145. Ext corridors. **Pets:** $5 one-time fee/pet. Service with restrictions, supervision.
[SAVE] ☒ ▣ 🏊

◆◆◆ **Comfort Inn** [M]
(970) 565-3400. **$59-$99.** 2321 E Main St. 1.3 mi e on US 160. Ext/int corridors. **Pets:** Accepted.
[SAVE] [SD] ☒ ▣ ☕ 🏊

[AAA] ◆◆ **Days Inn** [MI]
(970) 565-8577. **$59-$89.** 1.5 mi e on US 160, at jct SR 145. Ext/int corridors. **Pets:** Accepted.
[SAVE] [SD] ☒ 🍴

◆◆ **Econo Lodge** [M]
(970) 565-3474. **$45-$139.** 2020 E Main St. 1.3 mi e on US 160. Ext corridors. **Pets:** Accepted.
[SAVE] [SD] ☒ ▣ ☕ 🏊

[AAA] ◆◆◆ **Holiday Inn Express** [M]
(970) 565-6000. **$79-$149, 30 days notice.** 2121 E Main St. 1.3 mi e on US 160. Int corridors. **Pets:** Medium, other species. Designated rooms, supervision.
[SAVE] [SD] ☒ 👂 ▣ 🏊

[AAA] ◆◆ **Tomahawk Lodge** [M]
(970) 565-8521. **$37-$73.** 728 S Broadway. 1 mi sw on US 160 and 666. Ext corridors. **Pets:** Dogs only. $25 deposit/pet. Designated rooms, service with restrictions, supervision.
[SAVE] [SD] ☒ 🏊

[AAA] ◆◆ **Travelodge** [M]
(970) 565-7778. **$39-$79, 3 days notice.** 440 S Broadway. 0.8 mi sw on US 160 and 666. Ext corridors. **Pets:** $25 deposit/pet, $3 daily fee/pet. Service with restrictions, supervision.
[SAVE] [SD] ☒ ▣ ☕ 🏊

CRAIG

◆◆ **Bear Valley Inn** [M]
(970) 824-8101. **$49-$79.** 755 E Victory Way. 0.5 mi e on US 40. Ext corridors. **Pets:** Service with restrictions, supervision.
[A$K] [SD] ☒ ▣ ☕

[AAA] ◆◆ **Black Nugget Motel** [M]
(970) 824-8161. **$35-$59.** 2855 W Victory Way. 1.5 mi w on US 40, 0.3 mi w of jct SR 13. Ext corridors. **Pets:** Large, other species. $5 daily fee/pet. Supervision.
[SAVE] [SD] ☒ ▣ ☕

◆◆◆ **Craig Holiday Inn** [MI]
(970) 824-4000. **$81-$131.** 300 S Hwy 13. 0.3 mi s on SR 13 from jct US 40. Int corridors. **Pets:** Other species. $50 deposit/room. Service with restrictions, supervision.
[A$K] [SD] ☒ ♿ ▣ ☕ 🍴 🏊

[AAA] ◆◆◆ **Deer Park Inn and Suites** [M]
(970) 824-9282. **$69-$139.** 262 Commerce St. Jct US 40, just 0.3 mi s on SR 13. Int corridors. **Pets:** Large. $50 deposit/room. Supervision.
[SAVE] [SD] ☒ ♿[M] 👂 ▣ ☕ 🏊

CRESTED BUTTE

◆◆◆ **Sheraton Crested Butte Resort** [H]
(970) 349-8000. **$66-$395, 45 days notice.** 6 Emmons Rd. 2.5 mi n on SR 135; at Mt Crested Butte ski area. Int corridors. **Pets:** Accepted.
[A$K] [SD] ☒ ♿ ▣ ☕ 🍴 🏊 [AC]

DELTA

[AAA] ◆◆ **Best Western Sundance** [MI]
(970) 874-9781. **$65-$85, 14 days notice.** 903 Main St. 0.5 mi s on US 50. Ext corridors. **Pets:** Medium, other species. $5 daily fee/pet. Designated rooms, service with restrictions, crate.
[SAVE] [SD] ☒ ▣ ☕ 🍴 🏊

[AAA] ◆◆ **South Gate Inn** [M]
(970) 874-9726. **$45-$65.** 2124 S Main St. 1.5 mi s on US 50. Ext corridors. **Pets:** Dogs only. $5 daily fee/pet. Service with restrictions, supervision.
[SAVE] [SD] ☒ ▣ 🏊

DENVER METROPOLITAN AREA

AURORA

⚜ ♦♦♦♦ AmeriSuites (Denver/Airport) M
(303) 371-0700. **$103-$107.** 16250 E 40th Ave. I-70, exit 283 (Chambers Rd), just n, then 0.5 mi e. Int corridors. **Pets:** Small. Service with restrictions, supervision.

SAVE S🐾 ✕ 🖐M 🐾 🎦 🛏 💻 🏊

⚜ ♦♦♦♦ Holiday Inn DIA M
(303) 371-9494. **$89-$114.** 15500 E 40th Ave. I-70, exit 283 (Chambers Rd). Int corridors. **Pets:** $25 one-time fee/room. Service with restrictions, crate.

SAVE S🐾 ✕ 🖐M 🐾 🎦 🛏 💻 🍴 🏊

♦♦♦ Homestead Studio Suites-Denver/Aurora M
(303) 750-9116. **$39-$59.** 13941 E Harvard Ave. I-225, exit 5, just e of E Iliff Ave to Blackhawk St, then just s. Ext corridors. **Pets:** Other species. $100 one-time fee/room.

ASK S🐾 ✕ 🖐M 🐾 🎦 🛏 💻 🏊

♦♦♦ La Quinta Inn-Aurora M
(303) 337-0206. **$66-$82.** 1011 S Abilene St. I-225, exit 7, just e. Ext corridors. **Pets:** Medium, other species. Service with restrictions, crate.

SAVE ✕ 🖐M 🐾 💻 🏊

♦♦♦ Sleep Inn Denver Airport M
(303) 373-1616. **$72-$95, 3 days notice.** 15900 E 40th Ave. I-70, exit 283, from airport, Pena Blvd s to 40th Ave W. Int corridors. **Pets:** Small. $25 daily fee/pet. Service with restrictions, supervision.

SAVE ✕ 🖐M 🐾 🎦 🛏 💻 🏊

♦♦♦ Wellesley Inn & Suites M
(303) 337-7000. **$62-$85, 10 days notice.** 14095 E Evans Ave. I-225, exit 5, just e to Blackhawk St, then just n. Int corridors. **Pets:** Small. Service with restrictions, crate.

ASK S🐾 ✕ 🖐M 🐾 🎦 🛏 💻 🏊

DENVER

♦♦♦ Best Western Central Denver H
(303) 296-4000. **$87-$97.** 200 W 48th Ave. Int corridors. **Pets:** Other species. Service with restrictions, supervision.

SAVE S🐾 ✕ 🛏 💻 🍴 🏊

⚜ ♦ Cameron Motel M
(303) 757-2100. **$58-$68.** 4500 E Evans Ave. I-25, exit 203, then w. Ext corridors. **Pets:** $5 daily fee/pet. Designated rooms, service with restrictions, supervision.

SAVE S🐾 ✕ 🛏

⚜ ♦♦♦♦ Denver Marriott Hotel City Center H
(303) 297-1300. **$79-$169.** 1701 California St at 17th St. I-25, exit 210 (E Colfax Ave), to Welton St 0.5 mi ne, then left on 18th, then 1 blk. Int corridors. **Pets:** Accepted.

SAVE S🐾 ✕ 🐾 🎦 🛏 💻 🍴 🏊

⚜ ♦♦♦♦ Denver Marriott Southeast Hotel H
(303) 758-7000. **$149-$179.** 6363 E Hampden Ave. I-25, exit 201, just e. Ext/int corridors. **Pets:** Small. $50 one-time fee/room. Designated rooms, service with restrictions, supervision.

SAVE S🐾 ✕ 🖐M 🐾 🎦 💻 🍴 🏊

⚜ ♦♦♦ Denver Marriott Tech Center H
(303) 779-1100. **$160, 3 days notice.** 4900 S Syracuse St. I-25, exit 199, e to S Syracuse St, just n. Int corridors. **Pets:** Accepted.

SAVE S🐾 ✕ 🖐M 🐾 🎦 🛏 💻 🍴 🏊

♦♦♦ DoubleTree Hotel Denver H
(303) 321-3333. **$79-$159.** 3203 Quebec St. I-70, exit 278, 0.5 mi s; I-270, exit 4. Int corridors. **Pets:** Other species. $50 deposit/room. Service with restrictions, crate.

SAVE S🐾 ✕ 🐾 🎦 🛏 💻 🍴 🏊

♦♦♦ Drury Inn-Denver East M
(303) 373-1983. **$50-$95.** 4400 E Peoria St. I-70, exit 281, just n. Int corridors. **Pets:** Small. Service with restrictions, supervision.

✕ 🐾 🛏 💻 🏊

⚜ ♦♦♦ Embassy Suites-Denver International Airport H
(303) 375-0400. **$119-$149.** 4444 N Havana St. I-70, exit 280, just n. Int corridors. **Pets:** Accepted.

SAVE ✕ 🖐M 🐾 🛏 💻 🍴 🏊

♦♦♦ Hawthorn Suites M 🐾
(303) 804-9900. **$139, 30 days notice.** 5001 S Ulster St. I-25, exit 199, e to Ulster St, then just n. Int corridors. **Pets:** Large. $125 one-time fee/room. Service with restrictions.

ASK S🐾 ✕ 🖐M 🐾 🎦 🛏 💻 🏊

⚜ ♦♦♦ Holiday Chalet A Victorian Bed & Breakfast BB
(303) 321-9975. **$94-$160.** 1820 E Colfax Ave. I-25, exit 210, 1.3 mi e on US 40. Int corridors. **Pets:** Accepted.

SAVE ✕ 🛏 💻

♦♦♦ Homestead Studio Suites-Denver/Tech Center-North M
(303) 689-9443. **$64-$95.** 4885 S Quebec St. I-25, exit 199, just w to Quebec St, then just n; next to Mountain View golf course. Ext corridors. **Pets:** Accepted.

ASK S🐾 ✕ 🖐M 🐾 🎦 🛏 💻

⚜ ♦♦♦♦ Hotel Monaco Denver H 🐾
(303) 296-1717. **$139-$189.** 1717 Champa St. I-25, exit 212A, s to Curtis St, w to 19th St, 1 blk s to Champa St, then 2 blks w. Int corridors. **Pets:** Other species. Service with restrictions, supervision.

SAVE S🐾 ✕ 🖐M 🐾 🎦 💻 🍴

▼▼ ▼▼ Hotel Teatro 🅷 ✿
(303) 228-1100. **$255-$280.** 1100 14th St. I-25, exit 212 (Speer Blvd), s at jct Arapahoe St to Lawrence St, exit Auraria Pkwy, then e to 14th; northbound. Int corridors. **Pets:** Service with restrictions.

(ASK) (S🛏) (✕) (🔊) (🛗) (🖥) (🍴)

▼▼▼▼ La Quinta Inn & Suites DIA 🅼
(303) 371-0888. **$80-$120.** 6801 Tower Rd. I-70, exit 286, 4.2 mi n, 0.8 mi s of Pena Blvd. Int corridors. **Pets:** Accepted.

(SAVE) (✕) (🛗) (🔊) (🛗) (🖥) (≈)

▼▼▼▼ La Quinta Inn-Cherry Creek 🅼
(303) 758-8886. **$72-$96.** 1975 S Colorado Blvd. I-25, exit 204, just s. Ext corridors. **Pets:** Small. No service, supervision.

(SAVE) (✕) (🔊) (🖥) (≈)

▼▼▼▼ La Quinta Inn-Downtown 🅼
(303) 458-1222. **$66-$102.** 3500 Park Ave W. I-25, exit 213, take 38th Ave, just s, then left at Fox St. Ext/int corridors. **Pets:** Accepted.

(SAVE) (✕) (🛗) (🔊) (🖥) (≈)

▼▼▼▼ Magnolia Hotel-Denver 🅰
(303) 607-9000. **$99-$200.** 818 17th St. I-25, exit 212A, take Speer Blvd S, to Market St, then e to 17th St, then s to 17th and Stout sts. Int corridors. **Pets:** Medium. Service with restrictions, crate.

(ASK) (S🛏) (✕) (🛗) (🖥) (🛗) (🖥)

▼▼ ▼▼ Ramada Inn Airport 🅼🅸
(303) 388-6161. **$52-$79, 7 days notice.** 3737 Quebec St. I-70, exit 278, just s. Int corridors. **Pets:** Other species. $50 deposit/room. Service with restrictions.

(ASK) (S🛏) (✕) (🛗) (🖥) (🍴) (≈)

▼▼ ▼▼ Red Lion Denver Central 🅼🅸
(303) 321-6666. **$79-$99.** 4040 Quebec St. I-70, exit 278, just s. Ext/int corridors. **Pets:** Other species. $50 deposit/room. Designated rooms, service with restrictions.

(ASK) (S🛏) (✕) (🖥) (🖥) (🍴) (≈)

▲▲▲ ▼▼▼▼ Red Lion Hotel Denver-Downtown 🅼🅸
(303) 433-8331. **$79-$129.** 1975 Bryant St. I-25, exit 210B, just w. Int corridors. **Pets:** Medium. $50 deposit/pet. Service with restrictions, supervision.

(SAVE) (✕) (🖥) (🍴) (≈)

▲▲▲ ▼▼▼▼ Red Roof Inn & Suites 🅼
(303) 371-5300. **$69-$129, 5 days notice.** 6890 Tower Rd. I-70, exit 286, 4.2 mi n, 0.8 mi s of Pena Blvd. Int corridors. **Pets:** Accepted.

(SAVE) (S🛏) (✕) (🛗) (🔊) (🖥) (🛗) (🖥) (≈)

▲▲▲ ▼▼▼▼ Residence Inn by Marriott Denver Downtown 🅰 ✿
(303) 458-5318. **$152-$169.** 2777 Zuni St. I-25, exit 212B, just w. Ext corridors. **Pets:** Other species. $10 daily fee/pet, $50 one-time fee/pet.

(SAVE) (✕) (🔊) (🛗) (🖥) (≈)

▲▲▲ ▼▼▼▼ TownePlace Suites by Marriott-Denver Southeast 🅼
(303) 759-9393. **$85.** 3699 S Monaco Pkwy. I-25, exit 201, just e to Monaco Pkwy, then s. Int corridors. **Pets:** Accepted.

(SAVE) (S🛏) (✕) (🛗) (🛗) (🖥) (≈)

▲▲▲ ▼▼▼▼ TownePlace Suites by Marriott Downtown Denver 🅼
(303) 722-2322. **$69-$149.** 685 Speer Blvd. I-25, exit Speer Blvd S, 1.5 mi s, stay in right lane, just past Bannock St, exit towards Broadway, right onto Acoma St. Int corridors. **Pets:** Large, other species. $10 daily fee/room, $100 one-time fee/room. Service with restrictions.

(SAVE) (S🛏) (✕) (🛗) (🔊) (🖥) (🖥)

▼▼▼▼ The Warwick Hotel-Denver 🅷
(303) 861-2000. **$140-$150, 3 days notice.** 1776 Grant St at 18th Ave. I-25, exit 210 (Colfax Ave), to Logan, then n to 18th, just w. Int corridors. **Pets:** Large. $200 deposit/room, $15 daily fee/room. Designated rooms.

(ASK) (S🛏) (✕) (🔊) (🔊) (🖥) (🍴) (≈)

▼▼▼▼ The Westin Tabor Center Denver 🅷
(303) 572-9100. **$139-$254.** 1672 Lawrence St. I-25, exit 212A (Speer Blvd S), to Lawrence St, then e. Int corridors. **Pets:** Accepted.

(✕) (🛗) (🔊) (🔊) (🖥) (🍴) (≈)

ENGLEWOOD

▲▲▲ ▼▼▼▼ AmeriSuites (Denver/Tech Center) 🅼
(303) 804-0700. **$49-$98.** 8300 E Crescent Pkwy. I-25, exit 199 (Bellview Ave), 0.4 mi e to Crescent Pkwy, then s. Int corridors. **Pets:** Accepted.

(SAVE) (S🛏) (✕) (🔊) (🔊) (🛗) (🖥) (≈)

▼▼▼▼ Drury Inn & Suites-Near Denver Tech Center 🅼
(303) 694-3400. **$60-$110.** 9445 E Dry Creek Rd. I-25, exit 196. Int corridors. **Pets:** Accepted.

(✕) (🔊) (🛗) (🖥) (≈)

▼▼▼▼ Holtze Executive Village 🅰
(303) 290-1100. **$69-$89.** 6380 S Boston St. I-25, exit 197, just e, then just n. Ext corridors. **Pets:** Medium, other species. $100 one-time fee/pet. Service with restrictions.

(ASK) (S🛏) (✕) (🛗) (🖥) (≈)

▼▼ ▼▼ Homestead Studio Suites-Denver/Tech Center-South 🅼
(303) 708-8888. **$50-$64.** 9650 E Geddes Ave. I-25, exit 196, 0.5 mi, then just e. Ext corridors. **Pets:** Accepted.

(ASK) (S🛏) (✕) (🔊) (🔊) (🛗) (🖥)

▲▲▲ ▼▼▼▼ Residence Inn by Marriott-Denver South Tech Center 🅼 ✿
(303) 740-7177. **$79-$169.** 6565 S Yosemite St. I-25, exit 197, just w on Arapahoe Rd, then n. Ext corridors. **Pets:** Other species. $5 daily fee/room, $100 one-time fee/room.

(SAVE) (S🛏) (✕) (🔊) (🔊) (🛗) (🖥) (≈)

Residence Inn Park Meadows M
(720) 895-0200. **$129-$149.** 8322 S Valley Hwy. I-25, exit 195 (County Line Rd), just e to S Valley Hwy, then just s. Int corridors. **Pets:** Other species. $100 one-time fee/room. Service with restrictions.

TownePlace Suites Denver Tech Center M ✿
(720) 875-1113. **$55-$115.** 7877 S Chester St. I-25, exit 196, just w to Chester St, then 0.3 mi s. Int corridors. **Pets:** Other species. $100 one-time fee/room. Service with restrictions.

GLENDALE

Homestead Studio Suites-Denver/Cherry Creek M
(303) 388-3880. **$57-$89.** 4444 Leetsdale Dr. I-25, 1 mi n to E Virginia Ave, just e to S Birch St, then just n. Ext corridors. **Pets:** Other species. $25 daily fee/room, $100 one-time fee/room. Service with restrictions.

Loews Denver Hotel H ✿
(303) 782-9300. **$145-$169.** 4150 E Mississippi Ave. I-25, exit 204, 1 mi n on Colorado Blvd, just e. Int corridors. **Pets:** Other species. Service with restrictions, supervision.

GOLDEN

Denver Marriott West H
(303) 279-9100. **$134-$180.** 1717 Denver W Blvd. I-70, exit 263, just n, then w. Int corridors. **Pets:** Large. $10 daily fee/room. Designated rooms, supervision.

Holiday Inn Golden MI
(303) 279-7611. **$89-$107.** 14707 W Colfax Ave. I-70, exit 262, just e. Ext/int corridors. **Pets:** Medium. $150 deposit/room. Designated rooms, service with restrictions, supervision.

La Quinta Inn-Golden M
(303) 279-5565. **$66-$89.** 3301 Youngfield Service Rd. I-70, exit 264 (32nd Ave). Ext corridors. **Pets:** Medium. Service with restrictions, supervision.

Residence Inn Denver West/Golden M ✿
(303) 271-0909. **$107.** 14600 W 6th Ave Frontage Rd. US 6, exit Indiana Ave to frontage road, just e. Int corridors. **Pets:** Other species. $5 daily fee/room, $100 one-time fee/room. Service with restrictions.

Table Mountain Inn MI
(303) 277-9898. **$112-$184.** 1310 Washington Ave. US 6, exit 19th St, 0.5 mi n to Washington Ave, 0.5 mi w, downtown, just s of arch. Int corridors. **Pets:** Other species. $50 deposit/pet. Designated rooms, service with restrictions, supervision.

Williamsburg Inn Bed and Breakfast M
(303) 279-7673. **$95.** 1407 Washington Ave. US 6, exit 19th St, 0.5 mi n to Washington Ave, 0.5 mi w. Ext corridors. **Pets:** Accepted.

GREENWOOD VILLAGE

La Quinta Inn & Suites Denver Tech Center M
(303) 649-9969. **$86-$106.** 7077 S Clinton St. I-25, exit 197, just se. Int corridors. **Pets:** Small. Service with restrictions, supervision.

MainStay Suites Denver Tech Center M
(303) 858-1669. **$85-$110.** I-25, exit 197, just e on Arapahoe Rd, then se on Clinton St to Costilla St, then w. Int corridors. **Pets:** Accepted.

Sleep Inn Denver Tech Center M
(303) 662-9950. **$60-$90.** 9257 Costilla Ave. I-25, exit 197 (Araphoe Rd), just se on Clinton St to Costilla Ave, then w. Int corridors. **Pets:** Accepted.

Summerfield Suites by Wyndham-Denver Tech Center M
(303) 706-1945. **$68-$128.** I-25, exit 197 (Arapahoe Rd), just se on Clinton St. Int corridors. **Pets:** Medium. $150 one-time fee/pet. Service with restrictions, supervision.

Woodfield Suites Denver Tech Center M ✿
(303) 799-4555. **$59-$129.** 9009 E Arapahoe Rd. I-25, exit 197, just e. Int corridors. **Pets:** Large. Service with restrictions, crate.

HIGHLANDS RANCH

Residence Inn Denver South Highlands Ranch A
(303) 683-5500. **$149-$189.** 93 W Centennial Blvd. C-470, exit Broadway, just s, then w. Int corridors. **Pets:** $100 one-time fee/room. Service with restrictions, supervision.

LAKEWOOD

(AAA) ▼▼▼▼ Comfort Inn & Suites-SW Denver M
(303) 989-5500. **$57-$105.** 3440 S Vance St. Just ne of jct US 285 (Hampden Ave) and S Wadsworth Blvd, e on Girton Dr, then just s. Int corridors. **Pets:** Accepted.
[SAVE] [S◊] [✕] [█] [▦] [⇌]

(AAA) ▼▼▼▼ La Quinta Inn & Suites M
(303) 969-9700. **$72-$89.** 7190 W Hampden Ave. Just se of jct US 285 (W Hampden Ave) and Wadsworth Blvd, e on Jefferson Ave, just n, then e on frontage road. Int corridors. **Pets:** Small. Designated rooms, service with restrictions, supervision.
[SAVE] [S◊] [✕] [�ℊM] [🖉] [♨] [█] [▦] [⇌]

▼▼▼▼ Quality Suites Lakewood M
(303) 988-8600. **$59-$99.** 7260 W Jefferson Ave. Just se of US 285 (W Hampden Ave) and Wadsworth Blvd, then e. Int corridors. **Pets:** Accepted.
[SAVE] [S◊] [✕] [♨] [█] [▦] [⇌]

▼▼▼▼ Ramada Inn Denver West Conference Center M
(303) 238-1251. **$62-$85.** 7150 W Colfax. 3 blks e of jct Wadsworth Blvd and Colfax Ave. Ext corridors. **Pets:** Other species. $50 deposit/pet. Service with restrictions.
[ASK] [S◊] [✕] [♨] [█] [▦] [▥]

(AAA) ▼▼▼▼ Residence Inn by Marriott Denver SW/Lakewood M
(303) 985-7676. **$81-$110.** 7050 W Hampden Ave. Just se of jct US 285 (W Hampden Ave) and Wadsworth Blvd, then e on Jefferson Ave, then n on frontage road. Int corridors. **Pets:** Accepted.
[SAVE] [S◊] [✕] [ℊM] [🖉] [♨] [█] [▦] [⇌]

(AAA) ▼▼▼▼ TownePlace Suites by Marriott-Lakewood M ❀
(303) 232-7790. **$69-$104.** 800 Tabor St. US 6, exit Simms/Union, just n to 8th, then w. Int corridors. **Pets:** Other species. $10 daily fee/room, $150 one-time fee/room.
[SAVE] [S◊] [✕] [ℊM] [♨] [█] [▦] [⇌]

▼▼▼ Travelodge Denver West M
(303) 238-7751. **$69-$89, 3 days notice.** 11595 W 6th Ave. I-70, exit 261, 3 mi e on US 6; I-70 W, exit 269 (Wadsworth Blvd), s to US 6, then 6 mi w. Ext/int corridors. **Pets:** Accepted.
[ASK] [S◊] [✕] [█] [▦] [▥] [⇌]

LONE TREE

▼▼▼▼ Staybridge Suites Denver South-Lone Tree A
(303) 649-1010. **$118.** 7820 Park Meadows Dr. I-25, exit 194, w on County Line Rd to Acres Green, then s to E Park Meadows Dr, just w. Int corridors. **Pets:** Accepted.
[ASK] [S◊] [✕] [ℊM] [🖉] [♨] [█] [▦] [⇌]

NORTHGLENN

(AAA) ▼▼▼▼ Holiday Inn Denver-Northglenn M
(303) 452-4100. **$79-$109.** 10 E 120th Ave. I-25, exit 223, just e. Int corridors. **Pets:** Dogs only. Designated rooms, service with restrictions, supervision.
[SAVE] [S◊] [✕] [ℊM] [🖉] [♨] [█] [▦] [▥] [⇌]

THORNTON

(AAA) ▼▼▼ Sleep Inn North Denver M
(303) 280-9818. **$69-$99.** 12101 Grant St. I-25, exit 223 (120th Ave), e to Grant St, then n. Int corridors. **Pets:** Accepted.
[SAVE] [S◊] [✕] [ℊM] [🖉] [♨] [█] [⇌]

WESTMINSTER

(AAA) ▼▼▼▼ Double Tree Hotel Denver/Boulder H
(303) 427-4000. **$89-$109.** 8773 Yates Dr. US 36 (Boulder Tpke), exit Sheridan Ave, n to 92nd Ave, e to Yates Dr, then 0.5 mi s. Int corridors. **Pets:** Accepted.
[SAVE] [S◊] [✕] [🖉] [♨] [█] [▦] [▥] [⇌]

(AAA) ▼▼▼▼ Hawthorn Inn & Suites M
(303) 438-5800. **$121-$186.** 10179 Church Ranch Way. US 36 (Boulder Tpke), exit Church Ranch Blvd, just s to 103rd Pl, then e. Int corridors. **Pets:** Small. $50 deposit/pet. Designated rooms, service with restrictions, supervision.
[SAVE] [S◊] [✕] [ℊM] [♨] [█] [▦] [⇌]

(AAA) ▼▼▼▼ La Quinta Inn-Denver North M
(303) 252-9800. **$66-$92.** 345 W 120th Ave. I-25, exit 223, just w. Ext/int corridors. **Pets:** Medium. Designated rooms, service with restrictions, crate.
[SAVE] [S◊] [✕] [🖉] [█] [▦] [⇌]

(AAA) ▼▼▼▼ La Quinta Inn-Westminster Mall M
(303) 425-9099. **$66-$92.** 8701 Turnpike Dr. US 36 (Boulder Tpke), exit Sheridan Ave, just s, then left on Turnpike Dr at 87th Ave. Ext corridors. **Pets:** Medium, other species. Service with restrictions.
[SAVE] [S◊] [✕] [ℊM] [🖉] [▦] [⇌]

(AAA) ▼▼▼▼ Marriott Residence Inn, Westminster A
(303) 427-9500. **$76-$109, 14 days notice.** 5010 W 88th Pl. US 36 (Boulder Tpke), exit Sheridan Ave, n to 92nd Ave, e to Yates Dr, then s. Int corridors. **Pets:** Medium, other species. $5 daily fee/room, $125 one-time fee/room. Service with restrictions, crate.
[SAVE] [✕] [ℊM] [🖉] [♨] [█] [▦] [⇌]

▼▼▼ Super 8 Motel/Denver North Ⓜ ❀
(303) 451-7200. **$69-$74.** 12055 Melody Dr. I-25, exit 223, just w. Int corridors. **Pets:** Medium. $5.38 daily fee/pet. Service with restrictions, crate.
🅐🅢🅚 🆂🅓 ☒ 🗒 🖉 🖥 🖵

🔺🔺🔺 ▼▼▼▼ The Westin Westminster 🅷
(303) 410-5000. **$99-$269.** 10600 Westminster Blvd. US 36 (Boulder Tpke), exit 104th Ave, just n; opposite 24 screen movie complex. Int corridors. **Pets:** Small. $75 deposit/room. Service with restrictions, supervision.
🆂🅐🆅🅴 🆂🅓 ☒ 🆘ᴹ 🗒 🖉 🖥 🍴 🏊

❀   **END METROPOLITAN AREA**   ❀

DILLON

🔺🔺🔺 ▼◆▼◆▼ Best Western Ptarmigan Lodge Ⓜ🄸
(970) 468-2341. **$60-$145, 7 days notice.** 652 Lake Dillon Dr. I-70, exit 205, 1.3 mi se on US 6, then 0.3 mi s; opposite Lake Dillon. Ext/int corridors. **Pets:** Accepted.
🆂🅐🆅🅴 🆂🅓 ☒ 🖥 🖵 🍴 🄰🄲

DURANGO

🔺🔺🔺 ▼▼▼ Alpine Motel Ⓜ
(970) 247-4042. **$38-$84.** 3515 N Main Ave. 2.7 mi n of jct US 160 W and 550, on US 550. Ext corridors. **Pets:** Service with restrictions, supervision.
🆂🅐🆅🅴 🆂🅓 ☒ 🖥

🔺🔺🔺 ▼ Caboose Motel Ⓜ
(970) 247-1191. **$28-$68.** 3363 Main Ave. 2.5 mi n of jct US 550 and 160. Ext corridors. **Pets:** Dogs only. $3 daily fee/pet. Designated rooms, supervision.
🆂🅐🆅🅴 🆂🅓 ☒ 🖥 🖵

▼▼▼ Days Inn Durango Ⓜ🄸
(970) 259-1430. **$64-$114.** 1700 CR 203. 4.5 mi n on US 550; entry just s of establishment, then w. Int corridors. **Pets:** Other species. Service with restrictions, supervision.
🆂🅐🆅🅴 🆂🅓 ☒ 🏊

▼▼▼▼ DoubleTree Hotel Durango 🅷 ❀
(970) 259-6580. **$85-$184.** 501 Camino Del Rio. At jct of US 160 and 550. Int corridors. **Pets:** Medium, other species. $15 daily fee/room. Service with restrictions, supervision.
🆂🅐🆅🅴 ☒ 🆘ᴹ 🗒 🖉 🖥 🖵 🍴 🏊

🔺🔺🔺 ▼◆▼◆▼ Holiday Inn Ⓜ🄸
(970) 247-5393. **$64-$130, 3 days notice.** 800 Camino Del Rio. Just n of jct US 160 W and 550. Ext corridors. **Pets:** Other species. $10 daily fee/room. Service with restrictions, supervision.
🆂🅐🆅🅴 🆂🅓 ☒ 🗒 🖉 🖥 🖵 🍴 🏊

🔺🔺🔺 ▼◆▼◆▼ Iron Horse Inn Ⓜ🄸
(970) 259-1010. **$79-$209, 14 days notice.** 5800 N Main Ave. 4.5 mi n on US 550. Ext corridors. **Pets:** Accepted.
🆂🅐🆅🅴 🆂🅓 ☒ 🖥 🖵 🍴 🏊

🔺🔺🔺 ▼◆▼◆▼ Quality Inn & Suites Ⓜ
(970) 259-7900. **$69-$139.** 455 S Camino Del Rio. 1.5 mi e on US 160. Int corridors. **Pets:** Accepted.
🆂🅐🆅🅴 🆂🅓 ☒ 🆘ᴹ 🖉 🖥 🖵 🏊

🔺🔺🔺 ▼◆▼◆▼ Residence Inn by Marriott Ⓜ
(970) 259-6200. **$85-$211, 3 days notice.** 21691 Hwy 160 W. Just w on US 160. Int corridors. **Pets:** Small. $20 daily fee/room. Service with restrictions, supervision.
🆂🅐🆅🅴 🆂🅓 ☒ 🖉 🖥 🖵 🏊

▼◆▼◆▼ The Rochester Hotel 🄱🄱
(970) 385-1920. **$109-$209, 14 days notice.** 726 E 2nd Ave. Just e of Main Ave via 7th St, then just n. Int corridors. **Pets:** Medium. $20 daily fee/pet. Designated rooms, service with restrictions, supervision.
🅐🅢🅚 🆂🅓 ☒ 🖥

🔺🔺🔺 ▼▼▼ Rodeway Inn Ⓜ
(970) 259-2540. **$35-$109.** 2701 Main Ave. 2 mi n jct US 160 W and 550, on US 550. Ext corridors. **Pets:** Accepted.
🆂🅐🆅🅴 🆂🅓 ☒ 🖥 🏊

🔺🔺🔺 ▼▼▼ Travelodge Ⓜ
(970) 247-1741. **$88-$119.** 2970 Main Ave. 2.2 mi n jct US 160 and 550, on US 550. Ext corridors. **Pets:** Other species. $8 daily fee/pet. Designated rooms, service with restrictions, supervision.
🆂🅐🆅🅴 🆂🅓 ☒ 🖥 🖵

EAGLE

▼◆▼◆▼ AmericInn Lodge & Suites Ⓜ
(970) 328-5155. **$79-$129.** 0085 Pond Rd. I-70, exit 147, just n. Int corridors. **Pets:** Small. $25 one-time fee/room. Designated rooms, service with restrictions, supervision.
🅐🅢🅚 🆂🅓 ☒ 🆘ᴹ 🗒 🖉 🖥 🖵 🏊

🔺🔺🔺 ▼◆▼◆▼ Best Western Eagle Lodge &
Suites Ⓜ ❀
(970) 328-6316. **$75-$155.** 200 Loren Ln. I-70, exit 147, just s. Int corridors. **Pets:** Large, other species. $50 deposit/pet. Supervision.
🆂🅐🆅🅴 ☒ 🖉 🖥 🖵 🏊

▼◆▼◆▼ Holiday Inn Express Ⓜ
(970) 328-8088. **$59-$90.** 0075 Pond Rd. I-70, exit 147, just n. Int corridors. **Pets:** Other species. $20 one-time fee/room. Designated rooms, service with restrictions, supervision.
🅐🅢🅚 🆂🅓 ☒ 🆘ᴹ 🗒 🖉 🖥 🖵 🏊

EDWARDS

▼▼▼▼ Inn and Suites at Riverwalk [M]
(970) 926-0606. **$100-$1000, 14 days notice.** 27 Main St. I-70, exit 163, 0.3 mi s; in the Riverwalk Center. Int corridors. **Pets:** Large, other species. $25 one-time fee/pet. Designated rooms, service with restrictions.
[A$K] [S⅍] [✕] [🐾] [🛏] [💻] [🍴] [≈]

ESTES PARK

[AAA] ▼▼▽ Budget Host Four Winds Motor Lodge [M]
(970) 586-3313. **$43-$99, 3 days notice.** 1120 Big Thompson Ave. 1 mi e on US 34. Ext corridors. **Pets:** Designated rooms, supervision.
[SAVE] [S⅍] [✕] [🛏] [💻] [≈] [🐾]

[AAA] ▼▼▼ Castle Mountain Lodge [C] ❀
(970) 586-3664. **$65-$225, 30 days notice.** 1520 Fall River Rd. 1 mi w on US 34. Ext corridors. **Pets:** Dogs only. $15 daily fee/pet. Designated rooms, supervision.
[SAVE] [S⅍] [🛏] [💻] [🐾] [✿]

[AAA] ▼▼▼▼ Holiday Inn [M]
(970) 586-2332. **$79-$149, 3 days notice.** 101 S St Vrain Ave. 0.5 mi se; on SR 7 at jct US 36. Int corridors. **Pets:** Accepted.
[SAVE] [S⅍] [✕] [🐾] [🔑] [🛏] [💻] [🍴] [≈]

EVANS

[AAA] ▼▼▼ Sleep Inn Greeley/Evans [M]
(970) 356-2180. **$54-$84.** 3025 8th Ave. Just sw of jct US 34 and 85 Bypass. Int corridors. **Pets:** $15 one-time fee/room. Service with restrictions, supervision.
[SAVE] [S⅍] [✕] [♿M] [🐾] [🔑] [🛏] [💻] [≈]

EVERGREEN

▼▼▼▼ Quality Suites [M]
(303) 526-2000. **$60-$150, 7 days notice.** 29300 Hwy 40. I-70, exit 252, on west side of El Rancho Restaurant. Int corridors. **Pets:** Other species. $10 one-time fee/pet. Designated rooms, service with restrictions, crate.
[SAVE] [S⅍] [✕] [♿M] [🔑] [🛏] [💻] [≈]

FAIRPLAY

[AAA] ▼▼▼ The Western Inn [M]
(719) 836-2026. **$53-$73.** 490 Hwy 285. US 285, 0.3 mi n of jct SR 9. Ext corridors. **Pets:** Other species. $25 deposit/room, $5 one-time fee/pet. Supervision.
[SAVE] [S⅍] [✕] [🛏] [✿]

FORT COLLINS

▼▼▼▼ Fort Collins Comfort Suites [M]
(970) 206-4597. **$69-$109.** 1415 Oakridge Dr. I-25, exit 265, 3 mi w to McMurray Ave, just s, then w. Int corridors. **Pets:** Accepted.
[SAVE] [S⅍] [✕] [🐾] [🔑] [🛏] [💻] [≈]

▼▼▼▼ Hampton Inn [M]
(970) 229-5927. **$79-$125.** 1620 Oakridge Dr. I-25, exit 265, 3.3 mi w, then s on McMurray Ave to Oakridge Dr, just e. Int corridors. **Pets:** $25 one-time fee/room. Service with restrictions, supervision.
[SAVE] [✕] [♿M] [🔑] [🛏] [💻] [≈]

[AAA] ▼▼▼▼ Holiday Inn University Park [H]
(970) 482-2626. **$119.** 425 W Prospect Rd. 1 mi s on US 287, just w. Int corridors. **Pets:** Accepted.
[SAVE] [S⅍] [✕] [🐾] [🔑] [💻] [🍴] [≈]

▼▼▽ Quality Inn & Suites [M]
(970) 282-9047. **$94-$124.** 4001 S Mason St. I-25, exit 265, 4.6 mi w to Mason St, then 0.5 mi n. Int corridors. **Pets:** Other species. $25 deposit/room. Designated rooms, supervision.
[SAVE] [S⅍] [✕] [♿M] [🔑] [🛏] [💻] [≈]

[AAA] ▼▼▼▼ Residence Inn Fort Collins [A] ❀
(970) 223-5700. **$109.** 1127 Oakridge Dr. I-25, exit 265, 3.3 mi w on Harmony Rd to Lemay Ave, then s. Int corridors. **Pets:** Other species. $100 one-time fee/room. Designated rooms, service with restrictions.
[SAVE] [S⅍] [✕] [🔑] [🛏] [💻] [≈]

▼▼ Sleep Inn [M] ❀
(970) 484-5515. **$70-$120.** 3808 E Mulberry St. I-25, exit 269B, just nw. Int corridors. **Pets:** Other species. $10 one-time fee/pet. Service with restrictions, crate.
[SAVE] [S⅍] [✕] [🔑] [💻]

▼▼▼ Super 8 Motel [M]
(970) 493-7701. **$49-$114, 14 days notice.** 409 Centro Way. I-25, exit 269B, just w. Int corridors. **Pets:** Accepted.
[S⅍] [✕] [🛏]

FORT MORGAN

▼▼▽ Best Western Park Terrace Inn [M]
(970) 867-8256. **$54-$80.** 725 Main St. I-76, exit 80, 0.5 mi s. Ext corridors. **Pets:** $5 one-time fee/pet. Designated rooms, service with restrictions, supervision.
[SAVE] [S⅍] [✕] [🛏] [💻] [🍴] [≈]

[AAA] ▼▼▽ Central Motel [M]
(970) 867-2401. **$43-$61.** 201 W Platte Ave. I-76, exit 80, 0.4 mi s, then w on US 34. Ext corridors. **Pets:** Other species. $5 one-time fee/room. Designated rooms, service with restrictions, supervision.
[SAVE] [S⅍] [✕] [🛏] [💻]

FRISCO

[AAA] ▼▼▼ Best Western Lake Dillon Lodge [M]
(970) 668-5094. **$69-$159, 7 days notice.** 1202 Summit Blvd. I-70, exit 203, just s. Int corridors. **Pets:** Medium. $15 one-time fee/pet. Designated rooms, service with restrictions, supervision.
[SAVE] [S⅍] [✕] [🛏] [💻] [🍴] [≈]

▲▲▲ ▼▼▼ Holiday Inn Summit County M1 ☙
(970) 668-5000. **$62-$199.** 1129 N Summit Blvd. I-70, exit 203. Ext/int corridors. **Pets:** Large. $20 one-time fee/room. Designated rooms, service with restrictions, supervision.
[SAVE] [S6] [✕] [&M] [⊘] [&'] [🛏] [🖵] [¶] [🏊]

▲▲▲ ▼▼▼ New Summit Inn M
(970) 668-3220. **$50-$145.** 1205 N Summit Blvd. I-70, exit 203, just s, then just e. Int corridors. **Pets:** Other species. $20 deposit/pet. Service with restrictions.
[SAVE] [S6] [✕] [🛏]

▲▲▲ ▼▼▼ Snowshoe Motel M
(970) 668-3444. **$48-$125, 14 days notice.** 521 Main St. I-70, exit 203 westbound, 1 mi s to Main St, just w; exit 201 eastbound. Ext corridors. **Pets:** Medium. $10 deposit/pet, $10 one-time fee/pet. Designated rooms, service with restrictions, supervision.
[SAVE] [✕] [🛏] [Ⓐ]

FRUITA

▲▲▲ ▼▼ H-Motel M
(970) 858-7198. **$35-$55, 3 days notice.** 333 Hwy 6 & 50. I-70, exit 19, (use caution), 0.5 mi e. Ext corridors. **Pets:** Small, other species. $5 daily fee/pet. Designated rooms, service with restrictions, supervision.
[SAVE] [✕] [🛏]

▼▼ ▼▼ Super 8 Motel M
(970) 858-0808. **$50-$130.** 399 Jurassic Ave. I-70, exit 19, (use caution), 0.3 mi s; just e of Dinosaur Discovery Museum. Int corridors. **Pets:** Other species. $5 daily fee/room. Designated rooms, supervision.
[ASK] [S6] [✕] [&M] [⊘] [&'] [🛏] [🏊]

GEORGETOWN

▲▲▲ ▼▼ Georgetown Mountain Inn M
(303) 569-3201. **$46-$59.** 1100 Rose St. I-70, exit 228, just s, then 0.3 mi w. Ext corridors. **Pets:** $10 one-time fee/room. Designated rooms, service with restrictions, supervision.
[SAVE] [S6] [✕] [🛏] [🏊] [Ⓐ]

GLENWOOD SPRINGS

▼▼ ▼▼ Caravan Inn M ☙
(970) 945-7451. **$55-$109.** 1826 Grand Ave. I-70, exit 116, 1.3 mi s on SR 82. Ext corridors. **Pets:** Other species. $50 deposit/pet, $5 daily fee/pet. Service with restrictions, crate.
[ASK] [S6] [✕] [🛏] [🏊]

▲▲▲ ▼▼▼▼ Ramada Inn & Suites M1 ☙
(970) 945-2500. **$80-$130.** 124 W 6th St. I-70, exit 116, just w. Ext/int corridors. **Pets:** Medium. $10 one-time fee/room. Designated rooms, service with restrictions, supervision.
[SAVE] [S6] [✕] [🛏] [🖵] [¶] [🏊]

▲▲▲ ▼▼ ▼▼ Silver Spruce Motel M ☙
(970) 945-5458. **$45-$110.** 162 W 6th St. I-70, exit 116, just w on frontage road. Ext corridors. **Pets:** Other species. $5 daily fee/pet. Service with restrictions.
[SAVE] [S6] [✕] [🛏]

GRANBY

▲▲▲ ▼▼▼▼ The Inn at Silver Creek R
(970) 887-2131. **$59-$189, 30 days notice.** 62927 Hwy 40. 2 mi se on US 40. Int corridors. **Pets:** $12 daily fee/room. Service with restrictions, supervision.
[SAVE] [S6] [✕] [🛏] [🖵] [¶] [🏊] [✕🐾] [Ⓐ]

GRAND JUNCTION

▲▲▲ ▼▼▼▼ Best Western Clifton Inn M
(970) 434-3400. **$74-$99.** 3228 I-70 business loop. I-70, exit 37, on I-70 business loop at jct SR 141. Ext corridors. **Pets:** Accepted.
[SAVE] [S6] [✕] [🛏] [🖵] [🏊]

▲▲▲ ▼▼ ▼▼ Best Western Horizon Inn M
(970) 245-1410. **$51-$75.** 754 Horizon Dr. I-70, exit 31, 0.3 mi n. Ext corridors. **Pets:** Medium, other species. Service with restrictions, supervision.
[SAVE] [S6] [✕] [&M] [&'] [🛏] [🖵] [🏊]

▲▲▲ ▼▼ ▼▼ Budget Host Inn M
(970) 434-6050. **$55-$75, 7 days notice.** 721 Horizon Dr. I-70, exit 31, 0.3 mi s. Ext corridors. **Pets:** Dogs only. $50 deposit/room. Designated rooms, service with restrictions, supervision.
[SAVE] [S6] [✕] [🛏] [🖵] [🏊]

▲▲▲ ▼▼▼▼ Days Inn of Grand Junction M1
(970) 245-7200. **$61-$94.** 733 Horizon Dr. I-70, exit 31, just s. Int corridors. **Pets:** $50 deposit/room. Designated rooms, service with restrictions, supervision.
[SAVE] [S6] [✕] [🛏] [🖵] [¶] [🏊]

▲▲▲ ▼▼ ▼▼ Grand Junction Super 8 M
(970) 248-8080. **$45-$90.** 728 Horizon Dr. I-70, exit 31, just s. Int corridors. **Pets:** Accepted.
[SAVE] [S6] [✕] [🛏] [🏊]

▲▲▲ ▼▼▼▼ Grand Vista Hotel M1
(970) 241-8411. **$72-$79.** 2790 Crossroads Blvd. I-70, exit 31, 0.3 mi n. Int corridors. **Pets:** Accepted.
[SAVE] [S6] [✕] [🛏] [🖵] [¶] [🏊]

▲▲▲ ▼▼▼▼ Holiday Inn M1
(970) 243-6790. **$74-$84.** 755 Horizon Dr. I-70, exit 31, northwest corner. Ext/int corridors. **Pets:** Other species. Service with restrictions, supervision.
[SAVE] [S6] [✕] [⊘] [&'] [🛏] [🖵] [¶] [🏊]

▼▼▼▼ La Quinta Inns & Suites M ☙
(970) 241-2929. **$76-$106.** 2761 Crossroads Blvd. I-70, exit 31, n to Crossroads Blvd, just w. Int corridors. **Pets:** Medium. Service with restrictions, supervision.
[SAVE] [✕] [&M] [⊘] [&'] [🛏] [🖵] [🏊]

④④④ ▽▽▽ Mesa Inn M
(970) 245-3080. **$52-$80, 7 days notice.** 704 Horizon Dr. I-70, exit 31, 0.5 mi s. Ext corridors. **Pets:** Large, dogs only. $50 deposit/room. Designated rooms, service with restrictions, supervision.
SAVE S⊘ ✕ ⊟ ▣ ⊇

④④④ ▽▽▽ West Gate Inn M
(970) 241-3020. **$54-$74.** 2210 Hwy 6 & 50. I-70, exit 26, 0.3 mi se. Ext corridors. **Pets:** Other species. $50 deposit/room. Designated rooms, service with restrictions, crate.
SAVE ✕ ▣ ⑪ ⊇

GRAND LAKE

④④④ ▽▽▽ Spirit Lake Lodge M
(970) 627-3344. **$60-$140, 7 days notice.** 829 Grand Ave. Downtown; just e of US 34. Ext corridors. **Pets:** $10 daily fee/pet. Designated rooms, no service, supervision.
SAVE S⊘ ✕ ⊟ ⊇ 🄀

GREAT SAND DUNES NATIONAL MONUMENT

④④④ ▽▽▽ Great Sand Dunes Lodge M
(719) 378-2900. **$85-$99.** 7900 Hwy 150 N. From Alamosa, 16 mi e on US 160, 16 mi n on SR 150, at entrance to Great Sand Dunes National Monument. Ext corridors. **Pets:** $10 one-time fee/room. Service with restrictions, supervision.
SAVE ✕ ▣

GREELEY

▽▽▽ Holiday Inn Express M
(970) 330-7495. **$59-$85.** 2563 W 29th St. US 34 Bypass, exit 23rd Ave, just sw. Int corridors. **Pets:** Accepted.
S⊘ ✕ 🄜 ⑦ 🄵 ⊟ ⊇

▽▽ Microtel Inn & Suites M
(970) 392-1530. **$61-$71.** 5630 W 10th St. 5 mi w on US 34 business route. Int corridors. **Pets:** Other species. $50 deposit/room, $20 one-time fee/room. Designated rooms, service with restrictions, crate.
ASK S⊘ ✕ 🄜 ⑦ 🄵 ⊟ ▣

▽▽ Super 8 Motel M
(970) 330-8880. **$55-$90.** 2423 W 29th St. US 34 Bypass, exit 23rd Ave, just s, then just w. Int corridors. **Pets:** Other species. $20 one-time fee/room. Service with restrictions, supervision.
ASK S⊘ ✕ ⊟ ▣

GUNNISON

④④④ ▽▽▽ ABC Motel M
(970) 641-2400. **$49-$69.** 212 E Tomichi Ave. On US 50, near Western State College. Ext corridors. **Pets:** $5 daily fee/pet. Designated rooms, service with restrictions, supervision.
SAVE S⊘ ✕ ⊟

④④④ ▽▽▽ Hylander Inn M 🐾
(970) 641-0700. **$48-$82.** 412 E Tomichi Ave. On US 50, near Western State College; opposite Legion Park. Ext corridors. **Pets:** $5 one-time fee/room. Designated rooms, service with restrictions, supervision.
SAVE ✕

HOT SULPHUR SPRINGS

④④④ ▽ Canyon Motel M 🐾
(970) 725-3395. **$49-$79.** 221 Byers Ave. On US 40. Ext corridors. **Pets:** Other species. $8 daily fee/room. Supervision.
SAVE S⊘ ✕ ⊟ 🄰

HOTCHKISS

④④④ ▽▽▽ Hotchkiss Inn M
(970) 872-2200. **$35-$59.** 406 Hwy 133. 0.3 mi e jct SR 92 and 133. Ext corridors. **Pets:** Accepted.
SAVE S⊘ ✕

KEYSTONE

▽▽ Arapahoe Motel M
(970) 513-9009. **$79-$149, 14 days notice.** 22859 Hwy 6. I-70, exit 205, 6.5 mi e; opposite Keystone Ski Area. Int corridors. **Pets:** Accepted.
ASK S⊘ ✕ ⊟

LA JUNTA

▽▽▽ Holiday Inn Express M
(719) 384-2900. **$74-$99.** 27994 US Hwy 50 Frontage Rd. 0.8 mi w on US 50. Int corridors. **Pets:** Accepted.
ASK S⊘ ✕ ⑦ 🄵 ⊟ ▣

④④④ ▽ Travel Inn M
(719) 384-2504. **$33-$38.** 110 E First St. On US 50. Ext corridors. **Pets:** $5 one-time fee/pet. Designated rooms, service with restrictions, supervision.
SAVE S⊘ ✕ ⊟

LAMAR

④④④ ▽▽▽▽ Best Western Cow Palace Inn M
(719) 336-7753. **$84-$114.** 1301 N Main St. 0.8 mi n on US 50 and 287. Ext/int corridors. **Pets:** Other species. Service with restrictions, supervision.
SAVE S⊘ ✕ ⑦ 🄵 ⊟ ▣ ⑪ ⊇

④④④ ▽▽▽ Blue Spruce Motel M
(719) 336-7454. **$40-$45.** 1801 S Main St. 1.3 mi s on US 287 and 385. Ext corridors. **Pets:** Other species. $3 daily fee/pet. Service with restrictions, supervision.
SAVE S⊘ ✕ ⊟ ⊇

④④④ ▽ Passport Inn M
(719) 336-7746. **$40-$45.** 113 N Main St. Jct US 50 and 385, just e. Ext corridors. **Pets:** Small, other species. $5 daily fee/pet. Service with restrictions, crate.
SAVE S⊘ ✕ ⊟

LAS ANIMAS

🔺🔺🔺 Best Western Bent's Fort Inn **M**
(719) 456-0011. **$67-$73.** 10950 E US 50. 1.5 mi e on US 50. Int corridors. **Pets:** Medium. Service with restrictions, crate.
SAVE ⬛ ⬛ ⬛ ⬛ ⬛ ⬛

LEADVILLE

🔺🔺 Alps Motel **M**
(719) 486-1223. **$49-$89, 15 days notice.** 207 Elm St. Just s on US 24. Int corridors. **Pets:** Large. $10 daily fee/pet. Designated rooms, service with restrictions, supervision.
⬛ ⬛ ⬛

LIMON

🔺🔺🔺 Best Western Limon Inn **M**
(719) 775-0277. **$50-$99.** 925 T Ave. I-70, exit 359. Int corridors. **Pets:** Other species. $10 deposit/room. Supervision.
SAVE ⬛ ⬛ ⬛ ⬛

🔺🔺🔺 Preferred Motor Inn **M**
(719) 775-2385. **$40-$50, 5 days notice.** 158 E Main St. I-70, exit 361, just w. Ext/int corridors. **Pets:** Medium, dogs only. $4 daily fee/pet. Designated rooms, service with restrictions, supervision.
SAVE ⬛ ⬛ ⬛

🔺🔺🔺 Safari Motel **M**
(719) 775-2363. **$38-$66.** 637 Main St. I-70, exit 361, 0.8 mi w. Ext corridors. **Pets:** Other species. $10 deposit/pet. Service with restrictions, supervision.
SAVE ⬛ ⬛ ⬛

🔺🔺🔺 Super 8 Motel **M**
(719) 775-2889. **$44-$68.** 937 Hwy 24. I-70, exit 359. Int corridors. **Pets:** $10 one-time fee/room. Service with restrictions, supervision.
SAVE ⬛

🔺🔺🔺 Tyme Square Inn **M**
(719) 775-0700. **$65-$85.** 2505 6th St. I-70, exit 359, just s. Int corridors. **Pets:** Other species. $15 daily fee/pet. Service with restrictions, supervision.
SAVE ⬛ ⬛ ⬛ ⬛ ⬛ ⬛ ⬛

LONGMONT

🔺🔺🔺 Raintree Plaza Hotel Suites Conference Center **M**
(303) 776-2000. **$140.** 1900 Ken Pratt Blvd. 1 mi s on US 287, 1.3 mi sw on SR 119. Int corridors. **Pets:** $25 one-time fee/room. Service with restrictions, supervision.
ASK ⬛ ⬛ ⬛ ⬛ ⬛ ⬛ ⬛ ⬛

🔺🔺 Super 8 Motel **M** 🐾
(303) 772-0888. **$55-$86.** 10805 Turner Blvd. I-25, exit 240, at jct with SR 119; 7 mi e of town on SR 119. Int corridors. **Pets:** Other species. Service with restrictions, supervision.
ASK ⬛ ⬛

LOUISVILLE

🔺🔺🔺 Comfort Inn of Boulder County **M**
(303) 604-0181. **$84-$124.** 1196 Dillon Rd. US 36 (Boulder Tpke), exit Louisville/Superior, just n on McCaslin Blvd, then w; next to cinemas. Int corridors. **Pets:** Other species. $100 deposit/room. Designated rooms, supervision.
SAVE ⬛ ⬛ ⬛ ⬛ ⬛

🔺🔺🔺 La Quinta Inn-Boulder Louisville Area **M**
(303) 664-0100. **$66-$136.** 902 Dillon Rd. US 36 (Boulder Tpke), exit Louisville/Superior, just e on McCaslin Blvd, then s. Int corridors. **Pets:** Small, other species. Service with restrictions, crate.
SAVE ⬛ ⬛ ⬛ ⬛ ⬛ ⬛ ⬛

🔺🔺🔺 Residence Inn by Marriott-Boulder/Louisville **A**
(303) 665-2661. **$79-$129.** 845 Coal Creek Cir. US 36 (Boulder Tpke), exit Louisville/Superior, e on McCaslin Blvd to Dillon Rd, then 0.6 mi s. Int corridors. **Pets:** Medium, other species. $5 daily fee/room, $100 one-time fee/room. Service with restrictions, supervision.
SAVE ⬛ ⬛ ⬛ ⬛ ⬛ ⬛ ⬛

LOVELAND

🔺🔺🔺 Best Western Coach House **M**
(970) 667-7810. **$74-$115.** 5542 E US Hwy 34. I-25, exit 257B, just w. Ext/int corridors. **Pets:** Other species. $15 one-time fee/pet. Service with restrictions, crate.
SAVE ⬛ ⬛ ⬛ ⬛

MARBLE

🔺🔺🔺 Ute Meadows Inn Bed & Breakfast **BB** 🐾
(970) 963-7088. **$100-$150, 14 days notice.** 2880 CR 3. From SR 133, 3 mi toward Marble. Int corridors. **Pets:** Dogs only. $15 daily fee/pet. Service with restrictions, supervision.
⬛ ⬛ ⬛ ⬛

MESA VERDE NATIONAL PARK

🔺🔺🔺 Far View Lodge in Mesa Verde **M**
(970) 529-4421. **$89-$112.** 1 Navajo Hill. 10 mi e of Cortez; 8 mi w of Mancos on US 160, then 15 mi within the park; near park visitors center. Ext corridors. **Pets:** Medium. $50 deposit/pet. Service with restrictions, supervision.
SAVE ⬛ ⬛ ⬛ ⬛ ⬛ ⬛ ⬛

MONTE VISTA

🔺🔺🔺 Best Western Movie Manor Motor Inn **M**
(719) 852-5921. **$52-$110, 7 days notice.** 2830 W Hwy 160. 2 mi w on US 160. Ext corridors. **Pets:** Accepted.
SAVE ⬛ ⬛ ⬛

⚫⚫⚫ ▽▽▽▽ Comfort Inn M ✿
(719) 852-0612. **$99.** 1519 Grande Ave. 0.3 mi e on US 160. Int corridors. **Pets:** Other species. Service with restrictions, supervision.
[SAVE] [S6] [✕] [⤳]

MONTROSE

⚫⚫⚫ ▽▽▽▽ Best Western Red Arrow M
(970) 249-9641. **$64-$109.** 1702 E Main St. 1 mi e on US 50. Ext/int corridors. **Pets:** Accepted.
[SAVE] [S6] [✕] [🛏] [📺] [⤳]

⚫⚫⚫ ▽▽▽ Black Canyon Motel M ✿
(970) 249-3495. **$45-$95.** 1605 E Main St. 1 mi e on US 50. Ext corridors. **Pets:** Medium, other species. Designated rooms, supervision.
[SAVE] [S6] [✕] [🐾] [🛏] [📺] [⤳]

⚫⚫⚫ ▽▽▽ Canyon Trails Inn M ✿
(970) 249-3426. **$32-$50.** 1225 Main St. 0.8 mi e on US 50. Ext corridors. **Pets:** Small. $5 one-time fee/room. Designated rooms, service with restrictions, supervision.
[SAVE] [S6] [✕] [🛏]

▽▽▽▽ Comfort Inn M
(970) 240-8000. **$60-$90, 7 days notice.** 2100 E Main St. 1.3 mi e on US 50. Int corridors. **Pets:** $10 daily fee/pet. Designated rooms, service with restrictions, supervision.
[SAVE] [✕] [🐾] [🛏] [📺] [⤳]

⚫⚫⚫ ▽▽▽▽ Holiday Inn Express Hotel & Suites H
(970) 240-1800. **$89-$109.** 1391 S Townsend Ave. 1 mi s on US 550, turn e on Niagara Ave. Int corridors. **Pets:** Medium. Designated rooms, service with restrictions.
[SAVE] [S6] [✕] [🅜] [🌀] [🐾] [🛏] [📺] [⤳]

⚫⚫⚫ ▽▽▽ San Juan Inn M
(970) 249-6644. **$45-$75.** 1480 S Townsend Ave. 1 mi s on US 550. Ext corridors. **Pets:** Medium. $6 daily fee/pet. Designated rooms, service with restrictions, supervision.
[SAVE] [S6] [✕] [🛏] [⤳]

▽▽▽ Super 8 Motel M
(970) 249-9294. **$45-$65.** 1705 E Main St. 1 mi e on US 50. Int corridors. **Pets:** Medium. $20 deposit/room. Designated rooms, service with restrictions, supervision.
[ASK] [S6] [✕]

▽▽▽ Uncompahgre Bed & Breakfast BB
(970) 240-4000. **$60-$80.** 21049 Uncompahgre Rd. 8 mi s on US 550. Int corridors. **Pets:** Large. Service with restrictions, supervision.
[ASK] [S6] [✕] [🐾] [🖼]

⚫⚫⚫ ▽▽▽ Western Motel M
(970) 249-3481. **$40-$52.** 1200 E Main St. 0.8 mi e on US 50. Ext corridors. **Pets:** Small, dogs only. $25 deposit/pet, $5 daily fee/pet. Designated rooms, service with restrictions, supervision.
[SAVE] [S6] [✕] [🛏] [📺] [⤳]

OURAY

⚫⚫⚫ ▽▽▽▽ Ouray Victorian Inn & Resort Accommodations M
(970) 325-7222. **$65-$100.** 50 3rd Ave. Just w of US 550 via 3rd Ave. Ext corridors. **Pets:** Accepted.
[SAVE] [S6] [✕] [🛏] [📺] [🐾]

⚫⚫⚫ ▽▽▽ Rivers Edge Motel M
(970) 325-4621. **$50-$112.** 110 7th Ave. Just w of US 550 (Main St) via 7th Ave. Ext corridors. **Pets:** Dogs only. $10 daily fee/room. Supervision.
[SAVE] [S6] [✕] [🛏] [📺] [🐾]

⚫⚫⚫ ▽▽▽ Riverside Inn M ✿
(970) 325-4061. **$50-$105, 14 days notice.** 1805 N Main St. Just n on US 550. Ext corridors. **Pets:** Dogs only. $25 deposit/room. Designated rooms, service with restrictions, supervision.
[SAVE] [✕]

PAGOSA SPRINGS

⚫⚫⚫ ▽▽▽ Best Western Oak Ridge Lodge M
(970) 264-4173. **$70-$100.** 158 Hot Springs Blvd. SR 160, just s of SR 160. Int corridors. **Pets:** Small. $50 deposit/pet, $15 one-time fee/pet. Service with restrictions, supervision.
[SAVE] [S6] [✕] [🛏] [📺] [🍴] [⤳]

▽▽▽ Fireside Inn C ✿
(970) 264-9204. **$79-$180, 14 days notice.** 1600 E Hwy 160. 1.3 mi e on US 160. Ext corridors. **Pets:** Medium, other species. $5 daily fee/pet, $5 one-time fee/pet. Service with restrictions, supervision.
[ASK] [S6] [✕] [🛏] [📺] [🐾]

⚫⚫⚫ ▽▽▽ Pagosa High Country Lodge M ✿
(970) 264-4181. **$60-$160.** 3821 E Hwy 160. 3 mi e on US 160. Ext/int corridors. **Pets:** Large, other species. $15 one-time fee/pet. Designated rooms, service with restrictions, supervision.
[SAVE] [S6] [✕] [🛏] [📺]

⚫⚫⚫ ▽▽ Super 8 Motel M
(970) 731-4005. **$40-$100, 7 days notice.** 34 Piedra Rd. 2.5 mi w on US 160. Ext/int corridors. **Pets:** Accepted.
[SAVE] [S6] [✕] [🛏]

PUEBLO

⚫⚫⚫ ▽▽▽▽ Best Western Inn at Pueblo West M ✿
(719) 547-2111. **$47-$74.** 201 S McCulloch Blvd. I-25, exit 101, 8 mi w on US 50, 0.5 mi s. Ext/int corridors. **Pets:** Medium. $50 deposit/pet. Designated rooms, service with restrictions, supervision.
[SAVE] [S6] [✕] [🅜] [🐾] [🛏] [📺] [⤳]

⚫⚫⚫ ▽▽▽ Best Western Town House Motel M
(719) 543-6530. **$65-$75.** 730 N Santa Fe Ave. I-25, exit 99B, just w, then just s. Ext corridors. **Pets:** Accepted.
[SAVE] [S6] [✕] [🐾] [🛏] [📺] [🍴] [⤳]

▼▼▼ Hampton Inn M
(719) 544-4700. **$60-$90.** 4703 N Freeway. I-25, exit 102, just w. Ext corridors. **Pets:** $15 one-time fee/room. Service with restrictions, supervision.
(SAVE) (S6) (X) (🔒) (💻) (➜)

▼▼▼ Holiday Inn Pueblo MI ❀
(719) 543-8050. **$79-$109.** 4001 N Elizabeth St. I-25, exit 101 (US 50 W), 0.3 mi n on service road. Ext/int corridors. **Pets:** Other species. Designated rooms, service with restrictions, crate.
(A$K) (S6) (X) (🔒) (💻) (🍴) (➜)

⚑ ▼▼▼ Microtel Inn & Suites M
(719) 242-2020. **$45-$65.** 3343 Gateway Dr. I-25, exit 94. Int corridors. **Pets:** Other species. $50 deposit/room, $10 one-time fee/room. Service with restrictions, supervision.
(SAVE) (S6) (X) (🦽) (♿) (🔒) (💻)

PURGATORY

⚑ ▼▼▼ Best Western Lodge at Durango
Mountain MI
(970) 247-9669. **$89-$279, 30 days notice.** 49617 US 550 N. US 550; at base of Purgatory ski area. Int corridors. **Pets:** Accepted.
(SAVE) (S6) (X) (🔒) (💻) (🍴) (➜) (X) (⚒)

RIDGWAY

⚑ ▼▼▼ Ridgway-Telluride Super 8 Lodge M
(970) 626-5444. **$68-$78.** 373 Palomino Tr. On US 550, at jct with SR 62. Int corridors. **Pets:** Other species. $25 deposit/room. Designated rooms, service with restrictions, supervision.
(SAVE) (S6) (X) (🔒) (➜)

RIFLE

⚑ ▼▼▼ Rusty Cannon Motel M
(970) 625-4004. **$66-$72, 7 days notice.** 701 Taughenbaugh Blvd. I-70, exit 90, just s. Ext corridors. **Pets:** Accepted.
(SAVE) (S6) (X) (🔒) (➜)

SALIDA

⚑ ▼▼ Aspen Leaf Lodge M ❀
(719) 539-6733. **$35-$59.** 7350 Hwy 50 W. US 50, just w of Hot Springs Pool. Ext corridors. **Pets:** Medium. $5 daily fee/pet. Designated rooms, service with restrictions, supervision.
(SAVE) (S6) (X) (🔒)

⚑ ▼ Circle R Motel M ❀
(719) 539-6296. **$32-$75.** 304 E US Hwy 50 Blvd. US 50. Ext corridors. **Pets:** Large, other species. $5 one-time fee/room. Supervision.
(SAVE) (X) (🔒)

⚑ ▼▼▼ Silver Ridge Lodge M
(719) 539-2553. **$38-$75, 3 days notice.** 545 W Rainbow Blvd. US 50, just w of Chamber of Commerce and opposite Hot Springs Pool. Ext corridors. **Pets:** Medium. $5 daily fee/pet. Designated rooms, service with restrictions, supervision.
(SAVE) (S6) (X) (🔒) (💻) (➜)

⚑ ▼▼▼ Super 8 Motel M
(719) 539-6689. **$49-$109.** 525 W Rainbow Blvd. On US 50, opposite Hot Springs Pool. Ext corridors. **Pets:** Other species. Service with restrictions, supervision.
(SAVE) (X) (🔒) (💻) (➜)

⚑ ▼▼▼ Travelodge M
(719) 539-2528. **$49-$89.** 7310 Hwy 50. On US 50 W. Ext corridors. **Pets:** Other species. $8 daily fee/pet. Service with restrictions, supervision.
(SAVE) (S6) (X) (🔒) (💻) (➜)

⚑ ▼▼▼ Woodland Motel M ❀
(719) 539-4980. **$39-$96.** 903 W 1st. US 50 westbound, 1.5 mi on SR 291; US 50 eastbound, 1 mi ne on G St, then 6 blks w on SR 291; US 285 southbound, take SR 291 8 mi s and e. Ext corridors. **Pets:** Medium, other species. Supervision.
(SAVE) (X) (🔒) (💻)

SILVERTHORNE

▼▼▼ Quality Inn & Suites M ❀
(970) 513-1222. **$80-$280.** 530 Silverthorne Ln. I-70, exit 205, just n on SR 9, just e on Rainbow Rd, then just e on Tanglewood Ln. Int corridors. **Pets:** Medium. $50 deposit/room, $10 daily fee/pet. Designated rooms, service with restrictions, supervision.
(SAVE) (S6) (X) (♿) (🏊) (♿) (🔒) (💻) (➜)

SILVERTON

⚑ ▼▼▼ Silverton's Inn of the Rockies at the
Historic Alma House BB
(970) 387-5336. **$80-$130, 7 days notice.** 220 E 10th St. SR 110, off US 550 to 10th St, then just se. Int corridors. **Pets:** Accepted.
(SAVE) (S6) (X) (⚒) (☎)

▼▼ Villa Dallavalle B & B BB
(970) 387-5555. **$55-$100.** 1257 Blair. SR 110, off US 550, se on 12th to Blair sts, then just n. Int corridors. **Pets:** Accepted.
(X) (⚒)

⚑ ▼▼▼ The Wyman Hotel & Inn BB ❀
(970) 387-5372. **$100-$195, 14 days notice.** 1371 Greene (Main) St. Northeast corner of Greene (Main) and 14th sts. Int corridors. **Pets:** Other species. $15 daily fee/pet. Designated rooms, service with restrictions, supervision.
(SAVE) (X) (🔒) (⚒)

SNOWMASS VILLAGE

▼▼▼▼ Silvertree Hotel **H**
(970) 923-3520. **$105-$565, 30 days notice.** 100 Elbert Ln. 4 mi sw of SR 82 via Brush Creek and Snowmelt rds, Lot 8; in Upper Village. Int corridors. **Pets:** Designated rooms, service with restrictions, crate.

ASK Sb X 🐾 🖪 💻 🍴 ⛲ 🚫 🏋

AAA ▼▼▼▼ Snowmass Mountain Chalet **L**
(970) 923-3900. **$135-$299, 45 days notice.** 115 Daly Ln. 4 mi sw of SR 82 via Lower Village Rd, Lot 5. Ext/int corridors. **Pets:** $50 one-time fee/room. Service with restrictions, supervision.

SAVE X 🖪 ⛲ 🏋

SOUTH FORK

AAA ▼ Budget Host Ute Bluff Lodge **M**
(719) 873-5595. **$47-$68.** 27680 W Hwy 160. 2 mi e of jct US 160 and SR 149. Ext corridors. **Pets:** Medium. $5 daily fee/pet. Designated rooms, service with restrictions, supervision.

SAVE X 🖪 💻 🏋

AAA ▼▼▼ Comfort Inn **M**
(719) 873-5600. **$69-$109, 30 days notice.** 0182 E Frontage Rd. On US 160. Int corridors. **Pets:** Accepted.

SAVE Sb X 🖪 💻 ⛲

AAA ▼▼▼ Wolf Creek Ski Lodge **MI**
(719) 873-5547. **$58-$68, 14 days notice.** 31042 Hwy W 160. On US 160. Ext corridors. **Pets:** Other species. Service with restrictions, supervision.

SAVE Sb X 🖪 💻 🏋

STEAMBOAT SPRINGS

AAA ▼▼▼ The Alpiner Lodge **M**
(970) 879-1430. **$59-$149.** 424 Lincoln Ave. On US 40, just w of Hot Springs Pool. Ext/int corridors. **Pets:** $15 one-time fee/room. Service with restrictions, supervision.

SAVE Sb X 🖪 💻

AAA ▼▼ Comfort Inn **M**
(970) 879-6669. **$69-$169.** 1055 Walton Creek Rd. 2.8 mi e on US 40. Int corridors. **Pets:** $50 deposit/room, $5 daily fee/pet. Designated rooms, service with restrictions, crate.

SAVE Sb X 🔬M 🐾 🖪 💻 ⛲

AAA ▼▼▼ Holiday Inn Steamboat **MI**
(970) 879-2250. **$79-$149, 3 days notice.** 3190 S Lincoln Ave. 3 mi e on US 40. Int corridors. **Pets:** Other species. $25 deposit/room. Service with restrictions, supervision.

SAVE Sb X 🔬M 🐾 🐾 🖪 💻 🍴 ⛲

AAA ▼▼▼ Rabbit Ears Motel **M**
(970) 879-1150. **$75-$165, 3 days notice.** 201 Lincoln Ave. Just e on US 40, opposite Municipal Hot Springs Pool and adjacent to Yampa River Park. Ext corridors. **Pets:** Service with restrictions, supervision.

SAVE Sb X 🖪 💻

▼▼ Super 8 Motel **M**
(970) 879-5230. **$54-$94.** 3195 S Lincoln Ave. 3 mi e on US 40. Int corridors. **Pets:** Dogs only. $25 deposit/room. Designated rooms, service with restrictions, supervision.

ASK Sb X ⛲

STERLING

AAA ▼▼▼ Best Western Sundowner **M**
(970) 522-6265. **$84-$89.** 125 Overland Trail St. I-76, exit 125, just w. Ext/int corridors. **Pets:** Accepted.

SAVE Sb X 💻 ⛲

AAA ▼ Colonial Motel **M**
(970) 522-3382. **$41-$50.** 915 S Division. I-76, exit 125, 1.8 mi w on US 6 to 2nd traffic light (4th St), then s. Ext corridors. **Pets:** Accepted.

SAVE Sb X 🖪

AAA ▼▼▼ Ramada Inn **MI**
(970) 522-2625. **$63-$81.** 22246 E Hwy 6. I-76, exit 125, 0.5 mi e. Ext/int corridors. **Pets:** Other species. $25 deposit/room. Designated rooms, service with restrictions, supervision.

SAVE Sb X 🐾 🖪 💻 🍴 ⛲

STRATTON

AAA ▼▼▼ Best Western Golden Prairie Inn **MI**
(719) 348-5311. **$65-$99.** 700 Colorado Ave. I-70, exit 419, just n. Ext corridors. **Pets:** Accepted.

SAVE Sb X 🖪 💻 🍴 ⛲

TELLURIDE

AAA ▼▼▼ Hotel Columbia Telluride **H** 🐾
(970) 728-0660. **$125-$295, 30 days notice.** 300 W San Juan Ave. Just s of SR 145 Spur at Aspen and San Juan sts; opposite gondola. Int corridors. **Pets:** Dogs only. $15 daily fee/pet. Designated rooms, service with restrictions, supervision.

SAVE Sb X 🖪 💻 🍴

TRINIDAD

AAA ▼▼▼ Best Western Trinidad Inn **MI**
(719) 846-2215. **$59-$99.** 900 W Adams St. I-25, exit 13A, straight uphill and across bridge. Ext corridors. **Pets:** Medium. Designated rooms, service with restrictions, crate.

SAVE Sb X 🖪 💻 🍴 ⛲

AAA ▼▼▼ Budget Host Derrick Motel **M**
(719) 846-3307. **$56-$89.** 10301 Santa Fe Trail Dr. I-25, exit 11, just ne. Ext corridors. **Pets:** Accepted.

SAVE Sb X 🖪 💻

▼▼ Budget Summit Inn **M**
(719) 846-2251. **$55-$75, 10 days notice.** 9800 Santa Fe Trail Dr. I-25, exit 11, just se. Ext/int corridors. **Pets:** Accepted.

ASK Sb X 🐾 🐾 🖪

△△△ ▽▽▽ Days Inn M
(719) 846-2271. **$59-$99.** 702 W Main St. I-25, exit 13B. Ext/int corridors. **Pets:** Accepted.
[SAVE] [S6] [X] [Y1] [≈]

▽▽▽ Holiday Inn M
(719) 846-4491. **$90-$160.** 3125 Toupal Dr. I-25, exit 11. Int corridors. **Pets:** Accepted.
[A$K] [X] [B] [≡] [Y1] [≈]

▽▽ Super 8 Motel M
(719) 846-8280. **$55-$80, 7 days notice.** 1924 Freedom Rd. I-25, exit 15. Int corridors. **Pets:** Medium, other species. $10.80 one-time fee/room. Service with restrictions, supervision.
[A$K] [S6] [X] [B] [≡]

VAIL

△△△ ▽▽▽▽ Antlers at Vail CO 🐾
(970) 476-2471. **$210-$485, 60 days notice.** 680 W Lionshead Pl. I-70, exit 176, 0.5 mi w, just s on Lionshead Cir; at Lionshead Pl at Vail Ski area. Ext corridors. **Pets:** Other species. $15 daily fee/pet. Designated rooms, service with restrictions.
[SAVE] [S6] [X] [↗] [B] [≈] [K]

△△△ ▽▽▽ Roost Lodge M
(970) 476-5451. **$59-$200, 30 days notice.** 1783 N Frontage Rd W. I-70, exit 176, 1.5 mi w. Ext/int corridors. **Pets:** Other species. Designated rooms, service with restrictions.
[SAVE] [S6] [X] [B] [≈] [K]

△△△ ▽▽▽▽ Vail Marriott Mountain Resort and Spa H
(970) 476-4444. **$105-$429.** 715 W Lionshead Cir. I-70, exit 173 or 176, on south frontage road; in Lionshead Village at Vail ski area. Int corridors. **Pets:** Accepted.
[SAVE] [S6] [X] [&M] [↗] [s] [B] [≡] [Y1] [≈] [X]

WALSENBURG

△△△ ▽▽▽ Best Western Rambler M
(719) 738-1121. **$58-$93.** 457 US Hwy 85-87. I-25, exit 52. Ext corridors. **Pets:** Accepted.
[SAVE] [S6] [X] [≡] [Y1] [≈]

WINDSOR

▽▽▽ AmericInn Motel & Suites M
(970) 226-1232. **$89-$169.** 7645 Westgate Dr. I-25, exit 262, just se off SR 392. Int corridors. **Pets:** Small, other species. $5 one-time fee/pet. Designated rooms, service with restrictions.
[A$K] [S6] [X] [&M] [↗] [s] [B] [≡] [≈]

WINTER PARK

△△△ ▽▽▽▽ The Vintage Resort Hotel and Conference Center M 🐾
(970) 726-8801. **$60-$175, 30 days notice.** 100 Winter Park Dr. 2.5 mi se on US 40, near ski area. Int corridors. **Pets:** Other species. $25 one-time fee/room. Designated rooms, service with restrictions.
[SAVE] [S6] [X] [B] [≡] [Y1] [≈] [K]

△△△ ▽▽▽▽ Winter Park Mountain Lodge M
(970) 726-4211. **$65-$250, 30 days notice.** 81699 US Hwy 40. 2.3 mi se on US 40; near ski area. Int corridors. **Pets:** Other species. $25 deposit/room. Designated rooms, no service.
[SAVE] [S6] [X] [&M] [s] [B] [≡] [Y1] [≈] [X] [K]

BETHEL

 **Microtel Inn & Suites** **M**
(203) 748-8318. **$69-$119, 7 days notice.** 80 Benedict Rd. I-84, exit 8, 1 mi e on US 6. Int corridors. **Pets:** Medium. $100 deposit/room. Service with restrictions, supervision.

BRANFORD

Motel 6–1279 **M**
(203) 483-5828. **$50-$65.** 320 E Main St. I-95, exit 55, 0.3 mi n on US 1. Int corridors. **Pets:** Other species. Service with restrictions, supervision.

BRIDGEPORT

Bridgeport Holiday Inn & Convention Center **H**
(203) 334-1234. **$149-$179.** 1070 Main St. SR 8, exit 2 northbound, 0.7 mi se; exit 2 southbound, just s, then just e. Int corridors. **Pets:** Small, other species. $50 deposit/room. Service with restrictions, supervision.

BROOKFIELD

Twin Tree Inn **M**
(203) 775-0220. **$80-$95.** 1030 Federal Rd (Rt 7 & 202). Jct SR 25 and US 202, 1 mi n. Ext/int corridors. **Pets:** Medium. $10 one-time fee/room. Service with restrictions, supervision.

DANBURY

Holiday Inn **M** 🐾
(203) 792-4000. **$134-$139, 3 days notice.** 80 Newtown Rd. I-84, exit 8 (Newtown Rd), 0.5 mi s on US 6 W. Int corridors. **Pets:** Other species. Designated rooms, service with restrictions, supervision.

Radisson Hotel & Suites Danbury **H**
(203) 791-2200. **$129-$139, 3 days notice.** 42 Lake Ave Extension. I-84, exit 4, 0.5 mi w on US 6 and 202. Int corridors. **Pets:** Accepted.

Ramada Inn **M**
(203) 792-3800. **$79-$169.** 116 Newtown Rd. I-84, exit 8 (Newton Rd); northeast corner. Int corridors. **Pets:** Accepted.

Residence Inn by Marriott **M**
(203) 797-1256. **$152.** 22 Segar St. I-84, exit 4 eastbound, just n; exit 4 westbound, just e on Lake Ave Extension, then just s. Int corridors. **Pets:** Other species. $20 daily fee/pet. Service with restrictions, supervision.

DAYVILLE

Holiday Inn Express **M**
(860) 779-3200. **$99-$130.** 16 Tracy Rd. I-395, exit 94, just e. Int corridors. **Pets:** Medium. $10 one-time fee/room. Service with restrictions, supervision.

GROTON

Bestway Inn & Suites **M**
(860) 448-3000. **$59-$79.** 135 Gold Star Hwy. I-95, exit 86, 0.5 mi ne on SR 184. Int corridors. **Pets:** Large. $15 daily fee/pet. Designated rooms, service with restrictions, crate.

Clarion Inn **M**
(860) 446-0660. **$59-$179.** 156 Kings Hwy. I-95, exit 86, 0.3 mi ne on SR 184. Int corridors. **Pets:** Large, dogs only. $10 daily fee/pet. Service with restrictions, crate.

HARTFORD METROPOLITAN AREA

CROMWELL

▼▼▼ Comfort Inn M
(860) 635-4100. **$84.** 111 Berlin Rd. I-91, exit 21, just e on
SR 372. Int corridors. **Pets:** Accepted.
SAVE S₀ ✕ ☎ ▣

EAST HARTFORD

AAA ▼▼▼ Holiday Inn MI
(860) 528-9611. **$139, 14 days notice.** 363 Roberts St.
I-84, exit 58, just w. Int corridors. **Pets:** Other species.
Designated rooms, service with restrictions, supervision.
SAVE S₀ ✕ ⟲ ☎ ▣ ⑪ ⇌

EAST WINDSOR

AAA ▼▼▼ Best Western Colonial Inn M
(860) 623-9411. **$79-$189.** 161 Bridge St. I-91, exit 45, just
w. Int corridors. **Pets:** Accepted.
SAVE S₀ ✕ &M ▣ ⑪ ⇌

ENFIELD

AAA ▼▼▼ Red Roof Inn M
(860) 741-2571. **$53-$82.** 5 Hazard Ave. I-91, exit 47. Ext
corridors. **Pets:** Medium, other species. Service with restrictions, supervision.
SAVE ✕ &M ⟲ ☎

AAA ▼▼▼ Super 8 Motel-Enfield M
(860) 741-3636. **$60-$105.** 1543 King St. I-91, exit 46, 0.3
mi n on US 5. Ext corridors. **Pets:** Accepted.
SAVE S₀ ✕ ☎ ▣

FARMINGTON

▼▼▼ Centennial Inn Suites A
(860) 677-4647. **$145-$245.** 5 Spring Ln. US 6, 0.3 mi e of
jct SR 177. Ext/int corridors. **Pets:** Other species. $15 daily
fee/pet. Designated rooms, service with restrictions, crate.
ASK S₀ ✕ &M ⟲ ☎ ▣ ⇌

HARTFORD

▼▼▼ Crowne Plaza Hartford Downtown H
(860) 549-2400. **$84-$184.** 50 Morgan St. I-91, exit 32B;
I-84, exit 50 eastbound; exit 52 westbound. Int corridors.
Pets: Accepted.
ASK S₀ ✕ &M ⟲ ⟲ ☎ ▣ ⑪ ⇌

▼▼▼ Goodwin Hotel H
(860) 246-7500. **$109-$269.** 1 Haynes St. Downtown;
across from Civic Center Plaza, entrance on Asylum St. Int
corridors. **Pets:** Dogs only. $250 deposit/pet. Designated
rooms, service with restrictions.
ASK S₀ ✕ &M ⟲ ☎ ⑪

AAA ▼▼▼ Red Roof Inn M
(860) 724-0222. **$55-$77.** 100 Weston St. I-91, exit 33, just
w. Ext corridors. **Pets:** Accepted.
SAVE ✕ &M ⟲ ⟲ ☎

AAA ▼▼▼ Residence Inn by Marriott Downtown
Hartford A ❖
(860) 524-5550. **$99-$299.** 942 Main St. I-91, 29A northbound; exit 31 southbound. Int corridors. **Pets:** Other species. $25 daily fee/room, $250 one-time fee/room. Service
with restrictions, crate.
SAVE S₀ ✕ ⟲ ☎ ▣

MANCHESTER

AAA ▼▼▼ Residence Inn Manchester M
(860) 432-4242. **$119-$179.** 201 Hale Rd. I-84, exit 63, 0.5
mi nw, then 0.6 mi sw. Int corridors. **Pets:** Accepted.
SAVE S₀ ✕ &M ⟲ ⟲ ☎ ▣ ⇌

SIMSBURY

▼▼ The Ironhorse Inn M
(860) 658-2216. **$89.** 969 Hopmeadow St. On US 202/SR
10, 0.4 mi n. Ext corridors. **Pets:** $15 one-time fee/pet.
Designated rooms, service with restrictions, supervision.
ASK S₀ ✕ ☎ ⇌

WINDSOR

AAA ▼▼▼ The Residence Inn by Marriott
Hartford-Windsor A
(860) 688-7474. **$149-$159.** 100 Dunfey Ln. I-91, exit 37
(Windsor-Bloomfield), just w on SR 305 to Dunfey Ln, 0.3
mi n. Ext corridors. **Pets:** Accepted.
SAVE ✕ ⟲ ☎ ▣ ⇌

WINDSOR LOCKS

AAA ▼▼▼ Baymont Inn & Suites
Hartford-Airport M
(860) 623-3336. **$89-$99.** 64 Ella T Grasso Tpke. SR 75,
just n of SR 20. Int corridors. **Pets:** Medium. $50 deposit/
room.
SAVE S₀ ✕ &M ⟲ ☎ ▣

▼▼▼ Homewood Suites by Hilton M
(860) 627-8463. **$88-$150.** 65 Ella T Grasso Tpke. SR 75,
0.3 mi n of SR 20. Ext/int corridors. **Pets:** Accepted.
SAVE S₀ ✕ &M ⟲ ☎ ▣ ⇌

▼▼▼ Sheraton Hotel At Bradley International
Airport H
(860) 627-5311. **$229-$239.** 1 Bradley Int'l Airport. At Bradley International Airport terminal. Int corridors. **Pets:** Other
species. Supervision.
ASK S₀ ✕ &M ⟲ ☎ ▣ ⑪ ⇌

❖ END METROPOLITAN AREA ❖

LAKEVILLE

🆔 ▼▼▼▼ Inn at Iron Masters M ❖
(860) 435-9844. **$95-$185.** 229 Main St (Rt 44 & 41). 0.5 mi ne on US 44 and SR 41. Ext corridors. **Pets:** Dogs only. Designated rooms, supervision.
[SAVE] [✕] [🔊] [💻]

▼▼▼▼ Interlaken Inn Resort and Conference Center X ❖
(860) 435-9878. **$139-$319, 7 days notice.** 74 Interlaken Rd. SR 112, 0.5 mi w of jct SR 41. Ext/int corridors. **Pets:** Other species. $10 one-time fee/room. Designated rooms, service with restrictions, supervision.
[✕] [🔊] [🔊] [💻] [🍴] [≋] [✕]

LEDYARD

▼▼ The Mare's Inn B & B BB
(860) 572-7556. **$100-$165, 14 days notice.** 333 Colonel Ledyard Hwy. I-95, exit 89, 1 mi n to Gold Star Hwy, 0.6 mi w, then 0.7 mi n. Int corridors. **Pets:** Designated rooms.
[✕] [🔊] [💻] [☎]

MERIDEN

▼▼▼▼ Ramada Plaza Hotel H
(203) 238-2380. **$89-$159.** 275 Research Pkwy. I-91, exit 17 southbound; exit 16 northbound, 0.5 mi e, then 0.5 mi s. Int corridors. **Pets:** $50 deposit/room. Designated rooms, service with restrictions, supervision.
[ASK] [🔊] [✕] [🔊M] [🔊] [🔊] [💻] [🍴] [≋]

🆔 ▼▼▼▼ Residence Inn by Marriott A ❖
(203) 634-7770. **$144-$179.** 390 Bee St. I-91, exit 17 southbound; exit 16 northbound, just e on E Main St, 0.7 mi n. Ext/int corridors. **Pets:** Other species. $200 one-time fee/room. Designated rooms.
[SAVE] [🔊] [✕] [🔊] [🔊] [💻] [≋]

MYSTIC

🆔 ▼▼▼▼ AmeriSuites (Mystic/I-95 & Seaport) M
(860) 536-9997. **$79-$269.** 224 Greenmanville Ave. I-95, exit 90, just se. Int corridors. **Pets:** Very small, other species. Designated rooms, service with restrictions, supervision.
[SAVE] [🔊] [✕] [🔊M] [🔊] [🔊] [🔊] [💻] [≋]

NEW HAVEN

🆔 ▼ Days Inn M
(203) 469-0343. **$65-$100, 14 days notice.** 270 Foxon Blvd. I-91, exit 8, 0.5 mi e. Int corridors. **Pets:** Small. $7 daily fee/pet. Service with restrictions, supervision.
[SAVE] [🔊] [✕]

🆔 ▼▼▼▼ Omni New Haven Hotel at Yale H
(203) 772-6664. **$189-$219.** 155 Temple St. Downtown; center; adjacent to Yale Green. Int corridors. **Pets:** Accepted.
[SAVE] [🔊] [✕] [🔊M] [🔊] [🔊] [🔊] [🍴]

🆔 ▼▼▼▼ Residence Inn by Marriott A
(203) 777-5337. **$159.** 3 Long Wharf Dr. I-95, exit 45, 0.6 mi nw. Ext corridors. **Pets:** Small. $10 daily fee/pet. Service with restrictions, supervision.
[SAVE] [🔊] [✕] [🔊] [🔊] [💻] [≋]

NEW LONDON

▼▼▼▼ Radisson Hotel H
(860) 443-7000. **$99-$179.** 35 Governor Winthrop Blvd. I-95, exit 84, 0.7 mi s on US 1, then just e on Governor Winthrop Blvd. Int corridors. **Pets:** Small. Designated rooms, service with restrictions, supervision.
[ASK] [🔊] [✕] [💻] [🍴] [≋]

🆔 ▼ Red Roof Inn M
(860) 444-0001. **$60-$89.** 707 Colman St. I-95, exit 82A northbound (Colman St), 0.8 mi n, just w, then 0.6 mi s; exit 83 southbound, 0.6 mi s. Ext corridors. **Pets:** Accepted.
[SAVE] [✕] [🔊]

NORTH HAVEN

🆔 ▼▼▼▼ Holiday Inn MI
(203) 239-4225. **$89-$129.** 201 Washington Ave. I-91, exit 12, on US 5. Int corridors. **Pets:** Service with restrictions, crate.
[SAVE] [🔊] [✕] [🔊M] [🔊] [💻] [🍴] [≋]

NORWALK

▼▼ Homestead Studio Suites-Norwalk M
(203) 847-6888. **$99-$109.** 400 Main Ave. I-95, exit 15, 3.5 mi n via US 7, just e, then 1 mi s. Int corridors. **Pets:** Medium, other species. $100 one-time fee/pet. Service with restrictions, supervision.
[ASK] [🔊] [✕] [🔊] [🔊] [🔊] [💻]

OLD LYME

🆔 ▼▼▼▼ Old Lyme Inn CI
(860) 434-2600. **$135-$185, 10 days notice.** 85 Lyme St. I-95, exit 70 southbound, just n on US 1; exit 70 northbound, just n on SR 156, 0.5 mi e on US 1, then n. Int corridors. **Pets:** Accepted.
[SAVE] [✕] [🔊] [🍴]

PUTNAM

🆔 ▼▼ King's Inn MI
(860) 928-7961. **$68-$78.** 5 Heritage Rd. I-395, exit 96, just w. Int corridors. **Pets:** Medium. Service with restrictions, supervision.
[SAVE] [🔊] [✕] [🔊] [💻] [🍴]

RIVERTON

▼▼ Old Riverton Inn CI
(860) 379-8678. **$85-$205, 10 days notice.** 436 E River Rd (SR 20). Center. Int corridors. **Pets:** Medium, dogs only. $20 daily fee/pet. Designated rooms, service with restrictions, supervision.
[ASK] [🔊] [✕] [🔊] [🍴]

SHELTON

AAA ♦♦♦ AmeriSuites (Shelton/Corporate Towers) M
(203) 925-5900. **$89-$179.** 695 Bridgeport Ave. SR 8, exit 12, 0.3 mi w, then just s. Int corridors. **Pets:** Very small. Designated rooms, service with restrictions, supervision.
[SAVE] [S🐾] [✕] [🏋M] [🖥] [🍴] [📞] [💻] [🏊]

♦♦♦ Homestead Studio Suites Hotel A
(203) 926-6868. **$109-$129.** 945 Bridgeport Ave. SR 8, exit 11, 0.5 mi w. Int corridors. **Pets:** Accepted.
[ASK] [S🐾] [✕] [🏋M] [🍴] [📞] [💻]

AAA ♦♦♦ Ramada Plaza Hotel H
(203) 929-1500. **$69-$150.** 780 Bridgeport Ave. SR 8, exit 12, 0.3 mi w. Int corridors. **Pets:** Medium. $20 deposit/room. Service with restrictions, supervision.
[SAVE] [S🐾] [✕] [📞] [💻] [🍴] [🏊]

AAA ♦♦♦ Residence Inn by Marriott A
(203) 926-9000. **$129-$189.** 1001 Bridgeport Ave. SR 8, exit 11, 0.3 mi w. Ext corridors. **Pets:** Accepted.
[SAVE] [S🐾] [✕] [📞] [💻] [🏊]

TORRINGTON

AAA ♦♦♦ Days Inn M
(860) 496-8808. **$99-$150, 3 days notice.** 395 Winsted Rd. SR 8, exit 45, just w, then 0.6 mi s. Ext corridors. **Pets:** $15 daily fee/pet. Designated rooms, service with restrictions, crate.
[SAVE] [S🐾] [✕] [🍴] [📞] [🏊]

WATERBURY

♦♦♦ House on the Hill BB
(203) 757-9901. **$125-$175, 7 days notice.** 92 Woodlawn Terr. I-84, exit 21, 0.6 mi n on Meadow St, 0.4 mi ne on Pine St. Int corridors. **Pets:** Other species. Service with restrictions, supervision.
[ASK] [✕] [📞]

WILLINGTON

AAA ♦♦♦ Sleep Inn M
(860) 684-1400. **$75-$95.** 327 Ruby Rd. I-84, exit 71, just s. Int corridors. **Pets:** Supervision.
[SAVE] [S🐾] [✕] [🏋M] [🖥] [🍴] [📞] [🏊]

DELAWARE

CLAYMONT

∆∆∆ ▼▼▼▼ Holiday Inn Select Wilmington H
(302) 792-2700. **$119-$149.** 630 Naamans Rd. I-95, exit 11, just w on SR 92; I-495, exit 6 (Naamans Rd). Int corridors. **Pets:** Accepted.
[SAVE] [S⊘] [✕] [⅋M] [⌀] [⌀] [▮] [▭] [⊤⊤] [⇌]

DEWEY BEACH

∆∆∆ ▼▼▼▼ Atlantic Oceanside Motel M
(302) 227-8811. **$35-$199, 7 days notice.** 1700 Hwy 1. Jct of US 1 and McKinley St. Ext corridors. **Pets:** Other species. $5 daily fee/pet. Service with restrictions, crate.
[SAVE] [✕] [▮] [⇌]

∆∆∆ ▼▼▼ Bellbuoy Motel M
(302) 227-6000. **$42-$165, 10 days notice.** 21 Van Dyke St. US 1, on oceanside block of Van Dyke St. Ext corridors. **Pets:** Medium. $6 daily fee/pet. Designated rooms, service with restrictions, supervision.
[SAVE] [✕] [▮] [▭] [⌀]

∆∆∆ ▼▼▼▼ Best Western-Gold Leaf Hotel M
(302) 226-1100. **$79-$289, 3 days notice.** 1400 Hwy 1. On US 1. Int corridors. **Pets:** Accepted.
[SAVE] [S⊘] [✕] [⌀] [▮] [▭] [⇌]

∆∆∆ ▼▼▼ Sea-Esta Motel III M
(302) 227-4343. **$39-$189, 3 days notice.** 1409 Hwy 1. Jct US 1 and Rodney St. Ext corridors. **Pets:** Other species.
[SAVE] [▮]

∆∆∆ ▼▼ Sea-Esta Motel I M
(302) 227-7666. **$39-$149, 3 days notice.** 2306 Hwy 1. US 1 at Houston St. Ext corridors. **Pets:** Other species. $6 daily fee/pet. Service with restrictions, crate.
[SAVE] [▮]

FENWICK ISLAND

▼▼▼ Atlantic Coast Inn M
(302) 539-7673. **$49-$139, 5 days notice.** Lighthouse Rd & Coastal Hwy. Jct of US 1 and SR 54. Ext corridors. **Pets:** Small, dogs only. $10 daily fee/pet. Designated rooms, service with restrictions, supervision.
[✕] [▮] [▭] [⇌]

GEORGETOWN

∆∆∆ ▼▼▼▼ Comfort Inn M
(302) 854-9400. **$79-$169.** 507 N DuPont Hwy. On US 113, 0.5 mi n of jct SR 404. Int corridors. **Pets:** $5 daily fee/ room. Designated rooms, service with restrictions, supervision.
[SAVE] [S⊘] [✕] [⌀] [▮] [▭] [⇌]

LEWES

∆∆∆ ▼▼ Sleep Inn & Suites M 🐾
(302) 645-6464. **$59-$189, 3 days notice.** 1595 Hwy 1. 1.5 mi s on US 1. Int corridors. **Pets:** Dogs only. $10 daily fee/pet. Service with restrictions, supervision.
[SAVE] [S⊘] [✕] [⌀] [⌀] [▮] [▭] [⇌]

MILLSBORO

▼▼▼ Atlantic Budget Inn-Millsboro M
(302) 934-6711. **$69-$149.** 210 W DuPont Hwy. US 113, just s of SR 24. Ext corridors. **Pets:** Small. $10 one-time fee/room. Designated rooms, crate.
[✕] [▮] [⇌]

NEW CASTLE

∆∆∆ ▼▼▼ Quality Inn Skyways M
(302) 328-6666. **$74-$169.** 147 N DuPont Hwy. I-95, exit 5A, 0.6 mi s on SR 141, exit 1B, 1 mi s on US 13, 40 and 301. Ext corridors. **Pets:** Accepted.
[SAVE] [S⊘] [✕] [⌀] [▮] [▭] [⇌]

∆∆∆ ▼▼▼ Rodeway Inn M 🐾
(302) 328-6246. **$59-$79, 7 days notice.** 111 S DuPont Hwy. I-295, exit Dover/Shore Points, 2.5 mi s on US 13, 40 and 301. Ext corridors. **Pets:** Service with restrictions.
[SAVE] [S⊘] [✕] [▮]

NEWARK

∆∆∆ ▼▼▼ Best Western Delaware Inn M
(302) 738-3400. **$65-$75.** 260 Chapman Rd. I-95, exit 3A northbound; exit 3 southbound, 0.3 mi e on SR 273 E, then just n. Int corridors. **Pets:** $10 daily fee/pet. Designated rooms, service with restrictions, crate.
[SAVE] [S⊘] [✕] [▮] [▭] [⊤⊤] [⇌]

∆∆∆ ▼▼▼ Comfort Inn M
(302) 368-8715. **$62-$72.** 1120 S College Ave. I-95, exit 1B southbound; exit 1 northbound, 0.3 mi n on SR 896. Ext corridors. **Pets:** Medium, other species. $10 one-time fee/ room. Designated rooms, service with restrictions, supervision.
[SAVE] [S⊘] [✕] [▮] [▭] [⇌]

◆◆◆ Embassy Suites Newark/Wilmington South ☒

(302) 368-8000. **$114-$199.** 654 S College Ave. I-95, exit 1B southbound; exit 1 northbound, 0.8 mi n on SR 896. Int corridors. **Pets:** Small, other species. $100 one-time fee/room. Service with restrictions, supervision.

◆◆◆ Homestead Studio Suites-Newark/Christiana ☒

(302) 283-0800. **$78.** 333 Continental Dr. I-95, exit 4B, 0.3 mi n on SR 7, exit 166, 0.4 mi w on SR 58 (Churchman's Rd); at rear of Christiana Executive Campus. Int corridors. **Pets:** Small. $108 one-time fee/pet. Service with restrictions.

◆◆◆ Howard Johnson Inn & Suites ☒

(302) 368-8521. **$55-$65.** 1119 S College Ave. I-95, exit 1B southbound; exit 1 northbound, 0.3 mi n on SR 896. Int corridors. **Pets:** $10 daily fee/pet. Service with restrictions, supervision.

◆◆◆ Red Roof Inn-Wilmington ☒

(302) 292-2870. **$49-$69.** 415 Stanton Christiana Rd. I-95, exit 4B, 0.5 mi n on SR 7. Ext corridors. **Pets:** Other species. Service with restrictions.

◆◆◆ Residence Inn by Marriott ☒ ☙

(302) 453-9200. **$87-$169.** 240 Chapman Rd. I-95, exit 3A northbound; exit 3 southbound, 0.3 mi e on SR 273 E, then 0.5 mi s. Ext corridors. **Pets:** Large, other species. $50 daily fee/room.

REHOBOTH BEACH

◆◆ Atlantic Budget Inn-Downtown ☒

(302) 227-9446. **$59-$219, 7 days notice.** 154 Rehoboth Ave. Downtown; at Rehoboth Ave and 2nd St. Ext corridors. **Pets:** Large, dogs only. $10 daily fee/pet. Designated rooms, service with restrictions, supervision.

◆◆◆ Sea-Esta IV ☒

(302) 227-5882. **$37-$149, 3 days notice.** 3101 Hwy 1. 1 mi s. Ext corridors. **Pets:** Large, other species. $6 daily fee/pet. Service with restrictions, crate.

SEAFORD

◆◆◆ Best Western Seaford Inn ☒

(302) 629-8385. **$75-$91, 3 days notice.** 225 N Dual Hwy. 0.8 mi n on US 13 from SR 20. Ext corridors. **Pets:** Accepted.

WASHINGTON

Best Western-New Hampshire Suites Hotel [H]
(202) 457-0565. **$169-$189.** 1121 New Hampshire Ave NW. Just ne of 22nd and L sts NW. Int corridors. **Pets:** Accepted.
[SAVE] [Sb] [X] [⌀] [⌖] [■] [▣]

The Churchill [H]
(202) 797-2000. **$139-$289.** 1914 Connecticut Ave NW. Just n of DuPont Cir. Int corridors. **Pets:** Accepted.
[SAVE] [Sb] [X] [⌀] [■] [¶]

Doubletree Guest Suites, Washington DC [A]
(202) 785-2000. **$109-$215.** 801 New Hampshire Ave NW. Just sw at Washington Cir. Int corridors. **Pets:** Accepted.
[SAVE] [X] [&M] [⌀] [⌖] [■] [▣] [≈]

Four Seasons Hotel Washington [H]
(202) 342-0444. **$455-$635.** 2800 Pennsylvania Ave NW. In Georgetown. Int corridors. **Pets:** Accepted.
[SAVE] [Sb] [X] [⌀] [⌖] [■] [▣] [¶] [≈]

The Hay-Adams Hotel [H] ❖
(202) 638-6600. **$495.** 1 Lafayette Sq NW. 16th and H sts NW, just n of the White House. **Pets:** Service with restrictions, crate.
[X] [⌀] [■] [¶]

Henley Park Hotel [H]
(202) 638-5200. **$145-$160.** 926 Massachusetts Ave NW. 10th St and Massachusetts Ave NW. Int corridors. **Pets:** Accepted.
[ASK] [Sb] [X] [▣] [¶]

Hilton Washington [H]
(202) 483-3000. **$244-$284, 3 days notice.** 1919 Connecticut Ave NW. Just n of DuPont Cir at T St NW. Int corridors. **Pets:** Accepted.
[SAVE] [X] [⌀] [⌖] [■] [▣] [¶] [≈]

Holiday Inn-Central [H]
(202) 483-2000. **$99-$229.** 1501 Rhode Island Ave NW. Just e of Scott Cir. Int corridors. **Pets:** Accepted.
[SAVE] [Sb] [X] [⌀] [⌖] [▣] [¶] [≈]

Holiday Inn Downtown [H] ❖
(202) 737-1200. **$149-$229, 3 days notice.** 1155 14th St NW. Massachusetts Ave, at Thomas Cir NW. Int corridors. **Pets:** Small. $30 one-time fee/pet. Designated rooms, service with restrictions, supervision.
[SAVE] [Sb] [X] [⌀] [⌖] [■] [▣] [¶] [≈]

Hotel Washington [H]
(202) 638-5900. **$195-$275.** 515 15th St NW. 1 blk e of the White House, at Pennsylvania Ave and 15th St NW; 2 blks from Metro Center. Int corridors. **Pets:** Accepted.
[SAVE] [Sb] [X] [⌀] [⌖] [■] [▣] [¶]

The Jefferson, A Loews Hotel [H]
(202) 347-2200. **$259-$509.** 1200 16th St NW. 16th and M sts NW. Int corridors. **Pets:** Accepted.
[ASK] [Sb] [X] [&M] [⌖] [■] [▣] [¶]

Lincoln Suites Downtown [H]
(202) 223-4320. **$105-$175.** 1823 L St NW. Between 18th and 19th sts NW. Int corridors. **Pets:** Small, other species. $15 daily fee/pet. Designated rooms, service with restrictions, crate.
[SAVE] [Sb] [X] [⌀] [⌖] [■] [▣] [¶]

Loews L'Enfant Plaza Hotel [H]
(202) 484-1000. **$219-$289.** 480 L'Enfant Plaza SW. I-395, exit Maine Ave. Int corridors. **Pets:** Accepted.
[SAVE] [X] [⌀] [■] [▣] [¶] [≈]

The Madison Hotel [H]
(202) 862-1600. **$215-$315.** 1177 15th St NW. 15th and M sts NW. Int corridors. **Pets:** Accepted.
[SAVE] [Sb] [X] [⌀] [⌖] [■] [¶]

Marriott Wardman Park Hotel [H]
(202) 328-2000. **$209-$335, 7 days notice.** 2660 Woodley Rd NW. Just w of Connecticut Ave; at Woodley Park/Zoo Metro Station. Int corridors. **Pets:** Accepted.
[SAVE] [X] [&M] [⌀] [⌖] [■] [▣] [¶] [≈]

Monarch Hotel [H]
(202) 429-2400. **$235-$430.** 2401 M St NW. 24th and M sts NW. Int corridors. **Pets:** Accepted.
[SAVE] [Sb] [X] [⌀] [⌖] [¶] [≈]

Morrison-Clark Hotel and Restaurant [H]
(202) 898-1200. **$155-$225.** 1015 L St NW. 11th and L sts NW; just n of Massachusetts Ave. Ext/int corridors. **Pets:** Accepted.
[ASK] [Sb] [X] [¶]

Omni Shoreham Hotel [H]
(202) 234-0700. **$143-$224.** 2500 Calvert St NW. Just w of Connecticut Ave; adjacent to Rock Creek Park. Int corridors. **Pets:** Accepted.
[ASK] [Sb] [X] [⌀] [⌖] [■] [¶] [≈]

Park Hyatt Washington, D.C. [H] ❖
(202) 789-1234. **$230-$360.** 1201 24th St NW. 24th and M sts NW. Int corridors. **Pets:** Small. Designated rooms, service with restrictions, supervision.
[SAVE] [X] [&M] [⌀] [⌖] [¶] [≈]

Red Roof Inn Downtown [H]
(202) 289-5959. **$109-$174.** 500 H St NW. In Chinatown area; at 5th and H sts NW. Int corridors. **Pets:** Accepted.
[SAVE] [X] [⌀] [⌖] [■] [▣] [¶]

AAA ▼▼▼ **Residence Inn by Marriott-Dupont Circle** A
(202) 466-6800. **$199-$329.** 2120 P St NW. Between 21st and 22nd sts, northwest section of town, just w of DuPont Cir. Int corridors. **Pets:** $200 one-time fee/room. Service with restrictions.
[SAVE] [✕] [&M] [🛋] [🛏] [▭]

AAA ▼▼▼ **Residence Inn by Marriott-Washington DC-Thomas Circle** A
(202) 898-1100. **$119-$329.** 1199 Vermont Ave NW. At Thomas Cir, jct on 14th St and Vermont Ave NW. Int corridors. **Pets:** Accepted.
[SAVE] [S▪] [✕] [&M] [🗐] [🛋] [🛏] [▭]

▼▼▼▼ **The Ritz-Carlton Washington, DC** H
(202) 835-0500. **$199-$450.** 1150 22nd St NW. At 22nd and M sts NW. Int corridors. **Pets:** Small. Service with restrictions.
[ASK] [S▪] [✕] [🗐] [🛋] [¶] [≈]

AAA ▼▼▼ **The River Inn** A
(202) 337-7600. **$109-$189.** 924 25th St NW. Between K and I sts NW. Int corridors. **Pets:** Accepted.
[SAVE] [S▪] [✕] [🗐] [🛏] [▭] [¶]

▼▼ ▼▼ **The St. Regis** H
(202) 638-2626. **$245-$500, 14 days notice.** 923 16th St NW. Just n of the White House, 16th and K sts. Int corridors. **Pets:** Accepted.
[ASK] [S▪] [✕] [🗐] [🛋] [¶]

▼▼ ▼▼ **Swissotel Washington–The Watergate** H
(202) 965-2300. **$475-$725.** 2650 Virginia Ave NW. Adjacent to The Kennedy Center. Int corridors. **Pets:** Accepted.
[✕] [🗐] [🛋] [🛏] [▭] [¶] [≈]

▼▼ ▼▼ **Travelodge Gateway** M
(202) 832-8600. **$120-$200.** 1917 Bladensburg Rd NE. US 50 and Alternate Rt 1; just w of entrance to Baltimore-Washington Pkwy, New York Ave. Ext/int corridors. **Pets:** Accepted.
[ASK] [S▪] [✕] [🗐] [🛋] [▭] [¶] [≈]

▼▼▼▼ **The Washington Court Hotel** H
(202) 628-2100. **$139-$299.** 525 New Jersey Ave NW. On Capitol Hill, 3 blks from Capitol grounds. Int corridors. **Pets:** Accepted.
[ASK] [S▪] [✕] [🗐] [🛏] [▭] [¶]

AAA ▼▼▼ **Washington Suites Georgetown** A ❀
(202) 333-8060. **$160-$219.** 2500 Pennsylvania Ave NW. Jct 25th St NW and Pennsylvania Ave; 2 blks from Foggy Bottom Metro Station. Int corridors. **Pets:** Medium, other species. $12 daily fee/pet. Designated rooms, service with restrictions, crate.
[SAVE] [S▪] [✕] [&M] [🗐] [🛋] [🛏] [▭]

▼▼▼ **The Westin Fairfax, Washington, D.C.** H
(202) 293-2100. **$249-$399.** 2100 Massachusetts Ave NW. At 21st St. Int corridors. **Pets:** Accepted.
[ASK] [S▪] [✕] [🗐] [▭] [¶]

▼▼ ▼▼ **The Willard Inter-Continental** H
(202) 628-9100. **$299-$850.** 1401 Pennsylvania Ave NW. Just e of the White House. Int corridors. **Pets:** Other species. Service with restrictions.
[S▪] [✕] [&M] [🗐] [🛋] [▭] [¶]

AAA ▼▼▼ **Wyndham Washington, D.C.** H
(202) 429-1700. **$94-$167.** 1400 M St NW. Just w of Thomas Cir. Int corridors. **Pets:** Accepted.
[SAVE] [✕] [🗐] [▭] [¶]

CITY INDEX

ALACHUA

 Comfort Inn/FL-339 🅜
(386) 462-2414. **$75, 7 days notice.** 15405 Martin Luther
King Blvd. I-75, exit 78, just e on US 441. Ext corridors.
Pets: Accepted.
ⓢ🅢🅧🅑🄻🄳

APALACHICOLA

🔺 ▽▽◆ The Gibson Inn 🄲🄸
(850) 653-2191. **$90-$140.** Market St & Ave C. On US 98
at west end of bridge. Int corridors. **Pets:** Accepted.
ⓢ🅢🅧🍴

ARCADIA

(AAA) ▼▼▼▼ Best Western Arcadia Inn [M] ✿
(863) 494-4884. **$55-$119.** 504 S Brevard Ave. 0.6 mi s of SR 70 on US 17. Ext corridors. **Pets:** Other species. $15 one-time fee/room. Crate.

[SAVE] [S6] [X] [🛏] [💻] [≈]

BOCA RATON

(AAA) ▼▼▼▼ Boca Raton Radisson Suite Hotel [MI]
(561) 483-3600. **$157-$279.** 7920 Glades Rd. Florida Tpke, exit 75 (SR 808/Glades Rd). Int corridors. **Pets:** Other species. $100 one-time fee/room. Designated rooms.

[SAVE] [S6] [X] [🗁] [🐾] [🛏] [💻] [≈]

▼▼▼▼ Doubletree Guest Suites-Boca Raton [MI] ✿
(561) 997-9500. **$109-$249.** 701 NW 53rd St. I-95, exit 40 (Yamato Rd), just w. Ext corridors. **Pets:** Medium. $50 one-time fee/room. Service with restrictions.

[SAVE] [S6] [X] [🗁] [🛏] [💻] [🍴] [≈]

▼▼▼ Homestead Studio Suites-Boca Raton/Commerce [M]
(561) 994-2599. **$55-$149.** 501 NW 77th St. I-95, exit 40C, just w of Congress Ave. Ext corridors. **Pets:** Medium, other species. $75 one-time fee/room. Service with restrictions.

[X] [🐾] [🛏] [💻]

(AAA) ▼▼▼▼ Residence Inn-By Marriott-Boca Raton [A]
(561) 994-3222. **$129-$184.** 525 NW 77th St. I-95, exit 40C, just w of Congress Ave. Ext corridors. **Pets:** Accepted.

[SAVE] [X] [🗁] [🐾] [🛏] [💻] [≈]

(AAA) ▼▼▼▼ TownePlace Suites by Marriott [M]
(561) 994-7232. **$59-$159.** 5110 NW 8th Ave. I-95, exit 40 (Yamato Rd), just w. Int corridors. **Pets:** Other species. $3 daily fee/pet, $70 one-time fee/pet. Service with restrictions, supervision.

[SAVE] [S6] [X] [🐾M] [🗁] [🐾] [🛏] [💻] [≈]

BRADENTON

(AAA) ▼▼▼ Econo Lodge Airport [M]
(941) 758-7199. **$50-$90, 7 days notice.** 6727 14th St W. US 41, 2 mi s of jct SR 70. Ext corridors. **Pets:** Dogs only. $10 daily fee/pet. Designated rooms, service with restrictions, supervision.

[SAVE] [S6] [X] [🛏] [≈]

(AAA) ▼▼▼ Park Inn & Suites [M]
(941) 795-4633. **$84-$134.** 4450 47th St W. 2 mi w of jct US 41 on SR 684 (Cortez Rd), just s. Int corridors. **Pets:** Accepted.

[SAVE] [S6] [X] [🗁] [🛏] [💻] [≈]

▼▼▼ Super 8 Motel-Bradenton [M]
(941) 756-6656. **$48-$99, 7 days notice.** 6516 14 St W. US 41, 1.5 mi s of jct SR 70. Ext corridors. **Pets:** Small, dogs only. $10 daily fee/pet. Service with restrictions, crate.

[ASK] [S6] [X] [🛏] [≈]

BRADENTON BEACH

(AAA) ▼▼▼▼ Tortuga Inn [M]
(941) 778-6611. **$145-$319, 14 days notice.** 1325 Gulf Dr N. SR 789, 0.3 mi n of jct SR 684. Ext corridors. **Pets:** Small. $25 one-time fee/room. Designated rooms, service with restrictions, supervision.

[SAVE] [S6] [X] [🛏] [💻] [≈]

(AAA) ▼▼▼▼ Tradewinds Resort [A]
(941) 779-0010. **$109-$309, 14 days notice.** 1603 Gulf Dr N. SR 789, 0.5 mi n of jct SR 684. Ext corridors. **Pets:** Small. $25 one-time fee/room. Designated rooms, service with restrictions.

[SAVE] [S6] [X] [🛏] [💻] [≈]

BROOKSVILLE

▼▼▼ Best Western Brooksville I-75 [MI]
(352) 796-9481. **$69-$85, 30 days notice.** 30307 Cortez Blvd. I-75, exit 61, just w on SR 50. Ext corridors. **Pets:** Accepted.

[SAVE] [S6] [X] [🗁] [🛏] [💻] [🍴] [≈]

BUSHNELL

(AAA) ▼▼▼ Best Western Guest House Inn [M]
(352) 793-5010. **$39-$79.** 2224 W SR 48. I-75, exit 63, just e. Ext corridors. **Pets:** Accepted.

[SAVE] [S6] [X] [🛏] [≈]

CAPE CORAL

(AAA) ▼▼▼ Quality Inn-Nautilus [M]
(941) 542-2121. **$65-$125.** 1538 Cape Coral Pkwy. I-75, exit 22, jct Del Prado Blvd. Int corridors. **Pets:** $8 daily fee/pet. Designated rooms, service with restrictions.

[SAVE] [S6] [X] [🗁] [🛏] [💻] [≈]

CARRABELLE

▼▼▼▼ The Moorings At Carrabelle [M]
(850) 697-2800. **$48-$90.** 1000 US 98. US 98, just e of bridge. Ext corridors. **Pets:** Other species. $10 daily fee/pet. Supervision.

[ASK] [S6] [🛏] [💻] [≈] [X]

CEDAR KEY

(AAA) ▼▼▼ Park Place Motel & Condominiums [C]
(352) 543-5737. **$65-$90.** 211 2nd St. At A St. Ext corridors. **Pets:** Medium, other species. $7 daily fee/pet. Designated rooms, service with restrictions, supervision.

[SAVE] [X] [🛏] [💻]

CHARLOTTE HARBOR

▼▼▼ Banana Bay Waterfront Motel [A]
(941) 743-4441. **$36-$80.** 23285 Bayshore Rd. At jct US 41. Ext corridors. **Pets:** Very small. Designated rooms, service with restrictions, supervision.

[ASK] [S6] [X] [🛏] [💻]

CHIEFLAND

⬥⬥⬥ ▼▼▼▼ Best Western Suwannee Valley Inn M
(352) 493-0663. **$70-$85.** 1125 N Young Blvd. On US 19/98, just n of jct US 129. Ext corridors. **Pets:** $10.70 daily fee/pet. Designated rooms, service with restrictions, supervision.

[SAVE] [S🐾] [✕] [🛏] [💻] [🏊]

CHIPLEY

▼▼ ▼▼ Super 8 Motel M
(850) 638-8530. **$49-$69.** 1700 Main St. I-10, exit 18, just n. Ext corridors. **Pets:** Medium, dogs only. $5 daily fee/pet. Designated rooms, service with restrictions, supervision.

[ASK] [S🐾] [✕] [🛏]

COCOA

⬥⬥⬥ ▼▼ ▼▼ Best Western M
(321) 632-1065. **$60-$109.** 4225 W King St. I-95, exit 75 (SR 520), 0.3 mi e. Ext corridors. **Pets:** Accepted.

[SAVE] [S🐾] [✕] [🗂] [🐾] [🛏] [🏊]

▼▼ ▼▼ Econo Lodge-Space Center MI
(321) 632-4561. **$60-$150.** 3220 N Cocoa Blvd. US 1, just n of jct SR 528. Ext corridors. **Pets:** Accepted.

[SAVE] [✕] [🛏] [💻] [🍴] [🏊]

⬥⬥⬥ ▼▼ ▼▼ Ramada Inn Cocoa-Kennedy Space Center MI
(321) 631-1210. **$59-$99.** 900 Friday Rd. I-95, exit 76 (SR 524), just w. Ext corridors. **Pets:** Small, other species. $25 deposit/room. Service with restrictions, supervision.

[SAVE] [S🐾] [✕] [🛏] [🍴] [🏊] [✕]

⬥⬥⬥ ▼▼ ▼▼ Super 8 Motel M
(321) 631-1212. **$49-$89.** 900A Friday Rd. I-95, exit 76, 0.5 mi sw. Ext corridors. **Pets:** Small, other species. $25 deposit/room. Service with restrictions, supervision.

[SAVE] [S🐾] [✕] [🛏] [🏊]

COCOA BEACH

▼▼▼▼▼ Best Western Oceanfront Resort M
(321) 783-7621. **$109-$229.** 5600 N Atlantic Ave. SR A1A, 0.8 mi n of jct SR 520. Ext/int corridors. **Pets:** Small. Designated rooms, service with restrictions, supervision.

[SAVE] [S🐾] [✕] [🐾M] [🗂] [🐾] [🛏] [💻] [🏊]

⬥⬥⬥ ▼▼▼▼▼ Days Inn Cocoa Beach M
(321) 784-2550. **$89-$199.** 5500 N Atlantic Ave. SR A1A, 0.8 mi n of jct SR 520. Ext corridors. **Pets:** Small. Designated rooms, service with restrictions, supervision.

[SAVE] [S🐾] [✕] [🗂] [🛏] [💻] [🏊]

▼▼▼▼▼ Holiday Inn Cocoa Beach Oceanfront Resort MI
(321) 783-2271. **$79-$159.** 1300 N Atlantic Ave. SR A1A, 1.8 mi s of jct SR 520. Ext corridors. **Pets:** Accepted.

[ASK] [S🐾] [✕] [🐾M] [🗂] [🐾] [🛏] [💻] [🍴] [✕]

▼▼ ▼▼ Surf Studio Beach Resort M
(321) 783-7100. **$60-$150, 7 days notice.** 1801 S Atlantic Ave. SR A1A northbound, 5 mi s of jct SR 520 at Francis St, 1.3 mi n of Partrick AFB. Ext corridors. **Pets:** Medium. $20 daily fee/pet. Service with restrictions, supervision.

[🛏] [💻] [🏊]

CRESCENT BEACH

⬥⬥⬥ ▼▼ ▼▼ Beacher's Lodge M ☘
(904) 471-8849. **$79-$189.** 6970 A1A South. Just s of jct SR 206. Ext corridors. **Pets:** Medium, other species. $15 one-time fee/pet. Designated rooms, service with restrictions, crate.

[SAVE] [S🐾] [✕] [🛏] [💻] [🏊]

CRESCENT CITY

▼▼ ▼▼ Lake View Motel M
(386) 698-1090. **$55-$75.** 1004 N Summit St. 1 mi n on US 17. Ext corridors. **Pets:** Small. $25 deposit/room. Designated rooms, service with restrictions, supervision.

[✕] [🛏] [💻] [🏊]

CRESTVIEW

▼▼ ▼▼ Holiday Inn MI
(850) 682-6111. **$56-$85.** 4050 S Ferdon Blvd. I-10, exit 12 (SR 85), 0.5 mi s. Ext corridors. **Pets:** Small. $25 one-time fee/room. Designated rooms, service with restrictions, supervision.

[ASK] [S🐾] [✕] [🐾] [🛏] [💻] [🍴] [🏊]

▼▼▼▼▼ Jameson Inn M
(850) 683-1778. **$55-$70.** 151 Cracker Barrel Dr. I-10, exit 12, just s. Int corridors. **Pets:** Accepted.

[✕] [🛏] [💻] [🏊]

⬥⬥⬥ ▼▼ ▼▼ Super 8 Motel M
(850) 682-9649. **$43-$63.** 3925 S Ferdon Blvd. I-10, exit 12, 0.3 mi s. Ext corridors. **Pets:** $5 one-time fee/room. Designated rooms, service with restrictions, supervision.

[SAVE] [S🐾] [✕] [🛏]

CROSS CITY

⬥⬥⬥ ▼▼ ▼▼ Carriage Inn M
(352) 498-0001. **$39-$49.** 280 E Main (US 19/98/27A). 0.5 mi s on US 19, 27A and 98. Ext corridors. **Pets:** Small, other species. $5 daily fee/pet. Supervision.

[SAVE] [S🐾] [✕] [🏊]

CRYSTAL RIVER

⬥⬥⬥ ▼▼ ▼▼ Best Western Crystal River Resort R
(352) 795-3171. **$73-$110.** 614 NW Hwy 19. On US 19/98, 0.8 mi n of jct SR 44. Ext corridors. **Pets:** Small, other species. $3 daily fee/pet. Service with restrictions, supervision.

[SAVE] [S🐾] [✕] [🗂] [🐾] [🛏] [💻] [🏊] [✕]

DAYTONA BEACH

(AAA) ♦♦♦ Breakers Beach Oceanfront Motel M ❀
(386) 252-0863. **$50-$90, 21 days notice.** 27 S Ocean Ave. Ext corridors. **Pets:** Medium. $10 daily fee/room. Service with restrictions, crate.
[SAVE] [$⏰] [✕] [🛎] [▭] [🛁]

(AAA) ♦♦ Budget Host Inn, The Candlelight M
(386) 252-1142. **$38-$44.** 1305 S Ridgewood Ave. I-95, exit 86A, 2.5 mi e on SR 400, 0.4 mi n on US 1 (Ridgewood Ave). Ext corridors. **Pets:** Other species. $5 one-time fee/pet. Designated rooms, service with restrictions, crate.
[SAVE] [$⏰] [✕] [🛎] [▭]

(AAA) ♦♦♦ La Quinta Inn M
(386) 255-7412. **$65-$115.** 2725 W International Speedway Blvd. I-95, exit 87 northbound; exit 87B southbound, just e. Int corridors. **Pets:** Small. Service with restrictions, supervision.
[SAVE] [✕] [🖥M] [🌀] [🖥] [🛎] [▭] [🛁]

(AAA) ♦♦♦♦ Radisson Resort H
(386) 239-9800. **$97-$329, 7 days notice.** 640 N Atlantic Ave. SR A1A, 1 mi n of jct SR 90. Int corridors. **Pets:** Accepted.
[SAVE] [$⏰] [✕] [🖥M] [🌀] [🖥] [🛎] [▭] [🍽] [🛁]

(AAA) ♦♦♦♦ Ramada Inn Speedway MI
(386) 255-2422. **$79-$89.** 1798 W International Speedway Blvd. I-95, exit 87A southbound; exit 87 northbound, 2 mi e on US 92. Ext corridors. **Pets:** Accepted.
[SAVE] [$⏰] [✕] [🌀] [🛎] [▭] [🍽] [🛁]

DAYTONA BEACH SHORES

(AAA) ♦♦♦ Atlantic Ocean Palm Inn M
(386) 761-8450. **$39-$149, 30 days notice.** 3247 S Atlantic Ave. SR A1A, 5 mi s of jct US 92. Ext corridors. **Pets:** Small. $15 one-time fee/pet. Designated rooms, service with restrictions, supervision.
[SAVE] [✕] [🛎] [▭] [🛁]

(AAA) ♦♦♦♦ Quality Inn Ocean Palms M
(386) 255-0476. **$60-$160, 30 days notice.** 2323 S Atlantic Ave. SR A1A, 2.5 mi s of jct US 92. Ext corridors. **Pets:** Medium. $10 daily fee/room. Service with restrictions, crate.
[SAVE] [$⏰] [✕] [🖥M] [🌀] [🖥] [🛎] [▭] [🛁]

DE FUNIAK SPRINGS

♦♦♦ Best Western Crossroads Inn MI
(850) 892-5111. **$59, 5 days notice.** 2343 Freeport Rd. I-10, exit 14, just s. Ext/int corridors. **Pets:** Accepted.
[SAVE] [$⏰] [✕] [▭] [🍽] [🛁]

(AAA) ♦♦♦ Days Inn M
(850) 892-6115. **$55-$95.** 472 Hugh Adams Rd. I-10, exit 14, just n. Ext corridors. **Pets:** Accepted.
[SAVE] [$⏰] [✕] [🛎]

DELAND

(AAA) ♦♦♦ Best Inn University M
(386) 734-5711. **$60-$155.** 644 N Woodland Blvd. US 17, 0.9 mi n of jct SR 44. Ext corridors. **Pets:** $10 daily fee/pet. Service with restrictions, supervision.
[SAVE] [$⏰] [✕] [🖥] [🛎] [▭] [🛁]

(AAA) ♦♦♦♦ Holiday Inn MI
(386) 738-5200. **$80-$122.** 350 E International Speedway Blvd. 0.3 mi ne on US 92 from jct US 17. Int corridors. **Pets:** Accepted.
[SAVE] [$⏰] [✕] [🛎] [▭] [🍽] [🛁]

DELRAY BEACH

(AAA) ♦♦♦♦ The Colony Hotel & Cabana Club H ❀
(561) 276-4123. **$89-$210, 3 days notice.** 525 E Atlantic Ave. Center; on SR 806 at jct US 1 northbound. Int corridors. **Pets:** Other species. $20 daily fee/pet.
[SAVE] [✕] [🌀] [🖥] [🍽]

ELKTON

(AAA) ♦♦♦ Comfort Inn St. Augustine M
(904) 829-3435. **$54-$199, 7 days notice.** 2625 SR 207. I-95, exit 94, just w. Ext corridors. **Pets:** Accepted.
[SAVE] [$⏰] [✕] [🛎] [▭] [🛁]

ELLENTON

♦♦♦ Ramada Limited M
(941) 729-8505. **$70-$110, 14 days notice.** 5218 17th St E. I-75, exit 43, 0.3 mi w on US 301, just n on 51st Ave E, just e. Ext corridors. **Pets:** Accepted.
[A$K] [$⏰] [✕] [🛎] [▭] [🛁]

FLAGLER BEACH

(AAA) ♦♦♦ Beach Front Motel M
(386) 439-0089. **$45-$59.** 1544 S A1A. On SR A1A, 1 mi s of SR 100. Ext corridors. **Pets:** Medium, dogs only. $15 one-time fee/room. Service with restrictions, crate.
[SAVE] [$⏰] [✕] [🛎] [▭]

(AAA) ♦♦♦ Topaz Motel M
(386) 439-3301. **$55-$145, 14 days notice.** 1224 S Oceanshore Blvd. 0.5 mi s of SR 100 on SR A1A. Ext/int corridors. **Pets:** Dogs only. $10.70 one-time fee/room. Designated rooms, service with restrictions, supervision.
[SAVE] [✕] [🛎] [▭] [🍽] [🛁]

FLORAL CITY

♦♦ Moonrise Resort C
(352) 726-2553. **$50-$75 (no credit cards), 14 days notice.** 8801 E Moonrise Ln, Lot 18. Just e on CR 48, 1.5 mi n on Old Floral City Rd. Ext corridors. **Pets:** Medium, other species. $20 one-time fee/pet. No service.
[🛎] [▭] [✕] [🌀]

FORT LAUDERDALE METROPOLITAN AREA

CORAL SPRINGS

▼▼▼▼ La Quinta Inn **M**
(954) 753-9000. **$65-$145.** 3701 University Dr. SR 817, just n of jct Sample Rd (SR 834). Int corridors. **Pets:** Accepted.
[SAVE] [✕] [&M] [🔊] [♿] [🛢] [🖥] [🏊]

[AAA] ▼▼▼▼ Radisson Resort Coral Springs **MI**
(954) 753-5598. **$129-$199, 3 days notice.** 11775 Heron Bay Blvd. From Sawgrass Expwy/SR 869, exit Coral Ridge Dr N, 0.3 mi, then left onto Heron Bay Blvd, then first right. Int corridors. **Pets:** Small. $50 deposit/room, $50 one-time fee/room. Designated rooms, service with restrictions, supervision.
[SAVE] [S&] [✕] [🔊] [♿] [🛢] [🖥] [🍴] [🏊]

[AAA] ▼▼▼ Wellesley Inn & Suites **M**
(954) 344-2200. **$69-$119.** 3100 N University Dr. SR 817, just s of jct Sample Rd (SR 834). Int corridors. **Pets:** Small, other species. Designated rooms, service with restrictions, supervision.
[SAVE] [✕] [🔊] [♿] [🛢] [🖥] [🏊]

DANIA BEACH

▼▼▼ Sheraton Fort Lauderdale Airport Hotel **H**
(954) 920-3500. **$119-$179.** 1825 Griffin Rd. I-95, exit 26. Int corridors. **Pets:** Small. $50 one-time fee/room. Service with restrictions, supervision.
[ASK] [S&] [✕] [&M] [🔊] [♿] [🛢] [🖥] [🍴] [🏊]

DAVIE

▼▼▼ Homestead Studio Suites-Plantation/Davie **M**
(954) 476-1211. **$60-$74.** 7550 SR 84 E. I-595, exit University Dr/SR 817, to SR 84 E, then 0.3 mi. Ext corridors. **Pets:** Supervision.
[ASK] [S&] [✕] [&M] [🔊] [♿] [🛢] [🖥]

DEERFIELD BEACH

[AAA] ▼▼▼ Comfort Inn-Oceanside **M**
(954) 428-0650. **$69-$150.** 50 SE 20th Ave. SR A1A, at jct SR 810 (Hillsboro Blvd). Int corridors. **Pets:** Accepted.
[SAVE] [S&] [✕] [🔊] [♿] [🛢] [🖥] [🍴] [🏊]

[AAA] ▼▼▼ Comfort Suites **M**
(954) 570-8887. **$79-$145.** 1040 E Newport Center Dr. I-95, exit 36C, jct SW 10th St to SW 12th Ave, then s. Ext corridors. **Pets:** Accepted.
[SAVE] [S&] [✕] [🔊] [🛢] [🖥] [🏊]

[AAA] ▼▼▼▼ La Quinta Inn **M**
(954) 421-1004. **$61-$125.** 351 W Hillsboro Blvd. I-95, exit 37, 0.3 mi e on SR 810. Ext corridors. **Pets:** Accepted.
[SAVE] [✕] [&M] [🔊] [🖥] [🏊]

[AAA] ▼▼▼ Ramada Inn Deerfield Beach East **MI**
(954) 421-5000. **$69-$149.** 1401 S Federal Hwy. On US 1, 1.3 mi s of jct SR 810 (Hillsboro Blvd). Ext/int corridors. **Pets:** Medium. $10 daily fee/pet. Designated rooms, service with restrictions.
[SAVE] [S&] [✕] [🛢] [🖥] [🍴] [🏊]

[AAA] ▼▼▼ Wellesley Inn & Suites **M**
(954) 428-0661. **$59-$119, 3 days notice.** 100 12th Ave SW. I-95, exit 37, just w on SR 810 (Hillsboro Blvd), then just s. Int corridors. **Pets:** Accepted.
[SAVE] [S&] [✕] [&M] [🔊] [♿] [🛢] [🖥] [🏊]

FORT LAUDERDALE

[AAA] ▼▼▼▼ AmeriSuites Fort Lauderdale/17th Street **M**
(954) 763-7670. **$79-$179.** 1851 SE Tenth Ave. From SR A1A/17th St Cswy, just s. Int corridors. **Pets:** Small, other species. Service with restrictions, supervision.
[SAVE] [S&] [✕] [&M] [🔊] [♿] [🛢] [🖥] [🏊]

▼▼ Birch Patio Motel **M** ❀
(954) 563-9540. **$35-$105, 14 days notice.** 617 N Birch Rd. 0.4 mi s on SR A1A from jct SR 838 (Sunrise Blvd), w on Aurumar St. Ext corridors. **Pets:** $10 daily fee/pet. Designated rooms.
[ASK] [S&] [✕] [🛢] [🖥] [🏊]

[AAA] ▼▼▼▼ The Doubletree Guest Suites/Galleria/Intracoastal Waterway **H** ❀
(954) 565-3800. **$71-$188, 3 days notice.** 2670 E Sunrise Blvd. Intracoastal Bridge on SR 838 (Sunrise Blvd), 3 blks w of jct SR A1A. Int corridors. **Pets:** Other species. $15 daily fee/room. Designated rooms, service with restrictions.
[SAVE] [S&] [✕] [🔊] [🛢] [🖥] [🍴] [🏊]

[AAA] ▼▼▼▼ Eighteenth Street Inn **BB** ❀
(954) 467-7841. **$110-$200, 21 days notice.** 712 SE 18th St. I-95, exit 27 (SR 84 E), 1.9 mi e on SR 84 to US 1, 0.4 mi n, just e. Ext corridors. **Pets:** Small. $25 one-time fee/room. Service with restrictions, supervision.
[SAVE] [S&] [✕] [🛢] [🖥] [🏊]

▼▼▼▼ La Quinta Inn-Cypress Creek **M**
(954) 491-7666. **$65-$135.** 999 W Cypress Creek Rd. I-95, exit 33 southbound, 0.8 mi; 33B northbound at Powerline Rd. Int corridors. **Pets:** Accepted.
[SAVE] [✕] [🔊] [🛢] [🖥] [🏊]

▼▼▼ Motel 6–55 **M**
(954) 760-7999. **$52-$66.** 1801 SR 84. I-95, exit 27 (SR 84 E), just e, then U-turn at light. **Pets:** Accepted.
[✕] [🔊] [🏊]

[AAA] ▼▼▼ Red Roof Inn **M**
(954) 776-6333. **$49-$94.** 4800 Powerline Rd. I-95, exit 32, just sw of jct Commercial Blvd. Int corridors. **Pets:** Small, other species. Service with restrictions, supervision.
[SAVE] [✕] [🔊] [♿] [🏊]

[AAA] ◆◆ **Royal Saxon Apartments** [M] 🐾
(954) 566-7424. **$45-$125, 14 days notice.** 551 Breakers Ave. Just w of SR A1A; 0.5 mi s of SR 838 (Sunrise Blvd) at corner of Breakers Ave and Terranar St. Ext corridors. **Pets:** $100 deposit/room. Designated rooms, service with restrictions, supervision.
[SAVE] [SD] ☎ 🏊

[AAA] ◆◆◆ **TownePlace Suites by Marriott** [M]
(954) 484-2214. **$49-$119.** 3100 Prospect Rd. I-95, exit 33, Cypress Creek Rd/SR 811, 2.7 mi w, then 0.5 mi s on NW 31st St. Int corridors. **Pets:** Accepted.
[SAVE] [SD] 🚭 🦻 ♿ ☎ 📺 🏊

HOLLYWOOD

[AAA] ◆◆ **California Dream Inn** [H]
(954) 923-2100. **$149-$189.** 300 Walnut St. Just s of Dania Beach Blvd/SR A1A, then e. Ext corridors. **Pets:** Accepted.
[SAVE] [SD] 🚭 ☎ 📺

[AAA] ◆◆◆ **Comfort Inn-Ft. Lauderdale/Hollywood Airport** [M]
(954) 922-1600. **$79-$149.** 2520 Stirling Rd. I-95, exit 25, just e, 2 mi s of airport. Ext corridors. **Pets:** $25 one-time fee/pet. Designated rooms, service with restrictions, crate.
[SAVE] 🚭 ♿M 🦻 ♿ ☎ 📺 🏊

◆◆◆ **Days Inn Fort Lauderdale/Hollywood Airport South** [M]
(954) 923-7300. **$79-$299, 3 days notice.** 2601 N 29th Ave. I-95, exit 24, just nw on SR 822 (Sheriden St). Int corridors. **Pets:** Accepted.
[SAVE] [SD] 🚭 🦻 ☎ 📺 🏊

◆◆◆ **La Quinta Inn & Suites** [M]
(954) 922-2295. **$95-$155.** 2620 N 26th Ave. I-95, exit 24 (Sheridan St/SR 822), just e to Oakwood, then just left. Int corridors. **Pets:** Small, other species. Service with restrictions, supervision.
[SAVE] 🚭 ♿M 🦻 ♿ ☎ 📺 🏊

LAUDERDALE BY THE SEA

[AAA] ◆◆◆ **Courtyard Villa On The Ocean** [M]
(954) 776-1164. **$105-$250, 30 days notice.** 4312 El Mar Dr. From Commerical Blvd (SR 870), just s. Ext corridors. **Pets:** Small. $200 deposit/pet. Designated rooms, service with restrictions, supervision.
[SAVE] [SD] 🚭 ☎ 📺 🏊 🚫🍴

[AAA] ◆◆ **The Pier Point Resort** [M]
(954) 776-5121. **$87-$199.** 4320 El Mar Dr. From Commerical Blvd (SR 870) just s. Ext corridors. **Pets:** Accepted.
[SAVE] [SD] 🚭 📺 🏊

PLANTATION

[AAA] ◆◆◆ **AmeriSuites Plantation** [M]
(954) 370-2220. **$89-$149, 14 days notice.** 8530 W Broward Blvd. I-595, exit 5 (Pine Island Rd), 1.3 mi n. Int corridors. **Pets:** Small. $10 daily fee/pet. Service with restrictions, supervision.
[SAVE] [SD] 🚭 ♿M 🦻 ♿ ☎ 📺 🏊

[AAA] ◆◆◆ **Holiday Inn Plantation/Sawgrass** [M]
(954) 472-5600. **$109-$159.** 1711 N University Dr. SR 817, just s of jct SR 838 (Sunrise Blvd). Ext/int corridors. **Pets:** Accepted.
[SAVE] [SD] 🚭 ♿ ☎ 📺 🍴 🏊

◆◆◆ **La Quinta Inn & Suites** [M]
(954) 476-6047. **$75-$135.** 8101 Peters Rd. I-595, exit 6 (University Dr/SR 817 N), just w. Int corridors. **Pets:** Accepted.
[SAVE] 🚭 ♿M 🦻 ♿ ☎ 📺 🏊

[AAA] ◆◆◆ **Residence Inn by Marriott-Plantation** [A]
(954) 723-0300. **$139-$209.** 130 N University Dr. University Dr (SR 817), just n of jct Broward Blvd (SR 842). Int corridors. **Pets:** $20 daily fee/room. Service with restrictions.
[SAVE] [SD] 🚭 ♿M 🦻 ♿ ☎ 📺 🏊

◆◆◆ **Staybridge Suites Ft-Lauderdale-Plantation** [M]
(954) 577-9696. **$109-$179.** 410 N Pine Island Rd. I-595, exit 5, 1.7 mi n on Pine Island Rd. Int corridors. **Pets:** Other species. $75 one-time fee/room. Service with restrictions, crate.
[A$K] [SD] 🚭 ☎ 📺 🏊

[AAA] ◆◆◆ **Wellesley Inn & Suites** [M]
(954) 473-8257. **$69-$139.** 7901 SW 6th St. 0.3 mi w of University Dr (SR 817); 0.5 mi sw of jct Broward Blvd (SR 842). Int corridors. **Pets:** Accepted.
[SAVE] [SD] 🚭 🦻 ♿ ☎ 📺 🏊

POMPANO BEACH

[AAA] ◆◆ **Sea Castle Resort Inn** [M]
(954) 941-2570. **$48-$195, 4 days notice.** 730 N Ocean Blvd. On SR A1A, 1 mi n of jct SR 814 (Atlantic Blvd). Ext corridors. **Pets:** Other species. $15 daily fee/room. Designated rooms, service with restrictions.
[SAVE] [SD] 🚭 ☎ 📺 🏊

[AAA] ◆◆◆ **Wellesley Inn & Suites** [M]
(954) 783-1050. **$79-$134.** 1401 SW 15th St. I-95, exit 33B, Cypress Creek Rd to Andrews Ave, just s, then turn left onto McNab St. Int corridors. **Pets:** Small, other species. Service with restrictions, supervision.
[SAVE] [SD] 🚭 🦻 ♿ ☎ 📺 🏊

SUNRISE

AAA ▼▼▼▼ Baymont Inn & Suites-Sunrise at
Sawgrass **M**
(954) 846-1200. **$89-$114.** 13651 NW 2nd St. SW 136th
Ave, 0.3 mi n of jct I-595, exit 1 and SR 84; 0.5 mi e of jct
I-75 and Sawgrass Expwy. Int corridors. **Pets:** Medium. $50
deposit/pet. Designated rooms, service with restrictions,
crate.
[SAVE] [S$] [X] [⌖] [⌂] [📞] [💻] [⇄]

AAA ▼▼▼▼ Wellesley Inn & Suites **M**
(954) 845-9929. **$69-$109.** 13600 NW 2nd St. SW 136th
Ave, 0.3 mi n of jct I-595, exit 1 and SR 84; 0.5 mi e of jct
I-75 and Sawgrass Expwy. Int corridors. **Pets:** Accepted.
[SAVE] [S$] [X] [⌖] [⌂] [📞] [💻] [⇄]

TAMARAC

AAA ▼▼▼ Baymont Inn & Suites Ft.
Lauderdale/Tamarac **M**
(954) 485-7900. **$59-$109.** 3800 W Commercial Blvd. SR
870 (Commercial Blvd), 0.8 mi e of Florida Tpke, exit 62,
just e of jct SR 7 and US 441. Int corridors. **Pets:** Accepted.
[SAVE] [S$] [X] [⌖] [📞] [💻] [⇆]

▼▼ ▼▼ Homestead Studio Suites-Ft
Lauderdale/Tamarac **M**
(954) 733-6644. **$54-$64.** 3873 W Commercial Blvd. SR
870 (Commercial Blvd), 0.7 mi e of Florida Tpke, exit 62,
then just e of jct SR 7 and US 441. Ext corridors.
Pets: Accepted.
[ASK] [S$] [X] [⌖] [⌂] [📞] [💻]

AAA ▼▼▼ Wellesley Inn & Suites **M**
(954) 484-6909. **$62-$89, 10 days notice.** 5070 N SR 7.
SR 7 and US 441, just n of jct SR 870 (Commercial Blvd);
0.5 mi e of Florida Tpke, exit 62. Int corridors.
Pets: Accepted.
[SAVE] [S$] [X] [⌖] [⌂] [📞] [💻] [⇄]

❖ **END METROPOLITAN AREA** ❖

FORT MYERS

AAA ▼▼▼ Baymont Inn-Fort Myers **M**
(941) 275-3500. **$50-$116.** 2717 Colonial Blvd. I-75, exit 22,
4 mi w on SR 884. Ext corridors. **Pets:** Medium, other
species. $25 one-time fee/room. Service with restrictions,
crate.
[SAVE] [S$] [X] [⌖] [📞] [💻] [⇄]

▼▼ ▼▼ Best Western Airport Inn **M**
(941) 561-7000. **$-$175, 3 days notice.** 8955 Daniels
Pkwy. I-75, exit 21, 0.6 mi w. Int corridors. **Pets:** Small,
other species. $10 daily fee/pet. Service with restrictions,
supervision.
[SAVE] [S$] [X] [⌂] [📞] [💻] [⇄]

AAA ▼▼▼ Best Western Springs Resort **MI**
(941) 267-7900. **$64-$124, 7 days notice.** 18051 S Tamiami Tr. On US 41 at jct Constitution Blvd. Ext corridors.
Pets: Medium. $8 daily fee/pet. Service with restrictions.
[SAVE] [S$] [X] [📞] [💻] [⏹] [⇄]

AAA ▼▼▼ Comfort Suites Airport **M**
(941) 768-0005. **$80-$199, 7 days notice.** 13651A Indian
Paint Ln. I-75, exit 21, just w. Int corridors. **Pets:** Medium.
$10 daily fee/pet. Service with restrictions, supervision.
[SAVE] [S$] [X] [⌖] [⌂] [📞] [💻] [⇄]

▼▼▼▼ Ft. Myers Comfort Inn **M**
(941) 694-9200. **$79-$125.** 4171 Boatways Rd. I-75, exit
25, just e on SR 80. Int corridors. **Pets:** Accepted.
[SAVE] [S$] [X] [⌅M] [⌖] [⌂] [📞] [💻] [⇄]

▼▼▼▼ Hawthorn Suites **M**
(941) 454-6363. **$110-$220, 7 days notice.** 9200 College
Pkwy. 1.3 mi w of US 41, at jct McGregor Blvd. Int corri-
dors. **Pets:** Small, other species. $50 one-time fee/room.
Service with restrictions.
[ASK] [S$] [X] [⌅M] [⌖] [⌂] [📞] [💻] [⇄]

▼▼▼▼ La Quinta Inn **M**
(941) 275-3300. **$65-$145.** 4850 S Cleveland Ave. On US
41, just s of jct N Aiport Rd. Ext corridors. **Pets:** Small,
other species. Service with restrictions, supervision.
[SAVE] [X] [⌅M] [⌖] [⌂] [📞] [💻] [⇄]

AAA ▼▼▼▼ Radisson Inn Sanibel Gateway **MI**
(941) 466-1200. **$74-$199, 3 days notice.** 20091 Summer-
lin Rd SW. I-75, exit 21, 3 mi e of Sanibel Cswy on SR 869.
Ext corridors. **Pets:** Small. $25 one-time fee/room. Desig-
nated rooms, service with restrictions, crate.
[SAVE] [S$] [X] [⌖] [⌂] [📞] [💻] [⏹] [⇄]

AAA ▼▼▼▼ Residence Inn by Marriott **A** ❖
(941) 936-0110. **$94-$199.** 2960 Colonial Blvd. I-75, exit 22,
3.5 mi w on SR 884. Int corridors. **Pets:** Other species.
$125 one-time fee/pet. Service with restrictions, crate.
[SAVE] [X] [⌖] [📞] [💻] [⇄]

▼▼ ▼▼ Sleep Inn Airport **M**
(941) 561-1117. **$65-$129, 7 days notice.** 13651 Indian
Paint Ln. I-75, exit 21, just w. Int corridors. **Pets:** Medium.
$10 daily fee/pet. Service with restrictions, supervision.
[SAVE] [S$] [X] [⌖] [⌂] [📞] [💻] [⇄]

◆◆◆ ▼▼▼ Ta Ki-Ki Riverfront Inn M
(941) 334-2135. **$44-$95, 7 days notice.** 2631 First St.
I-75, exit 25, 4.5 mi w on SR 80. Ext corridors. **Pets:** $9
daily fee/room. Service with restrictions, crate.
[SAVE] [✕] [🛏] [💻] [🏊]

FORT MYERS BEACH

◆◆◆ ▼▼▼ Best Western Beach Resort M
(941) 463-6000. **$109-$229, 7 days notice.** 684 Estero
Blvd. 0.5 mi n of Matanzas Pass Bridge. Ext corridors.
Pets: Small. $10 daily fee/pet. Designated rooms, service
with restrictions, crate.
[SAVE] [S🔒] [✕] [🏊] [🛏] [💻] [🏊] [✕]

▼▼ Silver Sands Villas ▲
(941) 463-6554. **$80-$195, 21 days notice.** 1207 Estero
Blvd. Just s of Matanzas Pass Bridge. Ext corridors.
Pets: Small, other species. $100 one-time fee/room. No
service, supervision.
[✕] [🛏] [💻] [🍴] [🏊]

FORT PIERCE

▼▼ Days Inn M
(561) 466-4066. **$59-$89.** 6651 Darter Ct. I-95, exit 65. Ext
corridors. **Pets:** Accepted.
[SAVE] [S🔒] [✕] [🏊] [🛏] [💻] [🏊]

▼▼▼ Holiday Inn Express M
(561) 464-5000. **$79-$99.** 7151 Okeechobee Rd. I-95, exit
65, 0.7 mi w on SR 70; at Florida Tpke, exit 152. Ext
corridors. **Pets:** Accepted.
[ASK] [S🔒] [✕] [🅼] [🏊] [🅢] [💻] [🏊]

◆◆◆ ▼▼▼ Royal Inn M
(561) 464-0405. **$49-$99.** 222 Hernando St. 2.5 mi e on SR
A1A, southbound to Hernando St, just s. Ext corridors.
Pets: Medium, dogs only. $25 one-time fee/room. Desig-
nated rooms, no service, crate.
[SAVE] [S🔒] [✕] [🛏]

FORT WALTON BEACH

◆◆◆ ▼▼▼ Marina Motel & Efficiencies M
(850) 244-1129. **$46-$95.** 1345 Miracle Strip Pkwy E. 1 mi
e on US 98. Ext/int corridors. **Pets:** Accepted.
[SAVE] [S🔒] [✕] [🛏] [💻] [🏊] [✕]

GAINESVILLE

◆◆◆ ▼▼▼▼ Baymont Inn &
        Suites-Gainesville M ❀
(352) 376-0004. **$74-$94.** 3905 SW 43rd St. I-75, exit 75,
just w. Int corridors. **Pets:** $10 daily fee/pet. Designated
rooms, service with restrictions, supervision.
[SAVE] [S🔒] [✕] [🅼] [🅢] [🛏] [💻] [🏊]

◆◆◆ ▼▼▼▼ Best Western Gateway Grand M
(352) 331-3336. **$79-$189.** 4200 NW 97th Blvd. I-75, exit
77, just n of SR 222, just w. Int corridors. **Pets:** Accepted.
[SAVE] [S🔒] [✕] [🅼] [🅢] [🛏] [💻] [🏊]

▼▼▼▼ La Quinta Inn M
(352) 332-6466. **$75-$101.** 920 NW 69th Terrace. SR 26,
ne of jct I-75, exit 76. Ext corridors. **Pets:** Accepted.
[SAVE] [✕] [🏊] [🛏] [💻] [🏊]

◆◆◆ ▼▼▼ Red Roof Inn-Gainesville M
(352) 336-3311. **$45-$65.** 3500 SW 42nd St. I-75, exit 75,
just ne. Int corridors. **Pets:** Medium, other species. Service
with restrictions, supervision.
[SAVE] [✕] [🅼] [🏊] [🅢] [🛏] [🏊]

HAINES CITY

◆◆◆ ▼▼▼ Best Western Lake Hamilton M
(863) 421-6929. **$59-$89.** 605 B Moore Rd. On US 27, just
s of jct SR 544, 2 mi s of jct US 17-92. Ext corridors.
Pets: $5 daily fee/pet. Designated rooms, service with
restrictions, supervision.
[SAVE] [S🔒] [✕] [🅼] [🛏] [💻] [🏊] [✕]

◆◆◆ ▼▼▼ Howard Johnson Inn M🛈
(863) 422-8621. **$45-$90.** 1504 US 27S. US 27, 1.8 mi s of
jct US 17-92. Ext corridors. **Pets:** Accepted.
[SAVE] [S🔒] [✕] [🛏] [💻] [🍴] [🏊]

HERNANDO

▼▼▼▼ Best Western Citrus Hills Lodge M🛈
(352) 527-0015. **$75-$95.** 350 E Norvell Bryant Hwy. On
CR 486 at jct Citrus Hills Blvd, 3.3 mi w of US 41. Ext
corridors. **Pets:** Small. $10 daily fee/pet. Designated rooms,
service with restrictions, supervision.
[SAVE] [S🔒] [✕] [🅼] [🏊] [🛏] [💻] [🍴] [🏊]

INDIALANTIC

◆◆◆ ▼▼▼ Guesthouse International Inn M🛈
(321) 779-9994. **$49-$159, 7 days notice.** 2900 N A1A
Hwy. 0.4 mi s of SR 518 (Eau Gallie Cswy). Ext corridors.
Pets: Small. $25 deposit/room, $10 daily fee/pet. Desig-
nated rooms, service with restrictions, crate.
[SAVE] [S🔒] [✕] [🛏] [🍴] [🏊]

▼▼▼▼ Hilton Melbourne Beach Oceanfront M🛈
(321) 777-5000. **$99-$189.** 3003 N SR A1A. N SR A1A, 3
mi n of jct US 192. Int corridors. **Pets:** Other species. $25
deposit/pet, $10 daily fee/pet. Service with restrictions,
supervision.
[SAVE] [S🔒] [✕] [🛏] [💻] [🍴] [🏊]

▼▼▼▼ Melbourne Quality Suites Oceanfront
        Hotel M🛈
(321) 723-4222. **$109-$199.** 1665 N SR A1A. SR A1A, 1.5
mi n of jct US 192. Ext corridors. **Pets:** $10 daily fee/pet,
$25 one-time fee/pet. Designated rooms, service with
restrictions, supervision.
[SAVE] [S🔒] [✕] [🏊] [🛏] [💻] [🍴]

▼▼▼ Oceanfront Cottages **C**
(321) 725-8474. **$110-$145, 60 days notice.** 612 Wavecrest Ave. Just s of east end of US 192. Ext corridors. **Pets:** Small. $15 daily fee/pet. Service with restrictions.

⊠ 🛏 💻 🌊

INDIAN HARBOUR BEACH

▼▼ Travelodge **M**
(321) 773-0325. **$49-$79.** 1894 S Patrick Dr. I-95, exit 72, 8 mi e, 1 mi n on SR 513. Int corridors. **Pets:** Accepted.

ASK S🗭 ⊠ 🗐 🖑 💻 ⊠

JACKSONVILLE METROPOLITAN AREA

BALDWIN

AAA ▼▼▼ Best Western Inn Baldwin **M**
(904) 266-9759. **$50-$95.** 1088 US 301 & I-10. I-10, exit 50, just s. Ext corridors. **Pets:** Small. $8 daily fee/pet. Service with restrictions, supervision.

SAVE S🗭 ⊠ 🌊

FERNANDINA BEACH

AAA ▼▼▼▼ Florida House Inn **CI** ❀
(904) 261-3300. **$89-$189, 7 days notice.** 22 S 3rd St. Just s of Centre St. Ext/int corridors. **Pets:** Other species. $10 daily fee/pet.

SAVE ⊠ 💻 🍴

AAA ▼▼▼▼ Hoyt House B&B **BB**
(904) 277-4300. **$139-$169, 14 days notice.** 804 Atlantic Ave. On Atlantic Ave/SR 200 at Centre and S 8th sts. Int corridors. **Pets:** Accepted.

SAVE ⊠

JACKSONVILLE

AAA ▼▼▼▼ AmeriSuites/BayMeadows **M**
(904) 737-4477. **$89-$119.** 8277 Western Way Cir. I-95, exit 100, just e. Int corridors. **Pets:** Medium, other species. Service with restrictions, crate.

SAVE S🗭 ⊠ 🗐 🖑 🛏 💻 🌊

AAA ▼▼▼ Baymont Inn &
Suites-Jacksonville **M**
(904) 268-9999. **$64-$74.** 3199 Hartley Rd. I-295, exit 2A northbound; exit 2 southbound, at SR 13. Int corridors. **Pets:** Accepted.

SAVE S🗭 ⊠ 🗐 🛏 💻 🌊

▼▼▼▼ Hampton Inn **M**
(904) 741-4980. **$79-$89.** 1170 Airport Entrance Rd. I-95, exit 127, jct Airport Rd. Ext corridors. **Pets:** Accepted.

SAVE S🗭 ⊠ 🗐 💻 🌊

▼▼▼▼ Holiday Inn Airport **MI**
(904) 741-4404. **$88.** 14670 Duval Rd. I-95, exit 127, just w. Ext/int corridors. **Pets:** Accepted.

ASK S🗭 ⊠ 🗐 🖑 🛏 💻 🍴 🌊

▼▼▼▼ Holiday Inn Baymeadows **MI**
(904) 737-1700. **$60-$80.** 9150 Baymeadows Rd. I-95, exit 100, 0.3 mi e. Ext/int corridors. **Pets:** Other species. $35 deposit/room.

⊠ 🗐 🛏 💻 🍴 🌊

AAA ▼▼▼▼ Holiday Inn Express Hotel and
Suites **M**
(904) 332-9500. **$59-$140.** 4675 Salisbury Rd. I-95, exit 101, just e, then s. Int corridors. **Pets:** Small. $10 daily fee/pet. Service with restrictions, supervision.

SAVE S🗭 ⊠ 🖑M 🗐 🖑 🛏 💻 🌊

▼▼▼▼ Homestead Studio
Suites-Jacksonville/Baymeadows **M**
(904) 739-1881. **$55-$90.** 8300 Western Way. I-95, exit 100, just e to Western Way, then just s. Int corridors. **Pets:** Medium, other species. $75 one-time fee/room. Service with restrictions, supervision.

ASK ⊠ 🗐 🖑 🛏 💻

▼▼▼▼ Homestead Studio
Suites-Jacksonville/Southside **M**
(904) 642-9911. **$55-$84.** 10020 Skinner Lake Dr. I-95, exit 101, 3.5 mi on JT Butler Blvd to Gate Pkwy, just ne. Ext corridors. **Pets:** Accepted.

ASK ⊠ 🖑M 🛏 🛏 💻

▼▼▼▼ Homewood Suites by Hilton **A**
(904) 733-9299. **$119, 14 days notice.** 8737 Baymeadows Rd. I-95, exit 100, 0.3 mi w. Ext/int corridors. **Pets:** Accepted.

SAVE S🗭 ⊠ 🛏 💻 🌊

AAA ▼▼▼ Inns of America **M**
(904) 281-0198. **$49-$69.** 4300 Salisbury Rd N. I-95, exit 101, 0.5 mi n of jct Butler Blvd. Ext corridors. **Pets:** Other species. Service with restrictions, supervision.

SAVE S🗭 ⊠ 🗐 🛏 🌊

▼▼▼▼ La Quinta Inn & Suites **M**
(904) 296-0703. **$85-$115.** 4868 Lenoir Ave S. I-95, exit 101, northwest corner. Int corridors. **Pets:** Medium, other species. Service with restrictions.

SAVE ⊠ 🖑M 🗐 🖑 🛏 💻

▼▼▼▼ La Quinta Inn-Baymeadows **M**
(904) 731-9940. **$65-$95.** 8255 Dix Ellis Tr. I-95, exit 100, southwest corner. Ext corridors. **Pets:** Accepted.

SAVE ⊠ 🛏 💻 🌊

▼▼▼▼ La Quinta Inn-North **M**
(904) 751-6960. **$61-$85.** 812 Dunn Ave. I-95, exit 25, southwest corner. Ext corridors. **Pets:** Accepted.

SAVE ⊠ 🗐 🛏 💻 🌊

AAA ▼▼▼▼ MainStay Suites-Jacksonville **M**
(904) 296-0661. **$80-$90.** 4693 Salisbury Rd S. I-95, exit 101, e on Butler, then s. Int corridors. **Pets:** Accepted.

SAVE S🗭 ⊠ 🗐 🖑 🛏 💻 🌊

▼▼▼▼ Masters Inn JTB **M**
(904) 281-2244. **$41-$49.** 4940 Mustang Rd. I-95, exit 101, just w. Int corridors. **Pets:** Accepted.
(ASK) (S☐) (✕) (Ĺ,M) (✍) (⊟)

◑◑◑ ▼▼▼▼ Quality Hotel Southpoint **MI**
(904) 281-0900. **$59-$169, 7 days notice.** 4660 Salisbury Rd. I-95, exit 101, just e. Int corridors. **Pets:** Medium. $10 daily fee/room. Designated rooms, service with restrictions.
(SAVE) (S☐) (✕) (⌖) (⊟) (▣) (¶) (✍)

▼▼▼▼ Ramada Inn Conference Center **MI**
(904) 268-8080. **$76-$83.** 3130 Hartley Rd. I-295, exit 2A northbound; exit 2 southbound, just n on SR 13. Ext corridors. **Pets:** Accepted.
(ASK) (S☐) (✕) (⌖) (⊟) (▣) (¶) (✍)

◑◑◑ ▼▼▼ Red Roof Inn **M**
(904) 296-1006. **$44-$59.** 6969 Lenoir Ave E. I-95, exit 101, northwest corner. Int corridors. **Pets:** Accepted.
(SAVE) (✕) (⌖) (Ĺ) (⊟) (▣) (✍)

◑◑◑ ▼▼▼▼ Red Roof Inn-Airport **M**
(904) 741-4488. **$41-$54.** 14701 Airport Entrance Rd. I-95, exit 127. Ext corridors. **Pets:** Accepted.
(SAVE) (✕) (✍)

◑◑◑ ▼▼▼▼ Residence Inn-Airport **M**
(904) 741-6550. **$623 (weekly).** 1310 Airport Rd. I-95, exit 127B, 0.3 mi w. Int corridors. **Pets:** Other species. $100 one-time fee/room. Service with restrictions.
(SAVE) (S☐) (✕) (⊟) (▣) (✍)

◑◑◑ ▼▼▼▼ Residence Inn by Marriott **A**
(904) 733-8088. **$109-$139.** 8365 Dix Ellis Tr. I-95, exit 100, sw off Baymeadows Rd. Ext corridors. **Pets:** Other species. $75 one-time fee/room. Service with restrictions.
(SAVE) (S☐) (✕) (⌖) (⊟) (▣) (✍)

JACKSONVILLE BEACH

◑◑◑ ▼▼▼ Surfside Inn **M**
(904) 246-1583. **$59-$129.** 1236 N 1st St. 1.2 mi n of US 90 (Beach Blvd). Ext corridors. **Pets:** Medium. $15 daily fee/pet. Designated rooms, service with restrictions, supervision.
(SAVE) (S☐) (✕) (⊟) (✍)

ORANGE PARK

◑◑◑ ▼▼▼ Comfort Inn **M**
(904) 264-3297. **$69.** 341 Park Ave. I-295, exit 3, just s on US 17. Ext corridors. **Pets:** Medium. $25 one-time fee/ room. Service with restrictions.
(SAVE) (S☐) (✕) (⊟) (▣) (✍)

◑◑◑ ▼▼▼ Days Inn **M**
(904) 269-8887. **$64.** 4280 Eldridge Loop. I-295, exit 3, just s on US 17. Int corridors. **Pets:** Medium. $25 one-time fee/room. Service with restrictions.
(SAVE) (S☐) (✕) (⊟) (▣)

◑◑◑ ▼▼▼ La Quinta Inn-Jacksonville/Orange Park **M**
(904) 778-9539. **$61-$85.** 8555 Blanding Blvd. I-295, exit 4, just se on SR 21. Ext corridors. **Pets:** Accepted.
(SAVE) (✕) (⌖) (⊟) (▣) (✍)

◑◑◑ ▼▼▼ Red Roof Inn-South **M**
(904) 777-1000. **$42-$56.** 6099 Youngerman Cir. I-295, exit 4, jct SR 21. Ext corridors. **Pets:** Small, other species. Service with restrictions, crate.
(SAVE) (✕)

❖ **END METROPOLITAN AREA** ❖

JENSEN BEACH

▼▼▼▼ River Palm Cottages **C**
(561) 334-0401. **$89-$199, 7 days notice.** 2325 NE Indian River Dr. On SR 707 (NE Indian River Dr) 1.4 mi s of jct SR 732 (Jensen Cswy). Ext corridors. **Pets:** Other species. $10 daily fee/pet. Designated rooms.
(ASK) (✕) (⊟) (▣) (✍)

JUNO BEACH

▼▼▼▼ Holiday Inn Express-North Palm Beach **M**
(561) 622-4366. **$59-$199, 7 days notice.** 13950 US Hwy 1. At jct Donald Ross Rd. Ext/int corridors. **Pets:** Small, other species. $25 one-time fee/pet. Designated rooms, service with restrictions, supervision.
(ASK) (S☐) (✕) (⌖) (⊟) (▣) (✍)

JUPITER

◑◑◑ ▼▼▼▼ Wellesley Inn & Suites **M**
(561) 575-7201. **$50-$129.** 34 Fishermans Wharf. SR 706 (Indiantown Rd); 0.3 mi w of jct US 1. Int corridors. **Pets:** Small, other species. Service with restrictions, supervision.
(SAVE) (S☐) (✕) (⌖) (⊟) (▣) (✍)

LAKE CITY

◑◑◑ ▼▼▼▼ Best Western Inn **M**
(386) 752-3801. **$50-$65.** 4720 US 90 W. I-75, exit 82, just w. Ext corridors. **Pets:** Medium. $5 daily fee/pet. Designated rooms, service with restrictions, supervision.
(SAVE) (S☐) (✕) (⊟) (▣) (✍)

▼▼▼ Days Inn I-10 **M**
(386) 758-4224. **$48-$69.** US 441. I-10, exit 44, just s. Ext corridors. **Pets:** Accepted.
(SAVE) (S☐) (✕) (⊟) (▣) (✍)

(AAA) ▼▼▼ Driftwood Inn M
(386) 755-3545. **$30-$37.** 4380 US Hwy 90. I-75, exit 82, 0.7 mi e. Ext corridors. **Pets:** Small. $5 daily fee/pet. Designated rooms, service with restrictions, supervision.
[SAVE] [X]

(AAA) ▼▼▼ Econo Lodge South M
(386) 755-9311. **$50-$100, 10 days notice.** I-75, exit 80, at US 441. Ext corridors. **Pets:** Small. Designated rooms, no service, supervision.
[SAVE] [S🐾] [X] [▣] [⇨]

▼▼▼▼ Jameson Inn M
(386) 758-8440. **$55-$70.** 1393 Commerce Blvd. I-75, exit 82, just e, then s. Int corridors. **Pets:** Small, other species. Service with restrictions.
[X] [&M] [🐾] [🎓] [📶] [▣] [⇨]

(AAA) ▼▼ Rodeway Inn M
(386) 755-5203. **$35-$55.** 4570 Commerce Blvd. I-75, exit 82, just e. Ext corridors. **Pets:** Other species. $5 daily fee/pet. Designated rooms, service with restrictions, crate.
[SAVE] [S🐾] [X] [📶] [▣]

(AAA) ▼▼ Scottish Inns M
(386) 755-0230. **$35-$39.** 4450 Hwy 90 W. I-75, exit 82, 0.6 mi e. Ext corridors. **Pets:** Medium. $5 daily fee/pet. Designated rooms, no service, supervision.
[SAVE] [S🐾] [X]

LAKE WORTH

(AAA) ▼▼ Lago Motor Inn M
(561) 585-5246. **$45-$72.** 714 S Dixie Hwy. US 1, just s of jct 6th Ave S; from jct I-95, exit 47, 0.7 mi e, just s on US 1. Ext corridors. **Pets:** Medium. Service with restrictions, crate.
[SAVE] [X] [📶] [⇨]

(AAA) ▼▼ Martinique Motor Lodge M
(561) 585-2502. **$55-$95, 7 days notice.** 801 S Dixie Hwy. US 1, just s of jct 6th Ave S, 0.5 mi e of jct I-95, exit 47. Ext corridors. **Pets:** Small, dogs only. $15 daily fee/pet. Designated rooms, service with restrictions, supervision.
[SAVE] [S🐾] [📶]

(AAA) ▼▼ White Manor Motel M
(561) 582-7437. **$38-$64, 14 days notice.** 1618 S Federal Hwy. I-95, exit 47, 1 mi e, 0.8 mi s on SR 5 (Federal Hwy). Ext corridors. **Pets:** Small. $50 deposit/room, $10 daily fee/room, $25 one-time fee/room. Designated rooms, service with restrictions.
[SAVE] [S🐾] [📶] [⇨]

LAKELAND

(AAA) ▼▼▼▼ AmeriSuites Lakeland Center M
(863) 413-1122. **$109-$129.** 525 W Orange St. I-4, exit 18, 3.2 mi s on US 98, just w. Int corridors. **Pets:** Small. Designated rooms, service with restrictions, supervision.
[SAVE] [S🐾] [X] [&M] [🐾] [🎓] [📶] [▣] [⇨]

(AAA) ▼▼▼ Baymont Inn & Suites-Lakeland M
(863) 815-0606. **$74-$94.** 4315 Lakeland Park Dr. Jct SR 33 and I-4, exit 19, just nw. Int corridors. **Pets:** Accepted.
[SAVE] [S🐾] [X] [&M] [🐾] [🎓] [📶] [▣] [⇨]

(AAA) ▼▼▼ Comfort Inn M
(863) 688-9221. **$10-$85, 3 days notice.** 1817 E Memorial Blvd. 2 mi e of jct US 98 and 92. Ext corridors. **Pets:** Medium, dogs only. $5 one-time fee/pet. Designated rooms, service with restrictions, supervision.
[SAVE] [S🐾] [X] [📶] [▣] [⇨]

▼▼▼▼ Jameson Inn M ❀
(863) 858-9070. **$55-$70.** 4375 Lakeland Park Dr. I-4, exit 19, just nw. Int corridors. **Pets:** Very small, other species. Service with restrictions.
[X] [&M] [🎓] [📶] [▣] [⇨]

▼▼▼▼ La Quinta Inn & Suites M
(863) 859-2866. **$75-$125.** 1024 Crevasse St. I-4, exit 18, just n on US 98. Int corridors. **Pets:** Accepted.
[▦] [X] [&M] [🐾] [🎓] [📶] [▣] [⇨]

(AAA) ▼▼▼ Royalty Inn M
(863) 858-4481. **$49-$95.** 3425 Hwy 98 N. I-4, exit 18, just ne. Int corridors. **Pets:** Medium. $10 daily fee/room. Service with restrictions, crate.
[SAVE] [S🐾] [X] [📶] [⇨]

(AAA) ▼▼▼ Super 8 Motel M 🐾
(863) 683-5961. **$48-$70, 7 days notice.** 601 E Memorial Blvd. Just e of jct SR 33. Ext/int corridors. **Pets:** Medium. $10 daily fee/room. Service with restrictions, crate.
[SAVE] [S🐾] [X] [📶]

(AAA) ▼▼▼▼ Wellesley Inn & Suites M
(863) 859-0100. **$57-$119.** 3520 Hwy US 98 N. I-4, exit 18, just nw on US 98. Int corridors. **Pets:** Accepted.
[SAVE] [S🐾] [X] [&M] [🐾] [🎓] [📶] [▣] [⇨]

LIVE OAK

(AAA) ▼▼▼ Econo Lodge M ❀
(386) 362-7459. **$54-$74.** 6811 N US 129 & I-10. I-10, exit 40, just s on US 129. Ext corridors. **Pets:** $10 one-time fee/room. Service with restrictions, supervision.
[SAVE] [S🐾] [X] [📶] [▣] [⇨]

(AAA) ▼▼▼ Suwannee River Best Western Inn M
(386) 362-6000. **$45-$115, 5 days notice.** 6819 US 129 N. I-10, exit 40, 0.3 mi s. Ext corridors. **Pets:** Small, other species. $10 daily fee/pet. Service with restrictions, supervision.
[SAVE] [S🐾] [X] [📶] [⇨]

LONGBOAT KEY

▼▼▼ Riviera Beach Resort A
(941) 383-2552. **$600-$1200 (weekly), 30 days notice.** 5451 Gulf of Mexico Dr. On SR 789, 5 mi s of jct SR 684 (Cortez Rd). Ext corridors. **Pets:** Accepted.
[ASK] [📶] [▣] [⇨]

MACCLENNY

(A)(A)(A) ▼▼▼ Econo Lodge M
(904) 259-3000. **$52-$72.** I-10 & SR 121. I-10, exit 48, just s of jct SR 121. Ext corridors. **Pets:** Small, other species. $10 one-time fee/pet. Service with restrictions.
[SAVE] [S♦] [⊠] [📶] [📺] [➜]

MARIANNA

(A)(A)(A) ▼▼▼ Comfort Inn M ✿
(850) 526-5600. **$56-$64.** 2175 Hwy 71 S. I-10, exit 21, just nw. Ext corridors. **Pets:** Small, other species. $12 daily fee/pet. Service with restrictions, supervision.
[SAVE] [S♦] [⊠] [📶] [📺] [➜]

MELBOURNE

(A)(A)(A) ▼▼▼ Baymont Inn & Suites-Melbourne M
(321) 242-9400. **$69-$94.** 7200 George T Edwards Dr. SR 509, just w of I-95, exit 73. Int corridors. **Pets:** Other species. Service with restrictions.
[SAVE] [S♦] [⊠] [🖉] [♿] [📶] [📺] [➜]

(A)(A)(A) ▼▼▼ Best Western Harborview MI
(321) 724-4422. **$70-$79.** 964 S Harbor City Blvd. 1 mi n of SR 192 on US 1 at jct Nasa Blvd. Int corridors. **Pets:** Accepted.
[SAVE] [S♦] [⊠] [📶] [📺] [❢❢] [➜]

▼▼▼ Crane Creek Inn Waterfront Bed & Breakfast BB
(321) 768-6416. **$75-$125, 14 days notice.** 909 E Melbourne Ave. From jct US 192, just s on Babcock, then 0.9 mi e. Ext/int corridors. **Pets:** Dogs only. $10 daily fee/room. Designated rooms.
[⊠] [📶] [📺] [➜] [⊠]

(A)(A)(A) ▼▼▼ Hilton Melbourne Airport H
(321) 768-0200. **$59-$119.** 200 Rialto Pl. 1 mi w of US 1, 0.8 mi n of US 192. Int corridors. **Pets:** Other species. $50 deposit/room. Service with restrictions.
[SAVE] [S♦] [⊠] [♿M] [🖉] [♿] [📶] [📺] [❢❢] [➜]

▼▼▼ Holiday Inn-Melbourne Riverfront MI
(321) 723-5320. **$69-$83.** 420 S Harbor City Blvd. US 1, 1.7 mi n of US 192. Ext corridors. **Pets:** Small. $20 deposit/pet, $25 one-time fee/pet. Service with restrictions, supervision.
[ASK] [S♦] [⊠] [♿] [📶] [📺] [❢❢] [➜]

(A)(A)(A) ▼▼▼ Super 8 M
(321) 723-4430. **$46-$60.** 1515 S Harbor City Blvd. I-95, exit 71, 7 mi e to US 1 on SR 192, then 0.5 mi n. Int corridors. **Pets:** Medium, other species. $20 deposit/pet. Service with restrictions, supervision.
[SAVE] [S♦] [⊠] [♿M] [♿] [📶]

MIAMI-MIAMI BEACH METROPOLITAN AREA

COCONUT GROVE

(A)(A)(A) ▼▼ ▼▼ Mayfair House Hotel H
(305) 441-0000. **$169-$800.** 3000 Florida Ave. Center; at Florida Ave and Virginia St. Ext/int corridors. **Pets:** Accepted.
[SAVE] [S♦] [⊠] [🖉] [❢❢]

CUTLER RIDGE

(A)(A)(A) ▼▼▼ Baymont Inn & Suites Miami-Cutler Ridge M
(305) 278-0001. **$69-$99.** 10821 Caribbean Blvd. Florida Tpke, exit 12 (US 1), northwest corner. Int corridors. **Pets:** Accepted.
[SAVE] [S♦] [⊠] [♿M] [🖉] [♿] [📶] [📺] [➜]

FLORIDA CITY

(A)(A)(A) ▼▼▼ Coral Roc Motel M ✿
(305) 246-2888. **$32-$88.** 1100 N Krome Ave. On SR 997; just w of US 1, 0.5 mi s of Homestead. Ext corridors. **Pets:** Small. $50 deposit/room. Service with restrictions, supervision.
[SAVE] [S♦] [⊠] [📶] [➜]

▼▼▼ Hampton Inn M
(305) 247-8833. **$85-$140.** 124 E Palm Dr. On US 1, 0.3 mi s of Florida Tpke terminus. Ext corridors. **Pets:** Accepted.
[SAVE] [⊠] [🖉] [📶] [📺] [➜]

HIALEAH

(A)(A)(A) ▼▼▼ Days Inn Miami Lakes/Westland Mall M ✿
(305) 823-2121. **$64-$114.** 1950 W 49th St. SR 826 (Palmetto Expwy), exit NW 103rd St, just e. Int corridors. **Pets:** Small. $10 daily fee/pet, $25 one-time fee/pet. Service with restrictions, supervision.
[SAVE] [S♦] [⊠] [📶] [📺]

(A)(A)(A) ▼▼▼ Ramada Inn-Miami Airport North MI
(305) 823-2000. **$69-$119.** 1950 W 49th St. SR 826 (Palmetto Expwy), exit NW 103rd St, just e. Int corridors. **Pets:** Accepted.
[SAVE] [S♦] [⊠] [🖉] [📶] [📺] [❢❢] [➜]

HOMESTEAD

▼▼ Days Inn Homestead M
(305) 245-1260. **$65-$109, 3 days notice.** 515 S Homestead Blvd, US 1 & 320 St. On US 1, 1.2 mi n of Florida Tpke, at jct 320 St SW and US 1. Ext corridors. **Pets:** Accepted.
[SAVE] [S♦] [⊠] [📶] [❢❢] [➜]

Everglades Motel M
(305) 247-4117. **$29-$78.** 605 S Krome Ave. Just w of US 1; between Lucy and 6th sts; on SR 997, 0.5 mi s of center of town. Ext corridors. **Pets:** Small. $5 daily fee/pet. Service with restrictions, supervision.

KENDALL

AmeriSuites M
(305) 279-8688. **$119-$179.** 11520 SW 88th St. Florida Tpke, exit 20 (SW 88th Kendall Dr), just e on SR 94, 0.3 mi s. Int corridors. **Pets:** Small. Service with restrictions.

Wellesley Inn & Suites M
(305) 270-0359. **$89-$159, 3 days notice.** 11750 Mills Dr. Florida Tpke, exit SW 88th (Kendall Dr), 0.3 mi e on SR 94, 0.3 mi n on SW 117 Ave. Int corridors. **Pets:** Small. Supervision.

MIAMI

AmeriSuites Airport West M
(305) 718-8292. **$84-$159, 5 days notice.** 3655 NW 82nd Ave. 0.4 mi w on NW 36th St from jct SR 826 (Palmetto Expwy). Int corridors. **Pets:** Other species. $10 daily fee/room. Service with restrictions, supervision.

Crowne Plaza Miami International Airport H
(305) 446-9000. **$125-$174.** 950 NW Le Jeune Rd. 1 mi s of terminal entrance, just s of jct SR 836, Dolphin Expwy. Int corridors. **Pets:** Accepted.

Hampton Inn-Miami Airport West M
(305) 513-0777. **$89-$129.** 3620 NW 79th Ave. SR 826 (Palmetto Expwy), exit NW 36th St, just s of jct NW 58th St, exit s at 79th Ave. Int corridors. **Pets:** Accepted.

Holiday Inn-Downtown MI
(305) 374-3000. **$89-$149.** 200 SE 2nd Ave. Just s of Flagler St on US 1 and 41, 0.8 mi e of I-95, exit 3. Int corridors. **Pets:** Large, other species. $35 deposit/pet. Service with restrictions, supervision.

Homestead Studio Suites-Miami Airport/Doral M
(305) 436-1811. **$64-$90.** 8720 NW 33rd St. SR 826 (Palmetto Expwy), 0.8 mi w on NW 36th St, then s on 87th St, 0.6 mi on right. Ext corridors. **Pets:** Accepted.

Homewood Suites by Hilton-Miami Blue Lagoon M
(305) 261-3335. **$-$224.** 5500 Blue Lagoon Dr. Se of jct SR 836 (Dolphin Expwy), exit Red Rd. Int corridors. **Pets:** Accepted.

La Quinta Inn & Suites M
(305) 436-0830. **$75-$135.** 8730 NW 27th St. From SR 836 (Dolphin Expwy), just n on 87th NW Ave. Int corridors. **Pets:** Accepted.

La Quinta Inn Miami Airport North M
(305) 599-9902. **$65-$125.** 7401 NW 36th St. Just e of jct SR 826 (Palmetto Expwy). Ext corridors. **Pets:** Small, dogs only. Service with restrictions, crate.

Miami River Inn BB 🐾
(305) 325-0045. **$89-$249, 3 days notice.** 118 SW South River Dr. I-95, exit 2 (SW 7th St), just w to SW 5th Ave, just n to SW 2nd St, then e. Ext/int corridors. **Pets:** Medium. $25 daily fee/room. Service with restrictions.

Quality Inn-South MI
(305) 251-2000. **$74-$135.** 14501 S Dixie Hwy (US 1). US 1 at SW 145th St. Ext corridors. **Pets:** Other species. Service with restrictions.

Summerfield Suites by Wyndham-Miami Airport M
(305) 269-1922. **$89-$149.** 5710 Blue Lagoon Dr. 2.5 mi sw of airport entrance; se of jct SR 836 (Dolphin Expwy), exit Red Rd, just w. Int corridors. **Pets:** Small. $150 one-time fee/room. Service with restrictions, crate.

TownePlace Suites by Marriott M
(305) 718-4144. **$69-$109, 3 days notice.** 10505 NW 36th St. Florida Tpke, exit 29, 1.2 mi e to 107th Ave, just s on 107th Ave. Int corridors. **Pets:** Small, other species. $125 one-time fee/room. Service with restrictions, supervision.

MIAMI BEACH

Breakwater Hotel H
(305) 532-1220. **$149-$249, 3 days notice.** 940 Ocean Dr. E of SR of SR A1A; between 9th and 10th sts. Int corridors. **Pets:** Small, other species. Service with restrictions, supervision.

Century Hotel H
(305) 674-8855. **$135-$190, 3 days notice.** 140 Ocean Dr. Just e of SR A1A (Collins Ave), just s of 2nd St. Int corridors. **Pets:** Medium. $250 deposit/room. Service with restrictions, supervision.

Comfort Inn On the Beach M
(305) 868-1200. **$105-$165.** 6261 Collins Ave. SR A1A/Collins Ave at 63rd St. Int corridors. **Pets:** Small, other species. $10 daily fee/pet, $25 one-time fee/pet. Service with restrictions.

(AAA) ▽▽▽ **Days Inn Art Deco/Convention Center** Ⓜ
(305) 538-6631. **$109-$159.** 100 21st St. SR A1A (Collins Ave) at 21st St. Ext/int corridors. **Pets:** Accepted.
(SAVE) (🕭) (✕) (🐾) (🖰) (🖪) (🖵) (🍴) (🏊)

▽▽ ▽▽ **Fontainebleau Hilton Resort** Ⓗ
(305) 538-2000. **$179-$499, 5 days notice.** 4441 Collins Ave. On SR A1A. Int corridors. **Pets:** Accepted.
(SAVE) (✕) (🐾) (🖪) (🖵) (🍴) (✕)

▽▽ ▽▽ **Loews Miami Beach Hotel** Ⓗ
(305) 604-1601. **$189-$349, 3 days notice.** 1601 Collins Ave. On SR A1A, at Collins and 16th aves. Int corridors. **Pets:** Accepted.
(ASK) (🕭) (✕) (🐾M) (🐾) (🖰) (🖪) (🖵) (🍴) (🏊)

▽▽ ▽▽ **The Marlin** Ⓜ ❀
(305) 604-5063. **$250-$435, 3 days notice.** 1200 Collins Ave. On SR A1A, at Collins Ave and 12th St. Int corridors. **Pets:** Small, dogs only. $25 daily fee/pet.
(🐾) (🖪) (🖵)

(AAA) ▽▽▽ **Radisson Deauville Resort Miami Beach** Ⓗ
(305) 865-8511. **$99-$199, 3 days notice.** 6701 Collins Ave. SR A1A at 67th St. Int corridors. **Pets:** Accepted.
(SAVE) (✕) (🐾) (🖪) (🖵) (🍴) (🏊) (✕)

MIAMI LAKES

(AAA) ▽▽▽▽ **Towne Place Suites by Marriott** Ⓜ ❀
(305) 512-9191. **$99-$109.** 8079 NW 154th St. From SR 826 (Palmetto Expwy), exit 154th St, then 0.4 mi w. Int corridors. **Pets:** Other species. $6 daily fee/pet, $120 one-time fee/room. Service with restrictions.
(SAVE) (✕) (🖰) (🖵) (🏊)

(AAA) ▽▽ ▽▽ **Wellesley Inn & Suites** Ⓜ
(305) 821-8274. **$99.** 7925 NW 154th St. Just w off jct SR 826 (Palmetto Expwy). Int corridors. **Pets:** Small. $10 one-time fee/pet. Designated rooms, service with restrictions, supervision.
(SAVE) (🕭) (✕) (🐾) (🐾) (🖰) (🖵) (🏊)

MIAMI SPRINGS

(AAA) ▽▽ ▽▽ **Baymont Inn & Suites-Miami/Airport** Ⓜ
(305) 871-1777. **$79-$114.** 3501 NW Le Jeune Rd. SR 953 (Le Jeune Rd) at jct SR 112. Int corridors. **Pets:** Accepted.
(SAVE) (🕭) (✕) (🐾) (🖰) (🖵) (🏊)

(AAA) ▽▽▽▽ **Comfort Inn & Suites-Miami International Airport** Ⓜ
(305) 871-6000. **$85-$145.** 5301 NW 36th St. Between Le Jeune Rd and SR 826 (Palmetto Expwy). Int corridors. **Pets:** Accepted.
(SAVE) (🕭) (✕) (🐾) (🖰) (🖵) (🏊)

(AAA) ▽▽ ▽▽ **Holiday Inn Express Miami International Airport** Ⓜ
(305) 887-2153. **$85-$145.** 5125 NW 36th St. Between Le Jeune Rd and SR 826 (Palmetto Expwy). Int corridors. **Pets:** Large. $25 one-time fee/room. Designated rooms, service with restrictions, supervision.
(SAVE) (🕭) (✕) (🐾) (🐾) (🖰) (🖵)

(AAA) ▽▽▽▽ **MainStay Suites-Miami Airport** Ⓜ
(305) 870-0448. **$90-$150.** 101 Fairway Dr. I-95 to SR 112 W, exit NW 36th St, then w, right on Palmetto Dr, then w; behind Clarion Hotel; between LeJeune Rd and SR 826 (Palmetto Expwy). Int corridors. **Pets:** Accepted.
(SAVE) (🕭) (✕) (🐾) (🖰) (🖵) (🏊)

(AAA) ▽▽▽▽ **Red Roof Inn Miami Airport** Ⓜ
(305) 871-4221. **$61-$116.** 3401 NW LeJeune Rd. 0.5 mi n of airport entrance; on SR 953 at jct SR 112. Int corridors. **Pets:** Accepted.
(SAVE) (✕) (🐾) (🏊)

(AAA) ▽▽ ▽▽ **Sleep Inn-Miami Airport** Ⓜ
(305) 871-7553. **$80-$140.** 105 Fairway Dr. I-95 to SR 112 W, exit NW 36th St, then w, right on Palmetto Dr, then w; behind Clarion Hotel; between LeJeune Rd and SR 826 (Palmetto Expwy). Int corridors. **Pets:** Accepted.
(SAVE) (🕭) (✕) (🐾) (🖰) (🖵) (🏊)

SUNNY ISLES

(AAA) ▽▽▽▽ **Newport Beachside Hotel & Resort** Ⓗ
(305) 949-1300. **$109-$159.** 16701 Collins Ave. SR A1A, at jct SR 826 and Sunny Isles Blvd. Int corridors. **Pets:** Small. Service with restrictions.
(SAVE) (🕭) (✕) (🐾) (🖰) (🖵) (🍴) (🏊) (✕)

❀   **END METROPOLITAN AREA**   ❀

NAPLES

Baymont Inn & Suites Naples M
(941) 352-8400. **$59-$99.** 185 Bedzel Circle. I-75, exit 15, just w. Int corridors. **Pets:** Large, other species. Designated rooms, service with restrictions, supervision.

The Hawthorn Suites of Naples M
(941) 593-1300. **$89-$234.** 3557 Pine Ridge Rd. I-75, exit 16, just w. Int corridors. **Pets:** Large, other species. $125 one-time fee/room. Service with restrictions.

Naples Hotel & Suites M
(941) 262-6181. **$60-$130.** 221 9th St S. I-75, exit 15 (US 41), just s of Central Ave. Ext corridors. **Pets:** Other species. $25 one-time fee/room. Designated rooms, service with restrictions, crate.

Residence Inn by Marriott, Naples M
(941) 659-1300. **$89-$179.** 4075 Tamiami Tr N. I-75, exit 16, on US 41. Int corridors. **Pets:** Large, other species. $3 daily fee/room, $85 one-time fee/room. Service with restrictions.

Staybridge Suites Hotel by Holiday Inn M
(941) 643-8002. **Call for rates.** 4805 Tamiami Tr N. I-75, exit 16, w on Pine Ridge Rd to US 41 (Tamiami Tr), turn left. Int corridors. **Pets:** Accepted.

Wellesley Inn & Suites M
(941) 793-4646. **$71-$107.** 1555 5th Ave S. I-75, exit 15, 1 mi s on US 41, at jct SR 84. Int corridors. **Pets:** Small. Service with restrictions, supervision.

NAVARRE

Comfort Inn & Conference Center M
(850) 939-1761. **$60-$123, 3 days notice.** 8700 Navarre Pkwy. US 98, 0.3 mi e of Navarre Beach Bridge. Ext corridors. **Pets:** Large, other species. $10 daily fee/pet. Designated rooms, service with restrictions, supervision.

NEW SMYRNA BEACH

Buena Vista Inn and Apartments M
(386) 428-5565. **$65-$80, 14 days notice.** 500 N Causeway. 2 mi e on Business 44, at west end of North Cswy Bridge. Ext corridors. **Pets:** Accepted.

NICEVILLE

Holiday Inn Express M
(850) 678-9131. **$80.** 106 Bayshore Dr. SR 85, just se on jct SR 20. Int corridors. **Pets:** Accepted.

NOKOMIS

Suntan Terrace Beach Resort A
(941) 488-1565. **$69-$159, 21 days notice.** 117 Casey Key Rd. 1.1 mi w on Albee Rd from jct US 41, just n. Ext corridors. **Pets:** Medium, other species. $10 daily fee/room. Designated rooms, no service.

NORTH FORT MYERS

Econo Lodge M
(941) 995-0571. **$65-$125, 14 days notice.** 13301 N Cleveland Ave. On US 41, 1.1 mi n of Caloosahatchee Bridge. Ext corridors. **Pets:** Accepted.

OCALA

Budget Host Inn M 🌼
(352) 732-6940. **$32-$62.** 4013 NW Blitchton Rd. I-75, exit 70, 0.3 mi n on US 27. Ext corridors. **Pets:** Other species. $6 daily fee/pet. Service with restrictions, supervision.

Comfort Inn M
(352) 629-8850. **$60-$85.** 4040 W Silver Springs Blvd. I-75, exit 69, just w on SR 40. Ext corridors. **Pets:** Small, other species. $5 daily fee/pet. Service with restrictions, crate.

Hilton Ocala H 🌼
(352) 854-1400. **$79-$139.** 3600 SW 36th Ave. I-75, exit 68, 0.3 mi e on SR 200. Int corridors. **Pets:** Medium, other species. Service with restrictions, supervision.

Holiday Inn Ocala M
(352) 629-0381. **$78-$127.** 3621 W Silver Springs Blvd. I-75, exit 69, just e on SR 40. Ext corridors. **Pets:** Small. $20 one-time fee/room. Designated rooms, service with restrictions, supervision.

La Quinta Inn & Suites M
(352) 861-1137. **$85-$115.** 3530 SW 36th Ave. I-75, exit 68, just e on SR 200. Int corridors. **Pets:** Accepted.

Steinbrenner's Ramada Inn & Conference Center M
(352) 732-3131. **$69-$129.** 3810 NW Blitchton Rd. I-75, exit 70, just w. Ext corridors. **Pets:** Accepted.

OKEECHOBEE

Budget Inn M
(863) 763-3185. **$49-$89.** 201 S Parrott Ave (US 441). US 98 and 441, just s of jct SR 70. Ext corridors. **Pets:** Small, dogs only. $10 one-time fee/pet. Designated rooms, service with restrictions, crate.

AAA ▼▼▼ Economy Inn **M**
(863) 763-1148. **$40-$79.** 507 N Parrott Ave (US 441). US 441, 0.3 mi n of jct SR 70. Ext corridors. **Pets:** Small. $10 daily fee/pet. Service with restrictions, supervision.
SAVE 🅢 ⊠ 🖪

▼▼▼▼ Holiday Inn Express **M**
(863) 357-3529. **$59-$155.** 3975 Hwy 441 S. US 98 and 441, 3 mi s of jct SR 70, 0.3 mi n of Lake Okeechobee and jct SR 78. Ext corridors. **Pets:** Accepted.
ASK 🅢 ⊠ 🕭 ⊘ 🖪 ⇆

OLD TOWN

AAA ▼▼▼ Suwannee Gables Motel **M** ✿
(352) 542-7752. **$69, 7 days notice.** HC 3 Box 208. US 19, 98 and 27A; 2 mi s of jct SR 349. Ext corridors. **Pets:** Small. $10 daily fee/pet. Designated rooms, service with restrictions, supervision.
SAVE 🅢 ⊠ 🖪 ⇆

ORLANDO METROPOLITAN AREA

ALTAMONTE SPRINGS

AAA ▼▼▼▼ Embassy Suites Orlando North **H**
(407) 834-2400. **$89-$149.** 225 E Altamonte Dr. I-4, exit 48, 0.3 mi e on SR 436, just n on North Lake Blvd. Int corridors. **Pets:** Accepted.
SAVE ⊠ 🕭 ⊘ 🕯 🖪 🖵 🍴 ⇆

AAA ▼▼▼▼ Hampton Inn **M**
(407) 869-9000. **$89-$99, 7 days notice.** 151 N Douglas Ave. I-4, exit 48, just nw. Ext corridors. **Pets:** Accepted.
SAVE 🅢 ⊠ 🕭 ⊘ 🕯 🖪 🖵 ⇆

▼▼▼▼ Homestead Studio Suites-Orlando/
Altamonte Springs **M**
(407) 332-9300. **$55-$65.** 302 S North Lake Blvd. I-4, exit 48, just e, then 0.3 mi s. Int corridors. **Pets:** Accepted.
ASK 🅢 ⊠ 🕭 ⊘ 🕯 🖪 🖵

AAA ▼▼▼▼ La Quinta Inn-Orlando North **M**
(407) 788-1411. **$65-$95.** 150 S Westmonte Dr. I-4, exit 48, 0.3 mi w, just s of SR 436. Ext corridors. **Pets:** Small, dogs only. Service with restrictions, supervision.
SAVE ⊠ ⊘ 🕯 🖪 🖵 ⇆

AAA ▼▼▼▼ Residence Inn by Marriott **A**
(407) 788-7991. **$139-$155.** 270 Douglas Ave. I-4, exit 48, just w on SR 436, just n. Ext corridors. **Pets:** Small. $5 daily fee/pet, $150 one-time fee/room. Service with restrictions, crate.
SAVE 🅢 ⊠ 🕭 ⊘ 🕯 🖪 🖵 ⇆

APOPKA

AAA ▼▼▼▼ Crosby's Motor Inn **M** ✿
(407) 886-3220. **$60-$100, 7 days notice.** 1440 W Orange Blossom Tr/Hwy 441. 1.8 mi nw on US 441. Ext corridors. **Pets:** Medium. $10 daily fee/pet. Service with restrictions, supervision.
SAVE 🅢 ⊠ 🖪 🖵 ⇆

DAVENPORT

▼▼▼▼ Comfort Inn Main Gate South **M**
(863) 424-2811. **$39-$129.** 5510 US 27 N. I-4, exit 23. Ext corridors. **Pets:** Small. $10 daily fee/pet. Designated rooms, service with restrictions, crate.
SAVE 🅢 ⊠ 🖪 🖵 ⇆

▼▼▼▼ Days Inn-South of Disney **M**
(863) 424-2596. **$49-$63.** 2425 Frontage Rd. I-4, exit 23, just s on US 27. Ext corridors. **Pets:** Accepted.
SAVE 🅢 ⊠ 🕭 🖪 ⇆

AAA ▼▼▼▼ Super 8 Motel Maingate
South **M** ✿
(863) 420-8888. **$39-$120.** 5620 US Hwy 27 N. I-4, exit 23, 0.5 mi n. Ext corridors. **Pets:** $10 one-time fee/room. Designated rooms, service with restrictions.
SAVE 🅢 ⊠ 🕯 🖪 ⇆

▼▼ ▼ Villas at Polo Park **CO**
(863) 420-3838. **$62-$135, 14 days notice.** 12727 US 27 N. US 27; 0.5 mi s of US 192. Ext corridors. **Pets:** Accepted.
ASK 🅢 ⊠ 🖪 🖵 ⇆

KISSIMMEE

AAA ▼▼▼▼ AmeriSuites at Calypso Cay **M**
(407) 997-1300. **$89-$134.** 4991 Calypso Cay Way. I-4, exit 27, 3 mi s on SR 535, just s of Osceola Pkwy and just n of US 192. Int corridors. **Pets:** Small. $25 one-time fee/room. Service with restrictions, crate.
SAVE 🅢 ⊠ 🕭 ⊘ 🕯 🖪 🖵 ⇆

AAA ▼▼ ▼ Best Western-Eastgate **MI**
(407) 396-0707. **$42-$158.** 5565 W Irlo Bronson Memorial Hwy. I-4, exit 25A, on US 192, 2 mi e. Ext corridors. **Pets:** Other species. $15 daily fee/room. Service with restrictions.
SAVE 🅢 ⊠ ⊘ 🖪 🍴 ⇆ ⊠

▼ ▼ Days Inn-Kissimmee **M**
(407) 846-7136. **$35-$90, 3 days notice.** 2095 E Irlo Bronson Memorial Hwy. Florida Tpke, exit 244, 1 mi w. Ext corridors. **Pets:** Accepted.
SAVE 🅢 ⊠ 🖪 🍴 ⇆

AAA ▼▼ ▼ Flamingo Inn **M**
(407) 846-1935. **$29-$39, 3 days notice.** 801 E Vine St. US 192, 0.3 mi e of jct 441 and 192. Ext corridors. **Pets:** Small, dogs only. $8 daily fee/pet. Service with restrictions.
SAVE 🅢 ⊠ 🕯 🖪 ⇆

Holiday Inn Kissimmee Downtown M
(407) 846-2713. **$69-$89, 7 days notice.** 2009 W Vine St. I-4, exit 25A, 8 mi e on US 192; 1.3 mi w of jct US 17-92 and 441. Ext corridors. **Pets:** Small, dogs only. $8 daily fee/pet. Designated rooms, service with restrictions, crate.

Holiday Inn Maingate West M
(407) 396-1100. **$59-$139.** 7601 Black Lake Rd. I-4, exit 25B, 2.8 mi w on US 192, then just n; 1 mi w of Disney World main gate access road. Ext corridors. **Pets:** Medium, dogs only. $50 deposit/room, $25 one-time fee/room. Designated rooms, service with restrictions, supervision.

Homewood Suites by Hilton
(407) 396-2229. **$109-$159.** 3100 Parkway Blvd. I-4, exit 25A, 0.3 mi e on US 192, 0.5 mi n. Ext/int corridors. **Pets:** Supervision.

Howard Johnson Hotel M
(407) 846-4900. **$-$89.** 2323 E Irlo Bronson Memorial Hwy. On US 192 and 441; 0.3 mi e of Florida Tpke, exit 244. Int corridors. **Pets:** Other species. $10 daily fee/room. Service with restrictions, crate.

Larson's Inn & Family Suites M
(407) 396-6100. **$49-$69, 3 days notice.** 6075 W Irlo Bronson Memorial Hwy. I-4, exit 25A, 1 mi e on US 192; between MM 8 and 9. Ext corridors. **Pets:** Medium. $150 deposit/pet, $10 daily fee/pet. Service with restrictions, supervision.

Magic Castle Inn & Suites Eastgate M
(407) 396-1212. **$32-$50.** 4559 W Hwy 192. 4.5 mi w of US 17-92 and 441; 6.5 mi e of Disney/Epcot entrance. Ext corridors. **Pets:** $25 deposit/room, $6 daily fee/pet. Designated rooms, service with restrictions.

Magic Castle Inn & Suites Maingate M
(407) 396-2212. **$35-$53.** 5055 W Irlo Bronson Memorial Hwy. I-4, exit 25A, 3.2 mi w on US 192; between MM 10 and 11. Ext corridors. **Pets:** Medium. $25 deposit/pet, $6 daily fee/pet. Designated rooms, service with restrictions.

Masters Inn-Kissimmee M
(407) 396-4020. **$42-$79, 3 days notice.** 5367 W Irlo Bronson Hwy. I-4, exit 25, 2.5 mi e on US 192. Ext corridors. **Pets:** Accepted.

Masters Inn-Main Gate M
(407) 396-7743. **$59-$99.** 2945 Entry Point Blvd. I-4, exit 25, 2.5 mi w on US 192; 1 mi w of Disney World main gate. Ext corridors. **Pets:** Accepted.

Motel 6—#0436 M
(407) 396-6422. **$30-$44.** 7455 W Irlo Bronson Hwy. I-4, exit 25B, 1.3 mi w on US 192. Ext corridors. **Pets:** Other species. Designated rooms, service with restrictions, supervision.

Motel 6 #0464 M
(407) 396-6333. **$30-$60, 30 days notice.** 5731 W Hwy 192. I-4, exit 25, 2 mi e. Ext corridors. **Pets:** Other species. Service with restrictions, supervision.

Ramada Inn Resort Maingate M
(407) 396-4466. **$49-$139.** 2950 Reedy Creek Blvd. I-4, exit 25B, 2 mi w on US 192, 1 mi w of Disney World access road. Ext corridors. **Pets:** Accepted.

Red Roof Inn M
(407) 396-0065. **$60, 15 days notice.** 4970 Kyngs Heath Rd. I-4, exit 25A, 3.7 mi e of jct of SR 192 and 535, between MM 11 and 12. Ext corridors. **Pets:** Accepted.

Royal Oaks of Kissimmee CO
(407) 390-8200. **$99-$156, 14 days notice.** 5075 W Irlo Bronson Hwy. I-4, exit 25A, 3.1 mi e on SR 192. Ext corridors. **Pets:** Small, other species. $50 one-time fee/room. Service with restrictions, crate.

Summerfield Resort
(407) 847-7222. **$149, 15 days notice.** 2422 Summerfield Way. SR 423 (John Young Pkwy), 0.8 mi w of US 192; Florida Tpke, exit 249, 2.5 mi w, 2.5 mi s. Ext corridors. **Pets:** Medium. $50 one-time fee/pet. Designated rooms.

Travelodge Hotel/Airport South H
(407) 846-1530. **$42-$55.** 201 Simpson Rd. Florida Tpke, exit 244, 0.3 mi w on US 192, just n. Ext corridors. **Pets:** Accepted.

LAKE BUENA VISTA

Comfort Inn Lake Buena Vista M
(407) 996-7300. **$39-$99.** 8442 Palm Pkwy. 0.5 mi n on CR 535 from jct I-4, exit 27, 0.5 mi e. Ext corridors. **Pets:** Medium, other species. $50 deposit/room, $6 daily fee/pet. Designated rooms, service with restrictions, crate.

Holiday Inn-SunSpree Resort-Lake Buena Vista M
(407) 239-4500. **$99-$169.** 13351 SR 535. I-4, exit 27, 0.3 mi se on SR 535. Ext corridors. **Pets:** Accepted.

LAKE MARY

La Quinta Inn & Suites M
(407) 805-9901. **$-$95.** 1060 Greenwood Blvd. I-4, exit 50, just se via Lake Mary Blvd. Int corridors. **Pets:** Small. No service, supervision.

MainStay Suites Hotel M
(407) 829-2332. **$75-$135.** 1040 Greenwood Blvd. I-4, exit 50, 0.5 mi s on Lake Emma Rd; in Commerce Park. Int corridors. **Pets:** Medium, other species. $100 deposit/pet, $10 daily fee/pet. Service with restrictions, supervision.

LEESBURG

Shoney's Inn & Suites Conference Center M
(352) 787-1210. **$42-$95.** 1308 N 14th St. At jct US 27 and 441. Ext corridors. **Pets:** Accepted.

Super 8 Motel M
(352) 787-6363. **$49-$79, 7 days notice.** 1392 North Blvd W. At jct US 27 and 441. Int corridors. **Pets:** $10 daily fee/pet. Service with restrictions, supervision.

LONGWOOD

Ramada Inn North-Orlando MI
(407) 862-4000. **$45-$95.** 2025 W SR 434. I-4, exit 49, just nw. Ext corridors. **Pets:** Accepted.

MAITLAND

Homewood Suites Orlando North ▲
(407) 875-8777. **$139-$189.** 290 Southhall Ln. I-4, exit 47 (Maitland Ave), just w, then just s on Lake Destiny. Int corridors. **Pets:** $75 one-time fee/pet. Service with restrictions, supervision.

ORLANDO

AmeriSuites Orlando Airport Northeast M
(407) 240-3939. **$69-$149.** 7500 Augusta National Dr. SR 528 (Bee Line Expwy), exit 11, 0.5 mi n on SR 436, just e on TG Lee Blvd, then just s. Int corridors. **Pets:** Large, other species.

AmeriSuites (Orlando/Convention Center) M
(407) 370-4720. **$149-$169, 3 days notice.** 8741 International Dr. I-4, exit 29A, just e, then 0.7 mi s of SR 482 (Sand Lake Rd). Int corridors. **Pets:** Small. Designated rooms, service with restrictions, supervision.

AmeriSuites Orlando/Universal M
(407) 351-0627. **$59-$129, 3 days notice.** 5895 Caravan Ct. I-4, exit 30B, 0.6 mi ne. Int corridors. **Pets:** Small, other species. Service with restrictions, supervision.

Baymont Inn & Suites-Orlando South M
(407) 240-0500. **$59-$79.** 2051 Consulate Dr. US 17-92 and 441, just s of SR 528 (Bee Line Expwy), off Florida Tpke, exit 254. Int corridors. **Pets:** Accepted.

Best Western Orlando West M
(407) 841-8600. **$59-$99, 3 days notice.** 2014 W Colonial Dr. I-4, exit 41, 1.5 mi w on SR 50, 0.4 mi e of SR 423. Int corridors. **Pets:** Small. $25 deposit/room, $5 one-time fee/pet. Designated rooms, service with restrictions, supervision.

Comfort Inn-North M
(407) 629-4000. **$59-$125.** 830 Lee Rd. I-4, exit 46, 0.4 mi w on SR 423. Int corridors. **Pets:** Small. $10 daily fee/pet, $25 one-time fee/pet. Service with restrictions, crate.

Hawthorn Suites Orlando Airport M
(407) 438-2121. **$69-$109.** 7450 Augusta National Dr. SR 528 (Bee Line Expwy), exit 11, 0.5 mi n on SR 436, just e, then just s. Int corridors. **Pets:** Accepted.

Holiday Inn & Suites At Universal Orlando MI
(407) 351-3333. **$79-$159.** 5905 S Kirkman Rd. I-4, exit 30B, 0.5 mi n on SR 435 (Kirkman Rd). Int corridors. **Pets:** Small, dogs only. $50 one-time fee/pet. Service with restrictions, supervision.

Holiday Inn Express M
(407) 351-4430. **$69-$139.** 6323 International Dr. I-4, exit 29, just e on Sand Lake Rd, then 0.7 mi n. Int corridors. **Pets:** Small. $25 one-time fee/room. Service with restrictions, supervision.

Holiday Inn-International Drive Resort MI
(407) 351-3500. **$79-$149.** 6515 International Dr. I-4, exit 29, just e on Sand Lake Rd, then 0.5 mi n. Ext/int corridors. **Pets:** $100 deposit/room, $25 one-time fee/room. Service with restrictions, supervision.

Homestead Studio Suites-Orlando/South M
(407) 352-5577. **$54-$80.** 4101 Equity Row. Just sw of jct SR 423 (John Young Pkwy) and 482 (Sand Lake Rd). Int corridors. **Pets:** Other species. $75 one-time fee/room. Service with restrictions.

▼▼ **Howard Johnson Plaza Resort Universal Gateway** Ⓜ

(407) 351-2000. **$55-$109, 3 days notice.** 7050 S Kirkman Rd. I-4, exit 30A, 0.8 mi s on SR 435. Int corridors. **Pets:** Accepted.

Ⓐ🅢🅚 🆂🅜 ✕ 🦽 ⊟ 💻 🍴 ⇌

▲▲▲ ▼▼▼▼ **La Quinta Inn & Suites** Ⓜ

(407) 345-1365. **$85-$135.** 8504 Universal Blvd. I-4, exit 29, 0.5 mi e on SR 482 (Sand Lake Rd), then 0.5 mi s. Int corridors. **Pets:** Small, other species. Service with restrictions, crate.

🆂🅐🆅🅴 ✕ 🦽 🐾 🦽 ⊟ 💻 ⇌

▼▼▼▼ **La Quinta Inn & Suites Orlando Airport North** Ⓜ

(407) 240-5000. **$75-$125.** 7160 N Frontage Rd. SR 528 (Bee Line Expwy), exit 11, 0.5 mi n on SR 436, just w. Int corridors. **Pets:** Small. Service with restrictions, supervision.

🆂🅐🆅🅴 ✕ 🦽 🐾 🦽 ⊟ 💻 ⇌

▲▲▲ ▼▼▼▼ **La Quinta Inn & Suites UCF** Ⓜ

(407) 737-6075. **$75-$125.** 11805 Research Pkwy. Just se of jct University Blvd and SR 434 (Alafaya Tr). Int corridors. **Pets:** Small. Service with restrictions, crate.

🆂🅐🆅🅴 ✕ 🦽 🐾 🦽 ⊟ 💻 ⇌

▲▲▲ ▼▼▼▼ **La Quinta Inn-Orlando International Drive** Ⓜ

(407) 351-1660. **$71-$105.** 8300 Jamaican Ct. I-4, exit 29, just e on Sand Lake Rd, then just s on International Dr. Ext corridors. **Pets:** Accepted.

🆂🅐🆅🅴 ✕ 🦽 🐾 🦽 ⊟ 💻 ⇌

▼▼ **Quality Inn International** Ⓜ

(407) 996-1600. **$50-$80.** 7600 International Dr. I-4, exit 29, just e on Sand Lake Rd, then just n. Ext corridors. **Pets:** Other species. $7 daily fee/pet. Service with restrictions, crate.

🆂🅐🆅🅴 🆂🅜 ✕ 🦽 🦽 ⊟ 💻 🍴 ⇌

▼▼ **Quality Inn-Plaza** Ⓜ

(407) 996-8585. **$39-$99.** 9000 International Dr. I-4, exit 29, just e on SR 482 (Sand Lake Rd), then 1 mi s. Ext corridors. **Pets:** Other species. $10 daily fee/room. Designated rooms, service with restrictions.

🆂🅐🆅🅴 🆂🅜 ✕ 🦽 🐾 🦽 ⊟ 💻 🍴 ⇌

▲▲▲ ▼▼▼ **Red Roof Inn Convention Center** Ⓜ

(407) 352-1507. **$39-$99.** 9922 Hawaiian Ct. I-4, exit 28, 0.9 mi e on Bee Line Expwy (SR 528) to exit 1, then just n. Ext corridors. **Pets:** Medium. No service, crate.

🆂🅐🆅🅴 ✕ 🦽 🦽 ⊟ ⇌

▼▼◆▼ **Red Roof Inn Universal Studios** Ⓜ

(407) 313-3100. **$50-$90.** 5621 Major Blvd. I-4, exit 30B, just n, then just e. Int corridors. **Pets:** Accepted.

Ⓐ🅢🅚 🆂🅜 ✕ 🦽 🐾 🦽 ⇌

▲▲▲ ▼▼▼ ▼▼▼ **Renaissance Orlando Resort at SeaWorld** Ⓗ

(407) 351-5555. **$109-$189, 3 days notice.** 6677 Sea Harbor Dr. I-4, exit 28, just e on Central Florida Pkwy, 0.3 mi n or 0.7 mi w of International Dr. Int corridors. **Pets:** Small, dogs only. $100 one-time fee/pet. Designated rooms, service with restrictions, supervision.

🆂🅐🆅🅴 🆂🅜 ✕ 🦽 🐾 🦽 🍴 ⇌ 🗙

▲▲▲ ▼▼▼▼ **Residence Inn by Marriott Orlando Convention Center** Ⓜ

(407) 226-0288. **$119-$179.** 8800 Universal Blvd. I-4, exit 29A, 0.5 mi e on SR 482 (Sand Lake Rd), then 0.8 mi s. Int corridors. **Pets:** Small, other species. $75 one-time fee/ room. Service with restrictions, supervision.

🆂🅐🆅🅴 🆂🅜 ✕ 🦽 🐾 🦽 ⊟ 💻 ⇌

▲▲▲ ▼▼▼▼ **Residence Inn by Marriott-Orlando International Dr** Ⓐ

(407) 345-0117. **$129-$189.** 7975 Canada Ave. I-4, exit 29, just e on Sand Lake Rd (SR 482). Ext corridors. **Pets:** Small, other species. $50 deposit/room, $10 daily fee/room, $50 one-time fee/room. Service with restrictions.

🆂🅐🆅🅴 🆂🅜 ✕ 🐾 🦽 ⊟ 💻 ⇌

▼▼▼ **Rodeway Inn International** Ⓜ

(407) 996-4444. **$95.** 6327 International Dr. I-4, exit 29, just e on Sand Lake Rd, then 0.7 mi n. Ext/int corridors. **Pets:** Medium, other species. $5.55 daily fee/room. Service with restrictions, supervision.

🆂🅐🆅🅴 🆂🅜 ✕ 🦽 🐾 🦽 ⊟ 💻 🍴 ⇌

▼▼▼ **Travelodge Orlando Downtown** Ⓜ

(407) 423-1671. **$49-$65.** 409 N Magnolia Ave. Corner of Magnolia Ave, Rosalind Ave and Livingston St. Ext/int corridors. **Pets:** Accepted.

Ⓐ🅢🅚 🆂🅜 ✕ ⊟ 💻 🍴 ⇌

▲▲▲ ▼▼▼ ▼▼▼ **Universal's Hard Rock Hotel** Ⓗ 🐾

(407) 503-7625. **$185-$345, 5 days notice.** 5800 Universal Blvd. I-4, exit 30A. Int corridors. **Pets:** Other species. Designated rooms, service with restrictions.

🆂🅐🆅🅴 🆂🅜 ✕ 🦽 🐾 🦽 ⊟ 💻 🍴 ⇌ 🗙

▲▲▲ ▼▼▼ ▼▼▼ **Universal's Portofino Bay Hotel** Ⓗ 🐾

(407) 503-1000. **$240-$359, 5 days notice.** 5601 Universal Blvd. I-4, exit 30B, 0.5 mi n on SR 435 (Kirkman Rd), then just w via Vineland Rd; at Universal Studios. Int corridors. **Pets:** Medium, other species. Designated rooms.

🆂🅐🆅🅴 🆂🅜 ✕ 🦽 🐾 🦽 ⊟ 💻 🍴 ⇌

▼▼▼ **Ventura Resort Rentals-Kissimmee** 🆒

(407) 273-8770. **$56-$220, 91 days notice.** 5946 Curry Ford Rd. 0.6 mi e of SR 436. Ext corridors. **Pets:** Small, other species. $100 deposit/pet, $100 one-time fee/pet.

Ⓐ🅢🅚 🆂🅜 ✕ ⊟ ⇌

▼▼▼▼ **Ventura Resort Rentals Orlando** [CO]
(407) 273-8770. **$651-$1505 (weekly), 91 days notice.**
5946 Curry Ford Rd. 0.6 mi e of SR 436. Ext corridors.
Pets: Small, other species. $100 deposit/pet, $100 one-time fee/pet.
[ASK] [S⭕] [🛏] [🏊] [☒]

(AAA) ▼▼▼ **Wellesley Inn & Suites** [M]
(407) 248-8010. **$69-$89.** 8687 Commodity Cir. Just sw of
jct of SR 423 (John Young Pkwy) and 482 (Sand Lake Rd).
Int corridors. **Pets:** Accepted.
[SAVE] [S⭕] [☒] [🍽] [⬚] [🛏] [💻] [🏊]

(AAA) ▼▼▼ **Wellesley Inn & Suites** [M]
(407) 370-5100. **$59-$79.** 5635 Windhover Dr. I-4, exit 30B,
1 mi n on SR 435 (Kirkman Rd), just e. Int corridors.
Pets: Accepted.
[SAVE] [S⭕] [☒] [&M] [🍽] [⬚] [🛏] [💻] [🏊]

(AAA) ▼▼▼ **Wellesley Inn &**
Suites-Orlando/Maitland [M]
(407) 659-0066. **$59-$69.** 1951 Summit Tower Blvd. I-4, exit
47, 1 mi w. Int corridors. **Pets:** Small, other species. Service
with restrictions, crate.
[SAVE] [S⭕] [☒] [&M] [🍽] [⬚] [🛏] [💻] [🏊]

(AAA) ▼▼▼ **Wyndham Orlando Resort** [X]
(407) 351-2420. **$116-$144, 3 days notice.** 8001 Interna-
tional Dr. I-4, exit 29, just e at Sand Lake Rd (SR 482).
Ext/int corridors. **Pets:** Medium. $50 one-time fee/room.
Service with restrictions, supervision.
[SAVE] [S⭕] [☒] [&M] [🍽] [⬚] [🛏] [💻] [🍴] [🏊] [☒]

❖   **END METROPOLITAN AREA**   ❖

ORMOND BEACH

(AAA) ▼▼▼ **Comfort Inn On The Beach** [M]
(386) 677-8550. **$70-$175, 10 days notice.** 507 S Atlantic
Ave. On SR A1A, 1 mi s of jct SR 40. Ext corridors.
Pets: Very small, dogs only. $10 daily fee/pet. Service with
restrictions, supervision.
[SAVE] [S⭕] [☒] [🛏] [💻]

(AAA) ▼▼▼ **Days Inn Ormond Beach I-95** [M]
(386) 672-7341. **$50-$250, 3 days notice.** 1608 N US 1 &
I-95. I-95, exit 89, just nw on US 1. Ext corridors.
Pets: Accepted.
[SAVE] [S⭕] [☒] [🛏] [🏊]

(AAA) ▼▼▼ **Driftwood Beach Motel** [M]
(386) 677-1331. **$50-$82, 14 days notice.** 657 S Atlantic
Ave. On SR A1A, 1.5 mi s of jct SR 40. Ext corridors.
Pets: Very small, other species. $20 daily fee/pet. Service
with restrictions, supervision.
[SAVE] [🛏] [💻] [🏊]

PALM BAY

▼▼▼ **Jameson Inn** [M]
(321) 725-2952. **$55-$70.** 890 Palm Bay Rd. I-95, exit 70A.
Int corridors. **Pets:** Very small, other species.
[☒] [&M] [🍽] [⬚] [🛏] [💻] [🏊]

SANFORD

▼▼ **Best Western Marina Hotel & Conference**
Center [M]
(407) 323-1910. **$59-$69.** 530 N Palmetto Ave. I-4, exit
51C, 4.8 mi e. Ext corridors. **Pets:** Accepted.
[SAVE] [S⭕] [☒] [💻] [🍴] [🏊]

TAVARES

(AAA) ▼▼ **Budget Inn** [M]
(352) 343-4666. **$46-$74, 14 days notice.** 101 W Burleigh
Blvd. On US 441, 0.3 mi e of jct SR 19 S. Ext corridors.
Pets: Small, dogs only. $8 daily fee/pet, $8 one-time fee/
pet. Service with restrictions, crate.
[SAVE] [S⭕] [☒] [🛏] [💻] [🏊]

(AAA) ▼▼▼ **Inn On The Green** [M] ❖
(352) 343-6373. **$65-$79.** 700 E Burleigh Blvd. On US 441,
1 mi e of jct SR 19. Ext corridors. **Pets:** Other species. $5
one-time fee/pet. Designated rooms, service with restrictions.
[SAVE] [S⭕] [☒] [🛏] [💻] [🏊]

PALM BEACH

(AAA) ▼▼▼ **The Chesterfield Hotel** [H] ❖
(561) 659-5800. **$99-$450, 7 days notice.** 363 Cocoanut
Row. Just w of SR A1A; at Australian Ave and Cocoanut
Row. Int corridors. **Pets:** Small, other species. $100
deposit/room. Supervision.
[SAVE] [☒] [🍽] [🛏] [🍴] [🏊]

(AAA) ▼▼▼▼ **The Four Seasons Resort, Palm**
Beach [H] ❖
(561) 582-2800. **$395-$725, 7 days notice.** 2800 S Ocean
Blvd. SR A1A, 0.3 mi n of jct SR 802. Int corridors.
Pets: Small. Service with restrictions, supervision.
[☒] [&M] [🍽] [⬚] [💻] [🍴] [🏊] [☒]

▼▼▼ **Heart of Palm Beach Hotel** [MI]
(561) 655-5600. **$89-$329, 3 days notice.** 160 Royal Palm
Way. Center; just e of SR A1A. Int corridors. **Pets:** Large,
other species. Service with restrictions, supervision.
[ASK] [S⭕] [☒] [🍽] [🛏] [🍴] [🏊]

▼▼▼ **Plaza Inn** [M] ❖
(561) 832-8666. **$115-$275, 7 days notice.** 215 Brazilian
Ave. Center; at Brazilian Ave and SR A1A (S County Rd).
Int corridors. **Pets:** Large. Designated rooms, service with
restrictions.
[ASK] [S⭕] [☒] [🍽] [🛏] [🏊]

PALM BEACH GARDENS

▲▲▲ ▼▼▼▼ **Doubletree Hotel In The Gardens** 🅗
(561) 622-2260. **$109-$189.** 4431 PGA Blvd. Just w from Florida Tpke, exit 109, 1.8 mi e. Int corridors. **Pets:** Accepted.

[SAVE] [S☷] [✕] [☷M] [✍] [☷] [🛏] [💻] [🍽] [⇌]

▲▲▲ ▼▼▼ **Inns of America** 🅜
(561) 626-4918. **$59-$109.** 4123 Northlake Blvd. I-95, exit 56. Ext corridors. **Pets:** Small. $50 deposit/pet. Service with restrictions, supervision.

[SAVE] [S☷] [✕] [🛏] [⇌]

PALM BEACH SHORES

▲▲▲ ▼▼▼ **Best Western Seaspray Inn** 🅜🅘
(561) 844-0233. **$70-$180, 14 days notice.** 123 S Ocean Ave. On Singer Island; 0.5 mi s of SR A1A. Int corridors. **Pets:** Accepted.

[SAVE] [S☷] [✕] [🛏] [💻] [🍽] [⇌]

PALM COAST

▲▲▲ ▼▼▼ **Palm Coast Villas** 🅜
(386) 445-3525. **$55-$75, 30 days notice.** 5454 N Oceanshore Blvd. I-95, exit 91C, 2.8 mi e to SR A1A, 1.8 mi n. Ext corridors. **Pets:** Accepted.

[SAVE] [✕] [🛏] [💻] [⇌]

PANAMA CITY

▲▲▲ ▼▼▼ **Days Inn Bayside** 🅜🅘
(850) 763-4622. **$49-$96, 7 days notice.** 711 W Beach Dr. Business US 98, 0.5 mi w of jct US 231. Ext corridors. **Pets:** Accepted.

[SAVE] [S☷] [✕] [🛏] [💻] [🍽] [⇌]

▼▼▼ **Howard Johnson Inn** 🅜
(850) 785-0222. **Call for rates.** 4601 W Hwy 98. On US 98, 0.8 mi e of Hathaway Bridge. Ext corridors. **Pets:** Accepted.

[ASK] [✕] [💻] [🍽] [⇌]

▲▲▲ ▼▼▼▼ **La Quinta Inn & Suites** 🅜
(850) 914-0022. **$81-$125.** 1030 E 23rd St. Jct US 231 and CR 390A. Int corridors. **Pets:** Small, other species. Service with restrictions.

[SAVE] [✕] [☷M] [☷] [🛏] [💻] [⇌]

▼▼▼ **Super 8 Motel** 🅜
(850) 784-1988. **$43-$75.** 207 Hwy 231 N. Just n of jct US 98. Ext/int corridors. **Pets:** Other species. $10 one-time fee/room.

[ASK] [S☷] [✕] [🛏] [⇌]

PENSACOLA

▲▲▲ ▼▼▼ **Comfort Inn-NAS Corry** 🅜
(850) 455-3233. **$57-$82.** 3 New Warrington Rd. Just n of jct US 98 and SR 292. Ext corridors. **Pets:** Accepted.

[SAVE] [S☷] [✕] [🛏] [💻] [⇌]

▼▼▼▼ **Crowne Plaza Pensacola Grand** 🅗
(850) 433-3336. **$135.** 200 E Gregory St. Jct I-110 and US 98. Int corridors. **Pets:** Small, other species. $50 one-time fee/room. Service with restrictions, crate.

[ASK] [S☷] [✕] [🛏] [💻] [🍽] [⇌]

▲▲▲ ▼▼▼ **Days Inn North** 🅜
(850) 476-9090. **$49-$119, 7 days notice.** 7051 Pensacola Blvd. I-10, exit 5, just n on US 29. Int corridors. **Pets:** Other species. $10 daily fee/pet. Service with restrictions, supervision.

[SAVE] [S☷] [✕] [🛏] [⇌]

▼▼▼ **Hospitality Inn** 🅜
(850) 477-2333. **$55-$60, 3 days notice.** 6900 Pensacola Blvd. I-10, exit 3A, 0.5 mi s on US 29. Ext/int corridors. **Pets:** Small. $25 one-time fee/room. Designated rooms, service with restrictions, supervision.

[ASK] [S☷] [✕] [🛏] [💻] [⇌]

▲▲▲ ▼▼▼▼ **La Quinta Inn** 🅜
(850) 474-0411. **$65-$95.** 7750 N Davis Hwy. I-10, exit 5, just n. Ext corridors. **Pets:** Accepted.

[SAVE] [✕] [☷] [🛏] [💻] [⇌]

▲▲▲ ▼▼▼▼ **Ramada Inn Bayview** 🅜🅘
(850) 477-7155. **$75-$85, 30 days notice.** 7601 Scenic Hwy. I-10, exit 6, just sw on US 90. Int corridors. **Pets:** Medium, other species. $25 one-time fee/pet. Designated rooms, service with restrictions.

[SAVE] [✕] [🛏] [💻] [🍽] [⇌]

▲▲▲ ▼▼▼ **Ramada Inn North** 🅜🅘
(850) 477-0711. **$64-$68, 3 days notice.** 6550 N Pensacola Blvd. I-10, exit 3, 1.2 mi s on US 29. Ext corridors. **Pets:** Other species. $25 one-time fee/room. Service with restrictions.

[SAVE] [S☷] [✕] [🛏] [💻] [🍽] [⇌]

▲▲▲ ▼▼▼ **Red Roof Inn** 🅜
(850) 476-7960. **$42-$55.** 7340 Plantation Rd. I-110, exit 5, just s. Ext corridors. **Pets:** Accepted.

[SAVE] [✕] [🛏]

▼▼▼ **Travelodge Inn & Suites** 🅜
(850) 473-0222. **$59-$89, 14 days notice.** 6950 Pensacola Blvd. I-10, exit 3A, just se on US 29. Int corridors. **Pets:** Medium. No service, supervision.

[ASK] [S☷] [✕] [🛏] [💻] [⇌]

PORT CHARLOTTE

▼▼▼ **Days Inn of Port Charlotte** 🅜
(941) 627-8900. **$52-$139.** 1941 Tamiami Tr. On US 41, just s of jct Toledo Blade Blvd. Ext corridors. **Pets:** Small. Designated rooms, service with restrictions, supervision.

[SAVE] [✕] [✍] [🛏] [💻] [⇌]

PUNTA GORDA

🐾🐾🐾 ▽▽▽▽ **Best Western Waterfront Inn** Ⓜ
(941) 639-1165. **$69-$146, 7 days notice.** 300 Retta Esplanade. On US 41; just s of Peace River Bridge. Int corridors. **Pets:** Large, other species. $25 one-time fee/pet. Service with restrictions.

[SAVE] [S🐾] [✕] [🦮] [🔋] [💻] [🍴] [🏊]

🐾🐾🐾 ▽▽▽▽ **Holiday Inn Harborside** Ⓜ
(941) 639-2167. **$79-$159.** 33 Tamiami Tr. On US 41; at Peace River Bridge. Int corridors. **Pets:** Small, other species. $40 daily fee/pet.

[SAVE] [S🐾] [✕] [🦮M] [♿] [🔋] [💻] [🍴] [🏊] [✕]

QUINCY

▽▽▽▽ **Allison House Inn** 🅱🅱 ❀
(850) 875-2511. **$85-$100, 14 days notice.** 215 N Madison St. Just e of town center. Int corridors. **Pets:** Small, dogs only. Designated rooms, service with restrictions, supervision.

[ASK] [S🐾] [✕]

SANIBEL

🐾🐾🐾 ▽▽▽ **Waterside Inn on the Beach** Ⓜ ❀
(941) 472-1345. **$138-$299, 60 days notice.** 3033 W Gulf Dr. From causeway, Periwinkle Way 4 mi w to Tarpon Bay Rd, 1 mi s, then 1 mi w. Ext corridors. **Pets:** Small. $5 daily fee/pet. Designated rooms, service with restrictions, supervision.

[SAVE] [✕] [🔋] [💻] [🏊]

SARASOTA

🐾🐾🐾 ▽▽▽ **The Calais Motel-Apartments** 🅰
(941) 921-5797. **$54-$99, 3 days notice.** 1735 Stickney Point Rd. On SR 72, 0.3 mi sw of jct US 41. Ext corridors. **Pets:** Accepted.

[SAVE] [S🐾] [✕] [🔋] [💻] [🏊]

🐾🐾🐾 ▽▽▽ **Comfort Inn** Ⓜ
(941) 921-7750. **$59-$139.** 5778 Clark Rd. I-75, exit 37, just w on SR 72. Int corridors. **Pets:** Accepted.

[SAVE] [S🐾] [✕] [🦮] [♿] [🔋] [🏊]

🐾🐾🐾 ▽▽▽ **Coquina on the Beach Resort** Ⓜ ❀
(941) 388-2141. **$89-$199, 14 days notice.** 1008 Benjamin Franklin Dr. On St Armands Key of Lido Beach, 0.9 mi s of St Armands Cir. Ext corridors. **Pets:** Other species. $30 one-time fee/room. Service with restrictions.

[SAVE] [S🐾] [🔋] [💻] [🏊]

🐾🐾🐾 ▽▽▽ **Days Inn-Airport** Ⓜ
(941) 355-9721. **$39-$149.** 4900 N Tamiami Tr. On US 41, just s of jct University Pkwy. Ext corridors. **Pets:** Dogs only. $10 daily fee/pet. Designated rooms, no service, supervision.

[SAVE] [S🐾] [✕] [🦮] [🔋] [💻] [🍴] [🏊]

🐾🐾🐾 ▽▽▽▽ **Holiday Inn-Airport/Marina** Ⓜ
(941) 355-2781. **$87-$179, 7 days notice.** 7150 N Tamiami Tr. On US 41, 2.4 mi n of jct University Pkwy. Ext/int corridors. **Pets:** Accepted.

[SAVE] [S🐾] [✕] [🦮] [🔋] [💻] [🍴] [🏊]

▽▽▽▽ **Holiday Inn Express Sarasota Siesta Key** Ⓜ
(941) 924-4900. **$89-$139.** 6600 S Tamiami Tr. On US 41, just s of jct SR 72 (Clark Rd). Ext corridors. **Pets:** Small, other species. $30 one-time fee/room. Service with restrictions.

[ASK] [S🐾] [✕] [🦮M] [🦮] [♿] [🔋] [💻] [🏊]

▽▽ **Ramada Limited** Ⓜ
(941) 921-7812. **$60-$119.** 5774 Clark Rd. I-75, exit 37, just w on SR 76. Int corridors. **Pets:** Small. $10 one-time fee/pet. Service with restrictions, supervision.

[ASK] [S🐾] [✕] [🦮] [♿] [🔋] [💻] [🏊]

▽▽ **The Sunset Lodge Motel** 🅰
(941) 925-1151. **$58-$95, 7 days notice.** 1765 Dawn St. Jct Stickney Point Rd, just s on Ave C, just w. Ext corridors. **Pets:** Small, dogs only. Crate.

[✕] [🔋] [💻] [🏊]

SATELLITE BEACH

🐾🐾🐾 ▽▽ **Days Inn** Ⓜ
(321) 777-3552. **$70-$130.** 180 SR A1A. 0.3 mi s of jct SR 404. Ext corridors. **Pets:** Other species. $10 daily fee/pet. Designated rooms, service with restrictions, crate.

[SAVE] [S🐾] [✕] [♿] [🔋] [🏊]

SEBRING

🐾🐾🐾 ▽▽▽▽ **Quality Inn & Suites Conference Center** Ⓜ
(863) 385-4500. **$89-$299, 3 days notice.** 6525 US 27 N. On US 27, 7 mi n of jct SR 17. Ext corridors. **Pets:** Medium. $25 one-time fee/room. Designated rooms, service with restrictions, supervision.

[SAVE] [S🐾] [✕] [🦮M] [🦮] [🔋] [💻] [🍴] [🏊]

SIESTA KEY

▽▽ **Gulf Terrace Vacation Apartments** 🅰
(941) 349-4444. **$375-$1300 (weekly), 30 days notice.** 1105 Point of Rocks Rd. 0.5 mi s of jct SR 72 (Stickney Point Rd) on Midnight Pass Rd, just w. Ext corridors. **Pets:** Accepted.

[ASK] [✕] [🔋] [💻] [🏊]

🐾🐾🐾 ▽▽ **Miramar Beach Apartments of Siesta Key** 🅰
(941) 349-6800. **$60-$300, 30 days notice.** 92 Avenida Messina. Just w of Ocean Blvd. Ext corridors. **Pets:** Accepted.

[SAVE] [S🐾] [✕] [🔋] [🏊]

🐾🐾🐾 ▽▽ **Tropical Breeze Inn** 🅰
(941) 349-1125. **$79-$350, 14 days notice.** 140 Columbus Blvd. Just w of Ocean Blvd via Avenida Messina. Ext corridors. **Pets:** Accepted.

[SAVE] [S🐾] [✕] [🔋] [💻] [🏊]

Turtle Beach Resort A
(941) 349-4554. **$185-$375, 90 days notice.** 9049 Midnight Pass Rd. 2.8 mi s of jct SR 72 (Stickney Pt). Ext corridors. **Pets:** Other species. One-time fee/pet (10% of room rate). No service, supervision.

SILVER SPRINGS

Sun Plaza Motel M
(352) 236-2343. **$40-$65, 7 days notice.** 5461 E Silver Springs Blvd. SR 40 at jct CR 35. Ext corridors. **Pets:** Large, other species. $10.60 one-time fee/pet. Service with restrictions, supervision.

ST. AUGUSTINE

Best Western Inn M
(904) 829-1999. **$52-$129, 3 days notice.** 2445 SR 16. I-95, exit 95, southwest corner. Ext corridors. **Pets:** Medium, dogs only. $6 daily fee/room. Designated rooms, service with restrictions.

Clarion Inn Historic Downtown MI
(904) 824-3383. **$69-$169.** 1300 Ponce de Leon Blvd. US 1, 1 mi n. Ext corridors. **Pets:** Small, dogs only. $25 one-time fee/room. Designated rooms, service with restrictions.

Conch House Marina Resort MI
(904) 829-8646. **$70-$180, 7 days notice.** 57 Comares Ave. 1 mi s of Bridge of Lions on SR A1A, then 0.3 mi n. Ext corridors. **Pets:** Other species. $50 one-time fee/pet. Service with restrictions.

Days Inn Historic M
(904) 829-6581. **$77, 3 days notice.** 2800 N Ponce de Leon Blvd. US 1 at SR 16. Ext corridors. **Pets:** Medium, other species. $10 daily fee/pet. Designated rooms, service with restrictions.

Days Inn-West MI
(904) 824-4341. **$44-$104.** 2560 SR 16. I-95, exit 95, northwest corner. Ext corridors. **Pets:** Dogs only. $10 one-time fee/pet. Service with restrictions.

Ramada Limited M
(904) 829-5643. **$49-$179, 7 days notice.** 2535 SR 16. I-95, exit 95, just w. Ext corridors. **Pets:** Other species. Designated rooms.

Scottish Inns M
(904) 824-2871. **$45-$89, 7 days notice.** 110 San Marco Ave. Center; Old Mission and San Marco aves. Ext corridors. **Pets:** Accepted.

ST. AUGUSTINE BEACH

Holiday Inn-St Augustine Beach MI
(904) 471-2555. **$89-$130.** 860 A1A Beach Blvd. 1.8 mi s of jct SR 312 and A1A, on Business Rt A1A. Ext/int corridors. **Pets:** Accepted.

STARKE

Best Western Motor Inn M
(904) 964-6744. **$56-$95, 30 days notice.** 1290 N Temple Ave. 1 mi n on US 301 from jct SR 100. Ext corridors. **Pets:** Small. $10.90 daily fee/room. Service with restrictions, supervision.

STEINHATCHEE

Steinhatchee Landing Resort C ❀
(352) 498-3513. **$-$300, 14 days notice.** SR 51 N. SR 51, 8 mi w of jct US 19/98. Ext corridors. **Pets:** Small. $100 deposit/room. Designated rooms, no service, crate.

Steinhatchee River Inn M
(352) 498-4049. **$60-$85, 14 days notice.** 1111 Riverside Dr. Center. Ext corridors. **Pets:** Accepted.

STUART

Hutchinson Island Marriott Beach Resort & Marina R
(561) 225-3700. **$129-$259, 3 days notice.** 555 NE Ocean Blvd. 4 mi ne on SR A1A, on south end of Hutchinson Island at east end of causeway. Ext/int corridors. **Pets:** $75 one-time fee/room. Designated rooms, service with restrictions.

Pirates Cove Resort & Marina MI
(561) 287-2500. **$125-$200.** 4307 SE Bayview St. 0.3 mi e of SR A1A. Ext corridors. **Pets:** Medium, other species. $20 daily fee/pet. Designated rooms, service with restrictions.

TALLAHASSEE

Best Western Seminole Inn M
(850) 656-2938. **$65-$120, 7 days notice.** 6737 Mahan Dr. I-10, exit 31A, just w on US 90. Ext corridors. **Pets:** Small. $5 one-time fee/pet. Service with restrictions, supervision.

La Quinta Inn-North M
(850) 385-7172. **$66-$95.** 2905 N Monroe St. I-10, exit 29, just s on US 27, east side. Ext corridors. **Pets:** Accepted.

ⒶⒶⒶ ◈◈◈ La Quinta Inn-Tallahassee South M
(850) 878-5099. **$66-$95.** 2850 Apalachee Pkwy. 3 mi se on US 27. Ext corridors. **Pets:** Accepted.
[SAVE] [✕] [♿] [🐾] [🛎] [🍴] [💻] [➳]

◈ Motel 6–420 M
(850) 668-2600. **$42-$66, 10 days notice.** 1481 Timberlane Rd. I-10, exit 30, just n, w on Timberlane. Ext corridors. **Pets:** Accepted.
[✕] [➳]

ⒶⒶⒶ ◈◈ Red Roof Inn M
(850) 385-7884. **$41-$55.** 2930 Hospitality St. I-10, exit 29, southwest side, just off US 27. Ext corridors. **Pets:** Medium, other species. Service with restrictions.
[SAVE] [✕] [♿] [🐾]

ⒶⒶⒶ ◈◈◈ Shoney's Inn & Suites M
(850) 386-8286. **$49-$99.** 2801 N Monroe St. I-10, exit 29, southeast side. Ext corridors. **Pets:** Accepted.
[SAVE] [💰] [✕] [🛎] [💻] [➳]

◈ Super 8 Motel M
(850) 386-8818. **$45-$65, 3 days notice.** 2702 N Monroe St. I-10, exit 29, 0.4 mi s on US 27. Int corridors. **Pets:** Accepted.
[ASK] [💰] [✕] [🛎] [💻]

TAMPA BAY & CLEARWATER
METROPOLITAN AREA

APOLLO BEACH

ⒶⒶⒶ ◈◈◈ Ramada Bayside Inn & Resort MI ❀
(813) 641-2700. **$55-$150.** 6414 Surfside Blvd. I-75, exit 47, 1.8 mi w on CR 672; US 41, 1.8 mi s to Apollo Beach Blvd, 2.4 mi w to Surfside Blvd. Ext corridors. **Pets:** Small, other species. $20 daily fee/pet. Service with restrictions, supervision.
[SAVE] [💰] [✕] [🐾] [🛎] [💻] [🍴] [➳]

BRANDON

◈◈◈ Behind the Fence Bed & Breakfast BB
(813) 685-8201. **$89 (no credit cards), 10 days notice.** 1400 Viola Dr. I-75, exit 49, just s on US 301 (northbound); 1.5 mi s on US 301 (southbound), 2.5 mi e on Bloomingdale Ave, just n on Countryside St; at jct Viola Dr. Ext/int corridors. **Pets:** $10 one-time fee/pet. No service.
[ASK] [💰] [✕] [🛎] [💻]

◈◈◈ Homestead Studio Suites-Tampa/Brandon M
(813) 643-5900. **$60-$80.** 330 Grand Regency Blvd. I-75, exit 51, just e on SR 60, 0.4 mi n. Ext corridors. **Pets:** Accepted.
[✕] [🐾] [🍴] [🛎] [💻]

◈◈◈ La Quinta Inn & Suites M
(813) 643-0574. **$85-$135.** 310 Grand Regency Blvd. I-75, exit 51, just e on SR 60, 0.4 mi n. Int corridors. **Pets:** Medium, other species. $5 daily fee/pet. Service with restrictions, crate.
[SAVE] [✕] [♿] [🐾] [🍴] [🛎] [💻] [➳]

CLEARWATER

◈◈◈ Homestead Studio Suites-Tampa/Clearwater A
(727) 572-4800. **$64-$94.** 2311 Ulmerton Rd. I-275, exit 18 southbound; exit 16 northbound, 1.5 mi w on SR 688. Ext corridors. **Pets:** Medium, other species. $75 one-time fee/ room. Service with restrictions, crate.
[ASK] [💰] [✕] [🐾] [🍴] [🛎] [💻]

◈◈◈ Homewood Suites by Hilton M ❀
(727) 573-1500. **$113-$200.** 2233 Ulmerton Rd. I-275, exit 18 southbound; exit 16 northbound, 1.3 mi w on SR 688. Int corridors. **Pets:** Small, other species. $150 one-time fee/room. Service with restrictions, supervision.
[SAVE] [💰] [✕] [♿] [🐾] [🍴] [🛎] [💻] [➳]

◈◈◈ La Quinta Inn Clearwater-Airport M
(727) 572-7222. **$75-$125.** 3301 Ulmerton Rd. I-275, exit 18 southbound; exit 16 northbound, 1.7 mi w on SR 688. Int corridors. **Pets:** Accepted.
[SAVE] [✕] [🐾] [🍴] [🛎] [💻] [➳]

ⒶⒶⒶ ◈◈◈ Residence Inn by Marriott A ❀
(727) 573-4444. **$89-$185.** 5050 Ulmerton Rd. On SR 688, 1 mi e of jct US 19. Ext corridors. **Pets:** Large. $150 one-time fee/pet. Service with restrictions, supervision.
[SAVE] [💰] [✕] [🐾] [🍴] [🛎] [💻] [➳]

ⒶⒶⒶ ◈◈◈ Super 8 Motel-St. Petersburg/Clearwater M
(727) 572-8881. **$35-$119.** 13260 34th St N. I-275, exit 18 southbound; exit 16 northbound, 1.8 mi w on SR 688, just s. Int corridors. **Pets:** Large, other species. $10 daily fee/ pet. Designated rooms, service with restrictions, supervision.
[SAVE] [💰] [✕] [🛎] [➳]

(AAA) ▼▼▼▼ Towne Place Suites by Marriott **M**
(727) 299-9229. **$89-$139, 3 days notice.** 13200 49th St
N. I-275, exit 18 southbound; exit 16 northbound, 3 mi w,
then just s; 1 mi e of US 19 on SR 688. Int corridors.
Pets: Other species. $75 deposit/room, $10 daily fee/room.
Service with restrictions.

[SAVE] [S⊘] [✕] [🛏] [🖵] [⊸]

HOLIDAY

(AAA) ▼▼ Best Western-Tahitian
Resort **M** ✿
(727) 937-4121. **$59-$99, 7 days notice.** 2337 US 19. US
19, 3 mi n of jct SR 582. 1.5 mi s of jct SR 54. Ext
corridors. **Pets:** Other species. $5 one-time fee/pet. Desig-
nated rooms, service with restrictions, supervision.

[SAVE] [S⊘] [✕] [🐾] [🛏] [🖵] [⊸]

MADEIRA BEACH

▼▼ The Lighthouse Bed & Breakfast
Motel **A** ✿
(727) 391-0015. **$60-$105, 21 days notice.** 13355 2nd St
E. Just e of jct SR 699 on 134th Ave. Ext corridors.
Pets: $10 daily fee/pet. Service with restrictions.

[ASK] [✕] [🛏] [✆]

NEW PORT RICHEY

(AAA) ▼▼ Econo Lodge **M**
(727) 845-4990. **$52-$100.** 7631 US 19. 0.8 mi n of jct
Main St. Ext corridors. **Pets:** Medium, other species. $6
daily fee/room. Designated rooms, service with restrictions,
crate.

[SAVE] [S⊘] [✕] [🛏] [🖵] [⊸]

PALM HARBOR

(AAA) ▼▼▼▼ Four Points Sheraton Tarpon
Springs **M** ✿
(727) 942-0358. **$108-$128, 7 days notice.** 37611 US 19
N. On US 19, 3 mi s of jct SR 582. Ext corridors.
Pets: Other species. $10 daily fee/room. Service with
restrictions, supervision.

[SAVE] [S⊘] [✕] [✍] [🛏] [🖵] [🍴] [⊸]

(AAA) ▼▼ Knights Inn-Clearwater/Palm
Harbor **M**
(727) 789-2002. **$30-$119, 7 days notice.** 34106 US 19 N.
1.8 mi n of CR 752 (Tampa Rd). Ext corridors.
Pets: Accepted.

[SAVE] [S⊘] [✕] [🛏] [🖵] [⊸]

(AAA) ▼▼▼▼ Red Roof Inn **M** ✿
(727) 786-2529. **$58-$88.** 32000 US 19 N. On US 19, 0.4
mi s of jct Tampa Rd. Ext corridors. **Pets:** Medium, other
species. Service with restrictions, supervision.

[SAVE] [S⊘] [✕] [🐾] [✍] [🛏] [🖵] [⊸]

PINELLAS PARK

▼▼ La Mark Charles Motel **M**
(727) 527-7334. **$42-$50.** 6200 34th St N. I-275, exit 15,
1.4 mi w on Gandy Blvd (SR 694), 0.8 mi s on US 19. Ext
corridors. **Pets:** Accepted.

[✕] [🛏] [⊸]

▼▼▼▼ La Quinta Inn-Pinellas Park **M**
(727) 545-5611. **$65-$95.** 7500 US Hwy 19N. I-275, exit 15,
1.4 mi s on Gandy Blvd (SR 694), just n. Ext/int corridors.
Pets: Accepted.

[SAVE] [✕] [&M] [🐾] [🛏] [🖵] [⊸]

PLANT CITY

(AAA) ▼▼ Days Inn Plant City **M**
(813) 752-0570. **$65-$95, 7 days notice.** 301 S Frontage
Rd. I-4, exit 13A, just se via Frontage Rd. Ext corridors.
Pets: Small, other species. $10 one-time fee/pet. Service
with restrictions, supervision.

[SAVE] [S⊘] [✕] [🛏] [🖵] [🍴] [⊸]

▼▼▼ Holiday Inn Express Plant City **M**
(813) 719-3800. **Call for rates.** 2102 N Park Rd. I-4, exit
14, just e. Int corridors. **Pets:** Small. $40 one-time fee/pet.
Service with restrictions, supervision.

[✕] [&M] [🐾] [✍] [🛏] [🖵] [⊸]

PORT RICHEY

▼▼▼ Comfort Inn **M**
(727) 863-3336. **$65-$89.** 11810 US 19. On US 19, just s of
jct SR 52. Ext corridors. **Pets:** Medium. $6 daily fee/pet.
Service with restrictions, supervision.

[SAVE] [S⊘] [✕] [🐾] [🛏] [🖵] [⊸]

RUSKIN

▼▼▼▼ Bahia Beach Island Resort & Marina **M**
(813) 645-3291. **$74-$119.** 611 Destiny Dr. 3.5 mi w of US
41 via Shell Point Rd, follow signs. Ext/int corridors.
Pets: Very small, other species. $25 one-time fee/room.
Designated rooms, service with restrictions, supervision.

[ASK] [S⊘] [✕] [&M] [🐾] [✍] [🛏] [🖵] [🍴] [⊸] [✕]

SAFETY HARBOR

(AAA) ▼▼▼▼ Safety Harbor Resort and Spa on
Tampa Bay **R** ✿
(727) 726-1161. **$99-$179, 3 days notice.** 105 N Bayshore
Dr. At jct SR 590 (Main St). Int corridors. **Pets:** Small. $35
daily fee/pet. Designated rooms, service with restrictions,
supervision.

[SAVE] [S⊘] [✕] [&M] [🐾] [✍] [🛏] [🖵] [🍴] [⊸] [✕]

ST. PETE BEACH

▼▼ Ritz Motel Ⓐ
(727) 360-7642. **$49-$85, 14 days notice.** 4237 Gulf Blvd.
On SR 699, 0.5 mi n of Pinellas Bayway. Ext corridors.
Pets: Medium, other species. Service with restrictions,
supervision.
Ⓐ⅃Ⓚ Ⓢⅅ ⬛ ⤳

ST. PETERSBURG

AAA ▼▼▼ Days Inn of St. Petersburg Ⓜ ❀
(727) 522-3191. **$54-$89, 14 days notice.** 2595 54th Ave
N. I-275, exit 14; exit 14B northbound, 0.3 mi w. Ext corridors. **Pets:** Medium, other species. $10 daily fee/pet. Des-
ignated rooms, service with restrictions.
Ⓢ⥁ Ⓢⅅ ✕ ⏰ ⬛ ⅋ ⤳

AAA ▼▼▼▼ La Quinta Inn Ⓜ
(727) 527-8421. **$65-$95.** 4999 34th St N. I-275, exit 14,
just w on 54th Ave N, just s on US 19 (34th St). Ext
corridors. **Pets:** Small. Service with restrictions, supervision.
Ⓢ⥁ ✕ ♿ ⏰ Ⓚ ⬛ ▣ ⤳

▼▼▼▼ St. Petersburg Bayfront Hilton Ⓗ
(727) 894-5000. **$85-$125, 3 days notice.** 333 1st St S.
Downtown. Int corridors. **Pets:** Accepted.
Ⓢ⥁ Ⓢⅅ ✕ ♿ ⏰ Ⓚ ⬛ ▣ ⅋ ⤳

SUN CITY CENTER

▼▼ Sun City Center Inn Ⓜ
(813) 634-3331. **$49-$79.** 1335 Rickenbacker Dr. I-75, exit
46B; exit 46 northbound, 2.1 mi e on SR 674. Ext corridors.
Pets: Dogs only. $7.50 one-time fee/pet. Service with
restrictions, supervision.
Ⓐ⅃Ⓚ Ⓢⅅ ✕ ⏰ Ⓚ ⬛ ▣ ⅋ ⤳ ⌧

TAMPA

AAA ▼▼▼ AmeriSuites Ⓜ
(813) 622-8557. **$89-$139.** 10007 Princess Palm Ave. I-75,
exit 52 southbound; exit 52B northbound, 0.5 mi w, just s
on Falkenburg Rd, just w. Int corridors. **Pets:** Small, other
species. Service with restrictions.
Ⓢ⥁ Ⓢⅅ ✕ ⬛ ▣ ⤳

AAA ▼▼▼ Amerisuites-Tampa Airport Ⓜ
(813) 282-1037. **$129-$159.** 4811 W Main St. I-275, exit 21,
0.5 mi w on Westshore; exit 20A northbound, 1 mi n on
Kennedy Blvd, 1 mi w on Westshore. Int corridors.
Pets: Accepted.
Ⓢ⥁ Ⓢⅅ ✕ Ⓚ ♿ Ⓚ ⬛ ▣ ⤳

AAA ▼▼▼ AmeriSuites Tampa Busch
Gardens Ⓜ
(813) 979-1922. **$99-$149.** 11408 N 30th St. I-275, exit 34,
1.8 mi e on SR 582, just s. Int corridors. **Pets:** Very small.
Designated rooms, service with restrictions, supervision.
Ⓢ⥁ Ⓢⅅ ✕ Ⓚ ♿ Ⓚ ⬛ ▣ ⤳

AAA ▼▼▼ Baymont Inn & Suites
Tampa-Brandon Ⓜ
(813) 684-4007. **$69-$99.** 602 S Falkenburg Rd. I-75, exit
51, just w at jct SR 60 and S Falkenburg Rd. Int corridors.
Pets: Medium. $10 daily fee/room. Designated rooms, serv-
ice with restrictions, supervision.
Ⓢ⥁ Ⓢⅅ ✕ ♿ ⬛ ▣ ⤳

AAA ▼▼▼ Baymont Inn & Suites Tampa/near
Busch Gardens Ⓜ
(813) 930-6900. **$69-$99.** 9202 N 30th St. I-275, exit 33, 2
mi e on SR 580, just n. Ext corridors. **Pets:** Medium, other
species. Designated rooms, service with restrictions, supervision.
Ⓢ⥁ Ⓢⅅ ✕ ♿ ⬛ ▣ ⤳

AAA ▼▼▼ Baymont Inn Tampa-Fairgrounds Ⓜ
(813) 626-0885. **$59-$89.** 4811 US 301 N. I-4, exit 6 westbound; exit 6A eastbound, just se. Int corridors.
Pets: Medium. $50 deposit/room. Designated rooms, serv-
ice with restrictions, supervision.
Ⓢ⥁ Ⓢⅅ ✕ ♿ ⬛ ▣ ⤳

AAA ▼▼▼▼ Best Western All Suites Hotel Behind
Busch Gardens Ⓜ
(813) 971-8930. **$89-$159.** 3001 University Center Dr.
I-275, exit 34, 1.8 mi e on SR 582, 0.5 mi s on N 30th St.
Ext corridors. **Pets:** Medium, other species. $10 daily fee/
room. Service with restrictions, crate.
Ⓢ⥁ Ⓢⅅ ✕ ♿ ⬛ ▣ ⅋ ⤳

▼▼▼▼ Chase Suite Hotel by Woodfin Ⓐ
(813) 281-5677. **$105-$115.** 3075 N Rocky Point Dr. I-275,
exit 20 southbound; exit 20B northbound, 3 mi w on SR 60,
just n. Ext corridors. **Pets:** Accepted.
Ⓐ⅃Ⓚ Ⓢⅅ ✕ ♿ ⬛ ▣ ⤳ ⌧

▼▼▼ Days Inn Airport Stadium Ⓜ
(813) 877-6181. **$85-$129.** 2522 N Dale Mabry. I-275, exit
23A, 0.6 mi n. Ext corridors. **Pets:** Small, other species.
$25 one-time fee/room. Service with restrictions.
Ⓢ⥁ Ⓢⅅ ✕ ♿ Ⓚ ⬛ ▣ ⤳

▼▼▼ Holiday Inn Express Hotel & Suites
Stadium/Airport Ⓜ ❀
(813) 877-6061. **$81-$107.** 4732 N Dale Mabry. I-275, exit
23A, 2 mi n. Ext corridors. **Pets:** Other species. $25 one-
time fee/room. Service with restrictions.
Ⓐ⅃Ⓚ Ⓢⅅ ✕ Ⓚ ⏰ ⬛ ▣ ⤳

▼▼▼ Holiday Inn Tampa Near Busch
Gardens Ⓜ
(813) 971-4710. **$140-$160.** 2701 E Fowler Ave. I-275, exit
34, 1.5 mi e on SR 582. Ext/int corridors. **Pets:** Small. $25
one-time fee/pet. Service with restrictions, crate.
Ⓐ⅃Ⓚ Ⓢⅅ ✕ Ⓚ ⏰ Ⓚ ⬛ ▣ ⅋ ⤳

▼▼▼▼ Howard Johnson Near Busch Gardens
MainGate Ⓜ
(813) 988-9191. **$39-$129.** 4139 E Busch Blvd. I-275, exit
33, 3 mi e on SR 580. Int corridors. **Pets:** Accepted.
Ⓐ⅃Ⓚ Ⓢⅅ ✕ ⏰ Ⓚ ⬛ ▣ ⅋ ⤳

▼ Howard Johnson Tampa Airport/Stadium 🅼 ✿

(813) 875-8818. **$59-$84.** 2055 N Dale Mabry. I-275, exit 23A, 0.5 mi n. Ext corridors. **Pets:** Accepted.

(A$K) (S🅳) (✕) (🌀) (🔋) (💻) (🍴) (🌊)

▼▼▼ La Quinta Inn & Suites USF 🅼

(813) 910-7500. **$76-$125.** 3701 E Fowler. I-275, exit 34, 2.2 mi e on SR 582. Int corridors. **Pets:** Other species. Service with restrictions.

(SAVE) (✕) (🅼) (🌀) (🗿) (🔋) (💻) (🌊)

▼▼▼ La Quinta Inn Tampa Airport 🅼

(813) 287-0440. **$76-$125.** 4730 Spruce St. I-275, exit 21 southbound; exit 20A northbound (Westshore Dr), 0.8 mi w. Ext corridors. **Pets:** Accepted.

(SAVE) (✕) (🌀) (🔋) (💻) (🌊)

▼▼ Motel 6 🅼

(813) 628-0888. **$42-$56.** 6510 N US 301. I-4, exit 6 westbound; exit 6A eastbound, 0.7 mi n. Ext corridors. **Pets:** Accepted.

(S🅳) (✕) (🗿) (🌊)

▼▼ Motel 6–483 🅼

(813) 932-4948. **$42, 14 days notice.** 333 E Fowler Ave. I-275, exit 34, just w on SR 582. Ext corridors. **Pets:** Accepted.

(S🅳) (✕) (🌊)

🔺🔺🔺 ▼▼▼ Ramada Airport Inn & Conference Center 🄷

(813) 289-1950. **$120-$139.** 5303 W Kennedy Blvd. I-275, exit 21 southbound, 0.4 mi e on Westshore, 0.5 mi s; exit 20B northbound, just e. Ext/int corridors. **Pets:** Large. $25 daily fee/room. Designated rooms, service with restrictions, supervision.

(SAVE) (S🅳) (✕) (🌀) (🔋) (💻) (🍴) (🌊)

🔺🔺🔺 ▼▼▼ Red Roof Inn 🅼

(813) 932-0073. **$39-$69.** 2307 E Busch Blvd. I-275, exit 33, 1.4 mi e on SR 580. Ext corridors. **Pets:** Medium, other species. Service with restrictions, crate.

(SAVE) (✕) (🌊)

🔺🔺🔺 ▼▼▼ Red Roof Inn-Brandon 🅼

(813) 681-8484. **$44-$85.** 10121 Horace Ave. I-75, exit 51, just w to S Falkenberg Rd, just n. Ext corridors. **Pets:** Medium, other species. Service with restrictions, supervision.

(SAVE) (✕) (🌀) (🌊)

🔺🔺🔺 ▼▼▼ Red Roof Inn-Fairgrounds 🅼

(813) 623-5245. **$39-$77.** 5001 N US 301. I-4, exit 6 westbound; exit 6A eastbound, just se. Ext corridors. **Pets:** Medium, other species. Service with restrictions, supervision.

(SAVE) (✕) (🌀)

🔺🔺🔺 ▼▼▼ Wellesley Inn & Suites 🅼

(813) 637-8990. **$69-$109.** 1805 N Westshore Blvd. I-275, exit 21 southbound, 0.5 mi n; exit 20A northbound, 0.5 mi e on Kennedy Blvd, 1.3 mi n. Int corridors. **Pets:** Accepted.

(SAVE) (S🅳) (✕) (🅼) (🌀) (🗿) (🔋) (💻) (🌊)

▼▼▼ Wingate Inn-USF Near Busch Gardens 🅼

(813) 979-2828. **$85-$145.** 3751 E Fowler Ave. I-275, exit 34, 2.2 mi e on SR 582. Int corridors. **Pets:** Medium. $40 one-time fee/room. Designated rooms, service with restrictions, crate.

(A$K) (S🅳) (✕) (🅼) (🌀) (🗿) (🔋) (💻) (🌊)

TEMPLE TERRACE

🔺🔺🔺 ▼▼▼ Residence Inn by Marriott Tampa North 🄷 ✿

(813) 972-4400. **$99-$179.** 13420 N Telecom Pkwy. I-75, exit 55, 1.1 mi w on Fletcher Ave. Int corridors. **Pets:** Other species. $125 one-time fee/room. Service with restrictions, supervision.

(SAVE) (S🅳) (✕) (🅼) (🌀) (🗿) (🔋) (💻) (🌊)

WESLEY CHAPEL

🔺🔺🔺 ▼▼ Masters Inn Tampa North 🅼 ✿

(813) 973-0155. **$45-$50.** 27807 SR 54 W. I-75, exit 58, just w. Ext corridors. **Pets:** Small, dogs only. $5 daily fee/pet. Designated rooms, service with restrictions, supervision.

(SAVE) (S🅳) (✕) (🌀) (🔋) (🍴) (🌊)

✿ **END METROPOLITAN AREA** ✿

THE FLORIDA KEYS

ISLAMORADA

 **Sands of Islamorada** **M**
(305) 664-2791. **$99-$250, 3 days notice.** 80051 Overseas Hwy. US 1, MM 80. Ext corridors. **Pets:** Other species. $15 daily fee/pet. Service with restrictions, crate.
(SAVE) (✎) 🛢 🖥 ⊃

KEY WEST

Ambrosia Too At Fleming St **BB** ❖
(305) 296-9838. **$110-$379, 15 days notice.** 622 Fleming St. Just n of Simonton St. Ext corridors. **Pets:** Other species. $25 one-time fee/room. Service with restrictions, supervision.
(SAVE) ✕ 🛢 🖥 ⊃

Center Court Historic Inn & Cottages **BB**
(305) 296-9292. **$98-$198, 30 days notice.** 915 Center St. 0.5 mi n of jct US 1, between Duval and Simonton sts. Ext/int corridors. **Pets:** Other species. $10 daily fee/pet. Designated rooms, service with restrictions.
✕ 🛢 ⊃

Chelsea House **BB** ❖
(305) 296-2211. **$85-$245, 10 days notice.** 707 Truman Ave. At the corner of Elizabeth St and Truman Ave. **Pets:** Medium. $15 daily fee/pet. Designated rooms, service with restrictions, supervision.
(SAVE) ✕ 🛢 🖥 ⊃

Courtney's Place Historic Cottages & Inn **C**
(305) 294-3480. **$75-$245, 21 days notice.** 720 Whitmarsh Ln. Just e from jct Petronia and Simonton sts. Ext corridors. **Pets:** Accepted.
(SAVE) 🛢 🖥 ⊃

The Cuban Club Suites **A**
(305) 296-0465. **$99-$349, 14 days notice.** 1108 Duval St. Corner of Duval and Amelia sts; registration at La Casa de Luces on Amelia St. Int corridors. **Pets:** Accepted.
(SAVE) ✕ 🛢

Curry Mansion Inn **BB**
(305) 294-5349. **$150-$275, 14 days notice.** 511 Caroline St. Just n of jct Duval St. Ext/int corridors. **Pets:** Accepted.
✕ ⊃

Frances St Bottle Inn **BB** ❖
(305) 294-8530. **$80-$175, 14 days notice.** 535 Frances St. From US 1/Roosevelt Blvd, right onto White St, then left onto Southard St; at corner of Frances and Southard sts. Int corridors. **Pets:** Other species. $25 one-time fee/pet. Designated rooms, service with restrictions.
(SAVE) ✕ 🛢 ☑

The Palms Hotel **BB**
(305) 294-3146. **$95-$195, 14 days notice.** 820 White St. Just w of Truman. Ext corridors. **Pets:** Small, other species. Designated rooms, service with restrictions, supervision.
(SAVE) (S✎) ⊃

❖ END AREA ❖

TITUSVILLE

Best Western Space Shuttle Inn **M** ❖
(321) 269-9100. **$72-$112.** 3455 Cheney Hwy. I-95, exit 79, just e on SR 50. Ext corridors. **Pets:** Other species. $5 daily fee/pet. Designated rooms, service with restrictions.
(SAVE) (S✎) ✕ 🛢 🖥 🍴 ⊃

Days Inn-Kennedy Space Center **M**
(321) 269-4480. **$69-$135, 30 days notice.** 3755 Cheney Hwy. I-95, exit 79 (SR 50). Ext corridors. **Pets:** Other species. $10 one-time fee/room. Service with restrictions, crate.
(SAVE) (S✎) ✕ 🛢 🖥 ⊃

Holiday Inn Riverfront-Kennedy Space Center **M**
(321) 269-2121. **$110-$140, 7 days notice.** 4951 S Washington Ave. US 1, 0.5 mi s of jct SR 50; 1.7 mi n of jct SR 405. Ext corridors. **Pets:** Other species. $15 deposit/room, $10 one-time fee/room. Designated rooms, service with restrictions.
(ASK) (S✎) ✕ (⚙M) (⌚) (♿) 🛢 🖥 🍴 ⊃

VENICE

Days Inn **M**
(941) 493-4558. **$72-$102.** 1710 S Tamiami Tr. US 41 at jct Shamrock Dr, just s of jct US Business 41. Ext corridors. **Pets:** Other species. $30 one-time fee/room. Service with restrictions, crate.
(SAVE) (S✎) ✕ (✎) 🛢 🖥 🍴 ⊃

Motel 6-364 **M**
(941) 485-8255. **$46-$66, 30 days notice.** 281 US 41 Bypass N. On US 41, just n of jct Venice Ave. Ext corridors. **Pets:** Small, other species. Service with restrictions, supervision.
✕ (⌚) (✎) ⊃

VERO BEACH

The Islander Inn **M**
(561) 231-4431. **$69-$120.** 3101 Ocean Dr. Just s of SR 60. Ext corridors. **Pets:** Accepted.
(SAVE) 🛢 🖥 ⊃

▼▼ **Vero Beach Resort** Ⓜ
(561) 562-9991. **$44-$49, 3 days notice.** 8800 20th St.
I-95, exit 68 (SR 60), 0.5 mi e. Ext corridors.
Pets: Accepted.
[ASK] [S🐾] [✕] [🐾] [¶] [🏊]

WEEKI WACHEE

ⒶⒶ ▼▼▼ **Best Western Weeki Wachee**
Resort Ⓜ
(352) 596-2007. **$49-$89.** 6172 Commercial Way. On US
19; at jct SR 50 (Cortez Blvd). Ext corridors. **Pets:** Large,
other species. Service with restrictions, supervision.
[SAVE] [S🐾] [✕] [🐾] [🏊]

▼▼▼ **Comfort Inn** Ⓜ
(352) 596-9000. **$85-$120.** 9373 Cortez Blvd. On SR 50,
just e of jct US 19. Ext corridors. **Pets:** Accepted.
[SAVE] [S🐾] [✕] [🐾] [🅱] [🏊]

WEST MELBOURNE

▼▼ **Howard Johnson** Ⓜ
(321) 768-8439. **$45-$79, 7 days notice.** 4431 W New
Haven Ave. I-95, exit 71, just e on SR 192. Ext corridors.
Pets: Medium. $20 one-time fee/room. Designated rooms,
service with restrictions, crate.
[ASK] [S🐾] [✕] [🅱] [🖥] [🏊]

WEST PALM BEACH

ⒶⒶ ▼▼▼ **Comfort Inn-on Palm Beach**
Lakes Ⓜ
(561) 689-6100. **$89-$129.** 1901 Palm Beach Lakes Blvd.
I-95, exit 53, just w. Int corridors. **Pets:** Medium, other
species. $10 daily fee/room, $35 one-time fee/room. Designated rooms, service with restrictions, crate.
[SAVE] [S🐾] [✕] [🐾] [🅱] [🖥] [🏊]

▼▼▼ **Hibiscus House Bed & Breakfast** [BB]
(561) 863-5633. **$65-$250, 14 days notice.** 501 30th St.
1.2 mi n on Flagler Dr from jct Palm Beach Lakes Blvd, 0.3
mi w. Int corridors. **Pets:** Other species.
[ASK] [S🐾] [✕] [🅱] [🏊].

ⒶⒶ ▼▼ **Red Roof Inn-West Palm Beach** Ⓜ
(561) 697-7710. **$47-$89.** 2421 Metro Center Blvd E. I-95,
exit 54 (45th St), just w on CR 702. Ext/int corridors.
Pets: Accepted.
[SAVE] [✕] [� M] [🐾] [🅱] [🏊]

ⒶⒶⒶ ▼▼▼▼ **Residence Inn by Marriott West Palm**
Beach 🄰 🐾
(561) 687-4747. **$109-$229.** 2461 Metrocenter Blvd. I-95,
exit 54, just w on 45th St. Int corridors. **Pets:** Other species.
$100 one-time fee/room.
[SAVE] [S🐾] [✕] [⅒M] [🐾] [🅱] [🖥] [🏊]

▼▼▼ **Sheraton Hotel** 🄷
(561) 833-1234. **$109-$219.** 630 Clearwater Park Rd. I-95,
exit 52, 0.8 mi e on Okeechobee Blvd E. Int corridors.
Pets: Accepted.
[ASK] [S🐾] [✕] [🐾] [🅱] [🖥] [¶] [🏊]

▼▼ **Studio 6 Extended Stay** Ⓜ
(561) 640-3335. **$63-$91.** 1535 Centrepark Dr N. I-95, exit
51 (Belvedere Rd), w to Australian Ave, then n to Centrepark Dr, e on Centrepark Dr, straight ahead. Ext corridors. **Pets:** Medium. $10 daily fee/room. Service with
restrictions, crate.
[S🐾] [✕] [⅒M] [🅱] [🖥]

WILLISTON

▼ **Williston Motor Inn** Ⓜ
(352) 528-4801. **$35.** 606 W Noble Ave. 0.5 mi n on US 27
Alt. Ext corridors. **Pets:** Accepted.
[✕] [🅱] [🖥] [¶] [🏊]

WINTER HAVEN

ⒶⒶ ▼▼▼ **Best Western Admiral's Inn** Ⓜ
(863) 324-5950. **$72-$125.** 5665 Cypress Gardens Blvd.
SR 540, 3 mi e of jct US 17; 3.9 mi w of jct US 27. Ext/int
corridors. **Pets:** Accepted.
[SAVE] [S🐾] [✕] [🅱] [🖥] [¶] [🏊]

ⒶⒶ ▼▼ **Cypress Motel** Ⓜ 🐾
(863) 324-5867. **$50-$75, 30 days notice.** 5651 Cypress
Gardens Rd. 1.7 mi w of US 27 on SR 540; or 2 mi e of
Cypress Gardens Theme Park, then 500 yds n. Ext corridors. **Pets:** Other species. $10 one-time fee/room. Supervi-
sion.
[SAVE] [S🐾] [✕] [🅱] [🖥] [🏊]

GEORGIA

CITY INDEX

ADAIRSVILLE

Comfort Inn M
(770) 773-2886. **$50-$85.** 107 Princeton Blvd. I-75, exit 306, just w. Ext corridors. **Pets:** Small. $5 daily fee/room. Service with restrictions, supervision.

Ramada Ltd M
(770) 769-9726. **$54-$99.** 500 Georgia North Cir. I-75, exit 306, 0.3 mi w. Ext corridors. **Pets:** Accepted.

ADEL

Hampton Inn M
(229) 896-3099. **$63-$69.** 1500 W 4th St. I-75, exit 39, northwest corner. Int corridors. **Pets:** Medium, other species. $10 one-time fee/room. Service with restrictions, crate.

Super 8 Motel I-75 M
(229) 896-2244. **$34-$39.** 1103 W 4th St. I-75, exit 39, southeast corner. Ext corridors. **Pets:** Accepted.

ALMA

Days Inn M
(912) 632-7000. **$50-$60.** 930 S Pierce St. Just s of jct SR 32 on east side. Ext corridors. **Pets:** Medium, dogs only. $10 deposit/room. Service with restrictions, supervision.

AMERICUS

1906 Pathway Inn Bed & Breakfast BB
(229) 928-2078. **$85-$129.** 501 S Lee St. 0.5 mi s of US 280 on SR 377. Int corridors. **Pets:** Small. $50 deposit/room, $20 daily fee/pet. Designated rooms, supervision.

Ramada Inn MI
(229) 924-4431. **$75.** 1205 Martin Luther King Jr Blvd. 1 mi w of downtown on US 19 S. Ext corridors. **Pets:** Small. $10 daily fee/pet. Designated rooms, service with restrictions, supervision.

ASHBURN

Days Inn M
(229) 567-3346. **$38-$42, 7 days notice.** 823 E Washington Ave. I-75, exit 82, just w on SR 112. Ext corridors. **Pets:** Small. $5 one-time fee/pet. Designated rooms, service with restrictions, crate.

ATHENS

Best Western-Colonial Inn M
(706) 546-7311. **$59-$79.** 170 N Milledge Ave. 0.5 mi w on SR 15; at jct US 78 business route (Broad St). Ext corridors. **Pets:** Other species. $10 daily fee/room, service with restrictions.

Holiday Inn Express M
(706) 546-8122. **$82, 7 days notice.** 513 W Broad St. Center; on US 78. Int corridors. **Pets:** Other species. $25 one-time fee/room. Service with restrictions, supervision.

ATLANTA METROPOLITAN AREA

ACWORTH

▼▼ Best Western Frontier Inn M 🐾
(770) 974-0116. **$55-$60.** 5155 Cowan Rd. I-75, exit 277, just w. Ext corridors. **Pets:** Medium, other species. $10 one-time fee/room. Designated rooms, supervision.
[SAVE] [S₀] [✕] [📼] [💻] [➰]

AAA ▼▼ Days Inn M
(770) 974-1700. **$50-$80.** 5035 Cowan Rd. I-75, exit 277, just w. Ext corridors. **Pets:** Accepted.
[SAVE] [S₀] [✕] [➰]

AAA ▼▼ Econo Lodge M
(770) 974-1922. **$50-$80.** 4980 Cowan Rd. I-75, exit 277, just sw. Ext corridors. **Pets:** Accepted.
[SAVE] [S₀] [✕] [💻] [➰]

AAA ▼▼ Red Roof Inn M
(770) 974-5400. **$50-$60, 7 days notice.** 5320 Glade Rd. I-75, exit 278, just w. Ext corridors. **Pets:** Accepted.
[SAVE] [S₀] [✕] [🔊] [📼] [➰]

AAA ▼▼ Super 8 Motel M
(770) 966-9700. **$49-$69.** 4970 Cowan Rd. I-75, exit 277, just sw. Ext corridors. **Pets:** $8 daily fee/pet. Service with restrictions, supervision.
[SAVE] [S₀] [✕] [🔊] [📼] [➰]

ALPHARETTA

AAA ▼▼▼ AmeriSuites M
(678) 339-0505. **$99-$129.** 12505 Nortel Pkwy. SR 400, exit 11, 0.5 mi w. Int corridors. **Pets:** Small. $50 one-time fee/room. Service with restrictions, supervision.
[SAVE] [S₀] [✕] [&M] [🔊] [🔊] [📼] [💻] [➰]

AAA ▼▼▼ AmeriSuites-Atlanta/Windward M
(770) 343-9566. **$129-$139.** 5595 Windward Pkwy. SR 400, exit 11, just w. Int corridors. **Pets:** Very small. Designated rooms, service with restrictions, supervision.
[SAVE] [S₀] [✕] [&M] [🔊] [🔊] [📼] [➰]

AAA ▼▼▼ AmeriSuites North Point Mall M
(770) 594-8788. **$98, 30 days notice.** 7500 North Point Pkwy. SR 400, exit 8, just e to North Point Pkwy, just n. Int corridors. **Pets:** Very small, dogs only. $10 one-time fee/room. Service with restrictions, supervision.
[SAVE] [S₀] [✕] [&M] [🔊] [🔊] [📼] [💻] [➰]

▼▼▼ Hampton Inn & Suites M
(678) 393-0990. **$99, 3 days notice.** 16785 Old Morris Rd. SR 400, exit 11, 1.2 mi nw, follow Deerfield Pkwy and Morris Rd. Int corridors. **Pets:** Accepted.
[SAVE] [S₀] [✕] [&M] [🔊] [🔊] [📼] [💻] [➰]

▼▼▼ Homewood Suites ▲
(770) 998-1622. **$134.** 10775 Davis Dr. SR 400, exit 8, northwest corner. Int corridors. **Pets:** Other species. $100 one-time fee/room. Service with restrictions, supervision.
[SAVE] [S₀] [✕] [&M] [🔊] [📼] [💻] [➰]

AAA ▼▼▼ La Quinta Inn & Suites M
(770) 754-7800. **$65-$115.** 1350 North Point Dr. SR 400, exit 9, 0.5 mi e. Int corridors. **Pets:** Accepted.
[SAVE] [✕] [&M] [🔊] [🔊] [📼] [💻] [➰]

AAA ▼▼▼ Residence Inn by Marriott ▲
(770) 664-0664. **$134-$155, 3 days notice.** 5465 Windward Pkwy W. SR 400, exit 11, 0.5 mi w. Ext/int corridors. **Pets:** Other species. $125 one-time fee/room. Service with restrictions, crate.
[SAVE] [S₀] [✕] [&M] [🔊] [🔊] [📼] [💻] [➰]

▼▼▼ Staybridge Suites M
(770) 569-7200. **$127-$150.** 3980 North Point Pkwy. SR 400, exit 10, 0.5 mi e. Int corridors. **Pets:** Accepted.
[ASK] [S₀] [✕] [&M] [🔊] [🔊] [📼] [💻] [➰]

AAA ▼▼▼ Wellesley Inn & Suites M
(770) 569-1730. **$74-$89.** 3329 Old Milton Pkwy. SR 400, exit 10, just e. Int corridors. **Pets:** Accepted.
[SAVE] [S₀] [✕] [&M] [🔊] [📼] [💻] [➰]

ATLANTA

AAA ▼▼ Baymont Inn & Suites-Atlanta Lenox/Buckhead M
(404) 321-0999. **$59-$79.** 2535 Chantilly Dr NE. I-85, exit 88 southbound; exit 86 northbound, 2 mi on Buford Hwy to Lenox Rd, just e, under highway. Int corridors. **Pets:** Accepted.
[SAVE] [S₀] [✕] [🔊] [📼] [💻]

AAA ▼▼▼ Best Western Granada Suite Hotel M
(404) 876-6100. **$104-$219.** 1302 W Peachtree St. I-75/85, exit 250, just e on 14th, just n on W Peachtree to 16th St. Int corridors. **Pets:** Medium. $40 one-time fee/room. Service with restrictions.
[SAVE] [S₀] [✕] [📼] [💻]

AAA ▼▼▼ Best Western Inn at the Peachtrees M
(404) 577-6970. **$95-$249.** 330 W Peachtree St. I-75/85, exit 248C northbound, 0.4 mi w to Peachtree St, 0.3 mi n; exit 249C southbound, just s to Peachtree Pl, just e. Ext/int corridors. **Pets:** Accepted.
[SAVE] [S₀] [✕] [📼] [💻]

▼▼ Beverly Hills Inn Ⓜ
(404) 233-8520. **$110, 3 days notice.** 65 Sheridan Dr NE.
From jct Piedmont and Peachtree rds, 1.1 mi s on Peachtree to Sheridan Dr, just e. Int corridors. **Pets:** $50 one-time
fee/room. Service with restrictions.

🖬 💻

▼▼▼ Crowne Plaza-Atlanta Powers Ferry Ⓗ
(770) 955-1700. **$69-$179.** 6345 Powers Ferry Rd NW.
I-285, exit 22, southeast corner. Int corridors.
Pets: Accepted.

Ⓐ🆂Ⓚ 🆂 ☒ 🆕 🖉 🅕 🖬 💻 🍽 🚭

▼▼▼ Four Points Hotel Atlanta Perimeter Ⓗ
(770) 394-5000. **$99-$159, 14 days notice.** 1850 Cotillion
Dr. I-285, exit 30, 0.5 mi w, northeast corner. Int corridors.
Pets: Accepted.

Ⓐ🆂Ⓚ 🆂 ☒ 🖉 🅕 🖬 💻 🍽 🚭

⦿ ▼▼◈▼▼ Four Seasons Hotel
        Atlanta Ⓗ ❀
(404) 881-9898. **$260.** 75 14th St. I-75/85, exit 250, 0.3 mi
e. Int corridors. **Pets:** Small. Designated rooms, service
with restrictions, supervision.

☒ 🆕 🖉 🍽 🚭

⦿ ▼▼ ▼▼ Grand Hyatt Atlanta Ⓗ
(404) 365-8100. **$224.** 3300 Peachtree Rd. Corner of
Peachtree and Piedmont rds. Int corridors. **Pets:** Small. $50
deposit/pet, $50 one-time fee/pet. Service with restrictions,
crate.

🆂 ☒ 🆕 🖉 🅕 🖬 💻 🍽 🚭

▼▼▼ Hawthorn Suites-Atlanta NW Ⓐ ❀
(770) 952-9595. **$109.** 1500 Parkwood Cir. I-75, exit 260,
0.5 mi e, 0.3 mi s on Powers Ferry Rd. Ext corridors.
Pets: Medium, other species. $100 one-time fee/room.
Service with restrictions.

Ⓐ🆂Ⓚ 🆂 ☒ 🅕 🖬 💻 🚭

▼▼▼ Holiday Inn Select Atlanta Perimeter Ⓜ
(770) 457-6363. **$79-$159.** 4386 Chamblee-Dunwoody Rd.
I-285, exit 30 eastbound, southwest corner; westbound follow access road 1.3 mi to Chamblee-Dunwoody Rd, just s,
northeast corner. Int corridors. **Pets:** Medium. $100 deposit/
room, $25 one-time fee/room. Service with restrictions,
supervision.

Ⓐ🆂Ⓚ 🆂 ☒ 🆕 🖉 🅕 🖬 💻 🍽 🚭

▼▼◈▼ Homestead Studio Suites-Atlanta/North
        Druid Hills Ⓜ ❀
(404) 325-1223. **$79-$89, 3 days notice.** 1339 Executive
Park Dr NE. I-85, exit 89, just e to Executive Park Dr, just s.
Ext corridors. **Pets:** Large, other species. $75 one-time fee/
room. Service with restrictions.

Ⓐ🆂Ⓚ 🆂 ☒ 🆕 🖉 🅕 🖬 💻

▼▼◈▼ Homestead Studio
        Suites-Atlanta/Perimeter Ⓜ ❀
(770) 522-0025. **$79.** 1050 Hammond Dr. I-285, exit 18
eastbound, 0.5 mi n to Hammond Dr, 0.5 mi e; exit 30
westbound, just n, then just w. Ext corridors. **Pets:** Medium,
other species. $75 one-time fee/pet. Service with restric-
tions, supervision.

Ⓐ🆂Ⓚ 🆂 ☒ 🆕 🖉 🅕 🖬 💻

▼▼▼ Homewood Suites-Cumberland Ⓐ
(770) 988-9449. **$129-$189.** 3200 Cobb Pkwy SW. I-285,
exit 19 eastbound; exit 20 westbound, 0.7 mi se on US 41
(Cobb Pkwy). Ext/int corridors. **Pets:** Accepted.

🆂🆅🅴 🆂 ☒ 🆕 🖉 🅕 💻 🚭

▼▼▼ La Quinta Inn & Suites Ⓜ
(770) 801-9002. **$71-$115.** 2415 Paces Ferry Rd SE. I-285,
exit 18, just w. Int corridors. **Pets:** Small, other species.
Service with restrictions, crate.

🆂🆅🅴 ☒ 🆕 🖉 🅕 🖬 💻 🚭

⦿ ▼▼▼ La Quinta Inn &
        Suites-Perimeter Ⓜ
(770) 350-6177. **$65-$125.** 6260 Peachtree-Dunwoody.
I-285, exit 28 westbound, 0.7 mi n; exit 26 eastbound, 0.5
mi n to Hammond Dr, 0.7 mi e, then 0.5 mi n. Int corridors.
Pets: Other species. Service with restrictions.

🆂🆅🅴 ☒ 🆕 🖉 🅕 🖬 💻 🚭

▼ Masters Inn Six Flags Ⓜ
(404) 696-4690. **$48-$58, 3 days notice.** 4120 Fulton
Industrial Blvd. I-20, exit 49, just n. Ext corridors.
Pets: Accepted.

Ⓐ🆂Ⓚ 🆂 ☒ 🖬 🍽 🚭

⦿ ▼▼ ▼▼ Park Inn-6 Flags Ⓜ
(404) 696-4391. **$59-$69, 14 days notice.** 4265 Shirley Dr
SW. I-20, exit 49, just s. Ext corridors. **Pets:** Accepted.

🆂🆅🅴 🆂 ☒ 🖉

▼▼ Ramada Inn & Conference Center Ⓜ
(404) 873-4661. **Call for rates.** 418 Armour Dr NE. I-85,
exit 86 to Monroe Dr, just e to Armour Dr, 0.3 mi w. Ext
corridors. **Pets:** Accepted.

Ⓐ🆂Ⓚ ☒ 🆕 🖉 🅕 💻 🍽 🚭

⦿ ▼▼ ▼▼ Red Roof Inn-Druid Hills Ⓜ
(404) 321-1653. **$54-$69.** 1960 N Druid Hills Rd. I-85, exit
89, just w. Ext corridors. **Pets:** Accepted.

🆂🆅🅴 ☒ 🖉

⦿ ▼▼▼ Residence
        Inn-Buckhead/Lenox Ⓐ ❀
(404) 467-1660. **$250.** 2220 Lake Blvd. I-85, exit 89, 1.6 mi
w on N Druid Hills which becomes E Roxboro, just n on
Lenox Park Blvd. Int corridors. **Pets:** Small, other species.
$150 one-time fee/room. Service with restrictions, crate.

🆂🆅🅴 🆂 ☒ 🆕 🖉 🅕 🖬 💻 🚭

⦿ ▼▼▼ Residence Inn by
        Marriott-Atlanta/Buckhead Ⓐ
(404) 239-0677. **$79-$195.** 2960 Piedmont Rd NE. I-85, exit
86, 1.5 mi n. Ext corridors. **Pets:** Medium. $150 one-time
fee/room. Service with restrictions.

🆂🆅🅴 🆂 ☒ 🖉 🅕 🖬 💻 🚭

⦿ ▼▼▼ Residence Inn by Marriott Atlanta
        Dunwoody Ⓐ
(770) 455-4446. **$99-$109.** 1901 Savoy Dr. I-285, exit 30,
just e. Ext corridors. **Pets:** Accepted.

🆂🆅🅴 ☒ 🖉 🖬 💻 🚭

Residence Inn by Marriott Midtown Ⓐ
(404) 872-8885. **$99-$174.** 1041 W Peachtree St. I-75/85, exit 250, just e to W Peachtree St, just n; corner of 11th St. Int corridors. **Pets:** Accepted.

Residence Inn by Marriott-Perimeter West Ⓐ ❀
(404) 252-5066. **$139-$179, 3 days notice.** 6096 Barfield Rd. I-285, exit 26 eastbound, 0.5 mi n on Glenridge to Hammond, 0.3 mi e to Barfield Rd; exit 28 westbound (Peachtree-Dunwoody Rd), 0.5 mi n to Hammond Dr, just w. Ext corridors. **Pets:** Medium, other species. $100 one-time fee/room. Service with restrictions.

Staybridge Suites Atlanta Perimeter Ⓜ
(678) 320-0111. **$169.** 4601 Ridgeview Rd. I-285, exit 29, 0.5 mi n, 0.5 mi w on Perimeter Center W, just n. Int corridors. **Pets:** Accepted.

Summerfield Suites by Wyndham-Atlanta/Buckhead Ⓐ
(404) 262-7880. **$115-$149.** 505 Pharr Rd. Pharr Rd and Maple Dr, just w of Piedmont. Ext/int corridors. **Pets:** Accepted.

Summerfield Suites by Wyndham-Atlanta/Perimeter Ⓐ
(404) 250-0110. **$105-$139.** 760 Mt Vernon Hwy NE. I-285, exit 25, 0.8 mi n on Roswell Rd, 1 mi e. Ext/int corridors. **Pets:** Accepted.

Swissotel Ⓗ ❀
(404) 365-0065. **$190-$240.** 3391 Peachtree Rd NE. Adjacent to Lenox Mall. Int corridors. **Pets:** Small. $50 one-time fee/room. Designated rooms, service with restrictions, crate.

University Inn at Emory Ⓜ ❀
(404) 634-7327. **$89-$134, 3 days notice.** 1767 N Decatur Rd. I-85, exit 91, 3.8 mi s on Clairmont Rd to N Decatur Rd, then 0.8 mi w. Ext corridors. **Pets:** $15 daily fee/pet.

W Atlanta Ⓗ
(770) 396-6800. **$109-$379.** 111 Perimeter Center W. I-285, exit 29, 0.3 mi n to Perimeter Center W. Int corridors. **Pets:** Accepted.

Wellesley Inn & Suites Ⓜ
(770) 226-0242. **$109.** 2225 Interstate North Pkwy W. I-75, exit 260, just e to Interstate North Pkwy, just s. Int corridors. **Pets:** Accepted.

The Westin Atlanta North Ⓗ
(770) 395-3900. **$89-$169.** 7 Concourse Pkwy. I-285, exit 28 westbound; exit 26 eastbound, just n to Hammond Dr, just e. Int corridors. **Pets:** Large, other species. $50 deposit/room. Service with restrictions.

AUSTELL

La Quinta-Atlanta West/Six Flags Ⓜ
(770) 944-2110. **$55-$95.** 7377 Six Flags Dr. I-20, exit 46, just n. Ext/int corridors. **Pets:** Small, other species. Service with restrictions.

COLLEGE PARK

AmeriSuites Ⓜ
(770) 994-2997. **$98.** 1899 Sullivan Rd. I-85, exit 71, 0.8 mi e on Riverdale Rd, 0.5 mi s; I-285, exit 60 (Riverdale Rd N), 1 mi to Sullivan Rd, 0.5 mi sw. Int corridors. **Pets:** Accepted.

Atlanta Airport Marriott Ⓗ
(404) 766-7900. **$89-$174, 3 days notice.** 4711 Best Rd. I-85, exit 71, just w, se on access road to Best Rd, just s. Int corridors. **Pets:** Medium. $50 one-time fee/pet. Service with restrictions, supervision.

La Quinta Inn Airport Ⓜ
(404) 768-1241. **$55-$75.** 4874 Old National Hwy. I-85, exit 69; I-285, exit 62, northeast corner. Ext corridors. **Pets:** Accepted.

Ramada Hotel Atlanta Airport South Ⓜ
(770) 996-4321. **$62, 3 days notice.** 1551 Phoenix Blvd. I-285, exit 60, just sw. Ext/int corridors. **Pets:** Accepted.

Red Roof Inn Airport Ⓜ
(404) 761-9701. **$42-$54.** 2471 Old National Pkwy. I-85, exit 69; I-285, exit 62, just s. Ext corridors. **Pets:** Accepted.

DECATUR

Days Inn I-20 East Ⓜ
(770) 981-5670. **Call for rates.** 4300 Snapfinger Woods Dr. I-20, exit 68, 0.3 mi e. Ext corridors. **Pets:** Accepted.

DORAVILLE

Masters Inn Ⓜ
(770) 454-8373. **$43-$53.** 3092 Presidential Pkwy. I-85, exit 94, just e, then n. Ext corridors. **Pets:** Medium. $5 daily fee/pet. Designated rooms, service with restrictions, supervision.

DOUGLASVILLE

▼▼▼▼ Comfort Inn **M**
(678) 504-2000. **$79-$99, 14 days notice.** 5487 Westmoreland Plaza. I-20, exit 37, northeast corner. Int corridors. **Pets:** Accepted.
🅂🄰🅅🄴 🆂🄳 ☒ 🖉 🕭 🖬 🖵 ⤶

DULUTH

▼▼ Days Inn Gwinnett Place **M**
(770) 476-8700. **$70-$90, 15 days notice.** 1920 Pleasant Hill Rd. I-85, exit 104, northwest corner. Int corridors. **Pets:** Other species. $10 daily fee/pet. Service with restrictions, crate.
🅂🄰🅅🄴 🆂🄳 ☒

▲▲▲ ▼▼▼▼ Hampton Inn & Suites-Gwinnett **M**
(770) 931-9800. **$109.** 1725 Pineland Rd. I-85, exit 104, 0.3 mi e to Crestwood, just s. Int corridors. **Pets:** Accepted.
🅂🄰🅅🄴 🆂🄳 ☒ �figM 🖉 🕭 🖬 🖵 ⤶

▲▲▲ ▼▼▼▼ Wellesley Inn & Suites **M**
(770) 623-6800. **$89.** 3390 Venture Pkwy NW. I-85, exit 104, just w to Venture Pkwy, just n. Int corridors. **Pets:** Small. Service with restrictions, crate.
🅂🄰🅅🄴 🆂🄳 ☒ �figM 🖉 🖬 🖵 ⤶

EAST POINT

▼▼▼▼ Crowne Plaza Atlanta Airport **H**
(404) 768-6660. **$89-$179.** 1325 Virginia Ave. I-85, exit 73 southbound; exit 73B northbound, just w. Int corridors. **Pets:** Accepted.
🄰🅂🄺 🆂🄳 ☒ �figM 🖉 🅲 🕭 🖬 🖵 🍴 ⤶

▼▼▼▼ Drury Inn & Suites Atlanta Airport **M**
(404) 761-4900. **$70-$120.** 1270 Virginia Ave. I-85, exit 73 southbound; exit 73A northbound, just e. Int corridors. **Pets:** Accepted.
☒ �figM 🖉 🅲 🕭 🖬 🖵 ⤶

▼▼▼▼ Holiday Inn Atlanta Airport North **MI**
(404) 762-8411. **$79-$139.** 1380 Virginia Ave. I-85, exit 73 southbound; exit 73B northbound, just w. Ext/int corridors. **Pets:** Accepted.
🄰🅂🄺 🆂🄳 ☒ �figM 🖉 🅲 🕭 🖬 🖵 🍴 ⤶

FOREST PARK

▲▲▲ ▼▼▼ Motel 6 **M**
(404) 363-6429. **$48.** 5060 Frontage Rd. I-75, exit 237, southeast corner. Int corridors. **Pets:** Accepted.
🅂🄰🅅🄴 🆂🄳 ☒

▲▲▲ ▼▼▼ Super 8 Motel **M**
(404) 363-8811. **$49-$59, 15 days notice.** 410 Old Dixie Way. I-75, exit 235, just e. Ext corridors. **Pets:** Accepted.
🅂🄰🅅🄴 🆂🄳 ☒ 🅲 🕭 ⤶

HAPEVILLE

▲▲▲ ▼▼▼ ▼▼▼ Hilton Atlanta Airport **H**
(404) 767-9000. **$75-$139.** 1031 Virginia Ave. I-85, exit 73 southbound; exit 73A northbound, just e. Int corridors. **Pets:** Large.
🅂🄰🅅🄴 ☒ �figM 🖉 🕭 🖬 🖵 🍴 ⤶

JONESBORO

▲▲▲ ▼▼▼▼ Holiday Inn Atlanta South Jonesboro **MI**
(770) 968-4300. **$79-$109.** 6288 Old Dixie Hwy. I-75, exit 235, just w. Int corridors. **Pets:** Accepted.
🅂🄰🅅🄴 🆂🄳 ☒ �figM 🖉 🅲 🖵 🍴 ⤶

▲▲▲ ▼▼▼ ▼ Shoneys Inn-Atlanta South **M**
(770) 968-5018. **$49-$53, 3 days notice.** 6358 Old Dixie Rd. I-75, exit 235, just w. Ext corridors. **Pets:** Small, other species. $6 daily fee/pet. Designated rooms, service with restrictions, supervision.
🅂🄰🅅🄴 🆂🄳 ☒ 🕭 🖵 ⤶

KENNESAW

▲▲▲ ▼▼▼ Best Western Kennesaw Inn **M**
(770) 424-7666. **$59-$79, 7 days notice.** 3375 Busbee Dr. I-75, exit 271, just e. Ext corridors. **Pets:** Accepted.
🅂🄰🅅🄴 🆂🄳 ☒ 🕭 🖵 ⤶

▲▲▲ ▼▼▼▼ Country Inn & Suites By Carlson **M**
(770) 423-7105. **$75-$89, 14 days notice.** 3192 Barrett Lakes Blvd. I-75, exit 271, just w to Barrett Lakes Blvd, just s. Int corridors. **Pets:** Accepted.
🅂🄰🅅🄴 🆂🄳 ☒ �figM 🖉 🕭 🖵 ⤶

▲▲▲ ▼▼▼ ▼ Red Roof Inn-Town Center Mall **M**
(770) 429-0323. **$44-$54.** 520 Roberts Ct NW. I-75, exit 269, southeast corner. Ext corridors. **Pets:** Medium, other species. Service with restrictions, supervision.
🅂🄰🅅🄴 ☒ �figM 🖉 🅲 🕭

▲▲▲ ▼▼▼ ▼ Residence In by Marriott Town Center **A** 🐾
(770) 218-1018. **$130.** 3443 Busbee Dr. I-75, exit 271, just e. Int corridors. **Pets:** Other species. $8 daily fee/room, $100 one-time fee/room.
🅂🄰🅅🄴 🆂🄳 ☒ �figM 🖉 🅲 🕭 🖵 ⤶

▲▲▲ ▼▼▼ Rodeway Inn **M**
(770) 590-0519. **$42-$60.** 1460 George Busbee Pkwy. I-75, exit 273, just e. Ext corridors. **Pets:** Accepted.
🅂🄰🅅🄴 🆂🄳 ☒ 🕭 🖵 ⤶

LITHONIA

▲▲▲ ▼▼▼▼ La Quinta Inn Panola Road **M**
(770) 981-6411. **$51-$75.** 2859 Panola Rd. I-20, exit 71, just n. Ext/int corridors. **Pets:** Accepted.
🅂🄰🅅🄴 ☒ 🖉 🕭 🖵 ⤶

MARIETTA

◈◈◈ ▽▽▽ Best Inn Marietta M
(770) 955-0004. **$61.** 1255 Franklin Rd. I-75, exit 261, 0.3 mi w to Franklin Rd, just s. Int corridors. **Pets:** Medium, other species. $10 one-time fee/room. Service with restrictions, supervision.
SAVE Sd ⊠ 🖥 💻 ⊇

▽▽▽ Drury Inn & Suites-Atlanta Northwest M
(770) 612-0900. **$60-$100.** 1170 Powers Ferry Pl. I-75, exit 261, just e. Int corridors. **Pets:** Medium, other species. Service with restrictions, crate.
⊠ &M 🗐 🖳 🖥 💻 ⊇

◈◈◈ ▽▽ Econo Lodge Northwest M
(770) 952-0052. **$49.** 1940 Leland Dr. I-75, exit 260, just e, then 0.3 mi n. Ext/int corridors. **Pets:** Small. No service, crate.
SAVE Sd ⊠ 🖥 💻

▽▽▽ Homestead Studio Suites-Atlanta/Wildwood/ Powers Ferry M
(770) 303-0043. **$69.** 2239 Powers Ferry Rd. I-285, exit 22, just n. Int corridors. **Pets:** Accepted.
ASK Sd ⊠ &M 🗐 🖳 🖥 💻

◈◈◈ ▽▽▽ La Quinta Inn Marietta M ✿
(770) 951-0026. **$55-$75.** 2170 Delk Rd. I-75, exit 261, 0.3 mi w. Ext/int corridors. **Pets:** Small. Service with restrictions, supervision.
SAVE ⊠ 🗐 🖥 💻 ⊇

◈◈◈ ▽▽ Masters Inn Marietta M
(770) 951-2005. **$43-$53.** 2682 Windy Hill Rd. I-75, exit 260, just w, Circle 75, then just w. Ext corridors. **Pets:** Accepted.
SAVE Sd ⊠ 🖥

▽▽▽ Ramada Inn-Atlanta North M ✿
(770) 952-3251. **$63.** 2767 Windy Hill Rd. I-75, exit 260, just e. Ext corridors. **Pets:** Medium, other species. $25 one-time fee/pet. Designated rooms, service with restrictions, supervision.
ASK Sd ⊠ &M 🖳 🖥 💻 🍴 ⊇

◈◈◈ ▽▽▽ Ramada Limited Suites M
(770) 919-7878. **$48-$59.** 630 Franklin Rd. I-75, exit 263, 0.3 mi w to Franklin Rd, 0.3 mi s. Ext corridors. **Pets:** Accepted.
SAVE Sd ⊠ 🗐 🖳 🖥 💻 ⊇

◈◈◈ ▽▽▽ Super 8 Motel M
(770) 919-2340. **$48-$59.** 610 Franklin Rd. I-75, exit 263, 0.3 mi w to Franklin Rd, then 0.3 mi s. Ext corridors. **Pets:** Accepted.
SAVE Sd ⊠ 🗐 🖥 ⊇

▽▽▽ Wyndham Garden Hotel-Atlanta Northwest H
(770) 428-4400. **$80-$115.** 1775 Parkway Pl NW. I-75, exit 263, southwest corner. Int corridors. **Pets:** Medium, other species. $50 one-time fee/pet. Service with restrictions, supervision.
ASK Sd ⊠ &M 🗐 🖥 💻 🍴 ⊇

MORROW

◈◈◈ ▽▽▽ Best Western Southlake Inn M
(770) 961-6300. **$59-$79.** 6437 Jonesboro Rd. I-75, exit 233, just e. Ext corridors. **Pets:** Accepted.
SAVE Sd ⊠ 🖥 ⊇

▽▽▽ Drury Inn & Suites-Atlanta South M
(770) 960-0500. **$70-$105.** 6520 S Lee St. I-75, exit 233, just e. Int corridors. **Pets:** Other species. Service with restrictions, crate.
⊠ &M 🗐 🖳 🖥 💻 ⊇

◈◈◈ ▽▽▽ Quality Inn M
(770) 960-1957. **$49-$69.** 6597 Hwy 54. I-75, exit 233, just w. Ext corridors. **Pets:** Accepted.
SAVE Sd ⊠ 🖥 💻 ⊇

◈◈◈ ▽▽ Red Roof Inn-South M
(770) 968-1483. **$44-$64.** 1348 Southlake Plaza Dr. I-75, exit 233, just e to Southlake Plaza Dr, then just n. Ext corridors. **Pets:** Accepted.
SAVE ⊠ 🗐

◈◈◈ ▽▽ Sleep Inn M
(770) 472-9800. **$63-$109, 3 days notice.** 2185 Mt Zion Pkwy. I-75, exit 231, just w to Mt Zion Pkwy, then just s. Int corridors. **Pets:** Accepted.
SAVE Sd ⊠ &M 🖥 ⊇

NORCROSS

▽▽▽ Amberley Suite Hotel M
(770) 263-0515. **$75-$109, 3 days notice.** 5885 Oakbrook Pkwy. I-85, exit 99, 0.5 mi e to Live Oak Pkwy, 0.8 mi n and w. Int corridors. **Pets:** Accepted.
ASK Sd ⊠ 🗐 🖥 💻 🍴 ⊇

◈◈◈ ▽▽▽ AmeriSuites Atlanta/Peachtree Corners M
(770) 416-7655. **$99-$109, 7 days notice.** 5600 Peachtree Pkwy. I-285, exit 31B, 4 mi n on SR 141, 1 mi n. Int corridors. **Pets:** Medium. Designated rooms, service with restrictions.
SAVE Sd ⊠ &M 🗐 🖳 🖥 💻 ⊇

▽▽▽ ClubHouse Inn & Suites M
(770) 368-9400. **$89-$109.** 5945 Oakbrook Pkwy. I-85, exit 99, 0.5 mi e to Live Oak Pkwy, 0.8 mi w. Int corridors. **Pets:** Accepted.
ASK Sd ⊠ 🖥 💻 ⊇

▽▽▽ Drury Inn & Suites-Atlanta Northeast M
(770) 729-0060. **$60-$106.** 5655 Jimmy Carter Blvd. I-85, exit 99, just w. Int corridors. **Pets:** Small, other species. No service, crate.
⊠ &M 🗐 🖳 🖥 💻 ⊇

▼▼▼ Homestead Studio
Suites-Atlanta/Norcross **M**
(770) 449-9966. **Call for rates.** 7049 Jimmy Carter Blvd. I-285, exit 31B, 4 mi n; I-85, exit 99, 4 mi n. Ext corridors. **Pets:** Accepted.

⊠ 🛄 🐾 🛎 💷

▼▼▼▼ Homewood Suites by Hilton **A**
(770) 448-4663. **$109, 14 days notice.** 450 Technology Pkwy. I-85, exit 99, 4 mi w to Peachtree Industrial Blvd, 0.4 mi n, w on Holcomb Bridge Rd, 2 blks n on Peachtree Pkwy; I-285, exit 23B, 5 mi n on SR 141. Ext/int corridors. **Pets:** Accepted.

🅂 🔊 ⊠ 🛄 🐾 🛎 💷 🏊

🅰 ▼▼▼ La Quinta Inn-Jimmy Carter **M**
(770) 448-8686. **$55-$75.** 6187 Dawson Blvd. I-85, exit 99, just e to McDonough Dr, just s. Ext corridors. **Pets:** Small. Service with restrictions, crate.

🅂 ⊠ 💷 🏊

🅰 ▼▼▼ La Quinta-Peachtree **M**
(770) 449-5144. **$55-$75.** 5375 Peachtree Industrial Blvd. I-285, exit 31B, 5.5 mi n; I-85, exit 99, 4 mi w to Peachtree Industrial Blvd, 1.5 mi n. Ext/int corridors. **Pets:** Small, other species. Service with restrictions.

🅂 ⊠ 🐾 🛎 💷 🏊

▼▼▼▼ Northeast Atlanta Hilton **H**
(770) 447-4747. **$74-$114.** 5993 Peachtree Industrial Blvd. I-285, exit 31B, 4.5 mi ne. Int corridors. **Pets:** Accepted.

🅂 🔊 ⊠ 🛄 🐾 🛎 💷 🍽 🏊

▼▼ Red Roof Inn & Suites **M**
(770) 446-2882. **$60-$80, 7 days notice.** 5395 Peachtree Industrial Blvd. I-285, exit 31B, 5.5 mi n; I-85, exit 99, 4 mi w to Peachtree Industrial Blvd, 1.5 mi n. Int corridors. **Pets:** Accepted.

🅰🅂🄺 🔊 ⊠ 🛄 🐾 🛎 💷 🏊

🅰 ▼▼▼ Red Roof Inn-Indian Trail **M**
(770) 448-8944. **$41-$49.** 5171 Brook Hollow Pkwy. I-85, exit 101, just w to Brook Hollow Pkwy, just s. Ext corridors. **Pets:** Small. Service with restrictions, supervision.

🅂 ⊠ 🐾 🛄

▼▼ Rodeway Inn **M**
(770) 449-7322. **$59-$79, 3 days notice.** 6045 Oakbrook Pkwy. I-85, exit 99, just e to Live Oak Pkwy, 1 mi n and w. Ext/int corridors. **Pets:** Accepted.

🅂 🔊 ⊠ 🛎 💷 🏊

🅰 ▼▼▼ Shoney's Inn of Atlanta
Northeast **M**
(770) 564-0492. **$49-$69.** 2050 Willowtrail Pkwy. I-85, exit 101, just e. Ext corridors. **Pets:** Small. $25 deposit/room. Service with restrictions, supervision.

🅂 🔊 ⊠ 🛎 💷 🏊

ROSWELL

🅰 ▼▼▼ Baymont Inn & Suites
Atlanta-Roswell **M**
(770) 552-0200. **$59-$69.** 575 Old Holcomb Bridge Rd. SR 400, exit 7B, just w. Int corridors. **Pets:** Small, other species. $50 deposit/room. Designated rooms, service with restrictions, supervision.

🅂 🔊 ⊠ 🛄 🐾 🛎 💷 🏊

🅰 ▼▼▼▼ Best Western Roswell Suites **M**
(770) 552-5599. **$69-$75, 30 days notice.** 907 Holcomb Bridge Rd. SR 400, exit 7B, 0.7 mi w. Int corridors. **Pets:** Small. $25 one-time fee/pet. Designated rooms, service with restrictions, supervision.

🅂 🔊 ⊠ 🛄 🐾 🛄 🛎 💷 🏊

🅰 ▼▼▼▼ Brookwood Inn **M**
(770) 587-5161. **$49-$69.** 9995 Old Dogwood Rd. SR 400, exit 7B, just w to Old Dogwood Rd, just n. Ext corridors. **Pets:** Accepted.

🅂 ⊠ 🐾 💷 🏊

SMYRNA

▼▼ ▼▼ Microtel Inn **M**
(404) 799-7000. **$65, 14 days notice.** 5300 S Cobb Dr SE. I-285, exit 15, just e. Int corridors. **Pets:** Accepted.

🅰🅂🄺 🔊 ⊠ 🛄 🛄 🛎

🅰 ▼▼▼ Red Roof Inn-North **M**
(770) 952-6966. **$44-$54.** 2200 Corporate Plaza. I-75, exit 260, just w to Corporate Plaza, just s. Ext corridors. **Pets:** Small, other species. Service with restrictions, supervision.

🅂 ⊠

SUWANEE

▼▼▼▼ Holiday Inn **MI**
(770) 945-4921. **$69, 5 days notice.** 2955 Hwy 317. I-85, exit 111. Ext corridors. **Pets:** Accepted.

🅰🅂🄺 🔊 ⊠ 🛄 🛎 💷 🍽 🏊

TUCKER

▼▼▼▼ Hawthorn Suites Ltd **M** ❀
(770) 496-1070. **$62-$89.** 2060 Crescent Centre Blvd. I-285, exit 37, 0.5 mi se. Int corridors. **Pets:** Small. $75 one-time fee/room. Service with restrictions, supervision.

🅰🅂🄺 🔊 ⊠ 🐾 🛎 💷 🏊

🅰 ▼▼ Masters Inn Tucker **M**
(770) 938-3552. **$39-$49.** 1435 Montreal Rd. I-285, exit 38, just w. Ext corridors. **Pets:** Medium. $5 daily fee/pet. Designated rooms, service with restrictions, supervision.

🅂 🔊 ⊠ 🛎

🅰 ▼▼▼ Red Roof Inn-Atlanta (Tucker NE) **M**
(770) 496-1311. **$42-$52.** 2810 Lawrenceville Hwy. I-285, exit 38, just w. Ext corridors. **Pets:** Large, other species. Service with restrictions, crate.

🅂 ⊠ 🐾

UNION CITY

▼▼▼▼ Holiday Inn Express Hotel & Suites M
(770) 969-4567. **$55-$99.** 6743 Shannon Pkwy. I-85, exit 64, 0.3 mi w, just n. Int corridors. **Pets:** Medium, other species. Service with restrictions, supervision.
☒ Ⓜ ⓢ 🖩 💻 🐾

▼▼ Red Roof Inn M
(770) 306-7750. **$56.** 6710 Shannon Pkwy. I-85, exit 64, 0.3 mi w, just n. Int corridors. **Pets:** Large, other species. $10 daily fee/pet. Service with restrictions, supervision.
ASK ⓢ ☒ ⓢ 🖩 🐾

❖ 🐾 **END METROPOLITAN AREA** 🐾 ❖

AUGUSTA

⟨AAA⟩ ▼▼▼▼ AmeriSuites M
(706) 733-4656. **$62.** 1062 Claussen Rd. I-20, exit 200 westbound, just nw; exit 199 eastbound, 0.6 mi ne on service road. Int corridors. **Pets:** Other species. $30 one-time fee/pet. Designated rooms, service with restrictions, crate.
SAVE ☒ ⓢ 🖩 💻 🐾

▼▼▼ Comfort Inn M
(706) 855-6060. **$65.** 629 Frontage Rd NW. I-20, exit 196B, 0.3 mi n to Scott Nixon Memorial, just w, then 0.3 mi s. Int corridors. **Pets:** Accepted.
SAVE ⓢ ☒ 🖩 💻 🐾

⟨AAA⟩ ▼▼▼▼ Comfort Inn Medical Center M
(706) 722-2224. **$51-$225, 14 days notice.** 1455 Walton Way. I-20, exit 200, 4.5 mi e on SR 104, then turn right on 15th St, 4 lights then left. Ext corridors. **Pets:** Small, other species. $50 deposit/room. Service with restrictions, supervision.
SAVE ⓢ ☒ ⓢ 🖩 💻 🐾

⟨AAA⟩ ▼▼▼▼ Holiday Inn Augusta-West MI
(706) 738-8811. **$79.** 1075 Stevens Creek Rd. I-20, exit 199, just ne on service road. Ext corridors. **Pets:** Medium. $25 one-time fee/room. Service with restrictions, crate.
SAVE ⓢ ☒ ⓢ 🖩 💻 ⫟ 🐾

▼▼▼ Holiday Inn Gordon Highway at Bobby Jones MI
(706) 737-2300. **$69-$80.** 2155 Gordon Hwy. I-520, exit 3A, at jct SR 78 and 278. Ext corridors. **Pets:** Other species. $35 one-time fee/room. Service with restrictions, supervision.
ASK ⓢ ☒ 🖩 💻 ⫟ 🐾

⟨AAA⟩ ▼▼▼▼ La Quinta Inn M
(706) 733-2660. **$55-$75.** 3020 Washington Rd. I-20, exit 199 (Washington Rd), just n. Ext/int corridors. **Pets:** Accepted.
SAVE ☒ Ⓜ 🎔 🖩 💻 🐾

▼▼▼ The Partridge Inn H
(706) 737-8888. **$109-$135.** 2110 Walton Way. 1.3 mi w off 15th St. Int corridors. **Pets:** Medium, other species. $25 one-time fee/room. Service with restrictions, supervision.
ASK ⓢ ☒ 🖩 💻 ⫟ 🐾

⟨AAA⟩ ▼▼▼▼ Radisson Riverfront Hotel H
(706) 722-8900. **$119.** 2 10th St. On Riverwalk at 10th and Reynolds. Int corridors. **Pets:** Medium. $25 one-time fee/room. Service with restrictions, crate.
SAVE ☒ Ⓜ 🎔 🖩 💻 ⫟ 🐾

⟨AAA⟩ ▼▼▼▼ Radisson Suites Inn MI
(706) 868-1800. **$75, 7 days notice.** 3038 Washington Rd. I-20, exit 199, 0.3 mi n. Ext corridors. **Pets:** Small. $25 one-time fee/room. Service with restrictions, supervision.
SAVE ⓢ ☒ 🖩 💻 ⫟ 🐾

⟨AAA⟩ ▼▼▼▼ Sheraton Augusta Hotel H
(706) 855-8100. **$89-$135.** 2651 Perimeter Pkwy. I-520, exit 1C (Wheeler Rd), entrance 0.3 mi w. Int corridors. **Pets:** Accepted.
SAVE ⓢ ☒ Ⓜ 🖩 💻 ⫟ 🐾

BAINBRIDGE

▼▼▼▼ Jameson Inn M
(229) 243-7000. **$55-$70.** 1403 Tallahassee Hwy. Just s of US 84 Bypass on US 27. Ext corridors. **Pets:** Very small, other species. Service with restrictions, supervision.
☒ 🎔 🖩 💻 🐾

BAXLEY

⟨AAA⟩ ▼▼ Scottish Inns M
(912) 367-3652. **$40-$45.** 1179 Hatch Pkwy S. US 1 S, just s of jct SR 15. Ext corridors. **Pets:** Other species. $5 daily fee/room. Service with restrictions, supervision.
SAVE ⓢ ☒ 🖩 🐾

BLAIRSVILLE

⟨AAA⟩ ▼▼▼ Misty Mountain Inn & Cottages X
(706) 745-4786. **$65-$90.** 4376 Misty Mountain Ln. 2.7 mi s on US 19/129, 3.7 mi e on Town Creek Rd. Ext/int corridors. **Pets:** Other species. $10 one-time fee/pet. Designated rooms.
SAVE 🖩 💻 🖼

BLUE RIDGE

▼▼▼ Days Inn M
(706) 632-2100. **$45-$75.** 4970 Applachian Hwy. On SR 515 and US 76. Ext corridors. **Pets:** Accepted.
SAVE ⓢ ☒ 🖩 🐾

▼▼▼ Douglas Inn & Suites M 🐾
(706) 258-3600. **$50-$80.** 1192 Windy Ridge Rd. Just off SR 515 and US 76. Ext corridors. **Pets:** Medium, other species. $10 daily fee/pet. Service with restrictions, supervision.
ASK ⓢ ☒ 🖩 💻 🐾

BRUNSWICK

Baymont Inn & Suites-Brunswick M
(912) 265-7725. **$64-$69.** 105 Tourist Dr. I-95, exit 36A, 0.3 mi se. Int corridors. **Pets:** Other species. Service with restrictions, supervision.
SAVE S X 🐾 🛏 💻 ➿

Best Western Brunswick Inn M 🐾
(912) 264-0144. **$59-$69.** 5323 New Jesup Hwy. I-95, exit 36B, just w on US 341. Ext corridors. **Pets:** Service with restrictions.
SAVE S X 🛏 ➿

Embassy Suites Hotel H 🐾
(912) 264-6100. **$99-$144.** 500 Mall Blvd. I-95, exit 38, 1.5 mi s on SR 25. Int corridors. **Pets:** $10 daily fee/room. Service with restrictions, crate.
SAVE S X 🐾 🛏 💻 ➿

Holiday Inn I-95 M
(912) 264-4033. **$69-$99.** 5252 New Jesup Hwy. I-95, exit 36B, northwest corner, on US 341. Ext corridors. **Pets:** Other species. $10 daily fee/room. Service with restrictions, supervision.
SAVE S X 🐾 💻 🍽 ➿

Ramada Inn I-95 M
(912) 264-3621. **$59-$67.** 3040 Scarlet St. I-95, exit 36A, just e on US 341 and 25. Ext corridors. **Pets:** Small, other species. $10 one-time fee/room. Designated rooms, service with restrictions, supervision.
SAVE S X 🐾 🛏 💻 🍽 ➿

Red Roof Inn & Suites M
(912) 264-4720. **$59-$75.** 121 Tourist Dr. I-95, exit 36A, southeast corner. Int corridors. **Pets:** Accepted.
ASK S X 🐾 🛏 ➿

Super 8 Motel M
(912) 264-8800. **$51-$56.** 5280 New Jesup Hwy. I-95, exit 36B, just w. Int corridors. **Pets:** Accepted.
ASK S X 🛏

BYRON

Best Western Inn and Suites M 🐾
(478) 956-3056. **$56.** 101 Dunbar Rd (Hwy 49). I-75, exit 149, southeast corner. Ext corridors. **Pets:** Medium. $10 daily fee/room. Service with restrictions, supervision.
SAVE S X 🐾 🛏 ➿

Holiday Inn Express Hotel & Suites M
(478) 956-7829. **$64-$82, 14 days notice.** 102 Holiday Ct. I-75, exit 149, just e. Int corridors. **Pets:** Small. $25 one-time fee/pet. Designated rooms, service with restrictions, supervision.
X 🐾 🐾 🛏 💻 ➿

CALHOUN

Budget Host Shepherd Motel M
(706) 629-8644. **$38-$42.** 1007 Fairmount Hwy SE. I-75, exit 312, just e. Ext corridors. **Pets:** Large, other species. Service with restrictions.
SAVE S X 🐾 🛏 ➿

Knights Inn of Calhoun M
(706) 629-4521. **$33-$36.** 2261 US 41 NE. I-75, exit 318, just e. Ext corridors. **Pets:** Accepted.
SAVE S X 🛏 ➿

Quality Inn M
(706) 629-9501. **$54-$60.** 915 Hwy 53 E SE. I-75, exit 312, just e. Ext corridors. **Pets:** Very small. $6 one-time fee/pet. Service with restrictions, supervision.
SAVE S X 🛏 💻 🍽 ➿

Ramada Limited M
(706) 629-9207. **$45-$59, 7 days notice.** 1204 Red Bud Rd NE. I-75, exit 315, just w. Ext corridors. **Pets:** Very small. $5 daily fee/room. No service, supervision.
SAVE S X 🐾 ➿

CARROLLTON

Best Western Crossroads M
(770) 832-2611. **Call for rates.** 1202 S Park St. Jct US 27 and SR 166. Ext corridors. **Pets:** Accepted.
ASK X 🛏 💻 🍽 ➿

Jameson Inn M
(770) 834-2600. **$55-$70.** 700 S Park St. Just s of downtown, on US 27. Ext corridors. **Pets:** Very small, dogs only. Service with restrictions, supervision.
M 🐾 🛏 ➿

CARTERSVILLE

Budget Host Inn M
(770) 386-0350. **$35-$45.** 851 Cass-White Rd. I-75, exit 296, just w. Ext corridors. **Pets:** Other species. $2 daily fee/pet. Service with restrictions, supervision.
ASK S X ➿

Comfort Inn M
(770) 387-1800. **$42-$55.** 28 SR 20 Spur. I-75, exit 290, 0.3 mi se. Ext corridors. **Pets:** Small. $5 daily fee/pet. Service with restrictions, supervision.
SAVE S X 🛏 💻 ➿

Days Inn-Cartersville M
(770) 382-1824. **$44-$88, 14 days notice.** 5618 Hwy 20 SE. I-75, exit 290, just w. Ext corridors. **Pets:** Accepted.
SAVE S X 🛏 ➿

Holiday Inn M 🐾
(770) 386-0830. **$58-$69, 30 days notice.** 2336 Hwy 411 NE. I-75, exit 293, southwest corner. Int corridors. **Pets:** Small. Service with restrictions.
SAVE S X M 🐾 🛏 💻 🍽 ➿

Howard Johnson Express [M]
(770) 386-0700. **$45-$50.** 25 Carson Loop NW. I-75, exit 296, northwest corner. Ext corridors. **Pets:** Accepted.

Knights Inn [M]
(770) 386-7263. **$50-$75, 14 days notice.** 420 E Church St. I-75, exit 288, 1.5 mi w. Ext corridors. **Pets:** Small. $10 one-time fee/pet. Service with restrictions, supervision.

Motel 6–4046 [M]
(770) 386-1449. **$42.** 5657 Hwy 20 NE. I-75, exit 290, 0.3 mi e. Ext corridors. **Pets:** Other species. No service, supervision.

Super 8 Motel [M]
(770) 382-8881. **$46-$52, 10 days notice.** 41 SR 20 Spur SE. I-75, exit 290, 0.3 mi e. Int corridors. **Pets:** Other species. $5 daily fee/pet. Supervision.

CHATSWORTH

Key West Inn [M]
(706) 517-1155. **$49.** 501 GI Maddox Pkwy. Jct SR 76 and US 411. Ext corridors. **Pets:** Accepted.

CLAYTON

Shoney's Inn & Suites [M]
(706) 782-2214. **$50-$109.** 834 Hwy 441 S. 0.8 mi s on US 441 S. Ext corridors. **Pets:** Accepted.

Stonebrook Inn [M]
(706) 782-4702. **$42-$99.** 698 Hwy 441 S. On SR 441, just s of jct SR 76. Int corridors. **Pets:** Small. $50 deposit/pet, $5 daily fee/pet. Service with restrictions, crate.

COLUMBUS

Baymont Inn & Suites-Columbus [M]
(706) 323-4344. **$54-$64.** 2919 Warm Springs Rd. I-185, exit 7 southbound; exit 7A northbound, just e. Int corridors. **Pets:** Medium, other species. $50 deposit/room. Service with restrictions, supervision.

Holiday Inn North (Airport) [M]
(706) 324-0231. **$94.** 2800 Manchester Expwy. I-185, exit 7 southbound; exit 7B nothbound, just w. Int corridors. **Pets:** Accepted.

Howard Johnson Express [M]
(706) 322-6641. **$70-$77.** 1011 Veterans Pkwy. Downtown. Ext corridors. **Pets:** $25 one-time fee/pet. Service with restrictions, supervision.

La Quinta Inn [M]
(706) 568-1740. **$55-$75.** 3201 Macon Rd. I-185, exit 6, just w. Ext corridors. **Pets:** Accepted.

Motel 6 #058 [M]
(706) 687-7214. **$46.** 3050 Victory Dr. On US 280. Ext corridors. **Pets:** Accepted.

Super 8 Motel of Columbus [M]
(706) 322-6580. **$50-$68, 5 days notice.** 2935 Warm Springs Rd. I-185, exit 7 southbound; exit 7A northbound, just e. Int corridors. **Pets:** Small. $25 deposit/pet. Service with restrictions, crate.

COMMERCE

Comfort Inn [M]
(706) 335-9001. **$65-$75.** 165 Eisenhower Dr. I-85, exit 149, just nw. Ext corridors. **Pets:** Accepted.

Guesthouse Inn [M]
(706) 335-5147. **$42-$185, 3 days notice.** 30934 US 441 S. I-85, exit 149, 0.3 mi e. Ext corridors. **Pets:** Accepted.

Holiday Inn Express [M]
(706) 335-5183. **$60-$83.** 30747 US 441 S. I-85, exit 149, just e. Ext corridors. **Pets:** Accepted.

The Jameson Inn [M]
(706) 335-3738. **$55-$70.** 267 Steven B Tanger Blvd. I-85, exit 149, just nw. Ext corridors. **Pets:** Accepted.

CONYERS

La Quinta Inn & Suites [M]
(770) 918-0092. **$75-$115.** 1184 Dogwood Dr. I-20, exit 82, just n to Dogwood Dr, just w. Int corridors. **Pets:** Accepted.

Ramada Limited [M]
(770) 760-0777. **$55-$99, 7 days notice.** 1070 Dogwood Dr. I-20, exit 82, just n on SR 138, 0.5 mi w. Ext corridors. **Pets:** Accepted.

CORDELE

Best Western Colonial Inn [M]
(229) 273-5420. **$49.** 1706 16th Ave E. I-75, exit 101, just w. Ext/int corridors. **Pets:** Accepted.

Days Inn [M]
(229) 273-1123. **Call for rates.** 2115 16th Ave E. I-75, exit 101, just e on US 280. Ext corridors. **Pets:** Accepted.

Quality Inn & Suites M
(229) 273-4117. **$48.** 1711 E 16th Ave. I-75, exit 101, just w on US 280. Ext corridors. **Pets:** Accepted.
🆂🅰🆅🅴 🆂 ⓧ 🖥 💻 ➥

Ramada Inn M
(229) 273-5000. **$48-$52.** 2016 16th Ave E. I-75, exit 101, just e on US 280. Ext corridors. **Pets:** Small. $10 daily fee/pet. Service with restrictions, supervision.
🆂🅰🆅🅴 🆂 ⓧ 🖥 💻 🍴 ➥

COVINGTON

Holiday Inn Express M
(770) 787-4900. **$72-$79.** 10111 Alcovy Rd. I-20, exit 92. Ext corridors. **Pets:** Small, dogs only. $25 one-time fee/room. Service with restrictions, supervision.
🆂🅰🆅🅴 🆂 ⓧ 🆖 🖥 💻 ➥

The Jameson Inn M
(770) 784-1849. **$55-$70.** 10225 Hwy 142 N. I-20, exit 93, just s. Ext corridors. **Pets:** Very small. Service with restrictions, supervision.
ⓧ 🆖 🖥 💻 ➥

DALTON

Best Inns M
(706) 226-1100. **$52-$62.** 1529 W Walnut Ave. I-75, exit 333, just e. Ext corridors. **Pets:** Medium. Service with restrictions, supervision.
🆂🅰🆅🅴 🆂 ⓧ 💻 ➥

Best Western Inn of Dalton M
(706) 226-5022. **$50-$55.** 2106 Chattanooga Rd. I-75, exit 336, just w. Ext corridors. **Pets:** Very small. Service with restrictions, supervision.
🆂🅰🆅🅴 🆂 ⓧ 🖥 🍴 ➥

Holiday Inn M
(706) 278-0500. **$67.** 515 Holiday Dr. I-75, exit 333, northwest corner. Ext corridors. **Pets:** Medium. $10 one-time fee/room. Service with restrictions, supervision.
🅰🆂🅺 🆂 ⓧ 🖥 💻 🍴 ➥

DARIEN

Comfort Inn M
(912) 437-4200. **$79-$99.** 703 Frontage Rd. I-95, exit 49, just w. Int corridors. **Pets:** Other species. $10 daily fee/pet. Designated rooms, service with restrictions, supervision.
🆂🅰🆅🅴 🆂 ⓧ 🖥 💻 ➥

Holiday Inn Express M
(912) 437-5373. **$69, 15 days notice.** I-95 & SR 251. I-95, exit 49, just w. Int corridors. **Pets:** Accepted.
🆂🅰🆅🅴 🆂 ⓧ 🖥 ➥

DAWSONVILLE

Best Western (Dawson Village Inn) M
(706) 216-4410. **$59-$159.** 76 N Georgia Ave. 0.5 mi s of jct SR 400 and 53. Int corridors. **Pets:** Medium. $5 daily fee/pet. Service with restrictions, supervision.
🆂🅰🆅🅴 🆂 ⓧ 🆖 🖥 💻 ➥

Comfort Inn M
(706) 216-1900. **$84.** 127 Beartooth Pkwy. 0.5 mi s of jct SR 400 and 53. Int corridors. **Pets:** Accepted.
🆂🅰🆅🅴 🆂 ⓧ 🖥 💻 ➥

DILLARD

Dillard House M
(706) 746-5348. **$59-$129, 03 days notice.** 768 Franklin St. US 441, just e via Old Dillard Rd. Ext corridors. **Pets:** Small. Supervision.
🆂🅰🆅🅴 ⓧ 🖥 💻 🍴 ➥ ⌧

DUBLIN

Best Western Executive Inn & Suites M
(478) 275-2650. **$84.** 2121 Hwy 441 S. I-16, exit 51, 0.3 mi n. Ext corridors. **Pets:** Small. Service with restrictions, crate.
🆂🅰🆅🅴 🆂 ⓧ 🖥 💻 ➥

EASTMAN

The Jameson Inn M
(478) 374-7925. **$55-$70.** 103 Pine Ridge Rd. 1 mi se on US 341 and 23. Ext corridors. **Pets:** Accepted.
ⓧ 🖥 💻 ➥

FITZGERALD

Jameson Inn M
(229) 424-9500. **$55-$70.** 111 Bull Run Rd. Just n of US 319/107, on US 129. Ext corridors. **Pets:** Accepted.
ⓧ 🖥 💻 ➥

FORSYTH

Best Western Hilltop Inn M
(478) 994-9260. **$46.** 951 Hwy 42 N. I-75, exit 188. Ext corridors. **Pets:** Accepted.
🆂🅰🆅🅴 🆂 ⓧ ➥

Hampton Inn M
(478) 994-9697. **$65, 10 days notice.** 520 Holiday Cir. I-75, exit 186, just w. Int corridors. **Pets:** Small, other species. Service with restrictions, supervision.
🆂🅰🆅🅴 🆂 ⓧ 🆖 🖥 ➥

Holiday Inn Forsyth M
(478) 994-5691. **$76.** 480 Holiday Cir. I-75, exit 186, southwest corner. Ext corridors. **Pets:** Accepted.
🅰🆂🅺 🆂 ⓧ 🖥 💻 🍴 ➥

GARDEN CITY

(AAA) ▼▼▼ Masters Inn Garden City **[M]**
(912) 964-4344. **$44-$54.** 4200 Hwy 21 N; Augusta Rd. On SR 21 N, 0.3 mi nw of terminus, I-516. Int corridors. **Pets:** Accepted.
[SAVE] [S⊘] [✕] [⌖] [🛏] [⊇]

GLENNVILLE

(AAA) ▼▼▼ Cheeri-O Inn **[M]**
(912) 654-2176. **$40-$42.** 0.8 mi s on US 25 and 301. Ext corridors. **Pets:** Small. $5 daily fee/pet. Service with restrictions, supervision.
[SAVE] [S⊘] [✕] [🛏] [💻]

GOLDEN ISLES AREA

JEKYLL ISLAND

(AAA) ▼▼▼▼ Clarion Resort Buccaneer **[M]**
(912) 635-2261. **$79-$209, 3 days notice.** 85 S Beachview Dr. 1 mi s of Ben Fortson Cswy. Ext/int corridors. **Pets:** Medium, other species. $10 daily fee/room. Service with restrictions, crate.
[SAVE] [S⊘] [✕] [⌖] [⌕] [🛏] [💻] [🍽] [⊇] [⊠]

(AAA) ▼▼▼ Comfort Inn Island Suites **[M]**
(912) 635-2211. **$75-$179, 4 days notice.** 711 N Beachview Dr. 1.5 mi n of Ben Fortson Cswy. Ext corridors. **Pets:** Other species. $10 daily fee/pet. Service with restrictions.
[SAVE] [S⊘] [✕] [⌖] [⌕] [🛏] [💻] [🍽] [⊇] [⊠]

(AAA) ▼▼▼ Jekyll Inn **[M]**
(912) 635-2531. **$53-$161, 3 days notice.** 975 N Beachview Dr. From jct SR 520 (Ben Fortson Cswy) and Beachview Dr, 3 mi n. Ext corridors. **Pets:** $10 daily fee/pet. Service with restrictions, supervision.
[SAVE] [S⊘] [✕] [⌖] [🛏] [💻] [🍽] [⊇] [⊠]

(AAA) ▼▼▼ Seafarer Inn & Suites **[M]**
(912) 635-2202. **$49-$149.** 700 N Beachview Dr. 1.5 mi n of Ben Fortson Cswy. Ext corridors. **Pets:** Accepted.
[SAVE] [S⊘] [✕] [🛏] [⊇]

❀ END AREA ❀

GRIFFIN

▼▼▼ Holiday Inn Express **[M]**
(770) 228-9799. **$60-$75.** 1900 N Expressway. 2.5 mi n on US 41 and 19. Int corridors. **Pets:** Accepted.
[ASK] [S⊘] [✕] [⌖] [🛏] [💻] [⊇]

HAHIRA

▼▼ Super 8 Motel I-75 **[M]**
(229) 794-8000. **$38-$43.** 1300 Georgia Hwy 122 W. I-75, exit 29, just w. Ext corridors. **Pets:** Accepted.
[ASK] [S⊘] [✕]

HELEN

(AAA) ▼▼▼ A Premier Vacation Rentals Inc **[C]**
(706) 348-8323. **$85-$595, 14 days notice.** 5156 Helen Hwy. 3.5 mi s on SR 75. Ext corridors. **Pets:** Medium, dogs only. $200 deposit/room, $15 daily fee/pet. Designated rooms, no service, supervision.
[SAVE] [🛏] [💻]

▼▼ The Helendorf River Inn & Conference Center **[M]**
(706) 878-2271. **$34-$104, 10 days notice.** 33 Munichstrasse. Center on SR 17 and 75. Ext corridors. **Pets:** Other species. $10 daily fee/pet. Designated rooms, service with restrictions, supervision.
[✕] [🛏] [💻] [⊇]

HIAWASSEE

▼▼ Enota B & B, Cabins & Conference Lodge **[X]**
(706) 896-9966. **$50-$70, 30 days notice.** 1000 Hwy 180. E on US 76 to SR 75/15, 6 mi s to SR 180, 3 mi w. Ext corridors. **Pets:** Other species. $50 deposit/room, $15 daily fee/pet. Designated rooms, no service, supervision.
[✕] [💻] [⊠] [☎]

HINESVILLE

▼▼▼ Hampton Inn **[M]**
(912) 876-4466. **$60, 3 days notice.** 706 E Oglethrope Hwy. On SR 84. Ext corridors. **Pets:** Accepted.
[SAVE] [S⊘] [⌖] [⌕] [🛏] [💻] [⊇]

HIRAM

▼▼▼ Country Inn & Suites By Carlson **[M]**
(770) 222-0456. **$69-$100.** 70 Enterprise Path. 0.3 mi w of jct SR 92/6 and US 278. Int corridors. **Pets:** Accepted.
[ASK] [S⊘] [✕] [⌕] [🛏] [💻] [⊇]

HOGANSVILLE

▼▼ Key West Inn **[M]**
(706) 637-9395. **$50-$75.** 1888 E Main St. I-85, exit 28, just w. Ext corridors. **Pets:** Medium, dogs only. $5 daily fee/pet. Designated rooms, service with restrictions, supervision.
[ASK] [S⊘] [✕] [🛏] [💻] [⊇]

KINGSLAND

⬥⬥⬥ ▼▼▼▼ Best Western/Kings Bay Inn M
(912) 729-7666. **$54-$62.** 1353 Hwy 40 E. I-95, exit 3, just e. Ext corridors. **Pets:** $10 deposit/pet. Service with restrictions, supervision.
[SAVE] [S⬥] [✕] [🐾] [🛏] [🖥] [⤳]

▼▼ Econo Lodge M
(912) 673-7336. **$45-$50, 5 days notice.** 1135 E King Ave. I-95, exit 3, 0.4 mi w. Ext corridors. **Pets:** Accepted.
[SAVE] [S⬥] [✕] [⌗M] [🐾] [⌗] [🛏] [🖥] [⤳]

⬥⬥⬥ ▼▼▼ Quality Inn & Suites M⬧
(912) 729-3000. **$50-$63.** 930 Hwy 40 E. I-95, exit 3, just w. Ext corridors. **Pets:** Large, other species. $10 daily fee/room. Service with restrictions, crate.
[SAVE] [S⬥] [✕] [🛏] [🖥] [⤳]

⬥⬥⬥ ▼ Super 8 Motel M
(912) 729-6888. **$30-$50.** 120 Edenfield Dr. I-95, exit 3, southeast corner. Int corridors. **Pets:** Medium. $5 daily fee/pet. Supervision.
[SAVE] [✕] [🛏] [🖥]

LA FAYETTE

⬥⬥⬥ ▼▼ Days Inn M
(706) 639-9362. **$55-$60.** 2209 N Main St. 2.5 mi n on US 27. Ext corridors. **Pets:** Medium. $5 daily fee/pet. Service with restrictions, supervision.
[SAVE] [S⬥] [✕] [🛏] [⤳]

LAGRANGE

⬥⬥⬥ ▼▼▼ Days Inn-La Grange/Callaway Gardens M
(706) 882-8881. **$55-$70.** 2606 Whitesville Rd. I-85, exit 13, just e. Ext corridors. **Pets:** $6 daily fee/pet. Service with restrictions, supervision.
[SAVE] [S⬥] [✕] [⌗] [🛏] [🖥] [⤳]

LAKE PARK

▼▼ Best Western Lake Park Inn M
(229) 559-4939. **$50-$70.** 6972 Bellville Rd. I-75, exit 2, northeast corner. Ext corridors. **Pets:** Accepted.
[SAVE] [S⬥] [✕] [🖥] [⤳]

▼▼ Days Inn M
(229) 559-0229. **$45-$49.** 4913 Timber Dr. I-75, exit 5, northwest corner. Ext corridors. **Pets:** Accepted.
[SAVE] [S⬥] [✕] [🖥] [⤳]

▼▼ Holiday Inn Express M
(229) 559-5181. **$60.** 1198 Lakes Blvd. I-75, exit 5, just e. Ext corridors. **Pets:** Accepted.
[ASK] [S⬥] [✕] [🛏] [🖥] [⤳]

⬥⬥⬥ ▼▼ Super 8 Motel M
(229) 559-8111. **$42.** 4907 Timber Dr. I-75, exit 5, just w, then n. Ext corridors. **Pets:** Accepted.
[SAVE] [S⬥] [✕] [🛏]

▼▼ Travelodge M
(229) 559-0110. **$42-$48, 7 days notice.** 4912 Timber Dr. I-75, exit 5, just w, just n. Int corridors. **Pets:** Supervision.
[ASK] [S⬥] [✕] [⌗M] [🛏] [🖥] [⤳]

LOUISVILLE

⬥⬥⬥ ▼▼▼ Louisville Motor Lodge M
(478) 625-7168. **$48-$51.** 308 Hwy 1 Bypass. 1 mi ne on US 1 Bypass. Ext corridors. **Pets:** Accepted.
[SAVE] [S⬥] [✕] [🛏]

MACON

▼▼ Best Inns & Suites M
(478) 405-0106. **$60-$80.** 130 Holiday North Dr. I-75, exit 169, then just s. Ext corridors. **Pets:** Accepted.
[ASK] [S⬥] [✕] [🛏] [🖥]

⬥⬥⬥ ▼▼▼ Best Western Inn & Suites M 🐾
(478) 781-5300. **$56.** 4681 Chambers Rd. I-475, exit 3, southwest corner. Ext corridors. **Pets:** Medium. $10 daily fee/room. Service with restrictions, supervision.
[SAVE] [S⬥] [✕] [⌗] [🛏] [⤳]

▼▼▼ Comfort Inn-North M
(478) 746-8855. **$61.** 2690 Riverside Dr. I-75, exit 167. Ext/int corridors. **Pets:** Accepted.
[SAVE] [S⬥] [✕] [⌗M] [⌗] [🛏] [🖥] [⤳]

▼▼▼ Holiday Inn Express M
(478) 743-1482. **$59.** 2720 Riverside Dr. I-75, exit 167, just nw. Int corridors. **Pets:** Accepted.
[ASK] [S⬥] [✕] [⌗M] [⌗] [🛏] [🖥] [⤳]

▼▼▼ Holiday Inn Macon Conference Center M⬧
(478) 474-2610. **$72.** 3590 Riverside Dr. I-75, exit 169. Ext corridors. **Pets:** Small, other species. $25 one-time fee/room. Service with restrictions.
[ASK] [✕] [🛏] [🖥] [🍴] [⤳]

▼▼ Jameson Inn M
(478) 474-8004. **$55-$70.** 150 Plantation Inn Dr. I-475, exit 9, just e. Ext corridors. **Pets:** Very small. No service, supervision.
[✕] [🛏] [🖥] [⤳]

⬥⬥⬥ ▼▼▼ La Quinta Inn & Suites M
(478) 475-0206. **$71-$101.** 3944 River Place Dr. I-75, exit 169, southeast corner. Int corridors. **Pets:** Medium, other species. $10 daily fee/room. Service with restrictions, crate.
[SAVE] [✕] [⌗M] [⌗] [🛏] [🖥] [⤳]

▼▼ Quality Inn & Conference Center M 🐾
(478) 781-7000. **$45-$55, 7 days notice.** 4630 Chambers Rd. I-475, exit 3, just se. Ext corridors. **Pets:** Small. $5 one-time fee/pet. Designated rooms, service with restrictions, supervision.
[SAVE] [S⬥] [✕] [🛏] [🖥] [⤳]

▼ **Ramada Inn and Conference Center** Ⓜ
(478) 474-0871. **$44, 3 days notice.** 5009 Harrison Rd.
I-475, exit 3, northwest corner. Ext corridors.
Pets: Accepted.
(ASK) (S&) (✕) (🛏) (🖥) (🍴) (🏊)

▼▼ **Ramada Inn North** Ⓜ
(478) 474-9902. **$50.** 3850 Riverside Dr. I-75, exit 169, just
w. Ext corridors. **Pets:** $10 daily fee/pet. Service with
restrictions, supervision.
(ASK) (S&) (✕) (🛏) (🏊)

Ⓐ ▼▼ **Red Roof Inn** Ⓜ
(478) 477-7477. **$40-$54.** 3950 River Place Dr. I-75, exit
169, at Arkwright Rd. Int corridors. **Pets:** Accepted.
(SAVE) (✕) (🔑) (🛏) (🏊)

Ⓐ ▼▼ **Rodeway Inn** Ⓜ ❀
(478) 781-4343. **$45.** 4999 Eisenhower Pkwy. I-475, exit 3,
0.3 mi e on US 80. Ext corridors. **Pets:** Medium. $10 one-
time fee/room. Service with restrictions, crate.
(SAVE) (S&) (✕) (🛏) (🖥) (🏊)

MANCHESTER

Ⓐ ▼▼ **Western Inn & Suites** Ⓜ ❀
(706) 846-4410. **$45-$52.** 1119 Warm Springs Hwy. Just n
of town center. Ext corridors. **Pets:** Medium. $5 daily fee/
pet. No service, supervision.
(SAVE) (S&) (✕) (🛏) (🏊)

MCDONOUGH

Ⓐ ▼▼ **Days Inn** Ⓜ
(770) 957-5261. **$54-$69.** 744 SR 155 S & I-75. I-75, exit
216, just e. Ext corridors. **Pets:** Medium. $7 one-time fee/
pet. Service with restrictions, supervision.
(SAVE) (S&) (✕) (🔑) (🛏) (🖥) (🏊)

Ⓐ ▼▼▼ **Holiday Inn McDonough** Ⓜ
(770) 957-5291. **$79-$150.** 930 Hwy 155 S. I-75, exit 216,
just w. Ext corridors. **Pets:** Other species. Designated
rooms, service with restrictions.
(SAVE) (S&) (✕) (🔑) (🛏) (🖥) (🍴) (🏊)

Ⓐ ▼▼ **Masters Inn** Ⓜ
(770) 957-5818. **$36-$46.** 1311 Hampton Rd. I-75, exit 218,
just w. Ext corridors. **Pets:** Small. $5 daily fee/pet. Service
with restrictions, supervision.
(SAVE) (S&) (✕) (🛏) (🏊)

METTER

▼▼ **Days Inn** Ⓜ
(912) 685-2700. **$60, 5 days notice.** 720 S Lewis St. I-16,
exit 104, 1 mi n on SR 121. Ext corridors. **Pets:** Accepted.
(SAVE) (✕) (🛏) (🏊)

MILLEDGEVILLE

▼▼ **Ramada Ltd and Conference
   Center** Ⓜ ❀
(478) 452-3502. **$34-$74.** 2627 N Columbia St. 4 mi nw on
US 441 and SR 24. Ext corridors. **Pets:** Other species. $4
daily fee/pet. Service with restrictions, supervision.
(ASK) (S&) (✕) (🔑) (🔑) (🖥) (🍴) (🏊)

NEWNAN

Ⓐ ▼▼ **Best Western-Shenandoah Inn** Ⓜ
(770) 304-9700. **$62-$68, 7 days notice.** 620 Hwy 34 E.
I-85, exit 47, just w. Ext corridors. **Pets:** Medium. $10 daily
fee/pet. Designated rooms, service with restrictions, supervision.
(SAVE) (S&) (✕) (📶) (🔑) (🛏) (🖥) (🏊)

OAKWOOD

▼▼▼ **Country Inn & Suites By Carlson** Ⓜ
(770) 535-8080. **$80-$90, 14 days notice.** 4535 Oakwood
Rd. I-985, exit 16, just sw. Int corridors. **Pets:** Accepted.
(✕) (🔑) (🛏) (🖥) (🏊)

PEACHTREE CITY

Ⓐ ▼▼▼ **Best Western Inn & Suites** Ⓜ
(770) 632-9700. **$69-$79.** 976 Crosstown Dr. From jct SR
74 and 54, 2.1 mi s on SR 74. Ext corridors. **Pets:** Medium.
$10 daily fee/pet. Designated rooms, service with restric-
tions, supervision.
(SAVE) (S&) (✕) (📶) (🌐) (🔑) (🛏) (🖥) (🏊)

PERRY

Ⓐ ▼▼▼ **Days Inn & Suites** Ⓜ
(478) 218-5200. **$66-$86, 3 days notice.** 205 Lect Dr. I-75,
exit 135, just e. Int corridors. **Pets:** Other species. $15
one-time fee/pet. Service with restrictions, supervision.
(SAVE) (S&) (✕) (🔑) (🛏) (🖥) (🏊)

▼▼▼ **Hampton Inn** Ⓜ
(478) 987-7681. **$65.** 102 Hampton Ct. I-75, exit 136,
southeast corner. Int corridors. **Pets:** Medium. $65 one-time
fee/room. Designated rooms, service with restrictions,
supervision.
(SAVE) (✕) (📶) (🔑) (🛏) (🖥) (🏊)

Ⓐ ▼▼ **New Perry Hotel-Motel** Ⓜ
(478) 987-1000. **$40-$80.** 800 Main St. I-75, exit 136, 0.8
mi se on US 341, just off US 41. Ext/int corridors.
Pets: Accepted.
(SAVE) (🍴) (🏊)

Ⓐ ▼▼▼ **Quality Inn** Ⓜ ❀
(478) 987-1345. **$55-$75, 30 days notice.** 1504 Sam Nunn
Blvd. I-75, exit 136, at US 341. Ext corridors. **Pets:** $7.50
daily fee/room. Service with restrictions, crate.
(SAVE) (S&) (✕) (🛏) (🖥) (🍴) (🏊)

(AAA) ▼▼▼▼ **Super 8 Motel** **M**
(478) 987-0999. **$45-$55.** 102 Plaza Dr. I-75, exit 136, 0.3 mi e. Ext corridors. **Pets:** Other species. $10 daily fee/pet. Service with restrictions.
(SAVE) (S) (X) (&) (B) (C)

PINE MOUNTAIN

▼▼ **White Columns Motel** **M** ❀
(706) 663-2312. **$45-$55.** 524 S Main St. 1 mi s on US 27. Ext corridors. **Pets:** Other species. $5 one-time fee/room. Designated rooms, service with restrictions, crate.
(ASK) (S) (X) (B) (C)

POOLER

▼▼▼ **Jameson Inn** **M**
(912) 748-0177. **$55-$70.** 125 Bourne Ave. I-95, exit 102, just e. Int corridors. **Pets:** Small, other species. Service with restrictions, crate.
(X) (Z) (&) (B) (C) (~)

▼▼ **Red Roof Inn & Suites** **M**
(912) 748-4050. **$65-$95.** 20 Mill Creek Cir. I-95, exit 104, just w. Int corridors. **Pets:** Small. Service with restrictions, supervision.
(ASK) (S) (X) (Z) (&) (B) (C) (~)

(AAA) ▼▼▼▼ **Travelodge Suites** **M**
(912) 748-6363. **$60-$80.** 130 Continental Blvd. I-95, exit 102, just e. Int corridors. **Pets:** Accepted.
(SAVE) (S) (X) (&) (B) (C) (~)

RINCON

▼▼ **Days Inn** **M**
(912) 826-6966. **$44-$99, 7 days notice.** 582 Columbia Ave. I-95, exit 109, on US 21. Ext corridors. **Pets:** Small. $10 daily fee/pet. Service with restrictions, supervision.
(SAVE) (S) (X) (&) (B) (C) (~)

RINGGOLD

▼▼ **Super 8 Motel** **M**
(706) 965-7080. **Call for rates.** 5400 Alabama Hwy. I-75, exit 348, just e. Ext corridors. **Pets:** Accepted.
(ASK) (X) (B) (~)

ROME

▼▼▼ **Holiday Inn-Sky Top Center** **MI** ❀
(706) 295-1100. **$64-$75.** 20 US 411 E. 2 mi e. Ext corridors. **Pets:** Other species. Service with restrictions, supervision.
(ASK) (S) (X) (&M) (Z) (B) (C) (¶) (~)

SAVANNAH

(AAA) ▼▼▼ **Baymont Inn & Suites-Savannah** **M**
(912) 927-7660. **$59-$69.** 8484 Abercorn St. 6.3 mi sw of historic district on SR 204. Int corridors. **Pets:** Medium, other species. Designated rooms, service with restrictions, supervision.
(SAVE) (S) (X) (Z) (B) (C) (~)

(AAA) ▼▼▼ **Best Western Central** **M**
(912) 355-1000. **$59-$89, 3 days notice.** 45 Eisenhower Dr. 5.8 mi sw of historic district on SR 204. Ext corridors. **Pets:** Accepted.
(SAVE) (S) (X) (Z) (B) (C) (~)

▼▼▼ **ClubHouse Inn & Suites** **M**
(912) 356-1234. **$99-$119.** 6800 Abercorn St. 5.5 mi s of historic district, via SR 204. Int corridors. **Pets:** Accepted.
(ASK) (S) (X) (B) (C) (~)

▼▼▼ **Days Inn-I-95/204** **M**
(912) 925-3680. **$49.** 4 Gateway Blvd. I-95, exit 94, just e on SR 204. Int corridors. **Pets:** Accepted.
(SAVE) (X) (Z) (C) (~)

(AAA) ▼▼▼ **East Bay Inn** **CI**
(912) 238-1225. **$169-$199, 7 days notice.** 225 E Bay St. Corner of Lincoln St. Int corridors. **Pets:** Dogs only. $35 one-time fee/pet. Designated rooms, service with restrictions, crate.
(SAVE) (S) (X) (C) (¶)

(AAA) ▼▼▼ **GuestHouse International Inn** **M**
(912) 927-2999. **$60-$70, 3 days notice.** 390 Canebrake Rd. I-95, exit 94, just se off SR 204. Ext corridors. **Pets:** Accepted.
(SAVE) (S) (X) (Z) (B) (C) (~)

▼▼ **Joan's on Jones B & B** **BB** ❀
(912) 234-3863. **$145-$160 (no credit cards), 7 days notice.** 17 W Jones St. Southeast corner Jones and Whitaker sts. Ext corridors. **Pets:** Dogs only. $50 one-time fee/room. Designated rooms.
(X) (B) (C)

▼▼▼ **La Quinta Inn** **M**
(912) 355-3004. **$65-$95.** 6805 Abercorn St. 5.5 mi sw of historic district, via SR 204. Ext corridors. **Pets:** Medium. Service with restrictions.
(SAVE) (X) (Z) (B) (C) (~)

(AAA) ▼▼▼▼ **Marshall House** **MI**
(912) 644-7896. **$149-$359.** 123 E Broughton St. Between Drayton and Abercorn sts. Int corridors. **Pets:** Accepted.
(SAVE) (S) (X) (C) (¶)

(AAA) ▼▼▼ **Olde Harbour Inn** **BB**
(912) 234-4100. **$139-$249, 7 days notice.** 508 E Factors Walk. On Factors Walk; Lincoln St ramp off E Bay St. Ext corridors. **Pets:** Small, other species. $35 one-time fee/pet. Designated rooms, service with restrictions, supervision.
(SAVE) (S) (X) (B) (C)

(AAA) ▼▼▼ **Savannah Residence Inn by Marriott** **M**
(912) 356-3266. **$109-$160.** 5710 White Bluff Rd. 5.5 mi s of historic district off Abercorn St (SR 204). Int corridors. **Pets:** Other species. $125 one-time fee/pet. Service with restrictions, supervision.
(SAVE) (S) (X) (&) (B) (C) (~)

ⓐ ▼▼▼▼ Savannah South Inn Ⓜ
(912) 925-2770. **$67-$105.** 3 Gateway Blvd S. I-95, exit 94,
southeast corner. Ext corridors. **Pets:** Medium. $15 one-
time fee/pet. Designated rooms, service with restrictions,
supervision.
SAVE Ⓢ ⊠ 🔌 💻 🍴 ⇌

ⓐ ▼▼▼ Shoney's Inn Ⓜ
(912) 925-7050. **$49-$89, 10 days notice.** 17003 Abercorn
St. I-95, exit 94, SR 204, northeast corner. Ext corridors.
Pets: Accepted.
SAVE Ⓢ ⊠ ▤ ⇌

STATESBORO

▼▼▼▼ Statesboro Inn & Restaurant Ⓒ
(912) 489-8628. **$85-$135.** 106 S Main St. Just s of town
center on US 301/25. Ext/int corridors. **Pets:** Accepted.
A$K ⊠ ▤ 🍴

STOCKBRIDGE

▼▼ Motel 6–1117 Ⓜ
(770) 389-1142. **$42-$60.** 7233 Davidson Pkwy N. I-675,
exit 1, northeast corner. Ext corridors. **Pets:** Accepted.
A$K ⊠ 🔌 💺 ▤ ⇌

▼▼ Shoney's Inn Ⓜ
(770) 389-5179. **$55-$70.** 110 Hwy 138. I-675, exit 1, just e.
Ext corridors. **Pets:** Small, other species. $25 deposit/pet.
Designated rooms, service with restrictions, supervision.
A$K Ⓢ ⊠ ▤ 💻 ⇌

SWAINSBORO

ⓐ ▼▼▼ Bradford Inn Ⓜ
(478) 237-2400. **$51-$58.** 688 S Main St. 2.2 mi s of jct US
80, SR 26 and US 1. Ext corridors. **Pets:** Small. $6 daily
fee/pet. Service with restrictions, crate.
SAVE Ⓢ ⊠ ▤ 💻

THOMASVILLE

**▼▼▼▼ Qualtiy Inn & Suites Conference
Center Ⓜ**
(229) 225-2134. **$73-$87, 30 days notice.** 15138 Hwy 19
S. 0.3 mi s of US 319. Ext corridors. **Pets:** Accepted.
SAVE Ⓢ ⊠ 💺 🔌 ▤ 💻 🍴 ⇌

THOMSON

**ⓐ ▼▼▼▼ Best Western White Columns
Inn Ⓜ**
(706) 595-8000. **$53-$93, 30 days notice.** 1890 Washington Rd. I-20, exit 172, just s. Ext corridors. **Pets:** Other
species. $10 daily fee/pet. Designated rooms, service with
restrictions, crate.
SAVE Ⓢ ⊠ ▤ 💻 🍴 ⇌

ⓐ ▼▼ Days Inn Ⓜ
(706) 595-2262. **$55-$185.** 2658 Cobb Ham Rd. I-20, exit
175, northeast corner. Ext corridors. **Pets:** Accepted.
SAVE Ⓢ ⊠ ▤

TIFTON

▼▼ Family Values Inn Ⓜ
(229) 386-9558. **$48.** 1103 King Rd. I-75, exit 63A (W 2nd
St), northwest corner. Ext corridors. **Pets:** $5 daily fee/room.
Service with restrictions, supervision.
A$K Ⓢ ⊠ ▤ 💻 ⇌

▼▼ Hampton Inn Ⓜ
(229) 382-8800. **$78-$84.** 720 Hwy 319 S. I-75, exit 62, just
e on US 319. Ext corridors. **Pets:** Accepted.
SAVE Ⓢ ⊠ ▤ 💻 ⇌

▼▼▼ Holiday Inn Ⓜ
(229) 382-6687. **$55-$65.** 1208 Hwy 82 W. I-75, exit 62, at
jct US 82 and 319. Ext corridors. **Pets:** $5 daily fee/room.
Designated rooms, service with restrictions, supervision.
A$K Ⓢ ⊠ ▤ 💻 🍴 ⇌

▼▼ Microtel Inns & Suites Ⓜ
(229) 387-0112. **$44-$68.** 196 S Virginia Ave. I-75, exit 62,
just ne. Int corridors. **Pets:** Small. $15 one-time fee/room.
Service with restrictions, supervision.
A$K Ⓢ ⊠ 💺 💺 ▤ 💻 ⇌

ⓐ ▼▼ Motel 6 Ⓜ
(229) 388-8777. **$37-$39.** 579 Old Omega Rd. I-75, exit 61,
just w. Int corridors. **Pets:** Small. Service with restrictions,
supervision.
SAVE ⊠ ⇌

UNADILLA

ⓐ ▼▼ Scottish Inn Ⓜ
(478) 627-3228. **$36, 4 days notice.** 1062 Pine St (US 41).
I-75, exit 121, just e. Ext corridors. **Pets:** $5 daily fee/pet.
Service with restrictions, supervision.
SAVE Ⓢ ⊠ ⇌

VALDOSTA

ⓐ ▼▼▼▼ Best Western King of the Road Ⓜ
(229) 244-7600. **$54-$60.** 1403 N St Augustine Rd. I-75,
exit 18, northwest corner off of SR 94. Ext corridors.
Pets: Accepted.
SAVE Ⓢ ⊠ 🔌 ▤ 💻 🍴 ⇌

**ⓐ ▼▼▼ Comfort Inn Conference
Center Ⓜ ❀**
(229) 242-1212. **$61-$70.** 2101 W Hill Ave. I-75, exit 16,
southwest corner. Ext/int corridors. **Pets:** Medium. Designated rooms, service with restrictions, supervision.
SAVE Ⓢ ⊠ ▤ 💻 🍴 ⇌

▼▼ Days Inn Conference Center Ⓜ
(229) 249-8800. **$39-$49.** 1827 W Hill Ave. I-75, exit 16,
southeast corner on US 84. Ext corridors. **Pets:** Accepted.
SAVE Ⓢ ⊠ 💺 💺 ▤ ⇌

▼▼ Days Inn I-75 North Ⓜ
(229) 244-4460. **$38-$45.** 4598 N Valdosta Rd. I-75, exit
22, northwest corner. Ext corridors. **Pets:** Accepted.
SAVE Ⓢ ⊠ ⇌

 **Holiday Inn** Ⓜ
(229) 242-3881. **$59, 3 days notice.** 1309 St Augustine Rd.
I-75, exit 18, just e on SR 94. Ext corridors. **Pets:** Other
species. $10 daily fee/room. Service with restrictions.
SAVE Ⓢ Ⓧ 🖥 💻 🍴 🏊

 **Quality Inn North** Ⓜ
(229) 244-8510. **$45.** 1209 St. Augustine Rd. I-75, exit 18,
0.3 mi e on SR 94. Ext corridors. **Pets:** Accepted.
SAVE Ⓢ Ⓧ ♿ 🖥 💻 🏊

 **Quality Inn South** Ⓜ
(229) 244-4520. **$38-$54.** 1902 W Hill Ave. I-75, exit 16,
just e on US 84. Ext corridors. **Pets:** Other species. Service
with restrictions, crate.
SAVE Ⓢ Ⓧ 💻 🏊

 **Ramada Limited** Ⓜ
(229) 242-1225. **$49, 7 days notice.** 2008 W Hill Ave. I-75,
exit 16, just e on US 84. Ext corridors. **Pets:** Other species.
$5 daily fee/room. Service with restrictions, supervision.
ASK Ⓢ Ⓧ 🖥 💻 🏊

▼▼ **Super 8 Motel I-75** Ⓜ
(229) 249-8000. **$39-$49.** 1825 W Hill Ave. I-75, exit 16,
southeast corner on US 84. Int corridors. **Pets:** Accepted.
ASK Ⓢ Ⓧ ♿ 🏊

VIDALIA

 **Days Inn** Ⓜ
(912) 537-9251. **$50-$55.** 1503 Lyons Hwy, 280 E. 1 mi e
on US 280. Ext corridors. **Pets:** $10 one-time fee/room.
Service with restrictions, supervision.
SAVE Ⓢ Ⓧ 🍴 🖥 💻 🏊

WARNER ROBINS

 **Best Western Peach Inn** Ⓜ
(478) 953-3800. **$47-$60.** 2739 Watson Blvd. I-75, exit 146,
4.1 mi e. Ext corridors. **Pets:** Medium, other species. $5
daily fee/pet. Designated rooms, service with restrictions,
supervision.
SAVE Ⓢ Ⓧ ♿ 🖥 🏊

▲▲▲ ▼▼▼▼ **Comfort Inn & Suites** Ⓜ
(478) 922-7555. **$60-$74.** 95 S SR 247. I-75, exit 146, jct
US 129/SR 247 and Russell Pkwy on northwest corner;
I-75, exit 146 (Rt 247 Connector), 1.3 mi e to SR 247/US
129, then 1.6 mi s. Ext/int corridors. **Pets:** Other species.
$25 one-time fee/room.
SAVE Ⓢ Ⓧ 🍴 ♿ 🖥 💻 🏊

▼▼▼▼ **Country Inn & Suites** Ⓜ
(478) 971-1660. **$79-$110, 14 days notice.** 220 Margie Dr.
I-75, exit 146, 3.2 mi e. Int corridors. **Pets:** Accepted.
ASK Ⓢ Ⓧ 🍴 ♿ 🖥 💻 🏊

▼▼ **Super 8 Motel** Ⓜ
(478) 923-8600. **$45, 7 days notice.** 105 Woodcrest Blvd.
I-75, exit 146, 5.7 mi e. Int corridors. **Pets:** Accepted.
ASK Ⓢ Ⓧ 🍴 🖥

WAYCROSS

▼▼ **Days Inn** Ⓜ
(912) 285-4700. **$44, 5 days notice.** 2016 Memorial Dr. 2
mi se on US 1 and 23. Ext corridors. **Pets:** Very small,
dogs only. $6 daily fee/pet. Designated rooms, service with
restrictions, supervision.
SAVE Ⓢ Ⓧ 🖥 🏊

▼▼▼▼ **Holiday Inn Waycross** Ⓜ
(912) 283-4490. **$65-$75.** 1725 Memorial Dr. At jct US 82
and 1. Ext corridors. **Pets:** Service with restrictions.
ASK Ⓢ Ⓧ 🍴 ♿ 🖥 💻 🍴 🏊

▼▼ **Jameson Inn** Ⓜ
(912) 283-3800. **$55-$70.** 950 City Blvd. Just e of US 1. Ext
corridors. **Pets:** Small, other species. Service with restrictions.
Ⓧ ♿ 🍴 🖥 💻 🏊

HILO

AAA ◈◈ Hale Kai Bjornen Bed & Breakfast BB
(808) 935-6330. **$95-$115 (no credit cards), 10 days notice.** 111 Honolii Pali. 2 mi n on SR 19, e on Paukaa Rd (towards ocean), just right. Int corridors. **Pets:** Medium. Designated rooms, service with restrictions, supervision.
SAVE ✕ 🛏 ➳ AC

KAUPULEHU

AAA ◈◈◈◈ Four Seasons Resort Hualalai at Historic Ka'upulehu R ❀
(808) 325-8000. **$475-$725, 21 days notice.** Off SR 19; 6 mi n of Kona International Airport. Ext corridors. **Pets:** Very small.
SAVE ✕ 🛎M 🅿 🌤 🖵 ❚❙ ➳ ✕

VOLCANO

AAA ◈◈◈ Volcano Inn BB ❀
(808) 967-7293. **$95-$115, 14 days notice.** 19-3820 Old Volcano Hwy. SR 11, MM 26 to Pearl Ave, then just n on Old Volcano Hwy to the dead end. Ext/int corridors. **Pets:** Other species. $50 deposit/pet. Designated rooms, service with restrictions, supervision.
SAVE 🛎 ✕ 🛏 🖵 AC

WAILEA

AAA ◈◈◈◈ Four Seasons Resort, Maui at Wailea R ❀
(808) 874-8000. **$315-$650, 21 days notice.** 3900 Wailea Alanui Dr. From end of SR 31, 0.5 mi s. Int corridors. **Pets:** Service with restrictions.
SAVE ✕ 🛎M 🅿 🌤 🛏 🖵 ❚❙ ➳ ✕

IDAHO

BLACKFOOT

 Best Western Blackfoot Inn M
(208) 785-4144. **$50-$90, 7 days notice.** 750 Jensen Grove Dr. I-15, exit 93, just e on Bergener, 0.4 mi n on Parkway. Int corridors. **Pets:** Other species. Service with restrictions, supervision.

BLISS

Amber Inn Motel M
(208) 352-4441. **$39.** 17286 US Hwy 30. I-84, exit 141, just s. Int corridors. **Pets:** Other species. $4.28 daily fee/pet. Service with restrictions, supervision.

BOISE

AmeriSuites (Boise/Town Square Mall) M
(208) 375-1200. **$99-$109.** 925 N Milwaukee St. I-84, exit 49 (Franklin St), just w on Franklin St, 0.5 mi n. Int corridors. **Pets:** Small. Service with restrictions, supervision.

BestRest Inn M
(208) 322-4404. **$40-$50.** 8002 Overland Rd. I-84, exit 50A eastbound, just sw; exit 50A westbound, just s on Cole, then just w. Ext corridors. **Pets:** Dogs only. $10 one-time fee/pet. Service with restrictions.

Best Western Safari Motor Inn M
(208) 344-6556. **$80-$85, 3 days notice.** 1070 Grove St. City center; at 11th and Grove sts. Int corridors. **Pets:** Designated rooms, service with restrictions, supervision.

Boise Super 8 Lodge M
(208) 344-8871. **$55-$75.** 2773 Elder St. I-84, exit 53, just n. Int corridors. **Pets:** Other species. $25 deposit/room. Service with restrictions, supervision.

Doubletree Hotel Boise Downtown MI
(208) 344-7691. **$69-$95.** 1800 Fairview Ave. I-184, exit Fairview Ave, 1 mi n. Int corridors. **Pets:** Accepted.

Doubletree Hotel Riverside MI
(208) 343-1871. **$79-$179.** 2900 Chinden Blvd. I-184, exit Fairview Ave, just n, then just w on Garden. Int corridors. **Pets:** Medium. $15 one-time fee/room. Service with restrictions, supervision.

Econo Lodge Boise M
(208) 344-4030. **$50-$60.** 4060 Fairview Ave. I-184, exit Fairview Ave, just n. Int corridors. **Pets:** Very small, dogs only. $10 daily fee/pet. Service with restrictions, supervision.

Hampton Inn M
(208) 331-5600. **Call for rates.** 3270 S Shoshone St. I-84, exit 53, just n. Int corridors. **Pets:** Accepted.

Holiday Inn MI
(208) 344-8365. **$69-$99.** 3300 Vista Ave. I-84, exit 53, just n. Int corridors. **Pets:** Accepted.

Owyhee Plaza Hotel MI
(208) 343-4611. **$89-$149.** 1109 Main St. City center; at 11th and Main sts. Ext/int corridors. **Pets:** $25 deposit/room. Designated rooms, service with restrictions.

Rodeway Inn of Boise MI
(208) 376-2700. **$66-$110.** 1115 N Curtis Rd. I-184, exit 2, just se. Ext/int corridors. **Pets:** Accepted.

Shilo Inn-Boise Riverside M ❀
(208) 344-3521. **$55-$79.** 3031 Main St. I-184, exit Fairview Ave, 0.5 mi n, just w on S 30th St. Int corridors. **Pets:** Other species. $10 daily fee/pet. Service with restrictions, supervision.

Shilo Inn Suites-Boise Airport M ❀
(208) 343-7662. **$59-$99.** 4111 Broadway Ave. I-84, exit 54, just sw. Int corridors. **Pets:** Other species. $10 daily fee/pet. Service with restrictions, supervision.

▼▼▼▼ **WestCoast ParkCenter Suites** M
(208) 342-1044. **$79.** 424 E Parkcenter Blvd. I-84, exit 54,
2.3 mi n, just e on Beacon and Parkcenter Blvd. Int corridors. **Pets:** Accepted.

(ASK) (S♦) (✕) (&M) (∅) (&) (⊟) (⏻) (≈)

BONNERS FERRY

(AAA) ▼▼▼▼ **Best Western Kootenai River**
Inn MI
(208) 267-8511. **$77-$105.** 7160 Plaza St. City center; on
US 95. Int corridors. **Pets:** Very small. Service with restrictions, supervision.

(SAVE) (S♦) (✕) (&) (⊟) (⏻) (⎟⎟) (≈)

BURLEY

(AAA) ▼▼▼▼ **Best Western Burley Inn &**
Convention Center MI
(208) 678-3501. **$40-$59.** 800 N Overland Ave. I-84, exit
208, just s. Ext/int corridors. **Pets:** Medium. $25 deposit/
room. Designated rooms, service with restrictions, supervision.

(SAVE) (S♦) (✕) (∅) (&) (⊟) (⎟⎟) (≈)

(AAA) ▼▼▼ **Budget Motel of Burley** M
(208) 678-2200. **$50-$65.** 900 N Overland Ave. I-84, exit
208, just s. Ext corridors. **Pets:** Medium. $25 deposit/room.
Service with restrictions, supervision.

(SAVE) (S♦) (✕) (∅) (&) (≈)

CALDWELL

(AAA) ▼▼▼▼ **Best Inn & Suites** M ❖
(208) 454-2222. **$60-$75.** 901 Specht Ave. I-84, exit 29, just
s. Int corridors. **Pets:** Other species. $10 deposit/room.
Designated rooms, service with restrictions, supervision.

(SAVE) (S♦) (✕) (⊟) (⏻) (≈)

▼▼▼▼ **Best Western Caldwell Inn &**
Suites M ❖
(208) 454-7225. **$71.** 908 Specht Ave. I-84, exit 29, just s.
Int corridors. **Pets:** Dogs only. $50 deposit/room. Desig-
nated rooms, service with restrictions, crate.

(SAVE) (S♦) (✕) (&) (⊟) (⏻) (≈)

COEUR D'ALENE

(AAA) ▼▼▼▼ **Best Inn & Suites** M ❖
(208) 765-5500. **$49-$119.** 280 W Appleway Ave. I-90, exit
12, just ne. Int corridors. **Pets:** Large, other species. $10
one-time fee/pet. Designated rooms, service with restrictions, supervision.

(SAVE) (S♦) (✕) (&M) (∅) (⊟) (⏻) (≈)

(AAA) ▼▼▼▼ **Coeur d'Alene Inn & Conference**
Center MI
(208) 765-3200. **$64-$119.** W 414 Appleway Ave. I-90, exit
12, just n. Int corridors. **Pets:** Accepted.

(SAVE) (S♦) (✕) (&M) (&) (⊟) (⏻) (⎟⎟) (≈)

▼▼ ▼▼ **Days Inn-Coeur d'Alene** M
(208) 667-8668. **$54-$82.** 2200 Northwest Blvd. I-90, exit
11, just se. Int corridors. **Pets:** Other species. $25 deposit/
room. Service with restrictions, supervision.

(SAVE) (S♦) (✕) (&M) (∅) (&) (⊟) (⏻)

(AAA) ▼▼▼▼ **Hawthorn Inn & Suites** M
(208) 667-6777. **$45-$109.** 2209 E Sherman Ave. I-90, exit
15, just s. Int corridors. **Pets:** Medium, other species. Designated rooms, service with restrictions, crate.

(SAVE) (S♦) (✕) (&M) (⊟) (⏻) (≈)

(AAA) ▼▼▼ **Rodeway Inn Pines Resort** M ❖
(208) 664-8244. **$58-$99.** 1422 Northwest Blvd. I-90, exit
11, 0.8 mi s. Ext corridors. **Pets:** Service with restrictions,
supervision.

(SAVE) (S♦) (✕) (&M) (∅) (&) (⊟) (⏻) (⎟⎟) (≈)

▼▼▼▼ **The Roosevelt, A Bed & Breakfast**
Inn BB
(208) 765-5200. **$99-$119, 14 days notice.** 105 Wallace
Ave. I-90, exit 13, 2 mi s, just w. Int corridors.
Pets: Accepted.

(ASK) (S♦) (✕) (Ⓦ) (Z)

▼▼▼▼ **Shilo Inn Suites-Coeur d'Alene** M ❖
(208) 664-2300. **$69-$165.** 702 W Appleway Ave. I-90, exit
12, just w. Int corridors. **Pets:** Other species. $10 daily
fee/pet. Service with restrictions, supervision.

(ASK) (S♦) (✕) (&M) (∅) (&) (⊟) (⏻) (≈)

DRIGGS

(AAA) ▼▼▼ **Best Western Teton West Motel** M
(208) 354-2363. **$52-$100.** 476 N Main St. 0.7 mi n on SR
33. Int corridors. **Pets:** Accepted.

(SAVE) (S♦) (✕) (⊟) (⏻) (≈)

GRANGEVILLE

▼▼ **Monty's Motel** M
(208) 983-2500. **$44-$52.** W 700 Main. Jct SR 13 and US
95. Ext corridors. **Pets:** Medium. Service with restrictions,
supervision.

(ASK) (S♦) (✕) (⊟) (≈)

▼▼▼ **Super 8 Motel** M
(208) 983-1002. **$55-$149, 5 days notice.** 801 SW 1st St.
Jct SR 95 and 13. Int corridors. **Pets:** Other species. $10
daily fee/pet. Designated rooms, service with restrictions,
supervision.

(ASK) (S♦) (✕) (&M) (&) (⏻) (≈)

HAGERMAN

(AAA) ▼▼▼ **Hagerman Valley Inn** M
(208) 837-6196. **$45-$50.** 661 Frog's Landing. South end of
town on US 30. Ext/int corridors. **Pets:** $5 one-time fee/pet.
Service with restrictions, supervision.

(SAVE) (✕)

HAILEY

Airport Inn M ✿
(208) 788-2477. **$78-$98, 7 days notice.** 820 4th Ave S. Just n of SR 75 at 4th Ave; near airport. Ext corridors. **Pets:** Medium. $5 daily fee/pet. Designated rooms, service with restrictions, supervision.

SAVE ⊗ 🗎 💻

IDAHO FALLS

Best Western CottonTree Inn M
(208) 523-6000. **$71-$91.** 900 Lindsay Blvd. I-15, exit 119, just e. Int corridors. **Pets:** Small. $25 deposit/room. Designated rooms, service with restrictions, supervision.

SAVE S🔒 ⊗ 🗎 💻 ≈

Best Western Driftwood Inn M ✿
(208) 523-2242. **$65-$109.** 575 River Pkwy. I-15, exit 118, 0.5 mi e on Broadway, 0.3 mi n. Ext corridors. **Pets:** Medium, other species. $10 one-time fee/room. Service with restrictions, supervision.

SAVE S🔒 ⊗ 🗎 💻 ≈

Comfort Inn M
(208) 528-2804. **$67-$97.** 195 S Colorado Ave. I-15, exit 118, just w to Colorado Ave, then just s. Int corridors. **Pets:** Medium, other species. $5 one-time fee/pet. Service with restrictions, crate.

SAVE S🔒 ⊗ 🗎 💻 ≈

Shilo Inn Suites Conference Hotel MI ✿
(208) 523-0088. **$65-$115.** 780 Lindsay Blvd. I-15, exit 119, just se. Int corridors. **Pets:** Other species. $10 daily fee/pet. Service with restrictions, supervision.

ASK S🔒 ⊗ 🗎 💻 🍴 ≈

WestCoast Idaho Falls Hotel MI
(208) 523-8000. **$89-$109.** 475 River Pkwy. I-15, exit 118, 0.5 mi e on Broadway, then just n. Ext/int corridors. **Pets:** Accepted.

ASK S🔒 🗎 💻 🍴 ≈

JEROME

Best Western Sawtooth Inn and Suites M
(208) 324-9200. **$84-$99, 7 days notice.** 2653 S Lincoln. I-84, exit 168, just n on SR 79. Int corridors. **Pets:** Other species. $50 deposit/room. Service with restrictions, crate.

SAVE S🔒 ⊗ 🗎 💻 ≈

KAMIAH

Lewis Clark Resort & Motel MI ✿
(208) 935-2556. **$42-$46.** 1.5 mi e on US 12. Ext corridors. **Pets:** Other species. Designated rooms, service with restrictions, supervision.

ASK S🔒 ⊗ 🗎 💻 🍴 ≈

KELLOGG

Silverhorn Motor Inn MI ✿
(208) 783-1151. **$60-$65.** 699 W Cameron Ave. I-90, exit 49, just ne. Int corridors. **Pets:** Supervision.

⊗ 🗎 🍴

Super 8 Motel-Kellogg M
(208) 783-1234. **$50-$65.** 601 Bunker Ave. I-90, exit 49, 0.5 mi s. Int corridors. **Pets:** Accepted.

SAVE S🔒 ⊗ 🗎 🗎 ≈

KETCHUM

Best Western Tyrolean Lodge M ✿
(208) 726-5336. **$80-$140, 3 days notice.** 260 Cottonwood. South end of town, just w of SR 75 on Rivers St, just s on 3rd Ave. Int corridors. **Pets:** $10 daily fee/pet. Designated rooms, service with restrictions, crate.

SAVE S🔒 ⊗ 🗎 💻 ≈ 🐾

Clarion Inn of Sun Valley M
(208) 726-5900. **$84-$169, 3 days notice.** 600 N Main St. North end of downtown on SR 75 (Main St), corner of 6th and Main sts. Ext/int corridors. **Pets:** $25 deposit/room, $10 daily fee/pet. Designated rooms, no service.

SAVE S🔒 ⊗ 🗎 🗎 💻 ≈

KOOSKIA

Looking Glass Inn BB
(208) 926-0855. **$65-$85, 3 days notice.** HCR 75, Box 32, US Hwy 12. 11 mi e on US 12 (between MM 84 and 85). Ext corridors. **Pets:** Medium, dogs only. $10 daily fee/pet. Designated rooms, supervision.

SAVE ⊗ 🗎 💻 📺 🐾

LEWISTON

Comfort Inn M
(208) 798-8090. **$69-$120.** 2128 8th Ave. 1.2 mi s on US 12 from jct US 95, just s on 21st. Int corridors. **Pets:** Designated rooms, supervision.

SAVE S🔒 ⊗ 🗎ᴹ 🗎 🗎 🗎 💻 ≈

Howard Johnson Express M
(208) 743-9526. **$95.** 1716 Main St. 1.6 mi s on US 12 from jct US 95. Ext corridors. **Pets:** Medium. $15 one-time fee/room. Designated rooms, service with restrictions, supervision.

SAVE S🔒 ⊗ 🗎 💻 ≈

Red Lion Hotel MI
(208) 799-1000. **$99-$119.** 621 21st St. 1.2 mi s on US 12 from jct US 95, just s. Int corridors. **Pets:** Other species. Service with restrictions, supervision.

ASK S🔒 ⊗ 🗎ᴹ 🗎 🗎 🗎 💻 🍴 ≈

Sacajawea Select Inn MI
(208) 746-1393. **$57-$62.** 1824 Main St. 1.5 mi s on US 12 from jct US 95. Ext/int corridors. **Pets:** Medium, other species. $2 daily fee/pet. Designated rooms, service with restrictions, supervision.

SAVE S🔒 ⊗ 🗎 🗎 🗎 🗎 🍴 ≈

▼▼ Super 8 Motel M
(208) 743-8808. **$50.** 3120 North & South Hwy. Just e on US 12 from jct US 95. Int corridors. **Pets:** Accepted.
ASK S⚬ ✕ ☎

MACKAY

(AAA) ▼ Wagon Wheel Motel M
(208) 588-3331. **$40-$75.** 809 W Custer. 0.3 mi n on Hwy 93. Ext corridors. **Pets:** Accepted.
SAVE S⚬ ✕ ☎ ⌨ (K)

MCCALL

▼▼▼ Bear Creek Lodge X
(208) 634-3551. **$80-$175, 3 days notice.** 3492 SR 55. 4 mi n on SR 55 at MM 149. Ext corridors. **Pets:** $10 one-time fee/pet. No service, supervision.
ASK S⚬ ✕ & 🖋 ☎ ⌨ ¶ (K)

(AAA) ▼▼▼ Best Western McCall M
(208) 634-6300. **$75-$100.** 415 3rd St. SR 55, just s of jct of Lake St and SR 55. Ext/int corridors. **Pets:** Other species. Service with restrictions, supervision.
SAVE S⚬ ✕ &M 🖋 ☎ ⌨ ⊇

(AAA) ▼▼ McCall Super 8 Lodge M ❀
(208) 634-4637. **$56-$76.** 303 S 3rd St. South end of town on SR 55. Int corridors. **Pets:** Other species. $20 deposit/room, $6 daily fee/pet. Designated rooms, service with restrictions, supervision.
SAVE ✕ &M 🖋 ☎

MONTPELIER

(AAA) ▼▼▼ Best Western Clover Creek Inn M ❀
(208) 847-1782. **$67-$99, 3 days notice.** 243 N 4th St. Just n on US 30 from jct of US 89 S. Ext corridors. **Pets:** Dogs only. $10 one-time fee/pet. Service with restrictions, supervision.
SAVE S⚬ ✕ ☎ ⌨

(AAA) ▼▼ The Fisher Inn M
(208) 847-1772. **$35-$50.** 601 N 4th St. 0.8 mi n on US 30 jct of US 89 S. Ext corridors. **Pets:** Accepted.
SAVE ✕ ☎ ⊇ (K)

MOSCOW

(AAA) ▼▼▼ Best Western University Inn MI
(208) 882-0550. **$82-$112, 3 days notice.** 1516 Pullman Rd. 1 mi w on SR 8 from jct of US 95. Int corridors. **Pets:** Accepted.
SAVE S⚬ ✕ &M 🖋 ☎ ⌨ ¶ ⊇

(AAA) ▼▼ Mark IV Motor Inn MI
(208) 882-7557. **$59-$129, 14 days notice.** 414 N Main St. 0.4 mi n on US 95 from jct of SR 8. Ext/int corridors. **Pets:** Other species. $10 daily fee/pet. Designated rooms, service with restrictions, supervision.
SAVE S⚬ ✕ ☎ ¶ ⊇

MOUNTAIN HOME

(AAA) ▼▼▼ Best Western Foothills Motor Inn M
(208) 587-8477. **$66-$84.** 1080 Hwy 20. I-84, exit 95, just n. Ext corridors. **Pets:** Other species. $5 daily fee/pet. Service with restrictions, supervision.
SAVE S⚬ ✕ &° ☎ ⌨ ⊇

▼▼ Sleep Inn M
(208) 587-9743. **$64-$74.** 1180 Hwy 20. I-84, exit 95, just n. Int corridors. **Pets:** Other species. $5 daily fee/pet. Service with restrictions, supervision.
SAVE S⚬ ✕ ☎ ⌨ ¶

NAMPA

▼▼ Shilo Inn-Nampa Boulevard M ❀
(208) 466-8993. **$55-$79.** 617 Nampa Blvd. I-84, exit 35, just sw. Int corridors. **Pets:** Other species. $10 daily fee/pet. Service with restrictions, supervision.
ASK S⚬ ✕ 🖉 ☎ ⌨ ⊇

▼▼▼ Shilo Inn Nampa Suites MI ❀
(208) 465-3250. **$69-$99.** 1401 Shilo Dr. I-84, exit 36, just nw. Int corridors. **Pets:** Other species. $10 daily fee/pet. Service with restrictions, supervision.
ASK S⚬ ✕ 🖉 ☎ ⌨ ¶ ⊇

▼▼ Sleep Inn-Nampa M
(208) 463-6300. **$70-$99.** 1315 Industrial Rd. I-84, exit 36, just s. Int corridors. **Pets:** Small. $10 daily fee/pet. Designated rooms, service with restrictions, supervision.
SAVE S⚬ ✕ &M 🖉 &° ☎ ⌨ ⊇

NEW MEADOWS

(AAA) ▼▼▼ Hartland Inn & Motel M
(208) 347-2114. **$59-$200, 14 days notice.** 211 Norris St. US 95, just n of jct of SR 55. Ext/int corridors. **Pets:** Accepted.
SAVE S⚬ ✕ ☎ ⌨

OROFINO

(AAA) ▼▼▼ Konkolville Motel M
(208) 476-5584. **$50-$65.** 2000 Konkolville Rd. 2.7 mi e on Michigan Ave. Ext corridors. **Pets:** $5 daily fee/pet. Designated rooms, service with restrictions, supervision.
SAVE ✕ ☎ ⌨

POCATELLO

(AAA) ▼▼▼ Best Western CottonTree Inn M
(208) 237-7650. **$64-$78.** 1415 Bench Rd. I-15, exit 71, just e. Int corridors. **Pets:** Other species. $25 deposit/room. Designated rooms, service with restrictions, supervision.
SAVE S⚬ ✕ &° ☎ ⌨ ⊇

▼▼▼ Comfort Inn M
(208) 237-8155. **$56-$84.** 1333 Bench Rd. I-15, exit 71, just e. Int corridors. **Pets:** Other species. $7 daily fee/pet. Service with restrictions, supervision.
SAVE S⚬ ✕ 🖉 ☎ ⌨ ⊇

▼▼ Econo Lodge-University Ⓜ ❖
(208) 233-0451. **$50-$65.** 835 S 5th Ave. I-15, exit 67, 1.8 mi n; across from Idaho State University. Int corridors. **Pets:** Other species. $20 deposit/room. Designated rooms, service with restrictions, supervision.

[SAVE] [S♦] [✕] [⊟] [▭] [⑪]

▼▼▼ Holiday Inn-Pocatello Ⓜ
(208) 237-1400. **$63-$68.** 1399 Bench Rd. I-15, exit 71, just e. Ext/int corridors. **Pets:** Designated rooms, service with restrictions, crate.

[✕] [⌂] [⌂] [⊟] [▭] [⑪] [≈]

▼▼ Ramada Inn & Convention Center Ⓜ
(208) 237-0020. **$-$95.** 133 W Burnside. I-86, exit 61, just n. Int corridors. **Pets:** Small. $15 deposit/room. Designated rooms, service with restrictions, supervision.

[ASK] [S♦] [✕] [⌂] [▭] [≈]

⏣ ▼▼▼ Super 8 Motel Ⓜ
(208) 234-0888. **$55-$75, 5 days notice.** 1330 Bench Rd. I-15, exit 71, just e. Int corridors. **Pets:** Accepted.

[SAVE] [S♦] [✕] [⌂] [⊟]

▼ Thunderbird Motel Ⓜ
(208) 232-6330. **$48-$54.** 1415 S 5th Ave. I-15, exit 67, 1.3 mi n; just s of Idaho State University. Ext corridors. **Pets:** Other species. $5 daily fee/room. Service with restrictions, supervision.

[ASK] [S♦] [✕] [⊟] [≈]

▼▼ WestCoast Pocatello Hotel Ⓜ
(208) 233-2200. **$71-$137.** 1555 Pocatello Creek Rd. I-15, exit 71, just e. Int corridors. **Pets:** Medium, other species. Designated rooms, service with restrictions, supervision.

[ASK] [S♦] [✕] [⊟] [▭] [⑪] [≈]

POST FALLS

▼▼ Holiday Inn Express Ⓜ
(208) 773-8900. **$65-$95.** 3105 E Seltice Way. I-90, exit 7, just sw. Int corridors. **Pets:** Other species. $30 deposit/room. Service with restrictions.

[ASK] [S♦] [✕] [⌂ᴹ] [⊟] [▭]

⏣ ▼▼▼ Howard Johnson Express Ⓜ
(208) 773-4541. **$59-$109.** 3705 W 5th Ave. I-90, exit 2, just ne. Int corridors. **Pets:** Other species. $5 daily fee/pet. Service with restrictions, supervision.

[SAVE] [S♦] [✕] [⌂ᴹ] [⌂] [⊟] [▭] [≈]

▼▼ Sleep Inn Ⓜ
(208) 777-9394. **$50-$80.** 100 N Pleasant View Rd. I-90, exit 2, just s. Int corridors. **Pets:** Medium, other species. $15 one-time fee/room. Service with restrictions, supervision.

[SAVE] [S♦] [✕] [⌂] [▭] [≈]

⏣ ▼▼▼▼ WestCoast Templin's Resort Ⓜ
(208) 773-1611. **$82-$129.** 414 E First Ave. I-90 E, exit 5, just s to First Ave; I-90 W, exit 6, 1 mi w on Seltice Way to Spokane St, 0.5 mi s. Int corridors. **Pets:** Medium. $5 daily fee/pet. Designated rooms, service with restrictions, crate.

[SAVE] [S♦] [✕] [⌂ᴹ] [⌂] [⌂] [⊟] [⊟] [▭] [⑪] [≈] [⊠]

REXBURG

⏣ ▼▼▼ Best Western CottonTree Inn Ⓜ
(208) 356-4646. **$68-$85.** 450 W 4th St S. US 20, exit S Rexburg, 1 mi e. Int corridors. **Pets:** Medium. Designated rooms, service with restrictions, supervision.

[SAVE] [S♦] [✕] [⊟] [▭] [⑪] [≈]

⏣ ▼▼▼ Comfort Inn Ⓜ
(208) 359-1311. **$50-$90, 7 days notice.** 1565 W Main St. Just e of jct of US 20, exit Salmon/Rexburg and SR 33. Int corridors. **Pets:** Other species. Service with restrictions, supervision.

[SAVE] [S♦] [✕] [⊟] [▭] [≈]

⏣ ▼▼▼ Days Inn Ⓜ
(208) 356-9222. **$52-$64.** 271 S 2nd W. US 20, exit S Rexburg, 1.8 mi e, just n. Ext corridors. **Pets:** Medium. Designated rooms, service with restrictions, supervision.

[SAVE] [S♦] [✕] [⊟] [≈]

RIGGINS

▼ Pinehurst Resort Cottages 🅲
(208) 628-3323. **Call for rates, 7 days notice.** MM 182 on US 95. 13 mi s on US 95. Ext corridors. **Pets:** Accepted.

[✕] [⊟] [⋔] [📺] [🄩]

SAGLE

▼▼ Bottle Bay Resort & Marina 🅲
(208) 263-5916. **$75-$125, 30 days notice.** 115 Resort Rd. 8.3 mi e on Bottle Bay Rd from US 95. Ext corridors. **Pets:** Other species. $8 daily fee/pet. No service, supervision.

[⊟] [▭] [⑪] [✕] [⋔] [🄩]

SALMON

▼ Motel DeLuxe Ⓜ
(208) 756-2231. **$40-$55, 7 days notice.** 112 S Church St. just s of Main St. Ext corridors. **Pets:** Other species. Supervision.

[✕] [⊟]

⏣ ▼ Wagon's West Motel Ⓜ ❖
(208) 756-4281. **$50-$60, 14 days notice.** 503 Hwy 93 N. Just n on US 93 from jct of SR 28. Ext corridors. **Pets:** Other species. $50 deposit/room. Designated rooms, service with restrictions, supervision.

[SAVE] [S♦] [✕] [⌂ᴹ] [⊟]

SANDPOINT

▼▼▼ Best Western Edgewater Resort Ⓜ
(208) 263-3194. **$79-$139.** 56 Bridge St. just e of US 95 N. Int corridors. **Pets:** Accepted.

[SAVE] [S♦] [✕] [⊟] [▭] [⑪] [≈] [⊠]

⏣ ▼▼▼ Hawthorn Inn & Suites Ⓜ
(208) 263-9581. **$89-$109.** 415 Cedar St. at US 95 and 2. Ext/int corridors. **Pets:** Small, dogs only. Designated rooms, service with restrictions, supervision.

[SAVE] [S♦] [✕] [⊟] [▭] [⑪] [≈]

(AAA) ▼▼▼ Lakeside Inn M
(208) 263-3717. **$64-$135.** 106 Bridge St. just e of US 95 N. Ext corridors. **Pets:** Accepted.
[SAVE] [S/D] [✕] [▣] [⊠]

(AAA) ▼▼▼ Monarch Mountain Lodge M
(208) 263-1222. **$48-$75, 10 days notice.** 363 Bonner Mall Way. 0.5 mi n on US 95 N from jct SR 200. Int corridors. **Pets:** Accepted.
[SAVE] [S/D] [✕] [🔧]

▼▼ Quality Inn Sandpoint MI
(208) 263-2111. **$49-$99.** 807 N 5th. US 2/95, just s of jct SR 200. Int corridors. **Pets:** Accepted.
[SAVE] [S/D] [✕] [🔧] [▣] [🍴] [🏊]

▼▼ Sandpoint Motel 6–4163 M
(208) 263-5383. **$40-$51, 7 days notice.** 477255 Hwy 95 N. 1.2 mi n on US 95 from jct SR 200. Int corridors. **Pets:** Accepted.
[ASK] [S/D] [✕] [&M] [🐾]

▼▼ Super 8 Motel M
(208) 263-2210. **$40-$60.** 476841 Hwy 95 N. 0.7 mi n on US 95 from jct SR 200. Int corridors. **Pets:** Accepted.
[ASK] [S/D] [✕] [&M] [🔧]

SODA SPRINGS

(AAA) ▼ J-R Inn M
(208) 547-3366. **$47.** 179 W 2nd S. US 30. Ext corridors. **Pets:** Accepted.
[SAVE] [✕] [🐾]

ST. ANTHONY

▼▼▼▼ Best Western Weston Inn MI
(208) 624-3711. **$45-$55.** 115 S Bridge St. US 20, exit St Anthony, just n on US 30 business route. Ext corridors. **Pets:** Medium, other species. $25 deposit/room. Designated rooms, service with restrictions, supervision.
[SAVE] [S/D] [✕] [▣] [🍴]

STANLEY

▼▼ Mountain Village Lodge MI
(208) 774-3661. **$59-$79, 14 days notice.** Corner US 75 & SR 21. Jct US 75 and SR 21. Ext corridors. **Pets:** Large, other species. $8 daily fee/pet. Service with restrictions, supervision.
[ASK] [S/D] [✕] [🔧] [▣] [🍴] [🐾]

TETONIA

(AAA) ▼▼ Teton Mountain View Lodge M
(208) 456-2741. **$40-$85.** 510 Egbert Ave. On SR 33. Ext corridors. **Pets:** Other species. $5 deposit/pet. Designated rooms, service with restrictions, supervision.
[SAVE] [S/D] [✕] [🔧]

TWIN FALLS

(AAA) ▼▼▼ Best Western Apollo Motor Inn M 🐾
(208) 733-2010. **$55-$74, 15 days notice.** 296 Addison Ave W. I-84, exit 173, 5.7 mi s on US 93, 1.2 mi w. Ext corridors. **Pets:** Small. $50 deposit/room. Designated rooms, service with restrictions, supervision
[SAVE] [S/D] [✕] [🔧] [🐾]

▼▼▼▼ Comfort Inn M
(208) 734-7494. **$79-$129.** 1893 Canyon Springs Rd. I-84, exit 173, 3.5 mi s on US 93. Int corridors. **Pets:** $7 daily fee/pet. Service with restrictions, supervision.
[SAVE] [S/D] [✕] [🔧] [▣] [🐾]

(AAA) ▼▼▼ Days Inn M
(208) 324-6400. **$50, 3 days notice.** 1200 Centennial Spur. I-84, exit 173, just n on US 93. Int corridors. **Pets:** Accepted.
[SAVE] [S/D] [✕] [🐾] [🔧] [▣]

▼▼▼▼ Shilo Inn Suites-Twin Falls M 🐾
(208) 733-7545. **S-$90.** 1586 Blue Lakes Blvd N. I-84, exit 173, 3.7 mi s on US 93. Int corridors. **Pets:** Other species. $10 daily fee/pet. Service with restrictions, supervision.
[ASK] [S/D] [✕] [&M] [🔲] [🐾] [🔧] [▣] [🐾]

(AAA) ▼▼▼▼ WestCoast Twin Falls Hotel MI
(208) 734-5000. **$99-$117.** 1357 Blue Lakes Blvd N. I-84, exit 173, 4 mi s on US 93. Int corridors. **Pets:** Medium, other species. Service with restrictions.
[SAVE] [S/D] [✕] [🔲] [🔧] [▣] [🍴] [🐾]

WALLACE

▼▼▼▼ Best Western Wallace Inn MI 🐾
(208) 752-1252. **$72-$80.** 100 Front St. I-90, exit 61, just s. Int corridors. **Pets:** Other species. $10 daily fee/pet. Designated rooms, service with restrictions, supervision.
[SAVE] [S/D] [✕] [&M] [🐾] [🔧] [▣] [🍴] [🐾]

▼▼▼ Stardust Motel M
(208) 752-1213. **$50-$62.** 410 Pine St. I-90, exit 61 (Business Rt 90), 0.7 mi e. Ext corridors. **Pets:** Other species. $10 daily fee/pet. Designated rooms, service with restrictions, supervision.
[ASK] [S/D] [✕] [🔧] [▣]

WORLEY

(AAA) ▼▼▼▼ Coeur d'Alene Casino Resort Hotel MI
(208) 686-0248. **$80-$95.** 27068 S Hwy 95. 3 mi n on US 95. Int corridors. **Pets:** Medium, other species. $25 deposit/room.
[SAVE] [S/D] [✕] [🐾] [🔧] [▣] [🍴] [🐾]

CITY INDEX

ALTON

Comfort Inn M
(618) 465-9999. **$74-$86.** 11 Crossroads Ct. Jct SR 140, off SR 3. Int corridors. **Pets:** Service with restrictions, supervision.

Super 8 Motel M
(618) 465-8885. **$54-$72.** 1800 Homer Adams Pkwy. SR 111, 1.8 mi e of jct SR 67. Int corridors. **Pets:** Accepted.

BEARDSTOWN

Super 8 Motel M
(217) 323-5858. **$45-$52.** 1903 Grand Ave. US 67, just w from SR 125. Int corridors. **Pets:** Medium, other species. $25 deposit/pet. Service with restrictions, supervision.

BELLEVILLE

Super 8 Motel M
(618) 234-9670. **$50.** 600 E Main St. 0.4 mi e from SR 159. Ext corridors. **Pets:** Accepted.

BLOOMINGTON

Country Inn & Suites By Carlson-Bloomington/Normal-West M
(309) 828-7177. **$82-$116.** 923 Maple Hill Rd. I-55/74, exit 160B (SR 9), 0.3 mi w to Wylie Dr, just n, then just e. Int corridors. **Pets:** Small. Designated rooms, service with restrictions, supervision.

Days Inn M
(309) 829-6292. **$64-$79.** 1707 W Market St. I-55/74, exit 160A (SR 9), 0.5 mi e. Int corridors. **Pets:** Other species. $10 deposit/pet. Designated rooms, service with restrictions, supervision.

GuestHouse International Inn M
(309) 663-1361. **$65.** 1803 E Empire St. SR 9, just e of I-55 business route (Veterans Pkwy). Int corridors. **Pets:** Medium. $6 daily fee/pet. Designated rooms, service with restrictions, crate.

Jumer's Chateau M
(309) 662-2020. **$115-$119.** 1601 Jumer Dr. I-55 business route (Veterans Pkwy), 1.3 mi n of jct SR 9, 1 mi s of jct I-55. Int corridors. **Pets:** Medium, dogs only. $25 deposit/room. Service with restrictions, crate.

Microtel Inn & Suites M
(309) 828-0900. **$66-$107.** 919 Maple Hill Rd. I-55/74, exit 160B (SR 9), 0.4 mi w to Wylie Rd, just n, then just e. Int corridors. **Pets:** Accepted.

Radisson Hotel & Conference Center-Bloomington M
(309) 664-6446. **$109-$132.** 10 Brickyard Dr. I-55 business route (Veterans Pkwy), just n of US 150. Int corridors. **Pets:** Small, other species. $25 deposit/room. Supervision.

Wingate Inn M
(309) 820-9990. **$89.** 1031 Wylie Dr. I-55/74, exit 160B (SR 9), just w, then just n. Int corridors. **Pets:** Accepted.

BOURBONNAIS

Holiday Inn Express Hotel & Suites M
(815) 932-4411. **$83-$125.** 62 Ken Hayes Dr. I-57, exit 315 (SR 50). Int corridors. **Pets:** Small, dogs only. $50 deposit/room. Service with restrictions, supervision.

Lees Inn & Suites M
(815) 932-8080. **$89-$209, 7 days notice.** 1500 N SR 50. I-57, exit 315 (SR 50). Int corridors. **Pets:** Accepted.

CARBON CLIFF

Super 8 Motel-East Moline M
(309) 796-1999. **$56-$80, 7 days notice.** 2201 John Deere Rd. I-80, exit 4A (John Deere Rd), 5 mi w on SR 5. Int corridors. **Pets:** Accepted.

CARBONDALE

Best Inns M
(618) 529-4801. **$49-$70.** 1345 E Main St. I-57, exit 54B, 13 mi e on SR 13; next to University Mall. Ext corridors. **Pets:** Small. $25 one-time fee/room. Designated rooms, service with restrictions, supervision.

Holiday Inn Carbondale M
(618) 529-1100. **$63.** 800 E Main St. 1 mi e on SR 13. Int corridors. **Pets:** Accepted.

Super 8 Motel M
(618) 457-8822. **$54-$70.** 1180 E Main St. 1 mi e on SR 13. Int corridors. **Pets:** Accepted.

CARLINVILLE

Best Value Inn-Carlin Villa M
(217) 854-3201. **$47-$64.** 18891 Rt 4. 0.5 mi s from jct SR 108 and 4. Ext/int corridors. **Pets:** Medium, other species. $4 daily fee/room. Service with restrictions, supervision.

Holiday Inn-Carlinville M
(217) 324-2100. **$67-$77.** 19067 W Frontage Rd. I-55, exit 60 (SR 108), just w. Int corridors. **Pets:** Accepted.

CASEY

Comfort Inn M
(217) 932-2212. **$55-$65, 7 days notice.** I-70, exit 129, 0.3 mi se. Int corridors. **Pets:** Accepted.

CASEYVILLE

Best Inns M
(618) 397-3300. **$55-$85, 7 days notice.** 2423 Old Country Inn Dr. I-64, exit 9 (SR 157), just s. Int corridors. **Pets:** Accepted.

CENTRALIA

Bell Tower Inn M
(618) 533-1300. **$49.** 200 E Noleman St. Jct US 51 S and SR 161. Int corridors. **Pets:** Accepted.

CHAMPAIGN

Baymont Inn & Suites M
(217) 356-8900. **$65-$80.** 302 W Anthony Dr. I-74, exit 182 (Neil St), just nw. Int corridors. **Pets:** $50 deposit/room. No service, supervision.

Comfort Inn M
(217) 352-4055. **$54-$99, 7 days notice.** 305 Marketview Dr. I-74, exit 182B (Neil St), just n to Marketview Dr, then just w. Int corridors. **Pets:** Accepted.

Drury Inn & Suites-Champaign M
(217) 398-0030. **$73-$105.** 905 W Anthony Dr. I-74, exit 181 (Prospect Blvd). Int corridors. **Pets:** Accepted.

La Quinta Inn M
(217) 356-4000. **$62-$84.** 1900 Center Dr. I-74, exit 182B (Neil St), just n. Int corridors. **Pets:** Accepted.

Red Roof Inn #170 M
(217) 352-0101. **$40-$67.** 212 W Anthony Dr. I-74, exit 182B (Neil St), just n, then just w. Ext corridors. **Pets:** Accepted.

CHICAGO METROPOLITAN AREA

ALSIP

(AAA) ▼▼ Baymont Inn-Chicago Midway South M
(708) 597-3900. **$70-$95.** 12801 S Cicero Ave. I-294, exit Cicero Ave S. Int corridors. **Pets:** Medium, other species. $25 deposit/room. Designated rooms, service with restrictions.

(SAVE) (X) (&M) (🐾) (📱) (🛏) (💻)

(AAA) ▼▼▼ Radisson Hotel-Alsip MI
(708) 371-7300. **$119-$169, 14 days notice.** 5000 W 127th St at Cicero Ave. I-294, exit Cicero Ave S, just w. Int corridors. **Pets:** Other species. $50 deposit/pet. Service with restrictions, crate.

(SAVE) (S🐾) (X) (&M) (🐾) (🛏) (💻) (🍽) (🏊)

ANTIOCH

(AAA) ▼▼ Best Western Regency Inn M
(847) 395-3606. **$72-$107, 3 days notice.** 350 Rt 173. SR 173, 0.5 mi w of jct SR 83. Int corridors. **Pets:** Accepted.

(SAVE) (S🐾) (X) (🛏)

ARLINGTON HEIGHTS

(AAA) ▼▼▼ AmeriSuites (Chicago/Arlington Heights) M
(847) 956-1400. **$99-$109.** 2111 S Arlington Heights Rd. I-90, exit Arlington Heights Rd, 0.6 mi n. Int corridors. **Pets:** Accepted.

(SAVE) (S🐾) (X) (🐾) (🛏) (💻)

▼▼▼ La Quinta Inn-Arlington Heights M
(847) 253-8777. **$90-$129.** 1415 W Dundee Rd. SR 53, exit Dundee Rd, just e. Int corridors. **Pets:** Small. Service with restrictions, crate.

(SAVE) (X) (🐾) (🛏) (💻) (🏊)

▼ Motel 6–1048 M
(847) 806-1230. **$49-$67.** 441 W Algonquin Rd. I-90, exit Arlington Heights Rd, just n, then 0.5 mi w. Int corridors. **Pets:** Accepted.

(S🐾) (X) (&M) (🐾)

(AAA) ▼▼ Red Roof Inn #7102 M
(847) 228-6650. **$54-$81.** 22 W Algonquin Rd. I-90, exit Arlington Heights Rd, 0.5 mi n, then just w. Ext corridors. **Pets:** Large, other species. Service with restrictions, supervision.

(SAVE) (X)

BANNOCKBURN

(AAA) ▼▼▼ Woodfield Suites Chicago North Shore M
(847) 317-7300. **$99-$139, 7 days notice.** 2000 Lakeside Dr. I-94, exit Half Day Rd (SR 22), just e to Lakeside Dr, then just s. Int corridors. **Pets:** Small. $50 deposit/room. Designated rooms, service with restrictions, supervision.

(SAVE) (S🐾) (X) (&M) (🐾) (🐾) (🛏) (💻) (🏊)

BOLINGBROOK

(AAA) ▼▼▼ Holiday Inn Hotel & Suites MI
(630) 679-1600. **$129.** 205 Remington Blvd. I-55, exit 267, just n, then 0.4 mi sw. Int corridors. **Pets:** Accepted.

(SAVE) (S🐾) (X) (🐾) (🐾) (🛏) (💻) (🍽) (🏊)

BRIDGEVIEW

(AAA) ▼▼ Exel Inn of Bridgeview M
(708) 430-1818. **$64-$85.** 9625 S 76th Ave. I-294, exit 95th St, just s. Int corridors. **Pets:** Small, other species. $200 deposit/room. Designated rooms, service with restrictions, crate.

(SAVE) (S🐾) (X) (🛏) (💻)

BURR RIDGE

(AAA) ▼▼▼ AmeriSuites Chicago/Burr Ridge M
(630) 323-7530. **$99-$125.** 15 W 90 N Frontage Rd. I-55, exit 276B (County Line Rd), 0.3 mi n. Int corridors. **Pets:** Accepted.

(SAVE) (S🐾) (X) (&M) (🐾) (🐾) (🛏) (💻) (🏊)

CALUMET CITY

▼▼ Baymont Inn & Suites Chicago-Calumet City M
(708) 891-2900. **$79-$89.** 510 East End Ave. I-94, exit 71B (Sibley Blvd E). Int corridors. **Pets:** Accepted.

(ASK) (S🐾) (X) (&M) (🐾) (🐾) (🛏) (💻) (🏊)

CHICAGO

(AAA) ▼▼ Claridge Hotel H ❀
(312) 787-4980. **$129-$189.** 1244 N Dearborn St. Just s of Goethe St. Int corridors. **Pets:** Other species. Designated rooms, service with restrictions.

(SAVE) (S🐾) (X) (💻) (🍽)

(AAA) ▼▼▼▼ The Drake Hotel, Chicago H ❀
(312) 787-2200. **$265-$395.** 140 E Walton Pl. N Michigan Ave at Lake Shore Dr and Walton Pl. Int corridors. **Pets:** Medium, other species. $200 deposit/room. Service with restrictions, supervision.

(SAVE) (S🐾) (X) (🐾) (🐾) (🛏) (🍽)

▼▼▼ ▼▼▼ **The Fairmont Chicago** H
(312) 565-8000. **$214-$414.** 200 N Columbus Dr. Jct Michigan Ave and Wacker Dr, just e. Int corridors. **Pets:** Small. $25 daily fee/room. Supervision.
[A$K] [S☎] [✕] [🌙] [¶]

⚑ ▼▼▼▼ **Four Seasons Hotel**
Chicago H
(312) 280-8800. **$415-$575.** 120 E Delaware Pl. Jct Michigan Ave. Int corridors. **Pets:** Accepted.
[SAVE] [✕] [&M] [🌙] [&] [🛏] [💻] [¶] [⌒]

⚑ ▼▼▼▼ **Hilton Chicago** H
(312) 922-4400. **$154-$354.** 720 S Michigan Ave. I-290 (Congress Pkwy), just s; overlooking Lake Michigan and Grant Park. Int corridors. **Pets:** Accepted.
[SAVE] [✕] [🌙] [&] [💻] [¶] [⌒]

⚑ ▼▼▼▼ **Hilton Chicago O'Hare Airport** H
(773) 686-8000. **$174-$314.** Opposite and connected to terminal buildings at O'Hare International Airport, accessed via I-190. Int corridors. **Pets:** Accepted.
[SAVE] [✕] [🌙] [💻] [¶] [⌒]

▼▼▼▼ **Holiday Inn Chicago Mart Plaza** H
(312) 836-5000. **$245-$305.** 350 N Orleans. Atop the Apparel Center, at the Merchandise Mart, 14th-23rd floors. Int corridors. **Pets:** Accepted.
[A$K] [S☎] [✕] [🌙] [&] [🛏] [💻] [¶] [⌒]

▼▼▼▼ **Hotel Allegro Chicago** H
(312) 236-0123. **$279.** 171 W Randolph St. Jct Randolph and LaSalle sts. Int corridors. **Pets:** Accepted.
[A$K] [S☎] [✕] [🛏] [💻] [¶]

▼▼▼▼ **House of Blues Hotel A Loews Hotel** H
(312) 245-0333. **$129-$309.** 333 N Dearborn St. On Chicago River; between Dearborn and State sts. Int corridors. **Pets:** Accepted.
[✕] [🌙] [&] [🛏] [💻] [¶]

⚑ ▼▼▼ ▼▼▼ **The Palmer House**
Hilton H ✿
(312) 726-7500. **$154-$354.** 17 E Monroe St. Between State St and Wabash Ave. Int corridors. **Pets:** Large. $200 deposit/pet. Service with restrictions, supervision.
[SAVE] [✕] [🌙] [&] [💻] [¶] [⌒]

⚑ ▼▼▼▼ **Radisson Hotel & Suites**
Chicago H
(312) 787-2900. **$299-$389.** 160 E Huron St. Just e of N Michigan Ave. Int corridors. **Pets:** Medium. $75 deposit/room. Service with restrictions, supervision.
[SAVE] [✕] [🌙] [&] [🛏] [💻] [¶] [⌒]

⚑ ▼ **Red Roof Inn** H
(312) 787-3580. **$92-$146.** 162 E Ontario St. Just e of Michigan Ave. Int corridors. **Pets:** Small. Designated rooms, service with restrictions, supervision.
[SAVE] [S☎] [✕] [¶]

⚑ ▼▼▼ ▼▼▼ **Renaissance Chicago**
Hotel H ✿
(312) 372-7200. **$249-$319.** 1 W Wacker Dr. Jct State St and Wacker Dr. Int corridors. **Pets:** Small, other species. $75 one-time fee/room. Supervision.
[SAVE] [S☎] [✕] [&M] [🌙] [&] [💻] [¶] [⌒]

⚑ ▼▼▼▼ **Residence Inn by Marriott Chicago**
Downtown A
(312) 943-9800. **$155-$219.** 201 E Walton St. Just e of Michigan Ave at jct Walton and Mies van der Rohe. Int corridors. **Pets:** Accepted.
[SAVE] [S☎] [✕] [🌙] [&] [🛏] [💻]

⚑ ▼▼▼▼ **The Ritz-Carlton, Chicago (A Four**
Seasons Hotel) H
(312) 266-1000. **$425-$585.** 160 E Pearson St. Jct N Michigan Ave and E Pearson St; in Water Tower Place. Int corridors. **Pets:** Accepted.
[SAVE] [✕] [&M] [🌙] [&] [🛏] [💻] [¶] [⌒]

⚑ ▼▼▼▼ **Sheraton Chicago Hotel &**
Towers H
(312) 464-1000. **$169-$399.** 301 E North Water St. Columbus Dr at Chicago River, just e of Michigan Ave. Int corridors. **Pets:** Accepted.
[SAVE] [S☎] [✕] [🌙] [&] [💻] [¶] [⌒]

⚑ ▼▼▼▼ **The Sutton Place Hotel** H ✿
(312) 266-2100. **$169-$209.** 21 E Bellevue Pl. Jct of Rush St. Int corridors. **Pets:** Small, other species. $200 deposit/room. Service with restrictions, supervision.
[SAVE] [S☎] [✕] [🌙] [🛏] [¶]

▼▼▼▼ **W Chicago City Center** H
(312) 332-1200. **$149-$279, 7 days notice.** 172 W Adams St. Between LaSalle and Wells sts. Int corridors. **Pets:** Accepted.
[A$K] [✕] [🌙] [&] [🛏] [💻] [¶]

⚑ ▼▼▼▼ **Westin Chicago River North** H
(312) 744-1900. **$169-$399.** 320 N Dearborn St. Just n of Chicago River; between Dearborn St and Clark. Int corridors. **Pets:** Accepted.
[SAVE] [S☎] [✕] [🌙] [💻]

⚑ ▼▼▼▼ **The Westin Michigan Avenue**
Chicago H
(312) 943-7200. **$204-$424.** 909 N Michigan Ave. Across from John Hancock Center. Int corridors. **Pets:** Accepted.
[SAVE] [✕] [&M] [🌙] [&] [💻] [¶]

⚑ ▼▼▼ ▼▼▼ **Whitehall Hotel** H
(312) 944-6300. **$179-$359.** 105 E Delaware Pl. Just w of Michigan Ave. Int corridors. **Pets:** Very small. $100 deposit/pet. Service with restrictions, supervision.
[SAVE] [S☎] [✕] [¶]

CRYSTAL LAKE

▼▼ Super 8 Motel M
(815) 455-2388. **$60-$81.** 577 Crystal Point Dr. On US 14, 1 mi w of jct SR 31. Int corridors. **Pets:** Accepted.

ASK SA X 🖪 🖵

DEERFIELD

▲▲▲ ▼▼▼▼ Marriott Suites Deerfield H
(847) 405-9666. **$69-$179.** 2 Parkway Blvd N. I-94, exit Deerfield Rd northbound, just w; exit Lake Cook Rd southbound, 0.3 mi e to Saunders Rd, 0.5 mi n; in Parkway North Center. Int corridors. **Pets:** Accepted.

SAVE SA X 🖉 🖪 🖵 ❚❙ ⇌

▲▲▲ ▼▼▼▼ Residence Inn by Marriott ▲
(847) 940-4644. **$107-$161.** 530 Lake Cook Rd. I-94, exit Lake Cook Rd, 1.8 mi e, 3 blks n on Corporate 500 Dr Access Rd. Ext corridors. **Pets:** Accepted.

SAVE SA X 🖉 🖪 🖵 ⇌

DES PLAINES

▲▲▲ ▼▼ Travelodge Chicago O'Hare/Rosemont M
(847) 296-5541. **$99-$159.** 3003 Mannheim Rd. US 12 and 45, just n of jct SR 72 (Mannheim Rd). Ext/int corridors. **Pets:** Accepted.

SAVE SA X 🖪 🖵 ⇌

DOWNERS GROVE

▲▲▲ ▼▼▼ Red Roof Inn M
(630) 963-4205. **$44-$74.** 1113 Butterfield Rd. I-355, exit Butterfield Rd (SR 56), on frontage road; I-88, exit Highland Ave N, just w. Ext corridors. **Pets:** Other species. Service with restrictions, supervision.

SAVE X 🖉

ELGIN

▲▲▲ ▼▼▼ Baymont Inn M
(847) 931-4800. **$60-$85.** 500 Toll Gate Rd. I-90, exit SR 31 N, just n. Int corridors. **Pets:** Accepted.

SAVE SA X ᴸᴹ 🖉 ᵏ 🖪 🖵

▼▼ Ramada Inn Elgin MI
(847) 695-5000. **$62-$80.** 345 W River Rd. I-90, exit SR 31 S, 0.5 mi e. Int corridors. **Pets:** Accepted.

ASK SA X 🖉 🖪 🖵 ⇌

ELK GROVE VILLAGE

▲▲▲ ▼▼▼ Exel Inn of Elk Grove Village M
(847) 895-2085. **$56-$74.** 1000 W Devon Ave. I-290, exit Thorndale Ave, 0.5 mi w to Rohlwing Rd, 0.3 mi n to Devon Ave, then 0.3 mi e. Int corridors. **Pets:** Small, other species. Designated rooms, service with restrictions, supervision.

SAVE SA X 🖉 🖪 🖵

▲▲▲ ▼▼▼ Exel Inn of O'Hare M
(847) 803-9400. **$73-$91.** 2881 Touhy Ave. Jct SR 83 and 72, 1.5 mi e on SR 72 (Higgins/Touhy Ave). Int corridors. **Pets:** Small, other species. Designated rooms, service with restrictions, supervision.

SAVE SA X 🖉 🖪 🖵

▼▼▼▼ Holiday Inn of Elk Grove MI
(847) 437-6010. **$79-$119.** 1000 Busse Rd. SR 83 (Busse Rd), 0.3 mi s of jct Higgins Rd (SR 72). Int corridors. **Pets:** Small. Service with restrictions, crate.

ASK SA X 🖉 🖵 ❚❙ ⇌

▼▼▼▼ La Quinta Inn O'Hare Airport M
(847) 439-6767. **$90-$149.** 1900 Oakton St. Jct of Higgins and Busse rds with Oakton St. Int corridors. **Pets:** Accepted.

SAVE X 🖪 🖵 ⇌

ELMHURST

▲▲▲ ▼▼▼▼ AmeriSuites (Chicago/Elmhurst-O'Hare Area) M
(630) 782-6300. **$79-$109.** 410 W Lake St. I-290, exit 12, just w on US 20 (Lake St). Int corridors. **Pets:** Accepted.

SAVE SA X ᴸᴹ 🖉 ᵏ 🖪 🖵 ⇌

▲▲▲ ▼▼▼▼ Holiday Inn Chicago-Elmhurst MI ✿
(630) 279-1100. **$129.** 624 N York Rd. I-290, exit 12, just n. Int corridors. **Pets:** Medium. $25 deposit/pet. Designated rooms, service with restrictions, crate.

SAVE SA X 🖉 🖪 🖵 ❚❙ ⇌

FRANKLIN PARK

▼▼ Comfort Inn M
(847) 233-9292. **$99-$119.** 3001 N Mannheim Rd. Jct US 12/45 (Mannheim Rd) and Grand Ave, just n. Int corridors. **Pets:** Other species. $50 deposit/room. Designated rooms, service with restrictions, supervision.

SAVE SA X ᵏ 🖵 ⇌

GENEVA

▲▲▲ ▼▼▼ ▼▼▼ The Herrington Inn CI ✿
(630) 208-7433. **$159-$385.** 15 S River Ln. Banks of Fox River, just off SR 38, 0.5 mi w of jct SR 25. Int corridors. **Pets:** Medium, dogs only. $300 deposit/room, $40 one-time fee/room. Service with restrictions, supervision.

SAVE SA X 🖵 ❚❙

GLEN ELLYN

▼▼▼▼ Holiday Inn MI
(630) 629-6000. **$89-$109.** 1250 Roosevelt Rd. I-355, exit Roosevelt Rd, 0.8 mi e on SR 38. Int corridors. **Pets:** Small. $25 one-time fee/room. Service with restrictions, supervision.

ASK SA X ᴸᴹ 🖉 ᵏ 🖪 🖵 ❚❙ ⇌

GLENVIEW

⚠ ▼▼▼ Baymont Inn & Suites Chicago-Glenview **M**
(847) 635-8300. **$74-$84.** 1625 Milwaukee Ave. I-294, exit Willow Rd, 0.3 mi w to Sanders Rd, 1.3 mi s to Milwaukee Ave (SR 21), 0.5 mi se to Lake Ave. Int corridors. **Pets:** Accepted.

⌷ ⌷ ⌷ ⌷ ⌷ ⌷

▼ Motel 6-1040 **M**
(847) 390-7200. **$51-$67.** 1535 Milwaukee Ave. I-294, exit Willow Rd, 0.3 mi w to Sanders Rd, 1.3 mi s to Milwaukee Ave (SR 21), 0.5 mi se. Int corridors. **Pets:** Accepted.

⌷ ⌷ ⌷

GURNEE

⚠ ▼▼▼ Baymont Inn & Suites Chicago-Gurnee **M**
(847) 662-7600. **$89-$119.** 5688 N Ridge Rd. I-94, exit Grand Ave (SR 132 E), just e via service road. Int corridors. **Pets:** Medium, other species. Designated rooms, service with restrictions, supervision.

⌷ ⌷ ⌷ ⌷ ⌷ ⌷ ⌷ ⌷ ⌷

▼▼▼ Comfort Suites **M**
(847) 782-0890. **$79-$149.** 5430 Grand Ave. I-94, exit Grand Ave (SR 132 E), 0.5 mi e. Int corridors. **Pets:** Small. $50 deposit/room. Designated rooms, no service, supervision.

⌷ ⌷ ⌷ ⌷ ⌷ ⌷ ⌷ ⌷ ⌷

▼▼▼ Country Inn & Suites By Carlson **M**
(847) 625-9700. **$79-$149.** 5420 Grand Ave. I-94, exit Grand Ave (SR 132 E), 0.5 mi e. Int corridors. **Pets:** Accepted.

⌷ ⌷ ⌷ ⌷ ⌷ ⌷ ⌷ ⌷ ⌷

HARVARD

⚠ ▼▼▼ AmeriHost Inn-Harvard **M**
(815) 943-0700. **$109-$129, 14 days notice.** 1701 S Division St. Jct US 14 and SR 23. Int corridors. **Pets:** Accepted.

⌷ ⌷ ⌷ ⌷ ⌷ ⌷ ⌷ ⌷

HOFFMAN ESTATES

⚠ ▼▼▼▼ AmeriSuites (Chicago/Hoffman Estates) **M**
(847) 839-1800. **$69-$159.** 2750 Greenspoint Pkwy. I-90, exit Barrington Rd, 0.3 mi s. Int corridors. **Pets:** Accepted.

⌷ ⌷ ⌷ ⌷ ⌷ ⌷ ⌷ ⌷

⚠ ▼▼▼ Baymont Inn & Suites Chicago-Hoffman Estates **M**
(847) 882-8848. **$69-$89.** 2075 Barrington Rd. I-90, exit Barrington Rd, 0.3 mi s. Int corridors. **Pets:** Medium. $50 deposit/room. Designated rooms, service with restrictions, supervision.

⌷ ⌷ ⌷ ⌷ ⌷ ⌷

▼▼▼ La Quinta Inn **M**
(847) 882-3312. **$80-$129.** 2280 Barrington Rd. I-90, exit Barrington Rd, 0.3 mi s. Int corridors. **Pets:** Small, other species. Service with restrictions, supervision.

⌷ ⌷ ⌷ ⌷ ⌷ ⌷ ⌷

⚠ ▼▼▼ Red Roof Inn **M**
(847) 885-7877. **$51-$75.** 2500 Hassell Rd. I-90, exit Barrington Rd, 0.3 mi s. Ext corridors. **Pets:** Medium. Service with restrictions, supervision.

⌷ ⌷ ⌷ ⌷

ITASCA

⚠ ▼▼▼▼ AmeriSuites Chicago/Itasca **M**
(630) 875-1400. **$111.** 135 S Larkin Ave. I-290, exit Thorndale Ave, 0.6 mi e on Thorndale Heights Rd, 0.5 mi n. Int corridors. **Pets:** Very small. Designated rooms, service with restrictions, crate.

⌷ ⌷ ⌷ ⌷ ⌷ ⌷ ⌷ ⌷ ⌷ ⌷

JOLIET

▼▼ Comfort Inn-Joliet South **M**
(815) 744-1770. **$75-$135.** 135 S Larkin Ave. I-80, exit 130B, 0.5 mi n. Int corridors. **Pets:** Accepted.

⌷ ⌷ ⌷ ⌷ ⌷ ⌷

▼▼ Comfort Inn North **M**
(815) 436-5141. **$65-$75.** 3235 Norman Ave. I-55, exit 257, just e. Int corridors. **Pets:** Accepted.

⌷ ⌷ ⌷ ⌷ ⌷ ⌷

▼▼▼ Holiday Inn Express-Joliet **M**
(815) 729-2000. **$69-$119.** 411 S Larkin Ave. I-80, exit 130B. Int corridors. **Pets:** Small, dogs only. Designated rooms, service with restrictions, supervision.

⌷ ⌷ ⌷ ⌷ ⌷ ⌷ ⌷

▼▼ Motel 6 Joliet I-55-1296 **M**
(815) 439-1332. **$41-$57.** 3551 Mall Loop Dr. I-55, exit 257, 0.4 mi e on US 30, then 0.4 mi s. Int corridors. **Pets:** Accepted.

⌷ ⌷ ⌷ ⌷ ⌷

⚠ ▼▼ Red Roof Inn **M**
(815) 741-2304. **$39-$74.** 1750 McDonough St. I-80, exit 130B, just off Larkin Ave. Ext corridors. **Pets:** Accepted.

⌷ ⌷ ⌷ ⌷

▼▼ Super 8 Motel I-55 North **M**
(815) 439-3838. **$65-$87.** 3401 Mall Loop Dr. I-55, exit 257, 0.4 mi e on US 30, just s. Int corridors. **Pets:** Accepted.

⌷ ⌷ ⌷ ⌷ ⌷ ⌷ ⌷

LANSING

⚠ ▼▼ Red Roof Inn **M**
(708) 895-9570. **$44-$79.** 2450 E 173rd St. I-80/94, exit 161 (Torrence Ave), just n. Ext corridors. **Pets:** Other species. Service with restrictions, supervision.

⌷ ⌷ ⌷ ⌷

LIBERTYVILLE

▼▼▼ Candlewood Suites
Chicago-Libertyville M
(847) 247-9900. Call for rates. 1100 N US 45. I-94, exit SR 137 (Buckley Rd), 5.6 mi w to US 45, 1.4 mi s. Int corridors. Pets: Small. $150 one-time fee/room. Service with restrictions, supervision.

[ASK] [✕] [&M] [🐾] [🛁] [🖥] [💻]

♦♦♦ ▼▼▼ Days Inn M
(847) 816-8006. $68-$89. 1809 N Milwaukee Ave. Jct SR 137 and 21. Int corridors. Pets: Accepted.

[SAVE] [S🐾] [✕] [🐾] [🖥] [➳]

LINCOLNSHIRE

♦♦♦ ▼▼▼▼ Marriott's Lincolnshire
Resort R
(847) 634-0100. $89-$199. 10 Marriott Dr. I-94, exit Half Day Rd, 2 mi w to jct US 45, SR 21 and 22, just s. Int corridors. Pets: Small. $25 one-time fee/pet. Service with restrictions, crate.

[SAVE] [S🐾] [✕] [&M] [🐾] [🛁] [🖥] [💻] [🍴] [➳] [✕]

LISLE

♦♦♦ ▼▼▼▼ Wyndham Lisle/Naperville H
(630) 505-1000. $79-$165. 3000 Warrenville Rd. I-88, exit Naperville Rd, just n, then 0.3 mi e. Int corridors. Pets: Accepted.

[SAVE] [✕] [🛁] [🖥] [💻] [🍴] [➳]

LOMBARD

♦♦♦ ▼▼▼▼ AmeriSuites Chicago/Lombard M
(630) 932-6501. $69-$159. 2340 S Fountain Square Dr. I-88, exit Highland Ave, just n to Butterfield Rd (SR 56), 0.9 mi e, just n. Int corridors. Pets: Accepted.

[SAVE] [S🐾] [✕] [&M] [🐾] [🛁] [🖥] [💻] [➳]

▼▼▼▼ Homestead Studio Suites Hotel M
(630) 928-0202. $74-$99. 2701 Technology Dr. I-88, exit Highland Ave, just n, 0.6 mi e on Butterfield Rd (SR 53), just s. Int corridors. Pets: Medium, other species. $75 one-time fee/pet. Service with restrictions.

[ASK] [S🐾] [✕] [&M] [🐾] [🛁] [🖥] [💻]

MATTESON

♦♦♦ ▼▼▼ Baymont Inn & Suites
Chicago-Matteson M
(708) 503-0999. $69-$89, 18 days notice. 5210 W Southwick Dr. I-57, exit 340A, 0.3 mi e on US 30, 0.3 mi s on Cicero Ave to entrance. Int corridors. Pets: Small, other species. $50 deposit/room. Designated rooms, service with restrictions, supervision.

[SAVE] [S🐾] [✕] [🐾] [🛁] [💻]

NAPERVILLE

▼▼▼ Country Inn & Suites By Carlson M
(630) 548-0966. $80-$125, 14 days notice. 1847 W Diehl Rd. I-88, exit SR 59, just s. Int corridors. Pets: Very small. $10 daily fee/pet. Designated rooms, service with restrictions, supervision.

[ASK] [S🐾] [✕] [&M] [🐾] [🛁] [🖥] [💻] [➳]

♦♦♦ ▼▼▼ Exel Inn of Naperville M
(630) 357-0022. $55-$75. 1585 N Naperville Rd/Wheaton Rd. I-88, exit Naperville Rd, 0.5 mi s. Int corridors. Pets: Small. $50 deposit/pet. Service with restrictions, supervision.

[SAVE] [S🐾] [✕] [🛁] [💻]

▼▼▼▼ Hawthorn Suites-Naperville M
(630) 548-0881. $109-$129. 1843 W Diehl Rd. I-88, exit SR 59, just s to Diehl Rd, then just w. Int corridors. Pets: Other species. $100 one-time fee/room. Service with restrictions.

[ASK] [S🐾] [✕] [🐾] [🛁] [🖥] [💻] [➳]

▼▼▼ Homestead Studio
Suites-Chicago/Naperville M
(630) 577-0200. $84-$95. 1827 Centre Point Cir. I-88, exit Naperville Rd, just s to Diehl Rd, 0.8 mi w, then just n. Int corridors. Pets: Medium. $75 one-time fee/pet. Service with restrictions, crate.

[ASK] [S🐾] [✕] [&M] [🐾] [🛁] [🖥] [💻]

♦♦♦ ▼▼▼ Red Roof Inn M
(630) 369-2500. $53-$84. 1698 W Diehl Rd. I-88, exit SR 59, just s. Ext corridors. Pets: Accepted.

[SAVE] [✕] [🛁]

NORTH AURORA

♦♦♦ ▼▼▼ Baymont Inns & Suites North
Aurora M
(630) 897-7695. $76-$90, 7 days notice. 308 S Lincoln Way. I-88, exit SR 31, just s. Int corridors. Pets: Small. Service with restrictions, supervision.

[SAVE] [S🐾] [✕] [🐾] [🛁] [💻] [➳]

NORTHBROOK

♦♦♦ ▼▼▼ Red Roof Inn M
(847) 205-1755. $50-$79. 340 Waukegan Rd. I-94, exit SR 43 (Waukegan Rd). Ext corridors. Pets: Medium. Service with restrictions, supervision.

[SAVE] [✕]

OAKBROOK TERRACE

▼▼▼▼ La Quinta Inn-Oakbrook Terrace M
(630) 495-4600. $89-$129. 1 S 666 Midwest Rd. I-88, exit Midwest Rd, 0.4 mi n, just n of 22nd St/Cermak Rd. Int corridors. Pets: Small. Service with restrictions, supervision.

[SAVE] [✕] [🐾] [💻] [➳]

PROSPECT HEIGHTS

▲▲▲ ▼▼▼ Exel Inn of Prospect Heights Ⓜ
(847) 459-0545. **$46-$71.** 540 Milwaukee Ave. Jct SR 21 and US 45. Int corridors. **Pets:** Small, other species. Designated rooms, service with restrictions, supervision.
ⓈAVE Ⓢ Ⓧ 🔊 📂 🔒 💻

ROSEMONT

▼▼▼▼ Doubletree Hotel Chicago O'Hare Airport-Rosemont Ⓗ
(847) 292-9100. **$149-$189.** 5460 N River Rd. I-190, exit 1B, just s. Int corridors. **Pets:** Accepted.
ⓈAVE Ⓢ Ⓧ 🔊 📂 🔒 💻 🍴 🏊

▲▲▲ ▼▼▼▼ Residence Inn by Marriott O'Hare-Rosemont Ⓐ
(847) 375-9000. **$139-$189.** 7101 Chestnut St. At jct Touhy Ave and Mannheim Rd (US 12 and 45), 3 mi n of O'Hare Airport. Int corridors. **Pets:** Other species. $10 daily fee/room, $100 one-time fee/room.
ⓈAVE Ⓧ 🔊 📂 🔒 💻 🏊

▲▲▲ ▼▼▼▼ Sofitel Chicago O'Hare Ⓗ
(847) 678-4488. **$199.** 5550 N River Rd. I-190, exit 1B, just s. Int corridors. **Pets:** Other species. $25 daily fee/room. Service with restrictions, supervision.
ⓈAVE Ⓢ Ⓧ 🔊 🔒 🍴 🏊

SCHAUMBURG

▲▲▲ ▼▼▼▼ AmeriSuites (Chicago/Schaumburg) Ⓜ
(847) 330-1060. **$112, 30 days notice.** 1851 McConnor Pkwy. I-290, exit 1A (Woodfield/Golf Rd) northbound, just n to Golf Rd, just w to McConner Pkwy, just n; exit 1B (Woodfield/Golf Rd) southbound. Int corridors. **Pets:** Accepted.
ⓈAVE Ⓢ Ⓧ 🔊 📂 🔒 💻

▲▲▲ ▼▼▼▼ Chicago Marriott Schaumburg Ⓗ
(847) 240-0100. **$79-$209.** 50 N Martingale Rd. I-290, exit Higgins Rd W (SR 72), 0.5 mi s. Int corridors. **Pets:** Accepted.
ⓈAVE Ⓧ 🔊 📂 🔒 💻 🍴

▼▼▼▼ Drury Inn-Schaumburg Ⓜ
(847) 517-7737. **$70-$125.** 600 N Martingale Rd. I-290, exit Higgins Rd W (SR 72), just w, then just n. Int corridors. **Pets:** Small, other species. Service with restrictions.
Ⓧ 🔊 🔒 💻 🏊

▼▼▼▼ Holiday Inn Schaumburg/Hoffman Estates Ⓜ
(847) 310-0500. **$89-$139.** 1550 N Roselle Rd. I-90, exit Roselle Rd, then 0.8 mi s. Int corridors. **Pets:** Medium, other species. Service with restrictions, crate.
Ⓐ︎SK Ⓢ Ⓧ 🔊 🔒 💻 🍴 🏊

▼▼▼▼ Homestead Studio Suites-Chicago/Schaumburg Ⓜ
(847) 882-6900. **$84-$94.** 51 E State Pkwy. I-90, exit Roselle Rd, 0.8 mi s, then just e. Int corridors. **Pets:** Accepted.
Ⓐ︎SK Ⓢ Ⓧ 🔊 📂 🔒 🔒 💻

▼▼▼▼ Homewood Suites Schaumburg Ⓐ
(847) 605-0400. **$169-$189.** 815 E American Ln. I-290, exit Higgins Rd (SR 72), 0.5 mi w, 0.8 mi n on Meacham, then 0.8 mi w. Ext/int corridors. **Pets:** Accepted.
ⓈAVE Ⓢ Ⓧ 🔊 🔒 💻

▼▼▼▼ La Quinta Inn Schaumburg Ⓜ
(847) 517-8484. **$89-$139.** 1730 E Higgins Rd. I-290, exit Higgins Rd W (SR 72), just w. Int corridors. **Pets:** Small. $25 deposit/pet. Designated rooms, service with restrictions, supervision.
ⓈAVE Ⓧ 🔊 🔒 💻 🏊

▲▲▲ ▼▼▼▼ Summerfield Suites by Wyndham-Chicago/Schaumburg Ⓐ
(847) 619-6677. **$99-$165.** 901 E Woodfield Office Ct. Jct SR 53, 1.5 w on SR 72 (Higgins Rd), then 0.3 mi n on Plum Grove Rd. Ext/int corridors. **Pets:** Medium, other species. $150 one-time fee/room. Service with restrictions, crate.
ⓈAVE Ⓧ 🔊 🔒 💻 🏊

SCHILLER PARK

▲▲▲ ▼▼▼▼ Residence Inn by Marriott O'Hare-Schiller Park Ⓐ 🐾
(847) 725-2210. **$109-$179.** 9450 W Lawrence Ave. 0.5 mi e of US 12 and 45. Int corridors. **Pets:** Other species. $7 daily fee/room, $100 one-time fee/room. Service with restrictions, crate.
ⓈAVE Ⓢ Ⓧ 🔒 💻 🍴

SKOKIE

▼▼▼▼ Holiday Inn Northshore Ⓜ
(847) 679-8900. **$149-$189.** 5300 W Touhy Ave. I-94, exit 39A, 0.5 mi w. Ext/int corridors. **Pets:** Small. Designated rooms, service with restrictions, supervision.
Ⓐ︎SK Ⓢ Ⓧ 🔊 🔒 🔒 💻 🍴 🏊

▲▲▲ ▼▼▼▼ Howard Johnson Hotel-Skokie Ⓜ
(847) 679-4200. **$137-$164.** 9333 Skokie Blvd. On US 41, just n of Gross Point Rd. Int corridors. **Pets:** Other species. Service with restrictions, supervision.
ⓈAVE Ⓢ Ⓧ 🔒 🔒 💻 🍴 🏊

SOUTH HOLLAND

▼▼ Motel 6 Ⓜ
(708) 331-1621. **$40-$55.** 17301 S Halsted St. I-80/294, exit Halsted St N. Ext corridors. **Pets:** Accepted.
Ⓢ Ⓧ

ST. CHARLES

▼▼ Super 8 Motel-St. Charles M
(630) 377-8388. $75-$80, 14 days notice. 1520 E Main St. On SR 64, 1 mi e. Int corridors. Pets: Accepted.
ASK Sₒ ✕ 🖬

TINLEY PARK

AAA ▼▼▼ Baymont Inn & Suites Chicago-Tinley Park M
(708) 633-1200. $74-$94. 7255 W 183rd St. I-80, exit 148B, just n. Int corridors. Pets: Other species. $50 deposit/room. Designated rooms, service with restrictions, supervision.
SAVE Sₒ ✕ ␣M 🖉 ␣ 🖬 💻 🕹

VERNON HILLS

AAA ▼▼▼ AmeriSuites (Chicago/Vernon Hills) M
(847) 918-1400. $99-$159. 450 N Milwaukee Ave. SR 21, 0.3 mi s of jct SR 60. Int corridors. Pets: Service with restrictions, crate.
SAVE ✕ ␣M 🖉 ␣ 🖬 💻 🕹

▼▼▼ Homestead Studio Suites-Chicago/Vernon Hills M ❀
(847) 955-1111. $79-$104. 675 Woodlands Pkwy. I-94, exit SR 60 (Town Line Rd), 2.1 mi w to Milwaukee Ave (SR 21), 1.9 mi s to Woodlands Pkwy, then just w. Int corridors. Pets: Other species. $75 one-time fee/room. Designated rooms, service with restrictions.
ASK Sₒ ✕ 🖉 ␣ 🖬 💻

WARRENVILLE

AAA ▼▼▼ AmeriSuites (Chicago/Warrenville) M
(630) 393-0400. $79-$129. 4305 Weaver Pkwy. I-88, exit Winfield Rd, just s. Int corridors. Pets: Very small, other species. Service with restrictions, crate.
SAVE Sₒ ✕ ␣M 🖉 ␣ 🖬 💻 🕹

WAUKEGAN

▼▼ Best Inn M
(847) 336-9000. Call for rates. 31 N Green Bay Rd. I-94, exit Grand Ave (SR 132 E), 3.5 mi e to SR 131, 0.7 mi s. Int corridors. Pets: Accepted.
ASK ✕ 🖬 💻 🕹

▼▼▼ Candlewood Suites Chicago/Waukegan A
(847) 578-5250. $99-$119. 1151 S Waukegan Rd. I-94, exit Buckley Rd (SR 137), 0.5 mi e to SR 43 (Waukegan Rd), 1.9 mi n. Int corridors. Pets: Accepted.
ASK Sₒ ✕ 🖉 ␣ 🖬 💻

AAA ▼▼▼ Residence Inn by Marriott-Waukegan A
(847) 689-9240. $99-$179. 1440 S White Oak Dr. I-94, exit SR 137 (Buckley Rd), 0.5 mi e to SR 43 (Waukegan Rd), 1.5 mi n. Int corridors. Pets: Medium, other species. $5 daily fee/room, $75 one-time fee/pet. Service with restrictions, crate.
SAVE Sₒ ✕ ␣M 🖉 ␣ 🖬 💻 🕹

WEST DUNDEE

AAA ▼▼▼ TownePlace Suites A
(847) 608-6320. $58-$104. 2185 Marriott Dr. I-90, exit SR 31, 0.4 mi n to Marriott Dr, just e. Int corridors. Pets: Medium, other species. $100 one-time fee/room. Service with restrictions.
SAVE Sₒ ✕ ␣ 🖬 💻 🕹

WESTMONT

▼▼▼ Homestead Studio Suites-Chicago/Westmont/Oak Brook M
(630) 323-9292. $89-$119. 855 Pasquinelli Dr. SR 83, exit Ogden Ave (US 34), just w to Pasquinelli Dr, 0.5 mi n. Int corridors. Pets: Medium. $75 one-time fee/room. Service with restrictions, crate.
ASK Sₒ ✕ ␣M 🖉 ␣ 🖬 💻

WILLOWBROOK

AAA ▼▼▼ Baymont Inn & Suites Chicago-Willowbrook M
(630) 654-0077. $69-$89. 855 79th St. I-55, exit 274, just n. Int corridors. Pets: Small. Designated rooms, service with restrictions, supervision.
SAVE Sₒ ✕ 🖉 ␣ 💻

AAA ▼▼▼ Red Roof Inn M
(630) 323-8811. $57-$87. 7535 Robert Kingery Hwy. I-55, exit 274, 0.5 mi n on SR 83. Ext corridors. Pets: Medium. Service with restrictions, supervision.
SAVE ✕ 🖉 ␣

❖ END METROPOLITAN AREA ❖

CHILLICOTHE

▼▼▼ Super 8 Motel M
(309) 274-2568. $55-$65. 615 S Fourth St. 1.1 mi s on SR 29. Int corridors. Pets: Accepted.
ASK Sₒ ✕ ␣

COLLINSVILLE

▼▼▼ Drury Inn Collinsville M
(618) 345-7700. $82-$108. 602 N Bluff Rd. I-55/70, exit 11 (SR 157), just n. Int corridors. Pets: Accepted.
✕ ␣M 🖉 ␣ 🖬 💻 🕹

▼▼▼▼ **Holiday Inn Collinsville/St. Louis** Ⓜ
(618) 345-2800. **$121-$151.** 1000 Eastport Plaza Dr. I-55/70, exit 11 (SR 157), just nw. Int corridors. **Pets:** Medium, dogs only. Service with restrictions, supervision.
ASK Sⓓ ✕ 🖪 🖵 🍴 ⌁

▼▼ **Motel 6–1133** Ⓜ
(618) 345-2100. **$39-$61.** 295A N Bluff Rd. I-55/70, exit 11 (SR 157), just s. Int corridors. **Pets:** Other species. Service with restrictions, supervision.
Sⓓ ✕ 🖉 ✦

▼▼▼▼ **Pear Tree Inn by Drury** Ⓜ
(618) 345-9500. **$40-$79.** 552 Ramada Blvd. I-55/70, exit 11 (SR 157), just s. Ext corridors. **Pets:** Accepted.
✕ 🖤M 🖉 ✦ 🖪 🖵 ⌁

DANVILLE

ⒶⒶⒶ ▼▼▼ **Best Western Regency Inn** Ⓜ
(217) 446-2111. **$70-$90, 3 days notice.** 360 Eastgate Dr. I-74, exit 220 (Lynch Dr), just n. Ext/int corridors. **Pets:** Medium. $10 daily fee/pet. Designated rooms, service with restrictions, supervision.
SAVE Sⓓ ✕ 🖪 🖵

ⒶⒶⒶ ▼▼▼▼ **Best Western Riverside** Ⓜ
(217) 431-0020. **$75-$95.** 57 S Gilbert St. I-74, exit 215, 0.8 mi n, on US 150 and SR 1. Ext/int corridors. **Pets:** Medium. $10 daily fee/pet. Designated rooms, service with restrictions, supervision.
SAVE Sⓓ ✕ 🖪 🖵 ⌁

▼▼ **Comfort Inn** Ⓜ
(217) 443-8004. **$54-$84, 7 days notice.** 383 Lynch Dr. I-74, exit 220 (Lynch Dr), just n. Int corridors. **Pets:** Accepted.
SAVE Sⓓ ✕ 🖉 🖪 🖵 ⌁

▼▼ **Sleep Inn & Suites** Ⓜ
(217) 442-6600. **$70-$159.** 361 Lynch Dr. I-74, exit 220 (Lynch Dr), just n, then just e. Int corridors. **Pets:** Accepted.
SAVE Sⓓ ✕ 🖪 🖵 ⌁

▼▼ **Super 8-Danville** Ⓜ
(217) 443-4499. **$53-$60.** 377 Lynch Dr. I-74, exit 220 (Lynch Dr), just n. Int corridors. **Pets:** Accepted.
ASK Sⓓ ✕ 🖪 🖵

DECATUR

ⒶⒶⒶ ▼▼▼ **Baymont Inn-Decatur** Ⓜ
(217) 875-5800. **$59-$69.** 5100 Hickory Pt Frontage Rd. I-72, exit 141B (US 51 N), then s on frontage road. Int corridors. **Pets:** Accepted.
SAVE Sⓓ ✕ 🖉 🖪 🖵

▼ **Super 8 Motel-Decatur** Ⓜ
(217) 877-8888. **$55.** 3141 N Water St. I-72, exit 141A (US 51 S), 1.8 mi s. Int corridors. **Pets:** Accepted.
ASK Sⓓ ✕

DEKALB

ⒶⒶⒶ ▼▼▼▼ **Best Western DeKalb Inn & Suites** Ⓜ
(815) 758-8661. **$79-$89.** 1212 W Lincoln Hwy. I-88, exit Annie Glidden Rd, 2 mi n to W Lincoln Hwy (SR 38), then just w. Ext/int corridors. **Pets:** Medium. $10 daily fee/pet. Designated rooms, service with restrictions, supervision.
SAVE Sⓓ ✕ 🖉 🖪 🖵 ⌁

DIXON

ⒶⒶⒶ ▼▼▼ **Best Western Brandywine Lodge** Ⓜ
(815) 284-1890. **$70-$76.** 443 Illinois Rt 2. SR 2, 3.6 mi w of jct SR 26. Int corridors. **Pets:** Other species. $25 deposit/pet. Crate.
SAVE Sⓓ ✕ 🖪 🖵 🍴 ⌁

ⒶⒶⒶ ▼▼▼▼ **Comfort Inn** Ⓜ ❀
(815) 284-0500. **$64-$74.** 136 Plaza Dr. I-88, exit SR 26, just n, then just e. Int corridors. **Pets:** Medium. $15 daily fee/pet. Designated rooms, service with restrictions, supervision.
SAVE Sⓓ ✕ 🖪 🖵 ⌁

EAST PEORIA

▼▼ **Super 8 Motel** Ⓜ
(309) 698-8889. **$52-$72.** 725 Taylor St. I-74, exit 96, just e. Int corridors. **Pets:** Small. Designated rooms, service with restrictions, supervision.
ASK Sⓓ ✕ 🖪 🖵

EFFINGHAM

ⒶⒶⒶ ▼▼▼ **Best Western Raintree Inn** Ⓜ
(217) 342-4121. **$48-$65, 10 days notice.** 1811 W Fayette Ave. I-57/70, exit 159. Ext/int corridors. **Pets:** Medium. Designated rooms, service with restrictions, supervision.
SAVE Sⓓ ✕ 🖵 ⌁

ⒶⒶⒶ ▼▼▼▼ **Comfort Inn** Ⓜ
(217) 347-5050. **$48-$75, 10 days notice.** 1304 W Evergreen Dr. I-57/70, exit 160, just e, then just n. Int corridors. **Pets:** Accepted.
SAVE Sⓓ ✕ 🖤M 🖤 🖪 🖵 ⌁

ⒶⒶⒶ ▼▼▼▼ **Comfort Suites** Ⓜ
(217) 342-3151. **$59-$89, 10 days notice.** 1310 W Fayette Ave. I-57/70, exit 159, 0.4 mi e. Int corridors. **Pets:** Designated rooms, no service, supervision.
SAVE Sⓓ ✕ 🖤M 🖤 🖪 🖵

ⒶⒶⒶ ▼▼▼ **Days Inn** Ⓜ
(217) 342-9271. **$59-$69.** 1412 W Fayette Ave. I-57/70, exit 159, just e. Ext corridors. **Pets:** Other species. $5 one-time fee/pet. Service with restrictions, supervision.
SAVE Sⓓ ✕ 🖪 🖵 ⌁

▼▼▼ **Hampton Inn** Ⓜ
(217) 342-4499. **$66-$84, 10 days notice.** 1509 Hampton Dr. I-57/70, exit 160, just s. Int corridors. **Pets:** Medium. Designated rooms, service with restrictions, supervision.
SAVE Sⓓ ✕ 🖤M 🖤 🖪 🖵 ⌁

▼▼▼▼ **Holiday Inn Express** Ⓜ
(217) 540-1111. **$69-$139.** 1103 Ave of Mid-America. I-57/
70, exit 160 (SR 32/33), just n. Int corridors. **Pets:** $10 daily
fee/pet. Service with restrictions, supervision.

(ASK) (⅏) (✕) (ᴍ) (📖) (💻) (🏊)

▼▼▼▼ **Keller Inn** Ⓜ
(217) 342-2131. **$75-$149.** 1201 N Keller Dr. I-57/70, exit
160 (SR 32/33), just ne. Ext/int corridors. **Pets:** Accepted.

(ASK) (⅏) (✕) (📖) (💻) (🏊)

ⒶⒶⒶ ▼ **Paradise Inn** Ⓜ
(217) 342-2165. **$34-$39.** 1000 W Fayette Ave. I-57/70, exit
159, 1 mi e. Ext corridors. **Pets:** Medium. $20 deposit/pet,
$6 daily fee/pet. Designated rooms, service with restrictions,
supervision.

(SAVE) (⅏) (✕) (📖)

▼▼ **Super 8 Motel** Ⓜ ❀
(217) 342-6888. **$56-$76.** 1400 Thelma Keller Ave. I-57/70,
exit 160 (SR 32/33), 0.5 mi n. Int corridors. **Pets:** Other
species. Supervision.

(ASK) (⅏) (✕) (🔅) (📖) (💻)

FAIRVIEW HEIGHTS

▼▼ **Drury Inn-Fairview Heights** Ⓜ
(618) 398-8530. **$78-$108.** 12 Ludwig Dr. I-64, exit 12 (SR
159). Int corridors. **Pets:** Accepted.

(✕) (📖) (💻) (🏊)

ⒶⒶⒶ ▼▼▼▼ **Ramada Inn Fairview Heights** Ⓜ
(618) 632-4747. **$69-$89.** 6900 N Illinois Ave. I-64, exit 12
(SR 159), just n. Int corridors. **Pets:** Small. $25 one-time
fee/room. Service with restrictions, crate.

(SAVE) (⅏) (✕) (📖) (💻) (🍴)

▼▼ **Super 8 Motel** Ⓜ
(618) 398-8338. **$56-$77.** 45 Ludwig Dr. I-64, exit 12 (SR
159). Int corridors. **Pets:** Other species. Service with restrictions, supervision.

(ASK) (⅏) (✕) (🔅) (📖)

FORSYTH

▼▼▼▼ **Comfort Inn of Forsyth** Ⓜ
(217) 875-1166. **$54-$62, 7 days notice.** 134 Barnett Ave.
I-72, exit 141B (US 51), 0.5 mi n. Int corridors.
Pets: Accepted.

(SAVE) (⅏) (✕) (🔅) (📖) (💻) (🏊)

GALENA

ⒶⒶⒶ ▼▼▼▼ **Best Western Quiet House**
Suites Ⓜ ❀
(815) 777-2577. **$211.** 9915 US 20 W. On US 20, 1 mi e.
Ext/int corridors. **Pets:** Large, other species. $15 daily fee/
pet. Designated rooms, service with restrictions, supervision.

(SAVE) (⅏) (✕) (📖) (💻) (🏊)

GALESBURG

▼▼▼▼ **Comfort Inn** Ⓜ
(309) 344-5445. **$64-$99.** 907 W Carl Sandburg Dr. US 34,
exit US 150 E. Int corridors. **Pets:** Other species. $15 one-
time fee/room. Designated rooms, service with restrictions,
supervision.

(SAVE) (⅏) (✕) (ᴍ) (🔅) (📖) (💻)

▼▼▼▼ **Holiday Inn Express** Ⓜ
(309) 343-7100. **$75-$114.** 2285 Washington St. I-74, exit
48A (US 150), just w to Michigan Ave, just s to Washington
St, then just e. Int corridors. **Pets:** Accepted.

(ASK) (⅏) (✕) (ᴍ) (🔅) (📖) (💻) (🏊)

ⒶⒶⒶ ▼▼▼▼ **Jumer's Continental Inn** Ⓜ
(309) 343-7151. **$72-$80.** 260 S Soangetaha Rd. I-74, exit
48 (Main St), just e, then just s. Int corridors.
Pets: Accepted.

(SAVE) (✕) (🔅) (📖) (💻) (🏊)

GILMAN

ⒶⒶⒶ ▼▼▼ **Super 8 of Gilman** Ⓜ
(815) 265-7000. **$57-$69, 7 days notice.** 1301 S Crescent
St. I-57, exit 283, 0.3 mi e. Int corridors. **Pets:** Accepted.

(SAVE) (⅏) (✕) (🔅) (📖)

ⒶⒶⒶ ▼▼▼ **Travel Inn** Ⓜ
(815) 265-7283. **$50, 4 days notice.** 834 Hwy 24 W. I-57,
exit 283, just e. Ext/int corridors. **Pets:** Medium. $5 daily
fee/pet. Designated rooms, service with restrictions, supervision.

(SAVE) (⅏) (✕) (🏊)

GREENVILLE

ⒶⒶⒶ ▼▼▼ **Budget Host Inn** Ⓜ
(618) 664-1950. **$30-$47, 3 days notice.** 1525 S SR 127.
I-70, exit 45, 0.3 mi n. Ext corridors. **Pets:** $5 daily fee/pet.
Service with restrictions, supervision.

(SAVE) (⅏) (✕) (📖) (💻) (🏊)

JACKSONVILLE

ⒶⒶⒶ ▼▼▼ **Star Lite Motel** Ⓜ
(217) 245-7184. **$42-$48, 10 days notice.** 1910 W Morton
Ave. On US 67/SR 104, 1.8 mi w. Ext corridors.
Pets: Accepted.

(SAVE) (⅏) (✕) (📖)

▼▼ **Super 8 Motel** Ⓜ
(217) 479-0303. **$49-$79.** 1003 W Morton Ave. On US 67,
0.9 mi w. Int corridors. **Pets:** Other species. $10 daily fee/
room. Service with restrictions, supervision.

(ASK) (⅏) (✕) (📖) (💻)

LINCOLN

▼▼▼▼ **Holiday Inn Express** Ⓜ
(217) 735-5800. **$72-$125.** 130 Olson Dr. I-55, exit 126 (US
121), just e to Heitman Dr, just w to Olson Dr, then just n.
Int corridors. **Pets:** Other species. Designated rooms, service with restrictions, supervision.

(ASK) (⅏) (✕) (🔅) (📖) (💻) (🏊)

LITCHFIELD

(AAA) ▼▼▼▼ Baymont Inn of Litchfield M
(217) 324-4556. **$69-$79, 7 days notice.** 1405 W Hudson Dr. I-55, exit 52 (SR 16), just e to Ohren Ln, just s to W Hudson Dr, then just w. Int corridors. **Pets:** Small. Designated rooms, service with restrictions, supervision.

[SAVE] [S₀] [X] [🔌] [💻] [➷]

▼▼▼▼ Litchfield Comfort Inn M ❀
(217) 324-9260. **$61-$66, 3 days notice.** 1010 E Columbian Blvd N. I-55, exit 52 (SR 16), 0.7 mi e to Old SR 66, then 0.3 mi n. Int corridors. **Pets:** Other species. $10 one-time fee/room. Service with restrictions, crate.

[SAVE] [S₀] [X] [🔌] [💻] [➷]

MARION

▼▼▼▼ Drury Inn-Marion M
(618) 997-9600. **$52-$92.** 2706 W DeYoung St. I-57, exit 54 (SR 13), 0.5 mi w. Int corridors. **Pets:** Other species. Service with restrictions, supervision.

[X] [⬤M] [🔌] [🔌] [🔌] [💻] [➷]

▼▼▼▼ Hampton Inn-Marion M
(618) 998-9900. **$64-$76.** 2710 W DeYoung St. I-57, exit 54B (SR 13), 0.7 mi w to Williamson County Pkwy, just n to DeYoung St, then just e. Int corridors. **Pets:** Accepted.

[SAVE] [X] [🔌] [🔌] [💻] [➷]

▼ Motel 6 #1174 M
(618) 993-2631. **$39-$42.** 1008 Halfway Rd. I-57, exit 54B (SR 13), 0.3 mi w. Ext corridors. **Pets:** Other species. Supervision.

[X]

▼▼ Super 8 Motel M
(618) 993-5577. **$56-$76.** 2601 W DeYoung St. I-57, exit 54B (SR 13), just w. Int corridors. **Pets:** Accepted.

[ASK] [S₀] [X] [🔌] [🔌] [💻]

METROPOLIS

▼▼▼▼ Isle of View Bed & Breakfast BB
(618) 524-5838. **$70-$135, 7 days notice.** 205 Metropolis St. I-24, exit 37, 3 mi w, 0.3 mi s of US 45. Int corridors. **Pets:** Large, other species. Supervision.

▼▼▼ Super 8 M
(618) 524-8200. **$52-$70.** 2055 E 5th St. I-24, exit 37, just w. Int corridors. **Pets:** Accepted.

[ASK] [S₀] [X] [🔌] [🔌] [🔌] [💻]

MOLINE

▼▼▼▼ Comfort Inn M
(309) 762-7000. **$64-$99.** 2600 52nd Ave. In Moline, IL; I-280/74, exit 5B westbound; I-280, exit 18A eastbound, just s to traffic light, then 0.5 mi w, n on 27th St. Int corridors. **Pets:** Accepted.

[SAVE] [S₀] [X] [🔌] [💻] [➷]

(AAA) ▼▼▼ Exel Inn of Moline M
(309) 797-5580. **$43-$55.** 2501 52nd Ave. In Moline, IL; I-280/74, exit 5B westbound; I-280, exit 18A eastbound, just s on US 6 and 150, then 1 mi nw on 27th St. Int corridors. **Pets:** Accepted.

[SAVE] [S₀] [X] [🔌] [💻]

▼▼▼▼ Hampton Inn-Airport M
(309) 762-1711. **$79-$87.** 6920 27th St. In Moline, IL; I-280/74, exit 5B westbound; I-280, exit 18A eastbound, just s on US 6 and 150, then just nw. Int corridors. **Pets:** Accepted.

[SAVE] [S₀] [X] [🔌] [🔌] [💻] [➷]

▼▼▼▼ Holiday Inn-Airport Convention Center MI
(309) 762-8811. **$69-$98.** 6902 27th St. In Moline, IL; I-280/74, exit 5B westbound; I-280, exit 18A eastbound, just s on US 6 and 150, then just nw. Int corridors. **Pets:** Accepted.

[ASK] [S₀] [X] [🔌] [🔌] [🔌] [💻] [🍴] [➷]

▼▼▼▼ Holiday Inn Express-Moline Airport M ❀
(309) 762-8300. **$72.** 6910 27th St. In Moline, IL; I-280/74, exit 5B westbound; I-280, exit 18A eastbound, just s on US 6 and 150, then just nw. Int corridors. **Pets:** Other species. Service with restrictions, crate.

[ASK] [S₀] [X] [🔌] [💻]

(AAA) ▼▼▼▼ La Quinta Inn M
(309) 762-9008. **$56-$76.** 5450 27th St. In Moline, IL; I-280/74, exit 5B westbound; I-280, exit 18A eastbound, just s on US 6 and 150 to traffic light, just n, then w on 27th St. Int corridors. **Pets:** Other species. Designated rooms, service with restrictions.

[SAVE] [S₀] [X] [🔌] [💻]

MONTICELLO

(AAA) ▼▼▼▼ Best Western Monticello Gateway Inn M
(217) 762-9436. **$68-$88.** 805 Iron Horse Pl. I-72, exit 166, just s. Ext/int corridors. **Pets:** Small. $100 deposit/room. Designated rooms, service with restrictions, supervision.

[SAVE] [S₀] [X] [🔌] [💻] [➷]

MORRIS

▼▼▼ Best Western of Morris M
(815) 942-9000. **$55.** 80 Hampton Rd. I-80, exit 112, just n. Int corridors. **Pets:** Other species. Service with restrictions.

[SAVE] [S₀] [X] [🔌] [🔌] [➷]

▼▼▼ Holiday Inn MI
(815) 942-6600. **$81-$91.** 200 Gore Rd. I-80, exit 112, 0.3 mi nw. Int corridors. **Pets:** Designated rooms, service with restrictions, supervision.

[ASK] [S₀] [X] [🔌] [🔌] [💻] [🍴] [➷]

MOUNT VERNON

▼▼ Best Inns of America M
(618) 244-4343. **$45-$51.** 222 S 44th St. I-57/64, exit 95 (SR 15), just e to 44th, then just s. Ext corridors. **Pets:** Accepted.

[ASK] [S₀] [X] [🔌] [💻] [➷]

▼▼ **Drury Inn-Mount Vernon** Ⓜ
(618) 244-4550. **$48-$94.** 145 N 44th St. I-57/64, exit 95 (SR 15), just e, then just n (entry through restaurant parking lot). Int corridors. **Pets:** Accepted.

✕ ⊘ 🛏 ▣ ➹

▼▼ **Holiday Inn** Ⓗ
(618) 244-7100. **$71-$170.** 222 Potomac Blvd. I-57/64, exit 95 (SR 15), just w to Potomac Blvd, then just n. Int corridors. **Pets:** Medium. Designated rooms, service with restrictions, supervision.

🅰🆂🅺 🆂 ✕ 🅶ᴹ ⊘ 🛏 ▣ 🍴

▼ **Motel 6-1180** Ⓜ
(618) 244-2383. **$35-$51.** 333 S 44th St. I-57/64, exit 95 (SR 15), just e to Mateer Dr, then 0.4 mi s. Ext corridors. **Pets:** Accepted.

🆂 ✕ ➹

▼ **Super 8 Motel** Ⓜ
(618) 242-8800. **$49-$69.** 401 S 44th St. I-57/64, exit 95 (SR 15), just e, then just s. Int corridors. **Pets:** Other species. Service with restrictions, crate.

🅰🆂🅺 🆂 ✕ 🛏 ▣

▼▼ **Thrifty Inn-Mt. Vernon** Ⓜ
(618) 244-7750. **$40-$66.** 100 N 44th St. I-57/64, exit 95 (SR 15), just e. Ext corridors. **Pets:** Accepted.

✕ ⊘

NASHVILLE

🔷 ▼▼ 🔷 **Best Western U S Inn** Ⓜ
(618) 478-5341. **$50-$60, 7 days notice.** 11640 SR 127. I-64, exit 50 (SR 127), 0.3 mi s. Int corridors. **Pets:** Accepted.

🆂🅰🆅🅴 🆂 ✕ 🅶ᴹ 🐾 🛏 ▣

NORMAL

🔷 ▼▼▼ 🔷 **Best Western University Inn** Ⓜ
(309) 454-4070. **$74.** 6 Traders Cir. I-55, exit 165A (US 51), just s, then return on frontage road. Int corridors. **Pets:** Small. Service with restrictions, supervision.

🆂🅰🆅🅴 🆂 ✕ ⊘ 🛏 ➹

▼▼▼ **Comfort Suites of Bloomington** Ⓜ
(309) 452-8588. **$75-$95, 7 days notice.** 310 B Greenbriar Dr. I-55, exit 167, follow I-55 business route (Veterans Pkwy) 1.3 mi s; at Fort Jesse Rd intersection. Int corridors. **Pets:** Accepted.

🆂🅰🆅🅴 🆂 ✕ 🅶ᴹ 🐾 🛏 ▣ ➹

▼▼▼ **Holiday Inn**
Bloomington-Normal Ⓜ ✿
(309) 452-8300. **$106.** 8 Traders Cir. I-55, exit 165A, 0.5 mi e, return on service road. Int corridors. **Pets:** Large, other species. $15 one-time fee/room. Service with restrictions.

🅰🆂🅺 🆂 ✕ ⊘ 🛏 ▣ 🍴 ➹

▼▼▼ **Holiday Inn Express Hotel & Suites** Ⓜ
(309) 862-1600. **$99.** 1715 Parkway Plaza Dr. I-55, exit 167, follow I-55 business route (Veterans Pkwy), 1.7 mi s to Parkway Plaza Dr, then just e. Int corridors. **Pets:** Accepted.

🅰🆂🅺 🆂 ✕ ⊘ 🐾 🛏 ▣ ➹

O'FALLON

🔷 ▼▼▼ 🔷 **Comfort Inn** Ⓜ
(618) 624-6060. **$65-$89.** 1100 Eastgate Dr. I-64, exit 19B (SR 158), 0.5 mi n, then just sw. Int corridors. **Pets:** $50 deposit/pet. Service with restrictions, crate.

🆂🅰🆅🅴 🆂 ✕ 🛏 ▣ ➹

▼▼ **Econo Lodge** Ⓜ
(618) 628-8895. **$58-$69.** 1409 W Hwy 50. I-64, exit 14 (US 50), 0.4 mi w. Int corridors. **Pets:** Other species. $40 deposit/room, $10 one-time fee/room. Service with restrictions, supervision.

🆂🅰🆅🅴 🆂 ✕ 🐾 🛏 ▣ ➹

OGLESBY

▼▼▼ **Holiday Inn Express** Ⓜ
(815) 883-3535. **$59-$64.** 900 Holiday St. I-39, exit 54, just e. Int corridors. **Pets:** Accepted.

🅰🆂🅺 🆂 ✕ 🛏 ▣ ➹

OTTAWA

▼▼▼ **Holiday Inn Express** Ⓜ
(815) 433-0029. **$73-$83.** 120 W Stevenson Rd. I-80, exit 90 (SR 23), just n. Int corridors. **Pets:** Other species. Designated rooms, service with restrictions, supervision.

🅰🆂🅺 🆂 ✕ 🛏 ▣ ➹

PEKIN

▼▼▼ **Comfort Inn** Ⓜ
(309) 353-4047. **$62-$85.** 3240 Vandever Ave. Just n of SR 9, 3 mi e from jct SR 29. Int corridors. **Pets:** Medium. $10 daily fee/pet. Designated rooms, service with restrictions.

🆂🅰🆅🅴 🆂 ✕ ⊘ 🛏 ▣ ➹

▼▼ **Concorde Inn & Suites** Ⓜ
(309) 347-5533. **$49-$72, 7 days notice.** 2801 E Court St. 2.5 mi e on SR 9 from jct SR 29. Ext corridors. **Pets:** Accepted.

🅰🆂🅺 🆂 ✕ 🐾 🛏 ▣ 🍴 ➹

PEORIA

▼▼▼ **Comfort Suites** Ⓜ
(309) 688-3800. **$75-$95.** 4021 N War Memorial Dr. I-74, exit 89 (War Memorial Dr/US 150), just e, then just s. Int corridors. **Pets:** Accepted.

🆂🅰🆅🅴 🆂 ✕ ⊘ 🛏 ▣ ➹

▼▼▼ **Holiday Inn-Brandywine** Ⓜ
(309) 686-8000. **$79.** 4400 N Brandywine Dr. I-74, exit 89 (US 150/War Memorial Dr), just nw. Int corridors. **Pets:** Other species. $50 deposit/room. Service with restrictions.

🅰🆂🅺 🆂 ✕ ⊘ 🛏 ▣ 🍴 ➹

Jumer Hotels-Castle Lodge H
(309) 673-8040. **$79-$149.** 117 N Western Ave. I-74, exit 91 (University South), 1 mi s to Moss, 0.7 mi w. Int corridors. **Pets:** Accepted.

SAVE 🛏️ ✕ 🐾 🛎️ 💻 🍴 ⇒

Mark Twain Hotel H
(309) 676-3600. **$109-$129.** 225 NE Adams St. I-74, exit 98B (Adams St), just w; exit 93 eastbound. Int corridors. **Pets:** Other species. $50 deposit/room. Service with restrictions, supervision.

ASK 🛏️ ✕ 🛎️ 💻 🍴

Red Roof Inn M
(309) 685-3911. **$44-$62.** 4031 N War Memorial Dr. I-74, exit 89 (US 150/War Memorial Dr), just e. Ext corridors. **Pets:** Large, other species. Service with restrictions, supervision.

SAVE ✕ 🐾 🛎️

Residence Inn by Marriott A
(309) 681-9000. **$129-$149.** 4201 N War Memorial Dr. I-74, exit 89 (US 150/War Memorial Dr), just n; enter through Northlands Mall. Int corridors. **Pets:** Other species. $10 daily fee/room, $25 one-time fee/room. Service with restrictions, crate.

SAVE 🛏️ ✕ 🐾 🛎️ 💻 ⇒

Sleep Inn & Suites M
(309) 682-3322. **$63-$89.** 4244 Brandywine Dr. I-74, exit 89 (US 150/Memorial Dr), just w to Brandywine Dr, then just ne. Int corridors. **Pets:** Small. Designated rooms, service with restrictions, crate.

SAVE 🛏️ ✕ ⛆ 🐾 ⛆ 🛎️ 💻 ⇒

Super 8 Motel of Peoria M
(309) 688-8074. **$54-$76.** 4025 N War Memorial Dr. I-74, exit 89 (US 150/War Memorial Dr), just e. Int corridors. **Pets:** Other species. Designated rooms, service with restrictions, supervision.

ASK 🛏️ ✕ 🐾 🛎️ 💻

PERU

Ramada Limited M
(815) 224-9000. **$69-$99.** 4389 Venture Dr. I-80, exit 75 (SR 251), 0.5 mi s to 38th St, just w to Venture Dr, 0.9 mi nw. Int corridors. **Pets:** Small. Designated rooms, service with restrictions, supervision.

ASK ✕ 🛎️ 💻 ⇒

PONTOON BEACH

Best Western Camelot Inn M
(618) 931-2262. **$54-$75, 7 days notice.** 1240 E Old Chain of Rocks Rd. I-270, exit 6B (SR 111), just n. Int corridors. **Pets:** Small, other species. $10 one-time fee/pet. Service with restrictions, supervision.

SAVE 🛏️ ✕ 🛎️ 💻 ⇒

QUINCY

Comfort Inn M
(217) 228-2700. **$58-$84.** 4122 Broadway. I-172, exit 14 (SR 104), 1.3 mi w. Int corridors. **Pets:** Other species. $10 one-time fee/room. Service with restrictions, supervision.

SAVE 🛏️ ✕ 🛎️ 💻 ⇒

Holiday Inn-Quincy H
(217) 222-2666. **$72-$82.** 201 S 3rd St. 0.3 mi s on SR 57 from jct SR 104. Int corridors. **Pets:** Other species. $10 one-time fee/room. Designated rooms, service with restrictions, crate.

ASK 🛏️ ✕ 💻 🍴 ⇒

Super 8 Motel M
(217) 228-8808. **$47.** 224 N 36th St. I-172, exit 14 (SR 104), 1.8 mi w, then just s. Int corridors. **Pets:** Small. Service with restrictions, supervision.

ASK 🛏️ ✕ ⛆ 🛎️

RANTOUL

Best Western Heritage Inn M
(217) 892-9292. **$45-$50.** 420 S Murray Rd. I-57, exit 250 (US 136), 0.5 mi e to Murray Rd, then just s. Ext corridors. **Pets:** Accepted.

SAVE 🛏️ ✕ 🛎️ 💻 ⇒

ROBINSON

Best Western Robinson Inn M
(618) 544-8448. **$59-$65.** 1500 W Main St. 1 mi w on SR 33. Int corridors. **Pets:** Other species. $5 daily fee/room. Service with restrictions, supervision.

SAVE 🛏️ ✕ 🐾 🛎️ 💻 🍴

ROCHELLE

Comfort Inn & Suites H
(815) 562-5551. **$65-$185, 30 days notice.** 1131 N 7th St. I-39, exit 99 (SR 38), 2.5 mi w; at jct of SR 38 and 251. Int corridors. **Pets:** Other species. $15 daily fee/room. Designated rooms, service with restrictions, crate.

SAVE 🛏️ ✕ 🛎️ 💻 🍴 ⇒

ROCK FALLS

Holiday Inn MI
(815) 626-5500. **$65-$70.** 2105 First Ave. I-88, exit 41 (SR 40), 0.4 mi n. Int corridors. **Pets:** Small, other species. $20 one-time fee/room. Designated rooms, service with restrictions, supervision.

ASK 🛏️ ✕ 🛎️ 💻 🍴 ⇒

Rock Falls Super 8 M
(815) 626-8800. **$55-$57.** 2100 First Ave. I-88, exit 41 (SR 40), 0.3 mi n, just w on W 21st St. Int corridors. **Pets:** Other species. No service, supervision.

ASK 🛏️ ✕ 🛎️

ROCKFORD

(AAA) ▼▼▼ Baymont Inn & Suites M
(815) 229-8200. **$66-$86.** 662 N Lyford Rd. I-90, exit US 20 business route, just e, then just n. Int corridors. **Pets:** Accepted.
[SAVE] [S] [X] [] []

(AAA) ▼▼▼ Best Suites M
(815) 227-1300. **$75-$99.** 7401 Walton St. I-90, exit US 20 business route, just w to Bell School Rd, then just s. Int corridors. **Pets:** Small. Designated rooms, service with restrictions, supervision.
[SAVE] [S] [X] [] [] [] [] []

(AAA) ▼▼▼ Best Western Colonial Inn M
(815) 398-5050. **$49-$170.** 4850 E State St. I-90, exit US 20 business route, 3.5 mi w. Int corridors. **Pets:** Accepted.
[SAVE] [S] [X] [] [] [] []

(AAA) ▼▼ Exel Inn of Rockford M
(815) 332-4915. **$44-$65.** 220 S Lyford Rd. I-90, exit US business route 20, just e, then just s. Int corridors. **Pets:** Accepted.
[SAVE] [S] [X] [] []

(AAA) ▼▼▼ Red Roof Inn M
(815) 398-9750. **$43-$76.** 7434 E State St. I-90, exit US 20 business route, just w. Ext corridors. **Pets:** Accepted.
[SAVE] [X] [] []

(AAA) ▼▼▼ Residence Inn by Marriott A
(815) 227-0013. **$86-$144.** 7542 Colosseum Dr. I-90, exit US 20 business route, just w. Int corridors. **Pets:** Accepted.
[SAVE] [S] [X] [] [] [] [] []

(AAA) ▼▼▼ Sleep Inn-Rockford M
(815) 398-8900. **$59-$99.** 725 Clark Dr. I-90, exit US 20 business route, just w to Bell School Rd, just n to Clark Dr, then 0.4 mi ne. Int corridors. **Pets:** $15 daily fee/room. Designated rooms, service with restrictions, supervision.
[SAVE] [S] [X] [] []

SALEM

▼▼ Super 8 Motel of Salem M
(618) 548-5882. **$58-$78.** 118 Woods Ln. I-57, exit 116 (US 50), just w. Ext/int corridors. **Pets:** Other species. Service with restrictions, supervision.
[ASK] [S] [X] [M] [] [] []

SAVOY

(AAA) ▼▼ Best Western Paradise Inn Motel M
(217) 356-1824. **$65-$75, 7 days notice.** 1001 N Dunlap. I-57, exit 229, 1 mi e to US 45, then 2.5 mi n. Ext corridors. **Pets:** Small, other species. $5 daily fee/pet. Service with restrictions, crate.
[SAVE] [S] [X] [] [] []

SPRINGFIELD

(AAA) ▼▼▼ Baymont Inn M
(217) 529-6655. **$72-$77.** 5871 S 6th St. I-55, exit 90 (Toronto Rd), just e to 6th St, then just n. Int corridors. **Pets:** Small, dogs only. Designated rooms, service with restrictions, supervision.
[SAVE] [S] [X] [M] [] [] [] [] []

(AAA) ▼▼▼ Best Inns M
(217) 522-1100. **$70-$97, 30 days notice.** 500 N 1st St. Just n of Capitol; at 1st St and Carpenter. Int corridors. **Pets:** Large. $10 one-time fee/room. Designated rooms, no service, supervision.
[SAVE] [S] [X] [] [] []

▼▼▼ Comfort Inn M
(217) 787-2250. **$77-$94.** 3442 Freedom Dr. I-72, exit 93 (Veterans Pkwy), 0.7 mi n to Lindbergh Blvd, just w to Freedom Dr, then just s. Int corridors. **Pets:** Accepted.
[SAVE] [S] [X] [] [] []

▼▼ Days Inn M
(217) 529-0171. **$64-$85, 3 days notice.** 3000 Stevenson Dr. I-55, exit 94 (Stevenson Dr), just w. Ext corridors. **Pets:** Other species. $5 daily fee/pet. Service with restrictions, crate.
[SAVE] [S] [X] [] [] [] []

▼▼▼ Drury Inn & Suites-Springfield M
(217) 529-3900. **$72-$102.** 3180 S Dirksen Pkwy. I-55, exit 94 (Stevenson Dr), just w to Dirksen Pkwy, then just n. Int corridors. **Pets:** Small, other species. Service with restrictions, supervision.
[X] [M] [] [] [] [] []

▼▼ Howard Johnson Inn & Suites M
(217) 541-8762. **$60-$111.** 1701 J David Jones Pkwy. 1.5 mi n of Capital Airport on SR 29; opposite west entrance to Lincoln's tomb. Ext corridors. **Pets:** Dogs only. $25 one-time fee/room. Service with restrictions, crate.
[ASK] [S] [X] [] [] []

▼▼ Pear Tree Inn by Drury M
(217) 529-9100. **$50-$76.** 3190 S Dirksen Pkwy. I-55, exit 94 (Stevenson Dr), just w. Int corridors. **Pets:** Small, other species. Service with restrictions, supervision.
[X] []

▼▼ Ramada Limited (South) M
(217) 529-1410. **$69-$79.** 5970 S 6th St. I-55, exit 90, 0.3 mi e. Int corridors. **Pets:** Very small. $10 daily fee/pet. Designated rooms, service with restrictions, supervision.
[ASK] [S] [X] [] []

(AAA) ▼▼▼ Red Roof Inn M
(217) 753-4302. **$45-$59.** 3200 Singer Ave. I-55, exit 96B, just w. Ext corridors. **Pets:** Medium, other species. Service with restrictions, crate.
[SAVE] [X] []

▼▼ Sleep Inn M
(217) 787-6200. **$64-$94, 7 days notice.** 3470 Freedom Dr. I-72, exit 93 (Veterans Pkwy), 0.7 mi n to Lindbergh Blvd, just w to Freedom Dr, then just s. Int corridors. **Pets:** $25 one-time fee/room. Service with restrictions, crate.
SAVE S⊘ ✕ ⊘ ☁ ☐ ▣

▼▼ Super 8 Springfield South M
(217) 529-8898. **$65, 7 days notice.** 3675 S 6th St. I-55, exit 92A (Business US 55), just n to Hazel Bell, just w to Access Rd, then just n. Int corridors. **Pets:** Other species. $10 daily fee/pet. Designated rooms, service with restrictions, supervision.
ASK S⊘ ✕ ☐ ▣

STAUNTON

▼▼ Staunton Super 8 M
(618) 635-5353. **$60-$70, 7 days notice.** 1527 Herman Rd. I-55, exit 41, 0.3 mi w. Int corridors. **Pets:** Medium, other species. Service with restrictions, supervision.
ASK S⊘ ✕ ⊘ ☐

TUSCOLA

▼▼▼ Holiday Inn Express M
(217) 253-6363. **$70-$80.** 1201 Tuscola Blvd. I-57, exit 212 (US 36), 0.3 mi w to Progress Blvd, just s to Tuscola Blvd, then 0.4 mi se. Int corridors. **Pets:** Medium, other species. Designated rooms, service with restrictions, supervision.
ASK S⊘ ✕ ⚬M ☐ ▣ ☁

▼▼ Super 8 Motel-Tuscola M
(217) 253-5488. **$45-$70.** 1007 E Hwy 36. I-57, exit 212 (US 36), 0.4 mi w. Int corridors. **Pets:** Accepted.
ASK S⊘ ✕ ☐ ▣

URBANA

▲▲▲ ▼▼▼ Ramada
Limited-Urbana/Champaign M ✿
(217) 328-4400. **$85, 3 days notice.** 902 W Killarney St. I-74, exit 183 (Lincoln Ave), just s to Killarney St, then just w. Int corridors. **Pets:** Small. $50 deposit/pet. Service with restrictions.
SAVE S⊘ ✕ ☐ ▣ ☁

▼▼ Sleep Inn M
(217) 367-6000. **$69-$109.** 1908 N Lincoln Ave. I-74, exit 183 (Lincoln Ave), 0.5 mi s. Int corridors. **Pets:** Large, other species. $5 one-time fee/room. Designated rooms, service with restrictions.
SAVE S⊘ ✕ ☁ ☐ ▣

VANDALIA

▲▲▲ ▼▼ Days Inn M
(618) 283-4400. **$51-$89, 14 days notice.** 1920 Kennedy Blvd. I-70, exit 63 (US 51), 0.6 mi n, on US 51. Ext corridors. **Pets:** Other species. $10 deposit/room. Designated rooms, service with restrictions, supervision.
SAVE S⊘ ✕ ☐ ▣ ☁

▲▲▲ ▼▼▼ Jay's Inn M
(618) 283-1200. **$46-$58.** 720 Gochenour St. I-70, exit 63 (US 51), just s. Ext corridors. **Pets:** Other species. Service with restrictions.
SAVE S⊘ ✕ ☐ ▣

▲▲▲ ▼▼▼▼ Ramada Limited Vandalia M
(618) 283-1400. **$58, 30 days notice.** 2707 Veterans Ave. I-70, exit 61, just s. Int corridors. **Pets:** Large, other species. $10 deposit/room. Designated rooms, service with restrictions, supervision.
SAVE S⊘ ✕ ☐ ▣ ☁

▲▲▲ ▼▼▼ Travelodge of Vandalia M
(618) 283-2363. **$45-$55, 5 days notice.** 1500 N 6th St. I-70, exit 63 (US 51), just s. Ext corridors. **Pets:** Medium. $3 daily fee/pet. Service with restrictions, supervision.
SAVE S⊘ ✕ ☐ ▣ ☁

WASHINGTON

▼▼ Super 8 Motel M
(309) 444-8881. **$46-$53.** 1884 Washington Rd. On Business SR 24, 1.5 mi w. Int corridors. **Pets:** Medium. $5 daily fee/pet. Service with restrictions, supervision.
ASK S⊘ ✕ ⊘ ☐

WATSEKA

▲▲▲ ▼▼ Super 8 Motel M
(815) 432-6000. **$57-$69, 7 days notice.** 710 W Walnut. On US 24; in center of town. Int corridors. **Pets:** Small, other species. $5 daily fee/pet. Service with restrictions, supervision.
SAVE S⊘ ✕ ☐

WEST CITY

▲▲▲ ▼▼ Days Inn M
(618) 439-3183. **$49-$54, 10 days notice.** 711 W Main St. I-57, exit 71, just e. Int corridors. **Pets:** Accepted.
SAVE S⊘ ✕ ☁ ☐ ▣ ⊞

▼▼ Super 8 Motel of Benton/West City M
(618) 438-8205. **$50-$70, 10 days notice.** 711 1/2 W Main St. I-57, exit 71 (SR 14), just e. Int corridors. **Pets:** Other species. $5 daily fee/pet. Designated rooms, service with restrictions, supervision.
ASK S⊘ ✕ ☁ ☐

INDIANA

CITY INDEX

ANGOLA

▼▼ ▼▼ Best Western Angola Inn M
(260) 665-9561. **$75-$85, 5 days notice.** 3155 US 20. I-69,
exit 148 (US 20). Ext corridors. **Pets:** Accepted.
[SAVE] [🔊] [✕]

AUBURN

▼▼▼▼ Holiday Inn Express M
(260) 925-1900. **$81.** 404 Touring Dr. I-69, exit 129, just e
off SR 8. Int corridors. **Pets:** Accepted.
[ASK] [🔊] [✕] [🆔] [🎵] [♿] [🛏] [💻]

**▼▼▼▼ Ramada Limited & Suites & Conference
   Center M**
(260) 920-1900. **$81-$105.** 306 Touring Dr. I-69, exit 129,
0.5 mi e on SR 8. Int corridors. **Pets:** Medium. Designated
rooms, service with restrictions, supervision.
[ASK] [🔊] [✕] [🛏] [💻]

BEDFORD

▼▼▼▼ Holiday Inn Express M
(812) 279-1206. **$80-$90.** 2800 Express Ln. On US 50/SR
37, 1.4 mi s from jct SR 450. Int corridors. **Pets:** $10 daily
fee/room. Designated rooms, service with restrictions, crate.
[ASK] [🔊] [✕] [🎵] [♿] [🛏] [💻] [🏊]

BLOOMINGTON

▼▼▼▼ Hampton Inn M
(812) 334-2100. **$79-$99.** 2100 N Walnut St. 1 mi e of jct
SR 37 on SR 45/46 Bypass, just s on College Ave/Walnut
St. Int corridors. **Pets:** Medium. Service with restrictions,
supervision.
[SAVE] [🔊] [✕] [🎵] [🛏] [💻] [🏊]

**ⒶⒶⒶ ▼▼▼▼ TownePlace Suites By
   Marriott M 🐾**
(812) 334-1234. **$84-$124.** 105 S Franklin Rd. Just w from
SR 37 at Third St, 0.3 mi n. Int corridors. **Pets:** Medium.
$75 one-time fee/room. Service with restrictions.
[SAVE] [🔊] [✕] [🛏] [💻] [🏊]

BLUFFTON

▼ Budget Inn M
(260) 824-0820. **$39-$45.** 1090 N Main St. Jct SR 1 and
116; north side of town. Ext corridors. **Pets:** Accepted.
[ASK] [🔊] [✕] [🛏]

CHESTERTON

▼▼ ▼▼ Super 8 Motel M
(219) 929-5549. **$59-$64.** 418 Council Dr. I-94, exit 26A,
0.5 mi s; I-80/90, exit 31, 3 mi n on SR 49, just se. Int
corridors. **Pets:** Accepted.
[ASK] [🔊] [✕] [🎵]

CLARKSVILLE

▼▼ ▼▼ Best Western Green Tree Inn M
(812) 288-9281. **$69-$89.** 1425 Broadway. I-65, exit 4, just
w. Ext corridors. **Pets:** Small, dogs only. Service with
restrictions.
[SAVE] [🔊] [✕] [🛏] [💻] [🏊]

CLOVERDALE

▼▼▼▼ Holiday Inn Express M
(765) 795-5050. **$89-$90, 30 days notice.** 1017 N Main St.
I-70, exit 41. Int corridors. **Pets:** Medium, other species.
$25 one-time fee/room. Crate.
[ASK] [🔊] [✕] [🆔] [🎵] [🛏] [💻] [🏊]

COLUMBUS

AAA WW Days Inn Columbus M
(812) 376-9951. **$49-$59.** 3445 Jonathan Moore Pike. I-65, exit 68, just w. Int corridors. **Pets:** Accepted.
[SAVE] [S] [X] [H] [L] [~]

AAA WWW Holiday Inn Columbus-Conference Center MI
(812) 372-1541. **$80-$120, 3 days notice.** 2480 Jonathan Moore Pike. I-65, exit 68, just e on SR 46. Ext/int corridors. **Pets:** Accepted.
[SAVE] [S] [X] [&M] [D] [H] [L] [TI] [~]

AAA WW Ramada Inn & Plaza Hotel Conference Center MI
(812) 376-3051. **$85-$125.** 2485 Jonathan Moore Pike. I-65, exit 68, just e on SR 46. Int corridors. **Pets:** Accepted.
[SAVE] [S] [X] [H] [L] [TI] [~] [X]

CRAWFORDSVILLE

AAA WWW Comfort Inn M
(765) 361-0665. **$79-$125.** 2991 N Gandhi Dr. I-74, exit 34, just s on US 231. Int corridors. **Pets:** Accepted.
[SAVE] [S] [X] [H] [L] [~]

WWW Holiday Inn-Crawfordsville MI
(765) 362-8700. **$74-$79.** 2500 N Lafayette Rd. I-74, exit 34, 0.3 mi s on US 231. Ext corridors. **Pets:** Small. $5 daily fee/pet. Designated rooms, service with restrictions, supervision.
[S] [X] [H] [L] [TI] [~]

DALE

AAA WWW Baymont Inn & Suites M
(812) 937-7000. **$60-$120.** 20857 N US 231. I-64, exit 57 (US 231), just s. Int corridors. **Pets:** Accepted.
[SAVE] [S] [X] [&M] [L] [H] [L] [~]

DECATUR

AAA WW Days Inn M ✿
(260) 728-2196. **$49-$52.** 1033 N 13th St. On US 27 and 33, 0.5 mi n of jct US 224. Ext/int corridors. **Pets:** Dogs only. $5 daily fee/pet. Service with restrictions, crate.
[SAVE] [S] [X] [H] [L] [~]

ELKHART

AAA WW Econo Lodge M
(574) 262-0540. **$34-$49.** 3440 Cassopolis St. I-80/90, exit 92, 0.3 mi n. Ext corridors. **Pets:** Small, other species. $4 one-time fee/pet. Service with restrictions, crate.
[SAVE] [S] [X] [H] [~]

WWW Quality Inn & Suites M
(574) 264-0404. **$69-$169, 30 days notice.** 3321 Plaza Ct. I-80/90, exit 92, just n. Int corridors. **Pets:** Small, other species. $10 one-time fee/pet. Designated rooms, service with restrictions, crate.
[SAVE] [S] [X] [H] [L] [~]

AAA WW Red Roof Inn-Elkhart M
(574) 262-3691. **$44-$71.** 2902 Cassopolis St. I-80/90, exit 92, 0.5 mi s. Ext corridors. **Pets:** Accepted.
[SAVE] [X] [D] [L] [H]

WW Super 8 Motel-Elkhart M
(574) 264-4457. **$45-$139, 7 days notice.** 345 Windsor Ave. I-80/90, exit 92, just s. Int corridors. **Pets:** Accepted.
[ASK] [S] [X] [H] [L]

EVANSVILLE

AAA WWWW Casino Aztar Hotel H
(812) 433-4000. **$69-$115.** 421 NW Riverside Dr. SR 62 (Lloyd Expwy), just s on Fulton. Int corridors. **Pets:** Small, dogs only. $100 deposit/pet. Service with restrictions.
[SAVE] [S] [X] [&M] [L] [H] [L] [TI]

WWW Comfort Inn M
(812) 477-2211. **$59-$69.** 5006 Morgan Ave. I-164, exit 9, 1.5 mi w on SR 62. Int corridors. **Pets:** Accepted.
[SAVE] [S] [X] [D] [H] [L] [~]

WWW Comfort Inn Evansville M
(812) 476-3600. **$55.** 8331 E Walnut St. I-164, exit 7B (SR 66/Lloyd Expwy), 0.5 mi w to Eagle Crest Blvd, 0.3 mi se to Fuquay, just s to Walnut, then 0.4 mi e. Int corridors. **Pets:** Medium, other species. Service with restrictions.
[SAVE] [S] [X] [&M] [D] [L] [H] [L] [~]

WWW Drury Inn & Suites Evansville East M
(812) 471-3400. **$57-$92.** 100 Cross Pointe Blvd. I-164, exit 7B (SR 66/Lloyd Expwy), 0.5 mi w. Int corridors. **Pets:** Medium, other species. Service with restrictions, crate.
[X] [&M] [D] [L] [H] [L] [~]

WWW Drury Inn-Evansville North M
(812) 423-5818. **$60-$92.** 3901 US 41 N. US 41, 2.5 mi n of jct SR 62 and 66 (Lloyd Expwy), 3.3 mi sw of Regional Airport entrance. Int corridors. **Pets:** Accepted.
[X] [H] [L] [~]

WWW Holiday Inn Express East M
(812) 473-0171. **$64-$77.** 100 S Green River Rd. I-164, exit 7B (SR 66/Lloyd Expwy), 2 mi w. Ext corridors. **Pets:** Medium. Service with restrictions, crate.
[ASK] [S] [X] [D] [L] [H] [L] [~]

AAA WWW Residence Inn Hotel A
(812) 471-7191. **$96, 14 days notice.** 8283 E Walnut St. I-164, exit 7B (SR 66/Lloyd Expwy), 0.5 mi w to Eagle Crest Blvd, 0.3 mi se to Fuquay St, then 0.3 mi e. Int corridors. **Pets:** Other species. $200 one-time fee/room. Service with restrictions, supervision.
[SAVE] [S] [X] [&M] [D] [L] [H] [L] [~]

WW Super 8 Motel M
(812) 476-4008. **$40-$45.** 4600 Morgan Ave. I-164, exit 9 (SR 62 E/Morgan Ave), 1.7 mi w on SR 62. Int corridors. **Pets:** Accepted.
[ASK] [S] [X] [H]

FORT WAYNE

🔺 🔻🔻🔻 AmeriSuites (Ft Wayne) 🅼
(260) 471-8522. **$89.** 111 W Washington Center Rd. I-69, exit 112A, just w of Coldwater Rd. Int corridors. **Pets:** Small, other species. Supervision.

(SAVE) (S🔆) (✕) (🛢) (💻)

🔺 🔻🔻 Baymont Inn 🅼
(260) 489-2220. **$67-$74, 3 days notice.** 1005 W Washington Center Rd. I-69, exit 111B, 0.5 mi e. Int corridors. **Pets:** Medium, other species. $25 deposit/room. Designated rooms, service with restrictions, supervision.

(SAVE) (S🔆) (✕) (Ⓜ) (🌀) (🛢) (💻)

🔺 🔻🔻 Best Inn 🅼
(260) 483-0091. **$50-$60, 3 days notice.** 3017 W Coliseum Blvd. I-69, exit 109A, just s, then just w. Int corridors. **Pets:** Accepted.

(SAVE) (S🔆) (✕) (🛢)

🔻🔻 Econo Lodge 🅼
(260) 484-6262. **$44-$50.** 2908 Goshen Rd. I-69, exit 109A, 0.3 mi s of jct US 30 and 33. Int corridors. **Pets:** Other species. $25 deposit/room. No service, supervision.

(SAVE) (S🔆) (✕) (🛢) (💻)

🔺 🔻🔻🔻 Fort Wayne Marriott 🅷
(260) 484-0411. **$145-$175.** 305 E Washington Center Rd. I-69, exit 112A (Coldwater Rd). Int corridors. **Pets:** Small. $25 one-time fee/pet. Designated rooms, service with restrictions, supervision.

(SAVE) (S🔆) (✕) (🌀) (🛢) (💻) (🍴)

🔻🔻 Lees Inn & Suites 🅼
(260) 489-8888. **$79-$199, 7 days notice.** 5707 Challenger Pkwy. I-69, exit 111B. Int corridors. **Pets:** Accepted.

(ASK) (S🔆) (✕) (🛢) (💻)

🔺 🔻🔻🔻 Red Roof Inn-Fort Wayne 🅼
(260) 484-8641. **$41-$70.** 2920 Goshen Rd. I-69, exit 109A, at jct US 30 Bypass. Ext corridors. **Pets:** Medium. Service with restrictions, supervision.

(SAVE) (✕) (🐾)

🔺 🔻🔻🔻 Residence Inn by Marriott 🅰
(260) 484-4700. **$99-$159, 5 days notice.** 4919 Lima Rd. I-69, exit 111A, just s. Ext corridors. **Pets:** Accepted.

(SAVE) (S🔆) (✕) (🛢) (💻)

FRANKFORT

🔻🔻🔻 Holiday Inn Express 🅼
(765) 659-4400. **$58.** 592 S CR Rd 200 W. I-65, exit 158, 6.1 mi e; jct US 421/SR 38/39, 1.8 mi w. Int corridors. **Pets:** Other species. Designated rooms, service with restrictions, supervision.

(ASK) (S🔆) (✕) (🌀) (🐾) (🛢) (💻) (🌊)

🔻🔻 Super 8 Motel 🅼
(765) 654-0088. **Call for rates.** 1875 W SR 28. I-65, exit 158, 6.4 mi e; jct US 421/SR 38/39, 1.6 mi w. Int corridors. **Pets:** Accepted.

(ASK) (✕) (🛢) (🌊)

GOSHEN

🔺 🔻🔻 Best Western Inn 🅼
(574) 533-0408. **$64-$67.** 900 Lincolnway E. 1 mi se on US 33. Ext corridors. **Pets:** Accepted.

(SAVE) (S🔆) (✕) (💻)

GREENCASTLE

🔺 🔻🔻 College Inn 🅼
(765) 653-4167. **$38-$48.** 315 Bloomington St. I-70, exit 41, 8 mi n on US 231. Ext corridors. **Pets:** Accepted.

(SAVE) (S🔆) (✕) (🛢)

GREENSBURG

🔺 🔻🔻🔻 Best Western Pines Inn 🅼
(812) 663-6055. **$69-$89, 7 days notice.** 2317 N SR 3. I-74, exit 134A. Int corridors. **Pets:** Medium, other species. $5 daily fee/pet. Service with restrictions.

(SAVE) (S🔆) (✕) (🌀) (🛢) (💻) (🌊)

HAMMOND

🔻🔻 Holiday Inn Chicago Southeast/Hammond 🅼🅸 🐾
(219) 844-2140. **$86, 7 days notice.** 3830 179th St. I-80/94, exit Cline Ave, 0.6 mi s to frontage road, 0.6 mi n. Int corridors. **Pets:** Other species. $50 deposit/room. Service with restrictions, supervision.

(ASK) (S🔆) (✕) (🌀) (🛢) (💻) (🍴)

🔺 🔻🔻🔻 Residence Inn by Marriott 🅰
(219) 844-8440. **$129-$189.** 7740 Corinne Dr. I-80/94, exit 3 (Kennedy Ave S). Int corridors. **Pets:** Medium, other species. $5 daily fee/room, $75 one-time fee/room. Service with restrictions, crate.

(SAVE) (✕) (Ⓜ) (🌀) (🐾) (🛢) (💻) (🌊)

HAUBSTADT

🔺 🔻🔻🔻 Baymont Inn & Suites 🅼
(812) 768-5878. **$71-$97, 14 days notice.** RR 1 Box 252. I-64, exit 25B, 0.4 mi n to Warrenton Rd, just w to frontage road, then 0.3 mi s. Int corridors. **Pets:** $50 deposit/room. Designated rooms, service with restrictions, crate.

(SAVE) (S🔆) (✕) (🐾) (🛢) (💻) (🌊)

HOBART

🔺 🔻🔻 Comfort Inn 🅼
(219) 947-7677. **$84-$104.** 1915 S Mississippi St. I-65, exit 255 (61st St), then just e. Int corridors. **Pets:** Small. Designated rooms, service with restrictions, supervision.

(SAVE) (S🔆) (✕) (Ⓜ) (🐾) (💻) (🌊)

HOWE

🔺 🔻🔻 Super 8 Motel 🅼
(260) 562-2828. **$65-$85, 3 days notice.** 7333 N SR 9. I-80/90, exit 121, 0.5 mi s. Int corridors. **Pets:** Service with restrictions, supervision.

(SAVE) (S🔆) (✕) (Ⓜ) (🌀) (🐾) (🛢)

INDIANAPOLIS METROPOLITAN AREA

ANDERSON

Best Inns M
(765) 644-2000. **$49-$63.** 5706 Scatterfield Rd. I-69, exit 26, on SR 9. Int corridors. **Pets:** Accepted.

Comfort Inn-Anderson M
(765) 644-4422. **$59-$69.** 2205 E 59th St. I-69, exit 26, on SR 9. Int corridors. **Pets:** Large, other species. $15 one-time fee/pet. Designated rooms, service with restrictions, crate.

Lees Inn & Suites M
(765) 649-2500. **$79-$260, 7 days notice.** 2114 E 59th St. I-69, exit 26, on SR 9. Int corridors. **Pets:** Accepted.

CHESTERFIELD

Super 8 Motel M
(765) 378-0888. **$47-$57, 7 days notice.** I-69, exit 34. Ext/int corridors. **Pets:** Accepted.

EDINBURGH

Best Western Horizon Inn M
(812) 526-9883. **$59-$139.** 11780 N US 31. I-65, exit 76B, just n. Int corridors. **Pets:** Accepted.

FISHERS

Frederick-Talbott Inn BB
(317) 578-3600. **$124-$199, 7 days notice.** 13805 Allisonville Rd. I-465, exit 35 (Allisonville Rd), 6.2 mi n; I-69, exit 5, 1.5 mi w on 116th St to Allisonville Rd, then 2 mi n. Int corridors. **Pets:** Accepted.

Staybridge Suites
Indianapolis-Fishers M
(317) 577-9500. **$109-$169, 30 days notice.** I-69, exit 3, just nw. Int corridors. **Pets:** Medium, other species. $75 one-time fee/room. Service with restrictions, supervision.

GREENFIELD

Comfort Inn-Greenfield/Indianapolis M
(317) 467-9999. **$66-$199.** 178 E Martindale Dr. I-70, exit 104. Int corridors. **Pets:** Small, other species. $5 daily fee/room. Designated rooms, service with restrictions, supervision.

Lees Inn M
(317) 462-7112. **$69-$260, 7 days notice.** 2270 N State St. I-70, exit 104. Int corridors. **Pets:** Accepted.

GREENWOOD

Comfort Inn Greenwood M
(317) 887-1515. **$54-$200, 30 days notice.** 110 Sheek Rd. I-65, exit 99. Ext corridors. **Pets:** Large, other species. $5 daily fee/room.

Lees Inn & Suites M
(317) 865-0100. **$79-$500, 7 days notice.** 1281 S Park Dr. I-65, exit 99. Int corridors. **Pets:** Accepted.

INDIANAPOLIS

AmeriSuites
(Indianapolis/Airport) M
(317) 227-0950. **$89-$235.** 5500 Bradbury Ave. I-465, exit 11A, 0.3 mi e on Airport Expwy to Executive Dr exit. Int corridors. **Pets:** Other species. Service with restrictions.

AmeriSuites
(Indianapolis/Keystone) M
(317) 843-0064. **$99-$109.** 9104 Keystone Crossing. I-465, exit 33, 0.5 mi s on SR 431, just e on 86th St, then 0.5 mi n. Int corridors. **Pets:** Very small, other species. Service with restrictions, supervision.

Baymont Inn & Suites
Indianapolis-Airport M
(317) 244-8100. **$69-$84.** 2650 Executive Dr. I-465, exit 11, 0.3 mi e. Int corridors. **Pets:** Accepted.

Baymont Inn & Suites-Indianapolis
East M
(317) 897-2300. **$79-$89.** 2349 Post Dr. I-70, exit 91 (Post Rd), just n. Int corridors. **Pets:** Accepted.

Best Inns M
(317) 788-0811. **$45-$65, 14 days notice.** 450 Bixler Rd. I-465, exit 2B. Int corridors. **Pets:** Accepted.

Best Western Castleton Inn M
(317) 842-9190. **$76-$96, 10 days notice.** 8300 Craig St. I-69, exit 1, 0.5 mi w to Craig St, then just n. Int corridors. **Pets:** Small, dogs only. $25 one-time fee/pet. Designated rooms, no service, supervision.

Comfort Inn & Suites City Centre M
(317) 631-9000. **$119-$350, 4 days notice.** 530 S Capitol Ave. Downtown; just s of South St; across from RCA Dome. Int corridors. **Pets:** Accepted.

◆◆ **Comfort Inn-North** [M]
(317) 872-3100. **$50-$129, 30 days notice.** 3880 W 92nd St. I-465, exit 27, just s. Int corridors. **Pets:** Other species. $15 one-time fee/room. Service with restrictions, supervision.
[SAVE] [S D] ✗ 🧊 ☕ 🏊

◆◆◆ **Country Inn & Suites By Carlson-Indianapolis North** [M]
(317) 876-0333. **$78-$159.** 46032 N Michigan Rd. I-465, exit 27, 0.3 mi n on US 421. Int corridors. **Pets:** Small, other species. $25 daily fee/pet. No service, supervision.
[A$K] [S D] ✗ ♿ 🧊 ☕ 🏊

◆◆ **Days Inn & Suites** [M]
(317) 841-9700. **$64.** 8275 Craig St. I-69, exit 1, 0.5 mi w to Craig St, then just n. Int corridors. **Pets:** $5 daily fee/pet. Service with restrictions, supervision.
[SAVE] [S D] ✗ 🦻 🧊 ☕

◆◆◆ **Drury Inn-Indianapolis** [M]
(317) 876-9777. **$62-$95.** 9320 N Michigan Rd. I-465, exit 27, just s. Int corridors. **Pets:** Accepted.
✗ 🦻 🧊 ☕ 🏊

[AAA] ◆◆◆ **Four Points by Sheraton Indianapolis East** [MI]
(317) 897-4000. **$69-$99.** 7701 E 42nd St. I-465, exit 42 (Pendleton Pike), just e. Int corridors. **Pets:** Accepted.
[SAVE] [S D] ✗ ♿ 🧊 ☕ 🍴 🏊

◆◆◆ **Hawthorn Suites East** [M]
(317) 322-0011. **$89-$260.** 7035 Western Select Dr. I-70, exit 89; 0.5 mi w of jct I-465. Int corridors. **Pets:** Accepted.
[A$K] [S D] ✗ ♿ 🧊 ☕ 🏊

[AAA] ◆◆◆ **Holiday Inn East** [MI]
(317) 359-5341. **$129, 3 days notice.** 6990 E 21st St. I-70, exit 89; 0.5 mi w of jct I-465. Int corridors. **Pets:** Medium, other species. Service with restrictions, supervision.
[SAVE] [S D] ✗ 🦻 🧊 ☕ 🍴

◆◆ **Holiday Inn-Southeast** [MI]
(317) 783-7751. **$89-$250, 30 days notice.** 5120 Victory Dr. I-465, exit 52 (Emerson Ave). Int corridors. **Pets:** Accepted.
[A$K] ✗ ♿M ♿ ☕ 🍴 🏊

[AAA] ◆◆◆ **Indianapolis Marriott East** [H]
(317) 352-1231. **$100, 3 days notice.** 7202 E 21st St. I-70, exit 89 (Shadeland Ave), 0.3 mi se; 0.5 mi w of jct I-465. Int corridors. **Pets:** Other species. $75 deposit/room, $10 daily fee/room. Designated rooms, service with restrictions, supervision.
[SAVE] [S D] ✗ 🦻 🧊 ☕ 🍴 🏊

◆◆◆ **La Quinta Inn-Airport** [M]
(317) 247-4281. **$100-$122.** 5316 W Southern Ave. I-465, exit 11A, 0.5 mi e on Airport Expwy to Lynhurst Dr exit. Int corridors. **Pets:** Small. Designated rooms, service with restrictions, supervision.
[SAVE] ✗ 🦻 🧊 ☕ 🏊

[AAA] ◆◆◆ **La Quinta Inn-East** [M]
(317) 359-1021. **$66-$86.** 7304 E 21st St. I-70, exit 89 (Shadeland Ave), just s, then just e; 0.5 mi w of jct I-465. Int corridors. **Pets:** Small. Designated rooms, service with restrictions, supervision.
[SAVE] [S D] ✗ 🦻 ☕ 🏊

[AAA] ◆◆ **MainStay Suites-Indianapolis** [M] 🐾
(317) 334-7829. **$79-$99.** 8520 Northwest Blvd. I-465, exit 23, just e. Int corridors. **Pets:** Other species. $10 daily fee/pet. Service with restrictions, crate.
[SAVE] [S D] ✗ ♿M 🦻 ♿ 🧊 ☕ 🏊

[AAA] ◆◆◆ **Omni Indianapolis North Hotel** [H]
(317) 849-6668. **$89.** 8181 N Shadeland Ave. I-69, exit 1, just e. Int corridors. **Pets:** Accepted.
[SAVE] [S D] ✗ 🦻 ♿ 🧊 ☕ 🍴 🏊

[AAA] ◆◆◆◆ **Omni Severin Hotel** [H]
(317) 634-6664. **$115-$199.** 40 W Jackson Pl. Opposite Union Station. Int corridors. **Pets:** Small, other species. $50 one-time fee/room. Service with restrictions, supervision.
[SAVE] [S D] ✗ 🦻 ♿ 🧊 ☕ 🍴 🏊

[AAA] ◆◆ **Pickwick Farms Airport** [A]
(317) 240-3567. **$38-$85, 30 days notice.** 25 Beachway Dr. I-465, exit 13A, just ne. Ext corridors. **Pets:** Other species. $100 deposit/pet, $1.43 daily fee/pet, $50 one-time fee/pet. Service with restrictions, supervision.
[SAVE] [S D] 🧊 ☕ 🏊

[AAA] ◆◆ **Pickwick Farms Short-Term Furnished Apartments** [A] 🐾
(317) 872-6506. **$35-$90, 30 days notice.** 9300 N Ditch Rd. I-465, exit 31, just s to 96th St, 1.5 mi w to N Ditch Rd, then just s. Ext corridors. **Pets:** Large, other species. $100 deposit/pet, $1.25 daily fee/pet, $50 one-time fee/pet. Service with restrictions.
[SAVE] [S D] 🧊 ☕ ⛳

[AAA] ◆◆ **Red Roof Inn-South** [M]
(317) 788-9551. **$38-$64.** 5221 Victory Dr. I-465/74, exit 52 (Emerson Ave). Ext corridors. **Pets:** Other species. Supervision.
[SAVE] ✗ 🦻 ♿

[AAA] ◆◆ **Red Roof Inn-Speedway** [M]
(317) 293-6881. **$39-$61.** 6415 Debonair Ln. I-465, exit 16A, just se of jct US 136. Ext corridors. **Pets:** Small, other species. Crate.
[SAVE] ✗ 🦻

[AAA] ◆◆◆ **Residence Inn by Marriott/Indianapolis Airport** [A]
(317) 244-1500. **$109-$139.** 5224 W Southern Ave. I-465, exit 11A, 0.5 mi e on Airport Expwy to Lynhurst Dr exit. Int corridors. **Pets:** Small. $5 daily fee/room, $75 one-time fee/room. Service with restrictions, crate.
[SAVE] ✗ 🦻 ♿ 🧊 ☕ 🏊

AAA ◈◈◈◈ Residence Inn by Marriott Indianapolis/Fishers A ☙
(317) 842-1111. **$99-$129.** 9765 Crosspoint Blvd. I-69, exit 3, just nw. Int corridors. **Pets:** Small, other species. $75 one-time fee/room. Service with restrictions.
SAVE Sᴆ ✕ ᴳᴹ 🐾 🐾 🛏 💻 🌊

AAA ◈◈◈◈ Residence Inn by Marriott Indianapolis North A
(317) 872-0462. **$69-$105.** 3553 Founders Rd. I-465, exit 27, 1 mi s. Ext corridors. **Pets:** Large, other species. $7 daily fee/room, $50 one-time fee/room. No service, crate.
SAVE Sᴆ ✕ 🐾 🛏 💻 🌊

AAA ◈◈◈ Residence Inn Indianapolis on the Canal A
(317) 822-0840. **$129-$199.** 350 W New York St. Downtown; at New York St and Senate Ave. Int corridors. **Pets:** Small. $5 daily fee/pet, $50 one-time fee/room. Service with restrictions, crate.
SAVE Sᴆ ✕ ᴳᴹ 🐾 🐾 🛏 💻 🌊

AAA ◈◈◈ Wellesley Inn & Suites (Indianapolis Airport/Marion) M
(317) 241-0700. **$79-$109, 14 days notice.** 5350 W Southern Ave. I-465, exit 11A, just e to Lynhurst St, just s, then just w. Int corridors. **Pets:** Small. No service, supervision.
SAVE Sᴆ ✕ 🐾 🐾 🛏 💻 🌊

AAA ◈◈◈ Wellesley Inn & Suites (Indianapolis/North) M
(317) 471-0700. **$71-$81.** 9370 Waldemar Rd. I-465, exit 27, just s to 92nd St, just w to Waldemar Rd, 0.3 mi n. Int corridors. **Pets:** Small, other species. Service with restrictions, supervision.
SAVE Sᴆ ✕ 🐾 🐾 🛏 💻

LEBANON

◈◈ Super 8 Motel M
(765) 482-9999. **Call for rates, 30 days notice.** 405 N Mount Zion Rd. I-65, exit 140, just w. Int corridors. **Pets:** Accepted.
ASK ✕ 🐾 🛏 🌊

MARTINSVILLE

◈◈ Comfort Inn Martinsville M
(765) 342-1842. **$60-$80, 7 days notice.** 50 Bill's Blvd. Jct SR 37 and Ohio St, just w. Int corridors. **Pets:** $10 daily fee/pet. Service with restrictions, supervision.
SAVE Sᴆ ✕ 🛏 💻

PLAINFIELD

◈◈◈ Lees Inn & Suites M
(317) 837-9000. **$79-$409, 7 days notice.** 6010 Gateway Dr. I-70, exit 66, just n. Int corridors. **Pets:** Small, dogs only. $10 one-time fee/pet. Designated rooms, service with restrictions, supervision.
ASK Sᴆ ✕ 🐾 🐾 🛏 💻 🌊

SHELBYVILLE

◈◈ Comfort Inn M
(317) 398-8044. **$75-$175, 7 days notice.** 36 W Rampart Dr. I-74, exit 113. Int corridors. **Pets:** Accepted.
SAVE Sᴆ ✕ ᴳᴹ 🐾 🛏 💻 🌊

◈◈ Lees Inn M
(317) 392-2299. **$71-$260, 7 days notice.** 111 Lee Blvd. I-74, exit 116. Int corridors. **Pets:** Accepted.
ASK Sᴆ ✕ 🐾 🛏 💻

☙ END METROPOLITAN AREA ☙

JASPER

◈◈ Days Inn Jasper MI ☙
(812) 482-6000. **$65-$79.** 272 Brucke Strasse. On SR 162 and 164, 0.5 mi e of jct US 231. Ext/int corridors. **Pets:** Medium, other species. $7 daily fee/pet. Designated rooms, service with restrictions, crate.
SAVE Sᴆ ✕ 🐾 🛏 💻 🍴

KOKOMO

◈◈ Comfort Inn M
(765) 452-5050. **$66-$95.** 522 Essex Dr. US 31, just n of jct US 35. Int corridors. **Pets:** Designated rooms, supervision.
SAVE Sᴆ ✕ 🐾 🛏 💻 🌊

◈◈◈ Hampton Inn & Suites M
(765) 455-2900. **$86-$159.** 2920 S Reed Rd (US Hwy 31). US 31, 2 mi s of jct US 35. Int corridors. **Pets:** Accepted.
SAVE Sᴆ ✕ ᴳᴹ 🐾 🐾 🛏 💻

◈◈ Super 8 Motel M
(765) 455-3288. **$58.** 5110 Clinton Dr. US 31, 2.8 mi s of jct US 35. Int corridors. **Pets:** Accepted.
ASK Sᴆ ✕ 🐾 🛏 💻 🌊

LAFAYETTE

AAA ◈ Budget Inn of America M
(765) 447-7566. **$49-$79.** 139 Frontage Rd. I-65, exit 172. Ext corridors. **Pets:** Very small, dogs only. $5 one-time fee/room. Service with restrictions, supervision.
SAVE Sᴆ ✕

AAA ◈◈◈ Comfort Suites M
(765) 447-0016. **$85-$185, 14 days notice.** 31 Frontage Rd. I-65, exit 172, just e. Int corridors. **Pets:** Medium, other species. $10 one-time fee/pet. Designated rooms, service with restrictions, supervision.
SAVE Sᴆ ✕ ᴳᴹ 🐾 🐾 🛏 💻 🌊

(AAA) ▼▼▼▼ Holiday Inn Express M
(765) 449-4808. **$65-$220, 30 days notice.** 201 Frontage Rd. I-65, exit 172. Int corridors. **Pets:** Medium. Service with restrictions, crate.
[SAVE] [S🐾] [✕] [🛏] [💻]

▼▼▼▼ Homewood Suites M
(765) 448-9700. **$99-$179.** 3939 SR 26 E. I-65, exit 172, 0.8 mi w. Ext/int corridors. **Pets:** Accepted.
[SAVE] [✕] [🐾] [🛏] [💻] [🏊]

▼ Knights Inn M
(765) 447-5611. **Call for rates, 14 days notice.** 4110 SR 26 E. I-65, exit 172, 0.3 mi w. Ext corridors. **Pets:** Accepted.
[ASK] [✕] [🛏] [💻] [🏊]

▼▼▼ Lees Inn & Suites M
(765) 447-3434. **$79-$300, 7 days notice.** 4701 Meijer Ct. I-65, exit 172, just e on SR 26. Int corridors. **Pets:** Small, other species. Designated rooms, service with restrictions, crate.
[ASK] [S🐾] [✕] [🐾] [🦮] [🛏] [💻] [🏊]

(AAA) ▼▼▼▼ Radisson Inn-Lafayette M!
(765) 447-0575. **$78-$199, 30 days notice.** 4343 SR 26 E. I-65, exit 172, 0.3 mi n. Int corridors. **Pets:** Small. $15 daily fee/room. Designated rooms, service with restrictions, supervision.
[SAVE] [S🐾] [✕] [🐾] [🦮] [🛏] [💻] [🍴] [🏊]

(AAA) ▼▼▼ Ramada Inn-Lafayette M!
(765) 447-9460. **$82-$169.** 4221 SR 26 E. I-65, exit 172, 0.3 mi w. Int corridors. **Pets:** Medium, other species. Designated rooms, service with restrictions, supervision.
[SAVE] [S🐾] [✕] [🐾] [🛏] [💻] [🍴] [🏊]

(AAA) ▼▼▼ Red Roof Inn-Lafayette M
(765) 448-4671. **$42-$65.** 4201 SR 26 E. I-65, exit 72, 0.3 mi w. Ext corridors. **Pets:** Other species. Service with restrictions, supervision.
[SAVE] [✕] [🦮]

LAPORTE

▼▼▼ Ramada Inn M!
(574) 362-4585. **$69-$129, 14 days notice.** 444 Pine Lake Ave. 1.5 mi n on US 35. Int corridors. **Pets:** Other species. $25 one-time fee/room. Service with restrictions, supervision.
[ASK] [S🐾] [✕] [🛏] [💻] [🍴] [🏊]

LOGANSPORT

▼▼▼▼ Holiday Inn M!
(574) 753-6351. **$80-$90, 30 days notice.** 3550 E Market St. 2.5 mi e on US 24. Int corridors. **Pets:** Medium. Service with restrictions, crate.
[ASK] [S🐾] [✕] [🦮M] [🛏] [💻] [🍴] [🏊]

MARION

(AAA) ▼▼▼▼ Comfort Suites M
(765) 651-1006. **$79-$125, 3 days notice.** 1345 N Baldwin Ave. On SR 9, 1.5 mi n of SR 18. Int corridors. **Pets:** Other species. $10 one-time fee/pet. Designated rooms, service with restrictions, crate.
[SAVE] [S🐾] [✕] [🐾] [🦮] [🛏] [💻] [🏊]

▼▼ Holiday Inn-Marion M!
(765) 668-8801. **$66, 3 days notice.** 501 E 4th St. On SR 18, at corner of 4th and Shunk sts. Int corridors. **Pets:** Accepted.
[ASK] [S🐾] [✕] [🛏] [💻] [🍴] [🏊]

▼▼▼ Super 8 Motel Gas City M
(765) 998-6800. **$45-$65, 3 days notice.** 5172 S Kaybee Dr. I-69, exit 59. Int corridors. **Pets:** Medium, other species. $15 daily fee/room. Designated rooms, service with restrictions, crate.
[ASK] [S🐾] [✕] [🦮]

MARKLE

(AAA) ▼▼▼ Sleep Inn M
(260) 758-8111. **$59-$130.** 730 W Logan St. I-69, exit 86. Int corridors. **Pets:** Other species.
[SAVE] [S🐾] [✕] [🦮M] [🦮] [🛏] [💻]

▼▼ Super 8 Motel Fort Wayne South/Markle M
(260) 758-8888. **$52.** 610 Annette Dr. I-69, exit 86. Int corridors. **Pets:** Accepted.
[ASK] [S🐾] [✕] [🛏] [💻]

MERRILLVILLE

(AAA) ▼▼ Knights Inn M
(219) 736-5100. **$45-$65.** 8250 Louisiana St. I-65, exit 253A (US 30), 0.5 mi se. Ext corridors. **Pets:** $5 daily fee/room. Designated rooms, service with restrictions, supervision.
[SAVE] [S🐾] [✕] [🛏]

▼▼ Lees Inn & Suites M
(219) 942-8555. **$89-$259, 7 days notice.** 6201 Opportunity Ln. I-65, exit 255 (61st Ave), 0.3 mi e. Int corridors. **Pets:** Accepted.
[ASK] [S🐾] [✕] [🐾] [💻] [🏊]

(AAA) ▼▼▼ Red Roof Inn-Merrillville M
(219) 738-2430. **$40-$71.** 8290 Georgia St. I-65, exit 253B (US 30), 0.3 mi sw. Ext corridors. **Pets:** Other species. Service with restrictions, supervision.
[SAVE] [✕] [🐾] [🦮] [🛏]

(AAA) ▼▼▼▼ Residence Inn by Marriott A
(219) 791-9000. **$89-$129.** 8018 Delaware Place. I-65, exit 253B (US 30). Int corridors. **Pets:** Accepted.
[SAVE] [S🐾] [✕] [🦮M] [🐾] [🦮] [🛏] [💻] [🏊]

△△△ ▽▽▽ Super 8 Motel M
(219) 736-8383. **$47-$64, 8 days notice.** 8300 Louisiana St. I-65, exit 253A (US 30), 0.5 mi se. Int corridors. **Pets:** Service with restrictions, supervision.

SAVE S₀ ✕ &M ⌐ 🛏

MICHIGAN CITY

△△△ ▽▽ Knights Inn M
(219) 874-9500. **$35-$150.** 201 W Kieffer Rd. I-94, exit 34B, 0.3 mi n on US 421. Ext corridors. **Pets:** Other species. $10 one-time fee/pet. Service with restrictions.

SAVE S₀ ✕ 🛏 ▣ 🛏

△△△ ▽▽▽ Red Roof Inn-Michigan City M
(219) 874-5251. **$43-$71.** 110 W Kieffer Rd. I-94, exit 34B, 0.3 mi n on US 421. Ext corridors. **Pets:** Accepted.

SAVE ✕ & 🛏

MISHAWAKA

▽▽ ▽▽ Super 8 Motel M
(574) 247-0888. **$54-$67, 3 days notice.** 535 W University Dr. I-80/90, exit 83 to SR 23, 1.6 mi sw to Main St, just s, then just w. Int corridors. **Pets:** $25 deposit/room. Crate.

ASK S₀ ✕ &M

MONTGOMERY

▽▽▽▽ Gasthof Village Inn M
(812) 486-2600. **$60-$100.** CR 650 E, PO Box 60. US 50, 1 mi n. Int corridors. **Pets:** Other species. $50 deposit/room. Service with restrictions, supervision.

ASK ✕ ⌐ & 🛏 🛏

MOUNT VERNON

▽▽▽▽ Four Seasons Motel M ❀
(812) 838-4821. **$62-$95.** 70 Hwy 62 W. SR 62, 1.8 mi w of jct SR 69 N. Ext corridors. **Pets:** Small, other species. $20 deposit/pet. Service with restrictions, crate.

ASK S₀ ✕ 🛏 ▣ 🛏

▽▽ ▽▽ Super 8 Motel M
(812) 838-8888. **$56-$61.** 6225 Hwy 69 S. On SR 69 Bypass, just n from SR 62. Int corridors. **Pets:** Accepted.

ASK S₀ ✕ 🛏 🛏

MUNCIE

▽▽ ▽▽ Comfort Inn M
(765) 282-6666. **$59-$69.** 4011 W Bethel Ave. I-69, exit 41, 6.3 mi e on SR 332, just n. Int corridors. **Pets:** Accepted.

SAVE S₀ ✕ 🛏 ▣ 🛏

▽▽ ▽▽ Muncie Days Inn M
(765) 288-2311. **$46-$72.** 3509 N Everbrook Ln. I-69, exit 41, 6.3 mi e on SR 332, just n. Int corridors. **Pets:** Other species. $10 one-time fee/room. Service with restrictions, supervision.

SAVE S₀ ✕ 🛏 ▣

△△△ ▽▽▽▽ Radisson Hotel Roberts H
(765) 741-7777. **$110-$250.** 420 S High St. Opposite Horizon Convention Center. Int corridors. **Pets:** Medium. $25 deposit/pet. Service with restrictions, supervision.

SAVE S₀ ✕ 🛏 ▣ ¶¶ 🛏

▽▽▽▽ Super 8 Motel M
(765) 286-4333. **$46-$70.** 3601 W Fox Ridge Ln. I-69, exit 41, 6.3 mi n on SR 332. Int corridors. **Pets:** Medium. $10 one-time fee/room. Service with restrictions, supervision.

ASK S₀ ✕ 🛏

NEW ALBANY

▽▽▽▽ Holiday Inn Express Louisville Northwest M
(812) 945-2771. **$69-$99, 14 days notice.** 411 W Spring St. I-64, exit 123. Int corridors. **Pets:** Service with restrictions, crate.

ASK S₀ ✕ & 🛏 ▣ 🛏

NEW CASTLE

△△△ ▽▽▽ Best Western Raintree Inn MI
(765) 521-0100. **$58-$71.** 2836 S SR 3. I-70, exit 123, 2.5 mi n. Ext/int corridors. **Pets:** Small. $20 deposit/room. Service with restrictions.

SAVE S₀ ✕ & 🛏 ▣ ¶¶ 🛏

PLYMOUTH

▽▽ ▽▽ Ramada Inn MI
(574) 936-4013. **$60-$73.** 2550 N Michigan St. Jct US 30, 0.5 mi n on SR 17. Ext corridors. **Pets:** $10 daily fee/pet. Service with restrictions, supervision.

ASK S₀ ✕ 🛏 ▣ ¶¶ 🛏

△△△ ▽▽▽ Super 8 Motel M
(574) 936-8856. **$65-$120.** 2160 N Oak Rd. Just off US 30. Int corridors. **Pets:** Small. Service with restrictions, supervision.

SAVE S₀ ✕ &M 🛏 🛏

PORTAGE

▽▽ ▽▽ Comfort Inn M
(219) 763-7177. **$60-$129, 7 days notice.** 2300 Willow Creek Rd. I-80/90, exit 23; I-94, exit 19, 1.5 mi s. Int corridors. **Pets:** Accepted.

SAVE S₀ ✕ 🛏 ▣

PORTLAND

▽▽ ▽▽ Hoosier Inn M
(260) 726-7113. **$42-$50.** 1620 Meridian St. 0.5 mi n on US 27. Ext corridors. **Pets:** $4 daily fee/pet. Service with restrictions, supervision.

ASK ✕ 🛏 ▣

RENSSELAER

Holiday Inn Express M
(219) 866-7111. **$77-$87.** 4788 Nesbitt Dr. I-65, exit 215, just e. Int corridors. **Pets:** Accepted.
SAVE S X 6M &

RICHMOND

Best Western Imperial Motor Lodge M
(765) 966-1505. **$42-$60.** 3020 E Main St. I-70, exit 156A, 2 mi w. Ext corridors. **Pets:** Other species. $5 daily fee/pet. Service with restrictions, supervision.
SAVE S X & H

Holiday Inn-Richmond H
(765) 966-7511. **$86-$325.** 5501 National Rd E. I-70, exit 156A, 0.3 mi w. Int corridors. **Pets:** Accepted.
ASK S X 6M & H TI

Lees Inn & Suites M
(765) 966-6559. **$79-$209, 7 days notice.** 6030 National Rd E. I-70, exit 156A, jct SR 40. Int corridors. **Pets:** Accepted.
ASK S X H

ROCKVILLE

Billie Creek Village & Inn M
(765) 569-3430. **$49-$99, 3 days notice.** Billie Creek Dr. 1.4 mi e on US 36. Int corridors. **Pets:** $10 one-time fee/room. Service with restrictions, supervision.
SAVE X 6M H

ROSELAND

Best Inns of America/South Bend M
(574) 277-7700. **$48-$63, 31 days notice.** 425 Dixie Hwy N. I-80/90, exit 77, 0.8 mi n on US 933. Int corridors. **Pets:** Accepted.
SAVE S X

SCOTTSBURG

Best Western Scottsburg Inn MI
(812) 752-2212. **$67-$69.** 1525 West McClain St. I-65, exit 29, just w. Int corridors. **Pets:** Accepted.
SAVE S X H TI

Mariann Travel Inn MI
(812) 752-3396. **$55-$58.** SR 56. I-65, exit 29, just e. Ext corridors. **Pets:** Accepted.
SAVE S X H TI

SHIPSHEWANA

Super 8 Motel M
(260) 768-4004. **$59-$89, 14 days notice.** 740 S Van Buren. US 20, 0.8 mi n on SR 5. Int corridors. **Pets:** Accepted.
ASK S X

SOUTH BEND

Residence Inn by Marriott A
(574) 289-5555. **$99-$449.** 716 N Niles Ave. US 33, just e on Northshore Ave, 0.4 mi s. Ext corridors. **Pets:** Accepted.
SAVE S X H

TAYLORSVILLE

Comfort Inn M
(812) 526-9747. **$58-$200, 14 days notice.** 10330 US 31. I-65, exit 76A, just s. Ext corridors. **Pets:** Accepted.
SAVE S X H

TELL CITY

Ramada Limited M
(812) 547-3234. **$60.** 235 Orchard Hill Dr. Just off SR 66, 1.7 mi se of jct SR 37. Int corridors. **Pets:** Other species. $50 deposit/room. Service with restrictions, supervision.
ASK S X 6M & H

TERRE HAUTE

Comfort Suites M
(812) 235-1770. **$65-$125.** 501 E Margaret Ave. I-70, exit 7 (US 41/150), just ne. Int corridors. **Pets:** Other species. $15 one-time fee/pet. Designated rooms, service with restrictions, supervision.
SAVE S X 6M & H

Drury Inn-Terre Haute M
(812) 238-1206. **$64-$98.** 3040 Hwy 41 S. I-70, exit 7 (US 41/150), just n. Int corridors. **Pets:** Medium, other species. Service with restrictions, crate.
X 6M & H

Holiday Inn MI
(812) 232-6081. **$109.** 3300 US 41 S. I-70, exit 7 (US 41/150), just s. Ext/int corridors. **Pets:** Other species. Service with restrictions, supervision.
SAVE S X H TI

Knights Inn M
(812) 234-9931. **$44-$57.** 401 E Margaret Dr. I-70, exit 7 (US 41/150), just n to Margaret Dr, then e. Ext corridors. **Pets:** Other species.
ASK S X H

Pear Tree Inn by Drury M
(812) 234-4268. **$50-$88.** 3050 US 41 S. I-70, exit 7 (US 41/150), just n. Int corridors. **Pets:** Medium, other species. Service with restrictions, crate.
X &

Super 8 Lodge M
(812) 232-4890. **$48-$85.** 3089 S 1st St. I-70, exit 7 (US 41/150), just nw. Int corridors. **Pets:** Service with restrictions, crate.
ASK S X

VALPARAISO

AAA ▼▼▼ **Holiday Inn Express** M
(219) 464-8555. **$89-$119.** 760 Morthland Dr. 0.8 mi e on
US 30. Ext/int corridors. **Pets:** $15 daily fee/pet. Service
with restrictions, supervision.
SAVE ✕ 🐾 📶

WARREN

▼▼▼ **Ramada Limited Warren** M
(260) 375-4800. **$61-$89.** 7275 S CR 75 E. I-69, exit 78,
just n. Int corridors. **Pets:** Accepted.
ASK SD ✕ ♿ 🐾 📶 🖭 🌊

WARSAW

AAA ▼▼▼ **Ramada Plaza Hotel of Warsaw** M
(574) 269-2323. **$97-$101.** 2519 E Center St. 2.8 mi e of
SR 15 on US 30, just s. Int corridors. **Pets:** Medium. Service with restrictions.
SAVE SD ✕ 📶 🖭 🍴 🌊

WASHINGTON

AAA ▼▼▼ **Baymont Inn & Suites** M
(812) 254-7000. **$64-$94.** 7 Cumberland Dr. Just ne of jct
US 50 and SR 57. Int corridors. **Pets:** Small. $50 deposit/
pet. Service with restrictions, supervision.
SAVE SD ✕ 🐾 📶 🖭 🌊

WEST LAFAYETTE

AAA ▼▼▼ **Days Inn** M
(765) 567-2131. **$69.** 5600 SR 43 N. I-65, exit 178. Int
corridors. **Pets:** Accepted.
SAVE SD ✕ 🐾 📶 🖭 🍴 🌊

▼▼▼ **Super 8 Motel-West Lafayette** M
(765) 567-7100. **$53-$110.** 2030 Northgate Dr. I-65, exit
178, just n on SR 43. Int corridors. **Pets:** Other species.
$15 one-time fee/room.
ASK SD ✕ 🐾 🐾

IOWA

ADAIR

Adair Budget Inn
(641) 742-5553. **$39-$45.** 100 S 5th St. I-80, exit 76. Ext corridors. **Pets:** $20 deposit/room. Designated rooms, service with restrictions, supervision.

Adair Super 8
(641) 742-5251. **$49-$69.** 111 S 5th St. I-80, exit 76, just n. Int corridors. **Pets:** Very small. $20 deposit/room. Service with restrictions, supervision.

ALBIA

Indian Hills Inn
(641) 932-7181. **$52-$85.** 100 Hwy 34 E. Just e of jct US 34 and SR 5. Ext/int corridors. **Pets:** Medium. $10 daily fee/pet. Designated rooms, service with restrictions, supervision.

ALTOONA

Motel 6 Des Moines East
(515) 967-5252. **Call for rates.** 3225 Adventureland Dr. I-80, exit 142. Int corridors. **Pets:** Accepted.

Settle Inn & Suites-Altoona
(515) 967-7888. **$59-$89, 30 days notice.** 2101 Adventureland Dr. I-80, exit 142A, just se. Int corridors. **Pets:** Accepted.

AMANA

Amana Holiday Inn
(319) 668-1175. **$72-$89.** 2211 U Ave. I-80, exit 225 (US 151); in Little Amana Complex. Int corridors. **Pets:** Accepted.

Comfort Inn Amana Colonies
(319) 668-2700. **$55-$88.** 2185 U Ave. I-80, exit 225 (US 151), just n. Int corridors. **Pets:** Other species. $7 daily fee/pet. Designated rooms, service with restrictions, supervision.

Die Heimat Country Inn
(319) 622-3937. **$55-$85, 7 days notice.** 4430 V St. Just s of US 6, e on Main St, just e of jct US 151. Int corridors. **Pets:** Medium, dogs only. $10 daily fee/room. Designated rooms, no service, supervision.

AMES

Best Western Starlite Village
(515) 232-9260. **$80.** 2601 E 13th St. I-35, exit 113, 0.5 mi w. Int corridors. **Pets:** Small. Designated rooms, supervision.

Comfort Inn-Ames
(515) 232-0689. **$55-$90.** 1605 S Dayton Ave. Jct I-35 and US 30, just nw. Int corridors. **Pets:** Medium. $5 daily fee/pet. Designated rooms, service with restrictions, supervision.

Comfort Suites
(515) 268-8808. **$79-$119.** 2609 Elwood Dr. Jct I-35 and US 30, 3.5 mi w on US 30, exit 146 (Elwood Dr), then just s. Int corridors. **Pets:** Accepted.

The Hotel at Gateway Center
(515) 292-8600. **$119-$139, 7 days notice.** US 30 & Elwood Dr. Jct I-35 and US 30, 3.5 mi w on US 30, exit 146. Int corridors. **Pets:** Accepted.

(AAA) ▼▼▼ Howard Johnson Express Inn M ❀
(515) 232-8363. **$60.** 1709 S Duff Ave. Jct US 30 and exit 148 (Duff Ave), just n. Ext corridors. **Pets:** Medium, other species. $20 deposit/room, $5 one-time fee/pet. Designated rooms, service with restrictions.
SAVE S⊘ ✕ 🖥 💻 ⊇⊸

ANKENY

(AAA) ▼▼▼ Best Western Starlite Village of Ankeny M⊘
(515) 964-1717. **$99-$149.** 133 SE Delaware Ave. I-35, exit 92, just w. Int corridors. **Pets:** Medium. Designated rooms, service with restrictions, supervision.
SAVE S⊘ ✕ 🖥 💻 ⊨ ⊇⊸

ARNOLDS PARK

▼▼ Fillenwarth Beach R ❀
(712) 332-5646. **$55-$660 (no credit cards), 21 days notice.** 87 Lake Shore Dr. West Lake Okoboji; just w of US 71. Ext corridors. **Pets:** Other species. No service.
🖥 💻 ⊇⊸ ✕

ATLANTIC

▼▼ Econo Lodge M
(712) 243-4067. **$44.** 64968 Baston Rd. I-80, exit 60 (US 71), 0.5 mi s. Int corridors. **Pets:** Other species. Service with restrictions, supervision.
SAVE S⊘ ✕ 💻 ⊇⊸

▼▼▼ Super 8 Motel M
(712) 243-4723. **$50-$70, 30 days notice.** 1902 E 7th St. Jct US 6 and 71, just w on US 6; east side of town. Int corridors. **Pets:** Small, other species. Designated rooms, service with restrictions, supervision.
A$K S⊘ ✕ 🖥 💻 ⊇⊸

BETTENDORF

(AAA) ▼▼▼ Holiday Inn Hotel & Suites-Bettendorf M⊘
(563) 355-4761. **$75-$99, 30 days notice.** 909 Middle Rd. In Bettendorf, IA; I-74, exit 3, just w. Int corridors. **Pets:** Accepted.
SAVE S⊘ ✕ ⊠ 🖥 💻 ⊨ ⊇⊸

(AAA) ▼▼▼ Jumer's Castle Lodge-Bettendorf H
(563) 359-7141. **$81-$96.** 900 Spruce Hills Dr. In Bettendorf, IA; I-74, exit 2, just e, 3 mi s of jct I-74 and 80. Int corridors. **Pets:** $25 deposit/room. Service with restrictions, supervision.
SAVE ✕ ⊘ 🖥 💻 ⊨ ⊇⊸

BURLINGTON

(AAA) ▼▼▼ Best Western Pzazz Motor Inn M⊘
(319) 753-2223. **$80-$83, 3 days notice.** 3001 Winegard Dr. Jct US 61 and 34, just n. Int corridors. **Pets:** Other species. Designated rooms, service with restrictions.
SAVE S⊘ ✕ ⊠M ⊘ ⊠ 🖥 💻 ⊨

▼▼ Comfort Inn-Burlington M
(319) 753-0000. **$50-$75.** 3051 Kirkwood Ave. US 61, just n of jct US 34. Int corridors. **Pets:** $5 daily fee/pet. Service with restrictions, supervision.
SAVE S⊘ ✕ 🖥 💻 ⊇⊸

CEDAR FALLS

▼▼ University Inn M ❀
(319) 277-1412. **$46-$120.** 4711 University Ave. 2 mi w of US 218. Ext/int corridors. **Pets:** Large. $30 deposit/pet. Designated rooms, service with restrictions, crate.
S⊘ ✕ 🖥 💻

CEDAR RAPIDS

▼▼ Best Inn M
(319) 363-9999. **Call for rates, 5 days notice.** 3233 Southridge Dr SW. I-380, exit 17 (33rd Ave SW), just nw. Int corridors. **Pets:** Accepted.
A$K ✕ ⊠M ⊘ 🖥 ⊇⊸

(AAA) ▼▼▼ Best Western Cooper's Mill Hotel & Restaurant M⊘
(319) 366-5323. **$68.** 100 F Ave NW. I-380, exit 19C northbound, take a right at end of the exit, make an immediate U-turn and go under I-380; exit 20A southbound, cross river, right on 1st St NW. Int corridors. **Pets:** $5 daily fee/room. Service with restrictions, crate.
SAVE S⊘ ✕ 🖥 💻 ⊨ ⊇⊸

(AAA) ▼▼▼ Best Western Longbranch Hotel & Convention Center M⊘
(319) 377-6386. **$72-$81.** 90 Twixt Town Rd NE. I-380, exit 24A (SR 100/Collins Rd), 2.5 mi e, just n. Int corridors. **Pets:** $5 daily fee/room. Service with restrictions, crate.
SAVE S⊘ ✕ 🖥 💻 ⊨ ⊇⊸

(AAA) ▼▼▼ Collins Plaza Hotel & Convention Center H
(319) 393-6600. **$99, 3 days notice.** 1200 Collins Rd NE. I-380, exit 24A (SR 100/Collins Rd), 1 mi e on SR 100. Int corridors. **Pets:** Accepted.
SAVE S⊘ ✕ ⊘ ⊠ 🖥 💻 ⊨ ⊇⊸

▼▼▼ Comfort Inn of Cedar Rapids North M
(319) 393-8247. **$64-$89.** 5055 Rockwell Dr. I-380, exit 24A (SR 100/Collins Rd), 1.3 mi e on SR 100. Int corridors. **Pets:** Accepted.
SAVE S⊘ ✕ ⊘ 🖥 💻

▼▼ Comfort Inn-South M
(319) 363-7934. **$64-$84.** 390 33rd Ave SW. I-380, exit 17 (33rd Ave SW), just w. Int corridors. **Pets:** Small. Designated rooms, service with restrictions, supervision.
SAVE S⊘ ✕ 🖥 💻

▼▼▼ Days Inn of Cedar Rapids M
(319) 365-4339. **$49-$70, 7 days notice.** 3245 Southgate Pl SW. I-380, exit 17 (33rd Ave SW), just w. Int corridors. **Pets:** Accepted.
SAVE S⊘ ✕ ⊘ 🖥 ⊇⊸

(AAA) ◆◆◆ Exel Inn of Cedar Rapids M
(319) 366-2475. **$41-$51.** 616 33rd Ave SW. I-380, exit 17 (33rd Ave SW), 0.3 mi w. Int corridors. **Pets:** Small, other species. Designated rooms, service with restrictions, supervision.
[SAVE] [S] [X] [H] [▣]

(AAA) ◆◆◆ Four Points Sheraton H ☙
(319) 366-8671. **$93.** 525 33rd Ave SW. I-380, exit 17 (33rd Ave SW), just w. Int corridors. **Pets:** Medium. $50 deposit/room. Service with restrictions.
[SAVE] [S] [X] [↗] [H] [▣] [¶] [≈]

◆◆◆ Hawthorn Suites Ltd M
(319) 294-8700. **$98, 3 days notice.** 4444 Czech Ln NE. I-380, exit 24A (SR 100/Collins Rd), just s. Int corridors. **Pets:** Large, other species. Service with restrictions, supervision.
[ASK] [S] [X] [&M] [✦] [H] [▣] [≈]

(AAA) ◆◆◆ Red Roof Inn M
(319) 366-7523. **$39-$65.** 3325 Southgate Ct SW. I-380, exit 17 (33rd Ave SW), just sw. Ext corridors. **Pets:** Accepted.
[SAVE] [X] [&M] [↗]

(AAA) ◆◆◆◆ Residence Inn M
(319) 395-0111. **$145-$165.** 1900 Dodge Rd NE. I-380, exit 24A (SR 100/Collins Rd), just e. Int corridors. **Pets:** Medium, other species. $5 daily fee/pet, $50 one-time fee/pet. Designated rooms, service with restrictions, crate.
[SAVE] [X] [&M] [↗] [✦] [H] [▣] [≈]

(AAA) ◆◆◆ Shoney's Inn & Suites Cedar Rapids M
(319) 378-3948. **$62.** 2215 Blairs Ferry Rd NE. I-380, exit 24B, just e. Int corridors. **Pets:** Accepted.
[SAVE] [S] [X] [&M] [H] [▣] [≈]

◆◆◆ Super 8 Motel M
(319) 362-6002. **$54-$64.** 720 33rd Ave SW. I-380, exit 17 (33rd Ave SW), 0.4 mi w. Int corridors. **Pets:** $10 one-time fee/pet. Service with restrictions, supervision.
[ASK] [S] [X] [&M] [↗] [H]

◆◆ Super 8 Motel M
(319) 363-1755. **$49-$69.** 400 33rd Ave SW. I-380, exit 17 (33rd Ave SW), just w. Int corridors. **Pets:** Accepted.
[ASK] [S] [X] [↗] [H]

CHEROKEE

(AAA) ◆◆◆◆ Best Western La Grande Hacienda M
(712) 225-5701. **$70-$80, 3 days notice.** 1401 N 2nd St. 0.4 mi s of jct US 59 and SR 3, on US 59. Int corridors. **Pets:** Medium, other species. $50 deposit/room. Service with restrictions, supervision.
[SAVE] [S] [X] [&M] [↗] [▣] [¶] [≈]

CLARINDA

◆◆◆ Clarinda Super 8 Motel M
(712) 542-6333. **$60, 14 days notice.** 1203 S 12th St. Just e of jct US 71 and SR 2, on US 71 Bypass. Int corridors. **Pets:** Other species. Service with restrictions, supervision.
[ASK] [S] [X] [&M] [✦] [H] [▣] [≈]

CLEAR LAKE

(AAA) ◆◆◆ Best Western Holiday Lodge M
(641) 357-5253. **$72-$82, 3 days notice.** 2023 US Hwy 18. I-35, exit 194 (US 18), 0.3 mi w. Ext/int corridors. **Pets:** Accepted.
[SAVE] [X] [&M] [✦] [H] [▣] [¶] [≈]

(AAA) ◆◆◆ Budget Inn M
(641) 357-8700. **$40-$65.** 1306 N 25th St. I-35, exit 194 (US 18), just nw. Int corridors. **Pets:** Service with restrictions, supervision.
[SAVE] [S] [X] [▣] [≈]

◆◆ Lake Country Inn M
(641) 357-2184. **$35-$40.** 518 Hwy 18 W. I-35, exit 194 (US 18), 2 mi w. Ext corridors. **Pets:** Other species. Supervision.
[ASK] [S] [X] [H]

◆◆◆ Microtel Inn M
(641) 357-0966. **$56-$66.** 1305 N 25th St. I-35, exit 194 (US 18), just nw. Int corridors. **Pets:** Service with restrictions, supervision.
[ASK] [S] [X] [&M] [✦]

CLINTON

(AAA) ◆◆◆ Best Western-Frontier Motor Inn M
(563) 242-7112. **$69-$109.** 2300 Lincolnway. 3.5 mi w on US 30 and 67. Ext/int corridors. **Pets:** Small. $5 daily fee/pet. Service with restrictions, supervision.
[SAVE] [S] [X] [↗] [H] [▣] [¶] [≈]

(AAA) ◆◆◆ Country Inn & Suites By Carlson M
(563) 244-9922. **$69-$109.** 2224 Lincolnway. 3.5 mi w on US 30 and 67. Int corridors. **Pets:** Small. $5 daily fee/pet. Service with restrictions, supervision.
[SAVE] [S] [X] [&M] [↗] [✦] [H] [▣] [≈]

◆◆ Super 8 Motel-Clinton M ☙
(563) 242-8870. **$49-$65.** 1711 Lincolnway. 2.8 mi w on US 30 and 67. Int corridors. **Pets:** Other species. $10 daily fee/pet. No service, crate.
[ASK] [S] [X] [↗] [H]

CLIVE

(AAA) ◆◆◆ Baymont Inn & Suites-West Des Moines-Clive M
(515) 221-9200. **$64-$74.** 1390 NW 118th St. I-80/35, exit 124 (University Ave). Int corridors. **Pets:** Accepted.
[SAVE] [S] [X] [&M] [↗] [✦] [H] [▣] [≈]

▼▼▼ **Chase Suite Hotel by Woodfin** Ⓜ
(515) 223-7700. **$99.** 11428 Forest Ave. I-80/35, exit 124
(University Ave), just ne. Ext corridors. **Pets:** Other species.
$150 deposit/room, $5 daily fee/pet. Service with restrictions.

(A$K) (S✿) (✕) (🔊) (🌙) (🛏) (💻) (🏊)

(AAA) ▼▼▼ **Four Points by Sheraton Des Moines
West** Ⓜ
(515) 278-5575. **$75-$99.** 11040 Hickman Rd. I-80/35, exit
125, 0.3 mi e. Int corridors. **Pets:** Accepted.

(SAVE) (S✿) (✕) (&M) (🔊) (🌙) (🛏) (💻) (🍴) (🏊)

COLUMBUS JUNCTION
▼▼ **Columbus Motel** Ⓜ
(319) 728-8080. **$46-$53.** SR 92 E. 0.5 mi e. Int corridors.
Pets: Other species. $3 daily fee/pet. Service with restric-
tions, supervision.

(✕) (🛏) (💻)

CORALVILLE
▼▼▼ **AmericInn Motel & Suites** Ⓜ
(319) 625-2400. **$68-$130.** 2597 Holiday Rd. I-80, exit 240,
just n. Int corridors. **Pets:** Accepted.

(A$K) (S✿) (✕) (&M) (🌙) (🛏) (💻) (🏊)

▼▼▼ **Comfort Inn of Coralville** Ⓜ
(319) 351-8144. **$74-$99.** 209 W 9th St. I-80, exit 242, just
s. Int corridors. **Pets:** Small. Designated rooms, service with
restrictions, supervision.

(SAVE) (S✿) (✕) (🔊) (🛏) (💻) (🏊)

▼▼ **Super 8 Motel of Iowa City** Ⓜ
(319) 337-8388. **Call for rates.** 611 1st Ave. I-80, exit 242,
0.4 mi s. Int corridors. **Pets:** $10 daily fee/pet. Service with
restrictions, supervision.

(A$K) (✕) (&M) (🔊)

COUNCIL BLUFFS
(AAA) ▼▼▼ **Best Western Crossroads of the
Bluffs** Ⓜ
(712) 322-3150. **$59-$74.** 2216 27th Ave. I-80, exit 1B (24th
St). Int corridors. **Pets:** Accepted.

(SAVE) (S✿) (✕) (🔊) (🛏) (💻) (🍴) (🏊)

(AAA) ▼▼▼ **Comfort Suites** Ⓜ
(712) 323-9760. **$80-$135.** 1801 S 35th St. I-29, exit 52
(Nebraska Ave E). Int corridors. **Pets:** $10 daily fee/room.
Designated rooms, service with restrictions, supervision.

(SAVE) (S✿) (✕) (&M) (🔊) (🌙) (🛏) (💻) (🏊)

▼▼ **Days Inn** Ⓜ
(712) 323-2200. **$55, 45 days notice.** 3619 9th Ave. I-29,
exit 53A. Int corridors. **Pets:** $10 daily fee/pet. No service,
supervision.

(SAVE) (S✿) (✕) (🔊) (🛏) (💻)

▼▼ **Econo Lodge** Ⓜ ✿
(712) 366-9699. **$45-$66, 10 days notice.** 3208 S 7th St.
I-80, exit 3, just s. Int corridors. **Pets:** Medium. $10 one-
time fee/pet. Designated rooms, service with restrictions,
supervision.

(SAVE) (S✿) (✕) (🔊) (🌙) (🛏) (💻)

▼▼ **Motel 6 Council Bluffs, IA** Ⓜ
(712) 366-2405. **$45-$67.** 3032 S Expwy. I-29/80, exit 3
(US 92). Int corridors. **Pets:** Accepted.

(S✿) (✕) (🔊) (🌙) (🛏) (🏊)

(AAA) ▼▼▼ **Quality Inn Metro** Ⓜ
(712) 328-3171. **$69-$109.** 3537 W Broadway. Just e of
I-29 on US 6; I-29, exit 53A (9th Ave), just e, just n to
Broadway, then just w. Ext/int corridors. **Pets:** Other species. Designated rooms, no service, supervision.

(SAVE) (S✿) (✕) (🔊) (🌙) (🛏) (💻) (🏊)

▼ **Super 8 Motel** Ⓜ
(712) 322-2888. **$59-$61.** 2712 S 24th St. I-80, exit 1B
(24th St). Int corridors. **Pets:** Designated rooms, service
with restrictions, supervision.

(A$K) (S✿) (✕) (🔊)

▼▼ **Travelodge** Ⓜ
(712) 328-3881. **$50-$90.** 2325 Ave N. I-29, exit 55 (25th
St), just se. Int corridors. **Pets:** Small. $10 daily fee/room.
Designated rooms, service with restrictions, supervision.

(A$K) (S✿) (✕) (🔊) (🛏) (💻) (🏊)

CRESCO
(AAA) ▼ **Cresco Motel** Ⓜ
(563) 547-2240. **$50-$70.** 620 2nd Ave SE. On SR 9, on
the east side of town. Ext corridors. **Pets:** Other species.
$16 daily fee/room. Supervision.

(SAVE) (S✿) (✕) (&M) (🔊) (🛏)

DAVENPORT
(AAA) ▼▼▼ **Baymont Inn &
Suites-Davenport** Ⓜ
(563) 386-1600. **$64-$79.** 400 Jason Way Ct. In Davenport,
IA; I-80, exit 295A (US 61), just s to 65th St, 0.5 mi ne on
frontage road. Int corridors. **Pets:** Accepted.

(SAVE) (S✿) (✕) (🔊) (🌙) (🛏) (💻)

(AAA) ▼▼▼ **Best Western SteepleGate
Inn** Ⓜ ✿
(563) 386-6900. **$85-$159.** 100 W 76th St. In Davenport,
IA; I-80, exit 295A (US 61), just s to 65th St and frontage
road entrance. Int corridors. **Pets:** Small. $10 daily fee/pet.
Crate.

(SAVE) (S✿) (✕) (🔊) (🛏) (💻) (🍴) (🏊)

▼▼▼ **Country Inn & Suites By Carlson** Ⓜ
(563) 388-6444. **$69-$109.** 140 E 55th St. In Davenport, IA;
I-80, exit 295A (US 61), 1.4 mi s. Int corridors.
Pets: Medium. Designated rooms, service with restrictions.

(A$K) (S✿) (✕) (&M) (🔊) (🛏) (💻) (🏊)

(AAA) ▼▼▼ **Davenport Super 8 Motel** Ⓜ
(563) 388-9810. **$45-$85, 7 days notice.** 410 E 65th St. In
Davenport, IA; I-80, exit 295A (US 61), just e. Int corridors.
Pets: Very small. $5 daily fee/pet. Designated rooms, serv-
ice with restrictions, supervision.

(SAVE) (S✿) (✕) (🛏)

♦♦ ♦♦ Days Inn of Davenport **M**
(563) 355-1190. **$54-$84.** 3202 E Kimberly Rd. In Davenport, IA; I-74, exit 2, just w. Int corridors. **Pets:** Accepted.
(SAVE) (S&) (X) (🐾) (📶) (💻) (🏊)

♦♦♦ ♦♦ Exel Inn of Davenport **M**
(563) 386-6350. **$42-$62.** 6310 N Brady St. In Davenport, IA; I-80, exit 295A (US 61), 0.5 mi s. Int corridors. **Pets:** Small, other species. Designated rooms, service with restrictions, crate.
(SAVE) (S&) (X) (🐾) (📶) (💻)

♦♦♦♦ Hampton Inn-Davenport **M**
(563) 359-3921. **$65-$69.** 3330 E Kimberly Rd. In Davenport, IA; I-74, exit 2, just w, then just s. Int corridors. **Pets:** Accepted.
(SAVE) (X) (📶) (💻) (🏊)

♦♦♦ ♦♦♦♦ Residence Inn by Marriott **M**
(563) 391-8877. **$85-$95, 7 days notice.** 120 E 55th St. In Davenport, IA; I-80, exit 295 (US 61), 1.4 mi s. Int corridors. **Pets:** Large, other species. $100 one-time fee/room. Service with restrictions, crate.
(SAVE) (S&) (X) (🐾) (📶) (💻) (🏊)

♦♦♦ ♦♦♦♦ Rhythm City **H**
(563) 328-6000. **$75-$95.** 200 E 3rd St. In Davenport, IA; downtown; connected to River Center Convention Center, at 3rd and Perry sts. Int corridors. **Pets:** Accepted.
(SAVE) (X) (📶) (💻) (🍴)

DES MOINES ✓

♦♦ ♦♦ Bavarian Inn **MI**
(515) 265-5611. **$44.** 5220 NE 14th St. I-80/US 69, exit 136, 0.3 mi n. Int corridors. **Pets:** Accepted.
(ASK) (S&) (X) (📶) (💻) (🍴) (🏊)

♦♦♦ ♦♦♦♦ Best Inns of America **M**
(515) 270-1111. **$54-$69, 14 days notice.** 5050 Merle Hay Rd. I-80/35, exit 131, just n. Int corridors. **Pets:** Accepted.
(SAVE) (S&) (X) (&M) (🐾) (📶) (💻) (🏊)

♦♦♦ ♦♦ Best Western Colonial **M**
(515) 265-7511. **$51-$61.** 5020 NE 14th St. I-80/35, exit 136, just n on US 69. Ext/int corridors. **Pets:** Other species. Designated rooms, service with restrictions, crate.
(SAVE) (S&) (X)

♦♦ ♦♦ Best Western Starlite Village **MI**
(515) 282-5251. **Call for rates, 30 days notice.** 929 3rd St. I-235, exit 3rd St (downtown) westbound; exit 3rd St eastbound, across from Veterans Auditorium. Int corridors. **Pets:** Accepted.
(ASK) (X) (🐾) (📶) (💻) (🍴) (🏊)

♦♦ ♦♦ Comfort Inn **M**
(515) 287-3434. **$74-$94.** 5231 Fleur Dr. Across from airport. Int corridors. **Pets:** Accepted.
(SAVE) (S&) (X) (&M) (🐾) (&) (📶) (💻) (🏊)

♦♦♦ ♦♦♦♦ Des Moines Marriott Downtown **H**
(515) 245-5500. **$79-$189.** 700 Grand Ave. I-235, exit 7th St, 0.5 mi s. Int corridors. **Pets:** Other species. Service with restrictions, crate.
(SAVE) (X) (&M) (🐾) (&) (📶) (💻) (🍴) (🏊)

♦♦♦ ♦♦ Hickman Motor Lodge **M** 🐾
(515) 276-8591. **$48-$55.** 6500 Hickman Rd. I-80/35, exit 125, 2.5 mi e. Ext corridors. **Pets:** Other species. Designated rooms.
(SAVE) (S&) (X) (📶) (💻)

♦♦♦ ♦♦♦♦ Holiday Inn-Merle Hay **MI** 🐾
(515) 278-0271. **$85-$105.** 5000 Merle Hay Rd. I-80/35, exit 131, just s. Ext/int corridors. **Pets:** Medium. $20 one-time fee/room. Service with restrictions, supervision.
(SAVE) (S&) (X) (&M) (📶) (💻) (🍴) (🏊)

♦♦ ♦♦ Motel 6-30 **M**
(515) 287-6364. **$41-$57, 17 days notice.** 4817 Fleur Dr. I-35, exit 68 (SR 5/Army Post Rd), 5 mi e to Fleur Dr, then 0.5 mi n. Ext corridors. **Pets:** Accepted.
(S&) (X) (&)

♦♦ ♦♦ Quality Inn & Suites **M**
(515) 278-2381. **$69-$85.** 4995 Merle Hay Rd. I-80/35, exit 131, just s. Int corridors. **Pets:** Other species. $20 deposit/room. Service with restrictions, supervision.
(SAVE) (S&) (X) (&M) (🐾) (&) (📶) (💻) (🏊)

♦♦ ♦♦ Super 8 Lodge **M**
(515) 278-8858. **Call for rates.** 4755 Merle Hay Rd. I-80/35, exit 131, just s. Int corridors. **Pets:** $25 deposit/room. Service with restrictions, supervision.
(ASK) (X) (📶) (💻)

DUBUQUE

♦♦♦ ♦♦♦♦ Best Western Dubuque Inn **MI**
(563) 556-7760. **$79-$109.** 3434 Dodge St. US 20, 3 mi w of jct US 52/61/151 and Mississippi Bridge. Int corridors. **Pets:** Small. $50 deposit/pet. Designated rooms, no service, supervision.
(SAVE) (X) (🐾) (📶) (💻) (🍴) (🏊)

♦♦♦ ♦♦♦♦ Best Western Midway Hotel **MI**
(563) 557-8000. **$89-$99.** 3100 Dodge St. US 20, 2.3 mi w of jct US 52/61/151 and Mississippi Bridge. Int corridors. **Pets:** Medium. Service with restrictions, supervision.
(SAVE) (S&) (X) (🐾) (📶) (💻) (🍴) (🏊)

♦♦♦♦ Comfort Inn of Dubuque **M**
(563) 556-3006. **$69-$94.** 4055 McDonald Dr. US 20, 3.8 mi w of jct US 52/61/151 and Mississippi Bridge. Int corridors. **Pets:** Other species. $15 deposit/room. Service with restrictions, crate.
(SAVE) (S&) (X) (🐾) (📶) (💻) (🏊)

♦♦ ♦♦ Days Inn-Dubuque **MI**
(563) 583-3297. **$64-$99.** 1111 Dodge St. US 20, 0.8 mi w of jct US 52/61/151 and Mississippi Bridge, exit Hill/Bryant. Ext corridors. **Pets:** Other species. $5 daily fee/pet. Designated rooms, service with restrictions, crate.
(SAVE) (X) (📶) (💻) (🍴) (🏊)

 Holiday Inn Dubuque Five Flags **H**
(563) 556-2000. **$81-$90.** 450 Main St. Downtown; at Main and 4th sts; facing the Five Flags Civic Center. Int corridors. **Pets:** Accepted.

 MainStay Suites **M**
(319) 557-7829. **$75-$93, 30 days notice.** 1275 Associates Dr. Just n of jct US 20 and NW Arterial Rd. Int corridors. **Pets:** Accepted.

DYERSVILLE

 Comfort Inn-Dyersville **M**
(563) 875-7700. **$66-$87, 7 days notice.** 527 16th Ave SE. US 20, exit 294. Int corridors. **Pets:** Medium. $50 deposit/pet. Designated rooms, service with restrictions, supervision.

EVANSDALE

Ramada Limited M
(319) 235-1111. **$59-$150.** 450 Evansdale Dr. I-380, exit 68, just n. Int corridors. **Pets:** Other species. $30 deposit/room, $5 one-time fee/room. Service with restrictions, supervision.

FAIRFIELD

Best Western Fairfield Inn MI
(641) 472-2200. **$65-$110.** 2200 W Burlington Ave. On US 34, 1 mi w of jct SR 1. Int corridors. **Pets:** Small, other species. Designated rooms, service with restrictions, supervision.

FORT DODGE

Comfort Inn M
(515) 573-3731. **$54-$69.** 2938 5th Ave S. US 20, exit 124 (Coalville), 6 mi n on CR P59, 2 mi w on 5th Ave (Business Rt US 20). Int corridors. **Pets:** Other species. $10 one-time fee/pet. Designated rooms.

Super 8 Motel M
(515) 576-8000. **$46-$56.** 3040 5th Ave S. US 20, exit 124 (Coalville), 3.7 mi n on CR P59, 1.2 mi w on Business Rt US 20. Int corridors. **Pets:** Small, other species. $6 daily fee/pet. Designated rooms, service with restrictions, supervision.

FORT MADISON

 The Madison Inn Motel **M**
(319) 372-7740. **$45-$95.** 3440 Ave L. US 2 and 61, 2 mi w. Ext corridors. **Pets:** Medium. $10 daily fee/pet. Designated rooms, service with restrictions, supervision.

GLENWOOD

 Bluff View Motel **MI**
(712) 622-8191. **$42-$60.** 57902 190 St. I-29, exit 35 (US 34); adjacent to interstate. Int corridors. **Pets:** Accepted.

HAMPTON

AmericInn Lodge & Suites M
(641) 456-5559. **$76-$123.** 702 Central Ave W. On SR 3 (Central Ave W), 0.7 mi w of jct US 65 and SR 3. Int corridors. **Pets:** Accepted.

IDA GROVE

Delux Motel M
(712) 364-3317. **$40-$55.** 5981 US Hwy 175. Jct US 59 S and 175. Ext corridors. **Pets:** Large. $10 daily fee/pet. Designated rooms, service with restrictions, supervision.

INDEPENDENCE

Super 8 Motel M
(319) 334-7041. **$59-$100.** 2000 1st St W. US 20, exit 252, 1.4 mi n. Int corridors. **Pets:** Small. $10 daily fee/pet, $10 one-time fee/pet. Designated rooms, service with restrictions, crate.

JEFFERSON

 Budget Host Inn **M**
(515) 386-3116. **$40-$45.** 209 E Gallup Rd. Just e of jct US 30 and SR 4. Ext corridors. **Pets:** Accepted.

JOHNSTON

Ramada Inn-Des Moines North MI
(515) 276-5411. **$69-$89, 14 days notice.** 5055 Merle Hay Rd. I-80/35, exit 131 (Merle Hay Rd), just n. Int corridors. **Pets:** Small. $30 deposit/room, $10 one-time fee/room. Supervision.

KEOKUK

Econo Lodge M
(319) 524-3252. **$50-$55, 30 days notice.** 3764 Main St. 2.8 mi nw on US 218. Ext corridors. **Pets:** Medium. $5 one-time fee/pet. Designated rooms, service with restrictions, supervision.

LE CLAIRE

Comfort Inn Riverview M
(563) 289-4747. **$65-$85, 30 days notice.** 902 Mississippi View Ct. I-80, exit 306 (US 67), 0.5 mi n to Eagle Ridge Rd, then just se. Int corridors. **Pets:** Medium. $25 deposit/room. Service with restrictions, supervision.

▼▼▼▼ **Super 8 of Le Claire** M
(563) 289-5888. **$65-$75, 30 days notice.** 1552 Welcome Center Dr. I-80, exit 306 (US 67), 0.5 mi n to Eagle Ridge Rd, then just sw to Mississippi View Ct. Int corridors. **Pets:** Medium. $25 deposit/room. Service with restrictions, supervision.

ASK S⊘ ✕ ⌖M ⌑ ⬛ ⬜

LE MARS

▼▼ **Super 8 Motel** M
(712) 546-8800. **$49-$63.** 1201 Hawkeye Ave SW. 1.2 mi s of jct US 75/SR 3, on US 75, south end of town. Int corridors. **Pets:** Other species. $5 daily fee/pet. Designated rooms, service with restrictions, crate.

ASK S⊘ ✕ ⌖M ⬜ ⇌

MANCHESTER

▼▼ **Super 8 of Manchester** M
(563) 927-2533. **$58-$96.** 1020 W Main. Jct US 20 and SR 13, exit 275, 1.5 mi n, then 0.3 mi e. Int corridors. **Pets:** $5 daily fee/pet. Designated rooms, service with restrictions, supervision.

ASK S⊘ ✕ ⌖M ⬛ ⬜

MARION

▼▼ **Microtel Inn & Suites** M
(319) 373-7400. **$60-$65.** 5500 Dyer Ave. Jct of US 151 and SR 13. Int corridors. **Pets:** $50 deposit/room. Service with restrictions, crate.

ASK S⊘ ✕ ⌖M ⌑ ⬛ ⬜

MARQUETTE

▼ **The Frontier Motel** M
(563) 873-3497. **$55-$95.** 101 S 1st St. Just s of jct US 18 and SR 76; between Mississippi River Bridge and casino. Ext corridors. **Pets:** Medium. $10 one-time fee/pet. Designated rooms, service with restrictions, crate.

✕ ⬜ ⇌

MARSHALLTOWN

▼▼▼ **Best Western Regency Inn** M!
(641) 752-6321. **$74-$97.** 3303 S Center St. Jct US 30 and SR 14. Int corridors. **Pets:** Small, other species. $10 one-time fee/pet. Service with restrictions, supervision.

SAVE S⊘ ✕ ⌚ ⬛ ⬜ ⊓ ⇌

▼▼▼ **Comfort Inn** M
(641) 752-6000. **$63-$92.** 2613 S Center St. Jct US 30 and SR 14, 0.5 mi n. Int corridors. **Pets:** Large. $10 one-time fee/room. Service with restrictions, supervision.

SAVE S⊘ ✕ ⌖M ⌚ ⌑ ⬛ ⬜ ⇌

▼▼ **Econo Lodge** M
(641) 753-3333. **$50-$73, 7 days notice.** 3315 S Center St. Just n of jct US 30 and exit 185 (SR 14). Int corridors. **Pets:** Small, other species. $10 one-time fee/pet. Service with restrictions, supervision.

SAVE S⊘ ✕ ⌚ ⬛ ⬜

MASON CITY

▼▼ **Days Inn Mason City** M
(641) 424-0210. **$58-$78, 14 days notice.** 2301 4th St SW. I-35, exit 194 (US 18), 6 mi e. Int corridors. **Pets:** Supervision.

SAVE S⊘ ✕ ⌖ ⬛ ⬜

▲▲▲ ▼▼▼ **Holiday Inn** M!
(641) 423-1640. **$75-$82.** 2101 4th St SW (Hwy 122). 1.5 mi w of jct US 18 and 65, on SR 122 (Business 18); 8 mi e of jct I-35 and US 18. Ext/int corridors. **Pets:** Accepted.

SAVE S⊘ ✕ ⌖ ⬛ ⬜ ⊓ ⇌

▼▼ **Mason City Super 8 Motel & Suites** M
(641) 423-8855. **$59-$180, 7 days notice.** 3010 4th St SW. I-35, exit 194 (US 18), 6 mi e on SR 122. Int corridors. **Pets:** $5 daily fee/pet. Service with restrictions, supervision.

ASK S⊘ ✕ ⌖M ⌑ ⬛ ⬜ ⇌

▲▲▲ ▼▼▼ **Thriftlodge** M
(641) 424-2910. **$52-$69, 14 days notice.** 24 5th St SW. Just w of jct US 65 and SR 122 (Business 18). Ext/int corridors. **Pets:** Accepted.

SAVE S⊘ ✕ ⬛ ⇌

MONTICELLO

▼▼ **The Blue Inn** M!
(319) 465-6116. **Call for rates.** 250 N Main St. North end of town on US 151. Int corridors. **Pets:** Medium. $20 deposit/room. Designated rooms, service with restrictions, supervision.

ASK ✕ ⬜ ⊓ ⇌

MOUNT PLEASANT

▼▼ **Super 8 Motel-Mt Pleasant** M
(319) 385-8888. **$55-$89.** 1000 N Grand Ave. 1 mi n of the jct of US 34 and 218. Int corridors. **Pets:** Accepted.

ASK S⊘ ✕ ⌖M ⬛ ⬜

MUSCATINE

▼▼▼ **Holiday Inn Muscatine** M!
(563) 264-5550. **$89-$109, 7 days notice.** 2915 N Hwy 61. Jct US 61 and SR 38, just n. Int corridors. **Pets:** Medium, other species. $10 one-time fee/room. Service with restrictions, supervision.

ASK S⊘ ✕ ⬛ ⬜ ⊓ ⇌

NEWTON

▲▲▲ ▼▼▼ **Days Inn of Newton** M
(641) 792-2330. **$55-$62.** 1605 W 19th St S. I-80, exit 164 (SR 14), just n. Int corridors. **Pets:** Medium. $10 one-time fee/pet. Service with restrictions, supervision.

SAVE S⊘ ✕ ⌚ ⬛

▲▲▲ ▼▼▼ **Holiday Inn Express** M
(641) 792-7722. **$100-$105.** 1700 W 19th St S. I-80, exit 164 (SR 14), just nw. Int corridors. **Pets:** Medium. $25 one-time fee/room. Service with restrictions, supervision.

SAVE ✕ ⬛ ⬜ ⇌

Ramada Limited M
(641) 792-8100. **$45-$54.** 1405 W 19th St S. I-80, exit 164, just n. Int corridors. **Pets:** Medium, other species. $10 daily fee/pet. Service with restrictions, supervision.

OKOBOJI

AmericInn Motel & Suites M
(712) 332-9000. **$76-$165, 7 days notice.** 1005 Brooks Park Dr. Jct US 71 and SR 9, 2.5 mi s on US 71. Int corridors. **Pets:** Medium. $25 deposit/room. Service with restrictions, supervision.

Village East Resort R
(712) 332-2161. **$94-$169.** 1405 US 71. Jct US 71 and SR 9, 3 mi s. Ext/int corridors. **Pets:** Medium. Designated rooms, service with restrictions, supervision.

OSCEOLA

AmericInn Motel & Suites M
(641) 342-9400. **$70-$74, 5 days notice.** 111 Ariel Cir. I-35, exit 33. Int corridors. **Pets:** Small. $50 deposit/room. Designated rooms, service with restrictions, supervision.

OSKALOOSA

Comfort Inn M ❀
(641) 672-0375. **$77-$100, 30 days notice.** 2401 A Ave W. Just e of jct SR 163, exit 57 (SR 92). Int corridors. **Pets:** Designated rooms, service with restrictions, supervision.

Rodeway Inn M
(641) 673-8351. **$45-$60, 7 days notice.** 1315 A Ave E. SR 92 E. Ext/int corridors. **Pets:** Medium. Designated rooms, service with restrictions.

OTTUMWA

Colonial Motor Inn M
(641) 683-1661. **$38-$43.** 1534 Albia Rd. W on US 34 to Quincy St, 0.5 mi s, then just w. Ext/int corridors. **Pets:** Other species. $10 one-time fee/room. Service with restrictions, supervision.

PELLA

Comfort Inn & Suites M
(641) 621-1421. **$64.** 910 W 16th. SR 163, exit 40, just s. Int corridors. **Pets:** Accepted.

Super 8 Motel-Pella M
(641) 628-8181. **$45-$89.** 105 E Oskaloosa St. 1 mi s of jct SR 163, exit 42, 0.5 mi e. Int corridors. **Pets:** $5 deposit/pet. Designated rooms, service with restrictions, supervision.

PERRY

Hotel Pattee CI ❀
(515) 465-3511. **$110-$200, 3 days notice.** 1112 Willis Ave. I-80/35, exit 141, nw to Perry, right at First St, then n. Int corridors. **Pets:** Dogs only. $200 deposit/room. Service with restrictions.

RED OAK

Super 8–Red Oak M
(712) 623-6919. **$55-$65.** 800 Senate Ave. Jct US 34 and SR 48, just e on US 34. Int corridors. **Pets:** Other species. $15 one-time fee/room. Designated rooms, service with restrictions, supervision.

SIBLEY

Super 8 Motel M
(712) 754-3603. **$50-$60.** 1108 2nd Ave. On SR 60. Int corridors. **Pets:** Accepted.

SIOUX CITY

AmericInn Motel & Suites M ❀
(712) 255-1800. **$80-$105.** 4230 S Lewis Blvd. I-29, exit 143, just e. Int corridors. **Pets:** Large, other species. $25 deposit/room. Designated rooms, service with restrictions, supervision.

Baymont Inn M
(712) 233-2302. **$73-$78.** 3101 Singing Hills Blvd. I-29, exit 143, just e. Int corridors. **Pets:** Other species.

Best Western City Centre M
(712) 277-1550. **$63-$68.** 130 Nebraska St. I-29, exit 147B (business district), just w on Gordon Dr, then just n. Int corridors. **Pets:** $10 daily fee/pet. Designated rooms, service with restrictions, supervision.

Comfort Inn M
(712) 274-1300. **$69-$94.** 4202 S Lakeport St. I-29, exit 144A, 1 mi e on US 20, just s; do not use Business US 20. Int corridors. **Pets:** Other species. $5 daily fee/pet. Service with restrictions.

Hamilton Inn MI
(712) 277-3211. **$49-$89.** 1401 Zenith Dr. I-29, exit 149 (Hamilton Blvd). Int corridors. **Pets:** Accepted.

(AAA) ▼▼▼▼ Hilton Sioux City 🏨
(712) 277-4101. **$59-$89.** 707 4th St. Downtown. Int corridors. **Pets:** Accepted.
(SAVE) (S6) (✕) (🖫) (🗲) (▣) (Ⅱ) (≈)

▼▼▼▼ Holiday Inn 🅼
(712) 277-9400. **$64-$175, 30 days notice.** 701 Gordon Dr. I-29, exit 147B. Int corridors. **Pets:** Medium. $50 deposit/room. Service with restrictions, supervision.
(ASK) (S6) (✕) (🗲) (🖫) (▣) (Ⅱ) (≈)

▼ Motel 6-45 🅼
(712) 277-3131. **$35-$53.** 6166 Harbor Dr. I-29, exit 141, just w. Int corridors. **Pets:** Other species. Service with restrictions, supervision.
(S6) (✕) (🗲) (≈)

▼▼ Super 8 Motel 🅼
(712) 274-1520. **$49-$60, 14 days notice.** 4307 Stone Ave. I-29, exit 144A, 4.2 mi e on US 20, 1.2 mi n on SR 12 (Gordon Dr). Int corridors. **Pets:** Other species. $20 daily fee/pet. Designated rooms, service with restrictions, supervision.
(ASK) (S6) (✕) (🗲M) (🖫)

SLOAN

▼▼ Winna Vegas Inn 🅼
(712) 428-4280. **$47.** 1862 Hwy 141. I-29, exit 127, just e. Int corridors. **Pets:** Accepted.
(ASK) (S6) (✕) (🗲M) (🗲) (▣)

SPIRIT LAKE

▼ Oaks Motel 🅼
(712) 336-2940. **$35-$88, 10 days notice.** 1701 Chicago. Just e on US 71 and SR 9. Ext corridors. **Pets:** Other species. $20 deposit/room. Designated rooms, service with restrictions, supervision.
(✕) (🖫)

STORY CITY

▼▼ Viking Motor Inn 🅼
(515) 733-4306. **Call for rates.** 1520 Broad St. I-35, exit 124, just w. Int corridors. **Pets:** Accepted.
(ASK) (✕) (🖫) (≈)

STUART

▼▼ Super 8 Motel 🅼
(515) 523-2888. **Call for rates.** 203 SE 7th St. I-80, exit 93. Int corridors. **Pets:** Small. $25 deposit/pet. Service with restrictions, supervision.
(ASK) (✕) (🗲M) (🖫) (▣) (≈)

TOLEDO

▼▼ Super 8 Motel-Toledo 🅼
(641) 484-5888. **$49-$55, 10 days notice.** 207 Hwy 30 W. Just w of jct US 30 and 63. Ext/int corridors. **Pets:** Small. Designated rooms, service with restrictions, supervision.
(ASK) (S6) (✕) (🗲M) (🖫) (▣)

URBANDALE

(AAA) ▼▼▼▼ Comfort Inn of Urbandale 🅼
(515) 270-1037. **$65-$95.** 5900 Sutton Dr. I-80, exit 131, just s, then w. Int corridors. **Pets:** Accepted.
(SAVE) (S6) (✕) (🖉) (🖫) (▣) (≈)

▼▼ Days Inn-West 🅼
(515) 278-2811. **$52-$60.** 10841 Douglas Ave. I-35/80, exit 126, 0.3 mi e. Ext corridors. **Pets:** Accepted.
(SAVE) (S6) (✕) (🗲M) (🖫) (▣) (≈)

▼▼ Microtel Inn and Suites 🅼 ❧
(515) 727-5424. **$66.** 8711 Plum Dr. I-35/80, exit 129. Int corridors. **Pets:** Other species. $25 deposit/pet. Designated rooms, service with restrictions, supervision.
(ASK) (S6) (✕) (🗲M) (🗲) (🖫) (▣)

▼▼▼ Sleep Inn 🅼
(515) 270-2424. **$69-$79.** 11211 Hickman Rd. I-35/80, exit 125 (Hickman Rd), just ne. Int corridors. **Pets:** Small, other species. $5 daily fee/room. Designated rooms, service with restrictions, supervision.
(SAVE) (S6) (✕) (🗲M) (🖉) (🗲) (▣) (≈)

WALNUT

(AAA) ▼▼ Red Carpet Inn 🅼
(712) 784-2233. **$40-$95.** 1614 Antique City Dr. I-80, exit 46, just s. Int corridors. **Pets:** Medium. $5 one-time fee/pet. Designated rooms, no service, supervision.
(SAVE) (S6) (✕) (🖫)

WASHINGTON

▼▼ Super 8 Motel-Washington 🅼
(319) 653-6621. **$58-$63, 3 days notice.** 119 Westview Dr. 1.5 mi w on SR 1 and 92. Int corridors. **Pets:** $25 deposit/pet. Designated rooms, service with restrictions, supervision.
(ASK) (S6) (✕) (🖫)

WATERLOO

▼▼ Comfort Inn of Waterloo 🅼
(319) 234-7411. **$64-$94.** 1945 La Porte Rd. I-380 N, exit 72 (E San Marnan). Int corridors. **Pets:** Medium, other species. Designated rooms, service with restrictions, supervision.
(SAVE) (S6) (✕) (🖉) (🖫) (▣) (≈)

▼▼▼▼ Holiday Inn Convention Center 🏨
(319) 233-7560. **$149-$159, 30 days notice.** 205 W 4th St. Downtown; 4th and Commercial sts. Int corridors. **Pets:** Accepted.
(ASK) (S6) (✕) (🗲M) (🖉) (🖫) (▣) (Ⅱ) (≈)

▼▼▼ Motel 6-4081 🅼 ❧
(319) 236-3238. **$47-$56.** 2343 Logan Ave. 2 mi n of jct US 218 and 63, on US 63. Int corridors. **Pets:** Large, other species. Service with restrictions, supervision.
(✕) (🗲M) (🖫) (▣) (≈)

(AAA) ▽▽▽ **Quality Inn & Suites M**
(319) 235-0301. **$75-$225.** 226 W 5th St. Downtown. Int corridors. **Pets:** Other species. Service with restrictions, crate.
SAVE SÐ ✕ ᴥM ⬥ ⊟ ⬛

WAVERLY

(AAA) ▽▽▽ **Red Fox Inn Resort & Conference Center M** ❖
(319) 352-5330. **$69-$170, 3 days notice.** 1900 Heritage Way. SR 3, 2 mi e from jct US 218 and SR 3. Ext/int corridors. **Pets:** Medium, other species. $5 daily fee/room. Service with restrictions, supervision.
SAVE SÐ ✕ ⬥ ⊟ ⬛ ⊤⊤ ⬗ ✕

WEBSTER CITY

(AAA) ▽▽ **The Executive Inn M**
(515) 832-3631. **$53-$58.** 1700 Superior St. Jct US 20 and SR 17, exit 140, 0.5 mi n. Int corridors. **Pets:** Small. $35 deposit/pet. Designated rooms, service with restrictions, supervision.
SAVE SÐ ✕ ⊟ ⬛ ⬗

WEST BURLINGTON

▽▽▽ **AmericInn Motel & Suites M** ❖
(319) 758-9000. **Call for rates.** 628 S Gear Ave. US 34, exit 260 (Gear Ave), just ne. Int corridors. **Pets:** Large, other species. $50 deposit/room. Designated rooms, service with restrictions, supervision.
✕ ᴥM ⬥ ⬥ ⊟ ⬛ ⬗

WEST DES MOINES

(AAA) ▽▽▽ **Best Suites M**
(515) 223-9005. **$69-$99.** 1236 74th St. I-80, exit 121 (74th St), just s. Int corridors. **Pets:** Accepted.
SAVE SÐ ✕ ᴥM ⬥ ⬥ ⊟ ⬛ ⬗

▽▽▽ **Candlewood Suites-West Des Moines M**
(515) 221-0001. **$59-$109.** 7625 Office Plaza Dr N. I-80, exit 121 (74th St), just sw. Int corridors. **Pets:** Medium. $100 deposit/room. Designated rooms, service with restrictions, crate.
ASK SÐ ✕ ᴥM ⬥ ⊟ ⬛

▽▽▽ **Hawthorn Suites Ltd M**
(515) 223-0000. **$98, 3 days notice.** 6905 Lake Dr. I-80, exit 121 (74th St), just ne. Int corridors. **Pets:** Accepted.
ASK SÐ ✕ ⬥ ⊟ ⬛ ⬗

(AAA) ▽▽▽ **Holiday Inn-University Park M**
(515) 223-1800. **$69-$119.** 1800 50th St. I-80/35, exit 124 (University Ave). Int corridors. **Pets:** Medium. $50 deposit/room. Designated rooms, service with restrictions, crate.
SAVE SÐ ✕ ᴥM ⬥ ⬥ ⊟ ⬛ ⊤⊤ ⬗

▽▽ **Motel 6–1408 M**
(515) 267-8885. **$41-$57.** 7655 Office Plaza Dr N. I-80, exit 121 (74th St), just sw. Int corridors. **Pets:** Accepted.
SÐ ✕ ᴥM ⬥ ⬗

(AAA) ▽▽▽ **Valley West Inn M** ❖
(515) 225-2524. **$79-$99.** 3535 Westown Pkwy. I-235, exit 1 (35th St), just n. Int corridors. **Pets:** Large. $20 deposit/pet. Designated rooms, service with restrictions, crate.
SAVE SÐ ✕ ⬥ ⊟ ⬛ ⊤⊤ ⬗

(AAA) ▽▽▽ **West Des Moines Marriott H**
(515) 267-1500. **$69-$139.** 1250 74th St. I-80, exit 121 (74th St). Int corridors. **Pets:** Accepted.
SAVE SÐ ✕ ᴥM ⬥ ⊟ ⬛ ⊤⊤ ⬗

WEST LIBERTY

▽ **Econo Lodge M**
(319) 627-2171. **$53-$70.** 1943 Garfield Ave. I-80, exit 259, just sw. Ext corridors. **Pets:** Medium. $5 daily fee/pet. Service with restrictions, supervision.
SAVE SÐ ✕ ⬛

WILLIAMS

♦♦ **Best Western Norseman Inn M**
(515) 854-2281. **$48-$54.** 3086 220th St. I-35, exit 144, just e. Int corridors. **Pets:** Medium, dogs only. Service with restrictions, supervision.
SAVE SÐ ✕ ⊟ ⬛

WILLIAMSBURG

(AAA) ▽▽▽ **Best Western Quiet House Suites M**
(319) 668-9777. **$88-$157.** 1708 N Highland St. I-80, exit 220, 0.8 mi n; across from Tanger Outlet Mall. Int corridors. **Pets:** $15 daily fee/pet. Designated rooms, service with restrictions, supervision.
SAVE SÐ ✕ ⬥ ⬥ ⊟ ⬛ ⬗

▽▽ **Crest Country Inn M**
(319) 668-1522. **$45-$60, 7 days notice.** 340 W Evans St. I-80, exit 220, 0.3 mi w; across from Tanger Factory Outlet Mall. Ext corridors. **Pets:** Medium. $5 daily fee/pet. Designated rooms, service with restrictions, supervision.
✕ ⬥

(AAA) ▽▽▽ **Super 8 Motel M**
(319) 668-9718. **$66-$81.** 1708 N Highland St. I-80, exit 220, 0.8 mi n; across from Tanger Factory Outlet Mall. Ext/int corridors. **Pets:** $15 daily fee/pet. Designated rooms, service with restrictions, supervision.
SAVE SÐ ✕ ⬥

WINTERSET

▽▽ **Village View Motel M**
(515) 462-1218. **Call for rates.** 711 SR 92 E. Jct N US 169 and SR 92, 0.3 mi e. Int corridors. **Pets:** Accepted.
✕ ⊟

KANSAS

ABILENE

Best Western Abilene's Pride Ⓜ
(785) 263-2800. **$42-$74.** 1709 N Buckeye Ave. I-70, exit 275, 0.5 mi s. Ext/int corridors. **Pets:** Small. $20 deposit/room. Service with restrictions, crate.

Best Western President's Inn Ⓜ 🐾
(785) 263-2050. **$44-$60.** 2210 N Buckeye. I-70, exit 275, at jct SR 15. Ext corridors. **Pets:** Service with restrictions, supervision.

Diamond Motel Ⓜ
(785) 263-2360. **$30-$50, 14 days notice.** 1407 NW 3rd St. I-70, exit 275, 1.3 mi s, then 1 mi w. Ext corridors. **Pets:** Accepted.

Super 8 Motel Ⓜ
(785) 263-4545. **$48-$69, 15 days notice.** 2207 N Buckeye. I-70, exit 275, just s. Int corridors. **Pets:** Other species. $10 deposit/pet. Designated rooms, service with restrictions, supervision.

BAXTER SPRINGS

Baxter Inn-4-Less Ⓜ
(620) 856-2106. **$45-$49.** 2451 Military Ave. On US 69 Alt; 1 mi s from jct US 166. Int corridors. **Pets:** Small. $20 deposit/pet. Service with restrictions, supervision.

BELOIT

Super 8 Motel-Beloit Ⓜ
(785) 738-4300. **$46-$65.** 205 W Hwy 24. Just e of jct SR 14. Int corridors. **Pets:** Medium. Designated rooms, service with restrictions, supervision.

BURLINGTON

Country Haven Inn Ⓜ
(620) 364-8260. **$57-$64.** 207 Cross St. Just e of US 75, 1 mi n of center. Int corridors. **Pets:** Small, dogs only. $25 deposit/room. Designated rooms, service with restrictions, supervision.

CHANUTE

Chanute Safari Inn Ⓜ
(620) 431-9460. **$47.** 3428 S Santa Fe. US 169, exit 35th St, 1.5 mi e. Ext corridors. **Pets:** Accepted.

Guest House Motor Inn Ⓜ
(620) 431-0600. **$33-$37.** 1814 S Santa Fe. US 169, exit 35th St, 2.5 mi ne. Ext corridors. **Pets:** Very small. $5 one-time fee/room. Service with restrictions, supervision.

CLAY CENTER

Cedar Court Motel Ⓜ
(785) 632-2148. **$40-$60.** 905 Crawford. 0.5 mi e on US 24. Ext corridors. **Pets:** Small. Designated rooms, supervision.

COLBY

Best Western Crown Motel Ⓜ 🐾
(785) 462-3943. **$49-$79.** 2320 S Range. I-70, exit 53, just s on SR 25. Ext/int corridors. **Pets:** Other species. Supervision.

Comfort Inn Ⓜ
(785) 462-3833. **$59-$109.** 2225 S Range. I-70, exit 53, just s. Int corridors. **Pets:** Other species. $5 daily fee/pet. Designated rooms, supervision.

(AAA) ▼▼ Days Inn M
(785) 462-8691. **$53-$80, 14 days notice.** 1925 S Range. I-70, exit 53, 0.3 mi n on SR 25. Int corridors. **Pets:** Other species. $5 daily fee/pet. Service with restrictions, supervision.
[SAVE] [S6] [X] [T] [P]

▼▼▼ Holiday Inn Express M
(785) 462-8787. **$69.** 645 W Willow. I-70, exit 53, just ne. Int corridors. **Pets:** Accepted.
[ASK] [S6] [X] [D] [c6] [T] [P] [2w]

(AAA) ▼▼ Ramada Inn M
(785) 462-3933. **$56-$79.** 1950 S Range. I-70, exit 53, at jct SR 25. Ext/int corridors. **Pets:** Large, other species. Service with restrictions, crate.
[SAVE] [S6] [X] [c6] [T] [P] [T] [2w]

COTTONWOOD FALLS

(AAA) ▼▼▼▼ Grand Central Hotel CI
(620) 273-6763. **$139-$179, 4 days notice.** 215 Broadway. Center; just w of US 177. Int corridors. **Pets:** Accepted.
[SAVE] [S6] [X] [c6] [P] [T]

COUNCIL GROVE

(AAA) ▼▼ The Cottage House Hotel & Motel M
(620) 767-6828. **$55-$170, 7 days notice.** 25 N Neosho. Downtown; just n of Main St. Ext/int corridors. **Pets:** Accepted.
[SAVE] [S6] [X] [T] [P]

DODGE CITY

▼▼ Best Western Silver Spur Lodge M
(620) 227-2125. **$58-$70, 30 days notice.** 1510 W Wyatt Earp Blvd. 1 mi w on US 50 business route. Ext/int corridors. **Pets:** Accepted.
[SAVE] [S6] [X] [T] [P] [T] [2w]

(AAA) ▼▼ Econo Lodge of Dodge City M
(620) 225-0231. **$50-$80.** 1610 W Wyatt Earp Blvd. 1 mi w on US 50 business route. Int corridors. **Pets:** Small. $4 daily fee/pet. Designated rooms, service with restrictions, supervision.
[SAVE] [S6] [X] [D] [P] [T] [2w]

▼▼▼ Holiday Inn Express M
(620) 227-5000. **$90, 3 days notice.** 2320 W Wyatt Earp Blvd. 1.4 mi w on US 50 business route. Int corridors. **Pets:** Accepted.
[ASK] [S6] [X] [D] [c6] [T] [P] [2w]

▼▼ Super 8 M
(620) 225-3924. **$66, 3 days notice.** 1708 W Wyatt Earp Blvd. 1.2 mi w on US 50 business route. Int corridors. **Pets:** Other species. Service with restrictions, supervision.
[ASK] [S6] [X] [D] [T] [P] [2w]

EL DORADO

(AAA) ▼▼▼ Best Western Red Coach Inn M
(316) 321-6900. **$63-$110, 7 days notice.** 2525 W Central Ave. On SR 196 and 254, 0.8 mi e of turnpike, exit 71. Ext corridors. **Pets:** Medium. Designated rooms, service with restrictions, supervision.
[SAVE] [S6] [X] [D] [T] [P] [T] [2w]

▼▼ El Dorado Super 8 M
(316) 321-4888. **$45-$69.** 2530 W Central Ave. On SR 196 and 254, 0.8 mi e of turnpike, exit 71. Int corridors. **Pets:** Accepted.
[ASK] [S6] [X] [T] [P]

(AAA) ▼ Heritage Inn M
(316) 321-6800. **$50-$55, 7 days notice.** 2515 W Central Ave. On SR 196 and 254, 0.8 mi e of turnpike, exit 71. Ext corridors. **Pets:** Accepted.
[SAVE] [S6] [X] [T]

ELLSWORTH

▼▼ Best Western Garden Prairie Inn M
(785) 472-3116. **$60-$70.** 1400 N Hwy 156. 1 mi ne on SR 140 at jct SR 156. Ext/int corridors. **Pets:** Accepted.
[SAVE] [S6] [X] [P] [2w]

EMPORIA

▼▼ Days Inn M
(620) 342-1787. **$65-$80, 5 days notice.** 3032 W Hwy 50. On US 50, 0.3 mi e of turnpike; gate city route. Ext/int corridors. **Pets:** Other species. Service with restrictions.
[SAVE] [S6] [X] [D] [T] [P] [2w]

▼ Motel 6 M
(620) 343-1240. **Call for rates.** 2630 W 18th Ave. I-35, exit 128 (Industrial St), just s, then e. Int corridors. **Pets:** Small, other species. Designated rooms, service with restrictions, supervision.
[X] [T]

▼▼ Ramada Inn & Conference Center M
(620) 343-2200. **$59-$79.** 2700 W 18th Ave. I-35, exit 128 (Industrial St). Ext/int corridors. **Pets:** $10 daily fee/pet. Service with restrictions.
[ASK] [S6] [X] [P] [T] [2w]

FORT SCOTT

▼ 1st Interstate Inn M
(620) 223-5330. **$49-$78, 7 days notice.** 2222 S Main. On US 69, 2.5 mi s of US 54. Int corridors. **Pets:** Accepted.
[ASK] [S6] [X] [D] [T]

▼▼ Best Western Fort Scott Inn M
(620) 223-0100. **$64-$68.** 101 State St. On US 69 Bypass, exit US 54 southbound; exit 3rd St northbound. Ext/int corridors. **Pets:** Accepted.
[SAVE] [S6] [X] [T] [P] [T] [2w]

GARDEN CITY

AAA ▽▽▽ Best Western Red Baron Hotel 🅷
(620) 275-4164. **$64-$70.** 67846 E Hwy 50. 2.3 mi e on US 50 city route, at US 83 Bypass. Ext corridors. **Pets:** Accepted.
[SAVE] [S🔟] [✕] [🖉] [🅱] [🖵] [¶] [⇌]

AAA ▽▽▽ Best Western Wheat Lands Hotel &
Conference Center 🅷
(620) 276-2387. **$65-$78.** 1311 E Fulton. 1 mi e on US 50 city route. Ext corridors. **Pets:** Other species. Service with restrictions.
[SAVE] [S🔟] [✕] [🖉] [🅱] [🖵] [¶] [⇌]

▽▽ Days Inn 🅼
(620) 275-5095. **$65, 3 days notice.** 1818 Commanche Dr. W of US 50 and 83 Bypass on SR 156. Ext corridors. **Pets:** Accepted.
[SAVE] [S🔟] [✕] [🖉] [♿] [🅱] [⇌]

▽▽ Garden City Super 8 Motel 🅼
(620) 275-9625. **$49-$65.** 2808 N Taylor. 0.3 mi s of US 50 on US 83. Int corridors. **Pets:** Accepted.
[ASK] [S🔟] [✕] [🖉] [🅱] [🖵]

▽▽▽ Holiday Inn Express Hotel & Suites 🅼
(620) 275-5900. **$87, 3 days notice.** 2502 E Kansas Ave. At jct US 50, 83 and SR 156. Int corridors. **Pets:** Medium, other species. Service with restrictions.
[ASK] [S🔟] [✕] [🖉] [♿] [🅱] [🖵] [⇌]

▽▽ National 9 Inn 🅼 ❀
(620) 275-0677. **$49-$58.** 123 Honey Bee Ct. 2.3 mi e on US 50 city route, at US 83 Bypass. Ext corridors. **Pets:** Other species. Service with restrictions.
[ASK] [S🔟] [✕] [🅱] [⇌]

▽▽ Plaza Hotel 🅼
(620) 275-7471. **$73-$80.** 1911 E Kansas. 0.5 mi w of US 50 and 83 Bypass, on SR 156. Int corridors. **Pets:** Other species. Service with restrictions, crate.
[ASK] [S🔟] [✕] [♿] [🅱] [¶] [⇌]

GOODLAND

AAA ▽▽▽ Best Western Buffalo Inn 🅼 ❀
(785) 899-3621. **$48-$69.** 830 W Hwy 24. I-70, exit 17 or 19, n to jct US 24 and SR 27. Ext corridors. **Pets:** Large, other species. Designated rooms, service with restrictions, crate.
[SAVE] [S🔟] [✕] [🖵] [¶] [⇌]

AAA ▽▽▽ Comfort Inn 🅼
(785) 899-7181. **$75-$120, 7 days notice.** 2519 Enterprise Rd. I-70, exit 17, just n. Int corridors. **Pets:** Large, other species. $15 daily fee/pet. Designated rooms, service with restrictions, supervision.
[SAVE] [S🔟] [✕] [🔟M] [♿] [🅱] [🖵] [⇌]

GREAT BEND

AAA ▽▽▽ Best Western Angus Inn 🅼
(620) 792-3541. **$69-$79.** 2920 10th St. 0.8 mi w on US 56, SR 156 and 96. Ext/int corridors. **Pets:** Accepted.
[SAVE] [S🔟] [✕] [🖉] [🅱] [🖵] [¶] [⇌]

▽▽▽ Holiday Inn 🅼
(620) 792-2431. **$61-$74.** 3017 10th St. 1 mi w on US 56, SR 156 and 96. Ext/int corridors. **Pets:** Accepted.
[ASK] [✕] [♿] [🅱] [🖵] [¶] [⇌]

AAA ▽▽▽ Travelers Budget Inn 🅼
(620) 793-5448. **$46-$56.** 4200 W 10th St. 2 mi w on US 56, SR 156 and 96. Ext corridors. **Pets:** Small. $50 deposit/pet. Service with restrictions, supervision.
[SAVE] [S🔟] [✕] [🅱]

GREENSBURG

▽▽ Best Western J-Hawk Motel 🅼
(620) 723-2121. **$56.** 515 W Kansas Ave. 0.3 mi w on US 54. Ext corridors. **Pets:** No service, supervision.
[SAVE] [S🔟] [✕] [🅱] [🖵] [⇌]

HAYS

▽▽▽ Best Western Vagabond Motel 🅼
(785) 625-2511. **$52-$70.** 2524 Vine St. I-70, exit 159, 1 mi s on US 183. Ext corridors. **Pets:** Medium, other species. Designated rooms, service with restrictions, supervision.
[SAVE] [✕] [♿] [🅱] [🖵] [¶] [⇌]

AAA ▽▽▽ Budget Host Villa 🅼
(785) 625-2563. **$29-$51.** 810 E 8th. I-70, exit 159, 2 mi s on US 183. Ext corridors. **Pets:** Accepted.
[SAVE] [S🔟] [✕] [♿] [🅱] [🖵] [⇌]

▽▽▽ Hampton Inn-Hays 🅼
(785) 625-8103. **$59-$71.** 3801 Vine St. I-70, exit 159, just sw. Ext/int corridors. **Pets:** Other species. Service with restrictions, supervision.
[SAVE] [S🔟] [✕] [🖉] [♿] [🖵]

▽▽▽ Holiday Inn-Hays 🅼
(785) 625-7371. **$70-$80.** 3603 Vine St. I-70, exit 159, just s on US 183. Ext/int corridors. **Pets:** Other species. Service with restrictions, supervision.
[ASK] [✕] [♿] [🖵] [¶]

▽▽ Motel 6–167 🅼
(785) 625-4282. **Call for rates.** 3404 Vine St. I-70, exit 159, 0.3 mi s on US 183. Ext corridors. **Pets:** Accepted.
[✕] [⇌]

HAYSVILLE

AAA ▽▽▽ Haysville Inn 🅼
(316) 522-1000. **$42.** 301 E 71st S. I-35, exit 39, just w. Ext corridors. **Pets:** Medium. Service with restrictions, supervision.
[SAVE] [S🔟] [✕] [♿]

HILLSBORO

▼▼ Country Haven Inn–Highway 56 **M**
(620) 947-2929. **$54-$59, 3 days notice.** 804 Western Heights. SR 56. Int corridors. **Pets:** Small, other species. $25 deposit/room. Service with restrictions, supervision.
(ASK) (S✦) (✕) (☎)

HOLTON

▼▼ Red Roof Inn **M**
(785) 364-3172. **$71-$82, 10 days notice.** 115 S Hwy 75. Just s of jct US 75 and SR 116 on US 75. Ext/int corridors. **Pets:** Small. Designated rooms, service with restrictions, supervision.
(ASK) (S✦) (✕) (☎)

HUTCHINSON

⊕⊕ ▼ Astro Motel **M**
(620) 663-1151. **$40-$70.** 15 E 4th. Downtown; just e of Main St. Ext corridors. **Pets:** Small, dogs only. $5 daily fee/pet. Service with restrictions, supervision.
(SAVE) (S✦) (✕) (☎) (⟿)

▼▼ Comfort Inn **M**
(620) 663-7822. **$86, 3 days notice.** 1621 Super Plaza. 3 mi ne, just w of jct SR 61 and N 17th Ave. Int corridors. **Pets:** Accepted.
(SAVE) (S✦) (✕) (🖉) (🕹) (▢) (⟿)

▼▼▼ Holiday Inn Express Hotel Suites **M**
(620) 669-5200. **$87, 3 days notice.** 1601 Super Plaza. 3 mi ne, just w of SR 61. Int corridors. **Pets:** Very small, dogs only. Service with restrictions, crate.
(ASK) (S✦) (✕) (🕹M) (🖉) (🕹) (☎) (▢) (⟿)

▼▼ Microtel Inn & Suites **M** ❀
(620) 665-3700. **$69, 3 days notice.** 1420 N Lorraine. Jct SR 61 and N 11th Ave, 2.5 mi n. Int corridors. **Pets:** Other species. Service with restrictions, crate.
(ASK) (S✦) (✕) (☎) (▢)

▼▼ Quality Inn City Center **M**
(620) 663-1211. **$55-$150.** 15 W 4th St. Downtown; just e of SR 96. Ext corridors. **Pets:** Accepted.
(SAVE) (S✦) (✕) (🖉) (☎) (▢) (⟿)

INDEPENDENCE

▼▼▼ Appletree Inn **M**
(620) 331-5500. **$64.** 201 N 8th St. At 8th and Laurel sts. Ext/int corridors. **Pets:** Other species. Service with restrictions, supervision.
(✕) (☎) (⟿)

⊕⊕ ▼▼▼ Best Western Prairie Inn **M**
(620) 331-7300. **$51-$55 (no credit cards).** 3222 W Main. US 75. Ext corridors. **Pets:** Small. $10 one-time fee/pet. Service with restrictions, supervision.
(SAVE) (S✦) (✕) (▢) (⟿)

⊕⊕ ▼▼ ▼▼ Glencliff Farm Bed, Breakfast & Spa 🅱🅱 ❀
(620) 331-1277. **$79-$189, 14 days notice.** 448 Glencliff Rd. US 75. Int corridors. **Pets:** Large, other species. $10 one-time fee/pet. Designated rooms, service with restrictions, supervision.
(SAVE) (✕) (☎) (▢) (⟿) (✕)

▼▼ Microtel Inn & Suites **M**
(620) 331-0088. **$57-$68.** 2917 W Main. Jct US 160 and 75, 1.2 mi e on US 160. Int corridors. **Pets:** Accepted.
(ASK) (✕) (🕹M) (🖉) (🕹) (☎) (▢)

IOLA

⊕⊕ ▼▼▼ Best Western Inn **M**
(620) 365-5161. **$49-$55.** 1315 N State. 1 mi n on US 169. Ext corridors. **Pets:** Small. Service with restrictions, supervision.
(SAVE) (S✦) (✕) (🖉) (🕹) (☎) (▢) (🍴) (⟿)

JUNCTION CITY

⊕⊕ ▼▼ Days Inn **M**
(785) 762-2727. **$55-$70.** 1024 S Washington St. I-70, exit 296, just n. Ext/int corridors. **Pets:** Other species. Designated rooms, service with restrictions.
(SAVE) (S✦) (✕) (🖉) (☎) (▢) (⟿)

⊕⊕ ▼▼ Econo Lodge **M**
(785) 238-8181. **$35-$75.** 211 Flint Hills Blvd. I-70, exit 299 (Grandview Plaza). Int corridors. **Pets:** Accepted.
(SAVE) (S✦) (✕) (☎) (▢)

⊕⊕ ▼ Golden Wheat Budget Host **M**
(785) 238-5106. **$35-$65, 3 days notice.** 820 S Washington St. I-70, exit 296, 0.5 mi n. Ext corridors. **Pets:** Small, dogs only. $5 daily fee/pet. Service with restrictions, crate.
(SAVE) (S✦) (✕) (☎)

▼▼▼ Holiday Inn Express **M**
(785) 762-4200. **$64-$80, 15 days notice.** 120 N East St. I-70, exit 298, just nw. Int corridors. **Pets:** Accepted.
(ASK) (S✦) (✕) (🕹M) (🖉) (☎) (▢) (⟿)

▼▼ Ramada Limited **M**
(785) 238-1141. **$47-$62.** 1133 S Washington St. I-70, exit 296. Ext corridors. **Pets:** $10 daily fee/pet. Designated rooms, service with restrictions, supervision.
(ASK) (S✦) (✕) (☎)

KANSAS CITY METROPOLITAN AREA

DE SOTO

▼▼ ▼▼ **Super 8 Motel** **M**
(913) 583-3880. **$50-$81.** 34085 Commerce Dr. Just ne of jct SR 10 and DeSoto exit. Int corridors. **Pets:** Small, dogs only. $50 deposit/room, $10 one-time fee/pet. Service with restrictions, supervision.
[ASK] [S🐾] [✕] [🛏]

KANSAS CITY

🔺🔺 ▼▼▼▼ **Best Western Inn and Conference Center** **M**
(913) 677-3060. **$94.** 501 Southwest Blvd. I-35, exit 234, just s. Int corridors. **Pets:** Other species. Designated rooms, service with restrictions, crate.
[SAVE] [S🐾] [✕] [🛏] [💻] [⇌]

LENEXA

▼▼ ▼▼ **Days Inn Lenexa** **M**
(913) 492-7200. **$57-$77, 7 days notice.** 9630 Rosehill Rd. I-35, exit 224 (95th St), just e. Ext corridors. **Pets:** Small, dogs only. $25 deposit/pet. Service with restrictions, crate.
[SAVE] [S🐾] [✕] [⅋M] [♿] [🛏] [⇌]

▼▼▼▼ **La Quinta Inn** **M**
(913) 492-5500. **$65-$105.** 9461 Lenexa Dr. I-35, exit 224 (95th St), just ne; entrance left on Monrovia Rd off 95th St. Int corridors. **Pets:** Small. Service with restrictions, supervision.
[SAVE] [✕] [♿] [🛏] [💻] [⇌]

▼▼ ▼▼ **Super 8 Motel-Lenexa** **M**
(913) 888-8899. **$47-$60.** 9601 Westgate Dr. I-35, exit 224, just se. Int corridors. **Pets:** Medium. $10 daily fee/pet. No service, supervision.
[ASK] [S🐾] [✕] [⅋M] [🐾] [🛏] [💻]

🔺🔺 ▼▼▼▼ **Wellesley Inn & Suites (Kansas City/Lenexa)** **M**
(913) 894-5550. **$55-$75.** 8015 Lenexa Dr. I-35, exit 227 at 75th St, 1 mi s on east frontage road. Ext corridors. **Pets:** Small, other species. Service with restrictions, crate.
[SAVE] [S🐾] [✕] [⅋M] [🐾] [♿] [🛏] [💻] [⇌]

MERRIAM

🔺🔺 ▼▼ ▼▼ **Comfort Inn-Merriam** **M**
(913) 262-2622. **$65-$79, 7 days notice.** 6401 E Frontage Rd. I-35, exit 228B (Shawnee Mission Pkwy), just se. Int corridors. **Pets:** Medium. $5 one-time fee/pet. Service with restrictions, supervision.
[SAVE] [✕] [🐾] [🛏] [💻] [⇌]

▼▼▼▼ **Drury Inn Shawnee Mission/Merriam** **M**
(913) 236-9200. **$65-$100.** 9009 Shawnee Mission Pkwy. I-35, exit 228B (Shawnee Mission Pkwy). Int corridors. **Pets:** Accepted.
[✕] [⅋M] [🐾] [🛏] [💻] [⇌]

OLATHE

▼▼ ▼▼ **Sleep Inn** **M**
(913) 390-9500. **$80-$100, 10 days notice.** 20662 W 151st St. I-35, exit 215 (151st St), 0.4 mi sw. Int corridors. **Pets:** Medium. $10 one-time fee/pet. Designated rooms, service with restrictions, supervision.
[SAVE] [✕] [⅋M] [🐾] [♿] [🛏] [💻] [⇌]

OVERLAND PARK

🔺🔺 ▼▼▼▼ **AmeriSuites (Overland Park/Metcalf)** **H**
(913) 451-2553. **$89-$129.** 6801 W 112th St. I-435, exit 79 (Metcalf Ave), 0.6 mi s. Int corridors. **Pets:** Other species. Service with restrictions, supervision.
[SAVE] [S🐾] [✕] [⅋M] [🐾] [♿] [🛏] [💻] [⇌]

▼▼▼▼ **Chase Suites by Woodfin** **A** ❀
(913) 491-3333. **$159-$269.** 6300 W 110th. I-435, exit 79, 0.3 mi s on US 169, 0.5 mi e on College Blvd to Lamar Ave, just n. Ext corridors. **Pets:** Medium, other species. $150 deposit/room, $10 daily fee/pet. Service with restrictions, crate.
[ASK] [S🐾] [✕] [⅋M] [🐾] [♿] [🛏] [💻]

▼▼▼▼ **Drury Inn & Suites-Overland Park** **M**
(913) 345-1500. **$75-$120.** 10963 Metcalf Ave. I-435, exit 79 (Metcalf Ave), just se. Int corridors. **Pets:** Small, other species. Service with restrictions, crate.
[✕] [⅋M] [♿] [🛏] [💻] [⇌]

▼▼▼▼ **Holiday Inn of Mission-Overland Park** **MI**
(913) 262-3010. **$71-$81.** 7240 Shawnee Mission Pkwy. I-35, exit 228B (Shawnee Mission Pkwy), 1 mi e. Ext/int corridors. **Pets:** $25 one-time fee/room. Service with restrictions, supervision.
[ASK] [S🐾] [✕] [⅋M] [🐾] [♿] [🛏] [💻] [🍴] [⇌]

▼▼▼▼ **Holtze Executive Village** **M**
(913) 344-8100. **$109-$189.** 11400 College Blvd. I-435, exit 82 (Quivira Rd), 0.5 mi s, then just e. Ext/int corridors. **Pets:** Accepted.
[ASK] [S🐾] [✕] [⅋M] [🐾] [♿] [🛏] [💻] [⇌]

▼▼▼▼ **Homestead Studio Suites-Kansas City/Overland Park** **M**
(913) 661-7111. **$64-$74.** 5401 W 110th St. I-435, exit 77B (Nall Ave), just s. Int corridors. **Pets:** Other species.
[ASK] [S🐾] [✕] [⅋M] [♿] [🛏] [💻]

▼▼ ▼▼ **Microtel Inn and Suites of Overland Park/Lenexa** **M**
(913) 541-2664. **$65-$69.** 8750 Ballentine St. I-35, exit 225B, just se of jct. Int corridors. **Pets:** Medium. $25 deposit/pet. Service with restrictions, supervision.
[ASK] [S🐾] [✕] [⅋M] [♿] [🛏] [💻] [⇌]

▼▼▼ **Pear Tree Inn-Overland Park** 🅜
(913) 451-0200. **$55-$95.** 10951 Metcalf Ave. I-435, exit 79
(Metcalf Ave). Int corridors. **Pets:** Small, other species.
Service with restrictions, crate.
⊠ ᰀᴹ 🔌 🛢 💻 🏊

🅐🅐🅐 ▼▼▼ **Red Roof Inn-Overland Park** 🅜
(913) 341-0100. **$45-$73.** 6800 W 108th St. I-435, exit 79
(Metcalf Ave), just ne. Ext corridors. **Pets:** Accepted.
SAVE ⊠ ᰀᴹ

▼▼▼ **White Haven Motor Lodge** 🅜
(913) 649-8200. **$54-$58.** 8039 Metcalf Ave. I-435, exit 79
(US 169), 3.5 mi n on US 169 (Metcalf Ave) at 81st St. Ext
corridors. **Pets:** Medium. Designated rooms, supervision.
⊠ 🛢 🏊

❖ **END METROPOLITAN AREA** ❖

LANSING

🅐🅐🅐 ▼▼▼ **Econo Lodge** 🅜
(913) 727-2777. **$48-$56.** 504 N Main. On US 73 and SR
7, 10 mi n from jct I-70, exit Leavenworth. Int corridors.
Pets: Other species. $25 deposit/room. Service with restric-
tions.
SAVE S🌀 ⊠ 🛢 💻

▼▼▼ **Holiday Inn Express Hotel & Suites** 🅜
(913) 250-1000. **$85, 3 days notice.** 120 Express Dr.
Downtown; on SR 7, just s of jct SR 5. Int corridors.
Pets: Other species. $20 one-time fee/room. Service with
restrictions, crate.
ASK S🌀 ⊠ ᰀᴹ 🐾 🛢 💻 🏊

LARNED

🅐🅐🅐 ▼▼▼ **Best Western Townsman Inn** 🅜
(620) 285-3114. **$55-$65.** 123 E 14th. At jct US 56 and SR
156. Ext corridors. **Pets:** Medium. Service with restrictions,
supervision.
SAVE S🌀 ⊠ 🔌 🐾 🛢 💻 🏊

LAWRENCE

🅐🅐🅐 ▼▼▼ **Best Western Hallmark Inn** 🅜
(785) 841-6500. **$59-$69.** 730 Iowa St. 1 mi w on US 59, 1
mi s of W Lawrence Tpke exit. Ext corridors.
Pets: Accepted.
SAVE S🌀 ⊠ 💻 🏊

🅐🅐🅐 ▼▼▼ **Days Inn** 🅜
(785) 843-9100. **$65-$129.** 2309 Iowa St. On US 59 at jct
SR 10. Ext/int corridors. **Pets:** Large. Designated rooms,
service with restrictions, supervision.
SAVE S🌀 ⊠ ᰀᴹ 🐾 🛢 💻 🏊

🅐🅐🅐 ▼▼▼ **Holiday Inn** 🅜🅘
(785) 841-7077. **$79-$99.** 200 McDonald Dr. I-70, exit 202,
0.5 mi s on SR 59. Ext/int corridors. **Pets:** Accepted.
SAVE S🌀 ⊠ 🔌 🛢 💻 🍴 🏊

🅐🅐🅐 ▼▼▼ **Westminster Inn & Suites** 🅜 🐾
(785) 841-8410. **$59-$85, 14 days notice.** 2525 W 6th St.
W on US 40, 0.3 mi w of Tpke, exit 202. Ext corridors.
Pets: Medium. $50 deposit/room. Supervision.
SAVE S🌀 ⊠ 🛢 💻 🏊

LEAVENWORTH

🅐🅐🅐 ▼▼▼ **Village Lodge** 🅜
(913) 651-6000. **$57-$65, 14 days notice.** 3211 S 4th St.
On US 73 and SR 7. Ext corridors. **Pets:** Medium, other
species. Designated rooms, service with restrictions, supervision.
SAVE S🌀 ⊠ 🛢 💻

LIBERAL

🅐🅐🅐 ▼▼▼ **Best Western LaFonda Motel &**
Restaurant 🅜🅘
(620) 624-5601. **$54.** 229 W Pancake Blvd. On US 54, just
w of US 83 business route. Ext corridors. **Pets:** Small.
Service with restrictions, supervision.
SAVE S🌀 ⊠ 🔌 🛢 💻 🍴 🏊

🅐🅐🅐 ▼▼▼ **Liberal Inn** 🅜🅘
(620) 624-7254. **$49-$69.** 603 E Pancake Blvd. On US 54,
0.5 mi w of US 83. Int corridors. **Pets:** Service with restrictions, supervision.
SAVE S🌀 ⊠ 🛢 💻 🍴 🏊

LINDSBORG

▼▼▼ **Viking Motel** 🅜
(785) 227-3336. **$46-$51.** 446 Harrison. 1 mi ne on Business Loop I-135 and SR 4. Ext corridors. **Pets:** Small.
Designated rooms, service with restrictions, supervision.
⊠ 🏊

LYONS

▼▼▼ **Lyons Inn** 🅜
(620) 257-5185. **$45-$65.** 817 W Main. 1 mi w on SR 56
and 96. Int corridors. **Pets:** Accepted.
ASK S🌀 ⊠ 🛢

MANHATTAN

▼▼▼ **Hampton Inn** 🅜
(785) 539-5000. **$83, 3 days notice.** 501 E Poyntz Ave. SR
177, 0.3 mi e on US 24. Int corridors. **Pets:** Accepted.
SAVE S🌀 ⊠ 🐾 🛢 💻 🏊

(AAA) ▼▼▼▼ **Holiday Inn/Holidome** Ⓜ️
(785) 539-5311. **$105, 7 days notice.** 530 Richards Dr. 2.5 mi sw on SR 18, 0.3 mi e of jct SR 113. Ext/int corridors. **Pets:** Accepted.
[SAVE] [S🐦] [✖] [🐾] [🛢] [💻] [🍴] [🏊]

▼ **Motel 6–152** Ⓜ️
(785) 537-1022. **$41-$61.** 510 Tuttle Creek Blvd. 0.3 mi ne on US 24 and SR 177. Ext corridors. **Pets:** Small, other species. Service with restrictions, supervision.
[S🐦] [✖] [&M] [🐾] [🐾] [🏊]

(AAA) ▼▼▼ **Ramada Plaza Hotel** Ⓜ️
(785) 539-7531. **$90-$150.** 1641 Anderson. 1 mi n of SR 18; opposite Kansas State University. Int corridors. **Pets:** Accepted.
[SAVE] [S🐦] [✖] [🛢] [💻] [🍴] [🏊]

MARYSVILLE

▼▼ **Best Western Surf Motel** Ⓜ️ 🐾
(785) 562-2354. **$50.** 2105 Center St. 1 mi e on US 36 (Pony Express Hwy). Ext/int corridors. **Pets:** Small, other species. $5 daily fee/pet. Designated rooms, service with restrictions.
[SAVE] [S🐦] [✖] [🐾] [🛢] [💻]

(AAA) ▼▼▼ **Oak Tree Inn-Marysville** Ⓜ️
(785) 562-1234. **$55-$65, 7 days notice.** 1127 Pony Express Hwy. 1.6 mi e on US 36 (Pony Express Hwy). Int corridors. **Pets:** Accepted.
[SAVE] [S🐦] [✖] [🛢] [💻] [🍴]

▼▼ **Super 8 Motel** Ⓜ️
(785) 562-5588. **$47-$50.** 1155 Pony Express Hwy. 2 mi e on US 36 (Pony Express Hwy). Int corridors. **Pets:** Other species. $10 one-time fee/room. Designated rooms, service with restrictions, supervision.
[ASK] [S🐦] [✖] [🛢]

MCPHERSON

▼▼ **Best Western Holiday Manor Motel** Ⓜ️
(620) 241-5343. **$56-$64.** 2211 E Kansas Ave. I-135, exit 60, just w. Ext/int corridors. **Pets:** $10 daily fee/pet. Service with restrictions, supervision.
[SAVE] [S🐦] [✖] [🐾] [🛢] [💻] [🍴] [🏊]

(AAA) ▼ **Red Coach Inn** Ⓜ️
(620) 241-6960. **$54.** 2111 E Kansas Ave. I-135, exit 60, just w. Ext/int corridors. **Pets:** Other species. $15 one-time fee/room. Designated rooms, service with restrictions, supervision.
[SAVE] [S🐦] [✖] [🍴] [🏊]

MEADE

(AAA) ▼ **Dalton's Bedpost Motel** Ⓜ️
(620) 873-2131. **$36-$40.** 519 Carthage. On US 54. Ext corridors. **Pets:** Accepted.
[SAVE] [S🐦] [✖]

NEWTON

(AAA) ▼▼ **Best Western Red Coach Inn** 🅷
(316) 283-9120. **$55-$109, 7 days notice.** 1301 E 1st St. I-135, exit 31. Ext/int corridors. **Pets:** Other species. Supervision.
[SAVE] [S🐦] [✖] [🐾] [🛢] [💻] [🏊]

▼▼ **Days Inn Newton** Ⓜ️ 🐾
(316) 283-3330. **$56-$68.** 105 Manchester St. I-135, exit 31. Int corridors. **Pets:** Other species. $75 daily fee/room. Service with restrictions, supervision.
[SAVE] [S🐦] [✖] [🛢] [💻] [🏊]

OAKLEY

(AAA) ▼ **1st Travel Inn** Ⓜ️
(785) 672-3226. **$44-$48, 7 days notice.** 708 Center Ave. Center. Ext corridors. **Pets:** Accepted.
[SAVE] [S🐦] [✖] [🍴] [🏊]

(AAA) ▼▼▼ **Best Value Kansas Kountry Inn** Ⓜ️
(785) 672-3131. **$48-$68, 3 days notice.** 3538 US 40. I-70, exit 76, 1.5 mi w. Ext corridors. **Pets:** Other species. Service with restrictions, supervision.
[SAVE] [S🐦] [✖] [💻]

▼▼ **Best Western Golden Plains Motel** Ⓜ️
(785) 672-3254. **$58-$65, 7 days notice.** 3506 US 40. I-70, exit 76, 1.7 mi w. Ext corridors. **Pets:** Small. Service with restrictions, supervision.
[SAVE] [S🐦] [✖] [💻] [🏊]

OTTAWA

(AAA) ▼▼▼ **Days Inn** Ⓜ️
(785) 242-4842. **$55-$85, 7 days notice.** 1641 S Main. I-35, exit 183B (US 59), 1.5 mi n. Ext corridors. **Pets:** Accepted.
[SAVE] [S🐦] [✖] [&M] [🛢] [💻]

(AAA) ▼▼▼ **Econo Lodge** Ⓜ️
(785) 242-3400. **$50-$80, 7 days notice.** 2331 S Cedar Rd. I-35, exit 183B (US 59). Int corridors. **Pets:** Accepted.
[SAVE] [S🐦] [✖] [💻]

(AAA) ▼▼▼ **Holiday Inn Express** Ⓜ️
(785) 242-2224. **$70-$90.** 606 E 23rd St. I-35, exit 183B (US 59). Ext corridors. **Pets:** Small. Designated rooms, service with restrictions.
[SAVE] [S🐦] [✖] [&M] [🛢] [💻] [🏊]

▼▼ **Villager Lodge Ottawa** Ⓜ️
(785) 242-7000. **$50-$85.** 2209 S Princeton Rd. I-35, exit 183B (US 59). Ext corridors. **Pets:** Medium. $10 daily fee/pet. Designated rooms, service with restrictions, supervision.
[ASK] [S🐦] [✖] [🛢] [💻]

PHILLIPSBURG

♨♨♨ Cottonwood Inn **M**
(785) 543-2125. **$57-$87, 7 days notice.** 1200 State St. 2
mi e on US 36. Ext corridors. **Pets:** Accepted.
[SAVE] [S♦] [✕] [➰]

PRATT

♨♨ Best Western Hillcrest Motel **M**
(620) 672-6407. **$47-$51.** 1336 E 1st St. 1 mi e on US 54.
Ext corridors. **Pets:** Accepted.
[SAVE] [S♦] [✕] [🛏] [▣] [➰]

♨♨♨ Days Inn **M**
(620) 672-9465. **$55-$72.** 1901 E 1st. 1.7 mi e on US 54.
Ext corridors. **Pets:** Accepted.
[SAVE] [S♦] [✕] [▣] [➰]

♨♨ Economy Inn **M**
(620) 672-5588. **$34-$40, 4 days notice.** 1401 E 1st St. 1
mi e on US 54. Ext corridors. **Pets:** Small. $5 one-time
fee/room. Designated rooms, service with restrictions,
supervision.
[SAVE] [S♦] [✕] [🛏] [➰]

♨ Evergreen Inn **M**
(620) 672-6431. **$34-$45, 3 days notice.** 20001 W US Hwy
54. 3 mi w on US 54. Ext corridors. **Pets:** Accepted.
[ASK] [S♦] [✕] [🛏] [➰]

♨♨♨ Holiday Inn Express **M**
(620) 672-9433. **$80, 3 days notice.** 1401 W Hwy 54. 2 mi
w on US 54. Int corridors. **Pets:** Accepted.
[ASK] [S♦] [✕] [📶] [⛱] [🛏] [▣] [➰]

♨♨ Super 8 Motel of Pratt **M**
(620) 672-5945. **$48-$52.** 1906 E 1st St. 1.7 mi e on US
54. Int corridors. **Pets:** Small, dogs only. $10 deposit/pet.
[ASK] [S♦] [✕] [🛏]

QUINTER

♨ Budget Host Q Motel **M**
(785) 754-3337. **$50-$60, 3 days notice.** 1202 Castle Rock
St. I-70, exit 107, just n. Ext corridors. **Pets:** Other species.
[ASK] [S♦] [✕] [🍴]

RUSSELL

♨♨ Days Inn **M**
(785) 483-6660. **$54-$65, 5 days notice.** 1225 S Fossil St.
I-70, exit 184, just n. Ext corridors. **Pets:** Other species. $5
daily fee/pet. Designated rooms, service with restrictions,
supervision.
[SAVE] [S♦] [✕] [➰]

SABETHA

♨♨ Sabetha Country Inn **M**
(785) 284-2300. **$51-$61.** 1423 S 75 Hwy. On US 75, 1 mi
s of jct SR 246 and US 75. Int corridors. **Pets:** Accepted.
[S♦] [✕] [🛏]

SALINA

♨ 1st Inn Gold **M** 🐾
(785) 827-5511. **$45-$55.** 2403 S 9th St. I-135, exit 90
(Magnolia), just e. Ext corridors. **Pets:** Medium, other species. Service with restrictions, supervision.
[ASK] [S♦] [✕] [🛏] [▣] [➰]

♨♨♨ Best Western Mid-America Inn **M**
(785) 827-0356. **$56-$75.** 1846 N 9th St. I-70, exit 252, just
s. Ext corridors. **Pets:** Accepted.
[SAVE] [S♦] [✕] [⛱] [▣] [🍴] [➰]

♨ Budget King Motel **M**
(785) 827-4477. **$40-$46.** 809 N Broadway. I-70, exit 252,
1.5 mi s. Ext corridors. **Pets:** Medium. Service with restrictions, supervision.
[SAVE] [S♦] [✕]

♨ Comfort Inn **M**
(785) 826-1711. **$57-$105, 15 days notice.** 1820 W Crawford St. I-135, exit 92, just e. Int corridors. **Pets:** Small,
other species. $10 daily fee/pet. Designated rooms, service
with restrictions, supervision.
[SAVE] [S♦] [✕] [📶] [🛏] [▣] [➰]

♨♨♨ Hampton Inn-Salina **M**
(785) 823-9800. **$74-$99, 15 days notice.** 401 W Schilling
Rd. I-135, exit 89 (Schilling Rd), just e. Int corridors.
Pets: Very small, other species. $10 one-time fee/pet. Serv-
ice with restrictions, supervision.
[SAVE] [S♦] [✕] [⛱M] [📶] [⛱] [🛏] [▣] [➰]

♨♨♨ Holiday Inn Express Hotel &
Suites-Salina **M**
(785) 827-9000. **$55-$90.** 201 E Diamond Dr. I-70, exit 252,
just ne. Int corridors. **Pets:** Other species. $10 one-time
fee/room. Designated rooms, service with restrictions, crate.
[ASK] [S♦] [✕] [📶] [⛱] [🛏] [▣] [➰]

♨♨♨ Holiday Inn of Salina **M**
(785) 823-1739. **$74.** 1616 W Crawford St. I-135, exit 92,
0.5 mi e. Int corridors. **Pets:** Accepted.
[ASK] [S♦] [✕] [📶] [🛏] [▣] [🍴] [➰]

♨♨♨ Ramada Inn **M**
(785) 825-8211. **$66-$74, 7 days notice.** 1949 N 9th St.
I-70, exit 252, just s. Ext corridors. **Pets:** Accepted.
[SAVE] [S♦] [✕] [▣] [🍴] [➰]

♨♨♨ Red Coach Inn **M**
(785) 825-2111. **$59-$130.** 2110 W Crawford St. I-135, exit
92, just w. Ext/int corridors. **Pets:** Very small, other species.
$15 one-time fee/room. Designated rooms, service with
restrictions, supervision.
[SAVE] [S♦] [✕] [📶] [⛱] [🛏] [🍴] [➰] [✕○]

♨♨ Salina Super 8 Motel **M**
(785) 823-9215. **$54-$70.** 1640 W Crawford St. I-135, exit
92, 0.3 mi e. Int corridors. **Pets:** Accepted.
[ASK] [S♦] [✕]

Super 8 I-70 M
(785) 823-8808. **$60-$80, 7 days notice.** 120 E Diamond Dr. I-70, exit 252, just ne. Int corridors. **Pets:** Small. $5 daily fee/pet. Service with restrictions, supervision.

SHARON SPRINGS

Oak Tree Inn M
(785) 852-4664. **$66-$75.** US 40 & SR 27. At jct US 40 and SR 27. Ext/int corridors. **Pets:** Other species. $5 one-time fee/pet. Service with restrictions, supervision.

TOPEKA

AmeriSuites (Topeka/Northwest) M
(785) 273-0066. **$89-$99.** 6021 SW Sixth Ave. I-70, exit 356 (Wanamaker Rd). Int corridors. **Pets:** Accepted.

Best Western Candlelight Inn M
(785) 272-9550. **$57-$105.** 2831 SW Fairlawn Rd. I-470, exit 3. Ext corridors. **Pets:** Small. $5 daily fee/pet. Service with restrictions, crate.

Best Western Meadow Acres Motel M
(785) 267-1681. **$70-$90, 7 days notice.** 2950 S Topeka Blvd. I-470, exit 6 eastbound. Ext corridors. **Pets:** Small. $8 one-time fee/pet. Designated rooms, service with restrictions, supervision.

Capitol Plaza Hotel H
(785) 431-7200. **$109-$149.** 1717 SW Topeka Blvd. I-70, exit SE 8th Ave, 0.5 mi s, then 1.1 mi s; I-470, exit Topeka Blvd, 2.9 mi n. Int corridors. **Pets:** Medium, other species. Service with restrictions, crate.

ClubHouse Inn & Suites M
(785) 273-8888. **$79.** 924 SW Henderson. I-70, exit 356 (10th and Wanamaker Rd). Int corridors. **Pets:** Accepted.

Comfort Inn M
(785) 273-5365. **$64-$114.** 1518 SW Wanamaker Rd. I-470, exit 1 (Wanamaker Rd). Int corridors. **Pets:** Large, other species. $5 daily fee/pet. Designated rooms, service with restrictions, supervision.

Quality Inn M
(785) 273-6969. **$55-$89, 7 days notice.** 1240 SW Wanamaker Rd. I-470, exit 1 (Wanamaker Rd), just ne; I-70, exit 356A, 1 mi s. Int corridors. **Pets:** Very small. $25 deposit/pet, $5.60 daily fee/pet. Designated rooms, no service, supervision.

Ramada Inn Downtown H
(785) 234-5400. **Call for rates, 30 days notice.** 420 SE Sixth St. I-70, exit 362B, just e. Int corridors. **Pets:** Other species. Service with restrictions, supervision.

Residence Inn A
(785) 271-8903. **$90-$108.** 1620 SW Westport Dr. I-470, exit 1 (Wanamaker Rd). Int corridors. **Pets:** Accepted.

ULYSSES

Single Tree Inn M
(620) 356-1500. **$67, 3 days notice.** 2033 W Oklahoma St. 1.5 mi w on US 160. Int corridors. **Pets:** Accepted.

WAMEGO

Simmer Motel M
(785) 456-2304. **$46.** 1215 Hwy 24 W. 0.5 mi w on US 24 from jct SR 99. Ext corridors. **Pets:** Accepted.

WELLINGTON

Oak Tree Inn M
(620) 326-8191. **$65-$69.** 1177 E Hwy 160. I-35, exit 19, 2 mi w on US 160. Ext corridors. **Pets:** Accepted.

WICHITA

The Airport Plaza Hotel & Convention Center M
(316) 942-7911. **$79-$99.** 5805 W Kellogg. US 54, exit Dugan Rd; on S Frontage Rd. Int corridors. **Pets:** Small, other species. $25 one-time fee/room. Service with restrictions, crate.

Best Western Red Coach Inn M
(316) 832-9387. **$69, 3 days notice.** 915 E 53rd St N. I-135, exit 13. Ext/int corridors. **Pets:** Accepted.

Comfort Inn M
(316) 686-2844. **$70-$99.** 9525 E Corporate Hills. 6 mi e, just n of jct US 54, SR 96 and turnpike, exit 50. Int corridors. **Pets:** Accepted.

Comfort Inn M
(316) 522-1800. **$60.** 4849 S Laura. I-135, exit 1AB (47th St S), just e. Int corridors. **Pets:** Other species. $10 daily fee/room. Service with restrictions, supervision.

Comfort Suites Airport M
(316) 945-2600. **$91-$119.** 658 Westdale. Jct US 54 and I-235; adjacent to Towne West Square. Int corridors. **Pets:** Small, other species. Service with restrictions, supervision.

Hampton Inn M
(316) 686-3576. **$74-$99.** 9449 E Corporate Hills. 6 mi e, just n of jct US 54, SR 96 and turnpike, exit 50. Int corridors. **Pets:** Other species. Service with restrictions, crate.

Hawthorn Suites at Reflection Ridge M
(316) 729-5700. **$109, 3 days notice.** 2405 N Ridge Rd. I-235, exit 10, 2 mi w on Zoo Blvd/21st St N, then just n. Int corridors. **Pets:** Other species. $50 one-time fee/room. Service with restrictions, supervision.

Holiday Inn Express-North Wichita M
(316) 634-3900. **$74-$99.** 7824 E 32nd St N. SR 96 E, exit Rock Rd, just sw. Int corridors. **Pets:** Small. Service with restrictions, crate.

Holiday Inn Select H
(316) 686-7131. **$84-$104.** 549 S Rock Rd. On US 54 and SR 96, 0.5 mi w of turnpike, exit 50. Ext/int corridors. **Pets:** Other species. $25 one-time fee/room. Designated rooms, service with restrictions, supervision.

Holiday Inn Wichita/Airport MI
(316) 943-2181. **$79-$89.** 5500 W Kellogg. I-235, exit 7, just w. Int corridors. **Pets:** Accepted.

The Kansas Inn M
(316) 269-9999. **$58-$60.** 1011 N Topeka Ave. I-135, exit 8 (13th St), 0.7 mi w, then 0.3 mi s. Int corridors. **Pets:** $5 daily fee/pet. Designated rooms, service with restrictions, supervision.

La Quinta Inn M
(316) 681-2881. **$65-$105.** 7700 E Kellogg. On US 54 and SR 96, 0.5 mi w of turnpike, exit 50; northwest corner of Kellogg and Rock rds; adjacent to Towne East Shopping Mall. Int corridors. **Pets:** Small. Supervision.

Quality Inn-Airport MI
(316) 722-8730. **$60, 7 days notice.** 600 S Holland. I-235, exit 7, 0.5 mi w on US 54. Int corridors. **Pets:** Medium. $20 deposit/room. Designated rooms, service with restrictions, supervision.

Red Carpet Inn M
(316) 529-4100. **$46-$54.** 607 E 47th St S. I-135, exit 1B (47th St S), 0.3 mi w. Ext corridors. **Pets:** Accepted.

WINFIELD

Comfort Inn M
(620) 221-7529. **$63-$100.** Hwy 77 at Quail Ridge Dr. On US 77, 1 mi s. Ext/int corridors. **Pets:** $3 daily fee/pet. Service with restrictions.

YATES CENTER

Star Motel M
(620) 625-2175. **$32-$36.** 206 S Fry. On US 54 at jct US 75. Ext corridors. **Pets:** Medium, other species. Supervision.

KENTUCKY

CITY INDEX

ASHLAND

🔺🔺 ◈◈ Knights Inn M
(606) 928-9501. **$44-$49.** 7216 US Rt 60. I-64, exit 185, 5 mi sw on US 60, then 4.3 mi n. Ext corridors. **Pets:** Other species. $5 daily fee/room. Service with restrictions, supervision.

🅂🄰🅅🄴 🆂🅓 ⊠ 🖥 💻 🌊

BARDSTOWN

🔺🔺 ◈◈◈ Bardstown-Parkview Motel M🅸
(502) 348-5983. **$50-$70.** 418 E Stephen Foster Ave. 0.5 mi e on US 150; e of jct US 62. Ext corridors. **Pets:** Service with restrictions, supervision.

🅂🄰🅅🄴 🆂🅓 ⊠ 🖥 🍽 🌊

◈◈ Best Western General Nelson Motel M
(502) 348-3977. **$59-$79.** 411 W Stephen Foster Ave. 0.5 mi w on US 62. Ext corridors. **Pets:** Small. $10 one-time fee/room. Service with restrictions, crate.

🅂🄰🅅🄴 🆂🅓 ⊠ 🖥 💻 🌊

◈◈◈ Hampton Inn M
(502) 349-0100. **$64-$77.** 985 Chambers Blvd. Just s of US 245. Int corridors. **Pets:** Small, other species. Service with restrictions, supervision.

🅂🄰🅅🄴 ⊠ 🔹 📶 📶 🖥 💻 🌊

🔺🔺 ◈◈◈ Holiday Inn Convention Center M🅸
(502) 348-9253. **$69.** 1875 New Haven Rd. Blue Grass Pkwy, exit 21. Ext corridors. **Pets:** $10 one-time fee/room. Service with restrictions, supervision.

🅂🄰🅅🄴 🆂🅓 ⊠ 🖥 💻 🍽

🔺🔺 ◈ Old Kentucky Home Motel M
(502) 348-5979. **$35-$62.** 414 W Stephen Foster Ave. 0.5 mi w on US 62. Ext corridors. **Pets:** Accepted.

🅂🄰🅅🄴 🆂🅓 ⊠ 🖥 💻 🌊

◈◈ Ramada Inn M
(502) 349-0363. **$55-$85, 5 days notice.** 523 N Third St. 0.5 mi n on US 150. Ext corridors. **Pets:** Small, other species. $10 daily fee/room. Service with restrictions, supervision.

🄰🅂🄺 🆂🅓 ⊠ 🖥 💻 🌊

BEAVER DAM

◈◈◈ Days Inn Beaver Dam M
(270) 274-0851. **$64-$75, 7 days notice.** 1750 US Hwy 231. Kentucky Pkwy, exit 75, just n. Int corridors. **Pets:** Large, other species. $10 one-time fee/pet. Designated rooms, service with restrictions, supervision.

🅂🄰🅅🄴 🆂🅓 ⊠ 🖥 🌊

BENTON

◈◈◈ Holiday Inn Express Hotel & Suites M
(270) 527-5300. **$75-$85, 30 days notice.** 173 Carroll Rd. Purchase Pkwy, exit 47. Int corridors. **Pets:** Accepted.

🄰🅂🄺 ⊠ 🔹 📶 📶 🖥 💻 🌊

BEREA

🔺🔺 ◈◈◈ Boone Tavern Hotel-Berea College 🄷
(859) 985-3700. **$70-$100.** 100 Main St. I-75, exit 76, 1.5 mi ne on SR 21. Int corridors. **Pets:** $50 deposit/room. Service with restrictions.

🅂🄰🅅🄴 🆂🅓 ⊠ 🔹 💻 🍽

🔺🔺 ◈◈ Knights Inn Berea M
(859) 986-2384. **$40-$60, 14 days notice.** 715 Chestnut St. I-75, exit 76, 0.3 mi e. Ext corridors. **Pets:** Other species. $5 daily fee/pet, $5 one-time fee/pet. Supervision.

🅂🄰🅅🄴 🆂🅓 ⊠ 🖥

🔺🔺 ◈◈ Super 8 Motel M
(859) 986-8426. **$45-$64.** 196 Prince Royal Dr. I-75, exit 76, 0.3 mi e. Ext corridors. **Pets:** Other species. $5 daily fee/pet. Service with restrictions, supervision.

🅂🄰🅅🄴 🆂🅓 ⊠ 🖥 🌊

BOWLING GREEN

Baymont Inn & Suites-Bowling Green M
(270) 843-3200. **$64-$79.** 165 Three Springs Rd. I-65, exit 22 (Scottsville Rd), 0.3 mi w. Int corridors. **Pets:** Small, other species. $10 deposit/pet. Designated rooms, service with restrictions, supervision.
[SAVE] [S] [X] [figure] [figure] [figure]

Best Western Continental Inn M
(270) 781-5200. **$45-$65, 30 days notice.** 700 Interstate Dr. I-65, exit 28, 0.3 mi w. Ext corridors. **Pets:** Accepted.
[SAVE] [S] [X] [figure]

Country Hearth Inn M
(270) 783-4443. **$49-$65.** 395 Corvette Dr. I-65, exit 28, just w. Int corridors. **Pets:** Medium, other species. No service, crate.
[ASK] [S] [X] [figure] [figure] [figure]

Days Inn M ❀
(270) 781-6470. **$55-$65.** 4617 Scottsville Rd. I-65, exit 22 (Scottsville Rd), 0.3 mi e. Int corridors. **Pets:** Other species. $10 one-time fee/pet. Designated rooms, supervision.
[SAVE] [S] [X] [figure] [figure]

Drury Inn-Bowling Green M
(270) 842-7100. **$50-$96.** 3250 Scottsville Rd. I-65, exit 22 (Scottsville Rd), just w. Int corridors. **Pets:** Accepted.
[X] [figure] [figure] [figure] [figure] [figure]

News Inn of Bowling Green M
(270) 781-3460. **$39-$65, 3 days notice.** 3160 Scottsville Rd. I-65, exit 22 (Scottsville Rd). Ext corridors. **Pets:** Large. $5 daily fee/pet. Designated rooms, service with restrictions, supervision.
[SAVE] [S] [X] [figure] [figure]

Ramada Inn M
(270) 781-3000. **$64-$68.** 4767 Scottsville Rd. I-65, exit 22 (Scottsville Rd), 0.3 mi e. Int corridors. **Pets:** Small. $10 one-time fee/room. Designated rooms, service with restrictions, supervision.
[ASK] [S] [X] [figure] [figure] [figure] [figure] [figure]

Super 8 Motel M
(270) 781-9594. **$39-$55, 7 days notice.** 250 Cumberland Trace Rd. I-65, exit 22 (Scottsville Rd), just ne. Int corridors. **Pets:** Medium. $50 deposit/room. Designated rooms, service with restrictions, supervision.
[SAVE] [S] [X] [figure] [figure] [figure]

Travelodge Hotel M
(270) 781-6610. **$65-$75, 3 days notice.** 1000 Executive Way. I-65, exit 22 (Scottsville Rd), just ne. Int corridors. **Pets:** $10 one-time fee/room. Service with restrictions.
[ASK] [S] [X] [figure] [figure] [figure] [figure]

University Plaza Hotel & Conference Center H
(270) 745-0088. **$79-$99.** 1021 Wilkinson Trace. I-65, exit 22 (Scottsville Rd), 2.5 mi w, then just n. Int corridors. **Pets:** Medium. $25 one-time fee/room. Service with restrictions, crate.
[SAVE] [S] [X] [figure] [figure] [figure] [figure] [figure]

BURKESVILLE

Riverfront Lodge M
(270) 864-3300. **$50-$60.** 305 Keen St. 0.5 mi e on SR 90. Ext corridors. **Pets:** $5 daily fee/room. Service with restrictions, supervision.
[X] [figure]

CADIZ

Holiday Inn Express M
(270) 522-3700. **$70-$95, 10 days notice.** 153 Broad Bent Blvd. I-24, exit 65, just s. Int corridors. **Pets:** Accepted.
[ASK] [S] [X] [figure] [figure]

Super 8 Motel M ❀
(270) 522-7007. **$44-$69, 10 days notice.** 154 Hospitality Ln. I-24, exit 65. Ext corridors. **Pets:** Other species. $5 one-time fee/pet. Service with restrictions.
[ASK] [S] [X] [figure]

CAMPBELLSVILLE

Best Western Campbellsville Lodge M
(270) 465-7001. **$64-$69.** 1400 E Broadway. 2 mi e on US 68 and SR 55. Int corridors. **Pets:** Accepted.
[SAVE] [S] [X] [figure] [figure] [figure]

CARROLLTON

Days Inn Carrollton M
(502) 732-9301. **$55-$99, 7 days notice.** 61 Inn Rd. I-71, exit 44, just nw. Int corridors. **Pets:** Accepted.
[SAVE] [S] [X] [figure] [figure]

Holiday Inn Express M
(502) 732-6661. **$59-$109.** 141 Inn Rd. I-71, exit 44, just nw. Int corridors. **Pets:** Accepted.
[ASK] [S] [X] [figure]

Super 8 Carrollton M
(502) 732-0252. **$49-$99, 7 days notice.** 130 Slumber Ln. I-71, exit 44, just nw. Int corridors. **Pets:** Accepted.
[ASK] [S] [X] [figure]

CAVE CITY

Best Western Kentucky Inn M
(270) 773-3161. **$25-$99.** 1009 Doyle Ave. I-65, exit 53, just e. Ext corridors. **Pets:** Very small. $10 daily fee/pet. Designated rooms, service with restrictions, supervision.
[SAVE] [S] [X] [figure] [figure]

 Comfort Inn **M**
(270) 773-2030. **$45-$115, 3 days notice.** 801 Mammoth Cave St. I-65, exit 53, just ne. Ext corridors. **Pets:** Small. Designated rooms, service with restrictions, supervision.

Days Inn Cave City M
(270) 773-2151. **$37-$95.** 822 Mammoth Cave Rd. I-65, exit 53, just e. Ext/int corridors. **Pets:** Medium. $5 daily fee/pet. Designated rooms, service with restrictions, supervision.

Holiday Inn Express M
(270) 773-3101. **$40-$100.** 102 Happy Valley Rd. I-65, exit 53, just e. Ext corridors. **Pets:** Large. $10 daily fee/pet. Designated rooms, service with restrictions, crate.

Quality Inn M
(270) 773-2181. **$35-$90.** 1006 A Doyle Ave. I-65, exit 53, just se. Ext corridors. **Pets:** $6 daily fee/pet. Supervision.

Super 8 Motel M
(270) 773-2500. **$45-$89.** 799 Mammoth Cave St. I-65, exit 53, just ne. Ext corridors. **Pets:** Medium, other species. $5 daily fee/pet. Designated rooms, service with restrictions, crate.

CORBIN

Baymont Inn & Suites-Corbin M ❖
(606) 523-9040. **$55-$60.** 174 Adams Rd. I-75, exit 29. Int corridors. **Pets:** Medium. Designated rooms, service with restrictions, supervision.

Best Western-Corbin Inn M
(606) 528-2100. **$40-$80.** 2630 Cumberland Falls Rd. I-75, exit 25. Ext corridors. **Pets:** Other species. $10 daily fee/room. Service with restrictions.

Super 8 Motel M
(606) 528-8888. **$44-$48, 14 days notice.** 171 W Cumberland Gap Pkwy. I-75, exit 29, just e. Int corridors. **Pets:** Medium. $3 daily fee/pet. Designated rooms, service with restrictions, supervision.

COVINGTON

Embassy Suites Cincinnati RiverCenter H ❖
(859) 261-8400. **$109-$169.** 10 E River Center Blvd. I-75, exit 192, 0.8 mi e on 5th Ave, 0.3 mi n on Madison. Int corridors. **Pets:** Medium. $75 one-time fee/room. Designated rooms, service with restrictions, crate.

DANVILLE

Holiday Inn Express M
(859) 236-8600. **$50-$90.** 96 Daniel Dr. Just e of SR 127 on US 150 Bypass. Int corridors. **Pets:** Accepted.

Super 8 Motel M
(859) 236-8881. **$51-$65.** 3663 Hwy 150/127 Bypass. Just e of SR 127 on US 150 Bypass. Int corridors. **Pets:** Other species. $6 daily fee/pet. Service with restrictions, supervision.

DRY RIDGE

Holiday Inn Express M
(859) 824-7121. **$89.** 1050 Fashion Ridge Rd. I-75, exit 159, just nw. Int corridors. **Pets:** Accepted.

Microtel Inn and Suites M
(859) 824-2000. **$44-$83.** 79 Blackburn Ln. I-75, exit 159, just ne. Int corridors. **Pets:** Small. $10 one-time fee/pet. Service with restrictions, supervision.

EDDYVILLE

Holiday Hills Townhouses M
(270) 388-7236. **$100-$110, 30 days notice.** 5631 Kentucky 93 S. I-24, exit 45, 2 mi s on SR 93. Ext corridors. **Pets:** Accepted.

ELIZABETHTOWN

Best Western Cardinal Inn M
(270) 765-6139. **Call for rates.** 642 E Dixie Ave. I-65, exit 91 (US 31 W), 0.3 mi nw. Ext/int corridors. **Pets:** Small. $10 daily fee/pet. Service with restrictions.

Comfort Inn Atrium Gardens M
(270) 769-3030. **$69-$99.** 1043 Executive Dr. I-65, exit 94, just nw. Int corridors. **Pets:** Accepted.

Days Inn M
(270) 769-5522. **$62-$64, 10 days notice.** 2010 N Mulberry. I-65, exit 94, just ne. Ext corridors. **Pets:** Small, dogs only. $5 daily fee/pet. Service with restrictions, supervision.

Super 8 Motel M
(270) 737-1088. **$50-$71, 3 days notice.** 2028 N Mulberry St. I-65, exit 94, just ne. Int corridors. **Pets:** Accepted.

ERLANGER

Baymont Inn & Suites Cincinnati-Airport (Erlanger, KY) M
(859) 746-0300. **$69-$89.** 1805 Airport Exchange Blvd. I-275, exit 2. Int corridors. **Pets:** Accepted.

(AAA) ▼▼▼▼ **Residence Inn by Marriott, Cincinnati Airport** **A**
(859) 282-7400. **$109-$179.** 2811 Circleport Dr. I-275, exit 2. Int corridors. **Pets:** Other species. $100 one-time fee/pet. Service with restrictions.
[SAVE] [S☾] [✕] [&M] [&] [🛏] [💻] [⇌]

FLORENCE

(AAA) ▼▼▼▼ **AmeriSuites (Cincinnati Airport)** **M**
(859) 647-1170. **$89-$109, 30 days notice.** 300 Meijer Dr. I-75, exit 182, 0.4 mi sw. Int corridors. **Pets:** Small. Service with restrictions.
[SAVE] [S☾] [✕] [&M] [✍] [&] [🛏] [💻] [⇌]

▼▼▼▼ **Ashley Quarters** **M** ❀
(859) 525-9997. **$378-$534.** 4880 Houston Rd. I-75, exit 182, 0.6 mi w on Turfway and Houston rds. Int corridors. **Pets:** Other species. $50 one-time fee/room. Designated rooms.
[ASK] [S☾] [✕] [&] [🛏] [💻] [⇌]

(AAA) ▼▼▼▼ **Best Western Inn Florence** **M**
(859) 525-0090. **$55-$150, 7 days notice.** 7821 Commerce Dr. I-75, exit 181, just ne. Int corridors. **Pets:** Small. $10 daily fee/pet. Service with restrictions, supervision.
[SAVE] [S☾] [✕] [&M] [&] [🛏] [⇌]

(AAA) ▼▼▼ **Florence Super 8** **M** ❀
(859) 283-1221. **$64-$67.** 7928 Dream St. I-75, exit 180, just e on US 42, just n. Int corridors. **Pets:** Small. $5 daily fee/pet. Service with restrictions, supervision.
[SAVE] [S☾] [✕] [🛏]

(AAA) ▼▼▼ **Knights Inn Florence** **M**
(859) 371-9711. **$33-$99.** 8049 Dream St. I-71/75, exit 180, just e on US 42, then just n. Ext corridors. **Pets:** Medium. $10 one-time fee/pet. Service with restrictions, crate.
[SAVE] [✕] [🛏] [⇌]

FRANKFORT

(AAA) ▼▼▼ **Bluegrass Inn** **M**
(502) 695-1800. **$48-$60, 7 days notice.** 635 Versailles Rd. I-64, exit 58, 1 mi n on US 60. Ext corridors. **Pets:** Medium. $10 daily fee/pet. Designated rooms, service with restrictions, supervision.
[SAVE] [S☾] [✕] [🛏] [⇌]

(AAA) ▼▼▼ **Holiday Inn Capital Plaza** **H**
(502) 227-5100. **$80.** 405 Wilkinson Blvd. Adjacent to Frankfort Civic Center. Int corridors. **Pets:** Accepted.
[SAVE] [S☾] [✕] [&M] [✍] [&] [🛏] [💻] [🍴] [⇌]

▼▼▼ **Super 8 Motel** **M**
(502) 875-3220. **$45-$55.** 1225 US Hwy 127 S. I-64, exit 53B, 1.2 mi n on US 127. Int corridors. **Pets:** Accepted.
[ASK] [S☾] [✕] [💻]

FRANKLIN

(AAA) ▼▼▼ **Comfort Inn** **M**
(270) 586-6100. **$45-$85.** 3794 Nashville Rd. I-65, exit 2. Ext corridors. **Pets:** Medium. $5 daily fee/pet. Service with restrictions, supervision.
[SAVE] [S☾] [✕] [&M] [🛏] [💻] [⇌]

(AAA) ▼▼▼▼ **Days Inn** **M**
(270) 598-0163. **$45-$50.** 103 Trotter Ln. I-65, exit 6, just w. Ext corridors. **Pets:** Large, other species. $5 daily fee/pet.
[SAVE] [S☾] [✕] [&M] [&] [🛏] [⇌]

▼▼▼ **Holiday Inn Express** **M**
(270) 586-5090. **$64, 15 days notice.** 3811 Nashville Rd. I-65, exit 2, just w. Ext corridors. **Pets:** Accepted.
[ASK] [S☾] [✕] [&M] [🛏] [💻] [⇌]

GEORGETOWN

▼▼▼ **Country Inn & Suites By Carlson** **M**
(502) 868-6868. **Call for rates, 7 days notice.** 131 Darby Dr. I-75, exit 126, just nw. Int corridors. **Pets:** Accepted.
[ASK] [✕] [🛏] [💻] [⇌]

(AAA) ▼▼▼ **Days Inn of Georgetown** **M**
(502) 863-5000. **$36-$65.** 385 Cherry Blossom Way. I-75, exit 129, just se. Ext corridors. **Pets:** Other species. $5 daily fee/pet. Service with restrictions, supervision.
[SAVE] [S☾] [✕] [&] [🛏] [💻] [⇌]

▼▼▼ **Super 8 Motel** **M**
(502) 863-4888. **$49-$59.** 250 Shoney Dr. I-75, exit 126. Ext/int corridors. **Pets:** Medium, dogs only. $8 daily fee/pet. Service with restrictions.
[S☾] [✕] [&M] [🛏] [⇌]

GLASGOW

▼▼▼ **Comfort Inn** **M**
(270) 651-9099. **$57-$73, 10 days notice.** 210 Calvary Dr. Cumberland Pkwy, exit 11, just n. Ext corridors. **Pets:** Other species. $10 one-time fee/room. Service with restrictions, supervision.
[SAVE] [S☾] [✕] [&] [🛏] [💻] [⇌]

HARLAN

(AAA) ▼▼▼▼ **Best Western Harlan** **M**
(606) 573-3385. **$62-$87.** 2608 S Hwy 421. 2.8 mi s on US 421. Int corridors. **Pets:** Small, dogs only. Service with restrictions, supervision.
[SAVE] [S☾] [✕] [✍] [&] [🛏] [💻] [⇌]

HARRODSBURG

▼▼▼ **Country Hearth Inn** **M**
(859) 734-2400. **$49-$65.** 105 Commercial Dr. 0.6 mi n on College St. Int corridors. **Pets:** Accepted.
[ASK] [S☾] [✕] [🛏] [💻]

HEBRON

▼▼▼▼ **Radisson Hotel Cincinnati Airport** **M**
(859) 371-6166. **$89-$139.** Cincinnati N KY Airport. 4 mi w of I-71 and 75 via I-275, exit 4B from I-275 (SR 212), 1.3 mi w on SR 212. Int corridors. **Pets:** Medium. Service with restrictions, crate.
[ASK] [S☾] [✕] [✍] [🛏] [💻] [🍴] [⇌]

HOPKINSVILLE

▼▼▼ Holiday Inn Ⓜ
(270) 886-4413. **$62-$72.** 2910 Fort Campbell Blvd. Pennyrile Pkwy, exit 7A, 0.6 mi n on US 41A. Int corridors. **Pets:** Other species.
Ⓐ🆂�😠 ▣ 🖬 🍴 ➿

▼▼▼ Hopkinsville Best Western Ⓜ
(270) 886-9000. **$64-$69.** 4101 Fort Campbell Blvd. Pennyrile Pkwy, exit 7A, just s on US 41A. Int corridors. **Pets:** Accepted.
🆂🆂 🆂 😠 ▣ 🖬 ➿

HORSE CAVE

ⒶⒶⒶ ▼▼▼ Budget Host Inn Ⓜ
(270) 786-2165. **$33-$67.** I-65 & Hwy 218. I-65, exit 58, just ne. Ext corridors. **Pets:** Small, other species. $5 daily fee/pet. Designated rooms, service with restrictions, supervision.
🆂🆂 😠 ▣ 🍴 ➿

KUTTAWA

▼▼ Days Inn Ⓜ
(270) 388-4060. **$58-$72.** 139 Days Inn Dr. I-24, exit 40 (US 62), just s. Ext corridors. **Pets:** $10 one-time fee/room. Service with restrictions, crate.
🆂🆂 🆂 😠 🅜 🅔 ▣ 🖬 ➿

LEBANON

▼▼ Country Hearth Inn Ⓜ
(270) 692-4445. **$49-$65.** 720 W Main St. 1.4 mi s on SR 55 and US 68. Int corridors. **Pets:** Accepted.
Ⓐ🆂� 😠 🅜 ▣ 🖬

LEWISPORT

▼▼▼ Best Western Hancock Inn Ⓜ
(270) 295-3234. **$79.** 9040 US Hwy 60 W. US 60. Int corridors. **Pets:** Other species. $50 deposit/room. Service with restrictions, supervision.
🆂🆂 🆂 😠 ▣ 🖬 ➿

LEXINGTON

ⒶⒶⒶ ▼▼▼ Best Western Regency/Lexington Ⓜ
(859) 293-2202. **$49-$89, 7 days notice.** 2241 Elkhorn Dr. I-75, exit 110, 0.4 mi nw. Ext/int corridors. **Pets:** Accepted.
🆂🆂 🆂 😠 🅜 ▣ 🖬 ➿

▼▼ Days Inn-South Ⓜ
(859) 263-3100. **$50-$65.** 5575 Athens-Boonesboro Rd. I-75, exit 104, just e. Ext corridors. **Pets:** Small. $5 daily fee/pet. Designated rooms, service with restrictions, supervision.
🆂🆂 🆂 😠 🅜 ▣ 🖬

ⒶⒶⒶ ▼▼▼ Hampton Inn I-75 Ⓜ
(859) 299-2613. **$75-$95.** 2251 Elkhorn Rd. I-75, exit 110, 0.4 mi nw. Int corridors. **Pets:** Other species. Service with restrictions, crate.
🆂🆂 🆂 😠 🅜 ▣ 🖬 ➿

ⒶⒶⒶ ▼▼▼ Hilton Garden Inn Ⓜ
(859) 543-8300. **$72.** 1973 Plaudit Pl. I-75, exit 108, just sw. Int corridors. **Pets:** $10 daily fee/room. Service with restrictions, crate.
🆂🆂 🆂 😠 🅜 🅑 🅔 ▣ 🖬 🍴 ➿

ⒶⒶⒶ ▼▼▼ Holiday Inn-Lexington North Ⓜ 🐾
(859) 233-0512. **$96-$149, 14 days notice.** 1950 Newtown Pike. I-75, exit 115, just s. Ext/int corridors. **Pets:** Small. $100 deposit/room, $25 one-time fee/room. Designated rooms, service with restrictions, supervision.
🆂🆂 🆂 😠 🅜 🅑 ▣ 🖬 🍴 ➿

▼▼▼ Holiday Inn Lexington South Ⓜ
(859) 263-5241. **$59-$89.** 5532 Athens-Boonesboro Rd. I-75, exit 104, just e. Int corridors. **Pets:** Accepted.
Ⓐ🆂🆂 🆂 😠 🅜 ▣ 🍴 ➿

ⒶⒶⒶ ▼▼▼ La Quinta Inn Ⓜ
(859) 231-7551. **$66-$89.** 1919 Stanton Way. I-75/64, exit 115, just se off SR 922. Int corridors. **Pets:** Accepted.
🆂🆂 🆂 😠 ▣ 🖬 ➿

ⒶⒶⒶ ▼▼▼ Marriott's Griffin Gate Resort Ⓡ
(859) 231-5100. **$94-$210.** 1800 Newtown Pike. I-75/64, exit 115, 0.5 mi sw. Int corridors. **Pets:** Accepted.
🆂🆂 😠 🅜 🅑 🅔 ▣ 🖬 🍴 ➿ ❌

ⒶⒶⒶ ▼▼▼ Quality Inn Northwest Ⓜ
(859) 233-0561. **$50-$85.** 1050 Newtown Pike. I-75/64, exit 115, 1.5 mi w on SR 922. Ext corridors. **Pets:** Medium. $10 deposit/room. Service with restrictions, crate.
🆂🆂 🆂 😠 ▣ 🖬 ➿

ⒶⒶⒶ ▼▼▼ Radisson Plaza Hotel Lexington Ⓗ
(859) 231-9000. **$149-$179, 7 days notice.** 369 W Vine St. Corner of Vine and Broadway. Int corridors. **Pets:** Medium. $100 deposit/room, $40 one-time fee/pet. Service with restrictions, crate.
🆂🆂 🆂 😠 🅜 🅑 🅔 ▣ 🖬 🍴 ➿

ⒶⒶⒶ ▼▼ Red Roof Inn-North Ⓜ
(859) 293-2626. **$35-$60.** 1980 Haggard Ct. I-75/64, exit 113, 0.3 mi nw. Ext corridors. **Pets:** Other species. Service with restrictions, supervision.
🆂🆂 😠

ⒶⒶⒶ ▼▼ Red Roof Inn South Ⓜ
(859) 277-9400. **$54-$69.** 2651 Wilhite Dr. Jct US 27 and SR 4. Ext corridors. **Pets:** Medium, other species. Service with restrictions, supervision.
🆂🆂 😠 🅜 🅑

ⒶⒶⒶ ▼▼▼ Residence Inn by Marriott Ⓐ
(859) 231-6191. **$104-$159.** 1080 Newtown Pike. I-75/64, exit 115, 1 mi s on SR 922. Ext corridors. **Pets:** Other species. $75 one-time fee/room. Service with restrictions, supervision.
🆂🆂 🆂 😠 🅑 ▣ 🖬 ➿

▼▼ Shoney's Inn-Lexington M
(859) 269-4999. **$57, 14 days notice.** 2753 Richmond Rd.
I-75, exit 104, 5 mi w on US 25 (Richmond Rd). Ext corridors. **Pets:** Small, other species. $5 daily fee/room. Service
with restrictions, crate.
ASK S6 ✕ 🗄 ➽

▼▼ Super 8 Motel M
(859) 299-6241. **$44-$75.** 2351 Buena Vista Rd. I-75, exit
110. Int corridors. **Pets:** Accepted.
ASK S6 ✕ 🔥M 🗄

LIBERTY

♦♦♦ ▼▼ The Brown Motel M
(606) 787-6224. **$51-$60.** 579 Wallace Wilkinson Blvd. 1 mi
n on US 127; 0.5 mi n of jct SR 70. Ext corridors.
Pets: Accepted.
SAVE S6 ✕ 🗄 ➽

LONDON

▼▼ Budget Host Westgate Inn M ❀
(606) 878-7330. **$43-$49, 3 days notice.** 254 W Daniel
Boone Pkwy. I-75, exit 41, just w on SR 80. Ext/int corridors. **Pets:** Other species. Service with restrictions, supervision.
S6 ✕ 🔥M 🖐 🗄 ➽

♦♦♦ ▼▼▼ Red Roof Inn M
(606) 862-8844. **$64.** 110 Melcon Ln. I-75, exit 41, south-
west corner. Int corridors. **Pets:** Small. $6 one-time fee/pet.
Designated rooms, service with restrictions, supervision.
SAVE ✕ 🔥M 🗄 🖵 ➽

LOUISVILLE METROPOLITAN AREA

HURSTBOURNE

♦♦♦ ▼▼ Red Roof Inn Louisville–East
#034 M
(502) 426-7621. **$39-$54.** 9330 Blairwood Rd. I-64, exit 15,
0.3 mi nw of Hurstbourne Pkwy. Ext corridors.
Pets: Medium, other species. Service with restrictions,
supervision.
SAVE ✕ 🔥M

JEFFERSONTOWN

♦♦♦ ▼▼▼ AmeriSuites M
(502) 426-0119. **$89-$149.** 701 S Hurstbourne Pkwy. I-64,
exit 15, 1 mi n. Int corridors. **Pets:** Small. Service with
restrictions, supervision.
SAVE S6 ✕ 🔎 🗄 🖵 ➽

♦♦♦ ▼▼▼▼ Holiday Inn-Hurstbourne MI
(502) 426-2600. **$93.** 1325 S Hurstbourne Pkwy. I-64, exit
15 (Hurstbourne Pkwy). Ext/int corridors. **Pets:** Other species. $10 deposit/room. Service with restrictions.
SAVE ✕ 🔎 🗄 🖵 🍴 ➽

♦♦♦ ▼▼▼ MainStay Suites M ❀
(502) 267-4454. **$70-$250, 7 days notice.** 1650 Alliant Ave.
I-64, exit 17, just s. Int corridors. **Pets:** Other species. $10
daily fee/pet. Service with restrictions.
SAVE S6 ✕ 🔥M 🖐 🗄 🖵 ➽

▼▼ Microtel Inn M
(502) 266-6590. **$60, 3 days notice.** 1221 Kentucky Mills
Dr. I-64, exit 17. Int corridors. **Pets:** Small. $20 one-time
fee/pet. Service with restrictions, supervision.
ASK S6 ✕ 🔥M 🔎 🖐

♦♦♦ ▼▼▼ Residence Inn Louisville East ▲
(502) 425-1821. **$89-$139.** 120 N Hurstbourne Pkwy. I-64,
exit 15, 1.8 mi n. Ext corridors. **Pets:** Other species. $135
one-time fee/room. Service with restrictions.
SAVE ✕ 🗄 🖵 ➽

LOUISVILLE

▼▼▼ Aleksander House Bed and
Breakfast BB
(502) 637-4985. **$95-$169, 03 days notice.** 1213 S First
St. I-65, exit 135 (St Catherine St), just s. Int corridors.
Pets: Accepted.
ASK ✕ 🗄 🖵

♦♦♦ ▼▼▼▼ The Camberley Brown
Hotel H
(502) 583-1234. **$125-$179.** 335 W Broadway. I-65, exit
Jefferson St southbound; exit 136A (Broadway) northbound;
1.5 mi s on 4th, corner of 4th and Broadway. Int corridors.
Pets: Accepted.
SAVE S6 ✕ 🔎 🗄 🖵 🍴

▼▼ Executive West H
(502) 367-2251. **$74-$84.** 830 Phillips Ln. I-264, exit 11
(Fairgrounds/Expo Center Main Gate). Int corridors.
Pets: Other species. $100 one-time fee/room. Service with
restrictions.
ASK S6 ✕ 🔎 🗄 🖵 🍴 ➽

▼▼▼ Holiday Inn Airport East MI
(502) 452-6361. **$122-$151, 21 days notice.** 4004 Gardiner Point Dr. I-264, exit 15B westbound; exit 15 eastbound. Int corridors. **Pets:** $25 one-time fee/room.
Designated rooms, service with restrictions, supervision.
ASK S6 ✕ 🖐 🗄 🖵 ➽

♦♦♦ ▼▼▼ Holiday Inn Louisville
(Downtown) H
(502) 582-2241. **$121, 3 days notice.** 120 W Broadway.
Just w on US 60 business route and 150. Int corridors.
Pets: Accepted.
SAVE S6 ✕ 🔎 🖐 🖵 🍴 ➽

▼▼▼ Holiday Inn South-Airport MI
(502) 964-3311. **$89.** 3317 Fern Valley Rd. I-65, exit 128,
northeast corner. Int corridors. **Pets:** Accepted.
ASK ✕ 🔥M 🔎 🖐 🗄 🖵 🍴 ➽

△△△ ▼▼▼ Red Roof Inn-Airport-Fairgrounds M
(502) 968-0151. **$41-$64.** 4704 Preston Hwy. I-65, exit 130, northeast corner. Ext corridors. **Pets:** Accepted.
[SAVE] [X]

**△△△ ▼▼▼ Red Roof
Inn-Southeast-Fairgrounds M**
(502) 456-2993. **$44-$64.** 3322 Red Roof Inn Pl. I-264, 15B westbound, 0.3 mi s; exit 15 eastbound. Ext corridors. **Pets:** Accepted.
[SAVE] [X]

**△△△ ▼▼▼▼ The Seelbach Hilton
Louisville H**
(502) 585-3200. **$119-$169.** 500 Fourth Ave. I-65, exit 136C (Muhammad Ali), 0.3 mi w, then just s. Int corridors. **Pets:** $50 deposit/room.
[SAVE] [S] [X] [🖥] [🖴] [💻] [🍴]

▼▼ Sleep Inn Fairgrounds M
(502) 368-9597. **$54-$250.** 3330 Preston Hwy. I-264, exit 11 (Fairgrounds/Expo Center Main Gate), 0.5 mi e on Phillips, just n. Int corridors. **Pets:** Accepted.
[SAVE] [S] [X] [🖴] [🖪] [💻]

MIDDLETOWN

**△△△ ▼▼▼▼ Residence Inn by Marriott-Louisville
NE M**
(502) 412-1311. **$139-$179.** 3500 Spring Hurst Commons Dr. I-265, exit 32, 0.5 mi w on Westport Rd, just n. Int corridors. **Pets:** Accepted.
[SAVE] [S] [X] [🖴M] [🖴] [🖪] [💻] [🐾]

SHEPHERDSVILLE

△△△ ▼▼▼▼ Best Western South MI
(502) 543-7097. **$58-$62, 30 days notice.** 211 S Lakeview Dr. I-65, exit 117, just se. Int corridors. **Pets:** Small, other species. Service with restrictions.
[SAVE] [S] [X] [🐾]

ST. MATTHEWS

▼▼ Breckinridge Inn MI
(502) 456-5050. **$65-$85, 30 days notice.** 2800 Breckinridge Ln. I-264, exit 18A, just s. Int corridors. **Pets:** Accepted.
[ASK] [S] [X] [🖪] [💻] [🍴] [🐾]

━━━━━━━ ❀ **END METROPOLITAN AREA** ❀ ━━━━━━━

MADISONVILLE

▼▼ Days Inn Madisonville MI
(270) 821-8620. **$60.** 1900 Lantaff Blvd. Pennyrile Pkwy, exit 44. Int corridors. **Pets:** Small. $10 daily fee/pet. Service with restrictions, supervision.
[SAVE] [S] [X] [🖥] [🖪] [💻] [🍴] [🐾]

MAYFIELD

▼▼ Super 8 Motel M
(270) 247-8899. **$49.** 1100 Links Ln. Purchase Pkwy, exit 24, just s on SR 121. Int corridors. **Pets:** Accepted.
[ASK] [S] [X] [🖪] [💻]

MAYSVILLE

▼▼ Super 8 Motel, Maysville KY M
(606) 759-8888. **Call for rates.** 550 Tucker Dr. Just e of US 68. Int corridors. **Pets:** Accepted.
[X] [🖪]

MORTONS GAP

△△△ ▼▼▼ Best Western Pennyrile Inn M
(270) 258-5201. **$47-$56.** White City Rd. Pennyrile Pkwy, exit 37 (US 41). Ext corridors. **Pets:** Accepted.
[SAVE] [S] [X] [🖪] [💻] [🐾]

MOUNT VERNON

△△△ ▼▼▼ Kastle Inn Motel MI
(606) 256-5156. **$42-$62.** Hwy 25 S. I-75, exit 59. Ext corridors. **Pets:** Medium, other species. Supervision.
[SAVE] [S] [X] [🍴] [🐾]

MULDRAUGH

▼▼ Golden Manor Motel M
(502) 942-2800. **$62.** 116 S Dixie Hwy. Center; on US 31 W. Ext corridors. **Pets:** Medium. $10 daily fee/pet. Service with restrictions, crate.
[ASK] [X] [🖪] [💻] [🐾]

MURRAY

▼▼ Days Inn-Murray, KY M
(270) 753-6706. **$47-$57, 14 days notice.** 517 S 12th St. 1 mi s on US 641. Ext corridors. **Pets:** Other species. $10 daily fee/pet. Service with restrictions, crate.
[SAVE] [S] [X] [🖪] [💻] [🐾]

△△△ ▼▼ Murray Plaza Court M
(270) 753-2682. **$36-$39.** 504 12th St. 1 mi s on US 641. Ext corridors. **Pets:** Other species. Service with restrictions, supervision.
[SAVE] [X] [🖪]

OAK GROVE

▼▼▼▼ Days Inn Ft. Campbell M
(270) 640-3888. **$54-$79.** 212 Auburn St. I-24, exit 86, just s. Ext corridors. **Pets:** Accepted.
[SAVE] [S] [X] [🖴M] [🖥] [🖪] [🐾]

▼▼▼ Holiday Inn Express M
(270) 439-0022. **$59-$87.** 12759 Ft Campbell Blvd. I-24, exit 86. Int corridors. **Pets:** Accepted.
[ASK] [S] [X] [🖴M] [🖥] [🖪] [💻] [🐾]

OWENSBORO

▼▼ Owensboro Super 8 Motel **M**
(270) 685-3388. **$45-$60, 30 days notice.** 1027 Goetz Dr. US 60 Bypass, exit 4 at jct US 431. Int corridors. **Pets:** Accepted.

[ASK] [S&] [X] [&M]

PADUCAH

(AAA) ▼▼▼▼ Baymont Inn-Paducah **M**
(270) 443-4343. **$57-$74, 14 days notice.** 5300 Old Cairo Rd. I-24, exit 3 (SR 305), just w. Int corridors. **Pets:** Small, dogs only. $50 deposit/pet. Designated rooms, service with restrictions, supervision.

[SAVE] [S&] [X] [/] [&] [H] [L]

(AAA) ▼▼▼ Best Inns of America **M**
(270) 442-3334. **$48.** 5001 Hinkleville Rd. I-24, exit 4 (US 60), just w. Ext corridors. **Pets:** Small, other species. Designated rooms, service with restrictions, supervision.

[SAVE] [S&] [X] [/] [L]

▼▼▼▼ Drury Inn-Paducah **M**
(270) 443-3313. **$57-$94.** 3975 Hinkleville Rd. I-24, exit 4 (US 60), just e. Int corridors. **Pets:** Other species. Service with restrictions, supervision.

[X] [&] [H] [L] [L]

▼▼▼▼ Drury Suites-Paducah **M**
(270) 441-0024. **$68-$96.** 120 McBride Ln. I-24, exit 4 (US 60), just w. Int corridors. **Pets:** Accepted.

[X] [&M] [&] [H] [L] [L]

▼▼▼▼ Hampton Inn-Paducah **M**
(270) 442-4500. **$70-$100.** 4930 Hinkleville Rd. I-24, exit 4 (US 60), just w. Int corridors. **Pets:** Accepted.

[SAVE] [X] [&M] [/] [L] [L]

▼▼ Pear Tree Inn-Paducah **M**
(270) 444-7200. **$40-$77.** 4910 Hinkleville Rd. I-24, exit 4 (US 60), just w. Ext corridors. **Pets:** Accepted.

[X] [H] [L]

RICHMOND

(AAA) ▼▼▼ La Quinta Inn-Richmond **M**
(859) 623-9121. **$54-$74, 14 days notice.** 1751 Lexington Rd. I-75, exit 90 northbound; exit 90A southbound. Int corridors. **Pets:** Accepted.

[SAVE] [S&] [X] [/] [H] [L] [L]

▼▼▼ Red Roof Inn **M**
(859) 625-0084. **$46-$76.** 111 Bahama Ct. I-75, exit 90 northbound; exit 90A southbound. Int corridors. **Pets:** Medium, other species.

[ASK] [S&] [X] [H] [L]

SCOTTSVILLE

▼▼▼ Days Inn **M**
(270) 622-7770. **$56.** 57 Burnley Rd. On US 31 E; at jct SR 231 and 980. Ext corridors. **Pets:** Accepted.

[SAVE] [S&] [X] [H] [L]

SHELBYVILLE

(AAA) ▼▼▼▼ Best Western Shelbyville Lodge **M**
(502) 633-4400. **$64-$89, 7 days notice.** 115 Isaac Shelby Dr. I-64, exit 32, 0.5 mi n on SR 55. Int corridors. **Pets:** Other species. Service with restrictions, supervision.

[SAVE] [S&] [X] [H] [L] [L]

▼▼ Days Inn Shelbyville **M**
(502) 633-4005. **$50-$65.** 101 Howard Dr. I-64, exit 32, 0.8 mi n on SR 55. Ext corridors. **Pets:** Small. $10 one-time fee/room. Designated rooms, service with restrictions, supervision.

[SAVE] [S&] [X] [H]

SMITHS GROVE

(AAA) ▼▼▼ Bryce Inn **M**
(270) 563-5141. **$45-$53.** I-65, exit 38, 0.3 mi w. Ext corridors. **Pets:** Very small, dogs only. $5 one-time fee/pet. Designated rooms, service with restrictions, supervision.

[SAVE] [S&] [X] [H] [L] [L]

VERSAILLES

▼▼▼ 1823 Historic Rose Hill Inn [BB] ❀
(859) 873-5957. **$99-$149, 7 days notice.** 233 Rose Hill. Just s on SR 33 (S Main St), then just w. Ext/int corridors. **Pets:** Dogs only. $15 one-time fee/room. Designated rooms, service with restrictions.

[X] [H] [L]

WILLIAMSTOWN

(AAA) ▼▼ Days Inn **M**
(859) 824-5025. **$49-$66.** 211 SR 36 W. I-75, exit 154, just n. Ext corridors. **Pets:** Small. $5 daily fee/pet. Designated rooms, no service, supervision.

[SAVE] [S&] [X] [H] [L] [L]

WINCHESTER

(AAA) ▼▼▼ Best Western-Country Squire Motel **M**
(859) 744-7210. **$49-$99, 7 days notice.** 1307 W Lexington Rd. I-64, exit 94 (US 60), 0.9 mi se. Ext corridors. **Pets:** Very small. $5 one-time fee/pet. Designated rooms, service with restrictions, supervision.

[SAVE] [S&] [X] [H] [L]

▼▼▼ Days Inn **M**
(859) 744-9111. **$59-$64.** 1100 Interstate Dr. I-64, exit 96B westbound; exit 96 eastbound on southeast frontage road. Int corridors. **Pets:** Very small. $10 one-time fee/pet. Designated rooms, service with restrictions, supervision.

[SAVE] [S&] [X] [&M] [/] [H] [L] [L] [¶] [L]

LOUISIANA

CITY INDEX

ALEXANDRIA

◉◉ ▽▽▽ Best Western Inn & Suites Conference Center M
(318) 445-5530. **$75.** 2720 W MacArthur Dr. 0.9 mi n of jct SR 28 and US 71/165 (MacArthur Dr). Ext/int corridors. **Pets:** Accepted.
[SAVE] [S�] [✕] [🛏] [💻] [🍴] [➰]

▽▽ Days Inn M
(318) 443-1841. **$47-$49.** 1146 MacArthur Dr. 0.7 mi s jct SR 18 and US 71/165 (MacArthur Dr). Ext corridors. **Pets:** Accepted.
[SAVE] [S▷] [✕] [🛏] [💻] [➰]

▽▽▽▽ La Quinta Inn & Suites-Alexandria M
(318) 442-3700. **$65-$95.** 6116 West Calhoun Dr. I-49, exit 90 (Airbase Rd). Int corridors. **Pets:** Small, other species. Service with restrictions, crate.
[SAVE] [✕] [✦M] [🐾] [🛁] [🛏] [💻] [➰]

▽ Ramada Limited M
(318) 448-1611. **$47, 5 days notice.** 742 MacArthur Dr. 0.4 mi s of jct SR 28 and US 71/165 (MacArthur Dr). Ext corridors. **Pets:** Small. $20 one-time fee/room. Designated rooms, service with restrictions, supervision.
[ASK] [S▷] [✕] [🛏] [💻] [➰]

BATON ROUGE

◉◉ ▽▽▽ AmeriSuites (Baton Rouge/East) M
(225) 769-4400. **$119-$129.** 6080 Bluebonnet Blvd. I-10, exit 162. Int corridors. **Pets:** Accepted.
[SAVE] [S▷] [✕] [🐾] [🛁] [🛏] [💻] [➰]

◉◉ ▽▽▽ Baymont Inn & Suites-Baton Rouge M
(225) 291-6600. **$64-$69.** 10555 Rieger Rd. I-10, exit 163 (Siegen Ln), just n. Int corridors. **Pets:** Medium, other species. $50 deposit/room. Service with restrictions, supervision.
[SAVE] [S▷] [✕] [🐾] [🛏] [💻] [➰]

▽▽▽ Chase Suites by Woodfin A
(225) 927-5630. **$109-$154.** 5522 Corporate Blvd. I-10, exit 158, 0.5 mi ne. Ext corridors. **Pets:** Accepted.
[ASK] [S▷] [✕] [🛁] [🛏] [💻] [➰]

◉◉ ▽▽▽ Comfort Inn M
(225) 927-5790. **$64-$199, 3 days notice.** 2445 S Acadian Thruway. I-10, exit 157B, just n. Int corridors. **Pets:** $15 one-time fee/room. Service with restrictions, supervision.
[SAVE] [S▷] [✕] [🐾] [🛁] [🛏] [💻] [➰]

◉◉ ▽▽▽▽ La Quinta Inn-Baton Rouge M
(225) 924-9600. **$81.** 2333 S Acadian Thruway. I-10, exit 157B, at Acadian Thruway. Ext corridors. **Pets:** Medium. Designated rooms, service with restrictions, supervision.
[SAVE] [✕] [🐾] [🛏] [💻] [➰]

◉◉ ▽▽▽ Shoney's Inn and Suites of Baton Rouge M
(225) 925-8399. **$59-$199, 14 days notice.** 9919 Gwenadele Dr. I-12, exit 2B, just n on US 61. Ext corridors. **Pets:** Small, other species. $25 deposit/pet. Service with restrictions, supervision.
[SAVE] [S▷] [✕] [🛏] [💻] [➰]

BOSSIER CITY

▽▽▽ Hampton Inn M
(318) 752-1112. **$89.** 1005 Gould Dr. I-20, exit 21. Int corridors. **Pets:** Accepted.
[SAVE] [S▷] [✕] [✦M] [🐾] [🛁] [🛏] [💻] [➰]

▽▽▽ La Quinta Inn M
(318) 747-4400. **$95.** 309 Preston Blvd. I-20, exit 21, just w. Ext corridors. **Pets:** Accepted.
[SAVE] [✕] [🐾] [🛏] [💻] [➰]

▽▽ Quality Inn of Bossier City M
(318) 746-5050. **$74-$84.** 4300 Industrial Dr. I-20, exit 23 (Industrial Dr). Ext corridors. **Pets:** Accepted.
[SAVE] [S▷] [✕] [🛏] [💻] [➰]

▽▽ Ramada Inn Bossier M
(318) 746-8410. **$51-$73, 3 days notice.** 750 Isle of Capri Blvd. I-20, exit 20A. Ext corridors. **Pets:** Small, other species. $15 one-time fee/pet. Designated rooms, service with restrictions, supervision.
[ASK] [S▷] [✕] [💻] [🍴] [➰]

◉◉ ▽▽▽ Residence Inn by Marriott-Shreveport/Bossier City A
(318) 747-6220. **$89-$112.** 1001 Gould Dr. I-20, exit 21. Ext corridors. **Pets:** Accepted.
[SAVE] [S▷] [✕] [🐾] [🛏] [💻] [➰]

BREAUX BRIDGE

(AAA) ▼▼▼▼ Best Western Breaux Bridge M
(337) 332-1114. **$66-$95, 7 days notice.** 2088-B Rees St. I-10, exit 109. Ext corridors. **Pets:** Other species. $10 one-time fee/pet. Service with restrictions, crate.
(SAVE) (S🐾) (✕) (🏊)

CROWLEY

(AAA) ▼▼▼▼ Best Western-Crowley M
(337) 783-2378. **$65-$110.** 9571 Egan Hwy. I-10, exit 80. Ext corridors. **Pets:** $10 one-time fee/pet. No service, supervision.
(SAVE) (S🐾) (✕) (🏊)

DARROW

(AAA) ▼▼ ▼ Tezcuco Plantation B & B BB
(225) 562-3929. **$65-$165, 3 days notice.** 3138 Hwy 44. I-10, exit 179, 5.5 mi s. Ext/int corridors. **Pets:** Other species. $25 deposit/room. Designated rooms, no service, supervision.
(SAVE) (✕) (🏠) (💻) (🍴)

DELHI

▼▼▼▼ Days Inn M
(318) 878-9000. **$48, 14 days notice.** 113 Snider Rd. I-20, exit 153. Ext corridors. **Pets:** Medium, other species. $10.95 one-time fee/room. Designated rooms, service with restrictions, supervision.
(SAVE) (S🐾) (✕) (🏠) (💻) (🏊)

HAMMOND

(AAA) ▼▼ ▼ Best Western Hammond Inn & Suites M
(985) 419-2001. **$61-$81.** 107 Duo Dr. I-12, exit 40, just ne. Ext corridors. **Pets:** Accepted.
(SAVE) (S🐾) (✕) (🏠) (💻) (🏊)

HOUMA

(AAA) ▼▼▼▼ Hampton Inn M
(985) 873-3140. **$70.** 1728 Martin Luther King Blvd. 0.9 mi n of jct S Hollywood Rd and Martin Luther King Blvd. Int corridors. **Pets:** Accepted.
(SAVE) (S🐾) (✕) (💻) (🏊)

KINDER

(AAA) ▼▼▼▼ Best Western Inn At Coushatta M
(337) 738-4800. **$79-$180, 7 days notice.** 12102 US Hwy 165 N. 5.0 mi n of jct US 190 and 165. Int corridors. **Pets:** Very small, other species. $25 deposit/room. Service with restrictions, supervision.
(SAVE) (S🐾) (✕) (🏠) (💻) (🏊)

LAFAYETTE

▼▼▼▼ Comfort Inn Lafayette MI
(337) 232-9000. **$79-$82.** 1421 SE Evangeline Thruway. 3 mi s of I-10, at jct US 90 and Pinhook Rd. Int corridors. **Pets:** Other species. Service with restrictions, supervision.
(SAVE) (S🐾) (✕) (🎵) (🏠) (💻) (🍴) (🏊)

▼▼ ▼ Days Inn-Lafayette M
(337) 237-8880. **$54, 7 days notice.** 1620 N University. I-10, exit 101. Ext corridors. **Pets:** Other species. $10 daily fee/pet. Service with restrictions, crate.
(SAVE) (S🐾) (✕) (🏠) (💻) (🏊)

(AAA) ▼▼▼▼ La Quinta Inn-Lafayette M
(337) 233-5610. **$71.** 2100 NE Evangeline Thruway. I-10, exit 103A, 0.3 mi s on US 167. Ext corridors. **Pets:** Small, other species. Service with restrictions, supervision.
(SAVE) (✕) (🎵) (🏠) (💻) (🏊)

(AAA) ▼▼ ▼ Red Roof Inn M
(337) 233-3339. **$40-$52.** 1718 N University Ave (SR 182). I-10, exit 101, just n. Ext corridors. **Pets:** Accepted.
(SAVE) (✕)

LAKE CHARLES

(AAA) ▼▼▼▼ Best Suites of America M
(337) 439-2444. **$84-$150.** 401 Lakeshore Dr. I-10, exit 29 (business district/tourist bureau) eastbound; exit 30B (Ryan St business district) westbound, just s. Int corridors. **Pets:** Small. Service with restrictions, crate.
(SAVE) (✕) (🎵) (🐾) (🏠) (💻) (🏊)

LIVONIA

▼▼ Oak Tree Inn M
(225) 637-2590. **$53.** 7875 Airline Hwy. Jct SR 77 and US 190, 0.3 mi w. Ext corridors. **Pets:** Accepted.
(ASK) (S🐾) (✕) (🐾) (🏠)

MINDEN

(AAA) ▼▼▼▼ Best Western Minden Inn M
(318) 377-1001. **$50-$60.** 1411 Sibley Rd. I-20, exit 47, just n. Ext corridors. **Pets:** No service, supervision.
(SAVE) (S🐾) (✕) (🎵) (🐾) (🏠) (💻) (🏊)

MONROE

(AAA) ▼▼ ▼ Days Inn M
(318) 345-2220. **$52-$66.** 5650 Frontage Rd. I-20, exit 120, just s, 0.5 mi e on south service road. Ext corridors. **Pets:** Small. Service with restrictions, supervision.
(SAVE) (S🐾) (✕) (🏠) (💻) (🏊)

(AAA) ▼▼▼▼ La Quinta Inn-Monroe M
(318) 322-3900. **$55-$69.** 1035 Hwy 165 Bypass S. I-20, exit 118B, just ne on US 165 service road. Ext corridors. **Pets:** Accepted.
(SAVE) (✕) (🎵) (💻) (🏊)

NEW IBERIA

(AAA) ▼▼ ▼ Best Western Inn & Suites MI
(337) 364-3030. **$64-$80, 4 days notice.** 2714 Hwy 14. 0.3 mi e of jct US 90. Ext/int corridors. **Pets:** $50 deposit/room. Service with restrictions, supervision.
(SAVE) (S🐾) (✕) (🏠) (💻) (🍴) (🏊)

New Orleans Metropolitan Area

GRETNA

▼▼▼ La Quinta Inn-New Orleans Westbank M
(504) 368-5600. **$95.** 50 Terry Pkwy. S US 90 business route, exit 9A (Terry Pkwy); N US 90 (Westbank Expwy), exit 9 (Terry Pkwy/General DeGaulle). Ext corridors. **Pets:** Accepted.

KENNER

AAA ▼▼▼ Hilton New Orleans Airport H
(504) 469-5000. **$199.** 901 Airline Dr. On US 61. Int corridors. **Pets:** Other species. $25 one-time fee/pet. Service with restrictions, supervision.

▼▼▼ La Quinta Inn-New Orleans Airport M
(504) 466-1401. **$101.** 2610 Williams Blvd. I-10, exit 223A, 0.3 mi s. Int corridors. **Pets:** Small. Service with restrictions, crate.

LA PLACE

AAA ▼▼▼ Best Western of La Place M
(985) 651-4000. **$79-$179, 3 days notice.** 4289 Main St. I-10, exit 209 (US 51), just s. Ext corridors. **Pets:** Accepted.

METAIRIE

▼▼▼ La Quinta Inn-New Orleans Causeway M
(504) 835-8511. **$101.** 3100 I-10 Service Rd. I-10, exit 228 (Causeway Blvd). Ext corridors. **Pets:** Very small. Service with restrictions, supervision.

▼▼▼ La Quinta Inn-New Orleans Veterans M
(504) 456-0003. **$105.** 5900 Veterans Memorial Blvd. I-10, exit 225, just n. Ext/int corridors. **Pets:** Accepted.

NEW ORLEANS

AAA ▼▼▼ Ambassador Hotel H
(504) 527-5271. **$59-$225, 3 days notice.** 535 Tchoupitoulas. Between Poydras and Lafayette sts. Int corridors. **Pets:** Large, other species. $25 one-time fee/pet. Service with restrictions, crate.

▼▼▼ Drury Inn & Suites M
(504) 529-7800. **$140-$160.** 820 Poydras St. Between Baronne and Carondelet sts. Int corridors. **Pets:** Other species. Service with restrictions.

▼▼▼ The Fairmont New Orleans H
(504) 529-7111. **$109-$339.** 123 Baronne St. Between Canal and University sts; entrance on University. Int corridors. **Pets:** Accepted.

AAA ▼▼▼ French Quarter Courtyard Hotel M
(504) 522-7333. **$59-$239, 3 days notice.** 1101 N Rampart St. Between Ursulines and Governor Nicholls sts. Ext/int corridors. **Pets:** Accepted.

AAA ▼▼▼ Hilton New Orleans Riverside H
(504) 561-0500. **$265, 3 days notice.** 2 Poydras St. At the Mississippi River. Int corridors. **Pets:** Accepted.

▼▼▼ La Quinta Inn & Suites-Downtown New Orleans M
(504) 598-9977. **$169.** 301 Camp St. Corner of Gravier and Camp sts. Int corridors. **Pets:** Accepted.

AAA ▼▼▼ La Quinta Inn-New Orleans Bullard M
(504) 246-3003. **$95.** 12001 I-10 Service Rd. I-10, exit 245 (Bullard Rd). Ext corridors. **Pets:** Accepted.

AAA ▼▼▼ La Quinta Inn-New Orleans Crowder M
(504) 246-5800. **$95.** 8400 I-10 Service Rd. I-10, exit 242, 7 mi e at Crowder Blvd. Ext corridors. **Pets:** Small, other species. Service with restrictions, crate.

AAA ▼▼▼ Le Meridien Hotel New Orleans H
(504) 525-6500. **$365-$395, 3 days notice.** 614 Canal St. Registration and parking on Common St. Int corridors. **Pets:** Accepted.

▼▼ Rathbone Inn BB 🐾
(504) 947-2100. **$89-$259, 7 days notice.** 1227 Esplanade Ave. Just n of jct N Rampart and Esplanade. Ext/int corridors. **Pets:** Other species. $100 deposit/pet. Service with restrictions.

AAA ▼▼▼ Royal Sonesta Hotel New Orleans H
(504) 586-0300. **$245-$380, 3 days notice.** 300 Bourbon St. Garage entrance on Conti or Bienville sts. Int corridors. **Pets:** Small, other species. $50 one-time fee/room. Designated rooms, service with restrictions, crate.

▼▼▼▼ W French Quarter 🅷
(504) 581-1200. **$119-$199, 3 days notice.** 316 rue Chartres St. Between Bienville and Conti sts. Int corridors. **Pets:** Accepted.

🅰🅰🅰 ▼▼▼▼▼ Windsor Court Hotel 🅷 ❄
(504) 523-6000. **$360-$475.** 300 Gravier St. Between Magazine and Tchoucitoulas sts. Int corridors. **Pets:** Small. $150 one-time fee/room. Service with restrictions, crate.

SLIDELL

🅰🅰🅰 ▼▼▼ Guest Lodge 🅼
(985) 641-2153. **$35-$45.** 58512 Tyler Dr. I-10, exit 266, just e on US 190. Ext corridors. **Pets:** Accepted.

🅰🅰🅰 ▼▼▼▼ La Quinta Inn-New Orleans
Slidell 🅼
(985) 643-9770. **$85.** 794 E I-10 Service Rd. I-10, exit 266, just se. Ext corridors. **Pets:** Small. Service with restrictions, supervision.

OPELOUSAS

🅰🅰🅰 ▼▼▼▼ Best Western Opelousas 🅼
(337) 942-5540. **$66-$95, 7 days notice.** 5791 I-49 Service Rd S. I-49, exit 18 (Creswell Ln), on west service road. Ext corridors. **Pets:** Other species. $10 one-time fee/pet. Service with restrictions, crate.

RAYVILLE

🅰🅰🅰 ▼▼▼ Cottonland Inn 🅼
(318) 728-5985. **$44-$54.** 116 Cottonland. I-20 and SR 137, exit 138. Ext corridors. **Pets:** Small. Service with restrictions, supervision.

RUSTON

▼▼◆ Econo Lodge 🅼 ❄
(318) 255-0354. **$49, 3 days notice.** 1301 Goodwin Rd. I-20, exit 86, e of US 167 on frontage road. Ext corridors. **Pets:** Medium, other species. Service with restrictions, supervision.

▼▼◆ Ramada Inn 🅼🅸 ❄
(318) 255-5901. **$62, 3 days notice.** 401 N Service Rd. I-20, exit 85, on Frontage Rd, e of US 167. Ext corridors. **Pets:** Medium, other species. Service with restrictions, supervision.

SHREVEPORT

▼▼▼◆ La Quinta Inn & Suites-Shreveport 🅼
(318) 671-1100. **$115.** 6700 Financial Cir. I-20, exit 10. Int corridors. **Pets:** Small, other species. Supervision.

🅰🅰🅰 ▼▼▼ Red Roof Inn 🅼
(318) 938-5342. **$40-$60.** 7296 Greenwood Rd. I-20, exit 8. Ext corridors. **Pets:** Medium. Service with restrictions.

ST. FRANCISVILLE

▼▼◆ Green Springs Inn & Cottages 🅱🅱
(225) 635-4232. **$110-$195.** 7463 Tunica Trace. US 61, 4 mi n of jct US 61 and SR 10, to SR 66, 0.9 mi w. Ext/int corridors. **Pets:** Small. Designated rooms, service with restrictions, crate.

▼▼◆ Lake Rosemound Inn Bed & Breakfast 🅱🅱
(225) 635-3176. **$75-$125.** 10473 Lindsey Ln. 13 mi n on SR 61, 3 mi w using Rosemound Loop, Sligo Rd, Lake Rosemound Rd and Lindsey Ln, follow signs. Ext/int corridors. **Pets:** Service with restrictions, supervision.

SULPHUR

▼▼◆ Holiday Inn 🅼
(337) 528-2061. **$64, 3 days notice.** 2033 Ruth St. I-10, exit 20 (SR 27), just n. Ext corridors. **Pets:** Accepted.

▼▼◆ La Quinta Inn-Sulphur/Lake Charles 🅼
(337) 527-8303. **$75.** 2600 S Ruth St. I-10, exit 20 (SR 27). Ext corridors. **Pets:** Accepted.

WEST MONROE

🅰🅰🅰 ▼▼▼▼ Baymont Inn & Suites-West
Monroe 🅼
(318) 387-2711. **$65.** 503 Constitution Dr. I-20, exit 114 (Thomas Rd), just s to Constitution Dr, 0.6 mi w. Int corridors. **Pets:** Service with restrictions.

🅰🅰🅰 ▼▼▼ Red Roof Inn 🅼
(318) 388-2420. **$41-$55.** 102 Constitution Dr. I-20, exit 114 (Thomas Rd). Ext corridors. **Pets:** Accepted.

MAINE

CITY INDEX

AUBURN

▼▼ A Fireside Inn & Suites Ⓜ
(207) 777-1777. **$70-$100, 3 days notice.** 1777 Washington St. I-95 (Maine Tpke), exit 12, 5 mi s on US 202, SR 4 and 100. Ext/int corridors. **Pets:** Accepted.

AUGUSTA

ⒶⒶ ▼▼▼ Best Western Senator Inn & Spa Ⓜ
(207) 622-5804. **$99-$149.** 284 Western Ave. I-95 (Maine Tpke), exit 30 (Augusta-Winthrop) northbound; exit 30A southbound, on US 202, SR 11 and 100. Ext/int corridors. **Pets:** Other species. $50 deposit/room, $9 daily fee/pet. Designated rooms, service with restrictions, supervision.

▼▼ Motel 6–1270 Ⓜ
(207) 622-0000. **$49-$65.** 18 Edison Dr. US 202, SR 11 and 100; I-95 (Maine Tpke), exit 30 northbound; exit 30A southbound. Int corridors. **Pets:** Accepted.

ⒶⒶ ▼▼▼ Travelodge Hotel Ⓜ ❖
(207) 622-6371. **$79-$139.** 390 Western Ave. I-95 (Maine Tpke), exit 30B southbound; exit 30 northbound on US 202, SR 11 and 100. Ext corridors. **Pets:** Medium. Designated rooms, service with restrictions, supervision.

BANGOR

▼▼ Best Inn Ⓜ
(207) 942-1234. **$60-$90, 14 days notice.** 570 Main St. Jct I-395 and Main St. Int corridors. **Pets:** Service with restrictions, supervision.

ⒶⒶ ▼▼▼▼ Best Western White House Ⓜ ❖
(207) 862-3737. **$55-$110.** 155 Littlefield Ave. I-95, exit 44 (Coldbrook Rd), 5.5 mi s of downtown Bangor. Ext/int corridors. **Pets:** Other species. Service with restrictions, supervision.

▼▼ Comfort Inn Ⓜ
(207) 942-7899. **$69-$99.** 750 Hogan Rd. I-95, exit 49 (Hogan Rd), 0.5 mi w. Int corridors. **Pets:** Other species. $6 daily fee/room. Service with restrictions, supervision.

▼▼ Country Inn at The Mall Ⓜ
(207) 941-0200. **$50-$80, 10 days notice.** 936 Stillwater Ave. I-95, exit 49 (Hogan Rd), 0.5 mi w. Int corridors. **Pets:** Accepted.

▼▼ Days Inn Ⓜ ❖
(207) 942-8272. **$59-$109.** 250 Odlin Rd. I-95, exit 45B, 0.3 mi e on US 2 and SR 100. Int corridors. **Pets:** Other species. $6 one-time fee/room. Service with restrictions, supervision.

▼ Econo Lodge Ⓜ
(207) 945-0111. **$35-$89.** 327 Odlin Rd. I-95, exit 45B, just e on US 2 and SR 100. Int corridors. **Pets:** Large, other species. $6 one-time fee/pet. Supervision.

▼▼▼ Four Points by Sheraton Bangor Ⓗ
(207) 947-6721. **$99-$159.** 308 Godfrey Blvd. At Bangor International Airport. Int corridors. **Pets:** Accepted.

▼▼▼ Holiday Inn-Bangor Ⓜ
(207) 947-0101. **$90-$110.** 404 Odlin Rd. I-95, exit 45B; jct Odlin Rd and I-395. Int corridors. **Pets:** Accepted.

▼▼ Holiday Inn Bangor-Civic Center Ⓜ
(207) 947-8651. **$69-$200, 3 days notice.** 500 Main St. Center. Int corridors. **Pets:** Designated rooms, service with restrictions, supervision.

(AAA) ▼ Main Street Inn M
(207) 942-5282. **$49-$59.** 480 Main St. I-95, exit 45A to I-395, exit 3B. Ext/int corridors. **Pets:** Designated rooms, service with restrictions, supervision.
SAVE S6 ✕

▼▼ Ramada Inn MI
(207) 947-6961. **$89-$109.** 357 Odlin Rd. I-95, exit 45B; jct Odlin Rd and I-395. Int corridors. **Pets:** Accepted.
ASK S6 ✕ 🗗 🖵 🍴 🐾

▼▼ Riverside Inn M
(207) 973-4100. **$79-$109.** 495 State St. Adjacent to Eastern Maine Medical Center. Int corridors. **Pets:** Medium. $7 daily fee/pet. Designated rooms, service with restrictions, supervision.
✕ 🗗 🖵

▼ Rodeway Inn M
(207) 942-6301. **Call for rates.** 482 Odlin Rd. I-95, exit 45B. Ext corridors. **Pets:** Accepted.
ASK ✕ 🗗

BAR HARBOR

(AAA) ▼▼ Anchorage Motel M
(207) 288-3959. **$49-$109, 3 days notice.** 51 Mt Desert St. In town on SR 3. Ext corridors. **Pets:** Accepted.
SAVE ✕ 🗗

▼▼ A Wonder View Inn & Suites MI
(207) 288-3358. **$65-$199, 3 days notice.** 50 Eden St. 0.5 mi w on SR 3. Ext corridors. **Pets:** Accepted.
✕ 🗗 🍴 🐾

(AAA) ▼▼▼▼ Balance Rock Inn 1903 BB 🐾
(207) 288-2610. **$575, 14 days notice.** 21 Albert Meadow. Center; just s on Main St, then just e. Ext/int corridors. **Pets:** Other species. $30 daily fee/pet. Service with restrictions, supervision.
SAVE ✕ 🗗 🐾

(AAA) ▼▼▼ Best Western Inn M
(207) 288-5823. **$69-$125.** 452 State Hwy 3. 4.8 mi w. Ext corridors. **Pets:** Medium, other species. Designated rooms, service with restrictions, supervision.
SAVE S6 ✕ 🗗 🖵 🐾

▼▼ Days Inn M
(207) 288-3321. **$69-$155.** 120 Eden St. 1 mi w on SR 3. Ext corridors. **Pets:** Accepted.
SAVE S6 ✕ 🗗

▼ Hutchins Mountain View Cottages C 🐾
(207) 288-4833. **$40-$90, 14 days notice.** 286 SR 3. 4 mi w. Ext corridors. **Pets:** Other species. Service with restrictions, supervision.
🗗 🖵 🐾 🎿 ☎

(AAA) ▼▼▼ The Ledgelawn Inn BB
(207) 288-4596. **$75-$295, 14 days notice.** 66 Mt Desert St. Center. Ext/int corridors. **Pets:** Other species. $15 daily fee/pet. Service with restrictions, supervision.
SAVE ✕ 🐾

▼▼▼▼ Primrose Inn BB
(207) 288-4031. **$75-$185, 14 days notice.** 73 Mt Desert St. Center. Int corridors. **Pets:** Dogs only. $75 one-time fee/room. Designated rooms, no service, supervision.
✕ 🗗 🖵

BATH

▼▼▼ Holiday Inn Bath/Brunswick MI
(207) 443-9741. **$59-$149.** 139 Richardson St. 0.3 mi s on US 1. Int corridors. **Pets:** Medium. $50 deposit/pet. Designated rooms, service with restrictions, supervision.
ASK S6 ✕ 🏊 🗗 🖵 🍴 🐾

BELFAST

(AAA) ▼▼▼ Belfast Bay Meadows Inn BB
(207) 338-5715. **$65-$165, 14 days notice.** 192 Northport Ave (US 1). US 1, 2 mi s from jct SR 3. Ext/int corridors. **Pets:** Accepted.
SAVE ✕ 🗗

(AAA) ▼▼ Belfast Harbor Inn M 🐾
(207) 338-2740. **$49-$129.** 91 Searsport Ave (Rt 1). US 1, 1.2 mi n from jct SR 3. Ext/int corridors. **Pets:** Dogs only. $10 daily fee/pet. Designated rooms, service with restrictions, supervision.
SAVE S6 ✕ 🐾

(AAA) ▼▼▼ Comfort Inn Ocean's Edge M
(207) 338-2090. **$59-$149.** Rt 1. US 1, 2 mi n from jct SR 3. Int corridors. **Pets:** Other species. $10 daily fee/room. Designated rooms, service with restrictions, supervision.
SAVE S6 ✕ 🖶 🎿 🎦 🗗 🖵 🐾

(AAA) ▼▼ Gull Motel M
(207) 338-4030. **$39-$89, 3 days notice.** US Route 1. US 1, 3 mi n from jct SR 3. Ext corridors. **Pets:** Dogs only. $10 daily fee/pet. Designated rooms, service with restrictions, supervision.
SAVE ✕

(AAA) ▼▼ Seascape Motel & Cottages M
(207) 338-2130. **$49-$99, 3 days notice.** US Rt 1. US 1, 3 mi n from jct SR 3. Ext corridors. **Pets:** Accepted.
SAVE S6 ✕ 🗗

BETHEL

▼▼▼ The Briar Lea Inn & Restaurant CI
(207) 824-4717. **$59-$129, 14 days notice.** 150 Mayville Rd (US 2). 1 mi n of jct US 2, SR 5 and 26. Int corridors. **Pets:** Other species. $10 daily fee/room. Supervision.
ASK S6 ✕ 🍴

▼▼ The Inn At the Rostay M
(207) 824-3111. **$45-$120, 14 days notice.** 186 Mayville Rd (US 2). 2 mi e on US 2. Ext corridors. **Pets:** Accepted.
S6 ✕ 🗗 🍴

(AAA) ▼▼▼▼ L'Auberge Country Inn & Bistro **CI** ✿
(207) 824-2774. **$135, 14 days notice.** 22 Mill Hill Rd. Center of village; adjacent to Village Common. Int corridors. **Pets:** Other species. $20 daily fee/room. Service with restrictions, supervision.
(SAVE) ✕ ❨❩ ⓧ 🅟 (Z)

BOOTHBAY

▼▼ Hillside Acres Cabins & Motel **X**
(207) 633-3411. **$45-$75, 3 days notice.** 301 Adams Pond Rd. US 1, 9 mi s on SR 27, then just w. Ext/int corridors. **Pets:** Designated rooms, supervision.
✕ ❶ ❏ ⚊ ⓧ (Z)

▼▼▼ Kenniston Hill Inn **BB**
(207) 633-2159. **$70-$125, 14 days notice.** 988 Wiscasset Rd. US 1 to SR 27, 10 mi s. Ext/int corridors. **Pets:** Medium. Designated rooms, supervision.
(ASK) ⓢ ✕ ⓧ 🅟 (Z)

(AAA) ▼▼ White Anchor Inn **M**
(207) 633-3788. **$45-$79.** 609 Wiscasset Rd. US 1 to SR 27, then 7.5 mi s. Ext/int corridors. **Pets:** Accepted.
(SAVE) ✕ (Z)

BOOTHBAY HARBOR

(AAA) ▼▼▼ The Pines Motel **M**
(207) 633-4555. **$60-$90.** 30 Sunset Rd. 1 mi on east side of Boothbay Harbor. Ext corridors. **Pets:** Accepted.
(SAVE) ⓢ ✕ ❶ ⚊

BREWER

(AAA) ▼ Brewer Motor Inn **MI**
(207) 989-4476. **$49-$59.** 359 Wilson St. I-95, exit 45A to I-395, exit 4, just n on SR 15 to US 1A, then 0.7 mi e. Ext/int corridors. **Pets:** Designated rooms, service with restrictions, supervision.
(SAVE) ⓢ ✕ ❨❩

BRUNSWICK

(AAA) ▼▼▼ Viking Motor Inn **M**
(207) 729-6661. **$45-$94.** 287 Bath Rd. US 1, exit Cooks Corner, left on Bath Rd, then 1 mi. Ext/int corridors. **Pets:** Medium, dogs only. $10 daily fee/pet. Service with restrictions, supervision.
(SAVE) ✕ ❶

BUCKSPORT

▼▼ Best Western Jed Prouty Motor Inn **M**
(207) 469-3113. **$79-$139, 7 days notice.** 52 Main St. Center; on SR 15. Int corridors. **Pets:** Accepted.
(SAVE) ⓢ ✕ ❶ ❏

CALAIS

(AAA) ▼▼▼ Calais Motor Inn **MI**
(207) 454-7111. **$49-$74.** 293 Main St. 0.5 mi s on US 1. Ext/int corridors. **Pets:** Accepted.
(SAVE) ⓢ ✕ ❶ ❨❩ ⚊

(AAA) ▼▼▼ International Motel **M**
(207) 454-7515. **$50-$90.** 276 Main St. 0.5 mi s on US 1. Ext corridors. **Pets:** Accepted.
(SAVE) ⓢ ✕ ❶ ❏

CAMDEN

▼▼▼ Camden Harbour Inn **BB**
(207) 236-4200. **$135-$255, 7 days notice.** 83 Bayview St. Center; US 1, 0.3 mi e. Int corridors. **Pets:** Accepted.
✕ ❶ ⓧ

(AAA) ▼▼▼ Lord Camden Inn **BB** ✿
(207) 236-4325. **$90-$220, 7 days notice.** 24 Main St. Center. Int corridors. **Pets:** Service with restrictions, supervision.
(SAVE) ⓢ ✕ ❶ ❏

CAPE ELIZABETH

(AAA) ▼▼▼ ▼▼▼ Inn By The Sea **MI** ✿
(207) 799-3134. **$139-$549, 14 days notice.** 40 Bowery Beach Rd (SR 77). 7 mi s on SR 77. Ext/int corridors. **Pets:** Other species. No service, supervision.
(SAVE) ✕ ❶ ❏ ❨❩ ⚊ ⊗ ⓧ

CARIBOU

(AAA) ▼▼▼ Caribou Inn & Convention Center **M**
(207) 498-3733. **$60-$112, 14 days notice.** 19 Main St. 3 mi s on US 1. Int corridors. **Pets:** Other species.
(SAVE) ⓢ ✕ ❶ ❨❩ ⚊

CASTINE

▼▼ Pentagoet Inn **CI**
(207) 326-8616. **$75-$175, 14 days notice.** 26 Main St. Center. Int corridors. **Pets:** Medium. Service with restrictions, supervision.
✕ ❨❩ ⓧ 🅟 (Z)

CORNISH

▼▼▼ Midway Motel **M**
(207) 625-8835. **$44-$94, 7 days notice.** S Hiram Rd. 0.7 mi w on SR 25, just past corner of SR 25 and S Hiram Rd. Ext/int corridors. **Pets:** Accepted.
✕ ❶ ❏

EAGLE LAKE

▼▼ Overlook Motel & Lakeside Cabins **M**
(207) 444-4535. **$46-$125.** N Main St. Center; on SR 11. Ext/int corridors. **Pets:** Other species. Supervision.
❶ ❏

EAST BOOTHBAY

AAA 💎💎💎 **Smuggler's Cove Motor Inn MI**
(207) 633-2800. **$69-$189.** 727 Ocean Point Rd. Jct SR 27, 4.5 mi e on SR 96. Ext corridors. **Pets:** Accepted.
SAVE 🛏 💻 🍴 🏊 ☒

EDGECOMB

💎💎 **Sheepscot River Inn MI**
(207) 882-6343. **$66-$140.** 306 Eddy Rd. 1 mi w on US 1; on east side of Davies Bridge, 1 mi e of Wiscasset. Ext/int corridors. **Pets:** Accepted.
ASK 🎤 ☒ 🛏 💻 🍴 ☒

ELLSWORTH

💎💎 **Colonial Travelodge MI** 🐾
(207) 667-5548. **$68-$120.** 321 High St. 1.3 mi e on SR 3. Int corridors. **Pets:** Medium, dogs only. $50 deposit/room. Designated rooms, service with restrictions, supervision.
ASK 🎤 ☒ ♿ 🛏 💻 🍴 🏊

💎💎 **Comfort Inn MI**
(207) 667-1345. **$79-$139, 30 days notice.** 130 High St. Center. Int corridors. **Pets:** Medium, other species. $5 daily fee/pet. Service with restrictions, supervision.
SAVE 🎤 ☒ ♿ ♿ 🛏 💻

💎💎💎 **Holiday Inn MI**
(207) 667-9341. **$63-$150.** 215 High St. Jct US 1, 1A and SR 3. Int corridors. **Pets:** Other species. Designated rooms, supervision.
ASK 🎤 ☒ ♿ 🛏 💻 🍴 🏊

AAA 💎💎 **Jasper's Motel MI** 🐾
(207) 667-5318. **$59-$89, 3 days notice.** 200 High St. 1 mi e on US 1 and SR 3. Ext corridors. **Pets:** Other species. $15 one-time fee/pet. Supervision.
SAVE 🎤 ☒ 🛏 🍴

AAA 💎💎 **Twilite Motel M** 🐾
(207) 667-8165. **$50-$89, 3 days notice.** 147 Bucksport Rd. Jct US 1, 1A and SR 3, 1.1 mi w on US 1 and SR 3. Ext corridors. **Pets:** Medium, dogs only. $6 daily fee/room. Designated rooms, service with restrictions, supervision.
SAVE ☒ 🛏 💻

💎 **The White Birches MI**
(207) 667-3621. **$49-$99.** Rt 1. US 1, 1.5 mi n from jct SR 3. Ext corridors. **Pets:** Accepted.
ASK 🎤 ☒ 🛏 🍴

FARMINGTON

AAA 💎 **Mount Blue Motel M**
(207) 778-6004. **$48-$60.** 454 Wilton Rd. 2 mi w on US 2 and SR 4. Ext corridors. **Pets:** Accepted.
SAVE 🎤 ☒

FREEPORT

💎💎 **Coastline Inn M**
(207) 865-3777. **$60-$120.** 537 US Rt 1. I-95, exit 19, 0.3 mi s. Ext corridors. **Pets:** Service with restrictions, supervision.
☒ 🛏 💻

AAA 💎💎💎 **Freeport Inn MI** 🐾
(207) 865-3106. **$60-$130.** 31 US 1 S. I-95, exit 17, 1 mi n. Ext/int corridors. **Pets:** Other species. Designated rooms, service with restrictions.
SAVE ☒ 🛏 💻 🍴 🏊

AAA 💎💎💎 💎💎💎 **Harraseeket Inn CI** 🐾
(207) 865-9377. **$110-$275, 3 days notice.** 162 Main St. I-95, exit 20, 0.5 mi e. Int corridors. **Pets:** Dogs only. $25 daily fee/pet. Designated rooms, service with restrictions, supervision.
SAVE ☒ ♿ ♿ ♿ 🛏 💻 🍴 🏊

AAA 💎💎💎 **Isaac Randall House BB**
(207) 865-9295. **$90-$175, 7 days notice.** 10 Independence Dr. I-95, exit 19, 0.5 mi n on US 1, Independence Dr parallels US 1 on the west side. Ext/int corridors. **Pets:** Accepted.
SAVE 🎤 ☒ 🛏

FRYEBURG

AAA 💎💎💎 **The Oxford House Inn CI**
(207) 935-3442. **$110-$135, 10 days notice.** 105 Main St. US 302, just w of jct SR 113; in center of village. Int corridors. **Pets:** Accepted.
SAVE 🎤 ☒ 🍴 ☎

GILEAD

💎 **Evans Notch Motel & Cottages X**
(207) 836-2300. **Call for rates, 14 days notice.** Jct US 2 and SR 113, 9 mi w, then 9 mi e on US 2. Ext corridors. **Pets:** Accepted.
ASK ☒ 🛏 💻 ♿ ☎

GRAND LAKE STREAM

💎💎 **Leen's Lodge C** 🐾
(207) 796-2929. **$180, 21 days notice.** 10 mi w off US 1, 2 mi n on gravel entry road. Ext corridors. **Pets:** Dogs only. Service with restrictions, crate.
🛏 🍴 ☒ ♿ 🎦 ☎

GREENVILLE

AAA 💎💎 **Kineo View Motor Lodge M**
(207) 695-4470. **$59-$89.** SR 15. 2.5 mi s. Ext corridors. **Pets:** Accepted.
SAVE ☒

HOULTON

(AAA) ▼ Scottish Inns M
(207) 532-2236. **$50-$60.** US Rt 2A, Bangor St. I-95, exit 62, 1 mi s on US 1, 1 mi sw. Ext/int corridors. **Pets:** $6 one-time fee/room. Service with restrictions.

[SAVE] [S☼] [✕] [❚]

JACKMAN

▼▼ Sky Lodge Cabins & Motel ✕
(207) 668-2171. **$45-$175, 14 days notice.** 766 Main St. 1 mi n on US 1. Ext corridors. **Pets:** Small. $25 daily fee/pet. Service with restrictions, supervision.

[A$K] [❚] [✕] [⚖]

KENNEBUNK

(AAA) ▼▼ The Lodge at Kennebunk M ✿
(207) 985-9010. **$59-$109.** 95 Alewive Rd. I-95 (Maine Tpke), exit 3 (Kennebunk), just n on SR 35. Ext corridors. **Pets:** Medium, dogs only. $15 one-time fee/pet. Designated rooms, service with restrictions, supervision.

[SAVE] [✕] [❚] [▣] [⇝]

KENNEBUNKPORT

▼▼▼ The Captain Jefferds Inn BB ✿
(207) 967-2311. **$145-$295, 14 days notice.** 5 Pearl St. Dock Square; 0.3 mi e on Maine St, just s; corner of Pearl and Pleasant sts. Int corridors. **Pets:** Dogs only. $20 daily fee/room. Supervision.

[✕] [❚] [⚖]

(AAA) ▼▼ ▼▼ Captain Lord Mansion BB
(207) 967-3141. **$125-$399, 15 days notice.** 6 Pleasant St. Dock Square; 0.3 mi on Ocean Ave, left turn at sign. Int corridors. **Pets:** Accepted.

[SAVE] [✕] [❚]

(AAA) ▼▼▼▼ The Colony Hotel H ✿
(207) 967-3331. **$125-$430, 3 days notice.** 140 Ocean Ave. Dock Square; 1 mi s. Int corridors. **Pets:** Other species. $25 daily fee/pet. Supervision.

[SAVE] [✕] [⚲] [⊤] [⇝] [✕] [⚖]

▼▼▼ The Inn at Goose Rocks ◉
(207) 967-5425. **$60-$175, 14 days notice.** 71 Dyke Rd. I-95 (Maine Tpke), exit 3, 5 mi e on SR 35 to SR 9, 6 mi e to Dyke Rd, then just s on road toward Goose Rocks Beach (Dyke Rd). Int corridors. **Pets:** Accepted.

[✕] [❚] [▣] [⊤] [⇝]

(AAA) ▼▼▼▼ Lodge At Turbat's Creek M ✿
(207) 967-8700. **$79-$169, 14 days notice.** Turbat's Creek Rd. Dock Square, 0.5 mi e on Maine St, 0.6 mi ne on Wildes, then just se. Ext corridors. **Pets:** Other species. Service with restrictions, supervision.

[SAVE] [S☼] [✕] [⚒M] [❚] [⇝]

(AAA) ▼▼▼ ▼▼ The Yachtsman Lodge & Marina M
(207) 967-2511. **$159-$275, 14 days notice.** Ocean Ave. From Dock Square; 0.3 mi e. Ext corridors. **Pets:** Medium. Service with restrictions, supervision.

[SAVE] [✕] [❚] [▣] [✕]

KITTERY

▼▼ Enchanted Nights Bed & Breakfast BB ✿
(207) 439-1489. **$56-$270, 15 days notice.** 29 Wentworth St. I-95, exit 2 (Kittery), 1 mi s on SR 236, just w on SR 103. Ext corridors. **Pets:** Other species. $15 one-time fee/room. Service with restrictions, supervision.

[✕] [❚] [⚖]

LEWISTON

▼▼ Motel 6–1223 M
(207) 782-6558. **$45-$57.** 516 Pleasant St. I-495, exit 13, follow sign for Lisbon St, just w. Ext/int corridors. **Pets:** Accepted.

[S☼] [✕] [⚲] [⚐]

LINCOLNVILLE

▼ Abbingtons Seaview Motel & Cottages M
(207) 236-3471. **$55-$125, 3 days notice.** Rt 1. US 1, 4 mi n of downtown Camden; 1.5 mi s of Lincolnville Beach. Ext corridors. **Pets:** Other species. $10 daily fee/pet. Designated rooms, supervision.

[A$K] [S☼] [✕] [❚] [▣] [⇝]

▼▼ Pine Grove Cottages ◉
(207) 236-2929. **$50-$145, 7 days notice.** RR 3. 2 mi s on US 1. Ext corridors. **Pets:** Other species. $7 daily fee/pet. Service with restrictions, supervision.

[✕] [❚] [▣]

LUBEC

(AAA) ▼▼▼ The Eastland Motel M
(207) 733-5501. **$48-$65.** Jct US 1 and SR 189, 8 mi e on SR 189. Ext/int corridors. **Pets:** Medium, dogs only. $5 daily fee/pet. Designated rooms, service with restrictions, supervision.

[SAVE] [✕]

MACHIAS

(AAA) ▼▼▼ The Bluebird Motel M
(207) 255-3332. **$52-$64, 3 days notice.** 1 mi s. Ext corridors. **Pets:** Accepted.

[SAVE] [S☼] [✕] [⚒M] [❚]

(AAA) ▼▼▼ Machias Motor Inn M
(207) 255-4861. **$62-$68, 10 days notice.** 26 E Main St. 0.5 mi e on US 1. Ext corridors. **Pets:** Dogs only. $5 daily fee/pet. Service with restrictions, supervision.

[SAVE] [S☼] [✕]

MEDWAY

▼▼▼▼ Gateway Inn M
(207) 746-3193. **Call for rates.** Rt 157. I-95, exit 56, 0.3 mi w. Ext/int corridors. **Pets:** Accepted.
(ASK) ⊠ 🛏 🐾

▼▼ Katahdin Shadows Motel M
(207) 746-5162. **$49, 7 days notice.** I-95, exit 56, 1.5 mi w on SR 157. Ext corridors. **Pets:** Service with restrictions.
⊠ 🛏 🐾

MILFORD

▼▼ ▼▼ Milford Motel On The River M
(207) 827-3200. **$54-$89.** 154 Main Rd. 0.5 mi n on US 2. Ext corridors. **Pets:** Large. Service with restrictions, supervision.
⊠ 🛏

MILLINOCKET

▼▼ Best Western Heritage Motor Inn MI
(207) 723-9777. **$69-$102, 7 days notice.** 935 Central St. 0.8 mi e on SR 11 and 157. Int corridors. **Pets:** Accepted.
(SAVE) (S) ⊠ 🖤 (T)

▲▲▲ ▼▼▼ The Katahdin Inn M
(207) 723-4555. **$55-$80, 3 days notice.** 740 Central St. Center; on SR 157. Int corridors. **Pets:** Other species. Designated rooms, service with restrictions, supervision.
(SAVE) ⊠ 🛏 🐾

NEWPORT

▲▲▲ ▼▼ Lovley's Motel M
(207) 368-4311. **$40-$90.** 100 Pittsfield Rd. I-95, exit 39. Ext corridors. **Pets:** Other species. Supervision.
(SAVE) (S) ⊠ 🛏 🖤 🐾

OGUNQUIT

▼▼ Studio East Motor Inn M
(207) 646-7297. **Call for rates, 7 days notice.** 267 Main St. Center; on US 1. Ext corridors. **Pets:** Medium, other species. $10 one-time fee/pet. Designated rooms, service with restrictions.
⊠ 🛏

OLD ORCHARD BEACH

▼▼ Beau Rivage Motel M 🐾
(207) 934-4668. **$55-$170, 14 days notice.** 54 E Grand Ave. 0.3 mi e of Orchard St. Ext corridors. **Pets:** Small, dogs only. $25 deposit/pet, $10 daily fee/pet. Designated rooms, service with restrictions, supervision.
⊠ (🦮) 🛏 🖤 🐾

▼▼ Flagship Motel M
(207) 934-4866. **Call for rates, 7 days notice.** 54 W Grand Ave. 0.5 mi w on SR 9 (W Grand Ave). Ext corridors. **Pets:** Accepted.
⊠ 🛏 🐾

▲▲▲ ▼▼▼ Old Colonial Motel M 🐾
(207) 934-9862. **$60-$195, 10 days notice.** 61 W Grand Ave. 0.5 mi w on SR 9 (W Grand Ave). Ext corridors. **Pets:** Medium, other species. $5 daily fee/room. Service with restrictions.
(SAVE) (S) ⊠ 🛏 🖤 🐾

▲▲▲ ▼▼▼ Sea View Motel M 🐾
(207) 934-4180. **$50-$250, 3 days notice.** 65 W Grand Ave. 0.5 mi w on SR 9 (W Grand Ave). Ext corridors. **Pets:** Medium. $100 deposit/pet. Designated rooms, supervision.
(SAVE) (S) ⊠ 🛏 🖤 🐾

▼▼ ▼▼ Waves Oceanfront Resort M
(207) 934-4949. **$60-$185, 3 days notice.** 87 W Grand Ave. 0.5 mi w on SR 9 (W Grand Ave). Ext corridors. **Pets:** Small. Designated rooms, service with restrictions, supervision.
⊠ 🛏 🖤 (T) 🐾

ORONO

▼▼▼▼ Best Western Black Bear Inn & Conference Center M
(207) 866-7120. **$59-$119.** 4 Godfrey Dr. I-95, exit 51 (Stillwater Ave). Int corridors. **Pets:** Accepted.
(SAVE) ⊠ (&M) 🖤

▼▼ ▼▼ University Inn Academic Suites M 🐾
(207) 866-4921. **$59-$89.** 5 College Ave. 0.4 mi n on US 2, 8 mi n of Bangor; I-95, exit 50-51. Int corridors. **Pets:** Other species. Designated rooms, supervision.
⊠ 🐾

PORTLAND

▲▲▲ ▼▼▼▼ Eastland Park Hotel H 🐾
(207) 775-5411. **$109-$199.** 157 High St. Center; at Congress Square. Int corridors. **Pets:** Large, other species. $10 one-time fee/room. Service with restrictions.
(SAVE) (S) ⊠ 🛏 🖤 (T)

▲▲▲ ▼▼▼ Holiday Inn-West MI
(207) 774-5601. **$84-$164.** 81 Riverside St. I-95 (Maine Tpke), exit 8. Int corridors. **Pets:** Large. Designated rooms, service with restrictions, supervision.
(SAVE) (S) ⊠ (&M) (🦮) (🦮) 🛏 🖤 (T) 🐾

▲▲▲ ▼▼▼▼ Howard Johnson Plaza Hotel MI
(207) 774-5861. **$80-$145.** 155 Riverside St. I-95 (Maine Tpke), exit 8, jct SR 25. Int corridors. **Pets:** $50 deposit/room. Service with restrictions.
(SAVE) (S) ⊠ 🛏 🖤 (T) 🐾

PRESQUE ISLE

▲▲▲ ▼▼▼ Northern Lights Motel M 🐾
(207) 764-4441. **$46-$53.** 72 Houlton Rd. 2 mi s on US 1. Ext corridors. **Pets:** Other species. Designated rooms, service with restrictions, supervision.
(SAVE) ⊠ 🛏

(AAA) ▼▼▼ Presque Isle Inn & Convention Center MI ❧
(207) 764-3321. **$45-$125, 14 days notice.** 116 Main St. 1 mi s on US 1. Int corridors. **Pets:** Other species.
[SAVE] [S☉] [✕] [🛏] [🍴] [🏊]

ROCKLAND

(AAA) ▼▼ Navigator Motor Inn MI
(207) 594-2131. **$55-$115.** 520 Main St. On US 1. Ext corridors. **Pets:** Medium. Designated rooms, service with restrictions, supervision.
[SAVE] [✕] [🛏] [🍴]

(AAA) ▼▼▼ Trade Winds Motor Inn MI
(207) 596-6661. **$55-$145.** 2 Park Dr. Center; on US 1. Ext/int corridors. **Pets:** Designated rooms, service with restrictions, supervision.
[SAVE] [S☉] [✕] [🛏] [🍴] [🏊]

RUMFORD

(AAA) ▼▼▼ Linnell Motel & RestInn Conference Center M
(207) 364-4511. **$60-$75, 14 days notice.** 986 Prospect Ave. 2 mi w. Ext/int corridors. **Pets:** Accepted.
[SAVE] [S☉] [✕] [🛏]

▼▼ The Madison Motor Inn MI
(207) 364-7973. **$89.** 1257 US Rt 2. 4 mi w. Ext corridors. **Pets:** Other species. Service with restrictions.
[ASK] [S☉] [✕] [🛏] [💻] [🍴] [🏊] [✕]

SACO

(AAA) ▼▼▼ Hampton Inn M
(207) 282-7222. **$75-$150.** 48 Industrial Park Rd. I-95 (Maine Tpke), exit 5; I-195, exit 1. Int corridors. **Pets:** Other species. Service with restrictions, supervision.
[SAVE] [S☉] [✕] [⊾M] [⌖] [🛏] [💻] [🏊]

▼▼ Saco Motel M
(207) 284-6952. **$45-$75.** 473 Main St. I-95 (Maine Tpke), exit 5, 0.5 mi s on US 1. Ext corridors. **Pets:** Dogs only. $5 daily fee/pet. Service with restrictions, supervision.
[ASK] [S☉] [✕] [🛏] [🏊]

▼▼ Wagon Wheel Motel M
(207) 284-6387. **$45-$125, 3 days notice.** 726 Portland Rd. 1.8 mi n on US 1; 0.8 mi n of jct I-95. Ext corridors. **Pets:** Accepted.
[✕] [🛏] [💻] [🏊]

SANFORD

▼▼ Super 8 Motel M
(207) 324-8823. **$56-$95.** 1892 Main St (Rt 109). I-95 (Maine Tpke), exit 2, 7 mi w; adjacent to Sanford Airport. Int corridors. **Pets:** $15 daily fee/room. Service with restrictions, supervision.
[ASK] [S☉] [✕] [⌗]

SCARBOROUGH

▼▼ Pride Motel & Cottages [X] ❧
(207) 883-4816. **$40-$110.** 677 US 1. I-95 (Maine Tpke), exit 5, 0.5 mi e to US 1, 4.5 mi n. Ext corridors. **Pets:** Other species. $5 daily fee/room. Service with restrictions, supervision.
[✕] [🛏] [🏊]

(AAA) ▼▼▼ Residence Inn by Marriott M ❧
(207) 883-0400. **$59-$219.** 800 Roundwood Dr. I-95 (Maine Tpke), exit 6, 1.5 mi n on Payne Rd. Int corridors. **Pets:** Other species. $20 daily fee/room. Service with restrictions.
[SAVE] [✕] [⊾M] [⌗] [⌖] [🛏] [💻] [🏊]

(AAA) ▼▼▼ TownePlace Suites by Marriott M ❧
(207) 883-6800. **$84-$149.** 700 Roundwood Dr. I-95 (Maine Tpke), exit 6, 1.5 mi n on Payne Rd. Int corridors. **Pets:** Other species. $20 daily fee/room, $150 one-time fee/room. Service with restrictions.
[SAVE] [S☉] [✕] [⊾M] [⌖] [🛏] [💻] [🏊]

SKOWHEGAN

(AAA) ▼▼ Breezy Acres Motel M
(207) 474-2703. **$58-$68, 7 days notice.** 1.5 mi s on US 201. Ext corridors. **Pets:** Accepted.
[SAVE] [S☉] [✕] [🛏] [💻] [🏊]

SOUTH PORTLAND

(AAA) ▼▼▼ AmeriSuites–Portland/Maine Mall M
(207) 775-3900. **$119-$179.** 303 Sable Oaks Dr. I-95 (Maine Tpke), exit 7, just n on Maine Mall Rd, then just w on Running Hill Rd. Int corridors. **Pets:** Small. $20 one-time fee/room. Designated rooms, service with restrictions, supervision.
[SAVE] [S☉] [✕] [⊾M] [⌖] [🛏] [💻] [🏊]

(AAA) ▼▼▼ Best Western Merry Manor Inn MI
(207) 774-6151. **$90-$160.** 700 Main St. I-95 (Maine Tpke), exit 7, 3 mi e to US 1 jct, exit 7 spur road and US 1. Ext/int corridors. **Pets:** Other species. Service with restrictions, supervision.
[SAVE] [S☉] [⊾M] [⌖] [🛏] [💻] [🍴] [🏊]

(AAA) ▼▼▼ Howard Johnson Hotel MI
(207) 775-5343. **$94-$154.** 675 Main St. Jct US 1 and I-95 (Maine Tpke) access road, 1.3 mi e, exit 7. Int corridors. **Pets:** Other species. Designated rooms, service with restrictions, supervision.
[SAVE] [S☉] [✕] [🛏] [💻] [🍴] [🏊]

(AAA) ▼▼▼ Portland Marriott Hotel [H]
(207) 871-8000. **$139-$199.** 200 Sable Oaks Dr. I-95 (Maine Tpke), exit 7, just n on Maine Mall Rd, then just w on Running Hill Rd. Int corridors. **Pets:** Large. $20 one-time fee/room. Designated rooms, service with restrictions, supervision.
[SAVE] [S☉] [✕] [⊾M] [⌗] [🛏] [💻] [🍴] [🏊]

SOUTHPORT

⚑⚑ The Lawnmeer Inn ☒ ❀
(207) 633-2544. **$90-$190, 7 days notice.** 65 Hendricks Hill Rd. 2 mi s on Boothbay Harbor on SR 27, just s of bridge to Southport Island. Ext/int corridors. **Pets:** Medium. $15 daily fee/pet. Designated rooms, service with restrictions, supervision.

[SAVE] [☒] [¶]

SPRUCE HEAD

⚑⚑⚑ Craignair Inn [CI] ❀
(207) 594-7644. **$42-$125, 14 days notice.** At Clark Island Rd. 2.5 mi w on SR 73, 1.5 mi s on Clark Island Rd; 10 mi s of Rockland. Ext/int corridors. **Pets:** Medium. $10 daily fee/pet. Designated rooms, service with restrictions, supervision.

[☒] [₭]

WATERVILLE

⚑⚑ Best Western Waterville [MI]
(207) 873-3335. **$80-$145, 3 days notice.** 356 Main St. I-95, exit 34 (Main St) Int corridors. **Pets:** Service with restrictions, supervision.

[SAVE] [S▵] [☒] [▯] [▭] [¶] [⇌]

⚑⚑ Budget Host Airport Inn [MI] ❀
(207) 873-3366. **$40-$110.** 400 Kennedy Memorial Dr. I-95, exit 33, 0.3 mi s on SR 11 (Kennedy Memorial Dr). Ext/int corridors. **Pets:** Other species. $10 one-time fee/room.

[SAVE] [S▵] [☒] [▯] [¶]

⚑⚑ Econo Lodge [M]
(207) 872-5577. **$55-$95, 7 days notice.** 455 Kennedy Memorial Dr. I-95, exit 33, on SR 11 at Waterville-Oakland. Ext/int corridors. **Pets:** $5 daily fee/pet. Service with restrictions, supervision.

[SAVE] [S▵] [☒] [▭] [⇌]

⚑⚑⚑ Holiday Inn [MI]
(207) 873-0111. **$115-$135.** 375 Main St. I-95, exit 34 (Main St) on SR 104. Int corridors. **Pets:** Other species. Supervision.

[ASK] [S▵] [☒] [▯] [▭] [¶] [⇌]

WELLS

⚑⚑ Ne'r Beach Motel [M]
(207) 646-2636. **$36-$129, 10 days notice.** 395 Post Rd (Rt 1). US 1, 0.8 mi s of jct SR 9B. Ext corridors. **Pets:** Medium. $100 deposit/room. Service with restrictions, supervision.

[☒] [▯] [▭] [⇌]

WILTON

⚑⚑⚑ Whispering Pines Motel [M] ❀
(207) 645-3721. **$56-$104, 3 days notice.** 183 Lake Rd. SR 2, 1 mi w of jct SR 4. Ext corridors. **Pets:** $3 daily fee/pet. Designated rooms, service with restrictions, supervision.

[SAVE] [S▵] [☒] [▯] [▭] [☒]

YARMOUTH

⚑⚑ Down-East Village Motel [MI]
(207) 846-5161. **$65-$99.** 705 US Rt 1. I-95, exit 16 northbound; exit 17 southbound. Ext corridors. **Pets:** $7 daily fee/pet. Service with restrictions, supervision.

[SAVE] [S▵] [☒] [▯] [▭] [¶] [⇌]

YORK

⚑⚑⚑ The Cape Neddick House [BB]
(207) 363-2500. **$100-$145 (no credit cards), 7 days notice.** 1300 US 1. I-95, exit 4 (York-Ogunquit), 3.5 mi n. Int corridors. **Pets:** Accepted.

[☒] [PW] [Ⓩ]

⚑⚑ York Commons Inn [M]
(207) 363-8903. **$60-$155.** 362 US 1. I-95, exit 4 (York Ogunquit), 1 mi s. Int corridors. **Pets:** Accepted.

[SAVE] [S▵] [☒] [⅋M] [▯] [⇌]

MARYLAND

CITY INDEX

ANNAPOLIS JUNCTION

AAA ◆◆◆ TownePlace Suites by Marriott-Ft Meade/Baltimore M
(301) 498-7477. **$85-$109.** 120 National Business Pkwy. I-295, exit Dorsey Run Rd, 2 mi n. Int corridors. **Pets:** Other species. $100 one-time fee/room.
[SAVE] [S] [X] [&] [B] [C] [≈]

BALTIMORE METROPOLITAN AREA

ABERDEEN

AAA ◆◆◆ Four Points by Sheraton Aberdeen M
(410) 273-6300. **$89-$109.** 980 Hospitality Way. I-95, exit 85, just e on SR 22. Int corridors. **Pets:** Small, other species. Service with restrictions.
[SAVE] [S] [X] [&] [B] [C] [T] [≈]

AAA ◆◆◆ Holiday Inn Chesapeake House M
(410) 272-8100. **$105-$135.** 1007 Beards Hill Rd. I-95, exit 85, just e on SR 22. Int corridors. **Pets:** Medium. Service with restrictions, supervision.
[SAVE] [S] [X] [&] [B] [C] [T] [≈]

AAA ◆◆◆ Red Roof Inn M
(410) 273-7800. **$44-$69.** 988 Hospitality Way. I-95, exit 85, just e on SR 22. Ext corridors. **Pets:** Accepted.
[SAVE] [X] [&] [B]

ANNAPOLIS

AAA ◆◆◆ Loews Annapolis Hotel H ✿
(410) 263-7777. **$109-$269.** 126 West St. US 50 and 301, exit 24 eastbound; exit 24A westbound, 1.4 mi s on SR 70, just sw on Calvert St, just w. Int corridors. **Pets:** Other species.
[SAVE] [S] [X] [&] [&] [B] [C] [T]

AAA ◆◆◆ MainStay Suites Annapolis M
(410) 571-6600. **$106-$155.** 120 Admiral Cochrane Dr. 2.3 mi sw on US 50 and 301, exit 22, just s, then just e. Int corridors. **Pets:** Medium, other species. $100 deposit/pet, $10 daily fee/pet. Service with restrictions, crate.
[SAVE] [S] [X] [&M] [&] [&] [B] [C]

AAA ◆◆◆ Radisson Hotel Annapolis M
(410) 224-3150. **$129-$189.** 210 Holiday Ct. 2.3 mi sw on US 50 and 301, exit 22 to Riva Rd, then 0.3 mi n on Riva Rd. Int corridors. **Pets:** Medium. $25 one-time fee/room. Service with restrictions, supervision.
[SAVE] [S] [X] [&] [&] [B] [C] [T] [≈]

AAA ◆◆◆ Residence Inn by Marriott A
(410) 573-0300. **$189-$249.** 170 Admiral Cochrane Dr. 2.3 mi sw on US 50 and 301, exit 22 to Riva Rd, just s on Riva Rd, then just e. Ext corridors. **Pets:** $100 one-time fee/room. Designated rooms, service with restrictions, supervision.
[SAVE] [S] [X] [&M] [&] [&] [B] [C] [≈]

BALTIMORE

▼▼▼▼ Admiral Fell Inn 🇨🇮 ✿
(410) 522-7377. **$165-$265.** 888 S Broadway. Facing the waterfront in historic Fells Point; corner of Broadway and Thames sts. Int corridors. **Pets:** Dogs only. $35 daily fee/room. Designated rooms, service with restrictions, supervision.
[ASK] [S🐾] [✕] [🐾'] [🛗] [🍴]

▲▲▲ ▼▼▼ Holiday Inn-Baltimore West 🇲🇮
(410) 265-1400. **$129-$179.** 1800 Belmont Ave. I-695, exit 17, 0.3 mi nw. Ext corridors. **Pets:** Very small. $50 deposit/room. Designated rooms, service with restrictions, supervision.
[SAVE] [S🐾] [✕] [🐾'] [🛗] [💻] [🍴] [≈]

COLUMBIA

▼▼▼▼ Staybridge Suites by Holiday Inn Baltimore-Columbia 🇲
(410) 964-9494. **$139-$189, 30 days notice.** 8844 Columbia 100 Pkwy. I-95, exit 43B, 4 mi w on SR 100, exit 1B. Int corridors. **Pets:** Accepted.
[ASK] [S🐾] [✕] [🐾M] [🐾'] [🐾'] [🛗] [💻] [≈]

▲▲▲ ▼▼▼ Wellesley Inn & Suites (Columbia) 🇲
(410) 872-2994. **$109.** 8890 Stanford Blvd. I-95, exit 41B, 1.3 mi w on SR 175, 0.5 mi s on Snowden River Pkwy, just w on McGaw Rd, 0.3 mi nw. Int corridors. **Pets:** Accepted.
[SAVE] [S🐾] [✕] [🛗] [💻] [≈]

EDGEWOOD

▲▲▲ ▼▼▼▼ Best Western Invitation Inn 🇲
(410) 679-9700. **$69-$89.** 1709 Edgewood Rd. I-95, exit 77A, just e on SR 24. Ext corridors. **Pets:** Other species. $50 deposit/pet. Designated rooms, service with restrictions, crate.
[SAVE] [S🐾] [✕] [🐾'] [🐾'] [🛗] [💻] [≈]

ELLICOTT CITY

▲▲▲ ▼▼▼▼ Residence Inn by Marriott Columbia 🇦
(410) 997-7200. **$89-$114.** 4950 Beaver Run. I-95, exit 43B, 4 mi w on SR 100, exit 1B (Executive Park Dr). Int corridors. **Pets:** Accepted.
[SAVE] [S🐾] [🐾M] [🐾'] [🐾'] [🛗] [💻] [≈]

GLEN BURNIE

▲▲▲ ▼▼ Days Inn-Glen Burnie 🇲
(410) 761-8300. **$89-$109, 3 days notice.** 6600 Ritchie Hwy. I-695, exit 3B eastbound; exit 2 westbound, 0.5 mi s on SR 2. Ext corridors. **Pets:** Large. $10 daily fee/room. Service with restrictions.
[SAVE] [S🐾] [✕] [🐾'] [🐾'] [🛗] [💻] [≈]

HANOVER

▲▲▲ ▼▼▼ Red Roof Inn-BWI Parkway 🇲
(410) 712-4070. **$59-$79.** 7306 Parkway Dr S. 0.7 mi w of SR 295, exit 100, w to exit 8, 0.5 mi se. Ext corridors. **Pets:** Accepted.
[SAVE] [✕] [🐾']

HUNT VALLEY

▲▲▲ ▼▼▼ Embassy Suites Hotel 🇭
(410) 584-1400. **$149-$169.** 213 International Cir. I-83, exit 20A (Shawan Rd), just e. Int corridors. **Pets:** Accepted.
[SAVE] [S🐾] [✕] [🐾'] [🐾'] [🛗] [💻] [🍴] [≈]

JESSUP

▲▲▲ ▼▼▼ Red Roof Inn-Columbia/Jessup 🇲
(410) 796-0380. **$59-$74.** 8000 Washington Blvd. I-95, exit 41A, 0.5 mi w on SR 175; jct SR 175, 0.3 mi s on US 1. Ext corridors. **Pets:** Small. Designated rooms, service with restrictions, supervision.
[SAVE] [✕] [🐾']

LINTHICUM HEIGHTS

▲▲▲ ▼▼▼▼ AmeriSuites Baltimore/BWI Airport 🇲
(410) 859-3366. **$89-$118.** 940 International Dr. I-695, exit 7A, 1 mi s on SR 295, just e on W Nursery Rd. Int corridors. **Pets:** Small. Service with restrictions, supervision.
[SAVE] [S🐾] [✕] [🐾M] [🐾'] [🐾'] [🛗] [💻] [≈]

▲▲▲ ▼▼▼▼ Comfort Inn Airport 🇲
(410) 789-9100. **$130-$139.** 6921 Baltimore Annapolis Blvd. I-695, exit 6A eastbound; exit 5 westbound, at the jct of SR 170 and 648. Int corridors. **Pets:** Medium. Service with restrictions, supervision.
[SAVE] [S🐾] [✕] [🐾M] [🐾'] [🐾'] [🛗] [💻] [🍴]

▲▲▲ ▼▼▼▼ Comfort Suites-BWI Airport 🇲
(410) 691-1000. **$79-$139, 3 days notice.** 815 Elkridge Landing Rd. I-695, exit 7A, 1 mi s on SR 295, 1.3 mi e on W Nursery Rd. Int corridors. **Pets:** Small. $25 one-time fee/room. Designated rooms, service with restrictions, crate.
[SAVE] [S🐾] [✕] [🐾M] [🐾'] [🛗] [💻]

▼▼▼▼ Hampton Inn BWI Airport 🇲
(410) 850-0600. **$95-$121.** 829 Elkridge Landing Rd. I-695, exit 7A, 1 mi s on SR 295, 1.3 mi e on W Nursery Rd, then just w. Int corridors. **Pets:** Accepted.
[SAVE] [S🐾] [✕] [🐾'] [🛗] [💻]

▼▼▼▼ Homestead Studio Suites-Baltimore Washington Int'l Airport 🇲
(410) 691-2500. **Call for rates.** 939 International Dr. I-695, exit 7A, 1 mi s on SR 295, just e on W Nursery Rd. Ext corridors. **Pets:** Accepted.
[✕] [🐾M] [🐾'] [🐾'] [🛗] [💻]

 Homewood Suites by Hilton-BWI
Airport ▲
(410) 684-6100. **$134.** 1181 Winterson Rd. I-695, exit 7A, 1
mi s on SR 295, 0.7 mi e on W Nursery Rd, just n. Int
corridors. **Pets:** Accepted.

⅏ 🅂 ⊠ 🄴 🍳 🄴 🖥 📺 ⇌

🔷🔷 Red Roof Inn-BWI Airport Ⅿ
(410) 850-7600. **$69-$104.** 827 Elkridge Landing Rd. I-695,
exit 7A, 1 mi s on SR 295, 1.3 mi e on W Nursery Rd, then
just w. Ext corridors. **Pets:** Accepted.

⅏ ⊠ 🍳

⅏ 🔷🔷🔷 Residence Inn by Marriott-BWI
Airport ▲
(410) 691-0255. **$154-$189.** 1160 Winterson Rd. I-695, exit
7A, 1 mi s on SR 295, 0.7 mi e on West Nursery Rd, then
2 blks n. Int corridors. **Pets:** $10 daily fee/room, $100 one-
time fee/room. Service with restrictions.

⅏ 🅂 ⊠ 🄴 🄴 🖥 📺 ⇌

⅏ 🔷🔷🔷 Sheraton International Hotel On BWI
Airport Ⅿ
(410) 859-3300. **$109-$229.** 7032 Elm Rd. I-195, exit 1A,
0.5 mi n on SR 170, just e. Int corridors. **Pets:** Accepted.

⅏ 🅂 ⊠ 🍳 🄴 🖥 📺 🍴 ⇌

⅏ 🔷🔷 Sleep Inn & Suites Airport Ⅿ
(410) 789-7223. **$119-$129.** 6055 Belle Grove Rd. I-695,
exit 6A eastbound; exit 5 westbound, 0.3 mi n to jct SR
170/648. Int corridors. **Pets:** Medium. Service with restrictions, supervision.

⅏ 🅂 ⊠ 🄴 🍳 🄴 🖥 📺

OWINGS MILLS

⅏ 🔷🔷🔷 AmeriSuites-Owings Mills Ⅿ ✻
(410) 998-3630. **$113-$133.** 4730 Painters Mill Rd. I-795,
exit 4 (Owings Mills Blvd), 0.5 mi s, 0.7 mi e on Red Run
Blvd. Int corridors. **Pets:** Very small, other species. $50
deposit/room, $50 one-time fee/room. Service with restric-
tions, supervision.

⅏ 🅂 ⊠ 🄴 🍳 🄴 🖥 📺 ⇌

TIMONIUM

⅏ 🔷🔷 Red Roof Inn-Timonium Ⅿ
(410) 666-0380. **$54-$84.** 111 W Timonium Rd. I-83, exit
16A northbound; exit 16 southbound, just e. Ext corridors.
Pets: Accepted.

⅏ ⊠

TOWSON

⅏ 🔷🔷 Days Inn-Baltimore/Towson Ⅿ
(410) 882-0900. **$64-$139, 14 days notice.** 8801 Loch
Raven Blvd. I-695, exit 29B. Int corridors. **Pets:** $15 daily
fee/room. Service with restrictions, supervision.

⅏ 🅂 ⊠ 🍳 🖥 🍴

WESTMINSTER

🔷 The Boston Inn Ⅿ
(410) 848-9095. **$42-$58.** 533 Baltimore Blvd. 0.9 mi se on
SR 97/140 from jct SR 27. Ext corridors. **Pets:** Dogs only.
$50 deposit/room. Service with restrictions, crate.

⊠ 🖥 ⇌

✻   **END METROPOLITAN AREA**   ✻

CUMBERLAND

🔷🔷🔷 Holiday Inn Ⅿ
(301) 724-8800. **$59-$79, 3 days notice.** 100 S George St.
I-68, exit 43C, just n. Int corridors. **Pets:** Accepted.

Ⓐ🅂🅇 🅂 ⊠ 🖥 📺 🍴 ⇌

DISTRICT OF COLUMBIA
METROPOLITAN AREA

BETHESDA

(AAA) ▼▼▼▼ Residence Inn by Marriott-Bethesda A
(301) 718-0200. **$259.** 7335 Wisconsin Ave. I-495, exit 34, 2.5 mi s on SR 355; entrance on Waverly St. Int corridors. **Pets:** $5 daily fee/room, $100 one-time fee/room. Designated rooms, service with restrictions, supervision.

[SAVE] [X] [🖉] [🖳] [🛏] [🖵] [⌁]

GAITHERSBURG

(AAA) ▼▼▼▼ Comfort Inn Shady Grove M
(301) 330-0023. **$69-$119.** 16216 Frederick Rd. I-270, exit 8, 1 mi e on Shady Grove Rd at jct SR 355. Int corridors. **Pets:** Large, other species. Service with restrictions.

[SAVE] [S] [X] [🖉] [🛏] [🖵] [⌁]

(AAA) ▼▼▼▼ Hilton Washington DC North/Gaithersburg H
(301) 977-8900. **$80-$110, 3 days notice.** 620 Perry Pkwy. I-270, exit 11, then e. Int corridors. **Pets:** Accepted.

[SAVE] [X] [🖉] [🖳] [🛏] [🖵] [🍴] [⌁]

▼▼▼▼ Holiday Inn-Gaithersburg M
(301) 948-8900. **$79-$99.** 2 Montgomery Village Ave. I-270, exit 11, 0.3 mi e. Int corridors. **Pets:** Medium. Designated rooms, service with restrictions, supervision.

[ASK] [S] [X] [🖉M] [🖉] [🖳] [🛏] [🖵] [🍴] [⌁]

▼▼▼ Homestead Studio Suites-Gaithersburg/Rockville M
(301) 987-9100. **$58-$114.** 2621 Research Blvd. I-270, exit 8, just w, then just n. Int corridors. **Pets:** Accepted.

[ASK] [S] [X] [🖉M] [🖉] [🖳] [🛏] [🖵]

(AAA) ▼▼▼ Red Roof Inn-Gaithersburg M
(301) 977-3311. **$54-$79.** 497 Quince Orchard Rd. I-270, exit 10 northbound; exit 11B southbound, just w. Ext corridors. **Pets:** Small, other species.

[SAVE] [X]

(AAA) ▼▼▼▼ Residence Inn by Marriott-Gaithersburg A ✿
(301) 590-3003. **$169-$179.** 9721 Washingtonian Blvd. I-270, exit 9B, 0.9 mi s on Fields Rd, just ne. Int corridors. **Pets:** Other species. $6 daily fee/pet, $100 one-time fee/pet. Service with restrictions.

[SAVE] [X] [🖉M] [🖉] [🖳] [🛏] [🖵] [⌁]

▼▼▼▼ Summerfield Suites by Wyndham A
(301) 527-6000. **$109-$159.** 200 Skidmore Blvd. I-370, exit SR 355, just n to Westland Rd. Ext corridors. **Pets:** Small. $10 daily fee/pet, $200 one-time fee/pet. Designated rooms, service with restrictions, crate.

[X] [🖉M] [🖉] [🖳] [🛏] [🖵] [⌁]

(AAA) ▼▼▼▼ TownePlace Suites by Marriott-Gaithersburg M
(301) 590-2300. **$79-$99.** 212 Perry Pkwy. I-270, exit 11, just e on SR 124 to SR 355, 0.3 mi s, then 0.5 mi sw. Int corridors. **Pets:** Medium. $5 daily fee/room, $75 one-time fee/room. Service with restrictions.

[SAVE] [S] [X] [🖉M] [🖉] [🖳] [🛏] [🖵] [⌁]

GERMANTOWN

▼▼▼ Homestead Studio Suites-Germantown M
(301) 515-4500. **$58-$104.** 20141 Century Blvd. I-270, exit 15B, just w to Aircraft Dr, then just n. Ext corridors. **Pets:** Medium. $75 one-time fee/pet. Service with restrictions.

[ASK] [S] [X] [🖉M] [🖉] [🖳] [🛏] [🖵]

LANHAM

(AAA) ▼▼ Red Roof Inn-Lanham M
(301) 731-8830. **$54-$84.** 9050 Lanham Severn Rd. I-95/495, exit 20A, 0.3 mi e on SR 450. Ext corridors. **Pets:** Medium, other species. Service with restrictions, crate.

[SAVE] [X] [🛏]

LARGO

(AAA) ▼▼▼ Doubletree Club Hotel Washington DC-Largo M
(301) 773-0700. **$69-$149.** 9100 Basil Ct. I-95/495, exit 17A, jct SR 202; off Capital Beltway. Int corridors. **Pets:** Accepted.

[SAVE] [S] [X] [🖉M] [🖉] [🖳] [🛏] [🖵] [🍴] [⌁]

LAUREL

(AAA) ▼▼▼▼ Comfort Suites Hotel at Laurel Lakes M
(301) 206-2600. **$75-$159.** 14402 Laurel Pl. 1.4 mi s on US 1, from jct SR 198; adjacent to Laurel Lakes Mall. Int corridors. **Pets:** Medium, other species. $50 deposit/room. Service with restrictions.

[SAVE] [S] [X] [🖉] [🛏] [🖵] [⌁]

(AAA) ▼▼▼ Red Roof Inn-Laurel M
(301) 498-8811. **$49-$69.** 12525 Laurel Bowie Rd. SR 197, 0.3 mi w of SR 295, exit SR 197. Ext corridors. **Pets:** Accepted.

[SAVE] [X] [🖉] [🛏]

ROCKVILLE

AAA ▼▼▼▼ Best Western Washington Gateway Hotel M
(301) 424-4940. **$79-$169, 7 days notice.** 1251 W Montgomery Ave. I-270, exit 6B, just w on SR 28. Int corridors. **Pets:** Small, other species. $15 daily fee/pet. Service with restrictions, crate.

SAVE 🅂🄳 ✕ 🔊 🎦 🖥 💻 🍴 🏊

AAA ▼▼▼ Quality Suites and Conference Center M
(301) 840-0200. **$100-$180.** 3 Research Ct. I-270, exit 8, just sw. Int corridors. **Pets:** Large. $35 daily fee/pet. Designated rooms, service with restrictions, supervision.

SAVE 🅂🄳 ✕ 🔊 🎦 🖥 💻 🏊

AAA ▼▼▼ Red Roof Inn-Rockville M
(301) 987-0965. **$64-$89.** 16001 Shady Grove Rd. I-270, exit 8, 0.5 mi e. Ext corridors. **Pets:** Accepted.

SAVE ✕ 🄼 🔊 🎦 🍴 🏊

❀ END METROPOLITAN AREA ❀

EASTON

AAA ▼▼▼ Comfort Inn M
(410) 820-8333. **$99-$109.** 8523 Ocean Gateway. US 50, 0.7 mi n of jct SR 331. Ext corridors. **Pets:** Accepted.

SAVE 🅂🄳 ✕

AAA ▼▼▼▼ The Tidewater Inn and Conference Center H
(410) 822-1300. **$120-$186, 3 days notice.** 101 E Dover St. Center; on SR 331, 0.8 mi w of US 50. Int corridors. **Pets:** Accepted.

SAVE 🅂🄳 ✕ 🔊 🖥 🍴 🏊

FREDERICK

AAA ▼▼▼ Comfort Inn M
(301) 695-6200. **$85-$95.** 420 Prospect Blvd. US 15, exit Jefferson St, just se. Int corridors. **Pets:** Accepted.

SAVE ✕ 🔊 🖥 💻 🏊

AAA ▼▼▼ Comfort Inn Red Horse Frederick M
(301) 662-0281. **$69-$109.** 998 W Patrick St. Just w on US 40 from jct US 15. Int corridors. **Pets:** Accepted.

SAVE ✕ 🎦 🖥 🍴

AAA ▼▼ Econo Lodge M
(301) 698-0555. **$60-$80, 3 days notice.** 6005 Urbana Pike. Jct SR 85 and 355; behind Exxon station. Ext corridors. **Pets:** Accepted.

SAVE 🅂🄳 ✕ 🖥 💻 🏊

AAA ▼▼▼▼ Hampton Inn M ❀
(301) 698-2500. **$79-$89.** 5311 Buckeystown Pike (SR 85). I-270, exit 31B, 0.6 mi w via SR 85. Int corridors. **Pets:** Other species. $10 daily fee/pet. Designated rooms, service with restrictions, crate.

SAVE 🅂🄳 ✕ 🔊 🖥 💻 🍴 🏊

AAA ▼▼▼ Sleep Inn-Rockville M
(301) 948-8000. **$90-$120.** 2 Research Ct. I-270, exit 8, just sw. Int corridors. **Pets:** $35 one-time fee/pet. Designated rooms, service with restrictions, supervision.

SAVE 🅂🄳 ✕ 🄼 🔊 🎦 🖥

▼▼▼▼ Woodfin Suites Hotel M
(301) 590-9880. **$179.** 1380 Piccard Dr. I-270, exit 8, 0.3 mi s; 1 mi w of SR 355 via Redland Rd. Ext corridors. **Pets:** $50 one-time fee/pet. Designated rooms, service with restrictions.

ASK 🅂🄳 ✕ 🔊 🎦 🖥 💻 🏊

▼▼▼ Holiday Inn Express-FSK Mall M
(301) 695-2881. **$74-$84.** 5579 Spectrum Dr. I-270, exit 31A, just e on SR 85; in Francis Scott Key Mall. Int corridors. **Pets:** Small. $25 deposit/pet. Service with restrictions, supervision.

ASK 🅂🄳 ✕ 🔊 🎦 🖥 💻

▼▼▼ Holiday Inn-Francis Scott Key Mall M
(301) 694-7500. **$109.** 5400 Holiday Dr. I-270, exit 31A, just se of SR 85. Int corridors. **Pets:** Other species. Service with restrictions, crate.

ASK 🅂🄳 ✕ 🔊 🖥 💻 🍴

AAA ▼▼▼ Holiday Inn-Frederick/Ft Detrick M
(301) 662-5141. **$98-$108.** 999 W Patrick St. Just w on US 40 from jct US 15. Ext corridors. **Pets:** Accepted.

SAVE 🅂🄳 ✕ 🔊 🎦 🖥 💻 🍴 🏊

▼▼▼ MainStay Suites M
(301) 668-4600. **$119-$139, 7 days notice.** 7310 Executive Way. I-270, exit 31B. Int corridors. **Pets:** Other species. $150 deposit/room, $10 daily fee/pet. Service with restrictions, supervision.

ASK 🅂🄳 ✕ 🎦 🖥 💻 🏊

FROSTBURG

▼▼▼ Days Inn & Suites M
(301) 689-2050. **$69-$84, 10 days notice.** 11100 New Georges Creek Rd. I-68, exit 34, 1 mi n on SR 36. Int corridors. **Pets:** Accepted.

SAVE 🅂🄳 ✕ 🔊 💻

GRANTSVILLE

▼▼▼▼ Holiday Inn [MI]
(301) 895-5993. **$49-$89.** 2541 Chestnut Ridge Rd N. I-68, exit 22, just s on US 219; on south side. Int corridors. **Pets:** Other species. Designated rooms, service with restrictions, supervision.

[ASK] [✕] [📞] [💻] [🍴] [≋]

▼▼ Walnut Ridge Bed & Breakfast [BB]
(301) 895-4248. **$80-$150, 7 days notice.** 92 Main St. I-68, exit 19, just n on SR 495, then 0.5 mi e on US 40. Ext/int corridors. **Pets:** Accepted.

[ASK] [✕] [📞] [💻]

HAGERSTOWN

(AAA) ▼▼▼▼ Four Points by Sheraton Hagerstown [MI]
(301) 790-3010. **$89-$99, 3 days notice.** 1910 Dual Hwy. I-70, exit 32B, 0.5 mi n. Int corridors. **Pets:** Accepted.

[SAVE] [S🔊] [✕] [📞] [💻] [🍴] [≋]

▼▼ Motel 6–1259 [M]
(301) 582-4445. **$41-$57.** 11321 Massey Blvd. I-81, exit 5, 0.5 mi e, 0.5 mi n of jct I-81 and 70. Ext corridors. **Pets:** Accepted.

[S🔊] [✕] [♿] [≋]

(AAA) ▼▼▼ Quality Inn [M]
(301) 733-2700. **$69-$109, 7 days notice.** 1101 Dual Hwy. I-70, exit 32B, 2.2 mi w on US 40. Int corridors. **Pets:** Accepted.

[SAVE] [S🔊] [✕] [📞] [💻]

(AAA) ▼▼▼ Ramada Inn and Conference Center [MI] ☙
(301) 733-5100. **$94.** 901 Dual Hwy. I-70, exit 32B, 2.3 mi w on US 40. Int corridors. **Pets:** Small. $10 daily fee/room. Designated rooms, service with restrictions, crate.

[SAVE] [S🔊] [✕] [🔊] [📞] [💻] [🍴] [≋]

▼▼ Sleep Inn & Suites [M]
(301) 766-9449. **$79.** 18216 Col Henry K Douglas Dr. I-70, exit 29, just s. Int corridors. **Pets:** Medium, other species. $10 daily fee/pet. Service with restrictions, supervision.

[SAVE] [S🔊] [✕] [♿] [📞] [💻] [≋]

▼▼ Super 8 Motel Hagerstown [M]
(301) 739-5800. **$45-$57.** 1220 Dual Hwy. I-70, exit 32B, 2.1 mi nw on US 40. Int corridors. **Pets:** Accepted.

[ASK] [S🔊] [✕]

INDIAN HEAD

▼ Super 8 Motel [M]
(301) 753-8100. **$55.** 4694 Indian Head Hwy. On SR 210, 0.6 mi s of Jct SR 225. Int corridors. **Pets:** Medium. $10 one-time fee/pet. Service with restrictions, supervision.

[ASK] [S🔊] [✕] [📶] [📞]

LA PLATA

(AAA) ▼▼▼▼ Best Western La Plata Inn [M]
(301) 934-4900. **$55-$103.** 6900 Crain Hwy. 0.4 mi s on US 301 from jct SR 6. Int corridors. **Pets:** Small. $25 one-time fee/room. Service with restrictions, supervision.

[SAVE] [S🔊] [✕] [📶] [🔊] [📞] [≋]

LA VALE

(AAA) ▼▼ Oak Tree Inn [M]
(301) 729-6700. **$70.** 12310 Winchester Rd SW. I-68, exit 40, 0.6 mi s. Ext/int corridors. **Pets:** Medium, other species. $5 daily fee/pet. Service with restrictions, crate.

[SAVE] [S🔊] [✕] [🔊] [♿] [📞] [💻]

LEXINGTON PARK

▼▼ Days Inn Lexington Park [M]
(301) 863-6666. **$76-$82, 3 days notice.** 21847 Three Notch Rd. SR 235; opposite Patuxent Naval Station. Ext corridors. **Pets:** Large. $8 daily fee/pet. Designated rooms, service with restrictions, supervision.

[SAVE] [S🔊] [✕] [📶] [📞] [💻] [≋]

MCHENRY

▼▼ Comfort Inn [M]
(301) 387-4200. **$60-$100.** 2704 Deep Creek Dr. 1 mi s on US 219 from jct SR 42. Int corridors. **Pets:** Other species. $25 one-time fee/room. Service with restrictions, crate.

[SAVE] [S🔊] [✕] [📞] [💻]

▼▼ Wisp Mountain Resort/Hotel & Conference Center [R] ☙
(301) 387-5581. **$69-$199, 3 days notice.** 290 Marsh Hill Rd. 1 mi s on US 219 from jct SR 42, just w on Sang Run Rd, 0.3 mi s. Int corridors. **Pets:** Large, other species. $100 deposit/pet. $50 one-time fee/pet. Designated rooms, service with restrictions, supervision.

[ASK] [✕] [🔊] [📞] [💻] [🍴] [≋] [✕]

NORTH EAST

▼▼▼ Crystal Inn [M]
(410) 287-7100. **Call for rates.** 1 Center Dr. I-95, exit 100, 0.3 mi se on SR 272. Int corridors. **Pets:** Accepted.

[ASK] [✕] [🔊] [♿] [📞] [💻] [≋]

OCEAN CITY

(AAA) ▼▼▼▼ Clarion Resort Fontainebleau Hotel [H] ☙
(410) 524-3535. **$115-$319, 3 days notice.** 10100 Coastal Hwy. 101st St E Coastal Hwy. Int corridors. **Pets:** Medium. $25 daily fee/room. Designated rooms, service with restrictions.

[SAVE] [S🔊] [✕] [🔊] [📞] [💻] [🍴] [≋]

PERRYVILLE

 Comfort Inn **M** ✿
(410) 642-2866. **$59-$79.** 61 Heather Ln. I-95, exit 93, just
e. Ext corridors. **Pets:** Large, other species. $5 daily fee/
pet. Designated rooms, service with restrictions, crate.

PRINCESS ANNE

 Waterloo Country Inn **CI**
(410) 651-0883. **$105-$245, 7 days notice.** 28822 Mt Ver-
non Rd. 3.3 mi w on SR 362 from jct US 13. Int corridors.
Pets: Other species. Designated rooms, service with
restrictions, crate.

ROCK HALL

 Mariners Motel **M**
(410) 639-2291. **$60-$75.** 5681 S Hawthorne Ave. 0.3 mi e
of SR 20. Ext corridors. **Pets:** Dogs only. Service with
restrictions, supervision.

SALISBURY

 Best Western Salisbury Plaza **M**
(410) 546-1300. **$67-$135, 3 days notice.** 1735 N Salis-
bury Blvd. US 13 business route, 1.5 mi n of US 50. Ext
corridors. **Pets:** Other species. $10 daily fee/pet. Service
with restrictions.

Comfort Inn Salisbury **M**
(410) 543-4666. **$79-$109, 3 days notice.** 2701 N Salisbury Blvd. US 13, 0.5 mi n of jct US 13 business route and
Bypass. Int corridors. **Pets:** Service with restrictions.

Howard Johnson Inn-Salisbury **MI**
(410) 742-7194. **$49-$129.** 2625 N Salisbury Blvd. US 13,
0.5 mi n of jct US 13 business route and Bypass. Ext
corridors. **Pets:** Accepted.

SNOW HILL

River House Inn **BB** ✿
(410) 632-2722. **$150-$240, 7 days notice.** 201 E Market
St. 1 mi w on SR 394 from jct SR 113. Ext/int corridors.
Pets: Dogs only. $10 daily fee/pet. Designated rooms, serv-
ice with restrictions, supervision.

THURMONT

Rambler Inn **M**
(301) 271-2424. **$62-$72, 7 days notice.** US 15 at SR 550.
Ext/int corridors. **Pets:** Medium, other species. $10 daily
fee/pet. Service with restrictions, supervision.

WALDORF

Hampton Inn Waldorf **M**
(301) 632-9600. **$82-$159.** 3750 Crain Hwy. On US 301;
opposite St Charles Towne Plaza. Int corridors.
Pets: Accepted.

WILLIAMSPORT

Red Roof Inn **M**
(301) 582-3500. **$44-$54.** 310 E Potomac St. I-81, exit 2,
0.3 mi sw on US 11. Ext corridors. **Pets:** Medium. $5
one-time fee/pet. Designated rooms, service with restrictions, supervision.

MASSACHUSETTS

CITY INDEX

AMHERST

▼▼ University Lodge M
(413) 256-8111. **$69-$119.** 345 N Pleasant St. Center; 0.9 mi n. Ext corridors. **Pets:** Small. $20 daily fee/room. Designated rooms, service with restrictions, supervision.

ASK S❺ ✕ ▣

BARRE

⚠ ▼▼▼ Jenkins Inn CI ❖
(978) 355-6444. **$140-$185, 14 days notice.** 7 West St. Northeast end of town green on SR 122 and 32. Int corridors. **Pets:** Dogs only. $5 daily fee/pet. Service with restrictions, supervision.

SAVE S❺ ✕ ▣ ¶

BOSTON METROPOLITAN AREA

ANDOVER

▼▼▼ Hawthorn Suites-Andover M ❖
(978) 475-6000. **$103-$107.** 4 Riverside Dr. I-93, exit 45, 0.5 mi e; in Andover Research Park. Int corridors. **Pets:** Medium, other species. $10 daily fee/room, $50 one-time fee/room. Designated rooms.

ASK ✕ ⬆M ⌕ ⬥ ⬛ ▣ ⇄

▼▼ Ramada Inn and Conference Center MI
(978) 475-5400. **$119-$127.** 311 Lowell St. I-93, exit 43A (SR 133), just e; I-495, exit 40A, 1.3 mi s. Int corridors. **Pets:** $50 deposit/room, $10 daily fee/pet. Service with restrictions, crate.

ASK S❺ ✕ ⬥ ▣ ¶ ⇄

⚠ ▼▼▼ Residence Inn by Marriott
Boston-Andover M
(978) 683-0382. **$89-$159.** 500 Minuteman Rd. I-93, exit 45, 0.3 mi w, then 0.5 mi n. Int corridors. **Pets:** Other species. $10 daily fee/room, $100 one-time fee/room. Service with restrictions, crate.

SAVE S❺ ✕ ⬆M ⌕ ▣ ⇄

⚠ ▼▼▼ Staybridge Suites
Boston/Andover M
(978) 686-2000. **$80-$90, 30 days notice.** 4 Tech Dr. I-93, exit 45, just sw. Int corridors. **Pets:** Accepted.

SAVE S❺ ✕ ⬆M ⌕ ⬥ ▣ ⇄

⚠ ▼▼▼ Wyndham Andover H
(978) 975-3600. **$79-$155.** 123 Old River Rd. I-93, exit 45, just e on River Rd. Int corridors. **Pets:** Small. $50 deposit/room. Service with restrictions, crate.

SAVE ✕ ⌕ ⬥ ⬥ ▣ ¶ ⇄

BILLERICA

▼▼▼ Homewood Suites by Hilton M
(978) 670-7111. **$159-$189.** 35 Middlesex Tpke. I-95, exit 32B, 2.5 mi n via Middlesex Tpke. Int corridors. **Pets:** Small. $50 one-time fee/pet. Service with restrictions.

SAVE S❺ ✕ ⌕ ⬥ ⬥ ▣ ⇄

BOSTON

▼▼ ▼▼ Boston Harbor Hotel H
(617) 439-7000. **$295-$715.** 70 Rowes Wharf. At Rowes Wharf. Int corridors. **Pets:** Accepted.

✕ ⌕ ¶ ⇄

▼▼ ▼▼ The Eliot Suite Hotel H ❖
(617) 267-1607. **$255-$435.** 370 Commonwealth Ave. Corner of Commonwealth (SR 2) and Massachusetts (SR 2A) aves. Int corridors. **Pets:** Other species. Service with restrictions, supervision.

ASK ✕ ⌕ ¶

▼▼ ▼▼ **The Fairmont Copley Plaza**
Boston 🅷
(617) 267-5300. **$199-$389.** 138 St James Ave. At Copley
Sq. Int corridors. **Pets:** Accepted.
ⒶⓈⓀ Ⓢ🄳 ⊠ 🕖 🄴 🍴

🅰🅰🅰 ▼▼▼▼▼ **Four Seasons Hotel Boston** 🅷
(617) 338-4400. **$425-$815.** 200 Boylston St. At Boylston St
and Park Sq. Int corridors. **Pets:** Accepted.
ⓈⒶⓋⒺ ⊠ &ᴹ 🕖 🄴 🍴 ⇌

▼▼▼▼ **Hilton Boston Back Bay** 🅷
(617) 236-1100. **$119-$464, 3 days notice.** 40 Dalton St.
Adjacent to Copley Place; at Dalton and Belvidere sts. Int
corridors. **Pets:** Small. $40 one-time fee/room. Service with
restrictions, supervision.
ⓈⒶⓋⒺ ⊠ 🕖 🄴 🎴 🖳 🍴 ⇌

▼▼ ▼▼ **Howard Johnson Hotel Fenway** 🅼🅸
(617) 267-8300. **$105-$199, 3 days notice.** 1271 Boylston
St. I-90, exit Brookline Ave S. Int corridors. **Pets:** Accepted.
⊠ 🎴 🖳 🍴 ⇌

▼▼▼ ▼▼ **Le Meridien** 🅷
(617) 451-1900. **$355-$505.** 250 Franklin St. Center; on
Post Office Sq. Int corridors. **Pets:** Accepted.
ⒶⓈⓀ Ⓢ🄳 ⊠ 🕖 🄴 🖳 🍴 ⇌

🅰🅰🅰 ▼▼ ▼▼ **Ramada Inn Boston** 🅼
(617) 287-9100. **$99-$189.** 800 Morrissey Blvd. I-93, exit 13
northbound, 0.5 mi sw; exit 12 southbound, follow signs. Int
corridors. **Pets:** Service with restrictions, supervision.
ⓈⒶⓋⒺ Ⓢ🄳 ⊠ 🎴 ⇌

🅰🅰🅰 ▼▼ ▼▼ **Seaport Hotel** 🅷 ❋
(617) 385-4000. **$159-$289.** 1 Seaport Ln. At World Trade
Center/Commonwealth Pier. Int corridors. **Pets:** Medium.
Service with restrictions, supervision.
ⓈⒶⓋⒺ Ⓢ🄳 ⊠ &ᴹ 🕖 🄴 🖳 🍴 ⇌

▼▼▼▼ **Sheraton-Boston Hotel** 🅷
(617) 236-2000. **$249-$479.** 39 Dalton St. I-90, exit 22; at
Prudential Center. Int corridors. **Pets:** Accepted.
ⒶⓈⓀ Ⓢ🄳 ⊠ &ᴹ 🕖 🄴 🎴 🖳 🍴 ⇌

BOXBOROUGH

▼▼▼▼ **Holiday Inn Boxborough Woods** 🅼🅸
(978) 263-8701. **$99-$139.** 242 Adams Pl. I-495, exit 28,
just e on SR 111. Int corridors. **Pets:** Accepted.
ⒶⓈⓀ Ⓢ🄳 ⊠ 🕖 🎴 🖳 🍴 ⇌

BROOKLINE

▼▼▼▼ **Holiday Inn Brookline** 🅼🅸 ❋
(617) 277-1200. **$189-$239.** 1200 Beacon St. 1 mi sw of
Kenmore Square; at Beacon and St Paul sts. Int corridors.
Pets: $50 deposit/room, $15 daily fee/room. Designated
rooms.
ⒶⓈⓀ Ⓢ🄳 ⊠ &ᴹ 🕖 🄴 🎴 🖳 🍴

BURLINGTON

▼▼ ▼▼ **Homestead Studio**
Suites-Boston/Burlington 🅼
(781) 359-9099. **$84-$94.** 40 South Ave. I-95, exit 32B, just
n; in Northwest Park, opposite Burlington Mall. Int corridors.
Pets: Accepted.
ⒶⓈⓀ Ⓢ🄳 ⊠ 🕖 🄴 🎴 🖳

▼▼▼▼ **Staybridge Suites Boston-Burlington** 🅼
(781) 221-2233. **$69-$189.** 11 Old Concord Rd. I-95, exit
32B, just s on Middlesex Tpke. Int corridors. **Pets:** Large,
other species. $50 one-time fee/pet. Service with restric-
tions, supervision.
ⒶⓈⓀ Ⓢ🄳 ⊠ &ᴹ 🕖 🄴 🎴 🖳 ⇌

🅰🅰🅰 ▼▼▼▼ **Summerfield Suites by**
Wyndham-Boston/Burlington 🅼
(781) 270-0800. **$109-$199.** 2 Van de Graaff Dr. I-95, exit
33A, just s on US 3, then 0.5 mi w on Wayside Rd. Int
corridors. **Pets:** Medium. $10 daily fee/room, $250 one-time
fee/room. Service with restrictions, crate.
ⓈⒶⓋⒺ ⊠ &ᴹ 🕖 🄴 🎴 🖳 ⇌

CAMBRIDGE

▼▼▼ ▼▼ **The Charles Hotel, Harvard**
Square 🅷 ❋
(617) 864-1200. **$169-$259.** One Bennett St. Corner of
Bennett and Eliot sts; just s from Harvard Square. Int corridors. **Pets:** Large, other species. Service with restrictions,
crate.
ⒶⓈⓀ Ⓢ🄳 ⊠ &ᴹ 🕖 🎴 🍴 ⇌

▼▼▼▼ **Radisson Hotel Cambridge** 🅷
(617) 492-7777. **$139-$329, 3 days notice.** 777 Memorial
Dr. US 3 and SR 2; I-90 (Massachusetts Tpke), exit 18 via
River St Bridge. Int corridors. **Pets:** Accepted.
⊠ 🎴 🖳 🍴 ⇌

🅰🅰🅰 ▼▼▼▼ **Residence Inn by Marriott**
Cambridge 🅼
(617) 349-0700. **$189-$309.** 6 Cambridge Center. Corner of
Ames and Broadway sts. Int corridors. **Pets:** Accepted.
ⓈⒶⓋⒺ Ⓢ🄳 ⊠ &ᴹ 🕖 🄴 🎴 🖳

CONCORD

▼▼ ▼▼ **Best Western at Historic Concord** 🅼
(978) 369-6100. **$119-$149.** 740 Elm St. 1.8 mi w, just off
SR 2 and 2A. Int corridors. **Pets:** Other species. $10 daily
fee/room. Designated rooms, service with restrictions,
supervision.
ⓈⒶⓋⒺ Ⓢ🄳 ⊠ 🎴 ⇌

DANVERS

🅰🅰🅰 ▼▼▼▼ **Residence Inn by Marriott** 🅼
(978) 777-7171. **$134-$174.** 51 Newbury St (Rt 1). US 1 N,
just s of jct SR 114. Ext corridors. **Pets:** Accepted.
ⓈⒶⓋⒺ Ⓢ🄳 ⊠ 🄴 🎴 🖳 ⇌

TownePlace Suites by Marriott **M**
(978) 777-6222. **$69-$139.** 238 Andover St. Southwest corner of jct US 1 and SR 114; SR 114 eastbound, enter just w of US 1 (no westbound entrance); US 1 southbound, enter through shopping center. Int corridors. **Pets:** Accepted.

DEDHAM

Residence Inn by Marriott **A**
(781) 407-0999. **$120-$143.** 259 Elm St. I-95, exit 15A, 0.3 mi n on US 1, then 0.4 mi e. Int corridors. **Pets:** Other species. $10 daily fee/pet, $150 one-time fee/pet. Service with restrictions, crate.

EAST BOSTON

Hilton Boston Logan Airport **H**
(617) 568-6700. **$119-$464.** 85 Terminal Rd. At Boston Logan Airport. Int corridors. **Pets:** Other species. Designated rooms.

FOXBOROUGH

Foxborough Residence Inn by Marriott **M**
(508) 698-2800. **$99-$169.** 250 Foxborough Blvd. I-95, exit 7A, 0.6 mi s on SR 140, then 0.7 mi e, then just n; in Foxborough Business Center. Int corridors. **Pets:** Other species. $10 daily fee/room, $100 one-time fee/room. Service with restrictions.

FRAMINGHAM

Red Roof Inn **M**
(508) 872-4499. **$65-$107.** 650 Cochituate Rd. I-90 (Massachusetts Tpke), exit 13, on SR 30; SR 9 in Natick, 0.8 mi n on Speen St, then w on SR 30, follow signs for Massachusetts Tpke. Ext corridors. **Pets:** Small, other species. Service with restrictions, supervision.

Residence Inn by Marriott **M**
(508) 370-0001. **$199-$219.** 400 Staples Dr. I-90 (Massachusetts Tpke), exit 12, SR 9 W to Crossing Blvd, then s. Int corridors. **Pets:** Other species. $150 one-time fee/room. Service with restrictions.

FRANKLIN

Franklin Residence Inn by Marriott **M**
(508) 541-8188. **$99-$149.** 4 Forge Pkwy. I-495, exit 17, 0.7 mi s; in Forge Park office development. Int corridors. **Pets:** Other species. $10 daily fee/room, $100 one-time fee/room. Service with restrictions, crate.

Hawthorn Suites Ltd **M**
(508) 553-3500. **$99-$219.** 835 Upper Union St. I-495, exit 16, just s, then 0.3 mi e. Int corridors. **Pets:** Other species. $5 daily fee/room, $75 one-time fee/room. Service with restrictions, crate.

GLOUCESTER

Cape Ann Motor Inn **M**
(978) 281-2900. **$65-$145, 7 days notice.** 33 Rockport Rd. 2 mi n of the terminus of SR 128 via SR 127A. Ext corridors. **Pets:** Medium. Service with restrictions, supervision.

The Manor Inn **X**
(978) 283-0614. **$75-$144.** 141 Essex Ave. SR 133, 2.3 mi e of exit 14 (SR 128). Ext/int corridors. **Pets:** Accepted.

LAWRENCE

Hampton Inn Boston/North Andover **M**
(978) 975-4050. **$99-$139.** 224 Winthrop Ave. I-495, exit 42A, just s on SR 114. Int corridors. **Pets:** Other species. $10 daily fee/room, $25 one-time fee/room. Service with restrictions, supervision.

LEXINGTON

Battle Green Inn **M**
(781) 862-6100. **$89-$149.** 1720 Massachusetts Ave. I-95, exit 31A, 2 mi s on SR 4 and 225; center. Int corridors. **Pets:** Accepted.

MARLBOROUGH

Embassy Suites Hotel-Boston Marlborough **M**
(508) 485-5900. **$109-$254.** 123 Boston Post Rd W. I-495, exit 24B, 0.5 mi w, just off US 20. Int corridors. **Pets:** Other species. $10 daily fee/room. Designated rooms, service with restrictions.

Homestead Studio Suites Hotel **M**
(508) 490-9911. **$90-$110.** 19 Northborough Rd. I-495, exit 24B, just w on US 20. Int corridors. **Pets:** Medium, other species. $85 one-time fee/pet. Service with restrictions, crate.

NEWTON

Holiday Inn Newton **M**
(617) 969-5300. **$109-$189, 30 days notice.** 399 Grove St. I-95, exit 22, just e; 0.3 mi s of I-90 (Massachusetts Tpke). Int corridors. **Pets:** Small, other species. $25 daily fee/room. Supervision.

▼▼▼ Sheraton Newton Hotel 🄷
(617) 969-3010. **$99-$159.** 320 Washington St. I-90 (Massachusetts Tpke), exit 17 (SR 16). Int corridors.
Pets: Accepted.

(ASK) (✕) (⌕) (🖋) (🛏) (💻) (🍴) (🏊)

NORTH CHELMSFORD

▼▼▼ Hawthorn Suites, LTD 🅼 ❖
(978) 256-5151. **$79-$119.** 25 Research Pl. SR 3, exit 32,
0.3 mi ne on SR 4. Int corridors. **Pets:** Medium, other
species. $10 daily fee/room, $50 one-time fee/room. Designated rooms.

(ASK) (S🐾) (✕) (&M) (🖋) (🛏) (💻) (🏊)

PEABODY

(AAA) ▼▼▼ MainStay Suites 🅼
(978) 531-6632. **$125-$165.** 200 Jubilee Dr. SR 128, exit
28, just s to Centennial Dr, w to the end, n to Jubilee Dr,
then 1.1 mi e. Int corridors. **Pets:** Accepted.

(SAVE) (✕) (⌕) (🖋) (🛏) (💻)

REVERE

▼▼▼ Hampton Inn 🅼
(781) 286-5665. **$129-$219.** 230 Lee Burbank Hwy. On SR
1A; 1.9 mi n of Logan International Airport; 0.6 mi s of
terminus SR 60. Int corridors. **Pets:** Medium. Supervision.

(SAVE) (S🐾) (✕) (&M) (⌕) (🖋) (🛏) (💻) (🏊)

ROCKPORT

(AAA) ▼▼▼ Sandy Bay Motor Inn 🅼
(978) 546-7155. **$78-$150, 7 days notice.** 183 Main St. 0.5
mi s on SR 127. Ext/int corridors. **Pets:** Accepted.

(SAVE) (S🐾) (✕) (🛏) (🍴) (🏊)

SALEM

▼▼▼ Hawthorne Hotel 🄷
(978) 744-4080. **$132-$209, 3 days notice.** 18 Washington
Sq W. On SR 1A; adjoining the historical district and facing
the Salem Witch Museum. Int corridors. **Pets:** Other species. $7.50 daily fee/room. Service with restrictions, supervision.

(ASK) (S🐾) (✕) (🛏) (🍴)

▼▼▼ The Salem Inn 🆑
(978) 741-0680. **$129-$290, 7 days notice.** 7 Summer St.
On SR 114 at jct Essex St; SR 128, exit 25A, 3 mi e. Int
corridors. **Pets:** $15 daily fee/pet. Designated rooms, service with restrictions, supervision.

(ASK) (✕) (💻)

TEWKSBURY

(AAA) ▼▼▼ Residence Inn by
Marriott-Boston/Tewksbury 🅼
(978) 640-1003. **$89-$159.** 1775 Andover St. I-495, exit 39,
0.3 mi w on SR 133. Ext corridors. **Pets:** Other species.
$10 daily fee/pet, $100 one-time fee/room. Designated
rooms, service with restrictions, crate.

(SAVE) (S🐾) (✕) (&M) (⌕) (🖋) (🛏) (💻) (🏊)

(AAA) ▼▼▼ Townplace Suites by Marriott 🅼
(978) 863-9800. **$99-$179.** 20 International Pl. I-495, exit
39, 0.3 mi nw. Int corridors. **Pets:** Accepted.

(SAVE) (S🐾) (✕) (&M) (⌕) (🖋) (🛏) (💻) (🏊)

WALTHAM

▼▼ Homestead Studio
Suites-Boston/Waltham 🅼
(781) 890-1333. **$139.** 52 Fourth Ave. I-95, exit 27A, just
se. Int corridors. **Pets:** Accepted.

(ASK) (S🐾) (✕) (⌕) (🖋) (🛏) (💻)

(AAA) ▼▼▼ Summerfield Suites by
Wyndham-Waltham/Boston 🅼
(781) 290-0026. **$119-$219.** 54 Fourth Ave. I-95, exit 27A,
just e. Int corridors. **Pets:** Accepted.

(SAVE) (✕) (&M) (⌕) (🖋) (🛏) (💻) (🏊)

▼▼▼ The Westin, Waltham-Boston 🄷
(781) 290-5600. **$99-$295.** 70 Third Ave. I-95, exit 27A, just
se. Int corridors. **Pets:** Accepted.

(ASK) (S🐾) (✕) (&M) (⌕) (🖋) (💻) (🍴) (🏊)

❖   **END METROPOLITAN AREA**   ❖

BROCKTON

(AAA) ▼▼▼ Residence Inn by Marriott 🅼 ❖
(508) 583-3600. **$99-$209.** 124 Liberty St. SR 24, exit 17B,
just w, just s on Pearl St, then 0.3 mi se via Mill St Conn. Int
corridors. **Pets:** Other species. $10 daily fee/room, $150
one-time fee/room. Service with restrictions.

(SAVE) (S🐾) (✕) (🖋) (🛏) (💻) (🏊)

CAPE COD AREA

BUZZARDS BAY

(AAA) ▼▼▼ Bay Motor Inn [C]
(508) 759-3989. **$51-$109, 10 days notice.** 223 Main St. SR 25, 0.5 mi w of Bourne Rotary, exit 2. Ext corridors. **Pets:** $10 daily fee/room. Service with restrictions, supervision.
[SAVE] [Sᴅ] [🛏] [▣] [≈]

CENTERVILLE

(AAA) ▼▼▼ Centerville Corners [M]
(508) 775-7223. **$50-$140, 7 days notice.** 369 S Main St. 1 mi s of SR 28, at jct S Main St and Craigville Beach Rd. Ext corridors. **Pets:** Large, dogs only. $5 daily fee/pet. Service with restrictions.
[SAVE] [✕] [🛏] [▣] [≈]

FALMOUTH

(AAA) ▼▼▼ Mariner Motel [M]
(508) 548-1331. **$59-$159, 14 days notice.** 555 Main St. 0.5 mi e on SR 28. Ext corridors. **Pets:** Accepted.
[SAVE] [✕] [🛏] [≈]

HYANNIS

▼▼▼ Comfort Inn [M]
(508) 771-4804. **$85-$250.** 1470 Rt 132. US 6, exit 6, 1.3 mi se. Ext/int corridors. **Pets:** Large, other species. $50 deposit/room. Service with restrictions, crate.
[SAVE] [Sᴅ] [✕] [🐾] [🛏] [▣] [≈]

▼▼▼ Econolodge [M]
(508) 771-0699. **$39-$159, 7 days notice.** 59 Rt 28. US 6, exit 7, 2.4 mi s on Willow St, then 0.5 mi s on SR 28. Ext corridors. **Pets:** Small. $10 one-time fee/pet. Designated rooms, service with restrictions, supervision.
[SAVE] [Sᴅ] [✕] [🛏] [≈]

ORLEANS

(AAA) ▼▼▼▼ Skaket Beach Motel [M]
(508) 255-1020. **$58-$175, 10 days notice.** 203 Cranberry Hwy, Rt 6A. US 6, exit 12, just e. Ext corridors. **Pets:** Accepted.
[SAVE] [✕] [🛏] [▣] [≈]

PROVINCETOWN

▼▼▼▼ Bayshore [CO]
(508) 487-9133. **$75-$195.** 493 Commercial St. 0.8 mi e of Town Hall. Ext corridors. **Pets:** $15 daily fee/pet. Service with restrictions.
[🛏] [▣]

(AAA) ▼▼▼▼ Cape Inn [M]
(508) 487-1711. **$90-$180, 3 days notice.** 698 Commercial St. 1.5 mi se on SR 6A. Ext corridors. **Pets:** Other species. Service with restrictions, supervision.
[SAVE] [Sᴅ] [✕] [🐾] [🛏] [▣] [🍽]

▼▼▼ White Wind Inn [BB]
(508) 487-1526. **$85-$250, 14 days notice.** 174 Commercial St. Just w of Town Hall. Int corridors. **Pets:** Dogs only. $250 deposit/pet, $10 daily fee/pet. Designated rooms, service with restrictions, crate.
[✕] [🛏] [▣]

SANDWICH

▼▼▼ The Earl of Sandwich Motel [M]
(508) 888-1415. **$55-$109, 7 days notice.** 378 Rt 6A. At MM 5.1. Ext corridors. **Pets:** Accepted.
[✕] [🛏] [≈]

SOUTH YARMOUTH

▼▼ Motel 6–4042 [M]
(508) 394-4000. **$43-$93.** 1314 Main St (SR 28). 0.3 mi w of Bass River Bridge on SR 28. Int corridors. **Pets:** Medium. Designated rooms, service with restrictions, supervision.
[✕] [🛏] [≈]

WEST YARMOUTH

▼▼ Town 'N Country Motor Lodge [M]
(508) 771-0212. **$32-$109, 3 days notice.** 452 Main St (SR 28). 2.5 mi e of jct SR 132. Ext corridors. **Pets:** Accepted.
[✕] [🛏] [≈]

❧ END METROPOLITAN AREA ❧

GARDNER

▼▼ Super 8 Motel [M]
(978) 630-2888. **$79.** 22 Pearson Blvd. SR 2, exit 23, just n. Int corridors. **Pets:** $10.97 daily fee/pet. Service with restrictions, supervision.
[✕] [🛏]

GREENFIELD

(AAA) ▼▼▼▼ The Brandt House B&B [BB] ❀
(413) 774-3329. **$100-$225.** 29 Highland Ave. I-91, exit 26, 1.8 mi e on SR 2A, se via Cresent St. Int corridors. **Pets:** Dogs only. $25 one-time fee/pet. Supervision.
[SAVE] [✕] [🛏]

HADLEY

▼▼▼▼ Howard Johnson **M**
(413) 586-0114. **$79-$169.** 401 Russell St. I-91, exit 19 northbound, 4.3 mi e on SR 9; exit 24 southbound, 10 mi s on SR 116, then just w on SR 9. Int corridors. **Pets:** Small. $20 daily fee/room. Designated rooms, service with restrictions, supervision.

(ASK) (S/D) (✕) (&M) (⌀) (🛗) (🖥) (↝)

HANCOCK

AAA ▼▼▼▼ Jericho Valley Inn **M**
(413) 458-9511. **$48-$138, 14 days notice.** SR 43, 5 mi s of jct US 7. Ext/int corridors. **Pets:** Other species. Designated rooms.

(SAVE) (S/D) (✕) (🛗) (🖥) (↝)

LANESBORO

AAA ▼ Mt View Motel **M**
(413) 442-1009. **$49-$135, 7 days notice.** 499 S Main St. 1 mi s on US 7. Ext corridors. **Pets:** Large. $10 daily fee/pet. Designated rooms, service with restrictions, supervision.

(SAVE) (S/D) (✕) (🛗) (🖥)

AAA ▼ The Weathervane Motel **M**
(413) 443-3230. **$35-$110, 7 days notice.** 475 S Main St. 1.3 mi s on US 7. Ext corridors. **Pets:** $10 daily fee/pet. Service with restrictions, supervision.

(SAVE) (S/D) (✕) (🛗) (🖥)

LENOX

▼▼▼ Seven Hills Country Inn & Restaurant **CI** ❖
(413) 637-0060. **$85-$325, 31 days notice.** 40 Plunkett St. Jct US 7/20, 0.6 mi e on US 20, then 0.8 mi s. Ext/int corridors. **Pets:** Other species. $20 daily fee/pet. Designated rooms.

(✕) (&) (🛗) (🖥) (🍴) (↝)

MANSFIELD

AAA ▼▼ Red Roof Inn **M**
(508) 339-2323. **$75-$95.** 60 Forbes Blvd. I-95, exit 7A, 1.3 mi n; I-495, exit 12; in Cabot Business Park. Int corridors. **Pets:** Accepted.

(SAVE) (✕) (&) (↝)

MIDDLEBORO

AAA ▼▼ Days Inn-Plymouth/Middleboro **M** ❖
(508) 946-4400. **$89-$109.** 30 E Clark St. I-495, exit 4 at SR 105. Int corridors. **Pets:** Other species. $3 daily fee/pet. Service with restrictions, crate.

(SAVE) (S/D) (✕) (&) (🛗) (🖥) (↝)

ORANGE

AAA ▼ Executive Inn **M** ❖
(978) 544-8864. **$55-$85, 7 days notice.** 110 Daniel Shay Hwy. US 202, exit 16, just n of SR 2. Ext/int corridors. **Pets:** Medium. $7 daily fee/pet. Service with restrictions, supervision.

(SAVE) (S/D) (✕) (🛗)

RAYNHAM

▼▼ Days Inn Taunton **M**
(508) 824-8647. **$60-$90, 15 days notice.** 164 New State Hwy. SR 24, exit 13B, 0.8 mi w on US 44. Ext/int corridors. **Pets:** Small. Service with restrictions, supervision.

(SAVE) (S/D) (✕) (&) (↝)

REHOBOTH

▼▼▼▼ Five Bridge Inn Bed & Breakfast **BB** ❖
(508) 252-3190. **$89-$145, 7 days notice.** 154 Pine St. 1.6 mi n of US 44, 3.3 mi w of jct SR 118; US 44, n on Blanding, e on Broad, n on Salisbury, then w. Int corridors. **Pets:** Other species. $10 daily fee/room. Designated rooms, service with restrictions, crate.

(ASK) (S/D) (✕) (🛗) (🖥) (↝)

ROCKLAND

▼▼▼ Holiday Inn Express-Boston/Rockland **M** ❖
(781) 871-5660. **$117-$126.** 909 Hingham St. SR 3, exit 14, 0.3 mi sw on SR 228. Int corridors. **Pets:** $50 deposit/pet, $6 daily fee/pet. Service with restrictions, supervision.

(ASK) (S/D) (✕) (🛗) (🖥)

SEEKONK

▼▼ Motel 6-1289 **M**
(508) 336-7800. **$56-$81.** 821 Fall River Ave. I-195, exit 1, just n on SR 114A. Int corridors. **Pets:** Small, other species. Service with restrictions, supervision.

(✕) (&)

SOMERSET

▼▼ Quality Inn-Fall River/Somerset **M**
(508) 678-4545. **$79-$159.** 1878 Wilbur Ave. I-195, exit 4 eastbound; exit 4A westbound. Int corridors. **Pets:** Service with restrictions, supervision.

(SAVE) (S/D) (✕) (🛗) (🖥) (↝)

SOUTHBOROUGH

AAA ▼▼▼ Red Roof Inn **M**
(508) 481-3904. **$66-$92.** 367 Turnpike Rd. I-495, exit 23A, just e on SR 9. Ext corridors. **Pets:** Accepted.

(SAVE) (✕) (🛗)

STURBRIDGE

⬧⬧⬧ ▼▼▼ Comfort Inn & Suites at Pistol Pond M

(508) 347-3306. **$85-$209.** 215 Charlton Rd. I-90, exit 9, 0.5 mi e; I-84, exit 3A. Ext/int corridors. **Pets:** $15 daily fee/pet. Designated rooms, service with restrictions, crate.

SAVE 🔒 ✕ 🗄 🚭 🐾 ▤ 📺 🏊

⬧⬧⬧ ▼▼ Days Inn M ❀

(508) 347-3391. **$65-$140, 7 days notice.** 66-68 Old Route 15, Haynes St. I-84, exit 2, follow signs to SR 131, on I-84 service road. Ext/int corridors. **Pets:** Other species. $7 daily fee/pet. Service with restrictions, supervision.

SAVE 🔒 ✕ 📺 🏊

⬧⬧⬧ ▼▼ Green Acres Motel M

(508) 347-3496. **$65-$120, 3 days notice.** 2 Shepard Rd (SR 131). Just off SR 131, 1.4 mi s of jct US 20. Ext corridors. **Pets:** Accepted.

SAVE 🔒 ✕ ▤ 🏊

⬧⬧⬧ ▼▼ Publick House Historic Inn & Country Lodge X

(508) 347-3313. **$79-$165.** 295 Main St. I-90, exit 9; I-84, exit 3B, 0.5 mi s of jct US 20; on the Common. Ext/int corridors. **Pets:** Large. $5 daily fee/pet. Designated rooms, supervision.

SAVE ✕ ▤ 📺 🍴 🏊 ✕

⬧⬧⬧ ▼▼ Rodeway Inn M

(508) 347-9673. **$60-$150.** 172 Main St. 1.4 mi s of jct US 20 and SR 131. Ext corridors. **Pets:** $10 daily fee/pet. Service with restrictions, supervision.

SAVE 🔒 ✕ ▤ 📺

▼▼▼ Sturbridge Host Hotel and Conference Center on Cedar Lake M

(508) 347-7393. **$109-$169.** 366 Main St. I-90, exit 9, just w on US 20; I-84, exit 3B. Int corridors. **Pets:** Accepted.

ASK 🔒 ✕ 🚭 ▤ 📺 🍴 🏊 ✕

WEST SPRINGFIELD

⬧⬧⬧ ▼▼ Red Roof Inns M

(413) 731-1010. **$53-$82.** 1254 Riverdale (US 5) St. I-91, exit 13A. Ext corridors. **Pets:** Accepted.

SAVE ✕ 🗄 🚭

WEST STOCKBRIDGE

⬧⬧⬧ ▼▼ Pleasant Valley Motel M ❀

(413) 232-8511. **$39-$175, 14 days notice.** 42 Stockbridge Rd (Rt 102). I-90, exit B3 eastbound, 0.5 mi s on SR 22, 3.5 mi e on SR 102; exit 1 westbound, 0.4 mi e. Ext corridors. **Pets:** Large. $10 daily fee/pet. Designated rooms, service with restrictions, supervision.

SAVE ✕ ▤ 🏊

WESTBOROUGH

⬧⬧⬧ ▼▼▼ Residence Inn by Marriott Boston/Westborough M ❀

(508) 366-7700. **$99-$189.** 25 Connector Rd. I-495, exit 23B, just w; SR 9, exit Computer/Research Dr, 0.3 mi s. Ext/int corridors. **Pets:** Medium, other species. $150 one-time fee/room.

SAVE ✕ 🗄 🚭 🐾 ▤ 📺 🏊

⬧⬧⬧ ▼▼▼ Wyndham Westborough H

(508) 366-5511. **$119-$214.** 5400 Computer Dr. I-495, exit 23B, just w; SR 9, exit Computer/Research Dr. Int corridors. **Pets:** Medium. $50 deposit/room. Service with restrictions, crate.

SAVE ✕ 🗄 🚭 🐾 ▤ 📺 🍴 🏊

WILLIAMSTOWN

▼▼ Cozy Corner Motel M

(413) 458-8006. **$49-$125, 10 days notice.** 284 Sand Springs Rd (US 7). US 7, 1.5 mi n of jct SR 2. Ext corridors. **Pets:** Other species. $5 one-time fee/pet. Service with restrictions, supervision.

🔒 ✕ ▤

⬧⬧⬧ ▼▼ The Villager Motel M

(413) 458-4046. **$59-$109, 10 days notice.** 953 Simonds Rd. US 7, 1.7 mi n of jct SR 2. Ext corridors. **Pets:** Large. $10 daily fee/pet. Designated rooms, service with restrictions, supervision.

SAVE 🔒 ✕ ▤

MICHIGAN

CITY INDEX

ALGONAC

▼▼/▼▼ Linda's Lighthouse Inn 🅱🅱 ❧
(810) 794-2992. **$95-$125, 7 days notice.** 5965 Pointe
Tremble Rd (M-29). I-94, exit 243, 14 mi e on M-29. Int
corridors. **Pets:** $15 daily fee/pet.
[X] [X] [W] [Z]

ALPENA

⚫⚫⚫ ▼▼/▼▼ Holiday Inn Ⓜ🄸
(989) 356-2151. **$89-$119.** 1000 Hwy 23 N. 1 mi n on US
23. Int corridors. **Pets:** Other species. Service with restrictions, crate.
[SAVE] [S🄳] [X] [💻] [¶¶] [⇌]

ANN ARBOR

▼▼/▼▼ Hampton Inn-North Ⓜ
(734) 996-4444. **$79-$109.** 2300 Green Rd. US 23, exit 41
(Plymouth Rd), just nw. Int corridors. **Pets:** Small. $25 one-
time fee/room. Service with restrictions, supervision.
[SAVE] [X] [🄼] [🄰] [🄸] [💻] [⇌]

▼▼/▼▼ Hawthorn Suites Ⓜ
(734) 327-0011. **$130.** 3535 Green Rd. US 23, exit 41
(Plymouth Rd), just sw. Int corridors. **Pets:** $75 one-time
fee/room. Service with restrictions, supervision.
[ASK] [S🄳] [🄰] [🄵] [🄸] [💻] [⇌]

▼▼ Motel 6–1247 Ⓜ
(734) 665-9900. **$47-$65.** 3764 S State St. I-94, exit 177
(State St), just s, then just w on Airport Rd. Ext corridors.
Pets: Accepted.
[S🄳] [X] [🄵]

⚫⚫⚫ ▼▼/▼▼ Red Roof Inn Ⓜ
(734) 996-5800. **$54-$74.** 3621 Plymouth Rd. US 23, exit
41 (Plymouth Rd), just nw. Ext corridors. **Pets:** Accepted.
[SAVE] [X] [🄰] [🄸]

⚫⚫⚫ ▼▼/▼▼ Residence Inn by Marriott 🄰
(734) 996-5666. **$89-$119.** 800 Victors Way. I-94, exit 177
(State St), just ne. Ext corridors. **Pets:** Accepted.
[SAVE] [X] [🄰] [🄵] [🄸] [💻] [⇌]

AU GRES

⚫⚫⚫ ▼▼/▼▼ Best Western Pinewood Lodge Ⓜ
(989) 876-4060. **$69-$109, 3 days notice.** 510 W US 23.
Just w on US 23. Int corridors. **Pets:** Accepted.
[SAVE] [S🄳] [X] [🄸] [💻] [⇌]

BAD AXE

▼▼/▼▼ Best Western Bad Axe Hotel & Resort Ⓜ
(989) 269-3930. **$80-$90.** 898 N Van Dyke Rd. Downtown;
1 mi n. Int corridors. **Pets:** Very small, dogs only. $10
one-time fee/pet. Service with restrictions, supervision.
[SAVE] [X] [💻] [¶¶]

BARAGA

▼ Carla's Lake Shore Motel & Restaurant Ⓜ
(906) 353-6256. **$45-$52, 14 days notice.** 6 mi n on US 41. Ext corridors. **Pets:** Other species. $5 one-time fee/room. Supervision.
(ASK) (S⊘) (✕) (█) (¶¶)

▼ Super 8 Motel Ⓜ
(906) 353-6680. **$59-$64.** 790 Michigan Ave. 1 mi w on SR 38. Int corridors. **Pets:** Medium. $5 one-time fee/room. Supervision.
(ASK) (S⊘) (✕)

BATTLE CREEK

⊕ ▼▼▼ Battle Creek Inn Ⓜ
(616) 979-1100. **$72-$80.** 5050 Beckley Rd. I-94, exit 97, just s. Ext/int corridors. **Pets:** Other species. Service with restrictions, crate.
(SAVE) (S⊘) (✕) (█) (█) (¶¶) (➴)

⊕ ▼▼▼ Baymont Inn & Suites Ⓜ
(616) 979-5400. **$70-$87, 30 days notice.** 4725 Beckley Rd. I-94, exit 97, just sw. Int corridors. **Pets:** Accepted.
(SAVE) (S⊘) (✕) (⌗) (⌖) (█) (█) (➴)

⊕ ▼▼ Days Inn Ⓜ
(616) 979-3561. **$69-$110.** 4786 Beckley Rd. I-94, exit 97. Ext corridors. **Pets:** Other species. $25 one-time fee/room. Designated rooms.
(SAVE) (S⊘) (✕) (⚿ᴹ) (█)

▼▼▼ McCamly Plaza Hotel Ⓗ
(616) 963-7050. **$149.** 50 Capital Ave SW. Center. Int corridors. **Pets:** Medium. Service with restrictions, supervision.
(ASK) (S⊘) (✕) (⚿ᴹ) (⌗) (⌖) (█) (¶¶) (➴)

▼ Motel 6–1149 Ⓜ
(616) 979-1141. **$35-$51.** 4775 Beckley Rd. I-94, exit 97, just sw. Ext corridors. **Pets:** Accepted.
(S⊘) (✕) (⚿ᴹ) (⌖) (➴)

BAY CITY

⊕ ▼▼▼ AmericInn of Bay City Ⓜ
(989) 671-0071. **$64-$105.** 3915 Three Mile Rd. I-75, exit 164. Int corridors. **Pets:** Large, dogs only. Service with restrictions, supervision.
(SAVE) (S⊘) (✕) (⌖) (█) (█) (➴)

⊕ ▼ Delta Motel Ⓜ
(989) 684-4490. **$35-$55, 7 days notice.** 1000 S Euclid Ave. Jct I-75 and US 10, 1.8 mi e on SR 25, 0.8 mi s on SR 13. Ext corridors. **Pets:** Accepted.
(SAVE) (S⊘) (✕) (█) (█)

▼▼▼ Holiday Inn Ⓜ
(989) 892-3501. **$89-$99, 3 days notice.** 501 Saginaw St. Center line on I-75 business loop, SR 15 and 25. Int corridors. **Pets:** Other species. Service with restrictions, supervision.
(ASK) (S⊘) (✕) (⌖) (█) (¶¶) (➴)

BAY VIEW

⊕ ▼▼ Comfort Inn Ⓜ ☙
(231) 347-3220. **$58-$250.** 1314 US 31 N. Jct US 31 and SR 119. Int corridors. **Pets:** Other species. Service with restrictions, supervision.
(SAVE) (S⊘) (✕) (█) (█)

BENTON HARBOR

▼▼ Best Western T.C. Inn & Suites Ⓜ
(616) 925-1880. **$55-$99.** 1598 Mall Dr. I-94, exit 29, just n to Mall Dr, then just w. Int corridors. **Pets:** Small. $5 daily fee/pet. Service with restrictions, supervision.
(SAVE) (S⊘) (✕) (█) (➴)

▼ Motel 6 Ⓜ
(616) 925-5100. **$35-$61.** 2063 Pipestone Rd. I-94, exit 29, just nw. Ext corridors. **Pets:** Accepted.
(S⊘) (✕) (⚿ᴹ) (➴)

▼▼ Ramada Inn Ⓜ
(616) 927-1172. **Call for rates, 3 days notice.** 798 Ferguson Dr. I-94, exit 28, just sw. Int corridors. **Pets:** Other species. $25 deposit/room, $5 one-time fee/pet. Designated rooms, service with restrictions, crate.
(ASK) (✕) (█) (█) (¶¶) (➴)

⊕ ▼▼ Red Roof Inn Ⓜ
(616) 927-2484. **$39-$81.** 1630 Mall Dr. I-94, exit 29, just n, then just w. Ext corridors. **Pets:** Accepted.
(SAVE) (✕) (⚿ᴹ) (⚿) (█)

BEULAH

⊕ ▼ Pine Knot Resort Ⓜ
(231) 882-7751. **$85-$115, 14 days notice.** 171 N Center St. 1 mi ne on US 31 from jct SR 115. Ext corridors. **Pets:** Accepted.
(SAVE) (S⊘) (█) (█)

BIRCH RUN

⊕ ▼▼ Super 8 Motel Ⓜ
(989) 624-4440. **$45-$75.** 9235 E Birch Run Rd. I-75, exit 136, just e. Int corridors. **Pets:** Medium. Service with restrictions, supervision.
(SAVE) (S⊘) (█)

BOYNE FALLS

▼ Brown Trout Motel Ⓜ
(231) 549-2791. **$60, 3 days notice.** 2510 Nelson Ave. On US 131, just s of SR 75. Ext corridors. **Pets:** Accepted.
(ASK) (S⊘) (█) (█) (➴)

BREVORT

⊕ ▼ Chapel Hill Motel Ⓜ ☙
(906) 292-5534. **$44-$59, 3 days notice.** 4422 W US 2. Center. Ext/int corridors. **Pets:** Medium. Designated rooms, service with restrictions, supervision.
(SAVE) (✕) (█) (█) (➴)

BRIDGEPORT

AAA ▼▼▼ Villager Lodge **M**
(989) 777-2582. **$40-$60, 30 days notice.** 6361 Dixie Hwy.
I-75, exit 144B. Ext corridors. **Pets:** Medium, other species.
$30 deposit/room. Service with restrictions, supervision.
⟨SAVE⟩ ⟨S🛇⟩ ⟨✕⟩ ⟨🖉⟩ ⟨🖥⟩

CADILLAC

AAA ▼▼▼ Best Western of Cadillac **MI**
(231) 775-2458. **$58-$114.** 5676 E M55. On SR 55, 0.5 mi
w of jct SR 115. Ext corridors. **Pets:** Accepted.
⟨SAVE⟩ ⟨S🛇⟩ ⟨✕⟩ ⟨🖥⟩ ⟨🍴⟩ ⟨🏊⟩

AAA ▼▼ Econo Lodge **M**
(231) 775-6700. **$52-$85.** 2501 Sunnyside Dr. Jct SR 55
and 115. Ext/int corridors. **Pets:** Other species. Supervision.
⟨SAVE⟩ ⟨S🛇⟩ ⟨✕⟩ ⟨🖥⟩ ⟨🖥⟩

▼▼/▼ McGuires Resort **R**
(231) 775-9947. **$79-$199, 7 days notice.** 7880 Mackinaw
Tr. 0.5 mi w of US 131. Ext/int corridors. **Pets:** Medium. $15
daily fee/room. Designated rooms, service with restrictions,
crate.
⟨A$K⟩ ⟨✕⟩ ⟨🖉⟩ ⟨🖥⟩ ⟨🖥⟩ ⟨🍴⟩ ⟨🏊⟩ ⟨✕⟩

CASCADE

AAA ▼▼▼ Baymont Inn-Grand Rapids
       Airport **M**
(616) 956-3300. **$85, 30 days notice.** 2873 Kraft Ave SE.
I-96, exit 43B, just e. Int corridors. **Pets:** Accepted.
⟨SAVE⟩ ⟨S🛇⟩ ⟨🖥⟩ ⟨🖥⟩

▼▼▼ Country Inn & Suites By Carlson **M**
(616) 977-0909. **$80-$90.** 5399 28th St. I-96, exit 43B, just
e on SR 11. Int corridors. **Pets:** Accepted.
⟨A$K⟩ ⟨S🛇⟩ ⟨✕⟩ ⟨🖥M⟩ ⟨🗑⟩ ⟨🖉⟩ ⟨🖥⟩ ⟨🖥⟩ ⟨🏊⟩

AAA ▼▼▼ Exel Inn of Grand Rapids **M**
(616) 957-3000. **$46-$66.** 4855 28th St SE. I-96, exit 43A,
0.5 mi w on SR 11. Int corridors. **Pets:** Accepted.
⟨SAVE⟩ ⟨S🛇⟩ ⟨✕⟩ ⟨🖥⟩ ⟨🖥⟩

▼▼/▼ Hampton Inn **M**
(616) 956-9304. **$78-$90.** 4981 28th St SE. I-96, exit 43A,
0.5 mi w on SR 11. Int corridors. **Pets:** Service with restrictions, supervision.
⟨SAVE⟩ ⟨S🛇⟩ ⟨✕⟩ ⟨🗑⟩ ⟨🖥⟩ ⟨🖥⟩ ⟨🏊⟩

CEDARVILLE

AAA ▼▼▼ Comfort Inn **M**
(906) 484-2266. **$99-$139.** 106 W M-134. On SR 134, just
w of SR 129. Int corridors. **Pets:** Designated rooms, supervision.
⟨SAVE⟩ ⟨S🛇⟩ ⟨✕⟩ ⟨🖥⟩ ⟨🖥⟩ ⟨🏊⟩

CHARLEVOIX

▼▼▼ Sleep Inn **M**
(231) 547-0300. **$56-$136, 3 days notice.** 800 Petoskey
Ave. 1 mi n on US 31. Int corridors. **Pets:** Medium, other
species. $25 deposit/room. Service with restrictions, super-
vision.
⟨SAVE⟩ ⟨S🛇⟩ ⟨✕⟩ ⟨🖉⟩ ⟨🖥⟩ ⟨🖥⟩ ⟨🏊⟩

CHARLOTTE

AAA ▼▼▼ Super 8 Motel **M**
(517) 543-8288. **$55-$80.** 828 E Shepherd St. I-69, exit 60,
just w on SR 50. Int corridors. **Pets:** Accepted.
⟨SAVE⟩ ⟨S🛇⟩ ⟨✕⟩ ⟨🖥⟩

CHEBOYGAN

AAA ▼▼ Birch Haus Motel **M**
(231) 627-5862. **$40-$55.** 1301 Mackinaw Ave. On US 23,
0.8 mi nw. Ext corridors. **Pets:** Small. $5 daily fee/pet.
Service with restrictions, supervision.
⟨SAVE⟩ ⟨✕⟩ ⟨🖥⟩

AAA ▼▼ Pine River Motel **M**
(231) 627-5119. **$40-$60, 3 days notice.** 102 Lafayette. 0.5
mi e on US 23. Ext corridors. **Pets:** Accepted.
⟨SAVE⟩ ⟨S🛇⟩ ⟨✕⟩ ⟨🖥⟩

CHELSEA

▼▼/▼ Comfort Inn of Chelsea **M**
(734) 433-8000. **$89-$129, 3 days notice.** 1645 Commerce
Park Dr. I-94, exit 159, just n. Int corridors. **Pets:** Accepted.
⟨SAVE⟩ ⟨S🛇⟩ ⟨✕⟩ ⟨🖥M⟩ ⟨🖥⟩ ⟨🖥⟩ ⟨🏊⟩

COLDWATER

▼▼▼ Ramada Inn **MI**
(517) 278-2017. **$69-$119.** 1000 Orleans Blvd. I-69, exit 13,
0.3 mi w on E Chicago St (US 12), just n on N Michigan
Ave, then just e. Int corridors. **Pets:** Other species. $50
deposit/room. Service with restrictions, supervision.
⟨A$K⟩ ⟨S🛇⟩ ⟨✕⟩ ⟨🖥⟩ ⟨🖥⟩ ⟨🍴⟩ ⟨🏊⟩

AAA ▼▼▼ Super 8 Motel **M**
(517) 278-8833. **$65-$75, 5 days notice.** 600 Orleans Blvd.
I-69, exit 13, 0.3 mi w on E Chicago St (US 12), just n on N
Michigan Ave, then just e. Int corridors. **Pets:** Other spe-
cies. Service with restrictions, supervision.
⟨SAVE⟩ ⟨✕⟩ ⟨🖥M⟩ ⟨🖉⟩ ⟨🖥⟩

COMSTOCK PARK

▼▼▼ Swan Inn **MI**
(616) 784-1224. **$47-$80.** 5182 Alpine Ave. Jct I-96 and
Alpine Ave, 3 mi n on SR 37. Ext corridors. **Pets:** Medium,
dogs only. $5 daily fee/room. Service with restrictions, crate.
⟨✕⟩ ⟨🖥⟩ ⟨🖥⟩ ⟨🍴⟩ ⟨🏊⟩

COPPER HARBOR

Lake Fanny Hooe Resort & Campground [M]
(906) 289-4451. **$65-$80, 7 days notice.** 505 Second St. Just s on Manganese Rd. Ext corridors. **Pets:** Other species. $5 daily fee/pet. Service with restrictions, supervision.

☒ 🛏 🖵 ⊠ 🎞 🕿

Norland Motel [M]
(906) 289-4815. **$53-$57 (no credit cards), 7 days notice.** US 41, F # 172. 2 mi e on US 41; beyond entrance to Fort Wilkins State Park. Ext corridors. **Pets:** Accepted.

SAVE ☒ 🛏 🖵 ⊠ 🎞 🕿

DETROIT METROPOLITAN AREA

ALLEN PARK

Best Western Greenfield Inn [M]
(313) 271-1600. **$116.** 3000 Enterprise Dr. At jct I-94 and Oakwood Blvd, 2 mi from Greenfield Village. Int corridors. **Pets:** Small, dogs only. Designated rooms, service with restrictions, supervision.

SAVE 🔊 ☒ 🖉 🛏 🖵 🍴

Holiday Inn Express & Suites [M]
(313) 323-3500. **$109-$129.** 3600 Enterprise Dr. I-94, exit 206, jct Oakwood Blvd. Int corridors. **Pets:** Medium, dogs only. Designated rooms, service with restrictions, supervision.

SAVE 🔊 ☒ 🛏 🖵 🛶

AUBURN HILLS

AmeriSuites (Detroit/Auburn Hills) [M]
(248) 475-9393. **$99.** 1545 Opdyke Road. I-75, exit 79 (University Dr), just w, then n. Int corridors. **Pets:** Small, other species. Service with restrictions.

SAVE 🔊 ☒ 🖉 🖎 🛏 🖵 🛶

Hilton Suites Auburn Hills [H]
(248) 334-2222. **$99-$209.** 2300 Featherstone Rd. I-75, exit 79, w on University Dr, then 0.5 mi s on Opdyke Rd, just e. Int corridors. **Pets:** Small, dogs only. $50 deposit/pet. Service with restrictions, supervision.

SAVE 🔊 ☒ 🖉 🖎 🛏 🖵 🍴 🛶

Homestead Studio Suites-Detroit/Auburn Hills [A]
(248) 340-8888. **$76.** 3315 University Dr. I-75, exit 79, 0.9 mi e. Int corridors. **Pets:** Accepted.

ASK 🔊 ☒ 🛏 🖵

Staybridge Suites [M]
(248) 322-4600. **$69-$179, 14 days notice.** 2050 Featherstone Rd. I-75, exit 79, w on University Dr, 0.5 mi s on Opdyke Rd, just e. Int corridors. **Pets:** Accepted.

ASK 🔊 ☒ 🖎 🛏 🖵 🛶

Wellesley Inn & Suites (Detroit/Auburn Hills) [M]
(248) 335-5200. **$69-$89, 14 days notice.** 2100 Feather Stone Rd. I-75, exit 79, w on University Dr, then 0.5 mi s on Opdyke Rd, just e. Int corridors. **Pets:** Accepted.

SAVE ☒ 🛏 🖵 🛶

BELLEVILLE

Comfort Inn [M]
(734) 697-8556. **$79-$199.** 45945 S I-94 Service Dr. I-94, exit 190, just s. Int corridors. **Pets:** Small, other species. $10 daily fee/pet. Designated rooms, service with restrictions, supervision.

SAVE 🔊 ☒ 🖉 🖎 🛏 🖵 🛶

Red Roof Inn Metro Airport [M]
(734) 697-2244. **$55-$75.** 45501 N I-94 Expwy, Service Dr. I-94, exit 190 (Belleville Rd). Ext corridors. **Pets:** Accepted.

SAVE ☒ 🖉 🖎 🛏

BIRMINGHAM

Holiday Inn Express Birmingham [M]
(248) 646-7300. **$110-$170.** 34952 Woodward Ave. Center; on SR 1, jct Woodward Ave and Maple Rd. Ext/int corridors. **Pets:** Accepted.

ASK 🔊 ☒ 🖎 🛏 🖵

CANTON

Baymont Inn & Suites Detroit-Canton [M]
(734) 981-1808. **$74-$84.** 41211 Ford Rd. I-275, exit 25, just w on SR M153; behind White Castle. Int corridors. **Pets:** Small, other species. $50 deposit/room. Designated rooms, service with restrictions, supervision.

SAVE 🔊 ☒ 🖉 🛏 🖵

Motel 6–1070 [M]
(734) 981-5000. **$48-$63.** 41216 Ford Rd. I-275, exit 25, just w on SR M153. Ext corridors. **Pets:** Other species. No service, supervision.

🔊 ☒ 🖎

DEARBORN

Red Roof Inn-Dearborn [M]
(313) 278-9732. **$61-$92.** 24130 Michigan Ave. Jct US 12 and 24. Ext corridors. **Pets:** Accepted.

SAVE ☒ 🖉 🛏

The Ritz-Carlton, Dearborn [H] ❀
(313) 441-2000. **$139-$1500.** 300 Town Center Dr. SR 39 (Southfield Frwy), between Ford Rd and Michigan Ave exits, on Service Dr. Int corridors. **Pets:** Medium, other species. $50 one-time fee/room. Service with restrictions, supervision.

SAVE ☒ 🖉 🖎 🖵 🍴 🛶

DETROIT

④④④ ▼▼▼▼ Best Western-Detroit Downtown **MI**
(313) 887-7000. **$79-$119.** 1020 Washington Blvd. Downtown; at corner of Washington Blvd and Michigan. Int corridors. **Pets:** Small, other species. $25 deposit/pet. Service with restrictions, crate.
〔SAVE〕〔S6〕✕ 🖉 🛑 💻

④④④ ▼▼▼ Comfort Inn-Downtown Detroit **M**
(313) 567-8888. **$79-$229, 14 days notice.** 1999 E Jefferson Ave. I-375, exit E Jefferson Ave, 0.5 mi e. Int corridors. **Pets:** Small. Service with restrictions, supervision.
〔SAVE〕〔S6〕✕ 🖉 🛑 💻

▼▼▼▼ Hotel St. Regis-Holiday Inn **H**
(313) 873-3000. **Call for rates.** 3071 W Grand Blvd. W Grand Blvd and Cass. Int corridors. **Pets:** Accepted.
〔ASK〕✕ 🖉 🛑 💻 〔¶〕

④④④ ▼▼▼▼ Residence Inn By
            Marriott-Dearborn **A**
(313) 441-1700. **$85-$184.** 5777 Southfield Service Dr. Just n of Southfield Frwy at jct Ford Rd. Ext corridors. **Pets:** Accepted.
〔SAVE〕✕ 🖉 🛑 💻 🔁

FARMINGTON HILLS

④④④ ▼▼ Red Roof Inn-Farmington Hills **M**
(248) 478-8640. **$58-$74.** 24300 Sinacola Ct. I-96/275 and M-5, exit 165 (Grand River Ave); just w. Ext corridors. **Pets:** Small, other species. Service with restrictions, supervision.
〔SAVE〕✕ 🖉 🖉 🛑

LIVONIA

④④④ ▼▼▼▼ AmeriSuites-Detroit/Livonia **M**
(734) 953-9224. **$98-$109.** 19300 Haggerty Rd. I-275, exit 169A, just w on 7 Mile Rd. Int corridors. **Pets:** Accepted.
〔SAVE〕〔S6〕✕ 🖉 🛑 💻 🔁

④④④ ▼▼▼▼ Residence Inn
            Detroit-Livonia **A** 🐾
(734) 462-4201. **$89-$139.** 17250 Fox Dr. I-275, exit 170 (6 Mile Rd), just nw. Int corridors. **Pets:** Other species. $200 one-time fee/room. Designated rooms, service with restrictions, supervision.
〔SAVE〕〔S6〕✕ 〔S.M〕🖉 🖉 🛑 💻 🔁

MADISON HEIGHTS

④④④ ▼▼▼ Red Roof Inn **M**
(248) 583-4700. **$50-$72.** 32511 Concord Dr. I-75, exit 65A, just e, then just s. Ext corridors. **Pets:** Accepted.
〔SAVE〕✕ 🖉

④④④ ▼▼▼▼ Residence Inn by Marriott-Madison
            Heights **M** 🐾
(248) 583-4322. **$89-$139.** 32650 Stephenson Hwy. I-75, exit 65B, just w, then just s. Ext corridors. **Pets:** Other species. $240 one-time fee/room. Service with restrictions, supervision.
〔SAVE〕✕ 🖉 🛑 💻 🔁

NOVI

▼▼▼▼ Hilton-Novi **H**
(248) 349-4000. **$89-$229.** 21111 Haggerty Rd. I-275, exit 167, just w, then just s. Int corridors. **Pets:** Accepted.
〔SAVE〕〔S6〕✕ 🖉 🛑 💻 〔¶〕 🔁

PLYMOUTH

④④④ ▼▼▼ Red Roof Inn-Plymouth **M**
(734) 459-3300. **$58-$71.** 39700 Ann Arbor Rd. I-275, exit 28, just e. Ext corridors. **Pets:** Medium. Service with restrictions, crate.
〔SAVE〕✕ 🖉 🖉

PONTIAC

④④④ ▼▼▼▼ Residence Inn by Marriott
            Detroit/Pontiac **A**
(248) 858-8664. **$143-$170.** 3333 Centerpoint Pkwy. I-75, exit 75 (Square Lake Rd), w via Opdyke Rd. Int corridors. **Pets:** Large. $5 daily fee/pet. Service with restrictions, crate.
〔SAVE〕〔S6〕✕ 🖉 🖉 🛑 💻 🔁

ROCHESTER HILLS

④④④ ▼▼▼ Red Roof Inn **M**
(248) 853-6400. **$55-$77.** 2580 Crooks Rd. Jct M-59 and Crooks Rd. Ext corridors. **Pets:** Medium, other species. Service with restrictions.
〔SAVE〕✕ 🖉 🖉 🛑

ROMULUS

④④④ ▼▼▼ Baymont Inn & Suites
            Detroit-Airport **M**
(734) 722-6000. **$79-$89.** 9000 Wickham Rd. I-94, exit 198 (Merriman Rd). Int corridors. **Pets:** Accepted.
〔SAVE〕〔S6〕✕ 🖉 🛑 💻

④④④ ▼▼▼▼ Detroit Airport Marriott Hotel **H**
(734) 941-9400. **$189-$199.** Detroit Metro Airport. I-94, exit 198 (Merriman Rd). Int corridors. **Pets:** Small. $75 one-time fee/room. Service with restrictions, supervision.
〔SAVE〕✕ 〔S.M〕🖉 🖉 🛑 💻

④④④ ▼▼▼▼ Romulus Marriott At Detroit
            Airport **H**
(734) 729-7555. **$149-$164.** 30559 Flynn Dr. I-94, exit 198 (Merriman Rd). Int corridors. **Pets:** Other species. $75 one-time fee/room. Service with restrictions.
〔SAVE〕✕ 〔S.M〕🖉 🛑 💻 〔¶〕 🔁

ROSEVILLE

④④④ ▼▼▼▼ Baymont Inn & Suites
            Detroit-Roseville **M**
(586) 296-6910. **$79-$89.** 20675 13 Mile Rd. I-94, exit 232 (Little Mack Rd). Int corridors. **Pets:** Accepted.
〔SAVE〕〔S6〕✕ 〔S.M〕🖉 🛑 💻

(AAA) ▼▼▼▼ Georgian Inn Ⓜ
(586) 294-0400. **$76-$165.** 31327 Gratiot Ave. I-94, exit 27 eastbound (Gratiot Ave) just w; exit 232 westbound (Little Mack Rd), on SR 3, then n of 13 Mile Rd. Ext corridors. **Pets:** Medium, dogs only. Service with restrictions, supervision.
[SAVE] [S🐾] [X] [📠] [💻] [🍴] [🏊]

SOUTHFIELD

▼▼▼▼ Hilton Inn-Southfield Ⓜ
(248) 357-1100. **$169-$179.** 26000 American Dr. US 10 (Northwestern Hwy), just w on Beck Rd, then 0.3 mi s on Franklin Rd. Int corridors. **Pets:** Accepted.
[SAVE] [S🐾] [X] [🐾] [📠] [💻] [🍴] [🏊]

▼▼▼ Holiday Inn-Southfield Ⓜ
(248) 353-7700. **$129.** 26555 Telegraph Rd. I-696, exit 10, just s on US 24. Int corridors. **Pets:** Accepted.
[ASK] [S🐾] [X] [🐾] [📠] [💻] [🍴] [🏊]

▼▼▼ Homestead Studio
    Suites-Detroit/Southfield Ⓜ
(248) 213-4500. **Call for rates.** 28500 Northwestern Hwy. I-696, exit 9, just nw of jct US 24 (Telegraph Rd). Int corridors. **Pets:** Other species. $75 one-time fee/room. Service with restrictions.
[X] [♿M] [🐾] [🔧] [📠] [💻]

(AAA) ▼▼ Red Roof Inn-Southfield Ⓜ
(248) 353-7200. **$61-$81.** 27660 Northwestern Hwy. I-696, exit 9, just nw of Telegraph Rd. Ext corridors. **Pets:** Other species. Designated rooms, service with restrictions, supervision.
[SAVE] [X] [📠]

SOUTHGATE

(AAA) ▼▼▼▼ Baymont Inn & Suites
    Detroit-Southgate Ⓜ
(734) 374-3000. **$79-$89.** 12888 Reeck Rd. I-75, exit 37 (Northline Rd). Int corridors. **Pets:** Accepted.
[SAVE] [S🐾] [X] [🐾] [📠] [💻]

TAYLOR

(AAA) ▼▼▼ Red Roof Inn-Taylor Ⓜ
(734) 374-1150. **$56-$76.** 21230 Eureka Rd. I-75, exit 36 (Eureka Rd). Ext corridors. **Pets:** Accepted.
[SAVE] [X]

TROY

▼▼ Drury Inn Ⓜ
(248) 528-3330. **$65-$129.** 575 W Big Beaver Rd. I-75, exit 69 (Big Beaver Rd), 0.3 mi e. Int corridors. **Pets:** Large, other species. Designated rooms, service with restrictions, supervision.
[X] [🐾] [📠] [💻] [🍴] [🏊]

▼▼▼▼ Holiday Inn-Troy Ⓜ
(248) 689-7500. **$69-$139.** 2537 Rochester Ct. I-75, exit 67, 0.3 mi sw on Rochester Rd, just w. Int corridors. **Pets:** Large. Service with restrictions.
[ASK] [S🐾] [X] [📠] [💻] [🍴] [🏊]

(AAA) ▼▼▼ Red Roof Inn-Troy Ⓜ
(248) 689-4391. **$55-$76.** 2350 Rochester Ct. I-75, exit 67, 0.3 mi sw. Ext corridors. **Pets:** Accepted.
[SAVE] [X] [🐾]

(AAA) ▼▼▼▼ Residence Inn by Marriott Ⓐ
(248) 689-6856. **$139.** 2600 Livernois Rd. I-75, exit 69 (Big Beaver Rd), 0.5 mi e, then 0.5 mi s. Ext corridors. **Pets:** Accepted.
[SAVE] [S🐾] [X] [🐾] [📠] [💻] [🏊]

UTICA

(AAA) ▼▼▼ Baymont Inn & Suites
    Detroit-Utica Ⓜ
(586) 731-4700. **$99-$109.** 45311 Park Ave. At jct of Van Dyke (M-53) and Hall Rd (M-59). Int corridors. **Pets:** Medium. $100 deposit/room. Designated rooms, service with restrictions, supervision.
[SAVE] [S🐾] [X] [🐾] [♿] [📠] [💻] [🏊]

▼▼▼ Staybridge Suites-Utica Ⓜ
(586) 323-0101. **$112.** 46155 Utica Park Blvd. Int corridors. **Pets:** Accepted.
[ASK] [S🐾] [X] [📠] [💻] [🏊]

WARREN

(AAA) ▼▼▼ Baymont Inn & Suites Detroit-Warren
    Tech Center Ⓜ
(586) 574-0550. **$64-$74.** 30900 Van Dyke Rd. I-696, exit 23, 2 mi n, 12.5 mi n on SR 53. Int corridors. **Pets:** Accepted.
[SAVE] [S🐾] [X] [🐾] [📠] [💻]

(AAA) ▼▼▼ Red Roof Inn-Warren Ⓜ
(586) 573-4300. **$51-$72.** 26300 Dequindre Rd. I-696, exit 20, just ne. Ext corridors. **Pets:** Accepted.
[SAVE] [X] [🐾] [📠]

(AAA) ▼▼▼▼ Residence Inn by Marriott Ⓜ
(586) 558-8050. **$124-$134, 5 days notice.** 30120 Civic Center Blvd. I-696, exit 23, 2 mi n on Van Dyke Ave. Ext/int corridors. **Pets:** Other species. $75 one-time fee/room. Service with restrictions, crate.
[SAVE] [S🐾] [X] [🐾] [♿] [📠] [💻] [🏊]

WIXOM

▼▼▼ Baymont Inn & Suites Ⓜ
(248) 735-2781. **$54-$109.** 48953 Alpha Dr. I-96, exit 159, just n. Int corridors. **Pets:** Accepted.
[ASK] [S🐾] [X] [♿M] [♿] [📠] [💻] [🏊]

❖ **END METROPOLITAN AREA** ❖

DOUGLAS

▼▼▼▼ **AmericInn of Saugatuck/Douglas** **M**
(616) 857-8581. **$89-$249, 7 days notice.** 2905 Blue Star Hwy. I-196, exit 36, 1 mi n. Int corridors. **Pets:** Medium, dogs only. Designated rooms, service with restrictions, supervision.
(ASK) (S🐾) (X) (👓M) (🔌) (🐾) (📶) (💻) (🏊)

EAGLE HARBOR

🔷🔷 **Shoreline Resort** **M!**
(906) 289-4441. **$66-$77.** 201 Front St, F #2015. On SR 26. Ext corridors. **Pets:** Medium, other species. Supervision.
(SAVE) (S🐾) (💻) (🍴) (X) (🐾) (☎)

EAST LANSING

🔷🔷 ▼▼▼▼ **Residence Inn by Marriott** **🅰** ✿
(517) 332-7711. **$119-$225.** 1600 E Grand River Ave. US 127, exit Grand River Ave, 2.6 mi se on SR 43. Ext corridors. **Pets:** Other species. $100 one-time fee/room. Service with restrictions.
(SAVE) (S🐾) (X) (🐾) (📶) (💻) (🏊)

ESCANABA

▼ **Bay View Motel** **M**
(906) 786-2843. **$39-$60, 14 days notice.** 4.5 mi n on US 2/41 and SR 35. Ext/int corridors. **Pets:** Accepted.
(X) (📶) (🏊)

🔷🔷 ▼ **Hiawatha Motel** **M**
(906) 786-1341. **$40-$65.** 2400 Ludington St. 0.5 mi w on US 2/41. Ext corridors. **Pets:** Other species. $2 daily fee/pet. Service with restrictions, supervision.
(SAVE) (S🐾) (X) (📶)

FENTON

▼▼▼▼ **Holiday Inn Express Hotel & Suites** **🅷**
(810) 714-7171. **$70-$110.** 17800 Silver Pkwy. US 23, exit 78, just w, then 1 mi n. Int corridors. **Pets:** Small. Service with restrictions, supervision.
(ASK) (S🐾) (X) (👓M) (🔌) (📶) (💻) (🏊)

FLINT

🔷🔷 ▼▼▼ **AmericInn Flint** **M**
(810) 233-9000. **$69-$89.** 6075 Hill 23 Dr. US 23 and Hill Rd, exit 90; I-75 N, exit 475 to Hill Rd. Int corridors. **Pets:** Medium. Designated rooms, service with restrictions, supervision.
(SAVE) (S🐾) (X) (📶) (💻) (🏊)

🔷🔷 ▼▼▼▼ **Baymont Inn & Suites-Flint** **M**
(810) 732-2300. **$69-$89.** 4160 Pier North Blvd. I-75, exit 122, just w on Pierson Rd. Int corridors. **Pets:** Accepted.
(SAVE) (S🐾) (🔌) (📶) (💻)

▼▼🔷▼ **Holiday Inn Express** **M**
(810) 238-7744. **$82-$100.** 1150 Robert T Longway Blvd. I-475, exit 8A. Int corridors. **Pets:** Accepted.
(ASK) (S🐾) (X) (🐾) (📶) (💻)

🔷🔷 ▼▼ **Howard Johnson Lodge** **M**
(810) 733-5910. **$40-$65, 7 days notice.** G-3277 Miller Rd. I-75, exit 117 southbound; exit 117B northbound, just w. Ext corridors. **Pets:** Accepted.
(SAVE) (S🐾) (X) (📶) (💻) (🏊)

🔷🔷 ▼▼▼ **Red Roof Inn-Flint** **M**
(810) 733-1660. **$45-$66.** G-3219 Miller Rd. I-75, exit 117B (Miller Rd), just w. Ext corridors. **Pets:** Small. Service with restrictions, supervision.
(SAVE) (X) (🐾) (🔌) (📶)

FRANKENMUTH

▼▼▼▼ **Drury Inn & Suites** **M**
(989) 652-2800. **$69-$146.** 260 S Main St. Center; on SR 83. Int corridors. **Pets:** Small. No service, supervision.
(X) (👓M) (🔌) (📶) (💻) (🏊)

GAYLORD

🔷🔷 ▼▼▼▼ **Best Western Royal Crest Motel** **M**
(989) 732-6451. **$59-$99, 3 days notice.** 803 S Otsego Ave. I-75, exit 279, 2.3 mi ne on I-75 business loop. Int corridors. **Pets:** Supervision.
(SAVE) (S🐾) (X) (📶) (💻) (🏊)

🔷🔷 ▼▼ **Downtown Motel** **M**
(989) 732-5010. **$38-$68.** 208 S Otsego Ave. I-75, exit 282, 0.5 mi e and 0.3 mi s on I-75 business loop. Ext corridors. **Pets:** Other species. $5 daily fee/room. Service with restrictions, supervision.
(SAVE) (S🐾) (X) (📶)

▼▼ **Holiday Inn** **M!** ✿
(989) 732-2431. **$65-$84.** 833 W Main St. I-75, exit 282, 0.3 mi e on SR 32. Ext/int corridors. **Pets:** Other species. Designated rooms, service with restrictions, supervision.
(ASK) (X) (📶) (💻) (🍴) (🏊)

🔷🔷 ▼▼🔷 **Super 8 Motel** **M**
(989) 732-5193. **$49-$120.** 1042 W Main. I-75, exit 282 (SR 32), just w. Ext/int corridors. **Pets:** Accepted.
(SAVE) (S🐾) (X) (📶) (🏊)

🔷🔷 ▼▼ **Timberly Motel** **M**
(989) 732-5166. **$48-$84, 10 days notice.** 881 S Otsego Ave. I-75, exit 279, 2.5 mi n on I-75 business loop (Old US 27). Ext corridors. **Pets:** Large, other species. $8 one-time fee/room. Supervision.
(SAVE) (S🐾) (X)

GRAND MARAIS

▼▼ **Voyageur's Motel** **M**
(906) 494-2389. **$66-$70.** E Wilson St. 0.5 mi e of SR 77. Ext corridors. **Pets:** Small, dogs only. $5 daily fee/pet. Designated rooms, service with restrictions, supervision.
(ASK) (X) (📶) (💻) (🐾)

GRAND RAPIDS

▼▼ ▼▼ Days Inn-Downtown 🅗
(616) 235-7611. **$79-$89.** 310 Pearl St NW. US 131, exit Pearl St. Int corridors. **Pets:** Accepted.
🅢🅐🅥🅔 🆂🅓 ✖ 🈁 🖵 🍴 ➿

▼▼▼▼ Homewood Suites by Hilton 🅜
(616) 285-7100. **$69-$129.** 3920 Stahl Dr SE. I-96, exit 43A (28th St SW), 1.5 mi w to E Paris Ave, then just n. Int corridors. **Pets:** Accepted.
🅢🅐🅥🅔 🆂🅓 ✖ 🅓🅜 🄺 🈁 🖵 ➿

GRANDVILLE

🄰🄰🄰 ▼▼▼▼ Residence Inn by Marriott Grand Rapids West 🅜
(616) 538-1100. **$109.** 3451 Rivertown Point Ct SW. I-196, exit 67, 1.7 mi e. Int corridors. **Pets:** Accepted.
🅢🅐🅥🅔 ✖ 🈁 🖵 ➿

GRAYLING

🄰🄰🄰 ▼▼▼▼ Holiday Inn 🅜🄸 🐾
(989) 348-7611. **$79-$129.** 2650 S Business Loop. I-75 business loop, 0.8 mi s. Ext/int corridors. **Pets:** Other species. Service with restrictions.
🅢🅐🅥🅔 🆂🅓 ✖ 🅓🅜 🄺 🈁 🖵 🍴 ➿

🄰🄰🄰 ▼▼ North Country Lodge 🅜
(989) 348-8471. **$55-$175.** 617 N I-75 Business Loop. 1 mi n. Ext corridors. **Pets:** Other species. Designated rooms, supervision.
🅢🅐🅥🅔 ✖ 🈁

▼▼ ▼▼ Super 8 Motel 🅜
(989) 348-8888. **$54-$75.** 5828 Nelson A Miles Pkwy. I-75, exit 251. Int corridors. **Pets:** Other species. $50 deposit/pet. Service with restrictions, supervision.
🄰🅂🄺 ✖ 🚳 🈁 ➿

HANCOCK

▼▼ ▼▼ Best Western Copper Crown Motel 🅜
(906) 482-6111. **$60-$63, 7 days notice.** 235 Hancock Ave. On US 41 S. Ext/int corridors. **Pets:** Accepted.
🅢🅐🅥🅔 🆂🅓 ✖ 🖵 ➿

HART

▼▼ ▼▼ Budget Host Hart Motel 🅜
(231) 873-1855. **$49-$119.** 4143 Polk Rd. US 31, exit Mears/Hart, just e on US 31 business route. Int corridors. **Pets:** Very small, dogs only. $25 deposit/pet. No service, supervision.
🄰🅂🄺 🆂🅓 ✖ 🖵

🄰🄰🄰 ▼▼▼▼ Comfort Inn 🅜
(231) 873-3456. **$69-$175.** 2248 N Comfort Dr. US 31, exit Mears/Hart, just e on US 31 business route. Int corridors. **Pets:** Other species. $10 daily fee/pet. Service with restrictions, supervision.
🅢🅐🅥🅔 🆂🅓 ✖ 🄺 🈁 ➿

HOLLAND

🄰🄰🄰 ▼▼▼▼ Best Western Kelly Inn & Suites 🅜
(616) 994-0400. **$99-$149.** 2888 W Shore Dr. US 31, exit Felch St E, just n. Ext/int corridors. **Pets:** Service with restrictions, supervision.
🅢🅐🅥🅔 🆂🅓 🅓🅜 🄯 🄺 🈁 🖵 ➿

HONOR

🄰🄰🄰 ▼▼ Sunny Woods Resort 🅜
(231) 325-3952. **$55-$89, 3 days notice.** 14065 Honor Hwy. 3 mi e on US 31. Ext corridors. **Pets:** Accepted.
🅢🅐🅥🅔 ✖ 🈁 🖵 ⊠

HOUGHTON

🄰🄰🄰 ▼▼ ▼▼ Best Western-Franklin Square Inn 🅜🄸
(906) 487-1700. **$84-$169, 7 days notice.** 820 Shelden Ave. Center. Int corridors. **Pets:** $9 daily fee/room. Designated rooms, service with restrictions, supervision.
🅢🅐🅥🅔 🆂🅓 ✖ 🈁 🖵 🍴 ➿

▼▼ ▼▼ Best Western King's Inn 🅜
(906) 482-5000. **$65-$110, 48 days notice.** 215 Shelden Ave. Center; on US 41. Int corridors. **Pets:** Other species. $6 daily fee/room. Service with restrictions, crate.
🅢🅐🅥🅔 🆂🅓 ✖ 🈁 🖵 ➿

HOUGHTON LAKE

▼▼ Hillside Motel 🅜 🐾
(989) 366-5711. **$64-$74, 3 days notice.** 3419 W Houghton Lake Dr. On SR 55, 6 mi e of US 27; 10 mi w of I-75. Ext corridors. **Pets:** Other species. Service with restrictions, supervision.
🄰🅂🄺 🆂🅓 ✖ 🈁

🄰🄰🄰 ▼▼ Holiday On The Lake 🅜🄸
(989) 422-5195. **$60-$120, 7 days notice.** 100 Clearview Dr. On Old US 27, 0.5 mi n of SR 55. Ext corridors. **Pets:** Accepted.
🅢🅐🅥🅔 🆂🅓 ✖ 🈁 🖵 🍴 ⊠

HOWELL

🄰🄰🄰 ▼▼ ▼▼ Best Western Howell 🅜
(517) 548-2900. **$79-$125, 7 days notice.** 1500 Pinckney Rd. I-96, exit 137, just s on CR D19. Ext corridors. **Pets:** Small, dogs only. $10 daily fee/pet. Designated rooms, service with restrictions, supervision.
🅢🅐🅥🅔 ✖ 🈁 🖵 ➿

IMLAY CITY

🄰🄰🄰 ▼▼▼▼ Days Inn 🅜 🐾
(810) 724-8005. **$52-$70.** 6692 Newark Rd. I-69, exit 168, 0.3 mi n, then w. Int corridors. **Pets:** Large, other species. $8 one-time fee/room. Service with restrictions, supervision.
🅢🅐🅥🅔 🆂🅓 ✖ 🄯 🈁 ➿

▼▼ **Super 8 Motel-Imlay City** Ⓜ
(810) 724-8700. **$63-$75.** 6951 Newark Rd. I-69, exit 168, just n to Newark Rd, just e. Int corridors. **Pets:** Accepted.
Ⓐ$Ⓚ Ⓢ❄ ☒ 🖥

INDIAN RIVER

⨁ ▼ **Nor Gate Motel** Ⓜ
(231) 238-7788. **$40-$48, 3 days notice.** 4846 S Straits Hwy. I-75, exit 310, 0.3 mi w, then 2 mi s on Old US 27. Ext corridors. **Pets:** Accepted.
Ⓢ⃝ᴠᴇ ☒ 🖥 🖳

⨁ ▼ **Star Gate Motel** Ⓜ
(231) 238-7371. **$38-$52, 3 days notice.** 4646 S Straits Hwy. I-75, exit 310, 0.3 mi w, then 1.8 mi s on Old US 27. Ext corridors. **Pets:** Accepted.
Ⓢ⃝ᴠᴇ ☒ 🖥

IONIA

▼▼ **Super 8 Motel** Ⓜ
(616) 527-2828. **$56.** 7245 S State Rd. I-96, exit 67 (SR 66). Int corridors. **Pets:** Accepted.
Ⓐ$Ⓚ Ⓢ❄ ☒ 🔖ᴹ ⟲ 🖥

IRON MOUNTAIN

⨁ ▼▼ **Best Western Executives Inn** Ⓜ
(906) 774-2040. **$80-$105.** 1518 S Stephenson Ave. 0.8 mi e on US 2. Int corridors. **Pets:** Accepted.
Ⓢ⃝ᴠᴇ Ⓢ❄ ☒ 🖥 🏊

⨁ ▼ **Budget Host Inn** Ⓜ 🐾
(906) 774-6797. **$47-$53, 3 days notice.** 1663 N Stephenson Ave. 1.5 mi nw on US 2 and 141. Ext corridors. **Pets:** $5 daily fee/room. Designated rooms, service with restrictions, supervision.
Ⓢ⃝ᴠᴇ Ⓢ❄ ☒ 🖥 🏊

▼▼ **Days Inn** Ⓜ
(906) 774-2181. **$55-$95.** W8176 S US 2. 1.8 mi e on US 2. Ext/int corridors. **Pets:** Accepted.
Ⓢ⃝ᴠᴇ Ⓢ❄ ☒ 🖥 🏊

▼ **GH Guesthouse Inn** Ⓜ
(906) 774-6220. **Call for rates.** 1609 S Stephenson Ave. 1 mi e on US 2. Ext/int corridors. **Pets:** Accepted.
☒ 🖥 🖳

IRONWOOD

⨁ ▼ **Crestview Motel** Ⓜ 🐾
(906) 932-4845. **$40-$75, 7 days notice.** US 2. West edge. Ext corridors. **Pets:** Medium, other species. $5 daily fee/pet. No service, supervision.
Ⓢ⃝ᴠᴇ ☒ 🖥 🖳

⨁ ▼ **Royal Motel** Ⓜ
(906) 932-4230. **$36-$41, 7 days notice.** 715 W Cloverland Dr. 1 mi w on US 2. Ext corridors. **Pets:** Accepted.
Ⓢ⃝ᴠᴇ ☒

▼ **Super 8 Motel** Ⓜ
(906) 932-3395. **$75-$105, 10 days notice.** 160 E Cloverland Dr. Jct US 2 and US 2 business route. Int corridors. **Pets:** Other species. $25 deposit/room. Designated rooms, service with restrictions, supervision.
Ⓐ$Ⓚ Ⓢ❄ ☒ 🖥 🖳

ISHPEMING

⨁ ▼▼ **Best Western Country Inn** Ⓜ❗
(906) 485-6345. **$68-$90.** 850 US 41 W. On US 41, just n of town. Int corridors. **Pets:** Large. Designated rooms, service with restrictions, supervision.
Ⓢ⃝ᴠᴇ Ⓢ❄ ☒ 🖥 🍴 🏊

JACKSON

▼▼▼ **Holiday Inn** Ⓜ❗
(517) 783-2681. **$82-$95.** 2000 Holiday Inn Dr. I-94, exit 138, just nw. Ext/int corridors. **Pets:** Small. $15 daily fee/room. Designated rooms, service with restrictions, supervision.
Ⓐ$Ⓚ Ⓢ❄ ☒ ⟲ 🔖ᴹ 🖥 🖳 🍴 🏊 ☒

▼ **Motel 6–1088** Ⓜ
(517) 789-7186. **$43-$57.** 830 Royal Dr. I-94, exit 138, just se. Ext corridors. **Pets:** Accepted.
Ⓢ❄ ☒ ⟲ 🔖ᴹ

KALAMAZOO

▼▼ **Days Inn Airport** Ⓜ❗
(616) 381-7070. **$60-$82.** 3522 Sprinkle Rd. I-94, exit 80, just s. Int corridors. **Pets:** Accepted.
Ⓢ⃝ᴠᴇ Ⓢ❄ ☒ ⟲ 🖥 🏊

▼ **Knights Inn** Ⓜ
(616) 381-5000. **$31-$66.** 1211 S Westnedge Ave. I-94, exit 76B, 3 mi n, w on Park Place, then just s. Ext/int corridors. **Pets:** Accepted.
Ⓐ$Ⓚ Ⓢ❄ ☒ 🖥

▼▼▼ **Lees Inn & Suites** Ⓜ
(616) 382-6100. **Call for rates.** 2615 Fairfield Rd. I-94, exit 78, just s. Int corridors. **Pets:** Accepted.
☒ 🔖ᴹ 🖥 🏊

⨁ ▼▼ **Red Roof Inn-East** Ⓜ
(616) 382-6350. **$49-$71.** 3701 E Cork St. I-94, exit 80 (Sprinkle Rd), just nw. Ext corridors. **Pets:** Accepted.
Ⓢ⃝ᴠᴇ ☒ 🔖ᴹ 🔖

⨁ ▼▼▼ **Red Roof Inn-West** Ⓜ
(616) 375-7400. **$51-$68.** 5425 W Michigan Ave. US 131, exit 36B (Stadium Dr), just nw. Ext corridors. **Pets:** Accepted.
Ⓢ⃝ᴠᴇ ☒ 🖥

KENTWOOD

▼▼▼ **Comfort Inn** Ⓜ
(616) 957-2080. **$80-$100.** 4155 28th St SE. I-96, exit 43A, 1.5 mi w on SR 11. Int corridors. **Pets:** Large. Service with restrictions, crate.
Ⓢ⃝ᴠᴇ Ⓢ❄ ☒ 🔖 🖥 🖳

(A) ▼▼▼▼ Residence Inn by Marriott East **A**
(616) 957-8111. **$120-$159.** 2701 E Beltline. Jct SR 11 and
E Beltline (SR 37). Ext corridors. **Pets:** Accepted.
SAVE S X 🐾 🗄 💳 🛋

LAKE CITY

(A) ▼ Northcrest Motel **M**
(231) 839-2075. **$55-$80.** 1341 S Lakeshore. 1 mi s on SR
55 and 66. Ext corridors. **Pets:** Accepted.
SAVE S 💳 🛋

LANSING

(A) ▼▼▼ Best Western Midway Hotel **MI**
(517) 627-8471. **$85-$125.** 7711 W Saginaw Hwy. I-96/SR
43, exit 93B, just e. Int corridors. **Pets:** Accepted.
SAVE S X 🗄 💳 🍴 🛋

(A) ▼▼▼▼ Hampton Inn of Lansing **M**
(517) 627-8381. **$89-$119.** 525 N Canal Rd. I-96/SR 43,
exit 93B, just e on Saginaw St. Int corridors. **Pets:** Medium.
$100 deposit/room. Designated rooms, service with restrictions, crate.
SAVE S X 🐾 🗄 💳

▼▼▼▼ Lansing's Quality Suites Hotel **M**
(517) 886-0600. **$109-$199.** 901 Delta Commerce Dr.
I-96/SR 43, exit 93B, 0.8 mi e on Saginaw St. Int corridors.
Pets: Small, other species. $10 one-time fee/room. Designated rooms, service with restrictions, supervision.
SAVE S X 🗄 💳

(A) ▼▼▼ Red Roof Inn-East **M**
(517) 332-2575. **$55-$69.** 3615 Dunckel Rd. Just e of I-496
and US 127, exit 11 (Jolly Rd). Ext corridors.
Pets: Accepted.
SAVE X 🐾 🗄

(A) ▼▼▼ Red Roof Inn-West **M**
(517) 321-7246. **$55-$71.** 7412 W Saginaw Hwy. I-96, exit
93B (W Saginaw Hwy). Ext corridors. **Pets:** Small, other
species. Service with restrictions, supervision.
SAVE X

(A) ▼▼▼▼ Residence Inn-Lansing West **A**
(517) 886-5030. **$99-$139.** 922 Delta Commerce Dr.
I-96/SR 43, exit 93B, 0.8 mi e on Saginaw St. Int corridors.
Pets: Accepted.
SAVE S X 🗄 💳 🛋

LUDINGTON

▼▼▼▼ Holiday Inn Express **M**
(231) 845-7004. **$129-$209.** 5323 W US 10. 1.4 mi w of jct
US 10 and 31. Int corridors. **Pets:** Other species. $10 one-time fee/room. Service with restrictions, supervision.
ASK S X 🔧 🗄 💳 🛋

MACKINAW CITY

(A) ▼▼▼▼ Baymont Inn Suites **M**
(231) 436-7737. **$49-$175.** 109 S Nicolet St. I-75, exit 338.
Int corridors. **Pets:** Small. $50 deposit/room. Designated
rooms, service with restrictions, supervision.
SAVE S X 🔧 🗄 💳 🛋

(A) ▼ Beachcomber Motel on the Water **M**
(231) 436-8451. **$42-$125, 3 days notice.** 1011 S Huron
Dr. 1 mi s on US 23. Ext corridors. **Pets:** Small. $5 daily
fee/pet. Designated rooms, service with restrictions, supervision.
SAVE S X 🗄

(A) ▼ The Beach House **C**
(231) 436-5353. **$39-$160, 14 days notice.** 11490 W US
23 St. 1.3 mi s. Ext corridors. **Pets:** Medium. $15 one-time
fee/pet. Supervision.
SAVE S 🗄 🛋 📠

▼▼▼ Budget Host Mackinaw City **M**
(231) 436-5543. **$46-$138, 3 days notice.** 517 N Huron
Ave. I-75, exit 339, just n of town. Ext corridors.
Pets: Accepted.
ASK S X 🛋

(A) ▼ Capri Motel **M**
(231) 436-5498. **$35-$79.** 801 S Nicolet St. I-75, exit 338;
across from information center. Ext corridors. **Pets:** Large.
$5 daily fee/pet. Service with restrictions, supervision.
SAVE X 🛋

(A) ▼▼▼ Days Inn **MI**
(231) 436-5557. **$120-$194.** 825 S Huron St. I-75 N, exit
337, 0.5 mi n to US 23, 0.3 mi e to Huron St; I-75 S, exit
338, 0.8 mi se on US 23. Ext corridors. **Pets:** Accepted.
SAVE S X 🗄 💳 🍴 🛋

▼▼▼ The Grand Mackinaw Inn & Suites **M**
(231) 436-8831. **$59-$135, 3 days notice.** 907 S Huron St.
0.8 mi se on US 23. Ext corridors. **Pets:** Accepted.
ASK S X 🗄 💳 🛋

(A) ▼▼▼▼ Holiday Inn Express at the
Bridge **M**
(231) 436-7100. **$39-$229.** 364 Louvingney. I-75, exit 339;
at bridge. Int corridors. **Pets:** Accepted.
SAVE S 🗄 💳 🛋

(A) ▼ Kings Inn **M**
(231) 436-5322. **$29-$69, 3 days notice.** 1020 S Nicolet
St. I-75 N, exit 337, 0.5 mi n; I-75 S, exit 338, 0.5 mi s. Ext
corridors. **Pets:** Small, dogs only. $10 daily fee/pet. Designated rooms, service with restrictions, crate.
SAVE S X 🗄 💳 🛋

▼▼ Lighthouse View Motel **M**
(231) 436-5304. **$35-$95.** 699 N Huron St. I-75, exit 339.
Ext corridors. **Pets:** Very small, dogs only. Designated
rooms, service with restrictions, supervision.
ASK S X 🗄 💳 🛋

Motel 6-Downtown M
(231) 436-8961. **$35-$169.** 206 N Nicolet St. I-75, exit 339; at bridge. Ext/int corridors. **Pets:** Accepted.

Ramada Inn Convention Center MI
(231) 436-5535. **$40-$230.** 450 S Nicolet. I-75, exit 338. Int corridors. **Pets:** Accepted.

Starlite Budget Inns M ❀
(231) 436-5959. **$27-$98, 3 days notice.** 116 Old US 31. I-75 S, exit 338, 0.3 mi e; I-75 N, exit 337, then just ne. Ext corridors. **Pets:** Medium, dogs only. $15 deposit/pet. Service with restrictions, crate.

Super 8 Motel Bridgeview M
(231) 436-5252. **$37-$179, 3 days notice.** 601 N Huron Ave. I-75 N, exit 339 (Nicolet St), just n, then just e. Ext/int corridors. **Pets:** Accepted.

MANISTEE

Hillside Motel M
(231) 723-2584. **$35-$120.** 1675 US 31 S. 1.5 mi s on US 31. Ext corridors. **Pets:** Accepted.

MANISTIQUE

Best Western-The Breakers Motel M ❀
(906) 341-2410. **$59-$109.** 1199 E Lakeshore US 2 Dr. 2 mi e on US 2. Ext corridors. **Pets:** Medium, dogs only. $10 daily fee/pet. Designated rooms, service with restrictions, supervision.

Comfort Inn M
(906) 341-6981. **$69-$129.** 726 E Lakeshore Dr. 0.5 mi e on US 2. Int corridors. **Pets:** Other species. $10 daily fee/pet. Service with restrictions, supervision.

MARQUETTE

Birchmont Motel M ❀
(906) 228-7538. **$44-$58.** 2090 US 41 S. 4.3 mi s on US 41 and SR 28. Ext corridors. **Pets:** Large. $6 daily fee/pet. Designated rooms, service with restrictions, supervision.

Holiday Inn MI
(906) 225-1351. **$110-$120.** 1951 US 41 W. 1.8 mi w on US 41 and SR 28. Int corridors. **Pets:** Other species. Designated rooms, service with restrictions, supervision.

Ramada Inn MI
(906) 228-6000. **$104-$120.** 412 W Washington St. 0.5 w on US 41 business route. Int corridors. **Pets:** Other species. Service with restrictions.

Tiroler Hof Inn MI
(906) 226-7516. **$64-$74.** 1880 US 41 S. 1.8 mi se on US 41 and SR 28. Ext corridors. **Pets:** Medium, dogs only. Designated rooms, service with restrictions, supervision.

Travelodge M ❀
(906) 249-1712. **$58.** 1010 M-28 E. Jct US 41 S and SR 28 E. Int corridors. **Pets:** Other species. $5 daily fee/pet. Designated rooms, supervision.

MARSHALL

Arbor Inn of Historic Marshall M
(616) 781-7772. **$52-$62.** 15435 W Michigan Ave. I-69, exit 36, just w. Ext corridors. **Pets:** Medium, other species. $5 daily fee/pet. Designated rooms, service with restrictions, crate.

MENOMINEE

Howard Johnson Express M ❀
(906) 863-4431. **$55-$70.** 2516 10th St. 1 mi n on US 41. Int corridors. **Pets:** Service with restrictions, supervision.

MIDLAND

Best Western Valley Plaza Resort MI
(989) 496-2700. **$78-$90.** 5221 Bay City Rd. US 10, exit Midland/Bay City Rd. Int corridors. **Pets:** Accepted.

Fairview Inn M
(989) 631-0070. **$73-$89.** 2200 W Wackerly St. Jct US 10 and Eastman Rd. Int corridors. **Pets:** Accepted.

Holiday Inn MI
(989) 631-4220. **$86-$200.** 1500 W Wackerly. Jct US 10 and Eastman Rd. Ext/int corridors. **Pets:** Small, dogs only. Designated rooms, supervision.

Plaza Suites Hotel M
(989) 496-0100. **$95-$105.** 5217 Bay City Rd. US 10, exit Midland/Bay City Rd. Int corridors. **Pets:** Accepted.

Sleep Inn of Midland M
(989) 837-1010. **$69-$74.** 2100 W Wackerly. Jct US 10 and Eastman Rd. Int corridors. **Pets:** Medium. Designated rooms, service with restrictions, supervision.

MONROE

(AAA) ◆◆◆◆ Comfort Inn M
(734) 384-1500. **$59-$199.** 6500 Albain Rd. I-75, exit 11, just w on La Plaisance Rd. Int corridors. **Pets:** Other species. $7 daily fee/pet. Designated rooms, service with restrictions, supervision.

[SAVE] [⬡] [✕] [⬡] [⬛] [⬛] [⬷]

(AAA) ◆ Hometown Inn M ☙
(734) 289-1080. **$50-$108.** 1885 Welcome Way. I-75, exit 15 (SR 50). Ext corridors. **Pets:** Other species. $5 daily fee/room. Service with restrictions, supervision.

[SAVE] [⬡] [✕] [⬛]

MOUNT PLEASANT

◆◆◆◆ Holiday Inn M
(989) 772-2905. **$79-$149, 3 days notice.** 5665 E Pickard Ave. Jct US 27 and SR 20 E. Ext/int corridors. **Pets:** Medium, other species. Designated rooms, service with restrictions, supervision.

[ASK] [⬡] [✕] [⬡] [⬛] [⬛] [¶] [✕]

MUNISING

(AAA) ◆ Alger Falls Motel M
(906) 387-3536. **$35-$65.** E9427 E State Hwy M28. 2 mi e on SR 28 and 94. Ext corridors. **Pets:** Small, dogs only. Designated rooms, service with restrictions, supervision.

[SAVE] [✕] [⬛]

(AAA) ◆◆ Best Western M
(906) 387-4864. **$69-$119, 3 days notice.** M28. 3 mi e on SR 28. Ext/int corridors. **Pets:** Accepted.

[SAVE] [⬡] [✕] [⬛] [¶] [⬷]

◆◆ Comfort Inn M
(906) 387-5292. **$65-$115, 3 days notice.** M-28 E. 1.5 mi e on SR 28. Int corridors. **Pets:** Designated rooms, service with restrictions, supervision.

[SAVE] [⬡] [✕] [⬛] [⬷]

◆ Days Inn M
(906) 387-2493. **$55-$115, 3 days notice.** On M-28. 0.5 mi e on SR 28. Int corridors. **Pets:** Designated rooms, service with restrictions, supervision.

[SAVE] [⬡] [✕] [⬛] [⬛] [⬷]

(AAA) ◆ Sunset Motel M
(906) 387-4574. **$41-$57.** 1315 Bay St. 1 mi e on E Munising Ave (CR 58). Ext corridors. **Pets:** Dogs only. $5 one-time fee/pet. Designated rooms, service with restrictions, supervision.

[SAVE] [✕] [⬛] [✕] [🐾] [☎]

(AAA) ◆ Terrace Motel M ☙
(906) 387-2735. **$36-$52.** 420 Prospect. 0.5 mi e, just off SR 28. Ext corridors. **Pets:** Medium. $4 one-time fee/pet. Designated rooms, service with restrictions, crate.

[SAVE] [✕] [⬛] [🐾] [☎]

NORTON SHORES

(AAA) ◆ Bel Aire Motel M
(231) 733-2196. **$58-$74.** 4240 Airline Rd. At jct Business US 31 and I-96; US 31 northbound, exit Business US 31, exit 1A Airline Rd; US 31 southbound, exit Airline Rd; westbound I-96, exit Airline Rd. Ext corridors. **Pets:** Small, dogs only. $50 deposit/pet. Service with restrictions, supervision.

[SAVE] [✕]

NORWAY

◆◆◆ AmericInn of Norway M
(906) 563-7500. **$72-$89, 7 days notice.** W 6002 US Hwy 2. 0.7 mi w on US 2. Int corridors. **Pets:** Medium. $10 one-time fee/pet. Designated rooms, service with restrictions, supervision.

[ASK] [⬡] [✕] [⬛] [⬛] [⬷]

PAW PAW

(AAA) ◆◆◆ Quality Inn & Suites M
(616) 655-0303. **$65-$130.** 153 Ampey Rd. I-94, exit 60, just nw. Int corridors. **Pets:** $20 deposit/pet. Designated rooms, service with restrictions, supervision.

[SAVE] [⬡] [✕] [⬡M] [🐾] [⬡] [⬛] [⬛] [⬷]

PETOSKEY

(AAA) ◆◆ Green Roof Inn M
(231) 348-3900. **$39-$119.** 1420 US 131 S. 1.3 mi s on US 131. Ext corridors. **Pets:** Other species. $10 daily fee/pet. Supervision.

[SAVE] [⬡] [✕] [⬛]

PLAINWELL

(AAA) ◆◆◆ Comfort Inn M
(616) 685-9891. **$83-$180.** 622 Allegan St. US 131, exit 49A, just e. Int corridors. **Pets:** Medium, other species. $10 daily fee/room. Designated rooms, service with restrictions, supervision.

[SAVE] [⬡] [✕] [⬛] [⬛] [⬷]

PORTLAND

(AAA) ◆◆◆ Best Western American Heritage Inn M
(517) 647-2200. **$79-$89.** 1681 Grand River Ave. I-96, exit 77, just n. Int corridors. **Pets:** Small, other species. Designated rooms, service with restrictions, crate.

[SAVE] [⬡] [✕] [⬡] [⬛] [⬛] [⬷]

PRUDENVILLE

(AAA) ◆ Shea's Lake Front Lodge L
(989) 366-5910. **$42-$59, 10 days notice.** 125 12th St. I-75, exit 227, 8 mi w on SR 55. Ext/int corridors. **Pets:** Small. Service with restrictions, supervision.

[SAVE] [⬛] [⬛] [✕] [🐾] [☎]

SAGINAW

Best Western–Saginaw M
(989) 755-0461. **$49-$114.** 1408 S Outer Dr. I-75, exit 149B (SR 46). Int corridors. **Pets:** Large, other species. Service with restrictions, supervision.

Four Points by Sheraton Saginaw M
(989) 790-5050. **$78.** 4960 Towne Centre Rd. I-675, exit 6, just w on Tittabawassee Rd. Int corridors. **Pets:** Small. $50 deposit/room. Service with restrictions.

Red Roof Inn M
(989) 754-8414. **$37-$66.** 966 S Outer Dr. I-75, exit 149B (SR 46). Ext corridors. **Pets:** Large, other species. Service with restrictions, supervision.

SAULT STE. MARIE

Budget Host Crestview Inn M
(906) 635-5213. **$49-$79.** 1200 Ashmun St. I-75, exit 392, 2.8 mi ne on I-75 business loop. Ext corridors. **Pets:** Accepted.

Mid-City Motel M
(906) 632-6832. **$36-$58.** 304 E Portage Ave. Just e of town, on I-75 business loop. Ext corridors. **Pets:** Medium, other species. Service with restrictions.

Royal Motel M
(906) 632-6323. **$46-$52, 3 days notice.** 1707 Ashmun St. I-75, exit 392, 2 mi ne on I-75 business loop. Ext corridors. **Pets:** Medium, dogs only. Designated rooms, service with restrictions, supervision.

Super 8 Motel M
(906) 632-8882. **$52-$76.** 3826 I-75 Business Loop. I-75, exit 392, 0.5 mi ne. Int corridors. **Pets:** Large, other species. $50 deposit/room. Service with restrictions, supervision.

SILVER CITY

Best Western Porcupine Mountain Lodge M
(906) 885-5311. **$82-$125.** 120 Lincoln Ave. On SR 107, 0.3 mi w of SR 64. Int corridors. **Pets:** Small, dogs only. $10 daily fee/room. Designated rooms, service with restrictions, supervision.

Mountain View Lodges C
(906) 885-5256. **$115, 14 days notice.** 237 M-107. Jct SR 107 and 64, 0.8 mi w on SR 107. Ext corridors. **Pets:** Dogs only. $25 one-time fee/room. Designated rooms, no service, supervision.

Tomlinson's Rainbow Lodging M
(906) 885-5348. **$50-$120, 30 days notice.** 2900 M-64. SR 64, just e of jct SR 107. Ext corridors. **Pets:** Accepted.

SPRING LAKE

Holiday Inn Grand Haven-Spring Lake M 🐾
(616) 846-1000. **$99-$159.** 940 W Savidge St. On SR 104, just e of US 131. Int corridors. **Pets:** Dogs only. $25 daily fee/room. Designated rooms, service with restrictions, supervision.

ST. IGNACE

Bay View Motel M
(906) 643-9444. **$36-$72.** 1133 N State St. 3 mi n of bridge tollgate on I-75 business route. Ext corridors. **Pets:** Accepted.

Budget Host Inn M
(906) 643-9666. **$55-$115.** 700 N State St. 1.8 mi n of bridge tollgate on I-75 business route. Ext/int corridors. **Pets:** Other species. $20 deposit/room. Designated rooms, service with restrictions, supervision.

Howard Johnson Express Inn M
(906) 643-9700. **Call for rates, 7 days notice.** 913 Boulevard Dr. Jct I-75 and US 2 W. Int corridors. **Pets:** Accepted.

Wayside Motel M
(906) 643-8944. **$35-$75.** 751 N State St. 2 mi n of bridge toll gate on I-75 business route. Ext corridors. **Pets:** Dogs only. $5 daily fee/pet. Service with restrictions, supervision.

STEVENSVILLE

Baymont Inn & Suites-St. Joseph (Stevensville) M
(616) 428-9111. **$62-$72, 30 days notice.** 2601 W Marquette Woods Rd. I-94, exit 23, just w. Int corridors. **Pets:** Accepted.

Hampton Inn M
(616) 429-2700. **$84-$104.** 5050 Red Arrow Hwy. I-94, exit 23, just se. Int corridors. **Pets:** Service with restrictions, supervision.

Park Inn International M
(616) 429-3218. **$60-$99.** 4290 Red Arrow Hwy. I-94, exit 23 (Stevensville), 0.5 mi n. Ext/int corridors. **Pets:** $10 daily fee/room. Service with restrictions, crate.

STURGIS

Green Briar Motor Inn M
(616) 651-2361. **$38-$55.** 71381 S Centerville Rd (SR 66). I-90, exit 121, 0.4 mi n. Ext corridors. **Pets:** Small, dogs only. $5 daily fee/pet. Service with restrictions, supervision.

SUTTONS BAY

Red Lion Motor Lodge M
(231) 271-6694. **$85-$95, 3 days notice.** 4290 SW Bay Shore Rd. 5 mi s on SR 22. Ext corridors. **Pets:** Medium, dogs only. $10 daily fee/pet. Service with restrictions, supervision.

TAWAS CITY

Tawas Motel-Resort M
(989) 362-3822. **$65-$85, 3 days notice.** 1124 US 23 S. 1.8 mi s on US 23. Ext corridors. **Pets:** Other species. Service with restrictions, crate.

TECUMSEH

Tecumseh Inn Motel M
(517) 423-7401. **$60.** 1445 W Chicago Blvd. 1.5 mi w on SR 50, 15 mi w of US 23, exit Dundee. Ext corridors. **Pets:** Large, other species. $25 deposit/room.

THREE RIVERS

Three Rivers Inn MI
(616) 273-9521. **$53-$63.** 1200 W Broadway. 2 mi sw on US 131 and SR 60. Int corridors. **Pets:** $10 one-time fee/pet. Service with restrictions, supervision.

TRAVERSE CITY

Holiday Inn MI ❀
(231) 947-3700. **$99-$169.** 615 E Front St. 0.5 mi e on US 31. Int corridors. **Pets:** Medium, other species. $10 daily fee/room. Designated rooms, service with restrictions, supervision.

Motel 6–4065 M
(231) 938-3002. **$36-$100.** 1582 US 31 N. 4.3 mi e. Int corridors. **Pets:** $6 daily fee/pet. Service with restrictions, supervision.

Quality Inn M
(231) 929-4423. **$45-$160.** 1492 US 31 N. 3.3 mi e. Ext/int corridors. **Pets:** Large, other species. $10 one-time fee/pet. Designated rooms, service with restrictions, supervision.

WALKER

Baymont Inn & Suites M
(616) 735-9595. **$90, 30 days notice.** 2151 Holton Ct NW. I-96, exit 28 (Walker Ave), just s. Int corridors. **Pets:** Accepted.

WATERSMEET

AmericInn of Watersmeet-Lac Vieux Desert MI
(906) 358-4949. **$65-$75.** N5384 US Hwy 45. 1.8 mi n of US 2. Int corridors. **Pets:** Medium. $100 deposit/room. Designated rooms, service with restrictions, supervision.

WEST BRANCH

La Hacienda Motel M
(989) 345-2345. **$42-$62.** 969 W Houghton Ave. I-75, exit 215, 1.5 mi e on I-75 business loop. Ext corridors. **Pets:** Accepted.

Super 8 Motel M
(989) 345-8488. **$59-$87.** 2596 Austin's Way. I-75, exit 212 (Cook Rd). Int corridors. **Pets:** Medium, other species. Service with restrictions, supervision.

WHITEHALL

Lake Land Motel M ❀
(231) 894-5644. **$40-$75.** 1002 E Colby St. On US 31 business route, 0.8 mi w of US 31. Ext corridors. **Pets:** Other species. Supervision.

WHITMORE LAKE

Best Western Whitmore Lake M
(734) 449-2058. **$65-$99.** 9897 Main St. US 23, exit 53. Ext corridors. **Pets:** Small. $25 daily fee/pet. Designated rooms, service with restrictions, supervision.

WYOMING

Super 8 Motel M
(616) 530-8588. **$60-$65, 3 days notice.** 727 44th St SW. US 131, exit 79. Int corridors. **Pets:** Other species. $10 one-time fee/pet. Service with restrictions, supervision.

CITY INDEX

AITKIN

▼▼ 40 Club Inn
(218) 927-2903. **$59-$80.** 950 2nd St NW. SR 210, 1 mi w of jct US 169. Int corridors. **Pets:** Accepted.

▼▼ Ripple River Motel
(218) 927-3734. **$55-$75.** 701 Minnesota Ave S. US 169, 0.8 mi s of jct SR 210. Ext corridors. **Pets:** Other species. $5 one-time fee/pet. Designated rooms, service with restrictions.

ALBERT LEA

(AAA) ▼▼ Albert Lea Countryside Inn Motel
(507) 373-2446. **$48-$68, 3 days notice.** 2102 E Main St. I-35, exit 11, 1.3 mi w on CR 46. Ext/int corridors. **Pets:** Medium. $5 daily fee/pet. Service with restrictions, supervision.

(AAA) ▼▼▼ Budget Host Albert Lea Inn
(507) 373-8291. **$40-$69.** 2301 E Main St. I-35, exit 11, 1 mi w on CR 46. Int corridors. **Pets:** Medium, other species. $8 daily fee/pet. Designated rooms, service with restrictions, supervision.

(AAA) ▼▼▼ Country Inn & Suites By Carlson
(507) 373-5513. **$79-$99.** 2214 E Main St. I-35, exit 12 southbound; exit 11 northbound, 1 mi w. Int corridors. **Pets:** Small. $20 one-time fee/pet. Designated rooms, service with restrictions, supervision.

ALEXANDRIA

▼▼▼ Arrowwood-A Radisson Resort
(320) 762-1124. **$99-$134.** 2100 Arrowwood Ln. I-94, exit 103, 3 mi n, 0.8 mi w on CR 82, 2.5 mi n on CR 22. Int corridors. **Pets:** Dogs only. Designated rooms, supervision.

 **Country Inn & Suites By Carlson** M ❀
(320) 763-9900. **$62-$87.** 5304 Hwy 29 S. I-94, exit 103, just sw. Int corridors. **Pets:** Very small, other species. $10 daily fee/room. Designated rooms, service with restrictions, supervision.

 Super 8 Motel M
(320) 763-6552. **$55-$70.** 4620 SR 29 S. I-94, exit 103, 0.3 mi n. Int corridors. **Pets:** Service with restrictions, supervision.

AUSTIN

 **Country Side Inn** M
(507) 437-7774. **$45-$62.** 3303 Oakland Ave W. I-90, exit 175 (Oakland Ave), just nw. Int corridors. **Pets:** Other species. $5 one-time fee/room. Service with restrictions.

Days Inn M
(507) 433-8600. **$54-$62.** 700 16th Ave NW. I-90, exit 178A (4th St NW), just nw. Int corridors. **Pets:** Designated rooms, service with restrictions.

Holiday Inn & Austin Conference Center MI
(507) 433-1000. **$65-$159.** 1701 4th St NW. I-90, exit 178A (4th St NW), just nw. Int corridors. **Pets:** Medium, other species. $15 one-time fee/pet. Designated rooms, service with restrictions, crate.

BABBITT

Timber Bay Lodge & Houseboats C
(218) 827-3682. **$120-$135, 60 days notice.** 8347 Timber Bay Rd. 2.8 mi e of jct CR 21 via CR 70 and 623. Ext corridors. **Pets:** Other species. $14 daily fee/pet. No service.

BAUDETTE

AmericInn Lodge & Suites Lake of the Woods M
(218) 634-3200. **$70-$73, 5 days notice.** 0.5 mi w on SR 11. Int corridors. **Pets:** Medium. $200 deposit/room, $20 one-time fee/room. Designated rooms, service with restrictions, supervision.

BAXTER

 **Country Inn & Suites by Carlson** M
(218) 828-2161. **$75-$125.** 15058 Dellwood Dr N. Jct SR 371 and 210, 1 mi n on SR 371. Int corridors. **Pets:** Small, dogs only. Service with restrictions, supervision.

BEMIDJI

Bel Air Motel M
(218) 751-3222. **$36-$65, 7 days notice.** 1350 Paul Bunyan Dr NW. 0.4 mi e of the nw jct of US 2, 71 and SR 197. Ext corridors. **Pets:** Accepted.

 **Best Western Bemidji** M
(218) 751-0390. **$45-$75.** 2420 Paul Bunyan Dr. Jct US 2, 71 and SR 197. Int corridors. **Pets:** Other species. $25 deposit/room. Designated rooms, service with restrictions, supervision.

Ruttger's Birchmont Lodge R
(218) 444-3463. **$36-$246, 30 days notice.** 530 Birchmont Beach Rd. Jct SR 197 (Paul Bunyan Dr NW), 3.6 mi n on CR 21 (Bemidji Ave N). Ext/int corridors. **Pets:** Other species. $10 daily fee/pet. Designated rooms, service with restrictions, crate.

BLACKDUCK

AmericInn Motel M
(218) 835-4500. **$59-$120.** 81 Brandl Dr NW. Jct US 71 and SR 72, 0.3 mi s on US 71. Int corridors. **Pets:** Accepted.

BLUE EARTH

AmericInn of Blue Earth M
(507) 526-4215. **$85-$125.** 1495 Domes Dr. I-90, exit 119 (US 169), just se. Int corridors. **Pets:** Small. $5 one-time fee/pet. Service with restrictions, supervision.

Super 8 Motel M
(507) 526-7376. **$60-$70.** 1420 Giant Dr. I-90, exit 119 (US 169), just s. Int corridors. **Pets:** Other species. $5 one-time fee/pet. Service with restrictions, supervision.

BRAINERD

Days Inn M
(218) 829-0391. **$55-$75, 3 days notice.** 1630 Fairview Rd N. On SR 210 and 371; adjacent to Paul Bunyan Amusement Center. Int corridors. **Pets:** Other species. Supervision.

Ramada Inn Brianerd MI
(218) 829-1441. **$67-$86.** 2115 S 6th St. On SR 371 business route, 1.8 mi s of jct SR 210. Ext/int corridors. **Pets:** Accepted.

BRECKENRIDGE

△△△ ▼▼▼ Select Inn of
                Breckenridge/Wahpeton **M**
(218) 643-9201. **$46-$69.** 821 Hwy 75 N. Just sw of jct US 75 N and 210. Int corridors. **Pets:** Other species. $50 deposit/pet, $5 one-time fee/pet. Designated rooms, service with restrictions, supervision.
[SAVE] [S🐾] [✕] [🐾]

▼▼ ▼▼ South Haven Inn **M**
(218) 643-3125. **$160-$210, 14 days notice.** 1120 Buffalo Ave. 1 mi s on jct US 75 and Minnesota Ave. Ext corridors. **Pets:** Accepted.
[✕] [🖥] [🖥]

CALEDONIA

△△△ ▼▼▼▼ AmericInn Motel & Suites **M**
(507) 725-8000. **$68-$78.** 508 N Kruckow Ave. Just n of Main St on SR 44, then just w on Esch Dr. Int corridors. **Pets:** $50 deposit/room. Service with restrictions, supervision.
[SAVE] [✕] [🖥] [🖥]

CANNON FALLS

△△△ ▼▼▼▼ Best Western Saratoga Inn **M**
(507) 263-7272. **$64-$125.** 31591 64th Ave. 1 mi s on US 52. Int corridors. **Pets:** Small, dogs only. $15 daily fee/room. Designated rooms, service with restrictions, supervision.
[SAVE] [✕] [🖥] [🖥] [🐾]

CROOKSTON

▼▼ ▼▼ Northland Inn of Crookston **MI**
(218) 281-5210. **Call for rates.** 2200 University Ave. 1.5 mi n on US 2 W and 75 N. Int corridors. **Pets:** $10 one-time fee/room. Designated rooms, service with restrictions, supervision.
[ASK] [✕] [🍴] [🐾]

DETROIT LAKES

△△△ ▼▼▼▼ Best Western Holland House &
                Suites **M**
(218) 847-4483. **$59-$159, 3 days notice.** 615 Hwy 10 E. 1.3 mi se on US 10. Ext/int corridors. **Pets:** Accepted.
[SAVE] [✕] [🖥] [🖥] [🐾]

△△△ ▼▼ ▼▼ Budget Host Inn **M**
(218) 847-4454. **$43-$86.** 895 Hwy 10 E. 1.5 mi se. Ext corridors. **Pets:** $10 daily fee/room. Service with restrictions, supervision.
[SAVE] [S🐾] [✕] [🖥] [🖥]

▼▼▼▼ Country Inn & Suites By Carlson **M**
(218) 847-2000. **$59-$98.** 1330 Hwy 10 E. Just e of jct US 10 and CR 53 E. Int corridors. **Pets:** Accepted.
[ASK] [S🐾] [✕] [🖥M] [🖥] [🖥] [🐾]

DULUTH

▼▼▼▼ AmericInn Hotel & Suites of
                Duluth/Proctor **MI**
(218) 624-1026. **$68-$110.** 185 US Hwy 2. Jct I-35 and US 2, 0.8 mi n. Int corridors. **Pets:** Other species. $25 deposit/pet. Designated rooms, service with restrictions, supervision.
[ASK] [S🐾] [✕] [🖊] [🖥] [🖥] [🖥] [🍴] [🐾]

△△△ ▼▼ ▼▼ Best Western Downtown Motel **M**
(218) 727-6851. **$39-$105.** 131 W 2nd St. Center; 2nd St at 2nd Ave W. Ext/int corridors. **Pets:** Accepted.
[SAVE] [S🐾] [✕] [🖥]

△△△ ▼▼▼▼ Best Western Edgewater Motel **M**
(218) 728-3601. **$64-$149.** 2400 London Rd. I-35, exit 258 (21st Ave E), just nw. Ext/int corridors. **Pets:** Dogs only. $6 daily fee/room. Designated rooms, service with restrictions, supervision.
[SAVE] [S🐾] [✕] [🖊] [🖥] [🖥] [🖥] [🐾] [✕]

▼▼▼▼ Days Inn-Duluth **M**
(218) 727-3110. **$65-$125.** 909 Cottonwood Ave. SR 194, just n of jct US 53. Int corridors. **Pets:** Other species. Service with restrictions, supervision.
[SAVE] [S🐾] [✕] [🖊] [🖥]

△△△ ▼▼▼▼ Hawthorn Suites at Waterfront
                Plaza **H**
(218) 727-4663. **$90-$259, 10 days notice.** 325 Lake Ave S. In Canal Park area. Int corridors. **Pets:** Very small, dogs only. $75 deposit/pet. Designated rooms, service with restrictions, supervision.
[SAVE] [S🐾] [✕] [🐾M] [🖊] [🖥] [🖥] [🖥] [🍴] [🐾]

▼▼▼▼ Radisson Hotel Duluth-Harborview **H**
(218) 727-8981. **Call for rates.** 505 W Superior St. Center; Superior St at 5th Ave W. Int corridors. **Pets:** Accepted.
[ASK] [✕] [🖥] [🖥] [🍴] [🐾]

▼▼ ▼▼ Voyageur Lakewalk Inn **M**
(218) 722-3911. **$35-$150.** 333 E Superior St. I-35, exit 256 (Superior St), just n at jct 4th Ave E and Superior St. Ext corridors. **Pets:** Other species. $10 one-time fee/room. Service with restrictions, supervision.
[ASK] [S🐾] [✕] [🖥] [🖥]

FAIRMONT

▼▼▼▼ Comfort Inn **M**
(507) 238-5444. **$65-$77, 7 days notice.** 2225 N State St. I-90, exit 102 (SR 15), just sw. Int corridors. **Pets:** Designated rooms, service with restrictions, supervision.
[SAVE] [S🐾] [✕] [🐾M]

▼▼▼▼ Holiday Inn **MI**
(507) 238-4771. **$79-$99, 7 days notice.** 1201 Torgerson Dr. I-90, exit 102 (SR 15), just se. Int corridors. **Pets:** Designated rooms, service with restrictions, supervision.
[ASK] [S🐾] [✕] [🖥] [🖥] [🍴] [🐾]

▼▼ Super 8 Motel **M**
(507) 238-9444. **$49-$64, 7 days notice.** 1200 Torgerson Dr. I-90, exit 102 (SR 15), just se. Int corridors. **Pets:** Designated rooms, service with restrictions, supervision.
(ASK) (S⬤) (✕)

FARIBAULT

(AAA) ▼▼▼ AmericInn Motel **M**
(507) 334-9464. **$79.** 1801 Lavender Dr. I-35, exit 59, 0.3 mi e on SR 21. Int corridors. **Pets:** Large. Service with restrictions, supervision.
(SAVE) (S⬤) (✕) (🖊) (💺) (🍴) (💻) (⚊)

(AAA) ▼▼ Select Inn **M**
(507) 334-2051. **$45-$57, 7 days notice.** 4040 SR 60 W. I-35, exit 56, just w. Int corridors. **Pets:** Accepted.
(SAVE) (S⬤) (✕) (💺) (🍴) (💻) (⚊)

FERGUS FALLS

(AAA) ▼▼▼ AmericInn Motel **M**
(218) 739-3900. **$65-$128.** 526 Western Ave N. I-94, exit 54 (SR 210), just se. Int corridors. **Pets:** Medium. $50 deposit/pet, $10 one-time fee/pet. Designated rooms, service with restrictions, supervision.
(SAVE) (✕) (♿) (🖊) (💺) (🍴) (💻) (⚊)

FINLAYSON

▼▼ Super 8 Motel **M**
(320) 245-5284. **Call for rates, 3 days notice.** 2811 SR 23. I-35, exit 195 (SR 23), just ne. Int corridors. **Pets:** Accepted.
(✕)

FOSSTON

▼▼ Super 8 Motel **M**
(218) 435-1088. **$48-$53, 10 days notice.** 108 S Amber. US 2, 0.5 mi e. Int corridors. **Pets:** Dogs only. $5 daily fee/room. Supervision.
(ASK) (S⬤) (✕) (🍴)

GAYLORD

▼▼ Gold Leaf Inn & Suites **M**
(507) 237-5860. **$51-$64.** 330 Main Ave E. 1.5 mi e. Int corridors. **Pets:** Accepted.
(✕) (💺) (🍴)

GRAND MARAIS

(AAA) ▼▼▼ Aspen Lodge **M**
(218) 387-2500. **$39-$129, 3 days notice.** 310 E Hwy 61. SR 61, just ne of center. Ext/int corridors. **Pets:** Large. Designated rooms, service with restrictions, supervision.
(SAVE) (S⬤) (✕) (♿) (💺) (🍴) (⚊)

(AAA) ▼▼▼ Best Western Superior Inn & Suites **M**
(218) 387-2240. **$59-$229, 3 days notice.** 104 1st Ave E. SR 61, just ne of center. Ext/int corridors. **Pets:** Small. Designated rooms, service with restrictions, supervision.
(SAVE) (✕) (🖊) (💺) (🍴) (💻)

▼▼ Grand Marais Inn & Suites **M**
(218) 387-1585. **$39-$175, 7 days notice.** 1800 W Hwy 61. SR 61, 1 mi sw. Ext corridors. **Pets:** Service with restrictions, supervision.
(ASK) (S⬤) (✕) (🍴) (💻)

▼▼▼ Gunflint Lodge **R**
(218) 388-2294. **$158-$348, 60 days notice.** 143 S Gunflint Lake. 43 mi n of Grand Marais, 0.8 mi e of jct CR 12 (Gunflint Tr) and 50. Ext corridors. **Pets:** Accepted.
(♿M) (🍴) (💻) (🍸) (✕) (🐾) (☎)

(AAA) ▼▼ Nor'Wester Lodge and Outfitter **C**
(218) 388-2252. **$85-$220, 30 days notice.** 7778 Gunflint Tr. 30 mi nw on CR 12 (Gunflint Tr) from jct SR 61. Ext corridors. **Pets:** Other species. $10 daily fee/pet. Designated rooms, no service, supervision.
(SAVE) (🍴) (💻) (✕) (🐾) (⚊) (☎)

▼▼ Outpost Motel **M**
(218) 387-1833. **$39-$65.** 2935 SR 61 E. 9 mi ne. Ext corridors. **Pets:** Dogs only. $5 daily fee/pet. Supervision.
(✕) (🍴) (💻) (🐾)

(AAA) ▼▼▼ Super 8 Motel **M**
(218) 387-2448. **$39-$119, 3 days notice.** 1711 W Hwy 61. On SR 61, 1 mi sw. Ext/int corridors. **Pets:** Other species. Designated rooms, supervision.
(SAVE) (S⬤) (✕) (🍴)

(AAA) ▼▼ Wedgewood Motel **M**
(218) 387-2944. **$40-$45.** 1663 E Hwy 61. SR 61, 2.5 mi ne. Ext corridors. **Pets:** Accepted.
(SAVE) (S⬤) (✕) (🐾) (☎)

GRAND RAPIDS

(AAA) ▼▼▼ Budget Host Inn **M** 🐾
(218) 326-3457. **$60-$79.** 311 E Hwy 2. Jct US 2 E and US 169 N. Ext/int corridors. **Pets:** Other species. No service, crate.
(SAVE) (✕)

(AAA) ▼▼▼ Country Inn By Carlson **M**
(218) 327-4960. **$76-$81, 30 days notice.** 2601 Hwy 169 S. US 2, 2 mi s on US 169. Int corridors. **Pets:** Accepted.
(SAVE) (S⬤) (✕) (♿M) (🖊) (💺) (🍴) (💻) (⚊)

(AAA) ▼▼▼ Sawmill Inn **MI**
(218) 326-8501. **$75-$97.** 2301 S Pokegama Ave. US 2, 2 mi s on US 169. Ext/int corridors. **Pets:** Service with restrictions, supervision.
(SAVE) (S⬤) (✕) (🖊) (🍴) (💻) (🍴) (⚊)

HARMONY

▼▼ Country Lodge Motel **M**
(507) 886-2515. **Call for rates.** 525 Main Ave N. 0.4 mi n on US 52. Int corridors. **Pets:** Accepted.
(ASK) (✕) (💺) (🍴) (💻)

HIBBING

▽▽▽▽ Hibbing Park Hotel Ⓜ
(218) 262-3481. **Call for rates.** 1402 E Howard St. On US 169 and SR 73; near the Paulucci Space Theatre. Int corridors. **Pets:** Accepted.

ASK ⊠ 🖪 🖪 🖵 🏨 🌰

HINCKLEY

ⒶⒶⒶ ▽▽▽ Hinckley Gold Pine Inn Ⓜ ✿
(320) 384-6112. **$45-$70.** 325 Fire Monument. I-35, exit 183 (SR 48), just w. Ext/int corridors. **Pets:** Dogs only. $5 daily fee/pet. Service with restrictions, supervision.

SAVE Sₒ ⊠ 🖉 🖪 🖵

INTERNATIONAL FALLS

▽▽ Hilltop Motel Ⓜ
(218) 283-2505. **$49-$79.** 2002 2nd Ave W. US 53, 1 mi s of jct US 53 and SR 11. Ext corridors. **Pets:** Accepted.

ASK Sₒ ⊠

▽▽▽ Holiday Inn Ⓜ
(218) 283-8000. **$81-$98, 3 days notice.** 1500 Hwy 71 W. 1.5 mi w on US 71 and SR 11 W. Int corridors. **Pets:** Accepted.

ASK Sₒ ⊠ 🖪 🖪 🖵 🏨 🌰

JACKSON

ⒶⒶⒶ ▽▽ Budget Host Inn Praire Winds Ⓜ
(507) 847-2020. **$43-$55.** 950 US 71. I-90, exit 73 (US 71), 0.4 mi s. Ext corridors. **Pets:** Other species. $4 daily fee/pet. Service with restrictions, supervision.

SAVE ⊠ 🖪 🖪 🖵

▽▽ Super 8 of Jackson Ⓜ
(507) 847-3498. **$72-$106, 7 days notice.** 2025 Hwy 71 N. I-90, exit 73 (US 71), just n. Int corridors. **Pets:** $6 daily fee/pet. Designated rooms, supervision.

ASK Sₒ ⊠ 🖪 🖪 🖪

LITCHFIELD

▽▽ ScotWood Motel Ⓜ
(320) 693-2496. **$119, 30 days notice.** 1017 E Frontage Rd. On US 12. Int corridors. **Pets:** Accepted.

ASK Sₒ ⊠ 🖪 🌰

LITTLE FALLS

ⒶⒶⒶ ▽▽▽ Country Inn & Suites By Carlson Ⓜ
(320) 632-1000. **$70-$80.** 209 16th St NE. Just ne of jct SR 10 and 27. Int corridors. **Pets:** Small. Service with restrictions, supervision.

SAVE Sₒ ⊠ 🖪 🖪 🖪 🖵 🌰

LONG PRAIRIE

ⒶⒶⒶ ▽▽▽ Budget Host Inn Ⓜ
(320) 732-6118. **$47-$60, 7 days notice.** 417 Lake St. On US 71/SR 27, just s of jct SR 287. Ext corridors. **Pets:** Designated rooms, service with restrictions, supervision.

SAVE Sₒ ⊠ 🖪 🖵

LUTSEN

▽▽▽▽ The Mountain Inn at Lutsen Ⓜ
(218) 663-7566. **$54-$129, 46 days notice.** Ski Hill Rd. CR 36, 1.3 mi n of jct SR 61, on road to Lutsen Mountain Ski area. Int corridors. **Pets:** Other species. $15 one-time fee/pet. Designated rooms, service with restrictions, supervision.

ASK Sₒ ⊠ 🖪

ⒶⒶⒶ ▽▽▽ Solbakken Resort ☒
(218) 663-7244. **$54-$98, 14 days notice.** 4874 W Hwy 61. SR 61, 1.3 mi n of jct CR 4, (Caribou Tr). Ext corridors. **Pets:** Other species. $80 daily fee/pet. Designated rooms, supervision.

SAVE Sₒ ⊠ 🖪 🖪 🖵 ⊠ 🖩

MANKATO

ⒶⒶⒶ ▽▽▽▽ Best Western Hotel, Restaurant & Conference Center Ⓜ
(507) 625-9333. **$70-$109.** 1111 Range St. 1.3 mi n on US 169. Int corridors. **Pets:** $25 deposit/room. Designated rooms, service with restrictions, crate.

SAVE Sₒ ⊠ 🖪 🖪 🖵 🏨 🌰

▽▽▽ Comfort Inn of Mankato Ⓜ
(507) 388-5107. **$64-$99.** 131 Apache Pl. Just s of jct US 14 and SR 22 S. Int corridors. **Pets:** Accepted.

SAVE Sₒ ⊠ 🖪 🖪 🖵 🌰

▽▽▽ Holiday Inn Ⓜ
(507) 345-1234. **$72-$109.** 101 E Main St. Main St at Riverfront Dr. Int corridors. **Pets:** Accepted.

ASK Sₒ ⊠ 🖪 🖉 🖪 🖪 🖵 🏨 🌰

MARSHALL

ⒶⒶⒶ ▽▽▽▽ Best Western Marshall Inn Ⓜ ✿
(507) 532-3221. **$66-$80.** 1500 E College Dr. SR 19, just w of jct SR 23. Int corridors. **Pets:** Supervision.

SAVE Sₒ ⊠ 🖪 🖪 🖵 🏨 🌰

▽▽▽ Comfort Inn Ⓜ
(507) 532-3070. **$68-$88, 4 days notice.** 1511 E College Dr. SR 19, just w of jct SR 23. Int corridors. **Pets:** Accepted.

SAVE Sₒ ⊠ 🖪 🖉 🖪 🖪 🖵 🌰

▽▽ Super 8 Motel Ⓜ
(507) 537-1461. **$54-$64.** 1106 E Main St. 0.3 mi se on US 59 from jct SR 23. Int corridors. **Pets:** Accepted.

ASK Sₒ ⊠ 🖉 🖪

MCGREGOR

Country Meadows Inn M
(218) 768-7378. **$60-$74.** Jct SR 65 and 210. Int corridors. **Pets:** Accepted.

MILACA

Super 8 Motel M
(320) 983-2660. **Call for rates.** 215 10th Ave SE. Jct of SR 23 and 169. Int corridors. **Pets:** Accepted.

MINNEAPOLIS-ST. PAUL
METROPOLITAN AREA

BLOOMINGTON

AmeriSuites (Minneapolis/Mall of America) H
(952) 854-0700. **$109-$149.** 7800 International Dr. I-494, exit 1B (34th Ave), just sw. Int corridors. **Pets:** Accepted.

Baymont Inn Minneapolis-Airport (Bloomington) M
(952) 881-7311. **$69-$79.** 7815 Nicollet Ave S. I-494, exit 4A (Nicollet Ave), just s. Int corridors. **Pets:** Accepted.

Best Western Thunderbird Hotel MI
(952) 854-3411. **$99-$139.** 2201 E 78th St. I-494, exit 2A (24th Ave), just s. Int corridors. **Pets:** Accepted.

Bloomington Staybridge Suites By Holiday Inn M
(952) 831-7900. **$69-$199.** 8150 Bridge Rd. I-494, exit 6B (France Ave), just se of SR 100, 1 mi w on frontage road. Int corridors. **Pets:** $75 one-time fee/room. Service with restrictions, crate.

Clarion Hotel Bloomington MI
(952) 830-1300. **$79-$159.** 8151 Bridge Rd. I-494, exit 6B (France Ave), just se of SR 100, 1 mi w on frontage road. Int corridors. **Pets:** Medium, other species. $10 daily fee/room. Designated rooms, service with restrictions, supervision.

Exel Inn of Minneapolis M
(952) 854-7200. **$65-$91.** 2701 E 78th St. I-494, exit 2A (24th Ave), just se. Int corridors. **Pets:** Accepted.

Hilton Minneapolis-St. Paul Airport H
(952) 854-2100. **$125-$129.** 3800 E 80th St. I-494, exit 1B (34th Ave), just se. Int corridors. **Pets:** Accepted.

Minneapolis Airport Marriott MI
(952) 854-7441. **$159, 30 days notice.** 2020 E 79th St. I-494, exit 2A (24th Ave), just sw. Int corridors. **Pets:** Accepted.

Radisson Hotel South & Plaza Tower H
(952) 835-7800. **$99-$129.** 7800 Normandale Lake Blvd. I-494, exit 7 (SR 100). Int corridors. **Pets:** Accepted.

Sofitel Minneapolis H
(952) 835-1900. **$139-$229.** 5601 W 78th St. Just nw of jct I-494 and SR 100, access via SR 100 and Industrial Blvd. Int corridors. **Pets:** Small, dogs only. Service with restrictions, crate.

BROOKLYN CENTER

Baymont Inn & Suites Minneapolis-Brooklyn Center M
(763) 561-8400. **$69-$79.** 6415 James Cir N. I-94/694, exit 34 (Shingle Creek Pkwy). Int corridors. **Pets:** Medium, other species. $50 deposit/room. Designated rooms, service with restrictions, supervision.

Hilton Minneapolis North H 🐾
(763) 566-8000. **$80-$154.** 2200 Freeway Blvd. I-94/694, exit 34 (Shingle Creek Pkwy). Int corridors. **Pets:** Small. $50 deposit/room. Service with restrictions, supervision.

BROOKLYN PARK

Ramada Inn and Conference Center Northwest MI
(763) 566-8855. **$69-$129, 3 days notice.** 6900 Lakeland Ave N. I-94/694, exit 31, just nw on CR 81, then just e on W Broadway Ave, then just se. Int corridors. **Pets:** Small. $40 deposit/room, $10 one-time fee/room. Designated rooms, service with restrictions, supervision.

Sleep Inn M
(763) 971-8000. **$109.** 7011 Northland Cir. I-94/694, exit 30 (Boone Ave), just ne. Int corridors. **Pets:** Medium. $50 deposit/pet. Designated rooms, service with restrictions, supervision.

BURNSVILLE

▼▼▼▼ Hampton Inn M
(952) 435-6366. **$85-$105.** 14400 Nicollet Ct. Just n of jct I-35 and CR 42, off Nicollet Ave. Int corridors. **Pets:** Accepted.
SAVE S⊘ ⊠ 🔧 📧 💻 ⇌

ⒶⒶⒶ ▼▼▼ Red Roof Inn M
(952) 890-1420. **$39-$79.** 12920 Aldrich Ave S. I-35 W, exit 2 (Burnsville Pkwy), just sw. Ext corridors. **Pets:** Accepted.
SAVE ⊠ ⊘

▼▼▼ Super 8 Motel M
(952) 894-3400. **$50-$70.** 1101 Burnsville Pkwy. I-35 W, exit 2 (Burnsville Pkwy), just sw. Int corridors. **Pets:** Dogs only. $10 one-time fee/room. Service with restrictions, supervision.
ASK S⊘ ⊠

CHISAGO CITY

▼▼ Super 8 Motel-Chisago City/Lindstrom M
(651) 257-8088. **Call for rates.** 11650 Lake Blvd. 1.3 mi ne on US 8. Int corridors. **Pets:** Medium, dogs only. $10 daily fee/pet. Designated rooms, service with restrictions, supervision.
ASK ⊠ 🔧

COON RAPIDS

ⒶⒶⒶ ▼▼▼ Comfort Inn-Northtown M
(763) 785-4746. **$65-$119.** 9052 University Ave NE. Just ne of jct US 10, exit University Ave. Int corridors. **Pets:** Medium, other species. $80 deposit/room. Designated rooms, service with restrictions, supervision.
SAVE S⊘ ⊠ 🔧 💻 ⇌

ⒶⒶⒶ ▼▼▼ Country Suites By Carlson M
(763) 780-3797. **$119-$124.** 155 Coon Rapids Blvd. 0.5 mi e of SR 610. Int corridors. **Pets:** Small. $100 deposit/pet, $10 daily fee/pet. Designated rooms, supervision.
SAVE S⊘ ⊠ ⊘ 📧 🔧 💻 ⇌

EAGAN

▼▼▼ Homestead Studio Suites Hotel M
(651) 905-1778. **$74-$99.** 3015 Denmark Ave. I-35 E, exit 98 (Lone Oak Rd), just se. Int corridors. **Pets:** Other species. $75 one-time fee/room. Service with restrictions, supervision.
ASK S⊘ ⊠ ⊘ 📧 🔧 💻

ⒶⒶⒶ ▼▼▼ Residence Inn by Marriott-Mpls/St. Paul Airport A ❀
(651) 688-0363. **$129-$149.** 3040 Eagandale Pl. I-35 E, exit 98 (Lone Oak Rd), just sw; behind Lone Oak Plaza. Ext corridors. **Pets:** Other species. $5.33 daily fee/room, $100 one-time fee/room. Supervision.
SAVE ⊠ ⊘ 💻 ⇌

EDEN PRAIRIE

ⒶⒶⒶ ▼▼▼▼ AmeriSuites (Minneapolis/Eden Prairie) M ❀
(952) 944-9700. **$129.** 11369 Viking Dr. I-494, exit 11A westbound to Prairie Center Dr, then nw; exit 11A eastbound follow US 212. Int corridors. **Pets:** Small. Service with restrictions, crate.
SAVE S⊘ ⊠ ⊘M 📧 🔧 💻 ⇌

▼▼▼▼ Homestead Studio Suites-Minneapolis/Eden Prairie M
(952) 942-6818. **Call for rates.** 11905 Technology Dr. Just sw of jct I-494 and US 212 (Flying Cloud Dr). Int corridors. **Pets:** Accepted.
ASK ⊠ ⊘M 📧 🔧 💻

ⒶⒶⒶ ▼▼▼▼ The Residence Inn by Marriott-Minneapolis SW A
(952) 829-0033. **$79-$149.** 7780 Flying Cloud Dr. On US 169 S and 212 (Flying Cloud Dr), at jct I-494. Int corridors. **Pets:** Accepted.
SAVE ⊠ 🔧 💻 ⇌

ⒶⒶⒶ ▼▼▼▼ TownePlace Suites By Marriott M
(952) 942-6001. **$94-$129.** 11588 Leona Rd. I-494, at jct of US 212 (Flying Cloud Dr), southeast corner. Int corridors. **Pets:** Other species. $75 deposit/room, $5 daily fee/room.
SAVE S⊘ 🔧 💻 ⇌

EDINA

ⒶⒶⒶ ▼▼▼▼ Residence Inn Minneapolis-Edina H
(952) 893-9300. **$149-$199.** 3400 Edinborough Way. I-494, exit 6B (France Ave), 0.3 mi n to Minnesota Dr, just e. Int corridors. **Pets:** Accepted.
SAVE S⊘ ⊠ 🔧 ⊠

ELK RIVER

▼▼ AmericInn Motel M
(763) 441-8554. **Call for rates.** 17432 Hwy 10. 1.5 mi se on US 10/169. Int corridors. **Pets:** Accepted.
ASK ⊠ 📧 💻

FOREST LAKE

▼▼▼▼ Country Inn & Suites Forest Lake M
(651) 982-9799. **$74-$83.** 1959 Broadway Ave. I-35, exit 131 (CR 2), just sw. Int corridors. **Pets:** Small. $25 one-time fee/pet. Service with restrictions, supervision.
ASK S⊘ ⊠ ⊘M 📧 🔧 💻 ⇌

FRIDLEY

ⒶⒶⒶ ▼▼▼▼ Best Western Kelly Inn MI
(763) 571-9440. **$80-$95.** 5201 Central Ave NE. I-694, exit 38 (Central Ave/SR 65), 0.3 mi s. Ext/int corridors. **Pets:** Small. Designated rooms, service with restrictions, supervision.
SAVE S⊘ ⊠ ⊘ 📧 🔧 💻 ⇌

LAKEVILLE

▼▼▼▼ Comfort Inn M
(952) 898-3700. **$64-$109.** 10935 176th St W. I-35, exit 85
(SR 50), just se. Int corridors. **Pets:** Other species. $10
one-time fee/room. Designated rooms, service with restrictions, supervision.

⊕⊕ ▼▼▼ Super 8 Motel M
(952) 469-1134. **$60-$85.** 20800 Kenrick Ave. I-35, exit 81
(CR 70), just e. Int corridors. **Pets:** Accepted.

MAPLE GROVE

**▼▼▼▼ Staybridge Suites Minneapolis-Maple
Grove M**
(763) 494-8856. **$109-$129.** 7821 Elm Creek Blvd. Just ne
of jct I-94/494/694. Int corridors. **Pets:** Medium. $75 one-
time fee/room. Designated rooms, service with restrictions,
crate.

MINNEAPOLIS

⊕⊕ ▼▼▼▼ Hilton Minneapolis H
(612) 376-1000. **$119-$209.** 1001 Marquette Ave. Between
S 10th and S 11th sts. Int corridors. **Pets:** Accepted.

▼▼▼▼ Holiday Inn Minneapolis Metrodome H
(612) 333-4646. **$129-$185.** 1500 Washington Ave S.
Washington and S 15th aves. Int corridors. **Pets:** Accepted.

▼▼▼▼ The Marquette Hotel H
(612) 333-4545. **$99-$289.** 710 Marquette Ave. Marquette
Ave and S 7th St. Int corridors. **Pets:** Accepted.

▼▼▼▼ Millenium Hotel Minneapolis H
(612) 332-6000. **$79-$199.** 1313 Nicollet Mall. Jct of Nicollet
Ave and Grant St. Int corridors. **Pets:** $25 one-time fee/pet.
Service with restrictions, crate.

**⊕⊕ ▼▼▼▼ Minneapolis Marriott City
Center H**
(612) 349-4000. **$279-$299.** 30 S 7th St. Between Hennepin and Nicollet aves; in City Center shopping complex. Int
corridors. **Pets:** $250 deposit/room. Service with restrictions, supervision.

**⊕⊕ ▼▼▼▼ Radisson Plaza Hotel
Minneapolis H**
(612) 339-4900. **$79-$279.** 35 S 7th St. Between Nicollet
and Hennepin aves; in Radisson-Dayton Shopping Complex. Int corridors. **Pets:** Other species. $50 one-time fee/
room. Service with restrictions, crate.

MINNETONKA

⊕⊕ ▼▼▼▼ Minneapolis Marriott-Southwest H
(952) 935-5500. **$169-$204.** 5801 Opus Pkwy. Just nw of
jct US 169 and Cross Town Hwy 62, exit Bren Rd off US
169. Int corridors. **Pets:** $100 deposit/room. Service with
restrictions, supervision.

MONTICELLO

⊕⊕ ▼▼▼ Best Western Silver Fox Inn MI
(763) 295-4000. **$64-$131.** 1114 Cedar St. I-94, exit 193,
0.3 mi se. Int corridors. **Pets:** Accepted.

⊕⊕ ▼▼▼ Days Inn M
(763) 295-1111. **$69-$99.** 200 E Oakwood Dr. I-94, exit 193,
0.3 mi se. Int corridors. **Pets:** Medium. $10 daily fee/pet.
Designated rooms, service with restrictions, supervision.

OAKDALE

▼▼▼ Wingate Inn M ☙
(651) 578-8466. **$115-$135, 14 days notice.** 970 Helena
Ave N. I-694, exit 57, just e, then just s. Int corridors.
Pets: Very small, other species. $50 deposit/pet. Desig-
nated rooms, service with restrictions, crate.

PLYMOUTH

⊕⊕ ▼▼▼ Best Western Kelly Inn MI
(763) 553-1600. **$79-$119.** 2705 N Annapolis Ln. I-494, exit
22 (SR 55), just e. Int corridors. **Pets:** Designated rooms,
supervision.

**▼▼▼ Radisson Hotel & Conference
Center H ☙**
(763) 559-6600. **$85-$127.** 3131 Campus Dr. Jct of SR 55
and CR 61, 0.8 mi nw. Int corridors. **Pets:** Other species.
Service with restrictions, crate.

⊕⊕ ▼▼▼ Red Roof Inn M
(763) 553-1751. **$49-$79.** 2600 Annapolis Ln N. I-494, exit
22 (SR 55), just se. Ext corridors. **Pets:** Large, other species.

RICHFIELD

▼▼▼▼ Candlewood Suites M
(612) 869-7704. **$50-$140.** 351 W 77th St. I-494, exit 4B
(Lyndale Ave), just ne. Int corridors. **Pets:** Accepted.

ROGERS

▼▼ ▼▼ AmericInn Motel & Suites **M**
(763) 428-4346. **$64-$115.** 21800 Industrial Blvd. I-94, exit
207 (SR 101). Int corridors. **Pets:** Accepted.
(ASK) (S&) (✕) (🐾) (🖥) (💻) (⌐)

ROSEVILLE

🔷🔷 ▼▼▼▼ Residence Inn **M**
(651) 636-0680. **$89-$149.** 2985 Centre Pointe Dr. I-35 W,
exit 25A (CR C), just se. Int corridors. **Pets:** Medium, other
species. $150 one-time fee/room. Service with restrictions,
crate.
(SAVE) (✕) (&M) (🐾) (🖥) (💻) (⌐)

ST. LOUIS PARK

🔷🔷 ▼▼ Lakeland Inn **M**
(952) 926-6575. **$50-$65.** 4025 Hwy 7. SR 7, 0.5 mi e of
SR 100. Int corridors. **Pets:** Other species. $5 daily fee/pet.
Designated rooms, service with restrictions, supervision.
(SAVE) (S&) (✕)

🔷🔷 ▼▼▼▼ TownePlace Suites-Minneapolis
West **M** ❀
(952) 847-6900. **$79-$98, 7 days notice.** 1400 Zarthan Ave
S. I-394, exit 5 (Park Place/Xenia), 0.3 mi w on 16th, then
just n. Int corridors. **Pets:** $5 daily fee/pet. Service with
restrictions.
(SAVE) (S&) (✕) (🖥) (💻) (⌐)

ST. PAUL

🔷🔷 ▼▼▼▼ Best Western Kelly Inn-State
Capitol **MI** ❀
(651) 227-8711. **$99-$114.** 161 St. Anthony Ave. Jct I-35 E
and 94; near state capitol. Int corridors. **Pets:** Other species. Designated rooms, service with restrictions, supervision.
(SAVE) (S&) (✕) (🐾) (🖥) (💻) (¶) (⌐)

🔷🔷 ▼▼ ▼▼ Exel Inn of St. Paul **M**
(651) 771-5566. **$51-$76.** 1739 Old Hudson Rd. I-94, exit
245 (White Bear Ave), just nw. Int corridors. **Pets:** Designated rooms, supervision.
(SAVE) (S&) (✕) (🐾) (🖥) (💻)

STILLWATER

🔷🔷 ▼▼▼▼ Best Western Stillwater Inn **M**
(651) 430-1300. **$72-$92.** 1750 W Frontage Rd. SR 36 at
Washington Ave, 3 mi sw. Int corridors. **Pets:** Accepted.
(SAVE) (S&) (✕) (&M) (🐾) (🖥) (⌐)

TAYLORS FALLS

🔷🔷 ▼▼ ▼▼ The Springs Country Inn **M**
(651) 465-6565. **$45-$95, 3 days notice.** 361 Government
St. US 8 and SR 95, just w. Ext corridors. **Pets:** Accepted.
(SAVE) (✕) (🖥)

WACONIA

▼▼ ▼▼ Super 8 Motel **M**
(952) 442-5147. **$50-$65.** 301 E Frontage Rd. On SR 5 at
jct CR 10. Int corridors. **Pets:** Accepted.
(ASK) (S&) (✕) (🐾) (🐾) (🖥) (💻)

WHITE BEAR LAKE

🔷🔷 ▼▼▼▼ Best Western White Bear Country
Inn **MI**
(651) 429-5393. **$95-$120.** 4940 N Hwy 61. 1 mi n on US
61 from jct SR 96. Int corridors. **Pets:** $10 daily fee/pet.
Service with restrictions, supervision.
(SAVE) (S&) (✕) (🖥) (💻) (¶) (⌐)

WOODBURY

🔷🔷 ▼▼ ▼▼ Red Roof Inn **M**
(651) 738-7160. **$49-$79.** 1806 Wooddale Dr. I-494, exit 59
(Valley Creek Rd), just se. Ext corridors. **Pets:** Accepted.
(SAVE) (✕) (🐾)

❀ **END METROPOLITAN AREA** ❀

MONTEVIDEO

▼▼▼▼ Country Inn & Suites by Carlson **M**
(320) 269-8000. **$96.** 1805 E SR 7. On SR 7. Int corridors.
Pets: $200 deposit/room. Supervision.
(ASK) (S&) (✕) (🖥) (💻) (⌐)

MOORHEAD

🔷🔷 ▼▼ ▼▼ Motel 75 **M**
(218) 233-7501. **$43-$49.** 810 Belsly Blvd. I-94, exit 1A (US
75), 0.5 mi s. Int corridors. **Pets:** Large, other species.
Designated rooms, service with restrictions, supervision.
(SAVE) (S&) (✕)

▼▼▼▼ Red River Inn & Conference Center MI
(218) 233-6171. **Call for rates.** 600 30th Ave S. I-94, exit 1A (US 75), just w. Int corridors. **Pets:** Large. $10 one-time fee/pet. Designated rooms, service with restrictions, supervision.
(ASK) (✕) (¶) (≈)

MORA

▼▼▼▼ Americinn Motel & Suites M
(320) 679-5700. **Call for rates, 14 days notice.** 1877 Frontage Rd. Just s on SR 65. Int corridors. **Pets:** Accepted.
(ASK) (✕) (⅁M) (🐾) (🛏) (🖥) (≈)

MORRIS

▲▲▲ ▼▼▼ Best Western Prairie Inn MI
(320) 589-3030. **$60-$82.** 200 SR 28 E. Jct US 59 and SR 28, just sw. Int corridors. **Pets:** Accepted.
(SAVE) (S▵) (✕) (🛏) (¶) (≈)

NEW ULM

▼▼▼▼ Holiday Inn MI
(507) 359-2941. **Call for rates, 3 days notice.** 2101 S Broadway. SR 15/68, 1.8 mi se. Int corridors. **Pets:** Accepted.
(ASK) (✕) (🛏) (🖥) (¶) (≈)

▼▼ Super 8 Motel M
(507) 359-2400. **Call for rates, 3 days notice.** 1901 S Broadway. SR 15/68 at jct 20th St S, 1.5 mi se. Int corridors. **Pets:** $5 one-time fee/room. Service with restrictions, crate.
(ASK) (✕) (⅁M) (🐾) (🛏)

NISSWA

▼▼ Nisswa Motel M
(218) 963-7611. **$49-$76, 7 days notice.** 5370 Merrill Ave. Center; just sw of Main St. Ext corridors. **Pets:** Medium, dogs only. $5 daily fee/pet. Designated rooms, crate.
(ASK) (✕) (🛏) (🖥)

OLIVIA

▼▼ The Sheep Shedde Inn M
(320) 523-5000. **$55-$125.** 2425 W Lincoln Ave. Just e of jct US 71 and 212. Int corridors. **Pets:** Other species. $5 one-time fee/room. Service with restrictions, supervision.
(✕) (🛏) (🖥) (¶)

ONAMIA

▼▼ Econo Lodge M
(320) 532-3838. **$49-$99.** 40847 US 169. US 169, 6 mi n. Int corridors. **Pets:** Accepted.
(SAVE) (S▵) (✕) (🐾) (🛏) (🖥)

▼▼▼▼ Eddy's Lake Mille Lacs Resort M
(320) 532-3657. **Call for rates.** 41334 Shakopee Lake Rd. SR 26, 6 mi n on US 169. Int corridors. **Pets:** Accepted.
(ASK) (✕) (⅁M) (🛏) (🖥) (¶) (≈) (✕)

ORR

▼▼ North Country Inn M
(218) 757-3778. **$53-$58, 14 days notice.** 4483 Hwy 53. 0.3 mi s. Int corridors. **Pets:** $10 one-time fee/pet. Service with restrictions, supervision.
(✕) (⅁M) (🛏)

ORTONVILLE

▼▼ Econo Lodge M
(320) 839-2414. **$59-$65.** RR 2, Box 25D. Jct US 12 and 75, 0.3 mi n. Int corridors. **Pets:** Accepted.
(SAVE) (S▵) (✕) (🐾) (🛏) (🖥)

OWATONNA

▼▼▼ Country Inn & Suites By Carlson M
(507) 455-9295. **$69-$99.** 130 Allen Ave SW. I-35, exit 41 (Bridge St), just se. Int corridors. **Pets:** Small. $10 one-time fee/pet. Designated rooms, service with restrictions, supervision.
(ASK) (S▵) (✕) (⅁M) (🐾) (🐾) (🛏) (🖥) (≈)

PERHAM

▼▼ Super 8 Motel M
(218) 346-7888. **$58-$69.** 106 Jake St SE. SR 78, just nw of jct US 10. Int corridors. **Pets:** Accepted.
(ASK) (S▵) (✕) (🛏)

PINE RIVER

▼▼ Travelodge M
(218) 587-4499. **$69-$89.** 2684 SR 371 SW. 1 mi s. Ext corridors. **Pets:** Large, other species. $21.30 deposit/room. Service with restrictions, supervision.
(ASK) (S▵) (✕) (🖥)

RED WING

▲▲▲ ▼▼▼▼ Best Western Quiet House & Suites M
(651) 388-1577. **$122-$193, 7 days notice.** 752 Withers Harbor Dr. 1.5 mi n on US 61, at Withers Harbor Dr; opposite side of US 61 from Pottery Mall. Ext/int corridors. **Pets:** Medium. $15 daily fee/pet. Designated rooms, service with restrictions, supervision.
(SAVE) (S▵) (✕) (⅁M) (🐾) (🛏) (≈)

▼▼▼▼ Days Inn M
(651) 388-3568. **$46-$82.** 955 E 7th St. US 61/63, 1.7 mi se. Ext corridors. **Pets:** Accepted.
(SAVE) (S▵) (✕) (🛏) (🖥) (≈)

ROCHESTER

▼▼▼▼ Country Inn & Suites By Carlson M
(507) 285-3335. **$84-$104.** 4323 Hwy 52. US 52, exit 41st St NW. Int corridors. **Pets:** Small. $10 one-time fee/room. Designated rooms, service with restrictions, supervision.
(ASK) (S▵) (✕) (🐾) (🐾) (🛏) (🖥) (≈)

▼▼ Days Inn-South M
(507) 286-1001. $49-$69. 111 28th St SE. Jct US 52 and 63 (Broadway) 0.5 mi n. Int corridors. Pets: Small. Designated rooms, service with restrictions, crate.

🆂🅰🆅🅴 🆂🗗 ⊗ 🗐 🔥 🖬

▼▼ Econo Lodge M
(507) 288-1855. $49-$69. 519 3rd Ave SW. Just s of Mayo Clinic, 3rd Ave SW at 5th St SW. Ext corridors. Pets: Medium, other species. Designated rooms, service with restrictions, supervision.

🆂🅰🆅🅴 🆂🗗 ⊗ 🗐 🖃

▼▼ Econo Lodge-South M
(507) 282-9905. $49-$69. 1850 S Broadway. Jct US 52 and 63 (Broadway), 1 mi s. Int corridors. Pets: Accepted.

🆂🅰🆅🅴 🆂🗗 ⊗ 🗐 🔥 🖬 🖃

🅐🅐🅐 ▼▼ Executive Suites Hotel and Economy Inn by Kahler MI
(507) 289-8646. $79-$119. 9 NW 3rd Ave. Just n of Mayo Clinic; across from Methodist Hospital. Int corridors. Pets: Other species. Designated rooms, service with restrictions, supervision.

🆂🅰🆅🅴 🆂🗗 ⊗ 🗐 🔥 🖬 🖃 🍴 ⊶

🅐🅐🅐 ▼▼▼ Hilton Garden Inn Rochester Downtown M
(507) 285-1234. $94-$104. 225 S Broadway. US 63 (Broadway); downtown. Int corridors. Pets: Accepted.

🆂🅰🆅🅴 🆂🗗 ⊗ 🗐ᴹ 🗐 🔥 🖬 🖃 🍴 ⊶

▼▼▼▼ Holiday Inn South MI
(507) 288-1844. Call for rates. 1630 S Broadway. US 63 (Broadway), 0.5 mi s of jct US 14. Ext/int corridors. Pets: Accepted.

🅐🆂🅺 ⊗ 🗐 🔥 🖬 🖃 🍴 ⊶

🅐🅐🅐 ▼▼▼▼ The Kahler Grand Hotel 🅗 ❀
(507) 282-2581. $99-$139. 20 2nd Ave SW. Opposite Mayo Clinic and Methodist Hospital. Int corridors. Pets: Designated rooms, service with restrictions, crate.

🆂🅰🆅🅴 🆂🗗 ⊗ 🗐 🔥 🖬 🖃 🍴 ⊶

🅐🅐🅐 ▼▼▼▼ Marriott Hotel 🅗
(507) 280-6000. $179-$220. 101 1st Ave SW. Just e of Mayo Clinic. Int corridors. Pets: Accepted.

🆂🅰🆅🅴 🆂🗗 ⊗ 🗐 🔥 🖬 🖃 🍴 ⊶

▼▼ Microtel Inn & Suites M
(507) 286-8780. Call for rates, 3 days notice. 4210 Hwy 52 N. US 52, exit 41st St NW, just w. Int corridors. Pets: Accepted.

🅐🆂🅺 ⊗ 🗐ᴹ 🔥 🖬 🖃

🅐🅐🅐 ▼▼▼▼ Quality Inn & Suites M
(507) 282-8091. $79-$98, 7 days notice. 1620 1st Ave SE. On US 63 (Broadway) from jct US 14, 0.5 mi s, just e on 16th St, then just s. Ext/int corridors. Pets: Other species. Service with restrictions.

🆂🅰🆅🅴 🆂🗗 ⊗ 🗐 🔥 🖃

🅐🅐🅐 ▼▼▼▼ Radisson Plaza Hotel 🅗 ❀
(507) 281-8000. $109-$129. 150 S Broadway. On US 63 (Broadway). Int corridors. Pets: Service with restrictions.

🆂🅰🆅🅴 🆂🗗 ⊗ 🔥 🖬 🖃 🍴 ⊶

▼▼ Super 8 Motel-South #1 M
(507) 288-8288. $49-$69. 1230 S Broadway. Jct of US 63 (Broadway) and 14. Int corridors. Pets: Accepted.

🅐🆂🅺 🆂🗗 ⊗ 🔥 🖬 🖃 ⊶

▼▼ Super 8 Motel-West M
(507) 281-5100. $45-$59. 1608 2nd St SW. Just e of US 52, exit 2nd St SW; just w of St Mary's Hospital. Int corridors. Pets: Accepted.

🅐🆂🅺 🆂🗗 ⊗ 🔥ᴹ 🔥 🖬

SAUK CENTRE

🅐🅐🅐 ▼▼▼▼ AmericInn Motel & Suites M
(320) 352-2800. $63-$124. 1230 Timberlane Dr. I-94, exit 127, just ne. Int corridors. Pets: Medium. $50 deposit/room, $10 one-time fee/room. Designated rooms, service with restrictions, supervision.

🆂🅰🆅🅴 ⊗ 🔥 🖬 🖃 ⊶

SILVER BAY

🅐🅐🅐 ▼▼▼ Mariner Motel M ❀
(218) 226-4488. $45-$70, 3 days notice. 46 Outer Dr. Just w off SR 61; at traffic signal. Ext corridors. Pets: Dogs only. Service with restrictions, crate.

🆂🅰🆅🅴 ⊗ 🖬 🖃 🐾

SLEEPY EYE

▼▼▼▼ Best Western Inn of Seven Gables M
(507) 794-5390. $71-$95. 1100 E Main St. US 14, 0.8 mi e of jct CR 4 and US 14. Int corridors. Pets: Small. $8 daily fee/pet. Designated rooms, service with restrictions, supervision.

🆂🅰🆅🅴 🆂🗗 ⊗ 🖬 ⊶

SPICER

▼▼ Northern Inn Hotel & Suites M
(320) 796-2091. $50-$80. 154 Lake Ave S. Center; on SR 23. Int corridors. Pets: Accepted.

⊗ 🖬 🖃 ⊶

ST. CLOUD

🅐🅐🅐 ▼▼▼▼ AmericInn Motel & Suites M
(320) 253-6337. $60-$87. 4385 Clearwater Rd. I-94, exit 171 (CR 75), just ne. Int corridors. Pets: $10 daily fee/room. Service with restrictions, supervision.

🆂🅰🆅🅴 🆂🗗 ⊗ 🔥ᴹ 🔥 🖬 🖃 ⊶

🅐🅐🅐 ▼▼▼▼ Best Western Americanna Inn & Conference Center M ❀
(320) 252-8700. $61-$130. 520 S US Hwy 10. Jct US 10 and SR 23, 0.3 mi s. Ext/int corridors. Pets: Medium. $10 daily fee/room. Designated rooms, service with restrictions, supervision.

🆂🅰🆅🅴 🆂🗗 ⊗ 🗐 🔥 🖬 🖃 🍴 ⊶

(AAA) ▼▼▼ Best Western Kelly Inn **MI**
(320) 253-0606. **$75-$135.** 1 Sunwood Dr. Center; SR 23 at 4th Ave S. Int corridors. **Pets:** Accepted.
[SAVE] [S◐] [✕] [♿M] [♨] [❏] [▣] [¶] [≈]

▼▼▼ Holiday Inn Express **M**
(320) 240-8000. **$65-$100.** 4322 Clearwater Rd. I-94, exit 171 (CR 75), just ne. Int corridors. **Pets:** Other species. Service with restrictions, supervision.
[ASK] [S◐] [✕] [♿M] [♨] [♨] [❏] [▣] [≈]

▼▼▼ Holiday Inn Hotel & Suites **MI**
(320) 253-9000. **$79-$105.** 75 S 37th Ave. Jct SR 15 and 23. Int corridors. **Pets:** Other species. Service with restrictions, supervision.
[ASK] [S◐] [✕] [♨] [❏] [▣] [¶] [≈]

(AAA) ▼▼ Quality Inn Waterpark **M**
(320) 253-4444. **$39-$99.** 70 S 37th Ave. Jct SR 15 and 23, just e. Int corridors. **Pets:** Accepted.
[SAVE] [S◐] [✕] [♿M] [♨] [♨] [❏] [▣] [≈]

▼▼ Ramada Limited & Suites **M**
(320) 253-3200. **$70-$90.** 121 Park Ave S. Jct SR 15 and 23, just w. Int corridors. **Pets:** Medium. Designated rooms, service with restrictions, supervision.
[ASK] [S◐] [✕] [♿M] [♨] [❏] [▣] [≈]

▼ Thrifty Motel **M**
(320) 253-6320. **$36-$44.** 130 14th Ave NE. Jct US 10 and SR 23, 0.3 mi e. Int corridors. **Pets:** Accepted.
[✕] [♨] [❏]

(AAA) ▼▼ Travelodge **M**
(320) 253-3338. **$53-$73.** 3820 Roosevelt Rd. I-94, exit 171 (CR 75), 1 mi n. Int corridors. **Pets:** Accepted.
[SAVE] [S◐] [✕] [♨] [❏] [▣]

THIEF RIVER FALLS

▼▼▼ C'mon Inn **M**
(218) 681-3000. **$66-$72.** 1586 Hwy 59 SE. 1 mi se on US 59. Int corridors. **Pets:** Designated rooms, service with restrictions, supervision.
[ASK] [S◐] [✕] [❏] [▣] [≈]

(AAA) ▼ Hartwood Motel **M**
(218) 681-2640. **$33-$40.** 1010 N Main Ave. Jct US 59 and SR 32, 0.5 mi n on SR 32. Ext/int corridors. **Pets:** Accepted.
[SAVE] [✕] [▣]

TOFTE

(AAA) ▼▼▼ AmericInn Lodge & Suites **M**
(218) 663-7899. **$65-$165, 7 days notice.** 7261 W SR 61. On SR 61. Int corridors. **Pets:** Medium. $10 one-time fee/room. Designated rooms, service with restrictions, supervision.
[SAVE] [S◐] [✕] [♨] [❏] [▣] [≈]

(AAA) ▼▼▼ Bluefin Bay on Lake Superior **C** ☀
(218) 663-7296. **$79-$525, 7 days notice.** 7198 W SR 61. On SR 61. Ext corridors. **Pets:** Medium, other species. $20 one-time fee/room. Designated rooms, service with restrictions, crate.
[SAVE] [✕] [♨] [❏] [▣] [¶] [≈] [✕] [♨]

TWO HARBORS

(AAA) ▼▼▼ Superior Shores Resort **CO**
(218) 834-5671. **$49-$429, 14 days notice.** 1521 Superior Shores Dr. On SR 61, 1.5 mi n of center. Ext/int corridors. **Pets:** Other species. $25 deposit/room. Designated rooms, service with restrictions, supervision.
[SAVE] [S◐] [✕] [♨] [❏] [▣] [¶] [≈] [✕]

VIRGINIA

▼▼▼ AmericInn Lodge & Suites **M**
(218) 741-7839. **$65-$89.** 5480 Mountain Iron Dr. US 53, just s of jct US 169. Int corridors. **Pets:** Designated rooms, service with restrictions, supervision.
[✕] [♿M] [♨] [❏] [▣] [≈]

▼▼ Lakeshor Motor Inn Downtown **M**
(218) 741-3360. **$52-$64.** 404 6th Ave W. Center; just n of Chestnut St. Ext corridors. **Pets:** Accepted.
[S◐] [✕] [♨] [▣]

▼▼▼ Park Inn **MI**
(218) 749-1000. **$74-$84.** 502 Chestnut St. Downtown; at 5th Ave W and Chestnut St. Int corridors. **Pets:** Accepted.
[ASK] [✕] [♨] [❏] [▣] [¶] [≈]

▼▼ Ski-View Motel **M**
(218) 741-8918. **$40-$46.** 903 N 17th St N. Jct US 53 and 169, 0.5 mi n on US 53, 0.7 mi e on 9th St N, 0.5 mi n on 9th Ave W. Ext/int corridors. **Pets:** Service with restrictions, supervision.
[✕] [▣]

WARROAD

▼▼ Can-Am Motel **M**
(218) 386-3807. **$49-$65, 3 days notice.** 406 Main Ave NE. 1 mi w on SR 11, on the north side of railway tracks. Int corridors. **Pets:** Accepted.
[ASK] [S◐] [✕]

▼▼ The Patch Motel **M**
(218) 386-2723. **$45-$60.** Hwy 11 W. 1 mi w. Int corridors. **Pets:** Accepted.
[ASK] [S◐] [✕] [♿M] [≈]

WILLMAR

▼▼▼ Comfort Inn **M**
(320) 231-2601. **$80-$90.** 2200 E US 12. 1.8 mi e. Int corridors. **Pets:** Medium. Designated rooms, service with restrictions, supervision.
[SAVE] [S◐] [✕] [♨] [❏] [≈]

▼▼ **Days Inn-Willmar** Ⓜ
(320) 231-1275. **$48-$61.** 225 28th St SE. 2.3 mi e on US 12. Int corridors. **Pets:** Designated rooms, service with restrictions, crate.

🆂🆅 Ⓢ🗙 🗙 🖊 🛇 🖥 🖵

▼▼▼ **Holiday Inn & Willmar Conference Center** Ⓜ
(320) 235-6060. **$90-$130.** 2100 US 12 E. 1.8 mi e. Int corridors. **Pets:** Medium. Designated rooms, service with restrictions, supervision.

🅰🆂🅺 Ⓢ🗙 🗙 🖊 🖵 🍽 🏊

WINDOM

▼▼ **Super 8 of Windom** Ⓜ
(507) 831-1120. **Call for rates.** 222 3rd Ave S. Jct US 71 and SR 60, just n. Int corridors. **Pets:** Accepted.

🅰🆂🅺 🗙 🖥 🖵

WINONA

▼▼▼ **Best Western Riverport Inn & Suites** Ⓜ
(507) 452-0606. **Call for rates.** 900 Bruski Dr. Jct US 14/61 and SR 43. Int corridors. **Pets:** $10.70 one-time fee/room. Designated rooms, service with restrictions, supervision.

🅰🆂🅺 🗙 🖥 🖵 🍽 🏊

▼▼▼ **Holiday Inn Hotel and Suites** 🄷
(507) 453-0303. **$179.** 1025 Hwy 61 E. Jct US 61 and SR 43, just sw. Int corridors. **Pets:** $25 one-time fee/room. Designated rooms, service with restrictions, crate.

🅰🆂🅺 Ⓜ🗙 🗙 🖥 🖵 🍽 🏊

▼▼ **Quality Inn** Ⓜ🄸
(507) 454-4390. **$70-$90.** 956 Mankato Ave. Jct US 14/61 and SR 43. Ext/int corridors. **Pets:** Accepted.

🆂🆅 Ⓢ🗙 🖥 🖵 🍽 🏊

▼▼ **Super 8 Motel** Ⓜ
(507) 454-6066. **Call for rates.** 1025 Sugar Loaf Rd. Jct US 14/61 and SR 43. Int corridors. **Pets:** Accepted.

🅰🆂🅺 🗙

WORTHINGTON

▼▼▼ **AmericInn Motel** Ⓜ
(507) 376-4500. **$67-$79, 5 days notice.** 1475 Darling Dr. I-90, exit 43 (US 59), just se. Int corridors. **Pets:** Other species. Designated rooms, supervision.

🅰🆂🅺 Ⓢ🗙 🗙 Ⓜ🗙 🖊 🖎 🖥 🖵 🏊

▼▼ **Days Inn** Ⓜ
(507) 376-6155. **$52-$87.** 207 Oxford St. I-90, exit 42, 1 mi se on SR 266. Ext/int corridors. **Pets:** $6 daily fee/pet. Service with restrictions, supervision.

🆂🆅 Ⓢ🗙 🗙 Ⓜ🗙 🖎 🖥 🏊

MISSISSIPPI

CITY INDEX

ABERDEEN

Best Western Aberdeen Inn M ☘

(662) 369-4343. **$55-$74.** 801 E Commerce St. At jct US 45 and SR 25. Ext corridors. **Pets:** Medium. Service with restrictions, supervision.

BATESVILLE

Comfort Inn M

(662) 563-1188. **$75, 30 days notice.** 290 Power Dr. I-55, exit 243B, on SR 6. Ext corridors. **Pets:** Accepted.

BAY ST. LOUIS

Key West Inn M

(228) 466-0444. **$55-$80.** 1000 Hwy 90. 2.5 mi e of jct SR 603. Ext corridors. **Pets:** Small, other species. $5 daily fee/pet. Service with restrictions, supervision.

BILOXI

Father Ryan House Bed & Breakfast Inn BB

(228) 435-1189. **$100-$175, 7 days notice.** 1196 Beach Blvd. I-110, exit 1B, 0.8 mi w on US 90. Ext/int corridors. **Pets:** Accepted.

Gulf Beach Resort Hotel M

(228) 385-5555. **$60-$80.** 2428 Beach Blvd. US 90, 5 mi w of I-110. Int corridors. **Pets:** Large. $25 one-time fee/pet. No service, crate.

Holiday Inn Express M

(228) 388-1000. **$59-$119.** 2416 Beach Blvd. I-110, exit 1B, 5.5 mi w on US 90. Ext corridors. **Pets:** Accepted.

CANTON

Best Western-Canton Inn M

(601) 859-8600. **$55.** 137 Soldier Colony RD. I-55, exit 119. Int corridors. **Pets:** Accepted.

CLARKSDALE

Econo Lodge M

(662) 621-1110. **$51-$69.** 350 S State St. On US 61. Ext corridors. **Pets:** $5 daily fee/pet. Service with restrictions, supervision.

Hampton Inn M

(662) 627-9292. **$64.** 710 S State St. On US 61, 1 mi s of jct US 49. Ext/int corridors. **Pets:** Very small. $5 one-time fee/pet. Service with restrictions, supervision.

COLUMBUS

Ramada Inn M

(662) 328-5202. **$43-$62.** 506 Hwy 45 N. 0.3 mi n on US 45. Ext corridors. **Pets:** Accepted.

FOREST

Best Western Forest Inn M

(601) 469-2640. **$59, 3 days notice.** I-20, exit 88, just n on SR 35. Ext corridors. **Pets:** Accepted.

Comfort Inn M

(601) 469-2100. **$60-$65.** 1250 Hwy 35 S. I-20, exit 88, 0.3 mi n on SR 35. Ext corridors. **Pets:** Very small. $10 daily fee/pet. Service with restrictions, supervision.

GREENVILLE

Comfort Inn M

(662) 378-4976. **$69-$179.** 3080 US 82 E. 3 mi e. Ext corridors. **Pets:** Accepted.

GREENWOOD

Comfort Inn M

(662) 453-5974. **$59-$69.** 401 Hwy 82 W. On US 82. Ext corridors. **Pets:** Accepted.

▼▼▼▼ Hampton Inn M
(662) 455-5777. **$74, 10 days notice.** 635 Hwy 82 W. On US 82. Ext/int corridors. **Pets:** $5 daily fee/pet. Service with restrictions, crate.
SAVE S🐾 ✕ 🛏 💻 🕳

GRENADA

🅰️🅰️🅰️ ▼▼▼ Best Western Grenada M
(662) 226-7816. **$49-$65, 3 days notice.** 1750 Sunset Dr. I-55, exit 206, at jct I-55 and SR 7/8; on Frontage Rd. Ext corridors. **Pets:** Accepted.
SAVE S🐾 ✕ 🛏 💻 🍴 🕳

▼▼ Holiday Inn M
(662) 226-2851. **$62-$105.** 1796 Sunset Dr. I-55, exit 206, jct SR 7 and 8; on frontage road. Ext/int corridors. **Pets:** Medium. Supervision.
ASK ✕ 🛏 💻 🍴 🕳

GULFPORT

🅰️🅰️🅰️ ▼▼▼ Best Western Seaway Inn M
(228) 864-0050. **$40-$120.** 9475 Hwy 49. I-10, exit 34A, just s. Ext corridors. **Pets:** Medium. $10 daily fee/room. Service with restrictions.
SAVE S🐾 ✕ 👟 🛏 💻 🕳

▼▼▼▼ Holiday Inn Express M
(228) 864-7222. **$60-$120, 3 days notice.** 9435 Hwy 49. I-10, exit 34A, just sw. Ext corridors. **Pets:** Accepted.
ASK S🐾 ✕ 🔅 👟 🛏 💻

▼▼▼▼ Holiday Inn I-10/Airport M
(228) 868-8200. **$59-$134, 3 days notice.** 9415 Hwy 49 N. I-10, exit 34A, just sw. Ext corridors. **Pets:** Accepted.
ASK S🐾 ✕ 🛏 💻 🍴 🕳

🅰️🅰️🅰️ ▼▼▼ Shoney's Inn of Gulfport M
(228) 868-8500. **$59-$109.** 9375 Hwy 49. I-10, exit 34A, just sw. Ext corridors. **Pets:** Accepted.
SAVE S🐾 ✕ 🛏 💻 🕳

HATTIESBURG

🅰️🅰️🅰️ ▼▼▼ Baymont Inn &
      Suites-Hattiesburg M
(601) 264-8380. **$54-$114.** 123 Plaza Dr. I-59, exit 65, just nw. Int corridors. **Pets:** Accepted.
SAVE S🐾 ✕ 🔅 👟 🛏 💻 🕳

▼▼▼▼ Comfort Inn at Convention Center M
(601) 268-2170. **$65-$85.** 6595 Hwy 49 N. I-59, exit 67A, just se. Ext corridors. **Pets:** Accepted.
SAVE S🐾 ✕ 🛏 💻 🍴 🕳

🅰️🅰️🅰️ ▼▼▼▼ Hampton Inn of Hattiesburg M
(601) 264-8080. **$59-$89.** 4301 Hardy St. I-59, exit 65, just nw. Ext/int corridors. **Pets:** Small. Service with restrictions, supervision.
SAVE S🐾 ✕ 👟 🛏 💻 🕳

▼▼▼▼ Hawthorn Suites M
(601) 296-0302. **$99-$109.** 10 Gateway Dr. I-59, exit 67B, just n to Classic Dr, then just sw. Int corridors. **Pets:** Accepted.
ASK S🐾 ✕ 👟M 🔅 👟 🛏 💻 🕳

JACKSON

🅰️🅰️🅰️ ▼▼◆▼ Best Suites of America-Jackson M
(601) 899-9000. **$80-$130.** 5411 I-55 N. I-55, exit 102A northbound; exit 102 southbound, s on west service road. Int corridors. **Pets:** Small, other species. $37.80 daily fee/room. Service with restrictions, supervision.
SAVE S🐾 ✕ 🔅 👟 🛏 💻 🕳

🅰️🅰️🅰️ ▼▼▼ Best Western Metro Inn M
(601) 355-7483. **$60-$75, 3 days notice.** 1520 Ellis Ave. I-20, exit 42B, just ne. Ext/int corridors. **Pets:** Accepted.
SAVE S🐾 ✕ 🛏 🕳

▼▼▼▼ Clarion Hotel & Convention Center H
(601) 969-2141. **$79-$99.** 400 Greymont Ave. I-55, exit 96B, just w, then just s. Ext/int corridors. **Pets:** Accepted.
SAVE S🐾 ✕ 🛏 💻 🍴 🕳

▼▼▼▼ Crowne Plaza-Jackson H
(601) 969-5100. **$99-$109.** 200 E Amite St. I-55, exit 96B (High St), w to State St, then s, then w. Int corridors. **Pets:** Accepted.
ASK S🐾 ✕ 👟M 🔅 👟 🛏 💻 🍴 🕳

▼▼▼ Days Inn Coliseum M
(601) 352-7387. **$55-$65.** 804 Larison St. I-55, exit 96B, e to Greymont, then n, then e. Ext corridors. **Pets:** Accepted.
SAVE S🐾 ✕ 🛏 🕳

▼▼▼▼ Holiday Inn Hotel & Suites H
(601) 366-9411. **$85-$105.** 5075 I-55 N. I-55, exit 102A, s on west frontage road. Ext/int corridors. **Pets:** Other species. $100 deposit/room, $25 one-time fee/room. Service with restrictions, supervision.
ASK S🐾 ✕ 👟 🛏 💻 🍴 🕳

🅰️🅰️🅰️ ▼▼◆▼ La Quinta Inn-Jackson North M
(601) 957-1741. **$55-$75.** 616 Briarwood Dr. I-55 N, exit 102, just ne. Ext corridors. **Pets:** Small. Service with restrictions, supervision.
SAVE ✕ 🛏 💻 🕳

🅰️🅰️🅰️ ▼▼▼ La Quinta Inn-Jackson South M
(601) 373-6110. **$45-$66.** 150 Angle St. I-20, exit 43A, just w of Terry Rd. Ext corridors. **Pets:** Accepted.
SAVE ✕ 🛏 💻 🕳

🅰️🅰️🅰️ ▼▼▼ Red Roof Inn Fairgrounds M
(601) 969-5006. **$41-$57.** 700 Larson St. I-55 N, exit 96B, just w. Ext corridors. **Pets:** Medium. Service with restrictions, supervision.
SAVE ✕ 🔅 👟

🅰️🅰️🅰️ ▼▼▼ Residence Inn by Marriott ⬛
(601) 355-3599. **$109, 14 days notice.** 881 E River Pl. I-55, exit 96C, just e. Ext corridors. **Pets:** Accepted.
SAVE S🐾 ✕ 🔅 🛏 💻 🕳

KOSCIUSKO

🏧 ▽▽▽ Best Western Parkway Inn Ⓜ
(662) 289-6252. **$52-$66, 7 days notice.** 1052 Veterans Memorial Dr. At jct SR 35 and Natchez Trace Pkwy. Ext corridors. **Pets:** $5 daily fee/pet. Supervision.
🆂🅰🆅🅴 🆂🐾 ✖ 🔌 💻 🏊

MCCOMB

🏧 ▽▽▽▽ Days Inn McComb Ⓜ
(601) 684-5566. **$49-$79.** 2298 Delaware Ave. I-55, exit 17, just nw. Ext corridors. **Pets:** Accepted.
🆂🅰🆅🅴 🆂🐾 ✖ 🔌 💻 🍽 🏊

MERIDIAN

🏧 ▽▽▽ Baymont Inn & Suites-Meridian Ⓜ
(601) 693-2300. **$49-$59.** 1400 Roebuck Dr. I-20/59, exit 153, just s. Int corridors. **Pets:** Small. $25 deposit/room. Designated rooms, service with restrictions, supervision.
🆂🅰🆅🅴 🆂🐾 ✖ 🔌 💻 🏊

▽▽▽ Econo Lodge Ⓜ
(601) 693-9393. **$44-$49.** 2405 S Frontage Rd. I-20/59, exit 153, 0.5 mi sw. Ext corridors. **Pets:** Accepted.
🆂🅰🆅🅴 🆂🐾 ✖ 💻

▽▽▽ Holiday Inn Express Ⓜ
(601) 693-4521. **$70.** 1401 Roebuck Dr. I-20/59, exit 153, just s. Ext corridors. **Pets:** Accepted.
🅰🆂🅺 🆂🐾 ✖ 🦽 💻 🏊

▽▽▽ Holiday Inn Northeast Ⓜ
(601) 485-5101. **$85.** 111 US 11 & 80. I-20/59, exit 154 westbound, just n to frontage road, then just e; exit 154B eastbound. Ext corridors. **Pets:** Accepted.
🅰🆂🅺 🆂🐾 ✖ 🦽 🐕 🦽 🔌 💻 🍽 🏊

MOSS POINT

🏧 ▽▽▽▽ Holiday Inn Express Ⓜ
(228) 474-2100. **$50-$90, 7 days notice.** 4800 Amoco Dr. I-10, exit 69, just sw. Int corridors. **Pets:** Accepted.
🆂🅰🆅🅴 🆂🐾 ✖ 🦽 🐕 🦽 🔌 💻 🏊

NEWTON

🏧 ▽▽▽ Days Inn Ⓜ
(601) 683-3361. **$50-$75.** 261 Eastside Dr. I-20, exit 109, just s on SR 15. Ext corridors. **Pets:** Accepted.
🆂🅰🆅🅴 🆂🐾 ✖ 🔌 💻 🏊

OCEAN SPRINGS

▽▽▽▽ Comfort Inn Biloxi/Ocean Springs Ⓜ
(228) 818-0300. **$45-$159, 7 days notice.** I-10, exit 50, just nw on service road. Int corridors. **Pets:** Other species. $25 one-time fee/room. No service.
🆂🅰🆅🅴 🆂🐾 ✖ 🦽 🦽 🔌 💻 🏊

▽▽▽ Holiday Inn Express Ⓜ
(228) 875-7555. **$49-$109.** 7304 Washington Ave. I-10, exit 50, 0.4 mi s on SR 609. Ext corridors. **Pets:** Accepted.
🅰🆂🅺 🆂🐾 ✖ 🦽 🦽 🔌 💻 🏊

OLIVE BRANCH

▽▽▽ Whispering Woods Hotel and Conference Center Ⓡ
(662) 895-2941. **$100, 3 days notice.** 11200 E Goodman Rd. 3 mi e of jct US 78. Int corridors. **Pets:** Accepted.
🅰🆂🅺 🆂🐾 ✖ 🦽 🔌 💻 🍽 🏊 🐾

PASCAGOULA

🏧 ▽▽▽ La Font Inn Ⓜ
(228) 762-7111. **$55-$69.** 2703 Denny Ave. I-10, exit 69, 3.5 mi s on SR 63, 2 mi w on US 90. Ext corridors. **Pets:** Medium. Service with restrictions, supervision.
🆂🅰🆅🅴 🆂🐾 ✖ 🔌 💻 🍽 🏊 🐾

PEARL

▽▽▽ Jameson Inn Ⓜ
(601) 932-6030. **$55-$70.** 434 Riverwind Dr. I-20, exit 48, just nw. Int corridors. **Pets:** Accepted.
✖ 🦽 🦽 🔌 💻 🏊

PHILADELPHIA

▽▽ Key West Inn Ⓜ
(601) 656-0052. **$44-$89.** 1004 Central Dr. At jct of SR 15 and 16. Ext corridors. **Pets:** Accepted.
🅰🆂🅺 🆂🐾 ✖ 🦽 🔌 💻 🏊

PICAYUNE

▽▽▽ Days Inn Ⓜ
(601) 799-1339. **$59.** 450 S Lofton Ave. I-59, exit 4, just w. Ext corridors. **Pets:** Small. Designated rooms, service with restrictions, supervision.
🆂🅰🆅🅴 🆂🐾 ✖ 🦽 🔌 💻 🏊

RICHLAND

🏧 ▽▽▽ Days Inn Ⓜ
(601) 932-5553. **$55-$80, 3 days notice.** 1035 US Hwy 49 S. I-20, exit 47A, 4 mi s on US 49. Ext corridors. **Pets:** Medium, other species. $5 daily fee/pet. Service with restrictions.
🆂🅰🆅🅴 🆂🐾 ✖ 🔌

RIDGELAND

🏧 ▽▽▽ Red Roof Inn Ridgeland Ⓜ
(601) 956-7707. **$42-$52.** 810 Adcock Dr. I-55 N, exit 103, just ne on Frontage Rd. Ext corridors. **Pets:** Small. Service with restrictions, supervision.
🆂🅰🆅🅴 ✖

ⒶⒶⒶ ▼▼▼ **Shoney's Inn of Jackson** Ⓜ
(601) 956-6203. **$54-$119.** 839 Ridgewod Rd. I-55 N, exit
103, just ne on County Line Rd. Ext corridors. **Pets:** Small.
$25 one-time fee/room. Service with restrictions, supervi-
sion.
[SAVE] [S✱] [✕] [🛏] [💻] [≈]

ROBINSONVILLE

▼▼ **Key West Inn Tunica** Ⓜ
(662) 363-0021. **$50-$125, 3 days notice.** 11635 Hwy 61
N. On US 61, 0.3 mi n of SR 304. Ext corridors.
Pets: Accepted.
[ASK] [S✱] [✕] [🛏] [💻]

SOUTHAVEN

ⒶⒶⒶ ▼▼▼ **Best Western Inn** Ⓜ
(662) 393-4174. **$59-$79.** 8945 Hamilton Rd. I-55, exit 291,
just e. Ext corridors. **Pets:** Accepted.
[SAVE] [S✱] [✕] [🛏] [💻] [≈]

TUPELO

▼▼ **Days Inn** Ⓜ
(662) 842-0088. **$53-$60.** 1015 N Gloster St. From US 45,
w on McCullough Blvd (Old US 78) to N Gloster St, just n.
Ext corridors. **Pets:** $20 deposit/room. Service with restric-
tions, crate.
[SAVE] [S✱] [✕] [🛏] [💻] [≈]

▼▼▼ **Executive Inn** Ⓜ
(662) 841-2222. **Call for rates, 7 days notice.** 1011 N
Gloster St. From jct US 78 and 45, 1.3 mi s to McCullough
Blvd, then w. Int corridors. **Pets:** Accepted.
[ASK] [✕] [🛏] [💻] [🍴] [≈]

▼▼ **The Jameson Inn** Ⓜ
(662) 840-2380. **$55-$70.** 879 Mississippi Dr. US 45, exit
Barnes Crossing, 1 mi sw. Ext corridors. **Pets:** Very small,
other species. Service with restrictions, supervision.
[✕] [🛏] [💻] [≈]

ⒶⒶⒶ ▼▼▼ **Red Roof Inn Tupelo** Ⓜ
(662) 844-1904. **$41-$58.** 1500 McCullough Blvd. On SR
178, just w of jct SR 145 (Gloster St). Ext corridors.
Pets: Accepted.
[SAVE] [✕] [🛏] [💻]

▼▼ **Super 8 Motel** Ⓜ
(662) 842-0448. **$42-$55.** 3898 McCullough Blvd. US 78,
exit Belden, just ne. Ext corridors. **Pets:** Small, dogs only.
$5 daily fee/pet. Designated rooms, service with restrictions,
supervision.
[ASK] [S✱] [✕] [🛏]

VICKSBURG

ⒶⒶⒶ ▼▼▼ **Battlefield Inn** Ⓜ
(601) 638-5811. **$68-$73.** 4137 I-20 N Frontage Rd. I-20,
exit 4B, 1 mi e. Ext/int corridors. **Pets:** Other species. $5
daily fee/pet.
[SAVE] [S✱] [✕] [🛏] [🍴] [≈]

▼▼▼ **The Corners Bed & Breakfast Inn** ⒷⒷ
(601) 636-7421. **$90-$130, 3 days notice.** 601 Klein St.
I-20, exit 4B, 2.3 mi n on Washington, just w. Ext/int corridors. **Pets:** Accepted.
[ASK] [✕] [🛏] [💻]

ⒶⒶⒶ ▼▼▼ **Rainbow Hotel Casino an AmeriHost
Inn** Ⓜ
(601) 638-7111. **$74-$89.** 1350 Warrenton Rd. I-20, exit 1A,
1.4 mi s. Int corridors. **Pets:** Small. $50 deposit/pet. Desig-
nated rooms, service with restrictions, crate.
[SAVE] [✕] [♿] [🛏] [💻] [≈]

YAZOO CITY

▼▼ **Comfort Inn** Ⓜ
(662) 746-6444. **Call for rates.** 1600 Jerry Clower Blvd. On
US 49 E, 1.8 mi n of jct US 49 W. Int corridors.
Pets: Accepted.
[ASK] [✕] [🛏] [💻] [≈]

MISSOURI

CITY INDEX

ARNOLD

Drury Inn-Arnold
(636) 296-9600. **$70-$100.** 1201 Drury Ln. I-55, exit 191 (SR 141), 0.3 mi e. Int corridors. **Pets:** Accepted.

Microtel Inn & Suites-Arnold, MO
(636) 282-2400. **$59-$89.** 2121 Ridge Dr. I-55, exit 191 (SR 141), just se. Int corridors. **Pets:** Very small, other species. Service with restrictions, supervision.

BETHANY

Family Budget Inn
(660) 425-7915. **$40-$50, 5 days notice.** 4014 Miller St. I-35, exit 92. Int corridors. **Pets:** Other species. $20 deposit/room, $5.33 daily fee/pet. Designated rooms, service with restrictions, supervision.

BOLIVAR

Welcome Inn
(417) 326-5268. **$33-$55.** 4710 S 128th Rd, S Hwy 13. On Frontage Rd, 0.3 mi s of jct SR 13, 83 and 15 business route. Ext corridors. **Pets:** Medium, dogs only. $25 deposit/room, $5 daily fee/pet. Service with restrictions, supervision.

BRANSON

1st Inn Gold
(417) 334-7000. **$45-$65, 15 days notice.** 2719 W Hwy 76. 2.5 mi w of jct US 65. Ext/int corridors. **Pets:** Medium. $10 one-time fee/pet. Designated rooms, service with restrictions.

Atrium Inn
(417) 336-6000. **$48-$65.** 3005 Green Mountain Dr. 2.5 mi w on SR 76 from jct of US 65 and SR 76, 0.4 mi s. Ext corridors. **Pets:** Accepted.

Baymont Inn & Suites
(417) 336-6161. **$70-$170.** 2375 Green Mountain Dr. 2.5 mi w jct US 65 and SR 76, just s. Int corridors. **Pets:** Medium. $50 deposit/pet. Service with restrictions, crate.

Best Western Branson Rustic Oak
(417) 334-6464. **$35-$84.** 403 W Main (Hwy 76). 0.3 mi e from SR 76 and US 65. Ext corridors. **Pets:** Large. Service with restrictions.

Branson Inn M

(417) 334-5121. **$35-$75.** 448 SR 248. On SR 248, 0.3 mi w of jct US 65. Ext corridors. **Pets:** Medium. $10 deposit/pet. Service with restrictions, supervision.

The Branson Lodge M

(417) 334-3105. **$39-$60.** 2456 State Hwy 165. On SR 165, 3.2 mi s of jct SR 76. Ext corridors. **Pets:** Small, other species. $10 one-time fee/pet. Service with restrictions, crate.

Chateau on the Lake Resort Hotel & Convention Center H

(417) 334-1161. **$119-$269, 3 days notice.** 415 N State Hwy 265. Just n of jct SR 165 and 265. Int corridors. **Pets:** Small. Designated rooms, service with restrictions, crate.

Days Inn of Branson M

(417) 334-5544. **$45-$79.** 3524 Keeter St. Jct SR 376, 0.5 mi e on SR 76, then 0.3 mi w. Ext corridors. **Pets:** Small. $10 daily fee/room. Service with restrictions, supervision.

Dogwood Inn M

(417) 334-5101. **Call for rates.** 1420 Hwy 76 W. Jct US 65, 1 mi w on SR 76. Ext/int corridors. **Pets:** Accepted.

Hall of Fame Hotel M

(417) 334-5161. **$38-$70.** 3005 W Hwy 76. 2.5 mi w on SR 76. Ext/int corridors. **Pets:** Accepted.

Hotel Grand Victorian M

(417) 336-2935. **$60-$120, 3 days notice.** 2325 W Hwy 76. On SR 76, 2.6 mi w of US 65. Int corridors. **Pets:** Small. $10 daily fee/room. Designated rooms, service with restrictions, supervision.

Howard Johnson M

(417) 336-5151. **$45-$79.** 3027-A W Hwy 76. On SR 76, 3.5 mi w of jct US 65. Ext corridors. **Pets:** Accepted.

Peach Tree Inn M

(417) 335-5900. **$40-$70.** 2450 Green Mountain Dr. Jct US 65, 1.5 mi w on SR 76, then just s. Ext corridors. **Pets:** Accepted.

Ramada Limited M

(417) 337-5207. **$40-$80.** 2316 Shepherd of the Hills Expwy. Jct SR 76, 1.3 mi e. Ext corridors. **Pets:** Other species. $5 daily fee/room. Service with restrictions, crate.

Red Roof Inn #502 M

(417) 335-4500. **$40-$72.** 220 S Wildwood Dr. 2.5 mi w on SR 76, 0.3 mi s. Ext/int corridors. **Pets:** Accepted.

Residence Inn by Marriott A

(417) 336-4077. **$69-$99.** 280 Wildwood Dr S. 2 mi w on US 76, just s. Int corridors. **Pets:** Other species. $10 daily fee/room, $50 one-time fee/room. Service with restrictions, supervision.

Rock View Resort M

(417) 334-4678. **$51-$56, 21 days notice.** 1049 Parkview Dr. Jct US 65, 4.4 mi w on SR 165, then 0.3 mi s via Dale Dr, then 0.7 mi w. Ext corridors. **Pets:** Accepted.

Scenic Hills Inn M

(417) 336-8855. **$33-$55.** 2422 Shepherd of the Hills Expwy. Jct SR 76, 1.1 mi e. Int corridors. **Pets:** Medium, other species. $3 daily fee/room. Designated rooms, service with restrictions, crate.

Settle Inn Resort & Conference Center M

(417) 335-4700. **$55-$119.** 3050 Green Mountain Dr. Jct SR 76 and US 65, 3 mi w on SR 76, 0.8 mi s. Int corridors. **Pets:** Other species. $10 daily fee/pet. Service with restrictions, supervision.

Shoney's Inns & Suites M

(417) 336-1100. **$50-$70, 3 days notice.** 1970 W Hwy 76. 1.8 mi w of jct SR 65 and 76. Int corridors. **Pets:** $25 deposit/room. Designated rooms, service with restrictions, crate.

Taney Motel M

(417) 334-3143. **$35-$45.** 311 Hwy 65 N Business Rt. Just n on SR 65 business route, from jct SR 76. Ext corridors. **Pets:** Accepted.

Welk Resort Center M

(417) 336-3575. **$94-$99.** 1984 SR 165. On SR 165, 2.9 mi s of jct SR 76. Int corridors. **Pets:** Other species. $5 daily fee/room. Designated rooms, service with restrictions.

BRANSON WEST

Colonial Mountain Inn M

(417) 272-8414. **$55.** 10770 State Hwy 76. Jct SR 13, 0.3 mi e on SR 76. Ext corridors. **Pets:** Medium, dogs only. $5 daily fee/pet. Service with restrictions.

Shady Acre Motel M

(417) 338-2316. **$40.** 8722 Hwy 76. Jct SR 265, 1.1 mi w on SR 76. Ext corridors. **Pets:** Small, dogs only. $10 one-time fee/pet. Service with restrictions, supervision.

BUFFALO

[AAA] ♦♦ **Goodnite Inn** [M]
(417) 345-2345. **$39-$48.** 642 S Ash. US 65, just s of jct with SR 32. **Pets:** Medium, other species. $25 deposit/room, $5 daily fee/room. Service with restrictions, supervision.
[SAVE] [S/D] ⊠ ▣ 🏊

BUTLER

♦♦ **Days Inn** [M]
(660) 679-4544. **$45-$75.** 100 S Fran Ave. US 71, exit SR 52 W (Amoret and Butler). Int corridors. **Pets:** Other species. $5 daily fee/pet. Service with restrictions, supervision.
[SAVE] [S/D] ⊠ ▣ 🏊

♦♦ **Super 8 Motel–Butler** [M]
(660) 679-6183. **$46-$75.** 1114 W Fort Scott St. At jct US 71 and SR 52 W (Amoret and Butler). Ext corridors. **Pets:** Other species. $5 daily fee/pet. Service with restrictions, supervision.
[A$K] [S/D] ⊠

CAMERON

[AAA] ♦♦ **Best Western Acorn Inn** [M]
(816) 632-2187. **$59-$70.** US 36 and I-35. I-35, exit 54, 0.3 mi e on US 36. Ext corridors. **Pets:** Accepted.
[SAVE] [S/D] ⊠ 👂 ♿ ☕ 🏊

[AAA] ♦♦♦ **Comfort Inn** [M] 🐾
(816) 632-5655. **$59-$79, 7 days notice.** 1803 Comfort Ln. I-35, exit 54, just e. Int corridors. **Pets:** Small. Designated rooms, service with restrictions, supervision.
[SAVE] [S/D] ⊠ ▣ ☕ 🏊

[AAA] ♦♦ **Econo Lodge** [M]
(816) 632-6571. **$40-$58.** 220 E Grand. I-35, exit 54, 0.5 mi w on US 36, then just s on US 69. Ext corridors. **Pets:** Accepted.
[SAVE] [S/D] ⊠ ☕ 🏊

CAPE GIRARDEAU

♦♦ **Drury Lodge-Cape Girardeau** [MI]
(573) 334-7151. **$76-$91.** 104 S Vantage Dr. I-55, exit 96, just e. Ext/int corridors. **Pets:** Accepted.
⊠ 👂 ▣ ☕ 🍴 🏊

♦♦♦ **Drury Suites-Cape Girardeau** [M]
(573) 339-9500. **$72-$102.** 3303 Campster Dr. I-55, exit 96, just w. Int corridors. **Pets:** Accepted.
⊠ ♿M 👂 ♿ ▣ ☕

♦♦♦ **Holiday Inn of Cape Girardeau** [MI]
(573) 334-4491. **$85-$100.** 3257 William St. I-55, exit 96, just e. Ext/int corridors. **Pets:** Other species. $50 deposit/room. Service with restrictions, supervision.
[A$K] [S/D] ⊠ 👂 ▣ ☕ 🍴 🏊

♦♦ **Pear Tree Inn by Drury** [M]
(573) 334-3000. **$62-$76.** 3248 William St. I-55, exit 96, just e. Int corridors. **Pets:** Accepted.
⊠ 🏊

♦♦♦ **Hampton Inn-Cape Girardeau** [M]
(573) 651-3000. **$75-$100.** 103 Cape W Pkwy. I-55, exit 96 (William St), 0.3 mi sw. Int corridors. **Pets:** Accepted.
[SAVE] ⊠ ♿M 👂 ♿ ▣ ☕

♦♦ **Victorian Inn & Suites** [M] 🐾
(573) 651-4486. **$55-$85.** 3265 William St. I-55, exit 96, just e. Ext/int corridors. **Pets:** Other species. $50 deposit/room. Service with restrictions, crate.
[A$K] [S/D] ⊠ ♿M 👂 ♿ ▣ ☕ 🏊

CARTHAGE

[AAA] ♦♦ **Days Inn** [M]
(417) 358-2499. **$47-$54.** 2244 Grand Ave. Jct US 71, 0.7 mi e on SR HH. Ext corridors. **Pets:** Accepted.
[SAVE] [S/D] ⊠ ▣ 🏊

[AAA] ♦♦♦ **Econo Lodge** [M]
(417) 358-3900. **$55-$125.** 1441 W Central. On SR 96, at jct US 71. Ext/int corridors. **Pets:** $5 daily fee/pet. Service with restrictions, supervision.
[SAVE] [S/D] ⊠ ♿ 🏊

CASSVILLE

♦♦ **Budget Inn** [M] 🐾
(417) 847-4196. **$34-$48.** Hwy 112/248. Downtown; on SR 76, 86 and 112, just e of jct SR 248. Ext corridors. **Pets:** Very small. $20 deposit/room. Crate.
[A$K] [S/D] ⊠ ▣ ☕

♦♦ **Super 8 Motel** [M]
(417) 847-4888. **$51.** 101 S Hwy 37. Just s of jct 76, 86 and 37 business route. Int corridors. **Pets:** Accepted.
[A$K] [S/D] ⊠ ♿M ▣ 🏊

CHILLICOTHE

♦♦ **Best Western Inn & Suites** [M]
(660) 646-0572. **$50-$60, 10 days notice.** 1020 S Washington St. At jct US 36 and 65. Ext/int corridors. **Pets:** Large. $5 one-time fee/pet. Designated rooms, service with restrictions, crate.
[SAVE] [S/D] ⊠ ♿M ▣ ☕ 🏊

♦♦ **Chillicothe Super 8 Motel** [M]
(660) 646-7888. **$55.** 580 Old Hwy 36 E. Jct US 36 and 65, 0.8 mi e. Int corridors. **Pets:** Accepted.
[A$K] [S/D] ⊠

[AAA] ♦♦♦ **Grand River Inn** [MI]
(660) 646-6590. **$61-$68.** 606 W Business 36. On Old US 36, just e of jct US 65. Ext/int corridors. **Pets:** Other species. Service with restrictions, crate.
[SAVE] [S/D] ⊠ 👂 ▣ ☕ 🍴 🏊

CLINTON

♦♦♦ **Days Inn of Clinton** [M]
(660) 885-6901. **$47-$67.** Hwy 7 & Rives Rd. At north jct of SR 7 and 13. Int corridors. **Pets:** Accepted.
[SAVE] [S/D] ⊠ ▣ ☕ 🏊

(AAA) 🏨🏨🏨 **Knights Inn** M
(660) 885-2267. **$32-$55.** 1508 N 2nd. At north jct of SR 7 and 13. Ext corridors. **Pets:** Medium. $10 daily fee/pet. No service, supervision.
[SAVE] [S/D] [X] [🔌]

COLUMBIA

(AAA) 🏨🏨🏨 **Baymont Inn & Suites-Columbia** M
(573) 445-1899. **$64-$74.** 2500 I-70 Dr SW. I-70, exit 124 (Stadium Blvd), just w on frontage road. Int corridors. **Pets:** Large. Designated rooms, service with restrictions, supervision.
[SAVE] [S/D] [X] [🔌] [📺]

(AAA) 🏨🏨🏨 **Days Inn Conference Center** MI
(573) 445-8511. **$49-$89, 7 days notice.** 1900 I-70 Dr SW. I-70, exit 124 (Stadium Blvd), just e. Ext corridors. **Pets:** Medium. $5 daily fee/pet. Designated rooms, service with restrictions, supervision.
[SAVE] [S/D] [X] [🔌] [📺] [🍴] [🏊]

🏨🏨🏨🏨 **Drury Inn-Columbia** M
(573) 445-1800. **$90-$113.** 1000 Knipp St. I-70, exit 124 (Stadium Blvd), just s. Int corridors. **Pets:** Accepted.
[X] [🔌] [📺] [🏊]

🏨🏨🏨🏨 **Hawthorn Suites Ltd** M
(573) 442-8600. **$98, 3 days notice.** 805 Keene St. I-70, exit 128A, just se. Int corridors. **Pets:** Accepted.
[ASK] [S/D] [X] [&M] [🔌] [📺] [🏊]

🏨🏨🏨🏨 **Holiday Inn Express** M
(573) 449-4422. **$86, 3 days notice.** 801 Keene St. I-70, exit 128A, just se. Int corridors. **Pets:** Large, other species. Service with restrictions, crate.
[ASK] [S/D] [X] [&M] [🔌] [📺] [🏊]

🏨🏨🏨🏨 **Holiday Inn Select Executive Center** MI
(573) 445-8531. **$80.** 2200 I-70 Dr SW. I-70, exit 124 (Stadium Blvd), just w. Int corridors. **Pets:** Other species. Service with restrictions, supervision.
[ASK] [S/D] [X] [&M] [🔌] [📺] [🍴] [🏊]

🏨🏨 **Motel 6 #1152** M
(573) 445-8433. **$39-$55.** 1800 I-70 Dr SW. I-70, exit 124 (Stadium Blvd), just se. Ext corridors. **Pets:** Accepted.
[S/D] [X] [&M]

(AAA) 🏨🏨🏨 **Quality Inn Columbia** MI
(573) 449-2491. **$69-$79.** 1612 N Providence Rd. I-70 (Providence Rd), exit 126. Ext/int corridors. **Pets:** Accepted.
[SAVE] [S/D] [X] [&M] [🔌] [📺] [🍴] [🏊]

🏨🏨 **Ramada Inn & Conference Center** MI
(573) 449-0051. **$89.** 1100 Vandiver Dr. I-70, exit 127, on US 63. Ext/int corridors. **Pets:** Other species. $20 deposit/pet. Service with restrictions.
[ASK] [S/D] [X] [&M] [🔌] [📺] [🍴] [🏊]

(AAA) 🏨🏨🏨 **Red Roof Inn-Columbia** M
(573) 442-0145. **$45-$67.** 201 E Texas Ave. I-70, exit 126 (Providence Rd), just n. Ext corridors. **Pets:** Medium, other species. Service with restrictions, supervision.
[SAVE] [X]

🏨🏨🏨 **Travelodge** M
(573) 449-1065. **$49-$89, 7 days notice.** 900 Vandiver Dr. I-70, exit 127 (US 63), just n. Ext corridors. **Pets:** Small. $5 daily fee/pet. Designated rooms, service with restrictions, supervision.
[SAVE] [S/D] [X] [🔌] [📺] [🏊]

🏨🏨🏨🏨 **Wingate Inn** M
(573) 817-0500. **$89.** 3101 Wingate Ct. I-70, exit 128A, just s to I-70 Dr SE, 0.3 mi e to Keene St, 0.3 mi s, then just w. Int corridors. **Pets:** Accepted.
[ASK] [S/D] [X] [&M] [🔌] [📺] [🏊]

CONCORDIA

🏨🏨🏨 **Best Western Heidelberg Inn** M
(660) 463-2114. **$45-$60.** 406 NW 2nd St. I-70, exit 58, 0.3 mi sw. Int corridors. **Pets:** $20 deposit/pet, $5 daily fee/pet. Service with restrictions, supervision.
[SAVE] [S/D] [X] [&] [🔌] [📺] [🏊]

(AAA) 🏨🏨🏨 **Days Inn of Concordia** M
(660) 463-7987. **$44-$75.** 301 NW 3rd St. I-70, exit 58, just s to 3rd St, then just w. Ext/int corridors. **Pets:** Medium. $5 daily fee/pet. Service with restrictions, supervision.
[SAVE] [S/D] [X] [🔌] [🏊]

CONWAY

🏨🏨 **Budget Inn** M
(417) 589-2503. **$40-$50.** 101 Martingale Dr. I-44, exit 113. Ext corridors. **Pets:** Accepted.
[ASK] [S/D] [X] [🔌]

CUBA

(AAA) 🏨🏨🏨 **Best Western Cuba Inn** M
(573) 885-7707. **$55-$70.** 246 Hwy P. I-44, exit 208. Ext corridors. **Pets:** Very small, dogs only. $10 daily fee/pet. Designated rooms, service with restrictions, supervision.
[SAVE] [S/D] [X] [📺]

DEXTER

(AAA) 🏨🏨🏨 **Oak Tree Inn** M
(573) 624-5800. **$54-$64.** 1608 Hwy 60B W. US 60, exit One Mile Rd, just s to US 60B, then 0.5 mi w. Int corridors. **Pets:** Medium. $5 daily fee/pet. Service with restrictions, supervision.
[SAVE] [S/D] [X] [&M] [🔌] [&] [🔌] [📺]

DONIPHAN

🏨🏨 **Days Inn @ Current River** M
(573) 996-2400. **$58-$60.** 100 Oak Tree Village. Just e of jct US 160 and 142. Ext corridors. **Pets:** Accepted.
[SAVE] [X] [🔌] [📺] [🏊]

FESTUS

⚠️ ▼▼▼▼ Baymont Inn & Suites M
(636) 937-2888. **$60-$90.** 1303 Veterans Blvd. I-55, exit 175, just w. Int corridors. **Pets:** Accepted.
SAVE S✕ ✕ 🖥 💻

▼▼ Drury Inn Festus M
(636) 933-2400. **$52-$92.** 1001 Veterans Blvd. I-55, exit 175, just e. Int corridors. **Pets:** Small, other species. Service with restrictions, supervision.
✕ 🖥 💻 ⇌

FULTON

▼▼▼▼ Loganberry Inn Bed & Breakfast BB ❧
(573) 642-9229. **$85-$160, 14 days notice.** 310 W 7th St. 1 mi e of jct US 54 and CR F, then n on Westminster, then just e. Int corridors. **Pets:** Other species. Designated rooms, service with restrictions.
ASK ✕ 🖥

GRAY SUMMIT

▼▼▼ Best Western Diamond Inn Motel M
(636) 742-3501. **$59-$99, 3 days notice.** 2875 Hwy 100. I-44, exit 253. Ext corridors. **Pets:** Accepted.
SAVE S✕ ✕ 🌀 🖥 💻 ⇌

HANNIBAL

⚠️ ▼▼ Hannibal Travelodge M
(573) 221-4100. **$40-$76.** 500 Mark Twain Ave. I-72, exit 157, 0.6 mi se on US Business 36/SR 29. Ext corridors. **Pets:** Other species. Designated rooms, service with restrictions, crate.
SAVE S✕ ✕ 🖥 💻 ⇌

HARRISONVILLE

⚠️ ▼▼▼ Best Western Harrisonville M
(816) 884-3200. **$57-$82, 7 days notice.** 2201 N Rockhaven Rd. Jct US 71, just n on SR 291. Ext corridors. **Pets:** Small. $5 one-time fee/room. Designated rooms, service with restrictions, supervision.
SAVE S✕ ✕ 🖥 ⇌

⚠️ ▼ Budget Host Caravan Motel M
(816) 884-4100. **$39-$49.** 1705 Hwy 291 N. Jct US 71, just n. Ext corridors. **Pets:** Medium. $10 deposit/room. Designated rooms, service with restrictions, supervision.
SAVE S✕ ✕ ⇌

⚠️ ▼ Slumber Inn Motel M
(816) 884-3100. **$37-$47, 3 days notice.** 21400 E 275th St. Jct US 71 and SR 7 S (Clinton exit), just w. Ext corridors. **Pets:** $3 daily fee/pet. Supervision.
SAVE S✕ ✕ 🖥 ⇌

HAYTI

▼▼▼▼ Drury Inn & Suites-Hayti M
(573) 359-2702. **$67-$88.** 1317 Hwy 84. I-55, exit 19 (US 412/SR 84), just w. Int corridors. **Pets:** Accepted.
✕ 🌀 🖥 💻 ⇌

HIGGINSVILLE

▼▼ Best Western Camelot Inn MI
(660) 584-3646. **$55-$80, 3 days notice.** 6683 S Hwy 13. I-70, exit 49 (SR 13), just nw. Ext/int corridors. **Pets:** Accepted.
SAVE S✕ ✕ 🍴

▼▼ Super 8 Motel-Higginsville M
(660) 584-7781. **$57-$68.** 6471 Oakview Ln. I-70, exit 49 (SR 13), just se. Int corridors. **Pets:** Accepted.
ASK S✕ ✕

HOUSTON

▼▼ Southern Inn Motel M
(417) 967-4591. **$43-$50.** 1493 S Hwy 63. 1.3 mi s on US 63. Ext corridors. **Pets:** Medium. $6 daily fee/pet. Designated rooms, service with restrictions, supervision.
✕

JACKSON

▼▼▼ Drury Inn & Suites-Jackson M
(573) 243-9200. **$52-$80.** 225 Drury Ln. I-55, exit 105 (SR 61), 0.3 mi w. Int corridors. **Pets:** Accepted.
✕ ♿M 🐾 🖥 💻 ⇌

JEFFERSON CITY

⚠️ ▼▼▼▼ Capitol Plaza Hotel H
(573) 635-1234. **$99-$109.** 415 W McCarty St. On US 50 and 63 S, just e of jct US 54. Int corridors. **Pets:** Accepted.
SAVE S✕ ✕ 🐾 🖥 💻 🍴 ⇌

▼▼ Motel 6 M
(573) 634-4220. **$40-$50.** 1624 Jefferson St. US 54, exit Stadium Dr southbound; exit Ellis Blvd northbound. Int corridors. **Pets:** Accepted.
S✕ ✕ 🐾 🖥

⚠️ ▼▼▼ Ramada Inn-Jefferson City MI
(573) 635-7171. **$59.** 1510 Jefferson St. US 54, 0.5 mi nw of Ellis Blvd exit. Ext/int corridors. **Pets:** Other species. $10 daily fee/room. Designated rooms, service with restrictions.
SAVE S✕ ✕ 🐾 🖥 💻 🍴 ⇌

JOPLIN

⚠️ ▼▼▼ Baymont Inn & Suites M
(417) 623-0000. **$54-$74.** 3510 S Range Line Rd. I-44, exit 8B, just n. Ext/int corridors. **Pets:** Medium. $25 deposit/room. Designated rooms, service with restrictions, supervision.
SAVE S✕ ✕ 🐾 🖥 💻 ⇌

⚠️ ▼▼▼ Best Western Sands Inn M ❧
(417) 624-8300. **$49-$54, 3 days notice.** 1611 S Range Line Rd. I-44, exit 8B, 2 mi n. Ext corridors. **Pets:** Medium. Designated rooms, service with restrictions, supervision.
SAVE S✕ ✕ ⇌

▼▼▼ Drury Inn & Suites-Joplin M
(417) 781-8000. **$70-$100.** 3601 Range Line Rd. I-44, exit 8B, just ne. Int corridors. **Pets:** Medium, other species. Service with restrictions, supervision.

(AAA) ▼▼▼ Holiday Inn H
(417) 782-1000. **$95-$105.** 3615 Range Line Rd. I-44, exit 8 (US 71B). Int corridors. **Pets:** Medium, other species. $25 deposit/room. Designated rooms, service with restrictions, supervision.

▼ Motel 6–427 M
(417) 781-6400. **$39-$53.** 3031 S Range Line Rd. I-44, exit 8B, 1 mi n. Ext corridors. **Pets:** Accepted.

▼▼▼ Ramada Inn M
(417) 781-0500. **$78.** 3320 Range Line Rd. I-44, exit 8B, 0.3 mi n on US 71. Int corridors. **Pets:** Small. $10 daily fee/pet. Service with restrictions, supervision.

(AAA) ▼▼ Select Hallmark Inn M
(417) 624-8400. **$50-$58, 5 days notice.** 3600 S Range Line Rd. I-44, exit 8B, just nw. Ext corridors. **Pets:** Other species. $10 one-time fee/room. Designated rooms, service with restrictions, crate.

(AAA) ▼▼▼ Sleep Inn M
(417) 782-1212. **$55-$65.** I-44 & State Hwy 43 S. I-44, exit 4, just s. Int corridors. **Pets:** Medium, other species. $10 one-time fee/room. Service with restrictions, supervision.

(AAA) ▼▼▼ Solar Inn and Suites M
(417) 781-6776. **$40-$54.** 3508 S Range Line Rd. I-44, exit 8B, just n on US 71. Ext corridors. **Pets:** Medium. $50 deposit/room. Designated rooms, service with restrictions, supervision.

▼▼ Super 8 Motel-Joplin M
(417) 782-8765. **$47-$75, 7 days notice.** 2830 E 36th St. I-44, exit 8B, just n. Int corridors. **Pets:** Medium, other species. Designated rooms, service with restrictions, supervision.

KANSAS CITY METROPOLITAN AREA

BLUE SPRINGS

▼▼ Microtel Inn & Suites M
(816) 224-1122. **$49-$69, 15 days notice.** 3120 NW Jefferson Rd. I-70, exit 18, just ne. Int corridors. **Pets:** Accepted.

(AAA) ▼▼▼ Sleep Inn M
(816) 224-1199. **$60-$65, 30 days notice.** 451 NW Jefferson St. I-70, exit 20, just ne on frontage road. Int corridors. **Pets:** Accepted.

GRAIN VALLEY

(AAA) ▼▼▼ Travelodge M
(816) 224-3420. **$60-$70.** 105 Sunny Lane Dr. I-70, exit 24, just n. Ext corridors. **Pets:** Small. $7 daily fee/pet. Service with restrictions, supervision.

INDEPENDENCE

(AAA) ▼▼▼ Comfort Inn M
(816) 373-8856. **$59-$69, 30 days notice.** 4200 S Noland Rd. I-70, exit 12. Int corridors. **Pets:** Other species. $25 deposit/room. Service with restrictions, supervision.

(AAA) ▼▼▼ Independence Residence Inn by Marriott M
(816) 795-6466. **$110-$160, 30 days notice.** 3700 S Arrowhead Ave. Jct SR 291 and 39th St, just ne. Int corridors. **Pets:** Other species. $10 daily fee/pet, $50 one-time fee/room. Service with restrictions.

(AAA) ▼▼▼ Red Roof Inn-Independence M
(816) 373-2800. **$45-$71.** 13712 E 42nd Terrace. I-70, exit 12 (Noland Rd), just sw. Ext corridors. **Pets:** Accepted.

(AAA) ▼▼▼ Shoney's Inn-Independence M
(816) 254-0100. **$49-$74.** 4048 S Lynn Court Dr. I-70, exit 12 (Noland Rd). Ext corridors. **Pets:** Accepted.

KANSAS CITY

(AAA) ▼▼▼ AmeriSuites (Kansas City/Airport) M
(816) 891-0871. **$75.** 7600 NW 97th Terr. I-29, exit 10, just sw. Int corridors. **Pets:** Accepted.

Baymont Inn & Suites-Kansas City North M
(816) 221-1200. **$69-$79.** 2214 Taney Rd. At jct I-35, 29 and exit 6A. Int corridors. **Pets:** Accepted.
[SAVE] [S6] [X] [🐾] [🔌] [🖥]

Baymont Inn & Suites-Kansas City South M
(816) 822-7000. **$59-$69.** 8601 Hillcrest Rd. I-435, exit 69 (87th St). Int corridors. **Pets:** Accepted.
[SAVE] [S6] [X] [&M] [🐾] [🔌] [🖥]

Chase Suites by Woodfin A
(816) 891-9009. **$139.** 9900 NW Prairie View Rd. I-29, exit 10. Ext corridors. **Pets:** $50 deposit/pet. Service with restrictions, supervision.
[ASK] [S6] [X] [🐾] [🔌] [🖥] [≈]

Days Inn M
(816) 746-1666. **$70-$180, 7 days notice.** 11120 NW Ambassador Dr. I-29, exit 12, just e. Int corridors. **Pets:** Small, other species. $15 daily fee/pet. Designated rooms, service with restrictions, supervision.
[SAVE] [S6] [X] [&M] [🐾] [🔌] [🖥]

Days Inn-North M
(816) 421-6000. **$64-$85, 14 days notice.** 2232 Taney St. At jct I-35, 29 and exit 6A. Int corridors. **Pets:** Dogs only. $10 one-time fee/room. Service with restrictions, supervision.
[SAVE] [S6] [X] [&M] [🐾] [🔌] [🖥]

Drury Inn & Suites-Kansas City Airport M
(816) 880-9700. **$65-$110.** 7900 NW Tiffany Springs Pkwy. I-29, exit 10, just w. Int corridors. **Pets:** Small. Service with restrictions, crate.
[X] [&M] [🐾] [🔌] [🖥] [≈]

Drury Inn-Stadium M
(816) 923-3000. **$70-$110.** 3830 Blue Ridge Cutoff. I-70, exit 9, just n. Int corridors. **Pets:** Accepted.
[X] [&M] [🐾] [🔌] [🖥] [≈]

Econo Lodge KCI Airport M
(816) 464-5082. **$55-$80.** 11300 NW Prairie View Rd. At jct I-29 and exit 12 (112th St NW). Int corridors. **Pets:** Accepted.
[SAVE] [S6] [X] [🐾]

Embassy Suites Hotel KCI Airport H
(816) 891-7788. **$99-$179.** 7640 NW Tiffany Springs Pkwy. I-29, exit 10, just e. Int corridors. **Pets:** Small, other species. $50 deposit/pet. Service with restrictions, supervision.
[SAVE] [S6] [X] [&M] [🐾] [🔌] [🖥] [📶] [≈]

The Fairmont Kansas City at the Plaza H
(816) 756-1500. **$209.** 401 Ward Pkwy. In Country Club Plaza. Int corridors. **Pets:** Accepted.
[ASK] [S6] [X] [🐾] [📶] [≈]

Hampton Inn M
(816) 483-7900. **$69-$99.** 1051 N Cambridge Ave. I-435, exit 57, just sw. Int corridors. **Pets:** Small. $5 one-time fee/pet. Service with restrictions, supervision.
[SAVE] [S6] [X] [🐾] [🔌] [🖥] [≈]

Holiday Inn Kansas City South MI
(816) 765-4100. **$70-$80.** 5701 Longview Rd. I-435, exit US 71, 1 mi s. Int corridors. **Pets:** Accepted.
[SAVE] [S6] [X] [🔌] [🖥] [📶] [≈]

Holiday Inn KCI MI
(816) 464-2345. **$49-$129.** 11832 Plaza Cir NW. I-29, exit 13, just e. Int corridors. **Pets:** Small, other species. $25 deposit/room. Designated rooms, service with restrictions, supervision.
[ASK] [S6] [X] [🔌] [🖥] [📶] [≈]

Holiday Inn-Sports Complex MI
(816) 353-5300. **$79-$139.** 4011 Blue Ridge Cutoff. I-70, exit 9, just s; across from the Harry S. Truman Sports Complex. Int corridors. **Pets:** Large. Designated rooms, service with restrictions, supervision.
[SAVE] [S6] [X] [&M] [🐾] [🔌] [🔌] [🖥] [📶] [≈]

Homestead Studio Suites-Kansas City/ Country Club Plaza M
(816) 531-2212. **$69-$75.** 4535 Main St. Just ne of Country Club Plaza. Int corridors. **Pets:** Accepted.
[ASK] [S6] [X] [&M] [🔌] [🔌] [🖥]

Homewood Suites by Hilton M
(816) 880-9880. **$69-$129.** 7312 NW Polo Dr. I-29, exit 10, just e. Int corridors. **Pets:** Small, other species. $50 one-time fee/room. Service with restrictions.
[SAVE] [S6] [X] [🐾] [🔌] [🔌] [🖥] [≈]

Kansas City Marriott Downtown H
(816) 421-6800. **$149.** 200 W 12th St. Just s of I-70, US 24 and 40. Int corridors. **Pets:** Accepted.
[SAVE] [X] [🔌] [🖥] [📶] [≈]

MainStay Suites M
(816) 891-8500. **$99-$159.** 9701 N Shannon Ave. I-29, exit 10 (Tiffany Springs Pkwy). Int corridors. **Pets:** Small, other species. $100 deposit/room, $5 daily fee/pet. Service with restrictions, supervision.
[SAVE] [S6] [X] [&M] [🐾] [🔌] [🔌] [🖥] [≈]

Ramada Inn MI
(816) 741-9500. **$67, 7 days notice.** 7301 NW Tiffany Springs Pkwy. I-29, exit 10, 1 mi s on frontage road. Int corridors. **Pets:** Small. $20 one-time fee/room. Designated rooms, service with restrictions, crate.
[SAVE] [X] [🐾] [🔌] [🔌] [🖥] [📶] [≈]

Red Roof Inn-North M
(816) 452-8585. **$54-$76.** 3636 NE Randolph Rd. Just e of I-435 and SR 210, exit 55B northbound; exit 55 southbound. Ext corridors. **Pets:** Small. Service with restrictions, supervision.
[SAVE] [X] [&M] [🔌]

🔺 ▼▼💎 **Residence Inn by Marriott Union Hill** 🅰
(816) 561-3000. **$119-$149.** 2975 Main St. 1.8 mi s. Ext corridors. **Pets:** Large, other species. $5 daily fee/room, $50 one-time fee/room. Service with restrictions.
SAVE S X 🎵 🗎 💻 ⮆

▼▼▼ **Sleep Inn** Ⓜ
(816) 891-0111. **$70.** 7611 NW 97th Terrace. I-29, exit 10, just sw. Int corridors. **Pets:** Accepted.
SAVE S X 🚹 🎵 🗎 💻 ⮆

▼▼▼ **Super 8 Motel–NW Kansas City** Ⓜ
(816) 587-0808. **$54-$64.** 6900 NW 83rd Terrace. I-29, exit 8, just sw. Int corridors. **Pets:** $10 daily fee/pet. Service with restrictions, supervision.
ASK S X 🎵

▼▼▼ **Westin Crown Center** 🅷
(816) 474-4400. **$110.** 1 Pershing Rd. 0.5 mi s. Int corridors. **Pets:** Medium, other species. $20 daily fee/room. Service with restrictions.
ASK S X 🚹 🎵 🗎 💻 🍴 ⮆ ⊠

KEARNEY

🔺 ▼▼💎 **Econo Lodge** Ⓜ
(816) 628-5111. **$47-$63.** 505 Shanks Ave. I-35, exit 26, just w. Ext corridors. **Pets:** Medium, other species. $20 deposit/pet, $10 daily fee/pet. Designated rooms, no service, supervision.
SAVE S X 💻 ⮆

▼▼ **Kearney Super 8 Motel** Ⓜ ❀
(816) 628-6800. **$55-$65.** 210 Platte Clay Way. I-35, exit 26, just ne. Int corridors. **Pets:** Small, dogs only. $10 daily fee/room. Service with restrictions.
ASK S X 🗎

LIBERTY

🔺 ▼▼▼ **Villager Lodge-Liberty** Ⓜ
(816) 781-8770. **$55-$70, 7 days notice.** 209 N 291 Hwy. I-35, exit 16 (SR 152), 0.8 mi e on SR 152, just n. Ext corridors. **Pets:** Medium. $10 daily fee/room. Service with restrictions.
SAVE S X 🗎 💻 ⮆

NORTH KANSAS CITY

▼▼▼ **Harrah's North Kansas City Casino and Hotel** 🅷
(816) 472-7777. **$89-$169.** One Riverboat Dr. I-35, exit 6A, 1 mi e on SR 210 (Armour Rd). Int corridors. **Pets:** Accepted.
ASK S X 🚹 🎵 🗎 💻 🍴 ⮆

OAK GROVE (JACKSON COUNTY)

🔺 ▼▼▼ **Econo Lodge** Ⓜ
(816) 625-3681. **$60-$80.** 410 SE 1st St. I-70, exit 28, just se. Ext corridors. **Pets:** Small, dogs only. $5 daily fee/pet. Service with restrictions, supervision.
SAVE S X 🗎

PLATTE CITY

🔺 ▼▼▼ **Comfort Inn-KCI** Ⓜ
(816) 858-5430. **$71-$80.** 1200 Hwy 92. I-29, exit 18, 1 mi w. Int corridors. **Pets:** Medium. $3 daily fee/pet. Designated rooms, service with restrictions, supervision.
SAVE S X 🎵 🎵 🗎 💻 ⮆

▼▼ **Super 8 Motel** Ⓜ
(816) 858-2888. **Call for rates, 3 days notice.** 2500 NW Prairie View Rd. I-29, exit 18, just sw. Int corridors. **Pets:** Medium. Designated rooms, service with restrictions, supervision.
ASK X 🎵 🗎 ⮆

RIVERSIDE

▼▼ **Super 8 Motel–Riverside** Ⓜ
(816) 505-2888. **$63-$78 (no credit cards).** 800 NW Argosy Pkwy. I-635, exit 10 (Argosy Pkwy), follow signs. Int corridors. **Pets:** Accepted.
ASK S X 🗎 ⮆

❀ **END METROPOLITAN AREA** ❀

KENNETT

▼▼ **Days Inn** Ⓜ
(573) 888-9860. **$65-$69.** 110 Independence Ave. Jct US 412/SR 84 and 25, just n. Ext corridors. **Pets:** Medium. $10 daily fee/pet. Designated rooms, service with restrictions, supervision.
SAVE S X 🗎 💻 ⮆

KIMBERLING CITY

🔺 ▼▼▼ **Kimberling Heights Resort** Ⓜ ❀
(417) 779-4158. **$48-$59.** 9687 State Hwy 13. 1.5 mi s on US 13. Ext corridors. **Pets:** Medium, other species. Service with restrictions, supervision.
SAVE S 🗎 💻 ⮆ ⊠

▼▼ Kimberling Inn Resort & Conference Center ☒
(417) 739-4311. **$40-$160, 3 days notice.** 11863 St. Hwy 13. SR 13. Ext corridors. **Pets:** Other species. $100 one-time fee/pet. Service with restrictions, crate.
(ASK) 🔊 ☒ 🔲 💻 🍽 �'⌐ ☒

KINGDOM CITY

▼▼ Super 8 Motel-Kingdom City Ⓜ
(573) 642-2888. **$49-$65.** 3370 Gold Rd. I-70, exit 148 (US 54), 0.3 mi s. Int corridors. **Pets:** Accepted.
(ASK) 🔊 ☒ 🔲 🗑 🔲

KIRKSVILLE

▼▼ Best Western Shamrock Inn Ⓜ
(660) 665-8352. **Call for rates.** 2521 S Business 63. 0.3 mi w jct US 63 and Business 63. Ext corridors. **Pets:** Accepted.
(ASK) ☒ 🔲 💻 ➤

▼▼ Comfort Inn Ⓜ
(660) 665-2205. **$48-$74.** 2209 N Baltimore. US 63 N. Int corridors. **Pets:** Designated rooms, service with restrictions, supervision.
(SAVE) 🔊 ☒ 🗑 🔲 🔲 💻

KNOB NOSTER

▼▼ Whiteman Inn Ⓜ
(660) 563-3000. **$41-$63.** 2340 W Irish Ln. Jct US 50 and SR 23. Ext/int corridors. **Pets:** Medium, other species. $20 deposit/pet, $3 daily fee/pet. Designated rooms, service with restrictions, crate.
(ASK) 🔊 ☒ 🔲 🔲 💻 ➤

LAKE OZARK

◆◆◆ ▼▼▼ Holiday Inn Sun Spree Resort & Conference Center Ⓜ ❀
(573) 365-2334. **$85-$165.** 120 Holiday Ln. 2.6 mi s of Bagnell Dam on US 54 business route. Ext/int corridors. **Pets:** Other species. $50 deposit/pet. Service with restrictions, supervision.
(SAVE) 🔊 ☒ 🔲 🔲 🔲 🔲 💻 🍽 ➤

LAMAR

▼▼ Blue Top Inn Ⓜ
(417) 682-3333. **$46.** 65 SE 1st Ln. On US 160, just se of jct US 71. Ext corridors. **Pets:** Accepted.
(ASK) 🔊 ☒ 🔲 💻 ➤

LEBANON

◆◆◆ ▼▼ Best Western Wyota Inn Ⓜ
(417) 532-6171. **$64-$79, 3 days notice.** 1225 Milk Creek Rd. I-44, exit 130. Ext corridors. **Pets:** Small. $10 daily fee/pet. Designated rooms, supervision.
(SAVE) 🔊 ☒ 🔲 💻 🍽 ➤

▼▼ Econo Lodge Ⓜ
(417) 588-3226. **$34-$59.** 2125 W Elm St. I-44, exit 127, just n. Ext corridors. **Pets:** Other species. Supervision.
(SAVE) 🔊 ☒ 💻

▼▼▼ Holiday Inn Express Ⓜ
(417) 532-1111. **$79.** 1955 W Elm St. I-44, exit 127, just n. Int corridors. **Pets:** Accepted.
(ASK) 🔊 ☒ 🔲 💻 ➤

LOUISIANA

◆◆◆ ▼▼ River's Edge Motel Ⓜ
(573) 754-4522. **$48-$55.** 201 Mansion St. On US 54 at Champ Clark Bridge. Ext corridors. **Pets:** Medium, dogs only. $20 deposit/pet. Service with restrictions, supervision.
(SAVE) 🔊 ☒ 🔲 💻

MACON

▼▼ Best Western Inn Ⓜ
(660) 385-2125. **$50-$56.** 28933 Sunset Dr. On Outer Rd S at US 36 and Long Branch Lake exit. Ext corridors. **Pets:** Small. $20 deposit/room. Service with restrictions, supervision.
(SAVE) 🔊 ☒ 🔲 💻 ➤

▼▼ Super 8 Motel Ⓜ
(660) 385-5788. **$55.** 203 E Briggs Dr. Jct US 63 and 36. Int corridors. **Pets:** $25 deposit/room. Service with restrictions, supervision.
(ASK) 🔊 ☒ 🔲

MARSHFIELD

▼▼▼ Holiday Inn Express Ⓜ
(417) 859-6000. **$74-$78.** 1301 Banning St. I-44, exit 100, southeast corner. Int corridors. **Pets:** Accepted.
(ASK) 🔊 ☒ 🔲 🔲 💻 ➤

MARSTON

▼▼ Super 8 Motel Ⓜ
(573) 643-9888. **$53-$55.** 501 SE Outer Rd. I-55, exit 40, just se. Int corridors. **Pets:** Accepted.
(ASK) 🔊 ☒ 🔲 💻

MARYVILLE

▼▼ Super 8 Motel-Maryville Ⓜ
(660) 582-8088. **$43.** 222 Summit Dr. 2 mi s on US 71. Int corridors. **Pets:** Other species. $10 deposit/room. Service with restrictions, supervision.
(ASK) 🔊 ☒ 🔲 💻

MEXICO

▼▼ Villager Lodge Ⓜ
(573) 581-1440. **$48-$62, 14 days notice.** 1010 E Liberty St. 0.5 mi e on US 54. Ext corridors. **Pets:** Accepted.
(ASK) 🔊 ☒ 🔲 💻 ➤

MINER

Best Western Coach House Inn & Suites Ⓜ
(573) 471-9700. **$68-$148, 7 days notice.** 220 S Interstate Dr. I-55, exit 67, just e, 0.5 mi s on Interstate Dr (frontage road). Int corridors. **Pets:** Small. $25 one-time fee/room. Designated rooms, service with restrictions, supervision.
[SAVE] [S🐾] [✕] [🐾] [🛏] [💻] [🍴] [⌬]

Drury Inn-Sikeston Ⓜ
(573) 471-4100. **$66-$92.** 2602 E Malone. I-55, exit 67, just sw. Int corridors. **Pets:** Accepted.
[✕] [🛏] [🐾] [🐾] [🛏] [💻] [⌬]

Pear Tree Inn by Drury Ⓜ
(573) 471-8660. **$48-$76.** 2602 Rear E Malone. I-55, exit 67. Ext corridors. **Pets:** Accepted.
[✕] [🛏] [🐾] [⌬]

MONETT

Cambridge Inn Ⓜ
(417) 235-8039. **$43-$49.** 868 Hwy 60. On US 60, 1.3 mi e of jct SR 37. Ext corridors. **Pets:** Accepted.
[A$K] [S🐾] [✕] [🐾] [🛏] [⌬]

MONROE CITY

Rainbow Motel Ⓜ
(573) 735-4526. **$30-$40.** 308 5th St. Jct US 36 and 24, just s, then 1 mi w. Ext corridors. **Pets:** Small. $5 one-time fee/pet. Designated rooms, service with restrictions, supervision.
[✕] [🛏] [💻] [⌬]

MOUNT VERNON

Budget Host Ranch Motel Ⓜ
(417) 466-2125. **$46-$54.** 1015 E Mount Vernon Blvd. I-44, exit 46, just n. Ext corridors. **Pets:** Small, other species. $5 one-time fee/pet. Service with restrictions, supervision.
[SAVE] [S🐾] [✕] [⌬]

Super 8 Ⓜ
(417) 461-0230. **$55-$70.** 1200 Industrial Blvd. I-44, exit 46, just n, then just se. Int corridors. **Pets:** Small, dogs only. $10 one-time fee/pet. Service with restrictions, supervision.
[A$K] [S🐾] [✕] [🐾] [🛏] [⌬]

MOUNTAIN GROVE

Best Western Ranch House Inn Ⓜ
(417) 926-3152. **$46-$58.** 111 E 17th St. At jct US 60 and 95, just s. Ext corridors. **Pets:** Accepted.
[SAVE] [S🐾] [✕] [💻] [⌬]

Days Inn of Mountain Grove Ⓜ
(417) 926-5555. **$44-$56.** 300 E 19th St. At jct US 60 and 95, just se. Ext corridors. **Pets:** Accepted.
[SAVE] [S🐾] [✕] [⌬]

NEOSHO

Super 8 Motel Ⓜ
(417) 455-1888. **$48-$69.** 3085 Gardner/Edgewood Dr. US 71B, just s of jct US 60B and 71B. Int corridors. **Pets:** Very small. $10 daily fee/pet. Service with restrictions, supervision.
[A$K] [S🐾] [✕] [🐾] [⌬]

NEVADA

Rambler Motel Ⓜ ✿
(417) 667-3351. **$36-$59.** 1401 E Austin St. On US 71 business route, just e of jct US 54, 1 mi w of jct US 71, exit Camp Clark and Nevada. Ext corridors. **Pets:** $10 daily fee/pet. Service with restrictions, crate.
[SAVE] [S🐾] [✕] [🛏] [⌬]

Welk-Um Inn Ⓜ
(417) 667-6777. **$48-$65.** 2345 Marvel Dr. On US 71 business route, just w of jct US 71, Camp Clark and Nevada exit. Ext/int corridors. **Pets:** Small, dogs only. $25 deposit/pet. Service with restrictions, supervision.
[✕] [🛏] [💻] [⌬]

ODESSA

Parkside Inn Ⓜ
(816) 230-7588. **$55-$70.** 400 W 40 Highway. I-70, exit 37B, just s to US 40, then 0.4 mi e. Ext corridors. **Pets:** Small, dogs only. $25 one-time fee/pet. Service with restrictions, supervision.
[A$K] [S🐾] [✕] [🛏]

OSAGE BEACH

Lake Chateau Resort Ⓜ
(573) 348-2791. **$49-$135.** 5066 Hwy 54. Just s of Grand Glaize Bridge. Ext corridors. **Pets:** Medium. $10 one-time fee/pet. Designated rooms, service with restrictions, supervision.
[SAVE] [S🐾] [✕] [🛏] [💻] [🍴] [⌬] [✕]

Scottish Inns Ⓜ
(573) 348-3123. **$30-$65.** 5404 Hwy 54. 1 mi w of Grand Glaize Bridge. Ext/int corridors. **Pets:** Small. $5 daily fee/pet. Designated rooms, service with restrictions, crate.
[SAVE] [S🐾] [✕] [⌬]

OZARK

Comfort Inn Ⓜ
(417) 485-6688. **$55-$80.** 1900 W Evangel St. US 65, exit SR 14, southwest corner. Int corridors. **Pets:** Other species. $10 one-time fee/pet. Service with restrictions, supervision.
[SAVE] [S🐾] [✕] [🛏] [🛏] [💻] [⌬]

PERRYVILLE

Best Western Colonial Inn Ⓜ
(573) 547-1091. **$64-$69, 5 days notice.** 1500 Liberty St. I-55, exit 129 (US 51 S). Int corridors. **Pets:** Medium, other species. Service with restrictions, supervision.
[SAVE] [S🐾] [✕] [🛏] [💻] [⌬]

POPLAR BLUFF

▼▼▼▼ Comfort Inn M
(573) 686-5200. **$60-$79.** 2582 N Westwood Blvd. 1.3 mi s from jct US 60 E. Int corridors. **Pets:** Accepted.
[SAVE] 🇸🇩 ⊗ ⚙ 🐾 🛏 💻 ➴

▼▼▼▼ Drury Inn-Poplar Bluff M
(573) 686-2451. **$62-$92.** 2220 N Westwood Blvd. On US 67, 1.4 mi s from jct US 60 E. Int corridors. **Pets:** Accepted.
⊗ 🐾 🛏 💻 ➴

▼▼ Pear Tree Inn by Drury M
(573) 785-7100. **$52-$74.** 2218 N Westwood Blvd. On US 67, 1.4 mi s from jct US 60 E. Ext corridors. **Pets:** Accepted.
⊗ 🐾 ➴

PORTAGEVILLE

▲▲▲ ▼ TeRoy Motel M
(573) 379-5461. **$37-$39.** 903 N Hwy 61. I-55, exit 32, 0.5 mi w to US 61, then 0.8 mi n. Ext corridors. **Pets:** Accepted.
[SAVE] ⊗

RICH HILL

▲▲▲ ▼ Apache Motel M
(417) 395-2161. **$35-$38.** On CR B, just e of jct US 71. Ext corridors. **Pets:** Accepted.
[SAVE] 🇸🇩 ⊗

ROLLA

▲▲▲ ▼▼▼ Best Western Coachlight M
(573) 341-2511. **$48-$75.** 1403 Martin Springs Dr. At jct I-44 and Business Rt 44 S, exit 184. Ext corridors. **Pets:** Other species. Service with restrictions, supervision.
[SAVE] 🇸🇩 ⊗ 🛏 💻 ➴

▼▼ Days Inn M
(573) 341-3700. **$50-$80.** 1207 Kingshighway. I-44, exit 184, just s. Ext corridors. **Pets:** Service with restrictions, supervision.
[SAVE] 🇸🇩 ⊗ ➴

▼▼▼▼ Drury Inn M
(573) 364-4000. **$50-$93.** 2006 N Bishop. I-44, exit 186 (US 63), just ne. Ext/int corridors. **Pets:** Accepted.
⊗ 🛏 💻 ➴

▲▲▲ ▼▼ Econo Lodge M
(573) 341-3130. **$50-$60.** 1417 Martin Springs Dr. I-44, exit 184. Ext corridors. **Pets:** Medium, other species. Designated rooms, service with restrictions, crate.
[SAVE] 🇸🇩 ⊗ 🛏 ➴

▼▼▼▼ Holiday Inn Express M
(573) 364-8200. **$60-$90.** 1507 Martin Springs Dr. I-44, exit 184. Int corridors. **Pets:** Small. $10 daily fee/pet. Service with restrictions, supervision.
[ASK] 🇸🇩 ⊗ 🐾 🛏 💻 ➴

▲▲▲ ▼▼▼▼ Howard Johnson M
(573) 364-7111. **$49-$70.** 127 H J Dr. I-44, exit 184. Ext/int corridors. **Pets:** Accepted.
[SAVE] ⊗ 🛏 💻 🍽 ➴

SEDALIA

▼▼▼▼ The Hotel Bothwell H
(660) 826-5588. **$79-$229, 7 days notice.** 103 E 4th St. corner of 4th St and S Ohio. Int corridors. **Pets:** Small. $25 one-time fee/pet. Service with restrictions, crate.
[ASK] 🇸🇩 ⊗ 🛏 💻 🍽

SPRINGFIELD

▲▲▲ ▼▼▼ Baymont Inn & Suites M
(417) 889-8188. **$54-$74.** 3776 S Glenstone Ave. US 60. Int corridors. **Pets:** Accepted.
[SAVE] 🇸🇩 ⊗ 🐾 🐾 🐾 🛏 💻 ➴

▲▲▲ ▼▼▼ Best Western Coach House Inn M
(417) 862-0701. **$44-$69.** 2535 N Glenstone Ave. I-44, exit 80A, just s. Ext corridors. **Pets:** Service with restrictions, supervision.
[SAVE] 🇸🇩 ⊗ 🛏 💻 ➴

▲▲▲ ▼▼▼ Best Western Route 66 Rail Haven M
(417) 866-1963. **$44-$75.** 203 S Glenstone Ave. I-44, exit 80A, 3 mi s. Ext corridors. **Pets:** Accepted.
[SAVE] 🇸🇩 ⊗ 🐾 🛏 ➴

▼▼▼▼ Clarion Hotel H
(417) 883-6550. **$76-$99.** 3333 S Glenstone Ave. US 60, 0.5 mi n. Int corridors. **Pets:** Medium, other species. $10 daily fee/pet. Service with restrictions, crate.
[SAVE] 🇸🇩 ⊗ 🐾 🛏 💻 🍽 ➴

▲▲▲ ▼▼▼▼ Comfort Suites M
(417) 886-5090. **$80-$90.** 1260 E Independence St. US 60 (James River Expwy), exit National Ave. Ext corridors. **Pets:** Accepted.
[SAVE] 🇸🇩 ⊗ 🐾 🛏 💻 ➴

▼▼▼▼ Days Inn M ✿
(417) 862-0153. **$65-$146, 10 days notice.** 621 W Sunshine. US 65, exit Sunshine St, 3 mi w; across from the Bass Pro Shop. Int corridors. **Pets:** Other species. $10 daily fee/pet. Designated rooms, supervision.
[SAVE] 🇸🇩 ⊗ 🐾 🛏 💻 ➴

▼▼▼▼ Drury Inn & Suites-Springfield M
(417) 863-8400. **$70-$110.** 2715 N Glenstone Ave. I-44, exit 80A (Glenstone Ave), just s. Int corridors. **Pets:** Accepted.
⊗ 🐾 🐾 🐾 🛏 💻 ➴

▲▲▲ ▼▼▼▼ Econo Lodge-South M
(417) 882-2220. **$54-$125.** 3404 E Ridgeview. US 65, exit Battlefield Rd. Int corridors. **Pets:** Small, other species. $10 one-time fee/room. Service with restrictions, supervision.
[SAVE] 🇸🇩 ⊗ 🛏 💻 ➴

Holiday Inn University Plaza Hotel 🔆
(417) 864-7333. **$99-$129.** 333 John Q Hammons Pkwy. 0.5 mi e on St Louis St. Int corridors. **Pets:** $10 daily fee/room. Designated rooms, service with restrictions, supervision.

Howard Johnson Express Inn 🔆
(417) 890-6060. **$55-$70.** 2535 S Campbell. S on US 65 S to Sunshine Ave, then just s. Int corridors. **Pets:** Other species. $15 daily fee/pet. Service with restrictions, supervision.

Merigold Inn M
(417) 881-2833. **$44-$68.** 2006 S Glenstone Ave. On Business US 65, just s of CR D. Ext corridors. **Pets:** Small, dogs only. $10 daily fee/pet. Supervision.

Motel 6–1190 M
(417) 833-0880. **$37-$51.** 3114 Kentwood N. I-44, exit 80B, just nw. Ext corridors. **Pets:** Small. Service with restrictions, supervision.

Pear Tree Inn by Drury M
(417) 869-0001. **$50-$85.** 2745 N Glenstone Ave. I-44, exit 80A, just s. Ext/int corridors. **Pets:** Accepted.

Ramada Inn M
(417) 869-3900. **$54-$74.** 2820 N Glenstone Ave. I-44, exit 80A, just se. Ext/int corridors. **Pets:** Accepted.

Red Roof Inn M
(417) 831-2100. **$36-$54.** 2655 N Glenstone Ave. I-44, exit 80A, just s. Ext corridors. **Pets:** Accepted.

Scottish Inns M
(417) 862-4301. **$40-$45.** 2933 N Glenstone Ave. I-44, exit 80, just s, then 0.3 mi w. Ext corridors. **Pets:** Very small, dogs only. $10 one-time fee/room. Designated rooms, service with restrictions, supervision.

Sheraton Hotel H
(417) 831-3131. **$109-$119, 3 days notice.** 2431 N Glenstone Ave. I-44, exit 80A, just s. Int corridors. **Pets:** Accepted.

Sleep Inn of Springfield M
(417) 886-2464. **$48-$84, 3 days notice.** 233 E Camino Alto. US 60, exit Campbell Ave. Int corridors. **Pets:** Medium, other species. $25 one-time fee/pet. Service with restrictions, supervision.

ST. CLAIR

Budget Lodging M
(636) 629-1000. **$59-$79, 7 days notice.** 866 S Outer Rd W. I-44, exit 240, just w. Ext/int corridors. **Pets:** Other species. $5 daily fee/pet. Designated rooms, service with restrictions, supervision.

ST. JAMES

Comfort Inn M
(573) 265-5005. **$60-$120, 30 days notice.** 110 N Outer Rd. I-44, exit 195, southwest corner. Ext/int corridors. **Pets:** Accepted.

ST. JOSEPH

Drury Inn-St. Joseph M
(816) 364-4700. **$65-$95.** 4213 Frederick Blvd. I-29, exit 47 (SR 6). Int corridors. **Pets:** Accepted.

Holiday Inn Riverfront MI
(816) 279-8000. **$76.** 102 S Third St. I-229, exit Edmond St northbound; exit Felix St southbound; downtown. Int corridors. **Pets:** Small, dogs only. Designated rooms, service with restrictions.

Ramada Inn MI
(816) 233-6192. **$68-$83.** 4016 Frederick Blvd. I-29, exit 47. Int corridors. **Pets:** Medium, dogs only. $25 deposit/room. Designated rooms, service with restrictions, supervision.

ST. LOUIS METROPOLITAN AREA

BRIDGETON

Holiday Inn St. Louis Airport North H
(314) 731-2100. **$109-$139, 3 days notice.** 4545 N Lindbergh Blvd. I-70, exit 235B (US 67), just n. Int corridors. **Pets:** Small. $25 one-time fee/room. No service, supervision.

Red Roof Inn-Bridgeton M
(314) 291-3350. **$43-$69.** 3470 Hollenberg Dr. I-270, exit 20B (St Charles Rock Rd), 0.4 mi w. Ext corridors. **Pets:** Small. Designated rooms, service with restrictions, crate.

CLAYTON

▼▼▼▼ The Daniele Hotel 🅷 🐾
(314) 721-0101. **$119.** 216 N Meramec Ave. 1.5 mi n of I-64/US 40, exit 31 on Brentwood, e on Maryland, then just n; from I-170, exit 1F Ladue, 0.8 mi e on Maryland, then just n. Int corridors. **Pets:** Small, dogs only.
(A$K) (S🐾) (X) (🖂) (🍽) (⊒)

CREVE COEUR

▼▼▼▼ Drury Inn & Suites-Creve Coeur **M**
(314) 989-1100. **$80-$130.** 11980 Olive Blvd. I-270, exit 14 (Olive Blvd). Int corridors. **Pets:** Accepted.
(X) (&M) (🕅) (🖋) (🖂) (💷) (⊒)

EDMUNDSON

▼▼▼▼ Drury Inn-St. Louis Airport **M**
(314) 423-7700. **$82-$116.** 10490 Natural Bridge Rd. I-70, exit 236 (Lambert Airport), just se. Int corridors. **Pets:** Accepted.
(X) (&M) (🕅) (🖋) (🖂) (💷) (⊒)

EUREKA

🅐🅐🅐 ▼▼▼▼ Ramada Inn at Six Flags **MI** 🐾
(636) 938-6661. **$69-$229, 3 days notice.** 4901 Six Flags Rd. I-44, exit 261 (Allenton Rd). Ext/int corridors. **Pets:** Other species. $25 one-time fee/room. Designated rooms, service with restrictions, crate.
(SAVE) (S🐾) (X) (🖂) (💷) (🍽) (⊒)

🅐🅐🅐 ▼▼▼ Red Carpet Inn **M**
(636) 938-5348. **$40-$76.** 1725 W 5th St. I-44, exit 261, 0.8 mi ne. Ext corridors. **Pets:** Accepted.
(SAVE) (S🐾) (X) (🖂) (⊒)

FENTON

▼▼▼▼ Drury Inn & Suites Fenton **M**
(636) 343-7822. **$73-$111.** 1088 S Hwy Dr. I-44, exit 274 (Bowles Ave), just se. Int corridors. **Pets:** Accepted.
(X) (🕅) (🖂) (💷) (⊒)

▼▼▼▼ Pear Tree Inn by Drury-Fenton **M**
(636) 343-8820. **$56-$100.** 1100 S Hwy Dr. I-44, exit 274 (Bowles Ave), just s. Int corridors. **Pets:** Small, other species. Service with restrictions, supervision.
(X) (🕅) (🖂) (⊒)

FLORISSANT

🅐🅐🅐 ▼▼▼ Red Roof Inn-Florissant **M**
(314) 831-7900. **$42-$50.** 307 Dunn Rd. I-270, exit 26B (Graham/Hanley rds) eastbound, just n; exit 27 (Florissant Rd) westbound, 1 mi w on service road (Dunn Rd). Ext corridors. **Pets:** Designated rooms, service with restrictions, supervision.
(SAVE) (X) (🕅) (🖋)

FORISTELL

🅐🅐🅐 ▼▼▼ Best Western West 70 Inn **M**
(636) 673-2900. **$50-$60, 14 days notice.** 12 Hwy W. I-70, exit 203 (CR W), just n. Int corridors. **Pets:** Accepted.
(SAVE) (S🐾) (X) (🖂) (⊒)

HAZELWOOD

▼▼▼▼ La Quinta Inn-Airport **M**
(314) 731-3881. **$74-$81.** 5781 Campus Ct. I-270, exit 23 (McDonnell Blvd), just s. Int corridors. **Pets:** Accepted.
(SAVE) (X) (🕅) (🖂) (💷) (⊒)

KIRKWOOD

🅐🅐🅐 ▼▼▼▼ Best Western Kirkwood Inn **MI**
(314) 821-3950. **$89-$109, 7 days notice.** 1200 S Kirkwood Rd. I-44, exit 277B, just n. Int corridors. **Pets:** Medium. $10 daily fee/pet. Service with restrictions, crate.
(SAVE) (S🐾) (X) (🕅) (🖂) (💷) (🍽) (⊒)

MARYLAND HEIGHTS

🅐🅐🅐 ▼▼▼▼ Baymont Inn & Suites St. Louis-Westport **M**
(314) 878-1212. **$64-$74.** 12330 Dorsett Rd. I-270, exit 14, just w. Int corridors. **Pets:** Other species. Designated rooms, no service, supervision.
(SAVE) (S🐾) (X) (🖂) (💷)

🅐🅐🅐 ▼▼▼▼ Comfort Inn Westport **MI**
(314) 878-1400. **$55-$109.** 12031 Lackland Rd. I-270, exit 16A (Page Ave), just e to Lackland Rd, then just w. Int corridors. **Pets:** Medium, other species. $10 daily fee/pet, $25 one-time fee/room. Designated rooms, no service, supervision.
(SAVE) (S🐾) (X) (🕅) (🖋) (🖂) (💷) (🍽) (⊒)

▼▼▼▼ Drury Inn & Suites-Westport **M**
(314) 576-9966. **$70-$106.** 12220 Dorsett Rd. I-270, exit 17, just se. Int corridors. **Pets:** Accepted.
(X) (🕅) (🖂) (💷) (⊒)

▼▼▼▼ Harrah's Hotel at Riverport Casino Center 🅷
(314) 770-8100. **$89-$229.** 777 Casino Center Dr. I-70, exit 231 (Earth City Expwy), 1 mi s to Casino Center Dr, 1.2 mi nw. Int corridors. **Pets:** Small, other species. $25 one-time fee/room. Service with restrictions.
(A$K) (X) (&M) (🖋) (🖂) (💷)

▼▼▼▼ Holiday Inn Westport 🅷
(314) 434-0100. **$119-$159.** 1973 Craigshire Rd. I-270, exit 16A (Page Ave), just e to Lackland Rd, then 0.4 mi sw on Lackland and Craigshire rds. Int corridors. **Pets:** Large, other species. $50 deposit/room. Service with restrictions, supervision.
(A$K) (S🐾) (X) (🕅) (🖋) (🖂) (💷) (🍽) (⊒)

▼▼▼▼ **La Quinta Inn & Suites St. Louis Westport** Ⓜ
(314) 991-3262. **$80-$110.** 11805 Lackland Rd. I-270, exit 16A (Page Ave), 1.5 mi se via Lackland Rd exit. Int corridors. **Pets:** Small. Service with restrictions, supervision.
(SAVE) ⊠ ⓜ ⌁ ⌁ 🛢 🖥 ⇲

Ⓐ ▼▼▼ **Red Roof Inn-Westport** Ⓜ
(314) 991-4900. **$46-$68.** 11837 Lackland Rd. I-270, exit 16A (Page Ave), 1.5 mi se. Ext corridors. **Pets:** Small. Service with restrictions, supervision.
(SAVE) ⊠ ⓜ ⌁

Ⓐ ▼▼▼ **Residence Inn by Marriott-Westport** Ⓜ
(314) 469-0060. **$89-$109.** 1881 Craigshire Rd. I-270, exit 16A (Page Ave), 0.7 mi e, exit Lackland Rd, then 1 mi w, then s via Lackland and Craigshire rds. Ext corridors. **Pets:** Medium. $6 daily fee/room, $100 one-time fee/room. Service with restrictions, supervision.
(SAVE) ⓢ ⊠ ⌁ 🛢 🖥 ⇲

MEHLVILLE

▼▼▼ **Best Western 55 South Inn** Ⓜ
(314) 416-7639. **$70-$85.** 6224 Heimos Industrial Park Dr. I-55, exit 193 (Meramec Bottom Rd), just e to Heimos Industrial Park Dr, then just n. Int corridors. **Pets:** Very small, dogs only. $50 deposit/pet. Designated rooms, service with restrictions, supervision.
(SAVE) ⓢ ⊠ ⌁ 🛢 🖥 ⇲

▼▼▼ **Holiday Inn St. Louis-South I-55** Ⓜ ✿
(314) 894-0700. **$89-$119.** 4234 Butler Hill Rd. I-55, exit 195 (Butler Hill Rd), just se. Ext/int corridors. **Pets:** Service with restrictions, supervision.
(ASK) ⓢ ⊠ ⌁ 🛢 🖥 ⑪ ⇲

RICHMOND HEIGHTS

Ⓐ ▼▼▼ **Residence Inn By Marriott-St. Louis Galleria** 🅰 ✿
(314) 862-1900. **$124-$189.** 1100 McMorrow Ave. I-170 N, exit 1C (Brentwood Ave), 0.5 mi e of Galleria via Galleria Pkwy. Ext corridors. **Pets:** Large, other species. $10 daily fee/room, $50 one-time fee/room. Service with restrictions, crate.
(SAVE) ⊠ ⓜ ⌁ ⌁ 🛢 🖥 ⇲

ST. ANN

▼▼▼ **Hampton Inn-St. Louis Airport** Ⓜ
(314) 427-3400. **$75-$118.** 10800 Pear Tree Ln. I-70, exit 236, just sw. Int corridors. **Pets:** Accepted.
(SAVE) ⊠ 🛢 🖥 ⇲

ST. CHARLES

Ⓐ ▼▼▼ **Baymont Inn St. Charles** Ⓜ
(636) 946-6936. **$61-$81, 7 days notice.** 1425 S 5th St. I-70, exit 229B (5th St N), just n, then w. Int corridors. **Pets:** Medium, other species. $10 daily fee/pet. Designated rooms, service with restrictions, supervision.
(SAVE) ⓢ ⊠ ⌁ 🛢 🖥 ⑪ ⇲

Ⓐ ▼▼▼ **Red Roof Inn-St Charles** Ⓜ
(636) 947-7770. **$48-$67.** 2010 Zumbehl Rd. I-70, exit 227 (Zumbehl Rd), just s. Ext corridors. **Pets:** Accepted.
(SAVE) ⊠ ⌁

ST. LOUIS

▼▼▼ **Drury Inn & Suites Convention Center** Ⓜ
(314) 231-8100. **$92-$112.** 711 N Broadway. I-70, exit 250B, at Convention Center. Int corridors. **Pets:** Accepted.
⊠ 🛢 🖥 ⑪ ⇲

▼▼▼ **Drury Inn Union Station** Ⓜ
(314) 231-3900. **$92-$152.** 201 S 20th St. Just e of Jefferson Ave; between Market St and Clark Ave. Int corridors. **Pets:** Small. Service with restrictions, crate.
⊠ ⌁ 🛢 🖥 ⑪ ⇲

▼▼▼ **Drury Plaza Hotel** Ⓜ
(314) 231-3003. **$100-$171.** 14 S Fourth St. I-70, 250B (Stadium/Memorial Dr), just w on Pine to Broadway, just s to Walnut, just e to Fourth St, then just n. Int corridors. **Pets:** Accepted.
⊠ ⓜ ⌁ 🛢 🖥 ⑪ ⇲

▼▼▼ **Hampton Inn Union Station** Ⓗ ✿
(314) 241-3200. **$94-$130.** 2211 Market St. I-64/US 40, exit 39, just n on Jefferson Ave, then just e. Int corridors. **Pets:** Large. Service with restrictions, crate.
(SAVE) ⊠ 🛢 🖥 ⑪ ⇲

▼▼▼ **Holiday Inn-Forest Park** Ⓜ
(314) 645-0700. **$99-$130.** 5915 Wilson Ave. I-44, exit 286, just s. Int corridors. **Pets:** Other species. $75 deposit/room. Service with restrictions, supervision.
(ASK) ⓢ ⊠ ⓜ ⌁ ⌁ 🛢 🖥 ⑪ ⇲

Ⓐ ▼▼▼ **Red Roof Inn-Hampton** Ⓜ
(314) 645-0101. **$67-$107.** 5823 Wilson Ave. I-44, exit 286 (Hampton Ave), 0.3 mi se. Ext corridors. **Pets:** Medium, other species. Service with restrictions, supervision.
(SAVE) ⊠ ⌁

ST. PETERS

▼▼▼ **Drury Inn-St. Charles/St. Peters** Ⓜ
(636) 397-9700. **$78-$111.** 80 Mid Rivers Mall Drive Dr. I-70, exit 222 (Mid Rivers Mall Dr), just se. Int corridors. **Pets:** Other species. Service with restrictions, crate.
⊠ ⓜ ⌁ ⌁ 🛢 🖥 ⇲

▼▼▼ Holiday Inn Select of St. Peters/St.
Charles M
(636) 928-1500. **$72.** 4341 Veteran's Memorial Pkwy. I-70,
exit 225 (Cave Springs), 0.5 mi w. Int corridors.
Pets: Accepted.
[ASK] [S⬥] [✕] [🛏] [💻] [🍴] [⊃]

WENTZVILLE

⟨AAA⟩ ▼▼▼ Super 8 Motel-Wentzville M
(636) 327-5300. **$50.** 4 Pantera Dr. I-70, exit 208 (Pearce
Blvd), on S Outer Rd. Int corridors. **Pets:** Medium, dogs
only. $50 deposit/pet. Service with restrictions, supervision.
[SAVE] [S⬥] [✕] [♫] [⊃]

WOODSON TERRACE

▼ Motel 6–61 M
(314) 427-1313. **$46-$60.** 4576 Woodson Rd. I-70, exit 236
(Woodson Rd), at Natural Bridge Rd. Int corridors.
Pets: Other species. No service, supervision.
[S⬥] [✕] [🐾] [⊃]

❀ **END METROPOLITAN AREA** ❀

ST. ROBERT

⟨AAA⟩ ▼▼▼ Best Western Montis Inn M
(573) 336-4299. **$50-$70.** 14086 Hwy Z. I-44, exit 163, just
se. Ext corridors. **Pets:** Accepted.
[SAVE] [S⬥] [✕] [🛏] [⊃]

STE. GENEVIEVE

⟨AAA⟩ ▼▼ Family Budget Inn M
(573) 543-2272. **$50-$60.** 17030 New Bremen Rd. I-55, exit
143, just w on SR M. Ext/int corridors. **Pets:** Small, other
species. $3 one-time fee/pet. No service, crate.
[SAVE] [✕] [🛏] [⊃]

STOCKTON

⟨AAA⟩ ▼ Holliday Motel M
(417) 276-4443. **$50-$60, 3 days notice.** 400 Hwy 32 E.
SR 32, just e of jct SR 39. Ext corridors. **Pets:** Accepted.
[SAVE] [S⬥] [✕] [⊃]

STRAFFORD

▼▼ Super 8 Motel M
(417) 736-3883. **$60.** 315 E Chestnut St. I-44, exit 88,
southeast corner. Int corridors. **Pets:** Accepted.
[ASK] [S⬥] [✕] [🛏]

SULLIVAN

⟨AAA⟩ ▼▼▼ Super 8 Motel-Sullivan M
(573) 468-8076. **$50-$55.** 601 N Service Rd. I-44, exit 225,
just ne. Int corridors. **Pets:** Other species. $5 one-time fee/
room. Service with restrictions, supervision.
[SAVE] [S⬥] [✕] [🛏] [💻]

SWEET SPRINGS

⟨AAA⟩ ▼▼▼ People's Choice Motel M
(660) 335-6315. **$37-$41.** 1001 N Locust St. I-70, exit 66
(SR 127). Ext corridors. **Pets:** Other species. $20 deposit/
room. Supervision.
[SAVE] [S⬥] [✕]

TIPTON

▼ Twin Pine Motel M ❀
(660) 433-5525. **$38-$60.** 442 Hwy 50 W. On US 50 and
SR 5, just west. Ext corridors. **Pets:** Other species. Designated rooms, supervision.
[✕] [🛏]

WAPPAPELLO

▼▼▼ Millers Motor Lodge M
(573) 222-8579. **$42-$54, 7 days notice.** 8920 Hwy T. 2 mi
s of Wappapello Dam, on Hwy T. Ext corridors.
Pets: Accepted.
[🛏] [💻] [⊃]

WARRENSBURG

▼▼ University Inn M
(660) 747-5125. **$59-$89.** 403 E Russell Ave. Jct US 50
and SR 13. Ext corridors. **Pets:** Small, other species. $30
deposit/pet, $5 daily fee/pet. Designated rooms, service
with restrictions, supervision.
[ASK] [S⬥] [✕] [🛏] [🍴] [⊃]

WARRENTON

▼▼ Warrenton Super 8 M
(636) 456-5157. **$46-$50.** 1429 N Service Rd. I-70, exit
193, just n to N Service Rd, then 0.6 mi e. Int corridors.
Pets: Other species. $10 daily fee/pet. Service with restric-
tions, supervision.
[ASK] [S⬥] [✕] [⬥M] [🛏] [💻]

WEST PLAINS

▼▼ Ramada Inn M ❀
(417) 256-8191. **$62-$64.** 1301 Preacher Roe Blvd. 2 mi
sw at jct US 160 and 63 Bypass. Ext/int corridors.
Pets: $10 daily fee/room. Service with restrictions, supervi-
sion.
[ASK] [S⬥] [✕] [🛏] [💻] [🍴] [⊃]

MONTANA

BELGRADE

🔺 ♦♦♦ Belgrade Inn & Suites M
(406) 388-2222. **$59-$109, 14 days notice.** 6445 Jack Rabbit Ln. I-90, exit 298, just s on SR 85. Int corridors. **Pets:** Service with restrictions.
[SAVE] [S🄳] [✕] [🄴] [🅷] [💻] [⇌]

♦♦♦ Gallatin River Lodge L
(406) 388-0148. **$150-$300, 7 days notice.** 9105 Thorpe Rd. I-90, exit 298, 2.7 mi s on SR 85, 1 mi w on Valley Center Rd (gravel), then 0.5 mi s, follow sign. Int corridors. **Pets:** Other species. $25 one-time fee/pet. Designated rooms.
[✕] [🍴] [⊠] [🄰🄲]

🔺 ♦♦♦ Holiday Inn Express M
(406) 388-0800. **$90-$100, 15 days notice.** 6261 Jack Rabbit Ln. I-90, exit 298, just s on SR 85. Int corridors. **Pets:** Designated rooms, supervision.
[SAVE] [S🄳] [✕] [🄴🄼] [🄴] [🍴]

BIG SKY

♦♦♦ 320 Guest Ranch R🄰
(406) 995-4283. **$95-$321, 30 days notice.** 205 Buffalo Horn. 11.8 mi s on US 191. Ext corridors. **Pets:** Other species. $10 daily fee/pet. Service with restrictions, supervision.
[A$K] [S🄳] [✕] [🅷] [💻] [🍴] [⊠] [🄰🄲]

🔺 ♦♦♦ Best Western Buck's T-4 Lodge M
(406) 995-4111. **$69-$144, 7 days notice.** 46625 Gallatin Rd. US 191, 1 mi s of Big Sky entrance. Ext/int corridors. **Pets:** Other species. $5 daily fee/pet. Supervision.
[SAVE] [S🄳] [✕] [🄴] [🅷] [💻] [🍴] [⊠]

🔺 ♦♦♦ Comfort Inn at Big Sky M
(406) 995-2333. **$59-$169, 3 days notice.** 47214 Gallatin Rd. US 191, 0.7 mi s of Big Sky entrance. Int corridors. **Pets:** Accepted.
[SAVE] [S🄳] [✕] [🄴] [🅷] [💻] [⇌]

BIGFORK

🔺 ♦♦♦ Mountain Lake Lodge M
(406) 837-3800. **$85-$265, 7 days notice.** 1950 Sylvan Dr. On US 35, 5 mi s. Ext corridors. **Pets:** Medium. $15 daily fee/pet. Designated rooms, supervision.
[SAVE] [S🄳] [✕] [🄴🄼] [🅷] [💻] [🍴] [⇌]

🔺 ♦♦♦ Timbers Motel M 🐾
(406) 837-6200. **$42-$82, 7 days notice.** 8540 Hwy 35. Just n on SR 35 from jct of SR 209. Ext corridors. **Pets:** $50 deposit/room, $5 daily fee/pet. Service with restrictions, supervision.
[SAVE] [✕] [🄴] [💻] [⇌]

BILLINGS

🔺 ♦♦♦ Best Western Billings M
(406) 248-9800. **$75-$108.** 5610 S Frontage Rd. I-90, exit 446, just s. Ext/int corridors. **Pets:** Accepted.
[SAVE] [S🄳] [✕] [🄴🄼] [🄴] [🅷] [💻] [⇌]

🔺 ♦♦♦ Best Western Ponderosa Inn M
(406) 259-5511. **$65-$85.** 2511 1st Ave N. on I-90 business loop. Ext/int corridors. **Pets:** Accepted.
[SAVE] [S🄳] [✕] [🄵] [🅷] [💻] [🍴] [⇌]

🔺 ♦♦♦ Billings Hotel and Convention Center M
(406) 248-7151. **$89-$109.** 1223 Mullowney Ln. I-90, exit 446, just s. Int corridors. **Pets:** $75 deposit/room. Designated rooms, service with restrictions, supervision.
[SAVE] [S🄳] [✕] [🅷] [💻] [🍴] [⇌]

🔺 ♦♦♦ The Billings Inn M 🐾
(406) 252-6800. **$62-$72.** 880 N 29th St. I-90, exit 27th St, 2 mi n, just w on 9th Ave. Int corridors. **Pets:** Other species. $5 daily fee/room. Designated rooms, service with restrictions, supervision.
[SAVE] [S🄳] [✕] [🅷] [💻]

♦♦♦ Billings Super 8 Lodge M
(406) 248-8842. **$67-$97.** 5400 Southgate Dr. I-90, exit 447, just n on S Billings Blvd, 0.8 mi w on King Ave, then just s on Parkway Ln. Int corridors. **Pets:** Accepted.
[A$K] [S🄳] [✕] [🄴🄼] [🄵] [🅷] [💻]

⚑⚑⚑⚑ Cherry Tree Inn M
(406) 252-5603. **$48-$53.** 823 N Broadway. I-90, exit 450, 2 mi n on 27th St, just w on 9th Ave. Int corridors. **Pets:** Other species. Service with restrictions, crate.
SAVE S6 ✕ 🛋 💻

⚑⚑ Comfort Inn of Billings M
(406) 652-5200. **$60-$90.** 2030 Overland Ave. I-90, exit 446, n on King Ave W, just s on Overland Ave, first stoplight. Int corridors. **Pets:** $10 one-time fee/room. Designated rooms, supervision.
SAVE S6 ✕ 👪 🐾 🛋 💻 ⇌

⚑⚑ Days Inn M
(406) 252-4007. **$60-$90, 30 days notice.** 843 Parkway Ln. I-90 W, exit 447, just n on S Billings Blvd, 0.8 mi s on Parkway Ln, just s; I-90 E, exit 446, follow signs. Int corridors. **Pets:** Other species. Service with restrictions, supervision.
SAVE S6 ✕ 👪 🛋 💻

⚑⚑ Dude Rancher Lodge M
(406) 259-5561. **$-$57.** 415 N 29th St. just w of the 400 blk of N 27th st. Ext/int corridors. **Pets:** Other species. $5 daily fee/room. Designated rooms, service with restrictions, supervision.
SAVE S6 ✕ 🛋 💻 🍴

⚑⚑⚑ Hampton Inn M
(406) 248-4949. **$68-$89.** 5110 Southgate Dr. I-90, exit 447, just n on Billings Blvd, just w on King Ave, then 0.4 mi sw. Int corridors. **Pets:** Accepted.
SAVE S6 ✕ 👪 🐾 👪 🛋 💻 ⇌

⚑⚑⚑ Hilltop Inn M ☙
(406) 245-5000. **$62-$72.** 1116 N 28th St. I-90, exit 450, 2 mi n, just w on 11th Ave, then just n. Int corridors. **Pets:** Other species. $5 daily fee/room. Designated rooms, service with restrictions, supervision.
SAVE S6 ✕ 👪 🛋 💻

⚑⚑⚑ Holiday Inn Grand Montana Billings H
(406) 248-7701. **$89-$99, 3 days notice.** 5500 Midland Rd. I-90, exit 446. Int corridors. **Pets:** Accepted.
ASK S6 ✕ 👪 🐾 👪 🛋 💻 🍴 ⇌

⚑⚑⚑ Howard Johnson Express Inn M
(406) 248-4656. **$47-$81, 7 days notice.** 1001 S 27th St. I-90, exit 450, just n on SR 3 (S 27th St). Int corridors. **Pets:** Accepted.
ASK S6 ✕ 👪 🐾 👪 🛋 💻

⚑⚑ Kelly Inn M
(406) 252-2700. **$68-$78.** 5425 Midland Rd. I-90, exit 446, 0.5 mi se. Ext/int corridors. **Pets:** Accepted.
SAVE S6 ✕ 👪 🛋 💻 ⇌

⚑⚑⚑ The Northern Hotel H
(406) 245-5121. **$83-$103.** 19 N 28th St. Downtown. Int corridors. **Pets:** Large. Designated rooms, service with restrictions.
SAVE S6 ✕ 🐾 🛋 💻 🍴

⚑⚑⚑ Quality Inn Homestead M
(406) 652-1320. **$66-$99.** 2036 Overland Ave. I-90, exit 446, n on King Ave W, just s, 1st stoplight. Int corridors. **Pets:** Other species. $25 deposit/room. Supervision.
SAVE S6 ✕ 🛋 💻 ⇌

⚑⚑ Ramada Limited M
(406) 252-2584. **$57-$97.** 1345 Mullowney Ln. I-90, exit 446, just s. Int corridors. **Pets:** Accepted.
ASK S6 ✕ 🐾 👪 🛋 ⇌

⚑⚑⚑ Rimrock Inn M
(406) 252-7107. **$64-$68.** 1203 N 27th St. I-90, exit 450, 2.3 mi n. Ext/int corridors. **Pets:** Other species. $5 daily fee/room. Service with restrictions, supervision.
SAVE S6 ✕ 🍴

⚑⚑⚑ Rimview Inn M
(406) 248-2622. **$45-$60.** 1025 N 27th St. I-90, exit 450, 2 mi n. Ext/int corridors. **Pets:** Dogs only. $5 one-time fee/pet. Service with restrictions, supervision.
SAVE ✕ 🛋

⚑⚑⚑ Sheraton Billings Hotel H
(406) 252-7400. **$109.** 27 N 27th St. I-90 business loop and SR 3. Int corridors. **Pets:** Accepted.
ASK S6 ✕ 👪 🛋 💻 🍴 ⇌

BOZEMAN

⚑⚑⚑⚑ Best Western GranTree Inn M
(406) 587-5261. **$79-$109.** 1325 N 7th Ave. I-90, exit 306, just s. Int corridors. **Pets:** Service with restrictions, supervision.
SAVE S6 ✕ 💻 🍴 ⇌

⚑⚑⚑ Bozeman Inn M
(406) 587-3176. **$45-$79.** 1235 N 7th Ave. I-90, exit 306, just s. Ext corridors. **Pets:** $5 daily fee/room. Supervision.
SAVE S6 ✕ 🛋 💻 ⇌

⚑⚑ Bozeman Super 8 M
(406) 586-1521. **$45-$75.** 800 Wheat Dr. I-90, exit 306, just n, then just w. Int corridors. **Pets:** Other species. $5 daily fee/room. Designated rooms, service with restrictions, supervision.
ASK S6 ✕

⚑⚑⚑⚑ Bozeman's Western Heritage Inn M ☙
(406) 586-8534. **$46-$88.** 1200 E Main St. I-90 business loop, exit 309, 0.5 mi w. Int corridors. **Pets:** Dogs only. $25 deposit/room, $5 daily fee/pet. Service with restrictions, supervision.
SAVE S6 ✕ 🛋

⚑⚑⚑⚑ Holiday Inn M
(406) 587-4561. **$79-$109.** 5 Baxter Ln. I-90, exit 306, I-90 business loop, just s of jct I-90. Int corridors. **Pets:** Accepted.
SAVE S6 ✕ 👪 🛋 💻 🍴 ⇌

Motel 6 Bozeman M
(406) 585-7888. **$49-$89.** 817 Wheat Dr. I-90, exit 306, just n. Int corridors. **Pets:** Accepted.

Rainbow Motel M
(406) 587-4201. **$45-$70.** 510 N 7th Ave. I-90, exit 306, I-90 business loop, 0.8 mi s. Ext corridors. **Pets:** Accepted.

Ramada Limited M
(406) 585-2626. **$54-$99.** 2020 Wheat Dr. I-90, exit 306, just n, just w. Int corridors. **Pets:** Large, other species. Service with restrictions.

Royal "7" Budget Inn M
(406) 587-3103. **$44-$65.** 310 N 7th Ave. I-90 business loop, 0.8 mi s of jct I-90, exit 306. Ext corridors. **Pets:** Medium, other species. Designated rooms, supervision.

BROWNING

Western Motel M
(406) 338-7572. **$45-$90, 4 days notice.** 121 Central Ave E. Center of town on US 2. Ext corridors. **Pets:** Other species. Supervision.

BUTTE

Best Western Butte Plaza Inn MI
(406) 494-3500. **$69-$99.** 2900 Harrison Ave. I-90, exit 127 (Harrison Ave). Int corridors. **Pets:** Small. $50 deposit/room. Service with restrictions, supervision.

Comfort Inn of Butte M
(406) 494-8850. **$75-$99, 30 days notice.** 2777 Harrison Ave. I-90/15, exit 127, just s. Int corridors. **Pets:** Medium. $5 daily fee/room. Service with restrictions, supervision.

Days Inn M
(406) 494-7000. **$59-$109, 14 days notice.** 2700 Harrison Ave. I-90/15, exit 127, just n on Harrison Ave, e on Cornell St. Int corridors. **Pets:** Medium. Designated rooms, service with restrictions, supervision.

Ramada Inn Copper King MI
(406) 494-6666. **$89-$109.** 4655 Harrison Ave S. I-90/15, exit 127A, 2 mi s on SR 2 (Harrison Ave). Int corridors. **Pets:** Other species. $10 daily fee/room. Designated rooms, service with restrictions, supervision.

Red Lion Hotel MI
(406) 494-7800. **$69-$109.** 2100 Cornell Ave. I-90/15, exit 127B, just n on Harrison Ave, then just e. Int corridors. **Pets:** Medium. $8 daily fee/room. Designated rooms, service with restrictions.

Rocker Inn M
(406) 723-5464. **$48-$53.** 122001 W Brown's Gulch Rd. I-90/15, exit 122 (Rocker). Int corridors. **Pets:** Medium. $5 daily fee/room. Designated rooms, service with restrictions.

Super 8 Motel of Butte M
(406) 494-6000. **$58-$90, 3 days notice.** 2929 Harrison Ave. I-90/15, exit 127, just s. Int corridors. **Pets:** Dogs only. $60 deposit/room, $5 daily fee/room. Designated rooms, service with restrictions, supervision.

CHINOOK

Chinook Motor Inn MI
(406) 357-2248. **$58-$68.** 100 Indiana St. On US 2. Int corridors. **Pets:** Accepted.

CHOTEAU

Big Sky Motel M
(406) 466-5318. **$45-$65.** 209 S Main Ave. Just s of town center on US 89. Ext corridors. **Pets:** $5 daily fee/pet. Service with restrictions, supervision.

COLSTRIP

Super 8 Motel of Colstrip LLC M
(406) 748-3400. **$52-$89.** 6227 Main St. SR 39. Int corridors. **Pets:** Medium. $10 deposit/pet. Designated rooms, service with restrictions, supervision.

COLUMBIA FALLS

Meadow Lake Resort X
(406) 892-8700. **$89-$474, 30 days notice.** 100 St Andrews Dr. Jct US 2 and SR 40, 1.4 mi s on US 2, 1.1 mi n on Meadow Lake Blvd. Ext/int corridors. **Pets:** Other species. $15 daily fee/pet. Designated rooms, service with restrictions, supervision.

COLUMBUS

Super 8 of Columbus M
(406) 322-4101. **$65-$99, 30 days notice.** 602 8th Ave N. I-90, exit 408, just s on SR 78. Int corridors. **Pets:** Other species. $5 daily fee/pet. Service with restrictions, supervision.

CONRAD

Super 8 of Conrad M
(406) 278-7676. **$65-$99, 30 days notice.** 215 N Main. I-15, exit 339, just w. Int corridors. **Pets:** Other species. $5 daily fee/pet. Service with restrictions, supervision.

CUT BANK

△△△ ▼▼▼ Glacier Gateway Inn M
(406) 873-5544. **$54-$68.** 1121 E Railroad St. US 2, just e from town center. Int corridors. **Pets:** Accepted.
[SAVE] [S🔊] ✕ 🖥

△△△ ▼▼▼▼ Glacier Gateway Plaza M
(406) 873-5544. **$64-$74.** 1130 E Main St. Just e of town center on US 2. Int corridors. **Pets:** Accepted.
[SAVE] [S🔊] ✕ 🖥 ✍

DEER LODGE

▼▼▼▼ Coleman Fee Mansion Bed & Breakfast BB
(406) 846-2922. **$68-$158, 14 days notice.** 500 Missouri Ave. City center. Ext/int corridors. **Pets:** Accepted.
[ASK] ✕ 🐾 📺 🕹

△△△ ▼▼▼ Scharf's Motor Inn M
(406) 846-2810. **$50-$80.** 819 Main St. on I-90 business loop. Ext corridors. **Pets:** Other species. Service with restrictions, supervision.
[SAVE] ✕ 🖥

△△△ ▼▼▼ Super 8 Motel M
(406) 846-2370. **$69-$75, 10 days notice.** 1150 N Main St. I-90, exit 184, 0.3 mi s. Int corridors. **Pets:** Other species. $5 daily fee/pet. Designated rooms, service with restrictions, supervision.
[SAVE] [S🔊] ✕ 🖥 🖳

DILLON

△△△ ▼▼▼ Best Western Paradise Inn M
(406) 683-4214. **$52-$82.** 650 N Montana St. I-15, exit 63, 0.3 mi s on SR 41. Ext corridors. **Pets:** Accepted.
[SAVE] [S🔊] ✕ 🖳 🍴 ✍

△△△ ▼▼▼ Comfort Inn of Dillon M
(406) 683-6831. **$65-$99, 30 days notice.** 450 N Interchange. I-15, exit 63 (N Dillon). Int corridors. **Pets:** Other species. $5 daily fee/pet. Service with restrictions, supervision.
[SAVE] [S🔊] ✕ 🕹 🖥 🖳 ✍

▼▼▼▼ GuestHouse International Inns & Suites M
(406) 683-3636. **$53-$89, 7 days notice.** 580 Sinclair. I-15, exit 63. Int corridors. **Pets:** Other species. $10 one-time fee/room. Designated rooms, service with restrictions, supervision.
[ASK] [S🔊] ✕ [⅙M] 🃏 🖥 🖳 ✍

△△△ ▼▼▼ Sundowner Motel M
(406) 683-2375. **$38-$48.** 500 N Montana St. I-15, exit 63, just s. Ext corridors. **Pets:** Accepted.
[SAVE] [S🔊] ✕ 🖥

▼▼ ▼▼ Super 8 Motel M
(406) 683-4288. **$46-$66, 10 days notice.** 550 N Montana St. I-15, exit 63, just n on US 91. Int corridors. **Pets:** Other species. $25 deposit/room. Designated rooms, service with restrictions, supervision.
[ASK] [S🔊] ✕ 🖥

EAST GLACIER PARK

△△△ ▼▼ Dancing Bears Inn M
(406) 226-4402. **$45-$120, 4 days notice.** 40 Montana Ave. Center; just off US 2, follow signs. Ext/int corridors. **Pets:** Accepted.
[SAVE] ✕ 🖥

▼▼ ▼▼ Jacobson's Scenic View Cottages C
(406) 226-4422. **$49-$75.** 1204 Hwy 49. On SR 49, 0.8 mi n. Ext corridors. **Pets:** Small. $5 daily fee/pet. Service with restrictions, crate.
🖥 🖳 🃏 🕹

ENNIS

△△△ ▼▼▼▼ El Western Resort C
(406) 682-4217. **$60-$300, 3 days notice.** US Hwy 287 S. 0.8 mi s. Ext corridors. **Pets:** Large, dogs only. $10 daily fee/pet. Designated rooms, service with restrictions, supervision.
[SAVE] ✕ 🖥 🖳 🃏

△△△ ▼▼▼ Fan Mountain Inn M
(406) 682-5200. **$50-$65.** 204 N Main. US 287, just nw of city center. Ext corridors. **Pets:** Other species. $5 one-time fee/pet. Designated rooms, service with restrictions, supervision.
[SAVE] ✕ [⅙M] 🃏 🖥

△△△ ▼▼ Riverside Motel M
(406) 682-4240. **$40-$75, 14 days notice.** 346 Main St. US 287, e of town. Ext corridors. **Pets:** Other species. $5 daily fee/pet. Designated rooms, service with restrictions, supervision.
[SAVE] [S🔊] ✕ 🖥 🃏

▼▼ Sportsman's M
(406) 682-4242. **$55-$85, 10 days notice.** 310 US Hwy 287 N. US 287, just nw of city center. Ext corridors. **Pets:** Accepted.
[S🔊] ✕ 🖥 🍴

FORSYTH

△△△ ▼▼▼ Best Western Sundowner Inn M 🐾
(406) 356-2115. **$65-$80, 7 days notice.** 1018 Front St. I-94, exit 95, 0.5 mi nw on north frontage road. Ext corridors. **Pets:** Medium. $5 daily fee/pet. Service with restrictions, supervision.
[SAVE] [S🔊] ✕ 🖥 🖳

AAA ▼▼▼ **Rails Inn Motel** Ⓜ 🐾
(406) 356-2242. **$60-$65, 3 days notice.** 3rd & Front sts.
I-90, exit 93, just n, 0.5 mi e on frontage road. Int corridors.
Pets: Medium. $5 daily fee/room. Service with restrictions,
supervision.

[SAVE] [S🏊] [✕] [📶] [🍴]

AAA ▼ **Restwel Motel** Ⓜ
(406) 356-2771. **$39-$50.** 810 Front St. I-94, exit 95, 0.8 mi
nw on north frontage road. Ext corridors. **Pets:** $5 daily
fee/pet. Designated rooms, service with restrictions, supervision.

[SAVE] [S🏊] [✕] [📶]

AAA ▼ **Westwind Motor Inn** Ⓜ
(406) 356-2038. **$60-$65, 3 days notice.** 225 Westwind Ln.
I-94, exit 93, 0.3 mi n. Int corridors. **Pets:** Large. $5 daily
fee/pet. Service with restrictions, supervision.

[SAVE] [S🏊] [✕] [📶]

GARDINER

AAA ▼▼▼ **Best Western by Mammoth Hot**
Springs Ⓜ
(406) 848-7311. **$49-$115.** S Hwy 89. 0.5 mi n. Ext/int
corridors. **Pets:** Accepted.

[SAVE] [S🏊] [✕] [✏️] [📶] [📺] [🍴] [🏊]

▼▼ **Motel 6-4054** Ⓜ
(406) 848-7520. **$40-$85.** 109 Hellroaring Rd. North
entrance, just s on US 89, 0.5 mi n of Yellowstone north
gate. Ext corridors. **Pets:** Small. $15 one-time fee/room.
Service with restrictions, supervision.

[ASK] [S🏊] [✕] [✏️]

AAA ▼ **Yellowstone River Motel** Ⓜ
(406) 848-7303. **$40-$78.** 14 E Park St. Just e of US 89.
Ext corridors. **Pets:** Accepted.

[SAVE] [S🏊] [✕] [🛏️M] [📶] [📺]

▼▼ **Yellowstone Super 8-Gardiner** Ⓜ
(406) 848-7401. **$39-$99.** Hwy 89 S. On US 89. Int corridors. **Pets:** Medium. $50 deposit/room, $5 daily fee/pet.
Service with restrictions, supervision.

[ASK] [S🏊] [✕] [📶] [📺] [🏊]

GLASGOW

▼▼ **Cottonwood Inn** Ⓜ
(406) 228-8213. **$59-$66.** 45 1st Ave NE. 0.5 mi e of center
on US 2. Int corridors. **Pets:** Service with restrictions,
supervision.

[ASK] [S🏊] [✕] [📶] [🍴] [🏊]

GLENDIVE

AAA ▼▼▼ **Best Western Jordan Inn** Ⓜ
(406) 377-5555. **$62-$96, 5 days notice.** 223 N Merrill Ave.
I-94, exit 215, On I-94 business loop. Ext/int corridors.
Pets: Accepted.

[SAVE] [S🏊] [✕] [📶] [📺] [🍴] [🏊]

AAA ▼ **El Centro Motel** Ⓜ
(406) 377-5211. **$32-$37.** 112 S Kendrick Ave. I-94, exit
215, 1.4 mi sw on Merril Way, just n on Bell St, just w. Ext
corridors. **Pets:** Designated rooms, service with restrictions.

[SAVE] [S🏊] [✕] [📶]

▼▼ **Super 8 Glendive** Ⓜ
(406) 365-5671. **Call for rates.** 1904 Merrill Ave. I-94, exit
215, just n. Int corridors. **Pets:** Other species. Service with
restrictions, supervision.

[✕]

GREAT FALLS

AAA ▼▼▼ **Best Western Heritage Inn** Ⓜ
(406) 761-1900. **$89-$99.** 1700 Fox Farm Rd. I-15, exit
278, 0.8 mi e on 10th Ave S and US 87/89 and SR 3/200.
Int corridors. **Pets:** Accepted.

[SAVE] [S🏊] [✕] [✏️] [📶] [📺] [🍴] [🏊]

AAA ▼ **Budget Inn** Ⓜ
(406) 453-1602. **$55.** 2 Treasure State Dr. I-15, exit 278,
0.8 mi e on 10th Ave S and US 87/89/SR 3/200. Int corridors. **Pets:** Accepted.

[SAVE] [S🏊] [✕] [✏️] [📺]

AAA ▼▼ **Central Motel** Ⓜ
(406) 453-0161. **$45-$70.** 715 Central Ave W. I-15, exit 280,
0.7 mi e. Ext corridors. **Pets:** Small. $10 one-time fee/pet.
Designated rooms, service with restrictions, supervision.

[SAVE] [S🏊] [✕] [📶]

▼▼▼ **Comfort Inn Great Falls** Ⓜ
(406) 454-2727. **$65-$90.** 1120 9th St S. I-15, exit 278, 3 mi
e on 10th Ave S and US 87/89/SR 3/200, then just s. Int
corridors. **Pets:** Accepted.

[SAVE] [S🏊] [✕] [🛏️M] [✏️] [📶] [📺]

▼▼ **Days Inn of Great Falls** Ⓜ
(406) 727-6565. **$59-$84.** 101 14th Ave NW. I-15, exit 280,
1.3 mi e on Central Ave/Business 15, 0.8 mi n on 3rd St
NW, just w. Int corridors. **Pets:** Dogs only. $5 one-time
fee/room. Designated rooms, service with restrictions,
supervision.

[SAVE] [S🏊] [✕] [✏️] [📶] [📺]

AAA ▼▼▼ **The Great Falls Inn** Ⓜ 🐾
(406) 453-6000. **$59-$69.** 1400 28th St S. I-15, exit 278,
US 87/89 and SR3/200, 0.3 mi s on 26th St S, then just e
on 15th Ave S. Int corridors. **Pets:** Medium. $5 daily fee/pet.
Designated rooms, service with restrictions, supervision.

[SAVE] [S🏊] [✕] [🛏️M] [✏️] [✏️] [📶] [📺]

▼▼ **Great Falls Super 8 Lodge** Ⓜ
(406) 727-7600. **$50-$72.** 1214 13th St S. I-15, exit 278,
2.7 mi e on 10th Ave S and US 87/89 and SR 3/200, then
just s. Int corridors. **Pets:** Other species. Service with
restrictions, supervision.

[ASK] [S🏊] [✏️] [📺]

AAA ▼▼▼ **Guests First Howard Johnson** Ⓜ
(406) 761-3410. **$59-$79, 14 days notice.** 220 Central Ave.
Downtown. Ext/int corridors. **Pets:** Accepted.

[SAVE] [S🏊] [✕] [📶] [📺] [🍴] [🏊]

AAA ▼▼▼▼ Hawthorn Inn & Suites M
(406) 761-2600. **$79-$189.** 600 River Dr S. I-15, exit 278, 1.7 mi e on 10th Ave S, and US 87/89 and SR 3/200, then 0.8 mi n. Int corridors. **Pets:** Accepted.
SAVE S6 ✕ &M ✐ 🛏 💻 ⇌

AAA ▼ Plaza Inn M ❀
(406) 452-9594. **$40-$75, 3 days notice.** 1224 10th Ave S. I-15, exit 278, 2.4 mi e on 10th Ave S and US 87/89 and SR 3/200. Ext corridors. **Pets:** Small. $10 one-time fee/pet. Designated rooms, service with restrictions, supervision.
SAVE S6 ✕ 🛏

AAA ▼ Ski's Western Motel M
(406) 453-3281. **$45-$65, 3 days notice.** 2420 10th Ave S. I-15, exit 278, 5.2 mi e on 10th Ave S and US 87/89 and SR 3/200. Ext corridors. **Pets:** Accepted.
SAVE S6 ✕ 🛏

AAA ▼▼▼▼ TownHouse Inn of Great Falls MI
(406) 761-4600. **$75-$99, 30 days notice.** 1411 10th Ave S. I-15, exit 278, 2.6 mi e on 10th Ave S and US 87/89 and SR 3/200. Int corridors. **Pets:** Other species. $5 daily fee/pet. Service with restrictions, supervision.
SAVE S6 ✕ ✐ 💻 🍴 ⇌

HAMILTON

AAA ▼▼▼ Comfort Inn of Hamilton M
(406) 363-6600. **$65-$99, 30 days notice.** 1113 N 1st St. N of city center on US 93. Int corridors. **Pets:** Other species. $4 daily fee/pet. Service with restrictions, supervision.
SAVE S6 ✕ &M ✐ 🛏 💻

HARDIN

AAA ▼▼▼ American Inn of Hardin MI
(406) 665-1870. **$46-$79.** 1324 N Crawford Ave. I-90, exit 495, just s on SR 47. Ext corridors. **Pets:** Large. $5 daily fee/room. Designated rooms, service with restrictions, supervision.
SAVE S6 ✕ ✐ 🛏 🍴 ⇌

▼▼▼ Western Motel M
(406) 665-2296. **$45-$70.** 830 W 3rd St. I-90 E, exit 495, 1.3 mi s on SR 47 and Rt 313, just e; I-90 W, exit 497, 0.3 mi w on I-90 business loop, continue straight on 3rd St 0.7 mi. Ext corridors. **Pets:** Other species. $2.50 daily fee/pet. Designated rooms, service with restrictions, supervision.
✕ 🛏

HARLOWTON

▼ Corral Motel M
(406) 632-4331. **$40-$45.** 0.5 mi e at jct US 12 and 191. Ext corridors. **Pets:** Medium. Designated rooms, service with restrictions, supervision.
✕ 🛏

▼ Countryside Inn M
(406) 632-4119. **$49-$59.** 309 3rd St NE. US 12 E. Ext corridors. **Pets:** Medium. Designated rooms, service with restrictions, supervision.
ASK S6 ✕ 🛏

HAVRE

AAA ▼▼▼ TownHouse Inn of Havre M
(406) 265-6711. **$75-$99, 30 days notice.** 601 W 1st St. Just w of town center on US 2. Int corridors. **Pets:** Other species. $5 daily fee/pet. Service with restrictions.
SAVE S6 ✕ ✐ 🛏 💻 ⇌

HELENA

▼▼▼ Appleton Inn Bed & Breakfast BB
(406) 449-7492. **$95-$135.** 1999 Euclid Ave. I-15, exit 193, 1.3 mi w on Cedar St, 1.7 mi w at jct US 12 W (Lyndale Ave). Int corridors. **Pets:** Medium. Supervision.
✕

▼▼▼ Barrister Bed & Breakfast BB ❀
(406) 443-7330. **$95-$110, 3 days notice.** 416 N Ewing. 0.4 mi from Last Chance Gulch, 0.9 mi w of State Capitol on 6th Ave, just n. Int corridors. **Pets:** Other species.
ASK ✕ 💻

▼▼▼ Comfort Inn of Helena M
(406) 443-1000. **$60-$90.** 750 N Fee St. I-15, exit 192, just n. Int corridors. **Pets:** Accepted.
SAVE S6 ✕ &M 🛏 💻 ⇌

▼▼ Days Inn Helena M
(406) 442-3280. **$61-$95.** 2001 Prospect Ave. I-15, exit 192, just w. Int corridors. **Pets:** Medium. $25 deposit/room. Designated rooms, service with restrictions, crate.
SAVE S6 ✕ &M ✐ ✑ 🛏 💻

AAA ▼▼▼▼ Elkhorn Mountain Inn M ❀
(406) 442-6625. **$63-$68.** 1 Jackson Creek. I-15, exit 187 (Montana City), just w. Int corridors. **Pets:** $5 daily fee/pet. Supervision.
SAVE S6 ✕ &M ✑ 🛏 💻

AAA ▼ Lamplighter Motel C
(406) 442-9200. **$44-$64.** 1006 Madison. US 12 W, just s of Lundy Shopping Center. Ext corridors. **Pets:** Accepted.
SAVE S6 ✕ ✑ 🛏

AAA ▼▼▼ Shilo Inn-Helena M ❀
(406) 442-0320. **$45-$109.** 2020 Prospect Ave. I-15, exit 192, 2 mi, just w of I-15 interchange, enter from east on Prospect Ave. Int corridors. **Pets:** Other species. $10 daily fee/pet. Service with restrictions, supervision.
SAVE S6 ✕ 🛏 💻 ⇌

▼▼▼ Super 8 Motel M
(406) 443-2450. **$65-$72.** 2200 11th Ave. I-15 S, exit Capitol area; I-15 N, exit W business district on US 12. Int corridors. **Pets:** $25 deposit/room. Service with restrictions, supervision.
ASK S6 ✕ ✐ ✑ 🛏 💻

AAA ▼▼▼▼ WestCoast Colonial Hotel MI
(406) 443-2100. **$85-$109.** 2301 Colonial Dr. I-15, exit 192 southbound; exit 192B northbound. Int corridors. **Pets:** Small. Designated rooms.
SAVE S6 ✕ 🛏 💻 🍴 ⇌

▼▼▼▼ Wingate Inn M
(406) 449-3000. **$89-$150.** 2007 Oakes. I-15, exit 193, just sw. Int corridors. **Pets:** Accepted.
ASK S⌀ ✕ ⌂M 🌀 🛏 📖 ➿

HUNGRY HORSE

◈◈◈ ▼▼▼ Mini Golden Inns Motel M
(406) 387-4313. **$60-$96, 30 days notice.** 8955 US 2E. East end of town. Ext corridors. **Pets:** Accepted.
SAVE ✕ ⌂M 🛏 📖

KALISPELL

◈◈◈ ▼▼▼ Aero Inn M
(406) 755-3798. **$46-$76.** 1830 US 93S. 1 mi s on US 93 from jct of US 2. Int corridors. **Pets:** Other species. $10 deposit/room. Designated rooms, service with restrictions, supervision.
SAVE S⌀ ✕ 🛏 ⌀

▼▼ Days Inn Kalispell M
(406) 756-3222. **$48-$83.** 1550 Hwy 93 N. 1.3 mi n on US 93 from jct of US 2. Int corridors. **Pets:** Medium. $10 one-time fee/room. Designated rooms, service with restrictions, supervision.
SAVE S⌀ ✕

◈◈◈ ▼▼▼ Four Seasons Motor Inn M
(406) 755-6123. **$56-$90.** 350 N Main St. On US 93, just n of jct US 2. Ext/int corridors. **Pets:** Accepted.
SAVE S⌀ ✕ 🛏 📖 🍽

◈◈◈ ▼▼ Glacier Gateway Motel M
(406) 755-3330. **$50-$89.** 264 N Main St. Northwest corner of jct US 2 and 93. Ext corridors. **Pets:** Medium, dogs only. $8 daily fee/pet. Designated rooms, service with restrictions, supervision.
SAVE 🛏 📖

▼▼ Kalispell/Glacier Super 8 Motel M
(406) 755-1888. **$65-$123, 30 days notice.** 1341 1st Ave E. 1.2 mi s on US 93 from jct of US 2. Int corridors. **Pets:** Other species. $10 one-time fee/room. Supervision.
ASK S⌀ ✕ ⌂M 🌀 📖

◈◈◈ ▼▼▼ Kalispell Grand Hotel H
(406) 755-8100. **$71-$98.** 100 Main St. on US 93. Int corridors. **Pets:** Supervision.
SAVE S⌀ ✕ 🍽

◈◈◈ ▼▼▼▼ Kalispell Inn & Suites M
(406) 257-5255. **$69-$199.** 255 Montclair Dr. Jct US 93 and 2, 1 mi e. Int corridors. **Pets:** Other species. Designated rooms, service with restrictions, supervision.
SAVE S⌀ ✕ 🛏 📖 ➿

▼▼ Red Lion Inn Kalispell M
(406) 755-6700. **$59-$119.** 1330 Hwy 2 W. 1 mi w on US 2 from jct of US 93. Int corridors. **Pets:** Medium, other species. $15 one-time fee/room. Service with restrictions, supervision.
ASK S⌀ ✕ 🛏 📖 🍽 ➿

◈◈◈ ▼▼▼▼ WestCoast Kalispell Center Hotel M
(406) 751-5050. **$105-$140.** 20 N Main St. Just s on US 93 from jct of US 2. Int corridors. **Pets:** Accepted.
SAVE S⌀ ✕ ⌂M 🛏 📖 🍽 ➿

◈◈◈ ▼▼▼▼ WestCoast Outlaw Hotel M
(406) 755-6100. **$98-$125.** 1701 Hwy 93 S. 1.4 mi s on US 93 from jct US 2. Int corridors. **Pets:** Accepted.
SAVE S⌀ ✕ 🛏 📖 🍽 ➿ ✕

◈◈◈ ▼▼ White Birch Motel M
(406) 752-4008. **$29-$72.** 17 Shady Ln. 0.4 mi e on SR 35 from jct US 2, just s. Ext corridors. **Pets:** Accepted.
SAVE 🛏 📖 🌀

LAKESIDE

▼▼ ▼▼ Sunrise Vista Inn M
(406) 844-0231. **$50-$90, 10 days notice.** 7005 US 93. North edge of town on US 93. Ext corridors. **Pets:** Accepted.
ASK ✕ 🛏 📖 ✕

LAUREL

▼▼▼▼ Laurel Super 8 M
(406) 628-6888. **$68-$78.** 205 SE 4th St. I-90, exit 434, just n, just e. Int corridors. **Pets:** Accepted.
ASK S⌀ ✕ ⌂M 🌀 🛏 📖 ➿

LEWISTOWN

◈◈◈ ▼▼ B & B Motel M
(406) 538-5496. **$40-$53.** 520 E Main St. Downtown. Ext corridors. **Pets:** Large, dogs only. $3 daily fee/pet. Designated rooms, service with restrictions, supervision.
SAVE ✕ 🛏

LIBBY

▼▼ Sandman Motel M ✿
(406) 293-8831. **$38-$62.** 688 US Hwy 2 W. Just w on US 2 from jct SR 37. Ext corridors. **Pets:** Medium, other species. $20 deposit/room. Designated rooms, service with restrictions, supervision.
ASK S⌀ ✕ 🛏

◈◈◈ ▼▼▼ Super 8 Motel M
(406) 293-2771. **$50-$77.** 448 US 2 W. Just w on US 2 from jct SR 37. Int corridors. **Pets:** Other species. $10 one-time fee/pet. Service with restrictions, supervision.
SAVE S⌀ ✕ ➿

LINCOLN

◈◈◈ ▼▼ Leeper's Ponderosa Motel M
(406) 362-4333. **$47-$55.** Hwy 200 & 1st Ave. Just w on SR 200. Ext corridors. **Pets:** $5 daily fee/pet. Designated rooms, service with restrictions, supervision.
SAVE ✕ 🛏 🎿

LIVINGSTON

(AAA) ▼▼▼▼ Best Western Yellowstone Inn & Conference Center M ❖
(406) 222-6110. **$62-$98.** 1515 W Park St. I-90, exit 333, just n. Int corridors. **Pets:** Other species. $10 one-time fee/room. Service with restrictions, supervision.
SAVE S X 🛏 💻 🍴 ⇌

(AAA) ▼ Budget Host Parkway Motel M
(406) 222-3840. **$42-$78, 3 days notice.** 1124 W Park St. I-90, exit 333, 0.5 mi n on US 89. Ext corridors. **Pets:** Other species. $5 daily fee/pet. Designated rooms, supervision.
SAVE S X 🛏 💻

▼ Country Motor Inn M
(406) 222-1923. **$38-$60.** 814 E Park St. I-89, exit 337, 2.8 mi w. Ext corridors. **Pets:** Medium. $10 daily fee/room. Designated rooms, service with restrictions, supervision.
ASK S X 🛏 💻

(AAA) ▼▼ Del Mar Motel Inc M
(406) 222-3120. **$40-$75, 3 days notice.** 1201 Hwy 10 W. Just w of jct US 89 on I-90 business loop. Ext corridors. **Pets:** Large, other species. $5 daily fee/pet. Designated rooms, service with restrictions, supervision.
SAVE S X 🛏 💻 ⇌

(AAA) ▼▼▼▼ Econo Lodge M
(406) 222-0555. **$36-$99.** 111 Rogers Ln. I-90, exit 333, just n on US 89, then just w. Int corridors. **Pets:** Other species. $5 daily fee/room. Supervision.
SAVE S X ♿ 🎱 🖥 🛏 💻 ⇌

MILES CITY

(AAA) ▼▼▼▼ Best Western War Bonnet Inn M
(406) 232-4560. **$77.** 1015 S Haynes Ave. I-94, exit 138 (Broadus), 0.3 mi n. Ext corridors. **Pets:** Other species. Service with restrictions, supervision.
SAVE S X 🛏 💻 ⇌

▼▼▼▼ GuestHouse International Inn & Suites M
(406) 232-3661. **$62-$128.** 3111 Steel St. I-94, exit 138, just s. Int corridors. **Pets:** Large, other species. $10 daily fee/room. Designated rooms, service with restrictions, supervision.
ASK S X ♿ 🖥 🛏 💻 ⇌

MISSOULA

(AAA) ▼▼ Best Inn & Conference Center-South M
(406) 251-2665. **$64-$79.** 3803 Brooks St. I-90, exit 101 (Reserve St), 5 mi s to Brooks (US 93), just w. Int corridors. **Pets:** Large, other species. $7 daily fee/room. Designated rooms.
SAVE S X ♿ 🖥 🛏 💻

▼▼ Best Inn North M
(406) 542-7550. **$64-$79.** 4953 N Reserve St. I-90 W, exit 101, just s. Int corridors. **Pets:** Large, other species. $7 daily fee/room. Designated rooms.
ASK S X 🖥 🛏 💻

(AAA) ▼▼▼▼ Best Western Executive Inn M
(406) 543-7221. **$58-$75.** 201 E Main St. I-90, exit 104 (Orange St), 0.5 mi s to Broadway, 0.5 mi e to Washington, just s to Main St, just w. Ext corridors. **Pets:** Medium. $50 deposit/pet. Service with restrictions, crate.
SAVE S X 🛏 💻 🍴 ⇌

(AAA) ▼▼▼▼ Best Western Grant Creek Inn M
(406) 543-0700. **$89-$169.** 5280 Grant Creek Rd. I-90, exit 101, just n. Int corridors. **Pets:** Accepted.
SAVE X 🎱 🖥 🛏 💻 ⇌

▼▼ Campus Inn M ❖
(406) 549-5134. **$40-$80.** 744 E Broadway. I-90, exit 105 (Van Buren St), just s to Broadway, just w. Ext/int corridors. **Pets:** Medium, other species. $6 daily fee/pet. Service with restrictions, supervision.
ASK S X 🖥 🛏

▼▼▼ Comfort Inn M
(406) 542-0888. **$60-$150, 14 days notice.** 4545 N Reserve St. I-90, exit 101, 0.5 mi s. Int corridors. **Pets:** Small, other species. $10 daily fee/room. Service with restrictions, supervision.
SAVE S X ♿ 🖥 🛏 💻 ⇌

(AAA) ▼▼▼ Days Inn/Westgate M
(406) 721-9776. **$66-$74.** 8600 Truck Stop Rd. I-90, exit 96, just n. Int corridors. **Pets:** Accepted.
SAVE S X

(AAA) ▼▼▼ Doubletree Hotel Missoula/Edgewater M
(406) 728-3100. **$99-$275.** 100 Madison. I-90, exit 105 (Van Buren St), just s, then w on Front St. Int corridors. **Pets:** Accepted.
SAVE S X ♿ 🎱 🖥 🛏 💻 🍴 ⇌

(AAA) ▼ Downtown Motel M
(406) 549-5191. **$37-$45.** 502 E Broadway. I-90, exit 105 (Van Buren St), just w. Ext corridors. **Pets:** Medium, other species. $8 one-time fee/pet. Designated rooms, service with restrictions, supervision.
SAVE X 🛏 💻

(AAA) ▼ Family Inn M
(406) 543-7371. **$56-$60.** 1031 E Broadway. I-90, exit 105, just s, then just e. Ext corridors. **Pets:** Accepted.
SAVE S X ⇌

▼▼▼ Hampton Inn M ❖
(406) 549-1800. **$70-$99.** 4805 N Reserve St. I-90, exit 101, just s. Int corridors. **Pets:** Other species. $10 one-time fee/room. Designated rooms, service with restrictions, supervision.
SAVE X 🖥 🎱 🖥 🛏 💻 ⇌

▼▼▼ Holiday Inn Missoula-Parkside H
(406) 721-8550. **$69-$99, 10 days notice.** 200 S Pattee St. I-90, exit Orange St, 0.5 mi s to Broadway, just e to Pattee St, just s. Int corridors. **Pets:** Accepted.
ASK S X 🎱 🛏 💻 🍴 ⇌

▼▼▼▼ Microtel Inn & Suites M
(406) 543-0959. **$50-$120.** 5059 N Reserve St. I-90, exit 101, just s. Int corridors. **Pets:** Small, other species. $10 daily fee/pet. Designated rooms, service with restrictions, supervision.

⊠ ⌖ ⊘ ⌨ ⊟ ▣

⌬⌬ ▼▼▼ Orange Street Budget Motor Inn M
(406) 721-3610. **$53-$58.** 801 N Orange St. I-90, exit 104, just s. Int corridors. **Pets:** $5 one-time fee/room. Designated rooms, service with restrictions, supervision.

SAVE ⌑ ⊠ ⊟

▼▼▼ Red Lion Inn M
(406) 728-3300. **$54-$90.** 700 W Broadway. I-90, exit 104 (Orange St), just w. Ext corridors. **Pets:** Small. $5 daily fee/pet. Service with restrictions, supervision.

ASK ⌑ ⊠ ⊟ ▣ ⊵

⌬⌬ ▼▼▼ Redwood Lodge M
(406) 721-2110. **$60-$70.** 8060 Hwy 93 N. I-90, exit 96, just s. Ext corridors. **Pets:** Other species. Service with restrictions, supervision.

SAVE ⌑ ⊠ ⊟

⌬⌬ ▼▼ Royal Motel M
(406) 542-2184. **$32-$46.** 338 Washington St. I-90, exit 105, just s on Van Buren, 0.5 mi w on Broadway. Ext corridors. **Pets:** Accepted.

SAVE ⊠ ⊟

⌬⌬ ▼▼▼▼ Ruby's Inn & Convention Center MI
(406) 721-0990. **$65-$95.** 4825 N Reserve St. I-90, exit 101, just s. Ext/int corridors. **Pets:** Other species. $5 one-time fee/pet. Service with restrictions, supervision.

SAVE ⊠ ⌖ ⊘ ⌨ ⊟ ▣ ⌑⌑ ⊵

▼▼ Sleep Inn M
(406) 543-5883. **$55-$80.** 3425 Dore Ln. I-90, exit 101, 5 mi s on Reserve St, just e on Brooks St. Int corridors. **Pets:** Other species. Designated rooms, supervision.

SAVE ⌑ ⊠ ⌖ ⊘ ⌨ ⊟ ▣ ⊵

▼▼ Super 8-Brooks St M
(406) 251-2255. **$47-$70, 3 days notice.** 3901 Brooks St. I-90, exit 101, 5 mi s, just w. Int corridors. **Pets:** Small, dogs only. $3.50 daily fee/pet. Service with restrictions, supervision.

ASK ⌑ ⊠ ⊟

⌬⌬ ▼▼▼ Travelers Inn Motel M
(406) 728-8330. **$45-$65.** 4850 N Reserve St. I-90, exit 101 (Reserve St), just s. Ext corridors. **Pets:** Small, dogs only. $2 daily fee/pet. Designated rooms, service with restrictions, supervision.

SAVE ⌑ ⊠ ⊟

OVANDO

▼▼▼▼ Lake Upsata Guest Ranch RA
(406) 793-5890. **$1050-$3080 (weekly), 90 days notice.** 135 Lake Upsata Rd. 7.5 mi w on SR 200 to MM 38, 3.4 mi n on Woodworth Rd, 1 mi e. Ext corridors. **Pets:** Other species. $5 daily fee/pet. Service with restrictions, supervision.

⊠ ⊟ ▣ ⊠ ⌨ ⌶ ⊠

POLSON

▼▼ Bayview Inn M
(406) 883-3120. **$45-$74.** 914 Hwy 93. just s. Ext corridors. **Pets:** Accepted.

ASK ⌑ ⊠ ⊟ ▣

RED LODGE

▼▼ Best Western Lu Pine Inn M
(406) 446-1321. **$69-$89.** 702 S Hauser. 0.4 mi s, just w of US 212. Int corridors. **Pets:** Other species. Service with restrictions, supervision.

SAVE ⌑ ⊠ ⊟ ⊵

▼▼▼ Comfort Inn of Red Lodge M
(406) 446-4469. **$50-$150.** 612 N Broadway. Jct US 212 and SR 78, north entrance. Int corridors. **Pets:** $25 deposit/room. Designated rooms, service with restrictions, supervision.

SAVE ⌑ ⊠ ⌖ ⌨ ⊟ ▣ ⊵

⌬⌬ ▼▼▼ Super 8 of Red Lodge M
(406) 446-2288. **$55-$120, 30 days notice.** 1223 S Broadway Ave. Just s on US 212. Ext/int corridors. **Pets:** Accepted.

SAVE ⌑ ⊠ ⊟ ▣ ⊵

⌬⌬ ▼▼▼ Yodeler Motel M
(406) 446-1435. **$40-$78.** 601 S Broadway. Just s on US 212. Ext corridors. **Pets:** $5 one-time fee/pet. Designated rooms, service with restrictions, supervision.

SAVE ⌑ ⊠ ⊟ ▣

RONAN

▼▼ Starlite Motel M
(406) 676-7000. **$58-$70.** 18 Main St SW. Just w of jct US 93 and Main St. Ext corridors. **Pets:** $20 deposit/pet, $10 daily fee/pet. Designated rooms, service with restrictions, supervision.

ASK ⌑ ⊠ ⊟ ▣

SEELEY LAKE

⌬⌬ ▼▼▼ Wilderness Gateway Inn M ❧
(406) 677-2095. **$46-$61.** 2996 Hwy 83 N. South end of town on SR 83. Ext corridors. **Pets:** Other species. $5 daily fee/room. Service with restrictions, supervision.

SAVE ⊠ ⌨

SHELBY

⚫⚫⚫ 💎💎💎 Comfort Inn of Shelby M
(406) 434-2212. **$65-$99, 30 days notice.** 50 Frontage Rd. I-15, exit 363, just e, then just s on McKinley Ave. Int corridors. **Pets:** Accepted.
SAVE S🔒 ✕ 🖊 🖥 🖨 💻

⚫⚫⚫ 💎💎💎 Crossroads Inn M
(406) 434-5134. **$52-$66, 7 days notice.** 1200 Roosevelt Hwy. Just w of town center on US 2. Int corridors. **Pets:** Other species. $5.20 daily fee/pet. Service with restrictions, supervision.
SAVE ✕ 🖊 🖨 ⤚

⚫⚫⚫ 💎💎💎 O'Haire Manor Motel M
(406) 434-5555. **$50-$65.** 204 2nd St S. Just s of Main St via Maple St. Ext/int corridors. **Pets:** Large. $5 daily fee/room. Designated rooms, service with restrictions, supervision.
SAVE S🔒 ✕ 🖨

SHERIDAN

💎💎 Moriah Motel M
(406) 842-5491. **$43-$60, 7 days notice.** 220 S Main St. SR 287 S. Ext corridors. **Pets:** Other species. $6 one-time fee/pet. Service with restrictions.
✕ 🖨

SIDNEY

⚫⚫⚫ 💎💎💎 Richland Motor Inn M
(406) 433-6400. **$65-$78.** 1200 S Central Ave. 1.5 mi n of jct SR 200 and 16. Int corridors. **Pets:** Medium. Service with restrictions, supervision.
SAVE S🔒 ✕ 🖨 💻

ST. IGNATIUS

💎💎 Stoneheart Inn BB
(406) 745-4999. **$35-$65, 3 days notice.** 26 N Main. US 93, just s. Int corridors. **Pets:** Accepted.
A$K S🔒 ✕

💎 Sunset Motel M
(406) 745-3900. **$49-$59.** 32670 Hwy 93. Just s of downtown, exit on US 93. Ext corridors. **Pets:** Dogs only. $5 one-time fee/pet. No service, supervision.
A$K S🔒 ✕ 🖨 🐾

ST. REGIS

⚫⚫⚫ 💎 Little River Motel M 🌸
(406) 649-2713. **$35-$65.** 50 Old US Hwy 10 W. I-90, exit 33, just n to flashing light, just w, then just sw. Ext corridors. **Pets:** Small. $5 daily fee/pet. Designated rooms, service with restrictions, supervision.
SAVE S🔒 ✕ 🖨 🐾 📷

SUPERIOR

⚫⚫⚫ 💎💎💎 Budget Host Big Sky Motel M
(406) 822-4831. **$46-$58.** 103 4th Ave E. I-90, exit 47, just n. Ext corridors. **Pets:** Accepted.
SAVE S🔒 ✕

THOMPSON FALLS

💎💎 The Riverfront M 🌸
(406) 827-3460. **$69.** 4907 Scenic SR 200 W. 1 mi w of city center. Ext corridors. **Pets:** Medium, other species. $5 daily fee/pet. Service with restrictions, supervision.
✕ 🖨 💻

THREE FORKS

⚫⚫⚫ 💎💎💎 Broken Spur Motel M
(406) 285-3237. **$46-$60.** 124 W Elm (Hwy 2). I-90, exit 278 westbound, 1.3 mi sw on SR 2; exit 274 eastbound, 1 mi s on SR 287 to jct SR 2, 3 mi se on SR 2. Ext corridors. **Pets:** Other species. $5 daily fee/pet. Service with restrictions, supervision.
SAVE S🔒 ✕ 🖨

⚫⚫⚫ 💎💎 Fort Three Forks Motel & RV Park M
(406) 285-3233. **$46-$80.** 10776 Hwy 287. I-90, exit 274. Ext corridors. **Pets:** Accepted.
SAVE ✕ 🖨

WEST YELLOWSTONE

⚫⚫⚫ 💎💎💎💎 Best Western Cross Winds Motor Inn M
(406) 646-9557. **$35-$120, 3 days notice.** 201 Firehole Ave. Just w of US 191 and 287, on US 20 at Dunraven St and Firehole Ave; at end of city park. Ext corridors. **Pets:** Dogs only. Designated rooms, service with restrictions, supervision.
SAVE S🔒 ✕ 🖨 💻 🐾

⚫⚫⚫ 💎💎💎💎 Best Western Desert Inn M
(406) 646-7376. **$45-$145, 3 days notice.** 133 Canyon Ave. US 191 at jct US 20; corner of Canyon and Firehole aves. Int corridors. **Pets:** Accepted.
SAVE S🔒 ✕ 🔋M 🖊 🖥 🖨 🐾

⚫⚫⚫ 💎💎 Big Western Pine Motel M
(406) 646-7622. **$39-$110.** 234 Firehole Ave. Just w of Canyon Ave; corner Firehole Ave and Electric St; on US 20 and 191. Ext/int corridors. **Pets:** Other species. $5 daily fee/pet. Designated rooms, no service.
SAVE ✕ 🖨 💻 🍴 🐾

⚫⚫⚫ 💎💎💎💎 Days Inn West Yellowstone M
(406) 646-7656. **$64-$145, 14 days notice.** 301 Madison Ave. Just nw of park entrance; w off US 191. Ext/int corridors. **Pets:** Medium. $8 daily fee/pet. Designated rooms, service with restrictions, supervision.
SAVE S🔒 ✕ 🔋M 🖥 🖨 💻 🍴 🐾

(A) ▽ **Evergreen Motel** M
(406) 646-7655. **$39-$84, 5 days notice.** 229 Firehole Ave. Just w of Canyon; on US 20 and 191. Ext corridors. **Pets:** Accepted.

SAVE S× ⊘ ⊟ ⊑ X

(A) ▽▽▽ **Gray Wolf Inn & Suites** M
(406) 646-0000. **$45-$139.** 250 S Canyon Ave. Just w of Yellowstone National Park entrance. Int corridors. **Pets:** Other species. $5 daily fee/room. Service with restrictions, supervision.

SAVE S× ⊘ ⊑M ⊘ ⊑ ⊟ ⊑ ⊇

(A) ▽▽▽ **Kelly Inn** M
(406) 646-4544. **$59-$139, 6 days notice.** 104 S Canyon Ave. Just w of Yellowstone Park entrance; s of jct US 191, 287 and 20. Ext/int corridors. **Pets:** Other species. Service with restrictions, supervision.

SAVE S× ⊘ ⊑ ⊟ ⊑ ⊇

(A) ▽▽▽▽ **Three Bear Lodge Annex** M
(406) 646-7353. **$40-$80.** 217 Yellowstone Ave. Just w of park entrance. Ext corridors. **Pets:** Small. $5 daily fee/pet. Service with restrictions, supervision.

SAVE ⊘ ⊇

(A) ▽▽▽▽ **Three Bear Motor Lodge** M
(406) 646-7353. **$45-$90.** 217 Yellowstone Ave. Just w of park entrance. Ext/int corridors. **Pets:** Small. $5 daily fee/pet. Service with restrictions, supervision.

SAVE ⊘ ⊟ ⊑ ⊇

(A) ▽▽▽ **Travelers Lodge** M
(406) 646-9561. **$45-$84, 14 days notice.** 225 Yellowstone Ave. Just w of park entrance. Ext corridors. **Pets:** Accepted.

SAVE S× ⊘ ⊘ ⊟ ⊇

(A) ▽▽▽▽ **Yellowstone Lodge** M
(406) 646-0020. **$59-$139.** 251 Electric St. Just w of Yellowstone National Park entrance. Int corridors. **Pets:** Other species. $50 deposit/pet. Designated rooms, service with restrictions, supervision.

SAVE S× ⊘ ⊑ ⊟ ⊑ ⊇

WHITE SULPHUR SPRINGS

▽▽▽ **All Seasons Super 8 Motel** M
(406) 547-8888. **$56-$86, 3 days notice.** 808 3rd Ave SW. On US 89, south end of town. Int corridors. **Pets:** Accepted.

ASK S× ⊘ ⊑M ⊘ ⊟

WHITEFISH

(A) ▽▽▽▽ **Best Western Rocky Mountain Lodge** M
(406) 862-2569. **$73-$193.** 6510 Hwy 93 S. 1.3 mi s on US 93 from jct of SR 487. Ext/int corridors. **Pets:** Other species. $10 daily fee/pet. Designated rooms, service with restrictions, supervision.

SAVE S× ⊘ ⊑ ⊟ ⊑ ⊇

(A) ▽▽▽ **Chalet Motel** M ❧
(406) 862-5581. **$53-$95.** 6430 US 93S. 1 mi n on US 93 from jct SR 40. Ext corridors. **Pets:** Small, other species. $5 daily fee/pet. Designated rooms, service with restrictions, supervision.

SAVE S× ⊘ ⊟ ⊑ ⊇

▽▽ **Cheap Sleep Motel** M
(406) 862-5515. **$36-$65.** 6400 Hwy 93 S. US 93, 1 mi s. Int corridors. **Pets:** Medium, other species. $5 daily fee/pet. Service with restrictions, supervision.

× ⊇

(A) ▽▽▽▽ **North Forty Resort** C
(406) 862-7740. **$59-$195, 14 days notice.** 3765 Hwy 40 W. 2.5 mi e on SR 40 from jct of US 93. Ext corridors. **Pets:** $10 daily fee/pet. Designated rooms, service with restrictions, supervision.

SAVE × ⊟ ⊑ X

(A) ▽▽▽ **Pine Lodge** M ❧
(406) 862-7600. **$70-$140.** 920 Spokane Ave. 1 mi s on US 93. Int corridors. **Pets:** Supervision.

SAVE S× ⊘ ⊘ ⊑ ⊟ ⊑ ⊇

(A) ▽▽▽ **Super 8 Motel** M ❧
(406) 862-8255. **$62-$85.** 800 Spokane Ave. 1 mi s on US 93 from jct of SR 487. Int corridors. **Pets:** Medium. $5 daily fee/pet. Designated rooms, service with restrictions, supervision.

SAVE S× ×

CITY INDEX

AINSWORTH

AAA ◆◆◆ **Comfort Inn** **M**
(402) 387-1050. **$57-$94.** 1124 E 4th St. 0.5 mi e on US 20. Int corridors. **Pets:** $10 daily fee/pet. Designated rooms, service with restrictions, supervision.
[SAVE] [S♦] [✕] [♿M] [▧] [▨] [▭] [≋]

◆◆ **Super 8 Motel** **M**
(402) 387-0700. **$45-$50.** 1025 E 4th St. 0.5 mi e on US 20. Int corridors. **Pets:** $10 deposit/room. Designated rooms, no service, supervision.
[S♦] [✕]

ALLIANCE

◆ **Sunset Motel** **M**
(308) 762-8660. **$49-$59.** 1210 E Hwy 2. US 385, 1 mi e on SR 2. Ext/int corridors. **Pets:** $5 daily fee/pet. Designated rooms, supervision.
[S♦] [✕] [♿] [▭] [≋]

AURORA

AAA ◆◆ **Budget Host, Ken's Motel** **M**
(402) 694-3141. **$38-$40.** 1515 11th St. I-80, exit 332, 3 mi n on SR 14, then 0.3 mi w on US 34. Ext corridors.
Pets: Accepted.
[SAVE] [✕] [♿]

BEATRICE

◆◆◆ **Holiday Inn Express & Suites** **M**
(402) 228-7000. **$63.** 4005 N 6th. 1 mi n on US 77. Int corridors. **Pets:** Accepted.
[ASK] [✕] [♿M] [▧] [♿] [▭] [≋]

BELLEVUE

AAA ◆◆◆ **American Family Inn** **M** ❀
(402) 291-0804. **$52-$62.** 1110 Fort Crook Rd S. US 75, 0.3 mi n of jct SR 370 and Fort Crook Rd. Ext corridors. **Pets:** Medium. $7 daily fee/room. Designated rooms, service with restrictions.
[SAVE] [S♦] [✕] [♿M] [▧] [♿] [▭] [≋]

AAA ◆◆◆ **Settle Inn and Suites** **M**
(402) 292-1155. **$69-$84.** 2105 Pratt Ave. US 75, exit Cornhusker, just w. Int corridors. **Pets:** Small, other species. $10 daily fee/room. Service with restrictions, supervision.
[SAVE] [S♦] [✕] [♿M] [♿] [▭] [▭] [≋]

CHADRON

AAA ◆◆◆ **Best Western West Hills Inn** **M**
(308) 432-3305. **$50-$92, 14 days notice.** 1100 W 10th St. Jct US 385 and 20. Ext/int corridors. **Pets:** Service with restrictions, supervision.
[SAVE] [S♦] [✕] [▭] [▭] [≋]

◆◆ **Chadron Super 8 Motel** **M**
(308) 432-4471. **$44-$63.** 840 W Hwy 20. 0.8 mi w on US 20, just e of jct US 385. Int corridors. **Pets:** Service with restrictions, supervision.
[ASK] [S♦] [✕] [▭] [▭] [≋]

◆ **Grand Westerner Motel** **M**
(308) 432-5595. **$33-$49, 5 days notice.** 1050 W Hwy 20. 0.8 mi w on US 20, just e of jct US 385. Ext corridors.
Pets: Other species. Designated rooms, service with restrictions, supervision.
[ASK] [S♦] [✕] [▭]

AAA ◆ **Westerner Motel** **M**
(308) 432-5577. **$33-$49, 5 days notice.** 300 Oak St. US 20, 0.5 mi e of jct US 385 and SR 87. Ext corridors.
Pets: Other species. Designated rooms, service with restrictions, supervision.
[SAVE] [S♦] [✕] [▭]

COLUMBUS

◆◆ **Days Inn** **M**
(402) 564-2527. **$59-$65.** 371 33rd Ave. Jct US 30 and 81, 1 mi s. Int corridors. **Pets:** Medium. Service with restrictions, supervision.
[SAVE] [S♦] [✕] [▭]

AAA ◆◆ **Sleep Inn & Suites Hotel** **M**
(402) 562-5200. **$65-$95.** 303 23rd St. US 30, 2 mi e of jct US 30 and 81 east side of town. Int corridors.
Pets: Medium, other species. $10 daily fee/pet. Designated rooms, service with restrictions, crate.
[SAVE] [S♦] [✕] [♿M] [▧] [♿] [▭] [▭] [≋]

COZAD

AAA ◆◆◆ **Budget Host Circle S Motel** **M**
(308) 784-2290. **$45-$55.** 440 S Meridian. I-80, exit 222, 0.3 mi n. Ext corridors. **Pets:** Dogs only. Designated rooms, service with restrictions, supervision.
[SAVE] [S♦] [✕] [▭] [▥] [≋]

▼▼▼ Motel 6-Cozad–4091 **M**
(308) 784-4900. **$43-$50.** 809 S Meridian. I-80, exit 222, just s. Int corridors. **Pets:** Other species. Service with restrictions, supervision.

⊠ 🔧

FAIRBURY

🔺🔺🔺 ▼▼▼ Capri Motel **M**
(402) 729-3317. **$36-$40.** 1100 14th St. On US 136 at jct SR 15. Ext/int corridors. **Pets:** Small, other species. $25 deposit/pet. Service with restrictions, supervision.

SAVE ⊠ 🔧 ▨

FREMONT

▼▼▼ Comfort Inn **M**
(402) 721-1109. **$64-$94.** 1649 E 23rd Ave. 2 mi e on US 30, just e of Business US 275. Int corridors. **Pets:** Accepted.

SAVE S6 ⊠ ▨ 🔧 ▨ ➔

🔺🔺🔺 ▼▼▼ Holiday Lodge **MI**
(402) 727-1110. **$63-$83, 14 days notice.** 1220 E 23rd St. US 30, at jct Business US 275 and 30. Ext/int corridors. **Pets:** Medium. $25 deposit/room. Designated rooms, supervision.

SAVE S6 ⊠ ▨ 🍴 ➔

▼▼ Sleep Inn Fremont, NE **M**
(402) 721-8400. **$55-$75.** 120 W Cathy St. Jct US 275 and 77. Int corridors. **Pets:** Small, other species. $100 deposit/room. Designated rooms, crate.

SAVE S6 ⊠ 🅼 ▨ 🔧 ▨ ➔

FULLERTON

▼▼ The Fullerton Inn **M** 🐾
(308) 536-2699. **$50.** S Hwy 14. SR 14, just s of center. Int corridors. **Pets:** Medium. $5 daily fee/pet. Supervision.

ASK S6 ⊠ 🅼

GOTHENBURG

🔺🔺🔺 ▼▼▼ Gothenburg Super 8 **M**
(308) 537-2684. **$52-$75.** 401 Platte River Dr. I-80, exit 211, just n. Int corridors. **Pets:** Accepted.

SAVE S6 ⊠ 🔧 ▨ ➔

GRAND ISLAND

🔺🔺🔺 ▼▼▼ Best Western Riverside Inn & Conference Center **MI**
(308) 384-5150. **$60-$70, 10 days notice.** 3333 Ramada Rd. I-80, exit 312 eastbound; 5 mi n to US 34, 2 mi e to Locust St; exit 318 westbound, 3 mi n to US 34, 5 mi w to Locust St. Ext/int corridors. **Pets:** Accepted.

SAVE ⊠ 🔧 ▨ 🍴 ➔

▼▼ Days Inn **M**
(308) 384-8624. **$40-$65, 15 days notice.** 2620 N Diers Ave. 4.8 mi nw on US 281 at jct SR 2, off W Capital Ave. Ext/int corridors. **Pets:** Accepted.

SAVE S6 ⊠ ▨ 🗝 🔧

▼▼▼ Holiday Inn-Interstate 80 **MI**
(308) 384-7770. **$85.** 7838 S US Hwy 281. I-80, exit 312 (US 281). Int corridors. **Pets:** Other species. $15 daily fee/room. Service with restrictions, supervision.

⊠ 🗝 🗝 🔧 ▨ 🍴 ➔

▼▼ Super 8 **M**
(308) 384-4380. **$60-$63.** 2603 S Locust. I-80, exit 312 eastbound, 5 mi n to US 34, 2 mi e to Locust St, 0.5 mi n; exit 318 westbound, 3 mi n to US 34, 5 mi w to Locust St, then 0.5 mi n. Int corridors. **Pets:** Medium. Service with restrictions, supervision.

ASK S6 ⊠ 🔧 ▨

▼▼ Travelodge **M**
(308) 382-5003. **$58.** 1311 S Locust. I-80, exit 312 eastbound, 5 mi n to US 34, 2 mi e to Locust St, 1 mi n; exit 318 westbound, 3 mi n to US 34, 5 mi w to Locust St, then 1 mi n. Int corridors. **Pets:** Other species.

ASK S6 ⊠ 🗝 🔧 ▨

🔺🔺🔺 ▼▼▼ USA Inns of America **M**
(308) 381-0111. **$45-$60.** 7000 S Nine Bridge Rd. I-80, exit 312 (US 281). Ext/int corridors. **Pets:** Medium. $5 daily fee/pet. Designated rooms, service with restrictions, supervision.

SAVE S6 ⊠ 🔧 ▨

HASTINGS

▼▼ Holiday Inn-Hastings **MI**
(402) 463-6721. **$62-$97, 7 days notice.** 2205 Osborne Dr E. Jct US 34 and 281, 2 mi n on US 34. Ext/int corridors. **Pets:** Other species. $50 deposit/room. Service with restrictions, supervision.

ASK S6 ⊠ 🅼 🗝 🗝 🔧 ▨ 🍴 ➔

🔺🔺🔺 ▼▼▼ Midlands Lodge **M** 🐾
(402) 463-2428. **$39-$52, 7 days notice.** 910 West J St. Jct US 6/34/281. Ext corridors. **Pets:** Medium, other species. Designated rooms, service with restrictions, crate.

SAVE S6 ⊠ 🔧 ▨

▼▼ Super 8 **M**
(402) 463-8888. **$50-$65.** 2200 N Kansas Ave. Jct US 34 and 281, 2 mi n on US 34. Int corridors. **Pets:** Other species. Service with restrictions, supervision.

ASK S6 ⊠ 🗝 🗝 🔧 ▨

KEARNEY

🔺🔺🔺 ▼▼▼▼ Best Western Inn of Kearney **MI**
(308) 237-5185. **$49-$79.** 1010 3rd Ave. I-80, exit 272, 1 mi n on SR 44. Ext/int corridors. **Pets:** Other species. Service with restrictions, supervision.

SAVE S6 ⊠ 🗝 🔧 ▨ 🍴 ➔

KIMBALL

▼▼ Days Inn-Kimball **M**
(308) 235-4671. **$58-$130, 7 days notice.** 611 E 3rd St. I-80, exit 20, 1.5 ne on SR 71, then 0.5 mi e on US 30. Ext corridors. **Pets:** Accepted.

SAVE S6 ⊠ 🔧 ➔

LEXINGTON

Budget Host Minute Man Motel M
(308) 324-5544. **$38-$50, 5 days notice.** 801 Plum Creek Pkwy. I-80, exit 237, 2 mi n on US 283. Ext corridors. **Pets:** Accepted.

Days Inn M
(308) 324-6440. **$50-$65.** 2506 Plum Creek Pkwy. I-80, exit 237, 0.6 mi n on US 283. Int corridors. **Pets:** Dogs only. $6 daily fee/pet. Designated rooms, service with restrictions, supervision.

Holiday Inn Express Hotel & Suites M
(308) 324-9900. **$51-$62.** 2605 Plum Creek Pkwy. I-80, exit 237, 0.5 mi n on US 283. Int corridors. **Pets:** Large, other species. $10 one-time fee/room. Designated rooms, service with restrictions, supervision.

LINCOLN

Best Western Villager Courtyard & Gardens Hotel MI
(402) 464-9111. **$55, 30 days notice.** 5200 O St. 3 mi e on US 6 city route and 34. Ext corridors. **Pets:** Other species. Designated rooms, service with restrictions, supervision.

Chase Suites Hotel ⬛
(402) 483-4900. **$89-$109.** 200 S 68th St Pl. On US 34, 4.3 mi e, just s of jct 68th St. Ext corridors. **Pets:** Medium, other species. $150 deposit/pet, $5 daily fee/pet. Service with restrictions.

Comfort Inn of Lincoln M
(402) 475-2200. **$54-$94.** 2940 NW 12th St. I-80, exit 399 (airport); enter at Perkins Restaurant. Int corridors. **Pets:** Medium. $5 one-time fee/pet. Designated rooms, service with restrictions, supervision.

Comfort Suites M
(402) 476-8080. **$79-$104.** 4231 Industrial Ave. I-80, exit 403, 1.5 mi s on 27th St. Int corridors. **Pets:** Accepted.

Country Inns & Suites By Carlson M
(402) 476-5353. **$99-$105.** 5353 N 27th St. I-80, exit 403, 1.5 mi s. Int corridors. **Pets:** Small. $75 deposit/pet, $5 daily fee/pet. Designated rooms, service with restrictions.

Days Inn South M
(402) 423-7111. **$49-$80.** 1140 Calvert St. 2.5 mi s on SR 2. Ext/int corridors. **Pets:** Small. $5 daily fee/pet. Service with restrictions, supervision.

Hawthorn Suites Ltd M
(402) 464-4400. **$80-$120.** 216 N 48th St. 2.5 mi e on US 6 city route and 34; just ne of 48th and O sts; (entrance off of 48th St). Int corridors. **Pets:** Accepted.

Holiday Inn Express M 🐾
(402) 435-0200. **$77-$81.** 1133 Belmont Ave. I-80, exit 401A, mi s on I-180, exit 2 (Cornhusker Hwy), then just e. Int corridors. **Pets:** Other species.

Ramada Inn-Airport M
(402) 475-4971. **$59-$90.** 1101 W Bond St. I-80, exit 399. Int corridors. **Pets:** Small. $25 deposit/room. Designated rooms, no service, supervision.

Ramada Limited M
(402) 476-2222. **$63.** 4433 N 27th St. I-80, exit 403, 2 mi s. Int corridors. **Pets:** Small. $5 daily fee/pet. Service with restrictions, supervision.

Settle Inn & Suites M
(402) 435-8100. **$70-$100, 3 days notice.** 2800 Husker Cir. I-80, exit 403, just s to Wildcat Dr, just e, then just n. Int corridors. **Pets:** Small. $10 daily fee/pet. Supervision.

Staybridge Suites Lincoln-I-80 M
(402) 438-7829. **$79-$145, 7 days notice.** 2701 Fletcher Ave. I-80, exit 403, 0.4 mi s on N 27th St. Int corridors. **Pets:** Large, other species. $75 one-time fee/room. Service with restrictions.

Town House Motel ⬛
(402) 475-3000. **$57-$85, 7 days notice.** 1744 M St. Downtown. Int corridors. **Pets:** Accepted.

MCCOOK

Days Inn & Suites McCook M 🐾
(308) 345-7115. **$40-$55.** 901 N Hwy 83. Jct US 6 and 34, 0.3 mi n. Int corridors. **Pets:** Other species. Service with restrictions, supervision.

Holiday Inn Express M
(308) 345-4505. **$54.** 1 Holiday Bison Dr. Jct US 6 and 34, just n on US 83. Int corridors. **Pets:** Accepted.

Super 8 Motel M
(308) 345-1141. **$46-$49.** 1103 E B St. Jct US 6 and 34, 0.5 mi e. Ext corridors. **Pets:** Medium. Service with restrictions, supervision.

MORRILL

▼▼ Oak Tree Inn Ⓜ
(308) 247-2111. **$48-$67.** 80700 Hwy 26. 0.5 mi e. Ext/int corridors. **Pets:** Large. $5 one-time fee/room. Service with restrictions, supervision.
ASK S✦ ✕ 🄜 🞡 🖥 ¶¶

NEBRASKA CITY

⒜ ▼▼ Apple Inn Ⓜ
(402) 873-5959. **$50-$62.** 502 S 11th. Center. Ext/int corridors. **Pets:** Small, dogs only. $40 deposit/room, $7 daily fee/room. Designated rooms, service with restrictions, supervision.
SAVE S✦ ✕ 🞡 🖥 🖳 ➘

NORFOLK

⒜ ▼▼ Norfolk Country Inn Ⓜ ✤
(402) 371-4430. **$60.** 1201 S 13th St. Jct US 275 Bypass and US 81. Ext corridors. **Pets:** Medium. Designated rooms, service with restrictions.
SAVE S✦ ✕ 🖥 🖳 ¶¶ ➘

▼▼ Ramada Inn Ⓜ
(402) 371-7000. **$60-$70.** 1227 Omaha Ave. Jct US 275 and 81, just e. Ext/int corridors. **Pets:** $25 deposit/room. Service with restrictions, supervision.
ASK S✦ ✕ 🖥 🖳 ¶¶ ➘

▼▼ White House Inn Ⓜ
(402) 371-3133. **$53-$68.** 2206 Market Ln. On US 275 Bypass, 1 mi w of US 81. Int corridors. **Pets:** Accepted.
ASK S✦ ✕ 🄜 🞡 🖥 🖳

NORTH PLATTE

⒜ ▼▼ Best Western Chalet Lodge Ⓜ
(308) 532-2313. **$46-$70.** 920 N Jeffers St. I-80, exit 177, 2 mi n, US 83 and 30. Ext corridors. **Pets:** Other species. $3 daily fee/pet. No service, supervision.
SAVE S✦ ✕ 🖥 🖳 ➘

⒜ ▼▼▼ Holiday Inn Express Hotel & Suites Ⓜ
(308) 532-9500. **$59-$72.** 300 Holiday Frontage Rd. I-80, exit 177 (US 83), just s. Int corridors. **Pets:** Medium, other species. $10 one-time fee/room. Designated rooms, service with restrictions, supervision.
SAVE S✦ ✕ 🄜 🞡 🖥 🖳 ➘

▼▼▼ Quality Inn & Suites Ⓜ
(308) 532-9090. **$74-$149.** 2102 S Jeffers St. I-80, exit 177 (US 83), just s. Ext/int corridors. **Pets:** $10 daily fee/pet. Designated rooms, service with restrictions.
S✦ ✕ 🄜 🞡 🞡 🖥 🖳 ¶¶ ➘

⒜ ▼▼ Ramada Limited Ⓜ
(308) 534-3120. **$47-$77, 14 days notice.** 3201 S Jeffers St. I-80, exit 177 (US 83), 0.3 mi s. Int corridors. **Pets:** Medium. $5 daily fee/pet. Service with restrictions, supervision.
SAVE S✦ ✕ 🖳 ¶¶ ➘

▼▼ Travelers Inn Ⓜ
(308) 534-4020. **$45-$50.** 602 E 4th St. I-80, exit 177 (US 83), 1.5 mi n to E US 30, just e on US 30. Ext corridors. **Pets:** Medium, other species. Designated rooms, service with restrictions, supervision.
SAVE S✦ ✕ 🖥 ➘

O'NEILL

⒜ ▼ Elms Motel Best Value Inn Ⓜ ✤
(402) 336-3800. **$35-$41.** 414 E Hwy 20. 1 mi se on US 20/275. Ext corridors. **Pets:** Other species. Service with restrictions.
SAVE S✦ ✕

▼▼ Golden Hotel Ⓗ
(402) 336-4436. **$50.** 406 E Douglas. Center; jct US 20/275/281. Ext/int corridors. **Pets:** Accepted.
ASK S✦ ✕ 🖥 🖳

OGALLALA

⒜ ▼▼▼ Best Western Stagecoach Inn Ⓜ ✤
(308) 284-3656. **$53-$72, 14 days notice.** 201 Stagecoach Tr. I-80, exit 126, just ne on frontage road. Ext corridors. **Pets:** Other species. $5 daily fee/pet. Designated rooms, service with restrictions.
SAVE S✦ ✕ 🖥 🖳 ¶¶ ➘

⒜ ▼▼ Days Inn Ⓜ ✤
(308) 284-6365. **$45-$70.** 601 Stagecoach Tr. I-80, exit 126, just ne on frontage road. Int corridors. **Pets:** Dogs only. $6 one-time fee/room. Supervision.
SAVE S✦ ✕

▼▼▼ Holiday Inn Express Ⓜ
(308) 284-2266. **$69.** 501 Stagecoach Tr. I-80, exit 126, just n, then e on frontage road. Ext/int corridors. **Pets:** $10 one-time fee/room. Service with restrictions, supervision.
✕ 🞡 🞡 🖥

▼▼▼ Ogallala Comfort Inn Ⓜ
(308) 284-4028. **$55-$70.** 110 Pony Express Rd. I-80, exit 126, just s. Ext/int corridors. **Pets:** Small, other species. $10 daily fee/pet. Designated rooms, service with restrictions, supervision.
SAVE S✦ ✕ 🞡 🖳 ➘

▼▼ Ramada Limited Ⓜ
(308) 284-3623. **$40-$69.** 201 Chuckwagon Rd. I-80, exit 126, just nw. Ext/int corridors. **Pets:** Other species. $10 daily fee/pet. Designated rooms, service with restrictions, supervision.
ASK S✦ ✕ 🖳 ¶¶ ➘

OMAHA

⒜ ▼▼▼ Baymont Inn Omaha Ⓜ
(402) 592-5200. **$64-$74.** 10760 M St. I-80, exit 445, 0.3 mi e on L St, entry off 108th St. Int corridors. **Pets:** Accepted.
SAVE S✦ ✕ 🞡 🖥 🖳

♦♦♦ **Ben Franklin Motel M**
(402) 895-2200. **$50-$62.** 10308 Sapp Bros Dr. I-80, exit 440 (SR 50), just n to service road, then just w, follow signs. Ext corridors. **Pets:** Accepted.
ⒶⓈⓀ Ⓢⓓ ✕ 🏷️ 🛄 💻 ⇔

Clarion Hotel Executive Center MI
(402) 397-3700. **$79-$109.** 3650 S 72nd St. I-80, exit 449 (72nd St). Int corridors. **Pets:** Other species. $10 one-time fee/pet. Designated rooms, service with restrictions, supervision.
ⓈⒶⓋⒺ Ⓢⓓ ✕ ⓛⓜ 🎞️ 🏷️ 🛄 💻 🍴 ⇔

Crowne Plaza Omaha-Old Mill MI
(402) 496-0850. **$89-$129.** 655 N 108th Ave. I-680, exit 3 (Dodge St W), 0.7 mi to 108th St to 108th Ave and N Old Mill Rd exits, just n. Int corridors. **Pets:** Small. $100 deposit/room, $25 one-time fee/room. Service with restrictions, crate.
ⒶⓈⓀ Ⓢⓓ ✕ 🎞️ 🏷️ 🛄 💻 🍴 ⇔

Doubletree Guest Suites Omaha H
(402) 397-5141. **$89-$159.** 7270 Cedar St. I-80, exit 449 (72nd St), 1.3 mi n. Int corridors. **Pets:** Accepted.
ⓈⒶⓋⒺ Ⓢⓓ ✕ 🎞️ 🏷️ 🛄 💻 🍴 ⇔

Econo Lodge West Dodge M
(402) 391-7100. **$54-$90.** 7833 Dodge St. I-680, exit 3 (Dodge St E), 2.2 mi e. Ext corridors. **Pets:** Accepted.
ⓈⒶⓋⒺ Ⓢⓓ ✕ 🛄 💻 ⇔

Four Points by Sheraton Omaha MI
(402) 895-1000. **$71-$105, 7 days notice.** 4888 S 118th St. I-80, exit 445 (L St W), 0.3 mi w, US 275 and SR 92, then just s on 120th St. Int corridors. **Pets:** Small. $10 daily fee/room. Service with restrictions, crate.
ⓈⒶⓋⒺ Ⓢⓓ ✕ ⓛⓜ 🎞️ 🏷️ 🛄 💻 🍴 ⇔

Hawthorn Suites M
(402) 331-0101. **$89.** 11025 M St. I-80, exit 445, 0.3 mi e on L St, s on 108th St, then just w. Ext corridors. **Pets:** Medium, other species. $6 daily fee/pet. Service with restrictions, supervision.
ⒶⓈⓀ Ⓢⓓ ✕ 🎞️ 🛄 💻 ⇔

Holiday Inn Central MI
(402) 393-3950. **Call for rates.** 3321 S 72nd St. I-80, exit 449 (72nd St), just n. Int corridors. **Pets:** Accepted.
ⒶⓈⓀ ✕ ⓛⓜ 🎞️ 🛄 💻 🍴 ⇔

Homewood Suites M
(402) 397-7500. **$89, 30 days notice.** 7010 Hascall St. I-80, exit 449 (72nd St), just n, then just e. Ext/int corridors. **Pets:** Accepted.
ⓈⒶⓋⒺ Ⓢⓓ ✕ 🎞️ 🏷️ 🛄 💻 ⇔

La Quinta Inn M
(402) 493-1900. **$65-$81.** 3330 N 104th Ave. I-680, exit 4 (Maple St), just w to 108th St, just n to Bedford, then just e. Int corridors. **Pets:** Accepted.
ⓈⒶⓋⒺ Ⓢⓓ ✕ 🎞️ 🛄 💻 ⇔

Motel 6-161 M
(402) 331-3161. **$42-$57.** 10708 M St. I-80, exit 445 (L St E), 0.4 mi e, entry on 108th St. Ext corridors. **Pets:** Accepted.
Ⓢⓓ ✕ 🏷️ ⇔

Omaha Marriott Hotel H
(402) 399-9000. **$69-$159.** 10220 Regency Cir. I-680, exit 3 (Dodge St E), just s on Regency Pkwy, then just w. Int corridors. **Pets:** $30 one-time fee/room. Service with restrictions, crate.
ⓈⒶⓋⒺ ✕ ⓛⓜ 🎞️ 🏷️ 🛄 💻 🍴 ⇔

Ramada Inn-Airport MI
(402) 342-5100. **$77-$79, 15 days notice.** 2002 E Locust St. I-480 E, exit 14th St (downtown), via Capitol Ave and Abbott Dr, follow signs 2.5 mi. Ext/int corridors. **Pets:** Very small. Service with restrictions, supervision.
ⓈⒶⓋⒺ Ⓢⓓ ✕ 🎞️ 🛄 💻 🍴 ⇔

Ramada Limited M
(402) 896-9500. **$72-$75, 5 days notice.** 9505 S 142nd St. I-80, exit 440. Int corridors. **Pets:** Very small, dogs only. $10 daily fee/pet. Service with restrictions, supervision.
ⒶⓈⓀ Ⓢⓓ ✕ 🏷️ ⇔

Red Lion Hotel Omaha H
(402) 397-7030. **$99, 7 days notice.** 7007 Grover St. I-80, exit 449 (72nd St), just n, then just e. Int corridors. **Pets:** Other species. $30 one-time fee/room. Designated rooms, service with restrictions, supervision.
ⒶⓈⓀ Ⓢⓓ ✕ 🎞️ 🏷️ 🛄 💻 🍴 ⇔

Satellite Motel M
(402) 733-7373. **$46-$54.** 6006 L St. I-80, exit 450 (60th St), 0.8 mi s; on US 275 and SR 92. Ext/int corridors. **Pets:** Very small. $20 deposit/room, $5 daily fee/pet. Designated rooms, service with restrictions, supervision.
ⓈⒶⓋⒺ ✕ 🛄 💻

Sheraton Omaha Hotel H
(402) 342-2222. **$89-$189, 3 days notice.** 1615 Howard St. Downtown. Int corridors. **Pets:** Accepted.
ⒶⓈⓀ ✕ 🎞️ 🏷️ 🛄 💻 🍴

Super 8 Motel-Aksarben M
(402) 390-0700. **$59-$75.** 7111 Spring St. I-80, exit 449 (72nd St), 0.3 mi n. Int corridors. **Pets:** Accepted.
ⒶⓈⓀ Ⓢⓓ ✕ 🎞️

Super 8 Motel-Omaha M
(402) 339-2250. **$59-$89.** 10829 M St. I-80, exit 445 (L St E), just e on L St, entry off 108th St. Int corridors. **Pets:** Other species. $10 one-time fee/pet. Service with restrictions, supervision.
ⒶⓈⓀ Ⓢⓓ ✕ 🎞️

OSHKOSH

Shady Rest Motel M
(308) 772-4115. **$34-$40, 3 days notice.** 102 Main St. On US 26, jct Main St. Ext corridors. **Pets:** Accepted.
ⓈⒶⓋⒺ ✕

PAXTON

⟁⟁⟁ ▽▽▽ Paxton Days Inn M ✿
(308) 239-4510. **$50-$60.** 851 Paxton Rd. I-80, exit 145, just n. Ext corridors. **Pets:** Large. $10 daily fee/room. Service with restrictions, supervision.
SAVE S⊘ ✕ ⟁ ⊟ ▣ ⑪ ⊠

SCOTTSBLUFF

⟁⟁⟁ ▽ Capri Motel M
(308) 635-2057. **$32-$40, 3 days notice.** 2424 Ave I. 1.5 mi nw, just s of 27th St. Ext corridors. **Pets:** Other species. $6 daily fee/pet. Service with restrictions, supervision.
SAVE S⊘ ✕ ⊟ ▣

⟁⟁⟁ ▽▽▽ Days Inn MI
(308) 635-3111. **$54-$68.** 1901 21st Ave. 1.8 mi e on US 26. Int corridors. **Pets:** Other species. $5 daily fee/room. Service with restrictions, supervision.
SAVE S⊘ ✕ ⊟ ▣ ⑪ ⇌

▽▽ Lamplighter American Inn M ✿
(308) 632-7108. **Call for rates.** 606 E 27th St. US 26 business route, 0.5 mi e of jct SR 71. Int corridors. **Pets:** Dogs only. $6 daily fee/pet. Designated rooms, service with restrictions, supervision.
ASK ✕ ▣ ⇌

SEWARD

▽▽ Seward Super 8 M
(402) 643-3388. **$49-$56.** 1329 Progressive Rd. I-80, exit 379, 3 mi n on SR 15. Ext/int corridors. **Pets:** Accepted.
ASK S⊘ ✕ ⟁ ⊟

SIDNEY

⟁⟁⟁ ▽ Best Value Sidney Motor Lodge M
(308) 254-4581. **$44-$60.** 2031 Illinois St. On US 30, west edge of town. Ext corridors. **Pets:** Medium, other species. Service with restrictions, supervision.
SAVE S⊘ ✕ ⊟

⟁⟁⟁ ▽▽▽ Days Inn M ✿
(308) 254-2121. **$54-$80.** 3042 Silverberg Dr. I-80, exit 59, just n. Int corridors. **Pets:** Designated rooms, supervision.
SAVE S⊘ ✕ ⊟ ⇌

▽▽▽ Holiday Inn & Conference Center MI
(308) 254-2000. **$62-$85.** 664 Chase Blvd. I-80, exit 59, just s. Int corridors. **Pets:** Large, other species. $10 one-time fee/room. Service with restrictions.
ASK S⊘ ✕ ⟁ᴹ ⟁ ⟁ ⊟ ▣ ⑪ ⇌

SOUTH SIOUX CITY

▽▽▽ Marina Inn Conference Center MI
(402) 494-4000. **$89-$104, 3 days notice.** 4th & B sts. I-29, exit 148, on banks of Missouri River (turn e at stop light by Nebraska side of bridge). Int corridors. **Pets:** Accepted.
ASK S⊘ ✕ ⟁ᴹ ⟁ ⟁ ⊟ ▣ ⑪ ⇌

SYRACUSE

⟁⟁⟁ ▽▽▽ Sleep Inn & Suites M
(402) 269-2700. **$65-$122.** 130 N 30th Rd. 1 mi n on SR 50, jct SR 2. Int corridors. **Pets:** Large, other species. $10 daily fee/pet. Designated rooms.
SAVE S⊘ ✕ ⟁ᴹ ⟁ ⟁ ⊟ ▣

THEDFORD

⟁⟁⟁ ▽▽▽ Rodeway Inn M
(308) 645-2284. **$46-$75.** HC 58 Box 1D. 1 mi e on SR 2, just w of US 83. Int corridors. **Pets:** Other species. $50 deposit/room, $5 daily fee/room. Service with restrictions, supervision.
SAVE S⊘ ✕ ⟁ ⊟ ▣

VALENTINE

▽▽▽▽ Holiday Inn Express Hotel & Suites M
(402) 376-3000. **$65-$95, 30 days notice.** 803 E Hwy 20. Jct US 20/83, 0.5 mi se on US 20. Int corridors. **Pets:** Small. $10 daily fee/pet. Designated rooms, service with restrictions, supervision.
ASK S⊘ ✕ ⟁ᴹ ⟁ ⟁ ⊟ ▣

⟁⟁⟁ ▽▽ Motel Raine M
(402) 376-2030. **$42-$58.** US 20 W. On US 20, 0.5 mi sw. Ext corridors. **Pets:** Designated rooms, service with restrictions, supervision.
SAVE ✕ ▣

⟁⟁⟁ ▽▽▽ Trade Winds Lodge M
(402) 376-1600. **$43-$61.** E Hwy 20 & 83. Jct US 20/83, 1 mi se on US 20. Ext corridors. **Pets:** Other species. $3 daily fee/pet. Service with restrictions, supervision.
SAVE S⊘ ✕ ⇌

YORK

⟁⟁⟁ ▽▽▽ Best Western Palmer Inn M
(402) 362-5585. **$44-$69.** 2426 S Lincoln Ave. I-80, exit 353, 1 mi n on US 81. Ext corridors. **Pets:** Medium. $5 one-time fee/room. Designated rooms, no service, supervision.
SAVE S⊘ ✕ ⊟ ▣ ⇌

⟁⟁⟁ ▽▽▽ Yorkshire Motel M
(402) 362-6633. **$44-$70.** 3402 S Lincoln Ave. I-80, exit 353, 0.5 mi n on US 81. Ext/int corridors. **Pets:** Accepted.
SAVE S⊘ ✕

NEVADA

CITY INDEX

AMARGOSA VALLEY

▼▼▼▼ Longstreet Inn, Casino RV Park & Golf Club M

(775) 372-1777. **$59-$89.** 373 Stateline. 7 mi n of jct SR 127 and 190 (Death Valley Jct) on SR 373; 15 mi s of jct SR 95 and 373 on SR 373. Int corridors. **Pets:** Medium. $50 deposit/room. Service with restrictions.

⊠ ⑪ ⌁

BATTLE MOUNTAIN

⦿ ▼▼▼ Best Inn & Suites M ❀

(775) 635-5200. **$47-$52.** 650 W Front St. I-80, exit 229, 0.5 mi e. Ext corridors. **Pets:** $10 one-time fee/pet. No service, supervision.

SAVE 🕙 ⊠ 🛏 🖵

⦿ ▼▼▼ Big Chief Motel M

(775) 635-2416. **$42-$50.** 434 W Front St. I-80, exit 229 or 233, just n. Ext corridors. **Pets:** Other species. $5 one-time fee/pet. Designated rooms, supervision.

SAVE 🕙 ⊠ ⑦ 🛏 ⌁

⦿ ▼▼▼ Comfort Inn M

(775) 635-5880. **$54-$94.** 521 E Front St. I-80, exit 229 or 233, just n. Int corridors. **Pets:** Accepted.

SAVE 🕙 ⊠ ⑦ 🛏 🖵 ⌁

BEATTY

▼▼ Burro Inn MI

(775) 553-2225. **$40.** Third St & Hwy 95. 4 blks s on SR 95. Ext corridors. **Pets:** Other species. $25 deposit/room, $5 daily fee/pet. Service with restrictions, supervision.

⊠ ⑦ ⑪

▼▼ Phoenix Inn M

(775) 553-2250. **$28-$50.** 350 First St. Just off SR 95. Ext corridors. **Pets:** Accepted.

ASK 🕙 ⊠ 🛏

⦿ ▼▼▼ Stagecoach Hotel Casino & RV Park MI

(775) 553-2419. **$36-$44.** Hwy 95 N. North end of town, west side of US 95. Ext/int corridors. **Pets:** Medium, other species. $10 deposit/pet, $5 one-time fee/pet. Designated rooms, service with restrictions.

SAVE ⊠ 🦽 🛏 ⑪ ⌁

CARLIN

⦿ ▼▼▼ Best Inn & Suites M

(775) 754-6110. **$54-$104.** 1018 Fir St. I-80, exit 280, just s. Int corridors. **Pets:** Accepted.

SAVE 🕙 ⊠ 🦽M ⑦ 🦽 🛏 🖵

CARSON CITY

⦿ ▼▼ Best Value M

(775) 882-2007. **$33-$109.** 2731 S Carson St. 1.3 mi s on US 50 and 395. Ext corridors. **Pets:** Other species. $30 deposit/room. Service with restrictions, crate.

SAVE 🕙 ⊠ 🛏 ⌁

⦿ ▼▼▼ Best Western Trailside Inn M

(775) 883-7300. **$45-$159.** 1300 N Carson St. 0.5 mi n on US 395. Ext corridors. **Pets:** Other species. $10 daily fee/room. Service with restrictions, supervision.

SAVE 🕙 ⊠ 🛏 🖵 ⌁

⦿ ▼▼ Carson City Super 8 M

(775) 883-7800. **$35-$151.** 2829 S Carson. South end of town. Int corridors. **Pets:** $25 deposit/pet, $6 daily fee/pet. Designated rooms, service with restrictions, supervision.

SAVE 🕙 ⊠ 🛏

⦿ ▼▼▼ Days Inn M

(775) 883-3343. **$40-$140.** 3103 N Carson St. US 395 N, north end of city. Ext corridors. **Pets:** Dogs only. $10 daily fee/pet. Designated rooms, service with restrictions, supervision.

SAVE ⊠ 🛏

ELKO

▼▼▼▼ Best Western Elko Inn Express M

(775) 738-7261. **$64, 30 days notice.** 837 Idaho St. I-80, exit 301 or 303, 1 mi s. Ext corridors. **Pets:** Accepted.

SAVE 🕙 ⊠ ⑦ 🛏 ⌁

⦿ ▼▼▼ Best Western Gold Country Motor Inn MI ❀

(775) 738-8421. **$69-$109.** 2050 Idaho St. I-80, exit 303, just s. Ext corridors. **Pets:** Medium. $15 one-time fee/room. Designated rooms, service with restrictions, supervision.

SAVE 🕙 ⊠ 🦽M ⑦ 🦽 🛏 🖵 ⑪ ⌁

High Desert Inn M
(775) 738-8425. **$49-$59.** 3015 Idaho St. I-80, exit 303, just s. Ext/int corridors. **Pets:** Accepted.

Oak Tree Inn M
(775) 777-2222. **$45-$70, 3 days notice.** 95 Spruce Rd. I-80, exit 301, just n. Int corridors. **Pets:** Other species. $5 daily fee/pet. Service with restrictions, supervision.

Red Lion Inn & Casino M
(775) 738-2111. **$89-$119.** 2065 Idaho St. I-80, exit 303, just s. Int corridors. **Pets:** Accepted.

Shilo Inn M ❖
(775) 738-5522. **$69-$119.** 2401 Mountain City Hwy. I-80, exit 301, just n. Int corridors. **Pets:** Other species. $10 daily fee/pet. Service with restrictions, supervision.

Thunderbird Motel M
(775) 738-7115. **$53-$79.** 345 Idaho St. I-80, exit 301 or 303, 1 mi s. Ext corridors. **Pets:** Accepted.

ELY

Historic Hotel Nevada & Gambling Hall H
(775) 289-6665. **$38.** 501 Aultman St. Downtown. Int corridors. **Pets:** Accepted.

Ramada Inn-Copper Queen Casino X
(775) 289-4884. **$64-$110.** 805 Great Basin Blvd. 0.3 mi s of jct 6, 50 and 93. Ext/int corridors. **Pets:** Other species. Service with restrictions, supervision.

FALLON

Motel 6 M
(775) 423-2277. **$46-$56.** 1705 S Taylor St. 0.5 mi s of US 50. Ext corridors. **Pets:** Very small. Designated rooms, no service, supervision.

Western Motel M
(775) 423-5118. **$41.** 125 S Carson St. US 95, just e. Ext corridors. **Pets:** Small, dogs only. $5 daily fee/pet. No service, supervision.

FERNLEY

Best Western Fernley Inn M
(775) 575-6776. **$57-$87.** 1405 E Newlands Dr. I-80, exit 48, just s. Ext corridors. **Pets:** Other species. $7 daily fee/pet. Designated rooms, service with restrictions.

GARDNERVILLE

Topaz Lodge M
(775) 266-3338. **$39-$53.** 1979 US 395 S. US 395 S at Topaz Lake, 22 mi s of Garderville, NV. Ext corridors. **Pets:** Dogs only. $5 daily fee/pet. Designated rooms, service with restrictions.

Westerner Motel M
(775) 782-3602. **$40-$65.** 1353 US 395 N. US 395 S, end of town. Ext corridors. **Pets:** Dogs only. Designated rooms, service with restrictions, supervision.

HAWTHORNE

El Capitan Resort Casino M ❖
(775) 945-3321. **$45-$65.** 540 F St. Just n of US 95. Ext corridors. **Pets:** Medium, other species. $10 daily fee/room. Service with restrictions, supervision.

JACKPOT

Horseshu Hotel & Casino M
(775) 755-7777. **$29-$75.** 1385 Hwy 93. On SR 93. Int corridors. **Pets:** Accepted.

LAKE TAHOE AREA

STATELINE

Harrah's Hotel & Casino H
(775) 588-6611. **$109-$279, 03 days notice.** Hwy 50. In casino area. Int corridors. **Pets:** Accepted.

❖ END AREA ❖

LAS VEGAS METROPOLITAN AREA

BOULDER CITY

⨀ ▼▼ Best Western Lighthouse Inn M
(702) 293-6444. **$55-$75.** 110 Ville Dr. 1 mi e via SR 93. Ext corridors. **Pets:** Other species. $10 one-time fee/room. Service with restrictions, crate.
[SAVE] [$₀] [✕] [🛏] [📺] [≈]

▼ Super 8 Motel M
(702) 294-8888. **$45-$140.** 704 Nevada Hwy. On US 93. Ext corridors. **Pets:** Medium. $10 daily fee/pet. Service with restrictions, supervision.
[ASK] [$₀] [✕] [🛁] [🛏] [≈]

ECHO BAY

⨀ ▼▼ Echo Bay Resort MI
(702) 394-4000. **$60-$115, 3 days notice.** On Lake Mead; 4 mi e of SR 167. Int corridors. **Pets:** $25 deposit/pet. Service with restrictions.
[SAVE] [✕] [📺] [🍴] [✕]

HENDERSON

⨀ ▼▼▼ Hawthorn Inn & Suites H
(702) 568-7800. **$89-$160.** 910 S Boulder Hwy. Int corridors. **Pets:** Other species. $25 one-time fee/pet. Service with restrictions, supervision.
[SAVE] [$₀] [✕] [🛁] [🛏] [📺] [≈]

⨀ ▼▼▼ Residence Inn-Green Valley M
(702) 434-2700. **$114-$144.** 2190 Olympic Ave. I-215, exit Green Valley Pkwy N. Int corridors. **Pets:** Medium, other species. $50 one-time fee/room. Designated rooms, service with restrictions.
[SAVE] [$₀] [✕] [🛁M] [🛁] [🛏] [📺] [≈]

INDIAN SPRINGS

⨀ ▼ Indian Springs Motor Hotel M
(702) 879-3700. **$39-$42.** 300 Tonopah Hwy. On US 95, 45 mi n of Las Vegas. Int corridors. **Pets:** Medium. $50 deposit/pet, $5 daily fee/pet.
[SAVE] [$₀] [✕] [🛏] [🍴]

LAS VEGAS

⨀ ▼▼▼ AmeriSuites Las Vegas M
(702) 369-3366. **$89-$129.** 4520 Paradise Ave. Cross sts Harmon and Paradise, e of the Strip. Int corridors. **Pets:** Accepted.
[SAVE] [$₀] [✕] [🛁M] [�ô] [🛁] [🛏] [📺] [≈]

⨀ ▼▼ Best Inn & Suites M
(702) 632-0229. **$69-$125.** 4288 N Nellis Blvd. I-15, exit Craig St, e to N Las Vegas Blvd. Int corridors. **Pets:** Small. $10 daily fee/pet.
[SAVE] [$₀] [✕] [�ô] [🛁] [🛏] [📺]

⨀ ▼▼ Best Western Main Street Inn MI
(702) 382-3455. **$39-$149.** 1000 N Main St. I-15, exit 43E northbound; exit 44E southbound. Ext corridors. **Pets:** Other species. $8 daily fee/pet. Service with restrictions.
[SAVE] [$₀] [✕] [🛏] [🍴] [≈]

⨀ ▼▼ Best Western Nellis Motor Inn M
(702) 643-6111. **$39-$200, 7 days notice.** 5330 E Craig Rd. I-15, exit 48 eastbound, 7 mi ne; 0.3 mi from Nellis AFB. Ext corridors. **Pets:** Large. $10 daily fee/pet. Service with restrictions, supervision.
[SAVE] [$₀] [✕] [🛏] [📺] [≈]

⨀ ▼▼ Best Western Parkview Inn M
(702) 385-1213. **$39-$149, 7 days notice.** 921 Las Vegas Blvd N. I-15, exit US 93-95, 0.3 mi n at Washington. Ext corridors. **Pets:** Large, other species. $8 daily fee/pet. Service with restrictions, supervision.
[SAVE] [✕] [📺] [≈]

⨀ ▼▼▼ Comfort Inn M 🐾
(702) 399-1500. **$59-$250.** 910 E Cheyenne Ave. I-15, exit 46 (Cheyenne W). Int corridors. **Pets:** Other species. $5 daily fee/pet. Designated rooms, service with restrictions, supervision.
[SAVE] [$₀] [✕] [🛁] [🛏] [📺] [≈]

⨀ ▼▼▼ Crowne Plaza MI
(702) 369-4400. **$89-$185, 3 days notice.** 4255 S Paradise Rd. I-15, exit Flamingo Rd, 0.5 mi e to Paradise Rd, 0.3 mi s. Int corridors. **Pets:** Accepted.
[SAVE] [$₀] [✕] [🛁M] [🖊] [🛏] [📺] [🍴] [≈]

⨀ ▼▼▼▼ Four Seasons Hotel Las Vegas H 🐾
(702) 632-5000. **$200-$450.** 3960 Las Vegas Blvd S. I-15, exit E Tropicana, s on the Strip. Int corridors. **Pets:** Medium. Designated rooms, service with restrictions, supervision.
[✕] [🛁M] [�ô] [📺] [🍴] [≈]

⨀ ▼▼▼ Hawthorn Inn & Suites M
(702) 798-7736. **$69-$169.** 4975 S Valley View Blvd. I-15, exit 37, Tropicana Ave W.. Int corridors. **Pets:** Accepted.
[SAVE] [$₀] [✕] [🛁M] [�ô] [🛁] [📺] [≈]

▼▼▼ Hawthorn Suites-Las Vegas M 🐾
(702) 739-7000. **$120-$210.** 5051 Duke Ellington Way. I-15, exit E Tropicana Ave, 0.8 mi e to Duke Ellington Way, just s. Ext corridors. **Pets:** Other species. $100 deposit/room, $25 one-time fee/room. Designated rooms, service with restrictions.
[ASK] [$₀] [✕] [🖊] [�ô] [🛁] [📺] [≈]

⨀ ▼▼▼ Hawthorn Suites LTD M
(702) 243-0356. **$79-$150.** 9570 W Sahara. Just w of Fort Apache. Int corridors. **Pets:** Medium, dogs only. $20 one-time fee/pet. Designated rooms, service with restrictions, supervision.
[SAVE] [$₀] [✕] [🛁M] [�ô] [🛁] [📺] [≈]

(AAA) ◆◆◆ Holiday Inn Express M
(702) 256-3766. **$89-$156.** 8669 W Sahara Ave. I-15, exit Sahara, 6.5 mi w. Int corridors. **Pets:** Accepted.
[SAVE] [S⊘] [✕] [⌂] [⊞] [◻] [≈]

◆◆◆ Holiday Inn Express Hotel & Suites N Las Vegas M
(702) 649-3000. **$100-$130.** 4540 Donovan Way. I-15, exit W Craig Rd. Int corridors. **Pets:** Accepted.
[ASK] [S⊘] [✕] [⌂M] [⊞] [⌂] [◻] [≈]

(AAA) ◆◆◆ Howard Johnson Las Vegas Strip MI ❖
(702) 388-0301. **$49-$89.** 1401 Las Vegas Blvd S. I-15, to Las Vegas Blvd, then n. Ext/int corridors. **Pets:** Small. $10 daily fee/pet. Designated rooms, service with restrictions, supervision.
[SAVE] [S⊘] [✕] [⌂] [◻] [⋔] [≈]

◆◆◆ La Quinta Inn M
(702) 739-7457. **$72-$130.** 3782 Las Vegas Blvd S. 5.5 mi s on the Strip. Ext corridors. **Pets:** Accepted.
[SAVE] [✕] [◻] [≈]

◆◆◆ La Quinta Inn Convention Center M
(702) 796-9000. **$57-$110.** 3970 Paradise Rd. I-15, exit E Flamingo Rd, 0.8 mi s of convention center, 0.5 mi e of the Strip. Int corridors. **Pets:** Small. Designated rooms, service with restrictions, supervision.
[SAVE] [✕] [⌂] [⌂] [◻] [≈]

◆◆◆ La Quinta Las Vegas NW Tech Center M
(702) 360-1200. **$86-$96.** 7101 Cascade Valley Ct. I-95, exit 83, on W Cheyenne Ave. Int corridors. **Pets:** Accepted.
[SAVE] [✕] [⌂M] [⌂] [◻] [≈]

(AAA) ◆◆◆ Residence Inn-Hughes Center M
(702) 650-0040. **$89-$299.** 370 Hughes Center Dr. I-15, at Paradise Rd. Int corridors. **Pets:** Accepted.
[SAVE] [S⊘] [✕] [⌂M] [⌂] [⊞] [◻] [≈]

(AAA) ◆◆◆ Residence Inn Las Vegas Convention Center H ❖
(702) 796-9300. **$149.** 3225 Paradise Rd. Opposite convention center. Ext corridors. **Pets:** Medium, other species. $10 daily fee/room, $50 one-time fee/room. Service with restrictions.
[SAVE] [S⊘] [✕] [⌂] [◻] [≈]

◆◆ Super 8 Motel Las Vegas Strip MI
(702) 794-0888. **$58-$200.** 4250 S Koval Ln. I-15, exit S Koval. Int corridors. **Pets:** Large, other species. $15 daily fee/pet. Designated rooms, service with restrictions, supervision.
[ASK] [S⊘] [✕] [⌀] [⌂] [⌂] [≈]

(AAA) ◆◆ Thriftlodge M
(702) 643-9220. **$59-$99.** 4244 Las Vegas Blvd. I-15, exit Craig Rd W, 1.5 mi to Las Vegas Blvd, then s. Ext corridors. **Pets:** Accepted.
[SAVE] [S⊘] [✕] [⌂]

(AAA) ◆◆◆ Wellesley Inn & Suites M
(702) 731-3111. **$49-$149.** 1550 E Flamingo Rd. I-15, exit E Flamingo Rd, then 2 mi. Int corridors. **Pets:** Accepted.
[SAVE] [S⊘] [✕] [⌀] [⌂] [⌂] [◻] [≈]

LAUGHLIN

◆◆◆ Don Laughlin's Riverside Resort Hotel & Casino H
(702) 298-2535. **$25-$175, 7 days notice.** 1650 S Casino Dr. 2 mi s of Davis Dam. Int corridors. **Pets:** Accepted.
[ASK] [S⊘] [✕] [⌀] [⌂] [⌂] [⋔] [≈]

MESQUITE

◆◆ Budget Inn & Suites M
(702) 346-7444. **$60-$74.** 390 N Sandhill. I-15, exit 122. Ext corridors. **Pets:** Medium, other species. $10 daily fee/room. Designated rooms, service with restrictions, supervision.
[ASK] [S⊘] [✕] [⌂] [⌂] [≈]

(AAA) ◆◆◆ Oasis Resort Casino Golf and Spa R
(702) 346-5232. **$20-$99.** 897 W Mesquite Blvd. I-15, exit 120. Ext corridors. **Pets:** Accepted.
[SAVE] [✕] [⌂M] [⌂] [⋔] [≈] [✕]

◆◆ Virgin River Hotel Casino Bingo MI
(702) 346-7777. **$22-$75.** 100 Pioneer Blvd. I-15, exit 122, just w. Ext corridors. **Pets:** Accepted.
[✕] [⌂M] [⌂] [◻] [⋔] [≈]

OVERTON

◆◆◆ Best Western North Shore Inn at Lake Mead M ❖
(702) 397-6000. **$57-$75.** 520 N Moapa Valley Blvd. I-15, exit 93, 10 mi ne on SR 169. Int corridors. **Pets:** Medium. $50 deposit/room. Designated rooms, service with restrictions, supervision.
[SAVE] [S⊘] [✕] [⌂] [◻] [≈]

PAHRUMP

(AAA) ◆◆◆ Saddle West Hotel & Casino MI ❖
(775) 727-1111. **$44-$105.** 1220 S Hwy 160. Downtown. Ext corridors. **Pets:** Large, other species. $100 deposit/room. Designated rooms, service with restrictions, supervision.
[SAVE] [S⊘] [✕] [⌂] [⌂] [⋔] [≈]

❖   **END METROPOLITAN AREA**   ❖

LOVELOCK

▼▼▼▼ Ramada Inn-Sturgeon's Casino Ⓜ
(775) 273-2971. **$49-$89, 7 days notice.** 1420 Cornell Ave.
I-80, exit 105 or 107, just n. Ext corridors. **Pets:** Accepted.
(ASK) (S🐾) (✕) (🐾) (🛏) (💻) (🍴) (🌊)

MILL CITY

▼▼ Super 8 Motel Ⓜ
(775) 538-7311. **Call for rates.** 6000 E Frontage Rd. I-80,
exit 149 or 150, just n. Int corridors. **Pets:** Accepted.
(ASK) (S🐾) (✕)

MINDEN

(AAA) ▼▼▼▼ Best Western Minden Ⓜ
(775) 782-7766. **$46-$129.** 1795 Ironwood Dr. US 395, exit
Ironwood Dr W, 0.5 mi n of jct US 395 and SR 88. Ext
corridors. **Pets:** Medium, dogs only. $8 daily fee/pet. Desig-
nated rooms, service with restrictions, supervision.
(SAVE) (S🐾) (✕) (🐾) (🛏) (🌊) (📺)

▼▼ Holiday Lodge Ⓜ
(775) 782-2288. **$37-$48.** 1591 US 395 N. Center. Ext corridors. **Pets:** Medium, dogs only. $20 deposit/pet, $5 daily
fee/pet. Service with restrictions, supervision.
(✕) (🛏) (🌊)

RENO

(AAA) ▼▼▼ A&A's Rodeway Inn & Spa Ⓜ ❀
(775) 786-2500. **$49-$169, 7 days notice.** 2050 Market St.
I-395, exit W Mill St. Int corridors. **Pets:** Small, other species. $10 daily fee/pet. Designated rooms, no service,
supervision.
(SAVE) (S🐾) (✕) (🛏) (💻) (🌊)

▼▼ Days Inn Ⓜ
(775) 786-4070. **$43-$125.** 701 E 7th St. I-80, exit Wells
Ave, just s. Ext corridors. **Pets:** Other species. $10 one-
time fee/pet. Designated rooms, service with restrictions.
(SAVE) (S🐾) (✕) (🛏) (🌊)

(AAA) ▼▼ Easy 8 Motel Ⓜ
(775) 322-4588. **$29-$250.** 255 W 5th St. I-80, exit Keystone, 4 blks e. Ext corridors. **Pets:** Small. $25 deposit/
room. Designated rooms, service with restrictions, crate.
(SAVE) (S🐾) (✕)

(AAA) ▼▼ Holiday Inn-Downtown Ⓗ ❀
(775) 786-5151. **$79-$99.** 1000 E 6th St. I-80, exit Wells, 12
blks e. Int corridors. **Pets:** Other species. $10 daily fee/
room. Designated rooms, service with restrictions, supervision.
(SAVE) (S🐾) (✕) (🐾) (🛏) (💻) (🍴) (🌊)

▼▼▼ La Quinta Inn Ⓜ
(775) 348-6100. **$54-$95.** 4001 Market St. US 395, northbound exit airport; southbound exit Villanova Dr. Ext corridors. **Pets:** Accepted.
(SAVE) (✕) (♿M) (🐾) (🛏) (💻) (🌊)

▼▼▼ Miner's Inn (Super 8 Motel) Ⓜ
(775) 329-3464. **$40-$50, 15 days notice.** 1651 N Virginia
St. Opposite University of Nevada. Ext corridors.
Pets: Small. $50 deposit/room, $10 one-time fee/room.
Designated rooms, service with restrictions, supervision.
(ASK) (S🐾) (✕) (🛏) (🌊)

(AAA) ▼▼▼ Reno Downtown Travelodge Ⓜ
(775) 329-3451. **$29-$199.** 655 W 4th St. I-80, exit Keystone, just e. Ext corridors. **Pets:** Accepted.
(SAVE) (S🐾) (✕) (🛏) (💻) (🌊)

(AAA) ▼▼▼▼ Residence Inn by Marriott Ⓜ ❀
(775) 853-8800. **$109-$199.** 9845 Gateway Dr. 5 mi s; exit
US 395 at S Meadows Pkwy, e to Gateway Dr. Int corridors. **Pets:** Other species. $6 daily fee/pet, $90 one-time
fee/pet. Service with restrictions, supervision.
(SAVE) (✕) (♿M) (🛏) (💻) (🌊)

(AAA) ▼▼▼ Super 8 Motel at Meadow Wood
Courtyard Ⓜ ❀
(775) 829-4600. **$49-$119.** 5851 S Virginia St. US 395 at S
McCarran Blvd. Ext corridors. **Pets:** Small, other species.
$10 daily fee/pet. Designated rooms, service with restric-
tions, supervision.
(SAVE) (S🐾) (✕) (♿M) (🐾) (🛏) (💻) (🍴) (🌊)

▼▼ Truckee River Lodge Ⓜ ❀
(775) 786-8888. **$48-$120.** 501 W 1st St. I-80, exit Virginia,
just w. Ext/int corridors. **Pets:** Other species. $10 daily fee/
pet. Designated rooms, service with restrictions, supervision.
(ASK) (S🐾) (✕) (🛏) (💻) (🍴)

(AAA) ▼▼ Vagabond Inn Ⓜ
(775) 825-7134. **$50-$180.** 3131 S Virginia St. 2.5 mi s on
US 395. Ext corridors. **Pets:** $10 daily fee/pet. Designated
rooms, service with restrictions, supervision.
(SAVE) (S🐾) (✕) (🛏) (💻) (🌊)

TONOPAH

(AAA) ▼▼▼▼ Best Western Hi Desert Inn Ⓜ
(775) 482-3511. **$65-$79.** 320 Main St. On US 6 and 95. Int
corridors. **Pets:** Dogs only. Service with restrictions, supervision.
(SAVE) (S🐾) (✕) (🐾) (🛏) (💻) (🌊)

(AAA) ▼▼▼ Jim Butler Motel Ⓜ ❀
(775) 482-3577. **$49-$55, 3 days notice.** 100 S Main St.
On US 6 and 95. Ext corridors. **Pets:** Small, dogs only. $5
one-time fee/room. Designated rooms, service with restrictions, supervision.
(SAVE) (S🐾) (✕) (🛏)

WELLS

(AAA) ▼▼▼ Best Western Sage Inn Ⓜ
(775) 752-3353. **$49-$69.** 576 6th St. I-80, exit 352, 0.5 mi
n. Ext corridors. **Pets:** Accepted.
(SAVE) (S🐾) (✕) (🛏) (💻) (🌊)

[AAA] ♦♦ Super 8 Motel [M]
(775) 752-3384. **$49-$69.** 930 6th St. I-80, 0.5 mi w of jct US 93. Ext corridors. **Pets:** Small, dogs only. $5 daily fee/pet. Designated rooms, service with restrictions, supervision.
[SAVE] [S/D] 🚭 ☎ 🏊

WEST WENDOVER

♦♦ Wendover Super 8/Super 8 Motel [M]
(775) 664-2888. **$60-$70, 5 days notice.** 1325 Wendover Blvd. Int corridors. **Pets:** Medium, other species. $7 one-time fee/room. Designated rooms, service with restrictions, supervision.
[A$K] [S/D] 🚭 🦻 ☎

WINNEMUCCA

[AAA] ♦♦♦ Best Western Gold Country Inn [MI] 🐾
(775) 623-6999. **$89-$109.** 921 W Winnemucca Blvd. I-80, exit 176 or 178, just s. Int corridors. **Pets:** Other species. $10 one-time fee/pet. Designated rooms, supervision.
[SAVE] [S/D] 🚭 ☎ ☕ 🏊

[AAA] ♦♦♦ Best Western Holiday Motel [M]
(775) 623-3684. **$59-$64.** 670 W Winnemucca Blvd. I-80, exit 176 or 178, just s. Ext corridors. **Pets:** Other species. Service with restrictions, supervision.
[SAVE] [S/D] 🚭 ☎ ☕ 🏊

[AAA] ♦♦♦ Days Inn [M]
(775) 623-3661. **$59-$89.** 511 W Winnemucca Blvd. I-80, exit 176 or 178, just s. Ext corridors. **Pets:** Other species. $10 one-time fee/room. Service with restrictions, supervision.
[SAVE] [S/D] 🚭 ☎ ☕ 🏊

[AAA] ♦ Economy Inn [M] 🐾
(775) 623-5281. **$38.** 635 W Winnemucca Blvd. 0.5 mi w on I-80 (Business Rt), exit 176 or 178. Ext corridors. **Pets:** Medium. Designated rooms, no service, supervision.
[SAVE] 🚭 ☎ 🏊

♦♦ Holiday Inn Express [M]
(775) 625-3100. **$59-$89.** 1987 W Winnemucca Blvd. I-80, exit 176, just s. Int corridors. **Pets:** Accepted.
[A$K] [S/D] 🚭 [&M] 🦻 ♿ ☎ 🏊

[AAA] ♦♦♦ Red Lion Hotel & Casino [MI]
(775) 623-2565. **$89-$109.** 741 W Winnemucca Blvd. I-80, exit 176 or 178, just s. Int corridors. **Pets:** Other species. Service with restrictions, supervision.
[SAVE] [S/D] 🚭 🦻 ☎ ☕ 🍴 🏊

[AAA] ♦ Regency Inn & Suites [M]
(775) 623-4898. **$38-$59.** 705 W Winnemucca Blvd. center. Ext corridors. **Pets:** Accepted.
[SAVE] [S/D] 🚭 ☎ 🏊

♦♦ Santa Fe Inn [M]
(775) 623-1119. **$55-$65.** 1620 W Winnemucca Blvd. I-80, exit 176, just s, 0. mi e. Ext corridors. **Pets:** Other species. Supervision.
🚭 ☎ 🏊

♦♦ Super 8 Motel [M]
(775) 625-1818. **$47-$67.** 1157 W Winnemucca Blvd. I-80, exit 176, 0.5 mi e. Int corridors. **Pets:** Accepted.
[A$K] [S/D] 🚭 [&M] ☎

♦♦ Val-U Inn [M]
(775) 623-5248. **$45-$59.** 125 E Winnemucca Blvd. I-80, exit 176 or 178, just s. Int corridors. **Pets:** Accepted.
[A$K] [S/D] 🚭 ☎

BARTLETT

The Villager Motel M
(603) 374-2742. **$49-$139, 10 days notice.** US 302. 1 mi e on US 302; 1.3 mi w of Attitash Mountain. Ext corridors. **Pets:** Medium, other species. $8 daily fee/pet. Designated rooms, supervision.

CAMPTON

Super 8 Motel MI
(603) 536-3520. **$45-$139.** 1513 US 3. I-93, exit 27, just ne. Int corridors. **Pets:** Accepted.

CHESTERFIELD

Chesterfield Inn CI
(603) 256-3211. **$150-$300.** 399 Cross Rd. I-91, exit 3, 2 mi e on SR 9. Ext/int corridors. **Pets:** Accepted.

CLAREMONT

Best Budget Inn M
(603) 542-9567. **$52-$68.** 24 Sullivan St. Center; just n of jct SR 11/12/103/120. Ext corridors. **Pets:** Medium, dogs only. $25 deposit/pet, $15 daily fee/pet. Designated rooms, service with restrictions, supervision.

COLEBROOK

Northern Comfort Motel M
(603) 237-4440. **$60-$74, 3 days notice.** 1.3 mi s on US 3. Ext corridors. **Pets:** Accepted.

CONCORD

Best Western Concord Inn & Suites M
(603) 228-4300. **$59-$199.** 97 Hall St. I-93, exit 13, just n on Main St, then 0.5 mi w. Int corridors. **Pets:** Small. $10 daily fee/pet. Service with restrictions, supervision.

Concord Comfort Inn M
(603) 226-4100. **$79-$139.** 71 Hall St. I-93, exit 13, just n on Main St, then 0.3 mi w. Int corridors. **Pets:** Other species. $10 daily fee/pet. Supervision.

CONWAY

White Deer Motel M
(603) 447-5366. **$49-$159, 7 days notice.** 379 White Mountain Hwy. 2.1 mi s of jct US 302, 0.5 mi n of Village Center on SR 16. Ext/int corridors. **Pets:** Large, other species. $35 deposit/room. Designated rooms, service with restrictions, supervision.

DOVER

Days Inn M
(603) 742-0400. **$85-$165.** 481 Central Ave. Downtown; from Spaulding Tpke, exit 7, 2 mi n on SR 108. Ext/int corridors. **Pets:** Other species. $50 deposit/room. Service with restrictions, supervision.

DURHAM

Hickory Pond Inn & Golf Course BB
(603) 659-2227. **$59-$109, 3 days notice.** 1 Stagecoach Rd. 2.8 mi s on SR 108. Int corridors. **Pets:** Accepted.

FRANCONIA

Franconia Village Hotel Resort & Conference Center MI
(603) 823-7422. **$69-$129, 3 days notice.** 87 Wallace Hill Rd. I-93, exit 38, just e. Int corridors. **Pets:** Dogs only. $10 daily fee/room. Designated rooms, service with restrictions, supervision.

Gale River Motel M
(603) 823-5655. **$68-$95, 7 days notice.** 1 Main St. I-93, exit 38, 0.8 mi n on SR 18. Ext corridors. **Pets:** Medium, dogs only. $10 daily fee/pet. Designated rooms, service with restrictions, supervision.

GILMANTON

(AAA) ▼▼▼ Temperance Tavern BB
(603) 267-7349. **$75-$115, 10 days notice.** 506 Old Province Rd. Jct SR 140 and 107; in Gilmanton Historic District. Int corridors. **Pets:** Service with restrictions, supervision.

SAVE S♦ ⊠ ℀ ⚑ ☎

GORHAM

▼ Colonial Comfort Inn M
(603) 466-2732. **$90-$200, 3 days notice.** 370 Main St. Jct US 2 and SR 16. Ext corridors. **Pets:** Other species. Service with restrictions, supervision.

⊠ 🛏 ⑪

▼ Moose Brook Motel M
(603) 466-5400. **$39-$79, 7 days notice.** 65 Lancaster Rd. Jct SR 16, 0.5 mi w on US 2. Ext corridors. **Pets:** $5 one-time fee/pet. Designated rooms, service with restrictions, supervision.

⊠ 🛏 ▣ ⇥

▼▼ Mt Madison Motel M
(603) 466-3622. **$44-$108, 3 days notice.** 365 Main St. 1.2 mi n on US 2 and SR 16. Ext corridors. **Pets:** No service, supervision.

ASK S♦ ⊠ 🛏 ▣ ⇥

▼▼ Royalty Inn MI
(603) 466-3312. **$57-$100.** 130 Main St. Center; on US 2 and SR 16. Ext/int corridors. **Pets:** Other species. $5 daily fee/room. Designated rooms, service with restrictions, supervision.

⊠ ⓜ 🛏 ▣ ⑪ ⇥

(AAA) ▼▼ Top Notch Inn M 🐾
(603) 466-5496. **$54-$149.** 265 Main St. Center; on US 2 and SR 16. Ext corridors. **Pets:** Medium, dogs only. Designated rooms, service with restrictions, supervision.

SAVE S♦ ⊠ ⓚ 🛏 ▣ ⇥

▼▼ Town & Country Motor Inn MI
(603) 466-3315. **$60-$84.** US Rt 2. US 2, 0.5 mi e of jct SR 16. Ext/int corridors. **Pets:** Other species. $6 daily fee/pet. Designated rooms, service with restrictions, supervision.

⊠ 🛏 ⑪ ⇥ ⊠

HAMPTON FALLS

(AAA) ▼▼▼ Hampton Falls Inn M
(603) 926-9545. **$69-$169.** 11 Lafayette Rd (US 1). I-95, exit 1, 0.5 mi e on SR 107, 1 mi n on US 1. Int corridors. **Pets:** Accepted.

SAVE S♦ ⊠ 🛏 ⑪ ⇥

HANCOCK

▼▼▼ The Hancock Inn CI
(603) 525-3318. **$120-$250, 15 days notice.** 33 Main St. Center; jct of SR 123 and 137. Int corridors. **Pets:** Dogs only. Designated rooms, service with restrictions, supervision.

⊠ ⑪

HARTS LOCATION

▼▼▼ Notchland Inn CI
(603) 374-6131. **$180-$290, 14 days notice.** US 302. From Bartlett, 6.4 mi w. Int corridors. **Pets:** Other species. $150 deposit/room, $5 daily fee/pet. Designated rooms, service with restrictions, crate.

⊠ ⑪ ⊠ ⚑ ☎

JACKSON

▼▼▼ Whitneys' Inn CI
(603) 383-8916. **$78-$171, 14 days notice.** Rt 16B. 1.7 mi n. Ext/int corridors. **Pets:** Dogs only. $25 one-time fee/pet. Designated rooms, service with restrictions.

ASK ⊠ 🛏 ▣ ⑪ ⇥ ⊠ ☎

KEENE

▼▼▼ Best Western Sovereign Hotel MI
(603) 357-3038. **$89-$140.** 401 Winchester St. On SR 10, just s of jct SR 12 and 101. Int corridors. **Pets:** Other species. $10 one-time fee/pet. Service with restrictions, supervision.

SAVE S♦ ⊠ ⓓ 🛏 ▣ ⑪ ⇥

▼▼▼ Holiday Inn Express M
(603) 352-7616. **$95-$179.** 175 Key Rd. SR 101, just n, via Winchester St, then 0.3 mi w. Int corridors. **Pets:** Accepted.

ASK S♦ ⊠ ⓜ 🛏 ▣ ⇥

▼▼▼ Super 8 Keene M
(603) 352-9780. **$100-$130.** 3 Ashbrook Rd. Jct SR 9 and 12, just w. Int corridors. **Pets:** $20 one-time fee/room. Service with restrictions, supervision.

ASK S♦ ⊠

LEBANON

(AAA) ▼▼▼ Days Inn M
(603) 448-5070. **$89-$149.** 135 Rt 120. I-89, exit 18, 0.8 mi n. Ext/int corridors. **Pets:** Accepted.

SAVE S♦ ⊠ 🛏

LINCOLN

(AAA) ▼▼▼ Parker's Motel M
(603) 745-8341. **$39-$89, 3 days notice.** US 3. I-93, exit 33 (US 3), 2 mi ne. Ext corridors. **Pets:** $50 deposit/room, $5 daily fee/pet. Designated rooms, service with restrictions, crate.

SAVE S♦ ⊠ 🛏 ⇥

LISBON

▼▼ Ammonoosuc Inn CI
(603) 838-6118. **$80-$130, 15 days notice.** 641 Bishop Rd. SR 302 and 10, just nw on Lyman Rd, then 1 mi sw. **Pets:** Medium, dogs only. Designated rooms, service with restrictions, supervision.

ASK S♦ ⊠ ⑪ ⊠ ℀ ⚑ ☎

MANCHESTER

▼◆▼ Center of New Hampshire-Holiday
Inn �H
(603) 625-1000. **$139-$189.** 700 Elm St. Downtown; at jct
Granite St. Int corridors. **Pets:** Accepted.
🅰️🆂 🆂6 ☒ 🅼 🗐 🖝 🔋 💻 🍴 🌊

🔼 ▼◆▼ Towneplace Suites by Marriott 🅰
(603) 641-2288. **$116-$140.** 686 Huse Rd. I-293, exit 1, 0.5
mi se on SR 28. Int corridors. **Pets:** Other species. $175
one-time fee/room. Service with restrictions, supervision.
🆂🅰️🆅 🆂6 ☒ 🅼 🗐 🖝 🔋 💻 🌊

MERRIMACK

▼◆▼◆ Days Inn Merrimack 🅼
(603) 429-4600. **$50-$96.** 242 Daniel Webster Hwy. Everett
Tpke, exit 11, just e, then 0.7 mi s on SR 3. Int corridors.
Pets: Small. $25 one-time fee/pet. Service with restrictions,
supervision.
🆂🅰️🆅 🆂6 ☒ 🅼 🗐 🖝 🔋 💻

🔼 ▼◆▼◆ Residence Inn by Marriott 🅰
(603) 424-8100. **$119-$189.** 246 Daniel Webster Hwy. Everett Tpke, exit 11, just e, then 0.6 mi s on SR 3. Ext/int
corridors. **Pets:** Large, other species. $5 daily fee/pet, $75
one-time fee/room. Designated rooms, service with restrictions, crate.
🆂🅰️🆅 ☒ 🅼 🗐 🖝 🔋 💻 🌊

MOUNT SUNAPEE

🔼 ▼◆▼◆ Best Western Sunapee Lake
Lodge 🅼
(603) 763-2010. **$99-$149, 14 days notice.** 1403 Rt 103.
Jct SR 103B, just e. Int corridors. **Pets:** Other species. $8
daily fee/pet. Designated rooms, service with restrictions,
supervision.
🆂🅰️🆅 ☒ 🅼 🖝 🔋 🌊

NASHUA

🔼 ▼◆▼◆ Nashua Marriott 🅼🅸
(603) 880-9100. **$59-$159.** 2200 Southwood Dr. US 3, exit
8, just w; in Southwood Corporate Park. Int corridors.
Pets: Designated rooms, service with restrictions, supervision.
🆂🅰️🆅 ☒ 🅼 🗐 🔋 💻 🍴 🌊

🔼 ▼◆▼ Red Roof Inn 🅼
(603) 888-1893. **$57-$79.** 77 Spitbrook Rd. US 3, exit 1,
just e. Ext corridors. **Pets:** Small, other species. Service
with restrictions, supervision.
🆂🅰️🆅 ☒ 🅼 🗐 🔋

NORTH CONWAY

▼◆▼ Mt Washington Valley Motor
Lodge 🅼🅸 ❀
(603) 356-5486. **$59-$159.** 1567 White Mountain Hwy. Village Center; 2.5 mi s on US 302 and SR 16. Int corridors.
Pets: Medium, dogs only. $50 deposit/pet. Designated
rooms, supervision.
🅰️🆂 🆂6 ☒ 🔋 💻 🍴 🌊

🔼 ▼◆▼ North Conway Mountain Inn 🅼
(603) 356-2803. **$59-$169, 3 days notice.** 2114 White
Mountain Hwy. Center; 1 mi s on US 302 and SR 16. Ext
corridors. **Pets:** Supervision.
🆂🅰️🆅 ☒

PITTSBURG

▼◆▼ The Glen 🅻
(603) 538-6500. **$108-$200 (no credit cards), 7 days
notice.** 77 The Glen Rd. 8.5 mi n on US 3, then 1 mi e,
follow signs. Ext/int corridors. **Pets:** Large, other species.
Designated rooms, service with restrictions, supervision.
🔋 💻 🍴 ☒ 🅺 🅿 🆉

PORTSMOUTH

▼◆▼ Meadowbrook Inn 🅼
(603) 436-2700. **$45-$119.** 549 US Hwy 1 Bypass. I-95, exit
5, from Portsmouth Cir, US 1 Bypass. Ext/int corridors.
Pets: $50 deposit/room. Service with restrictions, supervi-
sion.
🅰️🆂 🆂6 ☒ 🔋 🌊

🔼 ▼◆▼◆ Residence Inn by Marriott 🅼
(603) 436-8880. **$169-$199.** 1 International Dr. SR 4/16,
exit 1, just s. Int corridors. **Pets:** Accepted.
🆂🅰️🆅 🆂6 ☒ 🅼 🖝 🔋 💻 🌊

ROCHESTER

🔼 ▼◆▼ Anchorage Inn 🅼
(603) 332-3350. **$42-$109.** 13 Wadleigh Rd. Jct Spaulding
Tpke and SR 125, exit 12. Ext corridors. **Pets:** $10 daily
fee/pet. Designated rooms, service with restrictions, supervision.
🆂🅰️🆅 🆂6 ☒ 🔋 🌊

SALEM

🔼 ▼◆▼ Red Roof Inn 🅼
(603) 898-6422. **$49-$91.** 15 Red Roof Ln. I-93, exit 2, just
se. Ext corridors. **Pets:** Medium. Service with restrictions,
supervision.
🆂🅰️🆅 ☒ 🅼 🗐

SUGAR HILL

▼◆▼ The Hilltop Inn 🅱🅱 ❀
(603) 823-5695. **$90-$195, 8 days notice.** 1348 Main St.
I-93, exit 38, 0.5 mi n on SR 18, then 2.8 mi w on SR 117.
Int corridors. **Pets:** Dogs only. $10 daily fee/room.
☒ 🔋 🅺 🅿

SUNAPEE

▼◆▼ Dexter's Inn 🅱🅱 ❀
(603) 763-5571. **$125-$195, 14 days notice.** 258 Stagecoach Rd. Jct SR 103B and 11, 0.4 mi w on SR 11, 1.75 mi
s (Winn Hill Rd). Ext/int corridors. **Pets:** Other species.
Designated rooms, service with restrictions, supervision.
☒ 🔋 💻 🌊 🆉

SWANZEY

▼▼ **Loafer Inn at the 1792 Whitecomb House B & B** 🅱🅱
(603) 357-6624. **$75-$90, 7 days notice.** 27 Main St. 4 mi s of Keene on SR 10. Int corridors. **Pets:** Small, dogs only. Service with restrictions, supervision.
⊠ 💻 🐕 📺 🗲

TAMWORTH

▼▼▼ **Tamworth Inn** 🆑 🐾
(603) 323-7721. **$115-$300.** 15 Cleveland Hill Rd. Jct SR 16 and 113, 3 mi w on SR 113; center of Tamworth Village. Int corridors. **Pets:** Dogs only. $10 daily fee/pet. Service with restrictions, supervision.
ASK ⊠ 🍴 🐕 🐾 📺 🗲

THORNTON

▼ **Shamrock Motel** M
(603) 726-3534. **$38-$73.** Rt 3. I-93, exit 29, 2.3 mi n on US 3; exit 30, 5 mi s. Ext corridors. **Pets:** Medium. $5 daily fee/room. No service, supervision.
ASK 🔋 🔌 🐕 📺 🗲

WEST LEBANON

🔷 ▼▼▼ **Airport Economy Inn** M
(603) 298-8888. **$55-$95.** 45 Airport Rd. I-89, exit 20 (SR 12A), just s, then just e. Int corridors. **Pets:** Other species. $10 daily fee/pet. Designated rooms, service with restrictions, supervision.
SAVE 🔋 ⊠ ♿ 🔌 🐕

▼▼▼ **Fireside Inn and Suites** MI
(603) 298-5906. **$110-$150.** 25 Airport Rd. I-89, exit 20 (SR 12A), just s. Int corridors. **Pets:** Large. $10 daily fee/pet. Designated rooms, service with restrictions, supervision.
ASK 🔋 ⊠ 🍴 🔌 💻 🍴 🐕

WOLFEBORO

▼▼ **The Lake Motel** M
(603) 569-1100. **$99-$114, 14 days notice.** 280 S Main St. 0.5 mi se on SR 28. Ext/int corridors. **Pets:** Accepted.
🔌 💻 ⊠

WOODSVILLE

🔷 ▼ **All Seasons Motel** M
(603) 747-2157. **$50-$75, 3 days notice.** 36 Smith St. Jct SR 10, 0.4 mi w on US 302, then 0.3 mi se. Ext corridors. **Pets:** Accepted.
SAVE 🔋 ⊠ 🔌 🐕

🔷 ▼▼ **Nootka Lodge** M
(603) 747-2418. **$60-$110.** Jct SR 10 & US 302. Ext corridors. **Pets:** Accepted.
SAVE 🔋 ⊠ 🔌 🐕

NEW JERSEY

CITY INDEX

ATLANTIC CITY METROPOLITAN AREA

SOMERS POINT

(AAA) ▼▼▼▼ Residence Inn by Marriott A
(609) 927-6400. **$119-$259.** 900 Mays Landing Rd. Garden
State Pkwy, exit 30 southbound; exit 29 northbound, 1 mi e.
Ext corridors. **Pets:** Medium, other species. $75 one-time
fee/room. Service with restrictions.

[SAVE] [X] [🏊] [📶] [🍴] [💻] [🐾]

❖ END METROPOLITAN AREA ❖

BASKING RIDGE

▼▼▼▼ The Inn at Somerset Hills M
(908) 580-1300. **$129-$245.** 80 Allen Rd. I-78, exit 33, 0.3
mi n on CR 525, then 0.3 mi w. Int corridors. **Pets:** Medium,
other species. $25 daily fee/room. Designated rooms, serv-
ice with restrictions, supervision.

[A$K] [🏊] [X] [📶] [🍴] [🍴] [💻] [🍴]

BEACH HAVEN

(AAA) ▼▼▼ Engleside Inn M
(609) 492-1251. **$88-$375, 30 days notice.** 30 Engleside
Ave. 6.9 mi s of SR 72 Cswy to Engleside Ave, just e. Ext
corridors. **Pets:** Other species. $10 daily fee/pet. Desig-
nated rooms, service with restrictions, supervision.

[SAVE] [X] [📶] [🍴] [💻] [🍴] [🐾]

COLESVILLE

▼▼ High Point Country Inn M
(973) 702-1860. **$70-$90.** 1328 SR 23 N. 1 mi n of Coles-
ville Village town center. Ext corridors. **Pets:** Other species.
$10 daily fee/pet. Designated rooms.

[X] [🍴] [🐾]

DENVILLE

▼▼▼▼ Hampton Inn/The Inn At Denville M
(973) 664-1050. **$109-$169, 7 days notice.** 350 Morris
Ave. US 80, exit 37 westbound, just s on Green Pond Rd,
then just e; eastbound, just n onto Hibernia Ave, then just e.
Int corridors. **Pets:** Medium. $20 daily fee/pet. Service with
restrictions.

[SAVE] [🏊] [X] [📶] [📶] [🍴] [🍴] [💻] [🐾]

EAST BRUNSWICK

▼▼▼▼ Hilton East Brunswick H
(732) 828-2000. **$109-$289, 3 days notice.** 3 Tower Center
Blvd. New Jersey Tpke, exit 9 (SR 18 N), first right on
service road. Int corridors. **Pets:** Accepted.

[SAVE] [🏊] [X] [📶] [📶] [🍴] [💻] [🍴] [🐾]

EAST HANOVER

**(AAA) ▼▼▼▼ Ramada Inn & Conference
Center M**
(973) 386-5622. **$60-$159.** 130 Rt 10 W. I-287, exit 39, 3
mi e. Int corridors. **Pets:** $50 deposit/room. Designated
rooms, service with restrictions, supervision.

[SAVE] [🏊] [X] [📶] [📶] [🍴] [🍴] [💻] [🍴]

EAST RUTHERFORD

▼▼ Homestead Studio
Suites-Meadowlands **M**
(201) 939-8866. **$105-$135.** 300 SR 3 E. New Jersey Tpke, exit 16W (from western spur), sports complex right after toll (SR 3 E). Int corridors. **Pets:** Medium, other species. $75 one-time fee/room. Service with restrictions, crate.

(A$K) (S₀) (✕) (&M) (🔊) (🖉) (🔋) (💻)

▼▼◆▼▼ Sheraton Meadowlands Hotel & Conference
Center **H**
(201) 896-0500. **$179-$199.** 2 Meadowlands Plaza. New Jersey Tpke, exit 16W (from western spur), sports complex right after toll (SR 3 E) to Sheraton Plaza Dr. Int corridors. **Pets:** Accepted.

(A$K) (S₀) (✕) (&M) (🔊) (🖉) (🔋) (💻) (🍴) (🏊)

EDISON

(AAA) ▼ Red Roof Inn **M**
(732) 248-9300. **$72-$86.** 860 New Durham Rd. I-287, exit 2A northbound, 0.3 mi w via Bridge St, then left; exit 3 southbound, just w. Ext corridors. **Pets:** Accepted.

(SAVE) (✕) (&M) (🔊)

ELIZABETH

(AAA) ▼▼◆▼▼ Hilton Newark Airport **H**
(908) 351-3900. **$129-$294.** 1170 Spring St. New Jersey Tpke, exit 13A on US 1 and 9 N, U-turn on McClellan St. Int corridors. **Pets:** Medium, other species. Service with restrictions, supervision.

(SAVE) (S₀) (✕) (&M) (🔊) (🔋) (💻) (🍴) (🏊)

ENGLEWOOD

▼▼◆▼▼ Radisson Hotel Englewood **H**
(201) 871-2020. **$-$165.** 401 S Van Brunt St. SR 4, exit Van Brunt westbound; 2nd exit Grand Ave/Englewood eastbound, just n, return to SR 4 westbound, next Van Brunt exit. Int corridors. **Pets:** Accepted.

(A$K) (S₀) (✕) (🔊) (🖉) (🔋) (💻) (🍴) (🏊)

FAIR LAWN

(AAA) ▼▼◆▼▼ AmeriSuites (Fairlawn/Paramus) **M**
(201) 475-3888. **$129-$199.** 41-01 Broadway (Rt 4 W). Garden State Pkwy, exit 161 northbound, 0.7 mi w; exit 163 southbound. Int corridors. **Pets:** Accepted.

(SAVE) (S₀) (✕) (&M) (🔊) (🖉) (🔋) (💻) (🏊)

FLEMINGTON

▼▼ The Ramada Inn **M**
(908) 782-7472. **$97-$135.** 250 Hwy 202 & SR 31. 0.5 mi s of the circle. Ext corridors. **Pets:** Small. $10 daily fee/pet. No service, supervision.

(A$K) (S₀) (✕) (🔊) (🔋) (🏊)

HAZLET

(AAA) ▼▼▼ Wellesley Inn & Suites **M**
(732) 888-2800. **$89-$159.** 3215 SR 35 N. Garden State Pkwy, exit 117, 1.5 mi s on SR 35, U-turn on Hazlet Ave. Int corridors. **Pets:** Accepted.

(SAVE) (S₀) (✕) (&M) (🔊) (🖉) (🔋)

LAWRENCEVILLE

(AAA) ▼ Red Roof Inn-Princeton **M**
(609) 896-3388. **$49-$69.** 3203 Brunswick Pike (US 1). I-295, exit 67A, just n on US 1. Ext corridors. **Pets:** Accepted.

(SAVE) (✕) (🔊) (🖉)

MAHWAH

(AAA) ▼▼◆▼▼ Sheraton Crossroads Hotel **H**
(201) 529-1660. **$114-$195, 14 days notice.** 1 International Blvd (Rt 17). I-287, exit 66, at jct SR 17 N. Int corridors. **Pets:** Accepted.

(SAVE) (S₀) (✕) (🔊) (💻) (🍴) (🏊) (✕)

MIDDLETOWN

(AAA) ▼▼▼ Howard Johnson Inn **M** ✿
(732) 671-3400. **$105-$165.** 750 Hwy 35 S. Garden State Pkwy, exit 114, 2 mi on Red Hill Rd, 1 mi s on King's Hwy to SR 35, then 0.3 mi s. Int corridors. **Pets:** Large, other species. $10 daily fee/room. Service with restrictions, supervision.

(SAVE) (S₀) (✕) (🔊) (🔋) (💻) (🏊)

MONMOUTH JUNCTION

(AAA) ▼ Red Roof Inn/North Princeton **M**
(732) 821-8800. **$54-$77.** 208 New Rd. US 1 S at New Rd. Ext corridors. **Pets:** Accepted.

(SAVE) (✕) (🔊)

(AAA) ▼▼◆▼▼ Residence Inn by Marriott **M** ✿
(732) 329-9600. **$159-$181.** 4225 Rt 1 S. 0.5 mi s of Raymond Rd. Int corridors. **Pets:** Other species. $175 one-time fee/room. Service with restrictions.

(SAVE) (✕) (🔊) (🔋) (💻) (🏊)

NEWARK

▼▼◆▼▼ Hilton Gateway **H**
(973) 622-5000. **$149-$289.** Raymond Blvd. New Jersey Tpke, exit 15E, 3 mi w via Raymond Blvd; connecting to Penn Station, New Jersey Transit, Path and Amtrak. Int corridors. **Pets:** Accepted.

(SAVE) (S₀) (✕) (🔊) (🖉) (🔋) (💻) (🍴) (🏊)

OCEAN CITY

(AAA) ▼▼▼ Crossings Motor Inn **M** ✿
(609) 398-4433. **$94-$180.** 3420 Haven Ave. Garden State Pkwy, exit 25, 3 mi e; 0.3 mi w of ocean beaches on the south end of town at 34th St. Ext corridors. **Pets:** Other species. $25 daily fee/pet. Designated rooms, service with restrictions, supervision.

(SAVE) (✕) (🔋) (💻) (🏊)

PARK RIDGE

(AAA) ▼▼▼▼ Park Ridge Marriott Hotel 🄷
(201) 307-0800. **$99-$224.** 300 Brae Blvd. Garden State Pkwy S, U-turn through Food Fuel Service Plaza; exit 172 northbound, right 300 yds on Grand Ave, 0.5 mi s on Mercedes. Int corridors. **Pets:** Large. Designated rooms, service with restrictions, supervision.
(SAVE) (✕) (🖉) (🖫) (🖬) (💻) (🍴) (🏊)

PARSIPPANY

▼▼▼▼ Hilton Parsippany 🄷 ✿
(973) 267-7373. **$89-$269.** 1 Hilton Ct. I-287, exit 39 northbound; exit 39B southbound, 1.3 mi w on SR 10; in Hilton Court. Int corridors. **Pets:** Medium. $50 deposit/room. Designated rooms, service with restrictions.
(SAVE) (S✦) (✕) (🖉) (🖫) (🖬) (💻) (🍴) (🏊) (✕)

PHILADELPHIA METROPOLITAN AREA

BORDENTOWN

(AAA) ▼ Imperial Inn 🄼 ✿
(609) 298-3355. **$50-$65.** 3312 Rt 206 S. New Jersey Tpke, exit 7, 0.8 mi s. Ext corridors. **Pets:** Medium, dogs only. $20 deposit/pet, $5 daily fee/pet. Service with restrictions, supervision.
(SAVE) (S✦) (✕) (🖫)

CHERRY HILL

▼▼▼▼ Holiday Inn-Cherry Hill 🄼
(856) 663-5300. **$94.** Rt 70 & Sayer Ave. I-295, exit 34B, 2.5 mi w; opposite Garden State Race Track. Int corridors. **Pets:** Small, other species. $75 deposit/pet. Service with restrictions, supervision.
(ASK) (S✦) (✕) (🖉) (🖫) (🖬) (💻) (🍴) (🏊)

(AAA) ▼▼▼▼ Residence Inn by Marriott 🄼
(856) 429-6111. **$125.** 1821 Old Cuthbert Rd. I-295, exit 34A, just e to Marlkress Rd jughandle, then back to Old Cuthbert Rd, just n. Ext corridors. **Pets:** Other species. $250 one-time fee/pet. Service with restrictions, crate.
(SAVE) (S✦) (✕) (🖉) (🖫) (💻) (🏊)

MOUNT HOLLY

(AAA) ▼▼▼▼ Best Western Burlington Inn 🄼
(609) 261-3800. **$74-$109, 3 days notice.** Box 2020, Rt 541, RD 1. New Jersey Tpke, exit 5, just n. Int corridors. **Pets:** Small, other species. $10 daily fee/pet. Service with restrictions, supervision.
(SAVE) (S✦) (✕) (🖉) (🖫) (💻) (🏊)

MOUNT LAUREL

(AAA) ▼▼▼▼ Radisson Mount Laurel Motel 🄷
(856) 234-7300. **$89-$139.** 915 Rt 73 N. New Jersey Tpke, exit 4, northeast corner; I-295, exit 36A, just se. Int corridors. **Pets:** Accepted.
(SAVE) (S✦) (✕) (🖉) (🖫) (🖬) (💻) (🍴) (🏊)

(AAA) ▼▼▼ Red Roof Inn 🄼
(856) 234-5589. **$49-$69.** 603 Fellowship Rd. New Jersey Tpke, exit 4, just nw on SR 73 to Fellowship Rd, just s; I-295, exit 36A, just se on SR 73 to Fellowship Rd, just s. Ext corridors. **Pets:** Accepted.
(SAVE) (✕) (🖉)

(AAA) ▼▼▼▼ Summerfield Suites by
Wyndham-Mount Laurel 🄼 ✿
(856) 222-1313. **$95-$129.** 3000 Crawford Pl. New Jersey Tpke, exit 4, 1 mi on SR 73 S; I-295, exit 36A, 1.5 mi on SR 73 S. Ext corridors. **Pets:** Medium, other species. $150 one-time fee/room. Designated rooms.
(SAVE) (✕) (S✦) (🖉) (🖫) (🖬) (💻) (🏊)

WINSLOW

▼▼ Winslow Inn & Suites 🄼
(609) 561-6200. **$40-$95.** 530 Rt 73. Atlantic City Expwy, exit 31 westbound; exit 33 eastbound, just nw. Ext corridors. **Pets:** Accepted.
(ASK) (S✦) (✕) (🖫)

▼▼ Ramada Limited 🄼
(973) 263-0404. **Call for rates.** 949 Rt 46 E. I-80, exit 47 westbound; exit 45 eastbound, 0.5 mi e. Int corridors. **Pets:** Accepted.
(ASK) (✕) (🖉) (🖫) (💻) (🏊)

(AAA) ▼ Red Roof Inn 🄼
(973) 334-3737. **$62-$81.** 855 US 46 E. I-80, exit 47 westbound; exit 45 eastbound, then 0.5 mi e. Ext corridors. **Pets:** Small, other species. Service with restrictions, supervision.
(SAVE) (✕) (🖉)

✿ END METROPOLITAN AREA ✿

PHILLIPSBURG

▼▼▼▼ **Clarion Hotel & Conference Center** Ⓜ
(908) 454-9771. **$100-$110, 30 days notice.** 1314 US Rt 22. I-78, exit 3, just n. Ext/int corridors. **Pets:** Supervision.

PISCATAWAY

▼▼ **Sierra Suites** Ⓜ
(732) 235-1000. **$79-$209.** 410 S Randolphville Rd. I-287, exit 7, 0.4 mi s. Int corridors. **Pets:** Accepted.

PRINCETON

ⒶⒶⒶ ▼▼▼▼ **AmeriSuites (Carnegie CenterWest)** Ⓗ
(609) 720-0200. **$99-$199.** 3565 US 1 S. 1.5 mi s of jct CR 526 and 571. Int corridors. **Pets:** Very small. Service with restrictions.

ⒶⒶⒶ ▼▼▼▼ **Holiday Inn Princeton** Ⓜ
(609) 520-1200. **$79-$129.** 100 Independence Way. I-295, exit 67 on US 1; 3 mi n of jct CR 526 and 571; in Princeton Corporate Center. Int corridors. **Pets:** Accepted.
ⓈⒶⓋⒺ Ⓢ ✕ ⓐ ⊟ Ⓣ ⤳

ⒶⒶⒶ ▼▼▼▼ **Summerfield Suites by Wyndham-Princeton** Ⓜ
(609) 951-0009. **$89-$189.** 4375 US 1 S. Just past Ridge Rd. Ext corridors. **Pets:** Medium. $150 one-time fee/room. Service with restrictions.
ⓈⒶⓋⒺ ✕ ⓐ ⊟ ⊡ ⤳

RAMSEY

ⒶⒶⒶ ▼▼ **Best Western** Ⓜ
(201) 327-6700. **$79-$169, 7 days notice.** 1315 Rt 17 S. Jct I-287 and SR 17 S, then 3 mi s. Int corridors. **Pets:** Medium. $10 daily fee/room. Service with restrictions, supervision.
ⓈⒶⓋⒺ Ⓢ ✕ ⊟ Ⓣ

ⒶⒶⒶ ▼▼ **Wellesley Inn** Ⓜ
(201) 934-9250. **$108-$120, 14 days notice.** 946 Rt 17 N. SR 17 at Airmont Rd. Int corridors. **Pets:** Accepted.
ⓈⒶⓋⒺ Ⓢ ✕ ⓜ ⓐ ⓔ ⊟ ⊡

SECAUCUS

ⒶⒶⒶ ▼▼▼▼ **AmeriSuites (Secaucus/Meadowlands)** Ⓜ
(201) 422-9480. **$209, 30 days notice.** 575 Park Plaza Dr. New Jersey Tpke, exits 16E, 17 or 16W via SR 3 to Harmon Meadow Blvd, then just w. Int corridors. **Pets:** Accepted.
ⓈⒶⓋⒺ Ⓢ ✕ ⓜ ⓐ ⓔ ⊟ ⊡

ⒶⒶⒶ ▼▼▼▼ **Crowne Plaza Meadowlands** Ⓗ
(201) 348-6900. **$109-$179.** 2 Harmon Plaza. Between eastern and western spurs of New Jersey Tpke, exits 16E, 17 or 16W to SR 3 W, exit Meadowlands Pkwy. Int corridors. **Pets:** Small. $50 one-time fee/pet. Service with restrictions, supervision.
ⓈⒶⓋⒺ Ⓢ ✕ ⓐ ⊟ ⊡ Ⓣ ⤳

ⒶⒶⒶ ▼▼▼▼ **MainStay Suites, Secaucus/Meadowlands** Ⓜ
(201) 553-9700. **$91-$199.** 1 Plaza Dr. New Jersey Tpke, exit 16E northbound; exit 17E southbound, 0.3 mi e. Int corridors. **Pets:** Accepted.
ⓈⒶⓋⒺ Ⓢ ✕ ⓜ ⓐ ⓔ ⊟ ⊡ ⤳

ⒶⒶⒶ ▼▼▼▼ **Radisson Suite Hotel Meadowlands** Ⓗ
(201) 863-8700. **$89-$141.** 350 Rt 3 W, at Mill Creek. In Mill Creek Mall; between eastern and western spurs of New Jersey Tpke, exits 16E, 17 or 16W via SR 3 W and Harmon Meadow Blvd. Int corridors. **Pets:** Accepted.
ⓈⒶⓋⒺ Ⓢ ✕ ⓐ ⊟ ⊡ Ⓣ ⤳

ⒶⒶⒶ ▼▼▼ **Red Roof Inn-Meadowlands** Ⓜ
(201) 319-1000. **$84-$109.** 15 Meadowlands Pkwy. Between eastern and western spurs of New Jersey Tpke, exits 16E, 17 or 16W via SR 3, exit Meadowlands Pkwy. Ext corridors. **Pets:** Accepted.
ⓈⒶⓋⒺ ✕ ⓔ

SOMERSET

ⒶⒶⒶ ▼▼▼▼ **Holiday Inn-Somerset** Ⓗ
(732) 356-1700. **$69-$169.** 195 Davidson Ave. I-287, exit 10, just n on CR 527 (direction Bound Brook), 0.5 mi sw. Int corridors. **Pets:** Large, other species. Service with restrictions.
ⓈⒶⓋⒺ Ⓢ ✕ ⓜ ⓐ ⓔ ⊟ ⊡ Ⓣ ⤳

ⒶⒶⒶ ▼▼▼▼ **Summerfield Suites by Wyndham-Somerset** Ⓜ
(732) 356-8000. **$89-$224.** 260 Davidson Ave. I-287, exit 10 (direction Bound Brook), just n on CR 527 to Davidson Ave, 0.8 mi sw. Ext corridors. **Pets:** Accepted.
ⓈⒶⓋⒺ ✕ ⓐ ⊟ ⊡ ⤳

SOUTH PLAINFIELD

▼▼ **Holiday Inn** Ⓜ
(908) 753-5500. **$144-$149.** 4701 Stelton Rd. I-287, exit 5, just s; adjacent to Middlesex Mall. Int corridors. **Pets:** Other species. Service with restrictions, supervision.
ⒶⓈⓀ Ⓢ ✕ ⓐ ⊟ ⊡ Ⓣ ⤳

SPRINGFIELD

▼▼ **Holiday Inn Springfield** Ⓜ
(973) 376-9400. **$130.** 304 Rt 22 W. 4 mi w of Garden State Pkwy, exit 140 northbound; exit 140A southbound. Int corridors. **Pets:** Service with restrictions, supervision.
ⒶⓈⓀ Ⓢ ✕ ⓐ ⊟ ⊡ Ⓣ ⤳

TINTON FALLS

Red Roof Inn M
(732) 389-4646. **$59-$89.** 11 Centre Plaza. Garden State Pkwy, exit 105, just right at 1st light after toll. Ext corridors. **Pets:** Accepted.
SAVE ✕ ⌖M ⌕

Residence Inn by Marriott M ❀
(732) 389-8100. **$134-$161.** 90 Park Rd. Garden State Pkwy, exit 105, 1st jughandle after toll, immediate left before Courtyard by Marriott, just n, then e. Ext corridors. **Pets:** Other species. $275 one-time fee/room.
SAVE ✕ ⌁ ⌕ ☰ ▣ ⇌

Sunrise Suites Hotel M
(732) 389-4800. **$89-$189.** 3 Centre Plaza. Garden State Pkwy, exit 105, 1st right at Hope Rd after toll. Ext/int corridors. **Pets:** Accepted.
✕ ☰ ▣ ⇌

TOMS RIVER

Holiday Inn M
(732) 244-4000. **$69-$149.** 290 Hwy 37 E. Garden State Pkwy, exit 82, 1.5 mi e. Int corridors. **Pets:** Accepted.
ASK S⌂ ✕ ☰ ▣ ⫴ ⇌

Howard Johnson Hotel-Toms River M
(732) 244-1000. **$70-$199.** 955 Hooper Ave. Garden State Pkwy, exit 82, 1 mi e on SR 37. Int corridors. **Pets:** Other species. $25 one-time fee/pet. Designated rooms, service with restrictions, supervision.
SAVE S⌂ ✕ ⌁ ☰ ▣ ⫴ ⇌

WARREN

Somerset Hills Hotel H
(908) 647-6700. **$129-$245.** 200 Liberty Corner Rd. I-78, exit 33, just n on CR 525. Int corridors. **Pets:** Medium, other species. $25 daily fee/room. Designated rooms, service with restrictions, supervision.
ASK S⌂ ✕ ⌁ ☰ ▣ ⫴ ⇌

WEEHAWKEN

Sheraton Suites On The Hudson H
(201) 617-5600. **$269-$349.** 500 Harbor Blvd. I-495 E toward Lincoln Tunnel, exit Weehawken/Hoboken, bear right on bottom of hill, then 0.4 mi e to Lincoln Harbor Complex. Int corridors. **Pets:** Small. $75 one-time fee/room. Designated rooms, service with restrictions, crate.
SAVE S⌂ ✕ ⌁ ⌕ ☰ ▣ ⫴ ⇌

WHIPPANY

Homestead Studio Suites Hotel M
(973) 463-1999. **$115.** 125 Rt 10 E. I-287, exit 39, 3.6 mi e. Int corridors. **Pets:** Small. $100 one-time fee/room. Service with restrictions, crate.
ASK S⌂ ✕ ⌖M ⌁ ⌕ ☰ ▣

Summerfield Suites by Wyndham-Parsippany/ Whippany M ❀
(973) 605-1001. **$99-$209.** 1 Ridgedale Ave. I-287, exit 39 (SR 10 W), just nw. Int corridors. **Pets:** Medium, other species. $10 daily fee/pet, $125 one-time fee/pet. Service with restrictions, supervision.
SAVE ✕ ⌖M ⌁ ⌕ ☰ ▣ ⇌

Wellesley Inn M
(973) 539-8350. **$89-$129.** 1255 Rt 10 E. I-287, exit 39B southbound; exit 39 northbound, just w. Int corridors. **Pets:** Very small. Service with restrictions, supervision.
SAVE S⌂ ✕ ⌁ ⌕ ☰ ▣ ⇌

WOODBRIDGE

Homestead Studio Suites Woodbridge M
(732) 442-8333. **$114.** 1 Hoover Way. New Jersey Tpke, exit 11, 1.4 mi to US 9 N, just w on King George Post Rd. Int corridors. **Pets:** Medium, other species. $75 one-time fee/pet. Service with restrictions.
ASK ✕ ⌖M ⌁ ⌕ ☰ ▣

ALAMOGORDO

⟨AAA⟩ ▼▼ All American Inn Ⓜ
(505) 437-1850. **$40.** 508 S White Sands Blvd. 1 mi s on US 54, 70 and 82. Ext corridors. **Pets:** Small. Designated rooms, service with restrictions, supervision.

[SAVE] ⊠ 🔲 🔲 🔲 ⇌

⟨AAA⟩ ▼▼▼ Best Western Desert Aire Motor Hotel Ⓜ
(505) 437-2110. **$52-$68.** 1021 S White Sands Blvd. 1.5 mi s on US 54, 70 and 82. Ext corridors. **Pets:** Other species. $50 deposit/room.

[SAVE] 🔲 ⊠ 🔲 🔲 🔲 ⇌

▼▼▼ Holiday Inn Express-Alamogordo Ⓜ
(505) 437-7100. **$59-$65.** 1401 S White Sands Blvd. US 70, 0.6 mi n of jct US 70, 54 and 82. Int corridors. **Pets:** Medium, other species. $50 deposit/room. Supervision.

[ASK] 🔲 ⊠ 🔲 🔲 🔲 ⇌

▼▼ Super 8 Motel-Alamogordo Ⓜ
(505) 434-4205. **$41-$59.** 3204 N White Sands Blvd. US 54, 70 and 82, 2 mi s. Int corridors. **Pets:** Small, other species. Designated rooms, service with restrictions, supervision.

[ASK] 🔲 ⊠ 🔲

ALBUQUERQUE

⟨AAA⟩ ▼▼▼ AmeriSuites (Albuquerque/Airport) Ⓜ
(505) 242-9300. **$69-$115.** 1400 Sunport Place Blvd SE. I-25, exit 221, 0.3 mi e to University Blvd exit, just n to Woodward Rd. Int corridors. **Pets:** Small, other species. Service with restrictions, supervision.

[SAVE] 🔲 ⊠ 🔲 🔲 🔲 🔲 🔲 ⇌

⟨AAA⟩ ▼▼▼ AmeriSuites (Albuquerque/Midtown) Ⓐ
(505) 881-0544. **$69-$125.** 2500 Menaul Blvd NE. I-40, exit 160, just n to Menaul Blvd, 0.6 mi w. Int corridors. **Pets:** Small. Service with restrictions, supervision.

[SAVE] 🔲 ⊠ 🔲 🔲 🔲 🔲 🔲 ⇌

⟨AAA⟩ ▼▼▼ AmeriSuites (Albuquerque/Uptown) Ⓜ
(505) 872-9000. **$69-$119.** 6901 Arvada Ave NE. I-40, exit 162 westbound; exit 162B eastbound, 0.7 mi n. Int corridors. **Pets:** Small. $25 one-time fee/room. Service with restrictions, supervision.

[SAVE] 🔲 ⊠ 🔲 🔲 🔲 🔲 🔲 ⇌

⟨AAA⟩ ▼▼▼ Baymont Inn & Suites-Albuquerque North Ⓜ
(505) 345-7500. **$49-$89, 10 days notice.** 7439 Pan American Frwy NE. I-25, exit 231, just w. Int corridors. **Pets:** Other species. Service with restrictions, supervision.

[SAVE] 🔲 ⊠ 🔲 🔲 🔲 ⇌

⟨AAA⟩ ▼▼▼ Best Western Airport Inn Ⓜ
(505) 242-7022. **$50-$90, 14 days notice.** 2400 Yale Blvd SE. I-25, exit 222 (Gibson Blvd) northbound; exit 222A southbound, 1 mi e, then just s. Int corridors. **Pets:** Accepted.

[SAVE] 🔲 ⊠ 🔲 🔲 🔲

⟨AAA⟩ ▼▼▼ Best Western American Motor Inn & RV Park Ⓜ
(505) 298-7426. **$59-$79, 7 days notice.** 12999 Central Ave NE. I-40, exit 167, 0.3 mi w on Central Ave westbound; exit 166 right on Juan Tabo, left on Central Ave, then 0.5 mi eastbound. Ext corridors. **Pets:** Other species. $5 daily fee/pet. Service with restrictions, supervision.

[SAVE] 🔲 ⊠ 🔲 🔲 ⇌

▼▼▼ The Blue Hotel Ⓜ
(505) 924-2400. **$60-$150.** 717 Central Ave NW. Center; 7th and Central Ave. Ext corridors. **Pets:** Medium. $25 one-time fee/pet. Service with restrictions.

[ASK] 🔲 ⊠ 🔲 🔲 🔲 🔲 🔲 ⇌

⟨AAA⟩ ▼▼▼ Brittania & W E Mauger Estate Bed & Breakfast Ⓑ ✿
(505) 242-8755. **$89-$189, 10 days notice.** 701 Roma Ave NW. I-25, exit 225 (Lomas Ave), 1 mi w, just s on 7th Ave. Int corridors. **Pets:** Dogs only. $30 one-time fee/room. Designated rooms, service with restrictions, crate.

[SAVE] 🔲 ⊠ 🔲 🔲

AAA ◇◇◇◇ Comfort Inn-Airport M
(505) 243-2244. **$40-$99, 3 days notice.** 2300 Yale Blvd SE. I-25, exit 222A (Gibson Blvd) southbound; exit 222 northbound, 1 mi n, just s. Ext/int corridors. **Pets:** Accepted.

[SAVE] [S☉] [✕] [∅] [☞] [≥]

◇◇◇◇ Comfort Inn & Suites M
(505) 822-1090. **$60-$85.** 5811 Signal Ave NE. I-25, exit 233, just e via Alaneda. Int corridors. **Pets:** Other species. $10 daily fee/room. Designated rooms, service with restrictions.

[SAVE] [S☉] [✕] [&M] [∅] [☞] [☐] [☞] [≥]

AAA ◇◇◇◇ Comfort Inn East M❘ ☙
(505) 294-1800. **$56-$74.** 13031 Central Ave NE. I-40, exit 167, just w. Ext corridors. **Pets:** Small, other species. $3 daily fee/room. Service with restrictions.

[SAVE] [S☉] [✕] [&M] [∅] [☞] [☐] [☞] [¶] [≥]

◇◇◇◇ Days Inn-Hotel Circle M
(505) 275-3297. **$55-$65.** 10321 Hotel Cir NE. I-40, exit 165 (Eubank Ave), just n on Eubank Ave. Ext corridors. **Pets:** $5 daily fee/pet. Service with restrictions, supervision.

[SAVE] [S☉] [✕] [≥]

◇◇◇◇ Days Inn West M
(505) 836-3297. **$50.** 6031 Iliff Rd NW. I-40, exit 155, just s on Coors Rd, then just w. Ext corridors. **Pets:** Accepted.

[SAVE] [S☉] [✕] [&M] [∅] [☞] [≥]

AAA ◇◇◇◇ Econo Lodge Old Town M
(505) 243-8475. **$45-$100.** 2321 Central Ave NW. I-40, exit 157A, 0.6 mi s on Rio Grande Blvd, 0.4 mi w. Ext corridors. **Pets:** Medium, dogs only. $10 daily fee/pet. Designated rooms, service with restrictions, crate.

[SAVE] [S☉] [✕] [☐] [☞] [≥]

AAA ◇◇◇◇ Hampton Inn-North M
(505) 344-1555. **$65-$77.** 5101 Ellison NE. I-25, exit 231, just w. Ext corridors. **Pets:** Other species. Designated rooms, service with restrictions, supervision.

[SAVE] [S☉] [✕] [&M] [∅] [☐] [☞] [≥]

◇◇◇◇ Hawthorn Inn & Suites M
(505) 242-1555. **$75-$85.** 1511 Gibson Blvd SE. I-25, exit 222 (Gibson Blvd) northbound; exit 222A southbound, just e. Int corridors. **Pets:** Large, other species. Designated rooms, service with restrictions, supervision.

[ASK] [S☉] [✕] [&M] [∅] [☞] [☐] [☞] [≥]

AAA ◇◇◇◇ Holiday Inn Express M ☙
(505) 275-8900. **$79-$115.** 10330 Hotel Ave NE. I-40, exit 165 (Eubank Ave), 2 blks n on Eubank Ave. Ext corridors. **Pets:** $5 daily fee/room. Supervision.

[SAVE] [S☉] [✕] [∅] [☞] [☐] [☞] [≥]

◇◇◇◇ Holiday Inn-Mountain View M❘
(505) 884-2511. **$99-$109.** 2020 Menaul Blvd NE. I-40, exit 160 (Carlisle Blvd), 0.3 mi n to Menaul Blvd, 1 mi w. Int corridors. **Pets:** Accepted.

[✕] [&M] [∅] [☞] [☐] [☞] [¶]

◇◇ Homestead Studio Suites-Albuquerque/Midtown A ☙
(505) 883-8888. **$54.** 2401 Wellsley Dr NE. I-40, exit 160, just n to Menaul Blvd, just w, then just s. Ext corridors. **Pets:** Medium. $75 one-time fee/room. Service with restrictions, supervision.

[ASK] [S☉] [✕] [☞] [☐] [☞]

AAA ◇◇◇◇ Howard Johnson Express M
(505) 242-5228. **$50.** 411 McKnight Ave NW. I-40, exit 159A, just s via 4th St N. Int corridors. **Pets:** Medium. $10 one-time fee/pet. Designated rooms, service with restrictions, supervision.

[SAVE] [S☉] [✕] [∅] [☐] [☞]

AAA ◇◇◇◇ Howard Johnson Express Inn M
(505) 828-1600. **$64-$69.** 7630 Pan American Frwy. I-25, exit 231, 0.8 mi n on frontage road. Int corridors. **Pets:** $5 daily fee/room.

[SAVE] [S☉] [✕] [∅] [☞] [☐] [☞] [≥]

◇◇◇ Howard Johnson Hotel & Convention Center M❘
(505) 296-4852. **$51-$69.** 15 Hotel Cir NE. I-40, exit 165 (Eubank Blvd), just n. Int corridors. **Pets:** Other species. $20 one-time fee/room. Service with restrictions, supervision.

[ASK] [S☉] [✕] [∅] [☞] [☐] [☞] [¶] [≥]

◇◇◇◇ La Quinta Inn-Airport M
(505) 243-5500. **$76-$82.** 2116 Yale Blvd SE. I-25, 222A (Gibson Blvd) southbound; exit 222 (Gibson Blvd) northbound, 1 mi e. Ext/int corridors. **Pets:** Medium, other species. Service with restrictions, crate.

[SAVE] [✕] [&M] [∅] [☞] [☐] [☞] [≥]

AAA ◇◇◇◇ La Quinta Inn North M
(505) 821-9000. **$66-$79.** 5241 San Antonio Dr NE. I-25, exit 231, just e. Ext corridors. **Pets:** Supervision.

[SAVE] [S☉] [✕] [&M] [∅] [☞] [☐] [☞] [≥]

AAA ◇◇◇◇ La Quinta Inn San Mateo M
(505) 884-3591. **$62-$66.** 2424 San Mateo Blvd NE. I-40, exit 161 westbound; exit 161B eastbound, just n. Ext corridors. **Pets:** Accepted.

[SAVE] [S☉] [✕] [∅] [☞] [☐] [☞] [≥]

◇◇◇◇ Le Baron Courtyard & Suites M
(505) 884-0250. **$59-$69.** 2120 Menaul Blvd NE. I-40, exit 160, just n to Menaul Blvd, 0.8 mi w. Ext corridors. **Pets:** $25 deposit/room. Supervision.

[ASK] [S☉] [✕] [∅] [☞] [☐] [☞] [≥]

◇◇ Motel 6-1349 M
(505) 243-8017. **$41-$53.** 1000 Avenida Cesar Chavez. I-25, exit 223, just w. Ext corridors. **Pets:** Accepted.

[S☉] [✕] [&M] [☞] [☐] [☞] [≥]

AAA ◇◇◇◇ Plaza Inn Albuquerque M❘
(505) 243-5693. **$89-$99.** 900 Medical Arts NE. I-25, exit 225, just e. Int corridors. **Pets:** Large. $25 one-time fee/room. Service with restrictions, crate.

[SAVE] [S☉] [✕] [☐] [☞] [¶] [≥]

▼▼▼ **Radisson Hotel & Conference Center** 🄷
(505) 888-3311. **$89-$185, 3 days notice.** 2500 Carlisle
Blvd NE. I-40, exit 160, just n. Ext/int corridors.
Pets: Accepted.

(ASK) (S🄳) (✕) (&M) (🖉) (🖇) (🖬) (💻) (🍴) (≈)

▼▼ **Ramada Inn Mountainview** 🄼🄸
(505) 271-1000. **$55, 7 days notice.** 25 Hotel Cir NE. I-40,
exit 165, just n via Hotel Cir. Ext/int corridors.
Pets: Medium. $25 one-time fee/room. Designated rooms,
service with restrictions, crate.

(ASK) (S🄳) (✕) (🖉) (🖇) (🖬) (💻) (🍴) (≈)

🄰🄰🄰 ▼▼▼ **Ramada Limited** 🄼
(505) 858-3297. **$79, 7 days notice.** 5601 Alameda Blvd
NE. I-25, exit 233, just w. Int corridors. **Pets:** Other species.
$10 daily fee/room. Service with restrictions.

(SAVE) (S🄳) (✕) (&M) (🖉) (🖇) (🖬) (💻) (≈)

🄰🄰🄰 ▼▼▼ **Red Roof Inn** 🄼
(505) 831-3400. **$42-$54.** 6015 Iliff Rd NW. I-40, exit 155,
just s on Coors Blvd, then just w. Ext corridors.
Pets: Accepted.

(SAVE) (✕) (&M) (🖉) (🖇) (≈)

🄰🄰🄰 ▼▼▼ **Residence Inn by Marriott** 🄰
(505) 881-2661. **$107-$189.** 3300 Prospect NE. I-40, exit
160, just n to Menaul Blvd, just w, then just s on Wellesley
Dr NE. Ext corridors. **Pets:** Accepted.

(SAVE) (S🄳) (✕) (🖉) (🖬) (💻) (≈)

▼▼ **Super 8 Motel East** 🄼
(505) 271-4807. **$52-$65.** 450 Paisano NE. I-40, exit 166,
just n to Copper, just s. Int corridors. **Pets:** Accepted.

(ASK) (S🄳) (✕) (🖇)

▼▼ **Super 8 Motel of Albuquerque** 🄼
(505) 888-4884. **$49-$69, 3 days notice.** 2500 University
Blvd NE. I-25, exit 227A, just s. Int corridors.
Pets: Accepted.

(ASK) (S🄳) (✕) (🖉) (🖇) (🖬)

▼▼ **Super 8 Motel West (Albuquerque)** 🄼
(505) 836-5560. **$52-$68.** 6030 Iliff Rd NW. I-40, exit 155
(Coors Rd), 0.5 mi s. Int corridors. **Pets:** Other species. $5
daily fee/pet. Service with restrictions, supervision.

(ASK) (S🄳) (✕) (🖬)

🄰🄰🄰 ▼▼▼ **Travelodge** 🄼
(505) 292-4878. **$40-$55.** 13139 Central Ave NE. I-40, exit
167, just w. Ext corridors. **Pets:** Accepted.

(SAVE) (S🄳) (✕) (💻)

ALTO

▼▼ **High Country Lodge** 🄲
(505) 336-4321. **$79-$149, 7 days notice.** Hwy 48. Center.
Ext corridors. **Pets:** Medium. $10.94 one-time fee/pet.
Crate.

(🖬) (💻) (≈) (✕) (🐾)

ANGEL FIRE

▼▼▼ **Angel Fire Resort Hotel** 🄡
(505) 377-6401. **$95-$379, 31 days notice.** 1 N Angel Fire
Rd. US 64, 2.6 mi s on SR 434, then 0.4 mi ne. Int
corridors. **Pets:** Other species. $25 one-time fee/pet. Serv-
ice with restrictions, supervision.

(ASK) (S🄳) (✕) (🖬) (💻) (🍴) (≈) (✕) (🐾)

ARROYO SECO

▼▼▼ **Adobe and Stars B & B** 🄱🄱
(505) 776-2776. **$115-$180, 15 days notice.** 584 SR 150.
1.1 mi ne on SR 150 at Valdez Rd. Ext/int corridors.
Pets: Designated rooms, supervision.

(ASK) (S🄳) (✕) (🖬) (🐾) (🖊)

ARTESIA

🄰🄰🄰 ▼▼▼ **Artesia Inn** 🄼
(505) 746-9801. **$45-$55.** 1820 S 1st St. 1.5 mi s on US
285. Ext corridors. **Pets:** Accepted.

(SAVE) (S🄳) (✕) (🖬) (💻) (≈)

▼▼▼ **Holiday Inn Express-Artesia** 🄼
(505) 748-3904. **$63-$69, 30 days notice.** 2210 W Main.
1.6 mi w of jct US 82 and 285. Int corridors.
Pets: Accepted.

(ASK) (S🄳) (✕) (&M) (🖉) (🖇) (🖬) (💻) (≈)

BELEN

🄰🄰🄰 ▼▼▼ **Best Western-Belen** 🄼
(505) 861-3181. **$70-$85, 7 days notice.** 2111 Camino del
Llano Blvd. I-25, exit 191, just w of jct. Ext/int corridors.
Pets: Medium, other species. $20 deposit/room, $5 daily
fee/room. Designated rooms, service with restrictions,
supervision.

(SAVE) (S🄳) (✕) (🖇) (🖬) (💻) (≈)

BLOOMFIELD

▼▼ **Super 8 Motel** 🄼
(505) 632-8886. **$50-$70.** 525 W Broadway Blvd. Jct of US
64 and SR 44. Int corridors. **Pets:** Small, dogs only. $10
one-time fee/room. Service with restrictions, supervision.

(ASK) (S🄳) (✕) (🖉) (🖬)

CAPITAN

▼▼ **Smokey Bear Motel** 🄼
(505) 354-2253. **$49-$59.** 316 Smokey Bear Blvd. Ext corridors. **Pets:** Small, other species. Designated rooms, service with restrictions, supervision.

(ASK) (S🄳) (✕) (🖬) (💻)

CARLSBAD

🄰🄰🄰 ▼▼▼ **Best Western Stevens Inn** 🄼🄸
(505) 887-2851. **$79-$99.** 1829 S Canal St. 1 mi s on US
62, 180 and 285. Ext corridors. **Pets:** Very small. Designated rooms, service with restrictions, supervision.

(SAVE) (S🄳) (✕) (🖇) (🖬) (💻) (🍴) (≈)

Carlsbad Inn
(505) 887-1171. **$34-$49.** 2019 S Canal St. 1.5 mi s on US 62, 180 and 285. Ext corridors. **Pets:** Small, other species. Service with restrictions, supervision.

Comfort Inn
(505) 887-1994. **$65-$85.** 2429 W Pierce St. N on US 285. Int corridors. **Pets:** Small. $5 daily fee/room. Designated rooms, service with restrictions, crate.

Continental Inn
(505) 887-0341. **$36-$55.** 3820 National Parks Hwy. 3.5 mi sw on US 62 and 180. Ext corridors. **Pets:** Small, other species. Service with restrictions, supervision.

Days Inn of Carlsbad
(505) 887-7800. **$70, 30 days notice.** 3910 National Parks Hwy. 3.5 mi sw on US 62 and 180. Ext corridors. **Pets:** Other species. $10 daily fee/pet. Service with restrictions, supervision.

Holiday Inn Carlsbad
(505) 885-8500. **$66-$69.** 601 S Canal. Center; on US 62/180 and 285, Canal St at Lee St. Ext corridors. **Pets:** Other species. $25 one-time fee/pet. Service with restrictions, supervision.

Quality Inn
(505) 887-2861. **$55-$79, 7 days notice.** 3706 National Park Hwy. 3 mi sw on US 62 and 180. Ext corridors. **Pets:** Other species. $100 deposit/room. Designated rooms, service with restrictions, supervision.

Stagecoach Inn
(505) 887-1148. **$40-$46, 7 days notice.** 1819 S Canal. 1 mi s on US 62, 180 and 285. Ext corridors. **Pets:** Other species. $5 daily fee/pet. Designated rooms, service with restrictions, supervision.

CHAMA

Branding Iron Motel
(505) 756-2162. **$69-$109.** 1511 W Main. 0.5 mi s. Ext corridors. **Pets:** Very small, dogs only. $7 one-time fee/pet. Designated rooms, service with restrictions, supervision.

Chama River Bend Lodge
(505) 756-2264. **$-$78.** 2625 Hwy 64/84. 0.5 mi s of SR 17. Ext corridors. **Pets:** Medium. $10 daily fee/pet. Designated rooms, service with restrictions, supervision.

CHIMAYO

Casa Escondida Bed & Breakfast
(505) 351-4805. **$80-$140, 14 days notice.** 64 CR 0100. From SR 68, 7.1 mi e on SR 76, then 0.5 mi nw on CR 0100 following signs. Ext/int corridors. **Pets:** $10 daily fee/pet. Designated rooms, service with restrictions, supervision.

CIMARRON

Cimarron Inn & RV Park
(505) 376-2268. **$44-$55.** 212 10th St. US 64. Ext corridors. **Pets:** $5 one-time fee/room. Service with restrictions, supervision.

CLAYTON

Best Western Kokopelli Lodge
(505) 374-2589. **$64-$99.** 702 S 1st St. US 87, 0.5 mi se of jct US 56 and 64. Ext corridors. **Pets:** Medium. $5 daily fee/pet. Designated rooms, service with restrictions, supervision.

Super 8 Motel
(505) 374-8127. **$51-$62, 4 days notice.** 1425 S 1st St. US 87, 1 mi se of jct US 56 and 64. Int corridors. **Pets:** Medium. $7 one-time fee/room. Service with restrictions, supervision.

CLOUDCROFT

The Lodge
(505) 682-2566. **$85-$145, 14 days notice.** 1 Corona Pl. US 82, 0.3 mi s. Int corridors. **Pets:** Accepted.

CLOVIS

Comfort Inn
(505) 762-4591. **$62-$67.** 1616 Mabry Dr. 1 mi e on US 60, 70 and 84. Ext corridors. **Pets:** Medium. $10 one-time fee/pet. Designated rooms, supervision.

Holiday Inn
(505) 762-4491. **$60-$105, 7 days notice.** 2700 E Mabry Dr. 1.5 mi e on US 60, 70 and 84. Ext corridors. **Pets:** Accepted.

DEMING

Anselment's Butterfield Stage Motel
(505) 544-0011. **$36-$38, 3 days notice.** 309 W Pine. I-10, exit 82, 0.4 mi w. Ext corridors. **Pets:** Accepted.

Days Inn ⬧ ❀
(505) 546-8813. **$42-$50.** 1601 E Pine St. I-10, exit 81, just
e. Ext corridors. **Pets:** Small. $5 daily fee/pet. Service with
restrictions, supervision.

Grand Motor Inn ⬧ ❀
(505) 546-2632. **$48.** 1721 E Pine St. 1.3 mi e on US 70
and 80 city route and I-10 business loop. Ext corridors.
Pets: Large, other species. $11 one-time fee/pet. Desig-
nated rooms, service with restrictions, supervision.

Holiday Inn ⬧
(505) 546-2661. **$59-$89.** 4600 Motel Dr. I-10, exit 85, just
w. Ext corridors. **Pets:** Service with restrictions, supervision.

Wagon Wheel Motel ⬧ ❀
(505) 546-2681. **$29-$33, 3 days notice.** 1109 W Pine St.
I-10, exit 81, just e. Ext corridors. **Pets:** Medium, dogs only.
Designated rooms, service with restrictions, supervision.

ELEPHANT BUTTE

Marina Suites Motel ⬧
(505) 744-5269. **$65-$105, 5 days notice.** 200 Country
Club Dr. I-25, exit 83, 4.7 mi e. Ext corridors. **Pets:** Supervision.

Quality Inn ⬧ ❀
(505) 744-5431. **$72-$92, 3 days notice.** 401 Hwy 195.
I-25, exit 83, 4 mi e. Ext corridors. **Pets:** Small. $10 one-
time fee/pet. Service with restrictions, crate.

ESPANOLA

Comfort Inn ⬧
(505) 753-2419. **$60-$75.** 604-B S Riverside Dr. US 84 and
285, just s of jct SR 68. Int corridors. **Pets:** Accepted.

FARMINGTON

Best Western Inn & Suites ⬧ ❀
(505) 327-5221. **$79-$109.** 700 Scott Ave. 0.8 mi e on US
64 at Bloomfield Blvd and Scott Ave. Int corridors.
Pets: $10 one-time fee/room. Designated rooms, service
with restrictions, supervision.

Comfort Inn ⬧
(505) 325-2626. **$69-$89.** 555 Scott Ave. 0.8 mi e on US 64
(Bloomfield Blvd), just n. Int corridors. **Pets:** Accepted.

Days Inn ⬧
(505) 325-3700. **Call for rates.** 1901 E Broadway. 1.7 mi e
on US 64. Int corridors. **Pets:** $50 deposit/room. Service
with restrictions, supervision.

Holiday Inn Express ⬧
(505) 325-2545. **$56-$95.** 2110 Bloomfield Blvd. 1.6 mi e on
US 64. Int corridors. **Pets:** Accepted.

Holiday Inn of Farmington ⬧
(505) 327-9811. **$75-$85.** 600 E Broadway. 0.8 mi e on US
64 at Bloomfield Blvd and Scott Ave. Int corridors.
Pets: Other species. $50 deposit/room.

La Quinta Inn ⬧
(505) 327-4706. **$70-$81.** 675 Scott Ave. 0.8 mi e on US 64
at Bloomfield Blvd and Scott Ave. Ext corridors.
Pets: Accepted.

Super 8 Motel ⬧
(505) 325-1813. **$48-$61.** 1601 E Broadway. Just n of jct
SR 44. Int corridors. **Pets:** Accepted.

GALLUP

Best Value Inn ⬧
(505) 863-9385. **$35-$39, 3 days notice.** 2003 US 66 W.
I-40, exit 20, 1 mi w. Int corridors. **Pets:** Accepted.

Best Western Inn & Suites ⬧
(505) 722-2221. **$75-$79, 7 days notice.** 3009 US 66 W.
I-40, exit 16, 1 mi e. Int corridors. **Pets:** Accepted.

Comfort Inn ⬧
(505) 722-0982. **$50-$80, 5 days notice.** 3208 US 66 W.
I-40, exit 16, 0.3 mi e. Int corridors. **Pets:** Accepted.

Days Inn East ⬧
(505) 863-3891. **$39-$59, 3 days notice.** 1603 W Hwy 66.
I-40, exit 20, 0.5 mi s to US 66, just w. Ext corridors.
Pets: Small. $5 daily fee/room. Designated rooms, service
with restrictions, supervision.

Days Inn-West ⬧
(505) 863-6889. **$49-$69, 3 days notice.** 3201 W Hwy 66.
I-40, exit 16, 0.3 mi e. Ext corridors. **Pets:** Small. $5 daily
fee/room. Designated rooms, service with restrictions,
supervision.

Econo Lodge ⬧
(505) 722-3800. **$34-$46.** 3101 US 66 W. I-40, exit 16, 0.8
mi e. Int corridors. **Pets:** Accepted.

Economy Inn ⬧
(505) 863-9301. **$25-$35.** 1709 US 66 W. I-40, exit 20, s to
US 66, 0.5 mi w. Ext corridors. **Pets:** Medium. $3 daily
fee/pet. Designated rooms, service with restrictions, supervision.

AAA ▼◆◆▼ Gallup Travelodge M
(505) 722-2100. **$39-$59, 3 days notice.** 3275 US 66 W. I-40, exit 16, just e. Int corridors. **Pets:** Small. $5 daily fee/room. Designated rooms, service with restrictions, supervision.
(SAVE) (S⬧) (✕) (&M) (&") (▦) (✍)

AAA ▼◆◆▼ Holiday Inn Holidome MI
(505) 722-2201. **$65-$85, 3 days notice.** 2915 US 66 W. I-40, exit 16, s to US 66, then 1 mi e. Ext/int corridors. **Pets:** Small. Service with restrictions, supervision.
(SAVE) (S⬧) (✕) (❚) (▦) (¶¶) (✍)

AAA ▼◆◆▼ Ramada Limited M
(505) 726-2700. **$59-$89, 3 days notice.** 1440 W Maloney Ave. I-40, exit 22, 1 mi w on frontage road. Int corridors. **Pets:** Small. $5 daily fee/room. Designated rooms, service with restrictions, supervision.
(SAVE) (S⬧) (✕) (&M) (❚) (▦) (✍)

AAA ▼◆ Road Runner Motel MI
(505) 863-3804. **$34-$44, 3 days notice.** 3012 Hwy 66 E. I-40, exit 26, 1 mi w. Ext corridors. **Pets:** Accepted.
(SAVE) (S⬧) (✕) (❚) (¶¶) (✍)

AAA ▼◆ ◆▼ Sleep Inn M
(505) 863-3535. **$50-$68.** 3820 E US 66. I-40, exit 26, just e. Int corridors. **Pets:** Small. $5 daily fee/room. Designated rooms, service with restrictions, supervision.
(SAVE) (S⬧) (✕) (&M) (&") (❚) (▦) (✍)

AAA ▼◆ ◆▼ Super 8 Motel M
(505) 722-5300. **$45-$52.** 1715 US 66 W. I-40, exit 20, s to US 66, 0.5 mi w. Int corridors. **Pets:** Accepted.
(SAVE) (S⬧) (✕) (❚) (▦) (✍)

GRANTS

AAA ▼◆◆▼ Best Western Inn & Suites of Grants MI
(505) 287-7901. **$61.** 1501 E Santa Fe Ave. I-40, exit 85. Int corridors. **Pets:** Accepted.
(SAVE) (S⬧) (✕) (🐾) (❚) (▦) (¶¶) (✍)

▼◆◆▼ Comfort Inn M
(505) 287-8700. **$49-$69, 3 days notice.** 1551 E Santa Fe Ave. I-40, exit 85. Int corridors. **Pets:** Small. $5 daily fee/room. Designated rooms, service with restrictions, supervision.
(SAVE) (S⬧) (✕) (&M) (❚) (▦) (✍)

AAA ▼◆◆▼ Days Inn M
(505) 287-8883. **$60-$90.** 1504 E Santa Fe Ave. I-40, exit 85, 0.3 mi n of e interchange. Ext corridors. **Pets:** Very small. Service with restrictions, supervision.
(SAVE) (S⬧) (✕)

AAA ▼◆◆▼ Grants Travelodge M
(505) 287-7800. **$44-$59, 3 days notice.** 1608 E Santa Fe Ave. I-40, exit 85. Ext corridors. **Pets:** Small. $5 daily fee/room. Designated rooms, service with restrictions, supervision.
(SAVE) (S⬧) (✕) (&M) (&") (▦) (✍)

AAA ▼◆◆▼ Holiday Inn Express M
(505) 285-4676. **$60-$90.** 1496 E Sante Fe Ave. I-40, exit 85, 0.3 mi n of e interchange. Ext/int corridors. **Pets:** Other species. Service with restrictions, supervision.
(SAVE) (S⬧) (✕) (❚) (▦) (✍)

AAA ▼◆ Leisure Lodge M
(505) 287-2991. **$32-$39.** 1204 E Santa Fe Ave. I-40, exit 85, 0.8 mi w on Business Loop 40. Ext corridors. **Pets:** $3 daily fee/pet. Service with restrictions.
(SAVE) (S⬧) (✕) (❚) (✍)

AAA ▼◆ ◆▼ Sands Motel M
(505) 287-2996. **$36-$46.** 112 McArthur St. I-40, exit 85, 1.5 mi w on Business Loop 40. Ext corridors. **Pets:** Large. $5 one-time fee/room. Service with restrictions, supervision.
(SAVE) (S⬧) (✕) (❚)

HERNANDEZ

▼◆◆▼ Casa del Rio BB
(505) 753-2035. **$90-$125, 21 days notice.** Hwy 84, MM 199.46. 2.3 mi n from jct US 285, then just e on gated drive. Ext/int corridors. **Pets:** Accepted.
(✕) (&") (❚) (𝒦) (𝒲) (✉)

HOBBS

AAA ▼◆ ◆▼ Days Inn M
(505) 397-6541. **$45-$55.** 211 N Marland Blvd. 2 mi e on US 62 and 180. Ext corridors. **Pets:** Small, dogs only. $10 one-time fee/pet. Service with restrictions, supervision.
(SAVE) (S⬧) (✕) (🐾) (&") (❚) (▦) (✍)

AAA ▼◆ ◆▼ Econo Lodge M
(505) 397-3591. **$39-$49.** 619 N Marland Blvd. 2.5 mi e on US 62 and 180. Ext corridors. **Pets:** Medium. Service with restrictions, supervision.
(SAVE) (S⬧) (✕) (❚) (▦) (✍)

AAA ▼◆ ◆▼ Howard Johnson-Hobbs M
(505) 397-3251. **$59.** 501 N Marland Blvd. 2.5 mi e on US 62 and 180. Ext/int corridors. **Pets:** $25 deposit/room. Service with restrictions.
(SAVE) (S⬧) (✕) (&") (❚) (▦) (¶¶) (✍)

▼◆ ◆▼ Travelodge Hobbs M
(505) 393-4101. **Call for rates.** 1301 E Broadway. 2 mi e on US 62 and 180. Ext corridors. **Pets:** Accepted.
(ASK) (✕) (❚) (▦) (✍)

LAS CRUCES

AAA ▼◆◆▼ Best Western Mesilla Valley Inn MI
(505) 524-8603. **$62-$84.** 901 Avenida de Mesilla. I-10, exit 140 (Mesilla), just n. Ext/int corridors. **Pets:** Medium, other species. Service with restrictions.
(SAVE) (S⬧) (✕) (🐾) (❚) (▦) (¶¶) (✍)

(AAA) ▼▼▼▼ Best Western Mission Inn ⓜ
(505) 524-8591. **$62-$72, 7 days notice.** 1765 S Main St. I-10, exit 142, 1 mi n. Ext corridors. **Pets:** Medium. $10 deposit/room. Designated rooms, service with restrictions, supervision.
[SAVE] [S♦] [✕] [🔒] [💻] [🍽] [⇌]

▼▼▼▼ Comfort Suites ⓜ
(505) 522-1300. **$65-$75.** 2101 S Triviz. I-25, exit 1. Int corridors. **Pets:** Accepted.
[SAVE] [S♦] [✕] [♿] [🔒] [🐾] [🔒] [💻] [⇌]

(AAA) ▼▼▼ Days Inn ⓜ
(505) 526-4441. **$50-$65.** 2600 S Valley Dr. I-10, exit 142 (University Ave). Int corridors. **Pets:** $10 one-time fee/room. Designated rooms, service with restrictions, supervision.
[SAVE] [S♦] [✕] [🔒] [🔒] [🍽] [⇌]

▼▼▼▼ Hampton Inn ⓜ
(505) 526-8311. **$60-$80, 10 days notice.** 755 Avenida de Mesilla. I-10, exit 140 (Mesilla). Ext corridors. **Pets:** Service with restrictions, supervision.
[SAVE] [✕] [🔒] [💻] [⇌]

▼▼▼▼ Hilton Las Cruces Ⓗ
(505) 522-4300. **$90-$125.** 705 S Telshor Blvd. I-25, exit 3 (Lohman Dr). Int corridors. **Pets:** Service with restrictions, crate.
[SAVE] [S♦] [✕] [♿] [🔒] [🔒] [💻] [🍽] [⇌]

▼▼▼▼ Holiday Inn de Las Cruces ⓜ
(505) 526-4411. **$63-$68, 5 days notice.** 201 E University Ave. I-10, exit 142, 2.8 mi s on US 80, 85 and 180. Int corridors. **Pets:** Accepted.
[✕] [♿] [🔒] [🐾] [🔒] [💻] [🍽] [⇌]

▼▼▼▼ Holiday Inn Express ⓜ
(505) 527-9947. **$49-$159.** 2200 S Valley Dr. I-10, exit 142, 2 blks w. Ext corridors. **Pets:** Very small. Service with restrictions, supervision.
[ASK] [S♦] [✕] [♿] [🔒] [🔒] [💻] [⇌]

(AAA) ▼▼▼▼ La Quinta Inn-Las Cruces ⓜ
(505) 524-0331. **$62-$67.** 790 Avenida de Mesilla. I-10, exit 140 (Mesilla). Int corridors. **Pets:** Other species. Service with restrictions, supervision.
[SAVE] [S♦] [✕] [♿] [🔒] [🔒] [💻] [⇌]

▼▼▼▼ Lundeen's Inn of the Arts ⒷⒷ
(505) 526-3326. **$72.** 618 S Alameda Blvd. Center. Int corridors. **Pets:** Large. $20 one-time fee/room. Service with restrictions.
[ASK] [S♦] [✕]

▼▼ Motel 6–363 ⓜ
(505) 525-1010. **$41-$51.** 235 La Posada Ln. I-10, exit 142, 2.8 mi s on US 80, 85 and 180. Ext corridors. **Pets:** Medium, other species. $10 daily fee/room, $25 one-time fee/room. Service with restrictions, supervision.
[S♦] [✕] [♿] [🔒] [🐾] [🔒] [💻] [⇌]

▼▼ Royal Host Motel ⓜ
(505) 524-8536. **$34-$38.** 2146 W Picacho St. I-10, exit 139, 1 mi n, then 0.5 mi e on I-10 business route (Picacho St). Ext corridors. **Pets:** Medium. $10 one-time fee/room. No service, supervision.
[✕] [🔒] [⇌]

▼▼▼▼ Sleep Inn ⓜ
(505) 522-1700. **$60-$70.** 2121 S Triviz. I-25, exit 1. Int corridors. **Pets:** $15 one-time fee/room. Designated rooms, service with restrictions, supervision.
[SAVE] [S♦] [✕] [♿] [🔒] [🔒] [🔒] [💻] [⇌]

▼▼▼▼ TRH Smith Mansion Bed and Breakfast ⒷⒷ
(505) 525-2525. **$63-$99, 7 days notice.** 909 N Alameda Blvd. Center. Int corridors. **Pets:** Medium, dogs only. $20 one-time fee/pet. No service, supervision.
[✕] [🐾]

LAS VEGAS

(AAA) ▼▼▼▼ Comfort Inn ⓜ
(505) 425-1100. **$60-$100.** 2500 N Grand Ave. I-25, exit 347, just sw, US 85 and I-25 business route. Int corridors. **Pets:** Designated rooms, service with restrictions, supervision.
[SAVE] [S♦] [✕] [⇌]

(AAA) ▼▼▼ El Camino Motel ⓜ
(505) 425-5994. **$45-$60.** 1152 N Grand Ave. I-25, exit 345, 0.3 mi w, US 85 and I-25 business route. Ext corridors. **Pets:** Small, dogs only. $6 daily fee/pet. Service with restrictions, supervision.
[SAVE] [S♦] [✕] [🍽]

▼▼ Inn on the Santa Fe Trail ⓜ
(505) 425-6791. **$59-$84.** 1133 N Grand Ave. I-25, exit 345, 0.5 mi n; I-25 business route and US 84, 0.3 mi w. Ext corridors. **Pets:** $5 daily fee/room. Service with restrictions, supervision.
[ASK] [S♦] [✕] [🔒] [💻] [🍽] [⇌]

(AAA) ▼▼▼▼ Plaza Hotel Ⓗ
(505) 425-3591. **$76-$79.** 230 Plaza. I-25, exit 343W, just w, follow signs to Old Town Plaza. Int corridors. **Pets:** Accepted.
[SAVE] [S♦] [✕] [💻] [🍽]

LORDSBURG

▼▼ Best Western American Motor Inn ⓜ ✿
(505) 542-3591. **$60-$69, 15 days notice.** 944 E Motel Dr. I-10, exit 24, just n on US 70/SR 90. Ext corridors. **Pets:** Other species. $5 daily fee/pet. Designated rooms, service with restrictions, supervision.
[SAVE] [S♦] [✕] [🔒] [🍽] [⇌]

(AAA) ▼▼▼ Best Western-Western Skies Inn ⓜ
(505) 542-8807. **$64-$68.** 1303 S Main St. I-10, exit 22, just s. Ext corridors. **Pets:** $7 one-time fee/pet. Service with restrictions, supervision.
[SAVE] [S♦] [✕] [🔒] [💻] [🍽] [⇌]

◆◆ ▼▼▼▼ **Days Inn & Suites** Ⓜ
(505) 542-3600. **$65-$75, 3 days notice.** 1100 W Motel Dr.
I-10, exit 20, just n. Int corridors. **Pets:** Other species. $10
deposit/pet, $5.58 daily fee/pet. Designated rooms, service
with restrictions, supervision.
⟦SAVE⟧ ⟦S⟧ ⟦✕⟧ ⟦♪⟧ ⟦▤⟧ ⟦⩘⟧

▼▼▼▼ **Holiday Inn Express** Ⓜ
(505) 542-3666. **$70.** 1408 S Main St. I-10, exit 22, just s.
Ext corridors. **Pets:** $50 deposit/room. Designated rooms,
service with restrictions, supervision.
⟦ASK⟧ ⟦✕⟧ ⟦M⟧ ⟦🦽⟧ ⟦▤⟧ ⟦▣⟧ ⟦⩘⟧

LOS LUNAS

▼▼ **Microtel Inn & Suites** Ⓜ
(505) 865-0001. **$59, 10 days notice.** 2258 Sun Ranch
Village Loop. I-25, exit 203, just n. Int corridors.
Pets: Small. $10 daily fee/pet. Designated rooms, service
with restrictions, supervision.
⟦ASK⟧ ⟦S⟧ ⟦✕⟧ ⟦M⟧ ⟦🦽⟧ ⟦⩘⟧

MESILLA

▼▼ **Meson de Mesilla** ⒸⒾ
(505) 525-9212. **$65-$175, 3 days notice.** 1803 Avenida
de Mesilla. I-10, exit 140 (Mesilla), then 0.4 mi s. Int corridors. **Pets:** Accepted.
⟦ASK⟧ ⟦S⟧ ⟦✕⟧ ⟦▤⟧ ⟦⫠⟧ ⟦⩘⟧

MORIARTY

◆◆ ▼▼▼ **Days Inn** Ⓜ
(505) 832-4451. **$43-$72.** US 66 W & I-40. I-40, exit 194.
Int corridors. **Pets:** Other species. $5 daily fee/pet. Service
with restrictions, supervision.
⟦SAVE⟧ ⟦S⟧ ⟦✕⟧ ⟦▤⟧

◆◆ ▼▼▼▼ **Holiday Inn Express** Ⓜ
(505) 832-5000. **$79.** 1507 Route 66. I-40, exit 194, 0.4 mi
e. Int corridors. **Pets:** Large, other species. $10 one-time
fee/pet. Designated rooms, service with restrictions, supervision.
⟦SAVE⟧ ⟦S⟧ ⟦✕⟧ ⟦M⟧ ⟦▤⟧ ⟦▣⟧ ⟦⩘⟧

◆◆ ▼▼▼ **Luxury Inn** Ⓜ
(505) 832-4457. **$40-$45.** 1316 Route 66 W. I-40, exit 194,
0.5 mi se on US 66 and I-40 business loop. Int corridors.
Pets: Other species. $3 daily fee/pet. Service with restric-
tions, supervision.
⟦SAVE⟧ ⟦S⟧ ⟦✕⟧ ⟦▤⟧ ⟦▣⟧

▼▼ **Motel 6** Ⓜ
(505) 832-6666. **Call for rates.** 109 Route 66 E. I-40, exit
197, 1 mi e, then 0.5 mi e. Int corridors. **Pets:** Accepted.
⟦✕⟧ ⟦M⟧ ⟦♪⟧ ⟦🦽⟧ ⟦⩘⟧

◆◆ ▼ **Sunset Motel** Ⓜ
(505) 832-4234. **$45.** 501 Old Route 66. I-40, exit 197, 1 mi
w, then 0.5 mi e. Ext corridors. **Pets:** Accepted.
⟦SAVE⟧ ⟦S⟧ ⟦✕⟧ ⟦▤⟧ ⟦▣⟧

▼▼ **Super 8 Motel** Ⓜ
(505) 832-6730. **Call for rates, 14 days notice.** 1611 W
Old Route 66. I-40, exit 194, then 0.5 mi e on Central Ave.
Int corridors. **Pets:** Accepted.
⟦ASK⟧ ⟦✕⟧ ⟦🦽⟧ ⟦▤⟧

PINOS ALTOS

▼▼ **Bear Creek Motel & Cabins** Ⓒ
(505) 388-4501. **$79-$159, 14 days notice.** 88 Main St. 1
mi n on SR 15. Ext corridors. **Pets:** Other species. $20
daily fee/pet. Service with restrictions, supervision.
⟦▤⟧ ⟦▣⟧ ⟦🐾⟧

POJOAQUE PUEBLO

▼▼▼ **Cities of Gold Hotel** ⓂⒾ
(505) 455-0515. **$49-$95.** 10A Cities of Gold Rd. On US
84/265, just n. Int corridors. **Pets:** Accepted.
⟦ASK⟧ ⟦S⟧ ⟦✕⟧ ⟦M⟧ ⟦🦽⟧ ⟦▤⟧ ⟦▣⟧ ⟦⫠⟧

RATON

◆◆ ▼▼ **Budget Host Raton** Ⓜ
(505) 445-3655. **$43-$53.** 136 Canyon Dr. I-25, exit 454,
0.8 mi s on I-25 business loop. Ext corridors.
Pets: Medium. Service with restrictions, supervision.
⟦SAVE⟧ ⟦S⟧ ⟦✕⟧ ⟦M⟧

◆◆ ▼ **The Pass Inn** Ⓜ
(505) 445-3641. **$38-$59.** 308 Canyon Dr. I-25, exit 454,
0.8 mi s. Ext corridors. **Pets:** Medium. Designated rooms,
no service, supervision.
⟦SAVE⟧ ⟦S⟧ ⟦✕⟧

RIO RANCHO

◆◆ ▼▼▼▼ **Best Western Rio Rancho Inn &**
Conference Center ⓂⒾ
(505) 892-1700. **$56-$71, 30 days notice.** 1465 Rio Rancho Blvd. I-25, exit 233 (Alameda Blvd), 6.5 mi w; I-40, exit
155, 10 mi n on Coors Rd/Coors Bypass to SR 528, 1 mi n.
Ext corridors. **Pets:** Small. $25 deposit/room. Service with
restrictions, supervision.
⟦SAVE⟧ ⟦S⟧ ⟦✕⟧ ⟦♪⟧ ⟦▤⟧ ⟦▣⟧ ⟦⫠⟧ ⟦⩘⟧

◆◆ ▼▼▼ **Days Inn** Ⓜ
(505) 892-8800. **$45-$59.** 4200 Crestview Dr. I-25, exit 233
(Alameda Blvd), then 8 mi w on SR 528; I-40, exit 155, then
8 mi n on Coors Rd (SR 448). Ext corridors. **Pets:** Small.
$5 one-time fee/pet. Service with restrictions, supervision.
⟦SAVE⟧ ⟦S⟧ ⟦✕⟧ ⟦▤⟧ ⟦⩘⟧

▼▼▼▼ **Ramada Limited Hotel** Ⓜ
(505) 892-5998. **$62-$75.** 4081 High Resort Blvd. I-25, exit
233, then 8 mi w on Alameda Blvd (SR 528); I-40, exit 155,
8 mi n on Coors Rd (SR 448). Int corridors. **Pets:** Accepted.
⟦ASK⟧ ⟦S⟧ ⟦✕⟧ ⟦▤⟧ ⟦▣⟧ ⟦⩘⟧

▼▼▼ **Rio Rancho Super 8 Motel** Ⓜ
(505) 896-8888. **Call for rates, 5 days notice.** 4100 Barbara Loop. I-25, exit 233, 0.5 mi w on Alameda Blvd, 3.8 mi
nw on SR 528, just e. Int corridors. **Pets:** Accepted.
⟦ASK⟧ ⟦✕⟧

(AAA) ▼▼▼ **Wellesley Inn & Suites (Albuquerque/North)** Ⓜ
(505) 892-7900. **$63-$99.** 2221 Rio Rancho Blvd. I-25, exit 233, 6 mi w on Alameda Blvd (becomes SR 528/Rio Rancho Blvd). Int corridors. **Pets:** Accepted.
[SAVE] [S◦] [✕] [🐾] [⚙] [✆] [🖵] [≈]

ROSWELL

(AAA) ▼▼▼ **Best Western El Rancho** Ⓜ
(505) 622-2721. **$46-$65, 7 days notice.** 2205 N Main St. 1.8 mi n on US 70 and 285. Ext corridors. **Pets:** Other species. Service with restrictions, supervision.
[SAVE] [S◦] [✕] [✆] [🖵] [≈]

(AAA) ▼▼▼▼ **Best Western Sally Port Inn & Suites** Ⓜ
(505) 622-6430. **$79-$99.** 2000 N Main St. 1.5 mi n on US 70 and 285. Int corridors. **Pets:** $10 one-time fee/pet. Designated rooms, service with restrictions, supervision.
[SAVE] [S◦] [✕] [✆] [🖵] [🍴] [≈]

(AAA) ▼▼▼ **Budget Inn-North** Ⓜ ❀
(505) 623-6050. **$35-$45, 10 days notice.** 2101 N Main St. 1.8 mi n on US 70 and 285. Ext corridors. **Pets:** Medium. $4 daily fee/pet. Designated rooms, service with restrictions, supervision.
[SAVE] [S◦] [✕] [✆] [≈]

(AAA) ▼▼▼ **Budget Inn West** Ⓜ
(505) 623-3811. **$32-$48.** 2200 W 2nd St. 2 mi w on US 70 and 380. Ext corridors. **Pets:** Small, dogs only. $2 daily fee/room. Service with restrictions, supervision.
[SAVE] [S◦] [✕] [✆] [≈]

(AAA) ▼▼▼▼ **Comfort Inn** Ⓜ
(505) 623-4567. **$75-$105.** 3595 N Main St. On US 70 and 285, 3 mi n. Int corridors. **Pets:** Medium. Service with restrictions, supervision.
[SAVE] [S◦] [✕] [Ⓖ] [⚙] [✆] [🖵] [≈]

(AAA) ▼▼▼ **Days Inn** Ⓜ
(505) 623-4021. **$52-$65, 14 days notice.** 1310 N Main St. 0.8 mi n on US 70 and 285. Ext corridors. **Pets:** Other species. Service with restrictions, supervision.
[SAVE] [S◦] [✕] [🐾] [✆] [🖵] [🍴] [≈]

▼▼▼ **Econo Lodge** Ⓜ
(505) 623-9425. **$43-$60.** 2331 N Main St. Ext corridors. **Pets:** Accepted.
[SAVE] [S◦] [✕] [✆] [🖵] [≈]

(AAA) ▼▼▼ **Frontier Motel** Ⓜ ❀
(505) 622-1400. **$32-$36.** 3010 N Main St. 2.5 mi n on US 70 and 285. Ext corridors. **Pets:** Service with restrictions, supervision.
[SAVE] [S◦] [✕] [✆] [≈]

(AAA) ▼▼▼ **Leisure Inn** Ⓜ
(505) 622-2575. **$42-$55.** 2700 W 2nd St. 2.5 mi w on US 70 and 380. Ext corridors. **Pets:** Small, dogs only. $4 daily fee/pet. Designated rooms, service with restrictions, supervision.
[SAVE] [S◦] [✕] [✆]

▼▼ **Motel 6 of Roswell** Ⓜ
(505) 625-6666. **Call for rates.** 3307 N Main St. US 70. Int corridors. **Pets:** Accepted.
[✕] [Ⓖ] [⚙] [✆] [≈]

(AAA) ▼▼▼ **National 9 Inn** Ⓜ
(505) 622-0110. **$37.** 2001 N Main St. 1.5 mi n on US 285 and 70. Ext corridors. **Pets:** Accepted.
[SAVE] [S◦] [✕] [✆] [≈]

▼▼▼ **Ramada Limited** Ⓜ
(505) 623-9440. **$73-$83, 3 days notice.** 2803 W 2nd. 2.5 mi w on US 70 and 380. Ext/int corridors. **Pets:** Medium, other species. $50 deposit/pet. Designated rooms, service with restrictions, supervision.
[ASK] [S◦] [✕]

RUIDOSO

▼▼▼ **Hawthorn Suites Golf & Convention Resort** Ⓜ ❀
(505) 258-5500. **$149-$169, 3 days notice.** 107 Sierra Blanca Dr. 2.5 mi n on SR 48. Int corridors. **Pets:** Medium. Service with restrictions, supervision.
[ASK] [S◦] [✕] [🐾] [⚙] [✆] [🖵] [≈]

▼▼ **Travelodge** Ⓜ ❀
(505) 378-4471. **$45-$120.** 159 W Hwy 70 W. Jct of US 70 and SR 48 (the "Y"). Ext corridors. **Pets:** Medium, other species. $10 daily fee/room. Service with restrictions, supervision.
[ASK] [S◦] [✕] [✆] [🖵] [≈]

▼▼▼ **Village Lodge Suites** 🅰
(505) 258-5442. **$89-$129, 7 days notice.** 1000 Mechem Dr. 2 mi n on SR 48. Ext corridors. **Pets:** Accepted.
[✕] [✆] [🖵]

SANTA FE

(AAA) ▼▼▼ **Alexander's Inn** 🅱🅱
(505) 986-1431. **$80-$185, 14 days notice.** 529 E Palace Ave. 6 blks e of Plaza. Ext/int corridors. **Pets:** $20 one-time fee/pet. Service with restrictions.
[SAVE] [✕] [✆] [🖵]

(AAA) ▼▼▼▼ **Best Western of Santa Fe** Ⓜ
(505) 438-3822. **$50-$110, 7 days notice.** 3650 Cerrillos Rd. I-25, exit 278B, 2.8 mi n. Int corridors. **Pets:** Accepted.
[SAVE] [S◦] [✕] [🐾] [✆] [≈]

(AAA) ▼▼ **Cactus Lodge Motel** Ⓜ
(505) 471-7699. **$38-$85.** 2864 Cerrillos Rd. 3.8 mi sw on US 85. Ext corridors. **Pets:** Medium, dogs only. Service with restrictions, supervision.
[SAVE] [S◦] [✕] [✆]

(AAA) ▼▼▼▼ **Camel Rock Suites** 🅰
(505) 989-3600. **$89, 3 days notice.** 3007 S St Frances Dr. I-25, exit 282, 0.8 mi n on S Saint Francis Dr, just e on Zia via access drive. Ext corridors. **Pets:** Small, dogs only. $100 deposit/room, $25 one-time fee/room. Service with restrictions, supervision.
[SAVE] [S◦] [✕] [Ⓖ] [🐾] [⚙] [✆] [🖵]

▼▼▼ **Casapueblo Inn** BB
(505) 988-4455. **$139-$229, 3 days notice.** 138 Park Ave. Center; intersection Guadalupe and Park. Ext corridors. **Pets:** Large. $50 one-time fee/room. Service with restrictions.

ASK S⊘ ✕ ⓘ ▤ ▦

AAA ▼▼▼ **Comfort Inn** M
(505) 474-7330. **$49-$149.** 4312 Cerrillos Rd. I-25, exit 278, 1.6 mi n. Int corridors. **Pets:** Medium. $20 deposit/room. Service with restrictions, supervision.

SAVE S⊘ ✕ ⓘ ⓘ ▤ ▦ ⇆

AAA ▼▼▼▼ **Eldorado Hotel** H
(505) 988-4455. **$159-$1500, 3 days notice.** 309 W San Francisco. Just w of The Plaza, at Sandoval St. Int corridors. **Pets:** Other species. $50 one-time fee/room. Supervision.

SAVE S⊘ ✕ ⓜ ⓘ ▤ ⑪ ⇆

AAA ▼▼▼ **El Paradero Bed & Breakfast** BB
(505) 988-1177. **$80-$125, 7 days notice.** 220 W Manhattan Ave. 0.3 mi s on Cerrillos Rd, 1/2 blk on E Manhattan Ave. Ext/int corridors. **Pets:** Dogs only. $10 daily fee/pet. Designated rooms, service with restrictions, supervision.

SAVE ✕ ⓘ ⓘ ▤

▼▼▼ **Hacienda Nicholas** BB
(505) 992-0888. **$95-$160, 14 days notice.** 320 E Marcy St. 4 blks e of The Plaza. Ext/int corridors. **Pets:** Accepted.

✕

AAA ▼▼▼ **Hampton Inn Santa Fe** M
(505) 474-3900. **$69-$119.** 3625 Cerrillos Rd. I-25, exit 278B (Cerrillos Rd), 2.5 mi n. Int corridors. **Pets:** Accepted.

SAVE ✕ ⓜ ⓘ ⓘ ▤ ⇆

AAA ▼▼▼ **Hotel Santa Fe** H ❀
(505) 982-1200. **$99-$459.** 1501 Paseo de Peralta. At Cerrillos Rd, 0.6 mi s of The Plaza. Int corridors. **Pets:** Medium, dogs only. $20 daily fee/pet. Service with restrictions, supervision.

SAVE S⊘ ✕ ⓘ ⑪ ⇆

▼▼▼▼ **Inn of the Anasazi** H ❀
(505) 988-3030. **$199-$459, 3 days notice.** 113 Washington Ave. Just w of The Plaza. Int corridors. **Pets:** Medium. $50 one-time fee/pet. Service with restrictions, supervision.

✕ ⓘ ▤ ⑪

AAA ▼▼▼ **Inn On The Alameda** M ❀
(505) 984-2121. **$157-$272, 3 days notice.** 303 E Alameda St. 4 blks e of The Plaza; at jct Paseo De Peralta. Ext/int corridors. **Pets:** Small, other species. $20 daily fee/room. Designated rooms.

SAVE S⊘ ✕ ⓘ ⓘ ⓘ

AAA ▼▼▼ **La Quinta Inn** M
(505) 471-1142. **$72-$106.** 4298 Cerrillos Rd. I-25, exit Cerrillos Rd, 1.8 mi n. Ext corridors. **Pets:** Medium, other species. Service with restrictions, supervision.

SAVE S⊘ ✕ ⓘ ⓘ ⓘ ▤ ⇆

▼▼▼ **Las Palomas** A
(505) 988-4455. **$139-$229, 3 days notice.** 460 W San Francisco St. Just w of jct Guadalupe St. Ext corridors. **Pets:** Accepted.

ASK S⊘ ✕ ⓘ ⓘ ⓘ ▤ ⇆

▼▼ **Motel 6-150** M
(505) 473-1380. **$45-$67.** 3007 Cerrillos Rd. I-25, exit 278B, 3.8 mi n. Ext corridors. **Pets:** Accepted.

S⊘ ✕ ⓘ ⓘ ⇆

AAA ▼▼▼ **Quality Inn** M
(505) 471-1211. **$60-$109.** 3011 Cerrillos Rd. I-25, exit 278B, 3.8 mi n. Int corridors. **Pets:** Medium. Service with restrictions, supervision.

SAVE S⊘ ✕ ⓘ ▤ ⑪ ⇆

AAA ▼▼▼ **Radisson Santa Fe** X
(505) 992-5800. **$89, 3 days notice.** 750 N St Francis Dr. 1.5 mi nw off US 64, 84 and 285. Ext/int corridors. **Pets:** Small. $150 deposit/room. Designated rooms, service with restrictions, supervision.

SAVE S⊘ ✕ ⓘ ⓘ ⓘ ▤ ⑪

▼▼▼ **Ramada Limited** M
(505) 471-4000. **Call for rates.** 3450 Cerrillos Rd. I-25, exit 278, 3 mi n. Int corridors. **Pets:** Accepted.

ASK ✕ ⓜ ⓘ ⓘ ▤ ⇆

AAA ▼▼▼ **Residence Inn by Marriott** A
(505) 988-7300. **$209.** 1698 Galisteo St. I-25, exit 282, 1.7 mi n on St Francis Dr to St Michaels Dr, just e. Ext corridors. **Pets:** Accepted.

SAVE ✕ ⓘ ⓘ ▤ ⇆

▼▼▼ **Rio Vista Suites** CO
(505) 982-6636. **$74-$179, 3 days notice.** 320 Artist Rd. 527 E Alameda St, 0.5 mi e of center. Ext corridors. **Pets:** Other species. $75 one-time fee/pet. Service with restrictions.

ASK S⊘ ✕ ⓘ ▤

SANTA ROSA

AAA ▼▼ **Best Western Adobe Inn** M
(505) 472-3446. **$49-$67, 3 days notice.** 1501 E Will Rogers Dr. I-40, exit 275. Ext corridors. **Pets:** Small, other species. Service with restrictions, supervision.

SAVE S⊘ ✕ ⇆

AAA ▼▼▼ **Best Western Santa Rosa Inn** M
(505) 472-5877. **$64, 30 days notice.** 3022 Will Rogers Dr. I-40, exit 277, 0.5 mi w. Ext corridors. **Pets:** Other species. Supervision.

SAVE S⊘ ✕ ⓘ ⇆

▼▼▼ **Comfort Inn** M
(505) 472-5570. **Call for rates.** 3343 E Will Rogers Dr. I-40, exit 277, 0.3 mi w. Ext corridors. **Pets:** Other species. $10 one-time fee/pet. Supervision.

ASK ✕ ▤ ⇆

Days Inn of Santa Rosa M
(505) 472-5985. **$63-$75.** 1830 Will Rogers Dr. I-40, exit 275, then just e. Ext corridors. **Pets:** Accepted.

Holiday Inn Express M
(505) 472-5411. **$55-$67, 5 days notice.** 3300 Will Rogers Dr. I-40, exit 277, 0.3 mi w. Int corridors. **Pets:** Small. $15 deposit/room. Designated rooms, service with restrictions, supervision.

Motel 6–273 M
(505) 472-3045. **$39-$57.** 3400 Will Rogers Dr. I-40, exit 277, 0.3 mi w on Will Rogers Dr (US 66). **Pets:** Accepted.

Ramada Limited M
(505) 472-4800. **$68-$80, 10 days notice.** 1701 Historic Route 66. I-40, exit 275, just e. Int corridors. **Pets:** $10 one-time fee/pet. Supervision.

Super 8 Motel-Santa Rosa M
(505) 472-5388. **Call for rates.** 1201 Will Rogers Dr. I-40, exit 275, just w. Int corridors. **Pets:** Accepted.

SILVER CITY

Copper Manor Motel MI
(505) 538-5392. **$50-$57, 3 days notice.** 710 Silver Heights Blvd. On US 180 and SR 90, 1.3 mi ne. Ext corridors. **Pets:** Accepted.

The Drifter Motel MI
(505) 538-2916. **$45-$50.** 711 Silver Heights Blvd. On US 180 and SR 90, 1.3 mi ne. Ext corridors. **Pets:** Accepted.

Econo Lodge Silver City M
(505) 534-1111. **$49-$70.** 1120 Hwy 180 E. 1.5 mi ne on US 180 and SR 90. Int corridors. **Pets:** Small. $30 deposit/room, $7 daily fee/pet. Designated rooms, service with restrictions, crate.

Holiday Motor Hotel M
(505) 538-3711. **$50-$65, 3 days notice.** 3420 Hwy 180 E. 3 mi ne on jct SR 180 and 90. Ext corridors. **Pets:** Accepted.

Super 8 Motel M ✿
(505) 388-1983. **$49-$69.** 1040 E Hwy 180. 1.5 mi ne on US 180 and SR 90. Int corridors. **Pets:** Small. $5 one-time fee/pet. Service with restrictions, supervision.

SOCORRO

Econo Lodge M
(505) 835-1500. **$35-$58.** 713 California Ave. I-25, exit 150, 1 mi s. Ext corridors. **Pets:** Small. $5 daily fee/pet. Designated rooms, service with restrictions, supervision.

Holiday Inn Express M
(505) 838-0556. **$81-$110.** 1100 California Ave NE. Center. Ext/int corridors. **Pets:** Accepted.

Motel 6 M
(505) 835-4300. **$40.** 807 S US 85. I-25, exit 147. Ext corridors. **Pets:** Accepted.

TAOS

American Artists Gallery House Bed & Breakfast BB
(505) 758-4446. **$89-$250, 14 days notice.** 132 Frontier Ln. SR 68, 1 mi sw of jct US 64 and Taos Plaza, 0.3 mi e. Ext/int corridors. **Pets:** Dogs only. $25 daily fee/pet. Designated rooms, service with restrictions, supervision.

Casa Encantada BB ✿
(505) 758-7477. **$99-$155, 10 days notice.** 416 Liebert St. 0.6 mi e on US 64 from jct SR 68 and Taos Plaza, just s. Ext corridors. **Pets:** Other species. $10 daily fee/room. Supervision.

Casa Europa Inn & Gallery BB
(505) 758-9798. **$105-$175, 14 days notice.** 840 Upper Ranchitos Rd. 1.7 mi s from jct SR 64. Ext/int corridors. **Pets:** Medium, other species. $10 daily fee/pet. Designated rooms, service with restrictions, supervision.

El Pueblo Lodge M
(505) 758-8700. **$59-$89, 7 days notice.** 412 Paseo del Pueblo Norte. US 64, 0.5 mi n of jct SR 68 and Taos Plaza. Ext corridors. **Pets:** Other species. $10 daily fee/pet. Designated rooms, service with restrictions, supervision.

Fechin Inn M ✿
(505) 751-1000. **$109-$209.** 227 Paseo Del Pueblo Norte. Center; just n on US 64 of jct SR 68 and Taos Plaza. Int corridors. **Pets:** Small, dogs only. $20 daily fee/pet. Designated rooms, service with restrictions, supervision.

Holiday Inn Don Fernando de Taos MI
(505) 758-4444. **$99-$185.** 1005 Paseo del Pueblo Sur. SR 68, 1.8 mi sw of jct US 64 and Taos Plaza. Ext corridors. **Pets:** Very small, other species. $75 deposit/pet. Supervision.

Inn On The Rio M
(505) 758-7199. **$139-$150, 14 days notice.** 910 Kit Carson Rd. US 64, 1.5 mi e of jct SR 68 and Taos Plaza. Ext corridors. **Pets:** Dogs only. $20 daily fee/pet. Designated rooms, service with restrictions, supervision.

Orinda Bed & Breakfast BB
(505) 758-8581. **$80-$130, 14 days notice.** 461 Valverde. Center; 0.5 mi ne of The Plaza. Ext/int corridors. **Pets:** Medium, dogs only. $10 daily fee/pet. Designated rooms, service with restrictions, supervision.

Quality Inn M
(505) 758-2200. **$90-$100, 3 days notice.** 1043 Camino del Pueblo Sur. SR 68, 2 mi sw of jct US 64 and Taos Plaza. Ext/int corridors. **Pets:** Other species. $7.80 one-time fee/pet. Designated rooms, no service, supervision.

Ramada Inn de Taos M
(505) 758-2900. **$69-$89.** 615 Paseo del Pueblo Sur. SR 68, 1 mi sw of jct US 64 and Taos Plaza. Ext corridors. **Pets:** Medium. $10 one-time fee/pet. Designated rooms, service with restrictions, supervision.

Sagebrush Inn M
(505) 758-2254. **$59-$165, 3 days notice.** 1508 Paseo del Pueblo Sur. SR 68, 3 mi sw of jct US 64 and Taos Plaza. Ext corridors. **Pets:** Other species. Designated rooms, supervision.

San Geronimo Lodge L
(505) 751-3776. **$95-$175, 10 days notice.** 1101 Witt Rd. Center; jct US 64 and 68, 1.3 mi e on US 64 E (Kit Carson Rd), 0.6 mi s. Ext/int corridors. **Pets:** Other species. $15 one-time fee/room. Designated rooms, service with restrictions, crate.

Sun God Lodge M
(505) 758-3162. **$58-$88, 4 days notice.** 919 Paseo del Pueblo Sur. SR 68, 1.8 mi sw of jct US 64 and Taos Plaza. Ext corridors. **Pets:** Accepted.

THOREAU

Zuni Mountain Lodge CI
(505) 862-7769. **$95 (no credit cards), 3 days notice.** 40 W Perch Dr. I-40, exit 53, 13 mi s on SR 612, then w. Ext/int corridors. **Pets:** Medium, other species. Supervision.

TRUTH OR CONSEQUENCES

Best Western Hot Springs Motor Inn M
(505) 894-6665. **$57-$79.** 2270 N Date St. I-25, exit 79. Ext corridors. **Pets:** Accepted.

Holiday Inn H
(505) 894-1660. **Call for rates, 14 days notice.** 2250 N Date St. I-25, exit 79. Int corridors. **Pets:** Accepted.

Super 8 Motel M
(505) 894-7888. **$49-$69.** 2151 N Date St. I-25, exit 79, just s. Int corridors. **Pets:** Other species. $15 deposit/pet. Service with restrictions, supervision.

TUCUMCARI

Americana Motel M
(505) 461-0431. **$30-$38.** 406 E Tucumcari Blvd. I-40, exit 332, 1.5 mi n on SR 18, 0.5 mi e on US 66. Ext corridors. **Pets:** Medium. $3 one-time fee/pet. Service with restrictions, supervision.

Best Western Discovery Inn M
(505) 461-4884. **$52-$76.** 200 E Estrella. I-40, exit 332. Ext corridors. **Pets:** Other species. $5 daily fee/room. Designated rooms, service with restrictions, supervision.

Best Western Pow Wow Inn M
(505) 461-0500. **$55-$69.** 801 W Tucumcari Blvd. I-40, exit 332, 1.5 mi n on SR 18, 0.5 mi w on US 66. Ext corridors. **Pets:** Medium, other species. $10 daily fee/room. Supervision.

Comfort Inn M
(505) 461-4094. **$52-$75, 7 days notice.** 2800 E Tucumcari Blvd. I-40, exit 335, 0.5 mi w. Ext corridors. **Pets:** Accepted.

Days Inn M
(505) 461-3158. **$45-$60, 7 days notice.** 2623 S First St. I-40, exit 332, just n. Ext/int corridors. **Pets:** Other species. Service with restrictions, supervision.

Hampton Inn M
(505) 461-1111. **$55-$89, 10 days notice.** 3409 E Tucumcari Blvd. I-40, exit 335, 0.7 mi w. Int corridors. **Pets:** Accepted.

Holiday Inn M
(505) 461-3780. **$85-$104.** 3716 E Tucumcari Blvd. I-40, exit 335, 0.3 mi w on US 66. Ext corridors. **Pets:** Medium, other species. $8 one-time fee/room. Service with restrictions, supervision.

Howard Johnson M
(505) 461-2747. **$55-$60.** 3604 E Tucumcari Blvd. I-40, exit 335, then 0.5 mi w. Int corridors. **Pets:** Other species. $6 one-time fee/room. Service with restrictions, supervision.

Microtel Inn-Tucumcari M
(505) 461-0600. **$35-$64.** 2420 S First St. I-40, exit 332, just n. Int corridors. **Pets:** Other species. $6 daily fee/pet. Designated rooms, no service, supervision.

Rodeway Inn East M
(505) 461-0360. **$45-$60.** 1023 E Tucumcari Blvd. I-40, exit 333 to Tucumcari Blvd, 0.6 mi w. Ext corridors. **Pets:** Other species. $5 deposit/pet. Service with restrictions, supervision.

Safari Motel M
(505) 461-3642. **$38-$44, 5 days notice.** 722 E Tucumcari Blvd. I-40, exit 332, 1.5 mi n on 1st St, 0.4 mi e on US 66. Ext corridors. **Pets:** Accepted.

Super 8 Motel M
(505) 461-4444. **$40-$70.** 4001 E Tucumcari Blvd. I-40, exit 335, just w. Int corridors. **Pets:** Accepted.

Tucumcari Travelodge M
(505) 461-1401. **$35-$50.** 1214 E Tucumcari Blvd. I-40, exit 333, 1.5 mi n on Mountain Rd, then 0.5 mi w. Ext corridors. **Pets:** Medium. $5 daily fee/pet. Designated rooms, service with restrictions, supervision.

VAUGHN

Bel-Air Motel M
(505) 584-2241. **$38-$42.** 1 mi e on US 54, 60 and 285. Ext corridors. **Pets:** Small, dogs only. Designated rooms, service with restrictions, supervision.

Oak Tree Inn M
(505) 584-8733. **$59-$79, 5 days notice.** 1.5 mi e on US 54, 60 and 285. Int corridors. **Pets:** Accepted.

WHITES CITY

Best Western Cavern Inn M
(505) 785-2291. **$65-$105.** 17 Carlsbad Caverns Hwy. US 62 and 180 at jct SR 7. Ext corridors. **Pets:** Medium. $10 daily fee/room. Service with restrictions, supervision.

NEW YORK

CITY INDEX

ALBANY

Albany Mansion Hill Inn & Restaurant BB
(518) 465-2038. **$145-$165, 5 days notice.** 115 Philip St at Park Ave. I-787, exit 3B (Madison Ave/US 20 W) to Philip St, then just s. Ext/int corridors. **Pets:** Other species.
[SAVE] [S⊘] [✕] [⊟] [⊟] [⍅]

Albany TownePlace Suites M
(518) 435-1900. **$100-$150, 3 days notice.** 1379 Washington Ave. I-90, exit 2, just s on Fuller Rd, then 0.6 mi e. Int corridors. **Pets:** Other species. $75 one-time fee/room. Service with restrictions.
[SAVE] [S⊘] [✕] [⅙M] [⍾] [⊟] [⊡] [⍅]

Best Western Albany Sovereign Hotel MI
(518) 489-2981. **$95-$135, 3 days notice.** 1228 Western Ave. I-87, exit 24, 0.7 mi se, 5 mi w on US 20; I-90, exit 2 (Fuller Rd) westbound, 0.7 mi s, follow signs to US 20. Int corridors. **Pets:** Accepted.
[SAVE] [S⊘] [✕] [⍪] [⍾] [⊟] [⊡] [⍅]

ALEXANDRIA BAY

Riveredge Resort-Hotel R
(315) 482-9917. **$98-$298, 14 days notice.** 17 Holland St. I-81, exit 50N, 4.9 mi n on SR 12, 0.6 mi e on Walton, then just ne. Int corridors. **Pets:** Small. $10 daily fee/pet. Service with restrictions, supervision.
[SAVE] [✕] [⍪] [⊟] [⍅] [⍅] [⊠]

ANGELICA

Angelica Inn B&B BB
(585) 466-3063. **$75-$100, 14 days notice.** 64 W Main St. SR 17, exit 31, 0.5 mi w. Int corridors. **Pets:** Small, other species. $10 daily fee/pet. Designated rooms, no service, supervision.
[ASK] [✕] [⊟] [⊡] [⊘]

APALACHIN

The Dolphin Hotel M
(607) 625-4441. **$61-$68.** 7666 Rt 434. SR 17, exit 66, just e. Int corridors. **Pets:** Medium. $5 daily fee/room. Designated rooms, service with restrictions, supervision.
[ASK] [S⊘] [✕] [⍾] [⊟]

AUBURN

AAA ▼▼▼ **Auburn Microtel Inn & Suites** Ⓜ
(315) 253-5000. **$45-$89.** 12 Seminary Ave. Center; jct SR
34/38, just e on US 20/SR 5. Int corridors. **Pets:** $15 one-
time fee/room. Designated rooms, service with restrictions,
supervision.

⟦SAVE⟧ ⟦S✿⟧ ⟦✕⟧ ⟦&M⟧ ⟦🔲⟧ ⟦✦⟧ ⟦🖬⟧ ⟦💻⟧

AAA ▼▼▼▼ **Holiday Inn-Auburn/Finger**
                Lakes Ⓜ
(315) 253-4531. **$70-$120.** 75 North St. SR 34, just n of US
20/SR 5. Int corridors. **Pets:** $10 daily fee/room. Designated
rooms, service with restrictions, supervision.

⟦SAVE⟧ ⟦S✿⟧ ⟦✕⟧ ⟦&M⟧ ⟦🖬⟧ ⟦💻⟧ ⟦🍴⟧ ⟦✦⟧

▼ **Sleepy Hollow Country Inn** Ⓜ ✿
(315) 704-0343. **$50-$99, 10 days notice.** 3401 E Genesee St. US 20, 1 mi e. Ext corridors. **Pets:** $15 one-time
fee/pet. Crate.

⟦✕⟧ ⟦🖬⟧ ⟦💻⟧

AVERILL PARK

▼▼▼▼ **La Perla at the Gregory House Country Inn**
              & Restaurant ⓒⒾ
(518) 674-3774. **$115-$125, 7 days notice.** 3016 Rt 43.
Center. Int corridors. **Pets:** Very small, dogs only. Service
with restrictions, supervision.

⟦ASK⟧ ⟦✕⟧ ⟦🍴⟧ ⟦✦⟧ ⟦🌊⟧

AVOCA

▼ **Caboose Motel** Ⓜ
(607) 566-2216. **$36-$52, 3 days notice.** 8620 SR 415.
I-390, exit 1, 2.2 mi n. Ext corridors. **Pets:** Small, dogs only.
Designated rooms, service with restrictions, supervision.

⟦✕⟧ ⟦🖬⟧ ⟦💻⟧

BATAVIA

AAA ▼▼▼ **Best Western Batavia Inn** ⓂⒾ
(585) 343-1000. **$89-$99.** 8204 Park Rd. I-90, exit 48, just
w. Int corridors. **Pets:** Accepted.

⟦SAVE⟧ ⟦S✿⟧ ⟦✕⟧ ⟦🍴⟧ ⟦✦⟧

AAA ▼▼▼ **Crown Inn** Ⓜ
(585) 343-2311. **$50-$110.** 8212 Park Rd. I-90, exit 48, just
w. Ext/int corridors. **Pets:** Accepted.

⟦SAVE⟧ ⟦S✿⟧ ⟦✕⟧

▼▼▼▼ **Holiday Inn** Ⓗ
(585) 344-2100. **$89-$124.** 8250 Park Rd. I-90, exit 48, just
w. Int corridors. **Pets:** Accepted.

⟦ASK⟧ ⟦S✿⟧ ⟦✕⟧ ⟦🖬⟧ ⟦💻⟧ ⟦🍴⟧ ⟦✦⟧

▼ **Park Oak Inn** Ⓜ
(585) 343-7921. **$55-$99, 3 days notice.** 301 Oak St. I-90,
exit 48, just n. Int corridors. **Pets:** Medium. $5 daily fee/
room. Service with restrictions, supervision.

⟦ASK⟧ ⟦S✿⟧ ⟦✕⟧ ⟦🖬⟧

BATH

▼▼▼ **Bath Super 8** Ⓜ
(607) 776-2187. **$60.** 333 W Morris St. I-86, exit 38, just n.
Int corridors. **Pets:** Accepted.

⟦ASK⟧ ⟦S✿⟧ ⟦✕⟧ ⟦🖬⟧

▼▼▼ **Days Inn** ⓂⒾ
(607) 776-7644. **$70-$115.** 330 W Morris St. SR 17, exit 38,
just n. Int corridors. **Pets:** Other species. Service with
restrictions, supervision.

⟦SAVE⟧ ⟦S✿⟧ ⟦✕⟧ ⟦🖬⟧ ⟦💻⟧ ⟦🍴⟧ ⟦✦⟧

BELLPORT

▼▼▼▼ **The Great South Bay Inn** ⒷⒷ
(631) 286-8588. **$99-$135, 10 days notice.** 160 S Country
Rd. Downtown; on Main St (S Country Rd). Int corridors.
Pets: Small. $15 daily fee/pet. Designated rooms, service
with restrictions, supervision.

⟦✕⟧ ⟦✉⟧

BINGHAMTON

AAA ▼▼▼ **Comfort Inn** Ⓜ
(607) 722-5353. **$45-$200.** 1156 Front St. I-81, exit 6, just n
of Broome Community College. Int corridors. **Pets:** Other
species. $10 one-time fee/room. Designated rooms, service
with restrictions, supervision.

⟦SAVE⟧ ⟦S✿⟧ ⟦✕⟧ ⟦🖬⟧ ⟦💻⟧

▼▼▼▼ **Days Inn** Ⓜ
(607) 724-3297. **$95-$100, 3 days notice.** 1000 Front St.
I-81 S, exit 6, 2 mi s on US 11; I-81 N, exit 5 (Front St), 1
mi n on US 11. Int corridors. **Pets:** $10 daily fee/room.
Designated rooms, service with restrictions, supervision.

⟦SAVE⟧ ⟦S✿⟧ ⟦✕⟧ ⟦&M⟧ ⟦🖬⟧ ⟦💻⟧ ⟦✦⟧

▼▼▼▼ **Holiday Inn Arena** Ⓗ
(607) 722-1212. **$94-$124.** 2-8 Hawley St. Downtown. Int
corridors. **Pets:** $25 one-time fee/room. Service with restric-
tions, crate.

⟦ASK⟧ ⟦S✿⟧ ⟦✕⟧ ⟦&M⟧ ⟦🖬⟧ ⟦💻⟧ ⟦🍴⟧ ⟦✦⟧

▼ **Motel 6–1222** Ⓜ
(607) 771-0400. **$43-$61.** 1012 Front St. I-81 S, exit 6, 2 mi
s on US 11; I-81 N, exit 5 (Front St), 1 mi n on US 11. Int
corridors. **Pets:** Accepted.

⟦S✿⟧ ⟦✕⟧ ⟦&M⟧ ⟦✦⟧

AAA ▼▼▼ **Ramada Limited** Ⓜ
(607) 724-2412. **$72-$92.** 65 Front St. I-81, exit 5, 2 mi s;
SR 17 E, exit 72, 1 mi s. Int corridors. **Pets:** Accepted.

⟦SAVE⟧ ⟦S✿⟧ ⟦✕⟧ ⟦🖬⟧ ⟦💻⟧ ⟦✦⟧

AAA ▼ **Super 8 Motel-Binghamton** Ⓜ
(607) 773-8111. **$43-$95.** 650 Old Front St. I-81, exit 5 to
access road. Int corridors. **Pets:** Large. $35 deposit/room.
Service with restrictions, crate.

⟦SAVE⟧ ⟦S✿⟧ ⟦✕⟧ ⟦🖬⟧

BOONVILLE

AAA ❤❤❤ Headwaters Motor Lodge M
(315) 942-4493. **$55-$65, 3 days notice.** 13524 Rt 12. Jct US 12 and 120, 0.7 mi n. Int corridors. **Pets:** Accepted.

SAVE 🅂🄳 ❌ 🅱

BRIGHTON

AAA ❤❤❤ Wellesley Inn-Rochester/South M
(585) 427-0130. **$54-$84.** 797 E Henrietta Rd. I-390, exit 16 northbound; exit 16B southbound. Int corridors. **Pets:** Medium. Designated rooms, service with restrictions, supervision.

SAVE 🅂🄳 ❌ 🕮 🛠 🅱 💻

BROCKPORT

AAA ❤❤❤ Econo Lodge of Brockport M
(585) 637-3157. **$58-$90.** 6575 4th Section Rd. Jct SR 19, just w on SR 31. Ext corridors. **Pets:** Other species. Service with restrictions, supervision.

SAVE 🅂🄳 ❌ 🅱 💻 🛳

AAA ❤❤❤❤ Holiday Inn Express M
(585) 395-1000. **$90-$140.** 4908 Lake Rd S. Jct CR 39 and 19, just s. Int corridors. **Pets:** Other species. $15 one-time fee/room. No service.

SAVE 🅂🄳 ❌ 🕮 🅱 💻

BUFFALO METROPOLITAN AREA

AMHERST

AAA ❤❤❤❤ Buffalo Marriott-Niagara H
(716) 689-6900. **$79-$174.** 1340 Millersport Hwy. I-290, exit 5B, 0.5 mi n on SR 263 (Millersport Hwy). Int corridors. **Pets:** $50 one-time fee/room. Designated rooms, service with restrictions.

SAVE 🅂🄳 ❌ 🕮 🛠 🅱 💻 🍴 🛳

AAA ❤❤❤ Lord Amherst Motor Hotel MI
(716) 839-2200. **$69-$99.** 5000 Main St. I-290, exit 7A, just w on SR 5. Ext/int corridors. **Pets:** Service with restrictions, supervision.

SAVE 🅂🄳 ❌ 🕮 🅱 💻 🍴 🛳

AAA ❤❤❤ Red Roof Inn M
(716) 689-7474. **$43-$86.** 42 Flint Rd. I-290, exit 5B, 0.5 mi n on SR 263 (Millersport Hwy). Ext corridors. **Pets:** Accepted.

SAVE ❌ 🕮 🅱

BOWMANSVILLE

AAA ❤❤❤ Red Roof Inn-Buffalo Airport M
(716) 633-1100. **$41-$77.** 146 Maple Dr. Just e of SR 78, just n of entrance to I-90 (New York Thruway), exit 49; behind Bob Evans Restaurant. Ext corridors. **Pets:** Accepted.

SAVE ❌ 🛠

BUFFALO

AAA ❤❤❤ Best Western Inn-On The Avenue M
(716) 886-8333. **$99-$129.** 510 Delaware Ave. Downtown; between Virginia and Allen sts. Int corridors. **Pets:** Medium, dogs only. $100 deposit/room. Designated rooms.

SAVE 🅂🄳 ❌ 🅱 💻

AAA ❤❤❤❤ Holiday Inn-Downtown H
(716) 886-2121. **$99-$125, 3 days notice.** 620 Delaware Ave. Downtown; between Allen and North sts. Int corridors. **Pets:** Accepted.

SAVE 🅂🄳 ❌ 🅱 💻 🍴 🛳

CHEEKTOWAGA

❤❤❤ Homewood Suites by Hilton M
(716) 685-0700. **$114-$189.** 760 Dick Rd. Jct SR 33, exit Dick Rd, 0.3 mi sw. Int corridors. **Pets:** Medium, other species. $85 one-time fee/room. Service with restrictions, supervision.

SAVE ❌ 🛠 🅱 💻 🛳

GRAND ISLAND

AAA ❤❤ Chateau Motor Lodge M
(716) 773-2868. **$35-$79, 3 days notice.** 1810 Grand Island Blvd. I-190, exit 18A northbound, 0.5 mi w on SR 324. Ext corridors. **Pets:** Medium. $8 daily fee/pet. Service with restrictions, supervision.

SAVE 🅂🄳 ❌ 🅱

❤❤ Cinderella Motel M
(716) 773-2872. **$48-$55, 3 days notice.** 2797 Grand Island Blvd. I-190, exit 19 northbound, 1.3 mi w on SR 324; exit 20B southbound, just e on SR 324. Ext corridors. **Pets:** Small. Service with restrictions, supervision.

❌ 🅱 💻

HAMBURG

AAA ❤❤❤❤ Comfort Inn & Suites M
(716) 648-2922. **$55-$130, 5 days notice.** 3615 Commerce Pl. I-90, exit 57, then just w on SR 75 S. Int corridors. **Pets:** Other species. $10 daily fee/room. Designated rooms, service with restrictions, supervision.

SAVE 🅂🄳 ❌ 🕮 🛠 🅱 💻 🛳

AAA ❤❤❤❤ Holiday Inn Hamburg MI
(716) 649-0500. **$59-$119.** 5440 Camp Rd. I-90, exit 57, 0.3 mi e se on SR 75 S. Int corridors. **Pets:** Accepted.

SAVE 🅂🄳 ❌ 🛠 🅱 💻 🍴 🛳

AAA ❤❤❤ Red Roof Inn M
(716) 648-7222. **$42-$75.** 5370 Camp Rd. I-90, exit 57, just se on SR 75 S. Ext corridors. **Pets:** Other species. Service with restrictions.

SAVE ❌ 🛠

▼▼ Tallyho-tel M
(716) 648-2000. **$38-$95, 14 days notice.** 5245 Camp Rd. I-90, exit 57, just nw on SR 75. Ext corridors. **Pets:** Accepted.

KENMORE

▼▼ Super 8-Buffalo/Niagara Falls M
(716) 876-4020. **$46-$74.** 1288 Sheridan Dr. I-190, exit 15, 1.5 mi e. Int corridors. **Pets:** Medium. Service with restrictions, supervision.

TONAWANDA

▼▼ Microtel-Tonawanda M
(716) 693-8100. **$39-$94, 3 days notice.** 1 Hospitality Centre Way. I-290, exit 1B westbound; exit 1 eastbound, 0.5 mi e on Crestmount Ave, then just n on SR 384 (Delaware St). Int corridors. **Pets:** Accepted.

WILLIAMSVILLE

▼▼ Microtel-Lancaster M ❖
(716) 633-6200. **$40-$65.** 50 Freeman Rd. Jct SR 78, just e on frontage road; I-90, exit 49, 0.3 mi n. Int corridors. **Pets:** Other species. $5 daily fee/room. Service with restrictions, supervision.

▲▲▲ ▼▼▼ Residence Inn by Marriott Buffalo/Amherst ◭
(716) 632-6622. **$119-$179.** 100 Maple Rd. I-290, exit 5B, just e on Maple Rd from jct SR 263 (Millersport Hwy). Ext corridors. **Pets:** Other species. $6 daily fee/pet, $50 one-time fee/room. Service with restrictions, crate.

❖ **END METROPOLITAN AREA** ❖

CAMBRIDGE

▼ Cambridge Inn Bed & Breakfast BB
(518) 677-5741. **$58-$75 (no credit cards), 7 days notice.** 16 W Main St. Jct SR 22 and 372, 0.3 mi w. Ext/int corridors. **Pets:** Accepted.

CANANDAIGUA

▲▲▲ ▼▼▼ Canandaigua Inn on the Lake MI
(585) 394-7800. **$84-$304.** 770 S Main St. Jct SR 332, just s on US 20 and SR 5. Int corridors. **Pets:** Small. Service with restrictions, supervision.

▲▲▲ ▼▼ Econo Lodge Canandaigua M
(585) 394-9000. **$44-$109.** 170 Eastern Blvd. Jct SR 332, 5 and US 20, 0.5 mi e. Int corridors. **Pets:** Other species. Service with restrictions, supervision.

CANASTOTA

▼▼ Days Inn M ❖
(315) 697-3309. **$69-$80, 14 days notice.** N Peterboro St. I-90, exit 34 on SR 13. Int corridors. **Pets:** Other species. Service with restrictions, crate.

CLINTON

▼▼▼ The Hedges BB ❖
(315) 853-3031. **$110, 5 days notice.** 180 Sanford Ave. College St, 0.3 mi n on Elm St. Int corridors. **Pets:** Dogs only. Supervision.

COBLESKILL

▲▲▲ ▼▼▼ Best Western Inn of Cobleskill MI
(518) 234-4321. **$79-$179.** 12 Campus Dr Ext. I-88, exit 21 eastbound on SR 7, 0.8 mi e of jct SR 10; exit 22 westbound. Int corridors. **Pets:** Accepted.

COLONIE

▲▲▲ ▼▼▼ Ambassador Motor Inn M
(518) 456-8982. **$60-$109.** 1600 Central Ave. I-87, exit 2W, 0.8 mi w, 5.4 mi w on SR 5. Ext corridors. **Pets:** Small, other species. $50 deposit/pet. Designated rooms, service with restrictions, crate.

▲▲▲ ▼▼▼ Best Western Albany Airport Inn MI
(518) 458-1000. **$89-$129.** 200 Wolf Rd. I-87, exit 4, 0.3 mi se. Int corridors. **Pets:** Small. Supervision.

▲▲▲ ▼▼▼ Red Roof Inn M
(518) 459-1971. **$47-$94.** 188 Wolf Rd. I-87, exit 4, 0.3 mi e. Ext corridors. **Pets:** Small. Service with restrictions, supervision.

COOPERS PLAINS

▲▲▲ ▼ Stiles Motel M
(607) 962-5221. **$47-$62.** 9239 Victory Hwy. SR 17, exit 42, 0.3 mi s to Victory Hwy (CR 415), then 0.3 mi n. Ext corridors. **Pets:** Other species. $3 daily fee/pet. Service with restrictions, supervision.

CORNING

♦♦♦♦ Radisson Hotel Corning 🄷
(607) 962-5000. **$78-$145.** 125 Denison Pkwy E. Center; on SR 17. Int corridors. **Pets:** Other species. Designated rooms, service with restrictions, supervision.

⊠ 🛗 🖵 🍴 ⚊

CORTLAND

♦♦ Comfort Inn 🄼🄸
(607) 753-7721. **$69-$169, 3 days notice.** 2 1/2 Locust Ave. I-81, exit 11, just e. Int corridors. **Pets:** $10 one-time fee/room. Designated rooms, service with restrictions, supervision.

🆂🅰🆅🅴 🆂🄳 ⊠ 🛗 🖵 🍴

♦♦ Holiday Inn Cortland 🄼🄸
(607) 756-4431. **$89-$109.** 2 River St. I-81, exit 11. Int corridors. **Pets:** Accepted.

🄰🆂🄺 🆂🄳 ⊠ 🖵 🍴 ⚊

CUBA

♦♦♦ Cuba Coachlight Motel 🄼
(585) 968-1992. **$49-$55.** 1 N Branch Rd. US 86, exit 28, just n to N Branch Rd, then e. Int corridors. **Pets:** Large, other species. $5 daily fee/pet. Service with restrictions, crate.

🆂🄰🆅🅴 🆂🄳 ⊠ 🛗

DE WITT

♦♦♦ Econo Lodge 🄼
(315) 446-3300. **$60-$120, 3 days notice.** 3400 Erie Blvd E. I-481, exit 3W, 1.2 mi w on SR 5 W. Ext corridors. **Pets:** Small. $10 daily fee/pet. Service with restrictions, supervision.

🆂🄰🆅🅴 🆂🄳 ⊠ 🛗 🖵

DELHI

♦♦ Buena Vista Motel 🄼
(607) 746-2135. **$64-$85, 7 days notice.** 18718 State Hwy 28. Jct SR 10, 0.8 mi e. Ext corridors. **Pets:** Accepted.

🆂🄰🆅🅴 ⊠ 🛗 🖵

DIAMOND POINT

♦♦ Diamond Cove Cottages 🄲
(518) 668-5787. **$65-$190, 30 days notice.** 3648 Lake Shore Dr. I-87, exit 22, 3.3 mi n on SR 9 N. Ext corridors. **Pets:** Small. Designated rooms, service with restrictions, supervision.

🛗 🖵 ⚊ ⊠

DUNKIRK

♦♦♦♦ Best Western Dunkirk/Fredonia 🄼
(716) 366-7100. **$69-$139.** 3912 Vineyard Dr. I-90, exit 59, just w. Int corridors. **Pets:** Medium. $10 daily fee/pet. Designated rooms, service with restrictions, supervision.

🆂🄰🆅🅴 🆂🄳 ⊠ 🄲 🛗 🖵 ⚊

♦♦♦♦ Comfort Inn 🄼
(716) 672-4450. **$55-$120.** 3925 Vineyard Dr. I-90, exit 59, just w of jct SR 60. Int corridors. **Pets:** Other species. $10 daily fee/pet. Designated rooms, service with restrictions.

🆂🄰🆅🅴 🆂🄳 ⊠ 🄲 🛗 🖵

♦♦♦♦ Days Inn Dunkirk-Fredonia 🄼🄸
(716) 673-1351. **$55-$90.** 10455 Bennett Rd. I-90, exit 59, just s on SR 60. Ext/int corridors. **Pets:** Other species. Designated rooms, service with restrictions.

🆂🄰🆅🅴 🆂🄳 ⊠ 🛗 🖵 🍴

♦♦♦♦ Ramada Inn 🄼🄸
(716) 366-8350. **$60-$140.** 30 Lake Shore Dr E. Jct SR 60, 0.3 mi w on SR 5. Int corridors. **Pets:** Accepted.

🆂🄰🆅🅴 🆂🄳 ⊠ 🄲 🛗 🖵 🍴 ⚊

♦♦♦ Southshore Motor Lodge 🄴
(716) 366-2822. **$55-$125, 3 days notice.** 5040 W Lake Rd (Rt 5). Jct SR 60, 4 mi w. Ext corridors. **Pets:** Dogs only. $50 deposit/pet. Service with restrictions, supervision.

🛗 🖵 🄯

EAST HAMPTON

♦♦ Dutch Motel & Cottages 🄼
(631) 324-4550. **$68-$260, 60 days notice.** 488 Montauk Hwy. 1.3 mi e on SR 27 E (Montauk Hwy). Ext corridors. **Pets:** Small, dogs only. $10 daily fee/pet. Service with restrictions, supervision.

🛗

EAST SYRACUSE

♦♦ East Syracuse Super 8 🄼
(315) 432-5612. **Call for rates, 10 days notice.** 6620 Old Collamer Rd. I-90, exit 35 (Carrier Cir), just e on SR 298, then just n. Int corridors. **Pets:** Small. $10 one-time fee/room. Service with restrictions, supervision.

🄰🆂🄺 ⊠ 🅼 🄲 🄲 🛗

♦♦♦ Holiday Inn East-Carrier Circle 🄼🄸
(315) 437-2761. **$69-$109, 3 days notice.** 6555 Old Collamer Rd. I-90, exit 35 (Carrier Cir) to SR 298 E, then to Collamer Rd, just n. Ext/int corridors. **Pets:** Small. $25 one-time fee/room. Designated rooms, service with restrictions, supervision.

🄰🆂🄺 🆂🄳 ⊠ 🄲 🛗 🖵 🍴 ⚊

♦♦♦ Microtel Inn Syracuse 🄼
(315) 437-3500. **$32-$73.** 6608 Old Collamer Rd. I-90, exit 35 (Carrier Cir) to SR 298 E. Int corridors. **Pets:** $5 daily fee/pet. Service with restrictions, supervision.

🄰🆂🄺 🆂🄳 ⊠ 🅼 🄲 🛗

♦♦♦♦ Residence Inn By Marriott 🄰 🐾
(315) 432-4488. **$115-$142.** 6420 Yorktown Cir. I-90, exit 35 (Carrier Cir) to SR 298 E, just e to Old Collamer Rd, 0.5 mi n. Ext corridors. **Pets:** Other species. $50 one-time fee/room. Service with restrictions.

🆂🄰🆅🅴 🆂🄳 ⊠ 🅼 🄲 🛗 🖵 ⚊

ELLICOTTVILLE

ⒶⒶⒶ ▼▼▼ Jefferson Inn 🅱🅱
(716) 699-5869. **$89-$159, 30 days notice.** 3 Jefferson St. Western jct US 219 and SR 242, just n; eastern jct US 219 and 242, 0.8 mi w. Int corridors. **Pets:** Dogs only. $15 daily fee/pet. Designated rooms, no service.
[SAVE] [✕] [📶] [💻]

ELMIRA

ⒶⒶⒶ ▼▼▼ Coachman Motor Lodge 🅼
(607) 733-5526. **$70, 4 days notice.** SR 17, exit 56, 1.8 mi on SR 352 W, then 1.4 mi s. Ext corridors. **Pets:** Other species. Service with restrictions, supervision.
[SAVE] [S🔒] [📶] [💻]

FARMINGTON

ⒶⒶⒶ ▼▼▼ Budget Inn 🅼
(585) 924-5020. **$43-$70, 3 days notice.** 6001 Rt 96. I-90, exit 44, 1 mi s on SR 332, then just e. Ext corridors. **Pets:** Small, dogs only. $15 one-time fee/pet. Service with restrictions.
[SAVE] [S🔒] [✕] [📶] [💻]

FISHKILL

ⒶⒶⒶ ▼▼▼▼ MainStay Suites Fishkill 🅼 ❄
(845) 897-2800. **$95-$135.** 25 Merritt Blvd. I-84, exit 13, just n. Int corridors. **Pets:** Large, other species. $10 daily fee/room. Service with restrictions.
[SAVE] [S🔒] [✕] [📷] [✎] [📶] [💻]

ⒶⒶⒶ ▼▼▼▼ Residence Inn by Marriott 🅰
(845) 896-5210. **$199.** 14 Schuyler Blvd. I-84, exit 13, just n. Ext corridors. **Pets:** Accepted.
[SAVE] [S🔒] [✕] [🅼] [📷] [📶] [💻] [🏊]

ⒶⒶⒶ ▼▼▼ Wellesley Inn & Suites 🅼 ❄
(845) 896-4995. **$109-$129, 7 days notice.** 20 Schuyler Blvd & Rt 9. I-84, exit 13, just n. Int corridors. **Pets:** Small. Designated rooms, service with restrictions, supervision.
[SAVE] [S🔒] [✕] [🅼] [📷] [✎] [📶] [💻]

GATES

ⒶⒶⒶ ▼▼▼ Comfort Inn Central 🅼
(585) 436-4400. **$69-$94, 3 days notice.** 395 Buell Rd. I-390, exit 18B (SR 204), 0.3 mi w; opposite entrance to Rochester-Monroe County Airport. Int corridors. **Pets:** Large. $25 deposit/room. Service with restrictions, supervision.
[SAVE] [S🔒] [✕] [📷] [📶] [💻]

▼▼▼▼ Holiday Inn-Rochester Airport 🅼🅸
(585) 328-6000. **$79-$129.** 911 Brooks Ave. I-390, exit 18A (SR 204). Int corridors. **Pets:** Accepted.
[ASK] [S🔒] [✕] [📷] [📶] [💻] [🍽] [🏊]

GENEVA

▼▼ ▼▼ Motel 6-1216 🅼
(315) 789-4050. **$45-$61.** 485 Hamilton St. Jct SR 14 and US 20/SR 5, 1.8 mi w. Int corridors. **Pets:** Accepted.
[S🔒] [✕]

▼▼▼▼ Ramada Inn Geneva Lakefront 🅼🅸
(315) 789-0400. **$89-$169.** 41 Lakefront Dr. I-90, exit 42, 8 mi s on SR 14. Int corridors. **Pets:** Accepted.
[ASK] [S🔒] [✕] [✎] [📶] [💻] [🍽] [🏊]

GREAT NECK

▼▼▼▼ Inn at Great Neck 🅷
(516) 773-2000. **$259-$379.** 30 Cutter Mill Rd. Jct Middleneck Rd, just w. Int corridors. **Pets:** Small, dogs only. $250 deposit/pet. Service with restrictions, supervision.
[ASK] [S🔒] [✕] [📷] [✎] [📶] [💻] [🍽]

GREECE

ⒶⒶⒶ ▼▼▼▼ Comfort Inn-West 🅼
(585) 621-5700. **$54-$84, 3 days notice.** 1501 W Ridge Rd. Jct SR 390 and 104 (Ridge Rd), 0.5 mi e. Int corridors. **Pets:** Large, other species. $10 deposit/room, $10 one-time fee/room. Service with restrictions.
[SAVE] [S🔒] [✕] [📶] [💻]

▼▼▼▼ Hampton Inn-Rochester North 🅼 ❄
(585) 663-6070. **$69-$104.** 500 Center Place Dr. I-390, exit Ridge Road E, just e on SR 104, then just n on Buckman Rd. Int corridors. **Pets:** Small, other species. Service with restrictions, supervision.
[SAVE] [S🔒] [✕] [🅼] [✎] [📶] [💻]

ⒶⒶⒶ ▼▼▼▼ Residence Inn by Marriott-West 🅼
(585) 865-2090. **$99-$210.** 500 Paddy Creek Cir. I-390, exit 24A, just e on SR 104 (Ridge Rd), then just s on Hoover Dr, then just w. Int corridors. **Pets:** Other species. $10 daily fee/pet, $150 one-time fee/pet. Service with restrictions.
[SAVE] [S🔒] [✕] [✎] [📶] [💻] [🏊]

ⒶⒶⒶ ▼▼▼▼ Wellesley Inn-Rochester/North 🅼
(585) 621-2060. **$60-$110.** 1635 W Ridge Rd. I-390, exit 24A, just e on SR 104. Int corridors. **Pets:** Other species. $10 daily fee/room. Service with restrictions, supervision.
[SAVE] [S🔒] [✕] [🅼] [📷] [✎] [📶] [💻]

HAMLIN

▼▼ ▼▼ Sandy Creek Manor House 🅱🅱 ❄
(585) 964-7528. **$70-$95.** 1960 Redman Rd. 2.3 mi w of SR 19 on SR 18, 0.3 mi n. Int corridors. **Pets:** Other species. $5 daily fee/pet. Crate.
[S🔒] [✕] [📷]

HANCOCK

ⒶⒶⒶ ▼▼▼ Smith's Colonial Motel 🅼
(607) 637-2989. **$58-$95.** 23085 State Hwy 97. SR 17, exit 87; SR 87A, to SR 97 S. Ext corridors. **Pets:** $5 daily fee/pet. No service, supervision.
[SAVE] [✕]

HAUPPAUGE

Wyndham Wind Watch Hotel & Hamlet Golf Club H
(631) 232-9800. **$159-$244.** 1717 Vanderbilt Motor Pkwy. I-495, exit 57, just n to Motor Pkwy, 1.3 mi ne. Int corridors. **Pets:** Small. $50 one-time fee/room. Designated rooms, no service, supervision.

[SAVE] [X] [&M] [⌂] [▪] [▯] [¶] [≈] [⊠]

HENRIETTA

Econo Lodge-Rochester South M
(585) 427-2700. **$49-$82, 3 days notice.** 940 Jefferson Rd. I-390, exit 14A, just w on SR 252 (Jefferson Rd). Int corridors. **Pets:** Small, other species. Designated rooms, service with restrictions, supervision.

[SAVE] [Sᴅ] [X] [▪] [▯]

Microtel-Rochester M
(585) 334-3400. **$39-$56.** 905 Lehigh Station Rd. I-390, exit 12 northbound; exit 12A southbound, just n on SR 253; jct SR 15, 0.3 mi e on SR 253. Int corridors. **Pets:** Other species. Service with restrictions, supervision.

[ASK] [Sᴅ] [X] [▪]

Ramada Inn Rochester M
(585) 475-9190. **$69-$129.** 800 Jefferson Rd. I-390, exit 14, 0.5 mi w on SR 252 (Jefferson Rd). Int corridors. **Pets:** Medium, other species. Service with restrictions, supervision.

[SAVE] [Sᴅ] [X] [▪] [▯] [¶]

Red Roof Inn-Henrietta M
(585) 359-1100. **$46-$72.** 4820 W Henrietta Rd. I-90, exit 46; jct SR 253, just s on SR 15. Ext corridors. **Pets:** Accepted.

[SAVE] [X] [▪]

Residence Inn by Marriott A
(585) 272-8850. **$89.** 1300 Jefferson Rd. I-390, exit 14A, 0.5 mi e. Ext corridors. **Pets:** Accepted.

[SAVE] [Sᴅ] [X] [⌂] [▪] [▯] [≈]

Rochester/Henrietta Homewood Suites M
(585) 334-9150. **$109-$129.** 2095 Hylan Dr. I-390, exit 13, just e. Int corridors. **Pets:** Other species. $75 one-time fee/room. Service with restrictions.

[SAVE] [Sᴅ] [X] [&M] [⌂] [▪] [▯] [≈]

Super 8 Motel M
(585) 359-1630. **$49-$64.** 1000 Lehigh Station Rd. I-390, exit 12 northbound, just n; exit 12A southbound; jct SR 15, 0.3 mi e on SR 253. Int corridors. **Pets:** Other species. Service with restrictions, crate.

[SAVE] [Sᴅ] [X] [▪]

HERKIMER

Herkimer Motel M
(315) 866-0490. **$68-$88.** 100 Marginal Rd. Jct SR 28 and I-90 (New York Thruway), exit 30. Ext/int corridors. **Pets:** Service with restrictions, supervision.

[SAVE] [Sᴅ] [X] [☇] [▪] [▯] [≈]

Inn Towne Motel M
(315) 866-1101. **$32-$68.** 227 N Washington St. I-90 (New York Thruway), exit 30, 1 mi n on SR 28, just w. Ext corridors. **Pets:** Very small. $10 daily fee/pet. Service with restrictions.

[SAVE] [Sᴅ] [X] [▪]

HORNELL

Econo Lodge M
(607) 324-0800. **$49-$69.** 7462 Seneca Rd. Jct I-86 and SR 36, exit 34, just s to SR 21, just e to Seneca Rd, just s to entrance. Ext/int corridors. **Pets:** Other species. $5 daily fee/room. Designated rooms, service with restrictions, supervision.

[SAVE] [Sᴅ] [▪] [▯] [¶]

HORSEHEADS

Motel 6 Horseheads–1217 M
(607) 739-2525. **$43-$65.** 4133 Rt 17. Jct SR 17 and 13, south side of SR 17, 0.5 mi w. Int corridors. **Pets:** Accepted.

[Sᴅ] [X] [&M] [☇] [▪]

HUNTER

Hunter Inn CI
(518) 263-3777. **$79-$235, 14 days notice.** Rt 23A. SR 23A. Int corridors. **Pets:** Accepted.

[X]

HUNTINGTON STATION

Huntington Country Inn M
(631) 421-3900. **$110-$120.** 270 W Jericho Tpke. Jct SR 110, just w on SR 25 (Jericho Tpke). Ext/int corridors. **Pets:** Accepted.

[SAVE] [Sᴅ] [X] [▪] [▯] [≈]

ITHACA

Holiday Inn-Executive Tower M
(607) 272-1000. **$81-$99, 30 days notice.** 222 S Cayuga St. Just n from SR 96B. Int corridors. **Pets:** Other species. $15 one-time fee/room. Designated rooms, service with restrictions, supervision.

[SAVE] [Sᴅ] [X] [⌂] [▪] [▯] [¶] [≈]

Meadow Court Inn M
(607) 273-3885. **$60-$195.** 529 S Meadow St. 1.5 mi s on SR 13 and 96. Ext/int corridors. **Pets:** $10 daily fee/pet. Service with restrictions.

[SAVE] [X] [&M] [▪] [¶]

JAMESTOWN

Comfort Inn M
(716) 664-5920. **$69-$169.** 2800 N Main St Extension. SR 17, exit 12 (SR 60). Int corridors. **Pets:** Accepted.

[SAVE] [Sᴅ] [X] [▪] [▯]

JOHNSON CITY

(AAA) ▼▼▼ Best Western of Johnson City M
(607) 729-9194. **$55-$65.** 569 Harry L Dr. SR 17, exit 70N, 0.3 mi n; opposite Oakdale Mall. Int corridors. **Pets:** Accepted.
⟦SAVE⟧ ⟦S🐾⟧ ⟦✕⟧ ⟦🛏⟧ ⟦💻⟧

(AAA) ▼▼ Red Roof Inn-Binghamton M
(607) 729-8940. **$39-$66.** 590 Fairview St. SR 17, exit 70N, 0.3 mi n, just n on Reynolds Rd. Ext corridors. **Pets:** Accepted.
⟦SAVE⟧ ⟦✕⟧ ⟦🛏⟧

JOHNSTOWN

▼▼▼ Holiday Inn M
(518) 762-4686. **$76-$135.** 308 N Comrie Ave. Jct SR 30A and 29 E, 1.3 mi n. Ext/int corridors. **Pets:** Accepted.
⟦ASK⟧ ⟦S🐾⟧ ⟦✕⟧ ⟦🐾M⟧ ⟦🐾⟧ ⟦🛏⟧ ⟦💻⟧ ⟦🍴⟧ ⟦🏊⟧

KINGSTON

(AAA) ▼▼▼ Holiday Inn M
(845) 338-0400. **$129-$179, 3 days notice.** 503 Washington Ave. I-87, exit 19, just e of traffic circle. Int corridors. **Pets:** Accepted.
⟦SAVE⟧ ⟦S🐾⟧ ⟦✕⟧ ⟦🛏⟧ ⟦💻⟧ ⟦🍴⟧ ⟦🏊⟧

LAKE GEORGE

▼▼ Balmoral Motel M
(518) 668-2673. **$42-$195, 14 days notice.** 444 Canada St. Jct SR 9 and 9 N, 0.3 mi n on SR 9. Ext corridors. **Pets:** Small. $15 daily fee/pet. Designated rooms, service with restrictions, supervision.
⟦ASK⟧ ⟦S🐾⟧ ⟦✕⟧ ⟦🛏⟧ ⟦💻⟧ ⟦🏊⟧

▼▼ Green Haven M
(518) 668-2489. **$44-$109, 10 days notice.** 3136 Lake Shore Dr. I-87, exit 22, 0.8 mi n, 1.8 mi n on SR 9 N. Ext corridors. **Pets:** Large, dogs only. $10 one-time fee/pet. Service with restrictions, supervision.
⟦✕⟧ ⟦🛏⟧ ⟦💻⟧ ⟦🏊⟧

(AAA) ▼▼▼ Travelodge of Lake George M 🐾
(518) 668-5421. **$49-$134, 3 days notice.** 48 Canada St. I-87, exit 21, just s on US 9. Ext/int corridors. **Pets:** Small, other species. $15 daily fee/pet. Designated rooms, service with restrictions, supervision.
⟦SAVE⟧ ⟦S🐾⟧ ⟦✕⟧ ⟦🍴⟧

LAKE LUZERNE

(AAA) ▼▼ Luzerne Court M
(518) 696-2734. **$85-$180, 14 days notice.** 508 Lake Ave. I-87, exit 21, 8.7 mi sw on SR 9 N, 1.1 mi ne. Ext corridors. **Pets:** Dogs only. $10 one-time fee/pet. Service with restrictions, supervision.
⟦SAVE⟧ ⟦🛏⟧ ⟦🍴⟧ ⟦🏊⟧ ⟦🗌⟧

LAKE PLACID

(AAA) ▼▼▼ Art Devlin's Olympic Motor Inn, Inc M
(518) 523-3700. **$48-$128, 14 days notice.** 350 Main St. 0.5 mi e on SR 86. Ext corridors. **Pets:** Dogs only. Supervision.
⟦SAVE⟧ ⟦✕⟧ ⟦🛏⟧ ⟦🏊⟧

(AAA) ▼▼▼ Best Western Golden Arrow Hotel M 🐾
(518) 523-3353. **$89-$189, 7 days notice.** 150 Main St. Center. Int corridors. **Pets:** Medium. $25 one-time fee/room. Designated rooms, service with restrictions, supervision.
⟦SAVE⟧ ⟦✕⟧ ⟦🐾⟧ ⟦🛏⟧ ⟦💻⟧ ⟦🍴⟧ ⟦🏊⟧ ⟦🗌⟧

(AAA) ▼▼▼ Edge of the Lake Motel M
(518) 523-9430. **$49-$109.** 56 Saranac Ave. 0.5 mi w on SR 86. Ext/int corridors. **Pets:** Accepted.
⟦SAVE⟧ ⟦🛏⟧ ⟦💻⟧ ⟦🏊⟧ ⟦🗌⟧

▼▼▼ Hilton Lake Placid Resort 🅷
(518) 523-4411. **$79-$249, 7 days notice.** 1 Mirror Lake Dr. 0.3 mi w on SR 86. Int corridors. **Pets:** Accepted.
⟦SAVE⟧ ⟦✕⟧ ⟦🐾M⟧ ⟦🐾⟧ ⟦🐾⟧ ⟦🛏⟧ ⟦💻⟧ ⟦🍴⟧ ⟦🏊⟧

(AAA) ▼▼▼ Howard Johnson Resort Inn M
(518) 523-9555. **$80-$180.** 90 Saranac Ave. 0.5 mi w on SR 86. Ext/int corridors. **Pets:** Other species. Service with restrictions, supervision.
⟦SAVE⟧ ⟦S🐾⟧ ⟦✕⟧ ⟦🐾⟧ ⟦🛏⟧ ⟦💻⟧ ⟦🍴⟧ ⟦🏊⟧ ⟦🗌⟧

(AAA) ▼▼▼ Lake Placid Ramada Inn M
(518) 523-2587. **$69-$140, 3 days notice.** 8-12 Saranac Ave. 0.3 mi w on SR 86. Ext/int corridors. **Pets:** Other species. Service with restrictions, crate.
⟦SAVE⟧ ⟦S🐾⟧ ⟦✕⟧ ⟦🐾⟧ ⟦🛏⟧ ⟦💻⟧ ⟦🍴⟧ ⟦🏊⟧

▼▼▼ Lake Placid Resort Hotel & Golf Club/ Holiday Inn M
(518) 523-2556. **$69-$229, 30 days notice.** 1 Olympic Dr. Center. Int corridors. **Pets:** Other species. $10 daily fee/room. Designated rooms, service with restrictions, supervision.
⟦✕⟧ ⟦🐾⟧ ⟦🛏⟧ ⟦💻⟧ ⟦🍴⟧ ⟦🏊⟧ ⟦🗌⟧

(AAA) ▼▼ Swiss Acres Inn and The Chalet Restaurant M
(518) 523-3040. **$35-$179, 7 days notice.** 189 Saranac Ave. 1 mi w on SR 86. Ext/int corridors. **Pets:** $50 deposit/pet, $20 one-time fee/room. Service with restrictions, supervision.
⟦SAVE⟧ ⟦S🐾⟧ ⟦✕⟧ ⟦🛏⟧ ⟦💻⟧ ⟦🍴⟧ ⟦🏊⟧

LANSING

▼▼ The Clarion University Hotel & Conference Center M
(607) 257-2000. **$89-$219, 3 days notice.** N of Ithaca on SR 13, exit Triphammer Rd, just s. Int corridors. **Pets:** Large, other species. $20 one-time fee/room. Designated rooms, service with restrictions, supervision.
⟦SAVE⟧ ⟦S🐾⟧ ⟦✕⟧ ⟦🛏⟧ ⟦💻⟧ ⟦🍴⟧ ⟦🏊⟧

(AAA) ▼▼ Econo Lodge 🅼
(607) 257-1400. **$56-$150, 14 days notice.** 3.5 mi n on SR 13, exit Triphammer Rd; adjoining Cayuga Mall. Int corridors. **Pets:** Small. $10 daily fee/pet. Designated rooms, service with restrictions, supervision.
[SAVE] [S₆] [✕] [❚] [💻]

▼▼ Ramada Inn-Airport 🅼
(607) 257-3100. **$89-$219, 3 days notice.** 2310 N Triphammer Rd. Jct SR 13 and 34, 3.5 mi n on SR 13, exit Triphammer Rd, just w. Int corridors. **Pets:** Other species. $20 one-time fee/room. Designated rooms, service with restrictions, supervision.
[ASK] [S₆] [✕] [✑] [❚] [💻] [🍴] [🌊]

LATHAM

(AAA) ▼▼▼ Century House Restaurant & Hotel 🅼
(518) 785-0931. **$115-$225.** 997 New Loudon Rd. I-87, exit 7 (SR 7), just e; 0.5 mi n on US 9 (New Loudon Rd). Int corridors. **Pets:** Accepted.
[SAVE] [✕] [❚] [💻] [🍴] [🌊] [🗙]

▼▼▼ Hampton Inn-Latham 🅼
(518) 785-0000. **$109-$129.** I-87, exit 7 (SR 7), just n on US 9. Int corridors. **Pets:** Designated rooms, service with restrictions, supervision.
[SAVE] [S₆] [✕] [♿M] [❚] [💻] [🌊]

(AAA) ▼▼▼ Microtel Inn 🅼
(518) 782-9161. **$44-$89, 3 days notice.** 7 Rensselaer Ave. I-87, exit 6, just w. Int corridors. **Pets:** Accepted.
[SAVE] [S₆] [✕] [♿M] [✑] [❚] [💻]

(AAA) ▼▼▼ Residence Inn by Marriott Albany Airport 🅰
(518) 783-0600. **$113-$161.** 1 Residence Inn Dr. I-87, exit 6, 2 mi w on SR 7. Ext corridors. **Pets:** Other species. $250 deposit/room, $50 one-time fee/room. Service with restrictions.
[SAVE] [S₆] [✕] [✑] [❚] [💻] [🌊]

LIBERTY

(AAA) ▼▼▼ Days Inn 🅼
(845) 292-7600. **$62-$110.** 52 Sullivan Ave. SR 17, exit 100, 0.3 mi e. Int corridors. **Pets:** Other species. $100 deposit/room. Designated rooms, service with restrictions, supervision.
[SAVE] [S₆] [✕] [❚] [🌊]

LITTLE FALLS

(AAA) ▼▼▼ Best Western Little Falls Motor Inn 🅼
(315) 823-4954. **$60-$90.** 20 Albany St. On SR 5 and 167. Int corridors. **Pets:** Other species. $10 deposit/pet. Service with restrictions.
[SAVE] [S₆] [✕] [💻] [🍴]

LIVERPOOL

▼▼▼▼ Holiday Inn Syracuse Airport 🅼
(315) 457-1122. **$92-$121.** 441 Electronics Pkwy. I-90, exit 37 (Electronics Pkwy); I-81, exit 25 (7th North St), 1.3 mi w. Int corridors. **Pets:** Designated rooms.
[ASK] [S₆] [✕] [♿M] [✑] [✑] [❚] [💻] [🍴] [🌊]

▼▼▼ Homewood Suites 🅼
(315) 451-3800. **$122-$183.** 275 Elwood Davis Rd. I-81, exit 25 (7th North St), 1 mi w; I-90, exit 36. Int corridors. **Pets:** Accepted.
[SAVE] [S₆] [✕] [❚] [💻] [🌊]

(AAA) ▼▼▼ Knights Inn 🅼 🐾
(315) 453-6330. **$44-$99.** 430 Electronics Pkwy. I-90, exit 37 (Electronics Pkwy), just s. Ext corridors. **Pets:** Medium. $8 daily fee/pet. Service with restrictions, supervision.
[SAVE] [S₆] [✕] [❚]

LONG LAKE

(AAA) ▼▼▼ Journey's End Cottages 🅲
(518) 624-5381. **$550-$700 (weekly), 60 days notice.** Deerland Rd, Rt 30. SR 30 and 28 N, 1 mi s. Ext corridors. **Pets:** Medium. $5 one-time fee/pet. Service with restrictions, supervision.
[SAVE] [❚] [💻] [🗙] [🎬] [🗙]

▼▼ Long View Lodge 🅲🅸
(518) 624-2862. **$55-$85, 7 days notice.** Rt 28 N & 30. SR 30 and 28 N, 3 mi s. Int corridors. **Pets:** Accepted.
[✕] [❚] [🍴] [🗙] [🎬]

LOWMAN

(AAA) ▼▼▼ Red Jacket Motor Inn 🅼🅸
(607) 734-1616. **$35-$62, 3 days notice.** Rt 17. SR 17, just e from CR 8; between MM 195 and 196. Ext corridors. **Pets:** Dogs only. $10 daily fee/pet. Service with restrictions, supervision.
[SAVE] [S₆] [✕] [✑] [❚] [🌊]

MALONE

(AAA) ▼▼▼ Four Seasons Motel 🅼
(518) 483-3490. **$45-$69, 3 days notice.** 236 W Main St. 1 mi w on SR 11. Ext corridors. **Pets:** Large, other species. Service with restrictions, supervision.
[SAVE] [S₆] [✕] [❚] [💻] [🌊]

▼▼ Sunset Inn 🅼
(518) 483-3367. **$55-$60.** 3899 US 11. 1.5 mi e on SR 11. Ext corridors. **Pets:** Supervision.
[ASK] [S₆] [✕] [❚] [💻] [🌊]

(AAA) ▼▼▼ Super 8 Motel at Jons 🅼
(518) 483-8123. **$60-$71.** Finney Blvd, Rt 30. On SR 30; just s of jct US 11. Int corridors. **Pets:** Medium. Service with restrictions, supervision.
[SAVE] [S₆] [✕] [♿M] [❚]

MASSENA

AAA **WWWW** Econo Lodge-Meadow View Motel **MI**
(315) 764-0246. **$73-$99.** 15054 SR 37. 2.7 mi sw on SR 37 W. Ext/int corridors. **Pets:** Small. $5 daily fee/pet. Designated rooms, service with restrictions.
[SAVE] [S6] [X] [8] [💻] [¶]

MCGRAW

AAA **WW** Cortland Days Inn **M**
(607) 753-7594. **$59-$125, 30 days notice.** 3775 US Rt 11. I-81, exit 10 (McGraw/Cortland). Int corridors. **Pets:** Small, dogs only. $10 daily fee/pet. Designated rooms, service with restrictions, supervision.
[SAVE] [S6] [X]

MIDDLETOWN

WW Super 8 Motel **M**
(845) 692-5828. **$75-$135, 30 days notice.** 563 Rt 211 E. I-84, exit 4W, 0.5 mi; jct SR 17, exit 120, 0.3 mi e. Int corridors. **Pets:** Accepted.
[ASK] [X] [8]

MONTOUR FALLS

AAA **W** Relax Inn **M**
(607) 535-7183. **$36-$89, 3 days notice.** 100 Clawson Blvd. Jct SR 14 and 224. Ext corridors. **Pets:** Dogs only. $10 daily fee/pet. Designated rooms, service with restrictions, supervision.
[SAVE] [S6] [X] [8] [💻]

NEW HAMPTON

WW Days Inn **M**
(845) 374-2411. **$49-$109.** Rt 17M. I-84, exit 3E, on US 6 and SR 17 W; 0.8 mi s of I-84; SR 17 W, exit 123, 3.8 mi w. Ext/int corridors. **Pets:** Accepted.
[SAVE] [S6] [X] [8] [≈]

NEW HARTFORD

WWW Holiday Inn Utica **MI**
(315) 797-2131. **$99-$159.** 1777 Burrstone Rd. I-90 (New York Thruway), exit 31, 4.5 mi w on SR 5 W, exit on Burrstone Rd, 1 mi nw. Int corridors. **Pets:** Large, other species. Service with restrictions, crate.
[ASK] [S6] [X] [🖉] [8] [💻] [¶] [≈]

NEW YORK METROPOLITAN AREA

JAMAICA

AAA **WWWW** Best Western Carlton House JFK Airport **H**
(718) 322-8700. **$129.** 138-10 135th Ave. In Jamaica; Belt Pkwy, exit 20 (Rockaway Blvd), 0.6 mi to 150th, just n to N Conduit, 0.4 mi to 140th, just n, then just w. Int corridors. **Pets:** Accepted.
[SAVE] [S6] [X] [💻] [¶]

MOUNT KISCO

AAA **WWW** Holiday Inn **MI**
(914) 241-2600. **$170-$190.** 1 Holiday Inn Dr. Saw Mill River Pkwy, exit 37, just e. Int corridors. **Pets:** $25 daily fee/room. Service with restrictions, supervision.
[SAVE] [S6] [X] [&M] [🖉] [8] [💻] [¶] [≈]

NANUET

WWW Candlewood Suites **M**
(845) 371-4445. **$79-$199.** 20 Overlook Blvd. I-287, exit 14, just n. Int corridors. **Pets:** Accepted.
[ASK] [S6] [X] [&] [8] [💻]

AAA **WW** Days Inn Nanuet **M** ❁
(845) 623-4567. **$79-$99.** 367 Rt 59. I-287/87, exit 14, just w. Ext/int corridors. **Pets:** Medium, other species. $8 daily fee/pet. Service with restrictions, crate.
[SAVE] [S6] [X] [8] [💻] [≈]

NEW YORK

WWW **WWW** The Benjamin Hotel **H**
(212) 715-2500. **$440-$585.** 125 E 50th St. Between Lexington and 3rd aves. Int corridors. **Pets:** Accepted.
[X] [🖉] [8] [💻] [¶]

WWW **WWW** The Carlyle **H**
(212) 744-1600. **$495-$875.** 35 E 76th St. At Madison Ave. Int corridors. **Pets:** Accepted.
[🖉] [&] [8] [¶]

WWWW Crowne Plaza at the United Nations **H**
(212) 986-8800. **$199-$589.** 304 E 42nd St. Between 1st and 2nd aves. Int corridors. **Pets:** Accepted.
[ASK] [S6] [X] [🖉] [&] [💻] [¶]

WWWW Crowne Plaza Manhattan **H**
(212) 977-4000. **$160-$500.** 1605 Broadway. 49th and Broadway. Int corridors. **Pets:** Small. $300 deposit/room. Service with restrictions, crate.
[ASK] [S6] [X] [&M] [🖉] [&] [8] [💻] [¶] [≈]

WW Eastgate Tower Hotel **H**
(212) 687-8000. **$290-$389.** 222 E 39th St. Between 2nd and 3rd aves. Int corridors. **Pets:** Other species. $250 deposit/pet. Service with restrictions, supervision.
[X] [&M] [🖉] [&] [8] [💻] [¶]

WWWW Four Seasons Hotel, New York **H** ❁
(212) 758-5700. **$625-$3025.** 57 E 57th St. Between Park and Madison. Int corridors. **Pets:** Very small. Service with restrictions, supervision.
[X] [&M] [🖉] [¶]

▼▼▼ Hilton New York 🄷
(212) 261-5870. **$209-$590.** 1335 Avenue of the Americas. Between 53rd and 54th sts. Int corridors. **Pets:** Small. Designated rooms, service with restrictions, supervision.

`SAVE` 🔊 ✕ 🅰 🎬 📺 🍽

▼▼▼ Hilton Times Square 🄷
(212) 840-8222. **$199-$499.** 234 W 42nd St. Between 7th and 8th sts. Int corridors. **Pets:** Accepted.

`SAVE` 🔊 ✕ 🅰 🎬 📺 🍽

▼▼▼ The Holiday Inn Martinique on Broadway 🄼🄸
(212) 736-3800. **$209-$399.** 49 W 32nd St. Corner of Broadway and 32nd St. Int corridors. **Pets:** Accepted.

✕ 🅼 🅰 🎬 📺 🍽

▼▼▼ Holiday Inn Wall Street Hotel 🄷 ☙
(212) 232-7700. **$159-$369.** 15 Gold St. Corner of Gold and Platt sts. Int corridors. **Pets:** $25 one-time fee/pet. Service with restrictions.

`ASK` 🔊 ✕ 🅼 🅰 🎬 📺 🍽

▼▼ ▼▼ Hotel Plaza Athenee 🄷 ☙
(212) 734-9100. **$515-$555.** 37 E 64th St. Between Madison and Park aves. Int corridors. **Pets:** Small.

✕ 📺 🍽

▼▼ ▼▼ Inter-Continental Central Park South New York 🄷
(212) 757-1900. **$265-$615.** 112 Central Park S. Between 6th (Ave of the Americas) and 7th aves. Int corridors. **Pets:** Accepted.

✕ 🅰 🍽

▼▼ ▼▼ Le Parker Meridien New York 🄷 ☙
(212) 245-5000. **$410-$630.** 118 W 57th St. Between 6th and 7th aves; vehicle entrance on 56th St. Int corridors. **Pets:** Other species. Service with restrictions, crate.

`ASK` ✕ 🅰 📺 🍽 🏊

▼▼ ▼▼ The Lowell Hotel 🄷
(212) 838-1400. **Call for rates.** 28 E 63rd St. Between Park and Madison aves. Int corridors. **Pets:** Accepted.

🅰 📺 📺 🍽

▼▼ ▼▼ The Mayflower Hotel On The Park 🄷
(212) 265-0060. **$230-$270.** 15 Central Park W. At 61st St. Int corridors. **Pets:** Accepted.

`SAVE` 🔊 ✕ 🅰 📺 🍽

▼▼ ▼▼ The Metropolitan 🄷 ☙
(212) 752-7000. **$169-$250.** 569 Lexington Ave. At E 51st St. Int corridors. **Pets:** Large. Service with restrictions.

`ASK` 🔊 ✕ 🅼 🅰 🎬 🍽

▼▼ ▼▼ Millennium Broadway 🄷 ☙
(212) 768-4400. **$220-$355.** 145 W 44th St. Between 6th and 7th aves. Int corridors. **Pets:** Large, other species. Service with restrictions.

`ASK` 🔊 ✕ 🅼 🅰 🎬 📺 🍽

▼▼ ▼▼ The Muse 🄷 ☙
(212) 485-2400. **$250-$440.** 130 W 46th St. Exit Between 6th and 7th aves. Int corridors. **Pets:** Other species. Service with restrictions.

`ASK` 🔊 ✕ 🎬 📺 📺 🍽

🄰🄰🄰 ▼▼ ▼▼ New York Marriott Marquis 🄷
(212) 398-1900. **$275-$555.** 1535 Broadway. Between 45th and 46th sts; motor entrance on 46th St. Int corridors. **Pets:** Accepted.

`SAVE` ✕ 🅰 🎬 📺 📺 🍽

🄰🄰🄰 ▼▼ ▼▼ The New York Palace 🄷
(212) 888-7000. **$475-$710.** 455 Madison Ave. Between 50th and 51st. Int corridors. **Pets:** Very small, other species. Service with restrictions, crate.

`SAVE` ✕ 🅼 🅰 🎬 📺 📺 🍽

🄰🄰🄰 ▼▼ ▼▼ Novotel New York 🄷
(212) 315-0100. **$199-$279.** 226 W 52nd St. At Broadway; motor access on 52nd. Int corridors. **Pets:** Medium. Service with restrictions, crate.

`SAVE` 🔊 ✕ 🅰 📺 🍽

🄰🄰🄰 ▼▼ ▼▼ The Peninsula New York 🄷 ☙
(212) 956-2888. **$560-$780.** 700 5th Ave. At 55th St. Int corridors. **Pets:** Very small, dogs only.

`SAVE` ✕ 🅰 🎬 📺 🍽 🏊

▼▼ ▼▼ The Pierre New York–A Four Seasons Hotel 🄷
(212) 838-8000. **$445-$945.** 2 E 61st St. At 5th Ave. **Pets:** Accepted.

✕ 🅼 🅰 🎬 📺 🍽

▼▼ ▼▼ Plaza Fifty Hotel 🄷
(212) 751-5710. **$229-$244.** 155 E 50th St. Between 3rd and Lexington aves. Int corridors. **Pets:** Small. Service with restrictions.

✕ 🅰 📺 📺

▼▼ ▼▼ The Regency Hotel 🄷 ☙
(212) 759-4100. **$180-$1300.** 540 Park Ave. At 61st. Int corridors. **Pets:** Other species. Service with restrictions, supervision.

✕ 🅼 🅰 🎬 📺 📺 🍽

🄰🄰🄰 ▼▼ ▼▼ Renaissance New York Hotel Times Square 🄷
(212) 765-7676. **$225-$450.** Two Times Sq, 7th Ave at W 48th St. Broadway and 7th Ave; auto access from 7th Ave, s of W 48th St. Int corridors. **Pets:** Accepted.

`SAVE` ✕ 🅰 📺 🍽

🄰🄰🄰 ▼▼ ▼▼ The Roosevelt Hotel 🄷
(212) 661-9600. **$279-$369.** 45 E 45th St. Between Madison and Vanderbilt aves. Int corridors. **Pets:** Small. Service with restrictions, supervision.

`SAVE` 🔊 ✕ 🅰 🎬 📺 📺 🍽

▼▼▼ The Shoreham Hotel 🅷 ❖
(212) 247-6700. **$279-$369.** 33 W 55th St. Between 5th and 6th aves. Int corridors. **Pets:** Other species. Designated rooms, service with restrictions, supervision.
(ASK) (S/D) (X) (&M) (&*) (🖬) (TI)

▼▼▼ Surrey Hotel 🅷
(212) 288-3700. **$284-$438.** 20 E 76th. 76th and Madison. Int corridors. **Pets:** Other species. Supervision.
(X) (&) (🖬) (🖵) (TI)

▼▼▼ Swissotel New York-The Drake 🅷
(212) 421-0900. **$575-$695.** 440 Park Ave. At 56th St; between Park and Madison aves. Int corridors. **Pets:** Accepted.
(X) (&) (&*) (🖬) (🖵) (TI)

PEEKSKILL

🔺 ▼▼ Peekskill Inn 🅼�ℹ
(914) 739-1500. **$111-$121.** 634 Main St. Jct SR 9 and 6, e to top of Main St. Ext corridors. **Pets:** Small. Service with restrictions, crate.
(SAVE) (S/D) (X) (🖬) (TI)

SUFFERN

🔺 ▼▼ Wellesley Inn 🅼
(845) 368-1900. **$99.** 17 N Airmont Rd. I-87, exit 14B, just s. Int corridors. **Pets:** Accepted.
(SAVE) (S/D) (X) (&M) (&) (&*) (🖬) (🖵)

TARRYTOWN

🔺 ▼▼▼ Hilton of Tarrytown 🅼ℹ
(914) 631-5700. **$139-$269.** 455 S Broadway. I-287/87, exit 9 (US 9 S). Int corridors. **Pets:** Medium. $100 deposit/room. Designated rooms, service with restrictions, supervision.
(SAVE) (S/D) (X) (&) (🖬) (🖵) (TI) (🖚) (X)

WHITE PLAINS

🔺 ▼▼▼ Renaissance Westchester Hotel 🅷
(914) 694-5400. **$109-$235.** 80 W Red Oak Ln. I-287, exit 9, left to Kenilworth Rd, left to Westchester Ave, then 0.5 mi to Red Oak Ln, follow signs. Int corridors. **Pets:** Accepted.
(SAVE) (X) (&M) (&) (🖬) (🖵) (TI) (🖚) (X)

🔺 ▼▼▼ Summerfield Suites By Wyndham-Westchester 🅼 ❖
(914) 251-9700. **$149-$259.** 101 Corporate Park Dr. I-287, exit 9A (Westchester Ave), 0.6 mi e, then n, continue through next light. Int corridors. **Pets:** Medium, other species. $10 daily fee/room, $150 one-time fee/room. Service with restrictions, crate.
(SAVE) (X) (&) (&*) (🖬) (🖵) (🖚)

❖ **END METROPOLITAN AREA** ❖

NIAGARA FALLS METROPOLITAN AREA

NEWFANE

▼ **Lake Ontario Motel** **M**
(716) 778-5004. **$49-$65, 7 days notice.** 3330 Lockport-Olcott Rd. 2.5 mi n of jct SR 104 on SR 78. Int corridors.
Pets: Other species. $5 daily fee/room. Supervision.
(A$K) (X) (☷)

NIAGARA FALLS

(AAA) **▼▼▼** **Best Western Summit Inn** **M**
(716) 297-5050. **$69-$139.** 9500 Niagara Falls Blvd. I-190, exit 22, 2.1 mi e on US 62 S. Int corridors. **Pets:** Medium, dogs only. $50 deposit/room, $8 daily fee/pet. Designated rooms, supervision.
(SAVE) (S☷) (X) (⫴) (⇌)

(AAA) **▼▼** **Howard Johnson Inn at the**
Falls **H** ❧
(716) 285-5261. **$55-$165.** 454 Main St. I-119 N, exit 21, 2 mi e on Robert Moses Pkwy (1st exit), just n to Rainbow Blvd, then just s. Int corridors. **Pets:** Medium, other species. $10 daily fee/pet. Designated rooms, service with restrictions, crate.
(SAVE) (S☷) (X) (☷M) (☷) (☐) (⇌)

(AAA) **▼▼** **Inn on the River** **M** ❧
(716) 283-7612. **$45-$149, 3 days notice.** 7001 Buffalo Ave. I-190, exit 21, just s on SR 384. Int corridors.
Pets: Small. $25 deposit/pet, $10 one-time fee/pet. Designated rooms, service with restrictions, supervision.
(SAVE) (S☷) (X) (☷) (⫴) (⇌)

▼▼ **Quality Hotel and Suites "At the Falls"** **M**
(716) 282-1212. **$69-$299.** 240 Rainbow Blvd. Downtown; adjoining Rainbow Shopping Center. Int corridors.
Pets: $20 daily fee/room. Service with restrictions, supervision.
(SAVE) (S☷) (X) (⟳) (☷) (☐) (⫴) (⇌)

(AAA) **▼▼** **Thriftlodge** **M**
(716) 297-2660. **$39-$179.** 9401 Niagara Falls Blvd. I-190, exit 22, 1.8 mi e on US 625. Ext corridors. **Pets:** Accepted.
(SAVE) (S☷) (X) (☷) (⇌)

(AAA) **▼** **Travelers Budget Inn** **M**
(716) 297-3228. **$35-$109, 3 days notice.** 9001 Niagara Falls Blvd. I-190, exit 22, 1.7 mi e on US 62 S. Ext corridors. **Pets:** Accepted.
(SAVE) (S☷) (X) (☷)

(AAA) **▼** **Travelodge Hotel Fallsview** **H**
(716) 285-9321. **$39-$169, 3 days notice.** 201 Rainbow Blvd. Downtown. Int corridors. **Pets:** Other species. $10 daily fee/pet. Service with restrictions, crate.
(SAVE) (S☷) (X) (☐) (⫴)

❧ END METROPOLITAN AREA ❧

NORTH SYRACUSE

▼▼▼ **Doubletree Club Hotel/Syracuse**
Airport **M**
(315) 457-4000. **$75-$139.** 6701 Buckley Rd. I-81, exit 25 (7th North St), 0.8 mi w; I-90, exit 36. Int corridors.
Pets: Large. Service with restrictions, supervision.
(SAVE) (S☷) (X) (⟳) (☷) (☐) (⫴) (⇌)

OGDENSBURG

▼▼ **Quality Inn Gran-View** **M** ❧
(315) 393-4550. **$72-$156.** 6765 State Hwy 37. SR 37, 3 mi sw of Ogdensburg on SR 37 W. Ext/int corridors.
Pets: Other species. $10 daily fee/room. Designated rooms, supervision.
(SAVE) (S☷) (X) (☷) (☐) (⫴) (⇌)

(AAA) **▼▼▼** **The Stonefence Resort & Motel** **C**
(315) 393-1545. **$70-$99.** 7191 SR 37. Jct SR 68 W, 0.5 mi w on SR 37. Ext/int corridors. **Pets:** $22.50 one-time fee/room. Designated rooms, service with restrictions, supervision.
(SAVE) (S☷) (X) (☷) (☐) (⫴) (⇌) (X̷)

OLD FORGE

▼▼ **Best Western Sunset Inn** **M**
(315) 369-6836. **$50-$189, 7 days notice.** SR 28. 0.3 mi s. Ext/int corridors. **Pets:** Accepted.
(SAVE) (S☷) (X) (☷) (☐) (⇌)

ONEONTA

(AAA) **▼▼▼** **Holiday Inn Oneonta/Cooperstown**
Area **M**
(607) 433-2250. **$89-$199.** Rt 23 Southside. I-88, exit 15, 1.5 mi e. Int corridors. **Pets:** Accepted.
(SAVE) (S☷) (X) (⟳) (☷) (☐) (⫴) (⇌)

▼▼ **Super 8 Motel** **M**
(607) 432-9505. **$70-$135.** 4973 SR 23. I-88, exit 15, 0.3 mi e. Int corridors. **Pets:** Large. Designated rooms, service with restrictions, supervision.
(A$K) (S☷) (X) (☷M) (☷)

OWEGO

🔺 ▼▼ Sunrise Motel **M**
(607) 687-5667. **$49-$53.** 3778 Waverly Rd. SR 17, exit 64, SR 96 N across river w to SR 17C, then 2 mi s. Ext corridors. **Pets:** Small. $5 daily fee/room. No service, supervision.
[SAVE] [S🐾] [✕]

PAINTED POST

🔺 ▼▼ Best Western Lodge on the Green **M**
(607) 962-2456. **$54-$100.** 3171 Canada Rd. SR 17, exit 44, s to Gang Mills exit, then n. Ext corridors. **Pets:** Medium, other species. Service with restrictions, crate.
[SAVE] [S🐾] [✕] [📧] [💻] [🍴] [🏊]

🔺 ▼ Erwin Motel **M**
(607) 962-7411. **$39-$69, 5 days notice.** Rt 417. US 15, exit Erwin Addison, 0.5 mi e. Ext corridors. **Pets:** Medium, dogs only. $5 daily fee/pet. Designated rooms, supervision.
[SAVE] [✕] [📧] [🏊]

PEMBROKE

▼▼ Darien Lakes Econo Lodge **M** 🐾
(585) 599-4681. **$44-$119.** 8493 SR 77. I-90, exit 48A, just s. Int corridors. **Pets:** Other species. Designated rooms, service with restrictions, supervision.
[SAVE] [S🐾] [✕] [📧] [💻]

PINE VALLEY

🔺 ▼▼▼ Best Western Marshall Manor **M**
(607) 739-3891. **$46-$83.** 3527 Watkins Rd. SR 17, exit 52, 5 mi n on SR 14. Ext corridors. **Pets:** Large, other species. $9 daily fee/pet. Supervision.
[SAVE] [S🐾] [✕] [📧] [💻] [🏊]

PLAINVIEW

🔺 ▼▼▼ Residence Inn by Marriott **M** 🐾
(516) 433-6200. **$199-$234.** 9 Gerhard Rd. Off Old Country Rd; opposite Central General Hospital; I-495 (Long Island Expwy), exit 44S, exit 10, just e. Int corridors. **Pets:** Other species. $20 daily fee/pet, $100 one-time fee/room. Service with restrictions.
[SAVE] [S🐾] [✕] [🦽M] [🔋] [🛗] [📧] [💻] [🍴] [🏊]

PLATTSBURGH

🔺 ▼▼▼ Baymont Inn & Suites-Plattsburgh **M**
(518) 562-4000. **$69-$79.** 16 Plaza Blvd. I-87, exit 37. Int corridors. **Pets:** Medium. $50 one-time fee/room. Designated rooms, service with restrictions, supervision.
[SAVE] [S🐾] [✕] [🦽M] [🔋] [🛗] [📧] [💻] [🏊]

🔺 ▼▼▼ The Inn at Smithfield by Best Western **M** 🐾
(518) 561-7750. **$69-$84.** 446 Rt 3. I-87, exit 37. Int corridors. **Pets:** Other species. Service with restrictions.
[SAVE] [S🐾] [✕] [📧] [💻] [🍴] [🏊]

PORT JERVIS

🔺 ▼▼▼ Comfort Inn **M**
(845) 856-6611. **$49-$149.** 2247 Greenville Tpke. I-84, exit 1. Int corridors. **Pets:** Medium. $50 deposit/room, $20 one-time fee/room. Designated rooms, service with restrictions, crate.
[SAVE] [S🐾] [✕] [📧] [💻] [🏊]

POTSDAM

🔺 ▼ The Nomad Motel **M** 🐾
(315) 265-6700. **$48-$68.** 7575 Hwy 11. 0.5 mi s on SR 11. Ext corridors. **Pets:** Medium, dogs only. $10 daily fee/pet. Designated rooms, service with restrictions, supervision.
[SAVE] [S🐾] [✕] [📧]

RHINEBECK

▼▼▼ Beekman Arms & Delamater Inn and Conference Center **CI**
(845) 876-7080. **$85-$165, 7 days notice.** 6387 Mill St (Rt 9). Jct SR 9 and 308. Ext/int corridors. **Pets:** Accepted.
[✕] [🛗] [📧] [💻] [🍴]

RIVERHEAD

▼▼▼ Best Western Riverhead **M**
(631) 369-2200. **$149-$229.** 1830 SR 25. I-495, exit 72 (SR 25 E). Int corridors. **Pets:** Medium, other species. $100 deposit/room. Service with restrictions, crate.
[SAVE] [S🐾] [✕] [📧] [💻] [🍴] [🏊]

ROCHESTER

🔺 ▼▼▼ Crowne Plaza Rochester **H**
(585) 546-3450. **$49-$99.** 70 State St. Downtown. Int corridors. **Pets:** $25 one-time fee/room. Designated rooms, service with restrictions, supervision.
[SAVE] [S🐾] [✕] [🎵] [📧] [💻] [🍴] [🏊]

ROCK HILL

🔺 ▼▼▼ The Lodge at Rock Hill **M**
(845) 796-3100. **$87-$169.** 283 Rock Hill Dr. I-17, exit 109, just e. **Pets:** Other species. $25 one-time fee/room. Service with restrictions.
[SAVE] [S🐾] [✕] [🎵] [🦽] [📧] [💻]

ROCKVILLE CENTRE

🔺 ▼▼▼ Holiday Inn **M**
(516) 678-1300. **$159-$169.** 173 Sunrise Hwy. On SR 27. Ext corridors. **Pets:** Large. $15 daily fee/pet. Service with restrictions, supervision.
[SAVE] [S🐾] [✕] [🦽M] [🎵] [📧] [💻] [🍴] [🏊]

ROME

▼▼ Adirondack Thirteen Pines Motel M
(315) 337-4930. **$35-$50, 3 days notice.** 7353 River Rd.
Jct SR 49, 9.5 mi e on SR 365. Ext corridors. **Pets:** Service
with restrictions, supervision.
🖥 🌊

AAA ▼▼▼ Inn at the Beeches MI
(315) 336-1776. **$63-$125.** 7900 Turin Rd. Jct SR 46, 2 mi
n on SR 26. Ext corridors. **Pets:** $5 daily fee/room. Service
with restrictions, crate.
SAVE 🖥 ✕ 🖥 🍴

ROSCOE

AAA ▼▼▼ Roscoe Motel M
(607) 498-5220. **$60, 7 days notice.** 2054 Old Rt 17. SR
17, exit 94, 0.5 mi n on SR 206, just w. Ext corridors.
Pets: Accepted.
SAVE 🖥

ROTTERDAM

▼▼ Super 8 Schenectady M
(518) 355-2190. **$55-$80.** 3083 Carman Rd. I-90, exit 25, at
jct Curry and Carman rds. Int corridors. **Pets:** Small. $10
daily fee/pet. Designated rooms, service with restrictions,
supervision.
ASK 🖥 ✕

SACKETS HARBOR

▼▼ Ontario Place Hotel M
(315) 646-8000. **$59-$175, 3 days notice.** 103 General
Smith Dr. Center. Int corridors. **Pets:** Other species. $10
daily fee/room. Designated rooms, service with restrictions,
supervision.
✕ 🖥 🖥

SARANAC LAKE

AAA ▼▼▼ Adirondack Comfort Inn MI
(518) 891-1970. **$65-$130.** 148 Lake Flower Ave. 0.8 mi e
on SR 86. Int corridors. **Pets:** Other species. $20 one-time
fee/room. Designated rooms, service with restrictions,
supervision.
SAVE 🖥 ✕ 🖥 🖥 🍴

AAA ▼ Adirondack Motel M
(518) 891-2116. **$55-$120.** 23 Lake Flower Ave. 0.5 mi e on
SR 86. Ext corridors. **Pets:** Dogs only. Service with restrictions, supervision.
SAVE ✕ 🖥 🖥 ✕

**AAA ▼▼▼ The Hotel Saranac of Paul Smith's
                College MI**
(518) 891-2200. **$69-$119, 3 days notice.** 101 Main St.
Center. Int corridors. **Pets:** $10 daily fee/pet. Designated
rooms, service with restrictions, supervision.
SAVE 🖥 ✕ 🎵 🖥 🖥 🍴

▼▼ Lake Flower Inn M
(518) 891-2310. **$48-$98, 14 days notice.** 15 Lake Flower
Ave. 0.6 mi e on SR 86. Ext corridors. **Pets:** Dogs only.
Supervision.
✕ 🖥 🌊

AAA ▼▼▼ Lake Side Motel M
(518) 891-4333. **$59-$109, 7 days notice.** 27 Lake Flower
Ave. 0.5 mi e on SR 86. Ext corridors. **Pets:** Accepted.
SAVE 🖥 ✕ 🖥 🌊 ✕

SARATOGA SPRINGS

▼▼▼ Holiday Inn MI
(518) 584-4550. **$99-$299.** 232 Broadway, Rt 9. Jct SR 50,
just s on US 9. Int corridors. **Pets:** Designated rooms,
service with restrictions.
ASK SAVE ✕ 🎵 🖥 🖥 🍴 🌊

AAA ▼▼▼ Playmore Farms Inn M
(518) 584-2350. **$55-$199, 3 days notice.** 3291 S Broadway. I-87, exit 13N, 1.5 mi n, 2.5 mi s on US 9. Ext/int
corridors. **Pets:** Medium. $10 daily fee/room. Designated
rooms, no service, supervision.
SAVE 🖥 ✕ 🖥 🌊

AAA ▼▼▼▼ Union Gables Bed & Breakfast BB
(518) 584-1558. **$110-$285, 14 days notice.** 55 Union Ave.
I-87, exit 14, 1.8 mi s. Int corridors. **Pets:** Accepted.
SAVE ✕ 🖥

SCHENECTADY

▼▼ Days Inn M
(518) 370-3297. **$89-$99.** 167 Nott Terr. Jct State St (SR 5)
and Nott Terr, 2 blks n. Int corridors. **Pets:** Small. $10 daily
fee/pet. Supervision.
SAVE 🖥 ✕ 🎵 🖥 🖥

▼▼▼ Holiday Inn-Downtown Schenectady MI
(518) 393-4141. **$104-$154.** 100 Nott Terr. Center; jct Nott
Terr and State St (SR 5), 2 blks n. Int corridors.
Pets: Accepted.
ASK 🖥 ✕ 🖥 🖥 🍴 🌊

AAA ▼▼ Ramada Inn MI
(518) 370-7151. **$80-$125.** 450 Nott St. I-90, exit 25 or 26;
I-890, exit 4B, 2 mi e on Erie Blvd to Nott St, then just e. Int
corridors. **Pets:** Accepted.
SAVE 🖥 ✕ 🖥 🖥 🍴 🌊

SCHROON LAKE

AAA ▼ Blue Ridge Motel M 🐾
(518) 532-7521. **$77-$88, 14 days notice.** 2455 US Rt 9. 6
mi n on US 9, exit 28, then 4 mi n. Ext/int corridors.
Pets: Other species. $6 daily fee/pet. Service with restric-
tions, supervision.
SAVE 🖥 ✕ 🖥 🖥 🌊 ✕

SENECA FALLS

▼▼ Microtel Inn & Suites **M**
(315) 539-8438. **Call for rates.** 1966 Rt 5 & 20. I-90, exit 41, 4 mi s on SR 414, just e. Int corridors. **Pets:** Accepted.
⊠ 🖾 🖉 🛢 ▣

SOUTH WORCESTER

▼▼ Charlotte Valley Inn B & B and
Antiques 🆎
(607) 397-8164. **$95-$165, 30 days notice.** 480 CR 40. SR 23, 5 mi n on Delaware CR 9/40. Int corridors. **Pets:** Accepted.
⊠ 🎿 🔟 ☎

SOUTHAMPTON

▼▼▼ Southampton Inn **M** 🐾
(631) 283-6500. **$109-$479, 30 days notice.** 91 Hill St. 0.3 mi n from corner of Main St and Job's Ln/Hill St. Int corridors. **Pets:** Medium. $25 daily fee/room. Service with restrictions, supervision.
🅰🆂🅺 🆂 ⊠ 🖉 🛢 ☎

SYRACUSE

▼▼ Comfort Inn Fairgrounds **M**
(315) 453-0045. **$69-$139, 7 days notice.** 7010 Interstate Island Rd. I-90, exit 39 to I-690 E, exit 2 (Jones Rd), just sw. Int corridors. **Pets:** Other species. $10 deposit/room. Service with restrictions, supervision.
🆂 🆂 ⊠ 🛢 ▣

▼▼▼ Days Inn University **M**
(315) 437-5998. **$50-$55.** 6609 Thompson Rd. I-90, exit 35 (Carrier Cir). Int corridors. **Pets:** Medium, other species. $10 daily fee/pet. Service with restrictions, crate.
🆂 🆂 ⊠ 🛢 ▣

▼▼▼ Ramada Limited-University/Carrier
Circle **M**
(315) 463-0202. **$49-$69.** 6390 Thompson Rd. I-90, exit 35 (Carrier Cir), just w. Int corridors. **Pets:** Other species. $10 daily fee/room. Service with restrictions, supervision.
🆂 🆂 ⊠ 🛢 ▣

▼▼▼ Red Roof Inn **M**
(315) 437-3309. **$43-$71.** 6614 N Thompson Rd. I-90, exit 35 (Carrier Cir), just n. Ext corridors. **Pets:** Medium, other species. Service with restrictions, supervision.
🆂 ⊠ 🔟

TICONDEROGA

▼▼▼ Circle Court Motel **M**
(518) 585-7660. **$52-$70.** 6 Montcalm St. US 9 N; at Liberty Monument traffic circle. Ext corridors. **Pets:** Large. Service with restrictions, supervision.
🆂 🆂 🛢 ▣

TROY

▼▼▼▼ Best Western-Rensselaer Inn **M**
(518) 274-3210. **$79-$109, 30 days notice.** 1800 6th Ave. I-787, exit 9E, 0.5 mi e, downtown exit, 0.5 mi s. Int corridors. **Pets:** Medium. $10 daily fee/pet. Designated rooms, service with restrictions, supervision.
🆂 🆂 ⊠ 🛢 ▣ 🍴 ☎

UTICA

▼▼▼ A-1 Motel **M**
(315) 735-6698. **$42-$60, 8 days notice.** 238 N Genesee St. I-90 (New York Thruway), exit 31, just s. Int corridors. **Pets:** Dogs only. $500 daily fee/room, $10 one-time fee/ room. Service with restrictions, supervision.
🆂 🆂 ⊠ 🛢

▼▼▼▼ Best Western Gateway Adirondack
Inn **M**
(315) 732-4121. **$85-$190, 3 days notice.** 175 N Genesee St. I-90, exit 31, 0.5 mi s. Int corridors. **Pets:** Other species. Designated rooms, service with restrictions.
🆂 🆂 ⊠ 🖉 🛢 ▣

▼▼▼▼ Radisson Hotel-Utica Centre **H**
(315) 797-8010. **$119.** 200 Genesee St. Downtown. Int corridors. **Pets:** Medium. $10 daily fee/pet. Service with restrictions, supervision.
🅰🆂🅺 🆂 ⊠ 🛢 ▣ 🍴 ☎

▼▼▼▼ Red Roof Inn **M**
(315) 724-7128. **$47-$93.** 20 Weaver St. I-90, exit 31. Ext corridors. **Pets:** Medium. Service with restrictions, crate.
🆂 ⊠ 🛢

VALATIE

▼▼▼▼ Blue Spruce Inn & Suites **M**
(518) 758-9711. **$70-$95, 3 days notice.** 3093 Route 9. 1 mi n. Ext corridors. **Pets:** Service with restrictions, supervision.
🆂 🆂 ⊠ 🛢 ▣ 🍴

VESTAL

▼▼▼▼ Holiday Inn at the University **M**
(607) 729-6371. **$100.** 4105 Vestal Pkwy. SR 17, exit 70S, 2.5 mi s on SR 201 to SR 434 W, right on Bunn Hill Rd. Ext/int corridors. **Pets:** Accepted.
🅰🆂🅺 🆂 ⊠ 🖾 🛢 ▣ 🍴 ☎

▼▼ Howard Johnson Express Inn (Binghamton
University) **M** 🐾
(607) 729-6181. **$59-$99, 3 days notice.** 3601 Vestal Pkwy E. SR 17, exit 70S, 1 mi s on SR 201 S, 0.5 mi w on SR 434 W. Int corridors. **Pets:** Medium, dogs only. $10 daily fee/pet. Designated rooms, service with restrictions, supervision.
🅰🆂🅺 🆂 ⊠ 🛢 ▣ ☎

Parkway Motel [M]
(607) 785-3311. **$49-$69, 14 days notice.** 900 Vestal Pkwy E Rt 434. SR 17, exit 67S to SR 434, then e. Ext corridors. **Pets:** Accepted.

Residence Inn
Binghamton-University [A] ❀
(607) 770-8500. **$109-$169, 14 days notice.** 4610 Vestal Pkwy. SR 17, exit 70S, 2.5 mi s on SR 201, 1 mi e on SR 434 E, right on Plaza Dr to service road. Ext corridors. **Pets:** Other species. $10 daily fee/room, $50 one-time fee/room. Service with restrictions.

WATERLOO

Holiday Inn Waterloo-Seneca Falls [MI]
(315) 539-5011. **$69-$199.** 2468 SR 414. I-90, exit 41, 4 mi s, just n of jct SR 414, US 20 and 5. Int corridors. **Pets:** Small, other species. Designated rooms, service with restrictions, supervision.

WATERTOWN

The Inn [M]
(315) 788-6800. **$60-$75, 14 days notice.** 1190 Arsenal St. I-81, exit 45, 0.3 mi e. Int corridors. **Pets:** Accepted.

Ramada Inn [MI]
(315) 788-0700. **$65-$90.** 6300 Arsenal St. I-81, exit 45, just w. Int corridors. **Pets:** Other species. $200 deposit/room. Designated rooms, service with restrictions, crate.

Travelodge [M]
(315) 786-8888. **$49-$65.** 652 Arsenal St. I-81, exit 45; on SR 3 (Arsenal St), 2 mi e. Int corridors. **Pets:** Very small. Service with restrictions, supervision.

WATKINS GLEN

Budget Inn [M]
(607) 535-4800. **$45-$125, 5 days notice.** 435 S Franklin St. On SR 14. Ext corridors. **Pets:** Medium, dogs only. $10 daily fee/pet. Designated rooms, service with restrictions, supervision.

Chieftain Motel [M]
(607) 535-4759. **$54-$134, 7 days notice.** 3815 State Rt 14. Jct SR 14A, 3 mi n. Ext corridors. **Pets:** Medium. $25 deposit/pet. Designated rooms, service with restrictions, supervision.

WEEDSPORT

Best Western Weedsport Inn [M]
(315) 834-6623. **$50-$140.** 2709 Erie Dr. I-90, exit 40, just s to jct SR 34 and 31, 0.3 mi w on SR 31. Ext corridors. **Pets:** Large, other species. $15 daily fee/pet. Service with restrictions, supervision.

WEST COXSACKIE

Best Western New Baltimore Inn [M] ❀
(518) 731-8100. **$59-$125.** 12600 Rt 9 W. I-87, exit 21B, 0.5 mi s. Int corridors. **Pets:** Other species. $5 daily fee/pet. Service with restrictions.

WESTMORELAND

Carriage Motor Inn [M]
(315) 853-3561. **$45-$65, 5 days notice.** SR 233 N. I-90, exit 32, just n. Ext corridors. **Pets:** Small. $20 deposit/room, $5 daily fee/room. Designated rooms, service with restrictions, supervision.

WILMINGTON

Grand View Motel [M]
(518) 946-2209. **$62-$99.** HC 2 Box 121 A, SR 86. 1 mi e. Ext corridors. **Pets:** Very small, dogs only. Designated rooms, service with restrictions, supervision.

Hungry Trout Motor Inn [MI] ❀
(518) 946-2217. **$97-$159, 14 days notice.** Rt 86. On SR 86, 2 mi w from town center. Ext corridors. **Pets:** Medium, dogs only. $5 daily fee/room. Service with restrictions, crate.

Ledge Rock at Whiteface Mountain [M] ❀
(518) 946-2379. **$59-$169, 10 days notice.** Placid Rd (SR 86). 3 mi sw on SR 86. Ext corridors. **Pets:** $10 one-time fee/room. Designated rooms, service with restrictions, supervision.

Mountain Brook Lodge [M]
(518) 946-2262. **$48-$95, 7 days notice.** Rt 86. Center; on SR 86. Ext corridors. **Pets:** Other species. Service with restrictions, supervision.

North Pole Motor Inn [M] ❀
(518) 946-7733. **$47-$89, 7 days notice.** SR 86. Jct SR 86 and CR 431, 1 mi sw. Ext corridors. **Pets:** Large, dogs only. $5 one-time fee/room. Service with restrictions, supervision.

ABERDEEN

Ⓐ ▼▼▼ Best Western Pinehurst Motor Inn M
(910) 944-2367. **$70, 30 days notice.** 1500 Sandhills Blvd. From jct of US 15 and 501, 0.3 mi s on US 1. Ext corridors. **Pets:** Accepted.

▼ Motel 6–1234 M
(910) 944-5633. **$50.** 1408 Sand Hills Blvd. From jct US 15 and 501, 0.3 mi s on US 1. Ext corridors. **Pets:** Accepted.

ASHEVILLE

Ⓐ ▼▼ Best Inns M
(828) 298-4000. **$47-$80, 3 days notice.** 1435 Tunnel Rd. I-40, exit 55, just n. Int corridors. **Pets:** Accepted.

▼▼▼ Comfort Inn River Ridge M 🐾
(828) 298-9141. **$69-$119.** 800 Fairview Rd. I-240, exit 8, jct I-40 and US 74. Int corridors. **Pets:** Service with restrictions, supervision.

▼▼▼ Comfort Suites M
(828) 665-4000. **$64-$129.** 890 Brevard Rd. I-26, exit 2, then 0.3 mi w. Int corridors. **Pets:** Medium. $20 daily fee/room. Designated rooms, service with restrictions, crate.

▼▼ Holiday Inn East/Blue Ridge Pkwy M
(828) 298-5611. **$65-$110.** 1450 Tunnel Rd. I-40, exit 55, just n. Int corridors. **Pets:** Medium, other species. Service with restrictions, supervision.

▼▼ Motel 6–1134 M
(828) 299-3040. **$44-$48.** 1415 Tunnel Rd. I-40, exit 55. Ext corridors. **Pets:** Accepted.

Ⓐ ▼▼▼ Red Roof Inn-West M
(828) 667-9803. **$39-$74.** 16 Crowell Rd. I-40, exit 44, just n on US 19 and 23, just w on old Haywood Rd, then just s. Ext corridors. **Pets:** Medium, other species. Service with restrictions, supervision.

Ⓐ ▼▼▼ Super 8 East M 🐾
(828) 298-7952. **$39-$94.** 1329 Tunnel Rd. I-40, exit 55, 0.3 mi w. Ext corridors. **Pets:** Other species. $15 one-time fee/pet. Service with restrictions, supervision.

BANNER ELK

▼▼▼ Banner Elk Inn Bed & Breakfast Ⓑ
(828) 898-6223. **$95-$140, 30 days notice.** 407 Main St E. Jct SR 184 and 194, 0.3 mi n on SR 194. Int corridors. **Pets:** Service with restrictions.

Ⓐ ▼▼▼ Holiday Inn/Banner Elk-Boone Area M
(828) 898-4571. **$70-$160, 3 days notice.** 1615 Tynecastle Hwy. 1 mi se on SR 184. Ext corridors. **Pets:** Other species. $25 deposit/room. Designated rooms, service with restrictions.

BREVARD

▼▼▼ Hampton Inn-Brevard M
(828) 883-4800. **$65-$129, 7 days notice.** 800 Forest Gate Ctr. 3.8 mi e on US 64, just e on SR 280. Int corridors. **Pets:** Accepted.

BURLINGTON

▼▼ Comfort Inn M
(336) 227-3681. **$69-$99.** 978 Plantation Dr. I-40/85, exit 145, just n, 0.3 mi w on service road. Ext corridors. **Pets:** Accepted.

(AAA) ▼▼▼▼ Holiday Inn [M]
(336) 229-5203. **$79-$159.** 2444 Maple Ave. I-40/85, exit 145, just n. Int corridors. **Pets:** $50 one-time fee/room. Service with restrictions, supervision.
[SAVE] [S◇] [✕] [&M] [∅] [▤] [▣] [¶] [⇌]

▼▼ Motel 6-1257 [M]
(336) 226-1325. **$41-$44.** 2155 Hanford Rd. I-40/85, exit 145, just s, then just w. Ext corridors. **Pets:** Accepted.
[S◇] [✕] [∅] [&] [⇌]

(AAA) ▼▼ Red Roof Inn [M]
(336) 227-1270. **$45-$125.** 2133 W Hanford Rd. I-40/85, exit 145, just s on SR 49, then just w. Int corridors. **Pets:** Other species. Service with restrictions, supervision.
[SAVE] [S◇] [✕] [▤] [▣] [⇌]

CARY

(AAA) ▼▼▼▼ La Quinta Inn & Suites [M]
(919) 851-2850. **$65-$105.** 191 Crescent Commons. US 1 and 64, exit 98A, 0.5 mi e on Tryon Rd, just n. Int corridors. **Pets:** Small. No service.
[SAVE] [✕] [&M] [∅] [&] [▤] [▣] [⇌]

(AAA) ▼▼ Red Roof Inn [M]
(919) 469-3400. **$49-$59.** 1800 Walnut St. I-40, exit 293, 0.3 mi sw on US 1 and 64 W; exit Cary-Walnut St, just e. Int corridors. **Pets:** Large, other species. Service with restrictions, supervision.
[SAVE] [✕] [∅] [&] [▤]

CASHIERS

▼▼▼ High Hampton Inn & Country Club [R]
(828) 743-2411. **$92-$118, 10 days notice.** 1525 Hwy S. 1.5 mi s on SR 107 from jct US 64. Ext/int corridors. **Pets:** Accepted.
[SAVE] [¶] [✕] [ℵ] [�®] [☎]

(AAA) ▼▼ Oakmont Lodge [M]
(828) 743-2298. **$55-$74, 3 days notice.** 173 Oakmont St. 0.4 mi n on SR 107 from jct US 64. Ext corridors. **Pets:** $10 one-time fee/pet. Service with restrictions, supervision.
[SAVE] [S◇] [✕] [▤] [ℵ]

CHAPEL HILL

(AAA) ▼▼▼▼ The Siena Hotel [M] ☙
(919) 929-4000. **$149-$179.** 1505 E Franklin St. I-40, exit 270, 2 mi s on US 15/501. Int corridors. **Pets:** Medium, other species. $50 one-time fee/room. Service with restrictions, crate.
[SAVE] [S◇] [✕] [&M] [∅] [▤] [¶]

CHARLOTTE METROPOLITAN AREA

CHARLOTTE

(AAA) ▼▼▼ AmeriSuites Arrowood [M]
(704) 522-8400. **$94.** 7900 Forest Point Blvd. I-77, exit 3 southbound, exit 3 southbound; exit 2 northbound, just e. Int corridors. **Pets:** Small, other species. Designated rooms, service with restrictions.
[SAVE] [S◇] [✕] [&M] [∅] [&] [▤] [▣] [⇌]

▼▼▼ Clarion Hotel [H]
(704) 523-1400. **$59-$99, 7 days notice.** 321 W Woodlawn Rd. I-77, exit 6B, just w. Int corridors. **Pets:** $10 daily fee/pet, $25 one-time fee/pet. Designated rooms.
[SAVE] [S◇] [✕] [&M] [∅] [&] [▤] [▣] [¶] [⇌]

(AAA) ▼▼▼ Comfort Inn Carowinds [M]
(704) 339-0574. **$59, 14 days notice.** 3725 Avenue of the Carolinas. I-77, exit 90, just w. Int corridors. **Pets:** Medium. $10 one-time fee/room. Service with restrictions, supervision.
[SAVE] [S◇] [✕] [∅] [▤] [▣] [⇌]

(AAA) ▼▼▼ Comfort Inn-Executive Park [M]
(704) 525-2626. **$66-$145, 3 days notice.** 5822 Westpark Dr. I-77, exit 5 (Tyvola Rd). Int corridors. **Pets:** Other species. $10 daily fee/room, $25 one-time fee/room. Service with restrictions.
[SAVE] [S◇] [✕] [∅] [&] [▤] [▣] [⇌]

▼▼▼ Drury Inn & Suites-Charlotte North [M]
(704) 593-0700. **$60-$110.** 415 W WT Harris Blvd. I-85, exit 45A, just e. Int corridors. **Pets:** Other species. Designated rooms, supervision.
[✕] [&M] [&] [▤] [▣] [⇌]

▼▼▼ Holiday Inn Airport [M]
(704) 394-4301. **$69-$79.** 2707 Little Rock Rd. I-85, exit 32, just e. Int corridors. **Pets:** Small, other species. $25 one-time fee/room. Designated rooms, service with restrictions, supervision.
[ASK] [S◇] [✕] [∅] [▤] [▣] [¶] [⇌]

▼▼▼ Holiday Inn at University Executive Park [M]
(704) 547-0999. **$69-$199.** 8520 University Executive Park Dr. I-85, exit 45A, 0.3 mi e. Int corridors. **Pets:** Small. $25 one-time fee/room. Designated rooms, service with restrictions.
[ASK] [S◇] [✕] [&M] [∅] [&] [▤] [▣] [¶] [⇌]

▼▼ Homestead Studio Suites-Charlotte/Coliseum [M]
(704) 676-0083. **$54.** 710 Yorkmont Rd. I-77, exit 6B, 0.3 mi w. Ext corridors. **Pets:** Accepted.
[ASK] [S◇] [✕] [&] [▤] [▣]

(AAA) ▼▼▼ La Quinta Inn-Airport [M]
(704) 393-5306. **$55-$75.** 3100 I-85 S Service Rd. I-85, exit 33, just w, then just n. Ext/int corridors. **Pets:** Accepted.
[SAVE] [✕] [&M] [∅] [▤] [▣] [⇌]

(AAA) ▼▼◆◆ La Quinta Inn & Suites-Charlotte Coliseum M
(704) 523-5599. **$65-$85.** 4900 S Tyron St. I-77, exit 6B, just w. Int corridors. **Pets:** Accepted.
[SAVE] [X] [&M] [⌀] [&] [🛏] [💻] [⇌]

(AAA) ▼▼ Red Roof Inn-Airport M
(704) 392-2316. **$44-$59.** 3300 I-85 S Service Rd. I-85, exit 33, just w, then just s. Ext corridors. **Pets:** Accepted.
[SAVE] [X] [&M] [⌀] [🛏]

(AAA) ▼▼ Red Roof Inn Coliseum M
(704) 529-1020. **$39-$54.** 131 Red Roof Dr. I-77, exit 4, just e. Ext corridors. **Pets:** Supervision.
[SAVE] [X] [&M] [⌀]

(AAA) ▼▼◆◆ Residence Inn by Marriott A
(704) 547-1122. **$109, 7 days notice.** 8503 N Tryon St. I-85, exit 45A, 0.3 mi e, then just s. Ext corridors. **Pets:** Other species. $100 one-time fee/room. Service with restrictions.
[SAVE] [S6] [X] [&M] [⌀] [&] [🛏] [💻] [⇌] [✕]

(AAA) ▼▼◆◆ Sheraton Charlotte Airport Plaza Hotel H
(704) 392-1200. **$89.** 3315 I-85 S at Billy Graham Pkwy. I-85, exit 33, just e. Int corridors. **Pets:** Accepted.
[SAVE] [X] [⌀] [🛏] [💻] [🍽] [⇌]

(AAA) ▼▼ Sleep Inn M
(704) 549-4544. **$49-$169, 10 days notice.** 8525 N Tryon St. I-85, exit 45A, 0.3 mi e on WT Harris Blvd, just s on US 29. Int corridors. **Pets:** Medium, other species. $25 one-time fee/room. Service with restrictions, supervision.
[SAVE] [S6] [X] [&M] [⌀] [&] [🛏] [💻]

(AAA) ▼▼◆◆ Summerfield Suites by Wyndham-Charlotte Airport M
(704) 525-2600. **$169-$189, 3 days notice.** 4920 S Tryon St. I-77, exit 6B, just w. Int corridors. **Pets:** Accepted.
[SAVE] [S6] [X] [&M] [⌀] [🛏] [💻] [⇌]

(AAA) ▼▼◆◆ TownPlace Suites by Marriott A
(704) 227-2000. **$59-$90.** 7805 Forest Point Blvd. I-77, exit 3 southbound; exit 2 northbound, just e. Int corridors. **Pets:** Other species. $10 daily fee/pet, $100 one-time fee/pet. Service with restrictions, supervision.
[SAVE] [S6] [X] [&M] [⌀] [&] [🛏] [💻] [⇌]

CORNELIUS

▼▼◆◆ Hampton Inn Lake Norman M
(704) 892-9900. **$75-$95, 7 days notice.** 19501 Statesville Rd. I-77, exit 28, just e, then just s. Int corridors. **Pets:** Accepted.
[SAVE] [S6] [X] [⌀] [🛏] [💻] [⇌]

(AAA) ▼▼◆◆ Holiday Inn Lake Norman MI
(704) 892-9120. **$69-$89, 7 days notice.** 19901 Holiday Ln. I-77, exit 28, just e, then just n. Ext corridors. **Pets:** Accepted.
[SAVE] [S6] [X] [&M] [⌀] [🛏] [💻] [🍽] [⇌]

PINEVILLE

▼▼◆◆ Staybridge Suites Charlotte-Ballantyne M ✿
(704) 248-5000. **$107.** 15735 John J Delaney Dr. I-485, exit 61, just s. Int corridors. **Pets:** Other species. $75 one-time fee/room. Service with restrictions, crate.
[ASK] [S6] [X] [&M] [⌀] [&] [🛏] [💻] [⇌]

✿   END METROPOLITAN AREA   ✿

CHEROKEE

(AAA) ▼▼ Best Western Great Smokies Inn MI
(828) 497-2020. **$45-$95.** 1636 Acquoni Rd. 2.5 mi n, just off US 441 N. Ext corridors. **Pets:** Accepted.
[SAVE] [S6] [X] [⌀] [🛏] [💻] [🍽] [⇌]

(AAA) ▼▼ Pioneer Motel M
(828) 497-2435. **$38-$78, 3 days notice.** 0.8 mi w on US 19 S. Ext corridors. **Pets:** Small, dogs only. $20 one-time fee/pet. Designated rooms, service with restrictions.
[SAVE] [S6] [X] [🛏] [💻] [⇌]

CLAYTON

▼▼ Jameson Inn M
(919) 661-1991. **$55-$70.** 101 Leone Ct. I-40, exit 312, just n. Ext corridors. **Pets:** Accepted.
[X] [&M] [🛏] [💻] [⇌]

▼▼ Sleep Inn M
(919) 772-7771. **$59-$69.** 105 Commerce Pkwy. I-40, exit 312, just s. Int corridors. **Pets:** Large, other species. $25 one-time fee/room. Designated rooms, service with restrictions, supervision.
[SAVE] [S6] [X] [&M] [⌀] [&] [🛏] [💻] [⇌]

DORTCHES

(AAA) ▼▼◆◆ Holiday Inn Dortches MI
(252) 937-6300. **$60, 10 days notice.** 5350 Dortches Blvd. I-95, exit 141, just w, then just n on service road. Ext corridors. **Pets:** Accepted.
[SAVE] [S6] [X] [⌀] [🛏] [💻] [🍽] [⇌]

DURHAM

(AAA) ▼▼ Best Western Skyland Inn M ✿
(919) 383-2508. **$62-$72, 7 days notice.** 5400 US 70 W. I-85, exit 170, 0.3 mi e on US 70, just n. Ext corridors. **Pets:** Large, other species. $10 daily fee/room. Service with restrictions, crate.
[SAVE] [S6] [X] [🛏] [💻] [⇌]

(AAA) ▼▼ ▼▼ Carolina Duke Motor Inn M
(919) 286-0771. **$52-$57.** 2517 Guess Rd. I-85, exit 175, just e. Ext corridors. **Pets:** Dogs only. $3 daily fee/pet. Designated rooms, service with restrictions, supervision.
SAVE ☒ ⊘ 🛈 ⇆

▼▼ ▼▼ Homestead Studio Suites-Raleigh/Durham/ Research Triangle Park M
(919) 544-9991. **$49-$74.** 4515 NC Hwy 55. I-40, exit 278, just s. Ext corridors. **Pets:** Accepted.
ASK S☉ ☒ ⊘ 🗜 🛈 ⊑

(AAA) ▼▼▼▼ La Quinta Inn & Suites M
(919) 401-9660. **$75-$95.** 4414 Chapel Hill Blvd. I-40, exit 270, 1.7 mi n on US 15/501. Int corridors. **Pets:** Small. Service with restrictions, supervision.
SAVE ☒ ♿M ⊘ 🗜 🛈 ⊑ ⇆

(AAA) ▼▼▼▼ La Quinta Inn & Suites Raleigh Durham RTP West M
(919) 484-1422. **$65-$95.** 1910 W Park Dr. I-40, exit 278, just n, then just e. Int corridors. **Pets:** Small. No service, supervision.
SAVE ☒ ♿M ⊘ 🗜 🛈 ⊑ ⇆

(AAA) ▼▼ ▼▼ Wellesley Inn & Suites M
(919) 998-0400. **$49-$99.** 4919 S Miami Blvd. I-40, exit 281, just s. Int corridors. **Pets:** Accepted.
SAVE S☉ ☒ ♿M ⊘ 🗜 🛈 ⊑ ⇆

▼▼▼▼ Wyndham Garden Hotel-RTP Airport MI
(919) 941-6066. **$63-$99.** 4620 S Miami Blvd. I-40, exit 281, 0.3 mi n. Int corridors. **Pets:** Accepted.
ASK S☉ ☒ ⊘ 🛈 ⊑ 🍴 ⇆

EDEN

▼▼ ▼▼ Jameson Inn M
(336) 627-0472. **$55-$70.** 716 Linden Dr. Just w of Moorehead Memorial Hospital. Ext corridors. **Pets:** Very small. Service with restrictions, supervision.
☒ ♿M 🛈 ⊑ ⇆

ELIZABETH CITY

▼▼ ▼▼ Quality Inn MI
(252) 338-3951. **Call for rates.** 522 S Hughes Blvd. 1 mi s on US 17 Bypass. Ext corridors. **Pets:** Accepted.
ASK ☒ ⊘ 🛈 ⊑ 🍴 ⇆

FAYETTEVILLE

(AAA) ▼▼ ▼▼ Comfort Inn I-95 M
(910) 323-8333. **$70-$80.** 1957 Cedar Creek Rd. I-95, exit 49, just w. Ext corridors. **Pets:** Medium, other species. Designated rooms, service with restrictions, supervision.
SAVE S☉ ☒ ⊘ 🛈 ⊑ ⇆

▼▼ ▼▼ Holiday Inn Bordeaux MI
(910) 323-0111. **$89.** 1707 Owen Dr. Jct I-95 business route and US 301, 2.3 mi w. Ext/int corridors. **Pets:** Medium. $100 deposit/room, $15 one-time fee/room. Service with restrictions.
S☉ ☒ ⊘ 🛈 ⊑ 🍴 ⇆

(AAA) ▼▼▼▼ Holiday Inn I-95 MI
(910) 323-1600. **$79.** 1944 Cedar Creek Rd. I-95, exit 49, just w on SR 53 and 210. Ext/int corridors. **Pets:** Accepted.
SAVE S☉ ☒ ⊘ 🛈 ⊑ 🍴 ⇆

(AAA) ▼▼ ▼▼ Radisson Prince Charles H
(910) 433-4444. **$55-$75, 30 days notice.** 450 Hay St. Center; just w of traffic circle. Int corridors. **Pets:** Accepted.
SAVE S☉ ☒ 🛈 ⊑ 🍴

(AAA) ▼▼▼▼ Red Roof Inn M
(910) 321-1460. **$49.** 1569 Jim Johnson Rd. I-95, exit 49, just w on SR 53, then just n. Int corridors. **Pets:** Medium. $10 daily fee/pet. Designated rooms, service with restrictions, supervision.
SAVE S☉ ☒ ♿M 🗜 🛈 ⇆

FLETCHER

▼▼▼▼ Holiday Inn Asheville-Airport MI
(828) 684-1213. **$69-$99.** 550 Airport Rd. I-26, exit 9, just e. Int corridors. **Pets:** Accepted.
ASK ☒ 🛈 ⊑ 🍴 ⇆

FRANKLIN

(AAA) ▼▼ Colonial Inn M ❀
(828) 524-6600. **$60-$65, 3 days notice.** 3157 Georgia Rd. 2.4 mi s on US 23/441 from US 441 Bypass. Ext corridors. **Pets:** Medium. Designated rooms, service with restrictions.
SAVE ☒ 🗜 🛈 ⊑ ⇆

▼▼ ▼▼ Days Inn-Franklin M
(828) 524-6491. **$49-$105.** 1320 E Main St. Just nw on US 441 business route, at jct US 23 and 441 Bypass. Ext corridors. **Pets:** Medium. $15 one-time fee/pet. Service with restrictions, supervision.
SAVE S☉ ☒ 🛈 ⇆

▼▼ ▼▼ Microtel M
(828) 349-9000. **$40-$90.** 81 Allman Dr. 0.4 mi s on US 23/441 from jct US 441 Bypass. Int corridors. **Pets:** Other species. $20 one-time fee/room. Service with restrictions, crate.
ASK S☉ ☒ 🗜 🛈 ⊑

▼▼ ▼▼ Mountainside Vacation Lodging A
(828) 524-6209. **$60-$75, 14 days notice.** 8356 Sylva Rd. 4.8 mi n on US 441 and 23. Ext corridors. **Pets:** Accepted.
☒ 🛈 ⊑ ☒

FUQUAY VARINA

▼▼ ▼▼ Comfort Inn M
(919) 557-9000. **$61-$121.** 7616 Purfoy Rd. 1 mi n on US 401 from jct SR 55, just e. Int corridors. **Pets:** Accepted.
SAVE S☉ ☒ 🗜 🛈 ⊑ ⇆

GOLDSBORO

▽▽▽▽ Best Western Goldsboro Inn
(919) 735-7911. **$66.** 801 US 70 E Bypass. 2 mi e on US 70 E Bypass, exit Williams St; follow service road. Ext corridors. **Pets:** Dogs only. $15 one-time fee/pet. Service with restrictions, supervision.
⟨SAVE⟩ ⟨S⟩ ⟨✕⟩ ⟨🖥⟩ ⟨💻⟩ ⟨🍽⟩ ⟨⇀⟩

GREENSBORO

◈◈◈ ▽▽▽▽ AmeriSuites
        Greensboro/Wendover
(336) 852-1443. **$89.** 1619 Stanley Rd. I-40, exit 214 westbound; exit 214B eastbound, just s, then just e. Int corridors. **Pets:** Medium, other species. Service with restrictions.
⟨SAVE⟩ ⟨S⟩ ⟨✕⟩ ⟨🔷⟩ ⟨🛏⟩ ⟨🖥⟩ ⟨💻⟩ ⟨⇀⟩

▽▽▽ Biltmore Greensboro Hotel 🅷 🐾
(336) 272-3474. **$85-$110, 4 days notice.** 111 W Washington St. Just s of town center on Elm St, then just w. Int corridors. **Pets:** Dogs only. Service with restrictions, crate.
⟨ASK⟩ ⟨S⟩ ⟨✕⟩ ⟨🖥⟩

▽▽▽ Drury Inn & Suites-Greensboro 🅼
(336) 856-9696. **$60-$97.** 3220 High Point Rd. I-40, exit 217, just s. Int corridors. **Pets:** Medium, other species. Designated rooms, service with restrictions.
⟨✕⟩ ⟨🔷⟩ ⟨🛏⟩ ⟨🖥⟩ ⟨💻⟩ ⟨⇀⟩

▽▽▽ Holiday Inn-Airport 🅼
(336) 668-0421. **$92-$98, 30 days notice.** 6426 Burnt Poplar Rd. I-40, exit 210, just n, then 0.5 mi e on service road. Int corridors. **Pets:** Large. Service fee. $25 one-time fee/room. Service with restrictions, supervision.
⟨ASK⟩ ⟨S⟩ ⟨✕⟩ ⟨🖥⟩ ⟨💻⟩ ⟨🍽⟩ ⟨⇀⟩

◈◈◈ ▽▽▽▽ La Quinta Inn & Suites 🅼
(336) 316-0100. **$75-$105.** 1201 Lanada Rd. I-40, exit 214 westbound; exit 214B eastbound, just s, then just e. Int corridors. **Pets:** Small, other species. Designated rooms, no service, supervision.
⟨SAVE⟩ ⟨✕⟩ ⟨🅼⟩ ⟨🔷⟩ ⟨🛏⟩ ⟨🖥⟩ ⟨💻⟩ ⟨⇀⟩

◈◈◈ ▽▽▽ Red Roof Inn Greensboro-Airport 🅼
(336) 271-2636. **$40-$59.** 615 Regional Rd S. I-40, exit 210, just s on SR 68 via service road. Ext corridors. **Pets:** Accepted.
⟨SAVE⟩ ⟨✕⟩ ⟨🔷⟩ ⟨🛏⟩

◈◈◈ ▽▽▽▽ Residence Inn by Marriott 🅡
(336) 294-8600. **$119-$149.** 2000 Veasley St. I-40, exit 217, 0.3 mi s, then 0.4 mi w. Ext corridors. **Pets:** Accepted.
⟨SAVE⟩ ⟨S⟩ ⟨✕⟩ ⟨🔷⟩ ⟨🛏⟩ ⟨💻⟩ ⟨🏊⟩

GREENVILLE

▽▽▽ The Jameson Inn 🅼
(252) 752-7382. **$55-$70.** 920 Crosswinds St. US 264, exit 273, 2 mi e on Stantonsburg, 0.5 mi s on Memorial Dr. Ext corridors. **Pets:** Very small. Service with restrictions, supervision.
⟨✕⟩ ⟨🅼⟩ ⟨🔷⟩ ⟨🛏⟩ ⟨💻⟩ ⟨⇀⟩

HENDERSON

▽▽ Jameson Inn 🅼
(252) 430-0247. **$55-$70.** 400 N Cooper Dr. I-85, exit 213, just w, then just n. Int corridors. **Pets:** Very small, other species. $5 daily fee/pet. Service with restrictions, supervision.
⟨✕⟩ ⟨🅼⟩ ⟨🔷⟩ ⟨🔷⟩ ⟨🛏⟩ ⟨💻⟩ ⟨⇀⟩

HENDERSONVILLE

◈◈◈ ▽▽▽▽ Comfort Inn 🅼
(828) 693-8800. **$60-$105, 15 days notice.** 206 Mitchell Dr. I-26, exit 18B, just w. Ext corridors. **Pets:** Large, other species. $10 daily fee/room. Service with restrictions, crate.
⟨SAVE⟩ ⟨S⟩ ⟨✕⟩ ⟨🛏⟩ ⟨💻⟩ ⟨⇀⟩

HICKORY

◈◈◈ ▽▽▽▽ Red Roof Inn Hickory 🅼
(828) 323-1500. **$45-$65.** 1184 Lenoir Rhyne Blvd. I-40, exit 125, just n. Ext corridors. **Pets:** Accepted.
⟨SAVE⟩ ⟨✕⟩ ⟨🔷⟩ ⟨🔷⟩ ⟨🛏⟩

HIGHLANDS

▽▽▽▽ Kelsey & Hutchinson Lodge 🅼 🐾
(828) 526-4746. **$82-$262, 7 days notice.** 450 Spring St. Just s of US 64 (Main St), just e of 4th St. Ext corridors. **Pets:** $15 daily fee/pet. Designated rooms, supervision.
⟨✕⟩ ⟨🛏⟩ ⟨💻⟩

◈◈◈ ▽▽▽ Mountain High Motel 🅼
(828) 526-2790. **$60-$205, 7 days notice.** 200 Main St. Downtown. Ext corridors. **Pets:** Accepted.
⟨SAVE⟩ ⟨✕⟩ ⟨🛏⟩ ⟨💻⟩

LAURINBURG

▽▽▽▽ Hampton Inn 🅼
(910) 277-1516. **Call for rates, 3 days notice.** 115 Hampton Cir. At jct US 15 and 401 Bypass. Int corridors. **Pets:** Medium, other species. Service with restrictions, supervision.
⟨✕⟩ ⟨🔷⟩ ⟨🔷⟩ ⟨🛏⟩ ⟨💻⟩ ⟨⇀⟩

▽▽▽ Jameson Inn 🅼
(910) 277-0080. **$55-$70.** 14 Jameson Inn Ct. Just n on US 15, 401 from US 74 and 501 Bypass. Ext corridors. **Pets:** Very small, other species. Designated rooms, service with restrictions, supervision.
⟨✕⟩ ⟨🛏⟩ ⟨💻⟩ ⟨⇀⟩

LENOIR

▽▽▽ Jameson Inn 🅼
(828) 758-1200. **$55-$70.** 350 Wilkesboro Blvd. 0.4 mi ne on SR 18 from jct US 321. Ext corridors. **Pets:** Very small, other species. Service with restrictions, supervision.
⟨✕⟩ ⟨🅼⟩ ⟨🔷⟩ ⟨🛏⟩ ⟨💻⟩ ⟨⇀⟩

Ramada Limited
(828) 758-4403. **$49-$65, 15 days notice.** 142 Wilkesboro Blvd SE. Just e on US 64/SR 18 from jct US 321. Ext corridors. **Pets:** Accepted.

LEXINGTON

Best Western Lexington Triad Inn
(336) 249-0111. **$53, 7 days notice.** 418 Piedmont Dr. I-85, exit 96, 3.5 mi w on US 64. Ext corridors. **Pets:** Small. $25 one-time fee/pet. Service with restrictions, crate.

LINCOLNTON

Days Inn
(704) 735-8271. **$54-$60.** 614 Clark Dr. US 321, exit 24, 1 mi w on SR 150. Ext corridors. **Pets:** Accepted.

LUMBERTON

Quality Inn and Suites
(910) 738-8261. **$55-$80.** 3608 Kahn Dr. I-95, exit 20, just e, enter at K-Mart entrance, then just w. Ext/int corridors. **Pets:** $10 daily fee/room. Designated rooms, service with restrictions, supervision.

MAGGIE VALLEY

Applecover Inn Motel
(828) 926-9100. **$35-$80, 7 days notice.** 4077 Soco Rd. On US 19, 4.5 mi w from jct US 276. Ext corridors. **Pets:** Accepted.

MORRISVILLE

Baymont Inn & Suites Raleigh-Airport
(919) 481-3600. **$59-$79.** 1001 Aerial Center Pkwy. I-40, exit 284 and 284A, 0.3 mi s. Int corridors. **Pets:** Accepted.

La Quinta Inn & Suites-Airport
(919) 461-1771. **$75-$125.** 1001 Hospitality Ct. I-40, exit 284 and 284A, just s. **Pets:** Small, other species. Service with restrictions, supervision.

Staybridge Suites Raleigh Durham Airport-Morrisville
(919) 468-0180. **$85-$145, 3 days notice.** 1012 Airport Blvd. I-40, exit 284 and 284A, just s; enter between Hampton Inn and Holiday Inn Express. Int corridors. **Pets:** Other species. $150 one-time fee/room. Service with restrictions, supervision.

MURPHY

Best Western of Murphy
(828) 837-3060. **$52-$109.** 1522 Andrews Rd. US 74, 19 and SR 129, exit Andrews Rd. Ext corridors. **Pets:** Small. $10 daily fee/pet. Service with restrictions, supervision.

Comfort Inn
(828) 837-8030. **$60-$109, 30 days notice.** 754 Hwy 64 W. On US 64 W, 19 S, 74 W and 129 S. Ext corridors. **Pets:** Accepted.

OUTER BANKS AREA

OCRACOKE

The Anchorage Inn
(252) 928-1101. **$59-$145, 3 days notice.** 205 Irving Garrish Hwy. Just n on SR 12 from Cedar Island Ferry, on south end of island. Ext corridors. **Pets:** Other species. $10 daily fee/room. Designated rooms, service with restrictions, supervision.

❀ END AREA ❀

PINE KNOLL SHORES

Amerisuites-Atlantic Beach
(252) 247-5118. **$59-$149.** 118 Salter Path Rd. On SR 58 at MM 5. Int corridors. **Pets:** Small, dogs only. $10 daily fee/pet. Designated rooms, service with restrictions, supervision.

RALEIGH

AmeriSuites
(919) 877-9997. **$89, 15 days notice.** 1105 Navaho Dr. I-440, exit 10 (Wake Forest Rd), just n, then just w. Int corridors. **Pets:** Accepted.

⊕ ▽▽▽ Fairfield Inn-Crabtree **M**
(919) 881-9800. **$89-$114.** 2201 Summit Park Ln. I-440, exit 7, just w on US 70, just s on Blue Ridge Rd, then just e. Int corridors. **Pets:** Accepted.
[SAVE] [S🅳] [✕] [♿M] [🐾] [🔋] [🍽]

▽▽▽ Holiday Inn-Crabtree **MI**
(919) 782-8600. **$116, 3 days notice.** 4100 Glenwood Ave. I-440, exit 7 (Glenwood Ave), just w on US 70. Int corridors. **Pets:** Small. $50 one-time fee/room. Service with restrictions, supervision.
[ASK] [S🅳] [✕] [♿M] [🐾] [🔋] [🖭] [🍴] [🍽]

▽▽▽ Homestead Studio
          Suites-Raleigh/North **M**
(919) 981-7353. **$50.** 3531 Wake Forest Rd. I-440, exit 10 (Wake Forest Rd), 0.5 mi n. Ext corridors. **Pets:** Accepted.
[ASK] [S🅳] [✕] [♿M] [🐾] [🛏] [🔋] [🖭]

⊕ ▽▽◈▽ La Quinta Inn & Suites **M**
(919) 785-0071. **$65-$95.** 2211 Summit Park Ln. I-440, exit 7B, just n to Blue Ridge Rd, then just e. Int corridors. **Pets:** Accepted.
[SAVE] [✕] [♿M] [🐾] [🛏] [🔋] [🖭] [🍽]

⊕ ▽▽◈▽ MainStay Suites **M**
(919) 807-9970. **$49-$89.** 2601 Appliance Ct. I-440, exit 11, just n on US 1, then just e. Int corridors. **Pets:** Accepted.
[SAVE] [S🅳] [✕] [🐾] [🛏] [🔋] [🖭] [🍽]

⊕ ▽▽▽ Red Roof Inn-North **M**
(919) 878-9310. **$39-$69.** 3201 Wake Forest Rd. I-440, exit 10, just n, then just w; enter behind Denny's. Ext corridors. **Pets:** Medium, other species. Designated rooms, service with restrictions, supervision.
[SAVE] [S🅳] [✕] [🐾] [🔋] [🍽]

⊕ ▽▽▽ Red Roof Inn-South **M**
(919) 833-6005. **$49-$64.** 1813 S Saunders St. I-40, exit 298B, just n on US 401 and 70. Int corridors. **Pets:** Medium, other species. Service with restrictions, supervision.
[SAVE] [✕] [♿M] [🐾] [🛏] [🔋]

⊕ ▽▽◈▽ Residence Inn by Marriott **A**
(919) 878-6100. **$79-$119.** 1000 Navaho Dr. I-440, exit 10 (Wake Forest Rd), just n, then sw. Ext corridors. **Pets:** $200 one-time fee/room. Service with restrictions, crate.
[SAVE] [S🅳] [✕] [♿M] [🐾] [🔋] [🖭] [🍽]

REIDSVILLE

▽▽ Ramada Inn **MI**
(336) 342-0341. **$65-$120, 3 days notice.** 2100 Barnes St. US 29 business route, exit 149 (Barnes St), just n. Ext corridors. **Pets:** Very small, other species. $10 daily fee/pet. Designated rooms, service with restrictions, supervision.
[ASK] [S🅳] [✕] [🔋] [🖭] [🍴] [🍽]

ROCKY MOUNT

⊕ ▽▽▽ Best Western Inn I-95 Gold Rock **M**
(252) 985-1450. **$58-$94, 15 days notice.** 7095 NC 4. I-95, exit 145, just w. Ext corridors. **Pets:** Small, other species. $5 daily fee/pet. Service with restrictions, supervision.
[SAVE] [✕] [🔋] [🍽]

⊕ ▽▽▽ Comfort Inn **M**
(252) 937-7765. **$73.** 200 Gateway Blvd. I-95, exit 138, 1 mi e on US 64, exit Winstead Ave. Int corridors. **Pets:** Other species. $25 one-time fee/room. Service with restrictions, supervision.
[SAVE] [S🅳] [✕] [🐾] [🔋] [🖭] [🍽]

⊕ ▽▽▽ Quality Inn & Suites **M**
(252) 977-0101. **$46-$76, 7 days notice.** I-95, exit 145, just e. Int corridors. **Pets:** Other species. $10 one-time fee/room. Service with restrictions.
[SAVE] [S🅳] [✕] [🔋] [🖭] [🍴] [🍽]

⊕ ▽▽▽ Red Roof Inn **M**
(252) 984-0907. **$40-$50.** 1370 N Weslyan Blvd. From jct US 64 Bypass, 1.5 mi n on US 301. Int corridors. **Pets:** Accepted.
[SAVE] [✕] [🐾] [🛏] [🔋] [🍽]

⊕ ▽▽◈▽ Residence Inn by Marriott **A** ✿
(252) 451-5600. **$119.** 230 Gateway Blvd. I-95, exit 138, 1 mi e on US 64, then just s on Winstead. Int corridors. **Pets:** Medium, other species. $100 one-time fee/room. Service with restrictions, crate.
[SAVE] [S🅳] [✕] [♿M] [🐾] [🛏] [🔋] [🖭] [🍽]

SALISBURY

⊕ ▽▽▽ Days Inn **M**
(704) 633-4211. **$60-$90, 7 days notice.** 1810 Lutheran Synod Dr. I-85, exit 75, just w. Ext corridors. **Pets:** $10 daily fee/pet. Service with restrictions, supervision.
[SAVE] [S🅳] [✕] [🐾] [🔋] [🖭] [🍽]

▽▽▽ Hampton Inn **M**
(704) 637-8000. **Call for rates.** 1001 Klumac Rd. I-85, exit 75, just w. Int corridors. **Pets:** Accepted.
[ASK] [✕] [🐾] [🔋] [🖭] [🍽]

SMITHFIELD

⊕ ▽▽▽ Super 8 Motel **M**
(919) 989-8988. **$53-$66.** 735 Industrial Park Dr. I-95, exit 95, just w on US 70, then just n. Int corridors. **Pets:** Medium. $4 daily fee/room. Designated rooms, service with restrictions, supervision.
[SAVE] [S🅳] [✕] [♿M] [🐾] [🛏] [🔋] [🍽]

STATESVILLE

⊕ ▽▽▽ Best Western Statesville Inn **M**
(704) 881-0111. **$55-$65.** 1121 Morland Dr. I-77, exit 49A, just e on US 70 E. Ext/int corridors. **Pets:** Accepted.
[SAVE] [S🅳] [✕] [🛏] [🔋] [🖭]

Red Roof Inn M
(704) 878-2051. **$42-$54.** 1508 E Broad St. I-77, exit 50, just w. Ext corridors. **Pets:** Medium, other species. Designated rooms, service with restrictions, supervision.
[SAVE] [X] [🐾]

Super 8 Motel M
(704) 878-9888. **$46-$120, 3 days notice.** 1125 Greenland Dr. I-77, exit 49A, just e. Ext/int corridors. **Pets:** Medium, dogs only. $5 daily fee/pet. Service with restrictions, supervision.
[SAVE] [Sb] [X] [🐾]

WADE

Days Inn Fayetteville M ❖
(910) 323-1255. **$44-$65, 7 days notice.** 3945 Goldsboro Rd. I-95, exit 58, just e. Ext corridors. **Pets:** $6 daily fee/pet. Designated rooms, service with restrictions, crate.
[SAVE] [Sb] [🐾] [🔒] [🍴] [🛏]

WASHINGTON

Econo Lodge M
(252) 946-7781. **$45-$62.** 1220 W 15th. 1.3 mi n on US 17 at jct US 264. Ext corridors. **Pets:** Other species. $5 daily fee/pet. Service with restrictions.
[SAVE] [Sb] [X] [🐾] [🔒] [🛏]

WELDON

Days Inn M
(252) 536-4867. **$55, 3 days notice.** 1611 Julian Allsbrook Hwy. I-95, exit 173, just e on US 158. Ext corridors. **Pets:** Accepted.
[SAVE] [Sb] [X] [🐾] [🔒] [🛏]

WILLIAMSTON

Holiday Inn M
(252) 792-3184. **$69-$89.** 101 E Blvd. Jct US 64 and 17. Ext/int corridors. **Pets:** Medium, other species. Designated rooms, service with restrictions, supervision.
[ASK] [Sb] [X] [🐾] [🛏] [🍴] [🛏]

WILMINGTON

Comfort Inn Wilmington M
(910) 791-4841. **$74-$119.** 151 S College Rd. Just s on SR 132 from jct US 17. Int corridors. **Pets:** Large. $25 one-time fee/pet. Designated rooms, service with restrictions, crate.
[SAVE] [Sb] [X] [🐾] [🔒] [🛏] [🛏]

Days Inn M
(910) 799-6300. **$49-$99.** 5040 Market St. 3.5 mi n on US 17 and 74. Ext corridors. **Pets:** Medium. $15 daily fee/room. Service with restrictions, supervision.
[SAVE] [Sb] [X] [🐾] [🔒] [🛏] [🍴]

Holiday Inn of Wilmington M
(910) 799-1440. **$69-$119.** 4903 Market St. On US 17 and 74. Ext corridors. **Pets:** Accepted.
[ASK] [X] [🐾] [🔒] [🛏] [🍴] [🛏]

WINSTON SALEM

Augustus T Zevely Inn BB
(336) 748-9299. **$80-$150.** 803 S Main St. In Old Salem Historical District. Ext/int corridors. **Pets:** Medium, other species. $15 daily fee/pet. Designated rooms, service with restrictions, crate.
[SAVE] [X] [🔒]

Holiday Inn Select M
(336) 767-9595. **$59-$149.** 5790 University Pkwy. US 52, exit 115B, just s. Int corridors. **Pets:** Other species. $25 one-time fee/room. Service with restrictions, crate.
[ASK] [X] [🐾] [🔒] [🛏] [🍴] [🛏]

La Quinta Inns & Suites M
(336) 765-8777. **$65-$95.** 2020 Griffith Rd. I-40, exit 189, just s on Stratford Rd, just e on Hanes Mall Blvd. Int corridors. **Pets:** Accepted.
[SAVE] [X] [SM] [🐾] [🔒] [🛏] [🛏]

Residence Inn by Marriott A
(336) 759-0777. **$89.** 7835 N Point Blvd. US 52 N, exit 115B, 2 mi s on University Pkwy, just e. Ext corridors. **Pets:** Accepted.
[SAVE] [Sb] [X] [🐾] [🔒] [🛏] [🛏]

Salem Inn M
(336) 725-8561. **$72-$129.** 127 S Cherry St. I-40 business route, exit 5D westbound; exit 5C eastbound, just s. Ext corridors. **Pets:** Other species. $25 one-time fee/room. Designated rooms, service with restrictions.
[ASK] [Sb] [X] [🔒] [🛏] [🛏]

YANCEYVILLE

Days Inn M
(336) 694-9494. **$55-$150, 3 days notice.** 1858 NC Hwy 86 N. SR 86 N, 2 mi from town. Ext corridors. **Pets:** Medium. $10 daily fee/pet. Service with restrictions, supervision.
[SAVE] [Sb] [X] [🔒] [🛏] [🛏]

BEULAH

AmericInn Motel & Suites M
(701) 873-2220. **$75-$125.** 2100 2nd Ave NW. Jct SR 49/200, 1.2 mi s. Int corridors. **Pets:** Service with restrictions, supervision.

BISMARCK

Best Western Doublewood Inn MI
(701) 258-7000. **$79-$99.** 1400 E Interchange Ave. I-94, exit 159 (US 83), just s. Int corridors. **Pets:** Medium. $10 daily fee/room. Service with restrictions, supervision.

Comfort Inn M
(701) 223-1911. **$52-$62.** 1030 Interstate Ave. I-94, exit 159 (US 83), 0.3 mi nw. Int corridors. **Pets:** Small. Service with restrictions, supervision.

Expressway Inn M
(701) 222-2900. **$55-$70.** 200 Bismarck Expwy. Jct I-94 business loop and S 3rd St; opposite Kirkwood Mall. Int corridors. **Pets:** Medium. $5 daily fee/room. Designated rooms, service with restrictions, supervision.

Holiday Inn Downtown Bismarck H
(701) 255-6000. **$89-$250.** 605 E Broadway Ave. Center (6th St and Broadway Ave). Int corridors. **Pets:** Accepted.

Kelly Inn MI
(701) 223-8001. **$59-$79.** 1800 N 12 St. I-94, exit 159 (US 83), 0.3 mi s. Int corridors. **Pets:** Medium. Designated rooms, service with restrictions, supervision.

Radisson Hotel Bismarck MI
(701) 258-7700. **$250.** 800 S 3rd St. Just s of jct I-94 business loop and S 3rd St; opposite Kirkwood Mall. Int corridors. **Pets:** $10 daily fee/room. Designated rooms.

Select Inn M
(701) 223-8060. **$43-$62, 7 days notice.** 1505 Interchange Ave. I-94, exit 159 (US 83), just se. Int corridors. **Pets:** $25 deposit/room, $5 daily fee/room. Designated rooms, service with restrictions, supervision.

BOWMAN

Budget Host 4U Motel M
(701) 523-3243. **$38-$46.** 704 Hwy 12 W. US 12 and 85, midway between US 85 N and 85 S. Ext corridors. **Pets:** Designated rooms, service with restrictions, supervision.

North Winds Lodge M
(701) 523-5641. **$40-$54.** 503 Hwy 85 S. US 85, just s of US 12. Ext corridors. **Pets:** Other species. Designated rooms, service with restrictions, supervision.

CARRINGTON

Chieftain Conference Center MI
(701) 652-3131. **$55-$75.** 60 4th Ave S. 0.5 mi e on US 52 and 281, just s of jct SR 200. Ext/int corridors. **Pets:** Small. $5 one-time fee/room. Designated rooms, service with restrictions, supervision.

Super 8 Motel M
(701) 652-3982. **$51-$58.** 101 4th Ave S. 0.5 mi e on US 52 and 281, just s of jct SR 200. Int corridors. **Pets:** Medium, other species. $5 daily fee/pet. Service with restrictions, supervision.

DEVILS LAKE

Comfort Inn M
(701) 662-6760. **$54-$77.** 215 Hwy 2 E. Jct US 2 and SR 20. Int corridors. **Pets:** Other species. $10 deposit/room. Service with restrictions, crate.

Days Inn Devils Lake M
(701) 662-5381. **$49-$56.** 1109 Hwy 20 S. On SR 20, just s of jct US 2. Ext corridors. **Pets:** Accepted.

Trails West Motel M
(701) 662-5011. **$38-$41, 7 days notice.** Hwy 2 W. 0.8 mi sw on US 2. Int corridors. **Pets:** $5 daily fee/pet. Service with restrictions, supervision.

DICKINSON

▼▼▼ AmericInn Motel & Suites of Dickinson M
(701) 225-1400. **$68-$105.** 229 15th St W. I-94, exit 61, just ne. Int corridors. **Pets:** Other species. Designated rooms, service with restrictions, supervision.

(A$K) (S◐) (✕) (ᵫM) (∅) (໒) (🛏) (💻) (➤)

▲▲▲ ▼▼ Best Western Badlands Inn M
(701) 225-9510. **$50-$70, 7 days notice.** 71 Museum Dr. I-94, exit 61, just se of jct SR 22. Int corridors. **Pets:** Medium. $50 deposit/room. Service with restrictions, supervision.

(SAVE) (S◐) (✕) (🛏) (💻) (➤)

▼▼ Comfort Inn M
(701) 264-7300. **$70-$80.** 493 Elk Dr. I-94, exit 61, just nw of jct SR 22. Int corridors. **Pets:** Other species. Designated rooms, service with restrictions, supervision.

(SAVE) (S◐) (✕) (ᵫM) (∅) (໒) (🛏) (💻) (➤)

▼▼ Hartfiel Inn BB
(701) 225-6710. **$69-$79.** 509 3rd Ave W. I-94, exit 61, 0.8 mi s on SR 22. Int corridors. **Pets:** Small, dogs only. Service with restrictions, supervision.

(✕)

FARGO

▲▲▲ ▼▼ Airport/Dome Days Inn & Suites M
(701) 232-0000. **$57-$84.** 1507 19th Ave N. I-29, exit 67, 1.2 mi e. Int corridors. **Pets:** Medium. $15 deposit/room. Designated rooms, service with restrictions, supervision.

(SAVE) (S◐) (✕) (∅) (໒) (🛏) (💻) (➤)

▲▲▲ ▼▼▼ AmericInn Lodge & Suites M
(701) 234-9946. **$62-$120.** 1423 35th St SW. I-29, exit 64 (13th Ave S), just se. Int corridors. **Pets:** Medium. $50 deposit/pet. Designated rooms, service with restrictions, supervision.

(SAVE) (✕) (∅) (໒) (🛏) (💻) (➤)

▼▼ Best Western Doublewood Inn MI
(701) 235-3333. **$84.** 3333 13th Ave S. I-29, exit 64 (13th Ave S), 0.3 mi e. Int corridors. **Pets:** Small, dogs only. Designated rooms, service with restrictions, crate.

(SAVE) (S◐) (✕) (ᵫM) (∅) (໒) (🛏) (💻) (🍴) (➤)

▲▲▲ ▼▼▼ Best Western Kelly Inn MI
(701) 282-2143. **$59-$99.** 3800 Main Ave. I-29, exit 65 (Main Ave), just w. Ext/int corridors. **Pets:** Small, other species. Supervision.

(SAVE) (S◐) (✕) (∅) (໒) (🛏) (💻) (🍴) (➤)

▼▼▼ Comfort Inn East M
(701) 280-9666. **$59-$94.** 1407 35th St S. I-29, exit 64 (13th Ave S), just se. Int corridors. **Pets:** Accepted.

(SAVE) (S◐) (✕) (∅) (🛏) (💻) (➤)

▼▼ Comfort Inn West M
(701) 282-9596. **$59-$94.** 3825 9th Ave SW. I-29, exit 64 (13th Ave S), just nw. Int corridors. **Pets:** Medium, other species. Designated rooms, service with restrictions, supervision.

(SAVE) (S◐) (✕) (🛏) (💻) (➤)

▼▼ Comfort Suites M
(701) 237-5911. **$69-$104.** 1415 35th St SW. I-29, exit 64 (13th Ave S), just se. Int corridors. **Pets:** Medium, other species. Designated rooms, service with restrictions, supervision.

(SAVE) (S◐) (✕) (ᵫM) (∅) (໒) (🛏) (💻) (➤)

▲▲▲ ▼▼▼ Country Suites By Carlson M
(701) 234-0565. **$81-$86.** 3316 13th Ave S. I-29, exit 64 (13th Ave S), 0.3 mi e. Int corridors. **Pets:** Small. $100 deposit/room, $10 daily fee/room. Designated rooms, service with restrictions, crate.

(SAVE) (S◐) (✕) (🛏) (💻) (➤)

▼▼ Econo Lodge of Fargo M
(701) 232-3412. **$39-$69.** 1401 35th St S. I-29, exit 64 (13th Ave S), just se. Int corridors. **Pets:** Designated rooms, service with restrictions, supervision.

(SAVE) (S◐) (✕) (∅) (໒) (💻)

▲▲▲ ▼▼▼ Flying J Inn M
(701) 282-8473. **$38.** 3150 39th St SW. I-29, exit 62, just nw. Int corridors. **Pets:** Medium. $10 one-time fee/room. Designated rooms, service with restrictions, supervision.

(SAVE) (S◐) (✕)

▼▼▼ Holiday Inn MI
(701) 282-2700. **$99-$149.** 3803 13th Ave S. I-29, exit 64 (13 Ave S), just nw. Int corridors. **Pets:** Service with restrictions, supervision.

(A$K) (S◐) (✕) (ᵫM) (∅) (໒) (🛏) (💻) (🍴) (➤)

▼▼▼ Holiday Inn Express Fargo M
(701) 282-2000. **$55-$80, 30 days notice.** 1040 40th St S. I-29, exit 64 (13th Ave S), just nw. Int corridors. **Pets:** Medium. Service with restrictions, supervision.

(✕) (ᵫM) (໒) (💻) (➤)

▲▲▲ ▼▼▼ Kelly Inn 13th Avenue M
(701) 277-8821. **$65-$104.** 4207 13th Ave SW. I-29, exit 64 (13th Ave S), just w. Ext/int corridors. **Pets:** Small. Service with restrictions, supervision.

(SAVE) (S◐) (✕) (ᵫM) (∅) (໒) (🛏) (💻) (➤)

▼ Motel 6 M
(701) 232-9251. **$38-$46.** 1202 36th S. I-29, exit 64 (13th Ave), just n, on east frontage road. Int corridors. **Pets:** Other species. Service with restrictions, supervision.

(✕) (໒) (➤)

▲▲▲ ▼ Motel 75 M
(701) 232-1321. **$43-$53.** 3402 14th Ave S. I-29, exit 64 (13th Ave), just se. Int corridors. **Pets:** Large, other species. Designated rooms, service with restrictions, supervision.

(SAVE) (S◐) (✕)

▼▼▼▼ **Radisson Hotel Fargo** 🄷
(701) 232-7363. **$74-$81.** 201 5th St N. Downtown; corner of 2nd Ave N and 5th St N. Int corridors. **Pets:** Medium. $25 deposit/room. Designated rooms, service with restrictions, crate.

ⒶⓈⓀ 🆂 ⓧ 🝣 🝙 🝓 🝒 🝕 ¶

▼▼ **Red Roof Inn** Ⓜ
(701) 282-9100. **$42-$53.** 901 38th St SW. I-29, exit 64 (13 Ave S), just nw. Int corridors. **Pets:** Service with restrictions, supervision.

ⒶⓈⓀ 🆂 ⓧ 🝒

⬥⬥⬥ ▼ **Select Inn** Ⓜ ☙
(701) 282-6300. **$41-$54, 7 days notice.** 1025 38th St SW. I-29, exit 64 (13th Ave S), just nw. Int corridors. **Pets:** Other species. $25 deposit/room, $5 daily fee/room. Designated rooms, service with restrictions, supervision.

🆂🄰🆅🄴 🆂 ⓧ 🝓 🝙 🝒

▼▼ **Sleep Inn** Ⓜ
(701) 281-8240. **$59-$79.** 1921 44 St SW. I-94, exit 348 (45th St), just n, then e. Int corridors. **Pets:** Accepted.

🆂🄰🆅🄴 🆂 ⓧ 🝣 🝙 🝒 🝕 ➣

▼▼ **Super 8 Motel** Ⓜ
(701) 232-9202. **$48-$62.** 3518 Interstate Blvd. I-29, exit 64 (13th Ave), just n on east frontage road. Int corridors. **Pets:** Small. $4 daily fee/room. Supervision.

ⒶⓈⓀ ⓧ 🝙 🝒 ➣

GRAND FORKS

▼▼ **Best Western Town House** Ⓜ🄸
(701) 746-5411. **Call for rates, 3 days notice.** 710 1st Ave N. I-29, exit 140, 3 mi e; downtown. Int corridors. **Pets:** Designated rooms, service with restrictions, supervision.

ⒶⓈⓀ ⓧ 🝣 🝙 🝒 ¶ ➣

▼▼▼ **Comfort Inn** Ⓜ
(701) 775-7503. **$59-$89.** 3251 30th Ave S. I-29, exit 138, 0.5 mi e. Int corridors. **Pets:** Other species. Designated rooms, service with restrictions, supervision.

🆂🄰🆅🄴 🆂 ⓧ 🝙 🝒 ➣

▼▼ **Days Inn** Ⓜ
(701) 775-0060. **$54-$84.** 3101 34th St S. I-29, exit 138, 0.5 mi e. Int corridors. **Pets:** Small. $5 one-time fee/room. Designated rooms, service with restrictions, supervision.

🆂🄰🆅🄴 🆂 ⓧ 🝙 ➣

▼▼ **Econo Lodge** Ⓜ
(701) 746-6666. **$45-$69.** 900 N 43 St. I-29, exit 141 (Gateway Dr), just se. Int corridors. **Pets:** Medium, other species. $50 deposit/pet, $10 daily fee/pet. Supervision.

🆂🄰🆅🄴 🆂 ⓧ 🝙 🝒

▼▼▼▼ **Holiday Inn Grand Forks** Ⓜ🄸
(701) 772-7131. **$79-$90, 3 days notice.** 1210 N 43rd St. I-29, exit 141 (Gateway Dr), just e on US 2. Ext/int corridors. **Pets:** Accepted.

ⒶⓈⓀ 🆂 ⓧ 🝣 🝙 🝒 ¶ ➣

▼▼ **Rodeway Inn** Ⓜ
(701) 795-9960. **$45-$65.** 4001 Gateway Dr. I-29, exit 141 (Gateway Dr), 0.3 mi e on US 2. Int corridors. **Pets:** Accepted.

🆂🄰🆅🄴 🆂 ⓧ 🝙 🝒

⬥⬥⬥ ▼ **Select Inn of Grand Forks** Ⓜ
(701) 775-0555. **$36-$46.** 1000 N 42nd St. I-29, exit 141 (Gateway Dr), just se of US 2. Int corridors. **Pets:** Accepted.

🆂🄰🆅🄴 🆂 ⓧ

▼▼ **Travelodge** Ⓜ
(701) 772-8151. **$51.** 3400 Gateway Dr. I-29, exit 141 (Gateway Dr), 0.8 mi e on US 2. Ext corridors. **Pets:** Supervision.

ⒶⓈⓀ 🆂 ⓧ 🝙 🝒 ➣

HANKINSON

▼▼▼▼ **Dakota Magic Casino & Hotel** 🄷
(701) 634-3201. **$40-$50.** 16849 102nd St SE. I-29, exit 1, just e. Int corridors. **Pets:** Accepted.

ⒶⓈⓀ 🆂 ⓧ 🝣 🝓 🝙 🝒 ¶ ➣

JAMESTOWN

▼▼ **Comfort Inn** Ⓜ
(701) 252-7125. **$64-$94.** 811 20 St SW. I-94, exit 258, just n, then w. Int corridors. **Pets:** Accepted.

🆂🄰🆅🄴 🆂 ⓧ 🝙 🝒 ➣

⬥⬥⬥ ▼ **Ranch House Motel** Ⓜ
(701) 252-0222. **$35-$46.** 408 Business Loop W. I-94, exit 258, 0.8 mi n on US 281. Ext/int corridors. **Pets:** $5 daily fee/pet. Designated rooms, service with restrictions, supervision.

🆂🄰🆅🄴 ⓧ 🝙 ➣

KENMARE

▼▼ **Quilt Inn** Ⓜ
(701) 385-4100. **$50.** 1232 N Central Ave. Just n on US 52. Int corridors. **Pets:** Accepted.

ⒶⓈⓀ ⓧ ➣

MANDAN

▼▼▼ **Best Western Seven Seas Inn & Conference Center** Ⓜ🄸
(701) 663-7401. **$79.** 2611 Old Red Tr. I-94, exit 152, just nw. Int corridors. **Pets:** $25 deposit/room. Service with restrictions, crate.

🆂🄰🆅🄴 🆂 ⓧ 🝣 🝙 🝒 ¶ ➣

MEDORA

AAA ▼▼▼▼ AmericInn Motel & Suites **M**
(701) 623-4800. **$61-$199.** 75 E River Rd S. I-94, exit 24, just se of downtown. Int corridors. **Pets:** Accepted.
[SAVE] [S🐾] [✕] [🅱M] [🐾] 🅱 🖵 ⊇

MINOT

AAA ▼▼▼▼ Best Western Kelly Inn **M**
(701) 852-4300. **$56-$125.** 1510 26th Ave SW. US 2 and 52 Bypass at 16th St SW; adjacent to Dakota Square Mall. Ext/int corridors. **Pets:** Other species. Designated rooms, service with restrictions, crate.
[SAVE] [S🐾] [✕] 🖵 ⊇

AAA ▼▼▼ Comfort Inn **M**
(701) 852-2201. **$58-$75.** 1515 22nd Ave SW. US 2 and 52 Bypass, at 16th St SW; adjacent to Dakota Square Mall. Int corridors. **Pets:** Other species. Service with restrictions, crate.
[SAVE] [S🐾] [✕] [🅱] 🅱 🖵 ⊇

AAA ▼▼ Dakota Inn **M**
(701) 838-2700. **$49-$54.** 2401 US 2 & 52 Bypass. Jct US 83, 1 mi w. Int corridors. **Pets:** Medium. Designated rooms, service with restrictions, supervision.
[SAVE] [S🐾] [✕] [🅱] [🐾] ⊇

AAA ▼▼ Days Inn **M**
(701) 852-3646. **$45-$61, 14 days notice.** 2100 4th St SW. Just n of jct SR 83, US 2 and 52 Bypass. Int corridors. **Pets:** Small, dogs only. $30 deposit/room. Designated rooms, service with restrictions, supervision.
[SAVE] [S🐾] [✕] [🅱] [🐾] 🅱 🖵 ⊇

▼▼▼ Holiday Inn Riverside Minot **MI**
(701) 852-2504. **$59-$93.** 2200 Burdick Expwy E. 1.3 mi e on US 2 business route (Burdick Expwy E). Int corridors. **Pets:** Very small, dogs only. Designated rooms, service with restrictions, supervision.
[ASK] [S🐾] [✕] [🐾] 🅱 🖵 [🍴] ⊇

AAA ▼▼▼▼ International Inn **MI**
(701) 852-3161. **$63-$89, 3 days notice.** 1505 N Broadway. 1.5 mi n on US 83. Int corridors. **Pets:** Large. Supervision.
[SAVE] [S🐾] [✕] [🐾] [🐾] 🅱 🖵 [🍴] ⊇

AAA ▼▼▼ Select Inn **M**
(701) 852-3411. **$38-$50, 7 days notice.** 225 22nd Ave NW. 2 mi n on US 83. Int corridors. **Pets:** Other species. $25 deposit/room, $5 daily fee/room. Designated rooms, service with restrictions, supervision.
[SAVE] [S🐾] [✕] [🐾] 🖵

NEW TOWN

AAA ▼▼▼ 4 Bears Lodge **MI**
(701) 627-4018. **$55, 4 days notice.** SR 23 W. 4 mi w. Int corridors. **Pets:** Accepted.
[SAVE] [S🐾] [✕] 🅱 🖵 [🍴] ⊇

VALLEY CITY

AAA ▼▼▼ Wagon Wheel Inn & Suites **M**
(701) 845-5333. **$50-$60.** 455 Winter Show Rd. I-94, exit 292, just ne. Ext/int corridors. **Pets:** Small, other species. Designated rooms, service with restrictions, supervision.
[SAVE] [✕] 🅱 🖵 ⊇

WAHPETON

▼▼▼ Comfort Inn **M**
(701) 642-1115. **$54-$84.** 209 13th St S. SR 13, 0.3 mi e of jct SR 210 Bypass. Int corridors. **Pets:** Other species. Designated rooms, service with restrictions, supervision.
[SAVE] [S🐾] [✕] 🅱 🖵 ⊇

▼▼▼ Holiday Inn Express **M**
(701) 642-5000. **$59-$69.** 1800 Two-Ten Dr. 1 mi n on SR 210 Bypass. Int corridors. **Pets:** Other species. Service with restrictions, supervision.
[ASK] [S🐾] [✕] [🅱M] [🐾] 🅱 ⊇

WATFORD CITY

AAA ▼▼ McKenzie Inn **M**
(701) 444-3980. **$41.** 132 SW 3rd St. US 85, just w of SR 23. Ext corridors. **Pets:** Medium, other species. Supervision.
[SAVE] [S🐾] [✕] 🅱

WEST FARGO

AAA ▼▼▼ West Fargo Days Inn **M**
(701) 281-0000. **$55-$67.** 525 Main Ave E. I-29, exit 65, 2.3 mi w. Int corridors. **Pets:** Medium. $15 deposit/room. Designated rooms, service with restrictions, supervision.
[SAVE] [S🐾] [✕] [🐾] 🅱 🖵 ⊇

WILLISTON

▼▼ El Rancho Motor Hotel **MI**
(701) 572-6321. **$48-$54.** 1623 2nd Ave W. US 2 and 85 N Bypass, 1 mi n. Ext/int corridors. **Pets:** Designated rooms, service with restrictions.
[ASK] [S🐾] [✕] 🅱 [🍴]

AAA ▼▼▼ Super 8 Motel **M**
(701) 572-8371. **$47-$57, 10 days notice.** 2324 2nd Ave W. 1.3 mi n on US 2 and 85 Bypass. Int corridors. **Pets:** $20 deposit/room. Designated rooms, service with restrictions, supervision.
[SAVE] [S🐾] [✕] [🐾] ⊇

CITY INDEX

AKRON

▼▼ **Days Inn Akron South/Airport** Ⓜ
(330) 644-1204. **$50-$70, 14 days notice.** 3237 S Arlington Rd. I-77, exit 120, just s. Ext corridors. **Pets:** Accepted.
[SAVE] [S$] [✕] [🖥] [🐾]

▼ **Econo Lodge** Ⓜ
(330) 644-1847. **$45-$70, 14 days notice.** 3237 1/2 S Arlington. I-77, exit 120, just s. Ext corridors. **Pets:** Accepted.
[SAVE] [S$] [✕] [🖥]

④④④ ▼▼▼ **Holiday Inn Express Akron South** Ⓜ
(330) 644-7126. **$79-$119, 3 days notice.** 2940 Chenoweth Rd. I-77, exit 120, just n. Int corridors. **Pets:** Accepted.
[SAVE] [S$] [✕] [🍴] [🖥] [💻] [🐾]

④④④ ▼▼▼ **Red Roof Inn-Akron South** Ⓜ
(330) 644-7748. **$41-$65.** 2939 S Arlington Rd. I-77, exit 120, just n. **Pets:** Small, other species. Service with restrictions, supervision.
[SAVE] [✕]

ALLIANCE

④④④ ▼▼▼ **Holiday Inn Express Hotel & Suites** Ⓜ
(330) 821-6700. **$75-$109.** 2341 W State St. 2 mi w on US 62. Int corridors. **Pets:** Medium, other species. $10 one-time fee/room. Designated rooms, service with restrictions, crate.
[SAVE] [S$] [✕] [🐕] [🍴] [💻] [🐾]

④④④ ▼▼▼ **Super 8 Motel** Ⓜ
(330) 821-5688. **$49-$67.** 2330 W State St. 2 mi w on US 62. Ext corridors. **Pets:** Accepted.
[SAVE] [S$] [✕] [🐕] [🐾]

ASHLAND

④④④ ▼▼▼ **Days Inn** Ⓜ
(419) 289-0101. **$45-$70.** 1423 CR 1575. I-71, exit 186, just w. Ext corridors. **Pets:** Other species. Service with restrictions, crate.
[SAVE] [✕] [🍴] [💻] [🐾]

 Holiday Inn Express Hotel &
Suites-Ashland **M**
(419) 281-2900. **$79-$139.** 1392 Montgomery Township Rd
743. I-71, exit 186, 0.5 mi w. Int corridors. **Pets:** Accepted.

ASHTABULA

 Cedars Motel **M**
(440) 992-5406. **$70-$80.** 2015 W Prospect Rd. Jct SR 11,
3 mi w on US 20. Ext corridors. **Pets:** Other species. $5
daily fee/pet. Service with restrictions, supervision.

Ho Hum Motel **M**
(440) 969-1136. **$55-$80.** 3801 N Ridge West. I-90, exit
223, 3 mi n on SR 45, 1 mi e on SR 20. **Pets:** Other
species. $5 daily fee/pet. Service with restrictions, crate.

ATHENS

 Days Inn-Athens **M**
(740) 592-4000. **$69-$85, 6 days notice.** 330 Columbus
Rd. Jct US 33, SR 550 and 13. Ext corridors. **Pets:** Small.
$5 one-time fee/room. Service with restrictions.

AUSTINBURG

Comfort Inn-Ashtabula **MI**
(440) 275-2711. **$78-$135.** 1860 Austinburg Rd. I-90, exit
223, just n. Int corridors. **Pets:** Service with restrictions,
supervision.

AUSTINTOWN

 Best Western Meander Inn **MI**
(330) 544-2378. **$60-$90.** 870 N Canfield-Niles Rd. I-80,
exit 223, 0.3 mi s on SR 46. Int corridors. **Pets:** $6 daily
fee/pet. Designated rooms, service with restrictions, supervision.

Motel 6–4066 **M**
(330) 793-9305. **$50-$70.** 5431 Seventy Six Dr. I-80, exit
223, just s on SR 46. Ext corridors. **Pets:** Other species.
Service with restrictions, supervision.

BELLEFONTAINE

Best Hotel **MI**
(937) 593-8515. **$69-$119, 15 days notice.** 1134 N Main
St. Jct US 33 and SR 68. Ext/int corridors. **Pets:** Accepted.

BLUFFTON

Comfort Inn **M**
(419) 358-6000. **$50-$100.** 117 Commerce Ln. I-75, exit
142, just w on SR 103. Int corridors. **Pets:** Accepted.

BOARDMAN

 Days Inn **M**
(330) 758-2371. **$36-$85, 7 days notice.** 8392 Market St.
I-76 (Ohio Tpke), exit 232, 1.8 mi n on SR 7. Ext corridors.
Pets: $5 daily fee/pet. Designated rooms, service with
restrictions, supervision.

Microtel Inn Youngstown **M**
(330) 758-1816. **$40-$60, 7 days notice.** 7393 South Ave.
Jct I-680 and US 224, 0.3 mi w. Int corridors. **Pets:** Other
species. $25 one-time fee/pet. Service with restrictions,
supervision.

BOWLING GREEN

 Days Inn **M**
(419) 352-5211. **$56-$129, 7 days notice.** 1550 E Wooster
St. I-75, exit 181, just w. Ext corridors. **Pets:** Medium. $10
one-time fee/pet. Service with restrictions, supervision.

BROOKVILLE

 Brookville Days Inn **M**
(937) 833-4003. **$50-$70, 30 days notice.** 100 Parkview
Dr. I-70, exit 21. Ext corridors. **Pets:** $10 daily fee/pet.
Service with restrictions, supervision.

BRUNSWICK

 Sleep Inn **M**
(330) 273-1112. **$65-$80, 7 days notice.** 1435 S Carpenter
Rd. I-71, exit 226, just w. Ext corridors. **Pets:** $10 daily
fee/pet. Service with restrictions, supervision.

CAMBRIDGE

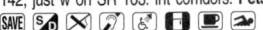 Best Western Cambridge **M**
(740) 439-3581. **$39-$79, 3 days notice.** 1945 Southgate
Pkwy. I-70, exit 178, 0.3 mi n on SR 209. Ext corridors.
Pets: Medium, other species. Service with restrictions,
crate.

Budget Host Deer Creek Motel **M**
(740) 432-6391. **$35-$59.** 2321 Southgate Pkwy. I-70, exit
178, just n on SR 209. Ext corridors. **Pets:** Other species.
$5 one-time fee/room. Designated rooms, service with
restrictions, supervision.

Budget Inn **M**
(740) 432-2304. **$30-$50.** 6405 Glenn Hwy. I-70, exit 176, e
on US 40. Ext/int corridors. **Pets:** Small. $10 daily fee/pet.
Designated rooms, service with restrictions, supervision.

▼▼▼ Comfort Inn M
(740) 435-3200. **$74-$114.** 2327 Southgate Pkwy. I-70, exit 178, just n on SR 209. Int corridors. **Pets:** Medium. $10 one-time fee/room. Designated rooms, service with restrictions, crate.

⟨SAVE⟩ ⟨S🐾⟩ ⟨✕⟩ ⟨✦⟩ ⟨🛏⟩ ⟨💻⟩ ⟨🏊⟩

▼▼▼ Holiday Inn Cambridge/Salt Fork Area M
(740) 432-7313. **$55-$79.** 2248 Southgate Pkwy. I-70, exit 178, just n on SR 209. Int corridors. **Pets:** Medium. Crate.

⟨ASK⟩ ⟨S🐾⟩ ⟨✕⟩ ⟨⌀⟩ ⟨🛏⟩ ⟨💻⟩ ⟨🍴⟩

CANTON

▼▼▼ Best Suites of America M
(330) 499-1011. **$73-$127, 14 days notice.** 4914 Everhard Rd. I-77, exit 109, 1 mi w. Int corridors. **Pets:** Accepted.

⟨SAVE⟩ ⟨S🐾⟩ ⟨✕⟩ ⟨⌀⟩ ⟨🛏⟩ ⟨💻⟩ ⟨🏊⟩

▼▼ Red Roof Inn M
(330) 499-1970. **$42-$68.** 5353 Inn Circle Ct NW. I-77, exit 109, just w on Everhard Rd. Ext corridors. **Pets:** Large. Service with restrictions, crate.

⟨SAVE⟩ ⟨✕⟩ ⟨⌀⟩

▼▼▼ Residence Inn By Marriott ▲
(330) 493-0004. **$68-$96.** 5325 Broadmoor Cir NW. I-77, exit 109, 0.5 mi e on Everhard Rd. Int corridors. **Pets:** Other species. $5 daily fee/pet, $100 one-time fee/room. Service with restrictions, supervision.

⟨SAVE⟩ ⟨S🐾⟩ ⟨✕⟩ ⟨⌀⟩ ⟨🛏⟩ ⟨💻⟩ ⟨🏊⟩

CINCINNATI METROPOLITAN AREA

BATAVIA

▼▼▼ Hampton Inn-Cincinnati Eastgate M
(513) 752-8584. **$71-$109.** 858 Eastgate North Dr. I-275, exit 63B (SR 32). Int corridors. **Pets:** Accepted.

⟨SAVE⟩ ⟨S🐾⟩ ⟨✕⟩ ⟨⌀⟩ ⟨✦⟩ ⟨💻⟩ ⟨🏊⟩

▼▼▼ Holiday Inn-Cincinnati Eastgate M
(513) 752-4400. **$79-$119.** 4501 Eastgate Blvd. I-275, exit 63B (SR 32) to Eastgate Mall exit. Int corridors. **Pets:** Small, dogs only. Service with restrictions, supervision.

⟨SAVE⟩ ⟨S🐾⟩ ⟨✕⟩ ⟨⌀⟩ ⟨🛏⟩ ⟨💻⟩ ⟨🍴⟩ ⟨🏊⟩

BLUE ASH

▼▼▼▼ AmeriSuites (Cincinnati/Blue Ash) M
(513) 489-3666. **$79-$119.** 11435 Reed-Hartman Hwy. I-275, exit 47, 0.8 mi s. Int corridors. **Pets:** Accepted.

⟨SAVE⟩ ⟨S🐾⟩ ⟨✕⟩ ⟨🔊M⟩ ⟨⌀⟩ ⟨🛏⟩ ⟨💻⟩ ⟨🏊⟩

CARROLLTON

▼▼▼ Carrollton Days Inn M
(330) 627-9314. **$69-$99, 7 days notice.** 1111 Canton Rd. On SR 43, 0.5 mi n of SR 39. Int corridors. **Pets:** Medium. $50 deposit/pet. Service with restrictions, supervision.

⟨SAVE⟩ ⟨S🐾⟩ ⟨✕⟩ ⟨🛏⟩ ⟨💻⟩ ⟨🏊⟩

CHILLICOTHE

▼▼▼ Christopher Inn M
(740) 774-6835. **$59-$79.** 30 N Plaza Blvd. US 35, exit Bridge St. Int corridors. **Pets:** $5 daily fee/room. Service with restrictions.

⟨SAVE⟩ ⟨S🐾⟩ ⟨✕⟩ ⟨✦⟩ ⟨🛏⟩ ⟨💻⟩ ⟨🏊⟩

▼▼▼ Comfort Inn M
(740) 775-3500. **$49-$79.** 20 N Plaza Blvd. Jct US 35 and US 23 business route. Int corridors. **Pets:** Other species. Service with restrictions.

⟨SAVE⟩ ⟨S🐾⟩ ⟨✕⟩ ⟨🛏⟩ ⟨💻⟩ ⟨🏊⟩

▼ Country Hearth Inn M
(740) 775-2500. **$45-$75.** 1135 E Main St. Jct US 35 and 50. Ext/int corridors. **Pets:** Accepted.

⟨ASK⟩ ⟨S🐾⟩ ⟨✕⟩ ⟨🛏⟩ ⟨💻⟩ ⟨🏊⟩

▼▼▼ Days Inn Chillicothe M
(740) 775-7000. **$50-$62, 3 days notice.** 1250 N Bridge St. US 35, exit Bridge St, 0.8 mi n. Int corridors. **Pets:** Other species. $5 daily fee/room. Service with restrictions, crate.

⟨SAVE⟩ ⟨S🐾⟩ ⟨✕⟩ ⟨🛏⟩ ⟨💻⟩ ⟨🏊⟩

▼▼▼ Clarion Hotel and Suites Cincinnati M
(513) 793-4500. **$69-$149.** 5901 Pfieffer Rd. I-71, exit 15, just w. Int corridors. **Pets:** Medium. Service with restrictions, supervision.

⟨SAVE⟩ ⟨S🐾⟩ ⟨✕⟩ ⟨⌀⟩ ⟨✦⟩ ⟨🛏⟩ ⟨💻⟩ ⟨🍴⟩ ⟨🏊⟩

▼▼▼ MainStay Suites-Blue Ash M
(513) 985-9992. **$65-$95.** 4630 Creek Rd. I-275, exit 47, 2.3 mi s on Reed-Hartman Hwy, just e. Int corridors. **Pets:** Accepted.

⟨SAVE⟩ ⟨S🐾⟩ ⟨✕⟩ ⟨⌀⟩ ⟨✦⟩ ⟨🛏⟩ ⟨💻⟩ ⟨🏊⟩

▼▼ Red Roof Inn Northeast (Blue Ash) M
(513) 793-8811. **$46-$76.** 5900 Pfeiffer Rd. I-71, exit 15, just w. Ext corridors. **Pets:** Large. Service with restrictions, crate.

⟨SAVE⟩ ⟨✕⟩ ⟨🔊M⟩ ⟨✦⟩ ⟨🛏⟩

▼▼▼ Residence Inn by Marriott-Blue Ash M 🐾
(513) 530-5060. **$119-$129.** 11401 Reed-Hartman Hwy. I-275, exit 47, 0.8 mi s. Ext corridors. **Pets:** Large, other species. $75 one-time fee/room. Service with restrictions.

⟨SAVE⟩ ⟨S🐾⟩ ⟨✕⟩ ⟨🔊M⟩ ⟨⌀⟩ ⟨✦⟩ ⟨🛏⟩ ⟨💻⟩ ⟨🏊⟩

CHERRY GROVE

(AAA) ▼▼▼ Red Roof Inn Cincinnati East M
(513) 528-2741. **$44-$79.** 4035 Mt Carmel-Tobasco Rd.
I-275, exit 65. Ext corridors. **Pets:** Other species. Service
with restrictions, crate.

SAVE ✕ ⬛

CINCINNATI

(AAA) ▼▼▼▼ Garfield Suites Hotel C
(513) 421-3355. **$149-$600.** 2 Garfield Pl. Corner of Vine
and 8th sts. Int corridors. **Pets:** Small, other species. $100
one-time fee/pet. Designated rooms, service with restrictions, supervision.

SAVE S⬛ ✕ ⬠ ⬛ ⬛ ⬚

▼▼▼▼ Hannaford Suites Hotel M
(513) 936-0525. **$79-$129.** 5900 E Galbraith Rd. I-71, exit
12, just w. Int corridors. **Pets:** Accepted.

ASK S⬛ ✕ ⬛ ⬛ ⬚

(AAA) ▼▼▼▼ Holiday Inn-Downtown MI
(513) 241-8660. **$69-$89.** 800 W 8th St. I-75, exit 1G;
entrance on 8th St. Int corridors. **Pets:** Accepted.

SAVE ✕ ⬛M ⬚ ⬚ ⬛ ⬚ ⬚

FOREST PARK

▼▼▼ Lees Inn & Suites Cincinnati M
(513) 825-9600. **$99-$129, 7 days notice.** 11967 Chase
Plaza Dr. I-275, exit 39, just s on Winton Rd. Int corridors.
Pets: Designated rooms, service with restrictions, crate.

ASK S⬛ ✕ ⬛M ⬚ ⬛ ⬛ ⬚

MASON

**(AAA) ▼▼▼▼ AmeriSuites (Cincinnati/Deerfield
Crossing)** M
(513) 754-0003. **$109-$129.** 5070 Natorp Blvd. I-71, exit 19,
0.5 mi w. Int corridors. **Pets:** Medium, other species. Service with restrictions, crate.

SAVE S⬛ ✕ ⬚ ⬛ ⬛ ⬚

**(AAA) ▼▼▼▼ Baymont Inn & Suites
Cincinnati-Mason/near Kings
Island** M
(513) 459-1111. **$64-$74.** 9918 Escort Dr. I-71, exit 19, just
w, then just s. Int corridors. **Pets:** Medium, other species.
$50 deposit/room. Designated rooms, service with restric-
tions.

SAVE S⬛ ✕ ⬚ ⬚ ⬛ ⬛ ⬚

**(AAA) ▼▼▼▼ Holiday Inn Express Kings
Island** M
(513) 398-8075. **$59-$275.** 5589 Kings Mills Rd. I-71, exit
25, just w, then just s. Ext corridors. **Pets:** Medium, other
species. Service with restrictions, crate.

SAVE ✕ ⬛M ⬚ ⬛ ⬛ ⬚

(AAA) ▼▼▼ Ramada Inn-Kings Island MI
(513) 398-8015. **$49-$129.** 9845 Escort Dr. I-71, exit 19,
just w. Int corridors. **Pets:** Other species. $10 daily fee/pet.
Supervision.

SAVE S⬛ ✕ ⬛ ⬛ ⬚ ⬚

▼▼▼ Red Roof Inn-Kings Island M
(513) 398-3633. **$35-$125, 10 days notice.** 9847 Bards
Rd. I-71, exit 19, just w. Ext corridors. **Pets:** Medium. $10
one-time fee/pet. Designated rooms, service with restrictions, supervision.

ASK S⬛ ✕ ⬛M ⬚ ⬚ ⬛ ⬛ ⬚

MIDDLETOWN

**▼▼▼ The Manchester Inn & Conference
Center** H
(513) 422-5481. **$82.** 1027 Manchester Ave. Just w of SR 4
and 73; at Middletown Civic Center. Int corridors.
Pets: Accepted.

ASK S⬛ ✕ ⬛ ⬛ ⬚

▼▼ Super 8 Motel M
(513) 422-4888. **$49-$79.** 3553 Commerce Dr. I-75, exit 32,
just e, then just n. Int corridors. **Pets:** $10 one-time fee/
room. Designated rooms, service with restrictions, supervision.

ASK S⬛ ✕ ⬛

MOUNT ORAB

▼▼▼ Holiday Inn Express-Mt. Orab M
(937) 444-6666. **$79-$169, 15 days notice.** 100 Leininger
St. Jct SR 32 and US 68, just n on US 68. Int corridors.
Pets: Service with restrictions.

ASK S⬛ ✕ ⬚ ⬛ ⬚

NORWOOD

▼▼▼ Howard Johnson East M ✿
(513) 631-8500. **$58-$80, 14 days notice.** 5410 Ridge Rd.
I-71, exit 8 southbound; exit 8B northbound, 4 mi nw. Int
corridors. **Pets:** Other species. $25 deposit/room.

ASK S⬛ ✕ ⬛ ⬛ ⬚

**(AAA) ▼▼▼ Red Roof Inn Cincinnati Central
(Norwood)** M
(513) 531-6589. **$44-$56.** 5300 Kennedy Ave. I-71, exit 8
southbound; exit 8B northbound; corner of Highland. Ext
corridors. **Pets:** Medium. No service, supervision.

SAVE ✕ ⬚

SHARONVILLE

▼▼ Days Inn Cincinnati/Sharonville M ✿
(513) 554-1400. **$45-$145.** 11775 Lebanon Rd. I-275, exit
46, just s. Ext/int corridors. **Pets:** Dogs only. Service with
restrictions.

SAVE S⬛ ✕ ⬛ ⬚

▼▼▼▼ Homewood Suites by Hilton-Cincinnati
　　North 🅰 ❖
(513) 772-8888. $109-$129. 2670 E Kemper Rd. I-275, exit
44, jct Mosteller Rd. Int corridors. Pets: Other species. $8
daily fee/room. Service with restrictions, crate.
[SAVE] [S🐾] ⨯ 🛢 💻 ⇋

🅰🅰🅰 ▼▼▼▼ Radisson Hotel Cincinnati 🄷
(513) 772-1720. $95, 3 days notice. 11320 Chester Rd.
I-75, exit 15, 0.3 mi w on Sharon Rd, 0.5 mi n. Int corridors.
Pets: Very small, other species. $25 one-time fee/room.
Service with restrictions, crate.
[SAVE] [S🐾] ⨯ 🗭 💺 🛢 💻 🍴 ⇋

🅰🅰🅰 ▼▼▼ Red Roof Inn Chester Rd 🅜
(513) 771-5141. $44-$64. 11345 Chester Rd. I-75, exit 15,
0.3 mi w on Sharon Rd, 0.5 mi n. Ext corridors.
Pets: Accepted.
[SAVE] ⨯ 🗭 💺 🛢

🅰🅰🅰 ▼▼▼ Red Roof Inn-Sharon Road 🅜
(513) 771-5552. $44-$64. 2301 E Sharon Rd. I-75, exit 15,
just e. Ext corridors. Pets: Accepted.
[SAVE] ⨯ 🗭 🛢

🅰🅰🅰 ▼▼▼▼ Residence Inn by Marriott 🅰
(513) 771-2525. $99-$109. 11689 Chester Rd. I-75, exit 15,
0.3 mi w on Sharon Rd, 1 mi n. Ext corridors. Pets: Large,
other species. $6 daily fee/room, $100 one-time fee/room.
Service with restrictions.
[SAVE] [S🐾] ⨯ 💺 🛢 💻 ⇋

🅰🅰 ▼▼▼▼ Woodfield Suites 🅜
(513) 771-0300. $99-$199. 11029 Dowlin Dr. I-75, exit 15,
just e. Int corridors. Pets: Small, other species. $50 deposit/
room, $10 one-time fee/room. Designated rooms, service
with restrictions, supervision.
[SAVE] [S🐾] ⨯ 🄼 🗭 💺 🛢 💻 ⇋

SPRINGDALE

🅰🅰🅰 ▼▼▼ Baymont Inn & Suites-Cincinnati
　　North 🅜
(513) 671-2300. $59-$69. 12150 Springfield Pike. I-275, exit
41, just n. Int corridors. Pets: Medium, other species. Designated rooms, service with restrictions, crate.
[SAVE] [S🐾] ⨯ 🗭 🛢 💻

🅰🅰🅰 ▼▼▼▼ Best Western Springdale Hotel &
　　Conference Centre 🅜🅸
(513) 671-6600. $59-$99. 11911 Sheraton Ln. I-275, exit
41, just nw on SR 4. Int corridors. Pets: Large, other species. $25 one-time fee/room. Service with restrictions, crate.
[SAVE] [S🐾] ⨯ 💻 🍴

WILMINGTON

🅰🅰🅰 ▼▼▼▼ Holiday Inn Express 🅜
(937) 382-5858. $79. 155 Holiday Dr. 1.6 mi e on US 22.
Int corridors. Pets: Accepted.
[SAVE] [S🐾] ⨯ 🄼 🗭 💺 🛢 💻 ⇋

❖　End Metropolitan Area　❖

Cleveland Metropolitan Area

BEACHWOOD

▼▼▼ Homestead Studio
　　Suites-Cleveland/Beachwood 🅜
(216) 896-5555. $94-$104. 3625 Orange Pl. I-271, exit
Chagrin Blvd, just w. Int corridors. Pets: Accepted.
⨯ 💺 🛢 💻

🅰🅰🅰 ▼▼▼▼ Residence Inn by Marriot
　　Cleveland-Beachwood 🅰
(216) 831-3030. $129-$165. 3628 Park East Dr. Jct US 422
and I-271, exit Chagrin Blvd, just w. Int corridors.
Pets: Accepted.
[SAVE] [S🐾] ⨯ 🄼 🗭 💺 🛢 💻 ⇋

CLEVELAND

🅰🅰🅰 ▼▼▼▼ Baymont Inn & Suites
　　Cleveland-Airport 🅜
(216) 251-8500. $74-$84. 4222 W 150th St. I-71, exit 240,
just n. Int corridors. Pets: $50 deposit/room. Designated
rooms, service with restrictions, supervision.
[SAVE] [S🐾] ⨯ 🗭 🛢 💻

🅰🅰🅰 ▼▼▼▼ Cleveland Airport Marriott 🄷
(216) 252-5333. $59-$169. 4277 W 150th St. I-71, exit 240,
just s. Int corridors. Pets: $50 one-time fee/room. Service
with restrictions, supervision.
[SAVE] ⨯ 🗭 💺 🛢 💻 🍴 ⇋

🅰🅰🅰 ▼▼▼▼ Radisson Hotel at
　　Gateway-Cleveland 🄷
(216) 377-9000. $139-$149. 651 Huron Rd. North side of
Jacob's Field. Int corridors. Pets: Very small. Designated
rooms, service with restrictions.
[SAVE] [S🐾] ⨯ 🄼 💺 🛢 💻 🍴

▼▼▼ ▼▼▼ The Ritz-Carlton, Cleveland 🄷
(216) 623-1300. $249-$269. 1515 W 3rd St. In Tower City
Center (3rd St side). Int corridors. Pets: Accepted.
⨯ 🗭 💺 🛢 🍴 ⇋

INDEPENDENCE

AAA ▼▼▼ **Amerisuites (Cleveland So/Independence)** **M**
(216) 328-1060. **$99-$119.** 6025 Jefferson Dr. I-77, exit Rockside Rd, just w to W Creek Rd, then just n. Int corridors. **Pets:** Medium. Designated rooms, supervision.
[SAVE] [S🐕] [✕] [🌁M] [🐾] [🐕] [📅] [💻] [🏊]

AAA ▼▼▼ **Baymont Inn & Suites Cleveland-Independence** **M**
(216) 447-1133. **$74-$84.** 6161 Quarry Ln. I-77, exit Rockside Rd, just e. Int corridors. **Pets:** Accepted.
[SAVE] [S🐕] [✕] [🐾] [📅] [💻]

AAA ▼▼ **Red Roof Inn** **M**
(216) 447-0030. **$53-$67.** 6020 Quarry Ln. I-77, exit Rockside Rd, just e. Ext corridors. **Pets:** Accepted.
[SAVE] [✕] [🐾] [🐕]

AAA ▼▼▼▼ **Residence Inn by Marriott** **M**
(216) 520-1450. **$125-$134.** 5101 W Creek Rd. I-77, exit Rockside Rd, just w to W Creek Rd, then just n. Ext corridors. **Pets:** Other species. $200 one-time fee/room. Service with restrictions, crate.
[SAVE] [S🐕] [✕] [🐾] [🐕] [📅] [💻] [🏊]

MAYFIELD HEIGHTS

AAA ▼▼▼ **Baymont Inn & Suites-Cleveland NE (Mayfield Heights)** **M**
(440) 442-8400. **$85-$95.** 1421 Golden Gate Blvd. I-271, exit Mayfield exit, 0.3 mi w off US 322. Int corridors. **Pets:** Accepted.
[SAVE] [✕] [🐾] [📅] [💻]

MEDINA

AAA ▼▼ **Days Inn Medina** **M**
(330) 722-4335. **$38-$85, 14 days notice.** 5200 Montville Dr. I-71, exit 218, just e. Ext corridors. **Pets:** Medium. $25 one-time fee/pet. Service with restrictions, crate.
[SAVE] [S🐕] [✕] [📅] [💻] [🏊]

▼▼ **Motel 6 4112** **M**
(330) 723-3322. **$44-$65, 3 days notice.** 3122 E Pointe Dr. I-71, exit 218, just w. Int corridors. **Pets:** Medium. Service with restrictions, supervision.
[A$K] [S🐕] [✕] [🏊]

MIDDLEBURG HEIGHTS

AAA ▼▼▼ **Comfort Inn-Cleveland Airport** **M**
(440) 234-3131. **$70-$150.** 17550 Rosbough Dr. I-71, exit 235, 0.3 mi w to Engle Rd, then 0.3 mi n. Int corridors. **Pets:** Large, other species. $10 daily fee/room, $35 one-time fee/room. Service with restrictions, supervision.
[SAVE] [S🐕] [✕] [📅] [💻] [🏊]

AAA ▼▼ **Red Roof Inn-Middleburg Heights** **M**
(440) 243-2441. **$51-$73.** 17555 Bagley Rd. I-71, exit 235, just w. Ext/int corridors. **Pets:** Accepted.
[SAVE] [✕]

AAA ▼▼▼ **Residence Inn by Marriott** **A**
(440) 234-6688. **$69-$119.** 17525 Rosbough Dr. I-71, exit 235, just w on Bagley Rd, just n on Engle Rd. Ext/int corridors. **Pets:** Other species. $200 one-time fee/room. Service with restrictions, crate.
[SAVE] [✕] [🐕] [📅] [💻]

NORTH OLMSTED

AAA ▼▼ **Hampton Inn** **M**
(440) 734-4477. **$69-$95.** 25105 Country Club Blvd. I-480, exit 6B, just n on SR 252. Int corridors. **Pets:** Other species. $25 one-time fee/room. Service with restrictions, crate.
[SAVE] [S🐕] [✕] [🐾] [💻]

▼▼ **Homestead Studio Suites-Cleveland/Airport/ North Olmsted** **M**
(440) 777-8585. **$59-$69 (no credit cards).** 24851 Country Club Blvd. I-480, exit 6B, just n on SR 252. Ext corridors. **Pets:** Accepted.
[A$K] [✕] [🐾] [📅] [💻]

STRONGSVILLE

AAA ▼▼ **Red Roof Inn-Strongsville** **M**
(440) 238-0170. **$45-$65.** 15385 Royalton Rd. I-71, exit 231A, just e; I-76 (Ohio Tpke), exit 161, 1 mi s. Ext corridors. **Pets:** Small. Service with restrictions, supervision.
[SAVE] [✕] [🐾]

WESTLAKE

AAA ▼▼ **Red Roof Inn-Westlake** **M**
(440) 892-7920. **$47-$76.** 29595 Clemens Rd. I-90, exit 156, just n. Ext corridors. **Pets:** Medium, other species. Service with restrictions, supervision.
[SAVE] [✕] [🐾] [📅]

AAA ▼▼▼ **Residence Inn by Marriott** **A**
(440) 892-2254. **$99-$119.** 30100 Clemens Rd. I-90, exit 156, just n. Ext corridors. **Pets:** Medium, other species. $200 one-time fee/room. Service with restrictions, crate.
[SAVE] [S🐕] [✕] [🐾] [📅] [💻] [🏊]

❧ **END METROPOLITAN AREA** ❧

COLUMBUS METROPOLITAN AREA

CIRCLEVILLE

🆔 🚩 Knights Inn M
(740) 474-6006. **$45.** 23897 US 23 S. 1.5 mi s. Ext corridors. **Pets:** $5 daily fee/pet. Designated rooms, service with restrictions, supervision.
SAVE 🔊 ✕ 🖥 💻

COLUMBUS

🆔 🚩🚩🚩 AmeriSuites
(Columbus/Worthington) M
(614) 846-4355. **$79-$114.** 7490 Vantage Dr. I-270, exit 23 (US 23 N), just ne. Int corridors. **Pets:** Very small, other species. Service with restrictions, supervision.
SAVE 🔊 ✕ 🖥 ♿ 🐾 🖥 💻 🏊

🆔 🚩🚩🚩 Columbus Marriott North 🅷
(614) 885-1885. **$64-$125.** 6500 Doubletree Ave. I-71, exit 117, 0.3 mi w on SR 161, 0.8 mi on Busch Blvd to Kingsmill Pkwy. Int corridors. **Pets:** Very small. $50 one-time fee/pet. Designated rooms, service with restrictions.
SAVE 🔊 ✕ 🖥 🐾 ♿ 🐾 🖥 💻 🍴 🏊

🆔 🚩🚩🚩 Days Inn Fairgrounds M
(614) 299-4300. **$50-$75.** 1700 Clara St. I-71, exit 111, just w. Ext corridors. **Pets:** Large, other species. $20 one-time fee/pet. Designated rooms, service with restrictions, supervision.
SAVE 🔊 ✕ 🐾 💻 🏊

🆔 🚩🚩🚩 Doubletree Guest Suites 🅷
(614) 228-4600. **$89-$139.** 50 S Front St. Downtown; corner of Front and State sts, just n. Int corridors. **Pets:** Accepted.
SAVE 🔊 ✕ 🐾 🖥 💻 🍴

🆔 🚩🚩 Holiday Inn City Center M🅸
(614) 221-3281. **$89-$119.** 175 E Town St. At 4th and E Town sts. Int corridors. **Pets:** Accepted.
SAVE 🔊 ✕ 🐾 🐾 ♿ 🐾 🖥 💻 🍴 🏊

🆔 🚩🚩🚩 Holiday Inn-Columbus/Worthington
Area M🅸
(614) 885-3334. **$79-$109.** 175 Hutchinson Ave. I-270, exit 23, just n of jct US 23 N. Int corridors. **Pets:** Accepted.
SAVE 🔊 ✕ 🐾 🐾 ♿ 🐾 🖥 💻 🍴 🏊

🚩🚩🚩 Holiday Inn East I-70 🅷
(614) 868-1380. **$109.** 4560 Hilton Corporate Dr. I-70, exit 107. Int corridors. **Pets:** Other species. Service with restrictions.
ASK 🔊 ✕ 🐾 🐾 🐾 🖥 💻 🍴

🆔 🚩🚩🚩 Holiday Inn on the Lane 🅷 🐾
(614) 294-4848. **$99-$119, 7 days notice.** 328 W Lane Ave. SR 315, exit Lane Ave, 0.5 mi e; opposite Ohio State University. Int corridors. **Pets:** Service with restrictions, supervision.
SAVE 🔊 ✕ 🐾 🐾 🐾 🖥 💻 🍴 🏊

🆔 🚩🚩🚩 Homewood Suites M
(614) 785-0001. **$109-$145.** 115 Hutchinson Ave. I-270, exit 23, just ne. Int corridors. **Pets:** Large. $10 daily fee/pet. Service with restrictions, supervision.
SAVE 🔊 ✕ 🐾 🖥 💻

🆔 🚩🚩🚩 Knights Inn-Columbus East M 🐾
(614) 864-0600. **$50-$90.** 4320 Groves Rd. I-70, exit 107, just sw. Ext corridors. **Pets:** Large. $25 deposit/room. Service with restrictions, crate.
SAVE 🔊 ✕ 🖥

🚩 Microtel Inn-North M
(614) 436-0556. **$37-$59.** 7500 Vantage Dr. I-270, exit 23, just n of US 23 N. Int corridors. **Pets:** Accepted.
ASK 🔊 ✕ 🐾

🆔 🚩🚩 Red Roof Inn Columbus North M
(614) 846-8520. **$42-$68.** 750 Morse Rd. I-71, exit 116. Ext corridors. **Pets:** Medium, other species. Service with restrictions, crate.
SAVE ✕ 🐾 🖥

🆔 🚩🚩🚩 Red Roof Inn-OSU M
(614) 267-9941. **$59-$69.** 441 Ackerman Rd. SR 315, exit Ackerman Rd, 0.3 mi e. Ext corridors. **Pets:** Accepted.
SAVE ✕

🆔 🚩🚩🚩 Red Roof Inn-West M
(614) 878-9245. **$45-$75.** 5001 Renner Rd. I-70, exit 91 eastbound; exit 91B westbound, just nw. Ext corridors. **Pets:** Accepted.
SAVE ✕ 🐾 🖥 🐾

🆔 🚩🚩🚩🚩 Residence Inn by Marriott M 🐾
(614) 880-0799. **$109.** 7300 Huntington Park Dr. I-270, exit 23, just e of Vantage. Int corridors. **Pets:** Large, other species. $100 one-time fee/room. Service with restrictions.
SAVE ✕ 🐾 🖥 💻 🏊

🆔 🚩🚩🚩 The Residence Inn by
Marriott-Columbus North 🅰
(614) 431-1819. **$99-$109.** 6191 W Zumstein Dr. I-71, exit 117, 0.3 mi w on SR 161, 0.4 mi n on Busch Blvd, Shapter, and Mediterranean. Ext corridors. **Pets:** Other species. $100 one-time fee/room. Service with restrictions.
SAVE 🔊 ✕ 🐾 🖥 💻 🏊

🆔 🚩🚩🚩🚩 Residence Inn by Marriott-Columbus
Southeast 🅰
(614) 864-8444. **$59-$149.** 2084 S Hamilton Rd. I-70, exit 107, just e. Ext corridors. **Pets:** $100 one-time fee/room. Service with restrictions.
SAVE 🔊 ✕ 🐾 🐾 🖥 💻 🏊

(AAA) ▼▼▼▼ **The University Plaza Hotel &**
Conference Center Ⓜ
(614) 267-7461. **$99-$149.** 3110 Olentangy River Rd. SR
315, exit N Broadway Rd, 0.5 mi s. Int corridors.
Pets: Large, other species. $20 deposit/room. Service with
restrictions, supervision.
[SAVE] [S🐾] [✕] [🛏] [💻] [🍽] [⊛]

(AAA) ▼▼▼ **Wellesley Inn & Suites**
(Columbus/Polaris) Ⓜ
(614) 431-5522. **$89-$109, 3 days notice.** 8555 Lyra Dr.
I-71, exit 121, just w on Polaris Pkwy. Int corridors.
Pets: Small. Service with restrictions, crate.
[SAVE] [S🐾] [✕] [♿M] [🐾] [🛏] [💻] [⊛]

(AAA) ▼▼▼ ▼▼▼ **The Westin Great Southern**
Columbus Ⓗ
(614) 228-3800. **$215.** 310 S High St. Downtown; corner of
Main and High sts. Int corridors. **Pets:** Accepted.
[SAVE] [S🐾] [✕] [🗝] [🐾] [💻] [🍽]

DELAWARE

▼▼ ▼▼ **Best Western Delaware Hotel** Ⓜ
(740) 363-1262. **$69-$85.** 351 S Sandusky St. 0.5 mi e. Int
corridors. **Pets:** Accepted.
[SAVE] [S🐾] [✕] [🛏]

(AAA) ▼▼ **Travelodge** Ⓜ
(740) 369-4421. **$48-$150.** 1001 US Rt 23 N. 0.5 mi n of
downtown. Ext/int corridors. **Pets:** Other species. $10 daily
fee/room. Service with restrictions, supervision.
[SAVE] [S🐾] [✕] [🛏] [💻]

DUBLIN

(AAA) ▼▼▼▼ **AmeriSuites-Columbus/Dublin** Ⓜ
(614) 799-1913. **$108, 3 days notice.** 6161 Park Center
Cir. I-270, exit 15 (Tuttle Crossing), just e. Int corridors.
Pets: Medium, other species. $50 deposit/pet. Designated
rooms, service with restrictions, crate.
[SAVE] [S🐾] [✕] [♿M] [🗝] [🐾] [🛏] [💻] [⊛]

(AAA) ▼▼▼ **Baymont Inn & Suites**
Columbus-Dublin Ⓜ
(614) 792-8300. **$74-$84.** 6145 Park Center Cir. I-270, exit
15 (Tuttle Crossing), just e. Int corridors. **Pets:** Medium,
other species. $50 deposit/room. Designated rooms, service
with restrictions, supervision.
[SAVE] [S🐾] [✕] [♿M] [🐾] [🛏] [💻]

(AAA) ▼▼▼▼ **Columbus Marriott Northwest** Ⓗ
(614) 791-1000. **$155-$179.** 5605 Paul Blazer Memorial
Pkwy. I-270, exit 15 (Tuttle Crossing), 0.3 mi e. Int corridors.
Pets: Accepted.
[SAVE] [S🐾] [✕] [♿M] [🗝] [🐾] [🛏] [💻] [🍽] [⊛]

(AAA) ▼▼▼ **Red Roof Inn-Dublin** Ⓜ
(614) 764-3993. **$52-$73.** 5125 Post Rd. I-270, exit 17A,
just ne. Ext corridors. **Pets:** Accepted.
[SAVE] [✕] [♿M] [🛏]

(AAA) ▼▼▼▼ **Residence Inn by Marriott** Ⓐ
(614) 791-0403. **$119-$149.** 435 Metro Place S. I-270, exit
17A, 0.5 mi s to Frantz Rd, 0.5 mi w. Ext/int corridors.
Pets: Other species. $100 one-time fee/room. Service with
restrictions, crate.
[SAVE] [S🐾] [✕] [♿M] [🗝] [🛏] [💻] [⊛]

(AAA) ▼▼▼▼ **Wellesley Inn & Suites**
(Columbus/Dublin) Ⓜ
(614) 760-0245. **$69-$99.** 5530 Tuttle Crossing Blvd. I-270,
exit 15, 0.3 mi w. Int corridors. **Pets:** Very small, other
species. Service with restrictions, supervision.
[SAVE] [S🐾] [✕] [♿M] [🐾] [🛏] [💻]

▼▼▼▼ **Woodfin Suites Hotel** Ⓐ
(614) 766-7762. **$99-$150.** 4130 Tuller Rd. I-270, exit 20,
0.3 mi s on Sawmill Rd via Dublin Center Dr. Ext corridors.
Pets: Other species. $50 one-time fee/room. Service with
restrictions, supervision.
[ASK] [S🐾] [✕] [🗝] [🛏] [💻] [⊛]

(AAA) ▼▼▼▼ **Wyndham Dublin** Ⓜ
(614) 764-2200. **$109-$154.** 600 Metro Place N. I-270, exit
17A, 0.5 mi s, then 0.5 mi nw. Int corridors. **Pets:** Other
species. $50 one-time fee/room. Service with restrictions,
supervision.
[SAVE] [✕] [🛏] [💻] [🍽] [⊛]

GAHANNA

(AAA) ▼▼▼ **TownePlace Suites by Marriott** Ⓜ
(614) 861-1400. **$95-$129.** 695 Taylor Rd. I-270, exit 37,
just w to Morrison Rd, just s to Taylor Rd, then just w. Int
corridors. **Pets:** $100 one-time fee/room. Service with
restrictions.
[SAVE] [S🐾] [✕] [🗝] [🐾] [🛏] [💻]

GROVE CITY

(AAA) ▼▼▼ **Best Western Executive Inn** Ⓜ 🐾
(614) 875-7770. **$57-$72.** 4026 Jackpot Rd. I-71, exit 100,
just e. Ext corridors. **Pets:** Small, dogs only. $9.26 daily
fee/pet. Designated rooms, service with restrictions.
[SAVE] [S🐾] [✕] [🛏] [💻] [⊛]

(AAA) ▼▼▼ **Red Roof Inn-South Columbus** Ⓜ
(614) 875-8543. **$46-$74.** 1900 Stringtown Rd. I-71, exit
100, just w. Ext corridors. **Pets:** Small, other species. Service with restrictions, supervision.
[SAVE] [✕] [🗝]

HEATH

(AAA) ▼▼▼ **Ramada Inn Newark/Heath** Ⓜ 🐾
(740) 522-1165. **$69-$110, 14 days notice.** 733 Hebron
Rd. I-70, exit 129B, 7 mi n on SR 79. Ext corridors.
Pets: Small. $5 daily fee/pet. Service with restrictions,
supervision.
[SAVE] [S🐾] [✕] [🛏] [💻] [🍽] [⊛]

HILLIARD

▼▼▼ **Comfort Suites** **M**
(614) 529-8118. **$88-$98, 5 days notice.** 3831 Park Mill Run Dr. I-270, exit 13A northbound; exit 13 southbound. Int corridors. **Pets:** Accepted.

▼▼▼ **Homewood Suites by**
   Hilton-Columbus/Hilliard **M**
(614) 529-4100. **$129-$149, 7 days notice.** 3841 Park Mill Run Dr. I-270, exit 13 southbound; exit 13A northbound. Int corridors. **Pets:** $10 daily fee/room, $95 one-time fee/room. Service with restrictions, supervision.

LANCASTER

⟨AAA⟩ ▼▼▼ Best Western Lancaster Inn **MI**
(740) 653-3040. **$65-$85, 3 days notice.** 1858 N Memorial Dr. 2 mi nw on US 33. Ext/int corridors. **Pets:** Medium. $10 one-time fee/pet. Service with restrictions, crate.

⟨AAA⟩ ▼ Knights Inn **M**
(740) 687-4823. **$63-$73, 3 days notice.** 1327 River Valley Blvd. 2 mi nw on US 33; at River Valley Mall entrance. Ext corridors. **Pets:** Small. $5 one-time fee/room. Service with restrictions.

[SAVE] [S₀] [✕] [📶]

MARYSVILLE

▼▼ **Days Inn Marysville** **M**
(937) 644-8821. **$69.** 16510 Square Dr. Just e of US 36, exit off US 33. Ext corridors. **Pets:** Medium. $10 one-time fee/pet. Designated rooms, service with restrictions, supervision.

[SAVE] [S₀] [✕] [📶] [💻]

REYNOLDSBURG

⟨AAA⟩ ▼▼▼ Best Western Columbus East **MI**
(614) 864-1280. **$61-$65.** 2100 Brice Rd. I-70, exit 110 westbound; exit 110B eastbound, just n. Int corridors. **Pets:** Other species. Service with restrictions.

[SAVE] [S₀] [✕] [🛏] [📶] [💻] [🍴]

❧ **END METROPOLITAN AREA** ❧

CONNEAUT

⟨AAA⟩ ▼ Days Inn of Conneaut **M**
(440) 593-6000. **$65-$150.** 600 Days Blvd. I-90, exit 241, 0.3 mi n. Int corridors. **Pets:** Medium, other species. $5 daily fee/pet. Designated rooms, service with restrictions, supervision.

[SAVE] [S₀] [✕] [💻] [🐾]

⟨AAA⟩ ▼▼▼ La Quinta Inn **M**
(614) 866-6456. **$62-$72.** 2447 Brice Rd. I-70, exit 110 westbound; exit 110B eastbound, 0.3 mi n. Int corridors. **Pets:** Accepted.

[SAVE] [✕] [🛏] [💻]

⟨AAA⟩ ▼▼▼ Red Roof Inn-East **M**
(614) 864-3683. **$52-$69.** 2449 Brice Rd. I-70, exit 110 westbound; exit 110B eastbound. Ext corridors. **Pets:** Accepted.

[SAVE] [✕] [💺]

SUNBURY

⟨AAA⟩ ▼▼▼ Days Inn of Sunbury **M**
(740) 362-6159. **$55-$70.** 7323 SR 37 E. I-71, exit 131, just w. Int corridors. **Pets:** Accepted.

[SAVE] [S₀] [✕] [💺] [🛏] [🐾]

WESTERVILLE

▼▼ **Knights Inn-Columbus/Westerville** **M**
(614) 890-0426. **$60.** 32 Heatherdown Dr. I-270, exit 29, 0.3 mi n on SR 3. Ext corridors. **Pets:** $10 one-time fee/pet. Service with restrictions, supervision.

[ASK] [S₀] [✕] [🛏] [💻] [🐾]

WORTHINGTON

⟨AAA⟩ ▼▼▼ Red Roof Inn-Worthington **M**
(614) 846-3001. **$44-$63.** 7474 N High St. I-270, exit 23, just n. Ext corridors. **Pets:** Accepted.

[SAVE] [✕] [🛏] [💻]

DAYTON

⟨AAA⟩ ▼▼▼ Dayton Marriott Hotel **H**
(937) 223-1000. **$69-$149.** 1414 S Patterson Blvd. I-75, exit 51 (Edwin C Moses Blvd), 1 mi e. Int corridors. **Pets:** $50 one-time fee/room. Designated rooms, service with restrictions, supervision.

[SAVE] [✕] [📶] [💺] [🛏] [💻] [🍴]

▼▼▼ **Howard Johnson Express Inn** Ⓜ
(937) 454-0550. **$68-$99.** 7575 Poe Ave. I-75, exit 60 northbound, just n; exit 60 southbound, n on Miller Ln, then n on Little York Rd. Int corridors. **Pets:** Accepted.

(A$K) (S🐾) (✕) (🌙) (🛡) (💻) (≈)

▼ **Motel 6–603** Ⓜ
(937) 898-3606. **$41-$53.** 7130 Miller Ln. I-75, exit 60 (Little York Rd). Ext corridors. **Pets:** Accepted.

(S🐾) (✕) (🛏) (≈)

▼▼ **Ramada Inn-North** Ⓜ
(937) 890-9500. **$50-$75, 10 days notice.** 4079 Little York Rd. I-75, exit 60, 0.5 mi s of jct I-70. Ext/int corridors. **Pets:** Other species. $10 one-time fee/room. Designated rooms, service with restrictions, supervision.

(A$K) (S🐾) (✕) (🌙) (🛡) (💻) (🍴) (≈)

◆◆◆ ▼▼▼ **Red Roof Inn-North** Ⓜ
(937) 898-1054. **$49-$73.** 7370 Miller Ln. I-75, exit 60; 0.5 mi s of jct I-70. Ext corridors. **Pets:** Other species. Service with restrictions.

(SAVE) (✕) (🌙) (🛏) (🛡) (💻)

◆◆◆ ▼▼▼▼ **Residence Inn by Marriott-Dayton North** Ⓐ
(937) 898-7764. **$119-$129, 7 days notice.** 7070 Poe Ave. I-75, exit 60. Ext corridors. **Pets:** Accepted.

(SAVE) (S🐾) (✕) (🌙) (🛏) (🛡) (💻) (≈)

DOVER

▼ **Hospitality Inn** Ⓜ 🐾
(330) 364-7724. **$40-$85, 7 days notice.** 889 Commercial Pkwy. I-77, exit 83, just e. Ext corridors. **Pets:** Other species. $10 daily fee/pet. Service with restrictions, supervision.

(A$K) (S🐾) (✕) (🌙) (🛡) (≈)

EATON

◆◆◆ ▼▼ **Econo Lodge** Ⓜ
(937) 456-5959. **$49-$55.** 6161 Rt 127 N. I-70, exit 10 (US 127). Ext corridors. **Pets:** Other species. $10 daily fee/pet. Designated rooms, service with restrictions, crate.

(SAVE) (S🐾) (✕) (🛡) (💻)

ELYRIA

◆◆◆ ▼▼▼ **Comfort Inn** Ⓜ
(440) 324-7676. **$60-$102.** 739 Leona St. I-80, exit 8, just n on SR 57, exit Midway Blvd. Int corridors. **Pets:** Medium. $8 daily fee/pet. Designated rooms, service with restrictions, supervision.

(SAVE) (S🐾) (✕) (🛡) (💻)

▼▼▼▼ **Super 8 Motel** Ⓜ
(440) 323-7488. **$52-$104.** 910 Lorain Blvd. I-80, exit 8, 0.5 mi s on SR 57. Int corridors. **Pets:** Accepted.

(A$K) (S🐾) (✕) (🛏) (≈)

ENGLEWOOD

▼▼▼ **Holiday Inn-Dayton Northwest Airport** Ⓜ
(937) 832-1234. **$65-$125.** 10 Rockridge Rd. I-70, exit 29. Int corridors. **Pets:** Small. $10 deposit/room, $15 one-time fee/room. Designated rooms, service with restrictions, supervision.

(A$K) (S🐾) (✕) (🛡) (💻) (🍴) (≈)

FAIRBORN

◆◆◆ ▼▼▼ **Comfort Inn-Wright Patterson** Ⓜ 🐾
(937) 879-7666. **$69-$84, 3 days notice.** 616 N Broad St. I-675, exit 24, 1.8 sw on SR 444. Int corridors. **Pets:** $75 deposit/room, $5 daily fee/room. Service with restrictions, crate.

(SAVE) (S🐾) (✕) (🌙) (🛡) (💻) (≈)

◆◆◆ ▼▼▼▼ **Homewood Suites-Fairborn/Dayton** Ⓐ
(937) 429-0600. **$113.** 2750 Presidential Dr. I-675, exit 17 (N Fairfield Rd). Ext/int corridors. **Pets:** Accepted.

(SAVE) (S🐾) (✕) (🌙) (🛡) (💻) (≈)

◆◆◆ ▼▼ **Red Roof Inn-Fairborn** Ⓜ
(937) 426-6116. **$52-$74.** 2580 Colonel Glenn Hwy. I-675, exit 17 (N Fairfield Rd). Ext corridors. **Pets:** Small, other species. Service with restrictions, supervision.

(SAVE) (✕) (🌙) (🛡)

FAIRLAWN

▼▼▼ **Best Western Inn & Suites** Ⓜ
(330) 670-0888. **$59-$2009.** 160 W Montross Ave. I-77, exit 137B, just w. Int corridors. **Pets:** Accepted.

(SAVE) (S🐾) (✕) (🛡M) (🛏) (🛡) (≈)

◆◆◆ ▼ **Red Roof Inn Akron North** Ⓜ
(330) 666-0566. **$34-$64.** 99 Rothrock Rd. I-77, exit 137A, just e. Ext corridors. **Pets:** Accepted.

(SAVE) (✕) (🌙)

◆◆◆ ▼▼▼▼ **The Residence Inn by Marriott** Ⓐ
(330) 666-4811. **$75-$115.** 120 W Montross Ave. I-77, exit 137B, just w. Ext corridors. **Pets:** Accepted.

(SAVE) (S🐾) (✕) (🛡) (💻) (≈)

FINDLAY

◆◆◆ ▼ **Rodeway Inn** Ⓜ
(419) 424-1133. **$39-$54, 3 days notice.** 1901 Broad Ave. I-75, exit 159, 0.5 mi e. Ext corridors. **Pets:** $10 one-time fee/pet. No service.

(SAVE) (S🐾) (✕) (🛡) (💻) (≈)

▼▼ **Super 8 Motel-Findlay** Ⓜ
(419) 422-8863. **$49-$51.** 1600 Fox St. I-75, exit 159, just e. Int corridors. **Pets:** Very small, other species. $5.28 daily fee/pet. Designated rooms, service with restrictions, crate.

(A$K) (S🐾) (✕) (🌙) (🛡)

FREDERICKTOWN

▼▼▼ Heartland Country Resort 🅱🅱 ❀
(419) 768-9300. **$105-$195, 7 days notice.** 2994 Township Rd 190. I-71, exit 151, 2 mi e on SR 95, 2 mi s on SR 314, then 1 mi e on SR 179. Int corridors. **Pets:** Other species. $15 daily fee/room. Designated rooms.
(A$K) ⊠ 🖥 💻 🏊

FREMONT

🔷🔷🔷 ▼▼▼ Comfort Inn & Suites 🅼 ❀
(419) 355-9300. **$83-$125.** 840 Sean Dr. I-80/90, exit 6, 2 mi s on SR 53. Int corridors. **Pets:** Other species. $15 one-time fee/pet. Service with restrictions, crate.
(SAVE) (S💰) ⊠ 🛋 🖥 💻 🏊

🔷🔷🔷 ▼▼▼ Holiday Inn-Fremont 🅼🅸
(419) 334-2682. **$87-$129.** 3422 Port Clinton Rd. Ohio Tpke, exit 91, on SR 53. Int corridors. **Pets:** Medium. Designated rooms, service with restrictions, supervision.
(SAVE) (S💰) ⊠ 🅼♿ 🖥 💻 🍽 🏊

GALION

▼▼ Hometown Inn 🅼
(419) 468-9909. **$60-$140, 3 days notice.** 172 N Portland Way. 1 mi w on SR 598, n of jct SR 309/61/19. Ext/int corridors. **Pets:** Accepted.
(A$K) (S💰) ⊠ 🖥

GALLIPOLIS

🔷🔷🔷 ▼▼ William Ann Motel 🅼
(740) 446-3373. **$50-$60, 3 days notice.** 918 2nd Ave. 0.8 mi n on SR 7. Ext corridors. **Pets:** Accepted.
(SAVE) (S💰) ⊠ 🖥

GREEN

▼▼ ▼▼ Super 8 Motel 🅼
(330) 899-9888. **$56-$76.** 1605 Corporate Woods Pkwy. I-77, exit 118, just w. **Pets:** Accepted.
(A$K) (S💰) ⊠ 🖥 💻 🏊

GREENVILLE

🔷🔷🔷 ▼▼▼ Greenville Inn 🅼🅸
(937) 548-3613. **$60-$80, 3 days notice.** 851 E Martin. Jct US 127 and 36, 0.3 mi w on SR 571. Int corridors. **Pets:** Small. $75 deposit/room. Service with restrictions, crate.
(SAVE) (S💰) ⊠ 🗗 🖥 💻 🍽

HAMILTON

▼▼▼ The Hamiltonian Hotel 🅷
(513) 896-6200. **$76-$81.** 1 Riverfront Plaza. Just off High St, on Front St. Int corridors. **Pets:** $50 deposit/room. Service with restrictions, crate.
(A$K) ⊠ 🗗 🖥 💻 🍽 🏊

HOLLAND

🔷🔷🔷 ▼▼ ▼▼ Cross Country Inn 🅼
(419) 866-6565. **$47-$54.** 1201 E Mall Dr. I-475, exit 8, just w on SR 2; behind the mall. Ext corridors. **Pets:** Accepted.
(SAVE) (S💰) ⊠ 🗗 🏊

🔷🔷🔷 ▼▼ ▼▼ Red Roof Inn Toledo/Holland 🅼
(419) 866-5512. **$44-$64.** 1214 Corporate Dr. I-475, exit 8, just e on Holland-Sylvania Rd, just n to Trust Dr. Ext corridors. **Pets:** Medium, other species. Service with restrictions.
(SAVE) ⊠ 🗗 🖥

🔷🔷🔷 ▼▼ ▼▼ Residence Inn by Marriott 🅰
(419) 867-9555. **$129-$159.** 6101 Trust Dr. I-475, exit 8, just e to Holland-Sylvania Rd, just n. Ext corridors. **Pets:** Accepted.
(SAVE) (S💰) ⊠ 🗗 🖥 💻 🏊

HUBER HEIGHTS

🔷🔷🔷 ▼▼ Travelodge 🅼
(937) 236-9361. **$55-$60.** 7911 Brandt Pike. I-70, exit 38, just s, at SR 201. Int corridors. **Pets:** Small. $25 deposit/pet. Service with restrictions, crate.
(SAVE) (S💰) ⊠ 🖥 💻 🏊

HURON

🔷🔷🔷 ▼▼ Plantation Motel 🅼 ❀
(419) 433-4790. **$38-$88, 3 days notice.** 2815 E Cleveland Rd. 3 mi e on US 6. Ext corridors. **Pets:** Other species. $7 daily fee/pet. Service with restrictions, supervision.
(SAVE) (S💰) ⊠ 🖥 💻 🏊

JACKSON

▼▼ Knights Inn 🅼
(740) 286-2135. **$46-$59.** 404 Chillicothe St. 0.7 mi n on US 35 business route. Ext corridors. **Pets:** Other species. $20 deposit/room.
(A$K) (S💰) ⊠ 🖥

KENT

▼▼ ▼▼ The Inn of Kent 🅼
(330) 673-3411. **$40-$80.** 303 E Main St. Just e on SR 59. Ext corridors. **Pets:** Small. Service with restrictions.
⊠ 🖥 🏊

▼▼▼▼ Ramada Inn-Akron/Kent 🅼🅸
(330) 678-0101. **$59-$99, 3 days notice.** 4363 SR 43. I-76, exit 33. Ext corridors. **Pets:** Large, other species. $50 deposit/room. Service with restrictions, supervision.
(A$K) (S💰) ⊠ 🗗 💻 🍽 🏊

▼▼ ▼▼ Super 8 Motel 🅼
(330) 678-8817. **$50-$90, 7 days notice.** 4380 Edson Rd. I-76, exit 33. Int corridors. **Pets:** Other species. $5.60 daily fee/pet. Service with restrictions, supervision.
(A$K) (S💰) ⊠ 🗗 🖥

LIMA

▼▼▼▼ **Holiday Inn Lima** **MI**
(419) 222-0004. **$79-$104.** 1920 Roschman Ave. I-75, exit 124A, at jct SR 117 and 309. Int corridors. **Pets:** Accepted.
A$K SD X ⌨ ⚹ 🛏 💻 🍽 ≈

▲▲▲ ▼ **Knights Inn** **M**
(419) 331-9215. **$50-$55, 7 days notice.** 2285 N Eastown Rd. 4.5 mi w of jct I-75, on SR 309; w of Lima Mall. Ext corridors. **Pets:** Accepted.
SAVE SD X 🛏 ≈

▼ **Motel 6–586** **M**
(419) 228-0456. **$41-$55.** 1800 Harding Hwy. I-75, exit 125, just e, at jct SR 117 and 309. Ext corridors. **Pets:** Accepted.
SD X ⌨

LISBON

▲▲▲ ▼▼▼▼ **Days Inn Lisbon** **M**
(330) 420-0111. **$72.** 40952 SR 154. SR 11, exit SR 154, just w. Int corridors. **Pets:** Accepted.
SAVE SD X ⌨ 🛏 💻

LOGAN

▲▲▲ ▼ **Shawnee Inn** **M**
(740) 385-5674. **$49-$70.** 30916 Lake Logan Rd. SR 664, just s of US 33. Ext corridors. **Pets:** Accepted.
SAVE SD X 💻

LOUDONVILLE

▼ **Little Brown Inn** **M**
(419) 994-5525. **$46-$66.** 940 S Market St. 1 mi s on SR 3. Int corridors. **Pets:** Medium, other species. $25 deposit/room, $5 daily fee/pet. Designated rooms, service with restrictions, crate.
X

MACEDONIA

▲▲▲ ▼▼▼▼ **Baymont Inn & Suites Cleveland-Macedonia** **M**
(330) 468-5400. **$99-$119.** 268 E Highland Rd. I-271, exit 18, just s; I-80/90 (Ohio Tpke), exit 180, just n. Int corridors. **Pets:** Medium, other species. $50 deposit/room. Designated rooms, service with restrictions, supervision.
SAVE SD X ⌨M ⌨ ⚹ 🛏 💻 ≈

▼ **Knights Inn-Cleveland/Macedonia** **M**
(330) 467-1981. **$45-$79.** 240 E Highland Rd. I-271, exit 18, just s; I-80/90 (Ohio Tpke), exit 180, 3 mi n. Ext corridors. **Pets:** Medium. $5 daily fee/room. Designated rooms, service with restrictions, supervision.
A$K SD X 🛏 💻 ≈

MANSFIELD

▲▲▲ ▼▼▼▼ **Baymont Inn & Suites-Mansfield** **M**
(419) 774-0005. **$69-$79.** 120 Stander Ave. I-71, exit 169. Int corridors. **Pets:** Medium, other species. Designated rooms, service with restrictions, supervision.
SAVE SD X ⌨M ⌨ ⚹ 🛏 💻 ≈

▲▲▲ ▼▼▼▼ **Comfort Inn** **M**
(419) 529-1000. **$130, 30 days notice.** 500 N Trimble Rd. Jct US 30 and Trimble Rd. Int corridors. **Pets:** Accepted.
SAVE SD X ⌨ 🛏 💻 ≈

▲▲▲ ▼ **Econo Lodge** **M**
(419) 589-3333. **$44-$60.** 1017 Koogle Rd. I-71, exit 176, just e. Int corridors. **Pets:** Medium. $6 daily fee/pet. Service with restrictions, supervision.
SAVE SD X 🛏 💻 ≈

▲▲▲ ▼ **Knights Inn** **M**
(419) 529-2100. **$49-$100.** 555 N Trimble Rd. Jct US 30 and Trimble Rd. Ext corridors. **Pets:** Other species. Service with restrictions, supervision.
SAVE SD X ⌨ 🛏 💻

▼▼ **Super 8 Motel** **M**
(419) 756-8875. **$55-$65, 30 days notice.** 2425 Interstate Cir. I-71, exit 169. Int corridors. **Pets:** Other species. $50 deposit/room. Designated rooms, service with restrictions, supervision.
A$K SD X ⌨ 🛏 💻

MARIETTA

▲▲▲ ▼▼▼ **Econo Lodge** **M**
(740) 374-8481. **$45-$75.** 702 Pike St. I-77, exit 1. Ext corridors. **Pets:** $5 daily fee/pet. Service with restrictions.
SAVE SD X 💻 ≈

▲▲▲ ▼▼▼ **Knights Inn** **M**
(740) 373-7373. **$50-$73.** 506 Pike St. I-77, exit 1. Ext corridors. **Pets:** $5 daily fee/pet. No service, supervision.
SAVE SD X 🛏 💻 ≈

▼▼ **Super 8 Motel-Marietta** **M**
(740) 374-8888. **$48-$54.** 46 Acme St. I-77, exit 1, just w. Int corridors. **Pets:** Accepted.
A$K SD X ⌨ 🛏

MARION

▼▼▼▼ **Marion Comfort Inn** **M**
(740) 389-5552. **$59-$89, 5 days notice.** 256 James Way. Jct SR 95 and US 23. Int corridors. **Pets:** Accepted.
SAVE SD X ⌨ ⚹ 🛏 💻 ≈

MASSILLON

▼▼▼ **Hampton Inn-Canton/Massillon** **M**
(330) 834-1144. **$79-$89.** 44 First St SW. Downtown. Int corridors. **Pets:** Other species. Service with restrictions, supervision.
SAVE X 💻

MAUMEE

▼▼▼ Country Inn & Suites By Carlson **M**
(419) 893-8576. **$75-$85, 5 days notice.** 541 W Dussel Dr. I-475, exit 6, just e. Int corridors. **Pets:** Accepted.
(ASK) (S6) (✕) (🔅) (🔋) (🛢) (💻) (🏊)

🅐🅐🅐 ▼▼▼ Days Inn Toledo Arrowhead **M**
(419) 893-9960. **$45-$80.** 150 Dussel Dr. I-80/90 (Ohio Tpke), exit 59, just s. Ext corridors. **Pets:** Accepted.
(SAVE) (S6) (✕) (🔅) (🔋) (💻) (🏊)

▼ Knights Inn-Toledo West **M**
(419) 865-1380. **$44-$150, 14 days notice.** 1520 S Holland-Sylvania Rd. I-475, exit 8, just e. Ext corridors. **Pets:** Medium. $50 deposit/pet. Service with restrictions, supervision.
(ASK) (S6) (✕) (🔋) (🏊)

🅐🅐🅐 ▼▼▼ Red Roof Inn-Maumee **M**
(419) 893-0292. **$43-$69.** 1570 S Reynolds Rd. I-80/90 (Ohio Tpke), exit 59, just s. Ext/int corridors. **Pets:** Medium. Service with restrictions.
(SAVE) (✕) (🔅) (🔅) (🔋)

▼▼▼ Toledo/Maumee Homewood Suites by Hilton **A**
(419) 897-0980. **$99-$119.** 1410 Arrowhead Rd. I-475, exit 6, just e. Int corridors. **Pets:** Medium. $10 daily fee/room, $100 one-time fee/room. Service with restrictions, crate.
(SAVE) (S6) (✕) (🔅) (🔋) (💻) (🏊)

MIAMISBURG

▼▼▼▼ Holiday Inn-Dayton Mall **MI**
(937) 434-8030. **$98-$107.** 31 Prestige Plaza Dr. I-75, exit 44, just e on SR 725. Int corridors. **Pets:** Small. Service with restrictions, supervision.
(ASK) (S6) (✕) (🔅) (🔋) (💻) (🍴) (🏊)

▼▼▼▼ Homewood Suites Hotel-Dayton Mall **A**
(937) 432-0000. **$129-$149.** 3100 Contemporary Ln. I-75, exit 44, just e on SR 725; in Prestige Plaza Complex. Int corridors. **Pets:** Other species. $200 deposit/room, $5 daily fee/room, $50 one-time fee/room. Service with restrictions, crate.
(SAVE) (S6) (✕) (🔅) (🔅) (🔋) (💻) (🏊)

🅐🅐🅐 ▼▼▼ Red Roof Inn-South **M**
(937) 866-0705. **$44-$66.** 222 Byers Rd. I-75, exit 44, just w on SR 725. Ext corridors. **Pets:** Medium. Service with restrictions, supervision.
(SAVE) (✕) (🔅) (🔅) (🔋) (💻)

🅐🅐🅐 ▼▼▼ Residence Inn by Marriott-Dayton South **A**
(937) 434-7881. **$140.** 155 Prestige Pl. I-75, exit 44, just e on SR 725. Ext corridors. **Pets:** Accepted.
(SAVE) (S6) (✕) (🔅) (🔋) (💻) (🏊)

MILAN

▼▼ Motel 6-4016 **M**
(419) 499-8001. **$36-$139, 3 days notice.** 11406 US 250 N. I-80/90 (Ohio Tpke), exit 118 1.5 mi n. Int corridors. **Pets:** Accepted.
(ASK) (S6) (✕) (🔅) (🏊) (📶)

MONTPELIER

▼▼ Ramada Inn **MI**
(419) 485-5555. **$99-$129, 3 days notice.** 13508 SR 15. I-80/90 (Ohio Tpke), exit 13, just s. Int corridors. **Pets:** Other species. Service with restrictions, supervision.
(ASK) (S6) (✕) (🔅) (💻) (🍴) (🏊)

MORAINE

▼▼▼ Holiday Inn Hotel & Suites **MI**
(937) 294-1471. **$79, 3 days notice.** 2455 Dryden Rd. I-75, exit 50A. Int corridors. **Pets:** Accepted.
(ASK) (✕) (🔅) (🔅) (🔋) (💻) (🍴) (🏊)

▼▼▼ Super 8 Motel-Moraine **M**
(937) 298-0380. **$49-$99, 10 days notice.** 2450 Dryden Rd. I-75, exit 50A. Ext corridors. **Pets:** Small. $10 one-time fee/room. Service with restrictions, supervision.
(ASK) (S6) (✕) (🏊)

MOUNT GILEAD

🅐🅐🅐 ▼ Knights Inn **M**
(419) 946-6010. **$50-$65.** 5898 SR 95. I-71, exit 151, 0.3 mi w. Ext corridors. **Pets:** Dogs only. $15 deposit/room. Designated rooms, service with restrictions, supervision.
(SAVE) (S6) (✕) (🔋)

MOUNT VERNON

▼▼▼ Holiday Inn Express **M**
(740) 392-1900. **$71-$80, 14 days notice.** 11555 Upper Gilchrist Rd. 3 mi e on US 36. Int corridors. **Pets:** Medium, other species. Designated rooms, service with restrictions.
(ASK) (S6) (✕) (🔅M) (🔅) (🔋) (💻) (🏊)

NEW PHILADELPHIA

🅐🅐🅐 ▼ Days Inn-New Philadelphia **M**
(330) 339-6644. **$53-$69.** 1281 W High St. I-77, exit 81, just e. Int corridors. **Pets:** Accepted.
(SAVE) (S6) (✕) (🔅) (🏊)

▼▼▼ Hampton Inn **M**
(330) 339-7000. **$69-$99, 7 days notice.** 1299 W High St. I-77, exit 81, just e. **Pets:** Medium. $50 deposit/room. Service with restrictions, supervision.
(SAVE) (S6) (✕) (🔋) (💻) (🏊)

▼▼▼ Holiday Inn-New Philadelphia/ Dover **MI**
(330) 339-7731. **$69-$99.** 131 Bluebell Dr SW. I-77, exit 81, 0.4 mi e. Int corridors. **Pets:** $15 one-time fee/pet. Service with restrictions, supervision.
(ASK) (S6) (✕) (🔋) (💻) (🍴) (🏊)

▼ Motel 6–254 **M**
(330) 339-6446. **$35-$61.** 181 Bluebell Dr SW. I-77, exit 81, 0.4 mi e. Ext corridors. **Pets:** Accepted.
⬛ ⬛ ⬛ ⬛

🔷 ▼▼▼ Schoenbrunn Inn by
        Christopher **M**
(330) 339-4434. **$69-$130, 30 days notice.** 1186 W High Ave. I-77, exit 81, 0.6 mi e. Int corridors. **Pets:** $10 one-time fee/room. Service with restrictions.
⬛ ⬛ ⬛ ⬛ ⬛ ⬛ ⬛

NEWTON FALLS

🔷 ▼ Rodeway Inn **M**
(330) 872-0988. **$35-$89.** 4248 SR 5. I-80, exit 209, just w. Ext corridors. **Pets:** Accepted.
⬛ ⬛ ⬛ ⬛

NORTH CANTON

▼▼ Super 8 Motel Canton North **M**
(330) 492-5030. **$60-$65.** 3950 Convenience Cir NW. I-77, exit 109 southbound, 0.3 mi e on Everhard Rd, 0.3 mi s on Whipple Ave; exit 109A northbound, 0.3 mi s on Whipple. Ext corridors. **Pets:** Other species. $5 one-time fee/pet. Service with restrictions, crate.
⬛ ⬛ ⬛ ⬛ ⬛ ⬛

NORTH LIMA

🔷 ▼ Rodeway Inn **M**
(330) 549-3988. **$50-$65.** 10650 Market St. I-76, exit 232, 0.3 mi s on SR 7. Ext corridors. **Pets:** Accepted.
⬛ ⬛ ⬛ ⬛ ⬛

🔷 ▼ Super 8 Motel **M**
(330) 549-2187. **$32-$85, 7 days notice.** 10076 Market St. I-76 (Ohio Tpke), exit 232, 0.7 mi n. Ext corridors. **Pets:** $5 daily fee/pet. Designated rooms, service with restrictions, supervision.
⬛ ⬛ ⬛ ⬛ ⬛

NORTHWOOD

▼▼ Microtel Inn & Suites **M**
(419) 662-1200. **$59-$79, 10 days notice.** 2600 Lauren Ln. I-75, exit 198, just e on Wales Rd, then just s on Oregon Rd. Int corridors. **Pets:** Small, other species. $25 deposit/room. Service with restrictions, supervision.
⬛ ⬛ ⬛ ⬛ ⬛ ⬛ ⬛ ⬛

OBERLIN

▼▼ Oberlin Inn **M**
(440) 775-1111. **$135-$215.** 7 N Main St. Center; on SR 58; at College and Main sts. Ext/int corridors. **Pets:** Accepted.
⬛ ⬛ ⬛ ⬛

OREGON

🔷 ▼▼▼ Comfort Inn East **M**
(419) 691-8911. **$69-$74.** 2930 Navarre Ave. I-280, exit 7, just n on access road, then 0.5 mi e on SR 2 (Navarre Ave). Int corridors. **Pets:** Other species. Designated rooms, service with restrictions, supervision.
⬛ ⬛ ⬛ ⬛ ⬛ ⬛ ⬛

🔷 ▼▼▼ Sleep Inn & Suites **M**
(419) 697-7800. **$74-$79.** 1761 Meijer Cir. I-280, exit 6. Int corridors. **Pets:** $20 one-time fee/pet. Designated rooms, service with restrictions, supervision.
⬛ ⬛ ⬛ ⬛ ⬛ ⬛ ⬛

PERRYSBURG

🔷 ▼▼▼ Baymont Inn & Suites
        Toledo-Perrysburg **M**
(419) 872-0000. **$64-$74.** 1154 Professional Dr. I-75, exit 193, just w. Int corridors. **Pets:** Other species. Designated rooms, service with restrictions, supervision.
⬛ ⬛ ⬛ ⬛ ⬛ ⬛ ⬛

▼ Days Inn of Toledo-Perrysburg **M**
(419) 874-8771. **$75-$90.** 10667 Fremont Pike. I-75, exit 193, just e on US 20 and 23. Ext corridors. **Pets:** Accepted.
⬛ ⬛ ⬛ ⬛ ⬛ ⬛ ⬛

🔷 ▼▼ Howard Johnson Inn Toledo
        South **M**
(419) 837-5245. **$39-$55.** I-280 & Hanley Rd. I-80/90 (Ohio Tpke), exit 71 to I-280, exit 1B. Ext/int corridors. **Pets:** Other species. Service with restrictions.
⬛ ⬛ ⬛ ⬛ ⬛ ⬛ ⬛ ⬛

🔷 ▼ Red Carpet Inn **M**
(419) 872-2902. **$45-$55.** 26054 N Dixie Hwy. I-475, exit 2, just s. Ext corridors. **Pets:** Accepted.
⬛ ⬛ ⬛ ⬛

PIQUA

▼▼▼ Comfort Inn-Piqua **M**
(937) 778-8100. **$74-$90.** 987 E Ash St. I-75, exit 82; in the Miami Valley Centre Mall. Int corridors. **Pets:** $25 deposit/room. Designated rooms, service with restrictions, supervision.
⬛ ⬛ ⬛ ⬛ ⬛ ⬛ ⬛

▼▼▼ Ramada Limited **M**
(937) 615-0140. **$70, 24 days notice.** 950 E Ash St. I-75, exit 82, just w. Int corridors. **Pets:** $50 deposit/room. Designated rooms, service with restrictions, crate.
⬛ ⬛ ⬛ ⬛ ⬛ ⬛

POLAND

🔷 ▼▼ Red Roof Inn **M**
(330) 758-1999. **$45-$72.** 1051 Tiffany S. I-680, exit 11, just w. Int corridors. **Pets:** Accepted.
⬛ ⬛ ⬛ ⬛ ⬛ ⬛

(AAA) ▼▼▼ Residence Inn M
(330) 726-1747. **$109-$159.** 7396 Tiffany S. I-680, exit 11, just w. Int corridors. **Pets:** Accepted.
🅂🅰🆅🅴 ⊠ 📷 ✒ 🔌 💻 ≈

PORT CLINTON

▼▼ Country Hearth Inn M
(419) 732-2111. **$50-$109.** 1815 E Perry St. 1.2 mi e on SR 163, w of jct SR 2. Ext/int corridors. **Pets:** Other species. Designated rooms, service with restrictions, supervision.
A$K 🆂🅾 ⊠ 🔌 💻 ≈

RIO GRANDE

▼ College Hill Motel M
(740) 245-5326. **$43.** 10987 State Rt 588. US 35, exit Rio Grande. Ext corridors. **Pets:** Accepted.
A$K 🆂🅾 ⊠

SANDUSKY

▼▼ Clarion Inn Sandusky M
(419) 625-6280. **$55-$130.** 1119 Sandusky Mall Blvd. 1.5 mi n of SR 2, on US 250; in Sandusky Mall. Int corridors. **Pets:** Medium, other species. $100 deposit/room. Service with restrictions.
🅂🅰🆅🅴 🆂🅾 ⊠ 📷 🔌 💻 🍴 ≈

▼ Cornado Motel M
(419) 625-2954. **$35-$117.** 4319 Venice Rd. 1 mi e of SR 2. Ext corridors. **Pets:** Accepted.
⊠ 🔌 ≈

SEVILLE

▼▼ Super 8 Motel-Seville M ❀
(330) 769-8880. **$61-$69.** 6116 Speedway Dr. Jct SR 224 and Lake Rd. Int corridors. **Pets:** Medium. $50 deposit/pet. Designated rooms, service with restrictions, crate.
A$K 🆂🅾 ⊠ ✒ 🔌

SIDNEY

(AAA) ▼▼▼ Comfort Inn M
(937) 498-9749. **$61-$95.** 1959 W Michigan Ave. I-75, exit 92, on SR 47. Int corridors. **Pets:** Accepted.
🅂🅰🆅🅴 🆂🅾 ⊠ 🔌 💻 ≈

(AAA) ▼▼▼ Days Inn M
(937) 492-1104. **$43-$75, 3 days notice.** 420 Folkerth Ave. I-75, exit 92, at SR 47. Ext corridors. **Pets:** Medium. $5 daily fee/pet. Service with restrictions, supervision.
🅂🅰🆅🅴 🆂🅾 ⊠ 🔌 🍴 ≈

(AAA) ▼▼▼ Holiday Inn M
(937) 492-1131. **$62.** 400 Folkerth Ave. I-75, exit 92, just w. Int corridors. **Pets:** Small. $20 deposit/pet. Designated rooms, service with restrictions, supervision.
🅂🅰🆅🅴 🆂🅾 ⊠ 📷 🔌 💻 🍴 ≈

SPRINGFIELD

(AAA) ▼ Knights Inn M
(937) 325-8721. **$40-$58.** 2207 W Main St. I-70, exit 47, just e of US 68 on US 40. Ext corridors. **Pets:** Accepted.
🅂🅰🆅🅴 🆂🅾 ⊠ 🔌 ≈

(AAA) ▼▼◆ Ramada Limited M
(937) 328-0123. **$75.** 319 E Leffel Ln. I-70, exit 54, just n. Int corridors. **Pets:** Accepted.
🅂🅰🆅🅴 🆂🅾 ⊠ 📷 🔌 💻 ≈

(AAA) ▼▼▼ Red Roof Inn M
(937) 325-5356. **$59-$99, 14 days notice.** 155 W Leffel Ln. I-75, exit 54, just n, then w. Int corridors. **Pets:** Medium, other species. $10 daily fee/room. Service with restrictions, supervision.
🅂🅰🆅🅴 🆂🅾 ⊠ 🔌 ≈

ST. CLAIRSVILLE

(AAA) ▼▼▼ Knights Inn-St. Clairsville/Wheeling M
(740) 695-5038. **$45-$66.** 51260 National Rd. I-70, exit 218, 0.5 mi ne on US 40. Ext corridors. **Pets:** Accepted.
🅂🅰🆅🅴 🆂🅾 ⊠ 📷 🔌 💻 ≈

(AAA) ▼▼▼ Red Roof Inn M
(740) 695-4057. **$42-$74.** 68301 Red Roof Ln. I-70, exit 218. Ext corridors. **Pets:** Large, other species. No service, supervision.
🅂🅰🆅🅴 ⊠ 📷 🔌

STOW

(AAA) ▼ Stow Inn M
(330) 688-3508. **$51-$91.** 4601 Darrow Rd. 2 mi n on SR 91. Int corridors. **Pets:** Service with restrictions, crate.
🅂🅰🆅🅴 🆂🅾 ⊠ 🔌

TOLEDO

(AAA) ▼▼▼ Comfort Inn-North M
(419) 476-0170. **$59-$89.** 445 E Alexis Rd. I-75, exit 210, 2 mi w on SR 184; just e of jct US 24 and SR 184. Int corridors. **Pets:** Other species. $5 daily fee/pet. Designated rooms, service with restrictions, crate.
🅂🅰🆅🅴 🆂🅾 ⊠ 📷 🔌 💻

(AAA) ▼▼ Crown Inn M
(419) 473-1485. **$62-$69.** 1727 W Alexis Rd. 2 mi w of jct US 24 and SR 184. Ext corridors. **Pets:** Other species. $40 deposit/room. Service with restrictions, crate.
🅂🅰🆅🅴 🆂🅾 ⊠ 🔌

(AAA) ▼▼▼ Radisson Hotel Toledo H
(419) 241-3000. **$135.** 101 N Summit St. Downtown; between Jefferson and Monroe sts. Int corridors. **Pets:** Large, other species. Service with restrictions, crate.
🅂🅰🆅🅴 ⊠ 💻 🍴

(AAA) ▽▼▽ Ramada Inn & Suites Ⓜ
(419) 242-8885. **$79-$139, 14 days notice.** 141 N Summit St. Downtown; between Jefferson and Monroe sts. Int corridors. **Pets:** Accepted.
[SAVE] [S🐾] [✕] [🔌] [🛏] [🖥] [🍴] [🏊]

(AAA) ▽▼▽ Red Roof Inn Secor Ⓜ
(419) 536-0118. **$49-$68.** 3530 Executive Pkwy. I-475, exit 17, 0.5 mi s on Secor Rd, then just e. Ext corridors. **Pets:** Accepted.
[SAVE] [✕] [🔌] [🖥] [🛏]

TROY

(AAA) ▽▼▽ Holiday Inn Express Hotel & Suites Ⓜ
(937) 332-1700. **$74-$79.** 60 Troy Town Dr. I-75, exit 74, just w on SR 41. Int corridors. **Pets:** Small, other species. Designated rooms, service with restrictions, supervision.
[SAVE] [S🐾] [✕] [🔌] [🖥] [🛏] [🖥] [🏊]

▽▼ Knights Inn Troy Ⓜ
(937) 339-1515. **$46-$50, 7 days notice.** 30 Troy Town Dr. I-75, exit 74, just w on SR 41. Ext corridors. **Pets:** Accepted.
[ASK] [S🐾] [✕] [🛏] [🖥]

(AAA) ▽▼▽ Residence Inn By Marriott 🅰 ❧
(937) 440-9303. **$84-$116.** 87 Troy Town Dr. I-75, exit 74, just w on SR 41. Int corridors. **Pets:** Other species. $200 one-time fee/room. Service with restrictions.
[SAVE] [S🐾] [✕] [🔌] [🖥] [🛏] [🖥] [🏊]

TWINSBURG

▽▼ Twinsburg Super 8 Motel Ⓜ
(330) 425-2889. **$50-$85.** 8848 Twins Hills Dr. I-480, exit 36, just w on SR 82. Int corridors. **Pets:** $5 daily fee/pet. Designated rooms, service with restrictions, supervision.
[ASK] [S🐾] [✕] [🛏]

UPPER SANDUSKY

(AAA) ▽▼▽ AmeriHost Inn-Upper Sandusky Ⓜ
(419) 294-3919. **$74-$189, 14 days notice.** 1726 E Wyandot Ave. Jct US 30 and 23. Int corridors. **Pets:** Accepted.
[SAVE] [S🐾] [✕] [🛏ᴹ] [🔌] [🖥] [🛏] [🖥] [🏊]

URBANA

(AAA) ▽▼▽ Logan Lodge Motel Ⓜ
(937) 652-2188. **$56-$60, 7 days notice.** 2551 S US Hwy 68. 1.3 mi s on US 68. Ext corridors. **Pets:** Other species. $15 daily fee/pet, $15 one-time fee/pet. Service with restrictions.
[SAVE] [S🐾] [✕] [🛏] [🏊]

VANDALIA

(AAA) ▽▼ Travelodge Dayton Airport Ⓜ
(937) 898-8321. **$55-$90, 10 days notice.** 75 Corporate Center Dr. Across from Dayton International Airport; off National Rd. Ext corridors. **Pets:** Accepted.
[SAVE] [S🐾] [✕] [🛏] [🖥] [🏊]

VERMILION

▽▼▽ Holiday Inn Express Ⓜ
(440) 967-8770. **$69-$139.** 2417 SR 60. Jct SR 60 and 2. Int corridors. **Pets:** Medium, other species. $50 deposit/room. Service with restrictions, crate.
[ASK] [S🐾] [✕] [🔌] [🖥] [🛏] [🖥] [🏊]

(AAA) ▽▼ Motel Plaza Ⓜ
(440) 967-3191. **$58-$89.** 4645 Liberty Ave. 2 mi e of SR 60; on US 6. Ext corridors. **Pets:** Dogs only. $20 deposit/pet. Supervision.
[SAVE] [S🐾] [✕] [🛏] [🖥]

WAPAKONETA

(AAA) ▽▼▽ Best Western Wapakoneta Ⓜ
(419) 738-8181. **$59-$85, 10 days notice.** 1510 Saturn. On I-75 business loop at jct I-75, exit 111. Int corridors. **Pets:** $10 one-time fee/room. No service, supervision.
[SAVE] [S🐾] [✕] [🔌] [🛏] [🖥]

▽▼ Super 8 Motel-Wapakoneta Ⓜ
(419) 738-8810. **$49.** 1011 Lunar Dr. I-75 business loop at jct I-75, exit 111. Ext/int corridors. **Pets:** Accepted.
[ASK] [S🐾] [✕] [🛏] [🖥]

WARREN

(AAA) ▽▼▽ Best Western Downtown Motor Inn Ⓜ
(330) 392-2515. **$55-$80, 7 days notice.** 777 Mahoning Ave. 0.3 mi n of Courthouse Square. Ext corridors. **Pets:** Other species. Service with restrictions, supervision.
[SAVE] [✕] [🔌] [🛏]

WASHINGTON COURT HOUSE

(AAA) ▽▼ Knights Inn Ⓜ
(740) 335-9133. **$46-$59.** 1809 Columbus Ave. 1.5 mi n on US 62 and SR 3. Ext corridors. **Pets:** $6 daily fee/pet. Service with restrictions.
[SAVE] [S🐾] [✕] [🛏]

WAUSEON

(AAA) ▽▼▽ Best Western Del Mar Ⓜ ❧
(419) 335-1565. **$64-$160, 3 days notice.** 8319 SR 108. I-80/90 (Ohio Tpke), exit 34, just s. Ext corridors. **Pets:** Medium. $17 one-time fee/room. Service with restrictions, supervision.
[SAVE] [S🐾] [✕] [🔌] [🖥] [🛏] [🖥] [🏊]

WILLOUGHBY

(AAA) ▽▼▽ Ramada Inn Cleveland East 🅷 ❧
(440) 944-4300. **$60, 12 days notice.** 6051 SOM Center Rd. I-90, exit 189, at jct SR 91. Int corridors. **Pets:** Small. Service with restrictions, supervision.
[SAVE] [S🐾] [✕] [🔌] [🛏] [🖥]

⚠️ ▽▽ Red Roof Inn-East M
(440) 946-9872. **$49-$72.** 4166 SR 306. I-90, exit 193, just
s. Ext corridors. **Pets:** Accepted.
SAVE ✕ 🐾 ♿

WOOSTER

⚠️ ▽▽▽ Econo Lodge M
(330) 264-8883. **$54-$79.** 2137 E Lincoln Way. 3 mi e on
US 30. Ext corridors. **Pets:** $10 daily fee/pet. Designated
rooms, service with restrictions, supervision.
SAVE S🐾 ✕ 🐾 🛏️ ☕

XENIA

▽▽ Best Western Regency Inn M
(937) 372-9954. **$45-$48.** 600 Little Main St. 1 mi w. Ext
corridors. **Pets:** Small. $6 one-time fee/pet. Service with
restrictions, supervision.
SAVE S🐾 ✕ 🛏️

ZANESVILLE

⚠️ ▽▽▽ Best Western Town House M▯
(740) 452-4511. **$54-$94.** 135 N 7th St. I-70, exit 155 on
SR 60, follow signs. Ext corridors. **Pets:** Large, other species. $10 one-time fee/room. Designated rooms, service
with restrictions.
SAVE S🐾 ✕ 🐾 🛏️ ☕ 🍽️

⚠️ ▽▽▽ Comfort Inn M
(740) 454-4144. **$64-$159.** 500 Monroe St. I-70, exit 155
westbound; exit 7th St eastbound, e on Elberon to light, just
n on Underwood. Int corridors. **Pets:** Large, other species.
$10 one-time fee/room. Designated rooms, service with
restrictions.
SAVE S🐾 ✕ 🐾 ♿ 🛏️ ☕ ☕

▽▽▽ Holiday Inn Conference Center M▯
(740) 453-0771. **$74-$129.** 4645 E Pike. I-70, exit 160 on
US 22 and 40. Int corridors. **Pets:** Medium. Designated
rooms, service with restrictions, supervision.
ASK S🐾 ✕ 🐾 ♿ 🛏️ ☕ 🍽️ ☕

⚠️ ▽▽▽ Red Roof Inn M
(740) 453-6300. **$49-$95.** 4929 E Pike. I-70, exit 160, just s.
Int corridors. **Pets:** Accepted.
SAVE S🐾 ✕ ♿M ♿ 🛏️ ☕

▽▽ Super 8 Motel-Zanesville M
(740) 455-3124. **$60-$90, 7 days notice.** 2440 National Rd.
I-70, exit 152, just n on SR 40 (National Rd). Int corridors.
Pets: $5 daily fee/pet. Crate.
ASK S🐾 ✕ 🐾 🛏️

OKLAHOMA

CITY INDEX

ALTUS

(AAA) ▼▼▼ Best Western Altus M
(580) 482-9300. **$62-$70.** 2804 N Main St. 2 mi n on US 283. Ext corridors. **Pets:** Large.
SAVE Sᴅ ✕ 🔒 💻 ➰

▼ Days Inn M
(580) 477-2300. **$43-$55.** 3202 N Main St. 2.3 mi n on US 283. Ext corridors. **Pets:** Accepted.
SAVE Sᴅ ✕ 🔒

ARDMORE

(AAA) ▼▼▼ Best Western Ardmore Inn M
(580) 223-7525. **$59, 3 days notice.** 6 Holiday Dr. I-35, exit 31A, just ne. Int corridors. **Pets:** Accepted.
SAVE Sᴅ ✕ 🔒 💻 ➰

▼▼ Comfort Inn M
(580) 226-1250. **$64-$125, 7 days notice.** 2700 W Broadway. I-35, exit 31A, just e on SR 199. Int corridors. **Pets:** Other species. Service with restrictions, supervision.
SAVE Sᴅ ✕ 🔒 💻 ➰

▼▼ Days Inn M
(580) 223-7976. **$55, 5 days notice.** 2432 Veterans Blvd. I-35, exit 33, just e on SR 142. Ext corridors. **Pets:** Accepted.
SAVE Sᴅ ✕ 🕙 🔒

▼▼▼ Holiday Inn, Ardmore MI
(580) 223-7130. **$69.** 2705 Holiday Dr. I-35, exit 31A, just e. Ext corridors. **Pets:** Other species. $10 one-time fee/room. Service with restrictions, supervision.
ASK ✕ 🕙 🔒 💻 🍴 ➰

▼▼ Super 8 Motel M
(580) 223-2201. **$38-$44, 7 days notice.** 2120 Hwy 142 W. I-35, exit 33, 0.3 mi e. Int corridors. **Pets:** Accepted.
ASK Sᴅ ✕ 🔒

BARTLESVILLE

▼▼ Holiday Inn MI
(918) 333-8320. **$72-$100.** 1410 SE Washington Blvd. On US 75, 0.3 mi n of jct US 60 E, 0.5 mi s of jct US 60 W. Int corridors. **Pets:** Accepted.
ASK ✕ 🔒 💻 🍴 ➰

▼▼ Super 8 Motel M 🐾
(918) 335-1122. **$45-$47.** Hwy 75. On US 75, 0.7 mi n of jct US 60 and 75. Ext/int corridors. **Pets:** Small. Service with restrictions, supervision.
ASK Sᴅ ✕ 🔒 💻

BIG CABIN

▼▼ Big Cabin Super 8 M 🐾
(918) 783-5888. **$45-$49, 5 days notice.** I-44 & Hwy 69. I-44, exit 283, just ne. Ext corridors. **Pets:** Small, dogs only. Supervision.
ASK Sᴅ ✕

BLACKWELL

(AAA) ▼▼▼ Comfort Inn M
(580) 363-7000. **$44-$70, 7 days notice.** 1201 N 44th St. I-35, exit 222, just ne. Int corridors. **Pets:** Accepted.
SAVE Sᴅ ✕ 🕙 🔒 💻 ➰

CHECOTAH

▼▼ Days Inn of Eufaula M
(918) 689-3999. **$54-$70.** Hwy 69 & 150. US 69, exit SR 150, just w. Ext corridors. **Pets:** Accepted.
SAVE Sᴅ ✕ 🕙 💻

(AAA) ▼▼▼ Lake Eufaula Inn M
(918) 473-2376. **$39-$79.** SR 150 & I-40. I-40, exit 259, just s. Ext corridors. **Pets:** Accepted.
SAVE Sᴅ ✕ ➰

CHEROKEE

▼▼▼ Cherokee Inn M
(580) 596-2828. **$60, 10 days notice.** 1720 S Grand. Jct US 64 and SR 58, 6.8 mi n. Ext corridors. **Pets:** Designated rooms, supervision.

[ASK] [S♦] [✕] [▭]

CHICKASHA

◈ ▼▼▼ Best Western Inn M
(405) 224-4890. **$55-$65.** 2101 S 4th St. I-44, exit 80, just w. Ext/int corridors. **Pets:** Very small. $10 one-time fee/pet. Designated rooms, service with restrictions, supervision.

[SAVE] [S♦] [✕] [🍴] [▭] [🍴] [≈]

DURANT

▼▼▼ Comfort Inn & Suites of Durant M
(580) 924-8881. **$67.** 2112 W Main St. US 75/69, exit US 70, just e. Int corridors. **Pets:** $10 one-time fee/room. Service with restrictions, supervision.

[SAVE] [S♦] [✕] [🌀] [🔌] [🍴] [▭] [≈]

ELK CITY

▼ Bedford Inn M
(580) 225-6775. **$40-$55, 10 days notice.** 2004 S Main. I-40, exit 38, just ne. Ext corridors. **Pets:** Accepted.

[ASK] [S♦] [✕] [🍴] [≈]

◈ ▼▼▼ Best Western Elk City Inn M
(580) 225-2331. **$59-$69.** 2015 W 3rd St. On US 66, 1.3 mi w of center. Ext corridors. **Pets:** Accepted.

[SAVE] [S♦] [✕] [≈]

▼ Budget Host Inn M
(580) 225-1811. **$45-$55.** 2000 W 3rd St. On US 66, 1.4 mi w of center. Ext corridors. **Pets:** Accepted.

[ASK] [S♦] [✕]

▼▼ Days Inn Elk City M
(580) 225-9210. **$40-$50.** 1100 Hwy 34. I-40, exit 41, just nw. Ext corridors. **Pets:** Other species. $5 daily fee/pet. Supervision.

[SAVE] [S♦] [✕] [🍴] [≈]

◈ ▼▼▼ Holiday Inn M 🐾
(580) 225-6637. **$59-$75.** 101 Meadow Ridge Dr. I-40, exit 38, just sw. Ext/int corridors. **Pets:** Other species. Service with restrictions, supervision.

[SAVE] [S♦] [✕] [🌀] [🍴] [▭] [🍴] [≈]

▼▼▼ Howard Johnson M
(580) 225-3111. **$70, 14 days notice.** 2606 E Hwy 66. I-40, exit 41, just nw. Ext/int corridors. **Pets:** $5 one-time fee/pet. Supervision.

[ASK] [S♦] [✕] [🍴] [▭] [🍴] [≈]

▼▼ Ramada Inn M
(580) 225-8140. **$49-$53.** 102 B J Hughes Access Rd. I-40, exit 38, just s. Ext corridors. **Pets:** Accepted.

[ASK] [S♦] [✕] [▭] [≈]

ENID

▼▼▼ Best Western Inn of Enid M
(580) 242-7110. **$59-$65.** 2818 S Van Buren St. Jct US 412 and 81, 1.7 mi s on US 81. Int corridors. **Pets:** Small, other species. $5 daily fee/pet. Supervision.

[SAVE] [S♦] [✕] [🍴] [🍴] [≈]

▼▼▼ Comfort Inn M
(580) 234-1200. **$69-$79, 30 days notice.** 210 N Van Buren St. 0.7 mi n on US 81. Ext/int corridors. **Pets:** Accepted.

[SAVE] [S♦] [✕] [🔌] [🍴] [▭] [≈]

▼▼ Days Inn M
(580) 234-0080. **$59-$69, 30 days notice.** 200 N Van Buren. 0.7 mi n on US 81. Ext corridors. **Pets:** Accepted.

[SAVE] [S♦] [✕] [🍴]

ERICK

◈ ▼▼▼ Comfort Inn M
(580) 526-8124. **$78-$108, 5 days notice.** 1001 N Sheb Wooley. I-40, exit 7, just nw. Ext corridors. **Pets:** Small. $6 daily fee/pet. Designated rooms, service with restrictions, supervision.

[SAVE] [S♦] [✕] [🌀] [▭] [≈]

FREDERICK

◈ ▼▼ Scottish Inns M
(580) 335-2129. **$45-$65.** 1015 S Main St. US 183, 1.1 mi s. Ext corridors. **Pets:** Designated rooms, service with restrictions, supervision.

[SAVE] [S♦] [✕] [🍴] [▭] [≈]

GUYMON

▼▼ Ambassador Inn M
(580) 338-5555. **Call for rates, 10 days notice.** Hwy 64 N at 21st. 1.5 mi n on US 64 and SR 136. Ext corridors. **Pets:** Medium. Service with restrictions, supervision.

[ASK] [✕] [▭] [🍴] [≈]

▼▼▼ Best Western Townsman Inn M 🐾
(580) 338-6556. **$55-$73.** 212 NE Hwy 54. 0.8 mi se on US 54. Ext corridors. **Pets:** Small, other species. Service with restrictions, supervision.

[SAVE] [S♦] [✕] [🔌] [🍴] [▭] [≈]

◈ ▼▼ Econo Lodge M
(580) 338-5431. **$41-$49, 3 days notice.** 923 Hwy 54 E. Just s of jct US 64. Ext corridors. **Pets:** Small, other species. $8 one-time fee/pet. Service with restrictions, supervision.

[SAVE] [S♦] [✕]

◈ ▼▼▼ Guymon Super 8 M
(580) 338-0507. **$54-$59.** 1201 Hwy 54 NE. Jct US 54 and 64. Int corridors. **Pets:** Other species. Service with restrictions, supervision.

[SAVE] [S♦] [✕] [🔌] [🍴]

HEAVENER

Green Country Inn ⛨
(918) 653-7801. **$54.** Rt 1, Box 1095. North end of town on SR 59. Ext corridors. **Pets:** Accepted.

HENRYETTA

Gateway Inn ⛨
(918) 652-4448. **$32-$38, 3 days notice.** 903 E Trudgeon St. I-40, exit 240B, 0.5 mi n. Ext/int corridors. **Pets:** Medium. $25 deposit/room. Service with restrictions, supervision.

LAWTON

Holiday Inn ⛨
(580) 353-1682. **$62-$70.** 3134 NW Cache Rd. I-44, exit 39A, 2.5 mi w. Ext corridors. **Pets:** Other species. $25 one-time fee/room. Service with restrictions, supervision.

Howard Johnson Hotel ⛨
(580) 353-0200. **$57-$61.** 1125 E Gore Blvd. I-44, exit 37, just e. Ext/int corridors. **Pets:** $25 one-time fee/room. Service with restrictions, crate.

Ramada Inn ⛨
(580) 355-7155. **$64-$70, 7 days notice.** 601 NW 2nd St. I-44, exit 37, 1.2 mi sw. Ext/int corridors. **Pets:** Medium. $15 daily fee/pet. Service with restrictions, supervision.

Super 8 Motel ⛨
(580) 353-0310. **$48-$58, 7 days notice.** 2202 NW Hwy 277. I-44, exit 40A, 0.5 mi sw. Ext corridors. **Pets:** Large. $6 daily fee/pet. Designated rooms, service with restrictions, supervision.

LOCUST GROVE

Holiday Inn Express Hotel & Suites ⛨
(918) 479-8082. **$69.** 106 Holiday Ln. On US 412 (Cherokee Tpke) and SR 82, just nw. Int corridors. **Pets:** Accepted.

MCALESTER

Best Western Inn of McAlester ⛨
(918) 426-0115. **$55-$62.** 1215 George Nigh Expwy. 6 mi s on US 69 Bypass, 3 mi n of Indian Nation Tpke. Ext corridors. **Pets:** Accepted.

Days Inn ⛨
(918) 426-5050. **$54-$65.** 1217 S George Nigh Expwy. 6 mi s on US 69 Bypass, 3 mi n of Indian Nation Tpke. Ext/int corridors. **Pets:** Accepted.

Super 8 Motel ⛨
(918) 426-5400. **$56-$64, 5 days notice.** 2400 S Main. 1.8 mi s on US 69 business route, 2.5 mi n of Indian Nation Tpke. Ext corridors. **Pets:** Accepted.

MUSKOGEE

Days Inn of Muskogee ⛨
(918) 683-3911. **$45-$55.** 900 S 32nd St. 3 mi s on US 64 and 69. Ext corridors. **Pets:** Very small. $5 daily fee/pet. Service with restrictions, supervision.

OKLAHOMA CITY METROPOLITAN AREA

DEL CITY

La Quinta Inn-East ⛨
(405) 672-0067. **$66-$92.** 5501 Tinker Diagonal Rd. I-40, exit 156A (Sooner Ave). Ext/int corridors. **Pets:** Accepted.

EDMOND

Ramada Plaza Hotel ⛨
(405) 341-3577. **$79.** 930 E 2nd St. I-35, exit 141, 2.3 mi w. Int corridors. **Pets:** Small. $25 deposit/pet. Service with restrictions, crate.

EL RENO

Best Western Hensley's ⛨
(405) 262-6490. **$50-$65.** 2701 S Country Club Rd. I-40, exit 123, just s. Ext corridors. **Pets:** Medium, other species. $20 deposit/room, $5 one-time fee/room. Service with restrictions, supervision.

GUTHRIE

Best Western Territorial Inn ⛨
(405) 282-8831. **$61-$69.** 2323 Territorial Tr. I-35, exit 157, just sw. Int corridors. **Pets:** Accepted.

MIDWEST CITY

▼▼▼▼ Comfort Inn & Suites M
(405) 733-1339. **$79-$84, 7 days notice.** 5653 Tinker Diagonal Rd. I-40, exit 156, just n. Int corridors. **Pets:** Small. $25 deposit/room. Service with restrictions, supervision.
SAVE S⊘ ✕ ⌨ 🛏 💻 ⊋

MOORE

▲▲▲ ▼▼ Microtel Inn & Suites M
(405) 799-8181. **$46-$69.** 2400 S Service Rd. I-35, exit 116, just s on east service road. Int corridors. **Pets:** Supervision.
SAVE S⊘ ✕ 🛏 💻 ⊋

▲▲▲ ▼▼ Super 8 Motel M
(405) 794-4030. **$47.** 1520 N Service Rd. I-35, exit 118 (12th St), just ne. Ext corridors. **Pets:** Medium. $50 deposit/pet, $8 daily fee/pet. Designated rooms, service with restrictions, supervision.
SAVE S⊘ ✕ 🛏

NORMAN

▲▲▲ ▼▼ Econo Lodge M
(405) 364-5554. **$60, 3 days notice.** 100 SW 26th Dr. I-35, exit 109 (Main St), just se. Ext corridors. **Pets:** Other species. $10 deposit/pet, $5 daily fee/pet. Service with restrictions, supervision.
SAVE S⊘ ✕ 💻

▼▼▼ La Quinta Inn & Suites M
(405) 579-4000. **$79-$135.** 930 Ed Noble Dr. I-35, exit 108B (Lindsey), just nw. Int corridors. **Pets:** Accepted.
SAVE ✕ ⌨M ⌨ 🛏 💻 ⊋

▲▲▲ ▼▼▼ The Residence Inn by Marriott A
(405) 366-0900. **$84-$135.** 2681 Jefferson St. I-35, exit 108A (SR 9 E), just se. Ext corridors. **Pets:** Accepted.
SAVE S⊘ ✕ ⊘ 🛏 💻 ⊋

▼▼ Thunderbird Lodge M
(405) 329-6990. **$40-$45.** 1430 24th Ave SW. I-35, exit 108A, just e to 24th Ave, then just n. Ext corridors. **Pets:** Accepted.
✕ 🛏

OKLAHOMA CITY

▲▲▲ ▼▼▼▼ AmeriSuites (Oklahoma City-Airport) M
(405) 682-3900. **$84.** 1818 S Meridian Ave. I-40, exit 145 (Meridian Ave), 1 mi s. Int corridors. **Pets:** Small. Service with restrictions, crate.
SAVE S⊘ ✕ ⌨M ⊘ ⌨ 🛏 💻 ⊋

▲▲▲ ▼▼▼▼ AmeriSuites (Oklahoma City/Quail Springs) M
(405) 749-1595. **$89-$94.** 3201 W Memorial Rd. SR 74 (Hefner Pkwy), exit Memorial Rd, 1.1 mi e on Service Rd to May, 0.4 mi w on N Service Rd. Int corridors. **Pets:** Small. Service with restrictions, supervision.
SAVE S⊘ ✕ ⌨ 🛏 💻 ⊋

▲▲▲ ▼▼▼▼ Best Western Saddleback Inn MI
(405) 947-7000. **$77-$82.** 4300 SW 3rd St. I-40, exit 145 (Meridian Ave), just ne. Ext/int corridors. **Pets:** Small, other species. $25 deposit/room. Designated rooms, service with restrictions, crate.
SAVE S⊘ ✕ ⊘ 🛏 💻 ⊓⊓

▼▼▼▼ Clarion Meridian Hotel and Convention Center M
(405) 942-8511. **$82-$95.** 737 S Meridian Ave. I-40, exit 145 (Meridian Ave), just s. Ext/int corridors. **Pets:** Small, dogs only. $25 deposit/room. Designated rooms.
SAVE ✕ ⌨M ⊘ ⌨ 🛏 💻 ⊓⊓ ⊋

▲▲▲ ▼▼▼▼ Comfort Inn North M
(405) 478-7282. **$60-$99.** 4625 NE 120th. I-35, exit 137 (122nd St), just sw. Int corridors. **Pets:** Medium, other species. $5 daily fee/pet. Service with restrictions, crate.
SAVE S⊘ ✕ ⌨ 🛏 💻 ⊋

▲▲▲ ▼ Days Inn M
(405) 942-8294. **$49, 7 days notice.** 504 S Meridian Ave. I-40, exit 145, just ne. Ext corridors. **Pets:** Small. $25 deposit/room. Service with restrictions, supervision.
SAVE S⊘ ✕ 🛏 💻 ⊋

▼▼▼▼ Days Inn & Suites North M
(405) 478-2554. **$55-$85, 15 days notice.** 12013 N I-35 Service Rd. I-35, exit 137, just sw. Ext/int corridors. **Pets:** Small, other species. Service with restrictions.
SAVE S⊘ ✕ 🛏 💻 ⊋

▼▼ Days Inn Northwest MI
(405) 946-0741. **$45-$50.** 2801 NW 39th St. I-44, exit 124, just n. Ext corridors. **Pets:** Accepted.
SAVE S⊘ ✕ ⊘ 🛏 💻 ⊓⊓ ⊋

▲▲▲ ▼▼▼ Econo Lodge M
(405) 942-5955. **$49, 10 days notice.** 4601 SW 3rd. I-40, exit 145 (Meridian Ave), just w. Ext corridors. **Pets:** Small. $5 one-time fee/pet. Service with restrictions, supervision.
SAVE S⊘ ✕

▼▼▼▼ Embassy Suites H
(405) 682-6000. **$139-$179.** 1815 S Meridian Ave. I-40, exit 145 (Meridian Ave), 1 mi s. Int corridors. **Pets:** Large. $35 one-time fee/room. Service with restrictions, crate.
SAVE S⊘ ✕ ⊘ 🛏 💻 ⊓⊓ ⊋

▲▲▲ ▼▼▼▼ Four Points by Sheraton Oklahoma City H
(405) 681-3500. **$89, 7 days notice.** 6300 Terminal Dr. Int corridors. **Pets:** Small. $50 one-time fee/room. Service with restrictions, supervision.
SAVE S⊘ ✕ ⌨ 🛏 💻 ⊓⊓ ⊋

Hampton Inn OKC Airport M
(405) 682-2080. **$79-$95, 14 days notice.** 1905 S Meridian Ave. I-40, exit 145, 1 mi s. Int corridors. **Pets:** Very small. $25 one-time fee/room. Service with restrictions, supervision.

SAVE ☒ ☒ 🖪 🖵 ⌂

Hilton Northwest H
(405) 848-4811. **$129-$149, 3 days notice.** 2945 Northwest Expwy. Jct SR 74 and 3, 0.5 mi e. Ext/int corridors. **Pets:** Accepted.

SAVE ⚿ ☒ ☒ ⚹ 🖪 🖵 ❌ ⌂

Howard Johnson Express Inn-Airport M
(405) 943-9841. **$51-$55, 15 days notice.** 400 S Meridian Ave. I-40, exit 145, just n. Int corridors. **Pets:** Accepted.

SAVE ⚿ ☒ ☒ 🖪 🖵 ⌂

La Quinta Inn & Suites M
(405) 773-5575. **$89-$105.** 4829 Northwest Expwy. Jct SR 74 and 3, 1.9 mi w. Int corridors. **Pets:** Small. Service with restrictions, crate.

SAVE ☒ ⚿M ☒ ⚹ 🖪 🖵 ⌂

La Quinta Inn-South M
(405) 631-8661. **$61-$91.** 8315 I-35 S. I-35, exit 121A (82nd St), just sw. Ext corridors. **Pets:** Other species. Service with restrictions, crate.

SAVE ☒ ☒ 🖪 🖵

La Quinta Oklahoma City Airport M
(405) 942-0040. **$68-$98.** 800 S Meridian Ave. I-40, exit 145 (Meridian Ave), just se. Ext/int corridors. **Pets:** Accepted.

SAVE ☒ ⚹ 🖪 🖵 ❌ ⌂

Microtel Inn and Suites M
(405) 942-0011. **$58, 14 days notice.** 624 S MacArthur. I-40, exit 144 (MacArthur), just s. Int corridors. **Pets:** Accepted.

ASK ⚿ ☒ 🖪 🖵 ⌂

Motel 6–1182 M
(405) 478-4030. **$35-$49.** 12121 Northeast Expwy. I-35, exit 137, just sw. Ext corridors. **Pets:** Accepted.

⚿ ☒ ☒ ⚹ ⌂

Motel 6 Airport–116 M
(405) 946-6662. **$41-$53.** 820 S Meridian Ave. I-40, exit 145 (Meridian Ave), just se. Ext corridors. **Pets:** Accepted.

⚿ ☒ ☒ ⚹

Motel 6 West–1128 M
(405) 947-6550. **$45-$57.** 4200 I-40 W. I-40, exit 145 (Meridian Ave), just e on south frontage road. Ext/int corridors. **Pets:** Accepted.

⚿ ☒ ⚿M ⚹ 🖪

Oklahoma City Marriott H
(405) 842-6633. **$159.** 3233 Northwest Expwy. Jct SR 74 and 3, just e. Int corridors. **Pets:** Service with restrictions, supervision.

SAVE ⚿ ☒ ⚿M ☒ ⚹ 🖪 🖵 ❌ ⌂

Quality Inn M 🐾
(405) 632-6666. **$59.** 7800 CA Henderson Blvd. I-240, exit 2A, just s. Ext corridors. **Pets:** Small, dogs only. $10 one-time fee/room. Designated rooms, service with restrictions.

SAVE ⚿ ☒ 🖪 🖵 ⌂

Quality Inn at Founders Tower M
(405) 810-1100. **$69-$149, 7 days notice.** 5704 Mosteller Dr. Jct SR 74 and 3, 0.5 mi e. Int corridors. **Pets:** Small. Service with restrictions, supervision.

SAVE ⚿ ☒ ⚹ 🖪 🖵

Quality Inn-North M
(405) 478-0400. **$49, 7 days notice.** 12001 N I-35 Service Rd. I-35, exit 137, just sw. Ext corridors. **Pets:** Small, other species. $10 one-time fee/room. Designated rooms, service with restrictions, supervision.

SAVE ⚿ ☒ ⚹ 🖪 🖵 ⌂

Residence Inn by Marriott-West A
(405) 942-4500. **$105-$135.** 4361 W Reno Ave. I-40, exit 145 (Meridian Ave), 0.3 mi n, then e. Ext corridors. **Pets:** Other species. $25 one-time fee/room. Service with restrictions.

SAVE ☒ ☒ 🖪 🖵 ⌂

Super 8-Frontier City M
(405) 478-8288. **$35-$55.** 12001 N I-35 Service Rd. I-35, exit 137, just sw. Ext corridors. **Pets:** Small, other species. $20 deposit/room. Service with restrictions, supervision.

ASK ⚿ ☒ 🖵 ⌂

The Waterford Marriott H
(405) 848-4782. **$99-$129.** 6300 Waterford Blvd. I-44, exit 125A, 1.4 mi n. Int corridors. **Pets:** Accepted.

SAVE ☒ ☒ ⚹ 🖪 🖵 ❌ ⌂

PURCELL

Econo Lodge M
(405) 527-5603. **$50-$55.** 2500 Hwy 74 S. I-35, exit 91, just w. Ext corridors. **Pets:** Small. $5 daily fee/pet. Service with restrictions, supervision.

SAVE ⚿ ☒ ☒ 🖪

SHAWNEE

Best Western Cinderella Motor Inn M
(405) 273-7010. **$55-$100.** 623 Kickapoo Spur. I-40, exit 185, 2.5 mi s, 0.3 mi w on Kickapoo Spur. Ext/int corridors. **Pets:** Other species. $10 daily fee/pet. Designated rooms, service with restrictions, crate.

SAVE ⚿ ☒ ☒ 🖪 🖵 ❌ ⌂

Motel 6–1236 M
(405) 275-5310. **$43-$55.** 4981 N Harrison. I-40, exit 186, just ne. Int corridors. **Pets:** Accepted.

⚿ ☒ ☒ ⚹ ⌂

YUKON

(AAA) ▼▼▼ Best Western Inn & Suites Yukon M
(405) 265-2995. **$56-$70.** I-40 and Hwy 4. I-40, exit 138, just sw. Ext/int corridors. **Pets:** Other species. $25 deposit/ room, $5 one-time fee/room. Designated rooms, service with restrictions, supervision.
[SAVE] [$⃠] [✕] [🐾] [&] [🛏] [💻] [🏊]

(AAA) ▼▼▼ Hampton Inn M
(405) 350-6400. **$69-$79.** 1351 Canadian Ct. I-40, exit 136, just se. Int corridors. **Pets:** Small. Designated rooms, service with restrictions.
[SAVE] [$⃠] [✕] [&] [🛏] [💻]

(AAA) ▼▼▼ Yukon Super 8 M
(405) 324-1000. **$60-$75, 7 days notice.** 321 N Mustang Rd. I-40, exit 138, just n. Ext corridors. **Pets:** Medium, other species. Service with restrictions, crate.
[SAVE] [$⃠] [✕] [🛏] [🏊]

❖ **END METROPOLITAN AREA** ❖

OKMULGEE

(AAA) ▼▼▼ Best Western Okmulgee MI
(918) 756-9200. **$65-$105.** 3499 N Wood Dr. Jct US 75 and N Loop 56, just n on US 75. Int corridors. **Pets:** $50 deposit/room. Service with restrictions, supervision.
[SAVE] [$⃠] [✕] [&] [🛏] [💻] [🍴] [🏊]

PAULS VALLEY

(AAA) ▼▼ Days Inn M
(405) 238-7548. **$70-$75, 30 days notice.** 3203 W Grant Ave. I-35, exit 72, just e. Int corridors. **Pets:** Accepted.
[SAVE] [$⃠] [✕] [🛏]

PERRY

(AAA) ▼▼▼ Best Western Cherokee Strip Motel MI
(580) 336-2218. **$50-$53.** I-35 & US 77. I-35, exit 185, just e. Ext corridors. **Pets:** Accepted.
[SAVE] [$⃠] [✕] [🍴] [🏊]

PRYOR

▼▼▼ Days Inn of Pryor M
(918) 825-7600. **$40-$50.** Hwy 69 S. 3.2 mi s on US 69. Ext corridors. **Pets:** Accepted.
[SAVE] [$⃠] [✕] [🐾] [🛏] [💻] [🏊]

ROLAND

▼▼▼ Days Inn of Roland M
(918) 427-1000. **$65.** 207 Cherokee Blvd. I-40, exit 325, just ne. Int corridors. **Pets:** Accepted.
[SAVE] [$⃠] [✕] [🐾] [&] [🛏] [🏊]

SALLISAW

(AAA) ▼▼▼ Super 8 Motel M
(918) 775-8900. **$40-$45, 7 days notice.** 924 S Kerr Blvd (US 59). I-40, exit 308, just n. Ext/int corridors. **Pets:** Accepted.
[SAVE] [$⃠] [✕] [&M] [&] [🛏] [💻] [🏊]

SAVANNA

(AAA) ▼▼ Travelodge M
(918) 548-3506. **$38-$42.** Hwy 69 & Panola. On US 69, 2 mi sw of Indian Nation Tpke. Ext corridors. **Pets:** Other species. $25 deposit/pet. Service with restrictions, supervision.
[SAVE] [$⃠] [✕] [🛏] [💻] [🏊]

STILLWATER

(AAA) ▼▼▼ Best Western Stillwater MI
(405) 377-7010. **$65-$90.** 600 E McElroy. 1 mi n on US 177 (Perkins Rd). Int corridors. **Pets:** Small. Service with restrictions.
[SAVE] [$⃠] [✕] [🐾] [🛏] [💻] [🍴] [🏊]

▼▼▼ Holiday Inn MI
(405) 372-0800. **Call for rates.** 2515 W 6th Ave. 1.8 mi w on SR 51. Ext/int corridors. **Pets:** Accepted.
[✕] [🛏] [💻] [🍴] [🏊]

TAHLEQUAH

▼▼ Oak Hill Motel and Suites MI ❖
(918) 458-1200. **$39-$65.** 2600 S Muskogee Pl. Just s on US 62 from jct SR 51, 10 and US 62. Ext corridors. **Pets:** Medium, other species. $7 daily fee/pet. Service with restrictions, supervision.
[ASK] [$⃠] [✕] [🛏] [💻] [🍴] [🏊]

Tulsa Metropolitan Area

BROKEN ARROW

◆◆◆◆ Holiday Inn Tulsa South M
(918) 258-7085. **$99.** 2600 N Aspen. Broken Arrow Expwy (SR 51), exit 145th Ave. Int corridors. **Pets:** Medium. Service with restrictions, crate.
🏧 💲 ✖ 🔗 🏨 📺 🏊

CATOOSA

◆◆◆ ◆◆◆ Super 8 M
(918) 266-7000. **$40-$60.** 19250 Timbercrest Cir. I-44, exit 240A, just nw. Ext corridors. **Pets:** Accepted.
💲 💲 ✖ 🏊

CLAREMORE

◆◆◆ ◆◆◆◆ Claremore Motor Inn M
(918) 342-4545. **$45.** 1709 N Lynn Riggs. On US 66. Ext/int corridors. **Pets:** Small. $25 deposit/room, $5 daily fee/pet. Designated rooms, service with restrictions, supervision.
💲 💲 ✖ 🏨

◆◆◆◆ Days Inn Claremore M
(918) 343-3297. **$63-$83.** 1720 S Lynn Riggs. On US 66, 2 mi s. Int corridors. **Pets:** Other species. $10 daily fee/pet. Designated rooms, service with restrictions, supervision.
💲 💲 ✖ 🔗 🏊

◆◆◆ ◆ Motel Claremore M
(918) 341-3254. **$40, 3 days notice.** 812 E Will Rogers Blvd. On SR 20, 0.5 mi w. Ext corridors. **Pets:** Accepted.
💲 💲 ✖

GLENPOOL

◆◆◆ ◆◆◆ Best Western Glenpool M
(918) 322-5201. **$54-$99.** 14831 S Casper St. I-44, exit 224, 9.5 mi s on US 75. Ext corridors. **Pets:** Other species. $50 deposit/pet. Service with restrictions, supervision.
💲 💲 ✖ 🏨 📺 🏊

SAND SPRINGS

◆◆◆ ◆◆◆ Best Western Sand Springs Inn & Suites M
(918) 245-4999. **$52-$83.** 211 South Lake Dr. Off SR 51, US 64 and 412, exit 81st W Ave, just sw. Ext/int corridors. **Pets:** $10 one-time fee/pet. Service with restrictions, supervision.
💲 💲 ✖ 🔗 🏨 📺 🏊

SAPULPA

◆◆◆ ◆◆◆ Sapulpa Super 8 M
(918) 227-3300. **$45-$49.** 1505 New Sapulpa Rd. 0.5 mi e on SR 66. Int corridors. **Pets:** Accepted.
🏧 💲 ✖ 🔗 🏨 🏊

TULSA

◆◆◆ ◆◆◆◆ AmeriSuites (Tulsa/Hyde Park) M
(918) 491-4010. **$65-$80.** 7037 S Zurich Ave. I-44, exit 229 (Yale Ave/SR 66), 3 mi s to 71st St, then just e. Int corridors. **Pets:** Accepted.
💲 💲 ✖ 🔗 🔗 🏨 📺 🏊

◆◆◆ ◆◆◆◆ Baymont Inn & Suites-Tulsa M
(918) 488-8777. **$64-$74.** 4530 E Skelly Dr. I-44, exit 229 (Yale Ave/SR 66), just s, then w. Int corridors. **Pets:** Accepted.
💲 💲 ✖ 🔗 🔗 🏨 📺 🏊

◆◆◆ ◆◆◆◆ Best Western Trade Winds Central Inn M
(918) 749-5561. **$59-$79.** 3141 E Skelly Dr. I-44, exit 228 (Harvard Ave), on northwest frontage road. Ext/int corridors. **Pets:** Very small. $10 one-time fee/room. Service with restrictions, crate.
💲 💲 ✖ 🔗 🏨 📺 🍴 🏊

◆◆◆ ◆ Days Inn-Tulsa West M
(918) 446-1561. **$45-$51.** 5525 W Skelly Dr. I-44, exit 222B, just w on south service road; I-44 W, exit 222A, just e on south service road. Ext/int corridors. **Pets:** Small. $8 daily fee/pet. Designated rooms, service with restrictions, supervision.
💲 💲 ✖ 🏨 🍴 🏊

◆◆◆◆ Doubletree Hotel At Warren Place H
(918) 495-1000. **$103-$123.** 6110 S Yale Ave. I-44, exit 229 (Yale Ave/SR 66), 1 mi s. Int corridors. **Pets:** Other species. $50 deposit/pet. Crate.
💲 💲 ✖ 🔗 🏨 📺 🍴 🏊

◆◆◆ ◆◆◆◆ Doubletree Hotel Downtown Tulsa H
(918) 587-8000. **$99-$129.** 616 W 7th St. 7th St and Houston. Int corridors. **Pets:** Accepted.
💲 💲 ✖ 🔗 🏨 📺 🍴 🏊

◆◆◆◆ GuestHouse International Suites Plus A
(918) 664-7241. **$299 (weekly).** 8181 E 41st St. Broken Arrow Expwy, exit Memorial Dr, 1 mi s, then just e. Ext corridors. **Pets:** Small. $8 daily fee/room. Designated rooms, service with restrictions, supervision.
🏧 💲 ✖ 🔗 🏨 📺 🏊

◆◆◆◆ Holiday Inn-International Airport M ❀
(918) 437-7660. **$74, 3 days notice.** 1010 N Garnett Rd. I-244, exit 14 (Garnett Rd). Int corridors. **Pets:** Other species. $20 one-time fee/room. Service with restrictions, crate.
🏧 💲 ✖ 🔗 🔗 📺 🍴 🏊

◆◆◆◆ Holiday Inn Select M
(918) 622-7000. **$75.** 5000 E Skelly Dr. I-44, exit 229 (Yale Ave/SR 66), on south frontage road. Ext/int corridors. **Pets:** Large, other species. $25 one-time fee/room. Service with restrictions, crate.
🏧 💲 ✖ 🔗 🏨 📺 🍴 🏊

La Quinta Inn 41st St Ⓜ
(918) 665-0220. **$64-$80.** 10829 E 41st St. US 169, exit E 41st St. Ext corridors. **Pets:** Accepted.

La Quinta Inn Airport Ⓜ
(918) 836-3931. **$58-$78.** 35 N Sheridan Rd. I-244, exit 11 (Sheridan Rd). Ext corridors. **Pets:** Accepted.

La Quinta Inn-Tulsa South Ⓜ
(918) 254-1626. **$64-$80.** 12525 E 52nd St S. Broken Arrow Expwy (SR 51), exit 129th and 51st sts. Ext corridors. **Pets:** Small. Service with restrictions, supervision.

Ramada Inn Ⓜ
(918) 743-9811. **$69.** 3131 E 51st. I-44, exit 228 (Harvard Ave), just sw. Ext/int corridors. **Pets:** Medium. $50 deposit/room. Service with restrictions, supervision.

Sheraton Tulsa Hotel Ⓗ
(918) 627-5000. **$74-$91.** 10918 E 41st St. Jct US 169 and 41st St, just e. Int corridors. **Pets:** Accepted.

Super 8 Airport Ⓜ
(918) 836-1981. **$40-$55.** 6616 E Archer. I-244, exit 11 (Sheridan Rd), just e. Ext corridors. **Pets:** Medium. $5 daily fee/pet. Service with restrictions, supervision.

Super 8 Motel Ⓜ
(918) 446-6000. **$45-$65.** 5811 S 49th West Ave. I-44, exit 222A, just e on south service road. Ext corridors. **Pets:** Medium, other species. Service with restrictions, supervision.

Tulsa Residence Inn Ⓐ
(918) 250-4850. **$79-$130.** 11025 E 73rd St. US 169, exit 71st St, just e. Int corridors. **Pets:** Accepted.

❖   **END METROPOLITAN AREA**   ❖

WEATHERFORD

Best Western Mark Motor Hotel Ⓜ
(580) 772-3325. **$49-$119.** 525 E Main St. I-40, exit 82, 0.5 mi n. Ext corridors. **Pets:** Small, other species. Designated rooms, service with restrictions, supervision.

WOODWARD

Northwest Inn Ⓜ
(580) 256-7600. **$62-$72.** Hwy 270 S & 1st St. 1 mi s on US 183, 270, SR 3 and 34. Ext/int corridors. **Pets:** Accepted.

OREGON

CITY INDEX

ALBANY

(AAA) ▼▼▼ Best Inn & Suites M
(541) 928-5050. **$65-$105.** 1100 Price Rd SE. I-5, exit 233, just e, then just n. Int corridors. **Pets:** Small, dogs only. $50 deposit/pet, $10 daily fee/pet. Designated rooms, no service, supervision.

(SAVE) (S) ✕ (♿) 🐾 ✆ 🍴 🖥 ➾

(AAA) ▼▼▼ Best Western Pony Soldier Inn M
(541) 928-6322. **$82-$90.** 315 Airport Rd SE. I-5, exit 234B southbound; exit 234 northbound, just w, then just s. Ext corridors. **Pets:** Accepted.

(SAVE) (S) ✕ 🐾 🍴 🖥 ➾

(AAA) ▼▼▼ Hawthorn Inn & Suites M
(541) 928-0921. **$79-$82.** 251 Airport Rd SE. I-5, exit 234B southbound; exit 234 northbound, just w. Int corridors. **Pets:** Other species. Service with restrictions, crate.

(SAVE) (S) ✕ 🐾 (♿) 🍴 🖥 ➾

(AAA) ▼▼ Motel 6 M 🐾
(541) 926-4233. **$63.** 2735 E Pacific Blvd. I-5, exit 234, 0.5 mi e. Ext corridors. **Pets:** Medium. Designated rooms, service with restrictions, supervision.

(SAVE) (S) ✕ (♿) (♿) 🍴

ASHLAND

(AAA) ▼▼▼ Best Western Bard's Inn M 🐾
(541) 482-0049. **$102-$168.** 132 N Main St. Just n on SR 99 (N Main St) from downtown plaza. Ext/int corridors. **Pets:** Medium. $15 daily fee/pet. Designated rooms, service with restrictions, supervision.

(SAVE) (S) ✕ (♿) 🍴 🖥 ➾

(AAA) ▼▼▼ Best Western Windsor Inn M
(541) 488-2330. **$89-$129.** 2520 Ashland St. I-5, exit 14, just e. Ext corridors. **Pets:** Accepted.

(SAVE) (S) ✕ (♿) (♿) 🍴 🖥 ➾

(AAA) ▼▼▼ Cedarwood Inn M
(541) 488-2000. **$56-$105, 3 days notice.** 1801 Siskiyou Blvd. I-5, exit 14, 0.5 mi w on SR 66, s on Tolman Creek Blvd, then n. Ext corridors. **Pets:** Accepted.

(SAVE) ✕ 🍴 🖥 ➾

(AAA) ▼▼▼ Flagship Inn of Ashland M
(541) 482-2641. **$56-$98, 3 days notice.** 1193 Siskiyou Blvd. I-5, exit 14, 1.1 mi w on SR 66, just n on US 99 (Siskiyou Blvd). Ext corridors. **Pets:** Other species. $10 daily fee/pet. Designated rooms, service with restrictions, supervision.

(SAVE) ✕ 🐾 🍴 🖥 ➾

(AAA) ▼▼▼ Hawthorn Inn & Suites M 🐾
(541) 482-6932. **$69-$155.** 434 Valley View Rd. I-5, exit 19, just w. Int corridors. **Pets:** Medium. Designated rooms, service with restrictions, supervision.

(SAVE) (S) ✕ 🐾 🍴 🖥 ➾

(AAA) ▼▼▼ Knights Inn Motel M 🐾
(541) 482-5111. **$44-$78, 3 days notice.** 2359 Hwy 66. I-5, exit 14, just w. Ext corridors. **Pets:** Other species. $50 deposit/room, $10 daily fee/pet. Designated rooms, supervision.

(SAVE) ✕ 🍴 ➾

▼▼ Super 8 Motel-Ashland M
(541) 482-8887. **$60-$150.** 2350 Ashland St. I-5, exit 14, just w. Int corridors. **Pets:** Other species. $25 deposit/room. Designated rooms, supervision.

(ASK) (S) ✕ 🍴 ➾

Windmill Inn & Suites of Ashland M
(541) 482-8310. **$61-$135.** 2525 Ashland St. I-5, exit 14, just e. Int corridors. **Pets:** Other species. Designated rooms, service with restrictions, supervision.
[SAVE] [S.] [X] [&M] [/] [&] [] [≈] [X]

ASTORIA

Crest Motel M ❀
(503) 325-3141. **$51-$107.** 5366 Leif Erickson Dr. 4 mi e of Astoria Bridge on US 30. Ext corridors. **Pets:** Other species. Service with restrictions, supervision.
[SAVE] [S.] [X] [] [] [/C]

Red Lion Inn MI
(503) 325-7373. **$72-$121.** 400 Industry St. Just w of Astoria Bridge on US 30, just n on Basin St (Caution: do not turn onto Astoria-Megler Bridge). Ext corridors. **Pets:** Accepted.
[ASK] [S.] [X] [/] [] [] [TI] [/C]

BAKER CITY

Geiser Grand Hotel H ❀
(541) 523-1889. **$89-$109.** 1996 Main St. I-84, exit 304, 0.9 mi w on Cambell St, then 0.3 mi s; downtown. Int corridors. **Pets:** Dogs only. $75 deposit/room, $10 daily fee/pet. Service with restrictions, crate.
[ASK] [S.] [X] [&] [TI]

BANDON

Best Western Inn at Face Rock M
(541) 347-9441. **$69-$234.** 3225 Beach Loop Rd. 1 mi s on US 101, 0.8 mi w on Seabird Rd, just s. Ext corridors. **Pets:** Accepted.
[SAVE] [S.] [X] [/] [&] [] [] [≈] [/C]

Driftwood Motel M
(541) 347-9022. **$60-$90.** 460 Hwy 101. Center; on US 101. Ext corridors. **Pets:** Dogs only. $10 deposit/room, $5 daily fee/pet. Designated rooms, service with restrictions, supervision.
[SAVE] [S.] [X] [] [] [/C]

BEND

Best Inn & Suites M
(541) 388-2227. **$65-$135.** 61200 S Hwy 97. Jct US 20 E, 3 mi s on US 97. Int corridors. **Pets:** Other species. Service with restrictions, supervision.
[SAVE] [S.] [X] [/] [] [] [≈]

Best Western Inn & Suites of Bend M
(541) 382-1515. **$69-$119.** 721 NE 3rd St. On US 97, just s of jct US 20. Ext corridors. **Pets:** $5 daily fee/pet. Designated rooms, service with restrictions, supervision.
[SAVE] [S.] [X] [/] [] []

Cricketwood Country Bed & Breakfast BB
(541) 330-0747. **$90-$130, 3 days notice.** 63520 Cricketwood Rd. 3.8 mi se on Deschutes Market Rd, 0.5 mi e on Hamehook Rd, 0.5 mi on Repine Rd, just n. Ext/int corridors. **Pets:** $10 daily fee/room. Designated rooms, no service.
[X] [] []

Econo Lodge M
(541) 318-0848. **$59-$99.** 20600 Grandview Dr. Jct US 20 W, just n on US 97. Int corridors. **Pets:** Small. $10 daily fee/pet. Designated rooms, service with restrictions, supervision.
[SAVE] [S.] [X] [&M] [/] [&] [] []

Hampton Inn M
(541) 388-4114. **$79-$109.** 15 NE Butler Market Rd. US 97, exit Butler Market Rd. Ext corridors. **Pets:** Accepted.
[SAVE] [S.] [X] [] [≈]

Holiday Inn Express Hotel & Suites M
(541) 317-8500. **$49-$149.** 20615 Grandview Dr. Jct US 20 W, 2.8 mi n on US 97. Int corridors. **Pets:** Other species. $10 daily fee/pet. Service with restrictions, supervision.
[SAVE] [S.] [X] [&M] [/] [&] [] []

Red Lion Inn/North MI
(541) 382-7011. **$64-$99.** 1415 NE 3rd St. US 97, just n of jct US 20. Ext corridors. **Pets:** Other species. Service with restrictions, supervision.
[ASK] [S.] [X] [&M] [/] [&] [] [] [TI]

Red Lion Inn/South M
(541) 382-8384. **$64-$99.** 849 NE 3rd St. US 97, just s of jct US 20. Ext corridors. **Pets:** Other species. Service with restrictions, supervision.
[ASK] [S.] [X] [&M] [/] [&] [] []

The Riverhouse Hotel MI ❀
(541) 389-3111. **$80-$123.** 3075 N Hwy 97. Jct US 20 E, 1.5 mi n on US 97. Ext/int corridors. **Pets:** Other species. Designated rooms, service with restrictions, supervision.
[SAVE] [X] [/] [&] [] [] [TI] [≈] [X]

Rodeway Inn M
(541) 382-2211. **$49-$91.** 3705 N US 97. 2 mi n. Ext corridors. **Pets:** Dogs only. $5 one-time fee/pet. Designated rooms, service with restrictions, supervision.
[SAVE] [S.] [X] []

Shilo Inn Suites Hotel-Bend MI ❀
(541) 389-9600. **$69-$189.** 3105 O B Riley Rd. Jct US 20 E, 1.5 mi n on US 97. Ext corridors. **Pets:** Other species. $10 daily fee/pet. Service with restrictions, supervision.
[SAVE] [S.] [X] [/] [] [] [TI] [≈]

Sleep Inn of Bend M ❀
(541) 330-0050. **$69-$99, 7 days notice.** 600 NE Bellevue. On US 20 E, 2 mi e of jct US 97. Int corridors. **Pets:** Large, other species. $8 one-time fee/room. Designated rooms, service with restrictions, supervision.
[SAVE] [S.] [X] [&M] [&] [] []

BOARDMAN

[AAA] ◆◆ Econo Lodge [M]
(541) 481-2375. **$62-$79.** 105 SW Front St. I-84, exit 164, just s. Ext corridors. **Pets:** Other species. Service with restrictions, supervision.
[SAVE] [S/D] 🚭 🦻 ▣ 📺 🏊

BROOKINGS

[AAA] ◆◆◆ Best Western Beachfront Inn [M]
(541) 469-7779. **$99-$175.** 16008 Boat Basin Rd. South end on US 101, 1 mi w on Lower Harbor Rd. Ext corridors. **Pets:** Other species. $5 daily fee/pet. Designated rooms, service with restrictions, supervision.
[SAVE] [S/D] 🚭 [♿M] 🦻 ♿ ▣ 📺 🏊 [AC]

BURNS

[AAA] ◆◆ Best Inn [M] 🐾
(541) 573-1700. **$47-$67.** 999 Oregon Ave. 1 mi w on US 395/20 from jct SR 78. Ext/int corridors. **Pets:** Small. $20 deposit/room, $5 one-time fee/pet. Designated rooms, service with restrictions, supervision.
[SAVE] [S/D] 🚭 ▣ 🏊

[AAA] ◆◆ Days Inn Ponderosa [M]
(541) 573-2047. **$67-$77, 7 days notice.** 577 W Monroe St. Just w on US 395/20 from jct SR 78. Ext corridors. **Pets:** Accepted.
[SAVE] [S/D] 🚭 ▣ 🏊

[AAA] ◆ Silver Spur Motel [M]
(541) 573-2077. **$50.** 789 N Broadway. US 395/20, n on Broadway to edge of town. Ext corridors. **Pets:** Dogs only. $5 one-time fee/pet. Designated rooms, no service.
[SAVE] [S/D] 🚭 ▣ 📺

CANNON BEACH

[AAA] ◆◆◆ Best Western Cannon Beach [M] 🐾
(503) 436-9085. **$134-$161, 3 days notice.** 3215 S Hemlock St. US 101, exit Tolovana Park, just w, then just n. Ext corridors. **Pets:** Other species. $10 daily fee/pet. Designated rooms, service with restrictions, supervision.
[SAVE] [S/D] 🚭 ♿ ▣ 📺 [AC]

◆◆ Cannon Beach Ecola Creek Lodge [M]
(503) 436-2776. **$95-$145, 3 days notice.** 208 5th St. 0.3 mi w of US 101 via north exit to Ecola State Park. Ext corridors. **Pets:** Dogs only. $10 daily fee/pet. Service with restrictions, supervision.
🚭 [♿M] ▣ 📺 [AC]

◆◆◆ Hallmark Resort at Cannon Beach [M]
(503) 436-1566. **$79-$410, 3 days notice.** 1400 S Hemlock St. US 101, exit Sunset Blvd, just s. Ext corridors. **Pets:** Accepted.
[A$K] [S/D] 🚭 [♿M] 🦻 ▣ 📺 🏊 [AC]

[AAA] ◆◆ Haystack Resort Motel [M] 🐾
(503) 436-1577. **$129-$219, 3 days notice.** 3339 S Hemlock St. US 101, exit Tolovana Park, just w. Ext corridors. **Pets:** Medium, other species. $10 daily fee/pet. Service with restrictions, supervision.
[SAVE] [S/D] 🚭 ♿ ▣ 📺 🏊 [AC]

[AAA] ◆◆ Ocean Lodge [A] 🐾
(503) 436-2241. **$249, 3 days notice.** 2863 Pacific St. On US 101, exit Tolovana Park, 1 mi s. Ext corridors. **Pets:** Other species. $10 daily fee/pet. Designated rooms, service with restrictions, supervision.
[SAVE] [S/D] 🚭 ▣ 📺 [AC]

[AAA] ◆◆◆ Surfsand Resort [MI] 🐾
(503) 436-2274. **$129-$339, 3 days notice.** Ocean Front & Gower. Downtown; US 101, exit 2nd Cannon Beach. Ext corridors. **Pets:** Other species. $12 daily fee/pet. Service with restrictions, supervision.
[SAVE] [S/D] 🚭 🦻 ♿ ▣ 📺 🍴 🏊 [AC]

[AAA] ◆◆◆ Tolovana Inn [CO] 🐾
(503) 436-2211. **$65-$165, 3 days notice.** 3400 S Hemlock St. 2 mi s off US 101 Beach Loop. Ext corridors. **Pets:** $10 daily fee/pet. Designated rooms, service with restrictions, supervision.
[SAVE] [S/D] 🚭 ▣ 📺 🏊 [AC]

CANYONVILLE

[AAA] ◆◆◆ Best Western Canyonville Inn & Suites [M]
(541) 839-4200. **$69-$83, 14 days notice.** 200 Creekside Rd. I-5, exit 99, just nw. Int corridors. **Pets:** Small. $15 daily fee/pet. Designated rooms, service with restrictions, crate.
[SAVE] [S/D] 🚭 ♿ ▣ 📺 🏊

CASCADE LOCKS

[AAA] ◆◆◆ Best Western Columbia River Inn [M]
(541) 374-8777. **$64-$119.** 735 WaNaPa St. I-84, exit 44. Int corridors. **Pets:** Other species. $10 daily fee/pet. Designated rooms, supervision.
[SAVE] [S/D] 🚭 [♿M] 🦻 ♿ ▣ 📺 🏊

COOS BAY

[AAA] ◆◆◆ Best Western Holiday Motel [M] 🐾
(541) 269-5111. **$67-$99.** 411 N Bayshore Dr. Downtown; just n on US 101. Ext/int corridors. **Pets:** Small, dogs only. $10 daily fee/pet. Designated rooms, service with restrictions, supervision.
[SAVE] [S/D] 🚭 ♿ ▣ 📺 🏊

[AAA] ◆◆◆ Edgewater Inn [M]
(541) 267-0423. **$75-$100.** 275 E Johnson St. Downtown; just s on US 101, then e. Ext/int corridors. **Pets:** Medium. $8 daily fee/pet. Designated rooms, service with restrictions, supervision.
[SAVE] [S/D] 🚭 [♿M] 🦻 ▣ 📺 🏊

▼▼ ▼▼ Motel 6–1244 **M**
(541) 267-7171. **$43-$65.** 1445 Bayshore Dr. Downtown;
0.6 mi n on US 101. Ext corridors. **Pets:** Other species.
Service with restrictions, supervision.
[S$ℓ] [✕] [⌀] [✆] [🛏] [💻]

▼▼ ▼▼ Red Lion Hotel **MI**
(541) 267-4141. **$74-$89, 7 days notice.** 1313 N Bayshore
Dr. Downtown; 0.5 mi n on US 101. Ext corridors.
Pets: Accepted.
[ASK] [S$ℓ] [✕] [ᴹ] [⌀] [🛏] [💻] [🍴] [🏊]

COQUILLE

▼▼ Myrtle Lane Motel **M**
(541) 396-2102. **$39.** 787 N Central Blvd. From SR 42, 0.4
mi n. Ext corridors. **Pets:** Small. $4 daily fee/room. Desig-
nated rooms, service with restrictions.
[✕] [🛏] [🏫]

CORVALLIS

▼▼▼▼ Holiday Inn Express On The River **M**
(541) 752-0800. **$81-$99.** 781 NW 2nd St. I-5, exit 228, 9.8
mi w on SR 34, 0.4 mi nw on SR 99 W, then just n. Int
corridors. **Pets:** Other species. $10 daily fee/room. Desig-
nated rooms, service with restrictions, supervision.
[ASK] [S$ℓ] [✕] [⌀] [✆] [🛏] [💻] [🏊]

▼▼ ▼▼ Motel Orleans **M**
(541) 758-9125. **$59-$89.** 935 NW Garfield. Downtown; 1.5
mi n on 9th St. Int corridors. **Pets:** Medium, other species.
$100 deposit/pet. Designated rooms, service with restric-
tions, supervision.
[SAVE] [S$ℓ] [✕] [ᴹ] [⌀] [✆] [🛏] [💻]

▼▼ ▼▼ Shanico Inn **M**
(541) 754-7474. **$60-$80.** 1113 NW 9th St. 1.3 mi n. Int
corridors. **Pets:** Medium, other species. $10 daily fee/pet.
Designated rooms, service with restrictions, supervision.
[SAVE] [S$ℓ] [✕] [⌀] [🛏] [🏊]

▼▼ ▼▼ Super 8 Motel **M**
(541) 758-8088. **Call for rates.** 407 NW 2nd St. On US 20,
just n of jct SR 34. Int corridors. **Pets:** Accepted.
[ASK] [✕] [⌀] [✆] [🛏] [🏊]

COTTAGE GROVE

▼▼ ▼▼ Best Western Village Green Resort **M**
(541) 942-2491. **$59-$89.** 725 Row River Rd. I-5, exit 174,
just e. Ext corridors. **Pets:** Accepted.
[SAVE] [S$ℓ] [✕] [🛏] [💻] [🏊]

▼▼ ▼▼ Comfort Inn **M**
(541) 942-9707. **$59-$79, 3 days notice.** 845 Gateway
Blvd. I-5, exit 174, just sw. Ext corridors. **Pets:** Accepted.
[SAVE] [S$ℓ] [✕] [⌀] [🛏] [💻] [🏊]

▼▼ ▼▼▼ Holiday Inn Express **M**
(541) 942-1000. **$80-$120, 3 days notice.** 1601 Gateway
Blvd. I-5, exit 174, just w. Int corridors. **Pets:** Medium, dogs
only. $10 one-time fee/pet. Service with restrictions, super-
vision.
[SAVE] [S$ℓ] [✕] [⌀] [🛏] [🏊]

CRESCENT

▼▼ ▼▼ ▼▼ Woodsman Country Lodge **M**
(541) 433-2710. **$43-$45.** 136740 Hwy 97 N. Center. Ext
corridors. **Pets:** Large, other species. $10 one-time fee/pet.
Service with restrictions, supervision.
[SAVE] [✕] [🛏] [💻]

CRESWELL

▼▼ ▼▼ Creswell Garden Inn **M**
(541) 895-3341. **$54-$67.** 345 E Oregon Ave. I-5, exit 182,
just w. Ext corridors. **Pets:** Accepted.
[SAVE] [S$ℓ] [✕] [🛏] [🏊]

DALLAS

▼▼ ▼▼▼ Best Western Dallas Inn &
　　　　Suites **M**
(503) 623-6000. **$79-$89.** 250 Orchard Dr. SR 223, just n.
Int corridors. **Pets:** Accepted.
[SAVE] [S$ℓ] [✕] [ᴹ] [⌀] [✆] [🛏] [💻]

DEPOE BAY

▼▼ ▼▼ ▼▼ Crown Pacific Inn **M**
(541) 765-7773. **$70-$88.** 50 NE Bechill St. Center. Ext/int
corridors. **Pets:** Medium, other species. $10 one-time fee/
pet. Designated rooms, service with restrictions, supervision.
[SAVE] [S$ℓ] [✕] [🛏] [💻] [🏫]

▼▼▼▼ Gracie's Landing Bed & Breakfast
　　　　Inn **BB** 🐾
(541) 765-2322. **$100-$150.** 235 SE Bay View Ave. US
101, just e on SE Bay St. Int corridors. **Pets:** Medium, dogs
only. $7 one-time fee/pet. Designated rooms, service with
restrictions, supervision.
[✕] [🏫] [☎]

ENTERPRISE

▼▼ ▼▼ Ponderosa Motel **M**
(541) 426-3186. **$62-$74.** 102 NE Greenwood St. Downtown;
town center across from City Hall. Ext corridors. **Pets:** Dogs
only. $10 daily fee/pet. Designated rooms, service with
restrictions, supervision.
[ASK] [S$ℓ] [✕] [ᴹ] [🛏] [💻]

▼▼ ▼▼ The Wilderness Inn **M**
(541) 426-4535. **$51-$65.** 301 W North St. Corner of NW
2nd. Ext corridors. **Pets:** Dogs only. $5 daily fee/pet. Super-
vision.
[ASK] [S$ℓ] [✕] [🛏] [💻]

EUGENE

▼▼ ▼▼▼ Best Western Greentree Inn **MI**
(541) 485-2727. **$76-$91.** 1759 Franklin Blvd. I-5, exit 194B
southbound to I-105, then University of Oregon Rt; exit 192
northbound, 1.2 mi w. Ext/int corridors. **Pets:** $50 deposit/
pet. Service with restrictions, supervision.
[SAVE] [✕] [🛏] [🍴] [🏊]

(AAA) ▼▼▼ Best Western New Oregon Motel M
(541) 683-3669. **$76-$91.** 1655 Franklin Blvd. I-5, exit 194B southbound to I-105, University of Oregon Rt; exit 192 northbound, 1.3 mi w. Ext/int corridors. **Pets:** $50 deposit/pet. Service with restrictions, supervision.
SAVE ✕ 🐾 🖥 🛁

(AAA) ▼▼▼ Hawthorn Inn & Suites M
(541) 344-8335. **$84-$114.** 155 Day Island Rd. I-5, exit 194B, 1.3 mi w on I-105, exit 2 (Coburg Rd), just s on Coburg Rd, just w on Centinnial Rd, then 0.5 mi se on Country Club Rd. Int corridors. **Pets:** Accepted.
SAVE S❄ ✕ 👤 🖥 🛁

(AAA) ▼▼▼ Hilton Eugene H
(541) 687-2395. **$120-$185.** 66 E 6th Ave. City Center; at 6th Ave and Oak St. Int corridors. **Pets:** Large, other species. $25 one-time fee/pet. Service with restrictions, supervision.
SAVE ✕ 🐾 🖥 🛁 🍴 🛁

▼ Motel 6–36 M
(541) 342-5201. **$45-$63.** 3690 Glenwood Dr. I-5, exit 191, just sw. Ext corridors. **Pets:** Other species. Service with restrictions, supervision.
S❄ ✕ 👤 🛁

(AAA) ▼▼ Quality Inn & Suites M
(541) 342-1243. **$77-$123.** 2121 Franklin Blvd. I-5, exit 192 northbound, just w; exit 194B southbound to I-105, exit University of Oregon Rt. Ext corridors. **Pets:** Accepted.
SAVE S❄ ✕ 🖥 🛁

(AAA) ▼▼▼ Ramada Inn-Eugene MI
(541) 342-5181. **$55-$145.** 225 Coburg Rd. I-5, exit 194B, 1.3 mi w on I-105, exit Coburg Rd, then just n. Ext/int corridors. **Pets:** $15 one-time fee/room. Service with restrictions, crate.
SAVE S❄ ✕ 🐾 👤 🖥 🍴 🛁

▼▼ Red Lion Hotel MI
(541) 342-5201. **$74-$89.** 205 Coburg Rd. I-5, exit 194B, 1.3 mi w on I-105, exit Coburg Rd, just n. Ext corridors. **Pets:** Accepted.
ASK S❄ ✕ 🐾 👤 🖥 🍴 🛁

(AAA) ▼▼ Travelodge M
(541) 342-6383. **$54-$105.** 1859 Franklin Blvd. I-5, exit 192 northbound, 1 mi w; exit 194B southbound to I-105, exit University of Oregon Rt. Ext/int corridors. **Pets:** Medium, other species. Designated rooms, service with restrictions, supervision.
SAVE S❄ ✕ 🖥 🖥

▼▼▼ The Valley River Inn MI 🐾
(541) 687-0123. **$114-$200.** 1000 Valley River Way. I-5, exit 194B, 2.5 mi w on I-105, exit 1, follow the Valley River Center signs; just s of mall. Int corridors. **Pets:** Other species. Service with restrictions, supervision.
ASK S❄ ✕ 🐾 👤 🖥 🍴 🛁

FLORENCE

(AAA) ▼ Money Saver Motel M
(541) 997-7131. **$45-$69.** 170 Hwy 101. SR 126, 0.5 mi s on US 101. Ext corridors. **Pets:** $10 one-time fee/pet. Designated rooms, service with restrictions, supervision.
SAVE S❄ ✕ 🐾

(AAA) ▼ Oceanbreeze Motel M
(541) 997-2642. **$45-$75.** 85165 Hwy 101 S. SR 126, 2 mi s on US 101. Ext corridors. **Pets:** Accepted.
SAVE S❄ ✕ 🖥 🖥 🐾

(AAA) ▼▼ Park Motel M 🐾
(541) 997-2634. **$48-$95.** 85034 Hwy 101 S. SR 126, 2.2 mi s on US 101. Ext corridors. **Pets:** Other species. $6 daily fee/pet. Service with restrictions, supervision.
SAVE S❄ ✕ 👤 🐾

GARIBALDI

▼▼▼ Western Royal Inn M
(503) 322-3338. **$40-$75.** 502 Garibaldi Ave. Center; on US 101 at jct 5th St. Int corridors. **Pets:** Other species. $10 one-time fee/pet. Designated rooms, supervision.
✕ 🐾 👤 🛁

GEARHART

(AAA) ▼▼▼ Gearhart By The Sea Resort CO
(503) 738-8331. **$158-$225, 3 days notice.** 1157 N Marion. US 101, exit City Center (Pacific Way), 0.6 mi w, then 0.5 mi n. Ext corridors. **Pets:** Medium. $11 daily fee/pet. Designated rooms, service with restrictions, supervision.
SAVE S❄ ✕ 👤 🖥 🛁 🐾

GLENEDEN BEACH

(AAA) ▼▼▼ ▼▼▼ The Westin Salishan Lodge & Golf Resort R 🐾
(541) 764-2371. **$119-$269, 5 days notice.** 7760 Hwy 101 N. Center; just e of US 101. Ext corridors. **Pets:** $25 one-time fee/room. Designated rooms, service with restrictions, supervision.
SAVE S❄ ✕ 🐾 🐾 👤 🖥 🍴 🐾 🐾

GLIDE

(AAA) ▼▼▼ Steelhead Run B & B and Fine Art Gallery BB 🐾
(541) 496-0563. **$58-$118, 7 days notice.** 23049 N Umpqua (Hwy 138). I-5, exit 124, 0.8 mi s, just n to SR 138, then 20 mi e to MM 20. Ext/int corridors. **Pets:** Other species. $20 deposit/room, $10 daily fee/room. Designated rooms, crate.
SAVE S❄ ✕

GOLD BEACH

▼ Econo Lodge At Gold Beach M 🐾
(541) 247-6606. **$40-$125.** 29171 Ellensburg Ave. South end on US 101. Ext corridors. **Pets:** $5 one-time fee/pet. Supervision.
SAVE S❄ ✕ 👤 🖥

Inn of The Beachcomber M
(541) 247-6691. **$65-$120.** 29266 Ellensburg Ave. South end on US 101. Ext/int corridors. **Pets:** Accepted.
SAVE [5b] X 🦮 🔲 💻 ⇌

Ireland's Rustic Lodges C
(541) 247-7718. **$45-$80.** 29330 S Ellensburg Ave. Center; on US 101. Ext corridors. **Pets:** Other species. $10 daily fee/pet. Designated rooms, service with restrictions, supervision.
SAVE X 🔲 💻 🅰 🗷

Jot's Resort MI 🐾
(541) 247-6676. **$50-$160.** 94360 Wedderburn Loop. W of US 101; at north end of Rogue River Bridge. Ext corridors. **Pets:** Other species. $10 daily fee/pet. Service with restrictions, supervision.
SAVE X 🅰 🔲 💻 ⇌ 🗷 🅰

Motel 6–4047 M
(541) 247-4533. **$36-$86.** 94433 Jerry's Flat Rd. North end of US 101. Ext corridors. **Pets:** Accepted.
X 🔲 💻 🅰

Sand 'n Sea Motel M 🐾
(541) 247-6658. **$39-$109.** 29362 Ellensurg Ave, Hwy 101. Center; on US 101. Ext corridors. **Pets:** $5 daily fee/pet. Designated rooms, service with restrictions, supervision.
ASK [5b] X 🦮 🔲 💻 🅰

Shore Cliff Inn M
(541) 247-7091. **$40-$80.** 29346 Ellensburg Ave. Center; on US 101. Ext corridors. **Pets:** Accepted.
SAVE X 🔲 💻 🅰

GOVERNMENT CAMP

Mt. Hood Inn M
(503) 272-3205. **$149-$179.** 87450 E Government Camp Loop. 0.5 mi w of center. Int corridors. **Pets:** Accepted.
ASK [5b] X 🗗 🔲 💻 🅰

GRANTS PASS

Best Western Grants Pass Inn M
(541) 476-1117. **$75-$115.** 111 NE Agness Ave. I-5, exit 55, just w. Ext corridors. **Pets:** Accepted.
SAVE [5b] X 🦮 🔲 💻 ⇌

Best Western Inn at the Rogue M
(541) 582-2200. **$55-$100, 3 days notice.** 8959 Rogue River Hwy. I-5, exit 48, just w. Int corridors. **Pets:** Small, other species. $30 deposit/room, $10 daily fee/pet. Designated rooms, service with restrictions, supervision.
SAVE [5b] X 🔲 💻 ⇌

Comfort Inn M
(541) 479-8301. **$70-$114.** 1889 NE 6th St. I-5, exit 58, just s on SR 99. Int corridors. **Pets:** Medium. $100 deposit/room. Service with restrictions, supervision.
SAVE [5b] X 🔲 ⇌

Hawthorn Inn & Suites M 🐾
(541) 472-1808. **$67-$150.** 243 NE Morgan Ln. I-5, exit 58, just s on SR 99, then just e; just n on SR 99, then just e. Int corridors. **Pets:** Other species. Service with restrictions, supervision.
SAVE X 🦮 🗗 🔲 💻 ⇌

Holiday Inn Express M
(541) 471-6144. **$69-$109.** 105 NE Agness Ave. I-5, exit 55, just w. Int corridors. **Pets:** $5 daily fee/pet. Designated rooms, service with restrictions, supervision.
SAVE [5b] X 🗗 🔲 💻

Motel 6–253 M
(541) 474-1331. **$45-$62.** 1800 NE 7th St. I-5, exit 58 (SR 99) southbound, 0.4 mi s. Ext corridors. **Pets:** Accepted.
[5b] X 🦮 🗗 ⇌

Redwood Motel M 🐾
(541) 476-0878. **$45-$160.** 815 NE 6th St. I-5, exit 58, 1.3 mi sw on SR 99. Ext corridors. **Pets:** Small, dogs only. $10 daily fee/pet. Service with restrictions, supervision.
SAVE [5b] X 🦮 🗗 🔲 ⇌

Riverside Inn MI 🐾
(541) 476-6873. **$69-$119.** 971 SE 6th St. I-5, exit 58 (SR 99) southbound, 2.5 mi sw. Ext corridors. **Pets:** Other species. $15 one-time fee/room. Service with restrictions.
SAVE [5b] X 🔲 💻 🍽 ⇌

Super 8 Motel-Grants Pass M
(541) 474-0888. **$62-$76, 7 days notice.** 1949 NE 7th St. I-5, exit 58, just s on SR 99, then just e; just n on SR 99, then just e. Int corridors. **Pets:** Other species. $25 deposit/room. Service with restrictions, supervision.
ASK [5b] X 🦮 🔲 ⇌

Travelodge M
(541) 479-6611. **$50-$60.** 1950 NW Vine St. I-5, exit 58, just s on SR 99. Ext corridors. **Pets:** Small, other species. $5 daily fee/pet. Designated rooms, service with restrictions, supervision.
SAVE [5b] X 🔲 💻 ⇌

HERMISTON

Oxford Suites M
(541) 564-8000. **$75-$109.** 1050 N First. 0.3 mi n on US 395. Int corridors. **Pets:** Small, other species. $10 one-time fee/pet. Designated rooms, service with restrictions, supervision.
ASK [5b] X 🦮 🅰 🗗 🔲 💻

HINES

Comfort Inn M
(541) 573-3370. **$84-$89.** 504 N Hwy 20. On US 20 (Hines/Burnes). Int corridors. **Pets:** Medium, other species. $50 deposit/room. Designated rooms, service with restrictions, supervision.
SAVE [5b] X 🅰 🗗 🔲 💻 ⇌

HOOD RIVER

AAA ♦♦♦♦ Best Western Hood River Inn MI
(541) 386-2200. **$79-$124.** 1108 E Marina Way. I-84, exit 64, just n, then just e. Int corridors. **Pets:** Dogs only. $12 daily fee/pet. Designated rooms, supervision.
[SAVE] [So] [X] [&M] [🐕] [🛏] [🖵] [🍴] [⌒]

AAA ♦♦♦ Meredith Gorge Motel M
(541) 386-1515. **$39-$79.** 4300 Westcliff Dr. I-84, exit 62, just n, then 0.8 mi w. Ext corridors. **Pets:** Medium. $10 one-time fee/room. Service with restrictions, supervision.
[SAVE] [So] [X] [🛏] [🖵]

JACKSONVILLE

♦♦♦ The Stage Lodge M ❀
(541) 899-3953. **$88-$165, 5 days notice.** 830 N 5th. 0.3 mi ne on SR 238 (N 5th). Ext corridors. **Pets:** Medium. $10 daily fee/pet. Designated rooms, service with restrictions, supervision.
[ASK] [So] [X] [🐕] [🛏] [🖵]

JOHN DAY

AAA ♦♦♦ Best Western John Day Inn M
(541) 575-1700. **$62-$106, 3 days notice.** 315 W Main St. Just w on US 26 and 395. Ext corridors. **Pets:** Medium, other species. $5 daily fee/pet. Designated rooms, service with restrictions, supervision.
[SAVE] [So] [X] [🐕] [🛏] [🖵]

AAA ♦♦ Dreamers Lodge M
(541) 575-0526. **$45-$63.** 144 N Canyon Blvd. Just n of jct US 26 and 395. Ext corridors. **Pets:** Other species. Service with restrictions, supervision.
[SAVE] [So] [X] [🛏] [🖵]

KLAMATH FALLS

AAA ♦♦♦ Best Western Klamath Inn M
(541) 882-1200. **$74-$104.** 4061 S 6th St. Just w on 6th St (SR 140) from jct SR 140 E/39 S and SR 39 N/US 97 business route. Ext corridors. **Pets:** Medium. Designated rooms, service with restrictions, supervision.
[SAVE] [So] [X] [🐕] [🐾] [🛏] [🖵] [⌒]

AAA ♦♦♦♦ Holiday Inn Express Hotel & Suites M
(541) 884-9999. **$83-$135.** 2500 S 6th St. 1.3 mi w on 6th St (SR 140) from jct SR 140 E/39 S and 39 N/US 97 business route. Int corridors. **Pets:** Accepted.
[SAVE] [So] [X] [&M] [🐕] [🐾] [🛏] [🖵] [⌒]

♦♦ Motel 6–226 M
(541) 884-2110. **$43-$65.** 5136 S 6th St. 0.5 mi e on SR 140 E from jct SR 39/US 97 business route. Ext corridors. **Pets:** Accepted.
[So] [X] [&M] [🐕] [🐾] [⌒]

AAA ♦ Oregon Motel 8 M
(541) 883-3431. **$48-$75.** 5225 Hwy 97 N. 3 mi n on US 97. Ext corridors. **Pets:** Medium, other species. $10 daily fee/room. Service with restrictions, supervision.
[SAVE] [So] [X] [🛏] [🖵] [⌒]

AAA ♦♦♦ Quality Inn M
(541) 882-4666. **$69-$89.** 100 Main St. Just e of US 97, exit City Center. Ext corridors. **Pets:** Service with restrictions, supervision.
[SAVE] [So] [X] [&M] [🐕] [🐾] [🛏] [🖵]

♦♦♦ Red Lion Inn MI
(541) 882-8864. **$59-$99.** 3612 S 6th St. 0.3 mi w on 6th St (SR 140) from jct SR 140 E/39 S, SR 39 N/US 97 business route. Ext corridors. **Pets:** Accepted.
[ASK] [So] [X] [🐕] [🐾] [🛏] [🖵] [🍴] [⌒]

♦♦♦♦ Shilo Inn Suites Hotel-Klamath Falls MI ❀
(541) 885-7980. **$99-$129.** 2500 Almond St. On Business 97, just s of jct US 97. Int corridors. **Pets:** Other species. $10 daily fee/pet. Service with restrictions, supervision.
[ASK] [So] [X] [&M] [🐕] [🐾] [🛏] [🖵] [🍴]

♦♦♦ Super 8 Motel M
(541) 884-8880. **$52-$60, 14 days notice.** 3805 Hwy 97. 2 mi n on US 97. Int corridors. **Pets:** Other species. $25 deposit/room. Service with restrictions, supervision.
[ASK] [So] [X] [&M] [🛏]

LA GRANDE

AAA ♦♦♦ Howard Johnson Inn M ❀
(541) 963-7195. **$77-$87.** 2612 Island Ave. I-84, exit 261, just e. Ext/int corridors. **Pets:** Medium, other species. $10 one-time fee/room. Designated rooms, service with restrictions, supervision.
[SAVE] [So] [X] [🐕] [🛏] [🖵] [⌒]

LA PINE

♦♦♦ Best Western Newberry Station M
(541) 536-5130. **$62-$132.** 16515 Reed Rd. North end of town, just off SR 97. Int corridors. **Pets:** Accepted.
[SAVE] [X] [&M] [🐾] [🛏] [🖵] [⌒]

LAKEVIEW

AAA ♦♦♦ Best Western Skyline Motor Lodge M
(541) 947-2194. **$89-$149.** 414 N G St. At jct US 395 and SR 140. Ext corridors. **Pets:** Small. $20 one-time fee/room. Designated rooms, service with restrictions, supervision.
[SAVE] [So] [X] [🐕] [🛏] [🖵] [⌒]

LINCOLN CITY

AAA ♦♦♦ Coho Inn M
(541) 994-3684. **$60-$152.** 1635 NW Harbor. US 101, exit N 17th St, just w. Ext corridors. **Pets:** Small. $7.49 daily fee/pet. Designated rooms, service with restrictions, supervision.
[SAVE] [X] [🛏] [🖵] [🎴]

♦♦♦ Inn on the Bay M
(541) 996-3996. **$50-$145.** 861 SW 51st St. US 101, exit 51st St, just w, south side. Ext corridors. **Pets:** Accepted.
[ASK] [So] [X] [🛏] [🖵] [🎴]

⨀ ◈◈◈ Lincoln City Inn M
(541) 996-4400. **$59-$109.** 1091 SE 1st St. On US 101 at D River. Int corridors. **Pets:** Medium, dogs only. $10 one-time fee/pet. Designated rooms, service with restrictions, supervision.

[SAVE] [S🐾] [✕] [🖨M] [🖋] [🍴] [💻]

⨀ ◈◈◈◈ The O'dysius Hotel M ❀
(541) 994-4121. **$145-$319, 3 days notice.** 120 NW Inlet Ct. Center; at D River on US 101. Int corridors. **Pets:** Very small, dogs only. $10 daily fee/pet. Designated rooms, service with restrictions, supervision.

[SAVE] [S🐾] [✕] [🖋] [🍴] [💻] [🏊]

⨀ ◈◈◈ Shilo Oceanfront Resort M ❀
(541) 994-3655. **$79-$209.** 1501 NW 40th Pl. US 101, exit NW 40th St, just w, north side. Ext/int corridors. **Pets:** Other species. $10 daily fee/pet. Service with restrictions, supervision.

[SAVE] [S🐾] [✕] [🖨M] [🖋] [🍴] [🍴] [💻] [🍴] [🏊]

MADRAS

⨀ ◈◈◈ Best Western Rama Inn M
(541) 475-6141. **$59-$79.** 12 SW 4th St. Downtown; on US 97/26 southbound. Ext corridors. **Pets:** Accepted.

[SAVE] [S🐾] [✕] [🖨M] [🖋] [🍴] [💻] [🏊]

MEDFORD

⨀ ◈◈◈ Best Inn & Suites M
(541) 773-8266. **$61-$101.** 1015 S Riverside Ave. I-5, exit 27, 0.4 mi n, just n on SR 99. Ext corridors. **Pets:** Small. $100 deposit/room, $5 daily fee/room. Designated rooms, service with restrictions, supervision.

[SAVE] [S🐾] [✕] [🖋] [🍴] [🍴] [💻] [🏊]

⨀ ◈◈◈ Best Western Pony Soldier Inn M
(541) 779-2011. **$86-$97.** 2340 Crater Lake Hwy. I-5, exit 30, just e on SR 62. Ext corridors. **Pets:** Accepted.

[SAVE] [S🐾] [✕] [🖋] [🍴] [💻] [🏊]

⨀ ◈◈◈ Cedar Lodge Motor Inn M
(541) 773-7361. **$49-$65.** 518 N Riverside Ave. I-5, exit 27, 0.5 mi w, then 1.2 mi n on SR 99. Ext corridors. **Pets:** Small. $20 deposit/pet. Designated rooms, service with restrictions, supervision.

[SAVE] [S🐾] [✕] [🍴] [🏊]

⨀ ◈◈◈ Knights Inn M
(541) 773-3676. **$40-$44.** 500 N Riverside Ave. I-5, exit 27, 0.5 mi w on Barnett Rd, then 1.2 mi n. Ext corridors. **Pets:** Accepted.

[SAVE] [S🐾] [✕] [🖋] [🍴] [🏊]

◈◈◈ Motel 6-Medford North–739 M
(541) 779-0550. **$48-$67.** 2400 Biddle Rd. I-5, exit 30, just e, then just n. Ext corridors. **Pets:** Accepted.

[S🐾] [✕] [🖋] [🍴] [🍴] [🏊]

◈ Motel 6-Medford South–89 M
(541) 773-4290. **$40-$44.** 950 Alba Dr. I-5, exit 27, just e, then just n. Ext corridors. **Pets:** Small, other species. Service with restrictions, supervision.

[✕] [🖨M] [🖋] [🍴] [🍴] [🏊]

⨀ ◈◈◈ Pear Tree Motel & RV Park M ❀
(541) 535-4445. **$54-$69.** 300 Pear Tree Ln. I-5, exit 24, just s on frontage road. Ext corridors. **Pets:** Small. $10 one-time fee/pet. Supervision.

[SAVE] [S🐾] [✕] [🖋] [🍴] [🏊]

◈◈◈ Red Lion Hotel M ❀
(541) 779-5811. **$69-$82.** 200 N Riverside Ave. I-5, exit 27, 0.5 mi w on Barnett Rd, then 1.5 mi n. Ext corridors. **Pets:** Other species.

[ASK] [✕] [🖨M] [🖋] [🍴] [💻] [🍴] [🏊]

⨀ ◈◈◈ Reston Hotel M
(541) 779-3141. **$64-$120, 7 days notice.** 2300 Crater Lake Hwy. I-5, exit 30, just e, then just s on Biddle Rd. Int corridors. **Pets:** Small. $20 one-time fee/pet. Designated rooms, service with restrictions, supervision.

[SAVE] [S🐾] [✕] [🍴] [💻] [🍴] [🏊]

◈◈ Shilo Inn-Medford M ❀
(541) 770-5151. **$59-$89.** 2111 Biddle Rd. I-5, exit 30, just e, then just s. Int corridors. **Pets:** Other species. $10 daily fee/pet. Service with restrictions, supervision.

[ASK] [S🐾] [✕] [🖋] [🍴] [💻]

⨀ ◈◈◈ Windmill Inn of Medford M ❀
(541) 779-0050. **$73-$98.** 1950 Biddle Rd. I-5, exit 30, just e, then just s. Int corridors. **Pets:** Other species.

[SAVE] [S🐾] [✕] [🖋] [🍴] [🍴] [🏊]

MYRTLE POINT

⨀ ◈◈ Myrtle Trees Motel M
(541) 572-5811. **$51-$57.** 1010 8th St (Hwy 42). 0.5 mi e on SR 42. Ext corridors. **Pets:** Accepted.

[SAVE] [S🐾] [✕] [🍴] [🏊]

NEWBERG

⨀ ◈◈◈ Shilo Inn Suites-Newburg M ❀
(503) 537-0303. **$49-$99.** 501 Sitka Ave. On SR 99 W. Int corridors. **Pets:** Other species. $10 daily fee/pet. Service with restrictions, supervision.

[SAVE] [S🐾] [✕] [🖋] [🍴] [💻] [🏊]

NEWPORT

⨀ ◈◈◈ The Best Western Agate Beach Inn H ❀
(541) 265-9411. **$74-$149.** 3019 N Coast Hwy. Jct US 20, 1.5 mi n on US 101. Int corridors. **Pets:** Other species. Designated rooms, supervision.

[SAVE] [S🐾] [✕] [🖋] [🍴] [💻] [🍴] [🏊] [🍴]

⨀ ◈◈◈ Econo Lodge M
(541) 265-7723. **$45-$90.** 606 SW Coast Hwy-101. 0.5 mi of SR 20. Ext/int corridors. **Pets:** Accepted.

[SAVE] [S🐾] [🖋] [🍴] [🍴]

🆎 ▽▽▽▽ Hallmark Resort Ⓜ️ 🌼
(541) 265-2600. **$89-$197.** 744 SW Elizabeth St. Jct US 20, 0.7 mi s, just w on SW Bay St. Ext corridors. **Pets:** Medium, dogs only. $10 daily fee/pet. Designated rooms, service with restrictions, supervision.

🆎 ▽▽▽▽ Hawthorn Inn & Suites Ⓜ️ 🌼
(541) 867-7727. **$75-$155.** 45 SE 32nd St. US 101, just s of Yaquina Bay Bridge. Int corridors. **Pets:** Medium, other species. $5 one-time fee/room. Designated rooms, service with restrictions, supervision.

▽▽▽ Shilo Inn Hotel-Newport Oceanfront Resort Ⓜ️ 🌼
(541) 265-7701. **$89-$159.** 536 SW Elizabeth St. Jct US 20, 0.5 mi s on US 101, just w on SW Falls St. Ext/int corridors. **Pets:** Other species. $10 daily fee/pet. Service with restrictions, supervision.

▽▽ Val-U Inn Ⓜ️ 🌼
(541) 265-6203. **$49-$79.** 531 SW Fall St. Jct US 20, 0.5 mi s on US 101, just w. Int corridors. **Pets:** Dogs only. $5 daily fee/pet. Designated rooms, service with restrictions, supervision.

🆎 ▽▽ Whaler Motel Ⓜ️
(541) 265-9261. **$79-$139.** 155 SW Elizabeth St. Jct US 20, just s on US 101, just w on SW 2nd. Ext corridors. **Pets:** Accepted.

OAKLAND

🆎 ▽▽▽ Best Western Rice Hill Inn Ⓜ️
(541) 849-2500. **$58.** 621 John Long Rd. I-5, exit 148, just e. Ext corridors. **Pets:** Medium, other species. $10 one-time fee/pet. Service with restrictions, supervision.

OAKRIDGE

🆎 ▽▽ Best Western Oakridge Inn Ⓜ️
(541) 782-2212. **$64-$76, 3 days notice.** 47433 SR 58. West end on SR 58. Ext corridors. **Pets:** Other species. Designated rooms, supervision.

ONTARIO

🆎 ▽▽▽ Best Western Inn & Suites Ⓜ️
(541) 889-2600. **$79-$110, 10 days notice.** 251 Goodfellow St. I-84, exit 376, just e. Int corridors. **Pets:** Small, dogs only. $50 deposit/pet. Service with restrictions, supervision.

🆎 ▽▽ Carlile Motel Ⓜ️ 🌼
(541) 889-8658. **$38-$67, 14 days notice.** 589 N Oregon St (SR 201 & 30). I-84, exit 374, 1.5 mi se; at jct Business Rt 30 and SR 201. Ext corridors. **Pets:** Small. $5 daily fee/pet. Designated rooms, service with restrictions, supervision.

🆎 ▽▽▽ Holiday Inn–Ontario, OR Ⓜ️
(541) 889-8621. **$72-$77.** 1249 Tapadera Ave. I-84, exit 376, just e. Int corridors. **Pets:** $10 one-time fee/room. Designated rooms, service with restrictions, supervision.

🆎 ▽ Holiday Motel Ⓜ️
(541) 889-9188. **$46-$50.** 615 E Idaho Ave. I-84, exit 376, just w. Ext corridors. **Pets:** Medium, other species. Service with restrictions, supervision.

🆎 ▽ Stockman's Motel Ⓜ️
(541) 889-4446. **$45-$50.** 81 SW 1st St. I-84, exit 376, 0.9 mi w on Idaho Ave, just s; just w of US 30 business route. Ext corridors. **Pets:** Other species. $10 deposit/room. Service with restrictions.

🆎 ▽▽ Super 8 Motel Ⓜ️
(541) 889-8282. **$57-$125.** 266 Goodfellow St. I-84, exit 376, just e. Int corridors. **Pets:** Accepted.

PACIFIC CITY

🆎 ▽▽▽ Inn at Cape Kiwanda Ⓜ️ 🌼
(503) 965-7001. **$109-$219.** 33105 Cape Kiwanda Dr. Just w on Pacific Ave, 1 mi n. Ext corridors. **Pets:** $15 daily fee/pet. Designated rooms, supervision.

PENDLETON

🆎 ▽▽▽ Best Western Pendleton Inn Ⓜ️
(541) 276-2135. **$66-$71.** 400 SE Nye Ave. I-84, exit 210, just se. Int corridors. **Pets:** Accepted.

🆎 ▽ Econo Lodge Ⓜ️
(541) 276-8654. **$53-$59.** 620 SW Tutuilla Rd. I-84, exit 209, just s on US 395. Ext corridors. **Pets:** Dogs only. $5 daily fee/pet. Designated rooms, service with restrictions, supervision.

▽▽▽ Holiday Inn Express Ⓜ️
(541) 966-6520. **$74-$120, 7 days notice.** 600 SE Nye Ave. I-84, exit 210, just se. Int corridors. **Pets:** Other species. $10 one-time fee/room. Service with restrictions, supervision.

▼▼▼ Oxford Suites **M**
(541) 276-6000. **Call for rates.** 2400 SW Court Pl. I-84, exit 209, just n on US 395, at northwest corner. Int corridors. **Pets:** Small. $15 one-time fee/room. Designated rooms, service with restrictions, supervision.

[ASK] [✕] [🛇M] [🖉] [🖾] [🖥] [💻] [🏊]

▼▼ Red Lion Hotel **M**
(541) 276-6111. **$54-$67.** 304 SE Nye Ave. I-84, exit 210, just s. Ext/int corridors. **Pets:** Other species. $25 deposit/room. Service with restrictions.

[ASK] [🛇] [✕] [🖉] [🖾] [🖥] [💻] [🍴] [🏊]

▼▼ Super 8 Motel **M**
(541) 276-8881. **$55-$102, 7 days notice.** 601 SE Nye Ave. I-84, exit 210. Int corridors. **Pets:** $10 one-time fee/room. Service with restrictions, supervision.

[✕] [🖉] [🖥] [🏊]

(AAA) ▼▼▼ Travelodge **M**
(541) 276-7531. **$59-$89.** 411 SW Dorion Ave. I-84, exit 209, just w of town center, on corner of SW 4th St; across from City Hall. Ext corridors. **Pets:** Other species. $10 daily fee/pet. Service with restrictions, supervision.

[SAVE] [🛇] [✕] [🖥] [💻]

▼▼ Wildhorse Resort & Casino Hotel **M**
(541) 276-0355. **$65-$70.** 72779 Hwy 331. I-84, exit 216, 0.6 mi n. Int corridors. **Pets:** Medium. $10 daily fee/room. Designated rooms, service with restrictions, supervision.

[ASK] [🛇] [✕] [🖾] [🖥] [💻] [🍴] [🏊]

PORT ORFORD

(AAA) ▼▼ Sea Crest Motel **M** 🐾
(541) 332-3040. **$47-$74.** 44 Hwy 101. 1 mi s on US 101. Ext corridors. **Pets:** Medium. $5 daily fee/pet. Designated rooms, service with restrictions, supervision.

[SAVE] [🛇] [✕] [🖥] [💻] [🎿]

PORTLAND METROPOLITAN AREA

BEAVERTON

(AAA) ▼▼▼▼ Greenwood Inn **M**
(503) 643-7444. **$138-$160, 3 days notice.** 10700 SW Allen Blvd. SR 217, exit Allen Blvd, just e. Ext/int corridors. **Pets:** $20 one-time fee/pet. Service with restrictions, crate.

[SAVE] [🛇] [✕] [🛇M] [🖉] [🖾] [🖥] [💻] [🍴] [🏊]

▼▼ Homestead Studio Suites-Beaverton **M**
(503) 690-3600. **$74-$94.** 875 SW 158th Ave. US 26, exit 65 westbound, just s on Cornell Rd, 1.1 mi se on 158th Ave; exit 65 eastbound, just straight on feeder road, then same directions as westbound. Ext corridors. **Pets:** Medium. $75 one-time fee/room. Designated rooms, service with restrictions, supervision.

[ASK] [🛇] [✕] [🖾] [🖥] [💻]

▼▼▼ Homewood Suites By Hilton **M**
(503) 614-0900. **$119-$169.** 15525 NW Gateway Ct. Int corridors. **Pets:** Accepted.

[SAVE] [🛇] [✕] [🛇M] [🖉] [🖾] [🖥] [💻] [🏊]

▼▼▼ Shilo Inn Hotel-Portland
Beaverton **M** 🐾
(503) 297-2551. **$65-$145.** 9900 SW Canyon Rd. SR 217, exit Canyon Rd/Beaverton Hillsdale Hwy, take feeder road, 0.3 mi e on SR 8 (Canyon Rd), then 0.6 mi e. Int corridors. **Pets:** Other species. $10 daily fee/pet. Service with restrictions, supervision.

[ASK] [🛇] [✕] [🖉] [🖾] [🖥] [💻] [🍴] [🏊]

CLACKAMAS

(AAA) ▼▼▼ Clackamas Inn **M**
(503) 650-5340. **$79.** 16010 SE 82nd Dr. I-205, exit 12A southbound; exit 12 northbound (SR 212). Int corridors. **Pets:** $10 daily fee/pet. Designated rooms, service with restrictions, supervision.

[SAVE] [🛇] [✕] [🖥] [🏊]

GLADSTONE

▼▼▼▼ Oxford Suites **M**
(503) 722-7777. **$85-$119.** 75 82nd Dr. I-205, exit 11, just w. Int corridors. **Pets:** Small, other species. $15 one-time fee/pet. Supervision.

[ASK] [🛇] [✕] [🛇M] [🖉] [🖾] [🖥] [💻] [🏊]

GRESHAM

(AAA) ▼▼▼ Best Inn & Suites **M**
(503) 661-5100. **$55-$63.** 121 NE 181st Ave. I-84, exit 13, 1.3 mi s. Int corridors. **Pets:** Small, other species. $10 daily fee/pet. Designated rooms, service with restrictions, supervision.

[SAVE] [🛇] [✕] [🖉] [🖥] [💻]

(AAA) ▼▼▼▼ Best Western Pony Soldier Inn **M**
(503) 665-1591. **$89-$99, 7 days notice.** 1060 NE Cleveland Ave. I-84, exit 16, 2.5 mi s on NE 238th, just w on Division St, then just n; I-205, exit 19, 5.5. mi e on Division St, then just n. Int corridors. **Pets:** Accepted.

[SAVE] [✕] [🖉] [🖥] [💻] [🏊]

Hawthorn Inn & Suites M
(503) 492-4000. **$72-$92.** 2323 NE 181st Ave. I-84, exit 13, just e. Int corridors. **Pets:** Medium. $10 one-time fee/pet. Designated rooms, service with restrictions, supervision.

Shilo Inn Hotel-Gresham M
(503) 907-1777. **$59-$124.** 2752 NE Hogan Dr. I-84, exit 16, 1.7 mi s on 238th/Hogan drs. Int corridors. **Pets:** Other species. $10 daily fee/pet. Service with restrictions, supervision.

Sleep Inn-Portland M
(503) 618-8400. **$60-$76.** 2261 NE 181st. I-84, exit 13, just s. Int corridors. **Pets:** Medium, other species. $10 daily fee/pet. Service with restrictions, crate.

HILLSBORO

Candlewood Suites M
(503) 681-2121. **$109-$129.** 3133 NE Shute Rd. US 26, exit 61, 1.2 mi s. Int corridors. **Pets:** Accepted.

Residence Inn by Marriott Portland West A
(503) 531-3200. **$149-$179.** 18855 NW Tanasbourne Dr. US 26, exit 64, just s. Ext/int corridors. **Pets:** Other species. $10 daily fee/pet.

TownePlace Suites by Marriott-Hillsboro M
(503) 268-6000. **$109.** 6550 NE Brighton Dr. US 26, exit 62, just s, 1 mi on Cornelius Pass Rd, 0.7 mi w on Cornell Rd, just n on 229th Ave, then just w. Ext/int corridors. **Pets:** Other species. $10 daily fee/room.

Travelodge M
(503) 640-4791. **$45-$58.** 622 SE 10th Ave. 0.5 mi e on SR 8. Ext corridors. **Pets:** Accepted.

Wellesley Inn & Suites (Portland/Hillsboro) M
(503) 439-0706. **$65-$95.** 19311 NW Cornell Rd. US 26, exit 64, 0.5 mi s on 185th, 0.4 mi w. Int corridors. **Pets:** Small. Service with restrictions, supervision.

WestCoast Hillsboro Hotel M
(503) 648-3500. **$84.** 3500 NE Cornell Rd. US 26, exit 62, 1.1 mi s on Cornelius Pass Rd, then 2.5 mi w; opposite Hillsboro Airport. Int corridors. **Pets:** Large, other species. $75 deposit/room, $5 daily fee/room. Service with restrictions, supervision.

KING CITY

Best Western Northwind Inn & Suites M
(503) 431-2100. **$84-$89.** 16105 SW Pacific Hwy. I-5, exit 292, just nw on SR 217, exit SR 99 W, then 2.5 mi s. Int corridors. **Pets:** Very small. $10 one-time fee/pet. Designated rooms, service with restrictions, supervision.

LAKE OSWEGO

Crowne Plaza H
(503) 624-8400. **$99-$149.** 14811 Kruse Oaks Dr. I-5, exit 292, just e. Int corridors. **Pets:** Other species. Service with restrictions, supervision.

Residence Inn by Marriott-Portland South A
(503) 684-2603. **$119-$169.** 15200 SW Bangy Rd. I-5, exit 292, just e, then 0.3 mi s. Ext corridors. **Pets:** Other species. $10 daily fee/pet.

OREGON CITY

Rivershore Hotel M
(503) 655-7141. **$81-$85, 7 days notice.** 1900 Clackamette Dr. I-205, exit 9, just n. Int corridors. **Pets:** Small. $5 daily fee/pet. Service with restrictions, supervision.

PORTLAND

5TH Avenue Suites Hotel H
(503) 222-0001. **$99.** 506 SW Washington. Downtown; at SW 5th Ave and Washington. Int corridors. **Pets:** Service with restrictions, supervision.

The Benson Hotel H
(503) 228-2000. **$170-$220.** 309 SW Broadway. Downtown; at SW Broadway and Oak. Int corridors. **Pets:** Medium. $50 one-time fee/room. Designated rooms, service with restrictions, supervision.

Best Inns & Suites-Portland Airport M
(503) 256-2550. **$60-$80, 3 days notice.** 3828 NE 82nd Ave. I-84, exit 5, 2.3 mi n. Ext/int corridors. **Pets:** Accepted.

Best Western Inn at the Convention Center M
(503) 233-6331. **$80-$110.** 420 NE Holladay. I-5, exit 302A, just e on Weidler, then just s on Martin Luther King Blvd. Int corridors. **Pets:** Accepted.

Ⓐ ♦♦♦♦ **Best Western Inn at the Meadows** Ⓜ
(503) 286-9600. **$89-$109.** 1215 N Hayden Meadows Dr. I-5, exit 306B, just e. Int corridors. **Pets:** Other species. $21.80 one-time fee/room. Service with restrictions, supervision.
SAVE S🐾 ✕ 🐾 🖥 💻

Ⓐ ♦♦ **Days Inn-Portland North** Ⓜ ❖
(503) 289-1800. **$65-$85.** 9930 N Whitaker Rd. I-5, exit 306B (Delta Park), just e. Int corridors. **Pets:** Other species. $15 one-time fee/room. Service with restrictions.
SAVE S🐾 ✕ 🐾 📠 🖥 💻

Ⓐ ♦♦♦♦ **Doubletree Hotel-Columbia River** Ⓜ
(503) 283-2111. **$119-$149.** 1401 N Hayden Island Dr. I-5, exit 308, just w; at Jantzen Beach. Int corridors. **Pets:** Accepted.
SAVE S🐾 ✕ 🖥 🐾 📠 🖥 💻 🍴 ➰

Ⓐ ♦♦♦♦ **Doubletree Hotel-Jantzen Beach** Ⓜ
(503) 283-4466. **$119-$149.** 909 N Hayden Island Dr. I-5, exit 308, just e; at Jantzen Beach. Int corridors. **Pets:** Small. $50 deposit/room. Service with restrictions, supervision.
SAVE S🐾 ✕ 🖥 🐾 📠 🖥 💻 🍴 ➰ ✕

Ⓐ ♦♦♦♦ **Doubletree Hotel Portland Downtown** Ⓜ
(503) 221-0450. **$79-$134.** 310 SW Lincoln. I-5 to I-405, exit 4th Ave, just n, then just e. Ext/int corridors. **Pets:** Medium, other species. $25 deposit/room. Service with restrictions.
SAVE S🐾 ✕ 🐾 🖥 🖥 💻 🍴 ➰

Ⓐ ♦♦♦♦ **Four Points Sheraton** Ⓜ
(503) 221-0711. **$117-$122.** 50 SW Morrison. Downtown; at Morrison and Naito Pkwy (formerly Front Ave). Int corridors. **Pets:** Other species. Service with restrictions.
SAVE S🐾 ✕ 🖥 🐾 🖥 🖥 💻 🍴

Ⓐ ♦♦♦ **Hawthorn Inn & Suites** Ⓜ
(503) 233-7933. **$79-$160, 7 days notice.** 431 NE Multnomah. I-5, exit 302A, just e, then just s on Martin Luther King Blvd. Int corridors. **Pets:** Other species. $10 daily fee/pet. Designated rooms, service with restrictions, supervision.
SAVE S🐾 ✕ 🐾 🖥 💻 ➰

Ⓐ ♦♦♦♦ **Hawthorn Inn & Suites** Ⓜ ❖
(503) 497-9044. **$81-$106.** 4319 NW Yeon. I-105, exit 3 northbound, 2.5 mi w on US 30; exit 302B southbound, 2.5 mi w n US 30. Int corridors. **Pets:** Other species. $7 one-time fee/room. Service with restrictions, crate.
SAVE S🐾 ✕ 🐾 🖥 💻 ➰

♦♦♦♦ **The Heathman Hotel** Ⓗ ❖
(503) 241-4100. **$169-$209.** 1001 SW Broadway. Downtown; at SW Broadway and Salmon. Int corridors. **Pets:** Medium. $25 one-time fee/pet. Supervision.
ASK S🐾 ✕ 🖥 🐾 🖥 🖥 🍴

♦♦♦♦ **The Hotel Lucia** Ⓗ
(503) 228-7221. **$118-$148.** 400 SW Broadway. Downtown; at SW Broadway and Stark St. Int corridors. **Pets:** Accepted.
ASK ✕ 🖥 🐾 🖥 🖥 🍴

Ⓐ ♦♦♦♦ **Hotel Vintage Plaza** Ⓗ
(503) 228-1212. **$99.** 422 SW Broadway. Downtown; at Broadway and Washington. Int corridors. **Pets:** Accepted.
SAVE S🐾 ✕ 🐾 💻 🍴

Ⓐ ♦♦♦ **Mallory Hotel** Ⓗ ❖
(503) 223-6311. **$95-$155.** 729 SW 15th. I-5 to I-405, exit Salmon St northbound; exit Couch-Burnside southbound; at SW 15th and Yamhill. Int corridors. **Pets:** Other species. $10 daily fee/room.
SAVE S🐾 ✕ 🖥 🐾 🖥 🖥 🍴

♦♦ **The Mark Spencer Hotel** Ⓐ ❖
(503) 224-3293. **$89-$149.** 409 SW 11th Ave. Downtown. Int corridors. **Pets:** Other species. $25 one-time fee/room. Designated rooms, service with restrictions, supervision.
ASK S🐾 ✕ 🖥 💻

Ⓐ ♦♦♦♦ **Marriott City Center** Ⓗ
(503) 226-6300. **$99-$169.** 520 SW Broadway. Downtown; at SW Broadway and Washington. Int corridors. **Pets:** $25 daily fee/pet. Service with restrictions, supervision.
SAVE S🐾 ✕ 🐾 🖥 🖥 💻 🍴

♦♦♦♦ **Oxford Suites** Ⓜ
(503) 283-3030. **$89-$199, 3 days notice.** 12226 N Jantzen Dr. I-5, exit 308, just e on Hayden Island Dr; at Jantzen Beach. Int corridors. **Pets:** Accepted.
ASK S🐾 ✕ 🖥 🐾 🖥 🖥 💻 ➰

Ⓐ ♦♦♦ **Portland Marriott Downtown** Ⓗ
(503) 226-7600. **$89-$179.** 1401 SW Naito Pkwy. Downtown; between Columbia and Clay. Int corridors. **Pets:** $50 one-time fee/room. Designated rooms, service with restrictions, crate.
SAVE ✕ 🖥 🐾 🖥 🖥 💻 🍴 ➰

Ⓐ ♦♦♦ **Quality Inn Portland Airport** Ⓜ
(503) 256-4111. **$76.** 8247 NE Sandy Blvd. I-84, exit 5, 1.5 mi n on 82nd Ave. Ext/int corridors. **Pets:** Accepted.
SAVE S🐾 ✕ 🖥 💻

♦♦♦ **Red Lion Inn & Suites-Portland Airport** Ⓜ
(503) 252-6377. **$69-$89.** 5019 NE 102nd Ave. I-205, exit 23A, just e on Sandy Blvd. Int corridors. **Pets:** Other species. $25 one-time fee/pet. Service with restrictions, supervision.
ASK S🐾 ✕ 🐾 🖥 🖥 🖥 💻 ➰

Ⓐ ♦♦♦♦ **Residence Inn by Marriott-Lloyd Center** Ⓐ
(503) 288-1400. **$119-$175.** 1710 NE Multnomah. I-5, exit 302A, 1.3 mi e on Weidler St, just s on 15th Ave; I-84 westbound, exit 1 (Lloyd Center), just n on 13th St, then just e. Ext corridors. **Pets:** Accepted.
SAVE S🐾 ✕ 🖥 🐾 🖥 🖥 💻 ➰

⚑⚑ ◈◈◈◈ Residence Inn Portland Downtown Riverplace 🅰 ❀
(503) 552-9500. **$79-$149.** 2115 SW River Pkwy. Downtown; at SW Moody and SW River Pkwy; on the Willamette River waterfront. Int corridors. **Pets:** Large, other species. $10 daily fee/pet.

SAVE Sᴏ ✕ 🖉 🖉 📵 💻 ⊇

⚑⚑ ◈◈◈◈ RiverPlace Hotel 🅷 ❀
(503) 228-3233. **$219-$259.** 1510 SW Harbor Way. Downtown; at Naito Pkwy (formerly Front Ave) and SW Harbor Way; on the Williamette River waterfront. Int corridors. **Pets:** Medium, other species. $45 one-time fee/room. Service with restrictions, crate.

SAVE Sᴏ ✕ ᴍ 🖉 🖉 📵 💻 🍴

⚑⚑ ◈◈◈ Staybridge Suites Portland-Airport 🅷
(503) 262-8888. **$99-$159, 7 days notice.** 11936 NE Glenn Widing Rd. I-205, exit 24B northbound; exit 24 southbound, just e. Int corridors. **Pets:** Other species. $10 daily fee/pet, $25 one-time fee/pet. Service with restrictions, crate.

SAVE Sᴏ ✕ ᴍ 🖉 🖉 📵 💻 ⊇

⚑⚑ ◈ Travelodge 🇲 ❀
(503) 244-0151. **$48-$54.** 10450 SW Barbour Blvd. I-5, exit 296A, 2.5 mi s. Ext corridors. **Pets:** Other species. $10 one-time fee/pet. Designated rooms, service with restrictions, supervision.

SAVE Sᴏ ✕ 📵 💻 ⊇

⚑⚑ ◈◈ Travelodge Suites Portland 🇲
(503) 788-9394. **$72-$87.** 7740 SE Powell Blvd. I-205, exit 19, 1 mi w. Ext/int corridors. **Pets:** Medium. $10 daily fee/pet. Service with restrictions, supervision.

SAVE Sᴏ ✕ 📵 💻

⚑⚑ ◈◈◈◈ The Westin Portland 🅷 ❀
(503) 294-9000. **$119-$169.** 750 SW Alder. Downtown; at Park Ave and Alder. Int corridors. **Pets:** Other species. $25 one-time fee/room. Service with restrictions.

SAVE Sᴏ ✕ ᴍ 🖉 🖉 📵 💻 🍴

TIGARD

◈◈◈ Embassy Suites Hotel-Portland Washington Square 🅷
(503) 644-4000. **$99-$169.** 9000 SW Washington Square Rd. SR 217, exit Progress/Scholls Ferry Rd, just e, then just s on Hall. Int corridors. **Pets:** Large, other species. $25 one-time fee/room. Designated rooms, service with restrictions, supervision.

SAVE ✕ ᴍ 🖉 🖉 📵 💻 🍴 ⊇

◈◈ Homestead Studio Suites Hotels 🇲
(503) 670-0555. **$69-$72.** 13009 SW 68th Pkwy. SR 217, exit 72nd St, just ne, just e on Hampton St, then just s. Ext corridors. **Pets:** Accepted.

ASK ✕ 🖉 📵 💻

⚑⚑ ◈◈ Ramada Limited 🇲 ❀
(503) 620-2030. **$54-$59.** 17993 Lower Boones Ferry Rd. I-5, exit 290, just n, then just s. Int corridors. **Pets:** Other species. $6 daily fee/room, $10 one-time fee/room. Service with restrictions, supervision.

SAVE Sᴏ ✕ ᴍ 🖉 📵 💻 ⊇

◈◈◈ Shilo Inn-Portland I-5 South 🇲 ❀
(503) 639-2226. **$69-$89.** 7300 SW Hazel Fern Rd. I-5, exit 290, just w, then just s. Ext corridors. **Pets:** Other species. $10 daily fee/room. Service with restrictions, supervision.

ASK Sᴏ ✕ 🖉 📵 💻 ⊇

◈◈ Shilo Inn-Tigard/Washington Square 🇲 ❀
(503) 620-4320. **$65-$145.** 10830 SW Greenburg Rd. SR 217, exit Greenburg Rd, just w. Int corridors. **Pets:** Other species. $10 daily fee/pet. Service with restrictions, supervision.

ASK Sᴏ ✕ 🖉 🖉 📵 💻

TROUTDALE

⚑⚑ ◈ East Portland/Gresham Travelodge 🇲 ❀
(503) 666-6623. **$49-$59.** 23705 NE Sandy Blvd. I-84, exit 16, just n. Int corridors. **Pets:** $5 daily fee/pet. Service with restrictions, supervision.

SAVE Sᴏ ✕ 🖉 📵 💻 🍴

◈ Motel 6-Portland Troutdale–407 🇲
(503) 665-2254. **$43-$67.** 1610 NW Frontage Rd. I-84, exit 17. Ext corridors. **Pets:** Accepted.

Sᴏ ✕ ᴍ 🖉 🖉 📵 ⊇

⚑⚑ ◈◈◈ Phoenix Inn Suites-Troutdale 🇲 ❀
(503) 669-6500. **$69-$89.** 477 NW Phoenix Dr. I-84, exit 17. Int corridors. **Pets:** Other species. $10 one-time fee/room. Service with restrictions, supervision.

SAVE Sᴏ ✕ 🖉 📵 💻 ⊇

TUALATIN

⚑⚑ ◈◈◈ The Sweetbrier Inn & Suites 🇲🇮 ❀
(503) 692-5800. **$74-$89.** 7125 SW Nyberg Rd. I-5, exit 289, just e. Ext/int corridors. **Pets:** Other species. $25 deposit/room.

SAVE Sᴏ ✕ ᴍ 🖉 🖉 📵 💻 🍴 ⊇

WILSONVILLE

⚑⚑ ◈◈◈ Best Western Willamette Inn 🇲
(503) 682-2288. **$80-$85.** 30800 SW Parkway Ave. I-5, exit 283, just e, then just s. Int corridors. **Pets:** Small. Designated rooms, service with restrictions, supervision.

SAVE ✕ ᴍ 📵 💻 ⊇

Comfort Inn M
(503) 682-9000. **$59-$99.** 8855 SW Citizens Dr. I-5, exit 283, just e, then just n on Town Center Loop W. Int corridors. **Pets:** $10 daily fee/pet. Service with restrictions, supervision.
[SAVE] [S] [X] [&M] [ ] [ ] [ ] [ ] [ ]

Holiday Inn-Wilsonville H
(503) 570-8500. **$99-$109.** 25425 SW 95th Ave. I-5, exit 286, just w. Int corridors. **Pets:** $10 daily fee/room. Service with restrictions, supervision.
[SAVE] [S] [X] [&M] [ ] [ ] [ ] [ ] [ ] [ ]

❀ **END METROPOLITAN AREA** ❀

PRINEVILLE

Stafford Inn M
(541) 447-7100. **$79-$99.** 1773 NE 3rd St. On US 26. Int corridors. **Pets:** $20 one-time fee/room. Designated rooms, service with restrictions, supervision.
[ASK] [S] [X] [ ] [ ] [ ] [ ]

PROSPECT

Prospect Historical Hotel-Motel & Dinner House M ❀
(541) 560-3664. **$50-$135.** 391 Mill Creek Dr. Center; off SR 62. Ext/int corridors. **Pets:** Other species. Designated rooms, service with restrictions, supervision.
[X] [ ] [ ] [ ]

REDMOND

Motel 6 Redmond-4076 M
(541) 923-2100. **$52-$70.** 2247 S Hwy 97. Jct SR 126 W, 1 mi s on US 97. Int corridors. **Pets:** Small. Service with restrictions, supervision.
[SAVE] [S] [X] [&M] [ ] [ ] [ ]

Redmond Inn M
(541) 548-1091. **$55-$70.** 1545 Hwy 97 S. Jct SR 126 W, 0.5 mi s on US 97. Ext corridors. **Pets:** Accepted.
[SAVE] [S] [X] [ ] [ ]

Redmond Super 8 Motel M ❀
(541) 548-8881. **$62-$85.** 3629 21st Place SW. US 97, exit Yew Ave. Int corridors. **Pets:** Other species. $25 deposit/room. Supervision.
[ASK] [S] [X] [&M] [ ] [ ] [ ]

REEDSPORT

Anchor Bay Inn M
(541) 271-2149. **$48-$75.** 1821 Winchester Ave (Hwy 101). On US 101, 0.8 mi s of jct SR 38. Ext corridors. **Pets:** Large, other species. $7 daily fee/pet. Designated rooms, service with restrictions, supervision.
[SAVE] [X] [ ] [ ] [ ] [ ]

Best Western Salbasgeon Inn M
(541) 271-4831. **$71-$185.** 1400 Hwy Ave 101 S. Jct SR 38, just s on US 101. Ext corridors. **Pets:** Medium, dogs only. $5 deposit/pet. Designated rooms, service with restrictions, supervision.
[SAVE] [S] [X] [ ] [ ] [ ]

Economy Inn M ❀
(541) 271-3671. **$35-$95.** 1593 Highway Ave 101. Center; on US 101. Ext corridors. **Pets:** Medium. $5 daily fee/pet. Designated rooms, service with restrictions, supervision.
[SAVE] [X] [ ] [ ] [ ]

Salbasgeon Inn of the Umpqua M
(541) 271-2025. **$65-$185.** 45209 Hwy 38. Jct US 101, 7.3 mi e on SR 38. Ext corridors. **Pets:** Medium, dogs only. $5 daily fee/pet. Service with restrictions, supervision.
[SAVE] [X] [ ] [ ] [X]

ROCKAWAY BEACH

Sea Treasures Inn M
(503) 355-8220. **$60-$75.** 301 N Miller St. Center; at jct 3rd Ave N. Ext corridors. **Pets:** Accepted.
[SAVE] [S] [X] [ ] [ ] [X]

Silver Sands Motel M
(503) 355-2206. **$76-$146.** 215 S Pacific St. US 101, exit S 2nd Ave, just w. Ext corridors. **Pets:** Dogs only. $5 one-time fee/pet. Designated rooms, service with restrictions, supervision.
[SAVE] [S] [X] [ ] [ ] [ ] [ ] [X]

Tradewinds Motel M ❀
(503) 355-2112. **$47-$95, 4 days notice.** 523 N Pacific St. US 101, exit N 6th Ave, just w. Ext corridors. **Pets:** Small, dogs only. $5 daily fee/pet. Designated rooms, service with restrictions, supervision.
[SAVE] [X] [ ] [ ] [X]

ROSEBURG

Best Inn & Suites M
(541) 673-5561. **$65-$105.** 427 NW Garden Valley Blvd. I-5, exit 125, just e. Ext corridors. **Pets:** Accepted.
[SAVE] [S] [X] [ ] [ ] [ ] [ ]

Best Western Garden Villa Motel M
(541) 672-1601. **$59-$89.** 760 NW Garden Valley Blvd. I-5, exit 125, just nw. Ext corridors. **Pets:** Other species. $10 deposit/room. Service with restrictions, supervision.
[SAVE] [S] [X] [ ] [ ] [ ] [ ]

Holiday Inn Express M ❀
(541) 673-7517. **$72-$99.** 375 W Harvard Blvd. I-5, exit 124, just se. Ext/int corridors. **Pets:** Other species. $5 daily fee/room. Designated rooms, service with restrictions.
[SAVE] [S] [X] [ ] [ ] [ ] [ ]

▼▼ **Howard Johnson Express Inn M**
(541) 673-5082. **$44-$64, 3 days notice.** 978 NE Stephen St. I-5, exit 125, 0.6 mi e on Garden Valley Blvd, then 0.4 mi s. Ext corridors. **Pets:** Small. $7 daily fee/pet. Designated rooms, service with restrictions, supervision.

SD X ☐ ▣

(AAA) ▼ Shady Oaks Motel M ❀
(541) 672-2608. **$40-$46, 3 days notice.** 2954 Old Hwy 99 S. I-5, exit 120, 0.5 mi ne. Ext corridors. **Pets:** Large, other species. Service with restrictions, supervision.

SAVE X

(AAA) ▼▼▼ Sleep Inn and Suites M ❀
(541) 464-8338. **$49-$69.** 2855 NW Edenbower Blvd. I-5, exit 127, just sw. Int corridors. **Pets:** Medium. $7 daily fee/pet. Service with restrictions.

SAVE SD X ☐ ☐ ☐ ▣ ☀

▼▼ **Super 8 Motel M**
(541) 672-8880. **$52-$59.** 3200 NW Aviation Dr. I-5, exit 127, just ne. Int corridors. **Pets:** Large, other species. $25 deposit/pet. Service with restrictions, supervision.

A$K SD X ☐ ☀

(AAA) ▼▼▼▼ Windmill Inn of Roseburg M ❀
(541) 673-0901. **$75-$91.** 1450 NW Mulholland Dr. I-5, exit 125, just ne. Int corridors. **Pets:** Other species. Service with restrictions, supervision.

SAVE SD X ☐ ☐ ☐ ▣ ☀

SALEM

(AAA) ▼▼▼▼ Best Western New Kings Inn M
(503) 581-1559. **$60-$70, 10 days notice.** 1600 Motor Ct NE. I-5, exit 256, just e. Ext corridors. **Pets:** Accepted.

SAVE SD X ☐M ☐ ☐ ☐ ▣ ☀

(AAA) ▼▼▼▼ Holiday Inn Express M
(503) 391-7000. **$75-$115.** 890 Hawthorne Ave SE. I-5, exit 253, just w, then just n. Int corridors. **Pets:** Other species. $15 daily fee/pet. Designated rooms, service with restrictions, supervision.

SAVE SD X ☐M ☐ ☐ ☐ ▣ ☀

(AAA) ▼▼ Holiday Lodge M
(503) 585-2323. **$44-$58.** 1400 Hawthorne Ave NE. I-5, exit 256, just w, then just s. Ext corridors. **Pets:** Small, dogs only. $7 daily fee/pet. Designated rooms, service with restrictions, supervision.

SAVE X ☐ ☐ ☀

▼▼ **Motel 6–1343 M**
(503) 371-8024. **$43-$57.** 1401 Hawthorne Ave NE. I-5, exit 256, just w, then just s. Ext corridors. **Pets:** Accepted.

SD X ☐ ☐ ☀

(AAA) ▼▼▼▼ Phoenix Inn Suites-North M
(503) 581-7004. **$79-$99.** 1590 Weston Ct NE. I-5, exit 256, just w, then just s. Int corridors. **Pets:** Accepted.

SAVE SD X ☐M ☐ ☐ ☐ ▣ ☀

(AAA) ▼▼▼▼ Phoenix Inn Suites-South M
(503) 588-9220. **$79-$99.** 4370 Commercial SE. I-5, exit 252, 1.5 mi w on Kuebler Rd, 0.7 mi n. Int corridors. **Pets:** Accepted.

SAVE SD X ☐M ☐ ☐ ☐ ▣ ☀

▼▼▼ **Red Lion Hotel MI**
(503) 370-7888. **$69-$99.** 3301 Market St NE. I-5, exit 256, just w. Int corridors. **Pets:** Accepted.

A$K SD X ☐ ☐ ☐ ☐ ▣ ☐ ☀

(AAA) ▼▼▼▼ Salem Inn M
(503) 588-0515. **$55-$129.** 1775 Freeway Ct NE. I-5, exit 256, just w. Int corridors. **Pets:** Other species. $50 deposit/room, $10 daily fee/pet. Service with restrictions, supervision.

SAVE SD X ☐ ☐ ☐ ☀

▼▼ **Salem Super 8 M** ❀
(503) 370-8888. **$59-$68, 10 days notice.** 1288 Hawthorne Ave NE. I-5, exit 256, just w, then just s. Int corridors. **Pets:** $25 deposit/pet. Designated rooms, service with restrictions.

X ☐ ☐ ▣ ☀

(AAA) ▼▼▼▼ Shilo Inn Suites-Salem M
(503) 581-4001. **$59-$95.** 3304 Market St NE. I-5, exit 256, just w. Int corridors. **Pets:** Small, dogs only. $15 daily fee/pet. Designated rooms, service with restrictions, supervision.

SAVE SD X ☐ ☐ ☐ ▣ ☀

(AAA) ▼▼ Travelodge Salem Capital M
(503) 581-2466. **$54-$69, 30 days notice.** 1555 State St. 0.5 mi e of Capital. Ext corridors. **Pets:** Small. $10 daily fee/pet.

SAVE SD X ☐ ☐ ☐ ▣ ☀

SANDY

▼▼▼ **Best Western Sandy Inn M**
(503) 668-7100. **$62-$78, 7 days notice.** 37465 Hwy 26. West side of town. Int corridors. **Pets:** Dogs only. $10 one-time fee/pet. Service with restrictions, supervision.

SAVE SD X ☐M ☐ ☐ ☐ ▣ ☀

SEASIDE

(AAA) ▼▼▼▼ Best Western Ocean View Resort MI
(503) 738-3334. **$89-$275.** 414 N Prom. US 101, exit 1st Ave, just w, just n on Necanicum Dr, then just w on 4th. Ext/int corridors. **Pets:** Medium. $15 daily fee/pet. Designated rooms, service with restrictions, supervision.

SAVE SD X ☐ ☐ ▣ ☐ ☀ Ⓐ

(AAA) ▼▼▼▼ Comfort Inn Boardwalk M ❀
(503) 738-3011. **$69-$199.** 545 Broadway. US 101, exit Ave A, just w. Ext/int corridors. **Pets:** Other species. $7 daily fee/room. Service with restrictions, supervision.

SAVE SD X ☐M ☐ ☐ ☐ ▣ ☀

△△△ ▽▽▽ Seaside Convention Center Inn M ☘
(503) 738-9581. **$99-$169, 3 days notice.** 441 2nd Ave. US 101, exit 1st Ave, 0.4 mi w. Ext/int corridors. **Pets:** $10 daily fee/pet. Service with restrictions, supervision.
[SAVE] [S♦] [✕] [🐾] [📠] [💻] [➤]

▽▽ Shilo Inn-Seaside East M ☘
(503) 738-0549. **$45-$119.** 900 S Holladay Dr. US 101, exit Ave G, just w, then just s. Ext/int corridors. **Pets:** Other species. $10 daily fee/pet. Service with restrictions, supervision.
[ASK] [S♦] [✕] [🐾] [📠] [💻] [➤]

SHADY COVE

△△△ ▽▽▽▽ The Edgewater Inn on the Rogue River M
(541) 878-3171. **$64-$155.** 7800 Rogue River Dr. Off SR 62. Ext corridors. **Pets:** $7 daily fee/pet. Service with restrictions, supervision.
[SAVE] [S♦] [✕] [🐾] [📠] [💻] [➤]

SISTERS

△△△ ▽▽▽▽ Best Western Ponderosa Lodge M
(541) 549-1234. **$79-$109, 30 days notice.** 500 Hwy 20 W. West end of town, just w on US 20 from jct SR 242. Ext corridors. **Pets:** Medium. $10 daily fee/pet. Designated rooms, service with restrictions, supervision.
[SAVE] [S♦] [✕] [🐾] [📠] [💻] [➤]

△△△ ▽▽ ▽▽ Comfort Inn at Sisters M
(541) 549-7829. **$90-$105.** 540 Hwy 20 W. West end of town, just w on US 20 from jct SR 242. Ext corridors. **Pets:** Other species. Designated rooms, service with restrictions, supervision.
[SAVE] [S♦] [✕] [🐾] [🐾] [📠] [💻] [➤]

SPRINGFIELD

△△△ ▽▽▽▽ Comfort Suites Eugene/Springfield M
(541) 746-5359. **$76-$88.** 969 Kruse Way. I-5, exit 195A, just e. Int corridors. **Pets:** Other species. $10 daily fee/room. Designated rooms, supervision.
[SAVE] [S♦] [✕] [🐾] [📠] [💻] [➤]

△△△ ▽▽ ▽▽ Doubletree Hotel/Eugene-Springfield M ☘
(541) 726-8181. **$89-$99.** 3280 Gateway St. I-5, exit 195A, just e, then just s. Ext/int corridors. **Pets:** Service with restrictions, crate.
[SAVE] [S♦] [✕] [🐾] [🐾] [📠] [💻] [🍴] [➤]

△△△ ▽▽▽ Holiday Inn Express M
(541) 746-8471. **$69-$89.** 3480 Hutton St. I-5, exit 195A, just e. Int corridors. **Pets:** Accepted.
[SAVE] [✕] [🐾] [📠] [💻] [➤]

▽▽ Motel 6 #418 M
(541) 741-1105. **$43-$57.** 3752 International Ct. I-5, exit 195A, just e, then just n on Gateway St. Ext corridors. **Pets:** Other species. Service with restrictions, supervision.
[S♦] [✕] [🐾M] [🐾] [➤]

△△△ ▽▽▽▽ Village Inn M ☘
(541) 747-4546. **$72-$82.** 1875 Mohawk Blvd. I-5, exit 194A (SR 126), 2.5 mi e, then just n. Ext corridors. **Pets:** Medium. Service with restrictions, supervision.
[SAVE] [S♦] [✕] [📠] [🍴] [➤]

ST. HELENS

△△△ ▽▽▽ Best Western Oak Meadows Inn M
(503) 397-3000. **$79-$99.** 585 S Columbia River Hwy. South end of town on US 30. Int corridors. **Pets:** Medium. $10 one-time fee/room. Service with restrictions, supervision.
[SAVE] [S♦] [✕] [🐾] [📠] [💻] [➤]

SUTHERLIN

▽▽ Sutherlin Inn M
(541) 459-6800. **$49-$99.** 1400 Hospitality Pl. I-5, exit 136, just se. Int corridors. **Pets:** Other species. $10 daily fee/room. Service with restrictions, supervision.
[✕] [🐾] [📠]

△△△ ▽▽▽ Umpqua Regency Inn M ☘
(541) 459-1424. **$67-$69.** 150 Myrtle St. I-5, exit 136, just ne. Ext corridors. **Pets:** $5 daily fee/pet. Designated rooms, service with restrictions, supervision.
[SAVE] [S♦] [✕] [📠] [💻] [➤]

SWEET HOME

△△△ ▽▽ Sweet Home Inn M
(541) 367-5137. **$59-$74, 3 days notice.** 805 Long St. Just e of jct US 20 and SR 228, just s on 10th Ave, then just w. Ext corridors. **Pets:** Medium, dogs only. $10 one-time fee/pet. Service with restrictions, supervision.
[SAVE] [S♦] [✕] [📠]

THE DALLES

△△△ ▽▽▽▽ Best Western River City Inn M
(541) 296-9107. **$62-$89.** 112 W Second. I-84, exit 84 eastbound; exit 85 westbound, just s. Ext/int corridors. **Pets:** Very small, other species. $10 daily fee/pet. Designated rooms, service with restrictions, supervision.
[SAVE] [S♦] [✕] [🐾] [📠] [💻] [🍴] [➤]

△△△ ▽▽▽▽ Comfort Inn M
(541) 298-2800. **$60-$140, 7 days notice.** 351 Lone Pine Dr. I-84, exit 87, just n. Int corridors. **Pets:** Accepted.
[SAVE] [S♦] [✕] [📠] [💻] [➤]

△△△ ▽▽▽▽ Quality Inn, Columbia River Gorge M
(541) 298-5161. **$64-$95, 3 days notice.** 2114 W 6th. I-84, exit 83 eastbound; exit 84 westbound, just s. Ext corridors. **Pets:** Accepted.
[SAVE] [S♦] [✕] [🐾M] [🐾] [🐾] [📠] [💻] [🍴] [➤]

▼▼ Shilo Inn Suites-The Dalles 🏨 ☙
(541) 298-5502. **$59-$109.** 3223 Bret Clodfelter Way. I-84, exit 87, just n. Int corridors. **Pets:** Other species. $10 daily fee/pet. Service with restrictions, supervision.

▼▼ Super 8 Motel 🏨
(541) 296-6888. **$51-$78.** 609 Cherry Heights Rd. Int corridors. **Pets:** Medium. $10 daily fee/pet. Designated rooms, service with restrictions, supervision.

TILLAMOOK

▼▼ Mar-Clair Inn 🏨
(503) 842-7571. **$55-$76.** 11 Main Ave. On US 101, just n of jct SR 6. Ext/int corridors. **Pets:** Small, dogs only. $6 daily fee/pet. Service with restrictions, supervision.

▼▼▼ Shilo Inn Suites-Tillamook 🏨 ☙
(503) 842-7971. **$69-$129.** 2515 N Main Ave. 1 mi n on US 101. Int corridors. **Pets:** Other species. $10 daily fee/pet. Service with restrictions, supervision.

WALDPORT

◈◈ ▼▼ Alsea Manor Motel 🏨
(541) 563-3249. **$43-$73, 3 days notice.** 190 SW Hwy 101. Downtown; SR 34, just s on US 101. Ext corridors. **Pets:** Small, dogs only. $5 daily fee/room. Designated rooms, service with restrictions, supervision.
[SAVE] 🆂 ✕ 🎾

WARRENTON

▼▼▼ Shilo Inn

Suites-Warrenton/Astoria 🏨 ☙
(503) 861-2181. **$69-$179.** 1609 E Harbor Dr. On US 26/101; near west end of Young's Bay Bridge. Int corridors. **Pets:** Other species. $10 daily fee/pet. Service with restrictions, supervision.
[ASK] 🆂 ✕ 🛏 🖥 🍴 ⊸

WINSTON

◈◈ ▼▼ Sweet Breeze Inn II 🏨
(541) 679-2420. **$60-$65.** 251 NE Main St. I-5, exit 119, 3 mi w. Ext corridors. **Pets:** Accepted.
[SAVE] 🆂 ✕ 🛎 🛏

WOODBURN

◈◈ ▼▼▼ Best Western Woodburn 🏨
(503) 982-6515. **$65-$85.** 2887 Newberg Hwy. I-5, exit 271, just e. Int corridors. **Pets:** Accepted.
[SAVE] 🆂 ✕ ♿ 🎾 🛎 🛏 🖥 ⊸

◈◈ ▼▼▼ Hawthorn Inn & Suites 🏨
(503) 982-1727. **$59-$75.** 120 NE Arney Rd. I-5, exit 271, just w. Int corridors. **Pets:** Medium. $50 deposit/pet, $5 daily fee/pet. Service with restrictions, supervision.
[SAVE] 🆂 ✕ 🎾 🛏 🖥 ⊸

YACHATS

◈◈ ▼▼▼ The Adobe Resort 🏨 ☙
(541) 547-3141. **$60-$125.** 1555 Hwy 101. 0.5 mi n on US 101. Int corridors. **Pets:** Other species. $10 daily fee/pet. Designated rooms, service with restrictions, supervision.
[SAVE] 🆂 ✕ 🎾 🛎 🛏 🖥 🍴 🎾

◈◈ ▼▼▼ Fireside Motel 🏨
(541) 547-3636. **$50-$120.** 1881 Hwy 101 N. 0.6 mi n on US 101. Ext corridors. **Pets:** Accepted.
[SAVE] 🆂 ✕ 🛏 🖥 🎾

▼▼ Shamrock Lodgettes 🅲
(541) 547-3312. **$75-$100, 3 days notice.** 105 Hwy 101 S. Just s on US 101. Ext corridors. **Pets:** Accepted.
✕ 🛏 🖥 🎾

PENNSYLVANIA

CITY INDEX

ABBOTTSTOWN

The Inn at the Altland House
(717) 259-9535. **$89-$125.** Center Sq Rt 30. Jct US 30 and SR 194. Int corridors. **Pets:** Accepted.

ALLENTOWN

Allenwood Motel
(610) 395-3707. **$50-$125.** 1058 Hausman Rd. I-476, exit 33, 0.5 mi e on US 22, 0.8 mi s on SR 309, w on Tilghman St to light, 0.8 mi n to dead end. Ext corridors. **Pets:** Medium. $8 daily fee/pet. Service with restrictions, supervision.

Days Inn Conference Center
(610) 395-3731. **$75-$150.** 1151 Bulldog Dr. I-476, exit 56, 0.5 mi e on US 22, 0.6 mi n on SR 309 via Bulldog Dr access road. Ext/int corridors. **Pets:** $15 daily fee/room. Designated rooms, service with restrictions, crate.

Four Points by Sheraton Hotel & Suites Lehigh Valley Airport
(610) 266-1000. **$174.** 3400 Airport Rd. SR 987 N (Airport Rd), 0.5 mi n of jct SR 22. Int corridors. **Pets:** Accepted.

Howard Johnson Inn & Suites M
(610) 439-4000. **$39-$149.** 3220 Hamilton Blvd. I-78, exit 54 (Hamilton Blvd), 0.8 mi n on US 222. Int corridors. **Pets:** Medium. $10 one-time fee/pet. Designated rooms, service with restrictions, supervision.

Microtel Inn M
(610) 266-9070. **$49-$74.** 1880 Steelstone Rd. US 22, exit Airport Rd S. Int corridors. **Pets:** Accepted.

Red Roof Inn M
(610) 264-5404. **$49-$69.** 1846 Catasauqua Rd. US 22, exit Airport Rd S, just s. Ext corridors. **Pets:** Accepted.

Staybridge Suites Allentown-Airport M
(610) 443-5000. **$89-$209.** 1787-A Airport Rd. US 22, exit Airport Rd S, 0.3 mi s. Int corridors. **Pets:** Accepted.

Super 8 Motel- Allentown M
(610) 435-7880. **$49-$89.** 1715 Plaza Ln. US 22, exit 15th St, just n. Int corridors. **Pets:** Accepted.

ALTOONA

Econo Lodge MI
(814) 944-3555. **$56-$63, 7 days notice.** 2906 Pleasant Valley Blvd. I-99/US 220, exit Frankstown Rd, 0.4 mi w, then 0.5 mi n. Ext corridors. **Pets:** Medium, other species. Service with restrictions.

Motel 6 M
(814) 946-7601. **$53-$63.** 1500 Sterling St. I-99/US 220, exit Plank Rd, just n. Ext corridors. **Pets:** Small, other species. Service with restrictions, supervision.

Super 8 Motel Altoona M
(814) 942-5350. **$48-$62.** 3535 Fairway Dr. I-99/US 220, exit Frankstown Rd, just w. Int corridors. **Pets:** Medium, other species. $6 daily fee/pet. Service with restrictions, supervision.

BARKEYVILLE

Days Inn M
(814) 786-7901. **$60-$70.** I-80, exit 29, just n on SR 8. Ext corridors. **Pets:** Other species. Service with restrictions.

Super 8 Motel-Barkeyville M
(814) 786-8375. **$48-$63, 3 days notice.** US 8. I-80, exit 29, just n. Int corridors. **Pets:** Other species. $5 one-time fee/pet. Designated rooms, service with restrictions, supervision.

BEDFORD

Best Western Bedford Inn MI
(814) 623-9006. **$64-$79.** 4517 Business Rt 220 N. I-70/76 (Pennsylvania Tpke), exit 146, 0.3 mi n. Ext/int corridors. **Pets:** Accepted.

Budget Host Inn M
(814) 623-8107. **$32-$78, 3 days notice.** 4378 Business Rt 220 N. I-70/76 (Pennsylvania Tpke), exit 146, just n. Ext corridors. **Pets:** $5 one-time fee/pet. Service with restrictions, crate.

Janey Lynn Motel M
(814) 623-9515. **$-$80, 3 days notice.** 3567 Business Rt 220. I-70/76 (Pennsylvania Tpke), exit 146, 1.6 mi s. Ext corridors. **Pets:** Small. $5 daily fee/pet. Designated rooms, service with restrictions, supervision.

Motel Town House M
(814) 623-5138. **$40-$65.** 200 S Richard St. I-70/76 (Pennsylvania Tpke), exit 146, 2.5 mi s on US 220 business route. Ext corridors. **Pets:** Small, dogs only. $6.36 one-time fee/pet. Designated rooms, service with restrictions, crate.

Quality Inn Bedford MI
(814) 623-5188. **$63-$80, 3 days notice.** 4407 Business Rt 220 N. I-70/76 (Pennsylvania Tpke), exit 146, just n. Ext/int corridors. **Pets:** Accepted.

Super 8 Motel M
(814) 623-5880. **$59-$69, 7 days notice.** 4498 Business Rt 220 N. I-70/76 (Pennsylvania Tpke), exit 11, 0.3 mi n. Int corridors. **Pets:** Accepted.

Travelodge M
(814) 623-7800. **$55-$75.** 4271 Business Rt 220. I-70/76 (Pennslyvania Tpke) exit 11, just s. Ext/int corridors. **Pets:** Other species. $7 daily fee/pet, $7 one-time fee/pet.

BETHEL

Comfort Inn-Bethel/Midway M
(717) 933-8888. **$69-$129.** 41 Diner Dr. I-78, exit 16. Int corridors. **Pets:** Other species. $10 daily fee/pet. Designated rooms, service with restrictions, crate.

BETHLEHEM

Comfort Inn M
(610) 865-6300. **$69-$99.** 3191 Highfield Dr. US 22, exit SR 191, just s. Ext/int corridors. **Pets:** Medium, other species. $10 daily fee/pet. Designated rooms, service with restrictions, crate.

Comfort Suites M
(610) 882-9700. **$69-$139.** 120 W 3rd St. Center; W 3rd and Brodhead sts (3rd St exit from SR 378). Int corridors.
Pets: Designated rooms, supervision.
[SAVE] [S6] [X] [∅] [B] [■] [¶]

Residence Inn by Marriott A
(610) 317-2662. **$114-$119.** 2180 Motel Dr. US 22, exit Aiport Rd S, 0.8 mi se on Catasauqua Rd. Int corridors.
Pets: Accepted.
[SAVE] [X] [∅] [ℰ] [B] [■] [∼] [X]

BLOOMSBURG

Econo Lodge at Bloomsburg M
(570) 387-0490. **$65-$90, 3 days notice.** 189 Columbia Mall Dr. I-80, exit 232, just n on SR 42. Int corridors.
Pets: Large, other species. $25 one-time fee/room. Designated rooms, service with restrictions, crate.
[SAVE] [S6] [X] [∅] [B] [■]

The Inn at Turkey Hill ℂℐ
(570) 387-1500. **$110-$207.** 991 Central Rd. I-80, exit 236 eastbound; exit 236A westbound, just s. Ext/int corridors.
Pets: Other species. $15 one-time fee/room. Designated rooms, supervision.
[X] [B] [■] [¶]

BLUE MOUNTAIN

Kenmar Motel M
(717) 423-5915. **$50-$75.** 17788 Cumberland Hwy. I-76 (Pennsylvania Tpke), exit 15, just e on SR 997 N. Ext corridors. **Pets:** Dogs only. $3 one-time fee/pet. Designated rooms, service with restrictions, supervision.
[SAVE] [S6] [X] [B] [∼]

BOYERTOWN

Mel-Dor Motel M
(610) 367-2626. **$52.** 1 Spring Garden Dr. SR 100, exit New Berlinville, 1 mi n. Ext corridors. **Pets:** Small, dogs only. $5 daily fee/pet. Service with restrictions, supervision.
[X] [B]

BRADFORD

Best Western Bradford Inn M
(814) 362-4501. **$70-$85.** 100 Davis St. US 219, exit Forman St southbound, just s; exit Elm St northbound. Ext/int corridors. **Pets:** Other species. $50 deposit/pet. Service with restrictions, crate.
[SAVE] [S6] [X] [B] [■] [¶] [∼]

Glendorn-A Lodge in the Country ℂℐ
(814) 362-6511. **$375-$715, 30 days notice.** 1032 W Corydon. Main and Corydon, 4.3 mi w to W Corydon, follow signs. Ext/int corridors. **Pets:** Accepted.
[SAVE] [B] [■] [¶] [∼] [X]

BREEZEWOOD

Comfort Inn of Breezewood M
(814) 735-2200. **$45-$75.** 16550 Lincoln Hwy. I-70 (Pennsylvania Tpke), exit 28, just n on US 30; I-76 (Pennsylvania Tpke), exit 12. Int corridors. **Pets:** Small. $10 daily fee/pet. Designated rooms, service with restrictions, supervision.
[SAVE] [S6] [X] [ℰ] [■] [∼]

Wiltshire Motel M
(814) 735-4361. **$44-$48.** 140 S Breezewood Rd. I-70 (Pennsylvania Tpke), exit 28, just w on US 30; I-76 (Pennsylvania Tpke), exit 12. Ext corridors. **Pets:** Small, dogs only. Designated rooms, service with restrictions, supervision.
[SAVE] [S6] [X] [■]

BROOKVILLE

Budget Host Gold Eagle Inn M
(814) 849-7344. **$55-$65.** 250 W Main St. I-80, exit 13, 0.5 mi s on SR 36. Ext corridors. **Pets:** Medium. Designated rooms, service with restrictions, crate.
[SAVE] [X] [B] [■] [¶]

Holiday Inn Express M
(814) 849-8381. **$59-$79, 7 days notice.** 235 Allegheny Blvd. I-80, exit 78, just s on SR 36. Int corridors. **Pets:** $10 one-time fee/pet. Service with restrictions, supervision.
[SAVE] [S6] [X]

Super 8 Motel M
(814) 849-8840. **$55-$65, 30 days notice.** 251 Allegheny Blvd. I-80, exit 78, just n on SR 36. Int corridors. **Pets:** Medium. Designated rooms, service with restrictions, supervision.
[ASK] [S6] [X] [B]

CAMP HILL

Radisson Penn Harris Hotel & Convention Center M
(717) 763-7117. **$159.** 1150 Camp Hill By-Pass. Jct US 11, 15 and Erford Rd. Ext/int corridors. **Pets:** Small, dogs only. $25 one-time fee/room. Designated rooms, service with restrictions, supervision.
[ASK] [S6] [X] [ℰM] [∅] [ℰ] [B] [■] [¶] [∼]

CARLISLE

Clarion Hotel and Convention Center ℍ
(717) 243-1717. **$75-$95.** 1700 Harrisburg Pike. I-81, exit 17 southbound; exit 17A northbound, 0.4 mi n; I-76 (Pennsylvania Tpke), exit 16, 1.2 mi n. Int corridors. **Pets:** Large. $10 daily fee/pet. Designated rooms, service with restrictions, supervision.
[SAVE] [S6] [X] [B] [■] [¶] [∼]

Comfort Suites Hotel M
(717) 960-1000. **$69-$159.** 10 S Hanover St. Downtown; just s of the square. Int corridors. **Pets:** Small. $10 daily fee/pet. Service with restrictions, crate.
[SAVE] [S6] [X] [ℰM] [ℰ] [B] [■] [¶]

⏀ ▼▼▼▼ Days Inn & Suites-Carlisle Ⓜ
(717) 258-4147. **$65-$129.** 101 Alexander Spring Rd. I-81, exit 45, just sw. Int corridors. **Pets:** Medium, other species. $6 daily fee/room. Designated rooms, service with restrictions, supervision.

[SAVE] [S⌀] [✕] [&M] [&] [🛏] [💻] [🕰]

⏀ ▼▼ Econo Lodge Carlisle Ⓜ
(717) 249-7775. **$44-$85.** 1460 Harrisburg Pike. I-81, exit 17 (US 11); I-76 (Pennsylvania Tpke), exit 16, 0.8 mi n. Ext corridors. **Pets:** Accepted.

[SAVE] [S⌀] [✕] [💻]

▼▼▼ Holiday Inn Carlisle Ⓜ
(717) 245-2400. **$79-$140.** 1450 Harrisburg Pike. I-81, exit 17 (US 11), just se; I-76 (Pennsylvania Tpke), exit 16, 0.8 mi n. Int corridors. **Pets:** Accepted.

[SAVE] [S⌀] [✕] [🛏] [💻] [🍴] [🕰]

▼ Motel 6–1297 Ⓜ
(717) 249-7622. **$39-$71.** 1153 Harrisburg Pike. I-76 (Pennsylvania Tpke), exit 16, just s. Ext corridors. **Pets:** Small, other species. Service with restrictions, supervision.

[✕] [&M] [&] [🛏] [🕰]

⏀ ▼▼▼▼ Quality Inn Carlisle Ⓜ 🐾
(717) 243-6000. **$59-$69.** 1255 Harrisburg Pike. I-81, exit 17 (US 11); I-76 (Pennsylvania Tpke), exit 16, 0.8 mi n. Int corridors. **Pets:** Other species. Service with restrictions, crate.

[SAVE] [S⌀] [✕] [&] [🛏] [💻] [🕰]

⏀ ▼▼ Ramada Ltd Ⓜ
(717) 243-8585. **$50-$80.** 1252 Harrisburg Pike. I-81, exit 17 (US 11); I-76 (Pennsylvania Tpke), exit 16, 1 mi n on US 11. Ext/int corridors. **Pets:** Medium. $10 daily fee/pet. Service with restrictions, crate.

[SAVE] [S⌀] [✕] [&] [💻]

⏀ ▼ Rodeway Inn Ⓜ
(717) 249-2800. **$55-$105, 7 days notice.** 1239 Harrisburg Pike. I-81, exit 17 (US 11), 0.3 mi s; I-76 (Pennsylvania Tpke), exit 16, 0.8 mi s. Ext corridors. **Pets:** Small. $5 daily fee/pet. Designated rooms, service with restrictions, supervision.

[SAVE] [✕] [🛏] [💻] [🕰]

⏀ ▼▼ Sleep Inn Carlisle Ⓜ
(717) 249-8863. **$69-$99.** 5 E Garland Dr. I-81, exit 14 northbound, just ne; exit 14E southbound. Int corridors. **Pets:** Medium, other species. $10 daily fee/pet. Service with restrictions, supervision.

[SAVE] [S⌀] [✕] [&M] [&] [🛏] [💻] [🕰]

▼▼ Super 8 Motel Ⓜ
(717) 245-9898. **$49-$98.** 100 Alexander Spring Rd. I-81, exit 45, just se. Int corridors. **Pets:** Other species. $5.30 one-time fee/pet. Designated rooms, service with restrictions, supervision.

[ASK] [S⌀] [✕] [&M] [🛏]

CHAMBERSBURG

⏀ ▼▼▼ Best Western Chambersburg Ⓜ
(717) 262-4994. **$69-$129.** 211 Walker Rd. I-81, exit 16, just w on US 30, then just n. Int corridors. **Pets:** Small. $9 daily fee/pet. Service with restrictions, supervision.

[SAVE] [S⌀] [✕] [&] [🛏] [💻] [🕰]

⏀ ▼▼▼ Chambersburg Travelodge Ⓜ▯
(717) 264-4187. **$39-$65, 15 days notice.** 565 Lincoln Way E. I-81, exit 16, 0.8 mi w on US 30. Ext corridors. **Pets:** Medium, other species. Service with restrictions, supervision.

[SAVE] [S⌀] [✕] [🛏] [💻] [🍴]

▼▼ Comfort Inn-Chambersburg Ⓜ
(717) 263-6655. **$59-$89.** 3301 Black Gap Rd. I-81, exit 20, just e, then just s on SR 997. Int corridors. **Pets:** Medium, other species. $10 daily fee/room. Designated rooms, service with restrictions, supervision.

[SAVE] [S⌀] [✕] [🛏] [💻] [🕰]

⏀ ▼▼ Days Inn Ⓜ
(717) 263-1288. **$56-$90, 21 days notice.** 30 Falling Spring Rd. I-81, exit 16, just e on US 30. Int corridors. **Pets:** Medium, other species. $5 daily fee/pet. Designated rooms, service with restrictions, supervision.

[SAVE] [S⌀] [✕] [🛏]

⏀ ▼▼▼ Econo Lodge Ⓜ
(717) 264-8005. **$55-$64.** 1110 Sheller Ave. I-81, exit 14, just w on SR 316. Int corridors. **Pets:** Other species. $10 daily fee/pet. Service with restrictions, supervision.

[SAVE] [S⌀] [✕] [🛏] [💻]

⏀ ▼▼▼ Quality Inn & Suites Ⓜ▯ 🐾
(717) 263-3400. **$72-$89.** 1095 Wayne Ave. I-81, exit 14, just w on SR 316. Ext/int corridors. **Pets:** Small. $10 daily fee/pet. Designated rooms, service with restrictions, supervision.

[SAVE] [S⌀] [✕] [🛏] [💻] [🍴] [🕰]

CLARION

▼▼▼▼ Holiday Inn Ⓜ▯
(814) 226-8850. **$70-$95.** 45 Holiday Inn Rd. I-80, exit 62, 0.5 mi n on SR 68. Int corridors. **Pets:** Service with restrictions, supervision.

[ASK] [S⌀] [✕] [&M] [&] [🛏] [💻] [🍴] [🕰]

▼▼▼ Microtel Inn & Suites-Clarion Ⓜ
(814) 227-2700. **$49-$79, 3 days notice.** 151 Hotel Dr. I-80, exit 62. Int corridors. **Pets:** Service with restrictions, supervision.

[ASK] [S⌀] [✕] [&M] [🐾] [&] [🛏] [💻]

▼▼ Super 8 Ⓜ
(104) 226-4550. **$43-$73, 7 days notice.** 135 Hotel Rd. I-80, exit 62, just n. Ext corridors. **Pets:** Other species. Designated rooms, service with restrictions, supervision.

[ASK] [S⌀] [✕] [🛏] [💻] [🕰]

CLARKS SUMMIT

△△△ ▼▼▼ Days Inn Scranton-North M
(570) 586-9100. **$65-$120.** 811 Northern Blvd. I-81, exit
194, on US 6 and 11; I-476 (Pennsylvania Tpke), exit 131.
Int corridors. **Pets:** Accepted.
[SAVE] [S♦] [X] [🐾] [📱]

△△△ ▼▼▼▼ Ramada Plaza Hotel MI
(570) 586-2730. **$74-$89.** 820 Northern Blvd. I-81, exit 194
on US 6 and 11; I-476 (Pennsylvania Tpke), exit 131, 0.3
mi w. Int corridors. **Pets:** Other species. $10 daily fee/pet.
Service with restrictions, supervision.
[SAVE] [S♦] [X] [📱] [💻] [🍴] [🏊]

CLEARFIELD

△△△ ▼▼▼ Best Western-Clearfield MI
(814) 765-2441. **$50-$90, 3 days notice.** Rt 879 E. I-80,
exit 120, 0.4 mi ne. Int corridors. **Pets:** $5 daily fee/pet.
Designated rooms, service with restrictions, supervision.
[SAVE] [S♦] [X] [💻] [🍴] [🏊]

△△△ ▼ Budget Inn M
(814) 765-2639. **$35-$59, 7 days notice.** Rt 322 E. I-80,
exit 120, 1.5 mi sw on SR 879, then 1.2 mi e. Ext/int
corridors. **Pets:** $5 daily fee/pet. No service, supervision.
[SAVE] [S♦] [X] [📱]

▼▼▼ Comfort Inn Clearfield M
(814) 768-6400. **$62-$89.** Industrial Rd. I-80, exit 120, just
s. Int corridors. **Pets:** Other species. No service, supervision.
[SAVE] [S♦] [X] [♿] [💺] [📱] [💻] [🏊]

▼▼▼ Super 8 Motel-Clearfield M
(814) 768-7580. **$50-$60, 10 days notice.** Rt 879. I-80, exit
120, just s. Int corridors. **Pets:** Accepted.
[ASK] [S♦] [X] [♿] [💺] [📱]

DICKSON CITY

▼▼ Quality Hotel H
(570) 383-9979. **$65-$149, 15 days notice.** 1946 Scranton-
Carbondale Hwy. I-81, exit 191A, 2 mi e on US 6; I-476
(Pennsylvania Tpke Northeast Extension), exit 131 (Clarks
Summit), 4.5 mi e on US 6. Int corridors. **Pets:** Accepted.
[SAVE] [S♦] [X] [💻] [🍴] [🏊]

DOUGLASSVILLE

▼▼ Econo Lodge M
(610) 385-3016. **$62-$89.** 387 Ben Franklin Hwy. From
Pottstown, 10 mi w on US 422; from Reading, 10 mi e on
US 422. Ext corridors. **Pets:** Large, other species. $12 daily
fee/pet. Service with restrictions, supervision.
[SAVE] [S♦] [X] [💺] [📱] [💻]

DU BOIS

△△△ ▼▼▼▼ Holiday Inn MI
(814) 371-5100. **$71-$75.** US 219 & I-80. I-80, exit 97, just
s. Int corridors. **Pets:** Medium, other species. Designated
rooms, service with restrictions.
[SAVE] [S♦] [X] [♿] [💺] [📱] [💻] [🍴] [🏊]

DUNMORE

△△△ ▼▼▼ Days Inn M
(570) 348-6101. **$57-$75.** 1226 O'Neill Hwy. I-81, exit 188,
just e at jct SR 347. Int corridors. **Pets:** Other species. $5
daily fee/pet. Service with restrictions, supervision.
[SAVE] [S♦] [X] [📱] [💻]

DUPONT

▼▼▼ Holiday Inn Express M
(570) 654-3300. **$69-$79.** 30 Concorde Dr. I-81, exit 178A,
just e. Int corridors. **Pets:** Small. Designated rooms, service
with restrictions.
[ASK] [S♦] [X] [♿] [🐾] [💺] [📱] [💻] [🏊]

EASTON

△△△ ▼▼▼▼ Best Western Easton Inn M
(610) 253-9131. **$79-$119.** 185 S 3rd St. I-78, exit 75, 1 mi
n, follow signs; US 22, exit 4th St (SR 611), just e to 3rd St,
0.5 mi s. Int corridors. **Pets:** Supervision.
[SAVE] [S♦] [X] [📱] [💻] [🏊]

▼▼ Days Inn M
(610) 253-0546. **$60-$125.** 2555 Nazareth Rd. US 22, exit
25th St, just e on N Service Rd. Int corridors.
Pets: Accepted.
[SAVE] [S♦] [X] [🐾] [📱]

EBENSBURG

▼▼▼ Comfort Inn M
(814) 472-6100. **$64-$130.** 111 Cook Rd. Jct US 219, just e
on US 22. Int corridors. **Pets:** Medium. $25 deposit/room,
$6 daily fee/pet. Designated rooms, service with restrictions,
supervision.
[SAVE] [S♦] [X] [♿] [💺] [📱] [💻] [🏊]

ERIE

△△△ ▼▼▼▼ Best Western M
(814) 864-1812. **$49-$125.** 7820 Perry Hwy. I-90, exit 7,
just n. Int corridors. **Pets:** $10 daily fee/room. Designated
rooms, service with restrictions, supervision.
[SAVE] [S♦] [X] [💺] [📱] [💻] [🏊]

△△△ ▼▼▼▼ Country Inn & Suites M
(814) 864-5810. **$59-$139, 3 days notice.** 8040 Old Oliver
Rd. I-90, exit 6, just s, then 0.5 mi w. Int corridors.
Pets: Very small. $25 one-time fee/pet. Designated rooms,
service with restrictions, supervision.
[SAVE] [S♦] [X] [📱] [💻] [🏊]

▼▼▼▼ Days Inn M
(814) 868-8521. **$60-$100.** 7415 Schultz Rd. I-90, exit 27,
just n. Int corridors. **Pets:** Large. $5 daily fee/pet. Desig-
nated rooms, service with restrictions, supervision.
[SAVE] [S♦] [X] [🏊]

▼▼▼▼ Hawthorn Suites M
(814) 866-8292. **Call for rates.** 2084 Interchange Rd. I-79,
exit 41, just e. Int corridors. **Pets:** Accepted.
[X] [📱] [💻] [🏊]

▼▼ **Microtel Inn-Erie** Ⓜ
(814) 864-1010. **$36-$63.** 8100 Peach St. I-90, exit 6, just s. Int corridors. **Pets:** Other species. $5 daily fee/room. Service with restrictions, crate.
A$K S🔒 ✕ 🌀 ✉

▼▼ **Motel 6** Ⓜ
(814) 864-4811. **$49-$99.** 7875 Peach St. I-90, exit 24, just n. Int corridors. **Pets:** Accepted.
A$K S🔒 ✕ 📶 ⇝

▼▼ **Quality Inn & Suites** Ⓜ!
(814) 864-4911. **$50-$110.** 8040 Perry Hwy. I-90, exit 27, just s. Ext/int corridors. **Pets:** Medium. Service with restrictions, supervision.
SAVE S🔒 ✕ 📶 💻 🍽 ⇝

▲▲▲ ▼▼ **Red Roof Inn** Ⓜ
(814) 868-5246. **$39-$81.** 7865 Perry Hwy. I-90, exit 27, just n. Ext/int corridors. **Pets:** Accepted.
SAVE ✕

▲▲▲ ▼▼▼▼ **Residence Inn by Marriott** Ⓜ
(814) 864-2500. **$121-$199.** 8061 Peach St. I-90, exit 6, just s. Int corridors. **Pets:** Other species. $7 daily fee/pet, $100 one-time fee/room. Service with restrictions, crate.
SAVE S🔒 ✕ 🌀 ⛽ 📶 💻 ⇝

▼▼ **Super 8 Motel** Ⓜ
(814) 864-9200. **$55-$90.** 8040 Perry Hwy. I-90, exit 27, just s. Ext/int corridors. **Pets:** Medium. Service with restrictions, supervision.
A$K S🔒 ✕ 📶

FAYETTEVILLE

▲▲▲ ▼ **Rite Spot Motel** Ⓜ
(717) 352-2144. **$35-$49.** 5651 Lincoln Way E. US 30, 1 mi w of jct SR 997. Ext corridors. **Pets:** Small, other species. $5 daily fee/pet. Service with restrictions, crate.
SAVE S🔒 ✕ 📶 💻

FOGELSVILLE

▼ **Cloverleaf Motel** Ⓜ 🐾
(610) 395-3367. **$40-$50.** I-78, exit 49A, 0.3 mi s on SR 100, left at first traffic light, then immediate left on service road, at end of service road. Ext corridors. **Pets:** Medium. Service with restrictions, supervision.
✕ 🌀 📶 💻

▲▲▲ ▼▼▼▼ **Comfort Inn-Lehigh Valley West** Ⓜ
(610) 391-0344. **$86-$136.** I-78, exit 49B (SR 100), just n on SR 100. Int corridors. **Pets:** $25 daily fee/pet. Service with restrictions, supervision.
SAVE S🔒 ✕ 🌀 📶 💻

▼▼▼▼ **Holiday Inn Conference Center** Ⓜ!
(610) 391-1000. **$99-$149.** 7736 Adrienne Dr. I-78, exit 49A, 0.3 mi s on SR 100. Int corridors. **Pets:** Other species. $10 daily fee/pet. Service with restrictions, supervision.
A$K S🔒 ✕ &M 🌀 📶 💻 🍽 ⇝

FRACKVILLE

▲▲▲ ▼▼▼ **Econo Lodge** Ⓜ
(570) 874-3838. **$45-$85.** 501 S Middle St. I-81, exit 124B, 0.4 mi n on SR 61. Ext corridors. **Pets:** Accepted.
SAVE S🔒 ✕ 📶

▲▲▲ ▼▼▼ **Granny's Motel &**
Restaurant Ⓜ 🐾
(570) 874-0408. **$47-$49, 7 days notice.** I-81, exit 124B. I-81, exit 124B, 0.3 mi nw on SR 61, 0.3 mi n on Altamont Blvd. Ext/int corridors. **Pets:** $30 deposit/room. Service with restrictions, crate.
SAVE ✕ 📶 💻 🍽

FRANKLIN

▼▼ **Franklin Super 8 Motel** Ⓜ 🐾
(814) 432-2101. **$56-$85.** 847 Allegheny Ave. 2 mi on SR 8. Ext/int corridors. **Pets:** Other species. Service with restrictions, supervision.
A$K S🔒 ✕ 📶

FRYSTOWN

▼ **Motel of Frystown** Ⓜ
(717) 933-4613. **$45.** 90 Fort Motel Dr. I-78, exit 2, just s on SR 645, just e on service road. Ext corridors. **Pets:** Accepted.
A$K S🔒 ✕

GALETON

▼ **Pine Log Motel** Ⓜ
(814) 435-6400. **$65-$75, 5 days notice.** 5156 US Rt 6 W. 9 mi w. Ext corridors. **Pets:** Other species. Service with restrictions, crate.
A$K ✕ 📶 🎿

GETTYSBURG

▲▲▲ ▼▼▼ **Best Inn** Ⓜ
(717) 334-1188. **$-$95.** 301 Steinwehr Ave. 1 mi s on US 15 business route, just s of jct SR 134. Ext/int corridors. **Pets:** Medium, other species. Service with restrictions, supervision.
SAVE S🔒 ✕ 📶 ⇝

▼▼ **Gettysburg Travelodge** Ⓜ
(717) 334-9281. **$69-$165, 30 days notice.** 613 Baltimore St. SR 97 at jct US 15 business route. Ext/int corridors. **Pets:** Accepted.
A$K S🔒 ✕ ⛽ 📶 💻

▼▼▼▼ **Holiday Inn-Battlefield** Ⓜ!
(717) 334-6211. **$59-$225.** 516 Baltimore St. Jct US 15 business route and SR 97. Ext/int corridors. **Pets:** Other species. Designated rooms, service with restrictions, supervision.
A$K S🔒 ✕ ⛽ 📶 💻 🍽 ⇝

GRANTVILLE

(AAA) ▼▼ Econo Lodge M
(717) 469-0631. **$40-$70.** 252 Bow Creek Rd. I-81, exit 80. Ext corridors. **Pets:** $6 daily fee/room. Designated rooms, service with restrictions, supervision.
[SAVE] [S🐾] [✕] [🔊] [🛏] [💻]

▼▼▼ Holiday Inn Harrisburg-Hershey Area, I-81 M
(717) 469-0661. **$96-$199.** 604 Station Rd. I-81, exit 80. Int corridors. **Pets:** Other species. Service with restrictions, supervision.
[ASK] [S🐾] [✕] [&M] [🔊] [&] [🛏] [💻] [🍴] [⊇]

GROVE CITY

▼▼ Lynnrose Bed and Breakfast BB
(724) 458-6425. **$65-$75, 10 days notice.** 114 W Main St. Just e. Int corridors. **Pets:** Service with restrictions, crate.
[✕] [ℳ] [🚗]

HARRISBURG

(AAA) ▼▼▼ Baymont Inn M
(717) 540-9339. **$82-$92.** 200 N Mountain Rd. I-81, exit 72. Int corridors. **Pets:** Other species. Supervision.
[SAVE] [S🐾] [✕] [🔊] [🛏] [💻]

(AAA) ▼▼ Baymont Inn & Suites Harrisburg-Airport M
(717) 939-8000. **$69-$94.** 990 Eisenhower Blvd. I-283, exit 2, just se; I-76 (Pennsylvania Tpke), exit 19, 1 mi n. Int corridors. **Pets:** Accepted.
[SAVE] [S🐾] [✕] [🔊] [🛏] [💻]

(AAA) ▼▼▼ Best Western Capital Plaza M
(717) 545-9089. **$72-$90.** 150 Nationwide Dr. I-81, exit 69, just n. Ext/int corridors. **Pets:** Accepted.
[SAVE] [S🐾] [✕] [🔊] [🛏] [💻] [⊇]

(AAA) ▼▼▼ Best Western Harrisburg/Hershey M
(717) 652-7180. **$64-$89.** 300 N Mountain Rd. I-81, exit 72. Int corridors. **Pets:** $5 daily fee/pet. Designated rooms, service with restrictions, supervision.
[SAVE] [S🐾] [✕] [🔊] [&] [🛏] [💻] [🍴] [⊇]

(AAA) ▼▼▼ Comfort Inn M ✿
(717) 540-8400. **$59-$129.** 7744 Linglestown Rd. I-81, exit 77, 0.5 mi w. Int corridors. **Pets:** Other species. $20 daily fee/pet. Service with restrictions, crate.
[SAVE] [S🐾] [✕] [🔊] [&] [🛏] [💻] [⊇]

▼▼▼ Comfort Inn East M
(717) 561-8100. **$89-$119.** 4021 Union Deposit Rd. I-83, exit 48, just w. Int corridors. **Pets:** Medium. Service with restrictions, crate.
[SAVE] [S🐾] [✕] [🔊] [&] [🛏] [💻] [⊇]

(AAA) ▼▼▼ Comfort Inn-Riverfront M
(717) 233-1611. **$69-$109.** 525 S Front St. I-83, exit 43, 0.5 mi n. Ext/int corridors. **Pets:** Accepted.
[SAVE] [S🐾] [✕] [🔊] [🛏] [💻] [⊇]

(AAA) ▼▼▼ Days Inn-Harrisburg Airport M
(717) 939-4147. **$69-$109.** I-76 (Pennsylvania Tpke), exit 247, just n; I-283, exit 1B (Highspire). Ext corridors. **Pets:** Medium, dogs only. Service with restrictions.
[SAVE] [S🐾] [✕] [🔊] [🛏] [💻] [⊇]

(AAA) ▼▼▼▼ Harrisburg-Hershey Marriott H
(717) 564-5511. **$69-$154, 3 days notice.** 4650 Lindle Rd. I-283, exit 2, just e. Int corridors. **Pets:** Other species. $50 one-time fee/room. Designated rooms, service with restrictions.
[SAVE] [✕] [&M] [🔊] [&] [🛏] [💻] [🍴] [⊇]

(AAA) ▼▼▼▼ Holiday Inn Express & Suites M
(717) 657-2200. **$89-$169.** 5680 Allentown Blvd. I-81, exit 72, just s on S Mountain Rd, then just w on SR 22. Int corridors. **Pets:** Other species. $10 one-time fee/room. Service with restrictions, supervision.
[SAVE] [S🐾] [✕] [&M] [🔊] [&] [🛏] [💻] [⊇]

▼▼ Ramada Limited M
(717) 545-6944. **$69-$129, 60 days notice.** 7965 Jonestown Rd. I-81, exit 77, just s. Int corridors. **Pets:** Accepted.
[ASK] [S🐾] [✕] [🛏] [💻] [⊇]

(AAA) ▼▼▼ Red Roof Inn-North M
(717) 657-1445. **$45-$82.** 400 Corporate Cir. I-81, exit 66, just n on Progress Ave. Ext/int corridors. **Pets:** Small. Service with restrictions, crate.
[SAVE] [✕] [🔊] [&] [🛏]

(AAA) ▼▼▼ Red Roof Inn-South M
(717) 939-1331. **$45-$79.** 950 Eisenhower Blvd. I-283, exit 2, just e. Ext/int corridors. **Pets:** Accepted.
[SAVE] [✕] [🔊] [&] [🛏]

(AAA) ▼▼▼ Residence Inn by Marriott Harrisburg-Hershey A ✿
(717) 561-1900. **$94-$179.** 4480 Lewis Rd. US 322, exit Penhar Dr, just e. Ext corridors. **Pets:** Large. $10 daily fee/room, $100 one-time fee/room. Service with restrictions, crate.
[SAVE] [S🐾] [✕] [🔊] [🛏] [💻] [⊇]

(AAA) ▼▼▼ Sleep Inn M
(717) 540-9100. **$57-$114.** 7930 Linglestown Rd. I-81, exit 77. Int corridors. **Pets:** Medium, other species. $10 daily fee/room. Service with restrictions, supervision.
[SAVE] [S🐾] [✕] [🔊] [🛏] [💻]

(AAA) ▼▼▼ Super 8 Motel-North M
(717) 233-5891. **$55-$129, 7 days notice.** 4125 N Front St. I-81, exit 66, 0.8 mi n. Ext corridors. **Pets:** Medium, dogs only. $10 daily fee/room. Service with restrictions, supervision.
[SAVE] [S🐾] [✕] [🛏] [🍴] [⊇]

▼▼▼ Wyndham Garden Hotel M
(717) 558-9500. **$78-$86.** 765 Eisenhower Blvd. I-283, exit 2, just w. Int corridors. **Pets:** Accepted.
[✕] [🔊] [&] [🛏] [💻] [🍴] [⊇]

HAZLETON

Best Western Genetti Motor Lodge ⚑ ❀
(570) 454-2494. **$65-$102.** I-32nd and N Church St. I-80, exit 262, 6 mi s on SR 309. Ext/int corridors. **Pets:** Designated rooms, service with restrictions, crate.

Hazleton Motor Inn ⚑
(570) 459-1451. **$38-$45.** 615 E Broad St. I-81, exit 143, 2 mi n on SR 924, then 1 mi s on SR 93. Int corridors. **Pets:** $5 daily fee/pet, $5 one-time fee/pet. Service with restrictions, supervision.

Ramada Inn Hazleton ⚑
(570) 455-2061. **$65-$85.** I-80, exit 262, 6 mi s on SR 309; I-81, exit 145, 0.5 mi n on SR 93, 1 mi e on Airport Rd, 0.7 mi s. Ext corridors. **Pets:** Accepted.

HERMITAGE

Holiday Inn-Sharon/Hermitage ⚑
(724) 981-1530. **$85.** 3200 S Hermitage Rd. I-80, exit 4B (SR 18), just n. Int corridors. **Pets:** Accepted.

HERSHEY

Hampton Inn & Suites ⚑
(717) 533-8400. **$99-$259.** 749 E Chocolate Ave. 0.9 mi e on US 422. Int corridors. **Pets:** Accepted.

Holiday Inn Express ⚑
(717) 583-0500. **$89-$179.** Just nw of jct US 322, 422 and SR 39; just off Hershey Park Dr. Int corridors. **Pets:** Accepted.

HUNTINGDON

Huntingdon Motor Inn ⚑
(814) 643-1133. **$51-$70.** Motor Inn Rd. On US 22 at jct SR 26. Ext corridors. **Pets:** Medium, other species. $20 daily fee/pet. Designated rooms, no service, supervision.

INDIANA

Best Western University Inn ⚑
(724) 349-9620. **$79-$109.** 1545 Wayne Ave. 0.6 mi n of US 422, exit Wayne Ave. Int corridors. **Pets:** Other species. $5 daily fee/pet. Service with restrictions, supervision.

Holiday Inn Holidome ⚑
(724) 463-3561. **$59-$94, 3 days notice.** 1395 Wayne Ave. US 422, exit Wayne Ave, 1 mi n. Ext/int corridors. **Pets:** Service with restrictions, supervision.

JONESTOWN

Days Inn Lebanon/Lickdale ⚑
(717) 865-4064. **$60-$120, 7 days notice.** 3 Everest Ln. I-81, exit 90. Int corridors. **Pets:** Medium. $10 one-time fee/room. Designated rooms, service with restrictions, supervision.

KITTANNING

Comfort Inn ⚑
(724) 543-5200. **$65-$89.** 13 Hilltop Plaza. SR 28, exit 19A. Int corridors. **Pets:** Small. $25 deposit/pet. Service with restrictions, supervision.

Quality Inn Royle ⚑
(724) 543-1159. **$59-$90.** 405 Butler Rd. SR 28, exit US 422 W (Belmont). Ext/int corridors. **Pets:** Accepted.

Rodeway Inn Kittanning ⚑
(724) 543-1100. **$56-$65.** US 422 E. E of jct US 422 and SR 66 and 28. Ext corridors. **Pets:** Small, dogs only. $25 deposit/room, $5 one-time fee/room. Service with restrictions, supervision.

KUTZTOWN

Campus Inn ⚑
(610) 683-8721. **$60-$75, 3 days notice.** 15080 Kutztown Rd. US 222, exit Kutztown Rd/Virginsville, 1 mi e. Ext corridors. **Pets:** Small. No service, supervision.

Lincoln Motel ⚑
(610) 683-3456. **$50-$70, 3 days notice.** 12 Lincoln Dr. US 222, exit Kutztown Rd/Virginsville. Ext corridors. **Pets:** Small. No service, supervision.

LAMAR

The Comfort Inn of Lamar ⚑
(570) 726-4901. **$85-$125.** 31 Comfort Inn Ln. I-80, exit 173, just n on SR 64. Int corridors. **Pets:** $10 daily fee/room. Designated rooms, service with restrictions, supervision.

LAUREL HIGHLANDS AREA

CHALK HILL

◆◆◆ ▼▼▼ The Lodge at Chalk Hill M
(724) 438-8880. **$60-$84.** Just w. Ext corridors. **Pets:** Other species. $10 daily fee/pet.
[SAVE] [X] [🛏] [💻] [X]

FARMINGTON

▼▼▼▼ Historic Summit Inn H
(724) 438-8594. **$89-$169, 3 days notice.** Center; on US 40. Int corridors. **Pets:** Accepted.
[X] [🛏] [💻] [🍴] [2~] [X]

GREENSBURG

▼▼▼▼ Four Points Hotel Sheraton H ❖
(724) 836-6060. **$69-$109.** 100 Sheraton Dr. I-76 (Pennsylvania Tpke), exit 76, 5.6 mi on SR 119 N, 3 mi e on US 30, then just n. Int corridors. **Pets:** Other species. $10 daily fee/room. Service with restrictions.
[ASK] [S🐾] [X] [🐾] [🛏] [💻] [🍴] [2~]

JOHNSTOWN

◆◆◆ ▼▼▼ Comfort Inn & Suites M
(814) 266-3678. **$75-$80.** 455 Theatre Dr. US 219, exit Elton (SR 756), just e. Int corridors. **Pets:** $15 daily fee/pet. Service with restrictions.
[SAVE] [S🐾] [X] [♿] [🐾] [🛏] [💻] [2~]

▼▼▼▼ Holiday Inn Downtown H
(814) 535-7777. **$85-$110.** 250 Market St. Downtown; corner of Market and Vine sts. Int corridors. **Pets:** Accepted.
[ASK] [S🐾] [X] [♿] [🛏] [💻] [🍴] [2~]

▼▼▼▼ Holiday Inn Express Johnstown M
(814) 266-8789. **$60-$75.** 1440 Scalp Ave. US 219, exit Windber (SR 56 E), just e. Int corridors. **Pets:** Other species. Service with restrictions, supervision.
[ASK] [S🐾] [X] [♿] [🐾] [♿] [🛏] [💻]

▼▼ Motel 6–4018 M
(814) 536-1114. **$46-$56.** 430 Napoleon Pl. Downtown; at jct SR 271 and 403. Int corridors. **Pets:** Medium, other species. Service with restrictions, supervision.
[S🐾] [X] [♿] [🐾] [♿] [🛏]

▼▼ Sleep Inn M
(814) 262-9292. **$70.** 453 Theatre Dr. US 219, exit Elton (SR 756), just e. Int corridors. **Pets:** $15 daily fee/room. Service with restrictions, supervision.
[SAVE] [S🐾] [X] [♿] [🐾] [♿] [🛏] [💻]

▼▼ Super 8 Motel Johnstown M
(814) 535-5600. **$43-$48.** 627 Solomon Run Rd. US 219, exit Galleria Dr, just w. Int corridors. **Pets:** Other species. Service with restrictions, supervision.
[ASK] [S🐾] [X] [♿] [🛏]

LIGONIER

◆◆◆ ▼▼▼▼ Lady of the Lake Bed & Breakfast BB
(724) 238-6955. **$75-$135, 30 days notice.** 157 Rt 30 E. US 30 E, just w of jct SR 711; beside Idlewild Park. Ext/int corridors. **Pets:** Medium, other species. $10 daily fee/pet. Designated rooms, service with restrictions, supervision.
[SAVE] [X] [🛏] [💻] [2~] [X] [📷]

NEW STANTON

◆◆◆ ▼▼▼ Ramada Inn of New Stanton M ❖
(724) 925-6755. **$58-$98.** 110 N Main St/Byers Ave. I-76 (Pennsylvania Tpke), exit 75, just w; I-70 (Pennsylvania Tpke), exit 57, just ne. Int corridors. **Pets:** Small, dogs only. $10 one-time fee/pet. Designated rooms, service with restrictions, supervision.
[SAVE] [S🐾] [X] [🛏] [🍴] [2~]

SOMERSET

◆◆◆ ▼▼▼ Best Western Executive Inn M
(888) 859-0609. **$50-$106.** 165 Water Works Rd. I-70/76 (Pennsylvania Tpke), exit 110, just e. Int corridors. **Pets:** Large, other species. $5 daily fee/pet. Designated rooms, service with restrictions, supervision.
[SAVE] [S🐾] [X] [♿] [🛏]

◆◆◆ ▼▼ Budget Host Inn M
(814) 445-7988. **$30-$75.** 799 N Center Ave. I-70/76 (Pennsylvania Tpke), exit 110, 0.3 mi s. Ext corridors. **Pets:** Medium. $5 daily fee/pet. Service with restrictions, supervision.
[SAVE] [S🐾] [X] [🛏]

◆◆◆ ▼▼ The Budget Inn M
(814) 443-6441. **$25-$55.** 736 N Center Ave. I-70/76 (Pennsylvania Tpke), exit 110, 0.4 mi s. Ext corridors. **Pets:** Other species. $3 one-time fee/room. Designated rooms, service with restrictions, supervision.
[SAVE] [S🐾] [X] [🛏]

▼▼ Days Inn-Somerset M
(814) 445-9200. **$35-$80, 5 days notice.** 220 Water Works Rd. I-70/76 (Pennsylvania Tpke), exit 110, just e. Ext corridors. **Pets:** Accepted.
[SAVE] [X] [🛏]

◆◆◆ ▼▼▼ Dollar Inn M
(814) 445-2977. **$30-$65.** 1146 N Center Ave. I-70/76 (Pennsylvania Tpke), exit 10, just e via Water Works Rd, then just n on SR 601, at top of hill. Ext corridors. **Pets:** $5 daily fee/pet.
[SAVE] [S🐾] [X] [🛏]

W W Glades Pike Inn BB ❖
(814) 443-4978. **$65-$105, 3 days notice.** 2684 Glades Pike. I-70/76 (Pennsylvania Tpke), exit 10, 7.9 mi w on SR 31. Int corridors. **Pets:** Other species. $5 daily fee/pet. No service, supervision.
[ASK] [S⬢] [✕] [☎]

❹ W W W Holiday Inn M
(814) 445-9611. **$79-$109.** 202 Harmon St. I-70/76 (Pennsylvania Tpke), exit 10, just s. Int corridors. **Pets:** Medium. Service with restrictions, supervision.
[SAVE] [S⬢] [✕] [✍] [🖬] [🖵] [🍴] [⊃]

W W W The Inn at Georgian Place BB
(814) 443-1043. **$95-$185, 10 days notice.** 800 Georgian Place Dr. I-70/76 (Pennsylvania Tpke), exit 110, just e via Water Works Rd, then 0.5 mi n on SR 601; at Horizon Outlet Center. Int corridors. **Pets:** Small. Service with restrictions, supervision.
[ASK] [S⬢] [✕] [🍴]

W W Knights Inn M
(814) 445-8933. **$43, 14 days notice.** 585 Ramada Rd. I-70/76 (Pennsylvania Tpke), exit 110, just s. Ext corridors. **Pets:** Other species. Service with restrictions, supervision.
[ASK] [S⬢] [✕] [🖬] [🖵]

❹ W W W W Ramada Inn M
(814) 443-4646. **$64-$125, 14 days notice.** 215 Ramada Rd. I-70/76, exit 110, just s. Int corridors. **Pets:** Other species. Service with restrictions, supervision.
[SAVE] [✕] [🖬] [🖵] [🍴] [⊃]

UNIONTOWN

W W Holiday Inn M
(724) 437-2816. **$64-$99.** 700 W Main St. 1.8 mi w on US 40. Int corridors. **Pets:** Large. Service with restrictions, crate.
[ASK] [S⬢] [✕] [✍] [⛐] [🖬] [🖵] [🍴] [⊃]

❖ **END AREA** ❖

LEWISBURG

❹ W W W Days Inn-Lewisburg M
(570) 523-1171. **$74-$140, 3 days notice.** US Rt 15. 0.5 mi n of jct SR 45. Ext corridors. **Pets:** Accepted.
[SAVE] [S⬢] [✕] [🖬] [🖵] [⊃]

LICKDALE

W W Super 8 Motel-Lickdale M
(717) 865-6600. **$55-$78, 3 days notice.** 16 Marsenna Ln. I-81, exit 30, just w. Int corridors. **Pets:** Accepted.
[ASK] [S⬢] [✕] [🖬] [🖵] [⊃]

LINCOLN FALLS

W W Morgan Century Farm BB
(570) 924-4909. **$78-$98, 3 days notice.** Rt 154. Ext/int corridors. **Pets:** Medium. $5 one-time fee/pet. Service with restrictions, supervision.
[S⬢] [✕] [🖬] [🖵] [☎]

MANSFIELD

❹ W W W Comfort Inn M
(570) 662-3000. **$75-$124, 3 days notice.** 300 Gateway Dr. Jct US 6 and 15. Int corridors. **Pets:** Medium. $10 one-time fee/room. Designated rooms, service with restrictions, supervision.
[SAVE] [S⬢] [✕] [🖬] [🖵]

❹ W W W Mansfield Inn M
(570) 662-2136. **$55-$75, 3 days notice.** 26 S Main St. Jct US 6, just s on Business Rt 15. Ext corridors. **Pets:** Accepted.
[SAVE] [S⬢] [✕] [🖵]

❹ W West's Deluxe Motel M
(570) 659-5141. **$50-$60.** Rt 15. 3.5 mi s. Ext corridors. **Pets:** Other species. Supervision.
[SAVE] [✕] [🖬] [🖵] [⊃]

MEADVILLE

W Days Inn M
(814) 337-4264. **$62-$96.** 18360 Conneaut Lake Rd. I-79, exit 147A, just e on US 322. Int corridors. **Pets:** Medium. $5 daily fee/room. Service with restrictions, supervision.
[SAVE] [S⬢] [✕] [🍴] [⊃]

W W Motel 6 M
(814) 724-6366. **$44-$99.** 11237 Shaw Ave. I-79, exit 147A, just e on US 322. Int corridors. **Pets:** Accepted.
[ASK] [S⬢] [✕] [⛐]

W W Super 8 Motel M
(814) 333-8883. **$55-$65, 30 days notice.** 17259 Conneaut Lake Rd. I-79, exit 147B, just w on US 322. Ext/int corridors. **Pets:** Small, other species. $50 deposit/room. Service with restrictions, crate.
[ASK] [S⬢] [✕] [🖬]

MERCER

❹ W W W Howard Johnson Inn M
(724) 748-3030. **$82-$85.** 835 Perry Hwy. I-80, exit 2, just n on US 19. Int corridors. **Pets:** Large, other species. Service with restrictions, supervision.
[SAVE] [S⬢] [✕] [✍] [🖬] [🖵] [🍴] [⊃]

MIFFLINVILLE

W W Super 8 Motel M
(570) 759-6778. **$50-$70.** 450 3rd St. I-80, exit 242, just n on SR 339. Ext corridors. **Pets:** $20 deposit/room. Service with restrictions, supervision.
[ASK] [S⬢] [✕]

MILESBURG

▼▼▼▼ Holiday Inn M!
(814) 355-7521. $65-$150, 7 days notice. Rt 150. I-80, exit 158, 0.4 mi n. Int corridors. Pets: Other species. Service with restrictions, supervision.
[ASK] [SD] [✕] [&M] [⏎] [&] [✎] [🖥] [¶] [≈]

MOOSIC

▲▲▲ ▼▼▼ Rodeway Inn M ❖
(570) 457-6713. $59-$85. 4130 Birney Ave. I-81, exit 182, 0.7 mi w, then 2.3 mi s on SR 11. Ext corridors. Pets: Other species. $5 one-time fee/pet. Service with restrictions, supervision.
[SAVE] [SD] [✕] [&] [✎] [🖥]

MORGANTOWN

▲▲▲ ▼▼▼▼ Holiday Inn M! ❖
(610) 286-3000. $79-$109. 6170 Morgantown Rd. I-76, exit 298, just s on SR 10. Int corridors. Pets: Small, other species. Designated rooms, service with restrictions.
[SAVE] [SD] [✕] [&] [✎] [🖥] [¶] [≈]

NEW CASTLE

▼▼ ▼▼ Super 8 Motel M
(724) 658-8849. $56-$70, 3 days notice. 1699 New Butler Rd. Jct SR 65, 1.1 mi e on US 422, 1 mi w on US 422 business route. Int corridors. Pets: Accepted.
[ASK] [SD] [✕] [✎]

NEW COLUMBIA

▲▲▲ ▼▼▼▼ New Columbia Comfort Inn M!
(570) 568-8000. $59-$84, 3 days notice. I-80, exit 210A (US 15/New Columbia), just s. Int corridors. Pets: Other species. $25 deposit/room.
[SAVE] [SD] [✕] [&M] [🖥] [¶] [≈]

NEW CUMBERLAND

▲▲▲ ▼▼▼▼ Days Inn Harrisburg South M! ❖
(717) 774-4156. $69-$85. 353 Lewisberry Rd. I-83, exit 39A, just ne; I-76 (Pennsylvania Tpke), exit 18, 0.5 mi s. Int corridors. Pets: Other species. $15 daily fee/room. Service with restrictions.
[SAVE] [SD] [✕] [✎] [🖥] [¶] [≈]

▲▲▲ ▼▼▼▼ Holiday Inn Hotel & Conference
Center-Harrisburg M!
(717) 774-2721. $83-$105. 148 Sheraton Dr. I-83, exit 40A, just se. Int corridors. Pets: Medium. $10 daily fee/pet. Designated rooms, service with restrictions, supervision.
[SAVE] [SD] [✕] [&] [✎] [🖥] [¶] [≈]

OIL CITY

▲▲▲ ▼▼ ▼▼ Arlington Hotel M!
(814) 677-1221. $64-$75. 1 Seneca St. Downtown. Ext/int corridors. Pets: Other species. $100 one-time fee/room. Service with restrictions.
[SAVE] [SD] [✕] [✎] [🖥] [¶] [≈]

PENNSYLVANIA DUTCH COUNTRY METROPOLITAN AREA

ADAMSTOWN

▲▲▲ ▼▼▼▼ The Barnyard Inn B & B and
Suites BB
(717) 484-1111. $85-$160, 10 days notice. 2145 Old Lancaster Pike. 1 mi ne via Main St/Old Lancaster Pike; SR 72, just w on Willow St to Main St, 1 mi n on Main St bearing left at fork, then just n of Adamstown. Int corridors. Pets: Medium, other species. $20 one-time fee/room. Designated rooms.
[SAVE] [✕] [W] [☎]

▲▲▲ ▼▼ ▼▼ Black Forest Inn M
(717) 484-4801. $55-$100. 500 Lancaster Ave. I-76 (Pennsylvania Tpke), exit 21, 2.8 mi n on SR 272. Ext corridors. Pets: Medium, dogs only. Designated rooms, service with restrictions, supervision.
[SAVE] [SD] [✕] [✎]

DENVER

▲▲▲ ▼▼▼▼ Black Horse Lodge and Suites M!
(717) 336-7563. $79-$129. 2180 N Reading Rd. I-76 (Pennsylvania Tpke), exit 286, 1 mi w to SR 272, then 0.3 mi n. Ext/int corridors. Pets: Other species. Service with restrictions, supervision.
[SAVE] [SD] [✕] [✎] [🖥] [¶] [≈]

▲▲▲ ▼▼▼▼ Comfort Inn M
(717) 336-4649. $69-$155, 3 days notice. 2015 N Reading Rd. I-76 (Pennsylvania Tpke), exit 286, 1 mi w to SR 272, then just s. Int corridors. Pets: Medium. $20 daily fee/pet. Service with restrictions, supervision.
[SAVE] [SD] [✕] [☊] [🖥]

EPHRATA

▲▲▲ ▼▼▼▼ Historic Smithton Country Inn BB
(717) 733-6094. $75-$160, 14 days notice. 900 W Main St. On US 322, just w of jct SR 272. Int corridors. Pets: Accepted.
[SAVE] [✕] [✎] [W] [☎]

LANCASTER

▼▼▼▼ Best Western Eden Resort Inn M!
(717) 569-6444. $49-$169. 222 Eden Rd. Jct US 30 (Lincoln Hwy) and SR 272 (Oregon Pike). Ext/int corridors. Pets: Medium, other species. Designated rooms, service with restrictions.
[SAVE] [✕] [&M] [☊] [&] [✎] [🖥] [¶] [≈] [✕]

◆◆◆ ▼▼▼▼ Comfort Inn-Sherwood Knoll Ⓜ
(717) 898-2431. **$82-$112.** 500 Centerville Rd. US 30 (Lincoln Hwy), exit Centerville, 5 mi w. Int corridors. **Pets:** Medium. $5 daily fee/pet. Designated rooms, service with restrictions, supervision.

[SAVE] [S🐾] [✕] [🐾] 🏠 🖥 ⍥ ⊶

▼▼▼▼ Hawthorn Inn & Suites Ⓗ
(717) 290-7100. **$59-$139, 7 days notice.** 2045 Lincoln Hwy E. Jct US 30 E and Lincoln Hwy. Int corridors. **Pets:** Medium. $25 one-time fee/room. Designated rooms, service with restrictions, crate.

[ASK] [S🐾] [✕] [🐾] 🏠 🖥

▼▼▼ Lancaster Host Resort & Conference
Center Ⓡ
(717) 299-5500. **$99-$159.** 2300 Lincoln Hwy E. 5 mi e on US 30 (Lincoln Hwy). Int corridors. **Pets:** Medium, other species. $75 deposit/room. Service with restrictions, supervision.

[ASK] [S🐾] [✕] [🐾] 🏠 🖥 ⍥ ⊶ ⊠

◆◆◆ ▼▼▼▼ Ramada Inn Brunswick Conference
Center Ⓗ
(717) 397-4801. **$89-$129.** 191 N Queen St. Center. Int corridors. **Pets:** Accepted.

[SAVE] [S🐾] [✕] [🐾] [🐾] 🏠 🖥 ⍥ ⊶

◆◆◆ ▼▼ Travel Inn Ⓜ
(717) 299-8971. **$35-$65.** 2151 Lincoln Hwy E. 4.5 mi e on US 30 (Lincoln Hwy). Ext/int corridors. **Pets:** Accepted.

[SAVE] [S🐾] [✕] ⊶

MANHEIM

◆◆◆ ▼▼ Rodeway Inn-Penns Woods Ⓜ
(717) 665-2755. **$52-$68, 3 days notice.** 2931 Lebanon Rd. I-76 (Pennsylvania Tpke), exit 266, just s on SR 72. Ext corridors. **Pets:** $5 one-time fee/pet. Service with restrictions, supervision.

[SAVE] [S🐾] [✕] ⊶

NEW HOLLAND

◆◆◆ ▼▼ The Hollander Motel Ⓜ
(717) 354-4377. **$42-$65, 3 days notice.** 320 E Main St. Just e on SR 23. Ext corridors. **Pets:** Medium. $20 deposit/pet. Designated rooms, service with restrictions, supervision.

[SAVE] [✕]

STRASBURG

◆◆◆ ▼▼▼▼ Historic Strasburg Inn Ⓒ
(717) 687-7691. **$139-$299, 3 days notice.** One Historic Dr. 0.5 mi n on SR 896; 2.5 mi s of US 30 (Lincoln Hwy). Ext/int corridors. **Pets:** Medium, dogs only. $25 deposit/room, $15 daily fee/pet. Designated rooms, service with restrictions.

[SAVE] [S🐾] [✕] 🏠 🖥 ⍥ ⊶ ⊠

❖ **END METROPOLITAN AREA** ❖

PHILADELPHIA METROPOLITAN AREA

BENSALEM

▼▼▼ Comfort Inn Ⓜ
(215) 245-0100. **$99-$119, 14 days notice.** 3660 Street Rd. I-276, exit 351 (Pennsylvania Tpke), just s on US 1, then just e on SR 132. Ext/int corridors. **Pets:** Other species. $20 deposit/room. Service with restrictions, crate.

[SAVE] [S🐾] [✕] [🐾] 🏠 🖥 ⊶

◆◆◆ ▼▼▼ Holiday Inn-Philadelphia
Northeast Ⓜ
(215) 638-1500. **$96.** 3499 Street Rd. I-276, exit 351 (Pennsylvania Tpke), just s on US 1, then 0.3 mi e on SR 132. Ext/int corridors. **Pets:** Accepted.

[SAVE] [S🐾] [✕] [🐾] 🏠 🖥 ⍥ ⊶

BERWYN

◆◆◆ ▼▼▼ Residence Inn by Marriott Ⓐ ❖
(610) 640-9494. **$169-$189.** 600 W Swedesford Rd. US 202, exit Valley Forge Rd, then 1 mi s on SR 252 (Swedesford Rd). Ext corridors. **Pets:** Large. $150 one-time fee/room. Service with restrictions, supervision.

[SAVE] [S🐾] [✕] [🐾] [🐾] 🏠 🖥 ⊶

CHADDS FORD

◆◆◆ ▼▼▼ Brandywine River Hotel Ⓜ
(610) 388-1200. **$125-$169.** Rt 1 & 100. Jct US 1 and SR 100, 2 mi w of US 202. Int corridors. **Pets:** Accepted.

[SAVE] [S🐾] [✕] [🐾] [🐾] 🏠 🖥

CONSHOHOCKEN

AAA ▼▼▼▼ Residence Inn by Marriott Philadelphia/Conshohocken M
(610) 828-8800. **$159-$179.** 191 Washington St. I-76, exit 332 (SR 23), proceed over Fayette Bridge, 0.3 mi to Elm St, then just se along the river. Int corridors. **Pets:** Other species. $25 daily fee/room.

[SAVE] [S🐾] [✕] [&M] [🐾] [🖼] [📁] [📠] [🏊]

EAST NORRITON

▼▼▼▼ Summerfield Suites Hotel by Wyndham M
(610) 313-9990. **$189-$209.** 501 E Germantown Pike. I-476, exit 20, 2.5 mi w. Int corridors. **Pets:** Accepted.

[ASK] [S🐾] [✕] [🐾] [🖼] [📁] [📠] [🏊]

ERWINNA

▼▼▼▼ Golden Pheasant Inn 🆑 🐾
(610) 294-9595. **$95-$225, 21 days notice.** 763 River Rd. SR 32, 0.5 mi n of jct Dark Hollow Rd. Ext/int corridors. **Pets:** Medium, other species. $20 daily fee/room. Designated rooms, service with restrictions, crate.

[ASK] [✕] [📁] [📠] [🍽] [✕]

ESSINGTON

AAA ▼▼▼ Comfort Inn Airport M
(610) 521-9800. **$68-$150.** 53 Industrial Hwy. I-95, exit 9A, 0.3 mi sw on SR 291. Int corridors. **Pets:** Accepted.

[SAVE] [S🐾] [✕] [&M] [🐾] [📁] [📠]

AAA ▼▼▼ Red Roof Inn-Airport M
(610) 521-5090. **$72-$96.** 49 Industrial Hwy. I-95, exit 9A, 0.3 mi sw on SR 291. Ext corridors. **Pets:** Small. Service with restrictions, supervision.

[SAVE] [✕] [🐾] [&]

EXTON

AAA ▼▼▼▼ Holiday Inn Express M
(610) 524-9000. **$100.** 120 N Pottstown Pike. I-76 (Pennsylvania Tpke), exit 312, 3 mi s at jct Business US 30 and SR 100. Int corridors. **Pets:** Small. $25 one-time fee/room. Designated rooms, service with restrictions, supervision.

[SAVE] [S🐾] [✕] [&M] [🐾] [📁] [📠] [🏊]

HORSHAM

▼▼▼▼ Horsham Days Inn M
(215) 674-2500. **$89-$129.** 245 Easton Rd. I-276, exit 343 (Pennsylvania Tpke), 1 mi n on SR 611 (Easton Rd). Int corridors. **Pets:** Accepted.

[SAVE] [S🐾] [✕] [🐾] [&] [📁] [📠]

AAA ▼▼▼▼ Residence Inn by Marriott-Willow Grove A
(215) 443-7330. **$149-$185.** 3 Walnut Grove Dr. I-276 (Pennsylvania Tpke), exit 343, 1 mi n on SR 611 (Easton Rd), 1.3 mi w on Dresher Rd. Ext corridors. **Pets:** Other species. $150 one-time fee/room. Service with restrictions.

[SAVE] [✕] [&M] [🐾] [&] [📁] [📠] [🏊]

KING OF PRUSSIA

▼▼▼ Homestead Studio Suites M
(610) 962-9000. **$94.** 400 American Ave. I-76 (Pennsylvania Tpke), exit 326 (Valley Forge); Schuylkill Expwy, exit Mall Blvd, 1.3 mi n on N Gulph Rd, 1 mi ne on 1st Ave. Int corridors. **Pets:** $100 one-time fee/room. Service with restrictions, crate.

[ASK] [S🐾] [✕] [&M] [&] [📁] [📠]

AAA ▼▼▼▼ MainStay Suites M
(484) 690-3000. **$89-$129.** 440 American Ave. I-76 (Pennsylvania Tpke), exit 326 (Valley Forge); Schuylkill Expwy, exit Mall Blvd, 1.3 mi n on N Gulph Rd, 1 mi ne on 1st Ave, just e. Int corridors. **Pets:** Accepted.

[SAVE] [S🐾] [✕] [&M] [&] [📁] [📠] [🏊]

KULPSVILLE

▼▼▼▼ Best Western-The Inn at Towamencin M
(215) 368-3800. **$110-$115, 3 days notice.** 1750 Sumneytown Pike. I-476, exit 31, just e. Int corridors. **Pets:** Accepted.

[SAVE] [S🐾] [✕] [🐾] [📁] [📠] [🍽] [🏊]

LANGHORNE

AAA ▼▼▼ Red Roof Inn-Oxford Valley M
(215) 750-6200. **$59-$102.** 3100 Cabot Blvd W. I-95, exit 46A (Oxford Valley Rd), just e off US 1 N; 0.5 mi n of Sesame Place. Ext corridors. **Pets:** Accepted.

[SAVE] [✕] [🐾] [&]

LIONVILLE

AAA ▼▼▼▼ Best Western Valley Forge/Exton Hotel & Conference Center M
(610) 363-1100. **$89-$119, 14 days notice.** 815 N Pottstown Pike. I-76 (Pennsylvania Tpke), exit 312, 2 mi s on SR 100. Int corridors. **Pets:** Other species. Service with restrictions, supervision.

[SAVE] [S🐾] [✕] [🐾] [📁] [📠] [🍽] [🏊]

AAA ▼▼▼▼ Exton Residence Inn By Marriott A
(610) 594-9705. **$110-$140.** 10 N Pottstown Pike. I-76 (Pennsylvania Tpke), exit 312, 1 mi s on SR 100. Int corridors. **Pets:** Accepted.

[SAVE] [S🐾] [✕] [&] [📁] [📠] [🏊]

▼▼▼▼ Hampton Inn M
(610) 363-5555. **$79-$119.** 4 N Pottstown Pike. I-76 (Pennsylvania Tpke), exit 312, 0.5 mi s, jct SR 113 and 100. Int corridors. **Pets:** Other species. Service with restrictions, crate.

[SAVE] [S♦] [✕] [♿M] [🐾] [🔒] [🖥] [🏊]

MALVERN

▼▼▼▼ Homewood Suites by Hilton A
(610) 296-3500. **$89-$179.** 12 E Swedesford Rd. US 202, exit SR 29 N, just w; opposite Great Valley Corporate Center. Int corridors. **Pets:** Accepted.

[SAVE] [S♦] [✕] [♿M] [🐾] [♿] [🔒] [🖥] [🏊]

⟨AAA⟩ ▼▼▼▼ MainStay Suites, Malvern M
(610) 695-9200. **$69-$109.** 8 E Swedesford Rd. Just w of US 202 and SR 29 N; opposite Great Valley Corporate Center. Int corridors. **Pets:** $100 deposit/room, $10 daily fee/pet. Service with restrictions, supervision.

[SAVE] [S♦] [✕] [🐾] [♿] [🔒] [🖥] [🏊]

⟨AAA⟩ ▼▼▼▼ Summerfield Suites by
Wyndham-Malvern/Great
Valley M ❀
(610) 296-4343. **$119-$209.** 20 Morehall Rd. Jct US 30 and SR 29, just nw. Ext/int corridors. **Pets:** Medium. $200 one-time fee/room. Service with restrictions, supervision.

[SAVE] [S♦] [✕] [🐾] [🔒] [🖥] [🏊]

NEW HOPE

▼▼▼▼ 1870 Wedgwood Inn of New Hope BB
(215) 862-2570. **$95-$260, 10 days notice.** 111 W Bridge St (SR 179). 0.5 mi w of SR 32. Ext/int corridors. **Pets:** Medium, dogs only. $20 daily fee/pet. Designated rooms, service with restrictions, supervision.

[✕] [🔒] [🖥]

▼▼▼▼ Aaron Burr House Inn & Conference
Center BB
(215) 862-2520. **$95-$245, 10 days notice.** 80 W Bridge St (SR 179). 0.5 mi w of SR 32; at W Bridge and Chestnut sts. Int corridors. **Pets:** Medium, dogs only. $20 daily fee/pet. Designated rooms, service with restrictions, supervision.

[✕] [🔒] [🐾]

⟨AAA⟩ ▼▼▼▼ Best Western New Hope Inn MI
(215) 862-5221. **$89-$169.** 6426 Lower York Rd. 2 mi s on US 202, 1 mi w of jct SR 179. Ext corridors. **Pets:** Small, other species. $20 daily fee/room. Designated rooms, service with restrictions, supervision.

[SAVE] [S♦] [✕] [🐾] [🖥] [🍴] [🏊]

⟨AAA⟩ ▼▼▼ New Hope Motel In The
Woods M ❀
(215) 862-2800. **$69-$139, 14 days notice.** 400 W Bridge St. 1 mi s on SR 179, e of jct US 202. Ext corridors. **Pets:** Medium, dogs only. $25 one-time fee/pet. Service with restrictions, supervision.

[SAVE] [S♦] [✕] [🔒] [🏊]

PHILADELPHIA

⟨AAA⟩ ▼▼▼ Best Western Center City Hotel MI
(215) 568-8300. **$119-$149.** 501 N 22nd St. Just n of Benjamin Franklin Pkwy. Int corridors. **Pets:** Medium. $10 daily fee/pet. Service with restrictions, supervision.

[SAVE] [S♦] [✕] [🐾] [🔒] [🖥] [🍴] [🏊]

⟨AAA⟩ ▼▼▼▼ Best Western Independence Park
Inn H
(215) 922-4443. **$150-$205, 7 days notice.** 235 Chestnut St. In Independence Park Historic District; between 2nd and 3rd sts. Int corridors. **Pets:** Small, other species. $50 one-time fee/room. Service with restrictions, supervision.

[SAVE] [S♦] [✕] [🐾] [🔒] [🖥]

⟨AAA⟩ ▼▼▼▼ Clarion Suites H
(215) 922-1730. **$109-$169.** 1010 Race St. In Chinatown; just e of Convention Center and 11th St. Int corridors. **Pets:** Medium, dogs only. $100 deposit/room, $10 daily fee/pet. Service with restrictions.

[SAVE] [S♦] [✕] [🐾] [🔒] [🖥]

⟨AAA⟩ ▼▼▼▼ The Conwell Inn BB
(215) 235-6200. **$125-$210.** 1331 W Berks St. On Temple University Campus, just e of Broad St on Beasley Walk. Int corridors. **Pets:** Small, other species. $25 deposit/pet. Service with restrictions.

[SAVE] [S♦] [✕] [♿]

▼▼▼ Crowne Plaza Philadelphia Center
City H
(215) 561-7500. **$189-$329.** 1800 Market St. Downtown; between 18th and 19th sts. Int corridors. **Pets:** Other species. $100 deposit/room, $50 one-time fee/room. Service with restrictions, supervision.

[ASK] [S♦] [✕] [🐾] [♿] [🔒] [🖥] [🍴] [🏊]

⟨AAA⟩ ▼▼▼▼▼ Four Seasons Hotel H
(215) 963-1500. **$350-$440.** 1 Logan Sq. Corner of 18th St and Benjamin Franklin Pkwy. Int corridors. **Pets:** Accepted.

[SAVE] [S♦] [✕] [♿M] [🐾] [♿] [🔒] [🖥] [🍴] [🏊]

⟨AAA⟩ ▼▼▼▼ Hampton Inn-Center City M
(215) 665-9100. **$99-$159, 3 days notice.** 1301 Race St. Downtown; at 13th and Race sts. Int corridors. **Pets:** Accepted.

[SAVE] [S♦] [✕] [🐾] [♿] [🔒] [🖥] [🏊]

▼▼▼▼ Hawthorn Suites Philadelphia at the
Convention Center H
(215) 829-8300. **$159-$179, 30 days notice.** 1100 Vine St. Downtown; 11th and Vine sts. Int corridors. **Pets:** Accepted.

[ASK] [S♦] [✕] [🐾] [♿] [🔒] [🖥]

▼▼▼▼ Loews Philadelphia Hotel H
(215) 627-1200. **$129-$139.** 1200 Market St. Corner of 12th and Market sts. Int corridors. **Pets:** Accepted.

[ASK] [S♦] [✕] [♿M] [🐾] [♿] [🔒] [🖥] [🍴] [🏊]

⟨AAA⟩ ▼▼▼ Philadelphia Airport Marriott H
(215) 492-9000. **$79-$230.** 1 Arrivals Rd. I-95, exit 10. Int corridors. **Pets:** Accepted.

[SAVE] [S♦] [✕] [♿M] [🐾] [♿] [🔒] [🖥] [🍴] [🏊]

(AAA) ▼▼▼▼ **Philadelphia Airport Residence Inn** M
(215) 492-1611. **$179.** 4630 Island Ave. I-95, exit 13 northbound; exit 15 southbound, 0.3 mi e on SR 291. Ext/int corridors. **Pets:** Accepted.
[SAVE] [S&] [✕] [&M] [🐾] [🐾] 🛏 💻 🏊

(AAA) ▼▼▼▼ **Philadelphia Downtown Marriott Hotel** H
(215) 625-2900. **$300.** 1201 Market St. Downtown; adjacent to Convention Center. Int corridors. **Pets:** Accepted.
[SAVE] [✕] [🐾] [🐾] 🛏 💻 🍴 🏊

(AAA) ▼▼▼▼ **The Radisson Plaza-Warwick Hotel Philadelphia** H
(215) 735-6000. **$99-$149.** 1701 Locust St. Jct 17th and Locust sts. Int corridors. **Pets:** Accepted.
[SAVE] [S&] [✕] [🐾] 🛏 💻 🍴

(AAA) ▼▼▼▼▼ **The Rittenhouse Hotel and Condominium Residences** H
(215) 546-9000. **$370-$410.** 210 W Rittenhouse Sq. Int corridors. **Pets:** Accepted.
[SAVE] [✕] [🐾] 🍴 🏊

(AAA) ▼▼▼▼▼ **The Ritz-Carlton Philadelphia** H ❀
(215) 735-7700. **$370-$455.** Ten Avenue of the Arts. Chestnut and Broad sts. Int corridors. **Pets:** Dogs only. $25 daily fee/room. Service with restrictions.
[SAVE] [S&] [✕] [🐾] [🐾] 🛏 🍴

▼▼▼ ▼▼▼ **Sofitel Philadelphia** H
(215) 569-8300. **$299.** 120 S 17th St. Jct Sansom and 17th sts. Int corridors. **Pets:** Small, dogs only. $25 one-time fee/room. Service with restrictions, supervision.
[ASK] [S&] [✕] [🐾] [🐾] 🍴

(AAA) ▼▼▼ ▼▼▼ **The Westin Philadelphia** H
(215) 563-1600. **$145-$240.** 99 S 17th St at Liberty Pl. Int corridors. **Pets:** Accepted.
[SAVE] [S&] [✕] [🐾] [🐾] 💻 🍴

POTTSTOWN

▼▼▼▼ **Comfort Inn** M
(610) 326-5000. **$69-$89.** 99 Robinson St. SR 100, 1 mi n of jct US 422. Int corridors. **Pets:** $25 deposit/pet. Service with restrictions, supervision.
[SAVE] [S&] [✕] [🐾] [🐾] 🛏 💻 🏊

(AAA) ▼▼▼ **Days Inn** M ❀
(610) 970-1101. **$42-$79.** 29 High St. Just off SR 663, 0.5 mi e of jct SR 100. Ext corridors. **Pets:** Other species. $5 daily fee/pet. Designated rooms, service with restrictions, supervision.
[SAVE] [S&] [✕] 🛏

▼▼▼▼ **Holiday Inn Express** M
(610) 327-3300. **$69-$80.** 1600 Industrial Hwy. US 422, exit Armand Hammer Blvd. Int corridors. **Pets:** Accepted.
[ASK] [S&] [✕] [&M] [🐾] 🛏 💻 🏊

QUAKERTOWN

(AAA) ▼▼▼ **Quakertown Rodeway Inn** M
(215) 536-7600. **$59-$89.** 1920 John Fries Hwy (SR 663). I-476 (Pennslyvania Tpke) exit 44, just e. Ext corridors. **Pets:** Other species. $5 daily fee/pet. Service with restrictions, supervision.
[SAVE] [S&] [✕] 🛏 💻

TREVOSE

(AAA) ▼▼▼ **Red Roof Inn** M
(215) 244-9422. **$54-$74.** 3100 Lincoln Hwy. I-276, exit 351 (Pennsylvania Tpke), 0.5 mi s on US 1 at jct US 132. Ext corridors. **Pets:** Accepted.
[SAVE] [✕] [&M] [🐾] [🐾]

WEST CHESTER

(AAA) ▼▼▼▼ **Holiday Inn West Chester** MI
(610) 692-1900. **$79-$119.** 943 S High St. 1.5 mi s on US 202 and 322; at jct US 322 business route. Int corridors. **Pets:** Other species. $25 daily fee/pet. Service with restrictions.
[SAVE] [S&] [✕] [&M] [🐾] [🐾] 🛏 💻 🍴 🏊

(AAA) ▼▼▼ **Microtel Inn & Suites** M
(610) 738-9111. **$74-$84.** 500 Willowbrook Ln. Just se of US 202, exit Matlack St. Int corridors. **Pets:** $10 daily fee/pet. Service with restrictions, supervision.
[SAVE] [✕] [&M] [🐾] [🐾] 🛏 💻

❀ **END METROPOLITAN AREA** ❀

PHILIPSBURG

(AAA) ▼▼ **Main Liner Motel** M
(814) 342-2004. **$36-$55.** US 322. 1 mi w of jct SR 53 N. Ext corridors. **Pets:** Medium. $6 daily fee/pet. Service with restrictions, crate.
[SAVE] [S&] [✕] 🛏

PIGEON

▼▼▼ **The Forest Lodge** M
(814) 927-6414. **$50-$56.** SR 66, 6 mi n of Marienville. Ext corridors. **Pets:** Other species. $6 daily fee/pet. Designated rooms, service with restrictions, supervision.
[ASK] [S&] [✕] 🛏 💻 [🎿] [✂]

PINE GROVE

▼▼ **Comfort Inn M**
(570) 345-8031. **$59-$119.** SR 443. I-81, exit 100. Int corridors. **Pets:** Other species. $10 one-time fee/pet. Service with restrictions, supervision.
[SAVE] [S🐾] [✕] [🖂M] [🐾] [🖳] [⇌]

▲▲ ▼▼▼ **Econo Lodge M**
(570) 345-4099. **$45-$80, 30 days notice.** 419 Sudberg Rd. I-81, exit 100, just e on SR 443. Ext/int corridors. **Pets:** Other species. $5.30 daily fee/pet. Service with restrictions, supervision.
[SAVE] [S🐾] [✕] [🐾] [🖳]

PITTSBURGH METROPOLITAN AREA

BEAVER FALLS

▼▼▼▼ **Holiday Inn M I**
(724) 846-3700. **$99-$105.** 7195 Eastwood Rd. I-76 (Pennsylvania Tpke), exit 2, just n. Int corridors. **Pets:** Small. Supervision.
[ASK] [S🐾] [✕] [🖑] [🖂] [🖳] [¶] [⇌]

BETHEL PARK

▼▼ **Holiday Inn Pittsburgh South M I**
(412) 833-5300. **$82-$89.** 164 Ft Couch Rd. 1 mi n on US 19; opposite South Hills Village Mall. Int corridors. **Pets:** Medium. Designated rooms, service with restrictions, supervision.
[ASK] [S🐾] [✕] [🐾] [🖑] [🖂] [🖳] [¶] [⇌]

BRADDOCK HILLS

▲▲ ▼▼▼▼ **Holiday Inn Parkway East M I**
(412) 247-2700. **$119.** 915 Brinton Rd. I-376, exit 11, 0.3 mi n. Int corridors. **Pets:** Accepted.
[SAVE] [S🐾] [✕] [🖑] [🖂] [🖳] [¶] [⇌]

BRIDGEVILLE

▲▲ ▼ **Knights Inn-Pittsburgh/Bridgeville M**
(412) 221-8110. **$55.** 111 Hickory Grade Rd. I-79, exit 54 (US 50). Ext corridors. **Pets:** Medium. $5 daily fee/pet. Designated rooms, service with restrictions, supervision.
[SAVE] [S🐾] [✕] [🐾] [🖑] [🖂] [🖳] [⇌]

BUTLER

▼▼▼ **Comfort Inn M**
(724) 287-7177. **$70-$100.** 1 Comfort Ln. 4 mi s on SR 8. Int corridors. **Pets:** Medium, other species. $50 deposit/room. Service with restrictions, supervision.
[SAVE] [S🐾] [✕] [🖑] [🖂] [🖳] [⇌]

▼▼ **Super 8 Motel M**
(724) 287-8888. **$50-$55.** 138 Pittsburgh/SR 8. 2 mi s on SR 8. Int corridors. **Pets:** Medium. $20 deposit/room, $5 daily fee/pet. Service with restrictions, supervision.
[ASK] [S🐾] [✕] [🖂]

CANONSBURG

▼▼ **Super 8 Motel M**
(724) 873-8808. **Call for rates.** 8 Curry Ave. I-79, exit 45, follow signs. Int corridors. **Pets:** Other species. Service with restrictions, crate.
[✕] [🐾] [🖂]

CORAOPOLIS

▼▼▼ **Hampton Inn Hotel Airport M**
(412) 264-0020. **$99-$109.** 1420 Beers School Rd. 0.5 mi n of Business Rt 60. Int corridors. **Pets:** Large. Service with restrictions, supervision.
[SAVE] [S🐾] [✕] [🐾] [🖂] [🖳]

▲▲ ▼▼▼▼ **Holiday Inn-Pittsburgh Airport H**
(412) 262-3600. **$59-$149.** 1406 Beers School Rd. 1 mi n of Business Rt 60. Int corridors. **Pets:** Accepted.
[SAVE] [S🐾] [✕] [🖂M] [🐾] [🖑] [🖂] [🖳] [¶] [⇌]

▼▼▼▼ **La Quinta Inn-Airport M** ❀
(412) 269-0400. **$73-$100.** 1433 Beers School Rd. 1 mi n of Business Rt 60. Int corridors. **Pets:** Service with restrictions, supervision.
[SAVE] [✕] [🖂M] [🖂] [🖳]

▲▲ ▼▼ **Red Roof Inn Pittsburgh Airport M**
(412) 264-5678. **$48-$65.** 1454 Beers School Rd. 0.5 mi n of Business Rt 60. Ext corridors. **Pets:** Accepted.
[SAVE] [✕]

DELMONT

▼▼ **Super 8 Motel M**
(724) 468-4888. **$52-$56.** 180 Sheffield Dr. SR 66, just s of US 22. Int corridors. **Pets:** Accepted.
[ASK] [S🐾] [✕] [🖂M] [🖂]

GIBSONIA

▼▼ **Comfort Inn Gibsonia M**
(724) 444-8700. **$53-$99.** 5137 Rt 8. I-76 (Pennsylvania Tpke), exit 39, just n. Ext corridors. **Pets:** Medium, other species. $6 daily fee/pet. Service with restrictions, supervision.
[SAVE] [S🐾] [✕] [🖑] [🖳]

GREEN TREE

▼▼▼▼ **Hampton Inn Hotel Green Tree** M
(412) 922-0100. **$89-$99.** 555 Trumbull Dr. I-279, exit 4A to jct US 22 and 30, 1 mi nw via Mansfield Ave. Int corridors. **Pets:** Accepted.

SAVE S6 ✕ ✐ 🖥 ▣

▼▼▼▼ **Hawthorn Suites** A
(412) 279-6300. **$129-$149, 7 days notice.** 700 Mansfield Ave. I-279, exit 4 to jct US 22 and 30, 1.5 mi nw via Mansfield Ave. Ext corridors. **Pets:** Accepted.

ASK S6 ✕ ✐ 🖥 ▣ ➿

◈◈◈ **▼▼▼▼** **Holiday Inn-Pittsburgh Central (Green Tree)** MI
(412) 922-8100. **$79-$109.** 401 Holiday Dr. I-279, exit 4 to jct US 22 and 30, 1 mi nw via Mansfield Ave. **Pets:** Small, other species. Designated rooms, service with restrictions, supervision.

SAVE S6 ✕ ⚐ 🖥 ▣ 🍴 ➿

MONROEVILLE

▼▼ **Days Inn-Monroeville** M
(412) 856-1610. **$45-$70.** 2727 Mosside Blvd. I-76 (Pennsylvania Tpke), exit 57; I-376, exit 14A, 1 mi s on SR 48. Ext corridors. **Pets:** Dogs only. $25 daily fee/room. Service with restrictions, crate.

SAVE S6 ✕ 🖥

▼▼▼▼ **Hampton Inn Monroeville/Pittsburgh** M
(412) 380-4000. **$99.** 3000 Mosside Blvd. I-76 (Pennsylvania Tpke), exit 57; I-376, exit 16A, 0.3 mi s on SR 48. Int corridors. **Pets:** Accepted.

SAVE S6 ✕ ✐ ⚐ 🖥 ▣ ➿

◈◈◈ **▼▼▼▼** **Holiday Inn Pittsburgh-Monroeville** MI
(412) 372-1022. **$69-$109.** 2750 Mosside Blvd. I-76 (Pennsylvania Tpke), exit 57, 0.4 mi s on SR 48; I-376, exit 14A, 0.4 mi s on SR 48. Int corridors. **Pets:** Small, other species. Service with restrictions, crate.

SAVE S6 ✕ ✐ ⚐ 🖥 ▣ 🍴 ➿

▼▼ **Ramada Inn and Conference Center-Pittsburgh East** MI
(412) 244-1600. **$59-$89, 30 days notice.** 699 Rodi Rd. Jct I-376 and US 22, exit 11, 8 mi e. Int corridors. **Pets:** Accepted.

ASK S6 ✕ 🖥 ▣ 🍴 ➿

◈◈◈ **▼▼▼** **Red Roof Inn-Monroeville** M
(412) 856-4738. **$53-$73.** 2729 Mosside Blvd. I-76 (Pennsylvania Tpke), exit 57; I-376, exit 16A, 0.8 mi s on SR 48. Ext corridors. **Pets:** Other species. Service with restrictions, supervision.

SAVE ✕

▼▼ **Super 8 Motel Pittsburgh/Monroeville** M
(724) 733-8008. **$54-$58.** 1807 Rt 286. I-76 (Pennsylvania Tpke), exit 57; I-376, exit 14A, 2 mi e on SR 22 E, then 2 mi e on SR 286. Int corridors. **Pets:** Other species. Supervision.

ASK S6 ✕ 🖥

MOON RUN

◈◈◈ **▼▼▼▼** **AmeriSuites (Pittsburgh/Airport)** M
(412) 494-0202. **$119-$124.** 6011 Campbells Run Rd. Jct US 22/30, exit Moon Run, just w. Int corridors. **Pets:** Accepted.

SAVE S6 ✕ ⚐M ✐ ✑ 🖥 ▣ ➿

◈◈◈ **▼▼▼** **Comfort Inn-Pittsburgh Airport** MI
(412) 787-2600. **$58-$104.** US 22/30; at jct SR 60; 4 mi w of jct I-279 and 79. Ext/int corridors. **Pets:** Medium. $7 daily fee/pet. Designated rooms, service with restrictions, supervision.

SAVE S6 ✕ ⚐ 🖥 ▣ 🍴

▼▼ **MainStay Suites Pittsburgh Airport** M
(412) 490-7343. **$79-$99.** 1000 Park Lane Dr. SR 60, exit 2 (Montour Run), then just w on Cliff Mine Rd, just s. Int corridors. **Pets:** Accepted.

ASK S6 ✕ ✑ 🖥 ▣

◈◈◈ **▼▼▼** **Red Roof Inn South Airport** M
(412) 787-7870. **$49-$63.** 6404 Steubenville Pike. I-179, exit 60A, 3.2 mi w on SR 60. Ext/int corridors. **Pets:** Accepted.

SAVE ✕ ✐ ✑ 🖥

◈◈◈ **▼▼▼▼** **Residence Inn-Pittsburgh Airport** M ✿
(412) 787-3300. **$59-$159.** 1500 Park Lane Dr. SR 60, exit 2 (Montour Run Rd), just w on Cliff Mine Dr to Summit Park Dr, just s to Park Lane Dr, then just e. Int corridors. **Pets:** Other species. $150 one-time fee/room.

SAVE S6 ✕ ⚐M ✐ ✑ 🖥 ▣ ➿

◈◈◈ **▼▼▼** **Sleep Inn Pittsburgh Airport** M
(412) 859-4000. **$59-$69, 7 days notice.** 2500 Marketplace Blvd. SR 60, exit 2 (Montour Run Rd), 0.5 mi e on Montour Run Rd, then 0.5 mi n. Int corridors. **Pets:** Accepted.

SAVE S6 ✕ ✐ ✑ ▣ ➿

◈◈◈ **▼▼▼▼** **Wyndham Pittsburgh Airport** H
(412) 788-8800. **$79-$169.** 777 Aten Rd. SR 60, exit 2 (Montour Run). Int corridors. **Pets:** Accepted.

SAVE ✕ 🖥 ▣ 🍴 ➿

NEW KENSINGTON

▼▼ **Clarion Hotel** MI
(724) 335-9171. **$73-$94, 3 days notice.** 300 Tarentum Bridge Rd. SR 366, 1.5 mi s of SR 28, exit 14; at south end of Tarentum Bridge. Int corridors. **Pets:** Accepted.

SAVE S6 ✕ ✑ 🖥 ▣ 🍴 ➿

PITTSBURGH

▼▼ **Best Western University Center** M
(412) 683-6100. **$89-$91.** 3401 Blvd of the Allies. Just w of jct Bates St. Int corridors. **Pets:** Accepted.

SAVE S6 ✕ ✐ 🖥 ▣ ➿

◈◈◈ **▼▼▼▼** **Hilton Pittsburgh** H ✿
(412) 391-4600. **$94-$149.** Gateway Center. In Gateway Center on Commonwealth, opposite Point State Park. Int corridors. **Pets:** Medium. Service with restrictions.

SAVE S6 ✕ ⚐M ✐ ✑ 🖥 ▣ 🍴

◆◆◆ ▼▼▼ **Holiday Inn Pittsburgh North Hills** M
(412) 366-5200. **$99-$129.** 4859 McKnight Rd. 7 mi n; adjacent and behind North Hills Village Mall. Int corridors. **Pets:** Medium, other species. $25 deposit/room. Designated rooms, service with restrictions, supervision.
SAVE SÓ ⊠ ⌀ 🕿 🖬 🖵 🍴 �

▼▼▼▼ **Holiday Inn Select University Center** M
(412) 682-6200. **$129, 7 days notice.** 100 Lytton Ave. Just nw of 5th Ave. Int corridors. **Pets:** Accepted.
ASK ⊠ ⌀ 🖬 🖵 🍴 �

▼▼▼▼ **Omni William Penn Hotel** H
(412) 281-7100. **$169-$209.** 530 William Penn Pl. Jct 6th St and William Penn Pl. Int corridors. **Pets:** Accepted.
SÓ ⊠ 🖧 🖬 🖵 🍴

◆◆◆ ▼▼▼▼ **Residence Inn by Marriott** M ❀
(412) 621-2200. **$129-$139, 3 days notice.** 3896 Bigelow Blvd. On SR 380. Int corridors. **Pets:** Medium, other species. $10 daily fee/room, $100 one-time fee/room. Service with restrictions, crate.
SAVE SÓ ⊠ 🖧 🖬 🖵 �

▼▼▼▼ **The Westin Convention Center Pittsburgh** H
(412) 281-3700. **$89-$189.** 1000 Penn Ave. At Liberty Center; adjacent to Convention Center. Int corridors. **Pets:** Small. $50 one-time fee/room. Service with restrictions, supervision.
ASK SÓ ⊠ ⌀ 🖬 🖵 🍴

◆◆◆ ▼▼▼▼ **Wyndham Garden Hotel Pittsburgh University Place** M
(412) 683-2040. **$119-$139.** 3454 Forbes Ave. Just w of Bundary St. Int corridors. **Pets:** Medium, other species. $50 deposit/pet. Service with restrictions, crate.
SAVE ⊠ 🖬 🖵 🍴

WARRENDALE

◆◆◆ ▼▼▼▼ **AmeriSuites (Pittsburgh/Cranberry)** M
(724) 779-7900. **$99-$114.** 136 Emeryville Dr. I-76 (Pennsylvania Tpke), exit 28; I-79, exit 79, 0.3 mi s on SR 19. Int corridors. **Pets:** Accepted.
SAVE SÓ ⊠ 🖧M ⌀ 🖧 🖬 🖵 �

◆◆◆ ▼▼▼ **Comfort Inn** M
(724) 772-2700. **$59-$91.** 924 Sheraton Dr. I-76 (Pennsylvania Tpke), exit 28, 0.5 mi s on US 19; I-79, exit 75 (US 19). Int corridors. **Pets:** Large. $15 one-time fee/room. Designated rooms, service with restrictions, crate.
SAVE SÓ ⊠ ⌀ 🖬

▼▼▼▼ **Hampton Inn Cranberry** M
(724) 776-1000. **$99.** 210 Executive Dr. I-76 (Pennsylvania Tpke), exit 28, 0.5 mi n on US 19, 0.3 mi w on Freedom Rd; I-79, exit 25 northbound, 0.5 mi w on Freedom Rd. Int corridors. **Pets:** Accepted.
SAVE SÓ ⊠ ⌀ 🖬 🖵 �

▼▼▼▼ **Holiday Inn Express** M
(724) 772-1000. **$84-$99.** 20003 Rt 19. I-76 (Pennsylvania Tpke), exit 28, jct SR 19 and Pennsylvania Tpke. Int corridors. **Pets:** Small. $10 daily fee/room. Service with restrictions, crate.
ASK SÓ ⊠ 🖬 🖵

◆◆◆ ▼▼▼ **Red Roof Inn-Cranberry Township-Pittsburgh North** M
(724) 776-5670. **$54-$70.** 20009 Rt 19. I-76 (Pennsylvania Tpke), exit 28; I-79, exit 76, SR 19. Ext corridors. **Pets:** Service with restrictions, supervision.
SAVE ⊠ ⌀

WASHINGTON

◆◆◆ ▼▼▼ **Holiday Inn-Meadow Lands** M
(724) 222-6200. **$99-$139.** 340 Race Track Rd. I-79, exit 41, 0.5 mi e. Int corridors. **Pets:** Accepted.
SAVE SÓ ⊠ 🖧M 🖧 🖬 🖵 🍴 �

▼▼▼ **Motel 6-1283** M
(724) 223-8040. **$41-$55.** 1283 Motel 6 Dr. I-70, exit 19A, 0.5 mi s on US 19. Ext corridors. **Pets:** Accepted.
SÓ ⊠ 🖧 �

◆◆◆ ▼▼▼ **Red Roof Inn** M
(724) 228-5750. **$44-$64.** 1399 W Chestnut St. I-70, exit 15, just e on US 40. Ext/int corridors. **Pets:** Accepted.
SAVE ⊠ 🖧 🖬

❀ **END METROPOLITAN AREA** ❀

PITTSTON

◆◆◆ ▼▼▼ **Knights Inn-Scranton/Pittston** M
(570) 654-6020. **$42-$46.** 310 SR 315. I-81, exit 175 northbound, just s on SR 315; exit 175A southbound; Pennslyvania Tpke NE Extension, exit 115. Ext corridors. **Pets:** Very small, other species. Service with restrictions, supervision.
SAVE SÓ ⊠ 🖬

POCONO MOUNTAINS METROPOLITAN AREA

BLAKESLEE

(AAA) ▼▼▼▼ Best Western Inn-Blakeslee/Pocono M
(570) 646-6000. **$65-$180.** New Ventures Business Park. I-80, exit 284, just n. Int corridors. **Pets:** Medium. $50 deposit/room. Service with restrictions, supervision.
(SAVE) (S&) (X) (&M) (🐾) (🛏) (▣)

(AAA) ▼▼▼▼ Blue Berry Mountain Inn BB
(570) 646-7144. **$90-$135, 30 days notice.** Thomas Rd. I-80, exit 284, 3 mi n on SR 115, just n on Thomas Rd, then to the end of Edmund Dr. Int corridors. **Pets:** Medium, other species. $20 daily fee/room. Designated rooms, service with restrictions, supervision.
(SAVE) (X) (🛏) (🛁) (X) (🇿)

EAST STROUDSBURG

(AAA) ▼▼▼▼ Budget Motel MI
(570) 424-5451. **$59-$84, 3 days notice.** I-80, exit 308, just se on Greentree Dr. Ext/int corridors. **Pets:** Medium, other species. $25 deposit/room. Designated rooms, service with restrictions, supervision.
(SAVE) (S&) (X) (🛏) (🍴)

HAMLIN

(AAA) ▼▼▼▼ Comfort Inn M
(570) 689-4148. **$70-$190.** SR 191. I-84, exit 17, just n. Int corridors. **Pets:** Large, other species. $15 daily fee/pet. Designated rooms, service with restrictions, crate.
(SAVE) (S&) (X) (🛏) (▣)

HAWLEY

(AAA) ▼▼▼ The Falls Port Inn & Restaurant CI
(570) 226-2600. **$65-$110, 3 days notice.** 330 Main Ave. At Main Ave (US 6) and Church St. Int corridors. **Pets:** Medium. $20 one-time fee/pet.
(SAVE) (X) (🍴) (🇿)

LAKE HARMONY

(AAA) ▼▼▼▼ Ramada Inn-Pocono MI
(570) 443-8471. **$75-$155.** I-80, exit 277; I-476, exit 95, 0.5 mi e on SR 940. Int corridors. **Pets:** Medium. $50 deposit/room. Service with restrictions, supervision.
(SAVE) (S&) (X) (🐾) (🛁) (🛏) (▣) (🍴) (🏊)

MATAMORAS

(AAA) ▼▼▼▼ Best Western Inn at Hunt's Landing MI
(570) 491-2400. **$89-$149, 45 days notice.** 120 Rt 6 & 209. I-84, exit 53. Int corridors. **Pets:** Other species. $30 deposit/room. Service with restrictions, supervision.
(SAVE) (S&) (X) (🐾) (🛏) (▣) (🍴) (🏊)

MILFORD

(AAA) ▼▼▼▼ Cliff Park Inn & Golf Course CI
(570) 296-6491. **$110-$170, 5 days notice.** 155 Cliff Park Rd. I-84, exit 46, 2 mi e on US 6, just s on 6th St, 1.5 mi w on SR 2001, then 0.5 mi s. Int corridors. **Pets:** Accepted.
(SAVE) (X) (🍴) (X)

(AAA) ▼▼ Milford Motel M
(570) 296-6411. **$50-$90, 3 days notice.** 591 Rt 6 & 209. 0.7 mi e on SR 6 E and 209 N. Ext corridors. **Pets:** Dogs only. Crate.
(SAVE) (S&) (X) (🛏) (🏊)

(AAA) ▼▼▼ Myer Motel C
(570) 296-7223. **$50-$90.** 600 Rt 6 & 209. 0.5 mi ne on US 6 and 209. Ext corridors. **Pets:** Accepted.
(SAVE) (S&) (X) (🛏)

(AAA) ▼▼▼ Red Carpet Inn-Milford M ❀
(570) 296-9444. **$60-$110, 7 days notice.** 240 Rt 6. I-84, exit 46, just s. Ext corridors. **Pets:** Medium. $5 daily fee/pet. Designated rooms, service with restrictions, supervision.
(SAVE) (S&) (X) (🛏)

(AAA) ▼▼ Scottish Inns M
(570) 491-4414. **$45-$89.** 274 Rt 6 & 209. I-84, exit 53, 1 mi s. Ext corridors. **Pets:** Medium. Designated rooms, service with restrictions, supervision.
(SAVE) (S&) (X) (🛏) (▣)

❀ END METROPOLITAN AREA ❀

PUNXSUTAWNEY

◆◆ Pantall Hotel ⬛
(814) 938-6600. **$57-$103.** 135 E Mahoning St. Downtown; on US 119 and SR 36, just across the park from "Punxsutawney Phil". Int corridors. **Pets:** Medium. $50 deposit/room. Designated rooms, service with restrictions.
(ASK) ✕ 🍴

READING

◆◆◆ Airport Lodge & Suites Ⓜ
(610) 736-0400. **$49-$99.** 2017 Bernville Rd. US 222, exit SR 183, 2 mi s. Int corridors. **Pets:** Medium. $50 deposit/pet, $5 daily fee/pet. Service with restrictions, supervision.
(ASK) ✕ 🔲 🖵

AAA ◆◆◆ Best Western Dutch Colony Inn & Suites Ⓜ ❀
(610) 779-2345. **$86-$106.** 4635 Perkiomen Ave. US 422, 0.3 mi e of jct US 422 business route. Ext/int corridors. **Pets:** Medium, other species. $10 daily fee/pet. Designated rooms, service with restrictions.
(SAVE) 🅢 ✕ 🔲 🖵 🍴 ⌷

◆◆ Econo Lodge Ⓜ
(610) 378-1145. **$54-$80.** 2310 Fraver Dr. Just off US 222 business route (5th St), s of Warren St Bypass (SR 12 E). Ext corridors. **Pets:** Small, dogs only. Designated rooms, service with restrictions, supervision.
(SAVE) 🅢 ✕ 🖵

◆◆◆ Ramada Inn @ The Outlets Ⓜ
(610) 929-4741. **$89-$149.** 2545 N 5th St. US 222 business route (5th St), just s of Warren St Bypass (SR 12 E). Ext/int corridors. **Pets:** Large, dogs only. $15 daily fee/pet. Crate.
(ASK) 🅢 ✕ 🔲 🖵 🍴 ⌷

SELINSGROVE

AAA ◆◆◆ Comfort Inn Ⓜ
(570) 374-8880. **$69-$129.** 710 S US Hwy 11 & 15. Just n of jct US 522. Int corridors. **Pets:** Medium, other species. $25 daily fee/pet. Service with restrictions, crate.
(SAVE) 🅢 ✕ 🔲 🖵 ⌷

SHAMOKIN DAM

AAA ◆◆◆ Hampton Inn Ⓜ
(570) 743-2223. **$99-$169.** 3 Stettler Ave. US 11 and 15, 1 mi s of jct SR 61. Int corridors. **Pets:** Other species. $25 one-time fee/room. Service with restrictions.
(SAVE) 🅢 ✕ 🖫 🖵 ⌷

SHARTLESVILLE

AAA ◆ Dutch Motel Ⓜ
(610) 488-1479. **$32-$45.** 1 Motel Dr. I-78, exit 23, just nw. Ext corridors. **Pets:** Dogs only. $3 daily fee/pet. Service with restrictions, supervision.
(SAVE) ✕

SHICKSHINNY

◆◆ The Blue Heron Bed & Breakfast ⬛⬛
(570) 864-3740. **$80 (no credit cards), 5 days notice.** 1270 Bethel Hill Rd. Jct SR 11, 6.2 mi n on SR 239, 2 mi n on CR 4016 (Harveyville/Bethel Hill Rd). Int corridors. **Pets:** Accepted.
✕ 🐾 🎦

SLIPPERY ROCK

◆ Evening Star Motel Ⓜ ❀
(724) 794-3211. **$44-$52.** 915 New Castle Rd. I-79, exit 105, 0.5 mi e on SR 108. Ext corridors. **Pets:** Medium. $5 daily fee/pet. Service with restrictions, supervision.
🅢 ✕ 🔲 🖵

SOUTH WILLIAMSPORT

AAA ◆◆ Ridgemont Motel Ⓜ
(570) 321-5300. **$43-$48.** 637 US 15 Hwy. 1.2 mi s. Ext corridors. **Pets:** Small, dogs only. $5 one-time fee/pet. Designated rooms, service with restrictions, supervision.
(SAVE) ✕ 🔲

ST. MARYS

◆◆◆ Comfort Inn Ⓜ
(814) 834-2030. **$59-$84.** 976 S St Marys Rd. SR 255, south end of town. Int corridors. **Pets:** Other species. Service with restrictions, supervision.
(SAVE) 🅢 ✕ 🎦 🔲 🖵 ⌷

STATE COLLEGE

AAA ◆◆ The Autoport Motel & Restaurant Inc Ⓜ
(814) 237-7666. **$60-$90.** 1405 S Atherton St. US 322 business route, 1.4 mi e of jct SR 26. Ext/int corridors. **Pets:** Accepted.
(SAVE) 🅢 ✕ 🔲 🖵 🍴 ⌷

AAA ◆◆◆ Days Inn Penn State ⬛
(814) 238-8454. **$59-$195, 30 days notice.** 240 S Pugh St. Downtown; just e of SR 26 northbound, 0.4 mi n of jct US 322 business route. Int corridors. **Pets:** Accepted.
(SAVE) 🅢 ✕ 🎦 🎦 🔲 🖵 🍴 ⌷

◆◆ Motel 6 State College Ⓜ
(814) 234-1600. **$45-$135.** 1274 N Atherton St. US 322 business route, 1 mi w of jct SR 26. Int corridors. **Pets:** Other species. Crate.
🅢 ✕ 🎦M 🎦 🎦 🔲

◆◆ Nittany Budget Motel Ⓜ
(814) 238-0015. **$245-$301 (weekly).** 2070 Cato Ave. SR 26, 2.6 mi s of jct US 322 business route. Ext corridors. **Pets:** Other species. $10 daily fee/pet. Designated rooms, service with restrictions, crate.
(ASK) 🅢 ✕ 🎦 🔲

▼▼▼▼ Ramada Inn-State College M
(814) 238-3001. **$95-$175.** 1450 S Atherton St. US 322 business route, 1.4 mi e of jct SR 26. Ext/int corridors. **Pets:** Medium. $10 daily fee/room. Designated rooms, service with restrictions, supervision.
⟨ASK⟩ ⟨S⟩ ⟨X⟩ ⟨▢⟩ ⟨¶⟩ ⟨≈⟩

TOWN HILL

⚿⚿ ▼▼▼ Days Inn M
(814) 735-3860. **$53-$58.** 9648 Old 126. I-70, exit 156, just n. Int corridors. **Pets:** Designated rooms, service with restrictions, supervision.
⟨SAVE⟩ ⟨S⟩ ⟨X⟩ ⟨¶⟩

WARREN

⚿⚿ ▼▼▼▼ Holiday Inn of Warren M
(814) 726-3000. **$72-$85.** 210 Ludlow St. 1.5 mi w on US 6, exit Ludlow St. Int corridors. **Pets:** Small. Service with restrictions, supervision.
⟨SAVE⟩ ⟨S⟩ ⟨X⟩ ⟨⊘⟩ ⟨▤⟩ ⟨▢⟩ ⟨¶⟩ ⟨≈⟩

▼▼ ▼▼ Warren Super 8 Motel M
(814) 723-8881. **$55-$65, 30 days notice.** 204 Struthers St. 1.5 mi w on US 6, exit Ludlow St, w on Allegheny, then s. Ext/int corridors. **Pets:** Other species. $25 deposit/room. Designated rooms, service with restrictions, supervision.
⟨ASK⟩ ⟨S⟩ ⟨X⟩ ⟨▤⟩ ⟨▢⟩

WAYNESBORO

⚿⚿ ▼▼ ▼▼ Best Western Waynesboro M
(717) 762-9113. **$72-$82, 3 days notice.** 239 W Main St. 0.5 mi w on SR 16. Ext corridors. **Pets:** Other species. $10 daily fee/pet. Designated rooms, service with restrictions, crate.
⟨SAVE⟩ ⟨S⟩ ⟨X⟩ ⟨▤⟩ ⟨▢⟩ ⟨¶⟩

WAYNESBURG

▼▼▼ Comfort Inn M
(724) 627-3700. **$59-$110, 10 days notice.** 100 Comfort Ln. I-79, exit 14, just e. Int corridors. **Pets:** Medium. Service with restrictions, supervision.
⟨SAVE⟩ ⟨S⟩ ⟨X⟩ ⟨⊘⟩ ⟨✦⟩ ⟨▤⟩ ⟨▢⟩

⚿⚿ ▼▼▼ Econo Lodge M
(724) 627-5544. **$50-$60.** 350 Miller Ln. I-79, exit 14, just w. Ext corridors. **Pets:** Other species. Service with restrictions.
⟨SAVE⟩ ⟨S⟩ ⟨X⟩ ⟨▤⟩ ⟨▢⟩

▼▼ ▼▼ Super 8 Motel-Waynesburg M
(724) 627-8880. **$51-$80.** 100 Stanley Dr. I-79, exit 14, just w. Int corridors. **Pets:** Accepted.
⟨ASK⟩ ⟨S⟩ ⟨X⟩ ⟨▤⟩ ⟨▢⟩

WELLSBORO

⚿⚿ ▼▼ ▼▼ Canyon Motel M
(570) 724-1681. **$55-$89.** 18 East Ave. Just e on US 6 and SR 660. Ext/int corridors. **Pets:** $10 daily fee/room. Designated rooms, service with restrictions, supervision.
⟨SAVE⟩ ⟨S⟩ ⟨X⟩ ⟨⅙M⟩ ⟨▤⟩ ⟨▢⟩ ⟨≈⟩

⚿⚿ ▼▼ Colton Point Motel M
(570) 724-2155. **$45-$60, 7 days notice.** Jct SR 287, 13 mi w on US 6. Ext/int corridors. **Pets:** Other species. $5 daily fee/pet. No service, supervision.
⟨SAVE⟩ ⟨S⟩ ⟨X⟩ ⟨¶⟩ ⟨X⟩ ⟨AC⟩ ⟨☎⟩

WEST HAZLETON

⚿⚿ ▼▼▼▼ Comfort Inn West Hazleton M ☙
(570) 455-9300. **$89-$160.** 58 St, Rt 93. I-80, exit 145, 0.3 mi se; I-80, exit 256, 3.8 mi se. Int corridors. **Pets:** Other species. Service with restrictions, supervision.
⟨SAVE⟩ ⟨S⟩ ⟨X⟩ ⟨⊘⟩ ⟨▤⟩ ⟨▢⟩ ⟨¶⟩

⚿⚿ ▼▼▼▼ Forest Hill Inn M
(570) 459-2730. **$55, 7 days notice.** 3 Forest Hill Rd. I-81, exit 145, 0.3 mi se; I-80, exit 256, 3.8 mi se. Ext corridors. **Pets:** Accepted.
⟨SAVE⟩ ⟨S⟩ ⟨X⟩

WEST MIDDLESEX

▼▼▼▼ Radisson Hotel Sharon M
(724) 528-2501. **$85-$129.** Rt 18 & I-80. I-80, exit 4B (SR 18), just n. Int corridors. **Pets:** Accepted.
⟨ASK⟩ ⟨S⟩ ⟨X⟩ ⟨⊘⟩ ⟨✦⟩ ⟨▤⟩ ⟨▢⟩ ⟨¶⟩ ⟨≈⟩

WILKES BARRE

⚿⚿ ▼▼▼▼ Best Western Genetti Hotel & Conference Center H
(570) 823-6152. **$84-$89.** 77 E Market St. At Market and Washington sts. Int corridors. **Pets:** Other species. $10 daily fee/pet. Designated rooms, service with restrictions.
⟨SAVE⟩ ⟨S⟩ ⟨X⟩ ⟨▤⟩ ⟨▢⟩ ⟨¶⟩ ⟨≈⟩

⚿⚿ ▼▼ ▼▼ Days Inn M ☙
(570) 826-0111. **$53-$65, 14 days notice.** 760 Kidder St. I-81, exit 170B, then exit 1 (SR 309 S business), just w; I-76 (Pennsylvania Tpke), exit 105, exit 1 (SR 115 N). Int corridors. **Pets:** Other species. $5 daily fee/pet. Service with restrictions.
⟨SAVE⟩ ⟨S⟩ ⟨X⟩ ⟨✦⟩

▼▼▼▼ Hampton Inn Wilkes-Barre at Cross Creek Pointe M ☙
(570) 825-3838. **$85.** 1063 Hwy 315. I-81, exit 170B, 0.3 mi n. Int corridors. **Pets:** Other species. Designated rooms, service with restrictions, supervision.
⟨SAVE⟩ ⟨S⟩ ⟨X⟩ ⟨⅙M⟩ ⟨▢⟩

▼▼▼▼ Holiday Inn M
(570) 824-8901. **$86.** 880 Kidder St. I-81, exit 170B, then exit 1 off expwy, 0.5 mi w. Ext corridors. **Pets:** Other species. Service with restrictions, supervision.
⟨ASK⟩ ⟨S⟩ ⟨X⟩ ⟨⅙M⟩ ⟨✦⟩ ⟨▤⟩ ⟨▢⟩ ⟨¶⟩ ⟨≈⟩

⚿⚿ ▼▼ ▼▼ Red Roof Inn M ☙
(570) 829-6422. **$45-$57.** 1035 Hwy 315. I-81, exit 170B, at jct SR 115, 0.7 mi w, exit 1 onto SR 315. Ext corridors. **Pets:** Medium, other species. Service with restrictions, supervision.
⟨SAVE⟩ ⟨X⟩ ⟨▤⟩

WILLIAMSPORT

(AAA) ▼▼▼ Genetti Hotel & Suites H
(570) 326-6600. **$56-$86.** 200 W Fourth St. Downtown; at W Fourth and William sts. Int corridors. **Pets:** Other species. Service with restrictions.
[SAVE] [✕] [🛏] [🖥] [🍴] [🏊]

▼▼▼ Holiday Inn-Williamsport MI
(570) 326-1981. **$66-$130.** 1840 E Third St. I-180, exit 25 (Faxon St), just e on Third St eastbound, 1 mi w of Third St westbound. Ext corridors. **Pets:** Other species. Service with restrictions, supervision.
[ASK] [S♦] [✕] [🛏] [🖥] [🍴] [🏊]

▼▼▼ Radisson Hotel Williamsport H
(570) 327-8231. **$99-$169.** 100 Pine St. Downtown; jct US 220 and SR 15 S. Int corridors. **Pets:** Medium. Designated rooms, service with restrictions, supervision.
[ASK] [S♦] [✕] [🛏] [🖥] [🍴] [🏊]

WIND GAP

(AAA) ▼▼ Travel Inn of Wind Gap M
(610) 863-4146. **$50-$90, 3 days notice.** 499 E Moorestown Rd. SR 512, e of jct SR 33, exit Bath. Ext corridors. **Pets:** Dogs only. $5 daily fee/pet. Designated rooms, no service, supervision.
[SAVE] [S♦] [✕] [🛏]

WYOMISSING

▼▼▼ Clarion/Inn at Reading MI
(610) 372-7811. **$99-$149.** 1040 Park Rd. US 422, exit Papermill Rd, 0.5 mi s, then just s on Spring St to Park Rd. Int corridors. **Pets:** Small. $10 daily fee/room. Designated rooms, service with restrictions.
[SAVE] [S♦] [✕] [🖉] [🛏] [🖥] [🍴] [🏊]

▼▼ Econo Lodge M
(610) 378-5105. **$54, 14 days notice.** 635 Spring St. Just off US 422, exit Papermill Rd. Int corridors. **Pets:** Dogs only. $10 daily fee/pet. Designated rooms, service with restrictions, supervision.
[SAVE] [S♦] [✕] [🖉] [🛏] [🖥]

▼▼▼ Sheraton Reading Hotel H ❀
(610) 376-3811. **$129-$169.** 1741 W Papermill Rd. US 422, exit Papermill Rd; opposite Berkshire Mall. Int corridors. **Pets:** Medium. Service with restrictions.
[ASK] [S♦] [✕] [🖉] [🖋] [🛏] [🖥] [🍴] [🏊]

(AAA) ▼▼▼▼ Wellesley Inn & Suites M
(610) 374-1500. **$92-$122.** 910 Woodland Rd. US 422 W, exit Papermill Rd, just e. Int corridors. **Pets:** Small. Service with restrictions, supervision.
[SAVE] [S♦] [✕] [🖋] [🖉] [🖋] [🛏] [🖥]

WYSOX

▼▼▼▼ Comfort Inn M
(570) 265-5691. **$89-$150.** US 6. Center. Int corridors. **Pets:** Large, other species. $10 one-time fee/pet. Service with restrictions.
[SAVE] [S♦] [✕] [🖋] [🖉] [🖋] [🛏] [🖥] [🏊]

YORK

▼▼▼ Holiday Inn Holidome & Conference Center MI
(717) 846-9500. **$79-$134.** 2000 Loucks Rd. I-83, exit 21B northbound, 2.5 mi w on US 30, then just n; exit 22 southbound, 0.5 mi s on SR 181, 2.2 mi w on US 30, then just n. Int corridors. **Pets:** Other species. Service with restrictions, crate.
[ASK] [S♦] [✕] [🖉] [🖋] [🛏] [🖥] [🍴] [🏊]

(AAA) ▼▼▼▼ Holiday Inn York I-83 & Rt 30 MI
(717) 845-5671. **$86.** 334 Arsenal Rd. I-83, exit 21A, just e on US 30. Ext corridors. **Pets:** Accepted.
[SAVE] [✕] [🖉] [🖋] [🛏] [🖥] [🍴] [🏊]

(AAA) ▼▼ Red Roof Inn M
(717) 843-8181. **$44-$64.** 323 Arsenal Rd. I-83, exit 21A, just e on US 30. Ext corridors. **Pets:** Accepted.
[SAVE] [✕]

▼▼ Super 8 Motel M
(717) 852-8686. **$48-$68.** 40 Arsenal Rd. I-83, exit 21B northbound, 0.3 mi w on US 30; exit 21A southbound, 0.5 mi s on SR 181 to US 30. Int corridors. **Pets:** Other species. $5 daily fee/room. Designated rooms, service with restrictions, supervision.
[ASK] [S♦] [✕] [🛏]

CRANSTON

△△△ ▽▽▽ Days Inn M
(401) 942-4200. **$79-$109, 14 days notice.** 101 New London Ave. I-95, exit 14A on SR 2. Ext corridors. **Pets:** Designated rooms, supervision.
[SAVE] [S▫] [✕]

MIDDLETOWN

▽▽ The Bay Willows Inn M
(401) 847-8400. **$39-$169, 3 days notice.** 1225 Aquidneck Ave. SR 138A, at jct of SR 138. Ext corridors. **Pets:** Accepted.
[✕] [🔌]

△△△ ▽▽▽ Howard Johnson Inn-Newport M
(401) 849-2000. **$49-$219.** 351 W Main Rd (SR 114). SR 114, 0.3 mi s of jct SR 138. Int corridors. **Pets:** Other species. $5 daily fee/pet. Designated rooms, supervision.
[SAVE] [S▫] [✕] [🔌] [💻] [≈]

▽▽ SeaView Inn M
(401) 846-5000. **$59-$199, 7 days notice.** 240 Aquidneck Ave (SR 138A). Jct SR 138A and SR 214. Ext corridors. **Pets:** Other species. $25 deposit/pet, $10 daily fee/pet. Designated rooms, service with restrictions.
[✕] [🔌] [💻]

PROVIDENCE

▽▽▽▽ The Westin Providence H
(401) 598-8000. **Call for rates.** One W Exchange St. I-95, exit 22A; downtown. Int corridors. **Pets:** Small. $50 deposit/room, $50 one-time fee/room. Designated rooms, service with restrictions, crate.
[ASK] [✕] [♿M] [🔌] [🐾] [💻] [🍴] [≈]

SOUTH KINGSTOWN

▽▽▽ The Kings' Rose Bed & Breakfast Inn BB
(401) 783-5222. **$130-$160 (no credit cards), 7 days notice.** 1747 Mooresfield Rd (SR 138). I-95, exit 3A, 11 mi e on SR 138, 3.3 mi w of US 1. Int corridors. **Pets:** Service with restrictions, supervision.
[✕]

WARWICK

▽▽▽▽ Crowne Plaza Hotel H
(401) 732-6000. **$179-$239.** 801 Greenwich Ave. I-95, exit 12A southbound; exit 12 northbound, 0.3 mi e on SR 5. Int corridors. **Pets:** Medium, other species.
[ASK] [S▫] [✕] [♿M] [🔌] [🔌] [💻] [🍴] [≈]

▽▽▽▽ Holiday Inn Express Hotel & Suites M
(401) 736-5000. **$119-$159.** 901 Jefferson Blvd. I-95, exit 13A, 0.6 mi e. Int corridors. **Pets:** Other species. Service with restrictions, crate.
[ASK] [S▫] [✕] [♿M] [🔌] [🐾] [🔌] [💻] [≈]

△△△ ▽▽▽▽ MainStay Suites, Warwick M
(401) 732-6667. **$90-$170.** 268 Metro Center Blvd. I-95, exit 12A, 0.4 mi e on SR 113, 0.4 mi n on SR 5, then 0.4 mi e. Int corridors. **Pets:** Accepted.
[SAVE] [S▫] [✕] [♿M] [🔌] [🐾] [🔌] [💻]

△△△ ▽▽▽▽ Residence Inn by Marriott A
(401) 737-7100. **$143-$215.** 500 Kilvert St. I-95, exit 13, 0.4 mi n on Jefferson Blvd, then 0.5 mi w. Ext corridors. **Pets:** Accepted.
[SAVE] [S▫] [✕] [🔌] [🔌] [💻] [≈]

▽▽▽▽ Sheraton Providence Airport Hotel H
(401) 738-4000. **$105-$269.** 1850 Post Rd. I-95, exit 13, on US 1. Int corridors. **Pets:** Accepted.
[ASK] [S▫] [✕] [♿M] [🔌] [🐾] [🔌] [💻] [🍴] [≈]

WOONSOCKET

▽▽▽▽ Holiday Inn Express Hotel & Suites M
(401) 769-5000. **$90-$120.** 194 Fortin Dr. I-295, exit 9, 3.5 mi n via SR 146/99/122. Int corridors. **Pets:** Other species. $100 deposit/room, $10 one-time fee/pet. Designated rooms, service with restrictions, supervision.
[ASK] [S▫] [✕] [♿M] [🐾] [🔌] [💻] [≈]

CITY INDEX

AIKEN

Comfort Inn & Suites M
(803) 641-1100. **$55-$75, 14 days notice.** 3608 Richland Ave W. 2.3 mi w on US 1 and 78. Ext corridors. **Pets:** Other species. $6 daily fee/pet. Service with restrictions.

Days Inn-Downtown M
(803) 649-5524. **$42-$175, 14 days notice.** 1204 Richland Ave W. 0.5 mi w on US 1 and 78. Ext corridors. **Pets:** Small. $10 daily fee/pet. Service with restrictions, supervision.

Holiday Inn Express M
(803) 648-0999. **$75-$195, 30 days notice.** 155 Colony Pkwy. US 78 and 1, 2 mi s on SR 19 off Whiskey Rd/SR 19. Ext corridors. **Pets:** Medium, other species. $30 one-time fee/pet. Service with restrictions.

Ramada Ltd M
(803) 648-6821. **$45-$229, 30 days notice.** 1850 Richland Ave W. 1.8 mi w on US 1 and 78. Ext corridors. **Pets:** $10 one-time fee/pet. Service with restrictions.

Sleep Inn M
(803) 644-9900. **$49-$79.** 1002 Monterey Dr. I-20, exit 19, 6.2 mi s to Whiskey Rd, then 2.6 mi s to Shanon Ln. Int corridors. **Pets:** Other species. $25 one-time fee/room.

Town & Country Inn BB
(803) 642-0270. **$70, 3 days notice.** 2340 Sizemore Cir. From US 1 downtown, 4.5 mi s on SR 19, just w. Int corridors. **Pets:** Accepted.

ANDERSON

Days Inn M
(864) 375-0375. **$65-$89, 10 days notice.** 1007 Smith Mill Rd. I-85, exit 19A, at jct US 76, just se. Ext corridors. **Pets:** Accepted.

Holiday Inn Express M
(864) 231-0231. **$75-$95.** 103 Anderson Business Park. I-85, exit 27, just s on SR 81. Int corridors. **Pets:** Other species. Supervision.

La Quinta Inn M
(864) 225-3721. **$65-$85.** 3430 Clemson Blvd. I-85, exit 19A, 2.5 mi se on US 76. Ext corridors. **Pets:** Accepted.

Royal American Motor Inn M
(864) 226-7236. **$42.** 4515 Clemson Blvd. I-85, exit 19A, just se on US 76/Clemson Blvd. Ext corridors. **Pets:** Accepted.

BEAUFORT

Holiday Inn of Beaufort MI
(843) 524-2144. **$89.** 2001 Boundary St. 2.5 mi nw on US 21 at Lovejoy St. Ext corridors. **Pets:** Large, other species. $25 one-time fee/room. Service with restrictions.

CAMDEN

Colony Inn M
(803) 432-5508. **$55-$59.** 2020 W DeKalb St. 1 mi w on US 1 and 601. Ext/int corridors. **Pets:** Medium. $10 one-time fee/room. Service with restrictions, supervision.

Lord Camden Inn BB
(803) 713-9050. **$85-$110, 5 days notice.** 1502 Broad St. On US 521, 0.5 mi n of jct US 601/US 1/SR 34. Int corridors. **Pets:** Medium, other species. $10 daily fee/pet. Service with restrictions, supervision.

CAYCE

Ramada Limited Airport M
(803) 794-7500. **$62-$72.** 3020 Charleston Hwy. I-26, exit 115; I-77, exit 1, just s on US 321. Ext corridors. **Pets:** Accepted.

Riverside Inn MI
(803) 939-4688. **$60, 5 days notice.** 111 Knox Abbott Dr. 1 mi w of downton on SR 321. Ext corridors. **Pets:** Medium. $20 one-time fee/room. Service with restrictions, supervision.

CHARLESTON METROPOLITAN AREA

CHARLESTON

Holiday Inn-Riverview
(843) 556-7100. **$85-$115, 14 days notice.** 301 Savannah Hwy. 1.8 mi w on US 17, s of bridge. Int corridors. **Pets:** Accepted.

Indigo Inn
(843) 577-5900. **$99-$235.** 1 Maiden Ln. Corner of Meeting and Pinckney sts. Ext corridors. **Pets:** Medium. $20 daily fee/pet. Designated rooms, service with restrictions.

Radisson Charleston
(843) 723-3000. **$89.** 170 Lockwood Dr. Just ne of Ashley River Bridge, on US 17. Int corridors. **Pets:** Medium. $50 deposit/room. Service with restrictions.

Town & Country Inn & Conference Center
(843) 571-1000. **$69-$129, 7 days notice.** 2008 Savannah Hwy. On US 17 S, 3.5 mi nw of Ashley River Bridge; I-526 W (end), US 17 N, just se. Ext corridors. **Pets:** Other species. $50 deposit/room. Service with restrictions.

MOUNT PLEASANT

Comfort Inn East
(843) 884-5853. **$69-$139.** 310 Hwy 17 Bypass. Just e of Cooper River Bridge. Ext corridors. **Pets:** Medium, dogs only. $10 one-time fee/pet. Service with restrictions, supervision.

Red Roof Inn #242
(843) 884-1411. **$44-$89.** 301 Johnnie Dodds Blvd. Just n of Cooper River Bridge on US 17 N. Ext corridors. **Pets:** Small. Service with restrictions, supervision.

Sleep Inn Mt Pleasant
(843) 856-5000. **$49-$149.** 299 Wingo Way, Hwy 17 Bypass. At Mt Pleasant exit, just w of Cooper River Bridge. Int corridors. **Pets:** Accepted.

NORTH CHARLESTON

Charleston Holiday Inn Airport
(843) 744-1621. **$59-$79.** 6099 Fain St. I-26, exit 211A (Aviation Ave), just sw. Ext corridors. **Pets:** Other species. $25 one-time fee/room. Designated rooms, service with restrictions, supervision.

Charleston Super 8 Motel
(843) 572-2228. **$60-$95, 7 days notice.** 2311 Ashley-Phosphate Rd. I-26, exit 209, just ne. Ext corridors. **Pets:** Small. $5 daily fee/pet. Service with restrictions, crate.

Comfort Inn Coliseum
(843) 554-6485. **$45-$109.** 5055 N Arco Ln. I-26, exit 213 (Montague Ave). Ext corridors. **Pets:** Small, dogs only. $20 one-time fee/pet. Designated rooms, service with restrictions, supervision.

La Quinta Inn
(843) 797-8181. **$61-$81.** 2499 La Quinta Ln. I-26, exit 209 (Ashley Phosphate Rd), just sw. Ext corridors. **Pets:** Accepted.

MainStay Suites
(843) 740-3440. **$80-$96.** 5045 N Arco Ln. I-26, exit 213A, just nw. Int corridors. **Pets:** Medium, other species. $50 deposit/pet, $5 daily fee/pet. Service with restrictions, supervision.

Red Roof Inn
(843) 572-9100. **$44-$64.** 7480 Northwoods Blvd. I-26, exit 209, just nw. Ext corridors. **Pets:** Accepted.

Sleep Inn Charleston North
(843) 572-8400. **$65-$85.** 7435 Northside Dr. I-26, exit 209 (Ashley Phosphate Rd), just sw. Int corridors. **Pets:** Other species. $10 one-time fee/room. Designated rooms, no service, supervision.

ST. STEPHEN

Econo Lodge
(843) 567-7397. **$61-$66.** 3986 Byrnes Dr. Center. Int corridors. **Pets:** Accepted.

SUMMERVILLE

Holiday Inn Express-Charleston/Summerville
(843) 875-3300. **$82-$93.** 120 Holiday Inn Dr. I-26, exit 199A, at jct US 17 Alt. Int corridors. **Pets:** Accepted.

CHERAW

Days Inn–Cheraw M
(843) 537-5554. **$45-$95, 3 days notice.** 820 Market St. Jct SR 9 and US 52 and 1. Ext corridors. **Pets:** Other species. $5 daily fee/pet. Designated rooms, service with restrictions, supervision.

Jameson Inn M
(843) 537-5625. **$55-$70.** 885 Chesterfield Hwy. On SR 9, 1.5 mi w of jct with US 1 and 52. Ext corridors. **Pets:** Accepted.

CLINTON

Comfort Inn M
(864) 833-5558. **$65-$90.** 12785 Hwy 56 N. I-26, exit 52, just e, then n. Ext corridors. **Pets:** Small. $10 daily fee/room. Designated rooms, service with restrictions.

Ramada Inn M
(864) 833-4900. **$63-$95, 5 days notice.** I-26, exit 52, just e on SR 56. Ext corridors. **Pets:** Accepted.

COLUMBIA

AmeriSuites M
(803) 736-6666. **$71.** 7525 Two Notch Rd. I-20, exit 74 (Two Notch Rd), 0.3 mi n; I-77, exit 17, just s. Int corridors. **Pets:** Accepted.

Baymont Inn & Suites Columbia Central/St. Andrews M
(803) 798-3222. **$54-$59.** 911 Bush River Rd. I-26, exit 108 (Bush River Rd). Int corridors. **Pets:** Accepted.

Baymont Inn & Suites Columbia NE/Ft. Jackson Area M
(803) 736-6400. **$54-$59.** 1538 Horseshoe Dr. I-20, exit 74 (Two Notch Rd), just n; I-77, exit 17 (Two Notch Rd), just s. Int corridors. **Pets:** Small, other species. Service with restrictions, supervision.

Days Inn M
(803) 754-4408. **$40-$52.** 133 Plumbers Rd. I-20, exit 71. Ext corridors. **Pets:** Large. $8 daily fee/pet. Service with restrictions.

Holiday Inn-Northeast M
(803) 736-3000. **$109-$119.** 7510 Two Notch Rd. I-20, exit 74 (Two Notch Rd), on US 1. Int corridors. **Pets:** Medium, other species. $25 one-time fee/room. Designated rooms, service with restrictions.

La Quinta Inn M
(803) 798-9590. **$45-$65.** 1335 Garner Ln. Jct I-20 and US 176, exit 65. Ext corridors. **Pets:** Accepted.

Microtel Inn M
(803) 736-3237. **$53.** 1520 Barbara Dr. I-20, exit 74, just n from I-77, then just s. Int corridors. **Pets:** $7 one-time fee/pet. Service with restrictions, supervision.

Ramada Plaza Hotel M
(803) 736-5600. **$75.** 8105 Two Notch Rd. I-77, exit 17 (Two Notch Rd), just n; I-20, exit 74 (Two Notch Rd), 0.5 mi n. Int corridors. **Pets:** Other species. Service with restrictions.

Red Roof Inn-West M
(803) 798-9220. **$39-$51.** 10 Berryhill Rd. I-26, exit 106A (St Andrews) westbound; exit 106 (St Andrews) eastbound. Ext corridors. **Pets:** Accepted.

Residence Inn by Marriott M
(803) 779-7000. **$79-$119.** 150 Stoneridge Dr. I-126, exit Greystone Blvd, 0.6 mi ne. Ext corridors. **Pets:** Other species. $100 deposit/room, $10 daily fee/room. Service with restrictions, crate.

Sheraton Hotel & Conference Center H
(803) 731-0300. **$145, 3 days notice.** 2100 Bush River Rd. I-20, exit 63 (Bush River Rd). Int corridors. **Pets:** Accepted.

Super 8 M
(803) 772-7275. **$120.** 773 St Andrews Rd. US 26, exit 106B, just s. Ext corridors. **Pets:** Small. $15 deposit/pet, $10 daily fee/pet. Service with restrictions, supervision.

DUNCAN

Comfort Inn Duncan M
(864) 433-1333. **$50-$62, 7 days notice.** 1391 E Main St. I-85, exit 63, just w at jct SR 290. Ext corridors. **Pets:** Medium. $15 one-time fee/room. Service with restrictions, supervision.

FLORENCE

Holiday Inn Express Civic Center M
(843) 664-2400. **$71-$79, 7 days notice.** 150 Dunbarton Dr. I-95, exit 160A (Business Rt 20), 0.3 mi e. Ext corridors. **Pets:** Large, other species. Service with restrictions, supervision.

Holiday Inn Hotel & Suites M
(843) 665-4555. **$69-$99.** 1819 W Lucas St. I-95, exit 164, just e on US 52. Ext corridors. **Pets:** Other species.

Howard Johnson Express Inn & Suites M
(843) 664-9494. **$65-$72.** 3821 Bancroft Rd. I-95, exit 157, 0.4 mi e on US 76. Ext corridors. **Pets:** Accepted.

Motel 6 M
(843) 667-6100. **$36-$46.** 1834 W Lucas St. I-95, exit 164, just e. Ext corridors. **Pets:** Accepted.

Ramada Inn MI
(843) 669-4241. **$60-$75.** 2038 W Lucas St. I-95, exit 164, just w on US 52. Ext/int corridors. **Pets:** Small. Designated rooms, supervision.

Red Roof Inn M
(843) 678-9000. **$40-$54.** 2690 David McLeod Blvd. I-95, exit 160A, 0.4 mi e I-20 business on service road. Ext corridors. **Pets:** Medium. No service, supervision.

Thunderbird Inn MI
(843) 669-1611. **$44-$49.** 2004 W Lucas. I-95, exit 164, just w. Ext corridors. **Pets:** Accepted.

GAFFNEY

Comfort Inn M
(864) 487-4200. **$69-$99.** 143 Corona Dr. I-85, exit 92, just w of SR 11. Ext corridors. **Pets:** Large, other species. $10 daily fee/room. Service with restrictions, supervision.

Jameson Inn M
(864) 489-0240. **$55-$70.** 101 Stuard St. I-85, exit 92, just e at jct SR 11. Ext corridors. **Pets:** Accepted.

Sleep Inn M
(864) 487-5337. **$50-$145.** 834 Winslow Ave. I-85, exit 90, just e on frontage road. Int corridors. **Pets:** Accepted.

GREENVILLE

AmeriSuites Greenville M
(864) 232-3000. **$80.** 40 W Orchard Park Dr. I-385, exit 39, just e on Haywood Rd, then n. Int corridors. **Pets:** Small. $25 one-time fee/room. Designated rooms, service with restrictions.

Crowne Plaza-Greenville H
(864) 297-6300. **$119-$139.** 851 Congaree Rd. I-385, exit 37, just w, then n. Int corridors. **Pets:** Accepted.

Days Inn M
(864) 288-6221. **$50-$125, 5 days notice.** 831 Congaree Rd. I-385, exit 37, just w, then n. Int corridors. **Pets:** Medium, other species. $15 one-time fee/pet.

GuestHouse International Suites Plus M
(864) 297-0099. **$80-$90, 3 days notice.** 48 McPrice Ct. I-385, exit 39, e on Haywood Rd, then s. Ext corridors. **Pets:** Small. $25 daily fee/room. Service with restrictions, supervision.

Hilton Greenville and Towers H
(864) 232-4747. **$89-$199.** 45 W Orchard Park Dr. I-385, exit 39, just e, then n. Int corridors. **Pets:** Accepted.

Holiday Inn Augusta Rd/I-85 MI
(864) 277-8921. **$99-$109.** 4295 Augusta Rd. I-85, exit 46, just s. Int corridors. **Pets:** Medium. $30 one-time fee/room. Service with restrictions, crate.

La Quinta Inn M
(864) 297-3500. **$55-$75.** 31 Old Country Rd. I-85, exit 51, just n on SR 146. Ext corridors. **Pets:** Accepted.

La Quinta Inns & Suites-Greenville Haywood M
(864) 233-8018. **$65-$95.** 65 W Orchard Park Dr. I-385, exit 39, just e, then n. Int corridors. **Pets:** Accepted.

Microtel Inn Greenville M
(864) 297-7866. **$50-$65.** 20 Interstate Ct. I-85, exit 54, just e, then s. Int corridors. **Pets:** Accepted.

The Phoenix Greenville's Inn MI
(864) 233-4651. **$95-$145.** 246 N Pleasantburg Dr. I-385, exit 40B, 0.6 mi w, on south side. Ext corridors. **Pets:** Other species. $10 deposit/room. Service with restrictions, supervision.

Red Roof Inn M
(864) 297-4458. **$41-$53.** 2801 Laurens Rd. I-85, exit 48A, just s on frontage road to dead end. Ext corridors. **Pets:** Small. Service with restrictions, supervision.

Sleep Inn M
(864) 240-2006. **$65-$95, 7 days notice.** 231 N Pleasantburg Dr. I-385, exit 40B, 0.6 mi w, on north side. Int corridors. **Pets:** Small. $20 one-time fee/pet. Designated rooms, service with restrictions, supervision.

GREER

▼▼▼▼ Comfort Suites–Greenville/Greer M
(864) 213-9331. **$69-$79, 7 days notice.** 2681 Dry Pocket Rd. I-85, exit 54, just nw on Pelham Rd, 0.3 mi ne on the Parkway to Parkway Rd, then 0.3 mi e. Int corridors. **Pets:** Other species. $15 one-time fee/room. Service with restrictions, supervision.

SAVE ✕ 🐾 💺 🔋 🖥 ➿

▲▲▲ ▼▼▼▼ MainStay Suites-Greenville M
(864) 987-5566. **$90.** 2671 Dry Pocket Rd. I-85, exit 54, 0.4 mi on The Parkway, just e on Parkway Rd. Int corridors. **Pets:** Small. $10 daily fee/pet. Service with restrictions, supervision.

SAVE 🆘 ✕ 🐾 💺 🔋 🖥 ➿

HILTON HEAD ISLAND

▲▲▲ ▼▼▼ Comfort Inn & Suites MI
(843) 842-6662. **$59-$179.** 2 Tanglewood Dr. Via US 278 E to Sea Pines Cir, 0.3 mi n via Pope Ave and S Forest Beach Dr. Int corridors. **Pets:** Small, other species. $10 daily fee/pet, $25 one-time fee/room. Service with restrictions, supervision.

SAVE 🆘 ✕ 🐾 🔋 🖥 🍴 🏊

▼▼▼▼ Quality Inn & Suites of Hilton Head Island M
(843) 681-3655. **$59-$79, 3 days notice.** 200 Museum St. On US 278 business, just e of Island Bridge on north side of road. Ext corridors. **Pets:** Small, dogs only. $25 one-time fee/room. Service with restrictions, supervision.

SAVE 🆘 ✕ 🐾 🔋 🖥 ➿

▲▲▲ ▼▼▼ Red Roof Inn-Hilton Head M
(843) 686-6808. **$39-$79.** 5 Regency Pkwy. On US 278; between Shipyard Plantation and Palmetto Dunes. Ext corridors. **Pets:** Medium. No service.

SAVE ✕ 🐾 🔋 ➿

IRMO

▲▲▲ ▼▼▼▼ AmeriSuites Columbia/I-26 M
(803) 407-1560. **$89.** 1130 Kinley Rd. I-26, exit 102B. Int corridors. **Pets:** Very small, dogs only. $25 one-time fee/room. Designated rooms, service with restrictions, supervision.

SAVE 🆘 ♿ 🐾 💺 🔋 🖥 ➿

▲▲▲ ▼▼▼▼ Wellesley Inn & Suites M
(803) 781-8590. **$71.** 1170 Kinley Rd. I-26, exit 102B. Int corridors. **Pets:** Accepted.

SAVE 🆘 ✕ ♿ 🐾 💺 🔋 🖥 ➿

LANDRUM

▼▼▼ The Red Horse Inn C ❀
(864) 895-4968. **$95-$165, 10 days notice.** 310 N Campbell Rd. 1 mi w on SR 11 from jct SR 14, 1 mi s on Tugaloo Rd to N Campbell Rd. Ext corridors. **Pets:** $50 deposit/pet, $20 one-time fee/pet. Designated rooms, supervision.

ASK 🆘 ✕ 🔋 🖥 🅿

LUGOFF

▼▼▼▼ Ramada Limited M
(803) 438-1807. **$56-$85, 14 days notice.** 542 Hwy 601 S. I-20, exit 92, just n. Ext corridors. **Pets:** Very small, cats only. $5 one-time fee/room. Service with restrictions, supervision.

✕ 🔋 ➿

MANNING

▲▲▲ ▼▼ Comfort Inn M ❀
(803) 473-7550. **$54-$89, 3 days notice.** Hwy 261 & I-95. I-95, exit 119 (SR 261). Ext corridors. **Pets:** Other species. Service with restrictions.

SAVE 🆘 ✕ 🐾 🔋 🖥 ➿

▲▲▲ ▼▼▼▼ Ramada Limited M
(803) 473-5135. **$46-$80.** 2816 Paxville Hwy. I-95, exit 119, just e. Ext corridors. **Pets:** Other species. Service with restrictions.

SAVE 🆘 ✕ 🐾 🔋 🖥

NEWBERRY

▲▲▲ ▼▼▼ Best Western Newberry Inn M
(803) 276-5850. **$52-$60.** 11701 S Carolina Hwy 34. I-26, exit 74, jct of SR 34. Ext corridors. **Pets:** Small. $5 daily fee/pet. Service with restrictions, supervision.

SAVE 🆘 ✕ 🔋 ➿

ORANGEBURG

▼▼ ▼▼ Jameson Inn Orangeburg M
(803) 534-1611. **$55-$70.** 2350 Chestnut St NE. At jct of SR 301 and 178, 2 mi w. Ext corridors. **Pets:** Accepted.

✕ 🔋 🖥 ➿

▲▲▲ ▼▼ ▼▼ Orangeburg Days Inn M
(803) 531-2590. **$65-$125.** 3691 St Matthews Rd. I-26, exit 145A, just s. Ext corridors. **Pets:** Other species. $7 daily fee/pet. No service, crate.

SAVE 🆘 ✕ 🔋 🖥 ➿

▲▲▲ ▼▼▼▼ Quality Inn & Suites MI
(803) 531-4600. **$55-$100.** 1415 John C Calhoun Dr. 0.8 mi w on US 301 and 601. Ext corridors. **Pets:** $10 one-time fee/pet. Service with restrictions, supervision.

SAVE 🆘 ✕ ♿ 🐾 🔋 🖥 🍴 ➿

POINT SOUTH

▼▼▼▼ Holiday Inn Express Point South/Yemassee M
(843) 726-9400. **$69-$79, 10 days notice.** 40 Frampton Dr. I-95, exit 33, just ne on US 17. Int corridors. **Pets:** $10 one-time fee/room. Service with restrictions, supervision.

ASK 🆘 ✕ ♿ 💺 🔋 🖥 ➿

RIDGELAND

▼▼▼▼ Comfort Inn M
(843) 726-2121. **$60-$85.** Hwy 336 and I-95. I-95, exit 21, just nw. Ext/int corridors. **Pets:** Accepted.

SAVE 🆘 ✕ 🐾 🔋 🖥 ➿

▼▼▼ **Ramada Limited Ridgeland** **M**
(843) 717-9595. **$49-$99, 3 days notice.** Hwy 336 & I-95.
I-95, exit 21, just nw. Ext corridors. **Pets:** $10 daily fee/pet.
Service with restrictions, supervision.

(ASK) (S🐾) (✕) (▣) (🏊)

ROCK HILL

(AAA) ▼▼▼▼ **Best Western Inn** **M**
(803) 329-1330. **$60-$90.** 1106 N Anderson Rd. I-77, exit
82B, 0.6 mi w on US 21 to US 21 Bypass. Int corridors.
Pets: Other species. $10 daily fee/room. Service with
restrictions.

(SAVE) (S🐾) (✕) (🔌) (🏊)

▼▼▼▼ **The Book & the Spindle** **BB**
(803) 328-1913. **$70-$85, 7 days notice.** 626 Oakland Ave.
I-77, exit 82B, 3.1 mi s on US 21; before Aiken. Int corridors. **Pets:** Accepted.

(✕) (🔌) (▣) (🚭)

▼▼▼▼ **Holiday Inn** **MI**
(803) 329-1122. **$65.** 2640 N Cherry Rd. I-77, exit 82A, just
e. Int corridors. **Pets:** Accepted.

(ASK) (S🐾) (✕) (♿) (🔌) (▣) (🍴) (🏊)

SANTEE

(AAA) ▼▼▼▼ **Comfort Inn** **M**
(803) 854-3221. **$45-$125.** 249 Britain St. I-95, exit 98 (SR
6). Ext corridors. **Pets:** Medium. $10 one-time fee/room. No
service, supervision.

(SAVE) (S🐾) (✕) (🐾) (♿) (🔌) (▣) (🏊)

▼▼ **Days Inn** **M**
(803) 854-2175. **$43-$50.** 9074 Old Hwy 6. I-95, exit 98
(SR 6). Ext corridors. **Pets:** Other species. $6 daily fee/pet.
Service with restrictions.

(SAVE) (S🐾) (✕) (🐾) (🔌) (▣) (🏊)

▼▼▼ **Hampton Inn** **M**
(803) 854-2444. **$90.** 9060 Old Hwy 6. I-95, exit 98, just sw.
Int corridors. **Pets:** Service with restrictions, supervision.

(SAVE) (S🐾) (✕) (🔌) (▣) (🏊)

(AAA) ▼▼▼▼ **Ramada Inn** **MI**
(803) 854-2191. **$68.** 123 Mall Dr. I-95, exit 98, just e. Ext
corridors. **Pets:** Accepted.

(SAVE) (S🐾) (✕) (▣) (🍴) (🏊)

▼▼ **Super 8 Motel** **M**
(803) 854-3456. **$38-$43.** 9125 Old Hwy 6. I-95, exit 98, 0.3
mi e on SR 6. Ext corridors. **Pets:** Accepted.

(ASK) (S🐾) (✕) (🔌) (🏊)

SIMPSONVILLE

▼▼▼ **Jameson Inn** **M**
(864) 963-7701. **$55-$70.** 45 Ray E Talley Ct. I-385, exit 27,
0.4 mi s, then just e. Ext corridors. **Pets:** Accepted.

(✕) (🔌) (▣) (🏊)

SPARTANBURG

▼▼▼▼ **Hampton Inn & Suites**
Greenville/Duncan **M**
(864) 486-8100. **$75-$105.** 108 Spartangreen Blvd. I-85,
exit 63, just e. **Pets:** Small, other species. $50 deposit/
room. Designated rooms, service with restrictions, supervision.

(SAVE) (S🐾) (✕) (🔌) (▣) (🏊)

(AAA) ▼▼▼ **The Quality Hotel & Conference**
Center **MI**
(864) 503-0780. **$76-$145, 14 days notice.** 7136 Asheville
Hwy. I-85 business route, exit 4 (US 56 Hearon Cir). Int
corridors. **Pets:** Accepted.

(SAVE) (S🐾) (✕) (🔌) (▣) (🍴) (🏊)

(AAA) ▼▼▼▼ **Ramada Inn** **MI** 🐾
(864) 576-5220. **$59.** 200 International Dr. I-85, exit 2C, just
s on frontage road. Ext/int corridors. **Pets:** Small. $25
deposit/pet, $10 daily fee/pet. Designated rooms, service
with restrictions, supervision.

(SAVE) (S🐾) (✕) (🐾) (🔌) (▣) (🍴) (🏊)

ST. GEORGE

(AAA) ▼▼▼ **Best Western-St. George** **M**
(843) 563-2277. **$56-$66, 5 days notice.** 104 Interstate Dr.
I-95, exit 77 (US 78), just w. Ext corridors. **Pets:** Accepted.

(SAVE) (S🐾) (✕) (🏊)

(AAA) ▼▼▼ **Comfort Inn** **M**
(843) 563-4180. **$65.** 139 Motel Dr. I-95, exit 77 (US 78),
just w. Ext corridors. **Pets:** Medium, other species. $20
one-time fee/room. Service with restrictions, supervision.

(SAVE) (S🐾) (✕) (▣) (🏊)

▼▼▼▼ **Holiday Inn-St George** **MI** 🐾
(843) 563-4581. **$49-$79.** 6014 W Jim Bilton Blvd. I-95, exit
77, just e on US 78. Ext corridors. **Pets:** Service with
restrictions.

(ASK) (S🐾) (✕) (♿) (▣) (🍴) (🏊)

(AAA) ▼▼▼ **St. George Economy Motel** **M**
(843) 563-2360. **$35-$55.** 125 Motel Dr. I-95, exit 77, on US
78. Ext corridors. **Pets:** Small. Designated rooms, service
with restrictions, supervision.

(SAVE) (S🐾) (✕) (🏊)

SUMTER

▼▼▼▼ **Magnolia House** **BB** 🐾
(803) 775-6694. **$85-$105.** 230 Church St. US 521/378 (N
Washington St), w on Calhoun, then right. Int corridors.
Pets: Other species. Designated rooms, supervision.

(✕)

(AAA) ▼▼▼▼ **Ramada Inn** **MI**
(803) 775-2323. **$69-$89, 3 days notice.** 226 N Washington St. 0.5 mi n on US 76 and 521 business route. Ext
corridors. **Pets:** Medium. $50 deposit/room. Designated
rooms, service with restrictions.

(SAVE) (S🐾) (✕) (🐾) (🔌) (▣) (🍴) (🏊)

THE GRAND STRAND AREA

GEORGETOWN

Clarion Carolinian Inn M
(843) 546-5191. **$59-$95.** 706 Church St. 0.5 mi ne on US 17. Ext corridors. **Pets:** Accepted.

MYRTLE BEACH

El Dorado Motel M
(843) 626-3559. **$26-$61, 21 days notice.** 2800 S Ocean Blvd. 28th Ave S and S Ocean Blvd. Ext corridors. **Pets:** Accepted.

La Quinta Inn & Suites M
(843) 916-8801. **$65-$155.** 1561 21st Ave N. Across from Broadway at the Beach on 21st Ave N, w of US 17 business route, just e of US 17 Bypass. Int corridors. **Pets:** Small. Service with restrictions, supervision.

Mariner M ❖
(843) 449-5281. **$39-$99.** 7003 N Ocean Blvd. 71st Ave N and N Ocean Blvd. Ext corridors. **Pets:** Dogs only. $100 deposit/room, $9 daily fee/pet. Service with restrictions.

Red Roof Inn & Suites M
(843) 626-4444. **$34-$99.** 2801 S Kings Hwy. US 17 business and 28th Ave S. Int corridors. **Pets:** Accepted.

St. John's Inn M
(843) 449-5251. **$35-$118, 7 days notice.** 6803 N Ocean Blvd. 68th Ave N and N Ocean Blvd. Ext corridors. **Pets:** Medium. $50 deposit/pet, $10 daily fee/pet. Service with restrictions, crate.

The Sea Mist Resort X
(843) 448-1551. **$33-$173, 7 days notice.** 1200 S Ocean Blvd. 12th Ave S and S Ocean Blvd. Ext/int corridors. **Pets:** Accepted.

Staybridge Suites Myrtle Beach-Fantasy Harbour M ❖
(843) 903-4000. **$58-$193, 14 days notice.** 3163 Outlet Blvd. 1 mi w on US 501; between Outlet Mall and Fantasy Harbour. Int corridors. **Pets:** Large, other species. $75 one-time fee/room. Service with restrictions.

❖ END AREA ❖

TURBEVILLE

Days Inn M
(843) 659-8060. **$42, 30 days notice.** Hwy 378. I-95, exit 135, just ne. Ext corridors. **Pets:** Accepted.

WALTERBORO

Best Western of Walterboro M
(843) 538-3600. **$45-$75, 7 days notice.** 1428 Sniders Hwy. I-95, exit 53, just ne on SR 63/US 17 Alt. Ext corridors. **Pets:** Small. $5 daily fee/pet. Designated rooms, service with restrictions, supervision.

Econo Lodge M
(843) 538-3830. **$40-$85.** 1145 Sniders Hwy. I-95, exit 53, 0.3 mi se on SR 63/US 17 Alt. Ext corridors. **Pets:** Accepted.

Holiday Inn M
(843) 538-5473. **$49-$79.** 1286 Snider's Hwy. I-95, exit 53 (SR 63). Ext corridors. **Pets:** Medium, other species. $10 one-time fee/room. Service with restrictions, supervision.

Rice Planters Inn M
(843) 538-8964. **$31-$35.** I-95 & SR 63. I-95, exit 53 (SR 63). Ext corridors. **Pets:** Very small. Service with restrictions, supervision.

Super 8 Motel M
(843) 538-5383. **$41-$55.** 1972 Bells Hwy. I-95, exit 57 (SR 64). Ext corridors. **Pets:** Accepted.

Thunderbird Inn M
(843) 538-2503. **$35-$40, 3 days notice.** I-95, exit 53 (SR 63). Ext corridors. **Pets:** Accepted.

WINNSBORO

Days Inn M
(803) 635-1447. **$45-$54, 8 days notice.** 1894 US Hwy 321 Bypass. At jct SR 213/34 and US 321 business/321. Ext corridors. **Pets:** Small. $5.35 daily fee/pet. Designated rooms, service with restrictions, supervision.

CITY INDEX

ABERDEEN

▼▼ Aberdeen East Super 8 Motel M
(605) 229-5005. **$50-$67, 14 days notice.** 2405 6th Ave SE. 1.8 mi e on US 12. Int corridors. **Pets:** Medium. $6 one-time fee/pet. Designated rooms, service with restrictions, supervision.
(ASK) (S/D) (X) (&M) (C/) (B)

▼▼ Aberdeen North Super 8 Motel M
(605) 226-2288. **$44-$54, 14 days notice.** 770 NW Hwy 281. 1.5 mi nw on US 281. Int corridors. **Pets:** Medium. $6 one-time fee/pet. Designated rooms, service with restrictions, supervision.
(ASK) (S/D) (X)

▼▼ Aberdeen West Super 8 Motel M
(605) 225-1711. **$44-$54, 14 days notice.** 714 S Hwy 281. Jct US 12 and 281. Int corridors. **Pets:** Medium. $6 one-time fee/pet. Designated rooms, service with restrictions, supervision.
(ASK) (S/D) (X) (B)

▼▼▼ AmericInn Motel & Suites M
(605) 225-4565. **$65.** 310 Centennial St. 2.2 mi e on US 12, then just n. Int corridors. **Pets:** Accepted.
(ASK) (S/D) (X) (&M) (C/) (B) (D) (Y) (≈)

▼▼▼ Best Western Ramkota Hotel M
(605) 229-4040. **$76.** 1400 8th Ave NW. 1.5 mi nw on US 281. Ext/int corridors. **Pets:** Accepted.
(SAVE) (S/D) (X) (&M) (∅) (B) (D) (Y) (≈)

◆◆◆ ▼▼▼ Comfort Inn M
(605) 226-0097. **$71-$159.** 2923 6th Ave SE. 2 mi e on US 12. Int corridors. **Pets:** Other species. $30 deposit/pet. Service with restrictions, crate.
(SAVE) (S/D) (X) (B) (D) (≈)

◆◆◆ ▼▼▼ Ramada Inn M
(605) 225-3600. **$80.** 2727 6th Ave SE. 2 mi e on US 12. Ext/int corridors. **Pets:** Accepted.
(SAVE) (S/D) (X) (D) (Y) (≈)

▼▼ The White House Inn M
(605) 225-5000. **$44-$50.** 500 6th Ave SW. 0.5 mi w on US 12 and 281. Int corridors. **Pets:** Other species. $5 daily fee/room. Designated rooms, service with restrictions.
(ASK) (S/D) (X) (C/) (B) (D)

BADLANDS NATIONAL PARK

▼ Cedar Pass Lodge C
(605) 433-5460. **Call for rates.** 1 Cedar St. I-90, exit 131, 8 mi s on SR 240; at visitor's center. Ext corridors. **Pets:** Accepted.
(X) (Y) (W) (Z)

BERESFORD

▼▼ Super 8 Motel M
(605) 763-2001. **$50-$65.** 1410 W Cedar. I-29, exit 47, just e. Int corridors. **Pets:** Other species. $25 deposit/room. Service with restrictions, supervision.
(ASK) (S/D) (X) (B) (D) (≈)

BLACK HILLS METROPOLITAN AREA

BELLE FOURCHE

⛟ Ace Motel M
(605) 892-2612. **$28-$48.** 109 6th Ave. 0.5 mi n via US 85, just e, just s of US 212 Bypass. Ext corridors. **Pets:** $4 one-time fee/room. Designated rooms, service with restrictions, supervision.
⊠ 🔧

⛟⛟ Lariat Motel M
(605) 892-2601. **$30-$40.** 1033 Elkhorn. 0.8 mi e of US 85 on Business 212 (State St). Ext corridors. **Pets:** Other species. $3 one-time fee/pet. Service with restrictions, crate.
SAVE 🔓 ⊠ 🔧

BLACK HAWK

⛟⛟⛟ Black Hawk Super 8 M
(605) 787-4844. **$65-$93.** 7900 Stagestop Rd. I-90, exit 48, just s. Int corridors. **Pets:** Small. $5 daily fee/pet. Designated rooms, service with restrictions, supervision.
ASK 🔓 ⊠ 🔧 💻 ➜

CUSTER

⛟⛟ American Presidents Cabins, Campgrounds & Resort C
(605) 673-3373. **$45-$89, 3 days notice.** Hwy 16 A. 1 mi e on US Alt 16. Ext corridors. **Pets:** Accepted.
SAVE 🔓 ⊠ 🔧 ➜ 🍴

⛟⛟⛟⛟ Bavarian Inn Motel MI
(605) 673-2802. **$39-$108, 3 days notice.** 1000 N 5th St. 1 mi n on US 16 and 385. Ext/int corridors. **Pets:** Accepted.
SAVE 🔓 ⊠ 🔧 💻 🍴 ➜ ⊠

⛟⛟ Chief Motel M
(605) 673-2318. **$39-$77.** 120 Mt Rushmore Rd. Just w on US 16. Ext corridors. **Pets:** Small, dogs only. $10 one-time fee/pet. Service with restrictions, supervision.
SAVE ⊠ 🔧 ➜

⛟⛟ The Roost Resort C ❀
(605) 673-2326. **$46-$72, 10 days notice.** US 16 A. 2 mi e on US Alt 16. Ext corridors. **Pets:** $7 daily fee/pet. Service with restrictions, crate.
SAVE 🔓 ⊠ 🔧 💻 🍴

DEADWOOD

⛟⛟ Budget Host Jackpot Inn M
(605) 578-7791. **$29-$70.** US Hwy 385. 0.3 mi s of jct US 385 and 85. Int corridors. **Pets:** Small, dogs only. $5 daily fee/pet. Service with restrictions, supervision.
SAVE 🔓 ⊠ ➜

⛟⛟⛟⛟ Days Inn at Deadwood Gulch Resort MI ❀
(605) 578-1294. **$45-$149.** 12 Timm Ln. 0.7 mi s on US 85 S. Ext/int corridors. **Pets:** Dogs only. $10 daily fee/pet. Designated rooms, crate.
SAVE 🔓 ⊠ 🔧 💻 🍴 ➜ ⊠

HILL CITY

⛟⛟ ⛟⛟⛟⛟ Best Western Golden Spike Inn MI
(605) 574-2577. **$55-$133.** 106 Main St. Just n on US 16 and 385. Ext/int corridors. **Pets:** Accepted.
SAVE 🔓 ⊠ 🔧 💻 🍴 ➜

⛟⛟⛟ Lantern Inn M
(605) 574-2582. **$42-$98.** 430 E Main St. On north side of town, on US 16 and 385. Ext corridors. **Pets:** Small. $5 daily fee/pet. Designated rooms, service with restrictions, supervision.
SAVE 🔓 ⊠ 🔧 ➜

⛟⛟ ⛟⛟⛟⛟ The Lodge at Palmer Gulch M
(605) 574-2525. **$60-$160, 10 days notice.** 12620 SR 244. 5 mi w of Mt Rushmore. Int corridors. **Pets:** Other species. Designated rooms, service with restrictions, supervision.
SAVE ⊠ 🔒 🔧 💻 ➜ ⊠

HOT SPRINGS

⛟⛟ ⛟⛟⛟ Budget Host Hills Inn M
(605) 745-3130. **$50-$140.** 640 S 6th St. 0.5 mi se off US 18 and 385. Ext corridors. **Pets:** Small. $5 daily fee/pet. Designated rooms, service with restrictions, supervision.
SAVE 🔓 ⊠ 🔧 💻 ➜

⛟⛟ ⛟⛟⛟⛟ Comfort Inn M
(605) 745-7378. **$69-$159.** 737 S 6th St. 0.5 mi se off US 18 and 385. Int corridors. **Pets:** Medium. Designated rooms, service with restrictions, supervision.
SAVE 🔓 ⊠ 🔒M 🔧 💻 ➜

⛟⛟ ⛟⛟⛟ Hot Springs Super 8 Motel M
(605) 745-3888. **$52-$112.** 800 Mammoth St. US 18 truck Bypass. Int corridors. **Pets:** Medium, other species. $25 deposit/room, $5 one-time fee/room. Service with restrictions, supervision.
SAVE 🔓 ⊠ 🔧

⛟⛟ Inn at Battle Mountain M ❀
(605) 745-3182. **$69-$99.** 402 Battle Mountain Ave. 1 mi n on US 385. Ext corridors. **Pets:** Medium. Designated rooms, service with restrictions, supervision.
ASK 🔓 ⊠ 🔧

KEYSTONE

⛟⛟ The First Lady Inn M
(605) 666-4990. **$62-$84.** 702 Hwy 16A. On US 16A, west side of town. Ext/int corridors. **Pets:** Small, other species. $10 daily fee/pet. Designated rooms, service with restrictions, supervision.
ASK 🔓 ⊠ 💻 ➜

⛟⛟ Keystone/Mt Rushmore Super 8 M ❀
(605) 666-6666. **$60-$110, 30 days notice.** 250 Winter St. Downtown; on US 16A. Ext/int corridors. **Pets:** Very small, dogs only. $10 daily fee/pet. Designated rooms, service with restrictions, supervision.
ASK 🔓 ⊠ 💻

▼▼▼ **Mt Rushmore's White House Resort** ꙮ
(605) 666-4917. **$70-$129, 3 days notice.** 111 Swanzey St. Jct US 16A and SR 40. Ext/int corridors. **Pets:** Other species. $10 daily fee/pet. Designated rooms, service with restrictions, supervision.

[ASK] [S▣] [✕] [&M] [&'] [🛏] [�╮]

ꙮꙮ ▼▼▼ **Powder House Lodge** ⊠
(605) 666-4646. **$65-$163.** 24125 Hwy 16A. 1.5 mi n. Ext corridors. **Pets:** Accepted.

[SAVE] [S▣] [🛏] [▣] [⑪] [➲]

ꙮꙮ ▼▼▼ **Rushmore Express** ꙮ
(605) 666-4483. **$55-$99.** 320 Old Cemetary Rd. S on US 16A to Tramway, then just e. Ext/int corridors. **Pets:** Medium, other species. $10 one-time fee/room. Designated rooms, service with restrictions, supervision.

[SAVE] [✕] [🌀] [🛏] [▣]

LEAD

ꙮꙮ ▼▼▼ **Palace Hotels, Golden Hills Inn** ⊞
(605) 584-1800. **$55-$179.** 900 Miners Ave. Center; US 85 and 14A. Int corridors. **Pets:** Accepted.

[SAVE] [S▣] [✕] [&M] [🌀] [🛏] [⑪]

ꙮꙮ ▼▼▼ **Palace Hotels, Palace Express** ꙮ
(605) 584-2000. **$29-$99.** 395 Glendale Dr. 0.3 mi n on US 14A. Int corridors. **Pets:** Accepted.

[SAVE] [S▣] [✕] [🌀] [&'] [🛏]

PIEDMONT

ꙮꙮ ▼▼▼ **Elk Creek Resort & Lodge** ꙮ 🐾
(605) 787-4884. **$59-$199, 14 days notice.** Elk Creek Rd. I-90, exit 46, 1 mi e. Ext corridors. **Pets:** Other species. $30 deposit/room, $7 daily fee/room. Service with restrictions, crate.

[SAVE] [S▣] [✕] [🛏] [▣] [➲] [✕]

RAPID CITY

ꙮꙮ ▼▼▼▼ **Alex Johnson Hotel** ⊞
(605) 342-1210. **$69-$160, 3 days notice.** 523 6th St. I-90, exit 57, s on I-190, left at Omaha; downtown. Int corridors. **Pets:** Small. $50 deposit/room, $50 one-time fee/room. Designated rooms, service with restrictions, supervision.

[SAVE] [S▣] [✕] [🌀] [🛏] [⑪]

ꙮꙮ ▼▼ **Big Sky Motel** ꙮ
(605) 348-3200. **$38-$64.** 4080 Tower Rd. 3 mi s on US 16, 0.3 mi n on Skyline Dr, take service road off US 16. Ext corridors. **Pets:** Accepted.

[SAVE] [✕] [☎]

▼▼▼ **Econo Lodge of Rapid City** ꙮ
(605) 342-6400. **$49-$119.** 625 E Disk Dr. I-90, exit 59 (La Crosse St), just ne. Ext/int corridors. **Pets:** Accepted.

[SAVE] [S▣] [✕] [🛏] [▣] [➲]

ꙮꙮ ▼▼▼ **Fair Value Inn** ꙮ
(605) 342-8118. **$38-$72.** 1607 La Crosse St. I-90, exit 59 (La Crosse St), 0.3 mi s. Ext corridors. **Pets:** Very small, dogs only. Service with restrictions, supervision.

[SAVE] [✕] [🛏] [▣]

ꙮꙮ ▼▼▼ **Foot Hills Inn** ꙮ
(605) 348-5640. **$69-$119, 4 days notice.** 1625 N La Crosse St. I-90, exit 59 (La Crosse St), just s. Int corridors. **Pets:** Large. $25 one-time fee/room. Service with restrictions, crate.

[SAVE] [S▣] [✕] [🛏] [➲]

ꙮꙮ ▼▼▼ **Gold Star Motel** ꙮ
(605) 341-7051. **$45-$68.** 801 E North. 2 mi ne on I-90 business loop, exit 59 or 60. Ext corridors. **Pets:** Other species. $5 daily fee/pet. Service with restrictions, supervision.

[SAVE] [S▣] [✕]

▼▼▼▼ **Holiday Inn Express Hotel & Suites, I-90** ꙮ
(605) 355-9090. **$70-$215.** 645 E Disk Dr. I-90, exit 59, just ne. Int corridors. **Pets:** Accepted.

[ASK] [S▣] [✕] [&M] [🌀] [&'] [🛏] [▣] [➲]

▼▼▼▼ **Holiday Inn Express-South** ꙮ
(605) 341-9300. **$73-$194.** 750 Cathedral Dr. 1.4 mi s on US 16, just e. Int corridors. **Pets:** Accepted.

[ASK] [✕] [&M] [🌀] [&'] [🛏] [▣] [➲]

▼▼ **Motel 6–352** ꙮ
(605) 343-3687. **$39-$77.** 620 E Latrobe St. I-90, exit 59 (La Crosse St) on corner. Ext corridors. **Pets:** Supervision.

[S▣] [✕] [&'] [🛏] [➲]

▼▼ **Quality Inn** ꙮ�
(605) 342-3322. **$49-$119.** 1902 La Crosse St. I-90, exit 59 (La Crosse St), just s. Ext/int corridors. **Pets:** Accepted.

[SAVE] [S▣] [✕] [&M] [🛏] [▣] [⑪] [➲]

ꙮꙮ ▼▼▼▼ **Ramada Inn** ꙮⒹ
(605) 342-1300. **$69-$139, 4 days notice.** 1721 N La Crosse St. I-90, exit 59 (La Crosse St), just s. Int corridors. **Pets:** $25 one-time fee/room. Service with restrictions, crate.

[SAVE] [S▣] [✕] [&M] [🛏] [▣] [➲]

ꙮꙮ ▼▼▼ **Rodeway Inn** ꙮⒹ
(605) 342-1303. **$49-$159.** 2208 Mt Rushmore Rd. 1 mi s on US 16. Ext corridors. **Pets:** Designated rooms, service with restrictions, supervision.

[SAVE] [S▣] [✕] [🛏] [▣] [⑪] [➲]

ꙮꙮ ▼▼▼▼ **Rushmore Plaza Holiday Inn** ⊞
(605) 348-4000. **$84-$250.** 505 N 5th St. I-90, exit 58, 1.3 mi s on Haines; adjacent to Civic Center. Int corridors. **Pets:** Accepted.

[SAVE] [S▣] [✕] [&M] [🌀] [&'] [🛏] [▣] [⑪] [➲]

▼▼▼ **Super 8 Motel** ꙮ
(605) 348-8070. **$42-$160, 14 days notice.** 2124 La Crosse St. I-90, exit 59 (La Crosse St), just n. Int corridors. **Pets:** Medium. $7 daily fee/pet. Service with restrictions, supervision.

[ASK] [S▣] [✕] [&M] [🌀] [&'] [🛏]

ꙮꙮ ▼▼ **Super 8 Motel** ꙮ
(605) 342-4911. **$40-$110.** 2520 Tower Rd. 1.4 mi s on US 16. Int corridors. **Pets:** Small, other species. Service with restrictions, supervision.

[SAVE] [S▣] [✕] [🛏]

ⒶⒶⒶ ▼▼▼ Thrifty Motor Inn Ⓜ
(605) 342-0551. **$38-$72.** 1303 La Crosse St. I-90, exit 59
(La Crosse St), 0.5 mi s. Ext corridors. **Pets:** Very small,
dogs only. Service with restrictions, supervision.
[SAVE] [✕] [🔒]

ROCKERVILLE

▼ Rockerville Trading Post & Motel Ⓜ ❀
(605) 341-4880. **$65-$75, 3 days notice.** 13525 Main St.
Center. Ext corridors. **Pets:** Other species. $5 daily fee/pet.
Service with restrictions, crate.
[Sᴆ] [✕] [🏊]

SPEARFISH

ⒶⒶⒶ ▼▼▼ Holiday Inn Hotel & Convention
         Center Ⓜ
(605) 642-4683. **$70-$120.** 305 N 27th St. I-90, exit 14
(Spearfish Canyon), just n. Ext/int corridors. **Pets:** $10 one-
time fee/room. Designated rooms, supervision.
[SAVE] [Sᴆ] [✕] [♿] [🅿] [✦] [🔒] [💻] [🍽] [🏊]

ⒶⒶⒶ ▼▼▼ Kelly Inn Ⓜ
(605) 642-7795. **$69-$109.** 540 E Jackson. I-90, exit 12,
just s. Ext/int corridors. **Pets:** Medium, other species. Service with restrictions, supervision.
[SAVE] [Sᴆ] [✕] [🅿] [🔒] [🏊]

ⒶⒶⒶ ▼▼ Royal Rest Motel Ⓜ
(605) 642-3842. **$30-$50.** 444 Main St. Downtown; on US
14/85. Ext corridors. **Pets:** Accepted.
[SAVE] [✕] [🏊]

ⒶⒶⒶ ▼▼▼ Travelodge Ⓜ
(605) 642-4676. **$44-$110.** 346 W Kansas St. Downtown;
follow signs off Main St. Ext corridors. **Pets:** Designated
rooms, service with restrictions, supervision.
[SAVE] [Sᴆ] [✕] [🔒] [💻] [🏊]

STURGIS

ⒶⒶⒶ ▼▼▼ Best Western of Sturgis Ⓜ!
(605) 347-3604. **$39-$99.** 2431 S Junction Ave. I-90, exit
32. Ext/int corridors. **Pets:** Designated rooms, service with
restrictions, supervision.
[SAVE] [Sᴆ] [✕] [🔒] [💻] [🍽] [🏊]

▼▼ Days Inn Ⓜ
(605) 347-3027. **$48-$90, 7 days notice.** I-90, exit 30, jct
US 14A. Ext/int corridors. **Pets:** $6 daily fee/pet. Service
with restrictions, supervision.
[SAVE] [Sᴆ] [✕] [🔒]

ⒶⒶⒶ ▼▼ National 9 Inn Ⓜ
(605) 347-2506. **$38-$70, 14 days notice.** 2426 Junction
Ave. I-90, exit 32, just n. Ext corridors. **Pets:** Small, dogs
only. $5 daily fee/pet. Service with restrictions, supervision.
[SAVE] [Sᴆ] [✕] [🔒] [💻]

❀ **END METROPOLITAN AREA** ❀

BRANDON

▼▼▼ Holiday Inn Express of Brandon Ⓜ
(605) 582-2901. **$72-$115, 5 days notice.** 1105 N Split
Rock Blvd. I-90, exit 406, just s. Int corridors. **Pets:** Large,
other species. $10 one-time fee/pet. Service with restric-
tions, supervision.
[ASK] [Sᴆ] [✕] [♿] [✦] [🔒] [💻] [🏊]

BROOKINGS

▼▼▼ Brookings Super 8 Motel Ⓜ
(605) 692-6920. **$49-$89.** 3034 Lefevre Dr. I-29, exit 132,
just e. Int corridors. **Pets:** Medium. $5 daily fee/pet. Service
with restrictions, supervision.
[ASK] [Sᴆ] [✕] [🔒] [🏊]

BUFFALO

▼ Tipperary Lodge Ⓜ
(605) 375-3721. **$40-$44, 5 days notice.** 604 1st St W. 0.5
mi n on US 85, turn at sign. Int corridors. **Pets:** Other
species. Designated rooms, service with restrictions, supervision.
[ASK] [Sᴆ] [✕]

CANISTOTA

ⒶⒶⒶ ▼▼▼ Best Western U-Bar Motel Ⓜ
(605) 296-3466. **$40-$80.** 130 Ash St. I-90, exit 368, 6 mi s,
follow signs. Ext corridors. **Pets:** Very small, dogs only. $20
one-time fee/pet. Service with restrictions, supervision.
[SAVE] [✕] [🔒] [💻]

CHAMBERLAIN

ⒶⒶⒶ ▼ Alewel's Lake Shore Motel Ⓜ
(605) 734-5566. **$27-$64.** 115 N River St. Just n of US 16
bridge (the northernmost bridge). Ext corridors.
Pets: Accepted.
[SAVE] [Sᴆ] [✕]

ⒶⒶⒶ ▼ Bel Aire Motel Ⓜ
(605) 734-5595. **$40-$64, 4 days notice.** 312 E King St.
Downtown; on US 16 and I-90 business loop, exit 263 and
265. Ext/int corridors. **Pets:** $5 daily fee/pet. Designated
rooms, service with restrictions, supervision.
[SAVE] [Sᴆ] [✕]

ⒶⒶⒶ ▼▼▼ Cedar Shore Resort Ⓡ ❀
(605) 734-6376. **$59-$139.** 1500 Shoreline Dr. I-90, exit
260, 2.5 mi e on Business 90, 1 mi ne on Mickelson county
road, follow signs. Int corridors. **Pets:** Other species. $10
daily fee/room. Service with restrictions, supervision.
[SAVE] [Sᴆ] [✕] [♿] [🅿] [✦] [🔒] [💻] [🍽] [🏊] [✕]

Oasis Inn M
(605) 734-6061. **$51-$109.** 1100 E Hwy 16. I-90, exit 260, 0.4 mi e on US 16 and I-90 business loop. Ext/int corridors. **Pets:** Other species. Service with restrictions, supervision.
SAVE | | | | | | | |

FAITH

Prairie Vista Inn M
(605) 967-2343. **$56-$65, 14 days notice.** Hwy 212 & E 1st. On US 212; at east city edge. Int corridors. **Pets:** Small. $40 deposit/room, $10 one-time fee/pet. Designated rooms, service with restrictions, supervision.
SAVE | | |

FAULKTON

Super 8 Motel M
(605) 598-4567. **$42-$63.** 700 Main St. Center; on US 212. Int corridors. **Pets:** Other species. $10 one-time fee/pet. Service with restrictions, supervision.
ASK | |

FORT PIERRE

Fort Pierre Motel M
(605) 223-3111. **$44-$52, 3 days notice.** 211 S 1st Ave. On US 83, 1.2 mi s of jct US 14. Ext corridors. **Pets:** Large, other species. Crate.
SAVE | | |

Holiday Inn Express Hotel & Suites M
(605) 223-9045. **$75-$95.** 110 E Stanley Rd. On US 83, just s of jct US 14 and 34. Int corridors. **Pets:** Accepted.
ASK | | | | | | | |

FORT THOMPSON

Lode Star Motel M
(605) 245-2899. **$63.** E Hwy 34. Just e of jct SR 47/34. Int corridors. **Pets:** Accepted.
ASK | | |

FREEMAN

Super 8 Motel M
(605) 925-4888. **$47-$57.** 1019 S Hwy 81. Just s on US 81. Int corridors. **Pets:** Other species. $10 daily fee/pet. Designated rooms, service with restrictions, crate.
ASK | | | |

HURON

Best Western of Huron M
(605) 352-2000. **$60, 7 days notice.** 2000 Dakota Ave. 1.3 mi s on SR 37. Ext/int corridors. **Pets:** Dogs only. Service with restrictions, supervision.
SAVE | | | | | | |

Holiday Inn Express M
(605) 352-6655. **$60-$70.** 100 21st St SW. 1.3 mi s on SR 37. Ext/int corridors. **Pets:** Accepted.
| | | | |

INTERIOR

Badlands Budget Host Motel M
(605) 433-5335. **$52-$58.** Jct SR 44 and 377, 2 mi s of Badlands National Park. Ext corridors. **Pets:** Other species. $5 daily fee/room. Service with restrictions, supervision.
SAVE | | |

KADOKA

Best Value Dakota Inn M
(605) 837-2151. **$35-$70.** I-90, exit 150, just n. Ext/int corridors. **Pets:** Other species. $5 daily fee/pet. Designated rooms, service with restrictions, supervision.
SAVE | | | | |

Best Western H & H El Centro Motel M
(605) 837-2287. **$50-$96, 7 days notice.** 105 E Hwy 16. 1.5 mi w on I-90 business route from exit 152, 1.3 mi e from exit 150. Ext corridors. **Pets:** Small, other species. Designated rooms, service with restrictions, supervision.
SAVE | | | | |

West Motel M
(605) 837-2427. **$36-$60, 3 days notice.** 306 Hwy 16 W. I-90, exit 150, 1 mi e on I-90 business route. Ext corridors. **Pets:** Accepted.
SAVE | |

MADISON

Super 8 Motel M
(605) 256-6931. **$48-$68, 3 days notice.** Jct US 34 and 81. Int corridors. **Pets:** Other species. $5 daily fee/room. Designated rooms, service with restrictions, supervision.
ASK | | |

MITCHELL

Econo Lodge M
(605) 996-6647. **$49-$75.** 1313 S Ohlman. I-90, exit 330, 0.3 mi n. Int corridors. **Pets:** Accepted.
SAVE | | |

Holiday Inn M
(605) 996-6501. **$70-$110.** 1525 W Havens St. I-90, exit 330, 0.5 mi n. Int corridors. **Pets:** Other species. $10 daily fee/room. Service with restrictions, supervision.
SAVE | | | | | | | |

MOBRIDGE

Best Value Wrangler Inn M
(605) 845-3641. **$64-$76.** 820 W Grand Crossing. 0.5 mi w on US 12. Ext/int corridors. **Pets:** Designated rooms, service with restrictions, supervision.
SAVE | | | | |

MURDO

Best Western Graham's M
(605) 669-2441. **$49-$99.** 301 W 5th. On I-90 business loop, 0.5 mi w of jct US 83; I-90, exits 191 and 192. Ext corridors. **Pets:** Accepted.
SAVE | | | |

NORTH SIOUX CITY

▼▼ Econo Lodge M
(605) 232-9600. **$45-$75.** 110 Sodrac Dr. I-29, exit 2, just w.
Int corridors. **Pets:** Accepted.
[SAVE] [S6] [X] [&] [H] [▣]

▼▼▼ Hampton Inn M
(605) 232-9739. **$63-$80, 7 days notice.** 101 S Sodrac Dr.
I-29, exit 2, just w. Int corridors. **Pets:** Accepted.
[SAVE] [S6] [X] [&M] [H] [▣] [≈]

▼▼ Super 8 Motel M
(605) 232-4716. **Call for rates.** 1300 River Dr. I-29, exit 2,
just w. Int corridors. **Pets:** Accepted.
[ASK] [X] [H]

PICKSTOWN

▲▲▲ ▼▼▼ Fort Randall Inn M
(605) 487-7801. **$57.** 103 Hwy 18/281. Just e of the dam,
on US 18/281. Ext corridors. **Pets:** Service with restrictions.
[SAVE] [S6] [X] [H]

PIERRE

▼▼▼▼ Best Western Ramkota Hotel M
(605) 224-6877. **$81-$90.** 920 W Sioux. 1 mi w on US 14
and 83. Ext/int corridors. **Pets:** Other species. Service with
restrictions, supervision.
[SAVE] [S6] [X] [&M] [🖉] [&] [H] [▣] [¶] [≈]

▼ Budget Host Inn/State Motel M
(605) 224-5896. **Call for rates, 30 days notice.** 640 N
Euclid Ave. 0.5 mi n on US 14 and 83. Ext corridors.
Pets: Accepted.
[X] [H] [≈]

▲▲▲ ▼▼▼ Comfort Inn M
(605) 224-0377. **$62-$79.** 410 W Sioux Ave. Just w on US
14, 83 and 34. Int corridors. **Pets:** Large, other species. $10
one-time fee/pet. Designated rooms, service with restrictions, supervision.
[SAVE] [X] [&M] [&] [H] [▣] [≈]

▼▼ Days Inn M
(605) 224-0411. **$47-$84.** 520 W Sioux Ave. On US 14, 83
and 34, just w. Int corridors. **Pets:** Accepted.
[SAVE] [S6] [X] [🖉] [&] [H] [▣]

▲▲▲ ▼▼▼▼ Governor's Inn M ❀
(605) 224-4200. **$59-$79.** 700 W Sioux Ave. On US 14, 83
and 34, just w. Ext/int corridors. **Pets:** Medium, dogs only.
$5 daily fee/room. Designated rooms, service with restric-
tions, supervision.
[SAVE] [S6] [X] [🖉] [&] [H] [▣] [≈]

▼▼ Kelly Inn M
(605) 224-4140. **$52-$69.** 713 W Sioux. 1 mi w on US 14
and 83. Int corridors. **Pets:** Other species. Service with
restrictions, supervision.
[ASK] [S6] [X] [&] [H]

▼▼ Kings Inn Hotel & Convention Center M
(605) 224-5951. **$64-$70.** 220 S Pierre St. Downtown; on
US 14 and 83. Ext/int corridors. **Pets:** Accepted.
[ASK] [S6] [X] [H] [▣] [¶]

▼▼ Super 8 Motel M
(605) 224-1617. **$42-$65, 14 days notice.** 320 W Sioux.
Just w on US 14, 83 and 34. Int corridors. **Pets:** Medium.
$5 daily fee/pet. Service with restrictions, supervision.
[ASK] [S6] [X] [&]

PLANKINTON

▼▼ Super 8 Motel M
(605) 942-7722. **Call for rates, 10 days notice.** 801 S
Main St. I-90, exit 308, just n. Int corridors. **Pets:** Accepted.
[ASK] [X]

SIOUX FALLS

▼▼▼ Best Western Ramkota Hotel M
(605) 336-0650. **$89-$139.** 2400 N Louise Ave. I-29, exit 81
(Airport/Russell St), just e. Ext/int corridors. **Pets:** Accepted.
[SAVE] [S6] [X] [&M] [🖉] [&] [H] [▣] [¶] [≈]

▼▼ Comfort Inn North M
(605) 331-4490. **$55-$139.** 5100 N Cliff Ave. I-90, exit 399
(Cliff Ave), 0.3 mi s. Int corridors. **Pets:** Other species. $10
daily fee/pet. Service with restrictions, supervision.
[SAVE] [S6] [X] [&M] [🖉] [≈]

▼▼ Comfort Inn South M
(605) 361-2822. **$64-$99.** 3216 S Carolyn Ave. I-29, exit 77
(41st St), just ne. Int corridors. **Pets:** $25 deposit/pet, $6
daily fee/pet. Designated rooms, service with restrictions,
supervision.
[SAVE] [S6] [X] [🖉] [H] [▣] [≈]

▼▼▼ Comfort Suites M
(605) 362-9711. **$74-$104.** 3208 S Carolyn Ave. I-29, exit
77 (41st St), just ne. Int corridors. **Pets:** Other species. $5
daily fee/room. Designated rooms, service with restrictions,
supervision.
[SAVE] [S6] [X] [🖉] [H] [▣] [≈]

▼▼▼ Country Inn & Suites By Carlson M
(605) 373-0153. **$76-$149.** 200 E 8th St. Downtown; just e
of Phillips Ave. Int corridors. **Pets:** Medium. $10 daily fee/
pet. Designated rooms, service with restrictions, supervision.
[ASK] [S6] [X] [&M] [🖉] [&] [H] [▣] [¶] [≈]

▼▼ Days Inn Airport M
(605) 331-5959. **$70-$125.** 5001 N Cliff Ave. I-90, exit 399
(Cliff Ave), just s. Int corridors. **Pets:** Accepted.
[SAVE] [S6] [X] [&M] [🖉] [&] [H] [▣]

▲▲▲ ▼▼▼ Homewood Suites By Hilton M
(605) 338-8585. **$109-$119, 30 days notice.** 3620 W Avera
Dr. I-229, exit 1C, just s. Int corridors. **Pets:** Other species.
$5 daily fee/pet, $25 one-time fee/pet. Service with restrictions, crate.
[SAVE] [S6] [X] [H] [▣] [≈]

▲▲▲ ▼▼▼ Kelly Inn M
(605) 338-6242. **$62-$81.** 3101 W Russell St. I-29, exit 81
(Airport/Russell St), just e. Ext/int corridors. **Pets:** Other
species. Service with restrictions, supervision.
[SAVE] [S6] [X] [🖉] [&] [H] [▣]

▼▼▼ MainStay Suites M
(605) 361-2626. **$69-$139.** 4545 W Homefield Dr. I-29, exit 78 (26th St), just w. Int corridors. **Pets:** Small, other species. $5 daily fee/room. Designated rooms, service with restrictions, supervision.

▼ Motel 6–0162 M
(605) 336-7800. **Call for rates.** 3009 W Russell St. I-29, exit 81 (Airport/Russell St), just e. Ext corridors. **Pets:** Accepted.

▼▼▼ Ramada Limited M
(605) 330-0000. **$75-$85.** 407 S Lyons Ave. I-29, exit 79 (12th St), just e. Int corridors. **Pets:** Medium. $15 deposit/room. Designated rooms, service with restrictions, supervision.

▼▼▼▼ Residence Inn by Marriott A
(605) 361-2202. **$80-$170, 14 days notice.** 4509 W Empire Pl. I-29, exit 77 (41st St), 0.5 mi se; in southwest corner of Empire Mall. Int corridors. **Pets:** Medium, other species. $5 daily fee/room, $25 one-time fee/room. Designated rooms, service with restrictions, supervision.

▼▼ Select Inn M
(605) 361-1864. **$43-$56, 7 days notice.** 3500 S Gateway Blvd. I-29, exit 77 (41st St), just w. Int corridors. **Pets:** Other species. $25 deposit/room, $5.30 daily fee/room. Designated rooms, service with restrictions, supervision.

▼▼ Sleep Inn M
(605) 339-3992. **$55-$75.** 1500 N Kiwanis Ave. I-29, exit 81 (Airport/Russell St), 0.7 mi e. Int corridors. **Pets:** Medium. $10 daily fee/pet. Designated rooms, service with restrictions, crate.

▼ Super 8/I-90/Airport East M
(605) 339-9212. **$59-$99.** 4808 N Cliff Ave. I-90, exit 399 (Cliff Ave), 0.3 mi s. Int corridors. **Pets:** Large, dogs only. $15 one-time fee/room. Designated rooms, service with restrictions, crate.

VERMILLION

▼▼ Comfort Inn M
(605) 624-8333. **$68-$70.** 701 W Cherry St. I-29, exit 26, 7.5 mi w Business SR 50. Int corridors. **Pets:** Medium, other species. $5 daily fee/pet. Service with restrictions, supervision.

WALL

▼▼▼▼ Best Western Plains Motel M ❀
(605) 279-2145. **$48-$140.** 712 Glenn St. I-90, exit 110, just n. Ext corridors. **Pets:** Other species. $10 daily fee/pet. Service with restrictions, supervision.

▼▼▼ Econo Lodge M
(605) 279-2121. **$59-$149, 3 days notice.** 804 Glenn St. I-90, exit 110, just nw. Ext corridors. **Pets:** Accepted.

▼▼ Sunshine Inn M
(605) 279-2178. **$46-$79.** 608 Main St. Downtown. Ext corridors. **Pets:** Other species. $5 one-time fee/room.

WATERTOWN

▼▼▼ Best Western Ramkota Hotel M
(605) 886-8011. **$70-$73.** 1901 9th Ave SW. I-29, exit 177, 4 mi w on US 212. Int corridors. **Pets:** Other species. Service with restrictions.

▼▼▼ Comfort Inn M ❀
(605) 886-3010. **$109.** 800 35th St Cir. I-29, exit 177 (US 212). Ext/int corridors. **Pets:** Other species. $10 one-time fee/room. Designated rooms, service with restrictions, supervision.

▼▼▼ Country Inn & Suites By Carlson M
(605) 886-8900. **$60-$90.** 3400 8th Ave SE. I-29, exit 177, just w. Int corridors. **Pets:** Small. $20 one-time fee/room. Designated rooms, service with restrictions, supervision.

▼▼▼ Travelers Inn Motel M
(605) 882-2243. **$48.** 920 14th St SE. I-29, exit 177, 1.5 mi w, then just s. Int corridors. **Pets:** Other species. $6 daily fee/pet. Designated rooms, supervision.

▼▼▼ Travel Host Motel M
(605) 886-6120. **$43-$48.** 1714 9th Ave SW. I-29, exit 177, 4 mi w on US 212. Int corridors. **Pets:** Small, dogs only. Designated rooms, service with restrictions, supervision.

YANKTON

▼▼▼ Best Western Kelly Inn-Yankton M
(605) 665-2906. **$85-$109.** 1607 Hwy 50 E. 1 mi e. Ext/int corridors. **Pets:** Other species. Designated rooms, service with restrictions, supervision.

▼▼ Lewis & Clark Resort M
(605) 665-2680. **Call for rates, 30 days notice.** 43496 Lake Shore Dr. 4 mi w on SR 52; in Lewis and Clark State Park, turn into park, just w of Marina. Ext corridors. **Pets:** Accepted.

▼▼ Ramada Limited M
(605) 665-8053. **$75-$125.** 2118 Broadway. US 81, 1.7 mi n. Int corridors. **Pets:** Small. $10 one-time fee/pet. No service, supervision.

CITY INDEX

ATHENS

▼▼ ▼▼ **Motel 6** Ⓜ
(423) 745-4441. **$40-$46.** 2002 Whittaker Rd. I-75, exit 49. Int corridors. **Pets:** Accepted.
🆂🅳 ⊠ ♿ 🛇 ➳

▼▼ ▼▼ **Ramada Inn** Ⓜ
(423) 745-1212. **$66-$108, 3 days notice.** 115 CR 247. I-75, exit 52. Ext corridors. **Pets:** Accepted.
🅐🆂🅚 🆂🅳 ⊠ 🛇 ▦ 🍽 ➳

BOLIVAR

🅐🅐🅐 ▼▼ **The Bolivar Inn** Ⓜ
(731) 658-3372. **$30-$40.** 626 W Market St. Jct US 64 and SR 18. Ext corridors. **Pets:** Other species.
🆂🅰🆅🅴 ⊠ 🛇

🅐🅐🅐 ▼▼ **Super 8 Motel** Ⓜ
(731) 658-7888. **$57-$68.** 916 W Market St. US 64 at jct of SR 18. Ext corridors. **Pets:** Accepted.
🅐🆂🅚 🆂🅳 ⊠ 🛇 ➳

BRENTWOOD

🅐🅐🅐 ▼▼▼ **AmeriSuites** Ⓜ
(615) 661-9477. **$69-$74.** 202 Summit View Dr. I-65, exit 74B. Int corridors. **Pets:** Accepted.
🆂🅰🆅🅴 🆂🅳 ⊠ ♿ 🛇 ▦ ➳

🅐🅐🅐 ▼▼▼ **Baymont Inn & Suites** Ⓜ
(615) 376-4666. **$65.** 111 Penn Warren Dr. I-65, exit 74B, 1.5 mi w. Int corridors. **Pets:** Designated rooms, supervision.
🆂🅰🆅🅴 🆂🅳 ⊠ ♿ 🖭 🛇 ▦ ➳

▼▼▼▼ **Hilton Suites Brentwood** Ⓗ
(615) 370-0111. **$79-$189.** 9000 Overlook Blvd. I-65, exit 74B, 0.5 mi s on US 31, e on Church St. Int corridors. **Pets:** Small. $75 deposit/room. Designated rooms, service with restrictions.
🆂🅰🆅🅴 🆂🅳 ⊠ ♿ 🖭 🛇 ▦ 🍽 ➳

▼▼▼ **MainStay Suites-Brentwood** Ⓜ
(615) 371-0100. **$40-$99.** 107 Brentwood Blvd. I-65, exit 74B, 1 mi w. Int corridors. **Pets:** Medium, other species. $100 deposit/room. Designated rooms, service with restrictions, supervision.
🅐🆂🅚 🆂🅳 ⊠ ♿ 🖭 🄲 🛇 ▦ ➳

🅐🅐🅐 ▼▼▼▼ **Residence Inn Brentwood** Ⓐ
(615) 371-9200. **$98.** 206 Ward Cir. I-65, exit 74B, 0.3 mi s on Franklin Pike (US 31 S), 0.5 mi w on Maryland Way. Ext/int corridors. **Pets:** Small. $100 one-time fee/room. Service with restrictions.
🆂🅰🆅🅴 ⊠ 🛇 ▦ ➳

▼▼ ▼▼ **Sleep Inn** Ⓜ
(615) 376-2122. **$49-$89, 7 days notice.** 1611 Service Blvd. I-65, exit 69 northbound, 0.4 mi, just n; exit 69W southbound, just n. Int corridors. **Pets:** Accepted.
🆂🅰🆅🅴 🆂🅳 ⊠ ♿ 🛇 ▦ ➳

BROWNSVILLE

▼▼ ▼▼ **Days Inn** Ⓜ
(731) 772-3297. **$60-$70.** 2530 Anderson Ave. I-40, exit 56. Ext corridors. **Pets:** Accepted.
🆂🅰🆅🅴 🆂🅳 ⊠ 🛇 ▦

BUCKSNORT

▼▼ **Travelodge** Ⓜ
(931) 729-5450. **$35-$50.** 5032 Hwy 230 W. I-40, exit 152. Ext corridors. **Pets:** Accepted.
🅐🆂🅚 🆂🅳 ⊠ ▦

BUFFALO

Best Western of Hurricane Mills M
(931) 296-4251. **$60-$90.** 15542 Hwy 13 S. I-40, exit 143. Ext corridors. **Pets:** Medium. $10 daily fee/pet. Service with restrictions, supervision.

Super 8 Motel M
(931) 296-2432. **$37-$80.** 15470 Hwy 13 S. I-40, exit 143. Ext corridors. **Pets:** Small, other species. $10 daily fee/room. Service with restrictions, supervision.

BUTLER

Iron Mountain Inn B&B and Creekside Chalet BB
(423) 768-2446. **$170-$250, 30 days notice.** 138 Moreland Dr. 1.6 mi w on Pine Orchard Rd from SR 67 at Stout Store, follow signs; 13 mi w on SR 67 from US 421 in Mountain City, then follow sign at Stout Store area. Ext/int corridors. **Pets:** Designated rooms, supervision.

CARYVILLE

Budget Host Inn M
(423) 562-9595. **$29-$46.** 115 Woods Ave. I-75, exit 134, just nw. Ext corridors. **Pets:** Medium. $6 one-time fee/pet. Designated rooms, service with restrictions, supervision.

Super 8 Motel of Caryville M
(423) 562-8476. **$44, 3 days notice.** 200 John McGhee Blvd. I-75, exit 134, just e, then just w on CR 116. Ext corridors. **Pets:** Medium. $5 daily fee/room. Service with restrictions, supervision.

CENTERVILLE

Days Inn M
(931) 729-5600. **$45-$55.** 634 David St. Jct SR 48, 2.5 mi w on SR 100. Int corridors. **Pets:** Other species. $5 daily fee/room. Supervision.

CHATTANOOGA

Baymont Inn and Suites M
(423) 821-1090. **$45-$145.** 3540 Cummings Hwy. I-24, exit 174, just s. Int corridors. **Pets:** Accepted.

Best Inn M
(423) 894-5454. **$52-$68.** 7717 Lee Hwy. I-75, exit 7B northbound; exit 7 southbound, 6.5 mi n of jct I-24. Ext corridors. **Pets:** Accepted.

Best Western Royal Inn M
(423) 821-6840. **$64-$75.** 3644 Cummings Hwy. I-24, exit 174, 5.5 mi w; jct US 64, 41 and 72. Ext corridors. **Pets:** Small, other species. $10 daily fee/pet. Service with restrictions, supervision.

Chattanooga/Aquarium Super 8 Motel M
(423) 821-8880. **$40-$90.** 20 Birmingham Hwy. I-24, exit 174. Int corridors. **Pets:** Small. $10 one-time fee/pet. Service with restrictions, supervision.

Days Inn-Lookout Mountain Tiftonia West M
(423) 821-6044. **$44-$62, 14 days notice.** 3801 Cummings Hwy. I-24, exit 174, at jct US 64, 41 and 72. Ext corridors. **Pets:** Other species. $7 daily fee/pet. Designated rooms, service with restrictions, supervision.

Holiday Inn I-75 Airport M
(423) 855-2898. **$79.** 2345 Shallowford Village Dr. I-75, exit 5 (Shallowford Rd), 0.3 mi w to Shallowford Village Dr, 0.3 mi n. Ext/int corridors. **Pets:** Small, other species. $100 deposit/pet. Service with restrictions, supervision.

Kings Lodge M
(423) 698-8944. **$50-$55.** 2400 Westside Dr. 3.5 mi se on US 41 and 76; just se of I-24, exit 181 westbound; exit 181A eastbound. Ext/int corridors. **Pets:** Medium, other species. $5 daily fee/pet. Designated rooms, service with restrictions, crate.

La Quinta Inn M
(423) 855-0011. **$56-$65.** 7015 Shallowford Rd. I-75, exit 5 (Shallowford Rd), 0.5 mi w. Ext corridors. **Pets:** Small. Designated rooms, service with restrictions, supervision.

Microtel Inn-Chattanooga M
(423) 510-0761. **$32-$49.** 7014 McCutcheon Rd. I-75, exit 5 (Shallowford Rd), 0.5 mi w to Shallowford Village Dr, 0.5 mi n, then just w. Int corridors. **Pets:** Medium, other species. Service with restrictions, supervision.

Motel 6 M
(423) 265-7300. **$40-$100.** 2440 Williams St. I-24, exit 178 (Market St). Int corridors. **Pets:** Accepted.

Red Roof Inn-Chattanooga M
(423) 899-0143. **$38-$53.** 7014 Shallowford Rd. I-75, exit 5 (Shallowford Rd). Ext corridors. **Pets:** Other species. Designated rooms, no service, supervision.

Rodeway Inn M
(423) 622-8353. **Call for rates.** 2000 E 23rd St. I-24, exit 181, just n on 4th Ave, just w. Ext corridors. **Pets:** Accepted.

CLARKSVILLE

⚜ ▽▽▽ Comfort Inn South M
(931) 358-2020. **$45-$58.** 1112 SR 76. I-24, exit 11. Ext corridors. **Pets:** Very small. $10 one-time fee/pet. Designated rooms, service with restrictions, supervision.
SAVE ⓢ ✕ 🛏 🖥 ☎

▽▽▽ Days Inn North M
(931) 552-1155. **$45-$65, 3 days notice.** 130 Westfield Ct. I-24, exit 4. Ext corridors. **Pets:** Accepted.
SAVE ⓢ ✕ ♿ 🛏 ☎

▽▽ Days Inn of Clarksville M
(931) 358-3194. **$45, 7 days notice.** 1100 Hwy 76 Connector Rd. I-24, exit 11. Ext corridors. **Pets:** Medium. Service with restrictions, supervision.
SAVE ⓢ ✕ 🛏 ☎

▽▽▽ Holiday Inn-I-24 M
(931) 648-4848. **$65-$79, 5 days notice.** 3095 Wilma Rudolph Blvd. I-24, exit 4. Ext corridors. **Pets:** Small, other species. $10 daily fee/room. Designated rooms, service with restrictions.
ASK ⓢ ✕ 🛏 🖥 🍴 ☎

▽▽ Ramada Limited M
(931) 552-0098. **$45.** 3100 Wilma Rudolph Blvd. I-24, exit 4. Ext corridors. **Pets:** Accepted.
ASK ⓢ ✕ 🛏 ☎

CLEVELAND

⚜ ▽▽▽ Comfort Inn M
(423) 478-5265. **$55-$75, 15 days notice.** 153 James Asbury Dr. I-75, exit 27, 0.5 mi w. Ext/int corridors. **Pets:** Accepted.
SAVE ⓢ ✕ 🛏 🖥 ☎

⚜ ▽▽▽ Holiday Inn Mountain View M
(423) 472-1500. **$69-$85.** 2400 Executive Park Dr. I-75, exit 25. Ext/int corridors. **Pets:** Accepted.
SAVE ⓢ ✕ ♿ 🛏 🖥 🍴 ☎

⚜ ▽▽▽ Ramada Limited M
(423) 472-5566. **$55-$75, 15 days notice.** 156 James Asbury Dr. I-75, exit 27. Ext corridors. **Pets:** Accepted.
SAVE ⓢ ✕ 🗲 🛏 🖥 ☎

CLINTON

▽▽▽ Best Western Clinton Inn M
(865) 457-2311. **$45-$120.** 720 Park Pl. I-75, exit 122, 0.5 mi w. Ext corridors. **Pets:** Medium. $5 daily fee/pet. Service with restrictions, supervision.
SAVE ⓢ ✕ ♿ 🛏 🖥 ☎

▽▽ Budget Inn M
(865) 457-3333. **$32-$40, 7 days notice.** 247 Main St. I-75, exit 122, 5 mi w on US 61 at jct US 25 W and 61. Ext corridors. **Pets:** Very small. $10 daily fee/pet. Designated rooms, service with restrictions, supervision.
ASK ⓢ ✕ 🛏

▽▽ Clinton Super 8 Motel M
(865) 457-0565. **$49-$75.** 2317 Sevver Blvd. I-75, exit 122, 0.5 mi w. Int corridors. **Pets:** Accepted.
ⓢ ✕ ♿ 🎧 🛏 🖥 ☎

▽▽▽ Holiday Inn Express Hotel & Suites M
(865) 457-2233. **$70, 3 days notice.** 141 Buffalo Rd. I-75, exit 122, 0.5 mi w. Ext corridors. **Pets:** Small. $10 daily fee/pet. Service with restrictions, supervision.
ASK ⓢ ✕ ♿ 🗲 🛏 🖥 ☎

COLUMBIA

⚜ ▽▽▽ Best Value Inn M
(931) 381-1410. **$45-$55.** 1548 Bear Creek Pike. I-65, exit 46, just w. Ext corridors. **Pets:** Accepted.
SAVE ⓢ ✕

⚜ ▽▽ James K Polk Motel M
(931) 388-4913. **$39.** 1111 Nashville Hwy. Jct SR 412 and US 31, just n. Ext corridors. **Pets:** $5 one-time fee/pet. Service with restrictions, supervision.
SAVE ✕ 🛏 ☎

▽▽ Ramada Inn M
(931) 388-2720. **$55.** 1208 Nashville Hwy. Jct SR 412 and US 31, 0.5 mi n. Ext corridors. **Pets:** Medium, other species. $5 deposit/pet. Designated rooms, service with restrictions, supervision.
ASK ⓢ ✕ 🛏 🖥 ☎

COOKEVILLE

⚜ ▽▽▽ Alpine Lodge & Suites M
(931) 526-3333. **$38-$54.** 2021 E Spring St. I-40, exit 290, just s. Int corridors. **Pets:** Other species. $5 daily fee/room. Designated rooms, service with restrictions, supervision.
SAVE ⓢ ✕ 🎧 🛏 ☎

⚜ ▽▽▽ Best Western Thunderbird Motel M
(931) 526-7115. **$50-$85.** 900 S Jefferson. I-40, exit 287. Ext corridors. **Pets:** Accepted.
SAVE ⓢ ✕ ♿ 🗲 🛏 ☎

⚜ ▽▽▽ Days Inn M
(931) 528-1511. **$45-$60, 7 days notice.** 1296 Bunker Hill Rd. I-40, exit 287. Ext corridors. **Pets:** Other species. $5 one-time fee/pet. Designated rooms, service with restrictions, crate.
SAVE ⓢ ✕ 🛏 🖥 ☎

⚜ ▽▽▽ Econo Lodge M ❀
(931) 528-1040. **$45-$65.** 1100 S Jefferson Ave. I-40, exit 287. Ext corridors. **Pets:** Small. $5 daily fee/pet. Designated rooms, service with restrictions, supervision.
SAVE ⓢ ✕ 🛏 🖥 ☎

▽▽▽ Hampton Inn M
(931) 520-1117. **$75-$115, 14 days notice.** 1025 Interstate Dr. I-40, exit 287, 0.5 mi n. Ext corridors. **Pets:** Service with restrictions, crate.
SAVE ⓢ ✕ ♿ 🎧 🗲 🛏 🖥 ☎

WWWW Holiday Inn **MI**
(931) 526-7125. **$86, 14 days notice.** 970 S Jefferson.
I-40, exit 287. Ext/int corridors. **Pets:** Small, other species.
$25 one-time fee/room. Service with restrictions, supervision.

(ASK) (S🐾) (✕) (க்M) (💻) (🍴) (🏊)

CORNERSVILLE

(AAA) WWW Econo Lodge **MI**
(931) 293-2111. **$55-$65.** 3731 Pulaski Hwy. I-65, exit 22, at
jct US 31A. Ext corridors. **Pets:** Small. $5 daily fee/pet. No
service, supervision.

(SAVE) (S🐾) (✕) (💻) (🏊)

CROSSVILLE

WW Ramada Limited **MI**
(931) 484-7581. **$62-$69, 15 days notice.** 4083 Hwy 127
N. I-40, exit 317, just n. Ext corridors. **Pets:** Other species.
$10 daily fee/room. Designated rooms, service with restrictions, supervision.

(ASK) (S🐾) (✕) (💻) (🏊)

CUMBERLAND GAP

WWWW Cumberland Gap Inn **MI**
(423) 869-9172. **$60-$80, 21 days notice.** 630 Brooklyn St.
US 25 E, exit 58E, 0.7 mi s to town. Ext corridors.
Pets: Accepted.

(ASK) (S🐾) (✕) (🍴) (💻) (🏊)

WW Ramada Inn of Cumberland Gap **MI** 🐾
(423) 869-3631. **$72-$92, 14 days notice.** Hwy 58. US 25
E, exit 58E. Int corridors. **Pets:** Other species. $25 one-time
fee/room. Service with restrictions.

(ASK) (S🐾) (✕) (🍴) (🏊)

DANDRIDGE

WW Tennessee Mountain Inn **MI** 🐾
(865) 397-9437. **$48-$100, 30 days notice.** 531 Patriot Dr.
I-40, exit 417, just n. Ext corridors. **Pets:** Small. $20 daily
fee/pet. Designated rooms, no service, supervision.

(S🐾) (✕) (🏊)

DAYTON

(AAA) WWW Best Western Dayton **MI**
(423) 775-6560. **$65-$105.** 7835 Rhea County Hwy. 1 mi n
on US 27. Ext corridors. **Pets:** Small, other species. $5
daily fee/pet. Designated rooms.

(SAVE) (S🐾) (✕) (🍴) (💻) (🍴) (🏊)

(AAA) WWW Days Inn **MI**
(423) 775-9718. **$55-$65.** 3914 Rhea County Hwy. 1 mi s
on US 27. Ext corridors. **Pets:** Accepted.

(SAVE) (S🐾) (✕) (🍴)

DECHERD

WW Jameson Inn **M**
(931) 962-0130. **$55-$70.** 1838 Decherd Blvd. Jct Main St
and SR 41A, just s. Ext corridors. **Pets:** Accepted.

(✕) (🍴) (💻) (🏊)

DICKSON

(AAA) WWW Days Inn **M**
(615) 740-7475. **$60-$80.** 2415 Hwy 46 S. I-40, exit 172,
just s. Ext corridors. **Pets:** Accepted.

(SAVE) (S🐾) (✕) (🏊)

(AAA) WWW Econo Lodge **M**
(615) 446-0541. **$40-$59.** 2338 Hwy 46. I-40, exit 172. Ext
corridors. **Pets:** Small, dogs only. $5 daily fee/pet. Service
with restrictions, supervision.

(SAVE) (S🐾) (✕) (🍴) (💻) (🏊)

(AAA) WWW Holiday Inn **MI**
(615) 446-9081. **$64-$74, 14 days notice.** 2420 Hwy 46 S.
I-40, exit 172. Ext corridors. **Pets:** Accepted.

(SAVE) (S🐾) (✕) (🔈) (🍴) (💻) (🍴) (🏊)

WW Super 8 Motel **M**
(615) 446-1923. **$49-$59, 7 days notice.** 150 Suzanne Dr.
I-40, exit 172. Int corridors. **Pets:** Very small, dogs only. $5
daily fee/pet. Designated rooms, service with restrictions,
supervision.

(ASK) (S🐾) (✕) (🍴) (🏊)

WW Value Inn **M**
(615) 446-2423. **$45, 3 days notice.** 2325 Hwy 46 S. I-40,
exit 172. Ext corridors. **Pets:** $5 daily fee/room. Designated
rooms, no service, supervision.

(ASK) (S🐾) (✕) (🔈) (🍴) (🏊)

DYERSBURG

WW Four Seasons Inn **M**
(731) 287-0044. **$38-$50.** 2331 Lake Rd. I-155, exit 13, 0.5
mi s. Ext corridors. **Pets:** $10 one-time fee/pet. Service with
restrictions, supervision.

(✕) (🍴)

WWWW Hampton Inn **M**
(731) 285-4778. **$69, 7 days notice.** 2750 Mall Loop Rd.
I-155, exit 13, just s. Int corridors. **Pets:** Service with restrictions, supervision.

(SAVE) (✕) (க்M) (🔈) (🍴) (🍴) (💻) (🏊)

EAST RIDGE

(AAA) WWWW Howard Johnson Plaza Hotel **MI**
(423) 892-8100. **$61-$76, 3 days notice.** 6700 Ringgold
Rd. 8.5 mi se on US 41 and 76, jct I-75, exit 1 (Ringgold
Rd). Int corridors. **Pets:** Accepted.

(SAVE) (S🐾) (✕) (🍴) (💻) (🍴) (🏊)

WW Knights Inn **MI**
(423) 894-1860. **$40-$80, 7 days notice.** 6650 Ringgold
Rd. I-75, exit 1 (Ringgold Rd). Ext/int corridors.
Pets: Accepted.

(ASK) (S🐾) (✕) (🏊)

⚠️ ▼▼▼ Ramada Inn South M ❀
(423) 894-6110. **$47-$51.** 6639 Capehart Ln. I-75, exit 1 (Ringgold Rd), 0.3 mi e. Ext/int corridors. **Pets:** Medium. $6 daily fee/pet. Service with restrictions, supervision.

ELIZABETHTON

▼▼▼ Comfort Inn M
(423) 542-4466. **$54-$200, 5 days notice.** 1515 US 19 E Bypass. 1 mi e on US 19 E Bypass and US 321. Int corridors. **Pets:** Small, other species. $10 daily fee/room. Designated rooms, service with restrictions, supervision.

ERWIN

▼▼▼ Holiday Inn Express M
(423) 743-4100. **$80.** 2002 Temple Hill Rd. Just e of exit 15, US 19 W and 23. Int corridors. **Pets:** Small. $14.95 one-time fee/pet. Service with restrictions, supervision.

▼▼ Super 8 Motel M
(423) 743-0200. **$49.** 1101 N Buffalo St. Just w of exit 18, US 19 W and 23. Int corridors. **Pets:** Small, dogs only. $5 daily fee/pet. Designated rooms, service with restrictions, supervision.

FARRAGUT

⚠️ ▼▼▼ Baymont Inn & Suites-Knoxville West M
(865) 671-1010. **$68-$70.** 11341 Campbell Lakes. I-40/75, exit 373 (Campbell Station Rd). Int corridors. **Pets:** Other species. Service with restrictions, supervision.

⚠️ ▼▼▼ Super 8 M
(865) 675-5566. **$54-$99.** 11748 Snyder Rd. I-40/75, exit 373 (Campbell Station Rd), just ne. Ext corridors. **Pets:** Small. $6 daily fee/pet. Service with restrictions, supervision.

FAYETTEVILLE

▼▼ Best Western-Fayetteville Inn M
(931) 433-0100. **$65-$85.** 3021 Thornton Taylor Pkwy. 0.7 mi e of US 431, on US 64 and 231 Bypass. Ext corridors. **Pets:** Other species. $10 daily fee/room.

FRANKLIN

⚠️ ▼▼▼ AmeriSuites M
(615) 771-8900. **$89-$119.** 650 Bakers Bridge Ave. I-65, exit 69 (Gallerria Blvd), 0.5 mi s, just e. Int corridors. **Pets:** Small, other species. $10 daily fee/pet. Service with restrictions, supervision.

⚠️ ▼▼▼ Baymont Inn & Suites-Nashville South (Franklin) M
(615) 791-7700. **$49-$69.** 4207 Franklin Commons Ct. I-65, exit 65, just e. Int corridors. **Pets:** Accepted.

⚠️ ▼▼▼ Best Western Franklin Inn M
(615) 790-0570. **$30-$80, 14 days notice.** 1308 Murfreesboro Rd. I-65, exit 65, just w. Ext corridors. **Pets:** Accepted.

⚠️ ▼▼▼ Comfort Inn M
(615) 791-6675. **$55-$125, 10 days notice.** 4206 Franklin Commons Ct. I-65, exit 65, just e. Ext corridors. **Pets:** Small. $10 daily fee/pet. Designated rooms, service with restrictions, supervision.

⚠️ ▼▼▼ Days Inn M
(615) 790-1140. **$55-$75.** 4217 S Carothers Rd. I-65, exit 65, just e. Ext corridors. **Pets:** Supervision.

▼▼ Holiday Inn Express Hotel & Suites M ❀
(615) 591-6660. **$75.** 4202 Franklin Commons. I-65, exit 65, just e. Int corridors. **Pets:** Other species. $15 daily fee/pet. Service with restrictions, supervision.

▼▼ Homestead Studio Suites-Nashville/Cool Springs/Brentwood M
(615) 771-7600. **$44-$48.** 680 Bakers Bridge Ave. I-65, exit 69 (Galeria Blvd). Ext corridors. **Pets:** Other species. $75 one-time fee/room. Service with restrictions, crate.

▼▼▼ Namaste Acres Country Ranch Inn BB
(615) 791-0333. **$95, 5 days notice.** 5436 Leipers Creek. SR 96, 5 mi w, SR 46, 6 mi sw, 1.9 mi s. Int corridors. **Pets:** Other species. No service, supervision.

▼▼ Super 8 M
(615) 794-7591. **$51-$85.** 1307 Murfreesboro Rd. I-65, exit 65, just w. Ext corridors. **Pets:** Accepted.

GALLATIN

▼▼ Super 8 Motel M
(615) 452-4521. **$43-$48.** Hwy 31/109 Business. I-31 E, corner of CR 109 Business. Ext corridors. **Pets:** Medium. $50 deposit/room. Designated rooms, service with restrictions, supervision.

GATLINBURG

▼▼ Highland Motel M
(865) 436-4110. **$25-$60.** 131 Parkway. US 441, just n of traffic light 1. Ext corridors. **Pets:** Accepted.

Holiday Inn Sunspree Resort M
(865) 436-9201. **$49-$109.** 520 Historic Nature Tr. US 441, 1 mi e at traffic light 8. Ext/int corridors. **Pets:** Other species. $6 one-time fee/pet. Service with restrictions, supervision.

SAVE 🏊 ✕ 🐾 🎦 📶 🖥 🖨 🍴 🍽

Microtel-Gatlinburg M
(865) 436-0107. **$28-$84, 3 days notice.** 211 Airport Rd. US 441, traffic light 8, just e. Int corridors. **Pets:** Medium, other species. $10 one-time fee/room. Designated rooms, service with restrictions, supervision.

SAVE 🏊 ✕ 🐾 🎦 🖥

Terrace Motel M
(865) 436-4965. **$49-$84, 7 days notice.** 396 Parkway. US 441, between traffic lights 2 and 3. Ext corridors. **Pets:** Small, dogs only. Service with restrictions.

ASK 🏊 📶 🍽

GREENEVILLE

Holiday Inn M
(423) 639-4185. **Call for rates.** 1790 E Andrew Johnson Hwy. US 11 E Bypass, 2.9 mi ne. Ext/int corridors. **Pets:** Accepted.

ASK ✕ 📶 🖥 🍴 🍽

HARRIMAN

Best Western Sundancer Motor Lodge M
(865) 882-6200. **$44-$59.** 120 Childs Rd. I-40, exit 347, just n. Ext corridors. **Pets:** Small. $5 daily fee/pet. Designated rooms, no service, supervision.

SAVE 🏊 ✕

Holiday Inn Express M
(865) 882-5340. **$62-$80.** 1845 S Roane St. I-40, exit 347, just s. Ext corridors. **Pets:** Other species. Designated rooms, no service, supervision.

ASK 🏊 ✕ 🐾 🎦 📶 🖥 🍽

Super 8 Motel M
(865) 882-6600. **$49-$54.** 1867 S Roane St. I-40, exit 347, 0.3 mi s on US 27/SR 61. Ext corridors. **Pets:** Medium. $5 daily fee/pet. Designated rooms, service with restrictions, supervision.

SAVE 🏊 ✕ 📶 🍽

HUNTSVILLE

Holiday Inn Express-Big South Fork M
(423) 663-4100. **$72-$77.** 11597 Scott Hwy. SR 63 and 27, just n. Ext corridors. **Pets:** Accepted.

ASK 🏊 ✕ 📶 🍽

HURRICANE MILLS

Holiday Inn Express M
(931) 296-2999. **$59-$69.** 15368 Hwy 13 S. I-40, exit 143, just ne. Int corridors. **Pets:** Accepted.

SAVE 🏊 ✕ 🎦 📶 🍽

JACKSON

Baymont Inn & Suites-Jackson M
(731) 664-1800. **$54-$59.** 2370 N Highland Ave. I-40, exit 82A. Int corridors. **Pets:** Accepted.

SAVE 🏊 ✕ 📶 🖥 🍽

Days Inn M
(731) 668-3444. **$53-$60, 14 days notice.** 1919 US 45 Bypass. I-40, exit 80A, just s. Ext corridors. **Pets:** Accepted.

SAVE ✕ 🍽

Days Inn-West M
(731) 668-4840. **$42-$49, 14 days notice.** 2239 Hollywood Dr. I-40, exit 79. Ext corridors. **Pets:** Small, other species. $20 deposit/room. Designated rooms, service with restrictions, supervision.

SAVE 🏊 ✕ 📶 🍽

Garden Plaza Hotel M
(731) 664-6900. **$81.** 1770 Hwy 45 Bypass. I-40, exit 80A, 0.5 mi s. Int corridors. **Pets:** Other species. $5 daily fee/pet. Designated rooms, service with restrictions, crate.

ASK ✕ 🎦 📶 🖥 🍴 🍽

Old Hickory Inn M
(731) 668-4222. **$54-$69.** 1849 Hwy 45 Bypass. I-40, exit 80A, 0.3 mi s. Ext corridors. **Pets:** Accepted.

ASK 🏊 ✕ 🍽

Travelers Motel M
(731) 668-0542. **$31-$55.** 2247 N Highland Ave. I-40, exit 82A, 1 mi s. Ext corridors. **Pets:** Accepted.

SAVE 🏊 ✕ 📶

JELLICO

Best Western Holiday Plaza Motel M
(423) 784-7241. **Call for rates.** 133 Holiday Dr. I-75, exit 160, just w. Ext corridors. **Pets:** Accepted.

ASK ✕ 🍽

Days Inn M
(423) 784-7281. **$46-$50.** US 25 W. I-75, exit 160, just w. Ext corridors. **Pets:** Accepted.

SAVE 🏊 ✕ 🖥 🍴 🍽

JOHNSON CITY

Comfort Inn of Johnson City M 🐾
(423) 928-9600. **$57-$160, 3 days notice.** 1900 S Roan St. I-181, exit 31, just n on US 321. Ext corridors. **Pets:** Medium. $80 deposit/room. Service with restrictions, supervision.

SAVE 🏊 ✕ 📶 🖥 🍽

Holiday Inn-Johnson City M
(423) 282-4611. **$69-$93.** 101 W Springbrook Dr. I-181, exit 35B northbound; exit 35 southbound, just e, then just s. Int corridors. **Pets:** Small. $50 deposit/pet. Service with restrictions.

ASK 🏊 ✕ 🎦 📶 🖥 🍴 🍽

▼▼▼ **Howard Johnson Plaza Hotel** Ⓜ ❀
(423) 282-2161. **$72.** 2406 N Roan St. I-181, exit 35B northbound; exit 35 southbound, just e. Ext/int corridors. **Pets:** Medium. $25 deposit/room. Designated rooms, service with restrictions, supervision.
(ASK) (S🔒) (✕) (🖑) 🔋 🖵 (¶) ⊶

🔺 ▼▼ **Red Roof Inn-Johnson City** Ⓜ
(423) 282-3040. **$39-$66.** 210 Broyles Dr. I-181, exit 35B northbound; exit 35 southbound, 0.5 mi w, then just s. Ext corridors. **Pets:** Accepted.
(SAVE) (✕) (🔊) 🔋

KINGSPORT

🔺 ▼▼▼ **La Quinta Inn-Kingsport** Ⓜ
(423) 323-0500. **$62-$76.** 10150 Airport Pkwy. I-81, exit 63, just e. Int corridors. **Pets:** Small, other species. Designated rooms, service with restrictions, supervision.
(SAVE) (S🔒) (✕) (🖑M) (🔊) (🖑) 🔋 🖵 ⊶

KINGSTON

🔺 ▼▼▼ **Comfort Inn of Kingston** Ⓜ
(865) 376-4965. **$55-$65.** 905 N Kentucky St. I-40, exit 352, 0.3 mi s. Ext corridors. **Pets:** Small, other species. $10 one-time fee/pet. Service with restrictions, supervision.
(SAVE) (S🔒) (✕) 🔋

🔺 ▼▼ **Days Inn** Ⓜ
(865) 376-2069. **$50-$90, 15 days notice.** 495 Gallaher Rd. I-40, exit 356, just n. Ext corridors. **Pets:** $5 daily fee/pet. Service with restrictions, supervision.
(SAVE) (S🔒) (✕) (🔊) 🔋 ⊶

KINGSTON SPRINGS

🔺 ▼▼▼ **Best Western Harpeth Inn** Ⓜ
(615) 952-3961. **$45-$85.** 116 Luy Ben Hills Rd. I-40, exit 188, just n. Ext corridors. **Pets:** Accepted.
(SAVE) (S🔒) (✕) (🔊) 🔋 🖵 ⊶

▼ **Scottish Inn** Ⓜ
(615) 952-3115. **$35-$65.** 116 Luy Ben Hills Rd. I-40, exit 188, just n. Ext corridors. **Pets:** Accepted.
(ASK) (S🔒) (✕)

KNOXVILLE

🔺 ▼▼ **Days Inn West** Ⓜ
(865) 966-5801. **$50-$70, 14 days notice.** 326 Lovell Rd. I-40/75, exit 374. Ext corridors. **Pets:** Medium. $6 one-time fee/pet. Designated rooms, service with restrictions, supervision.
(SAVE) (S🔒) (✕) (🔊) 🔋 🖵 ⊶

🔺 ▼ **Econo Lodge West** Ⓜ
(865) 693-6061. **$50-$110, 5 days notice.** 9340 Park West Blvd. I-40/75, exit 378 (Cedar Bluff), just n to Park West Blvd, then just w. Ext corridors. **Pets:** Medium. $5 daily fee/pet. Designated rooms, service with restrictions, supervision.
(SAVE) (S🔒) (✕) 🔋 🖵 ⊶

▼▼▼ **Hampton Inn-Knoxville West at Cedar Bluff** Ⓜ
(865) 693-1101. **$79-$98.** 9128 Executive Park Blvd. I-40/75, exit 378 (Cedar Bluff Rd). Ext/int corridors. **Pets:** Small.
(SAVE) (S🔒) (✕) (🖑M) (🔊) (🖑) 🔋 🖵 ⊶

▼▼▼ **Hilton Knoxville Downtown** Ⓗ
(865) 523-2300. **$129.** 501 W Church Ave. I-40, exit 388, 0.7 mi s on US 441, then just e; at Locust St. Int corridors. **Pets:** Accepted.
(SAVE) (S🔒) (✕) (🖑M) (🔊) 🔋 🖵 (¶) ⊶

▼▼▼ **Holiday Inn-Central/Papermill Road** Ⓜ ❀
(865) 584-3911. **$92-$109.** 1315 Kirby Rd. I-40/75, exit 383 (Papermill Rd). Int corridors. **Pets:** Medium, other species. $10 daily fee/pet. Service with restrictions, crate.
(ASK) (S🔒) (✕) (🖑M) (🔊) 🔋 🖵 (¶) ⊶

▼▼ **Howard Johnson-North** Ⓜ
(865) 688-3141. **$50-$90.** 118 Merchant Dr. I-75, exit 108 (Merchant Dr). Ext/int corridors. **Pets:** Medium, other species. $10 daily fee/room. Designated rooms, service with restrictions, supervision.
(ASK) (S🔒) (✕) (🔊) 🔋 🖵 (¶) ⊶

🔺 ▼▼▼ **Hyatt Regency Knoxville** Ⓗ
(865) 637-1234. **$87-$154.** 500 Hill Ave SE. I-40, exit 388A, 0.5 mi s on James White Pkwy. Int corridors. **Pets:** Medium, other species. $50 one-time fee/room. Service with restrictions.
(SAVE) (S🔒) (✕) (🔊) (🖑) 🔋 🖵 (¶) ⊶

▼▼ **Knights Inn-North** Ⓜ
(865) 687-3500. **$36-$44, 3 days notice.** 6730 N Central Ave Pike. I-75, exit 110 (Callahan Dr), just e. Ext corridors. **Pets:** Accepted.
(ASK) (S🔒) (✕)

🔺 ▼▼▼ **La Quinta Inn** Ⓜ
(865) 687-8989. **$55-$75.** 5634 Merchant Center Blvd. I-75, exit 108 (Merchant Dr), 0.5 mi w, then 0.5 mi n. Int corridors. **Pets:** Accepted.
(SAVE) (S🔒) (✕) (🖑M) (🔊) (🖑) 🔋 ⊶

🔺 ▼▼▼ **La Quinta Inn** Ⓜ
(865) 690-9777. **$55-$75.** 258 Peters Rd N. I-40, exit 378 (Cedar Bluff). Ext corridors. **Pets:** Medium, other species. Service with restrictions, crate.
(SAVE) (S🔒) (✕) (🖑M) (🔊) 🔋 🖵 ⊶

▼▼▼ **Masters Manor Inn** ⒷⒷ
(865) 219-9888. **$80-$200, 7 days notice.** 1909 Cedar Ln. I-75, exit 108 (Merchant Dr), 2 mi e. Int corridors. **Pets:** Accepted.
(ASK) (✕)

▼▼ **Microtel** Ⓜ
(865) 531-8041. **$43, 3 days notice.** 309 N Peters Rd. I-40/75, exit 378 (Cedar Bluff), 0.5 mi s, just w. Int corridors. **Pets:** Medium, other species. $10 one-time fee/pet. Designated rooms, service with restrictions.
(ASK) (S🔒) (✕) (🖑M) (🔊)

▼▼ Motel 6 **M**
(865) 689-7100. **$39-$49.** 5640 Merchant Center Blvd. I-75, exit 108 (Merchant Dr). Ext corridors. **Pets:** Accepted.
⟦Sᴅ⟧ ⟦X⟧ ⟦🐾⟧

▼▼ Motel 6–1252 **M**
(865) 675-7200. **$39-$50.** 402 Lovell Rd. I-40/75, exit 374. Ext corridors. **Pets:** Accepted.
⟦Sᴅ⟧ ⟦X⟧ ⟦&ᴹ⟧ ⟦🐾⟧ ⟦⛱⟧ ⟦≈⟧

▼▼ Quality Inn North **Mᴵ**
(865) 689-6600. **$50-$90.** 6712 Central Ave Pike. I-75, exit 110 (Callahan Dr), just e. Ext/int corridors. **Pets:** Accepted.
⟦SAVE⟧ ⟦Sᴅ⟧ ⟦X⟧ ⟦🛏⟧ ⟦💻⟧ ⟦🍴⟧ ⟦≈⟧

▼▼▼ Radisson Summit Hill **H**
(865) 522-2600. **$129.** 401 Summit Hill Dr. I-40, exit 388, just w. Int corridors. **Pets:** Medium. $25 one-time fee/room. Service with restrictions, crate.
⟦ASK⟧ ⟦Sᴅ⟧ ⟦X⟧ ⟦🐾⟧ ⟦⛱⟧ ⟦🛏⟧ ⟦💻⟧ ⟦🍴⟧ ⟦≈⟧

◆◆◆ ▼▼ Ramada Limited-East **M**
(865) 546-7271. **$49-$89.** 722 Brakebill Rd. I-40, exit 398 (Strawberry Plains), just n. Ext corridors. **Pets:** Small. $6 daily fee/pet. Designated rooms, service with restrictions, supervision.
⟦SAVE⟧ ⟦Sᴅ⟧ ⟦X⟧ ⟦&ᴹ⟧ ⟦🛏⟧ ⟦💻⟧ ⟦≈⟧

◆◆◆ ▼▼ Red Roof Inn-West **M**
(865) 691-1664. **$41-$54.** 209 Advantage Pl. I-40/75, exit 378 (Cedar Bluff Rd), just sw. Ext corridors. **Pets:** Accepted.
⟦SAVE⟧ ⟦X⟧ ⟦&ᴹ⟧ ⟦🐾⟧ ⟦🛏⟧

▼▼ Super 8 Motel-Knoxville **M**
(865) 584-8511. **$45-$69.** 6200 Papermill Rd. I-40/75, exit 383 (Papermill Rd), 0.3 mi e. Ext corridors. **Pets:** Other species. Service with restrictions, supervision.
⟦ASK⟧ ⟦Sᴅ⟧ ⟦X⟧ ⟦&ᴹ⟧ ⟦🐾⟧ ⟦🛏⟧ ⟦💻⟧ ⟦≈⟧

LAKE CITY

◆◆◆ ▼▼ The Lamb's Inn **M**
(865) 426-2171. **$39-$53.** 620 N Main. I-75, exit 129. Ext corridors. **Pets:** Other species. Service with restrictions, crate.
⟦SAVE⟧ ⟦X⟧ ⟦≈⟧

LAWRENCEBURG

◆◆◆ ▼▼▼ Best Western Villa Inn **M**
(931) 762-4448. **$58-$75, 5 days notice.** 2126 N Locust Ave. On US 43, 2.2 mi n of jct US 64. Ext corridors. **Pets:** $10 daily fee/pet. Designated rooms, service with restrictions, supervision.
⟦SAVE⟧ ⟦X⟧ ⟦🛏⟧ ⟦💻⟧ ⟦≈⟧

LEBANON

◆◆◆ ▼▼▼ Comfort Inn **M**
(615) 444-1001. **$49-$89.** 829 S Cumberland St. I-40, exit 238. Ext corridors. **Pets:** Medium. $5 daily fee/room. Designated rooms, service with restrictions, crate.
⟦SAVE⟧ ⟦Sᴅ⟧ ⟦X⟧ ⟦🛏⟧ ⟦💻⟧ ⟦≈⟧

▼▼ Days Inn **M**
(615) 444-5635. **$50-$80, 15 days notice.** 914 Murfreesboro Rd. I-40, exit 238. Ext corridors. **Pets:** $5 daily fee/pet. Service with restrictions, supervision.
⟦SAVE⟧ ⟦Sᴅ⟧ ⟦X⟧ ⟦🛏⟧ ⟦≈⟧

▼▼▼ Hampton Inn **M**
(615) 444-7400. **$54-$79.** 704 S Cumberland St. I-40, exit 238. Ext corridors. **Pets:** Accepted.
⟦SAVE⟧ ⟦Sᴅ⟧ ⟦X⟧ ⟦&ᴹ⟧ ⟦🐾⟧ ⟦🛏⟧ ⟦💻⟧ ⟦≈⟧

▼▼▼ Shoney's Inn **M**
(615) 449-5781. **$62-$110.** 822 S Cumberland St. I-40, exit 238. Ext corridors. **Pets:** $8 daily fee/pet. Service with restrictions, crate.
⟦ASK⟧ ⟦Sᴅ⟧ ⟦X⟧ ⟦🛏⟧ ⟦💻⟧ ⟦≈⟧

▼▼ Super 8 Motel **M**
(615) 444-5637. **$50-$80, 15 days notice.** 914 Murfreesboro Rd. I-40, exit 238. Ext corridors. **Pets:** $5 daily fee/pet. Service with restrictions, supervision.
⟦ASK⟧ ⟦Sᴅ⟧ ⟦X⟧ ⟦🛏⟧ ⟦≈⟧

LENOIR CITY

◆◆◆ ▼▼▼ Econo Lodge **M**
(865) 986-0295. **$49-$69.** 1211 Hwy 321 N. I-75, exit 81, just w. Ext corridors. **Pets:** Small. $6 daily fee/pet. Service with restrictions, supervision.
⟦SAVE⟧ ⟦Sᴅ⟧ ⟦X⟧ ⟦🐾⟧ ⟦🛏⟧ ⟦≈⟧

LOUDON

◆◆◆ ▼▼▼ Holiday Inn **H**
(865) 458-5668. **$70-$105.** 12400 Hwy 72 N. I-75, exit 72. Int corridors. **Pets:** Small, other species. Service with restrictions, supervision.
⟦SAVE⟧ ⟦X⟧ ⟦&ᴹ⟧ ⟦🛏⟧ ⟦💻⟧ ⟦≈⟧

◆◆◆ ▼▼ Knights Inn **M**
(865) 458-5855. **$42-$62, 3 days notice.** 15100 Hwy 72. I-75, exit 72. Ext corridors. **Pets:** Small. $3 daily fee/pet. Service with restrictions, supervision.
⟦SAVE⟧ ⟦Sᴅ⟧ ⟦X⟧ ⟦🛏⟧ ⟦≈⟧

◆◆◆ ▼▼▼ Super 8 Motel **M**
(865) 458-5669. **$55-$70, 10 days notice.** 12452 Hwy 72 N. I-75, exit 72. Ext corridors. **Pets:** Small, other species. Service with restrictions, supervision.
⟦SAVE⟧ ⟦Sᴅ⟧ ⟦X⟧ ⟦&ᴹ⟧ ⟦🐾⟧ ⟦💻⟧ ⟦≈⟧

MANCHESTER

◆◆◆ ▼▼ Days Inn & Suites **M**
(931) 728-9530. **$46-$66.** 2259 Hillsboro Blvd. I-24, exit 114, just w. Ext corridors. **Pets:** Medium, dogs only. $5 daily fee/pet. Service with restrictions, supervision.
⟦SAVE⟧ ⟦Sᴅ⟧ ⟦X⟧ ⟦🛏⟧ ⟦💻⟧ ⟦≈⟧

◆◆◆ ▼▼ Econo Lodge **M**
(931) 728-6023. **$45-$75.** 890 Interstate Dr. I-24, exit 110. Ext corridors. **Pets:** Accepted.
⟦SAVE⟧ ⟦Sᴅ⟧ ⟦X⟧ ⟦🛏⟧ ⟦💻⟧ ⟦≈⟧

Red Roof Inn M
(931) 728-5177. **$39-$69, 30 days notice.** 95 Expressway Dr. I-24, exit 114, just w. Ext corridors. **Pets:** Medium. $5 daily fee/pet. Service with restrictions, supervision.

Super 8 Motel M
(931) 728-9720. **$45-$55.** 2430 Hillsboro Hwy. I-24, exit 114. Ext corridors. **Pets:** Very small. $6 daily fee/pet. Designated rooms, service with restrictions, supervision.

MCMINNVILLE

Best Western McMinnville Inn M
(931) 473-7338. **$38-$80, 7 days notice.** 2545 Sparta Hwy. I-24, exit 111, n on SR 55 to US 70 S Bypass. Ext corridors. **Pets:** Medium, other species. $9 daily fee/pet. Service with restrictions.

MEMPHIS METROPOLITAN AREA

COLLIERVILLE

Comfort Inn M
(901) 853-1235. **$65.** 1230 W Poplar. 2.5 mi w on SR 57 and US 72. Ext corridors. **Pets:** Other species. $25 one-time fee/room. Service with restrictions, supervision.

CORDOVA

Best Suites of America-Memphis M
(901) 386-4600. **$72-$127.** 8166 Varnavas Dr. I-40, exit 16, 0.3 mi s on Germantown Rd, then e. Int corridors. **Pets:** Accepted.

COVINGTON

Best Western Inn M
(901) 476-8561. **$45-$55.** 873 Hwy 51 N. 0.8 mi n of jct US 59 W. Ext corridors. **Pets:** Medium. $5 daily fee/pet. Designated rooms, service with restrictions, supervision.

GERMANTOWN

Best Inns of America-Memphis M
(901) 757-7800. **$57-$82, 10 days notice.** 7787 Wolf River Blvd. I-40, exit 16, 5 mi s on Germantown Pkwy. Int corridors. **Pets:** Medium. Service with restrictions, crate.

Homewood Suites by Hilton-Germantown M
(901) 751-2500. **$99-$135.** 7855 Wolf River Pkwy. I-40, exit 16, 5.8 mi s on CR 177 at jct of Germantown and Wolf River pkwys. Int corridors. **Pets:** Accepted.

LAKELAND

Super 8 Motel M
(901) 372-4575. **$56-$70.** 9779 Huff & Puff Rd. I-40, exit 20. Ext corridors. **Pets:** Small, dogs only. $10 daily fee/pet. Designated rooms, service with restrictions, supervision.

MEMPHIS

Baymont Inn & Suites Memphis-Airport M
(901) 396-5411. **$54-$64.** 3005 Millbranch Rd. I-240, exit 24, just s. Int corridors. **Pets:** Small. $50 deposit/room. Designated rooms, service with restrictions, supervision.

Baymont Inn & Suites-Memphis East M
(901) 377-2233. **$64-$69.** 6020 Shelby Oaks Dr. I-40, exit 12, just n. Int corridors. **Pets:** Medium, other species. $50 deposit/room. Service with restrictions, supervision.

Best Suites Thousand Oaks M
(901) 365-2575. **$82-$127.** 2575 Thousand Oaks Dr. I-240, exit 18. Int corridors. **Pets:** Accepted.

Comfort Inn Airport/Graceland M
(901) 345-3344. **$55-$85, 7 days notice.** 1581 E Brook Rd. I-55, exit 5A (Brook Rd), 0.3 mi e. Ext corridors. **Pets:** $10 daily fee/pet. Service with restrictions, supervision.

Drury Inn & Suites-Memphis M
(901) 373-8200. **$60-$93.** 1556 Sycamore View. I-40, exit 12, just n. Int corridors. **Pets:** Accepted.

Hampton Inn & Suites M
(901) 762-0056. **$95.** 962 S Shady Grove Rd. I-240, exit 15A (Poplar Ave), 0.5 mi e. Int corridors. **Pets:** Accepted.

WWW Hawthorn Suites M
(901) 682-1722. **$99-$139, 7 days notice.** 1070 Ridge Lake Blvd. I-240, exit 15 (Poplar Ave), just e, then north under overpass. Int corridors. **Pets:** Accepted.

WWW Holiday Inn Memphis East MI
(901) 682-7881. **$139-$149, 7 days notice.** 5795 Poplar Ave. I-240, exit 15 (Poplar Ave), just e. Int corridors. **Pets:** Medium. $25 one-time fee/room. Service with restrictions, crate.

WWW Homestead Studio
Suites-Memphis/Airport M
(901) 344-0010. **$54-$69.** 2541 Corporate Ave E. I-240, exit 23B (Airways Blvd S), just s to Democrat Rd, just w to Nonconnah Blvd, 0.4 mi n to Corporate Ave, follow signs. Int corridors. **Pets:** Accepted.

WWW Homestead Studio
Suites-Memphis/Poplar M
(901) 767-5522. **Call for rates.** 6500 Poplar Ave. I-240, exit 15 (Poplar Ave), 1 mi e. Int corridors. **Pets:** Medium. $75 one-time fee/pet. Designated rooms, service with restrictions, supervision.

AAA WWWW Homewood Suites M
(901) 763-0500. **$129.** 5811 Poplar. I-240, exit 15A (Poplar Ave). Ext/int corridors. **Pets:** Accepted.

AAA WWWW La Quinta Inn & Suites M
(901) 374-0330. **$65-$95.** 1236 Primacy Pkwy. I-240, exit 15 (Poplar Ave), 0.3 mi e, s on Ridgeway, then w, just s. Int corridors. **Pets:** Small, dogs only. No service, supervision.

AAA WWWW La Quinta Inn-East M
(901) 382-2323. **$57-$77.** 6068 Macon Cove. I-40, exit 12, just s. Ext corridors. **Pets:** Accepted.

AAA WWWW La Quinta Inn-Medical Center M
(901) 526-1050. **$54-$71.** 42 S Camilla St. I-240, exit 30 (Union Ave), just w. Ext corridors. **Pets:** Accepted.

AAA WWWW Marriott Residence Inn A
(901) 685-9595. **$79-$129.** 6141 Old Poplar Pike. I-240, exit 15 (Poplar Ave), 0.5 mi e. Ext/int corridors. **Pets:** Accepted.

WWW Motel 6-459 M
(901) 382-8572. **$41-$53.** 1321 Sycamore View. I-40, exit 12, just e. **Pets:** Accepted.

AAA WWWW Red Roof Inn-East M
(901) 388-6111. **$42-$57.** 6055 Shelby Oaks Dr. I-40, exit 12, just n. Ext corridors. **Pets:** Accepted.

AAA WWWW Red Roof Inn
Memphis-Downtown M
(901) 528-0650. **$44-$69.** 210 S Pauline St. I-240 N, exit 30 (Union Ave W); I-240 S, exit 30 (Madison Ave). Ext corridors. **Pets:** Accepted.

AAA WWWW Red Roof Inn-South M
(901) 363-2335. **$45-$65.** 3875 American Way. I-240, exit 20A (Getwell Rd) eastbound; exit 20 westbound, then just s. Ext corridors. **Pets:** Accepted.

AAA WWWW Wellesley Inn & Suites M
(901) 380-1525. **$64-$99.** 2520 Horizon Lake Dr. I-40, exit 16B (Germantown), just n, then just w. Int corridors. **Pets:** Small, other species. Service with restrictions, supervision.

MILLINGTON

WW Best Western Inn M
(901) 873-2222. **Call for rates, 14 days notice.** 7726 Hwy 51 N. 0.3 mi s from jct of Navy Rd. Ext corridors. **Pets:** Accepted.

❀ **END METROPOLITAN AREA** ❀

MONTEAGLE

WWWW Best Western Smoke House Lodge MI
(931) 924-2091. **$60.** 850 W Main. I-24, exit 134. Ext corridors. **Pets:** Accepted.

MORRISTOWN

AAA WWWW Days Inn M
(423) 587-2200. **$45-$59, 30 days notice.** 2512 E Andrew Johnson Hwy. I-81, exit 8 (US 25 E), then 6 mi n, exit 2B (Greenville-Morristown). Ext corridors. **Pets:** Accepted.

▼▼▼ **Holiday Inn** Ⓜ
(423) 581-8700. **$65-$79.** 3304 W Andrew Johnson Hwy. 2.5 mi w on US 11 E. Ext corridors. **Pets:** Medium, other species. Service with restrictions.

(ASK) 🛒 ✕ 🌐 🛏 💻 🍴 🌊

▼▼▼ **Holiday Inn Morristown Conference Center** Ⓜ
(423) 587-2400. **$75-$105.** 5435 S Davy Crockett Pkwy. I-81, exit 8, just n. Int corridors. **Pets:** Medium, other species. Service with restrictions, supervision.

(ASK) 🛒 ✕ 🛏 💻 🍴 🌊

▼▼ **Super 8 Motel** Ⓜ
(423) 318-8888. **$44-$69.** 5400 S Davey Crockett Pkwy. I-81, exit 8, just n. Int corridors. **Pets:** Medium, other species. $9 one-time fee/pet. Service with restrictions.

(ASK) 🛒 ✕ 🖑 🖐

MURFREESBORO

▼▼▼▼ **Best Inn & Suites** Ⓜ
(615) 890-1006. **$55-$80.** 2135 S Church St. I-24, exit 81 westbound; exit 81B eastbound. Int corridors. **Pets:** Accepted.

(ASK) 🛒 ✕ 🖐 🛏 💻 🌊

🔷 ▼▼▼ **Best Western Chaffin Inn** Ⓜ 🐾
(615) 895-3818. **$55-$85, 10 days notice.** 168 Chaffin Pl. I-24, exit 78B. Ext corridors. **Pets:** Medium. $8 daily fee/pet. Designated rooms, service with restrictions, supervision.

(SAVE) 🛒 ✕ 🛏 💻 🌊

▼▼▼ **Hampton Inn** Ⓜ
(615) 896-1172. **$84-$139.** 2230 Armory Dr. I-24, exit 78B, just n. Ext corridors. **Pets:** Medium. Designated rooms, service with restrictions.

(SAVE) 🛒 ✕ 🌐 🌐 🛏 💻 🌊

🔷 ▼▼▼ **Holiday Inn Holidome** Ⓜ
(615) 896-2420. **$79-$129, 3 days notice.** 2227 Old Fort Pkwy. I-24, exit 78B. Ext/int corridors. **Pets:** Accepted.

(SAVE) 🛒 ✕ 🌐 🛏 💻 🍴 🌊

🔷 ▼▼ **Howard Johnson Express Inn** Ⓜ
(615) 896-5522. **$40-$79, 15 days notice.** 2424 S Church St. I-24, exit 81A. Int corridors. **Pets:** Small. $5 daily fee/pet. Service with restrictions, supervision.

(SAVE) 🛒 ✕ 🛏 💻 🌊

🔷 ▼▼ **Quality Inn** Ⓜ 🐾
(615) 848-9030. **$29-$69.** 118 Westgate Blvd. I-24, exit 81A. Int corridors. **Pets:** Large, other species. $5 one-time fee/room. Service with restrictions.

(SAVE) 🛒 ✕ 🛏 💻 🌊

🔷 ▼▼ **Ramada Limited** Ⓜ
(615) 896-5080. **$50-$90.** 1855 S Church St. I-24, exit 81. Int corridors. **Pets:** Other species. $10 daily fee/pet. Service with restrictions, supervision.

(SAVE) 🛒 ✕ 🌊

NASHVILLE METROPOLITAN AREA

GOODLETTSVILLE

🔷 ▼▼▼ **Baymont Inn & Suites-Nashville North** Ⓜ
(615) 851-1891. **$71-$125, 7 days notice.** 120 Cartwright Ct. I-65, exit 97 (Long Hollow Pike), just w. Int corridors. **Pets:** Small. Designated rooms, service with restrictions, supervision.

(SAVE) 🛒 ✕ 🖑 🌐 🖐 🛏 💻 🌊

▼▼ **Econo Lodge Rivergate** Ⓜ
(615) 859-4988. **$45-$70.** 320 Long Hollow Pike. I-65, exit 97 (Long Hollow Pike), 0.5 mi e. Ext corridors. **Pets:** Accepted.

(SAVE) 🛒 ✕ 🌊

🔷 ▼▼▼ **Red Roof Inn-Nashville North** Ⓜ
(615) 859-2537. **$33-$44.** 110 Northgate Dr. I-65, exit 97 (Long Hollow Pike), 0.5 mi e. Ext corridors. **Pets:** Accepted.

(SAVE) ✕ 🖑 🌐

🔷 ▼▼▼ **Shoney's Inn Nashville North** Ⓜ 🐾
(615) 851-1067. **$61-$85.** 100 Northcreek Blvd. I-65, exit 97 (Long Hollow Pike), 0.5 mi e. Ext corridors. **Pets:** Small. $25 deposit/pet. Service with restrictions, supervision.

(SAVE) 🛒 ✕ 🛏 💻 🌊

HERMITAGE

▼▼ **Ramada Limited** Ⓜ
(615) 889-8940. **$55-$70, 14 days notice.** 5770 Old Hickory Blvd. I-40, exit 221 westbound; exit 221B eastbound, just n. Ext corridors. **Pets:** Accepted.

(ASK) 🛒 ✕ 🛏 🌊

NASHVILLE

🔷 ▼▼▼ **AmeriSuites Nashville Airport** Ⓜ
(615) 493-5200. **$90-$100.** 721 Royal Pkwy. I-40, exit 216C (Donelson Pike). Int corridors. **Pets:** Medium. $50 deposit/room. Service with restrictions, supervision.

(SAVE) ✕ 🖑 🛏 💻 🌊

🔷 ▼▼ **Baymont Inn & Suites Nashville-Airport** Ⓜ
(615) 885-3100. **$59-$79.** 531 Donelson Pike. I-40, exit 216C (Donelson Pike), 0.3 mi n. Int corridors. **Pets:** Accepted.

(SAVE) 🛒 ✕ 🌐 🛏 💻 🌊

🔷 ▼▼▼ **Best Suites (Airport Area)** Ⓜ
(615) 391-3919. **$80-$130, 3 days notice.** 2521 Elm Hill Pike. I-40, exit 215, 1 mi n on Briley Pkwy, exit 7, 1 mi e. Int corridors. **Pets:** Accepted.

(SAVE) 🛒 ✕ 🖑 🌐 🛏 💻 🌊

Best Western Calumet Inn M
(615) 889-9199. **$40-$119, 15 days notice.** 701 Stewarts Ferry Pike. I-40, exit 219 (Stewarts Ferry Pike). Ext corridors. **Pets:** Accepted.

Comfort Inn Opryland M
(615) 889-0086. **$66-$85.** 2516 Music Valley Dr. I-40, exit 215, 4 mi n; I-65, exit 90, exit Magavock off Briley Pkwy. Int corridors. **Pets:** Accepted.

Days Inn Bell Road M
(615) 731-7800. **$50-$70.** 510 Collins Park Dr. I-24, exit 59 (Bell Rd). Ext corridors. **Pets:** Accepted.

Days Inn Vanderbilt M ✿
(615) 327-0922. **$80-$99.** 1800 West End Ave. I-40, exit 209A westbound; exit 209B eastbound. Ext/int corridors. **Pets:** Medium, other species. $10 daily fee/room. Service with restrictions, crate.

Doubletree Hotel Downtown Nashville H
(615) 244-8200. **$109-$189.** 315 Fourth Ave N. At corner of Union St and Fourth Ave. Int corridors. **Pets:** Accepted.

Drury Inn-Nashville South M
(615) 834-7170. **$40-$80.** 341 Harding Pl. I-24, exit 56 (Harding Pl). Ext corridors. **Pets:** Accepted.

Econo Lodge M
(615) 226-9805. **$35-$79, 3 days notice.** 2403 Brick Church Pike. I-65, exit 87 (Trinity Ln), just nw. Ext corridors. **Pets:** Large. $10 daily fee/pet. Designated rooms, service with restrictions, crate.

Embassy Suites H
(615) 871-0033. **$99-$149.** 10 Century Blvd. I-40, exit 215 (Briley Pkwy N), then exit 7 (Elm Hill Pike), 0.3 mi e to McGavock Pike, 0.3 mi s to Century Blvd, then 0.3 mi w. Int corridors. **Pets:** Small. $10 daily fee/pet. Service with restrictions, crate.

Hampton Inn Briley Parkway M
(615) 871-0222. **$69-$78.** 2350 Elm Hill Pike. I-40, exit 215B (Briley Pkwy), to exit 7 (Elm Hill Pike). Ext corridors. **Pets:** Accepted.

The Hermitage Hotel H ✿
(615) 244-3121. **$125-$185.** 231 6th Ave N. Center. Int corridors. **Pets:** Large, other species. $50 one-time fee/room. Service with restrictions.

Holiday Inn Select Opryland/Airport MI
(615) 883-9770. **$129-$149.** 2200 Elm Hill Pike. I-40, exit 215B (Briley Pkwy), 0.5 mi n. Int corridors. **Pets:** $100 deposit/room, $25 one-time fee/pet. Service with restrictions, supervision.

Holiday Inn-The Crossings MI ✿
(615) 731-2361. **$77-$84.** 201 Crossings Pl. I-24, exit 60, 0.5 mi e. Int corridors. **Pets:** Medium. Designated rooms, service with restrictions, supervision.

Homestead Studio Suites-Nashville/Airport M
(615) 316-9020. **$54-$69.** 727 McGavock Pike. I-40, exit 215B (Briley Pkwy), 1 mi n to exit 7 (Elm Hill Pike), just e. Ext corridors. **Pets:** Large, other species. $75 one-time fee/room. Service with restrictions, crate.

La Quinta Inn Nashville Airport M
(615) 885-3000. **$59-$79.** 2345 Atrium Way. I-40, exit 215B (Briley Pkwy), 1 mi n to exit 7 (Elm Hill Pike), e to Atrium Way, then 0.3 mi n. Int corridors. **Pets:** Small, other species. Service with restrictions, supervision.

La Quinta Inn-South M
(615) 834-6900. **$55-$75.** 4311 Sidco Dr. I-65, exit 78A. Ext corridors. **Pets:** Accepted.

Loews Vanderbilt Hotel Nashville H ✿
(615) 320-1700. **$139.** 2100 W End Ave. I-40, exit 209, 1.3 mi w. Int corridors. **Pets:** Other species. Service with restrictions, supervision.

Motel 6-156 M
(615) 333-9933. **$35-$45.** 95 Wallace Rd. I-24, exit 56 (Harding Pl). Ext corridors. **Pets:** Accepted.

Pear Tree Inn-Nashville South M
(615) 834-4242. **$35-$70.** 343 Harding Pl. I-24, exit 56 (Harding Pl). Ext corridors. **Pets:** Accepted.

Quality Inn MI
(615) 367-9150. **$53.** 981 Murfreesboro Rd. I-24, exit 52 (Murfreesboro Rd), 5 mi se. Ext corridors. **Pets:** Accepted.

The Quarters Motor Inn M
(615) 731-5990. **$49-$79.** 1100 Bell Rd. I-24, exit 59 (Bell Rd), just w. Ext corridors. **Pets:** Accepted.

Red Roof Inn M
(615) 889-0090. **$50-$79.** 2460 Music Valley Dr. I-40, exit 215B (Briley Pkwy), 4 mi n to exit 11 (McGavock Pike). Int corridors. **Pets:** Medium, other species. Crate.

Red Roof Inn Airport M
(615) 872-0735. **$42-$58.** 510 Claridge Dr. I-40, exit 216C (Donelson Pike), 0.3 mi n. Ext corridors. **Pets:** Accepted.
[SAVE] [X] [ᗌ]

Red Roof Inn South M
(615) 832-0093. **$43-$62.** 4271 Sidco Dr. I-65, exit 78. Ext corridors. **Pets:** Medium, other species. Service with restrictions, supervision.
[SAVE] [X] [&M] [ᗌ]

Sheraton Music City Hotel H
(615) 885-2200. **$89-$159.** 777 McGavock Pike. I-40, exit 215B (Briley Pkwy), 1 mi n to exit 7 (Elm Hill Pike), 0.5 mi e, then s. Int corridors. **Pets:** Service with restrictions.
[SAVE] [Sᗑ] [X] [&M] [ᗌ] [🖃] [📺] [🍴] [🏊]

Shoney's Inn-of Music Valley M
(615) 885-4030. **$64-$134.** 2420 Music Valley Dr. Briley Pkwy, exit 12B, 0.3 mi w, then 0.3 mi n. Int corridors. **Pets:** Other species. $100 deposit/room. Designated rooms, service with restrictions, crate.
[SAVE] [Sᗑ] [X] [🖃] [📺] [🏊]

Shoney's Inn Of Nashville M
(615) 255-9977. **$54-$124.** 1501 Demonbreun St. I-40, exit 209B. Ext corridors. **Pets:** Accepted.
[SAVE] [Sᗑ] [X] [🖃] [🏊]

Super 8 North M
(615) 226-1897. **$44-$64, 3 days notice.** 3320 Dickerson Pk. I-65, exit 90A southbound; exit 90B northbound. Int corridors. **Pets:** Medium, other species. $10 one-time fee/room. Crate.
[SAVE] [Sᗑ] [X] [&M] [🖃] [🏊]

Union Station-A Wyndham Historic Hotel H ❀
(615) 726-1001. **$124-$139.** 1001 Broadway. I-40, exit 209A, just ne. Int corridors. **Pets:** $50 one-time fee/room. Designated rooms, service with restrictions.
[SAVE] [Sᗑ] [X] [🖃] [📺] [🍴]

❀ **END METROPOLITAN AREA** ❀

NEWPORT

Best Western Newport Inn M
(423) 623-8713. **$44-$159, 7 days notice.** 1015 Cosby Hwy. I-40, exit 435, just w. Ext corridors. **Pets:** Medium, other species. Service with restrictions.
[SAVE] [Sᗑ] [X] [&M] [ᗌ] [🍴] [🏊]

Comfort Inn M ❀
(423) 623-5355. **$48-$109.** 1149 Smokey Mountain Ln. I-40, exit 432B. Int corridors. **Pets:** Large. $12 one-time fee/pet. Service with restrictions, supervision.
[SAVE] [Sᗑ] [X] [&M] [&] [🖃] [📺] [🏊]

Holiday Inn MI
(423) 623-8622. **$100.** 1010 Cosby Hwy. I-40, exit 435. Ext/int corridors. **Pets:** Accepted.
[ASK] [Sᗑ] [X] [ᗌ] [📺] [🍴] [🏊]

Motel 6-4090 M
(423) 623-1850. **$37-$81.** 255 Heritage Blvd. I-40, exit 435, just n, then turn right. Int corridors. **Pets:** Other species. Designated rooms, service with restrictions, supervision.
[Sᗑ] [X] [&M] [&] [🏊]

Relax Inn M
(423) 625-1521. **$28-$85, 3 days notice.** 1148 W Hwy 25-70. I-40, exit 432B. Ext corridors. **Pets:** Small. $5 one-time fee/pet. Crate.
[SAVE] [Sᗑ] [X] [🖃]

OAK RIDGE

Comfort Inn M
(865) 481-8200. **$72.** 433 S Rutgers Ave. 0.9 mi se of SR 95 on SR 62. Int corridors. **Pets:** Accepted.
[SAVE] [Sᗑ] [X] [🖃] [📺] [🏊]

ONEIDA

The Galloway Inn M
(423) 569-8835. **$36-$38.** 299 Galloway Dr. 2 mi s on US 27. Ext corridors. **Pets:** Small, other species. $3 daily fee/pet. Service with restrictions, supervision.
[SAVE] [Sᗑ] [X] [🖃]

OOLTEWAH

Super 8 Motel M
(423) 238-5951. **$45.** 5111 Hunter Rd. I-75, exit 11, jct US 11 and 64. Ext corridors. **Pets:** Accepted.
[ASK] [Sᗑ] [X] [🏊]

PIGEON FORGE

Grand Resort Hotel & Convention Center MI
(865) 453-1000. **$46-$120.** 3171 Parkway. On US 441. Ext/int corridors. **Pets:** Accepted.
[SAVE] [Sᗑ] [X] [🖃] [📺] [🍴] [🏊]

Holiday Inn Resort MI
(865) 428-2700. **$79-$159.** 3230 Parkway. Just w of US 441. Int corridors. **Pets:** Accepted.
[ASK] [Sᗑ] [X] [ᗌ] [🖃] [📺] [🍴] [🏊]

Microtel M
(865) 429-0150. **$28-$84, 3 days notice.** 202 Emert St. On US 441, just w between traffic light 7 and 8. Int corridors. **Pets:** Medium. $10 one-time fee/pet. No service, supervision.
[SAVE] [Sᗑ] [X] [&M] [🖃] [🏊]

▼▼ Motel 6 M

(865) 908-1244. **$25-$100.** 336 Henderson Chapel Rd. On US 441, just w of traffic light 1. Int corridors. **Pets:** Small. Service with restrictions, supervision.

ASK ⊠ &M 🐾 🛏 ➔

POWELL

▼▼ Comfort Inn M

(865) 938-5500. **$52-$90.** 323 E Emory Rd. I-75, exit 112. Ext corridors. **Pets:** $10 daily fee/room. Service with restrictions, crate.

SAVE S🏊 ⊠ 🛏 🖵 ➔

PULASKI

AAA ▼▼▼ Super 8 Motel M ❀

(931) 363-4501. **$47-$65.** 2400 Hwy 64 E. I-65, exit 14, just e. Ext corridors. **Pets:** Medium, other species. $5 daily fee/pet. Designated rooms, service with restrictions, supervision.

SAVE S🏊 ⊠ 🛏 ➔

ROGERSVILLE

▼▼▼ Holiday Inn Express M

(423) 272-1842. **$70-$90.** 7139 Hwy 11 W. Jct SR 66 and US 11, just sw. Int corridors. **Pets:** Very small, other species. $10 daily fee/pet. Designated rooms, service with restrictions, crate.

ASK S🏊 ⊠ 🐾 🛏 🖵 ➔

SELMER

▼▼ Super 8 Motel-Selmer M

(731) 645-8880. **$60-$150, 7 days notice.** 644 Mulberry Ave. Jct SR 64 and 45, just s on SR 45. Ext corridors. **Pets:** Medium. $25 deposit/room. Service with restrictions, supervision.

ASK S🏊 ⊠ 🛏 ➔

SEVIERVILLE

AAA ▼▼▼▼ Best Western Dumplin Valley Inn M

(865) 933-3467. **$39-$94.** 3426 Winfield Dunn Pkwy. I-40, exit 407, 0.3 mi s. Ext corridors. **Pets:** Medium. $10 daily fee/pet. Service with restrictions.

SAVE S🏊 ⊠ 🐾 🛏 ➔

▼▼▼ Holiday Inn Express Hotel & Suites M ❀

(865) 933-9448. **$50-$130.** 2863 Winfield Dunn Pkwy. I-40, exit 407, 2 mi s. Int corridors. **Pets:** Medium, dogs only. Service with restrictions, supervision.

ASK S🏊 ⊠ &M 🐾 🐾 🛏 🖵 ➔

SMYRNA

▼▼▼ Days Inn M

(615) 355-6161. **$62-$82, 3 days notice.** 1300 Plaza Dr. I-24, exit 66, 2 mi ne. Ext corridors. **Pets:** Dogs only. $10 daily fee/pet. Designated rooms, service with restrictions, supervision.

SAVE S🏊 ⊠ 🛏 ➔

SWEETWATER

AAA ▼▼▼▼ Best Western Sweetwater Inn M

(423) 337-3541. **$69-$115.** 1421 Murray's Chapel Rd. I-75, exit 60, just w. Ext/int corridors. **Pets:** Very small. Designated rooms, service with restrictions, supervision.

SAVE S🏊 ⊠ 🛏 🖵 🍴 ➔

AAA ▼▼▼▼ Comfort Inn M

(423) 337-6646. **$56-$75.** 731 S Main St. Jct SR 68 and US 11. Ext/int corridors. **Pets:** Small. $5 daily fee/pet. Designated rooms, service with restrictions, supervision.

SAVE S🏊 ⊠ 🛏 🖵 ➔

AAA ▼▼ Comfort Inn West M

(423) 337-3353. **$60-$85.** 249 Hwy 68. I-75, exit 60, just e. Ext/int corridors. **Pets:** Accepted.

SAVE S🏊 ⊠ 🛏 🖵 ➔

AAA ▼▼▼ Days Inn M

(423) 337-4200. **$54-$75, 3 days notice.** 229 Hwy 68. I-75, exit 60, just e. Ext corridors. **Pets:** $5 daily fee/pet. Service with restrictions, supervision.

SAVE S🏊 ⊠ 🛏 🖵 ➔

TOWNSEND

AAA ▼▼▼▼ Best Western Valley View Lodge M

(865) 448-2237. **$45-$120, 3 days notice.** 7726 E Lamar Alexander. Center; on US 321. Ext corridors. **Pets:** Small, dogs only. $10 one-time fee/room. Service with restrictions, crate.

SAVE S🏊 ⊠ 🐾 🛏 🖵 ➔

WHITE HOUSE

AAA ▼▼▼ Days Inn Whitehouse M

(615) 672-3746. **$40-$55.** 1009 Hwy 76. I-65, exit 108, just w. Ext corridors. **Pets:** Small. $5 daily fee/pet. Designated rooms, service with restrictions, supervision.

SAVE S🏊 ⊠ 🛏 ➔

▼▼▼ Holiday Inn Express M

(615) 672-7200. **$58-$89.** 354 Hester Ln. I-65, exit 108, just e. Ext corridors. **Pets:** Medium. $5 daily fee/pet. Service with restrictions, crate.

ASK S🏊 ⊠ &M 🐾 🛏 🖵 ➔

WHITE PINE

▼▼ Days Inn M

(865) 674-2573. **$53-$57.** 3670 Roy Messer Hwy. I-81, exit 4, just nw. Ext corridors. **Pets:** Accepted.

SAVE S🏊 ⊠ 🛏

WILDERSVILLE

AAA ▼▼▼ Best Western Crossroads Inn M

(731) 968-2532. **$42-$62.** 21045 Hwy 22 N. I-40, exit 108, just s. Ext corridors. **Pets:** Other species. $10 daily fee/pet. Service with restrictions, supervision.

SAVE S🏊 ⊠ 🛏 ➔

TEXAS

CITY INDEX

ABILENE

▼▼ Antilley Inn M
(915) 695-3330. **$46-$53.** 6550 S Hwy 83. From US 83/84, exit Antilley Rd. Ext corridors. **Pets:** Medium. $10 daily fee/pet. Service with restrictions, supervision.

▼▼▼ Best Western Abilene Inn & Suites M
(915) 672-5501. **$89-$99.** 350 I-20 W. I-20, exit 286C, just n. Int corridors. **Pets:** Accepted.

▲▲▲ ▼▼▼ Best Western Mall South M
(915) 695-1262. **$69-$78.** 3950 Ridgemont Dr. Just s of US 83/84, exit Ridgemont Dr. Ext corridors. **Pets:** Accepted.

▼▼ Budget Host Colonial Inn M
(915) 677-2683. **Call for rates, 3 days notice.** 3210 Pine St. Jct I-20 and US 83 business route, exit 286A. Ext/int corridors. **Pets:** Medium. $5 daily fee/pet. No service, supervision.

▼▼ Days Inn M ❀
(915) 672-6433. **$54-$59.** 1702 E Hwy 20. I-20, exit 288. Ext corridors. **Pets:** Medium, other species. $10 one-time fee/pet. Service with restrictions, supervision.

▼▼ Econo Lodge M ❀
(915) 673-5424. **$40-$45.** 1633 W Stamford. S Frontage Rd off I-20 and US 80, exit 285 eastbound; exit 286A westbound. Ext corridors. **Pets:** Small. $10 one-time fee/pet. Designated rooms, no service, supervision.
SAVE S⬚ ✕ 🖵

▼▼▼ Embassy Suites Hotel M
(915) 698-1234. **$109.** 4250 Ridgemont Dr. 0.3 mi s of US 83/84, exit Ridgemont Dr. Ext/int corridors. **Pets:** Medium. $25 one-time fee/room. Service with restrictions, supervision.
SAVE S⬚ ✕ 🖥 🖵 ¶¶ ⇌

▼▼ Executive Inn M
(915) 677-2200. **$45-$55, 5 days notice.** 1650 I-20 E. I-20, exit 288. Ext corridors. **Pets:** Other species. Supervision.
ASK ✕ 🖥 ⇌

◈◈◈ ▼▼ Quality Inn Civic Center M
(915) 676-0222. **$59-$75.** 505 Pine St. Downtown. Ext corridors. **Pets:** Small. $10 one-time fee/pet. Service with restrictions, supervision.
SAVE S⬚ ✕ 🖥 🖵 ¶¶ ⇌

▼▼ Ramada Inn M
(915) 695-7700. **$60, 30 days notice.** 3450 S Clack St. 5 mi sw on US 83/84, exit Southwest Dr. Int corridors. **Pets:** Accepted.
ASK S⬚ ✕ 🖥 🖵 ¶¶ ⇌

▼▼ Ramada Limited University M
(915) 673-5271. **$60-$90.** 1625 SR 351. I-20, exit 288. Ext corridors. **Pets:** Other species. $20 one-time fee/room. Service with restrictions, supervision.
ASK S⬚ ✕ ⬚M 🖉 🖵 🖥 🖵 ⇌

▼▼ Super 8 Motel M
(915) 673-5251. **$50-$65, 3 days notice.** 1525 E I-20. I-20, exit 288. Ext corridors. **Pets:** Large, other species. $5 daily fee/pet. Service with restrictions, supervision.
ASK S⬚ ✕ 🖥 🖵 ⇌

ALPINE

◈◈◈ ▼▼▼ Ramada Limited M
(915) 837-1100. **$95.** 2800 W Hwy 90. 2 mi n on US 90. Int corridors. **Pets:** Medium, other species. $20 deposit/pet. Service with restrictions, supervision.
SAVE S⬚ ✕ ⬚M 🖉 🖵 🖥 🖵

ALVIN

◈◈◈ ▼▼ Country Hearth Inn M
(281) 331-0335. **$59-$62.** 1588 S Hwy 35 Bypass. CR 35 Bypass, 0.5 mi sw of SR 6. Ext corridors. **Pets:** Accepted.
SAVE S⬚ ✕ 🖥 🖵 ⇌

AMARILLO

◈◈◈ ▼▼▼ Amarillo Residence Inn M
(806) 354-2978. **$99-$122, 14 days notice.** 6700 I-40 W. I-40, exit 66 (Bell St), 0.5 mi w on north frontage line. Int corridors. **Pets:** Accepted.
SAVE S⬚ ✕ 🖉 🖵 🖥 🖵 ⇌

▼▼▼ Ambassador Hotel H
(806) 358-6161. **$99-$139.** 3100 I-40 W. I-40, exit 68, just w on north frontage road. Int corridors. **Pets:** Medium. $75 one-time fee/room. No service, supervision.
ASK S⬚ ✕ 🖉 🖥 🖵 ¶¶ ⇌

◈◈◈ ▼▼▼ Best Western Amarillo Inn M
(806) 358-7861. **$62-$82, 30 days notice.** 1610 Coulter Dr. I-40, exit 65 (Coulter Dr), 0.6 mi n. Int/int corridors. **Pets:** Small, other species. $10 one-time fee/room. Service with restrictions.
SAVE S⬚ ✕ ⬚ 🖥 🖵 ¶¶ ⇌

◈◈◈ ▼▼▼ Best Western Santa Fe Inn M
(806) 372-1885. **$68-$81.** 4600 I-40 E. I-40, exit 73 (Eastern St) eastbound; exit 73 (Bolton St) westbound, U-turn on south frontage road. Int corridors. **Pets:** Accepted.
SAVE S⬚ ✕ 🖥 ⇌

◈◈◈ ▼▼▼ Big Texan Motel M
(806) 372-5000. **$60-$65.** 7701 I-40 E. I-40, exit 75 (Lakeside Dr), 0.3 mi w on north frontage road. Ext corridors. **Pets:** Other species. $30 deposit/pet. Designated rooms, service with restrictions, supervision.
SAVE S⬚ ✕ 🖥 ¶¶ ⇌

▼▼▼ Comfort Inn-East M
(806) 376-9993. **$49-$99.** 1515 I-40 E. I-40, exit 71 (Ross-Osage), just w on north frontage road. Ext corridors. **Pets:** $10 one-time fee/room. Supervision.
SAVE S⬚ ✕ 🖉 🖥 🖵 ⇌

▼▼▼ Days Inn H
(806) 379-6255. **$49-$99, 14 days notice.** 1701 I-40 E. I-40, exit 71 (Ross-Osage), just w on north frontage road. Int corridors. **Pets:** Other species. $1000 daily fee/room. Service with restrictions, crate.
SAVE S⬚ ✕ 🖉 🖥 🖵 ⇌

▼▼▼ Days Inn South M
(806) 468-7100. **$55-$79, 7 days notice.** 8601 Canyon Dr. I-27, exit 116, just n on east service road. Int corridors. **Pets:** Medium. $20 one-time fee/pet. No service, supervision.
SAVE S⬚ ✕ ⬚ 🖥 ⇌

◈◈◈ ▼▼▼ Hampton Inn M
(806) 372-1425. **$64-$114.** 1700 I-40 E. I-40, exit 71 (Ross-Osage), just e on south frontage road. Int corridors. **Pets:** Accepted.
SAVE S⬚ ✕ 🖥 🖵 ⇌

◈◈◈ ▼▼▼ La Quinta Inn-Amarillo-Medical Center M
(806) 352-6311. **$55-$101.** 2108 S Coulter St. I-40, exit 65 (Coulter Dr), just n. Ext corridors. **Pets:** Small, other species. Service with restrictions, crate.
SAVE S⬚ ✕ ⬚M 🖉 🖥 🖵 ⇌

◈◈◈ ▼▼▼ La Quinta Inn East-Amarillo M
(806) 373-7486. **$55-$101.** 1708 I-40 E. I-40, exit 71 (Ross-Osage), just e on south frontage road. Ext/int corridors. **Pets:** Medium, other species. Service with restrictions, supervision.
SAVE S⬚ ✕ 🖉 🖥 🖵 ⇌

♦♦ ♦♦ **Motel 6 Central #72** M
(806) 355-6554. **$35-$51.** 2032 Paramount Blvd. I-40, exit 68A (Paramount Blvd), just nw. Ext corridors. **Pets:** Accepted.

♦♦♦ ♦♦♦♦ **Quality Inn & Suites** M ❀
(806) 335-1561. **$89-$139.** 1803 Lakeside Dr. I-40, exit 287 (Lakeside Dr), just n. Ext/int corridors. **Pets:** Other species. $10 daily fee/pet. Designated rooms, service with restrictions, supervision.

♦♦ ♦♦ **Radisson Inn Amarillo Airport** M
(806) 373-3303. **$67.** 7909 I-40 E. I-40, exit 75 (Lakeside Dr), just nw. Int corridors. **Pets:** Other species. $100 deposit/room. Crate.

♦♦♦ ♦♦ ♦♦ **Red Roof Inn** M
(806) 374-2020. **$60-$70.** 1620 I-40 E. I-40, exit 71 (Ross-Osage), e on south frontage road. Ext corridors. **Pets:** Medium. Designated rooms, service with restrictions, supervision.

♦♦♦ ♦♦ ♦♦ **Sleep Inn Amarillo** M
(806) 372-6200. **$69-$110, 5 days notice.** 2401 I-40 E. I-40, exit 72A (Nelson), 0.3 mi w on north frontage road. Int corridors. **Pets:** Medium, other species. $10 one-time fee/pet. Supervision.

ANTHONY

♦♦ ♦♦ **Super 8 El Paso West-Anthony** M
(915) 886-2888. **Call for rates, 5 days notice.** 100 Park North Dr. I-10, exit 0. Ext corridors. **Pets:** Accepted.

ARLINGTON

♦♦♦ ♦♦♦♦♦ **AmeriSuites (Dallas/Arlington)** M
(817) 649-7676. **$134.** 2380 E Road to Six Flags St. I-30, exit 30 (SR 360), 0.5 mi sw. Int corridors. **Pets:** Small. Service with restrictions, supervision.

♦♦♦♦♦ **Arlington Homewood Suites** M
(817) 640-0077. **$119-$159.** 2401 East Rd to Six Flags St. I-30, exit 30 (SR 360), 0.5 mi sw. Int corridors. **Pets:** Small. $150 one-time fee/room. Service with restrictions, crate.

♦♦♦ ♦♦♦♦♦ **Baymont Inn & Suites-Arlington** M
(817) 633-2400. **$64-$119, 14 days notice.** 2401 Diplomacy Dr. I-30, exit 30 (SR 360), 0.5 mi s; off SR 360 exit Six Flags Dr northbound; exit Ave H/Lamar Blvd southbound, on southbound service road. Int corridors. **Pets:** Small. $50 deposit/pet. Designated rooms, service with restrictions, supervision.

♦♦♦ ♦♦ ♦♦ **Country Inn & Suites By Carlson** ▲
(817) 261-8900. **$80-$109.** 1075 Wet 'N Wild Way. I-30, exit 28 (SR 157/Collins St), Just ne of jct I-30 and SR 157, exit 28 (Collins St). Ext corridors. **Pets:** Small. $35 one-time fee/room. Service with restrictions, supervision.

♦♦♦ ♦♦ ♦♦ **Days Inn Ballpark at Arlington/Six Flags** M
(817) 261-8444. **$39-$95, 30 days notice.** 910 N Collins St. 1.5 mi ne on SR 157; 1 mi s of jct I-30, Collins St/SR 157, exit 28. Int corridors. **Pets:** Accepted.

♦♦ ♦♦ ♦♦ **Hawthorn Suites Hotel** M
(817) 640-1188. **$95-$199.** 2401 Brookhollow Plaza Dr. I-30, exit 30, just w of SR 360, exit Ave H/Lamar Blvd. Ext corridors. **Pets:** Accepted.

♦♦ ♦♦ **Homestead Studio Suites-Arlington** M
(817) 633-7588. **$50.** 1221 N Watson Rd. Jct US 360, at Ave K/Brown Blvd exit. Ext corridors. **Pets:** Accepted.

♦♦ ♦♦ **Howard Johnson Express Inn** M
(817) 461-1122. **$49-$75.** 2001 E Copeland Rd. I-30, exit 30 (SR 360) westbound, just s to Six Flags Dr, then just w to Copeland Dr, 0.9 mi w; exit 29 (Ball Pkwy) eastbound. Int corridors. **Pets:** Small. $50 deposit/room, $10 daily fee/pet. Designated rooms, service with restrictions.

♦♦ ♦♦ ♦♦ **La Quinta Inn & Suites South Arlington** M
(817) 467-7756. **$99-$115.** 4001 Scott's Legacy. I-20, exit 450 (Matlock Rd), on southbound service road. Int corridors. **Pets:** Small. Service with restrictions.

♦♦ ♦♦ ♦♦ **La Quinta Inn-Arlington-Conference Center** M
(817) 640-4142. **$71-$115.** 825 N Watson Rd. SR 360, just s of jct I-30, exit 30; off SR 360, Six Flags Dr exit northbound; Ave H/Lamar Blvd exit southbound. Ext corridors. **Pets:** Medium, other species. Service with restrictions, crate.

♦♦ **Motel 6-122** M
(817) 649-0147. **$40-$61.** 2626 E Randol Mill Rd. Jct of SR 360 and Randol Mill Rd. Ext corridors. **Pets:** Accepted.

♦♦♦ ♦♦ ♦♦ **Residence Inn by Marriott** M
(817) 649-7300. **$125-$140.** 1050 Brookhollow Plaza Dr. I-30, exit 30 (Six Flags Dr), just n on SR 360 to Lamar Blvd, then just w. Int corridors. **Pets:** Large. $5 daily fee/room, $100 one-time fee/room. Service with restrictions.

▼▼▼ Sleep Inn Main Gate-Six Flags 🅼
(817) 649-1010. **$65-$110.** 750 Six Flags Dr. I-30, exit 30 (SR 360), 0.5 mi s. Int corridors. **Pets:** Small. $10 daily fee/pet. Designated rooms, supervision.

SAVE 🔊 ⊠ 🗐 🔒 ▣ ≈

▼▼ Studio 6 🅼
(817) 465-8500. **Call for rates.** 1980 W Pleasant Ridge Rd. I-20, exit 449 (Cooper St), 0.3 mi n, then w. Ext corridors. **Pets:** Small, other species. $10 daily fee/room, $50 one-time fee/room. Service with restrictions.

ASK 🔊 ⊠ 🖭 🔒 ▣

AUSTIN

▲▲▲ ▼▼▼▼ AmeriSuites Arboretum 🅼
(512) 231-8491. **$169-$179.** 3612 Tudor Blvd. Jct of US 183 and SR 360, northwest corner. Int corridors. **Pets:** Small, other species. Service with restrictions, crate.

SAVE 🔊 ⊠ 🖭 🗐 🖭 🔒 ▣ ≈

▲▲▲ ▼▼▼▼ AmeriSuites (Austin/North) 🅼 🐾
(512) 323-2121. **$99.** 7522 N IH-35. I-35, exit 240A, on west frontage road. Int corridors. **Pets:** Small, other species. Designated rooms, service with restrictions, crate.

SAVE 🔊 ⊠ 🖭 🗐 🖭 🔒 ▣ ≈

▲▲▲ ▼▼▼▼ Austin Marriott at the Capitol 🅷
(512) 478-1111. **$215.** 701 E 11th St. I-35, exit 234B, 0.3 mi e on 11th St. Int corridors. **Pets:** Small. $50 deposit/pet. Service with restrictions.

SAVE ⊠ 🗐 🖭 🔒 ▣ 🍴 ≈

▲▲▲ ▼▼▼▼ Baymont Inn & Suites Austin-Round Rock 🅼
(512) 246-2800. **$74-$89.** 150 Parker Dr. I-35, exit 250, on west frontage road. Int corridors. **Pets:** Other species. Service with restrictions, supervision.

SAVE 🔊 ⊠ 🖭 🗐 🖭 🔒 ▣ ≈

▲▲▲ ▼▼▼ Best Western Atrium North 🅼
(512) 339-7311. **$59-$99.** 7928 Gessner Dr. I-35, exit 240A, 0.4 mi w on Anderson Ln. Int corridors. **Pets:** Medium. Service with restrictions, supervision.

SAVE 🔊 ⊠ 🔒 ▣ ≈

▼▼▼ Candlewood Suites-South 🅼
(512) 444-8882. **$119-$149.** 4320 I-35 Service Rd S. I-35, exit 230 northbound, exit 230B southbound; on southbound frontage road. Int corridors. **Pets:** Small. $100 one-time fee/pet. Service with restrictions, supervision.

ASK 🔊 ⊠ 🖭 🗐 🖭 🔒

▲▲▲ ▼▼▼ Days Inn University-Downtown 🅼
(512) 478-1631. **$64-$99.** 3105 N IH-35. I-35, exit 236A at 32nd St (from lower level). Ext corridors. **Pets:** Medium. $8 one-time fee/room. Service with restrictions, supervision.

SAVE 🔊 ⊠ 🔒 ▣ ≈

▲▲▲ ▼▼▼ Doubletree Guest Suites-Austin 🅷
(512) 478-7000. **$79-$179.** 303 W 15th St. Center; just nw of capitol. Int corridors. **Pets:** Small. $25 one-time fee/room. Service with restrictions, crate.

SAVE 🔊 ⊠ 🗐 🔒 ▣ 🍴 ≈

▲▲▲ ▼▼▼ Doubletree Hotel 🅷
(512) 454-3737. **$79-$149.** 6505 IH-35 N. I-35, exit 238 southbound; exit 239 northbound. Int corridors. **Pets:** Accepted.

SAVE 🔊 ⊠ 🖭 🗐 🖭 🔒 ▣ 🍴 ≈

▼▼▼▼ The Driskill 🅷 🐾
(512) 474-5911. **$285-$310.** 604 Brazos St. 6th at Brazos. Int corridors. **Pets:** Small. $50 one-time fee/room. Crate.

ASK 🔊 ⊠ 🗐 🖭 🍴

▼▼▼ Drury Inn & Suites-North 🅼
(512) 467-9500. **$65-$112.** 6711 IH-35 N. I-35, exit 238 southbound; exit 239 northbound, on east frontage road. Int corridors. **Pets:** Accepted.

⊠ 🖭 🔒 ▣ ≈

▼▼▼ Drury Inn Austin-Highland Mall 🅼
(512) 454-1144. **$60-$113.** 919 E Koenig Ln. I-35, exit 238B southbound; exit 238A northbound, on west frontage road. Int corridors. **Pets:** Accepted.

⊠ 🖭 🔒 ▣ ≈

▲▲▲ ▼▼▼ Exel Inn Of Austin 🅼
(512) 462-9201. **$49-$80.** 2711 IH-35 S. I-35, exit 231 (Woodward Ave) southbound; exit 232A (Oltorf St) northbound, on the northbound frontage road; just n of jct I-35 and US 290/SR 71. Int corridors. **Pets:** Accepted.

SAVE 🔊 ⊠ 🗐 🔒 ▣ ≈

▼▼▼ Four Points Hotel by Sheraton 🅼
(512) 836-8520. **$120-$128.** 7800 I-35 N. I-35, exit 240A, on west frontage road. Int corridors. **Pets:** Other species. $50 deposit/room. Service with restrictions, crate.

ASK 🔊 ⊠ 🖭 🔒 ▣ 🍴 ≈

▼▼▼ Four Seasons Hotel 🅷
(512) 478-4500. **$270-$350.** 98 San Jacinto Blvd. bordering Town Lake. Int corridors. **Pets:** Accepted.

⊠ 🖭 🔒 ▣ 🍴 ≈

▼▼▼ Habitat Suites Hotel 🄰
(512) 467-6000. **$127-$187.** 500 E Highland Mall Blvd. I-35, exit 238B, just w on SR 2222 to Airport Blvd, 0.6 mi n to Highland Mall Blvd, then 0.4 mi e. Ext corridors. **Pets:** $50 one-time fee/pet. Designated rooms, service with restrictions, supervision.

ASK 🔊 ⊠ 🗐 🔒 ▣ ≈

▼▼▼ Hawthorn Suites Austin Central 🄰
(512) 459-3335. **$139-$159.** 935 La Posada Dr. I-35, exit 238B southbound; exit 239 northbound, just off east frontage road. Ext corridors. **Pets:** Accepted.

ASK 🔊 ⊠ 🔒 ▣ ≈

▼▼▼ Hawthorn Suites Northwest 🄰
(512) 343-0008. **$129-$179.** 8888 Tallwood Dr. Just sw of jct US 183 and Loop 1. Ext corridors. **Pets:** Accepted.

ASK 🔊 ⊠ 🖭 🗐 🔒 ▣ ≈

▼▼▼ Hawthorn Suites South **M**
(512) 440-7722. **$99-$109.** 4020 I-35 S. I-35, exit 230 (Ben White Blvd/SR 71) southbound; exit 231 (Woodward Dr) northbound, just n of jct SR 71, US 290 and I-35, on southbound frontage road. Ext corridors. **Pets:** Small, other species. $10 daily fee/pet, $50 one-time fee/pet. Service with restrictions, crate.

[ASK] [S🐾] [✕] [🐾] [🖥] [📹] [🔁]

▲▲▲ ▼▼▼▼ Hilton Austin North & Towers **H**
(512) 451-5757. **$79-$149.** 6000 Middle Fiskville Rd. I-35, exit 238B, just off west frontage road. Int corridors. **Pets:** Small, other species. $25 one-time fee/pet. Service with restrictions, crate.

[SAVE] [S🐾] [✕] [🐾M] [🐾] [🐾] [🖥] [📹] [🍴] [🔁]

▲▲▲ ▼▼▼▼ Holiday Inn Airport South **MI**
(512) 448-2444. **$99.** 3401 I-35 S. I-35, exit 231 (Woodward St) southbound; exit 230 (Ben White Blvd) northbound, on northbound frontage road. Ext/int corridors. **Pets:** Accepted.

[SAVE] [S🐾] [✕] [🐾] [🖥] [📹] [🍴] [🔁]

▼▼▼▼ Holiday Inn-Highland Mall **M**
(512) 459-4251. **$65.** 6911 IH-35 N. I-35, exit 239 northbound; exit 238B southbound, on east frontage road. Ext corridors. **Pets:** Medium. $15 one-time fee/room. Service with restrictions.

[✕] [🐾] [🐾] [📹] [🔁]

▼▼▼▼ Holiday Inn Northwest/Arboretum **MI** 🐾
(512) 343-0888. **$129-$159.** 8901 Business Park Dr. At jct US 183 and Loop 1 (Mopac), on southwest corner. Ext corridors. **Pets:** Large, other species. $25 one-time fee/room. Designated rooms, service with restrictions, supervision.

[ASK] [S🐾] [✕] [🐾] [🖥] [📹] [🍴] [🔁]

▼▼▼▼ Holiday Inn-Town Lake **MI**
(512) 472-8211. **$99-$149.** 20 N IH-35. I-35, exit 233. Int corridors. **Pets:** $100 deposit/room, $25 one-time fee/room. No service.

[ASK] [S🐾] [✕] [🐾] [🐾] [📹] [🍴] [🔁]

▼▼▼▼ Homestead Studio Suites-Austin/Downtown/ Town Lake **M**
(512) 476-1818. **$70.** 507 S First St. I-35, exit 234B southbound; exit 234A northbound, 1.8 mi w on Caesar Chavez/E First St, then 0.5 mi s. Int corridors. **Pets:** Accepted.

[ASK] [S🐾] [✕] [🐾] [🐾] [🖥] [📹]

▲▲▲ ▼▼▼▼ La Quinta Capitol **M**
(512) 476-1166. **$103-$133.** 300 E 11 St. Just e of State Capitol Building. Ext/int corridors. **Pets:** Accepted.

[SAVE] [S🐾] [✕] [🐾] [📹] [🔁]

▲▲▲ ▼▼▼▼ La Quinta Inn & Suites at Austin-Airport **M**
(512) 386-6800. **$80-$130.** 7625 E Ben White Blvd. I-35, 230B (Ben White Blvd/SR 71), 3.8 mi e. Int corridors. **Pets:** Small. Service with restrictions.

[SAVE] [S🐾] [✕] [🐾M] [🐾] [🐾] [🖥] [📹] [🔁]

▲▲▲ ▼▼▼▼ La Quinta Inn & Suites-Austin North Mopac **M**
(512) 832-2121. **$110-$129.** 11901 N Mopac Expwy. US 183, 1 mi n on Mopac to Duval exit. Int corridors. **Pets:** Small. Service with restrictions, supervision.

[SAVE] [S🐾] [✕] [🐾M] [🐾] [🐾] [🔁]

▼▼▼▼ La Quinta Inn-Highland Mall **M**
(512) 459-4381. **$76-$92.** 5812 IH-35 N. I-35, exit 238B, on west frontage road. Ext corridors. **Pets:** Accepted.

[SAVE] [S🐾] [✕] [🐾] [🖥] [📹] [🔁]

▼▼▼▼ La Quinta Inn IH35 at Ben White **M**
(512) 443-1774. **$76-$92.** 4200 I-35 S. I-35, exit 230B (Ben White Blvd/SR 71) southbound; exit 230 northbound, just s of jct I-35, SR 71 and 290, on frontage road. Ext corridors. **Pets:** Small, other species. Service with restrictions, crate.

[SAVE] [S🐾] [✕] [🐾M] [🖥] [📹] [🔁]

▼▼▼▼ La Quinta Inn-North **M**
(512) 452-9401. **$76-$92.** 7100 IH-35 N. I-35, exit 239, on west frontage road. Ext corridors. **Pets:** Small. Service with restrictions, crate.

[SAVE] [S🐾] [✕] [🐾] [🖥] [📹] [🔁]

▲▲▲ ▼▼▼▼ La Quinta Inn Oltorf **M**
(512) 447-6661. **$76-$106.** 1603 E Oltorf Blvd. I-35, exit 232A (Oltorf Blvd), just s. Ext/int corridors. **Pets:** Small, other species. Designated rooms, service with restrictions, supervision.

[SAVE] [S🐾] [✕] [🐾] [🐾] [🖥] [📹] [🔁]

▲▲▲ ▼▼▼▼ La Quinta SW **M**
(512) 899-3000. **$120-$140.** 4424 S Loop 1 (Mopac). At jct of Loop 1 (Mopac), US 290 and SR 71 E, on southbound frontage road. Int corridors. **Pets:** Small, other species. Service with restrictions, supervision.

[SAVE] [S🐾] [✕] [🐾M] [🐾] [🐾] [🖥] [📹] [🔁]

▼▼▼ Motel 6 Austin North–360 **M**
(512) 339-6161. **$49-$65.** 9420 N I-35. I-35, exit 240 (Rundberg St), just w. Ext corridors. **Pets:** Accepted.

[S🐾] [✕] [🐾] [🔁]

▼▼▼ Motel 6 Central **M**
(512) 467-9111. **$49-$61.** 5330 I-35 N. I-35, exit 238B northbound; exit 238A southbound; on west frontage road. Ext corridors. **Pets:** Accepted.

[S🐾] [✕] [🐾] [🔁]

▼▼▼ Red Lion Hotel Austin **H**
(512) 323-5466. **$69-$129.** 6121 I-35 N. I-35, exit 238A northbound; exit 238B southbound, on east frontage road. Int corridors. **Pets:** Other species. $50 deposit/pet.

[ASK] [S🐾] [✕] [🐾] [🖥] [📹] [🍴] [🔁]

▲▲▲ ▼▼▼ Red Roof Inn Austin North **M**
(512) 835-2200. **$44-$60.** 8210 IH-35 N. I-35, exit 241, on west frontage road. Ext corridors. **Pets:** Small. Service with restrictions, crate.

[SAVE] [✕] [🐾] [🐾] [🔁]

🔺 ▽▽▽ Red Roof Inn-Austin South M
(512) 448-0091. **$59-$67.** 4701 IH-35 S. I-35, exit 203B
(Ben White Blvd) southbound; exit 229 (Stassney Rd)
northbound, on northbound frontage road. Int corridors.
Pets: Accepted.

⟦SAVE⟧ ⟦✕⟧ ⟦&M⟧ ⟦🖉⟧ ⟦&⟧ ⟦🛏⟧ ⟦≈⟧

🔺 ▽▽▽▽ Renaissance Austin Hotel H
(512) 343-2626. **$219-$249.** 9721 Arboretum Blvd. Jct of
US 183 and SR 360; southwest corner. Int corridors.
Pets: Small. Service with restrictions, supervision.

⟦SAVE⟧ ⟦S⟧ ⟦✕⟧ ⟦&M⟧ ⟦🖉⟧ ⟦🛏⟧ ⟦🖵⟧ ⟦¶⟧ ⟦≈⟧

**🔺 ▽▽▽▽ Residence Inn Austin
South A ❀**
(512) 912-1100. **$134.** 4537 S I-35. I-35, exit 229 (Stassney
Rd) southbound; exit 230 (Ben White Blvd) northbound, on
northbound frontage road. Int corridors. **Pets:** Other species. $125 one-time fee/pet. Service with restrictions, super-
vision.

⟦SAVE⟧ ⟦S⟧ ⟦✕⟧ ⟦🖉⟧ ⟦&⟧ ⟦🛏⟧ ⟦🖵⟧ ⟦≈⟧

**🔺 ▽▽▽▽ Residence Inn by Marriott-Austin
North A**
(512) 977-0544. **$129.** 12401 North Lamar Blvd. I-35, exit
245, just w. Int corridors. **Pets:** $5 daily fee/pet, $75 one-
time fee/room. Service with restrictions.

⟦SAVE⟧ ⟦S⟧ ⟦✕⟧ ⟦&M⟧ ⟦🖉⟧ ⟦&⟧ ⟦🛏⟧ ⟦🖵⟧ ⟦≈⟧

**🔺 ▽▽▽▽ Residence Inn by Marriott-Austin
Northwest/Arboretum A**
(512) 502-8200. **$89-$179.** 3713 Tudor Blvd. Northwest on
US 183 to Loop 360 exit. Int corridors. **Pets:** Accepted.

⟦SAVE⟧ ⟦S⟧ ⟦✕⟧ ⟦&M⟧ ⟦🖉⟧ ⟦&⟧ ⟦🛏⟧ ⟦🖵⟧ ⟦≈⟧

🔺 ▽▽ Rodeway Inn-North M
(512) 452-1177. **$50-$99.** 5656 I-35 N. I-35, 238B northbound; 238A southbound on frontage road. Ext corridors.
Pets: Large, other species. $25 deposit/pet. Designated
rooms, service with restrictions, supervision.

⟦SAVE⟧ ⟦S⟧ ⟦✕⟧ ⟦🛏⟧ ⟦🖵⟧ ⟦≈⟧

**▽▽▽▽ Sheraton Austin Hotel & Conference
Center H**
(512) 480-8181. **$149.** 500 N IH-35. I-35, exit 234B south-
bound; exit 234C northbound, on southbound frontage
road. Int corridors. **Pets:** Accepted.

⟦ASK⟧ ⟦S⟧ ⟦✕⟧ ⟦🖉⟧ ⟦&⟧ ⟦🛏⟧ ⟦🖵⟧ ⟦¶⟧ ⟦≈⟧

▽▽▽▽ Staybridge Suites Hotel A
(512) 349-0888. **$79-$129.** 10201 Stone Lake Blvd. Jct of
US 183 and SR 360; northwest corner. Int corridors.
Pets: Accepted.

⟦ASK⟧ ⟦S⟧ ⟦&M⟧ ⟦🖉⟧ ⟦&⟧ ⟦🛏⟧ ⟦🖵⟧ ⟦≈⟧

▽▽ Studio 6-Austin Midtown M ❀
(512) 458-5453. **$64-$74.** 937 Camino La Costa. I-35, exit
239 northbound; exit 238B southbound, on east frontage
road. Ext corridors. **Pets:** Small, other species. $10 daily
fee/room. Service with restrictions, crate.

⟦✕⟧ ⟦🖉⟧ ⟦&⟧ ⟦🛏⟧ ⟦🖵⟧

🔺 ▽▽ Super 8 Central M
(512) 472-8331. **$65-$85, 3 days notice.** 1201 N I-35. I-35,
exit 234, at 12th St. Ext corridors. **Pets:** Very small. $15
one-time fee/pet. Service with restrictions, supervision.

⟦SAVE⟧ ⟦S⟧ ⟦✕⟧ ⟦🛏⟧ ⟦🖵⟧ ⟦≈⟧

**🔺 ▽▽▽▽ Wellesley Inn & Suites (Austin/N
Mopac) M**
(512) 833-0898. **$89-$109.** 2700 Gracy Farms Ln. 2 mi n of
US 183 on Loop 1 (Mopac Blvd), exit Burnet Rd (FH 1325).
Int corridors. **Pets:** Accepted.

⟦SAVE⟧ ⟦S⟧ ⟦✕⟧ ⟦&⟧ ⟦🛏⟧ ⟦🖵⟧

**🔺 ▽▽▽▽ Wellesley Inn & Suites (Austin/North
Rutherford) M**
(512) 339-6005. **$85-$105.** 8221 N I-H 35. I-35, exit 241, on
east frontage road. Int corridors. **Pets:** Accepted.

⟦SAVE⟧ ⟦S⟧ ⟦✕⟧ ⟦🖉⟧ ⟦&⟧ ⟦🛏⟧ ⟦🖵⟧ ⟦≈⟧

**🔺 ▽▽▽▽ Wellesley Inn & Suites
(Austin/NW) M**
(512) 219-6500. **$99-$119.** 12424 Research Blvd. US 183,
exit Oak Knoll, on eastbound frontage road. Int corridors.
Pets: Accepted.

⟦SAVE⟧ ⟦S⟧ ⟦✕⟧ ⟦&M⟧ ⟦🖉⟧ ⟦&⟧ ⟦🛏⟧ ⟦🖵⟧ ⟦≈⟧

BANDERA

🔺 ▽▽ Bandera Lodge Motel MI
(830) 796-3093. **$52-$79.** 700 Hwy 16 S. 1 mi s on SR 16;
7 mi s of jct SR 173. Ext corridors. **Pets:** Accepted.

⟦SAVE⟧ ⟦S⟧ ⟦✕⟧ ⟦🛏⟧ ⟦¶⟧ ⟦≈⟧

BEAUMONT

🔺 ▽▽ Best Western Beaumont Inn M
(409) 898-8150. **$58, 7 days notice.** 2155 N 11th St. I-10,
exit 853B (11th St), just n. Ext corridors. **Pets:** Accepted.

⟦SAVE⟧ ⟦S⟧ ⟦✕⟧ ⟦🛏⟧ ⟦🖵⟧ ⟦≈⟧

🔺 ▽▽ Best Western Jefferson Inn M
(409) 842-0037. **$65-$69.** 1610 I-10 S. I-10, exit 851 (College St), westbound service road, 0.5 mi s of jct US 90. Ext
corridors. **Pets:** Accepted.

⟦SAVE⟧ ⟦S⟧ ⟦✕⟧ ⟦🖉⟧ ⟦🛏⟧ ⟦🖵⟧ ⟦≈⟧

🔺 ▽▽ Hilton Beaumont H
(409) 842-3600. **$80-$100.** 2355 I-10 S. I-10, exit 850
(Washington Blvd), on eastbound service road. Int corridors.
Pets: Medium. $50 deposit/room, $20 daily fee/room. Service with restrictions, supervision.

⟦SAVE⟧ ⟦✕⟧ ⟦🖉⟧ ⟦&⟧ ⟦🛏⟧ ⟦🖵⟧ ⟦¶⟧ ⟦≈⟧

🔺 ▽▽▽▽ Holiday Inn Beaumont Midtown MI
(409) 892-2222. **$59-$69.** 2095 N 11th St. I-10, exit 853B
(11th St), just n. Int corridors. **Pets:** Accepted.

⟦SAVE⟧ ⟦S⟧ ⟦✕⟧ ⟦&M⟧ ⟦🖉⟧ ⟦&⟧ ⟦🛏⟧ ⟦🖵⟧ ⟦¶⟧ ⟦≈⟧

AAA ▼▼▼▼ Holiday Inn Beaumont Plaza **H**
(409) 842-5995. **$99-$119.** 3950 I-10 S. I-10, exit 848 (Walden Rd), 0.8 mi sw of jct US 69/96 and 287. Int corridors. **Pets:** Medium, other species. $10 one-time fee/room. Supervision.
SAVE ✕ 🐾 🄫 🖥 💻 🍴 ⌁

AAA ▼▼▼▼ La Quinta Inn-Beaumont **M**
(409) 838-9991. **$62-$82.** 220 I-10 N. I-10, eastbound service road, exit 852B (Calder Ave) eastbound; exit 852A (Laurel Ave) westbound. Ext corridors. **Pets:** Accepted.
SAVE S🄪 ✕ 🐾 🄫 🖥 💻 ⌁

BEDFORD

AAA ▼▼▼▼ La Quinta Inn-Bedford **M**
(817) 267-5200. **$58-$78.** 1450 Airport Frwy. SR 121 and 183, 0.3 mi e of jct Bedford Rd/Forest Ridge Dr exit. Ext corridors. **Pets:** Accepted.
SAVE S🄪 ✕ 🐾 🖥 💻 ⌁

BEEVILLE

▼▼ ▼▼ Beeville Days Inn **M**
(361) 358-4000. **$55, 8 days notice.** 400 A S US 181 Bypass. 0.3 mi s of jct US 59 and 181. Ext corridors. **Pets:** $20 deposit/room. Service with restrictions, supervision.
SAVE S🄪 ✕ 🖥 ⌁

BELTON

AAA ▼▼▼ Budget Host Inn **M** 🐾
(254) 939-0744. **$42-$55.** 1520 S I-35. I-35, exit 292 southbound; exit 293A northbound. Ext corridors. **Pets:** Medium, other species. Service with restrictions, supervision.
SAVE S🄪 ✕ 🖥 💻 ⌁

▼▼ ▼▼ River Forest Inn **M**
(254) 939-5711. **$55-$75, 3 days notice.** 1414 E 6th Ave. Jct of FM 93 and I-35, US 81 and 190, exit 294B (6th St). Ext corridors. **Pets:** Service with restrictions, supervision.
ASK S🄪 ✕ 🖥 ⌁

BENBROOK

▼▼ ▼▼ Motel 6–4051 **M**
(817) 249-8885. **$47-$51.** 8601 Hwy 377 S (Benbrook Blvd). I-20, exit 429A, 0.7 mi s. Int corridors. **Pets:** Small. Service with restrictions, supervision.
✕ 🄬 🄫 ⌁

BIG SPRING

AAA ▼▼▼ Best Western Big Spring **M**
(915) 267-1601. **$53.** 700 W I-20 St. I-20, exit 177, just n. Ext corridors. **Pets:** Other species.
SAVE S🄪 ✕ 🐾 🖥 💻 ⌁

AAA ▼▼▼ Great Western Inn **M**
(915) 267-4553. **$45-$50.** 2900 E I-20. I-20, exit 179. Ext corridors. **Pets:** Accepted.
SAVE S🄪 ✕ 🖥 💻 ⌁

BOERNE

AAA ▼▼ ▼▼ Best Western Texas Country Inn **M**
(830) 249-9791. **$65-$90.** 35150 IH-10 W. Jct of I-10 W at US 46, exit 540. Ext corridors. **Pets:** $10 one-time fee/pet. Service with restrictions.
SAVE S🄪 ✕ 💻 ⌁

AAA ▼▼ ▼▼ Key To The Hills Motel **MI**
(830) 249-3562. **$50-$100, 3 days notice.** 1228 S Main St. Jct of I-10 and US 87 (Main St), 1 mi n. Ext corridors. **Pets:** Very small, other species. $8 daily fee/pet. Designated rooms, service with restrictions, supervision.
SAVE S🄪 ✕ ⌁

BONHAM

AAA ▼▼ ▼▼ Days Inn **M**
(903) 583-3121. **$46-$55.** 1515 Old Ector Rd. US 82 (SR 56) at w jct of SR 121. Ext corridors. **Pets:** Very small, other species. $10 deposit/pet. No service, supervision.
SAVE S🄪 ✕ 🖥 💻 ⌁

BORGER

▼▼ ▼▼ Select Inn **M**
(806) 273-9556. **$34-$80.** 100 Bulldog Blvd. Jct of US 207 and SR 136. Ext corridors. **Pets:** Small. $5 one-time fee/room. Service with restrictions, supervision.
S🄪 ✕ 🐾 🖥 💻 ⌁

BOWIE

AAA ▼▼ ▼▼ Days Inn **M**
(940) 872-5426. **$60-$65, 7 days notice.** SR 59 & US 287. On US 287 at jct SR 59. Ext corridors. **Pets:** Other species. $5 daily fee/pet. Designated rooms, service with restrictions, supervision.
SAVE S🄪 ✕ 🖥 ⌁

AAA ▼▼ Park's Inn **M**
(940) 872-1111. **$41-$55.** 708 W Wise St. 0.5 mi n of jct SR 59. Ext corridors. **Pets:** Small. $5 one-time fee/pet. Designated rooms, no service, crate.
SAVE S🄪 ✕ 🖥 ⌁

BRADY

AAA ▼▼ ▼▼ Days Inn **M**
(915) 597-0789. **$44-$95, 7 days notice.** 2108 S Bridge St. 1 mi s on US 87/377 at jct US 190. Ext corridors. **Pets:** Medium. $10 daily fee/pet. Service with restrictions, supervision.
SAVE S🄪 ✕ 🖥 💻 ⌁

BRENHAM

AAA ▼▼▼▼ Best Western Inn of Brenham **MI**
(979) 251-7791. **$69-$109, 3 days notice.** 1503 Hwy 290 E. 0.7 mi w of jct US 290 E and SR 577 eastbound; westbound 1.3 mi e of jct SR 36 and US 290. Ext corridors. **Pets:** Accepted.
SAVE S🄪 ✕ 🖥 💻 🍴 ⌁

BROWNSVILLE

▼▼▼▼ Four Points by Sheraton M!
(956) 547-1500. **$89-$159.** 3777 N Expwy. US 77 and 83, exit McAllen Rd, 0.5 mi s on west frontage road. Int corridors. **Pets:** Small. $100 one-time fee/room. Service with restrictions, supervision.

(ASK) (Sᴅ) (✕) (🖉) (🛏) (💻) (🍽) (≈)

(AAA) ▼▼▼▼ Residence Inn by Marriott A
(956) 350-8100. **$70-$144.** 3975 N Expwy. US 83 and 77 Expwy, exit McAllen Rd. Int corridors. **Pets:** Accepted.

(SAVE) (✕) (&M) (🖉) (🛏) (💻) (≈)

BROWNWOOD

▼▼ Best Western M
(915) 646-3511. **$49-$55, 7 days notice.** 410 E Commerce. On US 67, 84 and 377; just n of jct Main Ave. Ext corridors. **Pets:** Accepted.

(SAVE) (Sᴅ) (✕) (🖉) (🛏) (💻) (≈)

▼▼ Days Inn-Brownwood M
(915) 646-2551. **$49-$55, 5 days notice.** 515 E Commerce St. On US 67, 84 and 377, 0.4 mi n of jct Main Ave. Ext corridors. **Pets:** Accepted.

(SAVE) (Sᴅ) (✕) (🛏) (💻) (≈)

BURLESON

(AAA) ▼▼▼▼ Comfort Suites M
(817) 426-6666. **$71-$89.** 321 S Burleson Blvd. I-35 W, exit 36, just e. Int corridors. **Pets:** Medium. $10 daily fee/pet. Service with restrictions, crate.

(SAVE) (Sᴅ) (✕) (&M) (🖉) (🛏) (💻) (≈)

(AAA) ▼▼ Days Inn M
(817) 447-1111. **$59-$69.** 329 S Burleson Blvd. I-35, exit 36 (Renfro St), just w to east frontage road, 0.5 mi s. Ext corridors. **Pets:** Accepted.

(SAVE) (Sᴅ) (✕) (🛏) (≈)

CANTON

(AAA) ▼▼▼ Best Western Canton Inn M
(903) 567-6591. **$49-$129.** 2251 N Trade Days Blvd. Jct I-20 and SR 19, exit 527. Ext corridors. **Pets:** Accepted.

(SAVE) (Sᴅ) (✕) (🛏) (💻) (≈)

CANYON

(AAA) ▼▼▼▼ Holiday Inn Express Hotel & Suites M
(806) 655-4445. **$63-$89.** 2901 4th Ave. I-27, exit 106, 2 mi w. Int corridors. **Pets:** Other species. $10 one-time fee/room. Service with restrictions, supervision.

(SAVE) (Sᴅ) (✕) (&M) (🛏) (💻) (≈)

CEDAR PARK

▼▼ Comfort Inn M
(512) 259-1810. **$75-$95.** 300 E Whitestone Blvd. I-35, exit 256, 8 mi w on FM 1431. Int corridors. **Pets:** Other species. $10 daily fee/pet. Supervision.

(SAVE) (Sᴅ) (✕) (&M) (🖉) (🛏) (💻) (≈)

CENTER

▼▼ Best Western Center Inn M
(936) 598-3384. **$58-$69.** 1005 Hurst St. On US 96, e jct SR 87. Ext corridors. **Pets:** Medium, other species. $10 daily fee/room. Designated rooms, service with restrictions, supervision.

(SAVE) (Sᴅ) (✕) (🛏) (💻) (≈)

CHILDRESS

(AAA) ▼▼▼▼ Best Western Classic Inn, Childress M
(940) 937-6353. **$59-$65, 7 days notice.** 1805 Ave F NW. 1.5 mi w on US 287. Ext corridors. **Pets:** Small. $5 daily fee/pet. Service with restrictions, supervision.

(SAVE) (Sᴅ) (✕) (🛏) (💻) (≈)

(AAA) ▼▼▼▼ Comfort Inn M
(940) 937-6363. **$75-$79.** 1804 Ave F NW. 1.5 mi w on US 287. Ext corridors. **Pets:** Medium, other species. $5 daily fee/pet. Service with restrictions, supervision.

(SAVE) (✕) (&M) (🖉) (🛏) (💻) (≈)

(AAA) ▼▼ Econo Lodge M!
(940) 937-3695. **$48-$70.** 1612 Ave F NW Hwy 287. 1.3 mi w. Ext corridors. **Pets:** Accepted.

(SAVE) (Sᴅ) (✕) (💻) (≈)

CISCO

▼▼ Best Western Inn Cisco M
(254) 442-3735. **$59-$69.** 1898 Hwy 206 W. I-20, exit 330. Ext corridors. **Pets:** Small, other species. $10 one-time fee/pet. No service.

(SAVE) (Sᴅ) (✕) (💻) (≈)

CLARENDON

(AAA) ▼▼▼ Western Skies Motel M
(806) 874-3501. **$45-$50, 7 days notice.** 800 W 2nd St. 0.5 mi nw on US 287 and SR 70. Ext corridors. **Pets:** Small, dogs only. $49.50 daily fee/room. Designated rooms, service with restrictions, supervision.

(SAVE) (✕) (🛏) (≈)

CLAUDE

(AAA) ▼ L A Motel M! 🐾
(806) 226-4981. **$35-$45, 7 days notice.** Hwy 287/200 E 1st St. 0.3 mi s. Ext corridors. **Pets:** Small. $7 daily fee/pet. No service, supervision.

(SAVE) (Sᴅ) (✕) (🍽)

CLEBURNE

(AAA) ▼▼ American Inn M
(817) 641-3451. **$50-$60.** 1836 N Main St. On SR 174 (Main St), just e of jct US 67. Ext corridors. **Pets:** Small. $30 daily fee/room. Service with restrictions, supervision.

(SAVE) (Sᴅ) (✕) (🛏) (💻) (≈)

△△△ ▼▼▼ Comfort Inn **M**
(817) 641-4702. **$79-$89.** 2117 N Main St. On SR 174, just
e of jct US 67. Int corridors. **Pets:** Other species. $10 daily
fee/room. Service with restrictions, supervision.
[SAVE] [S△] [X] [&M] [🐾] [🖑] [🖥] [🖵] [➰]

△△△ ▼▼▼ Sagamar Inn **M** ❀
(817) 556-3631. **$60.** 2107 N Main. US 67, exit SR 174
(Main St), just e. Ext corridors. **Pets:** Small. $20 deposit/
room. Service with restrictions, crate.
[SAVE] [S△] [X] [🖑] [🖵] [➰]

CLUTE

△△△ ▼▼▼▼ La Quinta Inn **M**
(979) 265-7461. **$66-$79.** 1126 Hwy 332 W. 3.5 mi e on jct
SR 288 and 332. Ext corridors. **Pets:** Accepted.
[SAVE] [S△] [X] [🐾] [🖑] [🖵] [➰]

△△△ ▼▼▼▼ Mainstay Suites Clute/Lake
        Jackson **M**
(979) 388-9300. **$109-$129.** 1003 W Hwy 332. Just w of jct
SR 288. Int corridors. **Pets:** Small. $100 deposit/room.
Service with restrictions, supervision.
[SAVE] [S△] [X] [&] [🖑] [🖵] [➰]

COLLEGE STATION

▼▼ ▼▼ Holiday Inn-College Station **MI**
(979) 693-1736. **$75, 3 days notice.** 1503 S Texas Ave.
1.3 mi s of jct SR 60; on SR 6 business route (Texas Ave).
Int corridors. **Pets:** Medium, dogs only. $25 one-time fee/
room. Service with restrictions, crate.
[ASK] [X] [🐾] [🖑] [🖵] [🍴] [➰]

△△△ ▼▼▼▼ La Quinta Inn **M**
(979) 696-7777. **$76-$106.** 607 Texas Ave. Just s on jct SR
60/6 business route to Live Oak St, just e. Ext corridors.
Pets: Small. No service, supervision.
[SAVE] [S△] [X] [🖑] [🖵] [➰]

▼▼ ▼▼ Manor House Inn **M**
(979) 764-9540. **$63-$83.** 2504 Texas Ave S. 2.4 mi s of jct
SR 60; on SR 6 business route (Texas Ave). Ext corridors.
Pets: Accepted.
[ASK] [S△] [X] [🖑] [🖵] [➰]

△△△ ▼▼ ▼▼ Ramada Inn **MI**
(979) 693-9891. **$69-$125, 3 days notice.** 1502 Texas Ave
S. 1.3 mi s of jct SR 60; on SR 6 business route (Texas
Ave). Int corridors. **Pets:** Very small. $10 daily fee/pet. No
service, supervision.
[SAVE] [S△] [X] [🖑] [🍴] [➰]

COLUMBUS

△△△ ▼▼ ▼▼ Country Hearth Inn **M**
(979) 732-6293. **$62.** 2436 Hwy 71 S. I-10, exit 696 (SR
71), Jct I-10 and SR 71, exit 696 (Hwy 71). Ext corridors.
Pets: Accepted.
[SAVE] [S△] [X] [🖑] [🖵] [➰]

▼▼ ▼▼ Holiday Inn Express Hotel & Suites **M**
(979) 733-9300. **$89.** 4321 I-10. I-10, exit 696, just w on
westbound service road. Int corridors. **Pets:** $40 deposit/
room, $10 one-time/pet. No service, supervision.
[ASK] [S△] [X] [🖑] [🖵] [➰]

CONWAY

△△△ ▼▼ ▼▼ Budget Host S & S Motel **MI** ❀
(806) 537-5111. **$44-$50, 3 days notice.** I-40 & SR 207.
I-40, exit 96 (SR 207), Jct SR 207, 0.3 mi w on southbound
access road. Ext corridors. **Pets:** Very small. $20 deposit/
pet. Designated rooms, no service, supervision.
[SAVE] [S△] [X] [🍴]

COPPERAS COVE

▼▼ ▼▼ Howard Johnson Express Inn **M**
(254) 547-2345. **$59, 7 days notice.** 302 W US 190. On
US 190 at jct Georgetown Rd, 0.4 mi w of jct US 190 and
SR 116. Ext corridors. **Pets:** Medium, other species. $10
one-time fee/pet. Service with restrictions, supervision.
[ASK] [S△] [X] [🖑] [🖵] [➰]

CORPUS CHRISTI

△△△ ▼▼▼▼ Best Western Garden Inn **M**
(361) 241-6675. **$69-$94.** 11217 IH-37. I-37, exit 11B (Violet
Rd). Ext corridors. **Pets:** Medium. $5 daily fee/room. Serv-
ice with restrictions.
[SAVE] [X] [🖑] [🖵] [➰]

△△△ ▼▼▼▼ Christy Estate Suites **A**
(361) 854-1091. **$109-$189.** 3942 Holly Rd. 0.5 mi s of SR
358, exit Weber Rd. Ext/int corridors. **Pets:** Small, other
species. $300 deposit/pet. Designated rooms, service with
restrictions, crate.
[SAVE] [S△] [X] [🖑] [🖵] [➰]

▼▼ ▼▼ Days Inn **MI**
(361) 888-8599. **$40-$50.** 901 Navigation Blvd. I-37, exit 3A
(Navigation Blvd), Jct of Navigation Blvd and I-37, exit 3A.
Ext corridors. **Pets:** Small, other species. $10 daily fee/
room. Designated rooms, service with restrictions, crate.
[SAVE] [S△] [X] [🐾] [🖑] [🖵] [🍴] [➰]

▼▼ ▼▼ Days Inn Corpus Christi South **M**
(361) 854-0005. **$60-$149.** 2838 S Padre Island Dr. On SR
358 westbound access road, 0.4 mi w, exit Kostoryz Rd.
Ext corridors. **Pets:** Small. Designated rooms, service with
restrictions, supervision.
[SAVE] [S△] [X] [🖑] [➰]

▼▼▼▼ Drury Inn-Corpus Christi **M**
(361) 289-8200. **$56-$93.** 2021 N Padre Island Dr. Just s of
jct I-37; on SR 358 at Leopard St. Int corridors. **Pets:** Small,
other species. Designated rooms, service with restrictions,
crate.
[X] [🐾] [🖑] [🖵] [➰]

▼▼▼▼ Holiday Inn-Emerald Beach **MI**
(361) 883-5731. **$93-$169.** 1102 S Shoreline Blvd. 1.5 mi s
on bay. Ext/int corridors. **Pets:** Small. Service with restrictions, supervision.
[ASK] [S△] [X] [&M] [🐾] [🖑] [🖵] [🍴] [➰] [X]

Holiday Inn-Padre Island Drive H
(361) 289-5100. **$79-$119.** 5549 Leopard St. 5.5 mi w at jct SR 358 and Leopard St. Int corridors. **Pets:** Accepted.

La Quinta Inn-Corpus Christi-North M
(361) 888-5721. **$69-$91.** 5155 I-37 N. I-37, exit 3A (Navigation Blvd), 0.3 mi w. Ext corridors. **Pets:** Accepted.

La Quinta Inn-South M
(361) 991-5730. **$72-$113.** 6225 S Padre Island Dr. 7.5 mi se off SR 358 Expwy, exit Airline Rd. Ext corridors. **Pets:** Small, dogs only. Service with restrictions, supervision.

Motel 6 Lantana–231 M
(361) 289-9397. **$37-$51.** 845 Lantana St. I-37, exit 4B (Lantana St). Ext corridors. **Pets:** Other species. Service with restrictions, supervision.

Motel 6 SPI Drive–413 M
(361) 991-8858. **$41-$61.** 8202 S Padre Island Dr. South Padre Island Ave at Paul Jones St. Ext corridors. **Pets:** Accepted.

Ramada Limited MI
(361) 289-5861. **$62-$251, 4 days notice.** 5501 I-37 at McBride Lane. I-37, exit 3A (Navigation St), take loop around to McBride, then left. Int corridors. **Pets:** Accepted.

Red Roof Inn Corpus Christi Airport M
(361) 289-6925. **$54-$74.** 6301 I-37. I-37, exit 5 (Corn Products Rd), southbound access road. Ext corridors. **Pets:** Accepted.

DALHART

Best Western Nursanickel Motel M
(806) 244-5637. **$54-$74.** 102 Scott Ave. Just s of jct US 54 and 87. Ext corridors. **Pets:** Small, dogs only. Service with restrictions, supervision.

Budget Inn M
(806) 244-4557. **$39-$69.** 415 Liberal St. US 54, just e of US 87 and 385. Ext corridors. **Pets:** Very small. $10 deposit/pet. Designated rooms, service with restrictions, supervision.

Comfort Inn M
(806) 249-8585. **$80.** 1110 Hwy 54 E. 0.5 mi e. Ext corridors. **Pets:** Service with restrictions.

Days Inn M
(806) 244-5246. **$82-$119.** 701 Liberal. 0.5 mi e on US 54. Int corridors. **Pets:** $30 deposit/room. Service with restrictions, supervision.

Sands Motel M
(806) 244-4568. **$35-$59.** 301 Liberal St. US 54, just e of US 87 and 385. Ext corridors. **Pets:** Accepted.

DALLAS METROPOLITAN AREA

ADDISON

Crowne Plaza North Dallas/Addison Near The Galleria H
(972) 980-8877. **$129.** 14315 Midway Rd. 0.8 mi s of jct Beltline and Midway rds. Int corridors. **Pets:** Small. $100 deposit/pet, $25 one-time fee/pet. Designated rooms, service with restrictions.

Homewood Suites by Hilton A
(972) 788-1342. **$116-$136.** 4451 Beltline Rd. Just e of jct Beltline and Midway rds. Ext/int corridors. **Pets:** Accepted.

La Quinta Inn & Suites-Dallas Addison M
(972) 404-0004. **$60-$120.** 14925 Landmark Blvd. Jct of Beltline Rd and Landmark Blvd, just s. Int corridors. **Pets:** Medium, other species. Service with restrictions, supervision.

CARROLLTON

Red Roof Inn-Carrollton M
(972) 245-1700. **$37-$55.** 1720 S Broadway. I-35 E, exit 442 (Valwood Pkwy), just ne. Ext corridors. **Pets:** Small, other species. Service with restrictions.

DALLAS

The Adolphus H
(214) 742-8200. **$305-$455.** 1321 Commerce St. Int corridors. **Pets:** Accepted.

AmeriSuites (Dallas/North) M
(972) 716-2001. **$100.** 5229 Spring Valley Rd. I-635, exit Dallas Pkwy/Inwood Rd, 0.5 mi n to Spring Valley, just e. Int corridors. **Pets:** Small, other species. Service with restrictions, crate.

AmeriSuites (Dallas/Park Central) M
(972) 458-1224. **$79-$125.** 12411 N Central Expwy. US 75, exit 8B (Coit Rd) northbound; exit 8 (Coit Rd), on southbound access road. Int corridors. **Pets:** Accepted.

AmeriSuites (Dallas/West End) M
(214) 999-0500. **$149.** 1907 N Lamar St. I-35, exit Commerce St, just e, then just n. Int corridors. **Pets:** Small, other species. Service with restrictions.

Candlewood Dallas Market Center M
(214) 631-3333. **$77-$94, 3 days notice.** 7930 N Stemmons Frwy. I-35, exit 433B (Mockingbird Ln), just w. Int corridors. **Pets:** Accepted.

Comfort Inn South M
(972) 572-1030. **$70-$85, 15 days notice.** 8541 S Hampton Rd. I-20, exit 465, just s. Ext corridors. **Pets:** Accepted.

Crowne Plaza Dallas Market Center H
(214) 630-8500. **$159-$199.** 7050 Stemmons Frwy. I-35 E, exit 433B northbound; exit 432B southbound. Int corridors. **Pets:** Medium, other species. $100 deposit/pet, $25 onetime fee/pet. Service with restrictions, crate.

Crowne Plaza Suites-Dallas Park Central H
(972) 233-7600. **$159.** 7800 Alpha Rd. Just n of I-635, 0.3 mi nw of jct I-635 and US 75, exit 19C (Coit Rd) eastbound; exit 19B (Coit Rd) westbound. Int corridors. **Pets:** $25 onetime fee/room. Service with restrictions.

Dallas Marriott Suites Market Center H
(214) 905-0050. **$139.** 2493 N Stemmons Frwy. I-35, exit 431 (Motor St). Int corridors. **Pets:** Other species. $50 onetime fee/room. Service with restrictions.

Days Inn M
(972) 224-3196. **$55-$60, 7 days notice.** 8312 S Lancaster Rd. I-20, exit 470 (Lancaster Rd). Ext corridors. **Pets:** Accepted.

Drury Inn & Suites-Dallas North M
(972) 484-3330. **$60-$97.** 2421 Walnut Hill Ln. I-35E, exit 438 (Walnut Hill Lane). Int corridors. **Pets:** Accepted.

Embassy Suites Dallas-Market Center M
(214) 630-5332. **$129-$189, 3 days notice.** 2727 Stemmons Frwy. I-35 E, exit 432 (Inwood Rd). Int corridors. **Pets:** Accepted.

Embassy Suites Hotel-Dallas/Park Central H
(972) 234-3300. **$89-$145.** 13131 N Central Expwy. N off US 75, just n of I-635, 0.8 mi s of jct Midpark Rd; exit 22 (Midpark Rd) northbound; exit 21 (service road) southbound. Int corridors. **Pets:** Small. $25 one-time fee/pet. Service with restrictions, supervision.

Fairmont Hotel-Dallas H
(214) 720-2020. **$195-$330.** 1717 N Akard St. Uptown; corner of Ross Ave and N Akard St. Int corridors. **Pets:** Accepted.

The Harvey Hotel-Dallas H
(972) 960-7000. **$69-$99.** 7815 LBJ Frwy at Coit Rd. I-635, 0.3 mi w of jct US 75, exit 19C (Coit Rd) eastbound; exit 19B westbound. Int corridors. **Pets:** Accepted.

Hawthorn Suites Hotel-Dallas- Market Center A
(214) 688-1010. **$149, 3 days notice.** 7900 Brookriver Dr. I-35 E, exit 433B (Mockingbird Ln) northbound; exit 433B (Mockingbird Ln) southbound, just se. Ext corridors. **Pets:** Accepted.

Hawthorn Suites North Dallas M
(972) 248-2233. **$129-$189, 3 days notice.** 18470 N Dallas Pkwy. Dallas North Tollway, exit Frankford, just ne. Int corridors. **Pets:** Small, dogs only. $50 one-time fee/pet. Service with restrictions, crate.

Holiday Inn Express-Love Field M
(214) 350-5577. **$69.** 2370 W Northwest Hwy. I-35 E, exit 436 (W Northwest Hwy), 0.8 mi e. Int corridors. **Pets:** Accepted.

Homewood Suites by Hilton M
(972) 437-6966. **$129-$189, 7 days notice.** 9169 Markville Dr. I-635, exit 18A (Greenville Ave S), just s, then just e. Int corridors. **Pets:** Accepted.

Hotel St. Germain CI
(214) 871-2516. **$305-$700, 7 days notice.** 2516 Maple Ave. 0.3 mi n of Woodall Rogers Pkwy, exit Pearl St. Int corridors. **Pets:** Accepted.

La Quinta Inn-Dallas-City Place M
(214) 821-4220. **$82-$99.** 4440 N Central Expwy. N off US 75, exit 2 (Henderson-Knox) northbound; exit 1B (Haskell/Blackburn). Ext corridors. **Pets:** Small, other species. Service with restrictions, crate.

La Quinta Inn-Dallas-East M
(214) 324-3731. **$66-$83.** 8303 East R L Thornton Frwy. E off I-30, US 67 and 80, exit 52A (Jim Miller), 0.8 mi w of jct Loop 12. Ext corridors. **Pets:** Accepted.

▼▼▼▼ La Quinta Inn-Dallas-Love Field M
(214) 630-5701. **$68-$90.** 1625 Regal Row. I-35 E, exit 434B (Regal Row). Ext corridors. **Pets:** Medium. Service with restrictions.

▼▼▼▼ La Quinta Inn-Richardson M
(972) 234-1016. **$76-$93.** 13685 N Central Expwy. US 75 N, exit 22 (Midpark Rd). Ext corridors. **Pets:** Accepted.

▼▼▼▼ Le Meridien Dallas H
(214) 979-9000. **$119-$169.** 650 N Pearl St. 0.3 mi w of US 75/Central Expwy. Int corridors. **Pets:** $25 deposit/room. Service with restrictions.

▲▲▲ ▼▼▼▼▼ The Mansion On Turtle Creek H ✿
(214) 559-2100. **$465, 3 days notice.** 2821 Turtle Creek Blvd. 2 mi nw, entrance on Gillespie St. Int corridors. **Pets:** Other species. $100 one-time fee/pet. Supervision.

▼▼▼ The Melrose Hotel H
(214) 521-5151. **$265.** 3015 Oak Lawn Ave. I-35 E, exit 430, 0.8 mi n, entrance off Cedar Springs, just n. Int corridors. **Pets:** Accepted.

▼▼ Motel 6 #1479 M ✿
(214) 388-8741. **$42-$57.** 8108 E R L Thornton Frwy. I-30, US 67 and 80, exit 52A (Jim Miller Rd), 0.8 mi w of jct Loop 12. Ext corridors. **Pets:** Small. Service with restrictions, supervision.

▼ Motel 6 Forest Lane–South M
(972) 484-9111. **$43-$55.** 2660 Forest Ln. I-635, exit 26 (Josey Ln), 0.5 mi s to Forest Ln, just w. Ext corridors. **Pets:** Accepted.

▲▲▲ ▼▼▼▼ Radisson Hotel Dallas H
(214) 634-8850. **$119-$139.** 1893 W Mockingbird Ln. I-35 E, exit 433C (Mockingbird Ln), then 2 mi. Int corridors. **Pets:** Accepted.

▲▲▲ ▼▼▼ Red Roof Inn-Market Center M
(214) 638-5151. **$44-$59.** 1550 Empire Central Dr. I-35 E, exit 434A (Empire Central), 0.3 mi e. Ext corridors. **Pets:** Accepted.

▲▲▲ ▼▼ ▼▼ Red Roof Inn-Northwest M
(972) 506-8100. **$40-$54.** 10335 Gardner Rd. Just sw of jct Loop 12 (Northwest Hwy) and Spur 348, 0.8 mi w of I-35 E and US 77, exit 436. Ext corridors. **Pets:** Accepted.

▲▲▲ ▼▼▼▼ Residence Inn by Marriott at Central-Northpark A
(214) 750-8220. **$122.** 10333 N Central Expwy. I-75 N, exit 6 (Meadow Rd) northbound; exit 7 (Royal Ln) southbound. Ext corridors. **Pets:** Accepted.

▲▲▲ ▼▼▼▼ Residence Inn by Marriott-Dallas Market Center A ✿
(214) 631-2472. **$89-$129.** 6950 N Stemmons Frwy. I-35 E, northbound 433C (Mockingbird Ln); southbound exit 433A (Irving Blvd). Ext corridors. **Pets:** Other species. $50 one-time fee/room. Service with restrictions.

▲▲▲ ▼▼▼▼ The Residence Inn By Marriott-Dallas-North Central A ✿
(972) 669-0478. **$103-$149.** 13636 Goldmark Dr. US 75, exit 22 (Midpark Rd). Ext/int corridors. **Pets:** Other species. $60 one-time fee/room. Service with restrictions, supervision.

▲▲▲ ▼▼▼▼ Sheraton Dallas Brookhollow Hotel H
(214) 630-7000. **$49-$69.** 1241 W Mockingbird Ln. I-35 E, exit 433B, just nw of jct I-35 E and W Mockingbird Ln. Int corridors. **Pets:** $50 deposit/pet, $25 one-time fee/pet. Designated rooms, service with restrictions, supervision.

▼▼▼▼ Sheraton Suites Market Center-Dallas MI
(214) 747-3000. **$110.** 2101 Stemmons Frwy. Nw off I-35 E and US 77, exit 430D (Market Center Blvd). Int corridors. **Pets:** Medium. $50 deposit/pet. Service with restrictions, supervision.

▼▼▼▼ Staybridge Suites Dallas-Park Central M
(972) 391-0000. **$114-$129.** 7880 Alpha Rd. I-635, exit 19B (Coit Rd), 0.3 mi n, then just w. Int corridors. **Pets:** Medium. $125 one-time fee/room. Designated rooms, service with restrictions, crate.

▲▲▲ ▼▼▼ Wellesley Inn & Suites (Dallas/Park Central) M
(972) 671-7722. **$89-$109.** 9019 Vantage Point Rd. I-635, exit 18A (Greenville Ave), just sw. Ext corridors. **Pets:** Small, other species. Service with restrictions.

▼▼▼ ▼▼▼ The Westin Galleria, Dallas H
(972) 934-9494. **$294-$344.** 13340 Dallas Pkwy. Just n of jct I-635 and N Dallas Pkwy. Int corridors. **Pets:** Medium. Service with restrictions, supervision.

DENTON

(AAA) ▼▼▼ Exel Inn of Denton 🅼 🐾
(940) 383-1471. **$41-$65.** 4211 I-35 E N. Just n of jct US 380 and I-35, exit 469. Int corridors. **Pets:** Small, other species. Designated rooms, service with restrictions, supervision.

[SAVE] [S�D] [✕] [🏊] [🖥] [🖵] [🏊]

▼▼▼ Radisson Hotel Denton & Eagle Point Golf Club 🅼
(940) 565-8499. **$109-$119.** 2211 I-35 E N. 2.5 mi sw, off I-35 E and US 77, exit 466B (Ave D). Int corridors. **Pets:** Accepted.

[✕] [🖥] [🖵] [🍴] [🏊]

DESOTO

(AAA) ▼▼▼ Red Roof Inn Dallas/DeSoto 🅼
(972) 224-7100. **$49-$57.** 1401 N Beckley. I-35, exit 416. Ext/int corridors. **Pets:** Accepted.

DUNCANVILLE

▼▼▼ Ramada Inn-Dallas Southwest 🅼
(972) 298-8911. **$69-$89, 7 days notice.** 711 E Camp Wisdom Rd. I-20, exit 463, 0.3 mi w of jct I-20 and Cockrell Hill Rd; 2 mi w of US 67. Ext/int corridors. **Pets:** Accepted.

[A$K] [S�D] [✕] [🏊] [🖵] [🍴] [🏊]

FARMERS BRANCH

▼▼▼ Best Western Dallas North 🅼
(972) 241-8521. **$45-$95.** 13333 N Stemmons Frwy. I-35 E, exit 441 (Valley View Ln), on west side of frontage road. Ext corridors. **Pets:** Accepted.

(AAA) ▼▼▼ Days Inn–North Dallas 🅼
(972) 488-0800. **$44-$59, 14 days notice.** 13313 Stemmons Frwy. I-35 E, exit 441 (Valley View Ln), west side frontage road. Int corridors. **Pets:** Accepted.

[SAVE] [S�D] [✕] [🅲] [🖥] [🖵] [🏊]

▼▼▼ Doubletree Club Hotel 🅼
(972) 506-0055. **$139-$159.** 11611 Luna Rd. I-635, exit 28, just s. Int corridors. **Pets:** Small, other species. $25 one-time fee/pet. Service with restrictions, supervision.

[SAVE] [S🗄] [✕] [🏊] [🅲] [🖵] [🍴] [🏊]

(AAA) ▼▼▼ La Quinta Inn-Dallas-Northwest-Farmers Branch 🅼
(972) 620-7333. **$66-$82.** 13235 Stemmons Frwy N. I-35 E, exit 441 (Valley View Ln), west side of frontage road. Ext corridors. **Pets:** Accepted.

[SAVE] [S🗄] [✕] [🏊] [🖵] [🏊]

GARLAND

(AAA) ▼▼▼ Best Western Lakeview Inn 🅼
(972) 303-1601. **$59-$89.** 1635 E I-30 at Chaha Rd. I-30, exit 62 (Chaha Rd). Ext corridors. **Pets:** Medium, other species. $10 daily fee/pet. Service with restrictions, supervision.

[SAVE] [S🗄] [✕] [🅲] [🖥] [🖵] [🏊]

▼▼ Days Inn-Dallas/Garland 🅼
(972) 226-7621. **$49.** 6222 Belt Line Rd. I-30, exit 59, just s. Ext corridors. **Pets:** Small, dogs only. $10 one-time fee/pet. Service with restrictions, supervision.

[SAVE] [S🗄] [✕] [🏊]

(AAA) ▼▼▼ La Quinta Inn-Dallas-LBJ Northeast-Garland 🅼
(972) 271-7581. **$66-$85.** 12721 I-635. I-635, exit 11B (Northwest Hwy), just nw. Ext corridors. **Pets:** Small. Service with restrictions, supervision.

[SAVE] [S🗄] [✕] [🏊] [🖥] [🖵] [🏊]

GRAND PRAIRIE

(AAA) ▼▼▼ La Quinta Inn-Dallas-Grand Prairie (Six Flags) 🅼
(972) 641-3021. **$55-$85.** 1410 NW 19th St. I-30, exit 32, just se. Ext corridors. **Pets:** Accepted.

[SAVE] [S🗄] [✕] [🅶M] [🏊] [🅲] [🖥] [🖵] [🏊]

▼▼ Motel 6–446 🅼
(972) 642-9424. **$39-$55.** 406 E Safari Pkwy. I-30, exit 34 (Belt Line Rd), just n, then just w. Ext corridors. **Pets:** Accepted.

[S🗄] [✕] [🅲] [🖥] [🖵] [🏊]

GREENVILLE

▼▼▼ Holiday Inn Express Hotel & Suites 🅼
(903) 454-8680. **$79-$125.** 2901 Mustang Crossing. I-30, exit 93A. Int corridors. **Pets:** Accepted.

[A$K] [S🗄] [✕] [🅶M] [🅲] [🖥] [🖵] [🏊]

IRVING

(AAA) ▼▼▼ AmeriSuites (Dallas Las Colinas/Hidden Ridge) 🅼
(972) 910-0302. **$109-$140.** 333 W John Carpenter Frwy. SR 114, exit Hidden Ridge. Int corridors. **Pets:** Small. Service with restrictions, supervision.

[SAVE] [S🗄] [✕] [🅶M] [🏊] [🅲] [🖥] [🖵] [🏊]

(AAA) ▼▼▼▼ Omni Dallas Hotel Parkwest 🄷
(972) 869-4300. **$89-$209.** 1590 LBJ Frwy. Northwest off I-635 (LBJ Frwy), 1.5 mi w of jct I-35 E, exit 29 (Luna Rd). Int corridors. **Pets:** Small. $50 one-time fee/room. Service with restrictions, supervision.

[SAVE] [S🗄] [✕] [🏊] [🖥] [🖵] [🍴] [🏊]

AAA ▼▼▼▼ **AmeriSuites (Dallas Las Colinas/ Walnut Hill)** **M**
(972) 550-7400. **$93, 7 days notice.** 5455 Green Park Dr. SR 114, exit Walnut Hill Rd. Int corridors. **Pets:** Very small. $25 one-time fee/room. Service with restrictions, crate.
[SAVE] [S] [X] [&M] [⌀] [&] [▤] [▣] [↝]

▼▼ ▼▼ **Country Inn & Suites By Carlson** **A**
(972) 929-4008. **$65-$135.** 4100 W John Carpenter Frwy. Nw off SR 114, exit Esters Rd. Ext corridors. **Pets:** Other species. $50 deposit/room, $50 one-time fee/room. Service with restrictions.
[ASK] [S] [X] [⌀] [&] [▤] [▣] [↝]

AAA ▼▼▼▼ **Dallas Las Colinas TownePlace Suites** **H** ❀
(972) 550-7796. **$85-$135.** 900 W Walnut Hill Ln. SR 114, exit Walnut Hill Ln, then w. Ext corridors. **Pets:** Large, other species. $135 one-time fee/room. Service with restrictions.
[SAVE] [S] [X] [&M] [⌀] [&] [▤] [▣] [↝]

▼▼▼▼ **Drury Inn & Suites–DFW Airport** **M**
(972) 986-1200. **$60-$105.** 4210 W Airport Frwy. SR 183, exit Esters Rd, on south access road. Int corridors. **Pets:** Very small. No service, supervision.
[X] [⌀] [▤] [▣] [↝]

▼▼▼▼ **Four Seasons Resort & Club** **R** ❀
(972) 717-0700. **$335-$445.** 4150 N MacArthur Blvd. Se off SR 114, 1.5 mi s of MacArthur Blvd exit. Int corridors. **Pets:** Small. Service with restrictions, crate.
[X] [&M] [⌀] [▤] [▣] [¶] [↝] [X]

▼▼▼▼ **Hampton Inn-DFW Airport** **M**
(972) 986-3606. **$90-$100.** 4340 W Airport Frwy. SR 183, exit Valley View on south access road. Int corridors. **Pets:** Accepted.
[SAVE] [X] [⌀] [&] [▤] [▣] [↝]

▼▼▼▼ **Harvey Hotel-DFW Airport** **H**
(972) 929-4500. **$79-$189.** 4545 W John Carpenter Frwy. Nw off SR 114, exit Esters Rd. Int corridors. **Pets:** Accepted.
[ASK] [S] [X] [⌀] [▤] [▣] [¶] [↝]

▼▼▼▼ **Harvey Suites-DFW Airport** **M**
(972) 929-4499. **$69-$199.** 4550 W John Carpenter Frwy. SR 114, exit Freeport Pkwy on southbound service road. Int corridors. **Pets:** $100 deposit/room, $25 one-time fee/room. Service with restrictions.
[ASK] [S] [X] [&M] [⌀] [&] [▤] [▣] [↝]

▼▼ ▼▼ **Hearthside by Villager** **M**
(972) 929-3333. **$39-$99.** 7825 Heathrow Dr. From SR 114, exit Esters Blvd, then s to Plaza Dr, then w. Int corridors. **Pets:** Medium, other species. $100 deposit/room, $50 one-time fee/room. Service with restrictions.
[ASK] [S] [X] [▤]

▼▼▼▼ **La Quinta Inn & Suites DFW Airport North** **M**
(972) 915-4022. **$80-$150.** 4850 W John Carpenter Frwy. SR 114, exit Freeport on eastbound service road. Int corridors. **Pets:** Small. Service with restrictions, supervision.
[SAVE] [S] [X] [⌀] [&] [▤] [▣] [↝]

▼▼ ▼▼ **Motel 6 #1274 DFW North** **M**
(972) 915-3993. **$45-$57.** 7800 Heathrow Dr. Nw off SR 114, exit Freeport Pkwy. Int corridors. **Pets:** Accepted.
[S] [X] [↝]

AAA ▼▼ ▼▼ **Red Roof Inn/DFW Airport North** **M**
(972) 929-0020. **$47-$61.** 8150 Esters Blvd. SR 114, exit Esters Blvd, just n. Ext corridors. **Pets:** Medium. Designated rooms, service with restrictions, supervision.
[SAVE] [X] [⌀] [▤] [▣]

▼▼ ▼▼ **Red Roof Inn/DFW Airport South** **M**
(972) 570-7500. **$45-$57.** 2611 W Airport Frwy. SR 183, exit Story Rd. Int corridors. **Pets:** Accepted.
[S] [X] [&] [↝]

AAA ▼▼▼▼ **Residence Inn by Marriott at Las Colinas** **M**
(972) 580-7773. **$139-$149.** 950 W Walnut Hill Ln. SR 114, exit McArthur Blvd, 0.5 mi s, then e. Ext corridors. **Pets:** Medium. $5 daily fee/room, $100 one-time fee/room. Service with restrictions, crate.
[SAVE] [S] [X] [&M] [⌀] [&] [▤] [▣] [↝]

AAA ▼▼▼▼ **Residence Inn by Marriott-DFW/Irving** **M**
(972) 871-1331. **$197-$215, 7 days notice.** 8600 Esters Blvd. SR 114, exit Esters Blvd, then 0.9 mi e. Int corridors. **Pets:** Accepted.
[SAVE] [S] [X] [&M] [⌀] [&] [▤] [▣] [↝]

▼▼▼▼ **Sheraton Grand Hotel** **H**
(972) 929-8400. **$112.** 4440 W John Carpenter Frwy. SR 114, exit Esters Rd, just s. Int corridors. **Pets:** Accepted.
[ASK] [S] [X] [&M] [⌀] [&] [▤] [▣] [¶] [↝]

▼▼▼▼ **Staybridge Suites Dallas-Las Colinas** **M**
(972) 465-9400. **$79-$129.** 1201 Executive Cir. SR 114, exit MacArthur Blvd, just s to W Walnut Hill Ln, then just w. Int corridors. **Pets:** Accepted.
[ASK] [S] [X] [▤] [▣] [↝]

AAA ▼▼▼▼ **Wellesley Inn & Suites (Dallas Las Colinas)** **M**
(972) 751-0808. **$95-$115.** 5401 Green Park Dr. SR 114, exit Walnut Hill, just s. Int corridors. **Pets:** Accepted.
[SAVE] [S] [X] [&M] [⌀] [&] [▤] [▣] [↝]

▼▼ ▼▼ **Wilson World Hotel-DFW Airport South** **M**
(972) 513-0800. **$79, 14 days notice.** 4600 W Airport Frwy. 3.3 nw off SR 183, exit Valley View. Int corridors. **Pets:** Other species. Service with restrictions, supervision.
[X] [▤] [▣] [¶] [↝]

LEWISVILLE

▼▼▼ Comfort Suites M
(972) 315-6464. **$65-$95.** 755A Vista Ridge Mall Dr. I-35 E, exit 448A (Round Grove Rd), 0.5 mi s of jct I-35 and Round Grove Rd on southbound service road to Vista Ridge Mall Dr, just w. Int corridors. **Pets:** Accepted.
⛟ 🄢 ✕ 🄍 ⛌ 🚪 💻 ⇶

▼▼▼ Howard Johnson M
(972) 434-1000. **$71.** 200 N Stemmons Frwy. I-35 E, exit 452 (Main St), just ne. Int corridors. **Pets:** Medium, dogs only. $20 daily fee/pet. Service with restrictions, supervision.
A$K 🄢 ✕ 🄍 💻 ⇶

▲▲▲ ▼▼▼ La Quinta Inn-Dallas-Lewisville M
(972) 221-7525. **$69-$99.** 1657 S Stemmons Frwy. I-35 E, exit 449, just w. Ext corridors. **Pets:** Accepted.
⛟ 🄢 ✕ 🄜 🄍 🚪 💻 ⇶

▲▲▲ ▼▼▼ Microtel Inn & Suites M
(972) 434-0447. **$55.** 881 S Stemmons Frwy. I-35 E, exit 451, just w. Int corridors. **Pets:** Accepted.
⛟ 🄢 ✕ 🄍 🄍 🚪 💻

▼▼ Motel 6 M
(972) 436-5008. **$41-$49, 3 days notice.** 1705 Lakepointe Dr. I-35 E, exit 449, just n on access road. Int corridors. **Pets:** Accepted.
🄢 ✕ 🄍 🄍 ⇶

▲▲▲ ▼▼▼ Residence Inn M
(972) 315-3777. **$119-$154, 10 days notice.** 755C Vista Ridge Blvd. I-33 E, exit 448A (Round Grove Rd), 0.5 mi s on service road; jct I-35 and Round Grove Rd to Vista Ridge Rd, just w. Int corridors. **Pets:** Accepted.
⛟ 🄢 ✕ 🄜 🄍 🄍 🚪 💻 ⇶

▲▲▲ ▼▼ Super 8-Lewisville/Dallas North/Airport M
(972) 221-7511. **$50.** 1305 S Stemmons Frwy. I-35 E, exit 450, just sw. Ext corridors. **Pets:** Medium. $5 daily fee/pet. Designated rooms, service with restrictions, supervision.
⛟ 🄢 🚪 💻 ⇶

MCKINNEY

▲▲▲ ▼▼▼ Days Inn McKinney M
(972) 548-8888. **$60-$70.** 2104 N Central Expwy. US 75, 0.5 mi n of jct US 380, exit 41. Ext corridors. **Pets:** Medium, other species. $5 daily fee/pet. Service with restrictions.
⛟ 🄢 ✕ 🚪 ⇶

MIDLOTHIAN

▲▲▲ ▼▼▼ Best Western Midlothian Inn M
(972) 775-1891. **$64-$74, 3 days notice.** 220 N Hwy 67. 1 mi w on US 67, just n of jct US 287. Ext corridors. **Pets:** Medium. $25 deposit/pet. Service with restrictions, crate.
⛟ 🄢 ✕ 🚪 ⇶

PLANO

▲▲▲ ▼▼▼ AmeriSuites (Dallas/Plano North Tollway) M ✿
(972) 378-3997. **$119-$124.** 3100 Dallas Pkwy. Dallas Pkwy, northbound exit Park Blvd; southbound exit Parker Blvd, on northbound service road. Int corridors. **Pets:** Small, other species. Crate.
⛟ 🄢 ✕ 🄍 🄍 🚪 💻 ⇶

▲▲▲ ▼▼▼ Best Western Park Suites Hotel M
(972) 578-2243. **$105, 7 days notice.** 640 Park Blvd E. US 75, exit 29A northbound, just e; exit 29 southbound, 0.5 mi s on access road, just e on 15th St, 0.5 mi n on access road. Int corridors. **Pets:** $25 one-time fee/pet. Service with restrictions, supervision.
⛟ 🄢 ✕ 🄜 🄍 🚪 💻 ⇶

▼▼ Comfort Inn M
(972) 424-5568. **$65.** 621 Central Pkwy E. Just e of US 75; 0.3 mi ne of FM 544, exit 29A. Int corridors. **Pets:** Accepted.
⛟ ✕ 🚪 💻 ⇶

▼▼▼ Hampton Inn Plano M
(972) 519-1000. **$69-$89.** 4901 Old Shepherd Pl. I-635, exit 21 (Preston Rd), 6 mi n, then just e. Int corridors. **Pets:** Other species. $50 one-time fee/room. Service with restrictions, crate.
⛟ 🄢 ✕ 🄍 🚪 💻 ⇶

▼▼▼ Holiday Inn-Plano MI
(972) 881-1881. **$80-$129.** 700 Central Pkwy E. Just e of US 75; 0.3 mi ne of jct FM 544, exit 29A. Int corridors. **Pets:** Accepted.
A$K 🄢 ✕ 🄍 🚪 💻 🍴 ⇶

▼▼▼ Homewood Suites by Hilton M
(972) 758-8800. **$79-$129.** 4705 Old Shepherd Pl. US 75, exit 28A, 4.6 mi w, just n on Preston (SR 289), then just e. Int corridors. **Pets:** Accepted.
⛟ 🄢 ✕ 🄜 🄍 🚪 💻 ⇶

▼▼▼ La Quinta Inn & Suites-West Plano M
(972) 599-0700. **$80-$135.** 4800 W Plano Pkwy. US 75, exit 28A, 4.6 mi w at jct Preston (SR 289). Int corridors. **Pets:** Small. Designated rooms, service with restrictions, supervision.
⛟ 🄢 ✕ 🄜 🄍 🄍 🚪 💻 ⇶

▼▼▼ La Quinta Inn-Plano M
(972) 423-1300. **$66-$105.** 1820 N Central Expwy. US 75, exit 29A, just ne. Ext corridors. **Pets:** Accepted.
⛟ 🄢 ✕ 🄜 🄍 🄍 🚪 💻 ⇶

▲▲▲ ▼▼▼ MainStay Suites M
(972) 596-9966. **$105-$115.** 4709 W Plano Pkwy. US 75, exit 28A, 4.5 mi w. Int corridors. **Pets:** Small. $100 deposit/pet, $5 daily fee/pet. Service with restrictions, supervision.
⛟ 🄢 ✕ 🄍 🄍 🚪 💻 ⇶

▼▼ Motel 6–1121 M
(972) 578-1626. **$43-$55.** 2550 N Central Expwy. US 75, exit 29A (Park Blvd). Ext corridors. **Pets:** Accepted.
🄢 ✕ 🄍 🄍 ⇶

⚫⚫⚫ 〰〰 Red Roof Inn Dallas-Plano M
(972) 881-8191. $43-$64. 301 Ruisseau Dr. SR 75, exit 30 (Parker Rd), 0.5 mi w to Premier, then just n. Ext/int corridors. Pets: Accepted.
[SAVE] [✕] [♿M] [🐾] [📶] [🛎]

⚫⚫⚫ 〰〰〰 Residence Inn by Marriott
        Dallas/Plano ⚠
(972) 473-6761. $129. 5001 White Stone Ln. From Dallas, N Tollway, exit Spring Creek Pkwy, 1.9 mi e, then n on Preston Rd. Int corridors. Pets: Other species. $150 one-time fee/room. Service with restrictions.
[SAVE] [🔟] [✕] [🛎] [💻] [≋]

⚫⚫⚫ 〰〰 Sleep Inn Plano M
(972) 867-1111. $69, 10 days notice. 4801 W Plano Pkwy. US 75, exit 28A, 4.6 mi w at jct Preston (SR 289). Int corridors. Pets: Small. $10 daily fee/pet, $25 one-time fee/room. Service with restrictions, supervision.
[SAVE] [🔟] [✕] [♿M] [🐾] [💺] [💻] [≋]

⚫⚫⚫ 〰〰〰 Wellesley Inn & Suites
        (Dallas/Plano) M
(972) 378-9978. $89-$109. 2900 Dallas Pkwy. Dallas Pkwy, exit Park Blvd northbound; exit Parker Blvd southbound, on northbound service road. Int corridors. Pets: Small, other species. Service with restrictions.
[SAVE] [🔟] [✕] [♿M] [🐾] [💺] [🛎] [💻] [≋]

RICHARDSON

〰〰〰 Hampton Inn M
(972) 234-5400. $99. 1577 Gateway Blvd. US 75, exit 26, 0.4 mi s on access road, just w on Campbell Rd, 0.5 mi s. Int corridors. Pets: Accepted.
[SAVE] [🔟] [✕] [♿M] [🐾] [💺] [💻] [≋]

⚫⚫⚫ 〰〰〰〰 Renaissance Dallas-Richardson
        Hotel 🅷
(972) 367-2000. $179-$270. 900 E Lookout Dr. US 75, exit 26, e to Glenville Dr, 0.8 mi n to Lookout Dr, then w. Int corridors. Pets: Medium. $50 deposit/room. Service with restrictions, crate.
[SAVE] [🔟] [✕] [🐾] [💺] [🛎] [💻] [🍽] [≋]

⚫⚫⚫ 〰〰〰 Residence Inn by Marriott
        Richardson ⚠
(972) 669-5888. $129-$149. 1040 Waterwood Dr. US 75, exit 26, e to Greenville Ave, then just n. Int corridors. Pets: Other species. $8 daily fee/pet.
[SAVE] [🔟] [✕] [🐾] [💺] [🛎] [💻] [≋]

〰〰 Sleep Inn M
(972) 470-9440. $65. 2458 N Central Expwy. US 75, exit 27 northbound; exit 26 southbound, 0.8 mi n on access road. Int corridors. Pets: Accepted.
[SAVE] [🔟] [✕] [🛎] [💻]

〰〰〰 Wyndham Garden Hotel-Richardson Ⅿ
(972) 479-0500. $69-$114. 901 E Campbell Rd. US 75, exit 26 (Campbell Rd), just e. Int corridors. Pets: Very small. $35 one-time fee/room. Service with restrictions, supervision.
[✕] [♿M] [🐾] [💺] [🛎] [💻] [🍽] [≋]

ROWLETT

⚫⚫⚫ 〰〰〰〰 Comfort Suites Lake Ray
        Hubbard M
(972) 463-9595. $71-$117. 8701 E I-30. I-30, exit 64 (Dalrock Rd). Int corridors. Pets: Accepted.
[SAVE] [🔟] [✕] [♿M] [💺] [🛎] [💻] [≋]

TERRELL

⚫⚫⚫ 〰〰 Best Inn M
(972) 563-2676. $42-$65. 309 IH-20 E. Jct I-20 and SR 34, exit 501. Int corridors. Pets: Small, other species. $5 one-time fee/room. Service with restrictions, supervision.
[SAVE] [🔟] [✕] [🛎] [💻] [≋]

THE COLONY

⚫⚫⚫ 〰〰〰〰 Comfort Suites M
(972) 668-5555. $89, 10 days notice. 4796 Memorial Dr. Just n of jct SR 121. Int corridors. Pets: Accepted.
[SAVE] [🔟] [✕] [♿M] [🐾] [💺] [🛎] [💻] [≋]

WAXAHACHIE

⚫⚫⚫ 〰〰 Best Western M
(972) 937-4202. $72, 5 days notice. 200 N I-35 E. I-35 E and US 287 business route, 1.8 mi s of jct US 287, exit 401B. Ext corridors. Pets: Small, dogs only. Designated rooms, service with restrictions, supervision.
[SAVE] [🔟] [✕] [🛎] [💻] [≋]

⚫ END METROPOLITAN AREA ⚫

DECATUR

⚫⚫⚫ 〰〰 Best Western Inn of Decatur M
(940) 627-5982. $55-$75, 3 days notice. 1801 S Hwy 287. On US 287, 0.6 mi s of jct Business SR 380. Ext corridors. Pets: Small. $5 one-time fee/pet. Service with restrictions, crate.
[SAVE] [🔟] [✕] [🛎] [💻] [≋]

⚫⚫⚫ 〰〰〰 Comfort Inn M
(940) 627-6919. $59-$110, 7 days notice. 1709 S US 287 S. On US 287, 0.6 mi s of jct Business SR 380. Ext corridors. Pets: Small. $10 daily fee/room. Designated rooms, service with restrictions, supervision.
[SAVE] [✕] [🛎] [💻] [≋]

DEL RIO

(AAA) ▼▼▼▼ **Best Western Inn of Del Rio M**
(830) 775-7511. **$69, 7 days notice.** 810 Ave F. 0.8 mi nw on US 90, 277 and 377. Ext corridors. **Pets:** Accepted.
SAVE S✍ ✕ 🖥 💻 ➾

(AAA) ▼▼▼ **Days Inn and Suites M**
(830) 775-0585. **$57-$175.** 3808 Ave F. 3.5 mi nw on US 90. Ext corridors. **Pets:** Other species. $5 daily fee/room. Service with restrictions.
SAVE S✍ ✕ 🖥 💻 ➾

▼▼▼ **Holiday Inn Express M**
(830) 775-2933. **$63-$65.** 3616 Ave F. 3.2 mi nw on US 90. Ext/int corridors. **Pets:** Accepted.
ASK S✍ ✕ 🔊 🖥 💻 ➾

▼▼▼ **Howard Johnson La Siesta M**
(830) 775-6323. **Call for rates, 3 days notice.** 2000 Ave F. 1.5 mi nw on US 90, 277 and 377. Ext corridors. **Pets:** Accepted.
ASK ✕ 🖥 💻 ➾

(AAA) ▼▼▼▼ **La Quinta Inns-Del Rio M**
(830) 775-7591. **$72-$80.** 2005 Ave F. 1.8 mi nw on US 90, 277 and 377. Ext/int corridors. **Pets:** Accepted.
SAVE S✍ ✕ 🖥 💻 ➾

(AAA) ▼▼▼▼ **Ramada Inn M** ☙
(830) 775-1511. **$84-$99.** 2101 Ave F. 1.8 mi nw on US 90, 277 and 377. Ext/int corridors. **Pets:** Small. Designated rooms, service with restrictions, crate.
SAVE S✍ ✕ 🖥 💻 🍴 ➾

DUMAS

(AAA) ▼▼▼▼ **Best Western Windsor Inn M**
(806) 935-9644. **$59-$79, 7 days notice.** 1701 S Dumas Ave. US 287, 2 mi s of US 87 and SR 152. Ext corridors. **Pets:** Very small, dogs only. $5 daily fee/pet. Designated rooms, service with restrictions, supervision.
SAVE S✍ ✕ 🖥 💻 ➾

(AAA) ▼▼ **Econo Lodge M**
(806) 935-9098. **$45-$95.** 1719 S Dumas Ave. US 287, 2 mi s of US 87 and SR 152. Int corridors. **Pets:** Medium, other species. $5 daily fee/pet. Designated rooms, crate.
SAVE S✍ ✕ 🖥

▼▼▼ **Holiday Inn Express M**
(806) 935-4000. **$70-$120.** 1525 S Dumas Ave. US 87, 1.1 mi s. Int corridors. **Pets:** Accepted.
ASK S✍ ✕ 🖥 💻 ➾

▼▼ **Kona Kai Dumas Inn Motel M**
(806) 935-6441. **$60-$80, 3 days notice.** 1712 S Dumas Ave. US 287, 1.5 mi s from jct US 87 and SR 152. Ext/int corridors. **Pets:** Accepted.
ASK S✍ ✕ 🖥 💻 🍴 ➾

(AAA) ▼▼▼ **Super 8 Motel M**
(806) 935-6222. **$75-$110.** 119 W 17th St. Ext corridors. **Pets:** Accepted.
SAVE ✕ 🖥

EAGLE PASS

(AAA) ▼▼▼ **Best Western M**
(830) 758-1234. **$62-$72.** 1923 Loop 431. US 57, jct Loop 431. Ext corridors. **Pets:** Medium. Service with restrictions, crate.
SAVE S✍ ✕ 🔊 🖥 💻 ➾

(AAA) ▼▼▼▼ **Holiday Inn Express Hotel & Suites M**
(830) 757-3050. **$70.** 2007 Loop 431. 1.5 mi n on Loop 431. Int corridors. **Pets:** Small. Service with restrictions, supervision.
SAVE S✍ ✕ 🔊 🖥 💻 ➾

(AAA) ▼▼▼▼ **La Quinta Inn-Eagle Pass M**
(830) 773-7000. **$69-$90.** 2525 E Main St. US 57 and 277 at jct Loop 431. Ext corridors. **Pets:** Accepted.
SAVE S✍ ✕ 🔊 🖥 💻 ➾

(AAA) ▼▼▼ **Super 8 Motel M** ☙
(830) 773-9531. **$45-$53.** 2150 N US Hwy 277. 4 mi n on US 277. Ext corridors. **Pets:** Small. Service with restrictions, crate.
SAVE S✍ ✕ 🔊 🖥 🍴 ➾

EARLY

(AAA) ▼▼▼ **Post Oak Inn M**
(915) 643-5621. **$55-$60.** 606 Early Blvd. On SR 377 at jct Northline. Ext corridors. **Pets:** Accepted.
SAVE ✕ 🖥 💻 ➾

EASTLAND

(AAA) ▼▼ **Budget Host M**
(254) 629-3324. **$42-$46.** 2001 I-20 W. I-20, exit 343, on south service road. Ext corridors. **Pets:** Service with restrictions.
SAVE ✕ 🔊 🖥 💻 ➾

▼▼▼ **The Eastland** BB
(254) 629-8397. **$70-$90.** 112 N Lamar St. I-20, exit 343, 1.7 mi n to Lamar St, just e. Int corridors. **Pets:** Accepted.
ASK ✕ 💻 ✉

▼▼ **Super 8 Motel & RV Park M**
(254) 629-3336. **$55-$69.** 3900 I-20 E. I-20, exit 343, on north service road. Ext corridors. **Pets:** Accepted.
ASK S✍ ✕ 🖥 💻 ➾

EL PASO

(AAA) ▼▼▼▼ **AmeriSuites (El Paso/Airport) M**
(915) 771-0022. **$98, 5 days notice.** 6030 Gateway Blvd E. I-10, exit 24B (Geronimo St). Int corridors. **Pets:** Accepted.
SAVE ✕ 🔊 🔊 🔊 🖥 💻 ➾

Baymont Inn & Suites-El Paso East M
(915) 591-3300. $-$64. 7944 Gateway Blvd E. I-10, exit 28B. Int corridors. **Pets:** Small. $50 deposit/room. Service with restrictions, supervision.

Baymont Inn & Suites-El Paso West M
(915) 585-2999. $54-$64. 7620 N Mesa St. I-10, exit 11 (Mesa St). Int corridors. **Pets:** $50 deposit/room. Designated rooms, service with restrictions, supervision.

Best Western Airport Inn MI
(915) 779-7700. $64-$69, 14 days notice. 7144 Gateway E. I-10, exit 26 (Hawkins Blvd). Ext corridors. **Pets:** Medium, other species. Service with restrictions, supervision.

Best Western Sunland Park Inn M
(915) 587-4900. $59-$69. 1045 Sunland Park Dr. I-10, exit 13, just s. Ext corridors. **Pets:** Accepted.

Chase Suites by Woodfin A
(915) 772-8000. $119-$170. 6791 Montana Rd. I-10, exit Airway Blvd, 1 mi n, then just e. Ext corridors. **Pets:** Other species. $150 deposit/room, $5 daily fee/room. Service with restrictions, crate.

Comfort Inn Airport East M
(915) 594-9111. $64-$94. 900 Yarbrough Dr. I-10, exit 28B. Ext corridors. **Pets:** Accepted.

Comfort Inn West M
(915) 845-1906. $64-$74. 7651 N Mesa St. I-10, exit 11 (Mesa St). Int corridors. **Pets:** Accepted.

Comfort Suites M
(915) 587-5300. $59-$80. 949 Sunland Park Dr. I-10, exit 13. Int corridors. **Pets:** Accepted.

Days Inn M
(915) 595-1913. $49-$69. 10635 Gateway Blvd W. I-10, exit 28B. Ext corridors. **Pets:** Accepted.

Econo Lodge M
(915) 778-3311. $55. 6363 Montana Rd. 6 mi e on US 62 and 180. Ext corridors. **Pets:** Small. $10 one-time fee/pet. Service with restrictions, supervision.

Embassy Suites Hotel H
(915) 779-6222. $139. 6100 Gateway Blvd E. I-10, exit 24B (Geronimo St). Int corridors. **Pets:** Accepted.

Hilton Camino Real H
(915) 534-3000. $164-$184. 101 S El Paso St. Center. Int corridors. **Pets:** Accepted.

Hilton El Paso Airport MI
(915) 778-4241. $114. 2027 Airway Blvd. I-10, exit 25, 1.3 mi n. Int corridors. **Pets:** Accepted.

Howard Johnson Inn MI
(915) 591-9471. $62-$72. 8887 Gateway Blvd W. I-10, exit 26 (Hawkins Blvd). Int corridors. **Pets:** Service with restrictions, supervision.

La Quinta Inn-El Paso-Airport M
(915) 778-9321. $58-$81. 6140 Gateway Blvd E. I-10, exit 24B. Ext corridors. **Pets:** Accepted.

La Quinta Inn-El Paso-Cielo Vista M
(915) 593-8400. $57-$80. 9125 Gateway Blvd W. I-10, exit 28B westbound; exit 27 eastbound. Ext corridors. **Pets:** Medium, other species. Service with restrictions, supervision.

La Quinta Inn-El Paso-Lomaland M
(915) 591-2244. $57-$80. 11033 Gateway Blvd W. I-10, exit 29 eastbound; exit 30 westbound, 1 mi w. Ext corridors. **Pets:** Accepted.

La Quinta Inn-El Paso-West M
(915) 833-2522. $57-$84. 7550 Remcon Cir. I-10, exit 11 (Mesa St). Ext corridors. **Pets:** Accepted.

Microtel Inn & Suites M
(915) 772-3650. $51-$79. 2001 Airway Blvd. I-10, exit 25, 1.3 mi n. Int corridors. **Pets:** Small, other species. $100 deposit/room.

Red Roof Inn West M
(915) 587-9977. $39-$62. 7530 Remcon Circle. I-10, exit 11 (Mesa St). Ext/int corridors. **Pets:** Accepted.

Sleep Inn M
(915) 585-7577. $49-$68. 953 Sunland Park Dr. I-10, exit 13. Int corridors. **Pets:** Other species. $15 one-time fee/room. Service with restrictions.

Travelodge M
(915) 833-2613. $42-$52. 7815 N Mesa St. I-10, exit 11 (Mesa St). Ext corridors. **Pets:** Accepted.

Travelodge La Hacienda Airport M ❖

(915) 772-4231. **$62-$75.** 6400 Montana Ave. I-10, exit 25, 1.5 mi nw, then 6.3 mi e on US 62 and 180. Ext corridors. **Pets:** $10 daily fee/pet. Service with restrictions, supervision.

SAVE S🐾 ✕ 🍴 ≈

EULESS

La Quinta Inn-DFW Airport West-Euless M

(817) 540-0233. **$61-$71.** 1001 W Airport Frwy. SR 183, just e of FM 157, exit Industrial Blvd. Ext corridors. **Pets:** Small, other species. Service with restrictions, crate.

SAVE S🐾 ✕ 🍴 ≈

Microtel Inn and Suites M

(817) 545-1111. **$67-$77.** 901 W Airport Frwy. US 183, exit Industrial Blvd (FM 157), just e. Int corridors. **Pets:** Small, dogs only. $35 deposit/room. Service with restrictions, supervision.

ASK S🐾 ✕ ≈

FORT STOCKTON

Atrium West Inn M

(915) 336-6666. **$55-$65, 7 days notice.** 1305 N Hwy 285. I-10, exit 257, just s. Ext corridors. **Pets:** Accepted.

SAVE S🐾 ✕ ≈

Best Western Swiss Clock Inn MI

(915) 336-8521. **$68-$78, 10 days notice.** 3201 W Dickinson Blvd. I-10, exit 256, 0.5 mi e. Ext corridors. **Pets:** Accepted.

SAVE S🐾 ✕ 🍴 ≈

Comfort Inn of Fort Stockton M

(915) 336-8531. **$60-$65.** 3200 W Dickinson Blvd. I-10, exit 256, just s. Int corridors. **Pets:** Medium. $5 daily fee/room. Service with restrictions, crate.

SAVE S🐾 ✕ ≈

Days Inn M

(915) 336-7500. **$56-$76, 7 days notice.** 1408 N US Hwy 285. I-10, exit 257, just s. Ext corridors. **Pets:** Small. Supervision.

SAVE S🐾 ✕ ≈

Econo Lodge M ❖

(915) 336-9711. **$45-$55.** 800 E Dickinson Blvd. I-10, exit 261, 1.3 mi w on I-20 business route. Ext corridors. **Pets:** Accepted.

SAVE S🐾 ✕ ≈

Holiday Inn Express M

(915) 336-5955. **$54-$78.** 1308 N US Hwy 285. I-10, exit 257, just s. Ext corridors. **Pets:** Medium. $25 deposit/pet. Designated rooms, service with restrictions, supervision.

SAVE S🐾 ✕ ≈

La Quinta Inn-Fort Stockton MI

(915) 336-9781. **$55-$65.** 2601 W I-10. I-10, exit 257. Ext corridors. **Pets:** Accepted.

SAVE S🐾 ✕ ≈

FORT WORTH

AmeriSuites (Ft Worth/ City View) M

(817) 361-9797. **$89-$109.** 5900 City View Blvd. I-20, exit 431 (Bryant Irvin Rd). Int corridors. **Pets:** Very small, other species. Designated rooms, service with restrictions, supervision.

SAVE S🐾 ✕ ≈

Best Western InnSuites H

(817) 534-4801. **$60-$120.** 2000 Beach St. I-30, exit 16C (Beach St), just e. Ext/int corridors. **Pets:** Small. $25 one-time fee/room. Designated rooms, supervision.

SAVE S🐾 ✕ 🍴 ≈

Candlewood Suites M

(817) 838-8229. **$59-$89.** 5201 Endicott Ave. I-820, exit 17B, just s. Int corridors. **Pets:** Large. $100 deposit/room. Supervision.

ASK S🐾 ✕ ≈

Hampton Inn West Side/I30 M

(817) 560-4180. **$63-$70.** 2700 Cherry Ln. I-30, exit 7A, just s. Ext corridors. **Pets:** Very small. $25 deposit/pet. Service with restrictions, crate.

SAVE S🐾 ✕ ≈

Holiday Inn Express Hotel & Suites M

(817) 292-4900. **$84.** 4609 City Lake Blvd W. I-20, exit 431. Int corridors. **Pets:** Accepted.

ASK S🐾 ✕ ≈

Holiday Inn Ft. Worth South & Conference Center MI

(817) 293-3088. **$69-$99.** 100 Altamesa E Blvd. I-35, exit 44. Int corridors. **Pets:** Accepted.

SAVE S🐾 ✕ 🍴 ≈

Holiday Inn North/Conference Center MI

(817) 625-9911. **$89-$99.** 2540 Meacham Blvd. I-35 W, exit 56A. Int corridors. **Pets:** Accepted.

SAVE S🐾 ✕ 🍴 ≈

Homestead Studio Suites-Fort Worth M

(817) 338-4808. **$54, 7 days notice.** 1601 River Run. I-30, exit 12 (University Dr), just s. Ext corridors. **Pets:** Accepted.

ASK S🐾 ✕ ≈

La Quinta Inn & Suites-Fort Worth North M ❖

(817) 222-2888. **$75-$88.** 4700 N Frwy. N on I-35 at Meacham Blvd, exit 56A. Int corridors. **Pets:** Small, other species. Service with restrictions.

SAVE S🐾 ✕ ≈

▼▼▼ La Quinta Inn & Suites Fort Worth Southwest M
(817) 370-2700. **$81-$91.** 4900 Bryant Irving Rd. I-20, exit 431. Int corridors. **Pets:** Accepted.
🅂🄰🅅🄴 🛇 🖾 ⛕ ⛽ 🅿 💻 ⊇

⟁⟁⟁ ▼▼▼▼ La Quinta Inn-Fort Worth West Medical Center M
(817) 246-5511. **$56-$76.** 7888 I-30 W. I-30, exit 7A. Ext corridors. **Pets:** Accepted.
🅂🄰🅅🄴 🛇 ⛕ ⛽ 🅿 💻 ⊇

▼▼ Motel 6 East–1341 M
(817) 834-7361. **$41-$53.** 1236 Oakland Blvd. I-30, exit 18. Ext corridors. **Pets:** Accepted.
🛇 ⊇

▼ Motel 6 North–153 M
(817) 625-4359. **$41-$53.** 3271 I-35 W. I-35, exit 54C (33rd St) northbound; exit 54B (Paffort St) southbound. Ext corridors. **Pets:** Small. Designated rooms, service with restrictions, supervision.
🛇 🐾 ⊇

▼ Motel 6 South–405 M
(817) 293-8595. **$42-$57.** 6600 S Frwy. I-35, exit 44. Ext corridors. **Pets:** Accepted.
🛇 ⊇

⟁⟁⟁ ▼▼▼▼ The Renaissance Worthington Hotel H
(817) 870-1000. **$189-$245.** 200 Main St. northwest corner of 2nd and Main sts. Int corridors. **Pets:** Medium, other species. $200 deposit/room. No service.
🅂🄰🅅🄴 🛇 ⛕ ⛽ 🅿 💻 ⛺ ⊇ ⊗

⟁⟁⟁ ▼▼▼▼ Residence Inn-Alliance Airport M
(817) 750-7000. **$99-$149, 14 days notice.** 13400 N Frwy. I-35 W, exit 66. Int corridors. **Pets:** Medium. $6 daily fee/room, $175 one-time fee/room. Service with restrictions, supervision.
🅂🄰🅅🄴 🛇 ⛽ 🅿 💻 ⊇

⟁⟁⟁ ▼▼▼▼ Residence Inn By Marriott Fort Worth-River Plaza A
(817) 870-1011. **$119-$159.** 1701 S University Dr. I-30, exit 12 (University Dr), 0.4 mi s. Ext corridors. **Pets:** Accepted.
🅂🄰🅅🄴 🛇 🖾 ⛕ ⛽ 🅿 💻 ⊇

⟁⟁⟁ ▼▼▼▼ Residence Inn by Marriott-Fossil Creek M
(817) 439-1300. **$99.** 5801 Sandshell. I-35 W, exit 58 (Western Center), 0.7 mi e. Int corridors. **Pets:** Medium, other species. $5 daily fee/pet, $75 one-time fee/room. Service with restrictions, crate.
🅂🄰🅅🄴 🛇 🖾 ⛽ 🅿 💻 ⊇

FREDERICKSBURG

⟁⟁⟁ ▼▼▼ Budget Host Deluxe Inn M
(830) 997-3344. **$50-$80, 5 days notice.** 901 E Main St. 0.5 mi e on US 290. Ext corridors. **Pets:** Accepted.
🅂🄰🅅🄴 🛇 ⛽ 💻

⟁⟁⟁ ▼▼▼ Comfort Inn M
(830) 997-9811. **$70-$91.** 908 S Adams St. 0.8 mi sw on SR 16; 0.8 mi sw of jct US 87 and 290. Ext corridors. **Pets:** Accepted.
🅂🄰🅅🄴 🛇 ⛕ ⛽ 💻 ⊇

⟁⟁⟁ ▼▼ Dietzel Motel M
(830) 997-3330. **$44-$68.** 1141 W US 290. 1 mi w on US 290 at jct US 87. Ext corridors. **Pets:** $5 daily fee/pet. Service with restrictions.
🅂🄰🅅🄴 🛇

▼▼ The Full Moon Inn BB
(830) 997-2205. **$125-$200, 10 days notice.** 3234 Luckenbach Rd. 7 mi e to RR 1376, 4.5 mi s, then 0.5 mi e. Ext corridors. **Pets:** Medium, other species. $25 daily fee/room. Service with restrictions, supervision.
🄰🅂🄺 🛇 ⛽ 💻 🆆 🆉

⟁⟁⟁ ▼ Sunset Inn M
(830) 997-9581. **$47-$55.** 900 S Adams St. 0.8 mi sw of jct US 290 and SR 16. Ext corridors. **Pets:** Accepted.
🅂🄰🅅🄴 🛇 ⛽ 💻 🍽

FULTON

⟁⟁⟁ ▼▼▼▼ Best Western Inn by the Bay M 🐾
(361) 729-8351. **$85-$95, 3 days notice.** 3902 N Hwy 35. SR 35, 0.5 mi n of jct Business Rt 35 and FM 3063. Ext corridors. **Pets:** Other species. $4 deposit/pet, $5 daily fee/pet. No service, supervision.
🅂🄰🅅🄴 🛇 ⛕ ⛽ 💻 ⊇

GAINESVILLE

⟁⟁⟁ ▼ Budget Host Inn M
(940) 665-2856. **$40.** 1900 N I-35. I-35, exit 499 northbound; exit 498B southbound. Ext corridors. **Pets:** Accepted.
🅂🄰🅅🄴 🛇 ⛽

GALVESTON

⟁⟁⟁ ▼▼▼▼ La Quinta Inn M
(409) 763-1224. **$61-$166.** 1402 Seawall Blvd. Seawall Blvd at 14th St. Ext corridors. **Pets:** Accepted.
🅂🄰🅅🄴 🛇 ⛕ ⛽ 🅿 💻 ⊇

GEORGE WEST

⟁⟁⟁ ▼▼▼ Best Western Executive Inn M 🐾
(361) 449-3300. **$70-$75, 7 days notice.** 208 N Nueces St. Just n of US 59 on SR 281. Ext corridors. **Pets:** Small. Service with restrictions, supervision.
🅂🄰🅅🄴 🛇 ⛽ 🅿 💻 ⊇

GEORGETOWN

▼▼ Comfort Inn M
(512) 863-7504. **$70-$90.** 1005 Leander Rd. I-35, exit 260, on west frontage road. Ext corridors. **Pets:** Other species. $10 daily fee/pet. Service with restrictions, supervision.
🅂🄰🅅🄴 🛇 ⛽ 🅿 💻 ⊇

 **La Quinta-Georgetown-Sun City** **M**
(512) 869-2541. **$62-$85.** 333 I-35 N. I-35, exit 264 northbound; exit 262 southbound; on west frontage road. Ext corridors. **Pets:** Small, other species. Service with restrictions, crate.

[SAVE] [S/D] [X] [&] [🛏] [💻] [≈]

GIDDINGS

 **Ramada Limited** **M**
(979) 542-9666. **$50-$59.** 4002 E Austin St. 2.5 mi e on US 290. Ext corridors. **Pets:** Small. Service with restrictions, crate.

[SAVE] [S/D] [X] [🛏] [💻] [≈]

 **Super 8 Motel** **M**
(979) 542-5791. **$49, 7 days notice.** 3556 E Austin Rd. 2 mi e on US 290. Ext corridors. **Pets:** Accepted.

[SAVE] [S/D] [X] [🛏] [💻] [≈]

GRANBURY

Comfort Inn **M**
(817) 573-2611. **$70-$185.** 1201 Plaza Dr N. 2 mi e on US 377 Bypass. Ext corridors. **Pets:** Accepted.

[SAVE] [S/D] [X] [&] [🛏] [💻] [≈]

Days Inn of Granbury **M**
(817) 573-2691. **$59-$79.** 1339 N Plaza Dr. 2 mi e on US 377 Bypass. Ext corridors. **Pets:** Other species. $20 one-time fee/room. Service with restrictions, crate.

[SAVE] [S/D] [X] [&] [🛏] [💻] [≈]

Plantation Inn on the Lake **M**
(817) 573-8846. **$65-$90.** 1451 E Pearl St. 0.3 mi w of Business Rt 377 at jct US 377 Bypass. Ext/int corridors. **Pets:** Accepted.

[SAVE] [S/D] [X] [🛏] [≈]

GRAND PRAIRIE

AmeriSuites (Dallas/Grand Prairie) **M**
(972) 988-6800. **$49-$119.** 1542 N Hwy 360. On SR 360, exit J/K aves. Int corridors. **Pets:** Medium, other species. Service with restrictions, supervision.

[SAVE] [X] [&M] [&] [🛏] [💻] [≈]

GRAPEVINE

AmeriSuites (Dallas/DFW Airport N) **M**
(972) 691-1199. **$109-$126.** 2220 Grapevine Mills Cir W. SR 121 N, exit Bass Pro Dr. Int corridors. **Pets:** Medium. $50 one-time fee/room. Designated rooms, service with restrictions.

[SAVE] [S/D] [X] [&M] [🐾] [&] [🛏] [💻] [≈]

Embassy Suites Outdoor World **H** ❀
(972) 724-2600. **$209-$249, 3 days notice.** 2401 Bass Pro Dr. US 121, exit Bass Pro Dr. Int corridors. **Pets:** Very small, other species. $50 deposit/room. Designated rooms, service with restrictions, crate.

[SAVE] [S/D] [X] [🛏] [💻] [🍴] [≈]

HARLINGEN

Best Western Harlingen Inn **MI**
(956) 425-7070. **$54-$59, 7 days notice.** 6779 W Expwy 83. US 83, 2.3 mi w of jct US 77; at Stuart Place Rd exit. Ext corridors. **Pets:** Accepted.

[SAVE] [S/D] [X] [🛏] [💻] [🍴] [≈]

Country Inn & Suites by Carlson **M**
(956) 428-0043. **$64-$110, 7 days notice.** 3825 S Expressway 83. US 83/77 Expwy, exit Ed Carrey. Int corridors. **Pets:** Medium. $25 one-time fee/room. Service with restrictions, crate.

[ASK] [S/D] [&] [🛏] [💻] [≈]

La Quinta Inn-Harlingen **M** ❀
(956) 428-6888. **$85-$99.** 1002 US 83 S Expressway. US 83 and 77 Expwy, exit M St. Ext corridors. **Pets:** Small. Service with restrictions, crate.

[SAVE] [S/D] [X] [&M] [🐾] [🛏] [💻] [≈]

Super 8 Motel **M**
(956) 412-8873. **$50-$60, 3 days notice.** 1115 S Expressway 77/83. US 83 and 77 Expwy, exit M St, just n. Int corridors. **Pets:** $5 daily fee/pet. Service with restrictions, supervision.

[SAVE] [X] [🛏] [💻] [≈]

HENDERSON

Best Western Inn of Henderson **M**
(903) 657-9561. **$56-$84.** 1500 Hwy 259 S. 2 mi s on US 259. Ext/int corridors. **Pets:** Accepted.

[SAVE] [S/D] [X] [🛏] [💻] [≈]

HEREFORD

Best Western Red Carpet Inn **M**
(806) 364-0540. **$49-$53.** 830 W 1st St. Just w of jct US 385 and 60. Ext corridors. **Pets:** Service with restrictions, supervision.

[SAVE] [S/D] [X] [🛏] [💻] [≈]

HILLSBORO

Best Western Hillsboro Inn **M**
(254) 582-8465. **$65-$75.** 307 I-35. I-35, exit 368A northbound; exit 368B southbound, just w. Ext corridors. **Pets:** Medium. Service with restrictions, supervision.

[SAVE] [S/D] [X] [🛏] [≈]

HONDO

Whitetail Lodge **M**
(830) 426-3031. **$56-$86, 5 days notice.** 401 Hwy 90 E. US 90 at jct SR 173. Ext corridors. **Pets:** Small, dogs only. $10 one-time fee/pet. Designated rooms, service with restrictions, supervision.

[SAVE] [S/D] [X] [🛏] [≈]

HOUSTON METROPOLITAN AREA

BAYTOWN

Baymont Inn & Suites Houston-Baytown M
(281) 421-7300. **$49-$59.** 5215 I-10 E. I-10, exit 792. Int corridors. **Pets:** Accepted.

Holiday Inn Express M
(281) 421-7200. **$57-$105.** 5222 I-10 E. I-10, exit 792 (Garth Rd). Int corridors. **Pets:** Small. $10 daily fee/room. Designated rooms, service with restrictions, crate.

La Quinta Inn-Baytown M
(281) 421-5566. **$66-$79.** 4911 I-10 E. I-10, exit 792 (Garth Rd). Ext corridors. **Pets:** Other species. $25 deposit/room. Service with restrictions, supervision.

Motel 6–1136 M
(281) 576-5777. **$45-$54.** 8911 Hwy 146. I-10, exit 797 (SR 146). Ext corridors. **Pets:** Accepted.

Quality Inn Baytown M
(281) 427-7481. **$53, 7 days notice.** 300 S Hwy 146 business. 5 mi sw of jct I-10 and SR 146, exit 797, 2.2 mi s on Business 146 (Alexander Rd). Ext corridors. **Pets:** Service with restrictions, supervision.

CHANNELVIEW

Best Western Houston East M
(281) 452-1000. **$46-$80, 4 days notice.** 15919 I-10 E. I-10, exit 783 westbound; exit 784 eastbound. Ext corridors. **Pets:** Small. $10 deposit/pet, $10 one-time fee/pet. Service with restrictions, crate.

Travelodge Suites M
(281) 862-0222. **$55, 7 days notice.** 15831 2nd St. I-10, exit 783 (Sheldon Rd) eastbound, just n, just e on 2nd St; exit 783 (Sheldon Rd) westbound, 0.8 mi on Frontage Rd. Ext corridors. **Pets:** Accepted.

CONROE

Baymont Inn-Conroe M
(936) 539-5100. **$65-$70, 14 days notice.** 1506 I-45. I-45, exit 85 (Gladstell St) northbound; exit 84 (Frazier St) southbound. Int corridors. **Pets:** Medium. $50 deposit/room. Service with restrictions, crate.

Holiday Inn M
(409) 756-8941. **$79.** 1601 I-45 S. I-45, exit 84. Ext corridors. **Pets:** Accepted.

HOUSTON

AmeriSuites M
(281) 820-6060. **$116-$129.** 300 Ronan Park Pl. Sam Houston Pkwy (Beltway 8), exit Imperial Valley, 0.8 mi w on frontage road; exit Hardy Toll, turn under Pkwy, 1.2 mi w on west frontage road eastbound. Int corridors. **Pets:** Medium, other species. Service with restrictions, crate.

AmeriSuites (Houston/Hobby Airport) M
(713) 943-1713. **$99-$109.** 7922 Mosley Rd. I-45, exit 36 (Airport Blvd/College), off southbound service road. Int corridors. **Pets:** Accepted.

Baymont Inn & Suites Houston-Greenspoint M
(281) 875-2000. **$49-$64.** 12701 North Frwy. I-45, exit 61 (Greens Rd). Int corridors. **Pets:** $50 deposit/room. Service with restrictions, crate.

Baymont Inn & Suites-Houston Northwest M
(713) 680-8282. **$49-$64.** 11130 Northwest Frwy. I-45 N to I-610 N, then US 290 W, exit W 34th St, just ne. Int corridors. **Pets:** Small. $25 deposit/room. Service with restrictions, crate.

Baymont Inn & Suites-Houston Southwest M
(713) 784-3838. **$54-$64.** 6790 Southwest Frwy. Southwest Frwy (US 59), exit Hillcroft and W Park eastbound; exit Hillcroft westbound. Int corridors. **Pets:** Accepted.

Comfort Suites M
(713) 787-0004. **$108.** 6221 Richmond Ave. US 59, exit Hillcroft, 1 mi n on Hillcroft to Richmond, 0.6 mi e. Int corridors. **Pets:** Large, other species. $25 one-time fee/room. Service with restrictions, crate.

Days Inn-Houston North M
(281) 820-1500. **$47-$61.** 9025 North Frwy. I-45, exit 57A (Gulf Bank Rd). Ext corridors. **Pets:** Accepted.

Doubletree Guest Suites H
(713) 961-9000. **$239.** 5353 Westheimer Rd. I-610, 0.8 mi w off I-610, exit 8C (Westheimer Rd) northbound; exit 9A (San Felipe/Westheimer rds) southbound. Int corridors. **Pets:** Medium. $20 daily fee/pet.

Doubletree Hotel at Allen Center H
(713) 759-0202. **$119-$274.** 400 Dallas St. at Dallas and Bagby sts. Int corridors. **Pets:** Accepted.
⬛ ⬛ ⬛ ⬛ ⬛ ⬛ ⬛ ⬛

Drury Inn & Suites-Houston Hobby M
(713) 941-4300. **$60-$107.** 7902 Mosley Rd. Southbound service road, I-45 at Airport Blvd and College Rd, exit 36. Int corridors. **Pets:** Accepted.
⬛ ⬛ ⬛ ⬛ ⬛ ⬛ ⬛

Drury Inn & Suites Houston West M
(281) 558-7007. **$70-$102.** 1000 N Hwy 6. I-10, exit 751 (Addicks/Hwy 6), just n on SR 6. Int corridors. **Pets:** Small. Designated rooms, service with restrictions, supervision.
⬛ ⬛ ⬛ ⬛ ⬛

Drury Inn & Suites-Near Galleria M
(713) 963-0700. **$70-$132.** 1615 W Loop S. I-610, exit 9 (San Felipe Rd) northbound; exit 9A (San Felipe Rd) southbound, on east service road. Int corridors. **Pets:** Medium. Service with restrictions, supervision.
⬛ ⬛ ⬛ ⬛ ⬛ ⬛ ⬛

Four Seasons Hotel Houston H
(713) 650-1300. **$310-$385.** 1300 Lamar St. Lamar St and Austin. Int corridors. **Pets:** Accepted.
⬛ ⬛ ⬛ ⬛ ⬛ ⬛ ⬛ ⬛

Grant's Palm Court Inn M
(713) 668-8000. **$44-$66, 3 days notice.** 8200 S Main St. I-610, exit 2 (Main St), 1.4 mi ne. Ext corridors. **Pets:** Small, dogs only. Service with restrictions, supervision.
⬛ ⬛ ⬛

Hampton Inn I-10E M
(713) 673-4200. **$64-$84.** 828 Mercury Dr. I-10 E, exit 776A (Mercury Dr). Int corridors. **Pets:** Accepted.
⬛ ⬛ ⬛ ⬛ ⬛ ⬛ ⬛

Hawthorn Suites A
(713) 785-3415. **$79-$129.** 6910 Southwest Frwy. US 59 (Southwest Frwy), exit Hillcroft St. Ext corridors. **Pets:** Small, other species. $25 one-time fee/room.
⬛ ⬛ ⬛ ⬛ ⬛ ⬛

Hearthside by Villager M
(713) 895-8888. **$69, 7 days notice.** 12925 Northwest Frwy. US 290, exit Tidwell/Hollister, 1 mi e on Feeder Rd. Int corridors. **Pets:** Accepted.
⬛ ⬛ ⬛ ⬛ ⬛

Holiday Inn Hotel and Suites H
(713) 681-5000. **$75.** 7787 Katy Frwy. I-10, exit 762 (Antoine Dr) westbound; exit 762 (Silber/Post Oak Rd) eastbound, on eastbound service road. Int corridors. **Pets:** Other species. $25 one-time fee/room. Service with restrictions, supervision.
⬛ ⬛ ⬛ ⬛ ⬛ ⬛ ⬛ ⬛ ⬛

Holiday Inn Houston Intercontinental Airport H
(281) 449-2311. **$80-$170.** 15222 JFK Blvd. N Sam Houston Pkwy E and JFK Blvd intersection. Int corridors. **Pets:** Accepted.
⬛ ⬛ ⬛ ⬛ ⬛ ⬛ ⬛ ⬛ ⬛

Holiday Inn Select-Greenway Plaza H
(713) 523-8448. **$59-$99.** 2712 Southwest Frwy. US 59, exit Kirby Dr. Int corridors. **Pets:** Accepted.
⬛ ⬛ ⬛ ⬛ ⬛ ⬛ ⬛ ⬛

Holiday Inn Select I-10 H
(281) 558-5580. **$65-$115, 7 days notice.** 14703 Park Row. I-10, exit 751 (Addicks Rd/SR 6), just n. Int corridors. **Pets:** Accepted.
⬛ ⬛ ⬛ ⬛ ⬛ ⬛ ⬛ ⬛ ⬛

Homestead Studio Suites-Houston/Galleria Area M
(713) 960-9660. **$79.** 2300 W Loop S. I-10 W to 610 Loop S, exit 9A (San Felipe/Westheimer) southbound; exit 9 (San Felipe) northbound. Int corridors. **Pets:** Accepted.
⬛ ⬛ ⬛ ⬛ ⬛ ⬛

Homestead Studio Suites-Houston/Medical Center M
(713) 797-0000. **$59-$109.** 7979 Fannin St. I-610, exit 1B, 0.8 mi n. Ext corridors. **Pets:** Accepted.
⬛ ⬛ ⬛ ⬛ ⬛

Homestead Studio Suites-Houston/Willowbrook M
(281) 397-9922. **$274-$282 (weekly).** 13223 Champions Center Dr. Jct SR 249 and FM 1960 W, 0.9 mi e to Champion Center Dr, just n to Champion Center Plaza, just w. Ext corridors. **Pets:** Small. $100 one-time fee/room. Designated rooms, service with restrictions, supervision.
⬛ ⬛ ⬛ ⬛ ⬛ ⬛ ⬛ ⬛

Homestead Village Guest Studios M
(713) 785-8550. **Call for rates.** 3030 W Sam Houston Pkwy. Sam Houston Pkwy (Beltway 8), exit Westheimer Rd. Ext corridors. **Pets:** Accepted.
⬛ ⬛ ⬛ ⬛ ⬛

Homestead Village Guest Studios-Cypress Station M
(281) 580-2221. **Call for rates.** 220 Bammel-Westfield Rd. I-45, exit 66, southbound frontage road, then just n. Ext corridors. **Pets:** Accepted.
⬛ ⬛ ⬛ ⬛ ⬛

Homestead Village-Park 10 M
(281) 579-6959. **Call for rates.** 1255 Hwy 6 N. I-10, exit 751 (Addicks Rd), just n. Ext corridors. **Pets:** Accepted.
⬛ ⬛ ⬛ ⬛

Homewood Suites by Hilton M
(281) 486-7677. **$139-$179.** 401 Bay Area Blvd. I-45, exit 26 (Bay Area Blvd), 1 mi e. Int corridors. **Pets:** Accepted.
⬛ ⬛ ⬛ ⬛ ⬛ ⬛ ⬛

Homewood Suites Hotel-Willowbrook Mall M
(281) 955-5200. **$125-$159.** 7655 W FM 1960. Just e jct SR 249 and FM 1960. Int corridors. **Pets:** Accepted.

SAVE | S | X | &M | | | | |

Hotel Sofitel Houston H
(281) 445-9000. **$209.** 425 N Sam Houston Pkwy E. Beltway 8 (Sam Houston Pkwy), exit Imperial Valley westbound; exit Hardy Toll Rd eastbound, on westbound frontage road. Int corridors. **Pets:** Accepted.

ASK | S | X | | | | |

Houston Marriott Medical Center Hotel H
(713) 796-0080. **$89-$209.** 6580 Fannin St. I-610, exit 2 (Main St), 2.5 mi ne to Holcombe St, 0.3 mi e. Int corridors. **Pets:** Accepted.

SAVE | S | X | &M | | | | | | | |

La Quinta Inn & Suites M
(281) 646-9200. **$82-$92.** 15225 Katy Frwy. I-10, exit 748 (Barker-Cypress Rd) eastbound, 2.6 mi on eastbound service road; exit 751 (Hwy 6) westbound, just s to Grisby Rd, 0.5 mi w. Int corridors. **Pets:** Very small, other species. Service with restrictions, supervision.

SAVE | S | X | | | | | |

La Quinta Inn & Suites Houston-Galleria Area M
(713) 355-3440. **$76-$126.** 1625 W Loop S. I-610, exit 9 (San Felipe) northbound; exit 9A (San Felipe/Westheimer) southbound, on northbound service road. Int corridors. **Pets:** Small, other species. Service with restrictions, supervision.

SAVE | S | X | &M | | | | | |

La Quinta Inn-BrookHollow M
(713) 688-2581. **$56-$72.** 11002 Northwest Frwy. Nw on US 290, exit Magnum-Dacoma. Ext corridors. **Pets:** Accepted.

SAVE | S | X | | | | |

La Quinta Inn-Greenspoint M
(281) 447-6888. **$59-$79.** 6 N Sam Houston Pkwy E. I-45, exit 60A southbound; exit 60B northbound. Ext corridors. **Pets:** Accepted.

SAVE | S | X | &M | |

La Quinta Inn-Greenway Plaza M
(713) 623-4750. **$72-$86.** 4015 Southwest Frwy. Sw off US 59 (Southwest Frwy), Weslayan exit. Ext/int corridors. **Pets:** Small, other species. Service with restrictions, crate.

SAVE | S | X | | | | | |

La Quinta Inn-Houston-Astrodome M
(713) 668-8082. **$82-$102.** 9911 Buffalo Speedway. I-610, exit 2 (Buffalo Speedway/S Main St), just s. Ext corridors. **Pets:** Accepted.

SAVE | S | X | | | |

La Quinta Inn-Houston-Cy-Fair M
(281) 469-4018. **$82-$96.** 13290 FM 1960 W. SR 6, w of jct US 290 and FM 1960. Ext corridors. **Pets:** Accepted.

SAVE | S | X | | | | |

La Quinta Inn-Houston East M
(713) 453-5425. **$72-$86.** 11999 E Frwy. I-10, exit 778A (Federal Rd) eastbound; exit 776B (Holland Ave) westbound. Ext corridors. **Pets:** Accepted.

SAVE | S | X | | | |

La Quinta Inn-Houston-Gessner M
(713) 772-3626. **$59-$69.** 8201 Southwest Frwy. Sw on US 59, exit Gessner St. Ext corridors. **Pets:** Accepted.

SAVE | S | X | | | | |

La Quinta Inn-Houston-Hobby Airport M
(713) 941-0900. **$56-$89.** 9902 Gulf Frwy. I-45 S, exit 36 (Gulf Frwy), Airport Blvd-College Ave. Ext/int corridors. **Pets:** Accepted.

SAVE | S | X | &M | | | |

La Quinta Inn-Houston-I-45 North(Loop 1960) M
(281) 444-7500. **$59-$72.** 17111 North Frwy. I-45, exit 66, southbound service road, 0.4 mi s of jct FM 1960 and I-45. Ext corridors. **Pets:** Accepted.

SAVE | S | X | | | |

La Quinta Inn-Houston Wilcrest M
(713) 932-0808. **$52-$66.** 11113 Katy Frwy. I-10, exit 754 (Kirkwood Dr) westbound; exit 755 (Wilcrest Rd) eastbound, on eastbound service road. Ext corridors. **Pets:** Accepted.

SAVE | S | X | | | | |

La Quinta Inn-Wirt Rd M
(713) 688-8941. **$69-$96.** 8017 Katy Frwy. I-10, exit 761A (Wirt Rd), just w. Ext corridors. **Pets:** Accepted.

SAVE | S | X | | | | |

The Lovett Inn BB
(713) 522-5224. **$75-$175, 3 days notice.** 501 Lovett Blvd. I-610, exit Westheimer Rd, 4.5 mi e to Montrose Blvd, s to Lovett Blvd, just e. Ext/int corridors. **Pets:** Other species. Designated rooms, service with restrictions.

X | | | |

Motel 6–1140 M
(713) 937-7056. **$43-$53.** 16884 Northwest Frwy. US 290, westbound exit Jones Rd; eastbound exit Senate Ave on westbound frontage road. Ext corridors. **Pets:** Accepted.

S | X | | | |

Motel 6–1401 M
(713) 334-9188. **$47-$59.** 2900 W Sam Houston Pkwy S. Sam Houston Pkwy (Beltway 8), exit Westheimer Rd. Int corridors. **Pets:** Accepted.

S | X | &M | |

Omni Houston Hotel H
(713) 871-8181. **$119-$269.** Four Riverway. I-610, exit 10 (Woodway Dr), 0.5 mi w. Int corridors. **Pets:** Small, other species. $50 one-time fee/pet. Service with restrictions, supervision.

Omni Houston Hotel Westside H
(281) 558-8338. **$71-$171.** 13210 Katy Frwy. I-10, exit 753A (Eldridge St), just n. Int corridors. **Pets:** Small. $50 one-time fee/room. Service with restrictions, supervision.

Radisson Hotel & Conference Center H
(713) 943-7979. **$129-$135.** 9100 Gulf Frwy. I-45, exit 36 (Airport Blvd-College Rd), on west service road. Int corridors. **Pets:** Accepted.

Radisson Hotel Astrodome Convention Center H
(713) 748-3221. **$79-$129.** 8686 Kirby Dr. at jct I-610, exit 1C (Kirby Dr). Ext/int corridors. **Pets:** Accepted.

Ramada Plaza Hotel Near the Galleria M
(713) 688-2222. **$99-$109, 7 days notice.** 7611 Katy Frwy. I-10, exit 762 (Silber Rd). Int corridors. **Pets:** Accepted.

Red Roof Inn Hobby Airport M
(713) 943-3300. **$55-$65.** 9005 Airport Blvd. I-45, exit 36 (Airport Blvd/College Rd), just w. Int corridors. **Pets:** Accepted.

Red Roof Inn Houston West M
(281) 579-7200. **$44-$58.** 15701 Park Ten Pl. I-10, exit 751 (Addicks Rd/SR 6), 0.8 mi on west frontage road. Ext/int corridors. **Pets:** Accepted.

Red Roof Inns M
(713) 939-0800. **$44-$64.** 12929 Northwest Frwy. US 290, exit Hollister and Tidwell rds, on eastbound service road. Ext/int corridors. **Pets:** Accepted.

Red Roof Inns M
(713) 785-9909. **$49-$65.** 2960 W Sam Houston Pkwy S. Sw Sam Houston (Beltway 8), exit Westheimer Rd. Ext/int corridors. **Pets:** Medium, other species. Service with restrictions, supervision.

Residence Inn by Marriott M 🐾
(713) 840-9757. **$134-$197.** 2500 McCue. I-610, exit 8C (Westheimer Rd) northbound; exit 9A (San Felipe/Westheimer) southbound; just w to McCue, just n. Ext/int corridors. **Pets:** Medium. $5 daily fee/room, $25 one-time fee/room. Service with restrictions, supervision.

Residence Inn by Marriott Houston Westchase M
(713) 974-5454. **$124-$160.** 9965 Westheimer. Beltway 8 (Sam Houston Pkwy), exit Westheimer, 0.7 mi e to Elmside Dr, just s. Int corridors. **Pets:** Large, other species. $5 daily fee/pet, $50 one-time fee/room.

Residence Inn by Marriott-Medical Center/Astrodome A
(713) 660-7993. **$139.** 7710 Main St. I-610, exit 2 (S Main St/Buffalo Speedway), 1.5 mi n. Ext corridors. **Pets:** Medium. $7 daily fee/pet, $200 one-time fee/room. Designated rooms, service with restrictions, crate.

Residence Inn-Houston Clear Lake A
(281) 486-2424. **$99-$129.** 525 Bay Area Blvd. I-45 S, exit 26 (Bay Area Blvd), 1.2 mi e. Ext corridors. **Pets:** Accepted.

Robin's Nest Bed & Breakfast Inn BB
(713) 528-5821. **$110-$130, 7 days notice.** 4104 Greeley St. US 59 (Southwest Frwy), downtown exit Richmond Ave, just n. Int corridors. **Pets:** Accepted.

Rodeway Inn-Southwest Freeway M
(713) 526-1071. **$57-$69.** 3135 Southwest Frwy. Just se of US 59 (Southwest Frwy), exit Buffalo Speedway, on service road. Ext corridors. **Pets:** Small, dogs only. $20 deposit/pet. Designated rooms, service with restrictions, supervision.

The St. Regis Houston H 🐾
(713) 840-7600. **$322-$386.** 1919 Briar Oaks Ln. I-610, exit San Felipe, just e. Int corridors. **Pets:** Medium, other species. Service with restrictions, crate.

Sheraton Houston Brook Hollow H
(713) 688-0100. **$165-$365.** 3000 N Loop W. Just nw of jct I-610 and US 290, exit 13C (TC Jester). Int corridors. **Pets:** $50 deposit/room. Supervision.

Shoney's Inn & Suites Dairy Ashford M
(281) 493-5626. **$65-$105.** 12323 Katy Frwy. I-10, exit 753 (Dairy-Ashford Rd), on south service road. Int corridors. **Pets:** Accepted.

Shoney's Inn and Suites Houston Southwest M
(713) 776-2633. **$65-$105.** 6687 Southwest Frwy. US 59 N, exit Hillcroft Ave/West Park Dr, then just 0.7 mi eastbound; exit Hillcroft westbound. Int corridors. **Pets:** Accepted.

 **Shoney's Inn and Suites-Northwest** Ⓜ

(713) 690-1493. **$65-$105.** 7887 W Tidwell Rd. US 290 W, exit W Tidwell, 0.3 mi on service road to W Tidwell Rd; on se corner of eastbound service road and W Tidwell Rd. Int corridors. **Pets:** $25 one-time fee/pet. Service with restrictions, crate.

Ⓢ Ⓢ Ⓧ Ⓔ Ⓗ ▣ ≈

Star Inn & Suites Ⓜ

(713) 695-5552. **$54-$60.** 4515 Airline Dr. I-45, exit 53 (Airline Dr), just w. Ext corridors. **Pets:** Accepted.

Ⓢ Ⓢ Ⓧ Ⓗ

Staybridge Suites by Holiday Inn Houston-Near The Galleria Ⓜ ✿

(713) 355-8888. **$139-$169.** 5190 Hidalgo. I-610, exit 9A (San Felipe/Westheimer) southbound; exit 8C (Westheimer Rd) northbound, 0.4 mi w on Westheimer Rd to Sage Rd, just s. Int corridors. **Pets:** Medium, other species. $75 one-time fee/room.

Ⓐ Ⓢ Ⓧ Ⓜ Ⓗ ▣ ≈

Studio 6-Houston Hobby South Ⓜ

(281) 929-5400. **$50.** 12700 Featherwood. I-45, exit 33 (Fugua St), stay in right lane and cross over I-45, just e to Fugua St, just s. Ext corridors. **Pets:** Accepted.

Ⓧ Ⓔ Ⓗ ▣

Super 8 Motel Ⓜ

(281) 866-8686. **$70-$80.** 609 W FM 1960. I-45, exit 66 southbound; exit 66A northbound, just w. Int corridors. **Pets:** Accepted.

Ⓐ Ⓢ Ⓧ Ⓗ ≈

TownePlace Suites by Marriott-Westlake Ⓜ

(281) 646-0058. **$65-$100.** 15155 Katy Frwy. I-10, exit 751, just s on SR 6 to Grisby Rd, then w. Int corridors. **Pets:** Small, other species. $5 daily fee/pet, $100 one-time fee/room. Designated rooms, service with restrictions, supervision.

Ⓢ Ⓢ Ⓧ Ⓔ Ⓗ ▣ ≈

The Warwick Ⓗ

(713) 526-1991. **$179-$189.** 5701 Main St. Jct of Main and Ewing sts, just n of Herman Park. Int corridors. **Pets:** Accepted.

Ⓐ Ⓢ Ⓧ Ⓜ Ⓐ Ⓔ Ⓗ ▣ Ⓣ ≈

Wellesley Inn & Suites (Houston/Memorial) Ⓜ

(713) 263-9770. **$95-$115.** 7855 Katy Frwy. I-10, exit 762 (Antoine Dr) westbound; exit 762 (Sleber/Post Oak Rd) eastbound, on eastbound service road. Int corridors. **Pets:** Accepted.

Ⓢ Ⓢ Ⓧ Ⓔ Ⓗ ▣ ≈

KATY

 **Best Western-Houston West** Ⓜ

(281) 392-9800. **$60.** 22455 I-10 (Katy Frwy). I-10, exit 743 (Grand Pkwy), just e on eastbound service road. Ext corridors. **Pets:** Medium. $10 daily fee/pet. Service with restrictions, supervision.

Ⓢ Ⓢ Ⓧ Ⓗ ▣ ≈

LA PORTE

La Quinta Inn-La Porte Ⓜ

(281) 470-0760. **$72-$86.** 1105 Hwy 146 S. SR 146, exit Fairmont Pkwy, at jct SR 146 business route. Ext corridors. **Pets:** Accepted.

Ⓢ Ⓢ Ⓧ Ⓐ Ⓗ ▣ ≈

NASSAU BAY

Holiday Inn Houston/Nasa Ⓜ

(281) 333-2500. **$99-$109.** 1300 NASA Rd One. I-45, exit 25, 2.5 mi e. Ext/int corridors. **Pets:** Small. $50 one-time fee/room. Service with restrictions, supervision.

Ⓐ Ⓢ Ⓧ Ⓐ Ⓗ ▣ Ⓣ ≈

ROSENBERG

Holiday Inn Express Hotel & Suites Ⓜ

(281) 342-7888. **$79.** 27927 SW Frwy. US 59, exit #SH 36. Int corridors. **Pets:** Accepted.

Ⓐ Ⓢ Ⓧ Ⓜ Ⓔ Ⓗ ▣ ≈

STAFFORD

La Quinta Inn-Stafford Ⓜ

(281) 240-2300. **$66-$79.** 12727 Southwest Frwy. US 59 eastbound service road, exit Corporate Dr southbound; exit Airport Blvd/Kirkwood Rd northbound. Int corridors. **Pets:** Accepted.

Ⓢ Ⓢ Ⓧ Ⓐ Ⓗ ▣ ≈

Studio 6 Ⓜ

(281) 240-6900. **$43.** 12827 Southwest Frwy. US 59, exit US 90 and SR 41 alternate northbound, following frontage road; exit Corporate Dr southbound, following frontage road. Ext corridors. **Pets:** Accepted.

Ⓧ Ⓔ Ⓗ ▣

SUGAR LAND

Drury Inn & Suites-Houston/Sugar Land Ⓜ

(281) 277-9700. **$70-$107.** 13770 Southwest Frwy. Sw on US 59, exit Sugarland/Alternate 90/Spur 41 (Dairy Ashford/Sugarcreek Blvd). Int corridors. **Pets:** Small, other species. Service with restrictions, supervision.

Ⓧ Ⓐ Ⓔ Ⓗ ▣ ≈

▼▼ **Hearthside by Villager** Ⓜ ❄
(281) 494-6699. **$49-$99.** 13420 Southwest Frwy. US 59, exit Sugarcreek, just ne. Int corridors. **Pets:** Small. $100 deposit/pet, $10 daily fee/pet, $50 one-time fee/pet. Designated rooms, service with restrictions, supervision.

[⊠] [🛗] [💻]

Ⓐ ▼▼▼ **Residence Inn** Ⓜ
(281) 277-0770. **$119.** 12703 Southwest Frwy. US 59, exit Corporate Dr; southbound, exit Airport Blvd/Kirkwood Rd northbound. Int corridors. **Pets:** Accepted.

[SAVE] [🆘] [⊠] [🛗] [💻] [🏊]

Ⓐ ▼▼▼ **Shoney's Inn & Suites Houston-Sugar Land** Ⓜ
(281) 565-6655. **$65-$105.** 14444 Southwest Frwy. Sw on US 59, exit stafford/Sugarland (Dairy Ashford/Sugar Creek Blvd). Int corridors. **Pets:** $25 one-time fee/pet. Designated rooms, supervision.

[SAVE] [🆘] [⊠] [🍴] [🛗] [💻] [🏊]

THE WOODLANDS

▼▼▼ **Drury Inn & Suites-Houston The Woodlands** Ⓜ
(281) 362-7222. **$70-$107.** 28099 I-45 N. I-45, exit 78 southbound; exit 77 northbound on west service road. Int corridors. **Pets:** Accepted.

[⊠] [🛗] [🍴] [🖥] [🛗] [💻] [🏊]

Ⓐ ▼▼▼ **La Quinta Inn-Houston-Woodlands** Ⓜ
(281) 367-7722. **$66-$86.** 28673 I-45 N. I-45, exit 78 southbound; exit 79 northbound on southbound frontage road. Ext corridors. **Pets:** Accepted.

[SAVE] [🆘] [⊠] [🍴] [🖥] [💻] [🏊]

Ⓐ ▼▼▼▼ **The Woodlands Residence Inn** Ⓜ
(281) 292-3252. **$120-$170.** 1040 Lake Front Cr. I-45, exit 78 southbound; exit 79 northbound, 0.8 mi s of jct I-45 and Research Forest, just w. Int corridors. **Pets:** Accepted.

[SAVE] [🆘] [⊠] [🖥] [🛗] [💻] [🏊]

TOMBALL

▼▼▼ **Holiday Inn Express** Ⓜ
(281) 351-4114. **$75-$90.** 1437 Keefer St. Northeast corner, SR 249 and FM 2920. Ext corridors. **Pets:** Accepted.

[ASK] [🆘] [⊠] [🛗] [🏊]

WEBSTER

▼ **Motel 6 Houston Nasa/Clear Lake** Ⓜ
(281) 332-4581. **$43-$53.** 1001 W NASA Rd One. I-45, exit 25, just e. Ext corridors. **Pets:** Small, other species. Service with restrictions, supervision.

[🆘] [⊠] [🍴] [🖥] [🛗] [🏊]

Ⓐ ▼▼▼ **Wellesley Inn & Suites (Houston/NASA Clear Lake)** Ⓜ
(281) 338-7711. **$89-$109.** 720 W Bay Area Blvd. I-45, exit 26 (Bay Area Blvd), just e. Int corridors. **Pets:** Small. Service with restrictions, supervision.

[SAVE] [🆘] [⊠] [🍴] [🖥] [🛗] [💻] [🏊]

❈ **END METROPOLITAN AREA** ❈

HUNTSVILLE

▼▼▼▼ **Holiday Inn Express (Sam Houston)** Ⓜ
(936) 293-8800. **$74-$99.** 201 West Hill Park Cir. I-45, exit 116, just w on US 190 to West Hill Park Cir. Ext corridors. **Pets:** Accepted.

[ASK] [🆘] [⊠] [♿] [🛗] [💻] [🏊]

Ⓐ ▼▼▼▼ **La Quinta Inn-Huntsville** Ⓜ
(936) 295-6454. **$72-$86.** 124 I-45 N. I-45, exit 116. Ext corridors. **Pets:** Other species. Service with restrictions.

[SAVE] [🆘] [⊠] [🍴] [💻] [🏊]

HURST

Ⓐ ▼▼▼▼ **AmeriSuites (Ft Worth/Hurst)** Ⓜ
(817) 577-3003. **$98-$114.** 1601 Hurst Town Center Dr. SR 183, exit Precinct Line Rd, just n to Thousand Oaks, just w. Int corridors. **Pets:** Small. Service with restrictions, supervision.

[SAVE] [🆘] [⊠] [♿] [🍴] [🖥] [🛗] [💻] [🏊]

JASPER

Ⓐ ▼▼▼ **Best Western Inn Of Jasper** Ⓜ
(409) 384-7767. **$51.** 205 W Gibson. US 190 and SR 63, 0.5 mi w of jct US 96. Ext corridors. **Pets:** Small. $10 daily fee/room. Service with restrictions, crate.

[SAVE] [🆘] [⊠] [🛗] [🏊]

▼▼▼ **Holiday Inn Express** Ⓜ
(409) 384-8600. **$77.** 2100 N Wheeler. US 96, 1.8 mi n of jct US 190. Ext corridors. **Pets:** Accepted.

[ASK] [🆘] [⊠] [🛗] [💻] [🏊]

▼ **Ramada Inn Jasper** Ⓜ
(409) 384-9021. **$51.** 239 E Gibson (US 190). US 190 and SR 63, just w of jct US 96. Ext corridors. **Pets:** Accepted.

[ASK] [🆘] [⊠] [🛗] [💻] [🍽] [🏊]

JUNCTION

▼▼▼ Days Inn **M**
(915) 446-3730. **$59-$69.** 111 S Martinez St. I-10, exit 457, 0.3 mi s. Ext corridors. **Pets:** Medium, other species. $4 daily fee/pet. Service with restrictions, supervision.
🆂🆅 🆂🅾 ⊠ 🔋 💻 �というwait

▼▼ The Hills Motel **M**
(915) 446-2567. **$38-$42 (no credit cards), 3 days notice.** 1520 Main St. I-10, exit 456, 1.3 mi s on US 377. Ext corridors. **Pets:** Accepted.
🆂🅾 ⊠ 🔋 🍴 🌊

▼▼ La Vista Motel **M**
(915) 446-2191. **$34-$38.** 2040 N Main St. I-10, exit 456, 0.8 mi s. Ext corridors. **Pets:** Accepted.
🆂🆅 ⊠ 🔋 💻

KERRVILLE

▼▼▼ Best Western Sunday Inn **M**
(830) 896-1313. **$65-$120.** 2124 Sidney Baker St. I-10, exit 508 (SR 16). Ext corridors. **Pets:** Small. $10 daily fee/pet. Designated rooms, service with restrictions, supervision.
🆂🆅 🆂🅾 ⊠ 💻 🌊

▼▼ Budget Inn **M** 🐾
(830) 896-8200. **$45-$60.** 1804 Sidney Baker St. I-10, exit 508, 0.5 mi s on SR 16. Ext corridors. **Pets:** Small, dogs only. $5 daily fee/pet. Service with restrictions, supervision.
🆂🆅 🆂🅾 ⊠ 🔋 🍴 🌊

▼▼▼▼ Inn of the Hills Conference Resort **M**
(830) 895-5000. **$84-$109.** 1001 Junction Hwy. I-10, exit 505, 1.5 mi nw on SR 27. Ext corridors. **Pets:** Accepted.
🆂🆅 🆂🅾 ⊠ 🎾 🏌 🔋 💻 🍴 🌊 🏕

▼▼▼▼ Y. O. Ranch Hotel & Conference Center **H**
(830) 257-4440. **$99-$119, 3 days notice.** 2033 Sidney Baker St. I-10, exit SR 16, 0.3 mi s. Ext/int corridors. **Pets:** Accepted.
🅰🆂🅺 🆂🅾 ⊠ 🎾 🔋 💻 🍴 🌊 🏕

KILLEEN

▼▼▼ Holiday Inn Express **M**
(254) 554-2727. **$67-$85, 7 days notice.** 1602 E Center Expwy. US 190, exit Trimmier Rd. Ext corridors. **Pets:** Supervision.
🆂🆅 🆂🅾 ⊠ 🔋 💻

▼▼▼▼ La Quinta Inn-Killeen **M**
(254) 526-8331. **$65-$75.** 1112 Fort Hood St. 1.3 mi sw on RM 439 at jct US 190. Ext corridors. **Pets:** Accepted.
🆂🆅 🆂🅾 ⊠ 🎾 🔋 💻 🌊

KINGSVILLE

▼▼▼ Holiday Inn **M**
(361) 595-5753. **$65, 5 days notice.** 3430 Hwy 77 S. 1.5 mi s on US 77. Ext corridors. **Pets:** Accepted.
🅰🆂🅺 ⊠ 💻 🍴 🌊

▼▼▼ Howard Johnson **M**
(361) 592-6471. **$53-$59.** 105 S 77 Bypass. 0.8 mi e on US 77. Ext corridors. **Pets:** Very small. Service with restrictions, supervision.
🆂🆅 🆂🅾 ⊠ 🔋 💻 🌊

LAJITAS

▼▼▼ Lajitas On the Rio Grande **M**
(915) 424-3471. **Call for rates.** 1 Main Pl. Center. Ext/int corridors. **Pets:** Accepted.
🅰🆂🅺 ⊠ 🔋 💻 🍴 🌊 🏕

LAKE JACKSON

▼▼▼ Ramada Inn Lake Jackson **M**
(979) 297-1161. **$117-$137.** 925 Hwy 332. 2.8 mi e of jct SR 288 and 332. Int corridors. **Pets:** Large, other species. $100 deposit/room. Supervision.
🅰🆂🅺 ⊠ 🔋 💻 🍴 🌊

▼▼▼ Super 8 Motel Lake Jackson **M**
(979) 297-3031. **$50.** 915 Hwy 332. 3 mi e jct SR 288 and 332. Ext corridors. **Pets:** Very small. $10 daily fee/pet. Service with restrictions, supervision.
🅰🆂🅺 🆂🅾 ⊠ 🔋 💻 🌊

LAMESA

▼▼▼ Budget Host Inn **M**
(806) 872-2118. **$44, 3 days notice.** 901 S Dallas Ave. Jct US 180, 0.7 mi s on US 87. Ext corridors. **Pets:** Accepted.
🆂🆅 🆂🅾 ⊠ 🔋 🌊

▼▼▼ Shiloh Inn **M**
(806) 872-6721. **$42-$48, 3 days notice.** 1707 Lubbock Hwy. 1 mi n on US 87 from jct US 180. Ext corridors. **Pets:** Small. Designated rooms, no service, supervision.
🅰🆂🅺 ⊠ 🔋 💻 🌊

LAREDO

▼▼▼ Fiesta Inn **M**
(956) 723-3603. **$72-$77.** 5240 San Bernardo. I-35, exit 3B, 2.8 mi n on US 81 and 83. Ext corridors. **Pets:** Accepted.
🅰🆂🅺 🆂🅾 ⊠ 🔋 🌊

▼▼▼▼ La Quinta Inn-Laredo **M**
(956) 722-0511. **$95-$115.** 3610 Santa Ursula Ave. I-35, exit 3A (US 59). Ext corridors. **Pets:** Small. Service with restrictions, supervision.
🆂🆅 🆂🅾 ⊠ 🔋 💻 🌊

▼▼▼ Motel 6–1107 **M**
(956) 722-8133. **$52-$65.** 5920 San Bernardo Ave. I-35, exit 4 (Mines Rd). Ext/int corridors. **Pets:** Accepted.
🆂🅾 ⊠ 🏌 🌊

▼▼ Motel 6 South-142 M
(956) 725-8187. **$50-$63.** 5310 San Bernardo. I-35, exit 3B
(Mann Rd). Ext corridors. **Pets:** Accepted.

♦♦♦ ▼▼ Red Roof Inn Laredo M
(956) 712-0733. **$54-$72.** 1006 W Calton Rd. I-35, exit 3A,
0.3 mi w. Ext/int corridors. **Pets:** Accepted.

▼▼▼ Rio Grande Plaza Hotel H
(956) 722-2411. **$79-$84.** One South Main Ave. Just w of
International Bridge. Int corridors. **Pets:** Accepted.

LEAGUE CITY

▼▼ Super 8 Motel M
(281) 338-0800. **$54-$90.** 102 Hobbs Rd. I-45, exit 23, just
e to Hobbs Rd, just s. Int corridors. **Pets:** Accepted.

LITTLEFIELD

♦♦♦ ▼ Crescent Park Motel M
(806) 385-4464. **$42-$52.** 2000 Hall Ave. Jct US 84, 0.3 mi
n on SR 385. Ext corridors. **Pets:** Accepted.

LLANO

♦♦♦ ▼▼ Best Western M
(915) 247-4101. **$57-$72, 30 days notice.** 901 W Young
St. 1 mi w on SR 71 and 29. Ext corridors. **Pets:** Accepted.

LONGVIEW

♦♦♦ ▼▼▼ Days Inn of Longview M
(903) 758-1113. **$50-$60.** 3103 Estes Pkwy. I-20, exit 595,
0.3 mi n. Ext/int corridors. **Pets:** Accepted.

♦♦♦ ▼▼▼▼ La Quinta Inn M
(903) 757-3663. **$65-$75.** 502 S Access Rd. Jct Estes
Pkwy and I-20, exit 595. Ext corridors. **Pets:** Accepted.

LUBBOCK

**♦♦♦ ▼▼▼ Best Western Lubbock Windsor
        Inn M ✿**
(806) 762-8400. **$60-$90, 5 days notice.** 5410 I-27. 3.5 mi
s on I-27, exit 1B southbound; U-turn at exit 1A (50th St)
northbound. Int corridors. **Pets:** Medium. $25 deposit/pet,
$8 daily fee/pet. Designated rooms, service with restrictions,
supervision.

▼▼ Days Inn Texas Tech M
(806) 747-7111. **$49-$80.** 2401 4th St. I-27, exit 4 (4th St),
1.5 mi w. Ext corridors. **Pets:** Accepted.

▼▼▼ Four Points Sheraton Hotel H
(806) 747-0171. **$81-$92.** 505 Ave Q. I-27, exit 4, 0.9 mi w
to US 84, then just s. Int corridors. **Pets:** Accepted.

**♦♦♦ ▼▼▼▼ La Quinta Inn-Lubbock-Civic
        Center M**
(806) 763-9441. **$71-$81.** 601 Ave Q. 0.8 mi nw on US 84.
Ext corridors. **Pets:** Medium. $25 one-time fee/room. No
service, supervision.

**▼▼▼▼ La Quinta Inn-Lubbock-Medical
        Center M**
(806) 792-0065. **$76-$86.** 4115 Brownfield Hwy. 3.3 mi sw;
2.5 mi ne of Loop 289 on US 62 and 82. Int corridors.
Pets: Small, other species. Service with restrictions, crate.

▼▼ Lubbock Super 8 Motel M
(806) 762-8726. **$50-$80, 7 days notice.** 501 Ave Q. 1 mi
nw on US 84. Ext corridors. **Pets:** Other species. $25
deposit/pet, $6 daily fee/pet. No service, supervision.

▼▼▼▼ Ramada Inn Regency Hotel M
(806) 745-2208. **$84.** 6624 I-27. 3.8 mi s on I-27 and US
87; just w of jct Loop 289, exit 1B southbound. Int corridors.
Pets: Small. $10 daily fee/pet. Designated rooms, service
with restrictions, supervision.

♦♦♦ ▼▼▼▼ Residence Inn by Marriott A
(806) 745-1963. **$92.** 2551 S Loop 289. Loop 289, 3 mi w
of University exit, south frontage road. Ext corridors.
Pets: Other species. $50 one-time fee/room. Service with
restrictions, crate.

LUFKIN

▼▼▼▼ Comfort Suites M
(936) 632-4949. **$90-$150.** 4402 S 1st St. 2.2 mi s of jct US
59 and E Loop 287. Int corridors. **Pets:** Accepted.

▼▼ Day's Inn M
(936) 639-3301. **$65-$75.** 2130 S 1st St. 0.3 mi s of jct US
59 and Loop 287. Ext/int corridors. **Pets:** Medium. $25
deposit/pet. Service with restrictions, supervision.

♦♦♦ ▼▼▼▼ La Quinta Inn-Lufkin M
(936) 634-3351. **$58-$75.** 2119 S 1st St. US 59, Carriage-
way northbound, 0.3 mi s of jct S Loop 287 and US 59
business route. Ext corridors. **Pets:** Small. Service with
restrictions, crate.

MARBLE FALLS

♦♦♦ ▼▼▼▼ Best Western Marble Falls Inn M
(830) 693-5122. **$69-$119.** 1403 Hwy 281 N. 0.4 mi n of jct
SR 281 and CR 1431. Ext corridors. **Pets:** Accepted.

MCALLEN

▼▼▼▼ Drury Inn M
(956) 687-5100. **$70-$114.** 612 W Expwy 83. US 83 Expwy, exit 2nd St, northwest frontage road. Int corridors. **Pets:** Accepted.
⊠ 🖪 🖵 🌊

▼▼▼ Hampton Inn-McAllen M
(956) 682-4900. **$89-$109.** 300 W Expressway 83. US 83 Expwy, exit 2nd St, northwest frontage road. Int corridors. **Pets:** Small. Service with restrictions, supervision.
SAVE ⊠ 🖪 🖵 🌊

▼▼▼▼ La Quinta Inn-McAllen M
(956) 687-1101. **$74-$84.** 1100 S 10th St. 1.5 mi s on SR 336; just n of jct US 83 Expwy. Ext corridors. **Pets:** Accepted.
SAVE Sᴅ ⊠ 🔥ᴹ 🐾 🐾 🖪 🖵 🌊

▼▼▼ Thrifty-Inn-McAllen M
(956) 631-6700. **$40-$71.** 620 W Expwy 83. US 83 Expwy, exit 2nd St, northwest frontage road. Int corridors. **Pets:** Small. Service with restrictions, supervision.
⊠

MEMPHIS

▼▼▼ Executive Inn MI
(806) 259-3583. **$50-$55.** 1600 Boykin Dr. 0.5 mi nw. Ext corridors. **Pets:** Small. $5 daily fee/pet. Service with restrictions, supervision.
SAVE Sᴅ ⊠ 🖪 🍽 🌊

MIDLAND

▼▼▼ Best Inn & Suites M
(915) 699-4144. **$45.** 3100 W Wall St. 2 mi w on I-20 business loop. Int corridors. **Pets:** Medium, other species. $7 daily fee/pet. Service with restrictions, supervision.
SAVE ⊠ 🖪 🌊

▼▼▼▼ Best Western Atrium Inn M
(915) 694-7774. **$60-$65, 7 days notice.** 3904 W Wall St. I-20, exit 134, 1 mi n on Midkiff Rd, 0.3 mi w on Business Rt I-20. Ext/int corridors. **Pets:** $5 daily fee/pet. Service with restrictions, supervision.
SAVE Sᴅ ⊠ 🐾 🖵 🌊

▼▼▼ Days Inn M
(915) 697-3155. **$65, 7 days notice.** 1003 S Midkiff Rd. I-20, exit 134, 1 mi n. Ext corridors. **Pets:** Medium, other species. $10 one-time fee/pet. Service with restrictions, supervision.
SAVE Sᴅ ⊠ 🐾 🖪 🖵 🌊

▼▼▼ Holiday Inn MI
(915) 697-3181. **$75.** 4300 W Wall St. I-20, exit 134 (Midkiff Rd), 1 mi n to I-20 business loop, 0.7 mi w. Ext/int corridors. **Pets:** Other species. $20 one-time fee/room. Service with restrictions.
ASK Sᴅ ⊠ 🖪 🖵 🍽 🌊

▲▲▲ ▼▼▼▼ La Quinta Inn-Midland M
(915) 697-9900. **$61-$75.** 4130 W Wall St. I-20, exit 131, 0.9 mi n on SR 250 Loop to exit 1A; 1.2 mi e on I-20 business route. Ext corridors. **Pets:** Accepted.
SAVE Sᴅ ⊠ 🔥ᴹ 🖪 🖵 🌊

▲▲▲ ▼▼▼▼ Midland Hilton & Towers H
(915) 683-6131. **$119-$199.** 117 W Wall St. Wall and Loraine sts. Int corridors. **Pets:** Accepted.
SAVE Sᴅ ⊠ 🐾 🖪 🖵 🍽 🌊

▼▼▼ Sleep Inn M
(915) 689-6822. **$65.** 3828 W Wall. I-20, exit 134 (Midkiff Rd), 1 mi n to Wall St, just w. Int corridors. **Pets:** Very small. $30 deposit/room. Designated rooms, service with restrictions, supervision.
SAVE Sᴅ ⊠ 🖪 🖵 🌊

MONAHANS

▲▲▲ ▼▼▼ Best Western Colonial Inn MI
(915) 943-4345. **$49-$59.** 702 W I-20. I-20, exit 80, just s. Ext/int corridors. **Pets:** Accepted.
SAVE Sᴅ ⊠ 🐾 🍽 🌊

MOUNT PLEASANT

▲▲▲ ▼▼▼ Best Western Mt. Pleasant Inn M
(903) 572-5051. **$64, 5 days notice.** 102 Burton St. I-30 and Business Rt US 271, exit 162. Ext corridors. **Pets:** Small, dogs only. $10 daily fee/room. Designated rooms, service with restrictions, supervision.
SAVE Sᴅ ⊠ 🐾 🖪 🖵 🌊

▼▼▼ Ramada Inn-Mt. Pleasant MI
(903) 572-6611. **$67.** 2502 W Ferguson Rd. I-30, exit 160. Ext corridors. **Pets:** $10 one-time fee/pet. Service with restrictions, supervision.
ASK Sᴅ ⊠ 🖪 🖵 🍽 🌊

▼▼▼ Super 8 M
(903) 572-9808. **$54-$69.** 204 Lakewood Dr. I-30, exit 162 eastbound; exit 162A westbound. Ext corridors. **Pets:** Accepted.
SAVE Sᴅ ⊠ 🖪 🌊

MOUNT VERNON

▲▲▲ ▼▼▼ Super 8 Motel of Mount Vernon M
(903) 588-2882. **$50-$60.** 401 W I-30. I-30, exit 146 (SR 37). Ext corridors. **Pets:** $5 daily fee/room. Service with restrictions, supervision.
SAVE Sᴅ ⊠ 🐾 🖪 🖵

NACOGDOCHES

▲▲▲ ▼▼▼▼ La Quinta Inn-Nacogdoches M
(936) 560-5453. **$56-$76.** 3215 South St. US 59 at S jct Loop 224 and US 59 business route. Ext corridors. **Pets:** Small. Service with restrictions, supervision.
SAVE Sᴅ ⊠ 🐾 🖪 🖵 🌊

NEDERLAND

▼▼ Best Western-Airport Inn M
(409) 727-1631. **$64.** 200 Memorial Hwy 69. US 69, 96 and 287, exit Nederland Ave. Ext corridors. **Pets:** Small, other species. $20 one-time fee/room. Service with restrictions, crate.

[SAVE] [S✿] [✕] [🛏] [💻] [➥]

NEW BOSTON

▼▼ Best Western Inn of New Boston M
(903) 628-6999. **$49.** 1024 N Center. I-30 at jct SR 8, exit 201. Ext corridors. **Pets:** Accepted.

[SAVE] [S✿] [✕] [🖫] [🛏] [➥]

NOCONA

◆◆◆ ▼▼ Nocona Hills Motel and
Resort M ☙
(940) 825-3161. **$40-$46.** 100 E Huron Cir. 6 mi w of St Jo on US 82 to jct SR 1815, 4 mi n on SR 1815 to SR 1956; 2 mi w on SR 1956 to SR 3301. Ext corridors. **Pets:** Medium. $5 daily fee/pet. Service with restrictions, supervision.

[SAVE] [S✿] [✕] [🛏] [💻] [⊠]

NORTH RICHLAND HILLS

▼ Motel 6–1336 M
(817) 485-3000. **$41-$53.** 7804 Bedford Euless Rd N. Loop 820, 0.5 mi e of SR 121, exit 22A (Grapevine). Ext corridors. **Pets:** Accepted.

[S✿] [✕] [🖫] [➥]

▼▼▼ Ramada Limited M
(817) 485-2750. **$41-$68.** 7920 Bedford-Euless Rd. I-820, e of SR 121, exit 22A (Grapevine). Ext corridors. **Pets:** Accepted.

[ASK] [S✿] [✕] [🅿] [🛏] [💻] [➥]

▼▼ Studio 6 M
(817) 788-6000. **$48.** 7450 NE Loop 820. Loop 820 at Holiday Ln, exit 21, 0.3 mi e on south access road. Ext corridors. **Pets:** Accepted.

[✕] [🅿] [🖫] [🛏] [💻]

ODEM

◆◆◆ ▼▼▼ Days Inn-Odem M
(361) 368-2166. **$50-$100, 3 days notice.** 1505 Voss Ave (US 77). US 77, 1 mi s of jct 631. Ext corridors. **Pets:** Accepted.

[SAVE] [S✿] [✕] [🛏] [➥]

ODESSA

◆◆◆ ▼▼▼ Best Western Garden Oasis MI
(915) 337-3006. **$68-$78, 3 days notice.** 110 W I-20. Jct I-20 and US 385, exit 116. Ext/int corridors. **Pets:** Accepted.

[SAVE] [S✿] [✕] [🅿] [🛏] [💻] [🍽] [➥]

▼▼ Days Inn MI
(915) 335-8000. **$48-$56.** 3075 E Business Loop 20. I-20, exit 121, 0.7 mi n on Loop 338, then 0.5 mi w. Int corridors. **Pets:** Other species. No service, supervision.

[SAVE] [S✿] [✕] [🛏] [➥]

▼▼▼ Holiday Inn Express Hotel & Suites M
(915) 333-3931. **$57-$60.** 3001 E Business Loop 20. I-20, exit 121, 0.7 mi n on Loop 338, then 0.5 mi e. Ext/int corridors. **Pets:** Small, other species. Service with restrictions, supervision.

[ASK] [S✿] [✕] [🛏] [💻] [➥]

▼▼▼ Holiday Inn Hotel & Suites MI
(915) 362-2311. **$72.** 6201 E Business Hwy 80. I-20, exit 121, 0.8 mi n on Loop 338, then 1 mi e. Ext corridors. **Pets:** Medium, other species. Service with restrictions.

[ASK] [S✿] [✕] [🅿] [🛏] [💻] [🍽] [➥]

◆◆◆ ▼▼▼ La Quinta Inn-Odessa M
(915) 333-2820. **$55-$71.** 5001 E Business Loop I-20. I-20, exit 121, 0.8 mi n on Loop 338, then just w. Ext corridors. **Pets:** Accepted.

[SAVE] [S✿] [✕] [🅿] [🛏] [💻] [➥]

◆◆◆ ▼ Villa West Inn M
(915) 335-5055. **$35.** 300 W Pool Road. I-20, exit 116, just w on frontage road. Ext corridors. **Pets:** Small. $20 deposit/pet. Service with restrictions, supervision.

[SAVE] [S✿] [✕] [🛏]

ORANGE

▼▼▼ Holiday Inn Express M
(409) 988-0110. **$59.** 2900 I-10. I-10, exit 876 westbound, 1 mi w of jct SR 87 westbound; exit 877 eastbound, on westbound service road. Int corridors. **Pets:** Small. $10 one-time fee/pet. Designated rooms, crate.

[ASK] [S✿] [✕] [🅿] [🛏] [💻] [➥]

OZONA

◆◆◆ ▼▼ Best Value Inn M
(915) 392-2631. **$45-$59.** 820 11th St. 0.5 mi w on US 290 business route. Ext corridors. **Pets:** Other species. $5 daily fee/room. Designated rooms, service with restrictions, supervision.

[SAVE] [S✿] [✕]

◆◆◆ ▼▼ Travelodge M
(915) 392-2656. **$45-$50, 5 days notice.** 8 11th St. I-10 W, exit 368, 2 mi w; I-10 E, exit 365 to Loop 466, 1 me e. Ext corridors. **Pets:** Accepted.

[SAVE] [S✿] [✕] [🛏] [💻] [➥]

PALESTINE

◆◆◆ ▼▼▼ Best Western Palestine Inn MI
(903) 723-4655. **$50-$55.** 1601 W Palestine Ave. 0.7 mi sw jct US 287/SR 19 on US 79. Ext corridors. **Pets:** Accepted.

[SAVE] [S✿] [✕] [🖫] [🛏] [💻] [🍽] [➥]

PARIS

▼▼ Best Western Inn of Paris M
(903) 785-5566. **$50-$57.** 3755 NE Loop 286. Jct US 82 and E Loop 286, just n. Ext corridors. **Pets:** Medium, other species. Service with restrictions, supervision.
SAVE S✆ ✕ ⊘ ⌨ 🖥 🖨 🛏

▼▼▼ Holiday Inn MI
(903) 785-5545. **$79-$119.** 3560 NE Loop 286. E Loop 286, 0.3 mi n of jct US 82. Ext corridors. **Pets:** Accepted.
A$K S✆ ✕ ⊘ ⌨ 🖥 🖨 ⍾ 🛏

PECOS

ⒶⒶⒶ ▼▼▼ Best Western Swiss Clock Inn MI
(915) 447-2215. **$64-$74.** 133 S Frontage Rd, I-20 W. 1 mi w of jct US 285; 1 mi e of jct I-20 and SR 17, exit 40. Ext corridors. **Pets:** Accepted.
SAVE S✆ ✕ ⊘ ⌨ 🖥 ⍾ 🛏

ⒶⒶⒶ ▼▼▼ LAURA LODGE M
(915) 445-4924. **$38-$50, 4 days notice.** 1000 E Business 20. I-20 at US 285, exit 42, 1 mi e to Business 20. Ext corridors. **Pets:** Small. $10 daily fee/pet. Designated rooms, service with restrictions, supervision.
SAVE S✆ ✕ 🖥 🛏

▼▼ Quality Inn MI
(915) 445-5404. **$61-$86, 7 days notice.** 4002 S Cedar St. I-20, jct I-20 and US 285. Int corridors. **Pets:** Accepted.
SAVE S✆ ✕ 🖥 🖨 ⍾ 🛏

PLAINVIEW

ⒶⒶⒶ ▼▼▼▼ Best Western Conestoga Inn M
(806) 293-9454. **$65-$110.** 600 N I-27. I-27, exit 49, just s of US 70 on east access road. Ext corridors. **Pets:** Very small. $10 one-time fee/pet. Designated rooms, service with restrictions, supervision.
SAVE S✆ ✕ ⊘ 🖥 🖨

PORT ISABEL

ⒶⒶⒶ ▼▼▼ Southwind Inn M
(956) 943-3392. **$35-$120, 3 days notice.** 600 Davis St. Queen Isabella Cswy to Musina, then 3 blks n. Ext corridors. **Pets:** Small. $5 one-time fee/pet. Designated rooms, supervision.
SAVE S✆ ✕ 🖥 🖨 🛏

PORTLAND

ⒶⒶⒶ ▼▼▼▼ Comfort Inn M
(361) 643-2222. **$59-$84.** 1703 N Hwy 181. US 181 W access road, exit FM 3239 northbound; exit Lang St southbound. Ext corridors. **Pets:** Accepted.
SAVE ✕ ⌨ 🖥 🖨 🛏

ROBSTOWN

▼▼ Days Inn M
(361) 387-9416. **$50-$75.** 320 Hwy 77 S. 1 mi s on US 77. Ext corridors. **Pets:** Accepted.
SAVE S✆ ✕ 🖥 🛏

ROCKPORT

ⒶⒶⒶ ▼▼▼ Laguna Reef 🅰
(361) 729-1742. **$65-$275.** 1021 Water St. 0.5 mi s, just e of Business Rt 35; entrance on S Austin St. Ext corridors. **Pets:** Medium, other species. $50 deposit/pet, $7 daily fee/pet. Service with restrictions, supervision.
SAVE S✆ ✕ 🖥 🖨 🛏

ⒶⒶⒶ ▼▼▼ The Village Inn M
(361) 729-6370. **$50-$70.** 503 N Austin St. Just w of jct SR 35 and Business Rt 35. Ext corridors. **Pets:** Accepted.
SAVE S✆ ✕ 🖥 🖨 🛏

ROUND ROCK

ⒶⒶⒶ ▼▼▼ Best Western Executive Inn M
(512) 255-3222. **$55-$75.** 1851 N I-35. I-35, exit 253 northbound; exit 253A U-turn southbound. Ext corridors. **Pets:** Very small, other species. Service with restrictions.
SAVE S✆ ✕ 🚹 ⌨ 🖥 🖨 🛏

▼▼▼ La Quinta Inn-Austin-Round Rock M
(512) 255-6666. **$66-$78.** 2004 I-35 S. I-35, exit 254, on west rontage road. Int corridors. **Pets:** Accepted.
SAVE S✆ ✕ ⊘ 🖥 🖨 🛏

ⒶⒶⒶ ▼▼▼ Red Roof Inn M
(512) 310-1111. **$50-$60, 14 days notice.** 1990 I-35 N. I-35, exit 254, on west frontage road. Int corridors. **Pets:** Accepted.
SAVE S✆ ✕ 🖥 🛏

ⒶⒶⒶ ▼▼▼ Residence Inn by Marriott 🅰
(512) 733-2400. **$116-$125.** 2505 S IH-35. I-35, exit 250 southbound; exit 251 northbound, on east frontage road. Int corridors. **Pets:** $5 daily fee/room, $75 one-time fee/room. Service with restrictions, crate.
SAVE S✆ ✕ 🚹 ⊘ ⌨ 🖥 🖨 🛏

▼▼▼ Staybridge Suites Austin-Round Rock 🅰
(512) 733-0942. **$109.** 520 IH-35 S. I-35, exit 252B northbound; exit 252AB southbound; on west frontage road. Ext corridors. **Pets:** Large, other species. $75 one-time fee/room. Service with restrictions.
A$K S✆ ✕ 🚹 ⊘ ⌨ 🖥 🖨 🛏

SAN ANGELO

ⒶⒶⒶ ▼▼▼ Best Western San Angelo M
(915) 223-1273. **$75, 7 days notice.** 3017 W Loop 306. Loop 306, exit College Hills Blvd, just s. Ext corridors. **Pets:** Accepted.
SAVE ✕ ⌨ 🖥 🖨 🛏

▼▼ Days Inn M
(915) 658-6594. **$51-$70.** 4613 S Jackson. 2.8 mi s on US 87 and 277. Ext corridors. **Pets:** Accepted.
SAVE S✆ ✕ 🖥 🛏

▼▼▼ Holiday Inn Convention Center Hotel 🅷
(915) 658-2828. **$119-$179.** 441 Rio Concho Dr. 0.5 mi e. Int corridors. **Pets:** Large. $10 one-time fee/pet.
A$K S✆ ✕ ⊘ 🖥 🖨 ⍾ 🛏

Howard Johnson San Angelo Ⓜ
(915) 653-2995. **$56-$62, 3 days notice.** 415 W Beauregard. Just w on US 67 business route at jct US 87 southbound. Ext/int corridors. **Pets:** Accepted.

Inn of the Conchos Ⓜ
(915) 658-2811. **$45-$65.** 2021 N Bryant Blvd. 2 mi n on US 87. Ext corridors. **Pets:** Accepted.

La Quinta Inn-San Angelo Ⓜ
(915) 949-0515. **$65-$75.** 2307 Loop 306. Loop 306, exit Knickerbocker Rd, just s. Ext corridors. **Pets:** Small, other species. Service with restrictions, crate.

Ramada Limited Ⓜ
(915) 653-8442. **$58-$75.** 2201 N Bryant Blvd. 2.1 mi n on US 87 at jct N 23rd St. Ext corridors. **Pets:** Accepted.

SAN ANTONIO METROPOLITAN AREA

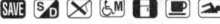

LIVE OAK

La Quinta-Inn-San Antonio-Toepperwein Ⓜ
(210) 657-5500. **$72-$98.** 12822 I-35 N. I-35, exit 170B (Toepperwein). Ext/int corridors. **Pets:** Accepted.

NEW BRAUNFELS

Holiday Inn Ⓜ
(830) 625-8017. **$89-$179.** 1051 IH-35 E. I-35, exit 189. Ext corridors. **Pets:** Accepted.

Rodeway Inn Ⓜ
(830) 629-6991. **$40-$130.** 1209 IH-35 E. I-35, exit 189, southbound access lane. Ext corridors. **Pets:** Small. Service with restrictions, supervision.

Super 8 Ⓜ
(830) 629-1155. **$44-$109.** 510 Hwy 46 S. I-35, exit 189 (SR 46), 0.3 mi e. Ext corridors. **Pets:** Small, other species. $5 daily fee/pet. Service with restrictions.

SAN ANTONIO

Aloha Inn Ⓜ ❀
(210) 828-0933. **$55-$90.** 1435 Austin Hwy. 0.8 mi s of jct I-410. Ext corridors. **Pets:** Small. Daily fee/pet (10% of room rate). Designated rooms, service with restrictions, supervision.

AmeriSuites (San Antonio/Airport) Ⓜ
(210) 930-2333. **$120-$150.** 7615 Jones Maltberger Rd. US 281, exit Jones Maltsberger Rd; inside Loop 410. Int corridors. **Pets:** Accepted.

AmeriSuites (San Antonio/Riverwalk) Ⓜ
(210) 227-6854. **$129-$169.** 601 S St Mary's St. I-35, exit Durango St, 0.9 mi e. Int corridors. **Pets:** Medium. Service with restrictions, crate.

Arbor House Inn & Suites 🅱🅱
(210) 472-2005. **$95-$175, 3 days notice.** 540 S St Mary's St. Near La Villita; just n of Durango St. **Pets:** Accepted.

Best Western Fiesta Inn Ⓜ
(210) 697-9761. **$46-$130.** 13535 I H 10 W. I-10, exit 557 westbound; exit 558 eastbound, on westbound access road. Ext corridors. **Pets:** Accepted.

Best Western Ingram Park Inn Ⓜ
(210) 520-8080. **$46-$130.** 6855 NW Loop 410. I-410, exit 10 (Culebra Rd) westbound; exit 11 (Ingram Rd) eastbound. Ext corridors. **Pets:** Accepted.

Best Western Lackland Inn & Suites Ⓜ
(210) 675-9690. **$55-$95.** 6815 Hwy 90 W. Jct US 90 and Military Dr, 1.5 mi e of Loop 410. Ext corridors. **Pets:** Accepted.

Brackenridge House B & B 🅱🅱
(210) 271-3442. **$115-$250, 14 days notice.** 230 Madison. King William Historic District. Ext/int corridors. **Pets:** Small. Designated rooms, service with restrictions.

Candlewood Suites Hotel Ⓜ
(210) 615-0550. **$119.** 9350 IH 10 W. I-10 W, eastbound access road between Wulzbach and Callaghan. Int corridors. **Pets:** Small. $75 one-time fee/room. Designated rooms, service with restrictions, supervision.

Clarion Hotel San Antonio Airport Ⓜ
(210) 494-7600. **$119-$129.** 12828 US Hwy 281 N. 2 mi n of airport on US 281; entrance at Countryside. Int corridors. **Pets:** Other species. Designated rooms.

Comfort Inn Airport Ⓜ
(210) 653-9110. **$52-$89.** 2635 NE Loop 410. Jct Loop 410 and Perrin-Beitel Rd. Ext/int corridors. **Pets:** Accepted.

ⒶⒶⒶ ▼▼▼ Comfort Inn Sea World M
(210) 684-8606. **$55-$109.** 4 Piano Pl. Loop 410, 0.5 mi e
jct Evers Rd. Ext corridors. **Pets:** Small. $10 daily fee/pet.
No service, supervision.

[SAVE] [S⌂] [✗] [💻] [⇌]

▼▼ ▼▼ Days Inn Coliseum M
(210) 225-4040. **$45-$120.** 3443 I-35 N. I-35, exit 160
(Splashtown). Ext corridors. **Pets:** Medium, other species.
$25 one-time fee/room. Designated rooms, service with
restrictions, supervision.

[SAVE] [S⌂] [✗] [💻] [⇌]

▼▼ ▼▼ Days Inn-Downtown Laredo St M
(210) 271-3334. **$40-$109.** 1500 IH-35 S. I-10/35, exit 154
(Laredo St). Ext/int corridors. **Pets:** Other species. $25 one-
time fee/pet. Service with restrictions, supervision.

[SAVE] [S⌂] [✗] [💻] [⇌]

▼▼▼▼ Drury Inn & Suites Airport M
(210) 308-8100. **$80-$118.** 95 NE Loop 410. Jct Jones
Maltsberger Rd at Loop 410, 1.8 mi w of airport. Int corridors. **Pets:** Accepted.

[✗] [⅋M] [⌕] [💻] [⇌]

▼▼▼▼ Drury Inn Northeast M
(210) 654-1144. **$67-$102.** 8300 IH-35 N. I-35, exit 165
(Walzem Rd), northbound access road. Ext/int corridors.
Pets: Accepted.

[✗] [⅋M] [💻] [⇌]

▼▼▼▼ Hampton Inn-Airport M
(210) 366-1800. **$89-$109.** 8818 Jones Maltsberger Rd.
I-410, exit 21B (Jones Maltsberger Rd) to airport exit. Int
corridors. **Pets:** Accepted.

[SAVE] [✗] [⌕] [💻] [⇌]

ⒶⒶⒶ ▼▼▼ Hampton Inn Six Flags Area M
(210) 561-9058. **$89-$99.** 11010 IH 10 W. I-10, exit 560
westbound; exit 559 (Huebner Rd) eastbound, just w, then
just s of jct I-10. Int corridors. **Pets:** Accepted.

[SAVE] [S⌂] [✗] [⌕] [💻] [⇌]

▼▼▼▼ Hawthorn Suites A
(210) 561-9660. **$109.** 4041 Bluemel Rd. I-10, exit Wurz-
bach Rd, 0.3 mi w. Ext corridors. **Pets:** Medium. $5 daily
fee/pet, $25 one-time fee/pet. Designated rooms, service
with restrictions, supervision.

[ASK] [S⌂] [✗] [💻] [⇌]

▼▼▼▼ Hawthorn Suites Riverwalk M
(210) 527-1900. **$109.** 830 N St Marys St. Just n of
Navarro St. Int corridors. **Pets:** Accepted.

[ASK] [S⌂] [✗] [⌕] [💻] [⇌]

▼▼▼▼ Hill Country Inn & Suites M ❀
(210) 599-4204. **$60.** 2383 NE Loop 410. Loop 410 W
access road at Starcrest exit. Ext corridors. **Pets:** Other
species. $75 one-time fee/room. Service with restrictions,
supervision.

[ASK] [S⌂] [✗] [⅋M] [⌕] [💻] [⇌]

▼▼▼ ▼▼▼ Hilton Palacio del Rio H
(210) 222-1400. **$169-$320.** 200 S Alamo St. Adjacent to
convention center. Int corridors. **Pets:** Medium. Service with
restrictions, crate.

[SAVE] [✗] [⅋M] [💻] [🍴] [⇌]

ⒶⒶⒶ ▼▼▼ Hilton San Antonio Airport H ❀
(210) 340-6060. **$199, 10 days notice.** 611 NW Loop 410.
Jct Loop 410, US 281 N exit (San Pedro Ave). Int corridors.
Pets: Small, other species. $25 daily fee/room. No service.

[SAVE] [S⌂] [✗] [⌕] [⌕] [💻] [🍴] [⇌]

ⒶⒶⒶ ▼▼▼ Holiday Inn Crockett Hotel H
(210) 225-6500. **$99-$169, 30 days notice.** 320 Bonham
St. Center. Ext/int corridors. **Pets:** Medium. $100 one-time
fee/room. Designated rooms, service with restrictions.

[SAVE] [S⌂] [✗] [💻] [🍴] [⇌]

▼▼▼ ▼▼▼ Holiday Inn-Downtown-Market Square MI
(210) 225-3211. **$99-$139.** 318 W Durango St. I-35, exit
Durango St. Int corridors. **Pets:** Accepted.

[ASK] [S⌂] [✗] [⅋M] [⌕] [💻] [🍴] [⇌]

▼▼▼▼ Holiday Inn Express M
(210) 599-0999. **$89-$199, 7 days notice.** 11939 N IH-35.
I-35, exit 170, on southbound access road, 0.5 mi s to
Judson Rd exit. Ext corridors. **Pets:** Very small. $25 one-
time fee/pet. Service with restrictions, supervision.

[ASK] [S⌂] [✗] [⌕] [💻] [⇌]

▼▼▼▼ Holiday Inn Express-Airport M
(210) 308-6700. **$89-$109.** 91 NE Loop 410. Loop 410, exit
21A eastbound; exit 20B westbound, on eastbound access
road between San Pedro Ave and Jones Maltsberger Rd.
Int corridors. **Pets:** Accepted.

[✗] [⅋M] [⌕] [💻] [⇌]

**▼▼▼▼ Holiday Inn Express-San Antonio
Northwest M**
(210) 561-9300. **$89-$109.** 9411 Wurzbach Rd. I-10 NW,
exit 561 (Huebner Rd). Int corridors. **Pets:** Small. No service, supervision.

[✗] [💻] [⇌]

▼▼▼▼ Holiday Inn-Northeast MI
(210) 226-4361. **$90, 5 days notice.** 3855 I-35 N. I-35, exit
Binz-Englemann Rd. Ext corridors. **Pets:** Medium. $50 one-
time fee/room. Designated rooms, service with restrictions,
crate.

[ASK] [S⌂] [✗] [💻] [🍴] [⇌]

▼▼▼▼ Holiday Inn Riverwalk H
(210) 224-2500. **$145-$165.** 217 N St. Mary's St. By the
San Antonio River; from Houston St, just s. Int corridors.
Pets: Accepted.

[ASK] [S⌂] [💻] [🍴] [⇌]

▼▼▼▼ Holiday Inn Select A
(210) 349-9900. **$99-$129.** 77 NE Loop 410. I-410, exit 20B
(McCullough St), on westbound access road. Int corridors.
Pets: Medium. $100 deposit/room, $25 one-time fee/room.
Service with restrictions, supervision.

[ASK] [S⌂] [✗] [⅋M] [⌕] [⌕] [💻] [🍴] [⇌]

▼▼ **HomeGate Studios & Suites** **M**
(210) 342-4800. **$59-$69.** 11221 San Pedro Ave. US 281 N, exit Nakoma, on west frontage road. Ext corridors. **Pets:** Large, other species. $100 one-time fee/room. Supervision.

(ASK) (S) (✕) (▣) (🐾)

▼▼ **Howard Johnson Coliseum** **M**
(210) 229-9220. **$40-$99.** 2755 I-35 N. I-35, exit 159B (Walters Ave), southbound access road. Ext corridors. **Pets:** Small. $25 one-time fee/pet. Designated rooms, service with restrictions, supervision.

(ASK) (S) (✕) (📱) (▣) (🐾)

▼▼ **Howard Johnson Express Inn Fiesta** **M**
(210) 558-7152. **$49-$99.** 13279 I-H 10 W. I-10 NW, exit 557 westbound; exit 558 eastbound, on westbound access road. Ext corridors. **Pets:** Large, other species. $20 deposit/room. Service with restrictions, crate.

(ASK) (S) (✕) (📱) (▣) (🐾)

▼▼ **Knights Inn Windsor Park** **M**
(210) 646-6336. **$52-$69.** 6370 IH-35 N. Just off Loop 410/I-35, exit Rittiman Rd, northbound access road. Ext corridors. **Pets:** Small. $10 one-time fee/room. Service with restrictions, crate.

(SAVE) (S) (✕) (🕹) (📱) (🐾)

▼▼ ▼▼ **La Mansion del Rio** **H** ❀
(210) 518-1000. **$199-$249, 3 days notice.** 112 College St. Just s on the riverwalk. Ext/int corridors. **Pets:** Service with restrictions, supervision.

(SAVE) (S) (✕) (🕹) (📱) (▣) (🍴) (🐾)

▼▼▼ **La Quinta Inn-Convention Center** **M**
(210) 222-9181. **$119-$149.** 1001 E Commerce St. 0.5 mi ne; opposite Hemisfair site, within walking distance of the Alamo. Ext/int corridors. **Pets:** Small. Service with restrictions, supervision.

(SAVE) (S) (✕) (📱) (▣) (🐾)

▼▼▼ **La Quinta Inn Market Square** **M**
(210) 271-0001. **$89-$135.** 900 Dolorosa. I-10 E or I-35 S, exit W Houston-Commerce, 0.5 mi sw. Ext corridors. **Pets:** Small. Service with restrictions.

(SAVE) (S) (✕) (♿M) (📱) (▣) (🐾)

▲▲ ▼▼▼ **La Quinta Inn-San Antonio-Ingram Park** **M**
(210) 680-8883. **$73-$132.** 7134 NW Loop 410. Loop 410, exit 10 (Culebra Rd), eastbound access road. Ext corridors. **Pets:** Small, other species. Service with restrictions, crate.

(SAVE) (S) (✕) (📱) (▣) (🐾)

▲▲ ▼▼▼ **La Quinta Inn-San Antonio-Lackland** **M**
(210) 674-3200. **$75-$99.** 6511 Military Dr W. Southwest jct of US 90 and Military Dr W; entrance on Military Dr. Ext corridors. **Pets:** Accepted.

(SAVE) (S) (✕) (📱) (▣) (🐾)

▲▲ ▼▼▼ **La Quinta Inn-San Antonio-Vance Jackson** **M**
(210) 734-7931. **$72-$92.** 5922 NW Expwy. I-10, exit Vance Jackson Rd, on eastbound access road. Ext corridors. **Pets:** Accepted.

(SAVE) (S) (✕) (📱) (🐾)

▲▲ ▼▼▼ **La Quinta Inn-San Antonio-Windsor Park** **M**
(210) 653-6619. **$72-$98.** 6410 I-35 N. I-35, on I-35 northbound access road between Rittiman and Eisenhauer rds, exit 163B northbound; exit 163 (Rittiman Rd) southbound. Ext corridors. **Pets:** Accepted.

(SAVE) (S) (✕) (📱) (▣) (🐾)

▼▼▼ **La Quinta Inn-San Antonio-Wurzbach** **M**
(210) 593-0338. **$72-$93.** 9542 I-10 W. I-10, exit Wurzbach Rd, just e on eastbound access road. Ext corridors. **Pets:** Small. Service with restrictions, supervision.

(SAVE) (S) (✕) (📱) (▣) (🐾)

▲▲ ▼▼▼ ▼▼▼ **Marriott Riverwalk** **H**
(210) 224-4555. **$294.** 711 E Riverwalk. Opposite convention center and Hemisfair Plaza. Int corridors. **Pets:** Accepted.

(SAVE) (S) (✕) (🕹) (🏊) (📱) (▣) (🍴) (🐾)

▼▼ **Motel 6–1122** **M**
(210) 225-1111. **$51-$75.** 211 N Pecos St. I-10/35, exit 155 B (Pecos). Ext corridors. **Pets:** Accepted.

(S) (✕) (🏊) (📱) (🐾)

▼▼ **Motel 6–134** **M**
(210) 650-4419. **$35-$57.** 9503 I-35 N. I-35, exit 167A (Randolf Blvd) southbound; exit 167 (Starlight Terrace) northbound. Ext corridors. **Pets:** Accepted.

(S) (✕) (🐾)

▼▼ **Motel 6–183** **M**
(210) 333-1850. **$41-$57.** 138 N W W White Rd. I-10, exit 580 (W W White Rd), just off westbound access road. Ext corridors. **Pets:** Accepted.

(S) (✕) (🐾)

▼▼ **Motel 6–651** **M** ❀
(210) 673-9020. **$41-$67.** 2185 SW Loop 410. I-410, exit 7 (Marbach Rd), on westbound access road. Ext corridors. **Pets:** Other species. No service, supervision.

(S) (✕) (🕹) (🏊) (📱) (🐾)

▼▼▼ **Pear Tree Inn Airport** **M**
(210) 366-9300. **$65-$106.** 143 NE Loop 410. Loop 410 W, exit 21 (Jones-Maltsberger), on westbound access road, between San Pedro Ave and Jones Maltsberger. Int corridors. **Pets:** Accepted.

(✕) (📱) (▣) (🐾)

▲▲ ▼▼▼ ▼▼▼ **Plaza San Antonio, A Marriott Hotel** **H**
(210) 229-1000. **$264-$274.** 555 S Alamo St. Opposite convention center and Hemisfair Plaza. Int corridors. **Pets:** Accepted.

(SAVE) (S) (✕) (♿M) (🕹) (▣) (🍴) (🐾) (🚫)

▼▼▼ **Quality Inn & Suites** M
(210) 359-7200. **$45-$95.** 222 S W W White Rd. I-10, exit 580, 0.4 mi s. Ext corridors. **Pets:** Accepted.

SAVE ⬚ ✕ ⬚ ⬚ ⬚ ⬚

◆◆◆ ▼▼▼ **Quality Inn & Suites Coliseum** M
(210) 224-3030. **$49-$120.** 3817 IH-35 N. I-35, Binz-Engleman exit, follow signs to I-35 S access road northbound, Binz-Engleman exit, continue straight southbound. Int corridors. **Pets:** Accepted.

SAVE ⬚ ✕ ⬚ ⬚

◆◆◆ ▼▼▼ **Quality Inn Northwest** M
(210) 736-1900. **$58-$139, 14 days notice.** 6023 NW IH-10 W. I-10, exit 565B eastbound; exit 565C (Vance Jackson Rd) westbound. Ext corridors. **Pets:** Medium, other species. $25 one-time fee/room. Designated rooms, service with restrictions, supervision.

SAVE ⬚ ✕ ⬚ ⬚ ⬚

◆◆◆ ▼▼ **Red Roof Inn-San Antonio Airport** M
(210) 340-4055. **$44-$64.** 333 Wolfe Rd. On southbound access road, just s of US 281 at Isam Rd. Ext/int corridors. **Pets:** Small. Service with restrictions, crate.

SAVE ✕ ⬚ ⬚ ⬚

◆◆◆ ▼▼▼ **Red Roof Inn San Antonio (Downtown)** M
(210) 229-9973. **$59-$94.** 1011 E Houston St. I-37, exit 141 northbound; exit 141B southbound. Int corridors. **Pets:** Accepted.

SAVE ✕ ⬚ ⬚

◆◆◆ ▼▼ **Red Roof Inn San Antonio (NW-SeaWorld)** M
(210) 509-3434. **$6-$75.** 6880 NW Loop 410. I-410, exit 10B, Alamo Downs Pkwy eastbound access road. Ext/int corridors. **Pets:** Accepted.

SAVE ✕ ⬚ ⬚ ⬚

◆◆◆ ▼▼▼ **Residence Inn by Marriott** A 🐾
(210) 231-6000. **$149-$209.** 628 S Santa Rosa. 0.5 mi e jct I-35 and Durango St. Ext corridors. **Pets:** Large, other species. $5 daily fee/room, $50 one-time fee/room.

SAVE ⬚ ✕ ⬚ ⬚ ⬚

◆◆◆ ▼▼▼ **Residence Inn San Antonio-Airport** A 🐾
(210) 805-8118. **$129.** 1014 NE Loop 410. On Loop 410, exit Broadway St, 0.4 mi e on access road. Ext corridors. **Pets:** Other species. $15 one-time fee/pet. Service with restrictions, crate.

SAVE ⬚ ✕ ⬚ ⬚ ⬚

◆◆◆ ▼▼▼ **Rodeway Inn-Six Flags Fiesta** M
(210) 698-3991. **$39-$120.** 19793 I-10 W. I-10, exit 554 (Camp Bullis). Ext corridors. **Pets:** Accepted.

SAVE ⬚ ✕ ⬚ ⬚ ⬚

▼▼▼ **Staybridge Suites San Antonio-Airport** M
(210) 341-3220. **$90-$120.** 66 NE Loop 410. Int corridors. **Pets:** Accepted.

✕ ⬚ ⬚ ⬚ ⬚

▼▼ **Studio 6** M
(210) 349-3100. **$53-$61.** 7719 Louis Pasteur Ct. Loop 410, 1.5 mi nw on Fredericksburg Rd to Louis Pasteur Dr. Ext corridors. **Pets:** Accepted.

✕ ⬚ ⬚

▼▼ **Super 8 Motel Downtown North** M
(210) 227-8888. **$38-$75.** 3617 N PanAm Expwy. I-35, exit 160, on southbound access road. Ext corridors. **Pets:** Very small. $50 deposit/pet, $7 daily fee/pet. Designated rooms, no service, supervision.

ASK ⬚ ✕ ⬚ ⬚ ⬚

▼▼ **Super 8 Motel of San Antonio Airport** M
(210) 637-1033. **$40-$75.** 11027 IH-35 N. I-35, exit 168 (Weidner Rd), southbound access road. Int corridors. **Pets:** Other species. $50 deposit/room. Designated rooms, service with restrictions, supervision.

ASK ⬚ ✕ ⬚

◆◆◆ ▼▼▼ **Super 8 Motel-Six Flags Fiesta** M
(210) 696-6916. **$49-$89.** 5319 Casa Bella. I-10, exit 557 westbound; exit 558 eastbound on westbound access road. Int corridors. **Pets:** Small. $10 daily fee/pet. Service with restrictions, supervision.

SAVE ✕ ⬚ ⬚

◆◆◆ ▼▼▼ **Town House Motel** M
(210) 826-6311. **$70-$80.** 942 NE Loop 410. I-410, exit 22, just se. Ext/int corridors. **Pets:** Accepted.

SAVE ⬚ ✕ ⬚ ⬚ ⬚

◆◆◆ ▼▼▼ **Woodfield Suites** M
(210) 212-5400. **$99-$169, 3 days notice.** 100 W Durango Blvd. I-35, exit 155B (Durango Blvd). Int corridors. **Pets:** Accepted.

SAVE ✕ ⬚ ⬚ ⬚ ⬚ ⬚

SEGUIN

◆◆◆ ▼▼▼ **Best Western of Seguin** M
(830) 379-9631. **$65-$99.** 1603 IH-10 & Hwy 46. I-10, exit 607 (SR 46). Ext corridors. **Pets:** Small. $10 daily fee/pet. Service with restrictions, supervision.

SAVE ⬚ ✕ ⬚

▼▼▼ **Holiday Inn Seguin** M
(830) 372-0860. **$72-$96, 3 days notice.** 2950 N 123 Bypass. I-10, exit 610 (SR 123). Ext corridors. **Pets:** Small. $25 deposit/room. Service with restrictions, supervision.

ASK ⬚ ✕ ⬚ ⬚ ⬚ ⬚ ⬚ ⬚

▼▼ ◆ **Super 8 Motel of Seguin** Ⓜ
(830) 379-6888. **$60-$89, 3 days notice.** 1525 N Hwy 46.
I-10, exit 607 (SR 46). Int corridors. **Pets:** Medium. $10
daily fee/pet. Service with restrictions, supervision.
ⒶⓈⓀ Ⓢ▱ ☒ 🖧 🖥

UNIVERSAL CITY

ⒶⒶⒶ ▼▼▼ **Clarion Suites Hotel** Ⓜ
(210) 655-9491. **$79-$149.** 13101 E Loop, 1604 N. Loop
1604 at Pat Booker Rd; 0.8 mi e of I-35. Ext corridors.
Pets: Medium. $25 one-time fee/room. Service with restric-
tions, supervision.
ⓈⒶⓋⒺ Ⓢ▱ ☒ 🖧 🖥 ➴

❖ **END METROPOLITAN AREA** ❖

SAN MARCOS

ⒶⒶⒶ ▼▼ **Days Inn** Ⓜ
(512) 353-5050. **$35-$95.** 1005 IH-35 N. I-35, exit 205
northbound; exit 204B southbound; on southbound frontage
road, at jct I-35 and SR 80. Ext corridors. **Pets:** Small. $25
deposit/pet. Designated rooms, service with restrictions,
supervision.
ⓈⒶⓋⒺ Ⓢ▱ ☒ 🖧 ➴

ⒶⒶⒶ ▼▼▼ **La Quinta Inn-San Marcos** Ⓜ
(512) 392-8800. **$66-$106.** 1619 IH-35 N. I-35, exit 206.
Ext/int corridors. **Pets:** Accepted.
ⓈⒶⓋⒺ Ⓢ▱ ☒ 🖧M 🖉 🖧 🖥 ➴

ⒶⒶⒶ ▼▼ **Ramada Limited** Ⓜ
(512) 395-8000. **$33-$139.** 1701 IH 35 N. I-35, exit 206
(Aquarina Spring). Ext corridors. **Pets:** Very small. $10 daily
fee/pet. Designated rooms, service with restrictions, supervision.
ⓈⒶⓋⒺ Ⓢ▱ ☒ 🖧 🖥 ➴

SANDERSON

ⒶⒶⒶ ▼ **Budget Inn** Ⓜ
(915) 345-2541. **$35-$40.** Hwy 90 E. Just e of center. Ext
corridors. **Pets:** Very small. $25 deposit/pet. Designated
rooms, service with restrictions, supervision.
ⓈⒶⓋⒺ Ⓢ▱ ☒

ⒶⒶⒶ ▼ **Desert Air Motel** Ⓜ
(915) 345-2572. **$34-$39.** 0.5 mi w on US 90, just e of jct
US 285. Ext corridors. **Pets:** Accepted.
ⓈⒶⓋⒺ Ⓢ▱ 🖧

SEMINOLE

ⒶⒶⒶ ▼▼ **Raymond Motor Inn** Ⓜ ❖
(915) 758-3653. **$40-$45.** 301 W Ave A. 0.3 mi w on US 62
and 180. Ext corridors. **Pets:** Other species. $5 daily fee/
room.
ⓈⒶⓋⒺ Ⓢ▱ ☒ 🖧

SHAMROCK

ⒶⒶⒶ ▼ **Budget Host-Blarney Inn** Ⓜ ❖
(806) 256-2101. **$34-$45.** 402 E 12th St, Rt 66. I-40, exit
164 westbound; exit 161 or 163 eastbound, just e of US 83.
Ext corridors. **Pets:** Other species. $3 one-time fee/room.
Service with restrictions, supervision.
ⓈⒶⓋⒺ Ⓢ▱ ☒ 🖧

ⒶⒶⒶ ▼▼ **Econo Lodge** Ⓜ
(806) 256-2111. **$48-$65.** 1006 E 12th St. I-40, exit 164
westbound; exit 161 or 163 eastbound, just e of US 83. Ext
corridors. **Pets:** Small. $5 one-time fee/room. Service with
restrictions, supervision.
ⓈⒶⓋⒺ Ⓢ▱ ☒ 🖧 🖥 ➴

ⒶⒶⒶ ▼▼▼ **Irish Inn Motel** Ⓜ
(806) 256-2106. **$54-$75.** 301 I-40 E. I-40, exit 163, 0.3 mi
e on north service road. Ext/int corridors. **Pets:** Accepted.
ⓈⒶⓋⒺ Ⓢ▱ ☒ 🖉 🖧 🖥 ⑪ ➴

ⒶⒶⒶ ▼ **The Western Motel** Ⓜ
(806) 256-3244. **$39-$59.** 104 E 12th St. Business I-40 and
US 83. Ext corridors. **Pets:** Accepted.
ⓈⒶⓋⒺ Ⓢ▱ ☒ ⑪

SHERMAN

ⒶⒶⒶ ▼▼▼ **La Quinta Inn & Suites**
Sherman Ⓜ
(903) 870-1122. **$80-$115.** 2912 US 75 N. US 75, exit 63,
jct US 82, just sw. Int corridors. **Pets:** Small. Service with
restrictions, supervision.
ⓈⒶⓋⒺ Ⓢ▱ ☒ 🖧 🖧 🖥 ➴

▼▼ **Sherman, Super 8 Motel** Ⓜ
(903) 868-9325. **$50-$80.** 111 E Hwy 1417. 3 mi s on US
75, exit 56. Int corridors. **Pets:** Other species. $5 daily
fee/pet. Service with restrictions, supervision.
Ⓢ▱ ☒

SNYDER

ⒶⒶⒶ ▼▼ **Purple Sage Motel** Ⓜ ❖
(915) 573-5491. **$50-$60.** 1501 E Coliseum. 2.5 mi se on
US 180. Ext corridors. **Pets:** Other species. Service with
restrictions, supervision.
ⓈⒶⓋⒺ Ⓢ▱ ☒ 🖧 🖥 ➴

SONORA

ⒶⒶⒶ ▼▼▼ **Best Western Sonora Inn** Ⓜ
(915) 387-9111. **$62-$88.** 270 Hwy 277 N. I-10, exit 400.
Ext corridors. **Pets:** Other species. $10 one-time fee/pet.
Supervision.
ⓈⒶⓋⒺ Ⓢ▱ ☒ 🖧 🖥 ➴

Days Inn M
(915) 387-3516. **$55-$65, 7 days notice.** 1312 N Service Rd. I-10, exit 400, just n. Ext corridors. **Pets:** Other species. $2 daily fee/room. Service with restrictions, supervision.
SAVE S☐ ✕ ☐ ▣ ❙❙ ⤻

Holiday Host Motel M
(915) 387-2532. **$34-$40.** 127 Loop 467 (Hwy 290). 3 mi w on Loop 467 exit 404 westbound; 3 mi e on Loop 467 exit 399 eastbound. Ext corridors. **Pets:** Service with restrictions, supervision.
SAVE ✕ ☐ ⤻

Twin Oaks Motel M
(915) 387-2551. **$40-$50, 3 days notice.** 907 N Crockett Ave. I-10, exit 400 westbound; exit 399 eastbound, 0.5 mi e, then 0.3 mi s on US 277. Ext corridors. **Pets:** Small. $10 deposit/room. Designated rooms, service with restrictions, supervision.
SAVE ✕

SOUTH PADRE ISLAND

Best Western Fiesta Isles M
(956) 761-4913. **$39-$249.** 5701 Padre Blvd. 3 mi n of Queen Isabella Cswy. Ext corridors. **Pets:** Large, other species. $25 deposit/room. Service with restrictions, supervision.
SAVE S☐ ✕ ☐ ▣ ⤻

Days Inn M
(956) 761-7831. **$39-$189.** 3913 Padre Blvd. 2.6 mi n of Queen Isabella Cswy. Ext corridors. **Pets:** Accepted.
SAVE S☐ ✕ ☐ ⤻

Econo Lodge M
(956) 761-8500. **$59-$320.** 3813 Padre Blvd. 2.6 mi n of Queen Isabella Cswy. Int corridors. **Pets:** Medium. $10 daily fee/pet. Service with restrictions, supervision.
SAVE S☐ ✕ ☐ ⤻

Super 8 Motel M
(956) 761-6300. **$49-$295.** 4205 Padre Blvd. 2.7 mi n of Queen Isabella Cswy. Ext corridors. **Pets:** Accepted.
ASK S☐ ✕ ☖ᴹ ☒ ☐ ⤻

The Tiki Condominium Hotel ⚠
(956) 761-2694. **$79-$275.** 6608 Padre Blvd. 3.8 mi n of Queen Isabella Cswy. Ext corridors. **Pets:** Small. $2 daily fee/pet, $35 one-time fee/pet. Designated rooms, service with restrictions, supervision.
✕ ☐ ⤻

STEPHENVILLE

Days Inn M
(254) 968-3392. **$55-$61.** 701 South E Loop. On US 377, just s of jct US 281. Ext corridors. **Pets:** Other species. Service with restrictions, crate.
SAVE S☐ ✕ ☐ ⤻

Holiday Inn Stephenville M
(254) 968-5256. **$78, 3 days notice.** 2865 W Washington St. 1.5 mi s on US 377/167. Ext corridors. **Pets:** Large. $100 deposit/room. Service with restrictions, supervision.
ASK S☐ ✕ ☒ ☐ ▣ ❙❙ ⤻

SULPHUR SPRINGS

Best Western Trail Dust Inn M
(903) 885-7515. **$59-$69, 14 days notice.** 1521 Shannon Rd. Jct I-30 and Loop 301, exit 127. Ext/int corridors. **Pets:** Medium. Service with restrictions.
SAVE S☐ ✕ ☒ ☐ ▣ ⤻

Comfort Suites M
(903) 438-0918. **$74-$89, 14 days notice.** 1521 E Industrial. I-30, exit 127, just n. Int corridors. **Pets:** Medium. Designated rooms, service with restrictions.
SAVE S☐ ✕ ☖ᴹ ☒ ☐ ▣ ⤻

Holiday Inn M
(903) 885-0562. **$69-$79, 3 days notice.** Interstate 30 E, exit 127. I-30, exit 127. Ext/int corridors. **Pets:** Medium. Service with restrictions.
ASK S☐ ✕ ☐ ▣ ❙❙ ⤻

SWEETWATER

Comfort Inn M
(915) 235-5234. **$69-$125, 14 days notice.** 216 SE Georgia Ave. I-20, exit 244. Ext corridors. **Pets:** Small. $25 deposit/pet. Service with restrictions, supervision.
SAVE S☐ ✕ ☒ ☐ ▣ ⤻

Mulberry Mansion BB
(915) 235-3811. **$72-$195.** 1400 Sam Houston St. I-20, exit 244, 0.4 mi n on Lamar St to Texas Ave, then 0.3 mi w. Ext/int corridors. **Pets:** Accepted.
ASK S☐ ☐ ▣

Ranch House Motel & Restaurant M
(915) 236-6341. **$48-$63.** 301 SW Georgia Ave. I-20, exit 244, just w of jct SR 70 on south access road. Ext/int corridors. **Pets:** Medium. Designated rooms, service with restrictions, crate.
SAVE ✕ ☐ ▣ ❙❙ ⤻

Sweetwater Inn M
(915) 236-6887. **$63, 30 days notice.** 500 NW Georgia St. I-20, exit 244, just w of jct SR 70 on north access road. Ext/int corridors. **Pets:** Other species. $25 one-time fee/ room. Service with restrictions, crate.
ASK ✕ ☐ ▣ ❙❙ ⤻

TAYLOR

Regency Inn M
(512) 352-2666. **$57.** 2007 N Main. 1.3 mi n on SR 95. Ext corridors. **Pets:** Accepted.
ASK S☐ ✕ ☐

TEMPLE

▼▼▼ Days Inn Ⓜ
(254) 774-9223. **$59.** 1104 N General Bruce Dr. I-35, exit 302 (Nugent Ave). Ext corridors. **Pets:** Accepted.
[SAVE] [S🐾] [✕] [🐾] [📱] [🏊]

ⒶⒶⒶ ▼▼▼▼ The Inn at Scott and White Ⓜ
(254) 778-5511. **$84.** 2625 S 31st St. 3 mi sw on FM 1741, 0.3 mi ne jct Loop 363, US 190 and SR 36. Ext/int corridors. **Pets:** Service with restrictions, crate.
[SAVE] [S🐾] [✕] [🐾] [📱] [🛎] [🏊]

▼▼▼ La Quinta Inn-Temple Ⓜ
(254) 771-2980. **$61-$76.** 1604 W Barton Ave. SR 53, just e, jct I-35 and US 81, exit 301. Ext corridors. **Pets:** Small, other species. Service with restrictions, crate.
[SAVE] [S🐾] [✕] [📱] [🏊]

▼▼ Motel 6–257 Ⓜ
(254) 778-0272. **$35-$47.** 1100 N General Bruce Dr. I-35, exit 302 (Nugent Ave), just s on access, follow signs. Ext corridors. **Pets:** Accepted.
[S🐾] [✕] [🏊]

ⒶⒶⒶ ▼▼ Super 8 Motel Ⓜ
(254) 778-0962. **$50-$55, 7 days notice.** 5505 S General Bruce Dr. I-35, exit 297 (Midway Dr). Ext corridors. **Pets:** Accepted.
[SAVE] [S🐾] [✕] [📱] [🏊]

TERLINGUA

ⒶⒶⒶ ▼▼ Big Bend Motor Inn Ⓜ
(915) 371-2218. **$70-$82, 7 days notice.** SR 118, 2 mi from entrance of Big Bend National Park. Ext corridors. **Pets:** Medium, other species. Designated rooms, service with restrictions, crate.
[SAVE] [✕] [📱] [🏊]

TEXARKANA

ⒶⒶⒶ ▼▼ Best Western Northgate Inn Ⓜ
(903) 793-6565. **$55-$65, 7 days notice.** 400 W 53rd St. I-30, exit 223B, on northwest frontage road. Int corridors. **Pets:** Accepted.
[SAVE] [S🐾] [✕] [📱] [🛎] [🏊]

ⒶⒶⒶ ▼▼ Four Points Hotel Sheraton Texarkana Ⓗ
(903) 792-3222. **$109-$129.** 5301 N State Line Ave. I-30, exit 223B. Int corridors. **Pets:** Small. $50 one-time fee/ room. Designated rooms, service with restrictions, supervision.

▼▼▼ Holiday Inn Express Ⓜ
(903) 792-3366. **$79.** 5401 N State Line Ave. I-30, exit 223B, 0.3 mi n on US 71. Int corridors. **Pets:** Small. $25 one-time fee/room. No service, supervision.
[ASK] [S🐾] [✕] [📱] [🏊]

ⒶⒶⒶ ▼▼▼▼ La Quinta Inn-Texarkana Ⓜ
(903) 794-1900. **$65-$75.** 5201 State Line Ave. I-30, exit 223A, sw of jct US 59 and 71. Ext corridors. **Pets:** Accepted.
[SAVE] [S🐾] [✕] [📱] [🏊]

▼▼ Motel 6–201 Ⓜ
(903) 793-1413. **$38-$42.** 1924 Hampton Rd. I-30, exit 222 (Summerhill Rd). Ext corridors. **Pets:** Accepted.
[✕] [🏊]

TEXAS CITY

ⒶⒶⒶ ▼▼▼ La Quinta Inn Ⓜ
(409) 948-3101. **$66-$116.** 1121 Hwy 146 N. Jct SR 146 S and FM 1764, 5 mi se of I-45, exit 16 southbound; exit 15 northbound. Ext corridors. **Pets:** Small, other species. Service with restrictions, supervision.
[SAVE] [S🐾] [✕] [🐾] [📱] [🏊]

THREE RIVERS

▼▼ Bass Inn Ⓜ
(361) 786-3521. **$46.** Hwy 72 W. SR 72, 7.5 mi w of jct US 281; adjacent to Choke Canyon Lake. Ext corridors. **Pets:** Accepted.
[ASK] [S🐾] [✕] [📱] [🏊]

TULIA

▼▼▼ Select Inn of Tulia Ⓜ
(806) 995-3248. **$54-$64.** Rt 1, Box 60. I-27, exit 74. Ext corridors. **Pets:** Accepted.
[ASK] [S🐾] [✕] [♿M] [📱] [🏊]

TYLER

ⒶⒶⒶ ▼▼ Best Western Inn & Suites Ⓜ
(903) 595-2681. **$59-$100.** 2828 W NW Loop 323. Jct US 69 N and Loop 323. Ext corridors. **Pets:** Medium. $10 daily fee/pet. Service with restrictions, supervision.
[SAVE] [S🐾] [✕] [📱] [🏊]

▼▼ Holiday Inn-Southeast Crossing Ⓜ
(903) 593-3600. **$89, 7 days notice.** 3310 Troup Hwy. 3.5 mi se on SR 110, 0.3 mi n of jct E Loop 323. Ext corridors. **Pets:** Accepted.
[ASK] [S🐾] [✕] [🐾] [📱] [🛎] [🏊]

ⒶⒶⒶ ▼▼▼ La Quinta Inn Ⓜ
(903) 561-2223. **$71-$81.** 1601 W SW Loop 323. 1 mi w of S US 69 on W Loop 323. Ext corridors. **Pets:** Accepted.
[SAVE] [S🐾] [✕] [🐾] [📱] [🏊]

▼▼▼ Radisson Hotel Tyler Ⓜ
(903) 597-1301. **$69, 14 days notice.** 2843 W NW Loop 323. On Loop 323, just w of jct US 69. Int corridors. **Pets:** Medium. $25 one-time fee/room. Designated rooms, service with restrictions, supervision.
[ASK] [S🐾] [✕] [♿M] [📱] [🛎] [🏊]

ⓐ ▼▼▼ Residence Inn by Marriott Ⓐ
(903) 595-5188. **$74-$113.** 3303 Troup Hwy. 3.5 mi se on SR 110, 0.3 mi n of jct E Loop 323. Ext corridors. **Pets:** Other species. $50 one-time fee/room. Designated rooms, service with restrictions, supervision.
SAVE Sⓓ ✕ 🛏 💻 🏊

▼▼▼ Sheraton Tyler Hotel Ⓜ
(903) 561-5800. **$109.** 5701 S Broadway. 1.1 mi s jct Loop 323 and US 69 (S Broadway). Ext/int corridors. **Pets:** Accepted.
A$K Sⓓ ✕ 🍽 🛏 💻 🍴 🏊

UVALDE

ⓐ ▼▼▼ Best Western Continental Inn Ⓜ
(830) 278-5671. **$56-$66.** 701 E Main St. 0.5 mi e on US 90. Ext corridors. **Pets:** Accepted.
SAVE ✕ 🛏 🏊

▼▼ Holiday Inn Ⓜ
(830) 278-4511. **$67-$95.** 920 E Main St. 0.5 mi e on US 90. Ext corridors. **Pets:** Large. $50 deposit/room. Service with restrictions, supervision.
A$K Sⓓ ✕ 🛏 💻 🍴 🏊

VAN HORN

ⓐ ▼▼ Best Western American Inn Ⓜ
(915) 283-2030. **$55-$95.** 1309 W Broadway. I-10, exit 138, 1 mi e. Ext corridors. **Pets:** Accepted.
SAVE Sⓓ ✕ 🛏 💻 🏊

ⓐ ▼▼ Best Western Inn of Van Horn Ⓜ
(915) 283-2410. **$49-$79.** 1705 W Broadway. I-10, exit 138, 0.3 mi e, 1 mi w on US 80. Ext corridors. **Pets:** Other species. Service with restrictions, supervision.
SAVE Sⓓ ✕ 🛏 💻 🏊

ⓐ ▼ Budget Inn Ⓜ
(915) 283-2019. **$30-$45.** 1303 W Broadway. I-10, exit 138, 0.7 mi e; US 80. Ext corridors. **Pets:** $4 one-time fee/room. Service with restrictions, supervision.
SAVE Sⓓ ✕ 🛏

ⓐ ▼▼ Days Inn Ⓜ
(915) 283-1007. **$44-$60.** 600 E Broadway St. I-10, exit 140B, just w. Ext corridors. **Pets:** Designated rooms, supervision.
SAVE Sⓓ 🛏 🏊

ⓐ ▼ Economy Inn Ⓜ
(915) 283-2754. **$25-$35, 30 days notice.** 1500 W Broadway St. I-10, exit 138, 0.5 mi e on US 80. Ext corridors. **Pets:** $5 deposit/pet. No service, supervision.
SAVE Sⓓ ✕ 🛏

ⓐ ▼▼▼ Holiday Inn Express Ⓜ
(915) 283-7444. **$65-$79.** 1905 SW Frontage Rd. I-10, exit 138 (Golf Course Dr). Ext corridors. **Pets:** Small, other species. Service with restrictions, supervision.
SAVE Sⓓ ✕ 🛗ᴹ 🍽 🛏 🏊

ⓐ ▼ Motel 6-4024 Ⓜ
(915) 283-2992. **$43-$63.** 1805 W Broadway St. I-10, exit 138. Ext corridors. **Pets:** Accepted.
SAVE Sⓓ ✕

ⓐ ▼▼ Ramada Limited Ⓜ ❀
(915) 283-2780. **$60-$75.** 200 Golf Course Dr. I-10, exit 138 (Golf Course Dr). Ext/int corridors. **Pets:** Medium, other species. $6 one-time fee/pet. Service with restrictions, supervision.
SAVE Sⓓ ✕ 🛏 🏊

ⓐ ▼▼ Van Horn Super 8 Ⓜ
(915) 283-2282. **$43-$46, 10 days notice.** 1807 E Service Rd. I-10, exit 138 (Golf Course Dr). Ext corridors. **Pets:** Accepted.
SAVE Sⓓ ✕ 🛏

VEGA

ⓐ ▼▼▼ Best Western Country Inn Ⓜ ❀
(806) 267-2131. **$59-$69, 7 days notice.** 1800 W Vega Blvd. 0.5 mi w on US 40 business loop. Ext corridors. **Pets:** Medium. Service with restrictions, supervision.
SAVE Sⓓ ✕ 💻 🍴 🏊

VERNON

▼▼ Best Western Village Inn Ⓜ
(940) 552-5417. **$54-$64.** 1615 Expwy. US 287, exit Main St, just w. Ext/int corridors. **Pets:** Small. Service with restrictions, supervision.
SAVE Sⓓ ✕ 🛏 💻 🍴 🏊

VICTORIA

ⓐ ▼▼▼ Comfort Inn Ⓜ
(361) 574-9393. **$75-$85, 30 days notice.** 1906 Houston Hwy. 3.5 mi ne on US 59. Ext corridors. **Pets:** $25 deposit/room. No service, supervision.
SAVE Sⓓ ✕ 🛏 💻 🏊

▼▼▼ Hampton Inn Ⓜ
(361) 578-2030. **$67.** 3112 E Houston Hwy (Business Rt 59). 2 mi ne on US 59. Ext corridors. **Pets:** Very small. Service with restrictions, supervision.
SAVE ✕ 🛏 💻 🏊

▼▼▼ Holiday Inn Holidome Ⓜ
(361) 575-0251. **$130, 5 days notice.** 2705 E Houston Hwy (Business Rt 59). 2.5 mi ne on US 59. Ext/int corridors. **Pets:** Accepted.
A$K ✕ 🛏 💻 🍴 🏊

▼▼▼ La Quinta Inn-Victoria Ⓜ
(361) 572-3585. **$76-$86.** 7603 N Navarro (US 77 N) St. 4 mi n on US 77 at jct Loop 463. Ext corridors. **Pets:** Other species. Service with restrictions, crate.
SAVE Sⓓ ✕ 🍽 🛏 💻 🏊

▼▼ **Ramada Inn** Ⓜ
(361) 578-2723. **$69, 7 days notice.** 3901 E Houston Hwy (Business Rt 59). US 59 business route, 2.3 mi ne of jct US 77. Ext corridors. **Pets:** Small, dogs only. Designated rooms, service with restrictions, supervision.

(ASK) (S🐾) (✕) (📱) (¶) (🏊)

WACO

▲▲▲ ▼▼ **Best Western Old Main Lodge** Ⓜ
(254) 753-0316. **$70-$77.** I-35 & 4th St. I-35 and US 81, exit 335A (4th-5th St). Ext corridors. **Pets:** Small. Service with restrictions, supervision.

(SAVE) (S🐾) (✕) (📱) (🖥) (🏊)

▲▲▲ ▼▼ **Best Western Waco Mall** Ⓜ
(254) 776-3194. **$66-$70.** 6624 Hwy 84 W. On US 84, 0.3 mi w of jct SR 6 and Loop 340. Ext corridors. **Pets:** Accepted.

(SAVE) (S🐾) (✕) (📱) (🖥) (🏊)

▲▲▲ ▼▼ **Days Inn** Ⓜ
(254) 799-8585. **$62-$82, 3 days notice.** 1504 I-35. I-35, exit 338B (Behrens Cir), N off I-35 at exit 338B (Behrens Circle). Ext corridors. **Pets:** Medium. $10 daily fee/pet. Designated rooms, service with restrictions, supervision.

(SAVE) (S🐾) (✕) (📱) (🖥) (🏊)

▼▲▼ **Holiday Inn-Waco I-35** Ⓜ
(254) 753-0261. **$100-$145.** 1001 Martin Luther King Blvd. N off I-35, exit 335C (Lake Brazos Dr). Int corridors. **Pets:** Other species. $100 deposit/room, $25 one-time fee/pet. Service with restrictions, crate.

(ASK) (S🐾) (✕) (📶) (🅯) (📱) (🖥) (¶) (🏊)

▼▲▼ **La Quinta Inn-Waco** Ⓜ 🐾
(254) 752-9741. **$71-$98.** 1110 S 9th St. E off I-35, exit 334 (17th St) southbound; exit 334A (18th St) northbound. Ext corridors. **Pets:** Other species. Supervision.

(SAVE) (S🐾) (✕) (📶) (📱) (🖥) (🏊)

▼▲▼ **Super 8 Motel-Waco** Ⓜ
(254) 754-1023. **$62-$74.** 1320 S Jack Kultgen Frwy. I-35, exit 334, just e. Int corridors. **Pets:** Accepted.

(ASK) (S🐾) (✕)

▲▲▲ ▼▲▼ **Waco Residence Inn** Ⓜ
(254) 714-1386. **$107-$117.** 501 S University Park Dr. I-35, exit 335B, 0.3 mi w. Int corridors. **Pets:** Accepted.

(SAVE) (✕) (📶) (🅯) (📱) (🖥) (🏊)

WEATHERFORD

▼▼ **Best Western Santa Fe Inn** Ⓜ
(817) 594-7401. **$69-$89, 4 days notice.** 1927 Santa Fe Dr. I-20, exit 409 (Clear Lake Rd), FM 2552, 0.3 mi nw of jct I-20, exit 409 (Clear Lake Rd). Ext corridors. **Pets:** Accepted.

(SAVE) (S🐾) (✕) (📱) (🖥) (¶) (🏊)

▼▲▼ **Hampton Inn** Ⓜ
(817) 599-4800. **$85-$140.** 2524 S Main St. I-20, exit 408. Int corridors. **Pets:** Medium. $10 daily fee/pet. Service with restrictions, supervision.

(SAVE) (S🐾) (✕) (📶) (🅯) (📱) (🖥) (🏊)

▼▼▼ **Holiday Inn Express** Ⓜ
(817) 599-3700. **$85-$150.** 2500 S Main St. I-20, exit 408. Ext corridors. **Pets:** Small. $10 daily fee/pet. Service with restrictions, supervision.

(ASK) (S🐾) (✕) (📶) (📱) (🖥) (🏊)

▲▲▲ ▼▼ **Ramada Limited** Ⓜ
(817) 599-8683. **$60-$95.** 809 Palo Pinto St. 0.8 mi w of Courthouse on US 80 and 180. Ext corridors. **Pets:** Accepted.

(SAVE) (S🐾) (✕) (📱) (🖥) (🏊)

WELLINGTON

▼ **Cherokee Inn & Restaurant** Ⓜ
(806) 447-2508. **$34-$48.** 1105 Houston. On US 83. Ext corridors. **Pets:** Accepted.

(ASK) (S🐾) (✕) (¶)

WESLACO

▲▲▲ ▼▲▼ **Best Western Palm Aire Motor Inn & Suites** Ⓜ
(956) 969-2411. **$54-$111.** 415 S International Blvd. US 83 Expwy, exit International Blvd. Ext corridors. **Pets:** Small. Service with restrictions, supervision.

(SAVE) (S🐾) (✕) (📶) (📱) (🖥) (¶) (🏊) (✕)

▼▲▼ **Super 8 Motel** Ⓜ
(956) 969-9920. **$50-$69.** 1702 E Expwy 83. US 83, exit Airport Dr. Ext corridors. **Pets:** Accepted.

(ASK) (S🐾) (✕) (📱) (🏊)

WEST COLUMBIA

▲▲▲ ▼▼ **Country Hearth Inn** Ⓜ
(979) 345-2399. **$61.** 714 Columbia Dr (Hwy 36). Jct SR 35 and 36 at Columbia Dr. Ext corridors. **Pets:** Accepted.

(SAVE) (S🐾) (✕) (📱) (🖥) (🏊)

WESTLAKE

▲▲▲ ▼▲▼ **Dallas-Fort Worth Marriott Solana** Ⓗ
(817) 430-3848. **$179.** 5 Village Cir. SR 114, exit Kirkwood Blvd, just s. Int corridors. **Pets:** Very small. Service with restrictions, supervision.

(SAVE) (✕) (♿M) (📱) (🖥) (¶) (🏊)

WICHITA FALLS

▲▲▲ ▼▼ **Best Western Towne Crest Inn** Ⓜ
(940) 322-1182. **$42-$52.** 1601 8th St. Just w of jct US 287. Ext corridors. **Pets:** Accepted.

(SAVE) (S🐾) (✕)

▼▲▼ **Comfort Inn** Ⓜ
(940) 322-2477. **$54-$64.** 1750 Maurine St. I-44, exit 2, just e. Int corridors. **Pets:** Accepted.

(SAVE) (S🐾) (✕) (♿M) (🅯) (📱) (🖥) (🏊)

▼▼▼ Hampton Inn M
(940) 766-3300. $47-$67. 1317 Kenley Ave. I-44, exit 2, just w. Int corridors. **Pets:** Accepted.

[SAVE] [S] [X] [H] [▣] [≈]

▼▼▼ La Quinta Inn-Wichita Falls M
(940) 322-6971. $61-$75. 1128 Central Frwy N. I-44, exit 2, just w. Ext corridors. **Pets:** Accepted.

[SAVE] [S] [X] [∂] [H] [▣] [≈]

▼▼ Motel 6 M
(940) 322-8817. $50. 1812 Maurine St. I-44, exit 2, just e. Ext corridors. **Pets:** Small. Service with restrictions, supervision.

[S] [X] [∂] [&] [≈]

⟪AAA⟫ ▼▼▼ Ramada Limited M
(940) 855-0085. $56-$59. 3209 Northwest Frwy (US 287). US 287, exit Beverly (CR 11), just w. Ext corridors. **Pets:** $10 daily fee/room. Designated rooms, service with restrictions, supervision.

[SAVE] [S] [X] [&] [H] [▣] [≈]

▼▼ Travelers Inn M
(940) 766-6881. $42-$66. 1032 Central Frwy. I-44, exit 2, just w. Ext corridors. **Pets:** Accepted.

[ASK] [S] [X] [H] [▣] [≈]

ZAPATA

⟪AAA⟫ ▼▼▼ Best Western Inn by the Lake M
(956) 765-8403. $65-$85, **14 days notice.** 0.5 mi se on US 83. Ext corridors. **Pets:** Accepted.

[SAVE] [S] [X] [H] [≈]

CITY INDEX

AMERICAN FORK

 **Quality Inn & Suites** M
(801) 763-8383. **$64-$109.** 712 S Utah Valley Dr. I-15, exit 279; in Utah Valley Business Park. Int corridors. **Pets:** Accepted.

BEAVER

Best Western Butch Cassidy Inn M
(435) 438-2438. **$54-$71.** 161 S Main St. I-15, exit 109 or 112, just e. Ext corridors. **Pets:** Medium, other species. $20 deposit/pet. Designated rooms, service with restrictions, supervision.

Best Western Paradise Inn M
(435) 438-2455. **$59-$77.** 1451 N 300 W. I-15, exit 109 or 112, just e, north end of town. Ext corridors. **Pets:** Other species. Service with restrictions, supervision.

DeLano Motel M
(435) 438-2418. **$30-$45, 7 days notice.** 480 N Main St. I-15, exit 109 or 112, just e, north end of town. Ext corridors. **Pets:** Small, dogs only. $5 daily fee/pet. Service with restrictions, supervision.

Motel 6 Beaver M
(435) 438-1666. **$38-$59, 7 days notice.** 1345 N 450 W. I-15, exit 109 or 112, just se of off ramp. Int corridors. **Pets:** Large, other species. Service with restrictions, supervision.

Quality Inn M
(435) 438-5426. **$53-$69.** 781 W 1800 S. I-15, exit 109 or 112, just w. Int corridors. **Pets:** Small. Designated rooms, service with restrictions, supervision.

BICKNELL

Aquarius Motel and Restaurant M
(435) 425-3835. **$34-$49.** 240 W Main St. Downtown; SR 24, 9 mi w of Capitol Reef National Park. Ext/int corridors. **Pets:** Other species. $25 deposit/room, $5 one-time fee/room. Service with restrictions, supervision.

BLANDING

Best Western Gateway Inn M
(435) 678-2278. **$40-$75.** 88 E Center St. East side on US 191. Ext corridors. **Pets:** Accepted.

Four Corners Inn M
(435) 678-3257. **$48-$70.** 131 E Center St. On US 191. Ext corridors. **Pets:** Other species. $3 daily fee/room. Designated rooms, crate.

BLUFF

Kokopelli Inn M
(435) 672-2322. **$38-$48.** US 191. Int corridors. **Pets:** Small, other species. $10 daily fee/pet. Service with restrictions, supervision.

Recapture Lodge M
(435) 672-2281. **$38-$56.** 220 E Main St. US 191. Ext corridors. **Pets:** Other species. Service with restrictions, supervision.

BOULDER

▼▼▼▼ **Boulder Mountain Lodge** Ⓜ️ ❀
(435) 335-7460. **$72-$160, 14 days notice.** 20 N Hwy 12. Jct SR 12 and Burr Trail. Ext/int corridors. **Pets:** $8.50 daily fee/pet. Designated rooms, service with restrictions, supervision.

🅧 🛢️ 🖥️ 🍴

BRIAN HEAD

▼▼▼ **The Lodge at Brian Head** Ⓜ️
(435) 677-3222. **$75-$129, 7 days notice.** 314 W Hunter Ridge Rd. Just s of SR 143, 2.2 mi n of Cedar Breaks National Monument. Int corridors. **Pets:** Accepted.

Ⓐ🆂🅺 🛦 🅧 🖑 🕜 🛢️ 🖥️ 🍴 ⊃ 🅧 🅰️

BRIGHAM CITY

Ⓐ🅐🅐 ▼▼▼ **Howard Johnson Inn** Ⓜ️
(435) 723-8511. **$49-$75.** 1167 S Main St. I-15 and 84, exit 364 (Logan and Brigham City), 2 mi e on US 89 and 91. Ext corridors. **Pets:** Service with restrictions, supervision.

Ⓢ🅐🆅🅔 🛦 🅧 🅗 🛢️ 🖥️ ⊃

BRYCE

Ⓐ🅐🅐 ▼▼◈◈◈ **Best Western Ruby's Inn** Ⓜ️
(435) 834-5341. **$46-$110.** UT Hwy 63. SR 63, 1 mi s of SR 12, 1 mi n of Bryce Canyon National Park entrance. Ext/int corridors. **Pets:** $100 deposit/room. Service with restrictions.

Ⓢ🅐🆅🅔 🛦 🅧 🛦🅜 🅗 🖑 🛢️ 🖥️ 🍴 🅧

Ⓐ🅐🅐 ▼▼◈◈◈ **Bryce Canyon Resorts** Ⓜ️
(435) 834-5351. **$39-$95.** 13500 E Hwy 12. Jct of SR 12 and 63. Ext corridors. **Pets:** Accepted.

Ⓢ🅐🆅🅔 🅧 🛢️ 🖥️ 🍴 ⊃

Ⓐ🅐🅐 ▼▼▼ **Bryce View Lodge** Ⓜ️
(435) 834-5180. **$44-$65.** SR 63. Ext corridors. **Pets:** $100 deposit/room. Service with restrictions.

Ⓢ🅐🆅🅔 🛦 🅧 🛢️ 🖥️ 🅧

CANNONVILLE

Ⓐ🅐🅐 ▼▼▼ **Grand Staircase Inn** Ⓜ️
(435) 679-8400. **$39-$79.** 105 N Kodachrome Dr. Center of town. Ext/int corridors. **Pets:** Accepted.

Ⓢ🅐🆅🅔 🛦 🅧 🅗

CEDAR CITY

Ⓐ🅐🅐 ▼▼▼ **Best Travel Inn** Ⓜ️
(435) 586-6557. **$28-$58.** 323 S Main St. Downtown; cross streets 300 S and Main sts. Ext corridors. **Pets:** Small. $5 daily fee/pet. Service with restrictions, supervision.

Ⓢ🅐🆅🅔 🛦 🅧 🛢️ ⊃

▼▼▼▼ **Cedar City Holiday Inn & Convention Center** Ⓜ️
(435) 586-8888. **$56-$72, 3 days notice.** 1575 W 200 N. I-15, exit 59, just w. Ext/int corridors. **Pets:** Medium. $25 deposit/room. Service with restrictions, crate.

Ⓐ🆂🅺 🛦 🅧 ⌀ 🛢️ 🖥️ 🍴 ⊃

Ⓐ🅐🅐 ▼▼▼ **Cedar Rest Motel** Ⓜ️
(435) 586-9471. **$35-$60.** 479 S Main St. I-15, exit 59, just e. Ext corridors. **Pets:** Medium. $5 daily fee/pet. Service with restrictions, supervision.

Ⓢ🅐🆅🅔 🛦 🅧 🅗

▼▼▼▼ **Comfort Inn** Ⓜ️
(435) 586-2082. **$45-$80, 7 days notice.** 250 N 1100 W. I-15, exit 59, just e. Ext corridors. **Pets:** Other species. Designated rooms, service with restrictions, supervision.

Ⓢ🅐🆅🅔 🛦 🅧 ⌀ 🅗 🖥️ ⊃

Ⓐ🅐🅐 ▼▼🅧 **Days Inn** Ⓜ️
(435) 867-8877. **$49-$89.** 1204 S Main St. I-15, exit 57, 0.4 mi e. Ext corridors. **Pets:** Small. $5 daily fee/pet. Service with restrictions, supervision.

Ⓢ🅐🆅🅔 🛦 🅧 ⌀ 🅗 🅗 ⊃

▼▼▼ **Motel 6 of Cedar City–4041** Ⓜ️
(435) 586-9200. **$49-$60.** 1620 W 200 N. I-15, exit 59, just w. Int corridors. **Pets:** Accepted.

🅧 🅗

▼▼▼ **Rodeway Inn** Ⓜ️
(435) 586-9916. **$48-$78.** 281 S Main St. I-15, exit 57, just e. Ext corridors. **Pets:** Medium, other species. No service, supervision.

Ⓢ🅐🆅🅔 🛦 🅧 🖥️ ⊃

Ⓐ🅐🅐 ▼▼▼ **Super 7 Motel** Ⓜ️
(435) 586-6566. **$35-$45.** 190 S Main St. I-15, exit 57, just e. Ext corridors. **Pets:** Accepted.

Ⓢ🅐🆅🅔 🛦 🅧 🅗

▼▼▼ **Super 8 Motel** Ⓜ️
(435) 586-8880. **$44-$53.** 145 N 1550 W. I-15, exit 59, just w. Int corridors. **Pets:** Medium, other species. Service with restrictions, supervision.

Ⓐ🆂🅺 🛦 🅧 🛦🅜 ⌀ 🅗 🅗

Ⓐ🅐🅐 ▼▼◈◈◈ **Travelodge** Ⓜ️
(435) 586-7435. **$39-$79.** 2555 N Main St. I-15, exit 62. Ext corridors. **Pets:** Small. $5 daily fee/pet. Service with restrictions, supervision.

Ⓢ🅐🆅🅔 🛦 🅧 🅗 🖥️ ⊃

Ⓐ🅐🅐 ▼▼▼ **Valu-Inn** Ⓜ️
(435) 586-9114. **$30-$70.** 344 S Main St. I-15, exit 57, just e. Ext corridors. **Pets:** Accepted.

Ⓢ🅐🆅🅔 🛦 🅧 🅗

CIRCLEVILLE

▼▼▼ **Butch Cassidy's Hideout** Ⓜ️
(435) 577-2008. **$42-$52.** 339 S Hwy 89. South end of town. Ext corridors. **Pets:** Accepted.

Ⓐ🆂🅺 🛦 🅧 🍴

CLEARFIELD

▼▼ Clearfield Super 8 **M**
(801) 825-8000. **$40-$60.** 572 N Main St. I-15, exit 338, just
w. Int corridors. **Pets:** Other species. $20 deposit/room.
Service with restrictions, supervision.

⊠ 🐾 🚦 🖪

DELTA

▲▲▲ ▼▼▼▼ Best Western Motor Inn **M**
(435) 864-3882. **$55-$64.** 527 E Topaz Blvd. US 6, at jct
US 50. Ext corridors. **Pets:** Other species. $10 deposit/
room. Designated rooms, service with restrictions, supervision.

SAVE 🖪 ⊠ 🐾 🚦 🖵 🚤

DUCK CREEK VILLAGE

▼▼ Duck Creek Village Inn **M**
(435) 682-2565. **$54, 14 days notice.** Hwy 14. 30 mi e of
Cedar City on SR 14; 10 mi w of US 89 on SR 14. Ext
corridors. **Pets:** Accepted.

ASK ⊠ 🚦 🖵 ¶¶ ℟ ☎

▲▲▲ ▼▼ Pinewoods Resort **X**
(435) 682-2512. **$85-$110, 30 days notice.** 121 Duck
Greek Ridge Rd. Just s of SR 14 via Cedar Mountain Rd,
31 mi e of Cedar City in Cedar Mountain Village; 10 mi w of
jct US 89. Ext/int corridors. **Pets:** Accepted.

SAVE ⊠ 🚦 🖵 ¶¶ ⊠ ℟ ☎

ESCALANTE

▼▼ Rainbow Country Bed & Breakfast **BB**
(435) 826-4567. **$45-$65, 3 days notice.** 586 E 300 S. Just
off SR 12, south end of town. Int corridors. **Pets:** Supervision.

ASK 🖪 ⊠ 𝒲 ☎

FILLMORE

▼▼▼▼ Best Inn & Suites **M**
(435) 743-4334. **$53-$94.** 940 S Hwy 99. I-15, exit 163, just
e. Int corridors. **Pets:** Accepted.

ASK 🖪 ⊠ 🐾 🚦 🖵 🚤

▲▲▲ ▼▼▼▼ Best Western Paradise Inn &
Resort **M**
(435) 743-6895. **$55-$77.** 905 N Main St. I-15, exit 167, just
e. Ext corridors. **Pets:** Small, other species. Service with
restrictions, supervision.

SAVE 🖪 ⊠ 🚦 🖵 ¶¶ 🚤

FRY CANYON

▲▲▲ ▼▼▼ Fry Canyon Lodge **MI**
(435) 259-5431. **$49-$99, 3 days notice.** Hwy 95. 22 mi w
of Natural Bridges National Monument at MM 71, SR 95.
Ext corridors. **Pets:** $10 daily fee/pet. Designated rooms,
service with restrictions, supervision.

SAVE ⊠ 🐾 ¶¶ 𝒲 ☎

GARDEN CITY

▼▼◆◆ Canyon Cove Inn **M**
(435) 946-3565. **$70.** 315 W Logan Hwy. Downtown; 3 blks
w. Int corridors. **Pets:** Accepted.

ASK ⊠ 🐾 🚦 🚤

GREEN RIVER

▼▼▼ Delux Inn **M** 🐾
(435) 564-8441. **$50-$60.** 1117 E Main St. I-70, exit 162, 1
mi nw. Ext/int corridors. **Pets:** Medium, other species. $5
daily fee/pet. Service with restrictions, supervision.

ASK 🖪 ⊠ 🚦 🚤

▼▼ Motel 6 **M**
(435) 564-3436. **$30-$60.** 946 E Main St. Ext corridors.
Pets: Accepted.

🖪 ⊠ 🐾 🚦 🚤

▼▼▼◆ Super 8 Motel **M**
(435) 564-8888. **$45-$75.** 1248 E Main St. I-70, exit 162. Int
corridors. **Pets:** Medium. $25 deposit/room, $5 daily fee/pet.
Designated rooms, service with restrictions, supervision.

ASK 🖪 ⊠ 🐾 🐾 🚦 🚤

HATCH

▲▲▲ ▼▼ Riverside Motel **M**
(435) 735-4223. **$45-$68.** 594 US Hwy 89. 1 mi n on US
89; at the Riverside Campground. Ext corridors.
Pets: Accepted.

SAVE 🖪 ⊠ 🚦 ¶¶

HEBER CITY

▲▲▲ ▼▼▼ National 9 High Country Inn **M**
(435) 654-0201. **$46-$54.** 1000 S Main St. On US 40 E. Ext
corridors. **Pets:** Accepted.

SAVE 🖪 ⊠ 🚦 🚤

▲▲▲ ▼▼▼ Swiss Alps Inn **M**
(435) 654-0722. **$55-$90.** 167 S Main St. On US 40. Ext
corridors. **Pets:** Service with restrictions, supervision.

SAVE ⊠ 🚦 🖵 🚤

HUNTSVILLE

▼▼ Jackson Fork Inn **BB**
(801) 745-0051. **$80-$120, 3 days notice.** 7345 E 900 S.
On SR 39. Int corridors. **Pets:** Small. $20 one-time fee/
room. Service with restrictions.

ASK 🖪 ⊠ ¶¶ ☎

HURRICANE

▲▲▲ ▼▼▼ Lamplighter Inn **M**
(435) 635-4647. **$34-$110.** 280 W State. Just w on SR 9.
Ext corridors. **Pets:** Small. $10 daily fee/pet. Designated
rooms, no service, supervision.

SAVE 🖪 ⊠ 🚦 🖵 🚤

⏢ ▽▽▽▽ Motel 6–4050 Ⓜ

(435) 635-4010. **$42-$85.** 650 W State. Just w on SR 9. Ext corridors. **Pets:** Small, dogs only. $20 one-time fee/pet. Designated rooms, service with restrictions, supervision.

(SAVE) ⊗ 🖥 ⊅

▽▽ Super 8 Ⓜ

(435) 635-0808. **$35-$64.** 65 S 700 W. Just s of SR 9. Ext corridors. **Pets:** Small. $10 daily fee/pet. Designated rooms, service with restrictions, supervision.

(S•) ⊗ (ﾟ) 🖥 🖳 ⊅

KANAB

⏢ ▽▽ Aikens Lodge National 9 Ⓜ

(435) 644-2625. **$33-$57.** 79 W Center St. On US 89. Ext corridors. **Pets:** Small, dogs only. $10 one-time fee/pet. Service with restrictions, supervision.

(SAVE) (S•) ⊗ (ﾟ) 🖥 ⊅

⏢ ▽▽▽ Best Western Red Hills Ⓜ

(435) 644-2675. **$47-$99.** 125 W Center St. Ext/int corridors. **Pets:** Other species. $10 one-time fee/room. Designated rooms.

(SAVE) (S•) ⊗ (𝒹) (ﾟ) 🖥 🖳 ⊅

⏢ ▽▽▽ Bob-Bon Inn Ⓜ

(435) 644-5094. **$28-$69, 3 days notice.** 236 Hwy 89 N. On US 89. Ext corridors. **Pets:** Accepted.

(SAVE) (S•) ⊗ 🖥 ⊅

▽ Color Country Inn Ⓜ

(435) 644-2164. **$45.** 1550 S US 89A. 1.5 mi s. Int corridors. **Pets:** Medium, other species. $10 deposit/room. Service with restrictions, supervision.

(A$K) (S•) ⊗

▽ Four Seasons Motel & Restaurant ⓂⅠ

(435) 644-2635. **$39-$69.** 36 N 300 W. Ext corridors. **Pets:** Accepted.

(A$K) (S•) ⊗ 🖥 (ﾟⅠ) ⊅

▽▽▽ Holiday Inn Express Ⓜ

(435) 644-8888. **$53-$99.** 815 E Hwy 89. Just e. Int corridors. **Pets:** Medium. $10 daily fee/room. Designated rooms, service with restrictions, supervision.

(A$K) (S•) ⊗ (𝒹) (ﾟ) ⊅

⏢ ▽ Kanab Mission Motel Ⓜ

(435) 644-5373. **$47-$52.** 386 E 300 S. Just e on US 89. Int corridors. **Pets:** Accepted.

(SAVE) (S•) ⊗

⏢ ▽▽ Parry Lodge Ⓜ

(435) 644-2601. **$35-$82.** 89 E Center St. Center; on US 89, corner of 100 E. Ext/int corridors. **Pets:** Medium, other species. $5 daily fee/room. Designated rooms, service with restrictions, crate.

(SAVE) (S•) ⊗ 🖥 🖳 (ﾟⅠ) ⊅

⏢ ▽▽ Quail Park Lodge Ⓜ

(435) 644-5094. **$28-$65, 3 days notice.** 125 Hwy 89 N. On US 89. Ext corridors. **Pets:** Accepted.

(SAVE) (S•) ⊗ 🖥 ⊅

▽▽▽ Shilo Inn Suites-Kanab Ⓜ ❀

(435) 644-2562. **$49-$149.** 296 W 100 N. On US 89. Int corridors. **Pets:** Other species. $10 daily fee/pet. Service with restrictions, supervision.

(A$K) (S•) ⊗ (𝒹) 🖥 🖳 ⊅

⏢ ▽ Sun N Sand Motel Ⓜ

(435) 644-5050. **$30-$50.** 347 S 100 E. Jct US 89 and 89A. Ext corridors. **Pets:** Other species. $10 deposit/room, $5 one-time fee/room. Designated rooms, service with restrictions, supervision.

(SAVE) (S•) ⊗ 🖥 ⊅

⏢ ▽▽ Super 8 Ⓜ

(435) 644-5500. **$43-$78.** 70 S 200 W. Just s off US 89. Ext corridors. **Pets:** Accepted.

(SAVE) (S•) ⊗ ⊅

LAKE POWELL

▽▽▽ Defiance House Lodge-Bullfrog Marina ⓂⅠ

(435) 684-3000. **$115-$125.** Bullfrog Marina. 70 mi s of Hanksville and 44 mi s off SR 95; on SR 276. Int corridors. **Pets:** No service.

(A$K) ⊗ 🖳 (ﾟⅠ) ⊗

LAYTON

▽▽▽ Hampton Inn Ⓜ

(801) 775-8800. **$70-$90.** 1700 Woodland Park Dr. I-15, exit 335, 0.3 mi se. Int corridors. **Pets:** Designated rooms, service with restrictions, supervision.

(SAVE) (S•) ⊗ (𝒹) (ﾟ) 🖥 🖳 ⊅

▽▽▽ Holiday Inn Express Ⓜ

(801) 773-3773. **$69-$109.** 1695 Woodland Park Dr. I-15, exit 335, 0.3 mi se. Int corridors. **Pets:** Accepted.

(A$K) (S•) ⊗ (𝒹) (ﾟ) 🖥 🖳 ⊅

⏢ ▽▽▽ La Quinta Inn Ⓜ

(801) 776-6700. **$65-$82.** 1965 N 1200 W. I-15, exit 335, 1 blk e; corner of Antelope Dr and Angel Rd. Int corridors. **Pets:** Accepted.

(SAVE) (S•) ⊗ (𝒹) 🖥 🖳 ⊅

⏢ ▽▽▽ TownePlace Suites Ⓜ

(801) 779-2422. **$74-$99.** 1743 Woodland Park Dr. I-15, exit 335, 0.3 mi se. Int corridors. **Pets:** Accepted.

(SAVE) (S•) ⊗ (𝒹) (ﾟ) 🖥 🖳 ⊅

LEHI

⏢ ▽▽▽ Best Western Timpanogos Inn Ⓜ

(801) 768-1400. **$70-$116.** 195 S 850 E. I-15, exit 282, southwest side. Int corridors. **Pets:** Other species. $10 one-time fee/room. Service with restrictions, supervision.

(SAVE) (S•) ⊗ (𝒹) (ﾟ) 🖥 🖳 ⊅

▽▽ Motel 6–1405 Ⓜ

(801) 768-2668. **$47.** 210 S 1200 E. I-15, exit 282, just e. Int corridors. **Pets:** Large, other species. Service with restrictions, supervision.

⊗ (𝒹) (ﾟ) 🖥 ⊅

△△△ ▽▽▽▽ Super 8 M
(801) 766-8800. **$50-$79.** 125 S 850 E. I-15, exit 282, southwest side. Int corridors. **Pets:** Accepted.
[SAVE] [S6] [✕] [✍] [🔥] [🛏] [🏊]

LOGAN

△△△ ▽▽▽▽ Best Western Weston Inn M
(435) 752-5700. **$55-$159.** 250 N Main St. US 89 and 91; downtown. Ext corridors. **Pets:** Accepted.
[SAVE] [S6] [✕] [✍] [🛏] [💬] [🏊]

▽▽ ▽▽ Logan Days Inn M
(435) 753-5623. **$38-$88.** 364 S Main St. US 89 and 91. Ext corridors. **Pets:** Accepted.
[SAVE] [S6] [✕] [🔥] [🛏] [🏊]

MEXICAN HAT

△△△ ▽▽ ▽▽ San Juan Inn & Trading Post M
(435) 683-2220. **$42-$70.** Hwy 163 & San Juan River. On US 163. Ext corridors. **Pets:** Designated rooms, service with restrictions, supervision.
[SAVE] [S6] [✕] [🛏] [💬] [🍴]

MIDWAY

▽▽▽▽ The Kastle Inn Bed & Breakfast BB
(435) 657-2755. **$89-$159, 7 days notice.** 1220 Interlaken Ln. Ext/int corridors. **Pets:** Accepted.
[ASK] [✕] [🛏] [ÆC] [Z]

MOAB

△△△ ▽▽ ▽▽ Apache Motel M
(435) 259-5727. **$32-$85.** 166 S 400 E. Just e off US 191. Ext corridors. **Pets:** Other species. $25 deposit/room. Service with restrictions, supervision.
[SAVE] [S6] [✕] [🛏] [🏊]

△△△ ▽▽▽▽ Big Horn Lodge M
(435) 259-6171. **$34-$89.** 550 S Main St. South end of town. Ext corridors. **Pets:** Medium. $5 daily fee/pet. Designated rooms, service with restrictions, supervision.
[SAVE] [S6] [✕] [🛏] [💬] [🍴] [🏊]

▽▽ ▽▽ Bowen Motel M
(435) 259-7132. **$55-$65.** 169 N Main St. Downtown. Ext corridors. **Pets:** Medium. $20 deposit/room, $5 daily fee/pet. Service with restrictions, supervision.
[ASK] [S6] [✕] [🛏] [🏊]

▽▽▽▽ Castle Rock Inn M
(435) 259-8700. **$63-$110.** 815 S Main St. South end of town. Int corridors. **Pets:** Small, other species. $25 one-time fee/room. Designated rooms, service with restrictions, supervision.
[ASK] [S6] [✕] [🛏] [💬] [🏊]

△△△ ▽▽▽▽ Cedar Breaks Condos CO
(435) 259-7830. **$72-$92, 7 days notice.** 400 East & Center St. Just s off US 191. Ext corridors. **Pets:** Dogs only. $10 daily fee/pet. Designated rooms, service with restrictions, supervision.
[SAVE] [✕] [🛏] [💬] [ÆC]

▽▽▽▽ Comfort Suites M
(435) 259-5252. **$69-$109.** 800 S Main St. Int corridors. **Pets:** Medium. $10 deposit/pet. Designated rooms, service with restrictions, supervision.
[SAVE] [S6] [✕] [✍] [🛏] [💬] [🏊]

▽▽▽▽ The Desert Chalet Bed & Breakfast BB
(435) 259-5793. **$55-$95, 7 days notice.** 1275 E San Juan Dr. 2.4 mi se. Int corridors. **Pets:** Accepted.
[ASK] [✕] [ÆC] [W] [Z]

△△△ ▽▽▽▽ The Gonzo Inn M
(435) 259-2515. **$125-$205, 14 days notice.** 100 W 200 S. Downtown. Ext/int corridors. **Pets:** $25 one-time fee/room. Service with restrictions, supervision.
[SAVE] [S6] [✕] [✍] [🛏] [💬] [🏊]

▽▽ Kokopelli Lodge M
(435) 259-7615. **$47-$76, 7 days notice.** 72 S 100 E. Downtown. Ext corridors. **Pets:** Dogs only. $10 daily fee/pet. Service with restrictions, supervision.
[ASK] [S6] [✕] [🛏] [💬]

▽▽▽▽ Microtel Inn M
(435) 259-5145. **$35-$65.** 71 W 200 N. Downtown; cross street 100 W and 200 N. Int corridors. **Pets:** Small. $10 one-time fee/room. Designated rooms, supervision.
[ASK] [S6] [✕] [🛏] [🏊]

▽▽▽▽ Moab Valley Inn M 🐾
(435) 259-4419. **$67-$135.** 711 S Main St. 1 mi s on US 191. Int corridors. **Pets:** Medium, other species. Service with restrictions, supervision.
[ASK] [S6] [✕] [🔥] [🛏] [💬] [🏊]

▽▽▽▽ Motel 6 Moab M
(435) 259-6686. **$35-$76.** 1089 N Main St. North end of town, west side of street. Int corridors. **Pets:** Medium. Designated rooms, service with restrictions, supervision.
[S6] [✕] [✍] [🔥] [🏊]

△△△ ▽▽ ▽▽ Red Rock Lodge M 🐾
(435) 259-5431. **$40-$125, 3 days notice.** 51 N 100 W. Just w of Main St. Ext/int corridors. **Pets:** Other species. $5 one-time fee/room. Service with restrictions, supervision.
[SAVE] [✕] [🛏] [💬]

△△△ ▽▽ ▽▽ Red Stone Inn M
(435) 259-3500. **$34-$70.** 535 S Main St. Int corridors. **Pets:** Other species. $5 daily fee/pet. Designated rooms, service with restrictions, supervision.
[SAVE] [S6] [✕] [🛏] [💬]

▽▽ ▽▽ Rustic Inn M
(435) 259-6177. **$30-$80.** 120 E 100 S. Ext corridors. **Pets:** Other species. $5 daily fee/room. Service with restrictions, supervision.
[✕] [🛏] [💬] [🏊]

▼▼ Sleep Inn **M**
(435) 259-4655. **$50-$95.** 1051 S Main St. South end of town. Int corridors. **Pets:** Large. Designated rooms, service with restrictions, supervision.

[SAVE] [S🐾] [✕] [🔥M] [🔊] [🛏] [🍴] [💻] [🏊]

◈◈◈ ▼▼◈ The Virginian Motel **M**
(435) 259-5951. **$30-$74.** 70 E 200 S. Just e of US 191. Ext corridors. **Pets:** Other species. $10 daily fee/pet. Service with restrictions, supervision.

[SAVE] [S🐾] [✕] [🛏] [💻]

MONTICELLO

▼▼◈◈ Super 8 of Monticello **M**
(435) 587-2489. **$45-$64.** 649 N Main St. North end of town. Int corridors. **Pets:** Small. $10 daily fee/pet. Designated rooms, service with restrictions, supervision.

[S🐾] [✕] [🛏] [🏊]

MOUNT CARMEL JUNCTION

◈◈◈ ▼▼◈▼ Best Western Thunderbird Resort **M**
(435) 648-2203. **$49-$98.** Jct US 89 and SR 9. Ext corridors. **Pets:** Small. $5 daily fee/room. Service with restrictions.

[SAVE] [S🐾] [✕] [💻] [🍴] [🏊]

◈◈◈ ▼▼◈ Golden Hills Motel **M**
(435) 648-2268. **$31-$49.** 4473 S State St. Jct US 89 and SR 9. Ext/int corridors. **Pets:** Medium. $3 one-time fee/pet. Crate.

[SAVE] [✕] [🍴] [🏊]

▼▼◈◈ Zion Mountain Resort **C**
(435) 648-2555. **$69-$119.** 9065 W SR 9. 3 mi e of Zion National Park entrance. Ext corridors. **Pets:** Small. $50 one-time fee/room. Service with restrictions, supervision.

[ASK] [✕] [🛏] [💻] [🍴] [✕] [▥] [🖊]

NEPHI

◈◈◈ ▼▼◈ Best Western Paradise Inn **M**
(435) 623-0624. **$45-$67.** 1025 S Main St. I-15, exit 222, 0.5 mi n. Ext corridors. **Pets:** Small, dogs only. $25 deposit/room, $5 one-time fee/pet. Designated rooms, service with restrictions, supervision.

[SAVE] [S🐾] [✕] [🛏] [🏊]

▼▼◈ Motel 6 **M**
(435) 623-0666. **$42-$46, 7 days notice.** 2195 S Main St. I-15, exit 222, just s. Int corridors. **Pets:** Accepted.

[ASK] [✕] [🔊] [🛏] [🏊]

◈◈◈ ▼▼◈ Safari Motel **M**
(435) 623-1071. **$38-$47.** 413 S Main St. I-15, exit 222, 3 mi nw. Ext corridors. **Pets:** Medium. $3 one-time fee/pet. Service with restrictions, supervision.

[SAVE] [S🐾] [✕] [🛏] [🏊]

OGDEN

▼▼◈▼ Ben Lomond Historic Suite Hotel **H**
(801) 627-1900. **Call for rates.** 2510 Washington Blvd. I-15, exit 344 (30th St), 2 mi ne via 31st St and Washington Blvd. Ext/int corridors. **Pets:** Large. $50 deposit/room. Service with restrictions.

[ASK] [S🐾] [✕] [🔊] [🛏] [💻] [🍴]

▼▼◈▼ Best Rest Inn **M**
(801) 393-8644. **$49-$59.** 1206 W 2100 S. I-15, exit 346, just e. Ext corridors. **Pets:** Accepted.

[ASK] [S🐾] [✕] [🔊] [🛏] [🛏] [🍴] [🏊]

◈◈◈ ▼▼◈▼ Best Western High Country Inn **M** ❀
(801) 394-9474. **$69-$79.** 1335 W 12th St. I-15, exit 347 (12th St), then e. Ext corridors. **Pets:** Other species. $25 deposit/room. Service with restrictions.

[SAVE] [S🐾] [✕] [🔊] [🛏] [💻] [🍴] [🏊]

▼▼◈▼ Comfort Suites of Ogden **H**
(801) 621-2545. **$72-$150.** 2250 S 1200 W. I-15, exit 346E. Int corridors. **Pets:** Accepted.

[SAVE] [S🐾] [✕] [🔊] [🛏] [🛏] [💻] [🍴] [🏊]

▼▼◈▼ Holiday Inn Express Hotel & Suites **M** ❀
(801) 392-5000. **$72-$150.** 2245 S 1200 W. I-15, exit 346E, just e of interstate. Int corridors. **Pets:** Large, other species. $50 deposit/room. Service with restrictions, supervision.

[ASK] [S🐾] [✕] [🛏] [💻] [🏊]

▼▼◈ Red Roof Inn **M**
(801) 627-2880. **$45-$72.** 1500 W Riverdale Rd. I-15, exit 343 southbound, 2 mi via Riverdale Rd; exit 342 northbound, 1 mi via Riverdale Rd. Ext/int corridors. **Pets:** Small, other species. Service with restrictions, supervision.

[ASK] [S🐾] [✕] [🛏] [🛏] [🏊]

▼▼◈ Sleep Inn of Ogden **M**
(801) 731-6500. **$65-$70, 10 days notice.** 1155 S 1700 W. I-15, exit 347, just w. Int corridors. **Pets:** Medium, other species. $10 daily fee/pet. Designated rooms, service with restrictions, supervision.

[SAVE] [S🐾] [✕] [🔊] [🛏] [🛏] [💻]

▼▼◈ Super 8 Motel **M** ❀
(801) 731-7100. **$42.** 1508 W 2100 South. I-15, exit 346, just w. Int corridors. **Pets:** Other species. $20 deposit/room. Service with restrictions, supervision.

[ASK] [S🐾] [✕] [🔊] [🛏]

▼▼◈ Travelodge-Ogden **M**
(801) 394-4563. **$49.** 2110 Washington Blvd. Downtown; cross street 21st St. Ext corridors. **Pets:** Accepted.

[ASK] [S🐾] [✕] [🔊] [🛏] [🛏] [💻] [🏊]

◈◈◈ ▼▼◈ Western Colony Inn **M**
(801) 627-1332. **$39-$47, 3 days notice.** 234 24th St. City center. Ext corridors. **Pets:** Small, dogs only. $10 deposit/pet, $10 one-time fee/pet. Service with restrictions, supervision.

[SAVE] [S🐾] [✕] [🛏]

OREM

Best Inn & Suites M
(801) 235-9555. **$59-$89.** 1100 W 780 N. I-15, exit 275, east side. Int corridors. **Pets:** Accepted.

La Quinta Inn & Suites M
(801) 226-0440. **$72-$91.** 521 W University Pkwy. I-15, exit 272, to 12th St S, 1 mi e. Int corridors. **Pets:** Accepted.

PANGUITCH

Adobe Sands Motel M
(435) 676-8874. **$35-$49.** 390 N Main St. Ext corridors. **Pets:** Small. $20 deposit/pet. Service with restrictions, supervision.

Bryce Junction Inn M
(435) 676-2221. **$29-$50.** 3068 E Hwy 12. 7 mi se on SR 12; 17 mi e of Bryce Canyon. Int corridors. **Pets:** Accepted.

Bryce Way Motel M
(435) 676-2400. **$35-$65.** 429 N Main St. On US 89. Ext corridors. **Pets:** Accepted.

Color Country Motel M
(435) 676-2386. **$35-$62.** 526 N Main St. On US 89. Ext corridors. **Pets:** Accepted.

Harolds Place Cabins C ❀
(435) 676-2350. **$45-$60.** 3066 Hwy 12. 7 mi se on SR 12; 17 mi e of Bryce Canyon. Ext corridors. **Pets:** Medium. $20 deposit/room. Designated rooms, service with restrictions.

Horizon Motel M
(435) 676-2651. **$29-$60.** 730 N Main St. US 89. Ext corridors. **Pets:** Small, dogs only. $10 one-time fee/room. Service with restrictions, supervision.

Marianna Inn Motel M ❀
(435) 676-8844. **$30-$75.** 699 N Main St. On US 89. Ext corridors. **Pets:** Dogs only. $5 daily fee/pet. Supervision.

PARK CITY

Best Western Landmark Inn M
(435) 649-7300. **$69-$169, 21 days notice.** 6560 N Landmark Dr. I-80, exit 145, 5 mi n of Park City at Kim Ball Jct. Int corridors. **Pets:** Accepted.

Holiday Inn Express Hotel & Suites M
(435) 658-1600. **$75-$269.** 1501 W Ute Blvd. I-80, exit 145, 5 mi n of Park City at Kim Ban jct. Int corridors. **Pets:** Large, other species. $50 deposit/room. Service with restrictions, supervision.

The Radisson Inn Park City MI
(435) 649-5000. **$129-$259, 30 days notice.** 2121 Park Ave. I-80, exit Kimball Junction, north end of town. Int corridors. **Pets:** Accepted.

PAROWAN

Days Inn M
(435) 477-3326. **$49-$85.** 625 W 200 S. I-15, exit 75, 1.5 mi e. Ext corridors. **Pets:** Accepted.

Swiss Village Inn M ❀
(435) 477-3391. **$49-$69, 10 days notice.** 580 N Main St. I-15, exit 78, just e. Ext corridors. **Pets:** Other species. $5 daily fee/pet. Service with restrictions, crate.

PAYSON

Comfort Inn M
(801) 465-4861. **$79-$130.** 830 N Main St. I-15, exit 254, just e. Int corridors. **Pets:** Other species. $20 deposit/room. Service with restrictions, supervision.

PRICE

Budget Host Inn M
(435) 637-2424. **$45-$55.** 145 N Carbonville Rd. US 6, exit 240, just e. Ext corridors. **Pets:** Accepted.

National 9-Price River Inn M
(435) 637-7000. **$39-$54.** 641 W Price River Dr. US 6, exit 240. Ext/int corridors. **Pets:** Medium. $50 deposit/pet, $5 daily fee/pet. Designated rooms, service with restrictions, supervision.

PROVO

Best Inn & Suites M
(801) 374-6020. **$59-$125, 3 days notice.** 1555 N Canyon Rd. I-15, exit 272, 3.5 mi e. Ext/int corridors. **Pets:** Accepted.

Colony Inn Suites-National 9 M
(801) 374-6800. **$45-$62.** 1380 S University Ave. I-15, exit 266. Ext corridors. **Pets:** Accepted.

▼▼▼ Days Inn M
(801) 375-8600. **$49-$99, 30 days notice.** 1675 N 200 W. I-15, exit 272, 3.5 mi e; at Village Green Square. Ext corridors. **Pets:** Accepted.
[SAVE] [S⬠] [✕] [⌖] [🌊] [▯] [💻] [⊃]

▼▼ Econo Lodge Provo Airport M
(801) 373-0099. **$39-$79.** 1625 W Center St. I-15, exit 268 southbound, exit 268B northbound, 0.3 mi w. Ext corridors. **Pets:** Medium, other species. $5 daily fee/pet. Service with restrictions, supervision.
[SAVE] [S⬠] [✕] [▯] [💻]

▼▼▼ Hampton Inn M
(801) 377-6396. **$69.** 1511 S 40 E. I-15, exit 266, just e. Int corridors. **Pets:** Medium. $7 daily fee/room. Service with restrictions, supervision.
[SAVE] [S⬠] [✕] [⌖] [🌊] [▯] [💻] [⊃]

▲▲▲ ▼▼ Provo Travelers Inn M
(801) 373-8248. **$39-$69.** 469 W Center St. I-15, exit 268A southbound; exit 268A northbound. Ext corridors. **Pets:** $5 daily fee/pet. Service with restrictions, supervision.
[SAVE] [S⬠] [✕] [▯] [⊃]

▲▲▲ ▼▼▼ Residence Inn by Marriott M ❀
(801) 374-1000. **$89-$125.** 252 W 2230 N. I-15, exit 272, 3.1 mi e via University Pkwy. Int corridors. **Pets:** Medium. $150 one-time fee/room. Service with restrictions.
[SAVE] [S⬠] [✕] [⬛M] [⌖] [🌊] [▯] [💻] [⊃]

▼▼ Sleep Inn M
(801) 377-6597. **$50-$80.** 1505 S 40 E. I-15, exit 266, just e. Int corridors. **Pets:** $7 one-time fee/room. Service with restrictions, supervision.
[SAVE] [S⬠] [✕] [⌖] [🌊] [▯] [💻]

RICHFIELD

▲▲▲ ▼▼▼ Best Western AppleTree Inn M
(435) 896-5481. **$49-$79.** 145 S Main St. I-70, exit 37 or 40, just s on US 89. Ext corridors. **Pets:** Large, other species. $6 daily fee/room. Supervision.
[SAVE] [S⬠] [✕] [⌖] [▯] [💻] [⊃]

▲▲▲ ▼▼▼ Budget Host Nights Inn M!
(435) 896-8228. **$36-$56.** 69 S Main St. I-70, exit 37 or 40, just s on US 89. Ext corridors. **Pets:** Accepted.
[SAVE] [S⬠] [✕] [▯] [🍴] [⊃]

▼▼▼ Comfort Inn M
(435) 893-0119. **$85-$105.** 1150 W 1250 S. I-70, exit 37. Int corridors. **Pets:** Small, dogs only. $20 deposit/room. Service with restrictions, supervision.
[SAVE] [S⬠] [✕] [▯] [💻] [⊃]

▲▲▲ ▼▼▼ Days Inn M!
(435) 896-6476. **$55-$89.** 333 N Main St. I-70, exit 40, just s on US 89. Int corridors. **Pets:** Small. $50 deposit/room. Designated rooms, service with restrictions, supervision.
[SAVE] [S⬠] [✕] [▯] [💻] [🍴] [⊃]

▲▲▲ ▼▼▼ Luxury Inn M
(435) 893-0100. **$39-$79.** 1335 N Main St. North end of town. Int corridors. **Pets:** Accepted.
[SAVE] [S⬠] [✕] [🌊] [▯] [⊃]

▼▼ New West Motel M
(435) 896-4076. **$34-$38.** 447 S Main St. I-70, exit 37 or 40, just s on US 89. Ext corridors. **Pets:** Accepted.
[ASK] [✕]

▼▼▼ Richfield Travelodge M!
(435) 896-9271. **$52-$90, 5 days notice.** 647 S Main St. South end of town. Int corridors. **Pets:** Small. $5 daily fee/room. Designated rooms, service with restrictions, supervision.
[ASK] [S⬠] [✕] [▯] [💻] [🍴] [⊃]

▲▲▲ ▼▼▼ Romanico Inn M
(435) 896-8471. **$34-$48.** 1170 S Main St. I-70, exit 37, just s. Ext corridors. **Pets:** Accepted.
[SAVE] [S⬠] [✕] [▯]

ROOSEVELT

▲▲▲ ▼▼▼ Frontier Motel M!
(435) 722-2201. **$45-$55.** 75 S 200 E. US 40. Ext corridors. **Pets:** Accepted.
[SAVE] [S⬠] [✕] [▯] [🍴] [⊃]

▲▲▲ ▼▼▼ Western Hills Motel M
(435) 722-5115. **$35-$60, 3 days notice.** 737 E 200 N. Ext corridors. **Pets:** Other species. $5 daily fee/pet. Supervision.
[SAVE] [S⬠] [✕] [▯]

SALINA

▲▲▲ ▼▼▼ Henry's Hideway M
(435) 529-7467. **$51-$60.** 60 N State St. I-70, exit 54, 2.5 mi n on US 89. Ext corridors. **Pets:** Accepted.
[SAVE] [✕] [▯] [💻] [⊃]

▼▼ Ranch Motel M
(435) 529-7789. **$38-$52.** 80 N State St. On US 89; near town center. Ext/int corridors. **Pets:** Accepted.
[ASK] [S⬠] [✕] [▯]

▼▼▼ Scenic Hills Super 8 M
(435) 529-7483. **$54-$62.** 75 E 1500 S. I-70, exit 54. Ext corridors. **Pets:** Accepted.
[✕] [▯] [⊃]

SALT LAKE CITY METROPOLITAN AREA

DRAPER

▼▼▼ Ramada Ltd M
(801) 571-1122. **$65-$119.** 12605 S Minuteman Dr. I-15, exit 294, 0.3 mi s is on Frontage Rd. Int corridors. **Pets:** Very small. $25 deposit/room. Designated rooms, service with restrictions, supervision.

⊠ 🐾 💺 🛑

▼▼▼▼ Travelodge Metropolitan Salt Lake M
(801) 572-1200. **$64.** 12117 S Factory Outlet Dr. I-15, exit 294, just ne. Int corridors. **Pets:** Accepted.

A$K 🐾 ⊠ 💺 🛑 💻 ≈

MIDVALE

◆◆◆ ▼▼▼▼ Best Western Executive Inn M
(801) 566-4141. **$69-$89, 3 days notice.** 280 W 7200 S. I-15, exit 301, just e. Int corridors. **Pets:** Other species. $15 daily fee/room. Service with restrictions, supervision.

SAVE 🐾 ⊠ 🐾 🛑 💻 ≈

◆◆◆ ▼▼▼▼ Discovery Inn M
(801) 561-2256. **$45-$74.** 380 W 7200 S. I-15, exit 301, just e. Ext corridors. **Pets:** Accepted.

SAVE ⊠ 🐾 🛑 💻 ≈

▼▼▼ Homewood Suites by Hilton H
(801) 561-5999. **$107-$180.** 844 E N Union Ave. I-15, exit 301, 1.5 mi e on 7200 S. Int corridors. **Pets:** Small. $75 one-time fee/room. Designated rooms, service with restrictions, crate.

SAVE 🐾 ⊠ 🐾 🐾 💺 🛑 💻 ≈

◆◆◆ ▼▼▼▼ La Quinta Inn M
(801) 566-3291. **$72-$82.** 7231 S Catalpa St. I-15, exit 301, just e. Int corridors. **Pets:** Accepted.

SAVE 🐾 ⊠ 🐾 💺 🛑 💻 ≈

MURRAY

◆◆◆ ▼▼▼▼ Quality Inn-Midvalley M
(801) 268-2533. **$60-$90.** 4465 S Century Dr. I-15, exit 304, just w. Int corridors. **Pets:** Other species. Service with restrictions.

SAVE 🐾 ⊠ 🐾 🛑 💻 ≈

▼▼▼ Reston Hotel MI
(801) 264-1054. **$71-$79.** 5335 College Dr. I-15, exit 303, 0.3 mi w. Int corridors. **Pets:** Other species. $30 one-time fee/room. Supervision.

A$K 🐾 ⊠ 🐾 🛑 ≈

▼▼▼ Studio 6 M
(801) 685-2102. **$47-$66.** 975 E 6600 S. I-215, exit 9, on 900 E, 0.5 mi. Ext corridors. **Pets:** Accepted.

A$K ⊠ 🐾 💺 🛑 💻

NORTH SALT LAKE

◆◆◆ ▼▼▼▼ Best Western Cotton Tree Inn M
(801) 292-7666. **$72-$139.** 1030 N 400E. I-15, exit 318, 10 mi n. Int corridors. **Pets:** Small. $25 deposit/room. Service with restrictions, crate.

SAVE 🐾 ⊠ 🐾 🛑 💻 ≈

SALT LAKE CITY

▼▼▼ Alpine Executive Suites A
(801) 533-8184. **$109, 30 days notice.** 150 S 900 E. Cross streets 200 S and 900 E. Int corridors. **Pets:** Medium, dogs only. $300 deposit/pet, $15 daily fee/pet. Service with restrictions, supervision.

A$K 🐾 ⊠ 🛑 💻

◆◆◆ ▼▼▼▼ Best Western Salt Lake Plaza H
(801) 521-0130. **$69-$129, 3 days notice.** 122 W S Temple. Downtown; w of Temple Square. Int corridors. **Pets:** Accepted.

SAVE 🐾 ⊠ 🐾 🛑 💻 🍴 ≈

▼▼▼▼ Chase Suite Hotel by Woodfin M
(801) 532-5511. **$99-$119.** 765 East 400 S. Ext corridors. **Pets:** Small. $50 deposit/room, $5 daily fee/room. Service with restrictions, crate.

A$K 🐾 ⊠ 🐾 💺 🛑 💻 ≈

◆◆◆ ▼▼▼ City Creek Inn M
(801) 533-9100. **$48-$74.** 230 W N Temple Dr. Downtown; cross street 200 W. Ext corridors. **Pets:** Accepted.

SAVE 🐾 ⊠ 💺

◆◆◆ ▼▼▼▼ Comfort Inn-Salt Lake City International Airport MI
(801) 537-7444. **$66-$90.** 200 N Admiral Byrd Rd. I-80, exit 113, 0.8 mi ne via 5600 W, Amelia Earhart, then s. Int corridors. **Pets:** Large, other species. $15 one-time fee/room. Service with restrictions, crate.

SAVE 🐾 ⊠ 🐾 🛑 💻 🍴 ≈

▼▼▼▼ Days Inn-Salt Lake City Airport M
(801) 539-8538. **$59-$109.** 1900W N Temple. Just w of Temple Sqare, 2.5 mi. Int corridors. **Pets:** Other species. $20 deposit/room. Designated rooms, service with restrictions, supervision.

SAVE 🐾 ⊠ 🐾 💺 🛑 💻 ≈

▼▼▼ Econo Lodge M
(801) 363-0062. **$49-$59.** 715 W N Temple. W from Temple Square, 2 mi. Ext corridors. **Pets:** Accepted.

SAVE 🐾 ⊠ 🐾 🛑 💻

Hilton Salt Lake City Airport M
(801) 539-1515. **$89-$189.** 5151 Wiley Post Way. I-80, exit 114 westbound, 0.4 mi nw via Wright Brothers and Wiley Post; exit 113 eastbound, 1.3 mi ne via 5600 W, Amelia Earhart then s on Charles Lindbergh Dr. Int corridors. **Pets:** $50 deposit/room. Service with restrictions, supervision.

Homestead Studio Suites-Salt Lake City/ Sugar House M
(801) 474-0771. **$74-$94.** 1220 E 2100 S. Cross streets 1300 E and 2100 S Sugarhouse. Ext corridors. **Pets:** Medium. $75 one-time fee/room. Designated rooms, service with restrictions, crate.

Hotel Monaco H
(801) 595-0000. **$199.** 15 W 200 S. Downtown; cross streets 200 S and Main St. Int corridors. **Pets:** Accepted.

Howard Johnson Express Inn M
(801) 521-3450. **$59-$79.** 121 N 300 W. At North Temple. Ext/int corridors. **Pets:** Medium. Designated rooms, service with restrictions, crate.

La Quinta Inn & Suites Salt Lake City Airport M
(801) 366-4444. **$52-$120.** 4905 W Wiley Post Way. I-80, exit 113 eastbound, 2 mi ne via 5600 W, Amelia Earhart Dr then s on Wright Brothers Dr, 2 mi to Wiley Post Way; exit 114 westbound, 0.3 mi nw. Int corridors. **Pets:** Medium, other species. Service with restrictions, crate.

Microtel Inn & Suites M
(801) 236-2800. **$68-$88.** 61 N Tommy Thompson Rd. I-80, exit 114 westbound, n on Wright Brothers Dr, e on Wiley Post; exit 113 eastbound, 2.4 mi ne via 5600 W, Amelia Earhard Dr, then s. Int corridors. **Pets:** Medium. $10 one-time fee/room. Service with restrictions, crate.

Quality Inn City Center MI
(801) 521-2930. **$59-$69.** 154 W 600 S. Between 100-200 W. Ext/int corridors. **Pets:** $50 deposit/pet. Service with restrictions.

Ramada Inn Downtown MI
(801) 364-5200. **$49-$59.** 230 W 600 S. Ext/int corridors. **Pets:** Small, other species. $10 one-time fee/pet. Service with restrictions, supervision.

Red Brick Inn BB
(801) 322-4917. **$60-$120, 7 days notice.** 1030 E 100 S. East side of town, cross street McClelland. Int corridors. **Pets:** Accepted.

Residence Inn by Marriott at The Cottonwoods M
(801) 453-0430. **$109-$135.** 6425 S 3000 E. I-215 S, exit 6200 S, 0.3 mi se to 3000 E. Int corridors. **Pets:** Accepted.

Residence Inn by Marriott Salt Lake City Airport M
(801) 532-4101. **$98-$149.** 4883 W Douglas Corrigon Way. I-80, exit 114 westbound, via Wright Brothers Dr; exit 113 eastbound, via Amelia Earhart and Wright Brothers Dr, just se 2.6 mi. Int corridors. **Pets:** Small. $10 daily fee/pet, $50 one-time fee/pet. Service with restrictions, crate.

Saltair Bed & Breakfast BB
(801) 533-8184. **$79-$129, 30 days notice.** 164 S 900 East. Cross streets 900 E and 200 S. Ext/int corridors. **Pets:** Medium, dogs only. $300 deposit/pet, $15 daily fee/ pet. Designated rooms, service with restrictions, supervision.

Salt Lake City Centre Travelodge M
(801) 531-7100. **$48-$75.** 524 S W Temple. Cross streets 500 S and Temple. Ext corridors. **Pets:** $10 daily fee/pet. Service with restrictions, supervision.

Salt Lake Travelodge At Temple Square M
(801) 533-8200. **$50-$80, 14 days notice.** 144 W N Temple. Just n of Genealogical Library. Ext/int corridors. **Pets:** Other species. Designated rooms, crate.

The Skyline Inn M
(801) 582-5350. **$59-$79.** 2475 E 1700 S. E off Foothill Dr, at 1700 S. Ext corridors. **Pets:** Accepted.

Sugar House Village-All Suites Inn M ❀
(801) 486-9976. **$124-$158, 3 days notice.** 1339 E 2100 S. Cross street 1400 E. Ext/int corridors. **Pets:** Medium, dogs only. $100 deposit/room. Designated rooms, service with restrictions, crate.

Super 8 Airport M ❀
(801) 533-8878. **$62-$95.** 223 N Jimmy Doolittle Rd. I-80, exit 113, 0.7 mi ne via 5600 W, Amelia Earhart Dr and Admiral Byrd Rd, then e. Int corridors. **Pets:** Other species. $50 deposit/room. Service with restrictions, supervision.

Super 8 Motel M
(801) 534-0808. **$46-$56, 14 days notice.** 616 S 200 West. Int corridors. **Pets:** Accepted.

SANDY

Best Western Cotton Tree Inn M
(801) 523-8484. **$85-$95.** 10695 S Auto Mall Dr. I-15, exit 297E, 0.3 mi e. Int corridors. **Pets:** Accepted.

Comfort Inn M
(801) 255-4919. **$65.** 8955 S 255 West. I-15, exit 298, just e via 150 W (Monrow St) and 2930 S (Harrison). Int corridors. **Pets:** Medium. $10 one-time fee/pet. Service with restrictions, supervision.

Quality Inn & Suites M
(801) 495-1317. **$89-$109, 14 days notice.** 10680 S Auto Mall Dr. I-15, exit 297E, 0.3 mi e. Int corridors. **Pets:** Medium, other species. $10 daily fee/room. Service with restrictions, supervision.

Residence Inn by Marriott M
(801) 561-5005. **$98-$152, 7 days notice.** 270 W 10000 S. W from Stare St, 0.3 mi on 10000 S. Int corridors. **Pets:** $150 one-time fee/pet. Service with restrictions, crate.

Super 8 Motel-South Jordan M
(801) 553-8888. **$50-$79.** 10722 S 300 W. 1 mi w on 106th to Jordan Gate Way, then s to Frontage Rd, n on Frontage Rd (300 W). Int corridors. **Pets:** Other species. $50 deposit/room. Designated rooms, service with restrictions, supervision.

SOUTH SALT LAKE

Days Inn-Central M
(801) 486-8780. **$59-$79.** 315 W 3300 S. W from State St, 0.3 mi. Ext corridors. **Pets:** Accepted.

TAYLORSVILLE

Homestead Studio Suites Hotel M
(801) 269-9292. **$59-$69.** 5683 S Redwood Rd. I-215, exit 13N, 0.5 mi n. Ext corridors. **Pets:** Small. $75 one-time fee/pet. Service with restrictions, supervision.

WEST JORDAN

River Oaks Apartments & Suites A
(801) 352-0900. **$99-$200.** 9035 S 1075 W. I-15, exit 298, 1.3 mi w via 90th S. Int corridors. **Pets:** Accepted.

WEST VALLEY CITY

Baymont Inn & Suites Salt Lake City-West Valley City M
(801) 886-1300. **$74-$84.** 2229 W City Center Ct. I-215, exit 18, just e. Int corridors. **Pets:** Small, other species. $25 deposit/room. Service with restrictions, supervision.

Hawthorn Inn & Suites M
(801) 954-9292. **$69-$89.** 3540 S 2200 W. I-215, exit 18, east side. Int corridors. **Pets:** Accepted.

Parkway Suites M
(801) 977-0800. **$45-$180.** 3580 W Parkway Blvd. Cross streets 2700 S and 3600 W. Ext corridors. **Pets:** Accepted.

Sleep Inn M
(801) 975-1888. **$55.** 3440 S 2200 W. I-215, exit 18, just e. Int corridors. **Pets:** Medium. $6 one-time fee/room. Designated rooms, service with restrictions, supervision.

WOODS CROSS

Hampton Inn M
(801) 296-1211. **$64-$84.** 2393 S 800 W. I-15, exit 318 W, just w of freeway. Int corridors. **Pets:** Service with restrictions, supervision.

❖ **END METROPOLITAN AREA** ❖

SPANISH FORK

Western Inn M
(801) 798-9400. **$55-$65.** 632 Kirby Ln. I-15, exit 261 southbound, 0.5 mi e; exit 260 northbound, 1 mi ne. Int corridors. **Pets:** Other species. $10 one-time fee/room. Service with restrictions, supervision.

SPRINGDALE

Best Western Zion Park Inn MI
(435) 772-3200. **$62-$109, 3 days notice.** 1215 Zion Park Blvd. 2 mi s of Zion National Park entrance. Int corridors. **Pets:** Medium. $25 one-time fee/room. Designated rooms, service with restrictions, supervision.

◆◆◆◆ Canyon Ranch Motel 🅲
(435) 772-3357. **$40-$88.** 668 Zion Park Blvd. SR 9, just s of south gate to Zion National Park. Ext corridors. **Pets:** $10 daily fee/pet. Service with restrictions, supervision.

⊠ 📧 🌣

ⒶⒶⒶ ◆◆◆ Driftwood Lodge Ⓜ
(435) 772-3262. **$62-$102.** 1515 Zion Park Blvd. SR 9, 2 mi s of south gate to Zion National Park. Ext corridors. **Pets:** Accepted.

ⓢⒶⓋⒺ 🆂 ⊠ 🍽 🌣

SPRINGVILLE

ⒶⒶⒶ ◆◆◆ Best Western CottonTree Inn Ⓜ
(801) 489-3641. **$55-$95.** 1455 N 1750 W. I-15, exit 265, just e, just s of Provo. Int corridors. **Pets:** $10 one-time fee/room. Service with restrictions, supervision.

ⓢⒶⓋⒺ 🆂 ⊠ ⓐ 🅱 🖥 🌣

◆◆◆ Days Inn Ⓜ
(801) 491-0300. **$59-$69.** 520 S 2000 W. I-15, exit 263. Int corridors. **Pets:** Accepted.

ⓈⒶⓋⒺ 🆂 ⊠ 🅱 🌣

ST. GEORGE

◆◆ Ambassador Inn Ⓜ
(435) 673-7900. **$43-$70.** 1481 S Sunland Dr. I-15, exit 6. Int corridors. **Pets:** Accepted.

ⒶⓈⓀ ⊠ ⓐ 🅱 🖥 🌣

◆◆◆ An Olde Penny Farthing Inn Bed & Breakfast Ⓑ Ⓑ
(435) 673-7755. **$60-$125, 3 days notice.** 278 N 100 W. Historical district. Int corridors. **Pets:** Accepted.

⊠ 🅱 ⓩ

ⒶⒶⒶ ◆◆◆ Atkin's Singletree Inn Ⓜ
(435) 673-6161. **$40-$58.** 260 E St George Blvd. I-15, exit 8, 1.5 mi w. Ext corridors. **Pets:** Other species. $50 deposit/room, $5 daily fee/room. Designated rooms, service with restrictions, supervision.

ⓈⒶⓋⒺ 🆂 ⊠ 🅱 🌣

◆◆ The Bluffs Inn & Suites Ⓜ
(435) 628-6699. **$50-$85.** 1140 S Bluff. I-15, exit 6 (Bluff St), just w. Ext corridors. **Pets:** Small, other species. $15 daily fee/pet. Designated rooms, service with restrictions, crate.

ⒶⓈⓀ 🆂 ⊠ 🅱 🌣

◆◆◆ Budget Inn & Suites Ⓜ
(435) 673-6661. **$50-$120.** 1221 S Main St. I-15, exit 6 (Bluff St), just w. Ext corridors. **Pets:** Accepted.

ⒶⓈⓀ 🆂 ⊠ 🅱 🖥 🌣

◆ Chalet Motel Ⓜ
(435) 628-6272. **$33-$40.** 664 E St George Blvd. I-15, exit 8, 0.3 mi w. Ext corridors. **Pets:** Accepted.

ⒶⓈⓀ 🆂 ⊠ 🅱 🌣

ⒶⒶⒶ ◆◆◆ ◆◆◆ The Coyote Inn at Green Valley Spa Ⓡ ❀
(435) 628-8060. **$550-$1150, 30 days notice.** 1871 W Canyon View Dr. From Bluff at S Main sts, 4 mi sw via Hilton Dr to Tonaquint Dr via Dixie Dr. Ext corridors. **Pets:** Small, dogs only. $500 deposit/room, $25 daily fee/pet. Service with restrictions, crate.

ⓈⒶⓋⒺ ⊠ 🆂 🅱 🖥 🌣 🕱

ⒶⒶⒶ ◆◆◆ Days Inn Ⓜ
(435) 673-6123. **$49-$99, 3 days notice.** 150 N 1000 E. I-15, exit 8, just w. Ext corridors. **Pets:** Medium. $5 daily fee/pet. Designated rooms, service with restrictions, supervision.

ⓈⒶⓋⒺ 🆂 ⊠ 🅱 🌣

◆◆ Econo Lodge Ⓜ Ⓘ
(435) 673-4861. **$40-$120.** 460 E St George Blvd. Downtown; cross streets 500 E and St George Blvd. Ext corridors. **Pets:** Accepted.

ⓈⒶⓋⒺ 🆂 ⊠ ⓐ 🆂 🅱 🖥 🍽 🌣

◆◆◆ Four Points by Sheraton St. George Ⓜ Ⓘ
(435) 628-0463. **$72-$124.** 1450 S Hilton Dr. I-15, exit 6, just w. Int corridors. **Pets:** Accepted.

ⒶⓈⓀ ⊠ ⓐ 🅱 🖥 🍽 🌣

◆◆◆ Holiday Inn/Holidome Ⓜ Ⓘ
(435) 628-4235. **$69-$99.** 850 S Bluff St. I-15, exit 6, just w. Ext/int corridors. **Pets:** Accepted.

ⒶⓈⓀ 🆂 ⊠ ⓐ 🆂 🅱 🖥 🍽 🌣 🕱

ⒶⒶⒶ ◆◆◆ Red Cliffs Inn & Suites Ⓜ Ⓘ
(435) 673-3537. **$44-$99.** 912 Red Cliffs Dr. I-15, exit 10, just e. Ext/int corridors. **Pets:** Accepted.

ⓈⒶⓋⒺ 🆂 ⊠ ⓐ 🆂 🅱 🖥 🍽 🌣

◆◆ Sunbird Inn Ⓜ
(435) 628-9000. **$45-$59, 14 days notice.** 750 E St George Blvd. Ext corridors. **Pets:** Accepted.

ⒶⓈⓀ ⊠ 🅱 🌣

◆◆ Suntime Inn Ⓜ
(435) 673-6181. **$40-$120.** 420 E St George Blvd. Downtown; cross streets 400 E and St George Blvd. Ext corridors. **Pets:** Accepted.

ⒶⓈⓀ 🆂 ⊠ 🅱 🌣

◆◆ Super 8 Motel Ⓜ
(435) 688-8383. **$35-$79.** 915 S Bluff. I-15, exit 6 (Bluff St), just w. Int corridors. **Pets:** Small. $10 daily fee/pet. Designated rooms, service with restrictions, supervision.

🆂 ⊠ 🌣

ⒶⒶⒶ ◆◆◆ Travelodge East Ⓜ
(435) 673-4621. **$36-$99, 14 days notice.** 175 N 1000 E. I-15, exit 8, just w. Ext corridors. **Pets:** $5 daily fee/pet. Service with restrictions, supervision.

ⓈⒶⓋⒺ 🆂 ⊠ 🅱 🖥 🌣

TICABOO

AAA ▼▼ Ticaboo Resort **M**
(435) 788-2110. **$49-$95.** 84533 Hwy 276. Jct SR 95 and 276, 28 mi s. Int corridors. **Pets:** $100 deposit/room. Supervision.
[SAVE] [✕] [◥] [⇌]

TORREY

▼▼ Cactus Hill Motel **M**
(435) 425-3578. **$45, 7 days notice.** 830 S 1000 E. 5 mi s of SR 24 at Teasdale; 5 mi w of SR 12, exit Teasdale; 13 mi w of Capitol Reef National Park, 2 mi se of Town Center. Ext corridors. **Pets:** Accepted.
[✕] [📶]

▼▼ Rim Rock Inn **MI**
(435) 425-3398. **$39-$59.** 2523 E Hwy 24. East end of town, 2.5 mi e of jct SR 12 and 24. Ext corridors. **Pets:** Accepted.
[ASK] [S🄳] [✕] [◥]

TREMONTON

AAA ▼▼ Sandman Motel **M**
(435) 257-5675. **$51-$59.** 585 W Main. I-15/84, exit 383. Ext corridors. **Pets:** Other species. $20 deposit/pet. Designated rooms, service with restrictions, supervision.
[SAVE] [S🄳] [✕]

TROPIC

▼ Doug's Country Inn Motel **MI**
(435) 679-8632. **$35-$50.** 141 N Main St. Center; on SR 12. Int corridors. **Pets:** Other species. $10 daily fee/pet. Service with restrictions, supervision.
[ASK] [S🄳] [✕] [◥]

AAA ▼▼ World Host Bryce Valley Inn **M**
(435) 679-8811. **$35-$70.** 199 N Main St. SR 12; 10 mi e of Bryce Canyon Park. Ext/int corridors. **Pets:** Large, other species. $10 daily fee/pet. Service with restrictions, crate.
[SAVE] [S🄳] [✕] [◥]

VERNAL

AAA ▼▼ Econolodge **M**
(435) 789-2000. **$40-$58, 7 days notice.** 311 E Main St. Ext corridors. **Pets:** Very small, other species. $5 daily fee/pet. Service with restrictions, supervision.
[SAVE] [S🄳] [✕] [♿] [📶] [▣]

▼▼ Motel 6 **M**
(435) 789-0666. **$56, 7 days notice.** 1092 W Hwy 40. Int corridors. **Pets:** Small. $5 daily fee/pet. Service with restrictions, supervision.
[ASK] [S🄳] [✕] [♫] [♿] [📶] [⇌]

▼▼ Rodeway Inn **MI**
(435) 789-8172. **$40-$69.** 590 W Main St. US 40. Ext corridors. **Pets:** Other species. $5 one-time fee/room. Service with restrictions, supervision.
[SAVE] [S🄳] [✕] [📶] [▣] [◥]

▼ Sage Motel & Restaurant **MI**
(435) 789-1442. **$37-$70.** 54 W Main. Center. Ext corridors. **Pets:** Other species. $5 daily fee/pet. Designated rooms, service with restrictions.
[✕] [📶] [◥]

WELLINGTON

▼▼ National 9 Inn **MI**
(435) 637-7980. **$39-$54.** 50 S 700 E. US 6. Ext/int corridors. **Pets:** Accepted.
[ASK] [S🄳] [✕] [📶] [◥] [⇌]

WENDOVER

▼▼▼ Days Inn of Wendover **M**
(435) 665-2215. **$49-$99.** 685 E Wendover Blvd. I-80, exit 2; in town. Int corridors. **Pets:** Accepted.
[SAVE] [✕] [♫] [♿] [📶] [⇌]

▼▼▼ Econo Lodge **M**
(435) 665-2226. **$39-$99.** 295 E Wendover Blvd. I-80, exit 2; in town. Ext/int corridors. **Pets:** Accepted.
[SAVE] [S🄳] [✕] [⇌]

VERMONT

ALBURG

◆◆ The Ransom Bay Inn BB
(802) 796-3399. $75. 4 Center Bay Rd. Jct SR 78 and US
2 E, 0.5 mi s, then 4 mi s. Int corridors. Pets: Accepted.
✕ 🎨 🗾 🖾

BARRE

AAA ◆◆◆ The Hollow Inn & Motel M
(802) 479-9313. $70-$145. 278 S Main St. Jct US 302, 1 mi
s on SR 14; I-89, exit 6, 4.3 mi e on SR 63, 0.7 mi n on SR
14. Ext/int corridors. Pets: Accepted.
SAVE S☉ 🖥 🖵 🖾

BENNINGTON

AAA ◆◆ Apple Valley Inn & Cafe MI
(802) 442-6588. $39-$85, 3 days notice. Jct SR 9, 2 mi s
on US 7. Ext/int corridors. Pets: Service with restrictions.
SAVE S☉ ✕ 🖥 🍴 🖾

AAA ◆◆◆ Bennington Motor Inn M
(802) 442-5479. $62-$102, 10 days notice. 143 W Main St
(SR 9). Jct US 7, 0.3 mi w. Ext corridors. Pets: Medium.
$20 daily fee/room. Designated rooms, service with restric-
tions, supervision.
SAVE S☉ ✕ 🖥 🖵

AAA ◆◆◆ Darling Kelly's Motel M
(802) 442-2322. $43-$102, 3 days notice. 357 US 7 S. 1.3
mi s of SR 9. Ext corridors. Pets: Dogs only. Designated
rooms, service with restrictions, supervision.
SAVE ✕ 🖥 🖾

AAA ◆◆◆ Fife 'N Drum Motel M
(802) 442-4074. $46-$108, 3 days notice. 693 US Rt 7 S.
Jct SR 9, 1.5 mi s. Ext corridors. Pets: Small, dogs only. $6
daily fee/pet. Designated rooms, service with restrictions,
supervision.
SAVE S☉ ✕ 🖥 🖵 🖾

◆◆ Knotty Pine Motel M
(802) 442-5487. $47-$89. 130 Northside Dr (SR 7A). Jct
SR 9, 1.2 mi n on US 7, then just n on Historic SR 7A. Ext
corridors. Pets: Medium, other species. Service with restrictions, supervision.
✕ 🖥 🖵 🖾

AAA ◆◆ South Gate Motel M ☙
(802) 447-7525. $44-$99, 3 days notice. 767 US 7 S. 1.5
mi s of jct SR 9. Ext corridors. Pets: $8 daily fee/pet.
Designated rooms, service with restrictions, supervision.
SAVE ✕ 🖥 🖾

BRATTLEBORO

AAA ◆◆◆ Colonial Motel & Spa MI ☙
(802) 257-7733. $69-$90. 889 Putney Rd (US 5). I-91, exit
3, 0.5 mi s on US 5. Ext corridors. Pets: Other species. $10
daily fee/pet. Service with restrictions, supervision.
SAVE S☉ ✕ 🖥 🍴 🖾

CAVENDISH

AAA ◆◆◆◆ Clarion Hotel at Cavendish
Pointe MI
(802) 226-7688. $89-$259, 14 days notice. SR 103. Jct
SR 103 and 131. Int corridors. Pets: $20 daily fee/room.
Supervision.
SAVE S☉ ✕ 🖥 🍴 🖾

CHESTER

◆◆ The Stone Hearth Inn CI ☙
(802) 875-2525. $89-$159, 14 days notice. 698 Rt 11 W. 1
mi w. Int corridors. Pets: Medium. $100 deposit/room, $50
one-time fee/room. Designated rooms, service with restrictions, supervision.
S☉ ✕ 🍴 🗾 🖾

COLCHESTER

◆◆ Days Inn M
(802) 655-0900. $50-$140. 23 College Pkwy. I-89, exit 15,
0.3 mi e on SR 15. Int corridors. Pets: Dogs only. $10 daily
fee/pet. Designated rooms, service with restrictions, crate.
SAVE S☉ ✕ 🖥 🖾

◆◆◆ Hampton Inn & Conference Center MI
(802) 655-6177. $84-$104, 3 days notice. 42 Lower Mountain View Dr. I-89, exit 16. Int corridors. Pets: Accepted.
SAVE S☉ ✕ 🐾 🖼 🖥 🖵 🖾

◆◆ Motel 6–1407 M
(802) 654-6860. $46-$78. 74 South Park Dr. I-89, exit 16,
just sw. Int corridors. Pets: Other species. Crate.
✕ 🔥M 🐾 🖼 🖥 🖾

CRAFTSBURY COMMON

▼▼▼▼ The Inn on the Common **CI**
(802) 586-9619. **$250-$310, 14 days notice.** 1162 N Craftsbury Rd. Center of village. Int corridors. **Pets:** Other species. $15 one-time fee/pet.
⊠ ▣ ¶¶ ➔ ⊠ ⬚ ⷞ ⓩ

ESSEX JUNCTION

▼▼▼ The Wilson Inn **M**
(802) 879-1515. **$94-$219.** 10 Kellogg Rd. I-89, exit 15, 2.1 mi e on SR 15, 0.5 mi n on Susie Wilson Rd, just w. Int corridors. **Pets:** Accepted.
ASK S⬚ ⊠ ⬚ ▣ ➔

FAIRLEE

▼▼ Silver Maple Lodge & Cottages **BB**
(802) 333-4326. **$59-$79, 14 days notice.** 520 US 55 S. I-91, exit 15, 0.5 mi s. Ext/int corridors. **Pets:** Other species. Designated rooms.
S⬚ ⊠ ⬚ ▣ ⓩ

FLETCHER

▼▼▼ The Inn at Buck Hollow Farm **BB**
(802) 849-2400. **$73-$93, 14 days notice.** 2150 Buck Hollow Rd. 6.1 mi n off SR 104. Int corridors. **Pets:** Other species.
ASK S⬚ ⊠ ➔ ⊠ ⓩ

JAMAICA

⚑ ▼▼▼ Three Mountain Inn **CI**
(802) 874-4140. **$125-$275, 10 days notice.** Rt 30. Center; on SR 30. Ext/int corridors. **Pets:** Dogs only. $75 deposit/room. Designated rooms, service with restrictions, supervision.
SAVE ⊠ ¶¶ ➔

JEFFERSONVILLE

⚑ ▼▼ Deer Run Motor Inn **M**
(802) 644-8866. **$85, 15 days notice.** 80 Deer Run Loop. 0.5 mi e on SR 15. Ext/int corridors. **Pets:** Medium. $10 daily fee/pet. Service with restrictions, supervision.
SAVE ⊠ ⬚ ▣ ➔

KILLINGTON

⚑ ▼▼▼ Butternut on the Mountain **M**
(802) 422-2000. **$75-$300, 30 days notice.** 63 Weathervane Rd. 1 mi s on Killington access road from US 4. Ext/int corridors. **Pets:** Accepted.
SAVE ⊠ ⬚ ▣ ¶¶ ➔

⚑ ▼▼▼ The Cascades Lodge **M**
(802) 422-3731. **$79-$229, 21 days notice.** 58 Old Mill Rd. 3.5 mi off US 4 on Killington Rd. Int corridors. **Pets:** Other species. $10 daily fee/room. Designated rooms, supervision.
SAVE S⬚ ⊠ ⬚ ⬚ ▣ ¶¶ ➔

⚑ ▼▼▼ Val Roc Motel **M**
(802) 422-3881. **$56-$130, 14 days notice.** 8006 US 4. Jct SR 100 S, 0.3 mi w. Ext/int corridors. **Pets:** Accepted.
SAVE S⬚ ⊠ ⬚

LOWER WATERFORD

⚑ ▼▼▼ ▼▼▼ Rabbit Hill Inn **CI**
(802) 748-5168. **$290-$460, 30 days notice.** Lower Waterford Rd. Village Center; I-93, exit 44 northbound, 2 mi n on SR 18; exit 1 southbound, 7 mi s. Ext/int corridors. **Pets:** Accepted.
SAVE ⊠ ⬚ ▣ ¶¶ ⊠ ⬚ ⓩ

LUDLOW

⚑ ▼▼▼ Timber Inn Motel **M**
(802) 228-8666. **$69-$199, 14 days notice.** 112 Rt 103 S. 1 mi e. Ext corridors. **Pets:** Accepted.
SAVE ⊠ ⬚ ➔

MENDON

▼▼▼ Cortina Inn and Resort **M** ❀
(802) 773-3333. **$124-$219.** 103 US 4. Jct SR 100 N, 3 mi w. Int corridors. **Pets:** Other species. $5 daily fee/pet. Designated rooms, service with restrictions, supervision.
ASK S⬚ ⊠ ⬚M ⬚ ▣ ¶¶ ⊠

⚑ ▼▼▼ Econo Lodge-Killington Area **M**
(802) 773-6644. **$44-$125, 7 days notice.** 51 US 4. Jct US 7, 5.3 mi e. Int corridors. **Pets:** Medium, other species. $5 daily fee/pet. Service with restrictions, crate.
SAVE S⬚ ⊠ ⬚ ▣ ➔

⚑ ▼▼ Edelweiss Motel & Chalets **M**
(802) 775-5577. **$54-$135, 14 days notice.** 119 Rt 4. Jct SR 100 N, 3 mi w. Ext corridors. **Pets:** Accepted.
SAVE S⬚ ⊠ ⬚ ➔

⚑ ▼▼▼ Mendon Mountainview Resort Lodge **M**
(802) 773-4311. **$45-$165, 7 days notice.** 78 US 4. 6 mi e of jct US 7. Int corridors. **Pets:** Accepted.
SAVE ⊠ ➔

MIDDLEBURY

⚑ ▼▼▼ The Middlebury Inn **CI**
(802) 388-4961. **$88-$385, 3 days notice.** 14 Court Square. Center; on US 7. Ext/int corridors. **Pets:** Other species. Designated rooms, service with restrictions, crate.
SAVE ⊠ ⬚ ⬚ ⬚ ▣ ¶¶

NEWFANE

▼▼▼ Four Columns Inn **CI**
(802) 365-7713. **$115-$340, 14 days notice.** 21 West St. Center; just w of SR 30. Int corridors. **Pets:** Accepted.
⊠ ¶¶ ➔ ⬚

NORTH HERO

AAA **WW** Shore Acres Inn **MI**
(802) 372-8722. **$75-$170, 10 days notice.** 237 Shore Acres Dr. 0.5 mi s on US 2. Ext corridors. **Pets:** Other species. $10 daily fee/pet. Service with restrictions, supervision.

[SAVE] [X] [🔒] [🍴] [X] [✆]

PERU

WW Johnny Seesaw's **L**
(802) 824-5533. **$90-$202, 14 days notice.** 3574 Vt Rt 11. Jct SR 30/11, 2.5 mi e on SR 11. Ext/int corridors. **Pets:** Medium, other species. $10 daily fee/pet. Designated rooms, service with restrictions, supervision.

[🔒] [🍴] [➳] [X]

PLYMOUTH

AAA **WWW** The Salt Ash Inn **CI**
(802) 672-3748. **$99-$169, 14 days notice.** 4758 Rt 100A. Jct of SR 100 and 100A. Int corridors. **Pets:** Medium, dogs only. $30 one-time fee/pet. Service with restrictions.

[SAVE] [X] [💻] [🍴] [➳] [X]

PUTNEY

AAA **WWW** The Putney Inn **MI**
(802) 387-5517. **$80-$160.** 57 Putney Landing Rd. I-91, exit 4, southbound follow US 5 just n, then just e on Putney Landing Rd; northbound, directly ahead after exit. Ext corridors. **Pets:** $10 daily fee/pet. Supervision.

[SAVE] [S🔒] [X] [💻] [🍴]

RUTLAND

WW Econo Lodge **M**
(802) 773-2784. **$39-$129, 14 days notice.** 238 S Main St (Rt 7 S). US 7, 2 mi s of jct US 4 E. Ext corridors. **Pets:** Small. Service with restrictions, supervision.

[SAVE] [S🔒] [X] [💻]

AAA **WW** Green Mont Motel **M**
(802) 775-2575. **$42-$119, 7 days notice.** 138 N Main St. US 7, 0.5 mi n of jct US 4 E. Ext corridors. **Pets:** Small. $10 daily fee/pet. Designated rooms, service with restrictions, supervision.

[SAVE] [S🔒] [X] [🔒] [➳]

AAA **WWW** Holiday Inn
Rutland/Killington **MI** 🐾
(802) 775-1911. **$129-$299.** 476 US Rt 7 S. 2.4 mi s on US 7 from US 4 W; 0.4 mi n, US 7 from US 4 E. Int corridors. **Pets:** Other species. $10 daily fee/pet. Service with restrictions, crate.

[SAVE] [S🔒] [X] [🔒M] [🛇] [🔒] [💻] [🍴] [➳]

AAA **WWW** Ramada Limited of Rutland **M**
(802) 773-3361. **$64-$169, 21 days notice.** 253 S Main St. 2 mi s on US 7. Int corridors. **Pets:** Accepted.

[SAVE] [S🔒] [X] [🔒] [💻] [➳]

AAA **WW** Royal Motel **M**
(802) 773-9176. **$47-$109, 7 days notice.** 115 Woodstock Ave. Jct US 7, 0.5 mi e on US 4 (Woodstock Ave). Ext/int corridors. **Pets:** Other species. $10 daily fee/pet. Service with restrictions, supervision.

[SAVE] [S🔒] [X] [🔒] [➳]

SHAFTSBURY

AAA **WW** Serenity Motel **C**
(802) 442-6490. **$55-$75, 3 days notice.** 4379 Rt 7A. 3.3 mi n on Historic SR 7A from SR 67. Ext corridors. **Pets:** Other species. Designated rooms, service with restrictions, crate.

[SAVE] [🔒]

SOUTH BURLINGTON

AAA **WW** Anchorage Inn **M**
(802) 863-7000. **$68-$108.** 108 Dorset St. I-89, exit 14 (US 2), just e, then 0.3 mi s. Int corridors. **Pets:** Dogs only. $50 deposit/room. Designated rooms, service with restrictions, supervision.

[SAVE] [S🔒] [X] [🔒] [💻] [➳]

AAA **WWW** Best Western Windjammer Inn &
Conference Center **MI** 🐾
(802) 863-1125. **$80-$195.** 1076 Williston Rd. I-89, exit 14E (US 2), 0.3 mi e. Int corridors. **Pets:** $5 daily fee/pet. Designated rooms, service with restrictions, supervision.

[SAVE] [S🔒] [X] [🛇] [🔒M] [🔒] [💻] [🍴] [➳]

AAA **WWW** Clarion Hotel and Conference
Center **MI**
(802) 658-0250. **$109-$189.** 1117 Williston Rd. I-89, exit 14E (US 2), just e. Int corridors. **Pets:** Medium. $50 deposit/room. Designated rooms, service with restrictions, supervision.

[SAVE] [S🔒] [X] [🛇] [🔒] [💻] [🍴] [➳]

AAA **WWW** Holiday Inn Burlington **MI**
(802) 863-6363. **$100-$165.** 1068 Williston Rd. I-89, exit 14E (US 2), just e. Int corridors. **Pets:** Medium. $10 one-time fee/room. Service with restrictions, supervision.

[SAVE] [S🔒] [X] [🛇] [🔒] [💻] [🍴] [➳]

WWW Sheraton-Burlington Hotel & Conference
Center **H**
(802) 865-6600. **$169-$269.** 870 Williston Rd. I-89, exit 14W (US 2), just w. Int corridors. **Pets:** Accepted.

[ASK] [S🔒] [X] [🛇] [🔒] [💻] [🍴] [➳]

AAA **WW** Town & Country Motel **M** 🐾
(802) 862-5786. **$59-$99, 3 days notice.** 490 Shelburne Rd. I-89, exit US 7, just n. Ext corridors. **Pets:** Dogs only. $5 daily fee/pet. Designated rooms, service with restrictions.

[SAVE] [X] [🔒] [💻]

SPRINGFIELD

▼▼▼▼ Holiday Inn Express Ⓜ ❖
(802) 885-4516. **$109-$149.** 818 Charlestown Rd. I-91, exit 7. Int corridors. **Pets:** Medium. $50 deposit/pet. Designated rooms, service with restrictions, supervision.
(ASK) (S&) ⊠ (&M) (🛋) 🔓 💻 🌊

ST. ALBANS

🔺 ▼▼▼ Econo Lodge Ⓜ
(802) 524-5956. **$56-$98, 7 days notice.** 287 S Main St. I-89, exit 19, 1 mi e to US 7, then 0.5 mi s. Ext/int corridors. **Pets:** Small. $10 daily fee/pet. Designated rooms, service with restrictions, supervision.
(SAVE) (S&) ⊠ 🔓 💻

ST. JOHNSBURY

▼ Aime's Motel Ⓜ ❖
(802) 748-3194. **$42-$90, 7 days notice.** 46 VT Rt 18. I-93, exit 1, 0.5 mi n on SR 18 at jct US 2. Ext corridors. **Pets:** Other species. Service with restrictions.
(ASK) (S&) ⊠

▼▼▼▼ Fairbanks Inn Ⓜ ❖
(802) 748-5666. **$59-$159.** 401 Western Ave. I-91, exit 21, 1 mi e, US 2. Ext corridors. **Pets:** Large, other species. $5 daily fee/room. Designated rooms, crate.
(ASK) (S&) ⊠ 🔓 💻 🌊

▼▼ Holiday Motel Ⓜ
(802) 748-8192. **$49-$129.** 222 Hastings St. Jct US 5 and Alternate US 5. Ext/int corridors. **Pets:** Medium, dogs only. $10 one-time fee/pet. Designated rooms, service with restrictions, supervision.
(ASK) (S&) ⊠ 🔓

STOWE

🔺 ▼▼▼▼ 1066 Ye Olde England Inne Ⓒ Ⓘ
(802) 253-7558. **$109-$199, 15 days notice.** 433 Mountain Rd. Jct SR 100, 0.5 mi w on SR 108. Int corridors. **Pets:** Accepted.
(SAVE) ⊠ (🛋) 🔓 💻 (🍴)

**🔺 ▼▼▼ Andersen Lodge-An Austrian
Inn** Ⓒ Ⓘ ❖
(802) 253-7336. **$68-$178, 14 days notice.** 3430 Mountain Rd. Jct SR 100, 3.5 mi nw on SR 108. Int corridors. **Pets:** Small, dogs only. Designated rooms, supervision.
(SAVE) (S&) ⊠ 🔓 (🍴) 🌊

▼▼ Commodores Inn Ⓜ Ⓘ
(802) 253-7131. **$156-$162, 7 days notice.** 823 Main St. Jct SR 108, 0.8 mi s on SR 100. Int corridors. **Pets:** Other species. $10 one-time fee/room. Service with restrictions, crate.
(ASK) (S&) ⊠ (🛋) 🔓 (🍴) 🌊 ⊠

▼▼▼▼ Edson Hill Manor Ⓒ Ⓘ
(802) 253-7371. **$139-$199, 14 days notice.** 1500 Edson Hill Rd. Jct SR 100, 3.5 mi w on SR 108, 2 mi n. Ext/int corridors. **Pets:** Designated rooms, service with restrictions, crate.
⊠ (🍴) 🌊 ⊠

🔺 ▼▼▼ Green Mountain Inn Ⓒ Ⓘ
(802) 253-7301. **$99-$259, 14 days notice.** 18 S Main St. Center; jct SR 108 on SR 100. Ext/int corridors. **Pets:** Accepted.
(SAVE) (S&) ⊠ 🔓 💻 (🍴) 🌊

🔺 ▼▼▼▼ Hob Knob Inn & Restaurant Ⓜ Ⓘ
(802) 253-8549. **$58-$110, 14 days notice.** 2364 Mountain Rd. Jct SR 100, 2.5 mi w on SR 108. Ext/int corridors. **Pets:** Accepted.
(SAVE) ⊠ 🔓 💻 (🍴) 🌊

🔺 ▼▼▼▼ Honeywood Country Lodge Ⓜ
(802) 253-4124. **$79-$149, 15 days notice.** 4527 Mountain Rd. Jct SR 100, 4.5 mi w on SR 108. Ext corridors. **Pets:** $10 daily fee/pet. Designated rooms, service with restrictions.
(SAVE) (S&) ⊠ 🔓 💻 ⊠

🔺 ▼▼▼ Innsbruck Inn at Stowe Ⓜ
(802) 253-8582. **$71-$169, 15 days notice.** 4361 Mountain Rd. Jct SR 100, 4.5 mi w on SR 108. Ext/int corridors. **Pets:** Accepted.
(SAVE) (S&) ⊠ 🔓 💻 🌊

**🔺 ▼▼▼ ▼▼▼ The Mountain Road Resort at
Stowe** Ⓜ
(802) 253-4566. **$105-$250, 15 days notice.** 1007 Mountain Rd. Jct SR 100, 1 mi w on SR 108. Ext corridors. **Pets:** $25 one-time fee/pet. Supervision.
(SAVE) (S&) ⊠ 🔓 💻 🌊 ⊠

▼▼ Notch Brook Condominiums Ⓒ Ⓞ
(802) 253-9129, **$50-$109, 15 days notice.** 1229 Notch Brook Rd. Jct SR 100, 5.3 mi w on SR 100, 1.3 mi n. Ext corridors. **Pets:** Accepted.
⊠ 🔓 💻 (♣)

▼▼▼▼ Ten Acres Lodge Ⓧ
(802) 253-7638. **$115-$440, 15 days notice.** 14 Barrows Rd. Jct SR 100, 2.1 mi w on SR 108, 0.5 mi s on Luce Hill Rd. Ext/int corridors. **Pets:** Accepted.
⊠ 🔓 💻 (🍴) 🌊

**🔺 ▼▼▼▼ Topnotch at Stowe Resort &
Spa** Ⓡ
(802) 253-8585. **$180-$420, 14 days notice.** 4000 Mountain Rd. Jct SR 100, 4 mi w on SR 108. Ext/int corridors. **Pets:** Accepted.
(SAVE) ⊠ 🔓 💻 (🍴) 🌊 ⊠

SUNDERLAND

(AAA) �winter �winter Arcady at the Sunderland Motor
Lodge **M**
(802) 362-1176. **$70-$130, 10 days notice.** On SR 7A, 6.3
mi s of jct SR 11. Ext corridors. **Pets:** Medium. $10 daily
fee/pet. Service with restrictions, supervision.
SAVE ☒ 🖵 🏊

WARREN

(AAA) �winter �winter PowderHound Inn &
Condominiums **X** ☘
(802) 496-5100. **$70-$115, 14 days notice.** 203 Powderhound Rd. SR 100, 0.3 mi s of jct Sugarbush Access Rd.
Ext corridors. **Pets:** Other species. $5 daily fee/pet. No
service.
SAVE 🔊 ☒ 🖬 🖵 🍴 🏊 🎿

(AAA) �winter �winter The Sugar Lodge **M**
(802) 583-3300. **$69-$125, 14 days notice.** 2197 Sugarbush Access Rd. Jct SR 100, 2 mi w. Int corridors.
Pets: Small, dogs only. $25 daily fee/pet. Designated
rooms, service with restrictions, supervision.
SAVE ☒ 🏊

WATERBURY

(AAA) �winter �winter The Old Stagecoach Inn **BB**
(802) 244-5056. **$60-$200, 14 days notice.** 18 N Main St.
I-89, exit 10, 0.5 mi se on SR 100. Int corridors.
Pets: Accepted.
SAVE ☒ 🖬 🖵

WEST BRATTLEBORO

�winter Molly Stark Motel **M** ☘
(802) 254-2440. **$40-$80, 14 days notice.** 829 Marlboro
Rd (Rt 9). I-91, exit 2, 3.3 mi w. Ext corridors. **Pets:** Large.
$5 daily fee/pet. Supervision.
☒ 🖬 🖵

WEST DOVER

(AAA) �winter�winter Snow Goose Inn **BB** ☘
(802) 464-3984. **$105-$135, 14 days notice.** 259 Rt 100. 1
mi n. Int corridors. **Pets:** Dogs only. $25 daily fee/pet. Des-
ignated rooms, service with restrictions, crate.
SAVE 🔊 ☒ 🖬 🎿 🆉

WESTMORE

(AAA) �winter �winter WilloughVale Inn on Lake
Willoughby **CI**
(802) 525-4123. **$79-$219, 14 days notice.** 793 Rt 5A. Jct
SR 16, just s on SR 5A; on Lake Willoughby. Int corridors.
Pets: Accepted.
SAVE 🔊 ☒ 🖬 🖵 🍴 ☒ 🆉

WHITE RIVER JUNCTION

(AAA) �winter�winter Best Western at the Junction **M**
(802) 295-3015. **$79-$149, 15 days notice.** 306 N Harland
Rd (US 5). Jct I-89 and 91, on US 5. Int corridors.
Pets: Other species. $10 daily fee/pet. Designated rooms,
service with restrictions, supervision.
SAVE 🔊 ☒ 🖬 🖵 🏊

�winter�winter Ramada Inn-White River Junction **M**
(802) 295-3000. **Call for rates.** 259 Holiday Dr. Jct I-89 and
91, just e. Int corridors. **Pets:** Accepted.
ASK ☒ 🖬 🖵 🍴 🏊

WILLISTON

(AAA) �winter�winter�winter Residence Inn by Marriott **A**
(802) 878-2001. **$99, 5 days notice.** 35 Hurricane Ln. I-89,
exit 12 (SR 2A), just s, then just e. Ext corridors.
Pets: Accepted.
SAVE 🔊 ☒ 🖉 🖬 🖵 🏊

(AAA) �winter�winter�winter TownePlace Suites by
Marriott **M** ☘
(802) 872-5900. **$85-$119.** 66 Zephyr Rd. I-89, exit 12 (SR
2A), 1.1 mi n. Int corridors. **Pets:** Other species. $75
deposit/room, $10 daily fee/pet. Service with restrictions.
SAVE 🔊 ☒ 🖬 🖵 🏊

WOODSTOCK

(AAA) �winter �winter Braeside Motel **M** ☘
(802) 457-1366. **$68-$108, 15 days notice.** Rt 4 E. 1 mi e.
Ext corridors. **Pets:** $10 one-time fee/pet. Designated
rooms, no service, supervision.
SAVE ☒ 🖬 🏊

(AAA) �winter�winter The Winslow House **BB**
(802) 457-1820. **$85-$165, 14 days notice.** 492 Woodstock
Rd. 1.2 mi w on US 4. Int corridors. **Pets:** Medium. Service
with restrictions, supervision.
SAVE ☒ 🖬

VIRGINIA

CITY INDEX

ALTAVISTA

▼▼▼ Comfort Suites Hotel M ❀
(434) 369-4000. **$75-$135, 7 days notice.** 1558 Main St.
US 29 business route, exit US 29. Int corridors.
Pets: Medium, other species. $10 one-time fee/room. Designated rooms, service with restrictions, supervision.
[SAVE] [S🐾] [✕] [🖥] [💻] [🏊]

BEDFORD

⬥⬥⬥ ▼▼▼ Days Inn M
(540) 586-8286. **$56-$66, 3 days notice.** 921 Blue Ridge
Ave. 1.5 mi w on US 221 and 460. Ext corridors.
Pets: Service with restrictions.
[SAVE] [S🐾] [✕] [🖥] [💻] [🍴] [🏊]

▼▼ Super 8 Motel M
(540) 587-0100. **$56-$95.** 842 Ole Turnpike Dr. 1.5 mi w on
US 221 and 460. Int corridors. **Pets:** Other species. $15
one-time fee/room.
[ASK] [S🐾] [✕] [🖥] [💻]

BIG STONE GAP

⬥⬥⬥ ▼ Country Inn Motel M
(540) 523-0374. **$48-$52.** 627 Gilley Ave. US 23, 1 mi w on
US 23 business route and 58A. Ext corridors. **Pets:** Small,
dogs only. $3 daily fee/pet. Service with restrictions, crate.
[SAVE] [S🐾] [✕] [🖥]

BLACKSBURG

▼▼ Best Western Red Lion Inn M
(540) 552-7770. **$75-$145, 7 days notice.** 900 Plantation
Rd. 1.7 mi w on SR 685; jct US 460 Bypass and Prices
Fork Rd. Ext corridors. **Pets:** Accepted.
[SAVE] [S🐾] [✕] [💻] [🍴] [🏊]

BRISTOL

▼ Econo Lodge M
(540) 466-2112. **$39-$130.** 912 Commonwealth Ave. I-81,
exit 3, 1.5 mi e. Ext corridors. **Pets:** $10 one-time fee/room.
Service with restrictions, supervision.
[SAVE] [S🐾] [✕] [🖥] [💻]

▼▼▼ Holiday Inn Hotel & Suites H
(540) 466-4100. **$90-$225.** 3005 Linden Dr. I-81, exit 7. Int
corridors. **Pets:** Other species. $10 one-time fee/room.
Service with restrictions.
[ASK] [S🐾] [✕] [🛠M] [🖥] [💻] [🍴] [🏊]

⬥⬥⬥ ▼▼▼ La Quinta Inn M
(540) 669-9353. **$55-$71.** 1014 Old Airport Rd. I-81, exit 7.
Ext corridors. **Pets:** Small, other species. Service with
restrictions, supervision.
[SAVE] [S🐾] [✕] [🛠M] [🐾] [🖥] [💻] [🏊]

▼▼ Motel 6 Ⓜ
(540) 466-6060. **$52-$62, 5 days notice.** 21561 Clear Creek Rd. I-81, exit 7, 0.3 mi w. Int corridors. **Pets:** Small. $10 daily fee/pet. Designated rooms, service with restrictions, supervision.
🆂🖏 ⊗ 🔥 🖊

▼▼ Super 8 Motel Ⓜ
(540) 466-8800. **Call for rates.** 2139 Lee Hwy. I-81, exit 5, just s. Int corridors. **Pets:** Medium, other species. $10 daily fee/pet. Service with restrictions, supervision.
ⒶⓈⓀ ⊗ 🔥

BUENA VISTA

ⒶⒶⒶ ▼ Buena Vista Motel Ⓜ
(540) 261-2138. **$36-$65, 7 days notice.** 447 E 29th St. I-81, exit 188A, 4.3 mi e on US 60, 0.4 mi w of Blue Ridge Pkwy. Ext corridors. **Pets:** Accepted.
🆂🅰🆅🅴 🆂🖏 ⊗ 🔥

CHARLOTTESVILLE

ⒶⒶⒶ ▼▼ Best Western-Mount Vernon Ⓜ
(434) 296-5501. **$68-$76, 30 days notice.** 1613 Emmet St. US 29, just n of jct US 250 Bypass. Ext corridors. **Pets:** Other species. Service with restrictions, crate.
🆂🅰🆅🅴 🆂🖏 ⊗ 🔥 🖊 🏊

ⒶⒶⒶ ▼▼▼ Comfort Inn Ⓜ
(434) 293-6188. **$75-$95.** 1807 Emmet St. Just n on US 29 from jct US 250 Bypass. Int corridors. **Pets:** Small. $10 daily fee/pet. Designated rooms, service with restrictions, supervision.
🆂🅰🆅🅴 🆂🖏 ⊗ ✒ 🔥 🖊 🏊

▼▼▼ Days Inn University Area Ⓜ⃒
(434) 293-9111. **$65-$95.** 1600 Emmet St. I-64, exit 118B (US 29), just n of jct US 250 Bypass. Ext corridors. **Pets:** Other species. $10 daily fee/pet. Service with restrictions.
🆂🅰🆅🅴 🆂🖏 ⊗ 🔥 🖊 🍴 🏊

▼ Econo Lodge-University Ⓜ
(434) 296-2104. **$46-$130.** 400 Emmet St. 1 mi s on US 29 business route from jct US 250 Bypass. Ext corridors. **Pets:** Small, dogs only. $10 one-time fee/room. Service with restrictions, supervision.
🆂🅰🆅🅴 🆂🖏 ⊗ 🔥 🖊

▼▼▼ Holiday Inn-Monticello/Charlottesville Ⓜ⃒
(434) 977-5100. **$65-$110.** 1200 5th St SW. I-64, exit 120, just n on SR 631. Int corridors. **Pets:** Other species. $7.50 daily fee/pet.
ⒶⓈⓀ 🆂🖏 ⊗ ✒ 🖊 🍴 🏊

▼▼▼ Quality Inn-University Area Ⓜ
(434) 971-3746. **$65-$95.** 1600 Emmet St. US 29, just n of jct US 250 Bypass, just e on Holiday Dr. Ext corridors. **Pets:** Other species. $10 daily fee/pet. Service with restrictions.
🆂🅰🆅🅴 🆂🖏 ⊗ 🔥 🖊

ⒶⒶⒶ ▼▼▼ Residence Inn by Marriott Ⓜ
(434) 923-0300. **$114.** 1111 Millmont St. I-64, exit 118B, 0.5 mi s on SR 29. Int corridors. **Pets:** Accepted.
🆂🅰🆅🅴 🆂🖏 ⊗ 🔥 🖊 🏊

CHRISTIANSBURG

ⒶⒶⒶ ▼▼▼ Econo Lodge Ⓜ
(540) 382-6161. **$48-$109.** 2430 Roanoke St. I-81, exit 118, just w on US 11/460. Ext corridors. **Pets:** Small. $5 daily fee/pet. Designated rooms, service with restrictions, supervision.
🆂🅰🆅🅴 🆂🖏 ⊗ 🔥 🖊 🏊

▼▼ Super 8 Motel-Christiansburg West Ⓜ
(540) 382-5813. **$57-$67, 3 days notice.** 55 Laurel St NE. I-87, exit 118, 1 mi w on US 11/460, then 3.5 mi nw on US 460 Bypass; at jct SR 114. Int corridors. **Pets:** Accepted.
ⒶⓈⓀ 🆂🖏 ⊗ 🔥

COLLINSVILLE

▼▼▼ Dutch Inn Ⓜ
(540) 647-3721. **$59-$64.** 2360 Virginia Ave. Jct US 58, 3 mi n on US 220 business route. Ext corridors. **Pets:** Small. $10 one-time fee/room. Designated rooms, service with restrictions, crate.
ⒶⓈⓀ 🆂🖏 ⊗ 🔥 🖊 🏊

ⒶⒶⒶ ▼▼▼ Knights Inn Ⓜ
(540) 647-3716. **$54-$60.** 2357 Virginia Ave. 3 mi n on US 220 business route from jct US 58. Ext corridors. **Pets:** Accepted.
🆂🅰🆅🅴 🆂🖏 ⊗ 🔥 🏊

COVINGTON

▼▼▼ Best Western Mountain View Ⓜ⃒
(540) 962-4951. **$79-$83.** 820 E Madison St. I-64, exit 16, just n. Ext corridors. **Pets:** Other species. $10 one-time fee/room. Service with restrictions, supervision.
🆂🅰🆅🅴 🆂🖏 ⊗ 🔥 🖊 🍴 🏊

▼▼▼ Comfort Inn Ⓜ
(540) 962-2141. **$79-$89.** 203 Interstate Dr. I-64, exit 16, just sw. Int corridors. **Pets:** Other species. $10 one-time fee/room. Service with restrictions, supervision.
🆂🅰🆅🅴 🆂🖏 ⊗ 🔥 🖊 🏊

▼▼▼ Knights Inn Ⓜ
(540) 962-7600. **$64-$79.** 908 Valley Ridge Rd. I-64, exit 16, just ne. Ext corridors. **Pets:** Other species. $10 one-time fee/room. Service with restrictions, supervision.
ⒶⓈⓀ 🆂🖏 ⊗ 🔥 🖊

CULPEPER

ⒶⒶⒶ ▼▼▼ Comfort Inn Ⓜ
(540) 825-4900. **$79-$89.** 890 Willis Ln. 2 mi s on US 29 business route, at jct US 29, just e. Ext corridors. **Pets:** Other species. $15 daily fee/pet. Designated rooms, service with restrictions.
🆂🅰🆅🅴 🆂🖏 ⊗ ✒ 🔥 🖊 🏊

DALEVILLE

AAA ▼▼▼ **Best Western-Coachman Inn Roanoke/Daleville** **M**
(540) 992-1234. **$59-$79.** 437 Roanoke Rd. I-81, exit 150B, just nw on US 220. Ext corridors. **Pets:** Accepted.
SAVE 🛇 ✕ 🅰 🔒 💻 🏊

DANVILLE

AAA ▼▼▼ **Stratford Inn** **M**
(434) 793-2500. **$72-$82.** 2500 Riverside Dr. US 58, just e of jct US 29 business route. Ext corridors. **Pets:** $25 one-time fee/room. Service with restrictions, supervision.
SAVE 🛇 ✕ 🅰 🔒 🔒 💻 🍴 🏊

DISTRICT OF COLUMBIA METROPOLITAN AREA

ALEXANDRIA

▼▼▼▼ **Executive Club Suites** **A**
(703) 739-2582. **$115-$155.** 610 Bashford Ln. Off George Washington Memorial Pkwy. Int corridors. **Pets:** $250 deposit/pet, $50 one-time fee/pet. Designated rooms, service with restrictions, supervision.
ASK 🛇 ✕ 🔒 💻 🏊

▼▼▼ **Hawthorn Suites LTD-Alexandria** **A**
(703) 370-1000. **$59-$119.** 420 N Van Dorn St. I-395, exit 3A, 0.3 mi e on SR 236 to S Van Dorn St, then 0.5 mi n. Int corridors. **Pets:** Medium. $100 one-time fee/room. Service with restrictions, supervision.
ASK 🛇 ✕ 🅰 🔒 🔒 💻 🏊

▼▼▼▼ **Hilton Alexandria Mark Center** **H**
(703) 845-1010. **$89-$269.** 5000 Seminary Rd. I-395, exit 4W, just w. Int corridors. **Pets:** Accepted.
SAVE 🛇 ✕ 🔒 🅰 🔒 🔒 💻 🍴 🏊 ✕

AAA ▼▼▼▼ **Hilton Alexandria Old Town** **H**
(703) 837-0440. **$129-$169.** 1767 King St. I-95/495, exit 176B, 0.5 mi n on SR 241, 0.5 mi e on SR 236, just ne on Diagonal Rd. Int corridors. **Pets:** Small, other species. $20 daily fee/room. Designated rooms, service with restrictions, supervision.
SAVE 🛇 ✕ 🅰 🔒 💻 🍴 🏊

▼▼▼▼ **Holiday Inn Eisenhower Metro** **M**
(703) 960-3400. **$109-$140.** 2460 Eisenhower Ave. I-95/495, exit 176, immediate e on Pershing Ave, then s on Stovall Rd, jct Telegraph Rd (SR 214 N) and I-95/495. Int corridors. **Pets:** Accepted.
ASK 🛇 ✕ 🅰 🔒 💻 🍴 🏊

AAA ▼▼▼▼ **Holiday Inn Select-Old Town** **H**
(703) 549-6080. **$183-$229.** 480 King St. In Old Town on SR 7; between S Pitt and S Royal sts; just sw of City Hall. Int corridors. **Pets:** Small. No service, supervision.
SAVE 🛇 ✕ 🅰 💻 🍴 🏊

▼▼ ▼▼ **Homestead Studio Suites-Alexandria** **M**
(703) 329-3399. **$89-$94.** 200 Blue Stone Rd. I-95/495, exit 174, just n to Eisenhower Ave, then 1.2 mi e. Int corridors. **Pets:** Medium. $75 one-time fee/pet. Service with restrictions.
ASK 🛇 ✕ 🔒 🅰 🔒 🔒 💻

AAA ▼▼▼ **Red Roof Inn-Alexandria** **M**
(703) 960-5200. **$69-$84.** 5975 Richmond Hwy. I-95/495, exit 1A, 0.5 mi s on US 1. Ext corridors. **Pets:** Medium. Service with restrictions, crate.
SAVE ✕

AAA ▼▼▼ **Washington Suites-Alexandria** **A**
(703) 370-9600. **$119-$199.** 100 S Reynolds St. I-395, exit 3A, 0.8 mi e on SR 236 E (Duke St), just s. Int corridors. **Pets:** Accepted.
SAVE 🛇 ✕ 🔒 🅰 🔒 🔒 💻 🍴 🏊

ARLINGTON

▼▼ ▼▼ **Best Western Key Bridge** **M**
(703) 522-0400. **$149-$189.** 1850 N Fort Meyer Dr. I-66, exit 73, just sw of Key Bridge; in Rosslyn area. Int corridors. **Pets:** $25 one-time fee/room. Designated rooms, service with restrictions, crate.
SAVE 🛇 ✕ 🔒 🍴 🏊

▼▼ ▼▼ **Executive Club Suites-Arlington** **A**
(703) 522-2582. **$115-$155.** 108 S Courthouse Rd. I-395, exit 8A northbound; exit 8 southbound, 1 mi nw on Washington Blvd to Second St, just 0.3 mi se of US 50. Ext corridors. **Pets:** $250 deposit/pet, $50 one-time fee/pet. Designated rooms, service with restrictions, supervision.
ASK 🛇 ✕ 🔒 💻 🏊

AAA ▼▼▼▼ **Quality Hotel Courthouse Plaza** **H**
(703) 524-4000. **$79-$129.** 1200 N Courthouse Rd. 1.5 mi sw of Theodore Roosevelt Bridge on US 50. Ext/int corridors. **Pets:** Accepted.
SAVE 🛇 ✕ 🅰 🔒 🔒 💻 🍴 🏊

AAA ▼▼▼ **Quality Inn-Iwo Jima** **M**
(703) 524-5000. **$105-$115, 10 days notice.** 1501 Arlington Blvd. 1 mi w of Theodore Roosevelt Bridge on US 50. Ext/int corridors. **Pets:** Medium. $10 daily fee/pet. Designated rooms, service with restrictions, supervision.
SAVE 🛇 ✕ 🔒 💻 🍴 🏊

CHANTILLY

◆◆ **Homestead Studio Suites-Dulles/Chantilly [M]**
(703) 263-3361. **$79-$109.** 4504 Brookfield Corporate Dr. I-66, exit 53, 3 mi n on SR 28; jct SR 28 and 50, 1 mi s. Ext corridors. **Pets:** Other species. $75 one-time fee/room. Service with restrictions.
[A$K] [SD] ✕ 👂 ♿ 🧊 ☕

DUMFRIES

[AAA] ◆◆◆ **Holiday Inn Express-Dumfries [M]**
(703) 221-1141. **$75-$99.** 17133 Dumfries Rd. I-95, exit 152, just w on SR 234 N. Ext/int corridors. **Pets:** Small. Designated rooms, service with restrictions, supervision.
[SAVE] [SD] ✕ 👂 🧊 ☕ 🏊

FAIRFAX

◆◆◆ **Holiday Inn-Fair Oaks [MI]**
(703) 352-2525. **$109-$189.** 11787 Lee Jackson Memorial Hwy. I-66, exit 57B, at jct US 50; adjacent to Fair Oaks Mall. Int corridors. **Pets:** Medium. Designated rooms, service with restrictions, crate.
✕ 👂 🧊 ☕ 🍴 🏊

◆◆ **Homestead Studio Suites-Fair Oaks [M]**
(703) 273-3444. **$94-$104.** 12104 Monument Dr. I-66, exit 57B, 0.8 mi w on US 50, then 0.3 mi s on SR 620 (West Ox Rd), just se. Ext corridors. **Pets:** Small. $75 one-time fee/pet. Service with restrictions, crate.
[A$K] [SD] ✕ ♿M 👂 ♿ 🧊 ☕

[AAA] ◆◆◆ **Residence Inn Fairlakes [A]**
(703) 266-4900. **$119-$165, 3 days notice.** 12815 Fairlakes Pkwy. I-66, exit 55 (Fairfax County Pkwy N), just w. Int corridors. **Pets:** Accepted.
[SAVE] ✕ ♿M 👂 ♿ 🧊 ☕ 🏊

[AAA] ◆◆ **Wellesley Inn [M]**
(703) 359-2888. **$69-$79.** 10327 Lee Hwy. I-66, exit 60, 0.7 mi s on SR 123, 0.3 mi e on US 29/50. Int corridors. **Pets:** $25 deposit/room. Service with restrictions.
[SAVE] [SD] ✕ 👂 ♿ 🧊 ☕

FALLS CHURCH

[AAA] ◆◆◆ **Fairfax-Merrifield Residence Inn by Marriott [A]**
(703) 573-5200. **$119-$204.** 8125 Gatehouse Rd. I-495, exit 50A, just w to SR 640 N. Int corridors. **Pets:** Other species. $150 one-time fee/room. Service with restrictions.
[SAVE] [SD] ✕ ♿ 🧊 ☕ 🏊

[AAA] ◆◆◆ **TownePlace Suites Falls Church [M]**
(703) 237-6172. **$74-$139, 3 days notice.** 205 Hillwood Ave. I-495, exit 50B, 2.5 mi e on US 50, 0.6 mi n on Annandale Rd, then e. Int corridors. **Pets:** Accepted.
[SAVE] [SD] ✕ ♿M ♿ 🧊 ☕ 🏊

HERNDON

◆◆◆ **Hawthorn Suites [H]**
(703) 437-5000. **$79-$189.** 467 Herndon Pkwy. SR 267 (Dulles Toll Rd), exit 11 (Fairfax County Pkwy). Int corridors. **Pets:** Accepted.
[A$K] [SD] ✕ 🧊 ☕ 🏊

[AAA] ◆◆◆ **Hilton Washington Dulles Airport [H]**
(703) 478-2900. **$79-$139, 7 days notice.** 13869 Park Center Rd. SR 267 (Dulles Toll Rd), exit 9, 3 mi s on SR 28. Int corridors. **Pets:** Accepted.
[SAVE] [SD] ✕ 👂 ♿ ☕ 🍴 🏊

◆◆◆ **Holiday Inn Express–Herndon [M]**
(703) 478-9777. **$59-$109.** 485 Elden St. 0.3 mi e on SR 606. Int corridors. **Pets:** Accepted.
[A$K] [SD] ✕ ♿M 👂 🧊 ☕

[AAA] ◆◆◆ **Residence Inn by Marriott-Herndon/Reston [M]**
(703) 435-0044. **$152-$161.** 315 Elden St. 0.5 mi e on SR 606. Int corridors. **Pets:** Other species. $6 daily fee/pet, $100 one-time fee/room. Service with restrictions.
[SAVE] [SD] ✕ 👂 🧊 ☕ 🏊

[AAA] ◆◆◆ **Summerfield Suites by Wyndham-Dulles Airport/Herndon [M]**
(703) 713-6800. **$99-$169.** 13700 Coppermine Rd. SR 267 (Dulles Toll Rd), exit 10, 0.7 mi s on Centerville Rd (SR 657), 0.4 mi w. Ext corridors. **Pets:** Small. $200 one-time fee/room. Service with restrictions, supervision.
[SAVE] ✕ 👂 🧊 ☕ 🏊

LEESBURG

◆◆◆ **Holiday Inn at Carradoc Hall [MI]**
(703) 771-9200. **$129.** 1500 E Market St. 2 mi e on SR 7. Int corridors. **Pets:** Medium, other species. Service with restrictions, supervision.
[A$K] [SD] ✕ ♿M 🧊 ☕ 🍴

LORTON

◆◆◆ **Comfort Inn Gunston Corner [M]**
(703) 643-3100. **$59-$109, 14 days notice.** 8180 Silverbrook Rd. I-95, exit 163, just w. Int corridors. **Pets:** Accepted.
[SAVE] [SD] ✕ 👂 ♿ 🧊 ☕ 🏊

MANASSAS

[AAA] ◆◆◆ **Best Western Battlefield Inn [MI]**
(703) 361-8000. **$89-$200.** 10820 Balls Ford Rd. I-66, exit 47A westbound; exit 47 eastbound, just s on SR 234, then w. Ext corridors. **Pets:** $10 daily fee/room. Service with restrictions, crate.
[SAVE] [SD] ✕ ♿ 🧊 ☕ 🍴 🏊

(AAA) ▼▼▼ Red Roof Inn-Manassas M
(703) 335-9333. **$64-$84.** 10610 Automotive Dr. I-66, exit 47 eastbound; exit 47A westbound, just s on SR 234, just e on Balls Ford Rd. Ext corridors. **Pets:** Large. Service with restrictions, crate.
[SAVE] [✕] [⌖]

MCLEAN

(AAA) ▼▼▼ Best Western Tysons Westpark Hotel H
(703) 734-2800. **$89-$189, 7 days notice.** 8401 Westpark Dr. I-495, exit 47B southbound; exit 47 northbound, 1.3 mi w on SR 7. Int corridors. **Pets:** Large, other species. Service with restrictions, crate.
[SAVE] [S⌀] [✕] [⌖] [📶] [🖥] [♨] [〰]

RESTON

▼▼▼ Homestead Studio Suites-Reston M
(703) 707-9700. **$90-$110.** 12190 Sunset Hills Rd. SR 267 (Dulles Toll Rd), exit 12 (Reston Pkwy), just n, then just w. Ext corridors. **Pets:** Medium, other species. $75 one-time fee/room. Service with restrictions.
[ASK] [S⌀] [⌖] [📶] [🖥]

SPRINGFIELD

▼▼▼ Comfort Inn Springfield M
(703) 922-9000. **$99-$129.** 6560 Loisdale Ct. I-95, exit 169A, just e on SR 644 E; 0.7 mi s of jct I-395 and 495; adjacent to Springfield Mall. Int corridors. **Pets:** Accepted.
[SAVE] [S⌀] [✕] [⌖] [📶] [🖥]

▼▼▼ Hampton Inn M
(703) 924-9444. **$99-$129.** 6550 Loisdale Ct. I-95, exit 169A, just e on SR 644 E; jct I-395 and 495, 0.6 mi s; adjacent to Springfield Mall. Int corridors. **Pets:** Accepted.
[SAVE] [S⌀] [✕] [⌂M] [📶] [⌖] [📶] [🖥] [〰]

STERLING

▼▼▼ Hampton Inn-Dulles/Cascades M ❁
(703) 450-9595. **$62-$109.** 46331 McClellan Way. I-267, exit 9, 5 mi to exit 7E, SR 7 to Cascade Pkwy. Int corridors. **Pets:** Other species. $25 one-time fee/room. Service with restrictions.
[SAVE] [S⌀] [✕] [⌖] [📶] [🖥] [〰]

▼▼▼ Hampton Inn Washington-Dulles Airport M
(703) 471-8300. **$62-$109.** 45440 Holiday Dr. SR 267 (Dulles Toll Rd), exit 9B, 1.8 mi n on SR 28, then just ne. Ext corridors. **Pets:** Accepted.
[SAVE] [S⌀] [✕] [📶] [🖥]

▼▼▼ Holiday Inn Washington Dulles International Airport MI
(703) 471-7411. **$69-$159.** 1000 Sully Rd. SR 28, 1.8 mi n of SR 267 (Dulles Toll Rd), exit 9B. Ext/int corridors. **Pets:** Accepted.
[ASK] [S⌀] [✕] [⌖] [📶] [🖥] [♨] [〰]

▼▼▼ Homestead Studio Suites-Dulles/Sterling M
(703) 904-7575. **$94-$99.** 45350 Catalina Ct. SR 267 (Dulles Toll Rd), exit 9B, 0.8 mi n on SR 28, then just w on CR 606. Ext corridors. **Pets:** Accepted.
[ASK] [S⌀] [✕] [⌖] [📶] [🖥]

(AAA) ▼▼▼ TownePlace Suites by Marriott at Dulles Airport M ❁
(703) 707-2017. **$79-$109.** 22744 Holiday Dr. SR 267 (Dulles Toll Rd), exit 9B, 1.8 mi n on SR 28, then just ne. Int corridors. **Pets:** $10 daily fee/room.
[SAVE] [S⌀] [✕] [⌖] [📶] [🖥] [〰]

VIENNA

(AAA) ▼▼▼ Comfort Inn Tysons Corner M
(703) 448-8020. **$90-$190, 7 days notice.** 1587 Spring Hill Rd. I-495, exit 47A, 1.8 mi w on SR 7, just s on Spring Hill Rd, just e of jct SR 267 (Dulles Toll Rd). Ext corridors. **Pets:** Small. $10 daily fee/room, $25 one-time fee/room. Service with restrictions.
[SAVE] [S⌀] [✕] [📶] [🖥] [〰]

(AAA) ▼▼▼ Residence Inn by Marriott-Tysons Corner A
(703) 893-0120. **$259.** 8616 Westwood Center Dr. I-495, exit 47A, 1.9 m w on SR 7, just s. Ext corridors. **Pets:** Accepted.
[SAVE] [S⌀] [✕] [📶] [🖥] [〰]

(AAA) ▼▼▼ Residence Inn by Marriott Tysons Corner-Mall A
(703) 917-0800. **$149-$189.** 8400 Old Courthouse Rd. I-495, exit 46A, 1.1 mi s on SR 123; 0.3 mi s of jct SR 7 and 123. Int corridors. **Pets:** Accepted.
[SAVE] [S⌀] [✕] [⌂M] [📶] [⌖] [📶] [🖥] [〰]

WOODBRIDGE

(AAA) ▼▼▼ Quality Inn at Potomac Mills M ❁
(703) 494-0300. **$49-$110.** 1109 Horner Rd. I-95, exit 161 southbound, 1.5 mi s on US 1, just n on SR 123, then just s; exit 160A northbound, 0.5 mi s on SR 123, then just s. Int corridors. **Pets:** Medium, other species. $15 daily fee/pet. Designated rooms, service with restrictions.
[SAVE] [S⌀] [✕] [📶] [🖥] [🖥] [〰]

❁ **END METROPOLITAN AREA** ❁

EMPORIA

(AAA) ▼▼◆ Best Western Emporia M
(434) 634-3200. **$55-$75, 7 days notice.** 1100 W Atlantic St. I-95, exit 11B, just w on US 58. Ext corridors. **Pets:** Other species. $10 one-time fee/room. Service with restrictions.
[SAVE] [S6] [✕] [✎] [🖥] [➔]

(AAA) ▼▼◆ Comfort Inn MI
(434) 348-3282. **$52-$70.** 1411 Skippers Rd. I-95, exit 8, just e on US 301. Ext corridors. **Pets:** Medium. Designated rooms, service with restrictions, supervision.
[SAVE] [S6] [✕] [🖥] [🍴] [➔]

▼ Days Inn-Emporia M
(434) 634-9481. **$49-$89.** 921 W Atlantic St. I-95, exit 11B, just w on US 58. Ext corridors. **Pets:** Medium. $4 one-time fee/pet. Designated rooms, service with restrictions, supervision.
[SAVE] [S6] [✕] [🖥] [➔]

(AAA) ▼▼◆ Hampton Inn M 🐾
(434) 634-9200. **$64-$76.** 1207 W Atlantic St. I-95, exit 11B, just w on US 58. Ext corridors. **Pets:** Other species. Service with restrictions, supervision.
[SAVE] [S6] [✕] [🔒] [🖥] [➔]

(AAA) ▼ Knights Inn M
(434) 535-8535. **$34-$49.** 3173 Sussex Dr. I-95, exit 17, 0.5 mi s on US 301. Ext corridors. **Pets:** Accepted.
[SAVE] [S6] [✕] [🖥] [➔]

FANCY GAP

(AAA) ▼▼◆ Doe Run Lodge C
(540) 398-2212. **$88-$275, 7 days notice.** MM 189.2 on Blue Ridge Pkwy; 10 mi n from US 52 (parkway entrance). Ext corridors. **Pets:** Other species. $25 one-time fee/room. Designated rooms, service with restrictions.
[SAVE] [S6] [✕] [🖥] [🖥] [🍴] [➔] [✕]

FREDERICKSBURG

(AAA) ▼▼◆ Best Western Central Plaza M
(540) 786-7404. **$59-$95.** 3000 Plank Rd. I-95, exit 130B, on SR 3; adjacent to Spotsylvania Mall. Ext corridors. **Pets:** Very small, other species. $25 deposit/room. Designated rooms, service with restrictions, supervision.
[SAVE] [✕] [🖥M] [🖥]

(AAA) ▼▼◆ Best Western Fredericksburg M
(540) 371-5050. **$50-$75.** 2205 William St. I-95, exit 130A, 0.3 mi e on SR 3. Ext corridors. **Pets:** Accepted.
[SAVE] [S6] [✕] [🖥M] [🖥] [➔]

(AAA) ▼▼◆ Dunning Mills Suites X
(540) 373-1256. **$59-$79.** 2305 C Jefferson Davis Hwy. I-95, exit 126, 3 mi n on US 1. Ext corridors. **Pets:** Other species. $200 deposit/room, $5 daily fee/pet. Designated rooms, service with restrictions, crate.
[SAVE] [S6] [✕] [🖥] [🖥] [➔]

(AAA) ▼▼ Econo Lodge Central M
(540) 786-8374. **$47-$56, 14 days notice.** 2802 Plank Rd. I-95, exit 130B, on SR 3. Ext corridors. **Pets:** Other species. $25 deposit/room. Service with restrictions, supervision.
[SAVE] [S6] [✕] [🖥] [🖥]

(AAA) ▼▼▼ Hampton Inn M
(540) 371-0330. **$76-$99.** 2310 William St. I-95, exit 130A, on SR 3 E. Ext corridors. **Pets:** Accepted.
[SAVE] [S6] [✕] [🖥] [🖥] [➔]

(AAA) ▼▼▼ Holiday Inn-Fredericksburg North MI
(540) 371-5550. **$65-$85.** 564 Warrenton Rd. I-95, exit 133, just nw on US 17. Ext corridors. **Pets:** Other species. Service with restrictions, crate.
[SAVE] [S6] [✕] [🖥] [🖥] [🍴] [➔]

(AAA) ▼ Holiday Inn Select Fredericksburg H
(540) 786-8321. **$109-$159.** 2801 Plank Rd. I-95, exit 130B, on SR 3; in Central Park. Int corridors. **Pets:** Accepted.
[SAVE] [S6] [✕] [🖥M] [📷] [🖥] [🖥] [🍴] [➔]

(AAA) ▼ Howard Johnson Hotel M
(540) 898-1800. **$65-$95, 7 days notice.** 5327 Jefferson Davis Hwy. I-95, exit 126. Int corridors. **Pets:** Medium, dogs only. $10 daily fee/pet. Designated rooms, service with restrictions, supervision.
[SAVE] [S6] [✕] [✎] [🖥] [🖥] [➔]

(AAA) ▼▼◆ Quality Inn Fredericksburg MI
(540) 373-0000. **$52-$70.** 543 Warrenton Rd. I-95, exit 133, n on US 17. Ext corridors. **Pets:** Other species. $8 daily fee/pet. Designated rooms, service with restrictions.
[SAVE] [S6] [✕] [🖥] [🍴] [➔]

(AAA) ▼▼◆ Ramada Inn MI
(540) 786-8361. **$64-$70, 14 days notice.** 2802 Plank Rd. I-95, exit 130B, on SR 3. Ext corridors. **Pets:** Other species. $25 deposit/room. Service with restrictions, supervision.
[SAVE] [S6] [✕] [🖥] [🍴] [➔]

▼▼◆ Ramada Inn South MI
(540) 898-1102. **$62-$85.** 5324 Jefferson Davis Hwy. I-95, exit 126, just n on US 1. Ext/int corridors. **Pets:** Accepted.
[ASK] [S6] [✕] [🖥] [🖥] [🍴] [➔]

FRONT ROYAL

(AAA) ▼▼ Bluemont Inn M
(540) 635-9447. **$48-$686, 3 days notice.** 1525 N Shenandoah Ave. I-66, exit 6, 1.8 mi s on US 340/522. Ext corridors. **Pets:** Accepted.
[SAVE] [S6] [✕] [🖥]

(AAA) ▼ Budget Inn M 🐾
(540) 635-2196. **$39-$75.** 1122 N Royal Ave. I-66, exit 6, 2.2 mi s on US 340/522 and SR 55. Ext corridors. **Pets:** Dogs only. $5 daily fee/pet. Service with restrictions, supervision.
[SAVE] [S6] [✕] [🖥]

▼▼ **Relax Inn** M
(540) 635-4101. **$50-$65.** 1801 Shenandoah Ave. I-66, exit 6, 1.5 mi s on US 340/522. Ext corridors. **Pets:** Accepted.
(ASK) (S&) (X) (H) (▣) (≈)

(AAA) ▼▼▼ **Scottish Inn** M
(540) 636-6168. **$46-$85.** 533 S Royal Ave. I-66, exit 6, 3.8 mi s on US 340, at jct SR 55. Ext corridors. **Pets:** No service, supervision.
(SAVE) (S&) (X) (H)

▼▼▼ **Super 8 Motel** M
(540) 636-4888. **Call for rates.** 111 South St. I-66, exit 6, 3.8 mi s on US 340, then just e on SR 55. Int corridors. **Pets:** Accepted.
(X) (H)

(AAA) ▼▼ **Twi-Lite Motel** M
(540) 635-4148. **$40-$79.** 53 W 14th St. I-66, exit 6, 2.3 mi s on US 340/522. Ext corridors. **Pets:** Small, dogs only. $5 daily fee/pet. Designated rooms, service with restrictions, supervision.
(SAVE) (X) (H) (≈)

GREENVILLE

(AAA) ▼▼▼ **Budget Host-Historic Hessian House** M
(540) 337-1231. **$40-$75, 7 days notice.** 3554 Lee Jackson Hwy. I-81, exit 213, 0.3 mi e. Ext corridors. **Pets:** Accepted.
(SAVE) (S&) (X) (H) (▣)

HAMPTON ROADS AREA

CHESAPEAKE

(AAA) ▼▼▼ **Days Inn-Chesapeake** M
(757) 487-8861. **$48-$75.** 1439 George Washington Hwy. I-64, exit 296A, 2.5 mi n on US 17. Ext/int corridors. **Pets:** Small. $10 daily fee/pet. Designated rooms, service with restrictions, supervision.
(SAVE) (S&) (X) (H) (▣)

(AAA) ▼▼▼ **Red Roof Inn** M
(757) 523-0123. **$39-$74.** 724 Woodlake Dr. I-64, exit 289A, just n to Woodlake Dr, just e. Ext corridors. **Pets:** Small. Service with restrictions, crate.
(SAVE) (X) (H)

▼▼▼ **Super 8 Motel** M ✿
(757) 686-8888. **$53-$65, 7 days notice.** 3216 Churchland Blvd. I-664, exit 9B, 1 mi s. Int corridors. **Pets:** Other species. Designated rooms, service with restrictions, crate.
(ASK) (S&) (X) (&M) (H)

(AAA) ▼▼▼▼ **TownePlace Suites By Marriott** M ✿
(757) 523-5004. **$75-$99.** 2000 Old Greenbriar Rd. I-64, exit 298A, just n. Int corridors. **Pets:** Other species. $10 daily fee/room. Service with restrictions.
(SAVE) (X) (&M) (🐾) (🛏) (H) (≈)

(AAA) ▼▼▼ **Wellesley Inn** M
(757) 366-0100. **$69-$99.** 721 Conf Center Dr. I-64, exit 289A, n to Woodlake Dr, 2 blks e. Int corridors. **Pets:** Accepted.
(SAVE) (S&) (X) (&M) (🛏) (H) (▣) (≈)

HAMPTON

▼▼▼▼ **Candlewood Suites** M
(757) 766-8976. **$89-$159.** 401 Butler Farm Rd. I-64, exit 261B eastbound; exit 261 westbound, then n. Int corridors. **Pets:** Accepted.
(ASK) (S&) (X) (&M) (🛏) (H) (▣)

(AAA) ▼▼▼▼ **La Quinta Inn** M
(757) 827-8680. **$55-$75.** 2138 W Mercury Blvd. I-64, exit 263B. Ext/int corridors. **Pets:** Small, other species. Service with restrictions, crate.
(SAVE) (S&) (X) (&M) (🐾) (🛏) (H) (▣) (≈)

(AAA) ▼▼▼▼ **Quality Inn & Suites Conference Center** H
(757) 838-5011. **$79-$159.** 1809 W Mercury Blvd. I-64, exit 263B, at jct SR 58. Int corridors. **Pets:** Accepted.
(SAVE) (S&) (X) (&M) (🐾) (🛏) (H) (▣) (🍽) (≈)

(AAA) ▼▼▼ **Red Roof Inn** M
(757) 838-1870. **$44-$79.** 1925 Coliseum Dr. I-64, exit 263B to Coliseum Blvd. Ext corridors. **Pets:** Accepted.
(SAVE) (X) (H)

NEWPORT NEWS

▼▼▼▼ **Comfort Inn** M
(757) 249-0200. **$79-$109.** 12330 Jefferson Ave. I-64, exit 225A, just s on Clarie Ln (mall parking lot); adjacent to Patrick Henry Mall. Int corridors. **Pets:** Designated rooms, service with restrictions, supervision.
(SAVE) (S&) (X) (&M) (🐾) (H) (▣) (≈)

(AAA) ▼▼ **Days Inn** M ✿
(757) 874-0201. **$53-$75.** 14747 Warwick Blvd. I-64, exit 250A, 2.5 mi to US 60 E. Ext corridors. **Pets:** Other species. $5 daily fee/pet. Service with restrictions, supervision.
(SAVE) (S&) (X) (H) (▣) (≈)

(AAA) ▼▼▼▼ **Days Inn-Oyster Point** M
(757) 873-6700. **$55-$95, 30 days notice.** 11829 Fishing Point Dr. I-64, exit 255A, 2.5 mi s to Thimble Shoals Dr E, 1 blk to property. Int corridors. **Pets:** Accepted.
(SAVE) (S&) (X) (🐾) (H) (▣) (≈)

Host Inn M
(757) 599-3303. **$45-$80, 3 days notice.** 985 J Clyde Morris Blvd. I-64, exit 258B, 0.8 mi n. Ext corridors. **Pets:** Small. $8 daily fee/pet. Designated rooms, service with restrictions, supervision.

Super 8 Motel M
(757) 595-8888. **$55-$65.** 945 J Clyde Morris Blvd. I-64, exit 258B, just n. Int corridors. **Pets:** Accepted.

TownePlace Suites by Marriott A
(757) 874-8884. **$79-$94.** 200 Cybernetics Way. I-64, exit 256B, e to Kiln Creek Pkwy. Int corridors. **Pets:** Accepted.

NORFOLK

Bed & Breakfast at the Page House Inn BB ❖
(757) 625-5033. **$125-$175, 7 days notice.** 323 Fairfax Ave. I-264, exit 264, 1.4 mi n on Waterside Dr to Olney Rd, just w to Mowbray Arch, then just s. Int corridors. **Pets:** Small, dogs only. $30 daily fee/pet. Service with restrictions, crate.

Clarion Hotel James Madison H
(757) 622-6682. **$99-$139.** 345 Granby St. Downtown; Granby St at Freemason St. Int corridors. **Pets:** Accepted.

Days Inn Marina M
(757) 583-4521. **$59-$99, 3 days notice.** 1631 Bayville St. I-64, exit 272 (Willoughby Spit), at east end of Hampton Roads Bridge-Tunnel. Ext corridors. **Pets:** Small, other species. $10 daily fee/pet. Designated rooms, service with restrictions, supervision.

Norfolk Waterside Marriott Hotel H
(757) 627-4200. **$149.** 235 E Main St. Center; corner of Main and Atlantic sts. Int corridors. **Pets:** Small, other species. $35 one-time fee/room. Service with restrictions, supervision.

Quality Suites Lake Wright M
(757) 461-6251. **$99-$159.** 6280 Northampton Blvd. I-64, exit 282, just w on US 13. Int corridors. **Pets:** Other species. $35 one-time fee/room. Service with restrictions, crate.

Radisson Hotel Norfolk H
(757) 627-5555. **$89-$129, 7 days notice.** 700 Monticello Ave. Downtown; at Brambleton Ave and St Pauls Blvd; across from Scope. Int corridors. **Pets:** Accepted.

Sleep Inn Lake Wright M
(757) 461-1133. **$79-$119.** 6280 Northampton Blvd. I-64, exit 282, just w on US 13. Int corridors. **Pets:** $25 one-time fee/room. Service with restrictions, crate.

Tazewell Hotel and Suites A Ramada Plaza H
(757) 623-6200. **$108-$118.** 245 Granby St. Downtown; at jct with Tazewell St. Int corridors. **Pets:** Other species. $25 deposit/room. Service with restrictions, supervision.

PORTSMOUTH

Holiday Inn-Olde Towne Portsmouth MI
(757) 393-2573. **$83-$129, 3 days notice.** 8 Crawford Pkwy. At Green St. Int corridors. **Pets:** Service with restrictions, supervision.

VIRGINIA BEACH

Days Inn Oceanfront MI
(757) 428-7233. **$55-$250, 3 days notice.** 3107 Atlantic. I-264, 0.8 mi n of terminus, just n of jct with Laskin Rd (SR 58) at 32nd St. Int corridors. **Pets:** Accepted.

Flagship Motel M
(757) 425-6422. **$45-$175.** 512 Atlantic Ave. I-264, 1 mi s of terminus at Atlantic Ave and 6th St. Ext corridors. **Pets:** $30 one-time fee/pet. Designated rooms, service with restrictions, supervision.

La Quinta Inn M
(757) 497-6620. **$55-$95.** 192 Newtown Rd. I-64, exit 284B to I-264 (Virginia Beach-Norfolk Expwy), exit Newtown Rd S. Int corridors. **Pets:** Small, other species. Service with restrictions.

Ocean Holiday Hotel M
(757) 425-6920. **$45-$195, 3 days notice.** 2417 Atlantic Ave. I-264, n of terminus; Atlantic Ave and 25th St. Int corridors. **Pets:** Small, dogs only. $20 daily fee/pet. Designated rooms, service with restrictions.

Ramada Inn Airport MI
(757) 464-9351. **$75-$110.** 5725 Northampton Blvd. I-64, exit 282, 1 mi n on US 13; 2.5 mi n of Norfolk International Airport. Ext corridors. **Pets:** Other species. $25 one-time fee/pet. Service with restrictions, supervision.

Ramada Plaza Resort Oceanfront H ❖
(757) 428-7025. **$80-$250, 3 days notice.** Atlantic Ave and 57th St. I-264, 2.2 mi n of terminus. Int corridors. **Pets:** Dogs only. $10 daily fee/room. Designated rooms, service with restrictions, supervision.

Red Roof Inn-Virginia Beach M
(757) 490-0225. **$44-$84.** 196 Ballard Ct. I-64, exit 284B (Newtown Rd). Ext corridors. **Pets:** Accepted.

The Thunderbird Motor Lodge M
(757) 428-3024. **$49-$189, 3 days notice.** 3410 Atlantic Ave. I-264, 1.2 mi n of terminus; at Atlantic Ave and 35th St. Ext/int corridors. **Pets:** Small. $20 daily fee/pet. Designated rooms, service with restrictions, crate.

TownePlace Suites By Marriott M ❖
(757) 490-9367. **$49-$159.** 5757 Cleveland St. I-64, exit 284B to I-264 (Virginia Beach-Norfolk Expwy), exit Newtown Rd N to Cleveland St. Int corridors. **Pets:** Other species. $100 one-time fee/pet. Service with restrictions, supervision.

❖ **END AREA** ❖

HARRISONBURG

Comfort Inn M
(540) 433-6066. **$70-$97.** 1440 E Market St. I-81, exit 247A, just e. Int corridors. **Pets:** Other species. Service with restrictions, crate.

Days Inn Harrisonburg M
(540) 433-9353. **$49-$120.** 1131 Forest Hill Rd. I-81, exit 245, just e. Int corridors. **Pets:** $10 daily fee/room. Service with restrictions, supervision.

Four Points by Sheraton Harrisonburg H
(540) 433-2521. **$70-$80.** 1400 E Market St. I-81, exit 247A, just e on US 33. Int corridors. **Pets:** Accepted.

Harrisonburg Econo Lodge M
(540) 433-2576. **$48-$84, 3 days notice.** 1703 E Market St. I-81, exit 247A, 0.5 mi e on US 33. Ext/int corridors. **Pets:** Designated rooms, service with restrictions, supervision.

Ramada Inn MI
(540) 434-9981. **$60-$85, 3 days notice.** 1 Pleasant Valley Rd. I-81, exit 243, just w, then just n on US 11. Ext corridors. **Pets:** Small, dogs only. $10 one-time fee/room. Designated rooms, service with restrictions, supervision.

Super 8 Motel M
(540) 433-8888. **$55-$69.** 3330 S Main St. I-81, exit 243, just e, then just s on US 11. Int corridors. **Pets:** Accepted.

The Village Inn MI ❖
(540) 434-7355. **$59-$67.** 4979 South Valley Pike. I-81, exit 240 southbound, 0.6 mi w on SR 257, then 1.5 mi n on US 11; exit 243 northbound, just w to US 11, then 1.7 mi s. Ext corridors. **Pets:** Other species. $5 daily fee/pet. Service with restrictions, supervision.

HILLSVILLE

Best Western Four Seasons South M
(540) 728-4136. **$62-$72, 10 days notice.** 57 Airport Rd. I-77, exit 14, just w on US 58 and 221. Ext corridors. **Pets:** Very small, other species. $5 daily fee/pet. Designated rooms, service with restrictions, supervision.

Holiday Inn Express M
(540) 728-2120. **$62-$150, 7 days notice.** 85 Airport Rd. I-77, exit 14, just w on US 58 and 221. Ext corridors. **Pets:** Small, other species. $5 daily fee/pet. Designated rooms, service with restrictions, supervision.

HOT SPRINGS

Roseloe Motel M
(540) 839-5373. **$60-$80, 3 days notice.** 590 US 220 N. 3 mi n. Ext corridors. **Pets:** Large. $10 one-time fee/room. Service with restrictions, supervision.

KESWICK

Keswick Hall at Monticello R
(434) 979-3440. **$450-$693, 14 days notice.** 701 Club Dr. Just n. Int corridors. **Pets:** Accepted.

KEYSVILLE

Sheldon's Motel MI
(434) 736-8434. **$50-$72.** 1450 Four Locust Hwy. 1.3 mi n on US 15 and 360 business route. Ext corridors. **Pets:** Other species. Service with restrictions, crate.

LEXINGTON

Best Western Inn at Hunt Ridge MI
(540) 464-1500. **$69-$150.** 25 Willow Springs Rd. I-81, exit 191, 0.6 mi w; I-64, exit 55, just n on US 11 to SR 39, then just w. Int corridors. **Pets:** Large. $25 one-time fee/room. Designated rooms, service with restrictions, supervision.

ⒶⒶⒶ ◆◆◆ Comfort Inn-Virginia Horse Center 🅼
(540) 463-7311. **$54-$125.** 62 Comfort Way. I-81, exit 191, 0.6 mi w; I-64, exit 55, just s on US 11. Int corridors. **Pets:** Medium, other species. Designated rooms, service with restrictions, supervision.
SAVE 🆂🅾 ✕ 🔲 💷 ⇆

ⒶⒶⒶ ◆◆◆ Days Inn Keydet General 🅼
(540) 463-2143. **$55-$80, 3 days notice.** 325 W Midland Tr. I-81, exit 188B, 4.5 mi on US 60 W; I-64, exit 50, 5 mi e on US 60. Ext/int corridors. **Pets:** Medium, other species. $5 daily fee/pet. Designated rooms, service with restrictions, supervision.
SAVE 🆂🅾 ✕ 🔲

ⒶⒶⒶ ◆◆◆ Econo Lodge 🅼 ❖
(540) 463-7371. **$50-$75.** 65 Econo Ln. I-81, exit 191, 0.6 mi w; I-64, exit 55, just s on US 11. Ext corridors. **Pets:** $8 daily fee/pet. Service with restrictions.
SAVE 🆂🅾 ✕ 🔲 💷

ⒶⒶⒶ ◆◆◆ Holiday Inn Express 🅼
(540) 463-7351. **$55-$130.** 850 N Lee Hwy. I-81, exit 191, 1.6 mi w; I-64, exit 55, just s on US 11. Ext corridors. **Pets:** Accepted.
SAVE 🆂🅾 ✕ 🄳 💷

ⒶⒶⒶ ◆◆◆ Howard Johnson Inn 🅼🄸
(540) 463-9181. **$65-$115.** 2836 N Lee Hwy. I-81, exit 195, just s on US 11. Int corridors. **Pets:** $5 one-time fee/room. No service, supervision.
SAVE 🆂🅾 ✕ 🄳 🔲 💷 🍴 ⇆

◆◆◆ Ramada Inn Lexington 🅼
(540) 463-6400. **$70.** 2814 N Lee Hwy. I-81, exit 195, just sw on US 11. Int corridors. **Pets:** $8 daily fee/pet. Service with restrictions, supervision.
ASK 🆂🅾 ✕ 🄳 🆁 🔲 🍴 ⇆

LURAY

ⒶⒶⒶ ◆◆◆◆ Best Western Intown of Luray 🅼🄸
(540) 743-6511. **$65-$100.** 410 W Main St. 0.3 mi w on US 211 business route. Ext corridors. **Pets:** Accepted.
SAVE 🆂🅾 ✕ 🔲 💷 🍴 ⇆

◆◆ Days Inn-Luray 🅼🄸
(540) 743-4521. **$49-$150.** 138 Whispering Hill Rd. US 211 Bypass, 1.7 mi e of jct US 340. Ext corridors. **Pets:** Medium. $10 daily fee/pet. Designated rooms, service with restrictions, crate.
SAVE 🆂🅾 ✕ 🍴 ⇆

LYNCHBURG

ⒶⒶⒶ ◆◆◆◆ Comfort Inn 🅼🄸
(434) 847-9041. **$79-$99.** 3125 Albert Lankford Dr. US 29, exit 7, 2.5 mi s. Int corridors. **Pets:** Medium, other species. $30 deposit/room. Designated rooms, service with restrictions, supervision.
SAVE 🆂🅾 ✕ 🔲 💷 🍴 ⇆

ⒶⒶⒶ ◆◆◆ Holiday Inn Select 🄷
(434) 528-2500. **$79-$109.** 601 Main St. US 29, exit 1; center. Int corridors. **Pets:** Accepted.
SAVE 🆂🅾 ✕ 🔲 💷 🍴 ⇆

MADISON HEIGHTS

ⒶⒶⒶ ◆◆ Knights Inn 🅼
(434) 929-6506. **$50-$60.** 3642 S Amherst Hwy. 5 mi n on US 29. Ext corridors. **Pets:** $5 daily fee/pet. Service with restrictions, supervision.
SAVE 🆂🅾 ✕ 🔲 ⇆

MARION

ⒶⒶⒶ ◆◆◆ Best Western-Marion 🅼🄸
(540) 783-3193. **$59-$79, 15 days notice.** 1424 N Main St. I-81, exit 47, 0.3 mi s on US 11. Ext corridors. **Pets:** Accepted.
SAVE 🆂🅾 ✕ 🄳 🔲 💷 🍴 ⇆

◆◆ Econo Lodge 🅼
(540) 783-6031. **$49-$54, 14 days notice.** 1424 N Main St. I-81, exit 47, 0.3 mi s on US 11. Ext corridors. **Pets:** Accepted.
SAVE 🆂🅾 ✕ 🄳 🔲 💷

MARTINSVILLE

ⒶⒶⒶ ◆◆◆ Best Lodge 🅼
(540) 647-3941. **$45-$60, 7 days notice.** 1985 Virginia Ave. 2.5 mi n on US 220 business route, from jct US 58. Ext corridors. **Pets:** Accepted.
SAVE 🆂🅾 ✕ 🔲 💷

◆◆◆ Best Western Martinsville Inn 🅼🄸
(540) 632-5611. **$69-$109.** US 220 Business S. 2.3 mi n on US 220 business route, from jct US 58. Ext corridors. **Pets:** Accepted.
SAVE 🆂🅾 ✕ 🔲 💷 🍴 ⇆

◆◆ Super 8 Motel 🅼
(540) 666-8888. **$54-$65, 14 days notice.** 1044 N Memorial Blvd. 1.5 mi n on US 220 business route, from jct US 58. Int corridors. **Pets:** Service with restrictions, supervision.
ASK 🆂🅾 ✕ 🔲

MAX MEADOWS

ⒶⒶⒶ ◆◆◆◆ Comfort Inn 🅼
(540) 637-4281. **$70-$80, 5 days notice.** 2594 E Lee Hwy. I-77/81, exit 80, just w. Int corridors. **Pets:** Accepted.
SAVE 🆂🅾 ✕ 🄼 🄳 🆁 🔲 💷 ⇆

MINT SPRING

◆ Armstrong Family Motel & Restaurant 🅼🄸 ❖
(540) 337-2611. **$35-$60.** 210 White Hill Rd. I-81, exit 217, just w on SR 654. Ext corridors. **Pets:** Other species. Service with restrictions.
ASK 🆂🅾 ✕ 🄳 🍴 ⇆

▼▼ Days Inn-Staunton Ⓜ
(540) 337-3031. **$89-$109, 5 days notice.** 372 White Hill Rd. I-81, exit 217, just e on SR 654. Ext corridors. **Pets:** Other species. $6 daily fee/pet. Designated rooms, service with restrictions, supervision.

🖼 🖼 🖼 🖼 🖼 🖼 🖼

NEW CHURCH

▼▼▼ The Garden & The Sea Inn Ⓒ 🐾
(757) 824-0672. **$85-$195, 10 days notice.** 4188 Nelson Rd. US 13, 0.3 mi s, then w on CR 710 (Nelson Rd). Int corridors. **Pets:** Other species.

🖼 🖼 🖼 🖼 🖼

NEW MARKET

Ⓐ ▼ Budget Inn Ⓜ
(540) 740-3105. **$29-$69, 3 days notice.** 2192 Old Valley Pike. I-81, exit 264, 1 mi n on US 11. Ext corridors. **Pets:** Small, other species. $10 deposit/room, $5 one-time fee/pet. Designated rooms, no service, supervision.

🖼 🖼 🖼 🖼 🖼

Ⓐ ▼▼ Days Inn Ⓜ
(540) 740-4100. **$39-$95.** 9360 George Collins Pkwy. I-81, exit 264, just w on US 211. Ext corridors. **Pets:** Service with restrictions, supervision.

🖼 🖼 🖼 🖼

PALMYRA

Ⓐ ▼▼▼ Palmer Country Manor Ⓒ 🐾
(434) 589-1300. **$77-$185, 10 days notice.** Rt 2 Box 1390. On SR 640, 1.8 mi w of jct US 15. Ext/int corridors. **Pets:** $15 daily fee/pet. Supervision.

🖼 🖼 🖼 🖼 🖼 🖼 🖼

PETERSBURG

Ⓐ ▼▼ Best Inn & Suites Ⓜ
(804) 733-1776. **$50-$65.** 405 E Washington St. I-85, exit 69. Ext corridors. **Pets:** Medium. $7 daily fee/pet. Service with restrictions.

🖼 🖼 🖼 🖼 🖼 🖼 🖼 🖼

Ⓐ ▼▼▼ Best Western-Steven Kent Ⓜ 🐾
(804) 733-0600. **$47-$77, 14 days notice.** 12205 S Crater Rd. I-95, exit 45, jct US 301. Ext/int corridors. **Pets:** Other species. $10 daily fee/room. Designated rooms, service with restrictions.

🖼 🖼 🖼 🖼 🖼 🖼 🖼 🖼 🖼

Ⓐ ▼▼▼ Comfort Inn Ⓜ
(804) 732-2900. **$51-$95, 14 days notice.** 11974 S Crater Rd. I-95, exit 45, n on US 301. Ext corridors. **Pets:** Medium. $10 daily fee/room. Designated rooms, service with restrictions, crate.

🖼 🖼 🖼 🖼 🖼

Ⓐ ▼▼▼ Days Inn Ⓜ
(804) 733-4400. **$49-$79, 14 days notice.** 12208 S Crater Rd. I-95, exit 45, jct US 301. Ext corridors. **Pets:** Accepted.

🖼 🖼 🖼 🖼 🖼 🖼

RADFORD

Ⓐ ▼▼▼ Best Western Radford Inn Ⓜ
(540) 639-3000. **$79-$99.** 1501 Tyler Ave. I-81, exit 109, 2.7 mi nw on SR 177. Int corridors. **Pets:** Accepted.

🖼 🖼 🖼 🖼 🖼 🖼

RAPHINE

▼▼ Days Inn-Shenandoah Valley Ⓜ
(540) 377-2604. **$49-$99, 15 days notice.** 584 Oakland Cr. I-81, exit 205, just sw. Int corridors. **Pets:** Large, other species. $5 one-time fee/pet. Designated rooms, service with restrictions, supervision.

🖼 🖼 🖼 🖼

RICHMOND METROPOLITAN AREA

ASHLAND

▼▼▼ The Henry Clay Inn Ⓑ
(804) 798-3100. **$90-$165, 7 days notice.** 114 N Railroad Ave. I-95, exit 92, 1.5 mi w on SR 54, then n; opposite Amtrak Station. Ext/int corridors. **Pets:** Accepted.

🖼 🖼 🖼 🖼

CHESTER

▼▼ Howard Johnson Hotel-Chester Ⓜ
(804) 748-6321. **$65-$95, 3 days notice.** 2401 W Hundred Rd. I-95, exit 61B, just e on jct SR 10. Int corridors. **Pets:** Other species. Supervision.

🖼 🖼 🖼 🖼 🖼 🖼 🖼 🖼

DOSWELL

Ⓐ ▼▼ Best Western-Kings Quarters Ⓜ 🐾
(804) 876-3321. **$34-$159, 3 days notice.** 16102 Theme Park Way. I-95, exit 98, just e on SR 30; at entrance to theme park. Ext corridors. **Pets:** Medium. $5 daily fee/room. Designated rooms, service with restrictions, supervision.

🖼 🖼 🖼 🖼 🖼 🖼 🖼 🖼 🖼

GLEN ALLEN

AmeriSuites (Richmond/Innsbrook) M
(804) 747-9644. **$95.** 4100 Cox Rd. I-64, exit 178B, 0.5 mi e to Dominion Blvd, just n; in Innsbrook Corporate Center. Int corridors. **Pets:** Accepted.

Homestead Studio Suites-Richmond/Innsbrook M
(804) 747-8898. **$45.** 10961 W Broad St. I-64, exit 178B, just e on W Broad St, just s on Cox Rd. Ext corridors. **Pets:** Small, other species. $75 one-time fee/pet. Service with restrictions, crate.

Homewood Suites Hotel Richmond West End M
(804) 217-8000. **$115-$125.** 4100 Innslake Dr. I-64, exit 178B, just e on W Broad St to Cox Rd, just n. Int corridors. **Pets:** Accepted.

Residence Inn by Marriott A
(804) 762-9852. **$134-$144.** 3940 Westerre Pkwy. I-64, exit 180, n on Gaskins Rd to W Broad St. Int corridors. **Pets:** Large, other species. $150 one-time fee/room. Service with restrictions.

TownePlace Suites by Marriott M
(804) 747-5253. **$76-$94, 3 days notice.** 4231 Park Place Ct. I-64, exit 178B, just e on W Broad St to Cox Rd, just n to Innslake Dr; in Innsbrook Corporate Center. Int corridors. **Pets:** Accepted.

RICHMOND

AmeriSuites (Richmond/Arboretum) M
(804) 560-1566. **$79-$129.** 201 Arboretum Pl. Jct Powhite Pkwy (US 76) and Midlothian Tpke (US 60), just w; enter at the Arboretum Pl. Int corridors. **Pets:** Small. Supervision.

Candlewood Suites M
(804) 271-0016. **$59-$109.** 4301 Commerce Rd. I-95, exit 69, just n. Int corridors. **Pets:** Accepted.

Commonwealth Park Suites M
(804) 343-7300. **$95-$169.** 901 Bank St. Downtown; at 9th and Bank sts; across the green from the State Capitol. Int corridors. **Pets:** Small. $25 one-time fee/room. Designated rooms, service with restrictions, crate.

Days Inn-Richmond/Broad St M
(804) 282-3300. **$51-$88.** 2100 Dickens Rd. I-64, exit 183B westbound; exit 183 eastbound, 0.3 mi e on W Broad St, just n. Int corridors. **Pets:** Medium. $5 daily fee/pet. Service with restrictions, crate.

Holiday Inn-Bells Road M
(804) 275-7891. **$62-$72.** 4303 Commerce Rd. I-95, exit 69, just n; adjacent to Philip Morris. Int corridors. **Pets:** Accepted.

Holiday Inn Central M
(804) 359-9441. **$69, 7 days notice.** 3207 N Boulevard. I-64/95, exit 78. Ext/int corridors. **Pets:** Accepted.

Homestead Studio Suites-Richmond/Midlothian M
(804) 272-1800. **$59-$79.** 241 Arboretum Pl. Jct Powhite Pkwy (US 76) and Midlothian Tpke (US 60), just w; enter at the Arboretum Pl. Int corridors. **Pets:** Accepted.

The Jefferson Hotel H
(804) 788-8000. **$255-$305.** 101 W Franklin St. Center; Franklin and Adams sts. Int corridors. **Pets:** $25 daily fee/ room. Service with restrictions, crate.

Quality Inn West End M
(804) 346-0000. **$69-$149.** 8008 W Broad St. I-64, exit 183C westbound; exit 183 eastbound, 1.5 mi w. Int corridors. **Pets:** Large, other species. $10 daily fee/room, $25 one-time fee/room. Service with restrictions, supervision.

Radisson Hotel Historic Richmond M
(804) 644-9871. **Call for rates.** 301 W Franklin St. Downtown; Franklin St at Madison. Int corridors. **Pets:** Accepted.

Red Roof Inn-Richmond South M
(804) 271-7240. **$39-$59.** 4350 Commerce Rd. I-95, exit 69. Ext corridors. **Pets:** Accepted.

Residence Inn by Marriott M
(804) 285-8200. **$99.** 2121 Dickens Rd. I-64, exit 183B, 0.3 mi e, just n of US 60 (Broad St). Ext corridors. **Pets:** Accepted.

Wyndham Richmond Airport H
(804) 226-4300. **$94-$119.** 4700 S Laburnum Ave. I-64, exit 195, 0.5 mi s. Int corridors. **Pets:** Medium. $50 one-time fee/room. Service with restrictions, supervision.

SANDSTON

Holiday Inn-Airport M
(804) 222-6450. **$84, 7 days notice.** 5203 Williamsburg Rd. I-64, exit 195, 1.5 mi s to Williamsburg Rd, then just e. Ext/int corridors. **Pets:** Small. $25 one-time fee/room. Service with restrictions, supervision.

Microtel Inn & Suites M
(804) 737-3322. **$55-$80.** 6000 Audubon Dr. I-64, exit 197A, just s. Int corridors. **Pets:** Other species. Service with restrictions, supervision.

Wingate Inn Richmond Airport M
(804) 222-1499. **$89-$145, 5 days notice.** 491 International Centre Dr. I-64, exit 197A, just s to Audobon Dr, just n. Int corridors. **Pets:** Small, other species. $15 one-time fee/pet. Designated rooms, service with restrictions, supervision.

❖ **END METROPOLITAN AREA** ❖

ROANOKE

AmeriSuites (Roanoke/Valley View Mall) M
(540) 366-4700. **$59-$149.** 5040 Valley View Blvd. I-581, exit 3E, just e, then just s via shopping center exit. Int corridors. **Pets:** Accepted.

Clarion Hotel Roanoke Airport M
(540) 362-4500. **$89-$139.** 3315 Ordway Dr. I-581, exit 3W, just w to Ordway Dr, then 0.6 mi n via service road. Int corridors. **Pets:** Other species. $25 deposit/pet. Designated rooms, service with restrictions.

Rodeway Inn-Civic Center M
(540) 981-9341. **$40-$100.** 526 Orange Ave NE. I-581, exit 4E, jct US 400 and 11, just n. Ext corridors. **Pets:** Other species. $10 one-time fee/room. Service with restrictions.

Super 8 Motel M
(540) 563-8888. **$54-$64, 14 days notice.** 6616 Thirlane Rd. I-581, exit 25, s on SR 117 (Peters Creek Rd), just w. Int corridors. **Pets:** Accepted.

Wyndham Roanoke Airport M
(540) 563-9300. **$94-$109.** 2801 Hershberger Rd. I-581, exit 3W, just w to Ordway Dr, just n via service road. Int corridors. **Pets:** Accepted.

ROCKY MOUNT

Franklin Motel M
(540) 483-9962. **$40-$60.** 20281 Virgil H Goode Hwy. 6.5 mi n on US 220. Ext corridors. **Pets:** Very small, dogs only. $10 deposit/pet, $10 one-time fee/pet. Service with restrictions, supervision.

SALEM

Baymont Inn Roanoke-Salem M
(540) 562-2717. **$64-$74, 7 days notice.** 140 Sheraton Dr. I-81, exit 141, 0.5 mi se on SR 419. Int corridors. **Pets:** Small. Designated rooms, service with restrictions, supervision.

Blue Jay Budget Host Inn M ❖
(540) 380-2080. **$35-$58, 3 days notice.** 5399 W Main St. I-81, exit 132, just e, then n on US 11/460. Ext corridors. **Pets:** $5 daily fee/pet. Designated rooms, service with restrictions, supervision.

Holiday Inn M
(540) 389-7061. **$79, 7 days notice.** 1671 Skyview Rd. I-81, exit 137, just w on SR 112, then just n. Ext corridors. **Pets:** Accepted.

Knights Inn-Roanoke/Salem M
(540) 389-0280. **$55-$65, 7 days notice.** 301 Wildwood Rd. I-81, exit 137, just e on SR 112. Ext corridors. **Pets:** Accepted.

Quality Inn Roanoke/Salem M
(540) 562-1912. **$60-$83, 14 days notice.** 179 Sheraton Dr. I-81, exit 141, 0.4 mi e on SR 419. Int corridors. **Pets:** Small. $15 daily fee/pet. Designated rooms, no service, supervision.

SCOTTSVILLE

High Meadows Vineyard Inn CI
(434) 286-2218. **$159-$350.** 55 High Meadows Ln. I-64, exit 121 (SR 20), 17 mi s, 1 mi n. Ext/int corridors. **Pets:** Accepted.

SOUTH BOSTON

Best Western Howard House Inn M
(434) 572-4311. **$67.** 2001 Seymour Dr. 1 mi e on US 360, from jct US 58, 501 and 360. Ext corridors. **Pets:** Accepted.

SOUTH HILL

Comfort Inn M
(434) 447-2600. **$55-$69.** 918 E Atlantic St. I-85, exit 12B, just e. Ext corridors. **Pets:** Other species. Service with restrictions, crate.

(AAA) (W)(W) Econo Lodge [M]
(434) 447-7116. **$55-$75, 7 days notice.** 623 E Atlantic St.
I-85, exit 12B, 0.5 mi w on US 58. Ext corridors.
Pets: Accepted.
[SAVE] [S] [X] [H] [P]

STAUNTON

(W)(W)(W) Ashton Country House [BB] ❀
(540) 885-7819. **$85-$150, 7 days notice.** 1205 Middlebrook Ave. I-81, exit 220, 1 mi to SR 252 (Middlebrook
Ave), 0.3 mi n. Int corridors. **Pets:** Other species. $10 daily
fee/room. Designated rooms, service with restrictions.
[ASK] [S] [X] [Z]

(W)(W)(W) Best Inn of Staunton [M]
(540) 248-5111. **$39-$75.** 96 Baker Ln. I-81, exit 225, just e
on SR 275 (Woodrow Wilson Pkwy). Ext corridors.
Pets: Other species. $6 daily fee/pet. Designated rooms,
service with restrictions, supervision.
[ASK] [S] [X] [H] [P] [≈]

(AAA) (W)(W)(W) Comfort Inn [M]
(540) 886-5000. **$69-$99.** 1302 Richmond Ave. I-81, exit
222, just w on US 250. Int corridors. **Pets:** Small, other
species. $10 daily fee/room. Designated rooms, service
with restrictions, supervision.
[SAVE] [S] [X] [Z] [H] [P] [≈]

(AAA) (W)(W) Econo Lodge Staunton [M]
(540) 885-5158. **$54-$84, 7 days notice.** 1031 Richmond
Ave. I-81, exit 222, 0.7 mi w on US 250. Ext/int corridors.
Pets: Large, other species. Service with restrictions, super-
vision.
[SAVE] [S] [X] [H] [P]

(AAA) (W)(W) Sleep Inn [M]
(540) 887-6500. **$49-$94.** 222 Jefferson Hwy. I-81, exit 222,
just e on US 250. Int corridors. **Pets:** Large. Service with
restrictions, supervision.
[SAVE] [S] [X] [⌂] [P]

(AAA) (W)(W)(W) Super 8 Motel [M]
(540) 886-2888. **$54-$84, 7 days notice.** 1015 Richmond
Rd. I-81, exit 222, 1.2 mi w on US 250. Int corridors.
Pets: Large, other species. Service with restrictions, super-
vision.
[SAVE] [S] [X] [H]

STEPHENS CITY

(AAA) (W)(W)(W) Comfort Inn-Stephens City [M]
(540) 869-6500. **$60-$85.** 167 Town Run Ln. I-81, exit 307,
just se. Int corridors. **Pets:** Accepted.
[SAVE] [S] [X] [Z] [H] [P] [≈]

STRASBURG

(AAA) (W)(W)(W) Hotel Strasburg [CI]
(540) 465-9191. **$81-$180.** 213 Holliday St. I-81, exit 298,
2.2 mi s on US 11, just s. Int corridors. **Pets:** Accepted.
[SAVE] [S] [X] [⌘]

THORNBURG

(W)(W)(W) Holiday Inn Express [M]
(540) 582-1097. **$79-$149.** 6409 Dan Bell Ln. I-95, exit 118
(SR 606). Ext corridors. **Pets:** Medium. $10 daily fee/pet.
Service with restrictions, supervision.
[ASK] [S] [X] [⌂M] [⌂] [H]

TROUTVILLE

(AAA) (W)(W)(W) Travelodge Roanoke North [M]
(540) 992-6700. **$35-$65.** 2619 Lee Hwy S. I-81, exit 150A,
just e, then just s on US 11. Ext corridors. **Pets:** Medium.
$6.39 daily fee/pet. Designated rooms, service with restric-
tions, crate.
[SAVE] [S] [X] [H] [P] [≈]

VERONA

(W)(W)(W) Ramada Limited [M]
(540) 248-8981. **$55-$95, 30 days notice.** 70 Lodge Ln.
I-81, exit 227, just w, then just n. Ext corridors. **Pets:** Other
species. $5 daily fee/pet. Designated rooms, service with
restrictions, supervision.
[ASK] [S] [X] [Z] [P] [≈]

WARRENTON

(AAA) (W)(W)(W) Comfort Inn [M]
(540) 349-8900. **$69-$95.** 7379 Comfort Inn Dr. 1.5 mi n on
US 15/29, on service road. Ext/int corridors.
Pets: Accepted.
[SAVE] [S] [X] [H] [P] [≈]

(AAA) (W)(W)(W) Hampton Inn [M]
(540) 349-4200. **$65-$99, 3 days notice.** 501 Blackwell Rd.
1 mi n on US 29 business route and 211. Ext corridors.
Pets: Large. Service with restrictions, supervision.
[SAVE] [X] [⌂M] [Z] [H] [P] [≈]

WARSAW

(W)(W)(W) Best Western Warsaw [M]
(804) 333-1700. **$63-$77.** 4522 Richmond Rd. US 360, just
w of town. Int corridors. **Pets:** Small. $10 daily fee/pet.
Service with restrictions, supervision.
[SAVE] [S] [X] [H] [≈]

WAYNESBORO

(AAA) (W)(W)(W) Comfort Inn Waynesboro [M]
(540) 942-1171. **$65-$89, 7 days notice.** 640 W Broad St.
I-64, exit 96, 3 mi w on SR 624; at jct US 250 and 340.
Ext/int corridors. **Pets:** Small. Designated rooms, service
with restrictions, crate.
[SAVE] [S] [X] [Z] [H] [P] [≈]

(W)(W) Super 8 Motel [M]
(540) 943-3888. **$55-$75.** 2045 Rosser Ave. I-64, exit 94, n
on US 340 to Lew DeWitt Blvd, just w to Apple Tree Ln. Int
corridors. **Pets:** Accepted.
[ASK] [S] [X] [Z] [H]

WILLIAMSBURG, JAMESTOWN & YORKTOWN AREA

WILLIAMSBURG

Best Inn M
(757) 220-2800. **$37-$94.** 600 Bypass Rd. US 60 Bypass, 0.5 mi w of jct SR 132. Int corridors. **Pets:** Small. $15 daily fee/pet. Designated rooms, service with restrictions, supervision.

Best Western Colonial Capitol Inn M
(757) 253-1222. **$59-$129, 3 days notice.** 111 Penniman Rd. Just n of jct US 60 and SR 5/SR 31. Int corridors. **Pets:** Medium. $10 one-time fee/room. Service with restrictions, crate.

Best Western Patrick Henry Inn H
(757) 229-9540. **$59-$179, 3 days notice.** 249 E York St NW. E on US 60 at jct SR 5 and 31, 1 blk from Colonial Williamsburg. Int corridors. **Pets:** Medium. $15 one-time fee/room. Designated rooms, service with restrictions, crate.

Best Western Williamsburg M
(757) 229-3003. **$69-$129, 3 days notice.** 7411 Pocahantas Tr. 2 mi e on US 60 at jct SR 199. Ext corridors. **Pets:** Medium. $10 one-time fee/room. Service with restrictions, crate.

Best Western Williamsburg Westpark Hotel M
(757) 229-1134. **$39-$99.** 1600 Richmond Rd. Jct US 60/Richmond Rd and SR 612/Ironbound Rd. Ext/int corridors. **Pets:** Large, other species. Service with restrictions.

Days Inn Colonial Downtown M
(757) 229-5060. **$33-$109.** 902 Richmond Rd. Just w of Colonial Williamsburg, on US 60. Ext corridors. **Pets:** $10 daily fee/pet. Service with restrictions, supervision.

Heritage Inn M
(757) 229-6220. **$50-$84, 3 days notice.** 1324 Richmond Rd. Just e of jct Richmond and Bypass rds. Ext corridors. **Pets:** Other species. Service with restrictions.

Holiday Inn 1776 M
(757) 220-1776. **$59-$159, 3 days notice.** 725 Bypass Rd. US 60 Bypass Rd, 0.5 mi w of jct SR 132. Int corridors. **Pets:** Medium. Service with restrictions.

Holiday Inn Patriot M
(757) 565-2600. **$49-$129.** 3032 Richmond Rd. I-64, exit 234 (SR 199 E) to US 60, 2 mi e. Int corridors. **Pets:** Medium, other species. $10 daily fee/room. Designated rooms.

The Inn at 802 BB
(757) 564-0845. **$130-$150, 7 days notice.** 802 Jamestown Rd. W of SR 199, 1 mi ne of SR 31 and 5; just w of College of William and Mary. Int corridors. **Pets:** Other species.

Quarterpath Inn M
(757) 220-0960. **$29-$85.** 620 York St. US 60 E, 0.5 mi se of jct SR 5. Ext corridors. **Pets:** Accepted.

Ramada Inn Historic M
(757) 220-1410. **$49-$114.** 500 Merrimac Tr. Jct SR 143 and 162, 0.8 mi e of US 60. Int corridors. **Pets:** Accepted.

Residence Inn Williamsburg X
(757) 941-2000. **$79-$299, 3 days notice.** 1648 Richmond Rd. On SR 60 just w of jct with Bypass Rd. Int corridors. **Pets:** Accepted.

Super 8 Motel-Colonial/Historical M
(757) 253-1087. **$43-$90, 3 days notice.** 1233 Richmond Rd. I-64, exit 238, 2 mi w of Colonial Williamsburg Historic area at the jct of Lafayette St. Int corridors. **Pets:** $10 daily fee/pet. No service.

❖ END AREA ❖

WINCHESTER

🔷 🔻🔻🔻 Best Western Lee-Jackson Motor Inn M|

(540) 662-4154. **$54-$66.** 711 Millwood Ave. I-81, exit 313B, just nw on US 50/522/17. Ext corridors. **Pets:** Accepted.

〔SAVE〕〔✎〕〔✕〕〔🛏〕〔💻〕〔🍴〕〔🏊〕

🔷 🔻🔻 Days Inn M|

(540) 667-1200. **$45-$69.** 2951 Valley Ave. I-81, exit 310, just w, then 1.8 mi n on US 11. Ext corridors. **Pets:** Medium. $5 daily fee/pet. Service with restrictions, supervision.

〔SAVE〕〔✎〕〔✕〕〔🛏〕〔🍴〕〔🏊〕

🔻 Mohawk Motel M

(540) 667-1410. **$43-$46, 5 days notice.** 2754 Northwestern Pike. I-81, exit 317, 3 mi s on SR 37, 1.7 mi w on US 50. Ext corridors. **Pets:** Accepted.

〔ASK〕〔✎〕〔✕〕

🔷 🔻🔻 Quality Inn East M

(540) 667-2250. **$61-$68.** 603 Millwood Ave. I-81, exit 313 northbound; exit 313B southbound, 0.5 mi nw on US 50/522/17. Ext corridors. **Pets:** Other species. $7 daily fee/pet. Service with restrictions.

〔SAVE〕〔✎〕〔✕〕〔🛏〕〔💻〕〔🏊〕

🔷 🔻 Tourist City Motel M

(276) 662-9011. **$36-$41, 5 days notice.** 214 Millwood Ave. I-81, exit 313 northbound; exit 313B southbound, 1 mi nw on US 50/522. Ext corridors. **Pets:** Other species. $5 daily fee/pet. Designated rooms, service with restrictions, crate.

〔SAVE〕〔✎〕〔✕〕〔🛏〕

🔷 🔻🔻🔻 Travelodge of Winchester M

(540) 665-0685. **$62-$77, 7 days notice.** 160 Front Royal Pike. I-81, exit 313 northbound; exit 313A southbound, just s on US 522. Int corridors. **Pets:** Medium, other species. $5 daily fee/pet. Service with restrictions, supervision.

〔SAVE〕〔✎〕〔✕〕〔✏〕〔🛏〕〔💻〕〔🏊〕

WOODSTOCK

🔷 🔻 Budget Host Inn M

(540) 459-4086. **$43-$48.** 1290 S Main St. I-81, exit 283, 0.8 mi se on SR 42, then 0.6 mi s on US 11. Ext corridors. **Pets:** Service with restrictions, supervision.

〔SAVE〕〔✎〕〔✕〕〔🛏〕〔🏊〕

🔷 🔻🔻🔻 Comfort Inn Shenandoah M

(540) 459-7600. **$75-$90.** 1011 Motel Dr. I-81, exit 283, just e. Int corridors. **Pets:** Other species. Supervision.

〔SAVE〕〔✎〕〔✕〕〔✏〕〔🛏〕〔💻〕〔🏊〕

🔷 🔻🔻🔻 Ramada Inn M|

(540) 459-5000. **$70-$85.** 1130 Motel Dr. I-81, exit 283, just e on SR 42. Int corridors. **Pets:** Small, dogs only. $10 daily fee/pet. Designated rooms, service with restrictions, supervision.

〔SAVE〕〔✎〕〔✕〕〔🛏〕〔💻〕〔🍴〕〔🏊〕

WYTHEVILLE

🔷 🔻🔻 Best Western Wytheville Inn M

(540) 228-5370. **$49-$79, 7 days notice.** 355 Nye Rd. I-77, exit 41, just e. Int corridors. **Pets:** $6 daily fee/pet. Designated rooms, service with restrictions, supervision.

〔SAVE〕〔✎〕〔✕〕〔🛏〕〔🏊〕

🔷 🔻🔻 Days Inn M

(540) 228-5500. **$50-$85.** 150 Malin Dr. I-81, exit 73, just w. Ext corridors. **Pets:** Medium. $5 daily fee/pet. Service with restrictions, supervision.

〔SAVE〕〔✎〕〔✕〕〔✎〕

🔷 🔻🔻 Econo Lodge M

(540) 228-5517. **$39-$100.** 1160 E Main St. I-81, exit 73, 0.8 mi w. Ext corridors. **Pets:** Medium, other species. $10 one-time fee/pet. Designated rooms, service with restrictions.

〔SAVE〕〔✎〕〔✕〕〔✎〕〔🛏〕〔💻〕

🔷 🔻🔻🔻 Holiday Inn M|

(540) 228-5483. **$69-$89.** 1800 E Main St. I-81, exit 73, just w. Ext/int corridors. **Pets:** Other species. Service with restrictions.

〔SAVE〕〔✎〕〔✕〕〔✎〕〔🖊〕〔🛏〕〔💻〕〔🍴〕〔🏊〕

🔷 🔻🔻🔻 Ramada Inn M| 🐾

(540) 228-6000. **$59-$74.** 955 Peppers Ferry Rd. I-77, exit 41, just e. Ext corridors. **Pets:** Large. Service with restrictions, supervision.

〔SAVE〕〔✎〕〔✕〕〔💻〕〔🍴〕〔🏊〕

🔷 🔻🔻 Red Carpet Inn M

(540) 228-5525. **$40-$120, 7 days notice.** 280 Lithia Rd. I-81, exit 73, just w. Ext corridors. **Pets:** Very small. $5 daily fee/pet. Designated rooms, service with restrictions, supervision.

〔SAVE〕〔✕〕

CITY INDEX

ABERDEEN

▼▼▼▼ GuestHouse International Inn & Suites M

(360) 537-7460. **$83-$145.** 701 E Heron St. Downtown; just e on US 12, then cross street to Kansas St. Int corridors. **Pets:** Small. $10 daily fee/pet. Service with restrictions, crate.

(ASK) (S🐾) (✕) (🌀) (🔥) (🔲) (💻) (🏊)

▼▼▼ Olympic Inn M

(360) 533-4200. **$59-$95.** 616 W Heron St. Downtown; 0.5 mi w. Ext corridors. **Pets:** Accepted.

(SAVE) (✕) (🔲) (🐾)

▼▼▼ Red Lion Inn M

(360) 532-5210. **$59-$69.** 521 W Wishkah. 0.5 mi w on US 101 N. Ext corridors. **Pets:** Other species. Service with restrictions, supervision.

(ASK) (S🐾) (✕) (🔥M) (🌀) (🔲) (💻)

AIRWAY HEIGHTS

▼▼▼ Microtel Inn & Suites M

(509) 242-1200. **$55-$84.** 1215 S Garfield Rd. I-90, exit 277 to SR 2, 4 mi w. Int corridors. **Pets:** Small, dogs only. $10 one-time fee/pet. Service with restrictions, crate.

(ASK) (S🐾) (✕) (🔥) (🔲) (💻)

ANACORTES

(AAA) ▼▼▼ Anacortes Inn M

(360) 293-3153. **$60-$77.** 3006 Commercial Ave. SR 20, 1.8 mi s. Ext corridors. **Pets:** Small, dogs only. $10 one-time fee/pet. Designated rooms, service with restrictions, supervision.

(SAVE) (S🐾) (✕) (🔲) (💻)

(AAA) ▼▼▼▼ Fidalgo Country Inn M

(360) 293-3494. **$89-$119.** 7645 SR 20. Ext/int corridors. **Pets:** Accepted.

(SAVE) (S🐾) (✕) (🔥M) (🌀) (🔲) (💻) (🏊)

BELFAIR

▼▼▼ Belfair Motel M

(360) 275-4485. **Call for rates.** NE 23322 SR 3. Downtown. Ext corridors. **Pets:** Accepted.

(ASK) (✕) (🔲) (💻)

BELLINGHAM

(AAA) ▼▼▼▼ Best Western Lakeway Inn 🏨 ❀

(360) 671-1011. **$79-$120.** 714 Lakeway Dr. I-5, exit 253, just se. Int corridors. **Pets:** Small. $5 daily fee/pet. Designated rooms, service with restrictions, supervision.

(SAVE) (S🐾) (✕) (🌀) (🔲) (💻) (🍽) (🏊)

Days Inn M
(360) 671-6200. **$55-$80.** 125 E Kellogg Rd. I-5, exit 256A, 1 mi n on Meridian St. Int corridors. **Pets:** Medium. $14 daily fee/room. Supervision.

Fairhaven Village Inn M
(360) 733-1311. **$99-$159.** 1200 10th St. I-5, exit 250, 1.5 mi w; in Fairhaven Historic District. Int corridors. **Pets:** Medium. $20 daily fee/pet. Service with restrictions, supervision.

Holiday Inn Express-Bellingham M
(360) 671-4800. **$80-$95.** 4160 Guide Meridian St. I-5, exit 256A, 0.7 mi e. Int corridors. **Pets:** Small, other species. $10 one-time fee/room. Designated rooms.

Motel 6-44 M
(360) 671-4494. **$43-$69.** 3701 Byron Ave. I-5, exit 252, just nw. Ext corridors. **Pets:** Accepted.

Quality Inn Baron Suites M
(360) 647-8000. **$85-$110.** 100 E Kellogg Rd. I-5, exit 256A, 1 mi ne via Guide Meridian St. Ext/int corridors. **Pets:** Medium. $25 one-time fee/room. Designated rooms, service with restrictions, supervision.

Rodeway Inn M
(360) 738-6000. **$49-$95.** 3710 Meridian St. I-5, exit 256A, just w. Int corridors. **Pets:** Medium, other species. $10 one-time fee/pet. Designated rooms, service with restrictions, supervision.

Shangri-La Downtown Motel M
(360) 733-7050. **$39-$59.** 611 E Holly St. I-5, exit 253 (Lakeway Dr), 0.3 mi nw. Ext corridors. **Pets:** Small. $5 deposit/pet. Service with restrictions, supervision.

Travel House Inn M
(360) 671-4600. **$39-$75, 3 days notice.** 3750 Meridian St. I-5, exit 256A, just w. Ext corridors. **Pets:** Other species. $5 daily fee/pet. Crate.

Val-U Inn M
(360) 671-9600. **$54-$80.** 805 Lakeway Dr. I-5, exit 253, just ne. Int corridors. **Pets:** Medium, dogs only. $5 daily fee/pet. Designated rooms, service with restrictions, supervision.

BLAINE

Resort Semiahmoo R ❖
(360) 318-2000. **$99-$259, 7 days notice.** 9565 Semiahmoo Pkwy. I-5, exit 270, on Semiahmoo Spit. Int corridors. **Pets:** Other species. $50 one-time fee/room. Designated rooms, service with restrictions, supervision.

BREMERTON

Dunes Motel M
(360) 377-0093. **$55-$65.** 3400 11th St. 2 mi w of ferry terminal; SR 3, exit Kitsap Way, 1 mi e. Ext corridors. **Pets:** Medium, other species. $25 one-time fee/room. Service with restrictions, supervision.

Flagship Inn M
(360) 479-6566. **$69-$99.** 4320 Kitsap Way. 3.5 mi w of ferry terminal; SR 3, exit Kitsap Way, 0.5 mi e. Int corridors. **Pets:** Medium. $6 daily fee/pet. Service with restrictions, supervision.

Howard Johnson Plaza Hotel & Conference Center MI
(360) 373-9900. **$89-$129.** 5640 Kitsap Way. US 303, exit Kitsap Way. Int corridors. **Pets:** Small. $25 one-time fee/room. Designated rooms, service with restrictions, supervision.

Illahee Manor Bed & Breakfast BB
(360) 698-7555. **$115-$250, 10 days notice.** 6680 Illahee Rd NE. US 3, exit E Bremerton, 4.9 mi se on Wheaton Way (SR 303), 1.2 mi e on McWilliams Rd, just n on East Rd, then 0.3 mi e on 3rd St, just n. Ext/int corridors. **Pets:** Accepted.

Midway Inn M
(360) 479-2909. **$55-$74, 3 days notice.** 2909 Wheaton Way. SR 303, 2 mi n; in E Bremerton. Int corridors. **Pets:** Small. $15 one-time fee/pet. Designated rooms, service with restrictions, supervision.

Oyster Bay Inn MI
(360) 377-5510. **$75-$80.** 4412 Kitsap Way. 3.8 mi w of ferry terminal; SR 3, exit Kitsap Way, 0.5 mi e. Int corridors. **Pets:** Accepted.

Super 8 Motel M
(360) 377-8881. **Call for rates.** 5068 Kitsap Way. 4.2 mi w of ferry terminal; SR 3, exit Kitsap Way, just ne. Int corridors. **Pets:** Large, other species. $25 deposit/room. Service with restrictions, supervision.

BUCKLEY

Mt View Inn M
(360) 829-1100. **$73-$89, 7 days notice.** 29405 SR 410 E. On SR 410 at jct SR 165. Int corridors. **Pets:** Small, dogs only. $20 one-time fee/pet. Designated rooms, service with restrictions, supervision.

CASHMERE

⬥⬥⬥ ▼▼▼ Village Inn Motel Ⓜ
(509) 782-3522. **$45-$64, 7 days notice.** 229 Cottage Ave. Downtown; on Business Rt US 2 and 97. Ext corridors. **Pets:** Small, dogs only. $5 daily fee/pet, $5 one-time fee/pet. No service, supervision.
SAVE ⬥ ✕ ▤

CASTLE ROCK

⬥⬥⬥ ▼▼▼▼ Timberland Inn & Suites Ⓜ
(360) 274-6002. **$55-$75.** 1271 Mount St. Helens Way. I-5, exit 49, just e. Ext corridors. **Pets:** Medium. $5 daily fee/pet. Designated rooms, service with restrictions, supervision.
SAVE ⬥ ✕ ▤

CENTRALIA

⬥⬥⬥ ▼▼▼ Centralia Travelodge Ⓜ
(360) 736-9344. **$65-$70.** 1325 Lakeshore Dr. I-5, exit 81, just nw. Ext corridors. **Pets:** Large. $5.49 daily fee/pet. Designated rooms, service with restrictions, supervision.
SAVE ⬥ ✕ ▤ ▭

▼▼ Motel 6–394 Ⓜ
(360) 330-2057. **$41-$51.** 1310 Belmont Ave. I-5, exit 82, 0.6 mi nw. Ext corridors. **Pets:** Accepted.
⬥ ✕ ⬥ ▭

CHEHALIS

⬥⬥⬥ ▼▼▼▼ Best Western Park Place Inn & Suites Ⓜ
(360) 748-4040. **$64-$82, 7 days notice.** 201 SW Interstate Ave. I-5, exit 76, just se. Int corridors. **Pets:** Small, dogs only. $10 daily fee/pet. Service with restrictions, supervision.
SAVE ⬥ ✕ ⬥ᴹ ⬥ ▤ ▭ ▭

⬥⬥⬥ ▼▼▼ Howard Johnson Inn Ⓜ
(360) 748-0101. **$71-$99.** 122 Interstate Ave. I-5, exit 76, just e. Ext corridors. **Pets:** Medium, other species. Service with restrictions, supervision.
SAVE ⬥ ✕ ▤ ▭ ▭

CHELAN

⬥⬥⬥ ▼▼▼▼ Best Western Lakeside Lodge Ⓜ
(509) 682-4396. **$159-$279, 7 days notice.** W 2312 Woodin Ave. West end of town. Ext corridors. **Pets:** Medium, dogs only. $10 daily fee/pet. Designated rooms, supervision.
SAVE ⬥ ✕ ⬥ ▤ ▭ ▭

CHEWELAH

⬥⬥⬥ ▼▼▼ Nordlig Motel Ⓜ
(509) 935-6704. **$54.** 101 W Grant Ave. North edge of town on US 395. Ext corridors. **Pets:** Accepted.
SAVE ⬥ ✕ ▤

CLE ELUM

⬥⬥⬥ ▼▼▼ Cle Elum Travelers Inn Ⓜ
(509) 674-5535. **$40-$110.** 1001 E 1st St. I-90, exit 85, 1 mi w on SR 903. Ext/int corridors. **Pets:** Medium, dogs only. $5 daily fee/pet. Service with restrictions, supervision.
SAVE ⬥ ✕ ▤

▼▼ Stewart Lodge Ⓜ
(509) 674-4548. **$48-$73.** 805 W 1st St. I-90, exit 84 eastbound, just n; exit 84 westbound, 0.6 mi w. Ext corridors. **Pets:** Accepted.
✕ ⬥ ▤ ▭

⬥⬥⬥ ▼▼▼ Timber Lodge Inn Ⓜ
(509) 674-5966. **$55-$65.** 301 W 1st St. I-90, exit 84 eastbound, 1 mi ne; exit 84 westbound, just w. Ext/int corridors. **Pets:** Medium, other species. $10 one-time fee/pet. Designated rooms, service with restrictions, crate.
SAVE ⬥ ✕ ▤

⬥⬥⬥ ▼▼ Wind Blew Inn Motel Ⓜ
(509) 674-2294. **$50.** 811 Hwy 970. I-90, exit 85, just w. Ext corridors. **Pets:** Accepted.
SAVE ✕ ⬥ ▤

COLVILLE

⬥⬥⬥ ▼▼▼▼ Colville Comfort Inn Ⓜ
(509) 684-2010. **$75-$125.** 166 NE Canning Dr. 1.5 mi n on US 395. Int corridors. **Pets:** $50 deposit/room, $5 daily fee/pet. Service with restrictions, supervision.
SAVE ⬥ ✕ ⬥ᴹ ⬥ ▤ ▭ ▭

COULEE DAM

⬥⬥⬥ ▼▼▼ Coulee House Motel Ⓜ
(509) 633-1101. **$55-$170.** 110 Roosevelt Way. Just e of river bridge. Ext corridors. **Pets:** $15 daily fee/pet. Service with restrictions, supervision.
SAVE ⬥ ✕ ▤ ▭ ▭

COUPEVILLE

⬥⬥⬥ ▼▼▼▼ The Victorian Bed & Breakfast 🅱🅱
(360) 678-5305. **$70-$100, 7 days notice.** 602 N Main St. Downtown; 0.3 mi n of jct SR 20. Ext/int corridors. **Pets:** $100 deposit/room, $10 one-time fee/room. Designated rooms, no service.
SAVE ✕ ▤ ▭ 🍴 Ⓚ 🖉

EAST WENATCHEE

▼▼▼▼ Cedars Inn, East Wenatchee Ⓜ
(509) 886-8000. **$72-$87.** 80 Ninth St NE. Just e of SR 28. Int corridors. **Pets:** Medium. $6 daily fee/room. Service with restrictions, supervision.
ASK ⬥ ✕ ▤ ▭

EATONVILLE

⬥⬥⬥ ▼▼▼▼ Mill Village Motel Ⓜ
(360) 832-3200. **$60-$75.** 210 Center St E. Downtown. Ext corridors. **Pets:** Accepted.
SAVE ✕ ⬥ ▤

ELLENSBURG

▼▼▼ Ellensburg Comfort Inn M
(509) 925-7037. $65-$153. 1722 Canyon Rd. I-90, exit 109. Int corridors. **Pets:** Large, other species. $10 one-time fee/room. Service with restrictions, supervision.

[SAVE] [S◇] [✕] [⊘] [☾] [🖥] [🖥] [⊇]

▼▼▼ Ellensburg Inn MI
(509) 925-9801. $60-$80. 1700 Canyon Rd. I-90, exit 109, just n. Int corridors. **Pets:** Accepted.

[ASK] [S◇] [✕] [🖥] [🖥] [¶] [⊇]

⚫⚫⚫ ▼▼▼ I-90 Inn Motel M
(509) 925-9844. $48-$68. 1390 Dollar Way Rd. I-90, exit 106, just n. Ext corridors. **Pets:** Accepted.

[SAVE] [S◇] [✕] [🖥]

▼▼ Nites Inn M ❀
(509) 962-9600. $51-$57. 1200 S Ruby. I-90, exit 109, 0.5 mi n. Ext corridors. **Pets:** Medium, other species. $7.70 one-time fee/pet. Service with restrictions, supervision.

[ASK] [S◇] [✕] [🖥] [🖥]

ENUMCLAW

⚫⚫⚫ ▼▼▼▼ Best Western Park Center MI
(360) 825-4490. $85. 1000 Griffin Ave. Downtown. Ext corridors. **Pets:** Small. $30 one-time fee/pet. Service with restrictions, crate.

[SAVE] [S◇] [✕] [🖥] [🖥] [¶]

FERNDALE

▼▼ Ferndale Super 8 M
(360) 384-8881. $59-$69. 5788 Barrett Ave. I-5, exit 262, just ne. Int corridors. **Pets:** $25 deposit/pet. Service with restrictions, supervision.

[ASK] [S◇] [✕] [☾M] [☾] [🖥] [⊇]

▼▼ Slater Heritage House BB
(360) 384-4273. $75-$105, 5 days notice. 1371 W Axton Rd. I-5, exit 262, 1 mi e. Int corridors. **Pets:** Medium. $15 daily fee/room. Service with restrictions, supervision.

[✕] [🖥] [🖥] [☾] [☎]

FORKS

⚫⚫⚫ ▼▼▼ Forks Motel M
(360) 374-6243. $50-$95. 351 US 101 (Forks Ave S). Just s on Forks Ave S (US 101). Ext corridors. **Pets:** Medium. $10 daily fee/room. Service with restrictions, supervision.

[SAVE] [✕] [🖥] [⊇]

▼▼ Manitou Lodge BB ❀
(360) 374-6295. $95-$150, 5 days notice. 813 Kilmer Rd. 8 mi sw on SR 110 (Lapush Rd), 0.8 mi w on Mora Rd, then 0.8 mi n. Ext/int corridors. **Pets:** Other species. $10 daily fee/room. Designated rooms, supervision.

[✕] [🖥] [☒] [☾] [☒] [☎]

▼▼ Miller Tree Inn Bed & Breakfast BB
(360) 374-6806. $55-$180, 4 days notice. 654 E Division St. Downtown; 0.3 mi e of US 101. Ext/int corridors. **Pets:** Other species. $10 daily fee/pet. Designated rooms, service with restrictions, crate.

[✕] [🖥] [🖥] [☾] [☎]

⚫⚫⚫ ▼▼▼ Olympic Suites Inn M
(360) 374-5400. $54-$94. 800 Olympic Dr. North end of town, just ne off US 101. Ext corridors. **Pets:** Dogs only. $150 deposit/room, $5 daily fee/pet. Designated rooms, service with restrictions, supervision.

[SAVE] [S◇] [✕] [🖥] [🖥] [☾]

FREELAND

▼▼ Harbour Inn Motel M
(360) 331-6900. $71-$96. 1606 Main St. Just e of SR 525. Ext corridors. **Pets:** Other species. $6 daily fee/pet. Designated rooms, service with restrictions, supervision.

[✕] [🖥] [🖥] [☾]

GOLDENDALE

⚫⚫⚫ ▼▼▼ Ponderosa Motel M ❀
(509) 773-5842. $55-$65. 775 E Broadway. US 97, exit SR 142 (Klickitat and Goldendale), 0.5 mi w. Ext corridors. **Pets:** Medium. $12 daily fee/room. Designated rooms, service with restrictions, supervision.

[SAVE] [✕] [🖥] [🖥]

KALALOCH

⚫⚫⚫ ▼▼▼ Kalaloch Lodge L
(360) 962-2271. $80-$190, 3 days notice. 157151 US 101. At MM 157. Ext/int corridors. **Pets:** Accepted.

[SAVE] [✕] [🖥] [🖥] [¶] [☾] [☎]

KELSO

▼▼ Best Western Aladdin M
(360) 425-9660. $58-$79. 310 Long Ave. West end Cowlitz Bridge. Int corridors. **Pets:** Other species. $10 one-time fee/room. Service with restrictions, supervision.

[SAVE] [S◇] [✕] [🖥] [🖥] [⊇]

▼▼▼ GuestHouse International Inn & Suites M
(360) 414-5953. $150. 501 Three Rivers Dr. I-5, exit 39, 0.3 mi w on Allen St, then 0.3 mi s. Int corridors. **Pets:** Medium. $10 daily fee/room. Service with restrictions, supervision.

[ASK] [S◇] [✕] [⊘] [☾] [🖥] [🖥] [⊇]

▼▼ Motel 6–43 M
(360) 425-3229. $43-$59. 106 Minor Rd. I-5, exit 39, 0.3 mi ne. Ext corridors. **Pets:** Small. Service with restrictions, supervision.

[S◇] [✕] [☾] [⊇]

▼▼▼ Red Lion Hotel Kelso/Longview MI
(360) 636-4400. $49-$99. 510 Kelso Dr. I-5, exit 39, 0.3 mi se. Int corridors. **Pets:** $10 one-time fee/room. Designated rooms, service with restrictions.

[ASK] [S◇] [✕] [⊘] [☾] [🖥] [🖥] [¶] [⊇]

▼▼ Super 8 Motel **M** ❄
(360) 423-8880. **$45-$85.** 250 Kelso Dr. I-5, exit 39, just sw. Int corridors. **Pets:** Other species. $25 deposit/room. Designated rooms, service with restrictions, supervision.
〔ASK〕 〔S⬟〕 ⊠ 〔&M〕 〔&ʳ〕 █ 〰

KENNEWICK

▼▼▼ Best Value Clearwater Inn **M**
(509) 735-2242. **$63.** 5616 W Clearwater Ave. US 395, 1.9 mi w. Int corridors. **Pets:** Accepted.
〔ASK〕 〔S⬟〕 ⊠ 〔∅〕 〔&ʳ〕 █ ▣

⬟⬟⬟ ▼▼▼ Best Western Kennewick Inn **M**
(509) 586-1332. **$84-$130.** 4001 W 27th Ave. I-82, exit 113, 0.8 mi n. Int corridors. **Pets:** $10 one-time fee/room. Designated rooms, service with restrictions, supervision.
〔SAVE〕 〔S⬟〕 ⊠ 〔&M〕 〔&ʳ〕 █ ▣ 〰

▼▼ Clover Island Inn **M**
(509) 586-0541. **Call for rates, 7 days notice.** 435 Clover Island. US 395, exit Port of Kennewick, 1 mi e on Columbia Dr, just n on Washington St. Int corridors. **Pets:** Accepted.
〔ASK〕 ⊠ █ 〰

▼▼▼ Comfort Inn **M**
(509) 783-8396. **$60-$120.** 7801 W Quinault Ave. From SR 240, 0.5 mi s on Columbia Center Blvd. Int corridors. **Pets:** Dogs only. $10 daily fee/pet. Service with restrictions, supervision.
〔SAVE〕 〔S⬟〕 ⊠ 〔&M〕 〔∅〕 〔&ʳ〕 █ ▣ 〰

⬟⬟⬟ ▼▼▼ Hawthorn Inn & Suites **M** ❄
(509) 736-3326. **$69-$99.** 4220 W 27th Pl. I-82, exit 113 (US 395), 0.8 mi n. Int corridors. **Pets:** Medium. $10 one-time fee/room. Service with restrictions, supervision.
〔SAVE〕 〔S⬟〕 ⊠ 〔&M〕 〔&ʳ〕 █ ▣ 〰

▼▼ Kennewick Super 8 **M**
(509) 736-6888. **$51-$61, 10 days notice.** 626 Columbia Center Blvd. 1.1 mi s of SR 240. Int corridors. **Pets:** $25 deposit/room. Service with restrictions, supervision.
〔ASK〕 〔S⬟〕 ⊠ 〔&M〕 〔∅〕 〔&ʳ〕 █ 〰

⬟⬟⬟ ▼▼ Tapadera Inn **M**
(509) 783-6191. **$50-$60, 5 days notice.** 300A N Ely St. On US 395 at jct Clearwater Ave. Ext corridors. **Pets:** Accepted.
〔SAVE〕 〔S⬟〕 ⊠ █ 〰

⬟⬟⬟ ▼▼▼▼ WestCoast Tri-Cities Hotel **MI**
(509) 783-0611. **$85-$126.** 1101 N Columbia Center Blvd. From SR 240, 0.5 mi s. Int corridors. **Pets:** $10 one-time fee/room. Service with restrictions, crate.
〔SAVE〕 〔S⬟〕 ⊠ 〔&M〕 〔∅〕 █ ▣ 〔¶〕 〰

LA CONNER

⬟⬟⬟ ▼▼▼▼ La Conner Country Inn **MI**
(360) 466-3101. **$89-$120.** 107 S 2nd St. Downtown; at 2nd and Morris sts. Ext/int corridors. **Pets:** $25 one-time fee/room. Designated rooms, service with restrictions, supervision.
〔SAVE〕 〔S⬟〕 ⊠ 〔&ʳ〕 ▣ 〔¶〕 〔AC〕

LACEY

⬟⬟⬟ ▼▼▼ Days Inn **M**
(360) 493-1991. **$59-$75.** 120 College St SE. I-5, exit 109, just sw. Int corridors. **Pets:** Large. $15 daily fee/pet. Service with restrictions, supervision.
〔SAVE〕 〔S⬟〕 ⊠ 〔∅〕 〔&ʳ〕 █

LEAVENWORTH

▼▼▼ Alpen Inn **M**
(509) 548-4326. **$59-$139, 14 days notice.** 405 W US 2. West end of town. Ext corridors. **Pets:** $50 deposit/room, $12 daily fee/pet. Designated rooms, service with restrictions, supervision.
〔ASK〕 〔S⬟〕 ⊠ █ ▣ 〰

⬟⬟⬟ ▼▼▼▼ Der Ritterhof Motor Inn **M**
(509) 548-5845. **$85-$175, 3 days notice.** 190 US 2. Just w. Ext corridors. **Pets:** Other species. $12 daily fee/pet. Service with restrictions, supervision.
〔SAVE〕 〔S⬟〕 ⊠ 〔∅〕 █ ▣ 〰

▼▼ The Evergreen Inn **M** ❄
(509) 548-5515. **$65-$95, 14 days notice.** 1117 Front St. US 2, just s. Ext corridors. **Pets:** Other species. $10 daily fee/pet. Designated rooms, supervision.
⊠ █ ▣

⬟⬟⬟ ▼▼▼▼ Obertal Motor Inn **M**
(509) 548-5204. **$59-$139.** 922 Commercial St. Center; off US 2. Ext corridors. **Pets:** Medium, other species. $10 daily fee/pet. Designated rooms, service with restrictions, crate.
〔SAVE〕 〔S⬟〕 ⊠ █ ▣

▼▼ River's Edge Lodge **M**
(509) 548-7612. **$66-$81, 10 days notice.** 8401 US 2. 3.5 mi e. Ext corridors. **Pets:** Accepted.
⊠ █ ▣ 〰

▼▼ Tyrolean Ritz Hotel **M**
(509) 548-5455. **$70-$95.** 633 Front St. Center. Ext/int corridors. **Pets:** Accepted.
〔ASK〕 〔S⬟〕 ⊠ █ ▣ 〔¶〕

LONG BEACH

⬟⬟⬟ ▼▼▼ Anchorage Cottages **C**
(360) 642-2351. **$82-$120, 7 days notice.** 2209 Boulevard N. Just w of SR 103. Ext corridors. **Pets:** Other species. $10 daily fee/pet. No service, supervision.
〔SAVE〕 〔S⬟〕 ⊠ █ ▣ 〔AC〕 〔Z〕

⬟⬟⬟ ▼▼▼ Edgewater Inn **MI**
(360) 642-2311. **$59-$139.** 409 10th St SW. Just w of SR 103. Ext/int corridors. **Pets:** $8 daily fee/pet. Designated rooms, service with restrictions, supervision.
〔SAVE〕 ⊠ 〔&ʳ〕 █ ▣ 〔¶〕 〔AC〕

⬟⬟⬟ ▼▼▼ Our Place at the Beach **M**
(360) 642-3793. **$42-$86.** 1309 South Blvd. South end of town. Ext corridors. **Pets:** Large. $5 daily fee/pet. Supervision.
〔SAVE〕 〔S⬟〕 ⊠ █ ▣ 〔AC〕

⚠⚠ ▼▼▼ Shaman Motel M
(360) 642-3714. **$54-$99, 7 days notice.** 115 3rd St SW.
Downtown. Ext corridors. **Pets:** Dogs only. $5.50 one-time
fee/pet. Service with restrictions, supervision.
[SAVE] [X] [🔒] [💻] [🐾] [🎶]

LONGVIEW

⚠⚠ ▼▼▼ Hudson Manor Inn M ❖
(360) 425-1100. **$40-$50, 3 days notice.** 1616 Hudson St.
Downtown. Ext corridors. **Pets:** Dogs only. $25 deposit/pet,
$5 daily fee/pet. Service with restrictions, supervision.
[SAVE] [S🔒] [X] [🔒] [💻]

▼▼▼▼ The Patrician Inn & Suites M ❖
(360) 414-1000. **$64-$99, 7 days notice.** 723 7th Ave. I-5,
exit 36, 3 mi w on SR 432. Int corridors. **Pets:** Other
species. $15 one-time fee/room. Designated rooms, service
with restrictions, supervision.
[ASK] [S🔒] [X] [🔒M] [🔒] [🔒] [🔒] [💻] [🐾]

⚠⚠ ▼▼▼ The Townhouse Motel M
(360) 423-7200. **$38-$52.** 744 Washington Way. Downtown.
Ext corridors. **Pets:** Medium. $5 deposit/pet. Supervision.
[SAVE] [S🔒] [X] [🔒] [💻] [🐾]

LYNDEN

▼▼▼ Windmill Inn Motel M
(360) 354-3424. **$47-$65, 3 days notice.** 8022 Guide
Meridian Rd. On SR 539, just s of jct Birch Bay-Lynden Rd.
Ext corridors. **Pets:** Small. $5 daily fee/pet. Service with
restrictions, supervision.
[ASK] [S🔒] [X] [🔒] [💻]

MOCLIPS

▼▼▼ Hi Tide Ocean Beach Resort CO ❖
(360) 276-4142. **Call for rates.** 4890 Railroad Ave. SR 109,
0.8 mi nw on beach; at 6th St and Railroad Ave. Ext corridors. **Pets:** Medium, dogs only. $12 daily fee/pet. Service
with restrictions, supervision.
[ASK] [S🔒] [X] [🔒] [💻] [🎶] [🔒]

⚠⚠ ▼▼▼ Ocean Crest Resort M
(360) 276-4465. **$50-$175, 7 days notice.** 4651 SR 109 N.
South edge of town. Ext corridors. **Pets:** Other species. $50
deposit/room, $15 daily fee/pet. Designated rooms, service
with restrictions, supervision.
[SAVE] [S🔒] [X] [🔒] [🔒] [💻] [🍴] [🐾] [🎶]

MORTON

⚠⚠ ▼▼▼▼ The Seasons Motel M
(360) 496-6835. **$60-$75.** 200 Westlake Ave. At jct SR 7
and US 12. Ext corridors. **Pets:** Accepted.
[SAVE] [X] [🔒]

MOSES LAKE

⚠⚠ ▼▼▼▼ Best Western Hallmark Inn MI ❖
(509) 765-9211. **$69-$99.** 3000 Marina Dr. I-90, exit 176,
just nw. Int corridors. **Pets:** Medium, other species. Service
with restrictions, supervision.
[SAVE] [S🔒] [X] [🔒] [🔒] [💻] [🍴] [🐾] [🔒]

▼▼▼▼ Holiday Inn Express M
(509) 766-2000. **$69-$99.** 1745 E Kittleson. I-90, exit 179,
just n. Int corridors. **Pets:** Medium. $20 deposit/room. Des-
ignated rooms, service with restrictions, crate.
[ASK] [S🔒] [X] [🔒M] [🔒] [🔒] [💻] [🐾]

▼▼▼ Inn at Moses Lake M
(509) 766-7000. **$70-$95.** 1741 E Kittleson. I-90, exit 179,
just n. Int corridors. **Pets:** Medium. $20 deposit/room. Des-
ignated rooms, service with restrictions, supervision.
[ASK] [S🔒] [X] [🔒]

▼▼▼▼ Shilo Inn Suites-Moses Lake M ❖
(509) 765-9317. **$73-$93.** 1819 E Kittleson. I-90, exit 179,
just n. Int corridors. **Pets:** Other species. $10 daily fee/pet.
Service with restrictions, supervision.
[ASK] [S🔒] [X] [🔒] [🔒] [💻] [🐾]

⚠⚠ ▼▼▼ Travelodge of Moses Lake M
(509) 765-8631. **$40-$100.** 316 S Pioneer Way. Downtown;
on Business Loop 90. Ext corridors. **Pets:** Medium, dogs
only. $10 deposit/room. Service with restrictions, supervi-
sion.
[SAVE] [S🔒] [X] [🔒] [💻] [🐾]

MOUNT VERNON

⚠⚠ ▼▼▼ Best Western College Way Inn M
(360) 424-4287. **$70-$90.** 300 W College Way. I-5, exit 227,
just w. Ext corridors. **Pets:** Accepted.
[SAVE] [S🔒] [X] [🔒] [🔒] [💻] [🐾]

⚠⚠ ▼▼▼▼ Best Western Cotton Tree Inn &
              Convention Center M ❖
(360) 428-5678. **$89-$99.** 2300 Market St. I-5, exit 227, 0.3
mi e on College Way, then 0.5 mi n on Riverside Dr. Int
corridors. **Pets:** Medium, dogs only. $10 one-time fee/room.
Designated rooms, service with restrictions, supervision.
[SAVE] [S🔒] [X] [🔒M] [🔒] [🔒] [💻] [🐾]

▼▼▼ Comfort Inn-Mount Vernon M
(360) 428-7020. **$80-$90, 14 days notice.** 1910 Freeway
Dr. I-5, exit 227, just w on College Way, then just n. Ext
corridors. **Pets:** Other species. $10 deposit/room. Desig-
nated rooms, service with restrictions, supervision.
[SAVE] [S🔒] [X] [🔒] [💻] [🐾]

OAK HARBOR

⚠⚠ ▼▼▼ Acorn Motor Inn M
(360) 675-6646. **$46-$98.** 31530 SR 20. On SR 20 at jct
300th Ave W (SE Barrington Dr). Int corridors. **Pets:** Other
species. $10 daily fee/room. Designated rooms, service
with restrictions, supervision.
[SAVE] [S🔒] [X] [🔒]

⚠⚠ ▼▼▼▼ Best Western Harbor Plaza M ❖
(360) 679-4567. **$90-$139.** 33175 SR 20. Just n. Int corridors. **Pets:** Medium. $15 daily fee/room. Designated rooms,
crate.
[SAVE] [S🔒] [X] [🔒M] [🔒] [🔒] [💻]

OCEAN PARK

⚠⚠ ▼▼▼ Ocean Park Resort M
(360) 665-4585. **$60-$98, 10 days notice.** 25904 R St. In
town; just e of SR 103. Ext corridors. **Pets:** Accepted.
[SAVE] [🔒] [💻] [🐾] [🎶] [🔒]

OCEAN SHORES

ꟲꟲꟲ ▼▼▼▼ The Grey Gull Resort 🆑
(360) 289-3381. **$80-$345.** 651 Ocean Shores Blvd NW. Just s of Shores Mall. Ext corridors. **Pets:** $10 daily fee/pet. Designated rooms, service with restrictions, supervision.
[SAVE] [S🐾] [✕] [📵] [💻] [🌊] [✗]

▼▼▼▼ Holiday Inn Express 🅼
(360) 289-4900. **$49-$169, 3 days notice.** 685 Ocean Shores Blvd NW. West side, near beach. Int corridors. **Pets:** Accepted.
[ASK] [S🐾] [✕] [📵] [💻] [🌊]

ꟲꟲꟲ ▼▼▼▼ The Nautilus 🆑 🐾
(360) 289-2722. **$70-$135.** 835 Ocean Shores Blvd NW. North end of town. Ext corridors. **Pets:** Dogs only. $20 one-time fee/pet. Supervision.
[SAVE] [✕] [📵] [💻] [✗]

ꟲꟲꟲ ▼▼▼▼ The Polynesian Condominium Resort 🆑 🐾
(360) 289-3361. **$99-$199.** 615 Ocean Shores Blvd NW. Just s of Shores Mall. Ext/int corridors. **Pets:** Medium, other species. $15 daily fee/pet. Designated rooms, service with restrictions, supervision.
[SAVE] [S🐾] [✕] [🏊] [📵] [💻] [🍴] [🌊] [✗]

OKANOGAN

ꟲꟲꟲ ▼▼▼ Ponderosa Motor Lodge 🅼 🐾
(509) 422-0400. **$44-$48.** 1034 S 2nd Ave. 0.3 mi n on SR 215 from jct SR 20. Ext corridors. **Pets:** Other species. Supervision.
[SAVE] [S🐾] [✕] [📵] [💻] [🌊]

OLYMPIA

ꟲꟲꟲ ▼▼▼▼ WestCoast Olympia Hotel 🅼
(360) 943-4000. **$108.** 2300 Evergreen Park Dr SW. I-5, exit 104, 0.5 mi nw via US 101 and Cooper Point Rd N exit; in Morris Business Park. Int corridors. **Pets:** Medium, other species. $100 deposit/room, $45 one-time fee/room. Service with restrictions, crate.
[SAVE] [S🐾] [✕] [📵] [💻] [🍴] [🌊]

OLYMPIC NATIONAL PARK

ꟲꟲꟲ ▼▼▼▼ Lake Crescent Lodge 🅻
(360) 928-3211. **$123, 3 days notice.** 416 Lake Crescent Rd. 22 mi w of Port Angeles on US 101. Ext/int corridors. **Pets:** Accepted.
[SAVE] [✕] [📵] [💻] [🍴] [✗] [✗] [🌊] [✗]

▼▼ Log Cabin Resort 🅻
(360) 928-3325. **Call for rates.** 3183 E Beach Rd. 3.3 mi nw of US 101 (MM 232); on Lake Crescent at Piedmont Recreation Area. Ext corridors. **Pets:** Accepted.
[✕] [📵] [💻] [🍴] [✗] [✗] [✗] [✗]

OMAK

ꟲꟲꟲ ▼▼▼ Motel Nicholas 🅼 🐾
(509) 826-4611. **$42-$46, 03 days notice.** 527 E Grape Ave. 0.8 mi n on SR 215 business route, 0.3 mi w of US 97, on north exit to Omak. Ext corridors. **Pets:** Dogs only. $3 one-time fee/room. Service with restrictions, supervision.
[SAVE] [✕] [📵] [💻]

ꟲꟲꟲ ▼▼▼▼ Omak Inn 🅼
(509) 826-3822. **$65-$75.** 912 Koala Dr. On US 97, just n of Riverside Dr. Int corridors. **Pets:** Accepted.
[SAVE] [S🐾] [✕] [📵] [💻] [🌊]

▼▼ ▼▼ Rodeway Inn & Suites 🅼
(509) 826-0400. **$44-$69.** 122 N Main St. Downtown. Ext corridors. **Pets:** Accepted.
[SAVE] [S🐾] [✕] [✗] [📵] [💻] [🌊]

OTHELLO

ꟲꟲꟲ ▼▼▼▼ Best Western Lincoln Inn 🅼
(509) 488-5671. **$69-$109.** 1020 E Cedar St. Just off Main St; at 10th and Cedar sts. Int corridors. **Pets:** Accepted.
[SAVE] [S🐾] [✕] [📵] [💻] [🌊]

PACIFIC BEACH

ꟲꟲꟲ ▼▼ ▼▼ Sandpiper Beach Resort 🆑
(360) 276-4580. **$55-$200, 14 days notice.** 4159 SR 109. 1.8 mi s. Ext corridors. **Pets:** Other species. $10 daily fee/pet. Service with restrictions, supervision.
[SAVE] [S🐾] [✕] [📵] [💻] [✗] [✗] [✗]

PASCO

▼▼ ▼▼ DoubleTree Hotel Pasco 🅼
(509) 547-0701. **$145-$180.** 2525 N 20th Ave. I-182, exit 12B, just n. Int corridors. **Pets:** Other species. Service with restrictions, crate.
[SAVE] [S🐾] [✕] [🆖M] [🏊] [✗] [📵] [💻] [🍴] [🌊]

PORT ANGELES

ꟲꟲꟲ ▼▼ The Pond Motel 🅼
(360) 452-8422. **$37-$78, 3 days notice.** 1425 W US 101. 2 mi w. Ext corridors. **Pets:** Accepted.
[SAVE] [S🐾] [✕] [📵] [💻] [✗] [✗]

ꟲꟲꟲ ▼▼ ▼▼ Portside Inn 🅼
(360) 452-4015. **$49-$119, 3 days notice.** 1510 E Front St. Front St at Alder, east side. Ext corridors. **Pets:** Medium. $25 deposit/pet. Designated rooms, service with restrictions, supervision.
[SAVE] [S🐾] [✕] [📵] [💻] [🌊]

ꟲꟲꟲ ▼▼ ▼▼ Red Lion Hotel Port Angeles 🅼
(360) 452-9215. **$79-$145.** 221 N Lincoln St. On US 101 westbound, at the ferry landing. Ext/int corridors. **Pets:** Other species. Service with restrictions, crate.
[SAVE] [S🐾] [✕] [🏊] [✗] [📵] [💻] [🍴] [🌊]

ꟲꟲꟲ ▼▼ Riviera Inn 🅼
(360) 417-3955. **$39-$89, 3 days notice.** 535 E Front St. Downtown; on US 101 W. Ext corridors. **Pets:** Small, dogs only. $10 daily fee/pet. Designated rooms, service with restrictions, supervision.
[SAVE] [S🐾] [✕] [📵] [💻] [✗]

PORT ORCHARD

GuestHouse International Inn M
(360) 895-7818. **$69-$150.** 220 Bravo Terrace. SR 16, exit Sedgwick, just e. Int corridors. **Pets:** Accepted.

PORT TOWNSEND

Bishop Victorian Guest Suites H
(360) 385-6122. **$89-$199, 3 days notice.** 714 Washington St. Corner of Washington and Quincy sts. Int corridors. **Pets:** Dogs only. $15 daily fee/pet. Supervision.

Harborside Inn M
(360) 385-7909. **$65-$105.** 330 Benedict St. Just e of SR 20. Ext corridors. **Pets:** Accepted.

Palace Hotel H
(360) 385-0773. **$59-$229.** 1004 Water St. Downtown. Int corridors. **Pets:** $10 daily fee/room. Service with restrictions, supervision.

Port Townsend Inn M
(360) 385-2211. **Call for rates.** 2020 Washington St. 0.5 mi s on SR 20. Ext corridors. **Pets:** Accepted.

The Swan Hotel M
(360) 385-1718. **$85-$365, 3 days notice.** 222 Monroe St. Downtown. Ext corridors. **Pets:** Dogs only. $15 daily fee/pet. Designated rooms, supervision.

PORTLAND METROPOLITAN AREA

VANCOUVER

Best Inn & Suites M
(360) 696-0516. **$62-$72.** 7001 NE Hwy 99. I-5, exit 4, 0.8 mi se. Int corridors. **Pets:** Accepted.

Best Inn & Suites M
(360) 256-7044. **$62-$77.** 221 NE Chkalov Dr. I-205, exit 28 (Mill Plain), just ne. Ext corridors. **Pets:** Medium. $15 one-time fee/pet. Service with restrictions, supervision.

Comfort Inn M
(360) 574-6000. **$59-$99.** 13207 NE 20th Ave. I-5, exit 7, just e; I-205, exit 36, just w. Int corridors. **Pets:** Other species. $10 daily fee/pet.

Ferryman's Inn M
(360) 574-2151. **$59-$63.** 7901 NE 6th Ave. I-5, exit 4, just nw. Ext/int corridors. **Pets:** $3 daily fee/pet. Designated rooms, service with restrictions, supervision.

Homewood Suites by Hilton A
(360) 750-1100. **$107.** 701 SE Columbia Shores Blvd. US 14, exit 1, just s. Ext/int corridors. **Pets:** Other species. $10 daily fee/pet, $25 one-time fee/room.

Red Lion Hotel at the Quay, Vancouver M
(360) 694-8341. **$94-$107.** 100 Columbia St. 0.5 mi s on dock at foot of Columbia St. Int corridors. **Pets:** Large. $25 one-time fee/pet. Designated rooms, service with restrictions, supervision.

Residence Inn Vancouver A
(360) 253-4800. **$109-$189.** 8005 NE Parkway Dr. I-205, exit 30 (SR 500 W), 0.5 mi w to Thurston Way, just n to NE Parkway Dr, then just w. Ext corridors. **Pets:** Other species. $15 daily fee/pet.

Shilo Inn-Downtown Vancouver M
(360) 696-0411. **$59-$99.** 401 E 13th St. I-5, exit 1C (Mill Plain), just w, then just s on D St. Int corridors. **Pets:** Other species. $10 daily fee/pet. Service with restrictions, supervision.

Shilo Inn-Hazel Dell/Vancouver M
(360) 573-0511. **$59-$89.** 13206 Hwy 99. I-5, exit 7, just e; I-205, exit 36, just w. Int corridors. **Pets:** Other species. $10 daily fee/pet. Service with restrictions, supervision.

Staybridge Suites Vancouver-Portland M
(360) 891-8282. **$89-$129.** 7301 NE 41st St. I-205, exit 30 (SR 500 W), 1 mi w to Andresen Rd, just n to 40th St, just e to 72nd St, just n to 41st St, then just e. Int corridors. **Pets:** Large, other species. $50 deposit/pet, $10 daily fee/pet. Supervision.

END METROPOLITAN AREA

POULSBO

 Poulsbo Inn M
(360) 779-3921. **$90-$100, 7 days notice.** 18680 SR 305. SR 3, 1 mi e. Ext corridors. **Pets:** Medium, other species. $10 daily fee/pet. Designated rooms, service with restrictions, crate.

PROSSER

 Best Western Prosser Inn M
(509) 786-7977. **$79-$99, 7 days notice.** 225 Merlot Dr. I-82, exit 80, just s. Int corridors. **Pets:** Accepted.

PULLMAN

 Hawthorn Inn & Suites M 🐾
(509) 332-0928. **$89-$99, 3 days notice.** 928 NW Olsen St. 1.6 mi e on SR 270 from US 195. Int corridors. **Pets:** Designated rooms, service with restrictions.

Holiday Inn Express Hotel & Suites M 🐾
(509) 334-4437. **$89-$129.** SE 1190 Bishop Blvd. US 195 business route, 0.5 mi s, 1 mi e on SR 270. Int corridors. **Pets:** Other species. Designated rooms, service with restrictions.

 Quality Inn Paradise Creek M
(509) 332-0500. **$75-$90.** 1400 SE Bishop Blvd. US 195 business route, 1 mi e on SR 270, just s. Int corridors. **Pets:** Accepted.

QUINAULT

 Lake Quinault Lodge L
(360) 288-2900. **$80-$180, 3 days notice.** 345 S Shore Rd. 2 mi of US 101. Ext/int corridors. **Pets:** Other species. $10 daily fee/pet. Designated rooms, service with restrictions, supervision.

QUINCY

Traditional Inns M
(509) 787-3525. **$58-$63.** 500 F St SW. West end of town on SR 28. Ext corridors. **Pets:** Accepted.

RAYMOND

Maunu's Mountcastle Motel M
(360) 942-5571. **Call for rates.** 524 3rd St. US 101, exit City Center, just w. Ext corridors. **Pets:** Accepted.

RICHLAND

 Best Western Tower Inn M
(509) 946-4121. **$80-$107, 10 days notice.** 1515 George Washington Way. I-182, exit 5B, 2.5 mi n. Int corridors. **Pets:** Large. $25 one-time fee/pet. Service with restrictions, supervision.

Red Lion Hotel Richland Hanford House MI
(509) 946-7611. **$69-$100.** 802 George Washington Way. I-182, exit 5B, 1.3 mi n on SR 240 business route. Ext/int corridors. **Pets:** Accepted.

Shilo Inn Hotel-Richland Conference Center MI 🐾
(509) 946-4661. **$69-$109.** 50 Comstock St. I-182, exit 5B, 0.5 mi n. Ext corridors. **Pets:** Other species. $10 daily fee/pet. Service with restrictions, supervision.

RIMROCK

Game Ridge Motel M
(509) 672-2212. **$67-$135, 7 days notice.** 27350 US Hwy 12. Ext corridors. **Pets:** Other species. $10 daily fee/pet. Service with restrictions, supervision.

RITZVILLE

Best Inn & Suites M
(509) 659-1007. **$59-$99.** 1513 Smitty's Blvd. I-90, exit 221, just n. Int corridors. **Pets:** Accepted.

Colwell Motor Inn M
(509) 659-1620. **$48-$75.** 501 W 1st Ave. I-90, exit 220, 0.9 mi n. Ext corridors. **Pets:** Medium. $5 daily fee/pet. Designated rooms, service with restrictions, crate.

SAN JUAN ISLANDS AREA

DEER HARBOR

▼▼▼ Deer Harbor Inn 🅛
(360) 376-4110. **$119-$219, 14 days notice.** 33 Inn Ln. 8 mi sw of ferry landing, 4 mi sw of Westsound Ln; in Deer Harbor. Ext/int corridors. **Pets:** Accepted.
⊠ 🛏 💻 🍴 🎿 🐾

FRIDAY HARBOR

▲▲▲ ▼▼▼ The Inn At Friday Harbor 🅜
(360) 378-4000. **$99-$200, 7 days notice.** 410 Spring St. 0.5 mi w of ferry dock; in Friday Harbor. Ext corridors. **Pets:** Medium, dogs only. $50 deposit/pet. Designated rooms, service with restrictions, supervision.
SAVE 🆂 ⊠ 🐾 🛏 💻 🐾

❖ END AREA ❖

SEATTLE METROPOLITAN AREA

ARLINGTON

▲▲▲ ▼▼▼ Crossroads Inn 🅜
(360) 403-7222. **$69-$99.** 5200 172nd St NE. I-5, exit 206, 1 mi e. Int corridors. **Pets:** Small. $20 one-time fee/pet. Designated rooms, service with restrictions.
SAVE 🆂 ⊠ 🛏 💻

▼▼ Smokey Point Motor Inn 🅜
(360) 659-8561. **$59, 3 days notice.** 17329 Smokey Point Dr. I-5, exit 206, just ne; adjoining the Smokey Point Shopping Center. Ext corridors. **Pets:** Accepted.
ASK 🆂 ⊠ 🛏 💻 🐾

AUBURN

▼▼▼ Days Inn 🅜 🐾
(253) 939-5950. **$65.** 1521 D St NE. SR 167, exit 15th St NW, just e. Ext corridors. **Pets:** Small, other species. $15 one-time fee/room. Service with restrictions, supervision.
SAVE 🆂 ⊠ 🐾 🛏 💻 🐾

▲▲▲ ▼▼▼ Microtel Inn & Suites 🅜
(253) 833-7171. **$61-$96, 14 days notice.** Nine 16th St NW. SR 167, exit 15th St NW, 0.3 mi e. Int corridors. **Pets:** Small, other species. $10 daily fee/room. Service with restrictions, supervision.
SAVE ⊠ 🅼 🐾 🐾 🛏 💻

▼▼▼ Val-U Inn 🅜
(253) 735-9600. **$60-$65, 7 days notice.** 9 14th St NW. SR 167, exit 15th St NW, just e. Int corridors. **Pets:** Small, dogs only. $5 daily fee/room. Service with restrictions, supervision.
ASK 🆂 ⊠ 🐾 🛏

BELLEVUE

▼▼▼▼ Candlewood Suites Hotel 🅜 🐾
(425) 373-1212. **$79-$149.** 15805 SE 37th St. I-90, exit 11A eastbound; exit 11 westbound, 0.9 mi se on south frontage road. Int corridors. **Pets:** Large, other species. $10 daily fee/pet, $75 one-time fee/room. Service with restrictions.
ASK 🆂 ⊠ 🐾 🐾 🛏 💻

▼▼ Doubletree Hotel-Bellevue Center 🅜🅸
(425) 455-1515. **$59-$129.** 818 112th Ave NE. I-405, exit 13B, 0.3 mi nw. Ext/int corridors. **Pets:** Other species. $20 one-time fee/room. Service with restrictions.
SAVE 🆂 ⊠ 🐾 🛏 💻 🍴 🐾

**▼▼ Homestead Studio
Suites-Bellevue/Factoria** 🅜
(425) 865-8680. **$109-$119, 7 days notice.** 3700 132nd Ave SE. I-90, exit 11A westbound; exit 10B eastbound, 0.5 mi se. Ext corridors. **Pets:** Small. $75 one-time fee/pet. Service with restrictions, supervision.
ASK 🆂 ⊠ 🐾 🐾 🛏 💻

**▼▼ Homestead Studio
Suites-Seattle/Redmond** 🅜
(425) 885-6675. **$119-$132, 7 days notice.** 15805 NE 28th St. I-405, exit 14 (SR 520), 3.3 mi e; exit 148th Ave NE (south), just e on 24th St, just ne on Bel-Red Rd, just n on 156th Ave, then just e. Ext corridors. **Pets:** Medium, other species. $75 one-time fee/pet. Service with restrictions, supervision.
ASK 🆂 ⊠ 🐾 🐾 🛏 💻

**▲▲▲ ▼▼▼▼ The Residence Inn By Marriott,
Seattle-Bellevue** 🅰 🐾
(425) 882-1222. **$185-$199.** 14455 NE 29th Pl. I-405, exit 14 (SR 520), 2.3 mi e to 148th Ave NE (north exit), just nw. Ext corridors. **Pets:** $15 daily fee/pet. Service with restrictions.
SAVE 🆂 ⊠ 🐾 🛏 💻 🐾

BOTHELL

Residence Inn by Marriott Seattle NE ⚑ ❀
(425) 485-3030. **$149.** 11920 NE 195th St. I-405, exit 24, just ne. Ext corridors. **Pets:** Medium. $10 daily fee/pet, $50 one-time fee/room. Service with restrictions.

DUPONT

GuestHouse Inn & Suites Ⓜ
(253) 912-8900. **$90-$135.** 1609 McNeil St. I-5, exit 118, 0.6 mi w. Int corridors. **Pets:** $10 daily fee/pet. Service with restrictions, supervision.

EDMONDS

Edmonds Harbor Inn Ⓜ
(425) 771-5021. **$89-$139.** 130 W Dayton St. Just s at Port of Edmonds; in Harbor Square Shopping Center. Ext/int corridors. **Pets:** Accepted.

Travelodge Seattle North Ⓜ
(425) 771-8008. **$64-$99.** 23825 Hwy 99. I-5, exit 177, 1 mi w, 0.3 mi n at jct SR 99 and 104. Ext corridors. **Pets:** Medium. $25 one-time fee/pet. Service with restrictions, supervision.

EVERETT

Holiday Inn Hotel & Conference Center Seattle/Everett Ⓜ
(425) 337-2900. **$95.** 101 128th St SE. I-5, exit 186, just e. Int corridors. **Pets:** Accepted.

FEDERAL WAY

Best Western Federal Way Executel Ⓜ
(253) 941-6000. **$59-$99.** 31611 20th Ave S. I-5, exit 143, 0.5 mi w, 0.3 mi n of S 20th Ave; across from Sea-Tac Mall. Int corridors. **Pets:** Accepted.

Federal Way Comfort Inn Ⓜ
(253) 529-0101. **$85, 3 days notice.** 31622 Pacific Hwy S. I-5, exit 143, 0.5 mi nw. Int corridors. **Pets:** Other species. $20 one-time fee/room. Service with restrictions.

Federal Way Super 8 Ⓜ
(253) 838-8808. **Call for rates.** 1688 S 348th St. I-5, exit 142B, just w. Int corridors. **Pets:** Accepted.

FIFE

Best Inn & Suites Ⓜ ❀
(253) 922-9520. **$57-$75.** 3100 Pacific Hwy E. I-5, exit 136, just nw. Ext corridors. **Pets:** Medium, dogs only. $50 deposit/pet, $10 daily fee/pet. Designated rooms, service with restrictions, supervision.

Best Western Executive Inn Ⓜ ❀
(253) 922-0080. **$74-$135.** 5700 Pacific Hwy E. I-5, exit 137, just ne. Int corridors. **Pets:** Other species. $35 one-time fee/room. Service with restrictions, crate.

Comfort Inn Ⓜ
(253) 926-2301. **$62-$89.** 5601 Pacific Hwy E. I-5, exit 137, just e. Ext corridors. **Pets:** Medium. $15 one-time fee/pet. Designated rooms, service with restrictions, supervision.

Ramada Limited Ⓜ
(253) 926-1000. **$60-$89.** 3501 Pacific Hwy E. I-5, exit 136B northbound; exit 136 southbound, just nw. Ext corridors. **Pets:** $10 daily fee/pet. Designated rooms, service with restrictions, supervision.

Royal Coachman Inn Ⓜ
(253) 922-2500. **$71-$84.** 5805 Pacific Hwy E. I-5, exit 137, just ne. Ext corridors. **Pets:** Accepted.

GIG HARBOR

Best Western Wesley Inn Ⓜ ❀
(253) 858-9690. **$99-$169.** 6575 Kimball Dr. SR 16, exit City Center, just e on Pioneer Way, 0.3 mi s. Int corridors. **Pets:** Other species. $10 daily fee/pet. Service with restrictions, crate.

The Inn at Gig Harbor Ⓗ
(253) 858-1111. **$93-$195.** 3211 56th St NW. SR 16, exit Olympic Dr, just w, then 0.4 mi n. Int corridors. **Pets:** $5 daily fee/room, $15 one-time fee/room. Service with restrictions, supervision.

ISSAQUAH

Motel 6–295 Ⓜ
(425) 392-8405. **$55-$77.** 1885 15th Place NW. I-90, exit 15, 0.3 mi n on Renton Issaquah Rd, then just w on NW Sammamish Rd. Ext corridors. **Pets:** Accepted.

KENT

Best Inn & Suites M
(253) 520-6670. **$69-$129.** 25100 74th Ave S. I-5, exit 149 (Willis St, Des Moines), 2.5 mi se via SR 516 to 74th Ave. Int corridors. **Pets:** Accepted.
[SAVE] [S] [X] [🐾] [🛎] [📶] [🛏] [💻] [🏊]

Days Inn South Seattle/Kent M
(253) 854-1950. **$70.** 1711 W Meeker St. I-5, exit 149 southbound; exit 149A northbound, 2.3 mi ne via Kent/Des Moines Rd (SR 516) and Meeker St. Int corridors. **Pets:** Accepted.
[SAVE] [S] [X] [🛏] [💻]

Howard Johnson Inn M
(253) 852-7224. **$59-$109.** 1233 N Central. SR 167, exit 84th Ave S, just s. Ext corridors. **Pets:** Accepted.
[SAVE] [S] [X] [🛏] [💻] [🏊]

Val U Inn M
(253) 872-5525. **$79-$129.** 22420 84th Ave S. SR 167, exit 84th Ave S, just n. Int corridors. **Pets:** Small, dogs only. $5 daily fee/pet. Service with restrictions, supervision.
[ASK] [S] [X] [🛏]

KIRKLAND

Best Western Kirkland Inn M
(425) 822-2300. **$77-$97, 7 days notice.** 12223 NE 116th St. I-405, exit 20A northbound; exit 20 southbound, just e; in Totem Lake area. Ext corridors. **Pets:** Small. $50 deposit/room. Designated rooms, service with restrictions, supervision.
[SAVE] [S] [X] [🐾] [🛏] [💻] [🏊]

La Quinta Inn M
(425) 828-6585. **$96-$115.** 10530 NE Northup Way. I-405, exit 14 (SR 520) via 108th Ave exit, n on 108th St, then w. Int corridors. **Pets:** Accepted.
[SAVE] [X] [🐾] [🛎] [🛏] [💻] [🏊]

Motel 6–687 M
(425) 821-5618. **$55-$77.** 12010 120th Pl NE. I-405, exit 20B northbound; exit 20 southbound, just se. Ext corridors. **Pets:** Other species. Service with restrictions, supervision.
[S] [X] [🐾] [🛎] [🏊]

LAKEWOOD

Best Western Lakewood Motor Inn M ❀
(253) 584-2212. **$65-$81, 10 days notice.** 6125 Motor Ave SW. I-5, exit 125, 2 mi nw via Bridgeport to Gravelly Lake Dr, just left. Ext corridors. **Pets:** Small, dogs only. $6 daily fee/pet. Designated rooms, service with restrictions, supervision.
[SAVE] [S] [X] [🚭] [🐾] [🛎] [🛏] [💻] [🏊]

Quality Inn M
(253) 588-5241. **$-$77.** 9920 S Tacoma Way. I-5, exit 127, 0.3 mi nw. Ext corridors. **Pets:** Accepted.
[SAVE] [S] [X] [🛏] [💻]

LYNNWOOD

Embassy Suites Hotels Seattle North/Lynnwood H
(425) 775-2500. **$129-$169.** 20610 44th Ave W. I-5, exit 181A northbound, just e; exit 181 southbound, just w on 196th St SW, then 0.4 mi s. Int corridors. **Pets:** Medium. $50 one-time fee/pet. Service with restrictions.
[SAVE] [S] [X] [🚭] [🐾] [🛎] [🛏] [💻] [🍽] [🏊]

Lynnwood Landmark Inn M
(425) 775-7447. **$59-$99.** 4300 Alderwood Mall Blvd. I-5, exit 181A northbound, just w; exit 181 southbound, 0.5 mi sw via 196th St and 44th SW, just e. Int corridors. **Pets:** Small. $25 daily fee/room. Designated rooms, supervision.
[SAVE] [S] [X] [🛏] [💻] [🏊]

The Residence Inn by Marriott-Seattle North A
(425) 771-1100. **$109-$139.** 18200 Alderwood Mall Pkwy. I-5, exit 183, just w on 164th St SW, then 1.5 mi se on 28th St W; just n of Alderwood Mall Shopping Center. Ext corridors. **Pets:** $10 daily fee/pet. Service with restrictions, supervision.
[SAVE] [S] [X] [🐾] [🛏] [💻] [🏊]

MARYSVILLE

Best Western Tulalip Inn M
(360) 659-4488. **$59-$109, 10 days notice.** 6128 Marine Dr. I-5, exit 199, just w. Int corridors. **Pets:** Accepted.
[SAVE] [S] [X] [🚭] [🐾] [🛎] [🛏] [💻] [🍽] [🏊]

The Village Motor Inn M
(360) 659-0005. **$54-$66.** 235 Beach Ave. I-5, exit 199, just se. Int corridors. **Pets:** Small. $12 daily fee/pet. Service with restrictions, supervision.
[SAVE] [S] [X] [🛏] [💻]

MONROE

Best Western Baron Inn M
(360) 794-3111. **$69-$109.** 19233 US 2. West end of town. Int corridors. **Pets:** Other species. $27.05 one-time fee/room. Service with restrictions, supervision.
[SAVE] [S] [X] [🛎] [🛏] [💻] [🏊]

MOUNTLAKE TERRACE

Studio 6 M
(425) 771-3139. **Call for rates.** 6017 244th St SW. I-5, exit 177, just nw. Ext corridors. **Pets:** Medium. $10 daily fee/pet, $50 one-time fee/pet. Service with restrictions, supervision.
[ASK] [X] [🚭] [🐾] [🛎] [🛏] [💻]

PUYALLUP

Best Western Park Plaza M
(253) 848-1500. **$102-$117.** 620 S Hill Park Dr. SR 512, exit S Hill/Eatonville, just w. Int corridors. **Pets:** $15 one-time fee/room. Service with restrictions, supervision.
[SAVE] [S] [X] [🚭] [🐾] [🛎] [🛏] [💻] [🏊]

 Holiday Inn Express Hotel & Suites
Puyallup **M**
(253) 848-4900. **$102-$117.** 812 S Hill Park Dr. SR 512,
exit S Hill/Eatonville, just w. Int corridors. **Pets:** Small, dogs
only. $15 one-time fee/room. Service with restrictions,
supervision.
[SAVE] [S6] [X] [/] [=] [=] [~]

REDMOND

 Residence Inn by Marriott Redmond
Town Center **A**
(425) 497-9226. **$169-$229.** 7575 164th Ave NE. I-405, exit
14 (SR 520), 5 mi e to Westlake Sammish Pkwy, just n to
Leary Way, just e to Bear Creek Pkwy, just n to 74th Ave,
just w to 163rd Ave, then just n. Int corridors. **Pets:** Other
species. $10 daily fee/pet, $50 one-time fee/room.
[SAVE] [S6] [X] [=] [=] [~]

RENTON

 Travelodge of Renton **M**
(425) 251-9591. **$59-$74.** 3700 E Valley Rd. SR 167, exit E
Valley Rd, just nw. Int corridors. **Pets:** $10 daily fee/pet.
Designated rooms, service with restrictions, crate.
[SAVE] [S6] [X] [=] [=]

SEATAC

Doubletree Hotel Seattle Airport **H**
(206) 246-8600. **$79-$149.** 18740 International Blvd. On SR
99. Int corridors. **Pets:** Accepted.
[SAVE] [X] [/] [&] [=] [=] [Ħ] [~]

Hawthorn Suites LTD Seatac **M**
(206) 824-0233. **$98-$119.** 19621 International Blvd. On SR
99. Int corridors. **Pets:** Accepted.
[SAVE] [S6] [X] [=] [=]

Holiday Inn Sea-Tac **H**
(206) 248-1000. **$129-$159.** 17338 International Blvd. On
SR 99. Int corridors. **Pets:** Small. $20 daily fee/room. Des-
ignated rooms.
[SAVE] [S6] [X] [&M] [/] [=] [=] [Ħ] [~]

La Quinta Inn-Sea Tac Intl **M**
(206) 241-5211. **$86-$116.** 2824 S 188th St. On SR 99. Int
corridors. **Pets:** Accepted.
[SAVE] [S6] [X] [/] [=] [=] [~]

Motel 6-90 **M**
(206) 241-1648. **$43-$65.** 18900 47th Ave S. I-5, exit 152,
just sw. Int corridors. **Pets:** Accepted.
[S6] [X] [/] [&] [=] [~]

Red Roof Inn **M**
(206) 248-0901. **$60-$85.** 16838 International Blvd. SR 99.
Int corridors. **Pets:** Other species. Service with restrictions,
supervision.
[SAVE] [S6] [X] [=]

Seattle Marriott Sea-Tac Airport **H**
(206) 241-2000. **$139-$169.** 3201 S 176th St. Just e of SR
99. Int corridors. **Pets:** Accepted.
[SAVE] [S6] [X] [/] [&] [=] [=] [Ħ] [~]

Super 8 Motel Sea-Tac **M**
(206) 433-8188. **$68-$95.** 3100 S 192nd St. Just e of SR
99. Int corridors. **Pets:** Large, other species. $25 deposit/
room. Service with restrictions, supervision.
[ASK] [S6] [X]

SEATTLE

The Alexis Hotel **H** ❀
(206) 624-4844. **$295-$315.** 1007 1st Ave. Corner of Madison St and 1st Ave. Int corridors. **Pets:** Other species.
Service with restrictions.
[SAVE] [S6] [X] [/] [&] [=] [Ħ]

Aurora Seafair Inn **M**
(206) 524-3600. **$65-$95.** 9100 Aurora Ave N. I-5, exit 172,
1.5 mi w on N 85th St, just n. Ext corridors. **Pets:** Medium.
$5 daily fee/pet. Service with restrictions, supervision.
[SAVE] [S6] [X] [=]

Crowne Plaza Hotel-Seattle **H**
(206) 464-1980. **$119-$180.** 1113 6th Ave. Corner of 6th
Ave and Seneca St. Int corridors. **Pets:** $50 one-time fee/
room. Service with restrictions, supervision.
[ASK] [S6] [X] [/] [=] [=] [Ħ]

The Edgewater **H** ❀
(206) 728-7000. **$210-$329.** 2411 Alaskan Way-Pier 67. On
waterfront at Pier 67. Int corridors. **Pets:** Dogs only. Designated rooms, service with restrictions, supervision.
[ASK] [S6] [X] [/] [=] [Ħ]

Four Seasons Olympic
Hotel **H** ❀
(206) 621-1700. **$365-$455.** 411 University St. Downtown;
at 4th Ave and University St. Int corridors. **Pets:** Small.
Service with restrictions.
[S6] [X] [/] [&] [=] [=] [Ħ] [~]

Hawthorn Inn &
Suites-Downtown **M**
(206) 624-6820. **$155-$168.** 2224 8th Ave. Downtown; at
8th Ave and Blanchard. Int corridors. **Pets:** Accepted.
[SAVE] [S6] [X] [/] [=] [=]

Homewood Suites Hotel by
Hilton-Seattle/Downtown **A** ❀
(206) 281-9393. **$149-$209.** 206 Western Ave W. I-5, exit
167, 0.3 mi w on Mercer St, 0.5 mi s on Fairview, 1 mi w on
Denny Way, just n. Int corridors. **Pets:** Other species. $20
daily fee/pet.
[SAVE] [S6] [X] [=] [=]

Hotel Monaco **H**
(206) 621-1770. **$315.** 1101 4th Ave. Downtown; corner of
4th Ave and Spring St. Int corridors. **Pets:** Service with
restrictions, supervision.
[SAVE] [S6] [X] [/] [=] [=] [Ħ]

◊◊◊ ▽▽ ▽▽ Hotel Vintage Park 🅷 ❋
(206) 624-8000. **$285-$315.** 1100 5th Ave. Corner of Spring St and 5th Ave. Int corridors. **Pets:** Other species. Service with restrictions, supervision.
(SAVE) (S🔄) (✕) (🏃) (🍴)

▽ Motel 6–736 🅼
(206) 824-9902. **$47-$59.** 20651 Military Rd. I-5, exit 151, just s. Ext corridors. **Pets:** Accepted.
(S🔄) (✕) (🏃) (🦮) (🏊)

◊◊◊ ▽▽ ▽ Ramada Inn Seattle at
Northgate 🅼 ❋
(206) 365-0700. **$97-$139.** 2140 N Northgate Way. I-5, exit 173, just w. Ext corridors. **Pets:** Other species. Service with restrictions.
(SAVE) (S🔄) (✕) (🏃) (🦮) (💻) (🏊)

◊◊◊ ▽▽ ▽▽ Residence Inn by Marriott Seattle
Downtown 🅰 ❋
(206) 624-6000. **$169-$329.** 800 Fairview Ave N. I-5, exit 167 (Mercer St), south end of Lake Union. Int corridors. **Pets:** Other species. $10 daily fee/pet. Service with restrictions.
(SAVE) (S🔄) (✕) (🏃) (🦮) (💻)

◊◊◊ ▽▽ ▽▽ Sorrento Hotel 🅷
(206) 622-6400. **$240-$265.** 900 Madison St. I-5, exit Madison St, just e; at 9th and Madison St. Int corridors. **Pets:** Medium. $50 one-time fee/room. Service with restrictions.
(SAVE) (S🔄) (✕) (💻) (🍴)

◊◊◊ ▽▽ ▽▽ Travelodge by the Space
Needle 🅼 ❋
(206) 441-7878. **$99-$169.** 200 6th Ave N. I-5, exit 167 (Mercer St), just n on Fairview Ave, just w via Valley and Broad sts, just s on 5th Ave, then just e on John St. Int corridors. **Pets:** Large, dogs only. $5 daily fee/pet. Service with restrictions, crate.
(SAVE) (S🔄) (✕) (🏃) (🦮) (💻) (🏊)

◊◊◊ ▽▽ ▽▽ University Inn 🅼 ❋
(206) 632-5055. **$112-$144.** 4140 Roosevelt Way NE. I-5, exit 169, 0.5 mi e, just s. Int corridors. **Pets:** Small, dogs only. $10 daily fee/pet. Designated rooms, service with restrictions, supervision.
(SAVE) (S🔄) (✕) (🏃) (🦮) (💻) (🍴) (🏊)

◊◊◊ ▽▽ ▽▽ The Westin Seattle 🅷
(206) 728-1000. **$159-$189.** 1900 5th Ave. Downtown. Int corridors. **Pets:** $50 deposit/room. Service with restrictions, crate.
(SAVE) (S🔄) (✕) (🔊) (🏃) (🦮) (🦮) (💻) (🍴) (🏊)

▽▽ ▽▽ W Seattle 🅷
(206) 264-6000. **Call for rates.** 1112 4th Ave. At 4th Ave and Seneca St. Int corridors. **Pets:** Accepted.
(A$K) (✕) (💻) (🍴)

SNOHOMISH

◊◊◊ ▽▽ ▽ Inn At Snohomish 🅼
(360) 568-2208. **$65-$105.** 323 2nd St. East end of town. Ext corridors. **Pets:** Medium. Supervision.
(SAVE) (S🔄) (✕) (🦮) (💻)

TACOMA

◊◊◊ ▽▽ ▽▽ Best Western Tacoma Inn 🅼🅸
(253) 535-2880. **$79-$129, 30 days notice.** 8726 S Hosmer St. I-5, exit 128 northbound, just se; exit 129 southbound, just e on 72nd St, 1.2 mi s. Ext corridors. **Pets:** Accepted.
(SAVE) (S🔄) (✕) (🏃) (🦮) (🦮) (💻) (🍴) (🏊)

◊◊◊ ▽▽ ▽▽ La Quinta Inn 🅼🅸
(253) 383-0146. **$80-$95.** 1425 E 27th St. I-5, exit 135 southbound; exit 134 northbound, just n. Int corridors. **Pets:** Small, other species. Service with restrictions, supervision.
(SAVE) (S🔄) (✕) (🏃) (🦮) (💻) (🍴) (🏊)

◊◊◊ ▽▽ ▽▽ Sheraton Tacoma Hotel 🅷
(253) 572-3200. **$209-$309.** 1320 Broadway Plaza. I-5, exit 133 to I-705 N (City Center), exit A St, left on 11th, then left; downtown. Int corridors. **Pets:** Medium, other species. $100 deposit/room. Service with restrictions, crate.
(SAVE) (S🔄) (✕) (🏃) (🦮) (💻) (🍴)

◊◊◊ ▽▽ ▽▽ Shilo Inn-Tacoma 🅼 ❋
(253) 475-4020. **$79-$125.** 7414 S Hosmer St. I-5, exit 129, just se. Int corridors. **Pets:** Other species. $10 daily fee/pet. Service with restrictions, supervision.
(SAVE) (S🔄) (✕) (🦮) (🦮) (💻) (🏊)

TUKWILA

◊◊◊ ▽▽ ▽▽ Best Western Southcenter 🅼🅸
(425) 226-1812. **$89-$124, 7 days notice.** 15901 W Valley Hwy. I-405, exit 1 (SR 181), just s; across from Boeing Longacres Park. Int corridors. **Pets:** Accepted.
(SAVE) (S🔄) (✕) (🏃) (🦮) (💻) (🍴) (🏊)

▽▽ ▽ Homestead Studio
Suites-Seattle/Southcenter 🅼
(425) 235-7160. **$69, 5 days notice.** 15635 W Valley Hwy. I-405, exit 1 (SR 181), just s. Ext corridors. **Pets:** Medium, other species. $75 one-time fee/room. Service with restrictions, supervision.
(A$K) (S🔄) (✕) (🔊) (🏃) (🦮) (🦮) (💻)

▽▽ ▽▽ Homewood Suites by Hilton 🅷
(206) 433-8000. **$139-$169.** 6955 Fort Dent Way. I-405, exit 1, just ne. Ext/int corridors. **Pets:** Accepted.
(SAVE) (S🔄) (✕) (🏃) (🦮) (💻)

◊◊◊ ▽▽ ▽ Red Lion Hotel Seattle Airport 🅼🅸
(206) 246-8220. **$69-$109.** 205 Strander Blvd. I-5, exit 153 northbound; exit 154B southbound; sw of Southcenter Shopping Mall. Int corridors. **Pets:** Medium, other species. $50 deposit/room. Service with restrictions, supervision.
(SAVE) (S🔄) (✕) (🏃) (🦮) (💻) (🍴) (🏊)

(AAA) ▼▼▼▼ Residence Inn by Marriott-Seattle South A
(425) 226-5500. **$105-$179.** 16201 W Valley Hwy. I-405, exit 1 (SR 181), just s; across from Boeing Longacre Park. Ext corridors. **Pets:** Accepted.

[SAVE] [Sᴅ] [X] [🖉] [🖬] [🖵] [〜]

VASHON

▼ The Swallow's Nest Guest Cottages C ✿
(206) 463-2646. **$65-$190.** 6030 SW 248th St. On Vashon Island; from north end ferry landing, 7.8 mi s on Vashon Hwy; from south end (Tahlequah) ferry landing, 5.8 mi n on Vashon Hwy, 1.4 mi w on Quartermaster Dr, 1.5 mi s on. Ext corridors. **Pets:** Other species. $10 daily fee/pet. Designated rooms, service with restrictions, supervision.

[X] [🖬] [🖵] [𝒦]

VASHON ISLAND

▼▼ Van Gelder's Retreat C
(206) 463-3684. **$85-$100 (no credit cards), 30 days notice.** 18522 Beall Rd SW. On Vashon Island; from north end ferry landing, 4.6 mi s on Vashon Hwy; from south end (Tahlequah) ferry landing, 9 mi n on Vashon Hwy, 0.5 mi e on SW Bank Rd, then 0.6 mi s. Ext corridors. **Pets:** Other species. No service, supervision.

[A$K] [Sᴅ] [X] [🖬] [🖵] [〜] [𝒦]

✿ END METROPOLITAN AREA ✿

SEDRO WOOLLEY

(AAA) ▼▼▼▼ Three Rivers Inn M ✿
(360) 855-2626. **$58-$108.** 210 Ball St. On SR 20, just w of jct SR 9 N. Ext corridors. **Pets:** Medium. $15 one-time fee/room. Designated rooms, service with restrictions, supervision.

[SAVE] [Sᴅ] [X] [&ᴍ] [🖬] [🖵] [🍴] [〜]

SEQUIM

(AAA) ▼▼ Econo Lodge M
(360) 683-7113. **$61-$99.** 801 E Washington St. East end of downtown. Int corridors. **Pets:** Other species. $10 daily fee/pet. Supervision.

[SAVE] [Sᴅ] [X] [🖉] [🖬]

(AAA) ▼▼ Ramada Limited M
(360) 683-1775. **$59-$119.** 1095 E Washington St. East end of downtown. Int corridors. **Pets:** Medium. $10 daily fee/room. Service with restrictions, supervision.

[SAVE] [X] [🖬] [〜] [𝒦]

(AAA) ▼▼ Sequim Bay Lodge M
(360) 683-0691. **$76-$102.** 268522 US 101. 3.2 mi se of town. Ext corridors. **Pets:** Other species. $10 daily fee/pet. Designated rooms, service with restrictions, supervision.

[SAVE] [Sᴅ] [X] [⅊] [🖬] [🖵] [〜]

SHELTON

(AAA) ▼▼ Shelton Inn Motel M
(360) 426-4468. **$55-$68, 3 days notice.** 628 Railroad Ave. 0.4 mi w of SR 3. Ext corridors. **Pets:** $7.70 daily fee/pet. Service with restrictions, supervision.

[SAVE] [Sᴅ] [X] [🖬] [🖵] [〜]

▼▼ Super 8 Motel of Shelton M ✿
(360) 426-1654. **$54-$69.** 2943 Northview Cir. US 101, exit Wallace-Kneeland Blvd, just se. Int corridors. **Pets:** Medium. $15 one-time fee/pet. Designated rooms, service with restrictions, supervision.

[X] [🖬] [🖵]

SILVERDALE

▼▼ Cimarron Motel M
(360) 692-7777. **$70.** 9734 NW Silverdale Way. Downtown. Int corridors. **Pets:** Small. $10 one-time fee/room. Service with restrictions, supervision.

[A$K] [Sᴅ] [X] [🖬] [🖵]

SKYKOMISH

(AAA) ▼▼ SkyRiver Inn M ✿
(360) 677-2261. **$73-$105, 14 days notice.** 333 River Dr E. 16 mi w of Stevens Pass on US 2; south end of Skykomish River Bridge. Ext/int corridors. **Pets:** Other species. $5 daily fee/pet. Service with restrictions.

[SAVE] [X] [🖬] [🖵]

SNOQUALMIE PASS

(AAA) ▼▼▼▼ Best Western Summit Inn M
(425) 434-6300. **$109-$299.** 603 SR 906. I-90 E, exit 52, 0.3 mi e; I-90 W, exit 53, 0.3 mi w. Int corridors. **Pets:** Large, other species. $10 one-time fee/room. Designated rooms, service with restrictions, crate.

[SAVE] [Sᴅ] [X] [🖬] [🖵] [🍴] [〜]

SOAP LAKE

▼▼▼ Notaras Lodge M
(509) 246-0462. **$65-$79.** 236 E Main Ave. Just w of SR 17. Ext corridors. **Pets:** Accepted.

[X] [🖬] [🖵]

SOUTH BEND

▼▼▼▼ The Russell House 🅱🅱
(360) 875-6487. **$65-$85, 7 days notice.** 902 E Water St. 0.5 mi s on Harrison. Int corridors. **Pets:** Small. $10 one-time fee/room. Designated rooms, service with restrictions, supervision.

🅰🆂🅺 🆂🔏 ✂ 🎿

SPOKANE

▼▼ Alpine Motel Ⓜ
(509) 928-2700. **$45-$65.** 18815 E Cataldo. I-90, exit 293, just n. Ext corridors. **Pets:** Medium, other species. $5 daily fee/pet. Designated rooms, service with restrictions, supervision.

🅰🆂🅺 🆂🔏 ✂ 🗝 🛗 🏊

▼▼▼ Apple Tree Inn Ⓜ
(509) 466-3020. **$49-$59.** 9508 N Division St. Jct US 2 and 395, just n. Ext/int corridors. **Pets:** Accepted.

🆂🅰🆅🅴 🆂🔏 ✂ 🛗 🏊

▼▼▼ Best Inn & Suites Ⓜ
(509) 535-7185. **$49-$89.** 6309 E Broadway. I-90, exit 286, just w. Ext/int corridors. **Pets:** Other species. Service with restrictions, supervision.

🆂🅰🆅🅴 🆂🔏 ✂ 🛗 💻 🏊

▼▼▼▼ Best Western Pheasant Hill Ⓜ 🐾
(509) 926-7432. **$79-$109.** 12415 E Mission. I-90, exit 289, just se. Int corridors. **Pets:** Medium. Designated rooms, service with restrictions.

🆂🅰🆅🅴 🆂🔏 ✂ 🗝 🛗 💻 🏊

▼▼▼ Best Western Thunderbird Inn Ⓜ
(509) 747-2011. **$65.** 120 W 3rd Ave. I-90, exit 281, just n, then just w on 2nd Ave. Ext corridors. **Pets:** Small, dogs only. $10 daily fee/pet. Service with restrictions, supervision.

🆂🅰🆅🅴 🆂🔏 ✂ 🎿 🛗 💻 🏊

▼▼▼ Best Western Trade Winds North Ⓜ 🐾
(509) 326-5500. **$74, 3 days notice.** 3033 N Division St. I-90, exit 281, 2.3 mi n on US 2 and 395 (Division St). Ext/int corridors. **Pets:** Other species. Service with restrictions, crate.

🆂🅰🆅🅴 🆂🔏 ✂ 🛗 💻 🏊

▼▼ Comfort Inn North Ⓜ
(509) 467-7111. **$79, 7 days notice.** 7111 N Division St. I-90, exit 281, 4.6 mi n. Int corridors. **Pets:** $5 daily fee/pet. Designated rooms, service with restrictions, supervision.

🆂🅰🆅🅴 🆂🔏 ✂ 💻 🏊

▼▼ Comfort Inn Valley Ⓜ
(509) 924-3838. **$49-$79, 10 days notice.** 905 N Sullivan Rd. I-90, exit 291, just s. Int corridors. **Pets:** Accepted.

🆂🅰🆅🅴 🆂🔏 ✂ 🛗 💻 🏊

▲▲▲ ▼▼▼ Days Inn Spokane Airport Ⓜ
(509) 747-2021. **$69-$129.** 4212 W Sunset Blvd. I-90, exit 277A eastbound, 1 mi on Garden Spring Rd; exit 277 westbound, just n on Rustle. Ext corridors. **Pets:** Small, other species. $10 deposit/pet. Designated rooms, service with restrictions, crate.

🆂🅰🆅🅴 🆂🔏 ✂ 🎿 🛗 💻 🍴 🏊

▼▼▼ Doubletree Hotel Spokane City Center 🅷
(509) 455-9600. **$184.** 322 N Spokane Falls Ct. I-90, exit 281, just n; downtown. Int corridors. **Pets:** Accepted.

🆂🅰🆅🅴 🆂🔏 ✂ 🗝 🛗 💻 🍴 🏊

▲▲▲ ▼▼▼ Doubletree Hotel Spokane Valley 🅷
(509) 924-9000. **$89-$139.** 1100 N Sullivan Rd. I-90, exit 291B, just s. Int corridors. **Pets:** Other species. $50 deposit/room. Service with restrictions, crate.

🆂🅰🆅🅴 🆂🔏 ✂ 🎿 🛗 💻 🍴 🏊

▲▲▲ ▼▼▼▼ Hawthorn Inn & Suites Ⓜ 🐾
(509) 893-0955. **$69-$89.** 3808 N Sullivan Rd. I-90, exit 291, 1.3 mi n. Int corridors. **Pets:** Other species. Service with restrictions, supervision.

🆂🅰🆅🅴 🆂🔏 ✂ 🔥 🎿 🗝 🛗 💻 🏊

▲▲▲ ▼▼▼ Howard Johnson Inn Ⓜ
(509) 838-6630. **$65-$78.** 211 S Division St. I-90, exit 281 (Division St), just n. Int corridors. **Pets:** Small. $10 daily fee/pet. Designated rooms, service with restrictions, supervision.

🆂🅰🆅🅴 ✂ 🛗 💻

▼▼▼ Quality Inn Oakwood Ⓜ
(509) 467-4900. **$78-$250.** 7919 N Division St. I-90, exit 281 (Division St), 8 mi n. Int corridors. **Pets:** Accepted.

🆂🅰🆅🅴 🆂🔏 ✂ 🔥 🎿 🗝 🛗 💻 🏊

▼▼▼ Quality Inn Valley Suites Ⓜ
(509) 928-5218. **$87, 30 days notice.** 8923 E Mission. I-90, exit 287. Int corridors. **Pets:** Medium. $50 deposit/room. Designated rooms, service with restrictions, supervision.

🆂🅰🆅🅴 🆂🔏 ✂ 🔥 🎿 🗝 🛗 💻 🏊

▼▼▼ Ramada Inn Airport Ⓜ
(509) 838-5211. **$84-$99.** 8909 Airport Dr. I-90, exit 277B eastbound; exit 277 westbound, 3.4 mi n. Int corridors. **Pets:** Accepted.

🅰🆂🅺 🆂🔏 ✂ 🛗 💻 🍴 🏊

▼▼▼ Ramada Inn & Suites Ⓜ
(509) 468-4201. **$75-$100.** 9601 N Newport Hwy. US 2 and 395, just n on US 2 (Newport Hwy). Int corridors. **Pets:** Medium. $10 deposit/room, $10 one-time fee/room. Service with restrictions, supervision.

🅰🆂🅺 🆂🔏 ✂ 🔥 🎿 🗝 🛗 💻 🏊

▼▼ Ramada Limited Ⓜ
(509) 838-8504. **$64-$84.** 123 S Post St. I-90, exit 280B (Lincoln St), just n to 1st Ave W, just e to Post St, then just s. Ext corridors. **Pets:** Small. $10 deposit/room, $10 one-time fee/room. Service with restrictions, supervision.

🅰🆂🅺 🆂🔏 ✂ 🎿 🛗 💻

Residence Inn by Marriott M
(509) 892-9300. **$109-$179.** 15915 E Indiana. I-90, exit 291 westbound, just e; exit 291B eastbound, just n, then just e. Int corridors. **Pets:** Small. $10 daily fee/pet, $50 one-time fee/room. Designated rooms, service with restrictions, supervision.

Shangri-La Motel M
(509) 747-2066. **$40-$45.** 2922 W Government Way. I-90, exit 277A eastbound; exit 277 westbound, Garden Springs Rd to Sunset Blvd, 1 mi e to Government Way, just n to Hartson. Ext corridors. **Pets:** Medium. Service with restrictions, supervision.

Shilo Inn Hotel-Spokane M ✿
(509) 535-9000. **$59-$79.** 923 E 3rd Ave. I-90, exit 281, just n to E 3rd Ave, 0.7 mi e. Int corridors. **Pets:** Other species. $10 daily fee/pet. Service with restrictions, supervision.

The Spokane House Hotel H
(509) 838-1471. **$58-$68.** 4301 W Sunset Blvd. I-90 E, exit 277A, 1 mi n on Garden Springs Rd; I-90 W, exit 277, just n on Rustle. Int corridors. **Pets:** Service with restrictions, supervision.

Super 8 Motel M
(509) 928-4888. **$49-$70.** N 2020 Argonne Rd. I-90, exit 287, just n. Int corridors. **Pets:** $25 deposit/room. Designated rooms, service with restrictions, supervision.

Super 8 West M
(509) 838-8800. **$59-$69.** 11102 W Westbow Blvd. I-90, exit 272 (Medical Lake), just s. Int corridors. **Pets:** Medium, other species. $10 deposit/pet, $10 one-time fee/pet. Service with restrictions, supervision.

Trade Winds Motel M
(509) 838-2091. **$35-$60.** 907 W 3rd Ave. I-90, exit 280 eastbound, e on 3rd Ave; exit 280B westbound. Int corridors. **Pets:** Other species. $25 deposit/room. Service with restrictions, crate.

Travelodge M ✿
(509) 623-9727. **$63-$78.** W 33 Spokane Falls Blvd. I-90, exit 281, 0.5 mi n on Division St, just w on Trent. Int corridors. **Pets:** Other species. $10 one-time fee/room. Service with restrictions, crate.

WestCoast Grand Hotel at the Park H
(509) 326-8000. **$85-$105.** 303 W North River Dr. I-90, exit 281, 1.5 mi n on US 195, just w. Int corridors. **Pets:** Medium, other species. Service with restrictions.

WestCoast Ridpath Hotel H
(509) 838-2711. **$74-$94.** 515 W Sprague Ave. Downtown. Int corridors. **Pets:** Accepted.

WestCoast River Inn M ✿
(509) 326-5577. **$78-$98.** N 700 Division St. I-90, exit 281 (Division St), 0.8 mi n. Int corridors. **Pets:** Other species. $50 deposit/room. Service with restrictions, supervision.

SULTAN

Dutch Cup Motel M
(360) 793-2215. **$59-$74, 7 days notice.** 918 Main St. US 2 and Main St. Ext corridors. **Pets:** Other species. $8 daily fee/pet. Service with restrictions, supervision.

SUNNYSIDE

Rodeway Inn M
(509) 837-5781. **$99.** 3209 Picard Pl. I-82, exit 69, just n. Int corridors. **Pets:** Accepted.

TOPPENISH

Best Western Lincoln Inn M
(509) 865-7444. **$75-$99.** 515 S Elm St. I-82, exit 50, 3.1 mi e. Int corridors. **Pets:** Very small, dogs only. $10 daily fee/pet. Designated rooms, service with restrictions, supervision.

TUMWATER

Best Western Tumwater Inn M
(360) 956-1235. **$70-$86, 10 days notice.** 5188 Capitol Blvd. I-5, exit 102, just e. Int corridors. **Pets:** Other species. $5 daily fee/room.

GuestHouse International Inn & Suites M
(360) 943-5040. **$92-$170.** 1600 74th Ave SW. I-5, exit 101, just e. Int corridors. **Pets:** Other species. $15 daily fee/pet. Service with restrictions, supervision.

Motel 6-77 M
(360) 754-7320. **$41-$55.** 400 W Lee St. I-5, exit 102, just e on Trosper Rd, just s on Capital Blvd, then just w. Ext corridors. **Pets:** Other species. Service with restrictions, supervision.

TWISP

Idle-A-While Motel M
(509) 997-3222. **$58-$81, 4 days notice.** 505 N SR 20. Just n of town. Ext corridors. **Pets:** Dogs only. $5 daily fee/pet. Service with restrictions, supervision.

UNION GAP

Quality Inn-Yakima Valley M
(509) 248-6924. **$69-$99.** 12 E Valley Mall Blvd. I-82, exit 36, just s. Ext corridors. **Pets:** Small, dogs only. $10 daily fee/pet. Designated rooms, service with restrictions, supervision.

Super 8 Motel Yakima M
(509) 248-8880. **$57-$70.** 2605 Rudkin Rd. I-82, exit 36, just s. Int corridors. **Pets:** Other species. $25 deposit/room. Service with restrictions, supervision.

WALLA WALLA

Best Western Walla Walla Suites Inn M
(509) 525-4700. **$79-$99.** 7 E Oak St. US 12, exit 2nd Ave, just s. Int corridors. **Pets:** Small. $10 one-time fee/pet. Service with restrictions, supervision.

Budget Inn M
(509) 529-4410. **$65.** 305 N 2nd St. US 12, exit 2nd St, 0.3 mi s. Ext corridors. **Pets:** $5 daily fee/pet. Service with restrictions, supervision.

Hawthorn Inn & Suites M
(509) 525-2522. **$59-$69, 7 days notice.** 520 N 2nd St. US 12, exit 2nd Ave, just s. Int corridors. **Pets:** Accepted.

Howard Johnson Express Inn M
(509) 529-4360. **$89-$129, 15 days notice.** 325 E Main. US 12, exit 2nd Ave, 0.5 mi s, just e. Ext/int corridors. **Pets:** Accepted.

Walla Walla Super 8 M ✿
(509) 525-8800. **Call for rates.** 2315 Eastgate St N. US 12, exit Wilbur, just s. Int corridors. **Pets:** Other species. $25 deposit/room. Service with restrictions.

Walla Walla Travelodge M
(509) 529-4940. **$55-$65.** 421 E Main. US 12, exit 2nd Ave, 0.5 mi s, just e. Ext/int corridors. **Pets:** Accepted.

WENATCHEE

Avenue Motel M
(509) 663-7161. **$45-$60.** 720 N Wenatchee Ave. On US 2 business loop, just nw of downtown. Ext/int corridors. **Pets:** Supervision.

Columbia River Comfort Inn M
(509) 662-1700. **$75-$99.** 815 N Wenatchee Ave. Downtown. Int corridors. **Pets:** Other species. $10 daily fee/room. Service with restrictions, supervision.

Hawthorn Inn & Suites M
(509) 664-6565. **$62-$99.** 1905 N Wenatchee Ave. West end of town. Int corridors. **Pets:** Other species. Service with restrictions, supervision.

Holiday Inn Express M
(509) 663-6355. **$79-$110, 30 days notice.** 1921 N Wenatchee Ave. Northwest side of town. Int corridors. **Pets:** Small, other species. Designated rooms, service with restrictions, supervision.

Orchard Inn M
(509) 662-3443. **$50-$55.** 1401 N Miller St. 1.5 mi n on US 2. Int corridors. **Pets:** $10 daily fee/pet. Designated rooms, service with restrictions, supervision.

Red Lion Hotel Wenatchee M
(509) 663-0711. **$59-$95.** 1225 N Wenatchee Ave. Just nw of downtown. Int corridors. **Pets:** Medium, other species. $50 deposit/room. Service with restrictions, supervision.

WestCoast Wenatchee Center Hotel M
(509) 662-1234. **$69-$85.** 201 N Wenatchee Ave. Downtown. Int corridors. **Pets:** $10 one-time fee/room. Service with restrictions, supervision.

WESTPORT

Coho Motel M
(360) 268-0111. **$51-$66, 3 days notice.** 2501 N Nyhus. Just e of boat basin. Ext corridors. **Pets:** Accepted.

WINTHROP

Best Western Cascade Inn M
(509) 996-3100. **$65-$159, 3 days notice.** 960 SR 20. 0.8 mi e. Ext corridors. **Pets:** Medium, dogs only. $10 daily fee/pet.

RiverRun Inn M
(509) 996-2173. **$70-$105, 7 days notice.** 27 Rader Rd. 0.5 mi w of town, just s of SR 20. Ext corridors. **Pets:** Medium. $10 daily fee/pet. Designated rooms, service with restrictions, supervision.

Winthrop Inn M ✿
(509) 996-2217. **$65-$95.** 960 SR 20. 0.8 mi e. Int corridors. **Pets:** Dogs only. $7 daily fee/pet. Supervision.

WOODLAND

(AAA) ▼▼▼▼ Lewis River Inn M
(360) 225-6257. **$56-$73.** 1100 Lewis River Rd. I-5, exit 21, just e. Ext corridors. **Pets:** $6 daily fee/pet. Designated rooms, supervision.
SAVE ⊠ ▯ ▭

(AAA) ▼ Scandia Motel M
(360) 225-8006. **$36-$40.** 1123 Hoffman St. I-5, exit 21, just nw. Ext corridors. **Pets:** Medium. $5.06 daily fee/room. Designated rooms.
SAVE ⊠ ▯

(AAA) ▼▼▼▼ Woodlander Inn Express M
(360) 225-6548. **$55-$70.** 1500 Atlantic St. I-5, exit 21, just ne. Ext corridors. **Pets:** Medium, other species. $10 daily fee/pet. Supervision.
SAVE S🐾 ⊠ ▯ ➰

YAKIMA

▼▼ Cedars Inn and Suites M
(509) 452-8101. **$59-$64.** 1010 E A St. I-82, exit 33B eastbound; exit 33 westbound, just w to 9th St, just n to A St, then just e. Ext corridors. **Pets:** Medium, other species. $6 daily fee/pet. Service with restrictions, supervision.
A$K S🐾 ⊠ ▯

(AAA) ▼▼▼▼ Comfort Suites-Yakima M
(509) 249-1900. **$89-$109.** 3702 Fruitvale Blvd. US 12, exit 40th Ave, just s. Int corridors. **Pets:** Very small, dogs only. $10 daily fee/pet. Designated rooms, service with restrictions, supervision.
SAVE S🐾 ⊠ 🅼 🗇 🐾 ▯ ▭ ➰

▼▼ Doubletree Hotel Yakima Valley MI
(509) 248-7850. **$64-$94.** 1507 N 1st St. I-82, exit 31, 0.5 mi s. Int corridors. **Pets:** Small. $15 one-time fee/pet. Service with restrictions, crate.
SAVE S🐾 ⊠ 🅼 🐾 ▯ ▭ 🍽 ➰

▼▼▼▼ Holiday Inn Express Yakima M
(509) 249-1000. **$86-$96.** 1001 East A St. I-82, exit 33B eastbound; exit 33 westbound, just w to 9th St, just n to A St, then just e. Int corridors. **Pets:** Small. $6 daily fee/pet. Designated rooms, service with restrictions, supervision.
A$K ⊠ 🅼 🗇 🐾 ▯ ▭ ➰

▼▼▼▼ Oxford Inn M
(509) 457-4444. **Call for rates.** 1603 Terrace Heights Dr. I-82, exit 33 westbound, just e; exit 33B eastbound. Int corridors. **Pets:** Accepted.
A$K ⊠ 🐾 ▯ ▭ ➰

▼▼▼▼ Oxford Suites M
(509) 457-9000. **$75-$199.** 1701 E Yakima Ave. I-82, exit 33 (Yakima Ave) westbound; exit 33B eastbound. Int corridors. **Pets:** Accepted.
A$K S🐾 ⊠ 🐾 ▯ ▭ ➰

▼▼▼▼ Red Lion Inn M
(509) 453-0391. **$79-$99.** 818 N 1st St. I-82, exit 31, 1.2 mi s. Ext corridors. **Pets:** Accepted.
A$K S🐾 ⊠ 🐾 ▯ ▭ ➰

(AAA) ▼▼▼ Sun Country Inn M
(509) 248-5650. **$57-$71, 5 days notice.** 1700 N 1st St. I-82, exit 31, just s. Ext corridors. **Pets:** $5 daily fee/pet. Service with restrictions, supervision.
SAVE S🐾 ⊠ ▯ ▭ ➰

▼▼▼▼ WestCoast Yakima Center Hotel MI
(509) 248-5900. **$95-$125, 7 days notice.** 607 E Yakima Ave. I-82, exit 33 westbound; exit 33B eastbound, 0.8 mi w. Ext/int corridors. **Pets:** Accepted.
A$K S🐾 ⊠ 🗇 ▯ ▭ 🍽 ➰

▼▼▼▼ WestCoast Yakima Gateway Hotel MI
(509) 452-6511. **$69-$125.** 9 N 9th St. I-82, exit 33 westbound; exit 33B eastbound, just s. Int corridors. **Pets:** Accepted.
A$K S🐾 ⊠ 🅼 ▯ ▭ 🍽 ➰

ZILLAH

▼▼▼ Comfort Inn M ❀
(509) 829-3399. **$79-$140.** 911 Vintage Valley Pkwy. I-82, exit 52, just n. Int corridors. **Pets:** Other species. $10 daily fee/room. Crate.
SAVE S🐾 ⊠ 🗇 🐾 ▯ ▭ ➰

CITY INDEX

BECKLEY

Best Western Four Seasons Inn M
(304) 252-0671. **$57-$64, 10 days notice.** 1939 Harper Rd. I-64/77, exit 44, just e on SR 3. Ext/int corridors. **Pets:** Small, other species. $5 daily fee/pet. Designated rooms, service with restrictions, supervision.

Comfort Inn M
(304) 255-2161. **$68-$90.** 1909 Harper Rd. I-64/77, exit 44, 0.3 mi e on SR 3. Ext/int corridors. **Pets:** Other species. Service with restrictions.

Country Inn & Suites By Carlson M
(304) 252-5100. **$89-$105.** 2120 Harper Rd. I-77, exit 44, just w on SR 3. Int corridors. **Pets:** Small. $25 one-time fee/pet. Designated rooms, service with restrictions, supervision.

Park Inn & Suites M
(304) 255-9091. **$89-$99.** 134 Harper Park Dr. I-64/77, exit 44, just w on SR 3. Int corridors. **Pets:** Accepted.

BLUEFIELD

Econo Lodge M
(304) 327-8171. **$43-$90.** 3400 Cumberland Rd. I-77, exit 1, 3.8 mi nw via US 52/460, 0.4 mi n on US 52. Ext corridors. **Pets:** Accepted.

Holiday Inn-On The Hill MI
(304) 325-6170. **$64-$104, 30 days notice.** 3350 Big Laurel Hwy. I-77, exit 1, 3.8 mi nw via US 52/460. Int corridors. **Pets:** Small. Service with restrictions.

Ramada Inn-East River Mountain MI
(304) 325-5421. **Call for rates, 3 days notice.** 3175 E Cumberland Rd. I-77, exit 1, 3.8 mi nw via US 52/460, then 0.7 mi n on US 52. Ext corridors. **Pets:** Accepted.

BRIDGEPORT

Holiday Inn Clarksburg-Bridgeport MI
(304) 842-5411. **$65-$80.** 100 Lodgeville Rd. I-79, exit 119, just e on US 50. Int corridors. **Pets:** Accepted.

Knights Inn-Clarksburg M
(304) 842-7115. **$54-$85, 3 days notice.** 1235 W Main St. I-79, exit 119, 0.3 mi e on US 50. Ext corridors. **Pets:** Other species. Service with restrictions.

Sleep Inn M
(304) 842-1919. **Call for rates.** 115 Tolley Dr. I-79, exit 119, just e on US 50. Int corridors. **Pets:** Accepted.

CHAPMANVILLE

Rodeway Inn M
(304) 855-7182. **$53-$55.** Rt 10/119. Just s on SR 10, from jct US 119. Ext/int corridors. **Pets:** Very small, dogs only. $5 daily fee/pet. No service, supervision.

CHARLESTON

Days Inn Charleston West M
(304) 925-1010. **$49-$69.** 6400 MacCorkle Ave. I-77, exit 95, just s on SR 61. Int corridors. **Pets:** Small, dogs only. Supervision.

Holiday Inn Express Civic Center M
(304) 345-0600. **$79-$129.** 100 Civic Center Dr. I-64, exit eastbound 58B; exit westbound 58C, just s. Int corridors. **Pets:** Small. $15 one-time fee/room. Designated rooms, supervision.

Knights Inn-Charleston East M
(304) 925-0451. **$50-$71.** 6401 MacCorkle Ave SE. I-77, exit 95, just s on SR 61. Ext corridors. **Pets:** $5 daily fee/room. Service with restrictions, supervision.

▲▲▲ ▽▽▽ Red Roof Inn-Kanawha City M
(304) 925-6953. **$43-$54.** 6305 SE MacCorkle Ave. I-77, exit 95, just s on SR 61. Ext corridors. **Pets:** Accepted.
[SAVE] [X]

DAVIS

▲▲▲ ▽▽▽▽ Deerfield Village Resort-Canaan
Valley C ❖
(304) 866-4698. **$130-$140, 10 days notice.** Cortland Ln. 7 mi s on SR 32. Ext corridors. **Pets:** Small. $50 one-time fee/pet. Designated rooms, no service, supervision.
[SAVE] [S6] [X] [B] [D] [Y1] [2] [X] [X]

ELKINS

▽▽ Econo Lodge M
(304) 636-5311. **$52-$73, 5 days notice.** US 33 E. 1 mi e on US 33. Ext/int corridors. **Pets:** Accepted.
[SAVE] [S6] [X] [B] [2]

▽▽▽ Elkins Days Inn M
(304) 637-4667. **$59-$95.** 1200 Harrison Ave. 1 mi w on US 33/250/SR 92. Int corridors. **Pets:** Dogs only. $5 daily fee/pet. Service with restrictions, crate.
[SAVE] [S6] [X] [&M] [B] [D] [Y1]

FAIRMONT

▲▲▲ ▽▽▽ Days Inn M
(304) 366-5995. **$47-$75, 10 days notice.** 228 Middletown Rd. I-79, exit 132, just se on US 250, then just s. Ext corridors. **Pets:** $10 one-time fee/pet. Designated rooms, service with restrictions, supervision.
[SAVE] [S6] [X] [B] [D] [Y1]

▲▲▲ ▽▽▽▽ Holiday Inn M
(304) 366-5500. **$59-$99.** 930 E Grafton Rd. I-79, exit 137, just e. Int corridors. **Pets:** Accepted.
[SAVE] [S6] [X] [&M] [2] [3] [B] [D] [Y1] [2]

▲▲▲ ▽▽▽ Red Roof Inn M
(304) 366-6800. **$42-$54.** 50 Middletown Rd. I-79, exit 132, 0.3 mi s on US 250, just w, then just s. Ext corridors. **Pets:** Accepted.
[SAVE] [X] [2] [B]

▽▽▽ Super 8 Motel M
(304) 363-1488. **$58-$65.** 2208 Pleasant Valley Rd. I-79, exit 133, just e. Int corridors. **Pets:** Medium. Service with restrictions.
[ASK] [S6] [X] [B]

FAYETTEVILLE

▽▽▽ Historic White Horse Bed &
Breakfast BB
(304) 574-1400. **$100, 14 days notice.** 120 Fayette Ave. US 19, 0.4 mi e on Court St, just n. Ext/int corridors. **Pets:** Accepted.
[ASK] [S6] [X] [X] [W] [2]

HUNTINGTON

▽▽▽▽ Holiday Inn Hotel & Suites M
(304) 523-8880. **$89, 7 days notice.** 800 3rd Ave. I-64, exit 11, 3 mi n on SR 10, then 0.9 mi w. Int corridors. **Pets:** Small. $20 one-time fee/room. Designated rooms, service with restrictions, crate.
[ASK] [S6] [X] [&M] [2] [3] [B] [D] [Y1] [2]

▲▲▲ ▽▽▽ Red Roof Inn M
(304) 733-3737. **$42-$64.** 5190 US Rt 60 E. I-64, exit 15, just s. Ext corridors. **Pets:** Accepted.
[SAVE] [X] [B]

HURRICANE

▽▽▽ Ramada Limited M
(304) 562-3346. **Call for rates, 7 days notice.** 419 Hurricane Creek Rd. I-64, exit 34. Ext corridors. **Pets:** Accepted.
[ASK] [X] [B]

▲▲▲ ▽▽▽ Red Roof Inn M
(304) 757-6392. **$44-$58.** 500 Putnam Village Dr. I-64, exit 39, just n on SR 34, just e; behind Liberty Square Shopping Center. Ext corridors. **Pets:** Medium, other species. Service with restrictions, supervision.
[SAVE] [X] [3] [B]

JANE LEW

▲▲▲ ▽▽▽ Wilderness Plantation Inn &
Restaurant M
(304) 884-7806. **$52-$63.** Rt 7 Berlin Rd. I-79, exit 105, just e, then 0.3 mi s. Ext corridors. **Pets:** Accepted.
[SAVE] [X] [3] [B] [Y1] [2]

KEYSER

▲▲▲ ▽▽▽ Keyser Econo Lodge M
(304) 788-0913. **$54-$76.** Rt 220 S. 2.3 mi s on US 220. Int corridors. **Pets:** $10 daily fee/room. Designated rooms, service with restrictions, supervision.
[SAVE] [S6] [X] [B] [D]

LEWISBURG

▲▲▲ ▽▽▽ Brier Inn M
(304) 645-7722. **$49-$73.** 540 N Jefferson St. I-64, exit 169, just s on US 219. Ext corridors. **Pets:** Medium, other species. $10 one-time fee/pet. Designated rooms, service with restrictions.
[SAVE] [X] [3] [B] [D] [Y1] [2]

▲▲▲ ▽▽▽ Days Inn M
(304) 645-2345. **$55-$125, 10 days notice.** 635 N Jefferson St. I-64, exit 169, 0.3 mi n on US 219. Ext corridors. **Pets:** Accepted.
[SAVE] [S6] [X]

▽▽▽ Fort Savannah Inn M
(304) 645-3055. **$49-$129.** 204 N Jefferson St. I-64, exit 169, 1.3 mi s on US 219. Ext/int corridors. **Pets:** $10 one-time fee/pet. Service with restrictions, supervision.
[ASK] [X] [B] [Y1] [2]

▼▼ Super 8 Motel **M**
(304) 647-3188. **$65-$96, 30 days notice.** 550 N Jefferson St. I-64, exit 169, just s on US 219. Int corridors. **Pets:** Other species. $10 deposit/pet. Service with restrictions, supervision.
ASK S✗ ✗ 🖉 🄵

MARTINSBURG

▼▼▼ Days Inn Shenandoah **M**
(304) 263-1800. **$49-$79.** 209 Viking Way. I-81, exit 13, just e on W King St (CR 15). Ext/int corridors. **Pets:** Accepted.
SAVE S✗ ✗ 🄵 🖵

◆◆ ▼▼ Econo Lodge **M**
(304) 274-2181. **$52-$71.** Rt 2, Box 208 N. I-81, exit 20, just e. Ext/int corridors. **Pets:** Other species. Service with restrictions, supervision.
SAVE S✗ ✗ 🖵 🍽 ⇔

◆◆ ▼ Economy Inn **M**
(304) 267-2994. **$36-$50.** 1193 Winchester Ave (US 11 S). I-81, exit 12, 0.3 mi e on SR 45, 0.3 mi s on US 11. Ext corridors. **Pets:** Small. $5 one-time fee/pet. Designated rooms, service with restrictions, supervision.
SAVE ✗ 🄵 ⇔

▼▼▼ Hampton Inn **M**
(304) 267-2900. **$69-$89.** 975 Foxcroft Ave. I-81, exit 12, just e on SR 45, then just n. Int corridors. **Pets:** Accepted.
SAVE ✗ 🖉 🐾 🖵 ⇔

▼▼▼ Holiday Inn Martinsburg **M**
(304) 267-5500. **$69-$99.** 301 Foxcroft Ave. I-81, exit 13, just e on W King St (CR 15). Int corridors. **Pets:** Other species. Supervision.
ASK S✗ ✗ 🖉 🄵 🖵 🍽 ⇔

◆◆ ▼▼ Knights Inn-Martinsburg **M** ✿
(304) 267-2211. **$55-$65, 5 days notice.** 1997 Edwin Miller Blvd. I-81, exit 16E, 0.4 mi e on SR 9. Ext corridors. **Pets:** Medium. $5 daily fee/pet. Designated rooms, service with restrictions, supervision.
SAVE S✗ ✗ 🄵

▼▼ Martinsburg Travelodge **M**
(304) 263-8811. **$69-$99, 7 days notice.** 94 McMillan Ct. I-81, exit 16E, just e. Ext/int corridors. **Pets:** Other species. $10 daily fee/pet. Designated rooms, service with restrictions, supervision.
ASK S✗ ✗ 🄵 🖵 ⇔

◆◆ ▼ Relax Inn **M** ✿
(304) 263-0831. **$30-$59, 3 days notice.** 1022 Winchester (US 11 N) Ave. I-81, exit 12, 0.3 mi e on SR 45, then just n on US 11. Ext corridors. **Pets:** Small. $5 daily fee/pet. Service with restrictions, supervision.
SAVE S✗ ✗ 🄵 ⇔

◆◆ ▼ Scottish Inns **M**
(304) 267-2935. **$42-$70.** 1024 Winchester Ave (US 11 N). I-81, exit 12, 0.3 mi e on SR 45, just n. Ext corridors. **Pets:** $5 daily fee/pet. No service, supervision.
SAVE S✗ ✗ 🄵 ⇔

MORGANTOWN

◆◆◆ ▼▼▼ Ramada Inn and Conference Center **M**
(304) 296-3431. **$80-$185, 3 days notice.** US Rt 119, I-68 & I-79. I-68, exit 1, 0.3 mi n. Int corridors. **Pets:** Medium. Designated rooms, service with restrictions, supervision.
SAVE S✗ ✗ 🄵 🖵 🍽 ⇔

MOUNT NEBO

▼ Days Inn-Mt Nebo **M**
(304) 872-5151. **$52-$66.** Rt 19, HC 76, Box 700. Jct US 19 and 41, just s. Ext corridors. **Pets:** Accepted.
SAVE ✗ 🄵 🍽 ⇔

NITRO

▼▼ Best Western Motor Inn **M**
(304) 755-8341. **Call for rates.** 4115 1st Ave. I-64, exit 45, 0.5 mi e on SR 25. Ext corridors. **Pets:** Accepted.
ASK ✗ 🄵 🖵

PARKERSBURG

◆◆◆ ▼ Expressway Motor Inn **M**
(304) 485-1851. **$48-$56.** 6333 Emerson Ave. I-77, exit 179, 0.4 mi sw on SR 68. Ext corridors. **Pets:** $5 daily fee/pet, $5 one-time fee/pet. Designated rooms, service with restrictions, crate.
SAVE ✗ 🄵

▼▼▼ Holiday Inn Parkersburg **M**
(304) 485-6200. **Call for rates, 3 days notice.** One Holiday Dr. I-77, exit 176, just e. Int corridors. **Pets:** Accepted.
✗ 🄵 🖵 🍽 ⇔

▼ Knights Inn **M**
(304) 420-2420. **$45-$65.** 3604 1/2 7th St. I-77, exit 176, just w. Ext corridors. **Pets:** Medium, other species. Service with restrictions, supervision.
ASK S✗ ✗ 🄵

▼▼ Red Roof Inn **M**
(304) 485-1741. **$42-$59.** 3714 E 7th St. I-77, exit 176, just w on US 50. Ext corridors. **Pets:** Small, other species. Service with restrictions, supervision.
✗ 🄵

PHILIPPI

▼▼ Philippi Lodging **M**
(304) 457-5888. **$59-$79.** Rt 4, Box 155. 2.5 mi s on US 250. Int corridors. **Pets:** Other species. Service with restrictions.
ASK S✗ ✗ 🄜 🖉 🄵

PRINCETON

◆◆◆ ▼▼▼ Days Inn **M**
(304) 425-8100. **$45-$65, 3 days notice.** 347 Meadowfield Ln. I-77, exit 9, 0.3 mi w on US 460, just s on Ambrose Ln, then just e. Ext corridors. **Pets:** Accepted.
SAVE S✗ ✗ 🖉 🄵 🖵 ⇔

Ramada Limited M
(304) 425-8711. **$39-$65, 3 days notice.** 1115 Oakvale Rd. I-77, exit 9, just w, then just ne via service road. Ext corridors. **Pets:** Accepted.

Sleep Inn M
(304) 431-2800. **$51-$100.** 1015 Oakvale Rd. I-77, exit 9, just w on US 460, then just n via service road. Int corridors. **Pets:** Small, other species. Service with restrictions, supervision.

Town-N-Country Motel M
(304) 425-8156. **$40-$60, 14 days notice.** 805 Oakvale Rd. I-77, exit 9, 0.3 mi w on US 460. Ext corridors. **Pets:** Accepted.

RIPLEY

Best Western McCoys Inn & Conference Center MI
(304) 372-9122. **$80-$150.** 701 W Main St. I-77, exit 138, just e. Ext/int corridors. **Pets:** Service with restrictions, supervision.

Ripley Super 8 Motel M
(304) 372-8880. **Call for rates.** 102 Duke Dr. I-77, exit 138, just e on SR 33. Int corridors. **Pets:** Small. Service with restrictions, supervision.

SOUTH CHARLESTON

Ramada Plaza Hotel Charleston MI
(304) 744-4641. **$59-$93.** 400 2nd Ave. I-64, exit 56, just nw. Int corridors. **Pets:** Small, other species. $50 deposit/room, $10 daily fee/room. Service with restrictions.

Red Roof Inn-S Charleston M
(304) 744-1500. **$44-$59.** 4006 MacCorkle Ave SW. I-64, exit 54. Ext corridors. **Pets:** Accepted.

STAR CITY

Econo Lodge-Coliseum M
(304) 599-8181. **$39-$59, 3 days notice.** 3506 Monongahela Blvd. I-79, exit 155, 1.4 mi s on US 119/SR 7. Ext corridors. **Pets:** Supervision.

Holiday Inn MI
(304) 599-1680. **$74-$129.** 1400 Saratoga Ave. I-79, exit 155, 1.7 mi s on US 119/SR 7. Ext corridors. **Pets:** Other species. $10 one-time fee/room. Service with restrictions, supervision.

SUMMERSVILLE

Best Western Summersville Lake Motor Lodge M
(304) 872-6900. **$56-$70.** 1203 S Broad St. US 19 and Broad St; 0.6 mi s of jct SR 39. Ext corridors. **Pets:** Medium, other species. $5 daily fee/pet. Service with restrictions, supervision.

Comfort Inn M
(304) 872-6500. **$55-$130, 30 days notice.** 903 Industrial Dr N. US 19, 1.9 mi n of jct SR 39. Int corridors. **Pets:** Accepted.

Sleep Inn of Summersville M
(304) 872-4500. **$50-$90, 30 days notice.** 701 Professional Park Dr. US 19, 1.7 mi n of jct SR 39; at Northside Plaza. Int corridors. **Pets:** Accepted.

TRIADELPHIA

Holiday Inn Express Wheeling East M
(304) 547-1380. **$59-$99.** I-70, exit 11. Int corridors. **Pets:** Other species. $10 daily fee/pet. Service with restrictions, supervision.

WEIRTON

Holiday Inn MI
(304) 723-5522. **$89-$129, 30 days notice.** 350 Three Springs Dr. 4.5 mi e on US 22, exit Three Springs Dr. Int corridors. **Pets:** Medium. $50 one-time fee/room. Designated rooms, service with restrictions, supervision.

WESTON

Comfort Inn MI
(304) 269-7000. **$48-$89.** I-79 & Rt 33 E. I-79, exit 33, just e on US 33. Ext corridors. **Pets:** Medium, other species. $10 daily fee/room. Designated rooms, service with restrictions, supervision.

CITY INDEX

ALGOMA

(AAA) ▼▼▼ Algoma Beach Motel & Condos ☒
(920) 487-2828. **$45-$239, 3 days notice.** 1500 Lake St. Jct SR 54, 0.4 mi s on SR 42. Ext/int corridors. **Pets:** Medium, dogs only. $15 daily fee/pet. Designated rooms, service with restrictions, crate.
⟦SAVE⟧ ⟦S⟧ ⟦☒⟧ ⟦⟧ ⟦⟧

▼ Scenic Shore Inn ⓜ
(920) 487-3214. **$44-$59, 3 days notice.** 2221 Lake St. Jct SR 54, 0.8 mi s on SR 42. Ext corridors. **Pets:** Accepted.
⟦☒⟧ ⟦⟧ ⟦⟧

ANTIGO

▼▼ Antigo Super 8 Motel ⓜ ☙
(715) 623-4188. **$49-$99.** 535 Century Ave. On US 45 at jct SR 64 E. Int corridors. **Pets:** $15 daily fee/pet. Designated rooms, service with restrictions, supervision.
⟦ASK⟧ ⟦S⟧ ⟦☒⟧ ⟦⟧ ⟦⟧ ⟦⟧ ⟦⟧ ⟦⟧

APPLETON

(AAA) ▼▼▼ Baymont Inn Appleton ⓜ
(920) 734-6070. **$74-$84.** 3920 W College Ave. US 41, exit 137 (SR 125), just e. Ext/int corridors. **Pets:** Accepted.
⟦SAVE⟧ ⟦S⟧ ⟦☒⟧ ⟦⟧ ⟦⟧ ⟦⟧

(AAA) ▼▼▼ Best Western Midway Hotel ⓜ
(920) 731-4141. **$99-$159.** 3033 W College Ave. US 41, exit 137 (SR 125), 0.5 mi e. Int corridors. **Pets:** Accepted.
⟦SAVE⟧ ⟦S⟧ ⟦☒⟧ ⟦⟧ ⟦⟧ ⟦⟧ ⟦⟧ ⟦⟧

(AAA) ▼▼▼ Comfort Suites Comfort Dome ⓜ
(920) 730-3800. **$102-$135.** 3809 W Wisconsin Ave. US 41, exit 138 (Wisconsin Ave), just e. Int corridors. **Pets:** Other species. Service with restrictions, supervision.
⟦SAVE⟧ ⟦S⟧ ⟦☒⟧ ⟦⟧ ⟦⟧ ⟦⟧ ⟦⟧

▼▼▼ Country Inn & Suites By Carlson ⓜ
(920) 830-3240. **$69-$175.** 355 Fox River Dr. US 41, exit 137 (W SR 125), just nw. Int corridors. **Pets:** Medium. Designated rooms, service with restrictions, crate.
⟦ASK⟧ ⟦S⟧ ⟦☒⟧ ⟦⟧ ⟦⟧ ⟦⟧ ⟦⟧

(AAA) ▼▼ Exel Inn of Appleton ⓜ
(920) 733-5551. **$42-$62.** 210 Westhill Blvd. US 41, exit 137 (SR 125), just e. Int corridors. **Pets:** Accepted.
⟦SAVE⟧ ⟦S⟧ ⟦☒⟧ ⟦⟧ ⟦⟧

(AAA) ▼▼▼ Residence Inn by Marriott ☒ ☙
(920) 954-0570. **$94-$109.** 310 Metro Dr. US 41, exit 137 (W SR 125), just nw on Mall Dr. Int corridors. **Pets:** Other species. $10 daily fee/room, $25 one-time fee/room.
⟦SAVE⟧ ⟦S⟧ ⟦☒⟧ ⟦⟧ ⟦⟧ ⟦⟧ ⟦⟧ ⟦⟧

(AAA) ▼▼▼ Woodfield Suites ⓜ
(920) 734-7777. **$115-$185.** 3730 W College Ave. US 41, exit 137 (SR 125), just e. Int corridors. **Pets:** Medium. $50 deposit/room, $10 daily fee/room. Designated rooms, service with restrictions, supervision.
⟦SAVE⟧ ⟦☒⟧ ⟦⟧ ⟦⟧ ⟦⟧

ARCADIA

◆ RKD Motel M
(608) 323-3338. **$40-$60.** 915 E Main St. On SR 95, 0.6 mi
w of jct SR 93. Ext corridors. **Pets:** Accepted.
ASK S✕ ⊠ ❒ ▣

ASHLAND

◆◆ ◆◆◆◆ AmericInn of Ashland M
(715) 682-9950. **$71-$133.** 3009 Lakeshore Dr E. On US 2,
2.1 mi e of jct SR 13 S. Int corridors. **Pets:** Other species.
$50 deposit/room, $6 daily fee/room. Designated rooms,
service with restrictions, supervision.
SAVE S✕ ⊠ ❒ ❒ ▣ ⊃

◆ Ashland Motel M
(715) 682-5503. **$25-$60.** 2300 W Lake Shore Dr. 2 mi w
on US 2. Ext corridors. **Pets:** Small. $5 one-time fee/pet.
Designated rooms, service with restrictions, supervision.
ASK S✕ ⊠ ❒

◆◆ Super 8 Motel M
(715) 682-9377. **$50-$120.** 1610 W Lakeshore Dr. On US 2
at jct 16th Ave. Int corridors. **Pets:** $50 deposit/room, $10
daily fee/pet. Supervision.
ASK S✕ ⊠ ⊾M ⊘ ❒ ❒ ▣

BALDWIN

◆◆ Super 8 Motel M
(715) 684-2700. **$73-$83.** 2110 10th Ave. I-94, exit 19 (US
63), just se. Int corridors. **Pets:** Medium. No service, supervision.
ASK S✕ ⊠ ❒ ❒ ⊃

BEAVER DAM

◆◆ Super 8 Motel M
(920) 887-8880. **$55-$58, 7 days notice.** 711 Park Ave. US
151, exit 132 (SR 33), just w. Int corridors. **Pets:** Accepted.
ASK S✕ ⊠ ⊘

BELOIT

◆◆ Comfort Inn of Beloit M
(608) 362-2666. **$55-$70.** 2786 Milwaukee Rd. I-90, exit
185A, just w, at jct I-43 and SR 81. Int corridors.
Pets: Medium. $10 daily fee/pet. Service with restrictions,
supervision.
SAVE S✕ ⊠ ⊘ ❒ ❒ ⊃

◆◆ Super 8 Motel M
(608) 365-8680. **$56-$76.** 3002 Milwaukee Rd. I-90, exit
185A, just w, at jct I-43 and SR 81. Int corridors.
Pets: Dogs only. $10 one-time fee/room. Service with
restrictions, supervision.
ASK S✕ ⊠ ⊾M ❒

BLACK RIVER FALLS

◆◆◆ ◆◆◆◆ Best Western-Arrowhead Lodge &
Suites M ✿
(715) 284-9471. **$59-$99.** 600 Oasis Rd. I-94, exit 116, at
jct SR 54. Int corridors. **Pets:** Large, other species. Designated rooms, service with restrictions, supervision.
SAVE S✕ ⊠ ⊘ ⊾ ❒ ❒ ❒❒ ⊃ ⊠

◆◆ ◆◆ Days Inn M
(715) 284-4333. **$69-$89.** 919 Hwy 54 E. I-94, exit 116, just
w. Int corridors. **Pets:** Small. Designated rooms, service
with restrictions, supervision.
SAVE S✕ ⊠ ⊾ ❒ ❒ ⊃

BOSCOBEL

◆◆ ◆ Sand's Motel M
(608) 375-4167. **$48-$62.** Hwy 61 N. 0.5 mi nw on US 61.
Ext/int corridors. **Pets:** Accepted.
SAVE ⊠

BOULDER JUNCTION

◆◆◆ White Birch Village R
(715) 385-2182. **$610-$1230 (weekly) (no credit cards),
21 days notice.** 8764 Hwy K. On CR K, 8 mi se. Ext
corridors. **Pets:** Other species. Supervision.
⊠ ❒ ❒ ⊠ ⊘

CABLE

◆◆ ◆◆◆ Lakewoods Resort R
(715) 794-2561. **$72-$500, 30 days notice.** HC 73, Box
715. 8 mi e on CR M. Ext/int corridors. **Pets:** $50 one-time
fee/pet. Designated rooms, service with restrictions, supervision.
SAVE ⊠ ⊘ ⊾ ❒ ❒ ❒❒ ⊃ ⊠

CAMERON

◆ Viking Motel M
(715) 458-2111. **$55-$65.** 201 S 1st St. On US 8 and CR
SS. Ext corridors. **Pets:** Other species. Service with restrictions, supervision.
S✕ ⊠ ▣

CAMP DOUGLAS

◆ K & K Motel M
(608) 427-3100. **$60.** 219 Hwy 12 & 16. I-90/94, exit 55,
just s. Ext corridors. **Pets:** Medium. $5 daily fee/pet. Desig-
nated rooms, service with restrictions, supervision.
ASK S✕ ⊠ ❒ ▣

CHIPPEWA FALLS

◆◆ ◆◆ AmericInn Motel & Suites M
(715) 723-5711. **$75-$126.** 11 W South Ave. 2 mi s on SR
124, access via CR J. Int corridors. **Pets:** Medium, other
species. $25 deposit/room. Designated rooms, service with
restrictions, supervision.
ASK S✕ ⊠ ⊘ ⊾ ❒ ❒ ⊃

▼▼ Park Inn **MI**
(715) 723-2281. **$87.** 1009 W Park Ave. Jct SR 124 and
CR J. Ext/int corridors. **Pets:** Small. $10 daily fee/pet. Serv-
ice with restrictions, crate.

(ASK) (S&) (✕) (🛏) (💻) (¶) (🏊)

CRIVITZ

▼▼ Shaffer Park Motel **MI**
(715) 854-2186. **$55-$70, 14 days notice.** N 7217 Shaffer
Rd. 5 mi w on CR W. Ext corridors. **Pets:** Small, dogs only.
$7 daily fee/pet. Designated rooms, service with restrictions,
supervision.

(🛏) (💻) (¶) (✕) (🏊)

DE FOREST

▼▼▼ Holiday Inn Express **M**
(608) 846-8686. **$99-$139.** 7184 Morrisonville Rd. I-90/94,
exit 126 (CR V), just e. Int corridors. **Pets:** Medium, other
species. $20 deposit/room. Service with restrictions, crate.

(ASK) (S&) (✕) (🔌) (🖥) (🛏) (💻) (🏊)

DE PERE

AAA ▼▼▼▼ Sleep Inn & Suites Green
Bay/DePere **M**
(920) 338-8800. **$66-$175.** 1600 Lawrence Dr. US 41, exit
161. Int corridors. **Pets:** Medium, dogs only. Designated
rooms, service with restrictions.

(SAVE) (S&) (✕) (♿M) (🔌) (🖥) (🛏) (💻) (🏊)

DODGEVILLE

AAA ▼▼▼▼ Best Western Quiet House &
Suites **M**
(608) 935-7739. **$97-$125.** 1130 N Johns St. On US 18,
just e of jct SR 23. Int corridors. **Pets:** Accepted.

(SAVE) (S&) (✕) (🔌) (🖥) (🛏) (💻) (🏊)

▼▼ Super 8 Motel of Dodgeville **M**
(608) 935-3888. **$49-$85.** 1308 Johns St. Just n of US 18.
Int corridors. **Pets:** $50 deposit/room. Supervision.

(ASK) (S&) (✕) (🔌) (🛏)

DOOR COUNTY AREA

FISH CREEK

▼▼ Julie's Park Cafe & Motel **MI** ❁
(920) 868-2999. **$41-$94, 10 days notice.** 4020 Hwy 42.
0.3 mi n on SR 42. Ext corridors. **Pets:** Other species. $15
daily fee/pet. Supervision.

(✕) (🛏) (¶)

GILLS ROCK

▼▼▼▼ Harbor House Inn **BB**
(920) 854-5196. **$45-$105, 21 days notice.** 12666 SR 42.
Center; on SR 42. Ext/int corridors. **Pets:** Accepted.

(✕) (🛏) (🏊)

▼ Maple Grove Motel **M** ❁
(920) 854-2587. **$60-$75, 15 days notice.** 809 State Road
42. 0.3 mi e on SR 42, 1.5 mi w of car ferry. Ext corridors.
Pets: Medium. $50 deposit/pet, $5 daily fee/pet. Supervision.

(✕) (🛏) (💻) (🏊)

SISTER BAY

▼ Edge of Town Motel **M**
(920) 854-2012. **$49-$69, 14 days notice.** 11092 Hwy 42.
1.5 mi n on SR 42. Ext corridors. **Pets:** Medium, other
species. $15 daily fee/pet. Service with restrictions, supervi-
sion.

(✕) (🛏) (🏊)

❁ END AREA ❁

EAGLE RIVER

AAA ▼▼▼ Best Western Derby Inn **M**
(715) 479-1600. **$70-$170, 3 days notice.** 1800 Hwy 45 N.
1 mi n. Int corridors. **Pets:** Small. $50 deposit/room. Desig-
nated rooms, service with restrictions, supervision.

(SAVE) (S&) (✕) (🖥) (🛏) (💻) (🏊)

AAA ▼▼ Days Inn **M**
(715) 479-5151. **$76-$97.** 844 Hwy 45 N. 0.5 mi n on US
45. Int corridors. **Pets:** Accepted.

(SAVE) (S&) (✕) (🖥) (🛏) (💻) (🏊)

EAST TROY

AAA ▼▼▼▼ Country Inn & Suites **M** ❁
(262) 642-2100. **$80-$145.** 2921 O'Leary Ln. I-43, exit 36,
at jct SR 120. Int corridors. **Pets:** Designated rooms, crate.

(SAVE) (S&) (✕) (♿M) (🖥) (🛏) (💻) (🏊)

EAU CLAIRE

AAA ▼▼▼ Americinn Motel & Suites **M**
(715) 874-4900. **$60-$129, 7 days notice.** 6200 Texaco Dr.
I-94, exit 59, at jct US 12. Int corridors. **Pets:** $10 one-time
fee/room. Service with restrictions, supervision.

(SAVE) (S&) (✕) (🖥) (🛏) (💻) (🏊)

Comfort Inn ⓜ
(715) 833-9798. **$59-$104.** 3117 Craig Rd. I-94, exit 65, 1.3 mi n on SR 37, just s of jct US 12. Int corridors. **Pets:** Dogs only. $50 deposit/pet. Designated rooms, service with restrictions, crate.

⬛⬛⬛⬛⬛⬛⬛

Country Inn & Suites By Carlson ⓜ
(715) 832-7289. **$69-$114.** 3614 Gateway Dr. I-94, exit 70, 0.8 mi n on US 50, just ne on CR AA. Int corridors. **Pets:** Small, dogs only. $10 daily fee/pet. Designated rooms, service with restrictions, supervision.

⬛⬛⬛⬛⬛⬛⬛⬛

Days Inn-West ⓜ
(715) 874-5550. **$58-$105.** 6319 Truax Ln. I-94, exit 59, at jct US 12. Int corridors. **Pets:** $25 deposit/room. Designated rooms, service with restrictions, supervision.

⬛⬛⬛⬛⬛⬛⬛

Econo Lodge ⓜ
(715) 833-8818. **$40-$125.** 4608 Royal Dr. I-94, exit 68, just n on SR 93, just w on Golf Rd, then just s. Int corridors. **Pets:** Accepted.

⬛⬛⬛⬛⬛

Exel Inn of Eau Claire ⓜ
(715) 834-3193. **$41-$65.** 2305 Craig Rd. I-94, exit 65, 1.3 mi n on SR 37, just w of jct US 12. Int corridors. **Pets:** Accepted.

⬛⬛⬛⬛⬛

Holiday Inn Campus Area ⓜⓘ
(715) 835-2211. **$62-$109.** 2703 Craig Rd. I-94, exit 65, 1.3 mi n on SR 37, just w of jct US 12. Int corridors. **Pets:** Other species. $15 one-time fee/room. Designated rooms, service with restrictions, crate.

⬛⬛⬛⬛⬛⬛⬛

Maple Manor Motel ⓜⓘ
(715) 834-2618. **$40-$50, 7 days notice.** 2507 S Hastings Way. I-94, exit 70, 3 mi n on US 53, exit US 12 (Clairemont Ave), just se. Ext corridors. **Pets:** Accepted.

⬛⬛⬛⬛⬛⬛

Park Inn & Suites International ⓜ
(715) 838-9989. **$89-$139.** 3340 Mondovi Rd. I-94, exit 65, just n. Int corridors. **Pets:** Other species. Designated rooms.

⬛⬛⬛⬛⬛⬛⬛

Ramada Inn & Conference Center ⓜⓘ
(715) 834-3181. **$89-$129, 30 days notice.** 1202 W Clairemont Ave. I-94, exit 65, 1.3 mi n on SR 37, just w of jct US 12. Int corridors. **Pets:** Other species. $15 daily fee/room. Designated rooms, service with restrictions.

⬛⬛⬛⬛⬛⬛⬛⬛⬛

EDGERTON

Comfort Inn ⓜ
(608) 884-2118. **$63-$120.** 11102 Goede. I-90, exit 163, just e. Int corridors. **Pets:** Accepted.

⬛⬛⬛⬛⬛⬛⬛

FENNIMORE

Fenmore Hills Motel ⓜ
(608) 822-3281. **$62-$70.** 5814 Hwy 18 W. 2.4 mi w. Int corridors. **Pets:** Service with restrictions, supervision.

⬛⬛⬛⬛

FITCHBURG

Quality Inn & Suites ⓜ
(608) 274-7200. **$99-$124, 3 days notice.** 2969 Cahill Main. US 12/18, exit 260 (Fish Hatchery/CR D), then 1.5 mi s at jct CR PD. Int corridors. **Pets:** Small. $25 one-time fee/room. Designated rooms, no service, supervision.

⬛⬛⬛⬛⬛⬛⬛

FOND DU LAC

Baymont Inn & Suites ⓜ 🐾
(920) 921-4000. **$65-$160.** 77 Holiday Ln. Sw of jct US 41 and 151. Int corridors. **Pets:** Designated rooms, service with restrictions, supervision.

⬛⬛⬛⬛⬛⬛

Holiday Inn ⓜⓘ
(920) 923-1440. **$98-$179, 3 days notice.** 625 W Rolling Meadows Dr. On US 151, just sw of jct US 41. Int corridors. **Pets:** $100 deposit/pet. Designated rooms, service with restrictions, supervision.

⬛⬛⬛⬛⬛⬛⬛⬛

Microtel Inn & Suites ⓜ
(920) 929-4000. **$51.** 920 S Military Rd. At jct US 41 and 151. Int corridors. **Pets:** Other species. $10 one-time fee/room. Designated rooms, service with restrictions, supervision.

⬛⬛⬛⬛⬛

Super 8 Motel ⓜ
(920) 922-1088. **$55-$61, 30 days notice.** 391 N Pioneer Rd. US 41, exit SR 23, just n on east frontage road (CR VV). Int corridors. **Pets:** Dogs only. $10 one-time fee/room. Designated rooms, service with restrictions, supervision.

⬛⬛⬛⬛⬛

GREEN BAY

AmericInn ⓜ
(920) 434-9790. **$65-$109, 30 days notice.** 2032 Velp Ave. US 41, exit 170, 0.3 mi w. Int corridors. **Pets:** Other species. $10 daily fee/room. Designated rooms, service with restrictions, supervision.

⬛⬛⬛⬛⬛⬛⬛⬛

Baymont Inn ⓜ
(920) 494-7887. **$60-$84.** 2840 S Oneida St. US 41, exit 164 (Oneida St), just e. Int corridors. **Pets:** Accepted.

⬛⬛⬛⬛

Bay Motel ⓜⓘ
(920) 494-3441. **$46-$70.** 1301 S Military Ave. US 41, exit 167 (Lombardi Ave), 0.4 mi e to Marlee, 0.6 mi n. Ext corridors. **Pets:** Accepted.

⬛⬛⬛⬛

▼▼▼ Exel Inn of Green Bay M
(920) 499-3599. **$46-$66.** 2870 Ramada Way. US 41, exit 164 (Oneida St), just e. Int corridors. **Pets:** Small. Designated rooms, service with restrictions, supervision.
SAVE S X 🔒 💻

▼▼▼ Holiday Inn City Centre MI
(920) 437-5900. **$109.** 200 Main St. Downtown; opposite Port Plaza Mall. Int corridors. **Pets:** Accepted.
ASK S X 🔒M 🖉 🖊 💻 🍴 🏊

▼▼▼ Residence Inn by Marriott A
(920) 435-2222. **$125-$161.** 335 W St Joseph St. SR 172, exit Riverside Dr, 1.1 mi n on SR 57, then just e. Ext corridors. **Pets:** Other species. $5 daily fee/pet, $150 one-time fee/room. Service with restrictions, crate.
SAVE S X 🔒 💻 🏊

▼▼▼ Super 8 Motel M
(920) 494-2042. **$60-$72, 30 days notice.** 2868 S Oneida St. US 41, exit 164 (Oneida St), just e. Int corridors. **Pets:** Other species. $25 deposit/room. Supervision.
SAVE S X 🖉 🔒

HAYWARD

▼▼▼ AmericInn of Hayward M
(715) 634-2700. **$65-$119.** 15601 US Hwy 63. On US 63, just n of jct SR 77. Int corridors. **Pets:** Medium. $6 daily fee/room. Designated rooms, service with restrictions, crate.
SAVE S X 🖊 🔒 💻 🏊

▼▼▼ Best Western Northern Pine Inn M
(715) 634-4959. **$59-$79, 3 days notice.** 9966 N Hwy 27. 1.7 mi s on SR 27 S from jct US 63. Ext/int corridors. **Pets:** $5 daily fee/pet. Service with restrictions, supervision.
SAVE S X 🔒 💻 🏊

▼▼▼ Comfort Suites M
(715) 634-0700. **$70-$165, 30 days notice.** 15586 Country Road B. On CR B, 0.5 mi s of jct SR 27. Int corridors. **Pets:** Other species. $50 deposit/room. Designated rooms, service with restrictions, supervision.
SAVE S X 🔒M 🖊 🔒 💻 🏊 ✕

▼▼▼ Ross' Teal Lake Lodge and Teal Wing Golf Club R
(715) 462-3631. **$130-$350, 21 days notice.** 12425 N Ross Rd. On SR 77, 20 mi ne of jct US 63. Ext corridors. **Pets:** Other species. $5 daily fee/pet. Service with restrictions.
SAVE X 🔒 💻 🍴 🏊 ✕ 🎾 🖋

▼▼▼ Super 8 Motel M
(715) 634-2646. **$58-$96, 3 days notice.** 10444 N SR 27. On SR 27, 0.3 mi s of jct US 63. Ext/int corridors. **Pets:** Other species. Designated rooms, service with restrictions, supervision.
SAVE S X 🏊

HUDSON

▼▼▼ Super 8 Motel of Hudson M
(715) 386-8800. **$89-$104, 7 days notice.** 808 Dominion Dr. I-94, exit 2 (CR F), 1 mi w on south frontage road (Crestview Dr). Int corridors. **Pets:** Accepted.
ASK S X 🔒 💻 🏊

HURLEY

▼▼▼ Days Inn of Hurley M
(715) 561-3500. **$69-$86.** 850 10th Ave N. S of jct US 2 and 51. Int corridors. **Pets:** Small. Designated rooms, service with restrictions, supervision.
SAVE S X 🔒 💻 🏊

JANESVILLE

▼▼▼ Baymont Inns & Suites M
(608) 758-4545. **$70-$150.** 616 Midland Rd. I-90, exit 175B (SR 11), just ne. Int corridors. **Pets:** Medium. $10 one-time fee/room. Designated rooms, service with restrictions, supervision.
SAVE S X 🖊 🔒 💻 🏊

▼▼▼ Best Western Janesville MI
(608) 756-4511. **$64-$89.** 3900 Milton Ave. I-90, exit 171A (SR 26), just e. Int corridors. **Pets:** Large, other species. $10 daily fee/room. Designated rooms, service with restrictions, supervision.
SAVE S X 🔒 💻 🍴 🏊

▼▼▼ Microtel Inn M
(608) 752-3121. **$44-$54.** 3121 Wellington Pl. I-90, exit 171C (US 14), just se. Int corridors. **Pets:** Other species. $10 one-time fee/room. Designated rooms, service with restrictions.
SAVE S X 🔒M 🖉 🖊 🔒

▼▼ Select Inn M
(608) 754-0251. **$42-$63, 7 days notice.** 3520 Milton Ave. I-90, exit 171A (SR 26), just sw. Int corridors. **Pets:** Accepted.
SAVE S X 🖊 🔒 💻

JEFFERSON

▼▼▼ Rodeway Inn M
(920) 674-4404. **$62-$94.** 1456 S Ryan Ave. On SR 26, 1.2 mi s of jct US 18. Int corridors. **Pets:** Accepted.
SAVE S X 🔒M 🖉 🖊 🔒 💻 🏊

JOHNSON CREEK

▼▼▼ Days Inn-Johnson Creek M
(920) 699-8000. **$57-$70.** W4545 Linmar Ln. I-94, exit 267 (SR 26), just ne. Int corridors. **Pets:** Accepted.
SAVE S X 🖊 🔒 💻 🏊

KAUKAUNA

◆◆ ◆◆ Settle Inn Ⓜ 🐾
(920) 766-0088. **$60-$80.** 1201 Maloney Rd. US 41, exit 148, just e. Int corridors. **Pets:** Other species. $3 daily fee/room. Designated rooms, service with restrictions, crate.
ⒶⓈⓀ Ⓢⓓ ⓧ 🛑 💻 ⌒

KENOSHA

◆◆◆◆ Holiday Inn Express-Harborside Ⓜ
(262) 658-3281. **$73-$100.** 5125 6th Ave. Downtown; just ne of jct SR 32 and 158. Int corridors. **Pets:** Accepted.
ⒶⓈⓀ Ⓢⓓ ⓧ 🥨 🛑 💻

KEWAUNEE

◆◆ ◆◆ The Historic Karsten Inn Ⓗ
(920) 388-3800. **$49-$129, 3 days notice.** 122 Ellis St. Center. Int corridors. **Pets:** Small, other species. $25 one-time fee/pet. Designated rooms, service with restrictions, crate.
ⒶⓈⓀ Ⓢⓓ ⓧ 💻 🍴

LA CROSSE

◆◆◆ ◆◆ Days Inn Hotel & Conference Center Ⓜ
(608) 783-1000. **$55-$94.** 101 Sky Harbour Dr. I-90, exit 2, then just sw; on French Island. Int corridors. **Pets:** Medium. $10 daily fee/pet. Designated rooms, service with restrictions, supervision.
🆂🅰🆅🅴 Ⓢⓓ ⓧ 🛑 💻 🍴 ⌒

◆◆◆ ◆◆ Exel Inn of La Crosse Ⓜ
(608) 781-0400. **$47-$67.** 2150 Rose St. I-90, exit 3, 0.8 mi s on US 53. Int corridors. **Pets:** Small, other species. Designated rooms, service with restrictions, supervision.
🆂🅰🆅🅴 Ⓢⓓ ⓧ 🛑 💻

◆◆◆ ◆◆◆ The Radisson Hotel La Crosse Ⓗ 🐾
(608) 784-6680. **$139-$179.** 200 Harborview Plaza. Downtown; just w of US 53. Int corridors. **Pets:** Other species. Designated rooms, service with restrictions, supervision.
🆂🅰🆅🅴 ⓧ 🥨 🛑 💻 🍴 ⌒

◆◆ ◆◆ Super 8 of La Crosse Ⓜ
(608) 781-8880. **$76-$98.** 1625 Rose St. I-90, exit 3, 1.2 mi s on US 53. Int corridors. **Pets:** Accepted.
ⒶⓈⓀ Ⓢⓓ ⓧ 🛑 💻 ⌒

LAND O'LAKES

◆◆◆◆ Sunrise Lodge Ⓒ
(715) 547-3684. **$68-$94, 3 days notice.** 5894 W Shore Dr. 2 mi s on US 45, 2.8 mi e on CR E, then 1 mi n. Ext corridors. **Pets:** Other species. Supervision.
ⒶⓈⓀ 🛑 💻 🍴 ⓧ ☎

LUCK

◆◆ ◆◆ Luck Country Inn Ⓜ Ⓘ
(715) 472-2000. **$40-$150.** 10 Robertson St. At jct SR 35 and 48. Int corridors. **Pets:** Designated rooms, service with restrictions, crate.
ⒶⓈⓀ Ⓢⓓ ⓧ 🛑 💻 🍴 ⌒

MADISON

◆◆◆ ◆◆◆ AmericInn of Madison South/Monona Ⓜ 🐾
(608) 222-8601. **$75-$150.** 101 W Broadway. US 12/18, exit 265 (Monona Dr), just nw. Ext/int corridors. **Pets:** $5 daily fee/room. Designated rooms.
🆂🅰🆅🅴 Ⓢⓓ ⓧ 🥨 🛑 💻 ⌒

◆◆◆ ◆◆◆ Baymont Inn & Suites Ⓜ
(608) 831-7711. **$79-$99, 7 days notice.** 8102 Excelsior Dr. US 12 and 14, exit 253 (Old Sauk Rd), just nw. Int corridors. **Pets:** Accepted.
🆂🅰🆅🅴 Ⓢⓓ ⓧ 🥨 🛑 💻 ⌒

◆◆◆ ◆◆◆ Best Western East Towne Suites Ⓜ
(608) 244-2020. **$80-$95.** 4801 Annamark Dr. I-90/94, exit 135A, just w on US 151. Int corridors. **Pets:** Medium, other species. $20 deposit/room. Designated rooms, service with restrictions, supervision.
🆂🅰🆅🅴 Ⓢⓓ ⓧ 🥨 🛑 ⌒

◆◆◆ ◆◆◆ Best Western West Towne Suites Ⓜ
(608) 833-4200. **$59-$109.** 650 Grand Canyon Dr. US 12 and 14, exit 255 (Gammon Rd), just e on Odana Rd, then just sw. Int corridors. **Pets:** $25 deposit/room. Designated rooms, service with restrictions, supervision.
🆂🅰🆅🅴 Ⓢⓓ ⓧ 🥨 🛑 💻

◆◆◆ ◆◆◆ Comfort Suites Ⓜ 🐾
(608) 836-3033. **$117-$257.** 1253 John Q Hammons Dr. US 12 and 14, exit 252 (Greenway Blvd), just sw. Int corridors. **Pets:** Service with restrictions.
🆂🅰🆅🅴 Ⓢⓓ ⓧ 🥨 🛑 💻 ⌒

◆◆◆ ◆◆◆ Crowne Plaza Ⓗ
(608) 244-4703. **$109-$149, 11 days notice.** 4402 E Washington Ave. I-90/94, exit 135A, 0.4 mi w on US 151. Int corridors. **Pets:** Medium, other species. Designated rooms, service with restrictions.
🆂🅰🆅🅴 Ⓢⓓ ⓧ 🥨 🛑 💻 🍴 ⌒

◆◆◆ ◆◆◆ Days Inn-Madison Ⓜ
(608) 223-1800. **$75-$95.** 4402 E Broadway Service Rd. US 12 and 18, exit 266 (US 51), just ne. Int corridors. **Pets:** Other species. $50 deposit/room. Service with restrictions, supervision.
🆂🅰🆅🅴 Ⓢⓓ ⓧ 🥨 🛑 💻 ⌒

◆◆◆ ◆◆ Exel Inn of Madison Ⓜ
(608) 241-3861. **$46-$72.** 4202 E Towne Blvd. I-90/94, exit 135A, 0.5 mi w on US 151. Int corridors. **Pets:** Designated rooms, supervision.
🆂🅰🆅🅴 Ⓢⓓ ⓧ 🛑 💻

🎖 ▼▼▼▼ Hawthorn Suites Ltd Ⓜ️
(608) 284-1234. **$88-$129.** 2110 Rimrock Rd. US 12 and 18, exit 262 (Rimrock Rd), just nw. Int corridors. **Pets:** Medium. $125 one-time fee/room. Service with restrictions, supervision.

[SAVE] [S] [X] [&] [📶] [💻] [🍴] [🏊]

🎖 ▼▼▼ Holiday Inn Express-Madison Ⓜ️
(608) 255-7400. **$85-$109.** 722 John Nolen Dr. US 12 and 18, exit 263 (John Nolen Dr), just ne. Int corridors. **Pets:** Medium. Designated rooms, supervision.

[SAVE] [S] [X] [🔊] [📶] [💻] [🏊]

🎖 ▼▼▼ Red Roof Inn-Madison Ⓜ️
(608) 241-1787. **$44-$74.** 4830 Hayes Rd. I-90/94, exit 135A, just w on US 151. Ext corridors. **Pets:** Accepted.

[SAVE] [X] [🔊]

🎖 ▼▼▼▼ Residence Inn Ⓐ
(608) 244-5047. **$89-$109.** 4862 Hayes Rd. I-90/94, exit 135A, just w on US 151. Int corridors. **Pets:** Medium. $10 daily fee/room, $25 one-time fee/room. Designated rooms, service with restrictions, crate.

[SAVE] [S] [X] [🔊] [&] [📶] [💻] [🏊]

🎖 ▼▼▼▼ Residence Inn By Marriott-Madison West Ⓐ
(608) 833-8333. **$101-$124.** 501 D'Onofrio Dr. US 12 and 14, exit 254 (Mineral Point Rd), 0.4 mi e, then just s. Ext corridors. **Pets:** Accepted.

[SAVE] [S] [X] [🔊] [📶] [💻] [🏊]

🎖 ▼▼ Select Inn Ⓜ️ 🐾
(608) 249-1815. **$45-$59, 7 days notice.** 4845 Hayes Rd. I-90/94, exit 135A, just w on US 151. Int corridors. **Pets:** Other species. $25 deposit/room, $5 daily fee/pet. Service with restrictions, supervision.

[SAVE] [S] [X] [&] [📶] [💻]

▼▼▼▼ Staybridge Suites Ⓜ️
(608) 241-2300. **$99-$159.** 3301 City View Dr. US 151, exit 98A, just e, then 0.5 mi s on High Crossing Blvd. Int corridors. **Pets:** Medium, other species. $75 one-time fee/room. Designated rooms, service with restrictions.

[ASK] [S] [X] [🔊] [&] [📶] [💻] [🏊]

▼▼▼ Super 8 Motel Ⓜ️
(608) 258-8882. **$71-$96, 7 days notice.** 1602 W Beltline Hwy. US 12 and 18, exit 260B (CR D), just w on north frontage road. Int corridors. **Pets:** Other species. $10 daily fee/room. Designated rooms, service with restrictions, supervision.

[ASK] [S] [X] [🔊] [&] [📶] [🏊]

▼▼▼▼ Wingate Inn Ⓜ️
(608) 224-1500. **$69-$119.** 3510 Mill Pond Rd. I-90, exit 142B, just e on US 12/18, then w on south frontage road. Int corridors. **Pets:** Other species. $25 deposit/room. Service with restrictions, supervision.

[ASK] [S] [X] [&] [📶] [💻] [🏊]

🎖 ▼▼▼ Woodfield Suites Ⓜ️
(608) 245-0123. **$99-$119.** 5217 E Terrace Dr. US 151, exit 98B (American Pkwy), then just sw. Int corridors. **Pets:** Accepted.

[SAVE] [S] [X] [&] [📶] [🔊] [📶] [💻] [🏊]

MANITOWOC

▼▼ Comfort Inn Ⓜ️ 🐾
(920) 683-0220. **$52-$110.** 2200 S 44th St. I-43, exit 149, just e. Int corridors. **Pets:** Other species. Service with restrictions, supervision.

[SAVE] [S] [X] [📶] [💻]

▼▼▼ Holiday Inn Ⓜ️
(920) 682-6000. **$104.** 4601 Calumet Ave. I-43, exit 149, just e. Int corridors. **Pets:** Other species. $200 deposit/room. Service with restrictions, crate.

[ASK] [S] [X] [&] [📶] [💻] [🍴] [🏊]

🎖 ▼▼▼ Inn on Maritime Bay Ⓜ️
(920) 682-7000. **$89-$119.** 101 Maritime Dr. I-43, exit 152, 4.2 mi e on SR 42 N, then 1 mi s. Int corridors. **Pets:** Other species. $25 one-time fee/room. Designated rooms, service with restrictions, supervision.

[SAVE] [S] [X] [🔊] [📶] [💻] [🍴] [🏊]

MAUSTON

🎖 ▼▼▼▼ Country Inn By Carlson Ⓜ️
(608) 847-5959. **$70-$95.** 1001 SR 82. I-90/94, exit 69, just ne. Int corridors. **Pets:** Other species. $5 daily fee/pet. Service with restrictions.

[SAVE] [S] [X] [📶] [💻] [🏊]

▼▼ Super 8 Motel Ⓜ️
(608) 847-2300. **$76-$96.** 1001A Hwy 82 E. I-90/94, exit 69, just ne. Int corridors. **Pets:** Medium, other species. $5 daily fee/pet. Service with restrictions, supervision.

[ASK] [S] [X] [📶] [💻] [🏊]

MENOMONIE

🎖 ▼▼▼▼ Country Inn & Suites Ⓜ️
(715) 235-5664. **$75-$149, 7 days notice.** 320 Oak Ave. I-94, exit 41 (SR 25), just se. Int corridors. **Pets:** $25 one-time fee/room. Service with restrictions, supervision.

[SAVE] [S] [X] [&] [📶] [💻] [🏊]

▼▼ Menomonie Motel 6 Ⓜ️
(715) 235-6901. **$44-$58.** 2100 Stout St. I-94, exit 41 (SR 25), just se. Int corridors. **Pets:** Small. Service with restrictions, supervision.

[X] [&]

▼▼ Super 8 Motel Ⓜ️
(715) 235-8889. **$54-$89.** 1622 N Broadway. I-94, exit 41 (SR 25), just s. Int corridors. **Pets:** $15 deposit/room. Designated rooms, service with restrictions, supervision.

[ASK] [S] [X] [🔊] [📶] [🏊]

MERCER

▼▼ Pine Noel Resort [C]
(715) 476-2539. **Call for rates (no credit cards), 30 days notice.** 5311 N Goettsche Rd. 0.3 mi s on US 51, just e on Clinic St, just se on Martha Lake Rd, then 0.4 mi ne to the end of Goettsche Rd. Ext corridors. **Pets:** Accepted.
[icons]

MERRILL

▲▲▲ ▼▼▼ Pine Ridge Inn [M]
(715) 536-9526. **$49-$64.** 200 S Pine Ridge. I-39, exit 208, just w. Int corridors. **Pets:** Small. Service with restrictions, supervision.
[icons]

▲▲▲ ▼▼▼▼ Super 8 Motel [M] ✿
(715) 536-6880. **$61-$97, 3 days notice.** 3209 E Main St. I-39, exit 208, 0.5 mi w on SR 64. Int corridors. **Pets:** Other species. $25 deposit/room. Service with restrictions, crate.
[icons]

MIDDLETON

▲▲▲ ▼▼▼▼ Marriott Madison West [H]
(608) 831-2000. **$89-$139.** 1313 John Q Hammons Dr. US 12 and 14, exit 252 (Greenway Blvd), then just w. Int corridors. **Pets:** Other species. Service with restrictions, supervision.
[icons]

MILWAUKEE METROPOLITAN AREA

BROOKFIELD

▲▲▲ ▼▼▼▼ Baymont Inn & Suites Milwaukee-Brookfield [M]
(262) 782-9100. **$69-$94.** 20391 W Bluemound Rd. I-94, exit 297, just e on US 18. Int corridors. **Pets:** Accepted.
[icons]

▼▼▼▼ Homestead Studio Suites-Milwaukee/Brookfield [A]
(262) 782-9300. **$49-$89.** 325 N Brookfield Rd. I-94, exit 297, 1.1 mi e on US 18, just e. Int corridors. **Pets:** Accepted.
[icons]

DELAFIELD

▲▲▲ ▼▼▼▼ Baymont Inn & Suites Milwaukee-Delafield [M]
(262) 646-8500. **$79-$104.** 2801 Hillside Dr. I-94, exit 287, just s on SR 83, then just e. Int corridors. **Pets:** Medium. Designated rooms, service with restrictions, supervision.
[icons]

GERMANTOWN

▲▲▲ ▼▼▼▼ Holiday Inn Express Milwaukee NW-Germantown [M]
(262) 255-1100. **$69-$129.** W 177 N9675 Riversbend Ln. US 41 and 45, exit CR Q (County Line Rd), then just w. Int corridors. **Pets:** Accepted.
[icons]

▼▼▼ Super 8 Motel-Germantown/Milwaukee [M]
(262) 255-0880. **$59-$99.** N96 W17490 County Line Rd. US 41 and 45, exit CR Q (County Line Rd), then just w. Int corridors. **Pets:** Accepted.
[icons]

GLENDALE

▲▲▲ ▼▼▼ Exel Inn of Milwaukee Northeast [M]
(414) 961-7272. **$56-$80.** 5485 N Port Washington Rd. I-43, exit 78A (Silver Spring Dr). Int corridors. **Pets:** Accepted.
[icons]

▲▲▲ ▼▼▼▼ Residence Inn by Marriott [A] ✿
(414) 352-0070. **$89-$239.** 7275 N Port Washington Rd. I-43, exit 80 (Good Hope Rd), just e. Ext corridors. **Pets:** Medium, other species. $6 daily fee/room, $175 one-time fee/room. Service with restrictions, supervision.
[icons]

▲▲▲ ▼▼▼▼ Woodfield Suites [M]
(414) 962-6767. **$90-$200.** 5423 N Port Washington Rd. I-43, exit 78A (Silver Spring Dr). Int corridors. **Pets:** Medium, other species. $50 deposit/room, $10 daily fee/room. Service with restrictions, supervision.
[icons]

MEQUON

▲▲▲ ▼▼▼▼ Best Western Quiet House & Suites [M]
(262) 241-3677. **$105-$135.** 10330 N Port Washington Rd. I-43, exit 85, just w on SR 167, 1 mi s on CR W. Int corridors. **Pets:** Other species. $15 daily fee/pet. Designated rooms, service with restrictions, supervision.
[icons]

MILWAUKEE

▲▲▲ ▼▼▼ Baymont Inn & Suites-Milwaukee NW [M]
(414) 535-1300. **$79-$99.** 5442 N Lovers Lane Rd. US 45, exit 46 (Silver Spring Rd), just se. Int corridors. **Pets:** Accepted.
[icons]

Best Western Inn Towne M ❀
(414) 224-8400. **$82-$119.** 710 N Old World 3rd St. Corner of Wisconsin Ave and N Old World 3rd St. Int corridors. **Pets:** Medium. Service with restrictions.
[SAVE] [S🐾] [✕] [🛏] [🔓] [🖥]

Hotel Metro-Milwaukee H
(414) 272-1937. **$180-$250.** 411 E Mason St. Corner of Mason and Milwaukee sts. Int corridors. **Pets:** Accepted.
[ASK] [S🐾] [✕] [🛏M] [🐾] [🔓] [🖥] [🍴]

OAK CREEK

Baymont Inn & Suites Milwaukee-Airport M
(414) 762-2266. **$69-$89.** 7141 S 13th St. I-94, exit 320, just se on Rawson Ave (CR BB). Int corridors. **Pets:** Accepted.
[SAVE] [S🐾] [✕] [🛏] [🖥]

Comfort Suites M
(414) 570-1111. **$94.** 6362 S 13th St. I-94, exit 319, just e on College Ave (CR 22), then just s. Int corridors. **Pets:** Other species.
[SAVE] [S🐾] [✕] [🛏M] [🐾] [🔓] [🛏] [🖥] [🏊]

Exel Inn of Milwaukee South M
(414) 764-1776. **$44-$73.** 1201 W College Ave. I-94, exit 319, just e on College Ave (CR 22). Int corridors. **Pets:** Small. Designated rooms, service with restrictions, supervision.
[SAVE] [S🐾] [✕] [🛏] [🖥]

MainStay Suites Oak Creek M
(414) 571-8800. **$70-$189.** 1001 W College Ave. I-94, exit 319, just e on College Ave (CR 22). Int corridors. **Pets:** Other species. $50 deposit/pet, $15 one-time fee/pet. Service with restrictions, supervision.
[ASK] [S🐾] [✕] [🔓] [🛏] [🖥]

Red Roof Inn-Milwaukee M
(414) 764-3500. **$40-$69.** 6360 S 13th St. I-94, exit 319, just e on College Ave (CR 22). Ext corridors. **Pets:** Accepted.
[SAVE] [✕] [🐾] [🛏]

PORT WASHINGTON

Best Western Harborside M
(262) 284-9461. **$99-$169.** 135 E Grand Ave. Downtown; on SR 43, waterfront of Lake Michigan. Int corridors. **Pets:** Small. $25 one-time fee/room. Designated rooms, service with restrictions, supervision.
[SAVE] [S🐾] [✕] [🔓] [🛏] [🖥] [🍴] [🏊]

WAUKESHA

Best Western Waukesha Grand M
(262) 524-9300. **$75-$95.** 2840 N Grandview Blvd. I-94, exit 293, just s on CR T. Int corridors. **Pets:** Small. Designated rooms, service with restrictions, supervision.
[SAVE] [S🐾] [✕] [🛏M] [🔓] [🛏] [🖥] [🏊]

Select Inn M
(262) 786-6015. **$48-$70, 7 days notice.** 2510 Plaza Ct. I-94, exit 297, just w on CR JJ (Bluemound Rd). Int corridors. **Pets:** Other species. $25 deposit/room, $5 daily fee/room. Designated rooms, service with restrictions, supervision.
[SAVE] [S🐾] [✕] [🔓] [🛏]

WAUWATOSA

Exel Inn of Milwaukee West M
(414) 257-0140. **$53-$76.** 115 N Mayfair Rd. I-94, exit 304B, just n on SR 100. Int corridors. **Pets:** Accepted.
[SAVE] [S🐾] [✕] [🛏] [🖥]

❀   **END METROPOLITAN AREA**   ❀

MINERAL POINT

Comfort Inn M
(608) 987-4747. **$50-$135.** 1345 Business Park Rd. On US 151, 0.6 mi n of jct SR 23 and 39. Int corridors. **Pets:** Medium. $25 deposit/room. Designated rooms, service with restrictions, crate.
[SAVE] [S🐾] [✕] [🔓] [🛏] [🖥] [🏊]

MINOCQUA

AmericInn of Minocqua M
(715) 356-3730. **$66-$161.** 700 Hwy 51. Downtown; on US 51. Int corridors. **Pets:** $50 deposit/room, $6 daily fee/room, $20 one-time fee/room. Designated rooms, service with restrictions, supervision.
[SAVE] [S🐾] [✕] [🔓] [🛏] [🖥] [🏊]

Comfort Inn M ❀
(715) 358-2588. **$50-$99.** 8729 Hwy 51 N. On US 51 at jct SR 70 w. Int corridors. **Pets:** $10 daily fee/room. Designated rooms, service with restrictions, supervision.
[SAVE] [S🐾] [✕] [🛏] [🖥] [🏊]

Lakeview Motor Lodge M
(715) 356-5208. **$41-$116.** 311 E Park Ave. North end of US 51 bridge. Ext/int corridors. **Pets:** $8 daily fee/pet. Service with restrictions, supervision.
[ASK] [S🐾] [✕] [🛏] [🖥]

Super 8 Motel M
(715) 356-9541. **$61-$77.** 8730 Hwy 51 N. On US 51 at jct SR 70 W. Ext/int corridors. **Pets:** Accepted.
[SAVE] [S🐾] [✕] [🛏] [🖥]

NEW LISBON

▲▲▲ ▼▼▼ Edge O' the Wood Motel 🏍
(608) 562-3705. **$61.** W 7396 Frontage Rd. I-90/94, exit 61 (SR 80), just e. Ext corridors. **Pets:** Designated rooms, service with restrictions, supervision.
[SAVE] [S🐾] [✕] [🔔] [💻] [🏊]

▲▲▲ ▼▼▼ Travelodge of New Lisbon 🏍
(608) 562-5141. **$53-$100, 3 days notice.** 1700 E Bridge St. I-90/94, exit 61 (SR 80), just ne. Int corridors. **Pets:** $50 deposit/room. Designated rooms, service with restrictions, supervision.
[SAVE] [✕] [🔔] [💻] [🏊]

NEW RICHMOND

▼▼▼ Americinn Motel 🏍
(715) 246-3993. **$65-$127.** 1020 S Knowles Ave. Just s on SR 65. Int corridors. **Pets:** Service with restrictions, supervision.
[ASK] [S🐾] [✕] [🔔] [💻] [🏊]

▼▼▼ Super 8 Motel 🏍
(715) 246-7829. **$59-$69.** 1561 Dorset Ln. Just s on SR 65. Int corridors. **Pets:** Large. $15 daily fee/room. Service with restrictions.
[ASK] [S🐾] [✕] [🔔]

ONALASKA

▲▲▲ ▼▼▼▼ Baymont Inn & Suites 🏍
(608) 783-7191. **$74-$159.** 3300 N Kinney Coulee Rd N. I-90, exit 5 (SR 16), just ne. Int corridors. **Pets:** Other species. $5 daily fee/pet. Designated rooms, service with restrictions, supervision.
[SAVE] [S🐾] [✕] [🔔] [💻] [🏊]

▼▼▼ Comfort Inn 🏍 🐾
(608) 781-7500. **$69-$99.** 1223 Crossing Meadows Dr. I-90, exit 4, just e on SR 157, then e on CR SS. Int corridors. **Pets:** Other species. Designated rooms, service with restrictions, supervision.
[SAVE] [S🐾] [✕] [🔔] [💻] [🏊]

▼▼▼ Microtel Inn 🏍
(608) 783-0833. **$43-$64.** 3240 N Kinney Coulee Rd. I-90, exit 5 (SR 16), just ne. Int corridors. **Pets:** Medium. $5 daily fee/room. Designated rooms, service with restrictions, supervision.
[ASK] [S🐾] [✕] [🔔]

OSCEOLA

▲▲▲ ▼▼▼ River Valley Inn 🏍
(715) 294-4060. **$66-$120.** 1030 Casade St. Just n on SR 35. Int corridors. **Pets:** Accepted.
[SAVE] [S🐾] [✕] [🔔] [💻] [🏊]

OSHKOSH

▲▲▲ ▼▼▼ Baymont Inn-Oshkosh 🏍
(920) 233-4190. **$64-$74.** 1950 Omro Rd. US 41, exit 119, at jct SR 21. Int corridors. **Pets:** Accepted.
[SAVE] [S🐾] [✕] [💻]

▲▲▲ ▼▼▼▼ Holiday Inn Express Hotel & Suites 🏍
(920) 303-1300. **$89-$189.** 2251 Westowne Ave. US 41, exit 119, 0.4 mi sw from jct SR 21. Int corridors. **Pets:** Accepted.
[SAVE] [S🐾] [✕] [🔔] [🔔] [💻] [🏊]

▼▼▼▼ Park Plaza Hotel & Convention Center 🅷
(920) 231-5000. **$94-$122.** 1 N Main St. Downtown; on shore of Fox River. Int corridors. **Pets:** Accepted.
[ASK] [S🐾] [✕] [🅿] [🔔] [💻] [🍴] [🏊]

PARK FALLS

▲▲▲ ▼▼▼ Super 8 Motel Park Falls 🏍
(715) 762-3383. **$56-$75, 3 days notice.** 1212 Hwy 13 S. Just s on SR 13. Int corridors. **Pets:** Dogs only. Service with restrictions, supervision.
[SAVE] [S🐾] [✕]

PEMBINE

▼▼▼ Grand Motel 🏍
(715) 324-5417. **$44-$54.** W 18379 Hwy 141. At jct US 141 and 8 W. Ext corridors. **Pets:** Service with restrictions, supervision.
[✕] [🔔] [💻]

PHILLIPS

▼▼▼ Super 8 Motel 🏍
(715) 339-2898. **$48-$68.** 726 S Lake Ave. 0.6 mi s on SR 13. Int corridors. **Pets:** Accepted.
[ASK] [S🐾] [✕]

PLATTEVILLE

▼▼▼ Mound View Inn 🏍
(608) 348-9518. **$50-$69, 3 days notice.** 1755 E Hwy 151. On US 151, 2 mi n of jct SR 80/81 N. Int corridors. **Pets:** $20 deposit/room. Service with restrictions, supervision.
[✕] [🅿] [🔔]

▲▲▲ ▼▼▼ Super 8 Motel 🏍 🐾
(608) 348-8800. **$58-$90.** 100 Hwy 80/81 S. At jct US 151 and SR 80. Int corridors. **Pets:** Other species. $10 daily fee/pet. Service with restrictions, supervision.
[SAVE] [S🐾] [✕] [🔔] [💻]

PLEASANT PRAIRIE

▲▲▲ ▼▼▼ Baymont Inn Kenosha-Pleasant Prairie 🏍
(262) 857-7911. **$69-$79.** 7540 118th Ave. I-94, exit 344 (SR 50), just e. Int corridors. **Pets:** Accepted.
[SAVE] [S🐾] [✕] [🅿] [💻]

▼▼▼▼ Hawthorn Suites LTD Hotel 🏍
(262) 942-6000. **$79-$149.** 7887 94th Ave. I-94, exit 344, 1.5 mi e on SR 50, 0.3 mi s. Int corridors. **Pets:** Other species. $50 one-time fee/room. Service with restrictions.
[ASK] [S🐾] [✕] [🔔] [🅿] [🔔] [💻] [🏊]

PRAIRIE DU CHIEN

Best Western Quiet House & Suites M
(608) 326-4777. **$97-$164.** 37268 US Hwy 18. On US 18, 1.9 mi e of jct SR 27 N. Ext/int corridors. **Pets:** Accepted.

Bridgeport Inn M
(608) 326-6082. **$87-$126, 10 days notice.** Hwy 18, 35 & 60 S. On US 18, 2.2 mi e of jct SR 27 N. Int corridors. **Pets:** Medium. $15 daily fee/pet. Service with restrictions, supervision.

Brisbois Motor Inn M
(608) 326-8404. **$54-$89.** 533 N Marquette Rd. On SR 35 N, 0.5 mi n of jct US 18/SR 35 S and 27 N. Ext/int corridors. **Pets:** Accepted.

Delta Motel M
(608) 326-4951. **$39-$69.** 1733 1/2 S Marquette Rd. On US 18, 1.6 mi e of jct SR 27 N. Ext corridors. **Pets:** Accepted.

Prairie Motel M
(608) 326-6461. **$35-$65.** 1616 S Marquette Rd. On US 18, 1.5 mi e of jct SR 27 N. Ext corridors. **Pets:** $10 one-time fee/room. Service with restrictions, supervision.

Super 8 Motel M
(608) 326-8777. **$63-$86.** 1930 S Marquette Rd. On US 18, 1.9 mi e of jct SR 27 N. Ext/int corridors. **Pets:** $15 one-time fee/room. Service with restrictions, supervision.

RACINE

Knights Inn M
(262) 886-6667. **$49-$69.** 1149 Oakes Rd. I-94, exit 333, 4 mi e on SR 20. Ext corridors. **Pets:** Service with restrictions, supervision.

Microtel Inn & Suites M
(262) 554-8855. **$62-$80, 7 days notice.** 5419 Durand Ave. On SR 11, 0.5 mi e of jct SR 31. Int corridors. **Pets:** Other species. $10 one-time fee/room. Designated rooms, service with restrictions.

Racine Marriott Hotel H
(262) 886-6100. **$150.** 7111 Washington Ave. I-94, exit 333, 4 mi e on SR 20. Int corridors. **Pets:** Accepted.

Super 8-Racine M
(262) 884-0486. **$49-$89.** 7141 Kinzie Ave. I-94, exit 333, 4 mi e on SR 20. Int corridors. **Pets:** Accepted.

REEDSBURG

Copper Springs Motel M ✿
(608) 524-4312. **$44-$68, 3 days notice.** E7278 Hwy 23 & 33. 2 mi e on SR 23 and 33. Ext corridors. **Pets:** Designated rooms, service with restrictions, supervision.

RHINELANDER

AmericInn M
(715) 369-9600. **$83-$92.** 648 W Kemp St. On Business Rt US 8, 0.3 mi e of jct SR 47. Int corridors. **Pets:** Other species. Designated rooms, service with restrictions, supervision.

Claridge Motor Inn, Best Western M
(715) 362-7100. **$70-$130.** 70 N Stevens St. Downtown; on SR 17. Int corridors. **Pets:** Medium, other species. $25 deposit/room, $10 daily fee/pet. Designated rooms, service with restrictions, supervision.

Comfort Inn M
(715) 369-1100. **$65-$110.** 1490 Lincoln St. On Business Rt US 8, 2.6 mi e of jct SR 47. Int corridors. **Pets:** $25 deposit/pet, $5 daily fee/pet. Designated rooms, service with restrictions, supervision.

Holiday Acres Resort X
(715) 369-1500. **$69-$269, 15 days notice.** 4060 S Shore Dr. 4.5 mi e on US Business Rt 8, 2.3 mi n on W Lake George Rd. Ext/int corridors. **Pets:** Accepted.

RICE LAKE

Currier's Lakeview Resort Motel M ✿
(715) 234-7474. **$49-$89, 7 days notice.** 2010 E Sawyer St. 1.5 mi n on CR SS from jct CR O, 1 mi e and n on CR C. Ext/int corridors. **Pets:** Dogs only. Service with restrictions, supervision.

Microtel Inn & Suites M
(715) 736-2010. **$50-$65.** 2771 Decker Dr. US 53, exit 140 (CR O), just ne. Int corridors. **Pets:** $10 daily fee/room. Service with restrictions, crate.

Super 8 Motel M
(715) 234-6956. **$55-$60.** 2401 S Main St. On CR SS, just n of jct CR O. Int corridors. **Pets:** Other species. $5 daily fee/room. Service with restrictions, supervision.

RICHLAND CENTER

Super 8 Motel-Richland Center M
(608) 647-8988. **$65-$80.** 100 Foundry Dr. 0.9 mi e on US 14. Int corridors. **Pets:** Accepted.

RIVER FALLS

▼▼ **Super 8 Motel** Ⓜ
(715) 425-8388. **$80-$92.** 1207 St Croix St. On SR 65, 0.5 mi w jct SR 35. Int corridors. **Pets:** Other species. Supervision.
Ⓐ Ⓢ ☒ ⬛ ⬛ ⥬

SHAWANO

▼▼ **Shawano Super 8 Motel** Ⓜ
(715) 526-6688. **$51-$90.** 211 Waukechon St. 1.2 mi e on SR Business 29. Int corridors. **Pets:** Other species. $25 deposit/room. Service with restrictions, supervision.
Ⓐ Ⓢ ☒ ⬛ ⬛ ⬛

SHEBOYGAN

◆◆ ▼▼▼ **AmericInn of Sheboygan** Ⓜ
(920) 208-8130. **$60-$160.** 3664 S Taylor Dr. I-43, exit 123, just e. Int corridors. **Pets:** $50 deposit/pet, $7 daily fee/pet. Designated rooms, service with restrictions, supervision.
Ⓢ ☒ ⬛ ⬛ ⬛ ⥬

◆◆ ▼▼ **Baymont Inn-Sheboygan** Ⓜ
(920) 457-2321. **$69-$79.** 2932 Kohler Memorial Dr. I-43, exit 126, 1 mi e on SR 23. Int corridors. **Pets:** Medium, other species. Designated rooms, service with restrictions, supervision.
Ⓢ Ⓢ ☒ ⬛ ⬛ ⬛

▼▼ **Comfort Inn** Ⓜ
(920) 457-7724. **$54-$139.** 4332 N 40th St. I-43, exit 128, 0.3 mi e on Business Rt 42. Int corridors. **Pets:** Other species. $25 one-time fee/pet. Designated rooms, service with restrictions, supervision.
Ⓢ Ⓢ ☒ ⬛ ⬛ ⬛ ⥬

▼▼ **Super 8 Motel** Ⓜ
(920) 458-8080. **$60-$80.** 3402 Wilgus Rd. I-43, exit 126, just ne. Int corridors. **Pets:** Dogs only. $10 one-time fee/room. Service with restrictions, supervision.
Ⓐ Ⓢ ☒ ⬛

SIREN

◆◆ ▼ **Pine Wood Motel** Ⓜ
(715) 349-5225. **$39-$44.** 23862 Hwy 35 S. On SR 35, 0.3 mi s of jct SR 70 W and CR B E. Ext corridors. **Pets:** Accepted.
Ⓢ ☒ ⬛

SPARTA

◆◆ ▼▼▼ **Country Inn By Carlson** Ⓜ
(608) 269-3110. **$83-$138.** 737 Avon Rd. I-90, exit 25 (SR 27), just n. Int corridors. **Pets:** Small, other species. $5 deposit/pet. Service with restrictions, crate.
Ⓢ Ⓢ ☒ Ⓜ ⬛ ⬛ ⥬

▼▼ **Super 8 Sparta** Ⓜ
(608) 269-8489. **$70-$110, 5 days notice.** 716 Avon Rd. I-90, exit 25 (SR 27), just n. Int corridors. **Pets:** Accepted.
Ⓐ Ⓢ ☒ ⬛ ⬛ ⥬

SPOONER

◆◆◆ ▼▼▼ **American Heritage Inn** Ⓜ
(715) 635-9770. **$79-$99.** 101 Maple St. On SR 70 at jct US 63, 1 mi w of US 53. Int corridors. **Pets:** Accepted.
Ⓢ Ⓢ ☒ ⬛ ⬛ ⥬

▼▼ ▼ **Country House Motel & RV Park** Ⓜ
(715) 635-8721. **$59-$109.** 717 S River St. On US 63, 0.5 mi s of jct SR 70. Ext/int corridors. **Pets:** Other species. $4 daily fee/pet. Designated rooms, service with restrictions, supervision.
☒ Ⓜ Ⓢ ⬛ ⬛ ⥬

ST. CROIX FALLS

◆◆◆ ▼▼▼▼ **Holiday Inn Express Hotel & Suites** Ⓜ
(715) 483-5775. **$65-$175, 3 days notice.** 2190 E US Hwy 8. On US 8, 1.3 mi e of jct SR 35 S. Int corridors. **Pets:** Medium. $15 daily fee/pet. Service with restrictions, supervision.
Ⓢ Ⓢ ☒ Ⓢ ⬛ ⬛ Ⓣ ⥬

ST. GERMAIN

▼ **North Woods Rest Motel** Ⓜ
(715) 479-8770. **$49, 3 days notice.** 8083 Hwy 70 E. 0.8 mi e on SR 70. Ext corridors. **Pets:** Accepted.
⬛ ⬛

STEVENS POINT

◆◆ ▼▼ **Baymont Inn & Suites** Ⓜ
(715) 344-1900. **$64-$74.** 4917 Main St. I-39, exit 158B (US 10), just w. Int corridors. **Pets:** Medium. $50 deposit/room. Designated rooms, service with restrictions, supervision.
Ⓢ Ⓢ ☒ Ⓜ ⬛ ⬛ ⥬

◆◆◆ ▼ **Point Motel** Ⓜ
(715) 344-8312. **$42-$46.** 209 Division St. 0.6 mi n on US 51 business route. Ext corridors. **Pets:** Medium. $5 one-time fee/pet. Designated rooms, crate.
Ⓢ Ⓢ ☒ ⬛ ⬛

STURTEVANT

◆◆ ▼▼▼▼ **Holiday Inn Express-Racine** Ⓜ
(262) 884-0200. **$74-$109.** 13339 Hospitality Ct. I-94, exit 333 (SR 20), just se. Int corridors. **Pets:** Small, other species. Designated rooms, service with restrictions, supervision.
Ⓢ Ⓢ ☒ Ⓜ Ⓢ Ⓢ ⬛ ⬛ ⥬

SUN PRAIRIE

◆◆ ▼▼ **McGovern's Motel & Suites** Ⓜ
(608) 837-7321. **$55-$98.** 820 W Main St. US 151, exit 101, 1.2 mi ne on US 151 business route. Ext corridors. **Pets:** Dogs only. $5 one-time fee/pet. Designated rooms, service with restrictions, supervision.
Ⓢ Ⓢ ☒ ⬛ ⬛ Ⓣ

SUPERIOR

(AAA) ▼▼▼ Barkers Island Inn MI
(715) 392-7152. **$60-$190.** 300 Marina Dr. Just ne of US 2/53 on Barkers Island. Int corridors. **Pets:** Medium. $50 deposit/room, $10 daily fee/room. Service with restrictions, supervision.
[SAVE] [S♦] [✕] [🔥] [▭] [🍴] [🏊]

▼▼▼▼ Best Western Bay Walk Inn M
(715) 392-7600. **$55-$99.** 1405 Susquehanna Ave. Just e of US 2 on Belknap. Int corridors. **Pets:** Small. Designated rooms, service with restrictions, supervision.
[SAVE] [S♦] [✕] [🔥] [🏊]

(AAA) ▼▼▼ Best Western Bridgeview Motor Inn M
(715) 392-8174. **$49-$125.** 415 Hammond Ave. 0.8 mi n at south end of Blatnik Bridge. Int corridors. **Pets:** Accepted.
[SAVE] [S♦] [✕] [🔥] [▭] [🏊]

▼ Stockade Motel M
(715) 398-3585. **$34-$75.** 1610 E 2nd St. On US 2/53, 2.8 mi se. Ext corridors. **Pets:** Medium, dogs only. Service with restrictions, supervision.
[✕] [▭]

(AAA) ▼▼▼ Superior Inn M
(715) 394-7706. **$49-$120.** 525 Hammond Ave. 0.8 mi n at south end of Blatnik Bridge. Int corridors. **Pets:** Accepted.
[SAVE] [S♦] [✕] [🔥] [🏊]

THORP

▼▼▼▼ AmericInn Lodge & Suites M
(715) 669-5959. **$65-$150.** 203 1/2 W Hill St. US 29, exit 108 (SR 73), just nw. Int corridors. **Pets:** Medium. $5 one-time fee/room. Service with restrictions, supervision.
[ASK] [S♦] [✕] [✍] [🔥] [▭] [🏊]

TOMAH

▼▼ Cranberry Suites M
(608) 374-2801. **$55-$175.** 319 Wittig Rd. I-94, exit 143 (SR 21), just w. Int corridors. **Pets:** Small. $5 daily fee/pet. Service with restrictions, supervision.
[ASK] [S♦] [✕] [🔥] [▭]

▼▼ Econo Lodge M ✿
(608) 372-9100. **$47-$155.** 2005 N Superior Ave. I-94, exit 143 (SR 21), just w. Ext/int corridors. **Pets:** Large, other species. $5 daily fee/pet. Service with restrictions, supervision.
[SAVE] [S♦] [✕] [🎾] [🔥] [▭] [🏊]

▼▼▼ Holiday Inn MI
(608) 372-3211. **$72.** 1017 E McCoy Blvd. I-94, exit 143 (SR 21), just e. Int corridors. **Pets:** Designated rooms, service with restrictions, supervision.
[✕] [🔥] [▭] [🍴] [🏊]

(AAA) ▼▼▼ Lark Inn M ✿
(608) 372-5981. **$52-$85.** 229 N Superior Ave. I-94, exit 143, 1.5 mi s on US 12; I-90, exit 41, 2 mi n on US 12. Ext/int corridors. **Pets:** Small. $6 daily fee/pet. Service with restrictions, supervision.
[SAVE] [S♦] [✕] [🔥] [▭]

▼▼▼ Super 8 Motel M
(608) 372-3901. **$45-$90.** 1008 E McCoy Blvd. I-94, exit 143 (SR 21), just e. Int corridors. **Pets:** Medium, other species. $10 one-time fee/pet. Designated rooms, service with restrictions, supervision.
[ASK] [S♦] [✕] [✍] [🔥] [▭]

▼▼▼ Tomah Comfort Inn M
(608) 372-6600. **$59-$104.** 305 Wittig Rd. I-94, exit 143 (SR 21), just w. Int corridors. **Pets:** Other species. Designated rooms, supervision.
[SAVE] [S♦] [✕] [🎾] [🔥] [▭] [🏊]

TOMAHAWK

▼▼ Super 8 Motel-Tomahawk M
(715) 453-5210. **Call for rates.** 108 W Mohawk Dr. On US 51 business route, 0.6 mi n of downtown. Int corridors. **Pets:** Other species. $25 deposit/room. Service with restrictions, supervision.
[ASK] [✕] [✍] [🔥] [🏊]

VERONA

▼▼ Rodeway Inn M
(608) 848-7829. **$69-$119.** 131 Horizon Dr. US 18 and 151, exit 94 southbound; exit 89 northbound, just n of US Business Rt 18 and 151. Int corridors. **Pets:** Accepted.
[SAVE] [S♦] [✕] [🔥] [▭] [🏊]

VIROQUA

▼ Doucette's Hickory Hill Motel M
(608) 637-3104. **$80.** US 14 S 3955. 1.8 mi se on SR 14, 27 and 82. Ext corridors. **Pets:** Accepted.
[ASK] [S♦] [✕] [🔥] [🏊]

WATERTOWN

▼▼▼▼ Holiday Inn Express M
(920) 262-1910. **$79-$102.** 101 Aviation Way. On SR 26, 1.5 mi s of jct SR 19. Int corridors. **Pets:** Accepted.
[ASK] [S♦] [✕] [✍] [🔥] [▭] [🏊]

▼▼ Super 8 Motel M
(920) 261-1188. **$65-$80.** 1730 S Church St. On SR 26, 1.5 mi s of jct SR 19. Int corridors. **Pets:** Other species. $50 deposit/room. Service with restrictions, supervision.
[ASK] [S♦] [✕] [🔥] [▭] [🏊]

WAUPACA

(AAA) ▼▼▼▼ Baymont Inn & Suites M
(715) 258-9212. **$105-$129.** 110 Grand Seasons Dr. At jct US 10 and SR 54. Int corridors. **Pets:** Medium, other species. $50 deposit/room. Service with restrictions, supervision.
[SAVE] [S♦] [✕] [🎾] [✍] [🔥] [▭] [🏊]

WAUPUN

▼▼ Inn Town Motel **M**
(920) 324-4211. **$43-$53.** 27 S State St. US 151, exit 146 (SR 49), 1.3 mi w. Ext corridors. **Pets:** Medium. $10 one-time fee/pet. Designated rooms, service with restrictions, supervision.

(ASK) ⊠ 🖪 💻

WAUSAU

⏣⏣⏣ ▼▼▼ Baymont Inn-Wausau **M**
(715) 842-0421. **$64-$74.** 1910 Stewart Ave. I-39, exit 192, just e. Int corridors. **Pets:** Large, other species. $50 deposit/room. Designated rooms, service with restrictions, supervision.

(SAVE) (S🔒) ⊠ 🖉 🖪 💻 ⇌

⏣⏣⏣ ▼▼▼ Exel Inn of Wausau **M**
(715) 842-0641. **$45-$57.** 116 S 17th Ave. I-39, exit 192, just e. Int corridors. **Pets:** Small. Designated rooms, service with restrictions, supervision.

(SAVE) (S🔒) ⊠ 🖪 💻

▼▼▼ Ramada Conference Center **MI**
(715) 845-4341. **$69.** 201 N 17th Ave. I-39, exit 193, just e. Int corridors. **Pets:** Accepted.

(ASK) (S🔒) ⊠ 🖉 🖪 💻 🍴 ⇌

▼▼ Rib Mountain Inn **M**
(715) 848-2802. **$69, 3 days notice.** 2900 Rib Mountain Way. I-39, exit 190 (CR NN), 1 mi w. Ext/int corridors. **Pets:** Accepted.

(ASK) (S🔒) 🖪 💻 (X)

▼▼ Super 8 Motel **M**
(715) 848-2888. **$58-$64.** 2006 Stewart Ave W. I-39, exit 192, just e. Int corridors. **Pets:** Accepted.

(ASK) (S🔒) ⊠ 🖉 🖭 💻

WAUTOMA

▼▼▼ AmericInn **M**
(920) 787-5050. **$65-$90.** W7696 SR 21/73. 1.2 mi e on SR 21/73. Int corridors. **Pets:** Accepted.

⊠ 🕭 🖭 🖪 💻 ⇌

▼▼ Super 8 Motel-Wautoma **M**
(920) 787-4811. **$61-$102.** W7607 State Rd 21 and 73. 1.5 mi e on SR 21 and 73. Int corridors. **Pets:** Accepted.

(ASK) (S🔒) ⊠ 🖪 ⇌

WEST SALEM

▼▼▼ AmericInn **M**
(608) 786-3340. **$90-$100.** 125 Buol Rd. I-90, exit 12, just sw on CR C. Int corridors. **Pets:** Accepted.

(ASK) (S🔒) ⊠ 🖭 🖪 💻 ⇌

WHITEWATER

▼▼▼▼ AmeriHost Inn & Suites **M**
(262) 472-9400. **$79-$149.** 1355 W Main St. On US 12, 0.5 mi w of jct SR 59 W. Int corridors. **Pets:** $10 deposit/room, $10 daily fee/room. Designated rooms, service with restrictions, supervision.

(ASK) (S🔒) ⊠ 🕭 🖉 🖭 🖪 💻 ⇌

WINDSOR

⏣⏣⏣ ▼▼▼ Days Inn **M**
(608) 846-7473. **$60-$75.** 6311 Rostad Dr. I-90/94, exit 131 (SR 19). Int corridors. **Pets:** Accepted.

(SAVE) (S🔒) ⊠ 🖭 🖪 💻 ⇌

⏣⏣⏣ ▼▼▼ Super 8 Motel-Windsor/North Madison **M**
(608) 846-3971. **$48-$74.** 4506 Lake Circle. I-90/94, exit 131 (SR 19). Int corridors. **Pets:** Accepted.

(SAVE) (S🔒) ⊠ 🖪 💻

WISCONSIN DELLS

⏣⏣⏣ ▼▼▼ Baker's Sunset Bay Resort **M**
(608) 254-8406. **$54-$132, 14 days notice.** 921 Canyon Rd. I-90/94, exit 92, 0.5 mi w on US 12, right on E Adams St, right on Canyon Rd, 0.8 mi on left. Ext/int corridors. **Pets:** Other species. $10 daily fee/room. Designated rooms, service with restrictions, crate.

(SAVE) (S🔒) ⊠ 🖪 💻 ⇌ (X)

⏣⏣⏣ ▼▼▼ Black Hawk Motel **M**
(608) 254-7770. **$35-$135, 3 days notice.** 720 Race St. I-90/94, exit 87, 2 mi e on SR 13, 16 and 23. Ext corridors. **Pets:** Accepted.

(SAVE) ⊠ 🖪 💻 ⇌

⏣⏣⏣ ▼▼ Bridge View Motel **M**
(608) 254-6114. **$49-$99, 3 days notice.** 1020 River Rd. Center; just n of SR 13 (Broadway). Ext corridors. **Pets:** Small, dogs only. $10 daily fee/pet. Designated rooms, no service, crate.

(SAVE) ⊠ 🖪 ⇌

⏣⏣⏣ ▼▼ Day's End Motel **M**
(608) 254-8171. **$34-$111, 3 days notice.** N 604 Hwy 12-16. I-90/94, exit 85 (US 12), 0.8 mi nw. Ext corridors. **Pets:** Designated rooms, service with restrictions, supervision.

(SAVE) (S🔒) ⊠ 🖪 💻 ⇌

⏣⏣⏣ ▼▼▼ Rodeway Inn **M**
(608) 254-6492. **$55-$109, 21 days notice.** 350 W Munroe Ave. I-90/94, exit 89 (SR 23 N), 0.4 mi e. Int corridors. **Pets:** Other species. $10.60 one-time fee/room. Service with restrictions, crate.

(SAVE) (S🔒) ⊠ 🕭 🖭 🖪 💻 ⇌

▼▼ Super 8 Motel **M**
(608) 254-6464. **$60-$139.** 800 Co Hwy H. I-90/94, exit 87 (SR 13), just e. Int corridors. **Pets:** Other species. Service with restrictions, supervision.

(ASK) (S🔒) ⊠ 🖉 💻 ⇌

WISCONSIN RAPIDS

Best Western Rapids Motor Inn M
(715) 423-3211. **$58-$70.** 911 Huntington Ave. 0.5 mi s on SR 13 from jct SR 54. Int corridors. **Pets:** Medium. Designated rooms, service with restrictions, supervision.

Hotel Mead H
(715) 423-1500. **$104-$114.** 451 E Grand Ave. Just e of downtown. Int corridors. **Pets:** Large. $15 daily fee/room. Designated rooms, service with restrictions, supervision.

Super 8 Motel M
(715) 423-8080. **$59-$79.** 3410 8th St S. 1.9 mi s on SR 13 from jct SR 54 W. Int corridors. **Pets:** Dogs only. $10 one-time fee/room. Service with restrictions, supervision.

WYOMING

CITY INDEX

AFTON

Best Western Hi Country Inn M
(307) 885-3856. **$95-$105, 5 days notice.** 689 S Washington. 0.8 mi s on US 89. Ext corridors. **Pets:** Accepted.

Lazy B Motel M
(307) 885-3187. **$55-$75.** 219 Washington. City center; on US 89. Ext corridors. **Pets:** Other species. Service with restrictions, supervision.

Mountain Inn M
(307) 885-3156. **$75, 7 days notice.** 83542 Hwy 89. 1.5 mi s on US 89. Ext corridors. **Pets:** Medium, dogs only. $5 daily fee/pet. Service with restrictions, supervision.

ALPINE

Best Western Flying Saddle Lodge M
(307) 654-7561. **$75-$180, 3 days notice.** 118878 Jct US 26 & 89. 0.5 mi e of jct US 26 and 89. Ext corridors. **Pets:** Accepted.

BUFFALO

Arrowhead Motel M
(307) 684-9453. **$42-$60.** 749 Fort St. Jct US 16, 87 and Business Loop 75, 0.6 mi w. Ext corridors. **Pets:** $5 daily fee/pet. Service with restrictions, supervision.

Canyon Motel M
(307) 684-2957. **$-$48.** 997 Fort St. Jct US 16/87/Business Loop 25, 0.9 mi w on US 16. Ext corridors. **Pets:** Other species. $3 daily fee/pet. Supervision.

Comfort Inn M
(307) 684-9564. **$50-$125, 3 days notice.** 65 Hwy 16 E. I-25, exit 299, just e; I-90, exit 58, 1.3 mi w. Ext/int corridors. **Pets:** Large, other species. $25 deposit/pet, $5 daily fee/pet. Designated rooms, service with restrictions, supervision.

Mountain View Motel & Campground M
(307) 684-2881. **$35-$59, 14 days notice.** 585 Fort St. Jct 16/87 and Business Loop I-25, 0.4 mi w on US 16. Ext corridors. **Pets:** Large, dogs only. $25 deposit/room, $10 daily fee/pet. Designated rooms, service with restrictions, supervision.

Super 8 Motel of Buffalo M
(307) 684-2531. **$44-$84, 3 days notice.** 655 E Hart St. I-25, exit 299 (US 16), just w; I-90, exit 58, 1.3 mi w. Int corridors. **Pets:** Large, other species. $5.25 daily fee/pet. Service with restrictions, supervision.

Wyoming Motel M
(307) 684-5505. **$27-$97.** 610 E Hart St. I-90, exit 299 (US 16), just w; I-90, exit 58, 1.3 mi w. Ext corridors. **Pets:** Accepted.

Z-Bar Motel C
(307) 684-5535. **$40-$65.** 626 Fort St. Jct US 16, 87 and Business Loop 25, 0.5 mi w on US 16. Ext corridors. **Pets:** Other species. $4 daily fee/pet. Service with restrictions, supervision.

CASPER

Days Inn Casper M
(307) 234-1159. **$60-$74.** 301 East E St. I-25, exit 188A, just w. Int corridors. **Pets:** Other species. Service with restrictions, supervision.

Holiday Inn M
(307) 235-2531. **$79-$109.** 300 West F St. I-25, exit 188A, just e. Int corridors. **Pets:** Other species. $50 deposit/room. Service with restrictions.

National 9 Inn Showboat M
(307) 235-2711. **$39-$52.** 100 West F St. I-25, exit 188A, just n. Int corridors. **Pets:** Accepted.

ⓐ ▼▼▼ Parkway Plaza Hotel & Convention Centre Ⓗ
(307) 235-1777. **$75.** 123 West E St. I-25, exit 188A, just w. Ext/int corridors. **Pets:** Other species. $25 deposit/room. Service with restrictions.
SAVE 🔥 ✕ 🌙 🐾 📶 🖥 🍽 🏊

ⓐ ▼▼▼ Quality Inn & Suites Ⓜ ✿
(307) 266-2400. **$65-$95.** 821 N Poplar St. I-25, exit 188B, just e. Ext/int corridors. **Pets:** Large, other species. Designated rooms, service with restrictions, supervision.
SAVE 🔥 ✕ 🐾 📶

▼▼▼▼ Radisson Hotel Casper Ⓗ
(307) 266-6000. **$81-$125.** 800 N Poplar St. I-25, exit 188B, just e. Int corridors. **Pets:** Medium. $35 deposit/room. Service with restrictions.
ASK 🔥 ✕ 🌙 🔊 🐾 📶 🖥 🍽 🏊

▼▼ Super 8 Motel Ⓜ
(307) 266-3480. **$60-$65, 30 days notice.** 3838 CY Ave. I-25, exit 188B, 1.7 mi w on S Poplar St (SR 220), 1.8 mi n. Int corridors. **Pets:** Accepted.
ASK ✕ 📶 🖥

ⓐ ▼▼ Westridge Motel Ⓜ ✿
(307) 234-8911. **$36-$49.** 955 CY Ave. I-25, exit 188B, 1.8 mi w on S Poplar St (SR 220). Ext corridors. **Pets:** Small. $7 one-time fee/pet. Designated rooms, service with restrictions, supervision.
SAVE 🔥 ✕ 📶

CHEYENNE

ⓐ ▼▼▼▼ Best Western Hitching Post Inn Resort & Conference Center Ⓜ ✿
(307) 638-3301. **$85-$139.** 1700 W Lincolnway. I-25, exit 9, 1 mi e on I-80 business loop/US 30. Ext/int corridors. **Pets:** Service with restrictions, supervision.
SAVE 🔥 ✕ 🌙 🔊 🐾 📶 🖥 🍽 🏊 ✕

▼▼ Comfort Inn Ⓜ ✿
(307) 638-7202. **$59-$200.** 2245 Etchepare Dr. I-25, exit 7, just w. Int corridors. **Pets:** $20 deposit/pet. Designated rooms, service with restrictions, supervision.
SAVE 🔥 ✕ 🌙 📶 🖥 🏊

▼▼ Days Inn Cheyenne Ⓜ
(307) 778-8877. **$58-$72, 14 days notice.** 2360 W Lincolnway. I-25, exit 9, just e on US 30/I-80 Business Loop. Int corridors. **Pets:** Medium, other species. $25 deposit/room. Designated rooms, service with restrictions, supervision.
SAVE 🔥 ✕ 🌙 🔊 🐾 📶 🖥

ⓐ ▼▼ Fleetwood Motel Ⓜ ✿
(307) 638-8908. **$47-$59.** 3800 E Lincolnway. I-80, exit 364, just n on N College Dr (SR 212), just w on I-80/US 30 Business Loop. Ext corridors. **Pets:** $7 daily fee/pet. Service with restrictions, supervision.
SAVE ✕ 📶 🏊

ⓐ ▼▼▼ Holiday Inn Ⓗ
(307) 638-4466. **$75-$98, 30 days notice.** 204 W Fox Farm Rd. I-80, exit 362, just s. Int corridors. **Pets:** Other species. $25 deposit/room, $25 one-time fee/room. Designated rooms, service with restrictions, supervision.
SAVE 🔥 ✕ 🌙 🐾 📶 🖥 🍽 🏊

ⓐ ▼▼▼ La Quinta Inn Cheyenne Ⓜ
(307) 632-7117. **$68-$86.** 2410 W Lincolnway. I-25, exit 9, just e. Int corridors. **Pets:** Accepted.
SAVE 🔥 ✕ 🌙 🔊 📶 🖥 🏊

ⓐ ▼▼▼ Lincoln Court Motel Ⓜ
(307) 638-3302. **$50-$80.** 1720 W Lincolnway. I-25, exit 9, 0.6 mi e on US 30/I-80 business loop. Ext/int corridors. **Pets:** Accepted.
SAVE 🔥 ✕ 📶 🏊

ⓐ ▼▼▼ Nagle Warren Mansion B & B ⒷⒷ
(307) 637-3333. **$108-$178, 3 days notice.** 222 E 17th St. I-80, exit 362, 1.2 mi n on Central Ave, just e. Int corridors. **Pets:** Medium, other species. $20 daily fee/pet. Designated rooms, service with restrictions, crate.
SAVE ✕ 🐾

ⓐ ▼▼▼ Oak Tree Inn Ⓜ
(307) 778-6620. **$59-$100.** 1625 Stillwater. I-25, exit 12, 0.7 mi e on Central, just n on Yellowstone Rd, 1.2 mi e on Dell Range, then just s. Ext/int corridors. **Pets:** Accepted.
SAVE 🔥 ✕ 📶 🍽

▼▼ Porch Swing Bed & Breakfast ⒷⒷ
(307) 778-7182. **$75.** 502 E 24th St. I-80, exit 362, 1.8 mi n on Central Ave, just e. Int corridors. **Pets:** Accepted.
✕ 🐾

▼▼▼ Windy Hills Guest House ⒷⒷ
(307) 632-6423. **$95-$190, 15 days notice.** 393 Happy Jack Rd. I-25, exit 10B, 22 mi w on SR 210 (Happy Jack Rd), 1 mi s on private gravel road. Ext corridors. **Pets:** Accepted.
ASK 🔥 ✕ 📶 🖥 ✕ 🐾

CHUGWATER

▼▼ Super 8 Motel-Chugwater Ⓜ①
(307) 422-3248. **$42-$80.** 100 Buffalo Dr. I-25, exit 54, just ne. Int corridors. **Pets:** Accepted.
ASK 🔥 ✕ 🍽 🏊

CODY

▼▼ Best Western Sunrise Motor Inn Ⓜ
(307) 587-5566. **$45-$110.** 1407 8th St. 0.8 mi w on US 14/16/20. Ext corridors. **Pets:** Small, dogs only. Service with restrictions, supervision.
SAVE ✕ 🔊 🏊

ⓐ ▼▼▼ Best Western Sunset Motor Inn Ⓜ①
(307) 587-4265. **$55-$129.** 1601 8th St. 0.8 mi w on US 14/16/20. Ext corridors. **Pets:** Medium, other species. Designated rooms, service with restrictions, supervision.
SAVE 🔥 ✕ 🐾 🖥 🍽 🏊

◇◇ ▽ Big Bear Motel M
(307) 587-3117. **$39-$70.** 139 W Yellowstone Hwy. 2 mi w on US 14/16/20, from city center. Ext corridors. **Pets:** Accepted.
[SAVE] [S▢] [✕] [☎]

▽▽ Cody Motor Lodge M ☙
(307) 527-6291. **$39-$100, 14 days notice.** 1455 Sheridan Ave. Just w on US 14/16/20 and SR 120. Ext corridors. **Pets:** Other species. $20 deposit/room. Designated rooms, service with restrictions, supervision.
[ASK] [S▢] [✕]

▽▽ Cody Super 8 Motel M
(307) 527-6214. **$50-$135.** 730 Yellowstone Rd. On US 14/16, 1 mi w of city center. Int corridors. **Pets:** Accepted.
[ASK] [S▢] [✕] [▨] [▤] [▣]

▽▽▽ Green Gables Inn M
(307) 587-6886. **$59-$99.** 1636 Central Ave. Just e on US 14/16/20 and SR 120. Ext corridors. **Pets:** Small, dogs only. Service with restrictions, supervision.
[ASK] [S▢] [✕]

◇◇ ▽▽▽ Kelly Inn of Cody M
(307) 527-5505. **$59-$130.** 2513 Greybull Hwy. 1.5 mi e on US 14/16/20. Ext/int corridors. **Pets:** Accepted.
[SAVE] [✕] [▤] [▣]

▽▽ Parkway Inn M
(307) 587-4208. **$59-$98.** 720 Yellowstone Hwy. 1.4 mi w on US 14/16/20. Ext corridors. **Pets:** Small, dogs only. Designated rooms, service with restrictions, supervision.
[ASK] [S▢] [✕] [➔]

◇◇ ▽▽▽ Skyline Motor Inn M
(307) 587-4201. **$32-$64.** 1919 17th St. 0.8 mi e on US 14/16/20 and SR 120. Ext corridors. **Pets:** Accepted.
[SAVE] [✕]

DOUGLAS

▽ Alpine Inn M
(307) 358-4780. **$45-$65.** 2310 E Richards St. I-25, exit 135, 0.8 mi e. Ext corridors. **Pets:** Accepted.
[ASK] [S▢] [✕] [▤]

◇◇ ▽▽▽ Best Western Douglas Inn & Conference Center M̄
(307) 358-9790. **$69-$93.** 1450 Riverbend Dr. I-25, exit 140, 0.8 mi e. Int corridors. **Pets:** Medium. Designated rooms, service with restrictions, supervision.
[SAVE] [S▢] [✕] [♿M] [▨] [▤] [▣] [¶] [➔]

▽ Super 8 Motel M
(307) 358-6800. **$50-$65.** 314 Russell Ave. I-25, exit 140, 1 mi e. Int corridors. **Pets:** Small, dogs only. $5 one-time fee/pet. Designated rooms, service with restrictions, supervision.
[ASK] [S▢] [✕]

DUBOIS

▽▽ Bald Mountain Inn M
(307) 455-2844. **$35-$90, 7 days notice.** 1349 W Ramshorn St. 1.6 mi w on US 26 and 287. Ext corridors. **Pets:** Accepted.
[ASK] [S▢] [✕] [▤] [▣] [♪]

◇◇ ▽ Black Bear Country Inn M
(307) 455-2344. **$35-$60.** 505 N Ramshorn St. 0.5 mi w on US 26 and 287. Ext corridors. **Pets:** Accepted.
[SAVE] [S▢] [✕] [▤] [♪]

◇◇ ▽ Branding Iron Inn C
(307) 455-2893. **$36-$64.** 401 W Ramshorn St. 0.3 mi w on US 26 and 287. Ext corridors. **Pets:** Accepted.
[SAVE] [S▢] [✕] [▤] [▣] [♪]

▽ Pinnacle Buttes Lodge & Campground M̄
(307) 455-2506. **$45-$70, 14 days notice.** 3577 US Hwy 26 W. 20 mi w on US 26 and 287; in Shoshone National Forest. Ext corridors. **Pets:** Accepted.
[ASK] [S▢] [▣] [¶] [✕] [♪] [☎]

▽▽ Riverside Inn M
(307) 455-2337. **$36-$49.** 5810 US Hwy 26. 3 mi e of town center on US 26 and 287. Ext corridors. **Pets:** Medium, dogs only. $5 daily fee/pet. Designated rooms, service with restrictions, supervision.
[S▢] [✕] [▤] [▣] [✕] [♪] [♬] [☎]

◇◇ ▽▽▽ Stagecoach Motor Inn M ☙
(307) 455-2303. **$44-$70.** 103 Ramshorn St. Center; on US 26 and 287. Ext corridors. **Pets:** Small. $5 daily fee/pet. Designated rooms, service with restrictions, supervision.
[SAVE] [✕] [✦] [▤] [▣] [➔] [♪]

◇◇ ▽▽▽ Trail's End Motel M
(307) 455-2540. **$39-$129, 3 days notice.** 511 Ramshorn St. 0.5 mi w on US 26 and 287. Ext corridors. **Pets:** Accepted.
[SAVE] [S▢] [✕] [▤] [▣] [♪]

EVANSTON

◇◇ ▽▽▽ Days Inn Evanston M̄
(307) 789-2220. **$55-$65, 5 days notice.** 339 Wasatch Rd. I-80, exit 3 (Harrison Rd), just n to Wasatch Rd. Int corridors. **Pets:** $10 one-time fee/room. Designated rooms, service with restrictions.
[SAVE] [S▢] [✕] [♿M] [▤] [▣] [¶]

◇◇ ▽▽▽ Prairie Inn M
(307) 789-2920. **$50-$65, 5 days notice.** 264 Bear River Dr. I-80, exit 6, 0.3 mi n. Ext/int corridors. **Pets:** Other species. $5 daily fee/pet. Designated rooms, service with restrictions, supervision.
[SAVE] [✕]

EVANSVILLE

▽▽▽ Casper Comfort Inn M
(307) 235-3038. **$60-$90.** 480 Lathrop Rd. I-25, exit 185, just e. Int corridors. **Pets:** Designated rooms, service with restrictions, supervision.
[SAVE] [S▢] [✕] [♿M] [▨] [✦] [▤] [▣] [➔]

AAA ▼▼▼ Shilo Inn-Casper/Evansville MI ☀
(307) 237-1335. **$49-$109.** 739 Luker Ln. I-25, exit 185, just e. Int corridors. **Pets:** Other species. $10 daily fee/pet. Service with restrictions, supervision.
SAVE S♂ ✕ 🛏 🐾 🛏 ¶ ➯

GILLETTE

AAA ▼▼▼▼ Best Western Tower West Lodge MI
(307) 686-2210. **$50-$134.** 109 N US Hwy 14-16. I-90, exit 124, just n. Int corridors. **Pets:** Small. $8 daily fee/pet. Designated rooms, service with restrictions, crate.
SAVE S♂ ✕ 🛏 🖃 ¶ ➯

GRAND TETON NATIONAL PARK

AAA ▼▼▼▼ Flagg Ranch Resort C
(307) 543-2861. **$110-$155, 7 days notice.** US 89 and 191; 2 mi s of Yellowstone National Park south entrance; 5 mi n of Grand Teton National park north entrance. Ext corridors. **Pets:** $5 daily fee/pet. Service with restrictions.
SAVE ✕ ♨M 🖉 🐾 🖃 ¶ ✕ 🏧 📶

AAA ▼▼ Hatchet Resort MI
(307) 543-2413. **$70-$210.** 19980 Hwy 287 Moran. 7.5 mi e on US 26 and 287, from Moran Jct. Ext corridors. **Pets:** Large. No service.
SAVE ✕ ✕ 🏧

▼▼▼▼ Jackson Lake Lodge H
(307) 543-2811. **$124-$225, 7 days notice.** 5 mi nw of Moran jct US 89 and 287. Ext/int corridors. **Pets:** Accepted.
✕ ♨M 🖉 🐾 🛏 🖃 ¶ ➯ ✕ 🏧 📶

AAA ▼▼▼ Signal Mountain Lodge X
(307) 543-2831. **$60-$225, 4 days notice.** Teton Park Rd, 2 mi s of US 89, 191 and 287. Ext corridors. **Pets:** Other species. $5 daily fee/room. Designated rooms, service with restrictions.
SAVE ✕ 🛏 🖃 ¶ ✕ 🏧 📶

GREEN RIVER

AAA ▼▼▼ Coachman Inn Motel MI
(307) 875-3681. **$38-$47, 10 days notice.** 470 E Flaming Gorge Way. I-80, exit 89, just e on I-80 business loop. Ext corridors. **Pets:** Accepted.
SAVE ✕ 🛏

AAA ▼▼▼ Oak Tree Inn MI
(307) 875-3500. **$69-$75.** 1170 W Flaming Gorge Way. I-80, exit 89. Ext/int corridors. **Pets:** Accepted.
SAVE S♂ ✕ ♨M 🖉 🐾 🛏 ¶

GREYBULL

▼▼ Antler Motel MI
(307) 765-4404. **$45.** 1116 N 6th St. 0.8 mi w on US 14/16/20. Ext corridors. **Pets:** Accepted.
✕ 🛏 🖃

AAA ▼▼▼ Yellowstone Motel M
(307) 765-4456. **$48-$78, 3 days notice.** 247 Greybull Ave. 0.4 mi e on US 14. Ext corridors. **Pets:** Small. $5 one-time fee/room. Designated rooms, service with restrictions, supervision.
SAVE S♂ ✕ 🛏 🖃 ➯

GUERNSEY

▼▼ ▼▼ The Bunkhouse Motel M
(307) 836-2356. **$49-$54, 45 days notice.** 350 W Whalen. Center; on US 26. Ext corridors. **Pets:** Other species. $3 daily fee/pet. Designated rooms, supervision.
✕ 🛏

HULETT

AAA ▼▼ Hulett Motel M
(307) 467-5220. **$65-$85.** 202 Main St. SR 24 at north end of town. Ext corridors. **Pets:** Accepted.
SAVE ✕

JACKSON

AAA ▼▼▼ Antler Inn M
(307) 733-2535. **$62-$118.** 43 W Pearl St. Just s of Town Square. Ext/int corridors. **Pets:** Designated rooms, service with restrictions, supervision.
SAVE ✕ 🛏 🖃

AAA ▼▼▼ Cache Creek Motel A
(307) 733-7781. **$65-$130.** 390 N Glenwood. US 26/89/191, n on Glenwood; w on Perry, just n. Ext corridors. **Pets:** Large, other species. $10 daily fee/pet. Service with restrictions, supervision.
SAVE ✕ 🛏 🖃

AAA ▼▼▼ Elk Country Inn M ☀
(307) 733-2364. **$50-$136, 14 days notice.** 480 W Pearl St. Just w then just s of town square. Ext corridors. **Pets:** Other species. Service with restrictions, supervision.
SAVE ✕ 🛏 🖃

AAA ▼▼▼ Jackson Hole Lodge X
(307) 733-2992. **$79-$304, 15 days notice.** 420 W Broadway. 0.3 mi w on US 26/89/191. Ext corridors. **Pets:** Other species. $50 deposit/room. Designated rooms, service with restrictions, supervision.
SAVE S♂ ✕ 🛏 🖃 ➯

AAA ▼▼▼▼ Painted Buffalo Inn MI
(307) 733-4340. **$75-$149.** 400 W Broadway. Just w of town square. Ext corridors. **Pets:** Medium. $10 one-time fee/room. No service, supervision.
SAVE S♂ ✕ ♨M 🛏 ¶ ➯

AAA ▼▼▼▼ Quality 49'er Inn and Suites M
(307) 733-7550. **$58-$199, 14 days notice.** 330 W Pearl St. Just w and just s of town square. Ext/int corridors. **Pets:** Other species. $25 deposit/room. Designated rooms, service with restrictions, supervision.
SAVE ✕ 🖉 🐾 🛏 🖃

Rawhide Motel M
(307) 733-1216. **$75-$129.** 75 S Millward St. Just s of US 26/89/191. Ext corridors. **Pets:** $20 one-time fee/room. Designated rooms, service with restrictions, supervision.

Red Lion Wyoming Inn of Jackson M
(307) 734-0035. **$109-$349, 3 days notice.** 930 W Broadway. 0.5 mi s on US 26/89/191. Int corridors. **Pets:** Other species. Designated rooms, service with restrictions, supervision.

Snow King Resort X
(307) 733-5200. **$120-$630, 3 days notice.** 400 E Snow King Ave. Just se of town square. Int corridors. **Pets:** Accepted.

LANDER

Baldwin Creek Bed & Breakfast C
(307) 332-7608. **$70-$95, 14 days notice.** 2343 Baldwin Creek Rd. 4.8 mi w on Baldwin Creek Rd from jct US 287. Ext/int corridors. **Pets:** $15 daily fee/room. Designated rooms, no service, supervision.

Budget Host Pronghorn Lodge M
(307) 332-3940. **$48-$74, 7 days notice.** 150 E Main St. Just n on US 287 at jct SR 789. Ext corridors. **Pets:** Accepted.

Holiday Lodge National 9 M
(307) 332-2511. **$40-$55.** 210 McFarlane Dr. On US 287 at jct SR 789. Ext corridors. **Pets:** Other species. $5 daily fee/pet. Service with restrictions, supervision.

Silver Spur Motel M
(307) 332-5189. **$35-$90.** 1240 Main St. 1.5 mi n on US 287. Ext corridors. **Pets:** $5 daily fee/pet. Service with restrictions, supervision.

LARAMIE

1st Inn Gold M
(307) 742-3721. **$57-$99, 7 days notice.** 421 Boswell. I-80, exit 313, just n n US 287. Ext/int corridors. **Pets:** Accepted.

Fosters Country Inn M
(307) 742-8371. **$66-$128.** 1555 Snowy Range Rd. I-80, exit 311, just s. Ext corridors. **Pets:** Other species. $10 daily fee/room. Designated rooms, service with restrictions, supervision.

Gas Lite Inn Motel M
(307) 742-6616. **$45-$65.** 960 N 3rd St. I-80, exit 313, 1.6 mi n on US 287. Ext corridors. **Pets:** Other species. $5 one-time fee/pet. Designated rooms, service with restrictions.

Holiday Inn of Laramie M
(307) 742-6611. **$87-$107.** 2313 Soldier Springs. I-80, exit 313, just s on US 287. Ext/int corridors. **Pets:** Other species. $10 daily fee/pet. Designated rooms, service with restrictions, supervision.

Sunset Inn M
(307) 742-3741. **$50-$70.** 1104 S 3rd St. I-80, exit 313, 0.3 mi n on US 287. Ext corridors. **Pets:** Accepted.

Travelodge Downtown M
(307) 742-6671. **$45-$75.** 165 N 3rd St. I-80, exit 313, 1 mi n on US 287 (downtown). Ext corridors. **Pets:** $50 deposit/room. Designated rooms, service with restrictions, supervision.

LOVELL

Horseshoe Bend Motel M
(307) 548-2221. **$49-$58.** 375 E Main St. 0.3 mi e on US 14A and 310. Ext/int corridors. **Pets:** Accepted.

LUSK

Town House Motel M
(307) 334-2376. **$45-$70.** 525 S Main St. On US 20/85, just n. Ext corridors. **Pets:** Other species. $5 daily fee/pet. Service with restrictions, supervision.

Trail Motel M
(307) 334-2530. **$42-$67, 7 days notice.** 305 W 8th St. 0.3 mi sw on US 20/18. Ext corridors. **Pets:** Very small. $10 daily fee/pet. Designated rooms, service with restrictions, supervision.

NEWCASTLE

Pines Motel M
(307) 746-4334. **$42-$75.** 248 E Wentworth St. just e from jct US Business Rt 16. Ext corridors. **Pets:** Medium. Service with restrictions, supervision.

Sage Motel M
(307) 746-2724. **$38-$58, 3 days notice.** 1227 S Summit Ave. 0.3 mi s of jct US 16 on US 85, just w. Ext corridors. **Pets:** Medium, other species. $5.35 daily fee/pet. Designated rooms, service with restrictions, supervision.

PAINTER

◆ Hunter Peak Ranch RA
(307) 587-3711. **$90-$130, 30 days notice.** 4027 Crandall Rd. SR 296, 5 mi s of US 212; 40 mi n of SR 120. Ext corridors. **Pets:** Dogs only. $10 daily fee/pet. Designated rooms, no service, supervision.

⊠ 🛏 💻 🍴 ⊠ 🗲 📵 🕿

PINEDALE

◆◆ ◆◆ Best Western Pinedale Inn M
(307) 367-6869. **$65-$110, 3 days notice.** 850 W Pine St. 0.5 mi n on US 191. Int corridors. **Pets:** Designated rooms, service with restrictions, supervision.

SAVE 🔊 ⊠ 🛏 🛋

◆◆ ◆◆ Sun Dance Motel M
(307) 367-4336. **$45-$75.** 148 E Pine St. US 191; in city center. Ext corridors. **Pets:** Service with restrictions, supervision.

SAVE ⊠ 🛏 🗲

◆◆◆◆ Window on the Winds B & B BB
(307) 367-2600. **$125, 7 days notice.** 10151 US 191. 2 mi n on US 191. Int corridors. **Pets:** Other species. Supervision.

⊠ 🛏 💻 🗲

POWELL

◆◆ Best Western Kings Inn MI
(307) 754-5117. **$-$80.** 777 E 2nd St. 0.3 mi e on US 14A. Ext corridors. **Pets:** Medium. Designated rooms, service with restrictions, supervision.

SAVE 🔊 ⊠ 🛏 💻 🍴 🛋

RAWLINS

◆◆ ◆◆◆◆ Best Western CottonTree Inn MI
(307) 324-2737. **$74-$109, 14 days notice.** 2221 W Spruce St. I-80, exit 211, just n. Ext/int corridors. **Pets:** Medium, other species. $10 daily fee/room. Designated rooms, service with restrictions, supervision.

SAVE 🔊 ⊠ 📶 🛏 💻 🍴 🛋

◆◆ ◆◆◆ Sleep Inn M
(307) 328-1732. **$60-$75.** 1400 Higley Blvd. I-80, exit 214, just sw. Int corridors. **Pets:** Other species. Designated rooms, service with restrictions, supervision.

SAVE 🔊 ⊠ 📶 🛏 💻

RIVERTON

◆◆ ◆◆ Days Inn M
(307) 856-9677. **$50-$70.** 909 W Main St. 0.5 mi nw on US 26. Ext corridors. **Pets:** Medium. $5 daily fee/pet, $5 one-time fee/pet. Service with restrictions, supervision.

SAVE 🔊 ⊠ 🗲 🛏

◆◆◆ ◆◆◆◆ Holiday Inn Convention Center MI
(307) 856-8100. **$69-$109.** 900 E Sunset Dr. 0.8 mi ne on US 26/SR 789. Int corridors. **Pets:** Accepted.

SAVE ⊠ 🗲M 🛏 💻 🍴 🛋

◆◆ ◆◆ Super 8 Motel M
(307) 857-2400. **$50-$70.** 1040 N Federal Blvd. 1 mi ne on US 26/SR 789. Int corridors. **Pets:** Accepted.

ASK 🔊 ⊠ 🛏

◆◆ Thunderbird Motel M
(307) 856-9201. **$36-$46.** 302 E Fremont. Just n of US 26. Ext corridors. **Pets:** Other species. $4 daily fee/pet. Service with restrictions, supervision.

⊠ 🛏

ROCK SPRINGS

◆◆◆ ◆◆ Budget Host Inn M
(307) 362-6673. **$43-$65, 3 days notice.** 1004 Dewar Dr. I-80, exit 102 (Dewar Dr), 1.3 mi se. Ext corridors. **Pets:** $5 daily fee/pet. Designated rooms, service with restrictions, supervision.

SAVE 🔊 ⊠ 🛏

◆◆◆◆ Comfort Inn M ❧
(307) 382-9490. **$56-$79.** 1670 Sunset Dr. I-80, exit 102 (Dewar Dr), 0.3 mi s, then just w. Ext corridors. **Pets:** Other species. $10 daily fee/room.

SAVE 🔊 ⊠ 🗲 💻 🛋

◆◆◆ Econo Lodge M
(307) 382-4217. **$50-$75.** 1635 N Elk St. I-80, exit 104 (Elk St), just n. Ext corridors. **Pets:** Medium. $5 one-time fee/pet. Designated rooms, service with restrictions, supervision.

SAVE 🔊 ⊠ 🛏 💻 🛋

◆◆◆ Holiday Inn MI
(307) 382-9200. **$73-$85, 30 days notice.** 1675 Sunset Dr. I-80, exit 102 (Dewar Dr), 0.3 mi sw. Ext/int corridors. **Pets:** Accepted.

ASK 🔊 ⊠ 🗲M 📶 🗲 🛏 💻 🍴 🛋

◆◆ Motel 6–395 M
(307) 362-1850. **$39-$57.** 2615 Commercial Way. I-80, exit 102 (Dewar Dr), n to Foothills Blvd, just e. Ext corridors. **Pets:** Accepted.

🔊 ⊠ 🗲 🛋

◆◆◆◆ Ramada Limited M
(307) 362-1770. **$60-$90.** 2717 Dewar Dr. I-80, exit 102 (Dewar Dr), just n. Int corridors. **Pets:** Medium. $5 one-time fee/pet. Designated rooms, service with restrictions, supervision.

ASK 🔊 ⊠ 📶 🛏 💻 🛋

◆◆◆ ◆◆ Springs Motel M
(307) 362-6683. **$38-$56.** 1525 9th St. I-80, exit 107, 0.3 mi w. Ext corridors. **Pets:** Accepted.

SAVE 🔊 ⊠

SARATOGA

◆◆ ◆◆ Hacienda Motel M
(307) 326-5751. **$54-$74, 7 days notice.** 1116 S First St. 0.5 mi s on SR 130. Int corridors. **Pets:** $5 daily fee/pet. Designated rooms, service with restrictions, supervision.

ASK 🔊 ⊠ 🛏

SHERIDAN

⬥ ⬥⬥ Guest House Motel M
(307) 674-7496. **$45-$65, 30 days notice.** 2007 N Main St. I-90, exit 20, 0.7 mi s; on I-90 business loop. Ext corridors. **Pets:** Medium. $5 one-time fee/pet. Designated rooms, service with restrictions, supervision.
⬛SAVE⬛ ⬛Ⓢ⬛ ⬛✕⬛ ⬛📱⬛ ⬛💾⬛

⬥⬥⬥ Holiday Inn M ❁
(307) 672-8931. **$-$89.** 1809 Sugarland Dr. I-90, exit 25, 0.3 mi nw. Int corridors. **Pets:** Other species. $50 deposit/room. Service with restrictions, supervision.
⬛ASK⬛ ⬛Ⓢ⬛ ⬛✕⬛ ⬛🌀⬛ ⬛♿⬛ ⬛📱⬛ ⬛💾⬛ ⬛🍴⬛ ⬛≋⬛

⬥⬥ Rock Trim Motel LLC M
(307) 672-2464. **$48-$52.** 449 Coffeen Ave. I-90, exit 25, w to Coffeen Ave, 1.3 mi n. Ext corridors. **Pets:** Accepted.
⬛SAVE⬛ ⬛✕⬛ ⬛📱⬛ ⬛💾⬛

SUNDANCE

⬥⬥ ⬥⬥⬥ Best Western Inn at Sundance M
(307) 283-2800. **$54-$109.** 2719 E Cleveland. I-90, exit 189, just n, then just w on I-90 business loop. Int corridors. **Pets:** Medium. $25 deposit/room. Service with restrictions, supervision.
⬛SAVE⬛ ⬛Ⓢ⬛ ⬛✕⬛ ⬛💾⬛ ⬛≋⬛

⬥⬥ ⬥⬥ Sundance Mountain Inn M
(307) 283-3737. **$44-$99.** 26 SR 585. I-90, exit 187, 0.4 mi n. Ext corridors. **Pets:** Large, other species. $25 deposit/room. Service with restrictions, supervision.
⬛SAVE⬛ ⬛Ⓢ⬛ ⬛✕⬛ ⬛💾⬛ ⬛≋⬛

THERMOPOLIS

⬥⬥⬥ Holiday Inn of the Waters M
(307) 864-3131. **$69-$125.** 115 E Park St. In Hot Springs State Park. Ext/int corridors. **Pets:** $30 deposit/room. Service with restrictions, supervision.
⬛ASK⬛ ⬛✕⬛ ⬛🌀⬛ ⬛♿⬛ ⬛💾⬛ ⬛🍴⬛ ⬛≋⬛

⬥⬥⬥ Hot Springs Super 8 M
(307) 864-5515. **$74-$99.** Lane 5, Hwy 20 S. On US 20, just se. Int corridors. **Pets:** $25 deposit/pet, $5 daily fee/pet. Service with restrictions, supervision.
⬛ASK⬛ ⬛Ⓢ⬛ ⬛✕⬛ ⬛♿M⬛ ⬛🌀⬛ ⬛♿⬛ ⬛📱⬛ ⬛💾⬛ ⬛≋⬛

TORRINGTON

⬥⬥ ⬥⬥ Kings Inn M
(307) 532-4011. **$50-$80.** 1555 Main St. On US 85; just s of jct US 26. Int corridors. **Pets:** Other species. $4 daily fee/pet. Designated rooms, service with restrictions, supervision.
⬛SAVE⬛ ⬛Ⓢ⬛ ⬛✕⬛ ⬛📱⬛ ⬛💾⬛ ⬛🍴⬛ ⬛≋⬛

⬥⬥ Maverick Motel M
(307) 532-4064. **$42-$46.** US 26 W. 1.7 mi w on US 26/85. Ext corridors. **Pets:** $5 one-time fee/room. Service with restrictions, supervision.
⬛SAVE⬛ ⬛Ⓢ⬛ ⬛✕⬛ ⬛📱⬛

UCROSS

⬥⬥ ⬥⬥⬥ The Ranch at Ucross RA
(307) 737-2281. **$119-$189, 3 days notice.** 2673 US Hwy 14 E. Jct US 14/16, 0.5 mi w on US 14. Ext/int corridors. **Pets:** Dogs only. Designated rooms, service with restrictions, crate.
⬛SAVE⬛ ⬛Ⓢ⬛ ⬛✕⬛ ⬛🍴⬛ ⬛≋⬛ ⬛☒⬛ ⬛🅆⬛

WAPITI

⬥⬥ ⬥⬥⬥ Elephant Head Lodge C ❁
(307) 587-3980. **$90-$120, 30 days notice.** 1170 Yellowstone Hwy. 19.8 mi w on US 14/16/20. Ext corridors. **Pets:** Large.
⬛SAVE⬛ ⬛Ⓢ⬛ ⬛✕⬛ ⬛📱⬛ ⬛💾⬛ ⬛🍴⬛ ⬛☒⬛ ⬛♿⬛ ⬛🅩⬛

⬥⬥ ⬥⬥ Wise Choice Inn M
(307) 587-5004. **$40-$70.** 2908 Yellowstone Hwy. 2.8 mi w on US 14/16/20. Ext corridors. **Pets:** Other species. $3 daily fee/pet. Service with restrictions, supervision.
⬛SAVE⬛ ⬛Ⓢ⬛ ⬛✕⬛ ⬛🅩⬛

WHEATLAND

⬥⬥ ⬥⬥⬥ Best Western Torchlite Motor Inn M
(307) 322-4070. **$48-$85.** 1809 N 16th St. I-25, exit 78, just e; 1.5 mi n on US 87/I-25 business loop (16th St). Ext corridors. **Pets:** Other species. $25 deposit/room. Service with restrictions, supervision.
⬛SAVE⬛ ⬛Ⓢ⬛ ⬛✕⬛ ⬛📱⬛ ⬛💾⬛ ⬛🍴⬛ ⬛≋⬛

⬥⬥⬥ Motel West Winds M
(307) 322-2705. **$49-$50.** 1756 South Rd. I-25, exit 78, just e; 0.4 mi n on US 87/I-25 business loop (16th St). Ext corridors. **Pets:** Service with restrictions, supervision.
⬛✕⬛ ⬛📱⬛

⬥⬥ ⬥⬥ Vimbo's Motel M
(307) 322-3842. **$44-$77.** 203 16th St. I-25, exit 78, just e; just n on US 87/I-25 business loop (16th St). Ext/int corridors. **Pets:** Other species. Designated rooms, service with restrictions.
⬛SAVE⬛ ⬛✕⬛ ⬛🍴⬛

WILSON

⬥⬥⬥ Sassy Moose Inn of Jackson Hole BB
(307) 733-1277. **$79-$204, 30 days notice.** 3859 Miles Rd. 2 mi n on SR 390 from jct SR 22, 5 mi s from Teton Village, 6 mi nw from Jackson. Int corridors. **Pets:** Accepted.
⬛✕⬛ ⬛♿⬛ ⬛🅩⬛

WORLAND

⬥⬥ ⬥⬥ Comfort Inn of Worland M
(307) 347-9898. **$58-$109.** 100 N Road 11. On US 16, 1.4 mi e. Int corridors. **Pets:** Accepted.
⬛SAVE⬛ ⬛Ⓢ⬛ ⬛✕⬛ ⬛♿⬛ ⬛📱⬛ ⬛💾⬛ ⬛≋⬛

⬥⬥ ⬥⬥ Days Inn M
(307) 347-4251. **$48-$78.** 500 N 10th St. 0.5 mi n on US 20. Ext corridors. **Pets:** Accepted.
⬛SAVE⬛ ⬛Ⓢ⬛ ⬛✕⬛ ⬛📱⬛

Canada

CITY INDEX

ATHABASCA

(CAA) ▼▼▼▼ Best Western Athabasca Inn [MI]
(780) 675-2294. $99-$119. 5211 41st Ave. 1 km s on Hwy 2. Int corridors. Pets: Accepted.
[SAVE] [S/b] [X] [🛏] [📺] [♨]

BANFF

▼▼▼▼ Banff Rocky Mountain Resort [X]
(403) 762-5531. $150-$295, 3 days notice. 1029 Banff Ave. Banff Ave at Tunnel Mountain Rd, just s of Trans-Canada Hwy 1. Ext corridors. Pets: $15 daily fee/pet. Designated rooms.
[ASK] [S/b] [X] [🛏] [📺] [♨] [⇌] [X] [AC]

(CAA) ▼▼▼▼ Best Western Siding 29 Lodge [M]
(403) 762-5575. $95-$205. 453 Marten St. 1.3 km ne off Banff Ave. Int corridors. Pets: Other species. Supervision.
[SAVE] [S/b] [X] [🛏] [📺] [⇌] [AC]

(CAA) ▼▼▼ Castle Mountain Chalets [C]
(403) 762-3868. $175-$350, 30 days notice. 32 km w on Trans-Canada Hwy 1, at Castle jct, 1 km ne on Hwy 1A (Bow Valley Pkwy). Ext corridors. Pets: $25 daily fee/pet. Service with restrictions, supervision.
[SAVE] [X] [✎] [🛏] [📺] [AC] [☎]

(CAA) ▼▼▼ ▼▼▼ The Fairmont Banff Springs [R]
(403) 762-2211. $167-$539, 3 days notice. 405 Spray Ave. Just s on Banff Ave over the bridge, 0.5 km e. Int corridors. Pets: Accepted.
[SAVE] [X] [✎] [🛏] [📺] [♨] [⇌] [X]

▼▼ ▼▼ Johnston Canyon Resort [C] ❀
(403) 762-2971. $89-$268. Hwy 1A. 24 km nw on Hwy 1A (Bow Valley Pkwy); at Johnston Canyon. Ext corridors. Pets: Other species. Supervision.
[X] [🛏] [📺] [♨] [AC] [☎]

(CAA) ▼▼▼ Red Carpet Motor Inn [M]
(403) 762-4184. $60-$160. 425 Banff Ave. 1 km ne. Ext/int corridors. Pets: Other species. Service with restrictions, supervision.
[SAVE] [X] [🛏] [📺]

BROOKS

▼▼▼ The Douglas Country Inn 2000 [CI]
(403) 362-2873. Call for rates. On Hwy 873, 6.5 km n of jct Trans-Canada Hwy 1. Int corridors. Pets: Accepted.
[X] [♨] [W] [☎]

▼▼ Heritage Inn [MI]
(403) 362-6666. $95-$100. 1217 2nd St W. On Hwy 873, 0.8 km s of jct Trans-Canada Hwy 1. Int corridors. Pets: Accepted.
[ASK] [S/b] [X] [🛏] [📺] [♨]

▼▼▼▼ Holiday Inn Express Hotel & Suites [MI]
(403) 362-7440. $105-$121. 1307 2nd St W. Trans-Canada Hwy 1, exit 2nd St W. Int corridors. Pets: Small. $25 one-time fee/pet. Designated rooms, service with restrictions, supervision.
[ASK] [S/b] [X] [⊘] [🛏] [📺] [⇌]

▼▼ ▼▼ Super 8 Motel-Brooks [M]
(403) 362-8000. $71-$84. 1240 Cassils Rd E. Trans-Canada Hwy 1, 0.3 km sw on SR 542 (exit E Brooks). Ext/int corridors. Pets: Other species. $5 daily fee/room, $5 one-time fee/room. Designated rooms, service with restrictions, supervision.
[ASK] [S/b] [X] [⌂M] [🛏]

CALGARY METROPOLITAN AREA

AIRDRIE

◆◆/◆◆ Super 8 Motel-Airdrie Ⓜ
(403) 948-4188. **$74-$104.** 815 E Lake Blvd. Hwy 2, exit E
Airdrie, 0.8 km e on Hwy 587 E, then 1.8 km s. Int corridors. **Pets:** Accepted.
Ⓢ Ⓧ 🏢

CALGARY

⟨CAA⟩ ◆◆/◆◆ Best Western Hospitality Inn Ⓜ🅸
(403) 278-5050. **$99-$164.** 135 Southland Dr SE. On Hwy
2 (Macleod Tr), corner of Southland Dr. Int corridors.
Pets: Accepted.
SAVE Ⓢ Ⓧ 🏢 🖥 🍴 🏊

⟨CAA⟩ ◆◆/◆◆ Best Western Village Park Inn Ⓜ🅸
(403) 289-0241. **$109-$149.** 1804 Crowchild Tr NW. Just ne
of jct Trans-Canada Hwy 1 and Crowchild Tr; in Motel Village. Int corridors. **Pets:** Designated rooms, service with
restrictions, supervision.
SAVE Ⓢ Ⓧ ⟨Ⓝ⟩ 🏢 🖥 🍴 🏊

⟨CAA⟩ ◆◆/◆◆ Blackfoot Inn Ⓜ🅸 ❀
(403) 252-2253. **$99-$165, 3 days notice.** 5940 Blackfoot
Tr SE. At 58th Ave SE; access to property from 58th Ave
only. Int corridors. **Pets:** Other species. Designated rooms,
service with restrictions, crate.
SAVE Ⓢ Ⓧ 👟 🏢 🖥 🍴 🏊

⟨CAA⟩ ◆◆/◆◆ Calgary Marriott Hotel 🄷
(403) 266-7331. **$185-$269.** 110 9th Ave SE. Across from
Calgary Tower. Int corridors. **Pets:** Accepted.
SAVE Ⓢ Ⓧ ⟨Ⓝ⟩ 👟 🏢 🖥 🍴 🏊

**⟨CAA⟩ ◆◆/◆◆ Calgary Westways Guest
House** 🅱🅱 ❀
(403) 229-1758. **$75-$130, 7 days notice.** 216 25th Ave
SW. 1.7 km s on MacLeod Tr S, 0.5 km w. Int corridors.
Pets: Other species. $5 daily fee/pet.
SAVE Ⓢ Ⓧ

⟨CAA⟩ ◆◆/◆◆ Carriage House Inn Ⓜ🅸
(403) 253-1101. **$89-$129, 3 days notice.** 9030 Macleod Tr
S. On Hwy 2, corner of 90th Ave SW. Int corridors.
Pets: Medium. $5 daily fee/pet. Service with restrictions,
crate.
SAVE Ⓢ Ⓧ 🏢 🖥 🍴 🏊

**⟨CAA⟩ ◆◆/◆◆ Coast Plaza Hotel & Conference
Centre** Ⓜ🅸
(403) 248-8888. **$109-$124.** 1316 33rd St NE. Just s of jct
16th Ave (Trans-Canada Hwy 1) and 36th St NE, just w on
12th Ave NE; adjacent to Pacific Place Mall. Int corridors.
Pets: Accepted.
SAVE Ⓢ Ⓧ �🄼 🏢 🖥 🍴 🏊

⟨CAA⟩ ◆◆/◆◆ Days Inn Calgary Airport Ⓜ
(403) 250-3297. **$99-$119.** 2799 Sunridge Way NE. Barlow
Tr, just e of Sunridge Way NE. Int corridors. **Pets:** Medium,
dogs only. $10 one-time fee/room. Designated rooms, serv-
ice with restrictions, crate.
SAVE Ⓢ Ⓧ 🄼 🏢 🖥 🏊

⟨CAA⟩ ◆◆/◆◆ Days Inn-Calgary West Ⓜ🅸
(403) 289-1961. **$59-$130, 14 days notice.** 1818 16th Ave
NW. 5.2 km nw on Trans-Canada Hwy 1. Int corridors.
Pets: Other species. $10 daily fee/pet. Designated rooms,
service with restrictions, supervision.
SAVE Ⓢ Ⓧ 🏢 🖥 🍴 🏊

◆◆/◆◆ Delta Bow Valley 🄷
(403) 266-1980. **$229-$259, 7 days notice.** 209 4th Ave
SE. 1st St SE and 4th Ave SE. Int corridors.
Pets: Accepted.
ASK Ⓢ Ⓧ 🖥 🍴 🏊

◆◆/◆◆ Delta Calgary Airport 🄷
(403) 291-2600. **$99-$209.** 2001 Airport Rd NE. At Calgary
International Airport. Int corridors. **Pets:** Supervision.
ASK Ⓢ Ⓧ 🖥 🍴 🏊

⟨CAA⟩ ◆◆/◆◆ Econo Lodge South Ⓜ🅸
(403) 252-4401. **$84-$124.** 7505 Macleod Tr. Corner of
Macleod Tr and 75th Ave. Ext/int corridors. **Pets:** Small.
$10 daily fee/room. Designated rooms, service with restric-
tions, supervision.
SAVE Ⓢ Ⓧ 🏢 🖥 🍴 🏊

⟨CAA⟩ ◆◆/◆◆ Elbow River Inn & Casino Ⓜ🅸
(403) 269-6771. **$79-$139.** 1919 Macleod Tr SE. Jct
Macleod Tr and 1st St SE; opposite Stampede Park. Int
corridors. **Pets:** Medium. Service with restrictions, supervision.
SAVE Ⓢ Ⓧ 🏢 🖥 🍴

◆◆/◆◆ The Fairmont Palliser 🄷
(403) 262-1234. **$159-$329.** 133 9th Ave SW. 9th Ave SW
at 1st St SW. Int corridors. **Pets:** Accepted.
ASK Ⓢ Ⓧ 🏢 🍴 🏊

◆◆/◆◆ Glenmore Inn and Convention Centre Ⓜ🅸
(403) 279-8611. **$119-$145.** 2720 Glenmore Tr SE. 3 km e
of Hwy 2 (Deerfoot Tr), exit Glenmore E; at Ogden Rd. Int
corridors. **Pets:** Accepted.
ASK Ⓧ 🏢 🖥 🍴

⟨CAA⟩ ◆◆/◆◆ Greenwood Inn Hotels Ⓜ🅸
(403) 250-8855. **$109-$149.** 3515 26th St NE. From Barlow Tr N, just e on 32nd Ave NE, then just n. Int corridors.
Pets: Accepted.
SAVE Ⓧ 👟 🏢 🖥 🍴 🏊

◆◆/◆◆ Hawthorn Hotel & Suites 🄷
(403) 263-0520. **$205-$305, 4 days notice.** 618 5th Ave
SW. Corner of 5th Ave and 6th St. Int corridors.
Pets: Medium, other species. $10 daily fee/pet. Designated
rooms, service with restrictions, supervision.
ASK Ⓢ Ⓧ 🏢 🖥 🍴 🏊

ⓒⒶ ▼▼▼ Holiday Inn Calgary Airport Ⓜ
(403) 230-1999. **$145-$165, 14 days notice.** 1250 McKinnon Dr NE. 1 km e of jct Hwy 2 (Deerfoot Tr) and 16th Ave NE (Trans-Canada Hwy 1). Int corridors. **Pets:** Large, other species. Service with restrictions.
[SAVE] [S✆] [✕] [▯] [Ⅱ] [≈]

ⓒⒶ ▼▼▼ Holiday Inn Calgary Downtown Ⓗ
(403) 266-4611. **$145-$155.** 119 12th Ave SW. Centre; at 1st St SW. Int corridors. **Pets:** Medium, other species. $25 one-time fee/room. Designated rooms, service with restrictions, supervision.
[SAVE] [S✆] [✕] [⅏] [✎] [✆] [▯] [Ⅱ] [≈]

▼▼▼ Holiday Inn Express Hotel & Suites Calgary South Ⓜ
(403) 225-3000. **$139-$159, 3 days notice.** 12025 Lake Frasier Dr SE. Deerfoot Tr, exit Anderson Rd w, then just s on Macleod Tr. Int corridors. **Pets:** Accepted.
[ASK] [S✆] [✕] [✆] [▯] [≈]

ⓒⒶ ▼▼▼ Holiday Inn Express University Ⓜ
(403) 289-6600. **$80-$175, 3 days notice.** 2227 Banff Tr NW. 16th Ave (Trans-Canada Hwy 1) and Banff Tr NW; in Motel Village. Int corridors. **Pets:** Accepted.
[SAVE] [✕] [⅏] [✎] [✆] [▯]

ⓒⒶ ▼▼▼ Marriott Residence Inn-Calgary Airport Ⓗ ✿
(403) 735-3336. **$139-$189, 10 days notice.** 2622 39th Ave NE. Corner of Barlow Tr and 39th Ave NE. Int corridors. **Pets:** Medium. $150 one-time fee/room. Designated rooms, service with restrictions, supervision.
[SAVE] [S✆] [✕] [⅏] [✎] [✆] [▯] [≈]

ⓒⒶ ▼▼▼ Quality Hotel & Conference Centre Ⓜ
(403) 243-5531. **$79-$129.** 3828 Macleod Tr S. Corner of Macleod Tr and 38th Ave SE. Int corridors. **Pets:** Small. $10 daily fee/pet. Designated rooms, service with restrictions, supervision.
[SAVE] [S✆] [✕] [✆] [▯] [Ⅱ] [≈]

ⓒⒶ ▼▼ Quality Inn Ⓜ
(403) 289-1973. **$89-$189, 3 days notice.** 2359 Banff Tr NW. Just n of jct Trans-Canada Hwy 1 and Crowchild Tr; in Motel Village. Ext/int corridors. **Pets:** Medium, other species. $100 deposit/room. Service with restrictions, supervision.
[SAVE] [S✆] [✕] [✆] [▯] [Ⅱ] [≈]

ⓒⒶ ▼▼▼ Radisson Hotel Calgary Airport Ⓜ
(403) 291-4666. **$124-$149.** 2120 16th Ave NE. 0.5 km e of jct Trans-Canada Hwy 1 and 16th Ave NE and Hwy 2. Int corridors. **Pets:** $35 deposit/room. Service with restrictions, supervision.
[SAVE] [S✆] [✕] [⅏] [▯] [Ⅱ] [≈]

ⓒⒶ ▼▼▼ Super 8 Motel Calgary Airport Ⓜ
(403) 291-9888. **$80-$159.** 3030 Barlow Tr NE. Corner of 32nd Ave and Barlow Tr NE. Int corridors. **Pets:** Dogs only. $10 daily fee/room. Service with restrictions, supervision.
[SAVE] [S✆] [✕]

ⓒⒶ ▼▼▼ Super 8 Motel-Motel Village Ⓜ
(403) 289-9211. **$60-$150.** 1904 Crowchild Tr NW. Just n of jct Trans-Canada Hwy 1 and Crowchild Tr; in Motel Village. Ext corridors. **Pets:** Small, dogs only. $10 deposit/pet. Service with restrictions, supervision.
[SAVE] [S✆] [✕] [✆] [▯] [≈]

ⓒⒶ ▼▼▼ Travelodge Hotel Calgary Airport Ⓜ
(403) 291-1260. **$101-$129.** 2750 Sunridge Blvd NE. Barlow Tr, then e. Int corridors. **Pets:** Large, other species. Service with restrictions, crate.
[SAVE] [S✆] [✕] [✆] [▯] [Ⅱ] [≈]

ⓒⒶ ▼▼▼ The Westin Calgary Ⓗ ✿
(403) 266-1611. **$169-$229.** 320 4th Ave SW. Corner of 4th Ave and 3rd St. Int corridors. **Pets:** Small. Service with restrictions, crate.
[SAVE] [S✆] [✕] [⅏] [♫] [▯] [Ⅱ] [≈]

COCHRANE

▼▼ Bow River Inn Ⓜ
(403) 932-7900. **$79-$119.** 3 Westside Dr. Hwy 1A, 1 km sw on Hwy 22. Ext corridors. **Pets:** Accepted.
[ASK] [✕] [✆] [▯]

OKOTOKS

▼▼ Okotoks Country Inn Ⓜ
(403) 938-1999. **$78-$95, 3 days notice.** 59 River Side Gate. On Hwy 2A (Northridge Dr), ne of Sheep River. Int corridors. **Pets:** Other species. $5 daily fee/pet. Designated rooms, supervision.
[ASK] [S✆] [✕] [✆] [▯]

STRATHMORE

ⓒⒶ ▼▼▼ Best Western Strathmore Inn Ⓜ
(403) 934-5777. **$75-$149.** 550 Hwy 1. Centre; on Trans-Canada Hwy 1, jct SR 817. Int corridors. **Pets:** Medium. $40 deposit/room, $5 daily fee/pet. Designated rooms, service with restrictions, supervision.
[SAVE] [✕] [✆] [▯] [≈]

▼▼ Super 8 Motel Ⓜ
(403) 934-1808. **$78-$120.** 450 Westlake Rd. Just n on SR 817. Ext/int corridors. **Pets:** Small, dogs only. $10 daily fee/pet. Designated rooms, service with restrictions, supervision.
[ASK] [S✆] [✕] [✆] [▯]

❖ **END METROPOLITAN AREA** ❖

CANMORE

Banff Boundary Lodge CO
(403) 678-9555. **$99-$269, 3 days notice.** 1000 Harvie Heights Rd. Just e of Banff National Park east gate, parallel to Hwy 1, exit Harvie Heights Rd. Ext corridors. **Pets:** Large, other species. $10 daily fee/room. Service with restrictions.

Canmore Regency Suites A
(403) 678-3799. **$90-$108, 5 days notice.** 1206 Bow Valley Tr. 5.8 km e of Banff National Park east gate; on Hwy 1A (Bon Valley Tr), via Canmore exit, from Trans-Canada Hwy 1. Ext corridors. **Pets:** Accepted.

Radisson Hotel & Conference Center M
(403) 678-3625. **$89-$249.** 511 Bow Valley Tr. 6 km e of Banff National Park east gate, on Hwy 1A (Bow Valley Tr), via Canmore exit from Trans-Canada Hwy 1. Ext/int corridors. **Pets:** Large, other species. $10 one-time fee/room. Designated rooms, service with restrictions, crate.

Residence Inn by Marriott L
(403) 678-3400. **$139-$249.** 91 Three Sisters Dr. Just w on Main St to 8th Ave, then se on 8th Ave. Int corridors. **Pets:** $85 deposit/room, $10 daily fee/pet. Service with restrictions, supervision.

Rocky Mountain Ski Lodge X
(403) 678-5445. **$55-$110.** 1711 Bow Valley Tr. 4.8 km e of Banff National Park east gate, on Hwy 1A (Bow Valley Tr), via Canmore exit from Trans-Canada Hwy 1. Ext corridors. **Pets:** Other species. Designated rooms, service with restrictions, crate.

Rundle Mountain Lodge M
(403) 678-5322. **$55-$135, 7 days notice.** 1723 Bow Valley Tr. 4.8 km e of Banff National Park east gate, on Hwy 1A (Bow Valley Tr); adjacent to Trans-Canada Hwy 1. Ext corridors. **Pets:** $7 daily fee/room. Designated rooms, service with restrictions, supervision.

Rundle Ridge Chalets C
(403) 678-5387. **$79-$154.** 1100 Harvie Heights Rd. 1 km e of Banff National Park east gate, on Trans-Canada Hwy 1, exit Harvie Heights. Ext corridors. **Pets:** Medium. $10 daily fee/pet. Designated rooms, service with restrictions, supervision.

The Stockade Log Cabins C
(403) 678-5212. **$78-$225, 14 days notice.** 1050 Harvie Heights Rd. 1 km e of Banff National Park east gate, on Trans-Canada Hwy 1, exit Harvie Heights. Ext corridors. **Pets:** Accepted.

CARDSTON

Flamingo Motel M
(403) 653-3952. **$55-$77.** 848 Main St S. 1 km s on Hwy 2, just s of Remington Carriage Center. Ext corridors. **Pets:** Accepted.

CLARESHOLM

Bluebird Motel M
(403) 625-3395. **$59-$70.** 5505 1st St W. 0.5 km n on Hwy 2. Ext corridors. **Pets:** Other species. Designated rooms, service with restrictions, crate.

DEAD MAN'S FLATS

Pigeon Mountain Motel M
(403) 678-5756. **$60-$115, 3 days notice.** 250 1st Ave. On Trans-Canada Hwy 1; at Dead Man's Flats Service Centre. Ext corridors. **Pets:** Accepted.

EDMONTON METROPOLITAN AREA

EDMONTON

Alberta Place Suite Hotel A
(780) 423-1565. **$89-$109.** 10049 103rd St. Just s of Jasper Ave. Int corridors. **Pets:** Accepted.

Argyll Plaza Hotel M
(780) 438-5876. **$65-$99.** 9933 63rd Ave. 63rd Ave at 99th St. Int corridors. **Pets:** Accepted.

Chateau Louis Hotel & Conference Centre M
(780) 452-7770. **$99-$129, 3 days notice.** 11727 Kingsway. On Kingsway and 117th St. Int corridors. **Pets:** Accepted.

Comfort Inn M
(780) 484-4415. **$89-$109, 3 days notice.** 17610 100th Ave. At 176th St. Int corridors. **Pets:** Designated rooms, service with restrictions, supervision.

(CAA) ▼▼▼ **Crowne Plaza-Chateau Lacombe** H
(780) 428-6611. **$109-$149.** 10111 Bellamy Hill. At jct 101st St, MacDonald Dr and Bellamy Hill. Int corridors. **Pets:** Small. Crate.

▼▼▼ **Delta Edmonton Centre Suite Hotel** H
(780) 429-3900. **$104-$149.** 10222 102nd St. At 102nd St at 103rd Ave. Int corridors. **Pets:** Accepted.

(CAA) ▼▼▼ **Delta Edmonton South Hotel and Conference Centre** H
(780) 434-6415. **$119-$189.** 4404 Gateway Blvd. At jct Calgary Tr (Hwy 2) and Whitemud Dr. Int corridors. **Pets:** Small. Service with restrictions, supervision.

▼▼ **Edmonton House Suite Hotel** H
(780) 420-4000. **$99.** 10205 100th Ave. Just se of jct 102nd St and 100th Ave. Int corridors. **Pets:** Accepted.

▼▼▼▼ **The Fairmont Hotel Macdonald** H
(780) 424-5181. **$133-$183.** 10065 100th St. Just s of Jasper Ave. Int corridors. **Pets:** Accepted.

(CAA) ▼▼▼ **Holiday Inn Convention Centre** M
(780) 468-5400. **$109.** 4520 76th Ave. Hwy 14, just s via 50th St exit, then just e. Int corridors. **Pets:** Very small. $15 daily fee/pet. Designated rooms, service with restrictions, supervision.

(CAA) ▼▼▼▼ **Holiday Inn Express Hotel & Suites** M
(780) 483-4000. **$109-$149, 14 days notice.** 10017 179A St. On 100th Ave, just w of 178th St. Int corridors. **Pets:** Accepted.

(CAA) ▼▼▼▼ **Holiday Inn The Palace** M
(780) 438-1222. **$99-$102, 14 days notice.** 4235 Calgary Tr N. Just s of Whitemud Dr. Int corridors. **Pets:** Accepted.

(CAA) ▼▼▼▼ **The Mayfield Inn & Suites, Edmonton** H ❀
(780) 484-0821. **$109-$229.** 16615 109th Ave. 1.6 km n of jct Hwy 2 and 16A on Mayfield Rd. Int corridors. **Pets:** Medium. $15 daily fee/room. Service with restrictions, supervision.

▼▼▼▼ **Ramada Hotel and Conference Centre** M
(780) 454-5454. **$149, 3 days notice.** 11834 Kingsway. 4 km nw on Kingsway at 119th St. Int corridors. **Pets:** $10 daily fee/pet. Service with restrictions.

▼▼▼▼ **Sheraton Grande Edmonton Hotel** H
(780) 428-7111. **$244-$284.** 10235 101st St. 102nd Ave at 101st St. Int corridors. **Pets:** $10 daily fee/room. Designated rooms, service with restrictions, supervision.

(CAA) ▼▼▼▼ **Thornton Court Hotel** H
(780) 423-9999. **$129-$219.** One Thornton Ct. Just s of Jasper Ave at Thornton Ct and 99th St. Int corridors. **Pets:** Large. $10 daily fee/pet. Designated rooms, service with restrictions, supervision.

(CAA) ▼▼▼ **Travelodge Beverly Crest** M
(780) 474-0456. **$79-$89.** 3414 118th Ave. 8 km e of Capilano Dr, 1 km s from W Hwy 16 (Yellowhead Tr) on Victoria Tr exit. Int corridors. **Pets:** Accepted.

▼▼▼▼ **The Varscona Hotel** M ❀
(780) 434-6111. **$205-$305.** 8208 106 St. Corner of 86th Ave. Int corridors. **Pets:** Medium. $35 one-time fee/pet. Designated rooms, service with restrictions, supervision.

▼▼▼▼ **The Westin Edmonton** H
(780) 426-3636. **$145-$205.** 10135 100th St. 101 Ave at 100th St. Int corridors. **Pets:** Service with restrictions.

LEDUC

▼▼ **Edmonton International Airport-Super 8 Motel** M
(780) 986-8898. **$74.** 8004 Sparrow Crescent. Hwy 2, exit N Business Section, 32 km s. Int corridors. **Pets:** Medium. $10 daily fee/room. Designated rooms, service with restrictions, supervision.

NISKU

▼▼ **Days Inn and Conference Centre-Edmonton Airport** M
(780) 955-7744. **$109-$169, 7 days notice.** 1103 4th St. Hwy 2, exit Edmonton International Airport/Nisku Business Park (10th Ave), 0.5 km e. Int corridors. **Pets:** Accepted.

SHERWOOD PARK

(CAA) ▼▼▼ **First Canada Inns** M
(780) 464-1000. **$84-$94.** 26 Strathmoor Dr. Just sw of Hwy 16, just e Broadmoor Blvd. Int corridors. **Pets:** Other species. $150 deposit/room, $50 one-time fee/room. Designated rooms, crate.

(CAA) ▼▼▼ **Franklin's Inn** M
(780) 467-1234. **$75, 3 days notice.** 2016 Sherwood Dr. At Granada Blvd. Int corridors. **Pets:** Large. $100 deposit/room. Designated rooms, service with restrictions, supervision.

Ⓐ ▽▽▽▽ **Ramada Limited-Edmonton East/ Sherwood Park** Ⓜ
(780) 467-6727. **$99-$109.** 30 Broadway Blvd. Hwy 14, 1.5 km e on Baseline Rd, 0.4 km n on Broadmoor Rd; from Hwy 16, exit Broadmoor Rd, 2.5 km s. Int corridors. **Pets:** Other species. $10 daily fee/room. Designated rooms, service with restrictions, crate.
〔SAVE〕 ⓢ ⓧ ⓛᴹ 🛑 🖵

STONY PLAIN

▽▽▽▽ **Ramada Inn & Suites** Ⓜ
(780) 963-0222. **$83-$200.** 3301 43rd Ave. From Hwy 16A, 2 km e. Ext/int corridors. **Pets:** Medium. $100 deposit/room, $4 daily fee/pet. Designated rooms, service with restrictions.
〔ASK〕 ⓢ ⓧ 🛑 🖵 ⓘ 🐾

▽▽ ▽▽ **Stony Convention Inn** Ⓜ
(780) 963-3444. **$67-$73.** 4620 48th St. Hwy 16A, exit Stony Plain, 0.8 km s. Int corridors. **Pets:** Medium. $4 daily fee/pet. Designated rooms, service with restrictions.
〔ASK〕 ⓢ ⓧ 🛑 🖵 ⓘ

━━━━━━━━ ❖ **END METROPOLITAN AREA** ❖ ━━━━━━━━

EDSON

▽▽▽▽ **Best Western High Road Inn** Ⓜ
(780) 712-2378. **$100-$120.** 300 52nd St. Centre; on 2nd Ave. Int corridors. **Pets:** Accepted.
〔SAVE〕 ⓢ ⓧ 🛑 🖵 ⓘ 🐾

▽▽ ▽▽ **Super 8 Motel** Ⓜ
(780) 723-2500. **$79-$85.** 4300 2nd Ave. 1.1 km e on Hwy 16. Int corridors. **Pets:** $50 deposit/room, $10 one-time fee/ pet. Designated rooms, service with restrictions, crate.
〔ASK〕 ⓢ ⓧ 🛑 🖵

FORT MACLEOD

Ⓐ ▽▽ **Sunset Motel** Ⓜ
(403) 553-4448. **$46-$64.** 104 Hwy 3W. 1 km w on Hwy 2 and 3. Ext corridors. **Pets:** Accepted.
〔SAVE〕 ⓢ ⓧ 🛑 🖵

FORT MCMURRAY

▽▽ ▽▽ **Super 8 Motel** Ⓜ
(780) 799-8450. **$89.** 321 Sakitawaw Tr. Just w of Hwy 63, 5 km. Int corridors. **Pets:** $10 daily fee/pet. Service with restrictions, crate.
〔ASK〕 ⓢ ⓧ 🛑 ⓘ

GRANDE PRAIRIE

▽▽▽▽ **Best Western Grande Prairie Hotel & Suites** Ⓜ
(780) 402-2378. **$109.** 10745 117th Ave. Corner of SR/US 107 and 117 Ave. Int corridors. **Pets:** Medium, other species. $10 one-time fee/room. Service with restrictions, supervision.
〔SAVE〕 ⓢ ⓧ 🗷 🛑 🖵 🐾

▽▽▽▽ **Service Plus Inns and Suites** Ⓜ ❖
(780) 538-3900. **$90-$250.** 10810 107th A Ave. 2.2 km w on Hwy 2, just n; adjacent to casino. Int corridors. **Pets:** Medium. $10 one-time fee/room. Designated rooms, service with restrictions, supervision.
〔ASK〕 ⓢ ⓧ ⓛ 🛑 🖵 🐾

▽▽ **Stanford Inn** Ⓜ
(780) 539-5678. **$80-$85.** 11401 100th Ave. 2.8 km w on Hwy 2. Ext/int corridors. **Pets:** $5.35 daily fee/pet. Service with restrictions, supervision.
〔ASK〕 ⓢ ⓧ 🛑 🖵 ⓘ

HIGH RIVER

▽▽ ▽▽ **Heritage Inn** Ⓜ
(403) 652-3834. **$89-$92.** 1104 11 Ave SE. Hwy 2, exit 23, 2 km w. Int corridors. **Pets:** Accepted.
〔ASK〕 ⓢ ⓧ 🛑 🖵 ⓘ 🐾

HINTON

Ⓐ ▽▽▽▽ **Crestwood Hotel** Ⓜ
(780) 865-4001. **$74-$104.** 678 Carmichael Ln. 1 km w on Hwy 16. Int corridors. **Pets:** Small. $10 daily fee/room. Designated rooms, service with restrictions, supervision.
〔SAVE〕 ⓢ ⓧ 🛑 🖵 ⓘ 🐾

▽▽▽▽ **Ramada Limited & Suites** Ⓜ
(780) 865-2575. **Call for rates.** 500 Smith St. 6 km e on Hwy 16. Ext/int corridors. **Pets:** Other species. $10 daily fee/room. Service with restrictions, crate.
ⓧ 🛑 🖵 ⓘ

▽▽ ▽▽ **Super 8 Motel** Ⓜ
(780) 817-2228. **$74-$110.** 284 Smith St. 1.6 km e on Hwy 16. Int corridors. **Pets:** Accepted.
〔ASK〕 ⓢ ⓧ ⓛᴹ 🛑 🐾

JASPER

Ⓐ ▽▽ ▽▽ **Amethyst Lodge** Ⓜ
(780) 852-3394. **$84-$208.** 200 Connaught Dr. 0.5 km e. Ext/int corridors. **Pets:** Accepted.
〔SAVE〕 ⓢ ⓧ 🖵 ⓘ

▽▽▽▽ **The Fairmont Jasper Park Lodge** Ⓡ
(780) 852-3301. **$119-$543, 3 days notice.** Lodge Rd. 4.8 km ne via Hwy 16; 3.2 km se off hwy via Maligne Rd, follow signs for lodge. Ext corridors. **Pets:** Medium, other species. $30 daily fee/pet. Service with restrictions, supervision.
ⓧ ⓛ 🛑 🖵 ⓘ 🐾 🗷 🎖

▼▼ **Jasper Inn Alpine Resort** Ⓜ
(780) 852-4461. **$105-$413, 3 days notice.** 98 Geikie St. 1.2 km ne at Geikie and Bonhomme sts. Ext/int corridors. **Pets:** Accepted.
[A$K] [S🐾] [✕] [🛢] [�«] [¶] [➔] [🅰]

Ⓐ ▼▼ **Lobstick Lodge** Ⓜ
(780) 852-4431. **$102-$208.** 94 Geikie St. 1.2 km ne at Geikie and Juniper sts. Int corridors. **Pets:** Accepted.
[SAVE] [S🐾] [✕] [🛢] [�«] [¶] [🅰]

Ⓐ ▼▼ **Marmot Lodge** Ⓜ
(780) 852-4471. **$94-$189.** 86 Connaught Dr. 1.6 km ne. Ext corridors. **Pets:** Accepted.
[SAVE] [✕] [🛢] [�«] [¶] [➔]

▼▼ **Patricia Lake Bungalows** 🅲
(780) 852-3560. **$56-$225, 7 days notice.** Pyramid Lake Rd. 4.8 km nw via Pyramid Lake Rd. Ext corridors. **Pets:** Medium, dogs only. $10 daily fee/pet. Designated rooms, service with restrictions, supervision.
[✕] [🛢] [�«] [✕] [🅰] [🄯]

▼▼ **Sunwapta Falls Resort** Ⓜ
(780) 852-4852. **$99-$169.** Hwy 93. 55 km s on Icefields Pkwy (Hwy 93). Ext corridors. **Pets:** Small, dogs only. $20 daily fee/room. Supervision.
[✕] [🛢] [�«] [¶] [✕] [🅰] [🄯]

Ⓐ ▼ **Tekarra Lodge** 🅲
(780) 852-3058. **$75-$190, 7 days notice.** Hwy 93A. From jct Hwy 93 and 16, 1.4 km s on Hwy 93, 1.2 km ne. Ext/int corridors. **Pets:** Other species. $25 daily fee/room. Designated rooms, service with restrictions, supervision.
[SAVE] [S🐾] [✕] [🛢] [�«] [¶] [✕] [🅰] [🎬] [🄯]

KANANASKIS

Ⓐ ▼▼▼ **Delta Lodge at Kananaskis** 🆁 ❀
(403) 591-7711. **$109-$319, 3 days notice.** Kanasaskis Village. Trans-Canada Hwy 1, 23.5 km s on Hwy 40 (Kananaskis Tr), then 3 km on Kananaskis Village access road, follow signs. Int corridors. **Pets:** $100 one-time fee/room. Designated rooms, service with restrictions, supervision.
[SAVE] [✕] [📠] [�«] [¶] [✕]

Ⓐ ▼▼▼ **Kananaskis Mountain Lodge** Ⓜ
(403) 591-7500. **$140-$230.** Trans-Canada Hwy 1, 23.5 km s on Hwy 40 (Kananaskis Tr), then 3 km on Kananaskis Village access road follow signs. Int corridors. **Pets:** Dogs only. $15 daily fee/pet. Designated rooms, service with restrictions, supervision.
[SAVE] [S🐾] [✕] [🛢] [�«] [¶] [🅰]

LAKE LOUISE

▼▼▼▼ **The Fairmont Chateau Lake Louise** 🆁
(403) 522-3511. **$174-$549, 3 days notice.** 111 Lake Louise Dr. 3 km up the hill from the village. Int corridors. **Pets:** Accepted.
[A$K] [✕] [�«] [¶] [➔] [✕] [🅰]

▼▼ **Lake Louise Inn** Ⓜ
(403) 522-3791. **$149-$270, 7 days notice.** 210 Village Rd. Just w of 4-way stop. Ext/int corridors. **Pets:** Other species. Designated rooms, service with restrictions, crate.
[✕] [🛢] [�«] [¶] [➔]

LETHBRIDGE

▼▼ **Days Inn Lethbridge** Ⓜ
(403) 327-6000. **$79-$89.** 100 3rd Ave S. Centre; corner of 3rd Ave and Scenic Dr. Ext/int corridors. **Pets:** Accepted.
[SAVE] [S🐾] [✕] [🛢] [�«] [➔]

Ⓐ ▼▼ **Econo Lodge-Lethbridge** Ⓜ
(403) 328-5591. **$70-$75, 7 days notice.** 1124 Mayor Magrath Dr S. From Hwy 3, 4 or 5, exit Mayor Magrath Dr S. Ext corridors. **Pets:** Accepted.
[SAVE] [S🐾] [✕] [🛢] [�«]

Ⓐ ▼▼▼ **Lethbridge Lodge Hotel and Conference Center** Ⓜ
(403) 328-1123. **$119-$139.** 320 Scenic Dr. Centre; Scenic Dr at 4th Ave S. Int corridors. **Pets:** Accepted.
[SAVE] [S🐾] [✕] [🛢] [�«] [¶] [➔]

LLOYDMINSTER

▼▼ **Best Western Wayside Inn** Ⓜ
(780) 875-4404. **$91-$113.** 5411 44th St. 0.8 km w on Hwy 16 from jct Hwy 17. Int corridors. **Pets:** $5 daily fee/pet. Designated rooms, service with restrictions, supervision.
[SAVE] [S🐾] [✕] [🛢] [�«] [¶] [➔]

Ⓐ ▼▼ **Tropical Inn** Ⓜ
(780) 875-7000. **$69-$85.** 5621 44th St. Jct Hwy 17 and 16, 1 km w. Ext/int corridors. **Pets:** Designated rooms, service with restrictions, crate.
[SAVE] [S🐾] [✕] [🛢] [�«] [¶] [➔]

▼▼ **West Harvest Inn** Ⓜ
(780) 875-6113. **$96.** 5620 44th St. Jct Hwy 17 and 16, 1 km w. Ext/int corridors. **Pets:** Small. $5 daily fee/pet. Designated rooms, service with restrictions, supervision.
[A$K] [S🐾] [✕] [🛢] [�«] [¶] [➔]

MEDICINE HAT

▼▼▼ **Best Western Inn** Ⓜ
(403) 527-3700. **$99-$199.** 722 Redcliff Dr. On Trans-Canada Hwy 1; 0.4 km w of jct Hwy 3 access 7th St SW. Ext/int corridors. **Pets:** Medium. Designated rooms, service with restrictions, supervision.
[SAVE] [S🐾] [✕] [🄼] [🛢] [�«] [➔]

Ⓐ ▼▼ **Imperial Inn** Ⓜ
(403) 527-8811. **$58-$74.** 3282 13th Ave SE. 3.6 km se; opposite Southview Shopping Mall; just n off Trans-Canada Hwy 1. Ext/int corridors. **Pets:** Other species. $100 deposit/room, $5 daily fee/room. Designated rooms, service with restrictions, supervision.
[SAVE] [S🐾] [✕] [🛢] [�«] [¶] [➔]

▼▼▼ **Medicine Hat Lodge Hotel Casino & Convention Centre** 🄷
(403) 529-2222. **$114.** 1051 Ross Glen Dr SE. East end approach to city on Trans-Canada Hwy 1, at jct Dunmore Rd. Int corridors. **Pets:** Other species.
[ASK] [S🄳] [✕] [🔲] [🍴] [🏊]

▼ **Ranchmen Motel** 🄼
(403) 527-2263. **$42-$44.** 1617 Bomford Crescent SW. On Trans-Canada Hwy 1 at 16th St SW. Ext corridors. **Pets:** Small. Service with restrictions, supervision.
[✕] [🔒] [🔲]

▼▼ **Super 8 Motel** 🄼
(403) 528-8888. **$60-$95.** 1280 Trans Canada Way SE. Trans-Canada Way at 13th Ave SE; just n off Trans-Canada Hwy 1. Ext/int corridors. **Pets:** Small, other species. $5 daily fee/room. Designated rooms, service with restrictions, supervision.
[ASK] [S🄳] [✕] [🄼] [🔒] [🔲] [🏊]

🄐🄐 ▼▼▼ **Travelodge Hotel Medicine Hat** 🄼🄸
(403) 527-2275. **$91-$121.** 1100 Redcliff Dr SW. 2.8 km sw on Trans-Canada Hwy 1 at jct Hwy 3. Ext/int corridors. **Pets:** Accepted.
[SAVE] [✕] [🔒] [🔲] [🍴] [🏊]

PEACE RIVER

🄐🄐 ▼▼▼ **Traveller's Motor Hotel** 🄼🄸
(780) 624-3621. **$53-$89.** 9510 100th St. Just off Hwy 2 southbound, exit town center. Ext/int corridors. **Pets:** Other species. Designated rooms, service with restrictions.
[SAVE] [S🄳] [✕] [🄼] [🔒] [🔲] [🍴]

PINCHER CREEK

▼▼ **Heritage Inn** 🄼🄸
(403) 627-5000. **$85-$92.** 919 Waterton Ave (Hwy 6). Hwy 3, 4.7 km s on Hwy 6. Int corridors. **Pets:** Accepted.
[ASK] [S🄳] [✕] [🔒] [🔲] [🍴]

▼▼ **Super 8 Motel-Pincher Creek** 🄼
(403) 627-5671. **$65-$93.** 1307 Freebairn Ave. Hwy 3, 2.6 km s on Hwy 6. Int corridors. **Pets:** Accepted.
[ASK] [S🄳] [✕] [🔒]

RED DEER

🄐🄐 ▼▼▼ **Holiday Inn Express-Red Deer** 🄼
(403) 343-2112. **$99-$109.** 2803 50th Ave. 1.8 km e on Hwy 2A (Gaetz Ave). Int corridors. **Pets:** Small. $100 deposit/room. Designated rooms, service with restrictions, supervision.
[SAVE] [S🄳] [✕] [🔒] [🔲] [🏊]

🄐🄐 ▼▼▼ **Holiday Inn Red Deer** 🄼🄸
(403) 342-6567. **$109-$119, 7 days notice.** 6500 67th St. 3.2 km nw, 0.8 km e of Hwy 2, exit 67th St. Int corridors. **Pets:** Small. $15 daily fee/room. Designated rooms, supervision.
[SAVE] [S🄳] [✕] [🔒] [🔲] [🍴] [🏊]

🄐🄐 ▼▼▼ **Service Plus Inns and Suites** 🄼
(403) 342-4445. **$94.** 6853 66th St. 3.6 km nw, 0.5 km e of Hwy 2, exit 67th St. Int corridors. **Pets:** Small. Designated rooms, service with restrictions, supervision.
[SAVE] [S🄳] [✕] [🔒] [🔲] [🏊]

🄐🄐 ▼▼▼ **Travelodge Red Deer** 🄼🄸
(403) 346-2011. **$95-$130.** 2807 50th Ave. 1.8 km s on Hwy 2A (Gaetz Ave). Ext/int corridors. **Pets:** Accepted.
[SAVE] [S🄳] [✕] [🔒] [🔲] [🍴] [🏊]

ROCKY MOUNTAIN HOUSE

▼ **Chinook Inn** 🄼
(403) 845-2833. **Call for rates.** 5321 59th Ave. 1.3 km w on Hwy 11, then s. Int corridors. **Pets:** $10 daily fee/room. Designated rooms, supervision.
[✕] [🔒]

TABER

▼▼ **Heritage Inn** 🄼🄸
(403) 223-4424. **$85-$89.** 4830 46th Ave. 1 km e of jct Hwy 3 and 36 S, on Hwy 3. Int corridors. **Pets:** Small, other species. Designated rooms, service with restrictions, supervision.
[S🄳] [✕] [🔒] [🔲] [🍴]

VALLEYVIEW

▼ **Raven Motor Inn** 🄼
(780) 524-3383. **$68-$78, 3 days notice.** 4606 50th St. Jct Hwy 49 and 43. Ext corridors. **Pets:** Accepted.
[ASK] [S🄳] [✕] [🔒] [🔲] [🏊]

WATERTON PARK

🄐🄐 ▼▼▼ **Bayshore Inn** 🄼🄸
(403) 859-2211. **$99-$145.** 111 Waterton Ave. Centre. Ext corridors. **Pets:** Service with restrictions.
[SAVE] [✕] [🔒] [🔲] [🍴] [🅇]

🄐🄐 ▼▼▼▼ **Waterton Lakes Lodge** 🅁
(403) 859-2151. **$110-$210, 3 days notice.** 101 Clematis Ave. Centre. Ext/int corridors. **Pets:** Accepted.
[SAVE] [S🄳] [✕] [🄼] [🄲] [🔒] [🔲] [🍴] [🏊] [✂]

WETASKIWIN

▼▼ **Best Western Wayside Inn** 🄼🄸
(780) 352-6681. **$79-$89.** 4103 56 St. Just n of Hwy 13 W, on Hwy 2A. Int corridors. **Pets:** $100 deposit/room. Designated rooms, service with restrictions, supervision.
[SAVE] [S🄳] [✕] [🔲] [🍴]

▼▼ **Super 8 Motel** 🄼
(780) 361-3808. **$75-$85.** 3820 56th St. On Hwy 2A, just s of jct Hwy 13 W. Ext/int corridors. **Pets:** Small. $100 deposit/room. Designated rooms, service with restrictions, supervision.
[ASK] [S🄳] [✕] [🄼] [🔒]

WHITECOURT

🄐🄐 ▼▼▼ **Quality Inn** 🄼🄸
(780) 778-5477. **$79-$91.** 5420 47th Ave. On Hwy 43, 0.5 km e of Hwy 32. Int corridors. **Pets:** Other species. Designated rooms.
[SAVE] [S🄳] [✕] [🔒] [🔲] [🍴]

CITY INDEX

100 MILE HOUSE

▼▼ 100 Mile House Super 8 Ⓜ
(250) 395-8888. **$79-$88.** 989 Alder Ave. 1 km s on Hwy 97. Ext corridors. **Pets:** Accepted.
Ⓐ🆂🅗Ⓧ🅗🅘

▼▼ Ramada Limited Ⓜ
(250) 395-2777. **$89-$95.** 917 Alder Rd. 1 km s on Hwy 97. Int corridors. **Pets:** Medium. $5 daily fee/pet. Designated rooms, service with restrictions, supervision.
Ⓐ🆂🅗Ⓧ🅗🅘

▼▼ Red Coach Inn Ⓜ
(250) 395-2266. **$65-$91.** 170 Cariboo Hwy N. On Hwy 97, north end of town. Int/int corridors. **Pets:** Other species. $6 daily fee/room. Service with restrictions.
Ⓐ🆂🅗Ⓧ🅛Ⓜ🅘Ⓨ

108 MILE HOUSE

Ⓒ ▼▼▼ 108 Resort Best Western Ⓡ
(250) 791-5211. **$70-$160.** 4816 Telqua Dr. 1.6 km nw on signed access road; in 108 Recreational Ranch. Ext corridors. **Pets:** Accepted.
🆂Ⓥ🆂🅗Ⓧ🅛Ⓜ🅗🅘Ⓨ🆇

ABBOTSFORD

Ⓒ ▼▼▼ Holiday Inn Express Ⓜ
(604) 859-6211. **$69-$109.** 2073 Clearbrook Rd. Trans-Canada Hwy 1, exit 87 (Clearbrook Rd). Ext/int corridors. **Pets:** $10 daily fee/pet. Service with restrictions, supervision.
🆂Ⓥ🆂🅗Ⓧ🅛Ⓜ🅗🅘Ⓨ🆇

▼▼▼ Ramada Inn-Abbotsford Ⓜ
(604) 870-1050. **$89-$99.** 36035 N Parallel Rd. Trans-Canada Hwy 1, exit 95 (Whatcom Rd). Int corridors. **Pets:** Accepted.
Ⓐ🆂Ⓧ🅛Ⓜ🅘🅘Ⓨ🆇

Ⓒ ▼▼▼ Super 8 Motel Abbotsford Ⓜ
(604) 853-1141. **$78-$115.** 1881 Sumas Way. Trans-Canada Hwy 1, exit 92 (Town Centre), just n on Hwy 11. Ext corridors. **Pets:** Medium, other species. $10 daily fee/pet. Designated rooms, service with restrictions, supervision.
🆂Ⓥ🆂🅗Ⓧ🅗🅘

BARRIERE

Ⓒ ▼▼▼ Mountain Springs Motel Ⓜ
(250) 672-0090. **$45-$61.** 4253 Yellowhead Hwy. 1 km s on Hwy 5 (Yellowhead Hwy). Ext corridors. **Pets:** Medium, dogs only. $5 daily fee/pet. Designated rooms, no service, supervision.
🆂Ⓥ🆂🅗Ⓧ🅗🅘

BLUE RIVER

▼▼ Glacier Mountain Lodge Ⓜ
(250) 673-2393. **$62-$97.** 869 Shell Rd. On Hwy 5 (Yellowhead Hwy) at Shell Rd, follow signs. Int corridors. **Pets:** Other species. $5 daily fee/pet. Designated rooms, service with restrictions, supervision.
Ⓧ🅗

▼▼▼ Mike Wiegele Helicopter Skiing Ⓡ
(250) 673-8381. **$145-$395, 4 days notice.** 1 Harrwood Dr. On Hwy 5 (Yellowhead Hwy) at Harrwood Dr, follow signs. Ext corridors. **Pets:** Medium, dogs only. $15 daily fee/room. Designated rooms, service with restrictions, supervision.
Ⓐ🆂🅗Ⓧ🅗🅘Ⓨ🆇

CACHE CREEK

Bonaparte Motel M
(250) 457-9693. **$60-$90.** 1395 Hwy 97 N. 1 km n of jct Trans-Canada Hwy 1. Ext corridors. **Pets:** Other species. $10 daily fee/pet. No service, supervision.

Tumbleweed Motel M
(250) 457-6522. **Call for rates.** On Trans-Canada Hwy 1, just e of jct Hwy 97. Ext corridors. **Pets:** Accepted.

CAMPBELL RIVER

Best Western Austrian Chalet M
(250) 923-4231. **$89-$169.** 462 S Island Hwy. 3.2 km s on Hwy 19. Ext/int corridors. **Pets:** Medium, other species. $5 daily fee/pet. Designated rooms, service with restrictions, supervision.

Campbell River Lodge Fishing & Adventure Resort M
(250) 287-7446. **$60-$94, 3 days notice.** 1760 Island Hwy. On Island Hwy 19, 2 km nw of downtown; or just e from Hwy 19 and 28. Ext/int corridors. **Pets:** $8 daily fee/pet. Designated rooms, service with restrictions.

Campbell River Super 8 M
(250) 286-6622. **$66-$90.** 340 S Island Hwy. 3 km s on Hwy 19. Int corridors. **Pets:** Medium, dogs only. $6 daily fee/pet. Designated rooms, service with restrictions, supervision.

CHASE

Chase Country Inn Motel M
(250) 679-3333. **$59-$95, 3 days notice.** 576 Coburn St. Trans-Canada Hwy 1 and Coburn St. Ext corridors. **Pets:** Accepted.

Quaaout Lodge Resort L
(250) 679-3090. **$75-$180.** Trans-Canada Hwy 1, exit Squilax Bridge, 2.5 km w on Little Shuswap Rd. Int corridors. **Pets:** Accepted.

CHEMAINUS

Chemainus Fuller Lake Motel M
(250) 246-3282. **$55-$85.** 9300 Smiley Rd. On Trans-Canada Hwy 1 and Henry Rd. Ext corridors. **Pets:** Very small, dogs only. $15 daily fee/pet. Service with restrictions, supervision.

CHILLIWACK

Best Western Rainbow Country Inn MI
(604) 795-3828. **$94-$130.** 43971 Industrial Way. Trans-Canada Hwy 1, exit 116 (Lickman Rd). Int corridors. **Pets:** Accepted.

Chilliwack Travelodge MI
(604) 792-4240. **$70-$85.** 45466 Yale Rd W. Trans-Canada Hwy 1, exit 119B eastbound; exit 119A westbound, just n. Int corridors. **Pets:** Medium. $5 one-time fee/pet. Designated rooms, service with restrictions, supervision.

Comfort Inn M
(604) 858-0636. **$82-$106.** 45405 Luckakuck Way. Trans-Canada Hwy 1, exit 119A eastbound; exit 119B westbound, s on Vedder Rd, then 1 km w. Int corridors. **Pets:** Medium, other species. Service with restrictions, supervision.

Rhombus Hotels & Resorts-Downtown Chilliwack MI
(604) 795-4788. **$89-$160, 7 days notice.** 45920 First Ave. Trans-Canada Hwy 1, exit 119B eastbound; exit 119A westbound, 3 km n, then just w. Int corridors. **Pets:** Accepted.

CHRISTINA LAKE

New Horizon Motel M
(250) 447-9312. **$60-$106, 15 days notice.** 2037 Hwy 3. Just e. Ext corridors. **Pets:** Accepted.

CLEARWATER

Jasper Way Inn Motel on beautiful Dutch Lake M
(250) 674-3345. **$56-$84.** 57 E Old N Thompson Hwy. 1 km w on Old N Thompson Hwy, just off Hwy 5 (Yellowhead Hwy). Ext corridors. **Pets:** Accepted.

COURTENAY

Best Western Collingwood Inn MI
(250) 338-1464. **$98-$137.** 1675 Cliffe Ave. 1 km n on Cliffe Ave (Hwy 19A) from jct Island Hwy connector. Ext corridors. **Pets:** Small. $8 daily fee/pet. Designated rooms, crate.

The Coast Westerly Hotel MI
(250) 338-7741. **$85-$129.** 1590 Cliffe Ave. 1 km n on Cliffe Ave (Hwy 19A) from jct Island Hwy connector. Int corridors. **Pets:** $200 deposit/room, $10 daily fee/pet. Service with restrictions, supervision.

▼▼▼▼ Kingfisher Oceanside Resort & Spa Ⓜ
(250) 338-1323. **$119-$139, 7 days notice.** 4330 S Island
Hwy. 1 km s on Island Hwy 19A from Island Hwy Connector. Ext corridors. **Pets:** Other species. $100 deposit/room,
$7 daily fee/room. Designated rooms, service with restric-
tions.
Ⓐ🅂🅚 ⓧ 🅛🅜 🄱 🄿 🄿 🍴 🏊 🄭 🐾

Ⓐ ▼▼ Travelodge Courtenay Ⓜ
(250) 334-4491. **$76-$86, 7 days notice.** 2605 S Island
Hwy. 1.8 km s of downtown, on Island Hwy 19; adjacent
Driftwood Mall. Ext corridors. **Pets:** Other species. $50
deposit/room, $25 one-time fee/room. Designated rooms,
service with restrictions.
Ⓢ🄰🅅🄴 🅂🄭 ⓧ 🄱 🄿 🏊 🐾

CRANBROOK

▼▼ Heritage Inn Ⓜ
(250) 489-4301. **$89-$102.** 803 Cranbrook St N. Centre;
Hwy 3 and 95. Int corridors. **Pets:** Accepted.
Ⓐ🅂🅚 🅂🄭 ⓧ 🄱 🄿 🍴 🏊

Ⓐ ▼▼ Model A Inn Ⓜ 🐾
(250) 489-4600. **$80-$150.** 1908 Cranbrook St N. 2.5 km n
on Hwy 3 and 95. Ext corridors. **Pets:** Medium. $10 daily
fee/pet. Designated rooms, service with restrictions, supervision.
Ⓢ🄰🅅🄴 🅂🄭 ⓧ 🄱 🄿

Ⓐ ▼▼ Ponderosa Motel Ⓜ
(250) 426-6114. **$45-$65, 3 days notice.** 500 Van Horne St
S. 2.5 km w on Hwy 3. Ext corridors. **Pets:** Accepted.
Ⓢ🄰🅅🄴 🅂🄭 ⓧ 🄱 🄿

▼▼ Super 8 Motel Ⓜ
(250) 489-8028. **$97-$109.** 2370 Cranbrook St N. Just w of
jct Hwy 93 and 95, corner of 30th Ave. Int corridors.
Pets: Accepted.
Ⓐ🅂🅚 🅂🄭 ⓧ 🅛🅜 🄱

CRESTON

▼▼ Downtowner Motor Inn Ⓜ
(250) 428-2238. **$42-$58.** 1218 Canyon St. Corner of 12th
Ave N. Int corridors. **Pets:** $4 daily fee/pet.
ⓧ 🄱

Ⓐ ▼▼ Sunset Motel Ⓜ
(250) 428-2229. **$66-$69.** 2705 Canyon St, Hwy 3 E. 1 km
e on Hwy 3. Ext corridors. **Pets:** Accepted.
Ⓢ🄰🅅🄴 ⓧ 🄱 🄿 🏊

DAWSON CREEK

Ⓐ ▼▼▼ Dawson Creek Super 8 Ⓜ
(250) 782-8899. **$72-$84.** 1440 Alaska Ave. Just s of jct
Hart Hwy (97 S) and Alaska Hwy (97 N). Int corridors.
Pets: Other species. $10 daily fee/pet. Designated rooms,
service with restrictions, supervision.
Ⓢ🄰🅅🄴 🅂🄭 ⓧ 🄱 🄿

▼▼ Ramada Limited Ⓜ
(250) 782-8595. **Call for rates.** 1748 Alaska Ave. Jct Alaska
and Hart (97 N) hwys. Ext corridors. **Pets:** Accepted.
Ⓐ🅂🅚 ⓧ 🄱 🄿

DUNCAN

**Ⓐ ▼▼▼ Best Western Cowichan Valley
Inn** Ⓜ 🐾
(250) 748-2722. **$85-$125.** 6474 Trans-Canada Hwy 1. 3
km n. Int corridors. **Pets:** Large. Service with restrictions,
supervision.
Ⓢ🄰🅅🄴 🅂🄭 ⓧ 🄱 🄿 🍴 🏊

▼▼ Falcon Nest Motel Ⓜ
(250) 748-8188. **$50-$67.** 5867 Trans-Canada Hwy 1. 1.5
km n. Ext corridors. **Pets:** Small, dogs only. $7 daily fee/pet.
Designated rooms, service with restrictions, supervision.
🅂🄭 ⓧ 🄱 🄿 🏊

▼▼ Travelodge Silver Bridge Inn Duncan Ⓜ
(250) 748-4311. **$88-$104.** 140 Trans-Canada Hwy 1. Just
n of the Silver Bridge. Ext corridors. **Pets:** Other species.
$10 daily fee/pet. Designated rooms.
Ⓐ🅂🅚 🅂🄭 ⓧ 🄱 🄿 🍴

ENDERBY

Ⓐ ▼▼ Howard Johnson Fortunes Landing Ⓜ
(250) 838-6825. **$70-$80.** 1510 George St. 1 km n on Hwy
97A. Ext corridors. **Pets:** Small, other species. $5.75 daily
fee/pet. Designated rooms, service with restrictions, supervision.
Ⓢ🄰🅅🄴 🅂🄭 ⓧ 🄱 🄿 🍴 🏊

FERNIE

**Ⓐ ▼▼▼ Best Western Fernie Mountain
Lodge** Ⓜ
(250) 423-5500. **$109-$149.** 1622 7th Ave. I-3, exit 7th Ave,
on Hwy 3; east end of Fernie. Int corridors. **Pets:** Accepted.
Ⓢ🄰🅅🄴 🅂🄭 ⓧ 🄱 🄿 🍴 🏊

Ⓐ ▼▼▼ Park Place Lodge Ⓜ
(250) 423-6871. **$89-$219.** 742 Hwy 3. At 7th St. Int corridors. **Pets:** Accepted.
Ⓢ🄰🅅🄴 🅂🄭 ⓧ 🄱 🄿 🍴 🏊

▼▼ Super 8 Motel-Fernie Ⓜ
(250) 423-6788. **$82-$98, 7 days notice.** 2021 Hwy 3. 1.5
km w on Hwy 3. Int corridors. **Pets:** Accepted.
Ⓐ🅂🅚 🅂🄭 ⓧ 🄱

FIELD

▼▼ Kicking Horse Lodge Ⓛ
(250) 343-6303. **$66-$172, 7 days notice.** 100 Centre St.
Centre. Ext corridors. **Pets:** Small, other species. $10 daily
fee/pet. Service with restrictions, crate.
ⓧ 🄿 🍴 🄭 🐾 🆉

FORT ST. JOHN

Best Western Coachman Inn ☒
(250) 787-0651. **$79-$104.** 8540 Alaska Rd. 2 km s on Hwy 97. Int corridors. **Pets:** Small. $15 daily fee/room. Service with restrictions, supervision.

Quality Inn Northern Grand ☒
(250) 787-0521. **$119-$139, 30 days notice.** 9830 100th Ave. Centre. Int corridors. **Pets:** Other species. $12 one-time fee/pet. Designated rooms.

Ramada Limited ☒
(250) 787-0779. **$103-$119.** 10103 98 Ave. Centre; corner of 100th St. Int corridors. **Pets:** Accepted.

FORT STEELE

Bull River Guest Ranch ☒
(250) 429-3760. **$95-$120.** Hwy 95, 21.9 km se of Fort Steele on Fort Steele-Wardner Rd, 12 km ne on gravel road follow signs; Hwy 3 W, 41 km e of Cranbrook, use Fort Steele Rd. Ext corridors. **Pets:** Accepted.

GIBSONS

Cedars Inn ☒
(604) 886-3008. **$84.** 895 Sunshine Coast Hwy. Hwy 101 and Shaw Rd opposite Sunnycrest Mall; 6 km n from ferry terminal. Ext/int corridors. **Pets:** Accepted.

GOLDEN

Best Western Mountain View Inn ☒
(250) 344-2333. **$99-$189.** 1024 11th St N. On Trans-Canada Hwy 1 south service road; 0.7 km w of jct Hwy 95 and Trans-Canada Hwy 1. Int corridors. **Pets:** Medium, other species. $20 one-time fee/room. Designated rooms, service with restrictions, supervision.

Golden Rim Motor Inn ☒
(250) 344-2216. **$59-$104, 3 days notice.** 1416 Golden View Rd. 1.5 km e on Trans-Canada Hwy 1 from jct Hwy 95. Ext corridors. **Pets:** Accepted.

Hillside Lodge & Chalets ☒
(250) 344-7281. **$90-$125, 5 days notice.** 1740 Seward Frontage Rd. 15 km w on Trans-Canada Hwy 1, follow signs n of highway. Ext corridors. **Pets:** Accepted.

GRAND FORKS

Ramada Limited ☒
(250) 442-2127. **$69-$89.** 2729 Central Ave. West end of town on Hwy 3. Ext corridors. **Pets:** $10 daily fee/pet. Service with restrictions, supervision.

Western Traveller ☒
(250) 442-5566. **$59-$79.** 1591 Central Ave. West end of town on Hwy 3. Ext corridors. **Pets:** Medium, dogs only. $7 daily fee/pet. Designated rooms, supervision.

❧ GULF ISLANDS AREA

QUADRA ISLAND

Taku Resort ☒
(250) 285-3031. **$34-$228, 30 days notice.** 616 Taku Rd. Campbell River ferry terminal, 8 km n on West Rd, then just w on Heriot Bay Rd, follow signs to Heriot Bay. Ext corridors. **Pets:** $7 daily fee/pet. Designated rooms, service with restrictions, supervision.

SALTSPRING ISLAND

Harbour House ☒
(250) 537-5571. **$59-$139.** 121 Upper Ganges Rd. 1 km n on Lower Ganges Rd, then just e, towards Long Harbour Ferry Terminal. Ext/int corridors. **Pets:** Accepted.

Seabreeze Inne ☒ ❧
(250) 537-4145. **$69-$165, 7 days notice.** 101 Bittancourt Rd. From Ganges, 1 km s on Fulford-Ganges Rd. Ext corridors. **Pets:** Dogs only. $25 daily fee/pet. Designated rooms, service with restrictions, supervision.

SATURNA

Saturna Lodge & Restaurant ☒
(250) 539-2254. **$120-$195, 14 days notice.** 130 Payne Rd. From BC Ferry Terminal, just s on Narvaez Bay Rd, then just e, follow signs. Int corridors. **Pets:** Small. $15 daily fee/pet. Designated rooms, service with restrictions.

❧ END AREA ❧

HARRISON HOT SPRINGS

(AA) ▼▼▼▼ **Harrison Hot Springs Resort & Spa** X
(604) 796-2244. **$159-$284, 7 days notice.** 100 Esplanade Ave. Just w on lakefront. Int corridors. **Pets:** Large, other species. Designated rooms, service with restrictions, supervision.
[SAVE] [S🌀] [X] [📠] [💻] [🍴] [⊶] [⊠]

HOPE

(AA) ▼▼▼ **Alpine Motel** M
(604) 869-9931. **$64-$80.** 505 Old Hope-Princeton Way. Hwy 5, exit 173 westbound; exit 170 eastbound, just n from lights. Ext corridors. **Pets:** Accepted.
[SAVE] [S🌀] [X] [📠] [💻]

(AA) ▼▼▼ **Inn Towne Motel** M ❖
(604) 869-7276. **$50-$110.** 510 Trans-Canada Hwy. Hwy 5, exit 170, 1 km n to downtown; near the south end of the Fraser River Bridge. Ext corridors. **Pets:** Medium. $5 deposit/pet, $5 daily fee/pet. Service with restrictions, supervision.
[SAVE] [S🌀] [X] [📠] [⊶]

(AA) ▼▼▼▼ **Quality Inn** M
(604) 869-9951. **$70-$92.** 350 Old Hope Princeton Way. Hwy 5, exit 173 westbound; exit 170 eastbound, just n from lights. Int corridors. **Pets:** Medium. Service with restrictions, supervision.
[SAVE] [S🌀] [X] [⊾M] [📠] [💻] [⊶]

(AA) ▼▼ **Swiss Chalets** C
(604) 869-9020. **$65-$75, 3 days notice.** 456 Trans-Canada Hwy. Hwy 5, exit 170, 1 km n to downtown; near the south end of the Fraser River Bridge.. Ext corridors. **Pets:** Accepted.
[SAVE] [S🌀] [X] [📠]

INVERMERE

(AA) ▼▼▼▼ **Best Western Invermere Inn** MI
(250) 342-9246. **$110-$140, 3 days notice.** 1310 7th Ave. Centre; 3 km w of Hwy 93 and 95 at Invermere exit. Int corridors. **Pets:** Other species. $10 daily fee/pet. Service with restrictions, supervision.
[SAVE] [S🌀] [X] [📠] [💻] [🍴]

KAMLOOPS

(AA) ▼▼▼▼ **Accent Inns** M ❖
(250) 374-8877. **$94-$119.** 1325 Columbia St W. Trans-Canada Hwy 1, exit 369 eastbound, Columbia St at Notre Dame Dr; exit Summit Dr westbound, exit 370 at Notre Dame Dr. Ext corridors. **Pets:** Other species. Service with restrictions, supervision.
[SAVE] [S🌀] [X] [⊾M] [📠] [💻] [⊶]

(AA) ▼▼ **A Super View Motel** M
(250) 374-8100. **$65-$85.** 1200 Rogers Way. Trans-Canada Hwy 1, exit 368, just n. Ext corridors. **Pets:** Medium. $5 daily fee/pet. Designated rooms, service with restrictions, supervision.
[SAVE] [S🌀] [X] [📠] [💻] [⊶]

(AA) ▼ **Casa Marquis Motor Inn** M
(250) 372-7761. **$42-$59.** 530 Columbia St. Just n, corner of 5th Ave and Columbia St downtown; via City Centre. Ext corridors. **Pets:** Small, dogs only. Service with restrictions, supervision.
[SAVE] [X] [📠] [💻]

▼▼▼ **Courtesy Motel** M
(250) 372-8533. **$54-$77.** 1773 Trans-Canada Hwy E. 2.4 km e on Trans-Canada Hwy 1, south side of service access road. Ext corridors. **Pets:** Accepted.
[ASK] [S🌀] [X] [⊾M] [📠] [💻] [⊶]

▼▼▼ **Days Inn** MI ❖
(250) 374-5911. **$89-$109.** 1285 Trans-Canada Hwy W. Trans-Canada Hwy 1, exit 368, just s. Int corridors. **Pets:** Large. $10 daily fee/pet. Designated rooms, service with restrictions, supervision.
[SAVE] [X] [📠] [💻] [🍴]

(AA) ▼▼▼ **Econo Lodge** M
(250) 372-8235. **$51-$75.** 775 Columbia St W. Trans-Canada Hwy 1, exit 369 eastbound, 2 km n on Columbia St; exit 370 (Summit Dr) westbound to Columbia St, via City Centre right. Ext corridors. **Pets:** $10 one-time fee/room. Service with restrictions, supervision.
[SAVE] [S🌀] [X] [📠] [💻] [⊶] [𝒲]

(AA) ▼▼ **Fountain Motel** M
(250) 374-4451. **$46-$68, 3 days notice.** 506 Columbia St. Corner of 5th Ave and Columbia St downtown; via City Centre. Ext corridors. **Pets:** Accepted.
[SAVE] [S🌀] [X] [📠]

(AA) ▼▼▼ **Grandview Motel** M
(250) 372-1312. **$55-$89.** 463 Grandview Terr. Trans-Canada Hwy 1, exit 369 eastbound, 2 km n on Columbia St; exit 370 (Summit Dr) westbound, to Columbia St, via City Centre Rt. Ext corridors. **Pets:** Medium. $5 daily fee/pet. Designated rooms, service with restrictions, crate.
[SAVE] [S🌀] [X] [📠] [💻] [⊶]

(AA) ▼▼▼ **Hospitality Inn** MI
(250) 374-4164. **$67-$89.** 500 W Columbia St. Trans-Canada Hwy 1, exit 369 eastbound, 2 km n on Columbia St; exit 370 (Summit Dr) westbound, to Columbia St via City Centre Rt. Ext corridors. **Pets:** $10 daily fee/room. Designated rooms, service with restrictions, supervision.
[SAVE] [S🌀] [X] [📠] [💻] [🍴] [⊶]

(AA) ▼▼▼ **Kamloops Super 8 Motel** M
(250) 374-8688. **$50-$90.** 1521 Hugh Allan Dr. Trans-Canada Hwy 1, exit 367 Pacific Way. Int corridors. **Pets:** Other species. Service with restrictions, supervision.
[SAVE] [S🌀] [X] [⊾M]

▼▼▼ **Kamloops Travelodge** MI
(250) 372-8202. **$71-$105, 3 days notice.** 430 Columbia St. Corner of 4th Ave and Columbia St downtown. Ext corridors. **Pets:** Small. $5 daily fee/room. Designated rooms, service with restrictions, supervision.
[ASK] [S🌀] [X] [💻] [🍴] [⊶]

Ⓐ ▼▼ Ramada Inn-Kamloops Ⓜ
(250) 374-0358. **$69-$109, 5 days notice.** 555 W Columbia St. Trans-Canada Hwy 1, exit 369 eastbound, 2 km n on Columbia St; exit 370 (Summit Dr) westbound, to Columbia St via City Centre Rt. Ext/int corridors. **Pets:** Service with restrictions, supervision.
SAVE 🏊 ✕ 🛏 💻 🍽

▼▼ Ranchland Motel Ⓜ
(250) 828-8787. **$49-$63.** 2357 Trans-Canada Hwy E. 4.5 km e on Trans-Canada Hwy 1, exit River Rd, then just w along service access road. Ext corridors. **Pets:** Accepted.
ASK 🏊 ✕ 🛏 💻

Ⓐ ▼▼ Scott's Inn & Restaurant Ⓜ
(250) 372-8221. **$56-$70.** 551 11th Ave. Trans-Canada Hwy 1, exit 369 eastbound, 5 km n on Columbia St; exit City Centre westbound, 1.6 km s on Colombia St. Ext corridors. **Pets:** Service with restrictions, supervision.
SAVE 🏊 ✕ 🛏 💻 🍽 🏊

▼▼ The Thompson Hotel & Conference Centre Ⓜ
(250) 374-1999. **$74-$122.** 650 Victoria St. Trans-Canada Hwy 1, exit 369 eastbound, follow Columbia St to City Centre; exit 370 westbound, then just n on 6th Ave. Int corridors. **Pets:** Accepted.
ASK 🏊 ✕ 🛏 💻 🍽 🏊

Ⓐ ▼ Thriftlodge Ⓜ
(250) 374-2488. **$32-$54.** 2459 Trans-Canada Hwy E. 4.8 km e on Trans-Canada Hwy 1, just e of jct River Rd along service access road, follow signs. Ext corridors. **Pets:** Accepted.
SAVE ✕ 🏊

KELOWNA

Ⓐ ▼▼▼ Accent Inns Ⓜ 🐾
(250) 862-8888. **$94-$129.** 1140 Harvey Ave. Corner of Hwy 97 N and Gordon Dr. Ext corridors. **Pets:** Large. Designated rooms, service with restrictions, supervision.
SAVE 🏊 ✕ ♿ 🛏 💻 🍽 🏊

Ⓐ ▼▼▼ Best Western Inn-Kelowna Ⓜ 🐾
(250) 860-1212. **$109-$239.** 2402 Hwy 97 N. 1 km s of jct Hwy 33 and 97 N, corner of Leckie Rd. Ext/int corridors. **Pets:** Medium. $15 daily fee/pet. Designated rooms, service with restrictions.
SAVE 🏊 ✕ ♿ 🛏 💻 🍽 🏊

▼▼▼▼ The Grand Okanagan Lakefront Resort & Conference Center Ⓗ
(250) 763-4500. **$189-$299, 3 days notice.** 1310 Water St. Hwy 97 (Harvey Ave), 1 km w. Int corridors. **Pets:** Medium. $10 daily fee/pet. Designated rooms, service with restrictions, supervision.
ASK 🏊 ✕ ♿ 🛏 💻 🍽 🏊 ✕

▼ Safari Inn Ⓜ
(250) 860-8122. **$49-$95.** 1651 Powick Rd. Just s of Hwy 97 N and 33. Ext corridors. **Pets:** Accepted.
✕ 🛏 💻 🏊

▼▼ Super 8 Motel Ⓜ
(250) 762-8222. **$63-$95.** 2592 Hwy 97 N. 0.5 km n on Hwy 97 N from jct Hwy 33. Ext corridors. **Pets:** Accepted.
ASK 🏊 ✕ 🏊

▼ Town & Country Motel Ⓜ
(250) 860-7121. **$53-$110.** 2629 Hwy 97 N. 0.5 km n on Hwy 97 N, from jct Hwy 33. Ext corridors. **Pets:** Small. $5 daily fee/pet. Designated rooms, service with restrictions, supervision.
✕ ♿ 🛏 💻 🏊

LADYSMITH

▼ Seaview Marine Resort Ⓒ
(250) 245-3768. **$70-$75, 14 days notice.** 11111 Chemainus Rd. 2.5 km s on Trans-Canada Hwy 1, 3 km se. Ext corridors. **Pets:** Medium, dogs only. No service, supervision.
✕ 🛏 💻 🐾 🏊

LOGAN LAKE

▼ Logan Lake Lodge Ⓜ
(250) 523-9466. **$60-$65, 7 days notice.** 111 Chartrand Ave. Centre of Meadow Creek Rd and Chartrand Cresent. Int corridors. **Pets:** Other species. $10 daily fee/room. Designated rooms, supervision.
ASK 🏊 ✕ 💻 🍽 🐾

MADEIRA PARK

▼▼ Sunshine Coast Resort Ⓒ 🐾
(604) 883-9177. **$70-$120, 7 days notice.** 12695 Sunshine Coast (Hwy 101). Just n of Madeira Park Rd, follow signs. Int corridors. **Pets:** $10 daily fee/pet. Designated rooms, supervision.
✕ 🛏 💻 ✕ 🐾 🏊

MANNING PARK

▼▼ Manning Park Resort Ⓛ
(250) 840-8822. **$69-$159, 14 days notice.** Hwy 3. Crowsnest Hwy 3, midway between Hope and Princeton. Ext/int corridors. **Pets:** Other species. $5 daily fee/room. Designated rooms, service with restrictions.
🏊 ✕ 🛏 💻 🍽 ✕ 🐾

MCBRIDE

Ⓐ ▼▼ North Country Lodge Ⓜ
(250) 569-0001. **$58-$99.** 868 N Frontage Rd. Just w of village main exit, on Hwy 16, north service road. Ext corridors. **Pets:** Medium. $50 deposit/room, $5 daily fee/pet. Designated rooms, service with restrictions, supervision.
SAVE 🏊 ✕ 🛏 💻 🍽

MERRITT

Ⓐ ▼▼▼ Best Western Nicola Inn Ⓜ
(250) 378-4253. **$78-$108.** 4025 Walters St. Hwy 5, exit 290, 1 km w. Ext corridors. **Pets:** Accepted.
SAVE 🏊 ✕ 🛏 💻 🍽 🏊

ⓐ ♦♦ **Merritt Motor Inn** Ⓜ
(250) 378-9422. **$60-$75.** 3561 Voght St. Hwy 5, exit 290, just w. Ext corridors. **Pets:** Accepted.
[SAVE] [🛏] [✕] [🔒] [🍴] [⊃]

♦♦ **Merritt Travelodge** Ⓜ
(250) 378-8830. **$70-$170.** 3581 Vought St. Hwy 5, exit 290, then just w. Int corridors. **Pets:** Accepted.
[ASK] [🛏] [✕] [🔒] [💻] [🍴] [⊃]

NAKUSP

ⓐ ♦♦ **The Selkirk Inn** Ⓜ
(250) 265-3666. **$45-$69.** 210 W 6th Ave. Just n. Int corridors. **Pets:** Medium. $5 daily fee/pet. Designated rooms, service with restrictions, supervision.
[SAVE] [✕] [🔒] [💻]

NANAIMO

ⓐ ♦♦ **Best Western Northgate Inn** Ⓜ
(250) 390-2222. **$89-$129.** 6450 Metral Dr. Hwy 19A, just w on Aulds Rd, then just s. Int corridors. **Pets:** $10 daily fee/pet. Designated rooms, service with restrictions, supervision.
[SAVE] [🛏] [✕] [🔒] [💻] [🍴]

♦♦ **Harbourview Days Inn** Ⓜ
(250) 754-8171. **$79-$105.** 809 Island Hwy S. 2 km s on Island Hwy 1. Int corridors. **Pets:** $10 daily fee/room. Designated rooms, service with restrictions, supervision.
[SAVE] [🛏] [✕] [🔒] [💻] [🍴] [⊃]

ⓐ ♦♦♦♦ **Ramada Limited On Long Lake** Ⓜ
(250) 758-1144. **$109-$169.** 4700 Island Hwy N. 5 km n on Hwy 19A from Departure Bay ferry terminal. Ext corridors. **Pets:** Other species. $20 one-time fee/pet. Supervision.
[SAVE] [🛏] [✕] [🔒ᴹ] [🔒] [💻] [✕]

ⓐ ♦♦♦ **Travelodge Nanaimo** Ⓜ
(250) 754-6355. **$78-$101.** 96 Terminal Ave N. At jct Hwy 19A and 1, access from either highway. Int corridors. **Pets:** Medium. $10 one-time fee/pet. Designated rooms, service with restrictions, supervision.
[SAVE] [🛏] [✕] [🔒] [💻]

NANOOSE BAY

♦♦ **Fairwinds Schooner Cove Resort** Ⓜ
(250) 468-7691. **$94-$159.** 3521 Dolphin Dr. Island Hwy, 8.5 km se, follow signs, via Powderpoint Rd (becoming Fairwinds Dr). Int corridors. **Pets:** Medium. $10 daily fee/room. Designated rooms, service with restrictions, supervision.
[ASK] [🛏] [✕] [🔒ᴹ] [💻] [🍴] [⊃] [✕] [ℳ]

NARAMATA

ⓐ ♦♦ **The Village Motel** Ⓜ
(250) 496-5535. **$48-$98, 14 days notice.** 244 Robinson Dr. 14 km n on Naramata Rd from Penticton. Ext corridors. **Pets:** Accepted.
[SAVE] [🛏] [✕] [🔒] [💻] [ℳ] [℥]

NEW DENVER

♦♦ **Sweet Dreams Guesthouse & Dining** Ⓒ🌼
(250) 358-2415. **$75-$90, 7 days notice.** 702 Eldorado St. 0.4 km w of Hwy 6, on Slocan Ave; across street from lake. Int corridors. **Pets:** Dogs only. $5 daily fee/pet. Service with restrictions, crate.
[ASK] [🛏] [✕] [🍴] [ℳ] [𝒲] [℥]

OLIVER

♦ **Southwind Inn** Ⓜ
(250) 498-3442. **$69-$109.** 1.2 km s on Hwy 97. Int corridors. **Pets:** Accepted.
[✕] [🔒] [💻] [🍴]

PARKSVILLE

ⓐ ♦♦♦ **Best Western Bayside Inn** Ⓜ
(250) 248-8333. **$69-$179.** 240 Dogwood St. Island Hwy 19 N, exit Parksville, 8 km n on Hwy 19A. Int corridors. **Pets:** $15 daily fee/pet. Service with restrictions, supervision.
[SAVE] [🛏] [✕] [🔒ᴹ] [💻] [🍴] [⊃]

♦ **Skylite Motel** Ⓜ 🌼
(250) 248-4271. **$59-$119.** 459 E Island Hwy. Island Hwy 19, exit Parksville, 3.5 km n on Hwy 19A. Ext corridors. **Pets:** Other species. Service with restrictions, supervision.
[ASK] [🛏] [✕] [🔒] [ℳ]

ⓐ ♦♦♦♦ **Tigh Na Mara Resort Hotel & Conference Centre** ⓧ
(250) 248-2072. **$83-$275, 5 days notice.** 1095 E Island Hwy. Island Hwy 19, exit N Parksville, 2 km n on Hwy 19A. Ext corridors. **Pets:** Other species. $2 daily fee/pet. Designated rooms, service with restrictions, supervision.
[SAVE] [🛏] [✕] [🔒] [💻] [🍴] [⊃] [✕] [ℳ]

♦♦ **Travelodge Parksville** Ⓜ
(250) 248-2232. **$80-$169.** 424 W Island Hwy. Island Hwy 19 N, exit Parksville, 8 km n on Hwy 19A. Int corridors. **Pets:** Other species. $10 daily fee/pet. Designated rooms, service with restrictions, supervision.
[ASK] [🛏] [✕] [🔒ᴹ] [💻] [⊃]

ⓐ ♦♦ **V.I.P. Motel** Ⓜ 🌼
(250) 248-3244. **$69-$114.** 414 W Island Hwy. Island Hwy 19 N, exit Parksville, 6.5 km n on Hwy 19A. Ext corridors. **Pets:** Service with restrictions, supervision.
[SAVE] [🛏] [✕] [🔒] [💻] [ℳ]

PENTICTON

ⓐ ♦♦♦♦ **Best Western Inn at Penticton** Ⓜ
(250) 493-0311. **$89-$145.** 3180 Skaha Lake Rd. 4 km s. Ext corridors. **Pets:** Small. $10 daily fee/pet. Designated rooms, service with restrictions, supervision.
[SAVE] [🛏] [✕] [🔒] [💻] [🍴] [⊃]

Days Inn Penticton M
(250) 493-6616. **$70-$160, 7 days notice.** 152 Riverside Dr. Hwy 97, just n. Int corridors. **Pets:** Medium. $5 daily fee/pet. Designated rooms, service with restrictions, supervision.

Penticton Lakeside Resort, Convention Centre & Casino H
(250) 493-8221. **$145-$210.** 21 Lakeshore Dr W. Main St at Lakeshore Dr W. Int corridors. **Pets:** Other species. $20 one-time fee/room. Service with restrictions, supervision.

Penticton Slumber Lodge M
(250) 492-4008. **$78-$130, 7 days notice.** 274 Lakeshore Dr W. Hwy 97, n on Riverside Dr, 1.5 km e. Ext corridors. **Pets:** Small, dogs only. $10 one-time fee/pet. Designated rooms, service with restrictions, supervision.

Spanish Villa Resort M
(250) 492-2922. **$58-$250, 7 days notice.** 890 Lakeshore Dr W. Corner of Power St and Lakeshore Dr W. Ext corridors. **Pets:** Other species. $10 daily fee/pet. Designated rooms, service with restrictions, supervision.

Waterfront Inn M
(250) 492-8228. **$50-$125, 30 days notice.** 3688 Parkview St. Hwy 97 to Channel Pkwy and Skaha Lake Rd, then just ne to Lee Ave, just s; adjacent to Skaha Park. Ext corridors. **Pets:** Medium, other species. $3 daily fee/pet. Designated rooms, service with restrictions, supervision.

PORT ALBERNI

Best Western Barclay Hotel M
(250) 724-7171. **$89-$139.** 4277 Stamp Ave. Just s on Gertrude St from Johnston Rd (Hwy 4). Int corridors. **Pets:** Small, other species. $20 one-time fee/room. Designated rooms, service with restrictions, supervision.

Coast Hospitality Inn M
(250) 723-8111. **$145, 3 days notice.** 3835 Redford St. 3.2 km sw of jct Hwy 4 via City Centre/Port Alberni South Rt. Int corridors. **Pets:** $10 daily fee/room. Designated rooms, service with restrictions, supervision.

Timberlodge & RV Campground M
(250) 723-9415. **$60-$90.** 5 km e on Hwy 4; at jct City Centre/Port Alberni South Rt. Ext corridors. **Pets:** $10 one-time fee/pet. Service with restrictions, supervision.

PORT HARDY

Airport Inn M
(250) 949-9434. **$75-$125.** 4030 Byng Rd. Hwy 19, 5 km ne, follow signs. Int corridors. **Pets:** Other species. Supervision.

Glen Lyon Inn M
(250) 949-7115. **$75-$120, 3 days notice.** 6435 Hardy Bay Rd. Hwy 19, 1.5 km n. Ext corridors. **Pets:** Accepted.

PRINCE GEORGE

Connaught Motor Inn M
(250) 562-4441. **$64-$91.** 1550 Victoria St. Corner of Victoria (Hwy 16) and Patricia Blvd, south end of downtown core. Ext corridors. **Pets:** Other species. $5 daily fee/pet. Designated rooms, service with restrictions, supervision.

PRINCE RUPERT

Aleeda Motel M
(250) 627-1367. **$48-$76.** 900 3rd Ave W. Corner of 3rd Ave W and 8th St. Int corridors. **Pets:** Service with restrictions, supervision.

PRINCETON

Best Western Princeton Inn M
(250) 295-3537. **$69-$139.** 169 Hwy 3. On Hwy 3. Ext corridors. **Pets:** Very small. $10 daily fee/pet. Service with restrictions, supervision.

QUESNEL

Talisman Inn M
(250) 992-7247. **$65-$81.** 753 Front St. 1 km n of Carson Ave, on Hwy 97. Int corridors. **Pets:** Designated rooms, service with restrictions, supervision.

RADIUM HOT SPRINGS

Cedar Motel M
(250) 347-9463. **$41-$72.** 7593 Main St W. Off Hwy 93 and 95, just s of jct Hwy 93, on service road (Main St). Ext corridors. **Pets:** Medium. $5 daily fee/pet. Designated rooms, service with restrictions, supervision.

Chalet Europe M
(250) 347-9305. **$69-$139, 7 days notice.** 5063 Madsen Rd. Just e of jct Hwy 93 and 95, 1 km off Hwy 93 up the hill. Ext corridors. **Pets:** Dogs only. $10 daily fee/room. Designated rooms, supervision.

Lido Motel M
(250) 347-9533. **$59-$275.** 4876 McKay St. Hwy 93 and 95 S, Stanley St w to Main St W, then s. Ext corridors. **Pets:** Other species. $20 deposit/room. Service with restrictions, supervision.

▼▼▼ **Sunrise Suites Motel** 🄰
(250) 347-0008. **$65-$135.** 7371 Prospective Ave. From jct Hwy 93/95, 0.7 km n on Hwy 95, just sw. Ext corridors. **Pets:** Accepted.

(ASK) [S🗲] [✕] [🛏] [💻] [🐾]

▼▼▼ **Sunset Motel** 🄼 🐾
(250) 347-9863. **$46-$70.** 4883 McKay St. Hwy 93 and 95 S, w to service road (Main St) and just s. Ext corridors. **Pets:** Other species.

(ASK) [S🗲] [✕] [🛏] [💻] [⊞]

REVELSTOKE

(CAA) ▼▼▼ **Best Western Wayside Inn** 🄼🄸
(250) 837-6161. **$89-$149.** 1901 LaForme Blvd. North side of Trans-Canada Hwy 1, at intersection nearest east end of Columbia River Bridge. Ext/int corridors. **Pets:** Other species. Designated rooms, service with restrictions, crate.

(SAVE) [S🗲] [✕] [🖦M] [🛏] [💻] [🍽] [➴]

(CAA) ▼▼▼ **The Coast Hillcrest Resort Hotel** 🄷 🐾
(250) 837-3322. **$95-$145.** 2100 Oak Dr. 4.3 km e on Trans-Canada Hwy 1, 0.9 km sw. Int corridors. **Pets:** Other species. $15 one-time fee/room. Designated rooms, service with restrictions, supervision.

(SAVE) [S🗲] [✕] [🛏] [💻] [🍽]

(CAA) ▼▼▼▼ **The Regent Inn** 🄼🄸
(250) 837-2107. **$99-$159.** 112 1st St E. 2 km s from Trans-Canada Hwy 1; at Victoria Rd in historic downtown adjacent to Grizzly Plaza. Int corridors. **Pets:** Accepted.

(SAVE) [S🗲] [✕] [🍽]

(CAA) ▼▼ **Swiss Chalet Motel** 🄼
(250) 837-4650. **$43-$77.** 1101 Victoria Rd. 0.9 km s from Trans-Canada Hwy 1. Ext/int corridors. **Pets:** Accepted.

(SAVE) [✕] [🛏] [💻] [🍽]

ROSSLAND

(CAA) ▼▼ **Thriftlodge-Swiss Alps Inn** 🄼🄸
(250) 362-7364. **$59-$89, 30 days notice.** 1199 Nancy Green Hwy. 1 km w on Hwy 3B, at jct of Hwy 22. Ext corridors. **Pets:** Other species. $5 daily fee/room. Designated rooms, service with restrictions, supervision.

(SAVE) [S🗲] [✕] [🛏] [🍽]

SALMON ARM

▼▼▼ **Super 8 Motel** 🄼
(250) 832-8812. **$-$82.** 2901 10th Ave NE. 1 km e on Trans-Canada Hwy 1. Int corridors. **Pets:** Accepted.

(ASK) [S🗲] [✕] [🖦M]

(CAA) ▼▼ **Travelodge-Salmon Arm** 🄼
(250) 832-9721. **$65-$85.** 2401 Trans-Canada Hwy W. 3 km w on Trans-Canada Hwy 1. Ext corridors. **Pets:** Medium. $5 daily fee/pet. Service with restrictions, crate.

(SAVE) [✕] [🖦M] [🖦] [🛏] [💻] [➴]

SICAMOUS

▼▼ **Sicamous Super 8 Motel** 🄼
(250) 836-4988. **$72-$110.** 1122 Riverside Ave. Trans-Canada Hwy 1, s on Hwy 97A, then just w on Main St to traffic circle, then just s. Ext corridors. **Pets:** Other species. Service with restrictions, supervision.

[S🗲] [✕] [🖦M] [🛏]

SILVERTON

▼▼ **William Hunter Cabins** 🄲
(250) 358-2844. **$75-$98, 10 days notice.** 303 Lake Ave. Centre. Ext corridors. **Pets:** Accepted.

[S🗲] [✕] [🛏] [💻] [⊠] [🐾]

SMITHERS

(CAA) ▼▼ **Aspen Motor Inn** 🄼🄸
(250) 847-4551. **$74-$85.** 4628 Yellowhead Hwy. 1.5 km w on Hwy 16. Ext corridors. **Pets:** Small. $5 daily fee/pet. Designated rooms, service with restrictions, supervision.

(SAVE) [S🗲] [✕] [🛏] [💻] [🍽] [➴]

SUMMERLAND

▼▼ **Summerland Motel** 🄼 🐾
(250) 494-4444. **$49-$99, 10 days notice.** 2107 Tait St. 5 km s on Hwy 97. Ext corridors. **Pets:** Small, dogs only. $10 daily fee/pet. Supervision.

(ASK) [S🗲] [✕] [🛏] [➴]

TERRACE

(CAA) ▼▼▼ **Best Western Terrace Inn and Conference Centre** 🄼🄸
(250) 635-0083. **$79-$114.** 4553 Greig Ave. Hwy 16, just e on Greig Ave, follow City Centre signs. Int corridors. **Pets:** $10 daily fee/pet. Designated rooms, service with restrictions, supervision.

(SAVE) [✕] [💻] [🍽]

(CAA) ▼▼▼ **Coast Inn of the West** 🄼🄸
(250) 638-8141. **$85-$115.** 4620 Lakelse Ave. Hwy 16 to City Centre, 0.5 km e to Emerson, just n. Int corridors. **Pets:** Medium, other species. Designated rooms, service with restrictions, supervision.

(SAVE) [✕] [💻] [🍽]

TOFINO

(CAA) ▼▼▼▼ **Wickaninnish Inn** 🄻 🐾
(250) 725-3100. **$210-$480, 7 days notice.** Osprey Ln at Chesterman Bch. 4.3 km e on Hwy 4. Int corridors. **Pets:** $20 daily fee/pet. Designated rooms, service with restrictions, crate.

(SAVE) [✕] [🖦M] [💻] [🍽] [🐾]

VALEMOUNT

▼▼ **The Canadian Lodge** 🄼
(250) 566-6222. **$99-$130.** 1501 5th Ave. Just e of Hwy 5 (Yellowhead). Ext corridors. **Pets:** Medium, other species. $10 one-time fee/pet. Designated rooms, service with restrictions, supervision.

(ASK) [S🗲] [✕] [🛏] [💻] [➴]

Vancouver Metropolitan Area

BURNABY

Ⓐ ▼▼▼▼ Accent Inns Ⓜ
(604) 473-5000. **$109-$119.** 3777 Henning Dr. Trans-Canada Hwy 1, exit 28 (Grandview Hwy), just n on Boundary Rd. Ext corridors. **Pets:** Very small, dogs only. Designated rooms, service with restrictions, supervision.
⟦SAVE⟧ ⟦S🐾⟧ ⟦✕⟧ ⟦&M⟧ ⟦⟧ ⟦█⟧ ⟦▣⟧ ⟦¶⟧

Ⓐ ▼▼▼ Best Western Kings Inn and Conference Centre Ⓜ
(604) 438-1383. **$86-$153.** 5411 Kingsway. Trans-Canada Hwy 1, exit Willingdon Ave S, 5 km e. Ext corridors. **Pets:** Other species. $10 daily fee/pet. Designated rooms, service with restrictions, supervision.
⟦SAVE⟧ ⟦S🐾⟧ ⟦✕⟧ ⟦█⟧ ⟦▣⟧ ⟦¶⟧ ⟦➴⟧

Ⓐ ▼▼▼▼ Hilton Vancouver Metrotown Ⓗ ❀
(604) 438-1200. **$130-$149.** 6083 McKay Ave. Kingsway at Willingdon Ave. Int corridors. **Pets:** Small. $75 one-time fee/room. Designated rooms, service with restrictions, supervision.
⟦SAVE⟧ ⟦S🐾⟧ ⟦✕⟧ ⟦&M⟧ ⟦⌖⟧ ⟦█⟧ ⟦▣⟧ ⟦¶⟧ ⟦➴⟧

▼▼▼ Lake City Motor Inn Ⓜ
(604) 294-5331. **$79-$104.** 5415 Lougheed Hwy. Boundary Rd, 3 km e on Lougheed Hwy at Holdom Ave, entrance on north side of highway. Ext corridors. **Pets:** Accepted.
⟦✕⟧ ⟦█⟧ ⟦➴⟧

COQUITLAM

Ⓐ ▼▼▼▼ Holiday Inn Coquitlam/Vancouver Ⓜ
(604) 931-4433. **$89-$159.** 631 Lougheed Hwy. E on Trans-Canada Hwy 1, exit 37 (Gaglardi Way), 3.5 km e on Lougheed Hwy (Hwy 7); west on Trans-Canada Hwy 1, exit 44 (Coquitlam), then 3 km w on Lougheed Hwy (Hwy 7). Ext/int corridors. **Pets:** Medium. $30 one-time fee/room. Designated rooms, service with restrictions, supervision.
⟦SAVE⟧ ⟦S🐾⟧ ⟦✕⟧ ⟦&M⟧ ⟦█⟧ ⟦▣⟧ ⟦¶⟧ ⟦➴⟧

DELTA

Ⓐ ▼▼▼ Best Western Tsawwassen Inn Ⓜ ❀
(604) 943-8221. **$89-$119.** 1665 56th St. Hwy 99, exit 28 Tsawwassen Ferries, then 8 km w on Hwy 17; only 5 km from the Island Ferry Terminal. Int corridors. **Pets:** $10 daily fee/room. Service with restrictions, supervision.
⟦SAVE⟧ ⟦S🐾⟧ ⟦✕⟧ ⟦&M⟧ ⟦█⟧ ⟦▣⟧ ⟦¶⟧ ⟦➴⟧

Ⓐ ▼▼▼▼ Delta Town & Country Inn Ⓜ
(604) 946-4404. **$89-$145, 7 days notice.** 6005 Hwy 17 at Hwy 99. Hwy 99 at jct Hwy 17, exit 28 Tsawwassen Ferries, 12 km ne on Hwy 17 of Tsawwassen-Victoria Ferry terminal. Int corridors. **Pets:** Small, dogs only. $15 daily fee/pet. Designated rooms, service with restrictions, supervision.
⟦SAVE⟧ ⟦S🐾⟧ ⟦✕⟧ ⟦▣⟧ ⟦¶⟧ ⟦➴⟧ ⟦✕⟧

▼▼▼ River Run Cottages ⒷⒷ
(604) 946-7778. **$125-$210, 21 days notice.** 4551 River Rd W. From Hwy 17, 2.5 km n on Ladner Trunk Rd which becomes 47A St and then becomes River Rd W; in Ladner Village. Ext corridors. **Pets:** Dogs only. $20 daily fee/pet. Designated rooms, supervision.
⟦ASK⟧ ⟦✕⟧ ⟦█⟧ ⟦▣⟧ ⟦✗⟧ ⟦➶⟧

LANGLEY

Ⓐ ▼ Best Value Westward Inn Ⓜ
(604) 534-9238. **$56-$72.** 19650 Fraser Hwy. Trans-Canada Hwy 1, exit 58 (200th St/Langley City), 5 km s on 200th St, 1 km w on Hwy 10, then just w. Ext corridors. **Pets:** Other species. $4 one-time fee/room. Service with restrictions, supervision.
⟦SAVE⟧ ⟦S🐾⟧ ⟦✕⟧ ⟦█⟧

Ⓐ ▼▼▼▼ Holiday Inn Express Hotel & Suites Ⓜ
(604) 882-2000. **$121-$131.** 8750 204th St. Trans-Canada Hwy 1, exit 58 (200th St/Langley City), 1 km e on 200th St. Int corridors. **Pets:** Small. $10 daily fee/pet. Designated rooms, service with restrictions, crate.
⟦SAVE⟧ ⟦S🐾⟧ ⟦✕⟧ ⟦&M⟧ ⟦⌖⟧ ⟦█⟧ ⟦▣⟧ ⟦➴⟧

Ⓐ ▼▼ Travelodge-Langley City Ⓜ
(604) 533-4431. **$76-$89.** 21653 Fraser Hwy. Trans-Canada Hwy 1, exit 58 (200th St/Langley City), 5 km s, 2.5 km e on Hwy 10, then 1.5 km e. Ext corridors. **Pets:** Medium, dogs only. $50 deposit/room, $10 daily fee/pet. Designated rooms, service with restrictions, crate.
⟦SAVE⟧ ⟦S🐾⟧ ⟦✕⟧ ⟦█⟧ ⟦▣⟧

MISSION

Ⓐ ▼▼▼ Best Western Mission City Lodge Ⓜ
(604) 820-5500. **$79-$106, 7 days notice.** 32281 Lougheed Hwy. Just w of Hwy 11, corner of Lougheed Hwy (Hwy 7) and Hurd St. Int corridors. **Pets:** Small. $10 daily fee/pet. Designated rooms, supervision.
⟦SAVE⟧ ⟦S🐾⟧ ⟦✕⟧ ⟦&M⟧ ⟦⌖⟧ ⟦█⟧ ⟦▣⟧ ⟦¶⟧ ⟦➴⟧

NORTH VANCOUVER

Ⓐ ▼▼▼ Holiday Inn Hotel & Suites North Vancouver Ⓜ ❀
(604) 985-3111. **$99-$179.** 700 Old Lillooet Rd. Trans-Canada Hwy 1, exit 22 (Mt Seymoor Pkwy), follow signs. Int corridors. **Pets:** Medium, dogs only. $25 daily fee/room. Designated rooms, service with restrictions, supervision.
⟦SAVE⟧ ⟦S🐾⟧ ⟦✕⟧ ⟦&M⟧ ⟦█⟧ ⟦▣⟧ ⟦¶⟧ ⟦➴⟧

RICHMOND

Ⓐ ▼▼▼▼ Accent Inns Ⓜ
(604) 273-3311. **$99-$119.** 10551 St Edwards Dr. Hwy 99 N, exit 39 (Bridgeport/Airport) to St Edwards Dr; Hwy 99 S, exit 39A (Richmond/Airport). Ext corridors. **Pets:** Small, other species. Designated rooms, service with restrictions.
⟦SAVE⟧ ⟦S🐾⟧ ⟦✕⟧ ⟦&M⟧ ⟦█⟧ ⟦▣⟧ ⟦¶⟧

▼▼ ▼▼ Best Western Richmond Inn Hotel & Convention Center Ⓜ
(604) 273-7878. **$89-$129.** 7551 Westminster Hwy. Corner of Minoru Rd and Westminster Hwy. Int corridors. **Pets:** Other species. Service with restrictions, supervision.
[SAVE] [S/D] [✕] [&M] [🛏] [💻] [🍴] [🚗]

ⓒ ▼▼ ▼▼ Comfort Inn-Airport Ⓜ
(604) 278-5161. **$79-$129.** 3031 #3 Rd & Sea Island Way. Hwy 99 N, exit 39 (Bridgeport/Airport); from Hwy 99 S, exit Bridgeport Rd to airport. Int corridors. **Pets:** Accepted.
[SAVE] [S/D] [✕] [💻] [🍴] [🚗]

ⓒ ▼▼ ▼▼ Delta Pacific Resort and Conference Centre Ⓗ
(604) 278-9611. **$99-$129.** 10251 St. Edwards Dr. From Vancouver; Hwy 99, exit 39A (Richmond/Airport) southbound; exit 39 (Bridgeport/Airport) northbound. Int corridors. **Pets:** Large, other species. $25 one-time fee/pet. Service with restrictions, supervision.
[SAVE] [S/D] [✕] [&M] [🐾] [🛏] [💻] [🍴] [🚗] [✕]

ⓒ ▼▼ ▼▼ Delta Vancouver Airport Ⓗ 🐾
(604) 278-1241. **$99-$129.** 3500 Cessna Dr. Corner of Russ Baker Way and Cessna Rd; near the Moray Bridge. Int corridors. **Pets:** Other species. Designated rooms, service with restrictions, supervision.
[SAVE] [✕] [💻] [🍴] [🚗] [✕]

▼▼▼ ▼▼▼ The Fairmont Vancouver Airport Ⓗ 🐾
(604) 207-5200. **$143-$159.** 3111 Grant McCamanhie Way. In Vancouver International Airport. Int corridors. **Pets:** Other species. $25 daily fee/room. Designated rooms, service with restrictions, supervision.
[ASK] [S/D] [✕] [&M] [🗝] [💻] [🍴] [🚗]

ⓒ ▼▼▼ ▼▼▼ Vancouver Airport Marriott Ⓗ
(604) 276-2112. **$149-$169.** 7571 Westminster Hwy. Corner of Minoru Rd and Westminster Hwy. Int corridors. **Pets:** Small, other species. $30 one-time fee/room. Service with restrictions.
[SAVE] [S/D] [✕] [&M] [🛏] [💻] [🍴] [🚗]

SURREY

ⓒ ▼▼ ▼▼ Days Hotel-Vancouver Surrey Ⓜ
(604) 588-9511. **$90-$122.** 9850 King George Hwy. Jct Fraser Hwy (1A) and 99A (King George Hwy). Int corridors. **Pets:** Other species. $10 daily fee/room. Designated rooms, service with restrictions, crate.
[SAVE] [S/D] [✕] [🛏] [💻] [🍴] [🚗]

▼▼▼ ▼▼▼ Ramada Limited Surrey-Langley Ⓜ 🐾
(604) 576-8388. **$79-$110.** 19225 Hwy 10. Trans-Canada Hwy 1, exit 58, 5 km s on 200th St, then 2 km w; corner of 192nd St and Hwy 10.. Int corridors. **Pets:** $10 daily fee/pet. Designated rooms, crate.
[ASK] [S/D] [✕] [&M] [🗝] [🛏] [💻] [🍴] [🚗]

ⓒ ▼▼ ▼▼ Sheraton Guildford Hotel Surrey Ⓗ
(604) 582-9288. **$99-$209.** 15269 104th Ave. Trans-Canada Hwy 1 E, exit 48, 1 km s on 152 St, then just e; Trans-Canada Hwy 1 W, exit 50, then just w. Int corridors. **Pets:** Medium, dogs only. $50 one-time fee/pet. Designated rooms, service with restrictions, supervision.
[SAVE] [S/D] [✕] [💻] [🍴] [🚗]

VANCOUVER

▼▼ ▼▼ 2400 Motel Ⓜ
(604) 434-2464. **$55-$125.** 2400 Kingsway. 7.2 km se on Hwy 1A and 99A (Kingsway). Ext corridors. **Pets:** $5 daily fee/pet. Designated rooms, service with restrictions, supervision.
[✕] [🛏] [🅰]

ⓒ ▼▼ ▼▼ Best Western Sands by the Sea Ⓜ 🐾
(604) 682-1831. **$119-$239.** 1755 Davie St. Between Bidwell and Denman sts. Int corridors. **Pets:** Medium, dogs only. $10 daily fee/room. Supervision.
[SAVE] [S/D] [✕] [💻] [🍴]

ⓒ ▼▼ ▼▼ Bosman's Hotel Ⓜ
(604) 682-3171. **$79-$129.** 1060 Howe St. Between Nelson and Helmecken sts. Int corridors. **Pets:** Other species. Service with restrictions.
[SAVE] [S/D] [✕] [🍴] [🚗]

▼▼▼ ▼▼▼ Crowne Plaza Hotel Georgia Ⓗ
(604) 682-5566. **$199-$399.** 801 W Georgia St. Between Howe and Hornby sts. Int corridors. **Pets:** Medium, other species. $500 deposit/room. Service with restrictions.
[ASK] [S/D] [✕] [&M] [🛏] [💻] [🍴]

ⓒ ▼▼▼ ▼▼▼ Delta Pinnacle Ⓗ 🐾
(604) 684-1128. **$159-$219.** 1128 W Hastings St. Between Thurlow and Bute sts. Int corridors. **Pets:** Medium, other species. Service with restrictions, crate.
[SAVE] [S/D] [✕] [&M] [💻] [🍴] [🚗]

ⓒ ▼▼▼ ▼▼▼ Delta Vancouver Suites Ⓗ
(604) 689-8188. **$159-$219.** 550 W Hastings St. Between Seymour and Richards sts; entrance in alley way. Int corridors. **Pets:** Other species. Designated rooms, service with restrictions, supervision.
[SAVE] [S/D] [✕] [&M] [💻] [🍴] [🚗]

▼▼▼ ▼▼▼ The Fairmont Hotel Vancouver Ⓗ
(604) 684-3131. **$169-$299.** 900 W Georgia St. Corner of Burrard at W Georgia St, enter from Hornby St. Int corridors. **Pets:** Accepted.
[✕] [&M] [💻] [🍴] [🚗]

▼▼▼ ▼▼▼ The Fairmont Waterfront Ⓗ
(604) 691-1991. **$169-$395.** 900 Canada Place Way. Opposite Canada Place at waterfront; motor entrance use Howe St. Int corridors. **Pets:** Accepted.
[ASK] [S/D] [✕] [&M] [💻] [🍴] [🚗]

ⓒ ▼▼▼ ▼▼▼ Four Seasons Hotel Vancouver Ⓗ 🐾
(604) 689-9333. **$300-$450.** 791 W Georgia St. Howe and W Georgia sts. Int corridors. **Pets:** Small. Designated rooms, service with restrictions, supervision.
[SAVE] [✕] [🐾] [🍴] [🚗]

▼▼▼ ▼▼▼ The Georgian Court Hotel Ⓗ
(604) 682-5555. **$115-$260.** 773 Beatty St. Between Georgia and Robson sts. Int corridors. **Pets:** $20 one-time fee/room. Service with restrictions, supervision.
[✕] [💻] [🍴]

▼▼▼ Granville Island Hotel H
(604) 683-7373. **$160-$230.** 1253 Johnston St. Granville Island; below the bridge, follow signs. Int corridors. **Pets:** $25 daily fee/room. Designated rooms, service with restrictions, supervision.
[A$K] [S☉] [✕] [▣] [¶]

ⓐ ▼▼▼ Holiday Inn Hotel & Suites Vancouver Downtown H ❧
(604) 684-2151. **$99-$169.** 1110 Howe St. Between Helmcken and Davie sts. Int corridors. **Pets:** Medium. Service with restrictions, supervision.
[SAVE] [S☉] [✕] [&M] [▤] [▣] [¶] [⊷]

▼▼▼ Holiday Inn-Vancouver Centre MI
(604) 879-0511. **$149-$199.** 711 W Broadway. Between Heather and Willow sts. Int corridors. **Pets:** Medium. Designated rooms, service with restrictions.
[A$K] [S☉] [✕] [▤] [▣] [¶] [⊷]

▼ The London Guard Motel MI
(604) 430-4646. **$49-$75.** 2227 Kingsway. 6.8 km se on Hwy 1A and 99A (Kingsway). Ext corridors. **Pets:** Accepted.
[✕] [▤] [AC]

ⓐ ▼▼▼▼ Metropolitan Hotel H ❧
(604) 687-1122. **$169-$625.** 645 Howe St. Between Georgia and Dunsmuir sts. Int corridors. **Pets:** Medium. Service with restrictions, supervision.
[SAVE] [S☉] [✕] [&M] [⌖] [▣] [¶] [⊷]

ⓐ ▼▼▼▼ Pacific Palisades Hotel H ❧
(604) 688-0461. **$290-$390.** 1277 Robson St. Between Jervis and Bute sts. Int corridors. **Pets:** Other species. Designated rooms, supervision.
[SAVE] [S☉] [✕] [&M] [⌖] [▤] [▣] [¶] [⊷]

ⓐ ▼▼▼▼ The Pan Pacific Hotel Vancouver H ❧
(604) 662-8111. **$390-$540.** 300-999 Canada Place. At Canada Place; motor entrance off Burrard St. Int corridors. **Pets:** Small. Service with restrictions, supervision.
[SAVE] [S☉] [✕] [&M] [▣] [¶] [⊷]

ⓐ ▼▼▼ Quality Hotel-Inn at False Creek MI ❧
(604) 682-0229. **$99-$229.** 1335 Howe St. Between Drake and Pacific sts. Int corridors. **Pets:** $15 daily fee/pet. Service with restrictions.
[SAVE] [S☉] [✕] [&M] [⌖] [▤] [▣] [¶] [⊷]

ⓐ ▼▼▼ Ramada Inn & Suites Downtown Vancouver MI
(604) 685-1111. **$89-$199.** 1221 Granville St. Between Davie and Drake sts. Int corridors. **Pets:** Other species. $20 one-time fee/pet. Designated rooms, service with restrictions, supervision.
[SAVE] [S☉] [✕] [▤] [▣] [¶]

ⓐ ▼▼▼ Ramada Vancouver Centre H
(604) 872-8661. **$85-$125.** 898 W Broadway. Between Laurel and Willow sts. Int corridors. **Pets:** Small, dogs only. $100 deposit/room, $10 daily fee/pet. Designated rooms, service with restrictions, supervision.
[SAVE] [S☉] [✕] [&M] [⌖] [▤] [▣] [¶]

ⓐ ▼▼◆ Renaissance Vancouver Hotel Harbourside H ❧
(604) 689-9211. **$139-$249.** 1133 W Hastings St. Between Bute and Thurlow sts. Int corridors. **Pets:** Large. $25 one-time fee/room. Service with restrictions, supervision.
[SAVE] [S☉] [✕] [&M] [▣] [¶] [⊷]

ⓐ ▼▼▼ Residence Inn by Marriott, Vancouver H ❧
(604) 688-1234. **$139-$229.** 1234 Hornby St. Between Drake and Davie sts. Int corridors. **Pets:** Small. $5 daily fee/pet, $75 one-time fee/pet. Service with restrictions, supervision.
[SAVE] [✕] [&M] [▤] [▣] [¶] [⊷]

ⓐ ▼▼▼▼ Sheraton Suites Le SoLeil Vancouver H
(604) 632-3000. **$300-$400.** 567 Hornby St. Between Dunsmuir and Pender sts. Int corridors. **Pets:** Accepted.
[SAVE] [S☉] [✕] [&M] [▣] [¶]

ⓐ ▼▼▼▼ Sheraton Vancouver Wall Centre Hotel H ❧
(604) 331-1000. **$159-$209.** 1088 Burrard St. At Burrard and Helmken sts. Int corridors. **Pets:** Medium. $60 one-time fee/room. Service with restrictions, supervision.
[SAVE] [S☉] [✕] [&M] [⌖] [▤] [▣] [¶] [⊷]

ⓐ ▼▼▼▼ The Sutton Place Hotel H
(604) 682-5511. **$179-$450, 3 days notice.** 845 Burrard St. Between Smythe and Robson sts. Int corridors. **Pets:** Accepted.
[SAVE] [S☉] [✕] [&M] [⌖] [¶] [⊷]

▼ Sylvia Hotel MI
(604) 681-9321. **$75-$175.** 1154 Gilford St. Beach Ave at Guilford St; across from English Bay. Int corridors. **Pets:** Other species. $15 one-time fee/room. Service with restrictions.
[¶] [AC]

ⓐ ▼▼▼▼ The Westin Bayshore Resort & Marina H
(604) 682-3377. **$159-$254.** 1601 Bayshore Dr. W Georgia at Cardero St. Int corridors. **Pets:** Small, dogs only. Designated rooms, supervision.
[SAVE] [✕] [&M] [⌖] [▣] [¶] [⊷] [✕]

❧ **END METROPOLITAN AREA** ❧

VERNON

◆◆ **Best Western Vernon Lodge & Conference Centre** [MI]
(250) 545-3385. **$94-$154.** 3914 32nd St. 1.5 km n on Hwy 97. Int corridors. **Pets:** Dogs only. $10 daily fee/room. Designated rooms, service with restrictions, supervision.
[SAVE] [S/D] ⊠ ♿ ▣ ☕ 🍴 🏊

[CAA] ◆◆ **Best Western Villager Motor Inn** [M]
(250) 549-2224. **$65-$105.** 5121 26th St. 2.5 km n on 27th St; across from Village Green Mall. Ext/int corridors. **Pets:** Small, dogs only. $10 one-time fee/room. Service with restrictions, supervision.
[SAVE] [S/D] ⊠ ▣ ☕ 🏊

◆◆ **The Maria Rose Bed & Breakfast** [BB] 🐾
(250) 549-4773. **$70-$85, 10 days notice.** 8083 Aspen Rd. From Hwy 97, 10 km e on Silver Star Rd; follow the Silver Star Resort signs. Ext corridors. **Pets:** Medium. $5 daily fee/pet. Service with restrictions, crate.
⊠ ☕ [AC] ☎

[CAA] ◆◆ **Schell Motel** [M]
(250) 545-1351. **$75-$85.** 2810 35th St. Centre; corner of 35th St and 30th Ave. Ext corridors. **Pets:** Small. $5 daily fee/pet. Designated rooms, supervision.
[SAVE] ⊠ ▣ ☕ 🏊

◆◆ **Vernon Travelodge** [M]
(250) 545-2161. **$69-$99.** 3000 28th Ave. Hwy 97 (32nd St), just e on 28th Ave, near Polson Park. Ext corridors. **Pets:** Medium, other species. $7 daily fee/room. Supervision.
[A$K] [S/D] ⊠ ▣ ☕ 🏊

VICTORIA METROPOLITAN AREA

MALAHAT

◆◆ **Malahat Bungalows Motel** [C]
(250) 478-3011. **$50-$128, 3 days notice.** On Trans-Canada Hwy 1 (Malahat Dr), 26 km n of Victoria. Ext corridors. **Pets:** Medium, other species. $6 daily fee/pet. Service with restrictions, supervision.
[A$K] ⊠ ▣ [AC] ☎

SAANICHTON

[CAA] ◆◆ **Quality Inn Waddling Dog** [MI]
(250) 652-1146. **$69-$129.** 2476 Mt Newton Crossroad. Corner of Hwy 17 and Mt Newton Crossroad. Int corridors. **Pets:** Other species. $5 daily fee/pet. Service with restrictions.
[SAVE] [S/D] ⊠ ☕ 🍴

[CAA] ◆◆ **Super 8 Victoria/Saanichton** [M]
(250) 652-6888. **$60-$130.** 2477 Mt Newton Crossroad. Just e of Hwy 17. Int corridors. **Pets:** Other species. $10 daily fee/room. Service with restrictions, supervision.
[SAVE] [S/D] ⊠ ♿ ▣

SIDNEY

[CAA] ◆◆◆ **Best Western Emerald Isle Motor Inn** [MI]
(250) 656-4441. **$119-$179.** 2306 Beacon Ave. Just e of Hwy 17, exit Sidney. Int corridors. **Pets:** Other species. $20 one-time fee/pet. Designated rooms, service with restrictions, supervision.
[SAVE] [S/D] ⊠ ▣ ☕ 🍴

◆◆◆ **The Cedarwood Inn & Suites** [M]
(250) 656-5551. **$79-$129, 7 days notice.** 9522 Lochside Dr. From Hwy 17, just e on McTavish Rd, then 1.4 km n. Ext corridors. **Pets:** Small, other species. $10 daily fee/pet. Designated rooms, service with restrictions, supervision.
⊠ ▣ ☕ [AC]

[CAA] ◆◆ **Victoria Airport Travelodge Sidney** [M]
(250) 656-1176. **$69-$145.** 2280 Beacon Ave. Just e of Hwy 17, exit Sidney. Int corridors. **Pets:** Other species. $100 deposit/room. Designated rooms, service with restrictions.
[SAVE] [S/D] ⊠ ☕ 🏊 [AC]

SOOKE

◆◆ **Ocean Wilderness Inn & Spa** [BB] 🐾
(250) 646-2116. **$99-$175, 7 days notice.** 109 W Coast Rd. 14 km w on Hwy 14. Ext/int corridors. **Pets:** Other species. $15 daily fee/pet. Designated rooms, service with restrictions, supervision.
[A$K] [S/D] ⊠ ▣ [AC] [DP] ☎

[CAA] ◆◆◆ **Sooke Harbour House** [CI] 🐾
(250) 642-3421. **$230-$555, 14 days notice.** 1528 Whiffen Spit Rd. 2 km w on Hwy 14. Ext/int corridors. **Pets:** Other species. $20 daily fee/pet. Service with restrictions.
[SAVE] ⊠ ♿ ♿ ▣ ☕ 🍴 [AC] [DP]

VICTORIA

◆◆◆ **Abbeymoore Manor Bed & Breakfast** [BB]
(250) 370-1470. **$70-$165, 10 days notice.** 1470 Rockland Ave. From Blanshard St; 2 km e on Front St, then just s on Pemberton St. Ext/int corridors. **Pets:** Accepted.
[S/D] ⊠ ▣ ☕ [AC]

(CAA) ▼▼▼ **Accent Inns** **M**
(250) 475-7500. **$94-$129.** 3233 Maple St. 3 km n on Blanshard St (Hwy 17); corner of Blanchard St and Cloverdale Ave. Ext corridors. **Pets:** Small, other species. Designated rooms, service with restrictions, supervision.
[SAVE] [S▲] [✕] [⚹M] [🛏] [▭]

(CAA) ▼▼▼ **Blue Ridge Inns** **M**
(250) 388-4345. **$69-$99.** 3110 Douglas St. 3.5 km n. Ext corridors. **Pets:** Medium, other species. Designated rooms, service with restrictions, supervision.
[SAVE] [S▲] [✕] [🛏] [▭] [🍴] [🏊] [🐾]

▼▼ **Dashwood Seaside Manor** **X** ✿
(250) 385-5517. **$80-$345, 14 days notice.** 1 Cook St. 1 km e of Douglas St on Dallas Rd. Int corridors. **Pets:** Medium, dogs only. $25 one-time fee/pet. Designated rooms, service with restrictions, supervision.
[ASK] [S▲] [✕] [🛏] [▭] [🐾] [🔌]

(CAA) ▼▼▼ **Days Inn on the Harbour** **MI** ✿
(250) 386-3451. **$89-$213.** 427 Belleville St. Entrance on Oswego at Quebec sts. Int corridors. **Pets:** $10 daily fee/room. Designated rooms, service with restrictions.
[SAVE] [S▲] [✕] [🛏] [▭] [🍴] [🐾]

(CAA) ▼▼▼▼ **Delta Victoria Ocean Pointe Resort & Spa** **H** ✿
(250) 360-2999. **$149-$209.** 45 Songhees Rd. Just w of Johnson St Bridge, Esquimalt at Tyee rds. Int corridors. **Pets:** Dogs only. Service with restrictions, supervision.
[SAVE] [S▲] [✕] [⚹M] [🛏] [▭] [🍴] [🏊] [🔌]

(CAA) ▼ **Dutchman Inn** **M**
(250) 386-7557. **$50-$105.** 2828 Rock Bay Ave. From Douglas St, just w, Gorge Rd and Rock Bay Ave. Ext corridors. **Pets:** Small, dogs only. $10 one-time fee/pet. Service with restrictions, supervision.
[SAVE] [S▲] [✕] [🛏] [▭] [🐾]

▼▼ **Executive House Hotel** **H**
(250) 388-5111. **$79-$179.** 777 Douglas St. Between Blanshard and Douglas sts. Int corridors. **Pets:** Other species. Designated rooms.
[ASK] [S▲] [✕] [🛏] [▭] [🍴] [🐾]

▼▼▼ **The Fairmont Empress** **H**
(250) 384-8111. **$159-$479.** 721 Government St. Government at Wharf St, just n of the Parliament buildings. Int corridors. **Pets:** Accepted.
[ASK] [✕] [⚹M] [🔌] [🛏] [▭] [🍴] [🐾] [🐾]

(CAA) ▼▼▼ **Harbour Towers Hotel and Suites** **H** ✿
(250) 385-2405. **$90-$230.** 345 Quebec St. Between Osweyo and Pendray sts. Int corridors. **Pets:** Medium. $15 daily fee/room. Supervision.
[SAVE] [S▲] [✕] [⚹M] [▭] [🍴] [🏊] [🐾]

(CAA) ▼▼▼ **Howard Johnson Hotel & Suites** **MI**
(250) 704-4656. **$99-$169.** 4670 Elk Lake Dr. Hwy 17, just w on Royal Oak Dr, then just n. Ext/int corridors. **Pets:** $10 daily fee/room. Service with restrictions, supervision.
[SAVE] [S▲] [✕] [⚹M] [🔌] [🛏] [▭] [🍴] [🐾]

(CAA) ▼▼▼ **The Magnolia Hotel & Spa** **H** ✿
(250) 381-0999. **$169-$309.** 623 Courtney St. Corner of Courtney and Gordon sts. Int corridors. **Pets:** Small. $60 one-time fee/room. Service with restrictions.
[SAVE] [✕] [⚹M] [▭] [🍴]

(CAA) ▼▼ **Oxford Castle Inn** **A**
(250) 388-6431. **$68-$158.** 133 Gorge Rd E. From Douglas St, 2 km w. Int corridors. **Pets:** Accepted.
[SAVE] [S▲] [✕] [🛏] [▭] [🐾] [🐾]

(CAA) ▼▼ **Robin Hood Motel** **M**
(250) 388-4302. **$51-$84.** 136 Gorge Rd E. From Douglas St, 2.4 km w. Ext corridors. **Pets:** Dogs only. $5 daily fee/pet. Designated rooms, service with restrictions, crate.
[SAVE] [S▲] [✕] [🛏] [▭] [🐾]

▼▼▼ **Ryan's Bed & Breakfast** **BB**
(250) 389-0012. **$105-$195, 10 days notice.** 224 Superior St. Between Montreal and Oswego sts. Int corridors. **Pets:** Accepted.
[✕] [🐾] [🔌]

(CAA) ▼ **Shamrock Motel** **A**
(250) 385-8768. **$70-$140.** 675 Superior St. Douglas and Superior sts. Ext corridors. **Pets:** Dogs only. $10 daily fee/pet. Supervision.
[SAVE] [S▲] [✕] [🛏] [▭] [🐾]

(CAA) ▼ **Travellers Inn City Center** **MI**
(250) 953-1000. **$59-$99.** 1961 Douglas St. Corner of Douglas and Discovery sts. Int corridors. **Pets:** Medium. $100 deposit/room. Service with restrictions, crate.
[SAVE] [✕] [🛏] [▭] [🍴] [🐾] [🐾]

✿ END METROPOLITAN AREA ✿

WESTBANK

▼▼▼ **Holiday Inn** **MI** ✿
(250) 768-8879. **$69-$119, 7 days notice.** 2569 Dobbin Rd. Hwy 97 (Dobbin Rd) and Herbert Rd. Int corridors. **Pets:** $10 daily fee/room. Designated rooms, service with restrictions, supervision.
[ASK] [S▲] [✕] [⚹M] [🛏] [▭] [🍴] [🐾]

WHISTLER

(CAA) ▼▼▼ **Best Western Listel Whistler Hotel** **MI**
(604) 932-1133. **$99-$299, 3 days notice.** 4121 Village Green. Hwy 99, just e on Village Gate Blvd, then follow Whistler Way. Int corridors. **Pets:** $15 daily fee/pet. Designated rooms, service with restrictions.
[SAVE] [S▲] [✕] [🛏] [🍴] [🐾]

ⓒⒶ ▼▼▼▼ **Crystal Lodge** 🅜🅘 ❖
(604) 932-2221. **$125-$304, 30 days notice.** 4154 Village Green. Hwy 99, just e on Village Gate Blvd, then follow Whistler Way. Int corridors. **Pets:** Medium, dogs only. $20 daily fee/pet. Designated rooms, service with restrictions.
[SAVE] [S₀] [✕] [📠] [💻] [🍴] [⇆]

ⓒⒶ ▼▼▼▼ **Delta Whistler Resort** 🄷
(604) 932-1982. **$145-$499, 14 days notice.** 4050 Whistler Way. Hwy 99, just e on Village Gate Blvd, then follow Whistler Way. Int corridors. **Pets:** Accepted.
[SAVE] [S₀] [✕] [📠] [💻] [🍴] [⇆] [✗]

▼▼▼▼ **Delta Whistler Village Suites** 🄷 ❖
(604) 905-3987. **$230-$820, 14 days notice.** 4308 Main St. Hwy 99, just e on Village Gate Blvd, then just n on Northlands Blvd, just e. Int corridors. **Pets:** Other species. $15 daily fee/room. Supervision.
[ASK] [✕] [♿] [📠] [💻] [🍴] [⇆]

ⓒⒶ ▼▼▼ **Edgewater Lodge** 🄻 ❖
(604) 932-0688. **$115-$320, 14 days notice.** 8020 Alpine Way. 4 km n of Whistler Village via Hwy 99, e on Alpine Way. Ext corridors. **Pets:** Dogs only. $20 daily fee/room. Supervision.
[SAVE] [✕] [🍴] [✗]

▼▼▼▼ **The Fairmont Chateau Whistler** 🄷
(604) 938-8000. **$169-$619.** 4599 Chateau Blvd. Hwy 99, 1 km e on Lorimer Rd, then just w on Blackcomb Way. Int corridors. **Pets:** Medium, dogs only. $25 daily fee/room. Service with restrictions, supervision.
[ASK] [S₀] [✕] [♿] [💻] [🍴] [⇆] [✗]

ⓒⒶ ▼▼▼ **Residence Inn by Marriott** 🄲🄾
(604) 905-3400. **$459-$799, 60 days notice.** 4899 Painted Cliff Rd. Hwy 99, 1 km e on Lorimer Rd (Upper Village), just se on Blackcomb Way, then just w, follow road all the way to the end. Int corridors. **Pets:** Accepted.
[SAVE] [✕] [📠] [💻] [⇆] [✗]

ⓒⒶ ▼▼▼▼ **Summit Lodge** 🄷 ❖
(604) 932-2778. **$170-$520, 14 days notice.** 4359 Main St. Hwy 99, just n on Village Gate Rd, then just w on Northland Blvd. Int corridors. **Pets:** Other species. $15 daily fee/pet. Designated rooms, service with restrictions, supervision.
[SAVE] [✕] [📠] [💻] [⇆]

ⓒⒶ ▼▼▼ **Tantalus Resort Lodge** 🄲🄾
(604) 932-4146. **$229-$350, 30 days notice.** 4200 Whistler Way. Jct Hwy 99 and Whistler Way. Int corridors. **Pets:** Accepted.
[SAVE] [S₀] [✕] [📠] [💻] [⇆] [✗]

WILLIAMS LAKE

▼▼▼ **Drummond Lodge Motel** 🅜
(250) 392-5334. **$66-$87.** 1405 Cariboo Hwy. 1 km s on Hwy 97. Ext corridors. **Pets:** Large. $5 one-time fee/pet. Crate.
[✕] [📠]

▼▼ **Williams Lake Super 8 Motel** 🅜
(250) 398-8884. **$63-$76, 5 days notice.** 1712 Broadway Ave S. 2 km s on Hwy 97. Int corridors. **Pets:** Other species. Supervision.
[ASK] [S₀] [✕] [♿] [📠]

YALE

▼▼ **Fort Yale Motel** 🅜
(604) 863-2216. **$50-$69.** 31265 Trans-Canada Hwy. On Trans-Canada Hwy 1, just n of main set of lights. Ext corridors. **Pets:** Accepted.
[S₀] [✕] [📠] [💻] [🎞]

BRANDON

▼▼ Comfort Inn **M** ❀
(204) 727-6232. **$69-$112, 30 days notice.** 925 Middleton Ave. North side Trans-Canada service road, between Hwy 10 N and 10 S, just e of MacDonalds Restaurant. Int corridors. **Pets:** Other species. $10 one-time fee/room. Designated rooms, service with restrictions, supervision.

CAA ▼ Rodeway Inn Motel **M**
(204) 728-7230. **$55-$59.** 300 18th St N. 3.2 km s of Trans-Canada Hwy 1, on Hwy 10 S. Ext/int corridors. **Pets:** Medium, other species. $3 daily fee/room. Service with restrictions, supervision.

SAVE ✕ 🛏

▼▼ Royal Oak Inn & Suites **MI**
(204) 728-5775. **$110-$180.** 3130 Victoria Ave. 5 km s of Trans-Canada Hwy 1, 1.4 km w of jct Hwy 10 (18th St) and Hwy 1A (Victoria Ave). Int corridors. **Pets:** Other species. Designated rooms.

✕ 🛏 💻 ⑪ ⇌

▼▼ Super 8 Motel Brandon **M**
(204) 729-8024. **$80-$85.** 1570 Highland Ave. On Trans-Canada Hwy 1, south service road, just e of Hwy 10. Int corridors. **Pets:** Accepted.

ASK S○ ✕ ⌖M 🛏 💻 ⇌

CAA ▼▼▼ Victoria Inn **MI** ❀
(204) 725-1532. **$86.** 3550 Victoria Ave. 5 km s of Trans-Canada Hwy 1; 1.8 km w of jct Hwy 10 (18th St) and Hwy 1A (Victoria Ave). Int corridors. **Pets:** $5 daily fee/room. Designated rooms, service with restrictions, supervision.

SAVE S○ ✕ 🛏 💻 ⑪ ⇌

CHURCHILL

▼▼ Polar Inn & Suites **M**
(204) 675-8878. **$125-$165.** 153 Kelsey Blvd. Centre. Int corridors. **Pets:** Service with restrictions.

ASK S○ ✕ 🛏 💻 ⌖

DAUPHIN

▼ Canway Inn & Suites **MI**
(204) 638-5102. **$68-$78.** 1601 Main St. 2.4 km s on Hwy 5A and 10A (Main St). Ext/int corridors. **Pets:** Accepted.

ASK S○ ✕ 💻 ⑪ ⇌

FLIN FLON

CAA ▼▼▼ Victoria Inn North **MI**
(204) 687-7555. **$78-$88.** 160 Hwy 10A N. Jct Hwy 10 and 10A, 1 km w, eastern approach to city. Int corridors. **Pets:** $5 daily fee/room. Service with restrictions.

SAVE ✕ 🛏 💻 ⑪ ⇌

HECLA

▼▼ Solmundson Gesta Hus **BB**
(204) 279-2088. **$50-$75.** On Hwy 8 in Hecla Village, in Hecla Provincial Park. Int corridors. **Pets:** Accepted.

ASK S○ ✕ ⌖ ⌖

NEEPAWA

▼▼ Neepawa Super 8 Motel **M** ❀
(204) 476-8888. **$89-$93.** 160 Main St W. Hwy 16, just w of jct Rt 5. Int corridors. **Pets:** Medium. Designated rooms, service with restrictions, supervision.

ASK S○ ✕ 🛏 ⑪ ⇌

PORTAGE LA PRAIRIE

▼▼ Super 8 **M**
(204) 857-8883. **$71-$83, 7 days notice.** 1.5 km w on Trans-Canada Hwy 1A. Int corridors. **Pets:** Other species. Service with restrictions.

ASK S○ ✕ 🛏 💻 ⇌

▼ Westgate Inn Motel **M**
(204) 239-5200. **$49-$54.** 1010 Saskatchewan Ave E. 1 km e on Trans-Canada Hwy 1A. Ext corridors. **Pets:** Accepted.

ASK S○ ✕ 🛏

RUSSELL

CAA ▼▼ The Russell Inn Hotel & Conference Center **MI**
(204) 773-2186. **$78-$98.** Hwy 16 Russell. 1.2 km se on Hwy 16 and 83. Ext/int corridors. **Pets:** Accepted.

SAVE S○ ✕ 🛏 💻 ⑪

STEINBACH

▼▼▼ Days Inn **M**
(204) 320-9200. **$80-$90.** 75 Hwy 12 N. Jct Trans-Canada Hwy 1 and Hwy 12, 20 km s. Int corridors. **Pets:** Other species. $10 one-time fee/room. Designated rooms, service with restrictions, crate.

SAVE ✕ ⌖ 🛏 💻 ⇌

THE PAS

(CAA) ▼▼▼ **Kikiwak Inn** Ⓜ️
(204) 623-1800. **$99.** Hwy 10 N. 0.6 km n on Hwy 10. Int corridors. **Pets:** Medium, other species. $10 one-time fee/pet. Designated rooms, service with restrictions, supervision.
[SAVE] [S🐾] [✕] [📶] [🖥️] [🍴] [🏊]

(CAA) ▼▼▼ **Wescana Inn** Ⓜ️
(204) 623-5446. **$79.** 439 Fischer Ave. Just s on Hwy 10. Ext/int corridors. **Pets:** Service with restrictions, crate.
[SAVE] [S🐾] [✕] [📶] [🖥️] [🍴]

THOMPSON

(CAA) ▼▼▼ **Country Inn & Suites By Carlson** Ⓜ️
(204) 778-8879. **$89-$99.** 70 Thompson Dr N. Just w of Hwy 6. Int corridors. **Pets:** $10 one-time fee/room. Service with restrictions, supervision.
[SAVE] [S🐾] [✕] [📶] [🖥️] [🏊]

WINKLER

▼▼ **Winkler Inn** Ⓜ️
(204) 325-4381. **$67-$79.** 851 Main St N. Center; Main St and Hwy 14. Int corridors. **Pets:** Small. $6 daily fee/pet. Supervision.
[✕] [📶] [🖥️] [🍴] [🏊]

WINNIPEG METROPOLITAN AREA

WINNIPEG

(CAA) ▼▼▼ **Best Western Victoria Inn** Ⓜ️
(204) 786-4801. **$102-$122.** 1808 Wellington Ave. At Berry St. Int corridors. **Pets:** $10 daily fee/room. Service with restrictions, crate.
[SAVE] [S🐾] [✕] [🍴]

(CAA) ▼▼▼ **Carlton Inn** Ⓜ️
(204) 942-0881. **$75.** 220 Carlton St. Just s off Metro Rt 85 (Portage Ave); opposite Convention Centre. Int corridors. **Pets:** Other species. Service with restrictions, crate.
[SAVE] [S🐾] [✕] [🖥️] [🍴] [🏊]

▼▼ **Comfort Inn** Ⓜ️
(204) 783-5627. **$84-$95.** 1770 Sargent Ave. At Sargent Ave and King Edward St. Int corridors. **Pets:** Accepted.
[SAVE] [S🐾] [✕] [🖥️] [📶] [🖥️]

▼▼ **Comfort Inn** Ⓜ️
(204) 269-7390. **$79-$95, 5 days notice.** 3109 Pembina Hwy. Just n of jct Perimeter Hwy 100 and 75. Int corridors. **Pets:** Small. Designated rooms, service with restrictions, supervision.
[SAVE] [S🐾] [✕] [📶] [🖥️]

(CAA) ▼▼▼ **Country Inn & Suites By Carlson** Ⓜ️
(204) 783-6900. **$105-$120.** 730 King Edward St. Just s of jct Wellington Ave. Int corridors. **Pets:** Medium, other species. $25 deposit/room. Service with restrictions.
[SAVE] [S🐾] [✕] [🖥️] [📶] [🖥️]

(CAA) ▼▼ **Days Inn** Ⓜ️
(204) 586-8525. **$119-$129, 14 days notice.** 550 McPhillips St. Just n of Logan Ave. Int corridors. **Pets:** Small. $10 daily fee/pet. Designated rooms, service with restrictions, supervision.
[SAVE] [S🐾] [✕] [📶] [🖥️] [🍴] [🏊]

(CAA) ▼▼▼ **Delta Winnipeg** 🄷
(204) 942-0551. **$89-$159.** 350 St Mary Ave. At Hargrave St; adjacent to Convention Centre. Int corridors. **Pets:** Dogs only. $20 one-time fee/room. Designated rooms, service with restrictions, crate.
[SAVE] [✕] [⅙M] [📶] [🖥️] [🍴] [🏊]

(CAA) ▼▼▼ **The Fairmont Winnipeg** 🄷 🐾
(204) 957-1350. **$99-$129.** 2 Lombard Pl. Just e of corner Portage Ave and Main St. Int corridors. **Pets:** Large, other species. $25 one-time fee/room. Designated rooms, service with restrictions, supervision.
[SAVE] [S🐾] [✕] [🌀] [📶] [🖥️] [🍴] [🏊]

(CAA) ▼▼ **Gordon Downtowner Motor Hotel** Ⓜ️
(204) 943-5581. **$80-$88.** 330 Kennedy St. Kennedy St at Ellice Ave. Int corridors. **Pets:** Accepted.
[SAVE] [S🐾] [📶] [🍴]

(CAA) ▼▼▼ **Greenwood Inn** Ⓜ️
(204) 775-9889. **$109-$179.** 1715 Wellington Ave. Wellington Ave at Broadford St. Int corridors. **Pets:** Small, dogs only. $10 one-time fee/room. Designated rooms, service with restrictions, supervision.
[SAVE] [✕] [📶] [🖥️] [🍴] [🏊]

▼▼▼ **Holiday Inn Winnipeg South** 🄷 🐾
(204) 452-4747. **$89-$99.** 1330 Pembina Hwy. At McGillivray Blvd. Int corridors. **Pets:** Other species. Designated rooms, service with restrictions, supervision.
[✕] [📶] [🖥️] [🍴] [🏊]

(CAA) ▼▼▼ **Place Louis Riel All-Suite Hotel** 🄷 🐾
(204) 947-6961. **$90-$125.** 190 Smith St. At St Mary Rd. Int corridors. **Pets:** Designated rooms, service with restrictions, crate.
[SAVE] [S🐾] [✕] [⅙M] [📶] [🖥️] [🍴]

▼▼▼ **Radisson Hotel Winnipeg Downtown** 🄷
(204) 956-0410. **$92-$179.** 288 Portage Ave. At Smith St. Int corridors. **Pets:** Medium. Service with restrictions, supervision.
[ASK] [S🐾] [✕] [🖥️] [🍴] [🏊]

▼▼ Ramada Marlborough Hotel 🔲
(204) 942-6411. **Call for rates.** 331 Smith St. Just n off
Metro Rt 85 (Portage Ave). Int corridors. **Pets:** Accepted.
ⒶⓈⓀ ⊠ 🔲 🖳 🍴

ⒸⒶⒶ ▼▼▼ Sheraton Hotel 🔲
(204) 942-5300. **$105-$159.** 161 Donald St. Donald St at
York Ave. Int corridors. **Pets:** Accepted.
SAVE ⓈⒹ ⊠ 🔲 🖳 🍴 🐾

▼ Twin Pillars Bed & Breakfast 🅱🅱
(204) 284-7590. **$55-$60 (no credit cards).** 235 Oakwood
Ave. 0.6 km e of Osborne St. Int corridors. **Pets:** Medium,
other species. $50 deposit/room. Designated rooms, service
with restrictions, crate.
ⒶⓈⓀ ⊠

▼▼ Viscount Hotel 🅼🅸
(204) 775-0451. **$85-$99.** 1670 Portage Ave. Portage Ave
at Rt 90. Int corridors. **Pets:** Medium. $25 one-time fee/
room. Designated rooms, service with restrictions, crate.
⊠ 🔲 🖳 🍴 🐾

❖ **END METROPOLITAN AREA** ❖

BATHURST

▼▼▼▼ Atlantic Host Hotel MI
(506) 548-3335. **$77-$95.** 1450 Vanier Blvd. Hwy 11, exit 310 (Vanier Blvd). Int corridors. **Pets:** Small. Designated rooms, service with restrictions, supervision.

▼▼ Comfort Inn M
(506) 547-8000. **$76-$85.** 1170 St Peter's Ave. 3.4 km n on Rt 134 (St Peter's Ave). Int corridors. **Pets:** Other species. Service with restrictions, supervision.

ⒶⒶ ▼▼▼▼ Country Inn & Suites By Carlson M
(506) 548-4949. **$60-$64.** 777 St Peter Ave. 3 km n on Rt 134 (St Peter's Ave). Int corridors. **Pets:** Accepted.

▼▼▼▼ Danny's Inn & Conference Centre MI
(506) 546-6621. **$74-$84.** Hwy 11, exit 310 northbound to Rt 134, 4 km n; exit 318 southbound to Rt 134, 3.8 km s. Ext/int corridors. **Pets:** Medium. $100 deposit/pet. Designated rooms, service with restrictions, supervision.

▼▼▼▼ Keddy's Le Chateau Bathurst MI
(506) 546-6691. **$50-$85, 14 days notice.** 80 Main St. Centre; on Rt 134 (St Peter's Ave) and 7. Ext/int corridors. **Pets:** Accepted.

CAMPBELLTON

▼▼ Comfort Inn M
(506) 753-4121. **$78-$104.** 111 Val D'amour Rd. Hwy 11, exit 415, 1 km e on Sugarloaf St W. Ext/int corridors. **Pets:** Accepted.

ⒶⒶ ▼▼ Howard Johnson MI
(506) 753-4133. **$89, 14 days notice.** 157 Water St. Hwy 134; in City Centre Complex. Int corridors. **Pets:** Accepted.

COCAGNE

▼▼ Cocagne Motel M
(506) 576-6657. **$50-$80.** Hwy 11, exit 15, 1 km n on Rt 535. Ext corridors. **Pets:** Service with restrictions, supervision.

EDMUNDSTON

▼▼ Comfort Inn M
(506) 739-8361. **$90-$112.** 5 Bateman Ave. Northwest quadrant off Trans-Cananda Hwy 2 and Herbert Blvd. Int corridors. **Pets:** Other species. Designated rooms, service with restrictions.

▼▼▼ Days Inn Edmundston M
(506) 263-0000. **$90-$160.** 10 rue Mathieu. Trans-Canada Hwy 2, exit 26. Int corridors. **Pets:** Accepted.

ⒶⒶ ▼▼▼▼ Howard Johnson Plaza Hotel H
(506) 739-7321. **$90-$130.** 100 Rice St. 1.6 km sw off Trans-Canada Hwy 2, exit 18 (Herbert Blvd), just w on Church Rd. Int corridors. **Pets:** Accepted.

FREDERICTON

▼▼ Auberge Wandlyn Inn MI
(506) 462-4444. **$120.** 958 Prospect St. Trans-Canada Hwy 2, exit 289 (Hanwell Rd) eastbound; exit 292B (Regent St) westbound. Ext/int corridors. **Pets:** Small. Designated rooms, service with restrictions, crate.

▼▼ Carriage House Inn BB
(506) 452-9924. **$85-$95.** 230 University Ave. Centre. Int corridors. **Pets:** Small. No service, supervision.

▼▼ Comfort Inn M
(506) 453-0800. **$90-$115.** 797 Prospect St. Trans-Canada Hwy 2, exit 289 (Hanwell Rd) eastbound; exit 291 (Smythe St) westbound. Int corridors. **Pets:** Other species. Designated rooms, service with restrictions, supervision.

ⒶⒶ ▼▼▼▼ Country Inn & Suites By Carlson M
(506) 459-0035. **$103-$121.** 665 Prospect St. Trans-Canada Hwy 2, exit 289 (Hanwell Rd), 0.4 km e. Int corridors. **Pets:** Other species. $50 deposit/room, $4 daily fee/pet. Designated rooms, service with restrictions.

Holiday Inn Fredericton Ⓜ ❖
(506) 363-5111. **$109-$149.** 35 Mactaquac Rd (Hwy 102). Trans-Canada Hwy 2, exit 289 (Hanwell Rd) westbound, 16 km w on Rt 102 at exit 274; exit 258 eastbound, 11 km e on Rt 102 at exit 274; 18 km w of Fredericton. Ext/int corridors. **Pets:** Large, other species. Designated rooms, service with restrictions, supervision.

ⒶⓈⓀ ⊠ 🅼 🔋 💻 🍽 ⌕ ⌧

Howard Johnson Hotel Ⓜ
(506) 460-5500. **$85-$129, 7 days notice.** Trans-Canada Hwy 2, north end of Princess Margaret Bridge. Int corridors. **Pets:** Accepted.

ⓈⒶⓋⒺ Ⓢ ⊠ 🔋 💻 🍽 ⌕ ⌧

Lord Beaverbrook Hotel Ⓗ
(506) 455-3371. **$150.** 659 Queen St. Centre. Int corridors. **Pets:** Small. Service with restrictions, supervision.

ⓈⒶⓋⒺ ⊠ 💻 🍽 ⌕

Sheraton Fredericton Ⓗ
(506) 457-7000. **$229-$284.** 225 Woodstock Rd. 1.6 km n on Rt 102. Int corridors. **Pets:** Other species. Service with restrictions, crate.

ⓈⒶⓋⒺ Ⓢ ⊠ 🅼 🔋 💻 🍽 ⌕

GRAND FALLS

Auberge Pres-du-Lac Inn Ⓜ
(506) 473-1300. **$80-$110.** 4 km w on Trans-Canada Hwy 2. Ext/int corridors. **Pets:** Small. Designated rooms, service with restrictions, crate.

Ⓢ ⊠ 🍽 ⌕ ⌧

MIRAMICHI

Comfort Inn Ⓜ
(506) 622-1215. **$78-$99, 3 days notice.** 201 Edward St. 1 km w on Rt 8. Int corridors. **Pets:** Service with restrictions, supervision.

ⓈⒶⓋⒺ Ⓢ ⊠ 🔋 💻

Country Inn & Suites By Carlson Ⓜ
(506) 627-1999. **$82-$108, 7 days notice.** 333 King George Hwy. 1.8 km w on Rt 8. Int corridors. **Pets:** Medium, other species. Designated rooms, service with restrictions, supervision.

ⓈⒶⓋⒺ Ⓢ ⊠ 🔋 💻

Rodd Miramichi River-A Rodd Signature Hotel Ⓜ
(506) 773-3111. **$90-$174.** 1809 Water St. Hwy 11, exit 120, 0.6 km e. Int corridors. **Pets:** Accepted.

ⒶⓈⓀ Ⓢ ⊠ 🅼 🅔 🔋 💻 🍽 ⌕

MONCTON

Beacon Light Motel Ⓜ
(506) 384-1734. **$60-$110.** 1062 Mountain Rd. Trans-Canada Hwy 2, exit 492 (Mapleton Rd), 2.8 km to Rt 126 (Mountain Rd), then just s. Ext/int corridors. **Pets:** Accepted.

⊠ 🔋 🍽 ⌕

Colonial Inns Ⓜ
(506) 382-3395. **$86-$98.** 42 Highfield St. Centre. Ext/int corridors. **Pets:** Small. Designated rooms, service with restrictions, supervision.

ⒶⓈⓀ Ⓢ ⊠ 🔋 🍽 ⌕

Comfort Inn Ⓜ
(506) 384-3175. **$65-$151.** 2495 Mountain Rd. Trans-Canada Hwy 2, exit 488A eastbound; exit 488B westbound. Int corridors. **Pets:** Other species. Service with restrictions, supervision.

ⓈⒶⓋⒺ Ⓢ ⊠ 🔋 💻

Comfort Inn Ⓜ
(506) 859-6868. **$90-$135.** 20 Maplewood Dr. Trans-Canada Hwy 2, exit 496A onto Hwy 115 S, left on Rt 134 E (Lewisville Rd). Int corridors. **Pets:** Designated rooms, service with restrictions, supervision.

ⓈⒶⓋⒺ Ⓢ ⊠ 💻

Country Inn & Suites By Carlson Ⓜ
(506) 852-7000. **$105-$165.** 2475 Mountain Rd. Trans-Canada Hwy 2, exit 488A eastbound; exit 488B westbound. Int corridors. **Pets:** Other species. $50 deposit/room, $5 daily fee/pet. Designated rooms, service with restrictions, crate.

ⓈⒶⓋⒺ Ⓢ ⊠ 🔋 💻

Holiday Inn Express Ⓜ
(506) 384-1050. **$99-$119.** Trans-Canada Hwy 2, exit 488A eastbound; exit 488B westbound. Ext/int corridors. **Pets:** Accepted.

ⒶⓈⓀ ⊠ 💻 🍽 ⌕

Howard Johnson Brunswick Plaza Hotel & Conference Centre Ⓗ ❖
(506) 854-6340. **$99-$139, 30 days notice.** 1005 Main St. Highfield and Main sts. Int corridors. **Pets:** Medium. Designated rooms, service with restrictions, supervision.

ⓈⒶⓋⒺ Ⓢ ⊠ 💻 🍽 ⌕

Keddy's Moncton Inn Ⓜ
(506) 854-2210. **Call for rates, 14 days notice.** 1510 Shediac Rd. Jct Trans-Canada Hwy 2 and Rt 134 S (Shediac Rd), exit 502 (Lakeville). Ext/int corridors. **Pets:** Accepted.

ⒶⓈⓀ ⊠ 💻 🍽 ⌕

Nor-West Motel Ⓜ
(506) 384-1222. **$95-$110.** 1325 Mountain Rd. Trans-Canada Hwy 2, exit 488A eastbound; exit 488B westbound, 5.2 km se on Rt 126; opposite Moncton Shopping Mall. Ext/int corridors. **Pets:** Accepted.

ⓈⒶⓋⒺ ⊠ 🍽

Rodd Park House Inn Ⓜ
(506) 382-1664. **$63-$151.** 434 Main St. 1 km e on Hwy 6. Ext/int corridors. **Pets:** Accepted.

ⓈⒶⓋⒺ Ⓢ ⊠ 💻 🍽 ⌕

SACKVILLE

▼▼ ▼▼ Coastal Inn Sackville 🅜
(506) 536-0000. **$70-$75.** 15 Wright St. Trans-Canada Hwy 2, exit 541. Int corridors. **Pets:** Medium. Designated rooms, service with restrictions, supervision.

(ASK) (S❄) (✕)

ⓐⒶ ▼▼▼▼ Marshlands Inn 🅒🅘
(506) 536-0170. **$79-$109.** 55 Bridge St. Centre; on Hwy 106. Int corridors. **Pets:** Accepted.

(SAVE) (✕) (¶¶) (🅐🅒)

SAINT JOHN

▼▼ Colonial Inns 🅜🅘
(506) 652-3000. **$86-$98.** 175 City Rd. Adjacent to Hwy 1, exit 112. Ext/int corridors. **Pets:** Accepted.

(✕) (📞) (¶¶) (🍴)

ⓐⒶ ▼▼ ▼▼ Comfort Inn 🅜
(506) 674-1873. **$105-$130.** 1155 Fairville Blvd. Hwy 1, exit 4 westbound; exit 107 eastbound, left turn to Fairville Blvd. Int corridors. **Pets:** Accepted.

(SAVE) (S❄) (✕) (▣)

ⓐⒶ ▼▼ ▼▼ Country Inn & Suites 🅜
(506) 635-0400. **$110-$150.** 1011 Fairville Blvd. Hwy 1, exit 107B eastbound, left on Catherwood Dr, left at lights. Int corridors. **Pets:** Medium. $15 one-time fee/room. Designated rooms, service with restrictions, supervision.

(SAVE) (S❄) (✕) (📞) (▣)

▼▼▼▼ Delta Brunswick 🅗
(506) 648-1981. **$115-$121, 3 days notice.** 39 King St. Centre; atop Brunswick Square Mall with connecting skywalk to Market Square. Int corridors. **Pets:** Accepted.

(ASK) (S❄) (✕) (▣) (¶¶) (🍴)

▼▼▼▼ Hilton Saint John 🅗
(506) 693-8484. **$110-$140.** 1 Market Square. At Market Square. Int corridors. **Pets:** Accepted.

(SAVE) (✕) (▣) (¶¶) (🍴)

ⓐⒶ ▼▼▼▼ Howard Johnson Hotel 🅜🅘
(506) 642-2622. **$120-$140.** 400 Main St/Chesley Dr. Hwy 1, 1 km w; north end Chesley Dr, exit off Harbour Bridge. Int corridors. **Pets:** Other species. Designated rooms, service with restrictions, supervision.

(SAVE) (S❄) (✕) (📞) (▣) (¶¶) (🍴)

▼▼ Island View Motel 🅜
(506) 672-1381. **$65.** 1726 Manawagonish Rd. 1.8 km w on Rt 100. Ext corridors. **Pets:** Accepted.

(✕) (🅐🅒)

▼▼ Regent Motel 🅜
(506) 672-8273. **$48-$63, 3 days notice.** 2121 Ocean West Way. Hwy 1, exit 112 eastbound, 2.4 km e on Rt 100; exit 101 westbound onto exit 96W, 0.5 km w on Rt 100. Ext corridors. **Pets:** Accepted.

(✕) (📞) (🅐🅒) (🆉)

▼▼▼▼ Shadow Lawn Inn 🅒🅘
(506) 847-7539. **$109-$195, 3 days notice.** 3180 Rothesay Rd. Hwy 1, exit 133B eastbound; westbound, follow signs for Rothesay Rd and Rt 100, 1.6 km left on Old Hampton Rd (Rt 100), then left onto Rt 100. Int corridors. **Pets:** Accepted.

(ASK) (✕) (📞) (▣) (¶¶)

ST LEONARD

ⓐⒶ ▼▼ ▼▼ Daigle's Motel 🅜🅘
(506) 423-6351. **$71-$89.** 68 rue DuPont. Hwy 17, 1 km s of Trans-Canada Hwy 2, exit 58. Ext corridors. **Pets:** Accepted.

(SAVE) (S❄) (✕) (¶¶) (🍴)

ST. ANDREWS

▼▼▼▼ The Fairmont Algonquin 🅗
(506) 529-8823. **$109-$349, 3 days notice.** 184 Adolphus St. Off Hwy 127. Int corridors. **Pets:** Small. $20 daily fee/room. Service with restrictions, supervision.

(ASK) (S❄) (✕) (📞) (▣) (¶¶) (🍴) (🅧)

ST. GEORGE

▼▼ ▼▼ Lake Digdeguash Four Season Chalets 🅒
(506) 755-2737. **$90 (no credit cards), 60 days notice.** Jct Hwy 1, 9 km w on Rt 760 to entry road, 1.5 km e on gravel entry road. Ext corridors. **Pets:** Accepted.

(S❄) (▣) (🅧) (🅐🅒) (🅟🅦) (🆉)

ST. STEPHEN

ⓐⒶ ▼▼ St. Stephen Inn 🅜🅘
(506) 466-1814. **$85-$120, 3 days notice.** 99 King St. Centre; on Hwy 1. Ext/int corridors. **Pets:** Large. $10 daily fee/pet. Designated rooms, service with restrictions, supervision.

(SAVE) (✕) (¶¶)

SUSSEX

▼▼ ▼▼ Econo Lodge 🅜🅘
(506) 433-2220. **$85-$105, 14 days notice.** 1015 Main St. Centre; Hwy 1 E, exit 192; Hwy 1 W, exit 198. Ext corridors. **Pets:** Accepted.

(SAVE) (S❄) (✕) (▣) (¶¶)

▼▼ ▼▼ Pine Cone Motel 🅜
(506) 433-3958. **$60-$70.** 12808 Rt 114. Trans-Canada Hwy 2, exit 418, 2 km e on Hwy 114 toward Penobsquis. Ext corridors. **Pets:** Small. Designated rooms, service with restrictions, supervision.

(✕) (🆉)

ⓐⒶ ▼▼▼▼ Quality Inn Fairway 🅜🅘
(506) 433-3470. **$85-$135, 14 days notice.** Hwy 1 at Sussex. Trans-Canada Hwy 2 at jct Hwy 1. Ext/int corridors. **Pets:** Very small. $10 daily fee/pet. Designated rooms, service with restrictions, supervision.

(SAVE) (S❄) (✕) (▣) (¶¶) (🍴)

WOODSTOCK

◆◆ Econo Lodge MI 🐾
(506) 328-8876. **$94-$139, 10 days notice.** 268 Rt 555. 4.8 km w on Trans-Canada Hwy 2, exit 188 (Houlton Rd) at jct Hwy 95. Ext/int corridors. **Pets:** Designated rooms, supervision.

◆◆ Panorama Motel MI
(506) 328-3315. **$79-$111, 14 days notice.** 4.8 km w on Trans-Canada Hwy 2, exit 188 (Houlton Rd) at jct Hwy 95. Ext/int corridors. **Pets:** Other species. Service with restrictions, supervision.

ⒶⒶ ◆◆ Stiles Motel Hill View MI
(506) 328-6671. **$70-$85, 3 days notice.** 827 Main St. Trans-Canada Hwy 2, exit 188 eastbound, 2.5 km e on Rt 103; exit 199 westbound, 8.5 km w on Rt 103 (Main St). Ext corridors. **Pets:** Accepted.

[SAVE] [S] [✕] [¶]

YOUNGS COVE ROAD

ⒶⒶ ◆◆ McCready's Motel MI
(506) 362-2916. **$55-$65.** 37343 Rt 2. Trans-Canada Hwy 2, exit 365, just w. Ext corridors. **Pets:** Accepted.

[SAVE] [¶] [AC] [☎]

CLARENVILLE

▼▼ St. Jude Hotel Ⓜ
(709) 466-1717. **$82.** Centre; on Trans-Canada Hwy 1. Int corridors. **Pets:** Designated rooms, service with restrictions, supervision.
(ASK) (S&) (✕) (▣) (¶)

CORNER BROOK

▼▼ Comfort Inn Ⓜ
(709) 639-1980. **$83-$99, 30 days notice.** 41 Maple Valley Rd. Trans-Canada Hwy 1, exit 5 eastbound; exit 6 westbound, via Confederation Ave. Int corridors. **Pets:** Other species. Service with restrictions, supervision.
(SAVE) (S&) (✕) (▣) (¶)

▼▼▼ Holiday Inn Ⓜ
(709) 634-5381. **$108-$118, 14 days notice.** 48 West St. Centre. Int corridors. **Pets:** Accepted.
(ASK) (S&) (✕) (▣) (¶) (≈)

COW HEAD

▼▼ Shallow Bay Motel & Cabins Ⓜ
(709) 243-2471. **$65-$77.** Hwy 430, 4 km w towards the ocean, follow signs. Ext/int corridors. **Pets:** Accepted.
(ASK) (S&) (✕) (🛏) (¶) (≈) (🐾)

GANDER

▼▼ Albatross Hotel Ⓜ
(709) 256-3956. **$83-$86.** On Trans-Canada Hwy 1. Ext/int corridors. **Pets:** Large, other species. Designated rooms, service with restrictions, crate.
(ASK) (S&) (✕) (▣) (¶)

▼▼ Comfort Inn Ⓜ
(709) 256-3535. **$99.** 112 Trans-Canada Hwy 1. Centre. Ext/int corridors. **Pets:** Very small, other species. Service with restrictions, supervision.
(SAVE) (S&) (✕) (🛏) (▣) (¶)

ⒶⒶ ▼▼▼ Hotel Gander Ⓜ
(709) 256-3931. **$74-$92, 30 days notice.** 100 Trans-Canada Hwy 1. Centre. Int corridors. **Pets:** Accepted.
(SAVE) (✕) (🛏) (▣) (¶) (≈)

▼▼ Sinbad's Hotel & Suites Ⓜ
(709) 651-2678. **$82-$160, 30 days notice.** Bennett Dr. Centre. Ext corridors. **Pets:** Other species. Service with restrictions.
(ASK) (S&) (✕) (🛏) (▣) (¶)

GRAND FALLS

▼▼ Mount Peyton Hotel Ⓜ
(709) 489-2251. **$101, 7 days notice.** 214 Lincoln Rd. 1 km ne on Trans-Canada Hwy 1. Ext/int corridors. **Pets:** Accepted.
(ASK) (S&) (✕) (▣) (¶)

ST. JOHN'S

▼▼ The Battery Hotel & Suites Ⓜ 🐾
(709) 576-0040. **$92-$109.** 100 Signal Hill Rd. 1.6 km e. Int corridors. **Pets:** Other species. Designated rooms.
(ASK) (S&) (✕) (🛏) (▣) (¶) (≈) (🐾)

▼▼ Best Western Travellers Inn, St. John's Ⓜ
(709) 722-5540. **$99-$119.** 199 Kenmount Rd. 4.8 km w on Trans-Canada Hwy 1. Ext/int corridors. **Pets:** Medium, other species. Designated rooms, service with restrictions, supervision.
(SAVE) (S&) (✕) (🛏) (▣) (¶) (≈) (🐾)

▼▼▼ Delta St John's Hotel and Conference Centre Ⓗ 🐾
(709) 739-6404. **$155-$160.** 120 New Gower St. Centre. Int corridors. **Pets:** Other species. $50 one-time fee/room. Supervision.
(✕) (▣) (¶) (≈)

▼▼▼ Holiday Inn-St. John's Ⓜ
(709) 722-0506. **$145-$162.** 180 Portugal Cove Rd. Trans-Canada Hwy 1, exit 47A, 1.4 km s. Ext/int corridors. **Pets:** Accepted.
(✕) (S&M) (🐾) (▣) (¶) (≈)

STEPHENVILLE

▼▼▼ Holiday Inn Ⓜ
(709) 643-6666. **$138.** 44 Queen St. Centre. Int corridors. **Pets:** Accepted.
(ASK) (S&) (✕) (▣) (¶)

YELLOWKNIFE

▼▼▼ Fraser Tower Suite Hotel 🅷
(867) 873-8700. **$147-$225.** 5303 52nd St. Corner of 52nd St and 53rd Ave. Int corridors. **Pets:** $5 daily fee/pet, $5 one-time fee/pet. Service with restrictions, crate.

(ASK) (S🔒) (✕) (🔋) (💻) (📶)

▼▼ The Regency Explorer Hotel 🅷
(867) 873-3531. **$184.** 4825 49th Ave. Downtown. Int corridors. **Pets:** Accepted.

(ASK) (S🔒) (✕) (💻) (🍴)

▼▼ Yellowknife Super 8 Motel Ⓜ
(867) 669-8888. **$107-$139, 30 days notice.** 308 Old Airport Rd. 2 km s on Franklin, 1 km w on Old Airport Rd; in Walmart Plaza. Int corridors. **Pets:** $25 daily fee/pet. Designated rooms, service with restrictions.

(ASK) (S🔒) (✕)

AMHERST

◆◆ Auberge Wandlyn Inn M
(902) 667-3331. **$120.** Trans-Canada Hwy 104, exit 3, 1 km w; at Victoria St. Ext/int corridors. **Pets:** Designated rooms, supervision.

(ASK) (S⬦) (✕) (🔌) (💻) (🍽) (⚓)

◆◆ Comfort Inn M
(902) 667-0404. **$102-$118, 14 days notice.** 143 Albion St S. Trans-Canada Hwy 104, exit 4, 1.5 km n on Hwy 2. Int corridors. **Pets:** Other species.

(SAVE) (S⬦) (✕) (💻)

ANTIGONISH

◆◆ Maritime Inn Antigonish M
(902) 863-4001. **$85-$145.** 158 Main St. Centre. Ext/int corridors. **Pets:** Other species. $50 deposit/room. Designated rooms, service with restrictions, supervision.

(✕) (💻) (🍽)

AULD'S COVE

(AAA) ◆◆ The Cove Motel & Mariner Dining Room ✕ ❀
(902) 747-2700. **$89-$99.** 1 km off Trans-Canada Hwy 104, 3 km w of Canso Cswy. Ext corridors. **Pets:** Small, dogs only. Designated rooms, service with restrictions, supervision.

(SAVE) (✕) (💻) (🍽) (✕)

BADDECK

◆◆◆ McIntyre's Housekeeping Cottages C
(902) 295-1133. **$62-$129, 4 days notice.** 8908 Hwy 105. Trans-Canada Hwy 105, 5 km w. Ext corridors. **Pets:** $5 daily fee/pet. Service with restrictions, supervision.

(✕) (🔌) (💻) (🎞) (☎)

◆◆◆ Silver Dart Lodge & MacNeil House ✕
(902) 295-2340. **$119-$139, 3 days notice.** 257 Hwy 205. Trans-Canada Hwy 105, exit 8, 1 km e on Shore Rd (Rt 205). Ext/int corridors. **Pets:** Accepted.

(✕) (🔌) (💻) (🍽) (⚓) (✕)

BLACK POINT

◆ Grand View Motel M
(902) 857-9776. **$49-$85, 7 days notice.** Hwy 3. Hwy 103, exit 5 westbound; exit 6 eastbound to Rt 3, 9 km e. Ext corridors. **Pets:** Small. $10 daily fee/pet. Service with restrictions, supervision.

(🎞) (☎)

BRIDGETOWN

◆◆ Bridgetown Motor Inn M
(902) 665-4403. **$65-$75.** 396 Granville St. Hwy 101, exit 20, 1 km w on Rt 1. Ext corridors. **Pets:** Accepted.

(ASK) (✕) (🍽) (⚓)

BRIDGEWATER

◆◆ Auberge Wandlyn Inn M
(902) 543-7131. **$120.** 50 North St. 1 km e on Hwy 325; adjacent to South Shore Shopping Mall; Hwy 103, exit 12. Int corridors. **Pets:** Supervision.

(ASK) (S⬦) (✕) (🔌) (💻) (🍽) (⚓)

◆◆ Comfort Inn M
(902) 543-1498. **$79-$119.** 49 North St. Hwy 103, exit 12, 1.7 km s on Rt 10. Int corridors. **Pets:** Service with restrictions, supervision.

(SAVE) (S⬦) (✕) (S.M) (💻)

CHESTER

◆ Windjammer Motel M
(902) 275-3567. **$50-$65.** 4070 Rt 3. 1 km w. Ext corridors. **Pets:** Medium, other species. Service with restrictions, supervision.

(S⬦) (✕) (🔌) (🍽)

CHETICAMP

◆◆ Cabot Trail Sea & Golf Chalets C
(902) 224-1777. **$109-$139, 7 days notice.** 71 Fraser Doucet Ln. Centre. Ext corridors. **Pets:** Medium, dogs only. $10 daily fee/pet. Service with restrictions, crate.

(✕) (🔌) (💻) (☎)

▽▽ Laurie's Motor Inn M
(902) 224-2400. **$85-$145, 7 days notice.** 15456 Laurie Rd. 1 km n, 7.2 km sw of West Gate Cape Breton Highlands National Park on the Cabot Tr. Ext/int corridors. **Pets:** Service with restrictions, supervision.

ASK SO X 🖶 🖵 🍴

CA ▽ Parkview Motel, Dining Room & Lounge M 🐾
(902) 224-3232. **$75-$80, 7 days notice.** 16546 Cabot Tr. 7.2 km n at West Gate Cape Breton Highlands National Park. Ext corridors. **Pets:** Designated rooms, service with restrictions, crate.

SAVE X 🍴 AC Z

CHURCH POINT

▽▽ Le Manoir Samson Inn M
(902) 769-2526. **$75-$92, 5 days notice.** 1768 Rt 1. Centre; on Hwy 1. Ext corridors. **Pets:** Accepted.

ASK SO X 🖶 🖵 AC

CLYDE RIVER

▽▽▽ Clyde River Inn Bed and Breakfast BB 🐾
(902) 637-3267. **$70-$100.** 10525 Main Hwy. Centre; on Trans-Canada Hwy 103. Int corridors. **Pets:** Other species. Service with restrictions, supervision.

X AC Z

DARTMOUTH

CA ▽▽ Best Western Mic Mac Hotel M
(902) 469-5850. **$69-$119.** 313 Prince Albert Rd. Hwy 111, exit 6A, 1 blk s. Int corridors. **Pets:** Designated rooms, supervision.

SAVE SO X 🖶 🖵 🍴

CA ▽▽ Comfort Inn M
(902) 463-9900. **$88-$135.** 456 Windmill Rd. Hwy 111, exit Shannon Park. Int corridors. **Pets:** Small, other species. Designated rooms, service with restrictions, supervision.

SAVE SO X 🖵

CA ▽▽▽ Holiday Inn-Harbourview H
(902) 463-1100. **$99-$149.** 99 Wyse Rd. Adjacent to Angus L MacDonald Bridge. Int corridors. **Pets:** Medium. Designated rooms, service with restrictions, supervision.

SAVE SO X 🖶 🖵 🍴 🐾

CA ▽▽▽ Park Place Ramada Plaza Hotel H
(902) 468-8888. **$99-$169.** 240 Brownlow Ave. From Murray Mackay Bridge, 1.2 km n on Hwy 111, exit 3 (Burnside Dr); in Park Place Centre. Int corridors. **Pets:** Small, dogs only. $50 deposit/pet. Designated rooms, service with restrictions, supervision.

SAVE SO X &M 🖵 🍴 🐾

DIGBY

CA ▽▽▽ Admiral Digby Inn M
(902) 245-2531. **$79-$99.** 441 Shore Rd. Hwy 101, exit 26, 2.5 km n, follow St John Ferry signs, 5 km w on Victoria Rd, 1 km e of ferry terminal. Ext corridors. **Pets:** Small. Designated rooms, service with restrictions, supervision.

SAVE X 🖶 🍴

HALIFAX

▽▽ Auberge Wandlyn Inn M
(902) 443-0416. **$79-$150.** 50 Bedford Hwy. 5.2 km w on Rt 2 (Bedford Hwy). Ext/int corridors. **Pets:** Accepted.

ASK SO X 🖵 🍴

▽ Bluenose Inn & Suites M
(902) 443-3171. **$56-$119.** 636 Bedford Hwy. Rt 2, 10.4 km nw. Ext corridors. **Pets:** Accepted.

ASK SO 🖶

▽ Chebucto Inn M
(902) 453-4330. **$75-$105.** 6151 Lady Hammond Rd. Jct Hwy 111 and Rt 2, 0.7 km e. Ext corridors. **Pets:** Accepted.

X 🍴

CA ▽▽▽ Citadel Halifax Hotel H
(902) 422-1391. **$99-$179.** 1960 Brunswick St. Centre. Int corridors. **Pets:** Service with restrictions, supervision.

SAVE SO X 🖶 🖵 🍴 🐾

CA ▽▽▽ Delta Barrington H
(902) 429-7410. **$129-$199.** 1875 Barrington St. Centre. Int corridors. **Pets:** Large. $50 deposit/room. Service with restrictions, supervision.

SAVE SO X 🖵 🍴 🐾

CA ▽▽▽ Delta Halifax H 🐾
(902) 425-6700. **$129-$189.** 1990 Barrington St. Corner of Cogswell and Barrington sts; in Scotia Square. Int corridors. **Pets:** Large, other species. $50 one-time fee/room. Service with restrictions, supervision.

SAVE SO X 🖶 🖵 🍴 🐾

CA ▽▽ Econo Lodge M 🐾
(902) 443-0303. **$69-$129.** 560 Bedford Hwy. 9.6 km w on Rt 2. Int corridors. **Pets:** $10 one-time fee/pet. Designated rooms, service with restrictions, supervision.

SAVE SO X 🍴 🐾

▽▽ Esquire Motel M
(902) 835-3367. **$55-$80.** 771 Bedford Hwy. Hwy 102, exit 4A, 5.3 km e on Rt 2 (Bedford Hwy). Ext corridors. **Pets:** Service with restrictions, supervision.

ASK SO X 🖶 🐾 AC

▽▽▽ Holiday Inn Express M
(902) 445-1100. **$119-$179.** 133 Kearney Lake Rd. Hwy 102, exit 2. Int corridors. **Pets:** Small. Designated rooms, service with restrictions, crate.

ASK SO X &M & 🖵 🐾

(CAA) ▼▼▼ **Holiday Inn Select-Halifax Centre H**
(902) 423-1161. **$129-$174, 18 days notice.** 1980 Robie St. Jct Quinpool and Robie sts. Int corridors. **Pets:** Medium. Designated rooms, service with restrictions, supervision.
[SAVE] [S✆] [✕] [▦] [¶] [≈]

(CAA) ▼ **Howard Johnson Hotel Halifax MI**
(902) 479-5611. **$98-$111, 3 days notice.** 20 St Margaret's Bay Rd. Hwy 3, 1 km w of Armdale Traffic Circle. Ext/int corridors. **Pets:** Small. Designated rooms, service with restrictions, supervision.
[SAVE] [S✆] [✕] [▦] [¶] [≈]

(CAA) ▼▼▼ **Lakeview Inn & Suites M** ❀
(902) 450-3020. **$115-$175.** 98 Chain Lake Dr. Hwy 102, exit 2A eastbound in Bayers Lake Business Park; from Hwy 103, exit 2. **Pets:** Medium. $100 deposit/room, $5 daily fee/pet. Designated rooms, service with restrictions, supervision.
[SAVE] [S✆] [✕] [≙M] [█] [▦] [≈]

(CAA) ▼▼▼ **The Lord Nelson Hotel & Suites H** ❀
(902) 423-6331. **$114-$154.** 1515 S Park St. Centre. Int corridors. **Pets:** Medium, other species. Designated rooms, service with restrictions, supervision.
[SAVE] [S✆] [✕] [█] [▦] [¶]

(CAA) ▼▼▼ **The Prince George Hotel H**
(902) 425-1986. **$-$149.** 1725 Market St. Centre; direct access to World Trade Centre. Int corridors. **Pets:** Other species. $50 deposit/room. Service with restrictions, supervision.
[SAVE] [✕] [≙M] [▦] [¶] [≈]

(CAA) ▼▼▼ ▼▼▼ **The Sheraton Halifax Hotel H**
(902) 421-1700. **$225-$300.** 1919 Upper Water St. Centre; adjacent to historic properties. Int corridors. **Pets:** Large, other species.
[SAVE] [S✆] [✕] [≙M] [█] [▦] [¶] [≈]

▼ **Travelers Motel M**
(902) 835-3394. **$69-$89.** 773 Bedford Hwy. Hwy 102, exit 4A, 5.3 km e on Rt 2 (Bedford Hwy). Ext corridors. **Pets:** Medium. Service with restrictions, supervision.
[✕] [█] [Ⓚ]

(CAA) ▼▼▼ ▼ **The Westin Nova Scotian H**
(902) 421-1000. **$109-$235.** 1181 Hollis St. Centre. Int corridors. **Pets:** Designated rooms, service with restrictions, supervision.
[SAVE] [S✆] [✕] [▦] [¶] [≈]

INGONISH BEACH

▼▼▼ **Keltic Lodge R**
(902) 285-2880. **$301-$316, 3 days notice.** Middle Head Peninsula. Inside the Cape Breton Highlands National Park; off Cabot Tr main highway. Ext/int corridors. **Pets:** Medium, dogs only. Service with restrictions, supervision.
[ASK] [✕] [█] [▦] [¶] [≈] [⊗]

KENTVILLE

(CAA) ▼ **Allen's Motel M**
(902) 678-2683. **$55-$70.** 384 Park St. Hwy 101, exit 14, 3 km e on Rt 1. Ext corridors. **Pets:** Accepted.
[SAVE] [S✆] [✕] [Ⓚ] [✆]

▼▼ **Auberge Wandlyn Inn MI**
(902) 678-8311. **$99-$109.** 7270 Hwy 1. Hwy 101, exit 14. Ext/int corridors. **Pets:** Other species. Designated rooms, service with restrictions.
[ASK] [S✆] [✕] [█] [▦] [¶] [≈]

(CAA) ▼ **Sun Valley Motel M**
(902) 678-7368. **$55-$70.** 905 Park St. Hwy 101, exit 14, 0.8 km e, then 3.2 km w on Rt 1. Ext corridors. **Pets:** Accepted.
[SAVE] [S✆] [✕] [▦] [Ⓚ] [✆]

LISCOMB

▼▼▼ **Liscombe Lodge X**
(902) 779-2307. **$145, 3 days notice.** Guysborough County. On Hwy 7. Ext/int corridors. **Pets:** Other species. Designated rooms, service with restrictions.
[✕] [█] [▦] [¶] [⊗] [Ⓚ]

LUNENBURG

▼▼ **Homeport Motel & Inn M** ❀
(902) 634-8234. **$75-$110, 3 days notice.** 167 Victoria Rd. 1 km w on Rt 3. Ext corridors. **Pets:** $10 one-time fee/room. Supervision.
[✕] [█] [▦]

MAHONE BAY

▼▼▼ **Bayview Pines Country Inn BB** ❀
(902) 624-9970. **$85-$100, 3 days notice.** 678 Oakland Rd Indian Point. Hwy 103, exit 10, 2 km w on Rt 3 to Kedy's Landing, 6 km e of Mahone Bay. Ext/int corridors. **Pets:** Medium. Designated rooms, service with restrictions, supervision.
[✕] [█] [▦] [Ⓚ] [✆]

MAVILETTE

▼▼ **Cape View Motel & Cottages M**
(902) 645-2258. **$53-$66.** Centre; Rt 1, 32 km ne of Yarmouth. Ext corridors. **Pets:** Service with restrictions, supervision.
[✕] [█] [Ⓚ] [✆]

NEW GLASGOW

▼▼ **Comfort Inn M**
(902) 755-6450. **$83-$110.** 740 Westville Rd. Trans-Canada Hwy 104, exit 23, just e on Hwy 289; opposite shopping mall. Int corridors. **Pets:** Accepted.
[SAVE] [S✆] [✕] [▦]

Ⓐ ▼▼▼ **Country Inn & Suites By**
    Carlson Ⓜ ❀
(902) 928-1333. **$87-$112.** 700 Westville Rd. Trans-Canada Hwy 104, exit 23, just e on Hwy 289; opposite shopping mall. Int corridors. **Pets:** Small. $5 daily fee/room. Designated rooms, service with restrictions, supervision.
[SAVE] [S🐾] [✕] [💻]

NORTH SYDNEY

Ⓐ ▼▼▼ **Clansman Motel** Ⓜ
(902) 794-7226. **$79-$99.** Hwy 125, exit 2, just e on King St. Ext/int corridors. **Pets:** Accepted.
[SAVE] [S🐾] [✕] [🍴] [⛱]

PORT HASTINGS

Ⓐ ▼ **Howard Johnson Inn Highland**
    Gateway Ⓜ
(902) 625-0460. **$109.** Just e of Canso Cswy on Trans-Canada Hwy 105 rotary; entrance through north side of church. Ext/int corridors. **Pets:** Small. Designated rooms, service with restrictions, supervision.
[SAVE] [S🐾] [✕] [💻] [🍴]

▼▼ **MacPuffin Motel** Ⓜ
(902) 625-0621. **$74-$119.** 373 Hwy 4. 1.6 km n on Hwy 4, 1.6 km s of Canso Cswy. Ext corridors. **Pets:** Other species. Designated rooms.
[A$K] [S🐾] [✕] [💻] [🍴] [⛱]

Ⓐ ▼ **Skye Lodge** Ⓜ
(902) 625-1300. **$69-$89, 14 days notice.** 160 Hwy 4. Jct of Hwy 105, Rt 104 and 19. Ext/int corridors. **Pets:** Accepted.
[SAVE] [S🐾] [✕] [💻]

PORT HAWKESBURY

▼▼ **Maritime Inn Port Hawkesbury** Ⓜ
(902) 625-0320. **$85-$145.** 717 Reeves St. 6.4 km e of Canso Cswy on Hwy 4; opposite shopping centre. Ext/int corridors. **Pets:** $50 deposit/room. Designated rooms, service with restrictions, supervision.
[✕] [💻] [🍴] [⛱]

SCOTSBURN

▼▼▼ **Stonehame Chalets** ❎
(902) 485-3468. **$96-$160, 7 days notice.** Rt 256, 12 km w of Pictou via Rt 376, last 2 km on gravel entry road. Ext corridors. **Pets:** Other species. Designated rooms, service with restrictions, supervision.
[✕] [💻] [⛱] [🎾]

SHELBURNE

Ⓐ ▼▼▼ **MacKenzie's Motel & Cottages** Ⓜ
(902) 875-2842. **$70-$85.** 260 Water St. Hwy 103, exit 26, 1.5 km e on Rt 3. Ext corridors. **Pets:** Accepted.
[SAVE] [S🐾] [✕] [💻] [⛱]

SMITHS COVE

▼▼ **Hedley House** Ⓜ
(902) 245-2500. **$79-$169.** RR 1. Hwy 101, exit 25 eastbound; exit 24 westbound. Ext corridors. **Pets:** Accepted.
[A$K] [S🐾] [✕] [💻] [🍴] [⛱]

Ⓐ ▼▼▼ **Mountain Gap Inn** ❎
(902) 245-5841. **$130, 3 days notice.** 217 Hwy 1. Hwy 101, exit 25 eastbound; exit 24 westbound, on Rt 1. Ext corridors. **Pets:** Other species. $10 daily fee/room. Service with restrictions, supervision.
[SAVE] [S🐾] [✕] [💻] [🍴] [⛱] [🎾]

SYDNEY

▼▼ **Comfort Inn** Ⓜ
(902) 562-0200. **$89-$121.** 368 Kings Rd. Hwy 4, 3.5 km e of jct Hwy 125, exit 6E. Int corridors. **Pets:** Large, other species. Designated rooms, service with restrictions, crate.
[SAVE] [S🐾] [✕] [💻]

Ⓐ ▼▼▼ **Days Inn Sydney** Ⓜ ❀
(902) 539-6750. **$119.** 480 Kings Rd. Hwy 4, 2.8 km e of jct Hwy 125, exit 6E. Int corridors. **Pets:** Large, other species. Service with restrictions, supervision.
[SAVE] [S🐾] [✕] [💻] [⛱]

Ⓐ ▼▼▼ **Delta Sydney** ❎
(902) 562-7500. **$129.** 300 Esplanade. Centre; on Hwy 4, 5.5 km e of jct Hwy 125, exit 6E. Int corridors. **Pets:** Accepted.
[SAVE] [S🐾] [✕] [💻] [🍴] [⛱]

SYDNEY MINES

▼▼▼ **Gowrie House Country Inn** ❎
(902) 544-1050. **$85-$295.** 139 Shore Rd. Hwy 105, exit 21E, 3 km n on Rt 305. Ext/int corridors. **Pets:** Accepted.
[✕] [💻] [🍴]

TRURO

▼▼ **Comfort Inn** Ⓜ
(902) 893-0330. **$116-$160.** 12 Meadow Dr. Trans-Canada Hwy 102, exit 14. Int corridors. **Pets:** Other species. Designated rooms, supervision.
[SAVE] [S🐾] [✕]

Ⓐ ▼▼▼ **Howard Johnson Hotel & Convention**
    Center Ⓜ
(902) 895-1651. **$95-$125, 3 days notice.** 437 Prince St. Centre. Ext/int corridors. **Pets:** Service with restrictions, crate.
[SAVE] [S🐾] [✕] [💻] [🍴] [⛱]

Ⓐ ▼ **The Palliser Motel** Ⓜ
(902) 893-8951. **$49-$65.** 103/104 Tidal Bore Rd. Trans-Canada Hwy 102, exit 14; Trans-Canada Hwy 104, exit 15, 3.2 km s. Ext corridors. **Pets:** Dogs only. Service with restrictions, supervision.
[SAVE] [S🐾] [✕] [🍴] [🎾]

WESTERN SHORE

ⒶⒶ ▼▼▼ Oak Island Resort & Marina ✖
(902) 627-2600. **$89-$129.** 55 Vaughn Rd. Hwy 103, exit 9 or 10, follow signs on Rt 3, then 10 km e of Mahone Bay. Int corridors. **Pets:** Service with restrictions.
[SAVE] [✖] [Ġᴹ] [🐾] [🖥] [💻] [🍴] [🏊] [✖]

WHITE POINT

▼▼ White Point Beach Resort ✖
(902) 354-2711. **$120-$130, 3 days notice.** White Point Beach. Hwy 103, exit 20A, 9 km w on Rt 3. Ext/int corridors. **Pets:** Other species. Designated rooms.
[✖] [🖥] [💻] [🍴] [🏊] [✖]

YARMOUTH

ⒶⒶ ▼▼▼ Best Western Mermaid Ⓜ
(902) 742-7821. **$79-$165, 7 days notice.** 545 Main St. On Hwy 1 at jct Hwy 3. Ext corridors. **Pets:** Accepted.
[SAVE] [Sᴅ] [✖] [💻] [🏊] [ĴC]

▼▼ Capri Motel Ⓜ
(902) 742-7168. **$79-$135.** 8-12 Herbert St. 1.6 km n on Hwy 1. Ext corridors. **Pets:** Accepted.
[ASK] [Sᴅ] [✖] [🖥] [💻]

ⒶⒶ ▼▼▼ Comfort Inn Ⓜ ✿
(902) 742-1119. **$68-$135.** 96 Starrs Rd. Jct Hwy 101 E and Rt 3. Int corridors. **Pets:** Other species. Designated rooms, service with restrictions, crate.
[SAVE] [Sᴅ] [✖] [💻]

ⒶⒶ ▼ Lakelawn Motel Ⓜ
(902) 742-3588. **$64-$79.** 641 Main St. 1 km n on Hwy 1. Ext/int corridors. **Pets:** Small. Designated rooms, service with restrictions, supervision.
[SAVE] [✖] [ĴC] [☎]

▼▼ Rodd Colony Harbour Inn Ⓜ ✿
(902) 742-9194. **$79-$129.** 6 Forrest St. At ferry terminal. Int corridors. **Pets:** Medium, other species. Service with restrictions, supervision.
[ASK] [Sᴅ] [✖] [🖥] [💻] [🍴] [ĴC]

▼▼▼ Rodd Grand Yarmouth-A Rodd Signature Hotel Ⓗ
(902) 742-2446. **$105-$190.** 417 Main St. Near centre. Int corridors. **Pets:** Accepted.
[ASK] [Sᴅ] [✖] [🖥] [💻] [🍴] [🏊] [ĴC]

▼▼ Voyageur Motel Ⓜ
(902) 742-7157. **$74-$98.** 4.8 km ne on Hwy 1. Ext corridors. **Pets:** Accepted.
[ASK] [Sᴅ] [✖] [🖥] [ĴC]

CITY INDEX

BANCROFT

Ⓐ ▽▽ Best Western Sword Motor Inn Ⓜ ❖
(613) 332-2474. **$93-$133.** 146 Hastings St. Centre; on Hwy 62 N. Ext/int corridors. **Pets:** Small. $15 deposit/room. Service with restrictions, supervision.
Ⓢᴬⱽᴱ Ⓢ❍ ⓧ 🔳 🔲 ⓣ 🏊

BARRIE

▽▽▽▽ Holiday Inn Barrie Ⓜ
(705) 728-6191. **$155-$169.** 20 Fairview Rd. 1.6 km s at jct Hwy 400 and 27, exit 94 (Essa Rd). Int corridors. **Pets:** Service with restrictions, supervision.
Ⓐˢᴷ Ⓢ❍ ⓧ Ⓜ 🔲 ⓣ 🏊

▽▽ ▽▽ Travelodge Barrie Ⓜ
(705) 734-9500. **$129-$139.** 55 Hart Dr. Hwy 400, exit 96A S (Dunlop St). Int corridors. **Pets:** Medium, other species. $20 deposit/room. Service with restrictions, supervision.
Ⓐˢᴷ Ⓢ❍ ⓧ 🔳 🔲 ⓣ 🏊

BARRY'S BAY

Ⓐ ▽ Mountain View Motel Ⓜ ❖
(613) 756-2757. **$59-$89.** 4 km e on Hwy 60. Ext corridors. **Pets:** Other species. Service with restrictions, supervision.
Ⓢᴬⱽᴱ Ⓢ❍ ⓧ 🔳 🔲

BAYFIELD

Ⓐ ▽▽▽ ▽▽▽ The Little Inn of Bayfield Ⓒ
(519) 565-2611. **$160-$710.** 26 Main St. Hwy 21, exit Main St, at jct Catherine. Int corridors. **Pets:** Medium, dogs only. $25 one-time fee/room. Designated rooms, service with restrictions, crate.
Ⓢᴬⱽᴱ ⓧ ⓣ

BELLEVILLE

Ⓐ ▽▽▽ Best Western Belleville Ⓜ
(613) 969-1112. **$99-$118.** 387 N Front St. Hwy 401, exit 543A, 0.5 km s on Hwy 62 (N Front St). Int corridors. **Pets:** Accepted.
Ⓢᴬⱽᴱ Ⓢ❍ ⓧ 🔳 🔲 🏊

Ⓐ ▽▽ Comfort Inn Ⓜ
(613) 966-7703. **$87-$116.** 200 N Park St. Hwy 401, exit 543A, 1 km s on Hwy 62 (N Front St). Int corridors. **Pets:** Accepted.
Ⓢᴬⱽᴱ Ⓢ❍ ⓧ 🔳 🔲

Ⓐ ▽▽ Quality Inn Belleville Ⓜ
(613) 962-9211. **$109, 14 days notice.** 407 N Front St. Hwy 401, exit 543A, just s on Hwy 62 (N Front St). Int corridors. **Pets:** Other species. Designated rooms, service with restrictions, crate.
Ⓢᴬⱽᴱ Ⓢ❍ ⓧ 🔳 🔲 ⓣ 🏊

▽▽▽▽ Ramada Inn on the Bay Ⓗ ❖
(613) 968-3411. **$180-$195.** 11 Bay Bridge Rd. Hwy 2, 0.5 km s; on E Zwick Island Park. Int corridors. **Pets:** Small. Designated rooms, service with restrictions, supervision.
Ⓐˢᴷ ⓧ 🔲 ⓣ 🏊 ⓧ

BRACEBRIDGE

Ⓐ ▽▽ Travelodge Bracebridge Ⓜ ❖
(705) 645-2235. **$89-$149.** 320 Taylor Rd. Hwy 11, exit 42 (Taylor Rd), 1 km w. Ext corridors. **Pets:** Medium. Service with restrictions, supervision.
Ⓢᴬⱽᴱ Ⓢ❍ ⓧ 🔳 🔲 🏊

BRAMPTON

[CAA] ◆◆◆ **Comfort Inn** [M]
(905) 452-0600. **$100-$120.** 5 Rutherford Rd S. Hwy 401, exit Hwy 410 N, 11 km to Hwy 7 E (Queen St), 1 km w. Int corridors. **Pets:** Accepted.
[SAVE] [S/D] ⊠ ▣ 🖥

[CAA] ◆◆◆ **Holiday Inn Select** [H]
(905) 792-9900. **$179-$209.** 30 Peel Centre Dr. Hwy 410 N, exit 7 (Queen St), 2 km e. Int corridors. **Pets:** Accepted.
[SAVE] [S/D] ⊠ ▣ 🖥 🍴 🏊

[CAA] ◆◆ **Motel 6** [M]
(905) 451-3313. **$71-$90.** 160 Steelwell Rd. Hwy 410, exit Steeles Ave E, s on Tomken, then just w. Int corridors. **Pets:** Small. Service with restrictions, crate.
[SAVE] ⊠

BRANTFORD

◆◆◆ **Comfort Inn** [MI]
(519) 753-3100. **$90-$113.** 58 King George Rd. Just s of jct Hwy 403 and 24. Int corridors. **Pets:** Other species. Designated rooms, supervision.
[SAVE] [S/D] ⊠ ▣ 🖥 🍴

[CAA] ◆◆◆ **Days Inn** [MI]
(519) 759-2700. **$81-$85.** 460 Fairview Dr. Hwy 403, exit Wayne Gretzky Pkwy, 0.8 km n. Int corridors. **Pets:** $10 one-time fee/room. Designated rooms, service with restrictions.
[SAVE] [S/D] ⊠ ▣ 🖥 🍴

BRIGHTON

◆ **Presquile Beach Motel** [M]
(613) 475-1010. **$52-$85.** 243 Main St W. Hwy 401, exit 509, 4 km s on Hwy 30, 2 km w on Hwy 2. Ext corridors. **Pets:** Other species. No service, crate.
⊠ ▣ ☎

BROCKVILLE

[CAA] ◆◆ **Best Western White House Motel** [M]
(613) 345-1622. **$69-$119.** RR 1 1843 Hwy 2 E. Hwy 401, exit 698, 1.7 km s on N Augusta Rd, 1.5 km e on Hwy 2 (King St W). Ext corridors. **Pets:** Small, other species. $10 daily fee/pet. Designated rooms, service with restrictions, supervision.
[SAVE] [S/D] ⊠ ▣ 🖥 🏊

BURLINGTON

[CAA] ◆◆ **Comfort Inn** [M]
(905) 639-1700. **$87-$119.** 3290 S Service Rd. QEW, exit Walker's Line Rd westbound, just s to Harvester Rd, then just w to S Service Rd; exit Guelph Line Rd eastbound, just s to Harvester Rd, then just e. Int corridors. **Pets:** Large, other species. Service with restrictions, supervision.
[SAVE] [S/D] ⊠ ▣ 🖥

[CAA] ◆◆ **Motel 6 Canada** [M]
(905) 331-1955. **$66-$82.** 4345 N Service Rd. QEW, exit Walker's Line N to N Service Rd. Int corridors. **Pets:** Medium, other species. Service with restrictions, supervision.
[SAVE] ⊠ ♿ ▣

[CAA] ◆◆◆ **Travelodge Hotel Burlington on the Lake** [MI]
(905) 681-0762. **$149-$179.** 2020 Lakeshore Rd. Jct of Brant St. Int corridors. **Pets:** Other species. $10 daily fee/room. Designated rooms, service with restrictions.
[SAVE] [S/D] ⊠ ▣ 🖥 🍴 🏊

CAMBRIDGE

◆◆ **Comfort Inn** [M] 🐾
(519) 658-1100. **$97-$113.** 220 Holiday Inn Dr. Hwy 401, exit 282, just n to Groh Ave. Int corridors. **Pets:** Other species. Service with restrictions, supervision.
[SAVE] [S/D] ⊠ ▣ 🖥

[CAA] ◆◆◆◆ **Langdon Hall Country House & Spa** [CI]
(519) 740-2100. **$229-$329, 7 days notice.** RR 33. Hwy 401, exit 275 to Homer Watson Blvd (Fountain St), 1 km s to Blair Rd, follow signs 1 km to Langdon Dr. Ext/int corridors. **Pets:** Accepted.
[SAVE] ▣ 🍴 🏊 🎾

CHAPLEAU

◆ **Riverside Motel** [M]
(705) 864-0440. **$75-$85.** 116 Cherry St. Northeast section of town; corner of Grey and Cherry sts; on Chapleau River. Ext corridors. **Pets:** Accepted.
[A$K] [S/D] ⊠ ▣

CHATHAM

[CAA] ◆◆◆ **Comfort Inn** [M]
(519) 352-5500. **$125.** 1100 Richmond St. Hwy 401, exit 81 (Bloomfield Rd), 5 km n to Richmond St (Hwy 2). Int corridors. **Pets:** Other species. $50 deposit/room. Service with restrictions, supervision.
[SAVE] [S/D] ⊠ ▣ 🖥

CHATSWORTH

◆◆ **Key Motel** [M]
(519) 794-2350. **$55-$75.** Hwy 6 and 10. Ext/int corridors. **Pets:** Accepted.
⊠ ▣ 🏊 🎾

COBOURG

[CAA] ◆◆◆ **Best Western Cobourg Inn and Convention Centre** [MI]
(905) 372-2105. **$118-$130, 3 days notice.** 930 Burnham St. I-401, exit 472 (Burnham St). Int corridors. **Pets:** Accepted.
[SAVE] [S/D] ⊠ ▣ 🍴 🏊

▼▼▼ Comfort Inn **M** ❀
(905) 372-7007. **Call for rates.** 121 Densmore Rd. Hwy 401, exit 474, just se. Int corridors. **Pets:** Other species. Designated rooms, supervision.
⊠ 🗄 💻

CORNWALL

Ⓐ ▼▼▼▼ Best Western Parkway Inn & Conference Centre **M**
(613) 932-0451. **$129-$149.** 1515 Vincent Massey Dr. Hwy 401, exit 789; from Brookdale Ave, just w on Hwy 2. Int corridors. **Pets:** Other species. Service with restrictions, supervision.
[SAVE] [S🐾] ⊠ 💻 ❬❙❭ 🌰

Ⓐ ▼ Econo Lodge **M**
(613) 936-1996. **$70-$100.** 1142 Brookdale Ave. Hwy 401, exit 789, 3 km s. Ext/int corridors. **Pets:** Medium. $10 daily fee/pet. Service with restrictions, supervision.
[SAVE] [S🐾] ⊠ 🗄

▼▼ Holiday Inn Express **M**
(613) 937-0111. **$118-$138.** 1625 Vincent Massey Dr. Brookdale Ave, just w on Hwy 2. Int corridors. **Pets:** Designated rooms, service with restrictions, supervision.
[ASK] [S🐾] ⊠ 🗄 💻 🌰

Ⓐ ▼▼▼▼ Ramada Inn & Conference Centre **M** ❀
(613) 933-8000. **$89-$149.** 805 Brookdale Ave. Hwy 401, exit 789, 4 km s. Int corridors. **Pets:** Small. Service with restrictions, supervision.
[SAVE] [S🐾] ⊠ 🗄 💻 ❬❙❭ 🌰

DRYDEN

Ⓐ ▼▼▼▼ Best Western Motor Inn **M**
(807) 223-3201. **$83-$90.** 349 Government St. Hwy 17. Ext/int corridors. **Pets:** Service with restrictions, crate.
[SAVE] [S🐾] ⊠ 🗄 💻 ❬❙❭ 🌰

▼▼ Comfort Inn **M** ❀
(807) 223-3893. **$75-$86, 14 days notice.** 522 Government St. Hwy 17. Int corridors. **Pets:** Other species. Designated rooms, service with restrictions, supervision.
[SAVE] [S🐾] ⊠ 💻

ELLIOT LAKE

▼ Dunlop Lake Lodge **M**
(705) 848-8090. **$75, 3 days notice.** 74 Dunlop Lake Rd. Hwy 17, 38.8 km n on Hwy 108, 0.8 km w, follow signs. Int corridors. **Pets:** Other species. $5 daily fee/pet. Designated rooms.
[ASK] [S🐾] ⊠ ❬❙❭ ⊠ ⒶⒻ

FONTHILL

▼ Hipwell's Motel **M**
(905) 892-3588. **$35-$75.** 299 Regional Rd 20. Town centre; 1.6 km w. Ext corridors. **Pets:** Other species. $4 daily fee/pet. Service with restrictions, crate.
[ASK] [S🐾] ⊠ 🗄 ❬❙❭ 🌰

GUELPH

Ⓐ ▼▼▼▼ Comfort Inn **M**
(519) 763-1900. **$99-$112.** 480 Silvercreek Pkwy. Jct Hwy 6 and 7 (Woodlawn Rd). Int corridors. **Pets:** Accepted.
[SAVE] [S🐾] ⊠ 🗄 💻

Ⓐ ▼▼▼▼ Holiday Inn-Guelph **M**
(519) 836-0231. **$129-$169.** 601 Scottsdale Dr. Jct Hwy 6 N and Stone Rd E, 8 km n of jct Hwy 401. Int corridors. **Pets:** Accepted.
[SAVE] [S🐾] ⊠ 🗄 💻 ❬❙❭ 🌰

Ⓐ ▼▼▼ Ramada Hotel & Conference Centre **H**
(519) 836-1240. **$109-$119.** 716 Gordon St. Jct Gordon St and Stone Rd, 8 km n of Hwy 401 via Brock Rd. Int corridors. **Pets:** Accepted.
[SAVE] [S🐾] ⊠ 🗄 💻 ❬❙❭ 🌰

HAMILTON

Ⓐ ▼▼▼▼ Sheraton Hamilton **H**
(905) 529-5515. **$260-$270.** 116 King St W. Downtown; at Jackson Square Shopping Centre; on Hwy 6 and 8 westbound. Int corridors. **Pets:** Small. $25 deposit/room. Designated rooms, service with restrictions, supervision.
[SAVE] [S🐾] ⊠ 🗄 💻 ❬❙❭ 🌰

HAWKESBURY

▼▼▼▼ Best Western Motel L'Heritage **M**
(613) 632-5941. **$85-$90.** 1575 Tupper St. 3 km e of jct Hwy 34, on Hwy 17. Int corridors. **Pets:** Accepted.
[SAVE] [S🐾] ⊠ 🗄 💻 ❬❙❭

HILTON BEACH

▼▼ Hilton Harbour Resort **M**
(705) 246-0063. **$63-$88, 7 days notice.** 3117 Marks St. Hwy 17 to Hwy 548, follow signs; in Hilton Beach. Ext corridors. **Pets:** Small, dogs only. Service with restrictions, supervision.
[ASK] [S🐾] ⊠ 🗄 💻 ⊠ ⒶⒻ

HUNTSVILLE

Ⓐ ▼▼ Comfort Inn **M**
(705) 789-1701. **$78-$143.** 86 King William St. Jct Hwy 60. Int corridors. **Pets:** Service with restrictions, supervision.
[SAVE] [S🐾] ⊠ 🗄 💻

▼ Tulip Inn **M** ❀
(705) 789-4001. **$80-$105, 3 days notice.** 211 Arrowhead Park Rd. Hwy 11, exit 226 (Muskoka Rd 3), follow signs for Arrowhead Park. Ext corridors. **Pets:** Other species. Service with restrictions, supervision.
⊠ 🗄 💻 ⊠

INGERSOLL

▼▼▼▼ Travelodge Ingersoll M
(519) 425-1100. **$90-$104.** 20 Samnah Crescent. Hwy 401, exit 216 (Culloden Rd). Int corridors. **Pets:** Accepted.
(ASK) (S&) (✕) (🛏) (💻) (🐾)

IRON BRIDGE

(CAA) ▼▼ Red Top Motor Inn MI
(705) 843-2100. **$50-$65.** 22133 Hwy 17. 0.5 km w. Ext corridors. **Pets:** Other species. Service with restrictions, supervision.
(SAVE) (S&) (✕) (🍴) (🐾)

JORDAN

(CAA) ▼▼▼ Best Western Beacon Harborside Resort
& Conference Centre MI
(905) 562-4155. **$59-$249, 30 days notice.** 2793 Beacon Blvd. QEW, exit 57. Int corridors. **Pets:** Accepted.
(SAVE) (S&) (✕) (🛏) (💻) (🍴) (🐾) (✕)

KAPUSKASING

▼▼ Comfort Inn M ❖
(705) 335-8583. **$99-$104, 14 days notice.** 172 Government Rd E. Hwy 11, corner of Burnell Rd. Int corridors. **Pets:** Designated rooms, service with restrictions, crate.
(SAVE) (S&) (✕) (🛏) (💻)

KENORA

▼▼▼ Best Western Lakeside Inn & Convention
Centre MI
(807) 468-5521. **$99-$124, 3 days notice.** 470 First Ave S. Centre. Int corridors. **Pets:** Small. Designated rooms, service with restrictions, supervision.
(SAVE) (S&) (✕) (💻) (🍴) (🐾)

▼▼ Comfort Inn M
(807) 468-8845. **$81-$92.** 1230 Hwy 17 E. 1.5 km e. Int corridors. **Pets:** Other species. Designated rooms, crate.
(SAVE) (S&) (✕) (💻)

(CAA) ▼▼▼ Kenora Travelodge MI
(807) 468-3155. **$88-$104.** 800 Hwy 17E. 1 km e. Int corridors. **Pets:** Designated rooms, service with restrictions, supervision.
(SAVE) (S&) (✕) (🛏) (💻) (🍴) (🐾)

(CAA) ▼▼ Whispering Pines Motel M
(807) 548-4025. **$58.** 5 km w of jct Hwy 17 and 71, on Hwy 17; 15 km e on Hwy 17 from Kenora Centre. Ext corridors. **Pets:** Service with restrictions, supervision.
(SAVE) (S&) (✕) (🛏) (💻) (Ⓩ)

KINGSTON

(CAA) ▼▼▼ Comfort Inn M
(613) 546-9500. **$82-$139.** 55 Warne Crescent. Hwy 401, exit 617 (Division St), 0.5 km s to Dalton Ave. Int corridors. **Pets:** Accepted.
(SAVE) (S&) (✕) (🛏) (💻)

▼▼ Comfort Inn M
(613) 549-5550. **$82-$139.** 1454 Princess St. Hwy 401, exit 613, 4 km se. Int corridors. **Pets:** Small. $100 deposit/room. Designated rooms, no service, supervision.
(SAVE) (S&) (✕) (💻)

(CAA) ▼▼ The Executive Motel M
(613) 549-1620. **$58-$98, 3 days notice.** 794 Hwy 2 E. Hwy 401, exit 623, 8 km s, then 2 km e. Ext corridors. **Pets:** Accepted.
(SAVE) (S&) (✕) (🛏) (🐾)

(CAA) ▼▼▼ Howard Johnson Confederation Place
Hotel M ❖
(613) 549-6300. **$100-$149.** 237 Ontario St. Centre. Int corridors. **Pets:** Medium. $15 one-time fee/room. Designated rooms, service with restrictions, crate.
(SAVE) (S&) (✕) (🛏) (💻) (🐾)

(CAA) ▼▼▼ Peachtree Inn M
(613) 546-4411. **$105-$120.** 1187 Princess St. Hwy 401, exit 615, 4 km sw. Int corridors. **Pets:** Designated rooms, supervision.
(SAVE) (S&) (✕) (🛏) (💻)

▼▼ Super 8 M
(613) 542-7395. **$55-$115.** 720 Princess St. Centre. Int corridors. **Pets:** Small, dogs only. $20 deposit/room. Designated rooms, service with restrictions, supervision.
(ASK) (S&) (✕) (🛏)

KIRKLAND LAKE

▼▼ Comfort Inn M
(705) 567-4909. **$72-$117.** 455 Government Rd W. Rt 66, just w of town centre. Int corridors. **Pets:** Accepted.
(SAVE) (S&) (✕) (🛏) (💻)

KITCHENER

▼▼ Aram's "Roots and Wings" BB ❖
(519) 743-4557. **$75-$100.** 11 Sunbridge Crescent. Hwy 86 N, exit University E, 1 km to Bridge St S, 0.5 km s to Bridal Tr, then just e. Int corridors. **Pets:** Accepted.
(✕) (🛏) (🐾)

(CAA) ▼▼▼▼ Comfort Inn M
(519) 894-3500. **$93-$149.** 2899 King St E. Jct Weber St, Fairway Rd and Hwy 8, 5.6 km n of Hwy 401 via Hwy 8 and Weber St. Int corridors. **Pets:** Medium. Designated rooms, service with restrictions, supervision.
(SAVE) (S&) (✕) (🛏) (💻)

(CAA) ▼▼▼▼ Four Points by Sheraton
Kitchener H
(519) 744-4141. **$99-$149.** 105 King St E. Downtown; opposite Kitchener Farmer's Market, corner of King and Benton sts. Int corridors. **Pets:** Accepted.
(SAVE) (S&) (✕) (🛏) (💻) (🍴) (🐾)

▼▼ The Howard Johnson Hotel Ⓜ
(519) 893-1234. **$79-$159.** 1333 Weber St E. Hwy 401, exit 278, 6.4 km w to Kitchener on Hwy 8 W, exit Weber St W. Ext/int corridors. **Pets:** Other species. Designated rooms, service with restrictions, supervision.

🔲 🔲 🔲 🔲 🔲 🔲 🔲

Ⓐ ▼▼▼ Radisson Hotel Kitchener Ⓜ
(519) 894-9500. **$114-$159.** 2960 King St E. Hwy 401, exit 35, 6 km w on Hwy 8 W, exit Weber St. Int corridors. **Pets:** Other species. Service with restrictions, crate.

🔲 🔲 🔲 🔲 🔲 🔲 🔲

LEAMINGTON

▼▼▼ Comfort Inn Ⓜ ❀
(519) 326-9071. **$100-$125, 14 days notice.** 279 Erie St S. Just s of jct Talbot and Erie sts; on direct route to Point Pelee National Park. Int corridors. **Pets:** Designated rooms, service with restrictions, supervision.

🔲 🔲 🔲

Ⓐ ▼▼ Sun Parlor Motel Ⓜ
(519) 326-6131. **$65-$90, 7 days notice.** 135 Talbot St W. Hwy 3, 1 km w of Erie St. Ext corridors. **Pets:** $25 deposit/ pet. Designated rooms, service with restrictions, crate.

🔲 🔲 🔲 🔲

LONDON

Ⓐ ▼▼▼ Best Western Lamplighter Inn &
       Conference Centre Ⓜ
(519) 681-7151. **$129-$199.** 591 Wellington Rd S. Hwy 401, exit 186, 3.7 km n. Ext/int corridors. **Pets:** Small. $5 daily fee/pet. Designated rooms, service with restrictions, supervision.

🔲 🔲 🔲 🔲 🔲 🔲 🔲

▼▼▼ Comfort Inn Ⓜ
(519) 685-9300. **$95-$120.** 1156 Wellington Rd. Hwy 401, exit 186B, just n. Int corridors. **Pets:** Other species. Designated rooms, service with restrictions, supervision.

🔲 🔲 🔲 🔲

Ⓐ ▼▼▼▼ Delta London Armouries Ⓗ
(519) 679-6111. **$99-$159.** 325 Dundas St. Hwy 2. Int corridors. **Pets:** Medium. Designated rooms, service with restrictions, supervision.

🔲 🔲 🔲 🔲 🔲 🔲

Ⓐ ▼▼▼ Marriott Residence
       Inn-London Ⓜ ❀
(519) 433-7222. **$127-$142.** 383 Colborne St. Jct of King St. Int corridors. **Pets:** Other species. $5 daily fee/room, $150 one-time fee/room. Service with restrictions, supervision.

🔲 🔲 🔲 🔲 🔲 🔲

Ⓐ ▼▼▼ Quality Suites Ⓜ ❀
(519) 680-1024. **$111-$126, 10 days notice.** 1120 Dearness Dr. Hwy 401, exit 186B (Wellington Rd N), 1.6 km. Int corridors. **Pets:** Other species. Service with restrictions, supervision.

🔲 🔲 🔲 🔲

Ⓐ ▼▼▼ StationPark All Suite Hotel Ⓗ
(519) 642-4444. **$119-$149.** 242 Pall Mall St. Hwy 401, exit 186B (Wellington Rd N), 9 km to Pall Mall St; jct Wellington Rd and Pall Mall St. Int corridors. **Pets:** Accepted.

🔲 🔲 🔲 🔲 🔲

MARATHON

Ⓐ ▼▼▼ Peninsula Inn Ⓜ
(807) 229-0651. **$63-$78, 3 days notice.** Hwy 17, 2.4 km w of jct Hwy 626. Ext corridors. **Pets:** Small. Designated rooms, service with restrictions, supervision.

🔲 🔲 🔲

MCKELLAR

Ⓐ ▼▼▼▼ The Inn at Manitou Ⓡ
(705) 389-2171. **$500-$836, 30 days notice.** 81 The Inn Rd. Hwy 124, exit McKellar Centre Rd, 8 km s, follow signs. Ext corridors. **Pets:** Accepted.

🔲 🔲 🔲 🔲 🔲 🔲

MIDLAND

▼▼ Comfort Inn Ⓜ
(705) 526-2090. **$72-$116.** 980 King St. Jct King St and Hwy 12. Int corridors. **Pets:** Cats only. Service with restrictions, supervision.

🔲 🔲 🔲 🔲 🔲

MISSISSAUGA

▼▼ Comfort Inn Ⓜ
(905) 858-8600. **$99-$119.** 2420 Surveyor Rd. Hwy 401, exit Erin Mills Pkwy, 2 km s. Int corridors. **Pets:** Medium. $10 daily fee/pet. Supervision.

🔲 🔲 🔲 🔲 🔲

Ⓐ ▼▼ Comfort Inn Airport West Ⓜ
(905) 624-6900. **$98-$219.** 1500 Matheson Blvd. Hwy 401, exit Dixie Rd, just s. Int corridors. **Pets:** Accepted.

🔲 🔲 🔲 🔲 🔲

Ⓐ ▼▼▼▼ Delta Meadowvale Resort and
       Conference Centre Ⓗ
(905) 821-1981. **$99-$179.** 6750 Mississauga Rd. Hwy 401 W, exit 336 (Mississauga Rd), just s. Int corridors. **Pets:** Large, other species. Service with restrictions, crate.

🔲 🔲 🔲 🔲 🔲 🔲

Ⓐ ▼▼▼ Four Points By Sheraton Toronto
       Airport Ⓗ
(905) 624-1144. **$119-$189.** 5444 Dixie Rd. 1 km s of jct Hwy 401 and Dixie Rd. Int corridors. **Pets:** $15 daily fee/ room. Service with restrictions, supervision.

🔲 🔲 🔲 🔲 🔲 🔲 🔲

Ⓐ ▼▼▼ Holiday Inn Toronto West Ⓜ
(905) 890-5700. **$105-$145.** 100 Britannia Rd E. Jct Hwy 401 and 10; from Hwy 401, exit Hwy 10 S. Int corridors. **Pets:** Small, other species. Designated rooms, service with restrictions, crate.

🔲 🔲 🔲 🔲 🔲 🔲 🔲

(CAA) ▼▼ Motel 6 M
(905) 814-1664. **$71-$106, 7 days notice.** 2935 Argentina Rd. Hwy 401, exit 333 (Winston Churchill Blvd), just s. Int corridors. **Pets:** Small. Designated rooms, service with restrictions, supervision.
[SAVE] [X]

▼▼▼ Novotel Hotel Mississauga H
(905) 896-1000. **$139, 7 days notice.** 3670 Hurontario St. Hwy 10 at Burnhamthorpe Rd; Hwy 401, exit Hwy 10 S, then 5 km. Int corridors. **Pets:** Small, other species. $50 deposit/room. Service with restrictions, crate.
[X] [YI] [≥]

(CAA) ▼▼ Ramada Hotel-Toronto Airport West MI
(905) 624-9500. **$85-$125, 7 days notice.** 5599 Ambler Dr. Hwy 401, exit 346 (S Dixie Rd), just w on Aerowood, then just n. Int corridors. **Pets:** Medium. $25 one-time fee/room. Service with restrictions, supervision.
[SAVE] [S6] [X] [B] [≥] [YI] [≥]

(CAA) ▼▼▼ Sandalwood Hotel & Suites M
(905) 238-9600. **$134-$135, 7 days notice.** 5050 Orbitor Dr. Jct Eglinton Ave and Renforth Dr, 2.3 km w on Eglinton Ave. Int corridors. **Pets:** $10 daily fee/pet. Designated rooms, service with restrictions, crate.
[SAVE] [S6] [X] [B] [≥]

(CAA) ▼▼▼▼ Sheraton Gateway Hotel In Toronto International Airport H
(905) 672-7000. **$209.** Box 3000. In Toronto International Airport. Int corridors. **Pets:** Very small. Designated rooms, crate.
[SAVE] [S6] [X] [ℒM] [≥] [YI] [≥]

▼▼ Studio 6 Mississauga M
(905) 502-8897. **$91-$97.** 60 Brittannia Rd E. Jct of Hwy 101 and 10; Hwy 401, exit 3, Hwy 10 S. **Pets:** Small. $25 one-time fee/room. Service with restrictions, supervision.
[X] [ℒ] [B] [≥]

▼▼▼ Toronto Airport Hilton H
(905) 677-9900. **$124-$450.** 5875 Airport Rd. Hwy 401, exit Dixon Rd, 3.5 km w; 1 km from Toronto Pearson International Airport. Int corridors. **Pets:** Other species. Designated rooms, service with restrictions, supervision.
[SAVE] [X] [≥] [YI]

MONETVILLE

▼▼ Memquisit Lodge C
(705) 898-2355. **$80-$105, 21 days notice.** 506 Memquisit Rd. 20.8 km ne on west arm of Lake Nipissing, on Hwy 64 and Memquisit Lodge Rd; 36.8 km sw off Hwy 17, on Hwy 64. Ext corridors. **Pets:** Designated rooms, no service, supervision.
[ASK] [S6] [B] [YI] [X] [ℐ] [≥]

MORRISBURG

(CAA) ▼▼▼ The McIntosh Country Inn & Conference Centre MI
(613) 543-3788. **$69-$99.** 12495 Hwy 2E. Hwy 401, exit 750, 2 km s on Rt 31, 1 km e on Hwy 2. Int corridors. **Pets:** Medium. $20 daily fee/pet. Designated rooms, service with restrictions, supervision.
[SAVE] [S6] [X] [B] [≥] [YI] [≥]

NEWMARKET

▼▼ Comfort Inn M
(905) 895-3355. **$107-$133.** 1230 Journey's End Cir. Hwy 404, exit Davis Dr. Int corridors. **Pets:** Accepted.
[SAVE] [S6] [X] [B] [≥]

NIAGARA FALLS METROPOLITAN AREA

FORT ERIE

▼▼ Comfort Inn M
(905) 871-8500. **$70-$150.** 1 Hospitality Dr. Just off Walden Blvd and QEW. Int corridors. **Pets:** Medium. $10 one-time fee/room. Service with restrictions, supervision.
[SAVE] [S6] [X] [B] [≥]

NIAGARA FALLS

(CAA) ▼▼▼ Best Western Fallsview Motor Hotel MI
(905) 356-0551. **$79-$229, 3 days notice.** 6289 Fallsview Blvd. Jct Niagara Pkwy, just n. Ext/int corridors. **Pets:** Service with restrictions, supervision.
[SAVE] [S6] [X] [≥] [YI] [≥]

(CAA) ▼▼ Camelot Inn M
(905) 354-3754. **$39-$229.** 5640 Stanley Ave. Just n of Hwy 20, then just n; just s of Hwy 420. Ext corridors. **Pets:** Medium. $10 one-time fee/room. Designated rooms, service with restrictions, supervision.
[SAVE] [S6] [X] [B] [≥] [≥]

▼▼ Econo Lodge Near the Falls M
(905) 358-6243. **$60-$240.** 6000 Stanley Ave. 1.3 km w on Hwy 20, just s. Ext/int corridors. **Pets:** Small. Designated rooms, no service, supervision.
[SAVE] [S6] [X] [B] [≥]

(CAA) ▼▼▼ Flamingo Motor Inn M
(905) 356-4646. **$49-$179, 7 days notice.** 7701 Lundy's Ln. QEW, 3.4 km w on Hwy 20. Ext corridors. **Pets:** Small. $10 daily fee/pet. Designated rooms, service with restrictions, supervision.
[SAVE] [S6] [X] [B] [≥]

(CAA) ♦♦♦ **Niagara Parkway Court Motel** M
(905) 295-3331. **$49-$199.** 3708 Main St. 2.5 km s of the falls on the Niagara Pkwy. Ext corridors. **Pets:** Medium. $10 daily fee/pet. Designated rooms, service with restrictions, crate.
[SAVE] [S🐾] [✕] [🔌] [💻] [✍]

(CAA) ♦♦♦ **Peninsula Inn & Resort** H
(905) 354-8812. **$69-$269.** 7373 Niagara Square Dr. QEW, exit McLeod Rd, just w. Int corridors. **Pets:** Very small. $10 daily fee/room. Designated rooms, service with restrictions, crate.
[SAVE] [S🐾] [✕] [🔌] [💻] [🍴] [🛋]

(CAA) ♦♦ **Stanley Motor Inn** M
(905) 358-9238. **$60-$150.** 6220 Stanley Ave. 2 blks from the falls, just w of Skylon Tower. Ext/int corridors. **Pets:** Very small. $10 daily fee/pet. Designated rooms, no service, crate.
[SAVE] [✕] [🔌] [🛋] [✍]

(CAA) ♦ **Thriftlodge Clifton Hill** M
(905) 357-4330. **$59-$369, 3 days notice.** 4945 Clifton Hill. Just s on jct Victoria Ave. Ext corridors. **Pets:** Small. $50 deposit/room. Service with restrictions, supervision.
[SAVE] [S🐾] [✕] [🔌] [💻]

(CAA) ♦♦♦ **Travelodge Bonaventure** M
(905) 374-7171. **$54-$199, 7 days notice.** 7737 Lundy's Ln. QEW, exit Hwy 20 W, 4.5 km w. Ext/int corridors. **Pets:** Accepted.
[SAVE] [S🐾] [✕] [🍴] [🛋]

NIAGARA-ON-THE-LAKE

♦♦♦ **Gate House Hotel** CI
(905) 468-3263. **$145-$230, 7 days notice.** 142 Queen St. Jct Gate. Int corridors. **Pets:** Medium. Designated rooms, service with restrictions, supervision.
[🍴]

(CAA) ♦♦♦♦ **The Pillar & Post Inn** CI
(905) 468-2123. **$170-$365.** 48 John St. 13 km from QEW, just n on Hwy 55, just e. Ext/int corridors. **Pets:** Accepted.
[SAVE] [✕] [🍴] [🛋]

ST. CATHARINES

(CAA) ♦♦♦ **Comfort Inn** MI
(905) 687-8890. **$96-$155.** 2 Dunlop Dr. QEW, exit 46 (Lake St), between Lake and Geneva sts. Int corridors. **Pets:** Accepted.
[SAVE] [S🐾] [✕] [♿M] [🔌] [💻] [🍴]

(CAA) ♦♦♦ **Holiday Inn St Catharines** MI
(905) 934-8000. **$99-$249.** 2 N Service Rd. QEW, exit 46 (Lake St), just e. Int corridors. **Pets:** Medium, other species. $25 deposit/room, $15 daily fee/room. Service with restrictions, supervision.
[SAVE] [S🐾] [✕] [🔌] [💻] [🍴] [🛋]

(CAA) ♦♦ **Howard Johnson Hotel & Conference Centre** MI
(905) 934-5400. **$79-$259.** 89 Meadowvale Dr. Jct QEW and exit 46 (Lake St). Int corridors. **Pets:** Medium. $25 deposit/room. Designated rooms, service with restrictions, supervision.
[SAVE] [S🐾] [✕] [🔌] [💻] [🍴] [🛋]

(CAA) ♦♦♦ **Ramada Parkway Inn and Conference Centre** MI
(905) 688-2324. **$79-$289.** 327 Ontario St. Jct QEW and Ontario St, exit 47, 0.8 km s. Int corridors. **Pets:** Other species. Designated rooms, service with restrictions, crate.
[SAVE] [S🐾] [✕] [🔌] [💻] [🍴] [🛋]

(CAA) ♦♦♦ **The Travelodge St. Catharines** M
(905) 688-1646. **$84-$169, 7 days notice.** 420 Ontario St. QEW, exit 47. Ext corridors. **Pets:** Medium. $10 daily fee/room. Designated rooms, service with restrictions, crate.
[SAVE] [S🐾] [✕] [🔌] [🍴] [🛋]

THOROLD

♦♦♦ **Four Points by Sheraton St. Catharines** MI
(905) 984-8484. **$119-$229.** 3530 Schmon Pkwy. Hwy 406, exit St. David's Rd W. Int corridors. **Pets:** Large, other species. Designated rooms, service with restrictions, supervision.
[ASK] [S🐾] [✕] [🔌] [💻] [🍴] [🛋]

WELLAND

♦♦ **Comfort Inn** M
(905) 732-4811. **$88-$129.** 870 Niagara St. 2.5 km n. Int corridors. **Pets:** Other species. $10 daily fee/room. Designated rooms, service with restrictions, supervision.
[SAVE] [S🐾] [✕] [🔌] [💻]

❖ **END METROPOLITAN AREA** ❖

NORTH BAY

(CAA) ♦♦♦ **Best Western North Bay** MI ❖
(705) 474-5800. **$109-$149.** 700 Lakeshore Dr. Hwy 11, exit Lakeshore Dr, 4 km n, on Hwy 11B. Int corridors. **Pets:** Large, other species. Service with restrictions.
[SAVE] [S🐾] [✕] [🔌] [💻] [🍴] [🛋]

(CAA) ▼▼▼▼ **Clarion Resort Pinewood Park** M
(705) 472-0810. **$101-$107.** 201 Pinewood Dr. Hwy 11, exit Lakeshore Dr, immediate turn s onto Hwy 113, then 1 km. Int corridors. **Pets:** Service with restrictions, supervision.
SAVE SB ⊠ 📵 💻 ¶¶ ⚓

▼▼ **Comfort Inn** M
(705) 494-9444. **$85-$110.** 676 Lakeshore Dr. Hwy 11B, exit Lakeshore Dr, 4 km n of jct Hwy 11. Int corridors. **Pets:** Accepted.
SAVE SB ⊠ 📵 💻

▼▼ **Comfort Inn-Airport** M
(705) 476-5400. **$86-$250.** 1200 O'Brien St. 3 km e on Hwy 11 and 17 Bypass at O'Brien St exit. Int corridors. **Pets:** Service with restrictions, supervision.
SAVE SB ⊠ 📵 💻

▼▼▼ **Super 8** M
(705) 495-4551. **$87-$96.** 570 Lakeshore Dr. Hwy 11, exit Lakeshore Dr, 4.5 km n, on Hwy 11B. Int corridors. **Pets:** Other species. Service with restrictions, supervision.
ASK SB ⊠ ⚿ 📵

▼▼▼▼ **Travelodge North Bay** M ✤
(705) 495-1133. **$109-$135.** 1525 Seymour St. Jct Hwy 11, 17 and Seymour St. Int corridors. **Pets:** Other species.
ASK SB ⊠ 📵 💻 ⚓

OAKVILLE

▼▼▼▼ **Holiday Inn Oakville Centre** M
(905) 842-5000. **$115-$165, 7 days notice.** 590 Argus Rd. Jct QEW and Trafalgar Rd, then just s. Int corridors. **Pets:** $15 daily fee/pet. Designated rooms, service with restrictions, supervision.
⊠ 📵 💻 ¶¶ ⚓

(CAA) ▼▼▼▼ **Quality Hotel & Suites-Oakville** M
(905) 847-6667. **$99-$159.** 754 Bronte Rd. QEW, exit 111 (Bronte Rd/Hwy 25), 0.4 km s. Int corridors. **Pets:** Accepted.
SAVE SB ⊠ 📵 💻 ¶¶ ⚓

ORILLIA

▼▼ **Comfort Inn** M ✤
(705) 327-7744. **$100-$122.** 75 Progress Dr (RR 1). Hwy 11 N, exit Hwy 12, just s on Memorial Ave, corner of Progress Dr and Memorial Ave. Int corridors. **Pets:** Medium, other species. Designated rooms, service with restrictions, crate.
SAVE SB ⊠ 📵 💻

(CAA) ▼▼ **Econo Lodge** M
(705) 326-3554. **$59-$109.** 265 Memorial Ave. 0.5 km n of Hwy 12. Int corridors. **Pets:** Medium. $20 deposit/pet. Service with restrictions, supervision.
SAVE SB ⊠ 📵 💻

OSHAWA

▼▼▼ **Comfort Inn** M
(905) 434-5000. **$99-$129, 3 days notice.** 605 Bloor St W. Hwy 401, exit 416 (Park Rd), just s to Bloor St, then 0.8 km w. Int corridors. **Pets:** Designated rooms, service with restrictions, supervision.
SAVE SB ⊠ 📵 💻

(CAA) ▼▼▼▼ **Holiday Inn Oshawa** M
(905) 576-5101. **$119-$169.** 1011 Bloor St E. Hwy 401, exit 419 (Harmony Rd). Int corridors. **Pets:** Service with restrictions, supervision.
SAVE SB ⊠ 📵 💻 ¶¶ ⚓

(CAA) ▼▼▼ **Oshawa Travelodge** M
(905) 436-9500. **$99-$139.** 940 Champlain Ave. Hwy 401, exit 412 (Thickson Rd N). Int corridors. **Pets:** Small. $25 one-time fee/pet. Designated rooms, service with restrictions, supervision.
SAVE SB ⊠ 📵 💻 ⚓

OTTAWA METROPOLITAN AREA

GLOUCESTER

▼▼ **Comfort Inn** M
(613) 744-2900. **$108-$130.** 1252 Michael St. Hwy 417, exit 115, St Laurent Blvd N to Lemieux St. Int corridors. **Pets:** Accepted.
SAVE SB ⊠ 💻

(CAA) ▼▼ **Travelodge** M
(613) 745-1133. **$99-$159.** 1486 Innes Rd. Hwy 417, exit 112 (Innes Rd), just e. Int corridors. **Pets:** Other species. Service with restrictions, supervision.
SAVE SB ⊠ 📵 💻 ¶¶ ⚓

NEPEAN

(CAA) ▼▼▼ **Best Western Barons Hotel** M
(613) 828-2741. **$124-$126.** 3700 Richmond Rd. Hwy 417, exit 130, 2 km s. Int corridors. **Pets:** Accepted.
SAVE SB ⊠ 📵 💻 ¶¶ ⚓

▼▼ **Rideau Heights Motor Inn** M
(613) 226-4152. **$89-$109.** 72 Rideau Heights Dr. Hwy 16, 0.5 km n of Hunt Club Rd. Ext corridors. **Pets:** Small, other species. $20 daily fee/pet. Designated rooms, supervision.
ASK SB ⊠ 📵 💻

OTTAWA

Days Inn-Downtown (Ottawa) M
(613) 789-5555. **$105-$139.** 319 Rideau St. Between Nelson St and King Edward Ave. Ext/int corridors. **Pets:** Medium, other species. Designated rooms, service with restrictions, supervision.

Delta Ottawa Hotel and Suites H
(613) 238-6000. **$119-$199.** 361 Queen St. Corner of Lyon St. Int corridors. **Pets:** Other species. $50 one-time fee/room. Service with restrictions.

Econo Lodge-Ottawa/Orleans M
(613) 745-1531. **$85-$115.** 2098 Montreal Rd. Hwy 417, exit 113, 2.5 km e on Hwy 174 to Montreal Rd W exit. Ext corridors. **Pets:** Medium, other species. $5 daily fee/pet. Service with restrictions, crate.

Fairmont Chateau Laurier H
(613) 241-1414. **$120-$359.** 1 Rideau St. Just e of Parliament buildings. Int corridors. **Pets:** Accepted.

Les Suites Hotel Ottawa A
(613) 232-2000. **$149-$209.** 130 Besserer St. Between Nicholas and Waller sts. Int corridors. **Pets:** $25 one-time fee/room. Designated rooms, service with restrictions, supervision.

Lord Elgin Hotel H
(613) 235-3333. **$160.** 100 Elgin St. Between Laurier Ave and Slater St; opposite National Arts Centre. Int corridors. **Pets:** Large. Designated rooms, service with restrictions, supervision.

Novotel Ottawa Hotel H
(613) 230-3033. **$143-$175.** 33 Nicholas St. Corner of Daly Ave. Int corridors. **Pets:** Small. Service with restrictions, supervision.

Ottawa Marriott H
(613) 238-1122. **$159-$225.** 100 Kent St. Corner of Queen St. Int corridors. **Pets:** Service with restrictions, supervision.

Quality Hotel Ottawa, Downtown M
(613) 789-7511. **$150-$165.** 290 Rideau St. Corner of King Edward Ave. Int corridors. **Pets:** Other species. $50 deposit/room. Service with restrictions.

Ramada Hotel & Suites H
(613) 238-1331. **$113.** 111 Cooper St. Corner of Cartier St. Int corridors. **Pets:** Accepted.

Residence Inn by Marriott M
(613) 231-2020. **$159-$279.** 161 Laurier Ave W. Corner of Elgin St. Int corridors. **Pets:** $150 one-time fee/room. Service with restrictions.

Sheraton Ottawa Hotel H
(613) 238-1500. **$139-$315.** 150 Albert St. Corner of O'Connor St. Int corridors. **Pets:** Small. Designated rooms, service with restrictions, supervision.

Southway Inn of Ottawa M
(613) 737-0811. **$110-$128, 3 days notice.** 2431 Bank St. Hwy 31, corner of Hunt Club Rd. Int corridors. **Pets:** Accepted.

Travelodge Hotel by Parliament Hill H
(613) 236-1133. **$109-$169.** 402 Queen St. Corner of Bay and Queen Sts. Int corridors. **Pets:** Accepted.

Webb's Motel M
(613) 728-1881. **$85-$95, 5 days notice.** 1705 Carling Ave. 0.5 km n on Maitland Ave from jct Hwy 417, exit 126, then 0.5 km e. Ext/int corridors. **Pets:** Accepted.

The Westin, Ottawa H
(613) 560-7000. **$139-$245.** 11 Colonel By Dr. Corner of Rideau St; adjacent to Rideau Centre Complex. Int corridors. **Pets:** Other species. Service with restrictions, crate.

❖ END METROPOLITAN AREA ❖

OWEN SOUND

Comfort Inn M
(519) 371-5500. **$89-$115.** 955 9th Ave E. Jct Hwy 6, 10, 21 and 26. Int corridors. **Pets:** Accepted.

Days Inn Hotel and Convention Centre M
(519) 376-1551. **$89-$155, 7 days notice.** 950 6th St E. Jct Hwy 6 and 10. Int corridors. **Pets:** Medium. $20 one-time fee/pet. Designated rooms, service with restrictions, supervision.

▼▼▼▼ Owen Sound Inn M
(519) 371-3011. **$40-$130.** 485 9th Ave E. Jct Hwy 6, 10, 26 and 21; follow Hwy 6 and 10, 1 km s. Int corridors. **Pets:** Large, dogs only. $10 one-time fee/pet. Service with restrictions, supervision.
SAVE SP ⊠ ▯

▼▼▼▼ Travelodge MI
(519) 371-9297. **$110-$150, 30 days notice.** 880 10th St E. Jct of Hwy 6, 10, 21 and 26. Int corridors. **Pets:** Accepted.
ASK SP ⊠ ▯ ▣ ⍚

PARRY SOUND

▼▼ Comfort Inn M
(705) 746-6221. **$99-$142, 7 days notice.** 120 Bowes St. Jct Hwy 69 and Bowes St. Int corridors. **Pets:** Accepted.
SAVE SP ⊠ ▣

PEMBROKE

▼▼ Best Western Pembroke Inn & Conference Centre MI
(613) 735-0131. **$117-$147.** One International Dr. Jct of Hwy 17 and 41. Int corridors. **Pets:** Accepted.
SAVE SP ⊠ ▯ ▣ ⍚ ⍦

▼ Colonial Fireside Inn M
(613) 732-3623. **$63-$88.** 1350 Pembroke St W. Jct Hwy 17, 5 km n on Forest Lea Rd, then just e. Ext corridors. **Pets:** Accepted.
⊠ ▯ ▣ ⍦

▼▼▼ Comfort Inn M ✿
(613) 735-1057. **$79-$89, 3 days notice.** 959 Pembroke St E. 1.8 km e of town centre on Old Hwy 17. Int corridors. **Pets:** Other species. Service with restrictions, supervision.
SAVE SP ⊠ ▯ ▣

PETERBOROUGH

▼▼▼▼ Comfort Inn MI
(705) 740-7000. **$130-$240, 15 days notice.** 1209 Lansdowne St W. 0.6 km w of jct Hwy 28. Int corridors. **Pets:** Accepted.
SAVE ⊠ ▯ ▣ ⍚ ⍦

▼▼ Holiday Inn Peterborough Waterfront MI
(705) 743-1144. **$100-$130.** 150 George St N. Charlotte and George (Clock Tower), 1 km s. Int corridors. **Pets:** $25 one-time fee/room. Designated rooms, service with restrictions, supervision.
ASK SP ⊠ ▯ ▣ ⍚ ⍦ ⊠

▼▼ King Bethune House BB ✿
(705) 743-4101. **$104-$176, 14 days notice.** 270 King St. Charlotte and George (Clock Tower), just s on George to King St, then just w. Int corridors. **Pets:** Other species. Supervision.
⊠ ▯ ▣

▼▼▼ Quality Inn M
(705) 748-6801. **$105-$125.** 1074 Lansdowne St W. 3 km from jct Hwy 115 and Bypass. Int corridors. **Pets:** Medium. Designated rooms, service with restrictions, supervision.
SAVE SP ⊠ ▯ ▣

▼ Robyn's Motel M
(705) 745-3225. **$55-$70.** 1136 Hwy 7E. Hwy 7, 2.5 km e of Television Rd. Ext corridors. **Pets:** Accepted.
ASK SP ⊠ ▯

PICKERING

▼▼▼ Comfort Inn M
(905) 831-6200. **$99-$135.** 533 Kingston Rd. Hwy 401, exit 394 N (White's Rd) to Hwy 2, 0.5 km w. Int corridors. **Pets:** Designated rooms, service with restrictions, supervision.
SAVE SP ⊠ ▯ ▣

PICTON

▼▼▼ Merrill Inn CI
(613) 476-7451. **$95-$185.** 343 Main St E. Centre; corner of Johnston St. Int corridors. **Pets:** Accepted.
⊠ ▣ ⍚

PLANTAGENET

▼▼ Motel De Champlain MI
(613) 673-5220. **$80.** 200 Hwy 17. Hwy 17 at jct CR 9. Ext/int corridors. **Pets:** Accepted.
ASK ⊠ ▯ ⍚

PORT HOPE

▼▼▼▼ Comfort Inn M
(905) 885-7000. **$95-$125, 30 days notice.** Hwy 401 & 28. Hwy 401, exit 464, just n. Int corridors. **Pets:** Accepted.
SAVE SP ⊠ ▯ ▣

PROVIDENCE BAY

▼▼ Huron Sands Motel M
(705) 377-4616. **$64-$73, 3 days notice.** 5216 Hwy 551 General Delivery. In Providence Bay; centre; Hwy 551, 27.2 km w of South Baymouth, via 10th Side Rd, follow signs. Ext corridors. **Pets:** Other species. Service with restrictions, supervision.
SAVE ⊠ ▯ ⍚ ⊠

RENFREW

▼▼▼ The Renfrew Inn MI
(613) 432-8109. **$89-$109.** 760 Gibbons Rd. Hwy 17, exit O'Brien Rd. Int corridors. **Pets:** Other species. $10 daily fee/pet. Designated rooms, supervision.
SAVE SP ⊠ ▯ ▣ ⍚

RICHARDS LANDING

▼ **The Clansmen Motel** Ⓜ
(705) 246-2581. **$55-$60.** 1430 Richard St. Hwy 17 to Hwy 548, follow signs. Ext corridors. **Pets:** Accepted.
�S✕🛏💻 🐾

ROSSPORT

▼▼ **The Willows Inn Bed & Breakfast** Ⓑ
(807) 824-3389. **$60-$125, 10 days notice.** 1 Main St. Centre. Int corridors. **Pets:** Accepted.
✕ 🐾

SARNIA

Ⓐ ▼▼▼ **Best Western Guildwood Inn** Ⓜ
(519) 337-7577. **$105-$110.** 1400 Venetian Blvd. 1 km e of Bluewater Bridge. Ext/int corridors. **Pets:** Service with restrictions, supervision.
SAVE S✕🛏💻 🍴🏊

▼▼▼▼ **The Drawbridge Inn and Spa** Ⓜ
(519) 337-7571. **$105-$129, 7 days notice.** 283 N Christina St. 1.5 km s of Hwy 402, Christina St exit. Int corridors. **Pets:** Accepted.
A$K S✕🛏💻 🍴🏊

SAULT STE. MARIE

Ⓐ ▼▼▼ **Algoma's Water Tower Inn** Ⓜ
(705) 949-8111. **$129-$165, 7 days notice.** 360 Great Northern Rd. Jct Hwy 17 (Great Northern Rd) and Second Line. Int corridors. **Pets:** Accepted.
SAVE ✕🛏💻 🍴🏊

▼ **Ambassador Motel** Ⓜ
(705) 759-6199. **$49-$89.** 1275 Great Northern Rd. 6.4 km n on Hwy 17. Ext corridors. **Pets:** Large, other species. $5 daily fee/pet. Designated rooms, service with restrictions, crate.
✕🛏💻🏊🐾

Ⓐ ▼ **Bel-Air Motel** Ⓜ
(705) 945-7950. **$60-$85.** 398 Pim St. 2 km n on Hwy 17B. Ext corridors. **Pets:** Medium. $5 daily fee/room. Service with restrictions, crate.
SAVE S✕🛏

Ⓐ ▼▼ **Catalina Motel** Ⓜ 🐾
(705) 945-9260. **$86-$105.** 259 Great Northern Rd. 3.2 km n on Hwy 17B. Ext corridors. **Pets:** $10 one-time fee/pet. Designated rooms, service with restrictions, supervision.
SAVE S✕🛏💻

▼▼ **Comfort Inn** Ⓜ
(705) 759-8000. **$80-$135.** 333 Great Northern Rd. 3.6 km n on Hwy 17B. Ext/int corridors. **Pets:** Large. Designated rooms, supervision.
SAVE S✕🛏💻

▼▼▼▼ **Glenview Vacation Cottages** Ⓒ 🐾
(705) 759-3436. **$115-$140, 5 days notice.** 2611 Great Northern Rd. 9.6 km n on Hwy 17. Ext corridors. **Pets:** Small, dogs only. $5 daily fee/room. Designated rooms, service with restrictions, crate.
✕🛏💻🏊🐾

Ⓐ ▼▼▼▼ **Holiday Inn** Ⓜ 🐾
(705) 949-0611. **$109-$159.** 208 St. Marys River Dr. On the waterfront; behind Station Mall. Int corridors. **Pets:** Designated rooms, supervision.
SAVE S✕🛏💻 🍴🏊

Ⓐ ▼ **Northlander Motel** Ⓜ
(705) 254-6452. **$50-$80.** 243 Great Northern Rd. 3 km n on Hwy 17B. Ext corridors. **Pets:** Accepted.
SAVE S✕🛏

▼ **Satelite Motel** Ⓜ
(705) 759-2897. **$50-$95, 3 days notice.** 248 Great Northern Rd. 3 km n on Hwy 17B. Ext corridors. **Pets:** Medium, other species. Service with restrictions.
✕🛏

Ⓐ ▼▼▼▼ **Travelodge** Ⓜ
(705) 759-1400. **$79-$120.** 332 Bay St. Opposite Station Mall. Int corridors. **Pets:** Medium. $50 deposit/room. Designated rooms, service with restrictions, supervision.
SAVE S✕🛏💻

SHARBOT LAKE

Ⓐ ▼▼▼ **Sharbot Lake Country Inn** Ⓜ
(613) 279-2198. **$65-$125.** Hwy 38. 3.5 km s of jct Hwy 7. Ext corridors. **Pets:** $10 one-time fee/pet. Service with restrictions.
SAVE S✕ 🍴📞

SIMCOE

▼▼ **Comfort Inn** Ⓜ 🐾
(519) 426-2611. **$84-$109.** 85 The Queensway E. 0.5 km e on Hwy 3. Int corridors. **Pets:** Other species. Service with restrictions, supervision.
SAVE S✕🛏💻

ST. THOMAS

▼▼ **Comfort Inn** Ⓜ
(519) 633-4082. **$85-$165.** 100 Centennial Ave. 6.5 km e on Hwy 3. Int corridors. **Pets:** Large, dogs only. $20 one-time fee/room. Service with restrictions, supervision.
SAVE S✕🛏💻

STRATFORD

▼▼▼ **Arden Park Hotel** Ⓜ
(519) 275-2936. **$92-$199.** 522 Ontario St. Jct of Romeo. Int corridors. **Pets:** Accepted.
✕🛏💻🍴🏊

SUDBURY

▼▼ Comfort Inn M ☙
(705) 522-1101. **$100-$150.** 2171 Regent St S. 5 km s on Hwy 46. Int corridors. **Pets:** Other species. Designated rooms, service with restrictions.
[SAVE] [S▲] [✕] [▭]

▼▼ Comfort Inn M
(705) 560-4502. **$90-$160.** 440 Second Ave N. The Kingsway at Second Ave. Int corridors. **Pets:** Medium, other species. Designated rooms, service with restrictions, supervision.
[SAVE] [S▲] [✕] [&M] [🛡] [▭]

▼▼ Ramada Inn & Convention Centre M ☙
(705) 675-1123. **$124-$139, 30 days notice.** 85 St. Anne Rd. Centre; jct St Anne Rd and Notre Dame Ave. Int corridors. **Pets:** Medium. Designated rooms, service with restrictions, supervision.
[ASK] [S▲] [✕] [🛡] [▭] [🍴] [🏊]

(CAA) ▼▼ Travelodge Hotel Sudbury M
(705) 522-1100. **$90-$125.** 1401 Paris St. 1.5 km n of jct Hwy 69. Int corridors. **Pets:** Other species. Designated rooms, service with restrictions, supervision.
[SAVE] [S▲] [✕] [🛡] [▭] [🍴] [🏊]

THESSALON

(CAA) ▼ Carolyn Beach Motor Inn M
(705) 842-3330. **$70-$89.** One Lakeside Dr. Just w on Hwy 17 at jct Hwy 17B. Ext corridors. **Pets:** Accepted.
[SAVE] [✕] [🛡] [▭] [🍴] [✕] [AC]

THUNDER BAY

(CAA) ▼▼ Best Western Nor'Wester Resort Hotel M
(807) 473-9123. **$116-$262.** 2080 Hwy 61. 9.2 km sw of jct Hwy 11, 17 and 61, exit Loch Lomond Rd. Int corridors. **Pets:** Other species. Designated rooms, service with restrictions, supervision.
[SAVE] [S▲] [✕] [🛡] [▭] [🍴] [🏊]

(CAA) ▼▼ Comfort Inn M
(807) 475-3155. **$110-$140, 3 days notice.** 660 W Arthur St. Jct Hwy 11, 17 and 61, just e. Int corridors. **Pets:** Other species. Designated rooms, service with restrictions.
[SAVE] [S▲] [✕] [🛡] [▭]

(CAA) ▼▼ Super 8 Motel M
(807) 344-2612. **$66-$76.** 439 Memorial Ave. North Metro area; 2.4 km s on Hwy 17B and 11B. Int corridors. **Pets:** Other species. Designated rooms, service with restrictions, supervision.
[SAVE] [S▲] [✕] [🛡]

(CAA) ▼▼▼ Victoria Inn M
(807) 577-8481. **$105.** 555 W Arthur St. 0.8 km e of jct Hwy 11B, 17B and 61 (western access to town). Int corridors. **Pets:** Other species. Designated rooms, service with restrictions, supervision.
[SAVE] [✕] [🛡] [▭] [🍴] [🏊]

TILLSONBURG

(CAA) ▼▼ Super 8 Motel-Tillsonburg M
(519) 842-7366. **$95-$99, 10 days notice.** 92 Simcoe St. Hwy 19, just e. Int corridors. **Pets:** Medium, other species. Service with restrictions.
[SAVE] [S▲] [✕] [🛡] [▭] [🍴]

TIMMINS

▼▼ Comfort Inn M
(705) 264-9474. **$85-$106, 15 days notice.** 939 Algonquin Blvd E. Hwy 101, 0.5 km e of Rt 655. Int corridors. **Pets:** Accepted.
[SAVE] [S▲] [✕] [🛡] [▭]

TORONTO METROPOLITAN AREA

DOWNSVIEW

(CAA) ▼▼▼ Montecassino Hotel & Suites M
(416) 630-8100. **$140.** 3710 Chesswood Dr. Chesswood Dr at Sheppard Ave. Int corridors. **Pets:** Small. Service with restrictions, supervision.
[SAVE] [S▲] [✕] [🛡] [▭] [🍴]

MARKHAM

▼▼▼ Comfort Inn M
(905) 477-6077. **$110-$129.** 8330 Woodbine Ave. Hwy 401, exit 375, 9 km n; Hwy 404, exit Hwy 7, just e, then just s. Int corridors. **Pets:** Small. $10 one-time fee/room. Designated rooms, service with restrictions, supervision.
[SAVE] [S▲] [✕] [🛡] [▭]

▼▼▼ Staybridge Suites M
(905) 771-9333. **$149.** 355 S Park Rd. Jct Hwy 404 and 7, just w on Hwy 7 (Times Ave S), then just e. Int corridors. **Pets:** Accepted.
[ASK] [S▲] [✕] [🐾] [🛡] [▭] [🏊]

TORONTO

(CAA) ▼▼ Carlingview Airport Inn M
(416) 675-3303. **$117-$169.** 221 Carlingview Dr. QEW, exit Hwy 427 N to Dixon Rd E, 1 km to Carlingview Dr, then just s. Ext/int corridors. **Pets:** Accepted.
[SAVE] [S▲] [✕] [▭] [🍴]

Colony Hotel Toronto
(416) 977-0707. **$109-$139.** 89 Chestnut St. Adjacent to City Hall. Int corridors. **Pets:** Accepted.

Comfort Inn
(416) 736-4700. **$105-$129.** 66 Norfinch Dr. Hwy 400, exit Finch Ave E, then just n. Int corridors. **Pets:** Designated rooms, service with restrictions, supervision.

Crowne Plaza Toronto Don Valley
(416) 449-4111. **$119-$240.** 1250 Eglinton Ave E. Don Valley Pkwy, exit 375 on Wynford Dr, jct Don Valley Pkwy and Eglinton Ave E. Int corridors. **Pets:** Small. $25 daily fee/room. Designated rooms, service with restrictions, supervision.

Days Inn & Conference Centre-Toronto Downtown
(416) 977-6655. **$109-$189.** 30 Carlton St. Adjacent to Maple Leaf Gardens. Int corridors. **Pets:** Accepted.

Delta Chelsea Hotel
(416) 595-1975. **$139-$279.** 33 Gerrard St W. W of Yonge St, just s of College St. Int corridors. **Pets:** Other species. Service with restrictions, supervision.

Delta Toronto Airport
(416) 675-6100. **$109-$199, 7 days notice.** 801 Dixon Rd. Jct Hwy 27 N and Dixon Rd. Int corridors. **Pets:** Medium. $50 deposit/room. Designated rooms, service with restrictions, supervision.

Delta Toronto East
(416) 299-1500. **$159-$299, 7 days notice.** 2035 Kennedy Rd. Just ne of jct Hwy 401 and Kennedy Rd, exit 379. Int corridors. **Pets:** Accepted.

The Fairmont Royal York
(416) 368-2511. **$159-$289.** 100 Front St W. Opposite Union Station; entrance on Wellington St; from QEW/Gardiner Expwy, exit n on York or Bay sts. Int corridors. **Pets:** Medium. $35 one-time fee/room. Service with restrictions, supervision.

Four Seasons Hotel
(416) 964-0411. **$345-$440.** 21 Avenue Rd. Corner of Avenue Rd and Cumberland Ave. Int corridors. **Pets:** Accepted.

Hilton Toronto
(416) 869-3456. **$239-$394.** 145 Richmond St W. Jct of University Ave. Int corridors. **Pets:** Accepted.

Holiday Inn On King
(416) 599-4000. **$209-$259.** 370 King St W. Between Spanish Ave and Peter St. Int corridors. **Pets:** Large, other species. Designated rooms, service with restrictions.

International Plaza Hotel & Conference Centre
(416) 244-1711. **$119-$278.** 655 Dixon Rd. Jct of Hwy 27 N, just w of jct Hwy 401. Int corridors. **Pets:** Other species. Service with restrictions, supervision.

Metropolitan Hotel
(416) 977-5000. **$305-$420.** 108 Chestnut St. Just s of Dundas St. Int corridors. **Pets:** Service with restrictions, supervision.

Novotel Toronto Centre
(416) 367-8900. **$225-$285.** 45 The Esplanade. Just ne of Gardiner Expwy via Yonge St. Int corridors. **Pets:** $20 one-time fee/pet. Service with restrictions, supervision.

Novotel Toronto North York
(416) 733-2929. **$137-$149, 3 days notice.** 3 Park Home Ave. Hwy 401, exit Yonge St, 2 km n, then just w. Int corridors. **Pets:** Accepted.

Park Hyatt Toronto
(416) 925-1234. **$187-$390.** 4 Avenue Rd. Corner of Bloor St W. Int corridors. **Pets:** Large, dogs only. $200 deposit/room. Designated rooms, supervision.

Quality Hotel & Suites Toronto Airport East
(416) 240-9090. **$90-$135.** 2180 Islington Ave. Hwy 401, exit 356. Int corridors. **Pets:** $12 daily fee/pet. Supervision.

Quality Hotel Downtown
(416) 367-5555. **$119-$249.** 111 Lombard St. West side of Jarvis St; between Adelaide and Lombard sts, 1 km n off Gardiner Expwy at Jarvis St exit. Int corridors. **Pets:** Small. Service with restrictions, supervision.

Quality Hotel Midtown
(416) 968-0010. **$130-$180.** 280 Bloor St W. Just w of St George. Int corridors. **Pets:** Large, other species. Service with restrictions, supervision.

Quality Suites
(416) 674-8442. **$99-$270.** 262 Carlingview Dr. 1 km w of jct Hwy 27 N and Dixon Rd. Int corridors. **Pets:** Designated rooms, service with restrictions, supervision.

[CAA] ▼▼▼▼ Radisson Suite Hotel Toronto Airport H
(416) 242-7400. **$119-$189.** 640 Dixon Rd. Just e of jct Dixon Rd and Hwy 27; 0.3 km w of jct Hwy 401 and Dixon Rd. Int corridors. **Pets:** Small. Designated rooms, service with restrictions, crate.
[SAVE] [S🐾] [✕] [▣] [¶]

[CAA] ▼▼▼▼ Renaissance Toronto Hotel at SkyDome H
(416) 341-7100. **$199-$249.** 1 Blue Jays Way. Jct Front St. Int corridors. **Pets:** Accepted.
[SAVE] [S🐾] [✕] [🔊] [▣] [¶] [🏊]

[CAA] ▼▼▼▼▼ The Sheraton Centre Toronto Hotel H
(416) 361-1000. **$155-$225.** 123 Queen St W. Opposite Toronto Civic Centre and City Hall. Int corridors. **Pets:** Accepted.
[SAVE] [S🐾] [✕] [🖐M] [🔊] [▣] [¶] [🏊]

[CAA] ▼▼▼▼▼ The Sutton Place Hotel H
(416) 924-9221. **$219-$370.** 955 Bay St. Jct of Wellesley. Int corridors. **Pets:** Accepted.
[SAVE] [✕] [🔊] [▣] [¶] [🏊]

[CAA] ▼▼▼ Travelodge Hotel Toronto Airport (Dixon Road) MI
(416) 674-2222. **$99-$115, 3 days notice.** 925 Dixon Rd. Corner of Carlingview and Dixon rds. Int corridors. **Pets:** Accepted.
[SAVE] [S🐾] [✕] [🔊] [▣] [¶] [🏊]

[CAA] ▼▼▼ Travelodge Toronto Airport Rexdale MI
(416) 740-9500. **$109-$199.** 445 Rexdale Blvd. Jct of Hwy 27 and Rexdale Blvd. Int corridors. **Pets:** Accepted.
[SAVE] [S🐾] [✕] [🔊] [▣] [¶] [🏊]

[CAA] ▼▼▼ Travelodge Toronto East MI
(416) 299-9500. **$109-$149.** 20 Milner Business Ct. Jct Hwy 401 and Markham Rd, just n on Markham Rd. Int corridors. **Pets:** Service with restrictions.
[SAVE] [S🐾] [✕] [🔊] [▣] [¶] [🏊]

▼▼▼▼ Windsor Arms H ✿
(416) 971-9666. **$425-$2000 (weekly).** 18 St Thomas St. Jct of Bloor St. Int corridors. **Pets:** Medium. $300 deposit/room. Service with restrictions, supervision.
[¶] [🏊]

✿ END METROPOLITAN AREA ✿

TRENTON

▼▼ Comfort Inn M
(613) 965-6660. **$85-$130.** 68 Monogram Pl. Hwy 401, exit 526 (Glen Miller Rd S). Int corridors. **Pets:** Small, other species. Designated rooms, service with restrictions, supervision.
[SAVE] [S🐾] [✕] [🖐M] [🔊] [▣]

▼▼▼▼ Holiday Inn Trenton MI
(613) 394-4855. **$130.** 99 Glen Miller Rd. Hwy 401, exit 526. Int corridors. **Pets:** Large, other species. Designated rooms, service with restrictions, supervision.
[ASK] [S🐾] [✕] [🔊] [▣] [¶] [🏊]

TWEED

▼▼ Park Place Motel M
(613) 478-3134. **$51-$55.** 43 Victoria St. Hwy 37, 0.5 km s of centre. Ext corridors. **Pets:** Service with restrictions, supervision.
[🔊]

WALLACEBURG

▼▼ Super 8 Motel M
(519) 627-0781. **$71-$85.** 76 McNaughton Ave. Hwy 40 (McNaughton Ave), south side of town. Int corridors. **Pets:** Accepted.
[ASK] [S🐾] [✕] [🔊]

WASAGA BEACH

▼ Kingsbridge Inn M
(705) 429-6364. **$60-$185, 30 days notice.** 268 Main St. Hwy 92, just n. Ext corridors. **Pets:** Medium. $100 deposit/room. Designated rooms, service with restrictions, crate.
[ASK] [✕] [🔊] [▣] [🖥]

WATERLOO

▼▼▼ Comfort Inn MI
(519) 747-9400. **$85-$120.** 190 Weber St N. East side off Weber St, 0.3 km s of University Ave (Hwy 86). Int corridors. **Pets:** Accepted.
[SAVE] [S🐾] [✕] [🔊] [▣] [¶]

[CAA] ▼▼▼ Les Diplomates B&B (Executive Guest House) BB
(519) 725-3184. **$88-$128, 3 days notice.** 100 Blythwood Rd. Hwy 86 N, exit King St, just s to Columbia, just w to Hazel St, then just e. Ext/int corridors. **Pets:** Accepted.
[SAVE] [S🐾] [✕]

▼▼▼ The Waterloo Inn & Conference Centre MI
(519) 884-0220. **$149.** 475 King St N. 3 km n on King St, at jct Hwy 86. Int corridors. **Pets:** Large, other species. $15 one-time fee/pet. Designated rooms, service with restrictions, supervision.
[ASK] [✕] [🔊] [▣] [¶] [🏊]

WAWA

▼▼ **Kinniwabi Pines Motel/Cottages** **M** ❀
(705) 856-7302. **$45-$60.** Hwy 17, 5.3 km s of jct Hwy 101.
Ext corridors. **Pets:** Medium. $8 one-time fee/pet. Designated rooms, service with restrictions, supervision.

[S🐾] [✕] [🛏] [💻] [✕] [🐾]

▼▼ **Parkway Motel** **M**
(705) 856-7020. **$50-$60.** Hwy 17, 4 km s of jct Hwy 101.
Ext corridors. **Pets:** Accepted.

[✕] [🛏] [💻] [✕] [🐾]

▼▼▼ **Sportsman's Motel** **M**
(705) 856-2272. **$60-$70.** 45 Mission Rd. Hwy 101, 2.4 km
e of jct Hwy 17. Ext corridors. **Pets:** Small. $10 daily fee/
room. Designated rooms, service with restrictions, supervision.

[S🐾] [✕] [🛏] [💻] [🐾]

ⒸⒶ **▼** **Wawa Northern Lights Motel &**
Chalets **M** ❀
(705) 856-1900. **$64-$79.** Hwy 17 N. 8 km n of jct Hwy
101. Ext corridors. **Pets:** Other species. Supervision.
[SAVE] [S🐾] [✕] [🛏] [🍴] [🐾]

WHITBY

ⒸⒶ **▼▼** **Motel 6** **M**
(905) 665-8883. **$71-$91.** 165 Consumers Dr. Hwy 401,
exit 410, just ne. Int corridors. **Pets:** Medium, other species.
Service with restrictions.

[SAVE] [✕] [🐾]

ⒸⒶ **▼▼▼** **Quality Suites** **M**
(905) 432-8800. **$164-$249.** 1700 Champlain Ave. Hwy
401, exit 412 (Thickson Rd), 0.5 km n to Champlain Ave,
just 1 km e. Int corridors. **Pets:** Accepted.
[SAVE] [S🐾] [✕] [🛏] [💻]

WHITEFISH FALLS

ⒸⒶ **▼▼▼** **The Island Lodge** **L**
(705) 285-4343. **$148-$165 (no credit cards), 21 days**
notice. In Whitefish Falls; parking and dock, just w of Hwy
6 (phone for boat at Espanola or Little Current). Ext corridors. **Pets:** Accepted.
[SAVE] [🛏] [💻] [🍴] [✕] [🐾] [☎]

WINDSOR

▼▼▼ **Comfort Inn** **M**
(519) 966-7800. **$110-$120, 7 days notice.** 2955 Dougall
Ave. 5.3 km s on Hwy 3B, off Hwy 401 via Tunnel exit. Int
corridors. **Pets:** Accepted.
[SAVE] [S🐾] [✕] [🛏] [💻]

ⒸⒶ **▼▼▼ ▼▼▼** **Hilton Windsor** **H**
(519) 973-5555. **$139-$209.** 277 Riverside Dr W. 1 km w of
Detroit-Windsor Tunnel; 1 km e of Ambassador Bridge. Int
corridors. **Pets:** Other species.
[SAVE] [S🐾] [✕] [💻] [🍴] [🐾]

ⒸⒶ **▼▼▼ ▼** **Holiday Inn Select** **H**
(519) 966-1200. **$144-$169.** 1855 Huron Church Rd. Jct
Huron Church and Malden rds; 1.5 km n of EC Row Expwy.
Int corridors. **Pets:** $10 daily fee/pet. Service with restrictions, supervision.
[SAVE] [S🐾] [✕] [🛏] [💻] [🍴] [🐾]

ⒸⒶ **▼▼▼** **Quality Suites** **M**
(519) 977-9707. **$119-$199.** 250 Dougall Ave. Downtown;
jct Dougall Ave and Chatham St. Int corridors. **Pets:** Other
species. $30 one-time fee/room. Service with restrictions,
supervision.
[SAVE] [S🐾] [✕] [💻] [🍴]

ⒸⒶ **▼▼▼ ▼** **Radisson Riverfront Hotel** **H**
(519) 977-9777. **$129-$199.** 333 Riverside Dr W. 1 km w of
Detroit-Windsor Tunnel; 1 km e of Ambassador Bridge. Int
corridors. **Pets:** Small. Service with restrictions, crate.
[SAVE] [S🐾] [✕] [💻] [🍴] [🐾]

WOODSTOCK

ⒸⒶ **▼▼▼ ▼** **Quality Hotel and Suites** **M**
(519) 537-5586. **$95-$229.** 580 Bruin Blvd. Hwy 401, exit
232, just n; w of Hwy 59. Int corridors. **Pets:** Service with
restrictions, crate.
[SAVE] [S🐾] [✕] [🛏] [💻] [🍴] [🐾]

▼▼▼ **Super 8 Motel** **M**
(519) 421-4588. **$80-$100.** 560 Norwich Ave. Jct Hwy 401
and 59, exit 232, just n. Int corridors. **Pets:** Accepted.
[ASK] [S🐾] [✕] [🛏]

WYOMING

▼▼▼ **Country View Motel and RV Camping**
Resort **M**
(519) 845-3394. **$54-$84, 3 days notice.** 4569 London
Line. Hwy 402, exit 25, 1 km s on Hwy 21 to Hwy 22, then
just e. Ext corridors. **Pets:** Accepted.
[✕] [🛏] [🐾] [✕]

CITY INDEX

ALBERTON

♦♦ **Briarwood Inn, Cottages & Lodge** [X]
(902) 853-2518. **$60-$125, 14 days notice.** 253 Matthews Ln. 3 km e on Rt 12, 1 km n on dirt entry road. Ext/int corridors. **Pets:** Accepted.
[A$K] [SD] ⊠ ▣ 📺 ✂ [AC] ☎

CAVENDISH

♦♦ **Bay Vista Motor Inn** [M]
(902) 963-2225. **$44-$89.** 9517 Cavendish Rd. Jct Rt 13, 4.8 km w on Rt 6. Ext corridors. **Pets:** Small. Designated rooms, service with restrictions, supervision.
⊠ 🏊 ☎

[CAA] ♦♦♦ **Cavendish Bosom Buddies Cottages** [C]
(902) 963-3449. **$80-$280, 14 days notice.** RR1. Jct Rt 6 and 13, 0.6 km e on Rt 6. Ext corridors. **Pets:** Medium. Designated rooms, service with restrictions, supervision.
[SAVE] [SD] ⊠ ▣ [AC] ☎

♦♦♦ **Cavendish Country Inn & Ocean Vista Cottages** [X]
(902) 963-2567. **$59-$325, 30 days notice.** Cavendish Rd, Rt 6. Jct Rt 6 and 13, 1.5 km e. Ext/int corridors. **Pets:** Accepted.
⊠ ▣ 🏊

[CAA] ♦♦♦ **Cavendish Maples Cottages** [C]
(902) 963-2818. **$100-$245, 14 days notice.** Jct Rt 6 and 13, 2.5 km w on Rt 6. Ext corridors. **Pets:** Accepted.
[SAVE] ▣ 🏊 [AC] ☎

CHARLOTTETOWN

[CAA] ♦♦ **Best Western Charlottetown** [MI]
(902) 892-2461. **$134-$179.** 238 Grafton St. Centre. Int corridors. **Pets:** Other species. $50 deposit/room. Designated rooms, service with restrictions, supervision.
[SAVE] [SD] ⊠ ♿M 👂 ♿ ▣ 📺 🍴 🏊

♦♦ **Comfort Inn** [M]
(902) 566-4424. **$103-$141.** 112 Trans-Canada Hwy 1. 4.5 km w. Int corridors. **Pets:** Other species. Service with restrictions, supervision.
[SAVE] [SD] ⊠ 📺

♦♦♦ **Delta Prince Edward** [H]
(902) 566-2222. **$129-$259.** 18 Queen St. Centre. Int corridors. **Pets:** Accepted.
[A$K] [SD] ⊠ 📺 🍴

♦♦ **Econo Lodge** [M]
(902) 368-1110. **$79-$175.** 20 Lower Malpeque Rd. 4.5 km w, jct of Trans-Canada Hwy 1 and Lower Malpeque Rd. Ext/int corridors. **Pets:** Small. Designated rooms, service with restrictions, supervision.
[SAVE] [SD] ⊠ ▣ 📺

[CAA] ♦♦♦ **Holiday Inn Express Hotel & Suites** [M]
(902) 892-1201. **$109-$155.** 200 Trans-Canada Hwy. 4.8 km w on Trans-Canada Hwy 1. Int corridors. **Pets:** Accepted.
[SAVE] [SD] ⊠ ♿M ♿ ▣ 📺 🏊

♦♦ **Quality Inn Charlottetown** [MI]
(902) 894-8572. **$109-$212.** 150 Euston St. Centre. Int corridors. **Pets:** Service with restrictions.
[SAVE] [SD] ⊠ ▣ 📺 🍴

♦♦♦ **Rodd Charlottetown-A Rodd Signature Hotel** [H]
(902) 894-7371. **$94-$212.** Kent & Pownal sts. Centre. Int corridors. **Pets:** Accepted.
[A$K] [SD] ⊠ ▣ 📺 🍴 🏊

♦♦ **Rodd Confederation Inn & Suites** [MI]
(902) 892-2481. **$67-$140.** Trans-Canada Hwy 1. 4 km w. Ext/int corridors. **Pets:** Medium. Service with restrictions, crate.
[A$K] [SD] ⊠ ▣ 📺 🍴 🏊

[CAA] ♦♦ **Rodd Royalty Inn** [MI]
(902) 894-8566. **$75-$158.** Intersection Hwy 1 & 2. 4 km w on Trans-Canada Hwy 1. Ext/int corridors. **Pets:** Accepted.
[SAVE] [SD] ⊠ ▣ 📺 🍴 🏊

CORNWALL

♦♦ **Sunny King Motel** [M]
(902) 566-2209. **$49-$116, 3 days notice.** Centre; on Hwy 1. Ext corridors. **Pets:** Accepted.
[A$K] [SD] ⊠ ▣ 📺 🏊 [AC]

MONTAGUE

♦♦♦ **Rodd Marina Inn & Suites** [M]
(902) 838-4075. **$69-$148.** 115 Sackville St. Centre. Int corridors. **Pets:** Large. $10 daily fee/room. Designated rooms, service with restrictions, supervision.
[A$K] [SD] ⊠ ♿M ▣ 📺

NORTH RUSTICO

▼ St. Lawrence Motel **M**
(902) 963-2053. **$42-$93, 7 days notice.** In PEI National Park on Gulf Shore Rd. Ext corridors. **Pets:** Accepted.

⊠ 🖥 🐾 ☎

RICHMOND

▼▼▼ Caernarvon Cottages, BB in Bayside **C**
(902) 854-3418. **$85-$150, 90 days notice.** RR 1. Jct Hwy 2 and Rt 131, 10 km e. Ext/int corridors. **Pets:** Designated rooms, service with restrictions, supervision.

🖥 🖵 🐾

ROSENEATH

▼▼▼ Rodd Brudenell River-A Rodd Signature Resort **X**
(902) 652-2332. **$75-$195, 3 days notice.** Jct Rt 4 and 3, 5.5 km e on Rt 3, Brudenell River Provincial Park. Ext/int corridors. **Pets:** Accepted.

(ASK) (S🄳) ⊠ 🖥 🖵 (Ⅱ) 🐾 (✗)

SUMMERSIDE

(AAA) ▼▼▼▼ Quality Inn Garden of the Gulf **M**
(902) 436-2295. **$89-$279.** 618 Water St. 1.6 km e on Hwy 11. Ext/int corridors. **Pets:** Designated rooms, service with restrictions, supervision.

(SAVE) (S🄳) ⊠ 🖥 🖵 🐾

WOODSTOCK

(AAA) ▼▼ Rodd Mill River Resort **MI**
(902) 859-3555. **$85-$222, 3 days notice.** Rt 180. Rt 136, just e of jct Rt 2; in Mill River Provincial Park. Int corridors. **Pets:** Accepted.

(SAVE) (S🄳) ⊠ 🖵 (Ⅱ) 🐾 (✗)

QUEBEC

CITY INDEX

ALMA

▼▼ Hotel Motel Les Cascades **MI**
(418) 662-6547. **$65-$75.** 140 ave du Pont N. Centre; on Hwy 169, just n of bridge. Ext/int corridors. **Pets:** Medium. Service with restrictions, supervision.
ASK SO ⊠ 🖪 🖵 ⑪

AYLMER

▼▼▼▼ Chateau Cartier Relais-Resort **R**
(819) 778-0000. **$149-$219.** 1170 chemin Aylmer. Hwy 148, 1 km w of Champlain Bridge. Int corridors. **Pets:** Accepted.
ASK SO ⊠ 🖪 🖵 ⑪ ⊅ ⊠

BAIE-COMEAU

▼▼ Comfort Inn **M**
(418) 589-8252. **$81-$88.** 745 boul Lafleche. Rt 138. Int corridors. **Pets:** Service with restrictions, supervision.
SAVE ⊠ 🖪

BAIE-ST-PAUL

CAA **▼▼▼** Hotel Baie-Saint-Paul **MI**
(418) 435-3683. **$59-$99.** 911 boul Mgr-de-Laval. Rt 138, 0.5 km e of Rt 362. Int corridors. **Pets:** Service with restrictions.
SAVE ⊠ 🖪 🖵 ⑪

BERTHIERVILLE

▼▼ Days Inn Berthierville **M**
(450) 836-1621. **$185-$205, 10 days notice.** 760 Gadoury. Hwy 40, exit 144. Int corridors. **Pets:** Accepted.
SAVE SO ⊠ 🖪 🖵

CHICOUTIMI

▼▼ Comfort Inn **M**
(418) 693-8686. **$80-$85.** 1595 boul Talbot. Jct Rt 170, 2.8 km n. Int corridors. **Pets:** Accepted.
SAVE SO ⊠ 🖪 🖵

[Hotel La Sagueneenne]

▼▼ Hotel La Sagueneenne **MI**
(418) 545-8326. **$85-$140.** 250 des Sagueneens. Just w of jct Rt 175 (boul Talbot). Int corridors. **Pets:** Accepted.
ASK SO ⊠ 🖪 🖵 ⑪ ⊅

DRUMMONDVILLE

CAA **▼▼▼▼** Best Western Hotel Universel **MI**
(819) 478-4971. **$89-$169, 14 days notice.** 915 rue Hains. Hwy 20, exit 177, 0.3 km s on boul St-Joseph, then just e. Int corridors. **Pets:** $75 deposit/room. Designated rooms, service with restrictions, supervision.
SAVE SO ⊠ 🖪 🖵 ⑪ ⊅

▼▼ Comfort Inn **M**
(819) 477-4000. **$80-$115.** 1055 rue Hains. Hwy 20, exit 177, 0.5 km s on boul St-Joseph, then just w. Int corridors. **Pets:** Other species. Designated rooms, service with restrictions, supervision.
SAVE SO ⊠ 🖪 🖵

GASPE

▼ Motel Adams **MI**
(418) 368-2244. **$89-$99.** 20 rue Adams. Centre; corner rue Jacques Cartier. Ext/int corridors. **Pets:** Small. Service with restrictions, supervision.
⊠ 🖪 🖵 ⑪

GATINEAU

▼▼ Comfort Inn **M**
(819) 243-6010. **$130-$150.** 630 boul La Gappe. Hwy 50, exit 140, 2 km e. Int corridors. **Pets:** Accepted.
SAVE ⊠ 🖪 🖵

HULL

▼▼▼ Holiday Inn Plaza la Chaudiere **H**
(819) 778-3880. **$108.** 2 rue Montcalm. 0.8 km w of Portage Bridge at jct Rt 148 and rue Montcalm. Int corridors. **Pets:** Medium. Service with restrictions, supervision.
ASK SO ⊠ 🖪 🖵 ⑪ ⊅

LA MALBAIE POINTE AU PIC

(AAA) ◆◆◆◆ Fairmont Le Manoir
Richelieu **R** ❀
(418) 665-3703. **$109-$299, 7 days notice.** 181 rue Richelieu. Rt 362, 4.1 km w of jct Rt 138. Int corridors. **Pets:** Medium. $25 daily fee/room. Designated rooms, service with restrictions, supervision.
[SAVE] [S🐾] [✕] [🛏] [💻] [▯] [🛶] [✕]

LA POCATIERE

◆◆ Motel Le Pocatois **MI**
(418) 856-1688. **Call for rates.** 235 Rt 132. Hwy 20, exit 439, 0.8 km s. Ext/int corridors. **Pets:** Small. Service with restrictions.
[✕] [🛏] [▯]

LENNOXVILLE

(AAA) ◆ La Paysanne Motel **MI**
(819) 569-5585. **$70-$80.** 42 rue Queen. On Rt 143. Ext/int corridors. **Pets:** Service with restrictions, supervision.
[SAVE] [S🐾] [✕] [▯]

LOUISEVILLE

◆◆◆ Gite du Carrefour et Maison historique
J.L.L. Hamelin **BB**
(819) 228-4932. **$75 (no credit cards), 15 days notice.** 11 ave St-Laurent ouest. Centre; on Rt 138; from Hwy 40, exit 174 westbound; exit 166 eastbound. Int corridors. **Pets:** Very small, dogs only. Supervision.
[ASK] [✕] [✕] [🐾] [☎]

MATANE

(AAA) ◆ Motel La Marina **M**
(418) 562-3234. **$49-$84.** 1032 ave du Phare ouest. On Rt 132. Ext corridors. **Pets:** Dogs only. Service with restrictions, supervision.
[SAVE] [🛏] [💻] [▯] [🛶] [✕]

MONT TREMBLANT

(AAA) ◆◆◆ Le Grand Lodge **R**
(819) 425-2734. **$159-$409, 8 days notice.** 845 chemin Principale. Jct Hwy 117 and 327, 1.5 km s. Int corridors. **Pets:** Small. $25 daily fee/room. Designated rooms, service with restrictions, supervision.
[SAVE] [S🐾] [✕] [🛏] [💻] [▯] [🛶] [✕]

(AAA) ◆◆◆◆ Le Westin Resort **H**
(819) 681-8000. **$215-$895, 30 days notice.** 100 chemin Kandahar. In Mont-Tremblant Resort Centre; Hwy 117 N, 10 km w on Montee Ryan, follow signs. Int corridors. **Pets:** Accepted.
[SAVE] [S🐾] [✕] [🛏] [💻] [▯] [🛶] [✕]

MONTEBELLO

◆◆◆ Fairmont Le Chateau
Montebello **R** ❀
(819) 423-6341. **$159-$329, 3 days notice.** 392 rue Notre-Dame. On Rt 148. Int corridors. **Pets:** Medium, dogs only. $50 daily fee/pet. Service with restrictions, crate.
[✕] [🛏] [💻] [▯] [🛶] [✕]

MONTREAL METROPOLITAN AREA

BOUCHERVILLE

◆◆ Comfort Inn **M**
(450) 641-2880. **$92-$125.** 96 boul de Mortagne. Hwy 20, exit 92. Int corridors. **Pets:** Small. Designated rooms, service with restrictions, supervision.
[SAVE] [S🐾] [✕] [💻]

BROSSARD

◆◆ Comfort Inn **M**
(450) 678-9350. **$95-$98.** 7863 boul Taschereau. Rt 134, 1.5 km w of Hwy 10, exit boul Taschereau ouest. Int corridors. **Pets:** Small. $50 deposit/pet. Service with restrictions, supervision.
[SAVE] [S🐾] [✕] [🛏]

DORVAL

◆◆ Comfort Inn **M**
(514) 636-3391. **$105-$135.** 340 ave Michel-Jasmin. Hwy 520, exit 2 eastbound; exit 1 westbound, 0.3 km along service road to ave Marshall, follow to ave Michel-Jasmin. Int corridors. **Pets:** Small. Designated rooms, service with restrictions, supervision.
[SAVE] [S🐾] [✕]

(AAA) ◆◆ Travelodge Dorval Airport **M** ❀
(514) 631-4537. **$106-$111.** 1010 chemin Herron. Hwy 20, exit 54 westbound, just s on boul Fenelon to ave Dumont, follow to chemin Herron; exit 54 eastbound, 1.7 km along service road. Int corridors. **Pets:** Other species. $40 deposit/pet. Designated rooms, service with restrictions.
[SAVE] [S🐾] [✕] [🛏] [💻]

LAVAL

◆◆ Comfort Inn **MI**
(450) 686-0600. **$97-$121.** 2055 Autoroute des Laurentides. Hwy 15, exit 8, e on boul St-Martin, 0.7 km n on boul Le Corbusier, w on boul Tessier. Int corridors. **Pets:** Other species. Service with restrictions, crate.
[SAVE] [S🐾] [✕] [🛏] [▯]

◆◆ Econo Lodge **M**
(450) 681-6411. **$59-$139.** 1981 boul Cure Labelle. Hwy 15, exit 8 northbound; exit 10 southbound, 1.8 km w on boul St-Martin ouest, then 0.6 km n. Ext/int corridors. **Pets:** Designated rooms, service with restrictions, supervision.
[SAVE] [S🐾] [✕] [🛏] [💻] [🛶]

☺☺ ▼▼▼▼ Quality Suites M
(450) 686-6777. **$113-$133.** 2035 Autoroute des Laurentides. Hwy 15, exit 8, e on boul St-Martin, 0.7 km n on boul Le Corbusier, w on boul Tessier. Int corridors. **Pets:** Other species. Service with restrictions, crate.
[SAVE] [S🐾] [✕] [▣]

LONGUEUIL

▼▼ Days Inn Longueuil M
(450) 677-8911. **$75-$94, 03 days notice.** 2800 boul Marie-Victorin. Hwy 20/Rt 132, exit 15 eastbound, follow signs for boul Marie-Victorin est; exit 90 westbound from Pont-Tunnel Louis-Hippolyte-Lafontaine. Int corridors. **Pets:** Small. Service with restrictions.
[SAVE] [S🐾] [✕] [▣] [¶]

▼▼▼▼ Holiday Inn Montreal-Longueuil H
(450) 646-8100. **$105-$159, 10 days notice.** 900 rue St-Charles est. Hwy 20/Rt 132, exit 11, to boul Rolland Therrien. Int corridors. **Pets:** Accepted.
[ASK] [S🐾] [✕] [🛏] [▣] [¶] [🌊]

☺☺ ▼▼▼▼ Hotel Motel Ideal La Barre M
(450) 677-9101. **$79-$99.** 2019 boul Taschereau. Hwy 20/Rt 132, exit 8, follow Hwy 134 E (boul Taschereau) to boul Jacques-Cartier, exit and loop around underpass to get back onto Hwy 134 E. Ext/int corridors. **Pets:** Accepted.
[SAVE] [S🐾] [✕] [🛏] [¶] [🌊]

MONTREAL

☺☺ ▼▼▼▼ Best Western Europa Downtown H
(514) 866-6492. **$129-$299.** 1240 rue Drummond. Between rue Ste-Catherine and boul Rene-Levesque. Int corridors. **Pets:** Very small. Service with restrictions, supervision.
[SAVE] [S🐾] [✕] [🛏] [▣] [¶]

▼▼▼▼ Crowne Plaza Metro Center H
(514) 842-8581. **$139-$219, 5 days notice.** 505 Sherbrooke E. Between rue Berri and St-Hubert. Int corridors. **Pets:** Other species.
[ASK] [S🐾] [✕] [▣] [¶] [🌊]

☺☺ ▼▼▼▼ Delta Montreal H
(514) 286-1986. **$149-$229.** 475 ave President Kennedy. Corner rue City Councillors. Int corridors. **Pets:** $30 deposit/room. Designated rooms, service with restrictions, crate.
[SAVE] [S🐾] [✕] [🛏] [▣] [¶] [🌊]

☺☺ ▼▼▼ ▼▼▼ Fairmont The Queen Elizabeth H ☺
(514) 861-3511. **$135-$279.** 900 boul Rene-Levesque ouest. Between rue Universite and Mansfield. Int corridors. **Pets:** Small. $25 daily fee/room. Service with restrictions, supervision.
[SAVE] [✕] [🛏] [▣] [¶] [🌊]

☺☺ ▼▼▼▼ Four Points by Sheraton Hotel & Suites, Montreal Centre-Ville H
(514) 842-3961. **$119-$159.** 475 rue Sherbrooke ouest. Between rue Durocher and Aylmer. Int corridors. **Pets:** Large. Service with restrictions, supervision.
[SAVE] [S🐾] [✕] [🛏] [▣] [¶]

☺☺ ▼▼▼ ▼▼▼ Hilton Montreal Bonaventure H
(514) 878-2332. **$145-$285.** 1 Place Bonaventure. Corner of Mansfield and de la Gauchetiere. Int corridors. **Pets:** Accepted.
[SAVE] [S🐾] [✕] [🛏] [▣] [¶] [🌊]

☺☺ ▼▼▼▼ Holiday Inn Montreal-Midtown H
(514) 842-6111. **$119-$189.** 420 rue Sherbrooke ouest. Between rue Bleury and City Councillors. Int corridors. **Pets:** Small. Service with restrictions, supervision.
[SAVE] [S🐾] [✕] [🛏] [▣] [¶] [🌊]

▼▼▼ ▼▼▼ Hotel Inter-Continental Montreal H
(514) 987-9900. **$245-$355.** 360 rue St-Antoine ouest. In Old Montreal; corner rue St-Pierre. Int corridors. **Pets:** Small. $30 one-time fee/room. Service with restrictions, supervision.
[ASK] [S🐾] [✕] [🛏] [▣] [¶] [🌊]

▼▼▼ ▼▼▼ Hotel Le Germain H ☺
(514) 849-2050. **Call for rates.** 2050 Mansfield St. Just n of President Kennedy. **Pets:** $25 one-time fee/pet. Service with restrictions, supervision.
[✕] [🛏] [▣] [¶]

▼▼ ▼▼ Hotel Lord Berri H
(514) 845-9236. **$86-$119.** 1199 rue Berri. Between boul Rene-Levesque and rue Ste-Catherine. Int corridors. **Pets:** Medium. $50 deposit/room. Designated rooms, service with restrictions, crate.
[ASK] [S🐾] [✕] [🛏] [▣] [¶]

☺☺ ▼▼▼▼ Hotel Maritime Plaza H
(514) 932-1411. **$179-$420.** 1155 rue Guy. Downtown centre; at corner of boul Rene-Levesque. Int corridors. **Pets:** Accepted.
[SAVE] [S🐾] [✕] [🛏] [▣] [¶] [🌊]

▼▼▼ ▼▼▼ Hotel Omni Mont-Royal H
(514) 284-1110. **$135-$227.** 1050 Sherbrooke ouest. Corner rue Peel. Int corridors. **Pets:** Small. $50 one-time fee/room. Service with restrictions, crate.
[ASK] [S🐾] [✕] [🎿] [🛏] [¶] [🌊]

☺☺ ▼▼▼ ▼▼▼ Le Centre Sheraton H
(514) 878-2000. **$169-$199.** 1201 boul Rene-Levesque ouest. Between rue Drummond and Stanley. Int corridors. **Pets:** Medium. Service with restrictions, supervision.
[SAVE] [✕] [🎿] [🛏] [▣] [¶] [🌊]

▼▼▼ ▼▼▼ Loews Hotel Vogue H ☺
(514) 285-5555. **$170-$440, 7 days notice.** 1425 rue de la Montagne. Between rue Ste-Catherine and boul de Maisonneuve. Int corridors. **Pets:** Large, other species. Designated rooms, service with restrictions, supervision.
[ASK] [S🐾] [✕] [🛏] [¶]

(CAA) ▼▼▼▼ Marriott Residence Inn-Montreal M
(514) 982-6064. **$124-$400.** 2045 rue Peel. Between rue Sherbrooke and boul de Maisonneuve. Int corridors. **Pets:** Medium. $250 one-time fee/room. Service with restrictions, crate.
[SAVE] [S&] [✕] [▣] [≈]

▼▼▼▼ Novotel Montreal Centre H
(514) 861-6000. **$119-$400.** 1180 rue de la Montagne. Between rue Ste-Catherine and boul Rene-Levesque. Int corridors. **Pets:** Other species. $15 daily fee/pet. Service with restrictions, supervision.
[ASK] [S&] [✕] [¶]

(CAA) ▼▼▼ Quality Hotel MI
(514) 849-1413. **$109-$210.** 3440 ave du Parc. Between rue Sherbrooke and Milton. Int corridors. **Pets:** Medium. Designated rooms, service with restrictions, supervision.
[SAVE] [S&] [✕] [¶] [▣] [¶]

**(CAA) ▼▼▼▼ Renaissance Montreal
Hotel H ❀**
(514) 288-6666. **$145-$189.** 3625 ave du Parc. Corner of rue Prince-Arthur. Int corridors. **Pets:** Dogs only. $50 deposit/pet. Service with restrictions, supervision.
[SAVE] [S&] [✕] [¶] [▣] [¶] [≈] [✕]

▼▼▼▼ Wyndham Montreal H
(514) 285-1450. **$149-$249.** 1255 Jeanne-Mance St CP 130. Corner rue Ste-Catherine. Int corridors. **Pets:** Accepted.
[✕] [&M] [¶] [▣] [¶] [≈]

POINTE-CLAIRE

▼▼ ▼▼ Comfort Inn M
(514) 697-6210. **$144-$165.** 700 boul St-Jean. Hwy 40, exit 52, 0.3 km s. Int corridors. **Pets:** Accepted.
[SAVE] [S&] [✕] [▣]

(CAA) ▼▼▼▼ Quality Suites MI
(514) 426-5060. **$149-$169.** 6300 Trans-Canada Hwy 40. Hwy 40, exit 52, south side service road; westbound, follow signs for boul St-Jean sud and Hwy 40 est to get onto south side service road. Int corridors. **Pets:** Other species. Designated rooms, service with restrictions, crate.
[SAVE] [S&] [✕] [&M] [¶] [▣] [¶]

ROSEMERE

(CAA) ▼▼▼▼ Hotel Le Rivage M
(450) 437-2171. **$75-$129.** 125 boul LaBelle. Hwy 15, exit 19, 0.5 km s of Rt 344. Int corridors. **Pets:** Small. Service with restrictions, supervision.
[SAVE] [¶] [▣] [≈]

ST-LAURENT

▼▼ ▼▼ Holiday Inn Aeroport Montreal MI
(514) 739-3391. **$104-$148.** 6500 Cote-de-Liesse. Hwy 520, exit 5 eastbound, on south side service road; exit 5 westbound to rue Ness, follow signs for rue Hickmore and Hwy 520 E. Ext/int corridors. **Pets:** Accepted.
[ASK] [S&] [✕] [&M] [¶] [▣] [¶] [≈]

(CAA) ▼▼▼▼ Quality Hotel Dorval MI
(514) 731-7821. **$132.** 7700 Cote-de-Liesse. Hwy 520, exit 4 eastbound, on south side service road; exit 4 (Montee-de-Liesse) westbound. Int corridors. **Pets:** Other species. Service with restrictions, supervision.
[SAVE] [S&] [✕] [▣] [¶] [≈]

(CAA) ▼▼▼▼ Ramada Montreal Airport Hotel MI
(514) 733-8818. **$129-$159.** 7300 Cote-de-Liesse. Hwy 520, exit 4 eastbound, on south side service road; exit 4 (Montee-de-Liesse) westbound. Int corridors. **Pets:** Other species. Service with restrictions, supervision.
[SAVE] [S&] [✕] [¶] [▣] [¶] [≈]

❀ **END METROPOLITAN AREA** ❀

NEW RICHMOND

▼▼ ▼▼ Hotel Motel Francis MI
(418) 392-4485. **Call for rates.** 210 chemin Pardiac. Just s of Rt 132. Ext/int corridors. **Pets:** Accepted.
[ASK] [✕] [¶] [▣] [¶] [≈] [✕] [⚿]

NORTH HATLEY

(CAA) ▼▼▼▼ Le Coeur d'Or B&B BB
(819) 842-4363. **$85-$250, 7 days notice.** 85 School St. Centre. Ext/int corridors. **Pets:** Accepted.
[SAVE] [✕] [¶] [▣] [✆]

PERCE

▼▼▼ Au Pic de l'Aurore C
(418) 782-2166. **$50-$117, 7 days notice.** 1 Rt 132. 2 km e from village centre. Ext corridors. **Pets:** Medium. Service with restrictions, supervision.
[✕] [¶] [▣] [⚿]

▼▼ ▼▼ Bonaventure Pavillon Cote Surprise MI
(418) 782-2166. **$51-$125, 7 days notice.** 367 Rt 132. On Rt 132, 0.7 km w of village. Ext/int corridors. **Pets:** Accepted.
[✕] [¶] [▣] [¶] [⚿]

▼▼▼▼ Hotel La Normandie MI
(418) 782-2112. **$89-$169.** 221 Rt 132. Centre. Int corridors. **Pets:** Accepted.
[✕] [¶] [⚿]

▼▼ Hotel Motel Manoir de Perce Ⓜ
(418) 782-2022. **$65-$128, 7 days notice.** 212 Rt 132. Centre. Ext/int corridors. **Pets:** Small, dogs only. Designated rooms, service with restrictions, supervision.
[ASK] [S₀] [✕] [†|]

PINE HILL

Ⓒ ▼▼▼ Hotel du Lac Carling Ⓡ
(450) 533-9211. **$225-$275.** 2255 Rt 327 Nord. 5 km n. Int corridors. **Pets:** Small. Supervision.
[SAVE] [✕] [📶] [💻] [†|] [🏊] [✕]

QUEBEC METROPOLITAN AREA

BEAUPORT

▼▼ Comfort Inn Ⓜ
(418) 666-1226. **$65-$140.** 240 boul Ste-Anne. Hwy 440, exit Francois-De-Laval. Int corridors. **Pets:** Designated rooms, no service, supervision.
[SAVE] [S₀] [✕] [💻]

L'ANCIENNE LORETTE

▼▼ Comfort Inn Ⓜ
(418) 872-5900. **$92-$104, 30 days notice.** 1255 boul Duplessis. Jct boul Duplessis and Wilfrid-Hamel (Hwy 138). Int corridors. **Pets:** Other species. Service with restrictions, supervision.
[SAVE] [S₀] [✕] [📶] [💻]

LEVIS

▼▼ Comfort Inn Ⓜ
(418) 835-5605. **$83-$160.** 10 du Vallon est. Hwy 20, exit 325S eastbound; exit 325 westbound. Int corridors. **Pets:** Accepted.
[SAVE] [S₀] [✕] [📶] [💻]

QUEBEC

Ⓒ ▼▼ ▼▼ Hilton Quebec Ⓗ
(418) 647-2411. **$154-$394.** 1100 boul Rene-Levesque est. Corner of ave Dufferin. Int corridors. **Pets:** Medium. Service with restrictions, supervision.
[SAVE] [✕] [📶] [💻] [†|] [🏊]

Ⓒ ▼▼▼ Hotel Quality Suites Quebec Ⓜ
(418) 622-4244. **$120-$170.** 1600 rue Bouvier. Hwy 40, exit 312 N (Pierre Bertrand nord), 2 km w of jct Rt 358. Int corridors. **Pets:** Other species. Supervision.
[SAVE] [S₀] [✕]

Ⓒ ▼▼▼ Hotel Radisson Quebec Ⓗ
(418) 647-1717. **$159-$209.** 690 boul Rene-Levesque est. Just w of Dufferin. Int corridors. **Pets:** Small, other species. Service with restrictions, supervision.
[SAVE] [S₀] [✕] [📶] [💻] [†|] [🏊]

Ⓒ ▼▼▼ L'Hotel du Vieux Quebec Ⓗ
(418) 692-1850. **$89-$259.** 1190 rue St-Jean. In Old Quebec; corner of rue de l'Hotel-Dieu. Int corridors. **Pets:** Designated rooms, service with restrictions, crate.
[SAVE] [✕] [📶] [†|]

Ⓒ ▼▼▼ ▼▼▼ Loews Le Concorde Ⓗ ❀
(418) 647-2222. **$120-$380.** 1225 Cours du General-de Montcalm. Corner of Grande Allee est. Int corridors. **Pets:** Designated rooms, service with restrictions, supervision.
[SAVE] [S₀] [✕] [📶] [💻] [†|] [🏊]

STE-FOY

▼▼ Comfort Inn Ⓜ
(418) 872-5038. **$77-$95.** 7320 boul Wilfrid-Hamel. Hwy 138, 1.5 km w of boul Duplessis. Int corridors. **Pets:** Other species. Service with restrictions, supervision.
[SAVE] [S₀] [✕] [📶] [💻]

▼▼▼ Hotel Clarion Ⓜ
(418) 653-4901. **$89-$109.** 3125 boul Hochelaga. Autoroute 73, exit 136 (Hochelaga ouest). Int corridors. **Pets:** Medium. Supervision.
[SAVE] [✕] [📶] [💻] [†|] [🏊]

▼ Motel Oncle Sam Ⓜ
(418) 872-1488. **$49-$99.** 7025 boul Wilfrid-Hamel. On Hwy 138 at jct boul Duplessis. Ext corridors. **Pets:** Designated rooms, service with restrictions, crate.
[✕] [📶] [🏊]

❀ END METROPOLITAN AREA ❀

RIMOUSKI

▼▼ Comfort Inn Ⓜ
(418) 724-2500. **$90-$100.** 455 boul St-Germain ouest. On Rt 132. Int corridors. **Pets:** Other species. Service with restrictions.
[SAVE] [S₀] [✕] [📶] [💻]

▼▼ Hotel L'Empress Ⓜ
(418) 723-6944. **$67, 10 days notice.** 360 Montee Industrielle. Hwy 20, exit 614, 3.4 km n. Int corridors. **Pets:** Accepted.
[ASK] [✕] [📶] [†|]

RIVIERE-DU-LOUP

▼▼ Comfort Inn M
(418) 867-4162. **$90-$160.** 85 boul Cartier. Hwy 20, exit 507, just sw on boul Cartier; Hwy 185, exit 96 (Fraserville). Int corridors. **Pets:** Other species. Designated rooms, service with restrictions.

(CAA) ▼▼ Days Inn-Riviere-du-Loup X
(418) 862-6354. **$80-$160.** 182 rue Fraser. Hwy 20, exit 503, then just 1 km e on Rt 132. Ext corridors. **Pets:** Accepted.

ROBERVAL

(CAA) ▼▼▼ Hotel Chateau Roberval H
(418) 275-7511. **$89-$149.** 1225 boul Marcotte. Centre on Hwy 169. Int corridors. **Pets:** Accepted.
SAVE ⊠ 🛢 💻 ‖ ⤸

ROCK FOREST

▼▼ Comfort Inn M
(819) 564-4400. **$76-$92.** 4295 boul Bourque. Hwy 410, exit 4, 1.5 km w on Rt 112. Int corridors. **Pets:** Medium. Designated rooms, service with restrictions, supervision.
SAVE S🐾 ⊠

ROUYN NORANDA

▼▼ Comfort Inn M
(819) 797-1313. **$79-$84, 10 days notice.** 1295 rue Lariviere. Rt 117, 4 km s from town centre. Int corridors. **Pets:** Accepted.
SAVE S🐾 ⊠ 🛢 💻

(CAA) ▼▼ Motel Mistral MI
(819) 762-0884. **$65, 7 days notice.** 903 rue Lariviere. Rt 117, 2 km s of town centre. Ext/int corridors. **Pets:** Accepted.
SAVE S🐾 ⊠ 🛢 ‖

SALABERRY DE VALLEYFIELD

▼▼▼ Hotel Plaza Valleyfield H
(450) 373-1990. **$87-$97.** 40 ave du Centenaire. Center; corner rue St-Laurent. Int corridors. **Pets:** Accepted.
ASK S🐾 ⊠ 🛢 💻 ‖ ⤸

SEPT ILES

▼▼ Comfort Inn M
(418) 968-6005. **$82-$98, 30 days notice.** 854 boul Laure. 4.5 km w on Rt 138. Int corridors. **Pets:** Designated rooms, service with restrictions, supervision.

SHAWINIGAN

▼▼ Auberge Escapade Inn MI
(819) 539-6911. **$64-$145.** 3383 rue Garnier. Hwy 55, exit 217, just n on Rt 351. Ext/int corridors. **Pets:** Other species. $5 daily fee/pet. Designated rooms, service with restrictions, crate.
⊠ 🛢 ‖

▼▼▼ Auberge Gouverneur & Convention Center Shawinigan H
(819) 537-6000. **$160.** 1100 Promenade-du-St-Maurice. Hwy 55 N, exit 211, then 4.4 km n on Hwy 153, follow signs. Int corridors. **Pets:** Small. $10 daily fee/pet. Designated rooms, no service, supervision.
ASK S🐾 ⊠ 🛢 💻 ‖ ⤸

SHAWINIGAN SUD

▼▼▼ Comfort Inn & Suites M
(819) 536-2000. **$86.** 500 boul du Capitaine. Hwy 55, exit 211, 4.4 km n on Hwy 153, then 2 km s on Rt 157. Int corridors. **Pets:** Small. Designated rooms, service with restrictions, supervision.
SAVE S🐾 ⊠ 💻

▼ Motel Safari M
(819) 536-2664. **$75.** 4500 12 Ave E. Hwy 55, exit 211, 4.4 km n on Hwy 153, then 7 km s on Rt 157. Ext/int corridors. **Pets:** Accepted.
ASK S🐾 🛢

SHERBROOKE

▼▼▼ Delta Sherbrooke Hotel and Conference Centre H
(819) 822-1989. **$87-$137.** 2685 rue King ouest. Hwy 410, exit 4E, 1 km e on Rt 112. Int corridors. **Pets:** Small. $15 one-time fee/room. Service with restrictions, supervision.
⊠ 💻 ‖ ⤸

ST-ANTOINE-DE-TILLY

▼▼▼ Manoir de Tilly CI
(418) 886-2407. **$129, 3 days notice.** 3854 chemin de Tilly. Centre; jct Hwy 20, exit 291, 8.5 km n on Rt 273. Int corridors. **Pets:** Accepted.
‖

ST-FAUSTIN-LAC-CARRE

▼ Motel sur la Colline M
(819) 688-2102. **$80-$172, 14 days notice.** 357 Rt 117. Rt 117, 4 km n of exit for city. Ext/int corridors. **Pets:** $15 daily fee/pet. Service with restrictions, supervision.
ASK S🐾 ⊠ 🛢 💻 ⤸

ST-FELICIEN

▼▼▼ Hotel du Jardin H
(418) 679-8422. **$84-$160.** 1400 boul du Jardin. On Hwy 167. Int corridors. **Pets:** Accepted.
ASK S🐾 ⊠ 🛢 ‖ ⤸

ST-FERREOL-LES-NEIGES

◆◆ Chalets-Village Mont-Sainte-Anne **C**
(418) 826-3331. **$225, 45 days notice.** 1815 boul Les Neiges. Village center, on north side of Hwy 360. Ext corridors. **Pets:** Other species. $100 one-time fee/room. No service, supervision.
🖻 ⊠

ST-HONORE

(CAA) **◆** Motel Jasper **MI**
(418) 497-2322. **$56-$66.** 657 Rt 185. On Rt 185. Ext corridors. **Pets:** Accepted.
[SAVE] [S🐾] ⊠ [¶]

ST-HYACINTHE

(CAA) **◆◆** Hotel des Seigneurs Saint-Hyacinthe **H**
(450) 774-3810. **$99-$119, 5 days notice.** 1200 Johnson. Just e on Gauvin St from Laframboise Blvd from Hwy 20, exit 130S. Ext/int corridors. **Pets:** Small. Service with restrictions, supervision.
[SAVE] [S🐾] ⊠ 🖪 🖻 [¶] 🏊

ST-JEAN-PORT-JOLI

◆◆ Auberge du Faubourg **X**
(418) 598-6455. **$65-$99, 10 days notice.** 280 ave de Gaspe ouest (Rt 132). 2.4 km w on Rt 132 from jct Rt 204; Hwy 20, exit 414. Ext corridors. **Pets:** Medium. $20 daily fee/pet. Designated rooms, no service, supervision.
[ASK] [S🐾] ⊠ 🖪 [¶] 🏊 [🦮]

ST-JEAN-SUR-RICHELIEU

◆◆ Comfort Inn **M**
(450) 359-4466. **$79-$129.** 700 rue Gadbois. Hwy 35, exit 9, e on rue Pierre-Caisse. Int corridors. **Pets:** Other species. Service with restrictions, supervision.
[SAVE] [S🐾] ⊠ 🖪 🏊

◆◆ Hotel Relais Gouverneur St-Jean-sur-Richelieu **H**
(450) 348-7376. **$89-$120.** 725 boul du Seminaire nord. Hwy 35, exit 7. Int corridors. **Pets:** Accepted.
[ASK] [S🐾] ⊠ 🖪 🖻 [¶] 🏊

STE-ANNE-DES-MONTS

(CAA) **◆◆** Motel Beaurivage **MI**
(418) 763-2291. **$50-$110, 5 days notice.** 245 1 ere ave ouest. Just off Rt 132. Ext/int corridors. **Pets:** Accepted.
[SAVE] ⊠ 🖪 🖻 [¶] [🦮]

STE-MARTHE

◆◆◆ Auberge des Gallant **CI**
(450) 459-4241. **$250-$350, 14 days notice.** 1171 chemin St-Henri. 8.5 km w on chemin St-Henri from jct Hwy 201. Int corridors. **Pets:** Accepted.
⊠ 🖻 [¶] 🏊 ⊠

THETFORD MINES

◆◆ Comfort Inn **M**
(418) 338-0171. **$88-$95, 5 days notice.** 123 boul Smith S. On Rt 112. Int corridors. **Pets:** Other species. Service with restrictions, crate.
[SAVE] [S🐾] ⊠ 🖪

TROIS-RIVIERES

◆◆◆ Delta Trois-Rivieres Hotel and Conference Centre **H**
(819) 376-1991. **$82.** 1620 rue Notre-Dame. Centre; corner of rue St-Roch. Int corridors. **Pets:** Accepted.
⊠ 🖻 [¶] 🏊

(CAA) **◆◆◆** Hotel Du Roy Trois-Rivieres **MI**
(819) 379-3232. **$70-$99.** 3600 boul Royal. Hwy 138, 2 km e of Pont Laviolette and jct Hwy 55. Ext/int corridors. **Pets:** Accepted.
[SAVE] [S🐾] ⊠ [¶] 🏊

TROIS-RIVIERES-OUEST

◆◆ Comfort Inn **M**
(819) 371-3566. **$77-$87.** 6255 rue Corbeil. Hwy 55, exit 183 (boul Jean XXIII), 2 km n of Laviolette Bridge. Int corridors. **Pets:** Medium. Designated rooms, service with restrictions, supervision.
[SAVE] ⊠ 🖪 🖻

(CAA) **◆◆◆** Days Inn **M**
(819) 377-4444. **$89-$139, 30 days notice.** 3155 boul St-Jean. Hwy 55 N, exit 183, then 0.5 km w on boul John XXIII, then 0.4 km n. Int corridors. **Pets:** Medium. $10 one-time fee/room. Designated rooms, service with restrictions, supervision.
[SAVE] [S🐾] ⊠ 🖪 🖻

VAL-D'OR

◆◆ Comfort Inn **M**
(819) 825-9360. **$91.** 1665 3 ieme ave. On Rt 117; in town centre. Int corridors. **Pets:** Other species. Service with restrictions, supervision.
[SAVE] [S🐾] ⊠ 🖪 🖻

◆◆◆ Motel L'Escale Hotel Suite **MI**
(819) 824-2711. **$78-$88.** 1100 rue L'Escale. Centre; on Rt 117 N. Ext/int corridors. **Pets:** Medium. Service with restrictions, supervision.
[S🐾] ⊠ 🖪 🖻 [¶]

WEST BROME

(CAA) **◆◆◆** Auberge West Brome **A**
(450) 266-7552. **$119-$280, 3 days notice.** 128 Rt 139. Hwy 10, exit 68 (Rt 139), 2.8 km s. Int corridors. **Pets:** Accepted.
[SAVE] [S🐾] ⊠ 🖪 [¶]

SASKATCHEWAN

CITY INDEX

CARONPORT

The Pilgrim Inn M
(306) 756-5002. **$69.** Hwy 1 W. Jct Main Access; on Trans-Canada Hwy 1. Int corridors. **Pets:** Other species. Designated rooms, service with restrictions, supervision.

ELBOW

Lakeview Lodge Motel M
(306) 854-4444. **$58.** 447 Saskatchewan St. Off Hwy 19, 1 km w. Ext corridors. **Pets:** $10 one-time fee/room. Designated rooms.

FOAM LAKE

La Vista Motel M
(306) 272-3341. **$52-$57.** Jct Hwy 16 & 310. On Hwy 16. Int corridors. **Pets:** Medium, other species. $7 daily fee/pet. Designated rooms, service with restrictions, crate.

MOOSE JAW

Heritage Inn MI
(306) 693-7550. **$90-$97, 14 days notice.** 1590 Main St N. 1.5 km s of jct Trans-Canada Hwy 1 and 2; access from Hwy 2 via Thatcher Dr. Int corridors. **Pets:** Accepted.

Prairie Oasis Motel M
(306) 693-8888. **$69-$75.** 955 Thatcher Dr E. Just s of jct Trans-Canada Hwy 1 and Thatcher Dr. Ext corridors. **Pets:** Designated rooms, service with restrictions, supervision.

Super 8 Motel-Moose Jaw M
(306) 692-8888. **$70-$80, 30 days notice.** 1706 Main St N. 1.5 km s of jct Trans-Canada Hwy 1 and 2; access from Hwy 2 via Thatcher Dr. Int corridors. **Pets:** Accepted.

NORTH BATTLEFORD

Super 8 Motel M
(306) 446-8888. **$67-$80.** 1006 Hwy 16 Bypass. 0.5 km se of jct Hwy 16. Int corridors. **Pets:** Accepted.

Tropical Inn MI
(306) 446-4700. **$66-$79.** 1001 Hwy 16 bypass. Corner of Battleford Rd and Hwy 16 Bypass. Int corridors. **Pets:** Accepted.

PRINCE ALBERT

Comfort Inn M
(306) 763-4466. **$87-$94.** 3863 2nd Ave W. 2.3 km s at jct Hwy 2 and Marquis Rd. Int corridors. **Pets:** Service with restrictions, crate.

Travelodge Prince Albert MI
(306) 764-6441. **$86.** 3551 2nd Ave W. 2.2 km s at jct Hwy 2 and Marquis Rd. Ext/int corridors. **Pets:** Other species. Service with restrictions, crate.

REGINA

Comfort Inn M
(306) 789-5522. **$72-$79.** 3221 East Eastgate Dr. Trans-Canada Hwy 1, 2 km e of Ring Rd, at eastern approach to Regina. Int corridors. **Pets:** Accepted.

Country Inn & Suites By Carlson M
(306) 789-9117. **$96-$98, 7 days notice.** 3321 Eastgate Bay. Trans-Canada Hwy 1, 2 km e of Ring Rd, at eastern approach to city. Int corridors. **Pets:** Medium, other species. Designated rooms, service with restrictions, crate.

Days Inn M
(306) 522-3297. **$82-$85, 30 days notice.** 3875 Eastgate Dr. Trans-Canada Hwy 1, exit Prince of Wales Dr, at eastern approach to city. Int corridors. **Pets:** Accepted.

Ramada Hotel & Convention Centre H
(306) 569-1666. **$95-$155.** 1818 Victoria Ave. Centre; Victoria Ave and Broad St. Int corridors. **Pets:** Accepted.

Regina Super 8 M
(306) 789-8833. **$68-$85, 14 days notice.** 2730 Victoria Ave E. Trans-Canada Hwy 1, 1.6 km e of Ring Rd at eastern approach to Regina. Int corridors. **Pets:** Other species. $10 one-time fee/room. Designated rooms, service with restrictions, supervision.

Travelodge Regina East M
(306) 565-0455. **$68-$87.** 1110 Victoria Ave E. Trans-Canada Hwy 1, just w of Ring Rd, at eastern approach to city. Int corridors. **Pets:** Other species. Designated rooms.

SASKATOON

Best Western Inn & Suites 🅜
(306) 244-5552. **$70-$92, 14 days notice.** 1715 Idylwyld Dr N. 2.6 km n on Hwy 16 and 11 (Idylwyld Dr). Ext/int corridors. **Pets:** Medium. Service with restrictions, supervision.

Colonial Square Motel 🅜
(306) 343-1676. **$79-$84.** 1301 8th St E. Just w of Cumberland St. Ext/int corridors. **Pets:** Accepted.

Comfort Inn 🅜
(306) 934-1122. **$82-$94.** 2155 Northridge Dr. 3 km n; just ne of jct Hwy 11 (Idylwyld Dr) and Circle Dr. Int corridors. **Pets:** Accepted.

Country Inn & Suites By Carlson
(306) 934-3900. **$83-$92.** 617 Cynthia St. Just w of jct Hwy 16 (Idylwyld Dr) and Circle Dr. Int corridors. **Pets:** Other species. Designated rooms.

Delta Bessborough 🄷
(306) 244-5521. **$149-$169.** 601 Spadina Crescent E. Centre; at 21st St E. Int corridors. **Pets:** Medium, other species. Designated rooms, supervision.

Quality Hotel 🄷
(306) 244-2311. **$95-$119.** 90 22nd St E. Just e of jct Hwy 11 (Idylwyld Dr), 1st and 22nd St. Int corridors. **Pets:** Accepted.

SWIFT CURRENT

Caravel Motel 🅜 ☙
(306) 773-8385. **$48-$59.** 705 N Service Rd E. Just e of Central Ave. Ext corridors. **Pets:** Small. Service with restrictions, supervision.

Comfort Inn 🅜
(306) 778-3994. **$78-$102.** 1510 S Service Rd E. Trans-Canada Hwy 1, just w of 22nd Ave NE. Int corridors. **Pets:** Medium. Designated rooms, service with restrictions, supervision.

Rodeway Inn Motel 🅜🄸
(306) 773-4664. **$50-$56.** 1200 S Service Rd E. Trans-Canada Hwy 1, just w of 22nd Ave NE. Ext/int corridors. **Pets:** Accepted.

Safari Motel 🅜
(306) 773-4608. **$45-$55, 3 days notice.** 810 S Service Rd E. 1 km e of jct Hwy 1 and 4, along Trans-Canada Hwy 1. Ext corridors. **Pets:** $40 one-time fee/pet. Supervision.

Super 8 Motel 🅜
(306) 778-6088. **$70-$91, 14 days notice.** 405 N Service Rd E. Just e of Central Ave. Int corridors. **Pets:** Accepted.

Swift Current Travelodge 🅜
(306) 773-3101. **$67-$120, 15 days notice.** Trans-Canada Hwy 1 E. Just e of Central Ave, on N Service Rd. Ext corridors. **Pets:** Accepted.

Westwind Motel 🅜 ☙
(306) 773-1441. **$56-$64.** N Service Rd W. Trans-Canada Hwy 1, 0.5 km w of Central Ave. Ext corridors. **Pets:** Small, dogs only. Designated rooms, service with restrictions, supervision.

WEYBURN

Perfect Inns 🅜
(306) 842-2691. **$56-$80.** 238 Sims Ave. Jct Hwy 35 and 39, 0.5 km w; beside McDonald's restaurant. Ext/int corridors. **Pets:** Accepted.

Weyburn Inn 🅜🄸
(306) 842-6543. **$54-$64, 7 days notice.** 5 Government Rd. Centre. Ext/int corridors. **Pets:** Accepted.

YORKTON

Comfort Inn & Suites 🅜
(306) 783-0333. **$69-$89, 30 days notice.** 22 Dracup Ave. Jct Hwy 9, 10 and 16 (Yellowhead Hwy), just w. Int corridors. **Pets:** $5 daily fee/pet. Designated rooms, service with restrictions, supervision.

Days Inn 🅜
(306) 783-3297. **$70.** 2 Kelsey Bay. Hwy 9, 10 and 16 (Yellowhead Hwy), just e. Int corridors. **Pets:** Small, dogs only. $10 one-time fee/pet. Designated rooms, service with restrictions, supervision.

Holiday Inn 🅜🄸
(306) 783-9781. **$73-$80.** 100 Broadway St E. On Hwy 10 and 16, downtown. Int corridors. **Pets:** Other species. Designated rooms, service with restrictions.

Imperial 400 Yorkton 🅜🄸
(306) 783-6581. **$64-$69.** 207 Broadway Ave E. At jct Hwy 9, 10 and 16 (Yellowhead Hwy). Ext/int corridors. **Pets:** Designated rooms, service with restrictions, supervision.

Travelodge Yorkton 🅜🄸
(306) 783-6571. **$69-$99.** 345 Broadway W. West end of town, just e of Agriplex (Hwy 10A). Ext/int corridors. **Pets:** Accepted.

DAWSON CITY

ⓦⓦ **Bonanza Gold Motel** Ⓜ
(867) 993-6789. **$89-$189.** 2.4 km s on Hwy 2.
Pets: Accepted.
✕ 🐾 🛏 💻 🎿

Ⓐ ⓦⓦ **Westmark Inn Dawson City** Ⓜ
(867) 993-5542. **$152.** At 5th and Harper sts. Ext/int corridors. **Pets:** Accepted.
ⓢⓐⓥⓔ ✕ 💻 🍽 🎿

ⓦ **White Ram Manor Bed & Breakfast** ⒷⒷ
(867) 993-5772. **$59-$109.** 813 7th Ave. 7th Ave and Harpert St. Int corridors. **Pets:** Accepted.
✕ 🎿 ⓩ

HAINES JUNCTION

Ⓐ ⓦⓦ **Alcan Motor Inn** Ⓜ
(867) 634-2371. **$107-$127.** Box 5460. Jct Alaska and Haines hwys (Hwy 1 and 3). Ext corridors. **Pets:** Accepted.
ⓢⓐⓥⓔ ✕ 🛏 💻 🎿

WHITEHORSE

Ⓐ ⓦⓦ **High Country Inn** Ⓜ 🐾
(867) 667-4471. **$109-$249, 3 days notice.** 4051 4th Ave. 0.6 km e of Main St. Int corridors. **Pets:** Other species. $15 daily fee/pet. Designated rooms, service with restrictions, supervision.
ⓢⓐⓥⓔ 🅢 ✕ 🛏 💻 🍽

Ⓐ ⓦⓦ **The Town and Mountain Hotel** Ⓜ
(867) 668-7644. **$69-$119.** 401 Main St. Downtown. Int corridors. **Pets:** Other species. $10 daily fee/pet. Designated rooms, service with restrictions.
ⓢⓐⓥⓔ 🅢 ✕ 🛏 💻 🍽 🎿

Ⓐ ⓦⓦ **Westmark Klondike Inn Whitehorse** Ⓜ
(867) 668-4747. **$125.** 2288 2nd Ave. Between Quartz Rd and 4th Ave. Int corridors. **Pets:** Accepted.
ⓢⓐⓥⓔ ✕ 🛏 💻 🍽

Ⓐ ⓦⓦ **Westmark Whitehorse Hotel & Conference Centre** Ⓜ
(867) 393-9700. **$116-$129.** 201 Wood St. Centre; 2nd Ave. Ext/int corridors. **Pets:** Other species.
ⓢⓐⓥⓔ ✕ 🅜 🚗 🛏 💻 🍽 🎿

NOTES